THE ENCYCLOPEDIA OF
MANITOBA

THE ENCYCLOPEDIA OF
MANITOBA
GREAT PLAINS PUBLICATIONS

GREAT PLAINS
PUBLICATIONS

Great Plains Publications
420 – 70 Arthur Street
Winnipeg, MB R3B 1G7
www.greatplains.mb.ca

Great Plains Publications gratefully acknowledges the financial support provided for its publishing
program by the Government of Canada through the Book Publishing Industry Development Program
(BPIDP); the Canada Council for the Arts; as well as the Manitoba Department of Culture, Heritage
and Tourism; and the Manitoba Arts Council.

Design & Typography by Relish Design Studios Ltd.
Printed in Canada by Friesens

CANADIAN CATALOGUING IN PUBLICATION DATA

Main entry under title:

    The enyclopedia of Manitoba / Ingeborg Boyens, managing editor

Includes bibliographical references and index.
  ISBN 978-1-894283-71-7

1. Manitoba—Encyclopedias.   I. Boyens, Ingeborg, 1955-

FC3354.E52 2007   971.27003   C2007-904011-X

TO THE PEOPLE OF MANITOBA

TABLE OF CONTENTS

A TO Z

E

PAGE 179

F

PAGE 209

G

PAGE 261

H

PAGE 301

M

PAGE 409

N

PAGE 489

O

PAGE 511

P

PAGE 519

U

PAGE 695

V

PAGE 707

W

PAGE 723

XYZ

PAGE 777

MESSAGE FROM THE PUBLISHER

"Man will never be free until the last king is strangled with the entrails of the last priest." So wrote Denis Diderot, French compiler of the world's first encyclopedia. Here in Manitoba, three centuries later, we don't feel quite as strongly about kings or priests. Diderot was a product of his times and so are we. Whereas Diderot had the world as his tapestry, we at Great Plains – compilers of this encyclopedia – have limited ourselves to Manitoba. But, where the Frenchman concentrated on ideas, we have embraced *everything* Manitoban, from rocks to events to people to insects.

Holding this volume in your hands, you know it is a big book. It is 800 pages long, with almost 2,000 entries and 1,000 illustrations. It took dozens of people working for three years to complete this, the largest publishing project in Manitoba history.

In an age of online reference material, the *Encyclopedia of Manitoba* is unabashedly a book. It has weight and heft. It smells of paper and glue. It is substantial and built to last. Most importantly, it is not anonymous, or re-writable, like Wikipedia and other online resources. Experts have compiled this information and are not afraid to sign their names to their material. And what a wealth of material! For the first time, just about anything you need to know about Manitoba has been collected in one place. We wanted to create something authoritative and accessible, and I think we have succeeded.

All right, you may ask, but how did you decide what gets in and what doesn't? Unlike the Internet, a book is finite. So what counts, and who decides? The question, and answer, define perfectly the difference between book culture and Web culture.

First we assembled a board of eminent Manitobans, people whose lives and careers have helped define the province. Then, we brought together a dozen academic experts who represented the major diciplines and institutions in the province. Finally, we all put our heads together and came up with a list of 2,000 things that, lined up from A to Z, spelled out Manitoba.

It wasn't that simple, of course. Things moved on and off the list. Experts made impassioned pleas, both for and against. Short entries became long entries and vice versa. But, and this is a big but, there was a process of discussion on every single entry. Things weren't added just because someone had a hobby horse, or because there was unlimited space. There was a process of evaluation, based on the principle that everything is *not* equal, and whereby recognized experts made the decision whether a subject deserved inclusion.

Is this book perfect? Of course not. Inevitably, there will be mistakes. Some will be outright errors, some will be oversights, some will be disagreements over tone or emphasis. Whatever the problem, if you find something wrong, we want you to be part of the discussion. Please email us at info@greatplains.mb.ca so that we can assess your concerns for subsequent printings.

Does this book follow some infallible plan or system? Again, no. The *Encyclopedia of Manitoba* is idiocyncratic, sometimes even a little eccentric. It was prepared and written by people, not machines. Occasionally we gave extra space to a person or a thing because we believed it had been under-appreciated in the past (*see* **MILITARY IN MANITOBA**). Sometimes we felt the claim for Manitoban status overstated (don't see Tom Cochrane). Often we wanted to learn more about something and assumed you would too (*see* **PENIS WORM**).

The issue of who we could claim as Manitoban was fiercely discussed by the editors. In the end, we decided that anyone spending their formative years here could be called a native son or daughter. We defined formative years as elementary and high school years, with university where applicable. That meant **MARSHALL MCLUHAN** could be included even though he was born in Edmonton and became famous in Toronto. This also – just barely–applies to **Neil Young**. Where the claim is more tenuous (*see* **DEANNA DURBIN, SANDFORD FLEMING, ANNA PAQUIN**), we have included only a photograph and caption.

As publisher, I came to discern peculiar patterns as I reviewed the hundreds of entries. For example, we expect our province to have produced a lot of world-class curlers (*see* **DON DUGUID, CONNIE LALIBERTIE, JENNIFER JONES**). But Manitoba has also spawned a lot of all-star NHL goalies (*see* **TURK BRODA, TERRY SAWCHUK, RON HEXTALL, ED BELFOUR**); a lot of best-selling Young Adult novelists (*see* **MARTHA BROOKS, SHELDON OBERMAN, CAROL MATAS**); a lot of national Aboriginal leaders (*see* **OVIDE MERCREDI, ELIJAH HARPER, PHIL FONTAINE**); and a lot of top generals (*see* **RAY CRABBE, WALTER NATYNCZWK, RAY HENAULT**). Why we specialize in these more arcane areas is a mystery to me, but it is worth some enjoyable speculation.

Flipping through the pages, one can't help noticing some pecularities as well. Why do we insist on calling any bump on the landscape higher than a grain elevator a "mountain?" Why is a trickle of water wider than a sidewalk automatically a "river?" And why do we annoit towns with more than 7000 people a "city?" It suggests an inferiority complex that we should have outgrown long ago. There are other negatives that can't be ignored: the shameful number of **WRONGFUL CONVICTIONS** in our court system; the continuing scourge of **CHILD WELFARE** disasters; the black mark of **RESIDENTIAL SCHOOLS.**

Generally, however, as you look at the amazing natural phenonema and human accomplishments recorded in this book, you can't help feeling proud to be a Manitoban. The resurgence of downtown **WINNIPEG**, the shimmering **AURORA BOREALIS** at **CHURCHILL**, our diverse Prairie and Shield **LAKES,** the business and population boom in **MENNONITE** southern Manitoba. I won't list all the highlights here because that is what an encyclopedia is for. Start at A, start at M, start wherever you want. But I can pretty much guarantee that after a few pages you won't stop. We hope you enjoy reading the *Encyclopedia of Manitoba* as much as we enjoyed creating it.

—GREGG SHILLIDAY

MESSAGE FROM THE MANAGING EDITOR

Like many Manitobans, I have lived and worked outside the province several times in my life. But like some trusty homing pigeon, I have always made it back to the place I know as "home." I kept coming back, not just for family and cheap housing prices, but because I knew Manitoba was much more than mosquitoes and long winters. I knew Manitoba was important; central to the nation's political, social and cultural development. Did we not produce Louis Riel, Nellie McClung and Margaret Laurence, not to mention latter-day worthies such as Elijah Harper, Carl Ridd and Guy Maddin?

However, over the course of my three years as managing editor of this encyclopedia, I found there was so much I didn't know. Conversations with the hundreds of contributors who wrote the nearly 2000 entries in this book gave me an endless supply of factoids. For example, did you know there is a frog in the province that copes with winter by freezing solid? That Winnipeg's Arlington Street Bridge was originally intended to span the Nile River? And (perhaps not something to brag about) the plastic green garbage bag was invented by a Manitoban? Beyond preparing me for the Trivial Pursuit circuit, this fact-finding journey has granted me vital information about the province's history, sports, science, geography, arts and economy – information that affirms why Manitoba deserves to be "home." I hope you too will be fascinated and informed by the broad scope of Manitoba people, places and things assembled here.

Compiling 800,000 words and 1000 pictures is a massive task. A task that couldn't have been achieved if this project had not reached out to the broader community beyond our core group at Great Plains Publications. Our first order of business was to set up an advisory board of Manitoba leaders to help ensure we were working from the appropriate list of entries. We subsequently pulled together an editorial board of experts who would identify and recruit authorities in their field of expertise. So the making of this encyclopedia was a kind of pyramid scheme – for all the right reasons. What we finally have is not a top-down exercise, not a single editorial voice imposed on all these pages. Rather, a whole choir of diverse and authentic voices contributed to make this encyclopedia an idiosyncratic, but harmonious whole.

The making of this book was a lengthy, complicated process. So it is no surprise our team members changed a bit as health challenges or unexpected time pressures interfered. Others, however, stepped up to the plate when deadlines loomed large – among them, Bob Wrigley, whose "encyclopedic" love of zoology shaped many of the pieces in this text; Patricia Bovey, who generously offered her vast knowledge about Manitoba art; Robert R. Taylor and his awesome array of nature photographs; Ruth DeGraves and Jim Shilliday who were the calm, competent generalists even in the face of near-panic; and Mildred Gutkin who contributed so much when the encyclopedia was just a good idea.

The story of Manitoba could fill many volumes. We thought a single book – albeit a hefty one – would be enough to pique the curiosity of the average reader. So our challenge was to decide what to put in and what to leave out. Our master list changed from day to day on the basis of sometimes heated conversations with our advisors, editors and curious observers. In the end, we simply had to make decisions about a broad range of subjects. You may disagree with some of those decisions. But be assured, our decisions were not taken lightly.

For example, we've included entries on all 14 sitting Manitoba Members of Parliament, but we decided that MLAs and provincial cabinet ministers warranted entries only with extraordinary achievement. We've provided entries on all 63 First Nations communities in Manitoba, often under their new, perhaps less-familiar, Aboriginal names.

Which communities to include proved to be a particular challenge. A town like Kane in southern Manitoba is still noted on the road by an official highway sign and a call for reduced speeds. Although it is in the heart of some of the province's most fertile farmland, Kane itself can hardly claim town status. The last store is now a private home. However, in 2000, several hundred people gathered in a blue-striped tent to pay tribute to their hometown. And a history of Kane, produced for the reunion, was almost as thick as this text. Should Kane be included? We finally decided "Sorry." Despite its role in the province's rural past, it's just not big enough now in the context of modern Manitoba.

We don't pretend to be infallible. You may feel some of our decisions were wrong. Or perhaps you've identified an entry that we somehow missed. These are things we want to hear about. Please do contact the editors so we can ensure future editions are complete. But for now, we invite you to step into a world that explores all things Manitoban – an exercise that proves Manitoba is indeed worth coming home to.

—INGEBORG BOYENS

Acknowledgments

In a book of this size and complexity, there are obviously many people and organizations we would like to thank. Unfortunately, to avoid a supplemental book almost as long as this one, we must limit ourselves to a few key friends of the *Encyclopedia of Manitoba*.

First, a tip of the hat to David G. Friesen and Friesens Printers of Altona who stepped in when we despaired finding anyone who shared our vision of a compendium of all things Manitoban. Friesens has not only manufactured the book with their usual sterling abilities, but they have also become a valuable partner in this enterprise.

We want to thank Richard Frost and the board of The Winnipeg Foundation who generously agreed to donate a copy of the *Encyclopedia* to every public and school library in the province. This demonstrates the commitment to Manitoba and to education for which The Foundation is justly famous.

The *Winnipeg Free Press* was media sponsor for this book and once again showed their ongoing dedication to literacy. Relish Design, especially Terry Corrigan and Suzanne Braun, worked long hours to convert words and pictures into something attractive and readable. David Carr and Professor J. M. Bumsted generously allowed us to reproduce biographical sketches from the University of Manitoba Press's *Dictionary of Manitoba Biography*. And, of course, we thank our advisory and editorial boards, our writers and photographers, and our researchers, proofers and indexers for their invaluable assistance.

—THE EDITORS

STAFF

Our strategy for the *Encyclopedia of Manitoba* has been to include as many writers as possible. This broad and inclusive approach calls on a group of in-house publishing professionals, a number of academic editorial advisors, and hundreds of expert contributors from around the province.

GREGG SHILLIDAY, Publisher

Gregg began Great Plains Publications in 1992 to bring the story of Manitoba's history to life in a popular, accessible format. The 3-volume *Manitoba 125* series has since become a Canadian bestseller, with more than 20,000 copies sold. Great Plains further honed its reputation as a big-book publisher by releasing titles like *Winnipeg: Heart of the Continent, The Lake: An Illustrated History*, and *A Store Like No Other: Eaton's of Winnipeg*. Before setting up Great Plains, Gregg worked as a journalist for newspapers, magazines, and television in Manitoba, Ontario and Alberta.

INGEBORG BOYENS, Managing Editor

Ingeborg has worked for newspapers and magazines across Canada and was with the CBC for more than a decade, working on national programs like *The Journal*. She most recently produced documentaries on food and agricultural issues for *Country Canada*. She has written two books that won national awards. Ingeborg has extensive managerial experience, overseeing newsrooms at CBC-TV and the *Winnipeg Free Press* and running a weekly current affairs program for the CBC.

ADAM J. LEVIN, Associate Editor

Adam has been employed by the Independent Learning Centre at TVOntario, Charlton Press, and McClelland & Stewart. He has written hundreds of articles, essays, and book reviews for such publications as *Books in Canada, Literary Review of Canada*, and *The Globe and Mail*. Adam earned a masters degree in philosophy from Oxford University.

JOEL TRENAMAN, Assistant Editor

Joel earned a BA in Political Studies from the University of Manitoba before becoming editor-in-chief of the *Manitoban* and Opinions Bureau Chief for the Canadian University Press. He is also the author of a history of Seven Oaks General Hospital.

RUSS GOURLUCK, Photo Editor

Russ has written two Canadian bestsellers: *A Store Like No Other: Eaton's of Winnipeg* (2004) and *Going Downtown: A History of Winnipeg's Portage Avenue* (2006). Great Plains will publish his third book, *Picturing Manitoba: Legacies of the Winnipeg Tribune*, in 2008.

MICHELLE DOBROVOLNY, Senior Writer

A graduate of the University of Winnipeg, Michelle gained media training as an intern at the *Winnipeg Free Press* and *Radio Prague* before joining Great Plains Publications as a staff writer.

TERRY CORRIGAN, Senior Designer

JILL CONDRA, Proofreading

JUDITH O'LEARY, Indexing

JEWLS DENGL, Administration

CATHARINA de BAKKER, TAMMY MARLOWE JOHNSON & ANITA DAHER, Marketing

See full list of contributors on page 781.

HOW TO USE THIS ENCYCLOPEDIA

We have tried to make this text as user-friendly as possible. Entries are arranged alphabetically, from A to Z, for the sake of simplicity. You will find radically different subjects sitting next to each other. "Charles Comfort" is next to "communism" is next to "Richard Condie" is next to "construction" is next to "Cook's Creek" and so on. The order of the entries follows the English alphabet, ignoring capital letters, accents or apostrophes. All headings beginning with Mac or Mc are listed together as if they were spelled `Mac`and are registered according to the next letter. So **MacKenzie, Gisele** comes before **McLuhan, Herbert Marshall** All names beginning with St. or Ste. are located under the spelling Saint.

If there is no specific heading to be found in the alphabetical listings, please check the index. Subjects that may not warrant their own entry are covered under other topics. There are also cross-references noted in the entries with **BOLD CAPS** that will lead the reader to other, related entries.

The entries in this encyclopedia are intended to be brief introductions to a subject. We have included a reader's list at the back of the book to direct the curious to more detailed sources. Although most entries provide only a taste of a subject, the *Encyclopedia of Manitoba* does include 12 feature-length essays written by an expert in that field.

Biographical subjects are alphabetized by the last name the individual was commonly known by. The maiden names of women are sometimes included in parentheses. The exact places and dates of birth and death are given when they are known. Numbers are numerical rather than spelled out. We have used many abbreviations in an effort to provide as much information as possible in a limited space. They are listed on page xvii. "Manitoba" is usually shortened to "MB," except in proper names. "Canadian" becomes "Cdn" when used as an adjective.

POPULATIONS: Statistics Canada released the initial findings of its 2006 census in time for inclusion in the encyclopedia. Population counts for MB's largest towns and cities are for the "census subdivision" (the best number to use according to StatsCan) as of 2006. Population for towns and villages not tabulated by the government agency were acquired the old-fashioned way – by a phone call to the people who live there. First Nations populations are based on the December 2006 analysis by the federal Department of Indian and Northern Affairs.

LANGUAGE: Over the past few decades, First Nation groups have changed their names, choosing designations they selected themselves rather than the names originally applied to them by Euro-Canadians. Whenever possible, we have decided to follow their example and use those current names. Although we recognize that language is always changing – particularly when it comes to First Nations communities – we have made no attempt to alter language in historical works, even if it feels uncomfortable by today`s standard.

BIOLOGICAL CLASSIFICATION: Currently, what used to be known as the plant and animal world is divided into 5 kingdoms – the Bacteria, Protoctista (or Protista), Fungi, Plant, and Animal. The Bacteria represent the earliest form of unicellular life and evolved between 3-4 bya (billion years ago). The Protoctista evolved about 1.5 bya, Fungi 1 bya, Animalia 700 mya (million years ago), and the Plantae 500 mya.

The reader will regularly come across technical words in naming and classifying organisms in this encyclopedia. Derived from Latin and Greek, these terms often describe some physical aspect of a species or its distribution, or to honour some person. While challenging to learn, scientific names are indispensable tools in naming, ordering and comprehending the relationships of the bewildering diversity of life, and in international communication among scientists. There are numerous levels possible within the classification system, but only the major ones (from comprehensive to specific) are used as follows, with the Human species used as an example.

Kingdom Animalia (cells with a nuclear membrane and no green chloroplasts or cellulose)

Phylum Chordata (Chordates, with a supporting rod of bone or cartilage)

Class Mammalia (Mammals, with hair and mammary glands)

Order Primates (Monkeys, Apes, and Humans)

Family Hominidae (Humans)

Genus Homo (Human)

ABBREVIATIONS

2Lt second lieutenant

AB Alberta

ACmdre air commodore

Adm admiral

Asst Assistant

Asst Comm Assistant Commissioner

Aug August

Ave Avenue (street name)

b born (only in biographical descriptions)

BA bachelor of arts

Batt battalion

BC British Columbia

BGen brigadier-general

Blvd Boulevard (street name)

BSc bachelor of science

BU Brandon University

ca circa

Capt army/air force captain, or non-naval ship's captain

Capt (N) naval captain

CBC Canadian Broadcasting Corporation

CCF Co-operative Commonwealth Federation

Cdn Canadian

Cdr commander

Cdt cadet

CEF Canadian Expeditionary Forces

CEO chief executive officer

CF Canadian Forces

CFB Canadian Forces Base

CFL Canadian Football League

cm centimetres

Cmdre commodore

CMU Canadian Mennonite University

CNR Canadian National Railway(s)

CNoR Canadian Northern Railway (1899-1918)

Col colonel

Comm commissioner

Const constable

CPR Canadian Pacific Railway/CP Rail

Cpl corporal

Cres Crescent

CSupt chief superintendent

CWB Canadian Wheat Board

CWO chief warrant officer

d died (only in biographical descriptions)

Dec December

DND Department of National Defence

Dr doctor (only in name, e.g. Dr Thorlaksson)

E east

Feb February

FLt flight lieutenant

FO flight officer

FRCPS (C) Fellow of the Royal College of Physicians and Surgeons (Canada)

FSgt flight sergeant

ft foot, feet

g gram

GCapt group captain

GDP gross domestic product

Gen general

gov governor

gov gen governor general

govt government

ha hectares

HBC Hudson's Bay Company

HIV human immunodeficiency virus

HM Her (or His) Majesty

HMCS Her (or His) Majesty's Canadian Ship

HRH His (or Her) Royal Highness

hwy highway

i.e. (id est) that is

in inch(es)

Inc Incorporated

Insp inspector

IR Indian Reserve

Jan January

KC King's Councillor

km kilometres, km^2 square kilometres

kW kilowatt(s)

kWh kilowatt hour(s)

l litre(s), etc. (ml, dl, cl)

LAC leading aircraftman

LCdr lieutenant-commander

LCol lieutenant-colonel

LCpl lance-corporal

LGen lieutenant-general

LS leading seaman

Lt lieutenant (army/air force)

Ltd Limited

Lt (N) naval lieutenant

lt gov lieutenant governor

m metres, m² square metres, etc.

MA master of arts

Maj major

MB Manitoba

M.B. Made Beaver (fur trade currency)

MCpl master corporal

MD medical doctor

MGen major-general

mi mile(s)

ml millilitre(s)

MLA Member of the Legislative Assembly

MLB Major League Baseball

MP Member of Parliament

MS master seaman

MSc master of science

MVP most valuable player

mW megawatt(s)

mWh megawatt hour(s)

MWO master warrant officer

mya million years ago

myo million years old

N north

NA North America(n)

NAFTA North American Free Trade Agreement

NATO North Atlantic Treaty Organization

NB New Brunswick

NCO non-commissioned officer

NDP New Democratic Party

NGO non-governmental organization

NHL National Hockey League

NL Newfoundland and Labrador

NORAD North American Aerospace Defense Command (not Defence)

No. number

Nov November

NS Nova Scotia

NU Nunavut

NT modern Northwest Territories (Since 1999)

NWC North West Company

NWT North-Western Territory (Before 1870)

NWTs North-West Territories (1870–1912), or Northwest Territories (1912-99)

NWMP North-West Mounted Police

Oct October

ON Ontario

PC Progressive Conservative (only on 2nd and subsequent uses in an entry)

PE Prince Edward Island

PhD doctor of philosophy

PM prime minister

PO pilot officer (RAF, former RCAF)

pop population (abbreviate only in initial description line of geographical entries)

POW prisoner of war

PPCLI Princess Patricia's Light Canadian Infantry

Pt point (in geographical names)

Pte private

QB Queen's Bench

QC Quebec

QC Queen's Councillor

RAdm rear-admiral

RAF Royal Air Force

RCAF Royal Canadian Air Force

RCMP Royal Canadian Mounted Police

RCN Royal Canadian Navy

Rd Road (street name)

Reg regiment

RM Rural Municipality

S south

SA South America

Sept September

Sgt sergeant

SgtMaj sergeant-major (obsolete rank)

SK Saskatchewan

SLdr squadron leader

Sqn squadron

SSgt staff sergeant

St street (only in formal name)

St. or Ste. Saint or Sainte

StatsCan Statistics Canada

Supt superintendent

U university (only in formal name, ex. Brandon U)

U of M University of Manitoba

U of W University of Winnipeg

UK United Kingdom

US United States

VAdm vice-admiral

VC Victoria Cross

W west

WCdr wing commander

WO warrant officer

WWI World War I

WWII World War II

yd yard and yards

YT Yukon Territory

AURORA BOREALIS,
see page 37

ABORIGINAL JUSTICE INQUIRY (AJI). The AJI was created by the MB govt to look into the deaths of Aboriginals **HELEN BETTY OSBORNE** and **JOHN JOSEPH HARPER**. The deaths, though 16 years apart, showed similar treatment of First Nations people by MB's **JUDICIAL SYSTEM**. The final report consisted of 296 recommendations aimed at the MB govt, the federal govt, and Aboriginal communities within the province. The recommendations made by commissioners **ALVIN HAMILTON** and **MURRAY SINCLAIR** covered 10 broad areas: Aboriginal rights; the **NORTHERN FLOOD AGREEMENT**; treaty land entitlement; **MÉTIS** issues; employment and cross-cultural training; policing; separate court system; violence toward women and children; **CHILD WELFARE**; and early support and crime prevention measures for youth.

Two central incidents acted as catalysts for the inquiry. First, Helen Betty Osborne, a teenager from **NORWAY HOUSE CREE NATION**, was sexually assaulted and murdered on Nov 13, 1971. She was found with multiple stab wounds outside the townsite of **THE PAS**. Four white men – Dwayne Archie Johnston, James Robert Paul Houghton, Lee Scott Colgan, and Norman Bernard Manger – were allegedly involved in this incident but were not taken to court until 1987. The inquiry refers to the racism and prejudices in The Pas

toward Aboriginal people. It was also referred to how widespread knowledge was in town about the murder. In Dec 1987, 16 years after her death, Johnston was convicted; Houghton was acquitted; and Colgan received immunity for testifying against Houghton and Johnston. Manger was never charged. The AJI's 1991 2-volume, 800-page report found that Osborne died because of a "racist and sexist act," and that she would likely still be alive today if she had not been Aboriginal and a woman.

Then, on March 9, 1988, an on-duty Winnipeg Police officer shot John Joseph Harper, a former director of Island Lake Tribal Council, the overseeing body for **GARDEN HILL, RED SUCKER LAKE, ST. THERESA POINT**, and **WASAGAMACK** First Nations communities. Const Robert Cross misidentified Harper as a car thief, perhaps due to racial profiling. Cross claimed that there was a physical confrontation and that his gun was fired accidentally, fatally injuring Harper. The internal Winnipeg Police Services investigation of the evidence surrounding the ordeal was not well received by the inquiry. For example, the AJI found irregularities with the handling of evidence, such as the seizing of Cross's gun and holster. As well, Cross was treated as the victim rather than as a suspect. The inquiry found other

A

WINNIPEG FREE PRESS

Robert Cross testifies at the AJI.

inconsistencies with note-taking, not following police protocol, the treatment of evidence, and the lack of forensic tests.

The AJI sat for 2 years, producing its report in 1991 after much travel and many consultations. The report did not mince words, stating the system had not only failed Aboriginal people, but had ignored their rights, and jailed them disproportionately to the general population. The commissioners called for a fundamental revamping of the justice system as it affected FIRST PEOPLES, including Aboriginal-run community courts. Most of these recommendations were not implemented, leading to concerns that the inquiry – like so many others – would be mere window-dressing. The Aboriginal Justice Implementation Commission was created late in 1999 to fast-track implementation of the original AJI recommendations. The new commission released its recommendations in June 2001, 10 years after the original report. Nothing substantive has since resulted and Aboriginal people continue to voice concerns about the time it has taken for the latest recommendations to be put into place. • WENDY ROSS

ABORIGINAL PEOPLES TELEVISION NETWORK is a WINNIPEG-based TV broadcaster dedicated to programming about – and primarily by – First Nations, MÉTIS, and Inuit peoples. Since Sept 1999, the cable and satellite channel has aired daily news, entertainment, cultural, youth, and educational programs for Aboriginals and non-Aboriginals, reaching an estimated 10 million Canadian homes. APTN programming is made up of at least 70% Canadian content, and features 55% in ENGLISH, 30% in Aboriginal languages, and 15% in FRENCH. The creation of the APTN was the result of a 2-decade-long effort by the Canadian Radio-television and Telecommunications Commission (CRTC) and lobby groups to improve broadcasting for an Aboriginal audience and for northern areas. Following a number of 1980s govt initiatives and technological upgrades, the CRTC approved the creation of Television Northern Canada in 1991. The regional (viewed in northern territories only) network became APTN in 1999 when the CRTC approved its bid to go national and made it a required channel for cable providers. APTN launched its daily news program in Oct 2002, featuring reports from bureaus located around the country. Requirements for original programming have helped foster a number of independent Aboriginal TV producers and documentary filmmakers. A 21-member national board of directors governs APTN, and about 75% of the staff is Aboriginal. The broadcaster's licence has been renewed by the CRTC until 2012. • JT

ABORIGINAL RIGHTS are those enjoyed by descendants of First Nations, the original occupants of this land. Such rights are in addition to the normal rights enjoyed by both Aboriginal and non-Aboriginal Canadians. While Manitobans of any culture are encouraged to maintain and enjoy their heritage, Aboriginal peoples are in a unique position: if their cultures disappear from MB, it will disappear from the world. MB is a homeland for a variety of CREE, OJIBWAY, DAKOTA, DENE, and MÉTIS peoples, many of whose distinct cultures and languages (such as MICHIF and Oji-Cree) can only be found here. Aboriginal rights are a way of enshrining additional protection for these First Peoples in the law.

Aboriginal rights have been built into the founding constitutional documents of Canada and MB. The Royal Proclamation of 1763, resulting from the Seven Years War between the British and French in Europe and eastern NA, recognized Aboriginal land ownership. The RUPERT'S LAND transfer of 1870, which transferred control of Rupert's Land from the HUDSON'S BAY COMPANY to the Dominion of Canada, included

AM. L.B.FOOTE COLLECTION 119, N1719

Premier Bracken meets with Native delegation at Legislative Building in 1929.

several statements ensuring that Aboriginal peoples would have some of their rights and interests protected. *The Manitoba Act*, negotiated by Métis leader **Louis Riel** in 1870, contained significant promises respecting Métis land rights. Treaties 1 (1871), 2 (1871), 4 (1874), and 5 (1875) were negotiated between the Crown and a variety of MB First Nations, establishing reserve lands, annual payments, and other promises and protections for treaty signatories. Other Treaties, including 3 (1873), 6 (1876), and 10 (1906), included a number of MB First Nations and Métis; as well, adhesions or additions to the treaties, especially Treaty 5, were signed in the first few decades of the 20th century with a variety of northern MB First Nations. The *Constitution Act* of 1982 included section 35, which "recognized and affirmed" Aboriginal and Treaty rights, and section 25, which ensured the equality rights of the Charter of Rights and Freedoms would not be interpreted in a manner that limits Aboriginal rights.

In spite of this strong constitutional history, Aboriginal rights (and the treaties they gave rise to) have more often been ignored than respected by a variety of provincial and federal govts. The *Natural Resource Transfer Act* (1930), by which the federal govt ceded control of natural resources to the MB govt, led to almost systematic curtailing of Aboriginal **Hunting** rights. Since 1982, the Supreme Court of Canada has rendered a series of strong decisions respecting both Aboriginal and treaty rights. It has argued that Aboriginal rights are meaningful and, when it comes to land and resource use, must take priority over commercial and recreation resource uses; that, in case of ambiguity, treaties must be interpreted in a way beneficial to Aboriginal people; that Aboriginal rights protect activities integral to the groups claiming them; that Aboriginal oral histories have significant weight in determining land and treaty rights; that Métis have rights as Aboriginal people; and that plans for resource use must involve consultation with affected Aboriginal peoples.

Aboriginal rights are particularly important to rural communities, where conflicts over resource use – such as whether a river should be dammed for **Hydroelectric** power or be kept as a fur trapping and **Fishing** lifeline – remain vital aspects of debates. Urban Aboriginals also strongly insist on their relevance. Decisions made by courts in MB regarding Aboriginal rights will likely be key in determining the future of Aboriginal peoples as distinct cultures. ● PETER KULCHYSKI

ABORIGINAL SPIRITUALITY AND MYTH,

though nuanced and regionally varied, has common elements crossing various First Nations.

There exists a shared worldview often represented through the concept of the Medicine Wheel, the Circle of Life. The circle is non-hierarchical and represents a belief in the equality and inter-relatedness of all things in the universe. It is a model for the cycle of the seasons and the individual life cycle. The 4 cardinal directions are indicated in the Medicine Wheel, with a colour, animal or spirit being, personal quality, and stage in the life cycle associated with each direction. For example, the East is the spring, the colour is yellow, the animal is the eagle, the personal quality is the physical, and the stage in the life cycle is child; the South is summer, red, buffalo, emotional, and youth; the West is fall, black, thunderbird, mental, and adult; and, the North is winter, white, bear, spiritual, and elder.

Other common elements include: shared cultural values exemplified by the seven sacred teachings (wisdom, love, respect, courage, truth, humbleness, and kindness); respect for the power of dreams; belief in the enduring influence of the souls of ancestors; belief in the spirit nature of all living things, and emphasis on the importance of dance and song (*see* **Powwows**). Some of the main ceremonies currently practised by First Nations people in MB include the sweatlodge, sundance, naming ceremonies, pipe ceremonies, **Midewiwin** ceremonies, and the vision quest. The ceremonies focus on health and healing and leading a good life, free from drugs and alcohol, and following the cultural values.

Much of the mythology or sacred narratives of MB **First Peoples** centres around the animals (or animal spirits) and other spirit beings; including the Sasquatch, the little people, the Thunderbirds, Windigo, and, Nanabozo. A common creation story type of narrative is called the "Earth Diver" which begins with an Earth covered by water, following a flood. In the **Ojibway** version, Nanabozo re-creates the earth by getting various animals to swim to the bottom of the waters to obtain some of the original earth. In the Earth Diver stories, Nanabozo is acting in the role of culture hero as opposed to a trickster. As a trickster, Nanabozo is more of an anti-hero fulfilling a dual role as a lascivious prankster.

While most figures of Aboriginal mythology are similarly envisioned as the embodiment of life's dual nature, the Ojibway Windigo is seen primarily as a force of evil. Commonly described as a giant, undead, humanlike monster that feeds on the meat of humans, the mythical Windigo is feared by all, said to prey on those who venture alone in the woods. The Windigo also serves as a symbolic creature that may usher in a period of famine, as its cry is reputed to scare creatures away. "Windigo fever" – the becoming of a

Windigo after encountering one – has been described by scientists and anthropologists as a sort of psychotic lust for cannibalism arising from hunger, or as a tool to teach Aboriginal children not to get lost in the woods.

The Thunderbird is another common figure in Aboriginal mythology. In the mythology of MB's First Peoples, thunderstorms are the result of a fight between the Thunderbird and a huge rattlesnake.

Unlike the world of nature spirits who held influence in daily life, a Supreme Being or creator, Gitche Manitou, was formless and had little contact with humans. Often translated as Great Spirit, Gitche Manitou represented the unknown power of life and the universe, and presided over all of Nature. Manitoba is a derivation of the spirit's name (*see* **Manitoba, Name Origin**). ● MARK RUML

ABORIGINAL WRITERS. Literature by First Nations and **Métis** writers is not usually discussed within a framework of regionalism as provincial (and national) boundaries were imposed upon Aboriginal cultural affiliations. Nonetheless, for the purposes of this book, there is a rich and growing tradition of Aboriginal writing within MB.

The autobiographical novel *In Search of April Raintree* (Pemmican Publications, 1983) by Métis author **Beatrice Culleton** (now Moisonier) became a milestone in the history of Aboriginal literature in Canada. Other well-known Aboriginal writers of this generation are **Tomson Highway**, Emma LaRocque, Duncan Mercredi, and Marvin Francis. Originally from the Métis community of Big Bay, AB, Métis poet Emma LaRocque now lives in **Winnipeg**, where she teaches at the **U of M**. Besides being well known for her extensive scholarly work, her poetry has appeared in anthologies such as *Native Poetry in Canada* and *Writing the Circle: Women of Western Canada*. Cree poet Duncan Mercredi, born in **Grand Rapids**, wrote largely about displacement – his generation experienced the first major **Hydroelectric** development in northern MB (*see* **Northern Flood Agreement**) – and finding a new place by building on old values in his 4 books, all with Pemmican: *Spirit of the Wolf: Raise Your Voice* (1990); *Dreams of the Wolf in the City* (1992), *Wolf and Shadows* (1995), and *The Duke of Windsor: Wolf Sings the Blues* (1997). Mercredi also deserves credit for founding the Aboriginal Writers Collective of Manitoba in 1999. The collective lost 3 prominent members to cancer in the early 21st century: Leonard Carriere, Marvin Francis, and Douglas Nepinak. Cree poet Marvin Francis, originally from the Heart Lake First

Nation in AB but a long-time Winnipeg resident, was praised for his ability to "write the street." Published in the anthologies like *A Shade of Spring* (1998), the 3ʳᵈ edition of *An Anthology of Canadian Native Literature in English*, and in literary **MAGAZINES**, he is best known for his poetry collection *City Treaty* (2002), for which he won the 2003 **JOHN HIRSCH** Award for Most Promising Manitoba Writer. The poetry of Doug Nepinak, who was born in **PINE CREEK FIRST NATION**, appeared in *Prairie Fire* and *Border Crossings*. He also produced a spoken-word CD with the help of the Aboriginal Writers Collective, and others, shortly before his 2005 death. Jordan Wheeler, another member of the collective, was born in Victoria but has spent much of his life in Winnipeg. His book of 3 novellas, *Brothers in Arms* (Pemmican, 1989), complements his 2 children's books. He now works mostly in video, **FILM**, and popular **THEATRE**. His mother, Bernalda Wheeler, was one of the earliest Aboriginal voices on radio in Canada, but is also well known for her literary contributions, especially her children's books.

Like all creative writers, Aboriginal authors work within a wide range of literary genres, but many prefer poetry. Though he now lives in BC, Greg Young-Ing, a member of the **OPASKWAYAK CREE NATION** in **THE PAS**, is both a poet – he wrote *The Random Flow of Blood and Flowers* (Ekstasis, 1996) – and a former **BOOK PUBLISHING** executive with the Aboriginal house Theytus Books. Rasunah Marsden, a Métis writer from **BRANDON**, edited a compilation of Aboriginal creative non-fiction entitled *Crisp Blue Edges* (Theytus, 2000). Her work also appears in *Native Poetry in Canada*. Randy Lundy, a Cree person affiliated with the **BARREN LANDS FIRST NATION**, is an English professor at the First Nations U of Canada in Regina as well as the author of 2 poetry volumes from Coteau Books, *Under the Night Sun* (1999) and *The Gift of the Hawk* (2004). Joanne Arnott, a Métis from Winnipeg, has lived on Canada's West Coast for most of her life. Her publications include 3 volumes of poetry, notably *Wiles of Girlhood* (Press Gang, 1992), for which she won the Gerald Lampert Memorial Award for best first book of Cdn poetry.

While *An Anthology of Canadian Native Literature in English* (Oxford University Press Canada, 1992) posits a canon of Aboriginal literature from across the country, region-specific anthologies often give voice to lesser-known writers by emphasizing their membership in a group. Examples include writers of the Prairies or of the West; women writers; and new writers. *Writing the Circle: Native Women of Western Canada* (NeWest, 1990), *A Shade of Spring: An Anthology of New Native Writers* (7ᵗʰ Generation, 1998),

and *Sky Woman* (Theytus, 2005) are among these. *Who Put Custer's Bloomers on the Pony? A Collection of Native Words* appeared in 1998 from Bearpaw Publishing at **BRANDON U**; though small, Bearpaw has proven itself committed to promoting Aboriginal voices and issues. In Winnipeg, Aboriginal and especially Métis writers get support from Pemmican Publications, which, for example, published collections by Métis poets Leonard Carriere (*White Eagle Speaks*, 2000) and Derek Garson (*mere observations*, 2002). Pemmican also issued *The 'Tobanz* (2003), a novel about an Aboriginal **HOCKEY** team by **ST. LAURENT**'s Edgar Danny Desjarlais. In general, however, Pemmican focuses on non-fiction and on children's books.

An Aboriginal classic

Among Aboriginal playwrights from MB, Tomson Highway and Ian Ross are the most well-known. Highway, from the **BARREN LANDS CREE NATION** in northern MB, today divides his time, after many years of residence in Toronto, between Northern ON and southern France. He gained national and international recognition with his play *The Rez Sisters* (1986). His acclaimed debut was followed by other plays/shows, notably the companion piece *Dry Lips Oughta Move to Kapuskasing* (1989). He also published 3 children's books written bilingually in Cree and in English, and his autobiographical novel *Kiss of the Fur Queen* (1998) was nominated for several awards. Ian Ross, from McCreary, is best known for his play *farewel* (1997), which won the Governor General's Award. In 1995, Ross received the John Hirsch Award for Most Promising MB Writer. Like his

more recent play *The Gap* (2001), *farewel* has been translated into Cree. Besides his work as a playwright, Ross is known to Manitobans as "Joe from Winnipeg." His weekly commentaries on CBC Radio One were published in 1998 (*Joe from Winnipeg*) and in 2004 (*Joe from Winnipeg: All My Best*). He is also the director of the Aboriginal theatre group *Red Roots*. Regarding theatre, Aboriginal performer, playwright, and educator. ● RENATE EIGENBROD

ABORTION. From the 1970s to the early 2000s, MB was at the forefront of the Cdn debate to decriminalize abortion. Featuring such big personalities as Dr. Henry Morgentaler and **JOE BOROWSKI**, the provincial argument between pro-life and pro-choice forces took the form of legal challenges, private clinics and dramatic demonstrations.

Canada's first Criminal Code deemed abortion illegal. However, in 1969, the federal govt allowed abortions in hospitals under special circumstances. Abortion anywhere else was still illegal. So women hoping to terminate an unplanned pregnancy in a hospital setting were required to obtain permission for the procedure from a "therapeutic abortion committee." The complicated process kept the number of abortions conducted in MB down. Montreal-based physician and abortion activist Henry Morgentaler challenged the Criminal Code provisions governing abortions repeatedly during the 1970s by opening a series of free-standing clinics across Canada. In May 1983, he opened such an abortion clinic in Winnipeg. The clinic was raided twice by police, with staff charged and equipment seized. But it stubbornly continued with business, offering abortions to women who were prepared to pay. In those days, former NDP MLA Joe Borowski devoted much of his time and energy to fighting Morgentaler and the pro-choice movement. In 1981, he went on a hunger strike to protest the absence of fetal rights in the Charter of Rights and Freedoms. Throughout the 1980s, he would clash frequently with Morgentaler, as in 1983 when the 2 engaged in heated debates at the **U OF W** and CJOB, over the opening of Morgentaler's clinic.

In Jan 1988, Morgentaler and Borowski's positions came head-to-head in a court of law. In the landmark case, the Supreme Court of Canada ruled existing abortion laws were unconstitutional. But because Parliament did not offer replacement legislation, Canada was effectively left in a legal vacuum when it came to abortion. Privately-paid abortion procedures continued to take place at Morgentaler's Winnipeg clinic while pro-life protestors demonstrated outside. Morgentaler continued to argue that the MB govt should pay for services at his clinic. Two anonymous women filed a lawsuit in a MB court requesting compensation for their procedures at the clinic. In late 2004, a Court of Queen's Bench judge agreed, ruling the province's funding system violated Canada's Charter of Rights and Freedoms by requiring women pay for a medically necessary procedure.

Also in 2004, Morgentaer sold his clinic to a group of women who pledged to run it as a non-profit centre called "Jane's Clinic." With the new proviso that all abortions would be paid for by the govt, Jane's Clinic became part of the Women's Health Clinic, funded by the Winnipeg Regional Health Authority. Although abortion continued to be a controversial issue, in the early 2000s, it became more routine. Statistics from MB Health showed 3670 abortions took place in 2003, nearly 15 % of live births. ● GPP

ADAMSON, Arthur, artist, poet, critic, scholar (b Jan 8, 1926, WINNIPEG) has made significant contributions to the MB art scene through his many exhibition reviews and critical articles on the visual arts in the **WINNIPEG FREE PRESS** and *Arts Manitoba* and with his own artistic output. A painter and printmaker, his work is spiritual, drawing from Biblical and mythological sources. Solidly rooted in his place, it portrays the landscape, its rhythms, light and space. Specific themes recur throughout his work, in all media, including acrylic, watercolour, ink, pencil, woodcuts and etchings. *Jacob and the Angel*, *Lazarus*, and *The Expulsion from the Garden* series each deal with the human experience and confrontation with others and with the inner self. Adamson studied fine art at the School of Art at the **U OF M** when he was teaching in the English dept. In 1957, he went to Emma Lake where he worked with members of the Regina 5. Throughout his artistic career, Adamson has been interested in process, technique, colour, texture and the strength of line. The resulting work is rich in spirituality, expressive in its message, and strong in its presentation. ● PATRICIA BOVEY

Raising of Lazarus by Arthur Adamson

ADOPTION in MB is the process whereby a child becomes legally and permanently cared for by a single adult, common-law partners, or a husband and wife who are not the biological parents of the child. The legislation outlining this process is the *Adoption Act* (1997). The act addresses 6 types of adoptions (called divisions), such as the adoption of a permanent ward, private adoption, and intercountry adoption.

The adoption process was first codified in the 1922 *Child Welfare Act*. Prior to that, adoption was based on legal principles derived from property arrangements. Attitudes have changed in this regard. One of these changes pertains to adoption and Aboriginal people.

Until the 1970s, little thought was given to the effects of adopting Aboriginal children into white, middle-class homes. Families who in no way shared their culture of origin regularly adopted children from First Peoples communities. In response to growing criticism from First Nations people in the 1970s, Judge Edwin Kimelman was asked to conduct a review of this adoption practice and other approaches to the placement of Aboriginal children. His report, *No Quiet Place* (1985), was scathingly critical of these cross-cultural placement practices, which he described as a form of "cultural genocide." In response to the report, the MB govt halted out-of-province adoptions and established requirements that child welfare agencies consult Aboriginal communities about such placements. In the 1980s, First Nations were given authority to develop their own child welfare agencies on-reserve. Returning children adopted outside of the culture to their home communities has been a high priority for these agencies.

Attitudinal shifts have also affected other aspects of adoption services. Unmarried pregnant women are no longer stigmatized, and many choose to keep their babies. There are more adoptive applicants than there are children available for adoption, especially since the advent of birth control and legal abortion. The voice of the biological father in these circumstances may also be heard, especially if his choices are different than the mother's. In private adoption, the parent(s) of the child exercise more choice in the selection of the adoptive parents. In MB, this process is codified in law; it requires a home study of prospective adoptive parents and approval by the court. Private adoption agencies began providing specialized adoption services in MB in the early 1990s, and these participate with the birth mother in the selection of the adoptive parents. Typically, private adoptions involve newborn babies and thus they are a popular alternative to the adoption of a permanent ward. Even so, the number of private adoptions in MB is relatively low. Between 1995 and 2005, the largest private adoption agency in MB, Adoption Options, placed an average of only 22 children per year.

Nevertheless, this number is higher than the number of private adoptions facilitated through child welfare agencies. These agencies place more emphasis on the adoption of older children (Division 1 adoption), many with special physical or emotional needs, and there is some public financial support for eligible adoptive parents of special-needs children. Few infants are available for adoption in MB, so international adoptions (Division 3 adoptions) have become popular. *The Intercountry Adoption Act,* commonly known as the "Hague Convention," is the international convention that guides international adoption. All costs associated with this process are borne by the adoptive parents.

Another shift in attitude relates to the relationship between the birth family and the adoptive parents. It is more common today that the birth mother, older birth siblings, grandparents, and sometimes the birth father maintain contact and some level of involvement with the adoptive parents and the child. This type of contact reflects what is described as an "open adoption." Open adoptions, which can be contrasted with "closed adoptions" (where the identity of one party is not disclosed to the other), have become more common since the 1980s. MB has legislation that supports openness in adoption, providing all parties agree. Children placed under closed adoption procedures knew nothing about their birth parents or other birth siblings. MB legislation and policy now provide for post-adoption services whereby grown adopted persons can be supported in actively searching for their birth families. If all parties agree, contact between the adult adoptee and birth family members can occur.
● DENNIS SCHELLENBERG/BRAD MCKENZIE

AEROSPACE in MB has roots that extend back to the turn of the 20th century, when entrepreneurs such as the Macdonald Brothers, Charles Pearce, and William Bickell founded Macdonald Brother Sheet Metal and Standard Machine Works, 2 companies that were later to gain renown as **BRISTOL AEROSPACE** and **STANDARD AERO**. From these modest beginnings, the industry has evolved into a state-of-the-art, high-tech sector vital to the economic growth of the province. The sector is the largest in western Canada and is home to a diversified range of manufacturing, repair and overhaul, and service firms. Manufactured products include composite aircraft assemblies, advanced alloy turbine engine components, and spacecraft systems. MB firms specialize in

SCISAT small satellite, manufactured by Bristol in Winnipeg

the repair and overhaul of turbine and reciprocating engines and commercial passenger aircraft. Aerospace services provided by MB companies cover a broad range from the training of military pilots to the integration of spacecraft payloads. In 2004, MB's aerospace industry earned approximately $800 million in revenue, with an estimated 4600 persons directly employed in the industry. Aerospace manufacturing, and repair and overhaul, account for approximately 80% of industry revenues with aerospace training and services providing 20%.

The industry is led by Boeing Canada, Standard Aero, Magellan Aerospace Limited-Winnipeg (Bristol Aerospace), and Air Canada Technical Services. The industry is supported by a large number of small- to medium sized aerospace suppliers including precision machine shops, tool and die makers, precision sheet metal fabricators, plating and coating operations, and electronics

companies. A sophisticated training, education and transportation infrastructure provides further industry support. MB's aerospace industry is intensely export oriented, serving hundreds of companies on every continent.

The Boeing composite manufacturing facility is the largest in NA. The new Composites Innovation Centre, located in Winnipeg near the **U OF M**, supports research, education, and training in the field of advanced composite materials, with applications for aerospace, automotive, civil infrastructure, and other industries. The centre provides access to advanced research tools, including highly sophisticated testing equipment.

Standard Aero Limited is the world's largest independent small-turbine-engine repair and overhaul company. Based in Winnipeg, Standard Aero operates facilities in the US, Europe, and Asia. In Mar 2003, the company opened a new

3700 m² (40,000 ft²) facility to house its new General Electric CF-34 overhaul cell and test facility. Standard Aero's proprietary component re-manufacturing processes allow the company to meet or exceed OEM specifications while reducing customers' direct operating costs.

Bristol Aerospace is the only Canadian company involved in the design and manufacture of small satellites. Bristol was the prime contractor for the design, development, and integration for the science satellite, SCISAT-1, that was successfully launched in August 2003. SCISAT-1 is a Canadian-led mission to help scientists from around the world better understand our ozone layer. Bristol is now designing a generic small satellite bus to meet the future requirements of a range of Canadian Space Agency (CSA) missions. The generic bus will provide low-cost access to space for science, Earth observation, and technology demonstration missions.

Military pilot training is delivered by a Kelowna Flighcraft consortium and 3 Canadian Forces Flying Training School, both located at the Southport Aerospace Centre. Stevenson Aviation and Aerospace Training Centre provides training programs for aircraft maintenance engineers at its $7.4 million Winnipeg facility and a leased facility at the Southport Aerospace Centre. ● GEORGE MANSON/MICHAEL BENNAROCH

AGRICORE UNITED was Canada's largest grain-handling and farm-supplies company. The Winnipeg-based agri-food giant was formed in 2001 with the merger of Agricore (a firm that was itself created in 1998 by the merger of 2 farmer-owned grain co-operatives, Manitoba Pool Elevators and Alberta Wheat Pool), and United Grain Growers, Canada's last farmer-owned grain co-operative. Partially owned by US agri-food giant Archer Daniels Midland, Agricore United provided Cdn grain farmers with a wide range of agricultural services, including grain storage and marketing, crop production products and analysis, livestock feed production, and financial services. Since its formation, the company went through a period of consolidation, with the sale of its Farm Business Communications division in 2003 and the closure of more than half of its Prairie grain elevators. Some of those elevators were subsequently replaced with high-throughput terminals to handle farmers' grain. As of 2003, the company had 75 grain elevators, 6 port terminals, 119 standalone farm service centres and stores, 2743 employees, and 49,000 farmer members. In 2007, SaskPool launched a hostile take-over bid which despite Winnipeg-based James Richardson International Ltd. counter-offer was accepted by shareholders. ● MM

AGRICULTURE IN MANITOBA
By John Morriss

A

Since the 1870s, agriculture has reshaped the landscape of the province and remains one of Manitoba's most important economic sectors. Farming itself accounted for only about 3.5% of MB's GDP in 2005, but for every $1 of net farm income, almost $2 is generated in the overall provincial economy through retail sales of products and services for farmers, handling, marketing, processing, and transportation of the food industry. In MB, 1 job in 11 depends on agricultural production. As well as stimulating local employment, agriculture in MB is directly responsible for thousands of jobs in other parts of Canada.

CHALRES SHILLIDAY

Straw bales waiting for stacking west of La Riviere

HISTORY: Agriculture has a long history in MB – an archaeological site on the bank of the **RED RIVER** near **LOCKPORT** found evidence of corn planted by Aboriginals in ground tilled with sticks and the shoulder blades of **BISON**. In the late 18th century, **HBC** fort master **PETER FIDLER**, who is cited in the Manitoba Agricultural Hall of Fame as "Manitoba's Johnny Appleseed," planted gardens in company forts across the West. **LORD SELKIRK**'s settlers, who arrived at the **RED RIVER SETTLEMENT** in 1812, were the earliest of what was to become a wave of immigrant farmers. That wave began in earnest with the Homestead Act of 1872, which allowed prospective farmers to claim, for a $10 fee, 160 ac (65 ha) on condition that they reside on the land for a least 6 months of the year, build a permanent residence, and break 40 ac (16 ha) over 3 years. This was part of an aggressive policy by the federal govt and the **RAILWAYS** to settle western Canada, a policy that successfully attracted thousands of immigrants from a number of countries. The particularly diverse ethnic mix in MB may explain 1 of the main modern attributes of the provincial farm economy. Immigrants from different regions carried on and adapted their traditions and specialties – Anglo Saxons with cattle farming, **Mennonites** and **Germans** with hog farming, **Icelanders** with sheep (*see* **Livestock, Alternative**), and Eastern Europeans with **Sunflowers, Ukrainian** cereal strains, and other specialty crops, which for a time included **Hemp** for rope and cooking oil. The 1st export of Prairie **Grain** was in 1876, when 857 bushels (23,300 kg) of **Wheat** left Winnipeg by steamer to eastern Canada via Minneapolis. The variety was Red Fife, the earliest of a series of high-quality wheats for which western Canada and particularly MB was to become famous worldwide. In 1885, Prairie wheat grades were officially designated as "Manitoba Hard" and later "Manitoba Northern," and while this was changed to "Canada Western Red Spring" in 1970, many buyers still refer to Cdn spring wheat as "Manitoba" wheat.

CLIMATE AND SOIL: According to StatsCan, 18.8 million ac (7.6 million ha) of land in MB was used for farming in 2001. That is about half of the land in the province judged to have agricultural potential. However, there are severe challenges to farming in some parts of the province. Crops need 3 basic ingredients to grow – sunlight, water, and soil. MB's relatively short frost-free period is balanced by long summer days with plenty of sunlight, making for vigorous growth. MB has higher rainfall than other parts of the Prairies, such as S Saskatchewan, but there are regional variations, with the highest moisture normally found in the SE and N **Interlake** and drier areas in the W and SW. Water is a varying challenge for MB farmers. Periodic droughts can cut yields sharply. The most famous such shortage was in the "Dirty '30s," but there also were severe droughts in 1961 and during the 1980s. On the other hand, excess moisture, even **Floods**, is also often a problem. Since many areas are so flat, water from excess rain or heavy spring melts can remain on fields for some time, delaying seeding or harvesting or causing crop damage during the growing season. Manitoba soils vary widely. Heavy black clay soils in the Red River Valley allow high yields of a variety of crops. Farther W, there are lighter-coloured and -textured soils, including sandy soils, which are ideal for producing potatoes. Farther N in the Interlake, soils are more thin and light, and there are many stones left by melting of glaciers during the last Ice Age (*see* **Glaciation**). These soils are generally not cultivated, but are rather left in permanent hayfields or pasture for the area's large cattle population. Prairie soils are susceptible to erosion, especially when tilled and subject to drought and high winds, or to water from heavy rainfall runoff. Like other provinces, MB saw massive dust storms during the dry years of the 1930s. These were largely due to the practice of summerfallow – leaving land unseeded for a year and tilling it to control weeds and conserve moisture. This prompted development of tillage equipment that would cut off or uproot weeds but leave crop residue on top of the soil to control erosion. It was once common for farmers to leave half their cropland in summerfallow but it now makes up only about 5% of MB's crop area. Because

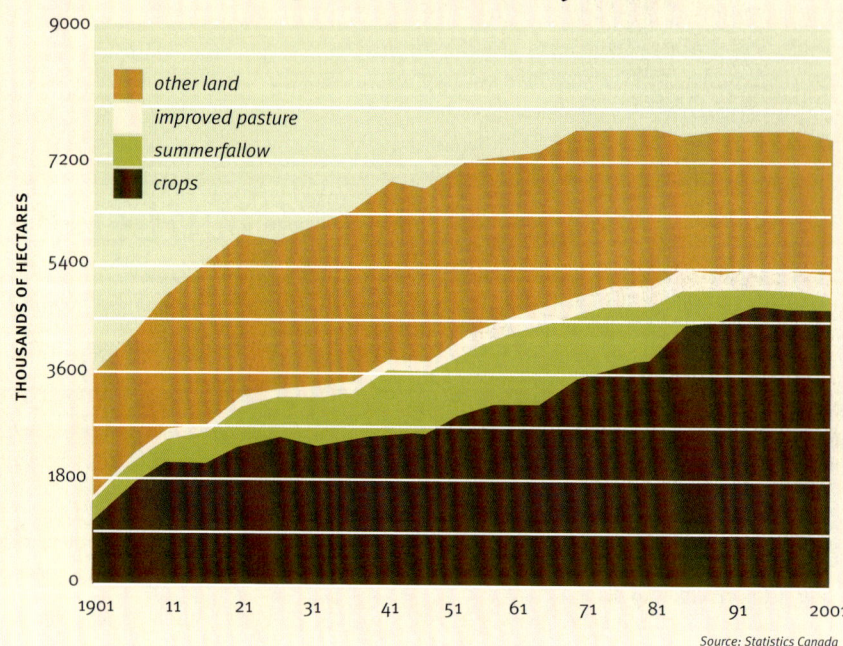

Agricultural Land Use, 1901-2001

- other land
- improved pasture
- summerfallow
- crops

THOUSANDS OF HECTARES

Source: Statistics Canada

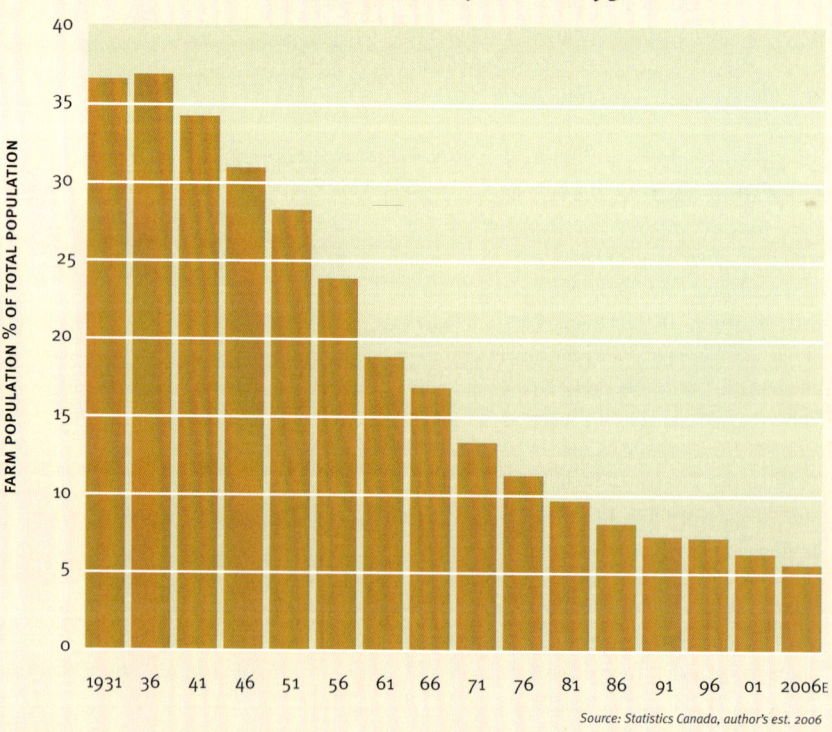

Manitoba's Farm Population: Percentage of Total Population, 1931-2006E

FARM POPULATION % OF TOTAL POPULATION

Source: Statistics Canada, author's est. 2006

weeds can now be controlled by herbicides, many fields are now "minimum-till," with only 1 cultivation done at the same time as seeding, or "zero-till," in which crops are seeded into last year's standing stubble.

CROPS: Most of the world's cereal and oilseed crops are "winter" crops, planted in the fall and growing briefly until going into dormancy until spring. Other than rye, which today is a relatively small crop, these varieties have not been hardy enough to survive a MB winter, so most crops in the province are seeded in spring. However, plant breeders have developed hardy winter wheat varieties, and their area has been increasing. Wheat, once "king" of the Prairies, is now less dominant but is still

Harvesting wheat in 1928

Value of Farm Production in Manitoba by Commodity, 2004

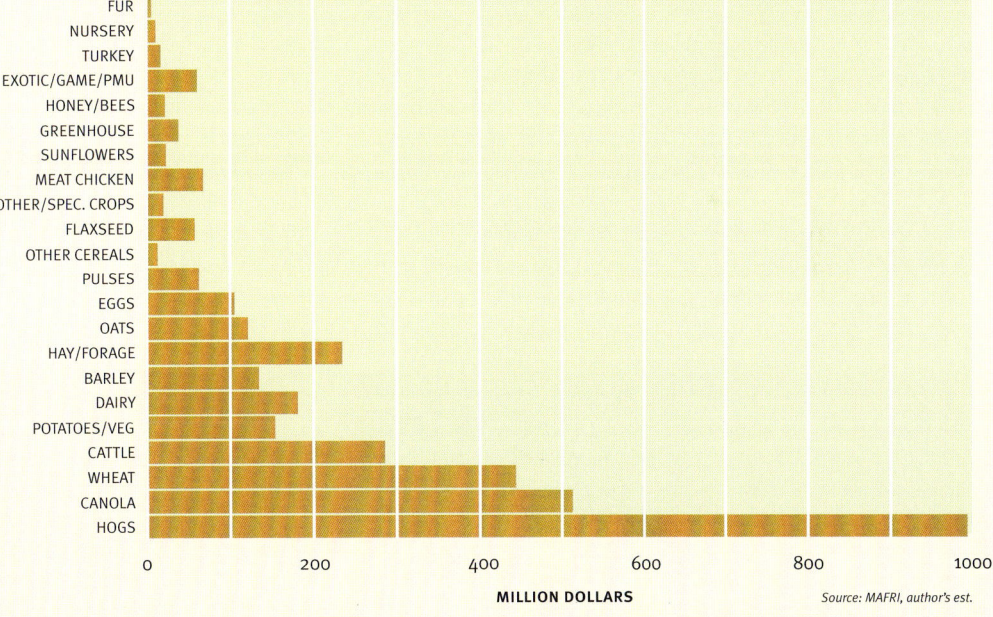

MILLION DOLLARS

Source: MAFRI, author's est.

A

the largest crop in MB by area, making up 25-30% of the 5.3 million ha (13 million ac) seeded to annual crops. The area seeded to **CANOLA** is now almost as large as wheat, but canola can sell at double the price of wheat, so the total crop value is higher. Barley, used for livestock feed and to make malt for brewing, makes up 8-10% of the annual crop area in MB, followed by oats, which is used for human food and livestock feed. MB farmers have traditionally produced smaller amounts of a wide range of "special" crops, such as edible beans, sunflowers, dry peas, and potatoes. In 2005, MB was the largest dry bean and faba bean producer in Canada. It was also the largest producer of sunflower seeds and buckwheat.

Development of shorter-season varieties of soybeans and corn have made them possible in the province, especially in the Red River Valley.

LIVESTOCK: By the 21st century, livestock – mainly hogs and **BEEF CATTLE** – generated more income than crops in MB. In 2002, the year before statistics were affected by an extended closure of the US border to live cattle due to a case of BSE (bovine spongiform encephalopathy) in AB, cash receipts were $715.4 million for hogs and $555.7 million for cattle. MB farmers also produce **DAIRY** products and **POULTRY**, mainly for the local market, most of which is sold through marketing boards. Sheep production is relatively small but growing. Grazing animals have always been part of the environment on the Cdn Prairies. Before settlement, bison, along with fire, recycled nutrients back to the soil and were part of a selection process to maintain diversity of the grasses and other native plants which grew so abundantly. Today, cattle and sheep have taken over that role, especially on lower-quality land that would be prone to erosion if

it were cultivated for crop production. MB is the country's 3rd largest beef producer. If left in native hay, or seeded to domestic perennial forage crops such as alfalfa, the land is protected from wind or water erosion. In recent years, many cattle producers have been much more scientific in their management, in effect attempting to recreate conditions when bison roamed the Prairies. Using "cross fencing" or moveable electric fences, pastures are divided into smaller parcels and animals are moved regularly to that a single area is not overgrazed, and given time to rest and regenerate new growth. Livestock are also fed grain, either grown specifically for feeding or lower-quality grain damaged by disease or excess rain during harvest, and which would not be desirable for human consumption. Cattle are often fed on pasture or hay for the 1st year or so of life, and then finished on grain until they reach slaughter weight. This usually results in more tender meat, but more producers are becoming interested in finishing completely on pasture or hay. By selecting the right

Hogs ready for processing.

A

breeds or crosses of different breeds, and by aging meat longer before sale, it is also possible to produce tender beef. Grass-fed beef has also been demonstrated to have higher content of Conjugated Linoleic Acid (CLA) which has benefits in preventing cancer and heart disease.

Winnipeg was once a large meat packing centre, with large packers such as Canada Packers, Swifts and Burns located near the former Winnipeg Livestock Yards in St. Boniface. These closed during the 1970s, as large packers, with the assistance of the AB govt, opened large plants in southern AB, where there are large concentrations of feedlots where cattle are fed to slaughter weight. MB became mostly a "cow-calf" industry, shipping calves for finishing to AB or the US. However, the closed US border due to BSE from 2003-2005 renewed efforts to built cattle slaughter plants in MB. In 2006, the MB govt established a Cattle Enhancement Council to collect voluntary levies on cattle sales and match them with govt funds to assist in the establishment of new plants. While MB's cattle feeding and processing industry declined during the 1970s and 1980s, the **Pork Industry** grew dramatically. High US and European subsidies on feed grain exports during the late 1980s and early 1990s made it unprofitable to export barley and feed wheat, and this was compounded by the end of the **Crow Freight Rate** subsidy in 1995. In 2005, MB was Canada's largest pig producer (more than 8.8 million head) and the largest pig exporter (148 million head).

FARM CHARACTERISTICS: There were about 21,000 farms in MB as of the 2001 Census, of which about half are considered full commercial operations with annual sales of over $50,000. Farm numbers peaked in the early 1940s and have declined since, though there are signs the trend is stabilizing. Almost 390,000 people lived in rural areas in 1946 – the last year that the number of rural residents would exceed urban residents. Farms have grown larger as farmers have sought economies of scale to offset low margins, especially in grain production. Larger and more efficient modern machinery also allowed a single operator to seed and harvest crops much more quickly. The average farm size in 2001 was about 360 ha (890 ac), but many grain and oilseed farms were 2000 ha (5000 ac) or larger. Farmers themselves own about 60% of farmland, but many rent land. Almost all farms remain family-operated. Operations range from "straight grain" to "straight livestock" with a range of "mixed" operations

in between, where farmers raise crops and 1 or more species of livestock. MB farms are among the most diversified on the North American Prairies: many farmers grow 5 or more crops each year. This helps diversify income and allows "rotation" of different crops on a field every year, which suppresses a buildup of insects or disease and halts nutrient depletion. Almost half of farmers rely on off-farm jobs to supplement their income. The average age of MB farmers has increased – in 2001, nearly 54% were between 35 and 54 years old and 33% were 55 and over. The average age was 48.8 years. In 2005, it was estimated that nationally, retirement or death of farmers would require sale of about $50 billion in farm assets over the next 15 years. This makes it a challenge to pass family farms to the next generation – older farmers need to sell to have enough to generate their retirement income, but raising new capital can be difficult for younger farmers entering a low-margin industry.

FUTURE: Diversity in MB agriculture has helped the province weather many storms throughout its history, but farmers continue to face many challenges, particularly in crop farming. Expectations that new trade agreements would lead to lower competitor subsidies and higher world prices have not been met. The loss of the Crow rate has reduced income for grain producers, and the benefits of the loss of the Crow for livestock producers are not as high as expected. Crop farmers have responded by growing higher-value crops rather than more low-price feed grain, and MB hog producers have responded by importing large amounts of subsidized US corn and soybeans. Relatively unsubsidized competitors, especially in Latin America and Eastern Europe, have increased production and exports. World grain markets, once sensitive to threats of short supply, have tended to expect supplies to be available from new exporters. Prices have not risen to the high levels of the "World Food Crisis" of the 1970s, even when supplies relative to demand have been tighter. MB farmers, as well as others in Canada, have been responding by continuing to look for higher-value crops, as well as by trying to cut production costs. One promising area for MB is more efficiency in beef cattle production, where modern forage and animal-management practices are showing dramatic improvements with relatively low capital investment. Farmers throughout Canada have also been challenging govts to provide support systems similar to their competitors, and are looking at ways to capture more of the retail food dollar. •

AIKINS, Sir James Albert Manning, lawyer, politician, lt gov (b Dec 10, 1851, Grahamsville, Peel Cty., Canada West [ON]; d March 1, 1929, **Winnipeg**). The son of James Cox Aikins, a federal Cabinet minister (1869-73, 1878-82) and lt gov of MB (1882-88) Aikins was educated at Upper Canada College and at the U of Toronto, graduating with a BA (1875) and LLB (1878). Aikins was called to the Law Society of Upper Canada in 1878 but moved shortly thereafter to MB with his father. Aikins began practising law in Winnipeg in Feb 1879, initially with the Department of Justice, later becoming the lawyer for the **CPR's** western department (1881-1911), and a QC in 1884. The founder of the oldest law firm in MB – now Aikins, MacAulay and Thorvaldson – Aikins was also bursar of the **U of M**, and co-founded a YMCA reading room. In 1900, shortly after becoming govt counsel and amid prompting by **Reform**-minded groups, he drafted the *Temperance Act* for the govt of Sir **Hugh John Macdonald**. In 1910, he helped found the Manitoba Bar Association and was its first president (1910-16). Aikins was knighted in 1914 for his work as a lawyer, the same year that he helped reorganize the Canadian Bar Association, of which he was president until 1923. Like his father, Aikins entered federal politics, becoming Conservative MP for **Brandon** in 1911, a constituency held the 4 previous elections by Liberal Sir **Clifford Sifton**, with whom Aikins had studied law. Aikins left his seat after Sir **Rodmond Roblin**'s govt was brought down by scandal and the Conservative Party of Manitoba needed a new leader. Aikins became that party's leader 1915-16, but the taint of scandal was too great, and the **Liberal Party** under **T. C. Norris** held on to power for years. Conservative PM Sir

Robert Laird Borden chose Aikins as lt gov of MB in 1916, an office to which he was reappointed in 1921. On Feb 25, 1929, Aikins was to throw a celebratory banquet for 450 guests to commemorate his 50 years at the Bar. He suffered a heart attack just before the event, and died a week later. Aikins's former house at Winnipeg's 630 Westminster Ave now houses Balmoral Hall School. ● MD

ALCOCK, Reginald B. "Reg," politician (b Apr 16, 1948, **Winnipeg**). After attaining his Master's Degree in Public Administration at Harvard U, Alcock began working as an organizer for the MB **Liberal Party** in the early 1980s. He was then director of MB Child and Family Services from 1983-85 and was the impetus behind changing the province's child protection legislation, making MB the first province in Canada to introduce official protocols to deal with instances of child sex abuse. As a member of the MB legislature for Osborne from 1988-1993, he acted as official Opposition house leader and finance critic. He won the federal Liberal nomination for Winnipeg South in 1993 and entered Parliament as a backbencher. Known for his interest in technology, Alcock was the first MP to launch a website. In 1995, he was appointed to the standing committee on foreign affairs and international trade and in 1997 was chair of the standing committee on transport. He went on to serve as parliamentary secretary to the president of the Queen's privy council for Canada and to the minister of intergovernmental affairs. Although he had supported Jean Chretien's bid for prime minister, Alcock was repeatedly passed over by Chretien for a cabinet post. He shifted his allegiances to Paul Martin and finally earned a cabinet post when Martin became prime minister in 2003. As president of the treasury board, minister responsible for the **Canadian Wheat Board** and political minister for MB, Alcock sat in the inner circle of cabinet. He was key in co-ordinating the govt's response to the sponsorship scandal in which monies were misappropriated by QC bureaucrats and agencies. Despite his acknowledged political savvy, Alcock lost his seat in the 2006 election to newcomer **Rod Bruinooge**. In Jan 2007, he took on a position as an executive in residence at the I.H. **Asper** School of Business at the **U of M**. ● RUTH DEGRAVES

ALDERFLY is an insect with a soft body, and 2 pairs of brown wings of similar shape and with numerous prominent veins, and held tent-like over the body at rest. There is only 1 species of alderfly in MB (*Sialis vagans*), but it is found abundantly in and near rivers and lake shores,

where the adults emerge in large numbers from land-based, over-wintering pupae. The adult has chewing mouthparts, but does not feed, living for only a few days. Mating occurs during nightly flights in May and June, and the female lays up to 900 orange eggs in clusters on vegetation above water, which hatch in a few weeks, swallow a bubble of air, and then drop into the water, where they drift in the current before settling to the bottom. The gilled aquatic larvae develop over 2-3 years, hiding under rocks and amid the bottom debris, and preying on insects, worms and other small creatures. All stages of alderflies are keenly sought after by fish, frogs and shorebirds. There about 25 species in Canada, 300 worldwide. Originating 250 mya (Permian period), alderflies and related snakeflies are the earliest insects to have developed a pupal stage. ● TDG, REW

ALDOUS, George Galt, BGen, soldier, (b Mar 26, 1920, **Winnipeg**; d Jan 29, 2005, Winnipeg) began his military service as a gunner with the Royal Cdn Artillery in 1941. He served in Europe during WWII, earning a Military Cross for valour in action. He was promoted from the ranks to Lt with the **Royal Winnipeg Rifles** in 1944. His promotion at the age of 43 to the rank of BGen made him one of the youngest to attain the army's top militia rank. Although he retired from the reserves in 1965, his military training led to leadership roles with the Cub Scouts, the Cdn Corps of Commissionaires, and the Royal Cdn Army Cadets. He devoted years of voluntary service with the Cdn National Institute for the Blind in 1982, winning the Cdn Volunteer Award in 1994, and in 2004, the Queen's Golden Jubilee Medal. ● AJL

ALIEN QUESTION. This controversy arose during and after WWI over the treatment of alien residents of Canada who had been born within the territory of the country's enemies, chiefly **Germans** and Austro-Hungarians. Among the huge stream of immigrants to MB before the war were many thousands from central and eastern Europe. **Immigration** of these people had been criticized on many grounds, chiefly that they could not easily assimilate into Cdn life; that they brought radical political ideas with them; and that they took away jobs from Cdn-born workers in tight labour markets. Their status in Canada had always been unclear because they were not British, but it did not occur to critics that these newcomers might prove a particular problem in wartime.

Nevertheless, as of 1914, over 60,000 Manitobans had been born within the boundaries of

Sir James Albert Manning Aikins, ca 1920

These children at Winnipeg's Aberdeen School in 1938 represented 21 nationalities.

A

the nations Canada was fighting, about 25,000 of whom were in Winnipeg. The 2 chief national groups were those born in Germany and those born in what is now Ukraine, which in 1914 was part of the Austro-Hungarian Empire. With the beginning of WWI, these people suddenly became "enemy aliens," people whose native state was at war with Canada. Most were not so much disloyal as suspected of potential disloyalty by patriots.

Developing policies, both official and unofficial, for dealing with the presence of these aliens was no easy matter. The problem was increased when large numbers of aliens abandoned the countryside and moved to the cities, where work might be easier to find. Officially, the federal govt responded to the wartime situation in 1914 by registering all enemy aliens with the police under the provisions of the Defence of the Realm Act (DORA). Many aliens responded by moving to the US, which did not join WWI until 1917. Eventually, the federal govt interned 8579 enemy-alien residents whom it regarded as dangerous in about 25 prison camps across Canada. Of these prisoners, 2009 were Germans and 5954 were Austro-Hungarians, mainly Ukrainian. Most were males, but a handful of women and children chose voluntarily to accompany their husbands and fathers into the camps. These internments paid little attention to the civil liberties of those involved, and would provide a political grievance for those arrested and their descendants – especially in the Ukrainian community – that would be harboured for the remainder of the 20th century.

In 1917, the federal govt also disenfranchised enemy alien voters, and in 1918, it suppressed the nation's foreign-language press. In MB, from 1914 onward, many aliens were dismissed from their jobs, and throughout the war, hostility was exhibited by the majority population, especially against **Ukrainians**. Ukrainian radicals were blamed for stirring up labour unrest, including the **Winnipeg General Strike** in 1919. Returning troops were especially active in calling for the deportation of aliens, since they saw them as standing in the ways of their own employment.

To ease the tension, the MB govt created an Alien Investigation Board early in 1919. Registration cards were issued only to those aliens who had been loyal during the war, based on the testimony of 2 reliable witnesses. Some criticized the AIB's hearings as being kangaroo courts, but over 3000 cases were processed before the board was phased out in summer 1919. The labour unrest of the spring of 1919 turned everyone's attention to the "radical alien," and the federal govt stepped in, raiding suspected radical centres in early July, seizing "incriminating" material, and arresting a number of people. Many were later deported.

The agitation against "enemy aliens" and especially "radical aliens" eventually died down, but it would scar MB's Ukrainian community for generations and provided an example of how civil liberties could easily be trampled upon in the course of wartime hysteria. ● J. M. BUMSTED

ALL PEOPLE'S MISSION provided for many of the immigrant poor of **Winnipeg**'s **North End**. It began in 1899 as a **Methodist** house run by Dollie McGuire, who taught Sunday school to **Immigrant** children. Though it was originally meant to promote the Protestant faith, the mission became focused on improving living conditions of the poor when **J. S. Woodsworth** became superintendent in 1907. The mission ran programs for children, including English and home economics classes. Woodsworth ran the mission until 1913, during which time he wrote *Stranger within Our Gates*, arguing that the success of immigrants depended on their ability to assimilate into mainstream **English** Protestant culture. The mission closed following Woodsworth's resignation, when funds for the program became limited with the outbreak of WWI. ● MD

ALLEN, Ralph, journalist, editor, writer (b Aug 25, 1913, **Winnipeg**; d Dec 2, 1966, Toronto). Born in Winnipeg, Allen was raised in Oxbow, SK, and began his journalism career as a sportswriter at the **Winnipeg Tribune**. He moved to Toronto and the *Globe and Mail* in 1938, where he was a war correspondent in Europe during WWII. Shortly after, Allen became editor of *Maclean's*, shepherding it through what were arguably its best years. Among the magazine's writers at the time were Pierre Berton, June Callwood, Peter Gzowski and Peter C. Newman. In fact, Allen "discovered" Gzowski, then a reporter in Moose Jaw, later a famed CBC Radio broadcaster. Allen is also credited with bringing high-calibre, well-crafted sports stories to the national magazine. Allen left *Maclean's* in 1959 and wrote sports articles for the *Toronto Telegram*. He drew on his experience as a war correspondent for 3 of his 5 novels, though his most famous was a satire of CBC, *The Chartered Libertine* (Macmillan, 1954). He also wrote several books of popular history, including *Ordeal by Fire: Canada 1910-1945* (Doubleday, 1961). His essay collection, *The Man from Oxbow: The Best of Ralph Allen* (McClelland & Stewart, 1967), appeared posthumously. ● AJL

ALLOWAY, William Forbes, entrepreneur, banker, philanthropist, (b August 20, 1852, Queen's County, Ireland; d February 2, 1930, Winnipeg). An immigrant to Canada at age 3, William Forbes Alloway lived with his family in Hamilton and Montreal before going west in 1870 as a young private in Col. Garnet Wolseley's expedition to the **Red River Settlement**. Alloway left the garrison force the next year, but remained in Manitoba and established a cigar and tobacco shop in Winnipeg. Soon after, he entered into the transport business, at one time owning and operating 6,000 Red River carts in a venture that stretched to Minnesota and Edmonton. Alloway's business interests over his lifetime were both many and varied; he operated a ferry over the **Assiniboine River** at Main Street, was a partner in Winnipeg's first flour mill, and was an amateur veterinarian who negotiated government purchases of horses. He was also a member

William Forbes Alloway

of Manitoba's first police force, served on Winnipeg's city council and was director of the Winnipeg General Hospital, in addition to his support of several other charitable institutions. In 1878, Alloway married Elizabeth McLaren, a member of a prominent Ottawa family. The Alloways lived on Assiniboine Ave., in a home known as "The Derries," and had one child, who died in early infancy. In 1879, Alloway, his younger brother Charles Valentine and a partner named Henry Thomson Champion, established Alloway and Champion Ltd., a private bank. The bank eventually had two Winnipeg locations: 362 and 667 Main Street, and a branch in **Portage la Prairie**. Specializing in services for immigrants and employing staff who could write and speak a number of languages, Alloway and Champion thrived. It competed with 18 chartered banks in the city and became one of the largest private banks in western Canada. In 1919, after Champion's death, the bank was sold to the Canadian Bank of Commerce. In 1921, Alloway established The **Winnipeg Foundation**, with a personal gift of $100,000, to provide perpetual support for the community in which he had prospered. During their lifetimes and through their estates, the Alloways contributed more than $2 million to the Foundation. The first community foundation in Canada, The Winnipeg Foundation continues to be a legacy to Alloway's vision and commitment. Today its work is felt throughout Winnipeg and the Foundation has distributed more than $175 million to charitable projects over its history.
● RICHARD FROST

ALTAMONT, pop 491, is an unincorporated community 110 km WSW of Winnipeg and 120 km ESE of Brandon. Originally founded as Musselboro in 1885, the name was changed to Alta in 1891 and to Altamont in 1894. It is thought the original name was in honour of the first postmaster, H. Mussel. The current town name means "top of the hill" in French. The area was immortalized in Gabrielle Roy's novel *The Road Past Altamont*. In the 21st century, the economy primarily centres on services for surrounding farms. ● GPP

ALTONA, pop 3600, is a town 100 km SSW of Winnipeg and 10 km N of the US border. Altona's diverse economy is supported by agriculture, printing, manufacturing, communications, and retail. Named after a NW German town of the same name, Altona was first settled in the 1870s by German-speaking Mennonites escaping persecution in E Europe. Today, Altona is a major service centre in southern MB, serving the needs of about 14,000 rural and town residents. Altona's largest employer is **Friesens** Printers. The community is also home to national headquarters of Red River Mutual Insurance and Golden West Broadcasting. The town was referenced in the *Guinness Book of World Records* for completing the largest painting on an easel. The giant replica of Vincent Van Gogh's *Sunflowers* is a town landmark. The replica was completed using 24 sheets of ¾-in (1.9 cm) plywood laminated to form the canvas and mounted on a 12,247 kg, 2316 cm

A giant relica of Van Gogh's *Sunflowers* greets visitors to Altona.

3-legged easel. Known as the "Sunflower Capital of Canada" and host to the annual Sunflower Festival, the choice of painting was fitting. ● GPP

AMABILE, George, educator, poet (b May 29, 1936, Jersey City, NJ). Joining the Faculty of English at the U of M as a lecturer in 1963, Amabile became a full professor in 1987. In 1968-69, he served a term as visiting writer-in-residence at the U of BC, and in 2000-2001 as writer-in-residence at the Winnipeg Centennial Library. He has published *Blood Ties* (1972), *Open Country* (1976), *Flower and Song* (1977), *Ideas of Shelter* (1981), *The Presence of Fire* (1982), *Four of a Kind* (1984), *Rumours of Paradise/Rumours of War* (1995), and he co-edited an anthology of poems about **Louis Riel** entitled *No Feather No Ink (1985)*. His work has appeared in anthologies and periodicals, and he has read at the **Manitoba Theatre Centre**, on radio and television, and at the 1976 Olympic Games in Montréal. Co-founder and editor of *The Far Point* and editor of *Northern Light*, he has edited *The Ivory Tower* and *The Penny Paper*. He is a director of the Canadian Periodical Publishers' Association and a member of the Western Canadian Publishers' Association, and has served on an artists' advisory committee to the Ministry of Tourism and Culture. Amabile is also known as a sympathetic mentor to several generations of young poets in MB.
● MILDRED GUTKIN

AMARANTH, pop 150, a community 110 km SE of **Dauphin**, near the W shore of **Lake Manitoba**. The local economy depends mainly on building trades and on servicing the local agricultural and fishing industries. Amaranth is named after the origin of one of its earliest settlers, Robert Johnson, of Amaranth Township, ON. The post office opened in 1911. It was also a **CNR** point. In May 1958, Amaranth was hit by a major tornado. ● GPP

AMBER is fossilized resin produced many millions of years ago by coniferous trees and served to thwart the attack of wood and bark feeding beetles and other insects. Much of what is known about the rich fossil history of insects during the Cretaceous Period (145-65 mya) derives from amber found in a number of sites in western NA, with one of the 3 main sites being Cedar lake, MB. This amber, aged 70 to 80 mya, is found on the beaches of Cedar Lake and was first described by J.B. Tyrrell in 1893. He estimated that 600 metric tons of amber were present in a single beach. Remarkably, the small, rounded pieces of amber presumably arrived in Cedar Lake after they were first eroded from coal seams (Foremost Formation) exposed near Medicine Hat,

AB, and transported down the Saskatchewan River system. The resin was produced from an extinct species of tree in the family Taxodiaceae (which includes redwoods, cedars and bald cypresses). Cedar Lake amber has exceptional clarity, revealing in great detail the structures (legs, antennae, wings, and eyes) of larval and adult insect life of the time. Represented in Cdn amber are over 150 species of hexapods (insects and several primitive types of arthropods with six pairs of legs) in 17 orders and 80 families, and many more species will be discovered in future finds. In greatest abundance are aphids, flies, midges, bugs, beetles, spiders and mites. When preliminary research appeared to extract DNA from insects preserved in amber, it attracted great attention by the public and media (e.g., the resurrection of dinosaurs from amber DNA in the popular film *Jurassic Park*), however it was soon discovered to be contaminant DNA, and current belief is that it is highly implausible that such a degradable molecule as DNA could ever survive fossilization in amber for millions of years. ● GY, REW

AMPHIBIAN is a group of aquatic vertebrates or back-boned animals that includes salamanders, frogs, and toads. The amphibians are an ancient group, arising over 350 mya in an age called the Silurian – a time of hot and wet climates supporting swamp vegetation. Evolving from fish, they were the first animals with backbones to inhabit the land. Not all amphibians were small and secretive; some were giant, predators resembling dinosaurs, which would have easily preyed on humans, had they been there. Since amphibians gave rise to reptiles, which in turn evolved into both mammal and bird lineages, we owe our very existence to our amphibian ancestors. This group is characterized by a thin moist skin which ties them to wet or moist habitats. Oxygen and carbon dioxide gas exchange occurs directly through the skin, although many amphibians also have lungs. Their eggs lack a tough coating, so they must be laid in freshwater or at least damp sites – usually in a pond. The young pass through a larval, usually aquatic stage (tadpole of frogs and toads) before they metamorphose into the adult. Amphibians are suffering alarming declines and extinctions as a result of habitat loss, pollution, increase in UV-radiation, and the world-wide spread of a deadly chytrid fungus – all man-caused factors.

Amphibians reach their greatest diversity in warm, moist climates and so there are relatively few species that are adapted to live in MB's cold climate (70 frost-free days in the N, 120 in the S). What the province lacks in numbers of species, it makes up for in species with fascinating adaptations, including a few species like the Wood Frog, Spring Peeper that can freeze solid and still revive, a feat few other vertebrates in the entire world can perform. Our fauna consists of 8 frogs, 4 toads, and 3 salamanders, for a total of 15 (Canada has 42 species). An experienced listener can identify each species of frog and toad by its characteristic call, supplemented with habitat and range information. In fact, local naturalists carry out annual breeding surveys to find out more about these interesting creatures, knowledge that is needed for ensuring their conservation (several species are at risk due to limited range and small populations).

The Plains Spadefoot (*Scaphiopus bombifrons*) is rare (fewer than 10 specimens from 3 locations) in extreme southwestern MB, and is noted for its remarkable breeding habits in temporary pools of rainwater; American Toad (*Bufo americanus*), found in mixed forests of southeastern MB; Canadian *Toad (Bufo hemiophrys*), in grassland, aspen parkland and boreal forests; Great Plains Toad (*Bufo cognatus*), rare and discovered only recently along the ND border in extreme southwestern MB; Spring Peeper (*Hyla crucifer*), tan with brown streaks, often in the shape of an X, and occuring in eastern coniferous and deciduous forests; Grey Treefrog (*Hyla versicolor*), a charmingly green and grey frog whose hands allow it to climb up even glass, and living in forests in south and eastern MB; Cope's Treefrog (*Hyla chrysoscelis*), closely related to the former, and identifiable only by its faster trill and chromosome complement, and found in south-central MB; Boreal Chorus Frog (*Pseudacris triseriata*), an abundant tiny frog with brown longitudinal stripes on a tan or green body, and inhabiting ponds and marshes throughout the province except the tundra; Green Frog (*Rana clamitans*), a large (10 cm) green or tan frog with black markings, known only from several specimens from ponds in the **WHITESHELL PROVINCIAL PARK**; Mink Frog (*Rana septentrionalis*), also green or tan frog with black markings, known only from several specimens from ponds in the Whiteshell and Nopiming provincial parks; Wood Frog (*Rana*

ROBERT R. TAYLOR

Spring peepers can be found in MB's eastern forests.

sylvanica), a medium-sized tan-colored frog with a dark mask, and which is found everywhere in the province except the extreme NE corner, on the tundra far from trees and shrubs; Northern Leopard Frog (*Rana pipiens*) is the large (9 cm) and familiar species, shiny-green with brown spots, often seen in marsh and meadows far from water, and which lives in the southern 2/3s of the province.

By far the largest amphibian in the province is the Mudpuppy (*Necturus maculosus*), which may reach 30-43 cm, is grayish-brown with large feathery red gills, and dwells throughout its life in lakes and rivers in the SE; Gray Tiger Salamander (*Ambystoma tigrinum diaboli*) is a 33 cm, grey-green, stocky animal with variable black markings, found in the grasslands of southwestern MB; Blue-spotted Salamander (*Ambystoma laterale*) is a thin and delicate little (13 cm) creature coloured black with beautiful light-blue spots, and found in mixed woods in southeastern MB. ● ROBERT E. WRIGLEY (REW)

AMPHIBIAN FUNGUS (*Batrachochytrium dendrobatidis*) causes a deadly disease in amphibians called chytridiomycosis, in which the fungus attacks the keratin in the sensitive skin of amphibians, with a 100% death rate. It has been decimating populations and species on an almost worldwide basis since the 1970s, and close to 200 species of frogs, toads and salamanders, including the famous Golden Toad (*Bufo periglenes*) of Costa Rica, have become extinct. Scientists have been searching for the causal agent of these sudden die-offs, and it now appears that the culprit is a chytrid fungal disease that is native to Africa and was spread globally by the shipment of African Clawed Frogs (*Xenopus laevis* and other species) for the pet trade (and subsequent escape to the wild). First discovered in 1938 in Africa, the chytrid fungus showed up in the native Green Frog (*Rana clamitans*) in QC in 1961. Then, infected American Bullfrogs (*Rana catesbeiana*) were traded worldwide as a food item. The fungus has since spread throughout the Americas and to other continents. Chytrid fungi and their relatives are parasites and saprophytes (devouring organic matter) in both aquatic and land habitats. Consequently they help the natural control populations of other creatures and biodegrade tough materials such as plant cellulose and the keratin and chitin of animals. In new environments however, and perhaps with the increased warmth and changes in humidity from global warming, the fungus is sadly decimating the world's amphibians, and may have been the cause of catastrophic frog deaths in MB in recent years. ● REW

Tramping Lake pictograph

ANCIENT ABORIGINAL ART of MB's **First Peoples** represents the production of objects and images that reflect beauty and symbolism through highly skilled craftsmanship, decoration, and/or spiritual symbolism (*see* **Aboriginal Spirituality and Myth**). Many First Nations' languages do not have a word for "art." The production of artistic items was the expected end result of producing something with great skill and an eye for beauty out of respect for the Creator and to bring pride and recognition to the family unit.

Artistic expression can be found in items made from a great variety of materials: decorated ceramic containers made from clay; delicately carved bone and antler (*see* **Ancient Aboriginal Technology**); stone items; and objects from **Birch** bark, wood, and leather. Although many of the ancient perishable objects have disintegrated, we can appreciate the range of items that were being produced from rare fortuitously recovered ancient caches and by looking at the ethnographic materials which represent traditional activities that have persisted into the early **Fur Trade** era and, in some cases, continue to the present. These include shell and bone beads, cradleboards, and **Medicine** and storage bags. In some cases traditional materials such as **Porcupine** quills continue to be used, but in other cases the tradition continued but the materials were changed such as glass beads replacing homemade pin cherry seed beads.

Artistic expression tends to be found on everyday items such as cooking vessels, **Fish** spears, knives, and jewellery. These utilitarian items were often decorated, e.g., the 4000-year-old fish spear having delicately carved barbs and rows of decorative notches along the length of the tool or geometric patterns of cord wrapped tool impressions around the upper part of a

1500-year-old Late **Woodland Period**, Blackduck culture cooking pot. A 3,000-year-old Old Copper culture spear or dart point would be hammered carefully into a thin-edged symmetrical tool or a 1000-year-old bone handle for a stone scraper tool would be carved as an ornately decorated sturgeon.

Art styles were formalized and persisted for hundreds or thousands of years. For example, the variety of decorative patterns and techniques found on Middle Woodland Laurel culture pottery, such as horizontal lines of notched-stick impressions, lasted for 800 years. Individuality was discouraged in the process of creating a persistent pattern from generation to generation that exemplified the importance of maintaining traditions and group identity.

One category of expression that has been called rock art includes sketches on vertical rock faces (**Pictographs**), cobble, or boulder alignments (**Petroforms**), and images pecked into flat rock surfaces (petroglyphs). Their portrayals are often simple but powerful spiritual icons and they often occur in dynamic clusters. Although these sites have often been referred to as rock art sites, a more suitable term might be sacred symbol sites on the sacred landscape.

The ancient Aboriginal art represents a dynamic and creative record that existed for thousands of years. There has been tremendous diversity through time and across the land. ● E. LEIGH SYMS

ANCIENT ABORIGINAL HORTICULTURE.
Agriculture was practised by First Nations in what is now MB for some 400 years before farming was introduced by the **French** and the **Lord Selkirk**'s settlers in the 18th and 19th centuries. Archaeologists use specific sets of characteristics to help them identify the ways in which

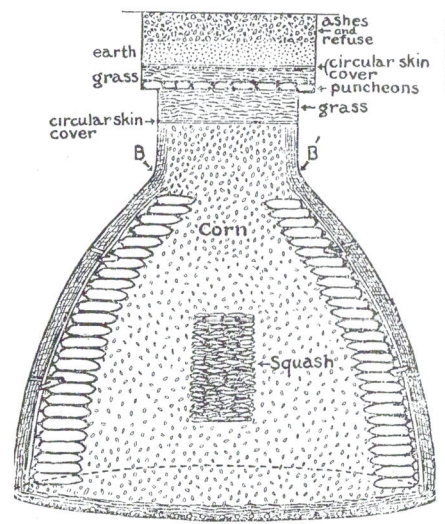

Pit used to store surplus foods such as corn

A past peoples obtained or produced their food. Horticultural sites (farming communities) from the pre-contact or **WOODLAND PERIOD** in MB are identified according to the presence of tools for farming and processing of farmed foods, storage facilities for crops, and the preserved remains of farmed produce. Based on what we know about pre-18th-century horticultural groups from farther S, such as the Siouan-speaking Mandan and Hidatsa peoples along the Missouri River, maize (corn), beans, and squash were the common crops. Horticultural groups tend to live in long-term villages, often pursuing a mixed economy that included farming, **HUNTING**, **FISHING**, and gathering. The presence of pottery vessels distinct from the pottery made by local **HUNTER-GATHERER CULTURES** is important in identifying horticulturalists in the archaeological record of MB.

The clearest evidence for pre-contact horticultural practices in MB comes from 2 related archaeological sites at **LOCKPORT** on opposite banks of the **RED RIVER**. At excavations of these sites, hoes made from the shoulder bones of **BISON** were recovered, as were bell-shaped storage pits containing maize kernels and cupules. In general, the pottery from the sites was minimally decorated, although there are occasionally more elaborate designs, including a bird motif, specifically the stylized tail feathers of Thunderbird. The Lockport pottery, identified as the Kenosewun Culture, dated to the early 15th century AD, is distinct from other pottery types common to the area, bearing similarities instead to pottery from other horticultural groups to the S along the Red River and to the SE, in what is now ND.

Sites such as Lovstrom, Lowton, and Randall, in the Pembina/**SOURIS** Plains of SW MB, have also provided intriguing evidence for horticulture

before European contact. Artifacts such as hoes, possible squash knives, and grinding stones were recovered from these sites. The pottery, identified as the Vickers Culture, dated to between the mid-15th to the late 17th century, is different again from the pottery recovered at Lockport, suggesting the presence of a separate and distinct group of agrarian people. The motifs and vessel shapes bear resemblances to pottery types produced by more-southerly horticultural groups.

Several storage pits, of which one deep pit was excavated, were discovered at the Snyder Site along the Gainsborough Creek S of **MELITA**. It dated to the late 17th century or early 18th century, when local First Nations initially encountered distant **FUR TRADERS**. The sudden appearance and disappearance of Precontact Period horticulturalists in MB suggests that their presence was the result of migrations to the area. It is unlikely that the hunter-gatherer people occupying southern MB suddenly abandoned their way of life in favour of farming and just as suddenly abandoned farming to return to hunting and gathering. Theories for the relatively brief relocation of pre-contact horticulturalists to MB include the possibility of environmental degradation farther S, and the possibility of inter-group hostilities. ● VALERIE MCKINLEY

ANCIENT ABORIGINAL MOUNDS are earthen mausoleums or tombs built by First Nations

people to honour their dead. With over 200 confirmed, probable, and possible structures, MB has the highest density of burial mounds in Canada. They occur mainly in the plains and parkland (*see* **ECOCLIMACTIC REGIONS**), clustering along the **SOURIS**, Pembina, and lower **RED** rivers. Mounds have also been discovered recently in the **WINNIPEG RIVER** drainage in SE MB.

Most are conical or dome-shaped, circular or elliptical structures, the former averaging 10.5 m in diameter and 0.6 m in height and the latter 16.7 m by 12.6 m in size and 0.8 m high. Linear mounds, restricted mainly to SW MB, average 100 m in length, but may be up to 258 m. Two Manitoba mounds appear to be effigy forms, representing a **TURTLE** or **BEAVER** and a **MUSKRAT**. Construction of the large structures in the tough prairie sod presented considerable challenges and required great effort. Some mounds were accretionary, having been built in several stages, and incorporating many burial episodes.

Though defining grave goods are relatively scarce, at least 2 major mound-building traditions are present. An earlier tradition, found in the E and centre of the province, bears similarities to the Arvilla and Rainy River cultures of northern MN and northwestern ON. It features beaver incisor tools, **BEAR** canine pendants, clamshell gorgets and pendants, clay smoking pipes, and miniature stamped or textile-impressed Woodland pottery vessels (*see* **WOODLAND PERIOD**).

Linear Mounds National Historic Site, SW Manitoba

Other mounds, particularly in the SW of the province, show strong connections to western MN and ND. Part of the Devil's Lake-Sourisford Burial Complex, their primary traits include miniature pottery vessels with lip tabs and incised spiral body decorations or animal forms, tubular stone pipes, and etched stone tablets. Exotic materials – including Lake Superior copper, pipes of catlinite (or pipestone) from southern MN, and beads and mask gorgets made from marine conch shell from the Gulf Coast – indicate participation in a widespread trade network. Some of the mask gorgets portray the "forked eye" motif, frequently found to the S, said by Elders to represent the face of thunderbirds, important spiritual beings. **Bison** bones were commonly buried in and beneath mounds.

Mounds occur singly or in small clusters. Many, like **Pilot Mound** and Star Mound, are in prominent locations near the edge of river valleys, atop large natural features, or on knolls or ridges. Many mounds lie on or near village or camp areas but are not necessarily related to them. Burial patterns include primary and secondary burials, extended, flexed or – rarely – seated burials, and sometimes cremation. Graves were often covered with boulders, limestone slabs, layers of clay, or wooden poles. Ash, burnt soils, and charred wooden elements suggest associated ritual fires.

Early antiquarians attributed the mounds to a mythical race of "Mound Builders." Scientific examination quickly determined that they were of First Nations origin. Since there were diverse groups in the area immediately before and after European contact, identifying the builders of the mounds with historically known groups is problematic. Analyses of skeletal remains have suggested both broad Siouan and Algonquian affiliations.

Mound explorations took place mainly be-tween the mid-19th and early 20th centuries. Though some excavations were conducted by scientists or trained archaeologists, most work consisted of crude recoveries by antiquarians and local residents using shovels and horse-drawn scrapers. The few surviving mounds stand as mute testimony to the rich burial ceremonialism of past times. ● DAVID ARTHURS

ANCIENT ABORIGINAL TECHNOLOGY

consisted of innovative and creative use of a wide variety of raw plant and animal materials and selective mineral products, such as copper, to produce tools necessary for daily life. Most of the ancient tools that have survived were made from durable materials, such as lithics (stone), ceramics, and – under the right conditions – bone and antler. The bulk of the other materials did not

Kame Hills cooking vessel, Intensive Diversification Point, replica bone harpoon

survive because MB's environment causes most perishable materials to disintegrate.

Lithic technology involved selecting or trading for the most workable stone materials. For much of the record of flintknapping – that is, making stone tools by flaking – the preferred materials were fine-grained materials containing silica, such as chert (a quartz with the properties of flint) or Knife River flint, originating primarily from trade with the Mandan and Hidatsa peoples of what is now ND. Flintknapping required modifying a stone in several stages. First, toolmakers used a stone hammer to remove large flakes from a rock, producing a core and flakes (hard hammer stage). They then struck flakes off the core with an antler billet (soft hammer stage). Next, they roughed large flakes into tool preforms or blanks with an antler billet. The tools were completed by removing tiny flakes with an antler tine flaker (pressure flaking) to produce thin, sharp edges. Some tools, such as hammerstones, were finished by pecking with a small stone hammer. Others, such as adzes and axes, were finished by grinding the sharp edges with hard, abrasive stones. All Aboriginal groups produced various functional and artistic tools.

Ceramic technology entailed mixing clay, water and some tempering material such as crushed granite, schist or shell to produce vessels for cooking and storage. The earliest pottery was made by building up coils of clay. Later, globular pottery was made inside flexible textile bags. The vessels tended to be decorated according to ancient traditions, left to dry, and then fired to make them durable. All First Nations east of the Rocky Mountains, except northern Athabaskan-speaking peoples of the Western Sub-Arctic – such as the Sayisi **Dene** – made pottery.

Surviving examples of bone and antler technology are scarce because of the relative perishability of these materials compared to stone. Antler, however, is durable, resists breaking, and can be bent when wet. The drawbacks of antler are that it becomes soft if placed in water, and does not hold a sharp edge for long. Bone is hard, can be carved into a sharp point, and does not bend when wet; on the other hand, bone is also fragile, and breaks easily under pressure. Given these properties, bone was often used for needles, harpoons, hide fleshers, and knives. Antler, meanwhile, was used to make woodworking tools (adzes, axes, wedges); pegs; scraper handles; picks; and flintknapping tools. Bone and antler could be cut and carved with stone tools and with incising tools made from rodent incisors, primarily the teeth of beaver, muskrat, and porcupine. ● C. GORDON HILL/E. LEIGH SYMS/KEVIN BROWNLEE

ANDERSON, David, bishop (b Feb 10, 1814, London, UK; d Nov 5, 1885, Clifton UK) was the first **Anglican** bishop in western Canada. After graduating from the U of Edinburgh and U of Oxford, Anderson served as vice-principal of St. Bee's College and as curate of All Saints' Church, Derby. He was sent to **Rupert's Land** in 1849 after receiving a doctorate of divinity and being consecrated primate. At the time, the newly formed Diocese of Rupertsland occupied the entire **Hudson Bay** watershed, though the diocese was soon subdivided and reorganized. Anderson was also chaplain to the **HBC**. His tenure, which lasted to 1864, was difficult, as many of the original **Scots** settlers were **Presbyterian**, and the **Métis** of the **Red River Settlement** were **Roman Catholic**. Respected as a preacher, he increased the number of Anglican clergy and founded the precursor of St. John's College (see **U of M**). After his 1864 resignation in the wake of the **Griffith Owen Corbett** scandal, Anderson returned to the UK, serving as vicar of Clifton, where he lived the remainder of his life. He wrote 2 works on the colony and published a number of his sermons. Some of his papers are deposited in the **Archives** of the U of M. ● MD

ANDERSON, George soccer player, sports administrator (b June 23, 1890, Aberdeenshire, Scotland; d May 30, 1985, **Winnipeg**) known in MB as "Mr. Soccer", he promoted soccer in MB through his work as a sports administrator. He immigrated to Souris in 1909, and began playing soccer recreationally for several local teams. He served with the **Royal Winnipeg Rifles** during WWI, and then became involved in the administration of minor and senior leagues, eventually serving on the exec of the Manitoba Soccer

Association. After the suspension of organized playing during WWII, Anderson helped revive Cdn soccer leagues in 1946 with the Dominion of Canada Football Association. He continued to work for the DCFA in various capacities from 1950 until his resignation in 1968. During this time, Anderson organized tours by European soccer teams, which brought professional-level playing to Canada. In 1956, he arranged a Cdn tour by the Russian team Moscow Locomotive, the first such athletic tour by a USSR sports team, and then arranged for a similar tour by the Cdn soccer team to the USSR in 1960. Anderson was also one of the main organizers behind Canada's first World Cup entry in 1957. For his work, Anderson was granted a lifetime membership to the Manitoba Junior Football Association (Manitoba Youth Soccer Association) in 1937, and to the Manitoba Soccer Association in 1978. In 1973, he was inducted into Canada's Sports Hall of Fame. ● MD

ANGLICAN CHURCH.

ANGLICAN CHURCH. The Church of England, separate from the Roman Catholic Church since 1534, arrived in MB long before Confederation. In 1670, the territory that now includes the province was ceded to the **HUDSON'S BAY COMPANY** and came to be known as **RUPERT'S LAND**. Chaplains were appointed (the first arrived in 1683), and officers of the company were instructed to read prayers on Sundays. It was not, however, until 1811 and the arrival of the **LORD SELKIRK'S** settlers to the **RED RIVER SETTLEMENT** that the Church of England began to be a strong presence in MB. Although the settlers were **SCOTS** and mainly **PRESBYTERIANS**, the land still belonged to the HBC, which provided such spiritual leadership as it saw fit. In 1820, it appointed John West as chaplain to Red River. West established the first church, Upper Church (now St. John's Cathedral in **WINNIPEG**), as well as the Red River Academy, the progenitor of the present-day St. John's College (*see* **U OF M**). One the academy's early students was **HENRY BUDD**, who became an important pioneer missionary in the West and the first person of Aboriginal descent to be ordained priest.

West was succeeded in 1823 by **WILLIAM COCKRAN**. Very much a man of his times, Cockran saw his mission as the "civilizing" of the First Nations and **COUNTRY-BORN** population; he is less kindly regarded now by historians, but in his day, he was an important and influential figure. He built the stone churches of St. Andrew's (**LOCKPORT**) and the original St. Peter's Dynevor, and, against the express wishes of HBC gov **GEORGE SIMPSON** and the HBC, established missions at **COOK'S CREEK** and **PORTAGE LA PRAIRIE**. In 1848, **DAVID ANDERSON**, the first Bishop of

Rupertsland, arrived in the colony. Urged by the Church Missionary Society to establish a training college for Aboriginal clergy, he acquired Red River Academy and renamed it St. John's College. Anderson stepped down in 1864 and was succeeded by Robert Machray. Machray was instrumental in the founding of the U of M, which began in 1870 as a consortium of 3 colleges: the Anglican St. John's, the **ROMAN CATHOLIC** St. Paul's, and the **METHODIST** Wesley College.

As MB continued to grow and prosper after joining Confederation, so did the church. In the process, it became the church of the MB establishment, overseeing the education of the children of the privileged through its 2 private boarding schools, St. John's College School for Boys (now part of St. John's–Ravenscourt School) and Rupertsland Ladies College. A flood of **ENGLISH** immigrants after both the Boer War and WWI led to a rapid expansion of the church and the creation of an ecclesiastical province of Rupertsland – covering NT (and NU), AB, SK, MB, and Northern ON – with a smaller Rupertsland diocese and 2 new sees. The first of these was Keewatin Diocese (1902), covering an area that included Northwestern ON and parts of northern MB. After 20 years as a missionary in **CHURCHILL**, Joseph Lofthouse was consecrated its first bishop. He chose Rat Portage (after 1904, called Kenora, ON) as his episcopal see, and this is where succeeding bishops of Keewatin have continued to reside.

In 1924, the Diocese of **BRANDON** came into being. It includes southwestern MB and extends as far N as **FLIN FLON** and **THE PAS**, where Henry Budd College undertakes to train Aboriginal people for various forms of ministry. Brandon's first Bishop was W. W. H. Thomas, founder of the Bishop's Messengers as well as St. Faith's Mission at **SWAN RIVER**. Both the Messengers and the staff of the Mission consisted of women licensed to conduct all church services (except the sacraments) in remote areas that had no priest. As a Bishop's Messenger slyly put it: "We go where the men can't." Bishop Thomas also recruited Eva Hasell, who, with Iris Sayle, became an iconic figure as the pair crisscrossed the Prairies in their rickety van as the "Canadian Sunday School Caravan." Women were admitted as priests in the Anglican Church of Canada in 1979, and as bishop in 1993. The church suffered a severe blow in 1932 when the diocese lost all its capital funds. This not only crippled the diocese but also affected the endowment funds of the college, the 2 private schools, and the funding of various missionary endeavours. Diocesan treasurer **JOHN ALEXANDER MACHRAY**, a nephew of the archbishop, was found criminally responsible and sentenced to prison.

During the '50s and '60s, the church underwent a building boom as it followed its parishioners into the new suburbs surrounding Winnipeg. This period also saw the renewal of St. John's

Old St. Andrews on the Red, 1960

The *Anson Northup* was the first steamboat on the Red River.

College and its migration to the campus of the U of M. Like all mainstream churches, the Anglican Church has seen its influence and its membership decline over the past half-century, with a corresponding loss of revenue. Exacerbating the financial difficulties were the substantial costs incurred by the payouts to **RESIDENTIAL SCHOOLS** claimants and the lawsuit resulting from the conviction of a priest for sexual abuse. But as its power declined, the church's involvement in various social issues has increased. Several parishes, for example, sponsor refugees, or operate and help support a variety of community ministries, including drop-ins, community gardens and kitchens, food distribution, and programs for both children and adults. • JUDY FLYNN

ANISHINABE. *See* OJIBWAY.

ANOLA, pop 200, is a community 20 km E of **WINNIPEG** on the **CN** main line. The post office opened in 1883, though the community was then known then as Richland. The name was changed to Anola in 1923, either named for a town in Finland or because the community is built on a hill or "knoll." Anola has a number of businesses that service local building and agricultural industries. However, its proximity to Winnipeg makes Anola largely a bedroom community. Every Sept, Anola hosts Canada's "Longest Yard Sale." The community is also the birthplace of **BASEBALL** player **COREY KOSKIE**. • GPP

ANSON NORTHUP was the first **STEAMBOAT** to travel the **RED RIVER**, ushering in a new era of trade for the **RED RIVER SETTLEMENT**. In 1858, the

chamber of commerce in St. Paul, MN, was seeking to improve trade with Fort Garry, and offered $1000 to the first person to launch a steamboat on the Red River. After negotiating the price to $2000, Minnesotan hotelier and speculator Anson Northup accepted the challenge. His vessel the *North Star* was disassembled and dragged 240 km overland from the headwaters of the Mississippi to the Red River, a task requiring 60 men, 13 yoke of oxen, and 17 horses. Reassembled and renamed the *Anson Northup*, the Red River's first steamboat was an ugly vessel, described by one capt as a lumbering old pine basket. Though she was hardly at the forefront of the steamboats of her time, the *Anson Northup* nonetheless cut travel time between St. Paul and Fort Garry in half. She embarked on her maiden voyage from Fort Abercrombie, MN, on May 19, 1859, and arrived in Fort Garry on June 10. Shortly after her first voyage, she was purchased by the **HBC** and entrepreneur J.C. Burbank, and renamed *Pioneer*. She sank over the winter of 1861-62 at Cook's Creek, N of Fort Garry. • MD

ANT is a small insect (family Formicidae) and would be hardly noticeable were it not for its remarkable abundance, constant activity, and highly developed social behaviour. Although diminutive (3-15 mm), ants' impact in all terrestrial ecosystems in MB, from the arctic tundra to grassland, is immeasurable. There are 61 species of ants recorded in MB, with 10 more probable and 8 more possible (i.e., occur nearby), for a potential total of 81 species (about 200 recorded in Canada). The largest at 13 mm is the Carpenter Ant (*Camponotus herculeanus*) often found

in rotting stumps and logs from Churchill to the S border; the smallest (1.3 mm) is the Thief Ant (*Solenopsis molesta*). The body is constructed in 3 units – the head, with sense organs like antennae and eyes, thorax with the 3 pairs of legs and wings, and the abdomen consisting of a thin stalk and the rounded part with the organs (called the gaster). Eyesight is useful only at close range and so it is pheromones (special odorous chemicals which stimulate instinctive behaviours) which are the main method of communication within the colony. Each chemical has its specific message, and it may be long or short lasting.

Co-ordinating group activity by chemical means has been of enormous importance for the evolution of ant societies. The red Slave-maker Ant (*Polyergus breviceps*) has become so dependant on slave ants, such as the black Formica fusca, that it can no longer survive on its own. The 1.5 mm Pharaoh Ant (*Monomorium pharaonis*), introduced from the tropics, survives here only inside heated buildings. Certain species are restricted to a certain soil type, such as Formica bradleyi occuring only in light, sandy soils around the Carberry Sandhills. While some species' nests are small and hidden under a log or rock, those of other species of enormous. The Mound-building ant (*Formica ulkei*) nest of soil may exceed 150 cm high, and 150 mounds may occur within 400 metres. The Thatching Ant (*Formica obscuripes*), common in southern MB, builds 50-150 cm piles of soil, pebbles, and conifer needles. Tunnels descend several metres underground, where inhabitants may number in the thousands. The nest keeps the ants cool in summer and warm in winter. In autumn, the average colony consists of about 100 queens and 40,000 workers. Activity drops over winter until late March, when the workers commence chores. The females begin laying eggs in April, which will become winged males and females (i.e., sexuals). The eggs hatch in May and grow through the larval stage in a week or two, and pupate in late May. These leave their cocoons in June and soon fly away to mate and find new colonies. Some females land on the nest of other colonies and join it, after shedding their wings. The males die immediately after mating, having served their sole function. In the meantime, the original queens continue laying more eggs in the nest from June to Aug, but these individuals all develop into non-sexual workers. These are all adults by Sept, and by return of cold weather in Oct, the colony again prepares for winter. When a colony reaches a certain size in summer, some of the workers and queens 'swarm' and march away to create a new colony, often within 20-100 meters from the original nest. This

A

Ants can be found from Churchill to Vita.

explains why one may see a whole series of nests in an area of Jack Pine forest.

During the warm months, the smaller workers in the colony care for the young, feeding them regurgitated meals. The larger workers are kept busy gathering food and building the nest. On cold or rainy days, they close the entrances, and expand the openings to aerate the tunnels during fair weather. The workers leave the nest daily to hunt for other insects, seeds and honeydew – a sweet excretion of aphid insects. In fact, a large colony of Formica ants may harvest 500 kg of honeydew in a year – far more honey than a bee colony can produce in that time. Marching ants leave little trails (and their chemical odour) on the ground, leading away from the nest to favorite plants with aphids. Some ant species raid the nests of other kinds of ants and steal their pupae, carry them back to their nest, and turn the adults into slaves. Ants aggressively protect themselves, feeding sites, their tended aphids, and their nests. Armed with a spray of formic acid and large jaws, they fight until they overcome their prey or foe, or die trying. Species of the Myrmica ants are also capable of attacking with their rear stinger. Bears and woodpeckers are major ant predators.

At least 14,000 ant species occur worldwide, and in unbelievable numbers (estimated at 10,000 trillion individuals). As one of the world's most-successful creatures for over 120 million years (Early Cretaceous), ants play dominant roles in all terrestrial ecosystems. As native terrestrial earthworms were eliminated from MB by glacial cold and scouring, ants have assumed their role as the chief tillers of the soil; their burrowing activities improve drainage, aeration, and fertility. As predators and scavengers, ants devour about 90% of dead land animals. Plants and animals have evolved to co-exist with ants in countless remarkable ways. • REW, WBP

AOKI, Fred Yoichi, physician, researcher (b March 2, 1942, Vancouver, BC). A recognized infectious disease expert, Aoki attended United College (now the **U of W**) from 1959-62 before completing his MD at the **U of M** in 1966. He went on to train at Toronto General Hospital and as a resident at the Montreal General Hospital in internal medicine and clinical pharmacology. Aoki taught at McGill U beginning in 1972, but left to complete a fellowship in infectious disease research at the Medical Research Council in the UK. He completed his research training at L'Institut Armand-Frappier in Laval-des-Rapides, QC before returning to McGill in 1977. In 1978, he took a position as associate professor at the U of M, and in 1988 became a full professor of **Medicine**, microbiology, pharmacology, and therapeutics. Aoki has conducted research into the clinical pharmacology of antiviral drugs for the treatment of infectious diseases, including clinical trials as well as animal studies. He has conducted studies of human papillomavirus and genital herpes vaccines for women. Another specialty has been research on drugs and vaccines to fight influenza. He is a member of the Canadian Pandemic Influenza Planning Committee, and has advocated for the Canadian govt to stockpile greater quantities of antiviral drugs. In 2005, Aoki received the Manitoba Medical Students Association Teaching Award, and in 2006, the Manitoba Medical Association Scholastic Award. • JOEL TRENAMAN

AQUACULTURE, or fish farming, is the cultivation of fish in a controlled environment. There were 4 major fish farm operations in MB in 2006, producing primarily rainbow **Trout** and arctic char, but as natural fish resources in MB are plentiful, aquaculture is mainly undertaken on hobby farms or to supplement supplies for **Sport Fishing**. The first fish operation began in the late 1960s when experimental studies supported by the MB govt were carried out in pothole lakes in SW MB. Extensive aquaculture, involving operations that are outdoors in natural and artificial lakes, is more common in MB than intensive aquaculture, which is often indoors in a controlled setting using large tanks, and involves high concentrations of fish. Intensive aquaculture can also be done in cages moored deep underwater. The deep lakes of northern MB would be suitable for cage aquaculture, but experimental farms in the early 1980s showed that transporting equipment N would be too expensive to be commercially viable. The possibility of cage culture farther S in MB is being studied. Roughly 30 commercial fish farmers in MB raise fish on private waters, though a few use govt-owned waters. In addition, about 600 hobby fish farmers raise fingerlings to stock waters for personal use. There are also 3 fee-for-fishing businesses, where customers who are unable to access natural fish resources pay to fish in privately stocked ponds. • MD

A favourite of fish farmers is the tasty rainbow trout.

ARACHNID is the name of the group containing **Spiders**, **Scorpions**, **Pseudoscorpions**, **Harvestmen**, **Ticks**, and **Mites**. It differs from the closely related class of insects (Insecta), in that their bodies have 2 rather than 3 segments, 4 instead of 3 pairs of legs, no wings, and no antennae. The ancestral group was the scorpion-like marine creatures called Eurypterids (class Meristomata – with 5 survivors, the Horseshoe and King crabs) of 435-400 mya (Silurian Period). The world total of named arachnids is 80,000, and Canada's fauna consists of an estimated 1400 spiders, 9500 mites, and including the other minor groups, totals about 11,000 species. With MB's central position in the country, possibly half of these will be found in the province. • REW

▶ (*See* **Spider**, **Mite**, **Tick**, **Lice**)

ARBORG, pop 1000, a town 110 km N of Winnipeg near the W shore of Lake Winnipeg. The area is rich in **Icelandic** history – in 1876, the federal govt set aside a reserve for Icelandic settlers along the W shore of Lake Winnipeg called **New Iceland**. By 1887, the settlers voted to become part of MB, and formed a municipality. Settlements along the shore gradually spread, approaching the present site of Arborg in 1890. By 1908, the first **Polish** and **Ukrainian** settlers arrived in the area. Numerous churches, ethnic foods, and social activities are evidence of the town's cosmopolitan makeup. Diverse farming plays an integral part in the local economy, and nearby **Lake Winnipeg** supports a strong year-round commercial fishing industry. The name "Arborg" is Icelandic meaning "river town." Originally named Ardal ("river valley" or "river dale"), the name was changed to Arborg when the railway arrived in 1910. The community was incorporated as a village in 1964 and attained town status in 1998. In 2006, Arborg unveiled a statue that it claims is the world's largest **Curling** rock in honour of the 1948 high school team that won a national championship. • GPP

ARCHAEOLOGY is the study of past peoples and communities based on the analysis of largely non-written records they have left behind. Acting as "time detectives," archaeologists reconstruct the lifestyles, technology, and social systems of ancient cultures based on the artifacts of their time. These materials include a variety of tools, containers, dietary items (such as animal bones and plant remains), spiritual articles, hearths, pits, and structural evidence. Archaeologists develop regional chronologies of ancient societies; describe in detail the traits that define and describe each of these cultures; and chart various processes such as stability, social change, migration, invention, and trade, using changes in the archaeological record to explain these occurrences. Since much of MB's archaeological record relates to the heritage and history of **First Peoples**, archaeologists draw upon traditional oral accounts, including ecological knowledge. For relatively recent times, such as the eras of the **Fur Trade**, European settlement, and industrial development, archaeologists also occasionally use written documents and records.

Most of MB's archaeological record consists of the vast Precontact (pre-European) Period or Prehistory Period. This period lasts from about 9500 BC, when the first known **Aboriginal** hunters followed the retreating glaciers, until the appearance of European traders and explorers around the 18th century AD. Since there was a great deal of relocation of First Nations during the early fur trade era, archaeologists cannot determine the exact link between many of the ancient Precontact Aboriginal cultures with historic groups, so archaeologists have given typological (place) names to these early cultures, often based on the first site that they have definitively linked to a culture. For example, the Blackduck Complex or culture (dating ca. AD 700-1000) is named after Blackduck, in northern MN, and is not a tribal name, although there is considerable agreement that this group's members were the ancestors of Algonquian speakers who were themselves ancestors to various **Ojibway** and/or **Cree** groups.

Other forms of archaeology include fur trade archaeology, such as **Upper** and **Lower Fort Garry;** industrial archaeology, such as the **Beausejour** Glass Works; ethnic archaeology, such as the **Riel** site of the **Métis**, and a **Ukrainian** farm; architectural archaeology, such as the log church in **St. Andrews**; and cultural resources management archaeology, which entails evaluating, salvaging, and protecting threatened archaeological sites. Within these broad areas are specialized studies, including flintknapping (stone tool production); faunal analysis (the study of animal-bone food remains); botanical studies of seeds, charcoal, phytoliths and starch grains; Precontact Aboriginal ceramic analysis; stone tool wear analysis; blood residue, stable isotope, and DNA analysis; and trade pattern and settlement analyses. A variety of studies on historic artifacts include commercial production and distribution patterns, urban garbage studies, underwater archaeology, makers' marks on ceramics and glassware, and analyses of metallurgy, clothing, architecture, hardware, and many other goods. An exciting specialty, and one that is new to MB, is replicative archaeology, in which tools, containers, and other items are made and used according to traditional techniques in order to understand and appreciate the skills of the original makers.

Archaeologists are known for their neat, square excavation units, but they study the human past through the discovery, analysis, and interpretation of archaeological cultural remains that exist in all contexts, both on and beneath Earth's surface. Following the recovery of an artifact, a vast amount of time is committed to cleaning, numbering, restoring, and documenting the item. The repetitive work of this phase is balanced by the exciting recoveries that occur. These usually include surprises, new insights, and an appreciation of the wonderful skills of the original makers. Rigorous analyses are usually substantiated by a variety of statistical techniques. The resultant interpretations and reconstructions are often a blend of rigorous science and creative inferences. • E. LEIGH SYMS

Excavations at The Forks National Historic Site

Variety of dart points.

MB MUSEUM

ARCHAIC PERIOD. The Archaic – or Intensive Diversification, Middle Precontact, or Middle Prehistoric – period lasted from about 7000 BC to AD 1. Major changes elsewhere in NA affected First Nations in what is now MB. Dart points for atlatls (dart throwers) became notched or stemmed; a variety of ground-stone woodworking tools, such as axes and adzes, were invented; and new survival strategies to increase the exploitation of plants and animals were developed. More sites date from this era than from the preceding **PALEO PERIOD** (Early Prehistoric or Paleoindian Period), indicating increasing population growth, but most sites were small with few dart points, suggesting that numerous groups existed in small numbers.

The forest region of SE MB remains poorly understood, though there are numerous collections from along the **WINNIPEG RIVER** and other waterways, because only limited efforts have been made to identify the wide range of dart points. Most have been lumped into a generic category called the Shield Archaic Culture, which is gradually being divided into several cultures. The 8000-year-old Sinnock Site (25 km N of the Town of **LAC DU BONNET**) was probably a **BISON**-kill site. Nearby, the 4000-year-old Two Eagles cache from the Lee River hints at the richness of the culture. Unearthed at this site were 2 ornate bone harpoons, an antler atlatl handle, a necklace of 7 **ELK** canine pendants, a bone sucking tube, a ceremonial **BEAR** claw, a **BEAVER** incisor chisel, a bone awl, 62 shell beads, 5 stone dart points, 1 spear point, a whetstone, a scraper, a flake, and an Old Copper decorative item. The Old Copper culture mined this metal in deep bedrock pits in the Lake Superior area from perhaps as early as 6000 or 5000 BC to 1000 BC. The copper was manufactured into hunting and **FISHING** tools and decorative items, and was traded widely.

In the northern boreal forest (*see* **ECOCLIMACTIC REGIONS**), the large concentration of over 800 sites recovered from the **CHURCHILL RIVER** Diversion has produced considerable insights into its rich heritage. An analysis of 500 dart points produced a typology of 77 cultural types. The majority of the points fell into 32 clusters representing Intensive Diversification types. Other major insights came from the 6 eroding burials, dating from 3000 BC to 1800 BC, which were analyzed and returned to the communities for reburial. These revealed a rich record of bone and antler tools, including long bone harpoons and fish spears, antler adzes, an ice scoop, ice picks, bone knives, a bark peeler, a quill flattener, bone awls, hide fleshers, antler pressure flakes, a bone bayonet, rodent incisor chisels, a stone polisher, a stone anvil, iron pyrite strike-a-light, and ochre (*see* **ANCIENT ABORIGINAL TECHNOLOGY**). Some of the surface sample of hundreds of stone adzes, scrapers, and bifaces – stone implements flaked on either side – belongs to this period.

In the Grasslands and Parklands of the southern part of the province, the Altithermal drought, ca 7000 BC to 4000 BC, apparently prevented migration into what is now MB until about 3500 BC, when the Mummy Cave Culture bison hunters, with their side-notched atlatl dart points, appeared. This evolved into the Oxbow Culture, ca 3000 BC to 1000 BC, which developed the first ceremonial medicine wheels and long-term cemeteries. The McKean Culture coexisted as bison hunters for some 2000 years, but is rarely found with Oxbow Culture sites, since they did not move into the northern areas, as the Oxbow hunters did. The Pelican Lake Culture emerged during the latter part of the period. It is noted for barbed dart points and communal bison kills in the form of traps, pounds, and jumps in MB, SK, and AB. This period was followed by the **WOODLAND PERIOD**. ● E. LEIGH SYMS/GARY ADAMS

ARCHAMBEAU, Robert, ceramic artist (b April 18, 1933, Toledo, OH) has strongly influenced ceramic artists, and the larger visual-arts sphere, of MB, Canada, and the world. His work has been exhibited and published internationally and is in public and private collections in Canada and the US. His inspiration for his forms, colours, and glazes comes from the natural environment around him and relate to the geology and landscape of MB, particularly **BISSETT**, where he has a studio. His interest in ceramics also extends to their international history, especially China and Asia as a whole. Archambeau's work is quiet and contemplative, strong and elegant. He uses salt glazes and a wood-fired kiln, and incorporates the ash deposits from the kiln as part of the surface decoration. A professor of Fine Arts at the **U OF M** and head of its Ceramics Dept 1968-91, Archambeau has lectured widely

A

and presented workshops and symposiums throughout Canada and the US. He received the Governor General's Award in Visual and Media Arts in 2003. • PATRICIA BOVEY

ARCHIBALD, Sir Adams George, politician (b May 3, 1814, Truro, NS; d Dec 14, 1893, Truro) was appointed the first lt gov of MB following the RED RIVER RESISTANCE. The Maritime lawyer earned the favour of PM Sir John A. Macdonald as a fervent supporter of Confederation. During federal debates over the formation of MB as a province in May 1870, Archibald made a speech defending the people involved in the resistance, and was offered a position as the first lt gov of the new province. Archibald had no interest in taking the position, and did so only on condition he be granted a patronage post following his term. This he was, as he became both lt gov of NS and director of the CPR. In the RED RIVER SETTLE-MENT, Archibald had the difficult job of easing tension between the MÉTIS and ON Protestant factions. Though he tried to remain neutral in disputes between the sides, he provoked the resentment of the Protestants just a year into his term by shaking LOUIS RIEL's hand. Archibald officially resigned following the incident, though he ended up staying another 2 years while Macdonald tried to find another suitable candidate. During his brief time in MB, Archibald negotiated the first treaties with the province's First Nations and attempted to settle the thorny issue of MÉTIS land SCRIP. • MD

Sir George Adams Archibald, ca 1889

AM, PERSONALITY FILES, A22/2, N12595

ARCHITECTURE IN MANITOBA
By David Butterfield

A

In Manitoba, post-settlement architecture has mostly followed trends and developments from Europe and from other parts of NA, offering many interesting subtexts on the grand themes that have described architectural history over the past 200 years.

FUR TRADE & RED RIVER (1812–69): The earliest buildings in MB recall the prov's FUR TRADE origins and the fledgling RED RIVER SETTLEMENT inaugurated by LORD SELKIRK. The grandest of these remnants are the great stone forts built by the HUDSON'S BAY COMPANY as the defensive, administrative, and working sites of the fur trade. The complexes at LOWER FORT GARRY (completed in 1837), near Selkirk, and FORT PRINCE OF WALES (completed in 1772), on the shores of Hudson Bay near CHURCHILL, are impressive reminders of the power and reach of the fur trade in Canada. Immense stone walls, battlements, and several large stone buildings make these some of Canada's most important historic sites.

The architectural legacy of the Red River Settlement is most impressively revealed in the collection of churches that were built to serve the first Anglican, Roman Catholic, and Presbyterian settlers. Nearly all of the settlement's churches still stand. The grandest, St. Andrew's Anglican (1845–49), the oldest church in western Canada, and St. Peter's Anglican (1865), built by its Aboriginal congregation, are simple, powerful, early Gothic Revival buildings carried out in local limestone. Even the few log churches built using a distinctive local log-building technology known as Red River frame, such as dainty St. James Anglican (1853), have survived.

The thousands of buildings that would have formed the architectural landscape of the province at this time – farmhouses, barns, outbuildings, and wind- and gristmills – have almost all been lost. Just a handful of these simple buildings survive, and almost all of these were

Upper Fort Garry

CHALRES SHILLADAY

Winnipeg's Exchange District is a good example of Romanesque Revival styles.

constructed using Red River frame, a technique in which short logs are squared and set between upright squared logs. The rarity of such buildings has often meant that they are carefully preserved as museum sites. The oldest house in the province, the William Fraser House (1837), is at Lower Fort Garry. The largest Red River frame building, the Grey Nuns' Convent in the St. Boniface (1846–51) area of **WINNIPEG**, is devoted to all aspects of early French-Canadian life in Manitoba.

TRANSITION (1870–80): Seminal events in the province's history, such as the entry of MB into the Cdn Confederation in 1870, brought only modest changes to the architectural landscape of the Red River Settlement. For the next 10 years, before the arrival of the **CPR** main line, the new province experienced a fitful and difficult existence. The old settlement society, along with its architecture, gradually faded, as upstart arrivals – mostly Ontarians – brought brash new ideas about commerce and buildings.

The City of Winnipeg lurched into formality in 1873, initially focusing on a small concentration of buildings about 1 km N of **UPPER FORT GARRY**. A flurry of building activity throughout the 1870s brought a new architectural aesthetic to the province. The early commercial nature of the community produced wood-frame rather than log buildings. Nevertheless, they were still rough and modest in their appearance – simple boxes with typical boomtown fronts for commercial enterprises. In 1878, the construction of a rail line from Pembina, ND, to St. Boniface allowed for the import of all kinds of goods, especially building materials. Those

products – brick, lumber, paint, wallpapers, architectural gewgaws – would transform the architectural character of the province. Substantial buildings began to rise in Winnipeg, as well as at other communities along the rail line, particularly **EMERSON** and **MORRIS**.

Beyond the familiar and supportive setting of the Red and Assiniboine rivers, a few Anglo-Ontarian pioneers began clearing land to make way for farms. Their buildings were typically rudimentary log structures, not appreciably different from those of the Red River era, except that they occasionally sported a rough interpretation of the Gothic Revival style that was gaining popularity in eastern Canada. At the edges of the new province, small but equally auspicious changes were being made to the old order, as exotic European building traditions were being used by other new arrivals. In the SE, **MENNONITES** arriving from Russia in 1874 brought a tradition of farm-village strips with distinctive house barns, simple churches, and windmills. Along the shores of **LAKE WINNIPEG**, where **ICELANDERS** first settled in 1875, the tall spires of the Lutheran faith appeared.

ESTABLISHMENT (1881–99): It was as if a decade's worth of pent-up energy was suddenly released when the CPR finally arrived in Winnipeg in July 1881, and in Brandon by Dec of that same year. The next 20 years were ones of turmoil, at least architecturally. A wild variety of buildings were thrown up, and in many cases just as quickly torn down and replaced. The first generation of significant MB public buildings rose between the early chaos of the early 1880s real estate boom and 1885.

Govt buildings were constructed in Winnipeg and in smaller developing communities like **BRANDON**, **NEEPAWA**, and **EMERSON**. With elaborate and exuberant Victorian styles, teeming with details inside and out, these new buildings were palpable symbols to citizens and newcomers alike of the "arrival" of the province. The firm of Barber and Barber helped change the face of downtown Winnipeg businesses. Charles Wheeler was also significant, designing buildings like **DALNAVERT** and Holy Trinity Anglican Cathedral.

By the mid-1880s, with a population of about 20,000, Winnipeg was a bona fide city, and its physical contours were gradually worked out. Neighbourhoods that had earlier contained a welter of activities – residential, commercial, manufacturing – gradually settled on one dominant function. The placement of the CPR's east-west line, and the opening for development of the old HBC compound along the Assiniboine, established the basic framework that the city would take: the commercial strip along Main St; the well-to-do in the south; the poor across the CPR tracks, in the North End; and the middle class south of the tracks and to the west. The buildings that accompanied the development of these neighbourhoods were typically Victorian. The homes of the wealthy sported the newest styles – dramatic Italianate, Gothic, and Second Empire revivals, usually in brick. Meanwhile, the more-modest wooden homes of the middle class assumed similar stylish pretensions without the level of detail or craftsmanship. And in the North End, poverty defined buildings that were made of the most rudimentary forms and materials.

Outside Winnipeg, in Brandon and other smaller towns, thriving commercial streets sprang up, and grand homes, large public schools, and impressive town halls confirmed their growth. In the country, pioneer log buildings were quickly removed and replaced by small but notable wooden buildings. By 1890, however, successful farmers deemed even these new farmhouses inadequate; large houses and barns began to replace earlier ones. Just as established farmers were upgrading to the latest NA architectural styles, a new wave of immigrants from Eastern Europe, mainly Ukrainians, were recreating their ancient architectural traditions. Their onion-domed churches and carefully constructed log houses were a striking contrast to prevailing trends.

CONSOLIDATION (1900–13): The 13 years following the tumultuous pioneer and settlement eras saw MB glide into a veritable golden age of optimism. Architecturally, it was a period of unsurpassed activity. Winnipeg especially grew, from a population of 42,000 in 1901 to 136,000 in 1911. Grand aspirations and grand buildings arrived in a big way. One effect was that buildings grew in size. With the introduction of new technologies – elevators and building cranes being the most important – it was possible to replace 2- and 3-storey commercial buildings typical of the previous decade. Office towers of 10 storeys or more rose along Main St. in Winnipeg, housing legions of workers in the burgeoning financial industry. These buildings invariably recalled the towers of Chicago. Indeed, many of the architects who worked on these new symbols of civic success were trained in the Chicago offices of trailblazers in tall building design.

Warehouses in Winnipeg's Exchange District attained great size and bulk, with robust Romanesque Revival styles. Some of the same architects who worked on the elegant towers also devoted their talents to these important new buildings. Classical Revival bank buildings, designed by top architects from Toronto, Montreal, and even New York, were carried out in marble, brass, and gold, and filled in gaps left by the new skyscrapers. Winnipeg saw the construction of two huge railway stations – one for the CPR, the other the Union Station of the CNoR and Grand Trunk Pacific, whose complex also included the nearby **HOTEL FORT GARRY**. Smaller centres also gained fine new stations.

Even if buildings didn't get taller, they often got more sophisticated and more expensive. Great mansions for Winnipeg's millionaires and the sub-millionaire strata dotted the S side of the Assiniboine River in Winnipeg, in the Roslyn Rd area, along Wellington Cres, and in a new area called Crescentwood. Usually designed by Winnipeg's "society" architects, these majestic buildings were the domestic extension of the power and prestige expressed in the skyscrapers downtown. In the city centre, as well as in the new suburbs of Elmwood, Wolseley, and Norwood, smaller, comfortable middle-class homes, with delicate Queen Anne flourishes, were rising rapidly.

Public buildings marked the pinnacle of the era's architectural advances. Grand Gothic and Romanesque revival churches, like the Presbyterian (now United) churches of Augustine (1904) and Westminster (1912), and the Roman Catholic Cathedral of St. Boniface (1906-8), expressed the tenor and wealth of the times. John Russell was the architect of choice for many of these churches. Impressive public school buildings, veritable mansions from the outside, rose in the province's largest centres. The provincial government undertook its own major building program, adding many excellent buildings to Manitoba's communities. An enormous and architecturally refined new Legislative Building was proposed for Winnipeg. New courthouses, land title offices, hospitals, and asylum complexes brought a whole new sense of grandeur and permanence to the province.

WARS AND DEPRESSION (1914–45): The outbreak of the Great War in 1914 slowed construction projects, and over the next 4 years, the province was brought to a virtual standstill. All energy went into the war effort. Building projects were shelved or abandoned, and it was not until the early 1920s that a revival of economic conditions created an environment that allowed for a modest resumption of architectural activity.

The early 1920s saw the completion of many of the delayed pre-war projects. The Legislative Building was finished, as was one of the largest churches in the province, Winnipeg's Knox Presbyterian. But the confidence that had defined the architecture of the first decade of the 20th century had been eroded. Modesty came to define many projects. When a whole raft of school buildings became a necessity in Winnipeg during the 1920s, architects looked to the examples of domestic architecture – the bungalow – or to a modest version of the Collegiate Gothic for inspiration. Optimism and ambition died hard for some, however. One of the grandest public school projects ever contemplated in MB –

Bank of Montreal at Portage and Main.

PETER TITTENBERGER

Daniel McIntyre Collegiate – was proposed in 1922, although only a small portion of it ever was built. Any glimmer of hope for a return to the grandeur of the decade before WWI was dashed as the Depression of the 1930s dried up land and dreams alike. Only a few major public works projects, like the Civic Auditorium and Federal Building in Winnipeg – striking Art Deco designs – allowed for any suggestion of activity. The entry of Canada into WWII prolonged this period of inactivity another 5 years. At its conclusion in 1945, it would be another 5 years before MB embarked on significant building projects.

MODERN (1946–PRESENT): The 1950s and '60s marked a return to the optimistic sensibility that had defined the first decade of the 1900s. The immediate engine of this change was the phenomenal birth rate – the Baby Boom – that accompanied the return of servicemen from the War. A complement was the institution of federal govt home-loans to veterans. MB, especially Winnipeg, was primed for a building boom that rivalled the one that had transformed the city in the 1880s.

New buildings of all sorts sprang up beginning in the early 1950s. The most visible manifestation of growth and prosperity were the new suburbs, with curving streets, low-slung ranch-style bungalows, International-style schools, and A-frame neo-Gothic churches. These buildings, along with various government structures and new commercial and industrial buildings of the same time, created a dramatic architectural contrast with those from the turn of the century. The source of this major shift in architecture was the acceptance of the modern movement, which after 1945 changed the way buildings looked. In MB, the rise of the School of Architecture at the **U of M** ensured that local expertise and sensitivity was brought to projects. The new approach to building design, however, also affected attitudes to old buildings, which were seen as symbols of decay and sentimentality. In an effort to renew downtown cores, in Winnipeg but also in smaller centres, entire blocks of old, sometimes-derelict buildings were removed; shiny new visions in steel and glass rose in their place. The most visible expression of this revolution occurred in the 1960s in Winnipeg, when City Hall and whole blocks of neighbouring commercial buildings were razed to make way for a major civic complex containing a city hall, police station, concert hall, theatre, museum, and planetarium. ETIENNE GABOURY designed several striking public buildings, including the Canadian Mint on Winnipeg's eastern outskirts.

In smaller communities throughout southern MB, these architectural developments were recast on a smaller scale but with similar results: many older buildings in commercial areas came down, and in new housing tracts beyond the old town boundaries, ranch-style bungalows rose. Northern MB, once an important hinterland for the fur trade of the 18th and 19th centuries, regained an economic base in the mid-20th century with the development of major mining sites, armed-forces bases, and huge hydroelectric projects. Major towns sprang up, including Thompson and Leaf Rapids, and a whole contingent of modern buildings was constructed. Leaf Rapids is notable, as its whole civic system – city hall, library, recreation facilities, and commercial services – was placed in one eye-catching, award-winning complex.

At the end of the 20th century and the beginning of the 21st, the architecture of MB responded to new challenges and opportunities. A respect for buildings of the late-19th and early-20th centuries has resulted in efforts by individuals and even governments to preserve many of these landmarks. And while hard commercial calculations continue to produce vast suburban "Big Box" developments and accompanying residential suburbs, there are also many new buildings that are completely modern in their aesthetic but which seem to reflect and respond in sensitive ways to the architecture of the past. •

Old and new on Winnipeg's Portage Avenue

Dauphin's stylish City Hall

Etienne Gaboury's Royal Canadian Mint

ARCHIVES in MB numbered 36 in 2005; however, half of them did not exist before 1976. They consist of: 1 commercial (insurance); 1 military (402 Squadron); 2 govt (MB and **Winnipeg**); 4 community (**Altona**, **Boissevain**, **Carberry Plains**, **Leaf Rapids**), 4 university (**U of M**, **U of W**, **College universitaire Saint-Boniface**, and **Brandon U**); 9 museums and galleries (**Brandon**, **Dugald**, **The Pas**, **Thompson**, and 5 in Winnipeg); 10 with religious affiliation (**Anglican**, **Jewish**, **Mennonite**, **Roman Catholic**, and **United Church**); and 5 others (Francophone, gay/lesbian, Girl Guides, Freemason, and **Ukrainian**). In MB, as elsewhere, archives can also mean records or documents kept as evidence of business or activity but not in current operational use. Archival records are thus always in the offing but not necessarily under specific archives' custody.

As organizational units, MB's archives are responsible for preserving and providing lawful access to archival records committed to their special care. Each archival entity reflects the record-keeping practices of its sponsoring parent and to a greater or lesser extent provides degrees of management in handling the information and records of the parent organization. This involvement varies widely from one archives to another, a few being closely connected to policymaking, current administration, and planning, others being more distant and passive in the long-term preservation of records. The intent of the archives is to provide a means for the protection and control of those records that should not be destroyed.

Archives of govt and educational institutions have extensively collected across a broad social spectrum, if records created or held by individuals and organizations are judged to be of archival value to society but have no ongoing protection from loss or damage. At times, acquisition of records from private sources, as opposed to publicly funded records, invites a purchase. Funds for the purchase of documents have never been readily available. Much more often, MB archives use the expert services of the National Archival Appraisal Board, which financially evaluates private records as donations eligible for income-tax relief.

The documentary holdings of MB archives mirror the particular reason for their foundation and operation. Most are paper-based with letters, files, reports, minutes, accounts, ledgers, maps, plans, drawings, and photographs. A small number, fewer than 2%-3% of MB's archival records, has been transferred to microfilm, which has a longer survival rate (more than 200 years) if stored and used judiciously. Yet, as technology for creating records advances at breakneck speed, moving from analog to digital forms, the archival capacity for identifying, capturing, and storing archival records in a sustainable medium is constantly challenged. Some MB archives have begun to mirror other Canadian archives by creating computer-run descriptive tools as part of a national network and exploring virtual exhibits through websites.

The Archives of Manitoba (AM), known before 2003 as the Provincial Archives, is the province's oldest public archival institution and holds one of the world's oldest business archives – dating from 1670, the Hudson's Bay Company Archives (HBCA) were donated to the people of MB in 1994. AM is charged under the *Archives and Recordkeeping Act* (2001) with identifying and preserving records of archival value to present and future generations. It is also responsible for promoting good record-keeping in govt to support public accountability and for making archival records known for public use. AM archival holdings amount to 24,600 m³ of paper records alone. There were 45 staff positions in the early 2000s, and annual expenditure topped $4 million.

AM's beginnings were not so promising. In 1885, the first librarian of the Legislature had begun to gather the few surviving records of the Council of the Assiniboia, the **Red River Settlement**, and early family papers predating the creation of MB. But the idea of setting up a provincial archives was mooted in 1914 and again at the end of WWI. The *Canadian Historical Review* referred to MB's archives in 1935 as "a bookcase in the office of the librarian." In 1946, a U of M historian was hired part-time for 5 years to attend to archival matters. MB's first full-time archivist was appointed only in 1952 with a staff of 2. He said sorting 75 years of assorted material would be a "slow and tedious process." His successor took over in 1968 with 2 archivists, 1 secretary, and 2 rooms in the Legislative Building.

The next 10 years were a time of progress. The Provincial Archives reached an independent status in govt (1971), private-sector records were actively sought out, and the HBCA was brought from London, UK, for deposit (as of 1974) in a newly refurbished Winnipeg Auditorium purchased from the City of Winnipeg and renamed the MB Archives Building.

From 1980, the govt's modern archives operation accelerated. Preservation expertise and a conservation laboratory were obtained. Over the next 25 years, records and information-management responsibilities grew progressively, especially with administration of citizen access to information rights (from 1988) and privacy rights (from 1999). Off-site records storage, especially for court records, with protective environmental standards has been developed. Since the 1990s, AM, like other archives in the province, has been faced with the scale of information technology evolution and how increasingly rapid changes will affect the integrity of future records.

Also in 1980, an Assoc of MB Archivists was formed, and 6 years later, the MB Council of Archives was set up. Subsequently, the 2 organizations joined forces to form the Assoc for Manitoba Archives. MB's archives have benefited from creative use of shared dollars obtained through the Canadian Council of Archives, set up in 1985 to enable joint federal-provincial funding partnerships for archival description and preservation initiatives. Since it began in 1991, AM especially, but also other archives in MB, have taken considerable value from the support and availability of graduate students in the U of M's archival studies program. ● GORDON DODDS

ARCTIC, ANCIENT PEOPLES OF. Between about 3000 and 2000 BCE, people reached Arctic NA, eventually occupying the area from Alaska to Greenland and as far S as the treeless Arctic coast of northern MB. Contemporary Inuit use the terms Tuniit and Inuit to refer to the 2 major groups of ancient Arctic peoples.

The Tuniit, whom archaeologists call the Pre-Dorset (2000 – 800 BCE) and Dorset (1000 BCE – 1400 CE) peoples, used small, finely made stone and bone tools, microblades, burins, harpoons, and projectile points, and, at the end of the continuum, excelled in carving artistic objects in bone, antler, and ivory. Pre-Dorset people hunted caribou and polar bear with bow and lance. The socketed toggling harpoon was used for hunting **Seal**, **Walrus**, and occasionally beluga and narwhal (*see* **Whale**). They lived in skin tents supported by driftwood poles, secured around the edge by an oval or ring of boulders, and warmed by a hearth fuelled by willow, driftwood, heather, and animal bone. Use of the snow house–inferred from the recovery of stone lamps used for burning blubber and the circular remains of dwellings without gravel or boulder borders–indicates that Pre-Dorset people may have lived on sea ice, exploiting the staple of ringed seal. Several families probably camped together seasonally for many generations. Often, Pre-Dorset sites are found at traditional hunting and fishing grounds used by later groups.

Sites marking the southernmost extent of Pre-Dorset occupation are found in MB on the North Knife River, Twin Lakes, Seahorse Gully near **Churchill**, and **Shamattawa**, 340 km S of Churchill. The Pre-Dorset occupation of MB dates from about 1700 BCE to 1000 BCE.

Artifacts from Seahorse Gully. Clockwise from top left: endblades, burins, burins spalls, scrapers, bifaces. Centre: notched

A

Excavations at the Seahorse Gully sites revealed an occupation from around 1100 BCE, at a time when the sites were on a small island. Ringed seal was the main prey, but bearded seal, polar **Bear**, **Wolf**, and **Birds** were also taken. The sites' location on a former island, the preponderance of seal bone, and the presence of migratory bird bone in the faunal assemblage imply a summer occupation and that the inhabitants used watercraft. The tool kit contained burins used for working bone, as well as a unique collection of large gouges, picks, adzes, and scraper planes, whose use may have been related to the accessibility of wood.

Around 500 BCE, the Arctic climate cooled, changing the seasonal distribution of animals and sea ice. Pre-Dorset people developed new ways of life, marking the emergence of the Dorset culture. Dorset people succeeded in the colder climate by increasingly relying on sea mammals for their diet and by developing suitable technology. Most Dorset settlements were located in coastal areas where sea mammals are abundant today. New types of harpoons and the crescent-shaped ulu blade were developed, as well as tools for living on sea ice—snow knives, ice crampons, and goggles to prevent snow blindness. It seems the Dorset did not use bows, though they used lances. The presence of sled shoes, dog bones, and boat ribs suggests that Dorset people used dog traction and watercraft. Ivory and bone needles and thimble holders used for tailoring skin clothing have been found, as well as many carvings that provide insight into the spirituality of the Dorset people.

Dorset dwellings were generally structures of stone and turf, 4 to 5 m wide, often excavated a few cm into the ground, and sometimes containing a mid-passage. Roofs were animal skins supported by driftwood poles. Soapstone lamps burned smokeless sea-mammal oil as a source of heat and light. Small boulder-covered caches near the dwellings protected a supply of frozen meat from scavenging animals. Dorset sites are found mainly along the W coasts of the Eastern and Central Arctic Archipelago, NL, Greenland, and also in MB on the Churchill West Peninsula. Here, Dorset people subsisted largely on seal and possibly Muskoxen, bear, eider, pintail, and arctic tern (*see* **Gulls and Terns**). Structural features of the few excavated houses were sub-rectangular outlines, slab pavements, and mid-passages. Artifacts include microblades, burin-like tools, an endblade, a knife blade, an adze blade, and a steatite vessel.

In the 12th or 13th century CE, people from northern Alaska moved E across the Cdn Arctic into areas occupied by the Dorset, displacing them. Known as the Thule, the ancestors of the modern Inuit, they developed a strong maritime economy based on whale hunting and the use of proficient dog traction and watercraft. There is little evidence of Thule settlement in MB,

PARKS CANADA, WNSC

although Churchill's Eskimo Museum contains artifacts collected by local residents, and possible house depressions have been noted in an aerial survey of the Churchill West Peninsula. By 1650-1800 CE, changing economic, social, and climatic conditions caused Thule people to contract into smaller groups to exploit regional resources. For the most part, these were the Inuit encountered by European explorers of the 18th and 19th centuries, although Thule people did persist until the 1700s in some areas.

The first European expeditions to reach the Churchill area (Thomas Button, 1612; **Jens Munk**, 1619-20; Luke Foxe, 1631-32) did not encounter local people. The HBC constructed a short-lived post at **Nelson River** by 1689 and on the **Churchill River** in 1717. At this time, James Knight observed a large winter Thule encampment at Eskimo Point and noted their extensive use of wood, required for making boats or umiak to hunt the abundant belugas. The building of **Fort Prince of Wales**, begun in 1732 at Eskimo Point, probably eradicated the remains of this settlement. After 1717, the Churchill Inuit retreated northward and Inuit on the western **Hudson Bay** coast began to rely more on the inland resources of **Caribou** and wood rather than sea mammals. Called the Caribou Inuit, they occupied the barren grounds and hunted with sinew-backed bows and hand-thrown lances. **Dog sleds** helped with winter hunting. **Fish** were taken with spears and leisters at stone weirs in rivers. Inuit groups near the coast continued to hunt sea mammals. By the late 1700s, Caribou Inuit trading parties were again travelling to Churchill.

On Churchill West Peninsula are 2 large sites with round and bilobate tent rings, caches, kayak rests, and graves. Artifacts found here were a mix of European and Indigenous – harpoon/lance/arrow shaft fragments, an iron ulu blade, paddle fragments, square nails, white clay pipe fragments, and glazed earthenware. Families who came to trade and hunt whales occupied these sites as, by 1795, the HBC employed Inuit at Churchill and Seal River. Inuit presence in the Churchill area appears in the archaeological record through the 1800s and early 1900s.
● MARGARET BERTULLI/TEIJA DEDI

ARCTIC GLACIER INC. is not only North America's second-largest packaged ice manufacturer and distributor, it is also one of MB's oldest companies, with roots dating back to 1882. That was the year Arctic Glacier's predecessor, Arctic Ice Services Ltd., was founded in **Winnipeg**.

In the 1980s Winnipeg businessman Robert Nagy acquired 3 Canadian packaged ice companies, including Arctic Ice. Nagy operated them as separate entities until 1996, when he founded The Arctic Group Inc. and brought all three firms under the new corporate umbrella. His intention was to take the new company public, which he did in 1997. By 2004, the company had acquired a total of 53 packaged-ice companies in Canada and the US, and owned and operated 25 production plants and 41 distribution centres in the 2 countries. By early 2005, it had become the second-largest packaged ice company on the continent, with annual revenues of about $130 million. ● MM

ARCTIC PLANTS. MB has a small Arctic zone, with characteristic plants and animals, in the far NE of the province and along the coast of **HUDSON BAY** (*see* **ECOCLIMACTIC REGIONS**). The bay creates Arctic conditions along its coast and inland for increasing distances as you go N. The northern treeline, beyond which trees can't grow and Arctic conditions occur, is just N of **CHURCHILL** on the coast and then goes inland at about a 50° angle toward the NU border. Farther N, many Subarctic plants grow, reaching their northern limits in MB, while true Arctic ones reach their southern limits.

Arctic plants are specifically adapted to a severe environment. Almost all are perennials, because of the short growing season, and most are short, hugging the ground as low clumps or layers or in hollows protected from wind and cold. Many have thick or fuzzy leaves, which botanists believe help retain heat from the Sun. Low, woody shrubs – including dwarf willows (*Salix* spp.), crowberry (*Empetrum* nigrum), bearberries (*Arctostaphylos* spp.), Lapland rosebay (*Rhododendron lapponicum*), and alpine azalea (*Loiseleuria procumbens*) – are common. Several maritime Arctic and Subarctic plants are adapted to high salt concentrations, and grow only along Hudson Bay coast. These include the edible fleshy-leaved sea-beach sandwort (*Honckenya peploides*), northern samphire (*Salicornia borealis*), and seaside lungwort (*Mertensia maritime*); thrift (*Armeria maritime*); sea lime grass (*Elymus arenarius*) and other grasses; Arctic chrysanthemum (*Chrysanthemum arcticum*); seashore chamomile (*Matricaria ambigua*); Egede's cinquefoil (*Potentilla egedii*); Greenland and erect primroses (*Primula egaliksensis* and *P. stricta*); and several sedges (*Carex* spp.).

Most of MB's saxifrages, low herbs with beautiful white-and-yellow flowers, are found only in this area. They include one of the earliest Arctic plants to bloom, purple saxifrage (*Saxifraga oppositifolia*), and yellow mountain saxifrage (*S. aizoides*); alpine brook saxifrage (*S. caespitosa*); and tall yellow saxifrage (*S. hirculus*).

The heath or heather family (Ericaceae, which includes various edible berries), also has many Arctic plants, including the showy pink-flowered native Lapland rosebay, and the commoner white dwarf Labrador tea (*Rhododendron decumbens*). Other heaths are alpine azalea (*Loiseleuria procumbens*) and the deciduous alpine and red bearberries (*Arctostaphylos alpina* and *A. rubra*). The 2 bearberries provide much of the red colour in the Arctic fall. Most louseworts (*Pedicularis* spp.), an unfortunate name for a lovely group of plants with intricate flowers, are not found S of Churchill. Other Arctic plants of interest include the white mountain avens (*Dryas integrifolia*), snow willow (*Salix reticulata*), broad-leaved fireweed (*Epilobium* latifolium), alpine milk vetch (*Astragalus alpinus*), alpine bluebell (*Campanula uniflora*), and bog asphodel (*Tofieldia pusilla*). Several Arctic plants occur only inland N of the treeline, including Lapland diapensia (*Diapensia lapponica*) and purple mountain heather (*Phyllodoce caerulea*).

The easiest place to see Arctic plants in MB is in exposed areas at Churchill, and in **WAPUSK NATIONAL PARK**. About 1/3 of the plants there are true Arctic species, while another 1/3 are Subarctic. ● KAREN JOHNSON

ARDEN, pop 150, a community 70 km NE of Brandon. The community was probably named by one of the town's first settlers for the country residence in Yorkshire of the same name. The Arden district was also called Beautiful Plains. The post office opened in 1884. Primarily an agricultural service centre, Arden was given the title of Crocus Capital of MB in 2001. It was home to the province's only dedicated organic grain elevator, however that elevator has closed and in 2006 was owned and operated by a local Hutterite colony. ● GPP

ARGUE, Robert FLETCHER, educator (b July 20, 1877, Stitsville, ON; d 1962, **WINNIPEG**). Known for being a favourite lecturer of his students, Argue was a professor and dean of residence at Wesley College (now the **U OF W**) and fought overseas during WWI. When he returned from service, he resigned from Wesley College after a dispute, and became professor of **ENGLISH** at the **U OF M** in 1923. From 1940-48 at the U of M's Broadway Ave campus, Argue was the dean of junior men, a group representing the rights of students on the smaller downtown campus (the older male students had moved on to the new Fort Garry campus). He was a member of the prominent **IRISH** Canadian Argue family, that also has also included Hazen Robert

Argue, Member of Parliament, national leader of the Co-operative Commonwealth Federation, senator, and federal cabinet minister; inventor Thomas Herbert Argue; and Andrew William Argue, a former chancellor of the U of Saskatchewan. The U of M's Fletcher Argue Building was completed in 1967. It houses the faculty of arts, other administrative offices, and lecture theatres. ● JT

ARGYLE, pop 100, is a hamlet 45 km NW of **WINNIPEG**. It was surveyed in 1872 and the first settlers came from Argylshire, Scotland, in the late 1870s. The first school was built in 1880. Argyle was connected to Winnipeg by rail in 1910. In 2003, the Brant-Argyle School, one of the last consolidated schools in MB, and the best example of its style, was designated a provincial historic site. ● GPP

ARMSTRONG, George, politician, labour activist (b April 17, 1870, Toronto, ON; d Feb 1956, Concord, CA) is the only Socialist Party of Canada (SPC) politician to become a MB MLA. Armstrong moved to **WINNIPEG** in 1905 with his wife **HELEN JURY ARMSTRONG** and their 3 daughters; their son Frank was born soon after their arrival. Armstrong was a master carpenter, and a member of the United Brotherhood of Carpenters and Joiners. His skill as an orator soon made him a leading spokesperson in the trade **UNION**, and he served as the representative to the Trades and Labour Congress. Armstrong was a staunch Marxist, and a founding member of the Winnipeg branch of the SPC, a party whose membership included both **COMMUNISTS** and **SOCIALISTS**. Armstrong ran to become Winnipeg West MLA as the SPC candidate in 1910, but lost to **LIBERAL** candidate Thomas Johnson by more than 2000 votes. He ran against Fred Dixon in 1914, but garnered only 953 votes to Dixon's 8105. In 1915, following the defeat of **RODMOND ROBLIN**'s govt, Armstrong ran against Dixon once more, again losing by a huge margin. Throughout WWI, Armstrong was a frequent soapbox orator in Winnipeg's Market Square, and his impassioned speeches would often incite crowds into an anti-capitalist frenzy. Though Armstrong played a minor role in organizing the 1919 strike, his speeches at rallies at the Walker Theatre (*see* **THEATRE**) and the Majestic Theatre made him a prominent figure, well known to members of the **CITIZENS' COMMITTEE OF 1000**. He was among 10 strike leaders – including **JOHN QUEEN** and **A. A. HEAPS** – arrested June 17, 1919. Though authorities had originally intended to deport Armstrong under a recently amended *Immigration Act* (*see* **ALIEN QUESTION**), they were embarrassed to find that, far from being an

"enemy alien," Armstrong was in fact Cdn-born. Armstrong was charged with 7 counts of seditious conspiracy, and appeared in a trial with 6 of the other strike leaders. He was convicted, and was sentenced to a year in prison. While serving his jail term in **STONY MOUNTAIN**, Armstrong was elected to the Legislature as a Socialist candidate on a "united labour" slate. He claimed his seat upon his release from prison Feb 17, 1920. After losing his seat in the 1922 election, he left with his family for Chicago in search of work. Armstrong later retired with Helen to Victoria, but they relocated to CA, where both died.
● MICHELLE DOBROVOLNY

ARMSTRONG, Helen Jury, labour activist (b 1875, Toronto; d Apr 17, 1947, Baldwin Park, CA) is recognized for her strenuous efforts to organize women workers and for her unconventional role as a strike leader in the run-up to the **WINNIPEG GENERAL STRIKE** of 1919. She was the eldest daughter of Toronto tailor Alfred Jury, a late-19th-century labour leader. Helen married **GEORGE ARMSTRONG**, a carpenter and radical member of the Socialist Party of Canada, with whom she had 3 daughters and a son. In search of work, George moved his family to Butte, MT, then New York, and, finally, to **WINNIPEG** in 1905. Helen campaigned in George's unsuccessful bid for a seat as a MB MLA in 1914, and later found her own political voice as an ardent advocate for the rights of working women. In 1917, she became president of the Women's Labour League, and led the organization of several female workers' unions, including housemaids, retail clerks, and biscuit factory worker's unions. Armstrong also played a crusading role in the 1918 campaign for an equitable minimum-wage scale for women. In Apr of that year, BC and MB became the first 2 provinces in Canada to pass a minimum wage act. Armstrong re-entered the public eye during the turbulent months of the Winnipeg General Strike of 1919. She was the lone female in the Strike Committee leadership, which included her own husband. Helen was on the front lines of the strike, organizing women workers, recruiting new union members, and organizing a soup kitchen for jobless female strikers. She had her own office in room 23 at the **UKRAINIAN** Labour Temple in the **NORTH END**, to which the various women's unions reported their strike activities. For her role as a labour agitator, Helen was arrested several times for disorderly conduct, and was eventually committed to trial for inciting 2 women to commit an indictable offence. She served 4 days in jail, and was released on $2000 bail. The end of the 1919 strike was triggered by the arrest of its leaders, including Helen's

DOROTHY DYER

Helen Armstrong

husband. In the trials that followed, Helen travelled to Toronto several times to enlist support and raise funds for the defence of the imprisoned strike leaders. One Toronto newspaper report remarked on Armstrong's resemblance to her father, who had been a well-known labour orator in his day. Helen later ran for a seat on the Winnipeg City Council in 1923, and was defeated. During the Depression years, she organized the Mothers Allowance Association to resist government reductions in the allowances for widows and single mothers. Thereafter, the Armstrongs withdrew from political activity, moving first to Chicago, then in 1945, to Victoria, and finally to CA, where both died. ● PAULA KELLY

ARNASON, David, writer and educator (b 1940, **GIMLI**), joined the Faculty of English, St. John's College, **U OF M**, in 1970, and became chair of the U of M English department and acting head of the university's Icelandic studies department. With a major interest in Prairie writing, he teaches Canadian literature and creative writing, and was the 2003 visiting lecturer for the Beck Lectures on Icelandic Literature of the **ICELANDERS** of Victoria Club, in Victoria. Arnason's published poetry includes *Marsh Burning* (1980) and *Skragg* (1987); his non-fiction, *The Icelanders* (1981) and *The New Icelanders* (1994); and his fiction, *Fifty Stories and a Piece of Advice* (1982), *The Circus Performers' Bar* (1984), *The Happiest Man in the World and Other Stories* (1989), *King Jerry* (2001), and *The Demon Love* (2002). He is founder and former editor of the *Journal of Canadian Fiction* and co-founder with **DENNIS COOLEY** and former editor of Turnstone Press. He has served as general editor of the Macmillan publishing series *Themes in Canadian Literature*, and edited **DOROTHY LIVESAY**'s *Right Hand, Left Hand*. Arnason's plays

include *Section 23/L'article 23, Welcome to Hard Times, The Hard Life Cabaret*, and *Dewline*, and he has also written *The Hard Times Cabaret* and adapted Henry Fielding's *Tom Jones* and Günter Grass's *The Tin Drum* for CBC Radio.
● MILDRED GUTKIN

ARNES, pop 381, is a cottage community 100 km N of Winnipeg just W of **LAKE WINNIPEG**. *Ár hnés* is Icelandic for "river points." Icelandic settlers arrived in 1876 and the community post office opened in 1877. The **CPR** arrived not long after. Arnes was the birthplace of noted Arctic explorer and writer Vilhjálmur Stefansson. Arnes is also the location of Camp Arnes, 19 km N of **GIMLI**, a summer camp for kids that also offers retreats and outdoor educational programs for adults. The area has several public camping sites. ● GPP

ARROW WORM is a small phylum, Chaetognatha, of only 100 species in arctic and sub-arctic marine waters, and found in the pelagic zone (mid water) and on the sea bottom. The body length ranges from 2-120 mm. There are 3 species recorded in **HUDSON BAY** (*Sagitta elegans, Sagitta maxima, Eukrohnia hamata*). Arrow Worms are a major component of the zooplankton, and are dominant predators of other small drifting species, mainly copepods. *Sagitta elegans* is the most-abundant species (1-30/m^3), occurring in Hudson Bay from the shallows to the greatest depths (over 150 m^3). The arrow-shaped, transparent body is gelatinous and 20-36 mm long, with 2 sets of lateral fins and a tail fin. The animal alternates swimming with floating, and ambushes prey with great speed. A voracious feeder, it uses its 9-11 spines on its head to capture prey. Arrow worms migrate vertically (usually near the surface at night and back down in the day) at about 30 m/hr, in response

JENNIFER LABELLA

Arrow worm

to light intensity and density of the zooplankton cloud. Sagitta is hermaphrodite, with both ovaries and testes clearly visible, but they mature at different times. There is only 1 brood produced annually in Hudson Bay, from July to Sept. The sperm packets are exchanged between 2 individuals, and the internally fertilized eggs (up to 1000) are released into the water, where they hatch in 48 hours and develop into tiny arrow worms (no larval form). These feed on zooplankton right though the winter, in spite of water temperatures as low as –1.8C. They live up to 2 years. Arrow worms are 2nd only to copepods in abundance in the zooplankton, and are eaten by fish and birds. They are especially susceptible to pollution (e.g., pesticide runoff from rivers, sewage dumping and oil spills). • REW

ARTHROPOD forms the largest group or phylum in the animal kingdom. They are characterized by bilaterally symmetrical (2 mirror-image sides) and segmented bodies with paired limbs, and a tough, protective exoskeleton (cuticle) which is moved by internal muscles. Its members are mostly small, but range from 1 mm mites to 4 m crabs. It includes insects, Springtails and relatives, **CRUSTACEANS**, **MILLIPEDES**, **CENTIPEDES**, **SPIDERS** and relatives. Due to sheer numbers of species, population sizes, and niches, these animals play the dominant role in all ecosystems, and represent critical links at several levels of the food web. Humans could not survive without them; crop pollination being just one vital role. Many of MB's arthropods are small and black – largely the result of adapting to the harsh northern climate, and to take advantage of absorbing heat rapidly from the sun. Some species take several summers to complete their life cycles, instead of one as in related species farther south. To date, 34,000 terrestrial species have been recorded in Canada, and biologists estimate the true total to be 66,610 species, to which must be added, when known, many thousands from aquatic and marine ecosystems, for a probable total of over 100,000 species. The number of arthropods living in MB's terrestrial, aquatic and marine habitats is unknown, but is estimated at over 10,000. This group may well number over 30 million species worldwide. Arthropods evolved almost 600 mya (Cambrian Era), most probably from an ancestral segmented worm (Annelida). The major groups are described in greater detail elsewhere. • REW

ARTIST-RUN CENTRES. As the name suggests, these centres differ from public and private galleries in that they are founded and run by artists in the community. **WINNIPEG**'s art community has been active since the 1970s in the development and creation of these organizations.

In 1972, a group of artists formed Plug In (now Plug In Institute of Contemporary Art). As one of the first artist-run centres on the Prairies, Plug In was a cutting edge institution showcasing everything from performance art to punk rock shows to avant garde work. **MENTORING ARTISTS FOR WOMEN'S ART** (MAWA) also started as an off-shoot organization of Plug In. They have since grown to be one of the best contemporary galleries in the country (although they are no longer considered an artist-run, but a public gallery). The programming has developed to include local, national and international contemporary programming.

When affordable video cameras were introduced to the market in late 1960s, a new world opened up for artists who wanted to make video work. Local artists such as Alex Poruchynk, Alethea Lahofer and Vern Hume were looking to work with this new media, and Plug In had recently acquired video equipment. Branching off of Plug In, VideoPool was formed and incorporated in Jan 1984 by artists working in the medium in the city. The premise behind the organization was for artists to "pool" together their resources in the new media so that artists who could not afford a video camera would be able to work. The organization, now called VideoPool Media Arts Centre, has since grown to include a 10-person staff, an extensive library of video art from across the globe, numerous funding opportunities for new media artists, and expanded facilities with dozens of equipment and several studios with state of the art editing equipment.

Although artists in Winnipeg had been working in photography for years, there was no single organization devoted solely to the practice. In June 1981, The Winnipeg Photographer's Gallery/The Floating Gallery Inc. was formed. Under the direction of then board of directors president **ROSALIE FAVELL**, the gallery became simply The Floating Gallery, and acquired a permanent exhibition space atop McDonald's Shoes on Main St. In the late 1980s, the Artspace building was designed to offer affordable space to arts community for both administrative and artistic work. Floating Gallery was one of the first organizations to move into the building. In 2002, the organization was re-named Platform: Centre for Photographic and Digital Arts Inc., with a broader focus to include not only photography but various forms of digital work such as audio, video and cyber art.

With more specialized artist-run centres starting in Winnipeg, it was only a matter of time before an all inclusive organization would start. In 1983, artists Donna Jones, Doug Melnyk, Larry Glawson, Janice Dehod, Gail Noonan, Gordon Arthur and Lorraine Wright were working together in a studio under the moniker Ace Art Manufacturing. Their common desire to have an exhibition space where emerging artists could exhibit their work saw the start of aceartinc. They moved into a space in the Bate Building at 221 McDermot Ave and moved down the road to 290 McDermot Ave where they resided in 2007. aceartinc. also had internship programs in addition to the exhibition programming, which saw Louis Ogemah through the program. He would later go on to be one of the founding members of **URBAN SHAMAN GALLERY**. The organization remains dedicated to showcasing emerging contemporary works, with a focus on local artists.

MANITOBA PRINTMAKERS ASSOCIATION (MPA) was established in 1988 to meet the needs of the city's print-based artists. Those artists working in lithography, intaglio and silkscreening had the facilities and support to work in their medium. After a change in location to Martha St, the organization expanded their facilities to a larger space in Jan 2000. Now also known as Martha Street Studio, MPA now has an exhibition space and programming that includes youth and Aboriginal mentorship programs. • STACEY ABRAMSON

Caricature of James Ashdown

ASHDOWN, James Henry, businessman, financier, civic leader (b Mar 31, 1844, London, England; d Apr 5, 1924, **WINNIPEG**). Ashdown came to Canada with his parents at age 8 and grew up in small-town ON. He was apprenticed to a tinsmith and first went west to Kansas. After coming to Winnipeg by oxcart in 1868 he bought out Winnipeg's tinsmith in 1869, establishing his small hardware store ("James H. Ashdown Hardware Merchant and Tinsmith") and building it into a major wholesale and retail business.

He supported **John Christian Schultz** in the **Red River Rebellion** of 1870 and was imprisoned by **Louis Riel**. He constructed his large house in Point Douglas in 1878. Real estate speculation added to his wealth. He built his second warehouse (today an apartment block) in 1896. An original member of the Winnipeg Board of Trade, he served as mayor of Winnipeg in 1907 and 1908. He was a prominent member of many boards of directors in both the business and the non-business world. ● JMB

ASHERN, pop 1513, a community 120 km E of **Dauphin** and 160 km NW of **Winnipeg**. Originally called Dodd's Siding after an early settler, the community was renamed after A. S. Hern, a timekeeper for the railway construction crews, in 1911. Ashern is the largest community in the RM of Siglunes in the province's **Interlake**. Located on hwy 6, it is the major trade centre for the NW Interlake. Agriculture is the dominant economic force in the area, specifically cattle production. Local beaches are popular with cottage-owners and seasonal campers. Ashern is also well known for its abundant wildlife. The Sharptail Grouse is common to the area and was adopted by the community as its mascot. Fishing also plays an important role in the local economy, particularly during the winter months. ● GPP

ASPEN (*Populus tremuloides*), also known as white poplar and trembling aspen, is the most common of the 4 native species of poplar in MB. It grows on moist sites throughout the province except for the far NE arctic area. The rustling of its heart-shaped leaves is a sure sign of spring and summer. Their delicate green in spring and gold in the fall provide much of MB's forest colour. Aspen's leaves rustle because their petioles (leaf stalks) are flat rather than round and so catch the wind more easily. Aspen is an unusual tree in many respects and very important ecologically. Its clumps are all clones, genetically identical individuals produced from a single original tree by suckers from underground roots. This allows it to recover easily after disturbances like fires, cutting and mowing, providing shelter, shade and food for many animals. It can also make it a nuisance if you are trying to keep an area open. Aspen has some claim to being the largest organism in the world, as some clumps cover several ha and have more biomass (living or former living tissue) than even redwoods. These clones all leaf out or change colour at the same time in spring and fall and so can easily be spotted. Aspen can be told from paper birch by its single trunks and greenish twigs whereas birch has several trunks from the same point

Aspen – also known as white poplar

and reddish twigs. The waxy coating on the aspen trunk is believed to protect it from sunburn and its greenish colour is chlorophyll that produces up to 25% of the tree's food by photosynthesis. Aspen, like other poplars in the Willow Family (Salicaceae), has male and female trees unlike most plants that have bisexual flowers. The female trees have long fuzzy clumps (catkins) of flowers that release millions of tiny fluffy seeds in late April or early May. These are carried kms by the wind, often covering the ground like snow. Aspen bark contains aspirin-like compounds (all poplars and willows do) and has been used by many native and immigrant peoples to treat a wide variety of ills. The inner bark is sweet and edible in spring and the wood had a variety of uses including canoe paddles, bowls and poles. Although not a major timber tree, MB's forest industry uses it. It makes up nearly 25% of MB's yearly forest harvest and is used mainly to make oriented strandboard. Aspen is the preferred food of beavers. Moose, deer and other animals eat its tender young twigs and its bark is an important emergency food for browsing animals. ● KAREN JOHNSON

ASPER, Israel Harold "Izzy," entrepreneur, politician, philanthropist and jazz pianist (b Aug 11, 1932, Minnedosa; d Oct 7, 2003, Winnipeg). The son of eastern European **Jewish** immigrants Leon and Cecilia, Asper grew up in the small town of **Minnedosa**, where his father, a former opera conductor in Ukraine, operated a movie theatre. The family relocated to **Winnipeg** in the late 1940s. Asper attended the U of M, receiving a BA in 1953, and then entered the U's law school. He received his law degree and was called to the

bar in 1957. Two years later, he founded his own law firm, Asper, Freedman & Company. He married Ruth Miriam "Babs" Bernstein in Winnipeg on May 27, 1956. They had 3 children – David, Gail, and Leonard.

Asper specialized in tax law and wrote a popular tax column for the *Globe and Mail* (Toronto) from 1966-77. He entered the political arena as a provincial Liberal in 1970 when he won the provincial party's leadership. During the 1973 provincial election, he campaigned for less govt involvement in the economy. But the Liberals came in 3rd, winning only 5 seats.

His business career and the roots of his media company **CanWest Global Communications Corp.** began in 1974 with the acquisition of North Dakota's KCND television station. Equipment was trucked north and the renamed CKND went on the air in Winnipeg in early Sept 1975. As CKND was launched, Asper became involved with the Global Television Network in Toronto, along with his partners in this and other ventures, Paul Morton, then the owner of Odeon-Morton movie theatres, and Seymour Epstein, a Toronto-based engineer.

In 1977, Asper and Winnipeg lawyer **Gerald Schwartz** (subsequently head of the Onex Corporation in Toronto) established an investment company, the CanWest Capital Corporation. Backed by a group of wealthy Manitobans, the firm made a number of profitable investments, including the purchase of the Monarch Life Assurance Company and a 54% stake in Crown Trust. In 1983, against Asper's wishes, the CanWest board opted to sell its interest in Monarch. After that, the Asper-Swartz partnership dissolved. Asper, however, kept the rights to the CanWest name. Asper eventually won total control of Global Television in 1989 after a court-ordered auction. By this time, he owned other television stations in SK and BC. Acquisitions of stations in the Maritimes and QC followed. His goal was to establish Canada's 3rd television network, a feat he did not accomplish until 2000, following CanWest's takeover of WIC Western International Communications. From his base in Winnipeg, Asper expanded into New Zealand, Australia, and Ireland. In August 2000, he engineered the biggest deal in Cdn media business history with CanWest's $3.2 billion acquisition of the Canadian newspaper and Internet assets of Hollinger International, then controlled by Conrad Black. This gave CanWest ownership of leading newspapers across the country, including the *Ottawa Citizen*, *Vancouver Sun* and the *Montreal Gazette*, in addition to a 50% stake in the *National Post*. Within a year, CanWest bought Hollinger's half-interest in the *Post* as well.

Asper was a colourful character. He once bought a building in Vancouver whose managers refused to allow him to smoke, he enjoyed the occasional martini, and he was an accomplished jazz pianist. Asper was also an ardent supporter of Winnipeg. He led the campaign to keep the **WINNIPEG JETS** in the city in 1996, though he was not a hockey fan. He lived his life according to axioms or "Izzoids," as his family and friends called them. His more noteworthy ones included: "Never start a war, but if you're in one, take no prisoners"; and "In negotiating, never give anything without getting something in return."

Israel Asper enjoys three of his favourite pastimes.

Asper was one of MB's great philanthropists. He founded the Asper Foundation in 1983, now overseen by his daughter Gail Asper. In the recent past, more than $103 million has been donated to various charitable causes through this family foundation as well as through his company's CanWest Global Foundation. The Asper Foundation has supported a variety of educational, health, and cultural projects, with an emphasis on Jewish causes in Canada and in Israel. It has supported the Asper Jewish Community Campus; the Hebrew U Scholarship Program; the I. H. Asper School of Business and the Asper Centre for Entrepreneurship at the U of M; the Asper Chair in International Business and Trade Law at the U of M's law school; the I. H. Asper Clinical Research Institute at the **ST. BONIFACE GENERAL HOSPITAL**; and the Lyric Theatre in **ASSINIBOINE PARK**, named after the first cinema owned by Asper's father Leon in Minnedosa.

Asper was inducted as Officer of the Order of Canada in 1995 and to the Canadian Business Hall of Fame in 1996. A year later, he received an honorary doctorate from the Hebrew U of Jerusalem; he was inducted into the Winnipeg Citizen's Hall of Fame; and was given the North American Broadcasters Association International Achievement Award. He was also inducted as a Member of the Order of Manitoba in 2000.

In 1997, on the occasion of CanWest Global's 20th anniversary, Asper stepped down as CEO, becoming executive chairman. Six years later, in Jan 2003, he relinquished that role and became non-executive chairman of the board of directors, leaving the company in the hands of his son Leonard, who became CEO in 1999. Asper planned to devote more of his time to the work of the Asper Foundation and, in particular, to ensure that his proposed Museum for Human Rights came to fruition. Before this could happen, Asper died at his home in Winnipeg on Oct.7, 2003. ● ALLAN LEVINE

ASPER FAMILY owns **CANWEST GLOBAL COMMUNICATIONS CORP.**, Canada's largest media conglomerate. The Aspers have become a dominant presence in Winnipeg through their support of various enterprises such as **CANWEST GLOBAL PARK** and the CanWest Global Performing Arts Centre. Through the Asper Foundation, the family also sponsors community organizations like the Asper Jewish Community Campus, and are driving the campaign to build the **CANADIAN MUSEUM FOR HUMAN RIGHTS** in Winnipeg. As the main shareholders of a company that operates 13 daily newspapers and 11 TV stations across Canada, the Aspers have sometimes been criticized for exerting too much control over Cdn media.

DAVID ASPER, lawyer, businessman (b 1958, Winnipeg) had his first experience in business at CKND, the TV station owned by his father, while still in high school. He went to university in BC, and studied at the California Western School of Law in San Diego. He was called to the MB bar in 1986, and soon after joined the legal team of **DAVID MILGAARD**, helping to win Canada's most prominent wrongful conviction case. In 1992, he left law to join CanWest, starting out at a TV station in SK and moving up company ranks to join the executive of his father's company in the late 1990s. As of 2007, he was exec VP of CanWest, and chair of the *National Post*. Among David's other involvements, he is on the board of governors for St. John's-Ravenscourt, and served as president of the **WINNIPEG FOLK FESTIVAL**. He was chair of the **WINNIPEG BLUE BOMBERS**, and vice-chair of the CFL. In 2007, he made an offer to purchase the Bombers franchise, and finance construction of a new stadium in Winnipeg.

GAIL ASPER, lawyer, businesswoman (b 1960, Winnipeg) attended Kelvin High School, and then the **U OF M**, graduating with a law degree in 1984. She articled and practised law in Halifax for 5 years while her husband Michael Paterson was attending Dalhousie U. She joined CanWest upon returning to Winnipeg in 1989, primarily doing legal work until the company went public in 1991, at which time she became corporate secretary. Gail is known for her community involvement. She has served on the board of the **MANITOBA THEATRE CENTRE**, and as chair for the United Way. She has received several awards for her volunteer efforts, including the Max Nathanson Young Leadership Award, the first Volunteer Centre of Winnipeg Award, and a YMCA/YWCA Women of Distinction Award for volunteerism. Through the Asper Foundation, Gail has led the fundraising drive for the $311-million Canadian Museum for Human Rights. She serves as director of CanWest, and oversees the corporation's charitable foundation.

(L to R) David, Gail, and Leonard Asper, 2002

LEONARD ASPER, lawyer, CEO (b 1964, Winnipeg) is the president and CEO of CanWest. Under his leadership, the company has acquired numerous TV and radio stations, and has expanded into newspapers with the purchase of Southam Inc.. Leonard studied political science at Brandeis U in MA, where he was capt of the school hockey team, and editor of the school newspaper. He then went to U of T law school, and articled at the Toronto law firm Cassels Brock & Blackwell. Upon joining the family company in 1992, Leonard worked in the legal department before heading up corporate development and acquisitions at CanWest's Winnipeg headquarters in 1994. Since taking over as CEO in 1999, Leonard has shown a different leadership style than his hardnosed father, and has made a name for himself as a strategist, with ambitious plans to "synergize" the company by maximizing the crossover benefits of owning so many different kinds of media outlets. Beyond his work at CanWest, Leonard serves on several boards, including with the University of Winnipeg Foundation and the Canadian Council of Chief Executives. ● MICHELLE DOBROVOLNY

ASSEMBLY OF MANITOBA CHIEFS is a provincial organization formed in 1988 to provide unified political representation for MB's First Nations. Governed by 63 chiefs-in-assembly elected by individual communities, the AMC is led by an executive council and a grand chief. There are 12 chiefs committees dedicated to issues like housing, treaties, justice, and child welfare, as well as a secretariat that carries out policy. From the late 1960s until 1981, the Manitoba Indian Brotherhood and its successor, the First Nations Confederacy, represented all MB First Nations. The organization split, however, and MB Keewatinowi Okimakanak acted for the Northern bands during the 1980s. The formation of the AMC brought the different groups back to the same table. The AMC is committed to principles of Aboriginal self-govt. The Framework Initiative Agreement, signed in 1994 by the AMC and the federal govt, began a process designed to dismantle the MB presence of the department of Indian affairs and northern development, and to restore Aboriginal peoples' jurisdiction over their own affairs. Current Grand Chief Ron Evans, elected in 2005, hails from **NORWAY HOUSE**. Previous chiefs include **DENNIS WHITE BIRD**, Rod Bushie, **PHIL FONTAINE**, and Louis Stevenson. The **WINNIPEG**-based AMC is affiliated with the national Assembly of First Nations. ● JT

ASSINIBOIA. Named after the Assiniboine tribe, Assiniboia is a term that has been used to describe several different historical and modern administrative land areas. It was first used as the official name for the section of **RUPERT'S LAND** territory granted to Thomas Douglas, 5th Earl of Selkirk (*see* **SELKIRK, LORD**) in 1811. In this context, Assiniboia was a vast region (more than 300,000 km²) stretching E from Lake Superior to the Prairies of present-day SK. The primary colony established by Lord Selkirk became better known as the **RED RIVER SETTLEMENT**. In 1834, the HBC purchased the territory back from Douglas' descendants, and reconstituted the administrative District of Assiniboia. The smaller district was a circular area with a 100 mi circumference, the centre of which was **LOWER FORT GARRY**. The pre-existing, **HBC**-appointed **COUNCIL OF ASSINIBOIA** governed the district until 1869 and the beginning of the **RED RIVER RESISTANCE**. In 1870, the founders of the second provisional govt established the legislative assembly of Assiniboia, and wanted the new province to be named as such until **RIEL** decided on Manitoba. The name resurfaced in May 1882 when the Canadian govt split the area known as the North-West Territories into 4 provisional districts: Alberta, Athabasca, Assiniboia, and Saskatchewan. Assiniboia

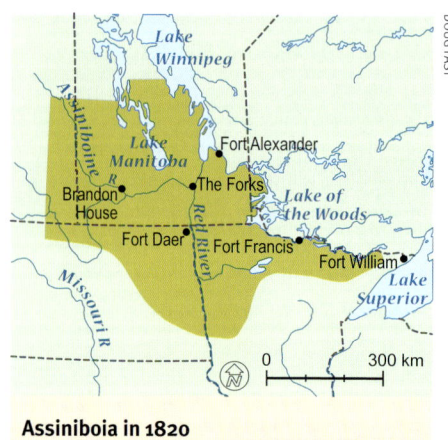

Assiniboia in 1820

was the southeastern district (present-day southern SK). In 1905, the federal govt chose to name its new province SK rather than Assiniboia, the moniker preferred by minister Sir **CLIFFORD SIFTON**. In 2007, the name Assiniboia remained in use in MB as both provincial and federal (Charleswood-St.James-Assiniboia) political districts, and also in SK as a town and a federal constituency. ● JOEL TRENAMAN

ASSINIBOIA DOWNS opened its doors June 10, 1958, and began a rebirth of **HORSERACING** in MB after Polo Park closed 2 years earlier. Built on the western fringe of Winnipeg by Jack Hardy, a local car dealer and horse owner, it was billed as the "Finest Racetrack in Western Canada." Through the years, Assiniboia Downs has been home to horseracing for most of the central northern prairies attracting fans from all over MN, ND, SD and MB. The Manitoba Derby was reinstituted in 1960 and has become the signature race for the track. Assiniboia Downs is also home to the Winnipeg Futurity, started in 1962, and races honouring the key players in MB horseracing such as **R. J. SPEERS**, founder of Polo Park, and Jack Hardy. In 1970, Assiniboia Downs hosted Queen Elizabeth II, Prince Phillip, and Princess Anne at the Manitoba Derby. The Queen presented the Queen's Cup to Derby winner, Franfreluche, the first filly to win since its inception in 1930. The Queen's Cup continues to be presented to each year's Derby winner.

Assiniboia Downs – at the gate

Purchased by Jim Wright in 1974, Assiniboia Downs became an innovator in the sport, introducing association colours and simulcast wagering. In 1993, horsemen formed a non-profit group called the Manitoba Jockey Club and purchased the track. It is now a year-round entertainment centre, offering simulcast thoroughbred and harness racing from around the world every day of the year, live racing from spring to fall, a large lounge containing VLTs and fine dining. Through changes in Cdn and US laws, betting pools at Assiniboia Downs are co-mingled with pools throughout NA, offering local bettors the opportunity to win big. Assiniboia Downs continues to be a major tourist attraction and employer for MB and contributes to the provincial agricultural economy. ● ALLAN GRAY

ASSINIBOINES. *See* **FIRST PEOPLES** essay

ASSINIBOINE COMMUNITY COLLEGE is an educational institution specializing in practical **NURSING** and agricultural training. It offers 32 primarily post-secondary programs such as culinary arts, Aboriginal community development, and media production. The ACC's main campus is located in **BRANDON**, but **DAUPHIN**, **WINNIPEG**, **NEEPAWA**, **RUSSELL**, and **SWAN RIVER** are home to regional training branches. Many programs are offered through distance education, and ACC features trade apprenticeships and co-op program options. Founded in 1961 as the Brandon Vocational Training Centre, it was renamed the ACC in 1969 when the MB govt also created **RED RIVER COLLEGE** and Keewatin College (now **UNIVERSITY COLLEGE OF THE NORTH**). During the 2005-06 academic year, ACC employed 500 staff, and had an enrolment of about 11,000 students, 2500 of which were full time. In 2007 the ACC planned to move its main campus to the former Brandon Mental Health Centre site. ● JT

ASSINIBOINE PARK, Winnipeg's largest and oldest park, attracts more than 1 million visits a year. Combined with the zoo and the forest, at 445 ha, Assiniboine Park is larger than New York's Central Park. In 1904, the city of Winnipeg purchased 115 ha of undeveloped woodland and prairie to become Assiniboine Park; the official opening ceremonies would not be held for another 5 years. By 1914, all major roadways, path systems, buildings, and landscape features had been created. That included the pavilion, constructed in 1908 for $19,000. The pavilion's dance and banquet halls, lunch, and catering facilities soon became the hub of Winnipeg's social life. The original pavilion was destroyed by fire on May 27,

ROBERT. R. TAYLOR

The Pavilion at Assiniboine Park

1929, and was rebuilt one year later. Between 1915 and 1950, there were few improvements made to the park. WWI, WWII, the **GREAT DEPRESSION** of the 1930s, and a flood in 1950 all placed great strain on the economy and posed major barriers to the park's development. Toward the end of the 1950s, an increase in economic prosperity allowed for greater attention to be given to park improvements. In 1961, the parks system was turned over to **METRO WINNIPEG**. During the 10 years of the corporation's existence, virtually every facility in the park was reconstructed or renovated, and locomotive 60433 – the last steam locomotive **CNR** used – found a home at the park. The park was expanded to include 287 ha of neighbouring urban forest; Assiniboine Forest is now one of the largest urban nature parks of its kind in Canada.

The Lyric Theatre, opened in 1999 thanks to a grant from **CANWEST**, is an outdoor bandshell used for performances given by musicians and by various arts groups, including the **ROYAL WINNIPEG BALLET** and **MANITOBA OPERA**. The Conservatory attracts 400,000 people annually and has been an integral part of the park since 1914. Showcasing a variety of plants and flowers even in the winter, it is the oldest facility of its kind in western Canada. For plant and flower enthusiasts, there are also a number of outdoor gardens throughout the park. The **LEO MOL** Sculpture Garden is another prominent feature of the park. The sculptures were donated by the renowned artist and are a celebration of his life's work. **ASSINIBOINE PARK ZOO** has been an important part of the park and has grown alongside the park since 1904. One hundred years after its founding, the city was struggling with how to best maintain

the park, considering such options as a condominium development on a little-used section of the park. ● JILL SEXSMITH

ASSINIBOINE PARK ZOO is the oldest surviving zoo in the country, and, with about 400,000 visitors a year, is a key attraction in the province. The zoo began modestly in 1904 by showcasing MB's native animals such as white-tailed **DEER**, **BISON**, and **ELK**. More than 100 years later, the zoo was home to 360 different species of **MAMMALS**, **BIRDS**, **REPTILES**, **AMPHIBIANS** and **INVERTEBRATES**. Collectively, the zoo houses over 1800 animals and commissions "guests" such as koalas, white tigers, giant pandas, and elephants to exhibit during summer months. The zoo's permanent collection includes favourites such as Polar Bears, Siberian tigers, and monkeys.

The zoo is located within **ASSINIBOINE PARK** in **WINNIPEG**. Much like the park itself, the zoo went through a series of growing pains. The financial stresses of WWI, WWII, the **GREAT DEPRESSION**, and a major flood in 1950 all hampered the zoo's development. Until its complete redevelopment in the 1960s, the zoo's growth was haphazard. In the early years, the donation of exotic animals merely highlighted the dilapidated conditions of the enclosures. The park superintendent warned that unless new enclosures were built, many of the popular animals would have to be disposed of. Despite the popularity of the zoo, and constant recommendations for improvement, it received little time and money for more than 40 years.

The 1950s marked a new era of revitalization. An advisory committee and the Zoological Society were formed. Under their guidance, the zoo was transformed from a simple collection of

animals to a more modern, professional operation. The zoo collection grew and became more diverse. The advisory committee also recommended obtaining a curator, and in 1959, the first full-time curator was hired. The children's zoo, known as Aunt Sally's Farm, after the first secretary of the **WINNIPEG HUMANE SOCIETY** opened in Aug 1959. On April 1, 1961, the responsibilities of the zoo were transferred to the Metropolitan Corporation of Greater Winnipeg. During the next decade, the zoo underwent more redevelopment than at any time throughout the previous 60 years. Virtually every building in the zoo was improved or rebuilt. In 2002, a continuing investment in the zoo's collection and the welfare of the animals was evident with a budget of just over $23 million.

The Assiniboine Park Zoo holds a number of longevity records – Debby the Polar Bear (*Ursus maritimus*), at 39 years in 2006, was the oldest known Polar Bear in the world. Animals in zoos are almost all born in captivity, often in organized breeding programs involving studbooks to avoid inbreeding. Individuals are selected to travel to other zoos around the world to pair up with other genetically valuable mates. Such programs have saved from extinction such Cdn species as the Black-footed Ferret and the Vancouver Island Marmot. The zoo contributes to over 50 official, international, endangered-species programs and studbooks. Success has been achieved in breeding the Lion-tailed Macaque (*Macaca silenus*), Amur Leopard (*Panthera pardus*), Snow Leopard (*Panthera uncia*), Vicuna (*Vicugna vicugna*), and European Bison (*Bison bonasus*). It is the only zoo in NA to display and breed all 6 members of the camel family (Camelidae).

The zoo allows people living in urban environments, who are seldom exposed to wild habitats and creatures, to regain some connection to the natural world. Zoos such as the Assiniboine Park Zoo remind us of our place in nature and demonstrate how we are still intimately connected to and dependant on it. ● JILL SEXSMITH / ROBERT E. WRIGLEY

ASSINIBOINE RIVER, more than 1000 km long, rises in eastern SK, crosses the MB border near **ROBLIN**, and flows S then E through **BRANDON** and **PORTAGE LA PRAIRIE** to join the **RED RIVER** at the **FORKS** in **WINNIPEG**.

The Assiniboine drains an area of 92,200 km² in MB, SK, and ND. Tributaries include the Shell, Qu'Appelle, Oak, Little Saskatchewan, **SOURIS**, and **CYPRESS** rivers. From the border to Brandon, it meanders across a flat-floored glacial spillway. From Brandon to just W of Portage la Prairie, it cuts across the Assiniboine Delta, and

A

Assiniboine River watershed

in the Portage la Prairie area, it flows across an alluvial fan where it has changed position several times. About 7000 years ago, it flowed N to **Lake Manitoba**. An eastward route to the Red River at St. Norbert was established about 3000 years ago, but the present route is less than 700 years old. Maximum discharge occurs in the spring – the highest discharge was recorded at Brandon at 651 m³/second on May 7, 1923. High spring discharge causes floods affecting settlements on the floodplain (**St. Lazare**, Brandon, Portage la Prairie, and Winnipeg) as well as First Nations reserves that border the river (**Gambler**, **Birdtail**, **Sioux Valley**, **Dakota Plains**, and **Long Plain**). The **Shellmouth** Dam, W of Roblin, completed in 1967, backs up **Lake of the Prairies**. It reduces flow in spring (for flood protection of downstream communities) and increases flow in summer (for municipal water supply). The Portage Floodway, W of Portage la Prairie, diverts water to Lake Manitoba, affording flood protection to Portage la Prairie and Winnipeg.

In 1738, **La Vérendrye** built **Fort la Reine** ("Queen's Fort") on the river near Portage la Prairie, and fur traders constructed Brandon House and Fort Assiniboine near the junction of the Assiniboine and the Souris. From 1878 to 1885, steamboats operated between Winnipeg and **Fort Ellice**, near the junction with the Qu'Appelle, but with the arrival of the railway line in 1882, river traffic declined rapidly. The Assiniboine provides water for residents,

businesses, and food processing plants in Brandon and Portage la Prairie, as well as for a thermal power plant in Brandon. Assiniboine water is also used for irrigation near Portage la Prairie, and its water is also pumped into the mill and **Elm** creeks and the **La Salle River** for irrigation supply. The Assiniboine is also used for recreation: boating, canoeing, water skiing, fishing (it provides habitat for 40 species of fish), and swimming are popular. Water-skiing competitions have been held at Brandon: the Western Canada Water Ski Championships (1981) and the Canada Summer Games (1997). Several provincial parks are located along its banks: **Asessippi**, at the Shell junction; **Spruce Woods**, near **Carberry**; and **Beaudry**, W of Winnipeg. Parks are also located in Brandon (Assiniboine River Corridor), Portage la Prairie (Island Park), and Winnipeg (**Assiniboine Park**). ● JOHN WELSTED

ASTRONOMY is one of the oldest sciences and was surely practised in some form by the very earliest inhabitants of what is now MB. Every culture throughout history has observed the motions and appearances of objects in the sky and has attempted to explain their significance. Many First Nations myths, for example, tell of celestial objects. Across the Prairies, great stone circles were constructed which seem to align with the rising and setting of the Sun and stars. None of these "medicine wheels" have been found in MB, but the peoples who built

them ranged across what is now MB as far back as 2000 BC. Although these **Petroforms** may have had other purposes, some suggest that they were an early form of astronomical observatory, marking the rising of the Sun at the summer solstice.

On June 3, 1769, a transit of Venus was observed from near **Churchill** by **English** astronomers William Wales and John Dymond. They arrived the previous summer and overwintered at Fort Prince of Wales, since ice prevented shipping for all but 2 months of the year. A transit of Venus occurs when Venus appears to move across the disc of the Sun as seen from Earth. By precisely measuring such a transit from widely separated locations, astronomers could work out the dimensions of the solar system. To the astronomers of the 18th century, this was one of the major questions of science to be solved. This observation was part of the first international scientific expedition, with observers sent out across the globe to measure this rare event. Capt (N) James Cook, in another, more-famous expedition, sailed his ship *Endeavour* to Tahiti to observe the same transit.

Nearly 2 centuries later, the US and Canada collaborated to build the Churchill Rocket Range, Canada's only space launch site. Many sub-orbital rocket launches occurred during the base's lifetime. Most were **Black Brant** rockets built by **Bristol Aerospace** (now Magellan) of **Winnipeg**, and were sent aloft to study the **Aurora Borealis**, easily seen from northern MB. The range closed in 1990. The Astronomical Society of Canada incorporated in Toronto in 1890 and received its Royal Charter from King Edward VII in 1903, making it the Royal Astronomical Society of Canada (RASC). The Winnipeg Centre of the RASC opened in 1911 and had over 140 members in 2006. The group is open to anyone with an interest in astronomy. MB is a great province to observe astronomical phenomena because of its low populations (meaning less light **Pollution**), clear skies, and northern latitude. Aurora Borealis, meteors, satellites and such atmospheric phenomena as sun dogs, halos around the Sun and Moon, and rainbows are all common and easily seen.

The **U of M** opened an astronomical observatory at their research station at Glenlea, about 35 km S of Winnipeg along the **Red River**. Its 0.4 m Evans telescope was the prototype for the proposed Queen Elizabeth telescope to be built on the summit of Mount Kobau, BC, and was used for a site survey before the program was cancelled. The telescope was then donated to the university and has been in operation since. The Winnipeg Centre of the RASC also operates its observatory there, with 0.37 m and 0.30 m telescopes. The **U of W** operates a 0.38 m telescope in a rooftop observatory on its downtown campus. There are several private observatories constructed and operated by amateur astronomers throughout the province.

There are 2 permanent planetariums in MB, both in Winnipeg. The **MANITOBA MUSEUM** operates a Zeiss Mark Vs ("Mark-Five-Ess") optomechanical star projector in an 18.3 m (60 ft) dome with 227 seats. This theatre is open to the public. The U of M operates the Lockhart Planetarium in University College. This theatre has a Spitz star projector in an 8 m (26 ft) dome. Used mainly for university teaching, it is also open to groups by pre-registration.

In 1987, Manitoban Ian Shelton discovered the brightest supernova seen in over 400 years. Shelton was working at the U of Toronto's telescope in Chile when he discovered a new star in the Large Magellanic Cloud, a companion galaxy to our own Milky Way Galaxy. Several Manitobans have asteroids named after them, including 5953 Shelton, named in honour of Ian Shelton; 12423 Slotin, named in honour of **LOUIS ALEXANDER SLOTIN**; and 14698 Scottyoung. The latter is named for Scott Douglas Young, who started going to schools and doing presentations in astronomy at age 16 with the RASC. He taught introductory astronomy labs for 4 years under Dr. Richard Bochonko and began a planetarium career working in the U of M's Lockhart Planetarium under Ian Cameron. From 1996 to 1999, he was director of the Alice G. Wallace Planetarium in Fitchburg, MA. In 2006, he was the manager of the Manitoba Museum's Planetarium in Winnipeg and was National President of the RASC. ● SCOTT YOUNG

ATHLETICS, also known as track and field, has its origins tens of thousands of years ago as casual challenges of speed or strength between amateur competitors. Modern athletics originated from the Olympic games of Ancient Greece, which awarded laurels for top male runners, horsemen, wrestlers, and pentathletes, among others. Early accounts of the **RED RIVER SETTLEMENT** report that foot races were held most summer evenings through the late 1870s, and often involved large wagers, with bettors trying to fix odds in their favour. In one such race in 1883, glass was spread on a track where an Aboriginal sprinter known for racing barefoot was scheduled to run. Also popular were pedestrian or "go-as-you-please" races, endurance events in which competitors walked a maximum distance within a fixed time, often over several days.

Track and field events were held at police and **MILITARY** sport days, at fairs, and on public holidays. **SCOTS** clubs were important to the

development of track and field, and in 1880, the St. Andrews Society of **WINNIPEG** held its first Dominion Day Games at Dufferin Park. Schools also held track-and-field events, and **JOE KEEPER** first started running while at **BRANDON**'s **RESIDENTIAL SCHOOL**. Upon moving to Winnipeg, he joined the North End Amateur Athletic Club, one of several athletic clubs that, through the first 3 decades of the 20th century, were the main institutions involved in athletics. The **NORTH END** club, under coach Walter Robertson, saw considerable success nationally and internationally, producing athletes such as sprinter Laurie Cohen and jumper Ken Aseltine. Brandonite **TOMMY TOWN** was one of the top distance runners at this time.

The first intercollegiate track meet between western Cdn universities was held in Winnipeg in 1920, with **U OF M** athletes winning 92 of the 126 points. The U of M team then travelled E to become the first Western university to compete in the Cdn university championships. **CYRIL COAFFEE** from the North End club qualified for the 100 m dash at the 1920 Olympics in Antwerp, Belgium. When a tight budget threatened his position on the Cdn team, Winnipeggers raised the money needed for his travelling expenses. Another track victory for western Canada came in 1927 when **JIMMY BALL**, after winning the 1925 Manitoban and western Cdn titles, won the gold medal in the 400 m race at the Dominion Championships in Toronto.

The 1930s saw considerable public support for track and field, with attendance often exceeding 10,000. Though the **GREAT DEPRESSION** restricted the number of athletes competing internationally, **ERIC COY** was a top athlete who set numerous Cdn and world records. The 1930s also saw the development of female track athletes such as Robina Higgins; Robina won 9 Cdn titles in javelin, shot put, and ball throw. Through WWII, track-and-field events were held in armed service competitions, or in exhibition races. One such, held at Winnipeg's Osborne Stadium in 1944, featured a race with famed US athlete Jesse Owens. **SVEIN OLAFUR SIGFUSSON**, a successful businessman who set a Cdn discus record at his first competition in 1938, won a total of 9 Cdn titles in competitions through 1954, often paying his way to meets so that athletic clubs could sponsor less-privileged athletes. Track and field relied less heavily on volunteerism and private funding after the passing of a 1961 federal *Fitness and Amateur Sport Act*, which led to further govt involvement in promoting sport. At the provincial level, Athletics Manitoba was incorporated in 1978.

The 1967 **PAN AM GAMES** saw the construction of a new track-and-field site at the U of M,

where MB's Janet Maddine Neale and Maureen Dowds won medals and Brian McLaren, who went on to compete at the 1972 Munich Olympics, won silver in the 4 × 400 relay and bronze in the 800 m. Competing at an international level, **ANGELA CHALMERS** won a bronze medal at the 1992 Barcelona Olympics, and **THERESA BRICK** was one of the first Cdn women to compete in the hammer throw, winning 10 national titles. Within Canada, MB track athletes mainly compete in the MTS Manitoba Games, Western Canada Summer Games, and the Canada Summer Games. ● MICHELLE DOBROVOLNY

AUCH, Susan, speed skater (b Mar 1, 1966, **WINNIPEG**) was an Olympic athlete and world champion. She won 3 Olympic medals during her 13 years on the national speed skating team: bronze in 1988 for the 3000 m relay, silver in 1994 for the 500 m, and silver in 1998 for the 500 m. Auch has also won 29 world titles, most notably at the 1986 World Short Track Championships in the 3000 m race, where she won a gold medal in record-setting time. She was voted the 1995 Female Athlete of the Year by the Canadian Press after her World Cup win over US rival Bonnie Blair, one of the top female speed skaters. Auch retired from speed skating following the 2002 Salt Lake City Games. She remains one of only 3 women in the world to have skated the 500 m in under 39 seconds without the use of energy-saving clap skates. The Sargent Park skating oval in Winnipeg where Auch first raced as a child is named in her honour. As of 2006, Auch was living in Calgary, where members of the national speed skating team train. ● MD

AURORA BOREALIS — or the northern lights — are one of the real benefits in living in MB. A spectacular sight in the night sky, the aurora borealis appears as glowing transparent curtains of green, blue, or pink lights and are often associated with winter nights. However, they are not related to seasons on Earth, but instead to the activity of the Sun.

Auroras are caused when high-energy atomic particles from the Sun – the "solar wind" – interact with upper parts of Earth's atmosphere. The solar wind streams outward from the Sun at high speeds and is collected and funnelled by Earth's magnetic field to the N and S magnetic poles. Here, these high-energy particles crash into the atoms and molecules making up the atmosphere – mainly nitrogen and oxygen. This excites these molecules, which then emit light as they return to their normal state. At altitudes of 100-300 km, interactions with oxygen molecules cause the common greenish auroral glow; at altitudes of about 100 km, interactions with nitrogen molecules occur. These produce a reddish colour. The aurora forms an auroral oval surrounding the magnetic poles. If solar activity is high, the auroral oval enlarges and pushes farther S, allowing aurora to be seen farther S. This is rare, however.

A The aurora can take many visible forms. Most commonly, it appears as a curtain of light in the northern sky, with red near the bottom and green higher up. The curtains can shift and "wave" in the solar wind, much as a window curtain blows in the breeze. When observers are at the same latitude as the auroral oval, they can look straight up into the curtain and see the pulsations and motions caused by solar activity. Although people associate auroras with winter, there is no real link to the seasons. You may see them more often in winter, but only because winter nights are longer and begin earlier. Auroras occur roughly equally in all seasons but can only be seen when the sky is dark; the light of a full moon or a city will make aurora invisible. The Sun's activity varies on an 11-year cycle, so there are times of greater or lesser auroral activity. The last solar maximum was in 2000, and the next (as of writing) was expected in 2011. The Sun's activity is more complicated than this, though, so some auroras can be seen in any year.

As of 2006, the N Magnetic Pole was in northern Canada, and MB thus had a front-row seat for viewing the northern lights. However, the north magnetic pole is not stationary, and was as of writing moving inexorably toward Siberia. In the meantime, **Churchill** is still world-renowned for the auroral displays that occur there on most clear nights. In the 1950s and '60s, sounding rockets were launched from the Churchill Rocket Range into the aurora to study them. Websites like <spaceweather.com> offer basic "aurora forecasts," but they are not easily predictable. The best way to see them is to watch the northern sky as often as possible from a dark location, especially in the few days after a solar flare has been observed. The farther N in MB you are, the better chance of observing the northern lights, but they can often be seen from Winnipeg and from the rest of southern MB. ● SCOTT YOUNG

AUSTIN, pop 450, is a community 75 km E of Brandon on the Trans-Canada Highway and Hwy 34. Austin was the 2nd **Railway** point established W of Winnipeg. The area was first settled in the 1870s, principally by those of **English**, **Scot**, and **Irish** background. Known originally as Three Creeks, a stopping point on the Fort Ellice trail, the community was renamed Austin in 1881 by

the gov gen, John George Edward Henry Douglas Sutherland Campbell, 9th Duke of Argyll and Marquess of Lorne. The gov gen was invited to name 6 stations along the **CPR** between **Portage la Prairie** and **Brandon**. He named Austin after Sidney Austin, a correspondent for the *London Graphic* who accompanied the party on their tour. Austin's economy is mainly based on serving surrounding farms. Canada's largest collection of operating vintage farm machinery is housed in the **Manitoba Agricultural Museum** here. Local tourist events include the Heartland Rodeo and the Thresherman's Reunion, a large country fair in which a parade of threshers, tractors, and other farm implements from early in the 20th century features prominently. ● GPP

AUSTIN, Albert William, entrepreneur, (b 1857, Toronto; d July 5, 1934, Toronto). The son of a prominent Toronto businessman, Austin arrived in Winnipeg in 1880, and quickly recognized the need for public transportation. He organized the **Winnipeg Street Railway Company**, and on June 12, 1882, was granted a 20-year franchise. Track was laid on Winnipeg's Main St, and the first run took place on October 20, 1882. By 1884, the company had 20 cars and over 100 horses in service. As the decade drew to a close, he finalized plans to replace the horse-drawn trolley cars (or, in winter, sleighs) with electric cars. On Jan 27, 1891, the first electric streetcar in Canada made its way over the Main St Bridge, and up River Ave to Osborne St. Austin petitioned city hall to allow electrification of the rest of his horse-drawn trolley system, which then extended from Kennedy and Broadway N to Portage Ave, E to Main St, and N to St. John's Ave. City hall responded by advertising for bids to operate the system. Thinking he was protected by his franchise, Austin did not put in an offer, and on February 1, 1892, the franchise was awarded to another firm, the Winnipeg Electric Street Railway Company. Austin appealed this decision all the way to the Privy Council in the UK, but it was dismissed. He continued to operate his horse-drawn cars along the same routes as the trolleys until 1894, when he sold his interests to the rival group for $175,000 and left MB, never to return. Austin eventually became president of both the Dominion Bank and the Consumers' Gas Co. ● DOUG ALLEN

AVIATION began in MB in July 1910 when US pilot Eugene B. Ely flew a Curtiss pusher biplane in **Winnipeg**. Exhibition flights and barnstorming can best describe the aviation scene in the province until 1924-32, when the newly formed RCAF set up bases in Winnipeg, **The Pas**, **Victoria Beach**, and **Norway House**, primarily to carry

out aerial surveying and forest fire patrol. MB was, and remains, unique, in that civil and military operations have shared Winnipeg's airport. MB took the lead in many aviation activities and was home to numerous innovations. In the 1930s and '40s, Winnipeg was seen as the crossroads of Cdn air travel, situated as it is, in mid-continent.

The first major commercial endeavour occurred in Dec 1926, when Winnipegger **James A. Richardson**, president of James Richardson & Sons, Limited, created Western Canada Airways (WCA). Richardson was the airline's president; Winnipeg was its headquarters, with its base on the **Red River** at Brandon Ave. Spurred by the gold rush at Red Lake, ON, Richardson's goal was to use aircraft to open up and develop the mineral resources of N Canada. WCA carried out Canada's first major winter airlift (to **Churchill**) in Mar 1927. The winter flights showed govt and mining officials the value of the airplane in peacetime. WCA was the first "airways" company in Canada to be run in a businesslike way. By 1929, it was the 2nd-largest airways company in the British Empire. WCA significantly affected aviation in Canada – it was the start of the nation's aviation industry.

In 1930, with the support of the federal govt in the form of airmail contracts, Richardson, using WCA as the nucleus, formed Canadian Airways Limited (CAL), the first transcontinental airline in Canada. Headquarters were in Winnipeg, Richardson was the president, and the vice-presidents were the presidents of **CPR** and **CNR**. The 1930s Depression and cancellation of the govt airmail contracts halted CAL's transcontinental development, forcing CAL to return to flying N "into the bush" to keep the company alive. Still, in the 1930s, CAL carried more freight than any other airline in the world. In 1931, CAL made headlines again with the purchase of the Junkers 52-1M ("the Flying Boxcar"), the largest single-engine aircraft in NA. In 1936, in anticipation of receiving a transcontinental contract, CAL introduced the modern Lockheed airliner (Lockheed 10A Electra) to Canada.

For his work in the development of the fledgling aviation industry, Richardson was posthumously inducted into Canada's Aviation Hall of Fame with the title of the "Father of Commercial Aviation in Canada." Significant is the fact that WCA spawned Canadian Airways Limited, which over time became Canadian Pacific Airlines, CP Air, and then Canadian Airlines International (bought by Air Canada in 2000).

In 1937, the federal govt created **Trans-Canada Air Lines** (Air Canada) as Canada's national carrier. The airline's operational headquarters and its overhaul base were both in Winnipeg.

"City of Winnipeg" aircraft and pilots on return of Churchill Expedition in 1927

TCA's formation was the start of the competition that characterized Canadian 20th-century airline history. In 1942, the Richardson family sold its aviation interests to CPR, which used them to form the nucleus of Canadian Pacific Airlines (CPA).

In the 1930s, other significant aviation ventures included the establishment of the Winnipeg Flying Club (1928) at Stevenson Field (Winnipeg International Airport); Lamb Airways (1935) at The Pas; Wings Ltd., MacDonald Brothers Aircraft (1930) in Winnipeg (now Bristol Aerospace); the Manitoba Government Air Services (1932); and **Standard Aero** Engines (1937), also at Winnipeg. All survived into the 21st century except Lambair, which went into bankruptcy in 1981.

Canada's first helicopter was made in MB in 1937 by brothers Douglas, Nicholas, and Theodore **Froebe** of **Homewood**. With no financing to make further improvements to their homemade helicopter, they abandoned it and returned to farming. The German-made Sikorksy helicopter, flown in 1939, is credited with being the world's first successful helicopter.

MB's blue skies and vast expanse of flat land made it an excellent training area for the **British Commonwealth Air Training Plan** (BCATP) during WWII. Airfields were built throughout the province, and industries such as MacDonald Brothers Aircraft tripled in size with war work.

MB's post-war aviation industry remained relatively strong. Mining-related flying was the bread and butter of most of the smaller companies. The most significant new companies in the 1940s, '50s and, '60s were Parsons Airways, Central Northern Airlines (CNA), MidWest Airlines, Northland Air, and Perimeter Aviation. MB's leading airline was Transair, formed out of CNA in 1955. Expanding through its Dewline opera-

tions and its 1957 takeover of CPA's scheduled routes, Transair developed into MB's regional airline. Transair made Canadian aviation history when it hired Canada's first female jet airline pilot (Rosella Bjornson) in 1973. Transair disappeared when Pacific Western Airlines bought it out in 1976.

Canada's first gold robbery at an airport happened in Winnipeg in Mar 1966 when **Ken Leishman**, the Flying Bandit, and 2 accomplices, dressed as Air Canada employees, stole $383,000 worth of gold bricks from one of Transair's DC-3s.

CPA became a stronger presence in Winnipeg in 1959, when the federal govt issued it a licence to operate a scheduled commercial air service to Vancouver, Winnipeg, Toronto, and Montreal. The CPA service broke TCA's transcontinental monopoly.

Bristol Aerospace of MB made world history in the 1970s when it began making the **Black Brant** sounding rockets, which it still manufactures. Bristol Aerospace's loss of the F-18 overhaul contract to a Montreal firm in the 1980s caused a political uproar, with accusations that QC was being favoured. MB was also home to many corporate air operators, one of the largest being the HBC, which began using aircraft in 1939 to keep in contact with its northern posts.

After WWII, the RCAF's presence declined, with bases only at **Gimli**, **Portage la Prairie**, and Winnipeg. Currently, bases remain only at Portage and Winnipeg. The amalgamation of air force, army, and navy into the Canadian Forces (CF) in 1975 saw Winnipeg emerge with Air Command headquarters at Winnipeg International Airport until 1997, when Air Command was transferred to Ottawa. The HQ building now houses 1 Canadian Air Division (operational HQ of Air Command), Canada/US NORAD HQ. The military side of the airport also hosts **17 Wing**, Canada's largest air force wing.

Winnipeg and Air Canada made world-wide news on July 23, 1982, when AC flight 143, a new Boeing 767 bound for Edmonton from Montreal, ran out of gas and lost all power and successfully glided and landed at a disused airstrip in **Gimli** (*see* **Gimli Glider**).

Winnipeg's main airport was Stevenson Airfield, named in honour of MB WWI ace **Fred Stevenson**, who died while testing a Canadian Airways plane at The Pas. It was renamed Winnipeg International Airport in 1958, and renamed again in 2006 to James Armstrong Richardson International Airport. Winnipeg's airport is one of the few in Canada to be open 24 hours a day, making it a key cargo centre. Building on its 24-hour-a-day status and its strategic position on the "the mid-continent trade corridor," private and public enterprise partnered to create Winnport in the mid-1990s to establish Winnipeg as a key air cargo link between NA and Asia. Although Winnport failed, the aviation/aerospace/avionics industry remains an important economic generator for MB in the 21st century. • SHIRLEY RENDER

AXWORTHY, Norman LLOYD, academic, politician (b Dec 21, 1939, North Battleford, SK). Lloyd Axworthy is the son of Norman and Gwen (née Thomas). Norman, the father, worked for **CNR** and later was an insurance agent and owner of an insurance agency; he served through **WWII** in the Royal Canadian Service Corps. Axworthy grew up in Winnipeg, in the old West End, and after 1950, in the **North End**. He was educated at General Wolfe School, Sisler High, United College (*see* **U of W**), and Princeton U, the last as a Woodrow Wilson Scholar.

In 1963, Axworthy wrote a letter to Lester Pearson, the national Liberal leader, protesting his decision to embrace the Bomarc nuclear-armed missile. He flirted with the newly formed NDP, but found the party dogmatic and too dominated by trade unions for his taste. His liberalism emanated from a tradition made famous by historian Frank Underhill. Like Underhill, Axworthy saw the essence of liberalism as a protest on behalf of the individual against big interests – in this case, "big" business and "big" unions. He ran unsuccessfully for the provincial Liberals in 1966 in the St. James riding and later, in 1968, worked for John Turner as a speechwriter in his campaign for the federal Liberal leadership. Axworthy enthusiastically embraced Pierre Elliott Trudeau's eventual leadership. He ran against Stanley Knowles in Winnipeg North Centre in June 1968 and was narrowly defeated.

The following year, he was appointed director of the Institute of Urban Studies at the **U of W**. His first successful foray into political office came in 1973, when he won a provincial seat in the constituency of Fort Rouge. In 1979, he was successful federally, running in Winnipeg–Fort Garry. When Trudeau returned as PM in Mar 1980, Lloyd entered the Cabinet as Minister of Employment and Immigration and Minister with responsibility for the Status of Women. He held as well a large informal authority over government activities in W Canada. He changed his portfolio in Aug 1983, becoming Minister of Transport and Minister responsible for the Wheat Board. At this time, he was involved in 2 important policy initiatives, the Core Area Initiative agreement in Winnipeg, and the phasing-out and deregulating of the CROW'S NEST PASS FREIGHT RATE, which had governed the costs of transporting western Cdn WHEAT and other grains since 1924.

Lloyd Axworthy, 1978

In opposition between 1984 and 1993, Axworthy went back into the Cabinet in Nov 1993 as Minister of Human Resources Development and Minister of Western Economic Diversification. He took on these portfolios until he was appointed Minister of Foreign Affairs and International Trade in Jan 1996, a position he held until he retired from federal politics in 2000.

While Foreign Affairs Minister, Axworthy oversaw a transformation of Cdn foreign policy. His initiatives cohered around the themes of "human security" and "soft power." The first oriented Canada's external policies to the notion of securing the physical and moral well-being of individuals throughout the world by expanding freedom, the rule of law, education, and social services. Part of this maturing policy was his advocacy of the "Responsibility to Protect" doctrine, which advanced the claim that there was justification for intervention – preferably by international bodies like the UN, but if necessary by other states – in another state's internal

affairs when the latter threatened the human security of its people. This, he believed, justified Canada's role in NATO's protection of the Kosovar Albanians in the war on Yugoslavia in 1999. "Soft power" conveyed the idea of a Canadian foreign policy that was much more about the utilization of civil society groups and non-government organizations (NGOs), international bodies like the UN and its agencies, and police and civilian personnel as the preferred vehicles for human security and peace-building rather than the military or coercive threats. Axworthy was a strong supporter of the UN; of initiatives to build international and multilateral agencies, such as the International Criminal Court; and of international treaty-making processes such as banning anti-personnel mines and dealing with war-affected children. Axworthy was nominated for the Nobel Peace Prize in 1998.

After retiring from politics, he served briefly as the director of the Liu Centre for the Study of Global Issues at the U of BC. Then, in May 2004, he returned to MB as president and vice chancellor of the U of W. Since then, he has been very active in attempting to raise the profile of the university, especially in the city's core area.

Axworthy is regarded by many as MB's most successful federal politician. His critics sometimes characterized him as the "Baron of Winnipeg" because of his ability to direct federal money to local initiatives like the Air Canada computer centre and the Core Area Initiative, but this never seemed to hurt his re-election bids. Public office for him was an opportunity to innovate and reform, and a chance to challenge entrenched bureaucracies and elites. His ultimate purpose was to move public policy in the directions of equality and of international co-operation. Administratively, he successfully recruited able and intelligent assistants who took his ideas and gave them practical shape and implementation. Axworthy was a rare example of a legislator who enjoyed both the rough and tumble of street politics and the heady world of national and international policy innovation.
● ALLEN MILLS

AXWORTHY, Thomas Sidney, academic, political advisor (b May 23, 1947, WINNIPEG), the younger brother of Lloyd, has achieved his own prominence in the Cdn political arena. The son of Norman and Gwen, Tom Axworthy grew up in Winnipeg, was educated at General Wolfe and Sisler High, and received his BA from the U OF W in 1968. He moved to Queen's U, earning his MA in 1970 and PhD in 1979. In 1974, Axworthy went to Ottawa as a special assistant. He joined the prime minster's office (PMO) in 1975, working

as special assistant and then policy advisor to Pierre Elliott Trudeau. After the Liberal defeat in 1979, Axworthy was named acting director of the office of the leader of the opposition. When Trudeau returned to power in Feb 1980, Axworthy became senior policy advisor. Appointed principal secretary to the prime minister in 1981, he held this position until 1984.

During his time at PMO, Axworthy was a key strategist in patriating the Cdn constitution, formulating the National Energy Program, reforming the Crow Rate system, and establishing the Royal Commission on Canada's Economic Union and Development Prospects. Virtually every major national policy topic benefitted from his political mind and tactical skills, including the prime minister's peace initiative of 1983-84. Axworthy also sought to smooth the transition to a successor to Trudeau in the summer of 1984.

In 1985, Axworthy was appointed visiting Mackenzie King Chair of Canadian Studies at Harvard U, joining the Kennedy School of Government the following year. While at Harvard, Axworthy also served as vice-president and then executive director for the Charles R. BRONFMAN Foundation. Under his leadership, the foundation created the "Heritage Minutes" dramatizing vignettes from Cdn history on TV and in cinemas. (About 60 of the Minutes involve MB, from Andrew Mynarski's Victoria Cross to WINNIE THE POOH.) He also co-authored the "Universal Declaration of Human Responsibilities" (1997) for the InterAction Council for the Former Heads of State and Government.

In 1999, Axworthy helped to create the Historica Foundation to improve teaching and learning of Canadian history, becoming its executive director until 2005. To recognize his achievements in Canadian heritage, Axworthy was invested as an Officer of the Order of Canada in 2002. Returning to Canada full time in 2003, he became Chair of the Centre for the Study of Democracy at Queen's U where he continues to pursue the themes of expanded human rights and responsibilities, democratic reform, Canada-US relations, and liberalism.

Following the Liberal defeat of Jan 2006, Axworthy was appointed co-chair of the Liberal Party Renewal Commission. Axworthy appears regularly on TV and radio as a political analyst, and contributes to both academic journals and newspapers. He also assisted with the Trudeau memoirs (book and television series) in 1992-1993. Axworthy maintains close ties to his MB roots, spending summers in the province. He lectures periodically at the U of W and he is an advisor to the proposed human rights museum in Winnipeg. ● DAVID CRENNA

BELUGA WHALES,
see page 61

BACHMAN, Randy, rock musician, singer/ songwriter, recording artist (b Sept 27, 1943, WIN- NIPEG). The son of a West Kildonan alderman and optician, Bachman started out playing violin until age 13 when, inspired by Elvis Presley, he took up the guitar. Bachman's dexterity on violin allowed him to progress quickly on the new instrument. Informal lessons from LENNY BREAU became piv- otal to Bachman's career as he, with schoolmate drummer Garry Peterson, joined his first band, The Embers, in 1958. Bachman later moved on to Mickey Brown and the Velvetones, then to The Jurymen. Spotted by East Kildonan singer Allan Kowbel (better known as Chad Allen), Bachman joined Allan's Silvertones, later Chad Allan and the Reflections. By 1964, the Reflections were the top band in Winnipeg and among the first local groups to release records; their single "Tribute to Buddy Holly" appeared in 1963. Their 1965 cover of British hit "Shakin' All Over" earned them a top- 10 hit across Canada and a place on the American *Billboard* charts at number 22, as well as a new name, GUESS WHO. The band toured the US and Canada for the next 4 years, releasing records to little success until 1969, when "These Eyes" – penned by Bachman and singer BURTON CUM- MINGS – became a North American million-seller. After adding 'The' to their name, The Guess Who

followed with "Laughing," "Undun," "No Time," and "American Woman."

After converting to the Mormon faith and rejecting the rock 'n' roll lifestyle, Bachman left The Guess Who, releasing a solo instrumental album *Axe* (1970) before forming the country- rock group Brave Belt with Chad Allan in 1971. Singer/bass player Fred Turner replaced Allan, and the band transformed into rock hitmakers Bachman-Turner Overdrive or BTO. Based out of Vancouver, BTO became one of the world's big- gest-selling bands 1973-76, with million-selling albums *BTO I* (1973), *BTO II* (1973), *Not Fragile* (1974), *Four Wheel Drive* (1975), and *Head On* (1975), and singles "Let It Ride," "Takin' Care of Business," "Roll On Down The Highway," "You Ain't Seen Nothin' Yet," "Hey You," and "Look- ing Out for No. 1." "You Ain't Seen Nothin' Yet," written and sung by Bachman, became a num- ber-1 single in over 20 countries, including Can- ada and the US. The band earned over 100 gold, silver, and platinum awards. They became the first Cdn group to be immortalized on *The Simpsons* (1999).

Bachman left BTO in 1977 over musical differences. Residing in Lynden, WA, with his first wife Lorayne and 6 children, he launched a solo career with *Survivor* (1979), later forming

Randy Bachman has received more than 100 gold records as both performer and producer.

the groups Iron Horse and Union (with Turner) before touring off and on throughout the '80s with a reunited BTO, interrupted by a The Guess Who reunion in 1983. In 1993, he released the solo album *Any Road*, teaming up with former Winnipegger **NEIL YOUNG** on "Prairie Town," a paean to Winnipeg. A much-heralded The Guess Who reunion for Winnipeg's 1999 **PAN AM GAMES** was followed by 2 tours; the release of his autobiography *Randy Bachman: Takin' Care of Business* (2000), written with Winnipeg author John Einarson; a CBC-TV *Life and Times* episode (2001); the release of his CD/DVD *Every Song Tells a Story* (2002); and *JazzThing* (2004), his tribute to mentor Breau. In 2005, Bachman began hosting popular CBC Radio series *Vinyl Tap* and teamed up with Burton Cummings for the CBC-TV special and DVD *First Time Around*, a national tour, and the album *The Bachman Cummings Songbook* (2006). With 2nd wife Denise, Bachman lives on Salt Spring Island, BC, where he writes and records at his home studio. He owns the largest collection of Gretsch guitars in the world, and holds the *Guinness Book of World Records* title for most performers playing one song, "Takin' Care of Business." • JOHN EINARSON

BADGER (*Taxidea taxus*) is a large and powerful member of the weasel family adapted to a life on the open prairies and deserts, ranging from southern MB to MEX. It has a stocky, flattened body weighing up to 12 kg, short limbs, and a wedge-shaped head ending in a tough, black nose pad. The limbs are heavily muscled and the claws are remarkably long – both adaptations for digging. The thick coat is coarse, with white and brown hairs. While seldom seen because it is mainly active at night, this species is common where ground squirrels and pocket gophers (its predominant prey) abound. The results of its burrowing are one or a series of large open holes in the ground, with several hundred litres of soil tossed aside. It has even been known to claw through roads of asphalt and concrete. The success rate of capturing prey is around 75%, but significant energy is expended in the process. The badger is a solitary animal, wandering over a home range of around 2.5 sq km. Since it is cut off from its prey by frozen ground for 5-6 months in the winter, the badger retires to an underground burrow in Oct, enters a deep sleep (but not true hibernation), and lives off its fat. The mating season occurs from Aug to Sept, the fertilized eggs postpone development until April, and 1-7 young are born in May or June. Few other predators will attempt to attack an angry badger, as it backs into a hole, bares its teeth, and growls convincingly. Its numbers are greatly reduced from over-trapping, habitat loss, and being struck by vehicles along highways. The American Badger closely resembles a number of other badgers on other continents, with which it shares a common ancestry originating in the forests of Asia. • REW

BAILEY, Norma, film director and producer (b 1949, **WINNIPEG**) Bailey grew up in **GIMLI** and graduated from the **U OF M**. She worked as a production assistant on David Cronenberg's *Rabid* before going on to direct documentaries and feature films. Her first film, *The Performer* (1980) – a 3-minute, day-in-the-life film about Roger Doucet as he prepares and sings *O Canada* at the Montreal Forum – won the Jury Prize for Short Film at the Cannes Film Festival. Her resumé includes more than 25 film entries, including theatrical features, television movies-of-the-week, and series-TV episodes such as *My Life as a Dog*, *The Atwood Stories*, and *The Shields Stories*. Her breakthrough as a filmmaker came with the 4-part series *Daughters of the Country*, which she produced; she also directed the one entitled "Ikwe." In 1996 and 1997, she produced and directed 2 films based on David Adams Richards novels – *For Those Who Hunt the Wounded Down* (1996) and *Nights Below Station Street* (1997) – which led to directing jobs on other dramatic TV movies. Her talent for translating stories based on real-life incidents led to her 2 most notable movies: *The Sheldon Kennedy Story* (1999), about a professional hockey player scarred by sexual abuse, and *Cowboys and Indians: The J. J. Harper Story* (2003), both of which have earned her numerous accolades, including several Gemini Award nominations. • GENE WALZ

BAIN, Donald Henderson "Dan," athlete, businessman (b Feb 14, 1874, Belleville, ON; d Aug 15, 1962, **WINNIPEG**) was one of Canada's most successful athletes and a wealthy Winnipeg businessman. His first athletic achievement came in 1887 at the age of 13 when he won the Three Mile Roller Skating Championship of Manitoba. He was MB's All Round Gymnastic Champion at 17, and that year also won his first of 3 consecutive provincial cycling championships. Bain began playing centre for the Manitoba Junior Hockey League's Winnipeg Victorias in 1895, and was made team captain. The following year, the Victorias won the Stanley Cup, which was then awarded to amateur championships. The team took home the cup again in 1901, after Bain scored the first-ever game-winning goal in overtime of a Stanley Cup match. That year, he also attracted media attention as the first player to wear a facemask during play, which he used to protect a broken nose. Bain retired from hockey in 1902, but continued to excel in various sports. He was considered one of MB's finest lacrosse players, won the Cdn trap shooting title in 1903, and claimed more than a dozen figure skating titles, earning a Cdn title in pairs competition. He was also a hunter who later championed **WATERFOWL** management, and he gave a large tract of marshland to **DUCKS UNLIMITED CANADA**.

He was chosen as Canada's outstanding athlete of the last half of the 19th century, and was one of the initial 12 players inducted into the Hockey Hall of Fame at the time of its establishment in 1945. As a businessman, Bain founded a successful grocery brokerage firm in Winnipeg with partner Edward Nicholson in 1905. He acquired sole ownership in 1917, and prospered with the development of a spur line from the **CNR** that facilitated the transportation of goods. His firm had 7 branches across the country. Bain became wealthy, and built himself a 3-storey mansion at 69 Eastgate in Winnipeg. He was a member of numerous secret societies, including the Ancient Landmark Masonic Lodge, the Prince Rupert Chapter of the Royal Arch Masons, the King Edward Preceptory Knights Templar, the Khartum Temple of the Shrine (of which he was a member for 57 years), and the Independent Order of Odd Fellows. When he died at the age of 88, Bain's estate was valued at over $1 million. ● MD

BALDUR, pop 477, is a community 75 km SE of **BRANDON** on highway 23. It was named by its **ICELANDIC** settlers for Baldur, the son of Odin and the god of innocence and summer sun in Scandinavian myth. Throughout the 1880s, Baldur's new homesteaders had no road or rail access to markets. In 1890, the community became a Northern Pacific (later **CN**) **RAILWAY** point, relieving farmers from the long hauls that were necessary to sell their **WHEAT**. More settlers came to the area, and by 1898, Baldur had a population of 400, though in the intervening century, the population has not grown. In an area dotted with seasonal sloughs and small lakes, Baldur depends mainly on retail and services for nearby farms, and is home to a school. Baldur's most famous son is hockey player **TOM JOHNSON**. The Grund Frireisis church, 7 km N of town, is the oldest Icelandic church in Canada. ● GPP

BALDWINSON, Baldvin Larus Baldvinsson, MLA (b Oct 26, 1856, Akureyri, Iceland; d Dec 7, 1936, Hayward, CA), immigrated to ON in 1873 and first settled in Toronto, where he worked as a shoemaker and served as bandsman with the Queen's Own Rifles from 1877-80. In 1882, he moved to Winnipeg, where he went into business and quickly assumed a leading role in community affairs. Appointed Dominion Icelandic Immigration Agent in 1883, he held this position until 1896, overseeing the immigration of 7000 of his countrymen to Canada and earning a reputation for integrity and reliability. Baldwinson was also publisher and editor of the Icelandic newspaper *Heimskringla* from 1898-1913, and he twice

served as Conservative MLA – for St. Andrews from 1899-1907, and for Gimli from 1910-13. He held the position of Deputy Provincial Secretary of Manitoba from 1913-22, and retired to California in 1934. He died in 1936 in Hayward, a suburb of San Francisco. ● NELSON GERRARD

BALDY MOUNTAIN, the highest point in MB, is 60 km NW of **DAUPHIN**, in the SE part of **DUCK MOUNTAIN PROVINCIAL PARK**. At 832 m above sea level, it is the highest elevation in the **MANITOBA ESCARPMENT**. In 1949, it received the name Baldy Mountain, as there are no **TREES** at the top. Visitors do not need to bring mountain-climbing gear as it is not really a mountain. Also, there is a road to the top. ● GPP

BALL, James A. "Jimmy," athlete (b May 7, 1903, **DAUPHIN**; d July 2, 1988) was a track and field star during the 1930s. He began his track and field career while studying pharmacy at the **U OF M**, winning his first major titles in 1925 at both the Manitoba and the Western Canadian Championships. He then went on to win gold in the 400 m race at the Dominion Championships in 1927. In 1928, Ball set a Cdn record at tryouts for the Olympic national team. He then broke his new record by almost a second in the same tryout's final race. He won silver at that year's Olympics in Amsterdam, where he also earned bronze as part of the Cdn relay team. Ball's last major competition was the 1932 Los Angeles Olympics where he earned a bronze medal as part of the Canadian One Mile relay team. He was awarded the Norton H. Crowe award for Male Athlete of the Year in 1933. He is also an inductee to the Canadian Sports Hall of Fame. ● MD

BALMORAL, pop 675, is a community 45 km NNW of Winnipeg. This community was named after Balmoral Castle, the Scottish home of the Royal Family in Aberdeenshire. The first settlers are believed to have arrived between 1874 and 1880. The post office was opened in 1879 and the community was also a **CPR** point. Most business in Balmoral serves surrounding farmers. Because it is within easy driving distance of both Winnipeg and **SELKIRK**, it also serves as a bedroom community to those larger centres. ● GPP

BALSILLIE, Gladys Eva "Gladdie," entrepreneur, burlesque agent (b March 27, 1919, RM of Franklin, MB; d Jan 9, 1987, **WINNIPEG**) was known as the "Queen of the Strippers," reigning over Winnipeg's exotic dance industry for nearly 20 years. Gladys Johnston attended St. Mary's Academy, a **ROMAN CATHOLIC** private school, and then took up flying at the Winnipeg Flying Club,

Gladys Balsillie, 1980

helping to form the Women's Auxiliary before marrying lounge musician Reginald Balsillie at age 21 and becoming his booking agent. The couple eventually saved enough from Reginald's shows to purchase a Main St restaurant called the Swinging Gate in 1961. The restaurant became a favourite hangout for **WINNIPEG BLUE BOMBERS** players. Gladys tended bar until the restaurant closed in 1967, after which she set up a bartending school. Around this time, she began booking go-go dancers in hotel lounges, expanding her business by recruiting women from other industries, including teachers and secretaries. She also became manager of the Airport Hotel's Continental Room, where many of her "girls" performed. Her husband led the house band at the hotel's lounge until his death in 1971. At the peak of her business, she managed roughly 100 exotic dancers, and was booking gigs in 45 Winnipeg hotels, giving her a virtual monopoly over exotic dancing. She introduced the first male exotic dancers to Winnipeg in 1980. She was a large woman known for her flamboyant style, but also a devout Catholic who made all her performers sign contracts forbidding drug use and prostitution. At the time of her death, Balsillie owed more than $600,000 to Revenue Canada in back taxes, resulting in the bankruptcy of her estate. ● MICHELLE DOBROVOLNY

BANKING was initially established in Canada shortly after Confederation in 1867. The first chartered bank branch in MB was set up in 1874, and over the next 20 years, the number of chartered bank branches in the province grew to 24. From its inception the banking industry in Canada has been highly regulated. Parliament has exclusive legislative authority over banks and the business of banking, as set out in the *Constitution Act*

(1867) and then the *Bank Act* (1871). Under this legislation, the federal Office of the Superintendent of Financial Institutions regulates chartered banks. The *Bank Act* and other relevant financial services legislation are updated periodically, usually every 5 years. The last major revision was completed in 2001.

B   Until 1858, a patchwork of money was in circulation. In 1858, the federal govt started issuing currency known as Dominion note (initially including ¢25, $1, and $2 notes), switching from the pound sterling to the new Canadian dollar in 1862. However, MB did not switch from the pound/shilling/pence system to the new dollar until entering Confederation in 1870, when the pound was valued at $4.87. From then until 1935, when the Bank of Canada was founded, Dominion notes co-existed with notes issued by private banks. The Bankers' Association of Canada regulated this currency. The federal govt gradually monopolized the issuing of currency, with private notes ceasing in 1944. Coins issued by the Bank of Canada are produced by the two ROYAL CANADIAN MINT branches – in Ottawa and WINNIPEG – under the supervision of the federal govt.

MB's rapid economic expansion in the late 19th century – brought on by vast immigration to the Prairies from the US and eastern Canada, the extension of the national railway network, an increase in agricultural production, and rapid growth in services – required the creation of extensive banking services. In the first decade of the 20th century, the number of bank branches nearly quadrupled from 52 to 192, the 4th-highest number of chartered bank branches in the Dominion, after ON, QC, and NT. A total of $614 million passed through the clearinghouse in Winnipeg in 1908.

Before this population and economic boom, MB's financial services were provided by a diverse group of private bankers and small banks, many of which were run as side enterprises by real estate and loan agents. The interest rate charged by these agents was high, ranging between 1.5 and 2% per month (18 to 24% per year) in most towns. The establishment of chartered banks in the province created a more competitive market that led to a decline in interest rates to about 8% per year. In addition to these small banks, there were also larger branches of banks in towns and cities throughout the province. These branches operated under each bank's head offices in ON or QC.

Around 1900, Winnipeg became the centre of banking in western Canada. Winnipeg's Main St was also known as "Banker's Row." There were over 20 banks and other financial institutions on Main St between City Hall and Portage Ave, including the Bank of Montreal, the Canadian

Current view of a section of Banker's Row on Winnipeg's Main Street

Bank of Commerce, and Imperial Bank (the last two of which merged to form the Canadian Imperial Bank of Commerce), the Royal Bank, and the Bank of Toronto, and the Dominion Bank (which merged to form the Toronto-Dominion Bank). Most of the banks had their Western regional headquarters in Winnipeg, and one, the Union Bank of Canada, moved its Canadian headquarters to the city. Two major banks, the Union Bank of Canada and the Canadian Bank of Commerce, accounted for about 1/3 of all branches in MB. In addition to these 2 banks, other banks operating in the province included the Merchant's Bank of Canada, Bank of Hamilton, the Northern Crown Bank, the Royal Bank of Canada, the Imperial Bank of Canada, the Bank of Montreal, the Bank of British North America, the Bank of Toronto, the Dominion Bank, the Bank of Ottawa, the Standard Bank of Canada, the Bank of Nova Scotia, the Molson's Bank, the Quebec Bank, and the Home Bank of Canada. Over time, many of these banks amalgamated or merged with other, larger banks.

MB had the first bank failure in the Dominion. The Commercial Bank of Manitoba, headquartered in Winnipeg, failed on July 3, 1893. The main reason for the bank failure was inadequate risk management, which subsequently led to mass withdrawals by depositors. Ultimately, however, all depositors and creditors were paid in full. The failure of the Commercial Bank led for the first time to banks in the Dominion accepting notes issued by a failed bank. These notes

remained in circulation and were exchanged at their face values.

Along with the chartered banks, a bank owned by the province, called the Saving Office, was founded in MB in 1920. Similar govt-owned banks were also established in ON and AB at that time. The aim of the govt bank was to fill a gap that existed in the provision of loans to agriculture by commercial banks. The intention was that deposits in the Saving Office were to be solely directed toward agriculture. The Manitoba Saving Office shut down in 1930.

In the last quarter of the 20th century, MB's banking industry grew dramatically. The total assets of the chartered banks grew almost 8-fold in the period between 1975-2004, reaching $28.5 billion by 2004. About 50% of the assets consist of loans, 30% of which are personal loans, 16% business loans, 40% residential mortgage, 3% non-residential mortgages, and 8% agricultural loans. As the banking industry has evolved, new technologies, such as bank machines and telephone or online banking, have allowed chartered banks to decrease employee numbers and branches in MB. Since 1997, the number of employees in chartered banks in Manitoba has been declining by 3% a year, on average, reaching 5370 in 2004.

Until the mid-1950s, the primary function of the chartered banks was to accept deposits and grant commercial loans. The scope of the banking industry has, however, changed considerably since then. Changes to the *Bank Act* in 1954 and 1967 allowed banks to offer new services, such

as mortgages and consumer loans, and a 1992 rewriting of the act allowed banks to own and operate trust companies and stock-brokerage services. Many chartered banks in MB now operate brokerage service subsidiaries, in addition to their traditional functions as chartered banks. ● SAEED MOSHIRI

▸ *See also* **CREDIT UNIONS**.

BANNATYNE, Andrew Graham Ballenden, fur trader, merchant, politician (b Oct 31, 1829, Orkney Islands [UK]; d May 18, 1889, St. Paul, MN). Bannatyne joined the **HBC** service at age 14, later becoming a Free Trader. According to Walter Traill, he quit the Company to marry Annie McDermott [see **ANNIE BANNATYNE**], since junior clerks were not allowed to wed. In 1857, he was arrested by the HBC for illegal trading, but was released by recorder [judge] Francis Johnson in a decision approved by the HBC's London Committee. By 1868, he was in partnership with Alexander Begg, running what quickly became the largest merchant firm in the **RED RIVER SETTLEMENT**. Bannatyne sought to act as a conciliator during the troubled times of 1869-70, serving as postmaster in **LOUIS RIEL**'s Provisional Govt on the condition that it seek terms from Canada. Although the English-speaking community was critical of him, he was appointed Winnipeg's first postmaster in 1871. That same year he helped found the St. Andrew's Society and an early lodge of Freemasons in MB. For several years, beginning in 1873, he supported Louis Riel's political pretensions and helped seek the release from prison of **AMBROISE LÉPINE**. He was himself elected to Riel's House of Commons seat in 1875, but he devoted most of his attention to business and local philanthropy, helping to organize the Winnipeg General Hospital, for example. He also played in Winnipeg's first curling match in Dec 1876. Although he became wealthy in the MB land boom of the early 1880s, he held on too long and lost virtually everything. He subsequently became involved in dubious dealings in **MÉTIS SCRIP**. He died on vacation in St. Paul, MN. ● JMB

BANNATYNE, Annie, hostess (b 1830; d May 14, 1908, SK). The **COUNTRY-BORN** daughter of **ANDREW MCDERMOTT** and wife of **A. G. B. BANNATYNE**, Annie was a noted hostess and charity organizer in the village of **WINNIPEG**. In Feb 1869 she famously horsewhipped poet **CHARLES MAIR** (either in her husband's store or on its front steps, depending on who tells the story) over slurs Mair had published in a Toronto newspaper about mixed-blood women in the **RED RIVER SETTLEMENT**. Her later energy was devoted to the Winnipeg General Hospital, built on land owned by her family. ● JMB

Cordell Barker's *The Cat Came Back* was nominated for an Oscar in 1988.

BARKER, Cordell, animator, filmmaker (b Sept 10, 1956, **WINNIPEG**). Like most of Winnipeg's animators, Cordell Barker apprenticed at Kenn Perkins Animation and began his career with *Sesame Street* inserts and **K-TEL** ads. By 2006, he had completed more than 100 hundred animated commercials and 2 multi-award-winning (Zagreb, Annecy, Hiroshima, New York, Los Angeles festivals) short **FILMS** through the **NATIONAL FILM BOARD**: *The Cat Came Back* (1988) and *Strange Invaders* (2002). Both were nominated for Oscars; *Cat* won the Genie for Best Animation in Canada in 1989. ● GENE WALZ

BARKER, William George "Billy," WWI pilot, **VICTORIA CROSS** winner (b Nov 3, 1894, **DAUPHIN**; d Mar 12, 1930, Ottawa). Barker was the most decorated Commonwealth serviceman of WWI and among the greatest flying aces Canada has produced. Mentioned in dispatches on three occasions, Barker also earned a Distinguished Service Order with Bar; Military Cross with 2 Bars; 2 Croix de guerre; and 3 Silver Medals for Valour from Italy. He enlisted in **WINNIPEG** in 1914 as an infantryman. After being gassed at Ypres as a Pte, he transferred to the RFC. He proved to be a natural pilot and a deadly shot. Flying on both the French and Italian fronts, he shot down 46 enemy aircraft. Barker's greatest exploit, for which he was awarded the VC, occurred near the end of WWI. Ordered back to England, Maj (later Lt Col) Barker was flying north when 15 German fighter planes ambushed him. Deciding that escape was impossible, Barker attacked. He managed to down 3 Fokkers before his bullet-ridden plane crashed near British lines. Miraculously, despite terrible wounds, he survived. After the war, Barker eventually became president of the Fairchild Aviation Corporation. He died after crashing a Fairchild plane during a test flight for Department of National Defence officials in Ottawa. Fellow Cdn ace Billy Bishop called Barker "the deadliest air fighter that ever lived." The Dauphin airport is named for Barker. ● R.G. ENFIELD

Dauphin's Billy Barker

BARNACLE is a type of crustacean found attached to rocks on seashores. There are 3 species of Acorn Barnacles reported in Hudson Bay – the Northern Rock (*Balanus balanoides*), Rough (*Balanus balanus*), and Notched (*Balanus crenatus*) – but several others will likely be found. These are sessile organisms, closely resembling molluscs, even down to having a "mantle" which secretes the calcareous shell plates. These plates are sharp-edged and can easily cut a predator or careless person. The 2-piece carapace is composed of 2 pairs of plates, which control the opening for the appendages, and 4 other pairs of plates. The shortened body is twisted inside so that the 6 pairs of feathery feeding appendages extend out the opening at the top, and these sweep tiny drifting animals and algae from the sea water into the mouth. Some groups of barnacles are parasitic or attach to other creatures such as lobsters, worms, or whales. The Hudson Bay barnacles species are 25-50 mm high and 13-50 mm wide, and often grow in bunches cemented to rocks and timbers by means of a tough base. They are abundant from the intertidal zone to shallow waters, although the Rough

B

Barnacle can also live to a depth of 165 m. Most barnacles specialize in living on wave-swept rocky beaches where competition for space is lessened by the rough conditions. When exposed to the atmosphere during twice-daily low tides, a barnacle seals itself inside its protective shells and awaits re-submergence before it opens again to resume feeding. Most species of barnacles are hermaphrodites, so they can fertilize their own eggs if necessary. However, since barnacles are often found in colonies, there is usually sexual breeding among them, with the highly extendable penis fertilizing the eggs inside the other member's mantle cavity. The eggs are brooded in an ovisac and hatch into nauplius larvae, which are released to drift and feed in the plankton. After moulting several times, the nauplius metamorphoses into a cypris larva, which continues to accumulate food reserves for about 3 months. How this larva selects a site to settle down is unknown, but it is often attracted to existing colonies. Once attached by its head, it cannot move again. The juvenile continues to feed and grow, eventually reaching the mature adult stage. A barnacle may survive 10 years. Barnacles are a fascinating part of the Hudson Bay fauna, and are eaten by a variety of fish and seabirds. • REW

BARREN LANDS FIRST NATION (formerly known as Brochet First Nation), on reserve pop 473, off reserve pop 452, is situated 928 km N of **WINNIPEG**, and 19 km E of the SK border. Treaty 10 was signed here in 1907. Access to Barren Lands First Nation is restricted to air travel, however, there is also a winter road to bring in construction material and fuel. In 2006, the people of Barren Lands were actively pursuing the building of an all-season road. The Frontier School Division administers schooling. This First Nation community goes from Nursery-Grade 9, and total enrolment for the year 2003-2004 was 130. Barren Lands' students attend high schools in nearby MB towns. One of this community's greatest accomplishments is that it has a very high post-secondary graduation rate in professions such as medicine, nursing, and teaching. The community of Barren Lands includes one reserve, called Brochet I.R. No. 197. It is a member of the Keewatin Tribal Council. The native languages in this community are Cree and Dene. Barren Lands' economic strength lies in commercial guided fishing, trapping, hunting, and construction. The playwright **TOMSON HIGHWAY** hails from Barren Lands area. Actor and writer **BILLY MERASTY**, also from the Barren Lands First Nation community, is known for productions such as *Fireweed: an Indigenous Fairy Tale*, *Le Confessional*, and *The Red Green Show*. • RK

BARROWS (pop 127) lies between **MAFEKING** and the MB-SK boundary, 95km NW of **SWAN RIVER**. It is the service centre for 5 communities: Baden, Powell, National Mills, Red Deer Lake and the Westgate cottage area. It was recognized as a community in 1984, and is governed by a mayor and council. The population has fallen from 176 in 1985. The local school handles students from all communities. There is a ball diamond, recreation hall, outdoor rink, restaurant, poolroom and post office. The economy depends on trapping, pulpwood harvesting and some milling. • GPP

BASEBALL has existed in MB since the early days of pioneer agricultural settlement. It fit well into the warm, long Prairie evenings between seeding and harvest, and offered a natural break after each pitch, so that one could watch a game while joking with friends or keeping an eye on the children. The sport also rewards several attributes that Manitobans have always applauded – including skill, teamwork, dedication, and sportsmanship. If baseball and **SOFTBALL** are lumped together, they are probably the most popular sport in MB's history.

Although First Nations peoples who inhabited MB for many centuries before Europeans arrived played several different types of ball games, none of them resembled baseball. The first signs of a game resembling baseball in MB appeared in the mid-19th century, when children in the **RED RIVER SETTLEMENT** amused themselves by playing a game they called "bat," which was a rudimentary form of baseball. In 1873, the first baseball clubs appeared in Winnipeg. Over the next few years, hundreds of clubs were established in the cities, towns, and villages of the rapidly growing province.

By the early 20th century, baseball was by far MB's most visible sport. Tiny villages, several school districts, and some rural townships had teams. Meanwhile, in the larger towns and cities, there were dozens of clubs, formed by trade unions, educational institutions, businesses, fraternal organizations, and neighbourhood groups. The better players in the towns and cities took part in senior or intermediate teams, which normally played in some kind of district league.

MB's golden years for baseball were the 1910s to the 1960s. In these decades, car use became more common, and a highway network was built up that allowed for the formation of leagues such as the Provencher, Border, Interlake, Midwest, Northern, or even, after WWII, the Polar. Teams in these leagues competed against each other at frequent tournaments or fairs around the province, especially on Victoria Day and Canada Day. From the 1920s forward, cars and highways also enabled high-calibre US barnstorming teams, such as the House of David, to visit, and the many teams – such as the Indianapolis Clowns or the Kansas City Monarchs – whose skilled **BLACK** players were not allowed into baseball's organized (white) major leagues. Some of the province's prominent players, such as **TERRY SAWCHUK** and **TONY TASCONA**, went on to be recognized for other endeavours.

Beginning in the 1960s and 1970s, rural depopulation combined with the growing popularity of sports such as soccer and golf caused

Great West Saddlery team, 1904

AM, SPORT - BASEBALL 5, N5156

smaller towns to lose their baseball teams. But the sport continued to be one of the most significant in the province, and crowds of hundreds or even thousands of spectators were likely to gather for games played in the Manitoba Senior Baseball League, formed in 1961. This league featured teams from **Brandon, Dauphin, Binscarth, Hamiota, Souris, Virden,** Riverside, Angusville, **Neepawa,** and other MB towns; and it paved the way for the RedBoine League, formed in 1970, with teams from **Winnipeg, Teulon, Carman,** Giroux, and other centres within an hour or so of the capital.

Winnipeg Goldeyes, 2006

Professional players have been a more consistent part of the MB scene in baseball than they have been in any other sport. Pro players have usually come from the US. Ever since 1878, it has been common for teams to import 1 or 2 pros, usually pitchers, to play alongside local amateurs. The first completely professional league was formed in 1886. It was comprised of 3 teams from Winnipeg and one from Portage la Prairie. It lasted only one season. Since early in the 20th century, several pro teams have come and gone. Several Winnipeg teams, usually called the Maroons or the Goldeyes, have been formed to play in leagues with teams from other cities in western Canada or from the northern US. At times, teams from Brandon or Carman have been part of these leagues. This was true especially in

the early 1950s, when both these centres, as well as Winnipeg had teams in the prestigious **Man-Dak League** (1950-57), a MB/ND league with some excellent former Negro League players. At present, the only professional team in the province is the Winnipeg Goldeyes of the independent Northern League.

Since late in the 19th century Manitobans, through their newspapers, then radios, then television sets, and now the Internet, have been keen followers of major-league baseball. However, only one Manitoban has been good enough to play at the major league level: **Corey Koskie** was born and raised in **Anola.**

Until the 1940s, baseball was a grown man's game. Boys played "scrub" or "500," or maybe the odd pick-up game, but rarely participated in highly organized matches. This changed in the 1940s, 1950s, and 1960s, as Little Leagues, PONY Leagues, Bantam or Midget, and other leagues, complete with umpires and scorekeepers and well-prepared diamonds, sprung up around MB. Soon, the youth teams from MB were competing in provincial, western Canadian, national, or even international championship events. MB's teams qualified for these events by registering with the Manitoba Baseball Association, created in 1968.

Since the 1960s, MB has played host to important national and international championships. Probably the most important of these were the tournaments held as part of the Pan American Games in both 1967 and 1999. The 1967 baseball games, played in Winnipeg, Portage, and Carman, drew a total of over 100,000 fans. Two other superbly organized and well-attended events were the World Youth Baseball Championships, held in Brandon in 1991 and 1994.

For over a century and a quarter, Manitobans have been demonstrating their love of baseball not only by playing and watching it, but also by committing time and money to the construction and maintenance of facilities. They have committed hundreds of thousands of dollars to spectator-oriented ball grounds such as River Park, Wesley Park, Sherburn Park, Osborne Stadium, Winnipeg Stadium, CanWest Global Park, all in Winnipeg, or to Brandon's Kinsmen or Westbran Stadiums, or to Fines Field in Stonewall, or "Red" Sangster Field in Thompson. ● MORRIS MOTT/ GLADWYN SCOTT

BASKETBALL, the game invented by Cdn-born James Naismith in 1891, was quickly adopted by Manitobans. The first known men's basketball game in the province was played in 1900, at Winnipeg's Broadway Drill Hall, at Broadway and Osborne. The final score was 4-1. The

players were members of the 90th Regt (the Winnipeg Rifles, later the **Royal Winnipeg Rifles**). In 1901, a military league was formed; sergeants were referees, the baskets were called goals, and the 5 positions were 2 forwards, 2 backs, and 1 goalie. The Crowe Trophy was awarded to the winning team.

By 1903, the **YMCA** had formed a Monday-night basketball league of 4 teams. Each team had 5 players, and there were no substitutes. All games were played at the Central YMCA gym. The fact that there was only room for 1 basketball court led to marathon basketball evenings. In order to get all the games played within 4 hours, play was continuous. Each game was divided into 15-minute halves. At the end of the first half, the second game started, while the players of the first game rested, and so on. Because there were no substitutes, injured players were expected to stay in the game.

Lady Wesmen celebrate winning 70th game in a row.

In 1909, the Red Cross Trophy, donated by the Dyson Co., was presented to the winner of the first provincial championship. Located in Winnipeg's Exchange District, the Dyson Building had a huge, red Maltese cross painted on one exterior wall: hence the name of the trophy. As the YMCA league expanded in 1911 to 24 teams, a Sunday-school boys' league of 18 teams was formed, with games played in church basements. No longer did players have to join the "Y" to play team basketball. During WWI, most senior players exchanged their sneakers for army boots. However, junior basketball continued. By 1919, senior men's basketball was back and thriving. In the 1920s and 1930s, the **Winnipeg Toilers** dominated

B

the senior league. **St. Andrews** (the Dunlops) also dominated from the mid-1930s through the 1940s. However, the Toilers were the first MB team to win national championships. It was not until 1954 that another MB senior team would win a national title.

In the 1949-50 season, the **U of M** Bisons defeated the mighty Winnipeg Paulins to win the provincial senior men's championship. The next year, the graduates of that team formed the Varsity Grads, which won the provincial championship in 1951, 1952, and 1953. It was only when the top players of the Varsity Grads donned the uniforms of the "Big Red Train" that the Paulins once again dominated the senior league, winning the Canadian championship in 1954, and representing Canada at the World Championships in Rio de Janeiro, placing 5ᵗʰ. From then on, most of the players in the Winnipeg men's and women's senior leagues were graduates of a local university.

The St. Andrews Super Saints arrived on the scene in the early 1960s, winning the MB championship in 1964. In the next 13 years, they were provincial champions 12 times, and were Canadian champions in 1972, 1975, and 1976. After Nicolett Inn entered the senior league in 1976 season, it took them only 2 seasons to end the domination of the St. Andrew's teams. In 1979, Nicolett defeated the "Saints" to win the provincial championship. They went on to win 4 consecutive provincial championships; they also won Canadian championships in 1979, 1980, and 1982.

In the mid-1950s, high school athletes had to choose between playing for their school or for a club team. Because the schools had the facilities and coaches who were also teachers, club teams found it difficult to attract quality players. Consequently, the club system withered, and high school basketball for both boys and girls flourished, becoming the feeder system for university basketball. Competition to determine Canadian club championships for men and women ended entirely in the late 1980s. This resulted in the death of club basketball at the competitive level.

It was not until the 1920s that a team representing the U of M as a whole had appeared on the basketball scene. From the 1920s until the 1950s, the U of M teams were in and out of play in the WICAA (Western Inter-Collegiate Athletic Association), in the city leagues (intermediate, senior B, and senior A), and with US teams from ND and MN. During that time, some university students played for both the university team and a team in the city league. The governing body of athletics at the U of M ended that situation in the late 1940s, by stipulating that a student

could play for only one team. MB universities dominated basketball in Canada in the 1980s and the 1990s. The **Brandon** Bobcats were Canadian Interuniversity Sport (CIS) champions in 1987, 1988, 1989, and 1996.

Club basketball made a comeback in MB in the fall of 1997. Then the Winnipeg Minor Basketball Association (WMBA), a community-based youth organization, began to offer competitive leagues for youth in Winnipeg. Starting with 40 teams from 8 community clubs, the leagues grew to more than 500 teams from 42 clubs by 2005. National championships made a return too. Each summer, Basketball Manitoba sends teams to national championships in the midget (under 15), juvenile (under 17), and junior (under 19) categories for both boys and girls. The midget and juvenile championships started in 2002, and the junior championship was inaugurated in 2005.

Winnipeg had a brief flirtation with professional basketball in the 1990s. The Winnipeg Thunder, in the National Basketball League, played their home games at the **Winnipeg Arena** in 1992, 1993, and 1994. The NBL folded mid-way through the 1994 season, to be replaced by the International Basketball League in 1995. The Winnipeg Cyclone played at the Winnipeg Convention Centre until 2001, when the IBL ceased operations.

In the 1920s, girls began playing basketball in church basements and on school playgrounds. By 1927, the CGIT (Canadian Girls in Training) of the United Church formed a league for girls aged 13-17, using church and mission basements for games. Initially, the girls' game involved 2 teams of 6 players: 2 centres or "rovers," who could go anywhere on the court; 2 forwards, restricted to the front court; and 2 guards, who could neither leave the back court nor shoot. Players could only dribble once, then they had to pass or shoot. There was also a jump ball after each score. During a jump ball, players had to hold their left hands behind their backs (as in the boys' game). In 1928, the girls began using boys' rules, freeing the players to move over the entire court. By the early 1930s, women's basketball was well established, with 5 organized leagues involving 750 players.

Among the many good women's teams over the years, there were some that clearly dominated play at the provincial level, such as the Flin Flon Legionettes/Kopper Kweens and the St. Vital Grads. A few teams, however, achieved honours beyond MB's borders. In 1936, the Olympias were the first MB senior women's team to win a W Cdn championship. In 1972, the Lady Wesmen of the **U of W**, in their first year of competition, were MB's first women's team to win a Cdn title, the junior championship. The team also set

the precedent of dropping the "ettes" from their university team name, such as the "Wesmenettes" and the "Bisonettes." In 1983, Team Manitoba, an all-star team, was the first women's team from the province to win a Cdn senior championship.

The Lady Wesmen from the U of W were CIS champions in 1992, 1993, and 1994. On March 5, 1994, the Lady Wesmen won their 70ᵗʰ game and broke the NA record for consecutive wins by a women's university team. Even more remarkable was the next step: their winning streak extended to 88 wins, which tied the National Collegiate Athletic Association (NCAA) record held by the UCLA Bruins men's team. The streak was broken by the Lady Bisons on December 2, 1994, at the U of W, in a packed gym and on national television, by a score of 64-62. • VIC PRUDEN

DOUGLAS WATKINSON

Smallmouth Bass

BASS is a fish in the Sunfish family (Centrarchidae) of which there are 5 native species in MB – Rock Bass (*Ambloplites rupestris*), Pumpkinseed (*Lepomis gibbosus*), Bluegill (*Lepomis macrochirus*), Black Crappie (*Pomoxis nigromaculatus*), and White Crappie (*Pomoxis annularis*). Smallmouth Bass (*Micropterus dolomieu*) and Largemouth Bass (*Micropterus salmoides*) have been introduced to lakes in southern MB. The introduced White Bass (*Morone chrysops*) is a member of the Temperate Bass family (*Moronidae*). There are 32 species of the Sunfish family in NA. Several of the group's distinguishing features include the joined 2 dorsal fins, the anal fin has 3 or more spines, and the caudal fin is slightly forked. Northern and western limits of species ranges in MB appear to be determined by the short warm season and by sudden periods of cold weather during the spawning period. Male centrarchids assume responsibility of building, guarding and cleaning the nest of fertilized eggs, and protecting the fry for a few days until they disperse. Cold fronts moving over the region from May to July may cause the male to abandon his duties, resulting in the loss of the eggs or at least lowered survival of the young. Members of this group are highly popular sport fishes and so have been widely introduced.

The Rock Bass is the most abundant member and has the largest range of the family in MB, in the watersheds of the **RED, ASSINIBOINE** and **WINNIPEG RIVERS**, and rivers emptying into **LAKE WINNIPEG**. It is a deep-bodied but small species in MB, mostly under 10 cm, with a record 21 cm in the Red River – compared to a length of up to 34 cm and a weight of 1.7 kg in the S USA. The colour is golden-brown to olive with dark and bronze blotches. This species prefers cold and clear shallow lakes and rocky streams with plenty of vegetation and logs for cover. It can also survive in some silt-filled waters, such as the Red and Assiniboine rivers. It is often found in small schools and in the company of other species of similar size. The Rock Bass feeds on aquatic insects, crustaceans (including crayfish), and small fish such as minnows and Yellow Perch. In turn it is preyed upon by Northern Pike, Bass, and Walleye. It is also a popular game fish.

The Pumpkinseed is a deep-bodied species, reaching 24 cm in length and with a red spot on the flap at the rear of the gill cover. It is rare and restricted to the Whiteshell and Lake of the Woods regions in extreme SE MB. The similar-looking Bluegill is distinguished by a black spot on the gill flap, and it grows to 23 cm. The Pumpkinseed is native to the Red River and its tributaries such as the La Salle River. Its appearance in the Whiteshell area is likely due to unintentional introduction during the release of non-native Largemouth Bass and Smallmouth Bass. The Bluegill is tolerant of silty waters and congregates in sites with plenty of cover like weeds, logs and boulders. Spawning of Pumpkinseed and Bluegill has not been reported, but juvenile fish have been collected.

The Black Crappie is silvery blue heavily mottled with black, has a thin body, and there are 6-7 spines in its broad anal fin. It may be distinguished from its close relative the White Crappie by having 7-8 spines in the dorsal fin rather than 6, and a less-elongated body. The Black Crappie averages 15 cm (max in Canada 43 cm and 1 kg; 2.3 kg in USA). It is found in the Red and Winnipeg River watersheds, and up the E side of Lake Winnipeg to Berens River. In Canada, this species reaches a length of 36 cm (max 44 cm, 2.7 kg in US) and lives 9 years.

The Smallmouth Bass was introduced into MB in 1900, the first of many releases. It now occurs in the Winnipeg River system, Lake Winnipeg tributaries (north to Wanipigow River), Lake Winnipeg near Hecla Island, the Red River, and up the west side of the province to the Saskatchewan River watershed. It can reach 56 cm and live 15 years. The Largemouth Bass was also introduced into a number of sites after 1942 and currently is found across S MB as far N as the Winnipeg River system, Red River, and the Shell

River S of Duck Mountain. The largest MB specimen measured 53 cm. This species is known to live 15 years. ● REW

BAT is a group of aerial mammals and among the most successful of all mammals in terms of species numbers (almost 1000 species worldwide), abundance (colonies may number 20 million), and specialization into a myriad of roles and habitats. Only the rodents are more abundant. Bats and flowering plants have shared a long history. For more than 50 million years of co-evolution, bats have fed on flowers and fruit, while providing the crucial service of pollination. Much of this success is based on bats' remarkable developments of flight and echolocation, permitting them to be active at night, and thereby avoiding competition with, and predation by, birds and other day-active predators. Bats' powered or flapping flight is made possible by wing and tail membranes – extensions of skin over the elongated bones of the arms, fingers, legs and tail. The knee and foot bones are rotated outward, which allows the bat to easily hang upside down from its root. It need only drop and spread its wings to quickly depart from its resting position.

Six species of bats – all members of the family of Plain-nosed Bats (*Vespertilionidae*), occur in MB during the summer, however the great majority migrate S to avoid the months of cold, when their insect prey is unavailable. The most common and widespread is the Little Brown Bat (*Myotis lucifugus*) with a 27 cm wingspan, which is generally the bat most-often seen in the evening flying over a pond or passing repeatedly past a light while capturing flying insects. This species is by far the dominant bat that hibernates in great numbers in limestone caves in MB's Interlake region. The Big Brown Bat (*Eptesicus fuscus*) is almost twice the size and has a 39 cm wingspan, but is rarely found here, and is usually discovered in buildings. Just as rare is Northern Long-eared Bat (*Myotis septentrionalis*) with a 25 cm wingspan; the most obvious difference from the Little Brown Bat being its longer ears. All 3 species are cave hibernators, with most individuals heading S and E to find hibernacula with just the right conditions of temperature (slightly above freezing) and high humidity (to prevent drying out).

The remaining 3 species are described as tree bats, since they prefer to roost during the day among tree leaves – hence their camouflaged

B

MANITOBA MUSEUM

Walk-through bat cave in the Manitoba Museum

coats, resembling dying leaves. Their common names well describe their appearance. The Red Bat (*Lasiurus borealis*) is an yellowish-red colour with a 33 cm wingspan, the Silver-haired Bat (*Lasionycteris noctivagans*) is black with silver-tipped hairs and 30 cm wingspan, while the Hoary Bat (*Lasiurus cinereus*) is yellowish-brown, mottled with white hair tips resembling frost, and has a 41 cm wingspan (MB's largest bat). All 3 species are impossible to see when suspended among a clump of leaves; they may also retreat under loose bark or in a tree cavity. Usually the only time they are discovered during the day is when a female with heavy young attached are blown to the ground in a storm. It is not a safe practice to touch a wild animal, and this is certainly true for bats, since they will defend themselves by biting, and a small percentage of the population may carry diseases like rabies. All 3 tree bats fly S in Sept or early Oct to the central and southern US, and even Mexico.

While most small creatures have a short life span, bats are an exception, with some surviving 10, 20, or even 30 years. They capture flying insects such as moths and mosquitoes – as many as several hundred a night, either scooped up initially by their tail membrane or directly by the mouth. This insect-control service is capitalized by some people who put up 'bat houses' in the hopes of attracting bats to their neighbourhood. Bats are capable of emitting over a dozen distinct calls, some of which can be heard by the human ear. However, ultrasonic calls (25-78 kHz frequencies and 5-200 pulses/second) are used to navigate and to pinpoint locations of insect prey within distances of 1-5 m, and some evidence suggests they can detect the humming of swarming insects several hundred metres away.

Copulation occurs in Aug and Sept, just prior to migration, and the sperm are stored in the female's uterus until fertilization the following spring. Some breeding may also occur during the winter in brief bouts of activity. The gestation period ranges from 50-80 days (depending on the species), and one offspring is the norm for the three cave-dwelling bats, but usually 2 (1-5) in the tree bats. The young are born in June, nurse for about 4 weeks and are capable of flying in 3-6 weeks – a remarkable rate of development and of mastering the complexities of flight. • REW

BATHGATE, Andrew James "Andy," hockey player (b Aug 28, 1932, **WINNIPEG**). Bathgate was a skilled rightwinger, and one of the first players in the NHL to use a slapshot. He also fired the infamous puck in Nov 1959 that hit Montreal Canadiens goaltender Jacques Plante so severely in the face that in all subsequent games, Plante

Andy Bathgate, 1963

wore a face mask, setting a trend that eventually spread throughout the NHL. Bathgate started out playing with the MJHL Winnipeg Black Hawks before signing with the Guelph Juniors for the 1951-52 season. He badly damaged his knee during his first game that season, and the injury required the insertion of a steel plate into his knee joint. Bathgate never fully recovered from the injury, and suffered recurring pain that often hindered his performance. Despite this setback, he went on to play in the NHL with the New York Rangers. Though he was a talented player, his skill was often overlooked because of the team's overall poor standings during the 1950s. His best personal season was 1958-59 when he scored 40 goals and 48 assists, earning him the Hart Memorial Trophy as MVP. Bathgate was traded to the Toronto Maple Leafs for 1964-65, and helped bring the team to a Stanley Cup victory. After one year, he was traded to the Detroit Red Wings, and then to the Pittsburgh Penguins. He scored 349 goals over his career, and was inducted into the Hockey Hall of Fame in 1978. • MD

BATTLE OF FORT WHYTE. This conflict arose between the **CPR** and a competing MB **RAILWAY** company in what is now part of suburban **WINNIPEG**. In 1888, the new Northern Pacific and Manitoba Railway Company proposed to cross the CPR's main line on its way to **PORTAGE LA PRAIRIE**. This would mean competition for the dominant national company, whose freight rates were substantially higher. In an attempt to thwart its new rival, the CPR sent **WILLIAM WHYTE** to seize the disputed crossing. In response, an angry provincial govt asked Winnipeg residents if they would like to "put the CPR in its place." A mob of concerned citizens hurried to the site, dubbed

"**FORT WHYTE**" by local **NEWSPAPERS**. Because the Northern Pacific's tracklayers had not yet arrived, the crowd left, but citizens returned 2 days later to see that the CPR had built a fence around its property, and had ditched an engine in the track-layers' path. The mob tore up part of the CPR tracks and installed a "diamond" to allow the Northern Pacific to cross the CPR line. Whyte's crew then arrived, and, after facing down the Winnipeggers, ripped out the diamond. Thereafter, the CPR installed 200 men to guard Fort Whyte, providing them with sleeping cars and meals, as well as a Sunday church service. Each evening, the 2 factions faced each other over a blazing bonfire. The matter was finally resolved when the Supreme Court of Canada ruled that the MB govt had the right to pursue alternatives to the CPR, so ending the "battle" of Fort Whyte without a single shot being fired. • MD

BAWLF, Nicholas, GRAIN merchant (b July 17, 1849, Smiths Falls, Canada West [ON]; d Dec 26, 1914, **WINNIPEG**). Bawlf moved to Winnipeg in 1877 and established a feed and flour business on Princess St. He helped found the Winnipeg Grain Exchange in 1887, serving as its president in 1887 and 1890. Active in the **GRAIN ELEVATOR** business, he joined with other Winnipeg merchants (including **RODMOND ROBLIN**) to form the Northern Elevator Company in 1893. He was Northern Elevator's president from 1903-09. Bawlf sold out to the Peavy Company of Minneapolis in 1909, then founded N. Bawlf Grain Company, and in 1912 became president of the Alberta Pacific Grain Company of Calgary. He was one of the first traders to ship grain to Japan via Pacific ports. Bawlf held many directorships of Canadian corporations. A devout Catholic, he opposed the *Manitoba School Act* of 1890 [see **MANITOBA SCHOOLS QUESTION**] and lobbied in Ottawa for more Anglo-Catholic senators. • JMB

BAY, The. *See* **HUDSON'S BAY COMPANY**.

BAYER, Mary Elizabeth, community, arts, and heritage activist (b Feb 10, 1925, AB; d Sept 7, 2005, Victoria), grew up and went to school in MB. She was a poet, educator, civil servant, and volunteer leader. Bayer was a 6th-generation descendant of the Red River settlers. Her educational attainments include an MA in English from the **U OF M** and an honorary doctorate from the **U OF W**. After WWII, she was the exec dir of the Volunteer Bureau, assisting war veterans. She went on to work for the United Way and UNESCO; she was the founding director of the MB Arts Council, founding chair of Heritage Winnipeg, and the executive director of the

Mary Elizabeth Bayer, 1968

Centennial Corporation of MB; and she worked for CBC Radio and Television for 10 years. She was the first female assistant deputy minister in MB, serving in the Department of Culture and Heritage. Bayer was the national president of the Heritage Canada, and served on the executive of Girl Guides Canada. Bayer was also a poet, and wrote the libretto for the 1967 Murray Adaskin opera, *Grant, Warden of the Plains*, based on the life of **CUTHBERT GRANT**. When she retired to Victoria in 1980, she continued to guide and advise heritage, arts, and community organizations. In June 1994, Bayer was appointed to the Order of Canada. In 2004, she received the Woman of Distinction Award for Lifetime Achievement. • RK

BEACH, Adam Reuben, OJIBWAY actor (b Nov 11, 1972, ASHERN), is one of the best-known and most prolific Aboriginal actors in NA. While growing up on the Dog Creek reserve of the

Hollywood star Adam Beach

LAKE MANITOBA FIRST NATION near Ashern, at the age of 8, Beach lost both of his parents to accidents within months. He moved to WINNIPEG and was raised by aunts and uncles. Though he became interested in drama at Gordon Bell High School, he has also spoken about being involved in a gang. His earliest acting experience was with the MANITOBA THEATRE FOR YOUNG PEOPLE and in the 1990 film *Lost in the Barrens*. One of Beach's breakthrough parts was in the CBC drama *North of 60*. He played a lead role in Cdn director Bruce McDonald's *Dance Me Outside* (1995), and carved out a niche S of the border with a number of TV roles. Beach was featured in the Sundance Award-winning, Canada-US co-production *Smoke Signals* (1998) – among the first films written and directed entirely by Native Americans – and the Cdn romantic comedy *The Art of Woo* (2001). His big break in Hollywood was starring opposite Nicholas Cage in *Windtalkers* (2002), a WWII story for which he learned the Navajo language. He returned to Canada for *Cowboys and Indians: The J.J. Harper Story* (2003), in which he portrayed the title character. He recently appeared in Clint Eastwood's *Flags of Our Fathers* (2006), portraying the Pima (Akimel O'odham) US Marine famous for raising the US flag on Iwo Jima. In Aug 2006, Beach ran for the position of chief of the Lake Manitoba First Nation. Though unsuccessful, he planned to continue on in politics. He has also travelled around NA speaking to Aboriginal youth. Beach moved to Ottawa in 1993, and also resides in Los Angeles. He has about 50 professional acting credits to his name. • JT

BEAL, William "Billy," pioneer (b 1874, Chelsea, MA, d 1968, THE PAS) was among MB's first BLACK homesteaders. Beal was a steam engineer, and arrived in MB in about 1907 to work at a sawmill in the SWAN RIVER area. He became a Cdn citizen in 1911, despite attempts by the Cdn govt to stop immigration by Black people. Beal earned a homestead in the Big Woody District, in the DUCK MOUNTAIN area, by clearing the 30 ac (12 ha) lot over 8 years, but he gave up farming in 1916 to return to work in the lumber mills. He was community leader, and helped set up the region's first library. He helped develop a local school division, and sat as a school board member for 37 years. Beal enjoyed intellectual pursuits, was a proficient photographer, and was a founding member of the region's literary society. He also built a telescope by fitting lenses into a stovepipe. He never married, and spent his last days in a retirement home in The Pas. Beal is the subject of a 1988 biography, *Billy: The Life and Photographs of William S. A. Beal*. • MD

BEAMISH, Robert Earl, physician, researcher (b Sept 16, 1916, SHOAL LAKE; d Feb 17, 2001, WINNIPEG). Cardiac specialist Beamish was educated at Shoal Lake Public School, McConnell High School, and Brandon College (now BRANDON U), graduating with a BA in 1937. In 1942, he earned his medical degree, and in 1944 a BSc in MEDICINE, both from the U OF M. He joined the Medicine faculty there in 1942 and was a professor from 1964 until his death. During WWII, Beamish completed a study of TUBERCULOSIS among soldiers. In 1947, he earned a 2-year fellowship to study in London, UK, at 2 of the city's most prestigious hospitals. He also joined (and was later a Fellow) of the Royal College of Physicians of London, gaining a specialty in cardiology. Upon his return in 1948, Beamish joined the Manitoba Clinic in Winnipeg, where he founded the department of cardiology. In the 1950s, Beamish pioneered research on arteriosclerosis, or hardening of the arteries. The prominent belief at the time was that the condition occurred as a natural part of the aging process, but Beamish advanced the theory that reducing cholesterol and fat in a person's diet would reduce the risk of artery deterioration and heart disease. He also promoted the use of anticoagulants – blood thinners – in the 1960s. Beamish worked at the Manitoba Clinic until 1970 and at Winnipeg General Hospital and HEALTH SCIENCES CENTRE (HSC) from 1957-88. In 1970, he took a position at GREAT WEST LIFE ASSURANCE CO. as medical director, and acted as vice president of underwriting and medical services 1975-81 in addition to his teaching and research commitments. In the 1980s, he began working at the ST. BONIFACE GENERAL HOSPITAL Research Centre alongside NARANJAN DHALLA. Beamish was the Manitoba Heart Foundation's founding director and a member for more than 30 years. He served as president for the College of Physicians and Surgeons of Manitoba (1960-61), the Canadian Cardiovascular Society from (1968-70), and the Manitoba Medical Association (1970-71). Some of Beamish's many awards include honorary doctorates from Brandon U in 1988 and the U of M in 1989; becoming a Member of the Order of Canada in 1990, and of the Order of Manitoba in 2000; and an HSC laureate of excellence in 1994. • JOEL TRENAMAN

BEAR (Family Ursidae) ancestors may be traced back in the fossil record to the Dawn Bear (Ursavus elmensis) – a raccoon-like carnivore that lived about 25 mya. Today's 8 species are the sole survivors of dozens of species classified within 3 ancient lineages – represented in recent times by the Giant Panda (Ailuropoda melanoleuca) of China, the Andean or Spectacled Bear (Tremarctos ornatus) of the SA, and the Brown (Ursus arctos), Black (Ursus americanus) and Polar (Ursus maritimus) Bears of Eurasia and NA. One of the most amazing bears was the Giant Short-faced Bear (Arctodus simus), which ranged throughout NA (including the plains of MB) during the Pleistocene Ice Ages (2 million-11,000 years ago). It weighed over 1 tonne, and with its long legs it was capable of running down bison. The Polar Bear and Brown Bear are now the largest living terrestrial carnivores in the world, although they would have been dwarfed by extinct relatives.

Gradually evolving a different body plan than other carnivores, bears developed massive skulls and jaw muscles, stout bodies, and a walking style in which they support their weight on the broad sole of the foot. This generates great stability and permits an upright stance when foraging for fruit and nuts and during aggressive encounters with other bears and predators. While some species like the Polar Bear are largely carnivorous, most bears are omnivores, devouring large amounts of plant material and insects, and playing a scavenger role. Bears have not incorporated cellulose-digesting bacteria in their gut, and consequently much of their plant food passes through undigested. Their cheek teeth have broad and rounded cusps, useful for grinding vegetation, whereas the long canines are employed for killing bites, ripping out chunks of flesh, and as weapons in battles with other bears.

In spite of their huge size, most bears (except Polar Bear and Grizzly) are excellent climbers, especially when young, aided by powerful limbs and long claws. Although they appear slow and lumbering, bears can readily outrun people, and are capable of travelling long distances without tiring. Home ranges are enormous – up to 2,000 sq km if food is scarce. Those bears dwelling in northern climates, where food becomes inaccessible for months, have adapted to limited resources by entering a deep sleep for the winter, approaching true hibernation, in which their heart, breathing and metabolic rates fall significantly.

Bears are especially known for their keen sense of smell, although their hearing and sight (including some colour vision) are also important in detecting food sources. The ever-present hunting activities for food often brings bears into conflict with people, and bears have suffered from both excessive hunting and habitat loss. There have also been significant numbers of attacks on humans, often resulting in fatalities, which further serve to promote destruction of these animals. Bears have been dominant creatures in the mythology and art of humans for over 25,000 years. Their size, strength and cunning

must have impressed prehistoric people, the bears acting as both predators and competitors of humans. Bears appeared frequently on cave wall paintings, petroglyphs, carvings, funeral rites, and even extended into the heavens as the constellations Ursa major and Ursa minor.

MB boasted 3 species of bears in historic times, but the plains race of the Grizzly (a type of Brown Bear) was exterminated here in the early 1800s, soon after the arrival of European trappers and settlers. The barren-ground race of Grizzly occasionally roams as far E as Hudson Bay and has been reported rarely in northern MB. The Polar Bear is found along the province's marine coast, while the Black Bear is common throughout undeveloped parts of the province.

Polar Bear near Churchill

ROBERT R. TAYLOR

POLAR BEARS (*Ursus maritimus*) evolved from brown bears about 250,000 years ago in Arctic Asia. Separated during a glacial period from the main range, this ancestral population adapted from an omnivorous diet to one based on seals. A male may weigh up to 800 kg; female 300 kg. This species was formerly common along the marine coast of MB – the Western Hudson Bay population traditionally numbering over 1500. The town of **CHURCHILL** became known as the 'Polar Bear Capital of the World' due to the number of bears passing through this coastal site where sea ice forms early in Nov. International tourists arrive each fall to ride the 'Tundra Buggies' out onto the coast in search of bears. When out on the Bay ice hunting seals, GPS/satellite surveys have shown that the bears move from 11-43 km/day within a home range averaging 107,000 sq km. The area of greatest concentration in winter lies offshore on the ice along the MB-Nunavut border. The most remarkable adaptation of the Polar Bear to an arctic marine lifestyle is the ability to alter its physiology to withstand months of fasting, at any time of the year, but especially during the summer when the bears are stranded and resting on land. No other

mammal can remain active without food for such an extended period – a necessity to survive in an environment where the major food source of seals is only seasonally available. Half the females in this region have 2 cubs every second year, and wean these at the early age of 1.5 years. The species inland denning area is mainly protected within **WAPUSK NATIONAL PARK**. This species seldom lives over 20 years in the wild. One famous bear – Debby at the **ASSINIBOINE PARK ZOO** – was the world's oldest Polar Bear at 40 years in 2006, and may well surpass the captive record of 43 years. Warmer temperatures, due to a temporary fluctuation or to **GLOBAL WARMING**, have resulted in fewer weeks of ice cover on the Bay, and consequently a shorter period of accessibility to seals basking on the ice. Breeding females are affected the most, since they are forced to go up to 8 months without eating while they are hibernating inland and returning to the sea with cubs from late Feb to early April. Accumulation of pesticides (organochlorines) are affecting immunity to disease, reproduction, and other biological functions. The bears almost exclusive diet of contaminated fat of Ringed Seal results in the bears further concentrating these deadly poisons. Feeding on milk, the cubs then become twice as contaminated as their mothers. MB's Polar Bear population fell from the mid-1980s to 2006 to less than 950 (37% decline), and some scientists project that the species will be eliminated from the entire Bay before the end of the century. It is only a matter of time before it reaches the endangered status.

BLACK BEARS (*Ursus americanus*) are well known to many Manitobans due to their common occurrence in recreational areas and along highways in remote regions. In years when berries and other natural foods are scarce, there are significant numbers of close encounters between bears and people, as the animals are drawn to the odour of food present around campgrounds and cottages. There have been occasional Black Bear attacks on people in MB over the years, including a few fatalities. Generally a bear will avoid human contact, unless attracted to a ready food source. However, this is a powerful and fast predator whose natural range has been invaded on all fronts by ever-increasing numbers of people. There is no way of identifying which bears are dangerous under certain conditions, so it is always prudent to back away slowly from a bear and to retreat to the safety of a vehicle or facility. This species' ancestors came to NA by crossing the Bering Land Bridge about 500,000 years ago. Black Bear males average 140 kg while females are smaller, at 110 kg. The coat is thick and coarse, protecting the skin from

Black Bear searches for grubs.

abrasion and exposure to the elements. The fur is so dark with the pigment melanin that it appears to absorb all light falling on it, rendering the bear hard to see in low light or the cover of darkness. Bears mate in summer, and following a delayed phase of development, the 1-5 embryos begin to grow in December. About 8 months later, 1-3 cubs are born, weighing only 300 grams. They instinctively nurse and gain warmth from the mother while she hibernates. Full size is reached by 4 years and most bears live less than 10 years in the wild. MB Conservation estimates that the Black Bear population is stable at around 30,000, of which 12% are killed annually during the licensed hunting season and by other people to protect personal safety, property and crops. The biology of the Black Bear differs significantly between populations in the boreal coniferous forest (with sparse, low-caloric foods) and in the interface between the boreal or mixed forest and agro-MB (with abundant, energy-rich food sources such as garbage, bird-feeders, bee hives, grain fields). The boreal forest bears average 1.8 cubs/litter, cub survival is less than 50%, adults breed first at 6-7 years, and seldom live beyond 20 years. The more-southern and better-nourished bears average 2.6 cubs/litter, cub survival is 80%, first breed at 4 years (a few mate at 2y and produce cubs at 3y), and some survive into their 30s.

GRIZZLY (Ursus arctos), a Brown Bear, also originated in the Old World, immigrating from Siberia following the last Ice Age. The plains race of the Grizzly was common on the prairies of MB, where it was first described by

European explorer Henry Kelsey in 1690. Skins were reported in the early 1800s by trader Alexander Henry from **Portage la Prairie**, Pembina River, Pembina Mountains, and the Red and Roseau rivers. Bison, both alive and scavenged, was likely an important source of food. This race was exterminated in MB by 1825, and 2 skulls from **Austin** and Turtle Mountain are the only surviving evidence that it lived here. The barren-ground race has occasionally been reported as far E as Hudson Bay in MB. There were several sightings near **York Factory** in 1991, and sightings in **Wapusk National Park** S of Churchill have been reported almost every 2nd year (likely several individuals) – one of which was photographed in 2004 at the mouth of the Broad River. One adult was shot in Sept 2005 at Smock River, 80 km NW of Churchill. Once covering much of the western half of NA, from Alaska to Mexico, this large and powerful terrestrial predator is now becoming endangered, with only remote areas of the northwest harbouring healthy populations. Trophy hunting is still permitted – a practice that is becoming ever-more controversial. Northern male Grizzlies weigh around 450 kg (maximum 780 kg), females 320 kg, but can still run up to 60 km/hr. ● REW, HH

BEARDY, Quentin Pickering JACKSON, artist (b Jul 24, 1944, **Garden Hill First Nation**; d Dec 8, 1984, **Winnipeg**). Born into a family of 13 children, Beardy was sent at age 7 to a **Residential School** in **Portage la Prairie**. He went on to study commercial art at Technical Vocational High School in Winnipeg in 1963-64, and began to create paintings and prints inspired by **Cree** myths and oral traditions. His later work delved deeper into spiritual and natural concepts. He exhibited in 1965 at the **Winnipeg Art Gallery**, and took classes in fine arts at the **U of M** in 1966. Beardy received commissions to produce work for the Cdn and MB centennial celebrations in 1967 and 1970 respectively. In 1972, he contributed to a major Aboriginal art display at the Winnipeg Art Gallery, and won the Canadian Centennial Medal. Along with fellow artist **Daphne Odjig**, Beardy became a member of the Professional Native Indian Artists Association – often referred to as the Indian Group of Seven or Woodlands Group of Seven – that formed in late 1972. A passion for teaching also led Beardy to instruct art students at **Brandon U**, the U of M, and in Winnipeg elementary schools. He consulted for the **Manitoba Museum** before moving to Ottawa to do the same for the federal Department of Indian Affairs and Northern Development. Beardy acted as senior advisor on art for the department 1982-84. The work left little time for personal projects, however, and he returned to Winnipeg in 1984, where he began a new set of paintings. Beardy had turned to alcohol at a young age to help deal with the cultural displacement and shock of residential school. He suffered through a myriad of health problems for much of his life. In 1984, he succumbed to a heart attack and subsequent infection. A large mural in memory of Beardy's work – *Peace and Harmony* – graces a building on Winnipeg's Selkirk Ave. ● JT

Jackson Beardy, 1971

BEAUSEJOUR, pop 2772, is a town 46 km NE of Winnipeg on hwy 44. "*Beau séjour*" is French for "good stopping-place." The town post office opened in 1881, and the **CPR** came soon after. First settled by people of Polish and Ukrainian, descent the town was incorporated in 1912. An RCAF/US air force Pinetree Radar Line station opened here in 1953, and was closed in 1986. Though the town is the primary grain-handling centre for the **Eastman** region of MB, tourism is also growing because of Beausejour's picturesque setting on the edge of **Whiteshell Provincial Park.** Much of the town's early economy was helped by the establishment of the first glass container factory in western Canada, built by Joseph Keilback in 1906. The old facility is now a historic site. Beausejour attracts many snowmobile and motocross enthusiasts thanks to a state-of-the-art racetrack that is home to the Canadian Power Toboggan Championship. A town by-law that allows snowmobiles to operate on snow-covered residential streets means that the sledded vehicles are an ever-visible presence in the community. The town also boasts a day lily garden that is the coldest day lily display garden in the world. The town is the birthplace of former gov gen and NDP premier **Edward Schreyer.** • GPP

BEAVER is our largest rodent (*Castor canadensis*), which holds a special place in the history and early development of MB. Beaver pelts, used mainly for felt hats and clothing in the Old World, became a valuable trade commodity and led to the establishment of fur-trade companies and exploration of the West by Europeans. In 1799, explorer David Thompson expressed concern about the decline of the beaver in MB. So relentless was the pursuit of this animal that during most of the 1800s, annual catches from central Canada averaged over 100,000 animals, and by the end of the century, populations of beaver were decimated across the country. Fortunately, the need for wildlife conservation was recognized in NA during the early 1900s, and the beaver, bison, and a host of other animals were finally afforded protection by hunting and trapping regulations. Beaver have once again reclaimed lost territory and their numbers have increased to the point where their activities have become a problem in some areas of the province.

When the beaver dives underwater, it closes its nose and ears, and covers its eyes with a transparent lid. The tongue blocks the back of the throat so that the animal can chew underwater without flooding its lungs. Most unusual for a rodent, the beaver is monogamous throughout life, and the pair may live 15 years. Mating occurs

Beavers have transformed MB's northern landscape.

in late winter and the several kits are cared for until the age of 2, when they are forced out to establish their own home range, up to 250 km away. Patrolling its aquatic world, the beaver slaps its tail hard on the water, often repeatedly, if it detects an intruder like a wolf or cougar hunting along the shore. The broad tail also serves as a storage depot of fat, drawn upon during winter, when the only food available is bark on branches cached underwater. Like other mammals, the beaver cannot digest the tough cellulose of plant-cell walls, and depends on microbial digestion to release nutrients.

The engineering feats of the beaver are legendary, and it is one of the few creatures in the world that can alter its own environment to meet its needs. With considerable effort and ingenuity, it constructs lodges and dams over a creek through careful placement of sticks, stones and mud. Water levels are monitored and allowed to expand into the surrounding meadow or forest, giving safe access to new food resources – the inner bark of shrubs and trees. The beaver is placed within the great order of rodents and is so distinct that it is given its own family (Castoridae). A related species – the Eurasian Beaver – occurs from France to eastern Russia, and is the ancestor of the NA Beaver. The two can no longer interbreed because of differing numbers of chromosomes. Averaging 25 kg (45 kg max) the beaver is second in size among rodents only to the Capybara of Panama and SA. Until 10,000 years ago, the beaver lived alongside the now-extinct Ice Age Giant Beaver (*Castoroides*), which at 320 kg was the size of a bear. • REW

BEDSON, Derek, public servant (b Oct 12, 1920, London, UK; d May 14, 1989, Regina) Bedson studied history at the **U of M** and served in WWII before attending Oxford. In 1947, he returned to Canada to work in the federal civil service, eventually acting as private secretary to PC leader John Diefenbaker. Bedson was hired as clerk of the executive council of the MB legislature by PC premier **Duff Roblin** in 1958, and continued in that capacity during **Walter Weir**'s administration. A political conservative known for his photographic memory and policy-drafting skills, Bedson was also known for his dry wit – he once said that Lester Pearson "wasn't the YMCA instructor he pretended to be" – and for his constant moaning during cabinet meetings, a habit he claimed to have picked up at Oxford. Bedson was – to the surprise of many – retained by NDP premier **Edward Schreyer** in 1969. When **Sterling Lyon** was elected premier of MB in 1977, Bedson sat in on the firing of 3 NDP-appointed deputy ministers: Lionel Orlikow (education), Willem "Bill" Janzen (agriculture), and Marv Nordman (public works). But when the NDP returned to power in 1981 under **Howard Pawley,** Bedson himself was finally let go. His dismissal was criticized in the **Winnipeg Free Press,** the *Globe and Mail*, and the *Ottawa Citizen*. The next year Bedson was hired by ON's PC government to serve as a counsellor in their Brussels consulate, but instead chose to serve under newly elected SK PC Premier Grant Devine as the clerk of the executive council of that legislature. Despite signing a 2-year contract, Bedson was let go after one year, due to a miscommunication with the premier over pay raises for 3 senior government officials. In November 1983 he was sent to Saskatchewan's Agricultural Development Corp. office in Vienna, where he worked until 1986, when he retired to **WINNIPEG**. Bedson was made an officer in the Order of Canada in 1978.

● TESSA VANDERHART

BEE is an insect specialized for feeding on flower pollen and nectar. In fact, bees are by far the most significant pollinator of flowering plants and crops, and consequently they are regarded as the most beneficial insects in the world. It is estimated that 1/3 of what we eat and drink comes from pollinated crops. Bees also play an important role in maintaining plant diversity in natural ecosystems, and have played prominent roles in people's diet and mythology for over 10,000 years. There are over 20,000 species of bees worldwide, 3500 in NA, 1300 in Canada, and 194 in MB. Although the fossil record of bees is meagre, they are believed to have developed from vegetarian-wasp ancestors 125 mya (early Cretaceous). Their diversity coincided with the radiation of flowering plants during the Cretaceous period, and these insects quickly developed intimate associations of feeding and pollination. Bees range from 4-25 mm long, and are coloured brown or black but with bands of yellow, orange, or white branched or feathery hairs. It is these hairs that pick up pollen and then deposit them from flower to flower. The pollen is usually combed into special baskets on the hind legs or abdomen. Many bees have a long lip in the form of a long tube for sucking nectar from flowers. This group is also characterized by a series of technical characters, but most people are able to identify a bee (usually Bombus or Apis) when they see one. While bees are famous for their social behaviour, ironically most species are solitary.

BUMBLE BEES AND HONEY BEES (family Apidae) are mostly social bees. The bumble

Bumble bee at work

©ROY ELLIS CARMAN MB

bees, of which there are 20 native species in MB, exist in small, closely knit colonies, founded by a single, mated, over-wintering queen. This queen initiates the nest in abandoned mouse nests or in natural cavities that contain suitable nest materials. The brood develops in small wax pots, which are also used for the storage of small reserves of honey. As the season progresses, males and virgin queens are eventually produced. The new queens mate and then seek a suitable over-wintering site, as the founding colony eventually breaks down and the members all die before winter. The 13 mm-long honey bee (*Apis mellifera*) is the well-known, domesticated bee, introduced into MB in the mid-1800s with the settlement by Europeans. MB is the third-largest honey-producing province in Canada. This species is normally managed in hives provided by bee keepers, but swarms occasionally escape and establish new colonies in sheltered sites. The honey bee is the most socially advanced species of bee. It has a complex division of labour among the sterile worker caste, and individuals are able to communicate sources of food using a sophisticated dance. It also has an extremely complex suite of chemical pheromones that affects colony status and well-being. Colonies may become very large, with over 50,000 worker bees, all under the influence of a single queen. Workers have special pollen baskets on their hind legs, and a modified crop – the honey stomach – to transport nectar. The queen, which develops from a normal larva that has been fed a special diet of royal jelly, has no such morphological features, and is dependent on the care of the workers for her survival. The drones develop from unfertilized eggs and contribute little to the colony except to fly out and fertilize virgin queens produced by overcrowded or failing colonies in the area. MB winters are too long and cold for the survival of unprotected honey bee colonies, therefore bee keepers either insulate the hives, or move them into buildings until spring.

YELLOW-FACED AND PLASTERER BEES (family Colletidae) are solitary bees with about 30 hard-to-identify species in MB. Colletids are inconspicuous, solitary nesters, and so records of species are few. There are only 2 genera in the province – *Colletes* and *Hylaeus*. *Colletes* are medium-sized, hairy bees, while *Hylaeus* are much smaller, without hair, but with characteristic yellow patches on the face, especially in the males. Females construct their nests in hollow twigs, holes in logs, cracks in rocks, and occupy holes in commercial leaf-cutting bee nests. Colletid nests are easily recognized because the female lines its cells with a transparent, parchment-like material. Colletids can be very

abundant and are important pollinators, but little research has been done on the group.

ANDRENID OR MINING BEES (family Andrenidae) is a large (10-15 mm) and mostly solitary and ground-nesting family with at least 40 species in MB, but another 20 are likely to be discovered here, particularly eastern and southern species whose ranges are known nearby. There are over 1200 species in NA. Andrenids are also very difficult to identify, being mostly medium-sized fuzzy bees. They can be quite abundant in many MB habitats, and consequently are probably important pollinators, but quantitative data on their precise role are lacking. Many species occur seasonally – closely timed with the period of flowering of their favoured host-plant species. Females excavate solitary burrows in a variety of soil types, and provision their nest with a mixture of pollen and nectar mixed together to form a paste.

SWEAT BEES (family Halictidae) are mostly solitary. An estimated 37 species of halictids are known in MB, but records are so poor that there could easily be another dozen present. This lack of data on these solitary pollinators is remarkable considering they are present in such large numbers, and their contribution as pollinators of native plants and crops is major. Nearly all species nest in the ground, but a few occupy cracks and holes in tree trunks and buildings. One species, the alkali bee (*Nomia melanderi*) has been domesticated, and in the southern US is used extensively to pollinate alfalfa. Most MB sweat bees visit a variety of plants, but a few species are attracted to only a few kinds of plants. Several species of Halictus are strongly attracted to human perspiration (perhaps for salt) and can at times be a nuisance, crawling around on exposed skin. The sting is not seriously painful. Sphecodes species are parasites, mainly of other sweat bees, and can be observed entering the nests of provisioning females. Because they are parasitic, they do not actually collect pollen and nectar themselves, though they are commonly seen feeding on flowers.

LEAFCUTTING BEES (family Megachilidae) receive their common name from the females' habit of cutting leaf and flower pieces with their mandibles to construct nests and to line the nest cells. Not all species use leaf pieces; there are several genera that use mud, tiny stones and plant resins as construction materials. Regardless of the nest material used, most species occupy pre-existing cavities for their nests. Several cells are built for eggs and provisions of pollen and nectar. Females carry pollen on a specialized brush of dense hairs (the scopa) on the ventral surface of the abdomen. Although most leafcutting bees are strictly solitary, some, like the alfalfa leafcutting bee (*Megachile rotundata*) are gregarious and can be found in dense colonies where conditions are suitable. Since this European bee was introduced to NA in the late 1930s, and to MB in 1966, it has been widely cultured, and is an important commercial species for alfalfa pollination in MB. One often sees large multi-coloured shelters in alfalfa fields especially installed for this species. There are over 40 species of leafcutting bees recorded for MB, but intensive collecting will almost certainly result in additional records. • TDG, RCL, REW

B

BEE-KEEPING. In MB, nectar-producing crops like alfalfa and a dry summer climate bolster beekeeping for honey production. In turn, honey-producing **Bee** hives help pollinate feed and food crops such as clover and buckwheat. Honeybees (*Apis mellifera* and *A. cerana*) are native to most of the Old World but not to the Americas, which is why First Nations used maple syrup as their sweetener. Beekeeping has nevertheless been practised in MB for over 100 years, and the Manitoba Beekeepers' Association was formed in 1903. Up until 1988, when the federal govt banned US bee stocks following the discovery of the parasitic mite *Varroa destructor*, most MB colonies were comprised of bees shipped in from the US South. Queen bees were a crucial import because of their vital role in a colony. As producing queen cells is a highly technical task, some MB honey producers resorted to importing queen and worker bees by jet from New Zealand when the US supply was cut off. Following the import ban, local production of queen bees was initiated by an apiarist in SW MB who had received training in CA. Using a grafting needle to transfer miniature larvae into special queen-cell cups suspended in the hives, where the larvae hatch as virgin queens, the apiarist successfully reared MB's first home-grown laying queens, and sold queen cells that could be raised to maturity by other beekeepers. Honey season runs from May-Aug, during which time beekeepers place colonies near flowering fields. Different crops will yield different honey; honey from alfalfa is white compared to the golden honey produced from the nectar of sunflowers. Roughly 1400 people are employed in apiaries during production season. There were 620 beekeepers in MB in 2006, operating roughly 80,000 bee colonies. The average colony production of 77 kg is among the highest in the world, and results in 6000 tonnes production each year, with a value of $10 million, most of which is exported to the US. MB is usually the 3rd-largest honey-producing province, behind AB and SK. • MD

AM. AGRICULTURE • LIVESTOCK • CATTLE 12. SHORTHORNS

Shorthorn cattle, ca 1915

BEEF CATTLE FARMING in MB is a significant agricultural sector in the province. MB's cow herd is the 3rd-largest in Canada, making up about 12% of the national total. SK has twice MB's amount, while AB has 3 times. The cattle feeding industry in AB produces 2/3 of the country's beef; over 40% of MB's production is fed or processed in AB.

Cattle production has contributed about 22% of the gross farm income since the 1950s. In 1970, 350,000 MB cows generated $90 million for farmers in the province. In 2006, the value of cattle production in the province was about $520 million, from a herd of 650,000 beef cattle. About half of MB farms have some cattle production – in 2006, 9000 farms. About 2/3 of those receive the majority of the their income from cattle. Dairy cows contribute over half of their calf production to the beef industry as well. Once the replacement females are selected from the calf crop, most farms sell the production as calves. Those animals would usually be up to half of their mature weight, and would have spent 4-6 months of their lives with their mothers on pasture.

Just over 1/3 of the land in MB is in **Forage** production, the grass or legume plants that cattle feed on during the winter months. A small portion of that land base would be on fields that could be cultivated for **Grain** crops but most of it would be pastures of native grasses. That grassland is not plowed because it has very shallow topsoil or because it is too sandy, dry, wet or stony to work with machinery.

Winter feed is the largest operating cost on the typical beef farm. Conventional practice has been to store forage for winter feeding as hay, the dried grasses and/or legumes such as alfalfa or clover that is compacted into bales. In the 1960s, when an average farm's cow herd numbered about 20, the bales would have been small rectangular ones weighing about 30 kg that were manually stacked to be dispensed by hand over the feeding period. With today's larger farms, most bales are round, weighing 500 kg or more, and have to be moved about by tractors with front-end loaders.

Silage is a winter feed storage system that requires more mechanization. A feed crop such as corn, alfalfa or barley is chopped by a silage harvester. Then it is trucked to a pile and compressed to remove as much air as possible. The pile is sealed by a large sheet of plastic. Or bales of the moist forage are put end-to-end and wrapped in multiple layers of thin plastic. After the sugars in the plant ferment in the sealed environment, the feed is more palatable to the cattle. Feeding a cow so that she can produce a calf each year will cost over a dollar per day using stored feed, making up more than half of the expenses to keep a cow for the year. Recent strategies to lower production costs include setting the calving season so that the cow's peak nutritional demands coincide with the peak of forage production. And more farms are using low-cost electric fences to intensively graze select portions of land while excluding the cattle from other areas to allow plants a longer period to regrow.

The beef industry has 3 segments: the cow-calf farm raises an annual crop of calves that is sold in the fall; a backgrounding operation takes younger calves and feeds them over the winter

to be put out on pastures for the summer, selling the yearlings at about 385 kg (850 lbs); and finishing feedlots use a high-energy, grain-based ration to grow muscle mass and fat cover needed to meet specifications for premium beef grades.
● GLEN NICOLL

BEEF PROCESSING in MB has gone from the hub of the western Cdn cattle business to being a spoke in AB's big wheel of beef feeding and processing. The industry began when an enterprising young man from **MINNEDOSA**, Pat Burns, saw the needs of the transcontinental **RAILWAY** construction crews as a great business opportunity and started supplying beef as part of his freighting business in 1886. The Burns Meats empire began building packing plants in 1890, and soon had a collection across the West.

Winnipeg's **ST. BONIFACE** Stockyards was the largest livestock-handling centre in the Commonwealth at its prime in the mid-20th century. It housed the sales, assembly, and forwarding facilities for a majority of livestock in western Canada. Surrounded by 6 packing plants, most of the larger ones slaughtering numerous species, the annual federally inspected beef slaughter was over 500,000 head. As the slaughterhouses closed in the 1980s due to aging equipment and infrastructure, the newly established feedlots and packing plants in AB pulled beef production westward. Small abattoirs across MB now process just 20,000 beef cattle a year.

MB cattle began to be processed elsewhere when the Cdn dollar entered world currency exchanges and lost its equivalency to the US dollar. Also in the 1970s, Canada's self-sufficiency in beef was lost, and imports flooded in from the countries such as Argentina, New Zealand, and Australia. The US cowherd was declining at that time as well, and its packing plants saw a supply just N of the border that could be purchased with a 20% advantage on the US dollar. Truck transport of cattle was then taking over from railways, and delivery times were shortened, adding to the incentive. Beef carcass weights went up almost 90 kg (200 lbs) during the period due to the importation of European beef breeds and improved feeding regimes. The resulting beef production filled in the supply deficit and Canada became a net exporter. By 1985, there were 60,000 head of MB feeder and slaughter cattle leaving for US destinations; by 1992 the currency incentive and demand sent 240,000 S as the last large Winnipeg packing plant closed.

MB's **BEEF CATTLE FARMING** industry began to grow in the early 1960s as small on-farm feedlots used large amounts of homegrown **GRAIN** to finish their calves. Large-scale feedlots started in the 1970s, working on economies of scale to feed animals by the thousands. The largest feedlot in MB at present feeds 10,000 head and there are estimated to be about 200 in the province, turning out about 160,000 finished cattle. That production is transported E to ON, W to AB, and S to the US for slaughter – packer prices and the exchange rate on the dollar determine the direction. Mature animals that can no longer be used for reproduction are slaughtered for use in processed foods. Some 60,000 head of cows would normally be marketed, and without a large MB plant, those animals have to be slaughtered outside the province.

In May 2003, the entire beef industry in Canada was turned on its ear when exports were shut off by the discovery of an AB cow that was infected with bovine spongiform encephalopathy (BSE or "mad cow"), the cause of variant Creutzfeldt-Jakob disease in humans. All countries stopped importing Cdn beef and with almost half of the country's beef production headed to export markets, the country had twice as much meat is it could consume. Cdn shoppers didn't shy away from beef, and consumption rose slightly. MB cattle producers, without any local large-scale beef plants to sell to, ended up at the end of the list at AB, ON, and QC slaughterhouses; the US closed its border to all shipments of live cattle. Returns from cattle sales were almost halved in the first year of BSE-influenced prices, from $500 million down to $290 million. Under a new set of slaughter procedures, boneless beef from young animals was allowed into the US in the first year, and young slaughter animals were allowed to be exported in the 2nd year, with access to some international markets regained in 3 years. Mature animals remained excluded, and with a closed market, the value stayed at about half of previous levels. Imported manufacturing beef slowed to a trickle. Cdn consumers had been eating about 33 kg (72 lbs) of bone-in carcass beef in 2005, a consistent level to the previous 25 years, but a decline of about 11 kg (25 lbs) from the 1960s.

Cattle producer initiatives to build some locally-owned packing plants began during the BSE crisis in an effort to give farmers some power in the marketplace. MB farmers invested about half of the producer equity in a Neudorf, SK plant that began processing 250 head per day in 2006. A planned 60,000 head-per-year co-op plant in Dauphin, called Ranchers Choice, ran out of interested producer members and commitments for cattle needed to make the plant viable. The provincial govt had promised just under half of the capital cost of the $26 million plant, but the co-op had been unable to find a financial institution to loan the rest of the money needed to get the plant built. In Feb 2007, the directors of Ranchers Choice gave up the dream and decided to return the producers' share monies.

So 2007 represented an ironic ending to what was once the home of a majority of western Canada's beef processing business. The industry is now made up of 20 small abattoirs across MB that process beef carcasses, some in conjunction with other species. The largest can handle about 50 head a day, with beef reaching the consumer through small retailers. One federally inspected plant does beef as part of its operation, and is the only plant that can sell product to other provinces or countries. AB processes almost 70% of the country's beef, and the largest plants there handle 5000 head a day. ● GLEN NICOLL

BEETLE is an insect characterized by a tough first set of wings which protect the delicate second, folded flying wings underneath, and forward projecting biting mouthparts in many species. Beetles are such a diverse group that it is difficult to characterize. Ranging in size from 0.25 mm – 20 cm, they come in countless shapes and colours (e.g., green, red, yellow, and even gold and silver). This group is the most successful of all non-microscopic organisms in terms of species diversity, population numbers, longevity over evolutionary time, and impact in all but marine permanent-ice ecosystems. Beetles fulfill the niches of predators, herbivores, scavengers, pollinators, decomposers, parasites, and economic pests. They occupy virtually every habitat in MB except permanent ice fields and the marine environments. In fact, entire ecosystems would collapse within a short period were it not for beetles, so integral in countless food webs have they become over 280 million years (early Permian) of evolution. More than 350,000 living species in 116 families have been named so far, but even a conservative estimate of actual species numbers exceeds 10 million, and could reach over 30 million. We truly live in the 'Age of Beetles' – 30% of all animal species and 40% of insect species are beetles. An estimated 112 families of 9125 species (7000 named) occur in Canada, 2351 species of which have been recorded in MB, but the actual number will no doubt surpass 2500 with additional surveys. They are represented within 83 families, the largest families being the ground beetles (Carabidae) 350 species, rove beetles (Staphylinidae) 278, leaf beetles (Chrysomelidae) 254, weevils (Curculionidae) 179, predaceous diving beetles (Dytiscidae) 145, longhorn beetles (Cerambyscidae) 100, click beetles (Elateridae) 99, scarabs (Scarabaeidae) 85, water scavenger beetles (Hydrophilidae) 64, and ladybird beetles (Coccinelidae) 56. Other common families in MB

Ladybeetles (Ladybugs) feed on aphids and mites.

are fireflies (Lampyridae), jewel beetles (Buprestidae), darkling beetles (Tenebrionidae), and blister beetles (Meloidae).

GROUND BEETLES (Carabidae) are represented by over 850 species in Canada (33,500 worldwide) and are characterized by a long, flattened, black body, long legs for rapid running and climbing, biting mandibles, and long threadlike antennae. Most hunt after dark, emerging from spaces in the soil, under logs and stones. They are often the most abundant beetles in numerous habitats, particularly in moist sites. A number of species of Carabus and Calosoma reach a length up to 20 mm and devour prodigious numbers of other insects, including many injurious to forests. Calosoma frigidum may become so numerous that they can often be seen wandering along forest trails in city parks during the day. They climb up the tallest trees along riverbanks to feed on caterpillars in the tree canopy. One of the most beautiful is the 25 mm Pasimachus elongatus found under debris in mixed-grass prairie. It is highly flattened and has a blue border around the edge of its shiny black body.

TIGER BEETLES (family Cicindela) are among the most voracious insects, running down their prey (mostly insects) and dispatching it with repeated bites of its long sickle-shaped jaws. Powerful digestive enzymes are then discharged into the wounds, and the soupy remains are then ingested, leaving only a hollow shell behind. There are 19 species in MB (109 for Canada and USA; 2600 worldwide), ranging from the 8 mm Variable Tiger Beetle (*C. terricola*) to the 20 mm Big Sand Tiger Beetle (*C. formosa*). Most have beautiful, intricate,

and identifying patterns on their wing covers (elytra) and colors ranging from blue-green, red, brown, and black. These day-active insects are highly specialized to live in specific habitats, like the Ghost Tiger Beetle (*C. lepida*) found in MB only in the bare sand dunes of the Spruce Woods Provincial Park, and the rare Salt Flat Tiger Beetle (*C. fulgida westbournei*), which occurs sparingly on salt flats. Tiger beetles are divided into spring-fall or summer species, based on when the adults emerge. Larvae live in deep burrows for 1-3 years, and ambush passing insect prey like ants.

ROVE BEETLES (family Staphylinidae) are flat, hairy and elongated beetles, 1-25 mm long. With a highly flexible body and short wing covers, they look anything but beetle-like. Most are black or brown, but some are brightly coloured with red or orange and black (*Oxyporus* species found in fungi) or are covered in silver or gold hair (*Ontholestes cingulatus*). Occuring in all types of land habitats, they can be extraordinarily abundant and are important predators and scavengers. They can run fast and fly well. Any animal carcass will have its share of rove beetles, feeding on larvae of flies and other insects. Some species can emit ill-smelling chemicals in the face of predators. There are likely over 350 species in MB (over 1000 in Canada; 30,000 worldwide), many of which await discovery. Rove beetles species may someday rival even the weevils in numbers.

LEAF BEETLES (family Chrysomelidae) are small (1-15 mm), colourful, domed, plant-eating beetles that can become extraordinarily abundant in natural ecosystems and in agricultural

crops. Often highly specific in host selection and niche, there are leaf feeders, leaf skeletonizers, leaf, root and stem miners, as well as root feeders. Some larvae live inside special cases they build for protection, while others heap their faeces onto their backs to ward off and disgust parasites and predators. Several species, whose larvae feed on willow, sequester defensive chemicals from the host plant. Some, like the Colorado potato beetle (*Leptinotarsa decimlineata*), are significant crop pests. There are also several major defoliators of trees grown for shade or shelter belts. Aphthona species, introduced from Europe, have been released in western MB for biological control of the invasive prairie weed Leafy Spurge. Exotic Galerucella species have also being released throughout the province as biological control agents for the wetland weed Purple Loosestrife. MB's leaf beetle fauna includes at least 254 species (38,000 worldwide), but many additional ones await discovery.

WEEVILS (family Curculionidae) are recognizable by the elbowed antennae and a down-turned snout, at the front of which are the mandibles. They are mostly under 10 mm long, but range from 0.7-80 mm. This is by far the largest family in the animal or plant kingdom, with 50,000 species named so far, and many thousands yet to be discovered. It has been stated by scientists that for every species of land plant on earth, there is at least one weevil that feeds on it. People likely eat weevil parts daily, since several species, such as the Grain Beetle (*Sitophilus granarius*) and Rice Weevil (*S. oryzae*) are ever-present in stored grain. Their great abundance is reflected in the major roles they play in natural ecosystems and with agricultural crops in MB. A common and interesting species is the Acorn Weevil (*Curculio pardalis*) whose female drills a deep hole into an acorn with her elongated snout to deposit an egg inside. Likely dozens of species remain to be discovered in the province.

PREDACEOUS DIVING BEETLES (family Dytiscidae) are smooth, flattened, oval-shaped aquatic beetles with about 150 species recorded so far in the province (267 in Canada and Alaska; 3000 worldwide). Usually black or brown, they range in size from 1.5 mm – 4.5 cm. The hind legs are flattened and lined with stiff hairs as an adaptation to swimming. They break the surface periodically to capture an air bubble for respiration. They are found in a wide variety of habitats, such as ponds, lakes, rivers, streams, springs and bogs. They range in size from 3 mm long (*Liodessus*) to 40 mm (*Dytiscus harrissii*). The aquatic larvae of Dytiscus species are aptly called 'water tigers' for their long and curved jaws and ability to take prey as large as minnows, tadpoles and insect life.

B

Digestion is partially external, and the liquefied contents are sucked up. Most species overwinter as adults and occasionally become trapped in the ice on the surface of ponds and stream, until spring melt releases them once again. Adults are excellent flyers and may reach isolated watercourses.

LONG-HORNED BEETLES (family Cerambyscidae) are small to large (10-31 mm) cylindrical beetles with long antennae and strong wings and limbs. In the tropics, several species can reach a length up to 20 cm. The larvae attack branches and stems of trees and shrubs, and are capable of boring with their well-developed mandibles through wood as tough as oak. The adults of smaller species may be seen feeding on the pollen and nectar of flowers. The body is often covered in scales or hairs, and coloured for camouflage (brown and grey) or to mimic wasps (yellow and black). Some species are banded or spotted with bright contrasting colors of red, white or black). The black, 27 mm White-spotted Sawyer (*Monochamus scutellatus*) is attracted to bright colors and not infrequently lands on campers in the woods, which can be quite disconcerting, since they hold on tightly with long powerful legs. The Red Milkweed Beetle (*Tetraopes tetrophthalmus*) is striking against the green leaves of milkweed and dogbane, and acquires protection from predators by sequestering distasteful chemicals from these plants. This is a huge family (over 35,000 species worldwide) and consequently plays a major role in forest ecology.

CLICK BEETLES (family Elateridae) are long (5-20 mm), thin beetles that have an interesting 'clicking' mechanism which repeatedly catapults the beetle into the air – an adaptation to escape the attention of predators. MB is host to about 100 species, found in many habitats in the soil, leaf litter, rotting wood, or moss. The adults of most species are secretive during the day, but fly actively at night, and are commonly collected at lights. The larvae, called wireworms, are mostly predacious, but a few species feed on the roots of plants and can cause damage to germinating seeds and potato tubers. The black and red *Ampedus nigricollis* is common inside rotting logs in aspen forest.

SCARABS (family Scarabaeidae) are robust beetles with clubbed antennae formed of leaf-like plates. They form a diverse group of about 85 species in MB (21,000 worldwide), many of which are scavengers such as dung beetles (e.g., the 8 mm *Onthophagus hecate*), which feed on animal wastes of all kinds. Some species (*Geotrupes semiopacus*) construct burrows beneath dung and carrion or other organic materials

and provision their larvae with resources from above. Geotrupes is a beautiful emerald green species occurring in sandy areas of MB. There are also 30 species of plant-eating scarab beetles in MB, including those species whose larvae feed on rotting logs or inside the nests of thatching ants. Scarab larvae are a characteristic C-shape, with the head and three pairs of legs at the anterior end, followed by a curved and bulbous abdomen. They emerge after 1 to 4 years (often feeding on plant roots), depending on the species, and devour herbs, shrubs and trees. June beetle (*Phyllophaga* species) larvae are often uncovered when digging in the garden, and after emerging the 20 mm brown adults are often attracted to lights at night and buzz against the screen or window. The 25 mm Goldsmith Beetle (*Cotalpa lanigera*) is an attractive yellow with a shiny green and hairy underside, found in deciduous forests.

WATER SCAVENGER BEETLES (family Hydrophilidae) are smooth, oval beetles generally colored black or greenish, and ranging in size from 1-40 mm. There are about 65 species in MB, 50 of which are aquatic and 14 terrestrial, found in decaying vegetation or faeces. The aquatic ones live in ponds and lakes, but are not adept at swimming; both adults and larvae paddle and tumble around in the water. The larvae are predacious, and some species hang at the surface, nabbing passing invertebrates. Adults are hampered by a large bubble of air carried in a ventral concavity of the body, but they are able to exchange air at the surface very efficiently. Where the predacious diving beetles (dytiscids) rise to the surface posterior-end first, the hydrophilids rise head first. They have long palps (mouthparts) which are used to break the surface tension, and to create an air channel connecting to the main ventral bubble. The adults are mainly scavengers of vegetation, and are capable of flight for dispersal.

LADYBEETLES OR LADYBUGS (family Coccinelidae) are familiar, colourful, domed beetles represented by about 56 species in MB (4500 worldwide). They specialize feeding on aphids, scale insects and mites, and so have been used successfully in biological control programs in agricultural fields and greenhouses. A European species (*Coccinella septempunctata*), referred to as C-7, was introduced into NA to control aphids, but it is now out-competing some native species. The multi-coloured Asian lady beetle (*Harmonia axyridis*) was first collected in Winnipeg in 2000, and may become a nuisance from its habit of entering homes in large numbers to find a place to spend the winter. Only time will tell if its occurrence in MB will also contribute

to a decline in native ladybird beetle species – an all too-frequent result of poorly conceived or accidental introductions of exotic species. Lady beetles can be very abundant, and vast numbers sometimes accumulate along the shorelines of lakes in spring and fall.

WHIRLIGIG BEETLES (family Gyrinidae) are shiny, black insects distinctly modified for living on the surface of ponds and lakes. The front legs are carried out in front of the body, while the other 2 pairs are reduced to form paddle-like appendages. The antennae are short and compact, and are used to detect vibrations created by insects trapped in the surface tension of water. Whirligig beetles secrete specialized surfactants that help keep the beetles afloat as they spin and twirl across the water surface. The compound eyes are among the most remarkable in the animal world in that they are divided horizontally so that the upper half views the terrestrial world while the lower half views underwater. The beetles seem to swim aimlessly on the surface, often in large aggregations of thousands of individuals in a multispecies swarm, and there may be many more swimming below the surface. It appears that they would be easy prey for fish, but they produce a potent defensive chemical secretion that deters most predators. There are 22 species in MB (700 worldwide). ● TDG, REW

BELFOUR, Edward John "The Eagle," goaltender (b Apr 21, 1965, Carman) is an all-star NHL goalie. At 21 he was still playing junior hockey for the Winkler Flyers. After being named top goaltender in the Manitoba Junior Hockey League in 1985-86, Belfour was offered a hockey scholarship at U of ND, where he first showed his potential. He won 29 of 34 games, attracting the attention of Chicago Blackhawks scouts who offered him a deal as a free agent for

Ed Belfour with his last NHL team, the Florida Panthers.

B

the 1988-89 season. His first year in the NHL was unremarkable. Belfour played 23 games, and had a 4-12-3 official record with a 3.87 GAA. The following season, he played 33 games with the Cdn national team. Belfour's best season came in 1990-91, when he became the Blackhawk's starting goalie and set a rookie record with 43 wins in 74 games. He won that year's Vezina Trophy for top goaltender, as well as the Calder Memorial Trophy for Rookie of the Year. In 1991-92, Belfour helped the Blackhawks advance to the Stanley Cup finals, where they lost to the Pittsburgh Penguins. The following season, he won his 2nd Vezina Trophy, as well as the Jennings Trophy for lowest-goals against, which he won another 3 times over the course of his career. Belfour was known as a quick-tempered player, who was arrested twice for drunken arguments with police. He was traded to the San Jose Sharks in the 1996-1997 season, then signed on with the Dallas Stars as a free agent the following year. He played with the Stars for 5 seasons, helping the team bring home the Stanley Cup in 1999. In 2002, he signed with the Toronto Maple Leafs. That year, Belfour also played on the gold medal-winning Cdn Olympic team at the Salt Lake Olympics. As of writing, Belfour had won 457 NHL games, placing him 3rd in the NHL for career wins. • MD

BELL, Charles Napier, trader, athlete, historian (b 1854, Perth, Upper Canada; d 1936, Minaki, ON). Bell first came W in 1870 as a bugler in the **Wolseley Expedition**. He stayed in the region first to trade and hunt before settling in **Winnipeg** to work as a Cdn customs officer. Bell became involved in the growing city's business community, serving on the Board of Trade (1887-1916) and Grain Exchange (1886), and earning money from real estate speculation. Also known for his athletic ability, Bell was an accomplished **Speed Skating** coach and one of the first to introduce **Figure Skating** to the West. He was a mason, fellow of the Royal Geographical Society, and a notable writer. Bell co-founded the Manitoba Historical and Scientific Society in 1889, twice serving as its president. He was the author of more than a dozen publications, including *Navigation of Hudson Bay and Straits* (1883), and *The Old Forts of Winnipeg* (1927). • JT

BELL, Gordon, ophthalmologist, bacteriologist (b 1863, Pembroke, Upper Canada; d 1923, Fox Lake). Born in Pembroke, Canada, he was educated at Pembroke Collegiate, the U of Toronto, and the Manitoba Medical College. He lost a leg as a result of a severe bout with diphtheria. He served as superintendent of the **Brandon** Hospital for the Insane from 1890 to 1893 before

becoming MB's first ophthalmologist. In 1896, he was appointed provincial bacteriologist, and in 1897 he set up a laboratory near the first Medical College building, which became the diagnostic and epidemiological centre for the province (became **Cadham Provincial Laboratory**). He was chair of the provincial Board of Health from 1913 to 1927. He resided at Fox Lake, MB from 1914 to 1923. He died of streptococcal sore throat, probably contracted from specimens he had examined in Brandon. A **Winnipeg** high school is named after him.

Gordon Bell

Gordon's son, Lennox Gordon "Buzz" Bell (1903-1973), graduated from U of M medical school in 1928. He was in charge of outpatients at Winnipeg General Hospital (*see* **Health Sciences Centre**) from 1933 to 1949. Appointed a professor of **Medicine** at the **U of M**, he became dean of the faculty in 1949, and physician-in-chief at Winnipeg General Hospital in 1950. During WWII he served as a wing commander in the medical branch of the RCAF. • JMB/GPP

BELL, Steve, Christian contemporary singer/songwriter (b Nov 17, 1960, Calgary AB). Moving to Drumheller, AB at age 8, Bell first received guitar lessons from inmates at the penitentiary where his father ministered. After relocating to **Stony Mountain** in MB in 1972, he and his family performed in churches as the Alf Bell Family Singers. After a stint with jazz fusion band Dega, Bell joined Tim Elias and John Schritt to form popular folk trio Elias, Schritt & Bell,

which recorded *Awakenings* (1980) for the CBC. Disbanding after 3 years, Bell backed up local singers Rhonda Hart, Rocki Rolletti (Peter Jordan), and Byron O'Donnell before returning to Christian music and embarking on a solo career. With financial help from friends, Bell recorded *Comfort My People* (1989), partnering with Mid-Ocean Studios owner Dave Zeglinski to form Signpost Music to record and distribute his recordings. *Deep Calls to Deep* (1992), *Burning Ember* (1994), and *The Feast of Seasons* (1995) all established Bell as the leading Christian contemporary singer/songwriter in Canada. *Romantics & Mystics* (1997) won a Best Gospel Album Juno Award, as did *Simple Songs* (2000). This latter album also won 2 Prairie Music Awards and 3 Vibe Awards. In 2003, *Sons & Daughters* featured daughter Sarah and sons Micah and Jesse. Signpost Music has 15 artists signed and markets their music worldwide making it one of the largest Christian contemporary music labels in NA. In 2006, Bell released *My Dinner With Bruce*, a tribute album to early mentor Cdn singer/songwriter Bruce Cockburn, and appeared with the **Winnipeg Symphony Orchestra**. • JOHN EINARSON

BELLAN, Ruben Carl, economist, professor, author (b Oct 2, 1918, **Winnipeg**; d Apr 17, 2005, Winnipeg) was an influential writer and speaker on the topic of economics. He was also known for pioneering a summer job program for university students in the 1950s, when there were no student loan programs. Through that program, hundreds of jobs were created, and many students credit Bellan's program for their being able to continue their studies. Bellan earned his BA from the **U of M** (1938), his MA from the U of Toronto (1941), and his PhD at Columbia U in New York (1958). He served in the RCAF during WWII and was stationed in Burma (now Myanmar), where he worked as an intelligence officer. In 1946, he joined the U of M's faculty of economics, where he also served as dean of studies at St. John's College. He retired in 1988, but stayed on as senior scholar and was elected a honorary fellow the following year. An economic nationalist, Bellan was sought after as a guest speaker, and wrote commentary for the **Winnipeg Free Press**, *Toronto Star*, *Financial Post*, and *Policy Options*. He also spoke on various TV and radio programs. Bellan advised or served as consultant to govt bodies and NGOs. He published several books, including *Principles of Economics and the Canadian Economy* (first ed 1960, 7th ed 1986); *The Evolving City* (1971); *Winnipeg First Century: An Economic History* (1978); *The Unnecessary Evil* (1986); and *Canadian Cities: A History* (2003). • JILL.SEXSMITH

BELMONT, pop 250, is a community 50 km SE of **Brandon** on highway 23. Settlement, mostly by eastern Canadians of **English**, **Scots**, and **Irish** stock, began around 1878. The community of Belmont was named after John Oliver Bell, who arrived from Nova Scotia in 1879. The community was named after his family, and "mount" or hills surrounding. A post office opened here in 1884. The local economy depends mainly on **Construction**, retail, and services for area farms. **Tourism** to nearby Spruce Woods Provincial Park (*see* **Provincial Parks**) is also important. • GPP

BENDER HAMLET is a ghost town 95 km NNW of Winnipeg. The post office opened in 1909 and was closed in 1916. Also known as Bender, the town was named after Jacob Bender, who, inspired by the Baron de Hirsch, tried to start an agricultural colony for Jewish settlers in 1903. Although the population in 1915 was 130, unproductive land and falling cattle prices forced the pioneers to leave in search of greater opportunities by 1918. All that remains of Bender Hamlet is a cemetery, some ruins, and a plaque. • GPP

BELUGA or White Whale is found in **Hudson Bay**. It reaches 3-5 metres in length and weighs about 700 kg (500-1500 kg), with males averaging larger than females. The Beluga's skin resembles white rubber and its smoothness reduces friction with the water. This whale has an appealing 'smile,' an enlarged forehead (melon), but a dorsal fin is lacking. A thick (3-10 cm) layer of blubber insulates the animal from the intensely cold water of the Bay, and the animal is capable of breaking through 20 cm of ice with its head or back in order to reach air. This species can swim over 20 minutes before having to surface for air. Dives for feeding often descend several hundred metres (max 1000 m). Belugas enter Hudson Bay as soon as spring ice conditions allow, and they gather in the estuaries of MB's **Nelson**, **Churchill** and Seal rivers from May to Aug in some of the largest concentrations (23, 000) in its circumpolar range. From Aug to Nov, the whales off the MB coastline follow the shoreline northward or head across Hudson Bay to their wintering areas in Foxe Basin, Hudson Strait and Ungava Bay; few remain all winter in either Hudson or James Bay.

Often hunting in pods of up to 12 individuals, the whales use sounds and echolocation to communicate and to hunt for fish and invertebrates, which are often concentrated in estuaries. The fresh water apparently softens the old outer layer of skin, and the stony or sandy bottom provides a convenient scratching surface to assist with the moult. Breeding occurs in April to May, births from May to Aug (following

a gestation of 14 months), and nursing for 20 months. A single, 1.5 metre young is usually born every third year. Dark brown to grey at birth, it becomes progressively lighter to age 6-8. The life span is estimated from 33-50 years, but few individuals survive past 16 years. Mortality is caused mainly by predation (Human, Orca, Polar Bear) and trapping by ice.

This was an important prey animal to a succession of early peoples that populated Hudson Bay, augmented after 1688 by Europeans. Like the Polar Bear, the Beluga is at the top of the food chain and its movements and feeding grounds are influenced by the distribution of ice cover. Consequently, bio-accumulation of human-generated pollutants and global warming, as well as over-harvesting, have placed this species of whale at risk. In the past, a number of animals were trapped alive near Churchill for shipment to aquariums. Many tourists currently flock to Churchill in summer to see the Belugas at close range. • REW, DBS, FOC

BENEDICTSSON, Margrét Jónsdóttir, suffragette, (b Mar 16, 1866, Iceland; d Dec 13, 1956, WA, US) was a central figure in the early suffrage movement. She immigrated to MB in 1887 after putting herself through college and business school. She was a firm believer in women's rights and was founding editor of the suffrage newspaper *Freyja* (meaning "woman"), which she published with her husband Sigfús. Canada's first suffrage newspaper grew to a 40-page monthly publication, reaching 500 homes. Benedictsson wrote most of the articles; *Freyja* was published for 12 years. The paper's aims were to advocate for "matters pertaining to the progress and rights of women" and to "support the betterment of social conditions." Articles stressed the importance of education for girls, economic independence for women, and equal pay for women. Influenced by the suffrage movement in Iceland, Benedictsson travelled and spoke to women of **Icelandic** origins throughout MB, SK, and northern ND. Although the **Reformist** Women's Christian Temperance Union (WCTU) is generally credited with starting the **Women's Movement** in MB, Icelandic women were active from the beginning and worked with the WCTU on suffrage petitions. Benedictsson also started the Icelandic Suffrage Association, the first organization of its kind in NA, and the Ladies' Aid Society of **Winnipeg's** Icelandic **Unitarian** Church. She co-ordinated women's delegations to the **Legislative Building** on the issue of women's suffrage. When the bill giving women the vote went through 3rd reading on Jan 27, 1916, it was moved by Attorney General and acting pre-

mier Thomas H. Johnson, whose mother was an Icelandic suffragist. • PENNI MITCHELL

BENHAM, Mary Lile, journalist, author, (b Oct 8, 1914, **Winnipeg**; d Jan 26, 1991, Winnipeg), was a former newspaper columnist as well as the author of numerous children's books about MB. Benham was born in Winnipeg and educated at Rupertsland School. She was the granddaughter of **Edward L. Drewry**, a Winnipeg brewer and Winnipeg city councillor. She was also the mother of former Winnipeg city councillor Donald Benham. While attending the **U of M**, Benham wrote for the student newspaper; she graduated in 1935. After graduation, she did freelance radio work before she started writing a column called "Victory People" in 1944 that appeared in both the **Winnipeg Tribune** and the **Winnipeg Free Press**. Benham authored numerous biographies of famous Canadians for schoolchildren, including Nellie McClung (1975), Paul Kane (1977), and La Verendrye (1980). She wrote a lot about local history, including a history of St. George's Church in Winnipeg's Crescentwood neighbourhood titled *Once More Unto the Breach* (1982). In 1974, she co-authored the book *Winnipeg*, and wrote *The Manitoba Club 100 Years: 1874-1974*. Her collection of written work also includes puppet plays, short stories, articles, book reviews, and poetry. Benham served as a director of the Canadian Writers' Federation, and was the recipient of the 1984 YWCA Woman of the Year Award. She died in 1991 at the age of 76. • AMANDA STEPHENS

BENITO, pop 415, a village 135 km NW of **Dauphin** and just E of the SK border. Founded by a variety of settlers – including Ontarians, **English**, and eastern Europeans – the area was first settled around 1900, and a post office opened in 1903. The postmistress decided the village's name, possibly after the protagonist of the novel *Benito Cereno* by Herman Melville. The **Railway** line came through in 1905. The local economy relies mainly on services for surrounding agriculture and logging. Myrna Dreidger, MLA for Charleswood, grew up in Benito, and the village is the birthplace of 1983 World Curling Championship-winning skip Ed "The Wrench" Werenich. • GPP

BERENS, Jacob, Ojibway chief, (b 1832, **Berens River** area; d July 7, 1916, Berens River). Also known as Nah-wee-kee-sick-quah-yash, meaning "Light Moving in the Centre of the Sky," Berens descended from a family that had travelled from the Lake Superior region in the 18th century. His father and grandfather were accomplished Medicine Men (*see* **Midewiwin**). As Berens was growing

B

Jacob Berens, ca 1909

up, settlers and missionaries were arriving at or passing through Berens River – probably known then as Omeemee Sibi, "Pigeon River") – on the E shore of **LAKE WINNIPEG**. **METHODIST** minister George McDougall baptized Berens on Feb 25, 1861, at **NORWAY HOUSE**. He became integrated with European settlers, marrying Scotswoman Mary McKay, as well as learning English and the newly introduced **CREE** syllabary. He worked for the **HBC** at an outpost in Canada West (later ON) and on **YORK BOATS**. In Sept 1875, Berens acted as a community leader for the signing of Treaty 5. The agreement, negotiated by govt commissioners **JAMES MCKAY** and **ALEXANDER MORRIS**, ceded Swampy Cree and Ojibway lands around **LAKE MANITOBA** and Lake Winnipeg, including Berens River and Norway House. Berens was elected as the first treaty chief, and initially oversaw a large region stretching into what is now Northwestern ON. As chief, he continued to co-operate with European settlers, including **ICELANDERS**, and supported Methodist missionary work that included a religious school. However, Berens also advocated on behalf of his people, including fighting for respect of cultural beliefs and against excessive **COMMERCIAL FISHING**. ● JT

BERENS RIVER FIRST NATION, on reserve pop 1693, off reserve pop 928, is located 270 km N of **WINNIPEG**, on the E shore of **LAKE WINNIPEG**. Berens River is the biggest community on the E side of the lake. There is no year-round road access; the community has a runway for air accessibility. The native language of the Berens River people is **OJIBWAY**. It is a member of the Southeast Tribal Council. The Frontier School Division administers education. Schooling in Berens River First Nation goes from Nursery-Grade 12, and

total enrolment for the year 2003-2004 was 353. This First Nation is comprised of 2 reserves: the Berens River Reserve No 13 and the more isolated, Pigeon River Reserve No 13A. Both reserves are named after the same river: the Berens River that was called the Pigeon River before it was named for a **HBC** Governor. Because of its location at the mouth of the Berens River, the area was a staging point for the HBC fur trade. Treaty 5 was signed at Berens River in 1875. The economy is based on fishing, trapping, and forestry. Since the mid-20th century, the main industry has been logging, and recent partnerships with industry and government have been designed to create a log-house-export industry. This First Nation has one of the world's biggest pickerel fisheries. In 2006, Berens River was facing several economic challenges. Fire had destroyed the community's water treatment plant in 2005. As a **WINNIPEG** insurance company refused to cover the full costs of its repair, the plant remained out of use and residents were under a boil-water advisory. As of July 2006, Berens River was $4.8 million in debt and the community was facing the threat of third-party management imposed by the federal Dept. of Indian and Northern Affairs. Although this First Nation may have to deal with poor housing conditions, water quality, roads, and health care, it is blessed with some of the most unspoiled wilderness in the province. Adjoining the First Nation is the non-treaty community of Berens River (pop 42), which is governed by a mayor and council and has a post office, public works employee, constable, volunteer fire chief and a recreation director. ● RK

BERGEN, David, author (b 1957, Prince Edward, BC). Now living in **WINNIPEG**, Bergen has worked as a teacher and a hospital orderly, and in the building trades. He won the John Hirsch Award for Most Promising MB Writer in 1993, the McNally Robinson Book of the Year Award in 1997 for his novel, *A Year of Lesser,* and the Canadian Literary Award for Short Story in 2000. He continues to work in the genre of fiction. His *The Case of Lena S.* (2003) won the Carol Shields Winnipeg Book Award and was nominated for the Governor General's Award. Bergen became the first Manitoban to win the Scotiabank Giller Prize for his novel *The Time in Between* in 2005. His work is gritty, not afraid to deal with sexuality and violence. Because of Bergen's interest in how characters respond to moral adversity, he has been compared by some critics to Graham Greene. ● MILDRED GUTKIN

BERRIES, FRUITS AND NUTS. MB has many kinds of edible native berries, a few poisonous ones, and 3 edible nuts, if you can beat **SQUIRRELS**,

BEAR, and **DEER** to them. Most edible berries come from the rose (Rosaceae), heath (Ericaceae), honeysuckle (Caprifoliaceae), and gooseberry (Grossulariaceae) families. All edible fruits in MB are borne on woody trees or shrubs. Most are found in moist forests or bogs, but some like open and dry or disturbed areas.

All fruits and berries of the rose family are edible, although some of the seeds – such as those of wild plums – are poisonous. MB has 2 kinds of wild strawberries, several kinds of tall and dwarf wild raspberries (including bakeapple berry or cloudberry), 2 kinds of wild plums, 3 kinds of wild cherries (chokecherry, pin cherry or fire-cherry, and sand-cherry) several kinds of hawthorns and roses and 2 kinds of mountain-ash in this family.

The heath family has 4 kinds of blueberries/bilberries with bluish berries; red-berried rock-cranberry/lingonberry; 2 kinds of true cranberries; 3 kinds of bearberries, the widespread mealy kinnikinnick/common bearberry (*Arctostaphylos uva-ursi*) and juicy northern red and alpine bearberries, and the wintergreen-tasting teaberry and creeping snowberry.

The honeysuckle family contains 2 kinds of wild honeysuckles with edible berries, as well as highbush cranberry, mooseberry and nannyberry. The gooseberry family contains 5 kinds

Chokeberries

of currants and a gooseberry. Currants are the wild black, northern black, and bristly black, wild red, and skunk species. This last type, though edible, tastes just like its namesake. Other edible berries include the northern crowberry, the widespread but tasteless bunchberry, soapberry, buffaloberry, wild grape, and the fuzzy sumac. Juniper has waxy "berries" with a strong gin-like smell and taste. A few are fine for flavouring, but more may cause stomach upset.

Poisonous or disagreeable berries include most of those found on non-woody vines or herbs, especially those of baneberry and blue cohosh. Poisonous berries found on shrubs include those of poison ivy, buckthorn, yew, snowberry/buckbrush, and some honeysuckles.

MB's 3 edible nuts include 2 kinds of hazelnut shrubs and the acorn of our native bur oak tree. All 3 are common in the southern half of MB, the hazelnuts in moist forests, and oak on drier sites or higher riverbanks. All are relished by people and by a variety of animals and birds. Hazelnuts can be eaten directly from the shell, but acorns usually require soaking and/or drying to remove the bitter tannins they contain. Of course, people also grow domesticated berries and fruits, such as raspberries, strawberries, grapes, crabapples, and plums, often derived from crosses with hardy native species. ● KAREN JOHNSON

BETHANY, pop 100, is a community 60 km NNE of **BRANDON**. First settled in 1879, a post office and **RAILWAY** point were established here in 1904. The community was originally known as Fotherby, after the landowner on whose land the community was situated. It was later changed, either to reflect that early settlers here who were from Bethany, ON, or after the biblical village of Mary (meaning "house of affliction" in Hebrew). The disassembled **CN** line through Bethany now forms part of the **TRANS-CANADA TRAIL**. ● GPP

BEYNON, Francis Marion, suffragist (b 1884, Streetsville, ON; d 1951, New York) was 5 when her family moved from southern ON to a farm in the **HARTNEY** area of MB. After her father's death, the family moved on to Winnipeg. Although Francis was trained as a teacher, she was hired by the **T. EATON COMPANY** as a catalogue writer. She moved in literary circles, and in 1908 she joined her older sister **LILLIAN BEYNON THOMAS** in forming the Quill Club, a group of intellectuals and journalists who gathered to discuss social and other issues. In 1912, Francis left Eaton's to become editor for the women's pages in the *Grain Growers Guide*. Beynon was an influential figure in establishing legal rights for women in MB, publishing groundbreaking articles for

Frances Marion Beynon

rural women in support of women's suffrage and other women's causes in the pages of the *Guide*. She also gave advice to rural women on how to organize and discuss social and political issues. Beynon advanced the idea that farmwomen were equal partners with their husbands. She was also an outspoken advocate for the rights of ethnic minority groups. Beynon, a socialist, was a strong opponent of conscription during WWI, believing any effort to disenfranchise "alien" voters who might not support conscription could influence women's right to the vote. Such a move would have given some women the right to vote, but not women classed as "aliens." At first, **NELLIE McCLUNG** supported the limited enfranchisement proposal as a temporary measure, but after Frances Beynon criticized the idea, McClung withdrew her support. In 1917, Frances moved to New York where her sister Lillian Beynon Thomas and husband Vernon Thomas had just moved. In 1919, Beynon's pacifist novel, *Aleta Dey* was published. She lived the rest of her life out of the public eye in the US. In 1984, playwright and MP Wendy Lill dramatized Beynon's life in *The Fighting Days*. ● PENNI MITCHELL

BEYNON THOMAS, Lillian, suffragist, (b 1874, Streetville, ON; d 1951, Winnipeg). Born in southern ON, Beynon Thomas lived with her family in **HARTNEY** until 1896, when they moved to Winnipeg. There she attended Normal School,

and went on to teach for 9 years in several rural communities. As a teacher, she became aware of the isolation, poverty, and abuse faced by many farmwomen, an experience that was to influence her later political life. In 1905, she became the editor of the women's pages for the *Manitoba Free Press*, where she created a forum for discussion on women's suffrage, the rights of domestic workers, and other legal and social reforms to aid women's equality efforts. Her column "Home Loving Hearts" was written under the pseudonym Lillian Laurie. The letters she published told stories about women who had been abused and abandoned and who had no legal right to their farms or custody of their children. She used the pages to lobby for new divorce and child-custody laws, for the protection of unwed mothers, for the property rights of farmwomen, and for legislation to prohibit the sale of liquor, which she saw as a cause of much of the misery and hardship facing women. Beynon Thomas was also the founding president of the Political Equality League in 1912, one of the first women's lobby groups in MB. The Political Equality League was comprised of both men and women and advocated for a dower law and homesteading right to give wives minimal authority to property upon death of a husband or upon divorce. It also lobbied for better working conditions and better wages for working women. Among the highlights of Thomas's public life was organizing the famous Women's Mock Parliament at Winnipeg's Walker Theatre (now the Odeon cinema) in Jan 1914, which satirized men by depicting their approach to an all-female legislature to ask for the right to vote. **NELLIE LETITIA McCLUNG**, playing the premier, answered the men seeking the franchise in almost the exact words that the real premier, **RODMOND ROBLIN**, had used in answering a deputation of women, to the audience's great amusement. Beynon Thomas was also an active member of the executive of the suffragist-leaning Canadian Women's Press Club, located in Winnipeg from 1913-20. Lillian married Alfred Vernon Thomas, who worked at the *Manitoba Free Press* as a legislative reporter until he was fired for his anti-conscription views in 1917. The couple moved to New York, returning to Manitoba in 1922, when Lillian Beynon Thomas became a novelist and playwright. ● PENNI MITCHELL

BEZAN, James, politician (b May 19, 1965, **RUSSELL**) is the Conservative MP for Selkirk-Interlake. He grew up on a farm near **INGLIS**. He received a diploma in agriculture production from Olds College in AB. Bezan worked for several companies in the agriculture industry, including the Manitoba Crop Insurance Corporation and as CEO

B

of the Manitoba Cattle Producers Association. In 1996, he established a livestock export and consulting company. Bezan has sat on numerous boards and committees, including the Canadian Cattlemen's Association, the Manitoba Forage Council, and the Manitoba Red Meats Forum. He was first elected to the House of Commons in 2004, and was re-elected in 2006. In early 2007, Bezan was selected as the chair of the standing committee on agriculture and agri-food. His family operates a farm near TEULON. ● MD

B

BIF NAKED, singer/songwriter (b June 17, 1971, New Delhi, India) was born to a Canadian teenager in India, and adopted by American missionaries and named Beth Torbert. She grew up in Minnesota and Kentucky, as well as the THE PAS and DAUPHIN, before moving to WINNIPEG at the age of 13. Torbert became interested in THEATRE during high school, and enrolled at the U OF W to study it further. She dropped out to join a band, Jungle Milk, and became known as Bif Naked while singing with the punk band Gorilla Gorilla. The name started out as a 1989 concert gimmick, but it stuck and has remained Torbert's stage name ever since. She also toured extensively with hard-edged bands Chrome Dog and Dying To Be Violent before deciding to start a solo career in 1994. That year she released and EP and a self-titled debut album. Torbert started her own label in 1995 – Her Royal Majesty's Records – and issued a spoken word release in 1996. She formed a band and went on to release *I Bificus* (1998) and *Purge* (2001), with the latter garnering a

Bif Naked

Juno Award nomination. *Superbeautifulmonster* followed in 2005. Bif Naked's most successful singles have been "Moment of Weakness," "Spaceman," and "I Love Myself Today," all of which were included on her retrospective album *Essentially Naked*. The tattooed singer has also maintained an acting career in television and feature films. ● JT

BIGELOW, Wilfred Gordon Jr "Bill," surgeon, inventor (b June 8, 1913, BRANDON; d Mar 27, 2005, Toronto). Bill was the son of Wilfred Bigelow Sr, one of the most prominent early doctors in Brandon. Wilfred Sr formed Canada's first group-practice medical clinic in that community in 1915. The younger Bigelow completed studies at Brandon College (now BRANDON U) in 1931, and went on to the U of Toronto, where he earned a BA in 1935, and an MD and MSc in 1938. During WWII, Bigelow served from 1941-45 as part of field transfusion and surgery units in Europe. Following the war, he became a research fellow at Johns Hopkins U (Baltimore, MD) from 1946-47, before returning to Toronto in 1947. He joined the staff at the Toronto General Hospital, and later the Department of Surgery and Banting Institute at the U of Toronto. Bigelow pioneered induced hypothermia as a surgery technique, finding that it slowed heart function, since the body requires less oxygen at low temperatures, enough to be able to perform major heart operations safely. He also experimented with electrical impulses, and in 1949, restarted a dog's heart during an experimental surgery. This research, and that of John C. Callaghan and fellow Manitoban JOHN HOPPS, led the 3 to develop the first working external pacemaker in 1950. These 2 techniques represented revolutionary changes in cardiovascular science. Bigelow became head of surgery at Toronto General in 1953, and in 1956, helped create Canada's first cardiac-surgery training program. He received an honorary doctorate from Brandon U in 1967; became an Officer of the Order of Canada in 1981, and a Fellow of the Royal Society of Canada in 1986; and was inducted to the Canadian Medical Hall of Fame in 1997. ● JOEL TRENAMAN

BINGO SCANDAL was the unscrupulous overestimation of ore value by a WINNIPEG mining company in the early 1920s. After gold was found at Herb Lake (140 km E of FLIN FLON), a Winnipeg-based syndicate of mine promoters, headed by New Zealander Joseph Myers, purchased the so-called Bingo claims in 1919. Myers was deceptive from the onset, purchasing the claims for $10,000, but presenting the price to his financial backers as $20,000. Unaware, the backers went

ahead with the deal, and formed Bingo Mines Ltd. in Dec 1919. Shortly after, Myers headed to the UK to secure funds to undertake shaft sinking. The ore mined from Herb Lake in 1920 was not worthwhile for a commercial mining operation, with assayers valuing the gold at only $1 per ton. Myers then hired new assayers, and "salted" the results by giving them only handpicked samples. Armed with the more valuable assessments, he headed back to the UK in search of more capital, and formed a new company, Bingo Gold Mines Ltd, in 1922. Soon, Herb Lake was booming, and the pop grew from 40 to 450 by 1924. The growth came to a standstill when Bingo's secretary, prominent Winnipeg Lawyer H. R. Drummond-Hay, filed charges against Myers in late 1924 after suspicious company officials had ore samples sent to an independent assayer, revealing the discrepancies in value. Myers was arrested on charges of fraud and brought to Winnipeg to stand trial early in 1925. Despite the evidence against him, he was acquitted on a technicality. To wary investors and developers, the charges were enough and they withdrew support from Herb Lake property. ● MD

BINSCARTH, pop 445, is a village located along hwy 16, 167 km NW of BRANDON, in the PARKLAND region. Binscarth was established by the Northwestern Railway in 1886. It was named after a farm established in the area by the Scottish Ontario and Manitoba Land Company, of which William Bain Scarth was founder and manager. The post office opened in 1883 as Binscarth. By 1890, the community boasted 2 hotels, a church, school, and 2 stores to support its growing population. It was incorporated in 1917 as a village. By 1964, Binscarth had a water and sewer system that supported its growing population. The area around Binscarth features rolling expanses of farmland that support a mix of livestock and agricultural crops. In addition to acting as a service centre for the agricultural sector, Binscarth residents also work in the service industry. The Binscarth and District Gordon Orr Memorial Museum boasts a collection of Aboriginal artifacts, vintage farm machinery, and a skull from an extinct species of BISON. ● GPP

BIOTECHNOLOGY is the use of micro-organisms or biological substances – such as bacteria, yeasts, DNA, or proteins – in the development or manufacture of a product. Biotechnology involves the integrated use of biological sciences, information technology, and engineering. The term *biotechnology* was coined in 1917, when it was used to refer to large-scale fermentation techniques that produced 2 critical by-products: carbon dioxide gas and alcohol. Today, biotechnology has applications in many fields, including pharmacology, medicine, agriculture, and the environment.

MEDICINE: In health sciences, MB biotechnology researchers have received international renown and made significant contributions in the areas of respirology, genetics, allergy and clinical immunology, neonatology, and Rh disease. Dr. **Henry G. Friesen**, a medical scientist from **Morden**, discovered the human hormone prolactin, and subsequently developed a simple blood test to identify patients with tumours secreting excessive amounts of this hormone. As a result, thousands of people with prolactin-related reproduction disorders have been successfully treated. Dr. **Bruce Chown**, a Winnipeg-born pathologist and researcher, and his team developed a vaccine known as Rh gamma globulin that prevents the RH disease from occurring in the human fetus. Chown's research led to the establishment of the Winnipeg company Rh Pharmaceuticals. In 1990, Rh Pharmaceuticals was purchased by **Apotex**, and in 1995 was renamed **Cangene**. Dr. **John (Jack) Maxwell Bowman**, a Winnipeg pediatrician, led the world-renowned MB Rh program.

Cangene Corporation represents the cornerstone of MB's biotechnology industry. Located in Winnipeg, it is a world leader in developing hyperimmune products. In March 2005, Cangene was awarded a 5-year contract by the US Center for Disease Control and Prevention (CDC) for the development of a maximum of 100,000 doses of Vaccinia immune globulin (VIG) to treat and prevent adverse reactions to the smallpox vaccine.

MB is home to numerous other biotechnology-related health organizations. The National Research Council's Winnipeg-based Institute for Biodiagnostics (IBD) is the most advanced facility in Canada for studying and developing non-invasive diagnostic tools. The Canadian Science Centre for Human and Animal Health (CSCHAH), also in Winnipeg, is the only facility in the world to have Level 2-4 biocontainment laboratories for both human and animal health under one roof, designed to analyze even the most deadly infectious organisms.

Well over 300 widely respected scientists work in the province's key infectious disease research and educational institutions. MB's infectious disease scientists have influenced global public health through groundbreaking work on BSE, HIV, West Nile Virus, and SARS. Winnipeg scientists Dr. Steven Jones and Dr. Heinz Feldmann have developed vaccines, released in June 2005, which fully protect monkeys against two of the world's deadliest viruses, Ebola and Marburg. In the US, the discovery is being hailed for its promise to defend against germ-based terrorism.

Most MB canola is now genetically modified.

AGRICULTURE: For several thousand years, farmers have selected the genetic makeup of the crops they grow. Despite limited understanding of genetics or biology, early plant breeders were highly successful at producing plants that matured more quickly and produced larger seeds, or sweeter or hardier fruit. In the early 20th century, the federal govt recognized the importance of gaining a better understanding of the genetic nature of wheat-stem rust races and developing rust-resistant varieties. Agriculture and Agri-Food Canada's (AAFC) Dominion Rust Laboratory (DRL) was established in Winnipeg in 1925. DRL went on to become the Cereal Research Centre. Dr. Margaret Newton and Dr. Thorvaldur Johnson, DRL researchers, were the first to demonstrate Mendelian inheritance of virulence in a plant pathogenic fungus. D. L. Bailey, C. H. Goulden, and K. W. Neatby, DRL plant breeders and pathologists, released the first rust-resistant wheat variety in 1936. R. F. Peterson released the wheat varieties Regent in 1939 and Redman in 1946, each with improved disease resistance and agronomic characteristics. A. B. Campbell released the variety Selkirk in 1953. The breeding of rust-resistant wheat varieties has been so successful that there has not been an epidemic of wheat stem rust in W Canada since 1954.

The Winnipeg program's wheat varieties have had desirable characteristics beyond stem rust-resistance and outstanding milling and baking qualities. Neepawa, which could withstand root rot, loose smut and bunt infection, was made available to the seed trade in 1969. Other varieties were designed so that sprouting would not occur in the swath even during prolonged wet harvest. By 1984, varieties developed in Winnipeg were seeded on 87% of the Canadian hard red, spring wheat area. Today, The Cereal

Research Centre is AAFC's lead centre for cereal genomics.

Triticale is a man-made crop developed by crossing wheat with rye. Although triticale was initially developed and researched in Europe in the late 1800s, the **University of Manitoba** began the first North American triticale breeding program in 1953.

In 1974, U of M developed the first low-erucic-acid, low-glucosinolate variety of rapeseed named Tower. At this time, the Rapeseed Council coined the name "canola," derived from "Canadian oil," and this new product became distinguished from other rapeseeds on the global market. **U of M** professor emeritus, Baldur Stefansson, won the 1998 Wolf Foundation Prize in Agriculture for his work in the development of canola and his innovative approaches to breeding and biocontrol. The U of M and the MB Canola Growers Association have funded research and development of high-erucic-acid rapeseed (HEAR).

MB remains internationally recognized for expertise in plant breeding to enhance both agronomic and quality traits for crops. Many agricultural companies, including **Agricore United**, Agriprogress, Brett Young Seeds, Monsanto, and Canterra Seeds Ltd., have established facilities within the province to further their plant-breeding research programs.

ENVIRONMENT: Environmental biotechnology is defined as the development, use, and regulation of biological systems for remediation of contaminated environments (land, air, water), and includes environmentally friendly products and processes such as green manufacturing technologies and biomonitoring. One of the earliest forms of environmental biotechnology was composting. In composting, organic wastes such as vegetation and manure are managed to create a valuable fertilizer. The city of **BRANDON** has provided leadership in municipal-scale composting in MB.

MB hosts excellent researchers and businesses using biotechnology in the environment sector. Nordevco Associates Ltd. develops new technologies and approaches to bio-remediation. Bio-remediation is the use of biological agents, such as bacteria or plants, to remove or neutralize contaminants in polluted soil or water. Nordevco's proprietary technology has been used around the globe, adapting to the specialized conditions encountered by livestock producers, multinational oil companies, utilities, and large engineering consulting companies in addressing organic pollution problems.

The U of M and the Biomass Energy Institute have conducted research in anaerobic digestion, a biological waste-treatment process where bacteria void of oxygen produce biogas as a by-product. The gas is easily combusted, creating a source of alternative energy. It can be used in factory boilers and in engine generator sets to produce electricity and heat. There are many ways to produce biogas from farm waste, whether the waste come from pigs, chickens, or cows. Anaerobic digestion at low temperatures may hold potential for MB, though the energy required to heat manure to be digested is greater than the energy that can be extracted from the manure.

The Avalon Institute of Applied Science Inc. is a private academic institution staffed by a network of international specialists that develop advanced biotechnology methodologies that are applied to projects, some of which have been sponsored by NATO and UNESCO. ● TARA MALTMAN

▶ *See also* **GENETIC ENGINEERING**

BIRCH. MB has 5 different native birch trees – 2 large trees, 1 small tree and 2 shrubs. All are deciduous and provide yellow or gold fall leaf colour. They bear their flowers in male and female clusters but on the same tree, not separate ones like the poplars and willows. The beautiful white flaky-barked trees (*Betula papyrifera* & *B. neoalaskana*) are called 'paper', 'canoe', 'white' or 'Alaska' birches and are very hard to tell apart. Birch can be told from aspens by its flaky bark, multiple trunks, reddish twigs and doubly toothed (teeth on teeth) leaves. It grows throughout MB except in the far NE arctic area, commonly on moist slopes or shorelines. Usually growing with other trees, one can find lovely pure stands around Moose Lake in SE MB and on north-facing slopes in southern MB valleys. It was the most useful tree to many early Aboriginal peoples. Birchbark was used to make everything from canoes to containers, bandages and paper.

The wood was used for sleds, snowshoes, paddles and a variety of other objects. Bark, buds and leaves were used as medicine, the inner bark for food. The sap was boiled to create syrup and produce birch beer and wine. A few people still make these today. Birch wood is prime firewood in MB, prized for its hardness and clean burning. It is also used in the production of oriented strandboard.

River or water birch (*Betula occidentalis*) is a small tree or large shrub with several stems, dark shiny smooth bark and small birch-shaped leaves. It grows on moist soils along streams, rivers and lakeshores and hollows in sandhills, usually with poplars, willows and alders. It is found throughout MB except for the far NE arctic area. The 2 shrub birches, bog or scrub birch (*Betula glandulosa*) and dwarf or swamp birch (*B. pumila* var.*gladulifera*), grow in wetlands (bogs, fens, swamps) and along rivers and streams. Bog birch occurs on acid soils in far-northern MB. It has nearly round 1-2 cm wide leaves on twigs covered with octopus-sucker shaped wart-like resin glands. It was used medicinally and gave useful dyes. The common taller southern dwarf birch occurs north to York Factory and has larger oval leaves (often angled at the base) and hairy rather than warty twigs. It was used medicinally and as a tea. Buds of both are a favourite winter food of grouse and ptarmigan. ● KAREN JOHNSON

BIRD (class *Aves*) is the only animal with feathers. Feathers not only enable birds to fly, but they also serve to protect them from the elements; to avoid detection, in the case of cryptically coloured females; and to advertise the presence of males during courtship. Although males of certain groups of birds, such as ducks, **FINCHES**, and **WARBLERS**, have brighter plumage than females, this is not the norm. Both sexes of most **HERONS**, **HAWKS**, **SHOREBIRDS**, **GULLS**, **FLYCATCHERS**, **SPARROWS**, **SWIFTS**, and other genera sport nearly identical plumage. In the case of phalaropes, a genus of small shorebirds, the females are more brightly coloured than the males. After laying eggs, female phalaropes abandon the nest, leaving the male to take care of incubation and rearing young.

The list of birds that have occurred in MB stands at nearly 400 species, which range in size from the diminutive Ruby-throated Hummingbird (*Archilochus colubris*) to the huge American White Pelican (*Pelecanus erythrorhynchos*) and Trumpeter Swan (*Cygnus buccinator*). Some are common and widespread, like the Canada Goose (*Branta canadensis*) or American Robin (*Turdus migratorius*), while others, like the White-winged

Tern (*Chlidonias leucopterus*) and Curve-billed Thrasher (*Toxostoma curvirostre*), have strayed only once to MB, and may never appear again. The vast majority of birds are protected at all times of the year by federal and provincial law. Only certain species may be taken during hunting seasons. Of these, geese, ducks, and grouse are the most sought-after by MB hunters.

Birds form an integral part of the food web and occur in every type of habitat found in the province. The greatest variety of species is found in the boreal forest and parkland **ECOCLIMACTIC REGIONS**, while tracts of monoculture farmland or areas in the far N harbour the least variety. For sheer numbers of individual birds, our marshes surpass all other habitats. A concerted one-day bird-finding effort in the south of the province in late spring or early summer can result in a list of 200 species. On the other hand, in winter, a good day's birding may turn up just 30 species.

ROBERT R. TAYLOR

Loon family

Birds played an important role in the lives of Aboriginal people long before the first Europeans arrived in MB in the 1600s. With the arrival of explorers and fur traders came the first written records; those of **HBC** employees, in particular, provided the basis for much of what was known about the region's birds well into the 19th century. Settlement of the south led to bird study as well, culminating in 1890 with the publication of the first *Birds of Manitoba* by **ERNEST THOMPSON SETON**.

In 1920, the Manitoba Natural History Society (now the Manitoba Naturalists Society) was formed; bird study was its most popular activity. Soon after, in 1921, the weekly column "Chickadee Notes" first appeared in the **WINNIPEG FREE PRESS**. Authored by A. G. Lawrence until 1955, and later by others, it enjoyed a wide readership. A similar column, "Wild Wings," later appeared in the **WINNIPEG TRIBUNE**.

Valuable sources of information on MB birds and where to find them include *The Birds of Manitoba*, by the Manitoba Avian Research Committee; *Manitoba Birds*, by Andy Bezener and Ken De Smet; *Birder's Guide to Southern and Central Manitoba*, by Manitoba Naturalists Society and Brandon Naturalists Society; and *A Birder's Guide to Churchill*, by Bonnie Chartier.

Ornithological research in the province has been carried out especially at Delta Marsh and Churchill, and has resulted in numerous publications. One group of birds, the owls, has been studied in depth since the late 1960s. Educational facilities, most notably the **MANITOBA MUSEUM**, Oak Hammock Marsh Interpretive Centre, and Fort Whyte Centre, have played an important role in showcasing our avian bounty. **DUCKS UNLIMITED**, in concert with the province of MB, has been instrumental in the restoration of many wetlands to their former state. Unfortunately, forested areas and tracts of native prairie have not received equal attention – unspoiled areas are dwindling rapidly. • RUDOLF KOES

BIRD MIGRATION is how most species of birds in MB cope with the cold **WEATHER** winter brings – they migrate to and from the province in spring and fall. Only a few species can find enough food during winter or can survive the cold. Birds that rely on insects or other invertebrates, or are bound to water, need to find warmer climes. Some species fly only a few hundred km S to find conditions to their liking, while others travel thousands of km. The greatest long-distance migrant is the Arctic tern (*Sterna paradisaea*), which breeds along the **HUDSON BAY** coast and farther N, and winters in the Antarctic region. Many of our shorebirds, flycatchers, and warblers make journeys that are nearly as impressive, as they spend the winter in Central or South America. Rock ptarmigans (*Lagopus mutus*) and snowy owls (*Nyctea scandiaca*) migrate into MB from their Arctic nesting grounds in fall.

Migrating birds can provide a stirring spectacle, especially in spring, when huge numbers of waterfowl and raptors may fill the skies during a warm front. Many species, however, migrate unnoticed at night and spend the daylight hours foraging. A city park or farm bluff may suddenly be filled with thrushes, warblers, and sparrows on the morning after such a night. At other times, inclement weather, such as a cold snap, may force birds down by the thousands. This phenomenon is called "fallout," and if poor conditions persist, mortality can be great. Snowstorms in May can be particularly devastating, reducing certain populations for years after.

Our earliest migrant in spring is the Horned **LARK** (*Eremophila alpestris*), which may return as early as Feb, when it can be seen along roads in rural areas of the S. Not long after, the first Canada Geese (*Branta canadensis*) and American **CROWS** (*Corvus brachyrhynchos*) arrive, staking out

Canada Geese heading south in autumn

their territories while snow still covers the ground. Then, in late March and early April, **WATERFOWL**, Raptors, and **GULLS** come pouring in, followed soon by a host of other species. The last to return are arctic-breeding shorebirds, **FLYCATCHERS**, vireos, and most **WARBLERS**, some arriving as late as early June.

Hardly has the northward migration ended when southbound shorebirds start to appear in July. The fall migration tends to be a more leisurely affair than the spring rush, with birds lingering to take advantage of abundant seeds, fruits, or insects. **SWALLOWS**, flycatchers, warblers, and other insect-eating birds move through en masse in Aug and early Sep, followed by **SPARROWS**, raptors, and waterfowl. If mild weather persists into Dec and little snow covers the ground, many waterfowl, raptors, and gulls may linger until a real cold spell forces them out. In some cases, a portion of a population will overwinter, while the majority will fly south. Examples of such "half-hardy" species are Mallard (*Anas platyrhynchos*), Common Goldeneye (*Bucephala clangula*), American Crow (*Corvus brachyrhynchos*), and Dark-eyed Junco (*Junco hyemalis*). • RUDOLF KOES

BIRD SANCTUARIES AND RESERVES are relatively common in MB. Some areas that afford protection for birds – such as **OAK HAMMOCK MARSH** Wildlife Management Area (WMA), near **STONEWALL**; Fort Whyte Centre, in **WINNIPEG**; and the Alf Hole Goose Sanctuary, at **RENNIE** – were created specifically with waterfowl in mind. Others aim to protect critical nesting spots for colonial birds. Still others, such as national and provincial parks, provide habitat not only for birds but also for a variety of other organisms. The interpretive centres at Oak Hammock Marsh and Fort Whyte Centre provide excellent educational opportunities related to bird study and conservation, while interpretive signage and brochures at parks and WMAs also helps to protect our avifauna. A recent development has been the federal creation of Important Bird Areas (IBAs). This initiative, under the management of Nature Canada and Bird Studies Canada, is meant to identify and protect key sites for birds. Identified sites in MB include **NETLEY-LIBAU** and **DELTA** marshes, Whitewater Lake, the Saskatchewan River Delta at **THE PAS**, and the region east of **CHURCHILL**. So far, the boreal forest **ECOCLIMACTIC REGION** is poorly represented, with few protected areas. • RUDOLF KOES

Oak Hammock Marsh

James Curtis Bird, oil on canvas
by V. A. Long, 1906

B

BIRD, James Curtis (b 1773, London UK, d 1856, **RED RIVER SETTLEMENT**) Fur trader. Born in England, he joined the **HBC** in 1788, serving at **YORK FACTORY** for 4 years before heading inland to Saskatchewan. He headed Carlton House from 1795 to 1799 and Edmonton House from 1799 to 1816, organizing the Peter Fidler expedition of 1799. Beginning in 1816, he acted as governor of **RUPERT'S LAND** until William Williams arrived in 1818. After the merger of the HBC and **NWC** he was made chief factor in charge of Lower **RED RIVER**. He served there only briefly, then was equally briefly in charge of Upper Red River. He retired in 1824 to Red River and received a large company grant (1,245 acres) on the east side of the Red River. The village of **BIRDS HILL** is named after him. He served on several early councils and was appointed a councillor of **ASSINIBOIA** in 1839. In 1836 he was made registrar for land sales and grants. Known for his harshness, he was never popular in the settlement. ● JMB

BIRDS HILL PROVINCIAL PARK, 25 km NE of **WINNIPEG**, is among the most visited of MB's **PROVINCIAL PARKS**, due to its proximity to the city. Established in 1964, it opened July 15, 1967, in celebration of Canada's Centennial. The park is named for the Bird family, in particular, **JAMES CURTIS BIRD**, who worked for the **HBC** for 36 years beginning in 1788. In 1824, the company granted Bird more than 1200 ha. His descendants continued to live in the **RED RIVER SETTLEMENT** area, and his son, prominent doctor Curtis J. Bird, became an MLA, as well as the Legislature's first speaker, in 1870. In the late 19th century, **GERMAN LUTHERANS** were the first among a group of European homesteaders, which included **POLES** and **UKRAINIANS**, to settle the land encompassed by the modern park.

Farming, forestry, and quarrying were the primary activities in the 1890s and early 20th century, and sand and gravel extraction continued into the 21st century. Due to its slight elevation above the surrounding prairie, settlers, **FUR TRADERS**, and animals from surrounding areas took refuge on the high ground during major **FLOODING** of the **RED RIVER** Valley. The **WINNIPEG FOLK FESTIVAL** has occupied a section of the park every year since 1974, using space for its facilities, stages, and thousands of campers. Birds Hill played host to Pope John Paul II on Sept 16, 1984, drawing between 125,000 and 200,000 visitors to an outdoor multi-faith celebration. In the early 21st century, the park faced controversy over water safety and lifeguard monitoring of the popular artificial beach/swimming area. Following the drownings of 6- and 7-year-old boys in summer 2000, and of an 18-year-old woman in 2001, a Feb 2002 inquest report by Judge Mary Kate Harvey led to an increase in beach patrol staffing. The terrain is classified as aspen/oak parkland, a mix of grasslands and forest (*see* **ECOCLIMACTIC REGIONS**). It is home to about 200 **BIRD** species and to a stable population of White-tailed **DEER**, as well as other wildlife. Popular recreational activities include horseback riding, swimming, hiking, cross-country **SKIING**, and **CYCLING**. The park offers 419 campsites in addition to group camping areas. ● JT

BIRDSELL, Sandra Louise, author (b April 22, 1942, **HAMIOTA**). The recipient of many honours, Birdsell's novels are acclaimed for their sensitive reflection of the human experience. Her short stories have been widely anthologized, with some translated into Spanish, Polish, French, Italian, and German. She is the author of 1 children's novel, 2 plays, and scripts for radio, TV, and films. She has taught creative writing as a mentor, workshop director, or writer-in-residence in several provinces. She has been a member of PEN International, the Writers Union of Canada, the Saskatchewan Writers Guild, the MB Métis Federation, and is a founder and lifetime member of the MB Writers Guild. Birdsell's writing is rooted in the western Prairie. Born of Métis and Mennonite heritage, she brings to her work her experience as an office worker, waitress, parent, and inner-city volunteer. Birdsell lived in Winnipeg for 30 years before moving to Regina in 1997. Birdsell's first collection of short fiction, *Night Travellers* (1982), announced Birdsell as an exciting, new literary voice. She followed up with *Ladies of the House* (1984) and *Agassiz Stor*ies (1987), a compilation of the previous two books. Birdsell's first novel, *The Missing Child* (1989), won the W. H. Smith/Books in Canada First Novel Prize. She followed up with

Agassiz: A Novel in Stories (1990); *The Chrome Suite* (1994); a children's story *The Town That Floated Away* (1997); *The Rüsslander* (2001); and *Children of the Day* (2005). *The Rüsslander* won 3 Saskatchewan Book Awards prizes and was shortlisted for the Giller Prize. Her theatre work includes *A Prairie Boy's Winter* (1986) and *The Revival* (1987). Birdsell has been nominated twice for the Gov Gen's Award – for her novel *The Chrome Suite* in 1992 and the her short-story collection *The Two-Headed Calf* in 1997. She has been the recipient of the Marion Engel Award, the Robert Kroetsch Scholarship (SK Arts Board), the Gerald Lampert Memorial Award (League of Canadian Poets), the National Magazine Award for Short Fiction, the 45 Below Award (Canadian Book Information Centre), the Joseph S. Stauffer Prize (Canada Council), the McNally Robinson Literature Award, and the City of Regina Book of the Year Award. ● MILDRED GUTKIN

BIRDTAIL SIOUX FIRST NATION, on reserve pop 470, off reserve pop 239, is a First Nation community located 96 km NW of Brandon. The native language of the Birdtail Sioux people is Dakota. This is one of handful of communities in western MB that have Dakota roots and have no treaties with the govt of Canada. The Dakota people migrated N from the US in the mid-1870s seeking refuge from the Indian wars in the US. Although they did not have official treaties, the Birdtail Sioux made a permanent home for themselves in MB. Birdtail Sioux First Nation was originally called "Can Kaga Otina," meaning "Log House Dwellers." The reason for this was at the community's beginnings, everyone lived in log houses after the tipi-dwelling days had passed. In the 1970s, Birdtail Sioux was one of the first First Nation communities to have a tribal officer working on the reserve, alongside the RCMP. He would wear a RCMP uniform when patrolling on the reserve. Chief Murray Clearsky was one of the first First Nation Chiefs to be the Chief of 2 First Nation communities at the same time (Birdtail and **WAYWAYSEECAPPO**). This community's education levels go from Nursery–Grade 12, and the total enrolment for 2003-2004 was 117. The Birdtail Sioux First Nation administers schooling. Children have the choice of attending school on or off reserve. The Birdtail Sioux First Nation is comprised of 3 reserves: Birdtail Creek I.R. No. 57, Birdtail Hay Lands I.R. No. 57A, and Fishing Station I.R. No. 62A. Birdtail Creek I.R. No. 57 is the most populated of the 3. The economy is based on agriculture and residential development. It is a member of the Dakota Ojibway Tribal Council. Track and field runner **ANGELA CHALMERS** comes from the

Birdtail Sioux First Nation. Riel Benn, a visual artist from the Birdtail Sioux First Nation, won various awards including the YTV Youth Achievement Award. Maxin Noel is another visual artist from Birdtail Sioux First Nation. • RK

BIRTLE, pop 715, is a town 100 km NW of **Brandon**. The town's name is probably a contraction of **Birdtail**, the name of the creek on which the town stands. Before permanent settlers started to arrive in 1879, the site was a stopping place on the Carlton Trail from **Upper Fort Garry** to Forts Ellice and Edmonton. Surveyors encouraged settlement in the area after rich, fertile soil and plentiful timber were discovered. The area also had a natural spring nearby that provided fresh, clear water. Settlers from ON started to arrive and following the construction of a sawmill, creamery, cheese factory, and cement-producing kilns, the local economy was largely self-sustaining. The town's post office opened in 1879. In the 2000s, agriculture forms the base of Birtle's economy. Cereal crops and oilseeds are the principal crops, while livestock and specialty animals are becoming increasingly important. Tourists are attracted to the area during summer months to golf and hike. • GPP

BISHOP, Heather, singer/songwriter, social activist (b April 25, 1949, Regina, SK). Bishop moved to Winnipeg in 1975, where she debuted the following year at the **Winnipeg Folk Festival.** She began playing the folk circuit in western Canada and beyond, often performing the songs of fellow Regina singer/songwriter Connie Kaldor. In 1979, Bishop formed Mother of Pearl Records to record and market her music, becoming an early pioneer in independent music. With producer Dan Donahue, Bishop recorded 13 folk-oriented albums and children's recordings, her best-known being *Belly Button* (1982; earning a gold record) and *Chickee's on the Run* (1997; nominated for a Juno Award for Best Children's Album). Bishop maintained a parallel career as a contemporary singer with *Grandmother's Song* (1979), *Taste of the Blues* (1987; nominated for a Juno for Most Promising Female Vocalist), *Old New Borrowed Blue* (1992), *Heather Bishop Live* (2000), and *A Tribute to Peggy Lee* (2004). For several years, she was a regular on CBC TV's *Fred Penner's Place*. In 1987, Bishop helped found MARIA (the Manitoba Audio Recording Industry Association) and sat on the board of Manitoba Film and Sound, her efforts earning her the Western Canada Music Award for Industry Builder of the Year (2005). Bishop's social activism for pay equity, gender equality, and gay and lesbian rights have earned numerous

honours, including the YM/YWCA Woman of Distinction (1997), the Order of Manitoba (2001), the Golden Jubilee Medal from HM Queen Elizabeth (2002), and the Order of Canada (2006). Bishop resides in Woodmore, about 20 km E of **Dominion City**, where she built her own solar-powered home. • JOHN EINARSON

BISON *(Bison bison)* is one of NA's most recognizable animals, and is classified in the cattle and even-toed ungulates, referring to the fact it walks on 2 digits in each hoof, protected by horny layers of keratin. Sometimes called the buffalo, the bison is a primary symbol of MB due to its importance as food for Aboriginal tribes and early settlers. So prominent has this species been to the history of this region that it was named the official mammal of MB and appears on the provincial logo, flag and crest.

The American Bison is the heaviest-surviving member of what is called 'mega-fauna' of NA; bulls weigh up to 1000 kg, females 450 kg. However, even the biggest bulls would have been dwarfed in comparison to other contemporary large mammals that were swept into extinction at the close of the last ice age (20,000 to 8000 years ago). A number of now-extinct bison species crossed over the Bering Land Bridge to North America over the last 1.5 million years. Some of these inhabited what is now MB, including the Giant Bison *(Bison latifrons)* with a 2-metre wide set of horns. The sole surviving Bison of the Ice

Age was Bison antiquus, which evolved into Bison bison only 10,000 years ago. Two geographic races are recognized – the Plains Bison of the east and the Wood Bison of the far west. The latter race did not reach MB, but a herd has been introduced in the **Interlake** region. It currently number 400 in captivity and 200 released in the wild.

In pre-European-contact time, the American Bison occurred over most of the continent and occupied the southern 1/3 of MB. Roaming in immense herds (estimates ranged from 50-75 million head), hundreds of thousands migrated into MB each spring to graze on prairie vegetation. Some herds over-wintered here, but most went south. The young explorer Henry Kelsey was the first European to describe the Bison, near the MB/SK border in 1690. There were descriptions of enormous herds crossing the Red River, only to break through the ice, causing the death of hundreds of individuals that were pushed into the water by the oncoming throng. From 1820-1860, the Métis hunts from Fort Garry killed about 200,000 annually. The last herd was reported near **Brandon** in 1861, and the last known wild MB Bison – an old bull – outdistanced hunters and escaped into SK. In the most appalling saga of wanton destruction (partly to force Aboriginal peoples off their land), the Bison herds in NA were shot and wasted, until fewer than 1000 survived (mostly in Canada). With a last-minute reprieve, several herds were saved in Canada and the US. The species now numbers

ROBERT R. TAYLOR

Bison in Riding Mountain National Park

over 200,000 in semi-wild managed herds and captive herds, some slaughtered for meat.

The American Bison is readily identified by its large size, broad head with sweeping black horns, shaggy brown coat, and large shoulder hump. Travelling an average of 3 km/day, a herd on the plains wandered over a range of about 30 sq km in summer and 100 sq km in winter, with movements dictated by weather, forage and water availability, and to avoid biting insects. The rut occurs from July to September or later, with the bulls approaching the cows to test their readiness to copulate. Cows still nursing last year's young mate later in the season. Rival bulls often battle at this time, and some are wounded or killed. Bison are gregarious animals, but there is considerable change in herd size and composition. The matriarchal herd typically consists of 10-60 individuals – cows, yearlings, calves, and a few old bulls. Bulls are sometimes solitary but often form small bands, which join the main herd during the rut. Most breeding is done by prime bulls ages 6-9 years. About 285 days later, 1 or 2 calves (weighing 18 kg) are born, usually in May or June. Guarded closely by the mother, offspring are up and running to follow the herd in 3 hours. Full size is reached at 4 years, but individuals continue to grow slowly thereafter, sometimes reaching 20 years old (but 41 in captivity). • REW

BISSETT, pop 125, is a community 250 km NE of **Winnipeg** and 35 km W of the ON border. The post office opened in 1927. The community was named after Dr. Edgar D. R. Bissett, who was the MP for the constituency of Springfield and a doctor in Pine Falls in the 1930s. Gold was discovered here in 1911. Bissett is the site of the Rice Lake Gold Mine (the historic San Antonio Gold Mine) and the San Gold Mine. The local economy centres on mining, exploration, forestry, and tourism. • GPP

BITING FLY is an insect, usually the female, that feeds on blood as a source of protein for egg development. When large animals evolved, they provided a new and inexhaustible supply of blood for biting insects, and entire families of recent flies now feed almost exclusively on vertebrate blood. Among **Black Flies**, **Mosquitoes**, biting midges, tabanids, and snipe flies, it is only the female that sucks blood; the non-biting males subsist only on sugars such as nectar or aphid honeydew. In contrast, both females and males of other flies (e.g., stable flies) bite and lap blood. Biting flies are extremely sensitive to carbon dioxide and have evolved the ability to detect and follow an odour plume of the gas (and possibly other odours) emanating from the potential

host for some distance. The fly is also sensitive to heat and moisture, and when approaching within a few metres of the host, vision comes into play. Female biting flies have modified mouthparts, with the mandibles and maxillae shaped into a blade- or sword-like structure with serrated edges, and their associated muscles thrust this organ into the skin. The presence of this feeding apparatus in all the above biting flies suggests they all arose from a common, blood-feeding ancestor.

The fly thrusts its maxillary blades into the skin to serve as anchors, and then the mandibles cut the skin like a pair of scissors until blood flows. The fly pumps saliva into the wound to prevent clotting, and it is this fluid that causes swelling, itching and allergic reaction. The fly then draws blood up through a channel along the underside of another mouthpart (the labrum). Only blood of the host is ingested; the belief that these flies can bite out a piece of flesh is false. Mosquitoes have evolved a further refinement in that the long sword-like mandibles are jabbed repeatedly deep into the skin to tap a blood capillary, from which blood is then pumped up by the labrum. Unlike nectar or other sugar solutions, which are stored in the crop, blood passes directly to the stomach. The abdominal walls of a biting fly are highly distensible – a mosquito may double or triple its weight with a single blood meal. With a full load of blood, the insect can barely fly, and so seeks a resting place for several days to digest its meal. About a week later, the eggs develop and the female then seeks a suitable place to deposit them. After laying, the female is ready to search for another blood meal to repeat the process. • TDG

BJARNASON, Jóhann Magnús, author, poet, and teacher, (b May 24, 1866, Meðalnes, Eastern Iceland; d Sept 8, 1945, Elfros, SK) immigrated to Canada at age 9 in 1875 and spent his formative years in NS where his parents homesteaded in the Markland (Mooseland Heights) Icelandic settlement. In 1882, at age 16, Jóhann migrated W to **Winnipeg** where he certified as a teacher. Beginning his career in 1889 at **Arnes**, he then settled in the Geysir district and taught there from 1892 to 1903. He became known as an inspirational and gifted educator and one of the principal writers and poets among the Icelandic people in NA. Awarded the Order of the Falcon (Iceland), he is commemorated by a cairn at *Arnheiðarstaðir* in Geysir, unveiled by the President of Iceland in 1989. His first book of prose and poetry, *Sögur og Kvæði*, was published in Winnipeg in 1892, and his novels include several semi-autobiographical adventures set in NS, Brazil, and MB: *Eiríkur Hansson*, 1899;

Brasilíufararnir (The Brazil Farers), 1905; *Vornætur á Elgsheiðum (Spring Nights on Mooseland Heights),* 1910; *Haustkvöld við Hafið (Autumn Evening by the Sea),* 1928; *Karl Litli (Little Karl),* 1935, and *Í Rauðárdalnum (In the Red River Valley),* partially published in serial in the MB periodical *Sýrpa* 1914-18 and later in its entirety in 1942. Bjarnason retired to Elfros, SK in 1922. • NELSON GERRARD

BLACK, Elinor Frances Elizabeth, physician, educator (b 1905, Nelson, BC; d Jan 30, 1982, **Winnipeg**). Known for her groundbreaking work in **Medicine**, Black moved to Winnipeg in May 1918 after spending her early years in Calgary and Scotland. She followed in the footsteps of brother Donald and entered medical school at the **U of M** in 1925. Black later said that in the difficult medical school environment at the time, women were expected to act just like men in order to fit in. She graduated in 1930, and did a 3-month residency at Winnipeg's Children's Hospital before continuing her training in England at the Royal Free Hospital and later at the South London Hospital for Women. In 1938, Black became the first Cdn woman member of the British Royal College of Obstetricians and Gynaecologists. In 1949, she was named a fellow of the Royal College of Physicians and Surgeons of Canada, and in 1951, became the first woman professor and head of a Cdn medical school department, taking charge of Obstetrics and Gynaecology at the U of M for the next 13 years. The Society of Obstetricians and Gynaecologists of Canada elected Black as its first female president in 1960. Throughout her career she also practiced and taught at the Winnipeg General Hospital (see **Health Sciences Centre**). • JT

▸ *See also* **Charlotte Ross**, **Amelia Yeomans**

BLACK, George Montegu II, businessman (b June 3, 1911, **Winnipeg**; d June 29, 1976, Toronto) was a prominent businessman and father of media mogul Conrad Black. During the 1950s, George was president of Canadian Breweries, then the world's largest brewing conglomerate. Black was exposed to the brewery business at a young age. In 1927, his father established Western Breweries Ltd., a conglomerate of 4 western Cdn breweries and a ginger ale plant. Though Black's family home was in Winnipeg, much of his youth was spent in eastern Canada, first at preparatory school in ON, followed by studies at McGill U, which were cut short by a bout of pneumonia. He then returned to Winnipeg to recuperate. Once well enough, Black enrolled at the **U of M**, where he met and fell in love with Jean Elizabeth Riley, the daughter of prominent businessman **Conrad**

RILEY. He graduated with a BA in 1933, and went on to earn an accountant's degree in 1937, the same year he married Riley. He was appointed comptroller at Western Breweries Ltd, where he worked until the outbreak of WWII. He enlisted in the RCAF, but was rejected because of poor eyesight. Black was then appointed to a civilian post with the National Defence for Air, where he helped implement the BRITISH COMMONWEALTH AIR TRAINING PLAN. After overseeing the launch of BCATP, Black was charged with setting up an aircraft propeller manufacturing operation in Montreal. It was around this time that Black was approached by wealthy industrialist E. P. Taylor about joining Canadian Breweries. Black moved to Toronto after the war, and proved himself a shrewd and sometimes ruthless business operator. He served as president of Canadian Breweries from 1951-58, during which time he oversaw its expansion, including the purchase of Western Breweries. He went on to serve as director of several firms, including the Toronto Dominion Bank, and was a governor of the Toronto Stock Exchange. ● MD

BLACK BRANT ROCKET. In 1957, the Cdn govt contracted the Bristol Aeroplane Company (*see* BRISTOL AEROSPACE LTD) of WINNIPEG to produce a rocket based on its anti-ballistic missile system designs. The first Black Brant was modified for use as a research rocket to study the effect of the AURORA BOREALIS on radio waves travelling in the ionosphere. This new design, named after the Brant goose, *Branta bernicla,* a species of WATERFOWL that summers in the Arctic, found its niche as a useful tool to reach an area of the outer atmosphere too high for balloons and too low for satellites. The first Black Brant was launched in Sept 1959 from Fort Churchill, a MILITARY base near CHURCHILL, active 1942-80. The rockets consisted of a solid propellant engine and a payload, and the first versions were able to reach a maximum height of 150 km above Earth. This success allowed Bristol to become the first company in Canada to mass-produce rockets. They later adapted the solid-fuel technology of the Brant to create the CRV7 rocket, the most-powerful air-to-surface rocket in existence. Many air forces internationally use the CRV7. Due to their low cost, short production time, small size, and reliability, Black Brants, now in their 12th version and produced at Bristol's space and defence facility in Rockwood, are still used in the early 21st century by NASA and other space agencies for suborbital research. These instruments later return to Earth with the help of parachutes. The modern version can reach a height of 1500 km – the International Space Station orbits at about

Black Brant 12 rocket launched in 1988

360 km – carrying payloads between 70 and 850 kg. Recent Cdn and international launch experiments have measured electric fields and waves, magnetic fields, and particles in the plasma of the ionosphere; the effects of micro, or reduced, gravity; and gathered telescopic images. The US military also uses Black Brants to test aspects of its ballistic missile defence program. By 2006, more than 800 Black Brants had been launched, with a 98% success rate. ● JOEL TRENAMAN

BLACK FLY is a biting insect characterized by small (2-4 mm), black, hunch-backed body with rounded wings. Black flies are most abundant in MB's forests and swamps from May to July. Members of the *Simulium venustum* species complex can be so numerous and can attack so persistently that outdoor activity during the day without some protection becomes almost impossible. Their numbers and their tendency to bite increase as sunset approaches. Black flies land and take off repeatedly, sometimes without biting, but their constant buzzing and crawling are highly irritating. Unlike mosquitoes and biting midges, black flies do not attack at night or indoors. Although they cannot bite through clothing, they have an uncanny ability to craw into hair or under clothing, and then biting in inaccessible places, such as ankles and belt line. Tucking trouser cuffs into socks helps prevent

them from getting at the ankles, and repellant discourages most from crawling under clothing or into hair. Black flies are strongly influenced by colour, finding dark hues more attractive than pale ones, so a light-colored shirt is recommended. Black flies are more selective in their choice of host than are mosquitoes, and comparatively few species take human blood. Most feed only on the blood of birds and some do not take blood at all, since their mouthparts have degenerated and appear useless for bloodsucking. Almost all MB and Canadian species of black flies have a single annual generation. Some (e.g., *Prosimulium* species) spend the winter in the larval stage under the ice, where they slowly mature. These pupate with the spring thaw and are therefore the first to appear as adults. After mating, the female lays eggs in the water, which pass the summer and early autumn in this stage. These hatch in October, or earlier in N MB. Of the remaining species of black flies, most remain in the egg stage throughout the summer, fall, and winter. Larval development is usually rapid the following spring, in shallow water and seepages that warm up quickly. Only a few species (e.g., *Simulium vittatum*) have more than one generation during the summer, and these overwinter as larvae. ● TDG, MAF, REW

BLACKBIRD (family Icteridae) is a diverse group of small to medium-sized songbirds that includes meadowlarks, cowbirds, and orioles. There are 11 species in MB. Although meadowlarks, blackbirds,

Red-winged Blackbird

and orioles bear a resemblance to some familiar Old World birds – hence their names – they are in fact not related, and occur only in the New World. The Western Meadowlark (*Sturnella neglecta*) is a favourite of many Manitobans, as it is one of the first birds to arrive in spring, and its pleasing song can be heard well into fall. The Brown-headed Cowbird (*Molothrus ater*) used to follow wandering herds of **Bison**, laying its eggs in nests of other species. This brood parasite is now found most often around domestic cattle. The Red-winged Blackbird (*Agelaius phoeniceus*) is a familiar roadside and marsh bird. In fall, it gathers in huge flocks and can cause considerable damage to cereal and sunflower crops. The Baltimore Oriole (*Icterus galbula*) is a striking bird with a loud, melodious song. Its nest is a marvel of engineering: a well-hidden pouch suspended from a branch, which becomes visible as the leaves drop in fall. • RUDOLF KOES

BLACKS. The majority of Black families who settled in MB prior to the 1950s had their roots in the southern US. Many of them were the descendants of slaves who had come N in search of freedom and had settled initially in AB and SK. Some of them had also come W from NS in search of work as porters on the **CNR** and **CPR** railways at a time when **Winnipeg** served as the central port for railway travel in Canada. In the early days, most of the 850 or so individual Blacks identified in the census of 1951 were connected to the railroad in one capacity or another. They worked as porters and red-caps as Blacks were then considered largely unsuitable for other forms of employment. They lived in rooming houses around Main, Broadway, Market and Sutherland Sts. They established a club, a small pool hall, a few barbershops and 2 fraternities (the Brotherhood of Elks and the Masonic Lodge). They also created 2 well-known orchestras, one led by Bill Moore and the other by Harold Green. The latter was perhaps the more famous and it kept its name even after the death of its founder.

The relaxation of Canada's immigration laws after 1955 brought thousands of Black immigrants from Africa and the Caribbean whom the mainstream welcomed as skilled craftsmen and/or professionals. The most visible among them were the West Indians who came in increasing numbers as students, domestics and nurses. They drew attention to themselves by founding an assortment of clubs, associations and societies and giving vigorous support to such organizations as the Bible Church of God, the Pilgrim's Baptist Church, the Black Educators' Association of Manitoba (BEAM), the Folk Arts Council of Winnipeg, the Manitoba Association of Rights

& Liberties (MARL), the Manitoba Intercultural Council, the Immigrant Women's Association of Manitoba (IWAM) and the Manitoba Cricket Association. Their protests over working conditions eventually led to radical changes in the provincial labour laws and customs so that Blacks could become equal members of trade unions and be eligible for promotion in such institutions as Via Rail.

Africa-Caribbean Pavilion, Folklorama 2006

Some of the early Black movements and clubs languished but many are still active in the 2000s. Almost every West Indian (Caribbean) country boasts a local association in Winnipeg and they operate under an umbrella known as the Council of Caribbean Organizations of Manitoba (CCOM). The oldest of these groups is the Afro-Caribbean Association of Manitoba (ACAM), founded in 1968 with its headquarters on Watt St. After years of struggle, CCOM has acquired a spacious Community Centre of its own at 1100 Fife Ave.

As a result of ongoing conflicts throughout Africa, MB saw many African refugees from Ethiopia, Eritrea, Congo, Rwanda, Sierra Leone, Zimbabwe, and Sudan arrive during the 1990s and thereafter. In 2006, the number of Africans in MB was estimated at about 15,000. As immigrants from Africa increased, so did the need to be organized. The newcomers came from different countries and often spoke different dialects

or languages. Ghanaians established a popular dance group which performs at a variety of social functions in Winnipeg. The Sudanese founded a community centre to assist immigrants and refugees from that war-torn country. But because the number of people from most African countries was not substantial, the leaders and members of the different associations needed to be united. This gave rise to the establishment of the Council of African Organizations in MB (CAOM). The CAOM served as an umbrella organization until 1997. In 2002, the Manitoba African Community Secretariat was established as an administrative office to help facilitate community relations, including community communications and public relations. By 2007, the African community was focused on developing an African-Canadian Cultural and Heritage Centre, which would serve as the anchor for the African community in MB.

In 1997, the African Communities of MB (ACOM) was formed to enable the African community to participate in **Folklorama**. As a result, the African Pavilion debuted in 1997 to represent Nigeria, Ghana, Uganda, Zambia, and the Democratic Republic of the Congo (Kinshasa). The establishment of this pavilion brought to 4 the number of Folklorama pavilions representing Blacks and West Indians: the African, Afro-Caribbean, Caribbean and Indo-Caribbean. These have generally attracted large audiences, exposing the mainstream to cultures much different from their own.

Under the direction of Wade Williams, the Winnipeg Black History Month Committee has staged numerous functions every Feb since 1981 with the view of drawing attention to the achievements of Blacks everywhere and which have traditionally been neglected by the White media and public.

It is always difficult to estimate the number of Blacks in MB at any point in the history of this province, but it is generally accepted that there were more than 40,000 in 2006. They have left an indelible impact on the society out of proportion to their numbers. So many African and Caribbean students remained in MB after obtaining their degrees that the province has boasted a solid cluster of Black accountants, bureaucrats, dentists, doctors, engineers, lawyers, nurses, social workers and teachers. Blacks have thus left a noticeable influence on MB architecture, cuisine, dance, education, literature, medicine and music. The steel-band orchestra, for instance, has become a regular feature in a number of Winnipeg schools and Winnipeggers are now very familiar with such culinary delicacies as roti, curried goat and jerk chicken. • KEITH A. P. SANDIFORD

Blaikie (centre) during his first election campaign in 1979

BLAIKIE, William Alexander "Bill," politician (b June 19, 1951, **Winnipeg**). First elected in 1979 as an NDP MP for Birds Hill, Blaikie was named "Dean of the House" in 2004 to recognize he was the longest continuously serving non-govt MP. Blaikie received a BA in philosophy and religious studies from the **U of W** in 1973. He received a MDiv. from the Toronto School of Theology in 1977 and was ordained as a **United Church** minister in 1978. Prior to entering politics, Blaikie worked in Winnipeg's **North End** as director of a special Outreach Ministry of the United Church. After his election, Blaikie has served in a number of critics' portfolios including health and social policy, the environment, external affairs and international trade, labour and democratic reform. He is acknowledged as being instrumental in the adoption of the *Canada Health Act* in 1984. Throughout the 1990s, Blaikie was a prominent critic of globalization and how it pertains to workers' rights. In particular he opposed the Multilateral Agreement on Investment and called for reform of the World Trade Organization. In 2000, Blaikie successfully encouraged the NDP caucus to support the *Clarity Act*, which remained contentious within the party during the 2004 federal election. In 2003, Blaikie sought the leadership of the NDP, but placed 2nd to Jack Layton. Layton named Blaikie deputy leader as well as parliamentary leader until 2004 when Layton was elected to the House of Commons. In 2006, Blaikie was elected as deputy speaker of the house. In 2007, he announced he would not be standing for re-election. As an ordained minister Blaikie was often viewed as continuing the social gospel tradition of **Tommy Douglas, J. S. Woodsworth** and **Stanley Knowles**. • CARSON JEREMA

BLAKE, Emily Hilda, murderer (b Jan 1877, Chedgrave, Norfolk, UK; d Dec 27, 1899, **Brandon**) was the only woman to be executed in

MB. Despite being a confessed murderer, Blake evoked much public sympathy, even counting Canada's then gov gen Gilbert John Minto among her defenders. Born into a working class family in England, Blake was left to state care at the age of 9 after the death of both her parents. Like thousands of other British orphans, she and her brother were sent to Canada, essentially to work for their "adoptive" family as an unpaid servants. Arriving in MB in 1888, Blake was placed on a farm at **Kola** near **Elkhorn**. She was unhappy with her situation in the household, and ran away, but returned after failing to find better circumstances elsewhere. When she was old enough to find paid employment as a maidservant, she worked with several different families, finally coming upon a position in the Brandon household of businessman Robert Lane in 1898.

Blake worked closely with the Lane family, making it all the more difficult to understand why, on June 5, 1899, she shot Lane's pregnant wife Mary in the back at close range. The murder of an affluent mother of 4 in her own kitchen, in the middle of the day, shocked and enraged Brandon's citizens. Blake initially told police that Mary had been shot by a tramp with a foreign accent, and a vigilante mob was soon scouring the Brandon area in search of the killer. The mob found a suspect matching Blake's description. However, when faced with the man, Blake admitted that he was not the killer.

Blake became the investigation's prime suspect after helping police locate the murder weapon. Investigators then discovered that a Winnipeg shop had sold a gun to a woman matching Blake's description just weeks prior to the murder. She was arrested on July 9. Faced with the evidence, Blake confessed to Brandon Police Chief James Kirkcaldy, saying that she had killed Lane because she was jealous of her loving relationship with her family. However, many have speculated that Blake had in fact been involved in a sexual affair with Robert Lane, an argument later supported by Blake's poem "My Downfall," which was printed in the **Brandon Sun** 2 weeks before her execution. In the poem, Blake hinted that she was provoked to kill because of temptation from a man.

At her trial, Blake ensured her execution by refusing legal counsel and confessing in court to the murder. She was sentenced to hang. A movement to have Blake's execution stayed was headed by **Amelia Yeomans**, and the debate over clemency for Blake reached national proportions, with federal politicians debating her case. Ultimately, the govt of PM Wilfrid Laurier upheld the court's sentence, and Blake was led to the gallows on Dec 27, 1899. Her story has inspired

the 2002 book *Walk Towards the Gallows: The Tragedy of Hilda Blake* by Tom Mitchell and Kramer Reinhold. • MICHELLE DOBROVOLNY

BLIZZARDS are winter storms defined by windchill, poor visibility, and long duration. Blizzards can occur when strong winds create near-whiteout conditions by blowing around existing snow on the ground. A blizzard is essentially a winter windstorm, as distinct from a snowstorm. That said, MB's famous blizzards have dumped substantial amounts of snow in our paths. In southern MB, the most severe blizzards arrive with "Colorado low" **Weather** systems. As the name suggests, these weather systems originate E of the Rockies in CO or WY, and track NE toward southern MB. Blizzards occur mainly in March, when warmer air from the Gulf of Mexico pushes N and meets a Colorado low tracking NE. Increased moisture in the air mass, combined with its relatively slow speed, can result in large amounts of snowfall for areas in its path. One of southern MB's most notable blizzards began March 4, 1966. In the 21-hour storm, **Winnipeg** reported 36 cm of snow and an average wind speed of 70 km/hour. The results were paralyzing. Hundreds of people spent the night in downtown department stores, buses and streetcars stopped running, and homes were snowed in, with drifts reaching the rooftops. Other significant blizzards occurred in **The Pas** on March 30, 1967; in Winnipeg on Nov 8, 1986; and in Winnipeg and southern MB on April 5, 1997. In the **Northern Region**,

The March 4, 1966 blizzard

the bare tundra landscape (*see* Physiographic Regions) along the shoreline of Hudson Bay also provides ideal topography for blizzards. Subject to "polar vortexes" or "Mackenzie Valley lows," Churchill experiences far more hours of blizzard conditions annually than other MB locations. • SHELLEY PENZIWOL

BLONDAL, Patricia, writer, (b Dec 12, 1926, Souris; d 1959, Montreal). The daughter of a railwayman, Patricia Jenkins moved to Winnipeg with her family at the age of 7. After graduating with a BA from United College (see U of W), where she was a classmate of Margaret Laurence, she worked as a broadcaster for the CBC, married, and spent a year in England, returning to live in Montreal with her husband and 2 children. She attempted unsuccessfully to write short stories, until *Chatelaine* magazine serialized one of her novels, *From Heaven With a Shout*. But Blondal gained acclaim only after her death of cancer, at the age of 32, with the posthumous publication in 1960 of her novel *A Candle to Light the Sun*, a possibly autobiographical account of life in a small town she called Mouse Bluffs. Described as "one of the most promising Canadian writing talents of the half-century," she left one book unpublished. • MILDRED GUTKIN

BLOODVEIN FIRST NATION, on reserve pop 884, off reserve pop 510, is located about 210 km N of Winnipeg. The native language in this community is Ojibway. Bloodvein First Nation signed Treaty 5 in 1875. The area is comprised of one reserve, called Bloodvein I.R. No. 12. Schooling in this community goes from Nursery-Grade 9, and total enrolment for the year 2003-2004 was tallied at 262. The Bloodvein First Nation administers schooling. This community has no permanent road; it relies on a Winter Road from Pine Dock on the W side of Lake Winnipeg, an airstrip and a summer-operational ferry/barge. The people here are in discussion with the MB govt to negotiate the classification of this area of land, with the govt pushing for it to be declared a protected geographical area. After having survived the damage caused by hydropower developments, the people of Bloodvein are concerned about any further disruption caused by external interest in the area's resources. Nonetheless since 2002, the community has begun to work with the govt on select projects, such as improved water quality. The main economic base of Bloodvein is commercial fishing and trapping. It is a member of the Southeast Tribal Council. Commissioner of the Manitoba Clean Environment Commission (CEC) Frank Young, comes from the Bloodvein First Nation community. • RK

Jack Blumberg, 1956

BLUMBERG, John "Jack," municipal politician (b Hull, UK, 1892; d Dec, 1961, Winnipeg). Blumberg came to Winnipeg in 1910. He worked as a streetcar motorman from 1912 until 1919, when he was elected to city council as an anti-communist. During WWI he served overseas in the King's Rifles. He served on the council almost continuously until his death, being defeated only in 1950. As acting mayor in Winnipeg in 1933 he refused to read the riot act to demonstrators against unemployment. He served as chair of the Greater Winnipeg Transit Commission from 1956. • JMB

BOBCAT. *See* cats.

Historic murals in Boissevain

BOEING CANADA TECHNOLOGY is Canada's largest Aerospace composite manufacturer. Although its mandate is to produce composite products for both the aerospace and non-aerospace industries, the division's specialty is producing composite products and sub-assemblies for aircraft built by its US-based parent company, Boeing Corporation. Its main product lines are wing-to-body fairings, which provide an aerodynamic shell between the wing and the fuselage of a jetliner; engine strut fairings, which protect the strut mechanisms that hold the engine on the airplane; a variety of aircraft doors, including nose gear, landing gear, shock strut, trunnion, and thrust-reverser blocker doors; and a variety of specialty ducts. The division had 50 employees when it opened for business in 1971, and by 2004, it had 900 workers and annual revenues of more than $200 million. • MM

BOIS-BRÛLÉ. *See* Métis.

BOISSEVAIN, pop 1495, is a town 65 km S of Brandon and 25 km N of the US border on the CPR line. The area first saw settlers come from ON and England in the 1870s. Mennonites also settled here. The CPR line came here in 1885. Originally known as Cherry Creek, the town name was changed in 1894, in honour of Dutch banker Adolf Boissevain. The post office opened in 1886, and the town was incorporated in 1906. Boissevain's economy is based primarily on mixed crop and livestock operations. Largely because of the town's proximity to Turtle Mountain Provincial Park and to the International Peace Garden, the town benefits from tourism. Boissevain also hosts several festivals, including Turtle Mountain Métis Days and a Festival of the Arts. It is also well known for its attractive outdoor murals that adorn several buildings in the town. • GPP

BOND, Eleanor, painter, (b March 25, 1948, **WINNIPEG**) is internationally acclaimed for her work, particularly her large scale paintings dealing with cities, their social settings and environmental impacts. She graduated from the School of Art at the **U OF M** in 1976; has lectured widely across Canada, taught at Concordia U, and held residencies in Banff, Paris, Australia, the Netherlands, New York and, in 2007, at Queen's U, Kingston, ON. Her unstretched, fluid, colour-filled paintings are metaphors, combining reality and fiction in destabilizing, birds-eye perspectives. They depict futuristic cities, pointing to contradictions in contemporary society. Series like *The Social Centers* examine the human impacts of technology in a post-industrial society and explore the issues through her juxtapositions of public and internal psychological spaces. Her works focusing on *Future Cities* present the issues of constant change in space, place and social activity, raising questions of the future global environment, physical and psychological. She has exhibited widely across Canada, and her many international exhibitions include those in the UK, the San Paulo Biennale, Turkey and the US. Her work is in many collections across Canada, including the National Gallery of Canada, The **WINNIPEG ART GALLERY**, and in many international collections. She has been profiled in many publications, including *Canadian Art, Border Crossings, Parachute* and *C Magazine* and *Social Centres: Eleanor Bond*, The Winnipeg Art Gallery 1993. ● PATRICIA BOVEY

BONNYCASTLE, Richard Henry Gardyne, publisher, entrepreneur, conservationist (b Aug 25, 1903, **BINSCARTH**; d Sept 29, 1968, Lake Winnipegosis) is best known for starting up **HARLEQUIN BOOKS**, now Harlequin Enterprises Ltd, a publisher of romantic and women's fiction and one of the largest publishers in the world. Bonnycastle was born near the towns of **RUSSELL** and **BIRTLE**, where his maternal grandfather, Maj Charles Boulton, formed Boulton's Scouts to serve in SK in the North West Resistance of 1885. Bonnycastle studied law at Oxford, playing on the U's hockey team with Lester Pearson and Roland Michener. However, after returning to MB, he practised law only briefly before accepting a job with the **HUDSON'S BAY COMPANY** in 1925. He worked first in the accounts department, then as manager of the Western Arctic District, and finally as secretary of the company's Cdn committee. In 1945, he resigned to become managing director of Advocate Printers in Winnipeg. Four years later, he started Harlequin to produce paperback reprints, using Advocate's presses when they were inactive. By 1959, most of the books published were romances.

Richard Bonnycastle, 1960

Bonnycastle sat on the boards of many corporations, serving as the pres of the **WINNIPEG** Chamber of Commerce, chairman of the Metropolitan Corporation of Greater Winnipeg (Metro) from 1960-66, and the first chancellor of the **U OF W** in 1967. From 1957 to 1968, he held various leadership positions on the board of **DUCKS UNLIMITED CANADA**. He died of heart failure in his floatplane after landing on a bay of **LAKE WINNIPEGOSIS**. ● CARON HART

BOOK PUBLISHING in MB grew mostly out of 2 developments: the new patriotism fostered by Canada's centenary in 1967; and the desire of Cdn regions to stimulate their own arts instead of relying on Toronto. Canada's regional publishers, like those in MB, have largely become the development arm of national publishing, finding and nurturing new talent that, if successful, moves on to the larger publishers. A prime example of this is Winnipeg's Turnstone Press, which published the first books of nationally bestselling authors **MIRIAM TOEWS** and **DAVID BERGEN**.

Expo '67 and the general national confidence of the 1960s made Canadians newly aware of their own art and **LITERATURE**, and of the potential for developing homegrown talent. The anglophone Cdn book-publishing industry was (and still is) centred in Toronto, and the federal govt came up with ways of subsidizing publishers while also giving grants to authors. But as this wave of nationalism spread across the country, entrepreneurs and writers in the provinces saw an opportunity to start their own publishing houses. Eventually, grant programs from the Canada Council and the MB Arts Council provided these businesses with essential working capital. Almost all MB book publishers are based in Winnipeg.

One of the first MB publishers was bookseller **MARY SCORER**, who started Peguis Publishers in 1967. Scorer concentrated on MB **HISTORY**, though her *Guide to Textiles for Interior Designers* proved among her top sellers. After taking over the company in 1985, Mary Dixon shifted the focus to educational books – books by teachers and for teachers rather than textbooks. Some of the most popular were those written by Marlene and Robert McCracken – such as *Spelling through Phonics*. Under the direction of Dixon, the house is now MB's biggest publisher. Recently, the name of the company was changed to Portage & Main Press.

Also begun in 1967 was the University of Manitoba Press, the first university press in western Canada. They publish books based on scholarly research for both academic and general audiences. Under the direction of David Carr, they have made First Nations and **ICELANDIC** studies their specialties.

Before Peguis Publishing and U of M Press appeared, there were 2 active book publishers on the MB scene. One was Prairie Publishing, run as a sideline by Ralph Watkins while he worked at the **WINNIPEG FREE PRESS**. The other was **HARLEQUIN BOOKS**, begun in 1949 as a reprint house by Winnipeg's **BONNYCASTLE** family, who ran a local printing company. Harlequin gradually turned to romance and became wildly successful in that genre, producing up to 70 titles a month that sold all over the world. Torstar Corporation, publishers of the *Toronto Star*, took over Harlequin in 1981.

Publishing in MB has been largely a labour of love. For example, Joan Parr started Queenston House in 1974 to publish some of the MB talent she felt was being ignored nationally. Her first book, a mass-market paperback called *Winnipeg Stories*, showcased short stories by 16 MB writers, and the book found its way into MB schools. Queenston House went on to publish debut novels of such award-winning authors as **JAKE MACDONALD** and **MARTHA BROOKS**. At one stage, Parr bought her own press and learned how to print her books.

Remarkably, the various MB publishers have found individual niches, each formulating an editorial vision. Though some compete in the fields of regional history and fiction, most have developed specialties. This allows them to be compatible with each other and work together for the promotion of MB books through the Assoc of Manitoba Book Publishers.

Turnstone Press, founded in 1976, started out publishing mostly **POETRY**. It has since evolved into a publisher of literary fiction, non-fiction,

B

and criticism as well as poetry, and, under its Ravenstone imprint, it produces mysteries and thrillers. A milestone was reached in 1992 when a Turnstone book called *Touch the Dragon: A Thai Journal*, by Toronto writer Karen Connelly, won a non-fiction Gov Gen's Award.

07 APRIL 22 – 28 AVRIL

~ SPREAD THE WORD ~
Manitoba Book Week
La semaine du livre du Manitoba
CELEBRATING 10 YEARS OF MANITOBA PUBLISHED BOOKS

PHONE 204 947-3335
EMAIL manitobabookweek@mts.net
WEB bookpublishers.mb.ca
Visit a bookstore or library near you for a calendar of events and more information about Manitoba-published books.
Visitez votre librairie ou bibliothèque pour découvrir les livres des éditeurs manitobains.

AMBP Association of Manitoba Book Publishers

Celebrating Manitoba published books.

Hyperion Press, established in 1977, features children's folk tales and how-to books. The latter category includes works on aerodynamics, gliding, kiting, cooking, mosaics, stained glass, puzzles, and the like. Their picture books are intended for children less than 8 years old. Interestingly, when the giant Disney corporation decided it wanted to name its new book division Hyperion (after the street in Los Angeles when they are headquartered) the tiny Winnipeg press struck a lucrative US distribution deal with Disney in return for sharing their name.

Signature Editions, begun in Montreal as Nuage Press and moved to Winnipeg by Karen Haughian, publishes literary fiction, non-fiction, drama, and poetry. They have recently branched out into mysteries as well.

In 1986, Gordon Shillingford co-founded Blizzard Publishing, which published stage plays such as Maureen Hunter's *Footprints on the Moon* and **Carol Shields**'s *Thirteen Hands*. Shillingford left Blizzard in 1992 to form his own company, J. Gordon Shillingford Publishing, which produces Cdn history, drama, poetry, and social history. He acquired Watson & Dwyer from its founder, Helen Burgess, in 1994, and publishes history under that imprint. His other imprints are Scirocco Drama and The Muses' Company.

Great Plains Publications was formed in 1992 by Gregg Shilliday and Ingeborg Boyens to specialize in Prairie history. Great Plains has since branched out into biography, fiction, and coffee-table books. Ideas for the latter often come from in-house, and writers are commissioned to provide the content. These full-colour, hardcover books (*Manitoba 125*, *Winnipeg: Heart of the Continent*, *The Lake* and *Blue & Gold*) have become bestsellers. Young adult novels are also becoming increasingly important to the firm.

Also in 1992, Heartland Associates was established by Barbara Huck. Heartland concentrates on non-fiction, with emphasis on history, nature, and travel. They have also published several political biographies.

Two French-language publishers have been active in St. Boniface since the 1970s: Les Éditions du Blé (founded in 1974), which produces literary fiction and non-fiction, and Les Éditions des Plaines (1979), which does fiction and non-fiction as well as poetry, drama, and children's books. Another company, Apprentissage Illimité, based in **St. Adolphe**, was formed in 1995 to produce books and kits designed to teach the French language.

Two publishers devote themselves to Aboriginal materials: Indian Life Books began in 1979 and features non-fiction and inspirational books. Pemmican Publications, founded in 1980, produces First Nations and **Métis** fiction and poetry, **Aboriginal Literature** for children, and books on Aboriginal studies. In 1983, Pemmican first brought out the popular novel *In Search of April Raintree*, by **Beatrice Culleton**.

Other MB publishers (publishing from a left-wing perspective) are Fernwood Publishing, which works in the social sciences and humanities; and Arbeiter Ring, which deals mainly with cultural studies.

Book publishing continues to flourish in MB, partly through shrewd promotion and distribution, partly through govt subsidy and grants, and partly through business acumen and an ability to find special markets. MB publishers do their part in making Manitobans aware of their own literature and bringing it to the attention of the outside world. • DAVE WILLIAMSON

BOREAL FOREST. *See* **Ecoclimactic Regions**.

BORGER, Alan A. Jr., lawyer, businessman (b June 17, 1961, **Winnipeg**) is the third-generation Borger to run the Winnipeg family-owned home-building and construction empire, Ladco Homes and Borland Construction. Founded in 1919 by Alan's grandfather, John Henry Borger, the real estate company began when the construction

company acquired land from customers who were unable to pay their bills. Ladco is the company responsible for building many of the new neighbourhoods in S Winnipeg during the last half of the 20th century and into the 21st, including Winnipeg's first planned communities in Windsor Park and Fort Richmond. The company pioneered the construction of manmade lakes in the Richmond West and Royal Wood neighbourhoods in SW Winnipeg. Partnering with the province, Ladco is a key player in the proposed development of 1200 ha (3000 ac) of land in the SW corner of the city, called Waverly West, where housing for 30,000 was being planned in 2005. In addition to home and infrastructure construction, the Borger family also owns several shopping centres in the Winnipeg communities where the company was the home builder, as well as 1000 apartment units. The family also owns the Holiday Inn, Airport West. Alan Jr. took over as chairman and CEO of the family-owned business when his father, Alan Borger, Sr. died in Aug 2000. • MARTIN CASH

BOROTSIK, Rick, politician, businessman (b Sept 8, 1950, **Brandon**) is a gregarious Brandon politician. Borotsik was born and raised in Brandon, and attended **Brandon U**, graduating in 1972. He was first elected to Brandon city council in 1978. He served 3 terms on council before running for mayor and defeating incumbent Ken Burgess in the 1989 civic election. During his time as mayor, Borotsik brought the Canada Games and the World Curling Championships to Brandon. He held office until 1997, when he entered federal politics as a **Progressive Conservative** MP. He was elected in the Brandon-Souris riding, and was the first PC to be elected in western Canada following the party's devastating defeat in the 1993 election. He was re-elected in 2000, defeating the Canadian Alliance candidate to become MB's only PC MP. He opposed merging the PC party with the Canadian Alliance, and chose not to run in the federal election of 2004. He openly criticized what he called Conservative Party leader Stephen Harper's social conservatism and regional ideology. A popular politician, Borotsik was wooed by both federal Liberals and provincial Conservatives following his departure. In 2006, he came out of retirement to let his name stand as a candidate in Brandon West which he won in 2007. • MD

BOROWSKI, Joseph P., "Joe," politician, activist (b Dec. 12 1933, Wishart SK; d Sept 23, 1996, **Winnipeg**). Joe Borowski was a controversial politician and anti-**Abortion** advocate, who almost single-handedly led the pro-life movement in Canada during the 1980s.

Joe Borowski, 1966

After growing up in SK, he moved to **THOMPSON** in 1958 where he worked as a miner and was instrumental in the campaign to have the town incorporated. In 1964-65, he served as vice-president of the United Steelworkers of America. Upon retiring from mining, Borowski opened a gift shop. However, by the late '60s, the always direct and often intemperate Borowski was back to public life. He camped out in front of the legislature to protest the low minimum wage, the PST and other issues. His notoriety would see him recruited by the **NDP**. After the party under newly minted leader **EDWARD SCHREYER** won the 1969 election, Borowski was named minister of transport. Though he was immensely popular due to his blue collar roots, Borowski's temperament would see him dropped from cabinet in 1971, sparked by comments he made on abortion.

Upon losing the 1973 election where he ran as an independent, Borowski opened a health-food shop. Beginning in 1977, Borowski devoted most of his energy to the anti-abortion cause. In 1981, Borowski went on an 80-day hunger strike to protest the absence of fetal rights in the Charter of Rights and Freedoms. He took his case to the SK court in 1983. The court eventually ruled against him in 1987. In Jan 1988, the landmark Henry Morgentaler case would see abortion laws ruled unconstitutional by the Supreme Court, creating an effective legal vacuum. Prior to this ruling, abortions were restricted to hospitals and only after a committee ruled that the procedure was necessary for the health of the woman. Borowski's own appeal – to have fetuses declared persons – was scheduled for the fall, but due to the Morgentaler ruling, Borowski's case was declared "moot" in 1989. One controversial action of many taken by Borowski was when he showed up to court with 2 aborted fetuses,

though his lawyer prevented him from bringing them in with him.

Throughout the 1980s, Borowski clashed frequently with Morgentaler, as in 1983 when they engaged in heated debates at the **U OF W** and CJOB, over the opening of a Morgentaler clinic in Winnipeg. He was arrested around 20 times during the course of his activities, including a 1985 incident where he refused to leave Morgentaler's Toronto clinic. Borowski was able to raise $800,000 for his cause and he was actually moved to ask people to stop giving him money. In the 1988 federal and MB elections, Borowski and other pro-life advocates publicly challenged politicians to state their stance on abortion, and Borowski was frequently quoted in the media with his characteristic remarks. Borowski died in 1996 of cancer. ● CARSON JEREMA

BOTTERILL FAMILY. The Botterills are a family of athletes, with many achievements in **SPEED SKATING** and **HOCKEY**.

CAL BOTTERILL (b Oct 17, 1947, **PORTAGE LA PRAIRIE**) is a well-known sports psychologist. He developed his love for sports as a player on the Cdn national hockey team, participating in the 1968 Grenoble Olympic Games. He studied physical education at the **U OF M**, where he met his wife Doreen, before taking sports psychology at the U of Alberta. He earned a professorship at the **U OF W** in 1980 while simultaneously working as a consultant for various sports teams. He has worked with 5 NHL teams, including the 1994 Stanley Cup-winning New York Rangers, and 8 Cdn Olympic teams.

DOREEN (NEE MCCANNELL) BOTTERILL (b July 29, 1947, Winnipeg) is a 2-time Olympic speed skater. She began her career as a figure skater at the age of 4, but switched to speed skating 7 years later. At 16, she represented Canada in the 1964 Olympics in Innsbruck, breaking into the top 15 in all 4 speed skating events despite being the youngest skater on Canada's team. She won the 1966 North American Senior Ladies Championship, and then competed again at the 1968 Olympic Games. By the time she retired from competition in 1969, Doreen held 31 Cdn records. Following her athletic career, she worked in Winnipeg as a physical education teacher. She was inducted into the Canadian Amateur Speed Skating Association Hall of Fame in 1978.

JASON BOTTERILL (b May 19, 1976, Edmonton) is a former NHL player, and member of the national junior team. He holds 3 gold medals from world junior hockey championships as a player on the Cdn junior team from 1993-96. During this period, Jason also played in the National Collegiate Athletic Association (NCAA) for the

U of Michigan Wolverines, helping the team win the 1996 championship. He first played in the NHL for the Dallas Stars in the 1997-98 season. He played 2 seasons, then was returned to the minor leagues. He bounced from team to team, with brief NHL stints with the Calgary Flames and the Buffalo Sabres. While playing for the American Hockey League's Rochester Americans, Jason suffered an injury that forced him into early retirement in 2005.

JENNIFER BOTTERILL (b May 1, 1979, Ottawa) is an Olympic hockey player. Jennifer started out playing ringette, switching to hockey at the age of 13. She was a prolific high school athlete at a special sports school in Calgary, earning provincial titles in 5 different sports. She began playing for the Cdn national hockey team in 1997, and despite being the youngest player on the Olympic squad at 18, her consistent scoring helped the Cdn team win a silver medal at the 1998 Olympics, and a gold medal at both the 2002 and 2006 Olympics. As a player at Harvard, Jennifer was twice awarded the Patty Kazmaier Award as the Top Female Player in NCAA Hockey, and she is the only player to have won the MVP award twice. ● MD

BOULTON, Charles Arkoll (1842-1899) Surveyor, soldier, politician. Born at Cobourg, Canada, Boulton was educated at Upper Canada College. He served with the Royal Canadian Regiment in Gibraltar and Wales before his appointment as a member of the Canadian survey party in **RED RIVER**. Boulton attempted to organize military support

Major C. A. Boulton, ca 1897

for Governor **WILLIAM MCDOUGALL** in December 1869 and reluctantly led an armed force from **PORTAGE LA PRAIRIE** in its attempt to free prisoners held by **LOUIS RIEL** in February 1870. Captured by Riel, he was threatened with execution. His reprieve was a major quid pro quo in the complex negotiations between Riel and Canadian envoy **DONALD A. SMITH**. After the rebellion, Boulton went back to Ontario, failed in business there, and then returned with his family to the Shellmouth region in 1880. In 1885 he raised Boulton's Scouts for service in the North-West Rebellion. After the uprising was suppressed, he immediately returned home, hired a stenographer, and dictated his best-selling *Reminiscences of the North-West Rebellion*, which led directly to his appointment as senator from Manitoba in 1889. ● JMB

BOUNDARY COMMISSION/NWMP TRAIL

is today a modern highway system that approximates the historically important trail used by the International Boundary Commission. The trail wound from **EMERSON** to what is now AB and was originally used by Aboriginal peoples. In 1873, the fed govt recognized the importance of opening up the West for settlement. The International Boundary Commission was sent from the UK to survey the official boundary between Canada and the US so that settlement disputes would be kept to a minimum. The trail was used again by the **NWMP** on their 1874 march westward to evict American whiskey traders from the NWTS. Early settlers in SW MB travelled with horse and wagon along this trail until the railway arrived in 1886. ● JS

BOUTAL, Pauline,

painter, theatre director, (b Sept 8, 1894, Lanhouarneau, France; d April 30, 1992, **ST. BONIFACE**). As a visual artist, Boutal is known for her oil portraits of local personalities, pastel portraits of children, and her views of historical buildings and urban landscapes. Boutal and her family emigrated to MB in 1907 from Brittany, settling first along **LAKE MANITOBA** before moving to St. Boniface. She was introduced to art at an early age. At 15, Boutal got her first job as an apprentice typographer at *Le Nouvelliste*, a St. Boniface newspaper; this is where her first caricatures were produced. She studied at the Winnipeg Art Club and Winnipeg School of Fine Arts in 1912. Later, in 1946, she continued her studies at the George Elmer Browne School of Fine Arts, then in Paris, at the studio of painter André Lhote and at the Académie de la Grande Chaumière. Boutal married Arthur Boutal while in France between 1916-1917. When they returned to St. Boniface, she worked as a fashion illustrator at **BRIGDENS** of Winnipeg

for the **EATON'S** catalogue from 1918-1941. From 1932 to 1975, she exhibited annually with the Manitoba Society of Artists, and the **WINNIPEG ART GALLERY** included her works in various group shows. She worked in oils, watercolors, pastels or pencil to produce landscapes, portraits, views and genre pictures. Her art was exhibited at the Cdn embassy in Paris, the National Gallery of Canada and the Manitoba Artists Society.

The Boutals joined the St. Boniface Franco-Manitoban theatrical group **LE CERCLE MOLIÈRE** at its founding in 1925. Arthur Boutal acted as its artistic director until his death in 1941. At that time, Pauline took over as artistic director from 1941-1968. Boutal directed about 30 Cercle Molière productions and went on several Western Cdn tours. She won 2 awards for her work as director. Boutal also designed sets and costumes for the Winnipeg Ballet in 1950. The Centre Culturel Franco-Manitobain in St. Boniface named its performing arts theatre the Salle Pauline Boutal in 1975. Boutal was a life member of Le Cercle Molière, and a member of the National Drama Festival Board of Governors, the Societé des Artistes of Manitoba, and the St. Boniface Historical Society. She won numerous awards, including "Woman of the Year" in 1962 from the Women's Advertising and Sales Club of Winnipeg, and Les Palmes Academiques and La Médaille de la Reconnaissance Française from the Government of France for her work in art and drama and services rendered to French culture. She was named a Member of the Order of Canada in 1973, was awarded an honorary degree by the **U OF M** in 1978, and was inducted by the govt of QC in 1981 into l'Ordre des francophones d'Amérique. Boutal continued to exhibit her art until her death in 1992. ● AMANDA STEPHENS

BOWLING

in MB is most popular as the Cdn 5-pin game, though the US 10-pin game was originally played when bowling leagues were first organized in **WINNIPEG** in 1906. Winnipeg's Senior City League sent 5 teams to the first International Bowling Association (IBA) tournament in 1907. MB bowler Charles Gibson and his partner were the first Manitobans to win an international tournament, claiming the IBA doubles championship in 1914. Gibson introduced 5-pin bowling to MB in 1923, using a different scoring system eventually adopted throughout western Canada with pins scored as 1-4-5-3-2 rather than the Eastern system of 4-2-1-3-5. A national system was adopted in 1959, using the present 2-3-5-3-2 system.

Some of MB's most notable 5-pin champions include Ollie Hyndiuk, who won national women's singles titles in 1955 and 1958. As a

coach, Hyndiuk led the MB women's team to the World 5-Pin Championship title when the tournament was held in Winnipeg in 1973. Hyndiuk received MB's Order of the Buffalo Hunt that year. Norman "Norm" Shanas started bowling after working as a pinsetter during the 1940s, and went on to win 7 Cdn titles between 1955-67. Dylis Turner won the Cdn title in 1980, and later coached the provincial team, twice winning the Canadian Coach of the Year Award. Bob McEachern was a member of 3 national champion men's teams, though his most notable achievement came in 1996, when he rolled a perfect game with 19 consecutive strikes.

Recreationally, 10-pin bowling is less popular in MB than the 5-pin version, though MB has several 10-pin bowlers competing at an elite level. For example, Edward "Ed" Sobie, set a record in 1938 as the first bowler to roll 300 in a Cdn tournament. Paul Yoshimasu was the Cdn singles champion in 1966, and was named that year's Manitoba Athlete of the Year. He became the first Cdn to compete at the World Bowling Cup. In 1970, the provincial 10-pin association named Yoshimasu the MB bowler who has made the most impact on the sport. Terry Quinn, another Winnipegger, became the first Cdn woman to compete in the World Bowling Cup in 1974. Michael Schmidt is one of the top 10-pin bowlers in the world, and won the World Bowling Cup in 2005, becoming the first Cdn man to do so since 1972. ● MD

BOWMAN, John "Jack,"

pediatrician, researcher (b May 24, 1925, **WINNIPEG**; d May 22, 2005, Winnipeg). Bowman graduated with the highest overall standing from **U OF M**'s medicine program in 1949. He practised in Oakville for 2 years before taking postgraduate training at Winnipeg's Children's Hospital, the Winnipeg General Hospital's Newborn Service, and at the Babies and Children's Hospital Columbia Presbyterian Medical Center in New York. He then practised and taught for a year at Queen's U, in Kingston, ON. Bowman returned to Winnipeg in 1957 and worked part-time at the U of M, as well as working at the MB Clinic, where he later became the medical director on the retirement of **BRUCE CHOWN**. He taught full-time at U of M starting in 1967. Bowman is best known for his work on the prevention and treatment of Rh disease in newborns. Under his guidance, amniocentesis and amniotic fluid spectrometry were added to the resources of the Winnipeg Rh Laboratory in 1961, and he and Dr. Rinehardt Friesen carried out the first fetal transfusion in NA in Winnipeg (1964). Millions of babies have been born safely as a result of Bowman's development of the Rh-immune globulin (antibody) WinRho in

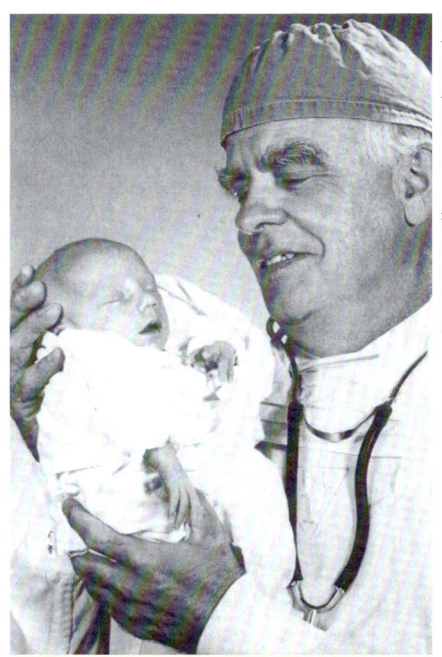

Jack Bowman, 1980

the 1950s. Before WinRho, mothers with Rh-negative blood would have an immune reaction to their Rh-positive babies, causing them to miscarry (maternal-fetal Rh disease or Rh hemolytic disease). Thanks to the product, annual mortality from Rh disease dropped from 50% in 1944 to 3% from 1982–92. WinRho is derived from human blood plasma and was developed in partnership with Dr. Bruce Chown and **Marion Lewis**. Bowman also made major contributions as Medical Director of the Red Cross Blood Transfusion Service in Winnipeg (1967–92), and Medical Director of Rh Pharmaceuticals (now **Cangene** Corporation) from 1991 to 1996. Cangene Corp of Winnipeg produces 80% of the Win-Rho in Canada. Bowman reinvested his profits from the development of Win Rho in the Rh Institute at the U of M to provide awards for promising researchers. Bowman retired from Rh Laboratory in 1996. In recognition of his contributions to the medical practice, Bowman was made an Officer of the Order of Canada in 1983 and was awarded the F. N. G. Starr Award in 1996. (The Starr Award is the highest award the Canadian Medical Association bestows.) He also received the Order of the Buffalo Hunt. ● JOHN HAMERTON

BOWSMAN, pop 320, is a village 50 km NW of **Brandon** in the picturesque Swan River Valley. The first surveyor to arrive at the spot of the original settlement named it "bowsman," after the first man out of the bow of the boat who touched the land. The community was originally known as "Bowsman River," but the name was later shortened to "Bowsman." The post office opened here in 1901. Bowsman was incorporated as a village in 1949. The village is nestled in a valley between the Duck and the Porcupine Mountains; rich agricultural farmlands meet natural prairie grasslands and forests here. Grain dealers, farm equipment suppliers and local bulk fertilizer dealers make Bowsman an important service centre for area farmers. Bowsman has a strong sense of community thanks to a curling rink, arena, community hall, various churches, and a variety of community clubs and organizations. The village also hosts an annual Father's Day picnic, a figure skating carnival and pickerel fish fry. ● GPP

BOYD, Alfred, merchant, politician (b UK, 1836, d 1908, UK). Born in England, Boyd was in the **Red River** by 1858. He owned a store in St. John's Parish that was managed by Maurice Lowman, and he engaged in fur trade with the Inkster interests. Boyd was elected as an English delegate to the 1870 Convention of Forty from St. Andrew's. Although Boyd was not a leading member, **Louis Riel** later described him as "one of the most decided against us." Boyd certainly opposed Riel's election as president and favoured territorial over provincial status. His critics later charged that he had received inflated reimbursement for "rebellion losses" (he claimed $55,500 in general damages and was awarded $2,505.18 for guns seized by the insurgents), but he always insisted that real goods had been involved. In any event, he was appointed provincial secretary in September 1870 and was elected to the Legislative Assembly from St. Andrew's North in December 1870. He resigned the secretaryship to become minister of public works and agriculture. He is sometimes regarded as Manitoba's first premier. Boyd was heavily criticized by incoming settlers for his failure to make public improvements, and he resigned in 1871 to be replaced by **John Norquay.** He subsequently became a founding member of the Council of the North-West Territories. He was a clever cartoonist, and according to J.H. O'Donnell he "drew many laughable sketches of members of the House that were grotesquely funny." He left Manitoba about 1889, dying in England a wealthy man. ● JMB

BRACKEN, JOHN, MB's longest-serving premier (b June 22, 1883, Ellisville, ON; d March 18, 1969, Ottawa). Bracken was educated as an agronomist at the U of Guelph. He taught at Saskatchewan Agricultural College before becoming president of the Manitoba Agricultural College (*see* **U of M**) in **Winnipeg**. In summer 1922, the Manitoba Liberal govt of **Tobias C. Norris** was defeated. It appeared that the United Farmers of Manitoba (UFM) were the winners of the election, even though they had failed to run candidates in several ridings. Nor did they have a leader or a universally accepted platform: such were the eccentric charms of the newer parties in that period. Once they realized that they had a mandate to govern, and hence would need someone to serve as premier, the UFM drew up a shortlist of prospects, one of whom was John Bracken whom farmers knew as an agricultural economist.

John Bracken, 1925

At first, Bracken was cool to the idea of being premier. He told those who came to lobby him that he hadn't even voted in the election, and did not wish to get involved in the highly risky engagement they put before him. In the end, the UFM, allegedly with the help of Bracken's wife, proved persuasive. The party's basic managerial instincts and highly practical approach reflected Bracken's own cautious nature. Bracken subsequently ran for a seat in **The Pas**, where the election had been deferred – a common practice in those days – becoming premier in Aug 1922. He would win re-election in 1927, 1932, 1936, and 1941, remaining in office for just over 20 years, the longest tenure of any MB premier. When he later resigned to become leader of the federal Conservative Party, he had been premier longer than any other serving head of govt in the British Empire.

Bracken's success seems bizarre to modern observers. Why was a reluctant leader who was devoid of charisma and who was frequently termed "dull" so successful? Secondly, how could he – and later, **Stuart Garson** and **Douglas Campbell**, his colleagues in the Liberal-Progressive coalition – continue to survive using a limited

79

store of policy and by sustaining into the 1940s a cautious **GREAT DEPRESSION**-era mentality when bolder action was becoming necessary. Bracken's success, despite a lack of vision, was largely due to his non-ideological politics. Bracken saw govt essentially as administration, and disliked what he saw as the excesses of partisan rhetoric. Bracken also benefited from a blatantly distorted distribution of the seats in the Legislative Assembly. The City of Winnipeg had just 10 MLAs for much of the Bracken period, whereas rural areas had more than 40. Clearly, it made excellent sense to show favour to the rural interest; this, Bracken did not fail to do.

Bracken's record was largely devoid of stirring legislative achievements. He pursued the goal of rural electrification (*see* **MANITOBA HYDRO**), and he revised his previous anti-Ottawa bias enough to endorse aspects of the Rowell-Sirois Report which led to equalization payments to the provinces. When the Depression came, he did not hesitate to use govt funds to ameliorate the situation. Overall, his contemporaries saw him as a good premier, by the standards of the day, and he was the only Cdn premier to be re-elected during the Depression. Yet some writers have, surprisingly, commented on his possessing the most "devious" mind in western Cdn politics, for he was able to survive by recruiting potential leaders of other parties, and by forming coalitions. He thus co-opted the opposition, and made a virtue of his pragmatic ideas.

Bracken was unable to find success as leader of the federal Conservative Party (1943-48). After running unsuccessfully for the **BRANDON** constituency in the 1949 federal election, he left politics. Bracken is the subject of a biography by John Kendle, *John Bracken* (1979). • GEOFF LAMBERT

BRAND, Oscar, folk singer, broadcaster, recording artist, writer (b Feb 7, 1920, **WINNIPEG**). Moving to Minneapolis in his teens, Brand left the US Navy in 1945 to take a position with a New York radio station, where he began his professional singing career hosting *Folksong Festival* and *The World of Folk Music*. Despite residing in the US, Brand, whose father hailed from **PORTAGE LA PRAIRIE**, retained his Cdn roots, hosting CBC-TV's popular folk music showcase *Let's Sing Out* (1963-66) and CTV's *Brand New Scene* (1966-67). As one of the world's pre-eminent folk music authorities, he has recorded over 70 albums, including several volumes of *Bawdy Songs & Back Room Ballads*, and published a number of collections of folk songs. Brand has shared stages with Woody Guthrie, Pete Seeger, Bob Dylan, Harry Belafonte, and others, and has written more than 300 songs, including

"Something to Sing About (This Land of Ours)" and "A Guy Is a Guy," a hit for Doris Day in 1952. He collaborated on several musical comedies, including *A Joyful Noise* and *The Education of Hyman Kaplan*, both produced on Broadway. He has hosted *Oscar Brand's Folksong Festival* for 60 years on WNYC-AM 820 in New York, and won 2 Peabody Awards (1982 and 1997, sharing the 2nd award with Oprah Winfrey) for his contributions to broadcasting. He also hosted the NBC-TV series *The Spirit of '76*. In 1983, Brand donated his **ARCHIVES** to the **U OF M**. He was inducted into the Canadian Songwriters Hall of Fame (2006). As of writing, he lived in Great Neck, NY.
• JOHN EINARSON

BRANDON, pop. 41,511, is in SW MB, along the Trans-Canada Highway, about 200 km W of Winnipeg. It is the 2nd largest of MB's 9 cities, and functions as a service centre for a surrounding trade area with a population of more than

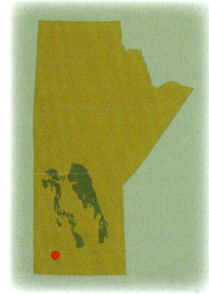

100,000. It covers about 43 km². The natural landscape of the area is flat to gently rolling, with characteristic parkland vegetation. The **ASSINIBOINE RIVER** meanders through the city just N of the downtown and **CPR** tracks.

In 1793, Donald McKay established Brandon House, a trading post for the **HBC** at a site near the confluence of the Assiniboine and **SOURIS** rivers, S of the present city's location. He may have named the post "Brandon House" because the

hills nearby reminded him of the Brandon Hill in James Bay, though most likely the post was named in memory of the Duke of Brandon, an ancestor of **LORD SELKIRK**. A party of Métis led by **CUTHBERT GRANT** ransacked Brandon House, then in the custody of Peter Fidler.

Apart from First Nations occupation, primarily **DAKOTA** and Assiniboine, and the temporary existence of **HBC** and **NWC** trading posts in SW MB, the Brandon area was first settled in 1877, when the McVicar brothers (Dougald and John) made a home on the N side of the Assiniboine River just E of the site the city currently occupies. The settlement that grew around their homestead became known as Grand Valley. Shortly after, William Currie, another early pioneer settler, established a competing settlement nearby. In addition to profiting from the small traffic plying the Assiniboine River (such as the SS *Marquette*), like many others in modern Prairie history, Currie and the McVicars waited in anticipation of the arrival of the railway. However, their locations were bypassed when, in May 1881, MGen **THOMAS LAFAYETTE ROSSER** selected a site just W of theirs and on the S side of the river as the first major divisional point W of Winnipeg for the **CPR**, which brought the first passenger train to the future city in Oct 1881.

The city was incorporated May 30, 1882, and the first meeting of city council was held on July 3, 1882, with Thomas Mayne Daly the first mayor. By this time, the population had already reached 1500 people. Once established, Brandon grew quickly, with notable periods of growth immediately after initial settlement (becoming a city without first being a village or town), and again

Brandon's 10th St. looking north, 1952

with the economic boom following the depression that ended in 1896. The date coincided with the completion of the settling of most of the better land in the interior of the US, increasing the attractiveness of the Cdn Prairies (and Brandon and area) as a destination for immigrants seeking a livelihood in the New World.

By 1900, Brandon's population had reached about 5000. By this time too, the Northern Pacific Railway had, like the CPR, made Brandon an important centre in its network, with Brandon, Saskatchewan, and Hudson's Bay Railway (part of Great Northern) following in 1906, and Grand Trunk Pacific a little after that. Northern Pacific's tracks in the area were taken over by CNoR, which, along with Grand Trunk Pacific, eventually became part of **CNR**.

In the early days, commercial development around the railway consisted mainly of wholesaling and retailing, grain elevators, and hotels. The city was performing the 3 basic functions of most early Prairie settlements: service centre for a surrounding agricultural hinterland; grain collection point; and stopover place for rail traffic, including workers and migrants travelling farther W.

The connection to the agricultural community has been a defining feature of the city since its inception. It is known colloquially as "The Wheat City," and its importance was confirmed when the federal govt chose the city as the location for one of the first branch farms in the Experimental Farm System, established in 1886. Agricultural fairs soon became major annual events in the city, so much so that Brandon was successful in its bid to host the national Dominion Exhibition of 1913. The railway and the surrounding agricultural hinterland clearly defined the role and evolution of the city for years to come.

Brandon's physical layout is typical of Prairie railway towns. Until the major wave of suburbanization of the 1970s, the main commercial structure consisted of development on one axis parallel and adjacent to the railway tracks, and another main commercial strip perpendicular to that, with the two "main streets" thus forming the "t" that is found in towns and cities throughout the Prairies. In the case of Brandon, there are 2 principal streets running parallel to the tracks – Pacific Ave. and Rosser Ave. – while the focus of the perpendicular strip has shifted from its initial location along 6th St. to its current concentration along 10th St, probably because the main CP station is on Pacific Ave at 10th.

The functions of the city include all of those typical of a mid-level service centre. There are numerous shopping opportunities, including the traditional downtown core, a suburban shopping

Brandon's skyline

mall ("The Shoppers Mall"), strip malls along major thoroughfares, and a relatively new "box store" development on the N side of the Assiniboine.

The city also offers a complete educational system, including Assiniboine Community College (est. 1961 as the Brandon Vocational Training Centre) and **Brandon U** (est. 1899 as Brandon College, with **Baptist** affiliation); the major regional health services for SW MB; public library and art gallery for the region; and a range of recreational and community facilities.

Brandon is also home to several major industries, most related in some way to agriculture: Maple Leaf (hog processing), McKenzie Seeds, Simplot Chemicals and Wyeth Organics (both agricultural chemical manufacturers), and Convergys (a large call-centre operation). The Maple Leaf plant continues a long tradition

of meat processing in the city. Another plant had been established by Donaldson in 1890, which evolved into Brandon Packers, then Burns. That plant eventually closed.

Culturally, Brandon was initially dominated by Anglo-Saxon Protestants, early settlers being primarily from ON and the UK. Shortly into the 20th century, a wave of immigrants from C and E Europe found their way here (primarily **Poles** and **Ukrainians**). Though no longer a homogeneous group, they still left their mark on the urban landscape. This is especially true in the working-class neighbourhood directly N of the downtown, between the CPR tracks and the Assiniboine, where there is a Ukrainian Orthodox Church, a Polish social club, and a variety of homes bearing colours or other indicators of the ethnic origin of their inhabitants.

Among its claims to fame, Brandon was the first city in Canada's West to be lighted by electricity (Feb 1889). Famous Brandonites include **Sir Clifford Sifton**, **James Ehnes**, **Glen Hanlon** and **Amanda Stott**. ● DERRECK EBERTS

BRANDON GENERAL STRIKE, or the Brandon Sympathy Strike, was the longest and most cohesive of sympathy strikes that erupted across Canada in support of the **Winnipeg General Strike**. In spring 1919, Winnipeg was the epicentre of a national labour protest that shook Canadian society. The Brandon sympathy strike began on May 20, 1919, and persisted until the end of June. It was preceded in late April by a dramatic and successful civic employees' strike, and followed at the end of June by an ill-conceived and futile general strike.

As in Winnipeg, the Brandon strike represented a struggle between 2 community coalitions: one included the Brandon business community, the *Brandon Sun*, the Law and Order League, and the city council allied with provincial and federal authorities; the other, the strikers and their supporters, the Brandon Trades and Labour Council, the Strike Committee, and the Peoples' Church, organized during the strike. While returned soldiers were prominent among the strikers, Brandon's Great War Veterans' Association, like its counterpart in Winnipeg, sought to play the role of mediator in the city's labour crisis.

The Brandon General Strike was the climactic event in a period of labour militancy dating from the reconstitution of the Brandon Trades and Labour Council in 1917. It was undertaken with the conviction that only through labour solidarity and direct action could labour achieve its legitimate aspirations for union recognition and improved economic conditions, and it was fuelled by economic grievances accumulated during WWI. The central purpose of the Brandon strike was the defence of labour's right to union recognition and collective bargaining. Nevertheless, the *Brandon Sun*, Brandon's Law and Order League, and the majority of the city council condemned the strike as part of an evil conspiracy to overthrow constitutional authority.

Following the collapse of the Winnipeg General Strike on June 25, 1919, the Brandon Strike Committee sought to orchestrate a continuation of the labour revolt in W cities. However, Brandon's call to labour in Regina, Moose Jaw, Saskatoon, and Calgary for a continuation of the general strike was a failure. The collapse of the June strikes left organized labour in Brandon in a state of turmoil and division. During fall and winter of 1919-20, the proponents of the One Big Union (OBU) struggled with the advocates of the Trades and Labour Congress and the international craft unions for control of Brandon's organized labour. In November 1919, a motion calling for the affiliation of the Brandon Trades and Labour Council with the OBU was referred to the council's affiliated locals. Though some organized workers in Brandon chose to affiliate with the OBU, by 1921, individuals loyal to the Trades and Labour Congress gained control of the Trades and Labour Council. While a small local of the OBU existed until 1923, the events of 1919 made them wary of striking again.

The labour crisis of 1919 was important both in shaping the evolution of Brandon's organized labour and in getting local workers to participate civically. In the aftermath of the strike, working-class solidarity and labour political action in Brandon was promoted through the People's Church, the Brandon Defence League, and, in 1920, the Brandon Labour Party. The vitality of the city's labour movement in the wake of the 1919 crisis was evident in the election of Brandon Labour Party candidate Albert Edward Smith as MLA in June 1920. ● TOM MITCHELL

BRANDON REGIONAL HEALTH CENTRE, formerly Brandon General Hospital (BGH), is the largest MB health-care facility outside of **Winnipeg** and the primary health services unit for the City of **Brandon** and the **Westman** area. Brandon's first doctor, Alexander Fleming, arrived via NB in 1881, and immediately began a movement for a hospital. John McDiarmid arrived later the same year, and both men were among the first governors of the hospital. The Brandon General Hospital was incorporated in 1883 by an act of the Legislature. Construction plans stalled, however, despite a $2500 city grant. The city had succumbed to a worldwide depression, and the hospital was a low economic priority until the late 1880s, when typhoid and diphtheria **Epidemics** were taking their toll. A temporary private hospital was established, and spirited community fundraising gave the fledgling board enough money for land and a building.

A small facility opened in April 1892. Within a few years, it had become overcrowded, especially as the epidemics continued. The hospital finally had enough funds to build a $7500 isolation wing in 1901. A surgical wing was added in 1904, and records note that 1620 patients were treated in 1905. BGH employed 8 doctors at the time, but Brandon had tripled its population over 10 years, and again the facility was too small. High debt, WWI, and the postwar influenza pandemic made expansion impossible until 1922, however. That year, a new 200-bed structure was completed. BGH's financial problems resurfaced with the onset of the **Great Depression**, and would not abate. The hospital barely fought off closure in 1951, and was saved only by fundraising and a systemic move to provincial-govt financing of hospitals in 1956. The federal and provincial govts also funded most of the $2.8-million cost for a new main building in 1962. A School of Nursing followed in 1968. In 1974, the hospital's Westman Laboratory took over lab services for the whole region.

As part of changes following the adoption of the provincial govt's *Regional Health Authorities Act* in 1997, the Brandon Regional Health Authority took over management of the hospital and renamed it the Brandon Regional Health Centre. A magnetic resonance imaging machine was added in 2004. By 2006, it was a 336-bed facility incorporating diagnostic, rehabilitative, and clinical services, as well as a full spectrum of inpatient and outpatient facilities. The hospital was scheduled to receive a new CT scanner in late 2006. ● JOEL TRENAMAN

BRANDON SUN. The daily **Newspaper** in **Brandon** had its start in 1882 – even before the city was incorporated – as *The Sun*, thanks to the efforts of Will White. White learned the printing trade by working with his father in Exeter, ON, and arrived in the little tent town taking shape in the **Assiniboine River** Valley with type cases and press. On Jan 19, 1882, he walked up and down Rosser Ave giving away copies of his paper's first edition. White published the paper until 1897, when he sold it to Gilbert Wilson, an educator who directed it until 1905. In that year, Joseph Whitehead purchased *The Sun* and became publisher. His son, **Ernest Christie Whitehead**, succeeded Joseph. Ernest was in turn succeeded by his son, Lewis D. ("L. D.") Whitehead. In the early 21st century, the newspaper was owned by the income fund FP Canadian Newspapers, also owner of the *Winnipeg Free Press*.

Coming as it did from a small city, *The Brandon Sun* has never had a large circulation, but it has enjoyed a longstanding reputation for the quality of its design and its editorials. For many years, it was a finalist in the annual design and typography competition for North American newspapers by the Inland Daily Press Association. As well, for many years Canadian Press rated the *Sun* the most-frequently quoted newspaper in Canada. In large part, this ranking was due to the writings of editor W. H. Noakes, a UK-trained editor/cartoonist. Noakes wrote a daily list of 1- and 2-line comments on national affairs of the day that were widely reprinted. On its 75th birthday, the *Winnipeg Tribune* saluted the Brandon daily for its "wit and pithy comment."

Other staff members earned a national reputation for journalistic excellence. Howard "Krug" Crawford, a lawyer who never practised, was the long-time sports editor whose observations on the sports scene were reprinted nationally. Over many years, *Sun* editorial writers who honed their writing skills in Brandon went on to positions of significance in related fields. Charles Magill became editor of *Reader's Digest*; William Morgan was appointed ombudsman of the CBC; Charles Gordon became an author and media columnist for the *Ottawa Citizen*; Haroon Siddiqi became editor of the *Toronto Star*'s editorial page.

While all those writers of editorials had complete freedom to express their opinions at *The Sun*, they also knew that Lewis Whitehead strongly believed in the special responsibilities of monopoly newspapers. He demanded political preferences be kept under control during elections. His repeated injunction was that, "on the morning after those votes are counted, I want all the political parties to be equally angry with us."

It is a tribute to this newspaper that, during its lifetime, 11 other daily newspapers challenged its position in the local marketplace, and all failed. In the early 1980s, George Bain, dean of journalism at U of King's College in Halifax, had his students undertake a critical examination of Canada's small dailies. They concluded that the *Sun* was the "Cadillac of Small Canadian Dailies."
● FRED MCGUINNESS

BRANDON UNIVERSITY is home to more than 30 academic departments that support a strong liberal arts and science tradition. Internationally, BU is best known for its music faculty, established in 1906. Students benefit from the custom-designed music building that was opened in 1983 featuring a 208-seat recital hall, organ room, 27 practice studios and a music library. In 1980, the first Master of Music Degree Program in MB was offered followed by the Master of Music Education in 1981.

There were several failed attempts to found colleges in the area before BU was established. However, these efforts are considered the foundation for what later became BU. When missionaries were first sent to SW Manitoba in 1869, they felt there was a need for a denominational college. In response to this need, Prairie College opened in 1880 in **RAPID CITY**. The college failed and a small academy tried to take its place. This later became McKee's Academy, and moved to Brandon in 1890 as the **CPR** mainline resulted in rapid growth of the city. In 1898, private donations helped to establish a Baptist college in Brandon. One year later, McKee's Academy

Brandon College in 1958

B

merged with the new Brandon College, which focused on liberal arts.

In 1938, the Baptist Union of Western Canada found it was no longer able to support Brandon College. Locals worked diligently and succeeded in keeping the college open. It became a non-denominational corporation that year. WWII saw students depart for service in the military, and enrolment therefore fell sharply. The 1950s, however, are considered rebound years as the facility, faculties, and student numbers grew. BU received its official charter on June 5, 1967.

The John R. Brodie Science Centre opened in 1972 and houses the departments of chemistry, physics, and math, among others. BU's small size accommodates undergraduate students' participation in research activities that would often be limited to graduate students in larger universities. As of 2005, BU faculty had won national awards for research in such areas as physics, astronomy, and mathematics and boasted a new, state-of-the-art microscopy and molecular systematics research lab.

BU is considered student-centred, offering mainly arts, sciences and fine arts programs at the undergraduate level. As of writing, the majority of BU students were enrolled in a bachelor of general studies, which allows for greater flexibility as students do not have to declare a major or minor. Also unique to BU is the 4-year bachelor of science in Psychiatric Nursing. Also, through the university's outreach programs, selected professors visit northern communities to teach for 5-week periods. BU, in conjunction

with the **U OF W** and the **U OF M**, has also formed an internet-based program to accommodate distance education.

In the early 21st century, more than half of all BU students were from small MB communities, including remote areas. To support the interests of its rural population, BU offers the only degree in rural and community studies in western Canada. BU's First Nations studies program was established in 1975; by 2005, about 30% of all students were Aboriginal. In 2004-05, BU had an enrolment of over 3300 full and part-time students and a faculty of over 200.
● JILL SEXSMITH

BRANDON WHEAT KINGS. Currently MB's only major junior **HOCKEY** team, the "Wheaties" have played in the Western Hockey League (originally the Western Canada Hockey League) since 1967, and at **BRANDON**'s **KEYSTONE CENTRE** since 1973. In 1904, a team called the Wheat Kings of the Manitoba and Northwestern Hockey League (MNHL) challenged the Ottawa Silver Seven for the Stanley Cup (*see* **WINNIPEG VICTORIAS**), losing 2 straight games in Ottawa. The Wheat Kings then began play in the Manitoba Hockey League in 1904 and also iced a team in the short-lived Manitoba Professional Hockey League in 1907-08. In 1949, as a member of the Manitoba Junior Hockey League (MJHL), the team played for their first Memorial Cup (national junior championship), losing to the Montreal Royals. The Wheat Kings were winners of 6 MJHL titles.

B

Brandon Wheat Kings

In the western league, the team's best season occurred in 1978-79 when future NHL players Laurie Boschman, Brian Propp, and Brad McCrimmon helped the Wheat Kings to a 58-5-9 record during the regular season, setting a Canadian major junior record for points. They defeated Portland in six games to capture the league championship (President's Cup), but lost the Memorial Cup to the Peterborough Petes. They also made it to the Memorial Cup tournament in 1995 and 1996 under successful head coach Bob Lowes (1992-2000). Former Wheat King player Kelly McCrimmon became general manager in 1988, team owner in 2000, and head coach in 2004.

Notable former Wheat Kings players include Bill Fairbairn, Dave Semenko, **GLEN HANLON**, Bill Derlago, Ron Hextall (see **HEXTALL FAMILY**), Ray Ferraro, Trevor Kidd, Marty Murray, Chris Dingman, Peter Schaefer, Mike Leclerc, Wade Redden, Bryan McCabe, Jordan Tootoo, and Eric Fehr. The 2006-07 season saw Brandon capture their 10th division title and set a single-season franchise attendance record, averaging more than 4000 fans per game. There is also a MB AAA Midget league hockey team that shares the Wheat Kings name. ● JOEL TRENAMAN

BRAY, Roger Ernest, socialist, veterans' leader (b Nov 19, 1875, Sheffield, England; d Oct 23, 1952, Vancouver, BC). Bray immigrated to **WINNIPEG** in 1903, working in the butcher trade. He was a former Methodist lay preacher and an active socialist, who had discovered "that Christianity was not the means of correcting social

injustice." Bray joined the Canadian army in 1916 while unemployed, later explaining he had "no job and a large family." He returned to Winnipeg from England on 31 December 1918, serving in 1919 as spokesman for a returned soldiers meeting in Victoria Park, and as chair of an informal group of returned soldier strikers (see **WINNIPEG GENERAL STRIKE**). On 14 June 1919 a secret agent of the RNWMP informed the superintendent of the Winnipeg District that Bray was "at the present time the most dangerous person in the City." He was arrested on 17 June 1919 by the government on charges of seditious conspiracy. He became vice-president of the Winnipeg Labour Council formed by the One Big Union on 5 August 1919. At his sedition trial in 1920, he was acquitted on most charges and convicted only on the charge of conspiracy to commit a common criminal nuisance. He was sentenced to six months in prison. Bray subsequently became an organizer for the One Big Union. He eventually moved to North Vancouver where he raised gladioli and was an organizer for the CCF. ● JMB

BREAU, Leonard Harold "Lenny" (or "Lone Pine Jr"), jazz guitarist (b Aug 5, 1941, Bangor, ME; d Aug 12, 1984, Los Angeles). Born to country and western performers Hal "Lone Pine" and Betty Cody, both of **FRENCH** Cdn descent, Breau began playing guitar at age 7, dropping out of school in Auburn, ME, at 14 to join his

Lenny Breau, 1964

parents' touring band billed as Lone Pine Jr. Moving to the **WINNIPEG** suburb of St. Vital in 1956, the family hosted the weekly CKY radio show *Caravan* and toured the Prairies. A prodigious talent, Breau quickly absorbed all country and western could offer, including a mastery of Chet Atkins's intricate finger-picking style, and began exploring jazz and flamenco guitar, incorporating all 3 into his own innovative approach that featured simultaneous lead, bass, and chord playing. Leaving his parents' band over musical differences in 1959, Breau found plenty of work at the **CBC** and in Winnipeg jazz clubs such as the Stage Door on Fort St. He also backed up local singer **RAY ST. GERMAIN** and married St. Germain's sister Val in 1959. The couple had 2 children, Chet and Melody; another daughter, Emily, was born in Edmonton. Young **RANDY BACHMAN** was a frequent visitor to Breau's house for lessons.

By 1962, Breau was playing coffeehouses in Toronto's Yorkville in a trio with bassist Ian Henstridge and actor/singer Don Francks, appearing in the 1962 **NATIONAL FILM BOARD** feature *Toronto Jazz* and on US television. He also recorded tracks backed by Levon Helm and Rick Danko, both from Ronnie Hawkins's Hawks (later "The Band"), released over 40 years later as *The Hallmark Sessions*. Breau also had his introduction to the underworld of drugs in Toronto.

Returning to Winnipeg in 1964, he appeared regularly on CBC shows *Music Hop* and *The George LaFleche Show*. Signed to RCA Records, Breau released *Guitar Sounds From Lenny Breau* (1969), produced by his mentor Chet Atkins, and *The Velvet Touch of Lenny Breau – Live!* (1969). For this last album, Winnipeggers Ron Haldorson (bass) and Reg Kelln (drums) accompanied him. Both albums set the jazz world on its ear, marking Breau as an innovative genius. CBC TV profiled Breau in *One More Take* (1968). He also backed jazz and pop artists such as Moe Koffman, Jimmy Dale, Beverly Glenn Copeland, and Anne Murray, with whom he toured Canada before his drug habit rendered him a liability.

By the 1980s, Breau lived in the US and was a regular on the jazz-club circuit, recording a number of albums – including *Five O'clock Bells* (1979), *Mo' Breau* (1981), and *Legacy* (1983) – for tiny independent labels in Nashville and Los Angeles. His increasing substance abuse led to erratic performances and a reputation for undependability. Relocating to Nashville in 1979, he again teamed up with Chet Atkins for *Standard Brands* (1981). Frequent trips to his birthplace, ME, to clean up inevitably failed. In the early 1980s, married to Jewel, Lenny moved to Los Angeles. There, he drew lineups at a regular gig at Donté's, where his innovative 7-string guitar technique wowed the jazz world. On Aug 12, 1984, Breau, age 43, was found dead at the bottom of the swimming pool on the roof of his apartment block. Investigators assumed foul play, and the case remains open to this day. His death brought tributes from around the world.

Breau's recorded work continues to be released posthumously by Art of Life Records, Favored Nations, and Guitarchives, Randy Bachman's label dedicated to preserving Breau's legacy for further generations of guitarists. In 1997, he was inducted into the Canadian Music Hall of Fame. Daughter Emily Hughes wrote the 1999 Bravo TV documentary *The Genius of Lenny Breau*. In 2006, author Ron Forbes-Roberts issued *One Long Tune: The Life and Music of Lenny Breau* (University of North Texas Press). ● JOHN EINARSON

BRELAND, Pascal, entrepreneur, politician, Métis leader, judge (b June 15, 1811, Saskatchewan River Valley; d Oct 24, 1896, St. Francois Xavier). Also a farmer, hunter, and Fur Trader, Breland moved from the Red River Settlement to Grantown (now St. Francois Xavier) with his family in 1832. In 1836, he married Maria Grant, daughter of Cuthbert Grant. The couple had 15 children. Breland became wealthy from farming and extensive trading at Forts across the plains, such as Fort Qu'Appelle, Fort Pitt, and Fort Ellice. He is said to have accumulated at least 152 ha (376 ac) of land, including all that had once belonged to his prominent father-in-law. His social and economic status afforded him considerable power. Breland, a free trader, protested the HBC trading monopoly at the 1849 trial of Pierre-Guillaume Sayer, and was appointed to various political roles, including magistrate – and later judge – for the White Horse Plain area, as well as member of the influential Council of Assiniboia (1857-68). Though his apparent unwillingness to take sides in the Red River Resistance (he left the area) may have cost him

Pascal Breland with Mrs. Breland, ca 1890

some influence in the Métis community, it did not prevent him from being elected to the first MB Legislative Assembly in 1870. He lost his bid for a seat in the federal riding of Marquette in 1872, however. At the start of his one term in provincial office, Breland also became part of the Cdn govt's new Council of the NWTs. He was sent to establish relationships with First Nations leaders, paving the way for the 1874 signing of Treaty 4 in what would become SK. He remained part of the Council until its dissolution in 1887. ● JOEL TRENAMAN

Alexander Brereton

BRERETON, Alexander Picton, Victoria Cross winner (b Nov13, 1892, Oak River; d July 1, 1976, Three Hills, AB), attended school in Hamiota, joined the 8th Battalion, Winnipeg Rifles (Little Black Devils) in 1916. On Aug 9, 1916, near Aubrecourt, France, his platoon was pinned down in the open by machine gun fire. Brereton single-handedly attacked, engaging in hand-to-hand combat. He took 9 prisoners. After the war, he farmed at Elnora, AB. He re-enlisted in WWII. ● JIM SHILLIDAY

BREWERIES have been operating in MB since the middle of the 19th century. While the history and extent of private brewing for household consumption, especially by early settlers, is almost impossible to uncover, facts about commercial breweries are well established.

Brewing did not spread through the Cdn Prairies as early or as quickly as it had done elsewhere in Canada. Three main reasons account for this. First, the vast space of the Prairies was, relative to other parts of the country, sparsely settled, with major communities at significant distances from each other. In the 1800s, before

artificial refrigeration and other means of preserving the product, beer could not withstand transportation over long distances. As a result, commercial brewing operations were found only in the major centres. Second, whisky was more popular for many consumers, in part because it was relatively cheap, especially if purchased in the grocery stores licensed to sell it, and in part because it had a much longer shelf life. Third, many of the settlers of this region of Canada came from C or E European countries that had well-established drinking cultures that favoured spirits over beer.

Probably the first brewery to operate in the province was run by the HBC at Lower Fort Garry, from about 1847 to 1868, when the settlement served as a supply centre for the fur trade throughout W Canada. The roots of the modern brewing industry in MB are traced to two early brewers: Henry Joachim, who had started brewing at the Red River Settlement about 1859, and Celestin Thomas, who set up a brewery near Middlechurch, on the banks of the Red, about 1860. Thomas moved his brewery to Colony Creek in 1873 as Winnipeg became an important commercial centre. (The creek is now gone; the brewery's site was approximately at the corner of Osborne and Broadway.) After several changes in ownership, Thomas's brewery was purchased by John McDonagh and Patrick Shea, eventually becoming Shea's Winnipeg Brewery.

As Winnipeg grew, so did the number of breweries operating in the city. In 1882, E. L. Drewry purchased the Redwood Brewery, which had been set up by Herchimer and Batkins in St. John's Parish in 1872. It eventually became Drewry's Manitoba Division of the larger Western Canada Breweries Ltd. There was a Silver Heights Brewery and Prairie Chicken Brewing Company by the 1880s, but there is no evidence that either survived Prohibition. Fort Garry Brewery succeeded MacPherson Brewing Ltd. (est. 1926) in 1930. Grant's Brewery Ltd., started as Edelweiss Brewing Ltd., becoming Riedle Brewing Ltd. (1925), and Grant's from 1950. Pelissier's Ltd. succeeded the Home Brewing Company Ltd. (established in the late 19th century), in 1925 (with a minor name change in 1936). The Kiewel Brewing Company Ltd. began operations in St. Boniface in 1925. In 1972, Uncle Ben's Tartan Brewery was opened in Winnipeg, only lasting about 5 years.

Shea's became famous for its Clydesdales, which were regular winners on the show circuit from 1921. When the company finally sold the horses in 1933, Anheuser-Busch, who introduced their first team that year, bought 8 of them. Outside Winnipeg, Brandon was the only centre with a significant commercial brewing industry. The Empire Brewing Company evolved from an earlier brewery established in 1885, and operated until 1931. The Brandon Brewing Company began operating in 1903 (as the Premier Brewing Company), and closed in 1932. William Ferguson ran an earlier brewery from 1884 to 1896. No other commercial brewing has since been undertaken in Brandon.

Prohibition was in effect in MB from 1916 to 1923, after which liquor became regulated at the provincial level; formerly, municipalities held jurisdiction over liquor production and sale. Many breweries survived this period by brewing "temperance beers" (up to 2% alcohol) and other alternatives to beer, as well as, in some cases, continuing to brew full-strength beer for export, and for local sale at hotels that were willing to risk being caught and fined. During this time, in MB as elsewhere, breweries often provided financial assistance to hotels for which the fines became unmanageable. A growing debt to the breweries led eventually to financial control, and by the mid-1950s, breweries owned 1/3 of the hotels in MB. The *Liquor Control Act* (1956) made this ownership illegal.

The wave of acquisition, merger, and consolidation that was taking place in the brewing industry across Canada arrived in Winnipeg in 1953. In that year, Shea's was purchased by Labatt, being renamed Labatt's Manitoba Brewery in 1958. Labatt also purchased Kiewel and Pelissier's in 1953, merging them in 1969 before shutting the operation down in 1976. When Western Canada Breweries was purchased by

Canadian Breweries in 1953, Drewry's became Carling Breweries (Manitoba) Ltd. Grant's was also purchased by Canadian Breweries in 1957, being operated as O'Keefe Brewing Company Ltd., renamed O'Keefe Old Vienna Brewing Company Ltd. in 1965. This plant was closed in 1969, and production of the two Canadian Breweries operations was consolidated at the Drewry's plant, then renamed Carling O'Keefe.

Molson entered Winnipeg by purchasing the Fort Garry Brewery in 1960. In 1989, Molson took over Carling O'Keefe and restructured its holdings by closing the former Fort Garry Brewery. By 1997, both Labatt and Molson closed their Winnipeg Breweries. Of note, Labatt's first attempt at a "national" brand – Pilsener Lager – introduced in 1951 elsewhere and later in the 1950s in MB, was eventually renamed "Blue", in part because of its association with the **Winnipeg Blue Bombers**, but largely because of the label colour.

As the rest of Canada experienced the microbrewing renaissance from the 1980s on, so too did MB. After a few decades of oligopoly by the national breweries operating in the province, Molson and Labatt were joined in 1994 by a revived Fort Garry Brewing Company (started by Richard Hoeschen, great-grandson of Ben Hoeschen, the owner of the original Fort Garry Brewery from 1930 to 1960). Agassiz Brewing Company and Two Rivers Brewing Company began production in 1999. In 2002, facing financial difficulty, Agassiz was restructured as New Manitoba Brewing, and production of the Agassiz brands was contracted out to Northern Breweries of Sault Ste. Marie, ON. In 2003, Fort Garry and

Two Rivers merged, and the company continues to operate under the Fort Garry name, making and selling products of both breweries (including Fort Garry Dark and Two Rivers Lager). As well, Winnipeg had, for a brief time, 2 brew pubs, both of which are now closed. ● DERREK EBERTS

WINNIPEG FREE PRESS

Theresa Brick

BRICK, Theresa, weightlifter, track & field thrower (b May 4, 1965, **Winnipeg**), has competed internationally in the discus and hammer throw, and is a pioneer in female competitive weightlifting. She began her athletic training in 1984. A natural athlete, she qualified for the discus throw at the Canada Games the following year. Though she didn't win any titles at her first national competition, the event introduced the young athlete to the hammer throw. As one of the first Cdn women to compete in the hammer throw, Brick took home 10 national titles in the event, as well as 3 titles in discus, between 1987-97. As her athletic prowess developed, Brick also took an increasing interest in the emerging sport of women's weightlifting. She was a competitor at the first World Weightlifting Championships for Women in 1987. She competed in the next 10 championships, and was consistently ranked as one of the top 10 female weightlifters in the world. Brick is also the only Cdn to have been invited to weightlifting's World Cup Gala, where she placed 4th in 1994. She retired from international competition following a run at entering the 2000 Olympics. As of 2006, Brick was active in promoting weightlifting as a sport for women. ● MD

BRIGDEN, William "Bill," paddler, canoe-builder (b Apr 11, 1916, **Winnipeg**; d Jan 16, 2005, Winnipeg) dominated Canada's paddling events for a decade before building hundreds of canoes in his St. Vital basement. Brigden won several national paddling competitions in the 1950s in both long and short races. At the Helsinki Olympics in 1952, he and his partner Jim Nickel placed 11th out of 18 teams that competed in the kayaking event. He took long distance titles in Flin Flon's Gold Rush Canoe Race, over 100 miles

Drewry's Brewery truck

long, in 1955 and 1956. Brigden's handmade canoes, known for their durability, were used by paddlers like **Don Starkell** on his long trips down the Amazon and Mississippi rivers and the Northwest Passage. Brigden was inducted into the MB Sports Hall of Fame in 1992. • MD

BRIGDENS OF WINNIPEG LTD., Designers and Engravers, was established in Winnipeg in 1914 by Arnold O. Brigden as the western branch of the Toronto family firm, Brigdens. The Toronto firm, one of Canada's oldest graphic arts companies, was founded in 1871, and by 1914 was run by Arnold Brigden's cousins. In 1920, the Winnipeg branch incorporated as a stand-alone company, Brigdens of Winnipeg Ltd., and run by Arnold until his retirement in 1956, when both firms were then taken over by the eastern Brigdens' nephew, Edward Nicholson. The Winnipeg firm's major contract from the outset was the design and production of the spring/summer and fall/winter issues of **Eaton's** Catalogue for Western Canada, which were to include "drawings depicting western sensibilities." Brigdens became a major employer of artists in Winnipeg – printmakers, painters and graphic designers – and was important throughout the first half of the 20th century in training artists and developing the Winnipeg art scene. Many Brigdens' artists were active Manitoba Society of Artists and Winnipeg Sketch Club members. Artists included **Charles Comfort, Walter J. Phillips**, Eric Bergman, **Pauline Boutal**, Alison Newton, Edgar Percy, Caven Atkins, Fritz Brandtner, **Hal Foster** (strip cartoonist) and **Charles Thorson** (Disney cartoon animator). Other clients included Birks Ltd and The **Winnipeg Art Gallery**. By the 1970s new advertising technologies and changing social patterns had spelled the end of mail-order catalogues; profits fell and Brigdens was sold. • PATRICIA BOVEY

BRISTLE WORM is a type of segmented worm related to the earthworm, and one of the most ancient forms of life, with fossils from 525 mya (middle Cambrian). They are characterized by bundles of bristles arising from paddle-like extensions (parapodia) of the body wall. Swimming forms have an impressive array of sense organs on the front part of the head (prostomium) – 4 eyes, tentacles and polyps. Bristle worms are relatively large worms, ranging from 1 cm to 3 m (most under 10 cm). This is a large group (over 8000 species) of mostly marine worms – only 50 species are restricted to freshwaters of the world, with several in NA, but not in MB. However, MB's marine waters of Hudson Bay boast an impressive 81 species, with more still undiscovered.

They are benthic dwellers, inhabiting the mud and sand sediments and spaces between rocks in shallow to deep marine waters, frequently in great numbers (>1000/sq metre), especially from low tide to a depth of 50 metres. Fine sediments are often riddled with burrows and tracks of bristle worms (e.g., Cistenides), while some species (*Onuphis conchylega*) remain semi-permanently at one site to feed from a constructed tube, into which they retreat rapidly from predators. A few species (e.g., *Manayunkia aestuarina*) are common in estuaries, where a lower and fluctuating salt concentration occurs. Some species of polychaetes feed on algae, bacteria, and organic detritus in the sediment or floating by in the current, captured by mucous and cilia lining several tentacles, or a beautiful feathery net originating near the mouth. Others, with strong jaws, tear at algal mats or fronds, while predatory species with a protrusible proboscis and sharp jaws capture invertebrates and small fish. They are preyed upon by echinoderms, fish, beluga, seals, shorebirds and waterfowl. • REW

BRISTOL AEROSPACE is one of the cornerstones of Manitoba's **Aerospace** sector, along with **Standard Aero** Limited, **Boeing Canada** Technology–Winnipeg Division, and the Air Canada maintenance base in **Winnipeg**. Owned by the Magellan Aerospace Company since 1997, Bristol's operations are divided into 3 major units. One is its Aerostructures business unit in Winnipeg, which specializes in the manufacturing of metal and composite aircraft structural components, the designing of aircraft tailcones, the repairing and overhauling of F-5 fighter jets, and the designing and manufacturing of the company's Wire Strike Protection System for helicopters. The second is its Aeroengine division, which is also in Winnipeg and specializes in the manufacture, repair, and overhaul of engine components. The third is its Defence and Space business unit in **Rockwood**. Canada's only large-scale manufacturing and test facility for composite propellant, the Rockwood plant manufacturers the CRV7 rocket system, **Black Brant** sounding rockets, and decoy flares. It also provides payload integration services and designs, manufactures, and integrates small satellites. Bristol, and the aerospace industry in general, went through some difficult years between 2000 and 2004. During that time, Bristol saw its workforce fall from 1100 to about 650 employees. However, in December 2004, the company announced it was purchasing $10 million worth of new equipment and had won strategic new contracts, which it felt would help to stabilize its workforce and get the company back on the right track. • MM

BRITISH COMMONWEALTH AIR TRAINING PLAN was a massive WWII aviation program in which Canada processed some 131,000 allied air force recruits and MB's wide-open spaces were regarded as ideal for training. Often referred to simply as "The Plan," BCATP was heavily supported by PM Mackenzie King as it gave Canada a prominent role in the war effort while putting off the need for a large expeditionary force. Our prairie was also considered an ideal location as it was beyond the reach of enemy aircraft, had ample air space, and was near US industry.

Even before the BCATP agreement was officially signed on Dec 17, 1939, turning Canada into what US president Franklin D. Roosevelt referred to as an "Aerodrome of Democracy," MB towns were lobbying govt to be selected as a site for a BCATP training school. With the extra spending of Air Force recruits from Canada, UK, Australia, and New Zealand, training schools gave a much-needed boost to the post-Depression economy of surrounding communities, providing civilian jobs in construction and labour, as well as flying instructor positions to civilian pilots. Many of MB's bush pilots were employed in this way (*see* **Aviation**). BCATP also bolstered MB's **Aerospace Industry**, with **Standard Aero** supplying the BCATP with roughly 7000 aircraft engines. The first training schools began operating in 1940, and MB's landscape was soon transformed as hangars, runways and tarmacs were erected throughout the province. In total, 14 BCAPT facilities were set up in MB.

Training was intensive, beginning with 4 weeks at the Manning Depot (No. 2) located in **Brandon** to learn military basics. Recruits who proved their potential as pilots, the most prestigious position, would then be sent to an Elementary Flying Training School (EFTS) in **Virden** (No. 19), **Neepawa** (No. 35), or **Portage la Prairie** (No. 14). At an EFTS, pilot trainees learned to fly single engine aircraft like Fleet Fawns, Fleet Finches, de Havilland Tiger Moths, and Fairchild Cornells. After 8 weeks at EFTS, successful graduates were sent to a Service Flying Training School in **Dauphin** (No. 10), **Souris** (No. 17), **Gimli** (No. 18), or **Carberry** (No. 33). Potential fighter pilots trained on single engine NA Harvards, while pilots selected for bomber, coastal, or transport operations trained on twin-engine Avro Ansons, Cessna Cranes, or Airspeed Oxfords.

Recruits chosen to be air observers received 2 months training at Air Observer School (No. 7) in Portage la Prairie and later, as the duties of an air observer evolved over the war, the Central Navigation School (No. 1) in **Rivers**. Bombing and Gunnery Schools were located in MacDonald (No. 3) and Paulson (No. 7). Winnipeg was home

Richard Burton trained at Dauphin's airbase.

B

to several facilities, including the No. 2 Training Command Headquarters, No. 4 Air Observer School, No. 3 Wireless School, No. 7 Equipment Depot, and the No. 8 Repair Depot.

The influx of thousands of Commonwealth air force recruits, including actor Richard Burton, had a significant impact on local communities. BCATP training schools became a centre for social activity, with local residents attending BCATP sporting events, open houses, graduation ceremonies, and dances. Many local women married Air Force trainees. The 216 airmen from Commonwealth countries who died while training in MB are memorialized in Winnipeg's Garden of Memories, opposite 17 Wing's southern gate, as well as by a statue on Memorial Blvd near the Legislature. A Commonwealth Air Training Plan Museum is located in **Brandon**.
● MICHELLE DOBROVOLNY

BROADCASTING in MB began in 1922 with the establishment of 3 AM radio stations. The first, CKZC, was built and operated by Lynn V. Salton from his **Winnipeg** home. Salton – an engineer and radio inspector for the 3 Prairie Provinces – went on the air 2 evenings a week, playing phonograph records to an audience as far as 1350 km away. Salton also helped the *Manitoba Free Press* (*see* **Winnipeg Free Press**) beat its rival, the **Winnipeg Tribune**, to air in early April as the first **Newspaper** on the Prairies to operate a radio station, CJCG. The *Tribune* followed later that month with the launch of CJNC. Both stations developed program formats that consisted of daily noon-hour news reports; weekday evening broadcasts of live concerts by local vocalists and instrumentalists, interspersed with phonograph recordings; and sacred music programs on Sunday evenings. These early radio stations were,

however, short-lived. Salton eventually stopped broadcasting as CKZC after he resigned as radio inspector, to take charge of the new radio department of the city's **Eaton's** store, where he set up his transmitter as an attraction for customers. Having failed to turn a profit, CJCG and CJNC ceased operating in March 1923, and relinquished control of radio in MB to the provincial govt's **Manitoba Telephone System** (MTS). Days later, MTS launched CKY, the country's first publicly owned broadcaster, offering programming similar to that of the stations it replaced, as well as the popular weekly *University Hour* educational program.

In 1924, CKY began to lease airtime to the **Canadian National Railway**, which broadcast CNR network programs and live items from Winnipeg, primarily for reception in its parlour cars. MTS established a 2nd station, CKX, in **Brandon** in 1928. In 1933, CKY became the provincial carrier of programming by the Canadian Radio Broadcasting Commission (after 1936, the **Canadian Broadcasting Corporation** or CBC), the national public radio network created in 1932 in response to the recommendations of the 1930 Aird Commission and intense lobbying from the Canadian Radio League, co-founded by **U of M** – educated Graham Spry.

Several important developments in MB radio occurred in the late 1940s. In 1946, CJOB went on the air from Winnipeg, soon becoming one of the province's highest-rated stations. CKSB, western Canada's first **French**-language station, also began broadcasting that year; the **St. Boniface** station was operated privately until the CBC's Francophone equivalent, Radio-Canada, purchased it in 1973. The province ceased to operate its own stations in 1948. The CBC purchased CKY, changing its call letters to CBW, while a group of Brandon businessmen headed by John B. Craig (*see* **Craig Family**) bought CKX. Lloyd Moffat took the call letters CKY for his new Winnipeg AM station in 1949. Nearly a decade later, rural southern MB got its first radio station, with the 1957 launch of CFAM in **Altona**.

FM radio was introduced to MB in 1948, with the creation of CJOB-FM. The station offered a simultaneous broadcast of CJOB-AM until 1962, when it was authorized to air distinct programming, and is now known as CJKR ("Power 97"). By the end of 1963, Winnipeg had 3 more FM stations: CFMW, CKY-FM, and CJQM-FM, the stations that would eventually become CBW ("CBC Radio Two"), CITI-FM, and CHIQ-FM ("Q-94 FM"), respectively. Also in 1963, the Craig family established MB's first stereo station in Brandon, CKX-FM. Since the early 1960s, nearly all new radio stations have been allocated FM

frequencies. These include the stations of Native Communications Inc. (NCI), an Aboriginal radio network; campus radio stations (the **U of M**'s CJUM, 1998; the **U of W**'s CKUW, 1999; **Red River College**'s CKIC, 2004; and **Assiniboine Community College**'s CJ-106, 2006); and Christian stations CFEQ (now rock station "FREQ-107," 1999) and CHVN (2000).

Television broadcasting came to MB when the CBC launched CBWT in Winnipeg in 1954, a year after the national public TV network was established. The station operated in both English and French until 1960, when the francophone CBWFT aired. The Craig family started CKX-TV in Brandon in 1955, a private affiliate of the CBC. A group of Winnipeg businessmen headed by Lloyd Moffat and Ralph Misener started CJAY-TV in 1960. CJAY joined 7 other new Cdn stations to form the Canadian Television Network in 1961 (CTV). Moffat Communications took full ownership of CJAY in 1973, changing its call letters to CKY-TV. CTV Inc. bought CKY in 2001. Winnipeg's 3rd English TV station signed on in 1975 as CKND. Former politician **Izzy Asper** and his business partners had bought out KCND, a ND border station that depended heavily on its Winnipeg audience for advertising revenue, moving the station's facilities to Winnipeg to save on start-up costs. CKND was rebranded as "Global Winnipeg" in 1997, as part of Asper's **CanWest Global Communications** nationwide Global Television Network. The Craig family started another station, CHMI, in 1986. Broadcasting from studios in **Portage la Prairie** and Winnipeg, it was

CJOB's George McCloy in 1964

first known as the Manitoba Television Network (MTN). It became the "A-Channel," after its sister stations in AB in 1999. CHMI was sold to Toronto's CHUM Ltd. in 2004, which gave the station its CITY-TV brand name the following year. Rogers Media launched CIIT ("OMNI.11") in 2006. Named after its cable channel position, the station also broadcasts on channel 35, making it MB's first UHF station. Since 1999, Winnipeg has also been home of the national **Aboriginal Peoples Television Network**.

Since the 1960s, Manitobans in select areas have been able to subscribe to cable television services. Videon Cable TV began serving Winnipeg neighbourhoods W of the Red River in 1967, while Greater Winnipeg Cablevision served the city's E side. Calgary-based Shaw Communications took over GWC's cable facilities in 1992, when it purchased its parent company, Cablecasting Ltd. In 2001, Shaw also purchased Videon when it acquired Moffat Communications. Today, Shaw serves many MB communities. Among the smaller cable companies operating in MB is Westman Communications Group, which serves Brandon and the surrounding towns and villages. Since 2002, MTS has also offered digital TV (and radio) services over its telephone wires. ● JEREMY WIEBE

BROADFOOT, Barry, oral historian, author (b Jan 21, 1926, **Winnipeg**; d Nov 30, 2003, Nanaimo, BC), chronicled the human face of historic 20th-century events by recording the stories told by hundreds of ordinary men and women across Canada. His first book *Ten Lost Years* (1973) vividly portrayed the experience of living through the Great Depression, and provided the basis for several films and stage productions. Other major works include: *Six War Years* (1975), about WWII; *The Pioneer Years* (1976), about homesteading in W Canada; and *Years of Sorrow, Years of Shame* (1977), about the internment of Japanese Canadians during WWII. Educated at the **U of M**, where he edited the student **Newspaper**, *The Manitoban*, Broadfoot worked as a journalist in Winnipeg, Edmonton, and Vancouver. He received the Order of Canada in 1988, an honorary LLD from the U of M in 1996, and BC's 3rd Terasen Lifetime Achievement Award for an Outstanding Literary Career in 1997. ● MILDRED GUTKIN

BROCHET, pop 226, is a community 330 km NW of **Thompson** on Brochet Bay at the N end of Reindeer Lake at the Cochrane River, adjoining **Barren Lands First Nation**. The community takes its name from the bay, itself called after the French word for **Pike**, which are abundant in

the area. Long home to both **Cree** and **Dene**, the area was permanently settled when an **HBC** post and a **Roman Catholic** mission were established here in the mid-19th century. In the 1930s and '40s, US anthropologist Prentice G. Downes used Brochet as a base for his travels among Cree and Dene people. He chronicled his journey in *Sleeping Island* (1943). **Thomas Lamb**'s Lamb Air operated here for much of its history. Brochet's current population remains almost exclusively Aboriginal, and mainly pursues traditional activities such as **Commercial Fishing**, subsistence hunting, and Fur Trapping. Some tourism occurs in the form of lodges for **Sport Fishing** and hunting. A fly-in community in summer, Brochet is connected by winter road to the S of the province. Unlike the majority of remote northern centres, Brochet's population grew slowly but steadily in the late 20th and early 21st centuries. ● GPP

BRODA, Walter Edward "Turk," hockey goaltender (b May 15, 1914, **Brandon**; d Oct 17, 1972, Toronto) was an exceptional and popular goalie for the Toronto Maple Leafs during the team's golden age through the 1940s. Broda tended net in the Manitoba Junior Hockey League for the Winnipeg Monarchs, then in the minor leagues for the Detroit Red Wings, where he was discovered by Leafs owner Conn Smythe. Smythe was so impressed upon seeing Broda's performance that he immediately called Red Wings coach Jack Adams, and paid $7500 cash to acquire the goalie. Broda played for the Leafs from 1936-51, seeing the team to 5 Stanley Cup victories. He won 3 Vezina trophies as the NHL's top goalie, in 1941, 1948 and 1951. His hockey career was interrupted when he joined the Armed Forces in 1943, though Broda kept up his skills by playing hockey in England. A boisterous and colourful personality, nicknamed "Turk" for the large freckles or "turkey eggs" on his face, Broda was a favourite with Leafs fans. He was once famously suspended from play because of his weight problem, which Conn Smythe then used as a publicity stunt. Despite his rotund build, Broda was an outstanding goalie and played in all games in 8 of his 11 seasons with the Leafs. He twice led the league in shutouts, and played 101 Stanley Cup games, a record for his time. When Broda retired in 1951, he had 62 shutouts and 302 wins, a record that still stands today. He was inducted into the Hockey Hall of Fame in 1967. ● MD

BRODSKY, Gerald Gregory, "Greg," defence counsel (b Apr 15, 1940, Melville, SK) has defended 600 murder cases, more than any other lawyer in Canada. Brodsky, whose parents owned a corner grocery store, graduated from the **U of M**

in 1963 and was called to the Manitoba Bar that year. He received his LLM in 1965, and was called to the ON bar in 1971 and the SK bar in 1977. He became a senior partner at the firm of Walsh Mickay & Co., and became a QC in 1976. He has chaired numerous committees for the Law Society of Manitoba. He started his own law firm, Brodsky & Co., to focus on criminal law. He has been involved with numerous precedent-setting cases, including *R. v. Lavallee*, creating a battered-wife defence; *R. v. Starr*, redefining reasonable doubt and clarifying Canada's approach to the admission of hearsay in court proceedings; and *R. v. Chalk*, modernizing the not-criminally responsible defence. He has worked on some of MB's most notorious cases, including the wrongful convictions of Thomas Sophonow and James Driskell, the murder trial of Aaron Molodowic, and the defence for physician and **Abortion** advocate Henry Morgentaler. ● MD

BROKENHEAD OJIBWAY NATION, on reserve pop 549, off reserve pop 1043, is located about 80 km N of **Winnipeg**. This First Nation community signed Treaty 1 in 1871. **Ojibway** is the native local language. There are all-weather roads; there is no air access, but there is float plane and boat docking available. The major economic base here is agricultural production. In 1995, Brokenhead signed a gaming agreement, and from that time on has its own gaming commission, governing on-reserve gaming. The Brokenhead Ojibway Nation administers education, through a local Board of Education and Chief and Council. Schooling in this FN community goes from Nursery-Grade 8, and the total enrolment for 2003-2004 was 164. Brokenhead is comprised of one reserve, called Brokenhead I.R. No. 4. It is a member of the Southeast Tribal Council. Since June 2005, this community, the MB govt, and orchid enthusiasts have designated an area in the Brokenhead Ojibway Nation as the Brokenhead Wetland Ecological Reserve. Sergeant **Thomas George ("Tommy") Prince**, a Canadian war hero and most decorated Aboriginal WWII and Korean War veteran, was born here. Tina Levesque is another important Aboriginal public figure that has served as Brokenhead Chief and has worked toward improving conditions for Aboriginal women. ● RK

BRONFMAN FAMILY. Bronfman patriarch Ekiel Bronfman, born in the **Jewish** town of Soroki, Bessarabia, in what is now Moldova, (d 1919, **Winnipeg**), was a successful tobacco farmer and miller. After suffering through pogroms, he brought his wife Minnie, (d 1918, Winnipeg) and their children to Canada, sponsored by the

B

same initiatives that saw the founding of Jewish agricultural settlements in BENDER HAMLET and NARCISSE. Ekiel tried his hand at WHEAT farming near Wapella, SK, not far from the MB border. When his initial wheat crop failed, the family moved to BRANDON, where Ekiel worked as a general labourer. He also ran a firewood business with his eldest son, Abraham "Abe" Bronfman (b March 15, 1882, Soroki; d March 16, 1968, Safety Harbor, FL) and 2nd son Harry Bronfman (b March 15, 1886, Soroki; d March 16, 1963, Montreal), who left school to help him. Ekiel had mixed success with these varied enterprises, and with the 2 sons, went into the hotel business in the border town of EMERSON in 1903. In those frontier days, hotels took most of their business from selling booze rather than renting beds. Interestingly, this may have once been the family business of the Bronfmans, since *bronfen* is Yiddish for *whisky*.

Thanks to the quick growth of the Northwest and RAILWAY expansion, their hotel proved a success. Ekiel's 3rd son and 4th child, Samuel Bronfman (b Feb 27, 1889, Soroki; d July 10, 1971, Montreal), who had joined his brothers' operation, bought several more hotels on Winnipeg's Main St – including the Bell Hotel. Sam also worked in the fur business. Thanks largely to Sam's success, most of the family moved to Winnipeg's NORTH END. While in Winnipeg, Sam met his future wife, U OF M student Saidye Bronfman (b Saidye Rosner, ca. 1897; d July 7, 1995), of PLUM COULEE. One of Sam's sisters would later marry Harry Druxerman, who owned Winnipeg's Savoy Hotel.

When PROHIBITION in SK (1915-24), MB (1916-23), and the US (1920-33) came into effect, the family operated a grey-market distillery business with a distribution centre in Montreal, as QC had no prohibition, and production of liquor for export from province to province was allowed until 1918. Their mail-order whisky outfit involved a Yorkton, SK moonshine operation in an old warehouse, and an outlet in Kenora, ON. By the time govts became more determined to stem the flow of liquor and dedicated significant manpower to stopping bootleggers, the Bronfmans found another way to sell alcohol: as medicine. Since liquor, with the addition of a few ingredients, was considered medicine, they founded the Canada Drug Pure Company to stock pharmacies and HBC stores with their drink. They also exported liquor to the US, which was legal under Cdn law until 1922.

In 1924, by which time most Cdn provinces had repealed prohibition – still in full swing in the US – the entire family relocated to Montreal and the nearby suburb of La Salle, where Sam

Bronfmans on the "Society Page", 1935

founded the Distillers Corporation Ltd., importing scotch such as Dewar's from a Glaswegian consortium and producing his own blends. He merged his company, by then publicly traded, with 70-year-old Waterloo, ON, whisky-maker Seagram's in 1928. Sam Bronfman proved the driving force behind the expansion of the family business. He had reputed links to Al Capone, and both had extensive dealings in the French territory of Saint-Pierre et Miquelon, S of NF, as these islands had no prohibition or export bans. The Bronfmans also allegedly had ties to Joseph Kennedy, father of US president John Kennedy, and with rumrunners associated with the Purple Gang, Meyer Lansky, and other US crime syndicates. With the end of prohibition in the US in 1933, Seagram's Cdn and scotch whiskies – including Crown Royal, Chivas Regal, and VO – remained among the most popular in the US for most of the 20th century.

Besides expanding the family's alcohol empire, making it the world's largest distiller by the time of his death, Sam was a renowned philanthropist, as was his wife Saidye. Sam served as president of the Canadian Jewish Congress 1939-62, and became a Companion of the Order of Canada in 1967. They founded the Samuel and Saidye Bronfman Family Foundation in 1952, which has contributed, among other things, to renewal projects in Plum Coulee, Saidye's birthplace. Sam's daughter, architect Phyllis Lambert, though born in Montreal, maintains ties to Plum Coulee, and sits on the Plum Coulee Community Foundation's board of trustees. ● A. J. LEVIN

BROOKER, Bertram Richard. painter, author, poet. (b March 31, 1888, Croydon, England; d March 22, 1955, Toronto). Brooker moved to PORTAGE LA PRAIRIE in 1905. His writing career

began in 1914 when he was editor of the *Portage Tribune*, and later he would contribute to the *Winnipeg Tribune* and the *Winnipeg Free Press*. He moved to Toronto in 1921 to take a position as an advertising exec, where he became involved with local artists such as Lawren Harris and his Arts and Letters Club. Although his work was not fully recognized at the time of its production, Brooker is now considered to be among the first abstract expressionists in the country. Paintings such as *Sounds Assembling* (1928) were the first abstract works to be shown in Canada. He was one of the founding members of the Canadian Group of Painters which was founded in 1933. His syndicated column "The Seven Arts" (1928-1930) saw Brooker examine and critique movements in all aspects of Canadian arts and culture. Fellow artist L.L. Fitzgerald was an inspiration to Brooker as both a friend and an artist. His book *Think of the Earth* won the first gov gen's award for fiction in 1936. Every major art gallery in Canada has a piece of Brooker's work in their collection. ● STACEY ABRAMSON

BROOKS, Martha, writer, (b July 15, 1944, NINETTE). Having grown up in a medical family practising in the MB Sanatorium for TUBERCULOSIS patients in Ninette (closed in 1972), Brooks is a self-taught author whose fiction for young adults has won wide recognition, frequently listed among the American Library Best Books. She has been nominated 4 times for the Governor General's Award and won the award in 2002 for her Young Adult novel *True Confessions of a Heartless Girl* (2002). She has received numerous other awards, including the Mr. Christie Book Award, the Ruth Schwartz Award, the Vicki Metcalf Award, the IBBY Honor Award, the McNally Robinson Book of the Year for Young People Award, the Chalmers Best Canadian Children's Play Award, and the Canadian Library Association Young Adult Book Award. Her published books include: *Paradise Cafe and other stories* (1988), *Two Moons in August* (1991), *Travelling on into the Light and Other Stories* (1994), *Bone Dance,* (1997), and *Being with Henry* (1999), all in the young-adult genre; as well as 2 dramas: *I Met a Bully on the Hill* (1995), co-written with Maureen Hunter, and *Andrew's Tree* (1996). Her novels are read worldwide and have been translated into Japanese, Italian, French, and German. Brooks is also a recognized jazz vocalist. In 2002, she won a Prairie Music Award for her debut CD *Change of Heart* (2001). She has given performances at the Jazz Winnipeg Festival, with Winnipeg Symphony Orchestra, at the Top o' the Senator in Toronto, and at the Berlin International Literary Conference in 2004. ● MILDRED GUTKIN

BROWN, Francis ROY, pioneer bush pilot, politician (b Sept 13, 1896, Stockton; d Nov 30, 1960, Winnipeg). Brown lived in Winnipeg until his WWI enlistment in the Cdn Cycle Corps. Brown served in France and Belgium at Ypres, Vimy Ridge, and Passchendaele until 1917, when he joined the RFC. He was a fighter pilot, though not the Roy Brown who shot down Capt Manfred Baron von Richthofen, the German "Red Baron." Returning to MB in 1923, Brown became a bush pilot for **JAMES A. RICHARDSON'S** Western Canada Airways, then superintendent and chief pilot of airmail operations, from 1930-32. Brown was a pilot for Macdonald Brothers Aircraft in Winnipeg, testing aircraft for the Commonwealth Air Training Plan during WWII. In 1947, he organized Central Northern Airways, a predecessor of TransAir Limited. In 1953, Brown became a Liberal-Progressive MLA, representing the northern constituency of Rupertsland. In 1975, Brown was admitted to Canada's Aviation Hall of Fame. ● JIM SHILLIDAY

BROWN, Shirley, multi-media artist. (b March 22, 1943, **TURTLE MOUNTAIN**) was raised in **DELORAINE** where she still resided in 2007. She married Murray Brown in 1964, and in the years following the couple had 2 children. She exhibited her paintings across rural MB, with her first solo exhibition in 1984 at the public library in **BOISSEVAIN**. After being involved in the mentorship program at **MENTORING ARTISTS FOR WOMEN'S ART** (MAWA) in 1986 in Winnipeg, she began to exhibit her work in a much broader arena. Approaching themes of weather and natural phenomenon, such as tornados and fire, she had solo exhibitions at Ace Art Inc. (1989) and the Art Gallery of Southwestern Manitoba (1990). She then began her humorous depictions of Queen Elizabeth II, through paintings, photographs, and 3-dimensional pieces. She was one of the founding members of Coterie of Malcontents in 1994, a group of artists including Barb Flemington and Michael Boss, who banded together to support each other's artistic practices in a rural setting. She was artist-in-residence at several

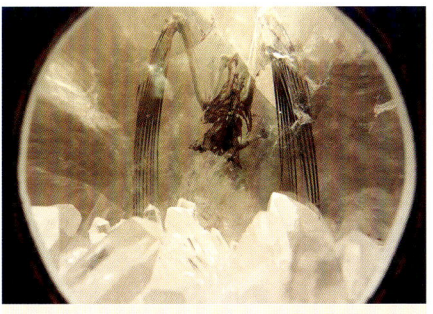

Lightbox #3, Crystals, 2004, mixed media, 25 x 18 x 18 cm, by Shirley Brown

organizations in Canada including Banff Centre for the Arts, Banff, AB (1993) and the Dunlop Art Gallery, Regina, SK (2002). Several of her works have been purchased by the Canada Council Art Bank and the Manitoba Arts Council Art Bank. Her examination and excavation of bird skeletons led to a 2005 solo exhibition at the Winnipeg Art Gallery, "Vestiges." ● STACEY ABRAMSON

BROWNE, Cecil "Cec," hockey player (b Feb 13, 1894, St. James; d Aug 13, 1985, **WINNIPEG**) was named Athlete of the Century (1870-1970) for the MB Centennial Celebration in 1970. Though he was most successful as a professional hockey player, Browne was also proficient in baseball, swimming, track and field, and football. As a hockey player, Browne was first noticed at the age of 18 when he scored 15 goals and 20 points in 5 games for the Winnipeg Strathconas in the World Junior Hockey League. He played in 3 Allan Cups; with the Winnipeg Monarchs in 1915-16, the Regina Victorias in 1923, and the Selkirk Fishermen in 1924. His only NHL season was 1927-28 when he played 13 games for the Chicago Black Hawks. As a result of injuries that hindered his performance, Browne was sold to the Seattle Eskimos in the Pacific Coast Hockey League (PCHL) the following year. He was the lead scorer in the PCHL from 1928-30. The Boston Bruins then purchased his contract in 1930, but Browne opted instead to play football for the Saskatchewan RoughRiders. While in SK, he was named the province's All-Around Track and Field Champion. He then retired to Winnipeg where he continued to stay active in sports as a junior hockey coach. He was inducted into the Manitoba Sports Hall of Fame in 1980. ● MD

BROWNE, Rachel, dancer, choreographer, (b Nov 6, 1934, Philadelphia) is the founder of MB's first modern dance company, Contemporary Dancers. Browne started the company in 1964 and served as the company's artistic director, choreographer, dancer, and teacher for more than 20 years. Under Browne's direction, the company quickly grew to a nationally recognized company. Browne got her start as a dancer in Philadelphia. After graduating from high school, she moved to New York, where she studied ballet and worked as a typist. While there, she studied with many teachers, including Robert Joffrey, Edward Caton, and teachers at the American Ballet Theatre. She worked obsessively to overcome a physical make-up that was considered less than ideal for classical ballet. After performing dance in the production *Oklahoma!* she earned her equity card.

In 1957, Browne accompanied her teacher and mentor Benjamin Harkarvy to Winnipeg

Rachel Browne (back left) instructing dance students, 1971

when he took on the directorship of the **ROYAL WINNIPEG BALLET** (RWB). Browne was offered a 6-month contract with RWB, which she accepted in hopes of returning to the NY dance scene with fresh ideas and performance experience. Browne never returned to NY. Instead, she stayed with the RWB until 1961, when she created Contemporary Dancers. Browne also served as resident choreographer and dancer for the company. Her single-mindedness and determination helped move the company forward, despite serious financial hurdles. Although Browne was dismissed as artistic director after 20 years, she maintains a cordial relationship with Contemporary Dancers. She also continues a close relationship with the professional program of the School of Contemporary Dancers, which she founded, and continues to work as an independent choreographer, teacher, and performer. She has amassed a body of choreography that includes over 70 modern dance pieces. In recognition of her contributions to dance she was appointed Member of the Order of Canada (1997), received a Jean A. Chalmers Award for Creativity in Dance (1995), Canada Council Jacqueline Lemieux Prize (2000), and the Manitoba Arts Council/ Great-West Life Lifetime Achievement Award (2001). ● JILL SEXSMITH

BRUINOOGE, Rod, politician (b 1973, **THOMPSON**) is the Conservative MP for Winnipeg South. Bruinooge is Aboriginal, and lived in **THOMPSON** until 1991. He has a BA in political science from

B

the **U OF M**. In 1995, he developed The Stone, a multiplayer Internet game that became popular internationally, attracting coverage from *Forbes* magazine. He made a documentary about the game and, while promoting the film at international festivals, began to make plans for a similar event to be held in Winnipeg, leading to the establishment of the Winnipeg International Film Festival. He ran unsuccessfully for fed office in 2004. In the 2006 fed election, he defeated incumbent **REG ALCOCK**. As of writing, he was parliamentary secretary to the Minister of Indian Affairs and Northern Development, and Federal Interlocutor for **MÉTIS** and Non-Status Indians. • MD

BRÛLÉ, Jayson TYLER, journalist, publisher (b 1968, **WINNIPEG**). The son of a **WINNIPEG BLUE BOMBERS** player and a local artist, Tyler Brûlé moved to England in 1989 to work as a journalist with the British Broadcasting Corporation (BBC). While covering the conflict in Afghanistan, he was shot in the arm in Mar 1994. While recovering from wounds that left him with limited use of his left arm, Brûlé launched the influential fashion and style magazine *Wallpaper* (1996). The publication became quite successful, and was purchased by Time Warner Inc. Brûlé remained as editor until 2002, during which time he launched unsuccessful titles *Spruce* and *Line*, and founded design and branding agency Winkmedia (now Winkreative). He has developed and produced 2 television shows for the BBC, *The Desk* and *Counter Culture,* and writes columns for several newspapers including the *International Herald Tribune*. In Mar 2007, Brûlé launched *Monocle*, an international design, business, and cultural affairs magazine. • JT

BRUNKILD, pop 105, is an unincorporated community 45 km SW of Winnipeg on the Morris River. Originally inhabited by various Algonquian peoples and later Métis, the area was first surveyed in 1872, and European settlers – primarily Germans and Poles – started to arrive in the 1880s. Local lore claims that the town was supposed to be named Sperling, but **RAILWAY** officials got the section numbers reversed, and "Sperling" was given to a nearby community instead. The community post office opened in 1903 and Brunkild became a **RAILWAY** point in 1903. The community's start was based on agriculture and in the 2000s, farming in the area is still the backbone of Brunkild's economy. However, many residents do commute to Winnipeg for work. • GPP

BRYCE, George, educator, author, clergyman (b 1844, Mount Pleasant [near Brantford], Canada West [ON]; d 1931, ON). After completing a degree at the U of Toronto in 1867 and his religious education in 1871, Bryce moved to MB as an ordained minister with a mandate to establish the first **PRESBYTERIAN** institutions. He began by creating Manitoba College (*see* **U OF M**), and went on to found **WINNIPEG**'s Knox Church (1872) and St. Andrew's Church (1881). In 1877, Bryce was elected to the first Winnipeg school board and became the inspector for public schools. That same year, at the urging of **ALEXANDER MORRIS**, Bryce agreed to combine Manitoba College with St. John's College and St. Boniface College. The 3 became the **U OF M**. Bryce taught science at the new university until 1904. He also played a key role on the university council. Bryce was an accomplished author, finishing 9 books and as many as 50 pamphlets, along with his sermons and speeches. He wrote biographies and area settlement histories, and about the **GEOGRAPHY** and **GEOLOGY** of MB. Bryce's most notable works include 1882's *Manitoba: Its Infancy, Growth, and Present Condition*, one of the first Cdn historiographies; *Canada: An Encyclopaedia of the Country* (1898), in which he wrote at length about the history, culture, and religion of First Nations in Canada; and 1906's *A History of Manitoba: Its Resources and People* (concerning settlement history as well as individual and family biographies). He also penned *The Remarkable History of the Hudson's Bay Company*. Bryce was a director of the Winnipeg General Hospital (later **HEALTH SCIENCES CENTRE**) 1874-79, including a stint as secretary and treasurer. A founder of the Manitoba Historical and Scientific Society, he served as its 4th president from 1884-87 and then again from 1905-13. He was elected to the Royal Society of Canada in 1902, becoming the scholarly organization's president in 1910. • JOEL TRENAMAN

BUCHWALD, Harold, lawyer, volunteer (February 22, 1928, **WINNIPEG**), is one of Manitoba's leaders in law, business, arts, and education. He obtained his LLB and LLM at the **U OF M**, was admitted to the Manitoba Bar in 1952, and was appointed Queen's Counsel in 1965. He is a co-founder of the firm Buchwald Asper (now Pitblado) where he practised for many years.

In addition to his legal practice Buchwald has worked on many community projects. He has served at various times as president of the Winnipeg Symphony Orchestra, the Jewish Foundation of Manitoba, the Law Society of Manitoba, and the Manitoba Bar Association. He was also founding director of the Business Council of Manitoba, director of the Winnipeg Hospital Authority, and chair of the **HEALTH SCIENCES CENTRE** Foundation.

Since his retirement from active practice in 2001, he has served as executive director of Arts Stabilization Manitoba and as a member of the board of the Jewish Foundation of Manitoba. Buchwald has received numerous awards including an Honorary Doctor of Laws from the U of M in 1994. He became a Member of the Order of Canada in 1993. • CATHERINA DE BAKKER

BUDD, Henry, cleric (b 1812, **NORWAY HOUSE**, d Apr 2, 1875, **THE PAS**). Budd was the son of an Indian and a **MÉTIS**. Educated in John West's school, he became a clerk in the **HBC** around 1827 and served in the Columbia River area. Returning to **RED RIVER**, he began teaching at the Upper Church (St. John's) parish school in 1837. In 1840 he was sent to Cumberland House District to teach and become a missionary, and in 1842 he moved to **THE PAS**, where he established the Devon Mission. Budd was ordained a deacon in 1850, the first Aboriginal in North America to be admitted to the Church of England ministry. He was ordained a priest in 1853. He moved to Nipawin, Saskatchewan, and remained there until 1867, when he returned to The Pas. Budd was a big man, an eloquent preacher, and a first-rate farmer. • JMB

BUDDHISM probably arrived informally in MB in the late 19th century with **CHINESE IMMIGRANTS** who worked on the **RAILWAY** and then settled in **WINNIPEG** or other towns, typically to run laundries or restaurants. The first formal Buddhists in MB, and Canada, were Japanese immigrants from what is now BC, where informal "dharma talks" were held as early as 1901. **JAPANESE CANADIANS** who were moved to MB during **WWII** established the Manitoba Buddhist Church in Winnipeg in 1946. In 2006, it had about 300 members who practise Japanese Pure Land Buddhism in both Japanese and English.

Buddhism, which has its origins in **HINDUISM**, bases itself on the teachings of Siddhartha Gautama, known as Shakyamuni Buddha. Born a wealthy prince in Nepal around 563 BC, Siddhartha led a sheltered and luxurious early life, but was later exposed to suffering, illness, and death. Gautama renounced his heritage to become a wandering ascetic, trying to find the secret of suffering and its cure. He followed many gurus and tried many spiritual practices, but none gave him the answers he was looking for. He finally achieved a state of perfect spiritual insight or enlightenment – bodhisattva – during meditation. Known thereafter as the Buddha ("Enlightened One"), he decided to share his insight with others. These disciples formed a monastic order (the *Sangha*) that followed his

Dharma or teachings. All Buddhists today still take refuge in the Buddha, the Dharma (teaching), and the Sangha. Buddhists also abide by 5 moral precepts, namely prohibitions against killing, stealing, lying, being unchaste, and becoming intoxicated. They believe that anyone can achieve enlightenment by following these teachings and precepts.

In the 21st century, there are 3 main schools of Buddhism, each arising from different geographical and cultural areas: Hinayana ("Lesser Vehicle") or Theravada ("Doctrine of the Elders"), Mahayana ("Greater Vehicle"), and Vajrayana ("Diamond Vehicle"). Mahayana split off from the earlier Theravada in about 100 BC, and Vajrayana developed later in Tibet. These divisions have never been as significant as the divisions found in Christianity, because Buddhism takes a pragmatic attitude toward doctrine. Buddhism can embrace very different doctrines provided practitioners are loyal to the essential spirit of the Buddha and to the Sangha. Theravada concentrates on individual enlightenment, and believes that the monastic life best exemplifies the original teaching of the Buddha. Mahayana, now the dominant form of Buddhism, emphasizes that laypersons as well as monks and nuns can achieve enlightenment through faith and devotion, and that spiritual practice and merit should be dedicated to the betterment of all beings, not just the individual practitioner. Vajrayana includes Mahayana practices and distinctive beliefs and rituals practised in and around Tibet. Buddhists do not believe in God in the sense of an ultimate being, but believe in reincarnation until enlightenment is achieved and in karma, the law of cause and effect.

At least 12 Buddhist groups, teaching and practising all 3 schools both formally and informally, are found in MB today. The 2001 Census listed 5745 Buddhists in MB, with an average age of 36. The majority of these are Asian but a strong minority of Westerners has also come to the religion since the 1970s. The largest Buddhist groups in the province are Vietnamese, Laotian, Japanese, and Chinese "Pure Land" Mahayana practitioners. Smaller Theravadan (Zen, Vihara, Vipassana) and Vajrayana (Tibetan Nyingma and other traditions) groups also exist. The number of Buddhists in the province grew by about 9% from 1991-2001, paralleling a growing interest across NA. However, in the early 21st century, Buddhists still made up only 0.5% of MB's population. ● KAREN JOHNSON

BUFFALO POINT FIRST NATION, on reserve pop 42, off reserve pop 67, is located 220 km SE of **WINNIPEG**, in the Lake of the Woods tourist area. Treaty 3 was signed here in 1873. **OJIBWAY** is the native language of this community. It is a member of the Southeast Tribal Council. There are 3 reserves in the First Nation community of Buffalo Point: Buffalo Point I.R. No. 36, Reed River I.R. No. 36A, and Agency I.R. No. 30. The Buffalo Point reserve has the largest harbour on Lake of the Woods, and in all of MB. It consists of 350 boat slips, 250 RV full service sites, an 18-hole golf course, and a community of 275 leased out cottage properties. Schooling for the Buffalo Point First Nation goes from Nursery-Grade 12, and total enrolment for the year 2003-2004 was 22. Students are bussed to Warroad to attend school. This community is accessible via paved road, near the Warroad-US border crossing. The economy in Buffalo Point First Nation is based on timber. The ecosystem includes a vast wildlife management program. Flora and fauna includes whitetail deer, wolves, red foxes, black bears, moose, beavers, muskrats, porcupines, purple fringed orchids, finches, grey owls, ospreys, and bald and golden eagles. ● RK

BUG is a very large group of insects whose representatives are commonly seen in the garden, on crops, around the cottage, and in native plant communities. Originating about 325 mya (Carboniferous Period), hemipterans are a highly successful line with an astonishing 1375 species in MB (3900 species in Canada, 82,000 worldwide). Due to their diversity and sheer numbers, they play prominent roles in all land and aquatic environments, as sap-suckers, predators, and a few blood-suckers. Bugs have piercing and sucking mouthparts, often in the form of a long, thin beak (rostrum). While displaying a bewildering variety of forms, many kinds can be distinguished from beetles and other insects by the large triangular, leathery shield (thorax segment called the scutellum) on the back, and the 'X'-shaped folds of the membranous wings. The front wings are thickened at the base; the second pair are membranous and used for flight. The 3-5-segmented antennae are long and project forward. Many bugs release defensive chemicals from glands on the thorax when disturbed or attacked. Bugs lay their eggs on plants or in the soil, and the nymphs grow through five stages. Some bugs produce live young, while a few other are able to reproduce without fertilization by a male. This group consists of 4 suborders, 3 of which contain familiar types of MB insects: true bugs (Heteroptera), leaf- and tree-hoppers and cicadas (Auchenorrhyncha), and aphids, plant lice and scale insects (Sternorrhyncha). Just a few of the major families common in the province are highlighted here.

Aphids on the march

APHIDS (family Aphidae and others) are small (2-6 mm), soft-bodied insects that frequent the growing tips of plants, where they suck juices. Great volumes of sap are ingested to obtain sufficient scarce amino acids that aphids must excrete excess suger and water as 'honeydew', droplets of which leave all surfaces under the aphids' trees covered in the sticky substance. Ants tend and protect aphids to feed on this honeydew. An aphid's rounded body ends in 2 tubes (cornicles) which secrete a noxious substance that deters predators. Females give birth to hundreds of nymphs from unfertilized eggs, which hatch inside her body. Winged adults leave their host plant and are dispersed in the wind many km to new food sources. This is a very large group with over 365 species in MB (806 species in Canada), which includes many serious pests on agricultural crops and ornament plants; other species specialize on conifers, mosses and ferns.

PLANT BUGS (family Miridae) are mainly sap-suckers, but some are predaceous. They are generally fragile, under 8 mm, with a slim or oval shape, and usually green or brown, and so blend in well on plants. They are often highly abundant, with hundreds easily swept up in a net. Over 241 species are known in MB (the most species of any hemipteran family).

AMBUSH BUGS (family Phymatidae) are highly camouflaged while resting in flowers and quickly grasp insect prey with their strong front legs. Their widened and flattened abdomen at the rear helps break up their insect's profile. There are 2 species in MB (*Phymata americana* and *P. vicina*).

STINK BUGS (families Pentatomidae and Acanthosomatidae) average 10-15 mm and are broadest at the shoulders-like thorax. They emit a smelly odour if handled. Some species are known for their dedicated maternal behaviour. They are common in meadows, prairie and woods, where they lay their eggs on tender plants and suck juices. At least 37 species have been recorded in MB.

SHIELD BUGS (family Scutelleridae) as the name implies are covered by a large shield or scutellum. Most are brown, and give off a noxious odour if handled. Some species are colourful and closely resemble small beetles. The nymphs and adults are sap-suckers. There are 6 species in MB.

SQUASH BUGS (family Coreidae) received their name from their frequent occurrence on the squash, but they often become pests on many kinds of vegetables. Most are a dull brown, but others can be colourful, sometimes with leaf-like expansions of the hind legs. The life cycle is rapid with eggs hatching into nymphs, which after 5 molts reach adulthood in only 3 weeks. There are 4 species in MB.

ASSASSIN BUGS (family Reduviidae) are 10-25 mm long, active predators, always on the alert to attempt to take a blood meal on vertebrates. With their sharp rostrum or beak (consisting of 3 segments), they can deliver a painful bite to the fingers if handled carelessly. There are 6 species are recorded for MB. The front legs are shorter but stronger, used to grasp its prey.

GIANT WATER BUGS (family Belostomatidae) are represented by of 3 aquatic members in MB, with the Toe-biter (*Lethocerus americanus*) being MB's largest insect at 5 cm, plus a long breathing siphon at the rear. It is sometimes found in swimming pools or on the ground under bright lights (such as at a gas station), where it astonishes observers by its huge size and menacing appearance. The flattened body is dull brown and the powerful front legs fold in front to grasp prey. Both the nymph and adult are aquatic and feed on insect larvae, fish, tadpoles, and even frogs, by means of a long piercing beak on the underside of the head. This beak can also inflict a painful bite to one's hand or foot. It is a strong flyer.

WATER SCORPIONS (family Nepidae) are represented in MB by 2 aquatic species (*Nepa apiculata, Ranatra fusca*), which resemble 3 cm stick insects. They hide among the stems of aquatic plants and pounce on passing insects and tadpoles with their long raptorial from legs. They are usually overlooked because they remain motionless and look like a dead plant stem.

BACK-SWIMMERS (family Notonectidae) are small (10-15 mm) aquatic bugs often seen swimming upside-down in ponds and quiet shores of lakes. They paddle rapidly with long, fringed hindlegs in search of tiny organisms in the water, which they locate with their large eyes. They break the surface to breathe with the tip of the abdomen. The male calls females by rubbing its front legs on the rostrum. Adults take to the air in late summer and autumn, often ending up in swimming pools, where they can deliver a painful but not dangerous bite. There are 8 species in MB (e.g., *Notonecta borealis*).

WATER BOATMEN (family Corixidae) are rapid swimmers in ponds and quiet margins of lakes. The 10 mm body is streamlined, with a flat back, and broad head and eyes. The hind legs are long and fringed for rowing. The middle legs for holding onto aquatic plants, while the front legs are modified into scoops for sweeping up tiny pond life, including algae. While built for swimming, these bugs also take to the air at night, and sometimes are attracted by the hundreds to a bright light. There are 40 species in MB.

WATER STRIDERS (family Gerridae) are fast, active predators that run on the surface of streams, ponds, lakes and even the ocean. They are buoyed up by a fine coating of unwettable silver hairs and surface tension of the water acting on their 6 thin legs. Averaging around 2 cm in length, there are 9 MB species, with a common example being *Gerris marginatus*. Most species lay eggs in the spring, the larvae mature by autumn, and adults overwinter.

FROGHOPPERS AND SPITTLEBUGS (family Cercopidae) are small (8 mm) stout insects found feeding on vegetation and which hop suddenly when disturbed. The larva feeds on a plant stem and creates a remarkable protective foam around itself, made by mixing a special fluid with air and expelling it from its anus. These foamy patches are commonly seen on plant stems in meadows. The Boreal Spittlebug (*Apthrophora gelida*) is a widespread species among the 11 recorded in MB (36 species in Canada).

LEAFHOPPERS (family Cicadellida) are small (5-9 mm) insects with a thin, streamlined shape and camouflaging striped pattern of green, blue, red, yellow and black. They are known for their great leaping ability when disturbed. Utilizing piercing-sucking mouthparts, they feed on plant juices. Excess sugary sap is sometimes excreted, which is highly attractive to ants and other insects. In fact, ants tenaciously guard leafhopper aggregations to ensure their crop of honeydew. Canada has at least 1262 species, 360 of which occur in MB.

TREEHOPPERS (family Membracidae) are small (10 mm) insects likely evolved from leafhoppers. With an elongated triangular shape, they are usually colored green or brown. In fact, they present some of the best examples of camouflage, and one would have to look closely on a stem to discover them. Many resemble thorns or buds. The front of the body (prothorax) often ends in sharp defensive spines, which also add to their cryptic appearance. The nymphs have a special tube at the rear which frequently presents droplets of honeydew (sweet, concentrated fruit sap) to ants, which in turn protect them from other predators. Canada has over 100 species, with 41 occuring in MB. • REW

BÜHLER, John "Johnny," businessman, philanthropist (b July 1, 1933, Haskett, MB), founded farm-machinery manufacturer Bühler Industries Inc. The son of a poor **IMMIGRANT MENNONITE** family in **MORDEN**, Bühler dropped out of the Morden Collegiate Institute in grade 10. He then drove a taxi, worked at a gas station, and sold cars. He joined the **CPR** as an assistant station manager at 17 years old, and later opened Bühler Motors, a Ford and Rambler dealership in Morden. In 1970, Bühler bought Standard Gas Engine Works from his father-in-law after acting as its secretary/treasurer. He renamed the company Farm King, and later gave it his own name. Bühler expanded the company in 1981, and has acquired many other companies including Allied Farm Equipment, Ideal Glass and Mirror, Craftech Manufacturing Inc., and Dominion Lumber. Bühler is known for his dynamic approach to business, which involves acquiring troubled businesses at a low price, restructuring them to make them profitable, and then either reselling them or retaining them. Bühler and his wife Bonnie are also well known across MB for their charitable giving. Examples of this include $500,000 donated toward a theatre and music hall at the Mennonite Collegiate Institute at **GRETNA**, $3.5 million to build the John Bühler Research Centre at the **HEALTH SCIENCES CENTRE**, and a $5 million donation to Morden Collegiate to build a performing arts centre in **MORDEN**. He has also made significant donations to **RED RIVER COLLEGE**'s Princess Street Campus and to both the **WINNIPEG SYMPHONY ORCHESTRA** and the Manitoba Chamber Orchestra. Bühler and his wife lived in **WINNIPEG** as of writing, where Bühler continues to act as chair and CEO of Bühler Industries Inc. • AMANDA STEPHENS

BÜHLER INDUSTRIES LTD. became Canada's last remaining tractor manufacturer when it purchased the Versatile tractor plant in Winnipeg from CNH Global (formerly New Holland) in July 2000. Less than 4 months after acquiring the plant, Bühler became involved in a bitter contract dispute with about 250 unionized workers at the plant. At one point, the company threatened to shut down the plant and relocate the operations to ND, and the dispute eventually ended up in front of the Manitoba Labour Board, which fined the company $6000 for bargaining in bad faith. The 9-month strike/lockout finally ended when the disgruntled workers accepted a $17.5-million compensation package in return for giving up their jobs at the tractor plant. The former Versatile plant, which produces 2- and 4-wheel-drive Genesis tractors, is only one of 10 production plants that Bühler Industries owns and operates. It also has 8 other plants in MB and one in Fargo, ND, which it acquired in 2002 from Deere & Co. The other plants produce various different types of agriculture equipment, including front-end loaders, cultivators, grain augers, mowers, landscape rakes, wheel loaders, and tractor-powered snow blowers. Although Bühler Industries is a publicly traded company, the firm's majority owner is **MORRIS**-born businessman **JOHN BÜHLER**, who got his start in the business in 1970 when he bought his father-in-law's agriculture equipment manufacturing plant in Morden. Bühler subsequently began acquiring other production plants in MB, and eventually moved his corporate headquarters to Winnipeg. As of 2004, Bühler Industries employed about 850 people and had approximately $160 million in annual revenues. • MURRAY MCNEILL

BUNIBONIBEE CREE NATION (formerly known as Oxford House First Nation), on reserve pop 2116, off reserve pop 352, is a largely Cree community located along the E shore of Lake Oxford and the Hayes River. It is about 950 km NE of **WINNIPEG**. The native languages here are **CREE** and **OJIBWAY**. An adhesion to Treaty 5 was signed here in 1909. The Bunibonibee Cree Nation has a runway for air travel, and is also equipped with boat and float plane docks. The Bunibonibee Cree Nation administers its own schooling. The community's levels of education range from Nursery-Grade 12, and total enrolment for the year 2003-2004 was 564. This Cree Nation has one reserve, called Oxford House I.R. No. 24 that is on the land between the W side of Oxford Lake, and the E side of Back Lake. The economic base of this Cree Nation community is derived from fuel wood, fishing, and trapping. It is a member of the Keewatin Tribal Council**.** • RK

BUNN FAMILY. The elder Thomas Bunn (b 1764, London, UK; d 1853, **RED RIVER SETTLEMENT**) joined the **HBC** in 1797 first as a clerk, and was posted to Brandon House (*see* **BRANDON**), and then **YORK FACTORY** in 1804. He left the HBC and moved to the Red River Settlement in 1822.

His **MÉTIS** son John Bunn (b c.1802; d 1861, Red River Settlement) went to medical school in Edinburgh, perhaps at the urging of his maternal grandfather, the **SCOTS** doctor – later HBC York Factory chief factor – John McNab. Before he had finished his training, however, he returned to **RUPERT'S LAND** to work for the HBC at Moose Factory [ON] in 1819. In about 1824, he moved to the Red River Settlement to join his father, and set up a medical practice in **MIDDLECHURCH**. From 1831-32, he revisited Scotland to upgrade his medical training. For long periods he was the only doctor to reside in the settlement. In 1835, he became a member of the Council of Assiniboia, and was magistrate of the district 1837-49. John Bunn's extensive public service record also includes the positions of sheriff and governor of the jail (1856-61), Board of Works chairman (1856-61), recorder (1858-61), and coroner (1849-61).

Dr. John Bunn

Thomas Bunn (b 1830, Middlechurch; d 1875) followed in the public service footsteps of his father John. He became the clerk of the Council of **ASSINIBOIA** in 1865, and a member of the council in 1868. At first, he seemed willing to accept the leadership of **WILLIAM MCDOUGALL**, but his skepticism and his Métis roots led him to support **LOUIS RIEL** and the **RED RIVER RESISTANCE** in 1869. Bunn chaired the famous meeting between Riel and **DONALD ALEXANDER SMITH**, and was one of the 40 members of the convention that was formed to negotiate with the Cdn govt. The convention nominated the provisional govt, and Riel named Bunn secretary of state. After Col **GARNET WOLSELEY** and his forces took control of the settlement, Bunn withdrew. He was elected to the new Legislature in 1870 representing St. Clements. • JOEL TRENAMAN

Burbot

BURBOT (Lota lota) is a freshwater member of the mostly marine cod-like fishes (family Gadidae, order Gadiformes, class Osteichthyes, phylum Chordata). Its unusual features include an elongated body resembling an eel, an odd-looking barbel projecting forward from the lower jaw, and tiny scales deeply sunken within the skin. The anal and dorsal fins run along the entire posterior portion of the body and the pelvic fins are placed far forward. It is yellowish-brown superimposed with a dark lacelike pattern. One of the most widely ranging fish in MB, it is absent only from most rivers emptying into Hudson Bay, but occurs in the Churchill and Nelson rivers. Its full range is enormous, covering the northern halves of both NA and Eurasia. Remarkably, the Burbot spawns under the ice in December and January, mainly in the shallows of lakes and rivers (e.g., including the Red and Winnipeg). During the night courtship, a swirling, intertwined mass of about a dozen individuals of mixed sexes moves along the bottom. From 45,000 to 1.4 million eggs are released from each female, fertilized externally by the males, and scattered over sand or gravel substrates. This species averages 40 cm and 1 kg in MB, but can grow up to a length of 99 cm and 8 kg in Canada (and even up to 120 cm and 34 kg in Eurasia). The life span may reach 15 years. This species feeds on insects, crustaceans and fish, including species like the Deepwater Sculpin, so Burbot can live at the bottom of MB's deepest lakes (over 200 m). In summer it prefers cold water (16C), but appears tolerant of warmer river waters up to a maximum of 23C. Burbot flesh is exceptional eating, but often anglers reject it, perhaps due to the fish's unusual appearance. • REW

BURKA, Sylvia, speed skater, cyclist (b May 4, 1954, **WINNIPEG**) was the top Cdn speed skater of her time. She was also a competitive cyclist, making her one of the first Cdn women to compete in 2 world championships in the same year. Burka, who was left with only 1 eye following a childhood accident, won her first national speed skating title in 1967 at the age of 15. Her first international title came at the world junior speed skating championships in 1973. She was Canada's top female speed skater through the 1970s, setting a total of 40 national speed skating records and winning 5 Cdn titles. At the 1976 Olympics, Burka

B

placed 4th in the 1500 m, but just 2 weeks later won the world speed skating championship, a title she claimed again in 1977. In total, Burka won 21 world speed skating titles over the course of her athletic career, and set 2 world records. Like many speed skaters, Burka was also a cyclist. In 1977, she finished 4th in the individual pursuit at the world championships. Her most noted accomplishment in cycling was her 1980 world record, which she set during a 1000 m time trial. She was named Manitoba Female Athlete of the Year a total of 6 times, and was named Manitoba's Amateur Female Athlete of the Century in 2000. She is a member of the Canadian Sports Hall of Fame. Burka moved to Toronto following her retirement from competitive sport, where she started an active wear company. • MD

BURKE-GAFFNEY, Chris, rock musician, singer/songwriter, producer, manager (b Sept 5, 1956, **Lynn Lake**). Burke-Gaffney moved to **Winnipeg** in 1957 and began his music career after meeting drummer Terry Norman Taylor at **Roman Catholic** St. Ignatius School in the early 1970s. With guitarist Lou Petrovich and Brent Diamond on keyboards, they formed the Pumps in '78, a popular power-pop band that released its debut album *Gotta Move* in 1980. A feature in *Maclean's* magazine and opening for AC/DC in a North American tour failed to generate sales, and a dispute with their label led to a 3-year hiatus. They returned in 1983 as Orphan with the album *Lonely at Night*, with Steve McGovern replacing Petrovich. "Miracle," written by Burke-Gaffney, became a Cdn hit. *Salute* followed in 1985, but the band broke up that year. Chris formed the Deadbeat Honeymooners before turning to production and representation, forming CBG Artist Management in 1996. He managed **Chantal Kreviazuk**'s early songwriting, as well as discovering and producing pop duo McMaster & James, Eagle & Hawk, Little Hawk (Troy Westwood), and blues guitar sensation Kyle Riabko. The Prairie Music Association (as it was then known) named Burke-Gaffney "Manager of the Year" 3 years running 2000-02, and he won a 2005 Western Canadian Music Award for Manager of the Year. He has written and recorded songs for several movies and television shows, including *Chicago Hope*, *Real World*, and *Providence*, and continues to develop Cdn talent • JOHN EINARSON

BURLAKOW, Klaus ("Patrick Burke"), bank robber, bureaucrat (b Mar 18, 1954, **Winnipeg**) embarked on a string of bank robberies in 2002-03 after serving nearly 30 years as a civic bureaucrat. Born to Russian parents, he earned a BA from the **U of W** before beginning a career with Winnipeg's Parks and Recreation Department, eventually landing a senior administrative position under Mayor **Glen Murray**. In this capacity, he helped plan the 1999 Pan American Games. Burlakow, often described by City Hall staff as an abrasive character, took an early retirement package in 2001. Burlakow began his robbery spree in Nov of the following year, hitting 6 Winnipeg banks by Feb. He became known as the "Fat Bandit" because of his ample girth. His spree ended on Feb 14, 2003, after he led police on a car chase that finished with his truck being stuck in a snow-filled ditch in rural MB. In a humorous incident, the 155 kg (340 lb) Burlakow then had to be pulled out of a car window, causing several police officers to stumble under his weight. Burlakow pled guilty to 7 charges of robbery, admitting to a Vancouver robbery as well, and was sentenced to 8 (later changed to 10) years in prison and ordered to pay $25,000 in restitution. Burlakow claimed he needed the money to pay off debts to US drug traffickers. After his arrest, it was soon discovered that Burlakow had led a double life, living lavishly while posing as a former Irish Republican Army member and businessman named "Patrick Burke" in Seattle. • MD

BURTNYK, Kerry & Team, curling (1995) overcame an initial losing streak in the 1994-95 season to bring home MB's first world title in men's curling since Orest Meleschuk's team in 1972. The team of Kerry Burtnyk, Jeff Ryan, Rob Meakin and Keith Fenton showed little promise after failing to win any titles in the first part of the season, but made a tremendous comeback in the 2nd half after winning the Eaton Trophy, gaining them a spot in the provincial championship. Wins at the Safeway Select in Winnipeg and the Cdn Brier in Halifax followed, earning the team a spot at the world championships in Brandon. In the final, Burtnyk performed a perfect double-takeout with his last stone to take home the title. At 21 years old, Burtnyk was the youngest man ever to skip world title-winning team. He continues to skip successful teams. • MD

BUS MANUFACTURING has become so significant in MB that the province is now the industry capital of NA. That status is due to the presence of 2 industry leaders – **New Flyer Industries** (NFI), a **Winnipeg**-based firm that designs and manufactures urban transit buses; and **Motor Coach Industries** (MCI), also Winnipeg-based, which designs and manufactures intercity highway coaches. In 2004, the latest year for which MB govt figures were available as of writing, New Flyer produced about 30% of the 4495 transit buses that were purchased that year in NA, making it the largest transit-bus manufacturer on the continent. That same year, Motor Coach manufactured about 45% of the 1668 intercity buses that were sold, which also made it the top player in its market segment. MCI also suffered an "off" year in 2004, because it traditionally produces more than 50% of all the intercity buses sold yearly in NA.

New Flyer diesel-electric hybrid, 2006

MCI and NFI both got their starts in the 1930s as auto body shops, subsequently branching out into the manufacture of buses. MCI – or Fort Garry Motor Body and Paint Works Ltd., as it was originally called – was first out of the starting block when its founder, Harry Zoltok, came up with a design for an 11-passenger bus in 1933. NFI (or Western Auto & Truck Body Works, as it was then known) followed Zoltok's lead 4 years later. New Flyer also started out producing inter-city buses and, like MCI, was a small regional player for its first few decades. Not until 1968, when it switched to making urban transit buses, did NFI gain an international presence, selling buses and trolley buses to public transit systems throughout Canada and the US.

MCI gained an international market after Greyhound Canada acquired full ownership of the firm in 1958 and developed the first 12 m motor coach, which it called the MC-6. Greyhound and the other owners that followed – including Grupo Dina, of Mexico, and JLL Partners, a US-based private equity firm – continued to improve on that groundbreaking product, introducing several other models, including a new luxury coach.

Their ability to come up with innovative new products has helped propel MCI and NFI to the head of the pack in the North American bus manufacturing industry. By 2005, MCI's D-series coaches were the most popular highway coaches on the continent, while NFI continued to win over new customers with its low-floor and articulated buses, as well as its environmentally friendly, alternate-fuel models, which run on such fuels as hydrogen cells, compressed natural gas, and liquid natural gas. NFI also developed various diesel-electric and gasoline-electric hybrid models, as well as buses made with composite materials and electronic controls – features which made them lighter, easier to maintain, and less costly to operate.

While MCI and NFI have become leaders within their market segments, they've also encountered their share of potholes along the way. MCI found itself in straits after the Sept 11, 2001, terrorist attacks, but has continued to succeed largely because of a worker-approved restructuring. New Flyer, meanwhile, went through several ownership changes between early 2002 and late 2003 before regaining a firm footing. It has a new lease on life thanks in part to its environmentally friendly alternative fuel engines. ● MURRAY MCNEILL

BUTTERFLY is the most familiar and best loved of all insects. The group is usually separated into the true butterflies (superfamily Papilionoidea) and skippers (superfamily Hesperioidea), but in reality there are intermediate families grading in features from true butterflies to skippers to moths. MB has 111 species of butterflies and 33 skippers, totalling 144 (293 in Canada, 750 in NA, 18,000 worldwide). Butterflies are well known due to their bright colours and conspicuous day-flying habits. Adults have 2 pairs of scale-covered wings, which are large relative to the thin hairy body. The wing scales (actually flattened setae or hairs) overlap one another like shingles on a roof, and are responsible for often-brilliant wing colour via reflection from pigments and/or diffraction of light. Scales also assist in thermoregulation and provide a means of escape (e.g., from sticky spider webs) by rubbing off easily. A large proportion of MB species are darkly coloured, allowing them to heat up quickly by basking in the sun on cold mornings. The mouthparts are long, tubular, and held in a tight coil prior to sucking up nectar from floral nectaries, juices from soft fruits, and fermenting sap, as well as moisture and salts from puddles and animal droppings. The two antennae are clubbed in butterflies, clubbed and hooked in skippers, and come in a great variety of shapes (often feathery) in moths. The feet have chemoreceptors which activate nerve impulses when in contact with appropriate food plants.

Butterfly development is described as complete metamorphosis, incorporating all 4 stages – egg, larva (caterpillar), pupa (chrysalis) and adult. The worm-like caterpillar is the herbivorous feeding stage, utilizing strong, chewing mouthparts. There are 6 hook-like legs on the thorax and up to 5 pairs of abdominal prolegs (pads with sticky surfaces), which disappear in the chrysalis stage. Caterpillars are either camouflaged while on food-plant leaves, flowers and stems, or brightly coloured, which warns predators of distasteful or toxic chemicals (manufactured or sequestered from food plants) stored in their bodies. Butterflies do not build a silk cocoon (like most moths), but form a naked chrysalis, inside which larval tissues are broken down chemically and reorganized into the adult. The chrysalis is usually attached to vegetation, but may be hidden in the ground litter. While adults of small species like Blues live only a week or two, most species survive for 2-4 weeks. Adult Monarchs may live up to 9 months. There are 5 families of butterflies found in MB, although some researchers split these into additional families based on patterns of wing veins and other features.

SKIPPERS (family Hesperiidae) are small-to-mid-sized (2-5 cm), moth-like butterflies with a stout body and head, antennae set far apart and ending in a club (most hook shaped), and brown to orange wings. They are fast darting flyers; hence the name skippers. At rest they keep the forewings at a 45-degree angle and the hind wings horizontal, unlike true butterflies which hold all 4 wings vertically or horizontally. The pupa is also unusual in that it is made with silk threads and leaves. There are 33 MB species, a number of which are known in MB from only a few specimens, either N strays or the result of habitat loss from agricultural activities. The rare Powesheik Skipper (*Oarisma powesheik*) is found in MB only in tall-grass prairie around **TOLSTOI**. The Uncas Skipper (*Hesperia uncas*), whose habitat is dry sandy hillsides and pastures, was last seen in MB in the Carberry area in 1978. The Ottoe Skipper (*Hesperia ottoe*) is found only in mixed-grass prairie in the Spruce Woods area (its only occurrence in Canada). MB holds the largest remaining population of the threatened Dakota Skipper (*Hesperia dacotae*). The bright-orange European Skipper (Thymelicus lineola), introduced accidentally to NA in 1910, was first found in MB at Winnipeg in 1972, and it now occurs throughout the S and C regions of the province. The Roadside Skipper (*Amblyscirtes vialis*) is the most-widely distributed skipper in NA and is common throughout the S half of MB in deciduous and coniferous forests and prairie.

SWALLOWTAILS (Papilionidae) are medium-to-large (5.5-14 cm) butterflies with hindwings each ending in a long 'tail.' Swallowtails are spectacular in bold patterns of yellow, black and orange – colours that warn predators of the frequent presence of toxic chemicals stored in their body and acquired from their larval plant foods. They are swift and strong fliers, often seen gliding over the tree canopy and patrolling back and forth over meadows and forest trails. They are quick to take erratic evasive action on the approach of a bird or person. There are 6 species recorded in MB, however the Pipevine Swallowtail (*Battus philenor*) is known from only one specimen taken at Killarney, and there are but 2 records of the Giant Swallowtail (*Papilio cresphontes*), taken at Winnipeg. The latter is the largest butterfly reported in MB, with a wingspan up to 14 cm. Both species' records represent windborne strays from the USA, as they cannot survive the winter here, and their larval food plants are absent. The Old World Swallowtail (*Papilio machaon*) and Tiger Swallowtail (*Papilio glaucus*) are widespread in forests, sometimes found as far N as **CHURCHILL**. Swallowtail caterpillars have a remarkable variety of defensive strategies, the most notable being a pair of fleshy orange glandular horns (osmeteria) behind the head capsule, which protrude and secrete protective, noxious chemicals (e.g., isobutyric and 2-methylbutyric acids) when attacked by predators. In some species the caterpillars posses large, staring eye spots (perhaps serving a defensive function) on the front of the body, while caterpillars of the Black Swallowtail (Papilio polyxenes) and Giant Swallowtail mimic black and white bird droppings. Swallowtails overwinter in the chrysalis stage, and there are 1 or 2 generations per year in the Black Swallowtail and1 per year in the Tiger and Old World Swallowtails.

WHITES, SULPHURS AND MARBLES (family Pieridae), represented in MB by 17 species, are coloured white, yellow, or orange, and with black or pink borders and dots. Males often have more ultraviolet-absorbing pigment in the wings than females, providing the butterflies with a means of sexual identification by means of different patterns, which are indiscernible by the human eye. The Western White (*Pontia occidentalis*), checkered with black and charcoal, is found in prairie settings and farmyards, where it searches out members of the mustard family to lay its eggs. Two annual broods on the wing from April to Sept, and populations are highest during hot, dry summers. The 11 species of Sulphurs are attractive medium-sized yellow or orange butterflies variously marked with black borders. Several of these are rare strays, such as the Mexican Sulphur (*Eurema mexicana*), while the Dainty Sulphur (*Nathalis iole*) is an irregular migrant into S MB. Others species, like the Arctic Sulphur (*Colias hecla*) and Palaeno Sulphur (*Colias palaeno*) are members of the tundra community in N MB. The largest is the Giant Sulphur (*Colias gigantea*) with a wingspan of up to 5.5 cm, being common in willow bogs in boreal forest. The Cabbage White (*Pieris rapae*), a native of Eurasia and North Africa, was introduced by accident in Quebec in 1860 and has since become one of the most abundant and widespread butterflies in NA. It is the white butterfly commonly seen in backyards and agricultural fields across the S third of MB. Its larvae, called the cabbage worm, is a serious pest of crops of the mustard (cruciferous) family such as broccoli, cabbage and cauliflower. There are several reasons behind this species' remarkable success including human assistance with the widespread planting of favoured food plants, the ability to produce 3 generations per year in MB, and defensive chemicals that deter predators in both adult and larval stages (e.g., mayolene lipids and pinoresinol secreted by glandular hairs along the caterpillar's back).

BRUSH-FOOTED BUTTERFLIES (family Nymphalidae) have reduced, brush-like forelegs that are not used for walking. There are 61 species present in MB. This group includes the famous Monarch (*Danaus plexippus*) and the orange

Butterfly feeding on Prairie wildflowers

and black Painted Lady (*Vanessa cardui*), both of which cannot survive MB's cold winters, and must repopulate southern Canada each spring via immigration from the S US. The White Admiral (*Limenitis arthemis*) is a common black species with blue and orange spots and white bars. It is often seen sipping at puddles along forest trails, slowly raising and lowering its wings. Its overwintering caterpillar, resembling a bird dropping, hibernates high up in its food-plant trees (poplars and birches), and the adults emerge from the chrysalis in June. The brownish-orange Macoun's Arctic (Oeneis macounii) is unusual in that it is found in Jack Pine-dominanted boreal forest only in even-numbered years E of the Red River and Lake Winnipeg, and in odd-numbered years in W MB. One of MB's most spectacularly coloured butterflies is the Great Spangled Fritillary (*Speyerai cybele*), with a dazzling pattern of orange, yellow, black, and silver spots. It has a wingspan up to 7 cm and its larva feeds on species of violets in forested meadows.

GOSSAMER BUTTERFLIES (family Lycaenidae) include the gems of the butterfly world – Blues, Hairstreaks, Elfins and Coppers, totalling 27 species in MB. These are small (12-45 mm wingspan) and delicately-built butterflies. The caterpillars of certain species have abdominal glands which produce a honeydew attractive to ants, thereby gaining the ants' protection, and sometimes feeding on nest debris and ant larvae. Other larva hide inside the food plant or under a rolled leaf. The silvery-blue Spring Azure (*Celastrina* argiolus), widespread throughout NA and EA, occurs all over the province and appears while there is snow lingering on the ground. As the season progresses, many other species of Blues appear, often marked with orange and black. Hairstreaks are named for the hair-like tails on the hindwings. The most-common species is the Striped Hairstreak (*Satyrium*

liparops) with white streaks on the brown undersides. The caterpillars feed mainly on wild cherry and adults peak in early July. The greyish-brown Hoary Elfin (*Callophrys polios*) is the most-abundant and widespread of several Elfins, reaching as far N as Churchill. Its bright-green larva feeds exclusively on Bearberry (*Arctostaphylos uva-ursi*). Coppers are mainly found in bogs, where the males are territorial and aggressively chase invading males away. An example is the tiny (20 mm) Bog Copper (*Lycaena epizanthe*) which feeds exclusively on cranberries and may be found in large numbers in a small bog or clearing. An eastern species, it reaches its W limits at Riding Mountain National Park.

LEPIDOPTERANS AND CADDISFLIES (Tricoptera) likely arose from a common ancestor about 200 mya (early Jurassic) and diversified 110-90 mya (middle Cretaceous period) with the proliferation of flowering plants (angiosperms). Today's butterflies and close relatives are more recent, likely appearing 65-70 mya (late Cretaceous period), but diversifying 60-15 mya (early to middle Tertiary period). Butterfly larvae are major herbivores in many biological communities, and many plants have evolved showy flowers and nectar treats to attract adult butterflies for pollination. Due to their conspicuousness, beauty, diversity, and the fact that certain species are serious crop pests, butterflies are among the best studied of all insects. They have played prominent roles in beliefs and mythologies of almost all human cultures. They attract the attention of poets, naturalists and artists; witness the abundance of butterfly field guides and use as motifs in decorative crafts and jewellery. These insects have also played a major role in ecological and environmental research. Increasingly, many species are becoming threatened (particularly those dependant on prairie ecosystems) from habitat loss and pesticides. ● REW

CATFISH (BROWN BULLHEAD),
see page 113

CADDISFLY is an insect that resembles a dull-brown moth, but has long, thin, forward-held antennae. There are 2 pairs of triangular, hairy wings. Caddisflies are found everywhere in the world (except polar regions) where there is clean water, but quickly die off with pollution. Most species are active at night, and remain hidden during the day. The males often swarm in the air, where they attract and mate with females, which then lay masses of eggs underwater, usually attached to plants. The great innovation of larvae is silk production, to weave food-capturing nets and to construct protective cases – tunnel-like, elaborate structures from pieces of plant debris, pebbles, sand, or a combination of these materials. These cases are often species specific in detail, and resemble beautiful mosaic works of art (straight to helical). The larva remains inside the case and captures food and feeds from the larger open end with its 3 pairs of legs and chewing mouthparts, while other families of caddisflies capture their food in a sticky net. Some cases are fixed with silk to the bottom, while others are portable. These marvellously crafted, well-camouflaged creations (3 mm to 5 cm) are well-worth searching for on stream and pond bottoms. They can be quite numerous in the shallows. The larvae eat plants (algae) or tiny animals (crustaceans), but the adults take only liquids. As the larva grows, it molts at five stages (instars) and one pupal stage, all inside the protective case. The mature insect then crawls to the surface where its wings complete development. Depending on the species, the life cycle may take 1, 2 or 3 years. There are 10 families totalling 150 species known in MB, however the actual number may approach 200 (750 in Canada; 8000 worldwide). Other predatory insects, fish, frogs and shorebirds seek out both larvae and adults as an important source of food. This is another ancient group of insects, closely related to moths and butterflies, and traceable back 280 mya (Permian Period). ● REW, TDG

CADHAM PROVINCIAL LABORATORY (CPL) is MB's largest provincial public-health laboratory. The CPL's main research activities included microbiology, the study of parasites, testing blood for antibodies, virus detection, bacteria research, newborn screening, and screening of at-risk populations. The lab employs research specialists trained to respond in crisis situations. CPL is the principle laboratory to respond in outbreak investigations. Each year, the lab investigates more than 60 outbreaks, including syphilis and hepatitis A in 2003. Every West Nile virus season, CPL conducts human and mosquito analysis. The

C

lab also performs regular tests for pathogens, diseases, viruses, and bacteria such as *Escherichia coli*, HIV, Lyme disease, and influenza. CPL also evaluates suspicious packages for biohazardous materials. Since 2001, CPL has investigated more than 50 suspicious packages and substances from all over MB. CPL is the central public-health microbiology reference laboratory for MB, and operates an infection control program in support of rural hospitals, long-term care facilities, and the Health Ministry's disease control programs. Originally known as the Board of Health Laboratory, the first facility was built in 1897. The lab served to identify carriers of infectious diseases and to test for bacteria in water and milk. CPL's original location was in the MB Medical College at Kate St. and McDermot Ave. in Winnipeg, and was run under the direction of Dr. **Gordon Bell**. Dr. Fred T. Cadham succeeded Dr. Bell following the latter's death in 1923. Upon Dr. Cadham's retirement in 1947, the laboratory was renamed the Fred T. Cadham Public Health Laboratory and was again renamed the Cadham Provincial Laboratory in 1980. The Cadham Provincial Laboratory is now on Winnipeg's William Ave. The facility has expanded to provide a range of public health services, including research, diagnostics, laboratory testing, referral, and consultations throughout MB and in SK. ● JILL SEXSMITH

CAMERON, Alastair Graham Walter, space scientist, (b June 21, 1925, **Winnipeg**; d Oct 3, 2005, Tucson, AZ), was a leading 20th-century astrophysicist. He conducted research in astrophysics, planetary sciences, and meteoritics. Born in Winnipeg to Canadians of **Scots** descent, Cameron began his career as an undergraduate at the **U of M**. He later earned a doctorate in nuclear physics at the U of Saskatchewan. Cameron developed an early theory of nucleosynthesis, the production of the chemical elements in stars. For 26 years, he worked at Harvard U, where he served as the head of the astronomy department. Over the last 30 years of his life, his studies greatly influenced the US Planetary Exploration program. Cameron chaired the Space Science Board of the US's National Academy of Sciences 1976-82. He was a strong advocate for academic freedom, and of the need of govt funding for research. In 1983, Cameron received NASA's Distinguished Public Service Medal; in 1988, he won the J. Lawrence Smith Medal from the National Academy of Sciences; and, in 2006, he was honoured with the Hans A. Bethe Prize from the Division of Nuclear Physics of the American Physical Society. Cameron became a leader and innovator in applying new computer technology to solve astrophysics quandaries. ● RK

Sir Douglas Colin Cameron, ca 1915

AM, PERSONALITY FILES, N21825.

CAMERON, Sir Douglas Colin, businessman, politician (b June 8, 1854, Hawkesbury, Canada West [ON]; d Nov 27, 1921, Toronto). Born and educated in eastern ON, Cameron migrated to **Brandon** in 1878, entering the lumber business and organizing the Rat Portage Lumber Company and the Maple Leaf Flour Mills. He was a millionaire by 1910, and the owner of a stable of prizewinning horses. He became mayor of Rat Portage (now Kenora, ON), and represented Fort William (later Thunder Bay) and Lake of the Woods in the ON Provincial Parliament 1902-05. He was subsequently defeated, and moved to Winnipeg in 1905. Cameron was made lt gov of MB 1911-16, and was knighted in 1913. While Cameron was in office, the **Legislative Building** scandal led to the demise of the govt of Sir **Rodmond Roblin**. Sir Douglas asked **Liberal Party** leader **T.C. Norris** to form a Cabinet, and called a Royal Commission to investigate the scandal. ● AJL

CAMERON, Duncan, fur trader, politician (b ca 1764, Glen Moriston, Highland, UK; d May 15, 1848, Williamstown, Canada West [ON]), was a key figure in the disputes between **Lord Selkirk**'s settlers and the **NWC**. The Scottish-born Cameron went to New York with his parents in 1773 and joined a Loyalist regiment in 1780. In 1785, he came to QC, and entered the **Fur Trade** in association with independent traders who were competing with the **HBC** northwest of Lake Nipigon. In 1795, he became a partner of the NWC, remaining in charge of the Nipigon Department until 1807, when he was sent to **Lake Winnipeg**. His clerks admired him very much. In 1814, he and Alexander Macdonell were put in charge of the Red River Department, in direct confrontation with the **Red River Settlement**. Cameron dressed in military uniform and insisted that he was "the chief of this Country." He and Macdonell convinced most of the Selkirk colonists to depart for Upper Canada [ON] in NWC canoes in 1815. A year later, he was arrested by **Colin Robertson** at **Fort Gibraltar**, sent to **York Factory**, and finally sent to the UK. He never stood trial for his actions, however, and after his return to Canada in 1820, he sued Robertson for false imprisonment. Cameron subsequently settled in Glengarry Cty, Upper Canada, representing Glengarry in the House of Assembly from 1825-28. ● JMB

CAMP MORTON, pop 379, is a community 95 km N of **Winnipeg** on **Lake Winnipeg**. Camp Morton was first named Faxa, presumably after the bay by the same name in Iceland, where the area's original settlers came from. In 1869, this area was purchased from the **HBC**; in 1870 it became part of MB. German settlers started to come into the area in 1901. The **CPR** began building a rail line in

The Champion Tower at Camp Morton.

1906 and after some delay was completed in 1914. In 1924, the Sisters of Service came to the area and took charge of the schools. Acreage along the lake shore was purchased by Monsignor Thomas W. Morton, rector of St. Mary's Cathedral of Winnipeg in 1919. A ROMAN CATHOLIC summer camp was established in 1920 for orphaned and underprivileged children. Shortly after this, the community became known as Camp Morton. Morton constructed a private residence on site, which became his retirement home. Many of the buildings used stackwall construction. Over the years, there were many additions to the camp such as a chapel, sunken garden, flower gardens, ponds, grotto, tennis courts, lawn bowling greens and many structures for houseguests and volunteer staff. The camp operated until the late 1960s, when a decline in interest and funding led to its closure. In 1974, the camp became a provincial recreational park, complete with log cabins and camping. Some of the original buildings have been preserved. ● TERILL ADAMIK

CAMPBELL, A. Lorne, lawyer (b Sept 18, 1920, **WINNIPEG**). Following service with the Canadian Army in WWII as a LCol with the Canadian Reserve Forces, he was called to the Bar in 1947. He practised with the firm of Campbell, Kelly & Mercury until 1964, when he joined Aikins, MacAulay & Thorvaldson, where he practised until his retirement in 2005. During his years in private practice he held the highest office of both provincial and national lawyer associations, as president of the Manitoba Bar Association (1960-61) and the Canadian Bar Association (1970-71). In between, he also served as president of the governing body of MB's legal profession, The Law Society of Manitoba (1966-67). Active in promoting the rights and interests of the disabled, he was the first president of the Canadian Rehabilitation Council for the Disabled (1962), and president of the Society for Manitobans with Disabilities (1962-63). In 1985 he was named an Officer of the Order of Canada. ● DOUG JOHNSTON

CAMPBELL, Douglas Lloyd, politician, premier, (b May 27, 1895, Flee Island; d Apr 23, 1995, **WINNIPEG**) was born in a small farming community near Delta Marsh, 25 km NE of Portage la Prairie. His parents had a large 480 ac (200 ha) farm originally homesteaded in 1880. Douglas was educated at Flee Island, at Portage la Prairie Collegiate Institute, and at **BRANDON COLLEGE**. A classic representative of MB's Anglo-Ontarian settlers, he was a member of the United Church and the Freemasons. Not long after he took over the family farm, he was nominated as a United Farmers of MB candidate in the 1922 election for

Lakeside constituency, which he would represent throughout his long political career.

From the outset, Campbell was an agrarian populist. He did not believe in any of the more extreme versions of agrarianism current in 1922, but instead held that farmers were experienced administrators who could and should run govts as they had to run their farms, efficiently and without running into debt. Campbell was a backbencher in the coalition govt of **JOHN BRACKEN** until 1936, when he was appointed MB's minister of Agriculture and Immigration. He served in this post quietly but competently, adding the responsibility for the MB Power Commission to his portfolio in 1942. It was under his guidance that MB began the process of rural electrification in 1945, beginning with 1000 farms as a test and then setting 5000 farms annually as a goal, until all the settled parts of the province were electrified more than a decade later.

Douglas Campbell, ca 1948

In 1948, he was chosen premier by his coalition colleagues, succeeding **STUART GARSON** as MB's second native-born premier. In 1949, he also was named the leader of the Liberal-Progressive Party. Campbell became premier at a critical juncture in MB's history. The province's farmers were gradually losing their dominant position in the economy and in the population as well, and the City of Winnipeg was becoming increasingly demanding. The equitable distribution of seats in the legislature would become an important issue. The Campbell govt stonewalled on issues of symbolic importance to farmers, like the **MARGARINE DEBATE**, throughout its period in office. Postwar MB had new needs for energy, an expanded educational system, increased social

services (including hospital and medical care), and northern development, while its economy and its tax base was changing little. In addition, the Campbell govt would soon face 2 unexpected crises – serious flooding threats in the Red River Valley in 1950, and an epidemic of polio in 1951 – that would test its credibility.

Within his own assumptions, which were that dealing with the **FLOOD** damage of 1950 required large amounts of federal assistance, Campbell did his best. He was an articulate speaker in the legislature, and effective on the hustings and elsewhere, defending his govt from charges of inaction and frugality by insisting that it was doing as much as the provincial revenue would allow and putting as much blame as possible on the federal govt for inequitable revenue-sharing arrangements.

Throughout his tenure, Campbell's strategy was delay as long as possible, then to appoint a Royal Commission to study a problem before acting on it, and then to respond to the commission's recommendations slowly and cautiously. One typical example was liquor reform. Campbell did not appoint a commission on the subject until 1954, headed by his old political mentor John Bracken, and his administration did not pass the new *Liquor Control Act* until 1956, when it accepted most of the Bracken commission's moderate recommendations. On flood control, Campbell delayed until 1956, then appointed a commission to make a cost-benefit analysis of possible actions. The **RED RIVER FLOODWAY** was not voted upon in the legislature until 1962 under **DUFF ROBLIN**'s administration, with Campbell and his rump of Liberals loudly in opposition.

It was not that the Campbell regime did nothing but it did fall further behind other provinces in important areas of social and economic policy. Ironically, the issue that most bedevilled Campbell throughout his administration and beyond it – the Red River Floodway – had no analogue in other provinces. In 1956, the Campbell govt signed an agreement with Inco for joint development of the nickel mine at Thompson, but in general, it allowed private enterprise its own way with the north.

The several Campbell govts – a coalition govt with the Conservatives in 1949, a Liberal govt in 1954 – contained few high-profile politicians. This cut down on dissent in the ranks, but cost Campbell heavily in his 1958 bid for re-election. His Liberals lost their majority. Campbell attempted to hang on through a coalition with the CCF, but the 2 parties finally agreed they had little in common. Campbell was not effective in opposition, and **GILDAS MOLGAT** replaced him as leader in 1961. In 1969, Campbell was appointed to the MB Hydro

Board, but resigned 1½ years later, claiming the board was wasting too much money.

One of his political opponents claimed that Liberal Douglas Campbell was the most consistently conservative politician he had ever encountered. In his later years – he lived a few days short of his 100th birthday, dying in 1995 – Campbell was often in the news supporting various neo-conservative movements. • J.M. BUMSTED

CAMPER, now essentially a ghost town, was one of the Prairie communities that was supposed to offer a new start to Jewish immigrants. Located 150 km NNW of Winnipeg, in 1911, the community was also known as New Hirsch, after Maurice Baron de Hirsch, a German **JEWISH** philanthropist who encouraged European Jews to immigrate to agricultural colonies in Canada (*see* **BENDER HAMLET**). Accordingly, Jewish families from Russia began to settle here around 1910. The name "Camper" came from a **ROMAN CATHOLIC** missionary, Rev Joseph Charles Camper, who worked in the area for more than 30 years. A post office and **RAILWAY** point were both established in 1911 a few years after settlement began. In its early years, the economy thrived on dairying and raising cattle. However, when prices declined after WWI, many residents were forced to leave. By 1924, the community had dissolved, and the last store in the community closed in 1980. • GPP

CAMPERVILLE, pop 650, is a community 100 km N of Dauphin on the W shore of Lake Winnipegosis. Named after Rev Joseph Charles Camper, this community is largely **MÉTIS**, and adjoins **PINE CREEK FIRST NATION**. The **HBC** established a post here by 1871, and the area was known then as Pine Creek. The post office was opened in 1905. Present economic activity centres on fishing and some trapping, and the community itself contains some retail and construction service outlets. There is a K-7 school in Camperville and a seniors' complex. Camperville is administered under the *Northern Affairs* Act. • GPP

CANAD INNS is the largest hotel firm in MB, with 7 hotels in **WINNIPEG**, one in **PORTAGE LA PRAIRIE**, and one in **BRANDON** (as of early 2006). The chain is owned and operated by Canad Corporation of Manitoba Ltd., a Winnipeg-based, family-owned firm that got its start in 1965 when Walter Ledohowski acquired a hotel in Yorkton, SK, and launched Ledohowski Hotels Limited. He was later joined by his sons, Leo and Ben, and in the 1970s, the family moved its operations to Winnipeg and began acquiring and building hotel properties here. The first was the Norlander Inn (now the Canad Inns–Express Fort Garry),

which was purchased in 1978. That was followed by the acquisition of the Golden Oak Inn (now Canad Inns–Transcona) in 1979 and The Windsorian (now Canad Inns–Windsor Park) in 1983; construction of the Garden City Inn (now Canad Inns-Garden City) in 1987; the purchase of the Ramada Inn (now Canad Inns–Fort Garry) in 1997 and the Polo Park Inn (now Canad Inns–Polo Park) in 1999; construction of the Canad Inns Club Regent Casino Hotel in 2001; the acquisition of the Westward Village Inn (now Canad Inns–Portage la Prairie) in 2003; and construction of the Canad Inns–Brandon, which opened in early 2005. In Dec 2005, construction began on the latest addition to the Canad Inns chain – a $50 million hotel and indoor water-park complex in Grand Forks, ND. The 3715 m² (40,000-sq-ft) water park was slated to open in summer 2006, and the 192-room hotel was expected to open in late 2006 or early 2007. In July 2006, the company also announced plans to build a new 19-storey hotel adjacent to Winnipeg's downtown **HEALTH SCIENCES CENTRE**. The project was described at the time as the first of its kind in Canada, and was expected to open in 2008. As of writing, the company employed more than 1900 people, mostly in MB. In 2001, the company purchased the naming rights to Winnipeg Stadium for 10 years, renaming it Canad Inns Stadium. • MURRAY MCNEILL

Ukrainian Festival in Dauphin

CANADA'S NATIONAL UKRAINIAN FESTIVAL. For 3 days every Aug, people come from all over the world to **DAUPHIN** to join **UKRAINIAN** Canadians celebrating their rich cultural heritage. The idea for the national festival was born in 1964, when a panel discussion on tourism proposed that local merchants capitalize on the area's substantial Ukrainian community and put aside assumptions that only larger centres could host such events. The first festival was organized 2 years later. Perhaps because ethnic heritage festivals were still novel at the time, the festival attracted crowds that peaked around 25,000 over the next decade. That initial popularity

has not been surpassed since; recently, attendance has averaged 4500. The festival brings in Ukrainian talent from all over the globe to perform. Visitors can see Ukrainian choral singing, traditional dance, and Cossack horsemanship. Colourful Ukrainian costumes abound, as well as traditional cuisine. There are workshops on cooking Ukrainian food and painting Easter eggs (*pysanky*), as well as cultural activities for children. A parade is held through the main street of Dauphin on Saturday night, and after a street dance, there is a *zabava*, or party. A talent competition that includes dance, instrumental and vocal music, and poetry is also part of the weekend festivities. A memorial park has tributes to Ukrainians interned in Cdn concentration camps as enemy aliens during WWI; to Ukrainian victims of Stalin's deliberately imposed 1932 famine; and to the unknown Ukrainian soldiers who have served in various wars. The best performer is chosen every year and featured in the afternoon grandstand show the next year. Some of the better-known guests have included the Kuban Cossacks from England, comedian Luba Goy, sculptor **LEO MOL**, Ukrainian Cossack horsemen, musician Ted Komar, and the **WINNIPEG**-based Rusalka Dance Ensemble. The festival operates with only one paid staff member and anywhere between 100 and 300 volunteers each year. • MAURICE MIERAU

CANADIAN FORCES BASE (CFB) SHILO, along with **17 WING**, is the only remaining Canadian Forces base operating in MB. CFB Shilo is located 35 km E of **BRANDON**. The base covers 40,000 ha and is home to 2 regular forces units: the **2ND BATT, PRINCESS PATRICIA'S CANADIAN LIGHT INFANTRY** and the **1ST REGT, ROYAL CANADIAN HORSE ARTILLERY**. Including civilian personnel, nearly 2000 persons work from the base. The surrounding area has been training troops since 1910, first as Camp Sewell, then Camp Hughes and finally as CFB Shilo. Many units have called the base home, including Cdn artillery units and the German army in the 1970s, '80s and '90s who trained their tanks corps in the rolling countryside. CFB Shilo was the winner when the fed govt in 2004 chose it rather than Winnipeg's Kapyong Barracks as the home for 2PPCLI. • GPP

CANADIAN FOSSIL DISCOVERY CENTRE (CFDC) is in **MORDEN**. Formerly called the Morden and District Museum, the CFDC has the biggest collection of ancient oceanic reptile fossils in Canada. Since the 1930s, fossils have been discovered in the Morden and **MIAMI** area, but it was not until recently that concentrated efforts to study them were made. In 1972, with the support of the

The plesiosaur had a long swan-like neck.

Morden Museum, 2 students – Henry Isaak and Don Bell – started collecting fossils from area quarries. Since then, it has grown into one of the largest and most interesting marine reptile collections in the world. All of CFDC's fossils have been unearthed from a nearby 109 ac (44 ha) site. In the summer, the centre runs several public digs and tours. Visitors can learn about how archaeologists locate, unearth, and dig for fossils, and can view and learn about the geology, geography, fossils, fish, birds, sharks, turtles, squids, mosasaurs (*see* **Dinosaur, Marine**), and plesiosaurs that lived in MB during the Cretaceous era, 80 million years ago. One section of the centre features a virtual tour of "Bruce," the centre's 13 m-long mosasaur. • RK

CANADIAN MENNONITE UNIVERSITY (CMU)

is a **Winnipeg**-based private post-secondary **Education** institution. The Christian university's degree programs concentrate on the arts, music, and theology. About 450 students study at CMU's main campus each year. Formed in 1998 by the merger of 3 colleges – the Canadian **Mennonite** Bible College, the Mennonite Brethren Bible College, and Menno Simons College – CMU is funded by the Mennonite Church of Canada and the Mennonite Brethren Church of Manitoba. The first Mennonite colleges in MB were founded in the 1940s when the Conference of Mennonites in Canada and the Mennonite Brethren churches each formed their own schools. Despite failed merger discussions in 1945, the colleges created lasting co-operative relationships. In 1980, the colleges and Mennonite organizations helped create Menno Simons College. After years of

planning in the mid-1990s, CMU received its provincial charter in 1998 and began instruction in 1999. In Sept 2000, CMU completed the move of its main campus to the 18 ha former site of the Manitoba School for the Deaf in Tuxedo, a provincial heritage building. In addition to its core programs, CMU includes an evangelical Anabaptist seminary, and the Outtatown youth discipleship program. CMU's Menno Simons College remains based at the **U of W**, and offers international development and conflict resolution courses utilized by about 1300 students. • JT

CANADIAN MUSEUM FOR HUMAN RIGHTS

will be the first national museum in western Canada. Originally envisioned by **Izzy Asper**, the ambitious project will exhibit the history of Canadian human rights, including MB histories such as the **Winnipeg General Strike**, **French Language Crisis** and **Métis** rights, and the **Women's Movement**. In the early stages of the proposal, it seemed unlikely that the project would go through. Gail Asper (*see* **Asper Family**) pushed forward the campaign and in 2007 completion of the $311 million project – located at **The Forks** in **Winnipeg** – was planned for 2011. As a national institution, the federal govt offered $100 million for the project, with the city of Winnipeg and the provincial govt contributing another $20 million each. Roughly half of the funding for the project has come from private sponsorship. Organizers are hoping the museum will attract 250,000 visitors annually.

In the initial planning stages, the museum had already been criticized on several fronts, from its high capital cost to the selection of a US design rather than a Cdn work. The symbolic structure

proposed by architect Antoine Predock was condemned as overly extravagant. Featuring a **Tyndall Stone** base from which a glass tower spirals 100 m upward, Predock's work is meant to present the struggle for universal human rights while serving as an internationally recognizable Winnipeg landmark. • MD

CANADIAN NATIONAL RAILWAY

(CNR). The CNR was created 1919-23 by the merger and nationalization of several **Railways** bankrupted by WWI and the recession that followed. These included the Canadian Northern Railway and the Grand Trunk, whose assets included **Winnipeg**'s Union Station, the splendid **Fort Garry Hotel**, and a sprawling complex at **The Forks**. Like rival **CPR**, the "National" was headquartered in Montreal but with a large **Winnipeg** base. Unlike its rival, however, CNR was comprised of a patchwork of primarily branch lines, though it did own the profitable Grand Trunk route from Winnipeg to Prince Rupert, BC, by way of Saskatoon and Edmonton, and a Chicago-to-Winnipeg route.

As **Aviation**, **Trucking**, and cars eclipsed the railways, CNR diversified to survive, just as the CPR did. In 1937, **Trans-Canada Air Lines** was founded as a branch of CNR, and was headquartered in Winnipeg until 1949. CNR further diversified into shipping and ferries by the 1940s, complementing its telegraph arm, known as CNT or CNTel. This company later merged with the CP telegraph operation to become CNCP. After name changes to Unitel and Allstream, the

The CNR depot, ca 1912

communications company – now devoted to long-distance telephone service and Internet provision – became part of **MTS** in 2004.

CNR's composition mainly of branch lines has been the bane of the railway through most of its history, but one line was to become the lifeblood of the Northern Region. Among its earliest initiatives, CNR helped finish the **Hudson Bay Railway**, connecting **The Pas** to **Churchill** in 1929. This project employed many surveyors, tracklayers, engineers, and others, but more lastingly opened the region to **Mining**, **Forestry**, and settlement. The CNR presence had its effects on southern MB, too, with construction of massive rail yards in Winnipeg, and employment of thousands in various professions.

In 1947, CNR's trans-Canada train, the Super Continental, was involved in the worst rail disaster in MB history when an excursion train bound from Minaki, ON, did not switch tracks, smashing headfirst into the CNR train at the **Dugald** station. There were no fatalities on the Super Continental, but 31 on the Minaki train died.

At its high point in the 1940s, CNR employed thousands of Manitobans and its workers made up the majority of the population in communities like Transcona and Fort Rouge. The 1970s were, however, a bleak decade for railways throughout NA. Branch-line closure became the norm everywhere. Lack of population density in MB, combined with lack of competitiveness with cars and commercial flights, conspired to erode passenger service, while demand for rail cargo fell as the trucking industry came of age, and pipelines were used to move petroleum rather than railcars. Intermodal transport, involving the trans-shipping of rail cars by flatbed or other trucks, helped keep the industry alive. A re-named CN created Via Rail to run its passenger operations – by then a small segment of its business – in 1978. A policy of demolishing branch and spur lines began that continued as of writing; one such line is now the Prairie Dog Central, a steam-locomotive excursion railway going from outside Winnipeg to **Warren**.

CN was privatized in 1995, expanding considerably into the US market, especially in the East and Midwest, including a merger with Illinois Central. The company maintains an office, an intermodal depot, their national call centre, and marshalling yards in Winnipeg (notably the Symington Yard), and employs 2200 Manitobans, including tradespeople, office staff, conductors, engineers, and police officers in the province. Several CN lines run through MB, though the company sold the Hudson Bay line to US-based firm OmniTRAX. Current routes include the national line running from Vancouver and Prince Rupert,

BC, to Halifax, also used by Via; the Duluth, MN, and Chicago line, with a spur to Thunder Bay, ON; and a web of smaller feeder lines, mostly in the S of the province. ● A.J. LEVIN

CANADIAN PACIFIC RAILWAY (CPR). The
Canadian Pacific Railway Company formed in 1881 with its headquarters in Montreal, inheriting the task to build a transcontinental **Railway**. Second only to the **Fur Trade** in its importance in settling MB, the CPR shaped the evolution of MB's agrarian and urban settlement, which had hitherto followed **Early Trails and Roads** or areas accessible by **York Boat** or **Steamship**. The CPR also shaped the Prairie landscape, with water towers, stations, and **Grain Elevators** all conforming to company standards.

With the establishment of CPR's western Cdn headquarters in the new city of **Winnipeg**, the population swelled, as did smaller rail centres such as **Brandon**. Would-be metropolises that the railway bypassed, such as **Emerson** or **Selkirk**, were relegated to town status or worse. Winnipeg's boom was a consequence of its being on a rail route and because of a demand for thousands of rail workers, for an economy to support them, and for manufacturing and warehousing firms that could take advantage of relatively inexpensive land close to a convenient means of shipping. While it was responsible for the success of Prairie grain farming, the CPR had its detractors among the early populace of MB. Some saw it as an annexationist imposition on the part of eastern

Canada, as there was no competition, forcing the federal govt to introduce a **Crow Rate** in 1897. The early CPR did initially stifle rivals until real competition came in the form of the CNoR in 1899, and the Grand Trunk Pacific, which built a line from Winnipeg to Edmonton in 1914.

Farmers, besides objecting to what they saw as high tariffs, resented the company's extensive land allotments, which prevented would-be farmers from settling on some of the new province's most fertile lands. On the other hand, the CPR brought an immensely diverse ethnic **Immigrant** mix, including **Chinese** workers, to the Northwest, and advertised the Cdn Plains to prospective migrants internationally, leading to a flood of primarily **English** and **Scots** pioneers, but also Americans. At its peak, the CPR was both the means of settlement in the province and its largest industry. It employed tracklayers, engineers, coalmen, porters, carpenters, conductors, welders, and a host of other trades in overhaul facilities, marshalling yards, and offices. The CPR can be credited with increasing Winnipeg's population from fewer than 2000 in 1873 to 20,000 in 1886, a population boom that would continue unchecked until the 1920s, when the area population crested above 200,000. By the 1940s, CPR employed tens of thousands of Manitobans and its workers made up most of the population in the Weston district of Winnipeg.

The CPR's operations extended beyond passengers and cargo rail service. It was involved in communications via telegraph lines; hotels and

View of CPR Yards from Salter Bridge, 1962

tourism, including Winnipeg's Royal Alexandra Hotel (1911-66); stores; ships; and sundry other industries. However, the CPR began to decline in importance by 1920, as did Winnipeg itself. The decline came from a combination of factors, including WWI, and the recession and international flu EPIDEMIC that followed it; increasing use of the Panama Canal as a shipping route after its 1914 opening; the mass-produced automobile; the 1919 WINNIPEG GENERAL STRIKE; and the founding of rival CNR, also in 1919. The drought and GREAT DEPRESSION of the 1930s led to a worldwide decrease in demand for wheat, and therefore lower prices and fewer markets.

CPR remained profitable for most of the 20th century only thanks to its parent company's diversification into AVIATION in the form of Canadian Pacific Air Lines (later CP Air and the principal founder of Canadian Airlines, bought out by Air Canada in 2001). The railway operations were known as CP Rail from 1968-96. Thanks in part to its pioneering of intermodal cargo – the carrying of rail cars on trucks – the firm's TRUCKING division also picked up business in the 1950s and later as railway fell out of favour. The widespread use of cars, aircraft, and buses led passenger service to migrate to Via Rail by the 1980s. By that decade, many branch lines were discontinued or dismantled, a process that was continuing as of writing. Even Winnipeg passenger stations were sold off; one is the basis of the McPhillips Street Station Casino, with another serving as the Aboriginal Centre of Winnipeg. In 1996, with a reorganization that saw the head office moving from Montreal to Calgary, the Winnipeg office decreased further in importance, though repair facilities continue to be located in the city. CPR maintains several main lines through MB: a route S from Winnipeg to Minneapolis; a route running E to Toronto and beyond; and routes going W to Regina and Saskatoon, and points W. In addition, there are still several CPR feeder lines. The CPR employed 1300 people in the province as of writing.

In 2001, Canadian Pacific split into 5 separate publicly traded entities to focus on shipping, rail, coal, petroleum, and real estate. While freight trucking outperformed rail for most of the last half of the 20th century, in the early 21st century, high fuel prices aggravated by international instability have led to a resurgence in rail trade.
● A.J. LEVIN

CANADIAN RANGERS. The Rangers were formally established in 1947 to provide a MILITARY presence in remote, isolated, and coastal areas of Canada that could not otherwise be covered by regular elements of the Canadian Forces. These men and women are part-time, non-combat reservists

responsible for reporting unusual activities and conducting SOV PATs – surveillance patrols to maintain Cdn sovereignty. Many Rangers belong to First Nations, and they often take on leadership positions within their communities. Easily recognizable by their red sweatshirts and ball caps, they give their time, provide local expertise, guidance, and advice, and are called upon to assist during emergencies and in other times of need.

As of 2006, MB had 9 patrols – in CHURCHILL, GILLAM, Lac Brochet, LITTLE GRAND RAPIDS, LYNN LAKE, SHAMATTAWA, SNOW LAKE, ST. THERESA POINT, and Tadoule Lake. Most patrol members serve at the rank of Ranger (equivalent to Pte), with section leaders serving at the rank of Cpl or MCpl, and patrol leaders holding the highest Ranger rank possible: that of Sgt. A Canadian Ranger Instructor, a high-ranking non-commissioned member or an officer in the regular or reserve CF, oversees each CRPG. Logistics and administration for MB's patrols are overseen by a provincial detachment based in WINNIPEG, established in 2000.

Among other duties, the province's Rangers have been called upon to conduct search and rescue operations for missing community members; assist with evacuations due to forest fires; reconstruct buildings for community and youth activities; and catch fish for distribution among elders. Each year, the Churchill patrol plays a vital role in the running of the Hudson Bay Quest, a 400 km DOGSLED race from Churchill to Arviat, NU. ● ANITA DAHER

CANADIAN SHIELD. *See* PHYSIOGRAPHIC REGIONS.

CANADIAN WHEAT BOARD (CWB), headquartered in WINNIPEG, is among the world's largest grain-marketing organizations and handles all sales for the more than 85,000 Prairie farmers who grow WHEAT, durum wheat, and barley

for export or for human consumption in Canada. All wheat and barley for these purposes must be delivered to the board, though the grains can be freely traded for domestic livestock feed. The revenue from those grain sales, minus the board's marketing costs, is passed back to the farmers. With annual sales of between $4 million and $6 million, the CWB is not only one of Canada's largest exporters, but also one of the biggest grain marketing organizations in the world.

Almost since the beginning of grain farming on the Prairies, farmers have had real or perceived grievances with grain merchants. Many were forced to sell shortly after harvest in order to raise cash, only to find prices were higher later in the year. WEATHER, poor roads, or poor communication often prevented deliveries when prices were higher. Farmers suspected grain elevator companies and futures traders colluded in keeping prices down. In 1905, a group of western Cdn farmers who wanted greater power and protection for themselves in the country's grain marketing system established the Grain Growers' Grain Company (GGGC), the predecessor of the CWB. Futures trading was suspended during WWI and the GGGC abolished. In 1919, as a transition back to the open market, the federal govt established the Board of Grain Supervisors to market the crop, though this was disbanded after only one year. It used a "pooling" system; farmers received an initial payment on delivery, and after the end of the year, average returns after expenses were calculated and the balance sent as a final payment. This system coincided with some of the highest prices on record, but farmers also liked the pooling system and the ability to deliver at any time of the year without fear of price penalty. This led to the formation of a voluntary pooling system through the MB, SK, and AB pools.

While the supervisors soon began to build country elevators, their initial purpose was to

Manitoba grows some of the highest quality wheat in the world.

CHARLES SHILLIDAY

form a central selling agency to sign farmers to a 5-year contract committing all their wheat and/or coarse (feed) grains for 5 years. The central selling agency was a spectacular success at first, soon handling the majority of wheat delivered on the Prairies. By 1929, it was Canada's largest business volume by dollar. After the stock market crash and plummeting grain prices that heralded the **Great Depression**, the agency found itself with an initial price higher than the selling price, and it was bankrupt in a year. A continued push for a pooling system with govt backing led to the formation of the Canadian Wheat Board in 1935. At first, participation was optional, but the CWB found that farmers tended to deliver only when the initial payment was above the market. The board lost $62 million in 1938-39, a huge sum then, which contributed to the decision to make wheat deliveries compulsory in 1943. The CWB's powers were extended to oats and barley in 1949, though its authority for oats was removed in 1989. The board continues to offer a pooling system with initial payments; interim payments, if prices are high enough; and a final payment at the end of the year. However, it now offers cash pricing options.

The board's monopoly powers have proved controversial, and in the late 20th century, a push for a "dual market" began, which would allow other companies to purchase export wheat and barley. However, many feel the CWB, which has no elevators or terminals, could not survive without the "single desk," which gives it a guaranteed ability to obtain enough grain to meet contracts, especially if grain companies offered full cash market premiums over an initial payment. On New Year's Eve, 1998, the governance of the CWB was changed from 5 appointed commissioners to a president/CEO with a 15-member board of directors, 10 of whom are elected by farmers, with the other 5 being federal appointments. Most elected directors have so far favoured a single-desk system, but they can recommend changes to the govt if enough vote in favour of a dual market. Although the change was designed to make the CWB more accountable to producers, some Western farmers have remained strongly opposed to the board's monopoly on the sale of wheat and barley in western Canada. They continue to press for the right to sell their grain to whomever they wish, and some have even been jailed for defying the board and selling their grain to the US without a board-issued permit.

The US has aggressively attempted to have the CWB's monopoly authority removed through World Trade Organization agreements or through other trade challenges. In 2003, the WTO ruled that the US complaints were without merit, though as of writing, grain continued to be one of the major thorns in Canada/US trade relations. The federal Conservative Party under Stephen Harper shared the perspective that the CWB's role in wheat and barley sales was wrong. When he won a minority govt in 2006, Harper's Agriculture Minister Chuck Strahl immediately began work to dismantle the board's monopoly. A plebiscite of Prairie barley producers was held in early 2007 and, in late March, results of that vote showed 62% wanted to end the board's status as the single-desk seller of barley. (In MB, slightly more than half of farmers wanted to maintain the CWB monopoly.)

At the time of writing, Strahl was hoping to change the board's barley power through regulations to take effect Aug 1, 2007. A similar effort in 1993 by then Agriculture Minister **Charlie Mayer** was overturned by the courts. Strahl vowed to continue his quest to allow dual marketing by holding another plebiscite on the more difficult question of whether the CWB should continue to be the sole marketer of Prairie wheat. ● JOHN MORRISS

CANGENE CORPORATION is one of Canada's largest **Biotechnology** companies, specializing in producing antibodies used to treat patients whose own immune systems are too weak to produce them naturally. For example, its leading product, WinRho, is used to treat blood irregularities in newborns. It also has developed plasma-based, hyperimmune drugs that may aid in the fight against infectious diseases such as smallpox, Ebola, anthrax, West Nile virus, and hepatitis. Headquartered in Winnipeg, Cangene was founded in 1984 as Rh Pharmaceuticals, based on the research of doctors **John Bowman** and **Henry Bruce Chown**, among others. In 1990, the manufacturer became a member of the Apotex group of companies, and has traded publicly as Cangene since 1995. However, Apotex retains majority control of Cangene. In addition to developing and producing its own products, Cangene offers contract research and manufacturing services to biopharmaceutical companies. Its operations include research and development facilities in Winnipeg and Mississauga, ON; manufacturing plants in Winnipeg and Baltimore; and plasma centres in Winnipeg, Frederick, MD, Maitland, FL, and Van Nuys, CA. The majority of the 600 people it employed, as of 2005, worked in its Winnipeg and Baltimore facilities. ● MM
▸ *See also* **Pharmaceutical Industry**.

CANID is the family of 35 living species of wolves, coyote, jackals, foxes and dogs, and occuring worldwide except on islands. Originating in NA during the Eocene (55-34 mya), this group specialized in running down prey in open country and in forests. Adaptations for this predatory way of life include long thin body with a large chest and lungs, long legs with non-retractable claws, and powerful jaws with numerous sharp teeth, especially the carnassials – specialized shearing sets of opposing premolars and molars in upper and lower jaws. The senses of sight, hearing and smell are remarkably keen. Many dozens of now-extinct canids roamed the region of what is now MB, and a relatively rich representation survives to this day with 6 species. The largest living canid at 50 kg is the Grey **Wolf** (*Canis lupus*) occuring in all terrestrial habitats of the province (but now driven out of the prairie region). The **Coyote** (*Canis latrans*) weighs 10 kg and lives on the prairie, aspen parkland and mixed forest. The Red **Fox** (Vulpes vulpes) is 5 kg and is widespread from prairie to tundra. The Grey Fox (*Urocyon cinereoargenteus*) is 4 kg and occurs in mixed woods of the extreme S. The Arctic Fox (*Alopex lagopus*) is 3.5 kg and inhabits the tundra, Hudson Bay ice, and forest-tundra transition. Finally, the smallest is the Swift Fox (*Vulpes velox*) at 2.5 kg and formerly common (but now extirpated) in mixed-grass prairie of SW MB. The Grey Fox line is known back to 6 mya, while the Swift and the Arctic foxes are the most-recently evolved from the Red Fox line, appearing only in the mid-Pleistocene (0.5 mya). ● REW
▸ *See also* **Coyote, Fox, Wolf**

CANOLA is a true Canadian crop, its name derived from the words "Canadian" and "oil." Canola started life as rapeseed – *Brassica napus*, a member of the mustard family – first grown in Canada as a source of industrial lubricants. Rapeseed oil was considered unsuitable for human consumption because it contained glucosinilates and erucic acid, both of which are slightly toxic. In the 1950s, Canadian plant breeders began work to eliminate these compounds from rapeseed oil. In 1974, U of M plant breeder Dr. **Baldur Stefansson** released "Tower," the first "double-low" variety (containing low levels of both components). Stefansson, along with U of SK researcher Keith Downey, became known as "fathers of canola." This was the first of many progressively improved varieties. The name "canola" was adopted in the 1970s, and is now known around the world. Today, canola is 2nd only to **Wheat** for returns to Prairie farmers, and is sometimes the highest-value crop in MB. In 2004, MB farmers earned $597 million from canola compared to $540 million for wheat. The year 2006 was a big year for canola across the Prairies, with more than 1.8 million ha in production in MB alone. Canola oil is recognized as one of the best for human consumption because

of its low level of saturated fats. Canola is now exported as seed around the world and crushed for oil in Cdn processing plants, including those in **Altona**, Harrowby, and **Ste. Agathe**. In 2006, one new crushing plant was being planned and several plant expansions were in the works on the Prairies. The canola meal remaining after crushing can be used for livestock feed.
● JOHN MORRISS

CANUPAWAKPA DAKOTA NATION (formerly known as Oak Lake First Nation), on reserve pop 320, off reserve pop 258, is 110 km SW of **Brandon**, on the SK-MB border. The native language of this community is Dakota, and there are 3 reserves here, including the Canupawakpa Dakota Nation I.R. No. 59, Oak Lake I.R. 59A, and Fishing Station I.R. No. 62A. The fishing station is held jointly by Canupawakpa, the **Birdtail Sioux** and **Sioux Valley First Nations**. This Dakota Nation community administers nursery and kindergarten levels of schooling; for grade levels beyond that children attend school in other nearby communities, such as **Virden**. Besides its internal roads, this Dakota Nation has all-weather roads that go out to hwys 1, 2, and 83. Agriculture is the primary economic base of Canupawakpa. This First Nation is a member of the Dakota Ojibway Tribal Council. It is not signatory to a treaty. In 2002, 40 horse riders from the Canupawakpa Dakota Nation represented members of the Unity Ride (a symbolic ride through Sioux land in a show of unity by Cheyenne, Oglala, Nakota, Lakota, and Dakota Sioux), at the 2002 North American Indigenous Games. ● RK

CANWEST GLOBAL COMMUNICATIONS CORP is a leading international diversified media company with interests in Canada, Europe, Australia, and New Zealand in television, film production, radio, the Internet, and print media. The company was founded in 1977 by **Israel Harold "Izzy" Asper**. Since 2000, the company has undergone a large expansion. By 2005, every major Canadian city was in some way connected to the CanWest system, whether through television, newspapers, the Internet, or, in most cases, all 3.

Although CanWest Global was officially born in 1977 as CanWest Capital Corporation, its roots go back further. In 1974, Asper had assembled a group of investors, including Paul Morton – then the owner of Odeon-Morton movie theatres – and Seymour Epstein, a Toronto-based engineer. The group was awarded the licence to establish a new Winnipeg television station. On Sept 1, 1975, CKND-TV Channel 12 was launched. Under the guidance of Don Brinton and Peter Liba, CKND was an instant success. Establishing

a pattern that later would be followed by other CanWest Global operations, costs were kept under control and the station found its niche in the marketplace.

The CanWest Global Building in Winnipeg

While CKND was being built, Asper, Morton, and Epstein also became involved with Toronto's Global Television Network. Established in Jan 1974 by broadcast promoter Al Bruner, Global ran into financial trouble soon after airing, the result of poor programming and weak advertising. The station was rescued by the Winnipeg group and by Allan Slaight of IWC Communications, based in Toronto. Owing to some astute programming choices – broadcasting such shows as *The Gong Show* and *Love Boat*, for example – Global was on better financial footing 2 years later. By that time, however, Slaight's partnership with Asper, Morton, and Epstein had soured. Following another round of negotiations, Asper, Morton, and Epstein bought out Slaight's shares. Global continued to grow under a successful business strategy conceived by its president David Mintz. Within a few years, disagreement about Global's future, and behind-the-scenes business wrangling, led to a bitter feud between Asper, on one side, and Morton and Epstein, on the other. The dispute culminated in a court-ordered auction of Global in Oct 1989, which Asper won.

By this time, Asper had embarked on a plan to acquire a string of independent television stations in W Canada. In September 1985, the CRTC granted CanWest licences for stations in Regina and Saskatoon. In the early 1980s, Asper

had also invested in CKVU, an independent Vancouver TV station. After protracted fights in court and at CRTC hearings, CanWest took over CKVU in 1988. This was another step toward Asper's overall plan to establish a 3rd television network in Canada to compete with the CBC and CTV. During the next decade, CanWest added television stations in Atlantic Canada and QC. The company's profits rose, in no small part due its strategy of rebroadcasting many popular US television shows.

Expanding into AB proved more difficult. In 1996, the CRTC did not approve CanWest's application for new stations in Calgary, Edmonton, Red Deer, and Lethbridge. A lengthy battle followed with Shaw Communications for control of Western International Communications (WIC) and its television properties in AB. It took until June 1998 before negotiations produced a deal both CanWest and Shaw found acceptable. In the end, CanWest assumed control of WIC's 9 conventional television stations – including those in Vancouver, Victoria, Kelowna, Calgary, Edmonton, Red Deer, Lethbridge, Hamilton, and Montreal. Before Izzy Asper's dream of a 3rd Canadian television network would become a reality, however, CanWest faced public opposition to its takeover of the WIC properties and had to win CRTC approval for the transfer. This approval did not come until the summer of 2000.

CanWest also expanded its broadcasting interests internationally. In 1992, the company purchased a 20% stake in New Zealand's TV3 and obtained management control as part of the deal. Under CanWest's leadership, TV3, which had been losing money, became profitable again. By the end of 1997, CanWest had bought out its partners and acquired 100% ownership of TV3. Since then, CanWest added TV4 – New Zealand's second privately owned, national, free-to-air television network – as well as a network of radio stations. New Zealand was followed in 1992 by a substantial investment in Australia's television Network Ten, one of CanWest's most successful ventures. The company, however, had to fight several regulatory and legal battles to prove it was not in violation of Australia's strict broadcasting rules. Through Network Ten, CanWest acquired 60% of Eye Corp, the 2nd-largest out-of-home advertising company in the country. Eye Corp had one of the largest networks of outdoor signage, airport advertising, visual advertising, point-of-purchase, and shopping centre advertising in Australia. Less successful television ventures were attempted in Chile and Romania. In 1994, CanWest mounted a campaign to broadcast in the UK, but lost out to a consortium led by the media conglomerate Pearson PLC.

A meeting between Izzy Asper and Irish broadcasting executive James Morris led to CanWest's expansion into Ireland. In Apr 1997, the company entered into an agreement with an Irish business group holding the exclusive right to become the Republic of Ireland's first private-sector national TV broadcaster. By fall 1998, TV3 was broadcasting from Dublin.

By far, the largest business undertaking in CanWest's history – and the biggest media transaction in Canadian history – took place in Aug 2000 with its $3.2-billion acquisition of Canadian newspaper and Internet assets from Hollinger International, then controlled by Conrad Black. By this time, Izzy Asper had handed control of the company to his youngest son Leonard, who became the CEO in 1999. This unprecedented deal gave CanWest ownership of the former Southam chain of 13 major daily newspapers – including *The Gazette* (Montreal), the *Ottawa Citizen*, the *Vancouver Sun*, the *Province* (Vancouver), the *Calgary Herald*, and the *Edmonton Journal*. As well, CanWest claimed a 50% stake in Black's *National Post*, as well as ownership of the Canada.com website. This joint Hollinger/CanWest operation of the *National Post* lasted only a year; by August 2001, CanWest bought out Black and assumed 100% ownership of the newspaper. Some critics complained of media concentration but Leonard Asper insisted that the "synergy" created by blending various media would benefit the public as well as shareholders.

The company also launched several speciality channels in recent years, including *Prime TV*, aimed at people 50 and older, and digital channels *Deja View*, a retro channel; *Lonestar*, a western-theme channel; and *Mystery*.

In 2006, CanWest Global recorded gross revenues of $2,878,625,000 – a slight drop from the previous year – and employed 600 people in MB.

CanWest has been generous in its philanthropic endeavours. In 1997, the CanWest Global Foundation was established with an initial contribution of $1 million. Its projects included CanWest Global Centre for Performing Arts and CANWEST GLOBAL PARK, the home of the WINNIPEG GOLDEYES baseball team. CanWest was designated "A Caring Company" by the Canadian Centre for Philanthropy's Imagine Program. It has been CanWest's policy to set aside a minimum of 1% of its pre-tax profits for donations to non-profit organizations and projects. In 2004, the CanWest Global Foundation and CanWest operating units donated $32.6 million and $13.4 million, respectively, in New Zealand, Australia, and Ireland.

● ALLAN LEVINE

CanWest Global Park

CANWEST GLOBAL PARK. A BASEBALL stadium located adjacent to THE FORKS in WINNIPEG, CanWest Global Park opened in June 1999 and has been the home of the WINNIPEG GOLDEYES ever since. The Goldeyes had been playing at WINNIPEG STADIUM, a facility not designed for baseball. In 1996, team owner SAM KATZ made a final 2-year lease agreement with Winnipeg Enterprises Corp, and began making plans for a new ballpark. His initial plan was to partner with the City of Winnipeg, who had committed to building a baseball facility for the 1999 PAN AMERICAN GAMES. However, Katz's appeal for public funding led to lukewarm support from mayor Susan Thompson and the city council. In the end, the $12 million park did receive more than $3 million in govt money and land concessions. The CROCUS INVESTMENT FUND and real estate developers Sandy and Robert Shindleman also made contributions. Potential names for the facility included "Riverside Park" and "Mind Field," before CANWEST GLOBAL paid $1.5 million for naming rights. "The Fishbowl," as it is sometimes called, opened with a seating capacity of 6140. Due to the consistent high demand for Goldeyes tickets, $6.5 million worth of renovations were completed in the spring of 2003. They saw the addition of 6 luxury suites, more concessions (including a restaurant), and about 1200 seats, raising the official capacity to 7481. ● JT

CAPELIN (*Mallotus villosus*) is a silvery, schooling fish in the smelt family. It is a small (16 cm), slim species (resembling a young trout) found in arctic and subarctic seas and estuaries, including those of HUDSON BAY. It is remarkable for its unusual breeding habits. During the spawning season of June and July, 2 pairs of ridges of scales develop along the male's sides and belly, giving the fish a more robust appearance. During the rest of the year the sexes are almost indistinguishable. The fish gather in estuaries such as the Churchill and Nelson rivers, where they are fed on heavily by other fish, seals, whales and seabirds. Spawning capelin prefer temperatures of 5.5 to 8.5°C and a pebbly bottom. Spawning normally occurs at night or on dull cloudy days over a 4-6 week period. Most spawning takes place on the beaches, but if water temperatures become too high, they will spawn in deeper water. During this season, the sexes are segregated, with males near the beach and females in deeper water. When ready to mate, the females join the males in the shallows, where eggs are released and fertilized by 1 or 2 males. The fish are washed back and forth in the waves. Females usually release all their eggs at one time, while males may mate more than once. Although most Capelin die after spawning, a greater proportion of females survive, perhaps because males undergo more physical damage during their extended stay in the turbulent water near the beach. Survivors move offshore in late summer and join immature fish to form feeding schools. Feeding on plankton is heavy from Aug to Nov. Capelin eggs stick to sand and gravel, with some buried up to 10 cm. Hatching begins in 15 to 20 days and the larvae remain in the gravel until released by waves;

without wind and waves, large numbers of larvae die while trapped in the gravel. Fry are 3-6 mm and by winter reach 3-4 cm. Capelin mature at 3-4 years and may survive to 7, reaching a length of 13-20 cm. Capelin is a major item in the diet of Arctic Cod, Arctic Char, seals, whales and marine birds. • DFO, REW

CARBERRY, pop 1513, is a town 45 km E of Brandon. Settlers attracted by free land started arriving from E Canada, England, and Scotland around 1878. In 1882, the **CPR** established a station at De Winton, 2 km E of the town's present site. Hoping to profit when the town grew, railway officials began to purchase much of De Winton's town-site property. As this was against CPR regulations, the company, using 100 hired men, physically moved the new station to the present site of the town of Carberry in the middle of the night. The name was changed to Carberry in 1883, after Carberry Tower in Musselburgh, UK, which belonged to Lord Elphinstone of the CPR. The landscape around Carberry has unique features. Thousands of years ago, the Carberry area and the **MANITOBA ESCARPMENT** formed the shore of **LAKE AGASSIZ**. As the lake dried, the **CARBERRY SAND HILLS** were left behind and the Spirit Sands "Desert," just outside of Carberry, is now 5 km² (1235 ac) of blowing sand dunes. The rolling hills and valleys are covered in fertile sandy soils. In the 1960s, soil specialists assured farmers in the area that their land was ideally suited for potato farming. Empty airport hangars – formerly an RCAF station used for the **BRITISH COMMONWEALTH AIR TRAINING PLAN** – were put to use by J. R. Simplot (*see* **SIMPLOT CANADA**) to establish a potato processing plant in 1961. The plant provided an economic boost to the community by providing both full-time and seasonal work opportunities. As of 2005, community developers were exploring ways to diversify the town's economy. Carberry is the birthplace of aviator Wilfrid Reid "Wop" May. • GPP

CARBERRY SAND HILLS (also Bald Head Hills, Spirit Sands) are MB's largest active sand dunes. They are in Spruce Woods Provincial Park (*see* **PROVINCIAL PARKS**), about 150 km SW of **WINNIPEG** and 15 km S of **CARBERRY**. Few areas in the province offer as much scenic splendour, historical interest, and biological diversity. Large areas of sand, up to 65 m thick, occur over much of SW MB, formed as a delta of the **ASSINIBOINE RIVER** when it flowed into glacial **LAKE AGASSIZ**. After this huge lake drained, strong winds heaped the exposed deltaic sands up into active dunes. About 40 km² of this former delta remain as large, active sand dunes, some of which are 20 m

tall. Plants have stabilized the rest, though you can easily site former dunes by the abrupt slopes and angles of the hills. These sandy areas are among the most unique and unusual landscapes in MB, with their rolling, small hills, eroded slopes, aspen clumps, and scattered mature white **SPRUCES** (*Picea glauca*).

The open dune area receives too much rainfall to count as true desert, but the sandy soil makes it very hot and dry, creating microhabitats of desert severity. As a result, plants and animals such as cacti, hognose **SNAKES**, and unusual **INSECTS** and other invertebrates especially adapted to desert conditions live there. Both of MB's native cacti – the rare pincushion or ball cactus or spiny star, *Corypantha vivipara*; and the more-common brittle prickly pear (*Opuntia fragilis*) – grow here, along with rare sand bluestem grass (*Andropogon hallii*), sand dock (*Rumex venosus*), and low Townsendia (*Townsendia exscapa*). Scattered white spruces, mats of low growing creeping juniper (*Juniperus horizontalis*) and bearberry (*Arctostaphylos uva-ursi; see* **BERRIES, FRUITS, AND NUTS**), and prairie sunflowers (*Helianthus petiolaris*) are more common. It is a great place to find MB's floral emblem, the **PRAIRIE CROCUS**, in spring. Uncommon "desert" animals include the olive-backed pocket mouse (*Perognathus fasciatus; see* **MOUSE**), the plains hognose snake (*Heterodon nasicus*), and the northern prairie skink, the province's only **LIZARD**. Invertebrates restricted to open sand areas include many interesting and unusual ones, such as the eastern sand **WASP** (*Bembix americana*), velvet **ANTS** (*Dasymutilla spp.*), burrowing **SPIDERS**, and the ghost and big sand **TIGER BEETLES** (*Cicindela lepida* and *C. formosa*). Large mammals found in the area include **COYOTES**, occasional **WOLVES** and **MOOSE**, **ELK**, **DEER**, red **FOX**, and **BADGERS**.

The sand hills have been known since the earliest First Nations migrated back into MB after the glaciers retreated several thousand years ago

(*see* **GLACIATION**). **MAMMOTHS** and giant **BISON** roamed there then, pursued by men armed with flint-tipped weapons (see **ANCIENT ABORIGINAL TECHNOLOGY**). They are still regarded as special and sacred places by local First Nations, and are therefore called "Spirit Sands." Early Europeans who took a special interest in the area included the **CRIDDLE FAMILY**, early naturalists and scientists who settled near the area, and **ERNEST THOMPSON SETON**. Seton roamed the sand hills in the 19th century and drew inspiration for his book *The Trail of the Sandhill Stag* from them. White-tailed deer have since replaced the mule deer featured in his book, but the area remains much the same.

The dune area was inaccessible to the public as part of **CFB SHILO** for many years, but became part of Spruce Woods Park in 1975. Frequent fires from military training on the adjacent base have helped maintain the open mixed-grass prairie (*see* **ECOCLIMACTIC REGIONS**) and dunes of the area. Several hiking trails run into and through the sand hills, or you can ride through them on a horse-drawn wagon in the summer. Spruce Woods Provincial Park has a campground nearby and several picnic areas. • KAREN JOHNSON

CARGILL LIMITED is the Canadian subsidiary of Cargill Inc., a Minneapolis-based international processor, marketer, and distributor of agricultural, food, financial, and industrial products. The Canadian subsidiary was launched in 1928 as a grain merchandising operation. It didn't make its first major capital investment until 1958, when it built a large grain export terminal in Baie Comeau, QC. It entered the grain-handling business 16 years later by acquiring National Grain, whose holdings included a grain-handling terminal in Thunder Bay, as well as feed- and seed-manufacturing operations. In 1988, the company further expanded its grain-handling operations with the acquisition of the Maple Leaf Mills' grain division, with several plants across

The Carberry Sand Hills look like a desert but actually receive too much rain to qualify.

S ON. It quickly followed that up with the 1989 acquisition of the retail and fertilizer distribution network Cyanamid Canada, and the 1990 purchase of Alberta Terminals with its 3 inland grain terminals. However, grain handling wasn't the company's only area of interest during the 1980s and 1990s. Other areas of business include salt, chocolate, and natural gas. In 1989, it also built a large beef processing plant in Hay River, AB, and 3 years later it purchased Trillium Meats, headquartered in Toronto. In 1996, it built the country's largest canola-crushing plant near Saskatoon, and the Hay River plant was expanded. The following year, Cargill acquired a 51% stake in Prairie Malt Ltd., one of the world's biggest malting companies, and a 50% stake of the Port of Vancouver's Cascadia Terminal grain export facility (Winnipeg-based **AGRICORE UNITED** owns the other 50%). Today, Winnipeg-based Cargill Ltd. is firmly established as one of Canada's largest agricultural merchandisers and processors, with more than 6000 employees and sales of more than $3.5 billion annually. • MM

CARIBOU (*Rangifer tarandus*) is a member of the **DEER** family, which plays a major role in the ecology of the N, much as the American **BISON** did prehistorically in the S. With different races inhabiting the western mountains, high arctic islands, barren-ground tundra, and the boreal forest, their immense numbers affect plant growth and serve as a main food supply for First Nations people, Grey Wolf, Wolverine, Black Bear and Raven. Antlers are usually present in both sexes – an unusual trait in modern members of the deer family. Along with the hooves, the antlers are used to dig through the snow for vegetation, as a defence against predators, and in dominance clashes between rival males. Group living in vast herds lessens each individual's probability of

being attacked by a predator. The bull, weighing up to 318 kg (females to 136 kg), comes into rut in late Sept–Oct and breeds as many cows as his dominance and strength permit. A single calf (weighing 5-9 kg) is born in May or June, and it is up, nursing, and keeping pace with the migrating herd in less than an hr. Survival of calves averages 30-50%. People and the Grey Wolf are the main predators. The average lifespan is 5 years, but can reach 20 in zoos. This species arrived in NA from Siberia during the Wisconsinan period of the last Ice Age, and without significant competition, numbers grew to 3.5-5 million. There are currently about 2 million caribou divided into 3 surviving races: the Barren-ground (*Rangifer tarandus groenlandicus*), Woodland (*R. t. caribou*) – the darkest and largest race – and Peary (*R. t. pearyi*) of the high arctic – the palest and smallest. The latter 2 races are endangered, suffering great reduction in numbers and distribution.

MB has only 2000 to 3000 individuals of the Woodland race (down over 60% from the mid-1900s), separated into a number of small isolated herds. When a population of large mammals becomes reduced to such low levels, and becomes isolated in small widely distributed groups, it deserves to be classified as "Endangered," since inbreeding and the likelihood of loss of each population without any opportunity for recruitment, work against survival. Woodland Caribou are known to recover slowly even with optimal conditions and conservation measures. Designated officially in MB and Canada at the lower-risk level of Threatened, the Woodland race's future is bleak without the permanent establishment of large areas of prime boreal forest, free from roads and human activity, habitat destruction (mainly from vast forestry and hydro operations) and hunting. Brain worm, contracted

by White-tailed Deer expanding into caribou range, has also destroyed many Caribou. Fire is also a limiting factor, destroying mature coniferous forest and slow-growing lichens, essential for winter survival.

The Barren-ground race (Beverley and Qamanirjuaq herds) in N MB is in good condition (relatively free from disturbance due to remoteness) and numbers around 275,000. It migrates long distances from birthing grounds on the tundra to wintering grounds in the taiga (forest-tundra transition). The herds' routes may vary greatly from year to year. Reindeer – domesticated from wild caribou for over 3,000 years in northern Eurasia – were introduced into NW Canada, but their range does not come as far E as MB. • REW

UMA, TRIBUNE, PERSONALITY FILES

Len Cariou, 1980

CARIOU, Len, actor, singer (b Sep 30, 1939, **WINNIPEG**) is perhaps best known for his title role in *Sweeney Todd: The Demon Barber of Fleet Street*, for which he won a Tony award (1979). His Broadway performances in *Applause* (1970) and *A Little Night Music* (1973) also earned him Tony award nominations. Cariou won a Canadian Genie for best actor in *One Man* (1977). Cariou got his professional start as an actor in Winnipeg while performing in the chorus of *Damn Yankees*. By 1962, he was cast in key roles for numerous Shakespearean plays. He moved on to the Tyrone Guthrie Theatre in Minneapolis, and then to Broadway in 1968. Cariou was artistic director of the **MANITOBA THEATRE CENTRE** for one season in the mid-1980s, and is an honorary lifetime

ROBERT R. TAYLOR

Manitoba hosts about 3000 Woodland caribou

member of that company. He was also the associate director of the Guthrie Theatre. Although the majority of his career has been spent onstage, Cariou made his film debut in the role of Fredrick Egerman, starring opposite Elizabeth Taylor in the 1977 film adaptation of A Little Night Music. He has performed in about 20 other films, including About Schmidt (2002) and Thirteen Days (2000). He has also made TV appearances on The West Wing, Law and Order, The Practice, and Murder, She Wrote. His more recent stage roles include MTC's production of The Dresser (2005). For his contributions to theatre, Cariou was awarded the **ORDER OF MANITOBA** in 2004. ● JS

CARLSON, Allan "Whitey," businessman, sports administrator (b Nov 14, 1919, **WINNIPEG**; d July 6, 2004, Winnipeg) is sometimes referred to as MB's "Mr. Basketball." During the 1950s, through his masterful marketing, Carlson turned **BASKETBALL** games at the Winnipeg Civic Auditorium into popular events that drew thousands. Carlson started out as an athlete, and first played basketball while attending Kelvin High School. Following graduation, he played on the Toilers junior and senior teams. Eventually, he became involved in the administrative side, and refereed senior and varsity games. In 1946, with funding from his employer Paulin Chambers Co. Ltd., Carlson founded the Paulins basketball team. He used clever advertising and promotions, including bringing in a 12-piece band, to turn the Paulins basketball games into a profitable attraction. The Paulins won the provincial championship in 1948 and 1949 and, in 1954, became the 2nd MB team to win the Cdn championship. The Paulins were then invited to represent Canada at the 2nd world basketball championships in Brazil, where they placed 5th. None of the team's accomplishments would have been possible without Carlson, who spearheaded the campaign to raise $7000 for the trip to Rio de Janeiro. He was one of the founders, and later an inductee, of the Manitoba Basketball Hall of Fame. He was inducted into the Manitoba Sports Hall of Fame in 1996. ● MD

CARMAN, pop 2831, is a town 75 km SW of **WINNIPEG**. The town was settled in 1870 when settlers from Winnipeg travelled the Missouri Trail (see **EARLY TRAILS AND PATHS**) SW to relocate around the Boyne River. It was named "Carman City" after Albert Carman, Bishop of the Episcopal **METHODIST** Church in Canada, though the name "Hazeldean" was also proposed. Carman was incorporated as a town in 1905. The majority of Carman settlers are of predominantly **ENGLISH**, **SCOTS**, **IRISH**, and **DUTCH** descent. The post office opened in 1880, and railway points were

established soon after. In the 1970s, Carman flooded 3 times. In 1992, a water diversion was erected, taking away the risk of continued annual flooding to this community. Today, Carman has one of the highest average personal incomes in MB, with many of the community's residents holding professional jobs. Various agricultural corporations as well as services and retail form Carman's economic backbone today. An expansion to a local industrial park in 2002 attracted a diverse client base, including a manufacturer of aerospace components and a grain vacuum manufacturer. The town has a large elderly population, but abundant recreational opportunities and a well-regarded education system have attracted younger families here as well. The **U OF M**'s Carman campus offers residents the opportunity to take postsecondary courses while remaining in the community. **HOCKEY** goaltender **ED BELFOUR** comes from Carman, as does Kelly Hand, who won a gold medal in sailing at the 1999 **PAN AM GAMES** in Winnipeg. ● GPP

CARNIVOROUS PLANTS. MB has 10 known kinds of carnivorous plants. Although commonly associated with tropical jungles, carnivorous plants occur widely around the world and as far N as the subarctic zone in MB. Plants use "meat eating" to gain nutrients, especially nitrogen, in environments like bogs, ponds, and lakes where nutrients are scarce. Carnivorous plants are also known, incorrectly, as insectivorous plants but they "eat'" many more kinds of animals than insects. Some of the larger tropical ones have captured small birds and the small aquatic bladderworts catch mainly very small crustaceans, nematodes and even protozoans.

Carnivorous plants don't really "eat" their prey. They trap it with specialized leaves, secrete digestive enzymes that break down its tissues and then absorb the nutrients they require from this fluid through their leaves. The variety of traps and their mechanisms is fascinating and the type of trap is one of the main ways by which these plants are classified. Passive traps can be ones in which the prey simply falls into a trap full of liquid and is digested. The purple pitcher plant (Sarracenia purpurea) is an example of this type. Others such as MB's 2 butterworts (Pinguicula vulgaris & P. villosa) have sticky leaves that trap prey like flypaper. Even more interesting are the active trappers. MB has three kinds of sundews (Drosera spp.) which use a combination of active and passive traps. Their leaves are covered with sticky hairs that first catch the prey like flypaper and then fold over it like a net. Then the leaf rolls up. MB's 4 species of bladderworts (Utricularia spp.) live mainly in quiet water.

They have tiny ingenious underwater traps. Water is absorbed out of the trap, leaving a negative pressure inside it. When prey hits a sensitive trigger hair, the door of the trap opens, causing water and prey to be sucked inside and the door to then close.

ROBERT R. TAYLOR

Butterwort ingesting mosquito

Pitcher plants, hairy butterwort (P. villosa) and round-leaved sundew (D. rotundifolia) grow in acid bogs, often in association with peat mosses (Sphagnum spp.). Common butterwort (P. vulgaris), oblong and slender-leaved sundews (D. anglica & D. linearis), and sometimes pitcher plants grow in fens with alkali or basic water. The famous 'Venus fly-trap' (Dionea muscipea) doesn't occur in MB, although you can often find it in garden stores and it is fairly easy to grow. The Conservatory in **ASSINIBOINE PARK** in Winnipeg is developing a collection of both native and exotic carnivorous plants. ● KAREN JOHNSON

CARP (Cyprinus carpio) is a prominent MB fish – the largest member of the minnow family. The Common Carp is a large, deep-bodied, laterally compressed species with an elongated dorsal fin and serrated spines on the leading edge of the dorsal and anal fins. Two barbells are present on each side of the upper jaw. Two forms are found in MB, the most common being golden tan to olive green, and with the body completely covered with large scales. The less-numerous form is known as the mirrored carp, which has only a few large scales scattered over an otherwise naked body. Average length is 38-47 cm, with some fish reaching 80 cm and 18 kg in Cdn waters (largest in MB was 108 cm in the **RED RIVER**). The Common Carp prefers warm waters of marshes, shallow lakes, and slow-moving rivers. It has exceptional tolerances and can thrive in many degraded aquatic habitats. Prior to spawning in May and early June, carp move upstream into shallows where they sometimes congregate in large numbers. A mature female averages 75,000 eggs (max 2.2 million eggs). Adults are bottom-feeding (benthic) omnivores, feeding on a variety of invertebrates, algae and plant material. Due to their feeding behaviour in soft sediments, and their often-high densities, carp uproot aquatic plants and contribute to increased water turbidity, which have negative impacts on native fish and waterbirds. Carp-control programs have been implemented in many countries and in MB, with mixed success. A native of Eurasia, the Common Carp has been successfully reared for centuries and has been introduced around the world for the aquaculture trade. It was introduced into MB in 1886 by English anglers, but no self-sustaining populations were found in MB until 1938, when wild specimens were caught in the Red River at Lockport. The species has since spread across much of S MB and is now established in the Nelson and Churchill river systems. Although initially introduced as a food fish, the Common Carp has only attracted limited attention commercially. Angling for carp is popular in some parts of the US and Canada, and is gaining popularity in MB. • DW

CARR, James Gordon, "Jim," politician, administrator (b Oct 11, 1951, **WINNIPEG**). Carr was educated at the **U OF M** and McGill U. He studied classical music, was an oboist and director with the **WINNIPEG SYMPHONY ORCHESTRA** and later served as executive director of the Manitoba Arts Council. Carr ran as a Liberal for a seat in the MB legislature in 1986, but lost to **GARY FILMON**. The following election, he ran again in the Fort Rouge riding, and defeated NDP cabinet minister Roland Penner. He was one of 20 Liberal MLAs to gain election under the leadership of **SHARON CARSTAIRS**. Carr was appointed deputy leader, and was a member of the Meech Lake and Charlottetown constitutional task forces. Though he maintained Fort Rouge in 1990, the Liberals lost more than half their seats, and he resigned in 1992. He then served on the editorial board of the **WINNIPEG FREE PRESS** from 1992-97. In 1998, he became the founding president of the Business Council of Manitoba, and in 2007 was serving as its CEO. He also sits on several boards, including the Canada West Foundation and the Winnipeg Airport Authority. • MD

CARSTAIRS, Sharon, politician, teacher (b April 26, 1942 Halifax). A dynamic politician, Carstairs is best known for her opposition to the **MEECH LAKE ACCORD** and for briefly bringing the provincial Liberal party back into contention. Carstairs began her working life as a teacher. She received a BA in political science and history from Dalhousie U before earning an MA in education from Smith College in Northampton

Sharon Carstairs, 1988

MA in 1963. She went on to teach in public, private and Catholic schools in AB, MA as well as MB. While she was unsuccessful in her bid for a seat in the AB legislature in 1975, her passion for politics led her to serve as president of the AB **LIBERALS** as well as sitting on the national executive of the federal wing of the party. After moving to MB, she became involved with the provincial Liberal party and worked during the 1981 election. With strong support from the party's youth wing, she used her oratorical and motivational skills to upset Bill Ridgeway and take the leadership in 1984. In the 1986 election, Carstairs won the River Heights riding but despite doubling the party's popular vote, she was the only Liberal elected. She sat as the only Liberal in the legislature for 2 years.

When disgruntled NDP MLA Jim Walding voted against the budget on March 8 1988, **HOWARD PAWLEY**'s govt unexpectedly fell. The Liberals had been building momentum since the beginning of 1988 with a robust advertising campaign, a convention and a number of rallies. Some referred to growing Liberal popularity as "Carstairsmania." **GARY FILMON**'s Tories formed a minority govt in April 1988 However, Carstairs' Liberals surged in the popular vote and found themselves the official opposition with 20 of the 57 seats in the legislature.

Carstairs' opposition to the Meech Lake Accord brought her to national prominence and put her at odds with many federal Liberal leaders. Carstairs and NDP MLA Elijah Harper were provided with bodyguards after they began receiving threats for their public opposition to the accord. Eventually, Carstairs supported the

agreement, out of fear that the country would fall apart if it was not implemented. However, when Meech died due to Harper's pivotal vote against it, Carstairs did not hide the fact that she was pleased with its defeat. In the 1990 prov election, the Liberals were reduced to 7 seats. In 1993, she resigned her seat in the legislature and in 1994, then PM Jean Chretien appointed her to the Senate. From 1997-99, she served as deputy leader of the govt in the senate, and leader of the govt in the senate from 2001-2003 when she also served as minister with special responsibility for palliative care. Carstairs wrote her autobiography, *Not One of the Boys* (1993). She also co-authored *Dancing backwards : a social history of Canadian women in politics*, published in 2004 with Tim Higgins. • CARSON JEREMA

CARTHER, Warren, artist, (b Aug 8, 1951, **WINNIPEG**) is an architectural glass artist of international repute. He received his BFA from the California College of Arts and Crafts in 1978. He has developed new techniques of laminating unlike glass surfaces to create large-scale sculptural and architectural works, some being more than 40 m in height. His many international commissions include the Anchorage International Airport (2004); Charles de Gaulle Airport, Paris (2000); Swire Properties Ltd. Lincoln House, Hong Kong (1999), the Ottawa International Airport (1999); Investors Group, Winnipeg (1994) and the Canadian Embassy, Tokyo, Japan, (1991). The imagery in each of these major installations draws on the geology of the region and its topography from aerial views, on which he overlays visual references to the respective cultures and philosophies. He uses heavy glass as the structural material, which he carves and sandblasts, onto which he glues various types of glass, clear, opaque and dichroic (which transmits different colours on each side). Using a wide range of colours, including metallics, the pieces are at once translucent and opaque. He received the Allied Arts Award from the Ontario Association of Architects in 1992; the American Craft Award in 1991; and has exhibited in the US, Canada, France and Switzerland. His work is in corporate and private collections in Canada and internationally and has been published worldwide including: Richard Yelle, *International Glass Art*, 2003; Andrew Moor, *Colours of Architecture*, 2006; Stephen Knapp, *The Art of Glass: Integrating Architecture and Glass*, 1998, and various periodicals. • PATRICIA BOVEY

CARTWRIGHT, pop 304, is a village 95 km SSE of Brandon and 10 km N of the US border. Originally built along the **BOUNDARY COMMISSION/NWMP**

TRAIL, and about 3 km N of its present location, the village's name was changed from Badger to Cartwright after Sir Richard Cartwright. (Sir Richard was then the Finance Minister for the federal govt, and owned land near the town) Residents moved to the railway site, the town's present location, when it was established between 1883 and 1885. The post office was opened in 1882. The village is primarily a service and retail centre for surrounding agriculture. A viewing area 6 km N of town allows visitors to see the Clay Banks, which were used as a **BISON** (buffalo) jump by Sonata and Besant cultures for thousands of years. • GPP

CAT is a family of carnivores represented in MB by 3 well-known members – the Cougar, Lynx and Bobcat. This family originated about 30 million years ago and evolved a great variety of forms both large and small, many of which became dominant predators in a wide variety of ecosystems in all regions except Australia and Antarctica. Unlike the wolf family (Canidae), whose large members run down their prey over long distances, cats exploited a strategy of ambush and lightening speed to capture their prey. Cats are characterized by a flattened face, teeth modified for tearing and cutting, large eyes, and retractile claws (which keep them sharp). The tongue is covered with rough bumps or papillae, which are used to rasp off flesh from carcasses or bones. Senses of sight, hearing and smell are highly developed and used in social interactions, prey detection, and avoidance of enemies.

COUGAR (*Felis concolor*) is a remarkably adaptive big cat, able to thrive in almost all habitats from the boreal and mountain forests of Canada, south through the tropics, to the southern tip of SA, from sea level to the alpine zone, as high as 3350 m elevation. Recent genetic evidence suggests that the Cougar is descended from the extinct American Cheetah. Males are considerably larger (averaging 80-136 kg) than females (50 kg). Rather surprisingly, early historical records of Cougars in MB are sparse, with few pelts recorded in fur-trade accounts (no certain localities), but with settlement of the prairie region, there are references to this animal (e.g., Tiger Hills south of Brandon). Records of Cougar up to 1940 are all in extreme southern Manitoba, within the former ranges of Mule Deer and American Elk – the Cougar's former main prey animals. With the subsequent great reduction in populations of these 2 species, and the influx of White-tailed **DEER** into the province, north to central MB, the Cougar's numbers and range expanded throughout the southern half of the province. There are many hundreds of acceptable sightings

and three kills recorded in the last two decades – evidence of several hundred Cougars resident here. Solitary for most of the year, the sexes come together in spring to mate, and about 90 days later (usually in June), 1-6 young are born in a rocky den or thicket. The young remain with the mother for up to 2 years, when she prepares to give birth again. Life expectancy is under 10 years in the wild, but may reach 19 years in a zoo. The Cougar is at the northern periphery of its range in MB, and no doubt it is severely tested to survive in our intensely cold winters.

ROBERT R. TAYLOR

Canadian Lynx

CANADIAN LYNX (*Felis canadensis*) is found throughout the province, from the prairies to the tundra, although it predominates in the boreal coniferous and mixed forests. Averaging 10 kg, exceptional individuals may reach 20 kg. The animal appears much larger than it is due to its cheek ruff, ear tufts, and luxuriant brown coat (longer in winter). The paws are enormous (approaching the size of a cougar), which help the Lynx float on top of the snow, and increase the chance of hooking prey animals with the long claws. Taking all kinds of small animals as food, its main diet consists of mice, snowshoe hares and birds. In fact, so dependant on the hare is the Lynx that its population cycles in slightly delayed synchrony with the 10-year cycle of the hare over large regions. Numbers may drop from 10 to 2 Lynx per 100 sq km in the years following a crash in hare populations. Highly secretive, the Lynx is a nervous and shy animal, preferring to live a solitary existence. With loud yowling and scent marking, the two sexes come together to mate in April, and quickly depart. The female gives birth 65 days later in June to 1-5 kittens in a hollow log or cave. Depending on food abundance, the Lynx wanders over a home range of from 10-300 sq km, covering from 5-19 km in a night. Longevity and average life span are unknown for wild Lynx, but individuals in zoos have lived for 21 years. Highly valued by the fur industry for several centuries, Lynx continue to be trapped widely in MB.

BOBCAT (*Felis rufus*) is often thought of as a small version of the Lynx (because the latter has longer fur), but it averages the same weight of 10 kg, and may reach 31 kg – far greater than any Lynx. The Bobcat does not have the Lynx's exaggerated ear tufts and cheek ruff, nor the black tip on the tail, but it does display black streaking on its equally shortened tail. The Bobcat's southern range complements that of the more-northerly Lynx. While a common species throughout all the contiguous US and most of Mexico, it is comparatively rare across southern Canada in mixed and deciduous forests, and has been found no farther north than Winnipeg. Remarkably, the Bobcat has been until recently a regular inhabitant along the riparian forest lining the Assiniboine River, well within the City of Winnipeg limits. It may be active during the day as well as night, and hunts over a home range of 1-200 sq km, travelling 1-12 km in a 12-hour period. Its numbers do not fluctuate significantly, averaging 1-3 /sq km. Both sexes may mate with several partners in March – the male grasping the back of the female's neck to protect himself during the noisy affair. About 62 days later, the female gives birth to 1-7 young, and the male occasionally stays nearby to help feed his offspring. The kittens travel with their mother until the end of winter, then strike out on their own. Like most cats, this species is an opportunistic hunter and feeds on a wide variety of small mammals, birds, fish, frogs and insects. While stalking a prey animal, the Bobcat concentrates so intently that it may ignore passing cars or hikers. • REW

CATFISH is a prominent MB fish featuring a rounded and stocky body without scales, sharp spines in the leading edge of the dorsal and pectoral fins, and a broad mouth surrounded by four pairs of whisker-like barbels. These mobile, fleshy structures, richly supplied with touch- and smell/taste-sensitive nerve cells, are the main means of detecting food items – a useful ability considering catfishes are active at night and often inhabit turbid water. Consequently, the eyes are small compared to other fish. Catfish play the roles of predator and scavenger, predominantly patrolling the bottom, and accepting opportunistically

DOUGLAS WATKINSON

Channel catfish

C

any creature they come across that they can fit into their large mouths. They also devour plant material. One must exercise caution in handling catfish, not from the teeth (which are small) but from the incredibly sharp and stout spines in some fins, which are thrust out to stab one's hand, or the mouth of any attacking predator. Although the Tadpole Madtom is small, its spines are used as an effective weapon, since they deliver a potent venom into the wound described as worse and longer lasting than a wasp sting. The use of this remarkable defensive adaptation usually results in the fish being rejected by predators, which may be left temporarily, partially paralyzed while the Madtom makes its escape, perhaps retreating into a discarded can or bottle. This secretive species and the Short-tailed Shrew (*Blarina brevicauda*) are the only venomous vertebrates in the province, although they pose no serious threat to people.

Catfish are represented in MB by 5 species with similar distributions in the **Red, Assiniboine** and **Winnipeg Rivers** and tributaries, **Lake Winnipeg**, and extreme southern **Lake Manitoba**. These are, in descending order of size: Channel Catfish (*Ictalurus punctatus*) averaging 10 kg and 90 cm in length; Brown Bullhead (*Ameiurus nebulosus*) 0.40 kg and 30 cm; Black Bullhead (*Ameiurus melas*); 0.3 kg and 23 cm; Stonecat (*Noturus flavus*) 0.28 kg and 20 cm; and Tadpole Madtom (*Noturus gyrinus*) 0.1 kg and 10 cm. All catfish are capable of living out of water for surprisingly long periods of time.

Mature Channel Catfish in MB waters are the largest catfish in Canada. The record MB specimen, taken in the Red River in 1992, was 20 kg and 118 cm. In spite of its considerable weight, it is a relatively slender species with an exceptionally wide and flat head. The tail is deeply forked. Mature individuals travel to gravel or rocky spawning sites in June, when water temperatures reach 21ºC. A nest, often with some kind of cover (such as a hole in a bank), is cleaned of debris and the female proceeds to lay 4,000 to 35,000 eggs, which are immediately fertilized by the male. Fanning and guarding the developing eggs is the responsibility of the male. The eggs hatch in 1-2 weeks and growth is rapid. Both young and adults accept a wide variety of plants and animals in their diet. The female matures at around age 10 and a length of 60 cm, and a few individuals may surpass 24 years. Breeding appears to take a toll on the fish, for the male's condition deteriorates during the activity, and females do not produce eggs every year. These catfish undergo remarkable journeys through connecting waterways – one tagged specimen travelled 350 km in Lake Winnipeg in

only 13 days. Angling for catfish is a highly popular sport in southern MB, but in spite of its excellent flavour and texture, catfish is not often eaten here. The reverse is true in the USA, where the Channel Catfish is the principal catfish raised in ponds for food, and its tender, white flesh is frequently served at home and in restaurants.

The 2 bullheads are often the first species caught by young anglers. They are distinguishable from the Channel Catfish by having a straight posterior border of the tail fin rather than the forked tail of the latter. The more-mottled Brown is often present in faster currents than the Black. In late May or June, when water temperatures reach around 21ºC, the Black Bullhead excavates a nest in or over a soft, muddy substrate, while the Brown prefers a nest on sand or gravel, although both will also use debris such as a tire or log. The nest is usually at depths of only 15-100 cm. During multiple releases, the female releases hundreds of eggs (although her ovaries may contain thousands) are fertilized by a single male, and he remains close by the female while the eggs develop and hatch in about 8 days. The pair keeps the eggs clean and oxygenated with the mouth and tail. In July and August, schools containing 500-800 small bullheads are often seen along the quiet shallows of streams and marshes, where they gobble up crustaceans, snail, leeches, insects and other small creatures. Fat and black, they resemble tadpoles, but they usually cruise continuously in a tight school, rather than wiggle in short bursts and independently like the amphibian larvae. The parents lurk nearby for several weeks, protecting their offspring from the attention of other large fish. Sexual maturity is reached in 3 years and maximum lifespan is 8 years. The Brown Bullhead in particular is a hardy species, capable of surviving for a short period in water as warm as 36º C, high dissolved carbon dioxide and low oxygen (critical in winter), and heavy levels of pollution. It may burrow into the mud to avoid some of these stressful conditions. • REW

CBC WINNIPEG COMEDY FESTIVAL. The annual festival brings together more Cdn comedians than any other festival in the country. It has taken place in Mar or Apr since 2001. Comedians perform stand-up comedy, sketches, and improvisational stage shows over 4 nights at venues around **Winnipeg**. Artists have included former Winnipegger and professional wrestler **"Rowdy" Roddy Piper**; Canadian Comedy Award winner Derek Edwards; *This Hour Has 22 Minutes* star Sean Majumder; UK comedian and TV writer Simon Evans; and Winnipeg-born **David Steinberg**. The festival is run by Winnipeg comic Al Rae. • GPP

CBWT was the Canadian Broadcasting Corporation's pioneer prairie television station, beginning its service out of **Winnipeg** on May 31, 1954. Only 22% of homes in Canada had a television set at that time. In its early years, CBWT programming was diverse and artistically adventurous. The station's signature news show *Spotlight* made local celebrities of newscaster Maurice Burchell, weatherman Ed Russenholt, who made his forecast by drawing a valentine in chalk over the MB area (the "heart of the continent"), and sportscaster "Cactus" **Jack Wells**, brother of Eric Wells, editor of the *Winnipeg Tribune*. The mobile unit of the news department was tested within a week of going on air by a massive fire at the Times Building fire. News director Norm Lacey devoted the entire 15-minute telecast to this event. The mobile unit would become a key part not only of news coverage but of sports and cultural reportage, broadcasting home games of the **Winnipeg Blue Bombers,** horseracing from the Polo Park grounds, the annual Santa Claus parade, the ice revue from the Winter Club, as well as openings from the **Winnipeg Art Gallery** and art classes from the **U of M** School of Art. *Country Calendar* with gardener Stan Westaway and farm commentator Vern McNair informed Manitobans about agricultural news and the mobile unit even telecast *The Cab Calloway Show* when the American entertainer played the Rancho Don Carlos nightclub in 1959.

The number of nationally broadcast shows was minimal and the isolation of Winnipeg prevented signals from American stations from being received locally. So CBWT shows drew upon and showcased local talent in music, dance, and drama. Although mostly short-lived, the resulting shows became models for longer-running and nationally broadcast shows in the next decade. *Cabaret* was a lively variety show hosted by the multi-talented Marsh Phimister, headlined by singers Maxine Ware and Reg Gibson, and backed by Reg Parks' orchestra. Employing an in-studio nightclub set complete with reception area and a cigarette girl circulating among patrons seated at tables, *Cabaret* offered up a half-hour of contemporary songs. Other music shows of the period included *Let's Sing* and the western-themed *Saddle Songs* and *Rope Around the Sun* (with Stu Phillips), both precursors of the popular *Red River Jamboree*.

Dance was also adapted for television. The **Royal Winnipeg Ballet** contributed a ballet series for youngsters called *Toes in Tempo* and revived a television version of Robert Service's *The Shooting of Dan McGrew* starring dancers Roger Fisher, Alex Yenko, Marina Katronis and Arnold Spohr. Spohr also partnered Kay Bird for

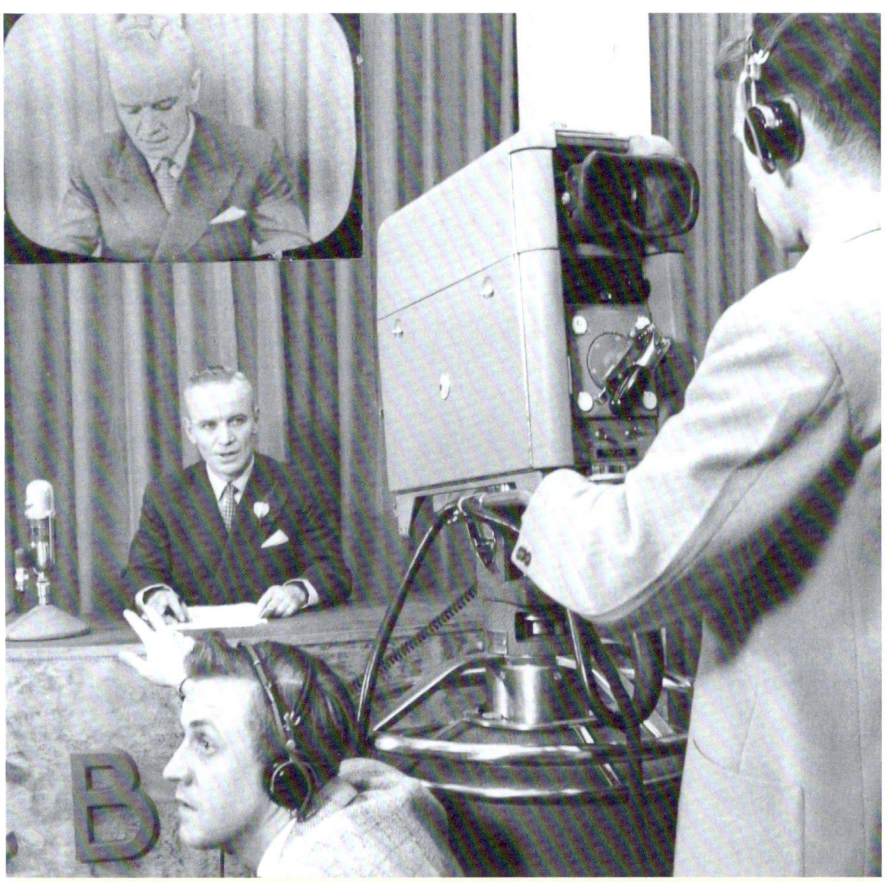

Maurice Burchell in a 1954 CBWT broadcast

ballroom dance guest spots on *Cabaret*. Drama had been a vital part of the national CBC schedule since the days of radio plays by Robert Allen and Lister Sinclair. CBWT televised original plays by Art Zigouras, Alfred Harris and Mary Fowler as well as John Hirsch's ambitious production of Anton Chekhov's 1-act play *The Anniversary* starring Victor Cowie.

In 1958, the new *Broadcasting Act* established a separate regulating body that permitted the entry of the private sector into television. Although the public network continued, the CBC had lost its monopoly at a time when 80% of Canadian households had televisions. Through the 1960s-1980s, CBWT was a significant player in the Cdn network, producing such national shows as *Hymn Sing*, *Fred Penner's Place* and *Country Canada* and a local hour-long daily news program featuring hosts like **JOHN HARVARD**, who would later become an MP and MB's lt gov. Many people who would go on to key positions in the CBC network, such as *The National*'s host Peter Mansbridge, not to mention CTV's Lloyd Robertson, also worked at CBWT. However, by the 1990s, govt funding became more uncertain and the network was challenged by the competition of a 200-channel universe. Local stations like CBWT did little of their own programming,

with the weekday news segment eventually cut to a half-hour. The vagaries of corporate decision-making in Toronto and Ottawa almost resulted in killing the local news altogether, but in 2007, a full-hour, supper news program was reinstated. It remained to be seen whether CBWT could make up ground lost to rival CTV and provide a viable alternative to the private stations. • HOWARD CURLE/INGEBORG BOYENS

CENTIPEDE is a multi-segmented, flattened arthropod related to millipede. It superficially resembles a worm, but there are numerous unique characteristics. Although the name implies 100 legs, they always have an odd number (15-191) of leg-bearing segments, with 1 pair of legs /segment, and with the last pair of legs longer and directed backwards, used for grasping prey. The antennae are long with 14 or more segments. Species can range from 2 mm-30 cm long – the largest ones being quite frightening in appearance and in their quick, sinuous movements (e.g., the 15 cm Scolopendra heros of the deserts of S US). MB species are generally under 3 cm long and harmless, but even these can startle a person when they appear suddenly. While there are some herbivorous species, most are active predators (often cannibalistic) armed

with a set of hollow, poison fangs on the first pair of legs, used for paralyzing insects, spiders, slugs, worms and other small creatures, which are then chewed up with a set of mandibles. Centipedes are common in grass and forested communities, especially in S MB. Entirely nocturnal, they are generally found during the day in crevasses in the soil, under logs and stones, and in decomposing plant litter. Most people only become aware of their presence when one is uncovered while digging in the garden, or moving items in the garage or basement. Centipedes overwinter as adults, and following courtship and mating, the female lays sticky eggs is the soil in spring and summer. This group contains over 3000 species worldwide, and about 105 species in Canada. Over 50 species occur in MB, including several exotics introduced from Europe. • REW

CENTRE FOR MENNONITE BRETHREN STUDIES. *See* MENNONITE HERITAGE CENTRE.

CENTRAL PLAINS, one of MB's 8 recognized provincial regions, is W of **WINNIPEG**, E of **BRANDON**, S of **LAKE MANITOBA**, and N of the **PEMBINA VALLEY**. It was home to about 44,000 people as of 1996. The region's landscape consists of flat land and isolated stands of trees, with sandy, rolling plains in the west. The **ASSINIBOINE** and La Salle rivers cross the district, which stretches to the S and SE shores of Lake Manitoba. The Trans-Canada and Yellowhead highways, as well as the main **CN** and **CPR** lines, traverse the region.

Nomadic Assiniboine, **DAKOTA**, and Plains **CREE** peoples followed and hunted huge prairie **BISON** herds throughout the region for thousands of years. **CUTHBERT GRANT** led one of the first **MÉTIS** settlements in the area, Grantown, at the site of what is now **ST. FRANCOIS XAVIER**. The town became MB's 2nd **ROMAN CATHOLIC** parish in 1834. The historic Fort Ellice Trail (the initial leg of the Carlton Trail to what is now Edmonton: *see* **EARLY TRAILS AND PATHS**) ran through the region from **UPPER FORT GARRY** to Fort Ellice near the MB-SK border. **ENGLISH**, **GERMAN** (including **HUTTERITES**), and **SCOTS** are the most common ethnic backgrounds of residents. In 1881-82, the completion of the CPR across the area led to speculation and inflated land prices for the prime, fertile land, though prices collapsed later in the decade.

In the 21st century, Central Plains is still dominated by **AGRICULTURE**, especially **GRAIN** farming. Most communities are regional service centres that support farming. In 1996, more than ¼ of area residents were employed in **AGRICULTURAL** and related services. The largest private-sector employer is McCain Foods in **PORTAGE LA PRAIRIE**.

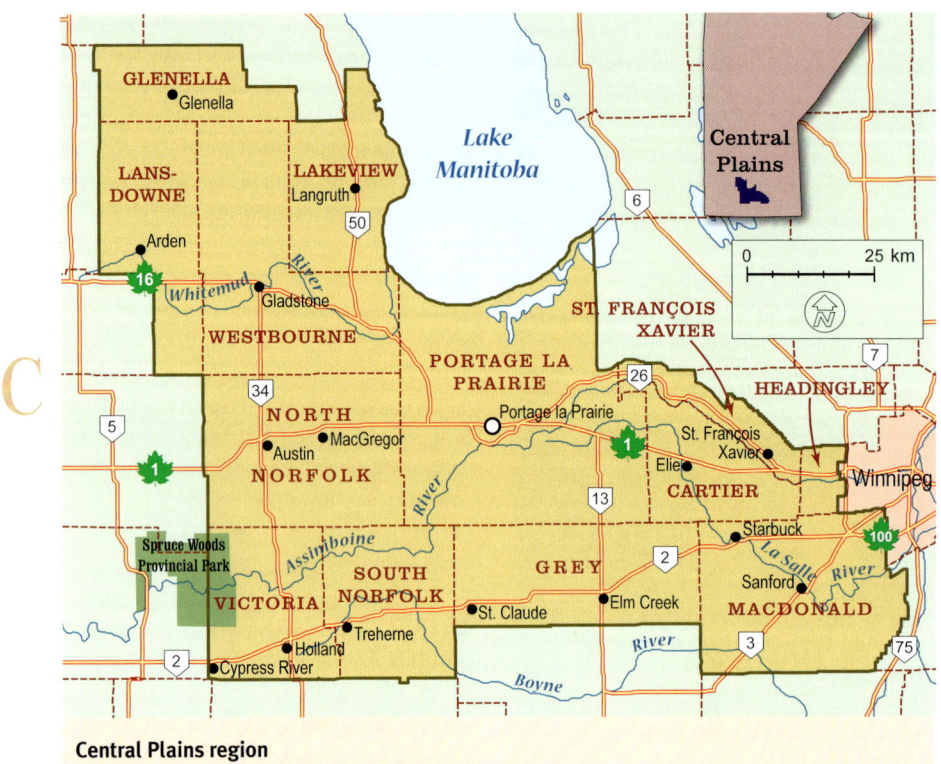

Central Plains region

DOUG FAST

Rural Municipalities in Central Plains

Cartier	Glenella
Grey	Headingley
Lakeview	Lansdowne
Macdonald	North Norfolk
Portage la Prairie	South Norfolk
St. Francois Xavier	Victoria
Westbourne	

The region is made up of 13 rural municipalities. The largest population centres include Portage la Prairie, **HEADINGLEY**, **MACGREGOR**, **GLADSTONE**, and **TREHERNE**. Central Plains also includes the First Nations communities of **DAKOTA TIPI**, **DAKOTA PLAINS**, **LONG PLAIN**, and **SANDY BAY**. ● JT

CERCLE MOLIÈRE, Le. MB's only professional French-language **THEATRE** company is also the oldest permanent theatre company in Canada. Founded by the Belgian André Castelin de la Lande (artistic director 1925-27), MB-born Raymond Bernier (secretary-treasurer), and the QC-born but MB-educated Louis-Philippe Gagnon (president 1925 27), Le Cercle Molière presented its inaugural play, a comedy of manners by a 19th-century Parisian playwright, at the Dominion Theatre on Apr 25, 1925. The theatre company's objective was to promote French culture and ideas to both French and English speaking audiences of MB.

Contrary to what its name might lead one to believe, it was only in 1950, to mark its 25th

anniversary, that the Cercle Molière presented a play by Molière. For its first 40 years, the Cercle Molière was an amateur theatre troupe without a permanent home. On the **WINNIPEG** side of the **RED RIVER**, the plays were staged at the Walker Theatre (*see* **CORLISS POWERS "C. P." WALKER**), the Pantages Playhouse, and the Civic Auditorium (*see* **ARCHIVES**). In **ST. BONIFACE**, the auditoriums of Provencher School, **COLLÈGE UNIVERSITAIRE SAINT-BONIFACE**, and Saint-Joseph Academy were the troupe's normal venues. The Cercle Molière's amateur years are closely identified with 2 artistic directors: Arthur Boutal, and his wife, Pauline Boutal. Arthur, a printer originally from France, was artistic director from 1926 to his death in 1941. **PAULINE BOUTAL** (née LeGoff), a fine portraitist and an illustrator at **BRIGDEN'S** – also originally from France – took over from 1941 until 1968.

The Cercle Molière has a long history of touring. The tradition started during the 1929-30 season, when the troupe took an Alphonse Daudet play to 30 Francophone communities in MB. From 1934 to 1974, the Cercle Molière was also a regular participant in the Dominion Drama Festival where it won many awards. By the late 1960s, with the coming of age of the baby boomers, changes were occurring in the francophone community. In 1968, after more than 40 years at the helm of the Cercle Molière, Pauline Boutal passed the torch to Roland Mahé, a **U OF M** fine arts graduate associated with the Cercle Molière since 1961. Roland Mahé became the first full-time artistic director of the

troupe. Under Mahé's direction, the Cercle Molière's vocation would no longer be to promote French culture and ideas through theatre, but rather to create the best professional French-language drama possible. In 1970, the Cercle Molière presented *Les Belles-sœurs* by Québécois playwright Michel Tremblay. For the first time, Franco-Manitoban spectators heard on stage a play "in their language." In 1975, the company's 50th anniversary year and their first season in their new permanent home at Salle Pauline-Boutal in the Centre culturel franco-manitobain, the Cercle Molière produced its first authentic Franco-Manitoban play. Written by Roger Auger, *Je m'en vais à Régina* (I'm leaving for Regina) presented a pessimistic look at the survival of the French community in MB. Auger would go on to write 3 more plays for the Cercle Molière, as well as a French-language adaptation of AB playwright George Ryga's *The Ecstasy of Rita Joe*. Other playwrights would follow, including Claude Dorge (later also an actor); Irène Mahé, Rhéal Cenerini, Jean-Pierre Dubé, and Marc Prescott. In 1986, the Cercle Molière presented its first "All Manitoban" season, where all the plays were by MB playwrights. It would repeat this feat for its 2000-01 season to commemorate the 75th anniversary of the company. ● LUCIEN CHAPUT

CF-18 SCANDAL was a pivotal political event in recent western Cdn history. In 1986 the federal Progressive Conservative govt of PM Brian Mulroney ignored the recommendation of a blue-ribbon panel of 75 civil servants and awarded a 20-year, $1.3-billion contract to overhaul Canada's new fleet of McDonnell Douglas (now Boeing) CF-18A Hornet fighter-bomber jets to Canadair of Montreal over a technically superior and cheaper bid by **BRISTOL AEROSPACE LTD.** of **WINNIPEG**. Announcing the decision, Treasury Board pres Robert de Cotret said the govt wanted the technology gained from the contract to remain in Cdn hands and not to go to a UK-owned company. But Manitobans and Westerners were instantly reminded of another, earlier, loss, when the headquarters of the nation's flag carrier, **TRANS-CANADA AIR LINES** (now Air Canada) was moved from its founding city of Winnipeg to Montreal in the 1960s.

Within hours of the Halloween announcement, Manitobans from all walks of life rallied around **HOWARD PAWLEY'S** **NDP** government. It was a political lifeline for an administration struggling to recover from a near loss in the Mar 18, 1986, election and a string of embarrassing scandals. Within days, a reinvigorated Pawley led a delegation of business, labour, municipal, and civic leaders to Ottawa to demand the govt listen to its own experts and rescind its decision. They got nowhere. Mulroney insisted his decision was in the national interest.

The controversy that engulfed the province spread to other parts of western Canada and was a significant factor in the creation of the Reform Party and the subsequent fracturing and destruction of the Progressive Conservatives in the 1993 federal election. That election was a political watershed. The party of Confederation and Sir John A. Macdonald plunged from govt and 169 seats to a minuscule 5th-party rump with just 2 MPs. Its place was taken by 2 regional entities: Reform in the West, and the separatist Bloc Québécois in Mulroney's home province.

Rhetoric was strong on all sides. A prominent Winnipeg businessman declared he wanted to see the PM "hanged, by the neck, on a rope." The premier called it "a royal shaft." Aware of the political minefield he now faced, **PC PARTY OF MANITOBA** Opposition leader Gary Filmon described it as a crass political decision that would cut at the root of Canada's national interest. "I am absolutely outraged," he said. The provincial PC party briefly considered changing its name to distance itself from its federal cousin. While that extreme was abandoned, MB PCs

did vote to condemn their federal cousins at their annual convention, held within days of the announcement.

Public calls went out to MB's 2 Cabinet representatives, Health Minister Jake Epp and **CANADIAN WHEAT BOARD** Minister Charlie Mayer, to resign. Learning that Conservatives across the province were ripping up their party cards, the Liberals offered half-price memberships to Tories willing to cut up their PC cards in Liberal offices. Not everyone climbed aboard the regional alienation bandwagon. **ST. BONIFACE** Tory MP Leo Duguay blasted his fellow Winnipeggers as "whiners." (He was sharply rebuked by Winnipeg mayor **WILLIAM "BILL" NORRIE**.)

For the vast majority of Manitobans and western Canadians, the issue was rubbing salt in an old wound, and a brand-new metaphor for all their grievances going back to the **CPR** and the National Energy Policy. The fact their betrayal had occurred at the hands of a govt whose party the West had faithfully backed since the John Diefenbaker era only intensified the anger and alienation. A poll conducted by the **WINNIPEG FREE PRESS** in Jan 1987 found Mulroney's approval rating had plunged to a dismal 4%. It also reported the federal Conservatives at a new low, a mere 16%.

YOU HAVE TO PLACE THE CONTRACT WHERE IT WILL DO THE MOST GOOD.

BALLOTS

CF-18 CANADAIR

Winnipeg Free Press **cartoon by Dale Cummings**

Winnipeg did get a consolation prize – the refitting of Canada's fleet of CF-5 fighter-trainers, and the building of helicopter parts and rocket components. But insistence by some Conservatives that these contracts were worth more than the CF-18 prize didn't impress Manitobans. They were more impressed by a Jan 1988 federal evaluation that found the awarding of the contract to Canadair cost taxpayers 13% more in the first 4 years and 1.8% each year after that. But the report was not released for 15 months – well after the 1988 federal election, in which Mulroney won another majority on the single issue of his free trade deal with the US – a long-cherished western Cdn dream. The seeds of the defeat of the federal Progressive Conservative Party in 1993 were sown with that 1986 Halloween decision. The CF-18 fiasco, pitting the West against central Canada, particularly, QC, is now seen by many as a defining, and nation-changing, event in Cdn politics. ● FRANCES RUSSELL

CHALMERS, Angela, distance runner (b Sept 6, 1963, **BRANDON**) is an Aboriginal Olympic athlete. Born to a **DAKOTA** mother and **SCOTS** father, Chalmers grew up on the **BIRDTAIL SIOUX FIRST NATION**. She began competing in track and field events in high school, and her MB records in the 800 m and 1500 m junior and senior events have never been broken. In 1981, she represented MB at the Canada Summer Games, winning 2 silver medals. She attended Northern Arizona U on an athletic scholarship, and won the All-American title 8 times. Her first international victory came in 1984 at the World University Games. She then joined Canada's national track and field team, and was a silver medallist at the 1987 **PAN AM GAMES**. At the 1990 Commonwealth Games, Chalmers became the first athlete to win gold in both the 1500 m and 3000 m events. She was named Manitoba Female Athlete of the Year, and was also awarded the Phil Edwards Memorial Trophy as Canada's top track and field athlete. Her crowning achievement came as a bronze medal winner at the 1992 Summer Olympics in Barcelona, Spain. She went on to win the 1500 m at the 1993 world championships. She won another gold medal in the 3000 m at the 1994 Commonwealth Games in Victoria, BC, and was awarded an Aboriginal Achievement Award the following year. A leg injury while training for the 1996 Olympics ended her career prematurely. She is considered an important Aboriginal role model. ● MD

CHAMPION, George, park planner, landscaper (b 1870, Frampton, Dorsetshire, UK; d 1946, Toronto) was employed at the Royal Gardens at

Kew before coming to Canada in 1897. He moved to **Winnipeg** in 1907 to become superintendent of the parks board. He retired in 1935 and returned to Toronto. Champion was responsible for the execution of the design of **Assiniboine Park** and for the design of **Kildonan Park** (1911), as well as for the creation of a number of smaller parks and municipal **Golf** courses. From the beginning, Champion envisioned an integrated park system linked with broad boulevards in the "City Beautiful" manner. He had some problems with the flatness of the landscape, although he designed the English Garden at Assiniboine Park. Champion was firmly opposed to commercial amusements in parks. • JMB

CHAR, ARCTIC (*Salvelinus alpinus*) is a member of the salmon family and holds the distinction of being the most northerly of all freshwater fish. It has a circumpolar range and occurs throughout **Hudson Bay** and inland in MB for about 100 km in rivers and lakes. It occurs in both land-locked and anadromous (migrating between freshwater to marine) populations. The latter migrate downstream with the break-up of river and Hudson Bay ice in June and early July and spend the summer feeding in marine waters. The ability to adapt to both fresh and salt water (particularly regarding kidney function) greatly increases the success of this species. Char range widely in search of prey concentrations during the summer in the Bay, with movements up to 33 km/day and over 800 km (Nunavut to ON). Prey such as crustaceans and fish are far-more abundant in marine waters than in fresh, so these Char grow faster and larger, and are in better body condition (also host to fewer parasites), and therefore produce more eggs. From mid-Aug to mid-Sept, they return to freshwater, thereby avoiding the sub-zero temperatures of the Bay waters (salt water can drop several degrees below 0° C without freezing). They do not necessarily select their natal rivers, until they are ready to spawn. Char mate and spawn in rivers and lakes from late Aug-early Oct (even under the ice) over a gravel bottom in a lake or river where the depth and current help keep the eggs from freezing and being covered by debris. Eggs hatch from April to May and the fry spend several years feeding on insects and crustaceans in freshwater before migrating to the Bay (at 15-20 cm length). After 2-4 seasons feeding in marine waters, the Char becomes mature (range between 5-12 years) and usually breeds in alternate years. It may reach 88 cm, 7.2 kg, and live 30 yrs. Char is an important prey species for seals, belugas and birds, and also for subsistence, commercial and sport fishing. • REW

CHEMAWAWIN CREE NATION, on reserve pop 1254, off reserve pop 283, located 120 km SE of **The Pas** and 500 km NW from **Winnipeg**. Chemawawin has 3 reserves, but only 2 are populated. Flooding forced the community to move from Reserve No. 1 on the S shore of Cedar Lake, W of **Easterville**, to Reserve No. 2, adjacent to **Easterville** on the SE shore of Cedar Lake. In 1963, **MB Hydro** built a dam in **Grand Rapids**, which caused extensive flooding in the area. The Chemawawin people were moved to their present location with promises from the MB govt that their life would be better. However, the Chemawawin Cree Nation's new home was a rocky terrain, where prospects for **Hunting**, gardening, and trapping were minimal. As well, because of the flooding, debris in nearby Cedar Lake and mercury contamination made **Fishing** difficult. The people of Chemawawin Cree Nation have had to deal with addictions, criminal behavior, welfare reliance, financial failure, and health problems. The native language of this community is **Cree**. Chemawawin signed Treaty 5 in 1875. The Chemawawin Cree Nation has access to a small runway in Easterville, along with float-plane and boat dock access. Education here goes from Nursery-Grade 9, and total enrolment for the year 2003-2004 was 458. The economic foundation of the Chemawawin Cree Nation includes heavy equipment contracting, logging, fishing, and residential development. It is a member of the Swampy Cree Tribal Council. • RK

AM, WINNIPEG FREE PRESS 18, N5384, AUGUST 2, 1913

Empress WHERE EVERYBODY GOES

Three Shows Daily: 3, 8, 9.30. Mats.: 10c to 25c. Evgs.: 10c to 35c.

CHAS. CHAPLIN

AS HE IS

NEXT WEEK

THEY'RE BACK AGAIN AFTER MAKING MILLIONS LAUGH.

KARNO'S LONDON COMEDIANS

With CHARLES CHAPLIN and a Company of Fourteen, in

"A NIGHT IN A LONDON CLUB"

The Noted Character Comedian	Musical Comedy's Cleverest Pair	Remarkable Human Salamanders
GEO. F. HALL	BRIERRE & KING	THE NAGYFYS

ROLAND WEST ANNOUNCES THE NEW FROLICSOME FARCE

"THE TAMER" With MABEL FLORENCE AND BERESFORD LOVETT

A FEATURE FILM AND THE EMPRESS ORCHESTRA

CHAPLIN, Charlie visited **Winnipeg** several times as a vaudeville performer before hitting it big in Hollywood. Fellow comedian Groucho Marx claimed he saw Chaplin for the first time in Winnipeg, when he was performing with his brothers on Fort St. There were several vaudeville theatres on Fort St., including the Orpheum, but the biggest shows usually played the Walker Theatre on Notre Dame. •

CHESS tournament activity in MB dates back to 1895, when 8 men gathered at Austen's Shorthand College on McDermot Ave in **WINNIPEG** to found the Winnipeg Chess Club. The club's earliest recorded tournament was a 6-board match against the **SCOTS** St. Andrews Society. The strongest MB player of the era was **ICELANDER** Magnus Smith. Smith, who was born in Iceland in 1867 and immigrated to Canada at the age of 18, won the Cdn championship in 1899, 1904, and 1906. He defeated several international players who gave simultaneous exhibitions in Winnipeg, including American Harry Nelson Pillsbury in 1899 and then-world champion Emanuel Lasker of Germany in 1907. There were many avid players among Winnipeg's **JEWISH** population, and in 1919, the Winnipeg Jewish Chess Club was founded. Although the province produced strong players over the years, the first to win the Cdn championship since 1906 was **DANIEL ABRAHAM "ABE" YANOFSKY**, in 1941. He went on to earn the international grandmaster title – the first from Canada to do so – and won 8 Cdn championships, becoming MB's strongest player for a half-century.

MB's greatest chess-problem composer was Jacob Funk, an **ALTONA** farmer born in 1889. Funk, who was also a skilled carpenter, guitar player, mathematician, and puzzle inventor, had his first problem published in 1918. For more than 40 years, his original problems were printed in international periodicals from the *Christian Science Monitor* to *Australian Chess Magazine*.

By the 1950s, MB had begun to organize important national events, including the Canadian Chess Championship in 1953 and the Canadian Open in 1958. In 1967, Winnipeg organized the strongest international tournament ever held in the country. The Canadian Centennial Grandmaster's Tournament had 10 participants, including 2 excellent players from the USSR, the Russian Boris Spassky and the Estonian Paul Keres. Klaus Darga of West Germany and Bent Larsen of Denmark were joint winners, with Yanofsky finishing 9th. Although MB produced no other players of Yanofsky's calibre, Peter Biyiasas learned the game in Winnipeg as a child and spent 10 years in the city, eventually moving to Vancouver, where he became a grandmaster. In 1974, Winnipeg organized the Pan American International, bringing together national champions of North, Central, and South America. The Canadian Open in 1986 featured the world's 3rd-highest ranking player, Artur Yusupov, who won the tournament with fellow-Soviet Viktor Kupreichik. The biggest tournament in MB history was the Canadian Open in 1997, with 188 players and 11 grandmasters. ● CECIL ROSNER

CHIEF MEDICAL EXAMINER. The CME is given the responsibility for investigating all violent, unexpected, unexplained, or unattended deaths occurring in the province. Hospitals and institutions are also investigated if an individual dies within 24 hours of admission, within 10 days of surgery, or while under or recovering from anaesthesia. The CME is appointed by the Lieut Gov to serve the province and is mandated by *The Manitoba Fatality Inquiries Act* and the *Vital Statistics Act*. The medical examiner and medical examiner's system evolved from duties that were originally assigned to coroners. The common-law powers of a coroner to indict someone after an inquest for murder or manslaughter, to commit them for trial, and to certify evidence were incorporated as part of the Canadian Criminal Code in 1892. With the advancements being made in forensics, the departure from using a coroner – often a physician with no special training in pathology – to a system that used qualified medical persons was a logical one. *The Manitoba Fatality Inquiries Act* replaced *The Coroner's Act* in 1971. Medical doctors throughout MB are appointed as medical examiners, and carry out investigations on behalf of the CME's office. The central office is in Winnipeg and is staffed with 14 permanent members. Other key functions of the CME are to supervise the work of medical examiners and investigators, establish and maintain professional standards for medical examiners and investigators, and regulate and provide education and training. The need for a court hearing or inquest to examine the death of an individual is determined by the CME. An inquest will be called if the CME determines that the public may benefit from information arising from the hearing. The initial inquiry is carried out by a medical examiner, while the inquest, if deemed necessary, is conducted by a provincial judge without a jury. ● JS

CHILD CARE in MB, outside the home, began when the Mothers' Association established the first day nursery in Winnipeg in 1901. For the next 70 years, only women's groups and charities provided child-care services. By the 1970s, the provincial govt began to monitor and subsidize programs. In 1983, the govt passed the *Community Child Day Care Standards Act*, and its corresponding regulations. In 2004, the act was renamed the *Community Child Care Standards Act* in order to recognize that early childhood education is often more than "daycare."

In 2004, MB had 25,634 regulated spaces in licensed child-care centres, nursery schools, and family daycare homes to serve infants and children up to the age of 12. Licensed child-care services are provided to 14.3% of the province's 179,400 young children (slightly lower than the national average of 15.5%). The number of spaces has grown slowly but steadily over recent years. In 1992, for example, there were licensed spaces for just 9.1% of the province's children.

Child care in MB is paid for directly by the parents who use the service. The fee varies by the age of the child and may be as high as $7280 per year for an infant or as low as $3138 per year for a school-age child. MB is one of only 2 provinces (QC being the other) where fee rates are set by the provincial govt. Parents pay the same fee regardless of income. In cases where parents have a very low income (well below the poverty line) and meet strict eligibility criteria, fee subsidies are available. Close to 45% of children in licensed child care received a fee subsidy in 2004, but no child received "free" care – all parents, even those on social assistance, must pay a portion of the cost.

The MB Child Care Program (operated through the Ministry of Family Services and Housing, under Child and Family Services) provides funding to child-care facilities. Provincial funding supports facilities and stabilizes parents' fees. The total budget for the MB Child Care Program, including the Children with Disabilities program, was $103 million in 2005-06. Nearly all of MB's child-care centres are non-profit, and MB Child Care Program funding is generally restricted to non-profit programs. However, some commercial facilities are eligible for partial payment.

In 2002, MB released its first Five Year Plan for Child Care, the only province outside QC to announce multi-year child-care planning. In the 2004 and 2005 federal elections, child care was a major social-policy issue. In 2005, the minority federal govt moved forward on its interest in developing a national system of early learning and child care by committing $5 billion, nationwide, over 5 years. MB was the first province to sign on to the innovative bilateral model. Highlights of the agreement include commitments to quality, universality, and developmentally appropriate services, with funding restricted to the community-based non-profit sector.

Other forms of early childhood care and education exist in MB. Under federal law, family-related leaves provide parents with up to 54 weeks of maternity and parental leave to care for newborn and adopted infants. Less than half of new mothers, however, are able to take an EI-paid maternity leave, while slightly more families are able to take a parental leave.

At age 5, many MB children have access to kindergarten. Kindergarten is a part-time (usually 2.5 hours), publicly funded program in schools, available without any direct parent fee. A few school divisions also provide a part-time "nursery" program, which, in other jurisdictions, is called "junior kindergarten."

Despite the abovementioned, there are not enough licensed spaces to meet the needs of MB children and parents. The best-served age group is preschoolers: those aged 2-5. There are fewer spaces available for infant and school-aged children. Most facilities are targeted to the standard Mon-Fri workweek of 9:00 am-5:00 pm. This leaves out the growing number of families where evening, weekend, seasonal, and shift-work care is needed. Children in rural, remote, and northern regions are particularly underserved, and the crisis of rural child care is becoming more urgent as the accident and injury rate remains unacceptably high. Aboriginal and Francophone communities need more culturally appropriate and accessible programs.

The area receiving the most attention is the labour force of early childhood educators. Child care, like most other female-dominated professions, has long been underpaid. Wages for child-care workers fell between 9-12% over the 1990s.

Key organizations working to improve MB's child-care system are the MB Child Care Association (which represents professional educators) and the Child Care Coalition of MB (a broad-based organization representing parents, programs, and social-justice groups). The trade-union movement is increasingly interested in child care, and the MB Government Employees Union (MGEU) and the Canadian Union of Public Employees (CUPE) represent a growing number of unionized facilities. ● SUSAN PRENTICE

CHILD WELFARE first became a govt concern in MB with the passage of the *Act for the Better Protection of Neglected and Dependent Children* (1898, also known as the *Children's Protection Act*), which permitted the development of private, voluntary societies to provide child-protection services. The Children's Aid Society (CAS) of Winnipeg was established in the same year and other societies were established over time in BRANDON, ST. BONIFACE, PORTAGE LA PRAIRIE, and DAUPHIN. The CAS of St. Adelard (later Eastern MB) was established in 1904 to serve the French ROMAN CATHOLIC population of ST. BONIFACE. The Hebrew Ladies' Home Association, formed in 1913, later became Jewish Child and Family Services, and provided specific services to JEWISH children and families. Religious or humanitarian organizations also formed orphanages, and institutional care evolved as the primary form of alternate care until after WWII. Growing concerns about high infant-mortality rates, particularly for infants in institutions in the early 20th century, also led to the boarding-out of some children

with other families. This form of alternate care was a forerunner of current foster care.

The *Children's Protection Act* was minimalist in intent, and it was the influence of the social-gospel and women's movements of the early 20th century that helped to ensure the passage of the *Child Welfare Act* (1922). This legislation was more comprehensive, and reflected both the humanitarian and social-control impulses associated with the child-saving movement. While there was a genuine concern to improve care for children at risk, there was also a concern about the need to control what was regarded as "uncivilized influences of wayward immigrant children." Provisions in the new act were implemented slowly, although the legislation remained the framework for provincial child-welfare services until the 1974 *Child Welfare Act*. The 1974 act introduced the notion of the "best interests" of the child as a basis for decision-making, and the option of providing early intervention and family-support services.

In the 1940s, services, provided directly by govt, were extended to rural and northern areas of MB, with the exception of First Nations (FN) reserves. Child welfare services, including the use of foster homes, expanded significantly following the introduction of fed/provincial cost sharing in the *Canada Assistance Act* (1966). The expansion of services coincided with an increase of children in care from 1250 in 1951 (a rate of 0.44%) to 5412 in 1992 (a rate of 1.88%).

The 1980s was a period of significant change in MB child welfare. In 1985, services previously offered through Winnipeg CAS were decentralized to 6 regional agencies in the city, and a more community-based service model evolved. While early intervention services were expanded, there was an unanticipated growth in the number of children in care, and regional agencies were disbanded in 1991. In 1985, the *CFS Act* was passed. It introduced mandatory reporting of suspected cases of abuse or neglect and a set of principles, including respect for cultural and linguistic heritage, to guide service provision.

The most important change in the 1980s was the delegation of service responsibility for child welfare on reserves to First Nations communities. This was in response to growing concerns about the overrepresentation of FN and other Aboriginal children in care, and the practice of placing these children outside their communities and culture. The delegated authority model involved FN management and control over service delivery, federal funding for on-reserve services, and the provision of services in compliance with provincial laws and standards. MB took a lead role in establishing

these arrangements in Canada, and the first agreement to provide fully mandated services to reserves was signed with the Dakota Ojibway CFS in 1981. Agreements with other FNs across MB followed over the next few years. More than half of the Aboriginal population in MB live off-reserve, and the 1991 ABORIGINAL JUSTICE INQUIRY recommended that Aboriginal child-welfare agencies be established to serve these families. In 1999, the Aboriginal Justice Inquiry Child Welfare Initiative was launched. Following a collaborative policy-making process, the *CFS Authorities Act* was passed in 2002, creating 4 authorities: a northern, a southern, a Métis, and a general one.

The case-transfer process to new authorities occurred in 2005. Intake procedures are designed to ensure Aboriginal families can receive culturally appropriate child-protection and family-support services. Although each authority has delegated responsibility for services and standards for agency providers under its mandate, overall responsibility for child welfare rests with the Ministry of Family Services and Housing. The distribution of child welfare caseloads between authorities, including caseloads on reserves, in 2005 was: Southern FN Authority – 40%; Northern FN Authority – 25%; Métis Authority – 7%; and General Authority – 28%.

As of Mar 2004, there were 5782 children in care within the MB child-welfare system, of whom 83% were Aboriginal. More than 8400 families or adolescent parents were receiving services from the 21 CFS agencies in MB in Mar 2004. More than 66% of the children in care were in foster care; 6% were in residential care (group homes or residential treatment centres); 18% were in designated places of safety; and 8% were in other living arrangements.

The cost of delivering child-welfare services by MB in 2003-04 was $150 million, excluding funding provided directly to FN agencies by the federal govt. Most of the resources in child welfare are devoted to the investigation of child maltreatment and the cost of maintaining children in alternate care. ● BRAD MCKENZIE/DENNIS SCHELLENBERG

CHINESE Canadians settled in MB in modest numbers in the 1880s, though the very first Chinese arrived from the US in 1877. The 1881 Census recorded only 4 residents of Chinese origin in MB, but successive waves of IMMIGRATION had created a vibrant Chinese community in the province of more than 14,000 by 2001.

The first major group of Chinese immigrants arrived in BC from the US West Coast in pursuit of gold, starting with the Fraser River

The Dynasty Building on King Street in Winnipeg.

Valley rush in 1858. They were joined by greater numbers from overseas and began to build the **CPR** in 1880. About 17,000 Chinese workers laboured under dangerous conditions for half the pay of whites. Following the completion of the line in 1885, many immigrants set out E to look for new opportunities. Due to language barriers, discrimination in other trades, and experience gained from CPR labour camps, most took work in laundries, or as cooks, domestic servants, grocers, and fruit and vegetable vendors. A small business culture began to take root. In 1901, the MB Census accounted for 167 Chinese; the number had risen to 885 in **WINNIPEG** by 1911, of a total population of 140,000. Also in 1885, the federal govt moved to restrict further Chinese migration by instituting the *Chinese Immigration Act*, which applied a head tax of $50 on new arrivals. It did not have the desired effect of stemming immigration, and the govt increased the tax to $100 in 1900, and to $500 in 1903. More than 82,000 Chinese immigrants paid the tax between 1885 and 1923, when xenophobia took an even-worse form: the 1923 *Chinese Immigration Act* prevented the admission of any new Chinese immigrants into Canada.

In the early 20th century, Winnipeg's Chinatown began to develop in the downtown warehouse district, where it can still be found today. Quong Chong Tai – the first Chinese store – opened in 1905 on King St. Chinese immigrants ran nearly all of the laundry houses. The 1921 Census counted 464 laundries in MB, compared with a Chinese population of only 1300. Most Chinese in Canada at that time were men who had immigrated without their spouses or families. Census data from 1931 show there were more than 12 men for every one woman in Chinese communities. For example, Ho King, owner of Central Laundry in Winnipeg, had left his wife and daughter in China in 1918, and was not able to fully reunite his family until 1981.

Discrimination was another constant challenge. A 1913 provincial law prevented white females from working for Chinese employers, partly due to fears that the women would be forced into prostitution. Chinese were not allowed into some buildings, such as theatres, and were reportedly mocked openly on the streets. The Chinese Benevolent Association was formed in part to help advocate on behalf of the community. Despite the widespread racism exemplified by national and local policies, many Chinese in MB were able to make the most of their limited opportunities. The Mar family moved to Winnipeg from BC after WWI expressly because the **U OF M** was one of the few schools in Canada that would admit Chinese. Three of the Mar's 4 sons completed their education at the university. The oldest son was the university's first Chinese Cdn graduate, completing a science degree in 1922. The 2nd was Canada's first Chinese graduate in engineering, while the 3rd brother earned his medical degree in 1935. Dr. Mar went on to serve in WWII and later created the Mar Foundation for Chinese Studies at the U of M.

During the immigration exclusion period, MB's Chinese population shrank, as only 1248 Chinese were counted in the 1941 Census, with 762 in Winnipeg. Chinese had spread throughout southern MB, often operating Cantonese restaurants or laundries. As Allies in WWII, relations between China and Canada improved, influencing the govt to repeal the ban on Chinese immigrants in 1947.

Chinese citizens were also given the right to vote for the first time. As institutional racism declined, immigration from China slowly began to pick up. Though the majority of Chinese settled in ON or BC, MB also attracted thousands of newcomers.

In the 1970s, Winnipeg's Chinatown was deteriorating, and newcomers settled in other areas of the city, especially Fort Richmond. Initial plans for reconstruction stalled due to a lack of funds and disagreements among citizens. In 1979-80, an influx of 4000 SE Asian refugees to MB (mainly ethnic Chinese Vietnamese), along with the govt Core Area Initiative, increased momentum for an improved infrastructure. In 1981, a Chinatown Development Corporation launched a $20-million makeover of the area. All 3 levels of govt contributed, as well as private developers. The city and provincial govt sold a parcel of land in the old Chinatown for a nominal $1. The improvements included a decorative gate across King St, a garden, the Mandarin Building, the Harmony Housing project, and the Dynasty Building, home to the Winnipeg Chinese Cultural and Community Centre (WCCCC). The centre, completed in 1987, includes recreation and conference facilities, as well as a 600-book library. It remained the focal point of Chinese cultural activities into the 21st century.

As early as the 1980s, fears about the planned 1997 handover of Hong Kong to China led wealthy, educated residents of the UK colony to seek options abroad. Cdn immigration rules encouraged entrepreneurs to move in with their investment dollars. Winnipeg was able to attract a number of these prosperous new arrivals. The decade also saw increasing immigration from Taiwan. In the late 1990s, increasing numbers of international students from Chinese families that benefited from the booming economy began coming to MB. In 2004-05, 1070 students from China and 42 from Taiwan were enrolled at the U of M, making up about ½ of the total number of international students.

In 2001, the Chinese Canadian National Council launched a class-action suit against the federal govt on behalf of relatives of those who paid the head tax. The Supreme Court rejected the claim. In Dec 2003, Chinese Manitoban MP Inky Mark introduced Bill C-333, asking for recognition and restitution. Mark and others eventually got their wish in June 2006, when PM Stephen Harper offered a national apology to those who paid the tax and for the exclusion policy. Redress cheques began going out in Oct 2006.

Today, the monthly **NEWSPAPERS** *Manitoba China Times* and the *Manitoba Indochina Chinese News*; the bi-monthly *Manitoba Chinese Tribune* magazine; as well as 2 radio programs serve the community. Prominent Chinese Manitobans include former Winnipeg city councillors Ken Wong and Joe Yuen, architect Raymond Wan, immigration lawyer Eva Luk, and the late restaurant owner, real estate developer, and philanthropist Hung Yuen Lee. Chemist Philip Lee (1977) and paediatrician Joseph Du (1984) each ran unsuccessfully for provincial and federal seats, respectively.

Educational institutions include the Manitoba Chinese Language and Art Institute, Manitoba Academy of Chinese Studies, and the Manitoba Indochina Chinese School. The Chinese UNITED CHURCH, Chinese Alliance Church, Chinese Mandarin Church, the Chinese MENNONITE and Mennonite Brethren churches, as well as the Huaguang and Huasing BUDDHIST temples, provide services for religious Chinese. The Manitoba Chinese Dramatic Society and Manitoba Great Wall Performing Arts Inc. hold cultural performances to help promote and preserve Chinese culture. ● JOSEPH DU/JOEL TRENAMAN

CHIPEWYAN. *See* DENE.

CHIPMAN FAMILY. Robert M. "R. M.," entrepreneur (b Aug 3, 1926, Vancouver), is chairman and founder of Megill-Stephenson Co, Ltd. the parent company to Birchwood Auto Group, the largest automobile dealership company in MB. Chipman's father owned a Studebaker dealership in Vancouver that went bankrupt, and the family moved to Winnipeg in the early 1930s because it was the largest city in the West and was thought to have the most opportunities. Chipman started Birchwood Pontiac in 1963 at the corner of Portage Ave and Moray St in Winnipeg. The family-owned operation had 15 dealerships by 2005, most located at Pointe West Auto Park, the Chipman-owned auto mall at the W edge of the city. He also started what was to become the largest Canadian-owned equipment leasing company, Winnipeg-based National Leasing Co. Ltd., which operates across the country. The family-owned enterprises generate more than $300 million in annual sales and employ close to 800 people.

The 3rd son, Mark Chipman (b Oct 8, 1960, Winnipeg), CEO of Megill-Stephenson, was the driving force in the development of the 15,000-seat MTS Centre that opened on Portage Ave in downtown Winnipeg in 2004. Megill-Stephenson owns 33% of the entity that operates the MTS Centre and the MANITOBA MOOSE Hockey Club, called True North Sports and Entertainment Centre, and Mark is its chairman.

His older brother, Jeoff Chipman (b May 22, 1953, Sault Ste. Marie, ON) runs the family-owned real estate enterprises, including one of the city's largest commercial leasing and management firms, Stevenson and Co. Their oldest brother, Stephen Chipman (b Aug 10, 1950, Winnipeg), is president of the Birchwood Group. Their sister, Susan Millican (b Dec 12, 1951, Winnipeg), is the president and CEO of the Winnipeg's National Screen Institute, a film and television training school. R. M. Chipman is a former director of the Royal Bank of Canada, **MTS**, and several other public and private corporations, and chaired the United Way and the Associates of the U of M's business school. ● MARTIN CASH

CHIPMUNK. *See* SQUIRREL.

CHIROPRACTIC. Manipulation of the spine has been around for centuries, but it wasn't until 1895 – when Cdn-born healer D. D. Palmer restored Harvey Lillard's hearing by adjusting a cervical vertebra – that chiropractic entered the realm of science. Palmer investigated the effects of spinal adjustments on the body, and began teaching others. His son, B. J. Palmer, continued developing and expanding chiropractic.

The first known chiropractor in MB, William Kelly, was active by 1904; a newspaper clipping with his advertisement was found recently. Chiropractors began arriving in greater numbers after 1910 and they located throughout MB. As early as 1912, chiropractors were charged with practising medicine without a licence. For more than 3 decades, chiropractors, their patients, and their supporters lobbied for legislation enable chiropractors to practise without fear of prosecution. Finally, in 1945, the Legislature passed *The Chiropractic Act*. However, that act was accompanied by the *Basic Sciences Act*, under which the Manitoba College of Physicians and Surgeons (MCPS) controlled examinations of would-be practitioners. No chiropractor passed the Basic Science exams, until the examiners were found to be biased. The *Basic Sciences Act* was repealed in 1952.

Due to the influence of the Manitoba Federation of Labour (*see* UNIONS), the Workman's Compensation Board of Manitoba included chiropractic in their benefits in 1950. Gradually, acceptance of chiropractic increased, and chiropractors became the 3rd-largest health care profession, behind allopathic (Western) MEDICINE and dentistry. In 2006, there were about 250 licensed chiropractors in MB. In 1979, when the Manitoba Health Services Commission (MHSC) came into being, chiropractic was included, in spite of vigorous opposition from the MCPS. In 1972, the Manitoba Provincial Insurance Corporation included chiropractic in its benefits package.

In 1980, the Chiropractic Foundation for Spinal Research was founded in MB. It has grown to become a significant funding organization for chiropractic in Canada. Chiropractors practise a drug-free, manual approach to health care that includes patient assessment, diagnosis, and treatment. In particular, chiropractors assess their patients for disorders related to the spine, pelvis, and extremity joints, and their effect on the nervous system. Chiropractors are also trained to recommend therapeutic exercise, to use other non-invasive therapies, and to provide nutritional, dietary, and lifestyle counselling. ● R. H. COLLETT

CHOWN, Henry Bruce, paediatrician, researcher (b Nov 10, 1893, Winnipeg; d July 3, 1986, Victoria) was the founder of the Rh Laboratory in Winnipeg. The son of pioneering MB surgeon Henry Havelock Chown, who was also dean of the MB College of Medicine, Bruce grew up in Winnipeg and studied at McGill U until the outbreak of WWI, when he enrolled in the Canadian Field Artillery, earning a Military Cross for his gallantry in France. Following his graduation as a medical doctor from U of M in 1922, Chown spent 3 years at Columbia U, Cornell U, and Johns Hopkins U, where he completed his specialty training in paediatrics. Upon his return to Winnipeg in 1926, he became a pathologist at the Children's Hospital until 1949, when he became head of paediatrics at U of M. Chown left in 1954 to devote himself to the **WINNIPEG RH INSTITUTE**, which he had established in 1944 with **MARION LEWIS**.

Henry Bruce Chown, 1954

Chown's interest in the Rh (Rhesus) factor stemmed from his experiences in seeing babies die before they were 2 weeks old of neonatal jaundice from an unknown cause. Eric J. Werner and Philip Levine discovered the Rh factor in 1940 in New York. Chown soon became the Canadian authority and a world leader in the diagnosis, prognosis, and management of hemolytic disease of the newborn. Chown established an unsurpassed lab and clinical service in Winnipeg. The first fetal blood-replacement and intrauterine transfusions were instituted under his direction, and women travelled from all over Canada and from farther abroad to be cared for under his supervision. Chown co-ordinated Canadian clinical trials that led to preventive treatment for all Rh-negative Cdn women during pregnancy and following the birth of an Rh-positive infant.

Along with **John Bowman,** Marion Lewis, and David Bowles, Chown founded the Winnipeg Rh Institute in 1969, a non-profit organization that provided Rh-immune globulin throughout Canada. He retired as director of the Rh laboratory in 1975 at the age of 82. Chown is credited with saving millions of lives around the world. His work led to the creation of Rh Pharmaceuticals, now **Cangene.** Chown became an Officer of the Order of Canada in 1967, and held the Order of the Buffalo Hunt. In 1987, the Bruce Chown Professorship in Paediatrics was created by the Children's Hospital of Winnipeg Research Foundation, and he was inducted into the Winnipeg Citizen's Hall of Fame in 1988. • JOHN HAMERTON

CHURCHILL, pop 963, is a town 1000 km NNE of Winnipeg on Hudson Bay and at the mouth of the **Churchill River,** from which the town takes its name. The only seaport in the Prairies, the only inland seaport in Canada, and one of the earliest settlements in W Canada, Churchill was an **HBC** port and base, though it later developed because of the **Hudson Bay Railway;** as an air hub for remote flights; and as a centre for medical aid to the north (1929-present).

Lying at the junction of several geological formations and 3 major **Ecoclimactic Regions** – the Arctic tundra, boreal forest, and Arctic marine biomes – it contains the most diverse natural landscape in MB. This includes animals and plants characteristic of each, the most famous being the maritime polar bears and beluga whales. Grey-purple rocks of ancient Precambrian Churchill quartzite underlie the region and form small cliffs and outcrops along the bay's coast here. This rock is why Churchill became MB's port, as there is less silting-up here than on the **Nelson River** at **York Factory.** Much younger light-coloured Ordovician and Silurian

An early map of Churchill Harbour

limestones overlie the quartzite, as do dolomites that are visible in places at low tide, and which contain interesting and unusual fossils including corals, brachiopods, and the largest trilobite ever found. Churchill's marine location results in twice-daily saltwater tides that vary from 3.4 to 4.3 m in height and uncover tidal flats up to several km wide along the coast. The bay and intertidal pools support a variety of marine life, including "seaweeds" (marine algae), scallops, sea anemones, shrimp, and fish such as arctic char, capelin, and sculpin, as well as seals, marine birds, beluga whales, and, perhaps most importantly, polar bears on their migratory route. Churchill is also near the tree line for spruce, poplar, and larch.

Present-day climate, soils, and vegetation of the area are determined by Hudson Bay, which creates a gigantic "cold warp" in the region and causes Arctic conditions to extend much farther south than in continental areas to the E and W. Frost and snow may occur in any month of the year, but are unusual in July and Aug, while Churchill records the fewest hours of sunshine per year in MB because of its short winter days and frequent fogs. It lies in the zone of continuous permafrost; ice has been found in bedrock cracks as deep as 44.5 m. Permafrost greatly influences the landscape and vegetation around Churchill, creating large, poorly drained areas of bog and muskeg.

Between 18,000 and 25,000 years ago, the Churchill area was covered with glacial ice that depressed the land over 300 m. When the ice melted, this compressed land started to rise, a process called isostatic rebound that is only about

50% completed. This process continually creates new coastal landscapes of "fossil" beach ridges and intervening peatlands or bogs, which are then uplifted and "moved" inland. All plants, land animals, and people in the area have returned since the first bare rocks appeared from under the post-glacial Tyrell Sea around 3000 BC.

Churchill has been inhabited for about 4000 years. The first humans to live in the Churchill area were Asiatic peoples called the pre-Dorsets and Dorsets. Their distinctive tools, soapstone lamps, and house sites date from 1500 BC to AD 1000. The Thule culture, ancestors of the present Inuit, arose from a second migration of Asiatic peoples around 1800 BC. They and modern Inuit always lived mainly N and W of Churchill with only seasonal visits to the area. The current population includes people of First Nations, Inuit, and European origins (mostly from Scotland and England). Henry Hudson was the first European to arrive in the area in 1608. A Danish group wintered here in 1619-20, but most died. Soon after the HBC was formed in 1670, an HBC post was founded in 1689 on the W side of the river.

The present town of Churchill was built around the railhead on the E side of the Churchill River. Some buildings were moved across the river from an earlier settlement associated with the HBC's **Fort Prince of Wales,** which was built ca. 1700-71, and named after George, Prince of Wales (later George II). The grain terminal was developed about the same time as the railway was completed in 1929. Though ice-covered for much of the year, Churchill's port offers ships the shortest sea route to Europe, and grain has travelled this way ever since.

The rocky shore of Hudson Bay at Churchill

C

In 1942, the US air force established a base east of the Churchill River, also called Fort Churchill. With the development of the Cold War, Fort Churchill became strategically important as the headquarters for the DEW Line and a large Cdn/US base radically increased the population to over 10,000. Though the UK planned to test about a dozen Blue Danubes – 25-kiloton nuclear warheads – in the area in the 1950s, the plan was fortunately scrapped. The base closed in Aug 1980, and all that is left of it today are a few buildings that have been converted into a polar bear "jail" and storage/research facility. With the withdrawal of military personnel, the town dwindled significantly, and continues to suffer slow depopulation. Northern federal govt services were relocated to the former NT (including what is now NU) in 1975, and the town suffered. A few grain ships were not enough to support a viable community.

Revitalization of the small community in the 1980s and '90s owes much to the determination of the local residents and the development of ecotourism as an industry. Churchill is on the N-S migration route of many birds, from the rare Arctic **Tern** and both Ross's and Sabine's **Gulls** to the abundant ducks and both Canada and snow geese (*see* **Waterfowl**). In June, avid birders frequent the town and the surrounding tundra, binoculars at the ready. They are soon followed by whale-watchers, who come to see and hear the beluga **Whales**. The Churchill area is also visited by wildflower experts, who find a variety of Arctic and sub-Arctic plants, including white mountain avens (*Dryas integrifolia* M. Vahl); several Lady's Slipper species (*Cyprepedium spp.*); and Lapland rose-bay (*Rhododendron lapponicum* [L.] Wahlenb.), MB's only native rhododendron.

It is, however, Oct and early Nov that bring visitors from all over the world to see the polar bears. Churchill is the most accessible location in the world for viewing the magnificent creatures. In early fall, the bears congregate along the **Hudson Bay** shore, waiting for the ice to develop so they can make their way onto ice floes and hunt, primarily for seals. They have little fear of humans – polar bears are the only animal in North America that will deliberately seek humans as prey – so it is possible to get close to the bears in the safety of specially modified "tundra buggies."

Today, the town is small but flourishing. The port facility is upgrading and trains carry grain across the muskeg to the port where it is loaded into ships bound for the European market. The port saw a slight increase in grain shipping in 2006, with a movement of 489,000 tonnes of wheat, durum, peas and canola. In addition to grain shipment, the port is used as a transshipment point for goods going to communities in NU and recently, luxury cruise ships have visited the community. There is a large town centre with schools, medical facilities, govt, and community services all under one roof. The original railway station has been reconstructed and is home not only to the passenger service, but also a National Parks interpretive centre for Fort Prince of Wales, **Wapusk National Park**, and **York Factory National Historic Site**. A short distance from the town site is the Churchill Northern Studies Centre, housed on the former Churchill Rocket Research Range (1956-84). The centre is home to various research and educational programs. Climate change would cause less ice in the bay and therefore more sea trade from the port. However, the extinction of polar bears is

an imminent threat, and would cause a massive drop in the town's tourism revenue. ● KAREN JOHNSON/GERRI SWEET

CHURCHILL FOREST INDUSTRIES (CFI)

was one of the great financial scandals in the history of MB. The project was first conceived in 1965 by the Progressive Conservative govt of **Duff Roblin** and announced on the eve of the 1966 provincial election. It was presented as a major new private investment by Monaco AG, a Swiss-based company, and involved the construction of a pulp and paper mill, a saw-mill, a machine shop, and a paper-making plant, to be located in **The Pas**. The total private investment was to be $100 million in 1965 dollars, the equivalent of close to $450 million in present-day terms. In the end, all of the money for the project came from the govt of MB and its Manitoba Development Fund (MDF). The PC govt presented the project as the "answer to the development and employment problems of MB's northern residents."

From the beginning, critical voices were raised about the mysterious nature of the companies involved and the lack of transparency about the original contract. The project involved very large subsidies in terms of reduced stumpage fees, forgiven taxes, subsidies for road building, hydro-electric power and exclusive timber harvesting rights over vast areas of the North, some 102,000 sq km in total.

The govt had contracted for the project with what turned out to be unscrupulous entrepreneurs who already had been identified for false and inflated invoicing, the use of front companies and the charging of excessive fees in building a pulp and paper plant in Catania, Italy. The govt tried to get Monaco AG to reveal its beneficial ownership but the company refused. In fact, Monaca had only one shareholder, Alexander Kasser, the owner of Technopulp AG.

Kasser, an American naturalized citizen with Austrian and Swiss residency rights, was the moving force behind the development. His credentials were impossible to verify and he was surrounded by equally mysterious partners. In the end, it was revealed that Kasser either owned or controlled all of the many companies involved in the project as well as a number of secret companies used to funnel money and fraudulent management fees.

The trail led from The Pas to Montclair, New Jersey, the home base for Technopulp AG to Switzerland and to Liechtenstein where secret bank accounts were located and front companies incorporated and, finally, to Catania. Both Monaca and Technopulp were owned by Kasser and his family. This common ownership was not known at the time. In fact, the original contract in 1965 had only involved Oscar Reiser and his lawyer Baxter Holland. No one in the govt in Sept 1965 had even heard of Kasser and Technopulp or any of the other companies that were subsequently involved

Investigative journalism by the CBC, *Financial Post* reporter Phillip Mathias and by the student newspaper *The Manitoban* raised many questions about the project, the principal persons behind it, the financial terms, the security of the government's monies, etc. However, Kasser still managed to convince the govt to pay him large amounts of money in advance of the actual work. In July 1969, the PC govt of **WALTER WEIR** was replaced by a **NDP** govt under **ED SCHREYER**. Schreyer vowed to honour the contract with CFI but at the same time attempted to improve it by increasing the private corporation's equity contribution and reducing the govt's debt exposure, as well as increasing transparency. After being briefed by Rex Grose, head of the MDF, Schreyer pronounced himself satisfied that due diligence had been followed. He continued the payment of millions of dollars to the company. Later Schreyer began to develop serious doubts.

In Oct 1969, Schreyer appointed a special auditor, NDP stalwart Allister Stewart, to review the project. Stewart privately recommended to the govt that it consider firing MDF officers and staff, and consider freezing the project and taking over its assets. However, he died suddenly in April 1970 of a heart attack at the airport in New Jersey while investigating the project and its headquarters in Montclair. The NDP govt was very reluctant to act on Stewart's recommendations.

On Mar 10, 1970 a special joint issue of *Omphalos*, a community newspaper, and *The Manitoban* was published on the CFI project. It provoked a special debate in the MB legislature in which it became clear that the govt could not answer most of the critical questions about the project and its principals. In early Mar, an engineering company, Stothert Engineering, was appointed to conduct an audit of the engineering work done on the project. On May 20, it issued its preliminary report in which it complained about inadequate data, incomplete controls, excessive fees and the fact that monies were paid out by MDF in large amounts in excess of the disbursements by CFI. Finally the govt acted. In Jan 1971, the govt placed the complex under receivership and appointed a commission of inquiry chaired by Chief Justice Rhodes Smith assisted by Prof Murray Donnelly and lawyer Leon Mitchell. The Commission reported in Oct 1974.

Its report was 5 volumes and 2171 pages long and essentially confirmed what the critics had alleged. Roblin's government was found to have made "ill-considered and improvident decisions" and Rex Grose was blamed for inadequate controls over the payment of loans. Schreyer too was found to have displayed a "lamentable lack of precision" in dealing with the company. As to the money lost, at the time the project was put into receivership, the report estimated that the total provincial investment amounted to $98 million while the value of the assets of the plant was only $72 million. The difference between the 2 amounts was explained, the report asserted, by mismanagement, excess fees and simple disappearance. The CFI scandal was a massive fraud committed by using false and inflated invoices, excessive fees, as many as a hundred secret bank accounts, many of them off-shore, front and shell companies and promoting the falsehood that the various companies involved were at arms-length when in fact they had been either owned or controlled by Kasser.

Alexander Kasser in 1976.

None of the principals accused of fraud was ever tried because they could not be extradited from their refuge in Austria or Switzerland. Most of the monies misappropriated were not recovered although the govt later negotiated for the return of a small portion of it from Kasser. The actual pulp and paper complex was taken over and operated on a much more modest scale than the original project envisaged. • HAROLD CHORNEY

CHURCHILL RIVER flows 1600 km ENE from its rise out of Lac La Loche in NW Saskatchewan to its mouth at **CHURCHILL** on **HUDSON BAY**. Though overshadowed by the Nelson and **HAYES** rivers to the S, it acted as a significant **FUR TRADE** route. The oldest recorded (Cree) name for the river is Missinipi, meaning great waters, or big water. It drains a 283,000 sq km watershed that stretches W into AB. Its main tributary is the Beaver River.

In 1619, Danish explorer **JENS MUNK** entered what would later become known as Churchill

Bay. Munk's survey of the harbour and shoreline resulted in the first map of MB's land mass. In 1686, Capt John Abraham named the river after John Churchill, **HBC** governor from 1685 to 1691 and later the first Duke of Marlborough. The HBC established an outpost near its mouth in 1688-89, but it burnt. Rebuilt in 1717, it was renamed **FORT PRINCE OF WALES** in 1719.

To protect against a potential sortie by France, a more substantial limestone fortress was built over about a 40-year period beginning in 1732. An attack did occur in 1782, and the French forces were able to raze the undermanned fortification. The massive star-shaped structure was restored in the 1930s and declared a National Historic Site.

In 1966, **MANITOBA HYDRO** declared its intention to reroute the river's course into the **NELSON RIVER**, via the Burntwood River system, in order to concentrate its **HYDROELECTRIC POWER** development on the more accessible Nelson. Completed in 1977, the $220 million diversion caused regional flooding, including a 3 m increase in Southern Indian Lake water levels. Control dams and channels were designed to redirect over 60%, or up to 850 m³/s, of the flow. The changes had substantial environmental impacts, particularly on wildlife habitats and commercial fishing. As a result of these impacts and the terms of the **NORTHERN FLOOD AGREEMENT**, in the 1990s Manitoba Hydro negotiated compensation agreements with effected First Nations communities and the town of Churchill. • JOEL TRENAMAN

CICADA is an insect that emits a prolonged, high-pitched buzzing on hot days – a sound that can be heard 1 km away. Few people ever see a cicada, since it usually perches high up in a tree or shrub, its camouflage is outstanding, and it takes off like a rocket when approached. This insect has a large head with prominent eyes and a stout segmented body coloured black, brown and green. A white powder is present on the undersides. The broad transparent wings extend well beyond the body when folded. The male's song (the loudest of all insects) attracts the silent females from long distances. The sound is generated by rapid clicking (over 100/sec) of a stiff plate in the thorax, and the resulting buzz is amplified by resonating air sacs in the abdomen. A cicada can turn off its hearing by tightening a muscle beside the eardrum. Following mating, the female deposits her eggs into twigs, and these either hatch soon after or overwinter, eventually dropping to the soil. The nymph inserts its beak into a tree root's vessels and begins to feed on sap. This diet is widely available but so low in nutrients (but augmented by bacteria in the gut), the nymphal stage takes 2 years. It has greatly enlarged front legs for digging. When it finally reaches maturity, it crawls to the surface in May or June and molts into the adult reproductive stage. In MB, some cicadas mature and emerge each year, unlike the 17-year cicada in the eastern USA which emerges by the trillions all at once every 17 years. Adult Cicadas live for only 3-4 weeks and die off by the end of August. There are 5 species in southern MB (21 in Canada), inhabiting mixed and coniferous forests and shrubby areas. The 2 most-common are the Dog-day Cicada (*Tibicen cunicularis*) with a body/total length of 25/50 mm, and Okanagana canadensis, 20/30 mm. • REW

CITIZENS' COMMITTEE OF 1000 was the ad hoc organization created by business and political leaders in 1919 to oppose the Winnipeg General Strike. Its secretive behaviour brought it much opprobrium. In contrast to the 1918 Citizens' Committee of 100, organized during the general strike of 1918, which proudly listed its membership in the pages of the local newspapers, the 1919 Citizens' Committee of One Thousand never made public its membership list or the names of those on its executive committee, and it preserved no record of its deliberations.

The Citizens' Committee was organized at a meeting on May 15, 1919. It was spearheaded by leaders of the Winnipeg Board of Trade, the Winnipeg branch of the Canadian Manufacturers Association, and the MB Bar Association. Whether it was supported by as broad a spectrum of community leaders as had been the case for its 1918 predecessor is not clear, given the absence of a membership list. In its organizing meeting, the committee declared that its principal aim was to oppose "sympathetic strikes by employees in Public Utilities, Department of Public Service, and those which affect the distribution of milk and food." It also objected to public unions having "outside" affiliations, and while recognizing the right of unions to bargain with their employers, insisted that unions in positions of public trust should in case of disagreement appeal to a duly constituted Board of Authority rather than to the mechanism of the strike. Many of its members believed that the strike was not merely an industrial action but an attempt at Soviet-style government.

The Citizens' Committee appears at first to have devoted itself to attempting to keep essential services running, beginning by providing volunteers to operate the fire department. But staffing fire halls was not enough. The reduced water pressure that was produced under orders of the strike committee was inadequate to reach

Citizens' Committee of 1000 were either thugs or patriots, depending on your point of view.

the second floor of buildings or to fight any serious fire. The Citizens' Committee therefore took over the pressure pumps, as well as the auxiliary steam plant necessary to generate these facilities, in 8-hour shifts. Moreover, since the volunteer firemen might be exhausted by false alarms rung by strikers or pranksters, the committee formed a patrol organization to guard more than 350 fire-alarm boxes, and to walk Winnipeg's streets at night. The committee also provided volunteers – mainly women – to pump gasoline and sell newspapers. It began publishing and distributing its own free newspaper, the *Winnipeg Citizen*, in response to the strike committee's closure of the daily newspapers. • J.M. BUMSTED

CLAM is a large group of sedentarym, 2-shelled molluscs which live in bottom sediments of streams and lakes. The matching pair of shells consists of layered calcium carbonate, which is covered by a protective organic layer called the periostracum. The shells are joined by a strong ligament at the hinge, and a muscular foot is used for digging in the sediment.

Freshwater clams consist of sphaeriids (family Sphaeriidae) and mussels (family Unionidae). Sphaeriids are grouped into Fingernail Clams (Sphaerium) and Pea or Pill Clams (Pisidium). Sphaeriids are hermaphroditic (have both sex organs) and incubate their young in a brood pouch until they are large enough to be released as shelled crawlers. Of the 9 species in MB, the largest is the Grooved Fingernail Clam (*Sphaerium simile*), up to 25 mm. Pea Clams are smaller, the 16 species in MB ranging from 12 mm for the Giant Northern Pea Clam (*Pisidium idahoense*) to <2 mm for the Perforated Pea Clam (*Pisidium punctatum*).

Freshwater mussels are large (>15 cm in some MB species), have separate sexes, and may survive for many decades. They are by far the longest-living invertebrates in MB waters, with some individuals reaching at least 150 years. Their long lifespan and sedentary lifestyle render them extremely vulnerable to pollution, siltation from erosion, habitat disturbance, and water-level fluctuation. Older individuals accumulate heavy metals and pesticides to toxic levels in their tissues. These negative factors, combined with overharvesting for buttons and seed pearls (artificial-pearl industry), have made freshwater mussels the single most-endangered group of animals in NA, and many species have already been driven into extinction and many others expected to follow. In MB, 13 freshwater mussels have been recorded historically, and these were once widespread, particularly in the **Assiniboine** and **Red River** systems, and **Lake Winnipeg**. Perfectly preserved mussel shells thousands of years old were found over 10 m underground in drill cores during construction at **The Forks** in **Winnipeg**. In the last 3 decades, mussels have declined catastrophically in MB due to habitat degradation. In the Assiniboine River, mussels were decimated in 1991 by commercial harvesting and poaching for the Asian seed-pearl industry. Currently in

Lampsilis radiata siliquoidea

MB, 98% of surviving freshwater mussel communities consist of only the 2 most-tolerant species – Fat Mucket (*Lampsilis radiata siliquoidea*) and Common Floater (*Pyganodon grandis*).

While the foreign, highly invasive Zebra Mussel (*Dreissena polymorpha*) has not yet reached MB, it has eliminated native mussels in the Great Lakes region. Monitoring and public-education programs are in effect in MB to guard against this species. At least 45 species of marine clams and mussels, belonging to numerous families, have been recorded in the Hudson Bay marine ecosystem along the MB coast. Information is incomplete due to taxonomic uncertainties and scarcity of collections, particularly from deep water. Scallops (family Pectinidae), like the Iceland Scallop (*Chlamys islandicus*) live in deep waters, but their attractive, 100 mm shells can often be seen washed up on the shore. Others mollusks, like edible mussels (family Mytilidae) live in the intertidal zone and offshore waters, attached to rocks with tough threads (byssus). A typical marine mussel of Hudson Bay is the Blue Mussel (*Mytilus edulis*), which is widespread along ocean coasts in the Northern Hemisphere. Often occuring in dense colonies, the mussels attach themselves to any solid object. The shell is a black and a rounded-triangle shape (100 mm long and 500 mm high). This species and others are included in the diet of northern indigenous peoples and the Polar Bear. ● EP, REW

CLANDEBOYE, pop 598, is a community 45 km ENE of Winnipeg. The name was supposedly suggested by a local resident because the area reminded her of Sir Walter Scott's expression "the lovely woods of Clandeboye," referring to the Irish area from which Frederick Temple Hamilton-Temple-Blackwood, Lord (later Marquess of) Dufferin, hailed. A post office opened in 1876 and the community was also a **CPR** point. Clandeboye is one of 3 villages in the RM of St. Andrews. Although it acts as a service centre for surrounding farms, its proximity to Winnipeg also makes it a commuter village. ● GPP

CLARKE, Henry Joseph Hynes, journalist, politician (b July 7, 1833, Cty. Donegal, Ireland; d Sept 13, 1889, Medicine Hat, AB) came to Lower Canada (QC) at the age of 3. He spent his early years as a journalist, criminal lawyer, and writer. Clarke moved to MB in Nov 1870 as an assistant to lt gov **SIR ADAMS GEORGE ARCHIBALD,** and soon became Attorney General. He clashed with Archibald over the issues of admission to the Manitoba Bar and the establishment of courts, but continued to lead the govt in the House of Assembly into the regime of **ALEXANDER MORRIS.**

Although he was never formally premier, he is sometimes described as such. He was active in various political intrigues and court cases, including the trial of **"LORD" GORDON GORDON'**s kidnapper. In 1885, he acted as counsel for a number of **LOUIS RIEL'**s followers. He was the author of *Sketch of the Life of Thomas D'Arcy McGee* (1868). ● JMB

CLARKE, Leo, war hero (b 1893, Waterdown, ON; d Oct 19, 1916, Étretat, Normandy, France), spent his early years in England, home of his parents, but later returned to Canada, living on Pine St (now Valour Rd) in **WINNIPEG**. When WWI started, he was working as a surveyor in the Canadian north. He returned to Winnipeg to enlist in the 27th Batt., and after arriving in England in June 1915, transferred to the 2nd Batt., Eastern Ontario Regiment, Canadian Expeditionary Force, to be with his brother. On Sep 9, 1916, in a battle near Pozières, Picardie, France, Acting Cpl. Clarke was the only Allied man left standing; the rest were all killed or wounded. He met a counterattack by 20 of the enemy, and was wounded in the leg, but returned to battle the next day. The Germans retreated, but Clarke pursued, killing 19 and capturing the remaining soldier. On Oct 11, 1916, Clarke was wounded by an artillery shell and taken to hospital in Étretat, where he died of his wounds 8 days later. In the spring of 1917, he was posthumously awarded the **VICTORIA CROSS**. It was handed to his father, in Winnipeg, by the gov gen, before a crowd of 30,000, the first time the VC was presented in Canada. Pine St was later renamed Valour Rd (the VC is awarded only rarely for conspicuous acts of valour) for Clarke and the two other VC winners who had lived there – Lt **ROBERT SHANKLAND** and SgtMaj **FREDERICK WILLIAM HALL**. ● JIM SHILLIDAY

CLARKE, Robert Earl "Bobby," hockey player (b Aug 13, 1949, **FLIN FLON**) is the all-time top scorer amongst MB-born NHL players with 1210 points, made up of 358 goals and 852 assists. Though Clarke was a leading scorer, he was also known for his aggressive style, and amassed 1453 penalty minutes during his 15 years with the Philadelphia Flyers. Clarke's talent was evident from the start of his career. Playing with the **FLIN FLON BOMBERS,** he scored 168 points with 51 goals and 117 assists in the 1967-68 season, making him the lead scorer in the Western Hockey League (WHL). However, he was only a 2nd-round draft pick for the Philadelphia Flyers in 1969 after NHL scouts became aware of his diabetes. After suffering 2 diabetic seizures during his first Flyers training camp, Clarke learned

Bobby Clarke, 1974

to manage his illness by drinking a bottle of soda with 3 added spoons of sugar before games, but many doubted that a diabetic would survive long as a pro hockey player. Though Clarke's first NHL season was unimpressive with 15 goals and 31 assists, he soon quelled any concerns over his physical condition. He improved in his 2nd season with 27 goals and 36 assists, and in 1971-72 was the leading scorer on the Flyers, setting a club record with 35 goals and 46 assists. He was awarded that season's Bill Masterton Trophy, as well as his first of 3 consecutive Hart Memorial trophies. In 1972-73, Clarke became the first player from an expansion team to break 100 pts with 37 goals and 67 assists. He became the Flyers' capt, and broke 100 pts in the following 2 seasons, scoring 89 assists both years, which was an NHL record until broken by Wayne Gretzky in 1981. He won the 1973 Lester Pearson Award as the most outstanding player in the NHL. He was one of the first players chosen for the Canada-USSR Summit Series of 1972, and is remembered for breaking Valeri Kharlamov's ankle with a slash in game 6. Along with coach **FRED SHERO** and fellow former Bomber player **REGGIE LEACH,** Clarke guided the Flyers to 2 Stanley Cup victories in 1974 and 1975, famously scoring the overtime winning goal in the 2nd game of the 1974 finals against the Boston Bruins. He retired from play in 1984 to become vice-president and general manager of the Flyers. He was inducted into the Hockey Hall of Fame in 1987. The trophy awarded to the WHL's leading scorer is named in his honour. ● MD

CLERK OF THE EXECUTIVE COUNCIL. The holder of this office is the senior public servant in the MB govt. The clerk is widely regarded as the deputy minister to the premier, but this understates the complexity of the role. The clerk is not only a servant of the premier but also the servant of the collective body of executive council or Cabinet. The clerk manages the pivotal interface between the collective, elected govt – represented by the premier and the executive council – and the professional public service, led by departmental deputy ministers. The clerk is the premier's chief advisor on the appointment of deputy ministers, and is responsible for advocating on behalf of what is supposed to be a non-partisan senior public service able to carry out the decisions of the elected govt, the premier appoints both ministers and deputy ministers. This prerogative is an important element in the shaping of a govt's policy direction. The clerk communicates the broad directions of the elected govt to the deputy ministers, who must assist their ministers in translating those directions into concrete policies and programs. The relationship between ministers and deputy ministers is complex and requires the clerk's attention. If ministers are "captured" by their officials, there is a danger to democratic accountability. Conversely, if a minister overpowers the managerial leadership of the deputy minister, there is danger to administrative integrity. The balance requires careful matching of deputies and ministers, and oversight by both the premier and the clerk. The clerk also has responsibility for a variety of other functions from time to time. These have included protocol, including royal and papal visits; French-language services; and even responsibility for overall govt communications. The role of the clerk in intergovernmental relations has also been significant. The premier's role in federal/provincial, inter-provincial, and international discussions and negotiations has necessitated an important supporting role for the clerk. In modern times, premier Duff Roblin appointed **Derek Bedson** clerk in 1958. Bedson would serve for 23 years, through the govts of premiers Roblin, Walter Weir, Edward Schreyer, and Sterling Lyon. Following Bedson, there have been 5 clerks: Michael Decter, George Ford, Don Leitch, Jim Eldridge, and Paul Vogt.
● MICHAEL DECTER

CLIMATE. MB's climate is a superb example of the effects of continentality – that is, its climate is very much affected by its location in the interior of a large landmass, far from the influence of oceans. MB does have over 900 km of maritime coastline along **Hudson Bay**;

however, the bay is frozen for much of the year, and very cold even when it isn't frozen. Its influence as a source of heat and moisture is therefore minimal, essentially limited to a narrow coastal zone. **Lakes Manitoba** and **Winnipeg**, though large in area, have relatively little influence on the climate, except along their shores during the open-water season; in the autumn, they occasionally enhance lake-effect snowfalls in the downwind direction.

The province's mid-continental location and its latitude produce what is arguably the most notable aspect of MB's climate: highly variable temperatures. In a typical year, all places in MB experience an extreme temperature range (that is, the difference between the highest and lowest observed temperatures) of between

70 and 80°C, and the difference between long-term record daily highs and lows is between 80 and 90°C for most locales. Clearly, MB has very pronounced seasonality in its temperatures, and is often described as having long, cold winters and short, hot summers. This is essentially true, but there are, of course, large differences between the lengths of summers and winters in the southern and northern parts of the province. For example, Winnipeg has an average 110 days a year with high temperatures above 20°C, and about 60 days a year with low temperatures below –20°C; in Churchill, the corresponding numbers are about 25 and 120, respectively.

The growing season in MB is obviously shortened by long winters. The average frost-free season in the province's north is about 70

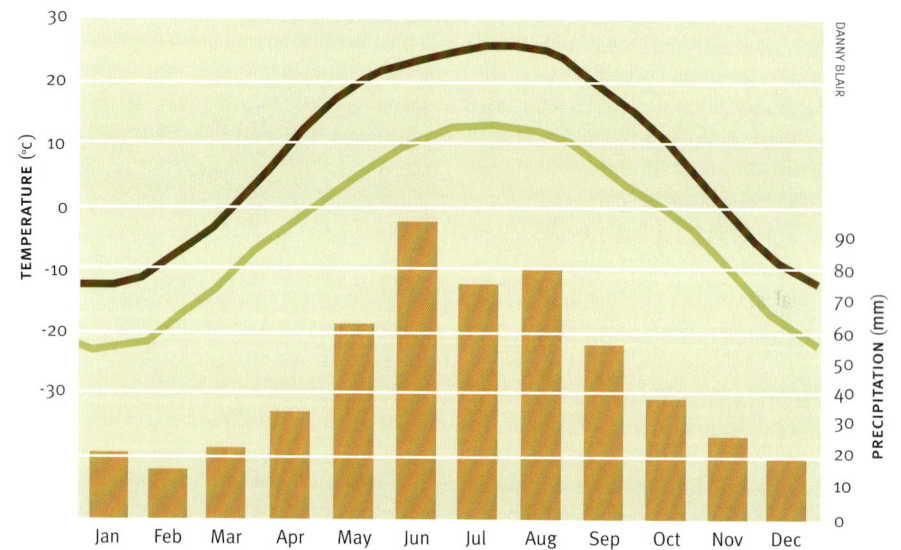

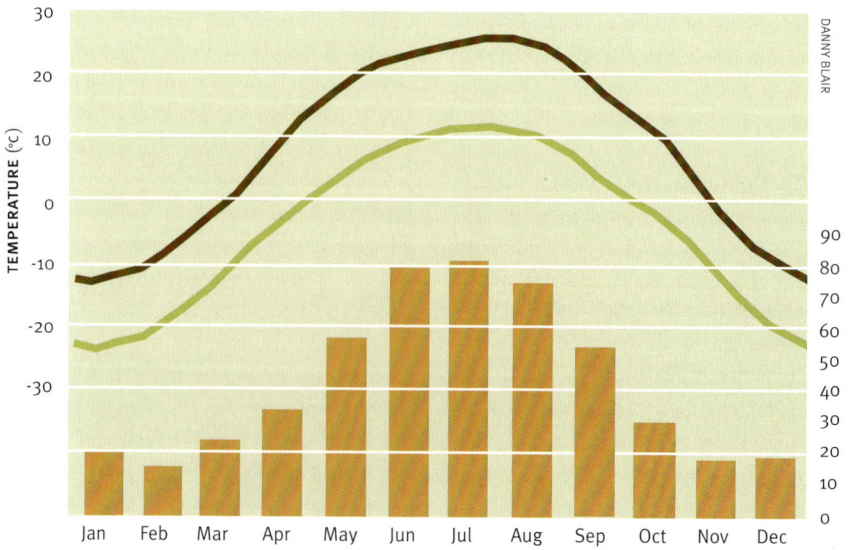

days, and in southern MB it is about 120 days, with local variations in areas of substantial relief, especially in the vicinity of the Manitoba Escarpment. Thus, temperature significantly limits **AGRICULTURAL** and horticultural activities; killing frosts in the spring and fall are especially problematic for farmers and gardeners. In the far south, the average last date of freezing temperatures in the spring is about May 25; in the fall, frosts occur on average after about Sept 15.

Because MB is situated in the heart of the continent, and because there is little relief to impede the movement of air masses embedded in the meandering westerly winds of the mid-latitudes, the province is frequently affected by air masses from the north, west, and south. A season with greater-than-normal numbers of intrusions of air masses from the north tends to be colder than normal, while a season affected by larger numbers of air masses from the west or south tends to be warmer than average. Thus, the westerly upper-level jet stream's shape and position are key determinants of the character of the **WEATHER** in MB, on a day-to-day basis and within a particular season.

Substantial year-to-year variability in winter temperatures is connected to the occurrence of global-scale El Niño and La Niña events. El Niño is associated with a large area of warmer-than-normal sea surface temperatures in the eastern equatorial Pacific, every 4 to 7 years or so; a La Niña is associated with these waters being colder than normal. Both events can temporarily distort global wind patterns. In a winter with a strong El Niño, temperatures across MB tend to be higher than normal, because El Niño usually causes the jet stream to move a larger-than-normal number of air masses from western NA into the Cdn Prairies, with fewer air masses brought into the region from the north.

Another consequence of MB's continental climate, along with its position in the downwind rainshadow of the Rocky Mountains, is aridity. In the southern half of the province, the average annual precipitation total increases toward the east, largely indicative of the diminishing influence of the rainshadow, to a maximum value of about 60 cm; the western margin of the southern region only receives about 47.5 cm of precipitation a year. Precipitation totals are slightly higher near the western uplands, such as those of Riding Mountain National Park. Precipitation totals generally decrease toward the north; the northern fringe of the province only receives about 40 cm of precipitation a year.

The influence of continentality is also expressed in the distribution of precipitation over the year. In typical MB locations, about 2/3 of the annual precipitation falls in the 5 months of May-Sept. The atmosphere in these warm months contains much more moisture than is present in the colder months, when the atmosphere is usually quite stable and consequently much less likely to produce deep, precipitation-rich clouds. Most of the precipitation throughout the year is associated with fronts within low-pressure systems that track across the region. Indeed, these travelling lows (or troughs), interspersed with travelling highs (or ridges), produce an irregular rhythm of sorts in the weather; a few days of cloudy and perhaps wet weather associated with low pressure systems is often followed by a few days of mostly clear and dry weather associated with high pressure systems, and this is then followed by another few days of low pressure weather, and so on. The coldest days of the winter are usually associated with the clear skies of high-pressure systems (allowing surface energy to escape); the hottest days of the summer are also usually associated with high-pressure systems, as the clear skies allow large amounts of strong sunlight to heat the surface. Humidity is generally low, especially in the winter, and occasionally very high in the summer when air masses originating from the Gulf of Mexico migrate into the province.

Most of the summer rain falls from thunderstorms, except in the north. The number of thunderstorms per year decreases toward the north; in the far south, the point frequency of thunderstorm days is about 30 per annum, about 2 or 3 of which produce hail. In the far north, the point frequency of thunderstorm days is less than 10 a year, with about 1 hail fall each year. Damaging hail is rare in the far north but quite common in the south. In an average year, crop-insurance companies report about 50 days with damaging hailstorms, and these storms typically account for annual crop-value losses amounting to many millions of dollars. Large property losses caused by hail are much less common, but single storms can produce hundreds of millions of dollars in losses when they occur in urban areas. For example, the Winnipeg hailstorm of July 16, 1996, resulted in over $100 million of insured losses to structures and vehicles. Severe thunderstorms, whether in the north or south, can also produce tornadoes. About 9 tornadoes are reported in a typical year in MB. Extreme rainfalls from thunderstorms are commonplace; many places have recorded daily amounts between 10 and 15 cm. Extended periods of above-normal precipitation are occasionally observed, but much more problematic are periods of below-normal precipitation: droughts. These can occur at any time of the year, but are most detrimental in the spring and summer, when they can profoundly affect the productivity of the farmed areas and dramatically increase the risk of fires in the forested regions.

Global warming is expected to change the climate of MB in very substantial ways throughout the 21st century. Indeed, even with significant reductions in global greenhouse gas emissions, all global climate model projections indicate that MB will warm by at least several degrees by 2100, with winters and springs warming considerably more than the rest of the year, especially in the north. The greater amounts of warming expected for the colder months of the year are largely associated with reductions in snow cover. Less snow cover means that less sunlight will be reflected and more will be absorbed, thereby warming the surface; this warming, in turn, will help to reduce the snow cover even further. Because of its sensitivity to these types of feedback processes and its proximity to the Arctic, where the feedback processes are even more pronounced, the climate of MB is expected to warm at a much greater rate than the globe as a whole. In fact, throughout the last few decades of the 20th century, average winter temperatures for most of MB rose by approximately 3°C, several times the global rate. The long-term consequences to other important aspects of the climate, particularly precipitation amounts and drought and **FLOOD** frequencies, are much less certain. • DANNY BLAIR

CNIDARIAN is a large group of more than 10,000 species worldwide which contains sea anemones, medusae, hydroids, soft corals and jellyfish. One feature in common is radial symmetry – a body plan organized around a central axis, and often cylindrical. These are relatively simple and ancient creatures, living solitarily or colonially. A total of 57 species of cnidarians have been reported to date in **HUDSON BAY**, however the list will grow as further studies are carried out. Sea anemones and soft corals (class Anthozoa) are represented by 10 species, hydroides and medusae (class Hydrozoa) by 46 species, and jellyfish (class Scyphozoa) by one species – the Lion's Mane Jellyfish (Cyanea capillata). This remarkable, crimson-coloured jellyfish is widely distributed in Arctic and temperate oceans, but is the only scyphozoan jellyfish in Hudson Bay. One-metre wide specimens have washed up on the shore in the Churchill and Nelson rivers estuaries. This species is the world's largest jellyfish, with a maximum weight of 450 kg, a bell diameter up 2.5 metres, and with up to 150 trailing tentacles 30 metres long. However, most specimens are much smaller. The organism swims slowly by contractile pulses of it bell, but it mainly drifts in the current. The tentacles are

C

richly supplied with stinging cells (nematocysts), which stun small prey like plankton and fish, but can severely injure a human with the injected toxin. The life span of this amazing creature is one year. Several jellyfish-like medusae (Aeginopsis laurenti and Aglantha digitale) commonly drift by the MB coast. Soft corals are colonies of individual polyps, and remain attached to the sea bottom, where they feed on passing plankton. All types of cnidarians protect themselves and capture food by stunning or killing other organisms with nematocysts. On contact, the nematocyst discharges its chemical contents into the skin of its attacker or prey. The tentacles then pull in and deposit the food item into the stomach-like interior of the animal. Reproduction may be accomplished asexually by budding or sexually by the release of eggs and sperm into the water. With amazing regenerative powers, some of these species can re-grow into many new individuals from the pieces of one damaged individual. Two freshwater (pond and stream) cnidarians are the small Hydra and Chlorohydra, which capture plankton, insects and fish fry with their outstretched tentacles. They look like a vertical hollow cylinder with tentacles on top. While they mainly remain attached to rocks and plants, they can move slowing to another location by gliding (on the pedal disc) or somersaulting in slow motion. ● REW

COAFFEE, Cyril, sprinter (b Feb 14, 1897, **Winnipeg**; d July 3, 1945, Winnipeg) was a national track and field star, considered at the height of his career to be one of the world's fastest humans. Coaffee began racing in 1915 after joining the North End Amateur Athletic Club. He soon made a name for himself as Winnipeg's top runner, known for his distinctive running style where he would lean his upper torso forward to compensate for the partial paralysis of his right arm. Competing at the 1920 Olympic trials in Montreal, Coaffee won the 100 yd dash. When he was prevented from joining the Cdn Olympic team because of limited funding, Winnipeg residents raised the money to send the talented athlete to the 1920 Antwerp Games. At the Cdn championships 2 years later, Coaffee ran the 100-yd dash in 9.6 secs, tying the world record set by US athlete Charlie Paddock. The record remained unbroken for more than 25 years. At the 1924 Olympic trials, Coaffee won the 100-yd dash, and was made capt of the Cdn track team. Following the 1924 Paris Olympics, Coaffee raced many top sprinters in the UK and NA, most notably winning 2 races in 1926 and 1927 against Cdn track legend Percy Williams. He was inducted into Canada's Sports Hall of Fame in 1956. ● MD

COCKRAN, Rev. William, cleric (b ca. 1796, Chillingham, Northumberland, UK; d Oct 1, 1865, **Portage la Prairie**). Though of **Scots** descent and raised a **Presbyterian**, Cockran converted to **Anglicanism** and was ordained deacon in 1824 and priest in 1825. That year, he came to the **Red River Settlement** with the Church Missionary Society as assistant to David Thomas Jones to minister to retiring **HBC** staff, many of them **Métis** who had worked with the former **NWC** before the 2 companies merged. Cockran, who had experience in **Agriculture** in the UK, founded a model farm as a means to attract the **Country-Born** to the church and its Sunday school. In 1829, he moved to **St. Andrews**, where he again started a farm and school in operation. In 1835, he joined the **Council of Assiniboia**. He tried both evangelizing and "civilizing" the Saulteaux **Ojibway** – largely unsuccessfully – and some **Cree** starting in 1831, though some later historians view his motivations as less than Christian, and he would eventually come to advocate that Aboriginal peoples return to a forest-based hunter-gatherer existence. Even at the time, Cockran was a controversial figure, in part for his support of **HBC** governor William Bletterman Caldwell and the judge **Adam Thom**, and in part because of his opposition to **Free Traders**, but largely because his wife Ann became embroiled in the **Foss-Pelly Case**. Cockran also antagonized the Kildonan Scots' Presbyterian church in a conflict over land use. Cockran suffered a hernia and a nervous breakdown and spent 1844-45 recuperating in Toronto, but returned to the Northwest. In 1851, Cockran moved to what became Portage la

Rev. William Cockran

Prairie, where he worked with both Europeans and First Nations people, and his son, Thomas Cochran, who also received Holy Orders in 1852, helped his efforts there. Cockran's son-in-law, Henry George, was also a vicar. Among other accomplishments, Cockran – created archdeacon by Bishop **David Anderson** in 1853 – designed the Anglican church in St. Andrews (built 1845-49), the oldest continually used church in western Canada, and St. Anne's Church, Poplar Point (1859). Cockran was buried in the St. Andrews churchyard. ● AJL

COCKROACH is an insect featuring a flattened body and 2 pairs of wings. An alternative classification places cockroaches with mantids into the order Dictyoptera. Many readers are only too aware that there are species of cockroaches in MB. Several are introduced exotics, such as the 2 cm German (*Blattela germanica*), 5 cm American (*Periplaneta americana*), 5 cm Oriental (*Blatta orientalis*), and 2 cm greenish *Pantchlora nivea* cockroaches that can inhabit local buildings. However, most people will be surprised to learn that MB has a native species – the pale reddish-brown Wood Cockroach (*Parcoblatta pennsylvanica*). It reaches a length of 22 mm and is found in the litter and under rocks, logs and bark in coniferous and mixed forests of the extreme SE MB. It was found here for the first time as recently as 1997. The diet is living and dead vegetation. After mating the female produces 20-50 eggs and retains them for a time in a leathery case (ootheca) projecting from the rear abdomen. The egg case is later deposited under bark or other debris. The nymphs hatch and molt up to a dozen times as they grow to maturity by the following spring, after hibernating overwinter. Adults are active from May to Oct, and may seek refuge in buildings over winter. This species can live 2 years. There are about 23 species in Canada, including many that have been introduced. While repulsive to people, even most entomologists, they are still fascinating creatures. They are among the oldest surviving land animals, originating in and remaining unchanged since the Carboniferous Period, over 320 million years ago. This incredible success is due to a combination of factors. They are extremely fast runners and jumpers, and disappear in a flash into tight cracks or holes in the ground. Vibration-sensitive hairs on a pair of terminal appendages on the abdomen activate giant nerve fibres that service the posterior nerve centre activating the legs, so the cockroach is running even before the signal reaches the brain. The long antennae pick up scents and direct the creature to food sources, and nourishment can be extracted from any plant or animal material. They can also survive without food for 6 months and moisture for many weeks, aided by the waterproofing in the cuticle covering the body and wings. If living conditions become unsuitable, they fly away on their large wings. They have a knack for avoiding many poisonous chemicals, including poison bait. Another reason for success is their great reproductive potential, with eggs laid in a tough waterproof egg case. ● REW

COD is a marine fish widespread in **HUDSON BAY** and other arctic waters. In fact, the Arctic Cod (*Boreogadus saida*) occurs farther N than any other fish. It is a small relative of the Atlantic Cod, distinguished by its slender body, deeply forked tail, projecting lower jaw, small size of the barbel on the lower jaw. It is brownish spotted with black spots, and silvery below. Individuals are found from off-shore to depths over 900 m, where temperatures may be as low as -1.4C. Temperatures of 0 to 4 C are optimal for the survival. During the spawning season the fish congregate in large numbers in coastal waters. Both sexes mature at 3 years when about 20 cm long. Spawning occurs in late autumn and winter, under the cover of ice. The female produces up to 21,000 eggs, which are fertilized externally by the male. Larval growth rate is highly dependant on how well timed their hatch is with the variable reproductive cycle and abundance of copepods – their main food item. At age one year, the cod is 9 cm long, and by 3 years it reaches 20 cm. Thereafter the growth rate slows, with old, 7-year individuals averaging 30 cm (max. 38 cm, about 180 g). Adults feed on copepods, amphipods, euphausiids, arrowworms and fish (including their own species). While not harvested commercially, this species plays a key role in the diet of seals, whales, seabirds and fish. ● DFO, REW

COHEN, Albert Diamond, entrepreneur, corporate executive, philanthropist (b Jan 20, 1914, Winnipeg). Cohen is often credited as being the first businessman to import Japanese transistor radios into North America after WWII. Through his Winnipeg-based company, **GENDIS** Inc., Cohen came to hold a majority stake in Sony Canada – the only Sony subsidiary not controlled by the parent company – until 1995. Born in 1914 to Alexander and Bereka (Diamond) Cohen, Albert first started selling shoes when he was 15. With his brothers, he started SAAN Stores (Surplus Army, Air Force, Navy) in 1947. The outfit grew to become a 220-outlet chain of junior department stores in western Canadian small towns. Before transistor radios, Cohen also struck it rich importing another novelty item – the Paper-Mate

ballpoint pen – in the '50s. In 1954, he married Irena, a dancer who had recently fled communist Czechoslovakia. SAAN stores eventually fell on hard times, and Gendis sold the chain, including Red Apple Clearance Centres, in 2004. Cohen was still the chairman and CEO of Gendis in 2005 when he was 91 years old, likely the oldest CEO of a public company in the country. He is the author of three books, including one about how he convinced the likes of Ross Perot, Richard Branson, Li Ka-Shing, and Martha Stewart to travel to Winnipeg to receive the International Distinguished Entrepreneur of the Year award, which Cohen himself received in 1983. Cohen was an early investor in the Canadian oil and gas industry, which remained the family's most enduring and lucrative investment. Cohen is a strong supporter of the business school at the **U OF M**, where a library is named in his honour, although he never attended post-secondary school himself. ● MARTIN CASH

COLDWELL, William, journalist (b 1834, London, UK; d 1907, Victoria) established several **NEWSPAPERS** in early MB settlements. Educated in Dublin, where he had experience as a typesetter and proofreader, Coldwell came to Canada in 1854 and worked on the *Toronto Leader*. He migrated to the **RED RIVER SETTLEMENT** with **WILLIAM BUCKINGHAM** in 1859 and founded the *Nor'-Wester*. He left the settlement for Toronto in 1865 to work on the Globe until 1869, when he again came W to begin the *Red River Pioneer* with James Ross, his brother-in-law. An excellent shorthand reporter, he served as UK secretary to the 1870 Convention of Forty (*see* **RED RIVER RESISTANCE**). In Sept 1870, he joined with **ROBERT CUNNINGHAM** in publication of the *Manitoban*, which merged with the *Manitoba Free Press* (*see* **WINNIPEG FREE PRESS**) in 1874. ● JMB

COLEMAN, James "Jim," sports journalist (b Oct 30, 1911, **WINNIPEG**; d Jan 14, 2000, Vancouver) was Canada's first nationally syndicated sportswriter, in a career that spanned 7 decades. Coleman inherited his love for hockey, horse racing and the CFL from his father, a **CPR** executive who took his son on business trips all over the country. After graduating from McGill U, Coleman began his writing career in 1931 at the *Winnipeg Tribune*. In 1943, after moving to the Toronto *Globe and Mail*, he invented the famous story of the Muldoon curse, supposedly invoked by former Black Hawks coach Peter Muldoon who was fired after the 1926-27 season, and angrily declared that the team would never finish first again. The myth endured until 1967, when the team finished first and Coleman finally confessed

Jim Coleman, 1980

that the curse had been his own invention. He wrote 3 books over the course of his career: *A Hoofprint on my Heart*, *Long Ride on a Hobby Horse* and *Hockey is Our Game*. Coleman continued writing for the *Vancouver Province* and the Southam chain of newspapers up to the time of his death. ● MD

COLLÈGE UNIVERSITAIRE DE SAINT-BONIFACE, or University College of St. Boniface (CUSB). An affiliated college of the **U OF M**, CUSB is a Winnipeg-based post-secondary institution featuring French-language instruction primarily for MB Francophones. It offers university level arts, science, education, and social work courses, as well as technical and vocational training in areas such as business administration, multimedia communications, and health care through its École technique et professionnelle (technical and professional school). Its translation program (English and French) is the only one of its kind in western Canada. CUSB also features a continuing education program. The oldest college in western Canada, CUSB originated as a **RED RIVER SETTLEMENT** school for boys founded by **ROMAN CATHOLIC** priest **JOSEPH PROVENCHER** in 1818. CUSB became incorporated by the province in 1871. It was 1 of 3 founding colleges of the U of M in 1877. Jesuit educators ran the school from 1885-1967. CUSB has occupied the same campus since 1922, after a fire destroyed the 1880 buildings. Marcien Lemay and **ETIENNE GABOURY**'s statue of Louis Riel has been on display at CUSB since 1995. The college unveiled a new $4.8 million student centre in 2002 to help accommodate its annual enrolment of about 1000 students. ● JT

COLVILE (b WEDDERBURN), Andrew, businessman (b Nov 6, 1779, UK; d Feb 3, 1856, RED RIVER SETTLEMENT) was pivotal in the merger of the **HBC** and the **NWC**. He was a West India sugar merchant who became the brother-in-law of **LORD SELKIRK**, in 1807, and was associated with Selkirk in the HBC and the Red River Settlement. He became a member of the HBC managing committee in 1810. Born Andrew Wedderburn, he assumed the name Colvile by royal licence in 1813. He secured **SIR GEORGE SIMPSON** to head the HBC, became a Selkirk trustee in 1820, and played a major role in the amalgamation of the HBC and NWC in 1821. He was deputy HBC governor 1839-52. ● JMB

COMB JELLY is a primitive marine group that resembles a rounded or ribbon-like jellyfish (both over 95% water), but the tentacles lack stinging cells and there is a more-developed digestive tract (but no anus). They are often common to abundant in the plankton (from the surface down to depths of 3000 m), where they drift in the current or swim feebly by beating waves of cilia (fine hairs) arranged on 8 rows called combs. These combs give off light (bioluminescence) which flashes in the dark, while the transparent body refracts sunlight like a jewel. They range in size from 1-100 cm in diameter. Comb Jellies feed on crustaceans, fish, jellyfish and other small creatures that become snared in lasso-like filaments of specialized cells lining the tentacles. When prey is captured, the tentacle contracts and wipes the food item into the mouth. Comb Jellies are hermaphrodites, shedding both eggs and sperm into the sea. The fertilized eggs develop into free-swimming larvae. There are only about 100 species in existence, divided into 2 classes – those with or without tentacles. Three species have been identified in Hudson Bay to date – the 50 mm Arctic Sea Gooseberry (*Mertensia ovum*), 28 mm Sea Gooseberry (*Pleurobrachia pilius*), and 115 mm, pinkish, Beroe's Comb Jelly (*Beroe cucumis*). The oldest Comb Jelly is found in fossils 400 myo (Devonian period) but they evolved much earlier, perhaps over 500 mya (Precambrian). ● REW

COMFORT, Charles Fraser, painter, arts administrator (b July 22, 1900, Cramond, Edinburgh; d July 5, 1994, Ottawa). The Scottish-born Comfort came to **WINNIPEG** as a child in 1912 and later studied art at the Winnipeg School of Art. Comfort began working for Brigden's, the graphic designer for **EATON'S**, in 1914, and in 1918 he won the Eaton's catalogue cover competition. In 1923, after a few years' study in New York, he co-illustrated W. J. Healey's *Women of Red River*

Prairie Road, 1925, by Charles Comfort

with Walter J. Phillips. He married Louise Irene Chase (1902-1998) in 1924. Comfort spent the next decade dividing time between Winnipeg and Toronto, often working briefly at Brigden's until he landed a teaching job at the Ontario College of Art. Comfort was known especially for his large portraits (including 3 of govs gen, and *Young Canadian*, a study of fellow painter Carl Schaefer), and for his murals, such as the one that graced the Canadian Pavilion at the 1937 Paris Exhibition. In 1938, Comfort began teaching at the U of Toronto, where he remained until 1960. When WWII came, Comfort became an OCdt and later Lt and Senior Official War Artist with the Cdn Army (1943-46), an experience

he chronicled in *Artist at War* (Ryerson Press, 1956). Over 200 of his wartime canvases, particularly his stark scenes showing the effects of the Battle of Ortona, Italy, hang in the Canadian War Museum. Comfort served as president of the Royal Canadian Academy of Arts (1957-60) and as director of the National Gallery of Canada (1960-65). He was a Fellow of the Royal Society of Arts (UK), and received the Order of Canada in 1972. The library of the National Gallery of Canada is named for him and his wife. ● AJL

COMMUNISM is a political theory most commonly identified with the writings of the 19th-century German philosopher Karl Marx, and the

20th-century political practices of Communist parties around the world that took their leadership from the Communist Party in the USSR. However, Communism had a foothold in MB throughout much of the province's history.

Although the Communist Party of Canada (CPC) was founded in 1921 – at which time it was an underground organization – it was preceded by a series of Marxist political parties, the two most notable being the Socialist Party of Canada and the less-doctrinaire Social Democratic Party. The SPC was formed in 1904 and had a **Winnipeg** local that recruited some of MB's most prominent trade unionists and had affiliations with **Jewish**, Polish, and Latvian socialist organizations in the city's **North End**. The SPC splintered in 1910 when Winnipeg members, dissatisfied with the party's dismissal of short-term reform, bolted to form the Social Democratic Party.

The CPC differed from these parties in that it was, from the outset, affiliated with the Communist International, which had been established by the USSR's Communist Party after the 1919 Russian Revolution. This association initially helped establish the CPC as a leading party of the political far left in Canada. However, in the long term, this connection – which required the Canadian party to follow the political direction set down by the USSR – was to be the party's greatest liability. It often made co-operation with the more moderately leftist Cooperative Commonwealth Federation, and its successor, the New Democratic Party, difficult.

During the 1920s and 1930s, the CPC enjoyed a large measure of political popularity in North Winnipeg. This was due to the role the party played in organizing trade unions, particularly in the garment and meat-packing industries, and the various ethnic federations that it established. Communists were rewarded for articulating the aspirations and anger of Eastern European immigrants who found themselves discriminated against and exploited in the workplace. In 1934, party activists organized miners in Flin Flon into the Mine Workers of Union of Canada and led them on a strike that was crushed when the provincial govt sent police to the community to arrest the union leaders. Communist Party members were also active in organizing a farmers' march on the MB legislature in 1931, the Winnipeg portion of the 1935 On-to-Ottawa Trek, and needle-trades workers in Winnipeg throughout the **Great Depression**.

While the party's intellectual life was always scarred by its ideological rigidity, during the 1920 and 1930s its members played a vital role in creating a series of popular economic and cultural institutions, ranging from a co-operative dairy and lumber yard, to benevolent associations and athletic clubs, to choirs and theatre groups. Many voters in north Winnipeg remained loyal to the Communists into the 1980s.

In 1926, Wasyl Kolisnyk became the first CPC member to win election to public office when he was elected to the Winnipeg City Council. In 1933, Winnipegger Jacob Penner was also elected to the council, joined soon after by Martin Forkin. In the 1930s, both William Ross, a future leader of the CPC in MB, and Andrew Bilecki were elected to the Winnipeg School Board. In the 1936 MB election, James Litterick became the first Communist to be elected to a provincial legislature. In September 1939, in keeping with Soviet policy, the CPC opposed Canada's participation in WWII. Many party leaders, including Penner and Bilecki, were interned under the *Defence of Canada Regulations*, while others, including Ross, were forced to go underground. The CPC's fortunes were reversed in 1941, following the German invasion of the USSR. The new party line called for complete support of the war effort, and party leaders were released from internment. In 1941, **Joseph Zuken**, a Winnipeg lawyer and the brother of Bill Ross, was elected to Winnipeg City Council. He would hold his position until 1983. Also in 1941, **William Kardash**, a veteran of the Spanish Civil War, was elected to the MB legislature, where he sat until his defeat in 1958. His wife, Mary Kardash, served several terms on the Winnipeg School Board, retiring in 1986.

The CPC's fortunes went into decline after WWII. The outbreak of the Cold War; revelations of Soviet anti-Semitism and the oppression of **Ukrainians** and other national groups in the USSR; and the USSR's disclosure after 1956 of Stalin's genocidal conduct in power led to mass abandonment of the party. However, at the civic and school-board levels, Communists continued to enjoy political success, based in large measure on their reputations for personal integrity and dedication to the community. In 1961, Joe Zuken replaced Jacob Penner on Winnipeg City Council. Zuken served as a councillor until he retired in 1983. As a councillor, he was a critic of the close relations between the governing group on city council and the development industry, and a strong advocate of improved services to North Winnipeg. In 1979, Zuken attracted international attention when he finished second in the city's mayoralty election.

While Communist Irene Haigh was elected to the Winnipeg School Board as late as 1989, by the early 1990s, the CPC in MB was in crisis. The USSR's collapse in 1991 led the party's national leadership to propose a liquidation of the CPC. While the proposal was rejected, many of the MB party's leading figures, including former leader Mike Gidora, left the party. ● DOUG SMITH

CONDIE, Richard, animator, film director (b 1942, Vancouver) is one of Canada's most celebrated animators. After graduating from the **U of M** with a BA, Condie worked as a teacher, social worker, performer, and musician. In 1975, he produced some animations for the Canadian edition of *Sesame Street*. In 1977, he was awarded a grant from the Canada Council for the Arts and used the money to produce *Oh Sure*. This film, which depicts men making fools of themselves in their efforts to impress one another, was the beginning of Condie's darkly comedic social commentary. The grant proved to be a turning point for Condie, as up until that time he considered drawing merely as a hobby. Condie's move to **Winnipeg** in 1974 was fortuitous, as it coincided with the National Film Board opening its Winnipeg studio. Condie and fellow artists worked with the studio and created a significant chapter in the history of Canadian animation that became known as Manitoba Animation. With the help of the NFB, Condie continued to produce semi-autobiographical animated films, often addressing themes of inadequacy, as in *Getting Started* (1979). These films won Condie national and international awards, but it was *The Big Snit* (1985) that earned Condie both an Oscar, and several Canadian and international awards. *La Salla* (1996) earned Condie a second Oscar nomination, and was his first computer-generated work. ● JS

"CONNOR, Ralph." *See* **Gordon, Charles William**

CONSTRUCTION is among MB's largest industries, as it provides most of the fixed assets and capital investment for all other industries and employs roughly 30,000 Manitobans. It involves the building of everything from houses, infrastructure, and shopping malls to large-scale projects such as the **Red River Floodway** and massive **Hydroelectric** projects such as Wuskwatim Generating Station.

The first major construction project in MB was the 2nd **Fort Prince of Wales**, built with stones quarried from the nearby **Churchill** area. Building began in 1731, and may have taken decades to complete, with some historians even debating the idea that the fort was ever finished. For most early settlers, however, even small stone buildings were costly and time-consuming. Many of MB's first **Métis** inhabitants built log structures, using a distinct technique called the

Road construction in Winnipeg, 2007

JOEL TRENAMAN

C

Red River frame, with squared logs cut with projecting tongues placed between upright logs cut lengthwise with mortises. The gaps between the logs were then filled with a combination of mud and clay, dung, or horsehair. Later settlers introduced their own construction techniques, such as the **MENNONITE** house barn and the **UKRAINIAN** sod house.

WINNIPEG's first major construction project – predating the incorporation of the city – was a general store built by **HENRY MCKENNEY** in 1862. In 1881, the arrival of the **CPR** led to a building boom in warehouse structures, mostly made with timber frameworks, though Winnipeg saw its first all-stone building in 1883. With the growth of the **GRAIN** trade, many office buildings were soon erected in Winnipeg. These structures were often built with bricks manufactured in the dozen-or-so brick factories operating in MB from 1890 until the 1920s.

In the early 20th century, Winnipeg was the fastest-growing city in NA, and the construction industry thrived. The 10-storey Union Bank Tower, built in 1903, was the first steel-framed skyscraper in western Canada, towering over the mainly 4-storey brick buildings that made up the city's downtown. In industrial construction, reinforced concrete replaced the heavy timbers previously used for warehouses. One of MB's first reinforced concrete buildings was the **MCKENZIE SEED COMPANY**'s **BRANDON** building.

The Winnipeg Construction Association, originally the Winnipeg Builders' Exchange, was founded in 1904 with 40 members. Because of Winnipeg's exponential growth, by 1910, the association had grown to 400 members, and was the largest builders' exchange in NA. In addition to a booming housing market, the establishment of public utilities – such as the first hydro-generating station and the **WINNIPEG AQUEDUCT** and its **RAILWAY** – provided lucrative projects for contractors. Construction reached a high in 1914, recording $10 million in building permits. The **GREAT DEPRESSION** halted most construction, though govt-initiated relief projects, including the Federal Building and the Winnipeg Civic

Auditorium, provided some contracts. In 1934, Winnipeg building permits were at an all-time low of just $700,000.

A baby boom followed WWII, creating a large market for residential and school construction. In the 1950s, winter construction through the coldest months became possible as MB contractors developed ways to work throughout the year. In 1963, contracts were awarded for the construction of the Red River Floodway, the largest earthmoving project to that point in Canada. In 1969, the 32-storey Richardson Building was erected, which remained the tallest building in MB until the TD Centre (now CanWest Global Place) was built in 1990. A mini-boom followed in the early part of the 21st century when both the MTS Centre and a new Manitoba Hydro headquarters were built in downtown Winnipeg. As of writing, the main MB-owned construction companies were Bockstael Construction Ltd., Bird Construction Company Ltd., M. D. Steele Construction Ltd., and Qualico Developments.

● MICHELLE DOBROVOLNY

COOKS CREEK, pop 90, is one of the oldest **UKRAINIAN** communities in Canada, located 20 km NE of **WINNIPEG**, on hwy 212. It was named after Joseph Cook, who established the community. Cooks Creek is best known for the Immaculate Conception Ukrainian Catholic church, parishioner-built in 1930, which is one of the largest hand-poured concrete buildings in the West, and a provincial heritage site featuring 9 onion domes and geometric designs. Nearby is the Grotto of Our Lady of Lourdes, a man-made monument containing an altar and cave-like wings housing the Stations of the Cross. There is also a Heritage Museum with traditional Slavic clothing, folk art and MB's smallest chapel. ● GPP

Cooks Creek Grotto, 1980

UMA, TRIBUNE, COOK'S CREEK GROTTO, GORDON AIKMAN PHOTO, 31-1244-6

COOLEY, Dennis Orin, educator, poet, (b Aug 27, 1944, Estevan, SK). From 1976, Cooley has taught in the dept of English, St. John's College, at the **U OF M**. As a teacher and scholar, he has been centrally concerned with the development of Prairie **POETRY**; as a poet, he has experimented with sound and with the visual effect of the poem on the page, exploring both personal and classical themes. Cooley's published poetry includes *Leaving* (1980), *Fielding* (1983), *Bloody Jack* (1984), *Soul Searching* (1987), *Dedications* (1988), *Perishable Light* (1988), *this only home* (1992), *burglar of blood* (1992), *gold finger* (1995), *Passwords: Transmigrations Between Canada and Europe* (1996), *sunfall* (1996), *the bentley poems* (2000), *Irene* (2000), *Seeing Red* (2003), *Translations* (2004), and *Country Music: New Poems* (2004). With **DAVID ARNASON,** he was co-founder in 1975 of Turnstone Press, and poetry editor in 1978-9 and 1992-3. He served as assistant editor of the *Journal of Canadian Fiction* in 1975-6, contributing editor of *Border Crossings* (formerly *Arts Manitoba*) in 1989, and editor of Pachyderm Press in 1993. Cooley was president of the Manitoba Writers Guild in 1989-91. ● MILDRED GUTKIN

CO-OPERATIVE COMMONWEALTH FEDERATION (CCF).

The CCF was founded in Calgary in 1932 as a federation of the Independent Labour Party (ILP), several farmers' organizations, the League for Social Reconstruction, and the Co-operative Commonwealth Youth Movement. By its first convention in 1936, the CCF had developed an identity of its own, separate from the long-established worker- and city-based ILP. Some prominent ILPers – including **WINNIPEG GENERAL STRIKE** leader and future mayor **JOHN QUEEN**, and MP **ABRAHAM ALBERT ("A. A.") HEAPS** – had been wary of the notion of a new party and its "broadening-out" strategy of courting farmers who had been ineligible to join the ILP. They were also suspicious of academic socialist intellectuals, but their opposition was insufficient to keep the CCF from taking root.

In the 1936 MB provincial election, the party's candidates in Winnipeg ran as ILP-CCF. By 1937, the Manitoba CCF was no longer a federation of groups; membership was now individual and handled directly through constituency associations. The party was the provincial section of the national CCF, led by **J. S. WOODSWORTH**. In 1934-5, the national CCF's founding declaration, the Regina Manifesto, appeared in MB in **ENGLISH, GERMAN, FRENCH, UKRAINIAN**, and Hungarian, but the party initially fared poorly among those of continental European backgrounds, other than Jewish people. The provincial party's membership and leadership drew heavily on British-born workers: 8 of the party's first 11 MLAs were British. Its first leader, S. J. Farmer, had emigrated from Wales in 1900, worked as a railway clerk, and served as Winnipeg's ILP mayor in 1922-3.

Initially, the party organ was the *Manitoba Commonwealth*. The paper advocated public ownership of natural resources, utilities, and major industries. It also called for govt planning, the creation of a provincial bank, support for co-operatives, a labour code, socialized health services, social insurance, free education, improved pensions, and a provincial construction program to combat unemployment. In 1940, the party joined the "non-partisan" coalition govt of Premier **JOHN BRACKEN**. Despite objections from the national party and from other provincial sections, Farmer sat at the Cabinet table with Conservatives, Liberals, Progressives, and a Social Crediter. He became Minister of Labour, making him the first social-democratic Cabinet member in North America.

The party fared poorly in the 1941 election, and the experience in govt proved difficult – Farmer came to describe it as "a fool arrangement." The CCF used Bracken's entry into federal politics in 1942 as an excuse to leave the coalition. CCF popularity surged during WWII as economic planning, the cornerstone of party thinking, proved necessary and acceptable. Party membership, which had hovered between 600 and 800 during its coalition venture, had grown to more than 5000 by 1945. In the 1945 provincial election, the CCF led in the popular vote but ran 3rd in number of seats because its votes were concentrated in Winnipeg, which was underrepresented in the legislature. The party's appeal in the southwestern wheat belt was so weak that, beyond **BRANDON**, it failed to nominate candidates in a number of ridings, and the govt won them by acclamation.

The party's support sagged during the Cold War, dropping to 26% in 1949 and 17% in 1953. Post-war economic recovery undercut the party's prediction that depression would be inevitable in the absence of socialist measures. The party retained its stature on the municipal level, and, although it elected aldermen, primarily from north, east, and central Winnipeg, it never captured Winnipeg's mayoralty. Party membership never exceeded 2000 between 1947 and 1957, and stood at a low of 717 in 1955.

The decline of the Liberal-Progressive govt, and aid from the federal CCF in the late 1950s, led to an increase in membership. The national party's ideology was updated in the 1956 Winnipeg Declaration, reducing emphasis on large-scale public ownership. The party's ties to organized labour became stronger as the newly created Canadian Labour Congress encouraged affiliation with the CCF. Some CCF officials, such as party secretary and MLA Donovan Swailes, held union positions, while some senior labour figures, such as the Manitoba Federation of Labour's Art Coulter, held party posts. The party picked up some support among former **UKRAINIAN** communists, but failed to achieve a rural breakthrough, despite informal support from the leadership of the upstart Manitoba Farmers' Union.

In the 1958 and 1959 elections under party leader **LLOYD C. STINSON** – a former United Church minister and insurance agent – the CCF gained 20% and 22% of the vote, and 11 seats (its highest ever) and 10 seats, respectively. The CCF held the balance of power in 1958, and Stinson negotiated a tentative coalition agreement with Liberal-Progressive Premier **D. L. CAMPBELL**, but opposition to it prevailed in both parties' caucuses.

Between 1958 and 1960, a joint CCF-MFL committee, paralleling a national CCF-CLC committee, negotiated a merged political effort known as the New Party, later named the **NEW DEMOCRATIC PARTY**. It attempted a broadened appeal to workers, farmers, co-operators, small businessmen, professionals, and "liberally minded" Canadians. It promised better economic management than the other parties, more social equality, and higher levels of social welfare. As in the 1930s, there was opposition to this "broadening-out" strategy. The leading national opponents of the NDP's creation were Al Mackling and Howard Pawley, who, a decade later, served in Manitoba's first NDP govt. The last leader of the CCF in 1960 and the NDP's first leader in 1961 was Russ Paulley, MLA for Transcona, a one-time member of the ILP youth group. ● NELSON WISEMAN

CO-OPERATIVES began in western Canada in the late 19th century when settlers recognized that they were dependent on national and international marketing networks dominated by a few large companies. Farmers were frustrated by the high prices charged by bankers, railways, elevator companies, implement manufacturers, and shopkeepers, so they began to use co-operatives to supply themselves with goods and to help them take control of handling and marketing their produce. They formed buying clubs to make bulk purchases of farm supplies and basic commodities, and in 1906, banded together to establish the "Grain Grower's Grain Company" to market their grain. In 1924, farmers formed the Manitoba and Saskatchewan Wheat Pools, with the aim of building an elevator system owned and controlled by farmer members. Livestock,

Visiting workplaces — a CCF tradition continued by Stanley Knowles and the NDP.

UMA, TRIBUNE, PC18-10269-006, 1965

dairy, and poultry producers formed their own marketing agencies a few years later. In 1935, the Wheat Pools gave up their central selling agency's marketing function to the **Canadian Wheat Board**.

Many of the co-operatives formed during and after WWI did not survive the **Great Depression**. Yet the hardships of the 1930s strengthened the co-op movement, and co-operative methods were used to meet a wide variety of needs, including marketing, banking, insurance, and the refining of oil and the providing of farm implements. Canadian Co-operative Implements, at its peak, was one of NA's largest farm machinery co-operatives.

In 1927, 13 retail consumer co-ops formed the Manitoba Co-op Wholesale to assist them in the bulk purchases of apples and coal, as well as other commodities. In 1955, Federated Co-operatives Ltd. was formed when the Manitoba Co-op Wholesale joined with a wholesale organization in SK. This new organization was expanded across western Canada with the addition of the Alberta Co-op Wholesale in 1961, and British Columbia in 1970.

A lack of financial services on the Prairies during the Depression led to the establishment of the co-operative financial sector. The first **Credit Union** in MB was established in **St. Malo** in 1937 by Father Benoit drawing upon the earlier success of Caisse Populaire and the Desjardins movement in Quebec. Today, credit unions and caisses populaires are serving their members throughout the province.

Co-operatives include organizations involved in areas such as housing, real estate development, employment, publishing (*see* **Book Publishing**), utilities, health, and **Childcare**. Housing co-operatives represent the largest category in this sector in terms of numbers and financial activity. Today in MB there are 46 housing co-operatives with 3030 active members. The Manitoba Worker Co-op Federation was formed in 2002 to assist in the development of the worker co-op business model. Westman Media Co-operative began operations on September 14, 1978, and serves over 28,000 members/customers in 36 western MB communities with a broad range of communication services.

Co-operatives in MB currently operate in conjunction with the Manitoba **Agriculture** Food and Rural Initiatives branch of the provincial government (MAFRI), and work very closely with the co-operative development department of MAFRI. The Agribusiness Chair in Co-operatives and Marketing at the **U of M** focuses on the major role that co-operatives have played in overall business development in Manitoba, especially agriculture. ● BARRY GOSNELL

COPEPOD is a torpedo-shaped crustacean found in both fresh and marine waters of MB. They have a dorsal shell, a pair of antennae, a segmented body, and a pair of long appendages at the rear. A characteristic pattern of bristles and the antennae help maintain the animal in the water column, but they often sink to the substrate. Many species are good swimmers, using their 5 pairs of thoracic appendages, beating antennae, and even mouth parts. Some common species undertake daily vertical migrations, usually from 1-20 m, rising at night and sinking during the day, in response to light levels. In the seas, daily migrations may be over 300 m, with the copepod swimming at a speed of 90 m/hr. Most copepods are only about 0.3-4 mm long (a few are as small as 250 micrometres), yet they make up the most-important component of the zooplankton (drifting animal life), even more so in marine waters. Up to 1000 per litre of water have been recorded. The majority filter feeds on minute plant life, but many others are predators or parasites on the gills of fish. Copepods may be intermediate hosts of tapeworms and flukes that infect fish, birds and mammals. During the breeding periods (more often in summer, but also in winter), the male clasps the female (sometimes for as long as 10 days) and transfers spermatophore packets to the female. A successive series of fertilized eggs (4-40 at a time) are carried in the female's single or double egg sac near the end of the body, and they hatch into a larval form called a nauplius. This molts 11 times as it grows, with appendages being added at various stages. The life cycle usually ranges from one week to 6 months, but individuals may survive for up to 3 years. Hostile environmental periods (winter or drought) may be passed in egg or cyst form, which disperse easily by water, on the wind, or on the feed of birds. Copepods play major roles in aquatic food webs in temporary sloughs, marshes, ponds, streams and lakes. At least 52 species (e.g., *Calanus hyperboreus*) have been reported in **Hudson Bay**, and an unknown number occur in MB's freshwaters. Over 12,000 species are known worldwide. ● REW

COPPINS, Frederick George, Victoria Cross winner (b Oct 25, 1889, London; d Mar 30, 1963, Livermore, CA). Coppins's family immigrated to Canada when he was young. He joined the 8th Batt of the CEF, Winnipeg Rifles, in WWI. On Aug 9, 1916, near the Bois de Hackett (Hackett Woods), close to Amiens, France, Coppins saved what remained of his platoon while pinned in the open by machine-gun fire. Leading 4 volunteers, he attacked. All 4 were killed, but Cpl Coppins, although wounded, silenced a machine-gun crew and took 4 prisoners. In 1919, reportedly as a special constable during the **Winnipeg General Strike**, he had 2 ribs broken in a fracas. He moved to California during the Depression, working in the construction industry in Oakland. While there, his VC disappeared; 38 years later, it was returned by mail from London, UK, and is now in the **Royal Winnipeg Rifles** Museum. ● JIM SHILLIDAY

CORBETT, Griffith Owen, Anglican clergyman, pamphleteer, physician (b ca. March 30, 1823, Littleworth, Gloucs., UK; d March 30, 1909, Lingfield, Surrey, UK). The son of Griffith Corbett, a weaver of probable Welsh ancestry, Griffith Owen Corbett was trained by the Church Missionary Society. The Colonial Church and School Society sent him to Montreal in 1851, where he was chaplain at the Montreal General Hospital. He applied for ordination from the Bishop of Montreal, Francis Fulford, who refused. In 1852, he was sent to **Rupert's Land**, where Bishop **David Anderson** ordained him in 1853. Corbett built Holy Trinity Church, christening the Parish **Headingley** in 1854, after the Leeds, UK-area church that had sponsored his mission. Corbett returned to the UK in 1855, studying medicine at King's College (U of London) while serving as a rural parson, and came back to Rupert's Land in 1857 after appearing before a British House of Commons committee to argue that the UK govt annex Rupert's Land. Corbett also established the Red River Settlement's first printing press in 1858 so that he could publish pamphlets arguing that Red River become a Crown colony. The English-speaking **Country-Born** supported this position, but Corbett got into trouble over his antipathy toward **Roman Catholicism**, Francophones in general, and **Métis** in particular. In Dec 1862, the married clergyman was arrested for attempting to induce an abortion on his mixed-blood servant, Maria Thomas. The trial the subsequent year – whose details were reprinted in the *Nor'-wester* – found that he had indeed tried to abort the foetus after impregnating her by repeated acts of adultery. Though he was sentenced to 6 months' jail time and was barred from the ministry, his supporters insisted that the charge had been trumped up by the **HBC**, of which Corbett was an outspoken opponent. A mob sprung Corbett from jail on April 20, 1863. The disgraced minister fled to the UK, leaving his wife and at least 2 children, as well as Thomas, who gave birth to Corbett's daughter shortly thereafter. After the **Red River Resistance**, Corbett published more pamphlets advocating Crown colony status for Red River. In 1877, after much petitioning, he was allowed to practise as a cleric again, though fresh charges of immorality in the early 1880s soon meant he was permanently defrocked. Corbett's wife, Abigail Corbett (née Budd or Butt), was apparently never granted a divorce. She remained in Red River, subsequently moving to **SWAN LAKE**, and died in 1918. Corbett's conduct, and the lawless aftermath, unquestionably damaged the Church of England's reputation in the Northwest and MB for decades, led to tensions between English- and French-speakers, and gave **LOUIS RIEL** reason to mistrust the intentions of the Canadians. ● AJL

CORMORANT, pop 450, is a community 50 km NE of **THE PAS**. This **HUDSON BAY RAILWAY** point was established in 1928. Today, the OmniTrax line runs through the community. Cormorant was named after a nearby lake of the same name. Economic activity in Cormorant in the 2000s is based on commercial fishing, forestry, wild rice cultivation, and outdoor tourism. The community lies in a flat, marshy area, however Tolko's logging area is close by. The community has basic services and a K-12 school, but RCMP and hospital services are in The Pas. Hopes for future growth have been fuelled by the discovery of mineral reserves within 80 km of the community. ● GPP

CORNISH, Francis Evans "Frank," QC, lawyer, politician (b Feb 1, 1831, London, Upper Canada [ON]; d Nov 28, 1878, **WINNIPEG**), Winnipeg's first mayor. Cornish, the son of **ENGLISH IMMIGRANT** William King Cornish, was called to the Bar in Canada West (ON) in 1855 and became mayor of London for 4 years before moving W in 1872 after he stuffed the mayoral ballot boxes and assaulted a British officer. In MB, he quickly allied with **SIR JOHN CHRISTIAN SCHULTZ**, and led a mob that ransacked the offices of 3 newspapers, whose coverage of the federal election he objected to. Cornish was among the first lawyers called to the Manitoba Bar, and Cornish was involved in the 1873 warrants on **LOUIS RIEL** and of **AMBROISE-DIDYME LÉPINE** for the execution of **THOMAS SCOTT**. An Orangeman antagonistic to **ROMAN CATHOLICS**, francophones, and **MÉTIS**, Cornish later received a share of the ON reward offered for the arrest of those responsible for the death of Scott. He was mainly noted as a defence lawyer, although in the Lépine case he was the prosecutor who successfully summed up for the jury the Crown's case. In 1874, he was elected first mayor of Winnipeg under suspicious circumstances – he received 383 votes from 382 eligible voters, to his opponent **WILLIAM FISHER LUXTON**'s 179. Cornish also served as city magistrate. In this capacity, he once pleaded guilty to driving his horse and buggy while intoxicated, fined himself $5, and promptly suspended his own sentence. He was elected to

Francis Evans Cornish

the MB **LEGISLATURE** as a "National" for the riding of Poplar Point that same year. He defended his friend, chief constable John Ingram, in the wake of calls for the chief's suspension over bad behaviour. Cornish himself suffered from vices: he was charged with stealing a poll book on election day in 1876. Ironically, a branch of the Winnipeg Public Library, and a nearby street, is named after the book-stealing mayor. He died of stomach cancer shortly before he was to face charges for interfering with his opponent's itinerary in a provincial election. ● AJL

CORRECTIONS. There is a long history of corrections in MB. Aboriginal communities practised their own forms of social discipline involving dispute resolution, shunning, and banishment. Contemporary ideas of corrections came with white settler society. Police and army enforced colonial laws and the courts generally used sanctions such as fines and corporal and capital punishment to regulate the local population. Offenders who needed restraining were housed for brief periods in holding cells in the military garrisons of forts operated by militia or the **NWMP**. The police often turned over delinquent youth and destitute adult offenders with little in the way of family support

to the church. The clergy were generally the only social institution engaged in efforts to reform and rehabilitate law-breakers. This often meant that the clergy encouraged Aboriginal people to abandon their culture in favour of European, Christian values.

In Western society, the 19th century saw corporal and capital punishment fall into disfavour. The penitentiary became the preferred means to manage offenders and to change behaviour. The first penitentiary in W Canada was built by the federal govt at **STONY MOUNTAIN** in 1870. **BRANDON** built a small multi-purpose jail in 1884. The **PORTAGE LA PRAIRIE** jail for women was built in 1906. A medium-security jail was constructed in **HEADINGLEY**, just W of Winnipeg, in 1930, while other provincial jails were built in **DAUPHIN** and **THE PAS**. The Vaughan St jail was opened in 1908 in downtown Winnipeg and housed remand inmates until it closed in the mid-1970s. Its replacement, the Winnipeg Remand Centre, was opened in 1986 but was soon filled.

The Headingley prison was rocked by 2 large-scale riots, one in 1956 and the other in 1996. The latter was one of the worst in Canadian history; inmates managed to take over the entire prison and hold off police for several days. No lives were lost, but several prisoners were tortured and mutilated. On the youth side, the Manitoba Home of Boys was built in Agassiz in 1899, while a Home for Girls was established in Winnipeg. In 1931, Agassiz assumed programming similar to the British borstal system, using tiered cottages. It offered different types of programming but has ended up as a high-security unit for high-risk youth and those with behavioural problems.

In 1909, the first juvenile court in Canada was established in Winnipeg, and in 1919 the first juvenile probation officer was appointed. It was not until 1957 that the first adult probation officer was hired, again in Winnipeg. The late 1950s and 1960s saw a shift in the structure and amount of correctional programming offered to adults and youth. In 1957, the provincial govt created the position of director of corrections,

Stony Mountain Institution – western Canada's first penitentiary

and the first to hold that office oversaw the expansion of provincial adult and youth probation services over the next 10 years. In 1962, a provincial chief probation officer was appointed. Adult probation services took off after 1969, with federal Criminal Code amendments that made repeat offenders eligible for supervision. The late 20th century saw MB move to more sophisticated classification systems and case management services for offenders.

In 1962, the first classification officer was hired at Headingley, marking a shift to what were thought to be more progressive correctional practices. The formal assignment of educational specialists and Protestant and Catholic chaplains also characterized the transition of the 1960s. The late 20th century saw efforts made to establish "unit management systems" within the institutions, promoting more interactive correctional officer supervision styles. These efforts have been hampered by the physical design of MB's prisons, which were built at a time when architectural styles emphasized surveillance, not interaction. The rise of inmate gangs has also impeded efforts to establish better inmate-staff relations.

The federal correctional service became more heavily involved in the use of parole with the creation of the National Parole Board in 1957. Rockwood Institution, a minimum-security facility built to ease the transition of inmates into the community, opened in 1962. The federal service has greatly expanded the use of classification and assessment in the last 30 years and added more programs both in the community and in the penitentiaries. They emphasize what is believed to be a more scientific system of risk classification and offer a larger range of programs for offenders in custody.

There has been an extensive growth in Aboriginal involvement in the MB corrections system since WWII. As Aboriginal peoples have had more contact with white society, they have been disproportionately represented in corrections, particularly in prisons. In the last 40 years, Aboriginal adults and youths have come to represent between 50%-80% of inmate populations, or 4-6 times their proportion of the general MB population. The ABORIGINAL JUSTICE INQUIRY (1989-91) clearly outlined many of the serious problems confronting the MB correctional system. The authors recommended a separate, Aboriginal-run system based on traditional First Nations values. Indeed, recently there has been a greater use of Aboriginal cultural programming within federal and provincial correctional systems, including the burning of sweetgrass, the use of sweat lodges, and access to elders. However, this programming has not resulted in any significant decrease in Aboriginal representation in probation, parole, or correctional institutions. To some, this makes the development of a separate, Aboriginal-run corrections system a top priority.
● MICHAEL WEINRATH

COSTUME MUSEUM OF CANADA (CMC), is the only dedicated apparel museum in Canada. The CMC, located in **DUGALD**, opened in 1983 as a result of the annual fashion show Dugald's **WOMEN'S INSTITUTE** had been running since 1953. The CMC still hosts period-focused fashion shows. CMC has a collection of 35,000 pieces from AD 1600 to present. These fashion items reflect the character and lifestyles of urban and rural Canadians through hand- and machine-made clothing, accessories, and textiles. The CMC also has pieces by renowned modern fashion designers such as Paco Rabanne and Coco Chanel.

1960s metal dress by Paco Rabanne at CMC

In addition, the museum's archives contain more than 4000 photos of clothing. The museum also offers several guided tours, including a wash-day tour, where visitors can learn how clothes were cleaned in the past, and a student tour highlighting the significance of clothing, dance, and **MUSIC** in relation to various eras. The CMC attracts thousands of visitors a year, including, in 1984, HM Queen Elizabeth. In 2007, the museum moved to Winnipeg's Exchange District. ● RK

CÔTÉ, Kirby, swimmer (b April 29, 1984, Winnipeg) is among the world's top Paralympic swimmers, having won 22 medals in international meets. She was born with an impairment that left her with just 10% of her vision. She started swimming at a young age as a means to improve her balance and coordination. When Côté began competing at age 8, she had to overcome the difficulties caused by her impairment, and find ways to swim within her lane boundaries and to sense the finish wall without using sight. Cote's eyes are also extremely sensitive to light. At the qualifying meet for the 2000 Sydney Paralympic Games, a large window caused a distracting glare in her lane, making it difficult for Cote to stay on-course. She managed to make the team, and went on to win 2 gold medals in Sydney, both in record time. Côté was named MB's Female Athlete and Youth Athlete of 2000. She then broke 3 records at the 2001 USA Swimming Disability Championships, winning 6 gold medals in total, and was named the meet's top swimmer. In 2001, she became the first impaired athlete to compete at the Canada Summer Games, racing against able-bodied swimmers. She won 5 gold at the International Paralympic Committee World Swimming Championships in 2002, and 6 gold medals at a 14-country Canadian Open for swimmers with a disability in 2003. At the 2004 Athens Paralympics, Cote won a medal in every event she entered, tallying 5 golds and 2 silvers. She was named Aquatic Canada's Female Swimmer of the Year. Côté briefly retired from competition following the Games, but decided to return to swimming, winning another gold at the 2006 IPC World Swimming Championships. ● MD

COTTAGE. *See* LAKE, GOING TO THE.

COTTON, Almon James, farmer, letter writer (b 1858, Port Hope, Canada West [ON]; d 1942, **SWAN RIVER**) was a successful grain farmer. He moved to **TREHERNE** in 1888, growing such successful **WHEAT** crops on rented land that he became known as the "Wheat King of Manitoba." One year, Cotton shipped over 17,000 bushels (46,000 kg) of Number 1 Hard. Concerned about inheritances for his sons, he began acquiring land in the Swan River Valley in 1898, and moved there in 1901. Although he was an unsuccessful politician, having run once for the **LEGISLATURE** in the valley as a **PROHIBITIONIST** candidate, Cotton was active in local govt. He served on the Harlington School Board and was Sunday-school superintendent for the Methodist church in Kenville. He was also a member of the board of governors of the **U OF M** from 1917-34. Cotton wrote thousands of letters to immigrants over the years, answering their questions and boosting both MB and the Swan River Valley. An ardent amateur photographer, he took many photographs that survive in family hands, as do most of his records and letter books. A 1985 selection of all these, *The Wheat King*, was edited by Wendy Owen. Cotton is a member of the Manitoba Agriculture Hall of Fame. ● JMB

COULTER, Arthur Edmund "Art," hockey player (b May 31, 1909, WINNIPEG; d Oct 14, 2000, Mobile, Al) played nearly 500 NHL games with the Chicago Black Hawks and the New York Rangers. He started out in Winnipeg with the senior league Pilgrims before playing 2 seasons with the Philadelphia Arrows, where he recorded the most penalty minutes in the Can-Am league for the 1930-31 season. Coulter played his first game with the Black Hawks during the 1931-32 season, earning a permanent spot on the team the following year. With defence partner Taffy Abel, Coulter helped the Black Hawks win their first Stanley Cup in 1934. He was then traded to the Rangers the following season and, as one of the team's most popular players, became captain in 1938. He joined the US Army during WWII, and played 2 seasons with the Coast Guard Clippers in the Eastern Hockey League, which won the Amateur Hockey Association's championship in 1943 and 1944. Coulter retired from play following his military service, and was inducted into the Hockey Hall of Fame in 1974. ● MD

COULTER, Garnet, municipal politician (b 1882, DOMINION CITY; d 1975, WINNIPEG) was a popular Winnipeg mayor. He came to the city in 1903 to article in law. He was called to the Manitoba Bar in 1907 and served overseas in WWI with the Canadian Forestry Corps as a transport officer. He resumed his legal career after demobilization, becoming KC in 1935. He served as a member of the Winnipeg School Board from 1924-36 (chair, 1932-33), and in 1936 was elected as alderman from Ward 2. On city council, he was an

Garnet Coulter, 1954

inveterate opponent of Mayor John Queen. He ran successfully for mayor as an Independent in 1942, and served until 1954. In the 1946 election, he received more than 62,000 votes. Mayor during the MB FLOOD of 1950, Coulter was responsible for the creation of the Manitoba Flood Relief Fund. As a mayor, he was regarded as fair but dull. After his defeat in 1954, he became chair of the Court of Revision. ● JMB

COULTER, James Arthur "Art," politician, activist (b Oct 20, 1916, WINNIPEG; d Apr 11, 2005, Winnipeg) was an advocate for labour rights and social justice. As part of a group of Western labour leaders with the Cooperative Commonwealth Federation (CCF), Coulter is credited with helping found the New Democratic Party (NDP). Coulter served as official agent for STANLEY KNOWLES for over 25 years. After graduating from Daniel McIntyre High School, Coulter began working as a power engineer for the former Canada Malting Company, later organizing the workers there. Sworn into the Winnipeg District and Labour Council in April of 1939, Coulter was active in the labour movement for 4 decades. Coulter was an alderman from 1956 to 1960, and sat as a city councillor from 1960 to 1970. He became executive secretary of the MB Federation of Labour in 1968, serving until a stroke in 1981 forced his early retirement. Coulter was an active member of several MB charities. He was a founding member of the United Way in Winnipeg, Meals on Wheels, Manitoba Blue Cross, the WINNIPEG CHAMBER OF COMMERCE, and the Social Planning Council of Winnipeg. He also served on the board of the Manitoba Medical Service, St. Boniface General Hospital, the WINNIPEG JETS, and as the chairman of the Manitoba Workers Compensation Board. In recognition of his contributions to MB, he was named to the ORDER OF MB in 2003. ● JS

COUNCIL OF ASSINIBOIA. The primary local administrative body of the **HBC** in the **ASSINIBOIA** territory (**RED RIVER SETTLEMENT**) from the arrival of European settlers until the creation of MB, the council was likely created in June 1813. **LORD SELKIRK**'s appointed governor, **MILES MACDONELL**, is said to have brought together an informal group of citizens at the Earl's request. Its initial purpose was to appoint a sheriff and to establish law and order in the fledgling colony. The council was formalized in 1815, when the HBC General Court recognized the council with Macdonell as governor of Assiniboia and **ROBERT SEMPLE** as governor-in-chief of the company's **HUDSON BAY**-area territories. Governance of the settlement proved impossible in the wake of

the **SEVEN OAKS INCIDENT** and **NWC** unrest, and the council was largely ineffective in the years immediately following.

By 1821, Lord Selkirk had died and the merger of the HBC and NWC led to the division of Rupert's Land into two departments – the Northern and Southern. The Northern encompassed the District of Assiniboia (including all lands W and N of present-day ON), and was headed by Governor-in-Chief **GEORGE SIMPSON**. Simpson made administrative changes, assigning company shares to HBC chief factors and chief traders, as well as granting them seats on the Council of Assiniboia. Through the 1820s, the council met infrequently, enacting limited municipal resolutions related to issues like livestock control. It acted as a dispute resolution body and employed part-time constables. Simpson kept a watchful eye on the colony.

In 1834, however, the HBC purchased Assiniboia from the Lord Selkirk's family and expanded the role of the council under Simpson and governor Alexander Christie. In 1835, its jurisdiction was officially declared within a roughly 50-mi (80 km) radius around newly constructed **UPPER FORT GARRY**. At its Feb 12 meeting that year, the council moved to create 4 administrative districts, each with a court and magistrate (later reduced to 3) to adjudicate minor criminal offences and civil matters. A General Quarterly Court was to handle appeals and more serious offences. The first four magistrates were **JAMES CURTIS BIRD**, **ROBERT LOGAN**, James Sutherland, and **CUTHBERT GRANT** (see **ADAM THOM**, **SAYER TRIAL**). Grant, the Métis "warden of the plains," was named a councillor in 1839. Bishop **JOSEPH-NORBERT PROVENCHER** was asked to advise the council – the first Francophone to do so. Donald Ross, Sheriff **ALEXANDER ROSS**, **JOHN BUNN**, and **ANDREW McDERMOT** were also added as advisors.

Also at the 1835 meeting – the turning point in the council's history – the councillors decided to impose a 7.5% duty on all exports and imports through York Factory, quickly adding to the grievances of the Métis and free traders. It was eventually lowered to 4%. A new Public Works committee arranged for the construction of a courthouse and jails, and began plans for a better land titles system and a postal service. The other significant plan was to create a 60-man police corps (later abandoned in favour of a constabulary system).

Despite the changes, the council was generally seen as unresponsive to concerns and unrepresentative of the settlement's population. The HBC always appointed councillors, without thought of elections. There was little Francophone representation until the early 1850s, when

UMA, TRIBUNE, PERSONALITY FILES, 1954

Provencher's influential successor **ALEXANDRE-ANTONIN TACHÉ** helped secure more appointments (Louis-François Lafleche and François-Jacques Bruneau for example). In 1848, William Bletterman Caldwell was named governor of Assiniboia. His appointment was another attempt by the HBC to give the impression of impartial govt (Caldwell had no HBC background). He is known for his oversight of the **FOSS-PELLY CASE** as the sole magistrate.

The authority of the council effectively disappeared in Dec 1869 when Riel seized Upper Fort Garry (and the colony's official land register documents) and declared the first provisional govt in direct opposition to the council (*see* **RED RIVER RESISTANCE**).

The governors of Assiniboia were: Miles Macdonell 1812-1815; Alexander Macdonell 1815 (acting), 1817-1822; Andrew Bulger 1822-25; Donald McKenzie 1825-32; Alexander Christie 1832-48; William Bletterman Caldwell 1848-55; Francis Godschall Johnson 1855-58; and William Mactavish 1858-70. Other prominent members of the Council of Assiniboia included **JAMES McKAY**, **PASCAL BRELAND**, and **ANDREW BANNATYNE**. ● JOEL TRENAMAN

COUNTESS OF DUFFERIN. The *Countess* was the first **RAILWAY** locomotive in the Cdn West. Philadelphia-based Baldwin Locomotive Works built the car in 1872 at a cost of $9850 US. The Northern Pacific Railway used her in MN and ND until 1875. After contractor Joseph Whitehead bought the engine, it arrived in St. Boniface on the **STEAMBOAT** Selkirk in Oct 9, 1877, although construction of the **CPR** line to **WINNIPEG** wasn't completed until 1881. About the time the locomotive arrived in Winnipeg, it was rechristened after the wife of the Gov Gen, the Earl of Dufferin, who had recently visited the MB capital. The locomotive was used in the construction of the Pembina Branch, as well as on sections of the CPR's original E-W line. The *Countess* then made the run between **EMERSON** and St. Boniface. After her retirement, the *Countess* was found in a lumberyard in BC in 1909 and was returned to MB, where she rests at the Winnipeg Railway Museum. ● MD

COUNTRY-BORN is a term historians use for people born in **RUPERT'S LAND** after 1670 to First Nations and especially **CREE** women – Country Wives – and **SCOTS**, **ENGLISH**, or **IRISH** fathers who worked in the **FUR TRADE**. It came into use when the older term "half-breed" began to be seen as pejorative. One of the distinguishing features of these mixed-bloods was their culture, which was based on that of the UK. English was their preferred language, they were typically **ANGLICAN** or **PRESBYTERIAN**, and they tended to think of themselves as British. Still, racist attitudes toward the country-born were often intense. Nowhere is this better illustrated than in the case of **JAMES ROSS** who, despite having a master's degree in law, was still never seen by the Canadians in the **RED RIVER SETTLEMENT** as anything other than a "half-breed." After 1890, the country-born tended to blend in with the waves of Cdn settlers in the West, and assimilated into mainstream Canada. Families unable or unwilling to do this gradually became mixed in with the predominantly **ROMAN CATHOLIC** and largely **OJIBWAY/FRENCH MÉTIS**, who were identified after **LOUIS RIEL**'s death as "half-breeds." In the 1960s, a political and cultural resurgence of the Métis and country-born began. Although most of their ancestors would not have described themselves as "Métis," many descendants of the country-born consider themselves such today. ● FRED J. SHORE

COUNTRYFEST. *See* **DAUPHIN'S COUNTRYFEST.**

COY, Eric, athlete (b May 17, 1911, Nottingham, UK; d Oct 28, 1985, **WINNIPEG**). Coy won numerous titles in track and field events over the course of an athletic career that spanned 20 years. His first Cdn championship title came in 1935 in the javelin throw. He won Cdn discus and shot put titles in 1938, earning him a spot at that year's British Empire Games (now known as the Commonwealth Games), where he won a gold medal with a record-setting discus throw, and a silver in shot put. He was awarded that year's Norton H. Crowe Trophy as Canada's Outstanding Amateur Athlete. Coy's athletic ability was not just limited to track and field. He was a competitive **SNOWSHOE** racer, and set numerous world records in the 100 and 200 yd sprints between 1933-40. While serving overseas during WWII, Coy played football for the RCAF Hurricanes, earning him a brief stint in the CFL. Returning to track and field events, in 1948 Coy set Cdn records in discus and shot put at the Olympic trials, and was named Capt of the national track and field team that competed in that year's Olympic Games in London. A Winnipeg arena in the Charleswood neighbourhood where Coy lived is named in his honour. He was inducted into Canada's Sports Hall of Fame in 1971, and the Manitoba Sports Hall of Fame in 1980. ● MD

COYNE, James Elliot, Rhodes Scholar, governor of the Bank of Canada (b July 17, 1910, **WINNIPEG**). A graduate of the **U OF M** and Oxford U, James Coyne began his career in the Bank of Canada's research department in 1938 before moving on to positions with the Central Mortgage Bank and the Cdn embassy in Washington. He joined the war effort in 1942 and served with the RAF for 2 years. Coyne was best known as the headstrong governor of the Bank of Canada from 1955 to 1961 whose public clashes with the Diefenbaker administration garnered nationwide headlines. As governor, he opposed interest cuts and increases in foreign investment and trade, arguing instead that the govt should focus on unemployment and domestic production. Coyne's infamous disputes with then minister of

Countess of Dufferin, 1923

finance, Donald Flemming, and the presidents of Canada's chartered banks led to an explosive political battle in the spring and summer of 1961 known as the "Coyne Affair." In response to his defiance and his public critiques of federal trade policies, the Diefenbaker administration began a parliamentary campaign to remove him from office. The House of Commons voted 129-37 in favour of his dismissal before the motion was rejected by the Senate. Although this decision helped to redeem his professional reputation, he resigned shortly thereafter. When asked by a newspaper reporter whether he had any last words as he left the offices of the Bank of Canada, an exhausted Coyne replied, "not for another 40 years." • LAURIE BERTRAM

Coyote

COYOTE (*Canis latrans*) is a medium-sized canine that was originally a western species, but with human alteration of the landscape, it has managed to spread far to the E, N and S (Alaska and QC south to Costa Rica). It is common in many regions in spite of several centuries of persecution. One reason for its remarkable success is its adaptability in exploiting vastly different habitats (boreal woodland to desert to tropical rainforest), including an ability to eat almost any animal, from a grasshopper to an elk, dead or alive. It has been known to co-operate in packs while hunting large prey like deer, sometimes capturing the prey in short chases, but at other times, pursuing their quarry for over 5 km. While some coyotes are small (10 kg), with a narrow snout and nose pad, others from northern populations such as in MB approach the size of a wolf (34 kg), and with only a fleeting glance, an observer would find it difficult to separate the two species. Then there is the challenge of identifying hybrids from coyote-dog matings. The animal follows regular trails over its home range of 10-30 sq km, travelling about 6 km per night, at speeds up to 32 km/hr. A pair often has a courtship of about 3 months, but occasionally a bond may form that lasts over a number of years. Matings, in which the animals are locked together for up to 25 minutes, results, 63 days later, in the birth of 1-19 young in an underground den. Most coyotes do not reach 8 years of age, but in

captivity, 18 years is possible. Large packs of coyotes and wolves on the prairies of MB caused early settlers significant problems – eating all food supplies and even devouring anything made of leather like saddles. • REW

CRABBE, Roy Raymond, "R. R.," soldier, businessman, writer (b Dec 31, 1944, NEEPAWA), is the former deputy chief of defence staff of Canada's MILITARY. Crabbe enlisted in the military in 1963. A graduate of U OF M with a bachelor's in mathematics and physics, he was posted to the UN mission in Cyprus and later with NATO forces in Germany. He trained at Canadian Land Force Command and Staff College, the Canadian Forces Staff College, and the US's Armed Forces Staff College (now the Joint Forces Staff College), in Norfolk, VA. In the early 1980s, as a LCol, he commanded the first Batt of the PRINCESS PATRICIA'S CANADIAN LIGHT INFANTRY. From 1986-89, he was Chief of Staff of the Prairie Militia Area. As a BGen, Crabbe headed the Special Service Force (SSF), a brigade-like command that included the elite Canadian Airborne Regt. Promoted to MGen, Crabbe was posted to the former Yugoslavia as Deputy Force Commander of the UN force there in 1994, as well as serving as commander of the Cdn contingent. On his return, he commanded Land Force Atlantic Area 1995-97. Promoted to LGen, from 1997-98 he was 2nd in command of Defence Staff at National Defence Headquarters. In this capacity, he appeared before the Standing Committee on National Defence and Veterans Affairs in 1997. Upon Crabbe's retirement in 1998, fellow Manitoban LGen RAY HENAULT succeeded him as deputy chief at NDHQ. Crabbe is a fellow of the Canadian Defence and Foreign Affairs Institute, acts as a consultant, and writes on military issues, sometimes critiquing the govt's lack of updating to army infrastructure. His writings occasionally appear in the *WINNIPEG FREE PRESS*. • A.J. LEVIN

CRAFTS have contributed to the artistic, social, and economic development of MB from the province's beginning. The province's Aboriginal peoples have rich heritages of leather, beadwork, clothing, basketry, and birch biting. As well, new Canadian settlers brought to Canada a wealth of craft traditions from overseas. In May 1928, the MB branch of the Canadian Handicraft Guild (CHG) was formed for the purpose of preserving crafts. Its mandate was to maintain quality standards of workmanship, to generate income from the sale of crafts, and to provide a solution to the problem of isolation in rural areas. To celebrate its launch, it held a handicraft festival at Winnipeg's Royal Alexandra Hotel. The festival featured colourful displays of fibre arts, including

embroidery, lace, crochet, weaving, and experimental dyes extracted from local plants. With the economic decline of the 1930s, families often crafted in order to supplement their meagre incomes. However, a large craft display, including woodcarvings, quilts, tapestries, rugs, pottery, weavings, and embroideries, was mounted as part of the Sept 1938 La Vérendrye Pageant, held to commemorate the 200th anniversary of the arrival at THE FORKS of LA VÉRENDRYE. After WWII, crafts were used extensively in rehabilitation programs for both polio victims and war veterans. Weaving, leather tooling, glove making, and rug hooking were taught as part of ongoing physiotherapy programs.

One interesting project produced by the CHG was an embroidery sampler in 1943. Each province was to contribute embroidery that would later become part of a travelling exhibition. The MB branch declined to use the canvas supplied for this project; arguing that if the sampler was to reflect the province accurately, the fabric had to be produced locally. Hence, a cotton/linen blend was woven by Inga Roos and Hattie Scott Bergman and the embroidered with of a map of MB depicting local flora and fauna, modes of transportation, and points of interest. Two other noteworthy projects of this time were the Red River Quilt and the creation of a MB tartan. The quilt was sewn in patterns of stylized wheat heads and prairie roses. Designed by Sophia May Osborne, it depicted items of local historical significance – a Red River cart, St. Boniface Cathedral, and a pioneer paddlewheel. The quilt won several awards and prizes, particularly in Montreal and Toronto. Hugh Kirkwood Rankine designed MB's tartan, which was adopted in 1962 to commemorate the Lord Selkirk settlers.

In 1979, the first juried crafts show in the province was held with the support of the WINNIPEG ART GALLERY and the Crafts Guild. In "Praise of Crafts" reflected the high quality of workmanship throughout the province in traditional and contemporary weaving, embroidery, batik, cornhusk dolls, and wheel-thrown pottery. Juried shows continued throughout the 1980s. At that time, teaching became an important function of the Crafts Guild. Stained glass, fibre arts, pottery, and doll-making were all explored, while weaving, quilting, and knitting all remained popular. Country workshops became an important extension of the guild's activities, with teachers travelling by bus to serve rural towns. However, as the decade ended, women's lifestyles changed dramatically, and paid work often left little time for serious craft studies. Long-time members of the MB Crafts Guild – those who had made significant contributions – retired, moved away, or died. To make matters worse, there was also a general lack of communication between the board, the volunteers, and the teachers at the guild shop. A long-range planning committee was struck in 1986 in an effort to try to overcome these problems. By the 1990s, volunteers were scarce. Sales within the guild crafts shop were inconsistent due to a poor economy. Board members reluctantly agreed to sell the building that had been the hub of activity for the crafts guild since its early days. The guild shifted its focus from retail to a crafts museum. Weaving looms, spinning wheels, textiles, and other education materials were distributed among dedicated craftspeople. In June 1999, the Manitoba Crafts Guild ceased to exist.

However, contemporary craft traditions remain strong throughout the province. In the early 2000s, more than 4500 MB residents derived an income from some form of fine craft. MB artisans worked in a great variety of media, including metal, stone, clay, ceramics, fibre, glass, leather, and wood, with mixed media also being popular. **Ione Thorkelson** is a major glassblower working in MB. Derek Boyda and Tim Boryes make fine wood furnishings, while Robert Wilson, Herman DeVries, and Ron Scott practise woodturning. Sculptors, like George Bird, and Ron Gorluck work in the North, while Reid Bricker, Don Golden and Maurice Marr are a few of the sculptors working in Winnipeg. Bronze casting by **Leo Mol** and Metro Dymetri is also notable. As well, there is an influential pottery collective working out of the Stoneware Gallery in Winnipeg, the more famous being Kathryne Koop, Valarie Metcalfe, Alan Lacovetsky, Kevin Stafford, and Ken Chernavitch. Others include Steve Jorgenson, Barbara Balfour, Janice Howarth, Merilyn Kraut, Marusia Foster, David Krindle, and Judy Marchand. Other notable artists working in clay are Jordon Van Sewell, Grace Nickel, Karen Dahl, Robert Archambeau, Duane Perkins, Steve Robinson, Claudia Bergen, Kevin Conlin, Tom Rroberts, and Joanna Lange. Contemporary fine craft is produced throughout MB in small villages, lakeside resorts, and urban centres. Hundreds of local craftspeople display their work at an annual craft fair/sale at the Winnipeg Convention Centre. MB craft is exhibited around the world. It is in the collections of the Smithsonian Institute and of the Japanese emperor, the Queen, and other royalty. As well, it is treasured in numerous private and public collections. ● DIANE PERREAULT

CRAIG MEDIA INC. From a single radio station in **Brandon**, the Craig family over the last half of the 20th century built a broadcasting network that spanned western Canada. The company's beginnings date to 1948, when John Craig organized a group of businessmen to purchase radio station CKX Brandon from the Manitoba Telephone System. Established as Western Manitoba Broadcasters Ltd., Craig's company brought television to Brandon in 1955, and in 1963 expanded into FM radio. WestMan remained Brandon's main broadcaster until 1972, when Moffat Communications Inc., owned by the **Moffat family**, finally gained entrance into the market with CKY-B.

In 1968, Stuart Craig succeeded his father as company president, and pursued the company's expansion beyond Brandon and rural MB into Winnipeg. After the rejection of several CRTC applications because of objections from Moffat Communications Inc. and **CanWest Global Communications Corp.**, WestMan was granted a license in 1986 for the new CHMI-TV, under the brand Manitoba Television Network (MTN), on the condition that it broadcast from **Portage la Prairie** and avoid seeking revenue from Winnipeg advertisers. Changing names in the 1990s to Craig Broadcast System Inc., the company acquired TV in Edmonton and Regina which were dubbed A Channel. The company moved its MB station to the Forks in Winnipeg, abandoning its original rural mandate. In 1996, the company launched digital signal SkyCable in southern MB.

The company was passed down to Drew Craig in 1999, with brothers Miles and Boyd also holding key positions in the company's operations. After a failed attempt to move into the ON market in 2003, Craig Media was sold to CHUM Ltd. in 2004 for $265 million. The family still owns and operates Craig Wireless Systems, which operates wireless Internet and cable in MB as SkyWeb. ● MD

CRANBERRY PORTAGE (pop 610) is a community 40 km SE of **Flin Flon**, just W of Grass River Provincial Park. The site played an important role in the early trade routes of the **Cree** people and their ancestors. In the fur-trade era, Cranberry Portage was used as a campsite and portage between Athapapuskow Lake – on whose shore it sits – and the North Saskatchewan River. By the 1780s, the community was named Cranberry Carrying Place because of the local profusion of lowbush cranberries, and after the historic portage between First Cranberry Lake and Goose Lake. The post office and a **CNR** station both opened here in the late 1920s, and the community is still a stop on the **Hudson Bay Railway/Via Rail** line. Thanks to mineral strikes in nearby Flin Flon and Sherridon, prospectors were lured here and the community boasted a population of 2000.

However, a massive fire destroyed most of the town in 1929, and no new lodes were found. In 1949, Highway 10 connected Cranberry Portage to Flin Flon, **The Pas**, and parts beyond. Soon after, the Department of National Defence took an interest in Cranberry Portage. The community's inconspicuous location was considered an ideal location for a back-up radar site for detecting Soviet aircraft, and in Jan 1958, it became one of the locations for a Mid-Canada Line installation. In Jan 1964, however, the govt ceased the operation, and the facility was sold to Frontier School Division. The facility ultimately became the Frontier College Institute's campus. The community's current economy centres on forestry, tourism, and wild rice. ● GPP

CRANE (family *Gruidae*) is a tall, stately bird that superficially resembles a **Heron**. They are often heard before they are seen, as their far-carrying calls reach us while they are mere specks in the sky overhead. In flight, their outstretched necks, as opposed to the S-curve in a heron's neck, make them easy to recognize. There are 2 species in MB: the Sandhill Crane (*Grus canadensis*), which is common, and the very rare Whooping Crane (*G. americana*). Sandhills breed throughout much of the province and may gather in large flocks during migration, especially in SW MB. Whooping Cranes, which bred in MB until around 1900, became nearly extinct during the early 20th century, but they have made a slow comeback and now appear relatively safe. Most breed in Wood Buffalo National Park in northern AB and winter in southern Texas. ● RUDOLF KOES

CRASH TEST DUMMIES was a rock group formed by lead singer/songwriter Brad Roberts in **Winnipeg** in 1987. The band's original lineup included Ellen Reid and Megan Saunders (who left soon after) on keyboards; Ben Darvill, harmonica; bassist George West; and drummer Vince Lambert. Dan Roberts and Mitch Dorge replaced the latter 2 by 1990. A 5-song demo tape in 1989 earned the group a contract with BMG Records. Their debut *The Ghosts that Haunt Me*, released 1991, sold over 1.5 million copies, boosted by the hit single "Superman's Song." The group won a Juno Award that year for Group of the Year. The Dummies toured NA releasing follow-up album *God Shuffled His Feet* (1993), which sold 4 million copies, with the quirky single "Mmm Mmm Mmm Mmm" rising to #2 on the *Billboard* charts. The album received 3 Grammy Award nominations. In 1994, they made 3 appearances on *Late Night with David Letterman*. Their cover of XTC's "The Ballad of Peter Pumpkinhead" (1995), sung by Reid, appeared in the *Dumb and Dumber* soundtrack, and became another hit. *A Worm's Life* (1995) and *Give Yourself a Hand* (1997) failed to maintain the momentum of previous albums, and BMG dropped the group. With the departure of Reid, Darvill, and Dorge, Roberts released *I Don't Care If You Don't Mind* (2001), *Crash Test Dude Live* (2001), and *Puss 'n Boots* (2003) independently. In 2005, Reid returned for *Songs for the Unforgiven*. Now residing in New York, Roberts continues to tour occasionally under the Crash Test Dummies' name. ● JOHN EINARSON

CRAWFORD, Mary Elizabeth, physician (b 1876, Lancs., UK; d 1953, **WINNIPEG**) was one of MB's earliest female physicians. She attended the Ottawa Normal School and the U of Toronto. She interned at the West Philadelphia Hospital for Women and Children. She came to Winnipeg in 1901, practising privately until she was appointed chief medical inspector of the public schools of Winnipeg. She served in this capacity from 1918-41. She was a founder and first president of the University Women's Club, and was president of the International Association of Women Physicians and the Women's Equity League. ● JMB

CRAYFISH is a member of the jointed-legged animals called crustaceans, which includes species ranging from microscopic to shrimps and lobsters. There are only 2 species adapted to live in MB's freshwaters – freezing to the bottom of waterbodies and oxygen depletion in winter prevent other species from surviving here. The uncommon Calico or Papershell Crayfish (*Orconectes immunis*) is grey-green and 9 cm long. It inhabits creeks, sloughs and ditches in the **RED RIVER** Valley, preferring slow-moving or still turbid waters with a muddy bottom, and is able to survive drying out of its home by burrowing into the mud, where it remains until water returns. The more-common and widely distributed Northern or Virile Crayfish (*Orconectes virilis*) is green to reddish-brown and extends throughout the boreal forest, where it requires permanent water with a rocky bottom, and a current to increase oxygen levels in the water. It can reach a size of 12 cm. The body of a crayfish is organized into regions with appendages specialized for specific duties. The head (with a pair of large, stalked eyes) and thorax are joined into a tough carapace (cephalothorax) which contains the large gills. There are 2 pairs of antennae, which are touch and chemically sensitive, and bear the organs of balance. A crayfish defends itself and captures and manipulates food (plants and small aquatic animals) with a pair of enlarged

Crayfish – only 2 species are adapted to live in Manitoba's freshwaters.

front legs (chelae) or pincers. It moves about on 4 pairs of legs (pereopods), but when a predator (fish, heron or mink) approaches, the crayfish contracts its wide tail several times and shoots rapidly backward, giving it time to seek cover under a rock or other debris. The male has larger pincers and a narrower abdomen. Mating may occur in fall (with the female storing the sperm) or spring, with the male turning over each potential mate (male or female) to check its sex. If a female is responsive, the male grasps her with his pincers and they join with their ventral sides together for sperm transfer. The fertilized egg mass is stored under the female's tail, secured by 5 pairs of swimmerets. These are laid on the bottom in late May and hatch by July, the youngsters resembling tiny copies of their parents. These are short-lived creatures which die at age 2 or 3, soon after completing their reproductive function. Their scavenging and algae-eating activities are important in the ecology of the waters they inhabit. Due to habitat destruction (mainly rising water pollution) 50% of North American species of crayfish are threatened. ● REW, WW

CREDIT UNIONS took root in MB when little else could – during the **GREAT DEPRESSION**. Several factors converged in the 1930s to spur their development. Credit from traditional lenders – to which the average citizen had limited access to begin with – became even scarcer during the Depression, and credit unions offered a way for people to help each other out. Every person who joined a credit union became a shareholder, with a single vote. They could use the union's deposit and loan services, and, ultimately, share in the profits.

In the early 20th century, many European immigrants had come to the Canadian Prairies already knowing about co-operatives and credit

unions, which had first been founded in 1844 and 1852 in the UK and Germany, respectively. One such man, Wasyl Topolnicky, founded the first Canadian-**UKRAINIAN** credit union in Saskatchewan, then moved on to MB, where he helped found 7 more.

By the mid-'30s, the credit union movement had caught the attention of the govt of premier **JOHN BRACKEN**. In 1937, an amendment to the *Companies Act* was passed that established the first legislation governing credit unions. (They were to get their own legislation in 1946.) The first credit union was chartered in 1937, in the southeastern farming community of **ST. MALO**. Local Roman Catholic priest Father (later Monsignor) Arthur Benoît saw that his parish – like most farmers on the continent – was suffering. He brought them together to help each other financially. The first loan to a member, $56.50 to be repaid in $2 monthly instalments, financed the purchase of a cream separator.

Bracken's govt did more than write the enabling legislation; it looked for people with expertise who could help promote and establish credit unions. In 1938, the premier wrote Arthur Béliveau, Archbishop of St. Boniface, to ask whether Benoît might be available "as an occasional lecturer on credit unions." The archbishop replied that Benoît could not be spared from his parish duties, but informed the premier, in a postscript, that 8 parishes were in the process of establishing credit unions.

The co-operative idea and how to put it into practice also reached Winnipeg by a weekly radio program – carried on Chicago radio station WCFL – from the extension services of St. Francis-Xavier U in Antigonish, NS. The first Winnipeg credit union was founded by the 4 men who comprised the Norwood Grove Study Group #1. David Harriman, Fred Everett, Walter Thomson, and Leonard Schaumloffel listened to the Antigonish broadcasts, worked through the material they'd sent away for, and, in 1938, formed the Norwood Credit Union. A Jan 1939 item in the *Winnipeg Tribune* reported that "the Antigonish idea has caught in the Maritimes and is sweeping westward. In its wake it is leaving a new philosophical mentality which (strictly off the official record) is viewed with alarm by stalwarts of the old-line parties."

In 1939, Bracken appointed a Commissioner of Credit Unions, who reported through the department of agriculture: 13 years later the govt would establish a Co-operative Services branch in the department. Credit unions would themselves form various organizations over the coming decades to provide education, organization and financing services – all of which would be consolidated in the Co-operative Credit Society (Credit Union Central) of MB in 1979.

While figures on the system's overall growth throughout the period are impressive (700% asset growth between 1950 and 1959, for example), the reality was that most of the province's credit unions were small. In 1953, 68% of credit unions had assets of less than $50,000 and fewer than 250 members, and 83% had either part-time or volunteer management, with the rest having but a single, full-time employee. The system had $11 million in total assets, but only 11 credit unions had more than $200,000. And most were closed-bond, meaning their members shared an occupation, employer, culture, or religion. Of the 76 with community bonds – known as open-bond today – only 6 were in Winnipeg, 42 had cultural or religious bonds, and 44 – including Winnipeg Housewives, Commercial Telegraphers, and MacDonald Brothers Aircraft Employees – were occupational. The number of credit unions peaked at 258 in 1963, after which resource pooling through amalgamations began to drive the number down. Member and asset growth continued to grow,

though, from 93,000 members and $42 million in 1960 to 184,000 members and $169 million by the end of the decade.

Ten years later, credit unions would be victims of their own success. Having kept pace with the heady growth of assets, long-term loans financed by short-term deposits squeezed margins and decimated profits when the prime rate climbed and climbed in the late 1970s and early '80s, eventually hitting 21.75% in September 1981. The system had very little equity to fall back on when the crisis hit. The provincial govt put a loan guarantee in place which, it turned out, the system never called on. Instead, credit unions, Central, and the regulator, the stabilization fund, put programs in place to build equity, accelerate amalgamations and strengthen controls.

From the early 1980s, credit unions' growth resumed its earlier momentum. While the number of credit unions fell with amalgamations, the number of branches continued to increase, as did the number of communities in which a credit union was the only financial institution available to businesses and consumers. By the end the end of the 20th century, a scant 60 years after their founding in MB, credit unions led all financial institutions in deposits and consumer and small-business lending in MB. ● JOHN HAMILTON

CREE are a numerous and widely dispersed **First People**. The 3 main groups of Cree were the Woods Cree of the western boreal forest, the Plains Cree of the northern plains, and the Swampy Cree on the east and west side of **Hudson Bay**. Cree can be found from Labrador through to the northern foothills of the Rocky Mountains in BC. There is some debate about where the word 'Cree' derives from; it is now thought to be an Algonkian language term (nabwe) *'kiristin,'* referring perhaps to a now-defunct band. Cree call themselves, depending on which sub group they belong to, as some version of *'ininiw'* (person).

Traditionally Cree were hunters, fishers and gatherers, relying on a wide range of bush or country food. Most of the year was spent in small hunting bands of 15 to 30 people, except in the summer when bands gathered together on a regional basis in groups of up to a few hundred people. Cree were among the main intermediaries during the **Fur Trade** epoch. They had direct contact with the **HBC**, which established itself directly in their territory from 1670. Cree were able to take advantage of their 'middleman' position to extend their traditional trading networks. Cree in MB are signatory to Treaty 1, Treaty 4, Treaty 5, Treaty 6 and Treaty 10, though Treaty 5 brings together the largest group of Cree.

Cree in contemporary times occupy communities from the W side of **Lake Winnipeg** (**Grand Rapids**), to the N of Lake Winnipeg (including **Cross Lake, Norway House, Nisichawayasihk**), N and W of the lake (including **Opaskwayak, Chemawawin, Mosakahiken**) and N and E of the lake (including **Tataskweyak, Bunibonibee, Manto Sipi**). Cree therefore have a large if not dominant position in northern Manitoba, especially N and W of Lake Winnipeg. Cree can be found in all walks of life, as lawyers, professors, politicians, entrepreneurs, workers, artists and so on. Cree artists like the writer **Tomson Highway** or the painter **Jackson Beardy**, among many others, have been able to add to the enormous cultural heritage that Cree contribute to MB. ● PETER KULCHYSKI

CREIGHTON, Thomas, prospector (b 1874, Dunedin, ON; d 1949, **Flin Flon**) is credited with naming Flin Flon. In 1914, after discovering a giant copper ore body, he decided to call the area after a character in a paperback novel he had found in the bush. The character's name – Flintabbatey Flonatin – was shortened to something more manageable. Creighton later worked as an executive with **Hudson Bay Mining and Smelting** and was president of the HB Air Transport Company. A town in SK, just across the border from Flin Flon is named for him. ● MD

CRERAR, Thomas Alexander, politician, grain dealer (b June 17, 1876, Molesworth, ON; d April 11, 1975, Victoria), the only politician to serve in federal Cabinet in both World Wars. Born in ON of Scottish ancestry, Crerar and his parents, William and Margaret, came to a homestead near **Russell** in 1881. He was educated in **Portage la Prairie**, obtained a teacher's certificate in 1894, and taught until 1902. He briefly farmed land his father had bought from the **CPR**, and some he himself bought from the **HBC**, as well as operating a lumber mill. He also became involved

Early photo of Steinbach Credit Union.

in the Independent Order of Odd Fellows – this may have sparked his interest in politics. He managed Russell's **GRAIN ELEVATOR** starting in 1904, and in 1907, became a director of the Grain Growers' Grain Company. He was subsequently president of it and if its 1917 successor, **UNITED GRAIN GROWERS** (UGG). Later that year, amidst WWI, he was made Minister of Agriculture in PM Sir Robert Laird Borden's Union govt, although he had never been elected to any office. However, he successfully ran for the Marquette constituency later that year, on the strength of his work to promote agricultural interests in Cabinet, such as lobbying for free trade with the US. Crerar resigned in 1919, as the govt would not lower tariffs on farm implements, despite the war's ending. In 1920, he founded and became parliamentary leader of the moderate and decentralized Progressive Party of Canada, allied with the Progressive Party of Manitoba. In the 1921 election, PM William Lyon Mackenzie King's Liberals won a minority govt, with the Progressive gaining support, especially in the Prairies. Though they had the 2nd-largest party and 21% of the popular vote, Crerar and many of his ex-Liberal MPs refused to become the Official Opposition, but neither would some Progressive elements allow him to join King's govt in a coalition.

Crerar managed to reintroduce the **CROW'S NEST PASS FREIGHT RATE**, but hamstrung by his own party at the same time his 8-year-old daughter succumbed to diphtheria, he resigned the leadership in 1922. He joined the Liberal Cabinet as Minister of Railways and Canals in 1929, resigning his presidency of UGG, but lost his **BRANDON** seat in a general election the next year. Crerar became part of King's govt in 1935 as the MP for **CHURCHILL**, and served prominently in Cabinet until the end of WWII, with portfolios including Mines, Immigration and Colonization, the Interior, and Indian Affairs. Immediately upon quitting his last Cabinet post, that of Mines and Resources, he was made a Senator (1945-66). He tirelessly advocated for Manitobans and their interests in Ottawa, and was inducted in the Manitoba Agricultural Hall of Fame. He was the first politician made Companion of the Order of Canada, in Dec 1973. He is the subject of the biography *T. A. Crerar: A Political Life* (McGill-Queen's University Press, 1997), by J. E. Rea, and he can be seen in the 1962 documentary *Crisis on the Hill* in the *Canada at War* series. ● AJL

CREWSON, Wendy, actor (b May 9, 1956, Hamilton, ON), is a television and feature film star. Born in ON, Crewson grew up in **WINNIPEG** and attended Westwood Collegiate before moving to Montreal. She graduated from Queen's U,

Wendy Crewson, 2006

in Kingston, ON, with a BA in drama in 1977, and received the Lorne Greene Award for outstanding work in the **THEATRE**. She then studied at the Webber Douglas Academy of Dramatic Art in London, UK. Crewson married actor Michael Murphy in 1988; they have 2 children, Maggie and Jack. Her most notable films include *The Good Son* (1993); *The Santa Clause* (1994) and its sequels; *To Gillian on Her 37th Birthday* (1996); *Air Force One* (1997); *The Sixth Day* (2000); and *What Lies Beneath* (2000). Crewson has won 3 Gemini Awards, with 2 for Best Actress in a Dramatic Program or Miniseries (1999, 2003), the other for Best Guest Actress (1998). Crewson's title-role performance in *At the End of the Day: The Sue Rodriguez Story* got her involved in fundraising for research into amyotrophic lateral sclerosis (ALS or Lou Gehrig's disease). The Winnipeg-born Rodriguez, who suffered from ALS, brought a challenge to the *Criminal Code* for its prohibition of euthanasia as far as the Supreme Court of Canada. In Feb 2007, ACTRA Toronto Performers honoured Crewson with their Award of Excellence. ● AMANDA STEPHENS

CRICKET is a bat-and-ball sport that slightly resembles **BASEBALL** and which likely originated in the Home Counties of the UK in the Middle Ages. Though more formally played over 4 days ("first-class" cricket), there is also a one-day version, generally limited to 50 overs. British soldiers garrisoned at Upper Fort Garry were probably the first to play cricket in MB. **WILLIAM COLDWELL** established the Northwest Cricket Club in 1864.

The earliest records of regular cricket matches in MB date from the early 1870s, and indicate that the sport was immensely popular, to the extent that PM John A. Macdonald declared it Canada's national sport in 1867. **MILITARY** units often formed teams, as did groups of **ENGLISH** professionals, such as bankers and lawyers. Prominent citizens of the **RED RIVER SETTLEMENT**, such as **A. G. B BANNATYNE** and J. H. McTavish, were among MB's earliest resident cricketers. Such local leaders helped form the Northwest Cricket

Association in 1896, though matches at this time were still organized after one side challenged another, following British tradition. The *Manitoba Free Press* (see **WINNIPEG FREE PRESS**) often printed accounts of these amateur matches. In 1882, a Winnipeg team travelled E for the first time to play a series of matches in ON and QC, winning against more established teams from Toronto, Ottawa, and Montreal. The Manitoba Cricket Association, founded in 1905, has mainly overseen matches between MB teams.

Games through the 1880s and '90s often occurred at **WINNIPEG**'s Dufferin Park. In 1908, a team of **CPR** employees played several Minneapolis sides, often on the fields of the mental hospitals at **SELKIRK** and **BRANDON**. **ASSINIBOINE PARK** became home to a cricket pitch with a pavilion in 1911. The following year, Winnipeg figured prominently in cricket, hosting a team from Philadelphia, at that time considered NA's cricket capital; in 1913, the Winnipeg Wanderers won the John Ross Robertson Trophy, the top prize for a Cdn cricket club, beating a preferred Toronto team and bringing the cup W for the first time. Winnipeg became a major centre for cricket, and there were 26 clubs in the city in 1914.

Cricket became less popular in eastern Canada following WWI, but was still widely enjoyed by western Cdn teams, who competed mainly against each other in inter-provincial championships until the onset of the **GREAT DEPRESSION**. Still, in 1932, Winnipeg cricket supporters raised enough money to host a famous Australian team. By WWII, cricketers were largely Australians, New Zealanders, and other Colonials attached to the **BRITISH COMMONWEALTH AIR TRAINING PLAN**, and the number of MB teams had dropped to just 3, all from Winnipeg. Recent **ENGLISH** arrivals occasionally organized matches, but they often switched to other sports as they adopted Cdn customs.

In 1966, the cricket fields in Assiniboine Park were renovated for field hockey events for the **PAN-AM GAMES**, but the city built a new cricket pavilion the following year. In 1968, the International Cricket Council (ICC, the world governing body of the sport) recognized the national team, a huge boost to Cdn cricketers. International cricket aspirations peaked in 1979, with Canada finishing 2nd to Sri Lanka for the ICC Trophy. Cricket is gradually spreading outside the confines of Winnipeg, with the first cricket pitch to be built in MB in over 30 years completed in **GIMLI** in 2001. **IMMIGRANTS** from **SOUTH ASIAN** and West Indian countries, where this sport is wildly popular, will have the task of reviving cricket in MB. Provincial teams are still competitive in domestic play, but MB sends few bowlers, batsman, and fielders to the national squad. ● MICHELLE DOBROVOLNY

CRICKETS are insects of prairies, meadows and agricultural fields. Appearing in the Permian Period (about 280 mya), there are now over 4085 species worldwide in this family of true crickets. They are dark brown or black, with a flattened body averaging 15-30 mm long, and with exceedingly long antennae, and 2 spines (cerci) at the end of the abdomen. Some have lost the ability to fly. These gregarious creatures are the virtuosos of insect world, with melodious chirping and intermittent trilling of the males calling the silent females. The sounds are generated by a tooth-and-comb adaptation – vigorous rubbing (stridulating) a roughened ridge on the underside of one front wing across a file on the upperside of the other wing. A cricket may create different sounds for calling, courting, and defending a female from the advances of a competitor. Females are silent, since they are carrying the eggs of the next generation, and calling could attract predators. Caged crickets are kept in some countries to enjoy the cheerful sounds. Many species produce sounds beyond human hearing (above 20 kHz). After mating, the female lays her eggs, by means of a long, needle-like ovipositor at the rear of the body, either singly or in masses, in moist ground. The nymphs grow an molt up to 10 times before reaching adult size. Population explosions occur when reproductive conditions allow, and they become so abundant that they swarm over the ground and often enter buildings in search of cover and to hibernate. While exceeded by grasshoppers in jumping ability, crickets also have powerful legs and can run and jump with remarkable speed. The mouthparts are adapted for chewing plant material, and they are prodigious eaters, capable of causing considerable losses to crops, particularly grains. There are 8 species in MB, including the Spring Field Cricket (*Gryllus veletis*), Fall Field Cricket (*Gryllus pennsylvanicus*), 3 species of Ground Cricket – Striped (*Allonemobius fasciatus*), Allard's (*Allonemobius allardi*) and Carolina (*Eunemobius carolinus*), and 3 species of Tree Crickets – Four-spotted (*Oecanthus quadripunctatus*), Prairie (*Oecanthus argentinus*), and Black-horned (*Oecanthus nigricornis*). The Mormon Cricket (*Anabrus simplex*) is actually a predaceous katydid and not a cricket.

● REW

CRIDDLE FAMILY were **English** homesteaders who lived near Aweme, several km N of **Wawanesa**, on a farm they named St. Alban's. The family was relatively wealthy and well educated, setting it apart from other settlers, who usually came from the impoverished underclass of their countries of origin. The Criddles' vari-

(L to R) Cecil, Elise, Evelyn, Edwy, Norman, Julia, Talbot, Alice, Alma, Percy, Maida, Harry, Beatrice, Stuart.

ous academic and recreational pursuits made St. Alban's a social hub as well as a centre for scientific research.

Patriarch Percy Criddle (b Nov 21, 1844, London, UK; d Apr 17, 1918) was a wine merchant in the UK. He studied law, medicine, and languages at several European universities, though he never received any degrees. He came to MB in 1882, accompanied by his legal wife Alice Criddle (née Nicol) (b Nov 24, 1849, London, UK; d May 6, 1918) and his mistress, Elise Harrer (b Nov 24, 1840, Germany; d Nov 2, 1903), and the children of both women. Ms Harrer adopted the surname Vane once in Canada. Percy met Elise while studying in Germany. She followed Percy to the UK after he left school, where they continued their relationship, which resulted in 6 children, of which 5 survived infancy. In 1874, he married Alice, who spoke 9 languages and was one of England's first female scholars, having studied at the University of Cambridge. Alice gave birth to 4 children in the UK before the Criddles and Vanes made the journey across the Atlantic. Much is known of the Criddles' pioneering life thanks to Percy's meticulous journal-writing. Though he was useless at farming and had to hire other homesteaders to construct his families' log house, Percy studied much of the flora and fauna surrounding his home, and kept daily logs of the weather.

Farm work fell to the oldest Vane children, especially Edwy (Edwin) Vane (1871-1955), whom Percy would refer to as "The Boy." The eldest Vane girls were sent to work as servants in Brandon. The Criddle children were kept largely unaware of their relation to the Vanes, though the former knew of their real parentage, as they had called Percy "Papa" in England and were only told upon their arrival in Canada that they must

call their father "Mr. Criddle." Some accounts of the family history relate that the parents were forced to admit the Vanes' real parentage to the Criddle children in order to circumvent a romantic relationship between siblings. Eventually, the Vanes built a separate residence for themselves on the edge of St. Alban's. The Criddle family prospered, and a new house, including a library and a billiards table, was built in 1905, allowing Percy to pursue the intellectual and recreational pastimes he had enjoyed in the UK. An avid sportsman, Percy also built a golf course and a tennis court on the property.

Percy's children inherited their father's passion for science. Norman Criddle (b May 14, 1875, Addlestone, Surrey, UK; d May 4, 1933) was Percy's eldest legitimate son. He became one of MB's most influential entomologists, publishing over 160 scholarly articles in his lifetime, as well as many detailed wildflower paintings. Norman was the entomologist for the Cdn govt from 1914-33. The insects he gathered and studied are part of many entomological collections throughout the world. During this time, Norman wintered in Ottawa, but returned every summer to his laboratory at St. Alban's. He was an authority on the **Grasshopper**, and developed MB's first poison bait, known as the "Criddle Mixture," to combat the insect.

Norman's brother Stuart Criddle (b Dec 4, 1877, Addlestone; d Oct 23, 1971, Sidney, BC) was also a noted naturalist. His fields of expertise were mammalogy and ornithology, and he published 18 papers. He also experimented in plant breeding, developing a new strain of lily, *Lilium stuart criddlei*, which still blossoms in small numbers around St. Alban's. He was awarded an honorary doctorate in science from **Brandon U**.

Maida Criddle (b May 2, 1884, Aweme, MB; d 1960) was the first Criddle to be born on the homestead. She lived all her life on the farm, keeping up the meteorological records started by her father until her death, which earned her a Centennial Award Plaque from the Canadian Meteorological Service in 1972. The continuous meteorological record log for Aweme from 1884-1960 is the 3rd-longest such record by a Cdn family. Talbot "Tolly" Criddle (b Aug 19, 1890, Aweme, MB; d Sep 1975) married and settled a farm in the area of his family's original homestead. He was also interested in natural sciences and helped his brother Norman to collect insects. He created the first "marrowkin," a cross between a pumpkin and a marrow.

The Criddle family sold the farm in 1960 and moved to Vancouver Island, where they now run a golf course. A 1973 book, *Criddle-de-Diddle-ensis*, was written by Percy's granddaughter, Alma Criddle, and is based on his journals. The Vanes remained in MB, where many of their descendants still live. The Criddle/Vane homestead has been made into a **PROVINCIAL PARK**.
• MICHELLE DOBROVOLNY

CROCUS. *See* **PRAIRIE CROCUS.**

CROCUS INVESTMENT FUND. Crocus was incorporated March 21, 1992, and was designed to participate in a provincial govt tax scheme to generate capital investment in mid-sized MB companies. Manitobans who invested up to $5000 a year in Crocus received 15% provincial and 15% federal tax credits. The goal of labour-sponsored investment funds (LSIFs), including Crocus, is to generate long-term capital appreciation by investing in growing companies and producing a return for its investors. Crocus also tried to make investments that would provide economic stability to the provincial economy, retain and create jobs in MB, and maintain local ownership of MB firms.

After enjoying some investment success and public support through the late 1990s Crocus' investment portfolio was valued at close to $200 million in 2000. In summer 2000, its shares peaked at $15.39, up from $10 when it was first launched. But after the collapse of several companies in its portfolio, management disputes over valuation, and damaging legal and regulatory actions, the fund was forced into receivership and a court-ordered liquidation in fall 2005. At that time, its shares were valued at $5.99.

In its heyday through the late 1990s and into the first years of the new century, the fund invested in such solid MB enterprises as Pollard Banknote, **MONDETTA**, National Leasing, Welling-ton West, and the **MTS CENTRE**. But some of its largest and most celebrated investments turned out to be its biggest money losers: Winnport, an international cargo hub concept that never got off the ground; Isobord (which became Dow BioChemicals), an **ELIE** factory that made fibreboard out of wheat straw, which closed in late 2005; Westsun International, a **WINNIPEG**-based theatrical lighting company that was a hit on Broadway but collapsed under heavy debt; and Maple Leaf Distillers, a Winnipeg liquor blender with big plans that disintegrated in a web of controversy. The losses from those companies cost Crocus investors close to $40 million.

Venture-capital funds are expected to offset their share of poor investments with big winners, but that was not to be for Crocus. Like many other Canadian venture-capital funds, the collapse of the high-tech market in 2000 meant a dramatic reduction in the value of Crocus' investment. The fund lost another $30 million from failed **INFORMATION TECHNOLOGY** companies. The fund devalued its portfolio by 10% in fall 2004. An internal conflict regarding the need for additional writedowns led to a suspension of trading in Dec 2004. The fund never recovered. A 30% devaluation in Apr 2005 preceded a damning provincial auditor general's report in May 2005 that detailed serious weaknesses in the fund's governance and operations. The auditor general cited a lack of oversight by the fund's board of directors, flaws in its investment procedures, abuse of the fund's expense policy, and concern that the value of its assets was overstated.

Before the report was released, the MB Securities Commission had commenced action against former members of the Crocus board of directors, alleging among other things, that the process that had been used to value the portfolio was not in the public's interest. Subsequent to the report, the RCMP began an investigation into potential criminal activity at Crocus. (No details on that investigation were available in early 2007.) In Jun 2005, a Crocus unit-holder launched a class action suit against the fund company and its officers, seeking up to $200 million in damages. That prompted the resignation of the entire board of directors, for fear that Crocus would not have sufficient director and officer liability insurance. The resulting absence of governance prompted the Securities Commission to apply for a court-appointed receiver to assume management of the fund at the end of Jun 2005. After much legal manoeuvring, and some 11th-hour protestations, the court directed the receiver to liquidate the fund in late Oct 2005.

The possibility that political mileage might be mined from the Crocus collapse kept the opposition provincial **PROGRESSIVE CONSERVATIVE PARTY** busy for much of 2006 and into 2007 calling for a public inquiry and trying to link the governing **NDP** to the fund's collapse. Experts believe the dearth of investment capital in MB has long been a challenge to the province's economy. Many of them believed the financial and political controversy that kept Crocus in the news for years exacerbated that problem. • MARTIN CASH

CROP CIRCLES are geometrical-pictorial designs appearing in nature, usually on crop or grass fields, but also on thin ice and over large tracts of forest. Their design can go well beyond the classic pie shape. Some are often extremely geometrically complicated, depicting parts of the solar system or religious images with multicultural symbols, while others remain obscure. Controversy surrounds crop circles, since hoaxers are known to have created some of them in the past, and may do so again in the future. However, there is a world of difference between man-made circles – which are rare, messy, and easy to spot – and the majority, which display precision seemingly beyond the realm of human capability.

Crop Circles

In Canada, the Canadian Crop Circle Research Network (CCCRN), with the help of numerous volunteers across the country, has been following the development of crop circles, studying and taking pictures, obtaining samples for lab testing, and compiling information trying to make sense of the phenomenon since 1995. Records at CCCRN show that 33 crop circles have been documented in Manitoba since the early 1900s. However, the records only show year and location, with no pictures or details of the design. Crop circles have been documented from almost every province, but Saskatchewan remains the Canadian "hot spot" by a large measure.

There are documented biological effects on plants in many crop circles. These effects include swollen nodes on plant stems, as well as tiny holes in the stems known as expulsion cavities. The plants commonly show effects of dehydration brought about by high heat. The soil around them commonly turns crusty and, under magnification, shows an increase in the size of crystals in the soil, a process that requires a very high temperature. The formation of about 25 crop circles has been witnessed in Europe and North America. All observers describe "balls of light" falling from the sky, creating the designs with extreme rapidity and violence, though little damage is found in the flattened plants.

In a crop circle formation in 2003 near **BOISSEVAIN**, the wheat plants were perfectly laid down in intricate yet regular patterns. Scientists reported that the ratios of areas of the circles were mathematically related to each other (being exactly 2, 3, and 5 times the smallest), in ratios similar to music notes. Insects such as grasshoppers were absent inside the circles.

When investigators arrive at a fresh crop circle, they frequently face malfunctioning of electronic equipment, such as watches, cameras, and videos. People nearby have also recounted health effects, like headaches, and animals are said to feel agitated by the phenomena and keep away. The forces creating these latter formations are unknown and cannot yet be explained. There is still resistance to mass acceptance, despite their effects, such as exquisite geometry or other designs pleasing to the eye; changes to plant matter; and effects on cameras and watches. Yet those who come close to the phenomenon are often profoundly affected. • MICHAEL ISSIGONIS

CROSS LAKE, pop 294, is a community 115 km S of Thompson on the SE shore of Cross Lake – after which the settlement is named – at the mouth of the **NELSON RIVER**. There are 2 closely-related, adjoining, but independent communities here. One is the Cross Lake **FIRST NATION,** the other is the community of Cross Lake found on provincial crown land. The 2 communities are linked by ferry across the Nelson. The post office opened here in 1921. Economic activities in the area centre on **COMMERCIAL FISHING,** Trapping, **WILD RICE,** and services. Cross Lake has an RCMP detachment, nursing station, gravel airstrip with scheduled plane service, and a school administered by the Frontier School Division. • GPP

CROW (family *Corvidae*) is our largest "songbird" – though its many calls could scarcely be described as tuneful. Five members of this family occur regularly, all of which can be found year-round. The American crow (*Corvus brachyrhynchos*) breeds throughout the province. In recent years, increasing numbers overwinter, particularly in Winnipeg and other urban centres in the south. Its larger cousin, the non-migratory common raven (*C. corax*), sometimes known as the "Thompson turkey," is more partial to forested areas, but it

has spread across the agricultural south in the last few decades. Blue jays (*Cyanocitta cristata*) and grey jays, Canada jays, or whisky jacks (*Perisoreus canadensis*), are common feeder birds, the latter species restricted to the boreal forest (*see* **ECOCLIMACTIC REGIONS**). The black-billed magpie (*Pica hudsonia*) is found mostly around farmyards, shelterbelts, and garbage dumps. Members of the crow family are often considered to be our most intelligent birds. Ravens, for example, have learned to patrol highways, looking for food in the form of roadkill, while grey jays may follow a trapper to steal bait from the traps. • RUDOLF KOES

CROWN CORPORATIONS (CCs) differ from their private sector counterparts in several important respects. CCs are govt-owned organizations that do not generally operate with a view to generating profit, whereas private sector corporations undertake market activity in pursuit of profit for shareholders. CCs are immune to bankruptcy since governments could cover operating losses indefinitely through general revenue whereas private sector corporations may, when liabilities exceed assets, be forced into bankruptcy.

What CCs and private sector corporations have in common is that both are legal entities controlled by a board of directors appointed or elected by owners, have the right to enter into contracts, sue or be sued in a court of law, own property and incur debts and limit owners' liability to the extent of their investment. The explanation for the proliferation of CCs in MB is that they have a highly flexible structure. This enables government to delegate a wide range of responsibilities to an autonomous organization while retaining considerable influence and ultimate control. The fact that there are currently 63 CCs in MB is a testament to their suitability and adaptability in discharging a myriad of tasks.

MANITOBA HYDRO is the monopoly supplier of electricity and natural gas in MB. It is the largest CC in terms of assets, revenues, and number of employees. Its long-term debt, incurred through large investments in **HYDROELECTRIC** dams, transmission lines and pipeline infrastructure, is almost half of the Government of MB's total debt. The government-appointed Manitoba Hydro-Electric Board governs Manitoba Hydro. The Manitoba Public Utility Board (PUB) regulates its rates. In applying for rate changes, Manitoba Hydro is expected by the PUB to satisfy financial targets such as maintaining sufficient reserves, meeting interest payment obligations, and meeting debt to retained earning targets.

The other three largest CCs are **MANITOBA PUBLIC INSURANCE CORPORATION** (MPIC), **MANITOBA LOTTERIES CORPORATION** (MLC), and the **MANITOBA**

LIQUOR CONTROL COMMISSION (MLCC). MPIC is the monopoly provider of mandatory motor vehicle insurance in MB. It is responsible for all vehicle and driver licensing in the province. Its mandate is to provide no-fault motor vehicle insurance at rates – regulated by the PUB – that enable it to cover its cost and maintain a reserve fund that can meet anticipated future claims. MLCC has a legal monopoly in the wholesale distribution of liquor in MB and in the retail distribution of hard liquor. Through its own stores, MLCC competes with private vendors in retail distribution. With the exception of relatively minor First Nations gambling operations, MLC has exclusive authority to operate casinos, lotteries, and video lottery terminals in MB. MLC and MLCC are essentially "government enterprises" which contributed $232 million and $176.25 million respectively to government coffers in 2004, net of PST and other taxes. Sales by MLCC additionally generated $16 million in provincial taxes and $32 million in federal taxes.

Apart from Manitoba Hydro, MPIC and MLCC, the other 61 CCs can be classified by 13 functional categories:

There are 11 regional health authorities in MB. Each is a CC responsible for healthcare delivery in its region. Three CCs that provide specialized medical services are CancerCare Manitoba, Manitoba Adolescent Treatment Centre Inc. and Addiction Foundation of Manitoba. Manitoba Health Research Council promotes medical research in the province.

Manitoba Health Services Insurance Plan provides financial administration for medical services and Manitoba Hospital Capital Financing Authority allocates funds for hospital construction.

U OF M, U OF W, BU, RED RIVER COLLEGE, UNIVERSITY COLLEGE OF THE NORTH, and **ASSINIBOINE COMMUNITY COLLEGE** are all organized as CCs.

The Council on Post-Secondary Education and the Public Schools Finance Board are responsible for capital budgeting for post-secondary education and public schools respectively.

Child and Family Services of Central Manitoba, Child and Family Services of Western Manitoba, Rehabilitation Centre for Children, Inc., Manitoba Housing and Renewal Corporation, MB Community Services Council Inc., Workers Compensation Board of Manitoba and Legal Aid Services are CCs dealing with a diverse range of social services, from social work services, to housing subsidies, to compensating workers who become disabled at work, to the provision of free legal services to those who qualify.

Manitoba Development Corporation, Manitoba Trade and Investment Corporation, Economic

Innovation and Technology Council, Communities Economic Development Fund, Special Operating Management Corporation, Cooperative Loans and Loans Guarantee Board, Cooperative Promotion Board, Leaf Rapids Town Properties Ltd., and Venture Tours of MB Ltd. are CCs with mandates ranging from fostering economic development to managing the Hecla Island Resort Centre.

MANITOBA ARTS COUNCIL, Centre Culturel Franco-Manitobain, Manitoba Film and Sound Recording Development Corporation and Manitoba Centennial Centre Corporation are CCs that fund or provide a venue for cultural activities.

Manitoba Lotteries Corporation operates provincial casinos, lotteries and video lottery terminals as a government revenue-generator.

Manitoba Water Services Board, MB Habitat Heritage Corporation, MB Floodway Expansion Authority Inc., and MB Hazardous Waste are CCs with a diversity of mandates that encompass environmental quality and infrastructure.

Manitoba Crop Insurance Corporation, MB Agricultural Credit Corporation are CCs that administer agricultural programs.

Manitoba Gaming Control Commission, Law Society of MB, Insurance Council of MB, Board of Administration under The Embalmers and Funeral Directors Act, Horse Racing Commission, and MB Boxing Commission are regulatory CCs with mandates that span the regulation of gambling, licensing of lawyers, insurance standards, funeral service standards, and monitoring horse racing and boxing activity.

Manitoba Foundation is a CC responsible for disbursing for charitable purposes a fund that arose from surplus government revenues.

Crown Corporations Council is a CC that facilitates mandate and performance measures with Manitoba Hydro, MPIC, MLC, MLCC, Communities Economic Development Fund, Centennial Centre Corporation, and Venture Tours of MB Ltd. and may address public complaints about these 7 CCs. ● IRWIN LIPNOWSKI

CROW'S NEST PASS FREIGHT RATE.

The "Crow," as it is commonly known, was born on June 29th, 1897, when Royal assent was given to *An Act to Authorize a Subsidy for a Railway through the Crow's Nest Pass*. For more than a century, the Crow was a fixture in ongoing debates about agriculture in western Canada. For many grain farmers, it became an article of faith, part of the West's historic right in Confederation. The Crow, they said, made it possible for them to compete in world grain markets because of cheap rail shipping. However, support for the Crow has never been unanimous. The livestock industry has often criticized it as a detriment, an unfair subsidy that

Rail line abandonment picked up steam with the death of the Crow's Nest Pass Freight Rate.

prevented Prairie agriculture from expanding and diversifying. Railways said it prevented them from maintaining and upgrading their facilities. In recent years, successive federal govts regarded it as a drain on the public purse, as well as contrary to international trade rules.

BEGINNINGS: The Crow takes its name from the Crow's Nest Pass – an access point through the mountains in SW Alberta. In the mid-1890s, there was pressure to construct a rail line from the Prairies into SE BC. Newly discovered mineral deposits attracted considerable interest from Canadians and Americans, and a railway was deemed to be the best way to exploit new economic opportunities. At the same time, the line would serve to protect Cdn interests from US encroachment. The contract was awarded to the **CPR**, which had completed the Transcontinental Railway in 1885. For a federal govt payment of close to $4 million, as well as running rights, the CPR agreed to construct a rail line from Lethbridge to Nelson, BC, through the Crow's Nest Pass. For its part, the CPR agreed to freight-rate reductions on farmers' goods and machinery, and on all wheat and flour. For a brief period in the early 1920s, the rates were suspended following an inflationary time after WWI. However, with considerable pressure from Western farmers, they were reintroduced in 1925, this time applicable to the new **CNR** as well.

FARMERS AND RAILWAYS: Grain produced for export markets makes Prairie farmers prisoners of geography. Just about every Western grain farm is thousands of km from an ocean port. From the beginning of Prairie agriculture, freight rates and transportation have been contentious. The monopoly enjoyed by the CPR made it a focus for the grievances of the thousands of farmers who settled the Prairies in the first decades of the 20th

century. They had a litany of complaints about service and what they saw as an unholy alliance between the railways, private grain companies, and the Winnipeg Grain Exchange. The railway monopoly was one of the factors leading to a farmer backlash and the creation of the farmer-owned grain co-operatives. Supporters of the Crow, on the other hand, claim it went partway to redressing the inequities of the Canadian economic system. In spite of the statutory Crow rates, many farmers felt freight rates were lower in central Canada, where there was more competition. There were also high tariffs that protected goods produced in central Canada. Those tariffs added to the costs of Prairie farmers. They also saw the Crow as redress for the huge business empire created by the CPR from public money and land grants. Crow critics, however, said it made Prairie agriculture too dependent on grain exports. Artificially low freight rates made it more attractive for farmers to sell their grain in export markets. This, they argued, stifled the development of the livestock industry and the creation of secondary processing on the Prairies. Prairie cattle producers, especially, felt that the Crow burdened them with high feed-grain prices because low freight rates gave an unfair advantage to export markets. They argued that exporting massive amounts of freight-subsidized grain amounted to an export of jobs and further economic opportunity.

THE DEATH OF THE CROW: Although a matter of some debate, the Crow rate probably covered the cost of grain transportation until the 1960s. Then – so claim the railways – a combination of increased costs and inflation saddled them with an unmanageable financial burden. That meant the railways cut back on upgrading and maintaining their grain-handling system. They

149

said the costs of running branch lines, where low grain volumes combined with the statutory Crow rate, made grain transportation uneconomical. Farmers became annoyed by a grain-handling system that was increasingly unreliable, as Canada's export reputation came under attack both at home and abroad. In 1984, the Liberal govt replaced the Crow with the *Western Grain Transportation Act*. The new act shifted the burden for any revenue shortfall from the railways to the public purse. The so-called "Crow benefit" was paid directly to the railways. In 1995, then-finance minister Paul Martin announced the elimination of the Crow benefit. At the same time, he announced a one-time payment to Prairie grain producers of $1.6 billion. After 98 years, the Crow was dead.

THE FALLOUT: The Crow disappeared at a time in the mid-1990s when grain prices were high, so farmers were cushioned from the immediate hike in freight rates. But in the late 1990s and the early 21st century, depressed world grain prices, combined with a substantial increase in freight rates, added to the woes of many Prairie grain producers. An argument for removing the Crow was that it violated international trade rules against unfair subsidies. However, as of writing, most foreign governments continue to subsidize their domestic agricultural industries. There is still an ongoing debate as to whether the end of the Crow has resulted in the development of more secondary industry on the Prairies. What has changed dramatically is the diversity of crops: CANOLA, soybeans, corn, canary seed, and sunflowers, to mention a few. How much credit is due to the demise of the Crow is still hotly debated. The disappearing Crow is only one of the many changes facing Prairie agriculture. Prairie branch lines have disappeared and, along with them, grain elevators, long a symbol of western Canada. In MB, wheat is no longer king. In 1999, hogs became the biggest source of income for MB's farmers. • SANDY CUSHON

CRUSTACEA is an enormous group of invertebrates, some well known and in the regular diet of humans (shrimp, lobster, crayfish), but most go about their aquatic lives without discovery by the public. The head has 5 pairs of appendages – 2 pairs of antennae, a pair of mandibles, and 2 pairs of maxillae, which function in the movement of water and food. The thorax and abdominal segments bear jointed appendages. The hardened body surface or skeleton occurs on the outside of the body and muscles lie within. Respiration occurs via substantial gills and through the body surface. There are over 26,000 species worldwide, and over 200 freshwater and marine species in MB. Due to great diversity and abundance of

species in both freshwater and marine ecosystems, crustaceans are dominant species in food webs, serving as herbivores, predators and scavengers. Most other groups of animals (e.g., fish and birds) depend heavily on crustaceans as their major source of food. There are 5 classes of crustaceans with freshwater representatives, all of which are present in MB: fairy shrimps, tadpole shrimps, clam shrimps and water fleas,(class Branchiopoda); seed shrimps (Ostracoda); copepods (Copepoda); fish lice (Branchiura); and sow bugs, scuds, sideswimmers, shrimps, crayfish, and lobsters (Malacostraca). Remarkably, 182 species of crustaceans have been reported in Hudson Bay, where they play the dominant invertebrate role in this marine ecosystem. These occur widely throughout the Arctic Ocean as well. Crustaceans occur in every habitat – the underside of sea ice floating in the current, swimming actively in the water column and on the sea floor. They are the main converter of plants into animals, which supply other larger animals (up to the Polar Bear and Bowhead Whale) either directly or indirectly with their food resources. There are also numerous carnivorous species and scavengers (especially amphipods) which rapidly consume any dead animal. The most important and abundant groups in species and population sizes are the amphipods.

AMPHIPODS are small, shrimp-like crustaceans also known as freshwater shrimp, scuds or sideswimmers. There are about 5 species in the freshwater habitats of the province (150 species in NA freshwaters), but an astounding 91 species in Hudson Bay (7,000 in marine and freshwaters worldwide). The body is laterally compressed, and consists of 4 regions; the cephalothorax (head fused with the first thoracic segment), the thorax (7 segments), the abdomen (6 segments), and the telson. Amphipods are 5-20 mm long and usually light brown to greenish. As an amphipod swims, it often rolls over on its side or back, thus the common name of sideswimmer. They live in lakes, ponds, streams, springs, and even subterranean waters, where they are usually found near the bottom, logs, and aquatic plants. Species may be herbivores, detritivores, predators and scavengers, and can quickly clean a carcass such as a dead fish. Amphipods are an important food source for many fish, amphibians and aquatic birds, particularly Lesser Scaup. Some species are found in a wide variety of habitats in MB (e.g., Hyalella azteca), while others are restricted to particular habitats, such as deep cold northern lakes.

FAIRY AND BRINE SHRIMP, or anostracans, are small, elongated, delicate crustaceans that lack the shell-like covering of the body typical of

most other crustaceans. There is one pair of large compound eyes. They glide through the water by beating their legs (11, 17 or 19 pairs thoracic legs, which) in wave-like motions from front to back. The legs are leaf-like and also function in respiration. Adults in MB freshwaters range from 7 to 40 mm. Fairy shrimp are found each spring in temporary freshwater pools, ponds and ditches that fill with snow melt. During the remainder of the year, these habitats are dry, and the shrimp survive as resting eggs, which are resistant to freezing and desiccation, and can remain viable for many years. Fairy shrimp typically produce only one generation per year, in about 3-4 weeks. Few predators are present in these temporary habitats, although waterfowl are known to feed on fairy shrimp. There is usually only one species present in a pond, but occasionally several species may occur. The number of species and their abundance can vary considerably among years within the same pond. Brine shrimp (Artemia species) differ from fairy shrimp in that they are found in more permanent saline waters, and can produce several generations per year. A variety of brine shrimp is sold as novelty pets under the brand name Sea-Monkeys. Both fairy shrimp and brine shrimp feed on microscopic organisms such as bacteria, protozoa and algae. There are about 10 species in MB (35 in NA).

WATER FLEAS or cladocerans are small (0.2-3.0 mm) crustaceans that take their common name from their jumping-like movements while swimming. Water fleas have a single large compound eye, a carapace or shell that covers the main part of the body, and 5-6 pairs of lobed or leaf-like thoracic legs. The second antennae are often large, branched appendages and are used for swimming. Some planktonic cladocerans show dramatic changes in body shape, with summer individuals looking very different from winter individuals (termed cyclomorphosis). Asexual (parthenogenesis) reproduction is common among the group, although many species also reproduce sexually. During some periods, the entire population consists entirely of females that are produced asexually. When environmental conditions deteriorate (e.g., pond drying), females will produce males. The eggs resulting from sexual reproduction enter a diapause (resting phase) and are protected by a modified part of the carapace. Resting eggs (called ephippia) are resistant to freezing and drying, and can remain viable for many years. Ephippia are an important means of survival, and also dispersal, as they can survive passage through the gut of a bird and can be blown on the wind. Some water fleas are benthic (associated with the bottom sediments and aquatic plants), but most are planktonic (living in the water column). They are filter feeders and consumer bacteria, fine detritus and algae. A few species are predators on smaller invertebrates. Water fleas are important components of aquatic food webs. They can consume a significant portion of the algal community in a waterbody, and are important food for invertebrates, fish and waterbirds. Water fleas are found in almost all freshwater habitats, but are not common in marine waters (not recorded in Hudson Bay). Being easy to culture in the lab, species like Daphnia are used in many types of research. Since they are excellent indicators of water quality , they are frequently used in biomonitoring. There are about 28 species in Lake Winnipeg (150 in NA). ● DW, REW

CRYSTAL CITY, pop 414, is a village 110 km SE of Brandon and 15 km N of the US border. Crystal City was established in 1879 when English-born **Thomas Greenway** brought homesteaders from around Exeter, ON, to the district. Greenway was subsequently elected to the MB Legislature, and went on to become the prov's 7th premier. He also established the Crystal City Print Shop, which is now a museum with the largest collection of working printing equipment from the 1900s in the West. The village was incorporated in 1948. In 2007, retail and service support for nearby agriculture formed the backbone of the village's economy. Crystal City had a farm machinery dealership, welding and repair shops, a hardware store, bulk fuel stations, 2 garages, an auto-body repair shop and a company that produces haying equipment. The village also had a K-4 elementary school, 3 parks, and a variety of shops.● GPP

CULLETON MOSIONIER, Beatrice, author, (b Aug 27, 1949, **St. Boniface**). Best known for her acclaimed novel *In Search of April Raintree*, Culleton Mosionier's early years inspired and informed her writing. After becoming a ward of the Children's Aid Society of **Winnipeg** (*see* **Child Welfare**) at the age of 3, she was separated from her 3 siblings and raised in foster homes. Both of her older sisters later committed suicide. She graduated from a clerical program at George Brown College in Toronto in 1970, and later completed a publishing program at Banff School of Fine Arts (now Banff Centre for the Arts, though the program is at Vancouver's Simon Fraser U) in 1983. She worked for Pemmican Publications – a non-profit **Book Publisher** of fiction, non-fiction, poetry, and children's titles founded in 1980 by the **Manitoba Métis Federation** – from 1982-87. Culleton Mosionier then moved to Toronto, where she wrote a script for the **National Film**

Board in 1991. Native Earth Performing Arts produced her play, *Night of the Trickster*. Culleton Mosionier also wrote *Spirit of the White Bison* (1985), *Christopher's Folly* (1996), *In Search of April Raintree: Critical Edition* (1999), *In the Shadow of Evil* (2000), and *Unusual Friendships: A Little Black Cat and A Little White Rat* (2002). Pemmican released her earliest 3 books, while the 2 most recent were published by Theytus Books of BC. *In Search of April Raintree* tells the tragic story of 2 **Métis** sisters growing up in foster care. It has become a part of the English and Native Studies curricula of many junior high, high school, and university courses in MB and elsewhere in Canada. Culleton Mosionier now resides in Winnipeg. ● JOEL TRENAMAN

CUMMINGS, Burton Lorne, rock musician, singer/songwriter (b Dec 31, 1947, **Winnipeg**). Raised by his single mother, Rhoda, on Bannerman Ave in Winnipeg's **North End**, Cummings took piano lessons as a child, discovering an early affinity for rock 'n' roll and joining his first band – The Deverons – at St. John's High School in 1962. The band had become a community-club favourite by 1964, and released 2 singles penned by Cummings, "She's Your Lover" and "Lost Love," the latter with Bruce Decker. In Dec 1965, the **Guess Who** invited Cummings to replace keyboard player Bob Ashley. He became their lead singer and front man, as the band worked steadily for 4 years to rebuild. After adding 'The' to their name, The Guess Who (especially Cummings and bandmate **Randy Bachman**) began writing songs,

Burton Cummings, 1979

ultimately crafting some of Canada's greatest hit tunes, including "These Eyes," "Laughing," "No Time," and "American Woman," all million-selling hit singles in 1969-70. After Bachman left the group, Cummings – either alone or partnering with bandmates Kurt Winter, Bill Wallace, **Greg Leskiw**, and Domenic Troiano – wrote further hits, including "Share the Land," "Rain Dance," "Albert Flasher," "Clap for the Wolfman," "Star Baby," and "Dancing Fool."

In 1975, Cummings folded The Guess Who and signed with US-based Portrait Records, launching his solo career in 1976 with the million-selling single "Stand Tall." He recorded this in Los Angeles with star producer Richard Perry and orchestration by Elton John's arranger, Paul Buckmaster. Further singles followed, including "I'm Scared," "Your Backyard," "My Own Way to Rock," "Break It to Them Gently," "Dream of a Child," "Fine State of Affairs," and "You Saved My Soul," as well as albums *Burton Cummings* (1976), *My Own Way to Rock* (1977), *Dream of a Child* (1979), *Woman Love* (1980), *Sweet Sweet* (1981), and *Heart* (1984). He starred in several TV specials, including *Burton Cummings West*, *My Own Way to Rock*, *Going for Gold*, and *Burton Cummings: Portage and Main*. Cummings won Juno Awards for Male Vocalist of the Year and Best New Male Vocalist (1977, 1980) and Best Selling Album Award (1979), in addition to hosting the annual event 4 times 1979-83.

Cummings starred in the 1980 feature film *Melanie* with Don Johnson and toured with friends Maclean & Maclean in the mid-1980s. He released a 1990 comeback album, *Plus Signs*; a *MuchMusic* TV concert special and the single "Take One Away" soon followed. Cummings toured with ex-Beatle Ringo Starr in 1992, then launched his *Up Close and Alone* tour and album in 1995. Cummings fulfilled a lifelong dream to host his own radio show in the latter '90s with Garry "Big Daddy" Maclean at CKY. In 1997, Cummings and Bachman reunited for the Red River Relief concert, a benefit for those affected by the **Red River**'s **Flood** that year; this set the stage for a The Guess Who reunion in 1999 for their Running Back Thru Canada tour, TV special, live album, and DVD. In 1990, Burton Cummings Community Club was named in his honour and in 2001 the Odeon Theatre (*see* **Theatre**) was renamed the Burton Cummings Theatre for the Performing Arts, with Cummings performing a benefit concert for the facility. He toured Canada with Bachman in 2006, appeared in the CBC-TV special *First Time Around*, and released the *Bachman Cummings Songbook*. As of writing, Cummings divided his time between Winnipeg and Los Angeles. ● JOHN EINARSON

CUNNINGHAM, Robert, journalist, politician (b May 12, 1836, Stewarton, Ayrshire, UK; d July 4, 1874, St. Paul, MN). The Scottish-born Cunningham was educated at Glasgow College and the U of London. Cunningham immigrated to Canada in 1868, and was sent W in 1869 as a special correspondent for the *Toronto Globe* and *Toronto Telegraph* to cover the **RED RIVER RESISTANCE**. He was expelled from the settlement by **LOUIS RIEL** shortly after his arrival, however. Nonetheless, after MB became a province in 1870, Cunningham started the *Manitoban* with **WILLIAM COLDWELL**. He was elected Liberal MP for Marquette in 1872, defeating **JOHN NORQUAY**, with support from Riel. In Ottawa, Cunningham spoke consistently on behalf of the **MÉTIS** community, supporting a general amnesty and the settlement of MB **LAND CLAIMS**. He remained unenthusiastically with the Liberals after his re-election in 1874. Cunningham was appointed to the Council for the NWTs in 1874, but died suddenly in St Paul, MN. • JMB

CURLING has been one of MB's most popular sports for 125 years. Furthermore, it is the one sport in which Manitobans have been consistently identified with excellence, having produced numerous national and international champions.

HISTORY: The sport we know, with brooms, houses, and prepared stones, evolved in Scotland and northern continental Europe between the 16th and 18th centuries. Curling came to various parts of the New World, primarily brought by **SCOTS** emigrants. In the 19th century, a few fur traders from the **HBC** curled on river ice, and so did a few individuals in the **RED RIVER SETTLEMENT**. However, it was not until after 1869-70, when the HBC's territories were incorporated into Canada, that curling became a significant sport. The first long-lasting club in the province's history was the Manitoba Curling Club, established in **WINNIPEG** in 1876. Soon, more clubs were formed in Winnipeg and in smaller centres such as **BRANDON**, **PORTAGE LA PRAIRIE**, and **GLADSTONE**.

In these first years of curling in the West, curlers used "stones" that were frequently made of iron or wood. At the time, iron stones were common in QC, and wooden stones in ON. However, it was becoming clear by this time that the best stones, especially for indoor play, were the granite ones manufactured in Scotland. As the railway network of the West was improved, granite stones were more frequently imported. By the end of the 19th century, iron and wooden rocks had all but disappeared from MB.

Early in the 20th century, curling had become one of the most popular sports in MB. In the cities and larger towns, separate facilities for the sport were constructed. In smaller towns and villages, the sport was played in the combined curling/skating/hockey facilities that became ubiquitous in rural MB before WWI. Most curling clubs in the province became affiliated with the Manitoba Branch of the Royal Caledonian Curling Club, formed in 1888. In 1908, this organization became the Manitoba Curling Association.

ORGANIZATION: In the pioneer years, curling was primarily a men's sport. Women participated intermittently, becoming more prevalent on the ice during WWI, when many men were overseas. By 1925, there were enough women's clubs to form a separate Manitoba Ladies' Curling Association. It existed as a separate entity until 2000, when the MCA and the MLCA united and became the (new) Manitoba Curling Association.

The early popularity of curling can be easily explained. First, a significant number of MB's pioneers were of Scottish ancestry. Second, MB's economy was based on commercial agriculture, and curling fit into a slow time of year, especially in the agricultural service centres of southern or western MB. Third, natural ice could be maintained in indoor facilities for 3 or 4 months each winter in MB. Fourth, both competitive and recreational players could enjoy curling. The sport rewarded concentration, skill, teamwork, and even, to some extent, physical strength and endurance. At the same time, non-athletes were attracted by the low risk of injury, by the high likelihood that even a novice would make a few successful throws, and by the natural pause after each shot that left time for visiting, mimicry, laughter.

Manitobans not only curled often, they also curled well. By early in the 20th century, Eastern Canadians and even Scots had participated in some MB bonspiels, and Manitobans frequently returned the visits. Once the MacDonald Tobacco Company established the Canadian championship event known as the Brier in 1927, the province's superiority was confirmed. MB won 15 of the first 28 Briers; AB won 6, and no other province won more than 2. At any time from the 1920s to the 1950s, about half of the top-10 teams in the world were from MB. They were led by the biggest names in the sport – **GORDON HUDSON**, **HOWARD "PAPPY" WOOD**, **KEN WATSON**, Jimmy Welsh, Ab Gowanlock, Bob Gourley, Jim Congalton, Leo Johnson, and Bill Walsh.

By the mid-20th century, curling was a well-established sport throughout the province, but it became even more popular once artificial-ice facilities became common. The technology of artificial ice was invented in the late-19th century, but not until the prosperous 1940s to 1960s could most curlers in MB and elsewhere afford to install ice plants in their rinks. Artificial ice meant longer seasons and heated rinks.

Artificial ice had other important consequences. It eliminated or at least neutralized the advantage that MB's top curlers had once enjoyed as a result of living in a cold climate. From the 1950s onward, in the Brier – as well as in other Canadian championship events that were established in the ladies', junior, mixed, and seniors' categories – Manitobans were always very competitive, but not as dominant as they had been. Though curling had been an official sport in the 1924 Olympic Games, it was not until the widespread availability of artificial ice that curling took hold internationally, and the world-championship events established in men's curling (unofficially in 1959, officially in 1966); ladies' curling (1979); junior men's (1975) and junior women's (1988); senior men's and senior women's (both in 2002); and wheelchair curling (2002) were won by Swedes, Germans, and Americans, as well as by Canadians.

AM. SPORT - CURLING 1 1, N972

Curling in 1955

Until well into the 1970s, in MB, as elsewhere, there were no professional curlers. Many of the competitive curlers, such as **DON DUGUID**, had won lucrative prizes at bonspiels and had approached their sport seriously, but they could not make a living at it. However, beginning in the 1980s, curling gained popularity thanks to cable television, and top MB teams, such as **CONNIE LALIBERTE**, **KERRY BURTYNK**, **JEFF STOUGHTON** and **JENNIFER JONES**, as well as the best teams from elsewhere, began to compete in Skins tournaments and other corporate-sponsored events. By early in the 21st century, there were perhaps half a dozen men's teams and 1 or 2 women's teams that were, in effect, professional,

MANITOBA'S CURLING CHAMPIONS

MB CANADIAN MEN'S CHAMPIONS

Year	Team
1928	Gordon Hudson, Sam Penwarden, Ron Singbusch, Bill Grant
1929	Gordon Hudson, Don Rollo, Ron Singbusch, Bill Grant
1930	Howard "Pappy" Wood, Jimmy Congalton, Victor Wood, Lionel Wood
1931	Bob Gourlay, Ernie Pollard, Arnold Lockerbie, Ray Stewart
1932	Jimmy Congalton, Howard "Pappy" Wood, Bill Noble, Harry Mawhinney
1934	Leo Johnson, Lorne Stewart, Linc Johnson, Marno Frederickson
1936	Ken Watson, Grant Watson, Marvin McIntyre, Charles Kerr
1938	Ab Gowanlock, Bung Cartmell, Bill McKnight, Tom McKnight
1940	Howard "Pappy" Wood, Ernie Pollard, Howard Wood Jr., Roy Enman
1942	Ken Watson, Grant Watson, Charlie Scrymgeour, Jim Grant
1947	Jimmy Welsh, Alex Welsh, Jack Reid, Harry Monk
1949	Ken Watson, Grant Watson, Lyle Dyker, Charles Read
1952	Billy Walsh, Al Langlois, Andy McWilliams, John Watson
1953	Ab Gowanlock, Jim Williams, Art Pollon, Russ Jackman
1956	Billy Walsh, Al Langlois, Cy White, Andy McWilliams
1965	Terry Braunstein, Don Duguid, Ron Braunstein, Ray Turnbull
1970	Don Duguid, Rod Hunter, Jim Pettapiece, Bryan Wood
1971	Don Duguid, Rod Hunter, Jim Pettapiece, Bryan Wood
1972	Orest Meleschuk, Dave Romano, John Hanesiak, Pat Hailley
1979	Barry Fry, Bill Carey, Gord Sparkes, Bryan Wood
1981	Kerry Burtnyk, Mark Olson, Jim Spencer, Ron Kammerlock
1984	Mike Riley, Brian Toews, John Helston, Russ Wookey
1992	Vic Peters, Dan Carey, Chris Neufeld, Don Rudd
1995	Kerry Burtnyk, Jeff Ryan, Rob Meakin, Keith Fenton
1996	Jeff Stoughton, Ken Tresoor, Garry Vandenberghe, Steve Gould
1999	Jeff Stoughton, Jonathan Mead, Garry Vandenberghe, Doug Armstrong

MB CANADIAN WOMEN'S CHAMPIONS

Year	Team
1965	Peggy Casselman, Val Taylor, Pat MacDonald, Pat Scott
1967	Betty Duguid, Joan Ingram, Laurie Bradawaski, Dot Rose
1978	Cathy Pidzarko, Chris Pidzarko, Iris Armstrong, Patty Vanderkerckhove
1984	Connie Laliberte, Chris More, Corinne Peters, Janet Arnott
1992	Connie Laliberte, Laurie Allen, Cathy Gauthier, Janet Arnott
1995	Connie Laliberte, Cathy Overton, Cathy Gauthier, Janet Arnott
2005	Jennifer Jones, Cathy Overton-Clapham, Jill Officer, Cathy Gauthier

WORLD CHAMPIONS (MEN'S AND WOMEN'S)

Year	Team
1970	Don Duguid & Team
1971	Don Duguid & Team
1972	Orest Meleschuk & Team
1984	Connie Laliberte & Team
1995	Kerry Burtnyk & Team
1996	Jeff Stoughton & Team

competing in national or international tour events across the country between 12 and 15 weekends a year.

FUTURE: Curling will probably remain an extremely popular participant and spectator sport in MB. Recent innovations such as time clocks (1989), use of microphones on players, and the free-guard zone to increase the likelihood of rocks in play (1991), have made curling increasingly attractive, especially on television. As a recreational sport, it is almost ideal: curling can be relatively inexpensive to play, and it can be enjoyed by men and women, young and old, robust and frail. The modern curling facility is warm, and typically has a canteen and a lounge. Manitobans will continue to believe that on chilly winter evenings there is no better place to gather. ● MORRIS MOTT

CURRIE, Andrew, athlete, civil servant, soldier (b June 5, 1911, **BRANDON**; d Aug 4, 1990, **WINNIPEG**) played and refereed in the CFL before serving in the league as an administrator. He graduated from the **U OF M**, and taught at St. John's College School before serving overseas with the Royal Canadian Army Service Corps, being awarded the Order of the British Empire. A football player, he played for the Regina (later Saskatchewan) Roughriders in 1928, and competed in the Grey Cup in 1928, 1930, and 1933. He coached Daniel McIntyre Collegiate to 4 straight Winnipeg football championships after WWII. From 1957-70, he was supervisor of officiating for the Western Conference of the CFL, and helped oversee a committee to revise the CFL rulebook 1965-67. After many years as director of physical education for Winnipeg (1951-57) and MB (1957-61), and a period as director of parks for Greater Winnipeg (1961-71), he served as MB Deputy Minister of Urban Affairs 1971-76. ● JMB

CURRY FAMILY. The Currys established their wealth in Winnipeg's booming real estate market in the 1880s, and survived near financial-ruin during the Great Depression to become a powerful family, wielding influence across NA.

DUNCAN STEELE CURRY (b Oct 31, 1852, Sydney, NS; d 1927, San Diego, CA) Duncan was a shrewd businessman, and wise investor. One of 8 children born to an Irish-Scottish family on the east coast, he started working at the age of 17 for the Glasgow & Cape Breton Coal and Railway Company. Seeing the vast opportunities to be found out West, he came to Winnipeg in 1874 as part of the 2nd contingent of the **NWMP** that was overseeing construction of the **CPR**. Although his contingent was travelling further W, Duncan left his position early, buying himself out of his contract in order to stay in Winnipeg. He found work with a lumber company, and then as a CPR purchasing agent, saving his money to buy up numerous properties throughout MB. He became a prominent businessman and, in 1884, was made Winnipeg's first city treasurer, a position he held for 21 years. In 1897, Duncan married an Icelandic woman named Bertha Laxdal. With his family, he retired to San Francisco, CA, in 1905, re-settling in San Diego following the disastrous earthquake and fire that destroyed the city. With millions of dollars at his disposal, Duncan became a world traveller. While vacationing in Tijuana, Mexico, he financed the restaurant that created the popular Caesar salad. He maintained his business interests in Winnipeg, constructing the Curry building in 1915, which still stands in the city's downtown.

PETER DUNCAN CURRY (b 1912, Snek-kersten, Denmark; d April 26, 1996, Montreal). Though raised in affluence, Peter had to re-build his family's fortune after his father died and the family's investments were lost in the 1930s. Peter was born while his parents were vacationing in Denmark. His father died when he was an adolescent, and Peter was sent to boarding school at Ridley College. He attended Bishop's U and Queen's U on athletic scholarships, but was forced to quit school in 1934 after the Great-West Life Assurance Company (*see* **GREAT-WEST LIFECO INC.**) threatened foreclosure of the Curry building in Winnipeg. Ironically, with his rise to prominence, Peter was later made chair of the Great-West Life board. Upon arriving in Winnipeg, a city he had seen little through his youth, Peter first earned a living selling real estate, and played one season with the **WINNIPEG BLUE BOMBERS**. His finances improved and, in 1944, he started an investment brokerage firm. He married Constance Noreen Murphy, the daughter of prominent businessman **WILLIAM A. MURPHY**, with whom he later purchased the Sovereign Life Assurance Company. As the company's president, he saw it triple in size before selling it in 1962. Among his other accomplishments, Peter assisted in the founding of the Delta Waterfowl Research Station (see **DELTA MARSH**), serving on its board for 26 years. He was president and part owner of the **WINNIPEG GOLDEYES**. He received an honourary degree from the **U OF M**, and served 2 terms as the chancellor. He was a school trustee, and later chair of the Winnipeg School Board. He served on numerous corporate boards, including CIBC, Ford of Canada, and International Nickel (see **INCO LIMITED**). He moved to Montreal in 1973 upon being appointed president of the aptly-named Power Corporation, which owned both Great-West Life and **INVESTORS GROUP**. ● MICHELLE DOBROVOLNY

CUTSCHALL, Colleen, painter, installation artist, university professor (b Aug 3, 1961, Pine Ridge, SD). Cutschall's tribal affiliation is the Oglala Lakota and the central theme in her artwork is the use and loss of rituals in native and non-native societies. During the 1990s, Cutschall produced a series of paintings, *Voices in the Blood* on Lakota cosmology. Her desire to pay respect to her roots is seen in her piece, *Catching the Sun's Tail* where she uses the medicine wheel as a focus for the re-emergence of spirituality in Aboriginal communities and she combines elements of nature: earth, rocks, animal bones and feathers with modern technological representations like recycled parachutes and halogen lights, linking the past, present and future. Her work is collected across the Prairies, Ottawa and in SD.

Hudson's Bay Co. Cycling Club ca 1890

AM. SPORT - BICYCLING 1, N21930

Over her academic career, she has been an education training specialist at the U of Utah in Salt Lake City, UT from 1977-78, a teacher orientation associate in Portland, OR in the North West Indian Reading Program, a curriculum developer at Standing Rock Community College in Fort Yates, ND, in 1981-82, a gallery manager at the Northern Lights Gallery, Deadwood, South Dakota and finally is Chair of the Fine Arts Program and Professor of Visual Arts for the **BRANDON U** beginning in 1984. ● RUTH DEGRAVES

CYCLING races were first organized in MB in the late 1870s. The Winnipeg Bicycle Club was founded in 1883 in order to oppose city by-laws that restricted bicycle use, though bikes were uncommon until mass production in the 1890s made them more affordable, leading to a bicycle craze throughout NA. Most towns in MB soon had a bicycle club, and many churches organized clubs for parishioners. Athlete **DONALD BAIN** was one of MB's top cyclists at this time, as was Jack McCulloch, who held the fastest Cdn times for 2 distances in 1895. In 1897, George Riddle of MB won the 1 mi, the ¼ mi, ½ mi, and 5 mi races at the Cdn championships, and was part of the pair that claimed the tandem title at the Canadian Wheelman's Association events held the following year in **WINNIPEG**. During WWI, a platoon of cyclists from Winnipeg was part of the Canadian Corps Cyclist Batt. Belgian **IMMIGRANTS** were especially fond of cycling, and formed the **ST. BONIFACE** Cycling Club in 1916. The club sponsored weekly races at a velodrome built in the 1930s. The Winnipeg-to-**WINNIPEG BEACH** road race was an important MB cycling event, and Theo Dubois holds the record for riding the 75 km distance in 1h 40 min in 1934, before the road had yet been paved. An annual 240 km (150 mi) road race from Winnipeg to Kenora, ON, was held annually 1937-52, and was the 2nd-longest amateur bike race in NA.

It was also the only Cdn championship open to riders who were not considered Cdn residents, meaning new **IMMIGRANTS** were able to race. With the ascendancy of the car, interest in cycling waned through the 1950s, until skiers and speed skaters seeking a training sport for summer revived cycling races with the Red River Road Race in 1961.

In 1973, in order to avoid a substantial import tariff, the Japanese-owned Sekine Company opened an assembly factory near **RIVERS**, which operated until the early 1980s. The high-end bicycles produced at this factory are now considered rare vintage items. Lindsay Gauld, who was on the 1972 Cdn Olympic cycling team, and opened a large ski/cycle store in Winnipeg in 1979. A new velodrome was built in Winnipeg for the 1967 **PAN AM GAMES**. It stood until the 1999 Games, when it was torn down and replaced by a portable track. Cycling is often used for off-season training by successful MB speed skaters, since it uses similar muscle groups to **SPEED SKATING**. **TANYA DUBNICOFF** won 2 gold medals in cycling events at the 1999 Pan Am Games. Other successful MB cyclists include **SYLVIA BURKA**, who set a world record in the 1000 m time trial in 1980, and **CLARA HUGHES**, who was an Olympic cyclist before switching to skates. ● MD

CYPRESS RIVER, pop 180, is a community 145 km WSW of **WINNIPEG**. Nestled between the Tiger Hills and Spruce Woods Provincial Park, this scenic agricultural community benefits from tourism. The community was originally located 2 miles NW and was known as Littleton in 1880. The **CPR** "missed the town by a mile," so the community moved to its present location and changed its name to Cypress River in 1885 after the nearby Cypress River, which rises in the Pembina Hills and flows N into the **ASSINIBOINE RIVER**. Today, the local economy relies primarily on surrounding farming operations. ● GPP

DINOSAURS, Marine
see page 165

DAFOE, Elizabeth, academic librarian (b Oct 22, 1900, Montreal; d April 25, 1960, **WINNIPEG**) was chief librarian of the **U OF M** Library from 1937 until her death. Educated at the U of M, at the Library School of the New York Public Library (now the Library School of Columbia U), and at the Graduate School of the U of Chicago, she joined the U of M library staff in 1925. In 1953, the new library on the Fort Garry campus was renamed in her honour, in recognition of her signal contribution to its professional excellence in collecting, cataloguing, and resource sharing. A tireless advocate for the importance of a national library for Canada, and highly influential in the development of library resources throughout Canada, she served on the National Library Advisory Board and the Canadian Library Council Inc. She was president of the Canadian Library Association in 1949, was a founding member of the Manitoba Library Association, and served on the Manitoba Library Board. She was also the daughter of journalist **JOHN WESLEY DAFOE**.
● MIRIAM GUTKIN

DAFOE, John Wesley, journalist (b March 8, 1866, Combermere, Canada West [ON]; d Jan 9, 1944, **WINNIPEG**) was the independent-minded editor of the **WINNIPEG FREE PRESS** from 1901-44.

Dafoe attended high school before beginning a journalistic career with the *Montreal Daily Star* in 1883. Converted to the merits of the federal Liberal Party, he edited the *Ottawa Journal* in 1885 and, a year later, joined the *Manitoba Free Press* (later the *Winnipeg Free Press*). Following another sojourn in Montreal journalism, he returned to Winnipeg to edit Sir **CLIFFORD SIFTON**'s *Free Press* in 1901, holding the position until his death. Dafoe made his newspaper the voice of Prairie Liberalism, as well as an international newspaper of record. He combined an advocacy of western Cdn issues, such as lower tariffs, lower

Dafoe dining at the Manitoba Club, 1941

D

freight rates, and provincial control of natural resources, with an international perspective that favoured the Commonwealth and the League of Nations. Dafoe helped found the Canadian Institute of International Affairs, and he was highly critical in the late 1930s of Mackenzie King's diffident foreign policy [toward Hitler's Third Reich]. He was a member of the Rowell-Sirois Commission on Dominion-provincial relations, and from 1934-44, was chancellor of the **U of M**. His books include *Laurier: A Study in Politics* (1922) and *Clifford Sifton in Relation to His Times* (1931). ● JMB

DAHL, Tracy Elizabeth, opera singer (b Nov 13, 1961, **Winnipeg**) is a coloratura soprano who has performed with every major Cdn orchestra, as well as in opera houses worldwide. Raised in Winnipeg, Tracy was a child actor for CBC Television, and sang with the Winnipeg Girls Choir. She performed in musical theatre productions such as *West Side Story* and *Grease* at the **Manitoba Theatre Centre**. Dahl studied at the Banff School of Fine Arts (now the Banff Centre) 1979-83, changing her focus from musical theatre to voice after making her operatic debut as Barbarina in Mozart's *Marriage of Figaro* for the **Manitoba Opera**. Dahl also graduated from the San Francisco Opera's Merola program in 1985, and the Western Opera Program. Dahl made her US opera debut in 1987 opposite Placido Domingo in Jacques Offenbach's *Tales of Hoffman*. Her European debut, also in 1987, was in France's Aix-en-Provence Festival. She appeared at New York's Metropolitan Opera in 1991 as Adele in Mozart's *Die Fledermaus*. The Manitoba Chamber Choir named Dahl the Artist of the Year in 1993, and her CBC recording *Glitter and Be Gay* was nominated for a Juno Award. Dahl now teaches in the Faculty of Music at the **U of M**. ● AMANDA STEPHENS

DAIRYING. Since it began in MB with European settlers, dairying has evolved from a small, cow-in-every-yard way of life to a dynamic industry, with specialized farms and processing plants. All Cdn dairy farmers operate under a supply management system, where they produce just enough milk to fill the national requirement. Each province is allotted a share of the national quota based on historical production. MB has Canada's 5th-largest dairy cow herd.

FARMING: The plan for a self-sustaining **Red River Settlement** depended on the settlers' ability to produce their own food; the 1821 establishment of a dairy farm there was a large step toward its independence. As the West developed, dairy cows became an essential component of the

Many dairies offered home delivery.

mixed farm. Milk not needed for drinking was used to make butter or cheese. Whatever was not consumed at home was then sold in local stores or bartered. The cream separator came into use in the 1880s, allowing farmers to mechanically separate fresh whole milk into cream and skim milk. The cream was often shipped to a local creamery to be made into butter, while skim milk was fed to livestock. With increased production capabilities, some rural farmers took advantage of the rapidly growing market in **Winnipeg**, delivering milk to the city by **Railway** in metal canisters. After WWII, the population in MB shifted to larger towns and cities, and there was an increased need for dairy products for urban consumers. The introduction of the labour-saving milking machine in the 1950s allowed dairy farms to increase in size and meet growing demand. Artificial insemination, introduced to MB dairy farming in the mid-1940s, also boosted production. Dairy cattle are now bred solely through artificial insemination so calves can be born throughout the year, not just in spring, as with beef cattle. This ensures a continuous supply of fresh milk. Mechanization, artificial insemination, and improved breeding have dramatically increased production. In 2006, there were 451 dairy farms in MB with an average herd size of 87 cows, producing 825,000 l of milk daily. Though the number of dairy cows has fallen from 92,000 in 1976 to about 40,000 in 2006, average milk production per cow has more than doubled over the same period. MB's Holstein genetics are

considered so good that embryos and semen are exported to several countries.

INDUSTRY: The dairy industry began to develop in the mid-1880s. The provincial govt, seeking to diversify Prairie agriculture, hired a "Professor of Dairying" in 1886 to promote the creation of dairy herds and creameries. That same year, the federal govt passed an act banning the manufacture and sale of margarine (*see* **Margarine Debate**), thus protecting the growth of commercial creameries. As the industry became increasingly regulated, a federal commission created rules for the grading of cream. Newer products, such as condensed milk, powdered milk, and ice cream, and the increased use of refrigeration, further bolstered the industry. In 1960, bulk milk hauling was established. Fresh whole milk collected in refrigerated bulk tanks on the farm was transported to processing plants by special bulk tanker trucks. During the **Great Depression**, about 70 creameries were in operation in MB, and the cream cheque was often the only reliable source of income for farmers. The Manitoba Co-Operative Dairies Ltd. was incorporated in 1920. Known as Manco, the co-op had acquired many MB creameries through the 1920s and '30s, and was one of the province's largest dairy producers until it was subsumed by Dairyworld Foods in 1996. In 2000, Dairyworld became a division of Saputo, a Montreal-based international company that has since closed the former Manco dairy in **Souris**. Consolidation of the industry continues; by 2005, there were just

9 milk and dairy product processors in the province. Parmalat – an Italian conglomerate whose Cdn brands include Astro, Beatrice, and Lactantia – was the largest of these. Although milk for consumption is processed in Winnipeg and other larger centres, creameries in smaller communities produce other dairy products. Notable in this regard is Bothwell Cheese Inc. in NEW BOTH-WELL, 35 km SSE of Winnipeg. Dairy Farmers of Manitoba is the regulatory agency that governs the production, transportation, and marketing of all raw milk produced in MB. All milk produced in MB is processed within the province. The production, processing, and distribution of dairy products employs roughly 2500 people. Dairy products made in MB such as milk, cream, butter, ice cream, and cheese were valued at over $614 million in 2005. ● MICHELLE DOBROVOLNY

DAKOTA. The term Dakota refers both to a specific people and to the larger nation they form with the Lakota and Nakota peoples, who live farther W. These groups have often been called "Sioux," a term they reject because it homogenizes 3 distinct cultures and also because it comes from an OJIBWAY word meaning "snakes" or "enemies."

The Dakota have long been treated as newcomers to the area that is now MB, but their history belies this notion. Archaeological evidence from pottery suggests that their ancestors had villages in the area at least 800 years ago. European records from the 17th and 18th centuries show Dakota territory stretching from western Lake Superior to the RED RIVER and INTERLAKE regions. Only in the later 18th century did they move farther S and W. The Dakota were active military allies of Britain in both the American Revolution and the War of 1812. Yet after the Revolution, British authorities labelled them "alien Indians," denying that they had any claim to lands north of the Canada-US border.

At least 3 Dakota bands returned to the Red River area in 1862-63, fleeing US Army reprisals for the Dakota Uprising of 1862 in MN. Despite settler opposition to their presence, the British government prohibited the US Army from entering its territory to crush the refugee Dakota, and eventually their permanent settlement was allowed. The Dakota obtained the consent of the Ojibway to use parts of their territory, and the federal govt granted them small reserves in what are now MB and SK.

The Dakota pursued different economic strategies according to their location, skills, and resources. One group around Turtle Mountain retained a hunting, fishing, and trapping economy, but was forced by govt agents to disperse to other reserves, and their reserve was sold. The groups around Birdtail, Oak Lake, and Oak River became successful farmers. Those around POR-TAGE LA PRAIRIE, who had been granted very small reserves, supported themselves largely through wage labour. In the 20th century, the Dakota experienced declining economic opportunities on and around their reserves, as demand for their labour diminished and the farming sector began to require increasing capital and larger farms, neither of which could be supplied by their small reserves. By the 2nd half of the 20th century, unemployment was a growing problem.

With increasing control of their own education and some govt assistance in building new economic ventures, the Dakota are making important steps toward improving their economic circumstances. Their strategies include improved EDUCATION, more intensive AGRICULTURE, and gaming. The Dakota live in the southwest, where they have 5 reserve communities: BIRDTAIL SIOUX, CANUPAWAKPA, DAKOTA TIPI, DAKOTA PLAINS, and SIOUX VALLEY. The total registered Dakota population in MB is about 4000. ● ROBIN JARVIS BROWNLIE

DAKOTA PLAINS FIRST NATION (formerly known as Wahpeton First Nation), on reserve pop 159, off reserve pop 73, is located approx 30 km SW of PORTAGE LA PRAIRIE, and 104 km SW of WINNIPEG. The native language of this community is Dakota. The community is made up of one reserve. It is a member of the Dakota Ojibway Tribal Council. Before 1972, the Dakota Plains First Nation community included the DAKOTA TIPI FIRST NATION population. The 2 communities separated due to cultural differences. Dakota Plains schooling, which the First Nation administers itself, goes from Nursery-Grade 6. Total enrolment for 2003-04 was 32. A new school was under construction in 2006. Besides internal roads, the Dakota Plains First Nation has a year-round gravel road access to hwys 1 and 2. Overland flooding is a problem for the Dakota Plains First Nation community, but since 2005, Indian and Northern Affairs Canada has been working with the community by putting in a drainage project to help bring the area's groundwater levels under control by installing pipes to relieve high water accumulation and standing water. The main economic activity generated by the Dakota Plains First Nation is agriculture and livestock. Until 1995, the First Nation community was in a reforestation program, which included planting about 10 million trees in the area. ● RK

DAKOTA TIPI FIRST NATION, on reserve pop 151, off reserve pop 151, is situated 2.5 km W of PORTAGE LA PRAIRIE, and 80 km W of WINNIPEG. The Dakota Tipi First Nation is one of the smallest First Nation communities in MB, in both the size of its land base and its population. It has only been in existence since 1972, when it broke away from the DAKOTA PLAINS FIRST NATION. Through much of the 1990s, Dakota Tipi was plagued with political instability. There was a conflict between the chief who had held the position – without elections – for 23 years, and a group in the community that wanted to depose him. Although the community won the right in 2001 to operate 25 video lottery terminals (VLTs), the MB public auditor identified accountability problems with the records. Indian and Northern Affairs intervened, invoking 3rd-party management of the First Nation. In Oct 2002, a new chief and council were elected. In 2006, Dakota Tipi was trying to build a more accountable govt structure and trying to find ways of taking advantage of the natural economic potential the community had by virtue of its location right next to a major population centre. ● RK

DALNAVERT MUSEUM, renovated home of MB premier Sir HUGH JOHN MACDONALD, is in downtown WINNIPEG. It is made of Victorian red brick, conveying a typical affluent 1900-era family home. The house is an early example of the whimsical Queen Anne Revival style, and was built in 1895. Since 1990, this museum has been designated a national and provincial historic site. It features an authentic Victorian Garden. The house was restored and reopened in 1974. The museum is named after the Macdonald's ancestral home (village) in Scotland. Various events and programs, such as conservationist and business meetings, and weddings are held there throughout the year. The Heritage Canada Foundation, in Sept 1974, awarded Dalnavert with the Prairie Regional Prize, in recognition of its outstanding restoration. Heritage Winnipeg, in Feb 1985, gave the house a "Preservation Award for Excellence." In 1995, a National Historic Sites and Monuments Board of Canada plaque was unveiled at the house. ● RK

The Dalnavert museum

GLENN MARQUEZ

D

Jim Daley in front of Pan Am Pool, 1977

DALY, James "Jim," sports organizer (b Feb 19, 1927, **WINNIPEG**). Daly's involvement in MB's sports community extends to 1949, when he helped establish a track and field program at the **U OF M**, but he is primarily known for leading the effort to bring the **PAN AMERICAN GAMES** to **WINNIPEG** in 1967. After organizing the failed attempt to attract the 1963 games, Daly stepped up the campaign in the following years with promotional speeches and attractive offers for participating nations. He secured the 1967 Pan Am Games for Winnipeg, and helped in the recruitment of the 9000 volunteers who made the event a success. Following the Games, the host committee led by Daly was recognized with an Olympic Cup for its outstanding organizational work. Daly also served as team manager for the 1964 Canadian Olympic team, and was Canada's Chef de Mission at the 1986 and 1990 Commonwealth Games. When the **U OF M** needed a new sports facility, he helped raise double the $6 million dollars needed for the arena. It is estimated that Daly has fundraised $130 million for various causes in MB. Daly helped with Winnipeg's bid for the 1999 Pan Am Games as well as the 2002 North American Indigenous Games. He was awarded the Order of Canada in 2001. ● MD

DALY, Thomas Mayne Jr, lawyer, politician, judge (b Aug 15, 1852, Stratford, Canada West [ON]; d June 24, 1911, **WINNIPEG**) was a Conservative MP and mayor of **BRANDON**. He was educated at Upper Canada College, was called to the ON Bar in 1876, and practised law in Stratford until he moved W to Brandon in 1881, where he became the community's first legal practitioner. When the railway arrived in 1882 to transform Brandon, he became its first mayor. He subsequently served as president of the Conservative Party of the Brandon electoral division, and was elected to Parliament from the riding of **SELKIRK** in 1887. He won again in 1891, beating **JOSEPH MARTIN**, the author of the *Manitoba School Act*. A year later, he became Minister of the Interior and

Superintendent-General of Indian Affairs, his portfolio responsible for federal immigration and settlement. He strongly supported Western settlement, and introduced in 1893 the *North West Immigration Act*. A supporter of Mackenzie Bowell, he was left out of the cabinet in the reshuffle that accompanied Charles Tupper's assumption of the PM's position in 1896. Rather than run in the 1896 election, he moved briefly to Rossland, BC. He soon returned to MB, settling in Winnipeg and becoming police magistrate in 1904. Daly wrote *The Canadian Spirit of the Northwest* (1907), *Canadian Criminal Procedure* (1911), and *The Magistrate's Manual* (1911). He ran for Parliament once more as a Conservative candidate for Brandon in 1908, but lost to **CLIFFORD SIFTON** and the Liberals by 69 votes. In 1909, Daly became Canada's first Juvenile Court judge. He was a prominent **ANGLICAN**, a member of the St. Luke's Church and of the advisory board of St. John's College (*see* **U OF M**). ● JMB

DALY HOUSE in **BRANDON** was built in 1882, the city's first decade of settlement. It was constructed for **THOMAS MAYNE DALY**, Brandon's first mayor, first MB MP to hold a cabinet portfolio, and Canada's first juvenile court judge (1909). This building subsequently housed "The Maples" orphanage, run by the City of Brandon from the 1920s to the mid-1960s. In 1976, the property was converted into the Daly House Museum, and opened year-round to the public. It has since been managed by the Brandon Museum. It is 4 stories high, and has historical exhibits displayed on each level. In the museum, there is an old fashioned general store, a butcher shop, and Brandon's first city council chambers. The house, a spacious, renovated structure, also has the Stephen Magnacca Research Centre within its walls – an archival centre that provides assistance in researching genealogy and Brandon history. ● RK

DANCE in MB had its origins in **POWWOWS**, the **SUN DANCE**, and other First Nations ceremonies, and in the folk dances of early European **IMMIGRANTS** to the **RED RIVER SETTLEMENT** (*see* **RED RIVER JIG**). However, nothing legitimized it within the province as a professional art form quite like the founding of the **ROYAL WINNIPEG BALLET** (RWB) in 1939 by **GWENETH LLOYD** and **BETTY FARRALLY**, the ballet company and school is internationally recognized as one of Canada's leading performing arts institutions.

RWB alumna **RACHEL BROWNE** established MB's first professional modern dance company – the **WINNIPEG CONTEMPORARY DANCERS** (WCD) – in February 1964, with an inaugural performance at the **U OF M**. Browne was the company's

instructor, choreographer, dancer, tour planner, fundraiser, publicist, and artistic director. In 2003, the troupe moved from its rented facility in an Osborne Village church into a studio with a 140-seat performance space in the Crocus Building on Winnipeg's Main St.

Just as RWB dancers such as Browne sometimes left the school or the company to pursue other forms of dance, many WCD company members or students from the school have gone on to create their own troupes. One of the most notable examples is Dance Collective, formed in 1989 by former WCD members Gaile Petursson-Hiley (now an independent **WINNIPEG** choreographer) and Ruth Cansfield. After creating or co-creating a repertoire of more than 20 original works, the company was dissolved. In 1995, Cansfield formed her own company, Ruth Cansfield Dance. Cansfield's groundbreaking company has performed across Canada, including performances at the Festival international de nouvelle danse, L'Agora de la danse, and the Canada Dance Festival, as well as in the US.

Other WCD alumni have helped expand MB's modern dance scene. Trip Dance Company, formed in 1997 by Karen Kuzak and Randy Joynt, has staged 10 successful productions to date. Young Lungs Dance Exchange (YLDE), formed in 2004 by a small group of recent graduates of the School of Contemporary Dancers in Winnipeg, is a network of photographers, actors, poets, musicians, and dancers whose members have collaborated on a series of 6 productions. YLDE also holds weekly improvisation jams. Acclaimed solo artist and choreographer Jolene Bailie, on the faculty of the School of Contemporary Dancers since 1997, has been mounting independent productions in Winnipeg and across Canada since 2003.

As suggested by YLDE, dance is, like other art forms in MB's melting pot, heterogeneous; artists of various genres and with backgrounds in classical, contemporary, and ethnic folk dance may mount multidisciplinary dance productions. The Sarah Sommer Chai Folk Ensemble, established in 1964 and produced by the Chai Folk Arts Council, is dedicated to preserving, promoting, and developing **JEWISH** and Israeli culture through performance and education in **MUSIC**, song, and dance. Among the oldest and best-known folk dance troupes in MB, Chai has performed across Canada, the US, Mexico, and, in 1998, Israel. They also operate the Lisa Cohen Chai School of Performing Arts.

Winnipeg is also famous for its high-flying **UKRAINIAN** dance troupe, the Rusalka Ukrainian Dance Ensemble, which was established in 1962. Rusalka was the first amateur troupe to share a stage with the RWB, and has performed around the world in places such as Mexico, the UK, Ukraine, Italy, and the US, and throughout Canada. The company has danced for HM Queen Elizabeth II, HRH Prince Phillip, Princess Margaret, HRH Prince Charles, and Pope John Paul II. In 2006, along with the Winnipeg Symphony Orchestra, Rusalka premiered a new original work, *The Legend of the Rusalka*, which was also seen by European audiences at Scotland's Aberdeen International Youth Festival.

Winnipeg's Manohar Performing Arts of Canada has brought **South Asian** dance to MB since 1991, often fusing Eastern folk-dance style with modern and classical Western styles. Manohar integrates classical Bharatanatyam and Kathak into the contemporary Cdn dance scene. Originally, the company was developed to foster greater cultural awareness of Indian history, heritage, and mythology, and to explore both traditional and modern aspects of Indian and Cdn culture through classical dance and drama. The company has produced 10 full-length productions, created, designed and produced by the artists of the company, and in 2005 produced its first Festival of Dance. Another company – Fusion Dance Theatre, founded 1989 by director/choreographer Rubena Sinha – blends Indian classical dance with other forms of expression, such as taiko drumming, **Irish** storytelling, and music.

Latin dance also thrives in MB, with 2 companies. These are Bolero Dance Theatre, founded by Pedro Aurelio in 1997 under the name of Hispanic Dance Theatre; and Theatre Flamenco, a dance collective co-founded by Winnipeg dancer and RWB instructor Claire Marchand and by Torontonian Claudia Carolina, Canada's most-esteemed flamenco choreographer. Bolero's original purpose was to present and preserve all aspects of Hispanic dance, from Spanish flamenco to Argentinean tango and from classical Spanish dance to tropical Latin dances. This brought many engagements around the time of the 1999 **Pan Am Games**. To date, Theatre Flamenco has created 7 productions exploring Flamenco dances and songs inspired by Latin America.

Dance in MB is not only supported by artists, audiences, and arts funding agencies, but also by cultural organizations that train new artists, provide a stage for them, and match them with mentors to aid in their development. Perhaps the most influential promoter of folk dance in MB is **Folklorama**, an annual, 2-week Winnipeg festival of culture in which more than 60 nations are represented. Folklorama has become a training ground for dancers since its inception in 1973. The Folk Arts Council, Folklorama's organizer, now operates FACES, a talent booking agency representing both ethnic and genre performers.

Dance Manitoba, born of a 1982 provincial govt initiative, produces an annual 12-day Manitoba Provincial Dance Festival and an annual Membership Showcase Concert, along with numerous educational workshops. The non-profit organization co-operates with other dance organizations, maintains a registry of Manitobans involved in dance, and provides a library related to this artistic form. As of writing, Dance Manitoba was developing an archive of dance in the province. ● GARTH A. BUCHHOLZ

DARLINGFORD, pop 225, is an unincorporated community 110 km SW of **Winnipeg** in the RM of Pembina. Several early area settlers came from

Darlingford War Memorial

Darlington, ON, and they were required to "ford" the Pembina River as they made their way to their new home. Or the community may have been named after C.R. Darlingford, one of the town's early residents. The first settlement was 3 km SW of the present site, but was moved when the **CPR** arrived. The post office opened in 1882. In the 21st century, Darlingford's biggest claim to fame is that it is home to the only freestanding memorial building in MB with the sole function of commemorating those who died in war. The Darlingford Memorial was built in 1921 on the initiative of Ferris Bolton, a local pioneer farmer and politician whose 3 sons were killed in France in 1917. Inside the memorial, 2 black marble tablets bear the names of the 199 local veterans and victims of WWI and WWII. Arthur A. Stoughton, the first head of the School of **Architecture** at the **U of M**, designed the Gothic-inspired memorial. The **Morden** Experimental Farm designed and landscaped the memorial park. Darlingford is also home to the Darlingford School Heritage Museum. ● GPP

DAUPHIN, pop 7906 and MB's 8th largest city, is located on the northern edge of **Riding Mountain National Park** at the junction of hwys 5 and 10. The community serves as the main trading and service centre for the Dauphin Valley which stretches between the Duck Mtns in the N and the Riding Mtns in the S. In 1739, **François de la Verendrye** established a fort near the shores of Lake Dauphin which he named in honour of the heir to the French throne. Fort Dauphin was

Ukraine-Kyiv Pavilion Folklorama, 2006

FOLKLORAMA - CANADA'S CULTURAL CELEBRATION; WHERE TO LOOK PHOTOGRAPHY

1 of 3 which La Verendrye established, the other 2 being Fort Bourbon on Cedar Lake and Fort Paskojac on the site of what is now the community of **THE PAS**. The settlement of the Dauphin Valley dates back to the early 1880s when a party of pioneers from the **GLADSTONE** area were enthralled by the description of the lake and valley provided by a **METIS** traveller and struck out on an expedition to explore the area. The group arrived on the shores of Lake Dauphin in mid-June 1883 and one of its members, John Edwards, chose a picturesque spot along a creek and broke a small plot of land on which he planted a crop of potatoes. Other members of the party continued W of the lake, choosing promising locations for future homesteads before heading back S to Gladstone. John Edwards returned with his family later that year to become the area's first official settler.

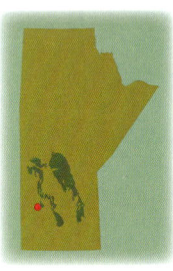

Dauphin came into being in 1897 when the railway arrived between the 2 early settlements of Gartmore to the S and Old Dauphin to the N, prompting residents of both communities to relocate in one settlement nearer the tracks. Dauphin was granted its village charter on July 11, 1899, and the first municipal election was held in Aug of that same year with George Barker being elected the village's first mayor. Less than 3 years later, Dauphin's pop had burgeoned to more than 1000 and the village was incorporated into a town on Nov. 21, 1901. George King served as the town's first mayor, taking office on New Year's Day 1902. Taking advantage of a change in the province's population requirements, Dauphin was incorporated as a city in 1998. Although the city's economy is based on agriculture, Dauphin is also a centre for health care and government servicing for a large geographic area. The city has become a tourist destination known for its summer festivals including **DAUPHIN'S COUNTRY-FEST**, **CANADA'S NATIONAL UKRAINIAN FESTIVAL** and Jesus Manifest. Given its proximity to national and provincial parks the city is also a destination for outdoor enthusiasts and is known for the world class hunting and fishing opportunities available in the area. ● SHAWN BAILEY

DAUPHIN RIVER FIRST NATION, on reserve pop 194, off reserve pop 78, is located 390 km N of **WINNIPEG**. The language here is **OJIBWAY**. There is one reserve. Dauphin River signed Treaty 2 in 1871; it is now a member of the Interlake Reserves Tribal Council. This area's Dauphin River is known for its record-breaking fishing over the years, winning many Master Angler

Awards for Walleye and Northern Pike catches. Residents say that some of the biggest Sturgeon have also been caught in this area. Schooling in this community, administered by Dauphin River, goes from Nursery-Grade 12. Total enrolment for the year 2003-2004 was 47. Besides interior roads, Dauphin River First Nation has all-weather road access to the provincial network. As well, this community has an airstrip for emergency air travel and dock facilities for float planes and boats. The local economy is based on commercial fishing, and hunting. ● RK

DAUPHIN'S COUNTRYFEST began in 1980 and is Canada's longest-running country **MUSIC** festival. Countryfest occurs annually around Canada Day on the N side of **RIDING MOUNTAIN NATIONAL PARK**, about 15 km S of **DAUPHIN**. The 4 day event features local, national, and international entertainment on 3 stages, with the picturesque Selo Amphitheatre acting as the main stage. The event features bluegrass, country, and rock 'n' roll music. Other features include a campground, a battle of the bands, perogy- and hot-wing-eating contests, a Countryfest mall that hosts approximately 40 exhibitions, and a talent contest. The talent show is part of a continuing effort to support and encourage amateur musicians from across the country; musicians such as **AMANDA STOTT** gained prominence this way. The festival was 1 of 5 events nominated at the 2002 and 2005 Canadian Country Music Association Awards in the Country Event of the Year category. As spectators come from across the province and beyond, Countryfest has sold out in the past few years and continues to be Dauphin's biggest annual party. ● AMANDA STEPHENS

Dauphin's Countryfest

DAVIS, Robert Atkinson, teacher, hotelier, politician. (b 1841, Upper Canada, d 1903, Phoenix, AZ). Born in Dudswell, Canada, he attended St. Francis College and became a school teacher. He and his brother spent several years after the American Civil War in the Rockies. In 1870, he came to **WINNIPEG**, arriving on 10 May while the provisional government was still in control of the settlement. He bought George Emmerling's hotel, renaming it Davis House. Its saloon became the social centre of the ON volunteers who came with the **WOLSELEY EXPEDITION**, and Davis was able to expand his operations to include a barbershop, billiard parlour, and store. Davis soon became a spokesman for the newcomers in the village, who struggled with the **HBC** for its control. In 1873, he took the lead in drafting a bill to incorporate Winnipeg. Soon afterward he became a leader of the Patrons of Husbandry, using this group's influence to gain election to the Assembly in April 1875. He soon became provincial treasurer under **MARC-AMABLE GIRARD** and, in the unstable political situation of the time, assumed the premiership as leader of the ON faction in the House of Assembly. Fluent in French, he managed to persuade the French faction that he supported French rights, and his ministry did uphold the system of dual education and maintain legislation limiting speculation in Métis lands, despite pressure to do otherwise. He lobbied successfully for the route of the transcontinental railroad to pass through Winnipeg rather than Selkirk. His government was responsible for the abolition of the Legislative Council in 1875. It also negotiated better financial terms with Ottawa. Having in 1875 married

Robert Atkinson Davis, 1874

an American resident of Illinois who did not move to MB, Davis joined her and their child in the US after his retreat from politics in 1878. The couple moved to Chicago in 1880, and Davis prospered in real estate speculation. His later years were marked by scandal. He was charged with breach of promise in 1890, and he publicly separated from his wife in 1896. • JMB

DAWSON, Simon James, surveyor, engineer, politician (b June 13, 1818, Redhaven, UK; d Oct 30, 1902, Ottawa) oversaw construction of the Dawson Road. Though **Scots** by birth, Dawson joined his family in Nepean Township, Upper Canada (ON), around 1840. He obtained govt appointments through the influence of his brother, and was appointed surveyor to the Dawson-Hind Expedition in 1857. In the expedition's report, he dealt at length with the Western route, proposing to use navigable waters in preparation for the **Railway**. After Confederation, Dawson was placed in charge of constructing the Cdn-financed road from Lake Superior to Lake of the Woods, with the section from there to **Fort Garry** under the supervision of John Allan Snow. This road is known as the Dawson Road. In 1870, Dawson used 1000 men to help expedite the passage of the **Wolseley Expedition**. Dawson and Col Garnet Joseph Wolseley disagreed over the road under construction. Dawson wanted to await its imminent completion to move men and material, while Wolseley insisted that since it was not finished, he would have to use a more difficult water route in order to guarantee the arrival of his troops in the summer of 1870. Dawson continued his disagreement with Wolseley in his *Report on the Red River Expedition of 1870* (1871). Because of the road-building, Dawson

became involved in negotiations with the Saulteaux (**Ojibway**) of Lake of the Woods. His concern over govt policy toward the region led him into politics, and he represented northern ON in the ON Provincial Parliament from 1875-78, and then in the House of Commons from 1878-91. He was suspected for his **Roman Catholicism**, and by 1889 was being dismissed as an "old fossil." Moreover, his support for bilingualism for the NWTs and for **Aboriginal Rights** were not well regarded by many of his constituents. • JMB

DECKERT, Mervin Harold, handballer (b Mar 9, 1949, **Winnipeg**) has won 11 Cdn handball titles and 3 world titles. He is one of a handful of Canadians to have mastered the difficult sport. While most handballers require years of training to acquire the ambidexterity needed for high-level competition, Deckert was competing nationally after just a few years of playing the sport recreationally. He won his first Cdn title in 1974, and remained at the top of the sport for nearly 3 decades, never placing less than 3rd at the national championships. In 1984, Deckert won the world championship, becoming only the 2nd Canadian to do so. He was named that year's Manitoba Male Athlete of the Year. He won world titles again in 1991 and 1997, and won the World Golden Masters Singles in 2000. He is a member of Manitoba's Order of the Buffalo Hunt, and the **Manitoba Sports Hall of Fame**. • MD

DEER is a member of the deer family Cervidae and is represented in MB by 2 species – the mule deer (*Odocoilius hemionus*) and the white-tailed deer (*Odocoilius virginianus*). They originated in NA, unlike the American Elk, caribou and Moose, which immigrated during the Pleistocene Ice Age from Eurasia. Few people are aware that only the mule deer was found in the province prehistorically, and it was only in 1881 that the first **White-Tailed** appeared – immigrating from ND and MN. The dramatic and rapid replacement of mule deer by the White-Tailed was likely due to habitat alteration during settlement of the prairie region, perhaps augmented by the former being more-easily shot, as it often paused to watch an approaching hunter. The mule deer was almost completely extirpated (i.e., eliminated) in this province by the mid-1900s, and its numbers have been slow to recover (estimated now at less than 1600), since hunters usually do not distinguish between the 2 species.

The mule deer is widespread in western NA (from the Yukon to Mexico) and extends into the SW corner of the province. Size varies greatly, with the largest individuals (males averaging 100 kg; maximum 215 kg) found in the N. Capable

of inhabiting a great variety of habitats over its large range, it generally prefers drier places than the Whitetail, and consequently is restricted to the mixed-grass prairie, **Aspen** parkland and mixed forests in southern MB. Compared to the White-Tailed, the male's antlers divide twice into equal branches, its ears are considerably larger, and the tail is smaller. Anything but a picky eater, it feeds on grasses, herbs, shrubs, and coniferous and deciduous trees. Winters with deep snow and intense cold severely stress the mule deer, and it continually loses weight and condition, with bark and buds its main food supply. The hairs of the coat are tubular and filled with air spaces, which offer excellent insulation, as well as buoyancy when swimming. This deer is known for its unusual high-bounding gait during which it takes off and lands with all 4 legs striking the ground simultaneously. While appearing awkward, this method assures good footing on loose terrain during jumps up to 8 m, and a top speed of 60 km/hr.

D

White-tailed deer

The White-tailed deer is truly remarkable in its adaptation to widely divergent habitats, from the boreal coniferous forest of N Canada through the grasslands and deserts of the US and Central America, to the steamy jungles and mountain slopes as far S as the N quarter of South America. It is characterized by a long bushy tail (which is flashed when the animal bounds away from danger) and antlers in the male that branch from one main beam. This species draws more hunters into the field each fall than any other mammal in MB and elsewhere (over 2 million are shot annually in NA). It is usually shy and elusive, using its acute senses of sight, smell and hearing to avoid people and predators such as the grey wolf, cougar, and black bear. Yet, it may become accustomed to living in close proximity to people, offering wonderful glimpses of a beautiful and graceful animal at close range even in cities. **Winnipeg**'s Assiniboine Forest harbours over 350 deer. Activity periods peak at dusk and dawn, and the deer browse while wandering over a 15-to-450 ha home range. Large numbers (20-80) occasionally gather in a field to take advantage of food supplies left on agricultural fields, but this generally means the animals are especially hungry. Summer is a time of plenty, when the spotted young are born. The female leaves her 1-2 offspring hidden in a forest glade or meadow, returning to feed them periodically. With little scent and strict immobility, they often go undetected by the close passage of people and predators. Sometimes people mistakenly think a fawn has been abandoned and 'rescue' it by carrying it away, but this usually results in the death of the animal. ● RWB

DEFEHR, Arthur A. "Art," entrepreneur, humanitarian (b Nov 10, 1942, **WINNIPEG**), DeFehr is the president and CEO of **PALLISER FURNITURE** Ltd., the largest furniture maker in Canada. Palliser Furniture was started in Winnipeg by Art's father, Abram Albert DeFehr, a Russian-born **MENNONITE** immigrant. DeFehr has an MBA from Harvard and is a recognized authority on refugee and disaster relief. That work has taken him to Cambodia, Bangladesh, and Somalia. (Kofi Annan was his colleague in Somalia in the early 1980s before the latter became secretary-general of the UN.) DeFehr started a Christian university in Lithuania in the 1990s, and has spent several months of every year undertaking relief efforts all over the world. Palliser is one of the largest domestic manufacturers of furniture, at a time when most other NA competitors have moved their production to less-expensive countries in the developing world. Combining production efficiency, excellent supply-chain management, and superior design, Palliser grew to about $600 million in annual sales in 2005 and remained one of the 5 largest private-sector employers in Winnipeg, with more than 3000 people on the payroll, including many of the city's newest international immigrants. The company launched its own retail division, EQ3, in the early 2000s. DeFehr is one of the Mennonite community's leaders in international humanitarian relief. He became an Officer of the Order of Canada in 2004. ● MARTIN CASH

DELORAINE, pop 977, is a town 80 km SSW of **BRANDON. LA VERENDRYE** was the first European to explore the area in the mid 1700s. He named the Turtle Mountains to the S. Over the years, several fur trading companies built forts in the area and on the nearby **SOURIS RIVER.** The **BOUNDARY COMMISSION TRAIL,** which was used by the NWMP heading W in 1874, cuts through Deloraine The town was originally 8 km SE of its present location and was called Zulu. Locals disliked this name and changed it to Deloraine in honour of the postman's home in Scotland. The town

moved to its present location in 1886 to coincide with the arrival of the **CPR.** The railway, the gently rolling hills and the rich, fertile soil, attracted settlers. Economic activity then and now in Deloraine centres on farming. However, there are vestiges around Deloraine of other economic pursuits: there is an old fieldstone bank vault in Old Deloraine, and nearby are old abandoned mine shafts, a tribute to the only commercial coal mining in MB. Deloraine is well serviced with a hospital, golf course, several churches, beaches, elementary and high school, and a massive Purple Martin tower. Favourite son and fashion mogul **PETER NYGARD** contributed to the town's millennium project, Nygard Park, and a 206-flag display called Flags of the World. Each year, the town hosts a town fair, gold tournaments and Métis Days, which celebrates **MÉTIS** culture with sash weaving, a roast beef and **BISON** supper, and Métis dancers. ● GPP

DELTA MARSH is situated 90 km WNW of **WINNIPEG** along the S shore of **LAKE MANITOBA,** near Delta Beach. It is an 18,500 ha (45,715 ac) freshwater coastal **WETLAND** made up of a series of interconnected large and small bays, channels, and isolated ponds, ranging in depth from less than 1 m-3 m. The marsh was formed about 500 BC when wind and wave action formed a barrier-beach ridge from sediments deposited from the once-northward-flowing **ASSINIBOINE RIVER.** Many of the marsh's present channels are remnants of the river's former course. Four openings or channels in the beach ridge permit the exchange of water between the marsh and Lake Manitoba. Strong winds over the lake result in fluctuating water levels. The marsh was named for a railway

station that opened at Delta Beach, then called Delta Station.

Delta Marsh is home to numerous species of aquatic plants, **AMPHIBIANS, FISH,** mammals, and **WATERFOWL.** Delta Marsh was known internationally for its abundant waterfowl and **HUNTING** opportunities. Several hunting lodges used by the rich and famous (including the Prince of Wales and Clark Gable) were a common feature around the marsh. Because of its historic abundance of waterfowl, Delta Marsh was designated a "Wetland of International Significance" under the Ramsar Convention in 1982, and a "Manitoba Heritage Marsh" by the MB govt in 1988. However, waterfowl numbers have nevertheless declined substantially in recent times.

The treed beach ridge that separates the marsh and the lake provides nesting habitat for numerous songbirds, including yellow **WARBLER** (*Dendroica petechia*), least **FLYCATCHER** (*Empidonax minimus*), and warbling vireo (*Vireo gilvus*), some of which are found in high densities. Chironomids (midges) emerging from Lake Manitoba and the marsh often form huge swarms over the treed ridge in summer, providing an abundant food resource for songbirds. In 1999, the marsh was designated an "Important Bird Area" due to the abundant songbirds. Since that year, the marsh has hosted an annual birding festival, timed to coincide with the peak of spring warbler **MIGRATION.**

Two scientific research stations, operated by the Delta Waterfowl Foundation and the **U OF M** respectively, are situated on the marsh: the Delta Waterfowl Research Station and the Delta Marsh Field Station. Both stations have contributed significantly to the knowledge of prairie

Delta Marsh near Lake Manitoba

CHARLES SHILLIDAY

wetlands and waterfowl. The Delta Marsh Bird Observatory, based at the Delta Marsh Field Station, studies songbirds as they migrate through central MB. It is one of the busiest songbird monitoring stations in Canada.

Several factors are thought to be contributing to the deterioration of Delta Marsh. Water levels on Lake Manitoba have been stabilized since 1961, and this has contributed to several changes in the marsh. Most notable is an expansion of the hybrid cattail (*Typha × glauca* Godr.) and associated loss of shallow peripheral ponds; loss of other aquatic plant species, especially *Scirpus* spp; loss of islands in the larger bays; and erosion of shorelines. Recent recommendations to deregulate lake water levels may help partially to restore the marsh. Another important concern is the abundant common carp (*Cyprinus carpio*). These introduced fish first appeared in the marsh in the late 1940s or early 1950s. Common carp have negative effects on wetland habitats, including uprooting aquatic plants and increasing water column turbidity. In the early 1960s, an attempt was made to keep common carp out of the marsh by installing screens on the 4 channels connecting the marsh with the lake. This attempt was abandoned after 3 years due to the high cost of cleaning, maintaining, and repairing the structures. Common carp are still considered a problem in the marsh. ● DALE WRUBLESKI/GORDON GOLDSBOROUGH

DEMPSEY, Shawna, performance artist (b April 30, 1963, Toronto). Dempsey attended York U, where she received an honours BA in 1986. Shortly after graduating, she began collaborating with **LORRI MILLAN**. The duo's first work was the informational video *We're Talking Vulva*, which became an international success in both artistic and educational circles. The pair showed their video when representing Canada in the 1992 International Istanbul Biennial. From here, they began to work in everything from books to videos to performance. Dempsey and Millan gained a strong reputation for their witty, fresh approaches to tackling issues of queer politics, domesticity, stereotypes, and feminism. Demspey has partaken in residencies since the early 1990s in several artist-run centres, including Banff Centre for the Arts and Queens U, where she was scholar-in-residence in Jan 1995. The duo began to produce numerous works that would give them the reputation of being 2 of Canada's best performance artists, such as *Lesbian National Parks*, which toured around the globe and gave rise to the book *Lesbian National Parks and Services Field Guide to North America*. Their works have been shown in venues as diverse as New York's

DON LEE, THE BANFF CENTRE

Shawna Dempsey and Lorri Millan

Museum of Modern Art, women's centres in Sri Lanka, and the **WINNIPEG ART GALLERY**. Although each of their works is collaborative, Dempsey is usually the performer or face of the works. She has received numerous awards and grants from the Winnipeg Arts Council, the Manitoba Arts Council, and the Canada Council for the Arts. ● STACEY ABRAMSON

DENATALE, Giuseppe "The Godfather," kickboxing and Muay Thai competitor (b May 12, 1973, **WINNIPEG**), is one of Canada's dominant and best-known **MARTIAL ARTS** competitors. DeNatale grew up in Winnipeg's West End. He began training in karate when he was 8, but was often disqualified from tournaments for excessive contact. In 1996, he began studying Muay Thai, a form of kickboxing originating in Thailand that incorporates the use of direct elbow and knee strikes. At 183 cm (6 ft) and 95 kg (210 lb), DeNatale is well suited for full-contact competition. His first major title wins came in 1998, when he won both the World Kickboxing Association's Canadian Golden Gloves championship and the Canadian International Federation Muay Thai Amateurs championship. In 2000, he turned professional, and started fighting with K-1, an organization that combines elements of several stand-up martial arts. In his first competition in Las Vegas, DeNatale triumphed as the underdog, beating out seasoned US fighter Kent "The Norseman" Hensley. DeNatale went on to become the 2000 International Kickboxing Federation Heavyweight Cdn champion. He was the champion of both the 2002 Heavyweight "King of the Gladiators" competition and the 2002 K-1

Milwaukee Grand Prix. He won the 2003 and 2004 International Sport Karate Association North American titles. In April 2006, DeNatale captured the IKF world heavyweight Muay Thai title at a highly publicized match in Winnipeg, knocking out Scottish 6-time world champion Duncan Airlie James despite sustaining an injury in the bout. DeNatale owns the Canadian Kickboxing and Muay Thai Centre in Winnipeg. Fans around the world know Giuseppe as "The Godfather," a nickname his trainer Duke Roufus coined because of DeNatale's **ITALIAN** heritage. ● MD

D

DENE are a distinct group of **FIRST PEOPLES**, speaking dialects of what linguists call the Athapaskan language. Dene are among the most geographically widespread of the Aboriginal peoples of NA. They can be found in remote NW Canada, as in the Gwi'chin of the NWT, as well as the SW US, as in the Navajo. Dene are often described by cultural anthropologists as being 'cultural borrowers,' meaning they take on the features of the other cultures that surround them. For example, the Witsuwit'en of BC practise potlatch and resemble many of the Pacific Northwestern First Peoples; northern Dene appear on the surface very similar to the Algonquian language speakers who bordered them. Yet, Dene themselves maintain that there is a coherent Dene identity, which links Dene from the American southwest to the far Cdn NW.

Two distinct groups of Dene occupy lands today in the NW corner of MB. Both are Chipweyan, the largest and most widespread of Cdn Dene, hence their language is mutually understood but they are also quite distinct from each other. One group is called the Sayisi Dene (rising sun people, as in the people of the east), the other is the Northlands Dene Band. Chipweyan are 'people of the caribou' occupying a territory from the SE of Great Slave Lake along a northern belt to where the **CHURCHILL RIVER** drains into **HUDSON BAY**. They traditionally lived in hunting bands; a regional band might involve a few hundred people who would gather for large spring or fall caribou hunts, then separate into smaller, local hunting bands of about 50 people. Although some accounts stress the particularly demeaning position of Chipweyan women, the single source for this understanding is **SAMUEL HEARNE**, whose diary has proven unreliable in many ways as a cultural description.

The Sayisi Dene experienced great hardship as a result of being relocated from Duck Lake to **CHURCHILL** in 1956. They eventually returned to their traditional territory and established the community of Tadoule Lake in the 1970s. They are signatories to Treaty 5. The Northlands Dene

D

were settled with **Cree** people in the community of **Brochet** in 1967, but moved to create their own community about a decade later which is still their centre, called **Lac Brochet**. They are signatories to Treaty 10. Both groups have outstanding land claims in their traditional barren ground hunting territories which in 1999 became a part of Nunavut. Dene stories, hand drums, powerful spiritual traditions, continuing bond with their land and many other elements of their culture have historically and in contemporary times enriched the cultural fabric of MB. ● PETER KULCHYSKI

DEPRESSION. *See* **Great Depression.**

DES GROSEILLIERS, Sieur Médard Chouart, explorer, fur trader (b July 31, 1618, near Château-Thierry, Brie, France; d 1696, New France [QC]) helped establish the **HBC**. Groseilliers came to Canada around 1641, and found work with Jesuit missionaries before becoming involved in the **Fur Trade** around 1646. By the early 1650s, he had begun exploring **Hudson Bay**. He married and had 2 children before his wife died. He remarried in 1653 to the half-sister of **Pierre-Esprit Radisson**. In 1660, des Groseilliers and Radisson led a successful fur trading expedition to Lake Superior, but were arrested for illegal trading upon their return to New France. Frustrated with French authorities, the pair decided to deal instead with the **English**, and ended up in London in 1665, where they argued that the best way to gain access to the rich trade of Hudson Bay was not over land but in large ships sailing directly to the heart of the continent. With the support of Prince Rupert, the pair left for Hudson Bay in 1668 aboard the *Nonsuch*. The success of Groseillier's first Hudson Bay expedition led to the founding of the HBC in 1670, and to his knighthood (*Sieur* is French for "Sir"). Over the following 5 years, he set up company posts in James Bay. He rejoined the French in 1676, and was tried for tax evasion in Paris in 1784, after which there are few records detailing the events of his life. ● MD

DESJARDINS, Laurent "Larry," politician (b Mar 15, 1923, St. Boniface). Desjardins was educated at St. Boniface College, St. Paul's College and the Cincinnati College of Embalming and went on to work as a funeral director. He entered political life at the municipal level and served as an alderman on St. Boniface city council from 1951-54. In the provincial election of 1959, Desjardins was elected to the MB legislature in the riding of St. Boniface as a **Liberal**-Progressive and was in the official opposition during **Duff**

Roblin's **Progressive Conservative** govt. Desjardins was returned in the elections of 1962 and 1966. During the provincial election of 1969 when he was re-elected as a Liberal, he crossed the floor to offer parliamentary support to the **NDP** so they could form a new govt. The NDP had won 28 out of 57 seats and there was talk of forming an anti-socialist coalition which would have excluded the NDP. Desjardins formed an alliance with Schreyer and he became his legislative assistant in 1969 and formally joined the NDP in 1971. That year he was appointed minister of tourism, recreation and cultural affairs. He was not re-elected in the general election of 1973, but regained his seat in a by-election the next year. He was re-admitted to cabinet as minister of health and social development and also given responsibility for the MB *Lotteries Act*. When the 1977 provincial election brought a victory for the PCs under **Sterling Lyon,** Desjardins was re-elected and sat as a member of the opposition. Under **Howard Pawley**, the NDP returned to power in 1981 and Desjardins was named minister of health and minister of recreation and sport with responsibility for *Lotteries and Gaming Control Act.* As a politician, he consistently worked to support francophone issues and throughout the 1908s he was a strong supporter of Pawley's efforts to expand French language services in MB. He was shifted to the ministry of urban affairs in Jan 1985. He was easily re-elected in 1986 and was appointed minister of health and sport. In Feb 1988, he resigned from his cabinet positions to take a job in the private sector as director of the Manitoba Hospital Association. In 2002, he participated in the Frontier Centre for Public Policy and argued that Canada's provinces should be allowed to enact user fees and expand the role of the private sector in health care provision. In 2007, he continued to live in **Winnipeg.** ● RUTH DEGRAVES

DEW DROP GANG, one of **Winnipeg's** first street gangs, was formed in the post-WWII period. The gang operated primarily in the **North End,** and was comprised of young men aged 18-22 who stole, committed vandalism, trafficked drugs, and bootlegged. The gang took its name from a restaurant they frequented. Gang members were distinguishable by their style of dress: grey fedoras and wide-legged, tapered pants called "drapes." News of the Dew Drop Gang appeared in Winnipeg **Newspapers** around 1949 after a series of fights and disturbances at teenage dance halls led to several Dew Droppers being arrested on weapons charges. The gang members were often armed with switchblades, knuckle rings, brass knuckles, and even nickel-plated revolvers. One

Dew Drops were dapper dressers.

of their specialities was mugging men returning home from bars late at night. Winnipeg police cracked down on the gang in 1950, making a series of arrests of high-profile members, which led to gang's demise around 1953. At its peak, the gang numbered roughly 100 members. ● MD

DEWAR, Archibald Stewart, policeman, lawyer, judge (b July 26, 1916, **Winnipeg**; d July 7, 2001, Winnipeg). Dewar worked as a constable with the Winnipeg Police Dept from 1938-40 before serving overseas with the Royal Canadian Artillery during WWII. Called to the bar in Winnipeg in 1948, he practised briefly as a solicitor with the Department of National Health and Welfare in Ottawa. He returned to Winnipeg in 1948, employed as a crown attorney until 1957, when he entered private practice. In 1973, he became chief justice of the Court of Queen's Bench, a position he held until his retirement in 1985. He was widely considered one of MB's premier litigation lawyers in the 1960s and early '70s. In honour of his skill as an advocate, following his death in 2001, a group of friends and former colleagues created the Archibald S. Dewar Award for Advocacy at the **U of M** Faculty of Law, awarded annually to the top 2 students in the law school's advocacy program. ● DOUG JOHNSTON

DHALLA, Naranjan, medical researcher (b 1936, Ghanieke, India). An international cardiac specialist, Naranjan's education includes a BSc from Panjab U in 1956, an MSc from the U of

Naranjan S. Dhalla, 1978

Pennsylvania in 1963, and a PhD in pharmacology from U of Pittsburgh in 1965. Dhalla began his professional career at St. Louis U before moving from MO to **Winnipeg** in 1968 to join the physiology faculty at the **U of M**. He became a full professor in 1974, and later a distinguished professor in 1991. Dhalla joined the International Society for Heart Research in 1967 and later served as its president (1992-95). In 1987, Dhalla founded and was named director of the Division (later institute) of Cardiovascular Sciences at the **St. Boniface General Hospital**. In 1987, he also became editor of the *Molecular and Cellular Biochemistry* journal. He founded the International Academy of Cardiovascular Sciences, a research and education body, in 1996, and has continued to serve as its executive director. As part of that role, Dhalla organized and chaired the 2000-delegate World Congress on Heart Health in Winnipeg in 2001. Dhalla's innovative research focuses on the effects of heart problems at the molecular, cellular, and biochemical levels. He found that imbalances in fatty acid and in sugar usage can cause heart problems in diabetics, and has examined the relationship between heart attacks, subcellular remodelling, and congestive heart failure. In March 2006, Dhalla stepped down as director of the Institute of Cardiovascular Sciences in part to focus more on a drug development company he co-founded, Medicure Inc. At the time, the company had 2 ischemic heart disease drugs in clinical trials. Dhalla has been an active member of the India Canada Culture and Heritage Association, and Panjab Foundation of Manitoba. In 1995, Dhalla was awarded an honorary doctorate by Charles U in Prague, and was named a Member of the Order of Canada in 1997, a fellow of the Royal Society of Canada in 2000, and a member of the Order of the Buffalo Hunt (1996) and Order of Manitoba 2002. By 2006, he had trained more than 145 scientists, published nearly 700 research papers, written or edited 40 books, lectured at more than 400 conferences in 65 countries, and received over 100 different honours. • JOEL TRENAMAN

DICKSON, Robert George "Brian," lawyer, judge (b May 25, 1916, Yorkton, SK; d Oct 17, 1998, Dunrobin, ON). Following his family's move to **Winnipeg**, he attended the **U of M** and graduated from its law school. Initially employed in Winnipeg in **Great-West Life** Assurance Co.'s investment division, he was called to the bar in 1940. However, before practising law, he enlisted in the **Military** and served overseas in WWII, during which he was severely wounded by enemy shellfire during the Normandy campaign. Following his recovery and demobilization, he returned to Winnipeg and the private practice of law at the firm of Aikins and MacAuley. In 1963, he was appointed to the Court of Queen's Bench of MB, and in 1967, he was elevated to the Court of Appeal. He was appointed to the Supreme Court of Canada in 1973, and became chief justice in 1984, a position he held until his retirement in 1990. His tenure as chief justice saw the enactment of Canada's *Charter of Rights and Freedoms* (1982). As a result, Dickson presided over a Supreme Court that morphed from a high court toiling in relative obscurity into a prominent national institution with the final say on some of the most controversial moral, legal, and political issues of the day. In 1991, he was named a companion of the Order of Canada. • DOUG JOHNSTON

DINOSAURS, MARINE lived in the vast tropical inland sea that covered much of NA until their extinction at the end of the Cretaceous Period, 70 million years ago. Fossils of marine dinosaurs are abundant in southern MB, and remains have been found in benthonite mines near **Morden**. The dominant predator of this era was the mosasaur. It was 20 m long and had mandibles with a joint in the middle to allow for extra-wide expansion, with one set of teeth to hold prey in place while another tore it apart. The plesiosaur, descended from air-breathing reptiles, also lived at this time. Plesiosaurs were surface feeders who may have used their long, swan-like necks to feed on sea birds, swallowing stones to grind up their food in their gizzard and provide ballast. Giant turtles, measuring up to 4 m in length, also roamed the seas of ancient MB, as well as some of the world's largest known prehistoric squid, with some fossils reaching up to 20 m in length. • MD

▸ *See also* **Canadian Fossil Discovery Centre**.

DIONISIO, Ma-Anne, singer, actress (b 1974, Manila, Philippines) is known as "Canada's *Miss Saigon*" for her performance as Kim in the musical. Dionisio emigrated with her family from the Philippines to **Winnipeg** in 1990, and lived in the north Winnipeg neighbourhood of Tyndall Park. One of 5 daughters, Dionisio attended Tech Voc High School and studied science at the **U of M**. Dionisio was 19 when she won the part in *Miss Saigon*, and spent 103 weeks with the Toronto production. She was nominated for the Dora Mavor Moore Award for Best Actress in a Musical for her performance. She reprised the role in Sydney, Australia and London, UK, before joining productions of *Les Miserables*, *West Side Story*, and *Grease*. Dionisio performed the role of Eponine in the international touring company of *Les Miserables*, travelling to Singapore, Korea, Hong Kong, and South Africa. She reprised the role in the US National touring company of *Les Miserables* in 2004. In 2001, Dionisio performed

D

The mosasaur, the most fearsome of the Cretaceous marine reptiles

Ma-Ann Dionisio

WINNIPEG FREE PRESS

D

several concerts with the WINNIPEG SYMPHONY ORCHESTRA. In 2007, Dionisio spent most of her time in Toronto, where she lives with her son, Nicholas. ● AMANDA STEPHENS

DISEASE IN WILDLIFE is a major force in nature. Pathogens are part of every ecosystem and do more good than harm ecologically. Ecosystems are stabilized and made resilient to disturbance by a richness of species, including pathogens. They contribute to the many alternative pathways for the flow of energy and the recycling of materials. But pathogens and diseases are troublesome too, as witnessed by the cost of the health care system, the growing toll of disease on farm animals, and the rising number and scale of economic and conservation issues associated with diseases in wild animals. Diseases in wild animals in MB are important issues in wildlife conservation and management, they have major economic affects on agriculture, and pose new threats to public health.

Disease is a state of physiological dysfunction due to parasitic invasion by some infectious organism, the effects of chemical or physical agents, malnutrition of various kinds, or defective genes. Yet, the mere presence of a pathogen in an animal does not mean that animal is diseased. For example, healthy humans are infected at all times with a variety of bacteria, and with mites in our eyelashes. Some of those bacteria are capable of causing fatal disease, but only in rare circumstances do they do so. Whether a pathogen results in disease depends on the interactions among the pathogen, the individual animal, and the environment in which they both live, making diseases in nature complicated subjects to understand.

MB's wildlife populations are sustained by ecosystems rife with pathogens; every animal

is, to some extent, challenged by disease. A few of these pathogens and diseases have become issues of concern to humans because they threaten our health, our quality of life, and the economy. Western equine encephalitis (WEE) and West Nile virus (WNV) are good examples of wildlife pathogens of concern because they threaten human health and cause disease in horses. Both are viruses of wild birds and certain species of bird-feeding mosquitoes. WEE is native to MB, while WNV is a new immigrant which arrived in MB only in 2002. Both can cause debilitating or fatal disease in humans, although most human infections result in no disease or mild disease. Both viruses are maintained in nature in cycles of infection between birds and mosquitoes. WNV also is a concern because it kills wild birds, especially CROWS, magpies and blue jays. It is also a new threat to rare species such as the Loggerhead Shrike. A number of rare native and exotic birds and mammals have died of the disease at the ASSINIBOINE PARK ZOO.

Several other wild-animal pathogens can cause serious disease in people. Rabies is perhaps the best known, and is caused by one of several strains of virus, each maintained in nature in a different mammalian host species. In southern MB, the predominant strain is the SKUNK strain, maintained in populations of the Striped Skunk. The FOX strain occurs in the N in Arctic Fox, and various species of bats also maintain their own strains. All of the strains can cause infection and disease in any species of mammal, including people, but they are maintained over the years only in the host species. There is no record of any human case of rabies contracted in MB. However, 100-200 wild and domestic rabid animals are identified each year here, mostly in skunks, but also cats, dogs, cattle, horses, bats, Arctic Fox, and other species.

Little is known about the range of human pathogens carried by small mammals in MB. Tularemia, a bacterial disease which is treatable and rarely now causes fatal disease in humans, is known to occur in rodents such as BEAVER, MUSKRAT, Deer MOUSE, Richardson's Ground SQUIRREL, and occasionally in people. The Sin Nombre (Spanish for "nameless") strain of hantavirus is present in Deer Mice, in which up to 11% of mice in regional MB populations have been found infected. The virus causes no disease in its rodent host, but severe and often-fatal disease in people. Only 2 cases of human disease caused by this virus have been detected in MB since the virus was first discovered in the US in 1993.

Bovine tuberculosis (the form of TB typically carried by cattle) is an important human

disease, and thus great effort was made in Canada to eradicate it from cattle. Eradication appeared achieved in the late 1980s but, starting in 1991, infected cattle were again detected near RIDING MOUNTAIN NATIONAL PARK. Subsequently, it was discovered that American ELK within the park had become infected and it appeared that contact between elk and cattle was maintaining the infection in both populations in the area. This threatened a large economic impact on the MB cattle industry through its loss of TB-free status in 1997. Factors contributing to bovine TB appeared to be high elk density, joint feeding of cattle and elk on hay bales on farms and at hunter-operated bait stations, and habitat changes within the park and on adjacent agricultural lands. A management plan is now in effect, and results to date are encouraging.

Newcastle disease is a devastating virus disease of poultry, with potential for enormous economic consequences from direct mortality and export restrictions. It occurs regularly and is probably maintained in Double-crested Cormorants, which can kill 20-60% of the young. Avian influenza viruses also are widespread in wild birds, especially ducks. In a 2005 survey, 18% of wild ducks sampled in MB were infected with 1 or more strains. Fortunately, in Canadian wild birds, only benign strains have been found thus far. Nonetheless, mild strains can undergo genetic changes and become important disease-causing strains if they become established in poultry populations.

Avian botulism regularly causes mortality among prairie-nesting water birds, and in outbreak years has killed hundreds of thousands of birds in SW MB. The brain worm (*Parelaphostrongylus tenuis*) of white-tailed DEER, which causes no disease in its normal host, causes fatal disease in MOOSE, American Elk, CARIBOU and mule deer, where their ranges overlap with the whitetail. The Winter Tick (*Dermacentor albipictus*) kills many yearling Moose in periodic outbreak years. Avian cholera (a bacterial disease unrelated to human cholera) causes regular losses in wild geese. An iridovirus of the Tiger SALAMANDER causes periodic massive mortality. Mercury has entered wildlife food chains from river impoundments, pulp mills, and metal mining and processing. A potent condensate of industrial pollutants rains down on the Hudson's Bay coast and waters, and is concentrated through the food chain and accumulates to toxic levels in the fat and milk of SEALS and Polar BEARS.

Changing patterns of pathogens and diseases are almost universal markers of ecosystem disturbance, and human activity has profoundly altered MB's environments. Native prairie has been reduced to a few remnant ha and most wetlands have been drained, resulting in new patterns of botulism and bovine tuberculosis. Chronic Wasting Disease has become established in wild deer in SK and AB and there is no barrier against its arrival in MB. Deer, American Elk, Moose and probably caribou will be severely impacted. More sweeping will be the inevitable impact of global warming. Thus, pathogens and diseases in wildlife will remain dynamic components of MB environments into the future. • FAL

DOC WALKER, country-rock group, was formed in 1991 in Westbourne (30 km NW of **PORTAGE LA PRAIRIE**) by singer/guitarists Chris Thorsteinson and Dave Wasyliw. Also in the group were drummer Mark Branconnier and bassist Blake Manley, later replaced by Chris Sutherland and Paul Yee, respectively. The group released *A Good Day to Ride* (1995) independently before signing with manger Ron Kitchener and Universal Music Canada for *Curve* (2001), produced by Cdn country star Joel Feeney. The album was the group's breakthrough, with top-10 singles "She Hasn't Always Been This Way," "Call Me a Fool," and "Rocket Girl" earning Juno Award nominations for Best New Country Artist/Group and Best Country Recording (2003). They also picked up nominations for Canadian Country Music Awards (CCMA) for Independent Group of the Year; SOCAN Song of the Year; Prairie Music Awards' 2002 Country Recording of the Year; and 6 Manitoba Country Music Association awards, including Entertainer, Song, Male Vocalist, Group, and both Recording Artist and Video of the Year Awards. With the addition of Portage la Prairie guitarist Murray Pulver, *Everyone Aboard* (2003) yielded further hit singles "The Show Is Free," "North Dakota Boy," and "Get Up," earning the band 5 CCMA nominations and Country Group of the Year, plus the Western Canada Music Awards Entertainer of the Year title (2004). In 2005, the group recorded in Nashville with noted producer Justin Neibank, releasing *Doc Walker* in fall 2006, including songs co-written with **RANDY BACHMAN.** • JOHN EINARSON

DR. BARNARDO'S HOME FOR BOYS, operated an industrial farm in **RUSSELL** from 1889-1908, bringing about 800 primarily **ENGLISH** orphans to MB. The enterprise was the brainchild of philanthropist Thomas John Barnardo (1845-1905), of mixed **JEWISH** and English extraction, who after becoming an **EVANGELICAL** Christian of the social gospel mode, started a charity in 1867 to educate impoverished London children. He later decided that the cure for poverty was to teach children

a trade, and to that end, founded numerous job training schools throughout the UK.

As part of the job training effort, Barnardo envisaged sending numerous children to the Colonies to learn **AGRICULTURE** and other skills. The first children – initially just boys – arrived at a receiving home in Peterborough, ON, in 1882; girls followed soon after, and went to a Toronto facility. About 1884, Barnardo bought land in the Shell River area – which would later become Russell – near the **ASSINIBOINE RIVER**, and an agricultural training centre opened there in 1887. Though Barnardo visited the facility several times, former **RAILWAYS** inspector E. A. Struthers oversaw its operations. At its furthest extent, the mixed-use farm covered about 40 km² (15 mi²). Throughout its history, the farm had, on average, 50 boys of about 16-18 years at any time, though it had sufficient capacity for 100 or more, at a time when Russell's population was under 200. Boys usually stayed for a year, working in the fields, in the vegetable gardens, or in the creamery or cheese factory. Most boys stayed in the Russell area, received land as homesteaders, or found work on farms elsewhere in MB or Canada.

Many dignitaries, including Premier **JOHN NORQUAY**, visited the farm or gave it public approval. Nevertheless, the operation had its dark sides: while **J. S. WOODSWORTH** applauded Dr. Barnardo's Christian motivations, he also believed the program was supplying Canada with slave labour. The Russell campus closed in 1908, a few years after the death of its founder, and the immigration program was discontinued nationally in the 1930s, but the charity has left its mark on the Russell area. The Barnardo Home building is now a museum. The National Archives also has much material from Barnardo's on deposit, while the

Archives of Manitoba and the Manitoba Genealogical Society have extensive holdings related to the Barnardo program. • A.J. LEVIN

DOER, Gary Albert, premier, trade unionist (b Mar 31, 1948, **WINNIPEG**), son of Albert and Gwen. Doer's father was a buyer in the **HBC**, and he grew up in his later youth in the South River Heights area of Winnipeg. The family was **CATHOLIC** and he went to St Paul's High School. He enrolled at the **U OF M** but left before earning a degree. He became the leader of a public-sector union, later entering politics, eventually to become premier. Married to Virginia "Ginny" Devine, they have two daughters.

In the early 1970s, Doer worked at the Vaughan St Detention Centre and the Manitoba Youth Treatment Centre, both in Winnipeg. He quickly came to the fore in the Manitoba Government Employees Association (MGEA), later called the Manitoba Government Employees Union. By 1977, he was its vice-president, becoming president 2 years later, a position he held until 1986. Doer was involved in several important initiatives, including establishing a provincial employees' day-care centre, and winning pay equity legislation in the MB civil service.

Politically, Doer was a pragmatist. He could have joined any of the 3 parties in MB politics, as he was moderately left-of-centre. In the mid-1980s, he was approached by the **PROGRESSIVE CONSERVATIVE** party to run provincially, and, by some accounts, Doer entertained the possibility. In the end, he was recruited by the NDP in March 1986 and he ran successfully in Concordia, a working-class constituency in NE Winnipeg. He was appointed in April 1986 as minister of urban affairs in **HOWARD PAWLEY**'s govt, which had won a small majority. He would later add other portfolios

AM, RUSSELL-SCHOOLS-BARNARDO HOME 3, N9290

Orphaned boys working at Dr. Barnardo's Home, Russell MB, 1892

D

Gary Doer has successfully positioned the NDP in the political centre.

Doer and his team won another majority in in May 2007, the first premier since Duff Roblin to do so.

Doer's administrations have been cautious and in many ways conservative, accepting initiatives of the previous Filmon govt. Blessed by abundant revenues from a buoyant economy and enlarged transfers from the federal govt, Doer had no difficulty in boosting spending on health care while offering modest tax decreases to the lower middle class. His govt kept its profile low, was acutely careful of its public image, and intentionally sought to avoid controversy.

Gary Doer was a telegenic politician who understood his province's politics intimately. He ran a personal, centralized govt, and the fortunes of his party depended mainly on him. He persisted in making the NDP successful at a time when social democracy was under intense pressure from neo-conservatism. ● ALLEN MILLS

DOERN, Russell "Russ," politician (b Oct 20, 1935, **WINNIPEG**; d Feb 19, 1987, **EMERSON**) opposed provincial bilingualism as a member of MB's first **NDP** govt. Doern was educated at Isaac Newton High School, United College (*see* **U OF W**), and the **U OF M**. In 1955, he came 2nd in the shot put and discus at the Junior Canadian Track and Field Competitions. From 1959-66, he taught English and history in various Winnipeg high schools until he was elected to the MB **LEGISLATURE** as an NDP member for Elmwood. Doern was re-elected in 1969, 1973, 1977, and 1981. In the House, he served as Deputy Speaker in 1969-70, and he was Minister of Public Works in the **EDWARD SCHREYER** govt from 1972-77. He resigned from the NDP in 1984 over his disagreement with the party's language

to his responsibilities: crown corporations, **MTS**, and liquor control.

In March 1988, the Pawley govt was brought down by a discontented backbencher, and the NDP was forced to the polls at the height of its unpopularity. Pawley resigned in mid-election, and after a hastily called leadership convention, Doer was elected leader. He did not then become premier. In the Apil 1988 election, Doer held on to his seat and led a reduced caucus of 12 NDP MLAs. The election saw the PCs come to power with a minority govt, facing a large Liberal caucus under **SHARON CARSTAIRS** in opposition.

Doer's task then was to ensure that the Liberals did not replace his own party as the ongoing voice of the centre-left in MB. He needed time to ensure that the NDP's unpopularity would fade. Though it was unspoken, an informal alliance with the provincial PCs of **GARY FILMON** ensued. Both wanted to dish the Liberals, and Doer ensured that Filmon's minority govt was not brought down over the budget of Aug 1988. Doer spoke volubly against the PCs' financial measures and supported the Liberals' opposition to the govt budget. However, he had arranged for his own caucus to abstain, and so 10 New Democrats did not vote, and Filmon's govt survived.

In the election of Sept 1990, the NDP improved their performance, and Doer became the opposition leader, but the PCs now had a majority govt. Throughout the 1990s, Doer bore down on the issues of the defence of medicare as

a public and accessible system, and was strident in his criticism of federal and provincial govt cutbacks. He hoped to win the 1995 election, but Filmon cannily exploited the "Save the Jets" campaign and won, in part with the overwhelming support of young male voters.

By 1999, Doer had been opposition leader for 9 years. He risked political irrelevance if he lost again. He cobbled together what was, for the NDP, a bold platform, which took many of its planks from Tony Blair's British success with "Third Way" policies. Doer emphasised that the NDP would respect balanced-budget legislation and would hold the line on taxes but would still be a strong defender of public medical care. This, combined with the PCs' loss of popularity over the scandal of vote-rigging in the Interlake in the 1995 election, gave the NDP its victory. Doer's party won 44% of the vote and took 32 of 57 seats, a large majority by MB's standards. He had convinced the public that, to the NDP's traditional emphasis on social programs, he could add a hard-headed, "sensible" position – that the economy should be left alone and that growth would be spearheaded by further hydroelectric development on the **NELSON RIVER**.

In June 2003, Doer's NDP won an even-larger majority in an election that was more about who could best run the province than about substantial political differences. The NDP won 35 seats and over 49% of the popular vote, an unprecedented measure of popularity.

Russell Doern, 1974

policy. Doern published 2 books: *Wednesdays are Cabinet Days: A Personal History of the Schreyer Administration* (1981) and *The Battle over Bilingualism: The Manitoba Language Question 1983-1985* (1985). He committed suicide in 1987. ● JMB

DOGSLEDDING started as an efficient way for **First Nations** and Inuit – later, for **Fur Trappers** and prospectors as well – to cross snow-covered terrain in Canada's North. However, the snowmobile has largely supplanted the millennia-old means of transport in MB, and mushing now survives primarily as a recreational sport. The first record of a dogsled race was in the late 1850s, with the informal organization of a race between **Winnipeg** and St. Paul, MN. Dogsledding is most common around **The Pas**, where a race was first organized in 1916 as The Pas Dog Derby, which covered 320 km (200 mi) to **Flin Flon**. It continues today as part of the **Northern Manitoba Trappers' Festival**. Some of the more prominent dogsledders in MB come from The Pas, such as **Emile St. Godard**, who won an Olympic gold medal in dogsledding when it became an exhibition sport in 1932. Albert Campbell, a **Métis** musher from the region, famously won a Winnipeg-St. Paul dogsled race in 1917. Campbell's win was fictionalized in the 1993 movie *Iron Will*. Skijoring, when 1 or 2 dogs pull a person on cross-country skis, and kick-sledding, which involved a maximum of 3 dogs pulling a lighter sled, are 2 new variations on traditional dogsledding. ● MD

DOGWOOD. MB has 5 species of native dogwoods (*Cornus* spp.), 4 medium-sized shrubs (one very common; 3 uncommon to rare) and one widespread low perennial. Red osier dogwood or red willow (not a true willow) (*Cornus stolonifera*) is one of the most common and easy to identify shrubs in the southern ⅔ of MB, growing in moist woods, thickets, clearings and on riverbanks. Its smooth stems are usually a distinctive bright red colour although they can be purple or green. It has opposite leaves and dense clusters of small white flowers and then bitter white berries. Red willow's inner bark was often smoked by itself or added to tobacco by Aboriginal peoples as 'kinnikinnick'. They used many parts of the plant for tea or medicines and the flexible branches to weave baskets or as rims for containers. Moose eat it as an important winter food and bears like the berries. The uncommon shrubby dogwoods are the grey (*C. racemosa*), round-leaved (*C. rugosa*), and alternate-leaved or green osier (*C. alternifolia*). All have similar clusters of small white flowers and bitter white berries and are found occasionally on moist

sites in southcentral and southeastern MB. The low dogwood (to 15 cm) is bunchberry (*Cornus canadensis*), which often forms large clumps in moist forests throughout MB. Its cluster of 4-7 evergreen oval leaves, 4-petalled white 'flowers' and clump of bright red 'berries' are common and distinctive. Its 'petals' are actually coloured leaves called 'bracts', more typical of tree dogwoods like the Pacific flowering dogwood (*C. nuttallii*), the floral emblem of BC. The actual flowers are in the center of the 4 bracts, small white ones similar to those found in the shrub dogwoods. The fruits are edible, although not very tasty to most people, and can be eaten fresh or cooked. Many small mammals and birds love them. ● KAREN JOHNSON

DOMINION CITY, pop 421, is an agricultural community 80 km S of **Winnipeg** and 15 km N of the US border on the **CPR** line. Originally known as Roseau because it was on the Roseau River, the town name was changed to Dominion City in 1880 to avoid confusion with Rosseau, ON. The Franklin Museum in Dominion City boasts a replica of what is believed to have been the largest freshwater fish ever caught in MB, a 185 kg sturgeon caught in the Roseau River. ● GPP

DOUGLAS, Thomas Clement "Tommy," politician, reformer, preacher (b Oct 20, 1904, Falkirk, UK; d Feb 24, 1986, Ottawa). Born to working-class **Scots**, Tommy moved with his family to the Point Douglas area of **Winnipeg** in 1910. Four years later, a leg injury turned into osteomyelitis, and after consulting a specialist who wanted to amputate the limb, a visiting doctor saved Douglas's leg at no charge on condition his students be allowed to witness the surgery. Historians often identify this moment as the genesis of national free medical care, which Douglas would later champion. The Labour-oriented family moved back to the UK during WWI, as Tommy's father, though a pacifist, volunteered in the Royal Army Medical Corps. They returned to MB just after the end of the war, this time to the Elmwood neighbourhood. Around this time, Tommy met **James Shaver Woodsworth** of **All People's Mission**. Another formative moment for him was the 1919 **Winnipeg General Strike**, where the teenaged Douglas witnessed RNWMP officers fire on and kill 2 protesters.

After leaving school at age 14, Douglas, unhampered by his childhood sickness, became an excellent light heavyweight boxer, briefly trod the stage, and worked as a printer's apprentice operating a Linotype machine. In 1924, he moved to **Brandon** to attend the **Baptist** Brandon College (*see* **Brandon U**), graduating in 1930. There,

Douglas further cemented his belief in the social gospel – a Protestant but ecumenical approach also seen in the thinking of classmate and friend **Stanley Knowles**. While studying in Brandon, he served as student preacher for a number of communities in SW MB, including **Austin** and **Carberry**. In Carberry, he met and married Irma Dempsey. After his graduation, they moved to Weyburn, SK, where he had been offered a job as a minister. The Douglases had one daughter, actor and activist Shirley, and later adopted a second girl, Joan.

In 1935, after an earlier unsuccessful campaign, Douglas became the Cooperative Commonwealth Federation MP for Weyburn, SK. Douglas stood down from his seat on becoming CCF leader of SK and, shortly thereafter, premier. As premier of SK (1944-61), federal NDP leader (1961-71), and NDP MP (1962-79), Douglas influenced both provincial and federal govts to pursue progressive policies, and Douglas is often called the "Father of Medicare." He also introduced public automobile insurance to SK; this later would serve as the model for Autopac. Douglas remained an outspoken critic of nuclear arms and of legislations that he viewed as curbing civil liberties, including PM Trudeau's use of the *War Measures Act* in 1970. After his 1979 retirement from politics, Douglas stayed in the Ottawa area, where he died of cancer in 1986.

Douglas is the subject of several documentaries, including *Tommy Douglas: In His Own Words* (2001), and of a number of books. Most notable among these are *Tommy Douglas: The*

Tommy Douglas, 1980

Road to Jerusalem (Fifth House, 2004) and Walter Stewart's *Tommy: The Life and Times of Tommy Douglas* (McArthur & Co., 2003). In a 2004 **CBC**-TV poll, over 1 million voters chose Douglas as the "Greatest Canadian," beating out such fellow Manitobans **Louis Riel** (11), **Nellie McClung** (25), and Sir **William Stephenson** (54). ● A.J. LEVIN

DOUGLAS MARSH, 15 km W of Brandon, is an 18 km² bog and wet-meadow system of ecological significance for breeding birds and several plant species. The marsh was formed toward the end of the Ice Age, between 9000 BC and 7000 BC. Before its formation, the "Douglas Distributary Channel" carried glacial meltwater flowing across the **Assiniboine** River delta into glacial **Lake Agassiz.** As water levels in Agassiz fell, the channel shifted. The original channel filled in with sediment, and Douglas Marsh was formed.

Douglas Marsh is maintained by groundwater seepage, resulting in a consistently wet environment. This characteristic has likely saved the marsh from human development beyond summer livestock grazing and hay crops in drier portions, even though the marsh is private land. Water drains W through Willow Creek, but does not drain fast enough to dry out the marsh.

The unique environmental conditions at the marsh have created a highly productive ecosystem with good biodiversity. Of particular importance is the predominance of a dense sedge (*Carex* spp.) community, which is the preferred breeding habitat for the yellow **Rail** (*Coturnicops noveboracencis*). The yellow rail is designated under Canada's *Species at Risk Act* (SARA) as being of special concern, suffering from habitat loss in both its northern breeding grounds and its southern wintering area. Douglas Marsh is thought to have the largest breeding population of yellow rails in southern MB, and perhaps in all of the Prairies. The marsh is also one of the few accessible breeding sites for yellow rail in NA, and is therefore an internationally renowned destination for birders.

The Douglas Marsh IBA Committee, composed of local researchers and concerned citizens, oversees the program at Douglas Marsh. Birders access the marsh on hwy 340, just S of the town of Douglas, on the northern edge of the marsh. The landowner does not use this area, and allows birders to enter the property. The Douglas Marsh IBA Committee has created a rough trail and erected interpretive signs for visitors. In 2004, the adjacent landowner placed a 1.5 km² portion of land into a conservation agreement through the Manitoba Habitat Heritage Corporation. This portion of land is now conserved in perpetuity.

Along with other birds and mammals, more than 200 species of plant have been recorded in Douglas Marsh, many of which are scarce in SW MB or the province as a whole. In particular, the small white lady slipper (*Cypripedium candidum*) is listed by both SARA and the *Manitoba Endangered Species Act* as endangered. The marsh felwort (*Lomatogonium rotatum*) is also a rare species; the only other records in MB are along the **Hudson Bay** coastline. Other notable plants include the pitcher plant (*Sarracina purporea*), scratch grass (*Muhlenbergia asperfolia*), prairie muhly (*M. cuspidate*), bog muhly (*M. glomerata*), bulb-bearing water hemlock (*Cicuta bulbifera*), flat-leaved bladderwort (*Utricularia intermedia*), marsh bellflower (*Campanula aparinoides*), Kalm's lobelia (*Lobelia kalmii*), and flat-topped white aster (*Aster umbellatus*). ● CHRISTOPHER MALCOLM

▸ *See also* **Delta Marsh**, **Netley-Libau Marsh**.

DOUPE, Joseph "Joe," physician, educator (b March 10, 1910, **Winnipeg**; d Aug 26, 1966, Winnipeg). As a youth, Doupe attended Laura Secord, Earl Grey, and Kelvin schools in Winnipeg. His grandfather, David Young, was MB's first psychologist. Doupe's early academic years were marked by low grades and an unsuccessful attempt at a **U of M** BSc in **Medicine** in 1930. He persevered, however, and achieved his MD in 1934. Doupe pursued postgraduate training at the Royal College of Physicians in London, England, and upon completion in 1936, was the recipient of a research fellowship. He went on to work in the department of physiology at the U of Pennsylvania in 1938, and moved to the U of Toronto's Banting Institute in 1939. With his British physician wife, Nona Wright, Doupe returned to London in 1940 and enlisted in the Royal Army Medical Corps. He served in France, Belgium, India, and Burma during WWII. Doupe and his colleagues conducted research on soldiers experiencing nerve damage. They used innovative heat and surgical cutting methods to ease painful injuries.

While in India in 1945, Doupe learned that the U of M was searching for a professor to head a research program in experimental medicine. Doupe proposed that the position be structured in an unusual way, that the head should be an advisor not an administrator, work with undergraduates, support a wide range of research, and maintain his or her own medical practice. After some negotiation, Doupe was hired on those terms in 1946 and returned to Winnipeg. During his tenure, Doupe made a number of upgrades to the U of M programs that reflected his unique approach to medicine. His changes integrated the physiology discipline into medicine, and allowed students to

do more research, participate in seminars, and have more rigorous individual attention from instructors. Some of the notable U of M trained doctors to graduate during Doupe's career included **Arnold Naimark**, **Barry Posner**, **Allan Ronald**, **Henry Friesen**, and **Frank Gunston**. The colourful, charismatic Doupe also practised at Winnipeg General Hospital (*see* **Health Sciences Centre**), and was a member of the National Research Council and its offshoot, the Medical Research Council. ● JOEL TRENAMAN

DOYLE, Jimmy "Jumbo," golfer (b Feb 28, 1933, **Winnipeg**; d April 6, 1991, **Sandy Hook**) was a prominent figure in MB golf for 40 years. Doyle was born into golf, playing as a child at Sandy Hook Golf Course, which his father later purchased after WWII. Doyle's first title came at the Manitoba Junior Championship in 1951. He won the 1957 Saskatchewan Open, and was runner-up at that year's Manitoba Open. After his father's death in the late '50s, Doyle continued to run the family's golf course while competing in golf tournaments. Doyle was thus considered a professional golfer since he made his living at golf, which prevented him from playing in amateur competitions. After taking work with an insurance company, he applied to have his amateur status reinstated in 1963, a request that was finally granted by the Royal Canadian Golf Association in 1968. He won the 1968 Canadian Amateur title, earning him that year's Male Athlete of the Year from the MB Sportswriters and Sportscasters Association. He went on to win 4 provincial amateur championships, and played on 11 Willingdon Cup teams, a national event where MB is represented by a team of the province's 4 top players. His nickname "Jumbo" stems from his considerable physical stature. Doyle never retired from competitive play and, fittingly, died while working on Sandy Hook Golf Course. ● MD

DRAGONFLY AND DAMSELFLY are predatory insects of the order Odonata, typically found near water, since they have an aquatic stage in their development. They must be recognized as one of the most successful groups of animals due to their long lineage, traceable back over 300 million years ago (Carboniferous period), and to their diversity and abundance in the world's many ecosystems. Among the earliest of land dwellers, they also were among the first to fly, and this invention is a main reason they have flourished to modern times. They have so mastered the technology of flight that they can hover endlessly and even fly backwards. **Fossils** reveal that dragonflies evolved some real giants like *Meganeura monyi* (the world's largest insect)

Dragonfly waits for tasty mosquito snack.

Dragonflies and damselflies can be hugely abundant under prime conditions near ponds and marshes, with one sweep of a butterfly net through the grass yielding a dozen specimens of several species. Single dragonflies on patrol are experts at avoiding capture, swerving away and departing at great speed. These insects are unable to bite and so they cannot harm people. They are important players in aquatic and land food webs, and perform the valuable function controlling biting insects, especially **MOSQUITOES**. Increasingly they are being used as an indicator of water quality. Biologists are currently investigating the diversity and distribution of dragonflies in the province, and new species are still being discovered. The current list includes 95 species in 9 families, and will no doubt exceed 100 species through the work of the MB Dragonfly Survey coordinated by Manitoba Conservation. About 200 species are known in Canada and 6000 species worldwide. ● RBW

DRAINAGE, AGRICULTURAL is the process of removing surface water, usually artificially. Although some of southern MB was naturally well-drained when settlers first arrived, particularly those lands lying immediately alongside the **RED RIVER**, not far inland was land that was swampy or peat bog or, in wet years, mostly ponds and sloughs. As early as 1859, **HENRY YOULE HIND** had recognized the potential of the vast wetlands of the Prairies, once they were cleared of groundwater. Settlement quickly took up the good land, and by the later years of the 19th century, many began to look to the wetter land for farming. The province recognized the need to reclaim these wetlands, while appreciating that the expense of their drainage was beyond the capacity of either individuals or the small municipalities of the time. Although the wetlands provided a natural habitat for wildlife and were part of the natural order of the geography of the region, little concern was given to the possible environmental implications of drainage.

Although some primitive ditches were dug in the early years, serious drainage began only in 1880, with the passage of the first provincial *Drainage Act*. This act created 3 drainage districts, one east of the Red, a 2nd W of the Red and S of the **ASSINIBOINE RIVER**, and a 3rd W of the Red and N of the Assiniboine. A sum of up to $50,000 was promised for drainage work in these districts, to be executed by the public works dept. As an added incentive, the Dominion govt turned over marshland to the province on the understanding that such land would be drained to make it arable. The early drainage under this act was scattered, involving shallow and therefore ineffectual

from France, with a wingspan up to 70 cm. Compared to dragonflies, which rest with the 2 sets of wings held out sideways, damselflies sit with the wings held together and raised vertically above the back, plus the body is considerably smaller and narrower. Dragonflies are also more robust and stronger fliers.

These insects spend the majority of their lives underwater, hatching from a submerged egg within 3 weeks into a nymph called a naiad. As the naiad feeds on small pond life and grows, it moults to rid itself of its tight skin. It may spend a few months to 3 years in this stage, depending on the species and food availability. The naiad demonstrates 2 most unusual abilities – it takes in water through the anus into the rectum, where gills exchange oxygen for carbon dioxide, and rapid expulsion of the water jettisons the naiad away in time of attack. This naiad becomes a fearsome-looking predator (resembling the creature from the movie *Alien*), with a lower lip that shoots far forward, punctures prey on a pair of sharp hooks, and then retracts the meal back into the mouth, where digestive enzymes flow over it and turn it into a soup. Insect larvae, tadpoles and even small fish are captured in this fashion. When mature, the naiad climbs out of its aquatic world, moults one last time into the adult form, fills its wings with clear blood, and begins its reproductive stage. To accomplish this important function, it requires additional nutrients, which it accumulates by eating aerial

insects. By having the 2 life stages separated – first in water and then in air – a wider range of food sources is exploited, greatly improving the chances of survival. The mating system is quite complicated, involving the transfer of a sperm package from the male to the reproductive tract of the female, while the two are attached in a mating circle (i.e., in tandem) for hours or even days, and often in flight. After they separate, the female deposits her fertilized eggs into the water, where the cycle begins anew.

These 2 groups are famous for their spectacular colours of the body (often blue, green and black), and some also sport distinctive patches of red, purple or black at the wing base, or spots along the wings. They have remarkably good eyesight, made possible by up to 25,000 minute lenses in each of their 2 prominent compound eyes, meeting at the top of the head. Swivelling on a narrow stalk, the eyes can see almost 360° – useful in detecting the insect prey and the rapid approach of a predator like a bird, from up to 20 m away. Alternate beating of the double set of wings, at a rate of around 30 beats/second, generates a speed up to 50 km/hr and allows a rapid change direction at a sharp angle. These aerial predators patrol back and forth over a set path along a bank or trail, intercepting any passing insect, and collecting it up with a basket formed by their 6 spiny feet. At other times, they can be seen resting on a stick or sedge stem, perhaps 'tail-hoisting' to control body heat absorbed from the sun.

D

ditches. Thus, in 1895, a more comprehensive *Land Drainage Act* was passed, which provided the first major organized drainage in MB.

The purpose of drainage was to fit an area for occupation and cultivation. Wetland areas were organized into new, consecutively numbered drainage districts. Once a drainage district was organized, the act provided for ways in which financing of the drainage could be arranged. The first drainage district under this act was in the municipalities of Rockwood and **St. Andrews**, and involved what was popularly known as "St. Andrew's Bog." By 1914, there were 21 drainage districts in MB, and by 1920, the dept of public works reported that over 800,000 ha (2 million ac) of land in the province had "benefited" from 4060 km (2522 mi) of drains constructed.

Complaints about the inequalities of assessment and taxation under the 1895 act led to the creation of the Manitoba Drainage Commission, which sat from 1919-21. It recommended the appointment of a permanent board to administer the *Land Drainage Act*; the extension of district boundaries to include all lands with surplus water entering the district and being carried away by drains; the equitable distribution of assessments; and govt assumption of responsibility for general maintenance of ditches. The last was never fully implemented.

In the later 1920s, 3 more districts were added, and by 1934, the total lands benefiting from drainage was 850,000 ha (2,109,154 ac) and there were over 5850 km (3642 mi) of drains. Problems of maintenance and distribution of drainage levies continued to be a problem, and another commission recommended that the provincial govt take over some of the indebtedness of the municipalities, organize maintenance districts, and contribute 33% of the cost of maintenance. The first 2 recommendations were confirmed in the *Land Drainage Arrangement Act* (1935). A govt report of 1949 recommended that the province pay 66% of the cost of future maintenance and construction of drains carrying "foreign water," and 33% of the cost of future maintenance of other drains. These recommendations were accepted by the govt for the fiscal year 1952. By 1965, there were 28 districts encompassing nearly 1 million ha (2.5 million ac).

The legal character of water is changed when it is collected in an artificial drain, and the collector becomes liable to make sure the water is carried to an adequate outlet, as well as acquiring other liabilities. Concern for the environmental effects of drainage has gradually become an important issue, both in terms of the maintenance of wetlands as natural habitats and because drainage carries not only water but also

a good deal of fertilizer and other chemicals from the land into the larger water systems. Scientists and environmentalists associate drainage with much of the pollution problem of lakes **Winnipeg** and **Manitoba**, for example. ● J. M. BUMSTED

Edward L. Drewry, 1909

DREWRY, Edward Lancaster "E. L.," brewer (b Feb 6, 1851, London, UK; d Nov 2, 1940, **Winnipeg**) was a prominent Winnipeg businessman. He moved with his parents to St. Paul, MN, in 1860. In 1875, he brought his family to Pembina, ND, just across the border from **Emerson**, and they settled in Winnipeg in May 1877. He took over the Herchmer and Batkin Brewery, which was idle, and operated it until he sold out in 1924. Along with the brewery, Drewry assumed possession of the home connected with it, Redwood, which had been built in 1857 by William Inkster. He was a member of city council in 1883-84, and advocated the introduction of street lighting and fire alarms. He later served as Conservative MLA for North Winnipeg from 1886-89, and as the first chair of the parks board from 1894-99. For 40 years he was a member of the board of the Winnipeg General Hospital, and he was one of the founders of Rupert's Land Ladies' College. ● JMB

DRIEDGER, Irwin, jockey (b July 25, 1956, **Altona**). Driedger is the only rider to win Canada's top jockey award while racing in MB. He started racing at the age of 11, at the urging of prominent **Winnipeg** trainer "Shorty" Grey,

who saw potential in Driedger's slight frame. Driedger was racing professionally by 16, and became MB's most successful jockey until **Todd Kabel** started racing. Driedger was named the MB Athlete of the Year in 1979. In 1981, he set a MB record of 214 season wins, and was awarded the national Sovereign Award. He moved E in 1982, and continued a successful career, winning the 1985 Prince of Wales Stakes, and the 1984 Canadian Oaks. Over 11,412 mounts, Driedger won 1661 races, and had 1549 2nd place finishes and 1508 3rd place finishes. He retired from racing in 1990. ● MD

DRISKELL, James. *See* **Wrongful Convictions.**

DRUNKEN POINT was a point along the SW shore of **Lake Winnipeg,** about 100 km N of Winnipeg. There are several theories about how the point got its name. One theory is that many rounds of rum were drunk here by voyageurs while travelling along their trade route. Another theory holds that the river here was the boundary S of which liquor could not be sold to Aboriginals. Treaty 1, drawn up in 1871, identified the northern boundary as Drunken River. Consequently the small settlement on the legal or N side of the river became the site of liquor trade and consumption. Drunken Point is what Icelandic settlers called **Arnes** (literally "River Point") when they arrived in 1875-76. At that time the river was called Drunken River, but the Icelanders renamed it Huldua (meaning "Hidden") River as it had a sandbar blocking its entrance at low water times. ● GPP

DU, Joseph, physician (b Apr 10, 1933, Hai Phong, Vietnam), is a long-time pediatrician and prominent member of MB's **Chinese** community. Du faced a difficult upbringing in war-torn northern Vietnam. An American bomb killed his father during WWII, and he was forced to leave his home and family as a refugee in 1954. Du ended up in Taiwan, where he set to work on his dream of becoming a doctor. He graduated from medical school in 1961, and chose Canada as the place to continue his training. After a short stint in a Regina hospital, Du moved to **Winnipeg** to take a position at the Misericordia Hospital. He became a Cdn citizen in 1967, and was hired by the Winnipeg Clinic a year later. Soon after, he began volunteering to travel to northern MB to provide medical services to Aboriginal communities such as **Norway House** and **Cross Lake**. Du took part in these trips for a total of 33 years.

In 1979, when migrants began leaving Vietnam en masse, Du was asked to help groups of refugees settle in Winnipeg. He helped dozens

AM. PERSONALITY FILES, FROM COLLECTIVE PERSONALITIES 3/186

of individuals and families establish themselves with housing, medical care, and basic skills. There were a number of doctors among the groups of refugees, and Du worked with the Manitoba College of Physicians and Surgeons to form a re-accreditation program that went on to assist immigrants of other nationalities.

The 1980s were a time of change for MB's Chinese community. Du was one of many individuals to work with govt and business leaders on the redevelopment of Winnipeg's Chinatown district. His negotiation skills also bore fruit in 1989, when he arranged for 2 Chinese pandas to be housed at the **Assiniboine Park Zoo**, attracting more than one million visitors. Du received the Order of Canada in 1985 and the **Order of Manitoba** in 2003. He is the president of the Winnipeg Chinese Cultural and Community Centre, and a member of the **St. Boniface General Hospital** board of directors. ● JT

DUBNICOFF, Tanya, cyclist (b Nov 7, 1969, **Winnipeg**) is an Olympic and world champion sprint cyclist. At age 12, Dubnicoff had her first taste of victory, racing BMX bicycles in a Cdn championship, and winning for her age group. When she entered university, she switched to sprint cycling and, after winning gold at the 1991 **Pan-American Games** in Havana, Cuba, worked her way to the 1992 Olympics in Barcelona, Spain, where she placed 6th. Dubnicoff continued to dominate cycling internationally throughout the 1990s. She set a new standard in Canada when she won the World Championship in 1993, the first Cdn female cyclist to earn the title. Her other wins include gold at the Commonwealth Games in 1994 and 1998, and at the Pan-Am Games in 1995. The 1999 Pan-Am Games in Winnipeg saw her win 2 gold medals in front of a home crowd. She placed 8th at the 1996 Atlanta Olympics, and 7th at the 2000 Sydney Olympics, after which she retired from competitive cycling. ● MD

DUBOIS, Theodore, rower (b May 19, 1911, Brussels, Belgium) is an icon in **Winnipeg's Rowing** community. Dubois started rowing as a teenager at the Winnipeg Rowing Club. He won 4 gold medals at the 1934 Northwestern International Rowing Association Regatta, and went on to win the competition's singles event 5 times. In 1939, Dubois captured the singles and, with partner Ab Riley, senior doubles titles at the Royal Canadian Henley Regatta. Though he twice qualified for the Olympics, Dubois never got the chance to compete; the 1940 summer Olympics were cancelled because of WWII, and though Dubois again qualified in 1948, Cdn Olympic officials felt that Dubois, at age 37, was too old to compete, though his race time was faster than the eventual

winner in the Olympic singles event. Dubois was awarded the Lou Marsh Trophy as Canada's athlete of the year in 1941. He became a coach at the Winnipeg Canoe Club in 1950, and was made honorary president in 1978. ● MD

Sir Joseph Dubuc, ca 1910

DUBUC, Sir Joseph, journalist, politician (b Dec 26, 1840, Sainte-Martine, Lower Canada [QC]; d Jan 7, 1914, St. Boniface) was an advocate for the rights of **Roman Catholic** Francophones. He worked in the US before attending Montreal College, where he met **Louis Riel**, and McGill U. Shortly after his graduation from McGill in 1869, he was called to the bar and came to the **Red River Settlement**, joining Riel's Provisional Government and engaging in journalism. He sat in the first MB **Legislature** for St. Norbert, and subsequently served briefly as Attorney General and as Speaker. He was appointed to the Council of the NWTs in 1872. He served as one of the defence counsel in the trial of **Ambroise Lépine** in 1873-74. In 1878, he was elected as a Conservative from Provencher to the House of Commons. A year later, he was appointed to the Court of Queen's Bench, becoming chief justice in 1903 and retiring in 1909. He suffered heavy financial losses from land speculation after 1880. In 1912, he became the first French Canadian from western Canada to be knighted. ● JMB

DUCHARME, Theresa, activist (b March 10, 1945, **Winnipeg**; d June 7, 2004, Winnipeg) was an outspoken advocate for the equal participation of those living with disabilities. Polio left Ducharme

confined to a wheelchair and forced to rely on a ventilator. Concerned that her husband, transit driver Clifford Ducharme, would have to quit his full-time job in order to take care of her, Ducharme's first political battle was to champion for homecare. In 1981, Ducharme became the first person requiring a life-support system to fly as a regular passenger on a Cdn commercial airplane. She was also one of the first ventilator-dependent people to live outside of a hospital. Ducharme was a frequent visitor to Winnipeg's city hall, often staging colourful one-woman protests. She once showed up with a paper chimney on her head in support of a total smoking ban. She also ran for mayor in 2002, but ill health forced her to drop out of the race. She founded People in Equal Participation (PEP) in 1981, an organization that aimed to improve the quality of life for the severely disabled by making it possible for them to leave institutions and live independently in their communities. Ducharme's core activist activity was to oppose assisted suicide. She spoke out on behalf of Tracy Lynn Latimer, whose father euthanized her in 1993. Ducharme used the Latimer case as a platform to express her belief that ability or disability should not affect the value of a life. She pleaded with politicians not to make it easier for the disabled to end their lives, but rather to make it easier for them to live their lives. Ducharme also championed wheelchair accessibility, public transit services for the disabled, and

Theresa Ducharme was known for dramatic demonstrations in favour of equal access.

public education on the topic of those living with physical disabilities. For her efforts, Ducharme earned the praise of the late Pope John Paul II. Ducharme's self-published autobiography, *Life and Breath: A Love Story*, includes a preface by **LLOYD AXWORTHY**. ● JILL SEXSMITH

DUCK. *See* **WATERFOWL.**

DUCK MOUNTAIN PROVINCIAL PARK, 60 km NW of **DAUPHIN**, is a 1424 km² **PROVINCIAL PARK** made up of forests, wetlands, and valleys along the **MANITOBA ESCARPMENT**. The highest point in MB, treeless **BALDY MOUNTAIN** – which rises 831.2 m – stands in the park's SE corner. The park has few developed roads for its size, helping ensure an abundance of wildlife, including **MOOSE**, white-tailed **DEER**, black **BEAR**, lynx (*see* **CATS**), **WOLVES**, **COYOTES**, and **ELK**. There are 4 campgrounds in the park. Recreation is based around the area's clear and deep glacial **LAKES**, most notably East Blue, Childs, Wellman, and Singush. They attract scuba divers, **TROUT** fishermen, and canoeists. Other points of interest include the Tunstell cabin site, Shining Stone Self-guiding Trail, and Wapiti Self-guiding Trail. (The English word *wapiti* derives from the Cree for "elk," and refers to the animal's whitish hindquarters). The park's extensive network of trails is used for hiking, horseback riding, and cross-country **SKIING**. The park, which was designated in 1961, is nicknamed "The Ducks." Assiniboine, **OJIBWAY**, and **CREE** peoples hunted in the area, and it became important in the **FUR TRADE** following the construction of nearby Fort Dauphin. The govt classifies Duck Mountain as a "natural" provincial park, and about 60% of its lands are open to resource development, primarily logging. In Aug 2003, Manitoba Parks released an updated draft management plan for the area, and cottage development continued under the terms of a lot-draw program in the early 21st century. ● JT

Oak Hammock Marsh Interpretive Centre with marsh in background

DUCKS UNLIMITED CANADA (DUC) is a private, non-profit, charitable organization that conserves, restores and manages wetlands and associated habitats for NA waterfowl. These habitats also benefit other wildlife and people. The organization is active in every province and territory. Since its inception in 1938 – the year DUC established its first conservation project at Big Grass Marsh near Gladstone – DUC has completed over 1100 habitat-conservation projects in MB. An active research program across NA guides habitat programs. DUC employs scientists, biologists, agrologists, engineers, and technical staff specialized in the conservation of wetlands and associated habitats. It also partners with other non-profit organizations, all levels of government, landowners, and industry to help reach its conservation goals. MB is home to DUC's national headquarters, located at the **OAK HAMMOCK MARSH** Conservation Centre, E of Stonewall. Nestled at the W edge of the restored wetland, the Conservation Centre also houses the Oak Hammock Marsh Interpretive Centre, jointly managed by DUC and the province of MB. DUC's MB field office is located in the Riverbank Discovery Centre in **BRANDON**, and operates an office in **THE PAS**, where staff oversees wetland-conservation projects in the boreal forest and Saskatchewan River Delta regions. ● LP

West Blue Lake in Duck Mountain

Henry Duckworth

DUCKWORTH, Henry Edmison "Harry," physicist, educator, administrator (b Nov 1, 1915, **Brandon**). After spending his youth in **Rivers** and **Winnipeg**, Duckworth began his studies at the **U of M**, but switched to Wesley College (*see* **U of W**) in 1932. He graduated with a BA (1935) and BSc (1936) and became a schoolteacher in **Stonewall**. In 1938, Wesley College hired Duckworth as a physics lecturer, despite his **English**, Latin and mathematics background. He excelled in the field, and went on to complete a PhD at the U of Chicago in 1942. He worked for the Cdn federal govt during WWII. Following the war, Duckworth was hired by McMaster U, eventually becoming an internationally recognized nuclear physicist – a mass spectroscopy expert responsible for discovering platinum as a stable isotope.

Duckworth became vice president at the U of M in 1965, and oversaw academic programs there until he was chosen as president of the U of W in 1971. He expanded the school's programming and property, and was responsible for acquiring the school's 25 ton centennial rock and beginning the traditional Great Rock Climb. In 1981, Duckworth left the U of W and took up a position as professor emeritus

at the U of M. From 1986-92, he served as the university's chancellor. He created the university sports Duckworth Challenge in 1992, and the U of W's athletic centre bears his name. Duckworth has written a number of books, including the first textbook on mass spectroscopy, and his 2000 memoirs, *One Version of the Facts: My Life in the Ivory Tower*. He has been awarded 10 honorary doctorates, the Order of the Buffalo Hunt (1992) (see **Order of Manitoba**), and the Order of Canada (1976). Duckworth remains on the board of directors of the **Wawanesa Mutual Insurance Company** and the U of W Foundation.

Duckworth's son Henry William, also "Harry," is a McMaster U and Yale U-educated chemist who has taught at the U of M since 1972. His research interests include enzymes, proteins, genetics, and DNA-protein interactions. He is also a historian with an interest in the fur trade.
● JOEL TRENAMAN

DUGALD, pop 800, is an unincorporated community 20 km E of **Winnipeg**, on the **CN** main line in the RM of Springfield. The post office opened here in 1879 when the community was known as Sunnyside. The post office and community were renamed in 1892 after settler, storekeeper, and postmaster Dugald Gillespie. Dugald's economy is based on grain and dairy farming. Its location makes it a bedroom community for Winnipeg. Dugald made national headlines when the worst train crash in western Cdn history took place here on Sept 1, 1947. A passenger train with older equipment, on its way back to Winnipeg from the resort of Minaki, ON, collided with a Transcontinental passenger train. The crash killed 37. Dugald was the long-time home to the **Costume Museum of Canada**, which moved to Winnipeg in 2007. ● GPP

DUGUID, Don, curler (b Feb 25, 1935, **Winnipeg**). Duguid, one of the sport's most accurate hitters, won consecutive world titles in 1970 and 1971. Duguid started curling at the age of 9 at Winnipeg's Victoria Curling Club, where his father was the icemaker. He became seriously interested in the sport as a teenager, in part because his small stature prevented him from pursuing contact sports like hockey. He curled with **Howard "Pappy" Wood Sr.** as part of the Granite Club team, and in 1957 played 2nd on the team of Howard Wood, Jr. which placed 3rd at the at the Brier. He first skipped his own team in 1962-63, winning the 1963 Grand Aggregate at that year's Manitoba Curling Association Bonspiel, and again in 1969 and 1970. He had planned to take time off from competitive curling in 1969, but was coaxed into filling in as skip on the team of Rod Hunter, Jim Pettapiece, and Bryan Wood. Though they had little time to train together, Duguid's team dominated in 1970, winning the club championship at the Granite Curling Club, the Winnipeg City Playdowns, the Manitoba Consols, and the Canadian Brier. The team went on to win that year's Henry Birks Trophy, the CBC Curling Series, and the Crystal Trophy. Representing Canada in the Silver Broom Championship, the Duguid team defeated Scotland to claim the world title after an 8 game winning streak. The team had similar success in 1971, winning all of the same titles, with the exception of the CBC Series and the Crystal Trophy, from which they were absent. At that year's Silver Broom, the team bested their previous performance by going 9 games undefeated, and again triumphing over Scotland. The record of 17 consecutive Silver Broom wins remains unbroken. Duguid was inducted into the Canadian Curling Hall of Fame in 1974, and he is one of

The Dugald train wreck killed 37 cottagers in 1947.

only 6 curlers honoured in the Canadian Sports Hall of Fame. Following his retirement from competitive curling, Duguid became a curling commentator for the CBC. ● MD

DUHKS, The. This eclectic bluegrass/roots music group formed in **WINNIPEG** in 2001, with banjo/fiddle player Leonard Podolak (son of **WINNIPEG FOLK FESTIVAL** founder **MITCH PODOLAK**), singer Jessica Havey, Vancouver fiddle prodigy Tania Elizabeth, guitarist Jordan McConnell, and percussionist Scott Senior, after Podolak folded his previous group, Scruj MacDuhk. Scruj had recorded 2 albums, *Live at the West End* (1997) and *Road to Canso* (1999; winner of 2 Prairie Music Awards). The Duhks' debut album, *Your Daughters and Your Sons* (2003), was released independently with assistance from Manitoba Film and Sound, and led to the group signing with US roots specialists Sugar Hill Records, and with powerful management company Creative Artist Agencies, in 2005. *The Duhks* (2005), produced by bluegrass legend Bela Fleck, was released to positive reviews across Canada and the US, and a Juno Award for Best Roots and Traditional Album of the Year: Group (2006). The group won a Grammy Award in 2004 for Best Traditional Folk Album for their contributions to *Beautiful Dreamer: The Songs of Stephen Foster*, and were nominated again in 2006 for the song *Heaven's My Home*. As of writing, the group has attempted to focus more on US and overseas markets, and toured NA, Australia, and Europe extensively, releasing *Migrations* in 2006. ● JOHN EINARSON

DUKES, Caroline, artist, painter, (b May 19, 1929, Ujpest, Hungary; d June 8, 2003, **WINNIPEG**) is known for her extensive body of work initially influenced by her experiences during the Holocaust and as a resident of communist Hungary. She began her art education in Budapest at the Academy of Fine Arts (1951), but bristled at the constraints of her expression under the communist region. Dukes emigrated to Toronto from Hungary in 1958 and moved to **WINNIPEG** in 1967. She continued her art training at the School of Art at the **U OF M** from 1968-72 and then began a career that would span 30 years. Her paintings are organized into series dealing with nature landscapes, interiors, nudes and architecture. *At the Focus of Forces Series* (1989) revolved around scenes of Jerusalem, peeling back layers of civilization. *Remember…Relate…Retell* (1992) is Dukes' most personal work, and recalls her family's Holocaust experience through a multimedia work that includes drawings, photographs, text, ready-made objects, video, and audio. In 1993, Dukes and fellow Hungarian-

born artist **EVA STUBBS** returned to Budapest for an exhibition. Dukes has otherwise exhibited across Canada, the US, Munich, and Jerusalem. In Winnipeg, she has shown at the **U OF W**, the U of M, the **WINNIPEG ART GALLERY**, and at the legislative building. She was always involved in the Winnipeg artistic community; in 1995, she became a founding member of Site Gallery. As a tribute to her significant role as an artist and her contributions to the Winnipeg art scene, **MENTORING ARTISTS FOR WOMEN'S ART** developed the Caroline Dukes Legacy Fund after her death. ● AMANDA STEPHENS

As Lieutenant Governor, Yvon Dumont (right) presided over many formal events.

WINNIPEG FREE PRESS

DUMONT, W. Yvon, politician (b Jan 21, 1951, **ST. LAURENT**). The first **MÉTIS** lt gov of MB, Dumont began a long career in Aboriginal organizations in 1967 when he became involved with his local branch of the **MANITOBA MÉTIS FEDERATION** (MMF). He was first elected as an MMF board representative for the **INTERLAKE** in 1972, and then as exec vice-president in 1973. During those 2 years, he also co-founded the Native Council of Canada (which became the Congress of Aboriginal Peoples in 1994). Dumont went on to become MMF president, serving 4 terms between 1984 and 1993. At the national level, he was president of the Métis National Council from 1988-1993, a position that allowed him to advocate for Métis rights during constitutional reform debates and to press for the recognition of **LOUIS RIEL**. His profile led to his appointment in 1993 as MB's 21st lt gov, a role he fulfilled until 1999. Dumont

returned to the Métis National Council as a governor until early 2003, when he resigned in order to run again for MMF president. After losing to incumbent David Chartrand by 20 votes, Dumont filed suit against Chartrand and election Chief Electoral Officer Justice **A.C. HAMILTON**, alleging improper conduct. The MB Court of Appeal eventually ruled against Dumont in Oct 2004, and the election results stood. Dumont again challenged for the presidency in June 2006, with Chartrand winning his 4th consecutive term. Dumont has also been a councillor for the RM of St. Laurent, a small business operator, and a member of the **U OF M** board of governors. He was recognized with a National Aboriginal Achievement Award and an honorary doctorate from the U of M in 1996, as well as invested with the **ORDER OF MANITOBA** in 2001. ● JT

DUNCAN, Chester, teacher, pianist, composer, (b Strasbourg, SK, May 4, 1913; d **WINNIPEG** Mar 31, 2002). Duncan studied piano privately in Winnipeg, then studied literature at the **U OF M** and the U of Toronto. He developed his parallel interests, music and literature, throughout his life, regularly combining them. He taught in the U of M's department of English for 45 years, becoming professor emeritus upon retirement. Duncan developed a national reputation as a CBC radio commentator. He performed most often as a chamber musician, also as a duo-recitalist and soloist. With the CBC Winnipeg Orchestra he performed the North American premieres of George Dyson's *Concerto Leggiero* and Gordon Jacob's *Concerto No. 2*. As a composer he focused on song, creating some 200 settings of primarily British and Cdn poets. Other compositions included incidental music for W. H. Auden's plays *The Ascent of F6*, and *For the Time Being*, the latter expanded into a 2-hour oratorio-style form. He contributed articles to several magazines and journals, and wrote program notes for the WSO. He published a book of essays, *Wanna Fight, Kid?* in 1975. A CD featuring 24 of his songs (Cana 001) was released shortly after his death. ● DON ANDERSON

DUNNOTTAR, pop 487, is a community on the SW shore of **LAKE WINNIPEG**, 65 km N of Winnipeg. The village was named after Dunnottar Pt on Lake Winnipeg. The village was incorporated to include the beaches of Matlock, Whytewold, and Ponemah. Beautiful lakeside beaches make Dunnottar a popular destination for cottage owners and tourists in the summer. The economic base of the village is tourism and some commercial fishing. Dunnottar's population swells in the summer months. ● GPP

Durbin, Edna Mae "Deanna," "WINNIPEG'S Sweetheart," was born in the city in 1921, though her family moved to Los Angeles only a year later. An aspiring opera singer, she made an impressive acting debut in MGM's *Every Sunday* (1936) alongside Judy Garland. Durbin was snapped up by Universal Studios and became known for her sweet soprano and charming looks. *Three Smart Girls* (1936) and *One Hundred Men and a Girl* (1937) vaulted her to child stardom, and her films continued to enjoy immense popularity, making her the highest-paid actress in the world well into the 1940s. Never comfortable with her iconic status, in 1950 she married director Charles David and though not yet 30, retreated from the Hollywood spotlight for good. ●

DURKIN, Douglas Leader, novelist, educator (b July 9, 1884, Parry Sound, ON; d June 4, 1967, Seattle). Though born in ON, Durkin moved to the MINITONAS area with his METHODIST family while young, and his father attempted to open a cheese factory there in 1903. Durkin graduated from school in SWAN RIVER and worked numerous odd jobs before being educated, initially as a missionary, at Wesley College (*see* U OF W). He worked for the YMCA in Spokane, WA, and served as a minister in the NORTH region, but soon found he was unsuited to religious life. He taught in CARMAN and at Brandon College (*see* BRANDON U). In 1915, the married Durkin began teaching English at Wesley College, where he fell in love with his young student, MARTHA OSTENSO. Durkin took a position in New York at Columbia U in 1922.

Ostenso followed him and, living and working together, the pair collaborated on several successful novels, most notably *Wild Geese* (1925), which, though published solely under Ostenso's name, is now regarded as being co-authored by Durkin. The couple became well known in local artistic circles, and Durkin's friends included US playwright Eugene O'Neill. The pair built a summer home in Brainerd, MN in the 1930s, spending summers there while wintering in Los Angeles, where they wrote screenplays and partied with the rich and famous. The couple spent their last years in Seattle. Durkin wrote several other novels set in MB, based on his diverse work experience: *The Heart of Cherry McBain* (1919), *The Lobstick Trail: A Romance of Northern Manitoba* (1921), and *The Magpie* (1923). These novels signalled an end to escapist Prairie fiction and the beginning of a gritty portrayal of Manitoban individualism. ● A.J. LEVIN

DUTCH immigrants have been attracted to NA since the 17th century but did not come to western Canada in significant numbers until the late 1800s. When cheap land was no longer available in the US, many immigrants set their sights on the Cdn Prairies. The first significant group of Dutch settlers arrived in MB in 1893. Their voyage was underwritten by one of the religious emigration societies in the Netherlands. These organizations believed that the unemployment and poverty in the Dutch countryside could be alleviated through emigration. An additional incentive was provided by the aggressive recruiting policies of the Cdn govt.

Many Dutch settlers found homesteading difficult and so gravitated to the WINNIPEG area. Here they established themselves as vegetable peddlers and market gardeners in Elmwood and East Kildonan. The street names De Jong Cres, Degraff Place, and de Vries Ave in Winnipeg commemorate some these early market gardeners and their contributions to the community. Artist LEO MOL has further honoured the contributions of these early settlers in his sculpture *De Zaaier/The Sower*, which celebrates the centennial of their arrival. By 1911, MB had Canada's highest population of people of Dutch origin outside AB.

By the early 20th century, the population was substantial enough to allow for the establishment of Dutch Reformed churches in several MB communities. The church functioned not only as a centre of faith, but also as a nexus for youth clubs, social organizations, and a source of financial support. Although reliance on the church

A sculpture by Leo Mol honours the arrival of Dutch immigrants in Manitoba.

D

lessened as the Dutch population integrated into Cdn society, its presence was important both for encouraging immigration and for helping Dutch settlers adjust to life in Canada.

During the GREAT DEPRESSION and WWII, immigration restrictions prevented community growth, but interest in Canada was renewed in the post-war years when economic depression and destruction caused by WWII encouraged many Dutch people to seek their fortune elsewhere. The years following the end of the war saw the largest migration of Dutch people to Canada, whose Army had liberated much of the Netherlands in 1945 and whose govt provided a haven for the Dutch royal family 1940-45. Many met up with relatives who had settled in previous years; others made their own way. In these years, many of the migrants were skilled workers or professionals who were attracted to ON, rather than MB, which was perceived as an agricultural province.

Although a significant number of Manitobans identify themselves as Dutch, many identifying factors of ethnic identity – such as language, traditions, and organizations – have all but disappeared. The Dutch Calvinist church and its affiliated organizations remain the most visible reminders of Dutch ethnicity in MB, but cultural groups, ethnic food stores, and place names still exist as subtle markers of this group. According to the 2001 Census, 51,350 Manitobans identify themselves as being of Dutch origin (single and multiple responses), making it the 11th-largest ethnic group in the province. ● CATHARINA DE BAKKER

DUTTON, Mervyn "Red," hockey player, NHL president (b July 23, 1898, RUSSELL; d March 15, 1987, Calgary) Dutton is the only Manitoban to have served as NHL president. From an affluent family, he attended St. John's College School, but left early to join the PRINCESS PATRICIA'S LIGHT INFANTRY during WWI. After being blasted by shrapnel through his right leg and hip, doctors thought they would have to amputate his limb. Dutton stubbornly refused, and made a full recovery upon his discharge in 1919, regaining the strength in his leg by playing in 7 WINNIPEG hockey leagues in the following year. After a failed attempt to establish himself in business in Winnipeg, Dutton turned to professional hockey. He signed a contract with the Calgary Tigers in the Big Four Hockey League, and then played for the Montreal Maroons. A tough defenceman, Dutton held the most penalty minutes in the league in 1929 and 1932. In 1930, he signed with the New York Americans, a team often considered secondary to the popular New York Rangers. Dutton was regardless a devoted Americans supporter, often helping out financially as the team suffered through the Depression. A solid and consistent player, he played for 6 seasons, and then took over as coach until the team folded in 1942.

Dutton was made NHL president following the sudden death Frank Calder in 1943. He served until 1946, resigning after the NHL reneged on a deal they had made to allow Dutton to re-establish the Americans franchise. It is around this time that Dutton is supposed to have uttered what became known to Rangers fans as "The Curse," stating that the Rangers would never win another game in his lifetime. Oddly enough, they didn't. Dutton then moved to AB, where he became a successful contractor. He was inducted into the Hockey Hall of Fame in 1958, and was posthumously awarded the Lester Patrick Trophy in 1993. He is also a member of the Order of Canada, and the hockey arena at his alma mater St. John's-Ravenscourt is named in his honour. ● MD

DYCK, Aganetha, multimedia artist (b Sept 12, 1937, WINNIPEG), began her artistic career in 1976 with a mentorship in Prince Albert, SK, under George Glenn and master weaver Margaret Van Walsem. She also had her first group showing there. Dyck attended both Prince Albert Community College and the U OF W, where she took art classes and art history courses in the late 1970s and early '80s. She began to exhibit regularly in venues across the Prairies, including the WINNIPEG ART GALLERY (WAG) and the Banff Centre for the Arts, in the mid-1980s. Dyck also became involved with artistic organizations across Canada by sitting on several boards of directors, volunteering for mentorship programs, and delivering public lectures. Dyck's early work approached images and materials of domesticity, such as buttons, clothing, canning, and busywork.

In the early 1990s, she moved into wax-encased sculptures and drawings that exhibited her interest in bees and which examined interspecies communication. Her research with bees has seen her work with apiculturists and biologists from across Canada. These delicate works exhibited in numerous shows across the world, and in a touring exhibition commissioned by the WAG in 1995-97. The National Gallery of Canada in Ottawa acquired her work *The Extended Wedding Party*. Her work also is in the Canada Council Art Bank, Passage, France's Centre d'art contemporain, and private collections. ● STACEY ABRAMSON

DZAMA, Marcel, multimedia artist (b May 4, 1974, WINNIPEG), is among the most successful Manitoban artists in recent years. He received a BFA with top honours in 1997 from the U OF M. While in art school, Dzama and classmates Michael Dumontier and Neil Farber formed the artistic collective Royal Art Lodge. Exhibiting in strange venues, their crude style of drawings brought them success even before they graduated, garnering them a show a New York's hip Drawing Center Gallery a mere 2 years after graduating. Plug In ICA's then-curator Wayne Barewald showed a keen interest in Dzama's signature style of morbid, root-beer-coloured cartoons, and offered him his first solo show at the gallery. Dzama's debut appearance in the US came at the Richard Heller Gallery in Los Angeles in 1998. When celebrities such as comedian Jim Carrey and author Dave Eggers praised Dzama, Marcel's works began to sell, and he had numerous solo shows in galleries in locales such as the US, Italy, Brazil, the UK, and Sweden. He currently resides in New York, where the Richard Heller Gallery represents him. ● STACEY ABRAMSON

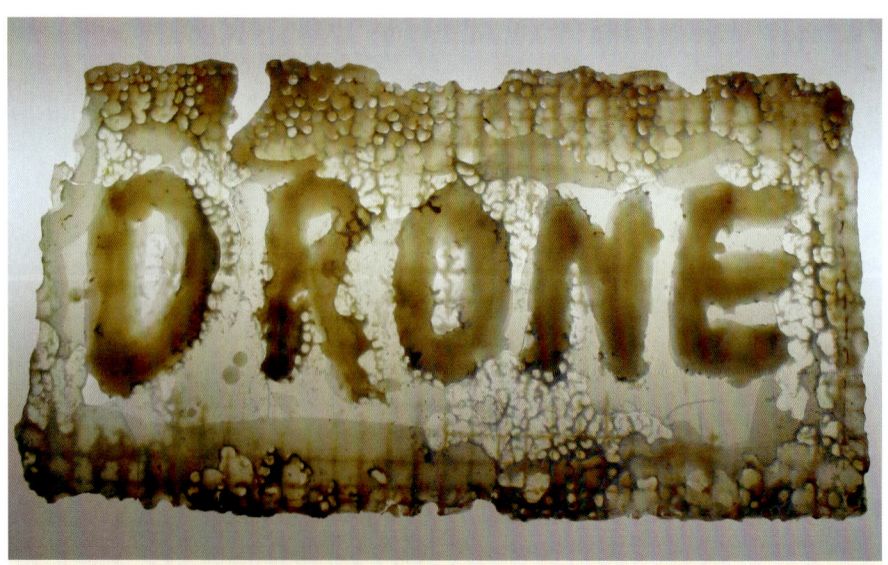

Profession, beeswax, 2006, 23 x 41 cm

EATON'S,
see page 181

E

EAGLE (family Accipitridae) forms part of a large group of raptors (birds of prey) that also include **Hawks** and harriers. Only 2 species occur in MB, of which the Bald Eagle (*Haliaeetus leucocephalus*) is the most widespread and best known. Adults, with their white heads and tails, are particularly striking, but even the brown young birds are majestic. Although the Bald Eagle is the national symbol of the US, it became almost extirpated in the mid-20th century due to the use of DDT and other highly toxic agricultural compounds. Fortunately, numbers have rebounded, and MB is home to a healthy breeding population, especially in areas near water. The Golden Eagle (*Aquila chrysaetos*) primarily occurs in open parts of Eurasia and the W of the US, and, in Canada, in BC, AB, and W SK, but a few are seen annually in MB on spring migration in late March and early April, and occasionally at other times of the year. ● RUDOLF KOES

EAKIN, William, photographer (b Aug 16, 1952, **Winnipeg**) was educated at the Vancouver School of Art and at the School of the Museum of Fine Arts in Boston, MA, completing his training as a photographer in 1974. Influenced by Andy Warhol's work, Eakin photographs pop objects and recontextualizes the everyday. He is an enthusiastic collector of society's cast-offs and photos such as

WILLIAM EAKIN

Night Garden, 2000, pigment ink jet print
on paper, by William Eakin

"Night Garden," a coloured photograph of painted flowers on a cookie tin from a thrift store, is characteristic and makes up part of one of his well-known exhibits, *William Eakin: The Visible World*. His photos can be found in many public collections including the Canadian Museum of Contemporary **Photography**, the Canada Council Art Bank, the **Winnipeg Art Gallery** and the Edmonton Art Gallery. Exhibitions of his work have taken place across Canada, in the US, the Netherlands, France, Japan and Taiwan. He has taught at the Dept of Visual Arts at the U of Victoria and the School of Art at the **U of M**. ● RUTH DEGRAVES

EARTHWORM is a soil- or aquatic-dwelling, segmented worm with species ranging in size from microscopic to 3.6 m. There are over 3200 species worldwide. The repeated movement of glaciers across MB destroyed all species of earthworms, and those species occurring here now have all been introduced from Europe or re-invaded from the US. Over 150 aquatic species have been recorded in Canada, and 18 terrestrial ones, all but one introduced. The most common of these exotics (especially in **WINNIPEG**) is the Night-crawler (*Lumbricus terrestris*), popular as fishing bait. This 8-14 cm worm arrived during European settlement. Earthworms feed by passing mud or earth through their tubular gut and extracting nutrients. Their burrowing activities turn over, enrich and aerate the soil, and improve its drainage – all-important functions which benefit plant growth. It is estimated that these worms move 20 tonnes/ha of plant material underground. Their passageways are used by many other kinds of soil organisms. A worm pushes its way through the soil by means of alternating contractions of muscles that encircle and run along the length of the body. Lacking eyes and ears, it is still sensitive to light and can detect vibrations of an approaching predator through the soil. These worms have both male and female sex organs (hermaphrodites), but most still mate to exchange sperm cells, while united by a band called the clitellum. The fertilized eggs are deposited in a mucous cocoon from which soon emerge tiny young (no larval stage). Earthworms breathe through the slimy skin, and quickly dry out if stranded above ground on a hot sunny day. Why they come out in such numbers after a rainy night is not clear, but they appear to dislike sitting in their water-logged tunnels. Many native species of animals appear to relish earthworms, and some like the American Robin, spend much effort hunting them down.

There are about 5 families of freshwater earthworms in MB, but the number of species is unknown. A total of 19 marine species has been identified in **HUDSON BAY**, with likely many more to be added. Most live in the mud and debris on the bottom and in filamentous algae, and range from 1-30 mm in size. The delicate body wall is so thin that the internal organs can be seen. Dissolved oxygen and waste carbon dioxide simply diffuse through the skin; some species also have gills. Minute bristles distributed on the body segments help the worms crawl through the slippery media, and happen to be a useful diagnostic feature. The feeding technique is similar to land forms, with algae, diatoms and organic debris providing nutrients. While all these worms are hermaphrodites, they can also reproduce by budding or by fragmenting into pieces with subsequent regeneration into several worms. Surely such reproductive strategies and abilities are a major reason why oligochaete worms are so successful. They are devoured in prodigious numbers by countless species (from insects to fish and aquatic birds) and help turn over and recycle nutrients in the sediments of freshwater and marine ecosystems. ● REW

EARWIG is an insect of the order Dermaptera, characterized by an elongated and flattened body (4-80 mm), chewing mouthparts, highly segmented antennae (sensitive to smell and touch), and a pair of forceps at the end of the abdomen (more curved and toothed in the male). The forceps are used in courting, grooming, to fold the wings, and as a defensive pinching mechanism. The legs are adapted for running. Earwigs have 2 pairs of wings – the outer leathery pair protects the delicate flying wings, although the insect seldom takes flight. Two species have been reported in MB, both exotics. The black, 7 mm *Labia minor* is a nocturnal scavenger living in the soil and leaf litter. It was introduced into NA over a century ago and has succeeded in invading southern MB. It hibernates as an adult underground or in heated buildings. The second species is the 30 mm European Earwig (*Forficula auricularia*), which is common in southern ON but rare in MB, where it is too cold for it flourish. Earwigs are omnivorous and may be observed at night crawling on plants and flowers, which they may damage by chewing. Most of the time they remain hidden under stones, bark, and even damp cellars, although they are occasionally attracted to lights at night. The mated female lays 30-50 eggs in a nest in the soil and remains nearby to guard her eggs and the nymphs as they hatch. She licks them to keep them free of fungi and brings them food. An odd myth is that this insect can crawl into one's ear (hence the name) while sleeping and bore into the brain, causing great pain and eventual death. ● REW

EASTERVILLE, pop 80, is a community near Cedar Lake, 125 km SE of **THE PAS**. The community and the **CHEMAWAWIN FIRST NATION** were relocated here in 1962-63 from Old Post due to flooding caused by the **GRAND RAPIDS** power project. The name Easterville was adopted in 1964 to honour Donald Easter, long-time chief of the Chemawawin Band. Before the move, fishing, hunting, and trapping allowed the population to be self-sufficient. The move to Easterville was considered by residents and elders to have eroded traditional ways of life, and the relocation created social and economic problems, including depopulation. A financial settlement was reached with **MANITOBA HYDRO** in 1990. Currently, commercial fishing on Cedar Lake is the primary industry. The post office opened in 1965. ● GPP

EASTMAN is a provincial region encompassing 17 rural municipalities in the SE corner of the province, directly E of **WINNIPEG**. One of 8 designated regions, it extends N to an arbitrary line marking the S end of **LAKE WINNIPEG**, E to the ON boundary, and S to the US border. The area has a wide range of **PHYSIOGRAPHIC REGIONS**. The rocky edge of the Precambrian Shield dominates the East, adjacent to the MB-ON border. Sandilands and Agassiz **PROVINCIAL FORESTS**, and **WHITESHELL PROVINCIAL PARK**, are the most significant wooded areas, and are popular for tourism and recreation. The flat farmland of the **RED RIVER** Basin dominates the S and W sections of Eastman. Between the Shield and the parkland is a transitional region, in which the physical geography, **TREES**, and fauna of both regions overlap.

The area was home primarily to **OJIBWAY**, but probably also to Siouan peoples, before **FRENCH** coureurs des bois came here in the 18th century following the **WINNIPEG RIVER**. The river had been a primary canoe route for First Nations for thousands of years, and when Europeans arrived, they helped make it an important transportation outlet for the **FUR TRADE**. The Seine, Whitemouth, and Brokenhead rivers are other major regional waterways. The Dawson Trail from Lake Superior to the **RED RIVER SETTLEMENT**, built in 1868, crossed the district, as did the La Vérendrye and Crow Wing trails. All 3 helped open the area to **IMMIGRATION** by Europeans. These early settlers engaged in **FORESTRY** as well as **AGRICULTURE**, and

RURAL MUNICIPALITIES in Eastman

Alexander
Brokenhead
De Salaberry
Franklin
Hanover
La Broquerie
Lac du Bonnet
Pinawa (Local Government District)
Piney
Reynolds
Ritchot
Springfield
Ste. Anne
Stuartburn
Taché
Victoria Beach
Whitemouth

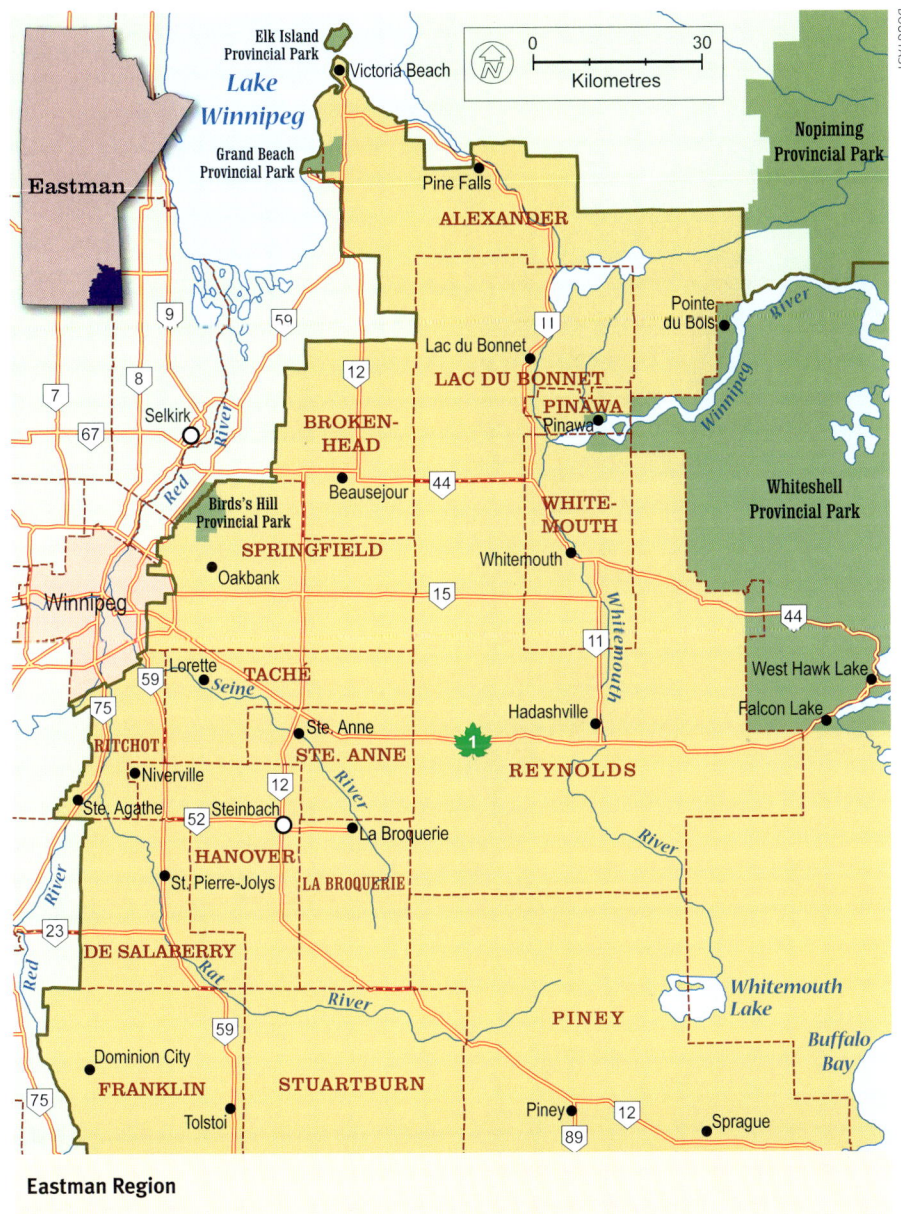

Eastman Region

DOUG FAST

quality products with superlative service at reasonable prices. In the process of making customer satisfaction its top priority, Eaton's provided employment for thousands of Manitobans.

EARLY YEARS: Eaton's Portage Ave store – at the time the largest building in Winnipeg – opened for business on July 17, 1905. Local newspapers estimated that 50,000 shoppers and browsers passed through its doors that day, even though the population of Winnipeg was only 78,000. Immediate plans were made to build additions, and more employees were hired. The 2.3 ha (5.5 ac), 5 storey redbrick department store and mail order service occupied the entire S side of Portage Ave between Hargrave and Donald streets. This was only the second Cdn outlet – the first was in Toronto – for the family-owned company that would eventually operate a chain of department stores across Canada.

Generations of bargain wise Manitobans looked forward to Eaton's sales events, such as Birthday Sales and Trans-Canada Sales. Customers' faith in the integrity of Eaton's was reinforced by the innovative Eaton Guarantee of "Goods Satisfactory or Money Refunded," which provided assurance that refunds or exchanges would be given virtually without question. The store became a destination for Manitobans regardless of whether they planned to shop there. The imposing bronze statue of the company's founder, Timothy Eaton, on the main floor was a traditional downtown meeting place for decades. Eaton's displays were a source of countless hours of free entertainment. The store was renowned for its almost-constantly changing windows along Portage, Donald, and Hargrave. Inside, displays within departments, fashion shows, MB Curling Bonspiel Fairs, and special events in the spacious assembly hall attracted millions of visitors over the decades. During Christmas seasons, Eaton's Toyland and its Santa Clauses were visited by millions of children. Extravagant annual Santa Claus Parades and magical Portage Ave display windows were essential ingredients of Christmas for generations of youngsters and their parents.

The downtown store housed numerous restaurants, and the elegant Grill Room, with its oak-panelled walls and wrought-iron chandeliers, provided many Manitobans with their first taste of genteel dining at reasonable prices. For others, the bustling Valley Room cafeteria offered respite during shopping expeditions. Among the foods associated with Eaton's of Winnipeg were chicken pot pies, toasted asparagus and cheese rolls, and red velvet cake. Eaton's was famous for its reliable and free home delivery service. Distinctive blue, red, and white trucks (or, in earlier years, delivery wagons pulled by sleek, athletic

NIVERVILLE became home to the first grain elevator in western Canada in 1878.

The largest settlements by population are **STEINBACH**, **LORETTE**, Landmark, **BEAUSEJOUR**, and Niverville. Population around Winnipeg consists primarily of bedroom communities. Eastman is known for its pockets of French (**STE. ANNE**, **ST-PIERRE-JOLYS**, **LA BROQUERIE**) and **MENNONITE** (Steinbach, Niverville) settlement. The RMs around Steinbach registered some of the biggest growth in the province from 2001-06. Hanover was the second fastest growing municipality in MB, swelling 42.9% to a population of 11,871. La Broquerie, on the other side of Steinbach, grew by 26%. As of the 1996 Census, a high number of residents (34%) had **GERMAN** – often meaning Mennonite – or French (22%) backgrounds. In fact, 15% of people identified German as their mother tongue, just ahead of French (12%). Some of these

Francophones are **MÉTIS**; local First Nations communities include **BUFFALO POINT**, Reed River, Northwest Angle, and Shoal Lake.

Manufacturing, **HYDROELECTRIC** power, **TOURISM**, transportation, retail, and agricultural industries predominate in Eastman. **LOEWEN WINDOWS** in Steinbach is the single largest employer. ● JOEL TRENAMAN

EATON'S achieved remarkable levels of commercial success in MB for most of the 20th century. The Timothy Eaton Co. and the people of MB established a unique relationship of mutual loyalty that saw generations of families make virtually all their retail purchases from Eaton's flagship **WINNIPEG** department store and mail order service. Estimates of the company's share of the Winnipeg market were as high as 80% because many Manitobans believed that Eaton's supplied

E

Eaton's was slowly dismantled to make room for the MTS Centre.

in the department store and another 12,000 in its mail order.

MAIL ORDER: Although rural MB residents made a point of visiting Eaton's department store if they travelled to Winnipeg, most relied on the mail order service. This aspect of the business was originally located in the company's Portage Ave department store, but it expanded to the point where by the early 1920s, a pair of 9-storey mail order buildings were erected on the S side of Graham Ave between Hargrave and Donald. The Winnipeg mail order operation served not only MB but also NW ON, SK, and AB. Catalogues printed at the company's plant on Alexander Ave offered a full range of merchandise, including clothing, appliances, furniture, hardware, agricultural needs, food, and even kits of pre-cut lumber and all of the other necessities to build a house. As telephone ordering became more prevalent, "the mail order" became known as "the catalogue," and by 1970, catalogue sales offices in 16 rural communities across MB provided a more personalized approach to shopping. Eaton's also had small department stores in communities such as **BRANDON, DAUPHIN,** and **PORTAGE LA PRAIRIE**. After catalogue sales across Canada slumped during the 1960s and '70s, the company decided to close this component of its operation in 1976. This resulted in the loss of nearly 9000 jobs, including 1600 in Winnipeg.

EXPANSION AND DECLINE: In 1968, Eaton's opened its first suburban mall outlet in Winnipeg with a 3-storey department store in the Polo Park Shopping Centre. This was followed by stores in the Garden City Shopping Centre (1976) and the St. Vital Mall (1979). A 60,000-m² warehouse – the size of more than 9 football fields – was erected at the corner of Wellington Ave and Berry St in the 1960s. By the 1980s, the downtown Eaton's share of the Winnipeg retail market had slipped considerably. Increased competition, the opening of shopping centres with free and convenient parking, and a general decline in the appeal of downtown Winnipeg contributed to an erosion of the loyalty that shoppers had previously felt for the huge Portage Ave store. Similarly, on a cross-Canada basis, the T. Eaton Co. faced severe financial difficulties as sales slipped and losses mounted. Finally, in 1999, the company went out of business. All Eaton's stores were closed, and the landmark downtown Winnipeg store was demolished to make way for the city's new arena and entertainment complex, the **MTS CENTRE**. ● RUSS GOURLUCK

EBB AND FLOW FIRST NATION, on reserve pop 1324, off reserve pop 996, is 83 km E of **DAUPHIN.** It signed Treaty 2 in 1871. The community

horses) and smartly uniformed, friendly drivers regularly confirmed the popular belief that a 5¢ spool of thread ordered by phone in the morning would be cheerfully delivered to the customer's front door that afternoon.

Many of the items sold by the T. Eaton Company were manufactured in its own factories, mostly located in ON. There were, however, some company-owned facilities in Winnipeg, including a shirt factory, a creamery, a candy

factory, an extensive bakery, and a large drug factory. The T. Eaton Co. was a major employer in MB, and in many instances 2 or 3 generations of family members worked for Eaton's. Careers of 40 or more years with the T. Eaton Co. were not unusual. The company's wide range of employee benefits inspired a high level of loyalty, although Eaton's was sometimes labelled as paternalistic and anti-union. It was estimated at one point in the 1950s that Eaton's employed 15,000 people

encompasses one reserve. It is a member of the West Region Tribal Council. The Ebb and Flow First Nation has year-round road access from **Ste. Rose du Lac**. The native language of Ebb and Flow is **Ojibway**. Education in this community, administered by Frontier School Division, runs from Nursery-Grade 12. Total enrolment for 2003-04 was 434. The economic backbone of the Ebb and Flow First Nation is agriculture. ● RK

EBOR, ghost town, 100 km W of **Brandon**, just E of the SK border. Travellers on PR 255 will easily miss the signs of the community that once flourished here. The village was founded in 1904 when pioneer Isaac Heywood opened a store. That store was followed by another, a post office, pool hall, bowling alley, and other signs of prosperity. Ebor, possibly named after the UK city of York (whose Latin name is Ebora), hosted sporting and social events. It benefited from being on the Reston-Wolseley line of the **CPR**. However, like other Prairie agricultural communities, it began to decline when increasing numbers of cars and trucks took people to larger towns. The post office closed in 1970. By 1980, all that was left of Ebor was the old school building. ● GPP

ECHINODERM is the animal group consisting of the starfish, sea urchins and sea cucumbers. They are characterized by radial symmetry – a body plan organized around a central axis, and often cylindrical; higher animals display bilateral symmetry – with 2 mirror-image sides. These are strictly marine organisms, living as adults on the sea bottom of **Hudson Bay**. Originating from the Arctic and Atlantic oceans, their distribution and abundance in MB marine waters are poorly known. They are represented here by about 39 species in 5 classes, and are found on mud, gravel and rock substrates from depths of less than 10 m down to the Bay's deepest troughs. Starfishes or class Asteroidea are represented by 17 species, sea lilies and feather stars or class Crinoidea by one species (*Heliometra glacialis*), sea urchins or class Echinoidea by only the Green Sea Urchin (*Strongylocentrotus droebachiensis*), sea cucumbers or class Holothuroidea by 6 species, and brittle stars or class Ophiuroidea by 10 species. The most abundant species in waters off MB are the Green Sea Urchin, several sea stars (*Urasterias lincki, Leptasterias polaris*, and *L. groenlandica*), and 2 sea cucumbers (*Cucumaria japonica* and *Psolus* fabricii), found from the lower intertidal zone to the depths.

These are tremendously ancient and successful marine creatures that have flourished for over 600 million years (since the Cambrian Era) in all the seas of the world, from the intertidal zone to over 6000 m deep. They live either attached on the substrate or are mobile, moving slowly on numerous tube feet (star fish) or by muscular contractions (sea cumbers). Most have protective bony plates covering the body (urchins also have spines) and some have arms (often 5). Crinoids feed by trapping plankton (algae, diatoms, protozoans) with sticky mucous, sea cucumbers extract organic matter from mud, while starfish are carnivorous – devouring crabs, mussels and carrion. Sexes are usually separate and shed the gametes (eggs and sperm) into the sea for fertilization. These develop into bizarre-shaped larvae which float and disperse in the currents. After feeding and growing in the planktonic fauna, they metamorphose and settle to the bottom, assuming a sessile life style. From egg to adult stages, echinoderms play a very important role in the food chain and are prey for countless animals from fish and sea birds to **Seals, Whales** and polar **Bears.** ● REW

ECKHARDT, Ferdinand Anton Ludwig, art historian, curator, educator, writer (b Apr 28, 1902, Vienna; d Dec 25, 1995, Winnipeg) Eckhardt's distinguished career was highlighted by his tenure as director of the **Winnipeg Art Gallery** (WAG), from 1953-74. In those 21 years, he achieved his vision of transforming the WAG from a small, provincial establishment into one of Canada's leading art institutions.

The son of a gifted printmaker and graphic artist, Ferdinand studied art history at the U of Vienna. In the late 1920s, he established himself in Berlin, working as a freelance writer and art critic. In 1930, while researching an article on post-WWI graphic artists, Eckhardt met his future wife, the composer and musician **Sophie-Carmen Eckhardt-Gramatté**. Sonia, as her friends called her, was still mourning the early death of her first husband, the German Expressionist artist Walter Gramatté. Eckhardt published a definitive catalogue of Gramatté's graphic works in 1932, and in the following year, organized a touring commemorative exhibition which exhibited in 10 cities before it was forcibly closed by the National Socialists as an example of newly outlawed "degenerate art."

Ferdinand married Sonia in 1934 after securing a job as advertising director for Bayer-Aspirin, a position he held for the next 8 years. When WWII broke out, he and Sonia relocated to Vienna. He was conscripted into the German military in 1942, but never saw active service.

UMA, TRIBUNE, PC18-10133-001

Ferdinand Eckhardt, 1965

His discharge came with the end of the war in 1945, after which he was hired to manage the art education programs of the state art museum of Austria. During this time, he co-founded the Austrian-American Society and was awarded a study grant to tour galleries all over NA. Through these new cultural associations, he was offered the position of gallery director in Winnipeg, a city completely unknown to him.

In 1953, the Eckhardts moved to Winnipeg. Thanks to his curatorial expertise, Ferdinand developed the gallery into one of NA's finest collections of Cdn art and Inuit sculpture. His passionate interest in art education resulted in the creation of an ongoing program of concerts, films, lectures, and other events to encourage a public understanding and appreciation of the arts. Eckhardt's leadership took the WAG in 1971 from its cramped quarters on the 2nd floor of what was then the Winnipeg Auditorium to its current facility, an elegant example of contemporary 20th-century architecture. He also persuaded the childless **Viscount Gort** to donate much of his collection to the gallery.

After the death of his wife in 1974, Dr. Eckhardt helped found the Eckhardt-Gramatté Music Competition to encourage the talents of young Cdn musicians and promote the works of contemporary composers. In 1983, he founded the Eckhardt-Gramatté Foundation, aimed at advancing and recognizing the music of Eckhardt-Gramatté as well as the artwork of her first husband. Two years later, he published a biography of Sonia, entitled *Music from Within*. Among Eckhardt's many published works are *150 Years of Art in Manitoba: Struggle for a Visual Civilization* (1970). He also published articles and essays on the works of Walter Gramatté. For his cultural contributions to the arts, Eckhardt received honorary doctorates from the **U of M** and **Brandon U**, as well as the Order of Canada in 1976 and the Order of the Buffalo Hunt in 1982. ● PAULA KELLY

ECKHARDT-GRAMATTÉ, Sophie-Carmen

"Sonia," composer, pianist, violinist, teacher (b ca Jan 6, 1899, Moscow; d Dec 2, 1974, Stuttgart). Eckhardt-Gramatté was a Cdn composer of European origin, whose body of work includes more than 175 compositions, ranging from short caprices for piano and violin, to chamber orchestra works, to full-length symphonies. Her turbulent life and career survived the wartime upheavals of 20th-century Europe, and later flourished after immigrating to **Winnipeg** in 1953, where she lived and worked for the last 20 years of her life.

Sonia, as she was usually known, was the daughter of Catherina de Kochevskaia, a talented pianist who taught music and French in the house of Count Leo Tolstoy for more than 20 years. Catherina married Russian businessman Nicolas de Fridman, but separated from him before Sonia was born. Sonia's true father remains unknown, because her birth was never registered. There has been speculation that Tolstoy himself was the father. Catherina sent Sonia to live in a Tolstoyan colony near Gloucester, England called Whiteway, where she remained for several years with a foster family. In 1904, Catherina took Sonia to live with her in Paris, where the little girl began her musical training. By age 6, she exhibited a precocious talent both on piano and violin, as well as writing her first early compositions. In 1908, Catherina enrolled her daughter at the Conservatoire de Paris, where the young girl quickly impressed the directors of the pre-eminent school of music. Sonia gave her first solo concerts at the age of 11 in Paris, Geneva, and Berlin, appearing as both pianist and violinist on an ambitious program of works by Bach, Beethoven, and Chopin. Her career as a concert performer showed great promise, but her teachers were unhappy with Sonia's insistent focus on composing instead of her music lessons. Sonia and her mother relocated to Berlin in 1914, just before WWI broke out. They soon found themselves destitute, and Sonia was forced to play in beer halls for food.

In 1920, Sonia met and married the German Expressionist artist Walter Gramatté, who promised her a new freedom to compose. Throughout the 1920s, Sonia composed works of a highly virtuosic nature, including several piano sonatas and her *Piano Concerto No. 1 for Solo Violin*. The Gramattés returned to Berlin in 1926. Two years later, Sonia received an invitation from the eminent conductor Leopold Stokowski to perform a concert program in the US that would feature her own compositions. However, this tour had to be postponed, owing to the serious illness that beset Gramatté and led to his early death in Feb 1929. Later that year, Sonia fulfilled her earlier commitment and travelled to the US to perform her works with the Philadelphia Orchestra and the Chicago Symphony. The following year, she met the Austrian-born art critic and historian, **Ferdinand Anton Ludwig Eckhardt**, who became a close confidante and supporter of her career as a composer. In 1934, they were married, and Sonia shifted her energies from performing to full-time composition.

In 1939, Sonia and her husband moved to Vienna. At this time, she began signing her compositions "S. C. Ekhardt-Gramatté," concerned that Vienna's conservative musical establishment would have difficulty with her identity as a female composer. WWII posed a series of new obstacles to her career, beginning with Ferdinand's forced conscription into the German military and culminating in the Allies' heavy bombing of Vienna. After the war ended, Sonia worked hard to re-establish herself as a serious

Sophie-Carmen Eckhardt-Gramatté, 1967

composer. She was rewarded in the years that followed with major composition prizes in 1948 and 1949, as well as winning an Austrian state prize for composition in 1950, a signal achievement for a female composer of the period.

However, Sonia was forced to re-establish her career when her husband accepted an appointment to become the director of the Winnipeg Art Gallery. The 2 emigrated to Canada in Oct 1953. Her first Canadian performance was at the invitation of CBC Radio's "Distinguished Artists" series in 1955. During the 1950s and '60s, Eckhardt-Gramatté's compositions matured to a dense, technically complex, yet still emotionally resonant style. Significant works commissioned during this period include her *Duo Concerto for Cello and Piano*, the *Symphony-Concerto for Piano and Orchestra*, and *Symphony II* ("Manitoba Symphony"). For her contributions to Canadian music as both a teacher and composer, Sonia Eckhardt-Gramatté received an honorary doctorate from **Brandon** U. During the last 2 years of her life, she was immersed in plans for a music competition to encourage young artists to play the works of contemporary composers. In 1974, while on a visit to Stuttgart, she died during an operation to repair a bone fracture. Two years later, the first S. C. Eckhardt-Gramatté Competition for the Performance of Canadian Music took place. ● PAULA KELLY

ECOCLIMATIC REGIONS

ECOCLIMATIC REGIONS are areas of Earth's surface characterized by distinctive ecological responses to climate, as expressed by vegetation and reflected in soils, wildlife, and water. Canada is grouped into 10 ecoclimatic provinces. Portions of 4 of these – the grassland, boreal, sub-Arctic, and Arctic – are found in MB. These portions are further subdivided into 8 ecoclimatic regions. Each region has a unique combination of vegetation, soil type, and wildlife. As climate is the most influential factor in determining both ecoclimatic classification and vegetation zonation, the NW-to-SE zonal pattern on both figures shows marked similarities.

THE GRASSLAND ECOCLIMATIC PROVINCE: Only 1 of the 3 ecoclimatic regions that make up Canada's grassland ecoclimatic province is found in MB, and this is transitional grassland. These are the grasslands of the SW and S portions of MB that have developed with low water, lightning and human-induced fire, strong winds, and grazing bison. Variations in these factors gave rise to 3 major ecosystem types: mixed-grass prairie, aspen parkland, and tall grass prairie. Tree-covered areas also developed where groundwater compensated for sub-humid climatic conditions. Such sites include treed

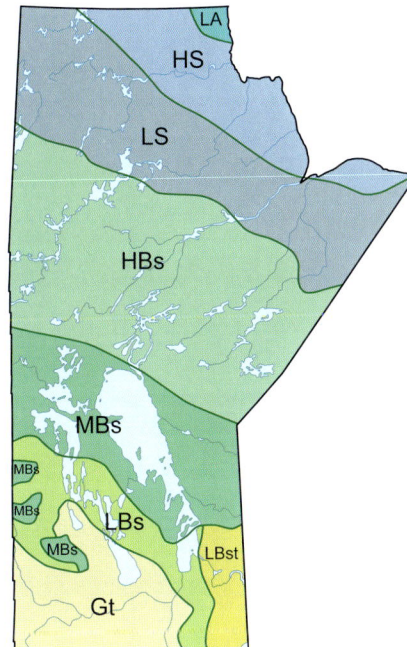

Arctic
LA Low Arctic

Subarctic
HS High Subarctic
LS Low Subarctic

Boreal
HBs Subhumid High Boreal
MBs Subhumid Mid-Boreal
LBs Subhumid Low Boreal
LBst Subhumid Transitional Low Boreal

Grassland
Gt Transitional Grassland

Ecoclimatic Regions

pothole and lake margins; riparian floodplains; hilly areas with broadleaf deciduous trees; and deltaic sands dominated by a prairie-conifer mix. Moisture stress has also limited the leaching of soil nutrients and promoted the humification of the large annual production of grass rooting systems. This produced the humus- and nutrient-rich black chernozemic soils that European farmers found so attractive.

MIXED-GRASS PRAIRIE: In the last 120 years, Mixed-Grass Prairie in MB has been greatly reduced by agricultural expansion and reduced burning. Typical mixed-grass cover includes attractive flowering broadleaf herbs and needle-and-thread (*Stipa comata*), June (*Koeleria cristata*), northern wheat (*Agropyron smithii*), and little bluestem (*Andropogon scoparius*) grasses. On drier sites, these are joined by blue grama (*Bouteloua gracilis*) and the evergreen shrub creeping juniper (*Juniperus horizontalis*), with its ground-hugging branches. In wetter sites, broadleaf herbs and sedges may be joined by willows (*Salix* spp.), reeds

(*Phragmites australis*), and trembling aspen (*Populus tremuloides*). Forest strips along river floodplains are dominated by willows and by the hardwood trees green ash (*Fraxinus pennsylvanica*), cottonwood (*Populus deltoides*), Manitoba maple (*Acer negundo*), and American elm (*Ulmus americana*).

TALL GRASS PRAIRIE: Before the spread of agriculture, the 6000 km² Red River Lowlands S of Winnipeg were dominated by a sea of Tall Grass Prairie. Today, however, less than 1% of the natural cover remains. Classic Tall Grass Prairie is dominated by big bluestem (*Andropogon gerardii*), Indian grass (*Sorghastrum nutans*), and switchgrass (*Panicum virgatum*), together with many of those species mentioned as typical of mixed-grass prairie. Large patches of big bluestem- and Indian grass-dominated prairie are also found around Tolstoi and Gardenton.

ASPEN PARKLAND: Following the reduction in burning at the end of the 19th century, both trembling **Aspen** and bur **Oak** (*Quercus macrocarpa*) became successful invaders of many mixed-grass areas. Aspen is particularly suited to this process, as its roots can radiate outward as much as 20 m just below the surface and sprout following fire or grazing by snowshoe hares or cattle. In the more elevated terrain of Turtle Mountain, broadleaf deciduous forest is dominated by trembling aspen, balsam poplar (*Populus balsamifera*), green ash, Manitoba **Maple**, and **Elm**. Here, undulating terrain limited the spread of prairie fires, and cooling caused by elevation has reduced moisture stress. In areas of sandy deltaic deposits, such as at Spruce Woods, scattered white **Spruce** (*Picea glauca*) have also been protected from fire, and have managed to tap groundwater in an otherwise physiological desert. Along parkland floodplains, broadleaf tree species are joined by basswood (*Tilia americana*), while nutrient-rich marshes formed where rivers enter lakes are dominated by cattails (*Typha* spp.), reeds, and bulrushes (*Scirpus* spp.). Most wetlands in the transitional grassland ecoclimatic region have been drained for agriculture, but where they remain, they form important wildlife habitat and staging areas for migratory waterfowl. They also support summer-resident waterfowl, muskrat (*Ondatra zibethica*), mink (*Mustela vison*), racoon (*Procyon lotor*), red fox (*Vulpes vulpes*), and the introduced white-tailed deer (*Odocoileus virginianus*). Non-waterfowl bird species, such as the blue jay (*Cyanocitta cristata*) and sharp-tailed grouse, (*Pedioecetes phasianellus*), have also adapted well to this managed parkland landscape.

BOREAL ECOCLIMATIC PROVINCE: Four of Canada's 26 boreal ecoclimatic regions are

185

E

Boreal forest display at Manitoba Museum

found within the boreal forest regions of MB; the subhumid low, mid-, and high boreal, and the subhumid transitional low boreal. The terms "low," "mid," and "high" reflect a shorter summer and cooler climate associated with increasing latitude, while "subhumid" emphasizes that there is just enough precipitation to support forest growth. "Transitional" refers to the presence of white and red **PINE** (*Pinus strobus* and *P. resinosa*) in the milder SE corner where boreal forest begins to form a gradual transition to E temperate deciduous forest in MN.

SUBHUMID LOW AND TRANSITIONAL LOW BOREAL: The southern fringes of the subhumid low boreal is a narrow transitional zone to prairie/aspen parkland dominated by broadleaf deciduous hardwood trees. Here at least 1, but not more than 3, of the 4 dominant central Cdn boreal softwood conifers – white spruce, black spruce *(Picea mariana)*, Jack pine (*Pinus banksiana*), and tamarack (*Larix laricina*) – are found. When all 4 are found, then the area is considered part of the classic northern coniferous forest, but this forest is still stressed climatically, and fires are common. Frequent forest fires ensure an important role for hardwood species such as trembling aspen and balsam poplar. As a result, the low and mid-boreal regions are often called mixed woods, to reflect this mix of hardwoods with typical boreal softwood conifers. Today, some of these areas are dominated by hardwood aspen, which support an oriented strand board (waferboard) mill near Swan River. Despite the subhumid climate, poorly developed drainage systems and impervious bedrock ensure the presence of large areas of fen and

bog dominated by black spruce and tamarack. Other significant tree species include eastern white cedar (*Thuja occidentalis*) in eutrophic swamps, and white birch (*Betula papyrifera*), found generally throughout the southern boreal forest. Balsam fir (*Abies balsamea*) increases in importance in the transitional zone to the southeast, where both white and red pine make an appearance.

SUBHUMID MID- AND HIGH BOREAL: Large expanses of typical northern coniferous forest, dominated by white spruce and Jack pine, are found here, as are some **BIRCH** and aspen. Jack pine does well on rocky outcrops and sandy sites, where it does not have to compete with the more

nutrient- and water-demanding spruces. Only following fire does Jack pine dominate on better-quality soils, and if succession-inhibiting fires are relatively frequent, as on the limestone/dolomite pavement areas N of Pine Falls, white spruce has difficulty replacing the pine. Carpets of feather-mosses (*Pleurozium* spp.) usually occur under spruce forests on better-drained soils; on more poorly drained conifer sites, sphagnum moss (*Sphagnum* spp.) and Labrador tea (*Ledum groenlandicum*) are the dominant ground cover. At these latitudes, however, intermittent permafrost begins to inhibit vegetation. Spruce, fir, and some Jack pine support several large pulp and paper mills, such as at **THE PAS** and **PINE FALLS**, and some softwood-lumber production. Typical wildlife species throughout boreal forests include black **BEAR** (*Ursus americanus*), **COYOTE** (*Canis latrans*), fisher (*Martens pennanti*), **LYNX** (*Lynx canadensis*), ermine (*Mustela erminea*), red **FOX**, timber **WOLF** (*Canis lupus*), and the occasional white-tailed **DEER**, while **MOOSE** (*Alces alces*), **BEAVER** (*Castor canadensis*), **MINK**, and **MUSKRAT** populations are common along rivers, marshes, or moister lowlands. Fourteen small herds of woodland **CARIBOU** (*Rangifer tarandus caribou*) are also found throughout the boreal, with 2 additional large herds of a separate variety (central Canada barren ground caribou, *R. tarandus arcticus*) that range peripheral to Hudson Bay in the high sub-Arctic.

SUB-ARCTIC ECOCLIMATIC PROVINCE: In MB, there are 2 sub-Arctic ecoclimatic regions: the low and high. The sub-Arctic coincides with the general location of the summer position of the polar front, so temperature-wise shows greatly increasing stress on tree species with

Arctic-Subarctic display at Manitoba Museum

increasing latitude. The low sub-Arctic is dominated by open spruce-lichen woodlands, and many vegetation zonation systems include it as part of the boreal forest. The high sub-Arctic is a forest-tundra transition zone where open spruce forest mosaics with treeless tundra.

LOW SUB-ARCTIC: This region marks the northern limit of the boreal forest and is variously described as "open spruce forest" or "open lichen woodland." The latter name is more accurate, because light-coloured fruticose (shrubby) lichens dominate the open ground between the white spruces. These open upland woodlands contrast with the more closely packed black spruce on poorly drained mid-slopes, and the scattered deciduous tamarack occupying lowland wetlands. Woodland caribou play an important part in modifying lichen cover as they migrate from the protection of their closed-forest overwintering areas to these summer grazing lands.

HIGH SUB-ARCTIC: Here, microclimates allow for tree growth only on more-favourable sites, while in more-exposed locations, tree species survive, if at all, only in the form of krummholz (German for "crooked wood"). This mosaic of forest stands, scattered throughout large expanses of tundra, has given rise to the area being called a forest-tundra transition region, with tree-stands sufficient in numbers that they can be called forest diminishing toward the boundary as tundra dissipates. Here, wetlands and numerous lakes take on particular significance, often dominating the landscape, especially where surface permafrost has recently melted. The treeline is where tree species can no longer grow over 5 m tall, and this line separates the forest-tundra from the shrub tundra to the low Arctic.

ARCTIC ECOCLIMATIC PROVINCE: While the Arctic ecoclimatic province is the largest ecoclimactic province in Canada, only small portions of the low Arctic region are found in the province. MB tundra is best described as shrub tundra because of the great significance of woody shrubs. Shrubs range from 1 to 3 m tall – from willows to dwarf shrubs, such as dwarf Labrador tea (*Ledum decumbens*) and dwarf birch (*Betula glandulosa*), to the prostrate ground-hugging alpine bearberry (*Arctostaphylos alpini*), Arctic avens (*Dryas integrifolia*) and Lapland rose-bay (*Rhododendron lapponicum*). These woody species, together with large expanses of lichen, provide important summer grazing grounds for caribou. Few annual herbs and grasses are found here – the short summer provides insufficient time for seeds to germinate, develop, flower, and set seed. ● GEOFF SCOTT

ECONOMY OF MANITOBA
By Michael Benarroch

E

O f all the western Canadian provinces, Manitoba's economy is the most diverse. Instead of relying on one resource (wheat, oil, lumber, etc.) MB has traditionally combined resource production with manufacturing and financial services. This is as true today as when Winnipeg was the gateway to the western hinterland at the turn of the 20th century. Diversity continues to be an economic theme as MB develops into a leader in aerospace, bus and furniture manufacturing; insurance and financial services; hydro-electric power; medical and bio-tech research; as well as more traditional activities like agriculture, transportation, forestry and mining.

HISTORY: Before the fur trade, southern MB's First Nation's economy was centred on the **BISON**. Hunts in the spring and autumn provided the groups with much of what was needed to survive. **PEMMICAN** was made of bison meat mixed with fat and berries, while tools, weapons, clothing, tents, and pouches were usually made from bison hide. Northern peoples such as the Swampy **CREE** and the **DENE** were also self-sufficient, with fish, birds, deer, and elk providing most staples.

MB's post-contact economy was initially centred on the **FUR TRADE**. More than 200 years before the creation of MB as a province, the fur trade and the **HUDSON'S BAY COMPANY** (HBC) dominated the economy. This domination began when Pierre-Esprit Radisson and Médard Chouart de Groseilliers determined that the fur trade would be far easier to conduct by setting up posts along Hudson Bay, rather than travelling inland from the East. On May 2, 1670, King Charles II granted the HBC monopoly rights over all trade from land draining into the bay. This land mass

Agriculture remains an important part of the economy of Manitoba.

PETER TITTENBERGER

The CanWest Global and Richardson buildings demonstrate the role of Manitoba families in the economy of the province.

With the construction of inland forts came the need for a permanent food supply. This led to the establishment of farms in the proximity of the **LORD SELKIRK**'s settlement at Red River. As the population located along the Red River grew, a diversified economy based on agriculture, hunting, and the fur trade evolved. The inhabitants were self-sufficient in food, while furs were exported and other goods imported through the HBC, which held on to its monopoly until 1849.

By the middle of the 19th century, trade with the US was taking hold. The first steamboat connecting MB to MN arrived via the Red River in 1859. This was followed by a north-south railway, which allowed the HBC to conduct trade by rail instead of via Hudson Bay.

By the late 1860s, there were 10,000 inhabitants in the Red River Settlement, and in 1870, a relatively small parcel of land in what is now southern MB was granted provincial status. However, the deal that made MB a province saw Ottawa retain power over all natural resources, including agricultural land, minerals, forests, rivers, and lakes. This severely restricted opportunities for the province to raise revenue and retain its wealth, and was inconsistent with the rules governing the 4 eastern provinces, which all maintained control over their natural resources. Ottawa signed similar deals with AB and SK in 1905, and did not relinquish control over resources until after the **GREAT DEPRESSION**.

With the advent of increased immigration, especially after the completion of the transcontinental railway in 1885, agriculture developed as the major sector in the provincial economy, replacing the fur trade. MB began to export Red Fife wheat, which required a shorter growing season and was ideally suited for MB and the West. Bulk storage and transport of wheat, by pouring from grain elevators into boxcars, vastly improved the economy of grain production.

Winnipeg shrewdly offered the transcontinental **CPR** permanent tax-free status in exchange for building a bridge across the Red River at Winnipeg rather than at Selkirk. With this, Winnipeg evolved into the business and transportation centre of western Canada. This led to an increase in population, real estate prices, hotels, banks, warehouses, govt buildings, machine shops, small industry (such as textiles and machine shops), and retail stores. Initially, the CPR invested heavily in infrastructure. This boom was short-lived, however, and the tax concessions made to the CPR deprived the province of millions of dollars in tax revenue.

From 1896 to 1918, MB experienced a sustained period of economic growth. Fuelled by a wave of immigration from Europe and the US, MB's population rose from 150,000 in 1891 to 550,000 in 1916. As population grew, Winnipeg became a major North American transportation centre. Three railways – the CPR, Grand Trunk Pacific, and CNoR – set up regional centres in Winnipeg. Agriculture, primarily wheat sales, fuelled this growth. Winnipeg became home to a grain exchange and other agriculture-related industries, such as meat packing, farm implements, breweries, and so on. Winnipeg, known as "Chicago of the North," also became a major financial centre with banks, insurance and trust companies, stockbrokers, and real estate brokers establishing offices in the city.

MB's economic boom came to a halt between 1918 and 1930. Part of the reason was the construction of the Panama Canal which allowed ships to cut thousands of kilometres from the Atlantic-Pacific route. This curtailed Winnipeg's importance as a transportation hub to the West Coast.

During the earlier years of prosperity, both industry and the labour movement grew in power. As economic conditions worsened, however, unemployment rose and wages fell. With this came a struggle between industry and labour that led to the Winnipeg General Strike in 1919.

At this time, the agriculture sector fared no better than industry. The price of wheat fell significantly, due to increased supply from Europe

comprised of roughly 25% of NA, including all of MB. For the next 200 years, both the fur trade and HBC controlled MB's economy, with the vast majority of exports from MB to Europe travelling through Hudson Bay.

After the establishment of the HBC, the **ENGLISH** constructed forts along the bay and its tributaries. It was not until the 1730s that forts were built by the French on the Red River at Fort Rouge, now Winnipeg and farther West along the Assiniboine River. These settlements were built by **LA VÉRENDRYE** during his western explorations. But they also were the basis for an expanded French fur trade in the interior. Over the next 100 years, the rivalry between the French and English persisted with the HBC also building interior trading posts, including eventually **UPPER** and **LOWER FORT GARRY** along the Red River.

and Latin America, and the federal govt abandoned its marketing controls. As MB's wheat farmers faced greater competition and the federal govt provided less support, the agricultural sector and the province as a whole experienced a significant reduction in income.

Despite the slowdown in economic activity, the MB govt remained committed to continued infrastructure investment across the province. As the govt built railways and roads into northern MB, pulp and paper mills and mining in Flin Flon expanded. With the provincial govt providing the infrastructure, private industry, such as the Hudson Bay Mining and Smelting Co., provided the financial capital.

As electrical needs spread in the province, MB made use of its extensive river system by generating its own electricity. The first hydro-electric generating station in MB was built in 1900 on the Minnedosa River (Little Saskatchewan River) and served Brandon. In 1904, the first hydro-generating station on the Winnipeg River at the Pinawa Channel was constructed. Over the years, additional generating stations have been built, with the sector becoming a significant employer in the province.

In the 1930s, both the Depression and drought hit MB – and the Prairies as a whole – harder than most other regions of Canada. By 1931, the HUDSON BAY RAILWAY (HBRR) was completed, and small amounts of wheat were being shipped through CHURCHILL. Initially, shipping rates from Churchill were below those of other Cdn ports in Montreal and Vancouver, and business expanded. Over time, however, insurance rates were increased due to fears associated with the risk of shipping through the North, and Churchill's advantage diminished. Simultaneously, Winnipeg saw its advantage of lower railway freight rates decline. With this came a loss of trade through Winnipeg.

As the economy of MB declined in the early 1930s, govt tax revenue sagged. The provincial govt responded by cutting expenditures in an attempt to balance its budget. Unfortunately, this only exacerbated the difficult times for the province, and by 1933, the province was nearly bankrupt.

In the '30s and '40s, MB forged a new economic relationship with Ottawa that formed the foundation for current revenue-sharing arrangements between the province and the federal govt. The federal govt, finally, transferred control over natural resources to the province, and provided MB with much-needed subsidies and welfare relief. In return, MB transferred the responsibility for unemployment along with corporate and personal income taxes for the war period to Ottawa. This greatly alleviated the burden on the province.

In the 1950s, MB's economy began to recover. The entire education system was restructured and expanded; a major investment in roads was undertaken; the Red River Floodway was built; the govt invested heavily to subsidize industrial development; hydroelectric power generation was expanded on the Saskatchewan, Nelson, and Churchill rivers; and a major pulp and paper mill was constructed at THE PAS.

DIVERSITY AND STABILITY: Between 1960 and the present, MB's economy evolved into a highly diversified one, with no single sector dominating the economic landscape. The well-diversified nature of the economy has allowed MB to avoid many of the ups and downs of the business cycle, settling for a more even – albeit slower – rate of growth than the rest of Canada. While agriculture, natural resources, and transportation remain important sectors within the economy, manufacturing has become the single largest sector. As in other provinces, the service sector, driven in part by expenditures from all as 3 levels of govt, is a significant employer in MB.

Between 1981 and 2004, GDP – the value of all goods and services produced in the province – grew at an average annual rate of 2.2%, adjusted for inflation. This ranks slightly below the national average rate of growth of 2.7%. MB has grown steadily over this period, though the pattern of economic growth has had its ups and downs following trends experienced by the rest of Canada. While economic growth was negative in 1982 and 1991, it was positive in all other years since 1981. From 1995 to 2004, the GDP growth rate was 2.5%, compared to a lower growth rate of 1.5% from 1985 to 1995. The more rapid expansion in the later period was driven by strong performance in exports, business investment, personnel incomes, and corporate profits.

Between 1981 and 2004, growth in the MB economy, as in the rest of Canada, was led by exports and imports, which both expanded at over 4% a year. An improving competitive climate in the province, particularly in the manufacturing sector, and a weak Cdn dollar together created ideal conditions for expanding exports. Following behind exports and imports, business investments grew at 3.4% on the strength of average annual increase in corporate profits (7.7%) over this period. In contrast, personal expenditures (1.9%) and govt expenditures (1.4%) lagged behind these other sectors. Slow growth in govt expenditures was a result of successive provincial govts' aiming to balance budgets or generate surpluses.

MB's export growth has concentrated primarily on agriculture, manufacturing, and electricity. Exports are well balanced across many sectors in the economy. In manufacturing, for example, no single industry exported as much as agriculture. Still, manufacturing as a whole accounted for 65% of total exports in 2004. This is significantly higher than the 57% of exports in manufacturing in 1996. Expansion of exports in new products such as furniture, prepared meats, potato products, industrial

The Manitoba Economy

	SCALE	1981	1991	2001	2004	2006
Gross Domestic Product (GDP)	Millions $	22,700	26,395	33,108	35,442	37,133
Personal Expenditure	Millions $	13,852	16,526	20,123	21,688	23,083
Government Expenditure	Millions $	5,590	6,985	7,364	7,891	8,510
Government Capital Investment	Millions $	470	746	774	893	749
Business Investment	Millions $	3,494	3,073	4,981	6,526	7,783
Exports to Other Countries	Millions $	2,828	5,334	10,289	10,402	11,343
Exports to Other Provinces	Millions $	6,547	6,700	10,630	11,278	11,713
Imports from Other Countries	Millions $	3,271	5,448	9,706	11,492	12,425
Imports from Other Provinces	Millions $	7,098	7,727	11,434	11,852	13,623
Employment	Thousands	468.8	506.3	554.3	576	587
Unemployment Rate Percentage	Percentage	6.00%	8.7%	5.0%	5.3%	4.3%
Average Weekly Earnings	Dollars		503.83	593.97	635.90	676.83

Total Manitoba Exports 2006

BY INDUSTRY	2006 (MILLIONS OF $)
Manufacturing	
Primary Metal	1624.8
Transportation Equip.	1070.1
Food	1050.0
Chemical Products	955.3
Machinery	746.2
Wood	502.5
Paper	268.1
Plastics	248.4
Electrical & Electronic	220.0
Printing	189.4
Fabricated Metals	156.9
Petroleum and Coal	91.2
Furniture and Fixtures	76.2
Clothing and Textiles	65.6
Other Manufacturing	147.5
Total Manufacturing	**7409.8**
Agriculture	2065.6
Electricity	648.0
Other Primary	817.1
Other Exports	402.4
Total Exports	**11,343.0**

BY DESTINATION	2006 (MILLION $)
United States	8596.0
Japan	469.29
China	348.5
Mexico	208.9
Hong Kong	204.2
Taiwan	96.1
Belgium	92.3
South Korea	80.4
India	79.0
United Kingdom	76.9
Other Countries	1091.6
Total Exports	**11,343.0**

chemicals, plastics, pharmaceuticals, and printing and publishing have accounted for the significant rise in the share of manufacturing in exports. Within the manufacturing sector, the top 4 exporting industries in 2004 were food (11.5%), primary metals (9.8%), transportation equipment (9.5%), and machinery (7.4%). Other than manufacturing and agriculture, MB exports electricity and a variety of other primary products. The primary destination for MB exports outside of Canada is the US: 73% of MB's exports were sold to the US. Japan, the 2nd-largest market, accounted for only 5.2% of exports.

The growth of exports from MB, which is consistent with higher Canadian and global trade, is in large part attributable to the signing of the Canada-US Free Trade Agreement (FTA) in 1989 and the North American Free Trade Agreement (NAFTA) in 1994. Under the FTA and NAFTA, Manitoba's trade with US and Mexico is virtually tariff-free. Overall exports from MB to the US since the signing of these agreements have increased by 370% compared to 87% with the rest of the world. While the overall effect on the exports has been overwhelmingly positive for MB, certain sectors – transport equipment, food and beverages and primary

metals – benefited greatly while exports from other sectors – clothing, textiles, and furniture – have lagged.

REVENUE AND EXPENDITURES: In 2004, govt expenditures accounted for about 22% of provincial GDP. About 65% of provincial govt expenditures are financed from sources within the province: taxes, interest, fees, and revenue from Crown corporations. The remainder of the revenue is transferred from the federal govt. In 2004, MB received just over $1.7 billion in equalization payments, $705 million in health transfers, and $304 million from the Canada Social Transfer.

As in other Cdn provinces, the largest proportion of provincial govt expenditure is for health care (41.7%) followed by education (21.5%). Under the *Balanced Budget, Debt Repayment, and Taxpayer Accountability Act* (1996), the province of MB cannot run a provincial deficit and must make payments toward provincial debt every year. To insure that deficits do not result, the province created a Fiscal Stabilization Fund in 1989, from which it may draw to cover excess spending. The fund started with a govt transfer of $200 million, dipped as low as low as $29 million in 1993-94, and went as high as $577 million in 1996-97, when the govt made a special transfer of $205 million with revenue earned from the sale of **MTS ALLSTREAM**.

Unlike most other provinces, provincial accounting techniques and the Balanced Budget Act only consider general-purpose debt toward the definition of a deficit. This implies that other types of govt liabilities – for example, pension liabilities – are not included in the deficit calculations. From 1991 to 1995, the province continually ran a deficit, and the provincial debt reached a peak of $7.364 billion in 1995. By 2004, however, the debt had fallen by nearly $800 million to $6.59 billion, and debt-servicing costs (the amount of the budget spent on paying the debt) only comprised 3.3% of govt expenditure. Net general-purpose debt as a percentage of provincial GDP is now only 15.8%, among the lowest rates across the Cdn provinces.

ECONOMIC ENGINES: With economic growth in MB has come strong labour market performance. The unemployment rate has consistently ranked below the national average, and in 2004, it was the 2nd-lowest of any Cdn province. Though in some years this was due in large part to outmigration from the province, MB saw a net inflow of migrants in 2003 and 2004. MB's labour force participation rate, which stood at 69% in 2004, is also the second highest in Canada. In 2004, MB's unemployment rate was 5.3%, and average annual employment reached a high of 576,000. The main driver for this high employment was the goods-producing manufacturing sector, which accounts for 24% of the growth in total employment in the province.

While agriculture and resource extraction have traditionally been the cornerstones of the economy, these sectors no longer dominate in MB. Between 1984 and 2000, the mining sector, together with fishing, hunting, logging, and forestry, declined at average annual rates of about 3%. Over this same period, agriculture grew at an average annual rate of less than 1%. This trend away from resource and agricultural dependency has also occurred in other provinces and regions of NA. Nevertheless, while agriculture and natural resources directly contribute a smaller share to the economy than in the past, the provincial economy still relies heavily on these sectors, as much of the province's manufacturing occurs in industries dependent on agriculture and natural-resources production. Though growth in agriculture has lagged behind other sectors, it is still a significant driver in the provincial economy. Hogs and oilseeds have recently replaced wheat – traditionally the largest income generator in this sector. Moreover, consistent with the pattern observed for the MB economy since 1960, agriculture in the province has become highly diversified. No sector dominates the agricultural economy with hogs (23.5%), oilseeds (17.5%), wheat (14.1%), and cattle and calves (6.7%) the largest players in the market.

Manufacturing is now the largest sector of the economy, generating nearly more than 2.5 times the level of income that agriculture does. Mirroring the provincial economy, the manufacturing sector is well diversified. Manufacturing and information, and culture and arts, have had the highest growth rates from 1985 to 2004, with the accommodation and food sector lagging well behind. MB is NA's largest manufacturer of buses. Two companies control the sector, **Motor Coach Industries** and **New Flyer**. MB has the country's largest furniture manufacturing plant, owned by **Palliser Furniture**. Maple Leaf Foods operates one of the world's largest and most technologically advanced meat-processing plants in **Brandon**. MB is Canada's third-largest aerospace centre, as well as the country's third-largest apparel manufacturing centre. Over 22% of MB's growth in GDP between 1980 and 2000 can be attributed to the manufacturing sector. This expansion in manufacturing is largely due to the province's competitive business environment, its central geographic location, and its transportation links to the rest of NA. Low cost of both industrial and commercial land compared to other major metropolitan centres, and electricity costs that are the lowest in NA, have provided the province with a cost advantage that has attracted manufactures.

Though the mining sector has suffered since 1980, expanding markets in Asia, particularly China, have recently created new opportunities for the industry. Nickel remains the primary metal, with MB producing 25% of the nation's production. Other metals exported by MB include zinc, copper, and gold, with other primary products including crude oil, diamonds, and platinum.

MB's largest utility and Crown corporation is **Manitoba Hydro**, which accounts for all public electric power generated in the province. MB generates most of its electricity from hydro (with a few diesel and thermal plants), and has capabilities to generate roughly 5000 mW of power. MB Hydro currently has plans to double that capacity by 2025. Two-thirds of all electricity generated in MB is consumed within the province. The remainder is exported to the US and to other provinces in Canada. With an ample supply of electrical power, Manitobans pay among the lowest rates for electricity in the world.

The construction industry, including residential construction, directly generates as much income as the agricultural sector. The boom in residential housing since the late 1990s, boosted by low mortgage rates, has generated significant gains for this sector. Single-family housing starts and multiple-family units (duplexes, condominiums, and apartments) have grown consistently since the mid-1990s. Buoyed by the growth in housing starts and strong employment, retail sales in MB have been on an upward trend. In 2004, retail sales grew at a rate well above the national average. Sales of home furnishings and computers have led this growth. Hardware stores, in particular, experienced a 30% increase between 2003 and 2004.

Service industries accounted for 74% of MB's economy in 2004, well above the national average of 69%. MB is the headquarters to 2 major financial companies, **Great-West Life** and **Investors Group**, as well as companies such as the **Cdn Wheat Board** and **CanWest Global Communications**. About ¼ of all services in the province are provided directly or

Manitoba Government Financial Statistics (MILLIONS OF $)

FINANCIAL STATEMENTS	2006/07	2004/05	2000/01	1991/92
Revenue				
Own-Source Revenue	5,651	5,286	4,739	3,146
Federal Transfers	3,113	2,918	2,091	1,821
Total	8,764	8,204	6,830	4,967
Expenditure				
Program Expenditure	8,333	7,554	6,181	4,779
Public Debt Costs	289	237	511	492
Total	8,622	7,791	6,693	5,271
Net Revenue/(Expenditure)	142	413	137	(304)
Debt/Pension Repayment	(110)	(99)	(96)	0
Transfers from/(to) Fiscal Stabilization Fund	85	0	0	(30)
Restatement Adjustment	(113)	0	0	0
Balance under Balanced Budget Legislation	4	314	41	(334)
Net Direct and Guaranteed Debt				
General Purpose	6,563	6,594	6,537	5,295
Manitoba Hydro	6,632	6,726	6,053	4,979
Other	1,304	1,343	1,086	1,549
Health Facilities	790	542	220	0
Government Enterprises and Other	168	498	0	0
Capital Investments	749	363	260	0
Total	16,206	16,066	14,156	11,823
Other Obligations				
Pension Liability	4,164	3,787	3,050	1,495
Pension Assets	701	(383)	(21)	0
Net Pension Liability	3,463	3,404	3,029	0
Health Debt	325	100	359	528
Total	3,788	3,504	3,387	2,023
Total Obligations	19,994	19,550	17,543	13,846
Fiscal Stabilization Fund End-of-Year Balance	477	395	320	315

Top Twenty Private and Public Manitoba Corporations 2006

Rank	COMPANY	GROSS REVENUE 2006 (x$1,000)	NET INCOME (x$1,000)	# EMPLOYEES	# EMPLOYEES MB	NATURE OF BUSINESS
1	Great-West Lifeco Inc	23,871,000	1,616,000	18,600	3,000	Financial Services
2	Cargill Limited	4,300,000	N/A	7,663	454	Agri Business
3	Canadian Wheat Board	3,700,000	3,500,000	460	430	Grain Marketing
4	CanWest Global	3,072,542	720,237	13,400	600	Media
5	Agricore United	2,775,279	12,514	2,800	891	Agriculture
6	Manitoba Hydro	2,400,000	400,000	6,000	6,000	Energy Utility
7	IGM Financial Inc.	2,350,000	682,400	3,320	1,075	Financial Services
8	MTS Allstream	2,017,200	213,700	6,000	3,000	Telecommunications
9	Wawanesa Mutual Insurance Company	1,921,511	147,617	1,842	321	Property & Casualty Insurance
10	James Richardson & Sons	1,784,000	N/A	1,400	380	Holding Company
11	Ceridian Canada	1,459,000	N/A	1,450	320	HR and Payroll
12	Standard Aero	884,702	N/A	2,526	1,250	Aviation MRO
13	North West Company	849,700	42,900	5,236	1,471	Retail
14	Manitoba Public Insurance	779,316	47,809	1,700	1,700	Driver and Vehicle Liscencing
15	Hudbay Minerals	652,028	88,218	1,707	1,442	Mining
16	New Flyer Industries Canada	590,804	-13,947	1,868	1,101	Bus Manufacturer
17	Winpak Ltd.	530,165	28,076	1,723	580	Packaging
18	Ridley Inc.	479,000	10,700	1,080	175	Mfg Forumulated Livestock Feeds
19	Monsanto Canada	460,000	N/A	300	120	Agriculture
20	Manitoba Lotteries Corp	433,293	273,038	1,800	1,800	Gaming

MAGELLAN

The Cassiope Satellite, manufactured in Winnipeg by Bristol (Magellan), scheduled for launch in 2008

indirectly by all 3 levels of govt – federal, provincial, and local/municipal – as well as expenditures on health and education. MB remains a major transportation, trucking, rail and air, and storage hub, with several major trucking companies headquartered in the province.

Small businesses are a significant employer in MB, and in 2004, 94% of all business enterprises in MB were defined as small businesses, having 50 or fewer employees. Virtually $1/3$ of all employment in the province is in small businesses, and 25% of the provincial GDP is generated by small businesses. About 15% of the labour force, or 86,000 people, are self-employed small business owners. The vast majority of small businesses are in manufacturing, but financial services and real estate also have significant numbers of small businesses. Surprisingly, 60% of these businesses exported goods to the US, and 80% engaged in interprovincial trade.

SUMMARY: Though MB is not a rich province – its GDP per capita is 7th in Canada – it has developed into a diversified economy with an expanding manufacturing sector and low unemployment. The economy relies less on agriculture and mining than it has in the past, though these 2 sectors still play prominent roles. MB is among Canada's leading aerospace centres, and is the North American leader in bus manufacturing. While its provincial govt finances are strong, it relies heavily on federal transfer payments to balance its budget. The province sees itself as a future leader in the provision of hydroelectric power and plans to more than double its electrical generating capacity. As with its manufacturing sector, MB envisions strong demand for hydroelectricity from ON and the US as a means of generating significant wealth in the future. •

ED LEITH CRETACEOUS MENAGERIE at the Dept of Geological Sciences at the **U of M** brings visitors to the world of the Cretaceous period, 145 million years ago. The museum houses skeletal replicas of: a *Gorgosaurus*, a tyrannosaurid dinosaur; the massive, piranha-like fish *Xiphactinus*; the world's largest sea turtle, *Archelon*; and a gigantic sea lizard, *Platecarpus*. Ed Leith studied at U of M in the late 1920s, and did postgraduate work at Yale U, coming back to Winnipeg to teach geology at the U of M until his 1971 retirement. The museum was organized and established following his death in 1999. • RK

EDUCATION, POST-SECONDARY, in MB had its origin in the long-standing practice among mainstream Christian denominations in Canada to make provision for the preparation of locally trained professional clerics. Typically at these institutions, a science/liberal arts program was available for students who did not wish concentrated study in theology. Shortly after Confederation, 3 colleges of this sort were incorporated by the MB govt, and although the present institutional arrangement of post-secondary education is now generally thought of as more a regional issue, religious distinctions have always influenced university policy in the province.

There are 4 public universities in the province, all having long histories, 3 of them descended from theological colleges. **Brandon U** was initially a Baptist college; **Collège Universitaire de Saint-Boniface** was established for French-speaking Catholics; and the **U of W** was originally a Methodist institution, Wesley College, which had been later merged with Manitoba College to create United College. The lone exception, the **U of M**, was founded in 1877 to bring St. Boniface, St. John's (Anglican), and Manitoba (Presbyterian) Colleges under the framework of a single secular institution. There are now 4 colleges associated with U of M, with the original St. John's, St. Paul's (Catholic), St Andrew's (Ukrainian Orthodox), and the non-denominational University College.

By the 1960s, after having become the primary source of funding for their operation, the provincial govt introduced legislation that effectively secularized the oversight of each of the new universities in Brandon and Winnipeg by introducing the same institutional arrangements that were in place at the U of M – a bicameral structure consisting of a Board of Governors (or Regents) to oversee the management of operations and a Senate having authority over academic matters.

The 3 community colleges, **Assiniboine** in **Brandon**, **Red River** in **Winnipeg**, and Keewatin in **The Pas**, each has regional responsibilities

to provide training (typically 2-year programs) leading to certification or a diploma. The govt has recently restructured and renamed Keewatin, which became the University College of the North. This new category of institution, the university college, is only now being given definition.

Four religious institutions – the **Canadian Mennonite U,** and William and Catherine Booth College, in Winnipeg; **Steinbach** Bible College; and Providence College and Seminary, in Otterburne, 40 km S of Winnipeg – receive annual operating grants from the provincial govt. Since the raison d'être of each of these institutions is to promote a particular religious orientation, the traditional standards of collegial governance and academic freedom that apply to the public universities are less applicable at these schools. There are also private, profit-driven post-secondary institutions in MB, which operate without direct govt subsidy.

ECONOMIC DEVELOPMENT BRANDON

Brandon University

The University Grants Commission was established in 1967 to distribute govt funds and to serve as a buffer between the govt and the public universities. In 1996, the Council on Post-Secondary Education (COPSE) replaced it. The new body consisted of a small secretariat with an 11-member board to serve as a public sounding board between the policy-making Department of Advanced Education and Training and the academic and technical post-secondary institutions in the province. • DICK HENLEY

EDUCATION, PRIVATE, has existed in MB since the early **Red River Settlement** period. Indeed, given that the **Council of Assiniboia** was unwilling to provide regular funding to support

schools, it might be argued that all formal education prior to Confederation was private. This disinclination did not mean that officials didn't appreciate the value of education but that they considered its function to be primarily a moral undertaking and therefore a responsibility of the established Christian denominations in the community. As a result, the first public school legislation passed in 1871, establishing the dual school system with separate **Roman Catholic** and Protestant school authorities, represented a continuation of past practice.

Organized Catholic involvement began in 1818 when Bishop Plessis of QC dispatched 3 clerics, including the future Bishop of St. Boniface, **Joseph Provencher**, to establish schools. Under Provencher's direction, a system gradually emerged with the Oblate Order, later joined by the Christian Brothers charged with directing education for boys and the **Grey Nuns** for girls.

The initial Protestant schools were **Anglican** and were financially supported by the Church Missionary Society based in England. After a sporadic beginning, church involvement became more systemic following the arrival of Rev John West in Red River in 1820. With the support of the **HBC**, the Red River Academy was established in 1836 to provide a classical curriculum to the children of the company's officers and the wealthier members of the community. By 1844, the Anglicans had established 4 parish schools with a nearly 500 students. The **Presbyterians** began their school system in 1847.

A pattern developed wherein when the number of settlers of a particular denomination achieved sufficient population and wealth, the church would set up a school. Considered from this perspective, the initial post-Confederation state school system did not represent a radical departure from the prevailing practice of the preceding period. The dual system came under attack only after the tide of Protestant immigration overwhelmed the Catholic population.

After 1890, part of the Catholic population decided to operate schools outside the authority of the *Public Schools Act*, a circumstance that church officials and laity resolutely maintained was forced on them by the govt decision to violate the dual schooling clause of the *Manitoba Act*. Catholic parents were not the only people in the province who were paying for private education, however. For a variety of reasons, mostly having to do with considerations of religion and social status, many non-Catholic Manitobans have also chosen to place their children in private institutions. Over the course of the first half of the 20th century, it became convenient for private school supporters to adopt the Catholic double taxation (property

E

St. Mary's Academy, Winnipeg

plus tuition) claim, that they, too, were victims of the rigid regulations contained in the *Public Schools Act*. They tended to ignore the constitutional aspect of the Catholic position, however.

The product of a Royal Commission that examined the state of public education in MB, the 1959 MacFarlane Report, agreed that "parochial and private school" users deserved some relief from the burden of private tuition fees. It recommended that all private schools that were able to meet public school standards should receive govt funding, suggesting that the subsidy amount to 80% of that going to the public schools. The document carefully avoided making a judgement on the Catholic claim. The hesitancy on the part of govt to act on the recommendation brought about the founding of the Manitoba Association for Equality in Education in 1964, an organization that unified supporters of parochial and private schools. An initial shared service agreement between private and public school boards began in 1965. Nine years later, the Manitoba Federation of Independent Schools was organized, and its lobbying efforts led to the initiation of a direct provincial subsidy to private educational institutions in 1980. Throughout the first years of the 21st century, the govt has pegged the contribution at 50% of the public subsidies.

There were about 60 funded and 45 nonfunded private schools (supporters like to use the term "independent" schools) in MB in 2005 with a student population of around 12,000. A number of these schools are of recent vintage, products of religious communities that reject the secular orientation of contemporary public education. The Montessori Learning Centre

(1982) is unique in that it provides a secular educational experience to pre-schoolers. Other non-profit private schools have long histories and a few have become prestigious institutions. St John's-Ravenscourt, for example, dates itself to John West's school in 1820. Catholic institutions, St Mary's Academy (1869) and St Paul's High School (1926), fit this designation as does The Collegiate at the **U of W** (1873) and Balmoral Hall (1901). The Mennonite Collegiate (1885) at **Gretna** and the Jewish-operated Gray Academy (1902) are examples of educational institutions that were established not long after these ethnic groups became established in MB.
● DICK HENLEY

EDUCATION, PUBLIC. Public education has its origins in the *Public Schools Act* (1890) and the so-called Laurier-Greenway Compromise to the **MB Schools Question** of 1896, though the administrative machinery that called on communities to organize local school districts to oversee the construction and operation of public schools and pay the teacher's salary has been practised since MB's entry into Confederation. The *Manitoba Act* contained provisions that established the provincial Board of Education, composed of an equal number of **Catholic** and Protestant members, to oversee the management of a dual school system. Twenty years later, the arrangement appeared preposterous to self-conscious Protestants, whose numbers overwhelmed the Catholic section, and the majority decided to do away with duality because it was deemed inefficient, divisive, and contrary to the real purpose of public education.

The non-sectarian public education system featured what its sponsors called National Schools to emphasize that they were intended to be more attuned to the broader needs of modern civic society. The Board of Education gave way to the Advisory Board, an appointive body mandated to provide a program of studies, authorize and approve textbooks, prepare final examinations, and devise a body of regulations to guide the deliberations of locally elected school boards. In MB communities with a predominantly Catholic population, it was possible to provide a Catholic orientation to public education. Elsewhere, however, particularly in urban areas, that option was not available, and many Catholic ratepayers complied with the wishes of church authorities to send their children to what were, in effect, private schools. The 1896 compromise did not alleviate the situation of many Catholic parents, who continued to pay for both private tuition fees and the property tax that was levied in support of their local public school. In their view, this double billing represented a clear violation of the *Manitoba Act*. That circumstance has continued to have resonance.

The rapid growth of **Winnipeg** during the first 2 decades of the 20th century provided the context for the emergence of a modern urban education system through the authority of the Winnipeg Board of School Trustees. Board members distinguished themselves during the protracted campaign for compulsory school attendance laws in the province, the resolution of which did not take place until 1916. That year also brought the demise of the so-called bilingual (English and any other language) system of instruction, a feature of the 1896 compromise. English became the only permissible language of instruction in MB public schools. The new law had no effect in Winnipeg, however, because its school board had never acceded to the bilingual clause over the previous 2 decades.

Elsewhere in the province, some of the school boards that had adopted the bilingual model decided that their schools would ignore the new law. This kind of subversion shows that local school boards never relinquished the power to ignore provincial authority when it ran counter to the needs of their community. Moreover, officials in the Department of Education, including elected officials, were usually more interested in maintaining social peace than they were in enforcing the letter of the law. The disposition to countenance ethno-cultural aspirations of school trustees in the face of established provincial law has been an important feature of public school administration in MB.

Of course, school boards were not at odds with most govt policy. The tide of **Immigration** compelled school divisions, especially those in Winnipeg but in the smaller urban centres as well, to expand the scale of their operations quickly. A new class of educationist, charged with planning, co-ordinating, and supervising these local bureaucracies, entered the scene. These professionals tended to steer clear of the traditional political issues, concentrating on other pressing educational concerns of the day. American progressives provided a veritable smorgasbord of school policy options for MB educationists. Since Winnipeg was home to a growing body of educational administrators who oversaw the operation of the Department of Education (Robert Fletcher), the Winnipeg School Division (**DANIEL McINTYRE** and **J.B. MITCHELL**), and some higher education facilities, including the province's largest normal school (W. A. McIntyre), there was ample opportunity to collaborate about the development of public education in MB. Through monthly educational journals like *The Educational Journal of Western Canada* and its successor, *The Western School Journal*, ideas were cherry-picked from ready US models of school reform and publicized, and, in due course, many were adopted.

Montrose School, Winnipeg

Reform took place at every level of public education, but perhaps nowhere more dramatically than that in the high schools. Manual training shops and home economics rooms were introduced at the turn of the century not long after commercial classes had been introduced in the Winnipeg High School. The notion that the high school should provide more than the traditional academic fare was extended further in 1910 when a provincial commission was appointed to investigate how technical education could be incorporated into the program. The Winnipeg School Division was already constructing 2 new technical high schools by the time the investigation convened. There were 6 streams of program available to students in the provincial capital by 1915. Four years later, the city had a fully functioning junior high school system. The modern urban school system in Winnipeg set the standard for emulation in the smaller towns.

A long-term effect of modern administrative practices in public schools has been to depoliticize public education. Indeed, the silence of the educational experts on matters related to the Manitoba Schools Question lent credence to the view the matter had been settled, first in 1896 and again in 1916. Over the years since WWI, those charged with overseeing MB public education have had to deal with a succession of revisionist schemes, usually US in origin; politicians have usually left it to the educational experts to decide whether they merit adoption.

The most persistent problem faced by provincial school officials over the years has been to find ways to ensure that children growing up in the MB countryside have access to good public schooling. The resolution of the problem, initially proposed in 1904 legislation and supported by 3 provincial commissions – the most influential being the 1959 MacFarlane Report – all strongly advocated the consolidation of rural school divisions. The pooling of scarce resources was said to be a much more efficient way to manage public schooling, but the recommendation also promised to improve the education of rural children in more stimulating graded classrooms. The fact that one-room schoolhouses remained in service through the 1960s in many areas has often been attributed to apathy and indifference, traits all too often assigned to those who resist modernization. That interpretation is convenient, but it fails to consider the cultural significance of the schools, often the only public institution that many communities ever had. They were highly valued on that account. After mid-century, improved highways and the lure of the urban lifestyle finally brought the era of the one-room school to an end.

Real and personal property have never been distributed evenly across MB, and so it has been necessary for the provincial govt to continually readjust funding arrangements to meet the needs of those school divisions which have difficulty achieving departmental standards. The tendency in the direction of greater provincial funding for provincial education continued until 1980, when it peaked at 80% of the total expenditure. It has fallen steadily since then to the point where the provincial govt now contributes about 60% of the total public expenditure on education. Property tax has never been a particularly popular way to generate public revenue; as long as it remains a major generator of educational revenue, however, school trustees, organized through the Manitoba Association of School Trustees (MAST), will remain important players in provincial education. The Manitoba Teachers Society (MTS) serves as a second counterweight to provincial authority in public education.

Manitobans have generally shown over the years that they have confidence in the public education system. A key ingredient of that public support has been the capacity of the system to bend enough to meet local conditions and circumstances, and the tendency has been to seek resolution of differences in a spirit of conciliation. • DICK HENLEY

EGG FARMING. Egg production added about $85 million each year in the early 21st century to MB's economy. The 177 registered egg and pullet producers in MB in 2004 operated on a supply-management or quota system that regulates the number of eggs produced but not the type. Vitamin-enhanced (including omega-3), organic, and vegetarian eggs result from adjustments to the hens' diet. Free-run and free-range eggs reflect how much freedom hens have to move outside of cages used in conventional egg production. The average hen begins to lay eggs at 19 weeks and over the next year lays 300 eggs. That is 18% more than in the 1990s. Inspectors sort eggs into 3 grades: grade A for retail sales; B, for institutional sales; and C, for industrial use. At the end of their productive cycle, hens are killed and composted. Egg farms in MB are generally highly-mechanized, family-owned businesses. In 2004, MB produced 15% of the Cdn total. Eggs are also processed into frozen products and liquid eggs at Trilogy Egg Products Inc., based in **WINNIPEG** and owned by Michael Foods Inc. of MN, Canada's largest egg processor, Inovatech Inc. of Abbotsford, BC, and Manitoba Egg Producers Co-Op Ltd. Processed products represent the growth area in the sector; in 2000, a special market development program allowed producers to expand their flocks to supply this market. Turkey eggs are not sold commercially in MB. • ANNE COTE

EHNES, James, concert violinist (b Jan 27, 1976, **BRANDON**), is a musical prodigy who has performed worldwide and is especially well-known for his recording of Paganini's *24 Caprices*. The son of a trumpeter and music instructor at **BRANDON U**, Ehnes began studying the violin at the age of 4. At 9, he became a protégé of Cdn violinist Francis Chaplin. In 1988, Ehnes was the youngest musician to ever win first prize in Strings at the Canadian Music Festival. The next year he made his orchestral solo debut with the Orchestre symphonique de Montreal. He attended New York's Meadowmount School of Music, and graduated from the Julliard School in 1997. At Julliard, he won the Peter Mennin Prize for Outstanding Achievement and Leadership in Music. Ehnes has performed with renowned conductors and

ANNA KEENAN

James Ehnes

appeared with orchestras throughout Europe, Asia, the US, and Canada. He has performed several times with the Manitoba Chamber Orchestra. As a chamber musician, he has performed with Jan Vogler, Louis Lortie, Leif Ove Andsnes, and Yo-Yo Ma. He has released 20 recordings and has won numerous awards including Juno Awards in 2001 and 2002 for best classical recording. In 2002, Ehnes was also named Young Artist of the Year at the Cannes Classical Awards. In 2005, he was honoured with a Doctor of Music degree from Brandon U. In 2006, Ehnes lived in Florida and Philadelphia with his wife. ● AMANDA STEPHENS

ELDERLY POPULATION in MB was proportionally the 2nd highest of all provinces in 2001. The geographical concentration of residents age 65 (the Cdn retirement age) and over has strong implications for public policy in the 21st century.

SOCIO-DEMOGRAPHIC CHARACTERISTICS: In 2001, 156,415 Manitobans were "elderly" (aged 65 or over), accounting for 14% of the entire population of the province, compared to 13.4% in 1991. In 2001, 57.8% (90,415 persons) of the provincial elderly population were women, owing to the higher level of mortality among men. The life expectancy at birth for females in MB was 81.1 years in 2001, compared to 76.2 years for their male counterparts.

Overall, MB's 2001 elderly population exceeded the national rate of 13.0%. Of the other Cdn provinces and territories, only SK had a higher percentage at 15.1%. The relatively high proportion of elderly is due to several demographic factors, particularly the tendency of long-time residents to remain, and the emigration of younger people from the province. However, the number of elderly people in MB increased by 6.7% between 1991 and 2001, compared to 22.6% in Canada, primarily because of relatively rapid aging in-place in many other areas of the nation.

According to the 2001 Census, the "young old" (65-74 years) comprised 78,565 persons, or 50.2% of the elderly population of MB. The 56,875 persons aged 75-84 years and over (the "old-old") accounted for 36.4% of the provincial elderly, and of that, 20,975 persons aged 85 years and over (the "oldest-old") made up 13.4% of the total. Of the 2 oldest age brackets, 44,720 (57.4%) were women. Between 1991 and 2001, it is noteworthy that the percentage increase in the old-old/oldest-old elderly was no less than 21.7%, while the number of young-old elderly declined by 4.9%. This upward shift in the average age of the elderly suggests that in future increasing demands will be placed on providers of long-term care resources in the province. In 2001, 20.5% of elderly Manitobans were born outside Canada, compared to 12.1% of the overall population. The largest proportions of these came from Eastern Europe (31.7%), the UK (17.5%), and Northern and Western Europe (16.8%).

Nearly 2000 elderly persons moved to MB from other provinces with the most common provinces of origin including BC (31.6%), ON (28.8%), SK (18.6%), and AB (14.2%). Some of these persons included previous residents of the province who returned to MB in order to gain health-related assistance from relatives or formal care facilities. Return migration of the elderly is typically motivated by declining physical capability or by the loss of the spouse. Of the 3400 elderly persons who moved from MB to other provinces between 1996 and 2001, the most popular destinations were BC (36.2%), AB (24.3%), ON (22.1%), and SK (11.6%). These movers included many younger retiree couples, often moving to resort areas with attractive scenery and gentler climate.

Among the entire elderly population of MB in 2001, 67.5% identified one ethnic or cultural group to which their ancestors belonged, while 32.5% reported more than one ethnic group. Of those who identified one ethnic or cultural group only, the most frequently reported were British (25.1%), Ukrainian (16.3%), German (13.8%), and Cdn (11.7%). No fewer than 17.3% of Manitobans younger than 65 identified themselves as "Aboriginal," compared to only 3.3% of the elderly. This disparity reflects the lower life expectancy of Aboriginal Manitobans.

As of the Census, the overwhelming majority of elderly lived with their spouse or common-law partner (56.1%), or lived alone (34.3%). However, there are differences concerning living arrangements that clearly reflect lower male life expectancy; specifically, while elderly men (73.9%) were more likely to live with their spouse than elderly women (42.5%), 44.5% of elderly women lived alone, compared to only 20.5% of elderly men.

SOCIO-ECONOMIC ATTRIBUTES: Labour force participation among elderly men in MB was 16.9% in 2001, compared to only 5% for elderly females. Of employed elderly men, 70.7% worked full-time, compared to 41.2% of employed elderly females. The major occupational categories of employed elderly men were "primary industry," including farming, fishing, forestry, and mining (38.1%); "sales and service" (14.8%); and "trades, transport, and equipment operators" (13.8%). The major occupational categories of employed elderly women were "sales and service" (26.8%); "primary industry" (24.1%); and "business, finance, administration" (18.9%). In 2000, the average income of households with the "primary household maintainer" aged 65 years or over was $36,066. However, among elderly female primary household maintainers, 30.2% reported household incomes of less than $15,000, compared to only 7.5% of their male counterparts.

GEOGRAPHICAL PATTERNS: In 2001, significant concentrations of the elderly persons occurred in small rural towns of the extremity of SW MB (such as VIRDEN, MELITA, and BOISSEVAIN), with the elderly accounting for between 19-22% of the local population. This was due the aging in place of long-time residents, and shifts of younger persons to urban areas, particularly WINNIPEG. Further important concentrations of elderly people were located at the SW extremity of LAKE WINNIPEG; for example, 31.3% of the population of GIMLI and 28.7% of the population of WINNIPEG BEACH were elderly in 2001. In part, the in-migration of amenity-seeking retirees from Winnipeg and other urban settlements in MB account for the concentrations of older people in these lakeshore communities.

The most notable relative growth of elderly people between 1991 and 2001 occurred in SE MB, with the 5 census divisions immediately bounding Winnipeg registering increases from 17-27%. This growth was mainly due to the aging in place of people in small towns or rural areas. Compared to their urban counterparts, MB's dispersed rural elderly population often faces less access to social services, health care, and public transportation.

Northern MB has the lowest percentages of the provincial elderly. For example, in 2001, the elderly population of THOMPSON was 2.3%, while in 2003, only 53 older persons lived in the CHURCHILL Health Region. Clearly, the harsh climate and resource-based economy of northern

MB are unattractive to older people, and northern residents typically migrate either before or immediately after retirement. The relatively lower life expectancy of Aboriginal people also partly accounts for this statistic.

In 2001, 76.4% of elderly Manitobans were classed as "urban." Overall, the elderly accounted for 14.8% of the province's urban population in 2001, compared to 11.7% of the rural population. While the elderly comprised 15.9% of the population of **BRANDON**, they accounted for 17.4% of the population of **PORTAGE LA PRAIRIE**. In 2001, 92,170 elderly people resided in the Winnipeg Census Metropolitan Area (CMA), representing 58.9% of the provincial elderly population compared to 57.3% in 1991. This represents an increase of 9.7% (8160 persons) over the 10-year period. Factors contributing to the increase in the elderly within the Winnipeg CMA include aging in place, and rural-to-urban migration of older people who require health care and social supports. Overall, elderly persons accounted for 13.7% and 14.1% of the total population of Winnipeg CMA and the City of Winnipeg respectively in 2001. From a policy perspective, the increasing concentration of older people in Winnipeg has important implications for those responsible for sheltering and caring for the elderly in MB.
● GEOFFREY C. SMITH

ELECTORAL SYSTEM. MB elections have changed dramatically over the years. The province's first election was held Dec 27, 1870. The legislative assembly consisted of 24 representatives whom voters elected by declaring in public their candidate of preference. Ridings were designated to balance and reflect the French-speaking and English-speaking elements of the provincial population.

To qualify to vote, one had to be a property-owning male. Originally, candidates did not run under party banners. They either declared themselves as candidates for the govt or the Opposition. Party labels began to be applied in 1879, but not until the 1883 election did it become clear that candidates were expected to run on party slates. These early provincial party banners corresponded to federal equivalents, the Conservatives (officially "Liberal-Conservatives": *see* **PROGRESSIVE CONSERVATIVE PARTY**) and the **LIBERAL PARTY**.

The secret ballot was introduced in the 1888 election. Voters were no longer required to own property, but had to have resided in the province for 6 months, and for one month in their electoral division. Due to population growth and territorial expansion, by 1892, the Legislature grew to 40 sitting MLAs.

In 1914, the legislature expanded to 49 seats. Furthermore, with the explosive growth of **WINNIPEG**'s economy in the early 20th century, labour parties had appeared in a strong fashion. However, they were up against the fact that rural ridings were over-represented in the legislature – a fact that would not be properly rectified until the 1960s. In 1914, a new system was introduced in **WINNIPEG**. Three regions replaced the 4 city ridings: Winnipeg North, Winnipeg South, and Winnipeg Centre. Voters in each region received 2 ballots to cast, one for a preferred candidate in the "A" seat, with the 2nd for a candidate in the identical riding for what

was designated as the "B" seat. Candidates could not run for both "A" and "B" seats.

The govt of **TOBIAS NORRIS** extended the vote to women in 1916, making MB the first province in Canada to allow them the franchise. In 1920, the legislature was expanded to contain 55 seats, and Winnipeg-based MLAs were now elected by a city-wide proportional-representation system. Voters would rate their preferences for all the candidates offered, and the top 10 would then represent Winnipeg as a single multiple-member riding. This system remained in place until 1949.

In 1922, MB voters rejected the Liberals, electing 28 United Farmers of Manitoba as MLAs. The party was leaderless but soon recruited **JOHN BRACKEN** to serve as the new premier. The party operated as the Progressive Party in the 1927 election, which served as both an end and a beginning for two electoral oddities. Ended was the tradition of having MLAs who entered the cabinet resigning their seat in order to be re-elected in a by-election as an MLA (with, of course, new status). This year also signalled the beginning of an "alternative" balloting system in rural ridings by which candidates needed to win a majority rather than a simple plurality. Where used, voters listed their preferences when voting for their MLA. If no candidate won a majority of votes, the candidate with the least number of votes would be dropped and voter second preferences would then be tallied. Counting would proceed until a candidate achieved 50% of the total vote. The system fell into disuse by the 1940s.

In 1932, the Progressive Party "fused" with the Liberal Party. Then, by 1941 Bracken formed an all-party coalition government in order to better negotiate financial arrangements with Ottawa and to respond to wartime conditions. This arrangement lasted throughout the decade, with the exception of the **CO-OPERATIVE COMMONWEALTH FEDERATION**, which departed cabinet in 1942. In this period, many seats were uncontested.

In Jan 1946, elections were held for 3 special seats for members of the **MILITARY**. These were

Manitoba Elections 1870-78

Election Year	GOVERNMENT		OPPOSITION		UNDECLARED/UNKNOWN	
	% Votes	Seats	% Votes	Seats	% Votes	Seats
1870	56%	18	23%	4	21%	2
1874	19%	9	18%	6	63%	9
1878	9%	7	–	–	91%	91%

Figures compiled from Elections Manitoba Historical Tables

Manitoba Elections 1879-1903

Election Year	CONSERVATIVE		LIBERAL		OTHER/INDEPENDENT/UNKNOWN		PATRONS OF INDUSTRY	
	% Votes	Seats	% Votes	Seats	% Votes	Seats	% Votes	Seats
1879	34%	13	7%	2	66%	9	–	–
1883	55%	20	45%	10	–	–	–	–
1886	51%	21	48%	14	1%	0	–	–
1888	34%	5	57%	32	10%	1	–	–
1892	41%	9	50%	24	9%	7	–	–
1896	40%	5	50%	32	2%	1	8%	2
1899	44%	18	50%	17	7%	5	–	–
1903	48%	29	45%	9	8%	2	–	–

Figures compiled from Elections Manitoba Historical Tables

Manitoba Elections 1907-20

Election Year	CONSERVATIVE		LIBERAL		LABOUR OR SOCIALIST		OTHER/INDEPENDENT	
	% Votes	Seats	% Votes	Seats	% Votes	Seats	% Votes	Seats
1907	51%	28	48%	13	2%	0	–	–
1910	51%	28	44%	13	4%	0	1%	0
1914	47%	28	43%	20	5%	0	6%	1
1915	33%	5	55%	40	3%	0	9%	2
1920	19%	9	35%	21	21%	12	26%	13

Figures compiled from Elections Manitoba Historical Tables

Manitoba Elections 1922-36

Election Year	CONSERVATIVE		LIBERAL		UFM/PROGRESSIVE		LABOUR/FARMER-LABOUR/CCF		OTHER/INDEPENDENT	
	% Votes	Seats	% Votes	Seats	% Votes	Seats	% Votes	Seats	% Votes	Seats
1922	16%	7	23%	8	33%	28	16%	6	13%	6
1927	27%	15	21%	7	32%	29	11%	3	9%	1
			LIBERAL-PROGRESSIVE							
1932	35%	10	40%	38			17%	6	9%	1
1936	28%	16	35%	23			12%	7	23%	9*

*includes 5 Social Credit seats with 9% of the vote   Figures compiled from Elections Manitoba Historical Tables

eliminated in 1949. The 10-member riding of Winnipeg was converted into 3 separate constituencies for the 1949 election, with each containing 4 MLAs. St. Boniface was represented by 2 MLAs. The preferential ballot was used for these multiple-member elections. In this same year, the Legislature expanded to 57 seats, the same number it retained as of writing. The multi-member riding disappeared in 1958, when St. Boniface became a single-member riding and Winnipeg was divided into 20 single-member constituencies.

The status-First Nations population became fully enfranchised in 1952, though those serving in the military had had the vote since 1932. Another reform at the time was to correct disparities between rural and urban representation: in 1952, 40 rural MLAs represented 224,083 voters, while 17 MLAs represented 228,280 urban voters. Therefore, in 1957 the legislature implemented the recommendations from its newly established Electoral Divisions Boundaries Commission to rectify over-representation of rural voters in the legislature. It was a less-than-complete solution, with the rural-urban balance partially resolved at a 7:4 ratio.

In 1968, the Electoral Boundaries Commission put forward an adjustment to balance further the rural-urban ratio of seats. The result was that almost half of the province's ridings became located in Winnipeg and its suburbs. The 1969 **NEW DEMOCRATIC PARTY** breakthrough has often been linked to this change.

Several minor procedural changes were made in the 1970s, such as a requirement of 50 signatures from voters in the riding rather than

Manitoba Elections: Coalitions in 1941-49

1941 GOVERNMENT COALITION	Seats	Popular Support
Liberal-Progressive	27	35%
Conservative	12	16%
CCF	3	17%
Social Credit	3	2%
Independent	5	11%
1941 ANTI-GOVERNMENT COALITION		
Conservative	3	4%
Social Credit	0	6%
Independent	1	5%
Communist	1	3%
1945 GOVERNMENT COALITION		
Liberal-Progressive	25	32%
Progressive Conservative	13	16%
Social Credit	2	1%
Independent	3	5%
1945 ANTI- GOVERNMENT COALITION:		
CCF	9	34%
Social Credit	0	1%
Labour-Progressive	1	5%
Independent/Ind. CCF	2	6%
1949 GOVERNMENT COALITION		
Liberal-Progressive	30	38%
Progressive Conservative	9	12%
Ind. Lib/Lib. Prog.	1	4%
Independent	4	4%
1949 ANTI- GOVERNMENT COALITION		
CCF	7	26%
Cons & Ind. PC	4	7%
Ind. Lib/Lib. Prog.	1	3%
Others	1	6%

Manitoba Elections 1953-66

Election Year	PROGRESSIVE CONSERVATIVE		LIBERAL-PROGRESSIVE/LIBERAL		CCF/NDP		OTHER/INDEPENDENT/ SOCIAL CREDIT	
	% Votes	Seats	% Votes	Seats	% Votes	Seats	% Votes	Seats
1953	21%	12	43%	36*	16%	5	19%**	4
1958	40%	27	35%	19	20%	10	4%	1
1959	46%	36	30%	11	22%	10	1%	0
1962	45%	36	36%	13	15%	7	3%	1
1966	40%	31	33%	14	23%	11	4%	1

*Includes Independent Liberal-Progressives (3 seats)   ** Includes 13% for Social Credit (one seat)   Figures compiled from Elections Manitoba Historical Tables*

Manitoba Elections 1969-2007

Election Year	PROGRESSIVE CONSERVATIVE		NDP		LIBERAL		OTHER	
	% Votes	Seats	% Votes	Seats	% Votes	Seats	% Votes	Seats
1969	35%	22	38%	28	24%	5	2%	2*
1973	37%	21	42%	31	19%	5	–	0
1977	49%	33	38%	23	12%	1	–	0
1981	44%	23	47%	34	7%	0	–	0
1986	40%	26	41%	30	14%	1	–	0
1988	38%	25	24%	12	35%	12	–	0
1990	42%	30	29%	20	28%	7	–	0
1995	43%	31	33%	23	24%	3	–	0
1999	41%	24	44%	32	13%	1	–	0
2003	36%	20	49%	35	13%	2	1%	0
2007	38%	19	48%	36	12%	2	2%	0

Includes one Independent and one Social Credit   Figures compiled from Elections Manitoba Historical Tables

E

a $200 candidate-nomination fee. A number of new measures were implemented in 1980. Candidates would now need 100 signatures from voters in their riding. More significant was the formal establishment of a chief electoral officer, an independent officer of the legislature, and the *Elections Finances Act*. This act included spending limits for advertising on elections, tax credits for contributions to parties, and new requirements for financial disclosure by campaign managers. In 1985, new spending limits were introduced that included all campaign expenses, not just advertising. In part due to issues surrounding senior govt officials involved in the **INTERLAKE VOTING SCANDAL**, 1998 saw a number of changes to the *Elections Act* and the *Elections Finances Act*. These included expanding the investigative powers of the chief electoral officer, and strengthening regulations pertaining to the disclosure of contributions and expenses.

As in many other jurisdictions across the Western world, declining voter turnout in MB is a concern. During the 1990s, turnout was close to 70% of registered voters, and a lower percentage of those eligible to vote. More recently, the figure has dropped below 60% of registered voters, and is even lower among specific socio-demographic groupings such as Aboriginal people, women, and young adults. • CHRIS ADAMS

ELGIN, pop 273, is a community located about 60 km WSW of Brandon. The post office opened here in 1899. The community is believed to have been named by the Northern Pacific Railway after James B. Elgin, 8th Earl of Elgin and gov gen in 1846. The first settlers arrived here in 1881. Today, Elgin is a service centre for the surrounding agricultural lands, and home to the Elgin and District Historical Museum. • GPP

ELIE, pop 1129, is a community located 45 km W of Winnipeg on the **CN** main line. The post office and railway point were established here in 1898. It is unclear whether the community was named after Elie Chamberland, a hotelier who started a business here in 1899 and died that same year, or after both Chamberland and Élie Dufresene, one of the first settlers. Elie is now an agricultural centre for nearby **HUTTERITE** communities, and supports 2 **GRAIN ELEVATORS**. As of Nov 24 2005, the local Dow BioProducts plant, which had produced strawboard – a product similar to particleboard – closed its doors after having several changes of ownership. In 2007, the strongest tornado in Cdn history ripped through the town, damaging many buildings, but leaving no fatalities. • GPP

ELK or wapiti (*Cervus elaphus*) is a large member of the **DEER** family or Cervidae that is native temperate and boreal forests right across Eurasia and NA, including the SW third of MB. Historical records note the abundance of American Elk throughout the prairie and mixed-woods regions, and there was mention of a herd at Little Grand Rapids. The 1930s estimate for **RIDING MOUNTAIN** alone was 14,000. Sadly, the species' numbers and range have been decimated since the arrival of Europeans. The current estimate for MB is 6500 (72,000 in Canada), within the following populations: Riding (1700), Duck (1500), and Porcupine (800) mountains, Interlake (1500), and 1000 combined in Spruce Woods, the Tallgrass Prairie Reserve near **TOLSTOI**, and the Turtle Mountains.

ROBERT R. TAYLOR

Elk (Wapiti) bugling

The exceptionally large race occurring in MB has been given the name *Cervus elaphus manitobensis*. Males average 325 kg (females 225), but may reach a massive 590 kg. The crowning glory of the bull is a magnificent rack of antlers, which are replaced each year. Beginning to grow from a nubbin of bone on the forehead in May, the pair of antlers grow quickly through the summer, supplied with nutrients from the blood vessels running through the antler's fuzzy skin or 'velvet.' Antler growth is completed in Aug., reaching up from 100-160 cm long (with about 6 points), and each weighing up to 6.6 kg, depending on the animal's health and food quality. The antlers are used in defence against predators (grey **Wolf** and cougar), and in combat between rival males during the rounding up of a harem of females. The antler and reproductive cycles are influenced by day length, and mediated via the brain and hormones. A social animal, gathering in large herds for the winter, the elk has no distinct home range, but wanders in search of pasture. Population density averages from 3-9/km². It can gallop at speeds up to 48 km/hr – remarkably fast for such a huge animal. • REW, VC

ELKHORN, pop 470, is a village located 95 km W of **Brandon**, just E of the SK border on the Trans-Canada Highway and the CP line. Settlers came to Elkhorn in 1882 the same year the **CPR** laid down its tracks. Formerly known as Flat Creek, the name changed when a CPR crewman came across a large rack of elk antlers. The village was incorporated in 1906. In the 21st century, economic activity in the village centres on agriculture, including numerous cattle and hog productions. A much smaller part of the economy is fuelled by oil explorations and extractions. Elkhorn is home of the Manitoba Antique Automobile Museum. This project, operating since 1965, attracts many visitors each summer and is considered to house one of the finest car collections in the country. • GPP

ELM. White/American Elm (*Ulmus americana*) is the only native elm in MB, best known as the stately large **Trees** lining the streets and boulevards of our towns and cities. An excellent shade tree with an umbrella-like crown, white elm is a tall deciduous hardwood capable of surviving harsh climates and urban environments. Historically, it occurred fairly commonly on rich moist soils, especially along streams and rivers, in the southern ⅖ of MB, reaching as far N as **The Pas**. Although it can be nearly 40 m in height and 2 m in diameter, most mature MB trees are between 20-30 m tall and 1-1.5 m in diameter. Only the northern cottonwood (*Populus deltoides)* have larger trunks. Leaves are alternate, dark green, uneven at their base and doubly toothed (teeth on teeth);

Young elm saplings planted along Winnipeg's Broadway around 1890 have become a distinguishing feature of the area.

bark is brownish-grey with deep furrows and scaly ridges. Its inconspicuous greenish flowers in April or May are wind-pollinated and produce numerous oval hairy-fringed winged seeds. These seeds provide food for mice, squirrels, ruffed grouse and other upland game birds. Its light-coloured heavy wood is strong and durable and has been used in paneling, furniture and ships. First planted along roadways in the late 1800s in what would become the Wolseley area of **Winnipeg**, elms were more widely planted in the 1920s.

Elms are now sadly best known because of the Dutch elm disease (DED), the latest disease of wild and planted trees to hit NA. DED arrived in southern MB in the early 1970s along the **Red River**. It is caused by a fungus (introduced from Europe) carried by tiny dark-brown elm bark beetles that feed only on healthy elms and reproduce in diseased ones. They carry spores of the fungus from diseased to healthy trees where it produces toxins lethal to the tree and blocks the flow of water and nutrients from roots to leaves. DED has killed about 90% of the 20 million native elms that once grew in MB. Only elms growing in isolated situations such as The Pas or where **Insect Control** programs can be carried out (such as Winnipeg) can survive DED although plant breeders continue to try to develop resistant trees.

The Siberian Elm (*Ulmus pumila*) has been widely planted and naturalized throughout southern MB. A smaller and much less attractive tree than our native elm, its smooth, abundant, 1 cm wide seeds have a nearly round wing and its leaves are single toothed. It is immune or very resistant to DED. • KAREN JOHNSON

▶ *See also* **Vern Hildahl**

ELM CREEK, pop 325, is a community located about 40 km SSE of Portage la Prairie and 60 km WSW of Winnipeg, on a **CPR** line. This community

was named after a nearby creek of the same name, though the creek is now known as Elm River. Elm Creek was originally within the **Métis** land reserve, but settlers displaced them with the construction of the Manitoba and Southwestern Colonization Railway. Some Métis sold their land, while others gave it up for grants received elsewhere. Founded in 1892, Elm Creek now has an economy mostly centred on grain, cattle, horse, swine, dairy and chicken farming, and there are 2 grain elevators. Many residents also commute to jobs in Winnipeg. • GPP

ELPHINSTONE, pop 100, is a community located 110 km NNW of **Brandon**. In 1880, a granary went into operation, and the post office opened here in 1887. The community was named after William Elphinstone, 15th Lord Elphinstone and first Baron Elphinstone, who was a director of the **CPR**. The Canadian Northern Railway began construction of the railway in Dec 1904. Elphinstone is close to the **Keeseekoowenin Ojibway First Nation** and to the former Riding Mountain House HBC trading post, which was replaced by an HBC post in Elphinstone in the 1880s. • GPP

EMERSON, pop 655, is a town located 95 km S of Winnipeg on the US border, along the **Red River**, with MN on the E bank and ND on the W. The town was founded by Thomas Carney, who is believed to be the inventor of the cash register, and W. A. Fairbanks, both of Red Wing, MN. The post office was known originally as North Fort Pembina and was opened in 1871. The name changed to West Lynne in 1873 because mail was being mis-routed from Fort Pembina just 5 km S in the US. Then, in 1879, the name changed again to Emerson, after the American essayist and philosopher Ralph Waldo Emerson. Emerson was once poised to become MB's largest centre. Due to its location, the town

Flooding in Emerson, 1897

Species at Risk Act (SARA). COSEWIC maintains a national listing of Cdn species at risk, based on scientific evidence available for vertebrates, invertebrates (only molluscs, butterflies and moths thus far), and plants. Wildlife is described as a species, subspecies, variety, or geographically or genetically distinct population of animal, plant or other organism (but not a bacterium or virus) that is wild by nature and is either native to Canada, or has extended its range into Canada without human intervention, and has been present in Canada for at least 50 years.

Risk categories are similar to those of MB – extinct, extirpated, endangered, threatened, or vulnerable. In many cases, species are found to be not at risk or lack sufficient data to make a determination. Currently there are 529 species in Canada listed in various COSEWIC risk categories: 205 Endangered, 136 Threatened, 153 Special Concern, 22 Extirpated, and 13 Extinct; an additional 41 species are Data Deficient and remain under review.

MB Conservation operates a program of Parks and Natural Areas that offers varying levels of protection for MB wildlife, including at-risk species. These lands range from multi-use wildlife-management areas and provincial parks to ecological reserves (low to high protection, respectively). Environment Canada complements this park system with two national parks.

was the first that travellers came upon when entering the province from the US. It was soon known as "MB's First City." Its prosperity rose in 1879 when the Pembina branch of the **CPR** connected with the US line to St. Paul, MN, making Emerson the only rail link between E Canada and the NW US. Business boomed and the population quickly grew to more than 5000 people, threatening to best the provincial capital. The boom collapsed, however, when the CPR laid a direct E-W route through Winnipeg. In the 21st century, Emerson's location in the heart of the Red River Valley makes it a centre for agricultural services. Its placement on the N/S commerce corridor makes Emerson the busiest border crossing in Canada between Windsor and Vancouver. • GPP

ENDANGERED SPECIES is a popular term describing wildlife species whose conservation status is of ecological concern. More appropriate terminology is 'species at risk,' since endangered is used in science as a specific category within a rating system to designate imminent loss of a species to a jurisdiction. The *Manitoba Endangered Species Act* (proclaimed 1990, amended 1993) was enacted to ensure the survival of endangered and threatened species in the province; to enable the reintroduction of extirpated species; and to designate species as endangered, threatened, extinct or extirpated. Additions or deletions to lists of species under each designation are recommended to the Minister of Conservation by an Endangered Species Advisory Committee.

Manitoba Conservation has yet to consider most of its wildlife, but is moving toward reconciling its designations with those of the Committee On the Status of Endangered Wildlife In Canada (COSEWIC). The following table lists the 30 species currently designated by MB, and while the actual total is unknown, it likely exceeds 300 species if all biota were considered.

Status categories stated in the *Manitoba Endangered Species Act* (MBESA) are:

- Threatened – A species indigenous to MB that is likely to become endangered (due to low or declining numbers) if factors affecting its vulnerability are not reversed.
- Endangered – A species indigenous to MB that is threatened with imminent extinction or with extirpation throughout all or a significant portion of its MB range.
- Extirpated – A species formerly indigenous to MB that no longer exists in the wild in MB, but exists elsewhere.
- Extinct – A species formerly indigenous to MB that no longer exists here or elsewhere.

At the federal level, COSEWIC is mandated to recommend species to be added to Canada's

Species designated under the Manitoba Endangered Species Act.
(Total 30 species)

EXTINCT:
Passenger Pigeon *(Ectopistes migratorius)*

EXTIRPATED:
Riding's Satyr Butterfly *(Neominois ridingsii)*

Trumpeter Swan *(Cygnus buccinator)*

Long-billed Curlew *(Numenius americanus)*

Greater Prairie Chicken *(Tympanuchus cupido)*

Grizzly, Prairie population *(Ursus arctos horribilis)*

Swift Fox *(Vulpes velox)*

Pronghorn *(Antilocapra americana)*

Muskox *(Ovibos moschatus)*

ENDANGERED:
Great Plains Ladies'-tresses *(Spiranthes magnicamporum)*

Small White Lady's-slipper *(Cypripedium candidum)*

Western Prairie Fringed Orchid *(Platanthera praeclara)*

Uncas Skipper *(Hesperia uncas)*

Baird's Sparrow *(Ammodramus bairdii)*

Burrowing Owl *(Athene cunicularia)*

Eskimo Curlew *(Numenius borealis)*

Loggerhead Shrike *(Lanius ludovicianus)*

Peregrine Falcon *(Falco peregrinus)*

Piping Plover *(Charadrius melodus)*

Whooping Crane *(Grus americana)*

THREATENED:
Culver's-root *(Veronicastrum virginicum)*

Riddell's Goldenrod *(Solidago riddellii)*

Western Silvery Astor *(Symphyotrichum sericeum)*

Western Spiderwort *(Tradescantia occidentalis)*

Dakota Skipper *(Hesperia dacotae)*

Ottoe Skipper *(Hesperia ottoe)*

Great Plains Toad *(Bufo cognatus)*

Ferruginous Hawk *(Buteo regalis)*

Mule deer *(Odocoileus hemionus)*

Caribou, Woodland subspecies *(Ranger tarandus caribou)*

A number of private organizations, such as The Nature Conservancy of Canada and Ducks Unlimited Canada, add significantly to protected lands and wetlands, offering habitat to species at risk. ● REW

ENGLISH. The story of the English in MB is in many ways the story of the province's settlement, and people of English descent – wholly or in part – form the largest ethnic origin in MB, with 243,835 of the 2001 Census total of 1,103,695, or 22.1%.

The English, as distinct from the British (which include the English, **Scots**, Welsh, and Northern **Irish**), were key players in every stage of MB's development. Most of the early naval explorers in the North were English. The **HBC** (though employing many Scots) was owned and operated by the English. The majority of settlers who flooded into MB from ON after the province's admission into Confederation (and who radically changed the region's culture) were of English descent. Most of the institutional philosophies that MB maintains (parliamentary democracy, common law, separation of church and state) were imported from England. Hundreds of place names for new settlements recalled English sites. Significant congregations attended Anglican and Methodist churches. In fact, the English presence is so rooted in MB's history that for a long time it existed as a de facto cultural hegemony. Until recently, schoolchildren sang *God Save the Queen* daily; our provincial flag featured the Union Jack; and English writers and entertainers were as well known in Brandon as they were in London.

The Union Jack and George's Cross in MB's flag demonstrates the English influence on the province's history.

On the other hand, direct immigration from England to MB has never been that pronounced. Actual Englishmen who arrived in the frontier province were often derided as "greenhorns" who were too soft to withstand the rigours of prairie life. It was not uncommon to see signs outside **Winnipeg** shops stating "No Englishmen Need Apply." Particular disdain was reserved for "remittance men," the younger sons of the English upper class who were sent away to the colonies after some scandal in the home country. Even Sir **Clifford**

Sifton, the federal immigration minister, seemed to agree, opening up Canada's laws to encourage agricultural settlement from eastern Europe. Along with **Mennonites** and **Icelanders**, it was **Ukrainians** and **Germans** who successfully applied the plough to much of MB's rich prairie soil.

There were, of course, occasional surges of immigration from England. The 1880s saw many English respond to **CPR** advertising for new settlers. A large number of "war brides" accompanied Cdn servicemen home after both world wars in the 20th century. Some airmen who trained here as part of the **British Commonwealth Air Training Program** returned after WWII. And there has been an increase in English farmers emigrating to MB after the hoof and mouth and "mad cow" crises of the 1990s. Nonetheless, the importance of the English in MB is more a reflection of inherited values and institutions (and the westward migration of English Ontarians) than it is of actual numbers of English immigrants who have settled here over the years. ● R. G. ENFIELD

ENNS, Harry, politician (b Nov 30, 1931, **Winnipeg**) was a longtime **Progressive Conservative** MLA, serving as a cabinet minister under 4 different premiers. He worked as a rancher before he began his political career in 1966, winning his first election in the rural riding of Rockwood-Iberville. The constituency had been vacated by Agriculture Minister George Hutton, whose cabinet post Enns assumed the next year. Enns went on to be a cabinet minister under PC govts of **Duff Roblin**, **Walter Weir**, **Sterling Lyon** and **Gary Filmon**. Through the years, he also held the portfolios of highways, mines and natural resources, public works, and govt services. In 1969, redistribution changed the name of Enns's riding to Lakeside, held by former Liberal Premier **Douglas Campbell** for 47 years. Enns defeated Liberal leader Robert Bend, and won the riding in every election until Enns retired. A rural conservative, Enns contested the party leadership in 1971 to replace Weir. He was defeated by **Sydney Spivak**, an urban progressive, by just 46 votes. In 1993, Enns was named Filmon's agriculture minister, 25 years after his first appointment to that post, serving until 1999, when the govt was defeated. An opponent of **Communism**, Enns fought the Schreyer govt's plan to display Russian artwork in MB, later relenting. In the 1980s, he also opposed the **NDP** govt's policy of restoring French-language services in MB. He retired in 2003, after 37 years of service. ● JIM SHILLIDAY

EPIDEMICS are widespread diseases in a population. If they are sufficiently common among large enough numbers of people, they are pandemics.

Epidemics occurred in what is now MB from the beginning of human habitation, although they became more severe after Europeans came to NA. The newcomers brought with them diseases to which Aboriginal peoples had no exposure or immunity. Some experts think that is how the Aboriginal population of NA was reduced substantially by the end of the 16th century. The most volatile of the newly introduced diseases were the directly transmitted acute infectious diseases – including chickenpox, influenza, measles, mumps, smallpox, scarlet fever, and whooping cough – that depended on humans for their existence. Another whole set of diseases (typhus, malaria, yellow fever, bubonic plague) were spread by animals. Still other epidemics occur primarily or only in animals themselves, such as anthrax and chronic wasting disease.

All epidemics require a certain population density to sustain themselves, and patterns among Aboriginal populations were complex. More disease was probably carried into MB from eastern regions of the continent than brought directly to **Hudson Bay**, but early records are not precise about identifying disease, its incidence, or its patterns. A great smallpox epidemic reached Hudson Bay in 1737-38. Thereafter, respiratory epidemics occurred sporadically but in increasing numbers, until a smallpox pandemic made its way up from Mexico around 1779. Trade and war enabled the disease to spread rapidly, and many died.

New diseases soon followed, and the settlers brought by **Lord Selkirk** experienced both typhoid and typhus epidemics aboard ship while coming to the **Red River Settlement**. There were measles and whooping cough epidemics in 1819 and 1820. After 1830, many observers commented on the extent of sickness in the country. By this time, both Aboriginal and European people around the settlement were affected. The worst killer was smallpox, but **Tuberculosis** – while less obvious – was almost as deadly.

Large-scale immigration from eastern Canada to MB in the 1870s was joined by mass immigration from Europe in the 1880s. Many of the newcomers clustered in **Winnipeg**, which expanded rapidly and contained – especially in the immigrant **North End** – one of the unhealthiest environments anywhere in NA. With its combination of overcrowded housing and wretched sanitation, it was a perfect breeding ground for epidemics – between 1881 and 1901, the **St. Boniface Hospital** dealt with 2 eruptions of typhoid and one each of typhoid, diphtheria, scarlet fever, and smallpox.

Around 1900, Winnipeg was known as the typhoid capital of NA; in 1905, there were 138 deaths and more than 1000 cases. Better sanitation and

Free Press carriers wore masks to avoid contacting Spanish Influenza (1918-19)

was controversial in the socially conservative riding he represented. In 1988, Epp was appointed minister of energy, mines and resources. In 1991, he oversaw the privatization of Petro Canada. In 1992, the govt repealed a law requiring the oil industry in Canada be 50% domestically owned, effectively opening up the industry to foreign investment. After retiring in 1993, Epp took a position as a vice-president for TransCanada PipeLine Ltd, where he worked until 2000. Subsequently as a consultant, Epp authored a report for the ON government that identified serious flaws at the province's Pickering nuclear facility. Epp was then appointed to a panel to investigate Ontario Power Generation's (OPG) role in the ON's electricity market. Epp then became the chairman of the OPG board in 2004. Seen as a Red Tory, Epp was one of the high profile PC party members recruited to join the Canadian Alliance when it was formed. ● CARSON JEREMA

EQUESTRIAN SPORTS. Historically, riding horses in MB is associated with First Nations and Métis bison hunters, and the Manitoba Provincial Police and North West Mounted Police. However, MB is home to a thriving equestrian scene that embraces a variety of breeds and disciplines. Horse owners can be found across the province, however, the RM of Springfield (*see* **EASTMAN**) near Bird's Hill Park boasts the highest per-capita horse population in Canada. Modern equestrian sport can be divided into 2 distinct disciplines: English (based on an older European style) and Western (evolved from the introduction of horses to NA), with several sub-categories of sport within each. The Federation Equestre Internationale (FEI), focuses on English style, recognizes show jumping, dressage, eventing, reining, and endurance riding as Olympic calibre sports.

Dressage (**FRENCH** for training) is a style of riding where horse and rider are asked to demonstrate distinctive movements accurately in the form of a "test" in a 20 x 60m arena with few visible aids. Its fundamental purpose is to develop, through standardized progressive training methods, a horse's athletic ability, obediance, cadence, and willingness to perform.

Hunter/Jumper refers to riding over fences. Hunter-style riding is based on the fox hunt, converted to a course for modern competition. Horses are expected to be easy going, jump natural-looking obstacles with ease while their riders pilot them with style and grace in a general figure 8 pattern. Jumper, or show jumping, is very different. Horse and rider combinations are challenged to ride over wild-looking colourful obstacles with scope and speed.

Jonas Salk's vaccine gradually reduced the number of typhoid victims. Improved treatment of water and milk limited the damage from waterborne and milk-borne disease. Smallpox eventually responded to an active program of inoculation. Tuberculosis, which was endemic among First Nations and immigrants, eventually responded to improved treatment.

Most MB epidemics were local. But in 1918, the province was visited by the 20th century's greatest pandemic, caused by the supervirus called Spanish influenza. The Spanish flu was so named because it was at first thought to have begun in Spain, although it probably gestated in a British Army transient camp in France, where the possibility for the exchange of the virus between humans and animals was extremely high. The disease was brought to NA from Europe by troops returning from the war in Oct 1918. Within weeks, the entire city of Winnipeg was virtually closed to minimize human contact, and everyone routinely wore gauze masks. More than 1000 people died in the city, and at least another 1000 in rural MB, many in Aboriginal communities. Still, the province was let off lightly compared to other areas.

After WWII, MB was hit by an epidemic that was part of a larger national pattern but which had a particular virulence in this province. This was the sudden recurrence of crippling attacks of the poliomyelitis virus. Polio had visited the province in epidemic proportions in several years between 1928 and 1947, but had not been particularly serious. In 1953, however, several thousand Manitobans were stricken with the disease, and more than 100 had to be placed on respirators. Polio struck people of all ages, but was most prevalent among the young. For some unknown reason, MB was the Cdn province most affected by severe cases of polio.

Polio was the last epidemic disease that seemed especially to target Manitobans. The later outbreaks of AIDS were part of an international crisis. International health experts warned at the beginning of the 21st century of the possibility of the return of another supervirus, but as of writing, Manitobans have not had to face the prospect seriously. ● J.M. BUMSTED

EPP, Arthur Jacob, "Jake," politician, consultant (b Sept 1, 1939, St Boniface). After graduating from the **U OF M** in 1961, Epp worked as a high school teacher in **STEINBACH** and served as a town councillor in 1970-71. In 1972, Epp was elected to represent the Provencher riding in the House of Commons as a **PROGRESSIVE CONSERVATIVE**. He held the seat until his retirement from politics in 1993. During Joe Clark's brief minority govt in 1979, Epp was appointed minister of aboriginal and northern affairs. In Opposition, Epp was one of the most prominent voices criticizing the unilateral patriation of the constitution under the Pierre Trudeau Liberal govt. After the election of Tory Brian Mulroney in 1984, Epp was appointed minister of health and welfare. Under Epp's direction, the govt introduced the *Canada Health Act,* outlining conditions under which the federal govt would withhold health transfer payments to a province not respecting the provisions of the CHA. Epp's support of his govt's 1989 bill to decriminalize **ABORTION**, after the Supreme Court ruled the previous law unconstitutional,

Equestrian sports are popular in the Bird's Hill area.

Horse Trials, or 3-Day Eventing, are modern competitions of endurance and skill with historical roots in military cavalry training. Horse and rider are asked to compete in 3 phases: dressage, stadium jumping, and cross-country, one event per day. In the cross-country phase, horses are guided over roads and tracks and through a steeplechase.

Western style focuses on the partnership between the horse and rider, the obedience of the horse and the willingness to work. Western riders can compete in Western Pleasure (horse is judged on its gaits), Western Equitation (rider is judged on their position and skill), Horsemanship (horse and rider are judged together over a pattern), Halter (horse's confirmation is evaluated) and Western Riding. More specialized classes include reining and cutting. Reining riders put their horses through a set pattern that includes rein backs, circles, and sliding stops. Cutting is a trial in which horse and rider must separate or "cut" a specific cow from a herd.

The Manitoba Horse Council (MHC), established in 1974, develops and delivers programs for its athletes, officials, and coaches. A rider and coaching certification program is in place for both English and Western riders through Equine Canada. In 2005, MHC represented 32 associations that included a broad range of disciplines and breeds. Disciplines that fall under the MHC umbrella include sports such as dressage, polo, hunter/jumper, reining, driving, and barrel racing. The MHC owns and operates an Equestrian Centre at **BIRDS HILL PROVINCIAL PARK**. This facility was developed to host the 1990 Western Canada Summer Games and was upgraded to international standards to host the 1999 **PAN AMERICAN GAMES**. The centre also includes a 3-star, 3-day event course, the only one of its kind in Canada. As of 2007, the centre continued to host competitions, training clinics, and educational seminars. Other competitions take place at the **RED RIVER** Exhibition Park where superior rings are located for hunter/jumper competitions. Pine Ridge Equine Park hosts indoor and outdoor shows for English and Western riders year round.

With MB's harsh winter climate, indoor training facilities are a necessity for competitive riders, and are often part of a boarding stable. As many as 42 commercial stables for boarding and training exist in the **WINNIPEG** and surrounding area alone. Prominent riding schools include Copall Equestrian Centre for beginners, and Teske's Equestrian Centre for more competitive riders. More advanced stables include Hermann Schweizer's Northfield Farms, a prominent jumper stable, and Eric and Danae Martin's Eastridge Stable, which caters to hunter, jumper and dressage riders alike. Western riders find upper level training with Donny Rudko or WW Stable's Wendy Robinson.

Throughout summer, many clubs host horse shows giving members a chance to show off their skills, compete for recognition and earn prize money. The Manitoba 50/50 Superhorse Futurity is among the most lucrative competitions in western Canada. Rural towns across the province also host **4-H CLUB** and multi-discipline, multi-breed horse shows that are often the place for young riders and their horses to gain the necessary experience, confidence and skills to compete at larger shows. Communities such as **MORRIS**, **CARMAN**, and **ST. CLAUDE** host these types of competitions as part of their annual summer fairs. Dressage Winnipeg and **WESTMAN** CADORA host 7-8 nationally sanctioned dressage shows each season. The Manitoba Hunter Jumper Association celebrated 60 years of competition in 2007, with 15 shows in its regular season.

MB riders within the various disciplines have attained national and international success. Elaine Banfield, a dressage rider based in **OAKBANK** has studied in England, France, and Canada and competes at the FEI level. She is also a sought-after and well-respected level II coach and judge. Myna Cryderman of **BOISSEVAIN** is a 7-time member of the Canadian Endurance Team. In 2005, she was Canada's top finisher at the World Endurance Championship held in Dubai. Danae Martin, also a level II coach, has competed at the Pan Am level in eventing and qualified for the Sydney Olympics on MB thoroughbred horses. James Atkinson of **NEEPAWA** has competed in eventing at the Pan Am Games and at many FEI-level competitions. ● KIMBERLY FRANCEY

▸ *See also* **HORSE RACING**.

ERASMUS, Peter, interpreter, missionary (b June 27, 1833, **RED RIVER SETTLEMENT**; d May 1931, Whitefish Lake, AB). Born of a Danish father and a **CREE** mother, Erasmus trained at an **ANGLICAN** church at **THE PAS** beginning in 1849. Under the direction of his grandfather – **HENRY BUDD**, the first Aboriginal Anglican minister in NA – he translated religious texts into Cree. Erasmus went on to attend St. John's religious school in the Red River Settlement, but left in 1856 after deciding not to take up the cloth. He worked with **METHODIST** minister Thomas Woolsey until 1862, during which time he also guided James Hector as part of the Palliser mapping expedition in 1858-59, and mined gold in the Fraser Valley of BC. He then continued his interpreting and guiding work with missionaries George McDougall and Henry Steinhauer before marrying and settling at Whitefish Lake to trap and trade. Erasmus acted as an interpreter on behalf of area chiefs during the signing of Treaty 6 in 1876 at Fort Carlton, as they trusted him more than they did the federal govt commissioners. He took more translation work with the Cdn govt shortly after, and continued to work for the Crown in various capacities until his retirement in 1912. His memoirs, as told to **MÉTIS** journalist Henry Thompson (ca 1920), are entitled *Buffalo Days and Nights*. Mount Erasmus, near Banff, AB, bears his name. ● JOEL TRENAMAN

ERICKSON, pop 448, is a town located 75 km N of **BRANDON**, on hwy 10 just S of **RIDING MOUNTAIN NATIONAL PARK**. Known as the "Land of the Vikings," the town was first settled in the 1800s by Scandinavian immigrants. To commemorate their heritage, a statue of a Viking ship was built on Main St. A railway point was established here in 1905. The town was named then after Albert Erickson, whose home was also the post office since the 1890s. Nevertheless, the town was only incorporated in 1953. With an elevation of 625 m (2054 ft), Erickson is the highest town in MB. It is a centre for the surrounding agricultural production and, as gateway to the park, also benefits from tourism. ● GPP

ERIKSDALE, pop 833, is a town located 130 km NNW of Winnipeg and 20 km E of **LAKE MANITOBA** on hwy 6. Many of the original pioneers came from Sweden, although the community is now more diverse. The town is probably named after Jonas Erik Erickson, the first homesteader here in 1904. A post office and railway point were established here in 1911. In 1960, Percy Moggey became the first inmate to escape from **STONY MOUNTAIN PENITENTIARY**. He hid near Eriksdale in a cabin he built, surviving by trapping muskrats and breaking into the local Co-op. Moggey's cabin was re-created, and is open for public viewing. The Eriksdale Creamery Museum, which opened in 2000, is one of a kind in MB. The community's economy is based on agriculture, fishing, building trades, and tourism. The town has an active equestrian society, ranch rodeo teams and champion bull riders. Eriksdale is also the administrative centre of the RM of Eriksdale. ● GPP

ETHELBERT, pop 335, is a village located 50 km NNW of **DAUPHIN** on hwy 10. Settlers arrived here in 1900, when the railway began its service. **RAILWAY** magnate R.J. McKenzie named the town after his 2 daughters Ethel and Bertha. The post office also opened in 1900, and the village was incorporated in 1950. In 2007, the economy is primarily based on agriculture, including cattle operations and grain farming. Other industries include berry, honey, forestry, lumber, and pulp production. Nestled near the base of **DUCK MOUNTAIN PROVINCIAL PARK**, Ethelbert also enjoys tourism spin-offs. The village is the administrative centre of the RM of Ethelbert. ● GPP

EVANGELICALS define themselves as custodians of the Evangel or *evangelium*, the Gospel of the grace of God, and believe that God's grace is communicated to men through faith alone. Some church bodies incorporate the word *evangelical* into their official name, including the Evangelical **LUTHERAN** Church, the Evangelical Free Church, and the Evangelical **MENNONITE** Church. The term distinguishes such bodies from sacramental churches, which teach that the grace of God comes to a person through the sacraments and the offices of an officiating priesthood.

METHODIST, Baptist, Congregational, **LUTHERAN**, **PRESBYTERIAN**, Salvation Army, Mennonite, and Evangelical **ANGLICANS** came to MB and erected places of worship early in the province's history. Most of them would have been proud to be called "evangelical." Certainly, the Methodist circuit-riders preached the gospel and called people to repentance and faith in the 1880s as fervently as any evangelist of today. In 1907, real estate agent Andrew H. Argue held prayer meetings in his home on St. John's Ave in **WINNIPEG**; these led to Pentecostal or Full Gospel churches of various sorts being founded in every corner of MB. The most visible group is the Pentecostal Assemblies of Canada, now with 80 churches in the province, of which Winnipeg's Calvary Temple is the most recognizable.

Significant events in the history of Evangelicals in MB must include campaigns by Gypsy Smith and by Dr. Reuben A. Torrey at Elim Chapel; the Dr. Charles S. Price crusades in **BRANDON** and Winnipeg in 1924 and 1925; mass Youth for Christ rallies in the 1940s, chaired by Rev. Watson Argue in the Winnipeg Ice Rink (featuring such speakers as Dr. Charles Fuller and the young Billy Graham); and inter-church evangelism celebrations with Jack Schuller, Stephen Olford, Canon Green, Theodore Epp, Barry Moore, and others from the 1950s to the '70s. Most noteworthy was the Centennial Billy Graham Crusade of 1967, held in the **WINNIPEG ARENA** and Stadium.

The charismatic movement of the 1960s and '70s gave birth to several congregations of significance, such as Springs Church, the Rock Church, Gateway Christian Community, and other fellowships throughout the province. The influx of people from many nations in the last ¼ of the 20th century resulted in vibrant evangelical churches worshipping in their own native tongues.

In addition to Youth for Christ, the story of Evangelicals in MB must include recognition of the work of such inter-denominational agencies as Child Evangelism, Teen Challenge, Inter-Varsity, Campus Crusade, plus the Lighthouse, Siloam, and Union Gospel Missions, among others.

Evangelicals have had a significant involvement in radio and television ministries from the inception of these media. For example, the Mennonite Brethren operate Faith and Life Communications; Trinity Television, with Willard Thiessen, now completing more than 30 years on air; and the *Faith to Live By* telecast with Rev. H. H. Barber, launched in 1962. Contributions to education by Evangelicals include Wesley College (*see* **U OF W**), Providence Bible College and Seminary (since 1925), Western Bible College (Dr. J. E. Purdie, principal from 1925 to 1950), Nazarene College, the **CANADIAN MENNONITE U**, Living Word College in **SWAN RIVER** (**UKRAINIAN**), founded by Rev. J. D. Harabenko in 1952, as well as Bible schools in **WINKLER** and **STEINBACH**. ● H. H. BARBER

EVANKO, Edward Danylo "Ed," singer, actor, priest (b Oct 19, 1941, **WINNIPEG**) is an actor and singer who in 2005 became a Ukrainian Catholic priest. Evanko was born to **UKRAINIAN** immigrants and was raised in Winnipeg's **NORTH END**. He was a member of the Winnipeg Boys Choir and won his first trophy at 13 in the Manitoba Music Competition Festival. He studied with Herbert Belyea and Lucien Needham and sang professionally for the first time at **RAINBOW STAGE**. He earned a BA from the **U OF M** in 1959, and trained at the Bristol Old Vic Theatre School. He performed in the Stratford Festival in 1960-1, and sang with the English Opera Group, the Welsh National Opera Company, and the BBC singers. Evanko returned to Winnipeg in 1967 to host *The Ed Evanko Show* on CBC TV. His Broadway debut in *Canterbury Tales* earned him a Theatre World Award in 1969, a New Jersey Drama Critics Award, and a Los Angeles Ovation Award nomination. He has recorded several albums, including Broadway albums and Ukrainian recordings.

(L) Ed Evanko, 1966 , (R) Fr. Edward Evanko, 2007

In the 1980s and 1990s, Evanko appeared on many TV series, including *Ryan's Hope*, *Chicago*, and *3rd Rock from the Sun*. After moving to Vancouver, BC (from LA) in 1997, Evanko began to teach acting while he also guest starred on several TV series. However, after a 4-decade-long career in music and theatre, Evanko took a dramatic turn. After becoming actively involved with his local parish, Evanko enrolled as **ROMAN CATHOLIC** semarian at the Pontificio Collegio Beda in Rome. He then opted for the religion of his immigrant family, and was accepted as a Ukrainian Catholic semarian at St. Josaphat Seminary and Catholic U in Washington, DC, and at Holy Spirit Seminary and St. Paul U in Ottawa. He completed his MA in Theology in 2005 and returned to Winnipeg to serve. In 2006, a world away from the stage lights in New York and London, Ed Evanko was practising as a travelling priest in rural MB towns such as **ROSSBURN** and **RUSSELL**. ● AMANDA STEPHENS

EVANS, Edward GURNEY Vaux, politician (b Sept 3, 1907, **WINNIPEG**; d Jan 8, 1987, Winnipeg). The son of politician **WILLIAM SANFORD EVANS** and Mary Irene Gurney, Gurney Evans was schooled at Ridley College in St. Catharines, ON, and at the

U OF M, where he graduated with a BA, before working at his father's company, W. Sanford Evans & Co. Ltd./Sanford Evans Statistical Service. Evans served with the **ROYAL WINNIPEG RIFLES** in WWII, eventually becoming assistant director of the Army Ordnance Services, obtaining the rank of LCol by his 1946 demobilization. He was made an Officer of the Order of the British Empire. He became involved in political life by serving on boards and commissions struck in the wake of the **RED RIVER**'s 1950 **FLOOD** and served as chair of the Civil Service Commission of Manitoba. Evans had grown up with a mayor and, later, MLA as a father, and Gurney's friend **DUFF ROBLIN** persuaded him to run for the **PROGRESSIVE CONSERVATIVE PARTY**. He was a widely respected MLA for Winnipeg South/Fort Rouge 1953-69, serving in cabinet as minister of industry and commerce (1958-66); mines and natural resources (1958-59, 1966-67); and finance (1966-69), and as provincial secretary (1959-63), in the govts of Duff Roblin and **WALTER WEIR**. As finance minister, Evans introduced the innovation of separating capital and operating expenses and revenues from each other in the provincial budget. In the 1969 election, with the constituency reorganized as Crescentwood, Evans lost to Cy Gonick by a small margin and never sought re-election. ● AJL

EVANS, William Sanford, politician, publisher, journalist, (b Dec 18, 1869, Spencerville, ON; d June 27, 1949, **WINNIPEG**). The son of Ontarian **METHODIST** clergyman J. S. Evans, Sanford was educated in Hamilton, ON; in Cobourg, ON; and at Columbia U in New York, where he earned an MA. He came back to ON in 1897, working at the *Mail and Empire*, later subsumed by the *Globe and Mail*. He tried unsuccessfully running for the ON legislature in 1898 and moved to Winnipeg in 1901 with wife Mary Irene Gurney to publish and edit the conservative daily **NEWSPAPER** *The Winnipeg Telegram*. Also that year, he wrote a book on Canada in the Boer War, *The Canadian Contingents and Canadian Imperialism: A Story and a Study*. The *Telegram*'s writers under Evans included **EMILY GOWAN MURPHY**, the paper's literary editor for 8 years, and Norman Bethune. The paper, and Evans, argued strongly for a Cdn as opposed to British Imperial identity. Evans left as publisher in 1905 but retained ownership of the paper, and started a lucrative brokerage firm. Evans was mayor of Winnipeg 1909-11. He was also founder and president of the Canadian Club and of the short-lived University Club of Winnipeg. The **WINNIPEG TRIBUNE** bought out his *Telegram* in 1920, and Evans started W. Sanford Evans & Co. Ltd./Sanford Evans Statistical Services (now Sanford Evans Communications/Sanford Evans Research Group), a publishing

William Sanford Evans

company located on Winnipeg's McDermot Ave, which specialized in providing grain information. He sat as a **CONSERVATIVE** MLA for Winnipeg 1922-36, and led the Conservative Caucus in Opposition through the worst of the **GREAT DEPRESSION** when his predecessor was appointed as a judge. In 1931, he chaired a BC Royal Commission on the orchard industry in that province. Evans's son, **EDWARD GURNEY EVANS**, became a MB cabinet minister, and his brother, Harry Marshall Erskine Evans, was a mayor of Edmonton. ● AJL

EXOTIC ANIMALS are species inhabiting MB that arrived through the activities of humans, although the line blurs in cases where humans have altered the landscape to the degree that has permitted the apparently recent entry and establishment of dispersing non-native wildlife (for example, white-tailed deer) following the advent of agriculture. With the great natural dispersal abilities and adaptability of small life forms, countless organisms have invaded the province since the historical period, from viruses like West Nile to injurious insects such as the Elm Bark Beetle which carries the virulent fungus causing Dutch Elm Disease.

Exotics have also been used widely for agricultural purposes such as all crops and pollinators (such as the alfalfa-pollinating Leafcutter Bee, *Megachile rotundata*), in pest control (ladybird beetles to devour aphids), and to attack invasive exotic plants (flea beetles to eat Leafy Spurge and Purple Loosestrife weeds). Of course, livestock species – such as horses, cattle, pigs, goats, sheep, llamas, alpacas, chickens, and turkeys – are all exotics, often displacing

native wildlife over large regions. These domestic animals also broadcast weed seeds and parasites in their droppings and carry their share of non-native diseases such as anthrax and bovine tuberculosis, which all-too-often are transmitted to native wildlife. The threat of reverse infection, such as Tuberculosis-infected American Elk infecting cattle raised in the same area, has devastating consequences for both wild populations and the ranching industry, leading to calls for the culling and even eradication of the wild animals, even in conservation areas like Riding Mountain National Park.

No one has any idea how many non-native species of invertebrates (lower animals without a backbone) have been accidentally introduced and become part of the local fauna of MB, but they no doubt number in the thousands. For example, the introduced Pharaoh Ant (*Monomorium pharaonis*) lives only inside heated buildings, thereby avoiding the cold of winter. Earthworms, slugs, and other invertebrates are particularly common in disturbed areas like city yards. The Cabbage White Butterfly (*Pieris rapae*) was accidentally introduced from Europe to QC about 1860, and has become the most-common butterfly in MB, found in gardens, crops, and forest clearings as far N as Churchill.

There are 12 exotic species of fish in MB, introduced purposefully for sport fishing, or accidentally – Common Carp, Goldfish, Rainbow Smelt, Cutthroat Trout, Rainbow Trout, Kokanee Salmon, Brown Trout, Splake (Lake X Brook trout hybrid), Tiger Trout (Brook X Brown trout hybrid), White Bass, Smallmouth Bass, and Largemouth Bass. Quite likely others will be added to this list in the future through accidents, illegal release, or connecting of drainage systems (i.e., the Missouri system into the Red River in ND).

Over 100 species of birds have been released into NA, but fortunately most of these failed to become established. A few, like the Cattle Egret (*Bubulcus ibis*) from Africa and Eurasia, has spread throughout the New World on its own (with cattle ranching supporting the birds once here), and occurs sparingly in MB during the summer. Others were released by conservation departments and game associations for hunting opportunities, such as Grey Partridge, Ring-necked Pheasant and Wild Turkey – the latter two requiring supplemental food to survive a number of MB winters. The release of the House Sparrow, Starling, and Rock Dove (Pigeon) in the US in the late 19th century has caused unimaginable damage to ecosystems throughout NA. These birds devour huge amounts of natural and human foods and confiscate nesting sites formerly utilized by native species.

With mammals, the House Mouse and Norway (Brown) Rat are the supreme invaders, having colonized the entire world (except perhaps Antarctica) wherever humans have travelled. These 2 pests spread out in summer throughout MB into natural habitats, agricultural fields, and in urban alleys, but must retreat to human shelter for the winter period. Both these Old World residents invaded MB first at **CHURCHILL** more than 3 centuries ago via ships of the early explorers, whalers and traders. Their descendants still survive there in buildings and on upper beaches in summer to this day.

Prehistoric humans (*Homo sapiens sapiens*) first arrived in SW MB about 8000 years ago, soon after dry land was exposed from the melting Laurentide Glacier and glacial **LAKE AGASSIZ**. With successive immigration of these huntergatherers from E Asia around 13,000 years ago, they may also be viewed as an foreign element, in that they invaded an unoccupied continent. However, our species arrived here through natural dispersal (as did thousands of other wildlife species), and hence this case does not fit the definition of exotic. The appearance of humans had major repercussions in many NA ecosystems, mainly through hunting activities (with weapons and use of fire). Humans have contributed to the extinction of over one-half the large species of mammals and birds.

Releasing any foreign species of plant or animal into the wild is biologically indefensible and generally results in unforeseen negative consequences. While some introduced species have failed to become established, the invaders invariably out-compete similar native species, outright devour them, or introduce foreign-disease organisms. At the very least, they occupy habitat of native species, seldom providing food, cover, or other resources for native wildlife. It is naive and uniformed, whether instigated by a conservation department or a private person releasing an unwanted pet, to think that such a release will be a positive step for either the organism, the species, or the biotic community, and yet the practice continues. The problem may sometimes be compounded by introducing an exotic natural predator of an exotic pest, as is the current practice in biological control. While occasionally this proves helpful in reducing the primary pest, the fact remains that an additional exotic has been introduced, often without full knowledge of long-term effects in the ecosystem.

The release or escape of genetically modified (GM) varieties of crops and other organisms are exotics of major concern, since the results frequently have far-reaching effects, including the real possibility of altering the genetics and ecology of wild species. While no doubt a boon to food production and company profitability, transgenic (recombinant DNA) technology carries inherent risks for species, ecosystems and human health. This is a controversial issue, with many known and unknown factors to consider. ● REW

EXTINCT ANIMALS are species with no surviving members. The term extirpation refers to the elimination of species from a region like MB, but the species survives elsewhere. There are only 3 native animal species that are known to have become extinct in MB during the historical period – the Passenger Pigeon (*Ectopistes migratorius*) and its host-specific Passenger Pigeon Louse (*Lipeurus extinctus*), and the Rocky Mountain Locust (*Melanoplus spretus*). However, there are likely hundreds of small species that have vanished without our knowledge due to the great physical (habitat loss) and chemical (pollution) assaults inflicted on the landscape, especially in S and W areas of the province. The Passenger Pigeon nested widely throughout southern MB and ranged N to **CHURCHILL**. With unrelenting hunting and trapping over its range, it was eliminated from the province by 1898 and became extinct in the wild in 1900; the last individual died in captivity in 1914.

The Rocky Mountain Locust (along with several other species of grasshoppers) have ravaged the prairies and farms of S MB in periodic outbreaks. There is reference in the literature to a "10-year locust war of 1864-74," and then another from 1897-1901. The following year, this unbelievably abundant locust (estimated at 3.5 trillion) suddenly became extinct over its entire western range – a mystery remaining partially unsolved to this day. It is believed that ploughing, grazing, and irrigation in the locust's traditional breeding grounds in valleys of the Rockies, low temperatures, and wet conditions combined to destroy the entire breeding stock. Ironically, the pigeon and locust were 2 of the most abundant species in NA, yet both were eliminated with surprising ease by human activities.

There have also been several extinctions of geographic races (i.e., subspecies) of prairie-dwelling animals – the Grey **WOLF** (*Canis lupus nubilis*) and Plains Grizzly (*Ursus arctos horribilis*), at the hands of people who could not tolerate large, aggressive carnivores around their farms and settlements. The Plains Grizzly occurred in SW MB from the **RED RIVER** W to **PORTAGE LA PRAIRIE, BRANDON,** Turtle Mountain, and likely as far N as the Duck and Porcupine mountains. It was shot and trapped out of existence in the province by 1810, and only 2 skulls in museums remain as evidence. The 'Prairie Wolf' was a definite threat and pest around settlements, and the last individual was shot in 1943 at **MORRIS**. It is just a matter of time until additional species will be added to this list.

Unknown to most people, MB has a diminished fauna of large animals. We think of wildlife as a complete set of creatures existing during our brief life span, when in fact, following the last Ice Age ending 8000 years ago, there existed a wonderful variety of large mammals and birds on the Northern Plains, including the SW corner of the province which was the first region to become ice-free. This great diversity of what has been called 'mega-fauna' on the NA plains, forests and tundra was as rich as that on the African savannah in recent times. Woolly and Columbian **MAMMOTHS** (*Mammuthus primigenius, M. columbi*), American **MASTODON** (*Mamut americanum*), Woodland Muskox (*Symbos cavifrons*), Stag **MOOSE** (*Cervalces scotti*), Giant and Western **BISON** (*Bison latifrons, B. antiguus occidentalis*), Scott's Horse (*Equus scotti*), Yesterday's Camel (*Camelops hesternus*), Sabre-toothed **CAT** (*Smilodon fatalis*), American Lion (*Panthera leo atrox*), American Cheetah (*Miracinonyx trumani*), Jefferson's and Shasta ground sloths (*Megalonyx jeffersoni, Nothrotheriops shastensis*), Short-faced **BEAR** (*Arctodus simus*), Dire Wolf (*Canis dirus*), Bone-eating Dog (*Borophagus diversidens*), Leidy's Peccary (*Platygonus vetus*), and Giant **BEAVER** (*Castoroides ohioensis*) are only a few examples of species that suddenly became extinct – all by 8000 years ago. The reasons causing this wave of Pleistocene extinctions remain controversial, but there is general agreement that the rapidly changing climate affected ecosystems to such an extent that regional ecology (e.g., predator-prey relationships) became disrupted, driving surviving populations of large animals into limited refugia. As species numbers decreased to dangerously low levels, prehistoric hunters appeared on the scene, immigrating around 13,000 years ago from Siberia. Several millennia of hunting, with ever-improving technologies, wiped out all-easily hunted species with dramatic efficiency. This process of faunal and floral degradation and extinction is still continuing under the increasing resource demands of our expanding human population. ● REW

EYRE, Ivan Kenneth, artist, teacher, author (b April 15, 1935, Tullymet, SK) is renowned nationally and internationally for his paintings, drawings, sculpture, and prints. Eyre moved to **WINNIPEG** to study at the Winnipeg School of Art, graduating with a BFA in 1957. After postgraduate studies in ND, he returned to join the **U OF M** faculty, teaching painting until his retirement in 1993. At the same time, he maintained a full practice as a visual artist. His significant output is represented in private, corporate, and public collections across Canada, the most extensive being in the Pavilion Gallery at **ASSINIBOINE PARK**.

Eyre has never followed the mainstream. The vocabulary, structure, and meaning in his work are unique, as is his invitation to the viewer to enter into a dialogue. He masterfully combines myth with reality and imagination with autobiography. Creating surrealistic works in the 1960s, and large landscapes and figurative work in the 1970s, images and themes recur in each successive decade, shifting in meaning and juxtapositions. A quiet, keen observer, Eyre's work is thoughtful, imbued with rich depth and substance of ideas and execution.

His landscapes seemingly refer to specific places but are in fact from his imagination, based on his perceptions and personal world view. They are complex, drawn from his acute and accurate memory. Eyre internalized his images to allow the prairie landscape to become his subject, while it simultaneously accommodated and supported his equally important other subject – his personal mythology. A master of the micro and macro in a single work, he creates large spaces filled with minute details, each heightened by precise brushwork. Emphasizing shapes and directions and depicting roads leading nowhere, he magnifies the scale and roles of the figures and objects. Several seasons might appear in a single work. For instance, in *The Gold Box* (1985), autumn, winter, and summer are each depicted in various sizes on the sides of boxes, creating paintings within paintings, thus suggesting a confluence of time.

Through the decades, Ivan has repeated many images, riders on horseback, wheeled horses, riderless horses, floating figures, wrapped heads, and still lifes. These are coupled with the landscapes and interiors. He has modernized traditional academic imagery, thus presenting duplicate timeframes. The juxtaposition of unlike objects is disturbing, resulting in perplexing contexts and disquieting messages. These recurring images have different meanings in different works and periods.

He makes his still lifes as small, 3-dimensional paper sketches, then greatly enlarges them to become 2-dimensional objects and focal points in his paintings and drawings. He draws human figures – often based on himself or his wife Brenda – from memory. He reinvents all these elements as metaphors, some linked to his life and place, others to the wider world. He consciously seeks a degree of mystery and conflicting sensibilities by setting moods and opening layers of meaning. Balance between the spaces and shapes is critical for Eyre. He continuously adjusts these precisely articulated works while they are in progress. The ever-changing

March Past, 2000, acrylic on canvas, 173 x 192 cm, by Ivan Eyre

skies and light enchant him. He collapses interior and exterior spaces and shifts the near and the far. In the silhouette series, the figure acts as a window for a landscape, combining nearby objects and deep spaces. Wanting to integrate all the images within a work, he often brings faraway objects to the fore, pushing those close by to the distance. He combines the known with the ominous, as in *Moos-O-Men* (1975), in which figures move across the canvas repeating the rhythms of the plant leaves in the foreground. Nothing is accidental in his work. He enjoys creating the bizarre, rather than illustrating realities. Not only is balance achieved within each work; he has achieved balance throughout his overall output in each of the media he has used. Pieces in every medium stand alone, yet each feeds another. The drawings serve the paintings and the paintings serve the drawings, and so on with his prints and sculptures.

Among Eyre's other visual interests are birds and flight. These converge in paintings and drawings of wrapped heads, masks, and head dresses. As with all his subject matter, he executes these with detail and precision. Done from model paper constructions he makes, draws on, and dons, they contain landscapes and figures in the wrappings themselves.

Ivan's sense of colour is acute, as is his ability to use it poignantly and effectively to emphasize peace, angst, or the conundrums he poses. Creating

dynamic shapes in the landscapes by constructing spaces using wide ranges of tones and textures, he finds winter and the world of white particularly interesting. He masterfully portrays movement across and through his compositions. Urban themes address complexities within cities, and both relationships of people with cities and those between urban life and the wider landscape. Buildings suggest richness; helmet-shaped clouds suggest war; and the juxtaposition of enigmatic urban settings within a detailed landscape, as in *Annex* (1996), raises questions of place, roles, and relationships. In *Birdmen* (1981), the artist did 2 self-portraits, one masked, the other with a still-life headdress. The overall composition is of overlapping planes, angled and perpendicular. The precisely executed factory in the background, with an army of bird-masked men representing conflict, is both threatening and vulnerable. The precision of the land and building suggests order, yet a sense of chaos layers the work. Drawing on recurring images from the 1960s – the wheeled horses, riders, and figure drawings in the foreground – he achieves another mythology and meaning.

Eyre's work falls into iconographic themes, not chronological periods. Each theme evolves over time in each medium, and they all pose unanswerable questions in his mythologies of place, angst, and calm. He is a seminal figure in the visual arts in Canada, and is recognized in Europe, especially Germany, and throughout NA. ● PATRICIA BOVEY

FLOODS,
see page 229

F

FABRO, Ronald "Sam," businessman (b Dec 8, 1920, Udine, Italy) helped promote sports in MB as an athlete and through his career in sports administration. Fabro immigrated as a child to **WINNIPEG**, where he developed a talent for hockey, playing with the Winnipeg Rangers when the team won the 1941 Memorial Cup. He briefly played with the **WINNIPEG BLUE BOMBERS** before serving in the military during WWII. His biggest contributions to provincial sport came through his work developing sports programs. Fabro was the chairman of baseball at the 1967 **PAN AMERICAN GAMES**, and later on helped organize the first MB Marathon and the first Canoe-athon. He served in various capacities with the Manitoba Baseball Association, the Manitoba Hockey Players' Foundation, Winnipeg Enterprises, the Manitoba Hockey Hall of Fame, the **MANITOBA SPORTS HALL OF FAME** and the Wildlife Foundation of Manitoba. He was awarded the Order of the Buffalo Hunt in 1986, and the Order of Canada in 1974. • MD

FALCON (family Falconidae) is a bird of prey known for its great speed. Indeed, the Peregrine Falcon (*Falco peregrinus*) is one of the fastest birds on the wing, but even its smaller cousin, the Merlin (*F. columbarius*), is capable of plucking swallows and dragonflies out of the air. Peregrines suffered drastic declines in the 20th century, but have made a steady recovery since DDT and related pesticides were banned in NA. Offspring of captive-reared birds nest annually on a few tall buildings in **WINNIPEG** and **BRANDON**. Merlins are much more common in cities and towns, where they make their presence known by their loud calling. They nest in tall ornamental conifers, much to the chagrin of many nearby homeowners. Of the 3 other species found in MB, including gyrfalcon and prairie falcon, only the American kestrel (*F. sparverius*) is common. It is mainly a rural bird. Its former (and Latin) name – sparrow hawk

BOB McKAY

Merlin preparing to pounce

– is misleading on 2 counts: falcons are not true **Hawks**, and this little falcon eats largely mice, voles, and large insects. • RUDOLF KOES

F

Pierre Falcon

FALCON, Pierre, Métis, songwriter, farmer, judge (b June 4, 1793, Fort la Coude [Elbow Fort], **Swan River**; d Oct 26, 1876, **St. François Xavier**). The son of a Francophone **NWC** employee and a First Nations, probably **Cree**, woman, Falcon was educated in La Prairie, Lower Canada (QC). He returned W in 1808, worked for the NWC 1808-21, and with the **HBC** after the latter company bought out the former. He married Marie Grant, sister of **Cuthbert Grant**, in 1812, and went with Grant to the Seven Oaks area in 1816. Falcon was involved in Grant's 1816 capture of **Peter Fidler**'s **Brandon** House, and then aided Grant in founding Grantown (**St. François Xavier**), where he farmed sheep and became a magistrate. However, he was best known as a songwriter/poet who wrote lyrics poking fun at local events, including the **Seven Oaks Incident**. His song about this Métis rout of the HBC, "La bataille de Sept-Chênes" or "Chanson de la Grenouillère," became the *cri de guerre* and anthem of the Métis. Known as "Pierre the Rhymer" or "Rhymster," or by the diminutive "Pierriche," he described himself as "poète du canton" ("district poet"). Though an old man at the time of the **Red River Resistance**, he reputedly expressed a desire to join his son – Pierre Jr – in taking up arms in defence of his fellow Métis. Falcon Lake is likely named for him. • AJL

FANNYSTELLE, pop 100, is an unincorporated community 50 km WSW of **Winnipeg** on hwy 2. Fannystelle was originally a French settlement founded by the Countess of Albufera da Valencia,

descendant of a Naploeonic-era French general, in honour of Fanny Rives. Rives worked on behalf of the homeless in Paris and met Lady Albufera while doing humanitarian work. The countess convinced her husband to fund the emigration of poor Parisians to Canada. Rives continued her work in Canada and died in 1883. The countess founded the settlement 6 years later and called it Fannystelle for "Fanny's star." A **CPR** point and post office opened 6 years later, in 1889. In the 21st century, the economy is supported predominantly by grain farming. Because of the close proximity to **Winnipeg**, many residents commute to the city for work. Every July, the community holds an annual Fun Fest, when residents get together to enjoy music, food, and entertainment. • GPP

FARRALLY, Betty, dancer, (b May 5, 1915, Bradford, UK; d Apr 9, 1989, Kelowna, BC) played an integral role in starting Canada's first ballet company. Along with her teacher, business partner, and friend, **Gweneth Lloyd**, the pair transformed their Winnipeg Ballet Club into the world-renowned **Royal Winnipeg Ballet**. Born into a wealthy family, Farrally was sent to a lady's college, where a rebellious streak and poor grades in Latin kept her from becoming a veterinarian. In 1932, she demanded to be allowed to go to London to pursue dance. She enrolled in Gweneth Lloyd's new dance school in Leeds, Yorkshire, where she studied and would eventually teach. When Lloyd approached her about the possibility of moving to Canada to start a dance school, Farrally, in the throes of a difficult break-up, agreed, and the pair left a week later. Farrally was 23. Although Farrally danced until 1949, she was never considered particularly talented. Her onstage performances were often done out of necessity, as when there was a shortage of dancers. Her outgoing nature and acting skills, however, made her a company favourite. She eventually took over the roles of ballet mistress, teacher, coach, and disciplinarian. She was artistic director of the RWB until 1957, when she and Lloyd founded a new school in BC, where Farrally lived for the rest of her life. She was also the long-time co-head of the Banff Centre's summer dance programs. For her contributions to the art of dance, she was inducted into the Order of Canada in 1981. • JS

FAVELL, Rosalie, photographer. (b Feb 20, 1958, **Winnipeg**). In 1984, Favell received her BA in Photographic Arts from Ryerson Polytechnical Institute in Toronto and received her MFA, U of New Mexico in 1998. In 1986, she was instrumental in the growth of The Floating Gallery in

Winnipeg during her time as president of the board of directors. Her intricate and layered self-portraits examine her cultural and personal identity as an Aboriginal woman in a contemporary society. She has received numerous awards from the Canada Council for the Arts. Her work has travelled around Canada and the world in solo exhibitions such as *Living Evidence* (1995) and *Longing and Not Belonging* (1997-99). Her work can be found in several institutions including Canadian Museum of Contemporary Photography/National Gallery, Canada Council Art Bank, the **Winnipeg Art Gallery**, and the National Museum of the American Indian in New York. She is currently working on her PhD in Cultural Mediations, Institute for Comparative Studies in Art, Literature and Culture at Carleton U in Ottawa, ON. • STACEY ABRAMSON

FEHR, Brendan Jacob Joel, actor (b Oct 29, 1977, New Westminster, BC) is a popular film and television actor who grew up in **Winnipeg**. Fehr, his mother, and sisters moved to Winnipeg in 1990; his mother was a case manager at the prison in **Stony Mountain**. Fehr worked as a model for local catalogue companies while attending a **Mennonite** high school. On a 1997 trip to Vancouver, a talent scout spotted Fehr and got Brendan his first guest role on the TV show *Breaker High*. Fehr is best known for his roles in television shows *Roswell* (1999-2002) and *CSI: Miami* (2005-06). He has also appeared in feature films such as *Disturbing Behaviour* (1998), *Final Destination* (2000), and *The Forsaken* (2004), and Cdn films *Childstar* (2004) and *Sugar* (2004). He was nominated for his work on *Roswell* twice at the Teen Choice Awards for TV-Choice Sidekick, and once for a Saturn Award. Fehr was also nominated for Best Performance by an Actor in a Supporting Role at the 2005 Genie Awards for *Sugar*. In 2006, Fehr married music publicist Jennifer Rollin. As of writing, they lived in Los Angeles. • AMANDA STEPHENS

FESTIVAL DU VOYAGEUR, western Canada's largest winter festival, takes place in the St. Boniface area of **Winnipeg** over 10 days each Feb. The first instalment – Feb 26 to March 1, 1970 – acted as part of MB's centennial. Its purpose was to develop, highlight, and promote **French** heritage and culture by reflecting the era of the voyageurs, contracted employees who worked as labourers for **Fur Trade** firms from the 1690s to the 1850s. The Festival du Voyageur celebrates these traders through live entertainment, traditional French-Canadian dishes, **Dogsled** races, a *cabane à sucre* (maple-sugaring shack), and a snow-sculpting competition.

Ice sculptures provide a unique entrance to the Festival du Voyageur.

A sculpture of a toque atop a pair of boots won first prize in 1972's competition; this became the symbol and mascot for the festival. The festival's home is at Whittier Park, also known as Voyageur Park. Its main attraction is **Fort Gibraltar**, a reconstruction of the fort that was at the centre of the fur trade. Buildings include a blacksmith shop, a general store, and 2 towers flanking a footbridge. Other Festival attractions include trading posts; fireworks; the Governor's Ball, a prestigious costume party; and outdoor games. The Festival du Voyageur has won several provincial and federal awards, and continues to attract visitors, with more than 160,000 people from across Canada and from abroad attending annually. • AMANDA STEPHENS

FIA, Albert, aerospace engineer (b 1915, Lethbridge, AB; d Jun 5, 2004, **Winnipeg**). Sometimes called the "father of Canadian rocketry," Fia oversaw the development of the **Black Brant Rocket** while employed at **Bristol Aerospace Ltd** in Winnipeg. Fia attended the Royal Military College of Science in Oxfordshire, UK, and also Laval U, earning an engineering degree. He also served in the Army (*see* **Military**) during WWII. Fia left the military in 1958 to become director of the aerospace program at Bristol. He helped develop a number of versions of the Black Brant, and the rocket shot to international prominence in the 1960s. After a long career, he retired as vice-president of Bristol in 1980. In 1981, NASA gave

Fia its Public Service Award, making him the first non-American to receive the honour. • JT

FIDLER, Peter, fur trader, surveyor (b Aug 16, 1769, Bolsover, UK; d Dec 17, 1822, Dauphin Lake House.) Fidler joined the **HBC** in 1788. As someone with both education and steadiness, he soon advanced in the Company service. He was sent inland, and in 1790 was taught surveying and astronomy by Philip Turnor, who he was probably intended to succeed. Fidler accompanied Turnor to the Athabasca region in 1790-92, and did well. He subsequently went on several surveying and trading expeditions, constantly experiencing trouble with the **NWC**, but providing the HBC with much useful information. By 1810, the intimidation led Fidler to request a year's furlough in England, and he returned in 1812 to be transferred to the **Red River Settlement**. When **Miles Macdonell** became incapacitated in 1815, Fidler was in command when a capitulation had to be signed, and he led the loyal settlers N to be met by **Colin Robertson**. In 1816, he was in Brandon House (*see* **Brandon**) when the post was plundered by the Métis. He returned to the **Fur Trade** in 1817. By 1821, he had suffered a stroke, and he died shortly thereafter, leaving behind 11 children. Fidler was simultaneously pedantic and diffident. He was not regarded as a great leader, although he was a highly competent surveyor. He is a member of the Manitoba Agricultural Hall of Fame. • JMB

FIGURE SKATING. *See* **Skating, Figure**.

FILIPINOS are the fastest-growing and largest visible minority in MB. The 2001 Census listed 30,490 in MB, representing 2.7% of all Manitobans and 35% of MB's visible-minority population. Of these Filipinos, all but a few hundred call **Winnipeg** home, with Inkster, the downtown area, Point Douglas, and Seven Oaks as the primary communities of residence. Across Canada, MB ranks 4th to ON (156,515), BC (64,005), and AB (33,940) in overall Filipino population, but has the highest per capita rate among Cdn provinces. Tagalog (or Filipino) is the 5th-most-common mother tongue in the province, just ahead of the **Cree** language.

Filipino migration to MB started in 1959 and the early 1960s with the arrival of a few nurses, doctors, medical technologists, and teachers from the US and from elsewhere in Canada. The profile of the Filipino migrant has changed through the different waves of migration through the years. Labour demands necessitated the recruitment of hundreds of nurses between 1967 and 1973, and again in 2000; thousands of garment workers in 1968-69, the late '70s through the early 1980s and '90s; hundreds of domestic workers in the '80s; and live-in caregivers since the '90s. Motivated by the expectation of a good life in Canada, Filipinos took advantage of every favourable immigration policy. The removal of racial barriers and the introduction of the "points system" based on education, skills, and language qualifications in 1962, with amendments in 1967, 1971, and 1974 opened the floodgates for the arrival of Filipino professionals and skilled

Philippine-Canadian Centre of Manitoba on Keewatin Street in Winnipeg

workers from the Philippines, The Netherlands, the UK, and, by the mid-1990s, from the Middle East. Relatives of earlier immigrants came under the Family Reunification Program. As a major source country for immigrants, annual immigration statistics rank the Philippines in the top 10 since the mid-1970s and in the top 5 from the mid-1980s to the present. The current Manitoba Provincial Nominee Program and the increased annual provincial immigration target will be a significant factor in increasing the Filipino population beyond the current community estimate of 45,000.

Filipinos contribute to all facets of life in the province. They form a strong component in the labour force in public and private offices and in different industries. However, it is in the health care area that they have found a particular niche. Many of the early doctors and nurses served as supervisors and as unit and department heads in major Winnipeg hospitals, as well as instructors in medical and nursing schools. Presently, Filipino health care professionals/givers and home care workers staff health institutions, nursing homes while others operate personal care homes. In the spiritual realm, Filipinos fill **Roman Catholic** and other Christian churches, necessitating the recruitment of Filipino Catholic priests since 1975 and Protestant pastors as well. Filipino Manitobans have distinguished themselves from other Filipino-Canadian communities by having elected representatives to all levels of govt: MP and former senior cabinet member Dr. **Rey Pagtakhan**; MLAs Dr. Conrad Santos and Cris Aglugub; Councillor Mike Pagtakhan; and school trustees Ric dela Cruz and Florencio Antonio. In education, Dr. Romulo Magsino served as dean of education at the **U of M**. In the print media, the *Filipino Journal*, owned by Rod and Rosalinda Natividad Cantiveros, has been operating for 20 years. Other newspapers are more recent, but CKJS Radio's Filipino programs have dominated the airwaves for quite some time. While many second-generation Filipinos pursue traditional careers, quite a number, including Ma Anne Dionisio, Canada's "Miss Saigon," are venturing successfully into the theatre arts, and other entertainment. Filipino food – including *lumpia*, or egg roll; *pancit*, or noodles; *adobo* (meat stew); and pork barbecue – enriches the taste of MB, while the Philippine-Canadian Centre of Manitoba (PCCM), constructed in 2004, featuring a cultural icon, "salakot"-shaped dome diversifies the province's architectural landscape.

Vibrant and dynamic, the Filipino community has always responded to various challenges. Community leaders and/or activists initiate ad hoc groups to address specific problems on discrimination, racism, youth gangs, immigration, addiction, and other issues that arise. Currently, over 50 associations provide programs and services for professionals, businesses, seniors, youth, women, and families. Others promote religious, social, and sports activities, and engage in cultural heritage maintenance and preservation through language classes, the celebration of traditional rituals and festivals (such as Atiatihan and Mayuhan), and the annual Philippine Heritage Week, which commemorates Philippine independence in June. The Nayong Pilipino and Pearl of the Orient Philippine pavilions showcase Philippine culture during the 2-week **Folklorama** festival of nations. Family life, which emphasizes strong ties and Filipino values, including the celebration of important milestones (including the 1st, 7th, and 18th birthdays, and weddings) still remains strong. However, changing family structure, assimilation through intermarriage, and exposure to mainstream cultures are expected to widen the generational gap. ● LINDA CANTIVEROS

FILMMAKING began in MB just 2 years after the Lumière brothers opened the first moving-picture parlour in Paris in 1895. By fall 1897, **James S. Freer** had bought one of Thomas Edison's Vitascope machines, and was filming scenes around his farm S of **Brandon**. He was the first Manitoban, and the first resident Canadian, to make and show movies. In the process, he established patterns that were to dominate provincial filmmaking for at least 6 decades.

Freer made a series of short movies about everyday Prairie reality with titles such as *Harvesting Scene, With Trains Passing By* and *Premier Greenway Stooking Grain*. Financed by the **CPR** in 1898, and the federal govt in 1902, Freer took these movies and some still photographs on lecture-screening tours of his native England to promote the Cdn West to prospective immigrants – and to drum up business for the CPR. Newsreels, documentaries, and "home movies" like his, used for promotional or institutional purposes, were virtually the only kinds of films made in the province until the 1960s.

The only exceptions were a few very early "animated" movies, now lost, made by Jean Arsin (ca 1910) and Charles Lambly (*Romulus and Remus*, 1926) and 2 fiction features. The most sensational silent feature film was *God's Crucible*, made from a bestselling novel by local author Ralph Connor (see **Charles William Gordon**). In 1920, QC-born producer Ernest Shipman blew into Winnipeg and set up a production that captivated the local populace for months on end. Fresh from a successful venture centred in AB called *Back to God's Country*, featuring his wife,

British Columbian actress Nell Shipman, in a heavily publicized "nude" scene, Shipman bought the rights to Connor's *The Foreigner* and convinced local entrepreneurs to invest in it. The movie was shot in and around Winnipeg in summer 1920 and shown in the city in the fall, but it then disappeared from sight. "Ten-Percent Ernie" – so named because that was his commission as movie producer – headed eastward with the rights to a couple of other Connor novels and further unrealized plans for creating a Cdn film industry. More modest were the ambitions of the undergrads of the **U of M**, who in 1938 filmed a comedy about student life called *And So to College*.

Aside from these, the overwhelming majority of movies made in the province between 1897 and 1967 were fact-based. Stringers, locally based cameramen who filmed current events and "soft news" stories for international agencies like Fox Movietone News, created most of them. For instance, in 1910, J. A. King set up the Great West Film Company to make up to 3 hours of footage about MB, often involving politicians or public figures in popular places. By far the most successful stringer was Angelo Accetti, a massive 135 kg (300 lb) but energetic man who, between 1920-54 from his St. Boniface premises, supplied a steady stream of filmed material on everything from blizzards to floods and from visiting royalty to dog shows, sports events, and flowering gardens. Two other noteworthy filmmakers of this era were Francis J. S. Holmes and Ken Davey, both makers of industrial or promotional films. Beginning in 1926 with a 77 minute silent film about Port Nelson, a tiny community at the mouth of the **Nelson River** at **Hudson Bay**, Holmes completed almost 50 films for various govt agencies and businesses. Typical are *Prairie Conquest*, a visual history of wheat; *Unlimited Horizons*, which extolled the virtues of family farm life; and *Beyond the Steel*, an account of the movement by sled of the buildings of Sherridon Mines to **Lynn Lake**. Davey also made industrials, but he is credited with initiating the practice of using film of the **Winnipeg Blue Bombers** for coaching purposes. He also set up his own laboratory for processing film and, in 1954, successfully made the transition to television. Many Manitobans who wished to work in film left the province during this period. Some, such as **Charles Thorson** and Jack Carson, left for Hollywood, others for Ottawa, home of the **National Film Board of Canada** (NFB) 1939-56. NFB filmmakers, including **Roman Kroitor** and husband-and-wife team Morten and Gudrun Bjerring Parker, returned to the province to make some documentaries here. When television began in 1954, local film productions decreased (though

Filmmaking equipment has become a common sight on Winnipeg streets.

films whose style, tone, and success influenced a generation of imitators, especially **Guy Maddin**. Maddin's output, from *The Dead Father* (1985) and features such as *Tales from the Gimli Hospital* (1988), *Careful*, and *The Saddest Music in the World* (2004), has garnered both international acclaim and, sometimes, puzzlement.

Following the achievements of the early 1980s, the local industry received a further boost with a federal-provincial agreement (CIDO – Cultural Industries Development Office) in 1987 to fund production and distribution of local films. CIDO evolved into a provincially funded organization, Manitoba Film and Sound (MFS), which in the 1990s and the early 21st century transformed the province into a filmmaking centre. Without it, *The Last Winter*, and such made-for-television movies as *The Diviners* (based on a novel by **Margaret Laurence**); *Milgaard*; and *Cowboys and Indians* (an account of **Cree** activist **J. J. Harper**'s killing) would not have been possible. The tax-credit program encouraged offshore companies to produce, among many others, *Capote* and *Shall We Dance* here. More importantly, MFS established stability for the industry, allowing producers and production companies like Phyllis Laing at Buffalo Gal Pictures, Kim Todd at Original Pictures, Louis Paquin at Les Productions Rivard, Lisa Meeches at Eagle Vision, Lank/Beach, and **Frantic Films** to create documentaries, television series, and feature films with a distinctive Manitoban stamp.
● GENE WALZ

FILMON, Gary Albert, businessman, premier (b Aug 24, 1942, **Winnipeg**). Filmon attended Sisler High School and the **U of M**, where he was a gold medallist in engineering. He ran a business before his election to Winnipeg City Council in 1975. He entered the legislative assembly in Oct 1979 and the cabinet of **Sterling Lyon** in Jan 1981, and became **Progressive Conservative Party** leader in 1983. His party lost the election of 1986, but he became premier in 1988. Following the party's defeat in 1999, he left politics in 2000.

Filmon's administration was judicious and careful, especially in its first term. It was one of the administration's proudest boasts that it had been able to avoid imposing any new taxes. However, it did cut the size and cost of govt, and public-sector workers were forced to take unpaid holidays, which came to be known as "Filmon Fridays." As premier, Filmon worked hard to attract jobs to MB. But the returns in this regard were modest. What new jobs were created were primarily unskilled, poorly paid, and part-time service positions. Typically, these new jobs seemed to occur in call centres.

local sports, variety shows, and drama were all recorded on film).

It wasn't until cheaper equipment became available in the 1960s and "new waves" of filmmakers were rising around the world that filmmaking began in earnest. The new wave of filmmaking in Manitoba began with the 1967 short-feature *And No Birds Sing*. Written and directed by Shakespeare professor Victor Speirs Cowie and filmed on the U of M campus, it followed the amusing infatuations of a callow undergrad. Voted best picture at the Vancouver Film Festival, it was nominated for Best Screenplay and Best Film over 30 Minutes, and won a prize for Best Supporting Actor, at the Canadian Film Awards in 1969. Seven years later, Leonard Yakir (producer, director) and Joe Wiesenfeld (writer) made a full-length feature on a similar theme – but from a Jewish perspective. Unable to buck a national distribution system enamoured with Hollywood movies, *The Mourning Suit* went the way of most Cdn films of that era: it was praised by many, but seen by few.

Two 1974 events profoundly changed filmmaking in the province. The **Winnipeg Film Group** was established, and the NFB set up their Prairie Production Office in the city. Together, they put the province on the filmmaking map, the NFB making not just documentaries but animation and dramas, and the Film Group devoted to independent films of all descriptions. By the mid-1980s, films made by both organizations attracted attention across the country, and at film festivals and among film buffs around the world.

Four productions indicated a coming-of-age for the Prairie Production Office of NFB: *Getting Started* (1980), an off-beat animated film about a concert pianist's inability to practise made by **Richard Condie**; *Capital* (1981), a drama set in the **Interlake** about a shady used-car salesman and his son, written and directed by Allan Kroeker; *Ted Baryluk's Grocery* (1982), a look at an inner-city store through still photographs and documentary sounds by **John Paskievich;** and *Daughters of the Country* (1986), a series of 4 hour-long dramas on the history of relations between white society and First Nations women. These 4 dramas were produced by **Norma Bailey** and directed by her, by Kim Johnson, and by Derek Mazur. Condie would go on to get 2 Oscar nominations (for *The Big Snit* – 1985 and *La Salla* – 1996), and led to a Winnipeg renaissance in animation. After captivating the Cannes Film Festival with *Ted Baryluk's Grocery*, Paskievich, with 10 documentaries to his credit, continues to tackle world issues. Kroeker has moved on to US television work, mainly famous for his science-fiction work, though he has also made a name for himself with adaptations of Cdn literature, especially the feature movie *Tramp at the Door*, based on a **Gabrielle Roy** story. Norma Bailey has since become one of the top women directors in the country.

At the same time, and sometimes with the assistance of the NFB, the Winnipeg Film Group produced a series of quirky films that *Toronto Star* critic Geoff Pevere dubbed "Prairie postmodern." John Paizs lead the way with *The Three Worlds of Nick* (1983) and *Crime Wave* (1985), feature

Public spending was restrained, both as a result of the govt's own choice and as a result of the cuts in transfer payments made by the Liberal federal govt, which held power in Ottawa for the latter half of Filmon's administration. These cuts affected most areas of govt activity, particularly education. Responses from the govt included establishing a commission under former MB premier **Duff Roblin** to look into the province's post-secondary education. The contents of the report were predictable and led to little action. The govt also appointed former Winnipeg mayor **Bill Norrie** to recommend on reductions in the number of school boards in the province. On the most critical social policy of all, spending on health care, the govt took considerable and perhaps justifiable pride. The proportion of the budget spent on health increased every year until it was close to 40% of the total budget.

Gary Filmon, 1988

Two highly significant moves were the passage of balanced-budget legislation, in 1995, and the privatization of the phone company **Manitoba Telephone System** in 1996. The *Balanced Budget, Debt Repayment, and Taxpayer Protection Act* prohibited the govt from abandoning a balanced budget, unless in times of war, insurrection, or natural disaster, or if the people approved of the departure in a referendum. Otherwise, Cabinet ministers would lose part of their salary. The govt defended MTS's privatization on the basis that it was necessary if the company was to recapitalize.

The govt also was involved in attempts to save the **Winnipeg Jets**. For several years, the province assumed part of the team's losses. However, the key demand from the team's owners was for a brand new arena. This became an issue at the end of the truncated 1994-95 season, when it appeared that the city and the province would lose their beloved team. The question surfaced during the 1995 election. Contrary to its general opposition to state intervention, the Filmon govt communicated the clear impression that it would spend more than the other parties to keep the Jets in Winnipeg. The promise helped the PCs get elected, but ultimately the team left anyway.

The govt was more successful in getting the **Pan American Games** to MB in July and Aug 1999. Filmon, and to an even greater extent his wife Janice (nee Wainwright) had been keen supporters of this effort, which required the city to beat out Toronto for the prize. The games were highly successful, due to a combination of superb weather and excellent work by the 20,000 volunteers servicing the events.

Canada's constitution was a dominant issue during the Filmon administration. The **Meech Lake Accord** had been agreed to during the previous NDP administration, but had not been voted on. Filmon introduced the ratifying resolution late in 1988. Since he led a minority govt, and both opposition parties were opposed, he looked for a way out. It came when the QC govt invoked the Notwithstanding Clause of the federal Charter of Rights and Freedoms to legitimize its language legislation. Filmon withdrew the resolution, and established a task force to make appropriate recommendations. The task force travelled widely in the summer of 1989. It detected a distaste for Meech Lake, and for anything that smacked of concessions to QC. Its report added a condition to MB's support: that the rest of the country be recognized for its distinctiveness and diversity. But still, the legislature did not deal with the original resolution. The end of the accord came in the MB legislative assembly in June 1990. The first ministers' talks of a few weeks previously had ended, it appeared, with agreement. MB, all 3 of whose party leaders had attended the talks, would, it seemed, soon be on board. But an NDP MLA, **Elijah Harper**, killed the accord by withholding his consent from procedural motions which required unanimity. This outcome was perhaps symptomatic of the cool relations that existed between the provincial govt and the Mulroney federal govt. When the Filmon govt campaigned for re-election in 1990, its advertising gave a clear impression that it had no affiliation with the national wing of the party.

Filmon's administration won majority govts in 1990 and 1995, leading some to speculate whether Filmon would become MB's longest serving premier. But he was finally defeated in 1999 because of the **Interlake Voting Scandal**. The scandal arose when some govt advisors, including the premier's chief-of-staff, offered money to Aboriginal individuals during the 1995 election in an attempt to get them to run as independents in areas where they might split the vote with the NDP, thereby handing the seat to the PCs. The resulting inquiry under Justice Alfred Monnin in 1998-99 placed no blame on the premier, but the revelations were a major factor in ending the life of the Filmon administration. Filmon now sits on various boards and is a member of Canada's Security Intelligence Review Committee. • GEOFF LAMBERT

House Finch

FINCH (family Fringillidae) is a small, seed-eating songbird. Finches include such familiar feeder birds as grosbeaks, redpolls, and goldfinches. Like their relatives the sparrows, they have short, stubby bills that are used to crack open seeds. The black-and-yellow American Goldfinch (*Carduelis tristis*) is mainly a summer resident, while Pine Grosbeaks (*Pinicola enucleator*) and Common Redpolls (*Carduelis flammea*) visit the S of the province in late winter, after having bred in the north. Red crossbills (*Loxia curvirostra*) and white-winged crossbills (*L. leucoptera*) are highly erratic, their presence or absence dictated by the availability of cone seeds, which are their main food source. A recent addition to the province's avifauna is the house finch (*Carpodacus mexicanus*), a native of the US SW and parts of Mexico. First seen in MB in 1983, it has since become a common year-round resident of cities and towns across the southern ⅓ of MB. • RUDOLF KOES

FINKLEMAN, Ken, filmmaker, actor (b June 4, 1946, **Winnipeg**). Educated at University College, **U of M**, Finkleman has been the main force behind several highly rated CBC Television "dramedies" that focus on current events and the incompetence of the media. Finkleman first wrote for the TV comedy series *The Frankie Howerd Show* (1976) and *Van Dyke and Company* (1976). In the 1980s, he worked in Hollywood, writing *Grease 2* (1982), immediately following that with *Airplane II: The Sequel* (1982), *Head Office* (1985), and *Who's That Girl?* (1987), an update of *Bringing up Baby* that Madonna headlined. Finkleman has often referred to this period as the lowest point in his career. Ken directed and acted in *Married Life* (1995), a 4-part "mockumentary" series for CBC-TV. Beginning with *The Newsroom* in the 1996-97 season, Finkleman served as writer, director, and producer of *More Tears* (1998), *Foolish Heart* (1999), *Foreign Objects* (2000), and *The Newsroom* (2003, 2004). In the latter series, he has also played the main character, the savvy but comically self-absorbed George Findlay, a role he assayed in the 2002 movie-of-the-week *Escape from the Newsroom*. Ken's brother Danny Finkleman, also from **NORTH END** Winnipeg, was long-time host of *Finkleman's 45s*, a Saturday-night CBC Radio show of opinions, stories, and vintage rock 'n' roll music that ran 1985-2005. ● GENE WALZ

FIREBRAT or Bristletail (*Thermobia domestica*) is a 12 mm, primitive, wingless insect with a flattened, tapering body, 2 long antennae, and 3 'tails' (2 cerci and a central 15 mm filament) sensitive to touch. It is light-mottled with scales and tuffs of comb-like hairs. Most species are native to warm countries (preferring 32-40°C), where they inhabit leaf litter, bark, decomposing logs, caves, animal burrows and nests. In buildings in MB, they congregate in warm sites like around furnaces and heating pipes. A close relative is the 12 mm, nocturnal silverfish (*Lepisma saccharina*), which sometimes turns up mysteriously in sinks and bathtubs. It prefers temperatures from 21-27°C. These insects can run rapidly on their 6 legs. Most species reproduce sexually, with the male displaying in a courtship dance. The female picks up the male's spermatophore and then lays her fertilized eggs in crevices. The immatures moult 10 times before reaching the adult stage, which also continues to moult throughout life, up to 4 years. Both species have chewing mouthparts and can survive on meagre rations of food, devouring almost anything organic, especially starchy items. When abundant, they can do significant damage to cereals, books, photos, wallpaper and clothes made from cotton and wool. They have bladder-like structures on the abdomen with which they soak up moisture. Firebrats and silverfish are not native to MB, but they have accidentally been introduced from the US and Europe and occur in MB homes and other heated buildings. There are 47 species recorded in NA and 580 worldwide. This is an ancient group, appearing 325 million years ago (Carboniferous period). ● REW, TG

FIRST PEOPLES OF MANITOBA
by Robin Jarvis Brownlie

Aboriginal peoples have lived in the lands that now form Manitoba for thousands of years. Their flexible, mobile societies thrived through many climatic changes, always basing their lives and economies on resourcefulness and resilience, respect for the interconnectedness of all life, and the tending of relationships with other humans, animals, and spirits. They adapted themselves expertly to their environment, stewarding resources for future generations and developing their tools and technology from materials readily at hand. Since the intrusion of Europeans and Euro-Canadians into their territories, First Peoples have continued their pattern of cultural and economic adaptation, but have faced severe disruption of their economies and substantial attacks on their cultures. Currently, they are mounting a major cultural reinvigoration and performing leading roles nationally in politics, arts and culture, and communications.

FIRST NATIONS: There are 6 Aboriginal peoples who make MB their home: the **OJIBWAY** (also known as Anishnawbe and Saulteaux), **CREE**, **DAKOTA**, **DENE**, **MÉTIS**, and Oji-Cree (or Ojibway-Cree). The Assiniboine were important before migrating west, but numerically, the Cree and Ojibway are the largest groups, the Cree located mostly in the northern and northeastern parts of the province, the Ojibway in southern and central MB. The Dakota live in the southwest, where they have 5 reserve communities: **DAKOTA TIPI, DAKOTA PLAINS, CANUPAWAKPA, BIRDTAIL SIOUX,** and **SIOUX VALLEY.** There are 2 Dene reserve communities, both situated in the far north, Tadoule Lake and Lac Brochet. The Oji-Cree, who blend the languages and traditions of the Ojibway and Cree into a unique culture of their own, live in the northeast near **HUDSON BAY** and around the Island Lake area. In 2007, there were 63 First Nations communities in the province which combined 103 reserves. The **MÉTIS** have no reserves and are dispersed throughout the province, mostly in southern urban areas; a few towns, such as **ST. LAURENT,** are primarily Métis communities. Given the increasing urbanization of Aboriginal people, many people from all these nations live in southern urban centres.

STAN MILOSEVIC, WWW.MANITOBAPHOTOS.COM

Diorama at Manitoba Museum

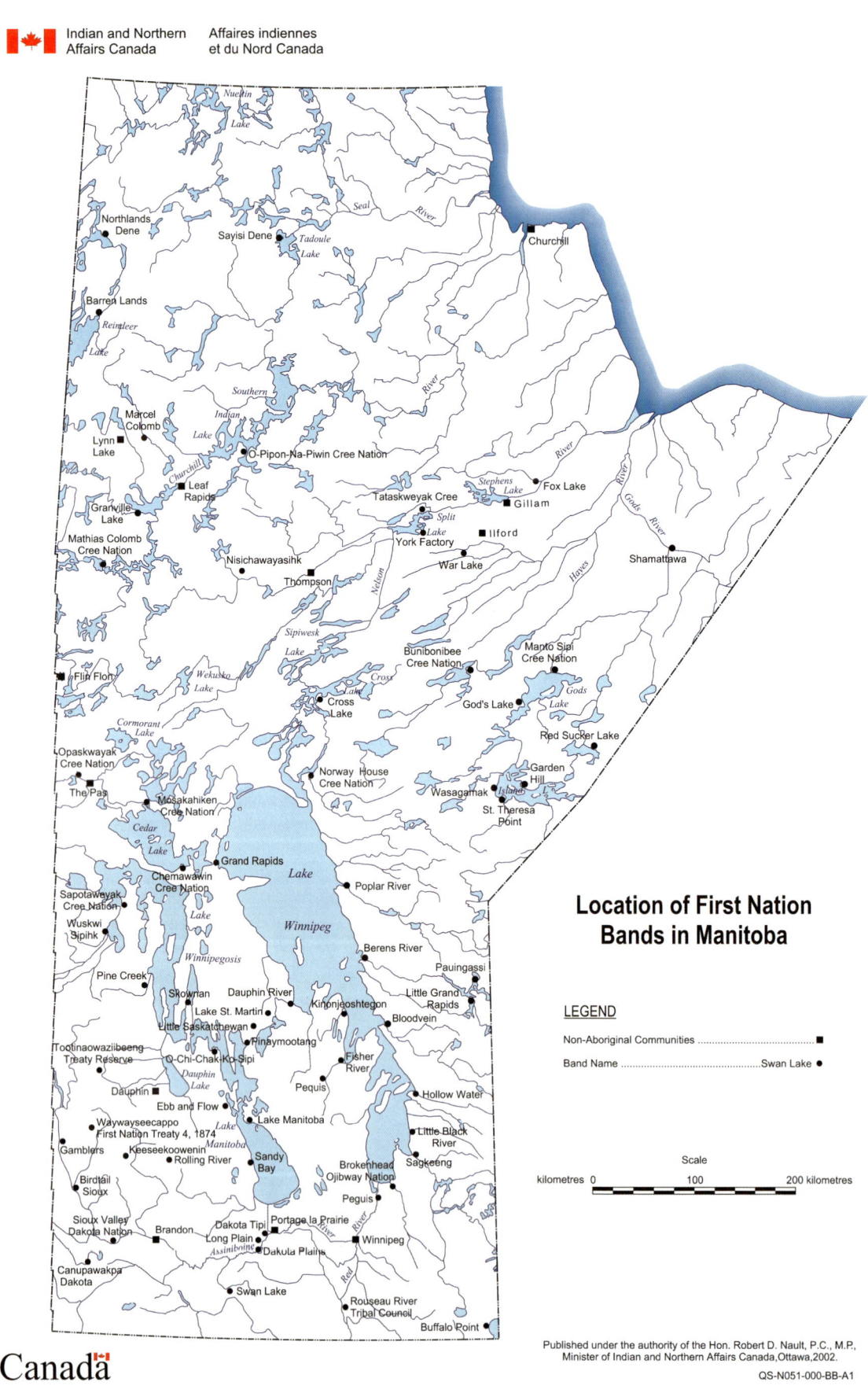

Indian and Northern
Affairs Canada

Affaires indiennes
et du Nord Canada

F

**Location of First Nation
Bands in Manitoba**

LEGEND

Non-Aboriginal Communities .... ■

Band Name ....Swan Lake ●

Scale

kilometres 0   100   200 kilometres

Canada

Published under the authority of the Hon. Robert D. Nault, P.C., M.P.,
Minister of Indian and Northern Affairs Canada,Ottawa,2002.

QS-N051-000-BB-A1

Each of these peoples has its own history, and, indeed, different branches of each have their own particular stories. The Cree, Dene, and Dakota have occupied parts of the territory that became MB for thousands of years; the Ojibway have been in this area for only 2½ centuries. The Oji-Cree are a blend of 2 long-established peoples, who began to intermarry and mingle their 2 languages in the late 18th century. As the descendants of Europeans as well as First Nations people, the Métis have a shorter history than their First Nations counterparts, but nevertheless they have over 2 centuries of history in the territory that is now MB.

The Ojibway, Dene, Cree, and Dakota have origin stories in which their distant ancestors arrive in their territory from another world, usually located in the sky. Most understand themselves as having originated in or near the territory where they presently are, in NA. Western scientists, by contrast, argue that all the Indigenous peoples of NA are the descendants of peoples who migrated to the Americas from northeastern Asia approximately 15,000 years ago. What is universally acknowledged is that Aboriginal peoples have lived in the Americas for thousands of years.

It is difficult to establish with any certainty exactly where the ancestors of any given Aboriginal group lived in the remote past. Territories shifted over time as a result of changing weather patterns, disputes with neighbours, internal divisions, and the availability of key resources. For example, Dene peoples are now scattered over an enormous distance, stretching from Hudson Bay in the northeast all the way across subarctic Canada, down into the BC plateau (the Chilcotin), and into the US west and southwest (Apache and Navajo, or Dinneh as they call themselves). The Dene's own traditions nearly universally state that they came from the northeast but began to move west and south as a result of internal disputes. Archaeological and geological research has shown that a disastrous volcanic eruption spread a layer of white ash about a metre thick across much of what is now the southern Yukon some time around 525 CE. The ash, combined with the noxious gases released at the same time, would have severely affected the availability of food for several years and undoubtedly forced people to migrate far from their home territories to survive. This event corresponds roughly with the time that the Dene peoples may have begun to separate and migrate.

Although the expressive cultural life of the Aboriginal peoples of MB varied quite remarkably, the underlying social and economic structures had a fundamental similarity. All can be characterized as hunting peoples. The activities of gathering, hunting, trapping and fishing provided for the dietary needs; by and large, agriculture was not practised. Hunting cultures are known for the rough equality that prevails in social relations, for the sustainable nature of their ecological interactions, for the strength of their narrative traditions, and as a flexible and enduring form of society. Hunting in early historic MB involved seasonal use of resources, which meant a degree of nomadic behaviour within a stable overall territory. For example, the Sayisi Dene might spend late summer and fall on the barren grounds, moving back to the forest for winter and spring; Plains Cree people might move into the forest for the winter and back out onto the plains for spring, summer and fall. Anthropologists have argued that hunters have been systematically under appreciated and that a less ethnocentric approach might characterize them as wealthy or 'affluent' rather than as engaged in mere survival. This characterization rests on the insight that hunters typically do not need to spend as much time as farmers working to meet their subsistence needs, partly because hunting and gathering were relatively efficient in obtaining food and partly because such societies do not require great quantities of material goods to satisfy their needs. Although outsiders long assumed that hunting peoples would disappear in the 20th century, in the 21st century it

Métis buffalo hunters waiting on horseback for word to advance.

is the remarkable persistence of hunters that has led to a reappraisal of their status and contributions.

THE FUR TRADE: The arrival of Europeans brought considerable changes in Aboriginal people's economies, cultures, environments, and territorial distributions. First Nations in the north were affected early, being drawn into the **FUR TRADE** when the **ENGLISH**-owned **HUDSON'S BAY COMPANY** (HBC) established itself in forts on **HUDSON BAY** from 1670 on. The local Swampy Cree (*muskekowuck athinuwick*, or "people of the swampy lands") became key suppliers to the company, trading furs they had trapped themselves, acquiring furs for trade from allies further inland, and providing "country food" (fish and game) to feed the company's employees. They also undertook seasonal wage labour, loading and unloading the supply ships and later helping transport goods inland on the large **YORK BOATS**, a gruelling, dangerous job that left many men disabled. Initially this relationship made the Cree more powerful than their neighbours, since they became the first group to own guns. They used this advantage to push neighbours such as the Dene out of prime fur lands and out of reach of the HBC's forts. By the early 18th century, however, the HBC had made direct contact with the easternmost Dene and began a long trading relationship with them. The Ojibway, who were mostly living to the north of Lakes Superior and Huron when the first Europeans entered their country, commenced trade with the **FRENCH** at the beginning of the 17th century, through their allies the Wendat (Huron), who lived farther south. They became very active participants in the fur trade, initially supplying furs and also serving as "middlemen" who obtained furs from inland allies and traded them to the French, passing on European goods to the inlanders at a sizable mark-up. Later, some began to work for the European traders as hunters, seasonal wage labourers, and travelling trappers who moved into new territories in search of furs.

Over time, the fur trade instituted tremendous changes. It introduced metal goods and firearms that were more durable and convenient than pre-existing Aboriginal technology, but gradually made First Nations people dependent on access to European goods. Guns required ammunition and repairs that the people were not able to make themselves. Devoting more time to trapping furs meant less time spent hunting for food, so that Aboriginal participants in the trade began to need imported European foods to survive, especially flour and lard, but also tea and sugar. These foods radically altered their diets, increasing carbohydrates and reducing protein intake. The great increase in animals harvested led to a decline in many animal species, presenting further problems for the food supply and also potential shortages of hides for clothing and shelter. European cloth and blankets began to replace the skin and fur clothing made of deer, beaver, rabbit, and hare. Moreover, the people's orientation to the land slowly changed, so that less time was spent in the stewardship

Treaties were necessary to facilitate settlement as early settlers and Aboriginals clashed over desirable lands.

formerly practised, such as breaking up beaver dams in spring for spawning fish to ascend the rivers, or burning off meadows for deer habitat. In many places, beaver were virtually eliminated through over-trapping, and other fur-bearing populations as well as large game were also compromised. These phenomena did not occur prior to the fur trade, because there was no incentive for obtaining excess meat or furs. Trading posts themselves consumed large quantities of local food, especially fish and large game, as well as forests for miles around. In the long term, the commercialization of the hunt introduced by the fur trade was unsustainable, depleting animal populations and leaving the local First Nations people dependent on European food, clothing, and equipment that they became increasingly unable to earn. When the HBC closed a trading post, often after several centuries of interdependence with the local First Nations, in many cases the people were left virtually destitute.

Another significant impact of the fur trade was that it spurred major migrations of peoples. The Ojibway, Cree, Dakota, and Dene all shifted territories, some of them dramatically, in response to fur trade developments. Indeed, the huge stretches of territory occupied in historic times by the Cree and Ojibway are a testimony to these 2 peoples' powerful association with the fur trade and the advantages they derived from it. With the guns they received from Europeans, both the Cree and Ojibway expanded far to the west of their original lands, pushing other peoples in front of them as they moved. From their original lands on both sides of Hudson and James Bays, the Cree expanded westward all the way across the prairies, developing new branches of their people known as the Plains Cree, though also leaving some Cree in their original locations, so that Cree people can be found from the eastern shores of Hudson Bay all the way to the Rockies.

The Ojibway seem to have been a relatively small group based on the northern shores of Lakes Superior and Huron when the first Europeans arrived. Moving with the fur trade, they began to migrate westward in the 18th century as their own lands became stripped of fur-bearing animals. Advancing first to the Lake of the Woods and Rainy River regions, they had established themselves in the **RED RIVER** area of MB by the mid-18th century. The Dakota, too, were originally a woodland group based around the western end of the Great Lakes, south of the Ojibway. They also moved westward onto the plains, establishing themselves in the areas that became MN. In moving, the Cree, Ojibway, and Dakota made a major shift from a woodland economy and culture to a plains economy and culture, learning new skills to adapt to a very different environment and adopting some elements of plains people's ceremonies, customs, and beliefs.

Finally, the fur trade gave birth to the "New People," the Métis. Born of fur trade unions between European trader men and First Nations women, the Métis gradually developed into a people distinct from both Europeans and First Nations. Although many children of such unions joined their mothers' people, others married amongst themselves, developing a distinctive culture blending European and Aboriginal traits, and creating specialized economic niches. The Métis were known for their work as voyageurs, carters, and boatmen who moved the goods of the fur trade through the continent's vast trails and waterways. They were also known for their role as bison hunters who provided a good portion of the pemmican that fuelled the trade. After the founding of the Red River colony at the forks of the Red and **ASSINIBOINE** Rivers, the Métis established themselves as the main population group in Red River and solidified their identity as a people and a nation.

COLONIZATION: A central concept for understanding the interaction of First Peoples and Europeans in what is now MB is "colonization." Colonization is a process in which one group of people intrudes into the territory of another people in order to exploit their lands and/or resources. While the process takes many forms, it necessarily involves the transfer of power from the Indigenous group to the colonizers, since Indigenous peoples always resist the appropriation of their land and subsistence base. Historically, colonizing groups have been backed by the power of nation states and have often enjoyed the advantage of a substantially larger population with which to overwhelm colonized peoples. Colonial powers justify the seizure of lands and resources through assertions of moral as well as technological superiority, creating negative stereotypes that further reinforce the subjugation of colonized peoples.

The fur trade can be usefully understood as a form of colonization, in that the fur and food resources of NA were commercialized and exploited for the benefit of Europeans, channelled into the profit-making systems of Europe. While many First Nations people willingly participated in the trade in order to obtain European goods, it became increasingly difficult for them to control the process and its impact on their societies and environment. At the same time, there were limits to the traders' power. Aboriginal people still controlled their own territories and governed their own communities, determined their own laws and institutions, and cultivated their own ceremonies, beliefs, and systems of thought.

With the onset of direct colonization by the Cdn state, beginning in 1870, much larger changes began to occur as the federal govt asserted administrative control over Aboriginal peoples and set about implementing its plans for the region. First Nations people lost their ability to manage the pace of change and to control their own territories and communities. From the 1870s on, the newly confederated Canada imposed its laws, police, education system, religion, and a special administrative regime to manage "Indians," run by the Dept of Indian Affairs. Canada's policy with regard to First Nations people was to obtain the surrender of their lands, confine them to small reserves, teach them farming and Christianity, and then assimilate them into Euro-Cdn society through absorption. The goal was to make Aboriginal peoples disappear as distinct peoples. Although govt officials believed that this disappearance would occur even without their intervention – Aboriginal peoples were long called "The Vanishing Race" because of the death toll taken by European diseases – they also took active measures to promote the termination of Aboriginal cultures and to make Aboriginal people culturally identical to Euro-Canadians.

TREATIES: In MB and the rest of the prairies, treaties were the mechanism by which land ownership was legally transferred from the First Nations to Canada. The Ojibway, Cree, Dene, and Oji-Cree all made such agreements with the govt of Canada between 1871 and 1910. Treaties 1, 2, 3, 4, 5, and 10 cover parts of MB. The first 5 of these were signed by the southernmost groups between 1871 and 1875, with subsequent "adhesions" to treaty by groups located farther north; these occurred between 1876 and 1910. Treaty 10 was signed in 1907. According to the written text of these agreements, the Aboriginal signatories gave up virtually all of their land in return for a small initial payment (usually $12 per person), perpetual annual payments ("annuities") of $5 per person, small reserves, and assistance to begin farming, including implements and farming instruction. In the North, the farming provisions were replaced by twine, ammunition, and other items geared toward hunting and fishing. Treaty texts also state that the First Nations will have the right to continue fishing and hunting on lands not yet occupied by newcomers, but add that govts will have the right to regulate these

practices. First Nations people state that such regulation was not part of the oral negotiations and that they were promised they could pursue their traditional harvesting activities. Written records of negotiating processes generally appear to substantiate this assertion, because the primary concern of every Aboriginal group in treaty negotiations was the preservation of their right to hunt, fish, and gather. It is most unlikely they would have signed the treaties if they had been told that these activities would be prohibited for most of the year. Indeed, the records show that govt negotiators repeatedly reassured them that they would be able to continue hunting and fishing as they always had. Not long after the treaties were signed, the province introduced game conservation regimes that criminalized Aboriginal hunting, imposing bag limits and closed seasons covering most of the year. It then began to prosecute Aboriginal hunters, punishing them with fines, jail terms, and/or the confiscation of their equipment and harvested food.

Not all Aboriginal groups in MB have treaty agreements with the Crown. The Métis were never asked to sign a treaty and were handled very differently than their First Nations relatives. Their Aboriginal title to land was acknowledged through the *Manitoba Act* of 1870 and also through the distribution of "**Scrip**," a piece of paper which was redeemable for a certain number of acres of land. Nevertheless, their title was also considered lesser than that of First Nations people, entitling them only to the one-time land allotment, with no other payments or benefits. The scrip entitled each Métis adult to 160 acres of land and each dependent child to 240 acres. The scrip for the Red River Métis was distributed in the 1870s in a flawed process that took so long, most Métis sold their scrip to land speculators for a fraction of its worth. In this way the vast majority of them were left landless and poor. During the treaty adhesion process in northern MB, scrip was again distributed to Métis people in the North, in a similarly problematic process that assigned them lands in the South, far from their homes. Virtually all the scrip handed out in this way was purchased at low prices by non-Aboriginal land speculators, some of whom used the treaty negotiators themselves as agents to purchase scrip as soon as it was distributed.

The Dakota also do not have treaties with Canada because they were deemed to be "American Indians," having lived south of the international border until 1862-63. In that year, they crossed the border into British territory (then called **Rupert's Land**) to escape US Army reprisals for the Dakota Uprising of 1862. Although local white settlers were reluctant to tolerate their presence, the British govt prohibited the US Army from entering its territory to crush the refugee Dakotas, and eventually their permanent settlement was allowed. The Dakota obtained the consent of the Ojibway to use parts of their territory, and the federal govt eventually granted them 4 small reserves on which to live. While one hunting group eventually disappeared, the other Dakota groups became successful farmers.

ECONOMIC ADAPTATION: The treaties ushered in the era of non-Aboriginal settlement, which quickly outnumbered Aboriginal people, especially in the arable lands around Red River and near the US border. The Ojibway living in the South were deprived of their old gathering, fishing and hunting lifeways long before Aboriginal groups in the North. After signing treaties, the southern Ojibway chose reserves and were quickly confined to these small spaces by white settlement of the surrounding areas. The goal for these southerly reserves was to found an economy based on agriculture, and this was moderately successful on some reserves where the land was suited to agriculture, gardening, or stock raising. In other places, reserve land was poorly suited to farming, and the people there focussed their energies more on wage labour. Farther north, around **Lakes Winnipeg** and **Manitoba**, the Ojibway and Cree often chose sites for reserves that were close to productive fisheries and also contained good hay lands, high ground, and timber. For a while they pursued extensive gardening and small farming while also maintaining some hunting and trapping activity, but by 1900 game populations and fur and hide prices had increased, enabling a return to hunting and trapping as the main livelihood. Many also cultivated potatoes and corn to supplement country food of fish, ducks, and moose. Other Ojibway and Cree around Lakes Winnipeg and Manitoba became employed in lumbering, commercial fishing, railway building, and transportation.

As capitalist development moved north, resources that Aboriginal people had once controlled were appropriated for private profit, including the trees, the fish, and the waterways. Aboriginal people became hired labourers and small commodity producers, supplying fish to fishing companies and various wood products to steamships and lumber companies. Indeed, Aboriginal labour was central to the development of the northern MB economy. Many sawmills and fishing stations were located on or near reserves in order to take advantage of Aboriginal labour. Participation in these industries provided reasonable incomes to many families, but often these were typical resource frontier industries, led from outside, export-oriented, and swiftly leading to exhaustion of the resource. The lumber industry in particular was a passing phenomenon, clearing each area of trees and moving on. Large-scale commercial fishing, particularly in the north end of Lake Winnipeg, severely decreased the amount of fish that could be caught near the shore using the small boats and nets Aboriginal people used. They objected strongly to this loss of their most reliable food source, but governments had no intention of curtailing the lucrative export of fish. As the industrial frontier moved north, Aboriginal people earned wages building railway lines and guiding survey and mineral prospecting parties. These, too, provided reasonable wages but were temporary pursuits.

By the 1930s, concern about the depletion of animal species was widespread. After the *NATURAL RESOURCES TRANSFER ACT* of 1930 gave the MB govt jurisdiction over resources, greater efforts were made to conserve game, including marsh rehabilitation projects around **THE PAS** to help restore muskrat populations. In the 1940s, the province imposed a registered trapline system that created a govt-controlled industry, forcing First Nations people to register specific areas for individual traplines, to apply for a trapline each year, and to produce a set quota of fur or lose the trapline to another trapper. The system overturned ancient, flexible, kinship-based Aboriginal methods of determining land use and opened large territories for non-Aboriginal trapping.

The most northerly parts of the province have been much less affected by industrial resource development. Those groups living north of the original territory surrendered in Treaty 5 (north of **NORWAY HOUSE**) experienced little of the economic development that brought wage labour to those south of the line. They remained for many years in an unequal economic relationship with the HBC, fur sales and wage labour for the company comprising their only options for cash income. In the Northeast, especially, technological change brought increasing isolation, as the railway to **CHURCHILL** transformed the fur trade transportation system from a water-based network using Aboriginal labour to a land-based system reliant on the railroad. Communities that had been built along the fur trade's main arteries were now bypassed and marginalized, resulting in significant loss of wage labour opportunities and greater remoteness from the outside world.

The Dene people of northern MB pursued their hunting economies into the 1950s. Though they participated in the commercial fur trade, they also retained considerable autonomy, largely because of the continuing viability of their caribou-based subsistence economy. In 1956, however,

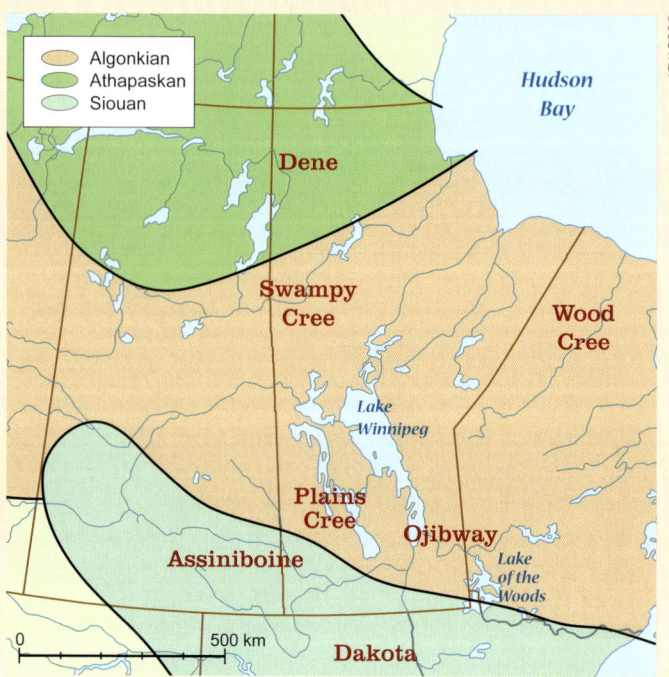

Aboriginal language groups of Manitoba

the federal govt decided to make a fateful intervention into the lives of a Dene group living at Little Duck Lake, known as the Sayisi ("eastern") Dene. The HBC was closing its post there, which led Indian Affairs officials to believe the Dene would face hardship. Meanwhile, the MB game branch had become convinced that the caribou population was declining and blamed the Dene winter caribou hunt. Because of these 2 considerations – and also in pursuit of assimilation – Indian Affairs officials decided to relocate the **SAYISI DENE** to a location near Churchill. Although the officials claimed to have gained the people's consent, the Dene state that no consultation occurred. In 1956, most of the people were airlifted from Little Duck Lake to North Knife River near Churchill, leaving behind their homes and virtually all their possessions. The govt failed to deliver the promised building supplies, and for the next 11 years the Sayisi Dene lived in shanties, most of them gradually moving into Churchill to obtain food. Without access to their traditional economy, the people became destitute, living off the town dump for food and turning to alcohol to escape their despair. The government eventually built houses for them in Churchill, but this did not solve the problems created by the relocation. After nearly 2 decades of alcohol-induced internal violence, the Sayisi Dene finally moved back to the land in 1973, establishing a community at Tadoule Lake, 400 km inland from Churchill. There they are currently working to overcome the painful legacy of the forced relocation.

Another phenomenon that has greatly affected Aboriginal peoples is the development of **HYDROELECTRIC** projects. The first damming project for hydroelectric power was the Island Falls power plant, constructed on the **CHURCHILL RIVER** on the MB-SK border in the late 1920s. Local Aboriginal people were employed in constructing the dam, which provided power for the smelter at nearby **FLIN FLON**. In the 1960s, the MB govt began to build increasingly large hydroelectric projects to generate cheap power for southerners and for planned exports to ON and the US. These projects involved damming and diverting several major rivers, and were commenced without consulting the First Nations whose territories were affected. The dams have had severe negative consequences for a series of Cree communities in central northern MB. Huge areas of land have been flooded, drowning and driving away large game, poisoning fish, filling the once-clean water with mercury and silt, and wreaking havoc in many ways with Aboriginal bush activities. Economic losses to these communities have run into the hundreds of millions of dollars, and the social costs are immeasurable. The **NORTHERN FLOOD AGREEMENT**, signed in 1978 between the province and 5 affected First Nations communities, was intended to lead to major compensation and assistance in rebuilding. Unfortunately, there has been substantial disagreement between the provincial government and the First Nations over the substantive meaning of its clauses, and to date little has been done to compensate or reconstruct these communities.

URBANIZATION: The period after WWII witnessed the beginnings of Aboriginal urbanization. Until this time, the vast majority of First Nations people lived on reserves or in the northern bush, although there have always been some First Nations people living in cities. Beginning in the 1950s, increasing numbers began to move to urban areas in search of jobs, health care, better housing, and improved services. In addition to such "pull" factors attracting people to towns and cities, there are also the "push" factors of reserve conditions: a rising population with a stagnant land base; a lack of employment opportunities; housing shortages; poor access to health care, post-secondary education, and almost all other services; and the social problems on many reserves. Access to television, beginning in the 1960s, also undoubtedly affected the trend, introducing youngsters to the attractions of city life. The federal government has tended to favour this movement, even providing some programs to encourage it, since urban Aboriginal people do not receive most of the services provided to reserve residents and smaller reserve populations thus translate into lower govt expenditures. Urbanization also advances the assimilation process, which remained the primary goal of federal Aboriginal policy until at least the 1970s.

Young hoop dancer at Folklorama First Nations Pavilion, 2006

Since the 1950s, urban Aboriginal populations have expanded steadily, largely through increasing migration, but also through natural increase and, since the 1980s, a growing tendency for people to identify as Aboriginal. By the 2001 census, almost exactly half of Canada's Aboriginal-identified population (49%) lived in urban areas. **BRANDON** and **THOMPSON** have Aboriginal populations of several thousand each, but by far the largest urban community is in **WINNIPEG**. The 2001 census showed 55,755 Aboriginal people living in Winnipeg, forming 8% of the city's population and the largest Aboriginal urban population in Canada. Of these, 22,955 were "registered" or "status Indians," again the largest urban population of that group in Canada. As of 1996, Winnipeg was also home to the largest Métis population in the country.

In general, non-Aboriginal people have regarded the Aboriginal movement into urban centres with ambivalence and even hostility; the colonial notion persists that Aboriginal people belong on reserves, apart from the rest of society. This unfriendly reception, combined with other adjustment difficulties, has contributed to the high unemployment, poverty, and segregation experienced by many urban Aboriginal people. For some, especially those from small communities and more remote areas, the transition to urban life has been difficult. Such migrants have to adjust to a large, impersonal community that is largely non-Aboriginal, often in circumstances where they have few acquaintances, few job skills, and inadequate education. Language barriers have existed for some. Urban (and non-urban) Aboriginal people have significantly lower average incomes than the general population, in fact the majority live below the poverty line. They experience high unemployment rates and, consequently, are much more likely to live in poor or substandard housing.

Despite these problems, or perhaps in response to them, Aboriginal people have built vibrant urban communities, especially in Winnipeg. Indeed, Winnipeg's Aboriginal community has a particularly large number of organizations run by and for Aboriginal people and catering to the community's social, cultural, and political needs. These include umbrella organizations such as the Aboriginal Centre of Winnipeg Inc. and before it the Winnipeg Native Family Economic Development Corporation, organizations that work to foster community development and coordinate services among different organizations. Winnipeg was the first city in Canada to have an Indian and Métis Friendship Centre, founded in 1958 to help Aboriginal people adapt to the city. The Centre is still in operation 5 decades later, offering a range of programs, from a youth drop-in to a computer lab to programs aimed at gang prevention, healthy babies, solvent abuse prevention, and help with parenting.

Winnipeg also boasts the Neeginan Development Corporation, an organization devoted to developing a kind of "campus" for Aboriginal people based on the Cree concept of "neeginan," meaning "our place." Neeginan was involved in the development of 2 important downtown institutions: the Aboriginal Centre of Winnipeg Inc. (ACWI) and Thunderbird House. The Aboriginal Centre, opened in the late 1990s in the renovated CPR station on Higgins Ave, is designed as an Aboriginal gathering place that houses a series of important services under one roof, especially health, educational, and human resource services. Located just across Higgins Avenue at the corner of Main St, Thunderbird House is a centre for Aboriginal spirituality and culture designed by renowned Cree architect Douglas Cardinal and completed in 2000. In 1999, the Manitoba Métis Federation chose to locate its provincial headquarters close to Thunderbird House and the Aboriginal Centre. These are only some examples of the numerous Aboriginal organizations in Winnipeg that pursue greatly varied mandates, from social service to community development, from political lobbying to educational and spiritual needs.

CONTEMPORARY DEVELOPMENTS: The Aboriginal population in Canada has grown significantly over the past 50 years, increasing its numbers by a factor of 7 between 1951 and 2001. In the same period, the whole Canadian population only doubled. In MB, the growth has been comparable, both in absolute numbers and as a percentage of the total. In 1981, there were 66,280 Aboriginal people in the province, forming 6.5% of the population. By 2001, 150,040 Aboriginal people lived in MB, making up 14% of the total population. This increase was the result of high birth rates, a decreasing mortality rate, especially among infants, and greater willingness to identify as Aboriginal. After the passage of Bill C-31 in 1985, permitting the reinstatement of many Aboriginal people who had lost Indian status, there was a major leap in Aboriginal population figures.

FOLKLORAMA – CANADA'S CULTURAL CELEBRATIONS; WHERE TO LOOK PHOTOGRAPHY

Although the Aboriginal birth rate has dropped considerably in recent years, it remains higher than the national average, which will ensure a growing proportion of the population. The proportion of Aboriginal people is particularly high in northern MB, where they make up about 57% of the population, largely because of the much lower population density.

Since the 1960s, Aboriginal peoples in MB have launched a major campaign to revitalize their cultures, have played an important role in provincial and national politics, and have founded a whole range of important artistic, political, social, and cultural institutions. In the political realm, key leaders on the national stage have come from MB, including **Ovide Mercredi** and **Phil Fontaine**, both of whom served terms as National Chief of the Assembly of First Nations. **Elijah Harper**, a Cree member of the provincial legislature originally from Red Sucker Lake, drew national attention when he refused to ratify the **Meech Lake Accord** in 1990, thus spelling the death of this constitutional agreement. In the late 1960s and early 1970s, Dave Courchene became prominent as head of the Manitoba Indian Brotherhood, which was involved in the campaign to defeat the Liberal federal govt's proposed drastic changes to Indian policy (which included terminating treaties, abolishing the *Indian Act* and the Indian Affairs Dept, and devolving responsibility for Aboriginal people to the provinces).

WINNIPEG FREE PRESS

Grand Chief Phil Fontaine

First Nations people received the provincial franchise in 1954, giving momentum to political activism on the provincial as well as the federal level. They have built and maintained a series of political organizations, including the Assembly of Manitoba Chiefs, the Southern Chiefs' Organization, and a series of tribal councils representing different parts of the province. The Manitoba Métis Federation, founded in 1967, serves as a prominent and vocal champion of Métis interests. Besides working to resolve First Nation land claims, a process that centres on the federal land claims process run by Indian and Northern Affairs Canada (INAC), these organizations have also negotiated with the provincial government on matters relating to treaty land entitlement, northern flooding from hydro-electric projects, problems with the justice and child welfare systems,

and other social and economic issues. In the 1980s, child welfare services for on-reserve First Nations children were transferred to First Nations-run agencies, beginning in 1981 with the Dakota-Ojibway Tribal Council, which was the first mandated Aboriginal child welfare agency in Canada. In 2002, the provincial govt introduced legislation to create Aboriginal-run child welfare agencies for off-reserve children and families. This process created 4 new child welfare authorities, 3 of them Aboriginal: the Metis Child and Family Services Authority, the First Nations of Southern Manitoba Child and Family Services Authority; the First Nations of Northern Manitoba Child and Family Services Authority; and the General Child and Family Services Authority (for all other families). These organizations have been gradually assuming their responsibilities since 2003.

One of the most far-reaching political developments for Aboriginal people in MB has been the Public Inquiry into the Administration of Justice and Aboriginal People, better known simply as the **Aboriginal Justice Inquiry**. This extensive inquiry into the administration of justice in the province has influenced developments and thinking across Canada. It was called by the MB govt in 1988 after pressure from Aboriginal groups to address problems of systemic discrimination in policing and the justice system. The immediate momentum came from 2 high-profile events that catalyzed the Aboriginal community's outrage at its treatment by police and the justice system: the 1987 trial of 2 men for the 1971 murder of **Helen Betty Osborne** and the 1988 police shooting of **J.J. Harper**, executive director of the Island Lake Tribal Council. The AJI report called for a fundamental transformation of the relationship between Aboriginal people and the rest of society, advancing dozens of recommendations to effect this change. Most of these recommendations have not yet been implemented.

Another significant success in recent years has been the Treaty Land Entitlement process, designed to provide additional land to First Nations that had not received as much land as they were entitled to under their treaties. Seven First Nations signed individual agreements of this type with the provincial government between 1994 and 1996, while the Treaty Land Entitlement Framework Agreement with 20 other First Nations was signed in 1997. The latter agreement specified that the First Nations involved could obtain up to 1,100,626 acres (445,408 ha) of land through the process, most of it Crown land. For the 6 most southerly groups, insufficient Crown land was available and privately owned land was to be purchased from willing sellers. By 2006, the Entitlement First Nations had selected 866,094 acres (350,496 ha) and purchased 5,465 acres (2212 ha). Although not all of this land had yet been transferred and converted to reserve status, the process was well underway and all but 3 of the First Nations signatories had completed their land selection.

Recent years have also seen the development of an urban Aboriginal middle class. The emergence of commercial Aboriginal-run companies such as Anokiiwin, an employment and training agency, is symptomatic of this phenomenon. Media and communications organizations such as the **Aboriginal Peoples' Television Network** (APTN), Native Communications Inc. (NCI), Aboriginal Peoples' Choice Music Awards and the Aboriginal Film and Video Festival have provided dynamic, well-paid jobs in which First Peoples can utilize technology to revitalize Aboriginal cultures.

The challenges for Aboriginal people remain considerable, as they work to overcome the legacies of colonization, to rebuild and reinvigorate their communities, and to achieve justice and redress for the many mistakes of the past. But these difficulties should not erase the successes already won by several generations of leaders and community activists, or the strength and resilience of First Peoples who have survived against all odds. •

FISH, FRESHWATER refers to the fish fauna breeding in MB's lakes, rivers and smaller water bodies, all within the **Hudson Bay** Drainage System. Two major groups are represented – the lampreys or class Cyclostomata, and the bony fishes, class Osteichthyes. These contain numerous families totalling 95 species, including 10 introduced species and 2 artificial hybrids. Like all other organisms, fish began to recolonize southern MB as soon as water bodies formed from the melting of the Laurentide Glacier, beginning about 11,000 years ago. Following the northward recession of the ice sheet, the massive glacial **Lake Agassiz** formed along its S edge, stretching across most of central Canada. At various times it drained to the S, E, and W, and it was during this period that 36 species of fish arrived via these routes. Then, 7800 years ago, Lake Agassiz finally breached the last remnant of ice in northern MB and it rapidly drained N into what is now Hudson Bay. About 43 species of fish are believed to have invaded provincial waters soon after this period. Fishes arrived from either the **Red River** watershed (from the upper Mississippi River), the **Winnipeg River** watershed (Great Lakes watershed), or by both routes.

Rainbow Smelt

Ten non-native species and 2 hybrids species have been introduced into MB or spread here from adjacent regions during historical times. This is now recognized by most biologists as an inappropriate practise, which often results in unforeseen, negative ecological consequences, particularly regarding the conservation of other aquatic life. The Rainbow Smelt (*Osmerus mordax*) from the Atlantic was illegally released in ON, appeared in Lake Winnipeg by 1991, reached Hudson Bay via the Nelson R by 1998, and spread N along the coast to the Churchill River by 2002. This species is a great concern, since it competes for invertebrate foods with native fishes and devours their eggs and young.

There are a number of other freshwater fishes that may in time reach MB, either through natural dispersal or with human assistance. Many of these already occur in watersheds draining into MB, and populations may be only short distances away. Perhaps the current warming trend will enable a number of these species to expand their ranges into the province. In general, fishes in N MB require cold, well-oxygenated water, while those in the S can tolerate higher temperatures of summer, lower oxygen levels, and often can withstand a higher load of sediment and pollution. Once ice cuts off the water's contact with air, decomposition processes deplete the available oxygen in the water, and fish begin to suffer and may even die in large numbers. This factor is one reason why some water bodies lack certain species.

For over 6000 years, MB's abundant waters provided First Nations peoples with a relatively secure source of food, and numerous camps have been found and excavated at choice fishing locations on lakes and rivers. The commercial fishing industry has played a prominent role in MB's economy for many decades, and the province is famous for its sports fishing. Substantial sums are paid annually by tourists to lodges and guides for the thrill of fishing in remote N waters, while countless local anglers wet their line during summer and winter fishing seasons, controlled by the Fisheries Branch of MB Conservation.

Since fish live in an underwater world so foreign to us, and lead such secretive lives, much remains to be discovered about species in MB. Unknown to the general public, fish first evolved many of our human characteristics – 4 limbs with terminal digits, the majority of internal organs such as a brain and lungs, and paired eyes, ears and nostrils. We acquired these traits through a direct line of evolution from fish, amphibian, reptile, and early mammals. A high percentage of the human genome is consequently derived from our fish ancestors. ● REW

FISH, MARINE is a term used to include a number of living and ancient vertebrate classes of marine fishes first appearing in the fossil record about 500 million years ago (Cambrian period). **Hudson Bay** is one of the largest inland seas in the world, and along with its estuaries, is host to at least 61 species of fish. Not all of these occur regularly along the shallow and slightly diluted coastal waters of MB. Some species are restricted to the deep waters of Hudson Strait and seldom venture S to MB and James Bay. In view of the fact that the annual freshwater discharge into Hudson Bay is more than double that of the St. Lawrence River, this magnitude of dilution of salt water (salt concentration decreases southward to James Bay) has a profound effect on the distribution fishes and their food supply. In Hudson Bay along the MB border, 49 species are listed – 22 species are classified as marine, 9 are marine but enter brackish water seasonally, one is estuarine year-round (Fourhorn Sculpin), 8 are anadromous (using freshwater to spawn and winter, but spend the summers in saltwater), one (Atlantic Salmon) is diadromous (spawns in freshwater but may winter in saltwater), and 8 are typically freshwater, but occasionally enter brackish waters (Lake Whitefish).

The ecologically most-important fish species are the anadromous Arctic Char (*Salvelinus alpinus*); Capelin (*Mallotus villosus*) – a small pelagic fish of deep waters and brackish coastal waters, with larvae abundant in the estuaries of the Churchill and Nelson rivers; Northern Sand Lance (*Ammodytes dubius*), and Stout Sand Lance (*A. hexapterus*) and Arctic Cod (*Boreogadus saida*). With the warming of Hudson Bay since the 1970s, some changes in fish populations have been detected – Arctic Cod has decreased while Capelin and Sand Lance have increased. (see Capelin, Cod, Char, Sand Lance)

Much remains to be discovered about fishes in Hudson Bay, and there are truly remarkable species to be studied. For example, the huge (max 7 m) Greenland Shark (*Somniosus microcephalus*) is common in Hudson Strait and has been reported occasionally throughout Hudson and James bays. Cruising from the surface to depths of 1200 m, it attacks and devours seals, fish, whales and sea birds, and in turn is harvested locally by residents around Baffin Bay and Greenland for meat, oil and hides. Capelin, Greenland Cod, Sculpins and Lumpfish (*Cyclopterus lumpus*) are also fished for subsistence by Cree and Inuit of the Hudson Bay region.

Around 400 million years ago (Devonian Period), MB was home to an amazing assortment of highly armoured, ancient marine fish called arthodires. Examples are *Eastmanosteus lundarensis*, *Ninichthys manitobensis*, and *Squamatognathus steeprockensis* (from Elm Point). The most famous is the giant (6-to-8 m-long, 3000 kg) *Dunkleosteus telleri*, whose massive head plate may be seen in the **Manitoba Museum**. It was truly the terror of the seas. Another giant (5 m-long) predatory fish named *Xiphactinus audux* lived in the inland seas that covered MB during much of the Cretaceous Period (144-65 million years ago). ● REW

FISH FLY. *See* **Mayfly.**

FISHER BRANCH, pop 450, is a village 150 km N of Winnipeg, in the **Interlake** Region. European immigrants inhabited the community in the early 1900s, naming it Wasoo, but the name was changed because it was beside a branch of the Fisher River. A rail spur connected the community to **Winnipeg** in 1914. Fisher Branch has a diverse economy, many residents being employed in agriculture. It is a service centre for the surrounding region, has 2 banks, a health clinic, senior citizens' home, schools, a RCMP detachment, 9-hole golf course, 4-sheet curling rink, skating rink and tennis courts. • GPP

FISHER RIVER FIRST NATION, on reserve pop 1715, off reserve pop 1389, is adjacent to the **PEGUIS FIRST NATION** reserve, 220 km N of **WINNIPEG**. The community signed Treaty 5 in 1875. Its native language is **CREE**. The Fisher River First Nation has 2 reserves. Schooling in this First Nation goes from Nursery-Grade 12, and total enrolment for the year 2003-04 was 431. Fisher River administers its education. Transportation for the Fisher River First Nation includes a year-round accessible road. The river is the other major means of transportation for the community. Economic activity in the Fisher River First Nation is based on commercial fishing and farming. Fisher River is an independent First Nation; therefore it is not a member of any tribal council. The Two Nations Sport Committee (Peguis and Fisher River First Nation communities) combined to bring about the first ever Manitoba Indigenous Winter Games in March, 2006. Rev Stanley John McKay, born and raised in the Fisher River First Nation, was the recipient of the National Aboriginal Achievement Award in the category of heritage and spirituality for building bridges between Aboriginal and Christian communities. • RK

FISHING, COMMERCIAL. This enterprise tentatively got underway in MB with the arrival of **HBC** fur traders. Although never as important a food source as **PEMMICAN** to the **FUR TRADE**, **FISH** caught by First Nations people (especially **CREE**) were often bartered to HBC and later **NWC** employees, as well as to Voyageurs. With the establishment of the **RED RIVER SETTLEMENT** in 1812, fish became a significant food source, especially in times of famine.

By 1872, J. P. Skaptason, deputy director of the federal fisheries department, indicated that commercial fishing had begun on a small scale when a few enterprising men in what would soon become **WINNIPEG** built a boat, equipped it with seine nets, and journeyed to the **LITTLE SASKATCHEWAN RIVER** to establish a station to supply Winnipeg with fresh and salted fish, chiefly whitefish. Commercial fishing received a boost with the arrival of **ICELANDERS** to the **GIMLI** area in 1875. It was reported that in 1879-80 settlers from **NEW ICELAND** sold between 15,000 and 20,000 whitefish. A few years later, the bulk of fishermen on **LAKE WINNIPEG** were Icelanders (3000) and Aboriginal people (2000).

Real exploitation of the fishery came with the opening up of the region immediately N of Winnipeg through rail transportation. Fish from

Boats in Gimli Harbour, 1956

Lake Winnipeg were brought by **STEAMBOAT** to **SELKIRK** and from there shipped to Winnipeg and then across NA, particularly Chicago. During this period, the important commercial fish species were sturgeon and whitefish. Sturgeon, besides being a food fish, was caught for its rich oil and caviar. It was valuable commodity, earning fishermen $1 for a fish (with an average weight of 12 kg) in 1902. Commercial sturgeon fishing reached its peak 1900-06, with over 272,700 kg caught annually; but due to overfishing, by 1910, the catch tumbled to 45,000 kg. Sturgeon had been regarded as so plentiful that their oil was even used to fuel the **STEAMBOATS** plying MB's lakes and rivers. Sturgeon in MB have still not recovered.

Whitefish and sturgeon were not the only fish species pressured by over-fishing. **GOLDEYE** and mooneye, when smoked, became a delicacy that attracted the taste of Eastern buyers. The *Manitoba Free Press* (now the ***WINNIPEG FREE PRESS***) reported that during this era, one million goldeye were caught each year, but only sold for less than half a cent a kg. In 1887, 65 sailboats and 7 tugs and barges operated on Lake Winnipeg, by then, as now, the primary source of commercial fish. According to the fisheries branch of the MB government, 1.1 million kg of fish were taken from the lake that year.

In this era, major US companies also began to take notice of the MB fishery because of the decline of Great Lakes commercial fish species. Booth Fisheries of Chicago set up a number of small companies that were to sell only to Booth, effectively creating a monopoly on Lake Winnipeg. This practice institutionalized a type of feudal system whereby the fishers were indebted to

smaller subsidiary companies, which were in turn indebted to the parent company – a subordination to US capital. Attempts were made to break the monopoly, including establishment of the Fishermen's Protective Union of Lake Winnipeg in Gimli in winter 1898. For a time, the union was able to market its own fish and receive better terms from the companies, which now included Armstrong Fish Company, but soon the companies again exercised their clout and reinstated their system. Disgruntled fishers went on strike in 1914, but the major companies broke the strike by hiring scabs from the Great Lakes. Some local fishers, such as the Sigurdson Brothers of **RIVERTON**, joined the ranks of the big companies and established fishing camps, hauling their own fish to market. Not until 1969, with the creation of the Crown **FRESHWATER FISH MARKETING CORPORATION**, did the hold of the big companies on MB finally end.

Transportation played an invaluable role in opening lakes to commercial fishing, especially in MB's **NORTHERN REGION**. The first **STEAMBOAT** reached **THE PAS**, within easy access to well-stocked lakes, in 1874. But the **RAILWAY** was the most important mode of freighting fish in the late 19th and early 20th centuries. McQueen predicted that the completion of the **HUDSON BAY RAILWAY** would "pass through a portion of the country in which are found in many lakes ... all said to contain an abundance of fish of various kinds." By 1908, the railway had reached The Pas and fish were being sent S by rail in cars cooled by ice. Later the rail cars would be refrigerated. The start of a **WINTER ROAD** system also allowed northern lakes – also communities not served by permanent links along Lake Winnipeg and **LAKE**

MANITOBA – to become part of the commercial fishery. Teams of horses moved ploughs along planned routes and then other teams of horses freighted fish to rail lines. LAKE WINNIPEGOSIS was opened to the winter fishery in this way. Air freight was also a major factor in expanding the commercial fishery. Air transportation commenced in winter of 1931-32 between GRAND RAPIDS on Lake Winnipeg and Lake Winnipegosis.

According to the MB Fisheries Branch, the province's commercial fisheries produce an average of 12 million kg of fish annually, using 295 commercially registered lakes in addition to lakes Winnipeg, Manitoba and Winnipegosis. Pickerel (walleye) comprises the greatest portion of production by weight at 27%, followed by mullet (suckers) at 24%, whitefish at 19%, PIKE at 12%, and sauger at 10%. The pickerel catch averages $14.6 million a year, or 57% of the landed species value. Sauger follows at 16% of landed value, while whitefish is next at 11%. Lake Winnipeg is the biggest commercial fishery, contributing over 40% of MB's total production and 58% of the landed value. Northern lakes contribute 24% of total production and 20% of landed value.

An average of 3222 licensed fishers and their helpers are employed annually in the commercial fishery, with over 30% of them employed on Lake Winnipeg. Of the 228 commercial fishers in the S basin of Lake Winnipeg, 131 operate out the lakeside community of Gimli. The FFMC, a single-desk marketing agency for all the Cdn inland fisheries in MB, AB, SK, and the NT as well as parts of Northern ON, buys all fish offered by MB fishers, although fishers are also allowed to sell directly to MB consumers. The FFMC either directly or indirectly operates 30 packing stations in MB during summer and 29 stations in the winter.

Challenges to the MB commercial fishery in recent decades range from POLLUTION to overfishing. In 1971, Lake Winnipeg was closed briefly to commercial fishing because of suspect concentrations of mercury in pickerel and sauger. Another major concern is massive algae blooms, which have intensified in the last few years on Lake Winnipeg, especially in the lake's large northern basin. High concentrations of phosphates and nitrates, originating primarily from municipal waste, industry, and agriculture, are to blame. The lower levels of the lake are being depleted of oxygen because of decaying algae. Algae bloom die-offs kill the micro-organisms and insects that feed smaller species of fish, which commercially viable fish species depend on for food.

There is also growing concern surrounding the Garrison diversion. This project (slated to begin in 2005) involves DRAINAGE into the already heavily polluted Sheyenne River of water from Devils Lake, ND. Devils Lake belongs to the Missouri/Mississippi watershed, and therefore houses different organisms from the RED RIVER's basin, leading to concerns that foreign biota will enter the ecosystem and adversely affect the multi-million-dollar MB commercial fishery. Environmental groups on both sides of the border have been unsuccessful in attempting to have this possibility addressed under the INTERNATIONAL BOUNDARY WATERS TREATY.

The lesson of the sturgeon has not been learned, and overfishing continues to be a problem. FLOODING resulting from HYDROELECTRIC dams built by MANITOBA HYDRO between the 1960s and '90s; the creation of the 3 major reservoirs (Lake Winnipeg, South Indian Lake/Notigi, and Cedar Lake); and 4 manmade bypass channels have dramatically reduced commercial production in communities such as CROSS LAKE and Pipestone. In recent years, Manitoba Hydro has negotiated compensation packages for those northern communities most affected by the decline in commercial fish species. • BRUCE CHERNEY

FISHING, SPORT, is distinguished in MB by the province's diverse and abundant fish species. Almost 100 species of fish make their home in MB, and many of them are valued by anglers, commercial fishers, and those who enjoy a good meal. The most popular game fish species are WALLEYE (pickerel), TROUT, northern PIKE, and channel CATFISH.

MB has huge prairie lakes like LAKE MANITOBA, Lake Dauphin, and LAKE WINNIPEGOSIS, and all are rich fisheries. LAKE WINNIPEG, the 11th-largest lake in the world, is home to the famous "greenback" walleye (*Sander vitreus*), often misnamed "pickerel." In the autumn, these big fish run into the mouth of the Red, attracting serious anglers who believe that this small stretch of river is the very best place in the world to catch a once-in-a-lifetime walleye of 5.5 kg (12 lb) or more.

Warm, turbid, winding rivers like the RED and the ASSINIBOINE are the home of the legendary Channel Catfish (*Ictalurus punctatus*), a large and hard-fighting fish that attracts anglers from the US, Britain, and Asia. It's possible to catch a 14 kg (30 lb) catfish off the riverbank right in the middle of Winnipeg, and anglers commonly while away the long summer days fishing for "cats" near the city's celebrated FORKS, or farther N, at the village of LOCKPORT, where the dam, the leafy picnic spots, and the colourful hot dog stands help attract catfish-minded anglers in the summertime.

Travelling N and E, one arrives in the Precambrian Shield, a region of evergreen forest, rocky granite ridges, and clear cold lakes. In this region, the Northern Pike (*Esox lucius*) is the premier aquatic predator. Jagged-toothed and deadly looking (like the medieval weapon after which the fish is named), pike cruise the edges of weedy points and boulder-strewn reefs, attacking lures with a ferocity that can shock the heart of even the most seasoned angler. Smaller pike in the 1 kg (2 lb) class, sometimes dismissed as "snakes" or "hammer handles," live in shallow weedy bays and provide reliable action for young anglers. Many young Manitobans will report that their first fish was precisely that generic, choleric 1 kg (2 lb) pike.

Jake MacDonald with a trophy lake trout.

Farther N yet, in the shallow lakes of the Hudson Bay lowlands, the Lake Trout (*Salvelinus namaycush*) is the apex game fish. In most regions of Canada, the lake trout is confined to a few deep, cold lakes. But in northern MB, hundreds of lakes are sufficiently oxygenated and cold to support lake trout. Growing at a rate of 225 g (0.5 lb) per year or faster, these fish attain great age, and the lucky angler who catches a lake trout of 14 kg (30 lb) or more may indeed be capturing (and, it is to be hoped, releasing) a fish older than himself. • JAKE MACDONALD

FITZGERALD, Lionel LeMoine, artist, teacher, (b March 17, 1890, WINNIPEG; d Aug 5, 1956, Winnipeg). The 'Painter of the Prairie', FitzGerald stood alone in 20th century Cdn art by virtue of geography, temperament and his individual visual expression. As Winnipeg offered little opportunity for art lessons, FitzGerald was primarily self-taught. His ability was evident early, and he fed his interest reading international art magazines, the works of Ruskin and writings of major modern artists. His childhood summers, spent on his grandparents' farm in Snowflake in southwestern MB gave him a lasting, profound understanding and respect of the vastness and subtleties of the Prairie. At 14, he left school, worked in commercial design at Stovel's Publishing and **EATON'S** display and, in 1909, took Hungarian art teacher, A. S. Keszthelyi's, evening class.

FitzGerald spent almost his entire life in Winnipeg, travelling relatively little. He studied at the Arts Student League in New York in the winter of 1921-22; spent the summer of 1924 in Banff; and, in 1930, visited New York, Montreal, Ottawa, and Toronto, meeting artists and seeing exhibitions. In 1938, he returned east; from 1947-49 he was in BC; and in 1951, Mexico.

FitzGerald taught at the Winnipeg School of Art, 1924-49, and was its principal 1929-49, the first Manitoban and second Canadian to do so. A member of the **MANITOBA SOCIETY OF ARTISTS** and the Winnipeg Sketch Club, in 1932 he became the only Western member of the Group of Seven. He was a founding member of the Canadian Group of Painters in 1933. FitzGerald was prolific, executing many oils and watercolours, thousands of pencil, ink and coloured pencil drawings, prints and some sculpture. Most of the drawings are finished complete works, not sketches. In all, his sensitivity of line is unique and his portrayals of space and application of colour are rhythmic and lyrical. Favoured subjects include landscape, back lanes, fences, trees and still lifes. Imbuing the ordinary with universality, coupling intimacy with strength, he created a body of work which is a testament of his place and time. An acute observer of nature, his letters and diaries chronicle the importance of the Prairie light to his work and the appeal of each season's unique palettes. He used value ranges masterfully to build shifting subtle contrasts, in snow, skies and trees, achieving harmony and unity in all media. His working method was deliberate and slow. Technique was a means, not an end; the subject being of primary importance. He gathered subject matter in good weather. He made preliminary composition notes for his paintings, drew the detailed image on the canvas and then, carefully and precisely, applied his colour. Some works took several years to complete, as commitments at the School of Art left only weekends and vacations for painting.

FitGerald's work falls into 4 phases: Early Years to 1921; the New York Impact to 1931; Experimentation and The School of Art to 1947; and the prolific Final period, 1947-56. The Early Years are characterized, first, by rather dark, pre-impressionist landscapes. Many, like *Late Fall, Manitoba,* 1918, were painted in East Kildonan. His application of paint was quick and thin, and volume and colour predominated over line. By 1920, and *Summer East Kildonan,* he had developed a new impressionist freedom of brushwork, achieving

Summer Afternoon the Prairie, 1921, oil on canvas, by Lionel LeMoine Fitzgerald

bold richness in colour and a strong sense of movement. Tree trunks become stabilizing anchors.

The New York Impact of the 1920s furthered the development of his unique style and strengthened his sense of line and form. *Potato Patch, Snowflake,* 1925, with its rhythmic flow of colours and shapes conveys his deep feeling for the land. The high horizon line, punctuated by the building and tree, coupled with the gently rolling clouds, suggest the expanse of the Prairie sky. The meticulous brushwork is the trademark of his mature style, incorporating small areas of raw canvas as subject details, adding greater depth.

In 1920, the FitzGeralds moved to Lyle St, St. James, the source of much subject matter. Window views to the neighbourhood provided the images for *Williamson's Garage,* 1927 and *Pritchard's Fence* c. 1928. Nearby Bruce Park, where he spent considerable time, inspired many drawings of trees. *Poplar Woods,* 1929 was an important transitional painting, for which he did several sketches.

The human-like energetic limbs cross the entire canvas, the saplings in the background forming a rhythmic frieze. The patterns and brushwork in the ground reflect the movement of the limbs and its reduced palette foreshadows FitzGerald's later interest in abstraction.

In his 3rd period, Experimentation and The School of Art, 1931-1947, he did few paintings, but many works on paper. These continued his interest in the MB landscape and still life. In *The Pool,* 1934, the lyrical parabolas of reeds in the foreground establish the rhythmic patterns for the brushwork throughout the painting. *The Jar,* 1938 and *From an Upstairs Window, Winter,* 1948, both painted from the landing of his house, show his interest in exploring the geometric forms of the window, sills and flat planes of the walls. Using his restrained pointillist technique, in *From an Upstairs Window, Winter* he combined elements from indoors and out, treating the trees as he had the saplings in *Poplar Woods.*

In these precisely executed works his technique balances and reflects the subject matter.

In the Final Period, 1947-1956, he moved into an abstraction based on reality. *Path over Hill (Abstract Landscape)* 1956, shows the landscape root for many of his geometric, yet fluid, abstract drawings. *Abstract in Green and Gold*, 1954, is based on still life. Its repeated flowing curved lines and forms, executed with modulated colours, are compelling and sensuous. While abstraction occupied him for most of his last several years, he returned to realism in his final works.

FitzGerald received an L.L.D. from the U of M in 1952; several posthumous memorial exhibitions and, in September 1958, 'FitzGerald Walk' was dedicated in Bruce Park, St. James, a spot central to his work. ● PATRICIA BOVEY

FLATWORM is simple type of worm (phylum Platyhelminthes) with no body cavity, and ranging in size from microscopic to a length of 15 m (parasitic forms). A few exotic species introduced into NA from SE Asia may reach 35 cm. The big freshwater ones resemble a leech in shape and colour. There may be green algal cells (zoochlorellae) living symbiotically inside the worm's body. As the name implies, these elongated worms are highly flattened, and most have a front region that looks like a head, often with 2 or more eyespots and a ventral mouth, which may contain a muscular, protrusible pharynx for engulfing food. There is no anus, the digested food being eliminated through the mouth. The diet consists of tiny invertebrates like rotifers, bacteria, plants, and dead organic matter. Several species devour large numbers of mosquito larvae and have been considered for biological control of these biting pests. Most are covered in tiny hairs (cilia). The common Planaria (*Dugesia tigrina*) often appears in home aquaria and has been used in science classes. Flatworms are bilaterally symmetrical (with a front and back, and two sides) – the first such animals to have evolved from radially symmetrical (like spokes of a wheel) creatures such as starfish. This invention of body organization has been incorporated in all higher forms of animals, including humans. Being soft-bodied, flatworms have left little fossil evidence, but they likely appeared over 500 million years ago (Cambrian Period).

There are 4 classes of flatworms totalling about 25,000 species worldwide. There is no current estimate of their number in MB, but it must exceed several thousand. The free-living planarians (class Turbellaria) are mostly marine (in **HUDSON BAY**), but also have freshwater and land representatives, and number about 5000 species

worldwide. The internal flukes (class Trematoda) are parasites, numbering 10,000 species. There are 6000 species of tapeworms (class Cestoda), all of which are parasitic. The 4th class is the monogenetic flukes (class Monogenea), which numbers about 4000 species. These latter are mostly ectoparasites on the skin and gills of fish, but also occurring in the esophagus and bladder of amphibians and turtles. Species of *Gyrodactylus* are serious pests in fish hatcheries. The internal flukes and tapeworms are serious disease-causing agents in humans and wildlife, and have evolved remarkably complex life cycles to find and infect hosts. The fish tapeworm (*Diphyllobothrium*) can grow to a length of 10 m in a human and is ingested by eating under-cooked infected fish.

While most species of free-living flatworms are hermaphrodites (with both testes and ovaries), others can also reproduce by splitting into 2 (a process named fission), which may remain attached to form a chain of individuals. Interestingly, splitting occurs more frequently as temperatures rise. Summer eggs hatch immediately, but in autumn, thick-walled winter eggs are produced which hatch the following spring. In a remarkable example of rejuvenation, a few species can fragment into many tiny pieces, each becoming covered in a mucus coating, and the resulting cysts can each grow into a whole flatworm. These creatures occur widely in many habitats, from freshwaters (puddles, marshes, lakes, streams), marine sediments of Hudson Bay, and on land. They produce a mucous which serves in locomotion or to hold the animal in place. They swim or glide on surfaces (even the underside of the water surface) by means of waves of the cilia, aided by the film of mucus. In MB's cold northern regions, freshwater and land flatworms may remain in a resting stage (diapause) for 8 months. A host of small predators prey on flatworms. ● REW

FLAX. Canada is the world's leader in the production and export of flax, and MB is one of only 3 provinces that grow the oilseed. Flax, with its distinctive blue blooms, is ideally suited to the cool, northern climate of the Prairie provinces. Flax is an ancient crop – its cultivation was depicted in burial chambers in Babylon. Flax was introduced to NA in the 1600s by way of New France. Cultivation in MB has fluctuated significantly – it peaked in 1983 with 1.35 million acres (.55 million ha) seeded. In its early years in MB, flax was grown primarily for industrial linseed oil, an ingredient used in the manufacture of paints and linoleum. By the late 20th century, flax was recognized as a healthy addition to the human diet. The seed contains Omega-3 fatty acids, high fibre, and supposed cancer-protective ingredients.

Crushed flax seed is used in baked goods and beverages and as enriched feed for livestock and egg-laying hens. About 90% of production is shipped to the US, Europe, Japan and South Korea. In 2005, MB produced 5.8 million bu from .33 million harvested acres (.13 ha). ● GPP

FLEA is an insect in the order Siphonaptera, which is a highly adapted as a blood-sucking ectoparasite of mammals and birds. Fleas are 1-9 mm long, wingless, and laterally flattened so that they can move easily among the hairs and feathers of their hosts. The body is covered with rows of backward-directed hairs, some of which on the head, thorax or abdomen may be thickened and modified to form combs (ctenidia), which ensure the flea is not dislodged from its host. The mouthparts are adapted for piercing the skin and sucking blood. The head of the male has a dorsal groove into which the ventral margin of the female's abdomen fits during mating. The antennae of the male are prehensile, and during mating are extended dorsally to clasp either side of the female's abdomen. The hind legs of most species are adapted for making incredible leaps, enhanced by the nearly perfect (97%-efficient energy storage) elastic protein called resilin. Jumping (as high as 34 cm) is made possible by a triggered click mechanism in a special structure (pleural arch) involving the thorax and legs, generating an acceleration described as '140 gravities.' Fleas are remarkably adept at finding hosts; a mouse or sparrow artificially cleansed of fleas will regain a full complement within 24 hours, with the fleas detecting the host's approach by its vibrations, heat, and carbon dioxide (most fleas are blind). A hungry flea can jump 600 times/hr for 3 straight days while searching for a suitable host.

There are about 57 species of fleas in 7 families recorded in MB (200 species in Canada; 2600 worldwide), with 46 species found in association with various mammals, and 11 attacking only birds. Some fleas are host specific (i.e., found on only one host species), such as the Beaver Flea (*Hystrichopsylla schefferi*) – the largest species of flea. Other species are less selective; for example, the Raccoon Flea (*Chaetopsylla lotoris*) infests the raccoon and all its family relatives. The flea family Ischnopsyllidae, with one species in MB, parasitizes **BATS**. At the other extreme, there are species that seem to be able to attack a wide variety of hosts. The European Hen Flea (*Ceratophyllus gallinae*) is an introduced species that readily infests native birds such as the American Robin, blue birds, House **SPARROW**, and Starling. Fleas may become household pests in MB, the **CAT** Flea (*Ctenocephalides* *felis*) being the common culprit. This species will readily feed on dogs, lizards, as well as humans, which may mislead people in identifying the flea. Surprisingly, the Dog Flea (*Ctencephalides canis*) has never been recorded in MB. The Human Flea (*Pulex irritans*) is most-often found in the province infesting the Red **Fox**. The Plague Flea (*Xenopsylla cheopis*) is the notorious vector of the Plague Bacterium (*Yersinia pestis*) – the cause of Black Death – transmitted primarily from rats and other rodents to humans by fleas. Several species of fleas in MB have also been shown to be effective plague vectors, however plague has never been found here, but is known in SK, AB, BC, and adjacent US – as close as Border County, ND. Richardson's or other ground squirrels (abundant in MB) were often implicated in carrying infected fleas. Fleas have complete metamorphosis (egg, larva, pupa, and adult), and are believed to have evolved about 160 million years ago (Jurassic period) from **Scorpionflies** (*Mecoptera*). ● TG, REW

Fleming, Sir Sanford. An internationally respected scientist and engineer, Fleming presented a petition in 1863 to Imperial authorities advocating the need for a railway connection linking the isolated Red River Settlement to the East. Later, as superintendent of engineering for the **CPR**, Fleming surveyed through MB. Fleming suggested a route through **Selkirk**, where higher riverbanks would preclude spring flooding. The CPR was instead swayed by **Winnipeg**'s greater political clout and, in a move that forever defined MB's geography, laid tracks through what then became the province's largest city. Also, as a result of requiring railway efficiency, Fleming invented Standard Time. ●

FLETCHER, Steven John, politician (b June 17, 1972 Rio de Janeiro, Brazil). Born in Brazil, where his father was working at the time, Fletcher was raised in **Winnipeg** and graduated from the **U of M** in 1995 with a bachelor of engineering degree. He was following his father's profession as a mining engineer in northern MB, when an automobile collision with a **Moose** in 1996 left him a wheelchair-dependent quadriplegic. The event might have prompted some to give up, but Fletcher, a former avid canoeist, preserved in the face of adversity. In 1997, he returned to the U of M to pursue an MBA, which he received in 2002. In 1999, he was elected president of the university's Students' Union. During his 2-term tenure, he oversaw the elimination of the union's debt. In 2000, he supported a council motion to limit funding for the left-leaning campus newspaper, the *Manitoban* that never came to fruition.

In Nov 2001, Fletcher was elected president of the **Progressive Conservative** Party of Manitoba and re-elected in 2003. After the Canadian Alliance merged with the federal PC party, he won the nomination for the new party in the Winnipeg riding Charleswood-St.James. Fletcher narrowly defeated the Liberal candidate, former Winnipeg mayor **Glen Murray**, by 734 votes. Fletcher is the first quadriplegic to serve as an MP and as such, has raised awareness about the ability of people with disabilities. He has metaphorically broken barriers in the House of Commons to the disabled. A wheelchair designed to elevate him has allowed Fletcher to "rise" in the House of Commons. And although rules prohibit a "stranger in the house," an assistant accompanies Fletcher at all times – even in the chambers. ● CARSON JEREMA

FLEURY, Theoren "Theo," hockey player (b June 29, 1968, Oxbow, SK) was a **Métis** hockey player who enjoyed a 15-year NHL career, despite problems with substance abuse. He grew up on a farm near **Russell**, and had a difficult upbringing. His father, a maintenance worker who drove the Zamboni at the local arena, struggled with alcoholism. Though Fleury was the star player on the local hockey team, he was often left to rely on teammates' families to feed him before games and drive him to the arena. At 15, Fleury moved to **Winnipeg** to play for the St. James Canadians midget team. The following year, he was selected to play in the Western Hockey League (WHL) for the Moose Jaw Warriors. He played in the WHL for 4 years, recording an impressive 201 goals and 271 assists. Fleury was then chosen to play for the Cdn junior team at the 1987 world junior championships, where he earned 5 pts in 6 games. In a now infamous game against the USSR, it was

a fight between Fleury and USSR player Pavel Kostichkin that initiated the 20 minute, bench-clearing fight that resulted in both teams being evicted from the championship.

Despite his success in the WHL, Fleury was only drafted to the Calgary Flames in the 8th round in 1987. At 5 ft 6 in and 145 lbs, Flames' management thought Fleury would be too small for the NHL, and he was sent to the farm team in Salt Lake City, UT. Fleury soon proved that his tough attitude more than made up for his small stature. The scrappy right winger recorded 37 goals and 37 assists in the first half of the 1988-89 season, and was then moved up to the Calgary Flames, helping them win the 1989 Stanley Cup. Over his 11 seasons with the Flames, he became the team's all-time leading scorer with 830 pts. He was traded to the Colorado Avalanche for the 1998-99 season, and then signed a $17 million contract as a free agent with the New York Rangers. Though Fleury was one of the top scorers in the NHL, he was also one of the league's most volatile players, once becoming embroiled in a brawl with "Sharkie," the mascot of the San Jose Sharks. He was suspended from the NHL for substance abuse in 2001. Despite his problems with alcohol, he was chosen for the Cdn team at the 2002 Salt Lake City Olympics, helping to win a gold medal. Nonetheless, the Rangers refused to re-sign the troubled player. Fleury then signed with the Chicago Blackhawks, but had to miss the first 25 games of the 2002-03 season because of his suspension. In 2003, after once more being suspended from the NHL for substance abuse, Fleury was dropped by the Blackhawks, ending his NHL career. In 1084 NHL career games, Fleury scored 455 goals with 633 assists, and appeared in 7 All-Star games. He also had 1840 penalty minutes. In 2005, Fleury made an unusual move by signing a contract to play in the UK for the Belfast Giants. He returned to Canada after one season to run a construction business. ● MD

FLIN FLON, pop 5594. Known as the "City Built on Rock," this mining town – the 11th-largest community in MB – is 125 km NNW of **The Pas**, on the SK border. Ore deposits were first discovered in the area in 1914, inspiring

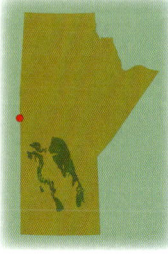

thousands of people to move N to face the challenges of a mining life. Although the first claim was made in 1915, almost 12 years passed before the mine was in production. In 1927, the Whitney family of New York created the **Hudson Bay Mining and Smelting Company** (HBMSC) and took control of the mine. Flin Flon's local economy continues to depend largely on the rich deposits of zinc, copper, silver, and gold in the area. The HBMSC continues to operate and is the city's largest employer. Forestry, agriculture – including, since 2001, medical marijuana for Health Canada, grown hydroponically in a disused copper and zinc mine – and light manufacturing are also important to the economic foundation. This trading base allows Flin Flon to offer a wide variety of retail services.

Because the city is surrounded by lakes, streams, and rivers, many tourists are attracted to the area for outdoor activities such as hunting, boating, and swimming. An annual Trout Festival attracts fishermen to the area, while the Flin Flon Tourist Park offers camping sites and modern amenities. The entrance of the park is marked by a 7 m statue of "Flinty" – Josiah Flintabbatey Flonatin, after whom the town is named – designed by Al Capp. Flintabbatey is the hero in J. E. Preston Muddock's novel *The Sunless City*. In the novel, Flonatin builds a submarine and travels to the centre of the earth, where he finds a city made of gold. Prospector **Thomas Creighton** and his party are believed to have read this novel shortly before discovering gold in what is now Flin Flon. Other attractions include the Flin Flon Heritage Museum, which houses historical information related to mining throughout the 20th century. The Flinty Boardwalk is also a popular city and tourist attraction. The boardwalk winds its way around Ross Lake and is marked with informative signs explaining the various types of indigenous rocks found in the area. In the winter, Flin Flon's groomed trails are a popular attraction for snowmobile enthusiasts. The city's

Flintabbatey Flonatin greets visitors to Flin Flon.

junior-league hockey players play in the Whitney Forum, a 3000-seat arena. Curling, cross-country, and downhill skiing facilities are also available in Flin Flon. Well-known Flin Flonners include NHLers **Bobby Clarke** and Ken Baumgartner.
● A.J. LEVIN

FLIN FLON BOMBERS is a junior 'A' **Hockey** team that plays in the SK Junior Hockey League (SJHL). Best known for their successful years as a team in the major junior Western Canada Junior Hockey League (WCJHL), the Bombers featured MB-born future NHL stars **Bobby Clarke** and **Reggie Leach** in the late 1960s. A **Flin Flon** team first took to the ice in 1927. The club, named the Bombers by a local miner in 1936, went on to play in a northern senior league, and the MB and SK senior leagues before joining the SJHL. They won 6 SJHL championships between 1952 and 1960, also reaching the Memorial Cup final in 1957. That year the Bombers defeated the Ottawa Canadians in a 7-game series to claim the trophy. Two players from that team, Teddy Hampson and Pat Ginnell, went on to the NHL. The Bombers switched over to the MB Junior Hockey League (MJHL), winning the league title in their only MJHL season, 1966-67 (also Clarke's and Leach's first full season). They entered the WCJHL for the 1967-68 season, and with Ginnell as coach, Clarke posted 168 points in 59 games and Leach scored 87 goals. The next year, with Clarke and Leach again dominant, the Bombers captured the WCJHL league championship, the first of 2 consecutive wins. The franchise relocated to Edmonton following the 1977-78 season. The Bombers resurfaced, first in the MB junior 'B' league and then as part of the NorMan Junior League in the early 1980s. In 1984, the SJHL granted a franchise to the Creighton Bombers, based in a SK town adjacent to Flin Flon (*see* **Thomas Creighton**). In 1986, the team moved back across the border to its original home, though it has remained a part of the SJHL. The Bombers won the Anavet Cup in 1993 as the best team from both the MJHL and SJHL. Other notable former Bombers players include Gerry Hart, Blaine Stoughton, Ken Baumgartner, and Reid Simpson. ● JT

FLOODS have presented residents of the Red River Valley in MB with some of the most costly environmental hazards in Canada and some of the most important milestones in the history of the region. For more than 200 years, written records document the periodic inundation of the valley, as in 1811 when William Auld of the **Hudson's Bay Company** wrote that Alexander Henry's post at Pembina was under water for 28 days in

the spring and the countryside on both sides of the river formed "a lake through its whole course of about 8 miles wide." Other early floods of varying magnitude are reported in historical sources from 1798, 1806, 1815, 1824, and 1825. These floods affected only parts of the valley and there were relatively few permanent structures to damage.

1800s: It was the epic flood of 1826 that established the true flood potential of the Red River and remains the largest known, significantly larger even than the 1997 "Flood of the Century." It nearly destroyed the fledgling Red River Settlement, precipitated the emigration of most of the de Meuron Swiss-German settlers, and caused the relocation of the Hudson's Bay Company headquarters from the Forks to Lower Fort Garry where flooding had not occurred. The 1826 flood was caused by the convergence of all of the factors which, in varying combinations, typically produce large spring floods on the Red River: abnormally wet conditions in the preceding summer and fall, strong freezing prior to the first major snowfall, a cold winter with little thawing, heavy snow cover over the watershed at the beginning of spring, a late spring followed by a rapid melt, a S-to-N progression of melt, abundant rainfall during the flood-formation period, and strong S winds which elevate the water level in the downstream section of the inundated area. The **Assiniboine** also made a significant contribution to several of the historical floods. These factors are exacerbated by the virtually flat slopes on the floor of former glacial **Lake Agassiz** which permit overbank flow to spread for great distances away from the river; the low gradients are also responsible for the slow buildup of floods and the long time they take to recede.

Small floods in 1827 and 1828 were followed by a lengthy flood-free period until 1850 when a series of large floods occurred in 1850, 1851, and 1852. The latter was the second largest on record until it was approximately equalled in 1997. Again the entire population was forced to flee beyond the flood margin (mostly to the W) and damage to buildings was extensive. On May 21, 1852, Bishop **David Anderson** described the river as "like that of a vast lake studded with houses, of many of which the projecting gable was the only part visible." Another large flood occurred in 1861. Although it was considerably smaller and much less damaging than the 1826 or 1852 events, it nevertheless remained the 3rd largest until 1997. The 1826, 1852, and 1861 floods led **Sanford Fleming** to argue strongly (but unsuccessfully) that the river crossing for the **Canadian Pacific Railway** should be located at **Selkirk** beyond the flood margin.

F

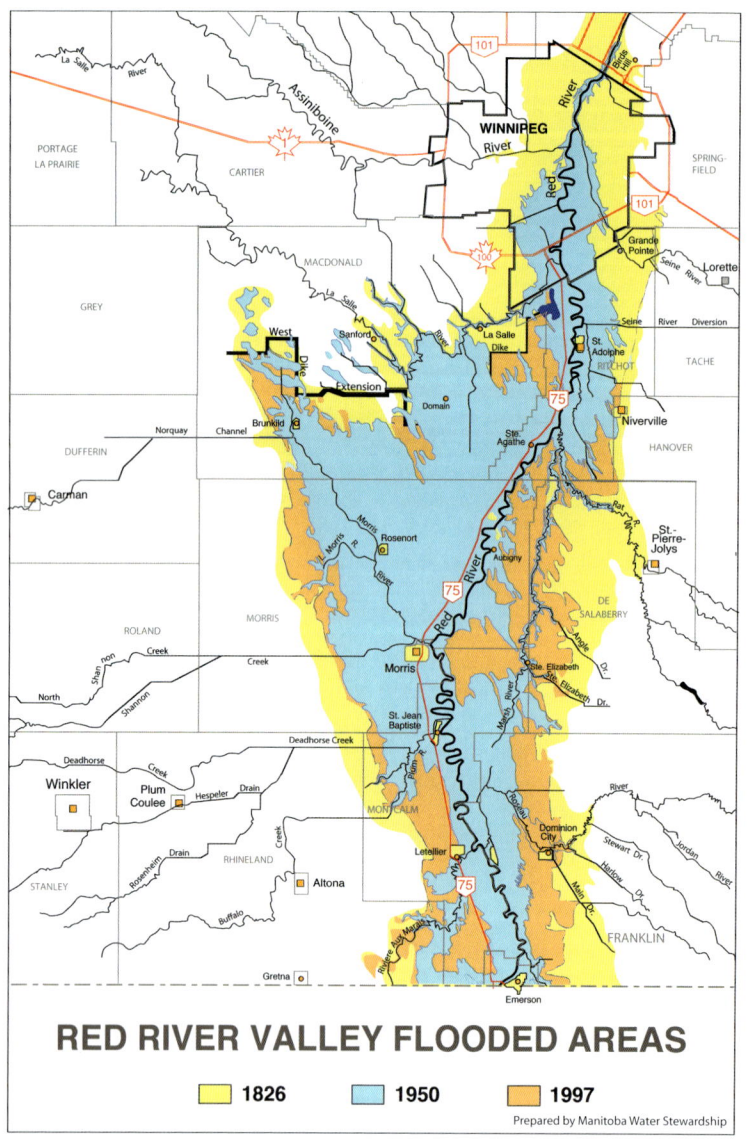

RED RIVER VALLEY FLOODED AREAS

■ 1826   ■ 1950   ■ 1997

Prepared by Manitoba Water Stewardship

Major Floods in the Red River Valley

YEAR	PEAK RIVER STAGE (feet above James Avenue datum)[1]	PEAK DISCHARGE ft³/sec	m³/sec
1826	36.6	225,000	6,372
1852	34.5	165,000	4,673
1861	32.2	125,000	3,540
1950	30.3	108,000	3,060
1997	34.3[2]	162,000[2]	4,588[2]

[1] The Imperial units are used for stage in keeping with local custom
[2] Calculated "natural" stage and discharge (that is, without the operation of the Red River Floodway, Assiniboine Diversion or Shellmouth Dam

1950: As time passed after 1861, the great 19th century floods gradually faded from public consciousness, particularly as the period from 1862 to 1950 saw only a few relatively small floods of little consequence. Because this period coincided with the main growth of Winnipeg, there was little public awareness of the hazard. Although a moderate flood in the valley in 1948 raised some alarms, Winnipeg was completely unprepared for the 1950 flood which became a

landmark in the city's history. That flood inundated about 1660 square km in the valley S of **WINNIPEG**, forcing the evacuation of all towns within the flooded area. In Winnipeg, despite a 7-week diking operation involving thousands of military and civilian personnel, 10,500 properties were flooded and 100,000 people were forced from their homes. Approximately $30 m was paid out in damages; the true cost of all aspects of the flood may have exceeded $100 m.

The immediate response to the 1950 disaster was to consolidate and extend the emergency dikes that had been built within Winnipeg during the flood; with subsequent additions this became the Primary Diking System, a 110 km complex of dikes parallel to the rivers, augmented by lower secondary dikes where lack of space or problems of bank stability prevented construction of the Primary Dike. Also in the aftermath of the flood, the Red River Basin Investigation (RRBI) was appointed to examine the history and causes of flooding and to propose solutions. The solutions which were available were constrained by a number of circumstances. First, most of the water during large floods originates beyond Canadian jurisdiction in the US, and thus such options as headwater storage or land management in the source area were not possible. Second, the established urban pattern and heavy occupation of the riverbanks in Winnipeg limited land use measures. Finally, the Assiniboine River joins the Red in the centre of the city; although it is much smaller than the Red, the Assiniboine has the potential to make critical contributions to large floods which cannot be controlled by measures on the Red itself. The investigation reported in 1953. An important result of the report was a better appreciation of the true magnitude of the 1826, 1852 and 1861 floods which the Investigation calculated. The incorporation of these floods into the frequency and damage curves greatly improved the awareness of the true magnitude of the hazard and contributed to the ultimate decision to design for protection from floods much larger than that of 1950.

ROYAL COMMISSION: No action was taken until 1956 when the threat of a large flood precipitated the creation of a Provincial Royal Commission to consider the benefits and costs of the alternative protection schemes identified by the RRBI and to recommend a course of action. The Commission's report, issued in December 1958, recommended the construction of the Red River Floodway, the Assiniboine Diversion, and the Shellmouth Dam, which in combination would protect Winnipeg from floods up to about 4800 cms (cubic metres per second), more than 50% greater than the 1950 peak. As would be expected for such an ambitious plan, the recommendations spawned a heated and at times acrimonious debate in the legislature, press, and public. The issues raised by the critics included the scheme's effectiveness in preventing flood damages and the advantages of alternative schemes, the enormous cost, cost-sharing arrangements with the federal government, and the lack of protection for residents of the valley south of Winnipeg. Despite this opposition, the project was endorsed by the minority government of **Duff Roblin**. After the 1959 election returned it with a strong majority, the legislation was approved by a vote of 38-11.

FLOOD PROTECTION: The **Red River Floodway** was the largest, most expensive, and most important component of the flood protection system. It is a 47 km excavated channel designed to divert Red River water around the E perimeter of the city, from St. Norbert on the S margin to Lockport 18 km N of the city where the channel is large enough to convey the entire flow. Gates in the floodway's control structure on the Red River regulate the discharge through the city. The floodway had a design capacity of 1700 cms and under emergency conditions could be made to convey as much as 2800 cms.

Second in cost and importance in the flood protection system is the Assiniboine Diversion, a 29 km long excavated and diked channel 3 km W of Portage la Prairie which can divert up to 700 cms from the Assiniboine to Lake Manitoba, thereby reducing the flow of Assiniboine water to Winnipeg and increasing the amount of Red River water which can be passed through the city.

The 3rd element is the Shellmouth Dam which impounds a 55 km long reservoir (**Lake of the Prairies**) in the upper Assiniboine valley, permitting further control over Assiniboine water flowing toward Winnipeg. The Dam also provides flood control along the Assiniboine and creates a pool of water for use during dry years.

The total cost of these components was $103 m and even with a federal contribution amounting to about 60% of the total, it was an exceptionally large financial undertaking for a province with fewer than 900,000 people. Construction of the Floodway began in 1962 and it was available for use in 1969. By 1972, all components had been completed. A further recommendation of the Royal Commission, that communities in the Red River valley upstream of Winnipeg be protected by ring dikes, was not acted upon until extensive flooding in 1966 led to the eventual construction of dikes around 8 communities which would provide protection up to the 1950 level.

The effectiveness of these structures was quickly demonstrated. From 1969-1979, the average flow of the Red River was the highest in the entire period of record and the system was used to manage spring discharges exceeding minimum flood level in 9 of the first 11 years. Most of these were relatively minor events but the 1974 and 1979 floods were large, comparable to 1950 in magnitude. In addition, in 1974 and 1976, flood discharges on the Assiniboine River exceeding previous records by about 50% and

150% respectively were accommodated by the Assiniboine Diversion with little flooding downstream. It has been estimated that by 1979, gross damage reduction achieved by the structures had exceeded $1 billion and that the entire cost of the control system had been recovered from foregone damages.

Until the 1970s, the emphasis in flood damage reduction was on structural measures and in most respects the system worked exactly as designed. In the 1970s, attention shifted to land-use controls. As was being realized elsewhere, the success of structural measures is usually compromised if they are not accompanied by effective measures to regulate building in flood-prone regions. After the 1950 flood, much of the growth of Winnipeg had been southward, directly into the area of maximum inundation. In 1970, a national cost-sharing formula for disaster assistance was negotiated whereby, in Manitoba, the federal government assumed 90% of the disaster relief costs above $5 m. Very large national flood damages in 1974 and 1975 raised concerns about the mounting disaster assistance being paid by Ottawa under this system. A federal/provincial Flood Damage Reduction Agreement, signed in 1976 (and extended in 1981 and thereafter) provided for the raising of community ring dikes to the 100-year flood level, mapping of flood hazard zones, and flood-proofing of buildings in the hazard zone; new buildings were required to meet flood-proofing standards. Implementation of the agreement was slow until 1979 when the consequences of inaction were once again demonstrated by the extensive emergency measures necessary to protect properties in the hazard zone. The measures in the original agreement

were modified and strengthened and financial assistance was provided to residents to flood-proof their structures by raising, diking or moving them. In 1996, another 1950 magnitude flood required evacuation of only 100 homes in the valley and total costs were less than $12 m. Thus, by 1996, the control system had prevented virtually all of the damages it was designed to prevent. However, all floods from 1969 to 1996 were well within the system's capacity.

1997: The "Flood of the Century" seriously tested the design capacity of the entire flood protection system for the first time. This catastrophic event was caused by a record blizzard in early April which added 58 cm of snow (at Winnipeg) to an already substantial late winter snowpack (which by itself might have led to 1950-level flooding). This was compounded by subsequent cold weather in MB which delayed melting as floodwaters were building in the United States. The peak "natural" discharge in Winnipeg (which would have occurred in the absence of the entire control system) on May 4 was 4588 cms, approximately the same as in 1852 and close to the capacity of the flood control system. The Manitoba portion of the flooded area created a 2000 km² water body with a maximum width of about 40 km which quickly became known as the "Red Sea." Despite the flood-proofing which had been done over the previous 20 years, a mandatory evacuation of 27,400 people in the valley was ordered. In what was described as the largest Canadian military operation since the Korean War, more than 8500 military personnel were deployed to assist a civilian "army" of several thousand provincial employees, innumerable engineers, surveyors, equipment operators, and

A protected farm house near Morris, 1997.

others with technical skills seconded from the private sector, and tens of thousands of volunteers who built and patrolled dikes, maintained pumps, managed evacuation centres, etc. One of the most dramatic of the emergency measures was the 26 km extension of the west wing dike to prevent water from bypassing it and entering the city. Construction of the extension was essentially completed within 4 days, involving more than 450 people using up to 400 pieces of earth-moving equipment to put in place 750,000 m³ of earth, 142,000 tonnes of limestone, 2000 one-tonne "super sandbags", and 4000 bales of straw. Once the dike was constructed, it was protected from wave action by 40 km of snow fence, 8 km of oil boom and 2.4 km of derelict vehicles. In all its aspects, the month-long emergency management operation was the largest in Canadian peacetime history to that date.

Despite the impressive performance of the control system for residents of Winnipeg and the exhausting efforts by individuals everywhere within the flooded zone, the consequences were tragic for many. Some buildings in low areas within Winnipeg were badly damaged but it was in the valley upstream of Winnipeg where the most serious losses occurred. **Ste. Agathe**, which was not protected by a ring dike, was inundated on April 29 when a combination of permanent and temporary dikes and road and railway embankments failed. Emergency dikes around many of the homes in Grande Pointe were overtopped as the river was nearing its peak and dikes failed around numerous individual buildings elsewhere in the valley. The mandatory evacuation and the operation of the floodway control structure remained controversial for many years afterward.

Although an estimated $500 m in damages and costs were incurred during the flood, the total would have been an order of magnitude greater without the control system and it is likely that much of the population of Winnipeg would have required evacuation. Furthermore, the situation could have been considerably worse since the blizzard which produced the record runoff throughout the Red River basin missed most of the Assiniboine basin and flows on the Assiniboine were easily managed. The weather during the flood was also generally favourable. Had there been considerable rainfall on the rising phase and/or if S winds had persisted for longer periods near the crest, it is likely that design conditions would have been exceeded. Even with these favourable circumstances, however, the strain on the control system and the resources of the population was severe.

From 1950 onward, every flood left a legacy of improvement in the region's ability to cope

with its greatest natural hazard. The original flood control system was designed to protect Winnipeg from floods of about 4800 cms, corresponding to a 1-in-169 year event. The remarkable series of floods after 1969 progressively reduced this Return Period to about 90 years and the narrow escape from disaster in 1997 demonstrated the urgency to upgrade the level of protection. In the wake of that flood, the design standard for flood-proofing property and ring dikes was increased again, to 0.6m above the 1997 peak level, numerous buildings were raised, diked, relocated or removed, and more ring dikes were constructed around previously unprotected communities in the Red River valley. Within Winnipeg, some dikes constructed during the flood were made permanent, some buildings were removed, riverbanks were protected at critical locations, and improvements were made to the storm sewer system. Most importantly, provincial and federal governments agreed to expand the floodway (mostly by widening) to more than double its capacity (from 1700 cms to 3960 cms). Together with other improvements, this would increase the level of protection for the city to the 1-in-700 year flood, thereby ensuring that the near disaster of 1997 would not be repeated.
● W. F. RANNIE

FLOUR MILLING, the process by which the endosperm of a **Wheat** (or other grain) kernel is separated from its other components and ground down, was once one of MB's largest industries. Most pioneer towns in MB had a flourmill, powered either by wind or water, to process grain grown by local farmers. The industry went into decline when it became cheaper to transport wheat rather than flour to centres of consumption. The first mill was built when **Lord Selkirk** sent out the parts for a windmill in 1825. Located at Point Douglas, the mill was in use until about 1870. **Métis** leader **Cuthbert Grant** built the first watermill in MB in 1829 at Sturgeon Creek in St. James. It failed, costing Grant $800, and closed down after 3 years. The grindstones were salvaged, and brought to Grantown (*see* **St. Francois Xavier**) for use in a windmill. **Louis Riel**'s father built a mill on the Seine River, and the millstones are now on display at the grounds of the **St. Boniface Museum**. In 1878, the Harrison Flour Mill was built in the Turtle Mountain area. Now in Holmfield, 15 km ESE of **Killarney**, it is MB's oldest mill still in operation.

A state-of-the-art commercial Ogilvie flourmill was built in **Winnipeg** in 1881. Lake of the Woods Milling Company, capitalizing on the abundance of **Hydroelectric** power in the area, was the 2nd-largest milling company in Canada at the

Ogilvie Flour Mill, Winnipeg, ca 1907

turn of the 20th century, producing the Five Roses brand of flour. As of 2006, only 3 commercial flour mills still operated in MB: A. D. M. Milling Co., in Winnipeg; Harrison Milling and Grain, in Holmfield; and **Elie**'s Prairie Flour Mills. The milling process is highly automated, and flour is extracted rather than ground down. Several smaller, sub-commercial mills persist, including the rebuilt "Grant's Old Mill" on Sturgeon Creek in the W of Winnipeg. ● MD

FLY is an insect in the order Dioptera characterized by only one set of flying wings; the hind pair is reduced to balance-sensitive clubs (halteres), which stabilize the fly during complex flight manoeuvres. This group boasts some of the finest flyers in the insect world, with remarkable feats involving great speed and endurance, powered by large muscles packed inside the mid-thorax. Wingbeats have been timed at 1000/sec in tiny midges. Flies can hover, fly backwards, and even swoop upside-down to land on the underside of objects. As expected in such masterful flyers, most flies have large compound eyes, providing relatively good vision. Their mouthparts are highly modified for sucking, sponging, lapping or piercing, but in some families the mouthparts are reduced or absent. Larvae and adults feed on fungi, dung, and dead and alive plants and animals, some species even gnawing on the flesh of living animals, under or on the surface of the skin. Flies fulfill roles of predators, scavengers, nectar feeders, and parasites, including internal, external, and blood-sucking habits. Manitobans are only too familiar with a myriad of blood-sucking species. This order contains some of the most-annoying pests of humans and animals, and are important vectors of numerous pathogens, many deadly to humans (malaria and yellow fever). In fact, along with fleas, flies have profoundly affected human evolution and history.

Ranging in size from .5-50 mm (with an 80 mm wingspan), flies are present in almost all land and freshwater habitats, and even some marine ones. The life cycle incorporates complete metamorphosis (i.e., stages of egg, larva, pupa and adult). The larvae or maggots are soft-bodied, headless, legless (but may have 'prolegs') grubs, which may occur singly (e.g., inside an apple) or in the thousands (on a corpse). Many types of flies have aquatic larvae in MB's wealth of watercourses and wetlands, which pupate into terrestrial adults, thereby exploiting the resources of both environments and avoiding competition. Flies also pollinate many kinds of plants, are major decomposers (cleaning up dead animals and plants), and serve as food for countless other animals and a few insectivorous plants. Flies are also among the most-destructive of agricultural pests, yet numerous other species are predators and parasitoids (i.e., ultimately killing their hosts) of pests such as aphids, grasshoppers and beetles. This is an ancient group, appearing in the fossil record 245 million years ago (early Triassic). There are 88 families of flies represented in MB, but no estimate of number of species is available, but it likely surpasses 6000. About 7100 species of flies have been recorded in Canada, with the estimated number at least 15,000 (120,000 worldwide). The following units highlight some of the dominant families in MB.

MOSQUITOES (family Culicidae) appear to be insignificant and fragile insects, but they deliver a big punch with their sting and they are notorious carriers of a myriad of disease organisms, several like malaria and yellow fever which kill many millions of people each year. The long, blood-sucking proboscis immediately identifies a mosquito. When resting, the mosquito lays its scale-covered wings tightly over the back, making it difficult for predators and hosts to see it in the foliage. Males feed only on plant juices, but to obtain sufficient nutrients for egg production, the female must seek out and find a blood meal. It uses its needle-like mouthparts to tap directly into a blood vessel of a host. Fertilized eggs are deposited in quiet ponds, sometimes in rafts, and hatch into larvae in several days. Larvae develop into pupae in 1-2 weeks, and these float and breathe just under the water's surface. Within a few days the adult emerges. One ha of muskeg in northern MB can produce over 10 million mosquitoes in the few brief months of summer.

BLACKFLIES (Simuliidae) are notorious biting pests in MB and much of Canada; in fact they have been immortalized in poems and songs. Attacking in small numbers or a swarm, they readily curtail outdoor activity. The female blackfly uses its mouthparts to create a wound in the skin, and then it laps up the pooling blood. MB's 50 or so species breed exclusively in running water. The larvae are highly adapted to survive in this challenging habitat, attaching themselves to the substrate using a circlet of hooks which latches into a patch of silk laid down specially for this purpose. The adult emerges from the cocoon into a gas bubble and rises to the surface, where it flies away. Some species of blackflies are partially or entirely able to produce eggs without a blood meal, but the blood feeders cause significant annoyance and economic losses to humans, livestock, and wildlife. *Simulium noelleri* is a common species in MB and throughout the N hemisphere.

MIDGES (Chironomidae) are small (1-10 mm), mosquito-like flies often seen hovering and heard humming in large mating swarms. They have thin bodies, feathery antennae in the male, and hold their wings to the side when at rest. There are biting and non-biting species, but even the latter may become a nuisance if a person becomes engulfed in a cloud of midges. They are most abundant near watercourses, since their larvae occur in the bottom sediments or in wet soil. These larvae are often called bloodworms due to the red pigment haemoglobin in their tissues. Midges are devoured by bats, and the larvae are a very important food source for many fish, birds and invertebrates.

BEE FLIES (Bombyliidae) are rounded, furry flies with a long, slim, forward-projecting proboscis. They resemble a small bee, and frequently one can hear their wings humming. Excellent flyers, they can hover motionless in the air above a flower, then take off at great speed. Adults feed on nectar, while most larvae are parasites of wasps, bees, and beetles, or are predacious on insect eggs and larvae, such as grasshoppers. After courtship and mating, the female drops eggs in the tunnels or nests of potential hosts or directly onto prey. Most species prefer dry, sunny habitats. Species of *Bombylius* (8-12 mm long) are common in MB.

HOVER FLIES (Syrphidae) are wasp and bee mimics, striped with the universal warning colours of yellow and black. They are usually found buzzing around and feeding on flowers, attracted to nectar. Sometimes many dozens will gather over flowers in a garden, with hovering males attempting to attract receptive females. They range in size from 5-18 mm. The exceptionally large eyes dominate the head. A common example, found over most of NA in fields with wild flowers is the Drone Fly (*Eristalis tenax*), which looks remarkably like a bee, with its brownish-yellow hair.

TACHINID FLIES (Tachinidae) are stocky flies with long but sparse bristles. Females deposit their eggs on other insects, which hatch and burrow into the host's body. As the larva completes its growth phases and prepares to pupate in the soil, the host dies. The Beelike Tachinid Fly (*Bombyliopsis abrupta*) is 13 mm long and has a bright-orange abdomen and legs with rows of black bristles. This group plays a significant role in controlling numbers of other insects, including pests.

ROBBER FLIES (Asilidae) range from 8-30 mm, and are characterized by large eyes, bulky thorax, and long, thin abdomen. The head is covered in bristles, which may help prevent being bitten by prey. Like a dragonfly, a Robber Fly sits on vegetation and ambushes passing insects. Its flying abilities are so well developed that it can snatch a passing fly out of mid-air. The legs (especially the hindlegs) are long, spiny and powerful, and are used to capture and subdue prey until

Hoverfly

it can be dispatched with a bite. The proboscis sucks up the victim's body juices. Many species are found in dry sandy areas, but other species prefer forests. Species of *Tolmerus* (20 mm long) are observed in fields and gardens in MB, and are grey with black markings. Larvae live in the soil where they feed on other insect larvae such as beetles. There are 6500 species worldwide.

MUSCID FLIES (Muscidae) include the housefly (*Musca domestica*), Stable Fly (*Stomoxys calcitrans*), and Face Fly (*Musca autumnalis*). House Flies are attracted to sources of organic matter (garbage, compost pile, manure) on which the female lays 75-150 eggs. She may produce up to 6 batches of eggs in her lifetime. This fly is frequently encountered on farms and in homes, and although it cannot bite, it remains bothersome, contaminates food, and may transmit bacterial and protozoan diseases, some a potential threat to humans and animals. Stable Flies pester and bite livestock, pets and sometimes people for a blood meal. Both sexes attack with a needle-like, piercing mouthpart, on bare skin or right through hair and clothing. A female lays up to 12 batches of 40-80 eggs on decaying organic material (lawn clippings, shore debris, wet hay bales). The life cycle can take as little as 3 weeks, and the fly over-winters as a larva or pupa. Face Flies do not bite but females feed on secretions of the eyes, nostrils and mouth of cattle, where they are extremely bothersome and spread pinkeye and other eye diseases. Males feed on nectar and dung. The females lays eggs on fresh cow manure and new adults are on the wing within 2 weeks. Muscid flies are strong flyers and may disperse hundreds of km with the aid of wind.

BLOW FLIES (Calliphoridae) are 9 mm long and often a beautiful, metallic colour. The Blue Bottle Fly (*Calliphora vomitaria*) and Green Bottle Fly (*Phaenicia sericata*) are widespread throughout MB and NA, and appear as if by magic soon after an animal dies. They can detect the odour of rotting flesh from great distances. The adults sponge-feed on rotting tissues of a carcass and the female lays hundreds of fertilized eggs on site, which hatch into larvae in 6-48 hours when sufficient moisture is present. These white grubs appear in large numbers and feed in a frenzy on liquids and flesh, using their hook-like mouthparts to tear at tissues. The larvae grow rapidly over 3-10 days, undergoing 4 stages marked by moults, and finally crawling away into the nearby soil to pupate. The adult fly emerges from 10-21 days later. These flies can clean up the soft parts of a bear or deer body in a week, leaving a dry shell of skin and bone. While disgusting for most people to witness, these flies are

an important part of the animal-decomposition process, helping to recycle nutrients into their bodies and into the soil.

HORSE FLIES, BULLDOGS AND DEER FLIES (family Tabanidae) comprise 50 species in MB. Horse flies (Hybomitra and Tabanus species) are large (up to 19 mm), robust, and attack mainly large animals, inflicting pain with their bite. Deer flies (Chrysops species) are smaller (13 mm), with darkly patterned wings, and sit at rest in a delta design. The females buzz annoyingly around one's head and also deliver a painful bite. Both types of flies are serious pests of cattle, horses, wildlife and humans. Other tabanids (e.g., *Atylotus* species) are rarely encountered and cause no economic concerns, and so have received little attention. Vertebrate blood is required for most species to lay mature eggs, and larvae are aquatic or live in wet soils. Many are predacious and have savage mouthparts capable of lacerating a finger. They feed on other invertebrates, including their own kind. Tabanids overwinter as larvae. Recent studies in MB have revealed that tiny (1 mm), newly discovered wasps (Telenomus species) are highly effective tabanid parasitoids, destroying a high percentage of tabanid eggs. The Manitoba Horsefly Trap, developed at the **U OF M** by A. J. Thorsteinson and his colleagues in the 1960s, is the standard means of collecting and studying this group of flies all over the world. ● TDG, MAF, RE, REW

▶ *See also* **MOSQUITOES**

FLYCATCHER (family Tyrannidae) is represented in MB by 14 species. As the name indicates, these birds obtain their food by catching insects rather than by gleaning from vegetation. Most are subdued in colour and many have similar plumages, making some species nearly impossible to identify if they do not vocalize. Most

Flycatcher – Eastern Kingbird

CORY LOEWEN

common is the Least Flycatcher (*Empidonax minimus*), which breeds in high densities along the beach-ridge of southern **LAKE MANITOBA**, and can be recognized by its "chebek" call. Better known, perhaps, is the Eastern Kingbird (*Tyrannus tyrannus*), dapper in its black-and-white plumage. The kingbird is so called because it will readily drive much larger birds, such as hawks or crows, from its territory. ● RUDOLF KOES

FOLKLORAMA, an annual festival that celebrates MB's multicultural heritage, is the province's premier tourist attraction. For 2 weeks every Aug, more than 400,000 visits are recorded at Folklorama pavilions in **WINNIPEG**. The provincial govt describes Folklorama as the world's largest multicultural festival, and travel writers have called it the "Manitoba Mardi Gras." In many ways, Folklorama symbolizes what makes Manitobans proud: a diverse group of people who have retained their heritage of unique foods, folkways, and languages.

Folklorama began modestly enough. In 1965, Winnipeg Mayor **STEPHEN JUBA** helped form the Community Folk Arts Council of MB, which in turn sponsored the Folkways Festival at the Red River Exhibition. The Folkways Festival evolved 5 years later into the first Folklorama, planned in 1970 as a one-week event commemorating MB's centennial, with 21 pavilions and 75,000 visitors. Audiences were attracted to the exotic foods, displays of arts and crafts, souvenirs, and varied entertainment. Visitors could soon expect everything from schnitzel to sushi, from Caribbean limbo to the Hungarian bottle dance, and from high-fashion saris to kimono-wrapping techniques.

Many of the early pavilions were hosted in church basements, community centres, and schools, as they are to this day. In 1970, the Chinese pavilion did not have a facility, and led visitors through the streets of Winnipeg's Chinatown to witness the Lion Dance. The popularity of Folklorama grew, thanks to Winnipeg's vibrant multicultural communities, active volunteerism, low ticket prices, free parking, and bus tours that boosted numbers. In 1988, Folklorama expanded into a 2-week event. Bus tours brought visitors to see Folklorama from all over Canada and from points in the US. The American Bus Association has named the festival "Canada's number 1 event."

The festival now attracts more than 400,000 pavilion visits each year to over 40 pavilions. The opening-night show has about 10,000 visitors. Folklorama commands the biggest volunteer corps of any festival in the province, with 20,000 dedicated volunteers doing everything from singing to cooking.

Nicaraguan Pavilion, Folklorama, 2006

More than a dozen dance groups and entertainers now travel from outside the province to perform in Folklorama pavilions. Recent guest entertainers have come from Ireland, Australia, Paraguay, China, and Ghana. Folklorama is operated by a non-profit umbrella group called the Folk Arts Council of Winnipeg Inc. The Department of Cdn Heritage, various provincial and civic agencies, and numerous corporate sponsors support the festival. ● MAURICE MIEREAU

FONSECA, William Gomez, merchant, politician, philanthropist (b Aug 26, 1823, Saint Croix, US Virgin Islands; d April 22, 1905, **WINNIPEG**). Fonseca was of Spanish origin and probably of Creole and partial Sephardic **JEWISH** heritage, but was raised an **ANGLICAN**. He moved to New York at age 17, working in a mercantile company. There he became a US citizen. He studied for the Episcopalian (**ANGLICAN**) ministry, but abandoned it because of vision problems. When in his 30s, he moved for a short time to St. Paul, MN, and, around 1859, to the **RED RIVER SETTLEMENT**. He married local resident Margaret Ann Logan the next year, and opened a dry goods shop in a building owned by his father-in-law, Thomas Logan. The couple had 10 children.

As a prominent businessman and engaging public speaker, the *NOR'-WESTER* put forward Fonseca's name for the post of American consul, which instead went to Oscar Malmros, who pushed for annexation of the Northwest by the US. On Dec 13, 1869, amidst the **RED RIVER RESISTANCE**, **LOUIS RIEL**'s provisional govt men arrested Fonseca, but he was released 2 days later after giving them his US citizenship papers. After MB entered Confederation, Fonseca worked in the ministry of agriculture and became involved in many local infrastructure projects, including

wells, sewers, and schools. He served 6 terms as alderman for the North Ward of Winnipeg, and as a trustee for the Protestant school board. He invested heavily in land, including apartment buildings and hotels, in the area: at one point, he owned most of Point Douglas, and he lived on Maple St in that neighbourhood. Indeed, after helping persuade the **CPR** to come through Winnipeg rather than **SELKIRK** in 1883, the CPR lines ran through what had been his property, and what is now Higgins Ave was called "Fonseca Ave" after him. Fonseca was inducted into the city's Citizens' Hall of Fame in 2001. ● AJL

FONTAINE, Larry Phillip "Phil," politician, Assembly of First Nations national chief (b Sept 20, 1944, **SAGKEENG FIRST NATION**). Fontaine's early education took place at 2 **RESIDENTIAL SCHOOLS** – Oblates of Mary Immaculate at Sagkeeng, and Assiniboia in **WINNIPEG**. In 1990, he testified that he and others were subject to physical and sexual abuse at those schools, making him one of the earliest First Nations leaders to speak publicly about the matter. He graduated from **POWERVIEW** Collegiate in 1961. Of **OJIBWAY** descent, he became an activist with the Canadian Indian Youth Council, a short-lived pressure group of the mid-1960s, and the Company of Young Canadians, a federally sponsored volunteer program.

In 1972, Fontaine was elected to the first of 2 consecutive terms as chief of Sagkeeng. During his tenure, the band was able to take control of its education system, child and family services, and on-reserve addictions treatment. The federal govt then hired Fontaine to be Indian and Northern Affairs Canada's regional director-general for YT. In 1980, he returned to Winnipeg to complete his BA in political science at the **U OF M**, and in 1982, he became an advisor for the Southeast

Resource Development Council, an organization founded in 1978 to assist 9 First Nations in SE MB. Fontaine then returned to electoral politics, first in the position of vice-chief representing MB for the Assembly of First Nations, and then in 1989, as grand chief of the **ASSEMBLY OF MANITOBA CHIEFS**. Over 3 terms, Fontaine organized against the **MEECH LAKE ACCORD** and led negotiations toward the Manitoba Framework Agreement Initiative. This accord with the federal govt worked at dismantling the MB department of Indian affairs and northern development, recognizing principles of self-rule, and transferring jurisdiction over their affairs to individual First Nations. It was signed in Dec 1994.

Having lost his first bid to become national chief of the Assembly of First Nations to **OVIDE MERCREDI** in 1991, Fontaine was elected to the role in 1997 after 4 ballots. While in office, his initiatives included the 1998 Statement of Reconciliation, which saw the federal govt recognize and apologize for the abuses of residential schools, as well as provide a $350 million fund for victims and the 1999 declaration of co-operation with the National Congress of American Indians. Fontaine has sometimes been perceived as, or criticized for, working too closely with the federal Liberal Party – a factor that contributed to his defeat by the more-confrontational QC **CREE** chief Matthew Coon Combe in 2000. PM Jean Chrétien appointed Fontaine chief commissioner of the Indian Claims Commission in Aug 2001. He helped resolve a longstanding land claim from 1907, securing $94.6 million for the Kahkewistihaw First Nation in SK. Fontaine was re-elected Assembly of First Nations chief in 2003, and again in July 2006. In 2005, he negotiated the $2.2 billion Indian Residential Schools

Phil Fontaine

Settlement Agreement. The IRSSA, which includes a Truth and Reconciliation Commission, was ratified by the newly elected federal Conservative government in May, 2006.

Fontaine was recipient of a 1996 National Aboriginal Achievement Award, and honorary doctorates from several universities. He was named a Member of the ORDER OF MANITOBA in 2004. • JOEL TRENAMAN

FOOD AND BEVERAGE PROCESSING is the largest manufacturing sector in MB. In 2003, the food and beverage sector generated $3.3 billion in sales and represented 28% of all manufacturing shipments for the province. The sector employed 8500 people throughout the province, with 5800 of the jobs in WINNIPEG. The industry's primary products include meat products, dairy, flour, feed, and other processed food and beverages. MB exports ⅓ of its food and beverage production to over 100 countries. Its principal export markets are the US (69%), Japan (20%), and Mexico (4%). Exports include pork and pork products, potatoes, honey, malt, beef, and eggs.

MB's strong food and beverage processing industry finds its roots in a successful and competitive provincial agricultural sector. Roughly 7.7 million ha (19 million ac) of agricultural land are employed for crop and livestock production in the province, and provincial agriculture represents 15% of Canada's primary agricultural production. Soil and climate conditions within the province allow for a large diversity of crops used in food and beverage processing. The success of MB's agriculture has provided the food and beverage sector with low-cost, high-quality raw materials. Combined with a stable provincial workforce and the lowest energy costs in NA, the province has developed a natural advantage in processing food and beverages.

MB's food and beverage processing consists of roughly 200 manufacturers. Most of these companies are small or medium-sized enterprises (SMEs), though large multinationals operate in the beverage, meat, frozen french fry, vegetable oil, and baking sectors. Some of the larger companies are Maple Leaf Meats (pork, processed meat), Pillsbury Canada Ltd. (frozen foods), PEAK OF THE MARKET (vegetables), Old Dutch Foods Ltd. (potato chips and snack foods), Consolidated/Canada Safeway (frozen foods), Pepsi Cola Canada (soft drinks), Coca-Cola Bottling Company (soft drinks), Granny's Poultry (poultry products), Parmalat Canada Inc. (dairy products), and Dunn-Rite Foods (poultry products). Other major companies are ARCTIC ICE GLACIER CDN WATER CO., Nestlé Canada Inc., CanAmera Foods, Parrheim Foods, Archer Daniels Midland,

Bunge Canada, McCain Foods Ltd., The J. R. Simplot Company, Diageo Canada Inc., Vantage Foods Inc., and Burnbrae Farms Ltd.

MB's food and beverage industry has developed an international reputation for high quality. The sector processes a wide range of products that include meats (pork, beef, poultry, luncheon meats, gourmet meats); eggs; dairy products (including cheese and ice cream); processed, frozen, canned, preserved, and ready-to-eat fruits and vegetables; confectionary products; snack foods; brewing/distilling; beverages; honey; vegetables oils; milling; commercial baking; pasta; perogies; nutraceuticals; and functional foods. MB has the largest and one of the most technologically advanced egg processing plants in the country, and boasts 3 potato processing plants, whose frozen potato products are exported internationally.

Peak of the Market offers prepared soups with a made-in-Manitoba flavour

The pork sector, with 3 technologically advanced, federally inspected, high-output hog processing plants, has earned a worldwide reputation. Hog processing has grown significantly since 2000, and is now the largest sector in the meat/poultry products business. Exports and new markets in South Korea, the Philippines, and Australia have primarily driven growth in hog processing. Hog processing employs 2000 people, with the largest companies being Maple Leaf Pork, The Landmark Group, Elite Swine Inc., and Maple Leaf Consumer Foods.

The success of the food and beverage industry in MB is largely due to the extensive network of research and development in agriculture and food processing within the province. There is a mix of both public (federal and provincial) and private organizations conducting research relating to agriculture and food processing. These

include Agriculture and Agri-Food Canada's research centres in BRANDON, Winnipeg, and MORDEN; Food Product Development Centre; Canadian International Grain Institute; U OF M's faculties of Agricultural and Food Sciences and Human Ecology; Manitoba Crop Diversification Centre; National Centre for Agri-Food Research in Medicine; Richardson Centre for Functional Foods and Nutraceuticals; Canadian Malting Barley Technical Centre; Canadian Grain Commission; and Grain Research Laboratory. Much of the research has concentrated on improved crop development, new food product development, regulatory compliance testing, and process development.

With future trends pointing toward annual sales of natural foods and food products that promote and maintain healthy living in the area of $500 billion, the industry has invested heavily in research and development relating to this field. Research facilities such as the Richardson Centre for Functional Foods and Nutraceuticals – which focuses its research on prairie-based plants – and the National Centre for Agri-Food Research in Medicine are working to develop functional and nutraceutical foods that are scientifically proven to be safe and effective. Research will assist food processors to identify opportunities in food sectors that are expected to enjoy significant growth. • MICHAEL BENARROCH, ALLEN STURKO, AND AL HANDFORD

FOODS AND BEVERAGES, MANITOBAN. Archaeological records indicate little evidence of early AGRICULTURE by First Nations peoples in what is now MB, unlike the Mandans of ND or the Iroquois of ON, as the CLIMATE here was mostly too harsh to allow for subsistence crops. A few crops, such as corn and pumpkins/squash, were grown, usually in small quantities, in the S of the province, especially by the DAKOTA. Without livestock, dairy products were unknown to Aboriginal peoples. Most early occupants here had a Hunter-Gatherer Culture that persisted until – and sometimes considerably beyond – the FUR TRADE era.

At the time of European arrival, the BISON and its derivative, PEMMICAN, were staples of the far S of MB, with CARIBOU the staple of the far N. The mule DEER (now extirpated from the province), ELK, and MOOSE constituted important food sources for much of MB's boreal forest (see ECOCLIMACTIC REGIONS). Numerous FISH, WATERFOWL, passenger pigeons, members of the GROUSE family, and other birds were crucial foods. Also eaten were BEARS and smaller MAMMALS, such as RABBITS and BEAVERS. These meats were typically jerked, smoked, sun-dried, or otherwise prepared so that they would last through times of scarcity.

PEAK OF THE MARKET

Perogies are a Manitoba staple.

Preserved fish was especially important for the **Cree** and **Dene** peoples. All Aboriginal peoples required higher fat levels than current medical guidelines suggest because of colder **Weather**, lack of artificial heating, and vigorous activity.

Though **Mushrooms** were not farmed, Aboriginal people harvested them wild. **Maple**, **Birch**, and other trees were also used for sugary syrup. Acorns, though they required processing, were nevertheless used as flour, and the nuts of many other trees provided much-needed nutrients, fat, and protein. Cattails were used for flour as well, with **Wild Rice** being so important to the **Ojibway** that it was considered a sacred plant. Many indigenous plants were food sources, including juniper berries; countless herbs and roots; fruits and berries, such as cranberries and saskatoons; and both the sunflower and its close relative, the Jerusalem artichoke, now also called the "sunchoke." Vegetables and fruits, as well as starches, were often eaten raw, but could be prepared together with meats, boiled, roasted, or otherwise prepared. The Assiniboines were so called by the Ojibway (in whose language the name means "stone boilers") because they appear to have cooked their soups and stews by heating rocks. While cold, fresh water was a primary drink, Aboriginal people drank innumerable herbal tisanes – such as wild mint, Labrador tea, rosehips, willow bark, and raspberry leaves – for nutritional, medicinal, social, and religious purposes.

With the arrival of Europeans, the diet of Aboriginal peoples came to rely more on what the HBC's stores carried. The reliance on dairy and grains as staples, and especially **Wheat**, has completely changed both the diet of the province's Aboriginal people and MB's physical appearance. Bannock or frybread made from wheat flour came to be the primary starch, and tea the primary drink, with the traditional diet falling out of fashion. But Europeans have also incorporated numerous local ingredients into their repertoire. These include pickerel and sauger; trout and Arctic char, both members of the salmon family; **Catfish**; and several often-oily varieties of fish eaten smoked, notably whitefish, **Bass**, cisco, and especially **Goldeye**. **Sturgeon** was once plentiful here, but was severely overexploited and is slow to rebound. Alongside Old World animals such as beef, chicken, and pork, native species including bison, elk, and turkey are ranched and eaten here, and **Sunflower** seeds have no stronger association than with MB. Although Aboriginal peoples here had no alcohol before European arrival, a Cree company now makes wines from native plants like blueberries, saskatoons, and birch.

The climate of MB continued to influence pioneers' diet, as early flash frosts and short growing seasons led by necessity to canning, pickling, jam making, and other forms of preserving. With widespread electricity and home refrigeration and freezing, and especially thanks to modern conveniences such as the automobile and the suburban supermarket, food preservation is now rare, except in remote locations. Thus, formerly common MB foods, such as vegetable aspics, have all but disappeared.

MB's ethnic patchwork has given rise to the popularity of perogies and kielbasa or kolbasa, from the **Ukrainian** and **Polish** peoples, and of smokies – a smoked sausage, generally made of pork. Several snack foods, like Old Dutch's potato chips, are strongly associated with, though not confined to, MB. Also typical of the Prairies is anything combining crabapples and rhubarb. Saskatoons are a popular pie, crumble, or crisp filling, and may appear alongside Bothwell cheese (*see* **New Bothwell**). A truly Manitoban dessert is shmoo (or schmoo) torte, a dessert rich and sweet enough to cause diabetes in a single serving. • A. J. LEVIN

FOOTBALL. The sport of football began in MB in the late 1870s as the unique brand of Cdn football evolved from **Rugby**. The first organized football club in western Canada was the **Winnipeg** Rugby Football Club, which was founded in 1879. At the time the sport was generally called 'rugby football' because its rules were similar to rugby.

The first organized competition occurred in 1888. In 1911, MB merged with AB and SK to form the Western Canada Rugby Football Union and adopted the rules of the Canadian Rugby Union (CRU). It was not until 1921 that the Western Canadian Rugby Football Union champion was allowed to challenge for the CRU championship trophy, the Grey Cup. Initially, the Western champions were not allowed to compete for the Grey Cup, because the CRU believed the calibre of the new competition to be inferior to those in the East. Finally in 1935, the Winnipeg team defeated the Hamilton Tigers 18-12 to capture the Grey Cup.

The Winnipeg Blue Bombers have won 10 Grey Cup championships – 1935, 1939, 1941, 1958, 1959, 1961, 1962, 1984, 1988, and 1990. Among the many legendary players to wear the Blue and Gold are: **Fritz Hanson**, **Jack Jacobs**, Herb Gray, **Ken Ploen**, **Gerry James**, **Leo Lewis**, **Joe Poplawski**, **Chris Walby**, James Murphy, Gregg Battle, and Milt Stegall.

U of M football dates back to 1907 and the St. Johns College Rugby Football Team. The team competed within a city of Winnipeg league against the YMCA and other Club teams. After a break for WW1, football resumed in 1919 with the U of M playing in the Winnipeg Senior Football League.

In 1927, the Bisons began playing in the Western Canada Intercollegiate Athletic Association (WCIAA) and won the championship in the first year. They competed in this league until 1933. In 1934, they played one season in ND under American Rules Football. From 1946-48, the Bisons were back in the WCIAA, however the football program then ceased operations until 1962. A key group of individuals, led by John Puchniak of St. Paul's College, managed to gather enough support to bring football back to the U of M campus after a 14-year absence.

2006 Grey Cup game, Winnipeg

Just 4 years later, the 1966 Bisons captured their first Western Intercollegiate Football Conference Championship. Then in 1969, they won what was their first national championship – the Canadian College Bowl – defeating McGill 24-15. They repeated as national champion in 1970 by beating Ottawa 38-11. The Bison program produced many players that went on to play in the CFL including Henry Janzen, Gord Patterson, Bob Toogood, Scott Coe and Matt Sheridan – and two players who made it to the NFL, Les Lear (1947), and **ISRAEL IDONIJE** (2003).

The first MB Junior football was played in 1919 when the Winnipeg Junior Football League (WJFL) was formed, comprised of the Tammany Tigers, St. Johns Juniors, and the Crestwood Juniors. The Tigers won the league but lost to the Regina Winners Rugby Club in the Western Canadian Championship.

Many other teams joined the WJFL over the years only to drop out after a few years of competition. Most notable were the Winnipeg Canoe Club, Winnipeg Victoria's, Deer Lodge, YMHA and the Winnipeg Native Suns who were the first Winnipeg team to play in the Canadian Championship losing to the Toronto Junior Argonauts in 1930.

During WWII, league play was suspended, but by 1948, the Manitoba Junior Football League formed and was comprised of 4 teams: Weston Wildcats (later Winnipeg Hawkeyes), St. John's Grads, Winnipeg Rods and the Winnipeg Light Infantry. In 1953 the Wildcats and the Rods joined with the Regina Bomber-Dales (later Rams) and Saskatoon Hilltops to form the Manitoba-Saskatchewan Junior Football League and thus began one of the most dominant leagues in Canada. The Winnipeg Rods won 3 Cdn championships over the next 25 years – 1955, 1956, and 1961.

Many players graduated to their local CFL teams, including Lorne Benson, Billy Cooper, Norm Hill, Harry Hood, Ed Kotowich, Harry Langford, Ron Latourelle, Cec Luining, Cornell Piper, Roger Savoie and Gord Sturtridge.

In 1976, the Manitoba Junior Football Conference (MJFC) was formed with the Fort Garry Lions, St. Vital Mustangs, Winnipeg Hawkeyes and the Winnipeg Rods (later St. James). In 1985 the Thunder Bay Giants joined the MJFC. The conference folded in 1995 leaving MB without a junior football team for the first time in over 75 years. Junior football returned to the province in 2002 when the Winnipeg Rifles (named after the Royal Winnipeg Rifles Regiment) joining the powerful Prairie Football Conference.

The first high school rugby football was played in 1927 with Daniel McIntyre, St. John's College, St. Paul's College, Wesley College, **PORTAGE LA PRAIRIE** High, and the YMHA fielding teams. The

Winnipeg High School Football League (WHSFL) was founded in 1933 with additional teams from Sisler, **GORDON BELL**, Tec Voc, Kelvin, and Isaac Newton. Play was suspended in 1935 and 1953 due to polio **EPIDEMICS**. In the 1960s, Churchill, Grant Park, and Elmwood entered the league and by the 1980's the WHSFL had expanded to 13 teams with the inclusion of Brandon, River East, Maples, Oak Park and Sturgeon Creek.

BRANDON moved to the Manitoba Rural Football League in 2001. Rural Manitoba has a long football history (9 man) with communities such as **BOISSEVAIN, VIRDEN, SOURIS, KILLARNEY, DELORAINE, MACGREGOR, WARREN, NEEPAWA,** and **DAUPHIN** fielding teams. 2001 saw significant changes as 3 teams from northern ON – Kenora, Dryden and Fort Frances – entered the league. In 2007, the league expanded by 4 more teams: Portage la Prairie, Murdock MacKay, West Kildonan and Garden City bringing the WHSFL to 25 teams.

Senior football started in Winnipeg in 1937, Juvenile in 1948, and Bantam in 1956. By 2007, there were 7 divisions beginning with Terminator (7 yr olds) all the way to Major (up to 21 yrs). Flag football is also hugely popular in Manitoba and is played by boys and girls from the ages of 9-16. ● TREVOR KENNERD

FOOTE, Lewis Benjamin "L.B.," photographer (b 1873, Foote's Cove, NL; d 1957, **WINNIPEG**) was a prolific Winnipeg photographer. He worked on the *Summerside Journal* (PEI), where he discovered a flair for **PHOTOGRAPHY**. He moved to Halifax, and then to Winnipeg in 1902, where he became a professional photographer. For more

L.B. Foote went to great heights for just the right photograph.

than 50 years, his photographs chronicled the development of the city. His most famous work was done in 1919 during the **WINNIPEG GENERAL STRIKE**, but he was also the official photographer to the Winnipeg coroner. ● JMB

FORAGE CROPS. About 2.6 million ha (6.4 million ac) of MB's farmland are used to grow crops such as timothy and alfalfa to feed cattle, sheep, horses, and other domestic animals throughout the winter. Forage crops also assist in soil conservation; alfalfa, for example, adds nitrates to the soil, reducing the need for fertilizers. Planting perennial and annual forage crops also allows farmers to rotate animals from one pasture to another. Rotation minimizes manure buildup, and allows pastures to rejuvenate quickly, facilitating more intensive feeding. MB's rich soil, abundant moisture, and moderate temperatures provide excellent conditions for the production of nutritious forage. MB operations export packaged products – such as timothy, hay and alfalfa pellets, and compacted hay – to Japan, Germany, and the Southern US. ● ANNE COTE

Thelma Forbes, 1963

FORBES, Thelma Bessie, politician (b Sept 26, 1910, **MANITOU**). Forbes was educated at the Manitou Collegiate and the Manitou Normal School and entered politics as a member of the **PROGRESSIVE CONSERVATIVE PARTY**. She was elected to the MB legislature in the 1958 by-election for the riding of Cypress and this made her the 3rd woman ever elected to serve the province. Under Premier **DUFF ROBLIN**, she was appointed speaker of the legislature in 1963 and held the post until 1966 when she became the first woman to serve in a cabinet position and was named minister of urban development and minister of municipal

affairs. This was her role until 1968 when she was appointed minister of public works. She did not seek re-election in 1969 as her riding was abolished. She was a member of the **WINNIPEG** Business and Professional Club and in 1975 was awarded an honorary doctorate by the **U OF W**.
• RUTH DEGRAVES

FORD, Russell William "Russ," baseball player (b April 25, 1883, **BRANDON**; d Jan 24, 1960, Rockingham, NC). Ford was the first player born in MB to play major league baseball. A right-handed pitcher, he also was the first Cdn player to win 20 games in the majors. Ford is credited with inventing the "emery" pitch. While with the Atlanta Crackers of the Southern Association, he accidentally discovered that a scuffed ball seemed to move differently. In Jersey City, he experimented by scuffing the ball first with a broken pop bottle and then with an emery cloth, and was able to make the ball hop and sail. The new pitch, which was declared illegal after the 1914 season, brought him great success in the majors, which helped him reach the American League where he won 26 games in his rookie season of 1910 with the New York Highlanders (later the Yankees). He pitched in the AL and the Federal League until 1917, compiling a 99-71 record with an ERA of 2.79. Ford was inducted into the Cdn Baseball Hall of Fame and Museum in 1989. When he was inducted into the MB Sports Hall of Fame in 2002, he was described as MB's "greatest unknown athlete." The MB Baseball Hall of Fame inducted him in 2004. • MD

FOREST, Georges, French language activist, insurance broker (b May 14, 1923 **LA SALLE**; d Feb. 14, 1990, St. Boniface). Protective of his French heritage, Georges Forest fought against St. Boniface's integration into the City of **WINNIPEG** in 1959. However, his real claim to fame came in 1975 when he received a simple traffic ticket. He refused to pay it as it was issued only in English. This set off a legal process that went all the way to the Supreme Court of Canada and provoked much debate with the Societe Franco-Manitobaine backing the challenge. The province's founding document, the 1870 *Manitoba Act*, gave equal status to French and English in provincial courts and the legislature, but in 1890, MB revoked French rights and made English the official language of the province. On Dec 13, 1979 the Supreme Court ruled than an English-only traffic ticket violated the *Manitoba Act* and that the legislature's subsequent amendment to the act was unconstitutional. The Supreme Court decision reversed 89 years of English linguistic practice in MB. This forced MB's NDP govt to

Georges Forest, 1978

drastically expand French-language services during the 1980s. Georges Forest died of a heart attack at the age of 65. • RUTH DEGRAVES

FORESTRY is the management of forests, including logging, the wood or forest products sector, forest health, and reforestation or silviculture activities. About half of MB's 54.8 million ha land base is forested. Aboriginal peoples practised forestry methods on the Prairies for centuries, employing controlled fires for renewal, felling trees, and using plants to meet their needs. Early European settlers in MB cleared trees for fuel and to create agricultural land throughout the S of the province. In response to over-cutting, the federal govt created its first timber reserve in MB in 1895. After it assumed responsibility over resources in 1930, the province created 15 provincial forests in order to manage the areas over the long term. Logging is also allowed in designated areas of many provincial parks. MB's forestry industry provides important economic benefits. In 2004, logging produced revenue of $119.6 million, wood product manufacturing $717.8 million, and paper manufacturing $511.8 million. About 7200 Manitobans worked in forestry in 2005, though the number varies throughout the year because of seasonal employment. The industry is also responsible for about $700 million of exports each year, nearly all of which goes to the US.

LOGGING: The provincial govt, which in 2005 owned 95% of forested lands (3% are privately owned and 2% belong to the federal govt), administers 10 forest sections, and oversees

UMA, TRIBUNE, JON THORDARSON PHOTO, PC18-10160-005

forestry policy through 6 pieces of legislation. MB's forests consist of 74% softwoods (like spruce, pine, and fir), 15% hardwoods (like elm, poplar, ash, aspen, and birch), and 11% mixed woods. About 1.3 million m³ of hardwoods and 2.6 million m³ of softwoods have been assigned for cutting annually. Large portions of the forested lands are in the N, and are not accessible by road, making further industry expansion cost prohibitive. The govt negotiates Forest Management License Agreements (FMLAs), logging arrangements of up to 20 years. Companies who hold or are seeking a licence are required to develop forest management plans and environmental impact statements. In 2007, there were 3 FMLAs in place in MB. The first, managed by Tembec Inc (the license was originally granted to Abitibi-Price Inc in 1979), covers a 900,000 ha area near **LAKE WINNIPEG** in **EASTMAN**. The 2ⁿᵈ was granted to Repap Manitoba Inc. in 1989, but was assumed by Tolko Industries Ltd in 1997. The largest by land area, the license stretches from Lake Winnipegosis to N of The Pas. Louisiana-Pacific Canada Ltd holds the 3ʳᵈ license (since 1994) in the **PARKLAND** region, S of the Tolko FMLA. Individuals and small enterprises also cut wood under Timber Sale Agreements (short-term arrangements that cover smaller wood harvesting areas), and Timber Permits (one-year personal or commercial licenses for even smaller volumes). As of writing, there were 185 timber sale agreement holders and 2928 timber permit holders in MB.

SILVICULTURE OR TREEPLANTING: This important work has been practised in MB since 1931. About 15 million seedlings are planted each year based on forest renewal standards set by the province. Surveyors monitor the level of success of re-growth. Many young people are attracted to this back-breaking but rewarding work.

AGROFORESTRY involves planting and managing woodlots on agricultural land for a range of purposes, including the reduction of erosion, restoration of wildlife habitat, or to provide timber. In MB, it dates back to at least 1919, when a campaign to begin reforesting the Prairies in this manner featured the "tree planting car," a boxcar that travelled the **CP** and **CN** rail lines. Alan B. Beaven was involved in the campaign from 1925-45 as an employee of the Canadian Forestry Association. He moved to MB in 1937 and also went on to become executive director of the Manitoba Forestry Association (MFA). The boxcar was in use until 1974. The govt and MFA continue to promote agroforestry today. • JOEL TRENAMAN

WOOD INDUSTRY: During the 20ᵗʰ century, MB developed a successful wood industry built on its abundant supply of wood. Primary wood products are converted into value-added finished products such as windows, cabinets, architectural millwork and furniture. The wood industry in MB produces a variety of products for both local and export use. It is the 5th largest manufacturing sector in the province and the 5th largest primary wood product producer in Canada after, BC, ON, PQ and AB. In 2004, the industry was made up of about 540 manufactures that generated $1.9 billion in sales. Over ⅔ of industry sales were exported, with $850 million worth of goods sent internationally to the US, Japan and Europe, and $450 million to other provinces. MB's industry directly employs 16,300 employees throughout the province. The Wood products industry can be divided into 3 subgroups: primary wood products, converted wood products, and furniture.

PRIMARY WOOD PRODUCTS: In 2004, this sector that produces paper and wood, consisted of 211 establishments that directly employed about 3300 people and generated shipments valued at about $530 million a year. The paper subgroup produces commodity grade paper products such as market pulp, newsprint, kraft paper, and paperboard. The wood sub-group, with 188 saw mill operators mostly located throughout Northern MB, produces commodity grade lumber, plywood, posts, beams, and OSB. The sector is dominated by a few large operators: Tembec in Pine Falls produces newsprint for major newspapers in Canada and the US. Tembec is MB's only newsprint mill and is the largest recycler of old newspapers and magazines in the province. The installation of a de-ink facility in 1995 allowed Tembec to use 100 tonnes per day of old newspapers and magazines in the pulping process. Since 1997, Tolko Industries has operated in **The Pas**. Tolko is a private, Cdn-owned company that produces lumber, specialty kraft paper and engineered wood products sold to world markets. The MB Tolko operations are comprised of 2 divisions, Kraft Papers and Solid Wood. The Manitoba Solid Wood Division consists of woodlands and a sawmill, which produce kiln-dried spruce/pine/fir lumber. Softwood fibre for both the sawmill and the kraft paper mill, located in The Pas, is supplied by Manitoba Woodlands. Louisiana Pacific, located in Swan Valley, produces oriented strand board (OSB).

CONVERTED WOOD PRODUCTS: MB's converted wood products sector includes companies which use or further process primary wood inputs into a wide range of products such as kitchen cabinets, windows, doors, manufactured housing, mobile homes, and architectural millwork products. In 2004, MB's converted wood products sector was comprised of 290 firms that generated roughly $950 million in revenues, employed 8700 people,

and shipped $650 million to inter-provincial and export markets. The intensely competitive nature of MB's converted wood products sector is characterized by a relatively small number of large firms that are responsible for the majority of industry shipments and a large number of smaller manufactures. The window and door sub-sectors comprise a quarter of the businesses in the sector yet are responsible for half of total industry shipments. The kitchen cabinet and vanity sub-sector accounts for more than 50% of the total number of businesses and 25% of total industry shipments. Other millwork industries represent 15% of sector shipments while wooden box/pallet, prefabricated buildings, etc. account for less than 10% of Manitoba industry output. Large Manitoba based companies in this sector are A&K Millwork, Décor Cabinets, Kitchen Craft, Loewen Windows, Bayridge Lumber, Mid-Canada, and Willmar Windows.

Lumberjacks (1990) by Leo Mol

FURNITURE MAKING: MB's furniture industry has recorded significant growth since the early 1990s. After the signing of the Canada-US Free Trade Agreement in 1989, MB furniture makers took advantage of the easier access to the US market to significantly expand their exports. This led to growth for the industry from 1990-2002. While the industry is now well-established, recent competition from China dampened the sector's growth. The furniture industry is primarily located in Winnipeg and in 2004 consisted of 35 establishments employing 4300 people. These companies generated approximately $415 million in revenues of which $300 million was shipped to export and inter-provincial markets. Excluding furniture re-upholstering, MB's furniture sector is made up of 3 sub-sectors. The household furniture sub-sector accounts for 81% of total furniture shipments and includes wooden, metal, and upholstered furniture for the residential market. The office furniture sub-sector represents 3% of total shipments and consists of a variety of commercial products such as desks, screens,

chairs, tables and filing cabinets. The miscellaneous furniture sub-sector represents 16% of provincial furniture shipments and includes various furniture types and accessories such as bed spring and mattresses, lamps and shades, pictures, mirrors, frames and components. The structure of MB's furniture industry has changed from one dominated by small family operations to an industry where the majority of sales and employees are generated from a small group of large companies. Approximately 60% of all furniture manufacturing establishments in MB employ fewer than 20 people and account for less than 7% of shipments. Two firms, Palliser, now the 13th largest manufacture in NA, and DeFehr Furniture, each employ more than 200 people while the remaining companies have from 21-200 employees and account for 18% of sector shipments. ● MICHAEL BENARROCH/PETER BOWES

THE FORKS is in the area surrounding the junction of the **RED** and **ASSINIBOINE** rivers in **WINNIPEG**. Today, it is a prominent tourist and commercial venue that each year receives thousands of visitors to its shops, restaurants, and heritage attractions. The Forks has an important place in the history of Aboriginal peoples, British and French fur traders, and thousands of newcomers from Europe and central Canada who arrived in Winnipeg after 1870.

BEGINNINGS: The Forks began to emerge as a geological feature around 8000 BC at the end of the last Ice Age. As the massive glaciers that covered much of northern and central NA receded, their melting waters created the massive **LAKE AGASSIZ**, which at its peak covered much of southern MB. The Red River cut its first channel S from the lake into the Mississippi River basin. Over many centuries, as the land released from the pressure of the ice rebounded and rose, Lake Agassiz shrank N to its present remnants of lakes **MANITOBA** and **WINNIPEG**. The Red River reversed its flow in response to this geological change, and gradually carved out its present channel to Lake Winnipeg. The origin of the Assiniboine also lies in the receding waters of Lake Agassiz. New research by historical geographers indicates that the river cut channels across southwestern MB. It flowed for many centuries N into Lake Manitoba, and only began its eastward direction to the Red River about 3000 BC. Its first junction with the Red River occurred considerably S of The Forks where the La Salle and Red Rivers now merge. The Assiniboine River carved its present channel to the Red River about AD 600 or 700, thus creating The Forks.

The first hunters in the area, whom researchers believe to be the ancestors of today's

First Nations, arrived from the S and W. The Red and its forested banks provided food and shelter for those first hunters. The remains of campfires with fragments of catfish bones date to this period. First Nations people were meeting and trading along the Red River before 1000 BC. Artifacts of tools for cleaning, cooking, and preparation of hides for clothing and shelter demonstrate that hunters harvested bison, whitetail deer, fox, rabbit, beaver, and squirrel along the river, and fished for the catfish, sucker, pike, walleye, goldeye, and sturgeon that thrived in the river. Evidence showing that corn was planted in the area suggests that some First Nations peoples stayed at encampments nearby, at least for the summer months. The oral narratives of First Nations peoples, combined with archaeological research, indicate that The Forks has been an important meeting and gathering site for many centuries.

FIRST NATIONS AND FIRST CONTACT: In Sept, 1738, **LA VÉRENDRYE**, an explorer and fur trader, and a small party of his men canoed from **LAKE WINNIPEG** to The Forks, where they were greeted by Assiniboine and **CREE** peoples. Their encampment consisted of 10 lodges, and was well provisioned with meat and other foodstuffs. La Vérendrye accepted an invitation from the First Nations peoples to feed and entertain his men. La Vérendrye established Fort Rouge (1738-49), the first of many company posts or forts to be built at The Forks during the **FUR TRADING** era. In 1810, the **NORTH WEST COMPANY** built **FORT GIBRALTAR**, a more permanent trading post. Its main purpose was to provide pemmican to the company's fur traders. Nakota (Assiniboine), **DAKOTA** (Sioux), **OJIBWAY**, and **CREE** camped regularly at The Forks. In 1815, Fort Gibraltar was destroyed during one of many the clashes between the North West Company and **HBC**. Rebuilt on the N side of the Assiniboine River in 1817 as Fort Gibraltar II, the fort was renamed **UPPER FORT GARRY** in 1821 when the HBC assumed control of the North West Company. In 1836, the HBC established the first of its experimental farms at The Forks. These demonstration farms were meant to encourage permanent farming in the area. Significant flooding in 1852 again forced the **HBC** to reconsider its plans for The Forks. Company officials decided that the fort would be rebuilt and expanded despite the constant concern with flooding. They calculated that growing trade and settlement and potential profits from provisioning British troops moving into the area justified their investments at The Forks. The HBC designated Fort Garry main administrative centre and trading depot into the 1870s. Later in the decade, however, the HBC dismantled the fort and replaced it with modern commercial

The Forks in Winnipeg continues to be a popular gathering place.

and warehouse buildings. The stone fort's main (north) gate, located in a small park at Broadway and Main in downtown Winnipeg, is all that remains of the once-bustling centre.

CONFEDERATION, MÉTIS RESISTANCE, AND THE FORKS: In 1869, negotiators for Canada and the HBC reached an agreement to transfer HBC lands in what is now Manitoba to Canada. The HBC still retained a significant amount of land, though, including a large reserve of 245 ha (600 ac) at The Forks. The agreement did not sufficiently recognize traditional Aboriginal land entitlements, and offered no guarantees for self-govt. Angry residents protested the agreement. The Métis, fearing for their very cultural and economic existence, took the most dramatic action. In Nov 1869, they crept across the frozen Assiniboine and seized Fort Garry. This **RED RIVER RESISTANCE** ultimately forced concessions from the Cdn govt, including provincial status for MB. The transfer of **RUPERT'S LAND** to Canada and the establishment of MB paved the way for the emergence of Winnipeg as a major political and commercial centre. The HBC surveyed its lands at The Forks for residential and commercial use to take advantage of the growth that provincial

status, and Winnipeg's designation as its capital, were expected to bring to the area. To the dismay of HBC officials, however, Winnipeg grew to the north of the HBC lands. Local merchants and residents showed little interest in The Forks, choosing instead to locate on less-expensive land outside the HBC reserve. In 1873, this rivalry between Winnipeg and the HBC intensified when Winnipeg built a commercial wharf on the Red River at the foot of Lombard and McDermott. It competed directly with the HBC's wharf and warehousing facilities at The Forks. At stake in the competition was control of the increasingly important riverboat trade on the Red River.

IMMIGRANTS AND RIVERBOATS: MB's isolation frustrated attempts to foster trade and immigration to the region. Transporting goods and people over the Dawson Trail across northern ON was slow and arduous work. The only alternative seemed to lie to the S, through the US. This route offered easier overland travel, and included a growing network of rail and water transportation. By summer 1859, this transportation network included **STEAMBOATS** operating on the Red for the first time. Commercial traders and immigrants now had easier access to southern MB.

241

Trade along the Red River was booming by the early 1870s, and in response, the HBC expanded its warehousing facilities, built a steam-powered grist mill, and welcomed the building by the federal govt of 2 IMMIGRATION sheds (1872), a post office, and a customs house at The Forks. The presence of the customs house and the post office increased commercial activity at The Forks. The first of the 2 immigration sheds measured about 0.2 ha (0.5 ac) and contained 30 small compartments for immigrant families. Cookhouses were away from the sheds to reduce the risk of fire, and crude washrooms were also built nearby. Govt officials did not winterize the sheds, because they assumed immigrant housing would be only needed in the summer, when the Red was open to navigation and that the newcomers would move on from The Forks before the onslaught of winter. This proved to be a serious miscalculation, as many immigrants ended up overwintering in the poorly insulated sheds. Living conditions never improved for immigrants at The Forks, though moderately better facilities on Higgins Ave., adjacent to the recently constructed CPR station, replaced the older sheds at The Forks.

SHANTYTOWN: In Oct 1875, a particularly nasty situation arose when 285 immigrants arrived from Iceland, later in the year than was expected. After a brief stay in the sheds at The Forks, the ICELANDERS moved N to GIMLI, but without the provisions promised to them by the federal govt. Ill-equipped for the harshness of a MB winter, many walked back to Winnipeg in search of shelter and work. In a desperate attempt to avoid a return to the miserable conditions in the immigration sheds, they salvaged building materials from around town and built a shantytown on the flats at The Forks. By the early 1880s, Shantytown was home to other immigrants and working-class sojourners attracted to Winnipeg by reports of plentiful jobs. Although jobs often were abundant in the growing city, accommodation was not so readily found. Immigrants and workers in the building trades – from highly trained crafts workers to unskilled labourers – found themselves living in Shantytown because they could either not afford or not find adequate housing elsewhere. Tents and shacks dotted the area. Shantytown became notorious for its frontier-town environment. Bawdy houses and unlicensed bars located in the area. These activities drew criticism from the city's commercial and cultural elites, who regularly condemned the residents of Shantytown but were not prepared to take the actions needed to improve the social conditions of those forced to live there. **JEWISH** immigrants often bore the brunt of such criticism, especially in the early 1880s, when hundreds of impoverished Jewish refugees lived in Shantytown. In 1885, city officials closed Shantytown when the federal govt moved the immigration sheds to Point Douglas.

RAILWAYS AND THE INDUSTRIAL AGE: In 1878, the **RAILWAY** industry began to alter the landscape of The Forks dramatically. Local merchants, with financial backing from the province, completed a rail line from Winnipeg to **EMERSON**/Pembina at the US border. Here, it connected with another line running N from St.Paul, called the St. Paul and Manitoba Railway. This supplied Winnipeg with its first year-round connection out of the region, providing immigrants, travellers, and shippers with dependable communication and transportation. The steam engine spelled the Prairie riverboat's obsolescence.

As the first trains headed N to Winnipeg, the federal govt finalized plans with the CPR to build a transcontinental railway. Following an intense campaign by local politicians and business interests, Winnipeg was designated as the CPR's Western regional centre. However, Winnipeg's victory over Selkirk, its chief rival for the railway, came at a considerable cost to the city. The CPR demanded and received construction subsidies, large land grants, and tax exemptions. In Winnipeg, HBC officials who tried to attract the CPR to The Forks found themselves frustrated by Winnipeg politicians and merchants. The CPR located its railyards, repair shops, and station on city land in Point Douglas and drew Winnipeg's commerce and industry toward it.

The HBC faced a dilemma. The company's earlier plans for residential and commercial development of its lands at The Forks had failed, and now it had lost the CPR to Point Douglas. Although the company continued to believe that the future of The Forks lay with the railway industry, it recognized that this goal would not be achieved easily. The CPR enjoyed a govt-imposed monopoly on railway construction in the West that would have to be broken if further rail expansion was to occur. With this goal in mind, the HBC joined the province of MB's lobby efforts to break the monopoly. The irony that the HBC – itself once the beneficiary of a trade monopoly – was now campaigning against the CPR's monopoly was not lost on local observers.

In 1888, shortly after the federal govt finally accepted Westerners' protests that the CPR monopoly was hindering expansion, the US-owned Northern Pacific Railway created the Northern Pacific and MB Railway by merging the St. Paul and MB Railway with 4 other short lines in southern MB. The NP&MR established its northern terminus at The Forks. Construction crews moved onto the flats to build a station, a 10-stall roundhouse for locomotives, engine and freight sheds, and machine and blacksmith's workshops. The NP&MR grew slowly, and by 1900, it suffered heavy debt loads.

The solution to its dire situation came in the form of the Canadian Northern Railway. The CNoR was emerging as Canada's second transcontinental railway and a serious competitor of the **CPR** in the West. In 1901, it purchased the NP&MR and merged it into its system, designating The Forks as its central terminus. The CNoR purchased much of the flats near the river junction from the HBC and built modern railway facilities at The Forks. Existing shops were renovated, new sheds constructed, and tracks laid for a major marshalling yard. By WWI, rail lines crisscrossed The Forks and factories and warehouses filled the land. Contributing to growing congestion in the area was another transcontinental railway company, the Grand Trunk Pacific. It shared facilities at The Forks with the CNoR. In 1923, it and the CNoR were merged by the federal govt to form the CNR. By converting The Forks into a bustling industrial area, the railway effectively barred local residents from the junction of the Red and Assiniboine rivers. Out of sight and out of mind, the citizens of Winnipeg turned their backs on the 2 rivers for much of the 20th century.

The Forks remained a busy industrial site into the 1960s, so few local residents ever stood at the junction of the city's 2 historic rivers. This situation slowly began to change in the early 1960s, when the CNR decided to abandon its crowded and confined operations at The Forks in favour of more modern facilities on the eastern edge of the city. Over the next several decades, as the vacated railway shops, warehouses, and car yards deteriorated, Winnipeg citizens began to rediscover The Forks and to debate the future of the historic meeting place.

THE GREENING OF THE FORKS: In the 1970s, citizen groups launched a campaign to convert the abandoned rail yards into a public green space that celebrated the natural beauty of The Forks and its place in Cdn history. This goal became a reality in the mid-1980s, when CN sold the land to the MB govt. A corporation of govt and business, with some citizen participation, was created to oversee the redevelopment of the area, and the federal govt declared The Forks a national historic site. Initially, redevelopment focused on the creation of an open green space at the junction of the rivers, and archaeological research to document its history. Archaeological digs, music and cultural festivals, and restaurants and boutiques in restored buildings from the railway era began attracting thousands Manitobans and tourists to The Forks.

In spring 1997, The Forks drew 30,000 weary but jubilant Manitobans to celebrate the receding floodwaters at the Red River Relief Concert.

RE-COMMERCIALIZATION: The 1997 concert marked the end to The Forks as an open public green space and historic site. The expansive green space has subsequently given way to commercial development, including a ballpark, a hotel, and a parking lot. Plans for a major human rights museum and new commercial ventures are quickly gobbling up remaining land. Supporters of commercial expansion argue that this is necessary to draw visitors and to make The Forks economically viable. Opponents lament the loss of The Forks' park-like setting, and the memory of The Forks' prominence in the region's history. ● NOLAN REILLY

FORT ALEXANDER FIRST NATION (formerly known as Sagkeeng First Nation), on reserve pop 3191, off reserve pop 3449, is situated about 145 km NE of WINNIPEG. There is one reserve located on the land of Fort Alexander. It is an independent First Nation; therefore it is not a member of any tribal council. The native language of this community is OJIBWAY. Fort Alexander signed Treaty 1 in 1871. Education goes from Nursery-Grade 12 at 3 First Nation-operated schools and a post-secondary program administered by the Sagkeeng Education Authority, and total enrolment for the year 2003-04 was 643. This community is accessible via year-round roads. There is a health centre here, personal care home, and 3 community health workers. The closest hospital is in PINE FALLS. The economic foundations of the Fort Alexander First Nation are trapping, fishing, hunting, govt services, and commercial businesses. Political leader PHIL FONTAINE was born here and was the acting chief of this First Nation community from 1973-1979. Fontaine's nephew, Jerry Fontaine, also from Fort Alexander, served as the First Nation's chief from 1989 to 1998, and ran as a MB Liberal party candidate in the 1998 elections. ● RK

FORT GARRY, LOWER. *See* LOWER FORT GARRY

FORT GARRY, UPPER. *See* UPPER FORT GARRY

FORT GARRY HORSE, The. This reserve armoured regt, formed in 1912, is part of the 38th Reserve Brigade Group located in Winnipeg. The unit has formally been known as:
- 34th Regiment of Cavalry (1912)
- 34th Fort Garry Horse (1913)
- The Fort Garry Horse (1920)
- 10th Armoured Regiment (Fort Garry Horse) (1941)
- The Fort Garry Horse (10th Armoured Regiment) (1949)

Fort Garry Horse, 1915

- 1st Fort Garry Horse (Regular) (1958)
- 2nd Fort Garry Horse (Reserve) (1958)
- The Fort Garry Horse (1970)

HISTORY: The Fort Garry Horse was formed in 1912 by using the Winnipeg Squadron of the 18th Mounted Rifles to be the nucleus of the 34th Regiment of Cavalry. The Fort Garry Horse placed details on local protective duty in Aug 1914. In Sept of that year, the 34th sent a large contingent to help form the 6th "Western Canada" Infantry Battalion, which later became the Canadian Cavalry Depot. In Jan 1916, the Fort Garry Horse CEF was formed from the cavalry depot in England and attached to the Canadian Cavalry Brigade. The regt took part in all actions of the brigade.

The Battle of Cambrai in 1917 was probably the finest cavalry action of the war for Canadians. On Nov. 20, one squadron of cavalry of the Fort Garry Horse led by Lt. Harcus Strachan attacked a German artillery battery. The squadron captured the guns and destroyed the battery, then proceeding inwards for two more miles cutting down retreating Germans. The "Garries" then fought their way back with only 43 men of the squadron returning to the Canadian lines. Lt. Strachan was awarded the VICTORIA CROSS for this action.

In Sept 1939, the regt was mobilized for active service in WWII. The unit was now mechanized and equipped with tanks as part of the 2nd Armoured Brigade. The regt took part in the Normandy landing on June 6, 1944, and in many actions, suffered horrendous casualties against the dug-in Germans. It served throughout the Northwest Europe campaign until VE Day.

In 1958, the regular army was expanded, with the Fort Garry Horse becoming an active regiment. The regiment saw service in Canada and West Germany with NATO. A reserve regiment was maintained during this period. In 1970, the regular component of the regiment was disbanded. Today, the Horse continues to serve, sending members on peacekeeping and military missions of the Canadian Forces. ● BRUCE TASCONA

FORT GARRY HOTEL is among WINNIPEG's oldest, and is designated as a National Historic Site. Built in 1913 by the former Grand Truck Pacific Railway (*see* CNR) to serve as luxury accommodations for RAILWAY travellers, the castle-like, 10-storey, steel, granite, and limestone structure is one of Winnipeg's most distinguished and recognizable landmarks. Modelled after another famous Cdn railway hotel, Ottawa's Château Laurier, the Fort Garry originally featured a large

Fort Garry Hotel, 2005

lobby area; 340 guest rooms; a spacious main-floor dining room (The Provencher Room, which is now used for banquets and large receptions); an elegant, oval-shaped public room called the Palm Room (originally used by guests to receive and entertain visitors, and which is now a lounge); a main-floor café (formerly called the Factor's Table Dining Room and now called the Broadway Room); a main-floor bar (which now houses a gift shop, deli, and hotel administration offices); and 2 large ballrooms (the Crystal Ballroom and the Concert Hall) on the 7th and 8th floors. During the 1990s, the ballrooms were converted to a provincial-govt-run casino (The Crystal Casino). When the casino moved out, at the urging of the owners, at the beginning of 2000, the ballrooms were restored to their original use.

The Fort Garry, which was named after **Upper Fort Garry**, the frontier fort that once stood at the nearby **Forks** of the **Red** and **Assiniboine** rivers, has passed through several owners' hands over the years. They included the Grand Truck Pacific Railway; the Perrin family; CN; QC entrepreneur Raymond Malenfant; and the Laberge family of Quebec. The City of Winnipeg also owned the facility briefly in the late 1980s after the then-owners ran up a $2.5 million unpaid tax bill. The hotel's current operators, the Winnipeg husband-and-wife team of Rick Bell and Ida Albo, became part owners in 1994, and then full owners. Over the years, they have spent millions of dollars on renovations and improvements to the historic building. Today, its amenities include 230 guest rooms on 9 floors, 16 guest suites, 16 meeting rooms, a pool, a whirlpool, a fitness centre, and a spa. Some of the famous guests at the hotel during its long history include King George VI, actor Sir Laurence Olivier, and entertainers Nelson Eddy, Harry Belafonte and Louis Armstrong . ● MURRAY MCNEILL

FORT GIBRALTAR. Built in 1809, Fort Gibraltar was a **NWC** trading post located at the junction of the **Red** and **Assiniboine Rivers**, strategically located near the **HBC** continental headquarters at Fort Douglas. It was an important warehouse for the NWC's vast stores of **Pemmican**, and was the site of numerous conflicts between the NWC and the HBC in the months following gov **Miles Macdonell**'s pemmican proclamation. Fort Gibraltar was twice captured by HBC agent **Colin Robertson**: first in 1815, and then again in 1816, when HBC supporters riled by the **Seven Oaks Incident** saw to its destruction. However, the British govt deemed the capture illegal, and the NWC rebuilt the fort in 1817. It was renamed Fort Garry in 1822, following the merger of the HBC and the NWC. It was later abandoned, and

Fort Gibraltar

then destroyed in the 1852 **Flood**. A reconstruction of Fort Gibraltar was built for the **Festival du Voyageur** in 1978. ● MD

FORT PRINCE OF WALES was built by the **HBC** to keep French rivals in the **Fur Trade** away from the rich resources of the **Hudson Bay** area. By securing this area, the HBC ensured a direct shipping route from Canada's North to the lucrative markets of Europe. In the event of a war with the French, all ships and men in the area were supposed to converge at the fort and man its 40 cannons. The fort was also to be used as a refuge for employees and company possessions. Initially built in 1717 at Eskimo Point, near the mouth of the **Churchill River**, and named "Churchill River Post" or "Fort Churchill," the name "Fort Prince of Wales" was given in 1719 to honour George Augustus, Duke of Cornwall, later King George II. Work on a massive, star-shaped replacement fort began in 1731. Difficult living conditions and the short building season meant that the building of the massive structure, with its 6.5 m-high and 11 m-thick walls, would drag on for decades.

In 1768, two Yorkshiremen, William Wales and Joseph Dymond, were sent by the UK's Astronomer Royal, Nevil Maskelyne, to the fort to observe a rare transit of Venus (when the 2nd planet can be seen passing before the sun) that would occur in spring 1769. This was part of a

series of observations – some of which were carried out by Capt James Cook, others by Charles Mason and Jeremiah Dixon, who surveyed the Mason-Dixon Line – that helped to calculate the distance between the sun and the earth. However important the fort proved to **Astronomy**, it was not crucial to the HBC's operations. Some historians believe that the fort was never completed, as construction lagged and repairs continued until Aug 8, 1782, when French navy ships under the command of Cmdre Jean-François Galaup, Comte de Lapérouse, reached the fort. As the HBC believed the post's isolation made it virtually impregnable, the fort had only 39 defenders at the time of the attack, though its capacity was 400. The fort's commander, **Samuel Hearne**, surrendered immediately, and no shots were fired. After expelling the fort's few occupants and seizing anything of value, the French burned the fort and blew up the outer walls. Lapérouse then continued along the coast and into the mouth of the **Hayes River**, sacking Fort York, before returning to Europe.

The fort's remnants were returned to the British a year later, and a new post with the same name was established on the original site. As inland waterways became the hub of the fur trade, however, and with increased competition from the **NWC**, the fort's importance was decreased. By the mid-1850s, a single postmaster manned the structure. The fort, now a **National Historic Site**, lay in ruins until the Cdn govt began restorations in the 1930s. The site is open to the public between June and Nov, but access depends on tides and **Weather**. ● AJL

FORT WHYTE. *See* **Battle of Fort Whyte**.

FORTWHYTE ALIVE, known until 2006 as the Fort Whyte Centre, is a non-profit centre for environmental education and outdoor recreation. It is located on Winnipeg's southern periphery in what was once the historical site of the **Battle of**

Drawing of Fort Prince of Wales attributed to Samuel Hearne

FORT WHYTE. Before being turned into a wildlife sanctuary, the area was a clay mine and cement factory for more than 40 years, leaving behind large excavations on the face of the landscape. The area's genesis into an environmental centre began with the employees of the Canada Cement Company Ltd., who formed a "Lucky 13 Rod & Gun Club" in 1955 to develop the exhausted quarry site into a waterfowl sanctuary. With funding from Canada Cement, the employees released pairs of geese and ducks into the region, built pens for waterfowls and later developed the first nature trails.

Employee Don Muir and lawyer Alan Scarth began seeking private donations outside Canada Cement, and established the Wildlife Foundation of Manitoba in 1966. By that time, the sanctuary was hosting growing populations of waterfowl, and the Fort Whyte Nature Centre as it was then known played a significant role in re-establishing Wood Ducks in the early 1970s. The original Fort Whyte structures, including an incubator room, were built in 1973, and an interpretive centre was built in 1983.

The centre was significantly expanded in 1999 to encompass 640 acres of forest and wetlands in addition to the original 5 excavation sites, now man-made lakes stocked with walleye, pike and rainbow trout for family fishing. One of MB's largest indoor aquariums is located in the centre's interpretive centre. A herd of 30 bison also lives in the park's sanctuary. The centre attracts about 100,000 visitors annually. ● MD

FORTS is the term commonly given to the more than 50 fur trading posts established in what is now MB by the various fur trading companies. The posts named "forts" usually had log stockades or palisades and heavy wooden gates around the outside of the buildings. This type of structure was not designed as military protection against armed attacks, but rather intended to keep Aboriginals from wandering in and out of the buildings at will. The French easily breached the gates and walls of the early posts of the **HBC** during the years of imperial warfare in the region. The utility of the structure as a barrier was increased at those posts that had bands of Aboriginals camped outside them. At many posts of the major fur trading companies, the Aboriginal families of the fur traders lived outside the walls, not within the post. The typical fur trading post consisted of several buildings within the walls or palisades. These buildings included a victual house, living quarters for the traders, a dedicated trading house, and a blacksmith's shop, as well as other out structures depending on the region and the function of the post. Some

of the posts of the HBC, both on the Bay and within the Red River Settlement, became extensive. ● J. M. BUMSTED

49th PARALLEL. The parallel of 49° N is one of 2 borders, 497 km long, that MB has with the US. The primary boundary runs along the 49th parallel, along the states of MN and ND. There is also a short N-S line at the North West Angle with MN. These boundaries pre-date the founding of MB, and have their origin in the 1783 Treaty of Paris (which ended the US's War of Independence) and the Convention of 1818, establishing the 49th parallel as the international boundary from Lake of the Woods to the Rocky Mountains.

One of the objectives of the Treaty of 1783 was to define the boundaries of the new US. The boundary was described as running along the water routes of the St. Lawrence River through the Great Lakes into Lake Superior, through the water route W to Lake of the Woods, and "Thence through the said Lake to the North-western Point thereof, and from thence on a due West Course to the River Mississippi," then through the Mississippi S to Spanish Florida. Unfortunately, the negotiators in Paris had a flawed knowledge of the central parts of the continent, and relied on an inaccurate 1755 map of NA by John Mitchell. That map showed the Mississippi River emerging from under an inset, and an accompanying note said the source of the Mississippi was presumed to be at 50° N. By the late 18th century, explorers and fur traders knew that the topography was much different.

In 1803 and 1807, UK and US diplomats attempted to deal with several problems arising out of the treaty, without success. The War of 1812 intervened and the Treaty of Ghent, which ended that war in 1814, created 4 **BOUNDARY COMMISSIONS** to resolve border disagreements from the Atlantic to Lake of the Woods. Survey crews under Article 7 of the Treaty of Ghent, including David Thompson as the chief British surveyor, reached Lake of the Woods in 1823, and by the following year came to an informal agreement that the "North-western Point" of the lake was near Rat Portage (now Kenora, ON). However, when the UK Foreign Office consulted with the deputy gov of the HBC, Nicholas Garry, who had travelled through Lake of the Woods in 1821, he urged that the lake be resurveyed so that the boundary not split the lake from N to S and obstruct canoe routes.

In 1803, the US acquired Louisiana from France, creating a whole new undefined boundary in the W between British NA and the republic. The French left the description of the boundaries deliberately vague, in the expectation that it

would generate border difficulties in the future. One immediate casualty was the 1803 King-Hawkesbury Convention, which had attempted to resolve the link between the Mississippi River and the Lake of the Woods. Further talks in 1807 also failed, but for the first time, the British mentioned the possibility of the 49th parallel of N Latitude as a boundary W of Lake of the Woods (a notion also raised by the British with the French in 1713). The matter was not taken up again until after the Boundary Commissions under the Treaty of Ghent had started their work and there was an expectation that all border disputes would be resolved.

The Convention of 1818 attempted to settle much of the border from Lake of the Woods W. The boundary was to run from the most NW point of Lake of the Woods (still undetermined) to "a Line drawn from the said Point due North or South, as the Case may be, until the said Line shall intersect with said [49th] Parallel of North Latitude" and extend W to the Rockies. The terms of this convention and of the Treaty of Paris clashed with the 1670 HBC charter, and specifically with the 1811 grant of land to **LORD SELKIRK**, but treaties superseded domestic law or legislation. Although the boundary commissioners under the Article 7 of the Treaty of Ghent failed to agree, the Webster-Ashburton Treaty of 1842 fixed the position identified in Angle Inlet by Dr. Tiarcks in 1825 as the NW point of Lake of the Woods.

The location of the 49th parallel became increasingly important to the settlement of **MÉTIS**, Swiss, and **SCOTS** at Pembina on the **RED RIVER** (now in ND near **EMERSON**), where unofficial astronomical sightings had placed the boundary at various locations. The Cdn govt's acquisition of **RUPERT'S LAND**, the **RED RIVER RESISTANCE** in 1869, the creation of the province of MB in 1870, and the so-called Fenian invasion in 1871 prompted a need to locate the boundaries between Canada and the US.

British and US boundary commissions were created in 1872, and work began in mid-Sept with the task of determining the location of the 49th parallel at Pembina. The surveyors found the HBC post to be about 100 yards N of the border and the Cdn customs house 165 m S. While work continued tracing out the line of latitude E of the Red, other surveyors began searching for the monument left by Thompson and Tiarcks in 1825 identifying the most NW point of Lake of the Woods. Aboriginal people helped locate the remains of the old monument and sightings were taken to register its position. Brush was cleared for roughly 26 km across the peninsula, known now as the North West Angle of MN, due south to

Buffalo Bay in Lake of the Woods. The due S line intersected with the 49th parallel in the lake, to be noted on markers on the shore. The following year, 1873, the survey crews proceeded W, marking the 49th parallel at 1 mile (1.61 km) intervals to the western boundary of MB, and at 3 miles (4.8 km) thereafter, continuing their work to the Rocky Mountains until 1876. As the surveying came to a close, the possibility of ceding the North West Angle of MN to Canada was raised but rejected by the US.

By this process, the southern border of MB with the US was established. The eastern border of MB with the US – the North West Angle – was the result of a complicated process by which the original 1870 boundaries of the province were expanded in 1881, although this led to a conflict with ON that was not resolved until a decision by the Judicial Committee of the Privy Council and new legislation in 1889 fixed the MB/ON boundary on a due N line drawn from the international boundary marker at the North West Angle. These boundaries were resurveyed, and new monuments set in place between 1910 and 1912, under the authority of a joint commission created through a 1908 treaty between Canada and the US. Technical problems concerning the slight curvature of the 49th parallel and the remote position of the NW-most point of the Lake of the Woods were adjusted in a treaty signed in Washington on Feb 24, 1925. The International Boundary Commission was also made permanent and given the responsibility for physical management of the boundary. ● FRANCIS M. CARROLL

FOSS-PELLY CASE was a civil suit heard between July 16-18, 1850, in the **RED RIVER SETTLEMENT** that highlighted the social and racial sensitivities of the community. In 1848, John Ballenden, the chief factor in charge of the HBC's Red River district, arrived with his mixed-blood wife Sarah. They settled in the mess at **UPPER FORT GARRY**, and quickly fit into the community's social life. The beautiful Sarah was popular in the mess, and by spring 1849, rumours circulated concerning a soldier, Capt Christopher Foss, and Sarah. By summer, these rumours grew to scandalous proportions. At this same time, Anne Clouston arrived to marry HBC clerk Augustus E. Pelly. As a white, English immigrant, she expected to take social precedence over women of partly Aboriginal background. However, Sarah, as wife of the chief factor, retained the pre-eminent position. To draw attention to herself, Anne affected illnesses and fainting in the mess – behaviour which Capt Foss mocked repeatedly.

The Pellys subsequently withdrew from the mess and refused to speak with the Ballendens.

Seeking justice, Anne approached Maj Caldwell, the Governor of **ASSINIBOIA**, and renewed the gossip concerning Sarah and Foss. She felt their behaviour could not be condoned, and demanded that Caldwell take action. As he was sensitive to John Ballenden's popularity, Caldwell waited until Ballenden had left Red River in June on furlough. With Ballenden gone, Caldwell instructed his family to shun Sarah, and other white families followed suit. At Sarah's request, Recorder [Judge] **ADAM THOM** investigated, and determined the allegations were unfounded. He advised Sarah and Foss to bring a civil suit against Pelly and others for circulating the rumours.

The trial divided the settlement along racial lines. Siding with Sarah were men of mixed ancestry or who had married mixed English/Aboriginal wives. Opposed were those of European stock only. Thom heard the case in his capacity as magistrate. His suitability was questioned, as he had advised Sarah to press the suit; however, he overrode the objections and the case proceeded. After 2 days of testimony – much of it hearsay – Thom found there was no substantive evidence of an affair between Mrs. Ballenden and Foss. The jury awarded substantial damages against Pelly for the slander.

In the fall of 1850, however, John Ballenden returned to the UK for medical treatment. In his absence, the white families in Upper Fort Garry continued to gossip about Foss, Sarah, and her "Native nature," and forced her to relocate to Lower Fort Garry. Shortly after Sarah moved, a note, allegedly from Sarah to her "darling Christopher," found its way to Thom. Once again, gossip forced Sarah to leave, and she moved in with friends outside the community. With her husband – and the protection he afforded – absent, this group seized on any hint of impropriety to marginalize Sarah and drive her out. In 1853, the Ballendens returned to England. Sarah died there that Dec, aged 35. ● STEVEN T. NAGY

FOSSIL is any evidence of past life, preserved in rock or sediment. This includes the organic remains of plants or animals and tracks, or traces made by animals. As well as providing the basic evidence for the history and evolution of life, fossils are also useful in the dating the age of rocks, and in studies of ancient environments, climate change, ancient geography, and plate tectonics (movements of continental plates). Scientists who study fossils are palaeontologists, and there are also many amateurs who enjoy collecting and studying fossils. Fossil-bearing rocks and sediments can be found in many parts of MB, however the fossil record is still poorly known, and new discoveries are made every year. The

following sections use the internationally recognized terms for the divisions of geological time.

PRECAMBRIAN (4500-543 million years ago): The world's oldest recognizable fossils are about 3.4-3.5 billion years old. These are the remains of primitive organisms that lived in the Archean Eon – the first part of the Precambrian. The Archean lasted from the origin of Earth, about 4.6 billion years ago, until 2.5 billion years ago. Most Archean fossils are stromatolites – simple mounds and mats of stone that were produced as layers of sediment were bound together by cyanobacteria (formerly called blue-green algae). Stromatolites in MB are poorly known, but they have been found at 2 sites – Wallace Lake near **BISSETT** (rocks 3 billion years old) and at **CROSS LAKE** (2.7 billion years old). The second division of the Precambrian, the Proterozoic, lasted from 2.5 billion years ago to 542 million years ago. During this time, life underwent a tremendous diversification, as multicellular life forms appeared, including complex algae and the first animals. Although Proterozoic rocks cover vast areas in N MB, fossils of this age have not yet been found here.

PALEOZOIC ERA (543 to 251 million years ago): After the Precambrian, geological time is divided into three major eras: the Paleozoic, Mesozoic, and Cenozoic. Each of these is broadly defined by the kinds of life forms found fossilized in the rocks. MB has fossils from all 3 eras, although records for the Paleozoic and Mesozoic are far richer and more varied than those for the Cenozoic. The Paleozoic and Mesozoic fossil-bearing rocks document the rise and fall of inland seas that covered middle NA many times over more than 400 million years of Earth history. They also record the movement of the NA plate as it has crawled across Earth's surface at a rate of a few cm per year.

CAMBRIAN PERIOD (543 to 490 million years ago): The oldest Paleozoic rocks in MB are from the Cambrian Period, known as a time of explosive diversification of life. Perhaps the most-famous Cambrian fossils are the many wonderful forms found in the Burgess Shale of BC. Unfortunately MB's Cambrian rocks do not have surface outcrops and are seen only in drill core in the SW part of the province, so few fossils are known.

ORDOVICIAN PERIOD (490-444 million years ago): MB has a huge and tremendously diverse fossil record from this time, when MB straddled the equator. This is one of the best places in the world to find fossils of this age. Limestones and dolostones outcrop in the Interlake of S MB, and date from about 444 to 450 million years ago. The most-famous fossil-collecting sites include the **TYNDALL STONE** quarries at Garson, Stony Mountain, and Stonewall. MB's Ordovician

Fossils in Tyndall stone

rocks have yielded hundreds of species of fossils including receptaculitids (an extinct group, possibly green algae; commonly called sunflower corals), sponges, corals, brachiopods (lamp shells), bryozoans (moss animals), cephalopods (relatives of squids and octopus), gastropods (snails), trilobites (joint-legged animals related to crabs), and sea lilies. These organisms lived in the warm, shallow seas that covered the province during most of this time. They represent many different life modes, including bottom-dwelling, crawling, free-swimming, and planktonic forms. Conodonts – the microscopic jaw elements of early chordate animals distantly related to fish – are very abundant in MB limestones. The cliffs near Cat Head on the W side of **LAKE WINNIPEG**'s North Basin possess some very unusual fossils, including trilobites, a great variety of fossil seaweeds, and conularids – an extinct group possibly related to jellyfish. The world's largest trilobite, the type specimen of the species *Isotelus rex*, was collected near Churchill in 1998, and is now in the **MANITOBA MUSEUM**. Also near **CHURCHILL**, fossilized shorelines have yielded fossils algae (*Chaetocladus*), sea scorpions (eurypterids), and the world's-oldest horseshoe crabs. One of the biggest mass extinctions in the history of life occurred near the end of the Ordovician Period (444 million years ago).

SILURIAN PERIOD (444-416 million years ago): Rocks from this period underlie much of the **INTERLAKE** region, the **GRAND RAPIDS** Uplands, and the **HUDSON BAY** Lowland. Silurian seas were often shallow and very salty, reflected by the common occurrence of stromatolites, sponges, corals, brachiopods, cephalopods, gastropods, crinoids and conodonts. Reef-like structures of dolostones in Wapusk National Park are composed sponges intergrown with corals. Fossil beds of a large brachiopod (*Virgiana decussata*) are found in several N localities.

DEVONIAN PERIOD (416-359 million years ago): Limestones and dolostones of this period are concentrated around **LAKE MANITOBA** and **LAKE WINNIPEGOSIS**, and in the easternmost part of the Hudson Bay Lowland. Coral and sponge reefs grew in these warm seas. The best-known MB reef is the Bluff Reef in the Dawson Bay area. Collectors have found corals, brachiopods, cephalopods, gastropods, trilobites, crinoids, conodonts, and, perhaps most famously, early fishes. Most fossil fishes occur around The Narrows and include *Eastmanosteus lundarensis* and the 6-to-8 m-long, 3000 kg armour-plated *Dunkleosteus telleri*. Another mass extinction took place in the Late Devonian Period, followed by 280 million years, for which there are few fossils in MB. Seas often drained away, so there was little sediment deposited here. Few fossils are known in MB from the *Mississippian Period* (359 to 345 million years ago) or *Pennsylvanian Period* (318 to 299 million years ago). The largest mass extinction in the history of life occurred 251 million years ago at the end of the *Permian Period* (299-251 million years ago). MB lacks fossil-bearing rocks from the Permian and the succeeding Triassic periods that would record this extinction.

MESOZOIC ERA (251-65 million years ago): Mesozoic fossils are dominated by organisms very different from those of the preceding Era, but the first period of the Mesozoic, the *Triassic Period* (251-200 million years ago) is not represented in MB rocks and fossils. *Jurassic Period* (200-145 million years ago) fossils are rare in MB but include belemnoids (cephalopods closely related to cuttlefish) and clams.

CRETACEOUS PERIOD (145-65 million years ago): The Cretaceous saw the deposition of some of the most fossil-rich rocks in MB. Alberta's diverse dinosaurs lived during the Late Cretaceous along a coastal floodplain that bordered the Western Interior Seaway – a body of water joining the Arctic Ocean to the Gulf of Mexico. Dinosaurs have not yet been found in MB because most rocks here were deposited as sediment on the seafloor of the seaway. There are however many wonderful marine fossils found along the Manitoba Escarpment – from the Pembina Hills to the Porcupine Hills. The most-famous sites are in the **MORDEN-MIAMI** area, where many fossil vertebrates have been collected from bentonite clay pits – 80-million-year-old deposits of volcanic ash deposited from eruptions farther west. Represented are giant carnivorous marine reptiles called mosasaurs and plesiosaurs, large sea turtles, sharks, bony fishes (e.g., 5 m-long *Xiphactinus audax*), early seabirds (*Hesperornis* and *Ichthyornis*), and invertebrates such as squid. Some of these fossils can be seen at the Canadian Fossil Discovery Centre in Morden, and at the Manitoba Museum. These life forms were members of a rich marine ecosystem existing in a warm sea. Perhaps the most-significant Cretaceous fossils from MB are insects in **AMBER** (fossilized tree resin) dating from 70-80 million years ago, washed up on the beaches of Cedar Lake. This amber was first described by J.B. Tyrrell in 1893, and he estimated that one beach contained 600 tonnes of amber. The small, rounded pieces of amber arrived here after being eroded from rocks farther W (possibly from coal seams near Medicine Hat, AB) and transported down the Saskatchewan River system. Cedar Lake amber is one of the most-important sources of Cretaceous fossil insects (flies, midges, aphids, bugs, beetles) and spiders, and exhibit remarkably fine preservation. Shortly before the end of this Period, the sea level dropped and the Western Interior Seaway receded from MB. Mosasaurs, plesiosaurs, and other marine life became extinct about 65 million years ago (end of the Cretaceous), in the mass extinction event that also marked the end of the last dinosaurs.

CENOZOIC ERA (65 million years ago to today): The first part of this era is the Tertiary Period (65-1.8 million years ago), also known as the Age of Mammals. Sandstones and shales from the Paleocene Epoch (65 to 60 million years old), the earliest part of the Tertiary, are found in the Turtle Mountain area. Lignite coal beds contain fossils including microscopic pollens and dinoflagellates (single-celled planktonic organisms),

F

and occasional plant fossils. MB lacks sedimentary rocks younger than the Paleocene, but much of the province is covered with sediments deposited either during the latter part of the Ice Age in the Pleistocene Epoch (1.8 million years ago to 10,000 years ago), or shortly after the ice ages in the early part of the Holocene or Recent Epoch (10,000 years ago to today).

PLEISTOCENE EPOCH (1.8 million years ago to 10,000 years ago): Ice Age fossils in MB are uncommon, but they include **MAMMOTHS**, **MASTODONS**, giant bison, horses and camels. These are members of the 'Pleistocene megafauna' which became extinct about 10,000 years ago. The causes are not well understood, but they appear to have resulted from rapid climate and ecosystem changes combined with hunting by prehistoric humans. Most of the fossils are robust bones and teeth that have been redeposited in gravels; these include teeth and tusks of Woolly Mammoth (*Mammuthus primigenius*) found in many parts of the province (from Gillam to Swan River and Bird's Hill), Scott's horse (*Equus scotti*) teeth, and very occasionally bones from animals such as North American camel (*Camelops hesternus*) and American Mastodon (*Mammut americanum*). Perhaps the most-exciting site is in gravel pits at Grunthal, where deep dredging has reached layers that sit beneath the gravels deposited by the last glaciation. These layers are more than 40,000 yo and were deposited in ponds and streams in boreal forest. Fossils include large mammoth bones and teeth, a muskox (*Ovibos*) skullcap, bones of extinct giant bison (similar to the Steppe Bison, *Bison priscus*), spruce wood (*Picea*), sedges (*Carex*), and the remains of predacious diving beetles, bark beetles, rove beetles (*Eucnecosum*), clams, and snails.

HOLOCENE EPOCH (10,000 ya-today): Fossils dating from the last 10,000 years are most-commonly found in the banks of rivers and along lakeshores, but also at excavation sites and in sinkholes such as those near Gypsumville. Most are bones and teeth of bison (*Bison* species), evidence of the immense herds that populated the grasslands. Other species are the Grey Wolf, Coyote, American Elk, and small mammals. Future research will almost certainly bring to light many new exciting species and associated ecological information on MB's rich fossil record. ● GY

▶ *See* **GEOLOGY**

FOSTER, Chip and Pepper, fashion designers (b Jan 25, 1964, **WINNIPEG**) are known for their 1980s sportswear line and their vintage denim clothing. Born in St. Boniface and raised in Winnipeg and in Burlington, ON, Chip and Pepper are identical twins. They began their fashion career selling tie-dyed clothing out of their car at **GRAND BEACH**. They launched Chip & Pepper Inc, based in Winnipeg, in 1987. The line was known for its bulldog-wearing-sunglasses logo, and at its height, generated $18 million in sales. The label was over-licensed by Chauvin International, putting the Chip & Pepper trademark on everything from running shoes to barbecue sauce; as a result, Chip & Pepper Inc. went into receivership in 1991. The pair moved to Los Angeles and hosted a Saturday-morning cartoon on NBC called *Chip and Pepper's Cartoon Madness* (1991-92). In a court case with Chauvin International, they were barred from using the Chip & Pepper trademark in anything other than entertainment ventures until 2002. In 1995, the twins opened the LA boutique Golf Punk, which specializes in vintage denim and T-shirts. In 2003, Chip and Pepper launched a high-end denim line that is sold in 42 countries around the world. Items in the line are named after family members and after Cdn – often Manitoban – references, such as the Lake of the Woods belt and a jacket named after the town of **FLIN FLON**. Sportswear International gave Chip and Pepper the award for Best Men's Denim in the 2005 Smirnoff International Fashion Awards (SIFA). The brothers also appear on Entertainment Television Inc.'s Style Network show *The Look for Less*. In 2006, they lived in Los Angeles. ● AMANDA STEPHENS

FOSTER, Harold Rudolf "Hal," comic artist (b Aug 16 1892, Halifax, NS; d July 25, 1982, Spring Hill, Florida). The creator of the Prince Valiant comic strip, one of the most beautiful, well-researched and well-paced comics of all time, spent his formative years (1905-1921) in **WINNIPEG**. After a stint at the Winnipeg School of Art where he met the artist H. Eric Bergman, who would become a lifelong friend, Foster was hired by **BRIGDEN'S** when it first opened in 1914 and became known there as "the best wrinkle artist in Winnipeg" because of his ability to draw underwear models wrinkle-free. He made frequent trips to Chicago (the first one by bicycle) where he was eventually hired to draw the Tarzan comic strip in 1928. The detailed realism of that strip prompted William Randolph Hearst to commission Foster to develop his own comic. Prince Valiant, the story of a fictitious knight in King Arthur's court, debuted in 1937. At the peak of its popularity in the 1950s, it appeared in over 200 international newspapers and inspired a movie starring Robert Wagner and Janet Leigh. ● GENE WALZ

4-H clubs are a network of agriculturally oriented youth branches across NA. The first Cdn club, modelled on examples in the US, started in the small town of **ROLAND** in 1913. The clubs were organized under the provincial department of agriculture to promote a farming lifestyle among youth. Seven other clubs started up in communities across MB by the end of the year.

In the program's early days, each new member would receive a dozen eggs from a good breed of laying hens, as well as seeds for fodder corn and seeds for potatoes. The youth then tended the livestock and vegetables for submission to annual competitions. Clubs also went on outings to agricultural fairs and exhibits, and sponsored lectures and essay contests. Such activities educated children in farming methods, and thus served to promote agriculture in rural communities where many of the original settlers were new **IMMIGRANTS** with limited knowledge of Prairie farming. The program saw an initial success and became an important part of rural life. By 1915, there were 4500 members across MB.

4-H logo

In 1952, Boys and Girls Club joined with the Homecraft Clubs from across Canada to become 4-H, after the US organization. The name "4-H" derives from the organization's pledge to improve community and country with their head, heart, hands, and health. The 4-H motto is "Learn to Do by Doing." As of 2001, 4-H in MB had about 4000 members and 1700 volunteers in 214 clubs. The average age of members is just under 12. The clubs' activities have broadened, though the aim is still to promote agriculture In the 21st century, members engage in activities ranging from baby-sitting to photography. ● MD

FOX is a medium-sized member of the carnivore family Canidae, characterized by a long, thin snout, large ears, long limbs with unretractible claws, and a bushy tail. The elongated face allows for enlarged nasal sinuses lined with odour-sensitive cells and for long rows of numerous sharp teeth with which to capture and dismember prey animals. Several premolars and molars (called carnassials) in the upper and lower jaw work against each other like scissors to cut tough hide, muscle and sinew. Foxes have developed an energy-efficient body form and physiology, enabling them to not only ambush prey in short bursts of speed, but to also run it down over long distances. Individuals have been know to run for many hours at a time, and to travel distances of over 1500 km over time. Foxes appear in many stories and fables of various cultures, generally characterized by cunning and resourcefulness. These characteristics are partly responsible for the great success of some species, in terms of huge natural ranges over several continents and the important role they play in their ecosystems. There are 4 species in MB – 1 widespread, and 1 each in prairie, deciduous forest, and tundra.

The **ARCTIC FOX** (*Alopex lagopex*) is a truly remarkable, diminutive carnivore that has managed to exploit one of the harshest environments on earth – the Arctic. Brownish grey in summer, it moults in Oct into a pure-white coat, making it nearly invisible against a background of snow. During years of low numbers of lemmings and voles, large number of foxes are driven by hunger to enter the forest-tundra transition and boreal forest, where deep and often-fluffy snow greatly hinders their movements. Although weighing only 3.5 kg (no bigger than a house cat), one individual is recorded to have trotted all the way from **HUDSON BAY** to the edge of the prairie at East Shoal Lake in S MB, no doubt taking advantage of wind-packed snow on large lakes and on snowmobile trails. With superb insulation of its long and dense coat, this fox does not have to increase its heat production until the temperature drops to -50°C. It only begins to shiver at -70°C and has even survived an experimental -80°C. There are records of individuals travelling 1120 km (on Hudson Bay) and 2000 km (in E Russia). Home ranges vary from 860-6000 ha. A pair of adults is monogamous during the breeding season, and prepares a den in a bank, which may be used for generations. About 52 days after mating, usually 6-12 pups are born in May or June. Many of these will survive when rodents are abundant, but in times of food shortage, the female produces no young that year, preserving her body resources and assisting her survival.

The **SWIFT FOX** (*Vulpes velox*) was once common on the prairies of SW MB (the northern periphery of its range), but was rapidly exterminated by the late 1800s due to habitat destruction from agriculture, and trapping, shooting and poison meant for wolves and coyotes. This beautiful little fox almost became extinct over its extensive range from the prairie provinces to Mexico, but it has rebounded since the 1950s in many areas with conservation initiatives and reintroductions. Populations are growing slowly in SK and AB, but MB has not attempted to bring it back, since few remnants of mixed-grass

ROBERT R. TAYLOR

Red fox hunting

prairie habitat remain. A study revealed that the **CARBERRY SAND HILLS** held the most promise for a potential reintroduction. This is MB's smallest fox, weighing only 2.5 kg. Its colour is buffygrey on the back and orangey-tan on the sides, blending in well with dead grass. It is rather timid and quickly retreats to its burrow. It is hunted by Red Fox, Coyote, Cougar, and many species of birds of prey. It has to be swift to survive – hence its name. The Swift Fox can dash at 40 km/hr and change direction quickly – generally giving it enough time when pursued to reach one of its many burrows. Its home range is about 25 km wide, over which it travels nightly for about 10 km in search of **MICE, RABBITS,** ground **SQUIRRELS, BIRDS** and **INSECTS**. One litter of 3-6 young is produced annually in May or June. Reaching adult size by late summer, they disperse to find their own home by Sept, and live an average of 5 years.

The **RED FOX** (*Vulpes vulpes*) has one of the largest distributions and habitat ranges of all the world's land animals, occupying almost all of Canada and the US, as well as most of Eurasia. In MB it is found from the tundra, boreal and deciduous forests, to the prairies, avoiding only dense forest. It is one of the few mammal species that has adapted remarkably well to great changes in the landscape, such as through agriculture. Some vegetative cover and a supply of rodents, rabbits, birds and insects are all it needs to flourish, even in close proximity to farms and towns. This species is most active at night, but it may be seen hunting anytime. It travels regular routes through a home range of 55-165 ha, often covering 8 km at a time, and with a burst of speed up to 48 km/hr if necessary. It marks its territory with urine and scent, which usually keeps other males away, but several females may occupy the same area. Often a pair will remain together for years, sharing underground dens. Mating occurs in Feb and March, with births in April and May

(gestation of 56 days). Generally there are about 5 young in a litter, but it can reach 13. At one month of age, the pups begin accompanying a parent on nightly forays and quickly pick up essential survival knowledge and hunting techniques. The animal's senses of hearing, sight and smell are acute. The Red Fox expresses its moods and communicates with a variety of yaps and howls. It weighs an average of 5 kg and sports a beautiful, long, yellowish-red coat, but other colour varieties are occasionally seen, such as a silver fox (black with silver-tipped hair).

The **GREY FOX** (*Urocyon cinereoargenteus*) spread into SW MB from MN as recently as 1946, with the first siting recorded at **SPRAGUE**, and the first specimen trapped at **ST. ADOLPHE** in 1957. A small population has been resident along the US border ever since. This range expansion may be related to the great influx of its main prey – the Eastern Cottontail. A fox of the deciduous forest and fields, at the N periphery of its distribution, it ranges S to Venezuela, and so is capable of living in a remarkable variety of habitats. The home range averages 3-28 km², and the boundaries are marked by urine, feces and strong scent. It is known for its climbing ability in trees, using its sharp claws to grasp the bark. This unusual habit permits the fox to exploit nesting birds, squirrels, insects and fruit not available to a ground-bound carnivore. With slightly shorter legs it looks smaller than a Red Fox, but weighs about the same, averaging 4 kg (3-7 kg). Its coat is a beautiful blend of grizzled grey and tawny, highlighted by a prominent black band on the muzzle, under the eyes, and on the top of the tail. These foxes pair off in Feb and 60 days after mating in April, 1-10 young, each weighing 100 g, are born in a den in June. The young add solid food to their milk diet at 6 weeks, and begin to hunt independently at 4 months of age. This species may survive 6-10 years in the wild, but can reach 15 years in captivity. • REW

Neepawa's Terry Fox Run, 2005

FOX, Terrance Stanley "Terry," athlete, activist, fundraiser (b July 28, 1958, WINNIPEG, d June 28, 1981, New Westminster, BC) attended Wayoata Elementary School in Transcona before moving to BC with his family at the age of 8. At 18, Fox was diagnosed with bone cancer that forced the amputation of his right leg 15 cm above the knee. Within 3 weeks of his surgery, Fox was walking with an artificial limb. Inspired by Dick Traum, an amputee who ran the New York City Marathon, Fox began a training schedule in preparation for his own marathon that he hoped would take him from coast to coast to raise $1 for every Cdn for cancer research.

In April 1980, with little fanfare, Fox dipped his leg in the Atlantic Ocean and began his *Marathon of Hope*, in St. John's. With a modified artificial limb made of out a pogo stick and a motorcycle shock absorber, Fox set a daunting pace, averaging 42 km per day. Enthusiasm for what he was trying to accomplish soon grew, as did the money collected for cancer research. After 143 days and 5373 km, however, Fox was forced to abandon his dream outside of Thunder Bay, ON as cancer had spread to his lungs. Before he died, he achieved his goal by collecting $24.1 million, the equivalent of $1 for every Cdn. In 2005, through the annual *Terry Fox Run*, more than $360 million had been raised worldwide for cancer research. *Terry Fox Runs* are held annually in 60 countries. In 2005, plans to rename his old Transcona school in his honour were voted down by the local school board. Afterward, students and members of the community stepped forward to protest the decision, claiming MB had done nothing to recognize Fox's contributions. The board stuck by its decision. ● JS

FOX LAKE CREE NATION, on reserve pop 273, off reserve pop 746, is located 192 km NE of THOMPSON, and 1053 km N of WINNIPEG. In 1947, 2 First Nation communities divided from the York Factory First Nation. Now, SHAMATTAWA and Fox Lake each have distinct status. The Fox Lake Cree Nation signed the 1910 union to Treaty 5. It is a member of the Keewatin Tribal Council. The native language here is Cree, and there are a total of 3 reserves located on the Fox Lake Cree Nation land. The Tribal Council administers education on Fox Lake from Nursery-Grade 8. Total enrolment for 2003-04 was 33. Transportation in this First Nation community includes an asphalt airstrip, and an airport in GILLAM. Fox Lake is one of the First Nations most deeply affected by northern hydro development. It is 1 of 5 communities that are signatories to the NORTHERN FLOOD AGREEMENT. Fox Lake is 1 of 19 First Nation communities in MB that is party to the Land Entitlement Framework Agreement (LEFA); but as of 2006, the community had yet to ratify the agreement. The Fox Lake Cree Nation community has seen a great deal of change in its economy over the last 30 years, with 3 hydro electric stations being built all within close proximity. This First Nation community will be affected if the proposed Gull (Keeyask) Generating Station being considered for construction by 2011/2012 does come to fruition. The Fox Lake Cree Nation is currently in negotiations with MANITOBA HYDRO to determine what role it will play and how it will be involved in this proposed generating station (other communities that would be affected by this proposed generating station are: TATASKWEYAK CREE NATION, WAR LAKE CREE NATION, YORK FACTORY FIRST NATION, and the Town of GILLAM.) ● RK

FOXWARREN, pop 269, is a town about 115 km NW of Brandon. Though primarily an agricultural community, Foxwarren is surrounded by rolling countryside and scenic valleys, making the town a popular destination for snowmobiling. There are several different theories about how Foxwarren got its name. The town may have been named after an English estate of the same name or after the numerous fox warrens in the banks of nearby Snake Creek. The railway reached this community in 1885, enabling pioneers to settle here more easily. The railway was taken over by CPR in 1894 and still offers freight services. The post office opened in 1889, with other services following shortly after. Albert Laycock is credited with building the earliest store, grain elevator, post office, and office building. Foxwarren is an active community and HOCKEY is considered the main sport for younger residents. Three players from this community have gone on to play in the NHL: Ron Low, Pat Falloon, and Mark Wotton. The arena is shared with the local figure skaters in the winter and is used by 4-H clubs in the summer to exhibit livestock in the annual Fat Stock Show. ● GPP

FRANTIC FILMS is an internationally acclaimed, WINNIPEG-based production company. Since its establishment in 1997, Frantic has played a large role in developing MB's successful FILMMAKING industry. Founded by computer animator Chris Bond and U OF M commerce graduate Ken Zorniak, with executive producer Jamie Brown joining the company in 2000, Frantic has grown rapidly, benefitting from Winnipeg's low overhead costs and a favourable US-Cdn exchange rate. As of 2006, Frantic was MB's largest film production house, employing over 100 people. The company has expanded from working solely in computer animation and visual effects, with the addition of divisions in film and TV programming, commercial production, and software design.

Some of Frantic's high-profile clients include Warner Bros., Sony Pictures, Paramount, 20th Century Fox, History Television, PBS, CTV, Global Television, Telefilm Canada, and Walt Disney. Frantic's visual effects can be seen in a number of widely-distributed and high-budget Hollywood films. The company is well regarded within the film community. In addition to numerous industry awards, Frantic received an Emmy nomination in 1999 for work in Stephen King's *Storm of the Century*, and was awarded a Gemini in 2006 for one of its TV documentary series. In 2006, 2 films for which Frantic produced visual effects, *Superman Returns* and *Poseidon*, were nominated for an Academy Award in visual effects. Frantic has offices in Vancouver, Los Angeles, and Sydney, Australia, but maintains its headquarters in Winnipeg. In 2006, it was one of the fastest growing firms in Canada, with revenue increasing from $431,000 to $9.2 million over 5 years, a growth rate of over 2000%. ● MD

FRASER, John Foster "Jack," businessman, (b 1930, Saskatoon) is best known for his role as president and CEO of the former Federal Industries Ltd (now Russel Metals Inc). Raised in Saskatoon, Fraser earned a BComm degree from the U of SK in 1952. Shortly after graduating, Fraser acquired a truck transportation company and served as its president for 9 years. In 1961, Fraser sold the company and moved to **WINNIPEG**, where he still lived in 2006. He acquired the menswear company Hanford Drewitt Ltd, and was president of Norcom Homes Ltd before he joined Federal Industries Ltd. as president and CEO in 1978, and was elected chairman of the board in 1992. Fraser has been the director and chairman of the board of Air Canada, and the director of numerous companies including the Bank of Montreal, Canada Development Investment Corporation, and Thomson Newspapers Limited. Fraser received the MB Chamber of Commerce Outstanding Business Achievement Award in 1984 for Business Citizen of the Year. He has been actively involved with the arts, including acting as past president of the **ROYAL WINNIPEG BALLET**, the **WINNIPEG SYMPHONY ORCHESTRA**, and the **MANITOBA THEATRE CENTRE**. He was a member of the Cultural Policy Review Committee of MB, and in 1980, he was 1 of 6 trustees responsible for restructuring and reorganizing the Winnipeg Symphony. In 1984, he was the first recipient of the Peter D. Curry Chancellor's Award from the **U OF M**, which is given for outstanding contributions to the development of the university; he has also received an honorary doctorate of law degree from the **U OF W**. In 1990, he was appointed as an Officer of the Order of Canada. In 2006, Fraser lived in Winnipeg. ● AMANDA STEPHENS

FRASERWOOD, pop 85, lies 15 km W of **GIMLI** near **LAKE WINNIPEG**. The first settlers to the area came from Germany, E Poland, and W Ukraine. From Gimli, where transportation ended, settlers carried their possessions to build their new homesteads at the site of Fraserwood. The heavy tree cover in the area offered settlers building materials and fuel. The post office opened in 1910 as Kreuzberg, German for "mountain of the cross." At the beginning of WWI, it was decided the name should be changed in response to anti-German sentiments. The postmaster set up a petition that could be signed when residents picked up their mail. In 1918, the name chosen was an amalgamation of the postmaster's last name, Wood, with his wife's maiden name, Fraser. Early settlers tried growing crops, but limestone bedrock made conditions unfavourable. New immigrants began working on the railways and cutting firewood for the city when the railway linked the community to **WINNIPEG** in 1911. In the 21st century, most residents farm or commute to nearby Gimli, **TEULON**, or **ARBORG**. A spacious new community hall opened here in 2005. The building, that some say is the most spectacular hall in rural MB features a tower, a fireplace in the lobby and space for 500 people. ● GPP

FREDERICKSON, Frank, hockey player (b June 11, 1895, **WINNIPEG**; d May 28, 1979) was captain of the **WINNIPEG FALCONS**, the first Cdn hockey team to win Olympic gold. Frederickson joined the team in 1913, and became Capt the following year, leading the team to the 1914-15 Manitoba Hockey League (MHL) title before the Falcons disbanded to fight overseas during WWI. Regrouping in 1919, the Falcons won the MHL championship, and then took on the Selkirk team in the rival Winnipeg Hockey League (WHL), winning 6-5 in an overtime game. Frederickson and the Falcons then beat the favoured U of Toronto team to claim the 1920 Allan Cup, earning the right to represent Canada in that year's Olympic hockey debut. Frederickson was crucial to the team's success, scoring both goals in the 2-0 victory over the US. His success at the Olympics led to an invitation to play in the Pacific Coast League. Frederickson played for the Victoria Cougars until 1926, ranking twice as the league's top scorer and helping the team win a Stanley Cup. He played in the NHL with the Boston Bruins for 2 seasons before being sold to the Pittsburgh Pirates in the 1928-29 season as the first ever player-coach in the NHL. After moving to the Detroit Falcons, a torn knee cartilage in the 1931-32 season ended his career. He retired to Winnipeg where he coached the junior and senior Falcon teams. He was inducted into the Hockey Hall of Fame in 1958. ● MD

FREDERICKSON, Friðjón Friðriksson, pioneer entrepreneur (b Aug 21, 1849, Hóll, Melrakkaslétta, Iceland; d Aug 17, 1913, **WINNIPEG**), immigrated to ON in 1873 and worked as a storekeeper at Kinmount (N of Peterborough, ON) until 1875. He then acted as translator and administrator for immigration agent John Taylor during the Icelandic migration from ON to **LAKE WINNIPEG** in 1875, and was vice-gov of New Iceland for a time, also playing a part in founding the settlement's newspaper, *Framfari,* in 1877. A merchant and postmaster at **GIMLI** from 1876-81 and at Möðruvellir, Icelandic River (**RIVERTON**), from 1881-84, Frederickson established an ambitious sawmill and shipping enterprise at Icelandic River together with **SIGTRYGGUR JÓNASSON** in 1880, and is thus credited with helping prevent the abandonment of New Iceland. In 1886, he became a merchant at **GLENBORO**, retiring to Winnipeg in 1906. ● AJL

FREEDMAN, Max, journalist (b June 15, 1914, Winnipeg; d Feb 26, 1980, Winnipeg) had a distinguished career in journalism. Raised in the **NORTH END** with his brother, **SAMUEL FREEDMAN**, his family could not afford to send Max to

university. Instead, he spent 4 years reading as many books as he could in the **U OF M** library, and he would later claim to be a "graduate" of the U of M library. He began his journalistic career with the *Edmonton Bulletin* (1880-1951), having been recommended for the job by Winnipeg's 3 chief librarians, and then served during WWII in the Corps of Royal Canadian Engineers and as education officer with the Royal Canadian Legion. After the war, Freedman worked briefly in the UK on London's Fleet St, and in 1946 joined the **WINNIPEG FREE PRESS** as the Ottawa correspondent. In 1949, he became the *Free Press*'s correspondent in Washington, then in 1952 served in Winnipeg as its senior editorial writer. In 1953, he returned to Washington as correspondent for the *Manchester Guardian* (since 1959, *The Guardian*), and he added work for the *Free Press* to his portfolio in 1954. His syndicated column for the *Chicago Daily News* was carried by more than 100 newspapers, and his advice sought by many politicians, including those on John F. Kennedy's staff. He retired in ill health in 1967. ● JMB

FREEDMAN, Samuel, lawyer, judge (b April 16, 1908, Zhytomyr Ukraine; d March 6, 1993, **WINNIPEG**). At age 3, Freedman moved with his **JEWISH** parents from what was then part of the Russian Empire. He was educated at Aberdeen School, St. John's High School, and the **U OF M**, where he graduated with a BA in classics (1929). He then entered the U of M Law School, where he was a skilled debater, teaming up with **WILLIAM LEWIS MORTON**. After finishing law school, he articled with Steinkopf and Lawrence, then served 4 years as editor of the *Manitoba Bar News*. He

Samuel Freedman, 1978

was president of the Manitoba Bar Association (1951-52) before being appointed to the Court of King's (Queen's) Bench (1952-60) and to the Manitoba Court of Appeal (1960). Freedman sat as Acting Chief Justice in 1966-67, and became MB's Chief Justice in 1971, retiring in 1983 at the mandatory age of 75. On Freedman's retirement, lawyer/professor Cameron Harvey selected some of the judge's rulings to be published as *Chief Justice Samuel Freedman: A Great Canadian Judge*. He served as chair of a commission investigating railway labour troubles in 1954-55. Freedman was chancellor of the U of M 1959-68, and received the Order of Canada in 1984. Sam's son, Martin Freedman, is also a judge, while his brother, **MAX FREEDMAN**, was a prominent journalist. ● AJL

FREER, James Simmons, pioneer filmmaker, (b Jan 4, 1855, Woodstock, Oxon., UK; d Dec 22, 1933, **WINNIPEG**) Less than 2 years after the Lumière brothers had presented their first moving-picture shows in Paris in Dec 1895, James Freer purchased one of their cinématographe machines, a combination movie camera and projector, and began making home movies on and near his farm in Brandon Hills, just W of **BRANDON**. The English-born farmer thus became the first Cdn to make movies in this country. His films were under 2 minutes' length and focused on local scenes and activities: farm work (stoking and harvesting), trains, and special events. In the spring of 1898, the **CPR** underwrote a trip for him back to the UK to help promote the Prairies (and the **RAILWAYS**) to prospective **IMMIGRANTS**. His program was entitled *Ten Years in Manitoba* (he had arrived in the province in 1888) and included his short films, magic lantern slides, and Freer's own gift with words. During his 6 month tour of the UK, he made films of that country, which he showed to MB audiences on his return. **SIR CLIFFORD SIFTON**, Freer's neighbour in Brandon and the federal Minister for the Interior, orchestrated a 2nd promotional trip, financed by the govt and much less successful, in 1902. Freer spent the last 20 years of his life as a reporter for the *Manitoba Free Press* (*see* **WINNIPEG FREE PRESS**). ● GENE WALZ

FRENCH in MB date back to the 18th century exploration of the western interior by Cdn-born explorers from New France. When Pierre Gaultier de Varennes et de **LA VÉRENDRYE**, accompanied by his sons Jean-Baptiste, Pierre and François set out for the West from Montreal in June, 1731, little was known about the land and the peoples of what would become the province of MB. A dozen years later, La Vérendrye, his sons and members of his party had built several **FORTS**, including Fort

Maurepas (1734) on the **RED RIVER**, a few kms above its mouth; Fort Rouge (**WINNIPEG**) and Fort La Reine (**PORTAGE LA PRAIRIE**) in 1738; and between 1741 and 1743, Fort Dauphin (**WINNIPEGOSIS**), Fort Bourbon, to the NW of **LAKE WINNIPEG**, and Fort Paskoya, to the NW of Cedar Lake.

French exploration during the 18th century did not initially result in the establishment of permanent francophone settlements in MB. However, when New France fell to the British in 1760, the **FUR TRADE** route using the lakes and rivers of the interior was mapped out for use by the voyageurs based in Montreal. This soon led to the establishment of a permanent French-speaking population in MB composed of French-Canadian voyageurs that stayed in the West with their First Nations wives and their children. These "free men" and their families eventually formed a new people, the **MÉTIS**.

By the beginning of the 19th century, 2 major fur trading companies, the **HUDSON'S BAY COMPANY** (HBC), headquartered in England, and the **NORTH WEST COMPANY** (NWC), based in Montreal, were at war. What started as a commercial rivalry led to sometimes violent confrontations in the field. On June 19, 1816, a party of Métis hunters under **CUTHBERT GRANT** reached the **RED RIVER SETTLEMENT** with a load of pemmican for the NWC. **ROBERT SEMPLE,** the territorial governor of the new HBC settlement at Red River, had imposed a blockade forbidding the Métis to sell pemmican to the NWC. A verbal altercation between Semple and the Métis led to the killing of the governor and 20 of his men. This episode, called the **SEVEN OAKS INCIDENT** in English, and "La bataille de la Grenouillère" (The battle of Frog Plains) by the Métis, marks the birth of Red River Métis nationalism. It also marks the birth of French-language literature in western Canada, for it inspired the song of Frog Plains composed by **PIERRE FALCON**, the Métis bard of the Prairies.

Fearing more unrest and violence, **LORD SELKIRK** asked the Catholic Church in 1816 to send missionaries to Red River. In 1818, QC Bishop Plessis sent Father **JOSEPH-NORBERT PROVENCHER**, Father Sévère Dumoulin and the seminarist William Edge to Red River. On the E bank of the Red River, opposite the mouth of the Assiniboine, the 3 men established the Mission of St. Boniface, the mother church of **ROMAN CATHOLICISM** in western Canada. The majority of the French-speaking population was still Métis, and would remain so until the end of the 1870s.

With the amalgamations of the HBC and the NWC and the creation of the **COUNCIL OF ASSINIBOIA** in 1822, life at Red River became relatively calm. Father Provencher, consecrated Bishop in 1820, would put into place the various

religious and educational institutions deemed essential. However, it was only after 1844, with the arrival of the **GREY NUNS** at Red River, and 1845, with the arrival of the Oblate Fathers that Catholic French-language schools and institutions achieved a permanent base.

On the political side, Bishop Provencher was appointed to the Council of Assiniboia in 1837, becoming the first French-speaking resident of Red River to hold political office at the colony. Cuthbert Grant, a Métis leader from St. François-Xavier, was appointed in 1839, becoming the first Métis named to the Council. Although Provencher was seen as the leader of the Catholic French-speaking population of Red River, the real political power resided with the Métis.

By 1869, thanks to the Métis community, the francophone fact is well established in the West, representing half of the population at Red River. Under the leadership of **LOUIS RIEL** and his provisional govt, this fact was underlined during the 1869 resistance to the unilateral transfer of the North-West to Canada. The *Manitoba Act*, which then created the province of MB in 1870, reflected the bilingual nature of Red River by stipulating that French and English could be used in the courts and legislature of the province, and that the laws and regulations must be adopted in English and in French. The *Manitoba Act* further guaranteed confessional schools financed by the province.

During the first years of the province, the francophone population participated fully in the political life of the province. French Canadians recruited by Bishop **ALEXANDRE-ANTONIN TACHÉ** came to MB to occupy positions of leadership. Joseph Royal, became the first speaker of the legislature in 1871. Marc-Amable Girard, another recruit, was named treasurer. Royal, with Joseph Dubuc, founded in May 1871, *Le Métis*, the first French-language newspaper in MB. Known as "Cartier's young men," these new Manitobans from QC pushed aside the original Métis leaders.

The bilingual and bicultural nature of the new province was severely tested in the first 2 decades of its existence. An influx of settlers of British descent, primarily from ON, changed the demographic balance of the province, which was further skewed by the exodus of many Métis to the North-West Territories. By 1881, Francophones, including French-speaking Métis, represented only 15% of the 66,000 residents of MB. The changing demographic balance had a huge impact on the provincial govt. In 1879, the English Party Caucus proposed the abolition of the publication of official documents in French. The issue was debated in the Legislature but Lieut Gov Joseph Cauchon refused to give his assent to the proposed bill. A decade later, with the adoption of the *Official Language Act* (1890), French would be suppressed as an Official Language in Manitoba, in spite of the guarantee provided by Section 23 of the *Manitoba Act*.

The various setbacks in minority language rights in MB hindered but did not stop the development of the francophone communities in the province. During the early 1870s, new settlers came primarily from QC. When the religious and political elites in QC shut the door to active recruitment in their province, efforts were deployed to repatriate French Canadians working in the New England states. Many families in the Letellier-St Jean Baptiste area of the Red River valley are descendants of these settlers. By the early 1890s, sometimes under the leadership of colonisation priests, francophone immigrants from Europe, primarily from France, Belgium and Switzerland, came to MB and established communities such as Notre Dame de Lourdes, St Claude, Bruxelles and Ste Rose du Lac.

In 1890, there were 74 Catholic schools with 3677 students in MB. The majority of these Catholic schools were French language. The *Manitoba Public Schools Act* of 1890 put an end to the financing of confessional schools. According to the new Act, and contrary to Section 22 of the *Manitoba Act*, no religious schools would receive public funding. Local trustees of francophone schools quickly found a way around the law. They realised that they could teach religion before and after school hours and still receive public financing for their school. And since the *Manitoba Public Schools Act* of 1890 did not specify a language of instruction, it was business as usual in most rural francophone communities.

The first 2 decades of the 20th century saw the creation of several provincial francophone associations which are still active today. The Société historique de Saint-Boniface, the second oldest French-language historical society in Canada, was founded in 1902 during an expedition to Lake to Woods to find La Vérendrye's Fort Saint Charles. The French weekly *La Liberté* was founded in 1913, ensuring that there was at least one French-language weekly published in MB since 1871. The **Cercle Molière**, Canada's oldest permanent theatre company with uninterrupted programming, was founded in 1925.

The francophone communities, most of which were rural and agriculturally based, were not immune to the effects of the **Great Depression** of the 1930s. However they were hit less severely than rural communities in SK, and benefited to a small extent from the out-migration of Saskatchewan francophones who "returned home" to Manitoba. The hardship of the Great Depression led also to the creation of a French-language cooperative movement and the creation of the first caisse populaire or French language credit union in **St. Malo** in 1937.

After WWII, rural out-migration to the urban centres posed new challenges for francophone community leaders. The biggest challenge was radio, which did not respect local boundaries. The francophone communities mobilized their efforts and on May 27, 1946, CKSB, the first French-language radio station created outside of Québec started broadcasting. A private radio station, it was funded by donations from francophone communities in MB and across the country. CKSB is bought by la Société Radio-Canada, the French section of the CBC in 1973.

The 1960s started on an upbeat note: the Manitoba French-language television of Radio-Canada was inaugurated on April 24, 1960. In 1967, **Duff Roblin**'s **Progressive Conservative** govt adopted *Bill 59* which allowed teaching in French for 50% of the school day. In 1968, St. Boniface College, under the direction of the Jesuits from 1885 to 1967, received postsecondary education funding for the first time. In 1970, Edward Schreyer's NDP government adopted *Bill 113*, which put the French language at an equal footing with the English language as a language of instruction in MB's public schools. Also in 1970, MB's centennial year, **Georges Forest**, a St. Boniface businessman who would contest the constitutionality of the 1890 *Official Language Act*, founded the **Festival du Voyageur**, a yearly tradition that has become the most important winter festival in western Canada.

If the 1960s can be identified with gains in French language education in MB, the 1970s and 1980s represent constitutional gains and the Manitoba French language crisis. Georges Forest set out to contest a unilingual English language parking ticket in 1975, to ensure that the terms of the amalgamation of the city of St. Boniface with Winnipeg and 10 other urban municipalities were respected. During its 4-year trip to the Supreme Court of Canada, the parking ticket had transformed into a challenge of the constitutionality of MB's *Official Language Act of 1890*. In 1979, the highest court in the country declared that the act was unconstitutional.

In another case, this one based on a unilingual speeding ticket received by the Franco-Manitoban lawyer Roger Bilodeau, it was the constitutionality of all of MB's laws that was put into doubt since they had not been adopted in French. In trying to find a compromise, **Howard Pawley**'s NDP government tried to negotiate with the francophone leaders which led to the MB French-language crisis. In 1985, the Supreme Court of Canada declared in the Bilodeau case that all of MB's laws unconstitutional and granted the government a 3-year time period for the translation of all laws and regulations.

The repatriation of the Cdn Constitution and the adoption of the Canadian Charter of Rights in 1982 marked a sea change in minority language rights in Canada and MB. Section 23 of the Charter guaranteed access to and governance of public schools by the official language minorities. It would, however, take a decade of lobbying and court challenges by francophone parents before Manitoba's francophone communities could benefit from this right. In 1993, the Supreme Court of Canada declared that Section 23 of the Charter does guarantee the right of Franco-Manitobans to govern their own schools. The same year, **Gary Filmon**'s Progressive Conservative govt adopted Bill 34, which created a provincial school division for schools offering instruction in French as a first language.

The St. Boniface Basilica is a French-Canadian landmark in MB.

Even with French language schools becoming a reality, and with the adoption in 1969 of the federal *Official Languages Act*, the demographic importance of MB Francophones continued its relative decline, dropping from 7% of the MB population in 1951 to 4.4% in 2001. In absolute numbers however, the francophone population has stabilized to around 45,000 people since the late 1980s, less than half of the 103,000 Manitobans who in 2001 are bilingual. And since the turn of the 21st century, the descendants of the Métis, French Canadian, French, Swiss, and Belgian pioneers who built the francophone communities welcome new Canadians from francophone Africa and Latin America. ● Lucien Chaput

FRENCH LANGUAGE CRISIS. The crisis over official bilingualism was one of the most intense, divisive debates in MB's history, a debate that virtually paralyzed the provincial **NDP** govt of Howard Pawley. A journalist even wrote that the period from May 1983 to the end of Feb 1984 was like an attempted legislative *coup d'état* by the minority Progressive Conservative Party.

The crisis had its roots in the *Manitoba Act*, the province's constitution adopted in 1870 after protracted negotiations between Louis Riel and his associates and the Cdn govt of Sir John A. Macdonald. Section 23 of the *Manitoba Act* provided that both English and French could be used in the MB and in the courts, and that all legislative documents must be adopted and published in both languages. In 1890, in an attempt to circumvent these provisions, the MB govt adopted the *Official Language Act*, making English the only official language in the province. The act was challenged twice in the courts, and twice the govt lost; however, the court rulings were ignored, and the law stood for almost a century.

In 1976, a Franco-Manitoban named Georges Forest received an English-only parking ticket from the City of Winnipeg, which he contested. A lower court judge declared that, by virtue of the 1890 *Official Language Act*, Forest was obligated to pay the ticket. Forest fought the ruling all the way to the Supreme Court of Canada, where he finally won on Dec 13, 1979. However, Forest had only won on principle. The court did not indicate whether this meant that all of MB's laws were now unconstitutional, and this omission meant that further court challenges were inevitable.

On May 29, 1980, young Franco-Manitoban lawyer Roger Bilodeau received a speeding ticket. He pleaded not guilty, on the grounds that the *Highway Traffic Act*, along with a related law, was unconstitutional, since it had not been adopted or published in French as well as English. On Nov 15, 1981, the Supreme Court of Canada agreed to hear his case. Two days later, the PC govt, led by Sterling Lyon was defeated in a provincial election, and the NDP under Pawley came into office.

Over the following year and a half, the Pawley govt entered into protracted and complex negotiations with the Franco-Manitoban community, which took the position that French language services were much more important to the community than the translation of hundreds, if not thousands, of legislative documents. In the later stages of negotiations, the federal govt became involved. Finally, in mid-May 1983, a tripartite package was announced. The package included provision for: a constitutional amendment declaring MB officially

bilingual; French-language services in areas with significant francophone populations; and guaranteed limited translation of existing acts and regulations, along with adoption of new laws in both official languages. The federal govt agreed to provide funds to implement the agreement.

The French language provoked demonstrations by advocates and opponents.

The Opposition PCs, still led by Lyon, immediately took a stand against the proposed amendment and led a populist charge against it, both in the legislature and in the streets. Citizen groups such as Manitoba Grassroots – aided by fringe right-wing elements in the province and elsewhere – organized scores of demonstrations in various MB locations over a period of months. The debate spilled into the municipal arena, though municipalities were explicitly excluded from the scope of the proposed constitutional amendment. Debate in the legislature became so heated – especially in Jan and Feb 1984 – that virtually no other lawmaking was possible. The PCs boycotted sessions of the legislature, and the bells rang continuously for them to attend. This gave every prospect of bringing the administrative machinery of govt itself to a standstill. Finally, the Pawley govt threw in the towel on Feb 27, 1984, and withdrew the legislation, fearing that funding for govt operations would otherwise be denied.

The opposition, both official and otherwise, had assumed that the Bilodeau case

would now proceed to the Supreme Court, but the Franco-Manitoban community had other ideas. During the weeks leading to prorogation, MB's francophone leaders had been meeting in Ottawa with senior Cabinet ministers, including PM Trudeau, to argue for a broad federal reference that would ask the Supreme Court to rule on the constitutionality of all MB laws, in light of the Forest case. A federal reference on the issue was hastily drafted, and the Supreme Court agreed to hear it. On July 13, 1985, the Supreme Court ruled that all MB's laws were invalid and had to be translated. However, the court also ruled that all laws would remain in effect temporarily while they were being translated, thereby avoiding the legal chaos that had been dreaded both by the govt and by the opposition. The parties had 120 days to work out a workable timetable for translation, to which they agreed in early Nov 1985. To their credit, the PCs adopted a strong provincial French-language-services policy shortly after they returned to power in 1988, to complement the Supreme Court's ruling on translation of legislation, thus ultimately giving a somewhat happy ending to an otherwise divisive episode in MB history. ● RAYMOND M. HÉBERT

FRESH I. E., Christian gospel-rap recording artist (b Robert Wilson, Oct 24, 1972, Winnipeg) attended Saughnessy Park School, St. John's High, and R. B. Russell Vocational School. Wilson adopted the name "Fresh E" while working as a dancer in Winnipeg. By age 18, he was living on the streets in Vancouver and later Toronto, and

Fresh I. E.

was involved in petty crime before beginning his career as a rapper in 1989 with Too Def Crew and working with members of Rascalz and Swollen Members. His life turned around in 1996 when he returned to Winnipeg and became a Christian, joining the Waves of Glory Church and counselling youth in Winnipeg's **NORTH END**. He founded the Living Bible Explorers (LBE) and the nationwide ministry Life Inc. (Resurrection and Life). Changing his moniker to Fresh I. E. (for "Fresh in Eternity"), he began gospel rapping, recording and releasing *The Revelation* (2000), *28:3* (2001), and the double CD *Tha Blacksmith & Tha Blade/ Tha Wordship & Tha Praise* (2002), earning him nominations for Hip-Hop Album of the Year and Song of the Year at the 2002 Vibe Awards in Calgary. In 2003, *Red Letterz*, released in the US on the SOAR (Sound of America Records) label, garnered a Grammy Award nomination for Best Gospel Rock Album. *Truth Has Fallen in the Streets* (2005) earned further praise for its positive-message hip hop. Fresh operates Kingdom Music and recording studios in Winnipeg, working with other local artists. ● JOHN EINARSON

FRESHWATER FISH MARKETING CORPOR-ATION. The FFMC is a self-sustaining federal crown corporation created in 1969 to buy, process, and market freshwater fish on behalf of fisheries in MB, SK, AB, the NT, and part of NW ON. Profits from the sale of its **FISH** products are distributed annually to participating fishers, who numbered about 2800 in 2004, including about 1500 in MB. The corporation sells its fish products, which are harvested from more than 400 lakes in W Canada and NW ON, in more than 25 countries. For example, the FFMC is one of the leading suppliers of pickerel in the US, and is the largest supplier of whitefish in Finland, whitefish caviar in Finland and Sweden, and Northern **PIKE** in France. Although participating fishers outside the province have the right to sell their fish either to the FFMC or directly to processors, those in MB must sell their catch to the FFMC. This is because the corporation was granted a monopoly in MB in 1969, in return for locating its headquarters in **WINNIPEG**. As of 2007, its future was in doubt due to proposed changes by the fed govt. ● MM

FRIESEN, Henry, physician, researcher (b Jul 31, 1934, **MORDEN**). Friesen earned his medical degree from the **U OF M** in 1958, and practised in **WINNIPEG** for 2 years before moving to Boston to pursue a specialty in endocrinology at the New England Medical Center. He went on McGill U from 1965-73, where his research and trials with human growth hormones led to treatments for

Dr. Henry Friesen, 1978

children suffering from dwarfism. Friesen is best known for identifying and isolating the hormone prolactin, whose main function is to stimulate the mammary glands. He discovered that too much of the hormone was to blame for cases of infertility in women. The drug bromocriptine was developed to counter these effects, helping thousands of women conceive. In 1973, Friesen returned to Winnipeg to work at the U of M. He eventually became head of the department of physiology and professor of **MEDICINE**, before resigning in 1991 to become president of the Medical Research Council of Canada. He oversaw the organization's conversion to the much-larger Canadian Institutes of Health Research in 2000. Also in 2000, he became the founding chairman of Genome Canada, a federal biomedical research grant agency, and again returned to Winnipeg to act as senior fellow at the Centre of Advancement of Medicine and distinguished professor emeritus at the U of M. Some of Friesen's many awards include Fellow of the Royal Society of Canada in 1978, Officer (1987) and Companion (2001) of the Order of Canada, an honorary science doctorate from the U of M in 1998, and membership in the **ORDER OF MANITOBA** (2004). He is a former president of both the National Cancer Institute of Canada and the Canadian Society for Clinical Investigation. He has published more than 460 articles in endocrinology. ● JOEL TRENAMAN

FRIESEN, Patrick, poet, playwright, filmmaker, producer (b 1946, **STEINBACH**). With the publication of his first 4 books – *the lands i am* (1976), *bluebottle* (1978), *The Shunning* (1980), and *Unearthly Horses* (1984) – Friesen was primarily known as a poet deeply rooted in the Mennonite traditions of his upbringing. He gained wider recognition when *The Shunning*, reworked as a play, was staged in 1985 by **WINNIPEG'S PRAIRIE THEATRE EXCHANGE**, and subsequently by drama companies elsewhere in Canada and in the US. His publications now include *Flicker and Hawk* (1987), *You Don't Get to Be a Saint* (1992), *Blasphemer's Wheel* (1994), *A Broken Bowl* (1997),

st. mary at main (1998), *carrying the shadow* (1999), *the breath you take from the lord* (2002), and *Bordello Poems* (2004). Friesen's work has also appeared in many anthologies; he has collaborated with Per Brask in translating Danish poetry into English; and some of his poems have been set to music. Increasingly multifaceted in his interests and his skills, Friesen has written, produced, and directed scripts for the stage, radio, films, and videos. He has collaborated in dance-poetry and multidisciplinary works with Montreal jazz pianist Marilyn Lerner; with **ALTONA**-born songwriter Cate Friesen; and with choreographers and dancers Ruth Cansfield, Gaile Petursson-Hiley, and Stephanie Ballard (all Winnipeggers), as well as Margie Gillis (of Montreal). A graduate in English of the U OF M, Friesen credits the late **VICTOR COWIE** as a mentor, and has himself been an effective force in the literary community of MB and the rest of Canada. He was a founder and president of the MB Writers' Guild, and has been a member of the executive of the League of Cdn Poets. He was the winner in 1994 of the **McNALLY ROBINSON** Book of the Year Award for *Blasphemer's Wheel*, and runner-up for the same work for the Milton Acorn Memorial People's Poetry Award. He has also been shortlisted for the Gov Gen's Award for Poetry. Having lived in Winnipeg for 30 years, Friesen now makes his home in Vancouver, where he teaches creative writing at Kwantlen University College. ● MILDRED GUTKIN

FRIESENS CORPORATION is one of Canada's largest book-printing operations, with a division that produces school yearbooks and local history books, and another that prints coffee-table books, trade books, children's books, and textbooks. The **ALTONA**-based, staff owned company began in 1907 as a small confectionery store owned and operated by businessman David Wiens Friesen. A couple of years later, the store also became the local post office and telephone agent, and in 1923, it purchased the local bookstore and began selling books, stationery, and office supplies. In 1933, it acquired its first small printing press, and by the 1950s it had begun to specialize in

Friesens Corporation in Altona

book printing. Through the 1980s and 1990s, the company completed its evolution from a general commercial printer to a book printer and manufacturer. By early 2005, Friesens was printing books for schools and publishers all over the world, although its primary markets continued to be MB, ON and the US. It employed about 500 people at its 1.25 ha (3.1 ac) printing plant in Altona, and also had sales representatives throughout Canada and in a few US locations. Over the years, the company has undergone several name changes. The latest occurred in 1995, when it changed its name from D. W. Friesen & Sons Ltd. to Friesens Corporation. ● MM

FROEBE HELICOPTER. Canada's first controlled manned vertical flight occurred on a farm in the Homewood area of MB. While Leonardo de Vinci was the first to design what we know as a helicopter, it was 3 brothers in southern MB who designed, built and flew the world's 2nd helicopter in 1937-38, a few months after a German-built helicopter was flown. The brothers, Douglas, Nicholas and Theodore Froebe had a keen interest in flight and learned to fly the aircraft of the day and then began to experiment with designing their own "flying machines," in early 1936, focusing on a helicopter rather than fixed wing.

Froebe Helicopter

They built the frame from aircraft chrome molybdenum steel tubing purchased from McDonald Aircraft Supply in **WINNIPEG**. Other parts were either handcrafted or taken from farm machinery. The finished product was left uncovered since they considered it experimental.

The brothers purchased a used 4-cyclinder air-cooled Gypsy engine from a plane dealer in Los Angeles for $100. It was installed in the forward section of the fuselage and connected it to the rotor shaft through a right-angled drive. Fuel was contained in a small tank behind the pilot's seat for better weight and balance. Two concentric counter-rotating blades located 5-6 feet above the fuselage provided lift, with directional control in the upper rotor assembly. Although the helicopter easily lifted off the ground, it vibrated severely and only short directional flights were achieved. Numerous flights were attempted

throughout 1937-39 with the last logbook entry being March 2, 1939. A total flying time of 4 hours and 5 minutes was logged. With no financial support and world war pending, further tests were suspended. In 1957 the National Research Council of Canada expressed interest.

The design was very similar to designs of the 1970s and 1980s – a tribute to the advanced thinking of the brothers. Unfortunately they never registered their design at the patent office with the result that Canada received no recognition of having designed one of the world's first helicopters. ● SHIRLEY RENDER

FROG is an instantly recognizable member of the class Amphibia, but few people can identify the species. Considering that the cold half the year in MB is entirely unsuited to the survival of frogs, it is remarkable that the group does so well here. But then, MB is the land of lakes and wetlands, and insects are everywhere, so these basic requirements are available in abundance. Frogs pass the hostile winter season in the time-honored fashion of avoiding it by hibernating – an energy efficient, life-suspending mode made possible through some remarkable chemical and physiological adaptations. When warmth returns and pools thaw and fill in the spring, frogs magically come back to life in a frenzy of activity, instinctively calling their own kind to come and breed. The combined chorus of frogs and toads makes the countryside ring, both day and night – a welcome sign for humans that spring has finally arrived. From a few hundred to over 5000 eggs may be laid in jelly clumps or strings, which soon hatch into larvae called tadpoles. Swarming in the warm shallows, these grow quickly on a diet of algae and other vegetation, and transform into the terrestrial adult a month to a year later, depending on the species, timing, and temperature. Full size and sexual maturity of the larger species require up to 3 years.

It may come as a surprise that MB has 4 species of treefrogs of the family Hylidae, even though they vigorously announce their presence through their peculiar calls. However, their camouflage is supreme in the animal world, and people often walk right by them without notice. Their climbing and leaping abilities are legendary, made possible by adhesive disks on the long fingers, and a light, lean body with elongated legs. The Spring Peeper (*Hyla crucifer*) is tan with brown streaks (often in the shape of an X) and is common in eastern coniferous and deciduous forests. The Boreal Chorus Frog (*Pseudacris triseriata*) is also an abundant tiny frog, with brown longitudinal stripes on a tan or green body, and inhabiting ponds and marshes

throughout the province except the tundra. The Grey Treefrog (*Hyla versicolor*) is lime-green and grey, and lives in forests in S and E MB, while its close relative, Cope's Treefrog (*Hyla chrysoscelis*), is found in SC MB. Only an expert is able to distinguish between these two attractive species, based on the trilling speed of their calls and their chromosome complement. Interestingly, the concealed side of their upper legs is bright yellow with black marbling – perhaps this flash of colour helps to startle a predator as the frog leaps away. Like an acrobat, only a few fingers of a treefrog need contact a landing platform to swing the airborne frog to a safe landing.

Northern Leopard Frog in Whiteshell

The other 4 MB species are members of the family Ranidae, several of which can grow to a large size (up to 11 cm). The Green Frog (*Rana clamitans*) may be green or tan with black markings, and is known only from several specimens from ponds in the Whiteshell Provincial Park. The Mink Frog (*Rana septentrionalis*) is similarly coloured, but has a smaller eardrum (tympanum), and lacks a fold of skin along the back and crossbands on the hindlegs, both characteristics present in the Green Frog. It too is known only from several specimens from ponds in the Whiteshell and Nopiming provincial parks; both species being mainly E and S in distribution, and barely entering MB. The Wood Frog (*Rana sylvanica*) is a medium-sized tan-coloured frog with a dark mask, and is found in forests and shrubby areas everywhere in the province except the extreme NE on the tundra. It is capable of hibernating on land and therefore experiences freezing, however cellular damage from ice crystals is mainly avoided by the production of a concentrated antifreeze called glycogen. This remarkable adaptation allows the frog to inhabit areas far from water during the summer, and to have a head-start on breeding in melt-water ponds in the spring.

The Northern Leopard Frog (*Rana pipiens*) is a large (6-10 cm), common and familiar species, shiny-green or light brown with brown spots, and white undersides. It is often seen in lawns, marshes, and even meadows far from water. Main items in the diet are beetles, grasshoppers, flies and small frogs. Living up to its name, it occurs as far N in the boreal coniferous forest as South Indian Lake, approaching the forest-tundra transition. Snakes, birds and mammals prey heavily on this species. The great abundance of this frog in certain areas like **NARCISSE** has long attracted commercial collectors for the biological-supply business, amounting to many thousands of kg of frogs annually. This activity is controlled by the province to ensure the conservation of the species.

Leopard frogs are common along lakes shores in spring and fall, and some swim far offshore (up to 18 km) in **LAKES WINNIPEG AND MANITOBA**, where they are occasionally taken in fishing nets. Leopard frogs migrate in the fall from foraging wetlands and woodlands to deep watercourses where they hibernate below the ice level. They cannot survive freezing like the Wood Frog. In April, these frogs emerge and begin calling, their air sacs bulging behind the head. During mating in May, 800-5000 eggs are deposited in the water, and these hatch in 9-20 days. The tadpoles transform into the adult form in 60-90 days. Few survive to 4 years in the wild, but captives may live 9 years. The Leopard Frog population across NA declined sharply in the 1970s, and while it is making a comeback in some regions like most of MB, it is still classified as endangered in some areas of its range. Many reasons have been proposed for the precipitous crash in numbers, but fungal disease, pollution from agriculture and human wastes, increased ultra-violet radiation, and habitat disturbance, and drought have all played roles. ● REW

FUNGUS *Tukahoe (stone-fungus or "Indian bread"):* The hard, underground resting part of this MB fungus (*Polyporus tuberaster*) is often mistaken for fossilized **PEMMICAN** by farmers and others who find it while digging in rich soil. Most of a terrestrial fungus lives underground or in decayed wood, with only the fruiting part appearing as a visible mushroom or other structure. Tuckahoe is parasitic on the roots of willows or other shrubs. It produces a large pore-bearing mushroom from an underground structure that can include soil and small stones. This hard, fibrous structure can reach more than 30 cm in diameter and weigh 6 kg or more. The word *tuckahoe* comes from an Algonquian word meaning "it is round." The roasted plant was a food source for First Nations, explaining its nickname "Indian bread." ● KAREN JOHNSON

THE FUR TRADE IN MANITOBA
By Frank J. Tough

F

The fur trade between Aboriginals and Europeans in Canada shaped relations between the 2 groups for several centuries. It also provided a means of accumulating commercial wealth which motivated French and British expansion into the northern half of the North American continent, contributed to the development of the Cdn nation, and was especially significant to the history of MB. Throughout most of Canada, the London-based **HUDSON'S BAY COMPANY** (HBC) was the central institution which dominated the development of this industry.

EARLY HISTORY: The HBC was founded in 1670 by a grant of a royal charter from **ENGLISH** monarch Charles II and was based on the model of the state-chartered joint stock trading companies that had successfully promoted the expansion of European mercantile trade in the Caribbean, Africa and Asia. Much of fur trade history has been identified with the HBC, although this powerful company was periodically challenged by traders from New France, the American Fur Company, and by independent Métis traders. The Montreal-based **NORTH WEST COMPANY** (NWC), ca. 1763-1821, was a group of merchants that led the expansion of this industry inland from Lake Superior all the way into the Mackenzie River drainage and British Columbia.

The ability to conduct trade relations between two distinct cultures over many decades was possible because of the adoption of a system of valuing pelts, provisions, goods, and services in a common unit of exchange known as the Made Beaver (M.B.). A M.B. was equal to the ideal of a single prime beaver belt. This system was used by the HBC and Natives to negotiate prices, to compare the value of things, and by the HBC as an accounting unit.

Bartering between fur traders and Natives often lasted well into the night.

Initially, the trade in fur was infrequent. Only beaver was wanted. The soft fur of the beaver pelt could be manufactured into felt and the European demand for felting material used for making fashionable hats meant that the beaver was almost the only product traded in the early years. Over time, all fur-bearers became commercially valuable, in part because the pelts of other animals, such as the muskrat, served as a substitute for diminishing beaver harvests. Along with beaver, important pelts included: marten, muskrat, mink, otter and fox; and in the late mid 19th century, a strong demand developed for buffalo robes. The trapping of fur for a fine fashion market becomes important only after 1900.

F The spatial structure of the fur trade developed from a limited and periodic contact to a well-organized system of posts, depots, district headquarters and transport networks which succeeded at bringing the furs of the most remote trapper to the London market. But for almost a century, the HBC conducted its trade from a few posts located on the shores of Hudson and James bays. Specialized Aboriginal traders, known as middlemen, obtained fur from distant groups by trading European goods secured at posts such as York Factory. The Cree and Assiniboine controlled river access to bay-side posts, thereby securing their roles as transporters and middlemen traders. In this period, indirect trade meant that the changes brought by engagement in this mercantile industry went beyond the local trade zone of the bay-side posts. When the HBC – provoked by the challenges of Montreal free-traders – moved inland after 1774, the services of middlemen were not needed.

Upper Fort Garry in 1859.

Trade was more sophisticated than the conventional view portraying a haphazard barter of a few beaver pelts for some useless trinkets. Not only did Natives provide a variety of animal pelts destined for external markets, but also trading systems created increasing demands for food and other raw materials. Aboriginals, and then the mixed-blood families of European fathers and Indian women, came to provision posts by hunting and fishing. The movement inland by trading companies, which displaced middlemen, also created greater needs: new posts had to be built and supported, and expansive transport systems demanded labour, food and materials. Pemmican – dried, pounded buffalo meat – was a major source of provisions for post employees and transport workers. Although posts did not have large resident populations, the provisioning demands were not trivial. Eight pounds of fresh meat or one and half pounds of pemmican constituted a daily ration for a man.

Contrary to what might be assumed, the earliest European goods were not always superior, and it took some time for trading companies to adapt technology to the extreme subarctic environment and to satisfy the technical demands and aesthetic tastes of Aboriginal consumers. In the 18th century for example, the HBC sold guns, ammunition (powder

and shot), tools (knives, hatchets, ice chisels), blankets and cloth, beads, alcohol and tobacco. Of special note, the work performed by Native women, which was vital to the success of the fur trade, was assisted by new goods, such as pots, referred to as kettles by traders, awls, knives and needles.

Ultimately, many of the goods provided by traders were designed to support a more efficient production of fur and food; for example, ice chisels made winter fishing with twine gill nets under the ice possible. This new tool was also used with setting nets at the entrances of beaver houses during the winter. The demands for guns was motivated by hunting and by territorial rivalry between Indian nations. Over time, European manufacturers replaced many items that Aboriginals had produced locally. In the scale of the world economy, Native demand for European manufactures was tiny. However, for certain firms, the contracts with the HBC to supply certain goods endured for decades. Significantly, the role of Natives as consumers of European manufactures, ca. 1600-1870, was consistent with a global economy in which Europe produced high valued products and the colonized regions provided cheaper raw material inputs.

ECONOMIC STRUCTURE: To this day, struggles by Native communities to protect a traditional livelihood (trapping, hunting, fishing) and land use from outside encroachment, such as corporate industrial exploitation of natural resources, entail an effort to preserve an economy that had been shaped by the fur trade. The traditional Native economy is generally described as a 2-sector mixed economy: (1) a domestic sector which involved hunting, fishing and gathering for direct consumption by the producers and their families; and (2) a commercial sector which produced pelts, food and other materials for trade by trapping, hunting, fishing and gathering. In several respects the domestic and commercial activities are distinct: the domestic sector activity is guided by use values, whereas the commercial sector is motivated by exchange values. However, the two sectors are interdependent and both are essential to satisfy needs for a Native livelihood based on the traditional economy. For example, many of the tools required for domestic production (guns, knives, nets) were acquired by trading pelts at a post. Protection for the traditional economy was provided by the Indian treaties between First Nations and the Canadian govt (ca. 1850-1930) and more recently by modern comprehensive land claim settlements.

Fundamentally, the fur trade involved the production of fur by Natives for export as a commodity under the control of European merchants. The fur trade was built upon the skills, knowledge and hard work of Native producers and the demand for pelts for felt, which was a classic long-distance trade requiring the financing and coordination of European merchants. Because the fur trade effectively combined elements of Aboriginal and European economies, it can be accurately described as a hybrid economy.

The success of mercantilism was predicated on this ability of monopoly traders to set prices based on ignorance between producers and consumers separated by long-distances. Native trappers had little notion of the London market value of furs they produced or the real cost of the goods they purchased from traders. To illustrate with an extreme example, in 1857, the price of a gun to a Cree producer was 20 M.B., worth £32 and 10 shillings (about 160 dollars) but the HBC purchased the gun in England for only 22 shillings (about five dollars). In other words, a commercial markup of 2,855%.

Similarly, in order to enhance or sustain a relationship with Aboriginal producers, traders gave goods away as presents. Other commodities did not have such high markups. The profit situation of the fur trade should also be viewed from the perspective of the HBC's entire operations. Between

Trappers often had to trek long distances through harsh conditions.

1738 and 1748, during a period of competitive pressure, total HBC sales amounted to £273,542, while costs totaled £194,174 or a profit rate of 40.9%. In the 19th century, the HBC aimed to price trade goods at 70% over all the costs required to get a trade good to a post. Between 1870 and 1900, fur prices were low, but the HBC came through this rough period because it was able to sell fertile Prairie land granted to it in 1870 under the Rupertsland Transfer and as part of MB entering Confederation. In the early 20th century, HBC shareholders were paid 40% dividends in some years.

When the HBC operated under monopoly conditions, it would attempt to maximize gains by pushing up the prices of trade goods and by buying furs and other products as cheaply as possible. When the HBC could purchase fur cheaply, its prospects for a strong return on the London fur market were good. In this sense, HBC profitability was based on an effort to gain on both sides of its business relationship with Natives. During the competitive periods, the situation was reversed and Native trappers drove up the price of furs relative to trade goods. When traders competed for the supply of furs (especially from 1783-1821), more alcohol was traded and the over-harvesting of fur-bearers occurred.

IMPORTANCE TO NATION-BUILDING: Because the fur trade was seldom conducted in a sustainable manner, the demand for pelts exceeded the capacity of local environments. In some regions, such as Atlantic Canada, the supply of beaver was quickly exhausted and the fur trade was not an enduring institution. Consequently, the competitively driven search for new sources of beaver pelts pushed the frontier of this industry out of Atlantic Canada and the St. Lawrence valley to the northern interior of the continent. In the wake of the search for new sources of supply came a European infrastructure of transport and settlement, and knowledge about the lands that would become part of Canada. European trading concerns also sought to push their operations inland in order to undermine the strategic position of middlemen traders. Thus the territorial expanse

of Canada was laid down by a search for new sources of beaver. The ties between the fur-producing hinterland and the London market were strong enough to counter the southern pull towards a continental integration with the expansionist American republic. The voyageur canoe and **YORK BOAT** transport systems and the North West Company were antecedents to a unifying national railway and Confederation.

Until the ability to supply a viable commodity for the world market developed, colonization efforts by Europeans of "new lands" usually floundered. While the cod fisheries of Atlantic Canada were a vital input to the European diets and dominated maritime regional development for centuries, the supply of pelts, such as the beaver of the interior, the sea otter of the west coast and the white fox of the arctic, meant the fur trade was truly national in scope. The beaver pelt provided the initial national staple export that gave an economic focus thereby ensuring a geographical foundation for Canada. Because of the diverse and vital economic roles (trapping, transporting, provisioning), First Nation and Métis peoples contributed significantly to the initial economic development of Canada. The perseverance of the beaver as a symbol for things Cdn is another legacy of the fur trade.

The pattern of economic development and trade set by the fur trade was followed by subsequent industries and consequently the study of the economic history of the fur trade has made an intellectual contribution known as the "staple thesis." This interpretation of Canadian economic history draws attention to the importance of different resources (e.g., beaver, timber, grain, minerals, hydro-power) for export-lead economic growth. A dependence on external markets means that an economic crises occurs when a staple is exhausted or export prices decline.

SIGNIFICANCE TO ABORIGINAL CULTURE: The fur trade influenced the course of Native history. The activities of the fur trade provided the basis of the central relationship between Aboriginal societies and Europeans

Muskrat pelts gained in popularity as beaver became scarce.

ROBERT R. TAYLOR

for decades, and in some cases centuries. Many Aboriginal communities have had longer contact with fur traders than with missionaries and government officials who arrived later. Thus, in some northern communities HBC also means "Here Before Christ."

Trapping and trading pelts represented an economic reorientation for Aboriginal economies. The over-harvesting of fur-bearers and game adversely affected Native well-being. The changing spatial structure of the fur trade and over-harvesting of resources resulted in regional migration. **OJIBWAY** movement from ON into southern MB reflected the importance of sustaining an adaptive relationship with the fur trade.

Native participation in the fur trade produced a form of economic integration, which was followed by political and legal subordination; the decline of the fur trade after 1870 gave impetus for First Nations to seek a treaty relationship with the Crown. Years of unequal trade, a characteristic of mercantilism, restricted the long-term economic prospects for Native peoples. However, it has been argued that the Canadian frontier was less violent than other parts of the New World because of the important economic relationship that had been created by decades of fur trade activity. This enduring relationship is often referred to as a "partnership." The development and perseverance of a new nation of Aboriginal people – the **MÉTIS** – is strongly associated with the fur trade.

DRIVING MB SETTLEMENT: The trade was a formative force in early MB. With the excursions of **LA VÉRENDRYE** in the 1730s, southern MB was in direct contact with the expanding St. Lawrence fur trade system. The centrality of the Saskatchewan/Nelson River system to the northern half of NA meant that strategic transport corridors passed through what is now MB. **YORK FACTORY**, as the main port for the HBC and the headquarters of the HBC's Northern Department, influenced the trading activities for a vast interior trade hinterland. For nearly two centuries, this now forgotten MB locale was the most important place in the northern fur trade.

Similarly, the **RED RIVER SETTLEMENT**, essentially a product of the fur trade, developed into a large and lively community which would become the City of **WINNIPEG**. While the settlement has an origin in dispossessed Highland Scots (i.e., the Selkirk Settlers), the in-migration of many employees laid off following the 1821 HBC/NWC merger and augmented by the Pembina Métis provided a predominately Métis population base that would continuously expand until 1870. York boat brigades were recruited at Red River and the large, organized Métis buffalo hunts supplied the settlement, northern posts and boatmen with pemmican.

NORWAY HOUSE – now one of the largest First Nations in MB – was not only an important trading post with a boatbuilding shop, but also served as a depot for HBC goods moving inland from York Factory. Today, Norway House annually celebrates York Boat Days. Significantly, a number of today's First Nations were located adjacent to HBC posts (e.g., Brochet, Nelson House, Cross Lake, Oxford House, Island Lake, Gods Lake, Norway House, Grand Rapids, Berens River, and Fort Alexander).

In 1912, MB's 1881 boundaries expanded northward and eastward, thereby incorporating Fort Churchill and York Factory on the Hudson Bay coast, as well as the old fur trade communities of Oxford House, Split Lake, Gods Lake and Island Lake. In order to counter ON's desire to annex this region, PM Sir Wilfrid Laurier argued that the old fur trade transport system gave Manitoba a stronger claim.

Because **LOUIS RIEL** could rely on the support and loyalty of a significant number of Métis buffalo hunters and boat men, his opposition to Canada's plan to appropriate the Northwest as a territory entirely subordinate to the Dominion government succeeded at bringing the Red River region into the federation as a province in 1870. The creation of a large settled community at Red River was a unique development in the fur trade country which gave Winnipeg a head start at urban and agricultural development in post-1870 western Canada. •

"CONTINENTAL" COCKED HAT. (1776)

"NAVY" COCKED HAT. (1800)

ARMY. (1837)

CLERICAL. (Eighteenth Century)

(THE WELLINGTON.) (1812)

CIVIL.

(THE PARIS BEAU.) (1815)

(THE D'ORSAY.) (1820)

(THE REGENT.) (1825)

Changing styles in beaver hats.

G

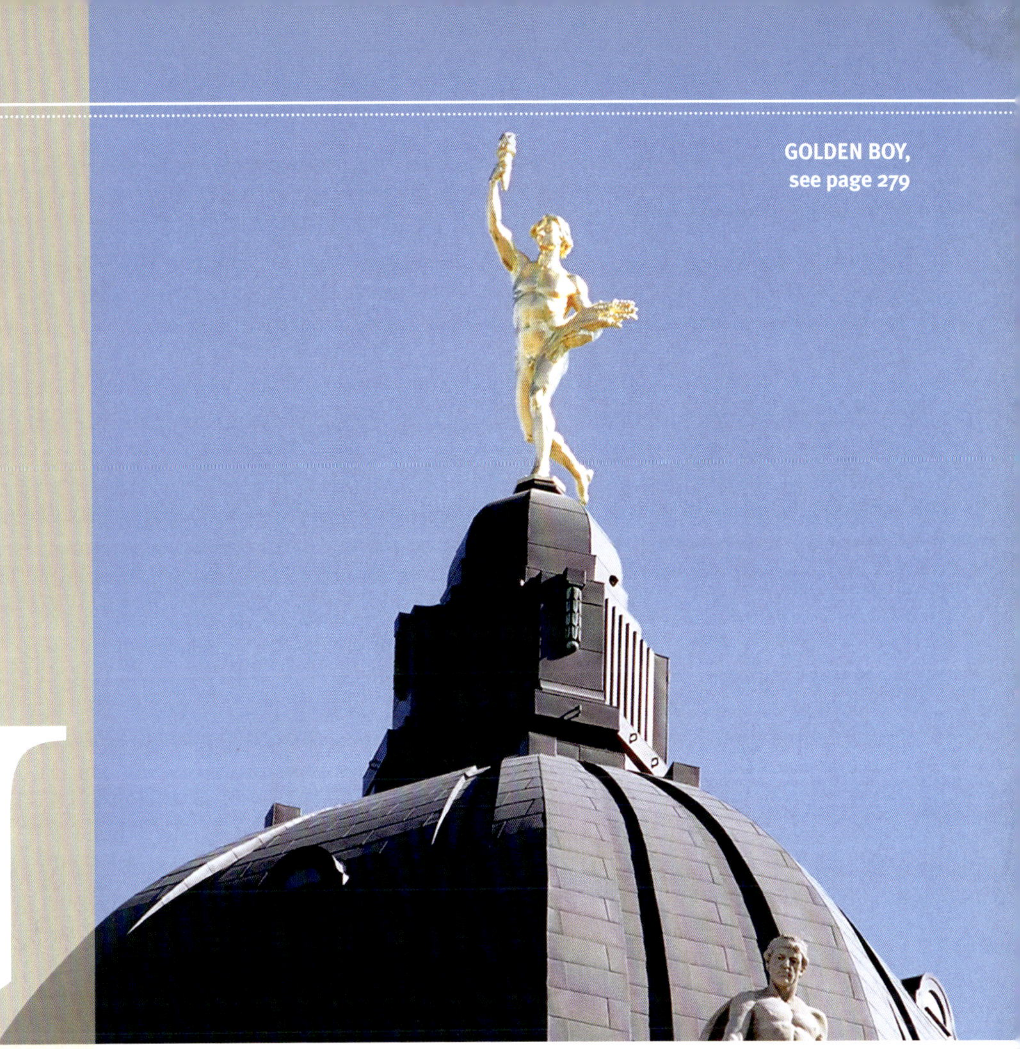

GOLDEN BOY,
see page 279

GABOURY, Étienne-Joseph, architect, sculptor (b Apr 24, 1930, Swan Lake) has had a greater influence on the modern skylines of St. Boniface and **Winnipeg** than that of any other architect. The youngest of 11 children of the Swan Lake farming couple Napoléon and Valentine (née Lafrenière) Gaboury, Étienne attended a local one-room schoolhouse before going to **Collège Universitaire de Saint-Boniface** in 1944. Upon his father's death in 1947, he interrupted his studies to help on the family farm. He returned in 1949 to the **U of M**, graduating in 1953 with a BA in Latin philosophy. Gaboury's intention was to study engineering, until his spiritual and career advisor, the Jesuit Lucien Hardy, noting Gaboury's artistic talents, suggested that he could combine the artistic with the technical by studying architecture. Gaboury graduated with a bachelor's from the U of M School of Architecture in 1958. With a bursary from the French govt, he attended the École des Beaux-Arts in Paris, completing his studies in 1959. The radical contrast between the strict functionalism of the Bauhaus movement of his MB studies, and the spiritual and emotional content of Le Corbusier's architecture experienced in his French studies, had a profound effect on Gaboury's style. For Gaboury, these elements must be fused: he has said "architecture must house both the body and the soul."

UMA, TRIBUNE, ROMAN CATHOLIC CHURCH, 59-4915-87, 1977

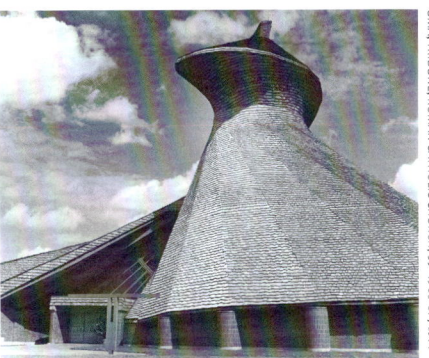

Precious Blood Church in St. Boniface

Gaboury returned to MB and was hired as a design architect with the Winnipeg firm Libling Michener Architects. Two years later, he opened his own office, with his brother Adrien as draftsman and manager. During the 1960s, Gaboury quickly established a reputation as a Prairie architect with a strong regionalist approach to design. The spiritual orientation of Gaboury's architectural philosophy fit in well also with the religious renewal of the 1960s brought upon by the Second Ecumenical Council of the Vatican (Vatican II). Gaboury received several religious commissions, beginning with the Saints-Martyrs Canadiens Church (1962) in the Windsor Park area of St. Boniface; the **Roman Catholic** church in **St Claude** (1963); the striking "teepee-style" Précieux-Sang (Precious Blood) Church in the Norwood area of St. Boniface (1968); the Messiah Lutheran Church in Winnipeg (1968); and the new St. Boniface Basilica, built in the ruins of the old Cathedral destroyed by fire in 1968.

Gaboury's works are not limited to religious edifices, nor are they limited to MB. Major projects undertaken during the 1970s and 1980s include the **Royal Canadian Mint** (1975), the Centre culturel franco-manitobain (1976), the Canadian Embassy in Mexico City (1982), and Abidjan's Hotel School in Côte d'Ivoire (1982). Projects undertaken in the subsequent decades include the PsycHealth Centre (1993) unit at Winnipeg's **Health Sciences Centre**, the Provincial Remand Centre (1994), the Students Centre at Collège universitaire de Saint-Boniface (2002), and the Helen Betty Osborne Ininiw Educational Resource Centre (2004) in **Norway House**. He was also the architectural design consultant for the Esplanade Riel/Pont Provencher Bridge across the **Red River** (2004).

Étienne Gaboury also had a hand in creating one of Winnipeg's more famous statues: the Louis Riel monument erected on the grounds of MB's **Legislative Building** for the province's centennial in 1970. The monument was the work of the artist/architect team of Marcien LeMay and Étienne Gaboury. LeMay's twisted existential nude figure of Riel was never popular with the general public and it was moved to the grounds of Saint-Boniface College in 1995. Gaboury's community involvement include terms as a board member for the **Royal Winnipeg Ballet**, the **Winnipeg Symphony Orchestra**, Heritage Canada, the **Manitoba Arts Council**, Canada World Youth, Société franco-manitobaine, and founding president of the Maison Gabrielle-Roy Corporation (see **Gabrielle Roy**). Étienne Gaboury is a Fellow of the Royal Architectural Institute of Canada, and has taught architecture at the U of M. He received an honorary doctorate from the U of M in 1987. ● LUCIEN CHAPUT

GABOURY, Marie-Anne, pioneer (b Aug 2, 1780, Maskinongé [QC]; d Dec 14, 1875, St. Boniface). The "first white woman to live in the West," Marie-Anne was the 5th child of Charles Gaboury (or Gabourie) and Marie-Anne Tessier (or Thésié). She was born near Trois-Rivières, QC. Her father died when she was 12, and she found work in a local parochial house until her marriage on April 21, 1806, to **Jean-Baptiste Lagimodière**. Atypically for the time, she insisted on

accompanying her voyageur/**Fur trading** husband on the long canoe route back to the Northwest, initially to **Fort Gibraltar**. On Jan 6, 1807, at an encampment outside the **HBC** post at Fort Daer (now Pembina, ND), she gave birth to a daughter, Reine, the first of their 8 children and likely the first white child born in the West. As they wandered the vast territory of **Rupert's Land** as far W as what is now Edmonton, settling for a few years along the Saskatchewan River, she raised the curiosity of the local Aboriginal peoples, who had never before seen a woman of European descent. Furthermore, she was a good shot and accompanied her husband on hunting trips, and may have saved several of her party by killing a bear. She also tolerated the fact that her husband had taken a "country wife," and was even well disposed toward their Métis daughters. In early 1812, they moved to **Lord Selkirk**'s new **Red River Settlement**. In 1816, Lagimodière – who had brought news of the **Seven Oaks Incident** to the Earl in Montreal – received a plot of land between the **Red** and **Seine** rivers. This area would become St. Boniface, where Marie-Anne lived for the rest of her long life. After **Roman Catholic** missionaries arrived in 1818, she became godmother to hundreds of Catholic children – including Franco-Manitobans, people of several First Nations, and Métis – and was grandmother to **Louis Riel**. She thus well deserves her sobriquet, "Godmother (or Grandmother) of Red River," and the descendants of "Manitoba's First Family" numbered about 50,000, as of writing. A Winnipeg school is named after her, as is a cultural centre in Edmonton, and she and her husband are honoured in Winnipeg's Lagimodière-Gaboury Historic Park. She is the subject of a biography by Agnès Goulet, *Marie-Anne Gaboury: Une femme dépareillée* (Édition des Plaines, 1989). ● AJL

GALLAGHER, John Patrick "Jack," geologist, business leader (b July 16, 1916, **Winnipeg**; d Dec 16, 1998, Calgary). After growing up in Winnipeg, Gallagher attended the **U of M** to study geology. In 1938, he began work as a petroleum geologist, and for 11 years, travelled to Egypt, Latin America, CA, and western Canada exploring on behalf of Shell, Standard Oil of New Jersey (now Exxon), and Imperial Oil. In 1950, with substantial US investment, he founded his own company, later known as Dome Petroleum (Western) Ltd. Dome developed oil and gas deposits in AB, but its major investments took place in the Arctic, including major drilling operations in the Beaufort Sea. It also acquired a number of Cdn junior oil companies. By the late 1970s, Dome was an expanding multi-billion-dollar firm, but was forced to accumulate billions more in debt in order to try

to exploit its resources. At its peak, it was one of Canada's largest oil companies. Gallagher resigned as Dome's CEO and chairman in 1983, as the company's debt became unmanageable, and founded Pauma Petroleum Ltd in 1984. In 1988, Amoco Canada Petroleum Co completed its $5.5-billion purchase of Dome. In 1973 and again in 1994, Gallagher donated funds for the Gallagher Library of Geology and Geophysics at the U of Calgary. He became an Officer of the Order of Canada in 1983, and a Fellow of the Arctic Institute of North America in 1999. ● JOEL TRENAMAN

GALT, George Frederick, businessman, sportsman (b March 1, 1855, Toronto; d April 15, 1928, **Winnipeg**). Galt came from an illustrious family: he was the grandson of **Scots** novelist John Galt; nephew of Sir Alexander Tilloch Galt, federal minister of finance and high commissioner to the UK; and son of John Galt Jr, registrar of Huron Cty. George was educated at Galt Collegiate Institute, in Galt, Canada West (now Cambridge, ON). The town Galt was named for John Sr, who had founded Guelph (ON). George came W, initially to Drumheller, AB, to invest in coal: by the 1870s, his uncle, Sir Alexander, and his cousin, Elliot T. Galt, set up the North Western Coal and Navigation Company to mine coal in the Lethbridge area. George moved to Winnipeg in 1882 to found, with cousin John Galt, the wholesale house of G. F. and J. Galt, whose subsidiaries included Blue Ribbon Manufacturing Company, a spice, coffee, and tea distributor. Blue Ribbon, which was housed at 87 King St in Winnipeg, also published a cookbook that went through more than 30 editions. The Galt Block, at the corner of Princess and Bannatyne, still stands. In 1883, he started the Winnipeg Rowing Club, for which he also captained and rowed ably. He later founded the Royal Lake of the Woods Yacht Club, in Kenora, ON, as well. He helped establish **Great-West Life**, and was president of the Winnipeg General Hospital (see **Health Sciences Centre**), of the Manitoba Curling Assoc, and of the Manitoba Red Cross Society. He was also a member of the **HBC**'s Cdn committee. In 1923, he helped **William Forbes Alloway** expand the banking firm of Alloway & Champion into SK, and in 1924, he hosted Edward, Prince of Wales (King Edward VIII), in his Wellington Cres home. He was married to Margaret, and the couple had 4 daughters and 1 son. A rowing trophy at the Royal Canadian Henley Regatta bears Galt's name. ● AJL

GAMBLERS FIRST NATION, on reserve pop 52, off reserve pop 100, is located 128 km NW of **Brandon.** This First Nation signed Treaty 4 in 1874. The native language here is Cree. It is a member of the West Region Tribal Council. The Gamblers First Nation community consists of 2 reserves: the Gambler IR No. 63 and the Treaty 4 Reserve Grounds IR No. 77. There are no schools in Gamblers First Nation, so young people in the community attend schools in nearby **Binscarth** or **Russell**. This community has an all-weather road access with full bus service. The economic activity of the Gamblers First Nation is based on farming. ● RK

GAMBLING is among the earliest forms of entertainment and remains a common pastime in most cultures, though some religious authorities prohibit it. Artifacts dating to 2300 BC confirm that various forms of gambling existed in ancient China, India, and Rome. Gambling was also part of First Nations cultures, including those in what is now MB, for at least 1000 years before European contact; gambling and games of chance were often played during festivals and ceremonies. Gambling's allure and addiction lies in the psychological gratification of competitors' trying to outwit their opponents, combining elements of both skill and luck. There has always been a physical connection between gamblers making their bet or move and the anticipation of material loss or gain.

MB, like many other Cdn provinces, has itself been "rolling the dice" with increasing involvement in regulating, managing, and profiting from gaming. The govt's substantial gaming revenues have been used to support social and economic development. However, this gain has not been without social costs – as more people are becoming addicted to gaming activities, the question remains, "Is it worth it?"

Historically, few gaming activities were regulated in MB. Most were under-the-table, contrary to the *Criminal Code*. However, in the 1980s, the MB govt took a more active role in promoting gaming as a revenue source to address increasing deficits. The Manitoba Lotteries Foundation was created in 1984. Two years later, the **Winnipeg Convention Centre** was named the permanent site for seasonal casinos in MB. In 1989, the Crystal Casino opened in **Winnipeg's Fort Garry Hotel**, becoming Canada's first permanent casino. By 1993, 2 large casinos were built in Winnipeg, and video lottery terminals (VLTs) had been distributed to licensed beverage premises throughout the province. Later that year, the govt formed a crown corporation, the **Manitoba Lotteries Corporation** (MLC), which would have complete control over all casinos and gaming in the province. Ironically, growing public concerns over gambling addiction also prompted, indeed necessitated, the creation of the Addictions Foundation of Manitoba (AFM). The AFM had

The MLC operates the McPhillips Street Station and the Club Regent casinos in Winnipeg.

as a mandate to address addictions associated with gambling. This evolved into a responsible gaming model, later adopted by other provinces. In 1997, the independent Manitoba Gaming Control Commission was created to regulate and control gaming activity in MB. In 2005, the MLC generated $271 million, almost 5% of provincial revenue. In spite of increased competition from gaming venues outside of MB, and the negative effects of a smoking ban introduced in 2003, gaming revenues continue to contribute significantly to provincial coffers. It is often said that govt is addicted to gaming and it is understandable when you consider the money donated in the form of unconditional grants to MB municipalities, rural and urban economic-development initiatives, and allocations to health care, to education, and to community and social services. In 2005, the economic contribution was almost $350 million, with over 2000 jobs directly supported by MLC activities, and $51 million in total tax income generated.

Not everyone wins. In a 2002 survey based on the Canadian Problem Gambling Index scores, 1.1% of adult Manitoban respondents were problem gamblers, 2.3% were moderate risk gamblers, and an estimated 3.4% may have been experiencing problems related to their gambling. In 2004-05, the Addictions Foundation of Manitoba Problem Gambling Helpline received 2908 calls, of which 1750 were calls for help. That same year, the AFM Rehabilitation programs admitted 543 clients, 86% of whom were seeking help for their own gambling; the rest were concerned about someone else's gambling. Revealingly, over 70% found VLTs most problematic. VLTs are among the most addictive forms of gambling because they offer gamblers a fast, highly stimulating rate of play. This faster play means that players make more bets and lose greater amounts of money

more quickly. VLTs are often referred to as the "crack cocaine" of gambling. The 2002 Canadian Community Health Survey on Mental Health and Well-being found that 25% of VLT players are at-risk problem gamblers. MB has a higher proportion of at-risk gamblers than any other province at 9.4%, largely attributable to the highest VLT participation rates in the country; among the highest casino participation rates; and above-average Aboriginal populations.

MB's First Nations have a special stake in the development of gambling operations. Aboriginal gaming in Canada began in 1984 when the **Opaswayak Cree Nation** held a federally sanctioned lottery. The lottery was later halted when regulation of gaming in First Nations communities became a provincial responsibility. Aboriginal communities have since been frustrated with the govt; after all, many Aboriginal gatherings included such games. More importantly, opportunities for economic development are considerable.

Internet gambling is rapidly setting gaming on an entirely different course. It allows anyone with a computer and credit card to gamble at any hour. According to a 2003 report in *Rolling Good Times*, a gambling information website, Canada is the top country for designing and providing gaming software, notwithstanding that operating an Internet gaming site in Canada is illegal. Govts face new challenges regulating offshore online casinos, and new legal, technological, and political solutions will have to be crafted to protect Canadians from the risks posed by Web gambling.

Internet gambling presents a particular concern for young people. In a 1999 study, 8% of youth were identified as at-risk for problem gaming, and 3% were identified as problem gamblers. More troubling was that 75% of adolescents viewed gambling as "potentially dangerous" compared with alcohol (60%), tobacco (64%), and

263

narcotics (75%). In a 2005 high school study, the AFM found 38% of students in grades 7-12 reported gambling in the past year. Youth interest in video gaming, coupled with the rapid growth of online gambling, makes this group potentially the most vulnerable.

The benefits and costs of govt-regulated gaming are complex. Aside from costs relating to addiction, govt-operated lotteries and gaming represent a form of regressive taxation, insofar as costs of gambling are often borne by those least able to afford it. However, financial benefits to govt make it unlikely that the govt will withdraw from the business. Regardless of the role govt plays in gaming, one thing remains certain: gambling is an integral part of our culture.
● BRENDA PROSKEN

GARDEN HILL FIRST NATION, on reserve pop 3507, off reserve pop 352, is situated on the N shore of Island Lake, 610 km NE of **WINNIPEG**. Until 1969, Garden Hill First Nation was a member of the Island Lake Band, which also included **WASAGAMACK, ST. THERESA'S POINT,** and **RED SUCKER LAKE FIRST NATIONS**. Garden Hill is signatory to Treaty 5. The native language here is Oji-Cree, the Island Lake dialect. Despite the remoteness of Garden Hill, English is commonly spoken here. The First Nation has several reserves – the Island Lake IR, Garden Hill First Nation, Pe-ta-wayga-mak IR, Seeseep Sakahikan IR, and Wesha Kijay Wasagamich IR. Schooling in Garden Hill goes from Nursery-Grade 12, and total enrolment for the year 2003-04 was 710. Garden Hill First Nation administers its own schooling. Transportation to the Garden Hill First Nation is limited to a winter road, an airstrip that runs from nearby Stevenson Island, and boat and float plane docks. The economic foundation of the Garden Hill First Nation is trapping and commercial fishing. In April 2006, this community had more than a dozen active cases of **TUBERCULOSIS**. Mike Birch, of the Garden Hill First Nation community, was the founder of the First Nations Buying Group, an Aboriginal business association that combines Canada's First Peoples for improved purchasing power. Closely associated with the First Nation is the non-treaty community of Island Lake (pop 59). ● RK

GARDINER, Charles Robert "Chuck," hockey goaltender (b Dec 31, 1904, Edinburgh, Scotland; d June 13, 1934, **WINNIPEG**) was one of the best goalies of his time, though his career was cut short by his premature death soon after leading the Chicago Black Hawks to their first Stanley Cup. Gardiner came to Winnipeg at the age of 7, and proved himself a prodigious athlete, playing goal for the **SELKIRK** intermediate team when he

was just 14. He began playing senior hockey with the Selkirk Fishermen in 1924, followed by one season with the Winnipeg Maroons in 1926-27 before being taken on by the fledgling Chicago Black Hawks. Though initially signed as back-up goalie, Gardiner proved himself worthy of more play in his rookie term with a 2.85 goals-against average and 3 shutouts. His game improved over the following seasons and in 1932, he was awarded the Vezina Trophy. Though Gardiner was battling intense headaches, an early warning sign of the brain hemorrhage that would kill him, he convinced coach Lionel Conacher to let him play in the final game of the 1934 Stanley Cup playoffs. In large part because of Gardiner's performance in goal, the Black Hawks overtook Detroit 1-0. He returned home to Winnipeg after the victorious game, and died a short time after. Over his brief 7 years in the NHL, Gardiner played 316 games with 42 shutouts and an average of 2.02 goals-against. He was voted into the Hockey Hall of Fame in 1957. ● MD

GARDINER, Herbert Martin "Herb," hockey player (b May 10, 1891, **WINNIPEG**; d Jan 11, 1972, Philadelphia). Gardiner reached the pinnacle of his career rather late in life, at the age of 36, but proved himself a seasoned and consistent player in professional play. Before playing pro hockey, Gardiner worked for the **CPR** and served in WWI. Upon his discharge, he signed with the Calgary Tigers in 1921-22, playing defence with fellow Manitoban **MERVYN "RED" DUTTON**. The defensive duo helped the Tigers win the 1924 Western Canada Hockey League championship. In 1926, he joined the Montreal Canadiens, and his performance earned him the Hart Memorial Trophy the following year. Already 35, Gardiner was past his peak years, and he played just 2 full seasons in the NHL. He then coached Philadelphia's first professional team. He was inducted into the Hockey Hall of Fame in 1958. ● MD

GARMENT MANUFACTURING is a vibrant industry that began production in MB at the turn of the 20th century. **JEWISH** immigrants from eastern Europe who came to the province with little English and little formal education were the catalyst to this industry. Their work ethic was fuelled by their need to survive and their desire to be successful in their new environment. This spawned several companies that made a variety of clothing items, including workwear for Western farmers and coats and jackets, notably bison coats for the Winnipeg Police.

One of the earliest such firms was the Dominion Garment Company, whose specialty was leather garments and bison coats. Others, like the

Monarch Overall Company, S. Stall & Son, Jacob & Crowley, Freed & Freed, soon followed. WWI led to high demand for military clothing of all types, and the **WINNIPEG** apparel industry played an important role in the war effort.

The years between the world wars saw the Winnipeg industry grow with the steady immigration to and development of western Canada. The industry imported fabrics and supplies from eastern Canada, the US, and Europe, and manufactured garments for distribution throughout the West. Large wholesale companies – such as McLeods, Robinson Little, Gaults, and Marshall Wells – became major customers of the many Winnipeg apparel manufacturers. The Timothy **EATON** Co. had its Western headquarters and a large mail-order facility in Winnipeg. It owned a garment manufacturing facility in Winnipeg, but also relied on the growing local apparel industry, which included newcomers like Peerless Garment, Western Glove, Rice Sportswear, United Garment, Junior Wear, Canadian Garment, Rich-lu, Olympic Pant, Crown Cap, and many others. The primary products manufactured at the time were work clothing, including denim and cotton twill pants and overalls. (Jeans were then considered workwear.) Warm winter jackets, parkas, leather jackets, and outerwear, all essential for Prairie living, were manufactured in Winnipeg, whereas fashion apparel was imported.

Immigration was the primary labour source for the industry; it grew with the population increase throughout western Canada. The apparel industry's infrastructure of support trades, including quilters, knitters, specialized cutters, accessory and trimming suppliers, fur suppliers, equipment suppliers, and service companies, all developed to create an "industry cluster" that gave the apparel industry lasting viability. The competition between manufacturers made certain that the challenge to improve was ever-present. The result was a viable industry with deep roots and a solid base of skilled and hard-working tradespeople.

With the start of WWII came another war effort that commanded the support of Winnipeg's apparel manufacturing industry. While men (and a few women) went to war, women worked in the factories. As a result, the Winnipeg industry continued to do all it could not only to supply Canada's military apparel needs but also to make whatever it could from the scarce civilian fabrics available to meet the needs of western Canadians.

At the end of WWII, another wave of immigration swelled the ranks of the industry. With the war effort over, civilian demands grew, and with them, the industry flourished. During the postwar period, there came an expansion in the scope and capability of the Winnipeg industry. Fashion entered the scene, and trade between eastern and western Canada became more 2-way than before the war. To workwear, the industry added fashion to attract buyers from all over Canada. In the late 1950s, The Monarch Overall Company became Monarch Wear, and Blue Jeans became TK's. Other companies, including Sterling Cloak, Jacob Fashions, Stall Sportswear, Panther Pant, and Victoria Leather, became established in the fashion side of Winnipeg's bustling apparel industry.

The industry experienced sustained growth throughout the 1950s and into the early 1960s. With the further development of commercial airlines, faster and better transportation and communication to E Cdn, US, and European markets, the Winnipeg industry faced increased competition and added pressures. The 1962 commission (TEDCO) of the MB govt that forecast the path of the provincial economy into the 1980s labelled MB's apparel businesses a "sunset industry." The govt felt the industry would not survive into the 1980s because it had no "real economic base" in the province, being distant from the major markets of both customers and suppliers, and had a small population from which to draw its labour resources. However, the industry did survive – in fact, it thrived and continued to expand. New companies like Gemini Fashions, Tan Jay, Standard Knitting, and Wescott Fashions – all creations of the late 1960s and early 1970s – became fashion and function powerhouses that continued into the 21st century. Older firms such as Western Glove changed their product lines from gloves to fashion jeans and sportswear. New management with degrees in commerce, law, accounting, engineering, and design took over from their more trade-skill-oriented predecessors in the industry.

The TEDCO economists and accountants who predicted gloom for the industry in 1962 did not consider the "hummingbird capabilities" of the Winnipeg industry nor the competitive advantage created by the cluster of manufacturers with its work ethic and extensive infrastructure. Satellite factories to the Winnipeg industry were established elsewhere in MB, including **Winkler**, **Steinbach**, **Miami**, **Altona**, and **Morden**. From 1976-81, the industry grew by 86% in jobs (from 6000 to over 11,000 workers), and became the 2nd-largest manufacturing employer in the province.

In 1982, Canada liberalized trade with low-cost, less-developed countries including Korea, Taiwan, Hong Kong, Malaysia, Indonesia, and so on. Offshore competition proved formidable, but the MB industry continued to adapt with better design, marketing, branding, and service capabilities. Foreign competition, however, began

taking its toll, notwithstanding all the effort of the industry "hummingbirds." Some of the largest and most successful companies in Winnipeg went out of business.

The survivors continued to adapt – Tan Jay became Nygard, Western Glove kept its name but moved further into the fashion jean business, Gemini began manufacturing offshore, Standard Knitting became Tundra, and Peerless Garments specialized in high-tech military garments for Cdn and NATO forces. The industry continues, but the number of jobs has decreased steadily with the implementation of a World Trade Organization agreement to remove all apparel quota restrictions on Jan 1, 2005.

Currently, the MB industry exists almost exclusively in Winnipeg, and most of the surviving companies have a major part of their production done offshore in developing countries in order to remain competitive and viable. The apparel industry continues to be an important part of the MB economy, employing 5000 people. The challenges of world competition and a global market continue to be met by MB's apparel entrepreneurs. While trade patterns, pushed by global economics, cause serious disruptions and changes in the industry, the 100-plus-year history of dealing with all types of vicissitudes has prepared the industry for survival well into the 21st century. ● GARY T. STEIMAN

GARSON, pop 350, is a community 45 km NE of **Winnipeg** on hwy 44. Incorporated in 1915 and originally known as Lydall, the village was renamed in 1927 to honour William Garson, who opened a limestone quarry in the area. William was the father of **Stuart S. Garson**, premier of MB (1943-48) and federal minister of justice (1948-57). A **CPR** point and post office were established here in 1902. Garson's limestone, known as **Tyndall stone**, is considered to be of the highest quality. The parliament buildings in Ottawa and the MB **Legislative Building** were both built using limestone from Garson. The stone quarry is the village's largest

employer. Otherwise, the economy relies on tourism and services, and some locals commute to Winnipeg. For recreation, village residents enjoy an arena, soccer and baseball fields, a playground, and a village drop-in centre. The village's largest tourist attraction is the Garson Sportfishing Park, which attracts anglers year round with stocked ponds and heated ice-fishing shacks. Since 2003, Garson gave up self-administration and became a part of the RM of Brokenhead. ● GPP

GARSON, Stuart Sinclair, lawyer, politician, premier (b Dec 1, 1898, St. Catharines, ON; d May 5, 1977, **Winnipeg**). Garson's father, William Garson, was a Liberal MPP in Oliver Mowat's ON govt. In 1901, the Garson family moved to MB, and William founded Garson Quarries, which extracted **Tyndall Stone** near **Garson**. That community was named for the elder Mr. Garson's quarrying enterprise. At a young age, Stuart was struck by polio, which left him with a permanent weakness in one leg. His father died in 1911, when Stuart was still young. The family business failed shortly thereafter, and, to support his family, Garson worked as a delivery boy, a summer guide at Lake of the Woods, and a farmhand during harvests. Because of the effects of the polio, Garson did not serve in WWI. He obtained his law degree from the **U of M** and was called to the bar in 1919. He practised law in **Ashern** from 1919-28.

Premier **John Bracken** recruited Garson in 1927 to run for the Progressives in that year's provincial election. He won the riding of Fairford by an 85-vote margin and held the riding until 1948. Although he did not enter Cabinet until 1936, he held a number of other influential positions. In 1932, he became chairman of a committee investigating the closing of the Provincial Savings Office, and in 1933, he chaired both the Metropolitan Mass Transportation and Private Bills committees. In the same year, he married Emily Topper, the daughter of F. E. Topper, the founder of Topper Grain Company in Winnipeg.

Distinctive Manitoba Tyndall stone is actually quarried in Garson, not nearby Tyndall.

Garson, who was already building a reputation for being careful with the public purse, became treasurer in 1936. The **GREAT DEPRESSION** had brought many provinces, including MB, to the brink of financial collapse, which led Bracken and Garson to pressure Ottawa for funds. This led to the establishment in 1937 of the Royal Commission on Dominion-Provincial Relations, also known as the Rowell-Sirois Commission. According to civil servant **JACK PICKERSGILL**, Garson was the "father of equalization," mainly through his presentations to the commission. In 1942, Ottawa entered into an arrangement with the provinces that involved transfer payments between the federal and provincial govts. This served as a precursor to the 1946 agreement between Ottawa and MB (and some other provinces) that allowed Ottawa to collect taxes while making fiscal transfers to the provinces, providing pensions, and offering support for developing frontier and **MINING** regions. Added to this was the cancellation of half the province's debt to the federal govt. Historian **W. L. MORTON** claimed that the new federal-provincial fiscal arrangements garnered approximately $5.5 million in annual revenues for MB.

Stuart Garson, 1941

In the 1940s, Garson continued to serve as treasurer as well as chairman of the Manitoba Power Commission (1940) and as minister of telephones (1941). The most notable moment in his career occurred when Bracken left provincial politics to become leader of the federal Progressive Conservative party. Chosen by the **LIBERAL**-Progressive caucus to be their new leader in Dec 1942, Garson was sworn in as premier on Jan 14, 1943. Under Garson's leadership, the **CONSERVATIVES** and Social Credit continued to support the Liberal-Progressive-led governing coalition Bracken had established, though the already disenchanted **CCF** soon left the coalition.

As wartime conditions abated, the provincial economy underwent a number of changes. This included an increasingly productive agriculture sector, the establishment of new industries, and developments in northern mining. A major challenge was to find a way to provide power to rural Manitoba. In 1941, only 480 farmers had Manitoba Power Commission lines. To address this problem, in 1946 the government established a rural electrification program. The program successfully connected 20,000 farms to the grid by 1950. The effects of electrification cannot be understated – it allowed farm families to use electrical motors for farm work, and connected rural areas to the world through radio and, later, television.

In the 1945 federal election, Garson expressed his support for Mackenzie King's Liberals against his former boss Bracken's Progressive Conservatives. At the 1948 national Liberal convention, some viewed Garson as a potential new leader for the national party. However, he withdrew his candidacy to support Louis St. Laurent. Garson resigned as premier the same year, and was sworn in as St. Laurent's new Minister of Justice and Attorney General on Nov 15, 1948. Garson became MP for Marquette in a Dec 20, 1948, by-election, and served as Solicitor General (1950-52), chairman of the Committee of Attorneys General (1950), and chairman of the Canadian delegation to the 1952 UN meeting in Paris. Following electoral defeat in 1957, he returned to law, practising in Winnipeg with Johnston, Garson, Forrester, Davison, and Taylor. In 1971, he became a Companion of the Order of Canada. • CHRIS ADAMS

GASTROTRICH is a common microscopic creature of the phylum Gastrotricha, found in all MB's freshwater environments – puddles and marshes to lakes and sandy beaches, but less so in streams and rivers. There are marine species as well, living in the spaces between the sand grains below the intertidal zone of **HUDSON BAY**. Gastrotrichs are seldom noticed because of their small size (<.5 mm). A gastrotrich consists of a head and arched trunk, covered with scales and numerous bristles or spines, and ending in 2 projections (furca). The ventral surface is flattened and lined with cilia (tiny hairs) on which the animal glides smoothly over aquatic plants and the bottom detritus of ponds and lakes. On occasion they leap with the aid of the long spines, or swim freely. They can also temporarily cement themselves to a support by means of secretions from the furca. Using a long proboscis, they suck up and devour bacteria, algae, diatoms, and protozoans. Beating cilia can create currents that also bring food items into the mouth. All freshwater gastrotrichs are apparently female, reproducing

parthenogenically, however it is possible that males may be discovered. A female produces only 1-5 large eggs in her lifetime, and these can withstand desiccation, freezing, high temperature, and a 2-year or longer dormancy. About 430 species are known worldwide; over 66 in NA. Species of *Chaetonotus* are found in MB and on all habitable continents. • REW

GEESE. *See* **WATERFOWL**.

GENDIS INC. is a publicly-traded, Winnipeg-based holding company whose majority shareholder is Alexander Prospects (1998) Inc., the investment arm of the **ALBERT COHEN** family of Winnipeg. Albert Cohen and his father, Alexander, founded General Distributors in 1934 as an importing and distribution firm. The company branched out into the retail sector 12 years later with the launch of the first SAAN (Surplus Army, Air Force, Navy) junior department store in Winnipeg. In the years that followed, the Cohen family built Gendis into a corporate powerhouse in Canada. By the mid-1980s, the firm's diversified portfolio of holdings included not only the SAAN chain, but also the Metropolitan, Greenberg, and Pomme Rouge (Red Apple) family clothing and junior department store chains; a 51% share in Sony Canada; and a variety of real estate and energy-industry holdings, including a 33% stake in Chauvco Resources Ltd. (a Calgary oil and gas company) and a 50% share in MB-based Tundra Oil and Gas. Although the company had always been profitable, its fortunes took a turn for the worse in 1995 with the bankruptcy of its Metropolitan and Greenberg chains. That led to the company recording its first annual loss, which was followed by even bigger losses in the following few years. That forced the company to begin selling off many of its oil and gas holdings, including the shares in Chauvco, Tundra, and Pioneer Natural Resources. By that time, its SAAN chain was also losing money, and after several unsuccessful attempts to sell it and a failed bid to turn it around, Gendis finally found a buyer for the chain in late 2004. The sale of SAAN reduced Gendis to a mere shadow of its former self. By mid-2005, its holdings consisted of 2.5 million shares in Fort Chicago Energy Limited Partnership, which owned a 50% stake in the $4.6-billion Alliance Pipeline (which runs from northern Canada to Chicago), and a 42% share of the $550-million Aux Sable Natural Gas Extraction Plant near Chicago; 50,000 shares in Opti Canada Inc., an AB firm which developed a new method for extracting oil from oil sands; 8 commercial real estate properties; a small amount of cash; and the company's Winnipeg headquarters/distribution centre. However, with the company once again turning a profit, Albert Cohen vowed to begin rebuilding it by expanding its holdings in the real estate and energy sectors. ● MURRAY MCNEILL

GENETIC ENGINEERING is the term that best describes the scientific alteration of natural life, generally for commercial purposes. Sometimes referred to as **BIOTECHNOLOGY** or genetic modification (GM), this process involves transferring a gene from one species to another in a manner that would not occur naturally. **WINNIPEG** is a centre of this emerging technology with the Cdn headquarters of Monsanto, the world's largest developer of engineered crops, located in the city. The company pursues crop research at the **U OF M**'s Smartpark in conjunction with university scientists.

Genetic engineering became possible as a result of recombinant DNA technology developed in the 1980s. It evolved into a scientific process that has been driven by the globalized corporate sector. The technology has been applied especially in agriculture, resulting in the arrival of the first engineered crops in 1996. Canada has consistently been a promoter of genetic engineering. Ten years after the introduction of the new crops – mainly corn and **CANOLA** – into the commercial marketplace, Canada is a world leader in GM production. And MB is a key player, with many farmers supporting the purported cost benefits of genetic engineering. For example, about 70% of the canola grown in MB is engineered to withstand the effects of a broad-spectrum herbicide like Monsanto's Roundup. This is accomplished (also for herbicide-resistant corn, cotton, and soybeans) by importing a gene from a tiny organism that lives in the soil.

The biotechnology industry launched its foray into the world of genetic engineering with talk of how nature could be improved and how global hunger could be eradicated by inventing more nutritious foods. However, the technology has focused primarily on creating crops that would be commercially successful for farmers in the industrialized world and, by extension, for corporate shareholders.

Although there have been no documented incidents of genetic engineering in food causing health problems, there has been evidence of environmental harm. "Genetic pollution" has become a commonly used phrase to describe how test-tube genes are spreading to nature's own plants, undermining natural diversity. In 2007, 2 SK organic farmers were attempting to launch a class action suit claiming engineered canola had contaminated their fields. ● INGEBORG BOYENS

▸ *See also* **BIOTECHNOLOGY**.

GEOGRAPHY OF MANITOBA
by John Welsted and John Everitt

The geography of Manitoba is more varied than many people think. Known as the "Keystone Province," Manitoba is close to the centre of NA. It extends from the US border at 49°N – the same latitude as both Vancouver and Paris – to 60°N, the same latitude as northern Labrador, Oslo, and St. Petersburg. It has geometric boundaries with its neighbours: NU, to the N; SK, to the W; the US (MN and ND), to the S; and ON, to the E. Only its northeastern border, the shore of **HUDSON BAY**, is natural. Its present size and shape evolved from the original "Postage Stamp Province" of 1870. Carved from the NWTs, this covered only a small part of the centre of today's province S of **LAKE WINNIPEG**. Expansion in 1881 extended the province N to 52° 50′ N (just S of Long Point in Lake Winnipeg) and E and W to today's ON and SK borders. Finally, in 1912, the present form was reached with a northern boundary at 60°N and an arbitrary northeastern border with ON that gave MB access to **HUDSON BAY**.

STAN MILOSEVIC, WWW.MANITOBAPHOTOS.COM

Clear Lake in Riding Mountain National Park

At 650,087 km², MB is the 6th-largest province in Canada (though 2 of 3 territories are larger than it), and has the 5th-largest population, with 1,148,401, as of the 2001 Census. France, which covers about the same area, has a population of just over 61 million. MB is the most easterly of the Prairie Provinces, but much of it is underlain by the Canadian Shield (*see* **PHYSIOGRAPHIC REGIONS**) and over 15% is inland water. The early-1970s licence-plate slogan "100,000 Lakes" is not an overstatement. Some of the **LAKES** are large: Lake Winnipeg is Canada's 6th-largest lake; **LAKE WINNIPEGOSIS**, 11th, and **LAKE MANITOBA**, the 13th. Parts of central and northern MB are a bewildering maze of bush and water that inspires admiration for the directional sense of First Nations travellers as well as the European explorers and early settlers who penetrated the province from the N.

GEOLOGY: The province consists of rocks that span the whole range of ages in the geological column. In the N, the Precambrian rocks of the Canadian Shield include some of the world's oldest, and some that contain rich ore deposits, the basis for several northern **MINING** settlements. The Shield's sharp southern boundary runs E-W just S of **FLIN FLON** and then

S along the E side of Lake Winnipeg. It is a dividing line between 2 areas with contrasting natural and cultural landscapes, historical evolutions, types of resource uses, and settlement systems. In contrast, the transition from the Shield to the Hudson Bay Lowlands – underlain by Palaeozoic rocks – in the NE features gentle topography and vegetation. In the SW, the bedrock is of the Palaeozoic, Mesozoic, and Cenozoic ages, decreasing in age to the SW, where the Tertiary rocks of Turtle Mountain are the youngest bedrock in the province. Westward-dipping, Cretaceous Age rocks have a sharply defined eastern edge along the **Manitoba Escarpment** with its "mountains" – Pembina Mountain, Riding Mountain, Duck Mountain, and the Porcupine Hills. These, together with Turtle Mountain, are the main upstanding landforms of "the south."

Today's land surface is a product of the latest Ice Age, 75,000-8000 years ago (*see* **Glaciation**), when what is now the province was entirely covered by ice. In the N, the main effect of the ice was erosional; loose surface sediments were scraped away to leave polished bare rock surfaces. In addition, sub-ice deposition left linear ridges (eskers) tens of km long, as well as more rounded landforms (drumlins). In the **Interlake** region, between Lake Winnipeg and lakes Winnipegosis and MB, ice erosion etched long, shallow NNW-to-SSE-trending grooves readily apparent on satellite images. Sediments eroded from the N mantle to the S, so that bedrock is now rarely visible at the surface. As the ice melted, its edge was at times stationary when forward movement within the ice was balanced by melting. At those times, ridges – called end moraines – were deposited at the ice front. Best known are the **Darlingford** moraine in the SW and S centre and **The Pas** moraine, which forms Long Point in Lake Winnipeg. Extensive areas are covered by hummocky ground moraine deposited beneath the ice. Eskers and drumlins are also found in the S but are not as obvious as in the N.

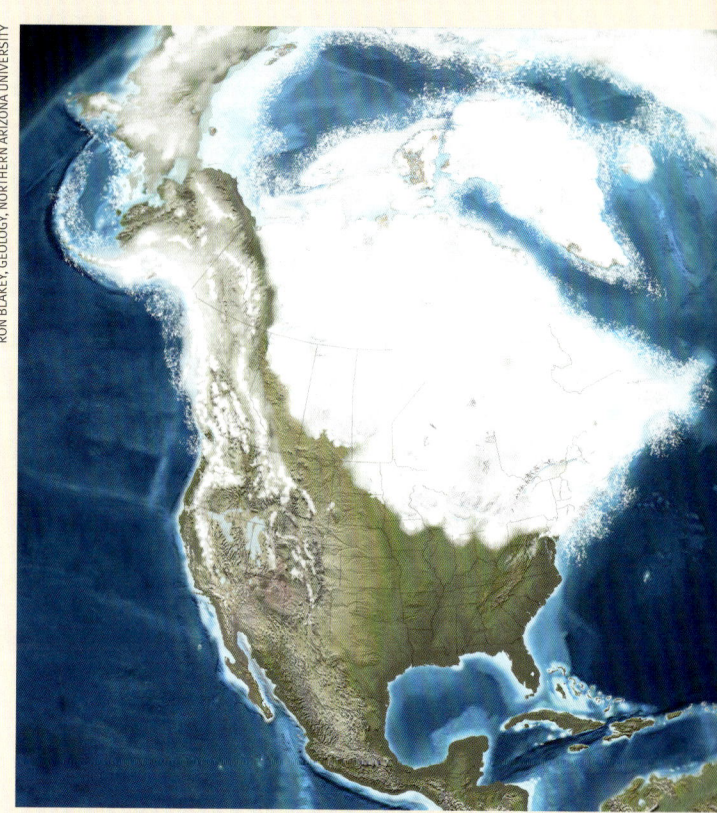

RON BLAKEY, GEOLOGY, NORTHERN ARIZONA UNIVERSITY

The Wisconsin ice sheet covered North America as recently as 12,000 years ago. When the ice retreated, the modern landscape appeared.

WATER: The legendary flatness of parts of the S results from the former existence of glacial lakes of which the present large lakes are remnants. Lakes resulted when ice in the N dammed northward-flowing rivers. They would rise until an outlet was found by which they would empty creating large, steep-sided, flat-floored valleys (spillways). **Lake Agassiz**, the largest, covered much of S-central MB. Sediments deposited on lake floors filled pre-existing hollows producing the flat land typified by the **Red River** Plain. Other indicators of the lakes are beaches deposited along former shores, deltas deposited where rivers entered the lakes (the largest is the **Assiniboine River** Delta fanning out E from **Brandon**), and spillways that carried water from one glacial lake to another: for example, the Qu'Appelle Valley, the Assiniboine Valley above Brandon, and the **Souris**-Pembina Trench. Spillways are spectacular gashes in otherwise flat terrain and may have been created quickly, perhaps in as little as weeks or months. In the NE, the Hudson Bay Lowlands were also recently below water – in this case, saltwater. The weight of the ice depressed Earth's crust, and when it melted, the sea flooded the depressed areas, forming shorelines. With the weight removed, the crust rose toward its former position, leaving behind staircases of former shorelines most visible N of **Churchill**, where some are 183 m above present sea level.

MB's geological history and its position on the North American continent result in it being "downstream from everybody else." Rivers enter from SK – the **Assiniboine**, Saskatchewan, **Churchill**, and Cochrane; from the US – the **Souris** and the **Red**; and from ON – the **Winnipeg**, Bloodvein, Berens, and Polar. Very rare are rivers that rise in MB and flow into another jurisdiction. This downstream location has its drawbacks; the province is vulnerable to **Pollution** resulting from the actions of upstream jurisdictions. Lake Winnipeg acts as a giant bathtub, collecting water from the W, S, and E and discharging it along the **Nelson River**, the outflow being controlled for maximum generating production for **Hydroelectricity**.

RON BLAKEY, GEOLOGY, NORTHERN ARIZONA UNIVERSITY

The late Cretaceous about 75 million years ago, showing the sea-water that covered much of the interior of North America.

CLIMATE: MB's continental location produces a **CLIMATE** of extremes, with low winter temperatures (in the S the Jan average is –12°C, and in the N, –23°C) and high summer temperatures (the July average in the S is 26°C, and in the far N, 17°C). Averages do not tell the whole story; the lowest ever recorded was –46.7°C and the highest 44.6°C, giving an extreme range of 91.3°C, a range rivalled by few places in the world. This temperature regime results in a short frost-free period, 115-125 days in southern MB, a challenge for **AGRICULTURE**; yet, by adopting the right crops, southern MB became one of the great agricultural regions of the world. Nor is the precipitation overly conducive to agriculture, with the S receiving only about 600 mm of precipitation a year. Droughts occur and, with recent crop diversification, irrigation has increased, especially in the **CARBERRY/PORTAGE LA PRAIRIE** area. Snow can occur in most months: in the S, only June, July, and Aug can be expected to be snow-free, while in the N, June is not exempt. Extremes occur; a blizzard in 1966 dumped 35.6 cm on **WINNIPEG** in a few hours, and on Feb 12, 1938, **MINNEDOSA** received 71.1 cm.

MB's great N-S extent results in several **ECOCLIMATIC REGIONS**. Whereas in the S, most of the natural vegetation has been removed for agriculture, much of the N remains in a near-natural state. Only small remnants of the tall-grass prairie and mixed-grass prairie remain in the S. Farther N were large areas of **ASPEN** parkland, also now mainly cleared, with islands of mixed woods on the "mountains." N of the parklands is a zone of mixed woods that gives way N and E of Lake Winnipeg to vast areas of northern coniferous forest dominated by **SPRUCE** trees. In the NE, this is replaced by open-lichen woodland and eventually by small areas of shrub tundra.

PEOPLE: Settlement of MB began soon after the ice retreated, with initial entry probably from the SW, since much of the S-centre and SE were covered by Lake Agassiz. When the first Europeans arrived, sparsely distributed First Nations groups inhabited the whole area. The principal groups in the central and southern forests and parklands were the Assiniboine (Nakota), **DAKOTA**, **CREE**, and **OJIBWAY**, with the **DENE** or Chipewyan in the far NW of MB. Other groups, including the Siouan-speaking Mandans and Gros Ventre (A'aninin), made occasional incursions to raid or trade. Fur companies brought in Iroquoian peoples from what is now ON and QC as voyageurs and hunters. Eventually, the depletion of animal resources and the introduction of new technology led to major social dislocation and upheaval within Aboriginal society. Events culminated in the reserve system fixed by treaties with the Cdn govt – although land claims resulting from these treaties are still being negotiated. The first European penetration was from the N with **FUR TRADING** posts and mission stations, beginning an important N-S orientation to activity in the region. Colonization began with the **LORD SELKIRK**'s settlers of the **RED RIVER SETTLEMENT**. They all followed the **HAYES RIVER** system to Lake Winnipeg and then S. Later **IMMIGRANTS**, attracted by the prospect of owning land, arrived from eastern Canada and the rest of the world in the late 19th century.

Since the beginning of European colonization, with the transformation of the grasslands and the parkland into productive agricultural regions and the establishment of a network of railway lines and service centres, the southern part of MB has become the demographic, economic, and political core of the province. The dominantly agricultural nature of this region has been reinforced and complemented by an industrial base, although this has tended to be mostly urban. Compared to the S of the province, the N has lagged behind in economic strength and development, especially in contrast to the early days of the fur trade, when European incursions originated along the shores of Hudson Bay and the large river and lake system draining to Hudson Bay.

With the building of the various trans-Cdn **RAILWAY** lines (initially the **CPR**, and later Canadian Northern and Grand Trunk Pacific) and the territorial evolution of the Dominion of Canada from "sea to sea," MB assumed a pivotal functional role as transportation link between E and W. This meant a clear reorientation of the transportation and economic linkages of the pre-Confederation, pre-railway era, during which the flows of people and goods had a distinct N-to-S trend. The railways influenced both the location of settlement and their internal configuration, with hundreds of Prairie communities having a similar plan. There was also a significant change in the rural cultural landscapes of the province with the implementation of the *Dominion Lands Act* with its distinctive section/township/range survey system, which was grafted onto the long-lot (seigneurial-system) landscape of the Red River Settlement.

This new agricultural settlement was superimposed on a region that had been Aboriginal and **MÉTIS**, for the most part. Early agricultural and urban settlers tended to come from ON and the UK, with some relocating from the US. But there were important minority groups, including early colonies of **MENNONITES**, **ICELANDERS**, and Scandinavians. Other early migrants came from QC and the Maritimes, often also settling as groups, but the new **FRENCH**-speaking settlement numbers never rivalled those of the Anglophones. From the 1890s, **UKRAINIAN** settlement began; this left an important imprint upon both urban and rural MB. Other eastern Europeans, such as Poles, Romanians, and Hungarians also arrived. Eastern European **JEWISH** pioneers tended to be urban, but at least one rural community (**BENDER HAMLET**, in the **INTERLAKE**) was set up. In most cases, chain migration was of considerable importance to growth of the culture groups, and this settlement process built a complex ethnic mosaic on the landscape. After 1917, other groups, such as the **HUTTERITES** – whose presence in MB has continued to increase in numbers, spatial distribution, and economic importance – supplemented it. In 2006, Old Order Mennonites from ON begun to settle in rural MB.

The 20th century also marked the opening up of MB's northern region, spurred by the discovery and large-scale exploitation of the key resources – **FORESTRY**, minerals, and **HYDROELECTRIC** power. In the wake of these developments, camps for workers and resource towns were quickly built, in either a planned or in an unplanned fashion. Some of these boom/bust towns soon declined or were abandoned after the exhaustion of the resources; when the major construction work was completed; or when the market price of minerals dropped drastically. The nickel-mining city of **THOMPSON** quickly expanded after the 1960s to become the major urban centre of northern MB and the 3rd-largest city in the province. Railway lines, highways, and air connections were also established to provide transportation links between the southern ecumene and the resource frontier. Although some northern towns have come and gone because of fluctuations in the mining industry (such as **LEAF RAPIDS**), others, including **FLIN FLON**, have persisted. One of the remarkable pioneer stories in transportation development of the N was the building of the **HUDSON BAY RAILWAY** and the foundation of the port of **CHURCHILL**.

Whereas 2 (or more) metropolitan centres characterize the other Prairie provinces, a single metropolis – Winnipeg – dominates and perhaps even overshadows MB. This city has a population of 633,461 (2006 Census) that is only 55% of the provincial total, although the Census Metropolitan Area has 60%. Even though the city has largely lost its major function as a gateway to western Canada, and the recent growth of Winnipeg has lagged behind that of most other western Cdn metropolitan centres, no other Prairie city exhibits the same level of urban primacy. By comparison, its nearest competitor, **BRANDON**, had a city population of 41,511 in 2006.

The trend toward population concentration in and around large cities during the 20th century is the result of several economic, social, and political adjustments and changes. Since the 1930s, the move toward larger farms, periodically occurring agricultural crises, and the lure of non-farm jobs have significantly reduced the number of farms. The reduction of rural infrastructures and services – justified based on an economic rationale that encouraged consolidation and concentration – eroded the attractiveness of rural living and the vitality of villages and small towns. Also, the decline of the economic and social viability of small settlements was spurred by the increased mobility of rural residents, by a dramatic expansion of private automobile ownership, by an improved road and highway network, and by the enhanced attractiveness of employment opportunities, shopping facilities, professional services, and entertainment choices in the larger centres. As these factors undermined the traditional service function of villages and small towns, they precipitated the exodus of people from these places. The sustainability of these non-metropolitan settlements remains a major challenge for the province.

CHARLES SHILLIDAY

Flat south-western Manitoba prairie stretches as far as the eye can see.

The present demographic and economic spatial patterns display a contrast between the contiguously, albeit sparsely, populated and economically dominant S and the economically weaker and more vulnerable N, with its patchy distribution of resources, towns, and First Nations communities. Many of the settlers 100 or more years ago came to MB lured by the prospect of establishing a farm, and the province still carries the image of widely dispersed farmsteads, small villages, and few towns. Nonetheless, the physiognomy of MB's present settlements is also characterized by the vertical growth of apartments and office buildings; by the sprawl of residential suburbs; by trailer parks, exurban estates, and cottages; and by industrial parks and large shopping complexes. Indeed, MB today is a highly urbanized province – in 2001, 71.9% of the population was urban – and agriculture and other resource-based industries account for only a small proportion of the provincial employment (8.4%) and GDP. Many of the remaining "rural" people have quasi-urban lifestyles because of better communications and transportation opportunities that make them more mobile and less isolated.

Immigration continues to be important, although today it mostly affects urban areas, particularly Winnipeg. Today's immigrants also come from new areas, such as **FILIPINOS** and those from other parts of Asia, as well as Latin America and the Caribbean, with chain migration still being important. Consequently, the face of MB is changing. As immigrants tend no longer to arrive as large, coherent cultural groups, and do not seek to establish "reserves" or other forms of group settlement along the lines of **NEW ICELAND**, they integrate more easily into the social fabric of Cdn society. Nevertheless, in Winnipeg, ethnic neighbourhoods populated largely by recent Latin American and Asian immigrants are noticeable. With the

drying-up of inflows of cultural groups that were significant in the past – for example, Ukrainians, Mennonites, Icelanders, and Scandinavians – the trend toward cultural assimilation and integration with a resulting loss of cultural identity for these groups has become more pronounced. This has led to a regrettable disappearance of a number of features of the material culture and to a disintegration of ethnic landscapes.

FUTURE: In spite of harsh environmental conditions and considerable constraints to the development of its resources, MB has a remarkable history of human achievements. However, the future of MB is uncertain. Its agriculture is changing, becoming more industrial, with wheat (and small grain) domination giving way, since the loss of the **CROW RATE**, to other forms of production. These newcomers include oilseed and other **SPECIALTY CROP** production, and increased cattle farming and, especially, hog farming (*see* **PORK INDUSTRY**). In addition, agricultural restructuring includes increasing off-farm employment, the performance of non-agricultural activities on the farm, and the addition of new commodities to existing farm operations. According to the Census, between 1996 and 2001, MB had a more-diversified agriculture than any other province. Its industrial base is important, particularly in urban areas, with manufacturing being significant; but as with mining, this industry continues to be subject to the fluctuations of external influences. Some of MB's industries are threatened by changing economic conditions, including the NAFTA deal with the US, but others, such as **TECHNOLOGY**, are growing.

The grain trade is still being reorganized as the old-style iconic crib **GRAIN ELEVATORS** disappear and the new huge concrete ones are fewer and farther between. In addition, companies continue to amalgamate, and new operations (some from the US) appear. Railway lines continue to disappear, or, in some cases, are converted to short-lines owned by non-traditional companies such as Denver-based OmniTRAX Inc. This company runs the old Hudson Bay line to Churchill, whose port is in a state of uncertainty. Although some suggest that **GLOBAL WARMING** might allow this settlement to achieve its long-promised status as inlet/outlet for the Prairies, the possible reorganization or elimination of the **CANADIAN WHEAT BOARD** might remove much of its shipping volume (80% is CWB grain) and remove its sustainability. Such a change would negatively affect most of MB N of The Pas. In addition, global warming will take its toll on the **WINTER ROADS** system that serves the North, causing greater instability of the roads and a shorter season for their use.

In addition to the rural depopulation of MB, the province's population is aging. Along with SK and Atlantic Canada, MB has one of the oldest average populations in the country, particularly in rural areas, as young people migrate out and the balance "age in place." The median age only remains as low as it does (36.8 years) because of relatively high birth rates in some of the immigrant groups, the Hutterites, and Aboriginal peoples. As a result, overall population growth is slow (0.5% from 1996-2001, compared to the national 4%), with most of the immigration that does occur being countered by emigration to other parts of the country (such as Alberta) that are perceived as more favourable. To counteract these changes, new occupations are being promoted, such as those associated with recreation and **TOURISM**. Tourism is arguably the largest industry in the contemporary world, but as with other industries, the wealth is unevenly distributed. Outsiders often see MB as a route rather than a destination, and although the landscape of the province is dotted with impressive **PROVINCIAL PARKS**, **RIDING MOUNTAIN** and **WAPUSK** national parks, and many other recreational offerings, the province still has challenges in attracting visitors. In the past few years, the rise of the Cdn dollar relative to its US counterpart has not helped this process. MB continues to live in interesting times. •

GEOLOGY. MB has a rich geological history, from some of the oldest rocks on earth to recent products of glacial processes that created most of its present day surface features. Rocks in MB form 3 natural groups based primarily on physical characteristics and age. The oldest date from the Precambrian Eon and contain an extremely diverse set of rock types, all of which have been recrystallized at high temperature and pressure deep within Earth's crust. These Precambrian rocks lie under the second group of sedimentary rocks that were deposited in the shallow seas covering the province throughout the Paleozoic and Mesozoic eras of the Phanerozoic Eon. Younger Cenozoic era sediments represent the 3rd natural group. These deposits are unconsolidated sediments that came from the continental GLACIATION of Pleistocene times.

PRECAMBRIAN: Ancient rocks in MB represent an almost astonishing record of early Earth. Over ½ of the 4.5 billion years of our planet's history is documented in MB's Precambrian rocks. They represent rocks formed from on the surface to depths as great as 25 km within the Earth's crust. The Precambrian is divided into 2 major eras Archean and Proterozoic, both well represented in MB. The Archean, Superior Geological Province consists of ancient rocks that formed into a continent roughly 2.7 billion years ago. The younger Proterozoic rocks of the Trans Hudson Orogen in northwestern MB formed from about 2.1 to 1.7 billion years ago.

ARCHEAN: The geological record of MB starts in the Precambrian Eon about 3.5 billion years ago in the eastern part of the Precambrian Shield in the Superior Province E and SE of THOMPSON. Ocean basins existed there then, with black-pillowed basaltic rocks being formed along ocean ridges much like those found in the Mid-Atlantic and Pacific today. Chains of volcanic islands known as island arcs were also being formed. Remnants of rocks formed during these times are preserved in long narrow belts called greenstone belts. Very old areas of continental granites are also present, indicating that some continents must have existed in the early Archean era. Geologic forces are imperceptibly slow but never idle and 2.7 billion year ago an event called an orogeny or mountain-building period began. During the next 60 million years, the forces that move continents were at work, moving various segments of the Earth's crust together to form the Superior Craton continent. In the process, high mountains were thrust up and great rivers ran through deep valleys. Gravel and sand deposited by these rivers are preserved in some of the greenstone belts. During this Kenoran Orogeny, many of the granitic rocks of the Superior Geologic Province were also formed deep in the crust. Under tremendous heat and pressure they, and the older granite and greenstone belts that they intruded, were metamorphosed beneath the high mountains. Thus, by the end of the Archean, 2.5 billion years ago, the Superior Geologic Province of MB had changed from the oceanic basin of some unnamed sea – similar to the East Indies of today – into a continent, with mountains along its western edge near where Thompson is now located. The eroded remains of this ancient mountain chain is preserved in the Precambrian Shield of western MB.

Limestone near Steep Rock has eroded into cliffs and caves.

PROTEROZOIC: There is evidence that a portion of the western edge of the Superior Geologic Province was rifted away westward about 2.2 billion years ago, creating an oceanic basin in the same way that the Atlantic Ocean opened and spread to separate the Americas from Africa and Europe. Within this new ocean, the cycle of ocean floor spreading, island arc development and sedimentation began again. The Thompson Nickel Belt was forming along the W coast of the old Archean Superior Province. The sands of the day were sitting on the granites and gneisses of the worn down mountains from the Kenoran orogeny about 600 million years before. Out in the seas to the W, deposits of mud and sand were building up on the bottom and new chains of volcanic islands were being formed in the basin. During this time, the FLIN FLON, LYNN LAKE, and Thompson ore deposits were being formed. Continents were again in motion and another old Archean continent to the N and W – the Rae-Hearne Geological Province – was closing in on the Superior Province. Just as India ran into Asia and pushed up today's Himalayas, this massive collision squeezed the Proterozoic sediments, volcanics, and ore deposits and created a chain of mountains during the Trans Hudson Orogen about 1.8 billion years ago. In the rolling outcrop areas NW of Thompson, the crustal roots of these eroded mountains are all that is left of this huge chain of mountains.

PHANEROZOIC: A long period of geological quiet occurred from about 1.7 billion years ago until the beginning of the Phanerozoic eon. During that time, the area that is now MB was eroded down to a relatively flat to undulating peneplain (almost-plain) located in the centre of the continent. Then the land sank and became the bottom of a shallow sea. Sediments deposited since have not been disturbed, except by periods of erosion when the land was above sea level. MB, unlike the mountainous areas of AB and BC, has not been disturbed by a more recent orogeny. This resulted in the preservation of abundant fossils and sedimentary features in rocks of the Paleozoic and Mesozoic eras.

PALEOZOIC: Paleozoic sedimentary rocks cover the Precambrian Shield in the Hudson Bay Lowland and southwestern MB. These rocks were formed in depressed areas in Earth's crust known as sedimentary basins. Two such basins influenced sedimentation in MB – the Hudson Bay basin, centred in Hudson Bay, and the Williston Basin, centred in northwestern ND. Within both basins, the Paleozoic rock strata dip gently toward their centres. These strata formed from about 570 million to 235 million years ago and are made up of limestones, dolomites, shales, sandstones, and some salt beds. The Williston Basin developed from the S as the seas advanced over the slowly subsiding Precambrian Shield. This advance of the sea, termed a transgression, left deposits of sandstone, (dominated by the quartz-rich sandstone of the Winnipeg Formation) as it flooded northward. As the Precambrian Shield continued to subside, sediments accumulated on the shallow bottom of the ancient sea at a rate that kept pace with the sinking of the crust. These sediments formed the dolomites and limestones of the Red River Formation. MB was near the equator then and the warm shallow seas teamed with newly developing life, resulting in the numerous fossils like corals, trilobites and brachiopods found in these rocks.

MESOZOIC: At the end of the Paleozoic era, the land rose. Shallow seas receded as the region was again raised above sea level and began to erode. This erosional surface was characterized by the development of sinkholes and caves in limestone and hills and valleys. Downward

BARTLEY KIVES

G

G

GEOLOGICAL TIME SCALE (selected highlights)

EON	ERA	PERIOD/EPOCH	BIOLOGICAL FEATURES	GEOLOGICAL EVENT IN MB
PRECAMBRIAN -4,500-543 million years ago (mya)\ Hadean Archean Proterozoic			First living things Algae, bacteria, land fungi Massive extinction	Hudsonian & Kenorian mountain bldg
PHANEROZOIC -543 mya-present				
	Paleozoic -543-251 mya			
		Ordovian -444-490 mya	First vertebrates Armoured, jawless fish Massive extinction event	Tropical seas
		Carboniferous -299-359 mya	First coniferous trees First reptiles, insects	Seas withdraw
	Mesozoic -251-65 mya			
		Triassic -200-251 mya	First mammals First dinosaurs First marine dinosaurs in MB Extinction event wipes out 35% of animal families	Shallow seas invade
		Cretaceous -65-145 mya	First flowering plants Last dinosaurs Extinction event	Meteorite strike at West Hawk Lake
	Cenozoic -65 mya-present			
		Paleocene Epoch -60-70 mya	First primates	Seas retreat
		Pleistocene Epoch -1.8 mya-10,000 ya	First true humans	Ice Age begins

movement of Earth's crust later led to a return of shallow seas and the accumulation of Mesozoic sediments on this surface from about 225 million to 65 million years ago. The contact between the eroded Paleozoic rocks is another example of an unconformity where rocks of intermediate ages are missing because of previous erosional cycles. Sediments deposited at this time came from the newly formed mountains in the W and are dominated by red siltstones, sandstones and shales as well as minor gypsum. With the return of the shallow seas, most of the species that had previously lived in the region returned, with some noteworthy exceptions, such as trilobites and graptolites, both of which were extinct by this time. However, fossils of large marine vertebrates, such as mosasaurs and plesiosaurs (*see* DINOSAURS, MARINE), occur in Mesozoic strata. This was the age of reptiles, and although fossils

of dinosaurs have not been found in the predominantly marine strata of MB, rocks of equivalent age to the W have abundant dinosaur remains. The possibility of finding fossil dinosaurs in southwestern MB remains.

CENOZOIC: Only a small part of MB contains rocks of early Cenozoic time, which began about 64 million years ago. Paleocene strata of the Turtle Mountain Formation are limited to a small cap on top of the Turtle Mountain in southwestern MB and consist primarily of fine sandy and silty shales. The past 55 million years has been a time of relative geological stability in central NA. The region was uplifted from the sea and became a flat plane. There was little sedimentation, and erosional patterns developed on these plains. Animal life diversified and flourished; dozens of species similar to those found on today's African plains were present. Grazing animals

such as horses and camels shared the grasslands with elephants, rhinoceroses, and tapirs. Fossil tortoises and alligators, which could not survive extended cold winters, indicate a warm climate. Carnivores, such as sabre-tooth cats and bears, found plenty of food on the plains. As the climate changed with the approach of the Ice Age, so did animal life. Woolly mammoths, bison, and other cold-tolerant species took the place of the savannah-dwelling species.

GLACIATION: During the last several-million years of the Pleistocene epoch, MB, along with much of the land in northern and southern latitudes, has been so cold that repeated advances of continental ice sheets covered vast areas. There have been numerous periods of GLACIATION, each lasting thousands of years. The most recent of these, termed the Wisconsinan, began about 75,000 years ago and ended 8000 years ago. The erosion and deposition from these episodes of glaciation and the significant sedimentary deposits formed by meltwater as the glaciers continued their slow, 3500-year process of melting and retreat are responsible for most of MB's present landscape. Features such as **Lake Agassiz** beach ridges, easily seen in the Agassiz and Sandilands Forest Reserves, our large and numerous lakes, the eskers and moraines underlying many northern routes such as Highway 10, the sand dunes of the **Carberry** area and the rich deposits of rocks and gravel found throughout the province (including in farmers' fields!) are all part of our rich heritage from past glaciers. ● TIM CORKERY

GERMANS have played a role in MB's history since Bavarian-born Prince Rupert of the Rhine (1619-82), cousin of King Charles II, became the **HBC**'s first governor in 1670. In 1817, 100 German and Swiss-German soldiers from the de Meuron and de Watteville regiments in **Lord Selkirk**'s employ protected the **Red River Settlement** and settled along "German Creek" (the present-day Seine) in St. Boniface, named for the Germans' patron saint, Winfried Bonifatius. About 200 Alsatian and Swiss settlers arrived in 1821, but left the settlement after the 1826 flood.

Of more lasting effect was the Germans' participation in the settlement of MB in the half-century after MB joined Canada in 1870. German immigrants were pushed from their home countries by increasing land shortages and pulled to the West by Cdn advertisements and letters sent by family and friends who had settled in MB. The immigrants were of diverse origins. Only 10% had been born in the German empire (so-called *Reichsdeutsche* or German nationals), including the immigration agent and land surveyor William Wagner (1820-1901), who wrote the first German-language publication on MB in 1872 and served as an MLA (1883-86). Most German immigrants, about 70%, were *Volksdeutsche* or ethnic Germans. They came from enclaves in eastern Europe settled by their ancestors in the 18th and 19th centuries, and formed settlements around their faith and church, like the 7000 **Mennonites** settling in southern MB in 1874-79. German **Lutherans**, **Roman Catholics**, Baptists, and Adventists from Russia's Black Sea and Volga regions, and Lutherans from the Ukrainian areas of Volhynia (Russia/Poland) and Galicia (Austria-Hungary), followed. About 20% of the German immigrants were second-or-later-generation Germans from the American Midwest, ON, and other places.

Germans continued to come to MB after 1900, but most now settled in SK and AB. Thus, by 1911, over half of MB's 35,000 Germans were Cdn-born. While German Catholics in MB, unlike in other Prairie provinces, did not establish rural settlements, Lutherans and Baptists lived amidst Mennonites or formed their own, small settlements, such as in **Beausejour**, **Brokenhead**, Thalberg, and **Whitemouth**, all E of **Winnipeg**; in Moosehorn and Grahamdale, in the **Interlake** region; in Waldersee, W of **Lake Manitoba**; and in **Inglis** and Friedfeld (Shevlin) on the SK border.

By 1911, ¼ of German Manitobans lived in urban centres, where they joined the industrial labour force, albeit often only temporarily to support their homesteads. Others established shops and businesses. Winnipeg's 9000 Germans concentrated S of the CPR tracks and in Point Douglas, and, after 1900, in the **North End** and Elmwood, where they formed Baptist, Lutheran, Catholic, **Evangelical**, and Reformed congregations with affiliated denominational immigrant aid societies. Like rural Mennonites, they established public bilingual and private German schools until their abolishment in 1916. They also built secular institutions to maintain their cultural heritage. The German Society of Winnipeg, still active today in its North End clubhouse, was founded in 1892 as a mutual benefit society and social club. Several other German clubs existed for shorter periods.

Among the contributors to the first German-language newspaper in MB, *Der Nordwesten* (1889-1969, circulation 25,000 in 1912), was **Frederick Philip Grove** (1879-1948), who lived in rural MB from 1912 to 1929, when he wrote *Settlers of the Marsh* (1925) and other novels. **Wilhelm Hespeler** (1830-1921), who had aided the initial Mennonite immigration, became the first German honorary consul for western Canada (1882-1908) and Speaker of the MB Legislature (1900-04).

Even before WWI, Anglo-Canadians increasingly identified German-speakers of diverse origins with the German empire. During and after the war, "Germans" were declared enemy aliens and forbidden to use German at school and in the press; recent immigrants had to register, and nationwide hundreds were interned and deported. Especially in the city, Germans were harassed, fired from jobs, and their clubs were vandalized and closed. In response, they organized self-help and kept a low profile. (*See* **Alien Question**.)

Tens of thousands of Germans immigrated to MB between 1923, when they were once again admitted into Canada (and recruited as "preferred immigrants" after 1927), and 1931, when Canada closed its borders because of the **Great Depression**. The **CPR** and **CNR**, in co-operation with denominational immigration agencies based in Winnipeg, brought Mennonite, Lutheran, and Catholic refugees from Russia; Catholics from the Banat (Romania, Hungary, Yugoslavia); and Sudeten Germans from Czechoslovakia to MB. A quarter of the 1920s German immigrants were *Reichsdeutsche*, including 100 Catholics from Westphalia and the Black Forest who built a short-lived co-operative settlement in Little Britain in 1927. By 1936, MB's 52,000 Germans made up 7% of the province's population.

Politically, German Manitobans were pro-Liberal and pro-labour, but never voted as a bloc, and elected few of their own as representatives. Although they had not played an active role in the **Winnipeg General Strike**, under the leadership of **Jacob Penner**, they established the communist German Workers and Farmers Assoc (1932-37), which had 2200 members nationwide. After the rise of the National Socialists in Germany, the German-Canadian Left warned the Cdn public about the Nazi movement, and, mostly in vain, lobbied the Cdn govt to admit Jewish refugees, many of whom were from Germany. Of the 5000 admitted, several hundred came to MB.

Ed Schreyer, whose family's origins are German, served as premier of Manitoba and governor general of Canada.

German-Canadian Nazi organizations had 3000 members nationwide. The German-Canadian Bund was the biggest, and catered to ethnic Germans. It had 2 active local groups in Winnipeg, and gained control of the "German Days" – summer festivals that had been held in MB since 1928 and which attracted up to 5000 Germans. The Bund was supported by prominent members of the Nazi Party (NSDAP), such as Winnipeg's German consuls, Heinrich Seelheim and Wilhelm Rodde, and Bernhard Bott, editor of a pro-Nazi paper in Winnipeg.

The Cdn govt disbanded these organizations in 1939 and interned some members. German Manitobans experienced less hostility than during the previous war, in part because the govt distinguished between Germans and Nazis. German Manitobans, including some Mennonites, served in the Cdn military.

Postwar German immigration began in 1947, with the immigration of German-Jewish displaced persons and ethnic German refugees. German nationals were once again admitted in 1950. Among the 318,000 Germans entering Canada in 1946-66, 75% were German-born; 9% came to MB. German immigration dropped significantly in the 1960s because of Canada's recession and West Germany's economic boom. By 1971, 123,000 Germans lived in MB.

Postwar immigrants were recruited as farm hands, miners, wood workers, and domestics, but soon moved from the countryside to towns and cities, and into manufacturing and service jobs. Half of all German Manitobans lived in Winnipeg, where many worked in the construction industry and some established successful businesses. Residential patterns shifted. Germans moved from the North End to North Kildonan, Elmwood, and the West End in the 1960s, and, from the 1970s, dispersed across the city and its suburbs. Politically, they continued to be mostly passive, although they helped elect German-Manitoban **EDWARD SCHREYER** as premier of MB (1969-77) and supported him as gov gen of Canada (1979-84).

Artists like H. Eric Bergman (1893-1958), composer **SOPHIE-CARMEN ECKHARDT-GRAMATTÉ** (1899-1974), the **WINNIPEG ART GALLERY** director **FERDINAND ECKHARDT** (1902-95), and **ROYAL WINNIPEG BALLET** artistic director **ARNOLD SPOHR** (b 1958), and other German Manitobans, contributed to the arts in the province and beyond.

In 2001, 200,000 Manitobans claimed German as one of their origins, among whom 40% claimed German as their sole ethnic origin. Since the late 1990s, immigration from Germany to MB has again increased to 5000 in the period 1998-2005, with Germany consistently being one of the top countries of origin for MB immigrants. This wave included German professionals, but mostly Russian Germans who, after some years in Germany, believed they could better pursue their dreams in MB. ● ALEXANDER FREUND

GIANT WATER BUG (*Lethocerus americanus*) is a true bug of the family Belostomatidae, and at a 5 cm length (plus a long breathing siphon at the rear) is the largest species of insect in MB. People come across this giant, flat and dull-brown bug in backyard swimming pools or on the ground under bright lights (like at a gas station), where it astonishes observers by its size and menacing appearance. The powerful pair of front legs, each armed with a sharp claw, fold in front, ready to impale prey. Both the nymph and adult are aquatic and feed on insect larvae, fish, tadpoles, and even frogs, by means of a long piercing beak on the underside of the head. This beak can also inflict a painful bite to one's hand or foot.

Digestive enzymes are pumped into the prey, and the liquefied remains are sucked back into the bug's stomach. In summer the female lays her fertilized egg mass on aquatic vegetation, but in a related MB species (*Belostoma flumineum*), the female cements her eggs on the male's back and departs, leaving him to unwittingly protect the brood until they hatch and swim away. In late summer, adults may take flight to find another deep pond, where they spend the winter under the ice. There are 3 species in MB. ● REW

Lillian Gibbons

GIBBONS, Lillian, journalist (b June 24, 1906, **WINNIPEG**; d Feb 13, 1996, Manaus, Brazil) was a reporter and feature writer for the *Winnipeg Tribune* from 1932 to 1972. A graduate in history of the **U OF M** and a 1928 gold medallist, Gibbons sought out and recorded in her newspaper work the human story embedded in MB places and place names. Her 1967 publication, *My Love Affair with Louis Riel*, introduced many readers for the first time to a significant MB figure, and *Stories Houses Tell* (1978) collected the best of her newspaper column under that name. She died, at the age of 89, on a trip up the Amazon River. ● MILDRED GUTKIN

GIBBONS, Walter Lee "Bubble Gum," BASEBALL player (b Oct 13, 1929, Tampa, FL) was a pitcher in the **MANDAK LEAGUE**. Gibbons first played professionally in the Negro League in 1941, starting with the Philadelphia Stars before joining the New York Black Yankees and then, in 1948, the Indianapolis Clowns. He began playing for the **BRANDON** Greys in the Manitoba Senior League the following year and, alongside fellow former Negro Leaguers such as **ARMANDO VÁSQUEZ**, helped the team win the league championship. In 1950, the Brandon Greys – now in the ManDak League – came in 2nd in the playoffs, and Gibbons was chosen for the all-star team. The following year, the Greys won the ManDak championship. Before switching to the Winnipeg Royals after the Brandon team took on too many pitchers in 1953, Gibbons's record for all games played for the Brandon Greys, including tournaments and playoffs, was 19-5. With the Royals, he pitched 10-6, before returning to Brandon the following year. In that season he inked an 11-7 record. Gibbons joined the Minot Mallards after the Brandon Greys folded in 1955, pitching for the ND team until the ManDak League ceased operations in 1957. Gibbons was inducted into the Manitoba Baseball Hall of Fame in 2006. ● MD

GIBSON, Ronald, organist, choirmaster, conductor (b May 28, 1903, Maidstone, Kent, UK; d **WINNIPEG**, Dec 14, 1993). Gibson arrived in **MORDEN** when he was 10. As a youngster, he performed as organist at Morden Presbyterian Church, then continued his studies on the instrument at Wesley College (*See* **U OF W**). He played viola and served as assistant conductor from 1924-34 in the Winnipeg String Orchestra and the **WSO**. He held musical posts with various churches (1920-87), and conducted ensembles including the Winnipeg Choral and Orchestral Society (1927-29) and the MB Schools Orchestra (1935-40). After serving overseas in the RCAF during WWII, Gibson conducted the CBC Winnipeg String Orchestra, then returned to England for additional studies. He served as director of the **U OF M**'s School of Music 1949-63, and continued to teach there until he retired in 1968. Among his students were teacher/composer Herbert Belyea and composer/conductor Victor Davies. Gibson wrote music criticism for the *Winnipeg Free Press* 1968-88, and contributed to the *Encyclopedia of Music in Canada*. He was the organist at Winnipeg's Holy Trinity Anglican Church for 53 years, and, beginning in 1968, he also composed music for church use. His honours included MB's Order of the Buffalo Hunt. ● DON ANDERSON

GILBERT PLAINS, pop. 800, is a town about 30 km W of **DAUPHIN** on hwy 5. Originally called Glenlyon, after **SCOTS** pioneer Glenlyon Campbell, the town was later renamed after **MÉTIS** Gilbert Ross, who was the first settler in the area. The town post office opened in 1892. Like nearby Dauphin, it was largely Ukrainians who settled Gilbert Plains. As the rolling plains surrounding the town hold some of MB's most fertile soil, farming forms the town's economic foundation.

Producers grow cereal grain, oilseed, and some specialty crops. Many agricultural-support businesses complement area farming. Gilbert Plains is home to the Negrych Pioneer Homestead, the best-preserved Ukrainian farmstead in Canada. For recreation, residents enjoy the Gilbert Plains Centennial Park and arena complex. An 18-hole golf course along the Valley River is a popular attraction. ● GPP

GILLAM, pop 1178, is a town along the historic NELSON RIVER, about 300 km ENE of THOMPSON. The community was named after Zachary Gillam and his son Benjamin, both sea captains who built posts along the Nelson in 1682. Both men were considered among the first Europeans to have travelled to the area. Gillam's population grew when the **HBC** established a post here in 1927 and when the railway arrived in 1929. The community remained a small outpost for traders, hunters, and trappers, and a base for wilderness lodges and outposts for many years. The construction of 3 HYDROELECTRIC dams in the mid-1960s resulted in an economic boom as well as population growth for Gillam. Two transmission lines run 895 km S from Gillam through the INTERLAKE to WINNIPEG. MANITOBA HYDRO's northern headquarters are in Gillam; hydro is the town's largest employer. The community continues to serve many small northern communities with retail and service centres. Supplies are transported to remote communities by truck or air. Gillam is also home to the FOX LAKE CREE NATION. ● GPP

GILLIES, Thomas Garnet "Gar," inventor (b Feb 28, 1921, WINNIPEG; d Dec 23, 2006, Winnipeg) was known as a founder of the "Winnipeg Sound" thanks to his invention of the Garnet amplifier. Gillies got his start as a musician in the 1930s playing the trombone in the Gar Gillies Jump Band. His first musical invention was a public address system, which he built in 1938 out of old radio parts and pieces to make himself better heard. Gillies was a father figure to the broader Winnipeg music scene of the 1960s; in fact, he was often known as "Papa Gar." His son Russell, who was a road manager for The GUESS WHO, complained the band wanted to be louder. So Gar Gillies built them a customized amp with a unique over-driven tone exemplified in the band's hit *American Woman*. In the 1960s, the radio and television repair business Gillies had been running evolved into the Garnet Amplifier Company, which he operated with the help of his sons. The Garnet Amplifier Company manufactured the famous Herzog and Guillotine guitar effects, Garnet guitar amplifiers, custom amps, and guitar cabinets. It is estimated that Gillies built more than 100 different

Gar Gillies, 1964

styles of amps for musicians and companies, and allowed many musicians to pay for the amps on credit. Gillies developed The Herzog exclusively for RANDY BACHMAN of The Guess Who and Bachman-Turner Overdrive; The Herzog became the signature sound of The Guess Who. The Garnet Amplifier Company closed in 1989 due to financial hardship, but Gillies continued to fix, upgrade and design amplifiers in his St. Matthews Ave. repair shop. In 2003, a mural was constructed in the likeness of Gillies on a building at 1349 Portage Ave. The local music hero died of cancer. ● AMANDA STEPHENS

GILSON, James Clayton "Clay," agricultural economist, educator (b Feb 7, 1926, DELORAINE; d June 11, 2000, WINNIPEG) was a prominent Cdn agricultural economist. Born and raised in southwestern MB, Gilson spent 2 years in the MILITARY before attending university. He graduated with a BSc in agriculture in 1950 and a MSc in 1952. After earning a PhD in agricultural economics from Iowa State U, Gilson returned to the U OF M in 1954 as a professor in the Agricultural Economics department. Gilson held various roles at the U of M, including head of the department, dean of the Graduate Studies faculty, and vice-president of academics. He was a member of the Manitoba Institute of Agrologists for nearly 50 years, and served as its president 1960-61. In 1966, Gilson was made a fellow of the Agricultural Institute of Canada; he was its president 1981-82. His appointments included the Joint Commission on Grain Trade, the Science Council of Canada, and the Manitoba Crop Insurance Corporation. Gilson became a Member of the Order of Canada in 1993, and was inducted into the Canadian Agricultural Hall of Fame in 1996. He died at the age of 74. ● AMANDA STEPHENS

GIMLI, pop 1891, is located along the W shore of LAKE WINNIPEG, 90 km N of WINNIPEG. Gimli was established in 1875 when the federal govt

granted land along Lake Winnipeg to ICELANDIC settlers as part of the NEW ICELAND reserve. The settlers established their own constitution, government, schools, and laws. In 1876, federal surveyors further divided New Iceland into 3 townsites, one of which became Gimli. In 1877, the first post office went into operation here. New Iceland retained its own governing system until 1887, when it became part of the province of MB. "Gimli," the name chosen by the Icelandic settlers, refers to the "Golden Hall of Gimli," the mythical paradise of Odin and the gods from Norse religion. In 1897, Gimli opened up to other settlers, attracting UKRAINIANS, POLES, Hungarians, and GERMANS. The arrival of the RAILWAY in 1909 made the lakeshore area accessible to tourists from Winnipeg. Gimli was incorporated as a village in 1908, and became a town in 1947. However, in 2003 the surrounding RM of Gimli annexed the town of Gimli, so that the town no longer exists officially and is now part of the rural municipality.

With the construction of an air force base during WWII and the establishment of an RCAF Flying Training School, the population of Gimli increased. The air force base closed in 1945, reopening in 1950 with the threat of the Cold War, and became a NATO jet fighter training school, where young men came from all over the world to learn to fly. The base was abandoned 21 years later, and has since been converted into an industrial park. Gimli has evolved as a thriving resort community, with the population swelling to well over 7000 each summer as vacationers move into their cottages. With its long sandy beaches and scenic harbour, the former town is among the most popular resort destinations in MB. The construction of a major hotel/conference centre has also boosted tourist activities. Tourism, a commercial fishery, farming, and the Crown Royal whisky distillery – one of the largest distilleries in Canada –support the economy. A vibrant and diverse arts community enhances the area's rich heritage. Gimli hosts an annual Icelandic Festival, ISLENDINGADAGURINN, a weekend celebrating the history and traditions of the largest Icelandic community outside Iceland. It also hosts the unique yearly Gimli Film Festival, one of whose venues is the beach itself, where an 11 m screen rises out of the lake and viewers line the sandy beach to see the films. The Gimli Yacht Club holds many regattas, and was the site of the sailing events for the 1999 PAN AM GAMES.

Gimli attracted national attention in July 1983 when it hosted the "Gimli Glider." Owing to a gauge malfunction and a confusion over whether fuel was measured in metric, an Air Canada Boeing 767 bound from Montreal to Edmonton began

G

Gimli's harbour shelters craft of all sizes.

G

running out of fuel near Red Lake, ON, 570 km NW of Thunder Bay and 225 km from Gimli. The first officer had been stationed at Gimli and knew the runways, while the pilot was an experienced glider flyer. With their combined expertise, they safely dead-stick-landed the huge plane with no loss of life, despite the fact that the tarmac – no longer part of an airbase – was now used as a public raceway. In an old hangar close by, 1150 former Gimli High School classmates were enjoying a reunion supper, and were very surprised with the added entertainment. • LORNA TERGESEN

GIRARD, Marc-Amable, politician, (b April 25, 1822, Varennes, Lower Canada [QC]; d Sept 12, 1892, St. Boniface) was a francophone MLA. Girard was educated at the Collège de Saint-Hyacinthe. A protegé of Sir George-Étienne Cartier, he was brought to MB in 1870 by Archbishop **A. A. Taché** to provide a **French**-Cdn presence in the new province, and especially to help protect the guarantees made to the francophones in the *Manitoba Act*. A Conservative, he was elected to

Marc-Amable Girard, 1880

represent St. Boniface in the legislature from 1870-78 and from 1879-83. He briefly served as "prime minister" in 1874. He was also was a member of the federal senate from 1871. He chaired a Senate Select Committee that studied the route of the **CPR** in 1877. From 1879-83, he served in the **John Norquay** govt as provincial secretary and then as minister of agriculture. A personable man, he did not provide strong leadership, and he gradually faded from the public scene. He was, however, the first president of the Société Saint-Jean-Baptiste de Manitoba. • JMB

GLACIATION, or the movement of Ice Age glaciers during the Pleistocene epoch, is the greatest force behind MB's present-day physical geography. Glaciers develop or advance when the annual addition of snow exceeds melting in summer. Conversely, when the climate is such that summer melts exceed winter ice accumulations, glaciers recede. Several periods of glacial advance and recession occurred during the Pleistocene epoch. At the maximum of the most recent glacial period, the Wisconsinan – which began about 75,000 years BC and ended about 6000 years BC – ice covered all of MB and extended S into the US, with 3-km-thick ice over Hudson Bay and 2-km-thick ice over what is now Winnipeg. As the ice shifted in order to form a level surface, the ice margins were pushed from behind as the glacier flowed to achieve equilibrium. The flowing ice eroded the rocks below it, subsequently depositing the eroded materials farther south. The ice sheet blocked preglacial drainage, creating new glacial lakes. Also, the weight of the ice depressed Earth's crust, and when the ice melted, the crust rebounded toward its former position in a process termed isostatic rebound. The erosion and deposition by ice and the erosion and sedimentation by glacial meltwater are

responsible for much of MB's topography. The effects of glaciation on the MB landscape can be grouped under 4 headings: erosion; deposition; glacial lakes, and their alteration of the preglacial drainage; and isostatic rebound.

EROSION: Though glacial erosion is usually associated with mountainous regions where fast-moving ice is channelled into valleys, it played a role in the evolution of MB's landscape, particularly in the province's north. Here, ice scraped surface materials off, leaving behind bare bedrock, much of which was subsequently covered by organic deposits. Scouring and etching at the base of the ice took the form of striations and gouges, on a small scale, and broad shallow grooves on a larger scale. The latter are common in the **Interlake** and the area just W of **Lake Manitoba**, where the NW-to-SE grooves are occupied by marshes or shallow lakes. In MB's south, evidence of erosion is mainly absent, or is covered by glacial deposits; however, ice flowing southward from a centre over Hudson Bay came into contact with the pre existing **MB Escarpment**, and may have scoured and steepened its edge. This hypothesis is supported by the fact that soils E of the escarpment contain trace elements derived from the escarpment's shale bedrock. An indirect erosive effect was the creation of valleys by glacial meltwater. Some rivers in southern MB are misfits; that is, the stream is too small to have eroded the valley in which it flows. This is the case with Shell River, Birdtail Creek, and Little Saskatchewan River, all of which emanate from the higher land of **Riding Mountain**. Toward the end of the Wisconsinan, melting ice on the "mountain" produced large quantities of water, which eroded correspondingly large valleys.

DEPOSITION: Much of central and southern MB is covered by glacial and fluvioglacial (water associated with ice) deposits that were derived by erosion in the north. Till – an unsorted, unstratified glacial deposit consisting of particles ranging in size from clay to boulders – and fluvioglacial deposits are widespread throughout the province, as are the landforms associated with a major ice sheet. A moraine is a landform composed of till. Various types of moraine are identified on the basis of their relationship to the depositing glacier: ground moraine was deposited under the glacier; end moraine, at the ice margin; and stagnation moraine, by stagnant ice (ice that is no longer moving). Ground moraine covers much of Turtle Mountain, **Riding Mountain**, **Duck Mountain**, and the Porcupine Hills. In these locations, it has the form of hummocky stagnation moraine that can reach a thickness of over 100 m. West of the "mountains" are extensive areas of ground moraine with an average local relief of only about 3 m. In the **MINNEDOSA** pothole region, the ground moraine surface has no clear pattern; numerous small sloughs, many of which have now been drained to increase arable land area, occupy depressions. In contrast, near Birdtail Creek First Nation in the W and **KILLARNEY** in the S, a variation of ground moraine has a corrugated form with low ridges and depressions – often water-filled – roughly parallel to the ice front. In the SW, near **DELORAINE**, sediment deposited by stagnant ice takes the form of circular ridges that are only clearly visible in aerial photographs. These ridges were probably formed by sediment sliding down the sides of isolated blocks of stagnant ice. They are remarkably uniform in diameter and height, being no more than 1 to 3 m above the land they encircle and the land surrounding them. Drumlins – low linear hills often described as being "inverted-spoon-shaped," with long axes parallel to the direction of ice movement – are not common in MB, but rock-cored streamlined hills similar to drumlins are found in the **HOLLAND/TREHERNE/NOTRE DAME DE LOURDES** area, as well as between **BINSCARTH** and **RUSSELL**. Similar features also occur in northern MB.

End moraines, of which 17 have been identified in MB, were deposited at the edges of ice sheets when forward motion balanced wastage. These end moraines represent successive positions of retreat of the ice front. In the S, the **DARLINGFORD** moraine, which extends from the **BRANDON** Hills, E through the Tiger Hills, to Pembina Mountain, was deposited on the W side

of an ice lobe in the **RED RIVER VALLEY**. To the E are Bedford Ridge and Milner Ridge, E of **STEINBACH**; and the Belair moraine on the E side of **LAKE WINNIPEG**. Fluvioglacial sediments also give rise to landforms, such as outwash plains that were deposited by glacial meltwater beyond the ice margin. On these areas of flat terrain, former stream channels can often be seen, especially in aerial photographs, for example between **PILOT MOUND** and **CRYSTAL CITY**. Subglacial or englacial streams in ice tunnels or between ice walls deposited eskers, sand, and gravel ridges anywhere from 100 m to over 100 km long, and between 3 m and 200 m high. They are prominent in the generally flat terrain of northern MB. Some are even named, as are the 130-km-long Robertson Esker in northwestern MB, and the 30-km-long Russell esker in N-central MB. In the south of the province, numerous small eskers occur S and W of **BALDUR**, between **CARTWRIGHT** and Crystal City, and SE of **BIRTLE**. The Arrow Hills, NW of Oak Lake; a ridge at the E end of the Brandon Hills; and a ridge that extends east from **BIRDS HILL** are also eskers. The Birds Hill deposit merges with deltaic sediments deposited into Lake Agassiz. Esker surfaces make good route ways, and eskers are excellent sources of sand and gravel for construction.

GLACIAL LAKES: Glacial lakes originated toward the end of the Ice Age, when the preglacial drainage to the E and N was blocked by ice. The largest of these lakes was **LAKE AGASSIZ**, which at its maximum covered much of MB and northern ON as well as parts of SK, ND, and MN.

Strandlines (beaches) at former lake levels, spillways that carried water from one glacial lake to another, deltas deposited into the lakes, and lake-bottom sediments all provide evidence of the existence of the lakes. These after-effects are most visible in the case of Lake Agassiz, but other, smaller lakes also left their imprint. In the extreme S, Lake Souris was mainly in ND, but extended just into MB in the **SOURIS RIVER** Valley, in the very SW corner of the province. North of it, extending to just east of **SOURIS**, was Lake Hind. These small lakes did not leave prominent beaches, as Lake Agassiz did, but some exist SE of **RESTON** on the W shore of Lake Hind. Glacial spillways are steep-sided and flat-floored. Once a lake had emptied – perhaps in only a few days – water flow along a valley was much reduced, culminating in small rivers now on the valley floors. The Qu'Appelle River Valley above **ST.-LAZARE** and the **ASSINIBOINE RIVER** Valley above **BRANDON** are glacial spillways. In the S, both the Souris and the **PEMBINA** rivers occupy spillways for part of their length. About 10,000 or 9000 years BC, Lake Regina (in SK) emptied SE into Lake Souris and from there into Lake Hind and through southern MB into Lake Agassiz. The outflow from Lake Hind followed the already existing Pembina Valley, which originated as the valley of a preglacial meltwater stream. The large outflow resulted in erosion through glacial deposits down to the underlying shales, and the creation of a typical steep-side, flat-floored spillway that is now occupied by a stretch of the Souris River SE of Souris and by Pelican Lake, Rock Lake, and **SWAN LAKE** along the course of the Pembina River. The Souris River used to flow aligned with what is now the Pembina Valley, but was diverted just N of Margaret to flow NE into the Assiniboine NW of **WAWANESA**. Although they were close to each other, a spillway between lakes Souris and Hind separated them. Between Coulter, 30 km ENE of the SK/ND border, and **MELITA**, this spillway splits into 2 separate channels easily seen on air photographs.

The Assiniboine delta deposited into Lake Agassiz is by far the biggest of its kind, but the flow that cut the spillway between Lake Souris and Lake Hind deposited a delta as it entered Hind. The land left behind when Lake Agassiz drained was extremely flat and marshy, as in the Red River Valley, where the marshes have since been drained for agriculture. A similar situation in the case of Lake Hind resulted in flat land W of Souris and marshland in the **OAK LAKE**/Plum Lakes/Marshy Lake area. Sands of the Assiniboine delta have been blown into dunes, forming the well-known Bald Head Hills (*see* **CARBERRY SAND HILLS**), while some of the Lake Hind

Full extent of glaciation during Wisconsinan period

Greenland
Ice Sheet

Laurentide
Ice Sheet

DOUG FAST

G

sediments created a less-well-known area of dunes – the Lauder Sand Hills, SW of **Hartney**.

ISOSTATIC REBOUND: The final, indirect effects of glaciation result from isostatic rebound. **Hudson Bay** was depressed by up to 1000 m, and its rebound is still in progress; when the process is complete, there will be little left of the bay. Old shorelines are found up to 183 m above sea level; the Hudson Bay coast N of **Churchill** is a staircase of elevated shorelines. Another indicator is found at Sloop Cover National Historic Site, near the mouth of the **Churchill River**, where iron mooring rings used by **HBC** ships in the 18th century are now several m above sea level. Rebound was greatest in the N, where ice was thickest. Consequently, Lake Agassiz beaches are tilted down to the S. Also, Lake Winnipeg is being tilted southward, which results in **Netley Marsh** at its S end, and erosion E and W of the marsh. Finally, the main branch of the Assiniboine now flows along the southern edge of the delta rather than its earlier, more northerly route via **Douglas Marsh** and Epinette Creek. ● JOHN WELSTED

GLADSTONE, pop 848, is a town 85 km ENE of **Brandon**. Settled in 1872, Gladstone was originally known as Third Crossing; the name changed to Palestine in 1871. It is not known why this name was chosen, but it may have alluded to bountiful harvests in the area comparable to the riches of the Promised Land. A school was built in 1873 and the settlement began to grow. The town was incorporated in 1882 and the name changed at that time to Gladstone in honour of UK PM William Ewart Gladstone. In the 21st century, visitors are welcomed to town by a large "happy rock" (Glad stone) statue. Agriculture is still the backbone of the town's economy, but tourism is a growing industry. Naturalists and wildlife enthusiasts come to appreciate Big Grass Marsh Refuge, 15 km N of Gladstone, which was the first **Ducks Unlimited** project in Canada in 1938. The town hosts an annual fair and rodeo in Aug. Gladstone's scenic Williams Park offers campers modern amenities and recreational facilities including a heated outdoor pool and tennis courts. An extensive walking trail originates in the campgrounds and follows the banks of the Whitemud River. And there are 2 museums – the Gladstone District Museum and the Third Crossing Museum. Gladstone celebrated its 125th anniversary in 2007. ● GPP

GLENBORO, pop 650, is a village 80 km SE of **Brandon**. The first settlers, Jonas Christie and James Duncan, arrived in 1879. It was not until after Christie and Duncan – encouraged by the prospect of the **CPR** establishing a stop in Glenboro – began to offer sections of their land to form a town site, that the village was settled in 1886. The village name was chosen by Duncan, and comes from the Scottish phrase "Borough of the Glen." Glenboro was incorporated as a village in 1950. Agriculture forms the economic base in Glenboro and much of the surrounding area. Rich soils support some of the grain and the close proximity of Spruce Woods Provincial Park generates tourism activity. Sara the Camel, a 5-m-tall statue on the outskirts of the village, emblematizes the nearby **Carberry Spirit Sands**. Glenboro also houses one of the oldest wooden railway water towers in Canada. ● GPP

STAN MILOSEVIC, WWW.MANITOBAPHOTOS.COM

Gladstone's "Happy Rock"

GLOBAL WARMING is a relatively recent phenomenon in which increasing emissions of greenhouse gasses (e.g., carbon dioxide, methane) and dusts from human activities have resulted in the trapping of excess solar heat in the atmosphere. This warming trend appears to be responsible for an alarming set of climatic consequences at local and global levels – changes in weather patterns and ocean currents, increases in number and intensity of violent storms and floods, droughts, and melting of glaciers and polar ice caps. With continued melting of glaciers and pack ice will come flooding of coastal cities, many of which are the largest in the world.

These effects are already apparent in MB, with a longer fire season in the boreal forest and the break-up of ice cover on Hudson Bay 3 weeks earlier than 30 years ago. The longer ice-free season has far-reaching results only now becoming apparent. Seals need a substantial ice and snow cover to successfully raise their pups, and it is these animals that nourish Polar Bears. Availability of seals is critically important to mother bears (after their 8-month fast on land) and their cubs. Both bear body weights and cub survival have dropped significantly since the 1970s from lessened accessibility to their main prey of seals. If this trend continues, it is likely that seals and the Polar Bear will be forced N of MB coastal waters, and perhaps Hudson Bay, within 40 years. Polar Bears are now being found that have drowned in failed attempts to reach distant shores from melting ice floes in the Arctic Ocean.

The worldwide extinction of 112 amphibians species and the decline in almost all populations have been linked to global warming. Changes in humidity and temperature since the 1970s have favoured the spread of a deadly chytrid fungus, which attacks and destroys the sensitive skin of amphibians. It is still not known if this or another infective agent is responsible for the population crash of frogs (particularly the Northern Leopard Frog) over the last several decades in MB and NA (see Amphibian Fungus). Likely new studies will show increasinly how global warming is affecting MB wildlife communities and individual species. For example, the Pitcher Plant Mosquito (*Wyeomyia smithii*) has already extended its breeding season and delayed the onset of hibernation by many days. With a number of fish species and other aquatic organisms occuring just outside MB borders (but still in provincial watersheds), an increase of only a few degrees in water temperature could set in motion a major influx of aquatic organisms, with unknown effects on native biota.

During periods of climatic change in the past, plant and animal communities have often been able to shift geographically without wholesale destruction of ecosystems, since the climate changed relatively slowly over many generations. The current warming trend is happening more rapidly, and habitats are already damaged and fragmented from human-induced changes of the landscape, leaving many species nowhere to retreat. On a broader scale, the northern hemisphere is in an interglacial period at the present time (maximum Wisconsinan glaciation was 20,000 years ago) – just one of a long series of glacial retreats and advances during the Pleistocene period (1.5 million years). The maximum warm-dry period was reached about 5000 years ago (hypsithermal), when MB biomes (major plant-animal communities such at Grassland) were several hundred km farther N, so we are well into the next cooling phase leading to a new glacial age. No one can determine how the natural course of events will change as a result of the current global-warming phenomenon. ● REW

GOD'S LAKE NARROWS, pop 100, is a community 224 km SE of **Thompson**. In 1824, a **HBC** post was established here, and development of the area began. The post was closed in 1832, re-established in 1865, and finally abandoned in 1872. Around 1888, the post was relocated to the N shore of the lake, remaining until 1964. A post office opened here in 1935. Around the same time, prospectors discovered gold in the area; soon much of the region had been staked. By the 21st century, mining was no longer viable and the local economy was dependent on commercial fishing and fly-in fishing lodges. This non-treaty community on crown land is closely related to the nearby **God's Lake First Nation**. ● GPP

GOD'S LAKE FIRST NATION, on reserve pop 1365, off reserve pop 926, is situated 258 km SE of **Thompson**, at the point of the narrows of God's Lake. The native language in this First Nation community is **Cree**. God's Lake is signatory to Treaty 5. It is a member of the Keewatin Tribal Council. There is one reserve in the God's Lake First Nation community. The narrows cross through the reserve and the main portion of the population is on the E side of the islands. The greater portion of the reserve land is located on the NW shore of the S area of God's Lake. Education, administered by the First Nation, goes from Kindergarten-Grade 8. Total enrolment in 2003-04 was 361. God's Lake has no access to all-weather roads, but there is a winter road. There is also an airstrip available year-round, serviced by scheduled flights. The economic foundation of God's Lake First Nation is trapping, hunting, and fishing. ● RK

GOERMANN, Monica, artistic gymnast (b Sept 1, 1964, **Winnipeg**) was one of Canada's top gymnasts. She received her training from her mother Elfriede Goermann, who founded the Winnipeg Gymnastics Centre. Goermann won a silver medal at the 1978 Commonwealth games where she averaged 9.0 in all events. She became Cdn champion in 1979. At that year's **Pan Am Games**, Goermann took home the all-around gold medal as well as 2 gold, one silver and one bronze. The Olympic Boycott of 1980 denied her Olympic glory, and a back injury at the 1981 World Championships ended her competitive career, after which she began work as a gymnastics coach and ballet instructor with the **Royal Winnipeg Ballet**. ● MD

GOLDEN BOY, a 5.25 m, 1650 kg statue that tops the cupola of the MB **Legislative Building** in Winnipeg, is one of MB's most recognizable symbols. After receiving a commission from the MB govt, the statue was sculpted in WWI by Parisian artist Georges Gardet (1863-1939), a member of the *Animalier* school. Gardet originally called his creation *Eternal Youth*, an auspicious name, as the statue has had a miraculous history. Emerging unharmed from the heavily bombed Ferdinand Barbédienne foundry in Paris, where the statue was cast in bronze in 1918, "The Golden Boy" was rushed to a seaport and laded on a cargo ship destined for the US. Before the ship could depart, however, it was commandeered as a troopship. For the remainder of the year, The Golden Boy, whether forgotten or merely useful as ballast, travelled thousands of kilometres in the ship's hold, miraculously avoiding torpedoes. At war's end, the statue was found, unloaded at Halifax, and shipped by rail to **Winnipeg**, where it was hoisted to the top of the MB Legislative Building on Nov 21, 1919. The statue had originally been purchased, along with the 2 bison statues that flank the legislature's main staircase, for about $14,000, and was part of the building's original design.

Eternal Youth is modelled after the *Mercury* of Giambologna (or Giovanni da Bologna, 1524-1608). Much like the Roman gods' courier Mercury (or, in Greek mythology, Hermes), *Youth* is a runner, captured mid-stride, with a message of coming prosperity for all Manitobans. Under his left arm is a sheaf of grain, representing the fruits of labour. In his right hand he holds a torch, with which he is said to call on the youth of MB to pursue a prosperous future. The statue faces N, toward MB's rich natural resources. The statue has seen its share of changes. Though originally made of bronze and gilt-painted, The Golden Boy was repainted gold in the 1940s, before being gilded with 23.5-kt gold leaf in 1951. To mark Canada's centenary in 1967, a light was installed in the statue's torch, and lit for the first time the night of Dec 31, 1966.

"The Golden Boy" under repair at The Forks, 2002.

Renovations to the Legislative Building in 2001 revealed that the statue's internal support post had corroded and would have to be replaced. The statue also needed a new gold coat and minor surface repairs. In Feb 2002, the statue was removed and publicly displayed in the **Manitoba Museum**, where an estimated 100,000 Manitobans took the rare opportunity to see this icon up-close, making it the largest attraction in the museum's history. The Golden Boy was dismantled and the $1-million repair and restoration began in March 2002. Repairs included installing monitors and gauges inside The Golden Boy so future wind and temperature stress on the statue and its support structures could be carefully monitored. To restore the statue's surface, it was blasted with crushed walnut shells then treated with 4 coats of a special, hand-applied

Monica Goermann, 1979

lead-based primer. Finally, the statue was again exhibited publicly, this time in a special glass case at **THE FORKS**, while technicians applied a 24-kt gold-leaf coat, before The Golden Boy returned to his dome atop the Legislative Building on Sept 5, 2002. ● A. J. LEVIN

GOFFMAN, Erving, sociologist, (b June 11, 1922, Manville, AB; d Nov 20,1982, Philadelphia) was raised in **DAUPHIN** and **WINNIPEG**, where he attended St. John's High School before enrolling in the **U OF M** in chemistry. After a 6-month stint at the **NATIONAL FILM BOARD**, he finished his BA at the U of Toronto, followed by an MA and PhD from the U of Chicago. Professor of Sociology at the U of California at Berkeley, he would become one of the most influential thinkers in the 2nd half of the 20th century. He is best known as the author of *The Presentation of Self in Everyday Life* (1959) and *Asylums* (1961). The U of M awarded him an honorary doctorate in 1976. ● GENE WALZ

GOLDEYE (*Hiodon alosoides*) and its close relative, the mooneye (*H. tergisus*), are important commercial fishes that are smoked and sold as the delicacy MB Goldeye. They are the only living members of the bony-tongued fish family Hiodontidae, which also includes the, extinct species *Xiphactinus audux* – a giant (5-m-long) predatory fish that lived in the inland seas that covered MB during much of the Cretaceous Period (144-65 mya). Both surviving species have numerous fang-like teeth on the tongue and roof of the mouth, large scales, large eyes, and a deeply forked tail fin. They are blue-green to silvery in colour. The Goldeye can be distinguished from Mooneye by its back-set (relative to the anal fin) dorsal fin and other characters. The Goldeye occurs in major rivers and lakes from the **RED** and **ASSINIBOINE** rivers N and W to the headwaters of the Churchill and Nelson rivers. The Mooneye is found N to the Saskatchewan and Nelson rivers and E into the Winnipeg River watershed. Both species average 40 cm (max 48 cm) and 0.7 kg. The fish over-winter in deep water and then travel to shallow water as ice breaks up. Spawning occurs in mid-water for 3-6 weeks, after water temperatures attain 10°C,

in May and June. A female lays 5000-25,000 eggs, which are semi-buoyant and quickly disperse in the current or waves. The eggs hatch in 2 weeks and the fry may reach 7cm by their first year. The usual lifespan is 8 years (max 15). Feeding mainly at night, they take insects (aquatic and others that fall into the water), minnows and crustaceans, and are important prey for **CHANNEL CATFISH, WALLEYE** and Northern Pike. ● REW

GOLF has played a large role in the MB sports community for more than a century and there has been a continual growth in participation in the game, competitively and in recreational play. Originating in Scotland, golf made its first appearance in Canada in 1860 on a makeshift 3-hole course in QC, with the first proper 9-hole course formed in 1873 at Montreal. The first appearance of golf in MB was in 1889 when a 9-hole course was established at **STONY MOUNTAIN PENITENTIARY** by the warden, Col Samuel Bedson. The **VIRDEN** Golf Club was the 2nd course formed in 1892 and is believed to be the province's oldest active club. The **WINNIPEG** Golf Club was formed in 1894. St. Charles Country Club in Winnipeg opened for play in 1905 and is the 2nd oldest active club in MB. MB was also involved with the national development of golf as the Winnipeg Golf Club was one of 10 from across the nation that formed the Royal Canadian Golf Assoc in 1895. The first national

men's amateur championship played outside of ON and QC was in 1921 at the Winnipeg Golf Club. The first women's amateur championship outside of ON and QC was in 1926 at the Elmhurst Golf Club. The Manitoba Golf Assoc was formed in 1915 with 5 clubs – St. Charles, Pine Ridge, Norwood, Winnipeg Hunt and Elmhurst. The Manitoba Ladies Golf Assoc was formed in 1922. The 2 associations were amalgamated in 2003 as Golf Manitoba, the governing body for the sport in the province. More than 100 golf clubs or courses were available to Manitobans in 2006, a majority of them members of Golf Manitoba. Most are available to the golfing public, though some private clubs allow only guests of members.

Despite a shorter playing season and smaller populations than provinces like ON, QC and BC, MB amateur golfers have made their mark on the national scene over the years. The men's Willingdon Cup team championship was won by MB teams 4 times, in 1974, 1986, 1995 and 1996, while the national women's team championship was won by a MB team in 1962. MB teams won the national junior men's interprovincial titles in 1967 and 1991. The Cdn men's mid-amateur team title was won by MB in 2005. The Cdn men's amateur honours were claimed by MB golfers Jim Doyle in 1968, Rob McMillan in 1996 and Dale Goehring in 1997. The national women's amateur title went to Mrs. John Rogers in 1932 and

Goldeye

Golfers at St. Charles Country Club, June 26, 1926

Aileen Robertson in 1994. National junior men's crowns for MB golfers went to Howard Bennett in 1939, George Knudson in 1955, Todd Fanning in1985 and 1986 and Rob McMillan in 1992, 1993 and 1994. Junior women's champions representing MB were Lynda Devine in 1968 and Brionie Brown in 1993. Juvenile men's national honours were won by MB golfers Bill Parker in 1973, Marc Chamberland in 1980, Dale Goehring in 1988 and Rob McMillan in 1990 and 1992. Two MB trained golfers won the Cdn women's senior championship, though not representing the province at the time. Jo-Ann Lindsay was playing out of MN when she took the national title in 1991 and Lynda Pahlaniuk was out of BC when she won the honours in 2003. Garth Collings was the national men's mid-amateur champion in 2003.

The Manitoba Golf Hall of Fame and Museum came into being in 2003 and 20 individuals were inducted in the first three years. Golfers in the Hall include Allan Boes, Jimmy Doyle, Dan Halldorson, George Knudson, Bobby Reith, Ann Tachan, June Bagley, Marj Edey, Marg Homenuik, Ted Homenuik, Merlene Netterfield, Bill Pidlaski, Don Gardner, Wilf Homenuik and Jo-Ann Lindsay, while the builder category has honoured Peggy Colonello, John Steel, Jack Blair, Aihlin Walker and W. Arthur Johnston. Many other golfers and builders became well known for their accomplishments within the province and the records are available through the various associations, but the main attraction for the sport of golf in MB is in the recreation mode. Thousands of Manitobans enjoy their summer months on the numerous courses throughout the province. Because the province's population is centred in Winnipeg, a majority of courses are located within the city or only a short drive away. However, many of the smaller towns in the province also boast layouts that attract golfers of all abilities, from the so-called duffer through to the top amateur and professional players. • RALPH BAGLEY

GOOD, Mary Ann, "The Tree Lady," amateur landscaper (b Dec 1, 1841, **RED RIVER SETTLEMENT**; d Jan 4, 1932, **WOODLANDS**). The daughter of **ENGLISH**-born **HBC** labourer Joseph Kirton and his wife Susanna, Mary Ann was born in Red River. Her mother died when she was 3, and a **SCOTS** woman raised her. Bringing home a sheep in 1857, young Mary Ann spotted a maple sapling in a drainage ditch and transplanted it next to her house. From her teenage years, she continued planting trees, especially maples and elms. In 1860, she married Joseph William Good (or Goode, 1838-1907), and they moved to what is now the Wolseley area of **WINNIPEG** along the

Wolseley area women defended the Wolseley Elm from destruction, 1957.

ASSINIBOINE RIVER at Newman and Wolseley. There they operated a market garden and had 3 sons, some of whom married into **MÉTIS** families. Mary Ann is credited with planting the Wolseley Elm about this time, and fought the city's attempts to remove the tree around 1910. She moved to Woodlands, 25 km WNW of **STONEWALL**, in 1905, died there in 1932, and was buried at Winnipeg's St. James Anglican Church, a parish with which she had long associations. • AJL

GOODEVE, Sir Charles Frederick, military scientist (b Feb 21, 1904, **NEEPAWA**; d April 7, 1980, London, UK), was instrumental in helping defeat the German navy during WWII. Goodeve grew up in **STONEWALL** and **WINNIPEG**, the son of an **ANGLICAN** clergyman. In 1923, his interest in boating led him to join the Royal Canadian Naval Volunteer Reserve Division in Winnipeg. Goodeve studied chemistry and physics at the **U OF M**, earning his BSc in 1935.

In 1927, Goodeve moved to England to study at the U of London's University College. He also became involved in the British navy reserves, training on submarines, minesweepers, battleships, and destroyers during the 1930s. At that time, his research led him to becoming a torpedo expert. When WWII erupted in 1939,

the German navy moved quickly to lay magnetic mines that soon paralysed **ENGLISH** ports. Goodeve devised a method to seek out underwater mines, called the "Double Longitudinal Sweep." Specially designed wooden minesweeping ships managed to clear hundreds of mines, greatly lessening the threat.

Goodeve was promoted to Cdr, but did not rest on his laurels. He conceived a way to protect ships from mines directly. Some ships had already begun carrying electrically charged cables to counteract their magnetic fields. Goodeve worked to perfect the method, setting up "degaussing" sites where rubber-insulated electric cables could be drawn along the side of a ship to create permanent magnetism in the hull.

With Goodeve's scientific acumen and take-charge attitude, he was chosen to lead a new Directorate of Miscellaneous Weapons Development in late 1940. He set to work on domestic production of the Oerlikon antiaircraft gun, a Swiss design that was being used with great success by the Nazis. Goodeve's organizational skills were credited for speeding up the process. He also designed the Hedgehog Antisubmarine Mortar, a new weapon that could attack submarines from the bow, rather than the stern, of a ship. Goodeve was then awarded the Order of the

G

British Empire and named head of all research and development for the navy.

Following the war, Goodeve was knighted, received the US Medal of Freedom, along with 5 honorary doctorates. He worked as director of the British Iron and Steel Research Association until his retirement in 1969. ● JOEL TRENAMAN

GOPHER. *See* SQUIRREL

GORDON, Charles William "Ralph Connor," clergyman, activist, author (b Sept 13, 1860, Glengarry Cty, Canada West [ON]; d Oct 31, 1937, WINNIPEG). The son of a fiery Free Kirk of Scotland minister and a gentler but equally devout mother, Gordon was educated at the U of Toronto and U of Edinburgh, and was ordained as a Presbyterian minister in 1890. He served for 4 years as a missionary out of Banff, AB, his territory extending to the mining and lumbering camps and the pioneers of the Cdn Northwest, and in 1894 was called to St. Stephen's parish in the rapidly expanding city of Winnipeg.

Rev. Charles William Gordon, 1920

Concerned with the **MB SCHOOLS QUESTION**, intensely involved in the temperance movement, and an ardent advocate of the social gospel movement and of progressive reform, Gordon became chairman of the MB Social Service Council in 1910, and his services were frequently in demand to mediate labour disputes. He served as chaplain to the Cameron Highlanders (*see* **THE QUEEN'S OWN CAMERON HIGHLANDERS OF CANADA**) in WWI, becoming senior Protestant chaplain to the Cdn Expeditionary Forces in 1917, and undertaking a speaking tour of the US on behalf

of the Allied govts to urge US participation in the war. A pacifist as a result of his war experience, he fought for the unification of the Protestant churches, partly in order to present a concerted Christian opposition against further slaughter, and he played a central role in the formation of the **UNITED CHURCH OF CANADA** in 1925.

Having retired from St. Stephen's in 1924, Gordon intensified his efforts on behalf of peaceful world relations, was invited to deliver the annual sermon to the League of Nations in 1932, and toured Spain as the guest of the newly established Spanish Republic. The nationwide distress of the **GREAT DEPRESSION** in the 1930s troubled him deeply, and he threw his support behind the embattled "On-to-Ottawa" marchers. An autobiography written just before his death in 1937 was edited by his son, King Gordon, and published a year later.

The Rev. Charles Gordon's career as an enormously successful author, under the pseudonym of Ralph Connor, came about not as the result of any literary ambitions but as an extension of his pastoral responsibilities. His first novel, *Black Rock: A Tale of the Selkirks* (1898), was an expansion of a series of magazine pieces written to stimulate support for the northern missions. Its initial printing of 5000 copies sold out; it was reissued in a dozen editions, some of them pirated; and its sales totalled half a million copies. The following year, *The Sky Pilot* doubled its predecessor's sales, and with the publication of *The Man from Glengarry* in 1902, Connor's readership for the 3 novels topped 5 million worldwide. Fast-paced and unabashedly melodramatic, Connor's stories of adventure, virtue, and heroism in the Cdn wilds showcased his own brand of strenuous, muscular Christianity. Didactic, perhaps turgidly moralistic – particularly in the many later works – they nevertheless have the ring of authenticity, affording distant readers an engaging taste of how life seemed to have been lived on the frontier.

The historic Gordon home on Winnipeg's Westgate Ave has been lovingly preserved as Ralph Connor House, the home of the University Women's Club. ● MILDRED GUTKIN

GORDON, "Lord" Gordon (a.k.a. Lord Glencairn, Hon. Mr. Herbert Hamilton, and numerous other aliases; real name unknown), confidence trickster (b ca 1840, UK; d Aug 1, 1874, HEADINGLEY). Little is known of "Gordon's" early life; indeed, even his real name and birthplace are uncertain. This con artist evidently learned to affect the manners of the aristocracy while serving as a butler in Scotland. Gordon's first reported crime occurred in 1868 when he cheated

Edinburgh jewellers Marshall & Son of £25,000 (then $122,000). He surfaced in the US around 1870, impersonating a **SCOTS** lord and investor. Gordon became a society darling in Minneapolis, where he spent much of 1871. In Pelican Rapids, MN, he claimed to have an option on hundreds of km² of railway land on which he was to start a Scottish colony similar to **LORD SELKIRK'S RED RIVER SETTLEMENT**. He conned local pioneer W. G. Tuttle, who was utterly ruined by Gordon: Tuttle spent most of the rest of his life in an insane asylum. Gordon then headed for New York, where he bilked Erie Railroad financier Jay Gould for hundreds of thousands of dollars, disappearing to Montreal when the matter was brought to court. From there, he went to Red River, claiming to be on a hunting trip. A Minnesotan in Red River on business happened to recognize Gordon in summer 1873, and alerted some of his countrymen. Shortly thereafter, a party of 5 MN bounty hunters, under the leadership of Capt Mike Hoy, abducted Gordon and headed for the US to collect their reward, but they were apprehended by Cdn customs officials at Pembina (now ND: *see* **EMERSON**), and were brought to trial in Red River. The MN governor applied to the lieut gov, **HENRY JOSEPH HYNES CLARKE**, for their release, but Clarke believed Gordon was a Scottish peer, not a confidence man. Claims of violated sovereignty by both sides led to escalating tensions between Canada and the US, and, amidst Fenian rumblings of invasion, PM Sir John A. Macdonald and US president Ulysses S. Grant exchanged urgent encrypted messages. The trial, over which Clarke presided, resulted in a plea bargain, and the bounty hunters were each sentenced a token day in jail, averting possible

Lord Gordon, 1870

war. However, the trial and its aftermath proved Gordon was not who he claimed to be, much to Clarke's embarrassment. Gordon remained in the area, but news of the trial reached Scotland. In 1874, when police tried to arrest Gordon for extradition to the UK at his Headingley rooming-house, the con man shot himself in the head. Gordon's criminal career is profiled in several books, and he is the subject of the opera *Let Us Pay Tribute to Gordon Gordon* by MB composer Victor Davies (1968). ● A. J. LEVIN

GORING, Robert Thomas "Butch," HOCKEY player, coach (b Oct 22, 1949, St. Boniface) is 1 of 3 Manitobans to be named most valuable player of the NHL playoffs (along with **REGGIE LEACH** and **RON HEXTALL**). Goring started out playing MB junior hockey for the West Kildonan North Stars, then the Winnipeg Rangers, **WINNIPEG JETS**, St. Boniface Mohawks, and **DAUPHIN** Kings. Drafted in the 5th round by Los Angeles, he played nearly 11 seasons with the Kings, winning the Bill Masterton and Lady Byng Memorial trophies in 1978. In 1980, a trade sent him to the New York Islanders.

In New York, Goring built upon his reputation as an all-around centre with outstanding speed and energy on the ice, though he was not a prolific regular-season scorer with the Islanders. However, he tallied 39 points in his first 41 playoff games with the team, winning the Conn Smythe Trophy following the 2nd of 4 consecutive Stanley Cup victories. Goring finished his career with the Boston Bruins in 1985 before succeeding Gerry Cheevers as the team's head coach. He was fired following a little more than one season, and moved on to coach in the American Hockey League and International Hockey League, where he won 2 championships with the Grizzlies, the New York affiliate. This earned Goring the head-coaching job with the Islanders in 1999, but the team performed poorly during his 2 seasons behind the bench.

Goring moved to Germany in 2001 to coach in the country's national league, where he won one championship. New York hired him yet again in early 2004, this time as assistant coach, but he returned to Germany later that year. During his NHL career, Goring accumulated 888 points and an incredibly low 102 penalty minutes in 1107 career NHL games. No other NHL player has ever appeared in more than 1000 games and taken so few penalties. Goring was also known for his trademark small helmet – he wore the same one from the age of 12 until the end of his career. ● JOEL TRENAMAN

GORT, (Lord) 7th Viscount, businessman, philanthropist, soldier (b Feb 12, 1888, Kenya,; d May 21, 1975, Isle of Man). Known as Col. Standish Robert Gage Prendergast Vereker or as "Lord Gort," Gort came from a family in the Anglo-**IRISH** aristocracy, though he lived mostly in England, having grown up in Rowlands Gill, Co. Durham. His father was John Gage Prendergast, the 5th Viscount Gort. As LCol commanding the 5th Durham Batt., he won a Military Cross, but lost his only son, in WWII. During the war, he sent most of his extensive late-Medieval and early-Renaissance art collection to Canada, where it would be safe from the Blitz. Standish inherited his viscountcy in 1946, after the passing of his older brother, the 6th Viscount, Field Marshal John Standish Surtees Prendergast Vereker, VC, also known as "Tiger." Gort invested initially in the coal industry in AB, later concentrating on Manitoba enterprises, especially real estate in **WINNIPEG**. The Viscount Gort Hotel is named for him, though he also owned apartment blocks in the Fort Rouge/Crescentwood area. While he remained a UK citizen and spent much of his time there and in Ireland, he had frequent dealings in Canada, often shopped at downtown Winnipeg clothiers, and became a Cdn citizen in 1963. **FERDINAND ECKHART** persuaded Gort – who by then had few surviving relatives – to donate much of his considerable collection of tapestries and panel paintings to the **WINNIPEG ART GALLERY**. ● AJL

GOTLIEB, Allan Ezra, public servant (b Feb 28, 1928, **WINNIPEG**). A graduate of Harvard Law School, where he edited the *Harvard Law Journal*, Gotlieb was named a Rhodes scholar and a university lecturer in Law at Oxford U, and was called to the bar of England in 1956. Returning to Canada in 1957, he joined the Dept of External Affairs, earning admiration for his acute grasp of constitutional and international law. A trusted advisor to the Liberal govt of Pierre Elliott Trudeau, Gotlieb became, successively, assistant undersecretary of state for external affairs in 1976-78; deputy minister of manpower and immigration in 1968-73; deputy minister of communications in 1973-77; and undersecretary of state for external affairs in 1977-81. It was his appointment from 1981-89 as Cdn ambassador to the US that brought him to the forefront of public attention. Along with his wife, **SONDRA GOTLIEB**, he ably represented Canada's interests among the multinational elite of Washington, DC. While in the US, he and his wife were as well known for their parties as their day work. Allan called this "public diplomacy" and argued that it was necessary in a capital where the media was as important as government in shaping policy. Gotlieb has since been appointed visiting fellow, All Souls' College, Oxford, and visiting professor

Alan Gotlieb, 1969

G

to both Harvard U and the U of Toronto. He has served as gov of the International Development Research Council; on the governing council of the International Institute for Strategic Studies (London, UK); as arbitrator on the Canada-France Tribunal on Maritime Boundaries; as chairman of the Canada Council for the Arts; on the National Film Board; and as honorary chairman of the ON Heritage Foundation. His publications include *Disarmament and International Law* (1965), *Canadian Treaty-Making* (1968), and *Impact of Technology on International Law* (1982), and *The Washington Diaries* (2006). Gotlieb has received awards and honorary degrees from several universities, including the U of W in 1982, and is a Companion of the Order of Canada. He lives in Toronto. ● MILDRED GUTKIN

GOTLIEB, Sondra, writer (b **WINNIPEG**, Dec 30, 1936). In 1981, Sondra Gotlieb arrived in Washington, DC, as the wife of the Canada's new ambassador to the US, **ALLAN GOTLIEB**. Already well known in Ottawa as a highly sought-after political hostess, Sondra Gotlieb put Canada in the media spotlight for her social acumen and her outspoken, irreverent comments on life in the elevated circles of diplomacy. A food expert and columnist, she published *The Gourmet's Canada* (1972) and *Cross Canada Cooking* (1976). Her 1978 novel *True Confections: How My Family Arranged My Marriage*, won the Stephen Leacock Medal for Humour. In 1981, the equally entertaining novel, *First Lady Last Lady*, appeared. Her bimonthly columns in the *Washington Post*, characteristically deflating the pretensions of notables, including herself, are collected in *Wife of –: An Irreverent Account of Life in Washington* (1985). Her take on the doings in the US capital appears once again in *Washington Rollercoaster* (1990). *Dogs, Houses, Gardens, Food, & Other Addictions* was published in 2002 and *When I Rises Up I Gets Confused* in 2004. She lives in Toronto. ● MILDRED GUTKIN

G

Scrap Bay by Steve Gouthro

GOUTHRO, Steve, painter, (b Pickton, ON, June 9, 1951) Gouthro moved to **WINNIPEG** when he was 12 years old. He received his BFA from the **U OF M** in 1975. Starting as a printmaker with Moosehead Press in 1979, he moved onto teaching at the School of Art in 1980 where he taught until 2006. Working in a variety of paper-based mediums, Gouthro's work has seen him depict everything from life stills to steel mills. His realist paintings are rich with colour and the subtleties of light on the objects, places and people he portrays. He has received numerous awards and grants from the Manitoba Arts Council, Canada Council for the Arts and received the University Teaching Services/University of Manitoba Students' Union Students' Teacher Recognition Award in 1998. He has had several solo exhibitions around the province, including *Through the Mill*, which was commissioned by The **WINNIPEG ART GALLERY** in 2004. In 2007, he taught at **BRANDON U.** ● STACEY ABRAMSON

GOVERNMENT, LOCAL is often described as tertiary (the 3rd order of) govt in Canada. Under the Constitution, the powers of local govts are not specified. Provincial govts have exclusive jurisdiction over local govts, with provincial laws prescribing their election processes, governing structures, functions, finances, and accountabilities. The trend in recent years has been to make provincial legislation less prescriptive, allowing local govts more freedom to run their own affairs.

The most important local govts in MB are municipalities. The main MB legislation governing municipalities is the *Municipal Act* (1996). Other important acts are the *Municipal Assessment Act*, the *Local Authorities Election Act*, the *Municipal Council Conflict of Interest Act*, and the *Planning Act*, which require municipalities to adopt development plans and to regulate the uses of land within their communities. **WINNIPEG** operates under its own legislation, *The City of Winnipeg Charter*, which contains its own requirements for a development plan. Both the *Planning Act* and the charter have been recently amended to reduce provincial control.

Including Winnipeg, there are 199 municipalities in MB, each with a council elected for 4 years. Councils vary in size, consisting of a mayor or reeve as head of council and at least 4 councillors. A chief administrative officer and additional administrative and operational staff support the council. Based upon population size and the concentration of settlements, MB's 199 local govts are divided into rural municipalities (116), villages (21), towns (51), cities (9), and local government districts (2). There are also elected school boards within local communities and, usually, appointed, semi-independent boards (such as library boards) and commissions (such as police commissions). These only add to the complexity of the local govt environment.

Portage la Prairie's historic city hall.

Historically, the main function of MB's municipalities has been to provide services to properties, such as sewer, water, garbage collection, road maintenance, firefighters, and police. In larger cities, such as Winnipeg and the other 8 cities in the province, local govts have gradually assumed responsibilities for new public services over the years, including economic development, housing, and cultural activities.

Municipalities rely on property taxes for most of their revenues. Typically, rural municipalities derive about 2/3 of their revenues from property taxes, whereas for urban municipalities, the reliance upon property taxes is typically 50% to 60%. MB is the only province unconditionally to share limited percentages of personal income tax and corporate income tax revenues with its municipalities (that is, there is no requirement that the municipality spend the money for a specified purpose). A share of revenue collected by the province from video lottery terminals is also transferred to the municipalities, but this must be used to foster economic development. A portion of fuel tax revenues is shared for the purposes of maintaining roads and public transit. Various special-purpose grants, which must be spent as the provincial govt designates, are also available. Finally, MB's Department of Intergovernmental Affairs and Trade provides property assessment, computer processing, and training services to local govt. The City of Winnipeg has a distinctive financial relationship to the province, because as MB's only large city, it has extra expenditure obligations and access to a greater variety of revenue sources and a broader range of special-purpose grants from the province. With a large, professional administrative branch, the City of Winnipeg does not rely to any great extent on service support from the provincial department.

With nearly 200 local govts for a province with about one million people, there have been pressures over the years to consolidate municipalities to achieve units with broader responsibilities. Some amalgamations of school divisions have taken place, but adjustments to municipal boundaries have been relatively minor. Municipal councils stand as a symbol of local identity and autonomy, and are not easily eliminated. The creation of regional bodies for specialized functions has been resisted as simply adding another tier of govt. It might also be the case that provincial govts have been reluctant to create local bodies that might rival them in power. These may be reasons why the present system of local govt is unlikely to change in the near future. ● PAUL THOMAS

GOVERNMENT OF MANITOBA is a Cabinet-Parliamentary system of govt. After each provincial general election, the **LIEUTENANT GOVERNOR** asks the leader of the political party with the most MLAs from the 57 constituencies in the province to appoint a Cabinet and take control over the direction and operations of govt. Under the leadership of the premier, the Cabinet formulates most bills, which become laws; initiates all taxing and spending; and oversees the implementation of all govt policies by the public

Provincial Premiers

NAME	TERM IN OFFICE	PARTY
BOYD, Hon. A.	Sept. 16, 1870 – Dec. 14, 1871	None
GIRARD, Hon. M. A.	Dec. 14, 1871 – Mar. 14, 1872	None
CLARKE, Hon. H. J. H.	Mar. 14, 1872 – Jul. 8, 1874	None
GIRARD, Hon. M. A.	Jul. 8, 1874 – Dec. 2, 1874	None
DAVIS, Hon. R. A.	Dec. 3, 1874 – Oct. 16, 1878	None
NORQUAY, Hon. J.	Oct. 16, 1878 – Dec. 24, 1887	Conservative
HARRISON, Hon. D. H.	Dec. 26, 1887 – Jan. 19, 1888	Conservative
GREENWAY, Hon. T.	Jan. 19, 1888 – Jan. 6, 1900	Liberal Party
MacDONALD, Hon. H. J.	Jan. 10, 1900 – Oct. 29, 1900	Conservative
ROBLIN, Hon. R. P.	Oct. 29, 1900 – May 12, 1915	Conservative
NORRIS, Hon. T. C.	May 12, 1915 – Aug. 8, 1922	Liberal Party
BRACKEN, Hon. J.	Aug. 8, 1922 – Jan. 14, 1943	Liberal-Progressive
GARSON, Hon. S. S.	Jan. 14, 1943 – Nov. 13, 1948	Liberal-Progressive
CAMPBELL, Hon. D. L.	Nov. 13, 1948 – Jun. 30, 1958	Liberal-Progressive
ROBLIN, Hon. D.	Jun. 30, 1958 – Nov. 27, 1967	Progressive Conservative
WEIR, Hon. W. C.	Nov. 27, 1967 – Jul. 15, 1969	Progressive Conservative
SCHREYER, Hon. E. R.	Jul. 15, 1969 – Nov. 24, 1977	New Democratic Party
LYON, Hon. S. R.	Nov. 24, 1977 – Nov. 30, 1981	Progressive Conservative
PAWLEY, Hon. H. R.	Nov. 30, 1981 – May 9, 1988	New Democratic Party
FILMON, Hon. G. A.	May 9, 1988 – Oct. 5, 1999	Progressive Conservative
DOER, Hon. G	Oct. 5, 1999 – present	New Democratic Party

service. Most of the powers of the premier and other Cabinet ministers rest on unwritten, well-established political conventions rather than on written constitutional or statutory provisions. Having concentrated authority in the hands of the premier and Cabinet, the system seeks to hold this small group of political insiders accountable by requiring the govt and individual ministers to retain the support of a majority of MLAs at all times. This arrangement is based on the largely unwritten principles of collective and individual ministerial responsibility.

Collectively the premier and the Cabinet are responsible for the overall performance of govt, being required to maintain majority support in the legislature at all times. Motions of non-confidence presented by the Opposition in connection with major govt initiatives test whether such support exists. Occasions for non-confidence votes include Throne Speeches, when the govt announces its legislative plans; and the budget speech, which announces a govt's planned taxing and spending. In addition to these occasions, the opposition parties provide continuous challenges to the govt through forums like question period, debates on bills, the examination of the estimates of expenditure, and the review of past spending by the public accounts committee.

With majority govts and party discipline, administrations seldom risk being forced to resign and call an election based on a vote of non-confidence. To preserve the image of Cabinet unity, to promote frank discussions internally, and to ensure the political survival of govts, established political conventions of Cabinet confidentiality and solidarity require ministers either to support Cabinet decisions publicly, or to resign. In this way, ministers individually answer to the premier and to the rest of Cabinet for their contribution to the govt's work. As well, ministers are responsible for the activities carried out under their individual authorities, and must answer to the Legislature for the actions of their departments. The pure doctrine of individual ministerial responsibility implies that ministers can be forced to resign for abuses of authority or mistakes made within their departments. In practice, ministers are only removed for personal misdeeds, for serious policy blunders, or for deliberately misleading the Legislature. Even then, their removal is up to the premier.

The premier decides on the structures and procedures for Cabinet's decision-making. Cabinet is primarily a political body, not a managerial one. Its functions consist of providing advice to the premier as leader of govt and of the governing party, securing agreement on priorities and arbitrating disputes among ministers and departments, reminding ministers of their obligations to the collective goals of the govt, planning the legislative and financial program, coordinating the implementation of policy through the civil service, and providing a forum for debate on current issues.

As Cabinets grew in size, one of the structural and procedural features adopted has been the greater use of Cabinet committees. Committees are used to reduce congestion on the agenda of the full Cabinet, to capture interdependencies among policies and programs operated by various departments, and to allow Cabinet members to deepen their policy knowledge. Under PROGRESSIVE CONSERVATIVE premier GARY FILMON, the highest number of Cabinet committees was 8, whereas under the NEW DEMOCRATS' GARY DOER, there were initially 3 committees, with a 4th added in 2003. Common to all Cabinet structures are a treasury board committee, to review expenditures and to promote good management in the civil service; a committee to deal with economic development issues; and a social policy committee.

As of writing, single-person rule by first ministers (whether called "premier" or "prime minister") was increasingly replacing collective decision-making by Cabinet. Arguments for this consolidation of power include: premiers' powers of appointment to Cabinet and other important posts; their control over Cabinet's agenda; their control over personal staff and central agencies serving Cabinet; their participation in intergovernmental meetings; their role in the media as the chief spokesperson for the govt; and their control over the timing of the election. These factors undoubtedly make the premier the most important figure in govt, but they do not eliminate premiers' need to gain Cabinet colleagues' support. To maintain the reputation of their govts and to preserve their political standing, premiers need the unforced support of their ministers. There are also practical constraints on the power of the premier, such as time, and not being present in all locations where significant decisions are made.

The premier and the Cabinet provide the initiative within govt. Most govt MLAs see their primary role as supporting the govt. It is left to the opposition parties to provide a critical review of govt action – or inaction. In short, in MB's Cabinet-Parliamentary system, the role of the Legislature is not to govern, but rather to require the premier and his Cabinet colleagues to boast and confess about their performance in office in order to secure re-election. Seeing the activities of the legislature as a permanent arena for electioneering may not fit exactly with constitutional theory, but it is a realistic description of what happens in practice. ● PAUL THOMAS

GRAIN ELEVATORS symbolize a way of life that defined southern MB for much of its history. The arrival of the railway accelerated the decline of the old order of a society based on the FUR TRADE and its replacement by a new order founded on AGRICULTURE, RAILWAYS, and a more complex

Grain elevator in western Manitoba

G

pattern of commerce: suddenly, grain farmers could access world markets in the nearest hamlet, village, or town on a railway line. Here, they sold to flour millers or elevator companies at the local country elevator. The elevator became the predominant structure of the Prairies, as it revolutionized the grain handling system and ensured the success of the region as a **WHEAT** producer. And, because of its looming height on an otherwise flat featureless landscape, the structure also become the vernacular symbol of the region, appearing on postage stamps, postcards, and magazine and book covers.

EARLY HISTORY: The elevator was invented in Buffalo, NY, in 1842, diffusing throughout the various states of the US Midwest and across the MB border in the 1880s as part of a wider modernization of the grain trade. Though the earliest elevator in MB appears to have been in **NIVERVILLE**, the first "standard" elevator was W. W. Ogilvie Milling Company's **GRETNA** elevator, built in 1881. The **CPR** defined a standard elevator as having not less than 25,000 bushels' capacity, having both elevation and cleaning machinery. The elevator soon sounded the death knell for its predecessor, the flat warehouse. Because of problems of capitalization, the CPR farmed out the elevator business, as did other railway companies. Still, the growth of the railway network remained a life-or-death matter to elevator companies. The CPR – and later the Northern Pacific and Manitoba, Great Northern, CNoR, and Grand Trunk Pacific systems – gave incentives for the construction of lines of standard elevators, so country elevators began to spread across the Prairies. A standard architectural form was ensured by the demands

of the railway companies. Once in place, the line of elevators allowed vast quantities of grain to be marketed cheaply and efficiently. Although individuals and small companies owned elevators, increasingly, groups that owned line elevator companies controlled the structures. Nicholas R. Bawlf organized the first of these, the Northern Elevator Company, in 1893. The major millers owned many more elevators. Chief among these were the Ogilvie Flour Mills, the Lake of the Woods Milling Company, and Western Canada Flour Mills, all of which used "lines" of elevators to obtain choice grain for flour production. These companies often received deals from the railways guaranteeing the rapid building of elevator lines. The major elevator syndicates soon formed a cartel, or a "syndicate of syndicates," and farmers came to believe that this cartel was taking advantage of them. The existence of a complex mesh of corporate linkages between railways, banks, flour milling, and grain and lumber companies gives some credence to this view. In time, farmer protests about the situation led to govt action, such as the *Manitoba Grain Act* (1900), as well as the formation of farmer-owned elevator companies that initially operated only a single elevator. After unsuccessful attempts to organize the handling of grain by farmers, the Prairie-wide Grain Growers Grain Company (later the United Grain Growers or UGG) was formed in 1906, but farmer ownership remained relatively unimportant until the provincially organized Wheat Pools were born in the 1920s. These pools were soon responsible for marketing over ½ of the Prairie crop.

RISE: In 1900, there were 6 line-elevator companies with 421 elevators, but by 1916, 302

companies with 3300 "houses," as the elevators were colloquially known, were in existence. These companies were centred in Winnipeg, mostly having offices in the Winnipeg Grain Exchange, which had quickly become the grain trade's headquarters. Such outfits often covered distinct regions of the province, or dealt exclusively with a specific rail company. Although Cdn entrepreneurs were foremost in the early trade, soon after 1900, farmers stereotyped the grain trade as "dominated largely...by American grain interests." Although this statement was an exaggeration (US ownership represented less than 1/3 of the total in 1921), the balance had swung toward American experience and capital. The explosive increase in the number of grain elevators illustrates the growth of the system, reflecting the development of the Prairies. From 90 elevators in the Prairie provinces in 1890, most of them in MB, the number rose to 2001 in 1911 and 4692 in 1927 (of which only 690 were in MB). The high-water mark for grain elevators came in the mid-1930s, with 5737 on the Prairies in 1934 and 5758 in 1936. Although elevators were first built in MB, the province had less than 13% of the total in 1933, with SK having 57%, reflecting its increasing importance in wheat production.

DECLINE: Since the 1930s, a process of elevator company amalgamation and geographic rationalization gained speed: from 5204 elevators in 1962-63, the total fell to 3324, owned by only 19 companies, by 1980. Moreover, 8 major firms owned 99.5% of the elevators, the UGG having 17.6% and the Pools owning 58.8%. So, 76.4% of the elevators were producer-owned. By 1999, the number of elevators was down to 1016, but as of Aug 2002, there were only 425 elevators left across the Prairies – almost the same number as there were in 1900. In June 2006, the total of licensed elevators had dropped to 340. On the farmer-owned side, UGG first privatized and then amalgamated with Agricore, (as **AGRICORE UNITED**), itself the result of the combination of the MB and AB Pools (84 licensed elevators in 2006). There has also been the spread of SK Pool–owned elevators (this company had 44 licensed elevators in 2006) into the neighbouring provinces, and subsequently the movement of other traditionally provincial operations (such as those of Agricore United) into SK. In each case, the companies are attempting to tap a Prairie-wide market. New inroads by private US companies into the Cdn grain trade reflected the increase in N-S traffic following the North American Free Trade Agreement. For example, Agricore United is now partially owned by US company Archer Daniels Midland (ADM). ADM has also bought into the Prairie flour milling trade. **CARGILL**, now with 32 elevators, has solidified the position it gained when it bought the National Elevator Company and other firms. Most of these new and reorganized companies have built massive modern elevators, with the smaller, older structures usually facing demolition. Some, however, are preserved as museum pieces, such as the Inglis Grain Elevators. Parrish and Heimbecker (20 elevators), Paterson (41), and Pioneer (59) remain as family-oriented companies, and thus as important remnants of the past. A handful of other companies own the balance of the licensed structures (60): Louis Dreyfus has 10; 25 other companies hold the balance. The Prairie landscape used to be symbolized by a wooden elevator – often farmer-owned – as its sentinel. A more accurate contemporary picture would show huge concrete elevators, mostly privately-owned. ● JOHN EVERITT

GRAINS are what the agricultural community calls the traditional cereal crops that MB farmers have planted since the Prairies were first settled. Although **WHEAT** is the primary grain grown, others include barley, oats, rye and mixed grains. Annual production has varied considerably along with markets and weather; however, yields improved steadily after WWII along with improved varieties. In 1883, 215,000 ac (87,000 ha) were planted to wheat, oats, and barley. In 2004, wheat and barley occupied more than 36% of the more than 11 million ac (4.5 million ha) of harvested crop area in the province. The area seeded to barley, used in beer and whisky, was the largest in 1981 at 2.4 million ac (1 million ha). MB normally produces about 10% of the Cdn barley crop. The area of oats seeded and harvested in MB was the greatest in 1921 at 2.2 million ac (.9 million ha) when oats were normally fed to animals. Demand fell off as the industry began to depend more on machinery than horses. In 2006, MB produced about 20% of the Cdn oats crop – about 1 million seeded ac (.45 million ha). MB producers also grow other grains, such as rye and mixed grains. In 2006, seeded acreage ran to 80,000 and 25,000 ac respectively. ● GPP

GRAND BEACH is on the eastern shores of **LAKE WINNIPEG** about 90 km N of **WINNIPEG**. In 1915, William Mackenzie of the CNoR acquired control of the locality and access to its 3 km of white sandy beach. Shortly after opening its line in 1916, the railway laid out a campground that was quickly converted into a cottage settlement and developed a number of beachfront attractions including a dance pavilion, carousel, boardwalk, bathhouses, and food concessions. Due to WWI, the bankruptcy of the CNoR and its takeover by

CNR, Mackenzie's plans for a prestigious hotel and a "Coney Island of the West" to compete with **WINNIPEG BEACH** did not materialize. However, during the years between the wars, the resort enjoyed huge popularity with holidaymakers and excursionists taking Moonlight Special trains over the course of the summer season. An annual highlight in July was the "Caterers' Picnic," a day-long celebration enjoyed by up to 8 trainloads of day-trippers taking in the parades, beauty pageants, races and dancing at the pavilion. After WWII, the resort lost popularity as the railway stopped running, the dance pavilion burned down, and the concessions closed. However, in 1961, the province took over, creating Grand Beach Provincial Park and beginning a long-term program of improvements including a modern campground, extensive nature reserve and year-round resort featuring summer beach related activities and cross-country skiing in the winter. The cottage settlement is again thriving with many owners using their

cottages through most of the year and upgrading or replacing the structures as now required by more stringent govt regulations. The community's white sand beach is considered one of the finest beaches in the world, even making *Playboy's* list of top beaches. On summer weekends the visiting population is thought to be close to 20,000. As Lake Winnipeg is full of long sandbars it makes for warm swimming and many areas for younger children to play on. ● GPP

GRAND MARAIS, pop 344, is a community 90 km NNE of Winnipeg, along the SE shore of **LAKE WINNIPEG**. In 1783, the French explorer **LA VÉRENDRYE** named the area Grand Marais ("Big Marsh"). The **CNR** line to Winnipeg was completed in 1916 and the area started to become a profitable resort attracting Winnipeggers, even in the throes of the **GREAT DEPRESSION**. Grand Marais is adjacent to Grand Beach, which was originally a resort owned and operated by the CNR. Grand Beach is now a **PROVINCIAL PARK**. ● GPP

G

Grand Beach featured in *Free Press* ad, 1916

GRAND RAPIDS, pop 355, is a town about 150 km ESE of **The Pas**, where the Saskatchewan River flows from Cedar Lake into **Lake Winnipeg**. The **Grand Rapids First Nation** is just S of the town. With many of the major fur trade routes converging here, Grand Rapids served as a busy trading centre in the years before MB became a province. **La Vérendrye** built Fort Bourbon here in 1741. Because portaging the 5 km of rapids just outside of town posed many hazards, the **HBC** built a horse-drawn tramway in 1877, which is considered the first railway in western Canada. Ironically, construction of the **CPR** brought an end to the importance of Grand Rapids as a transportation hub, and the HBC post was abandoned by 1900. A key economic base of Grand Rapids is tourism, as the rugged landscape and abundance of fish attract many tourists to the area. Commercial fishing, a forest products operation, and trapping also play important roles in the local economy.

The Grand Rapids dam was the first step in northern hydroelectric resources.

ARCHIVES OF MB, GOVERNMENT RECORDS, 62-631

However, the primary employer in the community is **Manitoba Hydro**'s Grand Rapids electric generating station. The Grand Rapids station was the cornerstone of MB Hydro's development of the North during the 1960s and '70s. When it was completed in 1963, it resulted in serious flooding along the Saskatchewan River. ● GPP

GRAND RAPIDS FIRST NATION, on reserve pop 888, off reserve pop 552, is situated 426 km N of **Winnipeg**, at the opening of the Saskatchewan River on **Lake Winnipeg**. The Grand Rapids First Nation community is located on the E and S banks of the Saskatchewan, just S of the town of **Grand Rapids**. Treaty 5 was signed here in 1875. It is a member of the Swampy Cree Tribal Council. The native language is Cree. There is all-weather road access to this community by way of hwy 6. There is also a runway for air transportation, plus docks, and Grey Goose Bus Lines service. The Frontier School Division administers schooling. Education in this First Nations community goes from Nursery-Grade 12, and total enrolment for the year 2003-04 was 249. This First Nation is located just down from the **Manitoba Hydro**'s Grand Rapids electric generating station. The Grand Rapids station is the cornerstone of MB Hydro's aggressive development of the North during the 1960s and '70s. When it was completed in 1963, the Grand Rapids station flooded the Saskatchewan River. Before the station was built, the community was self-sufficient, gathering its own food and making its own medicine as needed. Because of the flooding, the rapids have been destroyed and social problems are numerous. Although the First Nation received $5.05 million in compensation, serious problems persist. Politician, author, and lawyer **Ovide Mercredi** was born in the Grand Rapids First Nation community. ● RK

GRAND VALLEY, ghost town, was a community just E of **Brandon** on PR 457. The community began to develop in 1878, when Dougald and John McVicar, of Grenville, QC, began exploring less-popular MB locations not scheduled to be railway destinations. At first, the McVicars lived in a dugout home in the side of a hill on the N side of the **Assiniboine River**. By 1880, settlers began to form a town on the McVicars' land. By 1881, the population had grown to 400. There were 6 general stores, a jewellery shore, a harness shop, a bakery, brickyards, a tent hotel, and even a resident doctor. In early 1881, **CPR** surveyors began marking out a crossing for the line that would go to the Rockies. John McVicar, once indifferent to the prospect of his community becoming a railway point, arranged to have his land surveyed into lots. The

CPR offered $25,000 for the town site, but McVicar wanted $50,000. The CPR rejected his offer and built the point 3 km further W. That summer, Grand Valley was flooded as the **Assiniboine River** overflowed. Many residents, who had watched as their tents and shacks collapsed and floated away, moved on. The McVicars and others signed away in their lands in a desperate bid to secure a railway station. However, the trains would never stop in Grand Valley. In 1882, the Assiniboine flooded again. Many of the remaining people left for Brandon, including Dougald McVicar, and the deserted site was sold for $1500. The site is now marked with a fieldstone cairn. ● GPP

GRANDVIEW, pop 814, is a town 50 km W of **Dauphin**. Grandview lies in a valley with the **Riding Mountain National Park** to the S, the Duck Mountain Provincial Park to the N, and the Assessippi Provincial Park to the W. It is not known who was responsible for naming the town. However, according to popular accounts, someone is said to have stood looking W toward the Duck Mtns and exclaimed "What a grand view!" Settlement in Grandview – whose name was originally spelled "Grand View" – began around 1890. In 1900, the railway reached Grandview and the first surveyed lots were sold. The town was incorporated in 1905. Grandview was the 4th community in MB to install a piped water system. In 1902, T. A. Burrows decided to locate his sawmill here. A replica of the sawmill is now on display at the Watson Crossley Community Museum. Although forestry is still important to the community, Grandview is a thriving agricultural community with production of cereal grains, oilseeds, cattle and hogs. Local retail and service businesses support this base as well as catering to the increasing tourism sector. Abundant wildlife, such as moose, elk, and bear, has made viewing and photographing wildlife a popular pastime. The nearby **Ojibway** community of **Tootinaowaziibeeng** also relies on the town for retail and services. ● GPP

GRANT, Cuthbert James, "Wapistan," Métis leader, farmer, hunter, judge (b ca 1793, Fort de la Rivière Tremblante [near modern Kamsack, SK]; d July 15, 1854, Grantown [**St. Francois Xavier**]). Cuthbert was 1 of 5 children of **Scottish**-born **NWC** employee Cuthbert Grant (Sr) and a Métis mother about whom little is known, often called "Utiniwasis." After Cuthbert Sr died in 1799, the bilingual Cuthbert Jr was educated in Ville-Marie (Montreal) – where he was baptized as a **Presbyterian** – and possibly in Scotland, where his brother James had been sent. He returned to **Rupert's Land** as a trader for the

NWC on the Qu'Appelle River, where he was frequently called upon to organize **Bison** hunts. His strength – he was an avid wrestler – and hunting prowess combined with his white heritage earned him the Cree nickname of Wapistan or "Ermine."

The NWC appointed Grant to lead the Métis against the inhabitants of the **Lord Selkirk**'s **Red River Settlement**, especially after **HBC** gov **Miles Macdonell** issued the Pemmican Proclamation, cutting off the **Pemmican** trade routes the Métis relied on for food. In May 1816, Grant rode with an armed party that included his brother-in-law, **Pierre Falcon**, to take the HBC's Brandon House (*see* **Brandon**) and transport its pemmican to NWC posts. On June 19, Grant led the Métis into a confrontation with Red River settlers, under the command of gov **Robert Semple**, on Frog Plain, north of the settlement, in the **Seven Oaks Incident**. Though it is unclear who fired the opening – probably accidental – shot in this skirmish, Grant's side scored a decisive victory. They then took Fort Douglas. Falcon's song about the event has become part of Métis culture. Grant turned himself in to an authority from Lower Canada (QC) in 1817 and was sent there to be tried, but the charges were confusing and he was released. On his return to the Northwest the next year, he learned that his wife of 3 years, Elizabeth "Betsy" Grant (née McKay), and their son had disappeared, possibly murdered. He thereafter had a "country marriage" with Marie-Madeleine Desmaris. The couple had a daughter, Maria, but parted ways soon after.

After the merging of the 2 **Fur Trading** rivals in 1821 as HBC, company executives fired

Cuthbert Grant

Grant, until HBC gov **Sir George Simpson**, rather than showing animosity to Grant, appointed him a special constable of Red River in 1823. After Grant quit this post due to friction with Red River settlers, Simpson requested that Grant relocate the Métis of Pembina (now ND: *see* **Emerson**) to White Horse Plain, in a community initially known as Grantown (now St. François Xavier). Simpson's motives were complex. Grant had been exploited by the NWC, and had probably never intended to cause loss of life, and the grievances of the Métis were legitimate. Perhaps Simpson thought this would be a way to make an ally of a potentially dangerous enemy. In any case, a surveyors' party had revealed that Pembina would soon be ceded to the US as part of Dakota Territory, and the Métis had been warring intermittently with **Dakota** Sioux, an old enemy of the Métis' **Ojibway** ancestors, in the area. For his services, Grantown's founder was appointed "Warden of the Plains" by the HBC. This office, whose principal responsibility was to discourage increasingly bold US fur traders from entering HBC territory, came with a yearly stipend of £200 (then about $975). He settled into the agricultural life growing **Wheat** on the 43 ac (17.5 ha) he received along the Assiniboine River, and built a watermill. He became a **Roman Catholic** and married Métis Marie-Marguerite McGillis. The couple would have 11 children, several of whom did not survive infancy. Grant also served as advisor and doctor to his new community, which would soon be the 2nd Catholic parish in West, after St. Boniface.

Simpson's gamble worked: Grant became a friend both of **Red River** and of the HBC. From 1835-50, he was a member of the Council of **Assiniboia** and a sheriff and magistrate for the 4th District of Assiniboia. Around 1849, Grant fell out of favour with the Métis over the matter of free traders, and Jean-Louis Riel, father of **Louis Riel**, became the primary Métis spokesman during the trial of **Pierre-Guillaume Sayer**, over which Grant presided. Wealthy but with declining influence, Grant returned to hunt on the plains, sometimes accompanying Europeans touring the area. His long life ended on the Prairie after he fell off his horse. He was buried July 16, 1854, at the Catholic Church of Saint-François Xavier in the settlement he founded. Fittingly, his tomb near the altar listed his occupation as *écuyer*, with the double meaning of "horseman" and "knight."

While Grant was a moderate, diplomatic, influential leader, many Manitobans outside Métis and Franco-Manitoban circles have forgotten Grant's contributions. Grant can be credited perhaps as much as **Louis Riel** with cementing the Métis' status as a people in the West. ● A. J. LEVIN

Bud Grant, 1965

GRANT, Harry Peter "Bud," football coach (b May 20, 1927, Superior, WI) coached the **Winnipeg Blue Bombers** to 4 Grey Cup Titles. His athletic career began at the U of Minnesota where he played baseball, basketball and football. An all-around star athlete, Grant was drafted to both the NBA and the NFL in 1949. As part of the Minneapolis Lakers, he played on 2 consecutive NBA championship-winning teams. He left in 1951 to play in the NFL for the Philadelphia Eagles. Grant became the starting receiver in 1952, ranking 2nd in the NFL for receiving yardage with 997 yards on 56 catches. When Eagles' management refused to give him a pay raise the following season, Grant signed on with the Blue Bombers. Playing for both offence and defence, Grant set numerous CFL records for his time. However, Grant is best remembered as the team's successful head coach, a position he took over in 1956. During his 10-year reign, a time often referred to as the "Golden Years," Grant coached the Bombers to 102 wins, bringing home the Grey Cup consecutively in 1958-59 and again in 1961-62. In 1967, he was persuaded to take over the Minnesota Vikings. He coached the NFL team to 168 wins over the next 18 years, placing him among the top 10 most successful coaches in the league. He retired from the Vikings in 1983, coaching a final season in 1985 before leaving professional coaching permanently. He is a member of the Canadian Football Hall of Fame. ● MD

GRANT, Irene, women's rights activist (b Feb 1914, **Niverville**). For more than 70 years, Grant advocated to improve conditions for women in society. In 1945, after her marriage, she helped to break down the barrier stopping married women from teaching in Winnipeg. Grant subsequently served as a member of the Business and Professional Women's (BPW) Club of Winnipeg, and, beginning in the 1950s, was active with the MB Teachers Society. Grant worked toward changing the retirement policy which forced women to retire at age 60. She also lobbied for pay equity for women. Grant worked with the Family Law Reform Committee, which pressed for the *Family Maintenance Act* and the *Marital Property Act*. She was the citizen's advisor to Legal Aid Manitoba (1972-82), and helped found the Fort Garry Women's Resource Centre. She was an active member of the Land Use Committee of the MB Environmental Council, and chaired the Provincial Council of Women of MB's environment committee for 3 years. Grant received many accolades for her efforts, including the federal govt's Person's Day Award; a lifetime membership in both the **International Peace Gardens** and the Cdn Federation of Business and Professional Women's Clubs; and the Order of MB (2005). ● RK

GRAPHIC DESIGN INDUSTRY is comprised of designers who produce graphic art and other visual materials to communicate information. In 2006, there were just over 1000 designers in MB. Most worked for small-to-medium-sized studios, advertising agencies, or companies otherwise involved in the production of digital media. Many have an international clientele as the growth of **Information and Communications Technology** in the 1990s eliminated geographic boundaries, enabling MB designers to work with customers outside the province. The relatively low cost of living in MB also means that studios here have significantly lower overhead, making it often more affordable for companies from larger centres to hire a designer from here.

In the 1800s, graphic design played an important role in attracting the first settlers to MB, when lithographic posters advertising the "Last, Best West" were widely distributed in Europe. Within the province, the establishment of a substantial design industry began with the opening of a branch of the Toronto firm **Brigden's** Ltd. The **Winnipeg** office of Brigden's produced the artwork for **Eaton's** mail-order catalogues in western Canada, and employed a number of talented artists as designers, such as **Charles Thorson**, **Pauline Boutal**, and **Charles Comfort**. Many of these artists later received training from **Lionel**

LeMoine FitzGerald, who taught at the Winnipeg School of Art, established 1913. Painters often used the steady income from design work to support their fine art endeavours. It wasn't until Canada Council and Manitoba Arts Council grants became available in the 1960s that graphic design emerged as a profession rather than the bread and butter of starving artists.

Up until the 1970s, MacDonald, Michaleski and Associates was the province's most influential firm. As of 2007, advertising agency McKim Cringan George was among the largest MB firms involved in design work. The province has 2 designers, Robert L. Peters of Circle Design Inc. and Steven Rosenburg of Doowah Design, who are Fellows in the Society of Graphic Designers of Canada, the highest honour that can be given to a Cdn designer. ● MD

GRASSHOPPER is an insect of the order Orthoptera, characterized by long and powerful hind jumping legs, narrow, toughened forewings which protect the flying wings, and sound-producing organs in the male. Grasshoppers range in size from 10-150 mm and are frequently beautifully coloured – either cryptically for camouflage, or brightly to warn predators of distasteful chemicals. These insects have excellent sight and hearing, and leap or fly considerable distances when disturbed. If grasped, a grasshopper regurgitates its gut contents and releases noxious chemicals from glands lying under the cuticle. All grasshoppers are equipped with chewing, biting mouthparts. Some are capable of inflicting painful injuries to one's hand via bites and stabs from spines on the strong limbs.

Interestingly, the 'ears' of grasshoppers are located on the abdomen or front legs, and consist of a thin membrane which vibrates with incoming sound waves, and transmits this energy to internal receptors. Sounds produced by the male play a major role in courtship, and are generated by snapping the wings, or by rubbing the hind legs against the front wings (and not by rubbing the hind legs together as is often believed). Strikingly coloured patches (pink, red, yellow or black) on the rear set of wings of band-winged grasshoppers, such as the Northwestern Red-winged Grasshopper (*Arphia pseudonietana*) flash open when taking flight and to serve to attract the attention of females (and perhaps also to startle predators). Following courtship and mating, the female uses her long ovipositor to lay eggs in pods of 10-200 in the soil, within protective foam which prevents the eggs from drying out. The eggs hatch into tiny replicas of the adult called nymphs, which undergo 4-8 moulting stages (instars) as they grow, acquiring wings in the final moult into an adult. While most species have a one-year life cycle, overwintering as an egg, a few like the Coral-winged (*Pardalophora apiculata*) and Red-shanked (*Xanthippus corallipes*) grasshoppers live 2 years, over-wintering first as an egg, then the 2nd winter as a nymph.

There are an amazing 22,500 species of grasshoppers, katydids, crickets, and their relatives in the order Orthoptera, with close to 150 species in Canada. Over 68 species of grasshoppers occur

Grasshopper about to meet windshield near Wawanesa

in MB (over 600 in NA; 11,000 species worldwide), representing 4 families: True Grasshoppers and Locusts (Acrididae), Pygmy Grasshoppers (Tetrigidae), Frog Groundhoppers (Batrachideidae), and Pygmy Mole Crickets (Tridactylidae). Among MB Acrididae are several important subfamilies – Band-winged, Spur-throated, and Silent Slant-faced grasshoppers. Grasshoppers and their kin are dominant converters of plants into animal tissue, and supply countless species, from frogs and snakes to birds and mammals, with a stable and rich source of summer food.

Most grasshoppers may be described as neutral and even beneficial (by controlling weeds), such as the Meadow Purple-striped Grasshopper (*Hesperotettix viridis*). Several others, such as the Two-striped Grasshopper (*Melanoplus bivittatus*) and Clear-winged Grasshopper (*Camnula pellucida*) periodically become so numerous during warm, dry summers that they become major agricultural pests across S Canada. Pest status is reached at populations of 13/m², and may reach 200/m². MB Agriculture and Food provides annual grasshopper forecasts and maps showing the areas of species' abundance. Cool and wet conditions result in the death of large numbers of nymphs and adults, as well as eggs in the soil, due to disease from fungi and bacteria.

In the Rocky Mountain Locust (*Melanoplus spretus*) of MB and western NA, there are 2 distinct lifestyles, each tuned to environmental conditions. When feeding conditions are suitable, the grasshoppers develop into solitary adults, but when food sources disappear from drought, the nymphs develop through several moults a different coloration and adults become gregarious. A female detects crowding from having their legs being jostled by others, and this stimulates the release of a chemical pheromone that is passed into her eggs and subsequent offspring. These develop into gregarious locusts which join the swarm and devour every kind of plant and crop in their path over vast areas. During early settlement of prairie MB, there were periodic outbreaks lasting about 10 years. Locust 'wars', which devastated the settlers' crops, were recorded in 1864-74, and again from 1897-1901. The following year, this unbelievably abundant NA locust (estimated at 3.5 trillion) suddenly became extinct – a mystery remaining partially unsolved to this day. Likely plowing, grazing and irrigation in the locust's traditional breeding grounds in valleys of the Rockies, low temperatures, and wet conditions combined to destroy the entire breeding stock. The last live specimen in NA was picked up near Treesbank; preserved specimens can still be collected on glaciers in the Rockies. ● REW

Charles Gray, 1919

ARCHIVES OF MB, CHARLES F. GRAY COLLECTION 2, JUNE 7, 1919

GRAY, Charles Frederick, politician (b Dec 17, 1879, London, UK; d June 27, 1954, Victoria, BC) served as mayor during the **Winnipeg General Strike.** Gray was a consulting electrical engineer, with no apparent links to **Winnipeg**'s commercial elite, before his election to the Board of Control in 1917. He lived in the Elm Park neighbourhood. During the 1918 municipal workers' strike, he began by favouring a compromise with the unions, and ended up supporting a resolution denying all civic employees the right to strike. He ran for mayor in 1918 on a platform of honest govt, and was mayor during the Winnipeg General Strike in 1919. He was gradually persuaded that the strike was Bolshevism run rampant, and supported the efforts of city council to force its employees back to work through "yellow dog" tactics, issuing public proclamations against street demonstrations. On June 5, he ordered the use of special constables. On June 20 – "Black Friday" – when he was told the "specials" could not control the crowds, he personally drove to RNWMP headquarters to request that the Mounties intervene. He subsequently read the *Riot Act* to the demonstrators at city hall. In 1941, he moved to Ashland, BC, where he operated a salt mine. ● JMB

GRAY, James H., historian, journalist (b Aug 31, 1906, **Whitemouth**; d Nov 12, 1998, Calgary) wrote extensively about the Prairies. Brought up in Winnipeg, he attended Kelvin High School, leaving it after grade 9 to work in the **Winnipeg Grain Exchange.** Gray spent the **Great Depression** on relief until he became a reporter for the **Winnipeg Free Press** in 1935, working in the Ottawa press gallery until 1947, when he lost his job over his treatment of Cdn trade policy. Gray later worked as a journalist in many parts of Canada, editing the *Farm and Ranch Review* and the *Western Oil Examiner*. He took early retirement in 1963 to complete the manuscript of *The Winter Years* (1966), which had been rejected by Macmillan nearly 20 years earlier. He subsequently wrote a series of autobiographical social histories

of the Prairies, including *The Boy from Winnipeg* (1970) and *The Roar of the Twenties* (1975). Other historical works included *Men against the Desert* (1967), *Red Lights on the Prairies* (1971), and *Booze* (1972). Gray was at his best when he had some personal stake in the narrative, although his prose was always lucid. He won the Pierre Berton Award from Canada's National Historical Society for popularizing Cdn history. ● JMB

GREAT DEPRESSION. The Depression was hardly unique to MB or Canada. Triggered by the 1929 stock market crash, the 1930s were part of a massive contraction – the downward part of a periodical international economic cycle – that affected all nations, although industrialized and large-scale resource-exporting countries suffered more. However, the Depression was particularly severe in western Canada, where a combination of drought and the collapse of world commodity prices, especially grain, hit hard at the farm communities that had expanded for many years and were deeply in debt to the banks.

In 1930, farmers attempted, through their **Wheat** pools, to raise international prices by withholding wheat from sale, but the strategy backfired. Instead, harvests were greatly reduced by the absence of moisture in the wheat regions for 8 years. The dry soil blew away and grasshoppers covered the land – an infestation that often accompanied drought in MB. A ubiquitous dust blowing in the air, similar to the "Dust Bowl" phenomenon in the southern Great Plains, was the symbol of the times for many Manitobans. The resultant loss of income combined with a general lack of investment in the economy to produce high unemployment, particularly in Winnipeg, where the construction industry came to a virtual standstill. By 1932, **Winnipeg** had the 2nd-highest per capita unemployment in Canada. While those farmers able to keep their land out of the clutches of the bankers could at least eat some of their own products, the urban unemployed depended on the dole and handouts. Still, co-operation was key to farmers' survival, since the govt did not count independent farmers as unemployed. The jobless suffered from a political system that worked against them. Constitutionally, the provinces had almost all the responsibilities for social conditions, but they were not given commensurate powers of taxation and revenue-raising. Municipalities, moreover, had no constitutional existence whatever, and dispensed relief sparingly and with no effort to maintain recipients' dignity. For the half of the population that did not lose their jobs, however, life during the Depression could be comfortable. The cost of living was low, and houses repossessed or acquired by the

G

Great Depression soup kitchens

authorities for back taxes could be obtained for a pittance. Labour was also cheap, as servants vied for work and wages were low.

For many Manitobans, the economic collapse resulted in severe social dislocation. The young often rode the rails, becoming part of a virtual transient army of unemployed. This culminated in the 'On to Ottawa' trek, and the Regina Riots, in 1935. Husbands and fathers deserted their families en masse, leaving wives and mothers to cope with the difficult conditions as best they could. Others "left" in other ways. It is no accident that film came into its own in this age, and the radio was the last personal possession retained by the impoverished, for both media represented entertainment and an opportunity for escape into a fantasy world. For others, the experience of unemployment could be redemptive. Journalist James Gray, who described the experiences of the Winnipeg unemployed during the severe recession's depths in his book *The Winter Years*, pointed out that many turned to their local libraries and educated themselves. Some Manitobans used their free time for creative purposes, and drama, poetry, and art flourished because radical intellectuals found in them ideal media for expressing their discontent with the status quo. In Winnipeg, a Little Theatre movement grew in the **NORTH END**. Novelist **MARGARET LAURENCE** drew on her Depression-era childhood in both *Heart of a Stranger* and *The Diviners*.

Conservative premier **JOHN BRACKEN** made an alliance with the provincial Liberals in 1932, and went to Ottawa to demand more assistance from the federal govt. He got it, but in exchange was forced to balance his budget. Bracken remained in power throughout the Depression, usually heading a coalition govt and insisting that constitutional reform was the only way to save MB. Not until the end of the 1930s, with

the appointment of a Royal Commission to examine Dominion/provincial financial relations, was there a real sign of change. Not surprisingly, many across Canada turned to extreme political solutions. Except for a brief rise of Fascism in Winnipeg in 1935 and the election of socialist **JOHN QUEEN** as Winnipeg mayor in 1934, Manitobans generally eschewed political extremism. They resisted the blandishments of the Social Credit movement headed by William Aberhart in AB, as well as the **CCF**, headed by MB's own **J. S. WOODSWORTH**. A variety of political and economic changes, including the outbreak of WWII, finally led to the end of the Great Depression. ● J.M. BUMSTED

GREAT GREY OWL (*Strix nebulosa*), chosen as MB's provincial **BIRD** by naturalists and school groups, joined the **PRAIRIE CROCUS** as an emblem of MB in 1987. Although the species ranges across much of northwestern and north-central NA, great greys occur in stable populations – perhaps as high as several thousand – throughout MB, except for the very N and the very SW. They typically roost in mixed woods, often at or near

the edge, as they hunt over open areas. The **PINAWA** region, the **PROVINCIAL FORESTS** of **EASTMAN**, and the **WHITESHELL PROVINCIAL PARK** are among the best places in the world to see the birds.

The great grey is the largest **OWL** in NA, with an average wingspan of about 1.3 m, a length of about 70 cm, and a weight of about 1.3 kg for females, and 0.9 kg for males. It has a large, round, grey head with a black-and-white "beard," no "ear" tufts, and conspicuous facial rings. The greys' diet consists primarily of small-to-medium rodents, though small **WEASELS**, **FROGS**, **SNAKES**, **INSECTS**, and **BIRDS** as large as **CROWS** may form up to 15% of their diet. Their main threats are large, tree-based members of the **WEASEL** family, such as martens; great horned owls, which, though smaller in wingspan, are heavier; and human automobile drivers and poachers, although federal laws protect the grey in all its North American range. Goshawks may also take owlets when their main prey, **GROUSE**, is scarce.

Like other owls, the great grey is primarily nocturnal but may be about in daylight, particularly in winter toward the S of their range. The species generally ranges from the boreal forest and the edge of the tundra of the very W of QC and eastern Northern ON, through the N of the Prairie Provinces and S of the Territories, to most of AK. The owl occurs in the Rockies in WY and ID as well, with small, isolated populations in the interior of the Pacific coast states. The great grey, often called the "Lapland owl" in Eurasia, also occurs in Sweden, Finland, and Russia. Though not characterized as endangered, habitat loss has severely limited the species from parts of its historical range. In MB, the bird occurs typically in tamarack and poplar forests, near open meadows and muskeg. Stray owls, usually in pairs, may occur in the SW too, especially when populations stressed for food expand S of their usual range in winter.

Biologist Robert Nero rescued one great grey, "Lady Gray'l," when she was a hatchling

CORY LOEWEN

Great Grey Owl

in 1984. For 21 years, she visited countless schools, malls, and other public sites along with Nero, educating the public on conservation and fundraising for biological research. Nero subsequently wrote 9 books, many inspired by Lady Gray'l, including *Growing Old Together*, *The Great Gray Owl: Phantom of the Northern Forest*, and *Lady Gray'l: Owl with a Mission*. She was the subject of 3 entries in his **POETRY** book *Woman by the Shore* (Natural Heritage Books, 1990). After the owl's death in 2005, the Global Owl Project instituted the Lady Gray'l Award for the owl that has made the greatest contribution to raising awareness of these birds. MB is also home to a fund dedicated to conserving the great grey owl. ● A. J. LEVIN

GREAT WESTERN CANADIAN SCREEN-SHOP.

Founded in Winnipeg in 1968 by artist Bill Lobchuk, the goal of the Screen Shop was to provide facilities and technical assistance for western Cdn printmakers. It was the first of its kind and at the core of MB's contemporary printmaking development. Assisted by photographer Len Anthony, the Screen Shop expanded the technical limitations of silk screening, in size, complexity of numbers of colours and the inclusion of photography. Many major **WINNIPEG** artists were involved: **WINSTON LEATHERS**, Gordon Adaskin, **TONY TASCONA**, **KEN LOCHHEAD**, **BRUCE HEAD** and **DON PROCH**. The **WINNIPEG ART GALLERY** first exhibited the work of the Screen Shop in 1974. In the mid 1970s, the Screen Shop produced its first group portfolio, including MB and SK artists, pre-selling pieces at 'discount prices' to expand their market and raise necessary revenue. By 1975, they had outgrown their first premises on Princess St and moved to McDermott St. In Jan 1977, joined by Saskatoon artist David Umholtz, they added lithography and intaglio facilities, custom printing and presented classes and workshops, thus opening the Moosehead Press in Winnipeg. Together, the Great Western Canadian Screen Shop and Moosehead Press confirmed Winnipeg's position as a leading centre of printmaking in the 1970s and 1980s. Artists from across Canada were involved in both, including **KELLY CLARK**, **DON REICHERT**, **WANDA KOOP**, **ANDREW VOLKO** and Ron Shuebrook, Pierre Ayot and Naboru Sawai. Publications include Angela Davis, *The Grand Western Canadian Screen Shop*, 1992; and David Umholtz, *Moosehead Press: 10 Years: 1977-1987*, 1987. ● PATRICIA BOVEY

GREAT-WEST LIFECO INC.

is a **WINNIPEG**-based, publicly traded, financial services holding company with interests in the life insurance, health insurance, reinsurance, and investment and retirement savings businesses. A member of the Montreal-based Power Financial Corporation group of companies, Great-West Lifeco's holdings include some of the country's leading insurance firms, including Great-West Life Assurance Company of Winnipeg, London Life Assurance Company of London, ON, and Canada Life Assurance Company of Toronto. Outside Canada, G-W Lifeco owns Great-West Life & Annuity of Denver, CO. Its Canada Life subsidiary also has substantial life insurance operations in Europe and is among the UK's largest group life and health insurance companies.

G-W Lifeco's roots date back to 1891, when the Great-West Life Assurance Company was founded in Winnipeg. Great-West Life grew to become one of Canada's leading insurance companies. It also has been selling insurance products in the US since 1907 under the name Great-West Life & Annuity Insurance. Today, Great-West Life & Annuity, which is headquartered in Denver, is a significant player in the US life and casualty insurance industry. Great-West Lifeco Inc. was established in 1986 as the parent company for both G-W Life and G-W Life & Annuity. It became the largest life insurance conglomerate in Canada with the acquisition in 1997 of London Life for $2.94 billion, and the purchase in 2003 of Canada Life for $7.3 billion. As of writing, Great-West Lifeco was providing insurance for more than 13 million people in NA and had more than $164 billion in assets under its management. In June 2006, the company further bolstered is presence in the European market with the acquisition of London-based Equitable Life's pension annuity division. ● MURRAY MCNEILL

GREEN, Sidney, politician, labour lawyer (b Aug 1, 1929, **WINNIPEG**), served as a colourful and outspoken cabinet minister for **EDWARD SCHREYER**'s **NDP** govt and later established the Progressive Party. Green was born into a Jewish family in Winnipeg's **NORTH END**. He earned his law degree from the **U OF M**, articling under **JOE ZUKEN**, then a **COMMUNIST** school trustee. Despite his working-class background and Zuken's influence, Green chose to become involved with the NDP, not the Communist Party. He ran as a sacrificial candidate in the riding of Winnipeg South in the 1962 federal election. He began his true political career later that year with his election to Winnipeg's city council in a North End riding. He served on council until 1965, when he resigned to contest the federal election in the Winnipeg South constituency again. He once again lost that election, but was selected as president of the MB NDP in 1966 and elected to the provincial legislature on June 23, 1966, with the highest majority of any NDP candidate. In Sept 1968, he bid for the leadership of the MB party, but lost to incumbent Russell Paulley by 20 votes. Green ran for the party leadership again in 1969, this time against NDP MP **EDWARD SCHREYER**, who had been specially recruited as a young, new face to lead the party. Schreyer won the leadership, and the NDP, campaigning under Green's leadership slogan "Ready to Govern," and won its first ever majority govt. Green was re-elected to the legislature and served in Schreyer's cabinet from 1969-77 with the exception of a few months in 1972, when he resigned over Schreyer's decision to fund private denominational schools. Green was minister of health and social services (1969), mines and natural resources (1971),

G

Headquartered in Winnipeg, Great-West Lifeco is the largest life insurance conglomerate in Canada.

G

Sid Green, 1977

urban affairs (1971-72), and the Manitoba Development Corporation (1973-77).

After the NDP government was voted out of office and Schreyer was appointed gov gen in 1979, **Howard Pawley** took over as leader. Green became increasingly disillusioned with the party, leaving to sit as an independent in Dec 1979 in a disagreement over proposed anti-scab legislation. On March 3, 1981, he formed and led the Progressive Party with former NDP MLAs Ben Hanuschak and Bud Boyce, former NDP president Murdoch Mackay, and former party vice-president Max Hofford. The party was viewed as socialist, supporting traditional left-wing causes like full employment and increased taxation on resource industries. However, the party also borrowed from the right wing; Green strongly opposed the federal Charter of Rights and the **Meech Lake Accord**. The Progressives hoped to run a full slate of candidates in the 1981 election, but were unsuccessful. All the party's candidates were defeated, including Green. Green continued to act as party leader, repeatedly – without success – attempting to regain a seat in the legislature. Finally in 1995, Green dissolved the party. In 2003, Green published his memoirs, *The Rise and Fall of a Political Animal*. In 2007, he was retired and living in Winnipeg.
● TESSA VANDERHART

GREEN, Theodore Joseph "Terrible Ted,"

hockey player, coach (b March 23, 1940, Eriksdale). A hard-nosed defenseman and long-time NHL coach, Green got his start in the Manitoba Junior Hockey League in 1956 with the St. Boniface Canadiens. He won the Memorial Cup in 1959 while on loan to the **Winnipeg** Braves. He then moved up to play 2 seasons with the

Winnipeg Warriors of the Western Hockey League. Green began his NHL career in 1961 with the Boston Bruins. He quickly established himself as a valuable defensive defenseman known for his physical style of play. On Dec 26, 1968, Green set an NHL record for penalty minutes in a game when he was assessed 3 minors, 2 majors, and 2 game misconducts.

At the start of his 9th year with the team in 1969, during a preseason game, Green was involved in one of the most violent incidents in NHL history. A stick-swinging fight with Wayne Maki left Green near death with a fractured skull, brain damage, and temporary paralysis. Doctors inserted a metal plate in his head. Green made a full recovery, however, and returned to action with the team after missing the entire 1969-70 season. He won the Stanley Cup with the Bruins in 1972 before jumping to the World Hockey Association's New England Whalers. He played his final 4 professional seasons with the WHA **Winnipeg Jets**.

Green's coaching career began in 1979 in **Carman** with a minor league team named the Hornets. Former Bruins teammate Glen Sather of the Edmonton Oilers named him an assistant coach in 1981, and Green was part of each of their 5 Stanley Cup-winning teams. He became head coach in 1991, was fired in 1994, and remained part of the organization until 2000 when he followed Sather to the New York Rangers. He was a Rangers assistant coach until the end of the 2004 season. Green was inducted into the Manitoba Sports Hall of Fame in 2003. ● JT

GREENFELD, Sherman,

racquetball champion (b June 3, 1962, **Winnipeg**) has won 20 provincial and 10 national titles with 2 world championships in an athletic career that has spanned 22 years. Greenfeld was 16 when he first played racquetball at Court Sports Club. He instantly appreciated the individual nature of the sport, and began playing 6 hours a day, gaining the attention of the club's top players, who suggested that Greenfeld play competitively. He had his first major competition at the 1979 Canada Games in **Brandon**, where he won his first medal, followed 2 years later by his first MB title. Greenfeld went on to win his first Cdn championship in 1986, and claimed world championship titles in Mexico in 1994 and again in Bolivia in 1998, the only Cdn player to have 2 titles to his name. His last major international competition came in his hometown at the 1999 **Pan Am Games**. ● MD

GREENWAY, Thomas,

businessman, farmer, premier (b Mar 25, 1838, Cornwall, UK; d Oct 30, 1908, Ottawa). Greenway migrated to Canada with his family at age 6. He began his political

life in the early 1860s as a Reformer (Liberal) in ON, serving as an elected non-partisan official at the municipal level. He switched to the **Conservatives** later in the 1860s. After winning a federal seat by acclamation in 1875 as a Conservative, he switched affiliations yet again, joining the ruling **Liberal** govt of Alexander Mackenzie in 1876. After entering into a business arrangement with his chief rival for the Liberal nomination in 1878, he stepped aside, left ON for MB, and, using his former rival's investment capital, established himself as a colonization agent, land speculator, and farmer in the **Crystal City** area.

Thomas Greenway, 1888

Greenway entered provincial politics as a "non-partisan" in 1879, originally supporting the **Norquay** administration, but by 1882, he was its most severe critic. Instrumental in forming a "provincial rights" movement, Greenway became the leader of the opposition group in the MB assembly, and the first leader of the newly created **Liberal** Party of MB in 1885. The Liberals coalesced out of a mélange of "provincial rights" advocates, ON-style rural "Grits," and some urban Liberals in **Winnipeg** and **Brandon**. Greenway's primary issues were provincial rights (gaining better financial terms and local control over natural resources); lower tariffs; ending the **CPR** monopoly; acquiring more railways for MB; govt efficiency; and majority (English) rights. Greenway rode these issues to electoral victory after a scandal brought down premier John Norquay late in 1887, and many of these concerns defined his time in power (1888-1900).

Greenway's greatest fame would stem from his govt's controversies. In the name of economy and efficiency, of creating "national" schools for MB, and, later, for the sake of majority and provincial rights, French-language rights were abolished, as were funds for Catholic schools. This legislation, introduced in 1890, set off the **MB Schools Question**. The legal challenges and political wrangling over these issues would define Greenway's next 6 years of political life. As legal challenges to the school legislation worked their way through the courts in 1891-92, Greenway called an election that was in essence a provincial referendum on the MSQ, and won a renewed mandate. In 1895-96, when the federal govt threatened to force remedial legislation upon MB over the Schools Question, Greenway called yet another election, again running as the head of an administration dedicated to winning MB's "autonomy" and defending its provincial rights. The administration was returned to power. It was a smashing victory, as the Jan 1896 election reduced the Conservative opposition to 5 seats. But it was also clear that the Greenway administration was running out of steam – and issues. When Laurier's federal Liberals came to power later in 1896, a "compromise" on the MSQ was quickly worked out between MB Attorney General **Sir Clifford Sifton** and Cdn PM Sir Wilfrid Laurier (the Laurier-Greenway Compromise) allowing for some religious instruction and bilingual education.

By Dec 1899, Greenway was so out of touch with MB's voters that he was taken completely by surprise when his govt lost the election to Sir Hugh John Macdonald's Conservatives. Greenway spent 4 unhappy years as head of the Opposition, eventually bringing his party to its lowest level of electoral support since its inception in the 1903 election. He finally "escaped" provincial politics in 1904, winning a federal seat in Lisgar – but only to position himself for a well-paying federal appointment. This finally came in 1908, when he was appointed to the Railway Commission, which paid $7000 per year. Just as he arrived in Ottawa to take up his new post on Oct 30, he suffered a massive heart attack and died before serving a single day on the job.

For better or worse, the province had been altered to a staggering degree in the 12 years of the Greenway administration. Overt party politics had been introduced and accepted at the province level, the process of making MB more like ON in political and constitutional terms had nearly been completed, and MB's older communal and ethnic political compact was swept away. MB did have more railways and more "provincial rights" than 12 years earlier but some might ask if the price paid by minorities had been worth it. ● JIM MOCHORUK

GREENHOUSE INDUSTRY in MB is based primarily on the production of bedding plants. Greenhouse vegetable crops were once common in the province, but rising fuel costs through the 1970s made operating during the winter unprofitable.

As of 2006, most of MB's approximately 240 commercial greenhouses operated seasonally from Feb-Sept. A small number of greenhouses that grow specialty crops such as poinsettias operate year-round. The most common greenhouse structures in MB use a double layer of polyethylene, a type of thermoplastic, rather than glass in order to reduce heat loss. Flowers, ornamental plants, and bedding plants grown in MB greenhouses were valued at $31 million in 2005. ● MD

GRETNA, pop 563, is a town 105 km SSW of **Winnipeg** along the US border and on the CP/Burlington Northern line. Long a site of **Dakota** activity, Gretna was settled in 1883, following the linking of the **CPR** with the Great Northern Railway on the US side. The town was incorporated in 1886. Gretna continued to grow as the CPR not only established a stop here, but also encouraged the development of **Grain Elevators**. Gretna was renamed in honour of the man who built the first grain elevator, who was originally from Gretna Green, UK. Gretna also served as an important border crossing between Canada and the US. Both federal govts erected customs houses to help stop the flow of smuggled goods at the border. A town with a mainly Mennonite population, Gretna is home to western Canada's oldest private co-ed school, Mennonite Collegiate Institute. Education is also one of the leading industries, along a state-of-the-art concert hall, a book publishing company, and a polymer product fabrication company. The town hosts Sängerfest, an annual music festival that celebrates the talent of local musicians, and an annual family and sport festival known as Hot Spot. ● GPP

GREY NUNS are a group of **Roman Catholic** women dedicated to charitable work in health care, education, and social services. Formally known as the Congregation of the Sisters of Charity of Montreal, the organization was founded in 1737 when Marguerite d'Youville (b Marie Marguerite, 1701; d 1771) and 3 others dedicated themselves to serving the poor in God's name. When the order began to expand outside of Montreal in the 1840s, a group of 4 nuns arrived at the **Red River Settlement** from Canada East (QC) on June 21, 1844 at the request of Bishop **Joseph-Norbert Provencher**. Sisters Valade, Lagrave, Coutlée, and Lafrance settled in St. Boniface and worked alongside Provencher, mainly as teachers and nurses. In 1847, they opened a one-room hospital in their convent, and in 1871 the group bought a house in order to establish **St. Boniface General Hospital**, the first of its kind W of ON. The convent also housed an orphan asylum and a hospice until separate facilities were completed.

Two of the sisters opened Winnipeg's first school in 1869. **Louis Riel** was one of the attendees and his sister Sara later became a Grey Nun. The nuns founded St. Joseph's Orphanage in 1900 and operated it until 1937 when it was transferred to the Sisters of Providence order. In 1938, they helped build and staff the **Ste. Rose du Lac** hospital. Other Grey Nun-founded institutions that remain in operation include: **St. Amant**; Sara Riel Inc. (offering mental-health treatment programs since 1977); health education and resource facility Youville Centre; and long-term care units for the elderly, Foyer Valade (1988) and Taché Centre (1935).

In 2000, the Grey Nuns of MB transferred authority and ownership of their health-care institutions to the Catholic Health Corporation of MB, which in turn created the Catholic Health Network. The Grey Nuns' original convent is the oldest remaining building in Winnipeg, and now houses the **St. Boniface Museum**. There are also congregations of Grey Nuns across Canada and the US. In Dec 1990, Pope John Paul II canonized Marguerite d'Youville, making her a saint. ● JOEL TRENAMAN

Grey Nuns leaving Montreal for Red River

Spruce Grouse are found exclusively in the Boreal forest.

G

GREY OWL, born Archibald Stansfeld Belaney in 1888, was an Englishman who immigrated to ON at the age of 17 in order to live like Canada's **FIRST PEOPLES**. He did just that, assuming an Aboriginal identity and learning the skills of a trapper, canoeist, and forest ranger. In 1931, he lived in a cabin in MB's **RIDING MOUNTAIN NATIONAL PARK** while working for the Canadian parks service. He became a conservationist, filmmaker, and famous "Indian" writer, publishing many books and articles. His true origin was not revealed until after his death in 1938. ●

GROSSE ISLE, pop 565, is a community about 15 km NW of **WINNIPEG** on hwy 6. The name denotes a glacial ridge above marshland. The site was first temporarily occupied by **RED RIVER** settlers fleeing flooding in 1852. In the 1860s, William Inkster built a stopping-house here for traders and freighters. The earliest registered land-holder in 1863 was Winnipeg merchant Alfred Boyd. The last recorded shooting of a wild buffalo in MB was here in 1861. A rail line NW to Gypsumville was laid in 1904. Remnants of this line now are used by the Prairie Dog Central, a vintage tourist train from Winnipeg. A 116-km stretch of abandoned rail line N to Fisher Branch is now a spur trail of the Trans-Canada Trail. ● GPP

GROUSE and their relatives (family Phasianidae) are medium-sized to large chicken-like birds that feed mostly on the seeds, leaves, and buds of various plants. The group includes partridges, pheasants, grouse, ptarmigans, prairie chickens, and turkeys. Although many members of this group are locally known as "prairie chickens," the only true prairie chicken ever to have occurred in MB was the greater prairie chicken (*Tympanuchus cupido*), which became extinct in MB around

the middle of the 20th century due to changing agricultural practices and increased competition from sharp-tailed grouse (*T. phasianellus*). Ptarmigans are Arctic birds that are well camouflaged at most times, being white in winter and largely brown in summer.

Spruce grouse (*Falcipennis canadensis*) and ruffed grouse (*Bonasa umbellus*) use their cryp-tic colouration to avoid detection in their woodland habitat. Most members of this group are popular with hunters, and several Old World species have been introduced specifically with hunting in mind. Of these, two, the grey (or Hungarian) partridge (*Perdix perdix*) has adapted well to life on the Prairies, while the ring-necked pheasant (*Phasianus colchicus*), confined mainly to the SW of the province, suffers heavy losses during severe winters. The wild turkey (*Meleagris gallopavo*) occurs in much of the S of the province, and has even been recorded roosting in trees in **WINNIPEG**. Once almost extirpated from MB by overhunting and habitat loss, the turkey was reintroduced beginning in 1958, and has rebounded to several thousand pairs, expanding to its historical range and possibly beyond, thanks to conservation measures.
● RUDOLF KOES

GROVE, Frederick Philip, novelist, essayist, lecturer (b Feb 2, 1879, Radomno, West Prussia, Germany; d Aug 2, 1948, Simcoe, ON). In 1922 the schoolteacher from southwestern MB published *Over Prairie Trails,* depicting in vivid detail and considerable emotional intensity the Prairie landscape over which he journeyed in the course of his work. Having come from ND, and fluent in German, he had had been hired in 1912 to teach in the Mennonite village of Haskett,

near **WINKLER**, then as principal of the intermediate school at Winkler, and in 1916 as principal of the **GLADSTONE** high school. He had married a fellow-teacher, Catherine Wiens, and had moved in 1919 to a tiny school in the bush area NE of Gladstone, to devote himself increasingly to writing.

Grove's first modest volume was followed a year later by a 2nd book of sketches, *The Turn of the Year,* and then, in rapid succession, by his first 3 novels, *Settlers of the Marsh* (1925), *A Search for America* (1927), and *Our Daily Bread* (1928), the first in particular portraying in unforgiving detail the often tragic realities of homesteading on the raw Prairies. Hailed as contributing to the growth of a new, self-conscious Cdn identity, and particularly as the authentic voice of the West, his sombre themes and unsparing rigour attracted much critical attention, although his style was often deemed difficult and ponderous. In 1928-29 he carried out 3 much-publicized cross-Canada speaking tours, sponsored by the Canadian Club. His next novels, *The Yoke of Life* (1930) and *Fruits of the Earth* (1933) again won critical approval, but limited financial returns, and Grove moved E to Ottawa, to work briefly and unsuccessfully in a small publishing firm, and then to an equally unrewarding dairy farm near Simcoe, ON. *Two Generations* (1939) and *The Master of the Mill* (1944) were both set in ON, and he was granted several honorary degrees and elected to the Royal Society of Canada. He ran, unsuccessfully, for public office as a CCF candidate in the federal elections of 1942. With the publication in 1946 of his autobiography, *In Search of Myself,* Grove reached the pinnacle of his writing career, winning the Governor-General's Award for Non-Fiction in 1947. One more novel followed, *Consider Her Ways* (1947), an allegorical satire

Frederick Philip Grove

on humans as ants, and a curious addition to the genre of science fiction. He died at the age of 69, and a book of short stories, *Tales from the Margin*, was published posthumously in 1971.

In the years just before and after his death, scholarly assessment of the prolific author's importance was at its height, and spurred an increased curiosity about the shadowy details of his life before MB. *A Search for America* was apparently based, in part, on Grove's own travels in America, and on his attempt to re-make himself in a New World culture, and *In Search of Myself* offered some fascinating intimations of his aristocratic Swedish origins and distinguished early career. Subsequent research, by Douglas Pettigue and others, revealed that the author's early distinction was minor and his supposed aristocratic connections a fabrication, replacing a more sordid, if perhaps even more colourful reality. The distinguished writer was born Felix Paul Berthold Friedrich Greve to a working-class German family and grew up in Hamburg. He did indeed attend universities in Bonn and Munich, without graduating, and he published a book of poems and 2 novels in German, but after knocking about in Germany and Italy in search of intellectual fulfillment, was able to manage only a precarious livelihood as a translator of English writers into German. He threw himself into an extravagant affair with Else Ploetz, then married to architect August Endell, fell into serious debt, was jailed briefly for fraud, and then staged a false suicide and disappeared. In 1909, he surfaced again among the headline-grabbing artistic avant-garde of New York, joined by Else. Two years later, in Kentucky, the pair parted company, and Else re-married, to metamorphose into the flamboyant Dada poet, Baroness Else von

Freitag-Loringhoven, while the future Cdn laureate headed to ND as Fred Grove, and on to the obscurity of his prairie schoolrooms, to achieve at last something of the success he yearned for in his new identity.

Contemporary critical opinion has recognized the significance of Frederick Philip Grove as a founder of the realist tradition in modern Cdn fiction. His European influences, both classical and Romantic, have been analyzed, as have also the experiments in style and form that link him to the Modernist school. Considered a minor figure in turn-of-the-century German literature, he continues to be of major interest in the development of prairie writing. Of his books in English, never more than moderately popular, *Settlers of the Marsh* still retains its interest for the general reading public, a powerful evocation of pioneer existence. ● MILDRED GUTKIN

GRUNTHAL, pop 1200, is a community about 60 km SSE of **WINNIPEG**, in the RM of Hanover. Berghtal Mennonites settled the community in 1876. Originally called Grünthal – German for "Green Valley" – the name eventually became anglicized to Grunthal. A post office opened here in 1898, and the Mennonite church opened in 1936. The community may have been named after Grünthal, Bavaria, Germany; or after Grüntal, Austria. Current industry includes agriculture and related support industries, lumber/furniture manufacture, and welding/metal fabricating. Tourist attractions include the Grunthal Centennial Raceway, which hosts motocross races between June and Sept. Grunthal Annual Fair days are held in Aug, and feature a parade and rodeo. ● GPP

GUESS WHO, THE, were Canada's first rock superstars. Formed in **WINNIPEG** in 1962 as

Allan's Silvertones by guitarist/singer Allan Kowbel (Chad Allan), keyboard player Bob Ashley, bass player Jim Kale, guitarist **RANDY BACHMAN**, and drummer Garry Peterson, the quintet underwent several name changes – to Chad Allan and the Reflections, then Chad Allan and the Expressions – before becoming "Guess Who" in early 1965 with their 5th single, "Shakin' All Over." The new name was a gimmick to generate interest in the record. The single became a Top 10 hit across Canada and the name stuck. Released in the US, "Shakin' All Over" reached number 22 on the *Billboard* Hot 100, selling over 200,000 copies. The group toured the US in summer 1965 and released the albums *Shakin' All Over* and *Hey Ho (What You Do to Me)*, but failed to follow up their success. **BURTON CUMMINGS**, who later assumed lead-singer duties when Allan left in mid-1966, replaced Ashley on the keyboard in late 1965. Guitarist Bruce Decker briefly joined the group, but for the next 3 years, the quartet toured Canada relentlessly, even making an ill-fated trip to England that left them $25,000 in debt. They released further singles and hosted **CBC**-TV's Winnipeg episode of *Music Hop*. Spotted by Toronto-based record producer Jack Richardson and signed to his Nimbus 9 Productions, Richardson financed sessions for the group in New York that yielded an RCA Records contract and the album *Wheatfield Soul* (1969). "These Eyes," written by Bachman and Cummings, sold over 1 million copies, earning the group the first of 5 gold records. By 1970 (after adding 'The' to their name) and following hit singles "Laughing," "Undun," and "No Time," The Guess Who scored a number-1 single with "American Woman" (from the album of the same name), which topped the charts for 3 weeks. That year, the group earned more than $5 million, selling more records

The original "Guess Who" lineup

than the entire Cdn music industry had to that point, and closing out the year with the platinum album *The Best of the Guess Who*.

Bachman left the group in May 1970, replaced by Winnipeg guitarists Kurt Winter and **GREG LESKIW**, as the band continued to score hits with "Hand Me Down World," "Share the Land," "Hang on to Your Life," "Albert Flasher," "Rain Dance," and "Sour Suite." They played the White House and later toured Europe, Japan, and Australia, releasing the top-selling albums *Share the Land* (1970), *So Long Bannatyne* (1971), *Rockin'* (1972), and *Live at the Paramount* (1972). By 1972, guitarist Don McDougall and bassist Bill Wallace, both from Winnipeg, had replaced Leskiw and Kale as the group released *Artificial Paradise* (1973), *#10* (1973), and *Road Food* (1974), and the hit singles "Glamour Boy," "Orly," "Star Baby," and "Clap for the Wolfman." The latter, featuring famed DJ Wolfman Jack, restored the group to the *Billboard* Top 10. The band also hosted *The Midnight Special* in 1974. That same year, Winter and McDougall were replaced by Toronto-based guitarist Domenic Troiano, as the band released *Flavours* (1974) and *Power in the Music* (1975) and the hit single "Dancing Fool." Following a Sept 14, 1975, concert at the Montreal Forum, Cummings finally dissolved the group to pursue a solo career.

Kale acquired rights to the band name in 1978 and toured with several ex-members, including Winter, McDougall, and Peterson, on and off for the next 25 years. The 1969-70 quartet (including Bachman and Cummings) reunited for the closing ceremonies of Winnipeg's Pan Am Games in Aug 1999 for a televised audience of 100 million, and toured the next 2 years. They also joined the Rolling Stones and Neil Young, among others, at a Toronto "SARSstock" concert in summer 2003 following that city's severe acute respiratory syndrome scare.

Inducted into the Canadian Music Hall of Fame (1987), they were the first recipients of the Prairie Music Hall of Fame Award (1999), and were inducted into the Canadian Walk of Fame (2001) and the Canadian Broadcasters Hall of Fame (2002). That year, they also received the Governor General's Performing Arts Award. Guess Who songs have been featured in the movies such as *Almost Famous*, *Cable Guy*, *Austin Powers: The Spy Who Shagged Me*, *Jackie Brown*, and Academy Award–winner *American Beauty*. "These Eyes" earned a prestigious BMI Award from the US-based Broadcast Music, Inc., for over 1 million airplays. In 1999, American rocker Lenny Kravitz hit number 1 with his cover of "American Woman."

● JOHN EINARSON

Ross's Gull is now on Manitoba's endangered list

GULLS (family Laridae), and their relatives the terns (family *Sternidae*), are medium-sized to large birds that are mostly white. Although gulls are strongly linked to aquatic habitats, it is incorrect to call them all "seagulls," as several species breed inland, and many individuals never or only rarely venture near any marine habitat. Our large lakes and marshes harbour huge colonies of Franklin's Gulls (*Larus pipixcan*), herring gulls (*L. argentatus*), and ring-billed gulls (*L. delewarensis*), as well as smaller numbers of other gull species and terns. Perhaps most familiar to city-dwellers is the Ring-billed Gull, which has developed a fondness for hanging out at parking lots and fast-food outlets. Both it and the Franklin's Gull also frequently follows farmer's tractors as the fields are being ploughed. Arguably, the most famous of MB's gulls is the Ross's Gull (*Rhodostethia rosea*), which has nested annually in small numbers at **CHURCHILL** since 1980 and attracts birders from around the world. Terns are generally smaller and slenderer than gulls; they are sometimes referred to as "sea swallows." One common species is the Forster's Tern (*Sterna forsteri*), which has been the subject of several studies at **DELTA MARSH**. ● RUDOLF KOES

GUNN, Isabel, adventurer, cross-dresser (b 1780, probably near Kirkwall, Scotland; d Nov 7, 1861, Stromness, Scotland) was an Orkney girl who disguised herself as a man in order to travel to **RUPERT'S LAND**. Her scheme ultimately fell apart when she gave birth in front of a **NWC** employee near **EMERSON**. Though her stay in the Northwest was brief, Gunn was the first white woman to live in the **RED RIVER** area. Gunn was raised in the Orkney Islands, and her brother George was one of many Orkadians working for the **HBC**. In the summer of 1806, Gunn disguised herself as a man named John Fubbister and signed a 3-year contract with the HBC. Though her exact motive is unknown, in the most common version of the story, Gunn shipped out with the HBC to follow a faithless lover who had also signed up. Other accounts explain that one side of Gunn's face had been scarred by small pox. With little chance of finding financial support through marriage, she chose to go after the £8 offered annually in the HBC contract, far more than a single woman could expect to earn supporting herself.

Gunn set sail from Stromness in the *Prince of Wales* June 29, 1806, heading for Rupert's Land. If Gunn was indeed following her lover, she would have been disappointed upon her arrival in Moose Factory (ON), as Gunn was shipped to Fort Albany (ON), while her supposed lover was sent to Eastmain (QC), 300 km to the E of Albany. Nonetheless, at Fort Albany, Gunn successfully maintained her disguise, helping to ship goods inland and performing the same arduous work as other male employees. In May 1807, Gunn was part of a fur expedition to Martin Falls. Upon her return, she then embarked on a 2900-km canoe expedition that travelled from Martin Falls to Pembina (now ND, near **EMERSON**), still maintaining her disguise though she was already 4 months' pregnant when leaving Fort Albany.

The circumstances leading to the unmasking of "Fubbister" are well documented through the journals of Alexander Henry, the NWC chief at Pembina. Distressed and seeking shelter, Gunn appeared unexpectedly at Henry's door on the evening of Dec 28. Henry offered the young "man" a place by his fire, and returned to his bedroom. In the early morning of Dec 29, Henry was awakened by Gunn's screaming. He returned to the hearth and, much to his astonishment, found that the fur trader had given birth to a son. Once her true sex was revealed, Gunn became known as Mary, and was returned to Fort Albany in the spring, where she was forced into traditionally female work. Her son was baptized there as James Scarth, as Gunn claimed that she had become pregnant after being raped by a John Scarth. Though she did not want to return to the Orkney Islands, the HBC would not allow a white woman to remain at Fort Albany. She was discharged from service, and embarked on the return voyage on Sept 20, 1809. Gunn spent the rest of her life in poverty, working as a stocking and mitten-maker in Stromness until her death. Gunn's intriguing story was fictionalized into the novel *Isobel Gunn* by Audrey Thomas, as well as a poem by Stephen Scobie entitled *The Ballad of Isabel Gunn*. A documentary film by Anne Wheeler entitled *The Orkney Lad: The Story of Isabel Gunn* was released in 2001. ● MICHELLE DOBROVOLNY

GUNNARSON, Dean, escape artist, (b Jan 27, 1964, **Winnipeg**). At age 10, Gunnarson's mother gave him a book about Harry Houdini, and for the next 8 years, he immersed himself in Houdini's life and work. On Oct 31, 1982, he was strapped into a straitjacket and hoisted to the top of the old *Free Press* Building on Carlton St in **Winnipeg**. He wriggled free in record time, gaining national exposure. A year later, a crowd of about 10,000 gathered at the Alexander Docks on the **Red River**. He was bound with heavy chain, padlocked, and placed in a coffin, which was nailed shut. The coffin was slowly immersed into the river. When he didn't appear after almost 4 minutes, the coffin was dragged out and opened. He was pronounced dead at the scene, but was resuscitated at a hospital. This attempt gained worldwide attention. Since then, his underwater escapes have been performed in shark cages, barrels, and packing cases, and he has escaped from police jails and handcuffs all over the world. He is most famous for getting out of a straitjacket and handcuffs after jumping out of an airplane at 4000 m, and while hanging at 200 m from the Hoover Dam on the AZ/NV border. Gunnarson is the only escape artist to win the Houdini Award, which was presented in Tokyo

by Tony Curtis, star of the 1953 movie *Houdini*. He was the first Cdn, and the youngest person ever, to be named International Ambassador for the Society of American Magicians. In 2007, Gunnarson lived in Vancouver. ● DOUG ALLEN

GUNSTON, Frank, physician, inventor (b 1933, **Flin Flon**). With degrees in electrical engineering in 1957 and **Medicine** in 1963, both from the **U of M**, Gunston went to work for joint replacement specialist Sir John Charnley's Centre for Hip Surgery in Wrightington Hospital, near Wigan, UK. In 1968, Gunston developed a prosthetic knee made of stainless steel and plastic that would connect to bone using cement. It was the first biomechanical total knee replacement and allowed flexion, extension, and side movement of the joint, a revolutionary development for the time. Gunston published about the technology in 1971, but chose not to seek any patent for the prosthesis, believing it should be widely available without restriction. Gunston's invention remains the model for all modern knee replacements. He later moved to **Brandon** and worked as an orthopaedic surgeon at **Brandon General Hospital**. He also developed or improved hip and other joint replacements during his career. Gunston received a $100,000 Manning Innovation Award in 1989, and holds the Order of Canada. ● JT

UMA, TRIBUNE, JIM WALKER PHOTO, PC18-10198-015, 1979

Dr. Frank Gunston in 1979 with the artificial knee joint he developed.

GUNTON, pop. 550, is a community 50 km N of Winnipeg. Originally known as Gunview, in honour of the first postmaster, Donald Gunn, the community name changed to Gunton in 1906. The post office opened in 1905, and remains open. It is thought John Gunn purchased the 32 ha (80 ac) village site from Samuel Herron in 1906 and had the land surveyed into town lots, following which 22 English families settled in Gunton in 1909. A **CPR** point was established in Gunton with the opening of a limestone quarry in 1905. By 1914, about 500 people were employed at the quarry. However, it was forced to close when WWI started. There are no longer any major industries in Gunton, as most residents commute to Winnipeg or surrounding towns for employment. ● GPP

GUTKIN, Harry, cartoonist, businessman (b Aug. 10, 1915, Winnipeg; d May 17, 2004, Winnipeg). Gutkin studied in Winnipeg with **Lionel Lemoine Fitzgerald** and then at the Art Institute of Chicago, becoming a magazine illustrator and a political cartoonist before he was 20. With David Simkin, he founded Contemporary Publishers – which issued a number of paperbacks on social subjects – in the 1940s. His skill in the graphic arts and his talent for management led in 1948 to the founding of the advertising art and photography firm of Phillips-Gutkin and Associates, in partnership with John Phillips. PGA Films came into being 4 years later. With the co-operative movement as one of its chief clients, Gutkin, at the helm of PGA, wrote and directed several documentaries on the social significance of the movement. The firm is now recognized as one of the pioneers of animation in Canada. In the latter part of his life, Gutkin's interests turned to community service. Accepting an invitation by the newly constituted Jewish Historical Society of Western Canada (now the Jewish Heritage Centre), he produced *Journey into Our Heritage,* an exhibit on the western Cdn Jewish community that was shown for 6 months in 1976 at the MB Museum before travelling across Canada. He followed that exhibit with 19 years as president of the Jewish Historical Society. In 1997, the govt of MB awarded Gutkin the Prix MB Award – Heritage, for volunteer service to the community. Harry's wife, Mildred Gutkin, was a close collaborator in 2 books: *The Worst of Times, The Best of Times: Growing Up in Winnipeg's North End* (1987) and *Profiles in Dissent* (1997). ● INGEBORG BOYENS

GUTTORMSSON, Guttormur "Gutti" Jónsson, Icelandic poet, musician (b Nov 21, 1878, Icelandic River [**Riverton**]; d Nov 23, 1966,

G

Guttormur Jónsson Guttormsson, 1966

Riverton). Guttormur was born to Jón Guttormsson and Pálína Ketilsdóttir. In 1904, he married 19-year-old Jensína Julía Daníelsdóttir, a local resident. The couple had 6 children. Guttormur's only education was 3 years of primary school, and he worked almost his entire life as a farmer in the Riverton area. Nevertheless, his 5 volumes of **POETRY** – a talent he apparently inherited from his mother – became widely read by "West Icelanders," as North Americans of Icelandic descent call themselves, as well as by those in the motherland. His following in Iceland was such that that country's govt twice paid to bring him there. His poetic opus, often described as bitingly sarcastic yet playful, is collected in *Jón Austfirðingur og nokkur smákvæði* ("John of the East Fjords and Other Poems," 1909); *Bóndadóttir* ("A Farmer's Daughter," 1920); *Gaman og Alvara* ("Jest and Earnest," 1930); *Hunangsflugur* ("Honey Bees," 1944); and *Kanadapistill* ("Canada Thistle," 1958). He has become the object of critical interest since Roy St. George Stubbs wrote a study of him (*In Search of a Poet*, 1975), and a volume of his work was translated into English as *Aurora: English Translations of Icelandic Poems* (1993). An adept reader of his own work, Guttormsson was also a musician with a brass band, and was involved in the **UNITARIAN**

Church, for which he wrote at least one hymn. In 1994, a cairn commemorating Guttormur's work was placed in Riverton's Centennial Park, and his library is part of the Icelandic Collection at the **U OF M**. In 1998, the **ÍSLENDINGADAGURINN** festival staged a play dramatizing the author's biography, entitled *Sandy Bar*, after what is probably his best-known poem. He is also remembered for the "Icelanglish" poem "Winnipeg Icelander," in which he combines his ancestral language with that of his birthplace in a pidgin; the illustrative opening line reads "Eg fór on' í Main street með fimm dala cheque" ("I walk down Main Street with a five-dollar cheque"). ● AJL

GYMNASTICS comprises 2 separate disciplines: artistic and rhythmic. Artistic gymnastics began as athletic training for men, and was first practised in sports clubs, YMCAs, and university gyms. Competitions in MB were held as early as the 1890s, and **DONALD BAIN** was one of the first provincial champions. Men's competition comprises floor exercises as well as the vault, pommel horse, rings, parallel bars, and the high bar. Women's gymnastics, which didn't develop until the mid-1950s, involves the vault, balance beam, uneven parallel bars, and floor exercises. The Manitoba Gymnastics Association, formed

in 1960, became the 1st sports organization to separate from the Amateur Athletic Union and incorporate, following liability concerns arising from a serious accident at the 1966 national trials in **WINNIPEG**. The Panther Gymnastics Club was built the same year. At the 1967 **PAN AM GAMES**, Winnipeg's Jack Mowat was one of the international judges. An international meet held at the Winnipeg Arena in 1970 drew gymnasts from Japan, Russia, and France. The **U OF M** also trained gymnasts through its athletics program, which is where 1976 Montreal Olympic competitor Keith Carter developed his skill. A year after the Montreal games, Winnipeg Gymnastics Centre opened, providing a training facility for competitive MB athletes such as national champion **BONNIE WITTMEIER** and **MONICA GOERMANN**, who won several medals at the 1978 Commonwealth and the 1979 Pan Am Games, including several golds.

Rhythmic gymnastics differs from artistic gymnastics in its use of props, such as ribbons or balls, and the incorporation of dance techniques. It is also designated as a female sport. Zlatica Stauder introduced it to MB in the late 1960s. Stauder was trained in her native Czechoslovakia, where the sport had spread soon after its early development in the USSR. MB. In 1972, Stauder developed the 1st courses for judges and teachers in western Canada. She opened the 1st competitive rhythmic gymnastics club in MB in 1976, serving as head coach and training the province's 1st international competitors. In 1999, after winning the national team title, a MB rhythmic gymnastics team won the bronze medal at that year's Pan Am Games in Winnipeg. ● MICHELLE DOBROVOLNY

GYPSUMVILLE, pop. 285, is a community about 120 km NE of Dauphin, and near a complex of First Nations communities fronting **LAKE ST. MARTIN**, including **DAUPHIN RIVER**, **LAKE ST. MARTIN**, **LITTLE SASKATCHEWAN**, and **PINAYMOOTANG** First Nations. The town derives its name from the area gypsum deposits, which were discovered in 1888 and first mined in 1890. The gypsum was transferred by light rail to Davis Point on **LAKE MANITOBA**, then shipped to **DELTA BEACH**, at the lake's S end. The post office opened in 1905, and Gypsumville became the northern terminus of a branch line in 1912. In May 1961, the RCAF, under NORAD, began construction of a radar station as part of the Pinetree Line. The station went into operation in Jan 1964, making it the last Pinetree station to open. The station closed in July 1987, and the land was turned over to the local First Nations council. Current economic activities include tourism and hospitality. ● GPP

H

HOCKEY, ICE,
see page 322

The Canadian Women's National Team after their 2007 gold medal win in Winnipeg.

HADASHVILLE, pop 250, is a community 90 km ESE of **WINNIPEG**, just N of the Trans-Canada Highway. Hadashville was previously known as Reynolds, after which the RM of Reynolds is named. The town name was changed in honour of the first postmaster, Charles Hadash. Logistical problems prevented railway construction on the original site of Hadashville, so the community and the post office, which opened in 1912, had to move. Polish settlers made up much of the early population. The economy in the 21st century is supported by farming, logging, a tree nursery, and a peat moss operation. Hadashville is the administrative centre of the RM. The community's location on the edge of Sandilands Provincial Forest also leads to tourism in the area. ● GPP

HALL, Frederick William, VICTORIA CROSS winner (b Feb 8, 1885, Kilkenny, Ireland; d Apr 24, 1915, Ypres, Belgium). Hall emigrated to Canada around 1910, and lived on Pine St (now Valour Rd), **WINNIPEG**. Hall joined the 8th (Winnipeg Rifles) Batt in Sept 1914. As a Company SgtMaj near Ypres, he found that some of his men were missing. Hearing the cries for help of wounded men outside the trench, he retrieved many of them from no man's land. After daybreak, braving enemy fire, he twice attempted to rescue another wounded man, and was shot and killed while lifting the soldier to carry him to safety. ● JIM SHILLIDAY

HALL, Monty (b Maurice Halparin), entertainer, (b Aug 25, 1921, **WINNIPEG**) is best known as the host of the popular TV game show *Let's Make a Deal* (1963-1986, 1990). Hall attended the **U OF M**, where he performed in musicals and plays. He also served as an emcee of army shows during WWII. Intending to take medicine, Hall received his BSc from the U of M (1945) with a major in zoology and biology. After graduating, he moved to Toronto, where he resumed his career as an actor, singer, emcee, and sportscaster. In 1955, Hall moved to New York to work on NBC's *Monitor.* In 1960, he relocated to Hollywood, CA, to emcee CBS's *Video Village*. In Hollywood he sold his first production, *Your First Impression*, to the network. In 1963, Hall and writer-producer Stefan Hatos teamed up to create *Let's Make a Deal*, the show that would earn him star status. Hall has made guest appearances on numerous popular TV shows such as *The Dean Martin Show*, *Love Boat*, and *The Odd Couple*. He also starred in his own variety show specials on ABC. Hall was honoured with a star on the Hollywood Walk of Fame (1973).

H

Monty Hall, 1977

Interestingly, Hall has had a probability paradox named after him, though it was posed as early as the 1950s by logician Martin Gardner under a different name. In brief, the Monty Hall Problem posits, counter-intuitively, that the odds of game-show contestants' winning a grand prize from behind 3 doors increase if they switch their choice of door from Door 2 to Door 3 after the host shows that Door 1 holds nothing. Offstage, Hall is involved in numerous charities. He has travelled across Canada, the US, and Europe to speak and perform at numerous benefits for charity. His efforts have earned him over 500 awards, including the Variety Club International Humanitarian Award (1983), the Order of Canada (1988), and the **Order of Manitoba** (2002). ● AJL

HALLDORSON, Daniel Albert, golfer (b Apr 2, 1952, **Winnipeg**) was one of the most successful Cdn pro golfers. He spent 16 years on the PGA Tour, winning the 1980 Pensacola Open and the 1986 Deposit Guaranty Classic, and earning over $1 million. He was a strong supporter of Cdn golf, and frequently represented Canada in international competitions. Halldorson was raised in Shilo, where he first practised his swing at the Sandy Hook Golf Club located across from his house. His first title came in 1970 as Manitoba Junior Champion. He turned pro in 1971, and joined the Canadian Tour in 1973. In total, he has won 7 Canadian Tour events, including 4 Manitoba Opens, and was twice named the Canadian Professional

Golfers' Association's (CPGA) Player of the Year. He also won the 1986 CPGA Championship. He qualified for his first PGA tour in 1975, and was one of the tour's most consistent figures with a total of 28 top-10 finishes. In all, he has won 9 international victories, including 2 world cup titles in 1980 and 1985. He is the only Cdn to have twice won the title. Along with MB pro golfers **George Knudson** and **Jimmy Doyle,** Halldorson was an inaugural member of the Manitoba Golf Hall of Fame. He was inducted into the Canadian Golf Hall of Fame in 2002, and was named a lifetime member of the Canadian Tour in 2005. He lives in IL. ● MD

HALLDORSON, Elin Salome, MLA, teacher, activist (b Dec 29, 1887, **Lundar**; d May 31, 1970, **Winnipeg**), became the first **Icelandic**-Canadian/female MLA in MB when she was elected in the constituency of St. George in 1936 under the Social Credit banner. Born in the Lundar district to Halldór Halldorson and Krístin Pálsdóttir of Ísafjörður, Iceland, she was also sister to Liberal-Progressive MLA Christian (Kristján) Halldorson. Following her graduation from Wesley College, Halldorson gained prominence in the Icelandic community through her roles as languages instructor and dean of the Jón Bjarnason Academy in Winnipeg. Only the 2nd woman ever elected to the legislature, her political campaigns focused on increasing female political participation and economic reform. For women, she announced in 1937 to the legislative assembly, "government is only a larger housekeeping." Although initially a popular figure and media curiosity, her public image was tarnished by her pacifist stance and a series of radical political moves following the declaration of war in 1939. Alongside MLA **Lewis St. George Stubbs,** Halldorson co-ordinated an ill-fated motion of nonconfidence in the federal govt and split with her own party on the issue. She hoped that increased female political participation would ensure peace and criticized pro-war women's campaigns, including the Jón Sigurðsson IODE's knitting drives for soldiers. Lamented Halldorson: "it's so much easier to knit than to think about the business of our nation." Defeated by Liberal-Progressive Skuli Sigfusson in 1941, Halldorson continued to promote Social Credit in the province following her defeat and worked as a teacher and tutor of languages until the mid-1960s. ● LAURIE K. BERTRAM

HALTER, Gerald Sydney "Syd," lawyer, CFL exec (b Apr 18, 1904, **Winnipeg**; d Oct 24, 1990, Winnipeg), was the CFL's first commissioner. He became involved in sports administration as a

G. Sydney Halter, 1958

student at the **U of M** where he managed the hockey team while earning his law degree. He went on to serve as president for the Winnipeg Amateur Athletic Association Track & Field Club, and later as secretary of the Manitoba Athletic Union. He also became secretary of the Winnipeg Football Club in 1934, and was promoted to president in 1942. His sports career was interrupted by service in the RCAF during WWII, but he resumed his involvement upon his discharge. In 1952, he served as deputy commissioner and, the next year, as president for the Western Interprovincial Football Union. He was also the registrar for both the Eastern and Western Conferences, and had a hand in the 1958 merger with the Canadian Football Council that formed the CFL. He was appointed as the new league's commissioner, a position he held until 1968. Halter was also a horseracing enthusiast, and served as vice-chairman and chairman for the Manitoba Horse Racing Commission from 1966-82. He was awarded the Order of Canada in 1977, and is a member of the CFL Hall of Fame and the Canadian Horse Racing Hall of Fame. ● MD

HAMERTON, John Laurence, geneticist, administrator, sheep farmer (b Sept 23, 1929, Hove, Sussex, UK; d Feb 9, 2006, **Winnipeg**). The **English**-born Hamerton first studied genetics at Guy's Hospital, London, where he collaborated on research that would lead to bone marrow transplantation. With C. E. Ford, he confirmed the human chromosome number as 46. In 1969, he moved to MB to establish the first Human Genetics department at the Children's Hospital of Winnipeg (*see* **HEALTH SCIENCES CENTRE**). Through his work there and at the **U OF M**, he developed an international reputation as a researcher in many fields, including cytogenetics (the study of human chromosomes), prenatal diagnosis, and bioethical issues, especially those concerning the Human Genome Project. As one of the founders of the Canadian College of Medical Geneticists, and later its president, he was key in the establishment of medical genetics as an independent medical and scientific discipline. He also served as president of the American Society of Human Genetics and the Genetics Society of Canada, and as chair of the Manitoba Health Research Council.

At the U of M, he was the first chair of the Department of Human Genetics, and later encouraged the merger that formed the current Department of Biochemistry and Medical Genetics. Hamerton also served as associate dean of research in the Faculty of Medicine; on the senate and the board of governors; on Research Ethics Boards; and as mentor to many trainees and fellow faculty members. He was ultimately appointed Distinguished Professor Emeritus. He also received national acclaim, including fellowship in the Royal Society of Canada and an honorary fellowship in the Royal College of Physicians and Surgeons. In 2003, he was made an Officer of the Order of Canada. In addition to his academic work, John was a farmer, breeding pure Arcott sheep at his farm near Monominto, SE of **ANOLA**. He brought both scientific and administrative expertise to the industry and served as president of the Manitoba Sheep Association and chair of the Canada Sheep Council. Hamerton died in 2006 following complications from heart surgery. ● JANE EVANS

HAMILTON, Alvin Chown, lawyer, judge, author (b Aug 14, 1926, **WINNIPEG**), practised law privately 1951-971 in, successively, **ROBLIN**, Winnipeg, **MELITA**, and **BRANDON**. A president of the Brandon-Souris Liberal association, he ran unsuccessfully as the Liberal candidate in the 1963 federal election. In 1965, he was elected as the Manitoba Association of School Trustees' (MAST) first president. He was appointed a judge of MB's Court of Queen's Bench in 1971, and in 1983 became associate chief justice of that court, charged with heading up its newly created family division. From 1987-91, he was co-commissioner, with Associate Chief Judge **MURRAY SINCLAIR**, of the **ABORIGINAL JUSTICE INQUIRY**. The commission investigated 2 controversial deaths of **CREE** Manitobans: the long-unsolved murder of 19-year-old student **HELEN BETTY OSBORNE** in **THE PAS**, and the

Winnipeg death of Aboriginal leader **J. J. HARPER** at the hands of a Winnipeg Police Services officer. The commission's lengthy report dealt extensively with how the justice system serves, and fails to serve, Aboriginal people. Hamilton retired from the bench in 1993. In 2001, he wrote *A Feather, Not a Gavel: Working Towards Aboriginal Justice*, a book that considered the history of **TREATIES** and **ABORIGINAL RIGHTS**, and which recommended reforming how Canada's legal system treats First Nations and **MÉTIS** people. ● DOUG JOHNSTON

HAMILTON GROUP researched paranormal activities from 1918-34 in an effort to prove the existence of an afterlife. Comprised of prominent Winnipeg physician Thomas Glendenning Hamilton, his wife Lillian, and the medium Elizabeth Poole, the group adhered to a strict methodology in the hopes of finding scientific evidence that would confirm the reality of paranormal activities such as rappings, psychokinesis, ectoplasms, and materializations. The group's activities are thus well-documented as they kept meticulous records in an effort to prove the scientific merit of their work, many of which are verbatim accounts of the séances held in Dr. Hamilton's Elmwood home.

The group is best known, however, for its "spirit photography," of which 300 examples have been preserved at the **U OF M** archives. The photographs, known to spiritualists throughout the world, show Poole with ectoplasm oozing from her nostrils in which can be seen the faint outlines of

Hamilton Group - Ectoplasm

several spirits, among whom, the group believed, were the spirits of Robert Louis Stevenson and David Livingstone. Though the photographs are considered a rather peculiar side note to MB history, Hamilton's research at the time earned him a prestigious reputation as an expert on paranormal activity, and he gave over 80 lectures around the world, attracting the attention of well-known spiritualists such as UK author Sir Arthur Conan Doyle and Cdn PM William Lyon MacKenzie King. ● MD

HAMIOTA, pop 1072, is a town 60 km NW of **BRANDON** on hwy 21. Settlement first took place here in 1879. The post office opened SE of the current site of Hamiota in 1882, and was known as Hamilton after Thomas Hamilton who operated it. In 1884, the name changed to Hamiota to avoid confusion with Hamilton, ON. "Ham" was taken from Hamilton and "iota" meaning "many" was added. Hamiota relocated to its present site with the arrival of the railway in 1891. It became an incorporated village in 1907; a town in 1998. The local economy relies heavily on the local health care centre, the school division, the credit union, and a variety of local retail services and manufacturing businesses. The Hamiota Community Health Care Model, with its integrated, team-based system, has been recognized nationally. Ed Hudson received an Order of Canada for his work in developing the plans behind the small-town health centre concept that has managed to keep 5 physicians in Hamiota throughout the early 2000s. Sports have always been important for the town. The Hamiota Red Sox team, plus numerous individual players, have been inducted into the Manitoba Baseball Hall of Fame, supporting Hamiota's claim as "Baseball Capital of MB." Dallas Smith (Boston Bruins), Lyndon Johnson (Olympic pair's figure skating), Beth Cochran (national team basketball), Garth Strachan, Ross Fraser, Clair Hunter, Nelson Woods (national seniors curling) are all evidence of Hamiota's sporting success. In 2005, Hamiota received the top award for its size in the national Communities in Bloom competition. Nearby red **GARTER SNAKE** nests attract ecotourists. Annual events include the Triple H Rodeo and the Hamiota Agricultural Fair. ● GPP

HANLON, Glen, HOCKEY player, coach (b Feb 20, 1957, **BRANDON**). One of many NHL goaltenders to hail from MB, Hanlon enjoyed a 14-year playing career in the NHL before entering the coaching ranks. He played junior hockey with his hometown **BRANDON WHEAT KINGS** from 1974-77, and holds the franchise record for most career games played by a goaltender (172). The

H

Vancouver Canucks selected Hanlon in the 1977 NHL entry draft, making him the 40th player chosen. In his first year of professional hockey he was named the Central Hockey League's top rookie. He went on to play for the Canucks, as well as the St. Louis Blues, New York Rangers, and Detroit Red Wings (477 total NHL games). While tending goal for the Red Wings in 1987-88, Hanlon led the league in shutouts with 4. He is also known for allowing Wayne Gretzky's first NHL goal in 1979.

Hanlon retired as a player in 1991, and was named Vancouver's goaltending coach in 1992. He held that role until 1999, when the Washington Capitals hired him as the head coach of their American Hockey League (*see* **MANITOBA MOOSE**) affiliate. He coached the Portland Pirates for 3 seasons, earning a coach of the year award, and later, was promoted to assistant coach of the Capitals in July 2002. When the Capitals fired Bruce Cassidy, Hanlon became head coach of the team midway through the 2003-04 season, and remained in that role through the 2006-07 season. Hanlon also has international hockey experience, first as an assistant coach with Canada's 1998 world championship team, and then as head coach of Belarus at both the 2005 and 2006 World Hockey Championships. ● JT

HANSON, Melvin "Fritz," football player (b July 13, 1914, Perham, MN; d Feb 14, 1996, Calgary), was one of the first star players in the early days of the **WINNIPEG BLUE BOMBERS**. After attending the

Fritz Hanson – the "Galloping Ghost"

U of ND, Hanson signed with the Winnipeg Football Club in 1935 for $125 a game and free room and board. He quickly gained a reputation as a fast runner, and was dubbed the "Galloping Ghost" by sports media. His star presence brought a bright spot to the game for Depression-era fans. In 1935, the diminutive Hanson led the Winnipeg team to its first Grey Cup victory in a surprise win over the Hamilton Tigers. Hanson gained 300 yds in punt returns, a record which still holds for a Grey Cup game. Hanson then scored the winning touchdown with a 78 yd return for an 18-12 win. In 1938, he held the Western Inter-Provincial Football Union highest scorer title, and was with the team for 2 more Grey Cups wins in 1939 and 1941. He joined the Cdn army during WWII, playing for the Winnipeg Light Infantry Squad from 1942-45. After the war, Hanson joined the Calgary Stampeders for an undefeated, Grey Cup-winning 1947-48 season. Hanson stayed in Calgary following his retirement the next year, and worked at an insurance firm. He was inducted into the Canadian Football Hall of Fame in 1962. ● MD

HARGRAVE, Letitia, letter writer (b 1813, Edinburgh; d Sept 18, 1854, Sault Ste. Marie, Canada West [ON]) was the daughter of Sheriff Dugald MacTavish and Letitia Lockhart. She was courted in 1837 at her Scottish home by **HBC** chief trader **JAMES HARGRAVE**, who eventually proposed to her by mail. The couple were married in 1840 and, complete with a piano, sailed for **YORK FACTORY**. Like many women in her position, her first reaction upon her arrival was to "cry myself sick." But she soon recovered her natural ebullience and used letters to her family, later edited by **MARGARET ARNETT MCLEOD** and published by the Champlain Society under *The Letters of Letitia Hargrave*, as therapy. The letters offer a unique European female perspective on life in the trading posts and constitute her main claim to fame. At the same time, the letters demonstrate that Hargrave, the only white woman at York Factory for most of her stay there, was extremely privileged. She had a personal maid and was often indulged by her husband, who added a nursery to their house, for example. She bore 3 children at York Factory, 2 of whom survived. In constant ill health, she returned to Scotland in 1846, then came back to York Factory in 1847. She gave birth to 2 more children before Hargrave was transferred to Sault Ste. Marie in 1851. She died of cholera. ● JMB

HARLEQUIN BOOKS, now Harlequin Enterprises Ltd., the world's largest publisher of romantic fiction, was started in Winnipeg in 1949 by **RICHARD H. G. BONNYCASTLE**. In 1945, Bonnycastle

resigned a position with **HBC** to become managing director of Advocate Printers in Winnipeg. Four years later, he collaborated with 2 Toronto men – Doug Weld of Advocate's parent company, Bryant Press, and Jack Palmer of Curtis Distributing – to establish a publishing company that would produce paperback reprints, using Advocate's presses when they were inactive.

Harlequin cover

In the early years, Harlequin reprinted mysteries, westerns, thrillers, some non-fiction books, and a few romances. Bonnycastle's wife, Mary, who proofread many of the books and tried to ensure they met her standard of decency, and his secretary, Ruth Palmour, noticed that the romances sold best. When Palmer died and Weld ended his involvement with the company, the women's influence increased. They identified the British romance publisher, Mills & Boon, as a good source of the kind of books they wanted. In 1957, Palmour approached the publisher about reprint rights in Canada. That year, Harlequin's first Mills & Boon reprint, *The Hospital in Buwambo*, by Anne Vinton, was released. That book's exotic setting, doctor-and-nurse themes, and happy endings came to define Harlequin Romances for many readers. By 1964, all Harlequins published were Mills & Boon reprints.

After Bonnycastle's death in 1968, his son Richard Jr. moved the company to Toronto. He had already encouraged his father to distribute books in the US. Now, to raise funds for further expansion and to buy Mills & Boon, securing the supply of novels, he took the company public and hired sales and marketing experts to run it. To attract new readers, books were included in products women might use, like cleansers and detergents. They were advertised on television and in women's magazines, and sold in supermarkets and directly to readers through the Harlequin Reader Service.

In 1975, Torstar, the Cdn media corporation that owns the *Toronto Star*, bought the company. Harlequin has offices around the world and publishes over 100 books each month in 27 languages. Profits are down since 2005, and the company has responded by developing several new lines of women's fiction. ● CARON HART

Elijah Harper votes against Meech Lake

HARPER, Elijah, politician (b March 3, 1949, RED SUCKER LAKE FIRST NATION). The 2nd of 13 children, Harper attended high school in WINNIPEG and earned an anthropology degree at the U OF M. He worked for the Manitoba Indian Brotherhood – later the ASSEMBLY OF MANITOBA CHIEFS – as a community development worker and researcher, and then as a program analyst for the Department of Northern Affairs. At age 29, he became band chief at Red Sucker Lake, serving in that role until his 1981 election as MLA for Rupertsland. The first Status Indian MLA in MB, he represented the NEW DEMOCRATIC PARTY in the Legislature until 1992, and was named minister of native affairs in 1986 and later minister of northern affairs. He was removed from cabinet briefly in 1987 after admitting to leaving the scene of a car accident. In 1990, as the MB legislature was set to consider the MEECH LAKE ACCORD, Harper stood to oppose the agreement because it did not address ABORIGINAL RIGHTS. As a result, it failed to pass in MB, and was therefore doomed on the national stage.

After resigning his seat in 1992, Harper planned to run for the federal NDP in the 1993 election. He could not secure the party nomination, however, and made a controversial shift to the Liberal party, defeating the NDP candidate to become MP for the CHURCHILL riding. He served one term, and sat on the standing committee of Aboriginal Affairs. The NDP was able to regain the riding when Bev Desjarlais defeated Harper in 1997 and again in 2000. From Jan 1999 to Oct 2000, he was a commissioner with the Indian Claims Commission, and then moved on to become a consultant and speaker. Harper has also organized national gatherings to improve political and spiritual understanding between Aboriginal and non-Aboriginal Canadians. The first Sacred Assembly took place in Hull (now Gatineau), QC, in 1995, and a 2nd was held at the Sagkeeng First Nation in 1997. He has been the recipient of the STANLEY KNOWLES Humanitarian Award in 1991, and a 1996 National Aboriginal Achievement Award. Harper is also an honorary chief at Red Sucker Lake First Nation, his birthplace. CTV, Anagram Pictures, and Eagle Vision produced *Elijah* – a film about his life – in 2006. ● JOEL TRENAMAN

HARPER, John Joseph "J. J." CREE leader (b 1951, WASAGAMACK FIRST NATION; d March 9, 1988, WINNIPEG). Before his controversial shooting death, Harper had been the executive director of the Island Lake Tribal Council, a non-profit advisory organization for the GARDEN HILL, RED SUCKER LAKE, ST. THERESA POINT, and Wasagamack First Nations communities. Previously, he had been chief of Wasagamack. He was married, with 3 children. According to the sequence of events reported by the ABORIGINAL JUSTICE INQUIRY, Winnipeg Police Service Const Robert Cross was searching for a car thief when he approached Harper, who was on foot near the scene. Cross asked to see his identification; Harper refused. A struggle ensued, and both men ended up on the ground. Cross testified that they were struggling for control of his gun when it fired, wounding Harper in the chest and subsequently killing him. A coroner's inquest and police investigation initially ruled the shooting an accident, but the incident caused outrage in the native community over what many saw as a racist act indicative of systemic police bias against Aboriginal people.

Protests, vigils, and calls for justice led the govt to set up an inquiry. The Aboriginal Justice Inquiry, 1989-91, held Cross responsible, while also condemning the JUDICIAL SYSTEM's treatment of Aboriginal people. In 1992, the Law Enforcement Review Agency blamed Cross for using excessive force. The AJI report also criticized the police investigation, including the evidence-gathering process and the lenient treatment of Cross

by then-police-chief Herb Stephen. Though he moved to CO after the inquiry, Cross returned to MB in late 1998. He died in 1999, officially due to "acute alcoholism." In 2003, the CBC aired a film about the events. *Cowboys & Indians: The Killing of J. J. Harper* was directed by NORMA BAILEY and featured ADAM BEACH as Harper. ● JOEL TRENAMAN

HARRIS, Kitty, Soviet secret agent (b May 24, 1899, London, UK; d Oct 6, 1966, Gorky (now Nizhny Novgorod), USSR) Harris was part of a global Soviet espionage network during the 1930s and 40s. She was a fervent COMMUNIST, a political ideology she adopted while active in WINNIPEG's labour movement. Her parents were Jews who had fled persecution in Russia. She was born in London's East End, and came to Winnipeg with her family in 1908. Her father worked as a shoemaker, barely making enough to provide for his 10 children. Their impoverished circumstances forced Harris to drop out of school at age 12 to work in a cigarette factory, introducing her to the grim realities of factory conditions at an early age. Later working as a garment factory seamstress, she became an ardent supporter of the labour movement, and was part of the 1919 WINNIPEG GENERAL STRIKE. As secretary of the One Big Union (OBU), she had her first experience in covert intelligence work when a friend in the American Federation of Labour solicited her help in digging up information on OBU leaders. Through her espionage, Harris uncovered union ties with bootlegging and flagrant misuse of OBU funds in racetrack betting. The information helped the AFL discredit OBU leadership, leading to the eventual demise of the union.

In 1923, she moved with her family to Chicago, where she met and married Earl Browder, who would later became the general secretary of the American Communist Party. In 1927, the couple travelled to Shanghai, China, then a centre for communist activity, where Harris first became known to Soviet operatives. She was recruited by the KGB in 1931 and, following the dissolution of her marriage, moved to Europe where she began undertaking missions for Soviet foreign intelligence. Her secret career took her to Germany, Britain, France, China, Mexico, and the US. She went by several names, including Elizabeth Dreyfus, Alice Read, Mrs. Morris, and Elizaveta Stein. In KGB reports, she was codenamed GYPSY, NORMA, and ADA.

In 1938, Harris began working with British diplomat Donald MacLean, who was part of the infamous Cambridge spy ring. She took photographs of the internal documents MacLean secretly brought home from the British Foreign

Office, and served as his link to the KGB controller. MacLean was attracted to Harris, an experienced woman 13 years his senior who shared his communist idealism. The pair's working ties soon developed into a love affair. The intimate relationship, which ended in 1940 when MacLean married, was one of few allowed by Harris' double life, and she wore a locket given to her by MacLean for the rest of her life.

In 1941, Harris was sent to the US as a contact agent to help the Soviets penetrate the atom bomb Manhattan Project, followed by a period in Mexico City, where she organized a spy ring. By 1946, the strain of life as a secret agent was wearing on Harris. Unable to return to her family in the US, she sought refuge in the USSR. However, far from being welcomed into the regime she had served for so many years, Harris was treated as a threat by Soviet officials, who worried that she knew too much about secret Soviet operations. She was forcibly placed in a psychiatric hospital in 1952, where she was held for 2 years. Upon her release, she lived in isolation in the Russian city of Gorky, and died alone. • MICHELLE DOBROVOLNY

HART, Evelyn Anne, ballerina (b Apr 4, 1956, Toronto) is a world-renowned prima ballerina who danced professionally with the **Royal Winnipeg Ballet** (RWB) for 29 years. Known for her musicality and lyrical interpretations of both modern and classical ballet, she is considered among the finest ballerinas Canada has ever produced. Hart began her ballet training in 1970 at the Dorothy Carter School of Dance in London, ON. She briefly attended the National Ballet School in Toronto, but her struggle with anorexia nervosa forced her to leave. In 1973, after she had regained her strength and confidence, she began studying with David Moroni in the RWB's professional division. Hart made her debut with RWB in 1976 as a corps de ballet member. Her rise to soloist (1978), then principal dancer (1979) was considered meteoric. In 1980, Hart was awarded the bronze medal at the World Ballet Concours in Osaka, Japan. Later that year, Hart attracted international attention when she received a gold medal at the International Competition in Varna, Bulgaria, the first Western woman in the competition's history to do so. She was also awarded the Exceptional Achievement Award.

Hart appeared as a guest artist with numerous ballet companies around the world. Several of her signature pieces include Jiří Kylián's pas de deux *Nuages*, Norbert Vesak's pas de deux *Belong*, and the role of Tatiana in John Cranko's *Onegin*. After close to 3 decades with the RWB, Hart's contract was not renewed. Angry at the perceived rejection, she moved to Toronto,

Evelyn Hart, 1992

then London, ON, to pursue other performing opportunities. In recognition of her dancing and contributions made to the art form, Hart has received numerous awards, including the Order of Canada (1983, elevated from Officer to Companion in 1994); the Ontario Arts Council's Jean A. Chalmers Award (2000); Canada's Walk of Fame (2000); and the Gov Gen's Performing Arts Award (2001). Although Hart never completed her last year of high school, she holds honorary degrees from the U of M and McMaster U (both 1989). Despite these accolades, Hart's rise to fame was often plagued by self-doubt and crippling anxiety. Max Wyman captured her struggles and inspiring story in the biography *Evelyn Hart: An Intimate Portrait* (1991). She received the Order of Manitoba in 2007. • JILL SEXSMITH

HARTNEY, pop 400, is a town 50 km SW of **Brandon** in the **Souris River** Valley. The area had a rich role to play in the **Fur Trading** era, with a number of **Forts** built in the valley. Fort Desjarlais was built not far from what would become Hartney and **Cuthbert Grant** founded an independent fur trading fort which he modestly called Fort Mr. Grant. The town itself was founded in 1882 when the first settler, James H. Hartney, arrived from ON with his family and servants, purchased 2 full sections along the river, hired workers to plough and prepare the fields, built a smithy and general store, and became the first postmaster. The prosperity of Hartney's farm and business operations attracted more settlers. ON settlers moved W to take advantage of fertile soil and abundant wood for building houses. Farming and local Women's

Institutes are credited with shaping the identity of what locals call "The Little Town With a Lot of Heart." In the 21st century, the town services surrounding agriculture. Tourism is growing as an industry here, as sightseers are increasingly attracted to Fort Desjarlais, the Cam-Hart museum and uncommon bird and plant species at the nearby Lauder Sandhills. Archaeological digs are popular in the area and Hartney was the location site for a couple of feature films in 2006, including *The Stone Angel*. • GPP

HARVARD, John, politician, journalist (b June 4, 1938, **Glenboro**). Before becoming MB's 23rd lt gov in 2004, Harvard worked in broadcasting and was a Liberal MP for 16 years. He began his career as a radio announcer at CFRY in **Portage la Prairie** before moving on to CKX in **Brandon** and then to a station in Kitchener-Waterloo, ON. In 1960, he became a radio journalist at CJOB in **Winnipeg**, covering provincial politics and later hosting a popular call-in show. He moved to the CBC in 1970, and was a host for the TV supper-hour news show *24 Hours*, displaying an outspoken, colourful style. He made the move to federal politics in 1988 with his election to the House of Commons as a Liberal MP for the St. James riding. Although the constituency was redistributed and renamed, he was re-elected 3 times. Perhaps because he supported Paul Martin, Harvard was never given a cabinet position in Jean Chretien's govt. Instead, he chaired several committees and was a parliamentary secretary to the ministers of public works, agriculture and international trade. He was appointed lt gov just before the 2004 election in which former Winnipeg mayor **Glen Murray** unsuccessfully ran as the Liberal candidate in the St. James riding. In 2005, Harvard was awarded an honourary doctorate from the **U of M**. • MD

HARVESTMEN, or 'Daddy long-legs,' are members of a group of animals called arachnids, which also includes spiders and scorpions, but not insects. Placed in the order Opiliones, they range in body size from 1-13 mm and have 4 pairs of exceedingly slender legs (insects have 3 pairs), but no slender 'waist' between the forebody (cephalothorax) and the abdomen, as do spiders. They also lack typical spider features like fangs (they cannot bite hard with their tiny chelicerae), poison glands, and silk glands; consequently they make no webs. One pair of eyes is present. Harvestmen also differ from other arachnids in that they have internal fertilization. The male has a penis which is inserted into the female's oviduct during sperm transfer. The female subsequently lays 10-200 eggs into the soil with her ovipositor. The offspring mature over summer and die in the fall, after laying the eggs of the next generation. There are over 200 species in NA and 7000 species named worldwide (plus many yet unknown), but only a small number of species occur in MB. However, they are easily noticed and may be common in grassland and forest communities, and frequently turn up in disturbed sites such as around home foundations or in gardens. They usually take cover under logs and stones or leaf litter.

Some species nibble on plants, but most devour insects, snails and worms. Unlike other arachnids, they digest solid food (and not pre-orally digested fluids). The 4-8 mm Brown Harvestman (*Phalangium opilio*) is a common species throughout temperate NA (possibly introduced here) and Eurasia, and frequently inhabits fields of crops, city parks and gardens, where it serves a valuable service of devouring many kinds of insect pests. An interesting behaviour is the formation of aggregations of several to dozens of individuals, for reasons not entirely understood – perhaps a basking, resting, or hibernating strategy, or a defensive tactic, pulsing simultaneously on their legs or combining their warning secretions. On being discovered, they wave their second pair of legs menacingly, and then hobble off rather slowly on their long legs, which break off rather easily. Just like a detached lizard tail, the broken leg of a harvestman continues to twitch for several minutes or up to an hour, perhaps detracting the attention of a predator while the harvestman escapes. Another defensive feature is the secretion of distasteful chemicals from glands lying under the chitonous skin of the cephalothorax. This group evolved 325 million years ago. ● REW

HATSKIN, Benjamin, sports executive (b Sep 30, 1917, **Winnipeg**; d Oct 18, 1990, Winnipeg) formed the **Winnipeg Jets** and was co-founder of the World Hockey Association. Hatskin grew

Ben Hatkin (left) with the $1 million contract and Bobby Hull (right), 1972

up in Winnipeg's **North End**. A skilled athlete, Hatskin earned one of the first ever football scholarships awarded to a Cdn athlete, but his time at the U of Oklahoma ended early because of WWII. After service overseas, Hatskin returned to his hometown where he played 6 seasons with the **Winnipeg Blue Bombers**, helping bring home the Grey Cup in 1939 and 1941. Following his football career, Hatskin became involved in horseracing. Hatskin's Farms, built in 1957, produced the 1959 winner of the Louisiana Derby. Hatskin is best remembered for forming the Winnipeg Jets organization in 1966, originally as part of the Western Canada Hockey League, later as an entry in the World Hockey Association co-founded by Hatskin. The WHA posed a considerable threat to the NHL after the Jets lured Chicago Black Hawks superstar **Bobby Hull** to their franchise with a $1 million dollar contract. The 2 leagues continued to compete to attract the best talent until the 1979 merger that brought the Jets and 3 other WHA franchises into the NHL. ● MD

HAVENS, Betty, aging expert, scholar (b Oct 9, 1936, Omaha, NE; d Mar 1, 2005, **Winnipeg**). Havens was a professor and senior scholar in community health sciences at the **U of M** Faculty of Medicine before she initiated groundbreaking research on aging that has since been used around the world. Her breakthrough work was the *Aging in MB Study*, which she began in 1971 and continued to her death, interviewing nearly 9000 seniors. Havens also co-founded the Centre on Aging at the U of M, served as provincial gerontologist 1982-94, worked with the UN and the WHO, and was assistant deputy minister of MB's Continuing Care Program. Havens various awards and honorary degrees, including the Order of Canada on Feb 18, 2005, mere weeks before her death. ● GPP

HAWERCHUK, Dale, hockey player (b Apr 4, 1963, Toronto). After Hawerchuk joined the **Winnipeg Jets** in 1981, the team had a 48-point improvement, an NHL record for team turnaround. Hawerchuk began playing hockey as a toddler in Rexdale, ON. His professional career started with the Quebec Major Junior Hockey League as a star centre where he twice led the team to Memorial Cup victories. Hawerchuk was the first draft pick for the Jets the following season. He didn't disappoint, becoming the youngest player in NHL history to reach over 100 points, and earning the Calder Memorial Trophy for Rookie of the Year. He quickly became a favourite with Winnipeg fans by helping to turn the Jets into a winning team. He broke 17 club records

Dale Hawerchuck, 1983

and garnered over 100 points for 5 consecutive seasons. Hawerchuk remained one of the team's stars for 10 years until he was traded to the Buffalo Sabres. After stints with the St. Louis Blues and the Philadelphia Flyers, Hawerchuk retired following the 1996-97 season. Over his career, Hawerchuk recorded 518 goals, 891 assists and 1409 points. He is a member of the Hockey Hall of Fame. Hawerchuk married a MB girl and they maintain a cottage in the **Gimli** area. ● MD

HAWKS (family Accipitridae) are diurnal raptors, meaning they are birds of prey that hunt during the daylight hours. Harriers, **Eagles**, the Osprey (*Pandion haliaetus*), and so-called "accipiters" and "buteos" all belong in this family. Accipiters, such as the Northern Goshawk (*Accipiter gentiles*) and the Cooper's Hawk (*A. cooperii*), are frequently seen during migration, but they are unobtrusive during the breeding season, as they nest in dense woods. Buteos are

Red-tailed hawk

large hawks that feed primarily on rodents. The most common of these in MB is the Red-tailed Hawk (*Buteo jamaicensis*), which can often be seen soaring on broad wings over a farmer's field or perched on a roadside utility pole. Ospreys are large fish-eating hawks that reuse their nests, which can become massive structures, year after year. Regular visitors to Grand Beach Provincial Park will be familiar with a long-occupied nest on a local hydro transformer station. Harriers hunt by quartering low over marshes or pastures, on tilted wings. Of this group, only the Northern Harrier (*Circus cyaneus*) occurs in the province.
● RUDOLF KOES

▶ *See* EAGLES, FALCONS.

HAYES RIVER. The Hayes rises about 220 km SSE of THOMPSON at MOLSON LAKE, flowing NE into the HUDSON BAY at Marsh Point. Covering a distance of 485 km, it is the longest naturally flowing river in MB, in that it has remained virtually unaltered by damming or diversion. Before Europeans arrived, the river was an important trade and travel route for local First Nations. From the HBC's founding in 1670 until the early 20th century, when the railway became a more efficient means of transport, the river was significant as the main route for fur traders and settlers between York Factory and the rest of western Canada, as the route led, via the Echimamish and NELSON rivers to the N end of LAKE WINNIPEG at NORWAY HOUSE. The Hayes thus had an important influence on the development of Canada, though there are few settlements along its banks. The HBC established several key trading posts along the river, however, including YORK FACTORY. This post at the river mouth at Hudson Bay served as the company's centre of operations for over 200 years. In 1684, fur trader PIERRE-ESPRIT RADISSON named the river after Sir James Hayes, secretary to Prince Rupert and a charter member of the HBC.

The Hayes boasts several unique features, including a 17-km narrow gorge with high granite sides at Hell Gates and the 5 sets of falls at Robinson Falls. The river continues to be an important transportation route and source of traditional harvesting for MB's Swampy CREE people. The Hayes is also popular with adventurous canoeists and kayakers. In addition to natural highlights, travellers can stop at numerous historically significant points, including YORK FACTORY and several abandoned fur trading posts. Harbour seals and beluga whales inhabit the Hayes estuary, but as polar bears occur frequently around the river's northern reaches, camping here is imprudent. In 2000, the Hayes was nominated as a candidate to the Cdn Heritage Rivers System. ● AJL

Bruce Head

HEAD, Bruce, painter, sculptor, (b Feb 14, 1931, St. Boniface), is a member of the Royal Canadian Academy of Artists (RCA). Head graduated from the U OF M's School of Art in 1953. A graphic designer for the Canadian Broadcasting Corporation (1956-87) he brought a uniquely recognizable energy and bold strength to his work, an energy reflected consistently in his canvasses and sculptures, achieved through his integrity of the creative process. Colour has been core to Head's work, and the landscape and light is its foundation. Trips to Mexico have had a significant impact on his rich use of colour, and his abstracted images are predominantly based on the land, the horizon, and the geometry of the Prairie fields. The play of light and the juxtaposition of the abstract with soft linear forms imbue the work with magnetism. He uses a variety of materials in his painting, including metallic paint, stencils, cut outs and prints from found objects. All add texture, another important element Head's painting and sculpture. He has exhibited across Canada in group and one-man shows and is represented in public and private collections, including The WINNIPEG ART GALLERY, the Art Gallery of Greater Victoria and the National Gallery of Canada. Commissions include the Manitoba Law Courts Building and the Concourse at Portage and Main.
● PATRICIA BOVEY

HEADINGLEY, pop 1900, is a community located just 3 km W of WINNIPEG on the Trans Canada Highway and the ASSINIBOINE RIVER. Headingley was officially incorporated as a rural municipality in 1993, after it successfully seceded from Winnipeg. It consists of 107.47 km² of land, much

of which is farmland. The community was born in the 1850s when the Archdiocese of Rupertsland purchased 2 river lots just W of Winnipeg as a parish centre for the Church of England. In 1852, Rev Griffith Owen Corbett named Headingley after his former parish in Headingley, Leeds, Yorkshire. Although an attempt was made to create a municipality of Headingley in 1877, the application was turned down by the provincial govt. Headingley was then administered by the municipality of Assiniboia to the N and Charleswood to the S. It was annexed by the City of Winnipeg in 1972, and remained an outlying community until residents felt that they were not receiving the proper attention from the city and that the taxes they were paying outweighed the services they were provided. They voted to break away in 1993, and became an independent municipality that May.

In 2006, Headingley is a growing community because of its low residential tax, no business tax, and high quality of services. The community is predominantly English-speaking, youthful, and has experienced a housing boom in recent years with new developments built along Robin Boulevard. The major employers of the region include Shelmerdine's Nurseries, Taillieu Construction, Breezy Bend Golf Course, and the JOHN BLUMBERG Golf Course and Softball Complex. Headingley is known for its market gardeners along Portage Ave and Roblin Boulevard. Other attractions include the Gates on Roblin Restaurant, Thunder Rapids Fun Park, and the Headingley Heritage Centre. Headingley operates one elementary school and has one local weekly newspaper, the *Headingley Headliner*. Headingley landmarks include the Odeon Drive-In, the Holy Trinity ANGLICAN Church (originally built in 1853, but rebuilt several times), and the computer-monitored smart bridge, which is named for the Hon. John Taylor, a former prominent Headingley landowner and Member of Parliament. It is also home to the Headingley Correctional Centre, which acts as a minimum, medium and maximum-security provincial jail. ● AMANDA STEPHENS

HEALTH SCIENCES CENTRE. The HSC is the largest health-care institution in MB. It incorporates acute-care, educational, residential, research, administrative, clinical, rehabilitation, and specialized medical facilities over a 13-ha (32-ac) area in central WINNIPEG. The centre is among the largest health complexes in Canada, also serving northern MB, NW ON, and NU. It specializes in trauma care, transplant, and neurosurgery.

In 1972, ED SCHREYER's govt passed legislation to create the HSC, allowing for centralized planning and administration through a 27-member

PETER TITTENBERGER

board of a new organization that brought together the Children's Hospital of Winnipeg; the Manitoba Rehabilitation Hospital; the D. A. Stewart Centre, a respiratory hospital; and the main facility, which had long been known as the Winnipeg General Hospital.

Community planning for the "General" began Dec 1872, and it took only a week to open a 5-bed, one-room hospital on Main St. A typhoid fever **EPIDEMIC** was the immediate concern. *Manitoba Free Press* (later **WINNIPEG FREE PRESS**) editor **WILLIAM FISHER LUXTON** was among other prominent citizens behind the project. In 1875, **ANDREW MCDERMOT** and **ANDREW G. B. BANNATYNE** donated land on what was then the edge of the city, and fundraising allowed for the construction of a small building at what would later become the corner of Sherbrook St and McDermot Ave. In 1877, all 3 levels of govt began giving grants to the hospital. The associated Manitoba Medical College (*see* **U OF M**) was established in 1883, with a nursing school soon to follow in 1887. Construction was almost continuous, as site expansions occurred in 1884, 1888, 1897, 1903, and 1910. World wars and the **GREAT DEPRESSION** halted major development for a quarter-century, however. Growth continued in 1948 with the erection of the Women's Pavilion, as well as the N, S, and Service wings. The Children's Hospital moved from its Main St. location to a new building alongside the General in 1956, integrating its services with the new maternity ward. That same year saw construction begin on a 7-storey main building to replace the old edifice, and a new nursing school was completed. Other new and revamped buildings followed in the 1960s.

Construction at the HSC in 2007.

When the HSC began operations in 1973, it had a $43-million operating budget that funded 1350 beds and 4300 full-time-equivalent staff positions. It entered into an affiliation agreement with Manitoba Cancer Treatment and Research Foundation (now CancerCare Manitoba), and has made similar agreements with the U of M over the years. The faculties of medicine, pharmacy, and dentistry, as well as the schools of medical rehabilitation and dental hygiene, are located at the HSC. In 1994, an HSC department became the subject of controversy, as 12 infants died during or following heart surgery at the hospital. Judge **MURRAY SINCLAIR** presided over the Paediatric Cardiac Surgery Inquest (1995-98) and authored a 516-page report that was released in 2000. It found that most of the deaths had been preventable. In Apr 2000, the Winnipeg Regional

Health Authority (*see* **MEDICINE**) took over the administration and running of the HSC as part of a series of provincial govt reforms. A chief operating officer and an 11-member executive have since overseen day-to-day hospital operations.

Another period of significant growth began in May 2003, with the announcement of a 26,570 m², 4-level, $135-million critical services (surgical, emergency, and intensive-care) unit. It was completed in Sept 2006 and was named the Ann Thomas Building after one of the hospital's first and longest serving Aboriginal nurses. The Winnipeg Centre for Gamma Knife Surgery opened in late 2003, bringing Canada's first $6.7-million Leksell gamma knife to the province. The technology uses pinpoint radiation to treat cancers, tumours, and other brain disorders without the side effects of invasive surgery. In Mar 2005, HSC acquired MB's first positron emission tomography (PET) scanner, and in June of that year went ahead with plans for the Siemens Institute for Advanced Medicine, a $25-million neuroscience and infectious-disease research hub. A year later, in June 2006, the Manitoba Centre for Proteomics and Systems Biology – focused on cell biology and genomics – received the go-ahead after attracting nearly $8 million in grants. In addition, **CANAD INNS** decided in 2006 to build a 160-room hotel to accommodate hundreds of out-of-town patients and family members each year. The improvements continued in 2007, with the announcement in April of govt support for a $10.5 million non-invasive, high-energy X-Ray machine to cut cancer tumours in patients otherwise not eligible for surgery. The "Artiste" machine will be the first such technology in NA to adjust to the exact size of a tumour.

During the 2005-06 fiscal year, the HSC's 7817 staff and volunteers processed 31,194 admissions, 87,218 emergency visits, and 22,488 surgeries,

Winnipeg General Hospital, 1888

while maintaining 753 inpatient beds. Individuals that have made a significant contribution to the HSC or the Winnipeg General Hospital include **Robert Earl Beamish**, **Edith Rogers**, **Paul Thorlakson**, and Tannis Richardson (see **Richardson Family**). • Joel Trenaman

HEAPS, Abraham Albert "A. A.," politician (b Dec 24, 1885, Leeds, UK; d April 4, 1954, Leeds) was a prominent Socialist leader. Of **Polish Jewish** descent, he came to Canada in 1910, and to Winnipeg in 1911. He was a member of the Social Democratic Party and a pacifist, opposing conscription in 1917 with F. J. Dixon and **John Queen**. During the **Winnipeg General Strike** of 1919, he supervised the commissariat for the strike committee and, in council, advocated banning all parades. He was arrested on June 17, 1919, and he conducted his own defence against charges of seditious libel. He was found innocent on all counts on March 28, 1920, after a masterful address to the jury. He then started an insurance agency for **Great-West Life**, from which he resigned in 1925 when he was elected to the House of Commons from Winnipeg North as a Labour MP. He later became a **Co-operative Commonwealth Federation** MP. In 1926, he confronted **Arthur Meighen** in the House over govt policy at the time of the Winnipeg General Strike. Heaps was on friendly terms with PMs R. B. Bennett and Mackenzie King, but was cordially hated by Meighen and Tim Buck, the leader of the Communist Party of Canada. He served in the Commons as an unofficial critic on economic policy until 1940, when he retired. • JMB

HEARNE, Samuel, fur trader, explorer (b 1745, London, UK; d Nov 1792, London, UK) was one of the first European men to explore northern

Samuel Hearne

MB. He served in the RN before joining the **HBC** as a mate on the sloop *Churchill*. Hearne was soon singled out as an explorer, and beginning in 1769, made a series of attempts to reach the Coppermine River by an overland route. After several abortive efforts, Hearne accompanied the guide Matonabbee and his family on a lengthy journey to the North, becoming the first European to reach the Artic Ocean overland from NA, and the first to cross Great Slave Lake. He returned on June 30, 1772, and sent his journals back to England. In 1776, he was appointed head of **Fort Prince of Wales** at **Churchill**, and he surrendered it to the French in 1782. By 1787, he was ready to retire. He spent his last years in London working on his journals and maps. His *A Journey from Prince of Wales's Fort, in Hudson's Bay, to the Northern Ocean* was published in 1795 in London, going through several editions and translation into German, Dutch, and French. • JMB

HECLA (Hecla Island), 172 km² large, 165 km N of Winnipeg on the W shore of **Lake Winnipeg**, is a unique community with a history beginning in 1875 with the arrival of Icelandic land scouts from ON. Some 27 km long and previously known as Big Island, it became the most northerly part of an "Icelandic Reserve" known as **New Iceland** (*Nyja Island*), and the former name was translated as *Mikley*. Both names were used interchangeably over the next century, and following the establishment of the Hecla Post Office on the island in 1889, the community's association with the name *Hecla* began. Contrary to popular belief, however, the Icelandic volcano Hekla played no part in Icelandic emigration or settlement on Hecla Island.

Homesteading on the island began in 1876 with the arrival of both "old settlers" from Gimli and new immigrants directly from Iceland. Smallpox swept the fledgling settlement that winter, and the historic cemetery at *Kirkjubol* (Church Abode), toward the island's S end, dates from that time. Despite hardships, settlers soon claimed all suitable lands on the E and S shores of the island, and some later ventured to the marshy W side. In keeping with age-old Icelandic tradition, all homesteads were named, and settlers were associated with their farm names.

Following severe flooding in 1880, many settlers left for **Winnipeg**, **Baldur**, and the Dakota Territory in the US. In 1883, however, new arrivals from Iceland began reoccupying abandoned homesteads, and by 1891, the island was home to 31 families, for a total of 180 people. Many of the settlers were devout Lutherans, who re-organized the island congregation in 1886 and built a concrete church that was later replaced by the

present Hecla Church in 1928. The cemetery at that site dates from 1887. Literacy and culture were also priorities, and 3 schools were established: Big Island #589 (1889), Grund #627 (1891), and later South Hecla. Other organizations included the Women's Society *Undina* (1886); a reading society, *Morgunstjarnan* (1896), and an emergency fund called *Hjalp i Vidlogum*.

A living artifact of Hecla Village

Early on, settlement gravitated to the sawmill and pier built in Mylnuvik (Mill Bay) before 1875. A govt dock was later constructed at its present location, and during the 1890s enterprising islanders began establishing businesses nearby. A village formed as adjacent homesteads were subdivided into narrower lots to accommodate 2nd- and 3rd-generation descendants. By 1900, a cottage community had also taken root at Gull Harbour. At its peak, during the 1930-40s, Hecla was home to about 500 people who relied on fishing, farming, freighting, and logging. Adapting to both Lake Winnipeg's environment and Cdn society, *Mikleyingar* – as the islanders became known – developed a unique, colourful, and self-reliant culture. While they retained the Icelandic language and many traditions, many also spoke English and anglicized their names. In 1953, a ferry service at Grassy Narrows facilitated contact with the mainland, which had always been difficult and treacherous. This new link, however, also hastened a decline that became increasingly evident during the 1960s. The high school closed its doors in 1964, and when fishing on Lake Winnipeg was banned in the late 1960s (ostensibly due to high mercury levels), the population dropped to 78. Hecla was becoming a ghost town, and some islanders then began advocating development of the island's recreational potential.

In 1969, through the Fund for Rural Economic Development, the transformation of Hecla Island into a provincial park began. In 1970, a $1 million causeway spanning Grassy Narrows was started, and at Gull Harbour work began on a golf course/hotel with recreational facilities.

While the creation of Hecla Provincial Park promised employment and renewal for this island community, support quickly soured when officials withdrew promises of lifetime leases for residents wishing to remain. Aggressive expropriation of farmland, homes, and cottage properties ensued in 1971 – a move that would divide islanders and spawn bitter legal wrangles. Expropriation payments were so low that islanders could not acquire comparable properties on the mainland, and though plans called for an "historic Icelandic fishing village," only 4 island families remained by the time the park opened in 1975. Many also questioned the demolition of historic buildings on the island. More recently, in response to long-standing grievances and a desire to restore life to Hecla, leaseback deals on 5-ha (1.7-ac) lots were offered to descendants of expropriated landowners. This, together with the sale of lots on Hecla's N shore, has resulted in a flurry of building and renovation, signalling the beginning of yet another chapter in the history of this unique MB maritime community. ● NELSON GERRARD

HEMP. This plant, once discredited in the "reefer madness" period of the 1930s, enjoyed a resurgence in MB in the early 21st century. Although industrial hemp was legal to grow, a hefty tax discouraged farmers from attempting to farm it until 1998, when the Cdn govt introduced the *Industrial Hemp Act*. Producers in the **PARKLAND** region around **DAUPHIN** responded by growing about 4850 ha (12,000 ac) of hemp. When plans for a processing plant fell through, farmers banded together to form a co-op. In 2006, their efforts to develop the first hemp processing plant in NA were within reach, thanks to funding from all levels of govt.

Industrial hemp was commercially produced in the 1800s in many parts of the world. It was used to manufacture rope, cloth, sails, and paper. However, in the 1930s, it was lumped in with its cousin marijuana, although it had negligible levels of THC, the psychoactive compound tetrahydrocannabinol. For a brief period in WWII, farmers were encouraged to grow hemp for the war effort. Thereafter, plastics and synthetics replaced hemp, and the crop became too expensive to grow.

The resurrection of industrial hemp came about because it is both environmentally and economically efficient. As a renewable resource, it can be planted in the same fields year after year. The plants pull carbon out of the air. Moreover, every part of industrial hemp plants can be used for either fibre or oil. The processing plant proposed for Dauphin would not produce any waste, and would be heated by bricks made of the fibre.

Industrial hemp is a distinct variety of the plant species *Cannabis sativa*. It is an annual that can grow as tall as 3 m. Under federal legislation, it can only be grown under licence. In 2005, MB production expanded to more than 5000 ha (12,355 ac), largely to serve a small health-food market interested in the oil for the nutritive properties of its high content of unsaturated fatty acids such as omega-3. In 2004, hemp sold for $1100/tonne, outstripping the price of all conventional grain crops, except **WILD RICE**.
● INGEBORG BOYENS

HENAULT, Raymond, soldier (b April, 1949, **WINNIPEG**). Henault attended school in St. Jean Baptiste. As a teenager, his father taught him how to fly a crop duster. Henault enrolled in the air division of the newly unified Cdn Forces in 1968 to take more formal pilot training in Borden, ON, and **GIMLI**, where he learned to fly helicopters and jet fighters. A graduate of Paris's École supérieure de guerre aérienne, he also studied at the National Defence College in Kingston, ON, and completed a BA from the U of M in 1992. During his career with the Forces, Henault was promoted to the rank of Maj (1981), LtCol (1985), Col (1990), BGen (1994), MGen (1997), and LGen (1998). Once base commander of CFB **PORTAGE LA PRAIRIE**, he was appointed acting deputy chief of defence staff (1997) and chief of defence staff (2001), when he attained his present rank of Gen, the highest possible in the CF. After 36 years of service with the Cdn Forces, Gen Henault was elected chairman of NATO's military committee – the highest military decision-making post in the organization – in Nov 2004, largely on the strength of his poise during daily press briefings during NATO's 1999 Kosovo campaign, when Henault was the public face for Canada's air efforts. The bilingual Henault's savvy at handling Canada's role in Afghanistan solidified his reputation as a noteworthy negotiator and diplomat. As chief advisor to NATO's secretary-general (until Henault's retirement in June 2007), Henault stood atop a military hierarchy of more than one million troops from 26 nations. His honours include Commander of the Order of Military Merit, and Commander of both France's Legion of Honour and the US's Legion of Merit. ● JS

HENDERSON, Harold LLOYD, Presbyterian minister, politician (b 1907, Freeland, PEI; d Jan 18, 1993 **PORTAGE LA PRAIRIE**). Lloyd Henderson's early education took place in Prince Edward Island and he completed his studies in 1942 at the Presbyterian College in Montreal. On Jan 14, 1943 he was ordained and went on to become the

minister of the **PRESBYTERIAN** Church in Portage la Prairie. He served as mayor of Portage from 1947-1966 and again from 1971-1974. Although he was successful in municipal politics, he began a stubborn effort to attain higher office. In 1958, Henderson ran as a federal Liberal candidate in the riding of Portage-Neepawa. He was not elected. He then attempted a bid for leadership of the Liberal Party of Canada that same year and also in the 1968 leadership convention. Neither effort was successful. He persisted at the provincial level when he ran for leadership of the MB Liberal party 3 times, in 1961,1969 and in 1975 but was not successful. After his defeat as a Liberal candidate in the general election of 1958, Henderson ran in the same riding as an Independent in the 1962 and 1963 federal elections and came in last both times Early in 1993, Henderson died and was buried in his hometown on PEI.
● RUTH DEGRAVES

Tom Hendry, 1958

HENDRY, Thomas Best "Tom," playwright, actor (b June 7, 1929, **WINNIPEG**) is a writer and activist dedicated to the development of the arts in Canada. Although Hendry was expelled from the arts program at the **U OF M** for skipping too many classes, he later graduated as a chartered accountant in 1955. He began writing and acting in television and radio while at the U of M. The musical revue *Do You Remember?* – which he wrote – was televised in 1954 and was later produced at **RAINBOW STAGE**. Hendry became active in Winnipeg's growing arts community, especially **THEATRE**. In 1957, Hendry and **JOHN HIRSCH** co-founded Theatre 77, which merged with the Winnipeg Little Theatre to become the

Manitoba Theatre Centre (MTC). The MTC was the country's first regional theatre. Hendry managed both the MTC and Rainbow Stage before moving to Toronto in 1964. Hendry became secretary-general of the Canadian Theatre Centre, and consulted for Cdn performing arts until 1968. He was the first literary manager of the Stratford Festival. In the early 1970s, Hendry co-founded Playwrights Co-Op (now the Playwrights Guild of Canada), Toronto Free Theatre (now Canadian Stage Company), and the Playwrights' Colony and Playwrights Co-Op (now Playwrights Press, Inc.) at the Banff Centre. Hendry helped expand the Toronto Arts Council, and chaired a task force redefining the role of the National Arts Centre in Ottawa. Hendry has written 29 plays, including *Fifteen Miles of Broken Glass* (1966), *Satyricon* (1971), and *Byron* (1976). He won the Lieutenant-Governor of Ontario's Medal in 1969 for *Fifteen Miles of Broken Glass*. Hendry also wrote episodes of CBC's *King of Kensington*, radio plays and commentaries, articles, and short stories. Hendry became an Officer of the Order of Canada in 1995, and as of writing, remained treasurer of Playwrights Canada Press. ● AMANDA STEPHENS

HENNING, Douglas James, magician, entertainer (b May 3, 1947, **Winnipeg**; d Feb 7, 2000, Los Angeles). Henning grew up in the Wildwood Park area of Winnipeg before moving to Oakville, ON. He showed an early preoccupation with magic and tricks, giving his first performance when he was 14. After graduating with a psychology degree from McMaster U in Hamilton, ON, he abandoned plans to study medicine, and with the help of a grant from the Canada Council for the Arts, undertook a serious investigation of magic and magicians. He began to develop a stage show, and, in the early 1970s, he and Toronto film director Ivan Reitman produced the magic-themed rock musical *Spellound* in Toronto. The enormous success of this show led to *The Magic Show*, which debuted on Broadway in 1974 and ran for more than 4 years, earning Henning 2 Tony awards. He became an international star with his first TV special, *Doug Henning's World of Magic*. A version of this show aired each year for 7 years, and was nominated for 7 Emmys. Some of Henning's feats included walking through walls, making elephants disappear, and halving the time in which Houdini did his celebrated underwater escape. He was forced to stop airing live TV shows, however, when a tiger escaped from its cage and wandered through NBC's studios.

Henning created his own company, providing stage effects for music videos and concerts given by popular music performers such as Michael

Doug Henning, left, helping demonstrate Transcendental Meditation.

Jackson. In the 1980s, while continuing his show business career, Henning began exploring the Transcendental Meditation (TM) movement founded in 1955 by Maharishi Mahesh Yogi, the Indian mystic who once counted the Beatles and Beach Boys among his followers. As Henning's involvement deepened, he concentrated less on performing and more on developing Maharishi Veda Land, a theme park based on the principles of the TM movement. The park was originally planned for Niagara Falls, ON, but has not been built. In 1986, Henning quit show business altogether, selling his props to other illusionists. After studying TM in India, he ran in the 1993 Cdn federal election, in the Toronto riding of Rosedale, for the Natural Law Party, on the platform that yogic "flying," an advanced technique of TM, would heal the nation's ills. Henning is considered a pioneer in the art of illusion. Henning's long unruly hair, colourful sets, use of popular music, and flamboyant dress were a welcome departure from the staid magician in tails and top hat. Many credit Henning with reviving the public's interest in sleight-of-hand, paving the way for acts such as David Copperfield, Penn and Teller, and Winnipeg's **Dean Gunnarson**. Henning died in 2000 of liver cancer. ● DOUG ALLEN

HERONS (family Ardeidae) are tall birds with long necks and legs, most often found near water. There, they feed on a variety of small vertebrates and invertebrates. There are 14 heron species in MB. The most widespread heron is the American Bittern (*Botaurus lentiginosus*), which nests throughout the province. Being a mostly nocturnal marsh-dweller, it is more often heard than seen. The Great Blue Heron (*Ardea herodias*) nests in colonies throughout the southern half of the province. One such colony, at Dog Lake, also

harbours Black-crowned Night-Herons (*Nycticorax nycticorax*) and Great Egrets (*Ardea alba*). Egrets are largely white and some species were hunted almost to extinction about a century ago. Fortunately, they have rebounded and numbers have increased in MB recently. Cattle Egrets (*Bubulcus ibis*) were confirmed as breeders at **Oak Lake** in 2005. Scanning a herd of grazing cattle for this species may pay off, especially around Whitewater Lake or **Oak Hammock Marsh**. The White-faced Ibis (*Plegadis chihi*) is a related species that has also nested at Whitewater Lake. ● RUDOLF KOES

Great Blue Heron

Peter Herrndorf

HERRNDORF, Peter media administrator (b 1940, Amsterdam) is a prominent figure in journalism, **Broadcasting**, and the arts. Born in the Netherlands, his family immigrated to the US before settling in **Winnipeg**. He attended the **U of M** and edited the school **Newspaper** while he earned his BA in political science and English (1962). Herrndorf received a law degree from Dalhousie U in 1965, and returned to Winnipeg, where he got a job as a reporter for CBC Television. Later he moved to Edmonton, and, in 1967, to Toronto, all the while working as a current affairs producer for CBC. He attended Harvard Business School and earned an MBA in 1970. Herrndorf eventually became the CBC network VP. He left the CBC to become the publisher for the *Toronto Life* magazine in 1983. In 1992, Herrndorf became the chairman and CEO of TVOntario, and continued there until 1999, when he was appointed president and CEO of the National Arts Centre in Ottawa. In 2005, Herrndorf was appointed to the board of directors at the CBC for a 5-year term. He has received numerous awards for his work in several fields, including 6 honorary doctorates. Herrndorf was made an Officer of the Order of Canada in 1993, and in 1995 became the first recipient of the William Kilbourn Award for lifetime contribution to the arts in Toronto. In 1998, he received the John Drainie Award for significant contribution to broadcasting. In June 2002, Herrndorf was selected as one of Canada's 50 "Nation Builders" by *The Globe and Mail*. He is married to Eva Czigler, the acting head of CBC's network programming. They have 2 children, and as of 2006 they lived in Toronto. • AMANDA STEPHENS

HERSHFIELD, Earl, doctor (b May 17, 1934, **Winnipeg**), served as medical director of the tuberculosis control program for the **MB Sanatorium** Board (1966-2003) and taught as a professor of internal **Medicine** at the **U of M**'s medical school during the same time period. He was also executive director of the Canadian Lung Association from 1976-1982, and became an internationally recognized expert on the treatment of tuberculosis.

Hershfield grew up in Winnipeg's **North End** in a family of doctors. His father, Charles Sheppy Hershfield, practised family medicine from 1931-81, and wrote 2 memoirs about his professional and personal life. Sheppy's brother Harry was also a doctor, and so was Earl's brother Melvyn. In the early 1960s, Earl Hershfield studied lung disease at Albert Einstein College of Medicine in New York and at the Mayo Clinic in Rochester, MN, where he finished his medical studies. After a few years practising medicine with his father and uncle in Winnipeg, Hershfield became the 5th medical director of MB's TB control program in May 1967. He was jointly appointed to the U of M's School of Medicine, where he'd also been a student.

When Hershfield became medical director, the Sanatorium Board of MB (now known as the MB Lung Association) still ran the Ninette Sanatorium in southwestern MB. He presided over its closing as a TB sanatorium in 1971. At that point many Ninette patients were First Nations people. The standard treatment was lung removal surgery, when patients should have been getting inexpensive antibiotic treatment. Hershfield modernized the TB control program by standardizing drug regimens, centralizing control and monitoring, and by treating the disease within the larger medical system. He also ended virtually all TB-related lung surgery.

As part of Hershfield's work running the Canadian Lung Association, he became extensively involved in international TB treatment programs. This was partly because TB virtually disappeared from developed countries by the 1970s. Hershfield did research and consultative work in Bangladesh, Haiti, Nepal, Singapore, and Vietnam. He continues to be involved in the national TB control program in Guyana. Hershfield also sat on the Medical Immigration Review Board from 1978 until 2001. During his days with the Review Board, Hershfield wrote the new regulations for TB that became part of the 1976 Immigration Act. This act opened the country especially to Asian immigrants who came from areas of high TB incidence. • MAURICE MIERAU

HERSHFIELD, Leible, sports administrator (b Aug 30, 1909; d June, 1999, **Winnipeg**), contributed to Winnipeg's sports community through his work at the Young Men's Hebrew Association. Hershfield first became involved in sports as a track and field athlete at Isaac Newton Junior High School where he was a gold medallist at the 1924 high school city championships. At 16, Hershfield began playing senior league softball with the YMHA, a sport he played for the next 27 years, in addition to his involvement as a player or coach in volleyball, basketball, football and 10-pin bowling. Hershfield was appointed the YMHA's director of physical education in 1936, a position he held until 1942. He assumed the position again in 1952, conducting therapy classes for polio victims following the epidemic of the 1950s. Hershfield also coached a soccer team of Jewish orphans who had been rescued from the Holocaust and brought to Canada by the Canadian Jewish Congress. He retired in 1974, and was named Outstanding Jewish Athlete of the first half of the 20th century by the YMHA. His nephew is tuberculosis researcher Dr. **Earl Hershfield**. • MD

HESPELER, Wilhelm (William), merchant, immigration agent, politician (b Dec 29, 1830, Baden, Germany; d April 18, 1921, Vancouver) is credited with bringing **Mennonites** to MB. He was educated at the Institute of Technology at Karlsruhe (now the U of Karlsruhe). Hespeler came to Canada in 1850 and became a merchant in ON. In the late 1860s and early 1870s, he visited Germany and Ukraine to recruit Mennonites for the Cdn Prairies. He moved to MB, where he was a Dominion **Immigration** agent from 1870-82, and consul for Germany from 1883-1909. Although not a Mennonite himself, in 1873, he tried to settle a party of Mennonites in southern MB, but they went on to the Dakota Territory. Hespeler finally succeeded in attracting Mennonite families in 1874, and he is often regarded as the founder of **German** Mennonite settlements in southern MB. He was MLA for Rosenfeld from 1899-1903 as an independent Conservative, and was Speaker of the House for the same period. In 1903, Kaiser Wilhelm II gave him Prussia's Roter-Adler-Orden (Order of the Red Eagle). Streets in **Winkler** and **Winnipeg** are named for him. • JMB

HEXTALL FAMILY is a MB hockey dynasty with 3 generations of men playing in the NHL over a 50-year period.

BRYAN HEXTALL, SR. (b July 31, 1913, Grenfell, SK; d July 25, 1984, **Portage la Prairie**) was a legendary New York Rangers rightwinger. Born in SK, Bryan was raised in Poplar Point, MB, where he played hockey on the team that won the 1930 MB juvenile championship. He played in the Manitoba Junior Hockey League (MJHL) for **Winnipeg** and **Portage La Prairie** teams before moving west in 1934 to play for the Vancouver Lions of the North West Hockey League, leading the league in goals scored in the 1936-37 season. He accomplished the same the following season as a player for the Philadelphia Ramblers of the International-American Hockey League.

Bryan had his first taste of the NHL in the 1936-37 season with the New York Rangers, though he didn't become a permanent player until the following season. He scored the most goals in the NHL in the 1939-40 and 1940-41 seasons, and posted the NHL's highest score in 1942, earning him the Art Ross Trophy. A career highlight came in overtime during the 6th game of the 1940 Stanley Cup finals, when Bryan scored the series-winning goal. He was named the Rangers' MVP in 1943-44. Bryan retired following the 1947-48 season, and was inducted into the Hockey Hall of Fame in 1969.

BRYAN LEE HEXTALL, JR. (b May 23, 1941, Winnipeg) was born near the end of his father's career with the Rangers. He started out playing for the Brandon Wheat Kings in 1958. Bryan Jr. had a brief stint with the NHL New York Rangers in 1962. He bounced around the minor leagues before being signed with the Pittsburgh Penguins for 5 seasons. He retired from the NHL in 1976, having played in 549 games.

DENNIS HEXTALL (b April 17, 1943, **POPLAR POINT**) also made it to the NHL, though initially it seemed his small size would prevent him from playing in the major leagues. He first played for the Brandon Wheat Kings, and then accepted a hockey scholarship from the U of North Dakota, where he studied pre-dentistry. Dennis' ability on ice improved through his university years and, after graduating, he began playing professionally for minor league teams in Knoxville, Omaha and Buffalo. He had his first shot at the NHL with the New York Rangers in 1968, but returned to the minors following a mediocre season, bouncing around with different teams until he rejoined the NHL in 1971 with the Minnesota North Stars.

Dennis stayed on the team for 5 seasons before moving to the Detroit Red Wings for 4 seasons. He played with the Washington Capitals for the 1978-79 season, and retired from play the following year.

RON HEXTALL, son of Bryan Jr., (b May 3, 1964, **BRANDON**) was an NHL goaltender. He was the first 3rd generation player in NHL history. Ron was famous for his mobility, and revolutionized NHL goaltending by leaving the net and stickhandling the puck. In 1987, he became the first goalie in the league to score a goal, a feat he accomplished yet again in the 1989 playoffs. Ron was awarded the Vezina Trophy for best goalie, and the Conn Smythe Trophy for NHL playoff MVP in 1987. He was well known for his aggressive style, and received 3 suspensions in his career for foul play. Hextall was traded to the Quebec Nordiques for the 1992-93 season, followed by a year with the New York Islanders before returning to the Flyers in 1994. He retired from play in 1999 to take over the as the team's director of scouting operations. ● MD

HICKES, George, politician (b June 26, 1946, near Rankin Inlet, NT, now NU). The first Inuk speaker of a legislature, Hickes grew up in a family of 12 in what is now called the Kivalliq region of NU, as well as **CHURCHILL**, where he attended school. Hickes worked at various jobs in AB and northern MB before entering the New Careers adult education program in 1976. He then worked for the organization until taking a position as executive director for the Limestone Training and Employment Agency near **GILLAM**. In 1990, after Hickes moved to **WINNIPEG**, he was elected as an MLA representing the Point

Douglas constituency for the **NDP**. He was re-elected in 1995, 1999, 2003, and 2007. Hickes served as party whip from 1990-99, and when the NDP formed govt in 1999, he was elected speaker of the legislative assembly. Hickes' nephews are Hunter Tootoo, an MLA in NU, and NHL hockey player Jordin Tootoo. ● JT

HIEBERT, Paul Gerhardt, teacher, author, scientist (b July 17, 1892, **PILOT MOUND**; d Sept 7, 1987, **CARMAN**). Having grown up in **ALTONA**, the son of a local storekeeper, Hiebert was educated at United College (*see* **U OF W**), where he took a BA in philosophy, and at the U of Toronto, where he received an MA in Gothic and Teutonic philology, before switching to McGill U, where he earned an MSc in chemistry and physics and a PhD in chemistry. Hiebert initially taught in SK schools and was a school principal in **GIMLI** and Ochre River. A well-loved professor of chemistry at the **U OF M** from 1924 to 1953, he won a Gov Gen's Award for Science in 1924. But Hiebert also attracted a devoted circle of admirers for his mischievous humour. He gained near-iconic stature with the 1947 publication of *Sarah Binks*, his "biography" of the fictional poetess he dubbed "The Sweet Songstress of Saskatchewan," complete with generous helpings of her immortal doggerel. The book – whose protagonist many believe to be modelled after **GREAT DEPRESSION**-era SK poet Edna Jacques – won the 1947 Stephen Leacock Medal for Humour for its witty satire of Prairie social pretensions and literary criticism.

Hiebert followed with a sequel to *Sarah Binks* named *Willows Revisited* (1967), and another work of humour, *For the Birds* (1980). Indelibly associated now with his tongue-in-cheek creation, he considered his better work to be the serious moral philosophy of *Tower in Siloam* (1966), *Doubting Castle* (1976), and *Not As the Scribes* (1984). In 1968, Donald Harron began working on a musical stage comedy, for which Hiebert had written the script in 1953, entitled *Here Lies Sarah Binks*. Among his many other contributions, Hiebert was President of the Canadian Writers Association (Winnipeg) in 1948-49, a Fellow of the Canadian Institute of Chemistry, and a minister of the **UNITED CHURCH OF CANADA**. He was named to the Order of Canada in 1976. His Carman home has been designated a MB Heritage Site, and his wife Dorothy posthumously donated his papers, including the manuscripts of 2 unpublished works, to the archives at the **U OF M**. ● MILDRED GUTKIN

HIGHWAY, Tomson, playwright, novelist (b Dec 6, 1951, near **BARREN LANDS FIRST NATION**). Born on his family's trapline, the 11th of 12

CHARLES SHILLIDAY

Original Hextall family garage near Poplar Point

children, Highway grew up initially in the **LEAF RAPIDS** area, and spoke only **CREE** for the first 6 years of his life. Tomson's father, Joe Highway, was a hunter and champion dogsled racer. Later, as an adult living in cosmopolitan Toronto, Tomson described these earliest experiences in Canada's boreal forest as "a house built on solid rock," both in the lifestyle integrated with the land and in the dignity and emotional security of his family. Perhaps even more significantly, the traditional stories told by his parents remained embedded in his memory. He was taken away at the age of 6 and enrolled in the **ROMAN CATHOLIC**–run Guy Hill **RESIDENTIAL SCHOOL** in **THE PAS** until he was 15. There, Highway endured language deprivation, forced assimilation, and physical and sexual abuse, but came away, he says, able to move beyond the role of victim. Now fluent in French as well as English and Cree, he has absorbed the storytelling tradition of his heritage into his writing. In high school in **WINNIPEG**, Highway was identified as exceptionally talented in music. He studied piano for 2 years at the **U OF M**, and then spent a year in London, England, training under William Aide to be a concert pianist. Returning to Winnipeg and then to London, ON, he earned an Honours BMus degree at the U of Western ON in 1975 and a BA in English in 1976.

For the next few years, he travelled across Canada as a social worker among Aboriginal communities, setting aside his ambitions for a career at the piano, but increasingly finding in the performing arts a vehicle for Aboriginal self-realization. In 1982, he helped organize 3 major Aboriginal festivals, in London, ON; Window Rock, AZ; and Regina. He joined the faculty of ON's Native Theatre School (now the Centre for Indigenous Theatre). From 1984 to 1992, he was artistic director of Native Earth Performing Arts in Toronto, Canada's first Aboriginal theatre company. Highway's first play, *The Rez Sisters*, met with immediate acclaim, winning the Dora Mavor Moore Award for the best play performed in Toronto in 1986-87 and being shortlisted for the Ontario Arts Council's Floyd S. Chalmers Award. His *Dry Lips Oughta Move to Kapuskasing* (1989) won a Chalmers Award and was shortlisted for the Gov Gen's Award. Both plays deal with the tragicomic difficulties of life on a reserve, in language explicit and often crude. In both plays, a trickster figure from Cree myth underscores the painful encounter of 2 cultures. Highway has also written several other plays, including *New Song…New Dance* (1986), *Aria* (1987), *The Sage, The Dancer, and the Fool* (1989), *Annie and Old Lace* (1989), and a musical, *Rose* (2000).

Highway became the first Aboriginal writer to be inducted into the Order of Canada in 1994.

He sealed his position as one of Canada's foremost contemporary authors, and the master of a poignant, lyrical style, with the publication in 1998 of his novel, *Kiss of the Fur Queen*, a tale of 2 young Cree brothers whose lives once again are presided over by the mythical trickster figure. The novel draws on the experiences of Tomson and his brother, René Highway, who died of AIDS in 1990. Tomson Highway has also published a work of non-fiction, *Comparing Mythologies* (2003), and has entered the field of children's literature with 3 books in the *Songs of the North* series, bilingually in English and Cree: *Cariboo Song* (2001), *Dragonfly Kites* (2002), and *Fox on the Ice* (2003). • MILDRED GUTKIN

HILDAHL, Vern, forester, researcher (b Nov 4, 1917, Estevan, SK; d Aug 19, 2005, **WINNIPEG**). Known for mitigating the effects of Dutch **ELM** disease, Hildahl grew up in SK working on a farm and as a coalminer. He joined the air force in Winnipeg during WWII. Hildahl married and remained in the city following the war. The Canadian Forestry Service hired him as a forest entomologist in 1945, despite a lack of formal academic training. In the 1950s, elm trees (particularly American elms) in Canada and the US were dying in large numbers (though the problem reached the US from Europe in about 1930). At that time, Hildahl devoted considerable effort to researching the cause of Dutch elm disease, despite the fact that it did not appear in MB until 1975. He identified the elm bark beetle (*Hylurgopinus rufipes*) as the cause of the affliction. Two different species of the beetle spread a vascular wilt fungus, which completely chokes off a tree's water supply. Hildahl's work became internationally recognized, as his findings made saving the species possible. However, he also lobbied for cities to adopt strict pruning, tree removal, and insecticide programs to control the spread of the disease. Jurisdictions that did not follow his advice lost nearly all their elms. In total, Hildahl worked for the federal govt for 35 years, and in a split Winnipeg/MB govt position for another 10. He also conducted research on **TREES** and forests, including cankerworm, forest tent caterpillar, and **SPRUCE** budworm infestations, publishing a book and more than 30 academic papers. Hildahl was named a member of the Order of Manitoba in 2004. • JOEL TRENAMAN

HIND, Ella CORA, teacher, journalist, feminist reformer (b Sept 18, 1861, Toronto; d Oct 6, 1942, **WINNIPEG**). E. Cora Hind came W in 1882 to become a teacher, but her credentials were inadequate and she ended up as a typist in a law office. In 1893, she opened her own typing

Ella Cora Hind

bureau and first published in the *Manitoba Free Press* (see **WINNIPEG FREE PRESS**). She became Western correspondent for Eastern newspapers 2 years later. In 1901, she was hired as agricultural reporter for the *Manitoba Free Press*, and she became a noted journalist famed for her crop estimates, which usually contained less than a 1% margin of error. Hind was also involved in reform and women's issues. She was a member of the Women's Christian Temperance Union, wrote newspaper pieces on living and working conditions in Winnipeg, and in 1894 helped found the Manitoba Equal Franchise Club. She was involved in the Women's Institutes movement, and in 1912 was a founding member of the Political Equality League. Like many reformers of her generation, she feared the influx of non-British "foreigners." She wrote *Red River Jottings* (1905). Hind's account of agricultural conditions around the world, based on extensive travel, appeared in 1939 as *My Travels and Findings*. She was awarded an honorary doctorate from the **U OF M**, and in 1935 was made an honorary life member of the University Women's Club. In later years, she put much of her energy into the Red Cross Society. She is a member of the Manitoba Agricultural Hall of Fame. • JMB

HIND, Terrance "Terry," sports administrator (b July 23, 1920, **WINNIPEG**; d Jan 9, 2007), was involved in the development of several professional and senior league hockey, baseball and football teams in Winnipeg. His first love was baseball; Hind was a pitcher for MB junior and senior baseball leagues during the 1930s and '40s. In 1954, he became general manager for the **Winnipeg Goldeyes**, and helped the team win Northern League titles in 1957, 1959 and 1961. He was elected a City of Winnipeg councillor in 1962, and served for 3 years. During this time, he was also a manager for the Winnipeg Monarchs junior hockey team and acted as an executive for the Manitoba Junior Hockey League. As manager of the Winnipeg Maroons, Hind helped the team win the 1964 Allan Cup. Hind also worked as a manager for the **Winnipeg Blue Bombers** from 1965-69. From 1972-75, he helped **Ben Hatskin** with the development of the **Winnipeg Jets** and the **World Hockey Association**, while managing the triple A Winnipeg Whips in 1971-72. ● MD

HINDUISM may generally be considered the oldest living religion in the world. It had its first passing brush with MB on July 30, 1893, when the monk Swami Vivekanand happened to give a discourse in **Winnipeg** before proceeding on to Chicago. However, not until 1957 did a Hindu family arrive in the province.

Hinduism, established around 3000 BC, can perhaps better be described as a way of life than a religion. Hinduism was not started by any single person, and does not have any dogma, though Hindus regard non-violence as a supreme goal. The basic scriptures of Hinduism are the 4 Vedas ("Knowledges"): The Rig Veda, containing praises and hymns; the Sam(a) Veda, containing chants; the Yajur Veda, containing prayers; and the Atharva Veda, containing spells and incantations. Vedanta, a system of Hindu philosophy, is based primarily upon doctrine from ancient Sanskrit texts, originally taught by gurus, regarding the unifying relation between Atman, an individual's soul, and Brahman, the World Soul or Supreme Being.

The Naiter Mohan Chopra house, the home of the first Hindu family in Winnipeg, became the hub for the celebration of Hindu festivals in the city. In those days, the Chopra family took active part in introducing Hindu rituals in wedding and death ceremonies. Since the early 1960s, a small group of Hindus has met for puja (reverent worship of a god or goddess) and prayers in Winnipeg.

MB got a formal Hindu presence when Ram Gupta, of Edmonton, inaugurated the Hindu Society of Manitoba on May 23, 1970, at the residence of Pankaj Master. Officers were elected for the year 1970-71: Atish Maniar, Shriram Manohar, Pankaj Master, Tara Sampat, and Cyril Sankar. The society was officially incorporated in Feb 1971. Ushar Budh Arya, of the U of MN, delivered the first public lecture under the society's auspices on Oct 3, 1970. **Howard Pawley**, later

Hindu dancer

premier of MB, chaired the meeting. The first annual meeting of the Hindu Society – then with a membership of 51 – was held April 18, 1971, in Winnipeg. The general secretary of the Vishwa Hindu Parishad (the "World Hindu Conference," an international, India-based organization dedicated to the promotion of Hinduism) visited MB in 1971. The first international conference of Vishwa Hindu Parishad was held Aug 28-30, 1971, at **Lac du Bonnet**. Hindus from all over Canada and the US took part in that historic event. In Sept 1971, Swami Bhashyananda (1917-96) of the Chicago chapter of the Vivekananda Vedanta Society – an international organization affiliated with the Ramakrishna Order of India – gave a lecture to more than 200 people at the Planctarium (*see* **Manitoba Museum**). A dance drama entitled *Meera* was choreographed and staged by Rubena Sinha on April 7, 1972, for the benefit of the Hindu Society.

The opening ceremony of the Hindu Temple, located at 854 Ellice Ave in Winnipeg, took place on Oct 21, 1979, under the presidency of Mr Hasmukh Pandya. The society held its first

Youth Camp at Clear Lake in summer 1981. *Hindu Darshan* ("Hindu Vision"), a yearly magazine of the Hindu Society, was founded in 1982 under the editorship of Rajinder Goyal. In 1985, the Hindu Temple was expanded to accommodate the increasing number of devotees. Dr Rajendra Vyas, President of Blind Person's (formerly Blind Men's) Assoc, in Mumbai, in collaboration with the Somaiya Trust – an Indian educational charity founded in 1953 – donated deities of Laxmi or Lakshmi, the Goddess of wealth and beauty, which were installed in 1988. ● ATISH MANIAR

HIRSCH, John Stephen, theatre director (b May 1, 1930, Siófok, Hungary; d Aug 1, 1989, Toronto). Brought up in a cultured, secular Hungarian-Jewish family, Hirsch arrived in Winnipeg in 1947 at the age of 17 as part of a group of Jewish orphans displaced by the Holocaust. His immediate family, including both his parents and a brother, had perished at Auschwitz and elsewhere, and he himself had barely survived in the Budapest ghetto. After WWII, he had been smuggled into Romania, and had then spent time in a refugee camp in Germany and in a Paris orphanage. In the hope of being accepted by any country that would have him, he had made the rounds of various embassies, until, after passing through Greece and Palestine, the Cdn Jewish Congress brought him to **Winnipeg**. There, he was adopted into the home of **Sybil Shack** and her family. Winnipeg, in the middle of a continent, Hirsch would say later, seemed likely to be safe. Hirsch had read Shakespeare in German and knew something of European literature, and he acquired fluency in English at an extraordinary rate. Working part-time at a variety of jobs, he completed grade 12 at Winnipeg's St. John's High School, and 5 years after his arrival he graduated from the **U of M** with a BA in English literature, having been awarded a fellowship and prizes for the best short story and the best poem.

His bent for **Theatre** was already in evidence. At the refugee camp in Germany, he had helped produce a play to entertain the children, and during his university years, with **Thomas Hendry**, he organized a puppet theatre that toured the city's schools and community clubs, building all the sets and props in the Shacks' basement. He joined with James Duncan to mount a series of musicals in the bandstand at **Assiniboine Park**, he became the first paid director of Winnipeg's longstanding amateur Little Theatre, and in 1954, he was hired as director and then as producer of the new CBC television station in Winnipeg. In 1957, again with Tom Hendry, he founded Theatre 77 in the historic Dominion Theatre on Portage Ave, 77 steps east of the corner of Main St.

A year later, Theatre 77 and the Little Theatre came together as the **Manitoba Theatre Centre**, the first major regional theatre in NA, with John Hirsch as its first artistic director. Under his direction, a number of distinguished Cdn acting careers were launched, including those of Gordon Pinsent, **Len Cariou**, and Martha Henry. He was awarded the Order of Canada in 1967.

John Hirsch

From Winnipeg, Hirsch moved on to the Stratford Shakespeare Festival in Stratford, ON, to become associate artistic director with Jean Gascon from 1967-69. He was appointed the resident director of New York's Lincoln Center Repertory Theatre. He directed plays on and off Broadway; at Ottawa's National Arts Centre; at the Shaw Festival in Niagara-on-the-Lake, ON; and in Tel Aviv. He directed the New York City Opera in Verdi's *Masked Ball*, and won the Outer Circle Critics' Award for his production of Shaw's *Saint Joan*. In 1974, back home at the MTC, he mounted his own translation of the Yiddish classic *The Dybbuk*, and then took the much-acclaimed production to Toronto and Los Angeles, winning the Cdn Author's Association Literary Award and the Los Angeles Literary Critics' Award. He headed CBC television drama from 1974 to 1978, and in 1976, again at Stratford, he staged Chekhov's *Three Sisters*. In 1981, with Stratford enmeshed in a near-fatal entanglement of administrative and artistic cross-purposes, Hirsch resumed the reins as sole artistic director of the festival. In the next 5 years, he sought to place his own stamp of professional excellence and Cdn style on a valued national institution. His death of AIDS at the age of 59 cut short a remarkable career. Hirsch provided in his will for prizes to be awarded on a continuing basis to a Francophone and an Anglophone director, and to a MB writer of promise. ● MILDRED GUTKIN

HISTORY OF MANITOBA
by Gerald Friesen

H

The history of Manitoba began more than 3.5 billion years ago, according to geologists, and about 11,500 years ago, according to archaeologists. The dates underline 2 important aspects of the provincial past: the character of Manitoba's geological inheritance, the environmental foundation that shapes its human possibilities; and the great length of time – hundreds of generations – during which humans have occupied this land.

Early First Nation community

FIRST PEOPLES: Aboriginal hunting families moved into southwest MB from adjacent territories as glacial **Lake Agassiz** drained, between 11,000 and 7,700 years ago. For thousands of years their economic strategies relied on purposeful movement between resource zones as they conducted a seasonal harvest of plant and animal foods in plain, parkland, and forest. About 400 years before contact with Europeans, several Aboriginal groups also cultivated corn. Among all these peoples, an acceptance of law, understood as practices derived from "history," ensured the maintenance of community discipline. Their stories, probably told by firelight during long summer evenings and longer winter nights, ensured the communication of cultural memory. And their connection to neighbours throughout the Americas who occupied these 2 continents for at least 15,000 years, and perhaps millennia more, justified their conviction that their ancestors lived in this part of the world from "time immemorial."

"Contact" – sustained encounters with the civilization of Europe – changed all that. European capacities increased spectacularly between the 10th and the 17th centuries as a result of new developments in science, technology, law, government and communications. During this long era when Europeans explored and exploited the globe's resources, northern North America became the particular interest of ENGLISH and FRENCH entrepreneurs. Their goal was access to the rich fur resources of northern forests that sustained, among other industries, the manufacture of hats.

Two FUR TRADE strategies were employed in the lands of MB. One relied on a handful of posts on the shores of HUDSON BAY and was directed from 1670 by the HUDSON'S BAY COMPANY (HBC). The other was based in Montreal and conducted first by the French and, after their defeat by the British in the Seven Years' War (1756-63), by a succession of small Scots-English companies that federated under the name of the NORTH-WEST COMPANY (NWC) in the 1780s. Both strategies earned modest but quite steady returns for their European investors.

Aboriginal peoples were less affected by the trade than might be supposed. They continued their seasonal rounds, conducted their diplomatic relations with neighbouring groups, and maintained their beliefs about the ordering of the universe. On the rim of their world lived a few Europeans who introduced new items of material culture, lent new urgency to trade and trapping activities, and offered strikingly different conceptions of human capacities, particularly those arising from their utilization of literacy, markets, wage labour and private property.

Competition between the Bay Men and the Nor'Westers intensified in the late 18th and early 19th centuries. To prosecute the trade more effectively, the companies built several hundred fur trade posts, some short and others long-lived, throughout the northwestern interior of NA. The existence of these establishments brought about closer relations between the first peoples and the European and European-Cdn newcomers. Unions of Aboriginal women and European men resulted in the birth of children who became identified increasingly as a collective force in Prairie history, the MÉTIS people.

PERMANENT SETTLEMENT: Thomas Douglas, Earl of Selkirk, introduced a dramatic turn in the MB story by winning influence in the HBC and, in 1812, planting a colony of impoverished farmers, mainly SCOTS, at the forks of the RED and ASSINIBOINE rivers. The RED RIVER SETTLEMENT endured despite conflicts with the NWC and the deaths in 1816 of 21 male settlers at SEVEN OAKS in a confrontation with the Nor-Westers' allies, Métis hunters led by CUTHBERT GRANT. Peace was restored and the two companies merged in 1821.

The settlement became a magnet for retired fur trade families. It relied for its existence on desultory farming activities and intense buffalo hunts. By the 1860s the two economies were sufficient to sustain a chain of 24 parishes, half French-speaking and CATHOLIC, half English-speaking and ANGLICAN or PRESBYTERIAN, along the two rivers. About 10,000 residents hunted, traded, cultivated small plots, attended churches and schools, litigated in the quarterly courts, and gossiped about their neighbours.

North American and European exigencies during the mid-century decades challenged this seemingly stable picture. The American Civil War (1861-65) imposed stresses upon all parts of the continent but so, too, did immigrants seeking farmland and RAILWAY builders surveying new routes. Three British North American colonies responded to these pressures by creating a new country, Canada, in 1867. The next goal of the leaders of the Confederation movement, and especially George Brown of Canada West (Ontario), was to annex the vast northwestern interior of the continent before, as they imagined, the Americans did.

Residents of Red River, most of whom were of mixed Aboriginal and European heritage, felt considerable concern about this potential transfer of control from British to Cdn authorities. French-speaking Métis, in particular, believed their interests were threatened. Under the leadership of LOUIS RIEL, they seized control of Upper Fort Garry, declared the formation of a provisional government, and issued several lists of rights in the winter of 1869-70.

Clearing the land in pioneer days

PROVINCIAL STATUS: The Métis resistance provoked negotiations between Canada and representatives of the Red River government. Prime Minister Sir John A. Macdonald accepted most of their demands and secured the accession of Manitoba, the first new province of the Dominion, on July 15, 1870. A month later the military expedition Macdonald had dispatched arrived in the settlement. Henceforth, the province would develop within a Canadian institutional framework, including federal policies concerning parliamentary democracy, tariffs, a transcontinental railway, and land settlement. Aboriginal people then signed treaties, chose reserve lands, and – unbeknownst to them – were made subject to the rigid intrusive rule of a revised Indian Act (1876). The Métis and the French were increasingly thrust aside as a new, western version of Ontario was created. Nonetheless, the only Manitoba premier of mixed European and Aboriginal heritage, JOHN NORQUAY (1878-1887), administered the province when many of the crucial decisions that shaped economy and government were taken. [The tiny "postage stamp" province was only 160 by 100 kilometres square in 1870. It was enlarged in 1882, in 1884 (by a British court ruling on the Ontario boundary), and in 1912, when the present dimensions were determined.]

Divided equally into francophone and anglophone populations in 1870, Manitoba commenced as an officially bilingual community, meaning that both English and French could be used in the legislature. Its dual school system was administered in Protestant and Roman Catholic sections, the latter employing French in many of its schools. However, in 1890, by which time the provincial population was overwhelmingly of British stock, a new Liberal government under Premier THOMAS GREENWAY (1888-1899) abolished the official use of French in the legislature and ended public support for the Catholic school system. After battles with the federal government and several important court cases, the provincial government, in the so-called Laurier-Greenway compromise of 1897, recognized the right of Catholic students to have some instruction in their faith after regular school hours. It also accepted the introduction, where numbers of non-English-speaking students warranted, of instruction in English and another language "upon the bi-lingual system."

The issues raised by schools and language rights became even more pressing when thousands of immigrants, many of them from eastern Europe, arrived in the province around the turn of the century. Given the 1897 deal, their children had the right to instruction in their own language. Within a few years, schools operated not only in French but also in German, Polish and Ukrainian. After the right to a bilingual education was repealed in 1916 provincial schools became officially unilingual, though French instruction was offered unofficially. Finally in the 1960s, instruction in French became increasingly available, a practice that was extended to other languages in subsequent decades. And, in a famous 1979 ruling on Georges Forest's parking ticket, the Supreme Court of Canada declared the 1890 act outlawing the use of French in the legislature to be beyond the province's jurisdiction, thus restoring – if such a word can be used for justice so long delayed – the official bilingualism of the 19th century.

Arrangements for Aboriginal education reflected European-Cdn priorities. Aboriginal children were required to leave their families, relinquish their languages, and run the risk of high rates of disease in large, church-run residential schools between the 1890s and the 1960s. The effects of this disastrous political decision are still being felt in the province.

Development of a rural economy and society preoccupied the first 3 generations of Manitobans. Aboriginal people in southern MB took up farming in these years but were severely and unfairly handicapped by restrictions imposed by local agents and by federal Indian Department regulations. The growing farm population comprised large numbers of English-speaking immigrants from Ontario, Great Britain, and the United States, as well as communities of relative strangers, including Icelanders who were emigrating from their home island, French Canadians from New England, **MENNONITES** and **UKRAINIANS** and **JEWS** from eastern Europe, and many others. Hundreds of hamlets and towns anchored this wheat export economy. **WINNIPEG**, located at the forks of the Red and Assiniboine, became the seat of government, the crossroads of highways and railways, and the focus of commerce, finance, and education. All parts of the small province boomed in the first decade of the 20th century. The administration of Rodmond P. Roblin (1900-1915) attempted to ride this economic wave and did so effectively until the construction of a magnificent legislative building provoked allegations of fraud and the fall of his government.

WINNIPEG: Some of the hottest political issues of the early 20th century involved industrial relations in the capital city. With a population of 50,000 in 1900, and nearly 300,000 in 1940, Winnipeg was the metropolis of prairie Canada. It had a high degree of residential segregation by income and ethnicity. Working people, especially newcomers from Europe, lived in the **NORTH END** and the suburbs; British Canadian professionals and members of the prosperous business class lived in larger homes in the South End; in the West End lived members of the middle class – teachers, ministers, journalists, social workers – who acted as a bridge between the two and pressed for such reforms as child labour laws, a compulsory school leaving age, prohibition, and women's suffrage. The Liberal administration of **T.C. NORRIS** (1915-22), enacted many of these measures but this was not enough to avert conflicts between capital and labour that grew more intense during WWI (1914-18).

The world-wide influenza epidemic in the autumn of 1918 exacerbated these tensions. Then, in the spring of 1919, members of construction and metal trades unions adopted bargaining positions that set them at loggerheads with the owners and managers of their workplaces. Neither side was willing to back down. Leaders of the unions requested that the city's Trades and Labour Council call a general strike. On 15 May 1919 over 30,000 workers, half of them not in unions, walked off the job. The **WINNIPEG GENERAL STRIKE** lasted 6 weeks. It was broken by the combined weight of business leaders, in their Citizens' Committee of 1 000, and the federal and civic governments. Its legacy included hardship for working families in the short term and, in the longer term, a politicized urban community and an exceptional class consciousness and class loyalty among working people of Winnipeg.

RURAL MB: Stresses in the rural economy provoked another kind of political protest movement in the postwar years. Organized originally under the banner of a farm movement, the United Farmers of Manitoba administrations, later known as Liberal-Progressives, governed the province from 1922 until the 1950s. Under Premiers **JOHN BRACKEN** (1922-42), **STUART GARSON** (1942-48), and **D. L. CAMPBELL** (1948-58), the farmer progressive governments provided cautious, conservative leadership, resisting calls for government intervention in the economy, avoiding deficit financing, and encouraging the federal government to review its economic relations with the provinces. The latter campaign resulted in the creation of the Rowell-Sirois Royal Commission (guided by the great Winnipeg newspaperman, **JOHN W. DAFOE**), and, eventually, a national program for the partial equalization of government revenues among the Cdn provinces to ensure comparable levels of public services.

In the provincial economy diversification increased, though slowly, during the first half of the 20th century. **AGRICULTURE** accounted for about 40% of production by value but it ceased to be a major source of economic growth, its limits having been reached in the era of WWI. Manufacturing was a second locus of economic activity, accounting for about 30% of production by value, though only 10% of the workforce. The **HUDSON BAY RAILWAY**, completed in 1929, aided in opening the north, as did a rail line to a mine, zinc refinery and copper smelter at **FLIN FLON**. Hydro and paper production along the Winnipeg River also provided jobs and a little wealth. All of these activities, supplemented by the commercial, financial, communications and construction activities in the capital, ensured that Manitobans were able to keep abreast of changes in the wider world. They did not experience, however, the rates of economic growth that residents of ON enjoyed or that transformed petroleum-rich AB.

Such an account of politics and economics touches only indirectly upon the half of Manitoba's population that is female. Women's history between the 1870s and 1930s took place more often in the private or

A CPR pamphlet enticed new settlers to Manitoba.

domestic rather than public sphere. Women members of religious orders, such as Sara Riel, however, were often influential mediators in the community. In the intervening century, unlike Louis, her celebrated and scorned brother, Sara had been forgotten until women historians rediscovered her and her colleagues. This gendered amnesia did not occur in the case of the women who led the campaign for female suffrage. These Manitoba leaders, including NELLIE MCCLUNG, won the vote for women in Manitoba in 1916, ahead of any other Canadian jurisdiction. In the following generation, they made fewer headlines in the press but campaigned steadily and effectively to win respect for women's work, whether at home or in the waged labour market.

WWII (1939-45) constituted another watershed in provincial history. As in other parts of the prairies, rural depopulation commenced during the war. In the next half-century, the network of social institutions in rural Manitoba was drastically altered because many schools closed, many towns disappeared, and rail lines and grain elevators were abandoned. Paradoxically, agricultural production increased steadily, aided by new machinery and scientific breakthroughs in breeding, fertilizers, herbicides and pesticides. The diminishing number of families who remained in agriculture relied on the efficiencies created by such locally-inspired institutions as co-operatives, credit unions, the Canadian Wheat Board, and egg, poultry and dairy supply management systems.

The province became increasingly poly-ethnic in the post-war decades. New immigrants from Europe reinforced the ethnic cultures that had flourished before 1914, breathing new life into their churches, schools, arts groups, and social networks. At the same time, Manitobans began to think seriously about the reception of immigrants. During the 1950s they developed two responses, formal citizenship ceremonies and social services for immigrants, that offered bridges between the long-settled and the newcomers. A third approach emerged from the planning for the Canadian and provincial centennials: Folklorama (1970), an annual summer festival in which ethnic communities displayed their music, dance, cuisine and material culture, became a remarkable example of a people's educational activity designed to celebrate a multicultural society.

POLITICAL CHANGE: After the defeat of the Progressive administration in 1958, the provincial political system was dominated increasingly by 2 parties. The Conservatives were advocates of competitive capitalism and, particularly after the departure of Premier DUFF ROBLIN, opponents of social legislation and government activism. Conservative administrations included those led by Roblin (1958-67), WALTER WEIR (1967-69), STERLING LYON (1977-81) and GARY FILMON (1988-99). The New Democrats, descendants of the CO-OPERATIVE COMMONWEALTH FEDERATION (1933-61), were allies of the trade union movement and supporters of social legislation and co-operatives. They were also more inclined to consider state involvement in the economy. Their governments were led by ED SCHREYER (1969-77), HOWARD PAWLEY (1981-88) and GARY DOER (1999-2007). The 2 parties have shared power during this half-century more or less equally. A third party, the Liberals, governed in Ottawa for over half of this period, and consistently elected some Members of Parliament in MB, but had little success in provincial elections.

Aboriginal issues jumped to the top of the provincial agenda during these years. Over half of these "first peoples," who accounted for about 12% to 15% of the provincial population, and who in earlier decades resided almost exclusively in the North and on reserves, migrated into the cities, especially Winnipeg, Brandon, and THOMPSON, after 1960. Governments and Aboriginal leaders adopted a variety of tactics to deal with the resultant dislocations. Some advocated a greater degree of self-government. Others urged the pursuit of claims concerning land, forests, fish, game, and other resources wherein treaty entitlements, mostly dating

from the 1870s, had allegedly not been respected. Still others focused on the lingering problems stemming from the long, sad history of Aboriginal residential schools. All recognized the need for educational betterment and improved living standards. The flooding of vast acreages in north-central MB as part of the expansion of MANITOBA HYDRO's generating capacity in the 1960s and 1970s also added significant environmental stresses to this list of grievances. Since the 1982 patriation of the Canadian constitution, which included an entrenched Charter of Rights, Indian, Inuit, and Métis peoples have launched a series of court cases to clothe the Charter's recognition of their "Aboriginal and treaty rights" with greater meaning. Three Manitoba Aboriginal leaders, ELIJAH HARPER, PHIL FONTAINE, and OVIDE MERCREDI, have made a mark in national affairs while addressing these issues. A national institution, the ABORIGINAL PEOPLES' TELEVISION NETWORK (APTN), placed its headquarters on Winnipeg's main business street in 1999, a mark of the province's role in the life of first peoples.

MB was neither a very rich nor a very poor community. From the 1960s its public sector expenditures focused on health care (30-40% of the provincial budget) and education (20-25%). The province relied heavily on federal transfer payments, which accounted for approximately $\frac{1}{3}$ of provincial government revenues annually by the turn of the 21st century. Because of its diversified productive activities, including agriculture, resource development, manufacturing, and a wide range of services, the annual growth of Gross Domestic Product (GDP) was not subject to the sharp swings that occurred in some provinces, and averaged between 2% and 2.5% from 1981. Its unemployment rates were consistently below the national average. Its citizens developed specialties in aerospace, bus, window, and furniture manufacturing, in food and clothing and metal and wood products, in hydroelectric and agricultural and mineral exports, and in specialized financial services. Since the signing of the Free Trade Agreement in 1988, its export markets have been divided equally between the rest of Canada and the rest of the world, but ¾ of the latter shipments, by value, travelled to the United States, and half of the rest to Asia.

As Canada's 3rd largest city at the opening of the 20th century and 8th largest at its close, the provincial capital inevitably became the focus of cultural production and distribution. Winnipeg established a rich arts life early. Citizens and governments together maintained an array of institutions – art galleries, museums, theatres, orchestras, music festivals, universities, bookstores, archives and, most famously, the Royal Winnipeg Ballet – with admirable tenacity. They also relied on wealthy entrepreneurs, including the ALLOWAY, RICHARDSON, ASPER, and MOFFAT families, and a remarkable vehicle of community philanthropy, The WINNIPEG FOUNDATION, to sustain these expensive activities. They maintained such sports franchises as football's WINNIPEG BLUE BOMBERS and a series of baseball and hockey teams, though the WINNIPEG JETS of the World Hockey Association (1973-79) and the National Hockey League (1979-96) eventually departed for greener pastures, a measure of financial realities in "small market" cities. They could and did associate themselves with honours claimed in such diverse crafts as the writing of novels (MARGARET LAURENCE, CAROL SHIELDS) and the making of unusual cinema (GUY MADDIN, RICHARD CONDIE, FRANTIC FILMS). They won recognition for athletic, artistic, and cultural achievements, whether in speed skating (PETRA BURKA, CINDY KLASSEN, CLARA HUGHES), in ballet (EVELYN HART), in music (THE GUESS WHO), or in scientific research (BALDUR STEFANSSON on CANOLA, ALLAN RONALD and FRANCIS PLUMMER on Aids).

In the end, environment, communications, and a diversity of peoples distinguished the history of the province. Historian W. L. MORTON, a product of GLADSTONE, MB, ended his 1957 history with the observation: "The compulsions of geography alone would have taken its people on to

WINNIPEG FREE PRESS

Building dikes during the Flood of the Century

easier climes; the past alone would have invoked a sterile loyalty to an unresponsive northern land. Both had combined to set working a precise natural selection by which Manitobans had been made, as Canadians had been made, of those who by endurance in loyalty to older values than prosperity, had learned to wrest a living from the prairie's brief summer and the harsh rocks and wild waters of the north. Manitoba, like Canada, was the response to the challenge of the north, a challenge not quickly or easily met. And those who remained and met that challenge, generation on generation, might hope to see in the life of their country, by work of hand or word of spirit, some stubborn northern flowering."

THE PRESENT: In the early 21st century, one might find Morton's emphasis on the role of "older values than prosperity" less than persuasive. And yet these ideas touch upon inescapable aspects of MB life today. An economist's alternative phrasing might describe Manitobans as those who are willing to accept modest returns in exchange for remarkable economic stability and considerable advantages in ease of daily living. People who migrate to the province or, more often, do not leave, make their choices because they value the combination of small-town and bigger-town (but not truly metropolitan) society that it presents. They are aware of the attractions but also the inconveniences of places where greater economic growth, or milder climates, prevail. But they also value the combination of cultures, of outdoor life and urban refinements, of peoples' art and high art, of farm, north and city – and the ready movement between these spheres – that is possible here.

MB today is defined by the combination of its location, its communication institutions, its mix of peoples, and its history. Location takes us back to geology and environment and such matters as surface flooding and drainage which have involved a half-dozen catastrophic inundations and have probably been crucial in shaping southern MB's rural democracy.

Location also raises issues associated with ongoing agricultural production and potential hydroelectric developments. And, in an age when it is possible to reside in more than one place at a time (given seasonal movements), it has caused questions about whether one must always "freeze one's butt," as the saying has it, or will have the resources to spend part of the year (a week, a month, a season) in other places. Communication technology has permitted the development of a province-wide conversation and, given the biases associated with print, radio, television and the web, has shaped that exchange by endowing some parts of the province and some groups (Winnipeg, the wealthy) with more control over their fate than has been possible for others. Given that its citizens are Aboriginal, European, southern hemisphere – indeed, global – in origin, and that they speak native, French, English, and many other languages, it is striking that the mixing of peoples is a source of pride in the province.

Manitobans also know inequality, of wealth, of gender, and of opportunity for the children of some groups as opposed to others. They hold differing views on matters in the public sphere, including marriage, sexuality and the family. They continue to debate the relative merits of freer markets and government economic interventions. They know their good fortune in having inherited a vast land where lakes and rivers, forests and prairies have sustained life for some thousands of years. They probably recognize, too, that in the course of just one century they have squandered resources, polluted environments, and been party to a world-wide process of climate change. They have met sufficient challenges to be able to claim, as Morton suggested a half-century ago, that they have contributed to a "stubborn northern flowering" but they encounter further challenges with each passing year. As has been noted by students of other places and other times, histories such as this brief note have an end; history carries on. •

HOCKEY, ICE in all of its forms, amateur and professional, has captured the hearts of Manitobans more than any other sport. It is played by boys and girls, men and women, in big indoor city arenas and small town ponds and rinks. Famous MB players include **TERRY SAWCHUK**, **ANDY BATHGATE** and **BOBBY CLARKE**, along with referee **ANDY VAN HELLEMOND**, and coaches **FRED SHERO**, **BARRY TROTZ** and **ANDY MURRAY**.

EARLY YEARS: Hockey-like games were probably first played regularly in MB in the winter of 1886-87, and sporadically before that. The man who was most responsible in the 1880s for establishing the sport in MB was P. A. Macdonald. Macdonald was born in 1857 near Kingston, ON, and moved to **WINNIPEG** in 1880. He travelled to Montreal during the winter of 1885-86 over the newly completed **CPR**, and returned with hockey sticks, which were used the next season for shinny or hockey games. Over the next few winters, a few games of hockey or shinny were played in Winnipeg, mostly on outdoor ice. The sport was given a boost in 1889-90 when a well-prepared outdoor skating rink on the **ASSINIBOINE RIVER** became available for hockey matches. This was Austin's Rink, owned and operated by W. F. Austin, manager of Winnipeg's streetcar company. The next season, the first hockey clubs were formed, and the season after that, 1891-92, the first league – the Manitoba and North West Senior League – was organized.

The season of 1892-93 was important for several reasons. Hockey clubs were formed in **BRANDON**, **CARBERRY**, **PORTAGE LA PRAIRIE**, and in other centres; soon, there would be hockey clubs in most cities, towns, and villages. Secondly, late in the season, an all-star squad from the senior league went on an 11-game tour of eastern Cdn cities, and their record proved that MB was producing top players. Thirdly, in 1893 Lord Stanley of Preston, Gov Gen of Canada, donated a cup which would be awarded, initially, to the best team in the Dominion. The first such cup happened to be awarded to Montreal team, but MB's best players soon wanted to compete for it.

By this time, the highest-calibre hockey matches in MB were being played in an indoor facility in Winnipeg known as the McIntyre Rink, which had been a curling rink until 1892. The Auditorium Rink replaced the McIntyre Rink in 1898, and was in turn first supplemented and then replaced by the Winnipeg Amphitheatre, used for hockey 1912-55. The Amphitheatre gave way to the Winnipeg Arena, the main hockey venue from 1955 until 2004, when the **MTS CENTRE** opened. There were impressive facilities in Brandon, Portage la Prairie, and other locations, but the largest was always in Winnipeg. That meant

Stanley Cup champion Winnipeg Victorias

teams from rural MB or from Kenora, in the far NW of ON, frequently held their "home" games in Winnipeg when they were playing for a prestigious championship.

In the early 1890s, and for more than a decade thereafter, the top hockey club in MB was the Winnipeg Victorias. Early in 1896, the Vics challenged for the Stanley Cup, and won it in Montreal. They lost it later the same year but, after 2 unsuccessful challenges, claimed it back in 1901. They were defeated in 1902 in another challenge series. The Vics and other MB teams then fought for the cup several times over the next few years, but only the Kenora Thistles, who played in MB's top league, were successful, winning in 1907.

THE PROFESSIONAL GAME: After 1907, most of Canada's top teams were professional. Pro clubs operated in MB briefly (1906-09), but it quickly became obvious that major league pro hockey would not be financially viable in the province. For the next few decades, MB's top teams played for the Allan Cup, donated by Montreal businessman Sir Hugh Andrew Montague Allan in 1909 and emblematic of the Senior Amateur championship of Canada; and the Memorial Cup, established in 1919 and competed for by the best junior-aged teams. MB's teams still compete for these trophies. They have won the Allan Cup 12 times (including 3 victories by a team from Warroad, MN, which played in Manitoban leagues). They have won the Memorial Cup 12 times. Since the 1970s, most junior teams in MB, especially those from outside Winnipeg and Brandon, have

competed for the national championship; MB clubs have taken it twice.

These 3 national championships, as well as 2 others established more recently (the national midget championship, won once by a MB team, which began in 1979; and the national women's championship) are administered by Hockey Canada. This organization was founded in 1914 as the Canadian Amateur Hockey Association (CAHA), largely as a result of the efforts of Manitobans Claude Robinson and Dr. W. F. Taylor. The MB Amateur Hockey Association, now called Hockey MB, was established in the same year as the CAHA, and is the provincial branch of the national organization.

Professional hockey had become entrenched in NA in the 1910s and 1920s, and by the mid-1920s, there was one major professional league, the National Hockey League (NHL). Between 1927 and 1961, MB produced more players per capita for that league than any other province. Some of these players, including **TERRY SAWCHUK** and **BILL MOSIENKO**, were all-stars. However, the only professional teams in MB were minor league ones. In the 1920s, the Winnipeg Maroons played 2 seasons in an American Hockey Association, and in 1955, 2 MB teams – one from Brandon and one from Winnipeg – joined the Western Pro League. The Brandon Regals lasted one year, the Winnipeg Warriors 6.

Then, in 1972, the **WINNIPEG JETS** were established in a **WORLD HOCKEY ASSOCIATION** (WHA) that was a competing major league for the NHL.

The Jets were led by **Bobby Hull**, formerly of the Chicago Black Hawks (now the Blackhawks), considered by many to be the greatest left wing in the entire history of the sport. The team won the league's Avco Cup in 1976, 1978, and 1979. In the 1979-80 season, the Jets, along with 3 other WHA clubs, became part of the NHL. The team played 24 seasons, but by the mid-1990s, with a low Cdn dollar, the amount of money needed to run an NHL franchise was just too large for Winnipeggers and Manitobans to generate. The Jets moved to Phoenix in 1996. The **Manitoba Moose** entered the picture once the Jets left, and played in the International League until 2001, when the club joined the American Hockey League.

INTERNATIONAL HOCKEY: For several decades, Manitobans had a close connection to international hockey. The **Winnipeg Falcons**, made largely of Icelandic Canadians, won Olympic gold in 1920, and in 1932, the Winnipeg Hockey Club did so again. The Cdn National Hockey Team, which represented Canada in World and Olympic tournaments in the mid-to-late-1960s, was based in Winnipeg from 1965 to 1970. By the 1970s, Manitoban spectators had justifiably gained a reputation for receptivity to a "European" style of play, and the Winnipeg Jets of the WHA and NHL consciously recruited top European players (such as Anders Hedberg, Kent Nilsson, Lars-Erik Sjøberg, Veli-Pekka Ketola, **Thomas Steen**, and **Teemu Selanne**).

YOUTH: Until the 1950s, boys younger than 15 usually played hockey on pickup teams, and certainly not for prestigious championships. However, in the last half of the 20th century, youth hockey became "professionalized." By the 1990s, teams were organized for players as young as 5, and 10-year-olds could play for provincial championships. The first western Cdn championship event was for 13- and 14-year-olds; the first national championship was for those aged 15-17. The current prevalence of youth teams means that, on winter weekends, thousands of games are played across the province, usually in the ubiquitous community artificial ice rink.

SCHOOLS: Hockey teams have been associated with educational institutions since the 1890s, but high school hockey has become increasingly popular across the province, especially among boys who wish to play competitively in other sports as well as hockey. Meanwhile, inter-university hockey, which began in the 1920s, has in recent decades featured a much higher quality of play. This is partly because, since the 1970s, financial assistance has been available to student-athletes in hockey and other sports.

WOMEN'S: In recent years, in MB and elsewhere in Canada, women's hockey has increased dramatically in both popularity and quality. From the 1890s until the 1930s, women played the game frequently. Then, for half a century they participated only sporadically. However, since the 1980s, women's hockey has gained international prominence and has become a major part of Manitobans' winter life. This means that now, more than ever, hockey is the top sport in the province, if appeal to both participants and spectators is considered. ● ED SWEENEY/MORRIS MOTT

HOG FARMING. *See* **Pork Industry**

Women's Team Canada wins gold in 2007 at the MTS Centre.

Holland's windmill

HOLLAND, pop 400, is a community 80 km ESE of **Brandon**, at the junction of hwys 2 and 34. Primarily **Scots** and **English** initially settled this community, starting about 1877. The post office opened in 1880, adopting the name "Holland" after the first postmaster, Arthur Charles Holland. A **CPR** point was established nearby in 1884, requiring the post office and community to relocate about one km W. With the arrival of the railway, the settlement grew. In 2006, the local economy was supported by grain, dairy, beef and **PMU** farms. Holland's identifying landmark is a large windmill, located off hwy 2, which is surrounded by a park area. The community hosts a variety of activities each year, including a Santa Claus parade, a town-wide garage sale, and the MB Old Time Fiddling Championship. Holland has 2 grocery stores, 2 beauty salons, a Home Hardware, a liquor outlet, post office, insurance office, machinery dealership, motel, restaurant, garage and automotive truck repair service. Amongst other area attractions is the Our Lady of the Prairies Trappist Monastery, 8 km S of Holland. ● GPP

HOLLOW WATER FIRST NATION, on reserve pop 951, off reserve pop 569, is located about 190 km N of **Winnipeg**. Hollow Water was a signatory to Treaty 5 in 1875. It is a member of the Southeast Tribal Council. There is one reserve situated here. The native language of this First Nation is **Ojibway**. Education, administered by the Southeast Resource Development Council, goes from Nursery-Grade 12, and enrolment for 2003-04 was 544. Besides internal roads, access to Hollow Water First Nation consists of a year-round

323

road. The economic foundation of Hollow Water includes wild rice harvesting, hunting, fishing, and trapping. Like some other First Nations, Hollow Water has struggled with difficult issues such as addiction, suicide, violence, and sexual abuse. The First Nation has done so by putting into practice traditional Aboriginal healing methods, such as sentencing circles. Its approach on restorative justice earned it international attention. In 2004, the Hollow Water First Nation was 1 of 2 MB communities selected by the Smithsonian Institution in Washington, DC, to represent Aboriginal culture with an exhibit at the National Museum of the American Indian. And in 2000, the National Film Board of Canada released a documentary called *Hollow Water.* ● RK

HOLM, Torfhildur Thorsteinsdóttir, writer, poet, and folklorist (b Feb 2, 1845, Kálfafellsstaður, Southeast Iceland; d Nov 14, 1918, Reykjavík). Formally educated in Iceland and Denmark, Holm immigrated to **New Iceland** on **Lake Winnipeg** in 1876 as a young widow and lady companion to Rannveig Briem, bride of Sigtryggur Jónasson (Father of New Iceland). Resident with the Jónassons at Möðruvellir, **Riverton**, while this home was the centre of govt and cultural activity in the fledgling Icelandic reserve, she served as a teacher of fine arts and handwork there and took the unusual initiative of recording original folklore – both local and Icelandic – by interviewing her fellow settlers. Her manuscript was later published in Iceland under the title *Thjóðsögur og Sagnir (Folktales and Stories)* (1962). Torfhildur then lived in **Winnipeg**, learning painting and writing prolifically until returning to Iceland in 1889, after 13 years in MB. During this time she penned all her major novels and short story anthologies: *Sögur og Kvæði (Stories and Poems)* (1884); *Brynjólfur Sveinsson* (1886); *Kjartan og Guðrún* (1886); *Smásögur Handa Börnum (Short Stories for Children)* (1886); *Högni og Ingibjörg* (1889); *Elding (Lightning)* (1889); and *Barnasögur (Children's Stories)* (1889). After returning to Iceland, she edited the periodicals *Draupnir* (1891-1908) and *Dvöl* (1901-17). Mrs. Holm, as she was best known during her years in Canada, was the widow of Jakob Holm, a merchant at Hólanes, Iceland. ● NELSON GERRARD

HOLMES, Francis J. S. "Frank," filmmaker (b Aug 28, 1908, Carlyle, SK; d Oct 4, 1990, Toronto), was probably MB's most prolific filmmaker. He began his 40-year career in 1926 with a 77-minute silent film about the short-lived MB settlement Port Nelson called *Seaport of the Prairies.* He was quickly hired as a stringer for Fox Newsreel Presentations and assigned to film the gold rush in Red Lake, ON, that same year. As an independent film producer, he travelled from Sudbury, ON, to the Rockies in his own self-designed mobile film studio, making short industrial or promotional films and wildlife documentaries for businesses and govt agencies. Nearly all of the more than 50 films he made were about MB. Many were didactic, promoting such things as the **Manitoba Sanatorium** at **Ninette** (*Road to Recovery*, 1953), chemical weed-control (*Victory over Weeds*, 1956) or efficient **Dairy** farming (*The Magic of Milk*, 1960) or otherwise overlooked local places and occupations (*Forest Fire Fighters of the Sky*, 1927-28, and *Beyond the Steel*, 1953, about moving an entire northern town 250 km by sled). *Prairie Conquest* (1952), however, is a docudrama that provides a visual history of Canada's West by focusing on the evolution of **Wheat**, farm machinery, and distribution methods. He maintained a home studio in **Winnipeg** throughout his career. ● GENE WALZ

HOME REMEDIES in MB originated from a mixture of traditional **First Peoples** and European plant and mineral lore. Self-treatment for accidents and diseases was the norm among Prairie pioneers at a time when doctors were few, hard to reach, and expensive, and medical supplies were scarce. Aboriginal people used readily available organic materials to treat common ailments. **Dakota**, Assiniboine, and **Cree** all used sweet flag (*Acorus* spp.) to relieve pain, for example, though the Dakotas also used it to induce abortion. The **Ojibway** used a tea of juniper twigs to treat asthma, while the Cree used juniper bark as an antiseptic. **Birch** cambium was commonly used as a diuretic, and smoke produced by the seed cones was inhaled to help relieve catarrh. Some of these medications have entered the modern medical repertoire: Willow bark's pain-relieving properties, for instance, are now available in the form of acetylsalicylic acid (Aspirin), and purple coneflower (*Echinacea angustifolia*), a commonly used Dakota drug, is now taken by millions every flu season. Other common remedies included **Prairie Crocus** and water lilies.

European settlers also used numerous poultices, bandages, and herbal infusions to treat different ailments, some of which they learned from MB's Aboriginal peoples. Early **Railway** workers planted medicinal and food plants native to their homes in Europe and Asia along the tracks, and can be thanked (or blamed) for the spread of dandelion, chicory, mullein, plantain, chamomile, bladder campion, burdock, purslane, and numerous other traditional plant remedies across MB. Settlers used animal products as cures, as well; they might treat a severe infection with a poultice made from fresh cow manure. For a carbuncle boil, a cotton bag filled with onion, meat, and bread, chewed and mixed with sour cream, was left underground for a week. The fermented paste was then applied to the boil to draw out pus. **Bear** fat was often rubbed onto a weak and tired back, while **Skunk** fat was good for wounds that would not heal. Raw egg, or a generous amount of salt, was also used on burns to prevent blistering. A fried-onion poultice could be used to treat earache, though blowing cigarette smoke directly into the affected ear was another remedy, as was the application of the oil of mullein flowers. A poultice made of dry mustard or cayenne, flour, and water was the usual approach to chest colds, though rubbing camphor ointment directly onto the chest could treat them. An unwashed woollen stocking wrap around the throat at night was another cold treatment. ● MD

HOPPS, John Alexander "Jack," medical researcher (b May 21, 1919, **Winnipeg**; d Nov 24, 1998, Ottawa). After earning his electrical engineering degree from the **U of M** in 1941, Hopps joined the National Research Council of Canada (NRC) in Ottawa. His early research involved the use of microwaves and high-frequency radio waves to restore body temperature after the onset of hypothermia. His experiments also involved the use of electricity on the heart.

Hopps later joined the Banting Institute at the U of Toronto, where he worked alongside doctors **Wilfred Bigelow** and John Carter Callaghan, an early cardiac surgeon. In 1949, while studying the effects of cold on the heart during surgery, they found that gentle electrical current mimicked the normal neural stimulation of the heart. Hopps built on this research to develop the first functional cardiac pacemaker in 1950. It was a large device (30 cm long), was stored outside the body, and could also act as a defibrillator. It used catheter electrodes, and required 60 Hz of power delivered by vacuum tubes. Other researchers around the world improved on the design, and the first internal pacemaker was installed in 1957.

During his long career, Hopps was also involved in research to aid the blind, correct muscular disabilities, and improve ultrasound techniques. He went on to become head of the medical engineering section at the NRC until his retirement in 1979. In 1965, he founded and acted as the first president of the Canadian Medical and Biological Engineering Society, and became president of the International Federation for Medical and Biological Engineering in 1971. From 1985-88, Hopps served as secretary-general of the International Union for Physical and Engineering Science in Medicine. Some of Hopps' many awards over the years include an honorary DSc from the U of M in 1976, becoming an Officer of the Order of Canada in 1986, and his 2005 posthumous induction to the Canadian Science and Engineering Hall of Fame. Hopps himself was outfitted with 2 pacemakers during his life, in 1984 and 1997. • JOEL TRENAMAN

HORSE RACING

HORSE RACING is one of MB's oldest sports. Prairie Aboriginal groups competed with each other in what would become MB according to a set of rules and procedures established by their leaders. The early **RED RIVER SETTLEMENT** shared this pride of horsemanship. **HBC** governor **SIR GEORGE SIMPSON** introduced the stallion Fairway to improve the quality of the animals in the colony. Records show celebrations in 1860 featured racing events. Horse racing soon advanced beyond individual challenges to more formal competitions with rules of entry, rules of betting, and stewards to oversee the proceedings.

In 1873, the City of Winnipeg Charter gave city council power to pass laws to regulate horse racing. There were numerous equestrian opportunities in the city until WWI. The Winnipeg Race Course was set up 1.5 km W of the old courthouse building. James McKay, a prosperous **MÉTIS** member of the MB legislature, established Buffalo Park in the Deer Lodge area. In 1891,

Canada's Great Western Exposition grounds, with seating for 12,000, opened W of Winnipeg and became the focal point of racing with regular summer meets. River Park opened in 1892, with horse racing as part of its variety of entertainment, and in 1894, Fort Garry Park opened just north of the old **UPPER FORT GARRY**. In 1899, R. J. MacKenzie, president of the Manitoba Jockey Club, and Alex MacKenzie built a track N of Sturgeon Creek called Kirkfield Park. Racing continued with great enthusiasm until the war.

Racing was slow to return after WWI. But in 1921, the Winnipeg Driving Club was formed with the intent of breeding thoroughbred racehorses: until this time, all breeds had raced together. The Driving Club held a 3-day meet in late June, which the MB premier and the mayor of Winnipeg opened together. In an effort to control gaming, which had run rampant at the hands of bookies, a pari-mutuel system of betting was introduced.

In 1922, R. J. Speers arrived on the scene. Originally from ON, he frequented the Union Stock Yards as a prominent cattle buyer, often encountering the local racing set, and was invited to take part in the pastime. With a reputation for honest dealing, he said he'd only join the endeavours if all the bookies and touts were out. He cleaned house and, with Thomas Sumner and William Halpenny, took a 3-year lease on River Park. He knew that

if racing were to flourish, he'd need a long-term plan. So he obtained a 99-year lease for $1 from the railway for land N of Provencher Blvd in St. Boniface and built Whittier Park, which opened June 24, 1924. In 1925, Speers – who also owned racehorses – continued expansion with a new track at Polo Park, and raced at all 3 tracks with some 40 jockeys and 400 horses. Speers then approached the govt regarding legislation. MB passed the *Horse Racing Legislation Act* in 1925, giving it control over racing, and in 1926 ruled that no horses could race unless they were true registered thoroughbreds. A MB Stakes for horses bred in western Canada was inaugurated in 1930 and renamed the MB Derby. In 1941, it became the Cdn Derby, and ran in Winnipeg until the Polo Park track closed in 1956. The 1930s were the glory days for horse racing in MB. The first mechanical starting gate ever used on a recognized track was introduced here in 1939. HM Queen Elizabeth, The Queen Mother, had to see the gate herself during the Winnipeg stop on the Royal Canadian tour. A contemporary jockey riding in Winnipeg was Johnny Longdon, who went on to ride Count Fleet to win the Triple Crown. By 1943, all racing was held at Polo Park.

However, racing came to an end at Polo Park in 1956 shortly after R. J. Speers died suddenly and the land was deemed more suitable

Winnipeg's Polo Park Race Track, 1950

for commercial development. Jack Hardy, from one of the biggest automobile firms in Winnipeg, became involved in building a new racetrack W of Winnipeg. On June 10, 1958, **ASSINIBOIA DOWNS** opened a 42-day meet. By 1960, Assiniboia Downs was fast becoming a tourist destination and was the province's #1 tourist attraction for many years. In 1970, HM Queen Elizabeth was in attendance at the $70,000 MB Derby, the richest race to run in western Canada. In 1974, while attendance was falling off at other tracks, new owners Jim and Hazel Wright took over the Downs, planning many innovations, such as tractor wagering, that kept racing flourishing. In 1981, the Wrights sold the track, and it went into receivership in 1982. The MB govt became involved and put up the operating capital to keep the track in business. The track returned to the hands of Jim Wright, who continued with many racing innovations – the first in Canada to offer telephone account betting, the first in home-televised wagering, and the first to use the most advanced pari-mutuel system in Canada, where you could buy and cash at the same machine. In 1990, the explosion of govt gaming put private enterprise out of business, and the nonprofit Manitoba Jockey Club took over the management of Assiniboia Downs and, with the help of video lottery terminals, has kept thoroughbred racing alive to the present. ● HAZEL BOCHINSKI

HOSPITALITY forms a significant sector of MB's service industry. Including all hotels, restaurants, and bars, the hospitality industry is fundamentally linked to the growth of **TOURISM**.

HOTELS: The first hotel in MB was the Royal Hotel, opened in 1859 by **HENRY McKENNEY** in the area of what would one day become **WINNIPEG**. By the mid-1870s, though Winnipeg's population was less than 8000, there were roughly 32 hotels, mainly comprised of small, single rooms, which were ideal for the many bachelors flooding into the city.

As the city prospered, hotels became increasingly luxurious. Winnipeg's first "European-style" hotel, built in 1903 by Frank Mariaggi, included a Turkish bath and an oyster bar, followed 2 years later by the construction of the opulent Royal Alexandra Hotel, which remained one of MB's premier hotels until its demolition in the 1960s. Most such hotels were built by railway companies near train stations to provide accommodation for travellers and new immigrants. Grand Trunk Pacific Railway built the **FORT GARRY HOTEL** in 1913 as part of a chain of such hotels being erected across Canada. Similarly, in **BRANDON**, the **CNR** opened the Prince Edward Hotel. In most hotels, liquor sales formed a large part of the business, and the **BRONFMAN** family first entered the liquor trade by running a hotel in **EMERSON**.

Royal Alexandra Hotel dining room, 1959.

The location of hotels shifted as railway travel was gradually replaced with highway and air travel. Coupled with a general trend towards decentralization in MB urban centres, new hotels began to be constructed on the outskirts of cities rather than primarily in the city centre. Most of the Main St hotels that once formed the centre of Winnipeg's hotel industry consequently fell into disrepair. **CANAD INNS**, the largest hotel firm in MB, operates many hotels in the suburbs. As of 2006, there were 327 hotels in MB, making up about 14,000 guest rooms. MB hotels contribute over $30 million in property and business taxes, and employ approximately 7500 people.

RESTAURANTS: MB restaurants, including caterers, bars, and street vendors, had sales of $1.2 billion in 2005. In total, the restaurant industry accounted for 3.1% of MB's total GDP, and employed 37,800 people, of which 20,800 are under the age of 25.

For many Manitobans, work in the food-service industry is often their introduction to the workforce. New immigrants also find opportunity in the industry, establishing restaurants with cuisine from their country of origin. The restaurant industry is thus a reflection of MB's multicultural demographic, and over half of MB's 1840 restaurants and bars are independently owned. Notably, the restaurant chain **SALISBURY HOUSE** has maintained local ownership. The industry has seen brief drops in sales related to increased regulation and taxation, for example in 1991 when GST was introduced on food purchased in a restaurant. However, overall sales in MB are growing and increased by 8.1% in 2005, with Manitobans spending on average $1777 per year at restaurants and bars. ● MICHELLE DOBROVOLNY

HOULE, Robert, painter and multi-media artist, (b March 29, 1947, St. Boniface) received his BA at the **U OF M** in 1972, his BEd at McGill U in 1975 and studied in Salzburg, Austria. He was elected to the Royal Canadian Academy of Art in 2000. Houle has curated and written widely about the work of First Nations artists, including that for the Canadian Museum of Civilization, UBC Anthropology Museum and the National Gallery of Canada. Of **OJIBWAY** heritage, Houle addresses social, political and spiritual issues of the past and present in his art through narrative, continual cross-referencing of images and text, and by juxtaposing Native and Christian imagery. Issues of Aboriginal identity and history, as seen in the *Lost Tribes* and *Premises for Self-Rule* series, are fused with current concerns. *Sandy Bay*, for instance, with Houle's typical strong and symbolic abstracted colour, the inclusion of photographs and the depiction of the school building, veiled and without doors, poignantly portrays the history of the **RESIDENTIAL SCHOOL** and the subsequent social devastation. As the recipient of many national awards, including senior grants from Canada Council for the Arts and the Toronto Arts Award for Visual Arts, Houle has been artist in residence in New Mexico. His work has been in solo and group exhibitions across Canada, the US, Europe and Australia, and is in public and private collections including the National Gallery of Canada, The **WINNIPEG ART GALLERY** and the Art Gallery of Ontario. In 2007, Houle taught at the Ontario College of Art. ● PATRICIA BOVEY

HUDSON, Gordon, curler (b Jan 5, 1894, Kenora, ON; d July 10, 1959, Winnipeg) was the first

Winnipeg curler to skip a team at the national Brier, and introduced western Canada's style of curling to the E. At one time, he was considered the best curler in the world. He joined the Kenora Curling Club in 1908, and played his first Manitoba Curling Association Bonspiel in 1910. In 1914, at just 20 years old, Hudson skipped his team to a tie for the grand aggregate, earning himself the nickname "Boy Wonder." He served in WWI, and settled in Winnipeg upon his return. He joined the Strathcona Club with his brother Cliff, a talented curler in his own right, and the club was soon known as the "Home of the Champions." Through the 1920s, Hudson's teams won 3 grand aggregates and 11 bonspiel events. Hudson used a sliding delivery, and was often able to slide up to the front of the 12 ft ring by turning in his left ankle, leaving only the side of his shoe in contact with the ice. Hudson skipped his teams to 2 consecutive Brier wins in 1928 and 1929. He tied for a 5th grand aggregate in 1941, and his many trophies include the Henry Birks, Eaton, Dingwall, Tuckett, and the MacDonald Memorial. Strathcona Club members elected him as club's most illustrious curler in its first 50 years. He was inducted into the Canadian Curling Hall of Fame in 1974, and the **Manitoba Sports Hall of Fame** in 1985. ● MD

HUDSON, Henry, explorer (b 1570, UK; d 1611 Hudson Bay), first charted **Hudson Bay** for European exploration. Hudson was one of those figures who emerge from the darkness of obscurity with an international reputation already made, Hudson first entered the record as an employee of the English Muscovy Company in 1607, hired to find a short route to China over the North Pole. He failed in this, as in a 1608 search for a Northeast Passage through the Russia Arctic. The Dutch hired him in 1609 for another search for the Northeast Passage, but a recalcitrant crew forced him to head west instead, where he ascended the Hudson River. On his return, he was hired by the English for a venture aboard the *Discovery* to find a Northwest Passage. Again he had, from the beginning, a difficult crew, which, after a year's sailing and wintering in Hudson Bay – named for him – in conditions of great privation, mutinied and set Hudson and a few others adrift. They were never heard from again. The ringleaders of the mutiny went unpunished for this crime. A few were eventually arraigned for murder but acquitted. Despite his nautical achievements, Hudson was obviously not a good leader of men. ● JMB

HUDSON BAY is an immense inland sea penetrating deep into the centre of Canada. It takes its name from English explorer **Henry Hudson**, though for many generations, **Cree** have called the water body *Winipakw*. Hudson Strait connects the bay to the Atlantic Ocean, as Foxe Basin and the Fury and Hecla straits connect it to the Arctic Ocean. About 1500 km long and 830 km wide, Hudson Bay covers an area of 822,234 km². It is such a shallow basin that within 20-100 km from the shore, the "Bay" is generally less than 80 m deep. The maximum depth is a mere 125 m. The bottom is generally smooth, though it is frequently cut by several shallow troughs, and has many small banks.

The N shorelines are typically low and rocky, and are indented with small inlets and bays. In contrast, western and southwestern shorelines are characterized by expansive (up to 9-km-wide) tidal flats and drowned wetlands. Shorelines along the SE coast are rocky and low-lying. The Long-Nastapoka-Hopewell offshore island complex, extending for 600 km along the semicircular SE coast, is the longest island chain in Canada. A remarkable feature of the SE margin of Hudson Bay is a great semicircular bight apparently centred on the Belcher Islands. Many amateur meteorite impact scientists have asked if this feature represents a large structure caused by meteorite strikes.

The bay occupies a huge, saucer-shaped basin in the Canadian Shield, underlain by the Phanerozoic rocks of the Hudson Platform. The Hudson Platform was formed from 130 million years (488-359 million years ago) of deposition into 2 oceanic sedimentary basins – the Hudson Bay sedimentary basin, centred on the bay and its southern extension, and the Moose River sedimentary basin, centred E of James Bay. These late-Ordovician, Silurian, and early-Devonian coral reefs and sediments lithofied into fossiliferous carbonate rocks. These can be up to 1800 m thick in central Hudson Bay, and are exposed at several points along the cliffs of eastern shoreline. The sedimentary rocks of the Hudson Platform were uplifted during the late Palaeozoic and early Mesozoic era – about 350 million years ago – and now dip gently toward the NE. The mid-Mesozoic terrestrial environment brought 213 million years of rock weathering and erosion. The Cretaceous period, characterized by marine transgressions (flooding by the sea), followed. During the Palaeogene period of the early Cenozoic era (65.5-23 million years ago), plate tectonics formed the present-day continental configurations. In the Neogene period, the next 23 million years, Pleistocene glaciations scraped clean the Hudson Platform and most of the Canadian Shield. The 2.5-to-3-km-thick ridge/dome of glacial ice centred over the Hudson basin weighed heavily on the land and isostatically depressed the basin by an estimated 800-1000 m.

Immediately following the retreat of the last **Glaciation**, about 6000 BC, the seawater of the Tyrrell Sea inundated the depressed and, consequently, larger Hudson Bay basin. Since then, Hudson Bay and the associated lowland regions are isostatically readjusting, a process called postglacial uplift, initially rising at an estimated 9 cm/year and later at a rate of one cm/year. Today, the region is still rebounding, though only about 0.6 cm/year. The floor of Hudson Bay has risen about 250 m since 6000 BC, expelling the ancestral Tyrrell Sea around AD 1 and creating a staircase of raised beaches, the uppermost being 248 m above the current sea level. Present-day tides range from one m to just over 2 m.

Hudson Bay drains nearly 4 million km² of NA, including parts of ON, QC, SK, AB, NU, and the NT, all of MB, and parts of ND and MN. The volume of freshwater entering Hudson Bay (30,900 m³/second) is twice the flow from either the Mackenzie River or the St. Lawrence River. The *National Atlas of Canada* identifies 19 major river systems contributing a mean annual discharge of at least 2800 m³/second into Hudson Bay. The Thelon/Dubawnt and Kazan enter by way of Chesterfield Inlet along the NW shore. The Seal, **Churchill**, **Nelson**, **Hayes**, Severn, and Winisk enter the Bay from the SW, while the Attawapiskat, Albany, Moose/Abitibi, Harricanaw, Nottaway, Broadback, Rupert, Eastmain, and La Grande rivers drain into James Bay. Two major watersheds drain into the Bay from the E: Baleine Grande and the Povungnituk River.

The waters in Hudson Bay have relatively low salinity, ranging from 25-31 parts per trillion

Henry Hudson, right, with mutineers

(ppt) depending on spring and summer freshwater inflow. The higher-salinity (34.6 ppt) waters of the Atlantic do not mix with the brackish waters of Hudson Bay due to a strong outflow in Hudson Strait; consequently, Hudson Bay is considered part of the Arctic Ocean. Hudson Bay is the world's largest body of water that seasonally freezes over each winter and becomes ice-free each summer. Ice cover begins to form in the NW region by late Oct and continues to grow S and SE across the bay until a maximum ice cover is reached at the end of April. The bay, however, is never totally ice covered, as polynya – large open-water leads in the ice – occur along the NW and E coasts of Hudson Bay, both coasts of James Bay, and in the vicinity of the Belcher Islands throughout the winter months. The ice cover begins to decay in late May, and Hudson Bay is generally ice-free and navigable from mid-July to Oct. ● ROD MCGINN

HUDSON BAY MINING & SMELTING COMPANY LIMITED (HBMS) is one of the province's largest mining operations, employing about 1350 workers in **FLIN FLON** and **SNOW LAKE**. The Harry Payne Whitney interests of New York formed the company in 1927 to take over and operate a large copper and zinc ore body that had been discovered some years earlier in northern MB. Work began the following year on construction of a concentrator, a zinc recovery plant, a copper smelter, and a hydroelectric plant, and in the late 1930s, open-pit mining got underway in the Flin Flon area. In 1937, mining activities shifted underground, where the company continues to extract zinc, copper, and iron. HBM&S has undergone several ownership changes over the years, the latest occurring in Dec 2004, when

HBMS headframe at Flin Flon

Ontzinc Corp, a Toronto-based junior mining company that subsequently changed its name to HudBay Minerals Inc, acquired it from Anglo American International S.A. for $325 million. Before selling the operation, Anglo-American spent about $400 million to expand and upgrade the Flin Flon operations, including about $200 million on the development of its new Triple Seven mine. Although mining continues to be its core business, in the early 1990s, the company began diversifying its operations by joining forces with Prairie Plant Supplies Ltd to set up artificial growth chambers in some of its exhausted mine tunnels. The chambers have been used to grow a variety of crops, including **SASKATOONS**, roses, and herbs. The federal govt also has experimented with using the chambers to grow marijuana for medical purposes. ● MURRAY MCNEILL

HUDSON BAY RAILWAY (HBR) is a vital rail connection to **CHURCHILL**. From the moment that MB joined Confederation, railway connections to the outside world were a matter of crucial importance. Not surprisingly, even as the first rail lines were being built in the southern portions of the new province, a bold scheme was being developed to tie MB to the markets of Europe via the most direct route possible – a railway that would run N from **WINNIPEG** to a saltwater port on **HUDSON BAY**. By 1880, a charter for such a line was granted, the first of many to be issued for variations of this project. Public support for an HBR grew in western Canada not only because it seemed to be the shortest and most efficient way to ship Prairie grain to world markets, but because the HBR would also allow farmers to avoid paying the high freight rates on the monopolistic CPR. However, the HBR's earliest promoter, Hugh Sutherland, was unable to secure the financial backing that would make the railway possible. Still, the dream for such a railway remained alive and it even played a role in bringing down Premier **JOHN NORQUAY**'s provincial administration in 1887-88 when Sutherland applied for the land grant he had "earned" through the construction of the line's first 64 kms.

Donald Mann took over the charter in 1895, combined it (and its subsidies) with another railway charter and then, with his partner, William Mackenzie, began building the first sections of what would become the Canadian Northern Railway. By 1905, the CNoR had decided to build an extremely low quality extension from its mainline at Hudson Bay Junction, SK to **THE PAS**. (Although "completed" late in 1907 and inspected in Feb of 1908, until improvements were made

in 1909-10, it could only be operated when the ground was frozen solid!). Without substantive federal support there was no chance that the railway would be built any farther northwards. Bowing to considerable public pressure from western Canada, in 1908 the Laurier government agreed to finance the construction of the HBR from The Pas to the Bay through the sale of homestead and pre-emption lands in the West. The first earth was turned at The Pas in 1910 for this new HBR project and by 1911 a railway bridge across the Saskatchewan River was under construction and J.D. McArthur, one of western Canada's leading railway builders, was awarded the contract to build the first 300 kms of the line.

There was a setback, however. Soon after the federal election of 1911, the new Minister of Railways, Frank Cochrane, suspended all work on the HBR in order to re-examine the route and to determine the suitability of the 2 proposed terminal/harbour sites at Port Nelson and Fort Churchill. The public outcry in the West, however, was so great that the Conservative caucus overruled the minister and work was recommenced immediately. Soon afterwards, the closer site of Port Nelson was chosen as the terminus of the HBR.

Work on the HBR and the new terminal facilities at Port Nelson proceeded slowly in 1912 but then took off in 1913-14. Millions of dollars were expended and upwards of 2000 people were employed on the construction projects at any given time. The minister of railways was predicting that the HBR and Port Nelson would be shipping grain by the end of 1914. Neither the advent of WWI nor the revelation that a wharf complex on the mainland at Port Nelson was impractical served to derail the project – at least not at first. Instead, in the winter of 1914-15, it was decided that, to overcome the problem of silting along the banks of the Nelson River, an artificial island would be created. It was here that the wharf facilities would be built and then connected to the mainland by a one-km long railway bridge. These seemingly improbable projects at Port Nelson were in fact undertaken between 1915-17, but as war-related shortages of money, labour, and materials mounted, the federal govt's commitment to the project waned and all work was suspended for the duration of the war in January 1918. By this time, 534 kms of track had been laid – leaving only 148 kms of already graded line to be completed.

Burdened by war-related debts and the costs of railway nationalization, the post-war govt was unwilling to complete the project for several more years. However, in 1926, the Mackenzie King government – again bowing to western political pressure – agreed to have the new **CNR**

Laying track near Churchill in the winter of 1929 at Mile 510.

railway take on the project. After a new study of port sites it was decided to abandon Port Nelson and re-route the rail-line from near Kettle Rapids due N to Churchill. In total, another $40 million was spent on rehabilitating the existing track, building a new line from the end of steel to Churchill and constructing terminal facilities there between 1927 and 1931. The railway work was actually completed in the fall of 1929, and the first small (strictly symbolic) shipment of western grain sailed out onto Hudson Bay that same season. The terminal facilities were completed in 1931 and it was then that the first real shipments of grain were sent to England via Churchill.

Unfortunately, while the HBR was a technical success – pioneering new construction techniques such as the laying of track across frozen muskeg and then doing the ballasting afterwards – and while the terminal and port facilities at Churchill were of an excellent quality, the rail line never lived up to the expectations of its supporters. High maritime insurance rates on the Hudson Bay route and a very short shipping season in the summer and fall limited Churchill's value as a terminal for western producers. Still, there were some positive economic developments related to the construction of the HBR. Mineral exploration, mine development, timber-scouting, and hydroelectric investigations were spurred on by the construction of the HBR. Later, the HBR also played an important role in the establishment of the research-oriented rocket range in Churchill, which functioned sporadically from 1954 until the 1980s. Still, the railway proved to be enough of an ongoing liability for CN that in 1997 the decision was made to sell its operations in northern MB to a Denver-based firm, Omni-TRAX. This company also acquired control over the port facilities at Churchill and for the next few years worked diligently to increase the use of this route for both freight traffic and passenger/ tourist service – particularly in the field of "polar

bear" or eco-tourism. While company reports are positive about the long-term value of the HBR, economic success continues to elude Canada's "Arctic Outlet." ● JIM MOCHORUK

HUDSON'S BAY COMPANY ("The Governor and Company of Adventurers of England trading into Hudson's Bay") was granted, by royal charter on May 2, 1670, exclusive trading rights in all the lands draining into Hudson Bay. Although headquartered in London, UK, until 1970, the 18th century saw **YORK FACTORY** as its most important post and the centre of its NA operations. During the 19th century, the **RED RIVER SETTLEMENT** and, for a time, Ville-Marie (Montreal) took on increased administrative roles. In 1873, York Factory's importance ended when the northern department's headquarters was moved to **WINNIPEG**. Winnipeg's increasing dominance was recognized in 1970, when new supplemental charters granted by HM Queen Elizabeth II moved the

headquarters from the UK to Canada, and Winnipeg was chosen for the head office. In 1987, the head office moved to Toronto, where its operations had increasingly centred after 1979. However, Winnipeg remains the home for the archival records (**HUDSON'S BAY COMPANY ARCHIVES**) and the museum artifacts (the Hudson's Bay Company Gallery of the **MANITOBA MUSEUM**). Hbc (as it now brands itself) is the largest Cdn retailer and oldest corporation, operating over 500 stores including the Bay, Zellers, and Home Outfitters. In 2006 it was purchased by American Jerry Zucker.

EARLY HISTORY: During a successful **FUR-TRADING** trip N of Lake Superior in 1659-60, Médart Chouart, **SIEUR DES GROSEILLIERS**, and his brother-in-law **PIERRE-ESPRIT RADISSON** conceived the idea of a trading route to the heart of the NA continent through Hudson Bay. In New France, they met with castigation for trading without a licence, and in France, their proposal faced indifference. New England merchants were more receptive, but trial expeditions failed to reach their objective. However, the pair was encouraged to seek royal sponsorship in England, where a North-West Passage through the Arctic was as attractive as the prospect of fur trade. After a confrontation with the Dutch and a detour to Spain, the pair found their way to England and an enthusiastic reception in Oxford, where the court had taken refuge from the plague. Prince Rupert of the Rhine (1619-82, also known as the Duke of Cumberland); his cousin, King Charles II; and a group of merchants and noblemen agreed to provide capital and ships to explore the new route. After **DUTCH** interference and poor **WEATHER** prevented departures in 1666 and 1667, the ships set off in 1668. Radisson aboard the

***Nonsuch* leaving London on its way to Hudson Bay**

Eaglet was forced back by a storm, but des Groseilliers on the *Nonsuch* wintered on the eastern shore of Hudson Bay, and returned in 1669 with an impressive cargo of furs. On May 2, 1670, King Charles II granted the band of "adventurers" exclusive trading rights to a vast unexplored territory, named "**RUPERT'S LAND**" in honour of its first governor, Prince Rupert. It included almost 4 million km², including 40% of what is now Canada. Its boundaries stretched, from E-to-W, from present-day western and northern QC to the AB/BC border, and, N-to-S, from where ND and MN now lie into most of what is now NU and part of the present NT.

The joint stock company of bankers and entrepreneurs in London maintained a centralized control over the fur trade. Annual general courts of shareholders elected a governor and committee, who issued instructions to the ships' captains making the annual trip with men and supplies and to the council of officers in charge of the fur trade at the forts, referred to as "factories." They established posts at the mouths of rivers emptying into Hudson and James bays and traded with Aboriginal groups who travelled by canoe from their home territories to exchange furs for prized blankets, tobacco, and manufactured goods. In London, the furs were sold by auction, where **BEAVER** skins, in particular, were prized for felting, essential in the manufacture of hats.

EARLY CHALLENGES AND MERGER: The 1713 Treaty of Utrecht awarded control of Hudson Bay to the British, ending ¼ of a century of armed struggle on the bay. The French, led by men such as Pierre des Troyes and Pierre Le Moyne d'Iberville, had dominated during that time, limiting the HBC's financial success. York Factory was a "confused heap of old rotten houses" according to James Knight when he took possession for the HBC in 1714. His dream was to extend the trade beyond traditional Cree territory, and to attract their Chipewyan adversaries. Thanadelthur, a Chipewyan woman who had escaped from her Cree captors, accompanied an HBC expedition to her homelands and convinced the warring groups to make peace. Although she died in 1717, her efforts laid the groundwork for a trading post at **CHURCHILL RIVER**, later replaced by the impressive stone **FORT PRINCE OF WALES**. However, while HBC establishments remained on the shores of Hudson Bay, their French competitors increasingly cut off the HBC's fur supply, reaching the tribal territories directly using the St. Lawrence and Great Lakes routes. When British control of New France was confirmed by the Treaty of Paris in 1763, the situation only worsened. France briefly re-entered the picture in

1782 when Jean-François de Galaup, Comte de Lapérouse, captured both Fort Prince of Wales and York Factory. Peace treaties soon returned the damaged forts to the HBC, but QC traders proved more persistent foes. In 1774, the governor and committee in London ordered face-to-face confrontation in the interior where the HBC had previously only ventured in exploratory voyages by men such as Henry Kelsey and Anthony Henday. Samuel Hearne built the first inland HBC post at Cumberland House, SK. The free traders, based in London and in what would later become Montreal, established competing posts along the major waterways leading from Hudson Bay through MB into the interior, N along the Mackenzie River and W to the Rocky Mountains. In 1811, the HBC granted 185,000 km² to Committee member Thomas Douglas, Earl of Selkirk (*see* **SELKIRK, LORD**), for his **RED RIVER SETTLEMENT**. Here, **SCOTS** settlers were brought into the area around the junction of the **RED** and **ASSINIBOINE** rivers, a key link in the transport routes of both the **NORTH WEST COMPANY** and the HBC. The predictable result was violence, culminating in the 1816 battle known as the **SEVEN OAKS INCIDENT**. The NWC and the HBC, both overextended and exhausted from economic and physical conflict, united in 1821, extending the fur-trading monopoly beyond the bounds of Rupert's Land.

The merger brought together 2 different administrative styles. At the same time, Sir **GEORGE SIMPSON** arrived, charged with implementing the union. A structure of departments and districts based on the most efficient transportation connections was introduced, presided over by Simpson as NA governor after 1826. Unprofitable trading posts were closed, duplication eliminated, and redundant men dismissed. Officers shared in the profits as set out in the Deed Polls of 1821, 1834, and 1871. All information funnelled through Simpson, who acted as the eyes

and ears of the London committee. Until his death in 1860, his tireless travel and attention to detail controlled the vast domain that now stretched from sea to sea to sea.

DIVERSIFICATION: Fur trade remained the main focus of the HBC's activities, except where settlement forced adaptation. In the Red River Settlement, officers of the HBC participated in govt, granting land and enforcing the law. Attempts to protect its trading monopoly were challenged by independent traders. In 1849, because of strong public support for Métis Pierre-Guillaume Sayer, he was freed without punishment after being convicted of trading with the Indians. The trade in southern Rupert's Land was effectively "free." On the West Coast, traditional trading expanded and adapted: farm produce was traded to the Russian American Company (under a subsidiary Puget Sound Agricultural Company); timber and salmon was exported to the states of HI and CA and to Chile; horse brigades replaced canoes and **YORK BOATS**; and steamships joined the fleet shipping around Cape Horn and along the NW coast. American settlers were crowding out traditional HBC trade even before 1846, when the boundary established along the **49ᵀᴴ PARALLEL** placed former headquarters Fort Vancouver, WA, squarely in American territory, and showed the wisdom of the 1843 move to Fort Victoria on Vancouver Island. In 1849, the HBC was granted Vancouver Island as a crown colony and assumed formal responsibility for developing an agricultural settlement. As the administrative requirements became more onerous, Chief Factor James Douglas, who had been gov of Vancouver Island from 1851, relinquished his HBC commission in 1858 when he took on the expanded role of governor of the mainland colony of BC, and the HBC lessened its involvement in govt.

By the late 1840s, the HBC faced increased pressure to open the Western plains to settle-

HBC voyageurs enjoying a *pipeur* (a ten-minute break determined by the length of time it took to smoke one bowlful of pipe tobacco).

HBC store just outside Upper Fort Garry

ment, bolstered by the report of a select committee of the British House of Commons, appointed in 1857. The new shareholders of the International Financial Society, which bought a controlling interest in 1863, were more open to economic development and less wedded to the fur trade. Pressure from ON farmers only increased after Cdn Confederation in 1867. In 1869, after negotiations with the colonial office, the HBC relinquished its exclusive trading rights and vast territories to the Crown, in exchange for ownership of the lands around its posts, 5% of the land in the fertile belt (2.8 million ha), and £300,000 (about $1.2 million then, about $500 million in today's currency). In turn, the Crown transferred Rupert's Land (*see* **RUPERTSLAND TRANSFER**) to the new Dominion of Canada, and the *Manitoba Act* of 1870 extended its territory westward. This marked a significant watershed in HBC operations: after 200 years, the importance of the fur trade would be eclipsed by land sales, natural resource development, shipping, and retail sales.

The new business interests of the HBC required administrative changes and diversification, with operations increasingly centralized in Winnipeg. In 1871, the commissioner's office was created, under Donald A. Smith, in an effort to control communications and to manage change effectively. When the Northern Department headquarters moved from **YORK FACTORY** in 1873 in anticipation of railway and steamboat systems, Winnipeg became HBC command central in NA. Booming land sales, the railway, and **IMMIGRATION** efforts brought in settlers, whose trade replaced fur trade posts with sales shops in Canada's southern Plains. In 1881, the first HBC department store was built in Winnipeg, just N of where Fort Garry had stood until it was demolished to straighten Main St. Soon, every major city in western Canada boasted its own store, and mail-order catalogues served rural customers.

In 1874, the increasing importance of the sale of lands acquired under the Deed of Surrender led to the creation of a separate Land Commissioner's Office. The land office in Winnipeg auctioned town lots in Winnipeg and

PORTAGE LA PRAIRIE, and the HBC developed hotels, gristmills, and ferry and bridge service on a modest scale. The success of the land sales and the incorporation of Winnipeg in 1873 bolstered the retail business. Managing the resources discovered on these lands led to the founding in 1926 of Hudson's Bay Oil and Gas, the partial acquisition of Siebens Oil and Gas (1973), and of Roxy Petroleum (1980). While the Land Department closed in 1954, and the HBC sold off its resource-based businesses in 1987, real estate development continued through Markborough Properties until 1990, when it was spun off to shareholders.

THE 20ᵀᴴ CENTURY: As retail and wholesale operations increased in importance, the fur trade retreated farther N, moving into the Arctic in the 20th century. The nature of the trade also changed: raw furs of various categories had taken over from the dominance of beaver, and white trappers, including immigrants, increasingly participated with Aboriginals. As fur sources were depleted, and thanks to efforts by early conservationists **GREY OWL**, beaver and muskrat preserves were established in the 1930s and 1940s around James Bay and in MB and SK. Soaring fur prices and acquisitions such as Revillon Frères (51% in 1926, with the rest in 1937), C. M. Lampson (1930), and Maclure and McKinnon Fox Farms (1930) kept HBC as a dominant player in the fur trade until WWII. In 1987, HBC sold the London and Canadian fur sales operations, as well as the northern stores department, which now operates, from its headquarters in Winnipeg, as an independent company renamed the **NORTH WEST COMPANY INC.** While fur sales in the stores were discontinued at the same time, they have since been reinstated, but the famed HBC fur auction houses are no more.

Transportation and communication had always been an important aspect of the HBC operations, with sailing ships initially forming the vital link between London and NA. Telegraph, steamships, and railways soon became essential to business. Shipping expanded during WWI when a fleet of ships transported goods as far as wartime France and the Baltic under the subsidiary Bay Steam-

ship Company. As the Arctic fur trade developed, isolated posts required new means to keep in touch. Radio operators were first introduced at **NORWAY HOUSE** in 1921-22 and became an indispensable tool in the Arctic. The **HUDSON BAY RAILWAY** to **CHURCHILL** allowed shipment through this traditional HBC port – in 1931, blankets and china arrived and the first wheat left. In 1939, the HBC purchased its first airplane, a twin-engine Beechcraft, to found its air transport division. In conjunction with the annual ship – notably the *Nascopie*, which made the trip from 1911 until it foundered on a reef in 1947 – the airplanes provided crucial connections over the vast and sparsely populated expanse of the HBC's fur operations.

The HBC's dedication to communication provided the foundation for the famed **HUDSON'S BAY COMPANY ARCHIVES**, and the staff news magazine, *The Beaver*, which has evolved into a popular Cdn history publication. When the HBC received compensation for donating its archives and museum artifacts to the province of MB in 1994, it established the Hudson's Bay Company History Foundation to maintain collections at the Archives of MB and the MB Museum, as well as providing grants to Canada's National History Society, the new publisher of *The Beaver*, and other worthy projects promoting Cdn history. A separate Hudson's Bay Company Foundation, supplemented from the rewards program, provides support to a variety of charitable causes.

The Canadian Committee, established in Winnipeg as an advisory board, became involved in operational decisions by 1930, the first executive body outside of London. The directors met in Winnipeg, in their first meeting outside London, on Oct 16, 1958. When double taxation forced the HBC to become a Canadian company in 1970, the move to Winnipeg was natural. The new governor, George T. Richardson, was a prominent Winnipeg businessman, and the province proudly welcomed the head office and lobbied for the archives and museum artifacts. After Ken Thomson, 2nd Lord Thomson of Fleet, acquired a controlling interest in the HBC in a bidding battle with Galen Weston in 1979, operations gradually shifted to Toronto. The corporate office was located in the Simpson's Tower on Bay St, though Hudson's Bay House at 77 Main St in Winnipeg was listed as the registered head office until 1987.

THE FUTURE: The HBC now focuses on its retail operations, modernized in the early 20th century by advice from British retail experts. Large new downtown stores graced the major cities across the Canadian West following the 1926 construction of the new Winnipeg store at

Portage and Memorial, then considered the western outskirts of the city. HBC's reach extended across Canada with acquisitions such as Morgan's (1960), Freiman's (1971), Simpson's, Zeller's and Fields (1978), Robinsons (1979), Towers (1990), Woodwards (1993), Kmart (1998) and 17 **Eaton's** locations after that Cdn icon closed its doors. In 1965 a major re-branding had led to the retail stores using the name "The Bay" with the distinctive yellow ribbon design. Today, from its headquarters in Toronto, the HBC still uses this name, but relies on the blanket stripes (green, red, yellow and indigo) and the logo "Hbc" to distinguish its operations, including The Bay, Zellers, and Home Outfitters. The company continues to adapt to economic conditions, with new investments in electronics and e-commerce and efforts to compete with big-box US chains. The HBC in 2004 employed 70,000 people, with annual revenues exceeding $7 billion from more than 500 stores. Since the 2006 purchase of the company by American Jerry Zucker, speculation has increased regarding the future of Canada's oldest firm. • JUDITH HUDSON BEATTIE

HUDSON'S BAY COMPANY ARCHIVES are known internationally for their detailed documentation of early Cdn history. For a number of settlements in QC, ON, MB, SK, AB, and NU/NT they contain the only documentation for the 18th century. What makes them of particular interest to researchers is their continuity. For instance, all the **Hudson Bay Company** minute books have survived, except those for 1670-71 and 1674-79.

From its earliest days, the HBC instructed its men to "sende us home every yeare exact Journalls of what hath been Done both at the place where you shall reside your selfe and at all our other Factories." Men skilled in writing were hired and sent to the larger posts to help keep the books. The journal, account book, and other papers for the trading post's previous year were sent home by the annual ship. Considering the Company's peripatetic existence during its initial 12 years, maintaining the records could not have been easy. Meetings were held in various London venues where the management committee members had connections, such as in the Tower of London, where John Robinson was lieutenant; in Prince Rupert's Whitehall lodgings; or in local coffeehouses. Not all the records have survived. Some were lent and not returned. Fires, upset canoes, and lack of storage space in London also contributed to the gaps.

The archives contain many and varied documents, such as the London headquarters records, the daily post journals, ships' logs, the voluminous correspondence of **Sir George Simpson**, land records, retail trade, maps, photographic and art collections, films, and a small, highly specialized library. Some of the most valuable documents in the archives are those penned by employees who had a special interest in the country. Andrew Graham's and James Isham's 18th-century observations, and **Peter Fidler's** journals of travel and exploration, are invaluable to historians, geographers, and sociologists. For the 20th century, photographic collections, donated by staff who served in Arctic and Subarctic Canada, provide documentation for a way of life now vanished. For researchers interested in the indigenous peoples of Canada, the daily journals provide information on various aspects of their cultures. There are journals for more than 200 individual posts during the HBC's initial 200 years of operation, the earliest dating from 1705. Other documents – including ships' logs, meteorological journals, and account books – interest geographers, scientists, and business historians.

The HBC was a major contributor to the mapping of Canada, especially in the Northwest. More than 12,000 maps, charts, plans, and architectural drawings have survived, including over 50 maps from the famous London Arrowsmith firm. Many of the manuscript maps were drawn by well-known HBC employees, particularly Philip Turnor and Peter Fidler. A number of Fidler's maps were based on information received from Aboriginal people, the most famous being an 1801 derived from Siksika (Blackfoot) chief Ac ko mok ki ("The Feathers").

When the HBC relinquished its chartered territory, it received 2.8 million ha of agricultural land in the 3 Prairie provinces and 18,000 ha around its posts. For researchers interested in land settlement patterns and the development of towns and cities, the maps and records of the Land Department are a useful source.

The HBC's 250th anniversary in 1920 was the catalyst that brought attention to the archives, as people trying to stage anniversary events realized the significance of the records. Old files from the establishments in Canada were collected at Hudson's Bay House in **Winnipeg**, and then shipped to London. Sir William Schooling (1860-1936) was the first historian to have complete access to the records. His book *The Governor and Company of Adventurers of England Trading into Hudson's Bay during Two Hundred and Fifty Years 1670-1920* was given to employees and prominent friends of the Company as an anniversary memento. The HBC's first archivist, R. H. G. Leveson-Gower, was hired to organize the records. They were opened to the public in 1931. In 1938, the Hudson's Bay Record Society was incorporated and the first volume, *Simpson's Athabasca Journal*, was published. The first 12 volumes were published through an arrangement with The Champlain Society. The publishing continued during the adverse conditions of WWII. In 1983, when the Society ceased publishing, 33 volumes had been produced.

When HBC head office was transferred to Canada in 1970, it was evident that a decision had to be made about the archives. An agreement was signed with the province of MB on July 31, 1973, to deposit the archives in the Archives of MB. After a year of taking inventory, packing, and shipping, the archives arrived in Winnipeg in fall 1974, and were officially opened to researchers in Apr 1975. Since then, all the archive's textual records for the first 234 years have been microfilmed. The British govt, as one of its conditions of export, requested a microfilm copy of the archives from 1670-1904. Fortunately, under an arrangement with the National Archives of Canada, the records for the first 200 years had already been microfilmed, and the second phase, 1871-1904, was completed in 2001, though the microfilming of newer records is ongoing. Over 4000 microfilm reels of HBC archives are now available to researchers by inter-library loan. Copies of the microfilm are also available at the Library and Archives of Canada, in Ottawa, and the National Archives in Kew, Surrey, UK.

In 1994, the Company donated its archives to the province of MB. A conservative estimate of their value was $60 million. With the tax savings, the Company set up the Hudson's Bay Company Foundation to help support the archives and other projects of an historical nature. The HBC Archives operates as a separate division within the Archives of MB in the Winnipeg Auditorium building (*see* **Archives**). This vast array of documents, covering 3 centuries, is a rich research source for all Manitobans. • SHIRLEY SMITH

HUGHES, Clara, cyclist, speed skater (b Sep 27, 1972, Winnipeg) was the first Cdn, and 1 of only 4 athletes in the world, to have won medals at both Summer and Winter Olympic Games. Hughes began speed skating at 16, and in 1988 won her first Cdn junior title in the 3000 m. Like most speed skaters, she started cycling to cross-train in the summer. She decided to switch to cycling full time in 1990 at the encouragement of a local cycling association. The following year, she won a silver medal at the **Pan Am Games**, her first of 5 Pan Am medals. Over the course of her cycling career, she was a national champion 18 times, and won a silver medal at the 1995 world championships. She won her first Olympic medals at the 1996 Olympics in Atlanta, claiming bronze in both the cycling time trial and the road race.

In 2000, at the age of 28, Hughes made a successful return to speed skating, joining the national team after just 7 weeks of training. Meanwhile, she still competed in cycling events at the 2002 Commonwealth Games, winning a gold and bronze medal. At the 2002 Salt Lake City Olympics, Hughes' bronze medal win in speed skating made her the first Cdn athlete to win a medal in both summer and winter Olympic Games. She went on to win numerous speed skating medals in the 5000 m event: silver at the 2003 world single distance championships; bronze at the 2004 world all around championship; gold at the 2004 world single distance championship; and bronze at the 2005 world all around championship. Along with **Cindy Klassen** and Kristina Groves, Hughes set a world record in the team pursuit at the 2004 World Cup. At the 2006 Olympics, Hughes won gold in the 5000 m, and silver as part of the Cdn team in women's pursuit. She trains in Calgary. • MD

Bobby Hull, 1972

UMA, TRIBUNE, PERSONALITY FILES, GREGG BURNER PHOTO, 1972

HULL, Robert Marvin "Bobby," hockey player (b Jan 3, 1939, Pointe Anne, ON), became the first hockey player to earn a million-dollar contract when he signed on with the **Winnipeg Jets**. Hull debuted in the NHL with the Chicago Black Hawks in 1957 where his famed slap shot, which could travel over 160 kmph, helped the team win the 1961 Stanley Cup. He won the Hart Trophy in 1965, and a 2nd in 1966 after becoming the 3rd player in NHL history to score more than 50 goals in a season. In 1972, he was offered $1 million to play for the Jets in the World Hockey Association. Hull's superstar status gave the WHA the credibility to compete with the dominant NHL, and

paved the way for bigger contracts for hockey players in both leagues. Nicknamed the "Golden Jet" because of his blonde hair and speed, Hull helped the Jets win 3 Avco Cup WHA titles. After a brief stint with the Hartford Whalers, Hull retired and took up farming. Over his 23 years in the NHL, Hull scored 1018 goals. His brother Dennis and son Brett have also played in the NHL. • MD

HUMAN RIGHTS protection in MB has a history as old as the province itself. Legislation was initially developed piecemeal in response to various issues. Section 23 of MB's constitution, the *Manitoba Act* (1870), guarantees the use of the **French** language in the enactment of the province's legislation. The violation of this constitutional guarantee beginning in 1890 was finally rectified by a unanimous decision of the Supreme Court of Canada in 1985 (*see* **French Language Crisis**).

Nellie McClung led the **Women's Movement**, which championed equal rights for women, since before WWI. Their struggle resulted in 1916 in the right of Manitoban women to vote; MB was the first province to grant this right.

In 1934, responding to the anti-Semitic activities of William Whittaker's Nationalist Party, the Legislature passed its pioneering *Anti-Defamation Act*, often referred to as the "Hyman Act" because of the initiative of Jewish **Winnipeg** lawyer and leftist MLA Marcus Hyman. At the same time, Whittaker's followers, dressed in storm-trooper uniforms complete with the Nazi swastika, were routed in a street battle on Market Square with local **Communists** and the Jewish Anti-Fascist League. However, anti-Semitism remained a problem, as seen in an informal but widely known quota system that restricted the admission of Jewish students to the **U of M**'s Faculty of Medicine. Anti-Semitism existed alongside other forms of discrimination, against, for example, Aboriginal and **Chinese** people; women, despite the work of McClung and others; and, particularly in employment, **Immigrants** from eastern Europe. Not until the 1970 passage of the *Manitoba Human Rights Act* (*HRA*) by **Ed Schreyer**'s govt, following the example of a similar Ontario statute of 1967, did broad-based anti-discrimination legislation come into existence.

In a sense, the roots of the *HRA* originate with the UN's passage in 1948 of the Universal Declaration of Human Rights, drafted partly by a Canadian, John Peters Humphrey. The legally binding International Covenant on Civil and Political Rights followed it in 1966. The covenant provided the inspiration for domestic human rights legislation. In celebrating Human Rights

Day in Dec 1967, a new-formed, broad-based Manitoba Human Rights Committee (HRC) organized a Human Rights Conference in 1968 at the **U of W**. Subsequently, the HRC, together with the MB arm of the Canadian Civil Liberties Association, lobbied successfully for the *HRA*. This act essentially prohibited discrimination in employment, accommodation, and services generally available to the public on a number of grounds, including race, nationality, religion, age, sex, political belief, and physical or mental disability. Its prohibitions were enforced by a complaint-based procedure whereby, if the complaint was not otherwise resolved, either informally or by mediation, adjudication would follow. Adjudicators received a wide range of statutory enforcement procedures and penalties. The *Manitoba Human Rights Code* (1987) has since entirely replaced the *HRA*. This more-comprehensive statute now includes sexual orientation and failure to provide accommodation as prohibited grounds of discrimination.

Nationally, the *Charter of Rights and Freedoms* (1982) acts as a shield against statutes and law enforcement activities of both the federal and provincial govt. Constitutionally guaranteed rights and freedoms under the *Charter* include equality and political rights, such as freedom of expression and freedom of association. The *Charter* generally does not act as a substitute for human rights acts, which in the main operate against discrimination in the private sector.

Before the enactment of the *Charter*, the Supreme Court of Canada held that certain political rights – such as freedom of speech and the press and freedom of association, thought to be essential to the democratic process – were constitutionally guaranteed by implication. The implied bill of rights, the Supreme Court said in several landmark cases, was to be found in the preamble to the *Constitution Act* of 1867, which described Canada's constitution as being similar in principle to that of the UK. In addition to the *Manitoba Human Rights Code* and the *Charter of Rights and Freedoms*, various statutory safeguards – such as the *Fair Employment Practices Act* and the *Labour Relations Act* – protect Manitobans, particularly in the employment area. • ROLAND PENNER

▸ *See also* **Canadian Museum For Human Rights**

HUMMINGBIRDS (family Trochilidae) are NA's smallest birds. Only one member of this largely neotropical family is regularly found in MB – the Ruby-throated hummingbird (*Archilochus colubris*). After arrival from its CA wintering grounds around mid-May, it breeds most commonly along the edge of the boreal forest (*see* **Ecoclimactic Regions**), and is thus familiar to

CORY LOEWEN

Ruby-throated Hummingbird

H many cottagers. All but the occasional straggler will have departed by mid-Sept. Notwithstanding folk tales that hummingbirds migrate on the backs of Canada Geese (*Branta canadensis*; *see* **WATERFOWL**), "hummers" make the journey entirely under their own power. Due to their high metabolism, they need high-energy food, which is supplied by nectar, pollen, and small insects. They can often be easily attracted to feeders with sugar water. Look for hummingbirds in the English Gardens in Winnipeg's **ASSINIBOINE PARK** in Aug and early Sept. The Rufous Hummingbird (*Selasphorus rufus*), a Western species, has been documented about 20 times in MB, and has even reached **CHURCHILL** on several occasions. ● RUDOLF KOES

HUNTER, Robert "Bob," environmentalist, journalist, author, politician (b Oct 13, 1941, **WINNIPEG**; d May 2, 2005, Toronto). Named by *Time* magazine as one of the top 10 eco-heroes of the 20th century, Bob Hunter was the co-founder, president, and first member of the Greenpeace Foundation. Hunter led the organization from 1973-79, when Greenpeace International was formed.

The activist and journalist got his start in Winnipeg working for the **WINNIPEG TRIBUNE** in the early 1960s. A high-school dropout, Hunter worked his way up from copyboy to general reporter. After a few years, Hunter left the paper to hitchhike across Europe. In 1966, he left for Vancouver and took a job with the *Vancouver Sun*. He became the first counterculture newspaper columnist in Canada.

In Vancouver, Hunter met 2 former *Winnipeg Tribune* reporters, Dorothy and **BEN METCALFE**. The trio, along with a group of ecologists, Quakers, and US draft dodgers, established the Don't Make a Wave Committee, putting their lives on the line to protest the testing of nuclear bombs in AK by the US Atomic Energy Commission. To reflect the committee's interest in ecological peace, they later changed their name to the Greenpeace Foundation. Hunter coined the term "mind bomb." The use of images such as inflatable boats taking on whaling vessels and

warships, and the clubbing of baby seals, are examples of Hunter's "mind bomb." These images were used by Greenpeace to make a lasting impression and to create controversy.

In 1988, Hunter moved to Toronto, where he worked as an environmental reporter for CITY-TV and as a columnist for *eye weekly*. He gained notoriety in Toronto for a morning TV segment called *Paper Cuts*, in which he would appear in a bathrobe and comment on newspaper content. In 2001, Hunter ran for the Liberals in a provincial by-election, but lost to the NDP's Michael Prue. The author of 13 books, Hunter's first experimental novel, *Erebus* (1969), was loosely based on his experiences working in a St. Boniface abattoir, and earned him a Gov Gen's Award nomination. In 1991, Hunter was the co-recipient of the non-fiction Gov Gen's Award for his book *Occupied Canada: A Young White Man Discovers His Unsuspected Past* (1991). The follow-up to this title was *Red Blood: One (Mostly) White Guy's Encounters with the Native World* (1999). Hunter was first diagnosed with prostate cancer in 1999. Refusing surgery, he began years of treatment in a Mexican cancer clinic specializing in non-conventional treatments, but eventually succumbed to the disease. ● JILL SEXSMITH

HUNTING CULTURE is how anthropologists classify First Nations and many of the **MÉTIS** communities in MB. They describe hunting cultures as a set of social networks, values, economies, and practices quite distinct from farming peoples or from industrial society. Although gathering and hunting is the earliest form of society invented, contemporary anthropologists have rejected the notion that hunting peoples are lower on an evolutionary scale than other social forms.

Hunting as a way of life has been around for at least 60,000 years. In contrast, farming has been around for 10,000 to 12,000 years, industrialization a mere few-hundred years. Hence, hunting has proven the most sustainable form of society invented by humans. Furthermore, although the biased image of hunters is of near-starving primitives, Pulitzer Prize-winning scientist Jared Diamond has shown that, on average, hunters have more leisure time than is available in other social forms. Hunters are independent and self-reliant; in traditional times, they made all the tools they needed. They tended to travel within a fixed territory, making seasonal use of resources: for example, the Plains people often wintered in the forests and summered on the plains; northern First Nations like the Sayasi **DENE** often spent late summer and fall on the tundra, moving back into the subarctic forests for winter and spring.

Hunting involves dramatically different ways of seeing the world and the self. For example, because they were partly nomadic, hunters put less of a value on material objects: any object owned was also a burden to be carried. Hunting peoples use storytelling as a mode of creatively conveying knowledge and wisdom. Hunters tended to be organized in extended family groups; in such a face-to-face social context, equality prevailed and a form of participatory democracy often inflected decision-making. Hunters are still recognized for their vibrant and complex artistic productions.

MANITOBA HISTORIC RESOURCES

Early Clovis people killing a huge mammoth

Historically, the **FUR TRADE** relied enormously on the skills and knowledge of Aboriginal hunters. When the fur trade became less important to the economy of MB in the late 19th and early 20th century, hunting remained important to northern communities. The numbered treaties contained promises that Aboriginal people would be able to maintain their life ways, which for most meant hunting, but those promises were largely ignored by successive govts, which did not understand or respect the hunting way of life.

Many remote, northern communities in MB still rely on hunting (and the related activities of gathering, **FISHING**, and **FUR TRAPPING**) for subsistence, economic value, and cultural vitality. Yet, strikingly, almost no govt programs provide systematic support for hunters. Most resource use conflicts in MB's North can be seen as conflicts over land that may serve as a hunting territory or land that may be a source of revenue generation through exploitation of resources like rivers. At the beginning of the 20th century, most observers thought hunters were doomed to disappear within a generation or 2 because of the encroachments of modernization. However, as the 21st century takes hold, the notion of a surprising cultural persistence and resilience on the part of hunters has changed this view. Hunters appear to have found a place in the contemporary world, using new technologies to help perpetuate ancient values. • PETER KULCHYNSKI

HUTTERITES arrived on the Cdn Prairies in AB and MB from the US starting in 1918. The Hutterites originally emerged from the Austrian province of Tyrol, in what is today western Austria and northern Italy. Jacob Hutter, a leader of these Tyrolese Anabaptists, looked for a place of refuge for his followers after suffering persecution. Hutter and his followers sought adult baptism, separation of church and state, and non-resistance. In addition, they instituted a shared community of goods. Between 1874-79, communal and non-communal Hutterites – 1265 in total – left Ukraine for the Dakota Territory. However, by WWI, the pacifist Hutterites were again faced with persecution, this time for not joining US services; most left the US for Canada.

Unlike other Anabaptists, such as the **MEN-NONITES** and Amish, Hutterites live in communal groups. Baptized and married Hutterite men wear beards. Hutterite women are even more distinguishable, wearing ankle-length gathered skirts, a long apron, and a vest. Women wear black polka-dotted kerchiefs at all times, and wear their hair long. Radios, television, and magazines are banned to minimize influence from the modern secular world.

Hutterites are the longest surviving communal society in NA. They have grown from 3 colonies and less than 500 members in 1874, to more than 35,000 living in 368 colonies across NA in the early 21st century. There are an estimated 10,000 Hutterites living in MB.

A typical colony ranges in population from 75 to 150 persons, half of which are adults and half children under 15 years of age. MB's Schmiedeleut colonies average about 105 members. When colonies grow to about 150 residents, they usually subdivide, which usually happens about every 15 years. Colonies are typically located away from towns and main thoroughfares, and are surrounded by large areas of land, to minimize contact with outsiders. Colonies are hierarchical, with the minister at the top. The colony manager, in charge of the financial operations, is slightly below the minister. Men fill all these positions, although the head cook is a woman, and sometimes a woman heads the garden operations. The leaders are gatekeepers, and these leaders are in frequent contact with outsiders. In 1968, Manitoban Hutterites owned 35 ac (14 ha) per capita, or 250 ac (100 ha) per family, while the MB farm population owned 118 ac (48 ha) per capita and 500 ac (200 ha) per family. Since then, the Hutterites have adopted modern, mechanistic agricultural technology, keeping up with the latest machinery. For example, Hutterites today are a dominant presence in MB's **PORK INDUSTRY**.

Hutterites emphasize kindergarten, German-language school, English school, and Sunday school as part of the training process, to learn to read Scriptures and be able to give account of their faith. Education usually ends at grade 8. Provinces operate public schools on Hutterite colonies, with Hutterites providing school buildings and facilities while the school board supplies teachers. Because of their history of persecution, Hutterites are suspicious of rulers. Their idea of separation of church and state involves avoiding those who wield power whenever possible. Recently, some Hutterites have started to vote in elections if issues they consider locally important arise, but most do not. The modern welfare state, with its family allowances, income taxes, old-age benefits, and pension and medical plans, has caused Hutterites to pause, and make special arrangements in many instances. Canada's income-tax system also had to be modified to accommodate the Hutterites. • LEO DRIEDGER

HYDROELECTRIC POWER

HYDROELECTRIC POWER is one of MB's most important resources and one of its top exports. Its origins in the province, however, were modest. On Oct 16, 1882, the Manitoba Electric Light & Power Company provided a demonstration of electric street lighting. This was done with the aid of a small dynamo (a direct current variable speed generator) driven by the **HBC**'s gristmill steam engine in downtown **WINNIPEG**. A few years later MB's first electric street railway car made a demonstration run on Jan 28 on River Ave in Winnipeg. On Sept 5, 1892, regular service finally began, powered by the Winnipeg Street Railway Company's Assiniboine Ave 1000 hp steam-driven power plant.

The beginning of the 20th century marked the dawn of a new era starting with the first hydropower plant in MB on the Minnedosa River (now the **LITTLE SASKATCHEWAN RIVER**). This plant provided electricity to Brandon but could only operate 8 months of the year because of MB's harsh winter conditions. It was dismantled in 1924. In 1906, the Winnipeg Electric Railway Company (WERCo) took ownership of the Winnipeg, Selkirk, and Lake Winnipeg Railway Company and became the monopoly supplier of all public transit, power, street lighting, and gas distribution in and around Winnipeg. Finding this monopoly arrangement unacceptable, the City of Winnipeg formed the City of Winnipeg Hydro Electric System. The City of Winnipeg quickly began work on the Winnipeg River Pointe du Bois Generating Station which was completed in 1911 and eventually had a capacity of 72 MW. WERCo however, was initially far ahead of the city having already built the Pinawa plant, the first hydro plant in MB to operate year round. The first unit was in service by June 1906, and by 1912, the Pinawa plant was capable of 22 MW of output. The Pinawa plant operated reliably until it was retired in 1951 to make more efficient use of water flows for the newer Seven Sister's plant. The price of electricity in 1906 was about ¢20/kWh, which adjusted for inflation would be high by today's standards.

In 1919, the MB Power Commission (MPC) came into existence with a mandate to generate, purchase, transmit and distribute power throughout rural MB. MPC built transmission lines to move available power purchased from the City Hydro Point du Bois units at a cheaper cost. Its first line was built to Portage la Prairie in 1919. Following years saw many more towns joined to the MPC's growing provincial grid.

Hutterites awaiting a royal visit in 1970

The 1920s were years of strong growth in MB and in 1923 the WERCo delivered its first power from the Great Falls Generating Station on the Winnipeg River. By 1928, all units were on-line with a capacity of 132 MW. In 1924 City Hydro began production of power at the Amy St Steam Plant which produced both steam for downtown district heating in Winnipeg and electricity. With a capacity of 50 MW, Amy St operated until June 1990, and was fired by lignite coal mined at Estevan, SK. These power plants were major engineering and construction achievements for the time and required the use of much labour and materials. The Great Falls Generating Station pioneered the use of some design features that are now common in hydro power plants. It was the first hydro plant in NA to turn low-head, vertical shaft, fixed blade, propeller type turbines with a plant head (total distance the water can fall) of 10.6 m or greater. These units, at half the installed cost of alternatives, were substantially more economical than other technologies.

In the 1920s, the MB Power Commission faced a difficult situation as load growth on its transmission network was lower than had been expected. This caused revenue shortfalls. The MPC countered this by embarking on a load-building program which targeted farmers and suggested ways electricity would make life easier. It established a Business Development Department to sell electricity powered appliances to help build load. A more conservative approach to line extension also improved the commission's financial situation. The WERCo continued its building program generating its first output from the Seven Sister's GS on the Winnipeg River in

1931. When it was completed in 1952, the plant rating was 150 MW, the largest in MB. With the Seven Sister's plant now on-line, the MB Power Commission began to purchase power from WERCo for transmission throughout the province.

The war years of 1939-45 caused labour and material shortages, which necessitated efficient production methods. For many, this meant increasing use of electricity, especially on the farm. In 1942, only about 1000 of the province's 50,000 farms were electrified; the MB Farm Electrification Enquiry Commission recommended that a farm electrification program be implemented. By the time it ended in 1954, 75% of all MB farms were connected to the power grid. MB became the country's most completely electrified province. Under the program costs of building the distribution lines into farms were absorbed by the MPC and the farmer paid only $3.60 per month in fixed costs plus the power consumption cost.

Manitoba Hydro, MB's modern power utility, began in 1949 as the Manitoba Hydro Electric Board (MHEB), an agency of the govt of MB. When it was realized that a coordinated policy for power development and supply in the province was needed, MHEB immediately began construction of the Winnipeg River Pine Falls Generating Station which went on-line in 1951. On May18, 1951 the first Manitoba Hydro Electric Board members were appointed making that date the starting point for a board independent of govt. In 1953, MHEB amalgamated with the WERCo and the next year the Winnipeg River McArthur Falls Generating Station went into service. Over the following years more amalgamation occurred and Brandon GS was built. At the

beginning of 1960, electrical generating capacity in MB consisted of the 6 Winnipeg River hydro plants, the Amy St, and the Brandon coal fired plants for a total of 671 MW of capacity. In 1961, the Selkirk coal fired thermal generating station (132 MW) was completed.

The period from 1961-90 was an active one for power development in MB. MHEB and MPC were amalgamated in 1961 to form Manitoba Hydro. The power company's mandate was to supply electricity to any and all consumers throughout the province, excepting central Winnipeg, which was served by Winnipeg Hydro. By 1961, virtually all communities in MB (523) were connected to the power supply. As load growth increased, new plants were rapidly built with Kelsey (first on the **Nelson River** in 1960) and **Grand Rapids** being added by 1968.

The 1970s were a time of great expansion for hydro power in MB. Kettle Rapids (1272 MW), Jenpeg (126 MW), and Long Spruce GS (1010 MW) plants were all added in quick succession. In 1970, a trade link to the US was established with construction of a 230-KV transmission line to Grand Forks, ND. Two high-voltage direct-current transmission lines were also built (Bipoles 1 & 2) to allow high efficiency transmission of power from the Northern Nelson River plants to Winnipeg. Three important programs were undertaken in the 1970s. First, the Lake Winnipeg Regulation (LWR) guaranteed adequate minimum water flow for northern hydro plants through the construction of various channels and control structures. Secondly, the Churchill River Diversion (CRD) allowed enhanced water flow on the Nelson to feed the thirsty turbines of the Nelson River units, some of which are rated at 148,000 Hp each. Finally, the Northern Flood Agreement was signed to compensate Northern residents who were adversely affected by LWR and CRD.

In the 1980s, Limestone GS, MB's largest generating station project was begun, then halted due to falling load growth. Construction resumed in the late 1980s and was completed in 1990. Limestone's capacity is 1300 MW, impressive – even when compared to the US Hoover Dam Power Plant (2079 MW). With the addition of 2 natural gas fired combustion turbines at the Brandon GS, MB's power generation capability approached 5400 MW. In July 1999, MB acquired Centra Gas MB Inc. to become the one-stop energy provider in the province. MB Hydro became the province's only power utility when it took over Winnipeg Hydro on Sept 3, 2002. Manitoba Hydro typically produces 95% of its electricity from renewable hydroelectric generation and enjoys a reputation in and outside of MB for reliability, efficiency, and low electricity rates. ● BRIAN SUMNER

Dam at Seven Sisters Falls

ICELANDERS, one of the first European groups to settle in what is now MB, began arriving in 1875. By 1900, the province was home to some 10,000 Icelanders. Now, MB has the largest concentration of people of Icelandic descent outside their homeland, with an estimated 10% of Manitobans claiming some Icelandic ancestry.

The first Icelanders to make their way W to MB were scouts seeking land for group settlement on behalf of countrymen in ON and WI. In 1875, they secured the W shore of **Lake Winnipeg** as an Icelandic reserve called **New Iceland**. The first contingent of settlers bound for New Iceland arrived in Winnipeg in fall 1875, and in 1876, an additional 1200 immigrants, known as the "Large Group," arrived directly from Iceland. Severe hardships plagued the pioneers, and a major exodus south to Dakota Territory left the settlement depopulated and struggling by 1880. A hardy core of settlers remained, however, and beginning in 1883, a large influx of new immigrants from Iceland revived community life. **Sigtryggur Jónasson,** a leader and entrepreneur known as the "Father of New Iceland," and his business partner, **Friðjón Fridriksson Frederickson,** are credited with guiding the settlement through this critical time, thus retaining many Icelandic pioneers who would otherwise have left MB. In

STAN MILOSEVIC, WWW.MANITOBAPHOTOS.COM

Viking statue in Gimli

time, New Iceland thrived, and by 1900 it had a population of 2500.

Significant Icelandic immigration to MB continued until 1914, and numerous other settlements sprang up throughout the province. The Argyle Settlement, with **Baldur** and **Glenboro** as its principal towns and smaller centres at Grund, Bru, and Holar/Skalholt, dates from 1880. The Alftavatn (Shoal Lake) Settlement around **Lundar** was established in 1885. Other sites included Laufas (Sinclair/Melita), Brown (**Morden**), Piney, **Swan River**, **Winnipegosis**, Poplar Park, and several districts around **Lake Manitoba**: Big Point (**Langruth**), Marshland/Big Grass, **Gladstone**/Westbourne, Oak

Point, Oakview, Hayland, Siglunes, Vogar, Dog Lake, The Narrows, Steep Rock, Red Deer Point (Reykjavik), Bayend, Wapah, Asham Point, Silver Bay, Lonely Lake, Beckville, and others. Small pockets of Icelanders also formed in scattered locations such as Arbakka, Glenforsa (**Strathclair**), **Binscarth**, Fairford, and Grass River, while significant numbers lived in larger centres such as **Brandon**, **Selkirk**, and **Portage la Prairie**.

The largest concentration of Icelanders outside New Iceland, however, was in **Winnipeg**, which by 1900 had some 4000 Icelandic residents. Earlier, some Icelandic families occupied shanties on the Hudson Bay Flats along the **Red River**, but they soon gravitated to streets such as Ross, Elgin, and Pacific, N of Winnipeg's downtown. Later, they established homes, businesses, and churches in Winnipeg's West End, with an epicentre at Sargent and Victor. Like many of their rural countrymen, they quickly became prominent in public life, the professions, the arts, business, and construction.

One of the earliest achievements of the Icelandic people in MB was in the field of publishing. In 1877, scarcely 2 years after the first settlers arrived in New Iceland, *Framfari* ("Progress") rolled off the press in a log print shop at Icelandic River (**Riverton**). Edited and typeset locally, this newspaper set a high standard for Icelandic-language publications in NA. Though *Framfari* ceased publication in 1880, it was soon replaced by *Leifur*, published in Winnipeg 1883-86. *Heimskringla* ("The Circle of the World," named after a series of 13th-century Icelandic sagas) then commenced publication in 1886, with *Lögberg* ("The Law Rock") following soon after in 1888. These last 2 amalgamated in 1959 and now survive as *Lögberg-Heimskringla*, the oldest ethnic newspaper in Canada. Hundreds of Icelandic books and scores of periodicals were also published in MB, a notable example being *Ólafur Þorgeirssons Almanak* ("Olaf Thorgeirsson's Almanac," 1895-1954), which carried local histories in serial form. For years, the Icelandic language prevailed in print, but with time, English was adopted. Symbolic of this shift was the establishment in 1942 of *The Icelandic Canadian Magazine*, an English-language quarterly started by 2nd- and 3rd-generation Icelandic Canadians.

Given their proportionately small numbers and their early date of arrival in MB, the Icelandic people have preserved their language remarkably well. A diminishing number still speak Icelandic fluently. Through outstanding vision and determination, a chair in Icelandic was established at the **U of M** in 1951, and today the Icelandic Collection there is one of the largest in the world. Icelandic immigrants were Lutherans,

and wherever they settled, they formed congregations and built churches. The Icelanders tended to be freethinkers, however, and beginning in the 1880s, many embraced the Unitarian faith.

Early Icelandic societies in MB strove to promote education, Icelandic culture, and charitable endeavours. A significant example was the *Þjóðræknisfélags Íslendinga í Vesturheimi* (Icelandic National League of NA), a civic-oriented cultural organization founded in 1919 and still active today. Notably, one of its founding principles, along with the preservation of Icelandic culture, was the promotion of good citizenship among Canadians of Icelandic descent. As early as 1883, Icelanders in Winnipeg also became active in the temperance movement through the Good Templars, and by 1910, chapters of the IOGT had been established in virtually every Icelandic settlement in MB. Icelandic women undertook numerous charitable and educational ventures and played a significant role in the struggle for women's suffrage in MB. Chief among them was **Margret Jonsdottir Benedictsson** of Selkirk, publisher of the women's journal *Freyja*. Another priority was care for the aged, which in 1915 prompted the establishment of a care home called Betel. Also active in many Icelandic communities were athletic societies, including hockey clubs such as the **Winnipeg Falcons**, renowned for their gold medal at the 1920 Olympics.

Icelandic people in MB integrated well into the larger population. Though many actively espoused social reform, they were also devoted Canadians, UK subjects, and monarchists, and several, such as George Johnson and his daughter Janis, have played significant roles in mainstream politics. A large proportion of Icelandic Canadians also served in the 2 world wars. Today, the example set by MB's Icelandic pioneers has been followed by 5 successive generations of their descendants – proud Canadians who also cherish their Icelandic heritage. ● NELSON GERRARD

▸ *See also* **Gimli**, **Íslendingadagurinn**, **New Iceland**.

ICE ROADS. *See* **Winter Roads**.

IDONIJE, Israel "Izzy," football player (b Nov 17, 1980, Lagos, Nigeria). The first Manitoban to play in the National Football League (NFL), Idonije and his family immigrated to Canada when he was 5 years old. He grew up in **Brandon** and attended Vincent Massey High School where he first played **Basketball**, only taking up football in his senior year. It took only one year for the **U of M** Bison football program to recruit Idonije for the start of the 1998 season. He played 4 seasons with the Herd, reaching the Vanier Cup championship game in 2001. In 2002, after an

outstanding final season, Idonije was named team MVP, a Canada West All-Star and first-team All-Canadian, the recipient of the J.P. Metras Trophy for outstanding lineman in Cdn university football, and Manitoba Male Athlete of the Year. The 6'6", 275-lb defensive lineman was not selected in the 2003 NFL draft. However, the Cleveland Browns signed him to a free agent contract a week before the Ottawa Renegades chose him in the 2003 Canadian Football League draft.

WINNIPEG FREE PRESS

Chicago Bears lineman Israel Idonije, 2007

Idonije attended the Browns' 2003 training camp, but was placed on waivers following an injury. He was picked up by the Chicago Bears and spent most of the 2003 season on the team's practice squad. In 2004, he suited up for NFL Europe's Berlin Thunder before returning to Chicago. When the Bears reached the Superbowl following the 2006 season, Idonije gained international notoriety. In Jan 2007, he won his 2nd Manitoba Male Athlete of the Year (2006) award, and in March 2007 he was named to the Order of the Buffalo Hunt. In April 2007, Idonije visited US soldiers stationed in Iraq, and returned to Winnipeg for the launch of Football Manitoba's flag football intramural season. ● JOEL TRENAMAN

ÎLE DES CHÊNES, pop 960, is a community 13 km SE of **Winnipeg**. It was settled in 1874 by a group of colonists from QC and Massachusetts. In the 21st century, the majority of residents commute to work in Winnipeg. Annual Festival of the Stars, in July, attracts sport enthusiasts from all over the area. The community is home to the 9-hole Oak Grove Golf Course. ● GPP

ILFORD, pop 100, is a non-treaty community located on the rail line between **Thompson** and **Churchill**, 416 km by rail from **The Pas**. It was a material and service centre for the building of the **Hudson Bay Railway**; a gathering point for gold prospectors; and a marshalling point for winter road freighters. It is also closely affiliated with the **War Lake First Nation**. There is a community health worker, volunteer fire service and an airport. The local economy is based on fishing and trapping. ● GPP

IMMIGRATION is removal from one's native land to settle in another country. Since the end of the 19th century, the assumption has been that one's homeland was a clearly defined nation-state, but in earlier eras, national boundaries were a good deal less clear, if they existed at all. In any event, what is now MB has been settled by a succession of peoples who had departed their birthplaces.

The first of these were First Nations people, caught up in the westward movement of population instigated by the arrival of Europeans beginning in the 16th century. A whole new Aboriginal population at least partially displaced an existing one in what is now southern MB in the late 17th and 18th centuries. The earlier people were Assiniboine, long-time Prairie residents, and the new arrivals were CREE and OJIBWAY moving from the eastern woodlands onto the plains. The first European immigrants were the "freemen" employees of the early FUR TRADING companies who decided, beginning at the end of the 18th century, to remain in the West with their Aboriginal wives and their children.

The first orchestrated movement of European settlers into what is now MB occurred when LORD SELKIRK sent a small party to settle at THE FORKS in 1812, and was joined by several hundred more over the next few years. Most of these immigrants were Highland SCOTS, with a few IRISH. They were dispersed by the fur trade war between the NORTH WEST COMPANY and the HUDSON'S BAY COMPANY in 1815 and 1816, and were replaced by other immigrants recruited by Lord Selkirk and his estate: demobilized Swiss troops, French Canadians, and a large contingent of Swiss civilians who arrived in the RED RIVER SETTLEMENT in 1821. Most of the European arrivals chose to leave for the US after the devastating 1826 flood, to be replaced by mixed-bloods moving into the settlement from the plains and from the north. By 1840, 2 groups of mixed-bloods – the French-speaking MÉTIS and the English-speaking Country-Born – were the dominant population of the settlement.

In the 1850s and 1860s, the settlement received a small number of Cdn immigrants who intended to become the vanguard of an ultimate Cdn takeover of the West. These composed the Canadian Party, which opposed LOUIS RIEL and the Métis in the RED RIVER RESISTANCE of 1869-70. The first substantial movement of Canadians to MB were the Cdn volunteers who came with the WOLSELEY EXPEDITION in 1870 and 1871 and remained in the country to become the leaders of Winnipeg society. Canadian-born and UK farmers soon followed, mainly as individuals or in small parties.

The 2 most successful attempts to bring groups of settlers to MB in block settlements

ARCHIVES OF MB, ADVERTISING 67, N10094, C.1892

Cover of Department of Agriculture and Immigration publication, 1892.

occurred in this early period. The first saw successful negotiations between the Canadian govt and Russian-based MENNONITES in 1872 and 1873, offering exemption from military service, religious liberty, control of education, and free homesteads of 160 ac (65 ha). Canada set aside 2 blocks of townships for the Mennonites in southern MB, and about 8000 Mennonites settled there in the 1870s. The other effort involved ICELANDERS, who in 1875 were granted land on the W side of LAKE WINNIPEG, N of the boundary of the province of MB. The Canadian govt allowed the Icelanders a system of self-rule called New Iceland. This reserve became part of MB in 1881, but was largely autonomous until 1887. An effort to set up French Canadian colonies, as well, under the Société de colonisation, founded in St. Boniface and Montreal in 1874 and headed locally by Archbishop ALEXANDRE-ANTONIN TACHÉ as honorary president, was not so successful. A number of immigrants

from northern and central Europe also came to MB beginning in the 1880s, many settling in the NORTH END of Winnipeg. A small number of Highland crofter settlements were established in the same decade, but with limited success.

After 1896, Cdn immigration policy under Immigration ministers Sir CLIFFORD SIFTON and Frank Oliver changed in 2 ways. For one, the govt sought for the first time to keep out "undesirable" immigrants. The administrative apparatus of federal immigration increased (38 border crossings were set up on the Cdn-US border in 1908), and with the *Immigration Act* (1906), regulations excluded broad categories of unacceptable newcomers, including criminals, prostitutes, the mentally challenged, those with contagious diseases, and those impaired in hearing, sight, and speech. At the same time, the govt began deliberately recruiting large numbers of immigrants from outside the ranks of the UK and Northern

Europe, headed by the Ukrainians – peasants "in a sheepskin coat" – from the steppes of Russia who were deemed suitable to settle on the Prairies. Many of those who ended up in Winnipeg were Slavs and Jews from the Austro-Hungarian Empire. The period 1896-1914 saw Winnipeg's population triple, mainly thanks to the new immigrants, whom many also regarded as posing new problems of assimilation.

By 1914, the initial great wave of European immigration to MB was complete. Most of it had taken place without govt assistance, at least until immigrants arrived at their destination, when free land might be available. Over the 1920s, most immigration to MB occurred under various Empire Settlement schemes, in which former soldiers and other UK people could serve as the basis of state-assisted immigration schemes.

Large-scale immigration to Canada resumed after WWII, though MB was no longer a preferred destination. Thousands of war brides and hundreds of thousands of people from European refugee camps were brought to Canada from 1946-60. These people settled mainly in the big cities of ON, QC, and BC. MB received its biggest share between 1946-55 when agriculture was still deemed a desirable vocation. From 1955-76, rural depopulation and an economy still dependent on agriculture made MB less attractive to immigrants.

Canada had long used its immigration policies as a de facto means of racial and ethnic discrimination. However, criteria for immigration gradually changed, allowing people to come from Africa, Asia, and Latin America. MB, and especially Winnipeg, shared in the results of the new policies, but usually in levels below the national average. Canada began to open its borders to those fleeing strife around the world by creating a new class of immigration – the refugee. Refugees were welcomed from Hungary, Czechoslovakia, Chile and Uganda. MB played a big role in the new Private Sponsorship for Refugees program in the late 1970s when thousands of Southeast Asians arrived in the province. The "boat people" movement established a pattern of refugee support that continues to the present. In the early 2000s, MB continued to welcome about 20% of all of the privately sponsored refugees to Canada.

In the late 20th century, the MB govt initiated an aggressive new immigration policy to satisfy its economic requirements. It recognized the province was experiencing a drop in the birth rate that would put the population below the required replacement rate (2.1 live births for every woman of a child-bearing age). So it became a leader in Ottawa's new Provincial Nominee Program, initiated in 1998. Newcomers

who were skilled were "sponsored" by private community groups and businesses, fast-tracked by the govt, and supported by a number of provincial programs according to criteria reflecting local labour market conditions. The program was particularly successful in smaller, southern MB centres like WINKLER and STEINBACH. In early 2007, the provincial govt announced it had achieved the highest levels of immigration since 1957, much of it due to the nominee program. Fully half of all provincial nominees who came to Canada settled in MB. The province welcomed 9989 immigrants under the refugee, family reunification and economic classes in 2006 from Germany, the Philippines, India and China, an increase of 23.4% over 2005. In comparison, Canada overall saw a decrease of 4.1% in the numbers of newcomers.

Although very different strategies from the ones that saw MB achieve the country's highest immigration rates in the first 2 decades of the 20th century, immigration policies in the 2000s were once again shaping the province. • J. M. BUMSTED

INCO LIMITED, Manitoba Division, is the province's largest MINING operation and the largest employer in THOMPSON, with about 1500 workers as of mid-2005. Opened in 1961, the company's Thompson operation was the western world's first fully integrated nickel mining and processing complex, transforming nickel ore into finished electrolytic nickel, which is used mainly in the production of stainless steel. As of 2005, the MB division was producing approximately 45 million kg of nickel a year. Its operations included 2 underground mines (the Birchtree and Thompson mines), a mill, a smelter, and a refinery. With 2 mines in the Thompson area, it is Canada's 2nd-largest nickel mining operation next to the company's Sudbury, ON, operations. In the 1990s, the company spent nearly $300 million to develop other mining properties in the Thompson area, and in 2000, it announced plans to invest another $70 million to ensure at least another 15 years' supply of ore by deepening its Birchtree Mine. The division also continues to explore the Thompson Nickel Belt for other new nickel ore bodies. In mid-2005, it announced it would be spending $45 million over the next 2 years to develop a new ore body at its Thompson Mine. In 2005, it also spent another $100 million on infrastructure upgrades, including rebuilding its main smelter furnace. • MURRAY MCNEILL

INFORMATION AND COMMUNICATIONS TECHNOLOGY (ICT) INDUSTRY. This industry is comprised of companies that produce goods and offer services to manage and process

information electronically. ICT forms an important sector that enables other industries, as an increasingly wired society means computers and telecommunications are an essential part of all aspects of business, from inventory to sales to customer records. Products of the sector include broadband Internet and wireless services, biomedical informatics, software and related services, electronics and microelectronics, digital media, and geomatics, which deals with spatially referenced information. Centred in WINNIPEG, ICT employs just over 15,000 workers.

In 2003, the ICT sector produced revenue of $600 million, of which $227 million are exported from the province. The annual growth of ICT revenue averaged 5.2% between 1997 and 2004. MB companies account for a small portion of the total national industry, figuring somewhere under 4%. Most of the roughly 1500 companies in this industry are small or medium-sized firms employing fewer than 10 people. However, multinational companies, such as IBM and EDS, also operate in the province, and the 3rd-largest telecommunications provider in Canada, MTS, maintains its headquarters in Winnipeg. In 2005, MTS Allstream employed 6000 people (2800 in MB), and earned approximately $2 billion in revenue. MTS has led the way in the establishment of an extensive broadband communications infrastructure, including 75,000 strand-km of fibre-optic cabling and total digital-switching technology. Telecommunications companies also benefit from the province's low-cost electricity.

Several MB-based companies have made notable contributions to the industry, and operate on an international scale. AML Wireless Networks is a world leader in the design and manufacture of wireless transmission systems, serving roughly 60 million subscribers worldwide. Software developer Emerging Information Systems Inc. developed NaviPlan, the most widely used financial-planning software in NA. An electronics manufacturer in the AEROSPACE industry, Micropilot has created the world's smallest fully functional autopilot, and sells products to 6 branches of NASA. TelPay Inc. is Canada's largest independent electronic payment processor, and pioneered online bill payment. FRANTIC FILMS has created visual effects for several Hollywood productions, and, notably, designed new software that improved the computer animation of fluids.

There are more than 20 research institutions involved in ICT across the province, such as the Winnipeg branch of TRLabs, part of the largest not-for-profit research and development consortium in Canada. The U OF M has been a part of numerous research and education partnerships with govt and with other academic institutions, and opened the $52-million Engineering and Information Technology Complex in 2005. The U's Internet Innovation Centre has been a key player in Internet-related research projects. MRNet, formed by both private and public organizations and supported by the Canadian Network for the Advancement of Research, Industry, and Education (CANARIE Inc.), provides a high-speed communications network for research and education institutions within the province. • MD

INGALDSON, Fred, Basketball player (b Sep 2, 1932, Pontiac, MI) was one of MB's most prominent basketball players during the 1960s. Ingaldson first played basketball at Isaac Newton High School where he was named outstanding athlete upon graduation. He played for the junior league's Winnipeg Light Infantry, winners of the 1952 National Junior Championship. Ingaldson was then spotted by a scout from Montana State U, and accepted an athletic scholarship. He played for the university's basketball team from 1952-56. A leading scorer, Ingaldson was named the school's most outstanding basketball player in his graduating year. Ingaldson returned to **Winnipeg** and played in the Senior "A" league with the St. Vital Bulldogs before moving east and joining up with the Tillsonburg Livingstons. His performance in the senior leagues earned him a spot on the Cdn basketball team at 3 Olympic Games; 1960 Rome, 1964 Tokyo and 1968 Mexico. He was inducted into the Canadian Basketball Hall of Fame in 2002. • MD

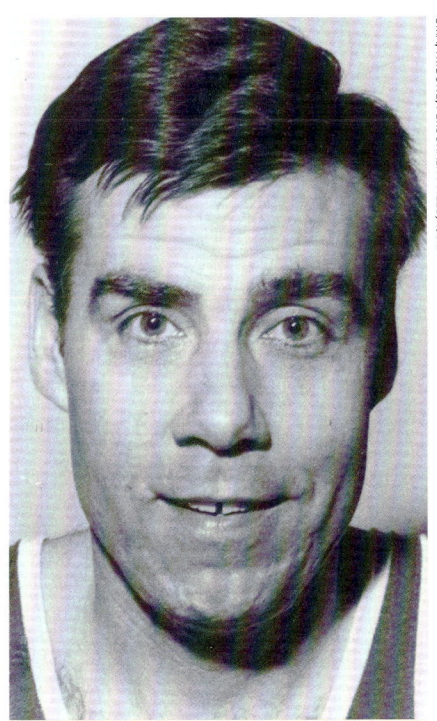

Fred Ingaldson, 1970

Looking south along the row of Inglis Grain Elevators with the Reliance Double Elevators in the forground.

INGLIS, pop 200, is a hamlet 90 km SW of **Dauphin**, near Asessippi Provincial Park and **Lake of the Prairies**. **Ukrainians**, **Germans**, **Scots**, **French**, **Poles**, and **Irish** settled here in the 1880s. The community was incorporated in 1956. Livestock and grain farming are the major industries in the area. Many residents commute to work in **Roblin** and **Russell**. When most historic grain elevators in western Canada were being demolished, Inglis looked ahead and preserved theirs for posterity. The Inglis Grain Elevators National Historic Site, is a tourist attraction of 5 rare wooden structures symbolizing the wheat economy of the early 20th century. The elevators are believed to be the last remaining row of 1920s-style grain elevators in Canada. Four of Inglis's 5 elevators ¬ the Paterson, the United Grain Growers, the National Elevator, and one of the double Reliance elevators – were built in 1922, when the railway line reached the community. The Paterson elevator is now an interpretive centre and museum; another serves as a gift shop. • GPP

INGRAM, Joan, athlete (b Feb 26, 1936, Oakville, MB). Ingram won Cdn championships in 2 sports, curling and softball. Her athletic career, which spanned 60 years, began with a senior women's softball team in **Brandon**. After moving to Winnipeg, she played shortstop for the Canadian Ukrainian Athletic Club (CUAC) Blues, helping the team win the provincial women's title every year from 1957-73, as well as 2 Western Canada titles in 1957

and 1959, and the first Cdn senior women's championship in 1965. Both the team and Ingram are inductees of the **Manitoba Sports Hall of Fame**.

Also an avid curler, Ingram played 3rd on the national title-winning team of Betty Duguid in 1967. She skipped her team to the Cdn final in 1973, winning 3rd place at the championship in 1981. Playing out of the Thistle Business Girls club, her team won the MB senior women's title every year from 1989-93, excepting 1991. She was named the All-Star skip at the 1990 and 1993 Cdn championships. In 2000, she played 3rd on the team that won the provincial masters championship and placed 2nd in the Cdn championship. She was the 2nd woman to be inducted into the Manitoba Curling Hall of Fame. • MD

INKSTER, Colin, sheriff (b Aug 3, 1843, **Red River Settlement**; d Sept 28, 1934, **Winnipeg**) worked as a boy on the farm belonging to his father, **John Inkster**. He attended St. John's College (*see* **U of M**) until 1863, and then freighted between MN and Red River from 1863-70. He met Bishop **Robert Machray** in MN in 1864. In 1871, he became a member of the Manitoba Legislative Council, serving until 1876 and becoming Minister of Agriculture and the council's president in 1874. He cast the deciding vote for abolition of the council in 1876. Upon the council's abolition, he was made high sheriff of MB, a post he held until the province was divided into 3 judicial districts in 1881, at which time he became sheriff of

Colin Inkster, 1920

the eastern district, which he served until 1928. An **ANGLICAN**, he was rector's warden of St. John's Cathedral for over 50 years. In later years, Inkster was always prepared to reminisce about the "early days." A boulevard in Winnipeg is named for him. • JMB

INSECT is a prominent class (Insecta) of jointlegged animals related to shrimps, spiders, centipedes and millipedes. The opposite of vertebrate animals, insects have a hard skeleton on the surface of the body, and musculature on the inside. This tough outer covering is made of chitin – a remarkable carbohydrate macromolecule (polysaccharide) related to the structural cellulose molecule of the plant cell. The insect body consists of 3 basic units – the head with 3 pairs of mouthparts, a pair of compound eyes and sometimes several simple eyes (ocelli), and a pair of antennae which are highly sensitive to touch and chemicals. The thorax is composed of 3 body segments each with a pair of legs (total of 6 legs), and on the upper part, 2 wings – functional in most insects, although some (many weevils) have lost the ability to fly. Finally, the abdomen represents a number of segments which carry the sexual and other organs. Valved openings (spiracles) running alongside the body connect to multi-branching breathing tubes (tracheae) which permit the diffusion and exchange of oxygen and carbon dioxide with the body fluids. A simple heart pumps blood to the head, which circulates slowly through the body, bathing the tissues with nutrients and picking up waste products.

Insects have been living on Earth for at least 420 million years (late Silurian period), making them among the earliest land animals

and the first to develop flight. The ancestors of insects remain unknown and controversial; however, most modern insect groups appeared by 250 mya (Permian period). Insects are unmatched in number of species (living and extinct), diversity of forms, adaptations, biomass (sheer weight of their bodies), and their ecological impact in all ecosystems except marine and polar. Insects owe their phenomenal success to a number of factors – small size which increases niche (role in nature) and habitat opportunities, high reproductive potential, ability to exploit nutrients from any organic source, adaptiveness to evolve to changing environmental conditions, and wings to carry the insects away when local conditions become unlivable. Temperature and daylight are the main stimuli that synchronize stages of the life cycle. Resting stages, which may be in the forms of egg, cyst, larva, pupa, or adult (imago), to pass temporary or extended periods of hostile environmental conditions, are particularly notable in MB's continental and N climate. Periods of activity, egg-laying and hatching are closely tied to daily and seasonal variables to ensure long-term survival in favoured and marginal habitats. Insect reproductive strategy is mainly sexual, which guarantees a high degree of genetic mixing. Typically large numbers of offspring are produced, with most lost before reaching adulthood.

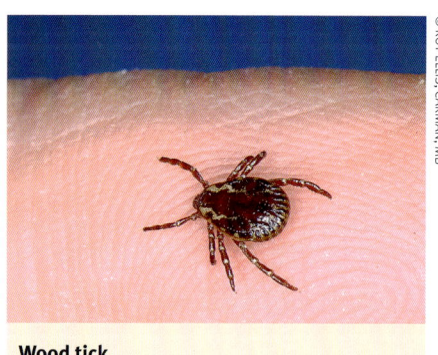

Wood tick

Many of the 29-32 orders of living insects are represented in MB, the more prominent of which are detailed elsewhere in this encyclopedia. About 80% of all insects are classified in only 4 orders – beetles (Coleoptera), flies (Diptera), wasps and ants (Hymenoptera), and butterflies and moths (Lepidoptera) – in which growth involves a transformation (metamorphosis) from cell to larva to pupa to adult (imago). The grublike larva's sole functions are eating and growing, by means of moulting, as each skin of chitin splits and is shed when it becomes too tight. The inactive pupal stage is a period of complete breakdown and reorganization of tissues in preparation for the emergence of the adult. The adult

stage is often abbreviated, just long enough for reproduction. In less advanced orders of insects (e.g., grasshoppers and bugs), metamorphosis is incomplete, meaning the larval stages (called nymphs) resemble the adult and there is no pupal stage. Many insects exploit different habitats when in the larval and adult stages, thereby reducing competition for food and susceptibility to predation.

There are more living species of insects than all other kinds of animals combined, and they also outnumber the plants. Almost one million species have been named worldwide and thousands of new species are described each year. Over 55,000 species have been documented in Canada so far (110,000 total for Canada and the US), but the true figure is likely more than double this figure. There is no reliable estimate on the number species of insects in MB, but it likely exceeds 10,000 and could reach 15,000. World estimates vary from 2-30 million (10 million may be realistic) of which 926,400 have been named to date. Even more remarkable is the belief that today's living fauna of insects is only a small percentage of the insect species that have lived in the past – recently estimated at 100 million. Such magnitude of uncertainty emphasizes just how little attention the group has received, except those that are damaging to human interests, such as agricultural and biting pests. Countless thousands of species, particularly tropical-forest dwellers, have been driven into extinction recently by the activities of our over-abundant species. As habitat destruction and pollution accelerate, so does the extinction rate of all wildlife, currently estimated at 100/day (mostly insects). Considering the critical role of insects in the world's ecosystems, such losses are ominous. For example, over 80% of flowering plants (angiosperms) and crops are dependant on insect pollinators, and in fact the incredible radiation of insects (especially beetles) occurred 100-65 mya (Cretaceous period) with the appearance and evolution of angiosperms. • REW

INSECT CONTROL. The City of **WINNIPEG** has the largest municipal **MOSQUITO**-control program in Canada. Some form of organized program has been in effect since 1927. During this period, nuisance mosquitoes have been the primary focus. There have been several periods, however, when the control of disease-vector mosquitoes was at the forefront. Western equine encephalitis, which was last present in 1983, and more recently, West Nile Virus (WNV), which was first discovered in MB in 2002, are some of the mosquito-borne diseases capable of infecting humans. A comprehensive integrated-pest-management program has been developed for the control of both nuisance and vector mosquitoes in Winnipeg and the surrounding 10 km. The Insect Control Branch considers larviciding, source reduction, and predator enhancement as the most-effective and most-environmentally acceptable methods of reducing larval mosquito numbers. Personal-protection measures are the best methodology for preventing mosquito bites. Larviciding is the largest component of the Insect Control Branch's mosquito control program, though the branch has other urban-pest programs that assist in improving overall quality of life for the city's residents. The 2 major such programs – targeting **ELM** bark beetles and fall and spring cankerworm larvae – are weather-dependant, as pest numbers are directly proportional to weather conditions. These **BEETLES** and cankerworms are serious pests to the health of urban forests.

MOSQUITO CONTROL: There are at least 48 species of mosquitoes in MB and 38 in Winnipeg, each of which has its own range of hosts and environments necessary for development. The main focus of mosquito control is on nuisance mosquitoes. Species like *Aedes vexans* and *Ochlerotatus dorsalis* are floodwater mosquitoes and are painful biters mainly present from dusk to dawn. These primarily nuisance mosquitoes develop rapidly in floodwater or temporary water bodies from summer rainfalls. Generally, nuisance mosquito species overwinter in the egg stage and not as adults. In 2005, Winnipeg's City Council approved a new Insect Control Strategy outlining new framework, direction, and policies for controlling nuisance mosquitoes. Methodologies were identified to shift the control program from mainly a chemically to a biologically based one, ie, the increased use of predators like dragonflies. A new policy was developed, determining that adult mosquito control be implemented only when conditions are conducive for a large mosquito emergence. The adulticiding factor analysis (AFA) guidelines are based on the following factors: soil conditions, daily city-wide average New Jersey Light Trap counts, predicted adult mosquito emergence and development, adult nuisance mosquito population, larval surveillance and predicted emergence, and the "current degree-day" model. These factors are analyzed daily and an AFA rating of low, medium, or high is documented. An AFA of low means operationally enhanced larviciding; medium means enhanced larviciding and barrier treatments for adult mosquitoes (where they rest during the day) with Permethrins; and high means implementing all methods used for AFA medium plus adult mosquito control using Malathion from

ULV (ultra-low volume) truck-mounted sprayers. A less-obvious but more-serious problem is a range of viruses transmitted by mosquitoes. The primary vector for West Nile virus in MB is *Culex tarsalis* – a primarily rural mosquito that develops in sunlit, highly organic waterbodies that are usually associated with animal farms. *Culex* mosquitoes overwinter as adults by entering a resting stage called diapause. The secondary vector is *Culex restuans*, a species that mainly feeds on birds. Determination of the health risk posed by WNV in the province is generally based on vector (risk) index; *Culex tarsalis* generation and age; human population at risk; time of year; and past and predicted weather conditions.

DUTCH ELM DISEASE: The fungus *Ophiostoma ulmi* causes DED. Two species of elm bark beetle, the native *Hylurgopinus rufipes* and the introduced European species *Scotylus multistriatus*, transmit this fungus. DED was initially detected in Winnipeg in 1975, and has since been spreading throughout the large urban American elms (*Ulmus americana*). In certain years, elm tree losses have been substantial, reaching 4-5% of the population. A comprehensive management program has kept losses minimal, and consequently a large elm population still survives in Winnipeg. The elm bark beetles have rapidly diffused across the country due to the movement of infected elm wood by humans. Natural means of disease transmission include root grafting and the natural feeding of the beetles in the tree canopy. The insects overwinter as adults at the base of elms, where females lay eggs in brood chambers. The larvae feed on the xylem and phloem tissues (water/nutrient-transmitting vessels) of the tree, while larval and pupal stages are spent between the bark and sapwood. If the

tree is infected with DED, the newly emerging adult beetles become covered with sticky fungal spores. The adults then fly to a nearby stressed elm and infect it. Monitoring for a DED symptom known as "flagging" occurs in summer, when elm trees grow rapidly. Flagging is the yellowing, curling, and then turning brown of the leaves on one or more branches of the tree. A branch sample is taken, and once the laboratory confirms a positive test for DED, the infected tree is destroyed. Additional prevention of the spread of DED by the bark beetles is accomplished by a basal-spray program (with Dursban Turf), treating the bottom 50 cm of the elm. This kills adult beetles entering the tree to overwinter as well as emerging new adults the following spring.

CANKERWORMS: Cankerworms are not worms but **MOTHS** that cause serious depredations of urban elms (*Ulmus americana*) and other ornamental trees. Two species are responsible – fall (*Alsophila pometaria*) and spring (*Paleacrita vernata*) cankerworms. Tree banding with adhesives prevents the wingless adult female from climbing up the trunk to lay its 50-200 eggs in the tree canopy. A tree band is a piece of insulation covered by plastic and coated with a sticky agent. Fall adult winged males and wingless females emerge in mid-Sept from the pupal stage. Generally, a hard frost activates the pupae, and the adults emerge to lay the eggs of the next generation. These eggs overwinter in the canopy and emerge in the spring when the tree buds break out. At the same time in the spring, adult spring cankerworm adults emerge to lay their eggs in the canopy. The spring cankerworm pupae remain in the ground over summer, fall, and winter, and emerge when temperatures rise the following spring. Both fall and spring larval

Insect control, 1927

cankerworms feed on the canopy vegetation and may defoliate trees in years of severe infestation. Trees respond after being defoliated with a 2nd generation of leaves, but over multiple years of heavy feeding, the tree will begin to die back. Cankerworm larvae live for about 3 weeks. During this feeding stage, the Insect Control Branch uses a bacterial spray (*Bacillus thuringiensis kurstaki*) applied with a high-pressure tree sprayer to control the feeding larvae biologically. Once an untreated larva has undergone 4 moulting stages (instars), it moves off the vegetation and hangs by a silken thread. Dropping to the ground, the larva burrows into the soil and pupates. Residents are encouraged to band trees early in Sept and to leave them on all winter, and then to reapply a sticky agent like Tanglefoot in the spring. The bands need to be removed by the end of June, since the bands will cause damage to the trunk of the trees if left on all summer.
● T. D. T. STUART

INTERLAKE is the provincially designated region found directly N of **WINNIPEG**, between the southern portions of **LAKE WINNIPEG** and **LAKE MANITOBA**. The area probably derived its name after the Interlachen area of Switzerland, and after the MB region's situation between the 2 large lakes. About 82,000 people inhabit the 16 rural municipalities and First Nations communities scattered throughout the district, though the population of cottagers, sightseers, and summer-camp attendees, mainly from Winnipeg, swells in summer. In the S of the region, the mouth of the **RED RIVER** forms the large **NETLEY-LIBAU MARSH** area. The flat central portion, dominated by mixed farming, gives way to marshland and more lakes in the N. Limestone bedrock is predominant, and the rock lines the shores of the lakes. The Lake St. Martin Impact Structure, a meteorite crater 24 km across, is near **GYPSUMVILLE**.

For thousands of years various Aboriginal tribes engaged in hunting, mostly **BISON**, but also fishing, **FUR TRAPPING**, and gathering. Plains Cree and **OJIBWAY**, who arrived in the area in the 18th century, still maintain settlements such as **PEGUIS**, **BROKENHEAD**, Dog Creek, **LITTLE SASKATCHEWAN**,

Rural Municipalities in Interlake	
Armstrong	Bifrost
Coldwell	East St. Paul
Eriksdale	Fisher
Gimli	Grahamdale
Rockwood	Rosser
Siglunes	St. Andrews
St. Clements	St. Laurent
West St. Paul	Woodlands

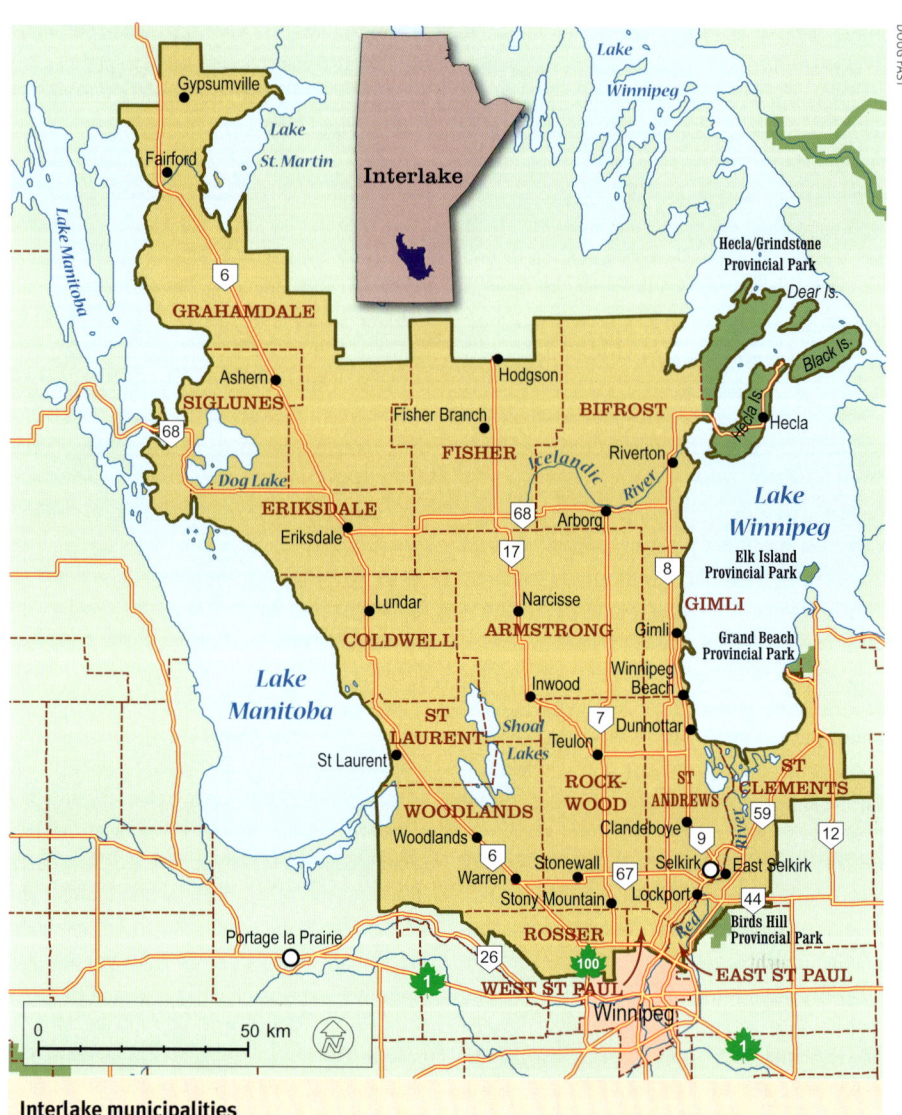

Interlake municipalities

DOUG FAST

LAKE MANITOBA, PINAYMOOTANG, FISHER RIVER, DAUPHIN RIVER, LAKE ST. MARTIN, and The Narrows. The region is also home to **ST. LAURENT**, perhaps the world's best-preserved **MÉTIS** community. In 1875, **ICELANDERS** made their way to MB and founded **GIMLI**, the capital of the **NEW ICELAND** reserve. In the rest of the region, however, people of **ENGLISH**, **UKRAINIAN**, and **SCOTS** descent are most numerous.

Cattle Farming and Hog Farming join **GRAIN** production as important staples of the regional economy, and Commercial Fishing and **TOURISM** are important to lakeshore communities. Ecotourism also draws wildlife-watchers to places such as **OAK HAMMOCK MARSH** and **NARCISSE**. Manufacturing is prevalent in Gimli and **SELKIRK**, though many residents of the southern Interlake commute to Winnipeg from bedroom communities N of the city. Selkirk remains the largest centre, but **STONEWALL** has experienced strong growth with a population increase of about 33% between 1991 and 2001. Gimli, **TEULON**, and **ARBORG** are the other important centres. ● JOEL TRENAMAN

INTERLAKE VOTE SPLITTING SCANDAL was a scheme developed and financed by leading members of the MB **PROGRESSIVE CONSERVATIVE PARTY** during the 1995 Manitoba election to run independent aboriginal candidates in three provincial ridings then held by the **NDP**. Since in previous elections, aboriginal people in these three ridings (**INTERLAKE**, **DAUPHIN** and **SWAN RIVER**) had voted in overwhelming numbers for NDP candidates, the Conservative strategists hoped that the candidates, who ran under banner of the Independent Native Voice (INV) party, would draw votes away from the NDP and provide the local PC candidates with the margin of victory. The plan failed to achieve its goal and all three ridings were held by the NDP. Following the election the NDP made allegations of improprieties. However, a provincial government investigation concluded that no election laws had been broken.

The issue lay dormant until the spring of 1998 when CBC Radio reporter Curt Petrovich revealed that the provincial investigation had failed to interview Darryl Sutherland, the INV candidate in the Interlake riding. In interviews Sutherland confirmed that the PC campaign manager for the Interlake riding, Allan Aitken, had recruited him, and that PC fundraiser Percival "Cubby" Barrett had paid for his campaign. Sutherland also said that he passed money from the PCs to two other INV candidates, Nelson and Carey Contois.

These allegations forced Premier **GARY FILMON** to appoint former Chief Justice **ALFRED MONNIN** to head a commission of inquiry into the allegations. During this inquiry it was revealed that leading members of the Filmon government and the PC Party had been involved in funding the INV campaign and subsequently covering up this fundraising activity. Filmon's principal secretary, Taras Sokolyk, and the Secretary of the Treasury Board, Julian Benson, both resigned as a result of their involvement in the scheme. Monnin's 1999 report called the scheme unethical and morally reprehensible but concluded that Filmon had not been aware of either the plot or the cover up. While Monnin identified a number of apparent violations of the Manitoba Elections Act, the Manitoba govt, based on the recommendations of a review of the case by an out-of-province lawyer, decided not to prosecute any of the individuals involved in the case. The Filmon government's public image was severely damaged by the information brought to light during the inquiry and it was voted out of office in 1999. ● DOUG SMITH

INTERNATIONAL BOUNDARY WATERS TREATY.

The 1909 agreement between Canada and the US regulates the use of lakes and rivers through which the international border runs (boundary waters), and rivers that flow across the international border (transboundary rivers). The treaty granted both countries freedom to navigate boundary waters and also established the International Joint Commission (IJC) to oversee disputes. The treaty prohibits any obstruction or diversion of boundary waters or transboundary rivers that would affect the level or flow on the other side (unless approved by the IJC). It also prohibits any obstructions on transboundary rivers on the downstream side that would cause a rise in level on the upstream side without IJC approval. Finally, there must be no pollution on one side "to the injury of health or property on the other."

MB has few transboundary lakes; in the SE, the border with MN extends 5 km into Buffalo Bay, an arm of Lake of the Woods (see North West Angle); and in the SW, the international boundary passes through some small lakes in Turtle Mountain. However, because MB's southern boundary – the international border – cuts across natural drainage lines, the province has several transboundary rivers, including the Antler, **SOURIS**, **PEMBINA**, **RED**, and Roseau.

The IJC scrutinizes projects that have an effect, or potential effect, on boundary waters and transboundary rivers. It considers "applications" for approval of projects and accepts "references" when a problem has arisen, in which case it is asked for a judgment, which the two countries usually accept, although the IJC's decision is not binding. Winnipeg was an early applicant, asking for permission to divert water from Shoal Lake, a bay off Lake of the Woods. In 1912, concerns about water levels on Lake of the Woods led to a reference to the IJC, resulting in the Lake of the Woods Convention and Protocol (1925), which established the International Lake of the Woods Control Board. This control board decides when to discharge from the lake when levels are high, as they were in 1985.

The Souris, Pembina, Red, and Roseau rivers have all been the subjects of references to the IJC, starting with the flood-prone Roseau River in 1929. In 1940, each country's federal govt asked the commission to investigate regulation, use, and flow of the Souris and its tributaries, and division of water between the two countries. Its recommendations were made in 1941 and revised in 1958, 1992, and 2000. It also established the International Souris River Board, to assist in preventing and resolving disputes. Flooding along the lower reaches of the Pembina River in the US resulted in a reference in 1962, but two recommended dams were never built. In 1964, the IJC was asked to study **POLLUTION** in the Red River. It created a Red River Pollution Board, which in 2001 was subsumed by the more inclusive International Red River Board. Following the 1997 **FLOOD** in the **RED RIVER VALLEY**, which caused damages approaching $5 billion USD, the Cdn and US govts asked the commission to examine floods in the Red's basin. Its final report, published in 2000, made 28 recommendations to avoid or reduce damages from future floods, and concluded that Winnipeg had narrowly averted disaster in 1997, and would be in danger from larger floods.

In 1975, the contentious Garrison Diversion Project in Devils Lake, ND, was referred to the IJC. The project aimed to provide water for irrigation and for rural, municipal, and industrial use. Because it would have resulted in the transfer of the Missouri water into the Hudson Bay drainage basin, with negative effects in MB, the IJC recommended that the project as originally planned should not proceed. However, this issue was not completely resolved. The original Garrison Diversion Project included provisions for an artificial increase in the level of Devils Lake, to improve its recreational potential, but between 1993 and 1999 the lake rose naturally by 7.6m causing flooding in the surrounding area. A suggested solution is artificial drainage of the lake into the Sheyenne River, a tributary of the Red River. In 2005, both the MB and the Canadian govts expressed opposition to this outlet for fear that foreign biota would make their way into the Red River system. MB's govt has argued strenuously for a reference to the IJC but to no avail. ● JOHN WELSTED

INTERNATIONAL PEACE GARDEN.

The International Peace Garden straddles the MB-US border S of **BOISSEVAIN**, adjacent to Turtle Mountain Provincial Park. Dedicated on July 14, 1932, the garden was conceived of in 1928 by Henry J. Moore, a horticulturalist from Islington, ON, to celebrate the vast undefended border between the US and Canada. Both the MB and the ND govts offered land that featured wheat fields and forest along the border, in the Turtle Mountain area. The agreements were signed in Dec 1931. In the 1930s, the Civilian Conservation Corps built many of the buildings, roads, and extensive gardens in the park. A Peace Chapel and a Veterans Memorial Bell Tower were constructed in 1976, using the chimes from the first United

STAN MILOSEVIC. WWW.MANITOBAPHOTOS.COM

Peace Towers in the International Peace Gardens near Boissevain

Church of Brandon, originally a memorial to Lady Arma Sifton. The State of ND adopted the nickname "Peace Garden State" in 1957, though the motto had previously been used unofficially on vehicle licence plates.

On the garden's 50th anniversary in 1982, 2 peace towers were erected: a 37-m-high pillar on each side of the border. The US Postal Service also issued a commemorative stamp that year. The grounds of the park constitute 947 ha (2339 ac), much of it featuring elaborate gardens of some 150,000 flowers. The park, which is open all day, year-round, is also used for conferences and music and athletic camps in the summer. The Peace Garden can be reached via MB Hwy 10. Customs posts allow the visitor to cross the border. A memorial of twisted steel girders marks the destruction of New York's World Trade Center in 2001. The park is run as a non-profit organization, whose 20 board members come in equal numbers from the US and Canada. ● GPP

INVERTEBRATE, FRESHWATER is a fauna of microscopic to small-sized creatures without backbones that live in MB's myriad of lakes, rivers, ponds, and sloughs. Various kinds of animal species are adapted to variables of the freshwater environment, such as great temperature fluctuations, ice cover, oxygen content, acidity, current, periodic or continual silting, pollution, and others. Consequently, freshwater is a more-challenging environment than saltwater – the ancestral habitat of almost all freshwater organisms (except insects, mites and pulmonate snails). Freshwater contains dissolved solids leached from the land, largely carbonates and bicarbonates, and so animal life living here is termed a 'carbonate fauna.' Freshwater may range from highly acidic (pH 4.4) to basic (pH 8.8). The latter are alkali or salt lakes and ponds, which carry a high load of dissolved carbonates, sodium chloride and sulphates. During periods of low rainfall, salt flats may be seen where ponds dried up, or along the shore of lakes. Relatively few life forms are specialized to thrive in such hostile conditions, such as single-celled life (ciliates, flagellates, amoebas), rotifers, midges, copepods, brine shrimp, and a few beetles. Some of these survive a dry period in the forms of resistant eggs, thick-walled cysts, or other resting stages. Moist sandy or muddy shores are host to a micro-fauna of rotifers, gastrotrichs, tardigrades, nematodes (roundworms), and copepods. These species feed on even-tinier creatures and graze on the organic slime in the spaces between the soil particles.

Extracting sufficient oxygen from freshwater is a major challenge for aquatic insects, since dissolved oxygen is at much lower levels than in air, and is highly variable (affected by temperature, dissolved solids, depth, current, etc) among different waterbodies and even the same one at different times of the year. In MB winters, organisms (especially fish) sometimes die from lack of oxygen due to the ice cover blocking oxygen renewal, creating lethal anaerobic conditions. Insects and other aquatic creatures have evolved many ways of efficiently absorbing oxygen – cutaneous respiration (through a thin outer layer), gills in various parts of the body, oral and rectal tissues, contractions of the internal tracheal system, capturing temporary air bubbles, body movements, and respiratory pigments like hemoglobin (which occurs in most animal phyla).

Freshwater environments present many habitable opportunities for small organisms, such as sediments at depths or in shallows; mud, sand and rock beaches; vertical water column, air/water film, shallow riffles, fast or standing water, ditches to vast lakes, and many sorts of substrates (plants and logs). Insects have been categorized by niche as skaters (on the surface), divers, active swimmers, floaters (planktonic), crawlers, climbers, and burrowers. Feeding types include predators, engulfers, net strainers, scrapers, shredders, piercers (sucking), parasites, and parasitoids (killing their hosts). Considering that there are over 1200 aquatic insects in MB alone, the entire freshwater fauna and flora of the province, from protozoans and algae to mammals, likely exceeds 10,000 species. ● REW

INVERTEBRATE, MARINE is a fauna of microscopic to small-sized creatures without back-bones that dwell in the enormous inland sea called the Hudson Bay Marine Ecosystem. Relatively little is known about these animals, since they are covered by 2-5 m of ice for 7 months of the year, and research in this harsh N climate is challenging and costly even in summer. However, there are well over 1000 species of animal life carrying out their complex and fascinating life cycles within a vast food web in the salt waters and estuaries off the MB coastline. (By comparison, there are about 14,000 marine species of plants and animals along the BC coast). No one has an idea of the full diversity of micro-organisms present in MB's marine waters, but they (e.g., bacteria and algae) are the food supply of over 557 species of multi-celled invertebrates (or metazoans) in at least 15 phyla (major animal groups), and 18 species of sea squirts Chordata) that have been recorded in W and central Hudson Bay. Over 132 additional species occur in the N Hudson Strait and in James Bay to the S. The majority of species arrived here as Arctic Ocean biota following the retreat of the Laurentide Glacier 7500 years ago, but some are representative of the Atlantic and rarely the Pacific faunas. In the coming years, many more species will be discovered and added to this diverse assemblage of animals.

The salt concentration of oceans, and hence Hudson Bay, varies from 3.3-3.7% (diluted near large rivers), over 80% of which consists of dissolved sodium chloride, giving rise to what is called a 'chloride fauna.' Salt water has a basic pH of 7.8-8.3. Both factors are important in the physiology of marine organisms. With a length of 1500 km, width of 830 km, and area of 637,000 km^2, Hudson Bay is one of the largest inland seas in the word. It is joined to the Arctic Ocean by Foxe Channel, through which pass many life forms. Creatures are carried in the counterclockwise current (.2 km/hr) coming from NW Hudson Bay, and passing S along the MB coastline. Countless rivers discharge 31,000 m^3/sec of freshwater – more than all the rivers flowing from NA into the Atlantic and Pacific oceans. During the ice-free period of July and Aug, the water warms to 10°C, resulting in a peak concentration of marine life. Few people standing on the shore and looking out over Hudson Bay could imagine the wealth of life in these waters.

The following is a list of the major groups of invertebrates recorded in this marine ecosystem: annelid worms, ribbon worms, phoronid worms, penis worms, peanut worms, crustaceans (copepods, amphipods, barnacles, shrimps, krill, crabs, isopod), sea spiders, aschelminthes (including round worms), bryozoans, arrow worms, cnidarians (jellies, medusae, hydroids, sea anemones, soft coral), comb jellies, echinoderms (sea stars, feather stars, sea urchins, sea cucumbers, brittle stars), sponges, lamp shells, and molluscs (snails, clams, mussels, scallops, chitins, tooth shells). Some species have yet to be identified.

Remarkably, a microfauna continues to survive for most of the year (Nov-June) within the lower few cm of the ice – the 'ice fauna' – consisting of rotifers, nematodes, protozoans, copepods and many other groups, feeding on each other and on ice algae, and greatly accelerating their feeding and reproduction with the spring algal bloom. The myriad of creatures of the zooplankton are fed upon by larger invertebrates and fish larvae, and these feed larger fish, which are in turn preyed on by sea birds, seals, whales, and these latter animals are food for top predators like the Polar Bear, Arctic Fox and Humans. All this wealth of life is carried along the MB coast by the steady current circulating around the Bay. Species composition and population sizes continue to fluctuate through the year in response to available sunlight, ice cover, temperature, nutrient levels, mixing of waters, and varying pulsations of salinity (brackish on the surface, saltier near the bottom). While not in sufficient abundance to support a commercial harvest, clams, scallops, the Green Sea Urchin, shrimps, crabs, and brittle stars are eaten by local people. ● DBS, FOC, REW

INVESTORS GROUP INC. is Canada's largest mutual funds company and a leader in providing financial planning advice and services to Canadians. As of mid-2005, the **WINNIPEG**-based firm was managing more than $48 billion in client assets through a network of 113 financial planning centres and approximately 3500 consultants. In addition to its own family of mutual funds and other investment vehicles, the company also offers a wide range of mortgage, insurance, brokerage and banking services. Investors Group traces its roots back to 1896, when Minneapolis lawyer John Tappan founded a new financial services company called Investors Syndicate because he felt consumers needed a better way to build their savings. For the first 30 years, Investors Syndicate operations were focused on the US. In 1926, the company expanded to Canada, and by 1940 its operations N of the border had grown to 13 sales offices in 7 provinces and nearly $10 million in client assets. That same year, the company created a new subsidiary, Investors Syndicate of Canada, to oversee its Cdn operations. Headquartered in Winnipeg, the new subsidiary, which later shortened its name to Investors Group Inc., soon became a leader in the financial planning industry in Canada and a pioneer in the establishment of mutual funds. Its first mutual fund, Investors Mutual of Canada, was launched in 1950 and remains the country's oldest active mutual fund. Today, Investors Group is a member of the IGM Financial Inc. group of companies. Winnipeg-based IGM Financial was formed in Apr 2004 as the publicly traded holding company for Investors Group, Toronto-based MacKenzie Financial Corporation, which Investors acquired in 2001, and IPC Financial Network, which it purchased in 2004. The company, along with **GREAT-WEST LIFE**, is owned by Montreal-based Power Corp. ● MURRAY MCNEILL

INWOOD, pop 200, is a community about 75 km NNW of **WINNIPEG** in the **INTERLAKE** region. Until 1912, Inwood was known as Cossette Post Office, named after early settlers. However, the settlers apparently changed the community's name to recognize the fact that train service went on a "turn around" into the woods. Rail service, plus the expansion of the Colonization Rd, attracted more settlers from diverse ethnic backgrounds – **UKRAINIANS**, Poles, Swedes, Danes, **GERMANS**, Norwegians, **FRENCH**, and **ICELANDERS**. In the 2000s, Inwood is a service centre for a mixed agricultural area and is home to many commuters and retirees. The community has a hotel, garage, K-12 school, golf course, and the offices of the RM of Armstrong. A 4.6-m statue of 2 intertwined red-sided garter snakes marks Inwood's location at the southern extreme of the snakes' denning area (*see* **NARCISSE**). Thousands of snakes can be seen in May as they make their way out of their dens. Local festivals include an annual Ice Carnival in early March. ● GPP

IRISH. There has been a strong Irish presence in MB since 1811. At that time, various labourers were brought over by **LORD SELKIRK** to help prepare his new colony at **RED RIVER**. **ANDREW MCDERMOT**, from Belanagare, County Roscom, Ireland, was hired by the **HBC** and arrived at Red River in 1812. He would later play a significant role in the **RED RIVER SETTLEMENT** as a fur trader and businessman. During the **SEVEN OAKS INCIDENT** on June 19, 1816, another Irish immigrant, John Palmer Bourke, was wounded in the groin. Unlike Gov **ROBERT SEMPLE** and 20 other colonists, Bourke survived the conflict.

Winnipeg's most famous street corner – Portage and Main – was created by **HENRY MCKENNEY**, who was born in Amherstburg, ON, to immigrants from Ireland. After his arrival in **WINNIPEG** in 1859, McKenney bought a store from McDermot and promptly converted it into the community's first hotel. On March 4, 1870, **LOUIS RIEL**'s provisional govt executed **THOMAS SCOTT**, a Protestant Orangeman born in Ireland. This action outraged Ontarians who convinced Cdn PM Sir John A. Macdonald to send an army to quell the uprising. Among the militia from eastern Canada arriving in the settlement in Aug 1870 were a number of Irish Orangemen, mainly from Northern Ireland, intent upon revenging the murder of Scott. In the months after their arrival, they created such havoc within MB that the eastern **NEWSPAPERS** began to describe a "reign of terror" existing in MB.

Fenians, Irish-Americans intent upon invading Canada, capturing the country and holding it for ransom until the British government granted Irish independence, created the first real panic in the new province. But the Fenians were engaged in a fool's errand, since Canadians vigorously fought back and the few invasions northward by Fenians were repulsed. A threatened 1871 Fenian invasion of MB was nipped in the bud when its ringleaders were captured near Pembina by American troops. Among the leaders was William O'Donoghue, an American who favoured annexation of western Canada to the US. He also was a former colleague of Riel in the provisional govt.

Thomas Sharpe, who was born in Sligo, Ireland, in 1866, was Winnipeg's mayor for 2 terms starting in 1903. **NELLIE MCCLUNG**, Manitoba's most famous suffragette, who helped women in the province get the vote in 1916, was another child of an Irish immigrant. MB's first and only PM of Canada, though only briefly, was Arthur Meighen, whose parents were born in Northern

Irish dancers at Folklorama pavilion

Ireland and settled in Ontario. Meighen was described as "Irish to the core" and delighted in Irish history and POETRY.

KILLARNEY, MB, named in 1883 after the town and lakes in County Kerry, Ireland, by Irish-born surveyor John Sidney O'Brien, holds its own St. Patrick's Day events on March 17. According to legend, O'Brien sat on the shore of the then-called Oak Lake and in a fit of home sickness for his native land, took out a bottle of "Good Irish" whiskey from his pack, poured a portion into the lake and christened it Killarney. The town of Killarney was incorporated in 1906.

The Irish had a great deal to do with the early social history of MB. It is said that the RED RIVER JIG is a descendent of an Irish dance. During her visit to Winnipeg in 1877 with her husband, Cdn gov gen Lord Dufferin, Lady Dufferin wrote in her journal after she saw the Red River Jig performed for the first time, she felt it was exactly the same as an Irish Jig. Irish immigrants and their descendants in MB have always celebrated St. Patrick's Day with song and dance. A dinner on the evening of St. Patrick's Day was a tradition that continued for years in Winnipeg. In 1894, 100 Irish-Canadians gathered at the Clarendon Hotel on the evening of March 17 for a feast in a banquet chamber artistically decorated with the insignia of England, and the banner of the St. Patrick's society. The celebration of St. Patrick's Day in MB remains a tradition. The Irish Club in Winnipeg on Erin Street has created what it calls a non-sectarian St. Patrick's Festival, with 3 evenings of MUSIC, DANCE, and song for members and non-members alike. ● BRUCE CHERNEY

ISAACS, Leonard, teacher, pianist, conductor, broadcaster (b Manchester, UK, Jan 3, 1909; d WINNIPEG, Dec 6, 1997). Isaacs studied piano initially with his father, concert pianist Edward Isaacs, then piano and horn at the Royal College of Music in London, 1925-29, plus piano in Paris with Alfred Cortot and in Berlin with Egon Petri. He toured Canada in 1931-32 as a pianist and assistant conductor for the English Light Opera Co. Returning to England, he freelanced as accompanist to cellist Maurice Hardy and orchestrated musicals and film scores for composer Richard Addinsell. In 1936, he joined the BBC, remaining with them as a distinguished radio producer for 26 years. Having become known in Winnipeg through adjudicating competitions during the 1950s, in 1963, Isaacs moved to Winnipeg and became director of the U OF M's School of Music, serving until 1974. He continued teaching at the U of Calgary, Carleton U, and the Banff School of Fine Arts, as well as giving private tuition. He gave many broadcasts on CBC Radio,

and contributed program notes and pre-concert lectures to the WINNIPEG SYMPHONY ORCHESTRA. His publications include a chamber orchestra arrangement of J. S. Bach's *The Art of Fugue* (1952), several times recorded. ● DON ANDERSON

ISABELLA is a ghost town 80 km NW of BRANDON. From Brandon, where the railway ended, early settlers of Isabella had to make their way up the ASSINIBOINE RIVER by steamer, then made the remaining 40-km journey in RED RIVER CARTS or by horse and buggy. Although the route was arduous, settlement continued in the district, though it would take until 1906 before a school and post office were built. The post office was named after the first postmistress, Isabella Taylor. The CNoR arrived in 1909 and was a relief for local farmers who until then had to make long hauls to sell their grain. A grain elevator was built the following year. Two more followed soon after. Community spirit was high with music, drama, a horticultural society, and a Women's Institute. However, that spirit was not enough to save a community that had been so hard to build. The population dwindled in the 1970s with the consolidation of schools, the loss of the railway, and the appeal of other, larger towns. ● GPP

ISBISTER, Alexander Kennedy, educator, ABORIGINAL RIGHTS reformer (b June, 1822, Cumberland House [SK]; d May 28, 1883, Barnsbury [now part of London], UK) defended RED RIVER SETTLEMENT residents in the British parliament. He was the son of an Orkney clerk of the HBC and a mixed-blood daughter of Alexander Kennedy and his CREE wife, Aggathas. He was originally schooled in the Orkney Islands, but he returned to RUPERT'S LAND to attend Red River Academy (1833-37). Isbister entered HBC service in 1838, but was unhappy with the lack of advancement granted to mixed-bloods. He resigned in 1841 and left for Great Britain in 1842. He attended King's College, Aberdeen, for 2 years, and the U of Edinburgh for one year. He joined the staff of East Islington Proprietary School in 1848, was headmaster in 1851, and moved to a series of more prestigious headmaster appointments.

Isbister became active with the College of Preceptors that oversaw the English teaching profession. He edited its magazine, the *Educational Times*, and was dean after 1872. He was a prolific author of school textbooks, receiving an MA from the U of Edinburgh in 1858 and an LLB from the U of London in 1866. Not surprisingly, he fought hard and long on behalf of his mixed-blood countrymen, whom he regarded as being under the tyranny of HBC. In 1847, he presented to the Colonial Office a petition from 1000 of the

Red River's inhabitants for status as a recognized colony, and he was an active lobbyist on behalf of the settlement with the public and the British authorities. He also wrote *A Proposal for a New Penal Settlement in the Uninhabited Districts of British North America* (1850) and, with A. W. Chesson, *The Red River Insurrection: Three Letters and a Narrative of Events* (1870). In 1857, Isbister testified before the parliamentary inquiry investigating the charter of the HBC. He endowed a schools prize for the Red River Settlement in 1867 (now awarded by St. John's College [*see* U OF M]) and a trust fund for scholars) at the U of M. In addition, he left his extensive collection of nearly 5000 books to the U of M. Regrettably, most were lost in a fire in 1898. ● JMB

ISLAM is an ancient and broadly based religion, spanning some 1400 years and stretching geographically from Indonesia to North Africa. The first centuries of Islam saw the development of many different schools of thought, such as the Sunni and Shi'i traditions, and witnessed varied divisions of opinion within the Muslim community. Some of Islam's central beliefs, institutions and practices include a belief in God's unity (*tawhid*), the revelation of the Qur'an to the Prophet Muhammad, the practice of 5 daily prayers (*salat*), giving alms (*zakat*), performing the pilgrimage to Mecca (*hajj*), with particular emphasis placed on the study of the Qur'an and the body of traditions (*hadith*) associated with the Prophet Muhammad.

The first Muslim communities in MB date back to the turn of the 20th century, when families arrived in the province from eastern Europe, Lebanon and the Caribbean Islands. In the 1950s, families of Indo-Pakistani and Arabic background begin to study and settle in MB, especially in the city of WINNIPEG. By 1966, Sunday noon prayer was held on a regular basis in the basement of one family's house: at the time, there were roughly 25 Muslim families in Winnipeg. In 1967, Muslims in Winnipeg formed an organization that would later become known as the Manitoba Islamic Association. As the population of Muslims grew in Winnipeg, the Sunday noon prayers were moved to a Unitarian church. Between the years 1969-1972, there were several developments within the Muslim community in Winnipeg: most markedly, the Manitoba Islamic Association was legally incorporated, fundraising for the first mosque (*masjid*) commenced, the Sunday noon prayer was moved from the Unitarian church elsewhere, and congregational Friday prayers (*Juma'ah*) began to be held on a regular basis at the U OF M. By 1975, the first Manitoba Islamic Association mosque had been constructed

JEWS,
see page 357
Honeymoon departure of Edward Kopstein
and Sybil Myers, CPR Station, 1912

J

JACKSON, Samuel Jacob "Stonewall," businessman, politician (b Feb. 18, 1848, Stradbally, Ireland; d May 29, 1942, **STONEWALL**). Born to Methodist Irish father Samuel Jackson Sr. and mother Elizabeth Sutcliffe, Jackson's family moved to Brampton, ON, in 1850, where the father opened a dry goods store. Jackson came to MB from ON in 1871 as part of a survey crew, taking the train from Port Huron to the terminus at Benson, MN, and walking the 645 km from Benson to the **RED RIVER SETTLEMENT**. Two years later, Jackson bought land 30 km NW of Red River, at the town of Stonewall's future site. The **CPR** arrived in Winnipeg in 1878, and the land Jackson purchased was supposed to be an important stopping point on Canada's main line. But the **RAILWAY** changed its mind, directing the main line straight W from Winnipeg. Undeterred, Jackson had his land resurveyed in 1880, divided it into 1000 lots, drew up a town map, and named many of the streets. He gave land and seed money to business operators. Building sites were free to those who promised to build a house to his specifications and to plant trees. The town's name probably was selected by its owner because his surname called to mind the US Confederate leader, LGen Thomas Jonathan "Stonewall" Jackson.

Samuel Jackson started *The Stonewall News*, **NEWSPAPER** (later the *Argus*) in 1882, its front page serving as his personal election pamphlet. He won his first provincial election in 1883 representing Rockwood for the **LIBERAL PARTY**, and took the next 6 elections. In the 1896 election – in which Jackson supported "national schools" rather than restoring separate schools taken away from French Roman Catholics in 1890 (*see* **MANITOBA SCHOOLS QUESTION**) – electors gave Jackson a 50-vote majority. He was speaker of the legislative assembly 1891-95. From 1904-1908, he served as MP for **SELKIRK**. He ran unsuccessfully in 1908, whereupon he quit politics. • JIM SHILLIDAY

JACKSON, Tom, singer/songwriter, actor, (b Oct 27, 1948, One Arrow First Nation, SK). Born to an **ENGLISH** father and a **CREE** mother, Jackson developed an affinity for music by age 7. Moving to **WINNIPEG** in 1963, he began performing 2 years later in folk clubs, including The Purple Pit at the Indian and Métis Friendship Centre on Donald St. He sang the traditional "Huron Carol" on CJAY-TV's *Christmas in a Global Village* (1965). Travelling E in 1969, Jackson performed at the Mariposa Folk Festival in Orillia, ON, and the Rainbow Bar and Grill in Montreal. In 1971, he recorded "White Man Listen" for the Manitoba Indian Brotherhood to commemorate the anniversary of the 1871 signing of Treaties 1 and 2. Throughout the '70s, he performed as Tom Jackson and Friends with Fred Dawes, Bill Merritt, Chris the Shark, Norm Dugas, Dave Wood, the Kozub sisters, and Dave Kramer. For a time, Jackson operated a restaurant and bar, TJ's 2 for 1 Steak House on Edmonton St, and opened a club, the Treble Clef, on River Ave.

Tom Jackson

An interest in acting led Jackson to perform with **Prairie Theatre Exchange** in 1979-80, which led to a recurring spot on *Sesame Street* and ultimately to roles in movies including *The Diviners* (based on a work by **Margaret Laurence**), *Grizzly Falls*, and *Water Giant*. His TV appearances include *Star Trek: The Next Generation*, *Longhouse Tales*, and a starring role in the long-running Cdn drama *North of 60*. Jackson has recorded 13 albums, including *The Huron Carol* (1988, 1994, and 1998); *Sally Ann* (1990); *Love, Lust, and Longing* (1992); *No Regrets* (1995); *That Side of the Window* (1997); *I Will Bring You Near* (2001); and *On the Holiday Train* (2003). In 1981, Jackson organized the first Huron Carol concert for food banks – the annual events have raised more than $3.8 million. He received the Canadian Aboriginal Music Award for Best Producer (1999), the Order of Canada (2000), a Lifetime Achievement Award from the Ontario Country Music Association (2000), the Queen's Jubilee Medal (2002), and Centennial Medals from AB and SK (2005). He has been named Canada's top activist by *Time* magazine, and has honorary degrees from the **U of W** and from several other Cdn institutions. • JOHN EINARSON

JACOBS, Jack "Indian Jack," football player (b Aug 7, 1919, Holdenville, Okla; d Jan 12, 1974, Greensboro, NC), is credited with introducing the forward pass to CFL football as a quarterback for the **Winnipeg Blue Bombers**. He played in the NFL for Cleveland, Washington and Green Bay before signing with the Bombers in 1950. Called

"Indian Jack" because of his full Cherokee ancestry, Jacobs quickly became one of the league's star players, helping improve the Bombers' 1950 record to 10-4 over the previous season's 2-12. Over the next 5 seasons, Jacobs completed 709 of 1130 passes for 11,094 yds, with 104 touchdown passes. In 1952, he won the Jeff Nicklin Trophy for Western Conference MVP. He went on to coach the London Lords in the Ontario Rugby Football Union, and was assistant coach for CFL teams Hamilton, Montreal and Edmonton. • MD

JAMES, Gerry, football and hockey player (b Oct 22, 1934, **Winnipeg**), is the only athlete in Cdn history to have played in both Stanley Cup and Grey Cup finals in the same season. He is the son of former Blue Bomber Eddie "Dynamite" James, and together they are the only father/son inductees in the Canadian Football Hall of Fame. James' athletic career began as a hockey player for the Winnipeg Monarchs in 1951. The following year, while still signed on as a junior league hockey player, James became part of the **Winnipeg Blue Bombers**. At 17, he was the youngest player ever to sign with a CFL team. He won his first of 2 Schenley awards as top player in 1954,

Gerry James, 1957

and was the team's leading rusher in 1954, 1955 and 1957. He was also the Western Conference's leading scorer in 1957 and 1960. In addition to his pro football career, James played in the NHL from 1955-60 for the Toronto Maple Leafs, with a one-year stint with the American Hockey League's Rochester Americans. He ended his hockey career with the Winnipeg Warriors for the 1960-61 season. James continued playing football for 2 more years, finishing a decade as a Blue Bomber with one year playing for the Saskatchewan Roughriders. When James retired from football in 1963, he had 5554 rushing yds to his credit. • MD

JAMES, June Marion Eleanor, physician (b June 17, 1939, Port of Spain, Trinidad & Tobago), immigrated to MB in 1960 in order to pursue **Medicine** at the **U of M**. When James completed her BSc in 1963, she became the first woman of African descent to be admitted to medical school in the province. Upon graduating with her MD in 1967, James interned at the **Health Sciences Centre** (HSC) and went on to complete specialist training in the areas of paediatrics and allergy, asthma, and immunology, including a Canada Medical Research Council Fellowship. In 1968 she joined Winnipeg's International Centre, an organization assisting with refugee settlement, later becoming its president. James started a private allergy, asthma, and immunology practice at the Winnipeg Clinic in 1976, and in 1980 began consulting in allergy at the HSC and was named an assistant professor in the U of M's Faculty of Medicine. She founded the Family Asthma Program, an innovative approach to asthma treatment that was accepted around NA, and is a recognized expert in her field.

James has served as president of the Manitoba Allergy Society, president of the Manitoba College of Physicians and Surgeons (2001-02), and chairman of the Winnipeg Clinic Medical Corporation (2003-2005). She formerly held positions in many community organizations, including: president of the **Manitoba Museum** (1998-2000); executive for the Caribbean Canadian Association; charter member of the Congress of **Black** Women (MB); founder and president of Harambee Housing Corporation (a Winnipeg housing **Co-Operative**); chairman of the Federal Judicial Advisory Committee for Manitoba; and president of CAA Manitoba.

James was also a member of the boards of St. John's-Ravenscourt School, the Community Legal Education Association, and the United Way, and as of writing held positions with the **Winnipeg Foundation**, CAA Manitoba, the Canadian Scholarship Trust Foundation, and the James Robinson Chair

Dr. June James

in Black Studies at Dalhousie University. She was named YWCA woman of the year in 1981, Manitoba Medical Association physician of the year in 2000, and was invested with the **ORDER OF MANITOBA** in 2004. James was married to the late teacher, publisher, and human rights advocate Dr. Ralph James.
● JOEL TRENAMAN

JAMES RICHARDSON & SONS, LIMITED, is a diversified company with operations in grain, shipping, farming, oil and gas, real estate investments, and financial services. Privately owned, the company has been controlled by **WINNIPEG**'s **RICHARDSON** family for 5 generations. Headquartered in Winnipeg since 1939, the company got its start in Kingston, Canada West (ON), in 1857, after tailor James Richardson began accepting grain as payment for tailoring services from some of his farm customers and discovered he could make more money buying and selling grain. Richardson soon established himself as one of ON's leading grain merchants, and was later joined in the business by his sons George and Henry.

In 1880, James Richardson & Sons expanded its operations into neighbouring MB, building several grain elevators and warehouses before finally establishing an office in Winnipeg in 1896. During WWI, the company branched out into the large-scale shipping business while still aggressively expanding its grain merchandising operations. By 1939, it controlled a grain terminal in Port Arthur (Thunder Bay), ON, and more than 200 **GRAIN ELEVATORS**. During that period, it also expanded into the stock brokerage business, and that venture went on to become one of the country's largest brokerage houses (Richardson Greenshields), acquired by the Royal Bank in 1996. Although no longer in the stock brokerage business, James Richardson & Sons remains a

player in the financial services sector, where its holdings include Richardson Financial Group Limited, which provides wealth-planning and management services to affluent individuals and families, and Richardson Capital Ltd, a registered investment advisor providing independent investment management services on a fee-only basis.

It also remains a major player in the grain and agrifood industry through its wholly owned subsidiary James Richardson International, whose holdings include Canada's largest private grain company (Winnipeg-based Pioneer Grain), one of its largest oilseed crushing, processing, and packaging operations (Canbra Foods, of Lethbridge, AB), the Green Valley fertilizer blending and packaging plant in Abbotsford, BC, and the 200 ha (500 ac) Kelburn Farm agriculture research and demonstration centre near Winnipeg. In 2007, JRI made an offer to merge with one of its main competitors, **AGRICORE** of Winnipeg but lost out to SaskPool.

The Richardson Building at Portage and Main

Its oil and gas division includes Richardson Oil & Gas Limited and MB's largest oil and gas company, Tundra Oil & Gas Limited. Its real estate division includes Lombard Realty Limited and Lombard Place Limited. James Richardson & Sons, Limited recorded gross revenues of $2,205,000,000 in 2006. ● MURRAY MCNEILL

JAPANESE Canadians arrived in MB in significant numbers during WWII. Before that, there were few people of Japanese heritage in the province. The 1941 Census listed 42 Japanese Canadians living in MB, 21 of them in **WINNIPEG**. The first Japanese settlers arrived in MB in 1906. Others came at different times as farmers and merchants. In Winnipeg, many Japanese men worked as redcaps for the railways and porters for hotels. Several families owned manufacturing and service-oriented businesses that employed other Japanese Canadians.

Following the attack on the US naval installation at Pearl Harbor, Oahu, HI, in Dec 7, 1941, the Cdn govt determined that the Japanese were a threat to national security, though most of them were naturalized citizens or born in Canada. When

the govt made plans to remove Japanese nationals from the coastal areas of BC, the MB govt was asked to provide work locations. Although the premier seemed willing, the politicians and public expressed concern about possible sabotage by the Japanese labourers, and the plans were scuttled. However, due to a labour shortage, sugar beet farmers in MB and AB made arrangements with the federal govt to allow the Japanese to work on their farms. Public reaction to this plan was mixed. Some municipalities lodged protests against having the Japanese come to their area. Many Japanese, especially from BC's Fraser Valley and the fishing village of Steveston, BC, chose to go to sugar beet farms when they were given assurances that the families would remain intact. By the end of 1942, about 1250 Japanese resided in MB.

Placed on sugar beet farms under the control of the BC Securities Commission, the Japanese faced a harsh life. Many families lived in shacks that lacked proper insulation from the harsh winters. Access to water, wood, and heating oil was often limited. However, the influx of the Japanese farm workers significantly increased the production of sugar beets for MB. Unable to become self-sufficient on sugar beet farms, many Japanese Canadians sought employment elsewhere. Prohibited from living within Winnipeg's city limits, many families settled on its outskirts, although some individuals received permission by the BC Securities Commission to work in Winnipeg. Most Japanese found employment with companies run by either **JEWISH** or **GERMAN** owners, because they appeared to be more sympathetic toward their plight. The men took manual labour jobs, working long hours for low wages. In the winter, some found employment as bush and lumber mill workers in northern MB and ON. Most of the women worked in sewing factories and tanneries.

In fall 1942, the YWCA organized a domestic employment program, and by Apr 1943, 61 young women worked and lived in Winnipeg homes as domestics. As people were given permission to move into Winnipeg, many of them had difficulty finding accommodation because of discrimination. In 1943, the MB Japanese Joint Council (MJJC) was formed, with leaders such as Harold Hirose and Shinji Sato, to assist Japanese Canadians moving into Winnipeg to find employment and housing, and to fight for fair treatment on the sugar beet farms. To demonstrate loyalty to Canada, 9 2nd-generation Japanese Canadians, offended by being treated as enemy aliens, enlisted in the Canadian army as interpreters and translators.

With the end of the war, the govt took steps to "repatriate" the Japanese in Dec 1945, though the majority of them were already citizens, or at least Cdn-born. In Jan 1946, 405, or 34.5% of, Japanese in MB had applied for repatriation, one of the highest numbers in the country. However, organizations such as the YWCA, church groups, the Civil Liberties Association of MB, lawyers, and the **Winnipeg Free Press** opposed the notion of deportation based solely on ancestry. The Supreme Court upheld the order in Feb 1946, and in May, the first group of 64 adults and 28 children left for Vancouver and Japan. In Mar 1946, the MB Japanese Canadian Citizens' Association (MJCCA) was formed to ensure that Japanese Canadians were not repatriated against their will. Finally, in 1947, the govt revoked the "repatriation" legislation. That same year, the federal govt established the Bird Commission to hold hearings to determine the compensation to claimants whose properties were confiscated by the govt. The MJCCA formed a Property Loss Committee to assist individual claimants to complete the form. Although many MB claimants were not satisfied with the settlement, they accepted the recommendations of their legal counsel.

In 1948, Japanese Canadians received full rights as Manitobans, including the right to live within Winnipeg and to own property. On Apr 1, 1949, the last of the wartime restrictions were lifted. By 1950, about half of the Japanese lived in or near Winnipeg, and a community was evolving. The **United Church** begun to hold services at Knox United Church in 1944, and a **Buddhist** temple was built in 1951. The Japanese Alliance Church took root in 1968. In the 1950s, social, cultural, sports, and educational activities became the responsibility of the MJCCA. The MJCCA newsletter, *Outlook*, was created in 1951 to communicate with its members. The MJCCA organized baseball and bowling leagues, and arranged community socials, concerts, and cultural activities.

The annual picnic, Keirokai (an event to honour seniors), children's parties; and **Folklorama** brought the community together.

The Japanese Canadian Centennial celebrations of 1977 raised awareness of the history, culture, and contributions of Japanese Canadians. In MB, the MJCCA organized seminars, reunions, and special events such as a historical photographic exhibit about Japanese Canadians. This interest created by the Centennial became the catalyst for the redress movement. The MJCCA Redress Committee co-ordinated community meetings and provided input to the national campaign undertaken by the National Association of Japanese Canadians. On Sept 22, 1988, PM Brian Mulroney, on behalf of the govt of Canada, acknowledged the injustices perpetrated upon Canadians of Japanese ancestry during and after WWII, and announced a comprehensive redress settlement.

Today, 3 major organizations are responsible for the activities within MB's Japanese Canadian community. The MJCCA is the umbrella organization and acts as the voice for the community. It is responsible for political, social, cultural and historical activities. Although the Japanese Canadian community had already established a modest cultural centre in 1987, the community fund from the redress settlement allowed for the purchase of a larger facility. The MB Japanese Canadian Cultural Centre administers cultural programs and activities within the cultural centre. The Horizons Club was formed in 1982, and co-ordinates programs for seniors.

Most of Japanese Canadians in MB were, or are descended from those who were, forcibly relocated from BC. With few immigrants from Japan to MB after WWII, a close-knit community was formed in Winnipeg, supported by active, dedicated volunteers. The high rate of intermarriage and assimilation resulting from the govt

dispersal policies during and after WWII is a critical issue that affects the future of the Japanese Canadian community. According to the 2001 Census, the number of Japanese Canadians in MB is about 1800, 55% of whom are of single ancestry.
● KEIKO MIKI

JAZZ WINNIPEG FESTIVAL began in 1989 as an incorporated, non-profit community organization. The founding artistic director was Neil Kimelman, who had volunteered at the Edmonton Jazz Festival and was inspired to try something similar in **Winnipeg** after cutting his teeth programming jazz and blues for the **U of W**'s student association. Dave Sherman became artistic director in 1993, and was succeeded by Chris Frayer (2004) and by Paul Nolin (2005). Of the festival's operating revenues, 14% are from govt sources, with the other 86% coming from sponsorships, ticket sales, and advertising.

For about 10 days every June, the festival produces a series of concerts by local and international jazz artists in Winnipeg venues. It also stages concerts, labs, and award presentations the rest of the year. Notable Cdn artists, such as Diana Krall, Denzel Sinclaire, Oliver Jones, and Molly Johnson, have appeared at the festival. Recent years have seen performances by bop-generation representatives, including Lew Tabackin and Sheila Jordan; Charlie Haden, Dave Holland, and other 1960s jazz heroes; and young musicians, including The Bad Plus and James Carter. Every festival has included high-profile concerts with internationally acclaimed jazz artists, as well as soul, blues, and middle-of-the-road fare designed to attract bigger box-office receipts. While jazz aficionados have criticized the amount of commercial music not clearly in the jazz genre, artistic directors have always pointed to the Winnipeg market's small size and geographic isolation as factors in booking acts like Aaron Neville or ND's Jonny Lang, who have sold many tickets, thus subsidizing the more purely jazz acts.

The festival always features both ticketed and free events. It kicks off every year with a 4-day opening weekend at Old Market Square in downtown Winnipeg, attracting more than 5000 people a day. The "Jazz for Lunch" series, with a variety of local, national, and international acts, is also free. In addition to concerts in larger venues, the festival also presents music in about 10 nightclubs every year, giving fans a chance to see jazz stars after hours and outside the formal concert setting. To attract younger audiences, the festival also runs a series that features everything from Cdn soul to world beat to Cuban rap and hip-hop. The Urban Groove Festival was also created by Jazz Winnipeg in 2000. This festival takes

Japanese drummers at Folklorama, 2006

FOLKLORAMA, CANADA'S CULTURAL CELEBRATION; WHERE TO LOOK PHOTOGRAPHY

Outdoor performance at Old Market Square in Winnipeg

place in several downtown Winnipeg venues and features free lunch hour events on various Winnipeg campuses. International acts appearing at the festival have included James Brown, Shaggy, and Soul Manifesto. Music varies from hip-hop to drum and bass. Over half the acts are Manitoban.

Since 1993, the festival has featured a MB All-Star High School Big Band with a special guest artist as conductor; the guests have included such musicians as Clark Terry, Phil Nimmons, Peter Appleyard, and Moe Koffman. The festival has also staged numerous jazz labs in schools and open to the public with luminaries like Wynton Marsalis, as well as jazz photo exhibits, and dozens of concerts outside the summer festival schedule. In addition, the festival has held an awards event since 1996, honouring local musicians and members of the jazz community, such as **Lenny Breau**, Ron Halldorson, Reg Kelln, Kerry Kluner, George Reznik, **Ron Paley,** Dave Young, and Ross Porter. The festival has been consistently able to attract headline performers, partly because of its block-booking with other jazz festivals in western Canada. The event itself attracts over 40,000 people annually, and has substantially affected local musicians, especially young performers interested in the genre. CBC radio broadcasted many of the concerts Canada-wide in 1999 and 2002. • MAURICE MIERAU

JEHOVAH'S WITNESSES is a worldwide faith known for its door-to-door activity and expectations of better conditions on earth by God's Kingdom. Followers believe that God, who is named Jehovah, is the Father of Christ Jesus, the Son. The name "Jehovah's Witnesses" is taken from the Isaiah 43:10-11. The Jehovah's Witnesses began in western PA in the 1870s, where Charles Taze Russell organized a Bible study group in an attempt to promote the basic teachings of the Bible and to return to the beliefs of early Christians.

The Jehovah's Witnesses have been active in MB dating to 1889, when William Flewweling of **Carberry** came into possession of the faith's main publication, *Watchtower*. Subsequently, he started spreading its message to others. The number of Witnesses in MB increased, and a congregation was formed in Winnipeg in 1905, with the first Witness convention in **Winnipeg** held in 1917. Similar conventions are now held annually in Winnipeg, **Brandon**, and **Selkirk**, each having an attendance of up to 5000. In 1914, Jehovah's Witnesses in the US produced the presentation *Photo-Drama of Creation*, designed to build appreciation for the Bible. It was shown that year in theatres and exhibition halls in Winnipeg, and contributed greatly to the increase of the Witnesses in the city. The presentation consisted of hand-painted photographic slides and motion-picture film accompanied by phonograph recordings of speech and music. *Photo-Drama* caused a sensation wherever it was shown, as it preceded Hollywood's first "talkie," *The Jazz Singer*, released in 1927. As the number of Witnesses grew across Canada, the need for an administrative building to oversee their work across the country became apparent. An office was established in Winnipeg on Jan 1, 1918. This administrative centre moved to Toronto in 1920.

Weekly meetings were arranged in rented facilities such as in theatres, dance halls, or behind restaurants until the first place of worship, called a Kingdom Hall, was built on Hespeler Ave, in Winnipeg's East Kildonan neighbourhood, in 1951. A 2nd place of worship was built on Main St N, also in Winnipeg. Later, Kingdom Halls were constructed throughout the city, as well as in various rural areas of MB. In 1970, the old College Theatre, located on Main St N, was purchased and renovated to accommodate gatherings of up to 800. This was the first Assembly Hall – a larger facility than Kingdom Halls, where

several congregations could meet simultaneously – of Jehovah's Witnesses in Canada.

In 1992, the Witnesses in southern Winnipeg built a 3-auditorium complex on Lakewood Blvd. It was designed to accommodate 1000 people, with the walls retracted. In 2006, there were about 3260 active members in MB, organized into 47 congregations, 23 of which meet in Winnipeg in 13 Kingdom Halls. The remaining 24 congregations meet in 23 Kingdom Halls in rural areas. Witnesses meet at these various locations for weekly Bible study sessions. The Theocratic Ministry School and Service Meetings are designed to provide training in public speaking, in reading, and in the door-to-door ministry. On Sundays, Bible discourses and various in-depth Bible-based studies are conducted. No collections are ever taken. All MB congregations are part of a worldwide association of active members, consisting of 6.6 million Witnesses organized in over 98,000 congregations in 235 countries, distributing Bibles and Bible-based literature in 413 languages. • WALLY SOPIWNYK

JELLYFISH is a jelly-like marine creature in the class Scyphozoa, phylum Cnidaria, and of truly ancient origin – about 700 million years old (Late Precambrian era). The group has a simple level of body organization, but surpassing sponges in complexity of cell and tissue types. Between the two basic layers of cells is the jelly (mesoglea) which maintains body shape and buoyancy. In jellyfish, the free-swimming, bell-like body stage (medusa) is dominant over the sessile polyp stage. The only true jellyfish or scyphozoan found in **Hudson Bay** is the crimson-coloured Lion's Mane Jelly (*Cyanea capillata*), which is wide ranging in arctic and temperate oceans. This remarkable species is the largest jellyfish in the world, with a maximum weight of 450 kg, a bell diameter up 2.5 m, and with up to 150 trailing tentacles 30 m long. Specimens drifting in Hudson Bay are generally smaller; one-m-wide specimens have washed up on the shore near Churchill and Nelson River. The organism can swim slowly by jet propulsion via pulses of its bell, but it is mainly dependant on currents for dispersal, which may lead to stranding on shore. The tentacles are richly supplied with stinging cells (nematocysts), which stun and snag prey like plankton and small fish. This species is dangerous to humans – the slightest contact with a tentacle produces severe burning and blistering of the skin, allergic reaction, muscle cramps, and difficulty breathing. A young Lion's Mane is pink or yellow, but with age, progressively darkens to reddish brown when mature. The life span of this amazing creature is one year. Several jellyfish-like medusae of hydro-zoans (class Hydrozoa), such as *Aeginopsis laurenti* and *Aglantha digitale*, are commonly found in MB coastal waters. There are over 110 species of jellyfish in Canada. • REW

JERICHO, Chris, wrestler (b Nov 9, 1970, Manhas-set, NY), is a professional wrestling entertainer. Though he was born in the US, where his father Ted Irvine played in the NHL for the New York Rangers, Jericho, then known as Chris Irvine, spent most of his childhood in **WINNIPEG**. He began watching pro wrestling on TV at the age of 12. He earned a journalism diploma from **RED RIVER COLLEGE**, but ultimately decided to pursue a career in wrestling, getting his start in the business by setting up rings for Winnipeg wrestling promoter Bob Holliday. He received training in 1990 at the Hart Brothers School of Wrestling in Calgary, and made his professional debut later that year with small organizations in Japan and Mexico before earning a spot in the World Wrestling Association and, in 1996, making it big with World Champion-ship Wrestling.

Taking his stage name from the title of a heavy metal album called "Walls of Jericho," he quickly became a popular WCW character, and won the Cruiserweight Championship the fol-lowing year. Though Jericho claimed the title another 4 times, he felt that his character wasn't getting enough attention in matches, and in 1999 he left for the World Wrestling Federation, where he claimed the WWF's Intercontinental Cham-pionship later that year. In 2001, the WCW was

merged with the WWF, giving Jericho the chance to hold titles from both organizations at once, and making him the first "Undisputed World Cham-pion." He left wrestling in 2005, but continues to work in the entertainment industry as a radio host and singer in a heavy metal band. Jericho was awarded MB's Order of the Buffalo Hunt in 2004 for his work with children's charities. • MD

JEWISH HERITAGE CENTRE OF WESTERN CANADA. The centre's mandate is to record the history and culture of Jewish people in Canada's West. Since 1999, it has been located in **WINNI-PEG**'s Asper Jewish Community Campus (*see* **ISRAEL ASPER**). The Heritage Centre consists of 4 components: the Marion and Ed Vickar Jewish Museum; the Freeman Family Foundation Holo-caust Education Centre; the Jewish Historical Society Archives; and the Genealogical Institute. The merging of these entities resulted from the merger of 3 organizations in 1999: the Jewish Historical Society of Western Canada, the muse-um, and the Holocaust education centre.

The museum opened in 1998, and contains a permanent exhibit called "Diversity and Vital-ity: The Jewish Experience in Western Canada." It covers about 150 years of Jewish experience in western Canada, with a special emphasis on Win-nipeg. Themes explored in the museum include immigration, urban and rural experience, reli-gious and communal life, and the role of **JEWS** in the broader Cdn community. Visitors can see a re-creation of various North End stores run by Jewish people.

The first major public exhibit of Western Jewish historical material was in 1972, when the Jewish Historical Society held an exhibit at the **MANITOBA MUSEUM** called Journey into Our Heritage. After a 6-month run in Winnipeg, the exhibit toured western Canada in 1976-77, also appearing at the Museum of the Jewish Dias-pora in Tel Aviv. Some of the material from this exhibit is now part of the permanent exhibit at the Marion and Ed Vickar Jewish Museum.The Freeman Family Foundation Holocaust Educa-tion Centre occupies a separate space within the museum. Visitors enter through a replica of the boxcar doors used by the Nazis to transport Holocaust victims to concentration camps. The permanent exhibit contains photographs, docu-ments, and artifacts related to MB survivors of the Holocaust and their families. The centre is used for educational presentations on the Holocaust for up to 50 people at a time. Visitors have included thousands of students, interfaith groups, service clubs, and seniors' groups. There is a kaddish corner for reflection and prayer, and a reading room of books on the Holocaust.

The Jewish Historical Society Archives began as a centennial project in 1967, when, under the auspices of the Canadian Jewish Congress, vari-ous members of the community began collecting historical photos and documents. The same year, the Jewish Historical Society needed to house its growing collection, finding a home at the Pro-vincial Archives of MB (PAM; *see* **ARCHIVES**). The PAM housed this collection for 30 years, until the opening of the Jewish Historical Society Archives on the Asper campus. The archives are a national resource for historians of western Canada, gene-alogists, authors, and the media. In addition to large manuscript and oral history collections, the archives house a searchable Jewish newspaper database and a research library. The newspaper database covers Anglo-Jewish and Yiddish publi-cations from 1911 until the present. The archives house a collection of more than 7000 historical photographs and over 600 artifacts.

Besides being important to researchers, the Genealogical Institute enables couples worldwide with ancestry in MB to get married in accor-dance with Jewish law. The institute provides workshops on Jewish genealogy, and has created a photographic record of Jewish cemeteries in MB, with over 15,000 gravestone photographs.

The Jewish Heritage Centre sponsors an annual lecture series and acts as a publisher. The JHC has brought out several historical publica-tions, including *Jewish Radicalism in Winnipeg, 1905-1960* (2003), which grew out of a confer-ence; and *Our Musical Heritage: A Century of Jewish Musicians and Music in Winnipeg*

WWF champion Chris Jericho

WINNIPEG FREE PRESS

(2000). The centre also provides outreach services, sending speakers and small exhibits on the Jewish experience in western Canada to schools and other organizations. • MAURICE MIERAU

JEWS began to settle in MB from about 1877, coming generally from Germany, England, and the US. A few venturesome merchants and trades people seeking new prospects in a new country, most of these newcomers opened various small enterprises in Winnipeg's business area around Logan and Main. By 1881, according to the census of that year, about 100 Jews resided in MB, with 21 families in **WINNIPEG** and the rest dotted across the province.

Events on the other side of the world precipitated the arrival in MB of the first major influx of Jewish immigrants, beginning in 1882. Under the regime of Alexander III, social and economic conditions for Jews in Czarist imperial Russia – never favourable – became intolerable. Jews were restricted to designated smaller towns and villages in the Pale of Settlement, and barred from owning land, from higher education, and from some occupations and professions; and, particularly after 1881, a wave of savage pogroms against Jews swept across the territory, condoned, encouraged, or instigated by the Czarist regime.

At just this time, the Cdn govt of Sir John A. Macdonald was embarked on an intensive policy of promoting immigration from Europe to the wide open lands of the Cdn West, partly at least to justify the controversial building of the **CPR**. Land for homesteading on the Prairies was offered to Jewish settlers, and the exodus from Eastern Europe began, aided by various charitable groups, both Jewish and non-Jewish. On May 26, 1882, 20 Jewish refugees from Czarist Russia reached Winnipeg, followed 6 days later by the rest of the party – 247 men, women, and children, the beginning of a steady flow of Jewish immigrants. Some eventually managed to obtain the promised farming acreage, and some gravitated to rural centres, but most settled in Winnipeg, to provide some of the goods and services the burgeoning city required.

A second major wave of Jews from eastern Europe to Winnipeg and the West followed the failed Russian Revolution of 1905, but before WWII, immigration to Canada was severely restricted, virtually blocking this country as a safe haven for Jews in flight from the Nazi terror. Holocaust survivors, among others, were admitted after WWII and some settled in MB, and in the 1990s the collapse of the USSR brought a further arrival of Russian Jews. By the beginning of the 21st century there were about 14,760 Jews in MB, down from an estimated peak of about 20,000 several decades earlier, and amounting to roughly 2% of the province's total population. At this time of writing, the Jewish community is actively encouraging the immigration of South American Jews to MB.

The initial expectation, in the 1880s, that the Jewish newcomers to the Prairies would become "agricultural settlers" was to prove unrealistic, since they had little or no knowledge of farming. Nevertheless, a number of Jewish farm colonies came hopefully into being in AB and SK, and in MB at **BENDER HAMLET** (near Narcisse) and **CAMPER**, and later at Bird's Hill, Pine Ridge, West Kildonan, Rosenfield, and Rosser. All of these are now extinct, partly because of their founders' inexperience, but generally because vital Jewish religious requirements and cultural institutions could not be sustained in the isolation of rural living. Equally, the small-town Jewish storekeeper, once as typical a figure as the Chinese restaurant-owner, has also virtually disappeared, under the same social pressures. Individual Jewish farms still operate throughout the West, often on land homesteaded by pioneer grandparents and great-grandparents, but the vast majority of MB Jews now live in Winnipeg, **BRANDON**, and **PORTAGE LA PRAIRIE**, engaged in trades, commerce, and professions.

RELIGION: Among the 3 major monotheistic religions still practised today – Christianity, Islam, and Judaism – all of which trace their origin to the patriarch Abraham, Judaism is the oldest and might be considered the ancestor, having arisen among the Semitic people of the Middle East thousands of years ago. Practising Jews base their belief on the Torah, which in its root sense denotes the Pentateuch, the first five books of what is commonly known as the Old Testament, with its foundation in the Ten Commandments, the Law of Moses. (Since Judaism does not recognize a "New" Testament, the reference in this context to an "Old" Testament is something of a misnomer.) In its widest sense the Torah includes the Pentateuch and the Talmud, the compendium of ancient and medieval rabbinic disputations and commentaries on *halakha*, the Law. These establish the hundreds of specific laws and practices (*mitzvoth*) that govern the life of the observant Jew. Among these, the most commonly known today are the keeping of Saturday as the Sabbath (*Shabbat*), the day of rest, and the restrictions of *Kashrut*, the determination of what foods are kosher (fit, proper) and may therefore be eaten. Most prayers are in the ancient Hebrew and Aramaic languages, although in some modern congregations in the English-speaking world English has been adopted instead.

Sephardic (Iberian, Balkan, and Greek/Turkish) and Oriental (Middle Eastern and African, largely Arabic- or Persian-speaking) Jews are rare in MB. Among the prevalent Ashkenazi (Central and East European) Jews, 3 major directions of worship have evolved. These are the Orthodox, which adheres most closely to Talmudic law; the Conservative, which incorporates a spectrum of more relaxed observances; and the Reform, which strives to adapt the ancient practices to the changing challenges of the contemporary world. All 3 Ashkenazi groups are represented among MB's Jews. In addition, the Jewish community also embraces an indeterminate number of secular-minded people, who observe few if any of the traditional beliefs and practices, but who identify closely with the community in its shared history, culture, and concerns.

J

(L to R) Sybil, Abe, and Sherman Grosney in front of 207 Selkirk Avenue 1941

Jewish religious services require, as a minimum, the presence of 10 adults (specifically men, for the Orthodox); and in sufficiently large centres, a synagogue is quickly perceived as a priority. In Winnipeg, the fledgling community dedicated its first synagogue, the Shaarey Zedek, in 1890, and its second, the Rosh Pina, in 1893. As the urban community rapidly expanded, divergent groups formed their own congregations; by the 1930s, with the Shaarey Zedek well established on Wellington Cres, just S of the **ASSINIBOINE**, there were 14 synagogues in the **NORTH END**. In smaller centres, however, a permanent house of worship could not be sustained, and over time, closures and amalgamations have taken place in Winnipeg as well. The North End Rosh Pina, for example, merged with 2 other synagogues early in the 21st century to become the Etz Chaim congregation.

J

Shaarey Zedek synagogue in Winnipeg's River Heights district

EDUCATION: From the outset, Jewish families, traditionally valuing education, enrolled their children in the public schools. Religious instruction was one of the essential services undertaken by the synagogues, at first for boys only, and then expanded to include girls as well, in classes held after school hours and on Sundays; and a group of secular-minded "cultural" Jews organized after-hours education in Jewish literature and history, in accordance with their own liberal precepts. By the 1920s, these classes had developed into 2 alternative elementary day schools, the religious-oriented Talmud Torah and the secular Peretz School, both covering the regular public school curriculum as well as Judaic subjects. Over the years, other educational ventures, both religious and secular, appeared. These competing schools merged in 1997 into a single kindergarten-to-grade-12 entity, the Gray Academy of Jewish Education.

POLITICS AND PUBLIC LIFE: In MB as elsewhere, Jews have struggled to combat the animosities and exclusions of anti-Semitism, and they began to participate in the political life of the province soon after their arrival. Over the years Jewish men and women have been elected to office on every level of govt, municipal, provincial, and federal. While Jewish voters tend to be broadly liberal in their ideology, the notion of an "ethnic vote" has been replaced by support for a range of political parties as Jews have moved into the mainstream. Most Cdn Jews have a particular interest in Israel, wholly compatible with their Cdn citizenship.

COMMUNITY AND CULTURAL INSTITUTIONS: An extensive system of communal self-help organizations mitigated the hardships of Jewish pioneer life. Newcomers from the same Old World town or area typically banded together into free-loan societies to provide emergency funding and support. Care for the aged and for orphans was organized as early as 1912: the Jewish Orphanage and Children's Home of Western Canada functioned until 1949, when foster care became the preferred alternative, and the longstanding Jewish Old Folks' Home has now become the Sharon Home, its 2 sites administered under the provincial Health Department. A free medical clinic for Jewish indigents opened in a North End house in 1926, expanding in 1929 into the **MOUNT CARMEL CLINIC**, which now serves the needy of every background.

Today, national and international organizations such as B'nai Brith and the Canadian Zionist Federation are active in MB, and the Jewish Federation of Winnipeg is the MB arm of the Canadian Jewish Congress. Jewish contribution to charity continues to be above the province's average; the Combined Jewish Appeal and the Winnipeg Jewish Foundation administer the collection and distribution of funds to a list of beneficiaries at home and abroad. The recently developed Asper Jewish Community Campus houses the Gray Academy and the offices of a variety of Jewish organizations. Among these, the **JEWISH HERITAGE CENTRE** includes the Holocaust Education Centre and holds an extensive archive of Jewish life in western Canada, presenting noteworthy cultural programs; and the Jewish Museum mounts both permanent and temporary displays. The Winnipeg Jewish Theatre provides an interesting addition to the local theatrical scene. ● MILDRED GUTKIN

JOHANNESSON, Konrad "Konnie," RFC/RAF pilot, flying instructor, airport administrator (b Aug. 10, 1896, **GLENBORO**; d Oct 25, 1968, **WINNIPEG**). The child of **ICELANDIC** immigrants, Konnie was raised in Winnipeg. He joined the Army in 1916, was sent to England and then Egypt, and trained as a pilot. On his return to Canada in 1919, Johannesson played defence for the **WINNIPEG FALCONS HOCKEY** team, which won the 1920 Allan Cup and Olympic gold. After hockey, between 1929-34,

Johannesson was the chief flying instructor with the Winnipeg Flying Club and administrator of Stevenson Field, now Winnipeg Airport. Turned down for service in WWII, Johannesson trained Icelandic-speaking pilots who wanted to join the Air Force, then opened an air service out of **FLIN FLON**. In 1947, he moved to establish Rivercrest Airstrip Ltd. airfield and floatplane facility in the RM of West St. Paul in the **INTERLAKE**, just N of Winnipeg. The municipality claimed the right to deny approval of the airport – a decision that was upheld by MB courts. In 1952, the Supreme Court of Canada disagreed, upholding federal over provincial authority in the case. The Johannesson ruling set precedence for all subsequent cases involving airports – or other conflicts of jurisdiction, such as urban sprawl – brought before the Supreme Court. Johannesson died in 1968 and was buried in Brookside Cemetery. ● JIM SHILLIDAY

JOHNSON, Frederick ROSS, corporate executive (b Dec 13, 1931, **WINNIPEG**) was one of NA's most controversial businessmen in the 1980s. As a young man, Johnson attended the **U OF M**, earning a commerce degree in 1952 before completing an MBA at the U of Toronto in 1956. He became an accountant at General Electric and a vice president at **EATON'S** before moving to the US to become president of Standards Brands Ltd in 1971.

Johnson rose quickly in the corporate ranks, and when R.J. Reynolds Tobacco Company and RJR Nabisco merged in 1985 he became the president of one of the US's largest companies. As CEO in 1988, Johnson, with partners Shearson Lehman Hutton Inc, initiated a leveraged buyout in an attempt to gain private ownership of RJR Nabisco, a bold, highly criticized move that led to no end of boardroom upheaval. Johnson's group was outbid by private equity firm Kohlberg Kravis Roberts & Co, who paid $31 billion, then a record-high price for a company. In a book about the takeover, *Barbarians at the Gate: The Fall of RJR Nabisco*, author Bryan Burrough described Johnson as a maverick – someone who had challenged the business establishment, a renegade corporate operator with a large expense account and little regard for business traditions. The story was also made into a movie.

After leaving Nabisco, Johnson founded and became chairman of the RJM Group (Ross Johnson Management), later run primarily by his son Neil. He has been a member of many corporate boards and advisory groups, including the U of Toronto President's International Alumni Council and Power Corporation. Johnson was appointed an officer of the Order of Canada in 1986, and lives in Jupiter, FL and Caledon, ON. ● JOEL TRENAMAN

JOHNSON, George, politician, physician, sailor (b **WINNIPEG**, Nov 18, 1920; d **GIMLI**, July 8, 1995). A Cdn of 3rd-generation Icelandic background, Johnson was raised in Winnipeg, where he attended public school and the **U OF M**. Johnson served in the navy (1941-45) as a navigation specialist on the North Atlantic, attaining the rank of Lt (N). In recognition of his war record and his lifetime of public service, Johnson was appointed Honorary Captain of the *HMCS Chippewa* in Winnipeg in 1988. After graduating from medical school in 1950, Johnson began a practice in Gimli, where he and his wife, Doris Blondal, lived and raised their family. In 1958, he was elected Progressive Conservative (PC) MLA for the Gimli constituency. He became the Minister of Health and Public Welfare, and Education in the govts of **DUFF ROBLIN** and **WALTER WEIR**. In these roles, he was instrumental in implementing universal medical care in MB (*see* **MEDICINE**); in creating **RED RIVER COLLEGE**; and in establishing both the **U OF W** and **BU**. Upon retiring from politics in 1969 after 4 consecutive election victories, Johnson practised medicine in Winnipeg until 1978, then served as senior medical consultant to the govt of MB. In 1986, he was appointed MB's 20th lieut gov, the first person of Icelandic descent so honoured. He served as lieut gov for 7 years, until 1993. In 1994, he was made an Officer of the Order of Canada. ● GPP

JOHNSON, Ivan Wilfred "Ching," hockey player (b Dec 7, 1897, **WINNIPEG**; d June 16, 1979, Silver Spring, MD), was one of the most popular original players for the New York Rangers. Johnson didn't start playing organized hockey until his late 20s, when he joined the Winnipeg Monarchs, following service in the army during WWI. In 1921, he played in the US Amateur League with the Eveleth Miners for 2 seasons before moving on to the Minneapolis Millers. He tried out for the New York Rangers when the team was first put together in 1926, though at 28 years old, he had to lie about his age to qualify for tryouts. Johnson made the team, and was part of the Rangers' NHL debut in 1926. Johnson was with the Rangers for 2 Stanley Cup victories in 1928 and 1933.

The 6 ft, 210-lb defenceman was a fan favourite, known for his solid body checks, as well as the occasional on-ice prank, such as when he would hide an extra puck in his gloves and drop it amidst the confusion of a multi-player scrum. His nickname does not refer to Johnson's actual ethnicity, but his willingness to cook meals for his friends on camping trips, at a time when it was common practice to hire a servant, usually of Chinese origin, to take over cooking on such

excursions. He played 11 seasons with the Rangers, and ended his career with their rival team, the New York Americans, for the 1937-38 season, though Johnson was such a favourite with Rangers fans that, in his first match going up against his old team at Madison Square Garden, they presented the new Americans player with a gold watch. He retired from the NHL in 1939, and was inducted into the Hockey Hall of Fame in 1958. ● MD

Janis Johnson in the Senate Chamber

JOHNSON, Janis Gudrun, Senator (b Apr 27, 1946, **WINNIPEG**) Johnson is the eldest child of the late **DR. GEORGE AND DORIS JOHNSON**. Educated at University College, **U OF M**, she received a BA in political science in 1968. Shortly thereafter, she began her political career as a policy researcher for federal PC leader Robert Stanfield and worked as a policy consultant for the PC Party of NL. Married in 1973, she lived in NL with her former husband, Frank Moores, Premier of that province, until 1980. Upon her return to MB, she founded the PC Women's Caucus of Winnipeg, and served as its president for three years. She co-directed the Brian Mulroney leadership campaign for MB in 1983, and became National Director for the PC Party of Canada, the first woman to hold this position. In 1985 she established Janis Johnson & Associates, a consulting firm in Winnipeg and remained involved with the federal and provincial parties as a strategist. From 1985 to 1990 she served as a CN director. Johnson was appointed to the Senate in 1990. Among her many volunteer accomplishments is the co-founding and production of the **GIMLI** Film Festival. She has one son, Tomas Stefan Moores. ● GPP

JOHNSON, Thorvaldur, agricultural researcher (b Oct 23, 1897, **ÁRNES**; d Sept 15, 1979, **WINNIPEG**). Born to Icelandic immigrants Sigurjón Jónsson and Guthrún Thorvaldsdóttir, Johnson taught school and attended university prior to

enlisting as a pilot in the Canadian Armed Forces in 1918. Following his graduation with a BSc from the U of SK, he earned an MA from the U of MN and eventually a PhD in plant pathology in 1930. In 1925, he began a long career with the newly established Dominion Rust Research Lab in Winnipeg, part of an international effort to address the issue of cereal crop rusts that plagued prairie agriculture and had resulted in the catastrophic Wheat Stem Rust epidemic of 1916 (destroying over 30 million bushels of wheat in Canada and the US). Alongside renowned rust researcher Margaret Newton, Johnson made major strides in the identification of the genetics, physiology, and epidemiology of these pathogens. Head of the then world-renowned Dominion Rust Research Lab from 1953 until his retirement in 1962, he wrote *Rust Research in Canada*, which was published by the federal department of agriculture in 1961 and was awarded the Gold Medal by the Public Service Institute of Canada in 1962. Following retirement, Johnson worked as an agricultural advisor to Pakistan under the Colombo Plan, an organization devoted to international co-operative economic and social development. He accepted an honorary Doctorate from the U of SK in 1967. ● LAURIE K. BERTRAM

JOHNSON, Tom Christian, hockey player (b Feb 18, 1928, **BALDUR**). One of the best defenceman to play in the NHL during the 1950s, Johnson won 6 Stanley Cups with the Montreal Canadiens. His playing career began with the junior level **WINNIPEG** Monarchs in 1946-47. The Toronto Maple Leafs scouted him first, but transferred his NHL rights to Montreal, who placed him with the Montreal Royals of the Quebec Senior League and then the Buffalo Bisons of the American Hockey League.

Johnson made his NHL debut during the 1950-51 season. The 2-way player and superb penalty-killer quickly became a key component of the team, though as the Canadiens' 2nd most important defenceman after Doug Harvey, his offensive contributions were overshadowed. The 2 often played as a pair, leading Montreal to Stanley Cup wins in 1953 and 5 straight from 1956-60. Johnson received more recognition as time went on, including a 1959 Norris Trophy victory and first-team all-star selection. He also gained a reputation around the league for his tough physical play.

In the early 1960s, Johnson suffered a serious eye injury. The Canadiens thought his career was over, but Johnson soon returned to action with the Boston Bruins. However, a 1965 skate accident left him with severed nerves in his leg, ending his playing days after 978 NHL games. Johnson then became an assistant to Bruins

J

president and general manager Harry Sinden. He was elected to the hockey hall of fame in 1970, and became the head coach of the Bruins in 1970. In 1972, he coached the team to the Stanley Cup. Johnson retired from hockey in 1999 as a Bruins vice president. • JOEL TRENAMAN

JOHNSTON, Lyndon, figure skater (b Dec 4, 1961, HAMIOTA). Johnston was an elite figure skater through the 1980s. He began his career at the Hamiota Skating Club, and went on to represent the province in 13 Cdn championships. He was the 1981 national junior champion with partner Melinda Kunhegyi in the pairs and fours events. Johnston is often credited with leading the brief revitalization of the fours event in national competition. He consistently ranked high in national competition through the 1980s, competing in the 1984 Olympics and, with partner Denise Benning, the 1988 Olympics. He appeared in 6 World Championships, and won silver in 1989 for his performance with partner Cindy Landry. He then toured internationally in World and Olympics tours before retiring from professional skating to coach in ON. • MD

JÓNASSON, Sigtryggur, "Father of New Iceland," politician, community leader, businessman, editor (b Feb 8, 1852, Bakki, Öxnadalur, Iceland; d Nov 26, 1942, ARBORG), the first Icelander to settle in Canada, immigrated at age 20 in 1872 and became a pioneer, governor, editor, entrepreneur, captain, politician, immigration agent, homestead inspector, and philanthropist. In 1874, the ON govt engaged him to assist in settling Icelandic immigrants in Kinmount, ON, and in 1875, as one of 3 scouts chosen by his countrymen, he helped select NEW ICELAND on the shores of LAKE WINNIPEG. Following a volcanic eruption in Iceland that year, the Cdn govt dispatched him to guide refugees from the stricken areas, and others wishing to emigrate – with the result that, in 1876, some 1200 Icelandic souls ("The Large Group") chose Canada as their destination. Instrumental in organizing NEW ICELAND as a unique Icelandic Cdn reserve, with its own council and constitution for the administration of local affairs, Jónasson was subsequently elected the first "governor," directly responsible to Ottawa. He spearheaded the founding of *Framfari* in 1877, and in 1880, he and FRIDJÓN FRIDRIKSSON FREDERICKSON launched an ambitious Lake Winnipeg transportation and lumber venture that operated for 11 years, providing New Iceland with economic stability at a crucial time. Master of various steamers during that time, he became known to many as "Captain." Moving to Winnipeg in 1881, Jonasson helped found

Sigtryggur Jónasson

Lögberg in 1888, which he edited 1896-1901. In 1920, he became editor and co-publisher of the publication *Syrpa*. He was twice elected Liberal MLA, for St. Andrews in 1896 and Gimli in 1907, and was instrumental in having railways built to the INTERLAKE. He also proposed several major innovations, including a shipping link with Iceland/Europe via HUDSON BAY. Jonasson spent his final 32 years at Arborg and RIVERTON. • NELSON GERRARD

JONES, Jennifer & Team, curler (b July 7, 1974, WINNIPEG), skipped the winning team at the women's 2005 Cdn curling championship. A corporate lawyer by day, she has one of the best career-winning percentages among active players in national competition. She saw success early in her career, winning 3 MB junior titles. Moving into women's competition, Jones won her first MB title in 2002 with the line-up of Dana Allerton (lead), Lynn Fallis-Kurz (2nd), and Karen Porritt (3rd). She went on to place 4th at the Cdn championship that year with a record of 8-3.

Jennifer Jones

Jones became a household name in MB at the 2005 Cdn championship where she skipped the line-up of Cathy Gauthier (lead), Jill Officer (2nd), and Cathy Overton-Clapham (3rd) to a 9-2 record in the round robin. In the 10th end of the final game, she made what has since been dubbed "The Shot," successfully making a double take-out of an ON team's stone on the outside edge of the rings, which ricocheted to knock the rival team's shot rock off the button. "The Shot" counted for 4 pts, and made the Jones team Cdn champions. It was MB's first national title since the 1995 victory of CONNIE LALIBERTE's team. As of writing, Jones had won her 3rd provincial women's title, and her first Strauss Canada Cup of Curling. • MD

JORGENSON, Warner Herbert, politician, farmer (b Mar 26, 1918 Canora, SK; d July 30, 2005, WINNIPEG) Jorgenson served during WWII with Royal Canadian Corps of Signals in the Mediterranean and Western Fronts. He returned to Canada to farm near MORRIS and became active in Manitoba Farmers Union. He began his long political career in 1957 with his election to the House of Commons for Provencher constituency as a PROGRESSIVE CONSERVATIVE; he was re-elected in 1958, 1962, 1963, 1965 and finally defeated in 1968. He served as parliamentary secretary to the minister of agriculture from 1960-63, and was a delegate to the Food and Agricultural Organization of the United Nations. He was elected to the MB legislature for the Morris constituency in a by-election in 1969 and subsequently re-elected in 1973, 1977. Jorgenson served as house leader in both opposition and govt. Under STERLING LYON's govt from 1977-81, he was variously minister of consumer and corporate affairs, government services, and minister without portfolio. Respected across party lines for his directness and for his skills as a speaker and debater, he did not seek re-election in 1981 but remained active in his community. • BILL NEVILLE

JUBA, Stephen, entrepreneur, politician (b July 1, 1914, WINNIPEG; d May 2, 1993, PETERSFIELD). Juba was Winnipeg's longest-serving mayor and the first non-Anglo-Saxon mayor in the city's history (1957-77). He also served as an MLA 1953-59. He was the 2nd son of UKRAINIAN immigrants Gregory Juba and Sophia (nee Mosata). Although he had planned to be a lawyer, and studied at United College (*see* U OF W), his plans were interrupted by the GREAT DEPRESSION. Juba was forced to leave school at age 15. He worked at odd jobs for several years, and also started 2 small businesses before he was 21: Weston Builders Ltd, and S. N. Juba & Co. He was largely unsuccessful as a businessman until 1945, when he started a wholesale distributing firm called Keystone Supply Ltd, which would make him wealthy.

Juba's first forays into electoral politics were also unsuccessful. In June 1949, he ran against **STANLEY KNOWLES** as an independent in Winnipeg North Centre in the federal election, receiving only 694 votes. In the Nov 1949 provincial election, Juba ran, again unsuccessfully, in Winnipeg Centre as an Independent Liberal, supporting the govt of **DOUGLAS CAMPBELL**. He lost in an election for Winnipeg's city council in 1950, and in 1952 challenged mayor **GARNET COULTER**, receiving 28,000 votes to Coulter's 38,000.

Juba ran again as an independent in the provincial election of 1953, this time victoriously, serving until 1959. Juba ran for mayor again in 1954, this time placing second to alderman George Sharpe. He was at last successful in 1957, after a campaign in which he referred to Sharpe as Premier Campbell's "trained seal," and promised to fight harder for the city's fair share of provincial revenues. (At the time, there was no perceived conflict in representing the city provincially while serving as mayor.) Juba received 46,197 votes to Sharpe's 44,266, most of his support coming from Winnipeg's ethnically diverse **NORTH END**. Juba was re-elected as an MLA in 1958, this time defeating **CCF** candidate Art Coulter in the single-member riding of Logan. He did not seek re-election again in 1959, choosing to concentrate on his responsibilities at City Hall.

Juba's terms as mayor were far from smooth. His unorthodox style antagonized many other council members. At the same time, Juba pursued his agenda for civic improvement, and, in the process, reinforced his image as the "people's mayor." In 1959, Winnipeg became the first area in NA to have a 3-digit emergency phone number – then 999 – after the UK model. He cajoled the provincial govt into contributing money for the Disraeli Bridge and Freeway, and launched an aggressive campaign for a new city hall, which opened in 1964. He helped liberalize liquor laws and legalize sweepstakes; fought for a bigger share of provincial tax revenue for Winnipeg, and lower property taxes; promoted tourism; and tried to get a monorail for public transportation.

Imaginative, colourful (he drove a bright-yellow Cadillac), and politically independent, Juba was one of the best promoters Winnipeg had ever seen. Juba aspired to establish Winnipeg on the world stage, and was instrumental in bringing the **PAN AM GAMES** to the city in 1967. The new sport facilities built for the games have served the city well. Other Juba projects were less successful. He was never able to establish gambling casinos, a covered stadium, parking lots on the tops of service stations, or a weatherproof cover

for downtown Winnipeg. One of Juba's greatest disappointments was his lack of success in developing mass rapid transit.

Juba supported the amalgamation of Winnipeg and the creation of **UNICITY** during the late 1960s, though he opposed the concept of Cabinet govt for it. He convinced the provincial govt of **EDWARD SCHREYER** to grant direct mayoral elections in the unified city, as opposed to the existing system of elected councillors appointing one of their members as mayor. Unsurprisingly, Juba himself became the first mayor of the unified city

Stephen Juba, 1960

in 1971. The city's right-wing Independent Citizens' Election Committee (ICEC) opposed him during the 1970s, and he frequently clashed with ICEC leader and deputy mayor **BERNIE WOLFE**. Still, while he presented himself as a spokesman for marginalized groups in the city's North End, he was not a social democrat, and often had a difficult relationship with the provincial CCF and its successor, the NDP. Some have referred to him as a "pro-business populist." Juba was a flamboyant mayor who was highly skilled at using the media to win support for his causes. His dramatic intervention to stop the cutting down of a giant elm tree on Winnipeg's Wolseley Ave in 1957 resulted in international exposure. Although the tree was destroyed, the effort to save it remained unforgettable. Similarly, in 1973, Juba protested the construction of a controversial provincially funded public washroom in Memorial Park by setting up a portable toilet on the MB Legislature grounds.

After he ceased to be mayor, Juba made a further foray into electoral politics in the provincial election of 1981, running as an independent candidate in his old riding of Logan. He was

resoundingly defeated by NDP candidate Maureen Hemphill, and did not attempt any additional comebacks. This populist mayor possessed the right combination of qualities: his background ensured him working-class support, and his policies won the favour of middle-class and business interests. ● TOM CARTER/MECHYSLAVA POLEVYCHOK

JUDICIAL SYSTEM. MB's judiciary comprises 3 levels of courts. The highest, or appellate, court, from which further appeals go to the Supreme Court of Canada, is the Manitoba Court of Appeal. Next is the Court of Queen's Bench (QB) or King's Bench (KB). The judges of both these courts, normally called "justices," are appointed by the federal govt and may hold office until age 75, being removed involuntarily only by joint resolution of the Senate and House of Commons. These courts are often referred to as the "superior courts of record." The Provincial Court of Manitoba is the 3rd tier. Its judges are appointed by the provincial govt, and are not subject to a mandatory retirement age. They may be removed from office at any time by the MB govt for appropriate cause, but this power is seldom exercised, and only after an inquiry and recommendation by the provincial judicial council.

While the various judges in each court are equal and independent in their decision-making, each court has a presiding judge for administrative purposes. In the Court of Appeal, that judge is the Chief Justice of Manitoba. In the QB, there are the Chief Justice of the Court of QB and 2 Associate Chief Justices: one for what is commonly known as the General Division, the other for the Family Division. In the Provincial Court, the designation is Chief Judge and there is statutory provision for the appointment of Associate Chief Judges.

The *British North America Act* of 1867 (now the *Constitution Act*) divides lawmaking powers between the provinces and Canada. Authority over criminal law and related procedure lies with the federal govt, while civil law and procedure is left to the provincial govts. Provinces must establish and maintain their courts, but the federal govt appoints and pays the judges of the superior courts. The *Constitution Act* of 1867 also gives Parliament the power to establish "a general Court of Appeal for Canada and any Additional Courts for the Better Administration of the Laws of Canada." Under this provision, federal legislation created the Supreme Court of Canada in 1875 to deal with appeals from the appellate courts of the provinces. The Supreme Court was subject to further appeals to the Judicial Committee of the Privy Council in Britain, which remained the final tribunal for criminal matters in Canada

The first Law Courts buildings on Winnipeg's Broadway

J

until 1933, following the *Statute of Westminster*. The UK's Privy Council continued to be the highest place of recourse for civil cases until 1949.

The Supreme Court has jurisdiction to hear appeals in all areas of law, including constitutional, administrative, criminal, and civil law. Generally, the Supreme Court will hear an appeal only after it has granted permission (or "leave") to bring the appeal. Leave is usually given only if the case raises a question of significant national or public importance, and pertains to an issue of law, or mixed law and fact. However, limited circumstances in which an appeal may be brought "as of right" without leave exist. Examples are criminal cases in which at least one judge has dissented in the Manitoba Court of Appeal, or where the Court of Appeal has substituted a guilty verdict for an acquittal entered at trial.

Before 1906, the judges of the Manitoba Court of Queen's Bench sat together ("en banc") as the final provincial appeal body. In 1906, the Legislature created the Manitoba Court of Appeal. It hears appeals from the QB and from the Provincial Court, and, in some circumstances, from administrative tribunals where legislation has authorized a direct appeal to the Court of Appeal. Legislation also allows the provincial govt to "refer" questions of constitutional law to the Court for an opinion. The Court does not retry cases that come before it, but is concerned only with errors of law or significant mistakes of fact that may have occurred in a lower court's process or decision. The Court usually sits with a quorum of 3 judges, but may sit with 5 – or even its full complement of 7 – judges.

The QB is the principal trial court of general jurisdiction in MB. MB is a common-law province, for which the basic law is the law of England as of July 15, 1870. Under common-law doctrine, the superior trial court has "inherent" jurisdiction over all manner of cases, with broad and flexible powers to fashion remedies to do justice in particular cases, unless those powers have been abridged or assigned to other tribunals by legislation. In MB, the QB accordingly has jurisdiction in almost all areas of law unless legislation, federal or provincial, has limited or removed its jurisdiction. The Court (or its judges) has also been assigned by legislation some authority historically exercised by other courts, as, for instance, in surrogate or probate matters.

The QB also has a varied appellate jurisdiction, hearing appeals from the Provincial Court of decisions for summary-conviction offences as well as hearings from judicial interim release (commonly called "bail") and youth justice court. The QB also receives appeals from hearing officers authorized to deal with civil disputes involving small claims of less than $7500 (as of 2006), and appeals from the Masters. These Masters are legally trained officers associated with the Court who adjudicate, at first instance, a wide range of legal and procedural issues. Small-claims and youth-justice-court appeals, and, for the most part, bail appeals, are in the nature of re-hearings of the cases appealed. The Court also has a "supervisory" jurisdiction over other tribunals, exercising "judicial review" of proceedings of the Provincial Court and of provincial boards, commissions, and tribunals alleged to have acted beyond their statutory powers; to have improperly exercised their powers; or to have failed to act in accordance with the principles of natural justice.

The Provincial Court of Manitoba has primarily criminal or quasi-criminal law jurisdiction. The Court deals with the vast majority of prosecutions for breaches of criminal law. The *Criminal Code of Canada* identifies most offences as summary conviction (less-serious) or indictable (more-serious) offences. All summary conviction offences are tried in the Provincial Court. Certain indictable offence charges that would otherwise be heard by the QB may be heard, by the choice or "election" of the parties, in the Provincial Court. The Provincial Court does not sit with a jury. Indictable offences that may not be heard by the Provincial Court are tried in the Court of QB, with or without a jury. Charges of indictable offences that are tried in the QB are subject to a preliminary hearing by a Provincial Court judge to determine whether the evidence is sufficient to warrant a trial.

The Provincial Court also deals with charges for offences under a range of federal, provincial, and municipal laws, by-laws, and statutes. Some are regulatory in purpose, while others – such as the *Highway Traffic* and *Liquor Control* acts – contain prohibitions and prescribe sanctions that closely resemble criminal law. As well, as inferred above, the Provincial Court deals with applications under the *Criminal Code* for "bail" (except murder and certain other designated offences, which must go directly to the QB), and is the designated court to conduct youth-justice proceedings under the federal *Youth Criminal Justice Act*. Judges of the Provincial Court also conduct inquests under the *Manitoba Fatality Inquiries Act* (*see* CHIEF MEDICAL EXAMINER); under the *Manitoba Law Enforcement Review Act*, they also review alleged police misconduct.
● D. TREVOR ANDERSON/W. SCOTT WRIGHT

JULIETTE, singer, television host (b Aug 27, 1926, WINNIPEG). Raised in the St. Vital area of Winnipeg, Juliette Augustina Sysak, the daughter of POLISH/UKRAINIAN immigrants, began her singing career at age 13 with the Dal Richards and at the Hotel Vancouver, making her national radio debut 2 years later on CBC's *Sophisticated Strings*. More radio shows followed, including *Here's Juliette* before moving to Toronto in 1954, guest starring on CBC Radio's *Holiday Ranch* and starring on *Gino and Juliette* with chorale arranger Gino Silvi. Married to manager Tony Cavazzi and taking his surname (though not on stage), she became known as "Our Pet Juliette" during a regular stint on Billy O'Connor's CBC-TV *The Late Show*. In 1956, she was given her own show, *Juliette*, which ran for 10 seasons as one of CBC's most popular TV shows – only *Hockey Night in Canada* and *The National* news hour topped her in ratings. With this show, she became one of Canada's most-recognized stars. Her "just folks" approach and closing "Good night, Mom" endeared her to fans, but by the mid-'60s, the music scene had changed. She later hosted *After Noon* (1969-71) and *Juliette and Friends* (1973-75) for CBC-TV. Juliette also recorded three albums for RCA Camden. In 1975, she received the Order of Canada; induction into the Walk of Fame in Toronto followed in 1999. CBC-TV's *Life and Times* profile Juliette in 2002. Having retired from music, as of writing, she lived in Vancouver. ● JOHN EINARSON

KLASSEN, CINDY, see page 369
Canada's most decorated Olympian

K

KABEL, Todd, "King Kabel," jockey (b Dec 7, 1965, **McCreary**), leads all current Cdn jockeys in purse earnings and career victories. He first started riding for Emile Corbeil, a MB businessman and trainer who, upon meeting the 96-lb, 14-year-old boy, recognized Kabel's potential as a jockey. Under Corbeil's tutelage, Kabel had his first career win at **Assiniboia Downs** in 1984. His 131 wins, mostly at **Winnipeg**'s racetrack, earned him the 1986 Sovereign Award as the country's Top Apprentice Jockey.

Kabel moved to Toronto the following year, where he would eventually become a leading jockey at Woodbine Racetrack. In 1992, he earned his first of 6 Sovereign Awards for Top Jockey. He won 193 races at Woodbine in 1995, the racetrack's 2nd highest number of wins in a season, as well as the first of 2 Queen's Plate victories. He broke the 2000 win mark in 1998. In 2003, Kabel set a new precedent for Cdn jockeys by recording over $11 million dollars in purse earnings, and winning a colony-best 29 stakes races. His best year at Woodbine came in 2004 with 36 stakes wins, tying a record set by the late Avelino Gomez in 1966. That year, Kabel also set a new Cdn record by winning the first 7 turf races of the year he had a mount in. He won his 2nd award as Manitoba Male Athlete of the Year in 2005. As of

Jan 1, 2007, Kabel had achieved 3113 wins from 16,917 mounts. ● MD

KAHANOVITCH, Rabbi Israel Isaac (or Yisroel Yitzchak), spiritual leader, educator (b ca. 1873, Wolpa, Grodno Uzed, Poland [now Voupa, Vawkavysk, Belarus]; d June 22, 1945, **Winnipeg**). After his ordination as an Orthodox rabbi at age 20, Kahanovitch served a number of congregations in Poland and in the US before he came to Winnipeg around 1906. From his office as rabbi of Beth Jacob Synagogue, and from his house on Flora St, he – together with his wife, Rebbetzin Chaie Rashel (Rachel) Kahanovitch – ministered to the burgeoning **Jewish** congregation of the **North End** and beyond. Most of this flock were recent **Immigrants** from Eastern Europe, escaping a wave of pogroms that followed the 1905 Russian Revolution. His involvement in the community included the founding of the Talmud Torah, or Winnipeg Hebrew School, and in 1911, the building of a new premises to house the school. Kahanovitch also helped establish a Jewish orphanage and a nursing home in Winnipeg, as well as the national Canadian Jewish Congress. Despite intermittent financial difficulties, all these institutions survived the **Great Depression**.

K

Rabbi Kahanovitch, centre, meets with Hashruth officials, 1907

The Talmud Torah is one of the schools that led to the founding of the Gray Academy at the Asper Jewish Community Campus; the Talmud Torah-Beth Jacob congregation (now simply Talmud Torah) continued, as of writing, as an Orthodox synagogue in a converted Main St cinema. Unlike many of his Orthodox contemporaries, Kahanovitch championed the creation of a Jewish state, and was therefore able to achieve broad consensus within western Cdn Jewry. Besides being the head of the Beth Din (the Jewish ecclesiastical court), he officiated at some 1500 weddings, and likely a similar number of funerals; the **Jewish Heritage Centre of Western Canada** archives his marriage records. Though it was an unofficial title, congregants widely considered him the first "chief rabbi of the West," as for a time he presided over the entire area from Fort William (now Thunder Bay, ON) to Victoria, travelling frequently. Kahanovitch died in 1945, and was buried in Winnipeg's Shaarey Zedek Cemetery near **Kildonan Park**. Rabbi Kahanovitch left a lasting mark on western Canada, and in 1989, the MB govt installed a plaque in the rabbi's honour at the Asper Community Campus in Winnipeg. ● A. J. LEVIN

KALEN, Henry, photographer (b Jan 20, 1928, **Winnipeg**; d Dec 25, 2004, Winnipeg) gained recognition for his book of photography titled *Henry Kalen's Winnipeg* (2000). As of 2005, the book, a collection of landmark photos, had been on **McNally Robinson Booksellers'** bestseller list for 4 years. Kalen graduated with an architecture degree from the **U of M** in 1957.

After 3 years of practice, he decided his love of **Photography** would bring him greater fulfillment. In 1960, he attended the summer session in art education at the Illinois Institute of Technology in Chicago. The same year, he joined the Faculty of Architecture at the U of M, where he taught photography, architectural drawing, graphic presentation, and fundamentals of design for 11 years. In 1973, Kalen started a postcard business, selling more than 12 million postcards in a 17-year period. Kalen was a founding member of the Professional Photographers of MB, holding the organization's first membership card. He was also the first photographer to have a one-man show at the **Winnipeg Art Gallery**, in 1966. In 1982, the

Henry Kalen, 1977

Royal Architecture Institute of Canada awarded him the Allied Arts Medal for architectural photography. He later became a member of the Royal Canadian Academy. At the time of his death, Kalen was working on a new book manuscript, *Henry Kalen's Manitoba*, which his friends and family are expected to complete. ● JS

KANE, Paul, artist (b Sept 3, 1810, Mallow, Cty. Cork, Ireland; d Feb 20, 1871, Toronto) documented Aboriginal life on the Cdn Prairies through his artwork during the 1850s. He spent much time in Toronto before touring the Cdn West from 1845-48. He travelled to several **HBC** posts, to OR, to New Caledonia (later BC), and to Vancouver Island, with a commission from **Sir George Simpson** for a series of paintings of Aboriginal life. He made hundreds of sketches, from which he derived 100 large canvases of a way of life on the edge of extinction, which offer much of our best visual record of the early West. Kane also wrote *Wanderings of an Artist among the Indians of North America* (1859), distinguished for its sparse narrative and translated into numerous languages. The originals of Kane's paintings are in Ottawa, Toronto, and Orange, TX, but his collection of Aboriginal artifacts is in the **Manitoba Museum**. ● JMB

KANEE, Solomon "Flour King," businessman, lawyer (b June 1, 1909, Melville, SK; d April 22, 2007, **Winnipeg**). A close friend of leading Liberal politicians such as PM Pierre Trudeau, Kanee's influence was far-reaching. His family moved to Winnipeg when he was 12. He received a BA and studied law at the **U of M** and then the U of Saskatchewan, graduating in 1932 and establishing a successful practice in Melville. He was one of the first Jewish Canadians to join the armed forces during WWII, enlisting in an officer's training program and ranking Maj by the end of the war. He then returned to Winnipeg and joined the firm Shinbane, Dorfman and Kanee. He practised law until 1951, when he took over his father's company, Soo Line Mills Ltd. A visionary businessman, Kanee revolutionized the Cdn **Flour Milling** industry by introducing the pneumatic flour conveying system, which eventually became the industry standard. He sold the company in 1969 to George Weston Bakeries Inc.

Kanee served on numerous boards, and is noted for sitting 17 years, the longest of any member, on the Bank of Canada board. He also served as president of the **Royal Winnipeg Ballet** and the United Way. An activist for **Jewish** causes, he was president of the Canadian Jewish Congress from 1971-74, and was on the executive of the World

Jewish Congress. He was a member of the Order of Canada and the **Order of Manitoba**. • MD

KARDASH, William Arthur, politician (b June 10, 1912, Hafford, SK; d Jan. 17, 1997, **Winnipeg**). A veteran of the Spanish Civil War, Kardash belonged to the MacKenzie-Papineau Battalion. He entered politics as a member of the **Communist** Party in 1941 and was elected to the legislature for the riding of **North End** Winnipeg. The Communist Party was banned in 1943 and he became the first leader of the Labour Progressive Party until 1948 when he resigned for health reasons. He was returned as a MLA in the 1945, 1949, 1953 and 1958 provincial elections. When he ran in Point Douglas in 1969 and was defeated, this marked the end of an LPP's presence in the legislative assembly. He remained active in the Ukrainian community for the remainder of his life. • RUTH DEGRAVES

KATYDID is an insect in the order Grylloptera, phylum Arthropoda, that features a short head, thin antennae usually longer than the body, large wings (reduced in some species but not absent), forewings (tegmina) that often resemble leaves, and a sword-like ovipositor or egg-laying organ at the back end. The group is sometimes called Long-horned Grasshoppers, but this term confuses their true relationships. There are 4 families in MB (e.g., Tettigoniidae) with about 16 species represented (6000 species worldwide). The Slender Meadow Katydid (*Conocephalus fasciatus*) is a 25-mm, green species often found in grass and weedy sites in S MB. The Mormon Cricket (*Anabrus simplex*), actually a katydid, is found in a variety of sparse vegetation in S MB.

In exceptional years, these insects can become super-abundant, and the soil may hold 30,000 eggs/m²; each female laying about 100 eggs. The brown, 20-mm Bog Katydid (*Metrioptera* or *Sphagniana sphagnorum*) is the N-most katydid and occurs across central Canada in sphagnum bogs of the boreal forest (not yet recorded in the US). Adults are active from July to Sept. The males attract females by singing, and mating occurs at night. The female deposits her fertilized eggs into the soil using her long ovipositor. Most species of katydids are herbivorous, but some are predaceous. The Mormon Cricket is omnivorous and will even turn to cannibalism. Katydids usually sit quietly on vegetation or the ground during the day, and will take flight when disturbed. Katydids are famous for their songs and remarkable camouflage (both shape and colour). In fact, everyone has walked past katydids on numerous occasions along meadow and forest trails in MB without observing their presence. • REW

KATZ, Samuel Michael, "Sam," 42nd mayor of **Winnipeg**, concert promoter, CEO of the **Winnipeg Goldeyes** baseball club, (b Aug 20, 1951, Rehovot, Israel). Sam Katz emigrated with his family to Winnipeg's **North End** shortly after his birth. He graduated with a BA from the **U of M**. He soon became a promoter. Through his company, Showtime Productions, he brought acts such as the Rolling Stones and Pink Floyd to Winnipeg. He also helped bail out the struggling Walker Theatre. In 1999, after years of wrangling with city hall over funding and land, Katz opened CanWest Global Park just north of **The Forks** to house his Goldeyes baseball club. In 2004, Katz was awarded the **Order of Manitoba**.

Sam Katz, 2007

WINNIPEG FREE PRESS

Katz was elected mayor of Winnipeg in June of 2004 after former Mayor **Glen Murray** stepped down in the middle of his term. Katz was a last-minute entry into the race, but his personal popularity as the little guy who built the ballpark propelled him to victory. Katz's first 2 years in office were marked by business-friendly policies. He trimmed the business tax, starting with businesses located downtown, and began to slash red tape at city hall. He also pledged to get tough on crime. His most controversial decision involved postponing construction of the city's first rapid transit system. He redirected millions in federal and provincial funding earmarked for transit to community clubs and recreation centres. He also faced significant community opposition to a plan to build a hog processing plant in St. Boniface. To quell critics who said he lacked a broad vision for the city, Katz hosted a city summit in 2006 that brought together some of Winnipeg's leading

thinkers. Known for his charm and accessibility, Katz was re-elected in Oct 2006, winning more than 61% of the popular vote. • MARY AGNES WELCH

KAY, Guy Gavriel, writer, (b Nov 7, 1954, Weyburn, SK) is the internationally acclaimed author of many speculative novels. Kay's family moved to **Winnipeg** when he was 3 so his father could take a position in the city as a surgeon. While attending the **U of M**, Kay met Christopher Tolkien, the son and literary executor of *Lord of the Rings* author J.R.R. Tolkien. In 1974 he went to Oxford, England, to assist with the editing of the senior Tolken's major manuscript, *The Silmarillion*. In 1976, Kay returned to Canada to finish his law degree at the U of Toronto. However, Kay could not give up the idea of writing. Between 1981-1989, he wrote scripts for the CBC, acting as associate producer for *The Scales of Justice*. He produced his first work of "high fantasy" in the Tolkien tradition in 1984. *The Summer Tree* became the first in a series of 3 books known as *The Fionavar Tapestry*. Kay's books blur the boundaries between history and fantasy by creating fictional realms that resemble real places during real historical periods like Moorish Spain, Renaissance Italy or ancient Byzantium. By 2007, Kay had written 10 books including *Tigana* (1990), *The Last Light of the Sun* (2004) and a collection of poetry *Beyond this Dark House* (2003). Kay has won numerous fantasy awards and his books have been translated into 20 languages. Kay is based in Toronto, but does much of his writing in Europe. • AMANDA STEPHENS

KEEPER, Joseph, runner (b Jan 17, 1886, Walker Lake, MB; d Sep 29, 1971, **Winnipeg**) was MB's top runner in the early 1900s. A member of the **Norway House Cree First Nation**, Keeper began running after being sent to **Brandon** Indian **Residential School** in 1899. He moved to Winnipeg in 1910, where he joined the **North End** Athletic Club. He soon grabbed the attention of Winnipeg's athletic community by winning his first major competition, a 7-mi road race with 40 seasoned runners. He won the same race again in 1911, and later that year set a Cdn record by running 10 mis in 54 minutes and 50 seconds. Keeper was then chosen to represent Canada at the 1911 Dominion Championship, where he placed 2nd in the 3-mi event. In 1912, he represented Canada at the Stockholm Olympics, finishing 4th in the 10,000 m final, which remains the highest finish of any Cdn runner in the event. Keeper served in the army during WWI. He was awarded the Military Medal for Bravery for his service. He then returned to northern MB where he worked for the **HBC**. • MD

K

Tina Keeper, 2006

K

KEEPER, Tina (Christina), actress, politician, activist (b Mar 20, 1962, **Norway House**). Keeper spent her early years in **Chemawawin Cree Nation**, where her father Joseph Irvine Keeper, a community activist and member of the Order of Canada, was working on hydro development. She developed an interest in acting after helping her sister in her Aboriginal theatre troupe. Her early film credits include *Mistress Madeleine* (1986) and *Smoked Lizard Lips* (1991). She graduated from the **U of W** in 1992 with a double major in theatre and Cdn history. Keeper had planned to pursue an academic career, but was then selected to play RCMP officer Michelle Kenidi on the CBC-TV series *North of 60*. She was nominated 3 times for a Gemini from 1994-96 for her work, finally winning the national award in 1997. She left the series the following year, and worked on the films *Heater* (1999) and *In the Blue Ground* (1999), for which she received the American Indian Film Festival award for Best Actress. Her other film credits include *Trial by Fire* (2000), *Dream Storm* (2001) and *Skins* (2002).

Keeper is an activist on issues facing the Aboriginal community, and has initiated various educational programs for Aboriginal youth, especially in regards to suicide prevention. She was made a member of the **Order of Manitoba** in 1999, and was awarded a National Aboriginal Achievement Award in 2004. In 2006, Keeper channelled her activism into politics and was elected the Liberal MP for **Churchill**. ● MD

KEESEEKOOWENIN FIRST NATION, on reserve pop 482, off reserve pop 527, is located 80 km NW of **Brandon**. The people of this First Nation also refer to themselves as the "Riding Mountain Band," due to their location just S of **Riding Mountain National Park** Over the years, many discussions between the federal govt and Keeseekoowenin First Nation have taken place on the subject of land rights. Treaty 2 was signed in 1871. Keeseekoowenin is a member of the West Region Tribal Council. The native language of this First Nation is **Ojibway**. Schooling, administered by the community, goes from Nursery-Grade 9. Total enrolment in 2003-04 was 122. There are 3 reserves in Keeseekoowenin First Nation: Keeseekoowenin IR No. 61, Clear Lake IR No. 61A, and Bottle Lake IR No. 61B. Keeseekoowenin First Nation is accessible by means of year-round roads and bus service, but no air service. The economic base of the Keeseekoowenin First Nation consists of agriculture and the potential for developing gravel deposits. ● RK

KELSEY, Henry, fur trader, explorer (b ca 1667, E Greenwich, UK; d 1724, E Greenwich, UK). The Englishman was apprenticed to the **HBC** in 1684 and posted to the **Nelson River**. He quickly achieved a reputation as an energetic young man. In 1689, he was sent to **Churchill River**, and he kept his first journal of the endeavour, which included an unsuccessful overland march. A year later, under orders from the Company, he began his trade expedition from York Fort. The journal he kept of this expedition is one of the most famous and controversial in the literature of Western exploration. It was published in 1929 by A. G. Doughty and Chester Martin as *The Kelsey Papers*. The notoriety is a result of the journal being written partly in rhyme. The controversy revolves around Kelsey's route, particularly how far N and W he got. Whatever his actual route, he was the first European to travel extensively W and N of the Bottom of the Bay, and the first to record descriptions of many things, including bison and grizzly bears. Kelsey remained at the Bay almost continuously until 1722, one of the most enigmatic of the early European figures of the region. He was well known for his expertise in Aboriginal languages, and he made several subsequent forays into the North. ● JMB

KEMPTON, Alonzo Fowler, entrepreneur, insurance executive (b Feb 11, 1863, Harmony Mills, NS; d June 28, 1939, Vernon, BC) was the founder of one of Canada's largest mutual insurance companies. He came to MB from NS with his parents in 1881. In his youth, Kempton was known as a smooth talker who shirked manual labour. He left school early to become a travelling salesman, and sold household goods to new **Immigrants**, visiting farmhouses in a horse and buggy. He became an insurance salesman and, seeing that the policies offered by eastern stock companies weren't suited to a western homesteader, he convinced his pioneer customers around **Wawanesa** to join him in forming the **Wawanesa Mutual Insurance Company**, a farmers' insurance

Henry Kelsey, first white man to see the Great Plains

Alonzo Fowler Kempton, centre front, always had the biggest car in town.

co-operative. At first, the company insured only threshing machines, but it soon branched out.

By 1910, it was the largest fire mutual in Canada, employing many Wawanesans, and paying for Kempton's fancy suits, imported barrels of raw oysters, a large house equipped with an electric generator, and Kempton's personal cook/chauffeur. Kempton launched other ventures, including a popular haemorrhoid cure and a manufacturing company for wagon seats and razor blades. He resigned from Wawanesa Mutual following a heated board meeting in 1922, and moved to BC, where he died a pauper, remembered by local residents for his wild rants about having started the insurance company. ● MD

KENNEDY, William, explorer (b 1814, Cumberland House, SK; d Jan 25, 1890, St. Andrews, MB) Born at Cumberland House in present-day SK to the **CREE** wife of an **HBC** chief factor, Kennedy was educated in Scotland before joining the HBC in 1833, spending a number of years in the Ottawa Valley and Labrador. He resigned from the company in 1846 because he objected to its liquor policy, and subsequently served as commander of Lady Franklin's second privately financed expedition to find her husband. He insisted on proper equipment (including Native outer-garments), and although he did not find Franklin, he expanded geographical knowledge of the Arctic and returned his crew to England without loss of life. He led a second expedition financed by Lady Franklin in 1853, but jailed its crew in Chile after a mutiny. Kennedy returned to Canada in 1856 and was one of the proponents of a Canadian annexation of **RUPERT'S LAND**.

He travelled overland from Toronto to Red River in the winter of 1857 to prove that it could be done, whatever the weather. In the **RED RIVER SETTLEMENT** he got 575 signatures to a petition requesting union with Canada. A year later he carried the first mail from Toronto to Red River. In 1860 Kennedy settled in St. Andrews. He was not very active at the time of the **RED RIVER RESISTANCE** in 1869-70, although at a parish meeting in St. Andrews in Oct 1869 he opposed welcoming gov **WILLIAM McDOUGALL** into the settlement, saying he was suspicious of the man's character and background. Kennedy on this occasion called for Confederation "on equal terms with other provinces." He was a founding member of the Historical and Scientific Society of Manitoba and an advocate in the 1880s of a **RAILWAY** to Hudson Bay. Kennedy was the author of *A Short Narrative of the Second Voyage of the Prince Albert in Search of Sir John Franklin* (1853). ● JMB

KENNEDY, William Nassau, soldier, businessman, mayor (b April 28, 1839, Newcastle, Upper Canada [ON]; d May 3, 1885, London, UK), founder and leader of the 90th Batt of Winnipeg Rifles (*see* **ROYAL WINNIPEG RIFLES**) and **WINNIPEG's** 2nd mayor. Kennedy left school at an early age, and worked as a contractor and then as a house painter. From a family with a long military history, Kennedy joined the newly organized 1st Company, Peterborough Rifles in Feb 1857. He progressed through the ranks, becoming Capt of the 57th Peterborough Batt in 1867. In 1869, Kennedy was chosen to travel W as part of the **WOLSELEY EXPEDITION** to quell the **RED RIVER RESISTANCE**. He travelled to **UPPER FORT GARRY** as a Lieut in the 1st Batt of Infantry (Ontario Rifles), developing

close ties with his commanding officer, Col Garnet Wolseley. Like many other soldiers who participated in the Expedition, Kennedy decided to stay in MB, and became a leading citizen.

During the Fenian offensive of 1871, he organized a volunteer unit to defend the Winnipeg garrison. The crisis then prompted Kennedy to form the Winnipeg Field Battery, in which he served as adjutant, and then commander until 1883. He was also a civil servant, and worked in a number of appointive positions. In 1875, he defeated the incumbent **FRANCIS CORNISH** to become the 2nd mayor of Winnipeg, serving a single term. His wife and family joined him in Winnipeg in 1876.

Kennedy was a supporter of **RAILWAY** companies, and participated in 11 railway charters between 1875-83. He was involved in the Manitoba South-Western Colonization Railway, and was vice-president of the Manitoba and Hudson's Bay Railway in 1884. His other involvements include serving on the Protestant section of the Manitoba Board of Education from 1876-81, and establishing the Winnipeg Philharmonic Society in 1880. He was a member of numerous fraternal societies, including the Orange Order, the Foresters, and Prince Rupert's Lodge, and was the deputy grandmaster of the Freemasons' Grand Lodge of MB at the time of its establishment in 1875.

In 1883, he established the 90th Winnipeg Rifles to protect western Canada. Kennedy was chosen to command the force, and promoted to LCol. When Kennedy learned that his former commander – now Gen Joseph Garnet, Lord Wolseley – was looking for Cdn boatmen to take Lord Kitchener's British expedition up the Nile River to relieve Gen Charles "Chinese" Gordon at Khartoum, he organized 100 Manitoban volunteers. In 1884, he led the MB contingent – the first Cdn

K

William Nassau Kennedy

force to serve overseas – into Sudan. Though the men were supposed to be voyageurs and York boatmen, Kennedy had also recruited many members of MB's professional elite, including 8 lawyers, which would cause numerous difficulties for the expedition.

Kennedy contracted smallpox on the return voyage, and was taken to a hospital in London, where he died. He was buried there, as it was feared that his contagious body might spread disease on a return voyage to MB. Winnipeg's Kennedy St is named for the soldier. • MICHELLE DOBROVOLNY

KENTON, pop 173, is a community 50 km WNW of **Brandon,** W of hwy 21. The post office opened in 1884 and was named Ralphtown, after postmaster W. J. Helliwell's son. In 1894, the post office moved to the home of A. W. Kent, where Annie Kent served as postmistress, and the community name was changed to Kenton. Kenton is the largest community in the RM of Woodworth. Agriculture is key to the local economy, with grain and traditional livestock farming being most common; however, elk, bee, and bison operations also occur within this diverse farming community, and some retail and services exist, as does an elementary school. The Kenworth Dam, about one km S of Kenton, is a popular recreational area for camping, fishing, and beach-going, and the Harding Agricultural Society's annual July fair, held in the nearby smaller community of Harding, brings visitors to the area. • GPP

KEYSTONE CENTRE in **Brandon** serves as the hub of entertainment and recreation for the city and the **Westman** region. With more than one million visitors each year, the centre sits on 32.7 ha (81 ac) on Brandon's busiest thoroughfare and hosts more than 1500 events annually. With an 8-sheet curling club, 2 regulation-sized ice rinks, 2787 m² (0.7 ac) of exhibition and meeting space, an indoor livestock show ring, stables, camping space, and a 160-room hotel, the centre is a one-of-a-kind facility.

The Keystone Centre – so named because MB's sobriquet is the Keystone Province (*see* **Nicknames**) – opened in April 1972 as a joint venture between the City of Brandon, the MB govt, the Provincial Exhibition of MB, and private donors. The centre was built as a replacement for the now-defunct Wheat City Arena, a fixture in the city for 60 years. To raise funds for the new centre, corporate donations were solicited from as far afield as **Winnipeg,** Toronto, and Montreal. Within Brandon, support of the Keystone Centre became almost a test of one's loyalty to the city and to the agriculture that supports

Brandonites cheer on the Wheat Kings at the Keystone Centre.

much of the region. Seniors signed over their pension cheques; schools held fundraisers; and **Brandon U** students collected pledges for the number of nights they could sleep out in igloos in –30°C temperatures. Their commitment paid off, as the Keystone Centre has proven to be a major economic catalyst to Brandon adding, in 2005, between $40 and $50 million annually to the local economy. Home to the **Brandon Wheat Kings,** the Brandon Curling Club, and the Royal Manitoba Winter Fair, these tenants, among others, play an integral role in the centre's success.

As the centre began to host an increasing number of regional, national and international events, the need for larger and improved facilities has been accommodated with 3 major expansions in 1982, 1991, and 2005. The Keystone Centre plays a key role in improving the quality of life for Westman residents by providing year-round entertainment and recreational opportunities. • JILL SEXSMITH

KILDONAN PARK is the 2nd-largest of the 8 major municipal parks in **Winnipeg.** The 77-ha (190-ac) park is along the W bank of the **Red River,** off Main St, in the N of the city. In 1909, public

Kildonan Park

parks superintendent **George Champion** took the first step to establish Kildonan Municipal Park with an initial purchase of 29 ha (72 ac). The park continued to expand and develop in the years leading up to WWI, with the addition of a pavilion, a formal flower garden, **Cricket** pitches, traffic and pedestrian bridges, and a floating dock. The region's first public **Golf** course opened here in 1921. In 1923, the Lord Selkirk Association dedicated a monument to **Chief Peguis,** an **Ojibway** leader and ally of the area's early **European** settlers. Along with other damage, the original bandstand was washed away in the 1950 **Flood.** The parks board agreed to build an elaborate new outdoor theatre, only the 2nd in Canada at the time. The inaugural concert took place in Sept 1953, and the 2000-seat **Rainbow Stage** officially opened in July 1954. In its opening year, the stage attracted more then 19,000 spectators to 19 performances. A dome built over the theatre in 1970 was one of many upgrades over the years. The Metro Winnipeg govt took over administration of the park in 1960 and began a series of improvements. The Peguis Pavilion was completed in 1965, erected alongside Lord Selkirk Creek to replace the original 50-year-old structure. An Olympic-sized swimming pool was built in 1966, and 1970 saw the completion of the German-Canadian Centennial Project, the Hansel and Gretel Fairytale House (later known as the Witch's Hut). The green space attracts about 500,000 car visits per year. Some of the oldest trees in the city can be found in the park, particularly **Elm** and cottonwood (*see* **Aspen**). • JT

KILLARNEY, pop 2199, is a town about 75 km SSE of Brandon, at the junction of hwys 18 and 3 about 20 km N of the US border. Killarney has

SANDY BLACK

STAN MILOSEVIC, WWW.MANITOBAPHOTOS.COM

a rich history. In the 1800s, the Boundary Trail Commission ran S of the community and was used by Northwest Mounted Police as they travelled W to the Rocky Mountains. The first post office opened here in 1883. The **CPR** reached Killarney in 1885. The community grew quickly: it was incorporated as a village in 1903; as a town in 1906. Local legend has it that Irish land surveyor John O'Brien christened the community and the lake it sits on "Killarney" after his hometown in Ireland by pouring whisky into the lake. The town has continued the Irish tradition by painting fire engines green, and naming local parks "Erin" and "Kerry."

In the 2000s, the town economy is based on both agriculture and tourism. Killarney is the self-declared "Wheat Capital of MB." There were more than 25 agriculturally based businesses in town in 2006 and 2 grain elevators. With a beach and wharf on Killarney Lake, the town also attracts tourists and cottagers. Killarney annually holds Pioneer Days and the Killarney Beach Festival in July. Town administrators like to note *Canadian Living* magazine once named Killarney as the best retirement community in Canada. ● PP

KINONJEOSHTEGON FIRST NATION (formerly known as Jackhead First Nation), on reserve pop 353, off reserve pop 335, is situated 235 km N of **WINNIPEG**. In 1875, after signing Treaty 5, the Kinonjeoshtegon First Nation people migrated from the Berens River to their current geographical location. It is now a member of the Interlake Reserves Tribal Council. There are 2 reserves here: Jackhead IR No. 43 and Jackhead IR No. 43A. The native language here is **OJIBWAY**. The Kinonjeoshtegon First Nation administers schooling; education goes from nursery-Grade 10, and enrolment for 2003-04 was 117. The Kinonjeoshtegon First Nation community has all-weather road access and Grey Goose Bus service. The economic base of this community is commercial trapping and fishing. ● RK

KLASSEN, Cindy, speed skater (b July 12, 1979, **WINNIPEG**). Klassen is Canada's most decorated Olympian with 6 medals. At the 2006 Turin Olympics, she became the first Cdn athlete to win 5 medals at one Olympics.

Klassen started out as a **HOCKEY** player, playing on boys' teams in AA and AAA leagues. In 1995, she played for Team Manitoba at the Canada Winter Games, and at 16 she was chosen for the Cdn junior team. When she failed to qualify for the 1998 Olympic women's team, she reluctantly agreed to try speed skating at the urging of her parents. Though at first Klassen was so embarrassed by her initial struggle with

Cindy Klassen with the 2006 Canadian Female Athlete of the Year award

the sport that she wouldn't let her family watch her skate, she quickly proved her ability on the track. After just one year of training, she qualified for the 1999 junior national team, winning first in the 1000 m and 3rd in the 500 m at the world junior championships.

The next year, Klassen was part of the national team. She won bronze at the 2001 world single distance championship, and a bronze in the 3000 m at the 2002 Olympics in Salt Lake City. In 2003, she won the overall title at the World Speed Skating Championships, becoming the first Cdn woman to do so in 27 years. In 2003, Klassen severely cut her forearm by crashing into a group of skaters while rounding a corner. She still managed to compete at the 2004 World Single Distance Championships, winning silver in the 1500 m and bronze in the 1000 m. In 2005, she took the title at the World Championships, and also won the 1500 and 3000 at the World Single Distance Championships. Her most momentous year came at the 2006 Turin Olympics, where Klassen won 1 gold, 2 silver and 3 bronze medals. With her previous Olympic bronze, she became the only Cdn to have won 6 Olympic medals.

Though now living in Calgary, the Winnipeg-born Klassen has a North Kildonan street and the Sargent Park recreation complex renamed in her honour. In 2006, she won the Lou Marsh Award. As of writing, she held the world record in the 1000 m, 1500 m, and 3000 m. ● MD

KLEEFELD, pop 500, is a community about 50 km SSE of Winnipeg. **MENNONITES**, who still predominate in the community, originally settled Kleefeld. In the late 1800s, more than 50 communities were established in the surrounding area of the East Reserve; however, many did not last. Kleefeld, along with **STEINBACH**, **NIVERVILLE**, Blumenort, and **GRUNTHAL**, became the key trading centres. The post office opened in 1896. Once

called Grünfeld ("green field"), Kleefeld was named after a Mennonite community in Russia of the same name. It means "clover field" in German. Agriculture forms the economic base of this community. Kleefeld is also home to a school and a few retail outlets. ● GPP

KNOWLES, Stanley Howard, politician (b June 18, 1908, Los Angeles, CA; d June 9, 1997, Ottawa). The longest-serving MB MP in Cdn history, Knowles acted as the **WINNIPEG** North Centre representative for nearly 38 years between 1942 and 1984.

Born in the US to Cdn parents, Knowles came to MB at the age of 16 and found work as a printer. He went on to earn a BA from Brandon College (*see* **BRANDON U**) in 1930 and a BDiv from United College (*see* **U OF W**) in 1933. His religious training, upbringing in the Methodist social gospel tradition, and early work experiences led him to become a **UNITED CHURCH** minister, but after seeing limited potential to enact social change, Knowles also joined the **CO-OPERATIVE COMMONWEALTH FEDERATION** (CCF) in 1935. He lost one provincial and 2 federal elections under the CCF banner before successfully winning a seat as a Winnipeg alderman in 1941. A year later, the death of **J. S. WOODSWORTH** gave Knowles the opportunity to run in a safer CCF riding. He never looked back, winning 13 elections in total, losing only in 1958 to the John Diefenbaker **PROGRESSIVE CONSERVATIVE** Party sweep.

Stanley Knowles

Knowles' first speech in the House of Commons focused on improving housing and employment conditions as well as pension benefits for Canadians, and his advocacy on these issues continued throughout his career. In 1948, he was successful in amending legislation to protect pension rights during labour disputes. In 1952, he helped ensure that the *Old Age Security Act* contained no income means test – that its benefits would be universal. Knowles also played an important role during the historic Pipeline Debate in 1956 that contributed to the fall of the St. Laurent govt.

K

While out of office from 1958-61, Knowles was instrumental in laying the foundations for the creation of the **New Democratic Party** (NDP). He worked for the Canadian Labour Congress, chaired a national organizing committee, and wrote a book on the process, *The New Party*. Knowles defeated the incumbent John Maclean to regain his seat in 1962, and due in part to his mastery of House of Commons rules and procedures, was named NDP house leader and deputy leader, positions he would occupy until the early 1980s.

Knowles was known for his routines, such as the consumption of plain roast beef sandwiches, tea, and arrowroot biscuits every day. He also boarded with the politically like-minded Mann family in Ottawa every year from 1942-80, leaving a deep influence on the household. Walter Mann was an unsuccessful CCF candidate, Gretchen Brewin (Mann) went on to become mayor of Victoria and a BC MLA, and Susan Mann Trofimenkoff completed a biography of Knowles.

In 1970, Knowles became Brandon U's chancellor, and in 1979 was named to the Privy Council. When he retired in 1984, Pierre Trudeau named Knowles an honorary officer of the House, a status that allowed him to maintain his office and long-time executive assistant, and to sit at the centre table while the house was in session (which he often did). Knowles lived with **Multiple Sclerosis** from 1946 onwards, and it was a 1981 stroke that forced him to reduce his commitment.

Knowles was invested as an officer of the Order of Canada in 1985. His death led to memorial services and tributes from coast to coast. An elementary school and a federal govt building in Winnipeg, a Toronto housing **Co-Operative**, and U of Waterloo and Brandon U professorships have all been named after the man. ● JOEL TRENAMAN

KNUDSON, George, golfer (b June 28, 1937, **Winnipeg**; d Jan 24, 1989, Toronto), was the first Cdn to win 8 PGA tour events. He began playing golf as a teenager at the St. Charles Country Club, eventually becoming the 1954 and 1955 Manitoba Junior Champion and winning 5 Cdn championships in 1954, 1967 and 1968. After turning pro in 1958, Knudson went on to win 8 PGA tour events between 1961-72, then the highest number of wins on a PGA tour by a Cdn golfer. Knudson was particularly admired for his superb swing. His weak point was his putting, which cost him the 1969 Masters when he missed a birdie putt by less than an inch on a final hole. A chain smoker, Knudson's plans to join the Senior PGA Tour came to an end when he was diagnosed with lung cancer at the age of 50. He made a brief recovery and managed to play in a

George Knudson, 1975

Komarno's famous mosquito

Legends of Golf Tournament before doctors realized that the cancer had spread to his brain. He died shortly thereafter. The Royal Canadian Golf Association named him Canada's Golfer of the Century in 2000. ● MD

KOLA, pop 175, is a community about 100 km W of **Brandon** and several km E of the SK border. A post office opened here in 1886. For many years, it was known as Butler Station, or Butler. It was attractive to **Mennonite** and British-Ontario settlers because of the rich agricultural soil. In 1884, the early settlers built the **Anglican** Church of the Advent, which was a municipal heritage site in 2006. Residents were reportedly the most generous givers to charity in MB in 2005, averaging $3380 per person. In the late 1990s, Kola was suffering from the rural depopulation that has sapped other small towns; the local school division threatened to close Kola's school. Community leaders struck an aggressive immigration committee and upgraded several vacant homes in an effort to save the school. Kola did enjoy a mini-population explosion with immigrants arriving from Belize, Bolivia, Paraguay and Germany. The school remained open in 2006-07, with 51 students from Grades 1-9. ● GPP

KOMARNO, pop 80, is an unincorporated community about 85 km N of Winnipeg in the **Interlake**. Settled largely by **Ukrainians** and **Poles**, Komarno's post office opened in 1907. A **CPR** point was established here in 1906. Bizarrely, the community celebrates its mosquitoes. The village landmark is a 4.6-m-tall statue of the biting insect. "Komarno" means "many mosquitoes" in

Ukrainian. There are 2 other places of the same name in the world – one in Slovakia, the other in the Ukraine. The MB community hosts a perogy fest each year, a Ukrainian New Year's Eve supper and dance in Jan, and a Mosquito Flea Market in the summer. ● GPP

KONANTZ, Margaret MacTavish (Rogers), politician (b April 30, 1899, **Winnipeg**; d May 11, 1967, Fredericton) was MB's first female MP. Konantz was educated at Bishop Strachan School in Toronto and at Miss Spence's School. Daughter of **Edith Rogers**, the first MB female MLA, Konantz kept a vow to her husband to remain out of public life that ended only with his death in 1954. In 1959, she was national vice-president of UNICEF, and in 1961, she became national vice-president of the UN Association. She ran for Parliament in 1962, and became MB's first female MP in 1963 when she was elected to represent Winnipeg South. She is buried in Winnipeg. ● JMB

KOOP, Wanda, painter, (b Nov 5, 1951, Vancouver), has exhibited, been purchased and published worldwide. She graduated from the **U of M** School of Art in 1973, was awarded the Order of Canada in 2006; an LLD from the **U of W** in 2002; the Queen's Golden Jubilee Medal, Canada Council and Manitoba Arts Council 'A' Grants and the Japan Fund Award and is a member of the Royal Canadian Academy of Artists. Koop's large-scale paintings and small works are landscape-based, exploring current issues of place and the peril human beings have caused the environment. These works are a quest for change. They represent places of the imagination with recognizable references to reality, presenting the dichotomies

Sightlines – panel 3 (2000), 3 x 4 m, acrylic on canvas, by Wanda Koop

of memory and the landscape, and of nature and human activity.

The artist adds images from new technology, circles, sight-lines, crosses and lines, onto these seemingly known places rendering them disconcerting and thought-provoking. In addition her compelling use of colour and constant horizons heighten the contrasted sense of the comfortable and surreal. Her series include *Sightline; Green Zone;* and *Paintings for Dimly Lit Rooms/Paintings for Brightly Lit Rooms*. Her work has been exhibited across Canada, Great Britain, the Netherlands, Germany, Brazil, Japan, the USA, Italy, India, and China and is in public and private collections including The Winnipeg Art Gallery and the National Gallery of Canada. It has been widely published in many periodicals, exhibition catalogues including *In Your Eyes, Books 1-3*, 2001; *See Everything/See Nothing*, 1998; *Sightlines*, 2002. In addition to her painting, Wanda Koop is the founder of Art City in **WINNIPEG**, a storefront creative visual art centre for youth at risk. • PATRICIA BOVEY

KOSKIE, Cordel Leonard "Corey," BASEBALL player (b June 28, 1973, **WINNIPEG**) is one of Major League Baseball's few Cdn players and the only Manitoban in recent times to crack the big leagues. Growing up in **ANOLA**, Koskie was an all-around athlete. As a goalie for the Manitoba Junior Hockey League's Selkirk Steelers, Koskie was scouted to play pro **HOCKEY**, but his mother discouraged him from signing a contract with the Western Hockey League until he graduated high school. He played in the Manitoba Junior Baseball League for the Elmwood Giants, but was primarily interested in **VOLLEYBALL** with the **U OF M** Bisons, helping the under-18 team win the 1991 Cdn championship as the tournament's

MVP. In 1992, he gained the attention of a US community-college baseball scout after running a 60-yd (55-m) dash in 6.9 seconds at a baseball camp at Winnipeg's Giants Field, home to the Elmwood Giants (now called Koskie Field). Originally, Koskie wasn't keen on the idea of playing baseball at a community college in Boone, IA; however, coach John Smith was persistent, calling every day until Koskie relented. After a year in IA, Koskie played for the MB baseball team at the 1993 Canada Summer Games, where he was scouted to train at the National Baseball Institute in Surrey, BC. At this specialized baseball school, Koskie focused his playing to 3rd base, and was then picked up by the Minnesota Twins in the 26th round of the 1994 Major League draft.

Corey Koskie, the only Manitoban in recent years to play big league baseball

After developing his talent as an infielder for several years on US minor league teams, in 1998 he played his first big-league game for the Twins. Koskie's best season was 2001 when he hit 26 home runs, drove in 103 runs, and batted .276. Though Koskie also had a strong 2003 season, he left the Twins in 2004 as a free agent after contract talks broke down. Koskie signed a 3-year, $16-million contract with the Toronto Blue Jays for the following season, fulfilling a childhood dream to play on native turf, and becoming the first Cdn player to hold an everyday position on the team since 1978. However, the Jays soon found themselves with a glut of 3rd-baggers, and Koskie's disappointing, injury-plagued season, with just 11 homers, 36 RBI, and a .249 average over 97 games, resulted in his trade to the Milwaukee Brewers. As of 2007, he was not playing, still plagued by the effects of a concussion. In 989 career games, Koskie had a .275 lifetime batting average with 124 home runs and 516 runs batted in. The only other MB athlete to play extensively in the Majors was **RUSSELL FORD**. Koskie was named MB's Male Athlete of the Year in 1999 and 2001. • MD

KRAFCHENKO, John Larry "Bloody Jack," outlaw (b 1881, Romania; d July 9, 1914, **WINNIPEG**) was one of MB's most notorious bandits, whose short life was spent in a series of crime sprees and daring prison escapes. Though described by some as a debonair and charismatic man, he was also possessed of a fierce temper. Nonetheless, his flagrant disregard for authority made him something of a folk hero to MB's marginalized immigrant community.

Born to **UKRAINIAN** parents, Krafchenko grew up in **PLUM COULEE**. His father was a gambler and carouser, and his mother had been an infamous horse thief in Europe. From an early age, Krafchenko also displayed a wild nature. At the age of 11, he had his first run-in with the law after stealing watches from a jewellery store, and at 15 he was imprisoned for stealing a bicycle. He briefly made a somewhat honest living as a professional wrestler in the US and Australia in his early twenties, making up for his small stature at 5 ft 6 in and 160 lbs with a brazen attitude. He was also endowed with a silver tongue, in addition to fluency in 5 languages, and in 1902 he toured the Prairies as a supporter of **PROHIBITION**. This was hardly a sign of moral reform: Krafchenko financed his proselytizing with fraudulent cheques, leading to his arrest in SK. Krafchenko, however, never served his sentence at the Prince Albert Penitentiary, making a bold prison escape by knocking out the jail guard with a paint can. On the lam, Krafchenko

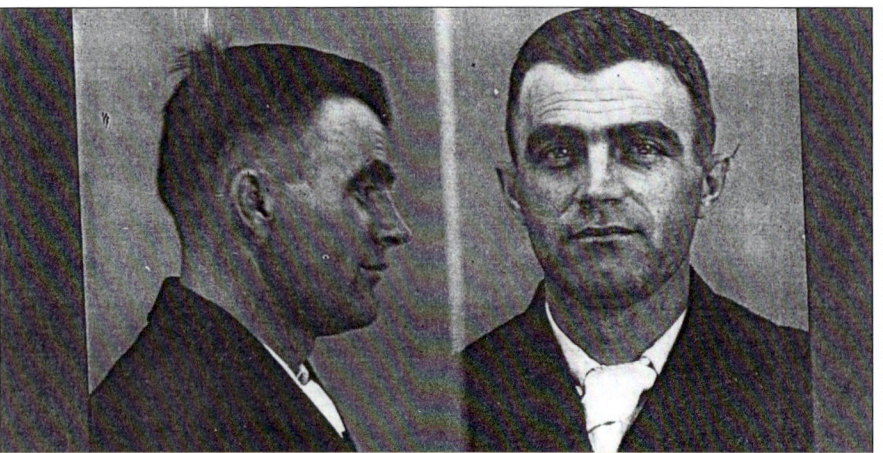

Jack Krafchenko's mugshot, just before his execution, 1914

K

embarked on a NA crime spree, committing robberies across the continent before stowing away on an Atlantic freighter bound for Europe. While there, he managed to evade arrest, despite making little attempt to keep a low profile. In one instance, having successfully robbed a bank in Milan, Krafchenko didn't even attempt to flee the scene, but rather slipped into the assembled crowd of curious spectators so that he could watch police investigate his crime.

Though an incorrigible ladies' man, Krafchenko married a Russian woman in 1905. The couple returned to the calm of Plum Coulee, but Krafchenko's restless spirit got the better of him, and he left his wife to once again plunder and pillage his way through NA, only returning to MB in 1908 to serve as a defence witness in a friend's murder trial. Krafchenko was then seized by Cdn authorities for his previous crimes and imprisoned. He served his time, though it did little to reform the career swindler. Upon his release, Krafchenko offered himself to the service of the Winnipeg police as a robbery consultant, convincing the chief to pay him an advance consultancy fee before taking off with the money. In a seeming attempt at something of a respectable life, Krafchenko then worked briefly as a railway labourer in ON. However, he despised manual labour and was even less amenable to taking orders from superiors. He was fired, and returned to Plum Coulee.

Krafchenko was well known in his hometown, and so the disguise he sported on Dec 3, 1913, in order to rob the town bank did little to conceal his true identity from his neighbours. Generally unashamed of his criminal exploits and preferring to utilize his wits rather than violence, Krafchenko that day made the most egregious error in judgement of his life. When bank manager Henry Arnold started chasing Krafchenko, the robber turned around and fired his gun,

killing the respected citizen instantly. A quick investigation resulted in Krafchenko's arrest for the murder. He made a final desperate escape from jail with the help of his lawyer and a prison guard, but was recaptured following a massive manhunt. Krafchenko's court case became a sensational media event that made front page news for a month. He was convicted and, though some supporters petitioned the fed govt for clemency, he was executed by hanging at Winnipeg's Vaughan Street Jail on July 9, 1914. Krafchenko is the subject of a long poem by **Dennis Cooley**, *Bloody Jack* (1984). ● MICHELLE DOBROVOLNY

KREVIAZUK, Chantal, pop singer/songwriter (b May 18, 1973, **Winnipeg**). In 1995, Kreviazuk was an unknown 21-year-old from suburban Charleswood, when she made headlines by signing a $1.5-million recording contract with Sony Music. The Balmoral Hall girls' school student had been honing her songwriting for several years under the tutelage of **Chris Burke-Gaffney** and producer Danny Schur. Her debut album, *Under These Rocks and Stars* (1997), recorded in Los Angeles with producer Peter Asher, was a critical and sales success. It featured hit singles "Wayne" and "Surrounded," inspired by the suicide of a close friend. She contributed "Feels Like Home" to the soundtrack for television series *Dawson's Creek* (1998-2003), and covered John Denver's "Leaving on a Jet Plane" for the 1998 film *Armageddon*. Her 2nd album, *Colour Moving and Still* (1999) included hits "Dear Life," "Faraway," and "Before You," inspired by her fiancé, Our Lady Peace singer Raine Maida, whom she married in Dec 1999. All 3 singles reached number 1 on *MuchMusic*. In 2000, Kreviazuk won 2 Juno Awards: Female Vocalist of the Year and Best Pop/Alternative Album for *Colour Moving and Still*. Her 3rd album, *What If It All Means Something* (2002), yielded the hit "In This Life." As a songwriter, Kreviazuk co-wrote several songs for Cdn pop star Avril Lavigne's 2004 album *Under My Skin*, and wrote "Meant To Fly" with Maida for 2006 *Canadian Idol* winner Eva Avila. *Ghost Stories*, her 4th album, was released in late 2006. ● JOHN EINARSON

KRINDLE, Ruth, lawyer, judge (b Feb 6, 1943, **Winnipeg**), practised labour law in Winnipeg 1968-71, when she became a prosecutor with the

Chantal Kreviazuk performing at Winnipeg's Centennial Concert Hall

Ruth Krindle, 1971

Attorney General's department (now the Department of Justice), becoming the province's first female Crown attorney. She was named chair of the Manitoba Labour Board in 1976, and returned to private practice the following year. Appointed a judge of the then–County Court of Winnipeg in 1980, she was the first woman in MB to be appointed to a federal judgeship. In 1984, she was appointed to the Court of Queen's Bench of MB. She retired from that court in 2002. After leaving the bench, she participated in a pilot project to reduce **Residential School** claims by First Nations and **Métis** people, and continues to act as the arbitrator for the **Northern Flood Agreement**. In 2002, the Canadian Bar Association presented her with its Sexual Orientation and Gender Identity Conference Hero Award. ● DOUG JOHNSTON

KROETSCH, Robert, writer, editor, teacher (b June 26, 1927, Heisler, AB). Kroetsch grew up on his father's farm, and this rural experience was to remain the backbone of his writing. After his graduation in 1948 from the U of AB, he spent 3 summers in the north, first as a labourer on the Slave River freight barges and then as purser on a Mackenzie River tugboat. His next job took him to the US Air Force base at Goose Bay, NL, in charge of information and education. In 1954, Kroetsch returned to graduate school at McGill U, to study under the noted NS/QC novelist Hugh MacLennan, and then to complete a master's degree at Middlebury College in Vermont and a doctorate at the U of IA. He joined the Faculty

of English at the State U of NY in 1961, remaining in the US for more than 20 years. In 1978, he came back to Canada to teach creative writing and Cdn literature at the **U of M**, where he was named a distinguished professor in 1985.

Kroetsch published his first short story in *The Montrealer* in 1950, and his first novel, *But We Are Exiles*, in 1966. He has written 9 nationally celebrated novels, as well as 12 books of poetry and a significant number of critical essays and other non-fiction works. He won the Gov Gen's Award for fiction in 1969 for *The Studhorse Man*, and with the publication in 2001 of *The Hornbooks of Rita K,* he was short-listed for the Gov Gen's Award for poetry. Among his many honours, Kroetsch received honorary doctorates from the **U of W** (1983) and the University College of the Cariboo (2002); was made a Fellow of the Royal Society of Canada in 1986; and was awarded the MB Arts Council Award of Distinction in 2004.

Kroetsch has frequently described his image of Canada, and especially of the north country and the western Prairies, as a complex, discontinuous land, composed of many different regions without a single, all-embracing identity; a sense of the ineffable multiplicity of all existence pervades his work. Accordingly, his writing, in both fiction and poetry, is postmodern, deliberately fragmented, confusing in its alternations between raucous comedy and mythic surrealism, breaking the categories of traditional forms, and denying the possibility of a single, clear interpretation. The founder in 1974 of a journal of postmodern writing, *Boundary 2*, he has been a central influence in the course of contemporary Cdn writing, and has mentored untold numbers of students. ● MILDRED GUTKIN

KROITOR, Roman, filmmaker, (b Dec 12, 1926, Yorkton, SK) was a member of the famed "Unit B" of the **National Film Board**, producing, directing, writing and/or editing some of the most memorable Canadian films of the 1950s and '60s, including film portraits of Glenn Gould, Igor Stravinsky, and Paul Anka. *Universe*, which he wrote and co-directed with Colin Low, was a major influence on Stanley Kubrick's *2001: A Space Odyssey*. Kroitor joined the NFB shortly after graduating with a BA from the **U of M** and created a 10-minute film portrait in 1954 called *Paul Tomkowicz: Street Railway Switchman*, which became one of the touchstones of the Cdn cinéma-vérité movement. Kroitor's skill as a technical innovator led to the Labyrinth project, also with Colin Low, a multi-screen presentation that was one of the hits of Expo 67. With partners Graeme Ferguson and Robert Kerr, he then

developed and founded the IMAX Corporation, for which he wrote and produced its first giant-screen, 70-mm film, *Tiger Child*, and many others. He was the driving force behind *Heartland* (1987), an IMAX film about MB. ● GENE WALZ

K-TEL INTERNATIONAL INC

K-TEL INTERNATIONAL INC was a family-run, **Winnipeg**-based music and consumer product corporation, known for its innovative television marketing strategies in the 1960s and '70s. K-Tel was famous for producing such items as the "Veg-O-Matic" food slicer, non-stick frying pans, and the "Miracle Brush" lint remover. It was one of the first companies to depend on television commercials to hard-sell its products. The distinctive, frantic style of the commercials was delivered by Bob Washington, a former DJ for Winnipeg's CKRC radio station.

K-Tel record

The company was the brainchild of Philip Kives, a son of Jewish farmers from SK. After completing high school in SK, Kives discovered he had a flair for salesmanship which he honed at fairs in rural Prairie towns. Moving to Winnipeg in 1962, he founded K-Tel (short for Kives Television.). His cousins Raymond and Harold Kives, along with Mickey Elfenbein, served as senior executives. In 1965, the company added to its household gadgets by marketing a line of "Greatest Hits" records, again pitching them on TV throughout North America. Within 10 years, the company was producing an average of 4 compilation records per month.

In the 1980s, K-Tel expanded into computer software, videogames, property investments, movie production and oil-and-gas development. In 1984, this rapid expansion led banks to call in their loans. In 1985, K-Tel closed its doors in Canada and went into receivership in the US. In Canada, Kives started a new company called K-5. He won the right to use the K-Tel name in Canada again in the early 1990s. K-Tel's stock price soared after Kives announced the company was going to sell music over the Internet, which was then a fledgling medium. But K-Tel was not successful in this endeavour, and became the subject of a massive class-action lawsuit that ultimately failed.

In the early 2000s, K-Tel then made a brief foray into selling pharmaceuticals over the Internet. In 2007, the principle focus of the company is on music distribution, licensing, and downloading, as well as consumer product marketing and distribution via mail-order, online, phone-in, and retail stores. • GPP

KU KLUX KLAN. The KKK had a brief presence in MB, especially around **SOURIS**, operating under the Protestant Orange Lodge. The first recorded meeting in MB was in 1928, organized by Klansman D. C. Grant from SK, where KKK membership once numbered 40,000. The Klan, founded in the Southern US in 1915 and modelled after an older organization of the same name, believed in the supremacy of white, Anglo-Saxon, Protestant society, and opposed immigration from Eastern Europe, especially by **JEWS**. The MB meeting was also vehemently anti–**ROMAN CATHOLIC**, inciting the wrath of priests from the **COLLÈGE UNIVERSITAIRE DE SAINT-BONIFACE**. The ultraconservative Grant also preached moral reform, seeking to eliminate **WINNIPEG** bordellos and public drunkenness. The KKK presence in MB quickly died out after Grant returned to SK, joining the CCF, and, in 1935, becoming an organizer for **TOMMY DOUGLAS** in the Weyburn constituency. Julian Sher documents this unpleasant chapter of Cdn history in *White Hoods: Canada's Ku Klux Klan* (Vancouver: New Star, 1983). • MD

KURELEK, William, painter, writer (b Mar 3, 1927, Whitford, AB; d Nov 3, 1977, Toronto). Kurelek was born the eldest of 7 children to a **UKRAINIAN** immigrant farming family in AB. The family lost the farm in the **GREAT DEPRESSION** and moved to **STONEWALL** when Kurelek was 7. He attended school there and in **WINNIPEG**, earning a BA from the **U OF M** in 1949. Kurelek dreamed of becoming an artist, against the wishes of his father whom he felt he could never please. He did begin his art education at the Ontario College of Art before studying at the Instituto Allende in San Miguel de Allende, Guanajuato, Mexico (1950). It was during his early adult years that he first began to show signs of depression and schizophrenia. He received treatment for his condition in England from 1952-57 as a patient and as an outpatient of a psychiatric hospital. At the same time, he studied art, worked at temporary jobs, and travelled to continental Europe

where he was influenced by museum collections. In 1957, he converted to the **ROMAN CATHOLIC** faith and returned to Canada, settling in Toronto. His spiritual quest prompted him to illustrate the Passion of Christ in 161 works, a project that took him to the Holy Land to retrace Jesus' steps. However, Kurelek is probably best known for the paintings and classic books that drew on his experiences as a youth on the Prairies. His emotional symptoms lessened and he was able to work prolifically – the Prairie landscape, lives of immigrants, the Ukrainians, Jews, Poles and Irish, and the key roles of women in the family were his subjects. His work, evocative and nostalgic, executed in minute detail, is imbued with Christian imagery and iconography. As the author and illustrator of children's books, he produced *Prairie Boy's Winter* and *Prairie Boy's Summer*. He also exhibited widely across Canada, the US and Europe, becoming internationally acclaimed during his lifetime. Kurelek completed his autobiography *Someone With Me*, before he died at the age of 50. In 1976, he received the Order of Canada. • PATRICIA BOVEY

KUZYK, Marilyn "Mimi," actor, dancer (b Feb 21, 1952, **WINNIPEG**), has appeared in numerous television shows and feature films. Kuzyk grew up in Winnipeg and attended the Immaculate Heart of Mary School. She wanted to be a song-and-dance artist on Broadway. After studying with the **ROYAL WINNIPEG BALLET**, Mimi danced for 12 years with the Rusalka Ukrainian Dance Ensemble (*see* **DANCE**). Kuzyk's screen debut was as an extra on a 1979 episode of *SCTV*. Her first feature performance was in 1984's *He's Hired, She's Fired*, but she has spent most of her career in TV playing supporting roles and occasional leads. Kuzyk's best-known role was that of Patsy Mayo on the 1980s police drama *Hill Street Blues*. She has also appeared in episodes of *L.A. Law, Street Legal, Traders, The Chris Isaak Show,* and *Navy NCIS: Naval Criminal Investigative Service.* Kuzyk's feature films include *Lost and Delirious* (2001), *The Human Stain* (2003), *The Day after Tomorrow* (2004), *Kardia* (2006), and *Camille* (slated for 2007). At the 2002 Genie Awards, Kuzyk was nominated for Best Supporting Actress for her role in *Lost and Delirious*. • AMANDA STEPHENS

KUZYK, Sylvia, TV personality (b 1950, Berlin, Germany) was one of the first female on-air TV news personalities in western Canada. Over the course of her 30-year career, she has become one of MB's most-recognized faces. Kuzyk immigrated to **WINNIPEG** with her family from Berlin at the age of 3. She initially pursued a career as a

nurse, and by age 19 was working in a Winnipeg hospital. The course of her life changed after Kuzyk enrolled in a community theatre course. Though innately shy, Kuyzk discovered she also had talent as a public speaker, and pursued acting as a hobby. While cast in a small dramatic role for a local TV production, Kuzyk learned of an opening as a weather anchor in the CKY news department. She auditioned on a whim and, to her surprise, was offered the position. She gave her first weather report in Feb 1974.

Her first years on the job were daunting as TV news at the time was still traditionally considered a male enterprise. Reaction to Kuzyk's first appearances was sometimes negative, and viewers unused to seeing a woman on a news program sent Kuzyk mail telling her to stay at home and cook supper for her family. Kuzyk also had to contend with co-workers and management who refused to take a female broadcaster seriously. She persisted, and over the years her career branched out into different segments of TV news and programming. Kuzyk has worked as an interviewer, producer, and a host on several daytime talk shows, all the while continuing as the weather anchor for CKY news, now CTV Winnipeg. Over the course of her lengthy career, she has seen weather reporting advance from plexi-glass weather board and greasepencil markers to state-of-the-art weather tracking technology. Kuzyk is also a supporter of numerous local charitable organizations, and has earned several awards for her community work, including the 2004 YM/YWCA Women of Distinction Award. • MD

UMA, TRIBUNE, PERSONALITY FILES

Sylvia Kuzyk, 1977

LAKES,
see pages 381-384

LA BROQUERIE, pop. 505, is a largely French-speaking community 80 km SE of Winnipeg on the Seine River and on a **CNR** line near Sandilands Provincial Forest. The first settlers arrived in the region in 1877, mainly from QC, and the majority of locals still claim **FRENCH** ancestry, with smaller, more-recent populations of **MENNONITE** and **DUTCH** descent. The community was named after the RM of the same name, which was in turn named for Joseph de la Broquerie, a direct descendant of **LA VÉRENDRYE** and a brother of **ALEXANDRE-ANTONIN TACHÉ**'s mother. The post office in the community opened in 1882. La Broquerie is a large service centre, catering to surrounding dairy and livestock operations. It also houses a water-bottling facility. Tourists, largely drawn to the nearby provincial forest, provide revenue. The community maintains its Francophone flavour, visible in its Fête Saint-Jean-Baptiste celebration every June 24. ● GPP

LA JEMERAIS, Christophe Dufrost de, cartographer, explorer (b Dec 6, 1708 Varennes, New France [QC]; d May 10, 1736, Roseau River [near **LETELLIER**]). Christophe Dufrost de la Jemerais, the youngest of a family of old **FRENCH** nobility that came to New France in 1685, entered the army at a young age. In 1731, after serving in various French posts, he went with his uncle, **PIERRE GAULTIER DE LA VÉRENDRYE**, as his 2nd-in-command on their first expedition towards the "Western Sea." That year, they built Fort St Pierre, at the W extremity of Rainy Lake, near present-day Fort Frances, ON. The following, year he accompanied La Vérendrye to Lake of the Woods and helped build Fort St Charles, near today's MN/ON border. In spring 1733, he and his cousin Jean-Baptiste Gaultier de La Vérendrye went to within a few km of **LAKE WINNIPEG** in search of a suitable site for a fort.

La Jemerais wrote to Charles, Marquis de la Boische, the gov gen of New France, in 1735 to inform him of the commercial activities of the posts. The marquis instructed him to visit the Mandans in the Missouri River region (around modern ND). He was sent to Fort Maurepas on the **RED RIVER**, just S of **NETLEY-LIBAU MARSH**, where, during winter 1735-36, he fell seriously ill. He died on May 10, 1736, while his 2 La Vérendrye cousins, who had been sent to his aid, were trying to bring him back to Fort St Charles, using the Roseau River/Savanne Portage route, which no other Frenchman had used before. He was buried where the Roseau joins the Red, on what is now the **ROSEAU RIVER FIRST NATION**, near the present village of Letellier. La Jemerais was a

skilled cartographer who knew how to "measure an elevation." He drew the first French map of the West, which is also the best of this era. His sister was St. Marie-Marguerite d'Youville, founder of the Sisters of Charity (**Grey Nuns**) of Montreal.
● LUCIEN CHAPUT

LA RIVIERE, pop 250, is an unincorporated community 120 km SW of **Winnipeg** on the Pembina River. A **CPR** point was established here in 1886, and a post office opened the following year. The community was named after Alphonse Alfred Clement la Rivière, who served as an area MLA, MP, and senator at the turn of the century. Located in a picturesque corner of the province, La Riviere is a recreational getaway. One of MB's few winter ski resorts lies one km SW of the community. A suspension bridge over the Pembina River leads to the resort. A 2.7-m-tall statue of "Tom the turkey" stands in the community as a tribute to those who introduced wild turkeys to the province through La Riviere. A passion play takes place each July at an outdoor theatre just outside of the community. ● GPP

LA SALLE, pop 1700, is a community 25 km SW of **Winnipeg** on the **La Salle River**. It was formerly named St. Hyacinthe by a local priest. The **CPR** built a railway station in 1882 and the post office opened in 1891. In the 21st century, La Salle's economy is based on supplying services to local **Agricultural** operations. The community was growing rapidly by 2007, partly due to being a bedroom community for Winnipeg. There is a golf and country club here. ● GPP

LA SALLE RIVER, a tributary of the **Red River**, rises near **Portage la Prairie**, probably following an ancient route of the **Assiniboine River**.

First used by and known to Assiniboine, **Cree**, and other First Nations peoples thousands of years ago, the La Salle was navigated by early European explorers and **Fur Traders**, including Alexander Henry. By the time Henry came to the area (around 1800), the river was known as Salé, French for *salted*, because of nearby saline springs or deposits; and as the Sale, French for *dirty*, because of the waterway's colour or its water's non-potable nature. The name was later changed to La Salle – a common name in NA, usually honouring the French-born explorer, René-Robert Cavalier, Sieur de la Salle. Regular **Flooding** of the La Salle has caused surrounding lands to be rich in nutrients, making them ideal for **Agriculture**. The same proneness to flooding caused the **Red River Floodway** to be less-than-effective, necessitating the construction of the **Brunkild** Dike. The river, which gives its name to the community of **La Salle**, is also a popular **Canoe** and kayaking route in spring and early summer, when snowmelt swells its levels. ● GPP

LA VÉRENDRYE FAMILY was a group of Canadian-born explorers who set out West to discover an overland route to the Pacific Ocean. In so doing, they became the first whites to visit what is now Manitoba, helped set the stage for the later emergence of Métis culture in the West, and created a new fur-trade empire for New France.

LA VÉRENDRYE, PIERRE GAULTIER DE VARENNES, SIEUR DE, officer, fur trader (b Nov 17, 1685, Trois-Rivières, New France [QC]; d Dec 5, 1749, Ville-Marie [Montreal], New France). Pierre Gaultier de Varennes, Sieur de la Vérendrye, was the son of **French** soldier René Gaultier de Varennes, who came to Canada as a Lt in the Carignan-Salières Regt, and Marie Boucher,

the daughter of Pierre Boucher, the local gov of Trois-Rivières. The youngest of 13 children, 8 of whom reached adulthood, Pierre studied at a seminary 1696-99 before choosing a military career. He saw action in MA in 1704, and in Nfld the following year. In 1708, Pierre decided to pursue his military career in France with the Régiment de Bretagne, and on Sept 11, 1709, was seriously wounded at the Battle of Malplaquet and was taken prisoner. Following his release in 1710, he was promoted to Lt. Unable to finance the social obligations that come with the rank, he returned to New France. On Oct 24, 1712, shortly after his arrival, he wed Marie-Anne Dandonneau DuSablé, the daughter of a substantial landowner in Trois-Rivières. The couple had 4 sons and 2 daughters: Jean-Baptiste (b 1713); Pierre Gaultier de la Vérendrye de Boumois; François la Vérendrye; Louis-Joseph de la Vérendrye; Marie-Anne (b 1721); and Marie-Catherine (b 1724). After ending his military career, La Vérendrye decided he was not cut out for the farming life. Thus, when in 1726 his brother Jacques-René received command of the *Poste du Nord*, headquartered at Kaministiquia (now Thunder Bay, ON), La Vérendrye joined the partnership as 2nd-in-command, becoming commander-in-chief in 1728. While commanding at the *Poste du Nord*, he questioned the First Nations people who came to trade. The **Cree** chief Pako told him about Lake Ouinipon (**Lake Winnipeg**) and its river system. Another Cree man, Auchagah, drew for him on a piece of bark a map of the western country. From this information, La Vérendrye concluded that the discovery of the Western Sea lay in the region of Lake Ouinipigon. In 1730, La Vérendrye was appointed commandant of the post to be built on Lake Ouinipigon, and received a monopoly of the area's fur trade for 3 years.

On June 8, 1731, La Vérendrye – accompanied by his sons Jean-Baptiste, Pierre, François, and some 50 *engagés* – set out from what is now Montreal, arriving Aug 26, 1731, at the Grand Portage, at the W extremity of Lake Superior. Under the command of La Vérendrye's nephew **Christophe la Jemerais** and his son, Jean-Baptiste, an advance party reached Rainy Lake, where they built Fort Saint-Pierre, the first of 8 posts eventually established by the La Vérendrye expedition in the Northwest. In spring 1732, the 2 groups, accompanied by Cree and Assiniboine, moved on to Lake of the Woods, where they built Fort Saint-Charles. This would serve as La Vérendrye's headquarters for the next several years. On June 21, 1735, after a visit to Quebec, La Vérendrye departed once more for the West accompanied by Louis-Joseph, the youngest of his sons, and the Jesuit Jean-Pierre Aulneau, arriving at Fort Saint-Charles on Oct 23.

La Salle River

STAN MILOSEVIC, WWW.MANITOBAPHOTOS.COM

During the following months, the worst series of setbacks of the commandant's career began. His nephew and second-in-command La Jemerais, stricken ill while commanding at Fort Maurepas on the **RED RIVER** (just S of **NETLEY-LIBAU MARSH**), died as he was being brought back to Fort Saint-Charles. Then, on June 8, 1736, an expedition led by his son Jean-Baptiste was attacked on an island in Lake of the Woods. All 20 were killed, including Jean-Baptiste and Père Aulneau. Despite these tragedies, La Vérendrye was determined to push on to Lake Winnipeg, and finally arrived at Fort Maurepas in Feb 1737.

La Vérendrye then decided to return to New France, where he received a cool reception from the gov, who extracted from him a promise that he would reach the Mandans (in what is now the ND area) the following year. Realizing that his future was at stake, La Vérendrye set out with new vigour. Arriving at Fort Maurepas Sept 22, 1738, he and his men would build Fort Rouge at **THE FORKS** in Winnipeg and Fort la Reine in what is now **PORTAGE LA PRAIRIE**. On Oct 16, accompanied by 20 men and his sons Louis-Joseph and François, he left for Mandan country, arriving at the main Mandan village, not far from the Missouri River, at the beginning of Dec. The journey to the Mandans left La Vérendrye physically exhausted and cash-strapped. In June 1740, he made a 3rd trip back to Quebec, hoping to straighten out his finances for another trip to the Missouri River country. Upon reaching Montreal, he learned that his wife, who was also his lawyer and procurator, had died the previous Sept.

In June 1741, after receiving the fur-trading monopoly of the posts he had founded, he set out on his 4th and last voyage to the West. With his headquarters now established at Fort la Reine, he sent Louis-Joseph and François in 1742-43 on a 14-month journey that took him to the Big Horn Mountains of WY. He also delegated his 3rd son, Pierre, the task of consolidating their control of the lakes in what is now MB. Between 1741 and 1743, Pierre would build Fort Dauphin (at what is now the Village of **WINNIPEGOSIS**) while members of his party would build Fort Bourbon, to the NW of **LAKE WINNIPEG** (*see* **GRAND RAPIDS**), and Fort Paskoya (*see* **THE PAS**). By then, the gov of New France was under pressure to remove La Vérendrye from the West. No doubt aware of this, La Vérendrye resigned effective 1744. He received an officer's commission and was named Capt of the Governor's Guards. In 1746, La Vérendrye was once again appointed commander of the western posts, and started planning another expedition, this time up the Saskatchewan River. He had planned to leave for the West in 1750, but died Dec 5, 1749. Though

La Vérendrye was penniless at the time of his death, he had pushed back the frontiers of New France as far as what is now MB. The posts he and his sons built W of the Great Lakes later diverted much of the fur of the Saskatchewan and **ASSINIBOINE RIVER** areas from **HUDSON BAY** to the St. Lawrence.

La Vérendrye statue in St. Boniface

LA VÉRENDRYE DE BOUMOIS, PIERRE GAULTIER DE, soldier, explorer (b Dec 1, 1714, Île aux Vaches [just W of modern Montreal]; d Sept 13, 1755, Ville-Marie [Montreal]). Pierre Gaultier de la Vérendrye, the 2nd son of Pierre Gaultier de Varennes et de la Vérendrye, was only 16 years old when in 1731 he left for the West with his father, 2 brothers and a cousin. In 1732, he accompanied his father to Lake of the Woods, where they built Fort Saint-Charles. When his father left for Montreal in 1734, Pierre was given command of the fort. A few years later, La Vérendrye Sr gave his son the necessary goods for an exploratory voyage into the Mandan and Pawnee country. Pierre went to Fort la Reine, at what is now Portage la Prairie, on the Assiniboine River, overwintering before leaving in spring 1741 with 2 other Frenchmen, going as far S as Pawnee territory in what is now NE. He returned to Fort la Reine with 2 horses, including possibly the first horse in MB. La Vérendrye Sr joined him there in Oct 1741, and immediately sent his son to build Fort Dauphin, N of Dauphin Lake, near present-day Winnipegosis. Pierre left the West in 1745 for what is now Montreal, and soon was engaged in various military operations in New England and Acadia. He would return to the West in 1748 to rebuild Fort Maurepas (on the Red River, just S of Netley-Libau Marsh), which had fallen into ruins. He died in Montreal, a bachelor, in Sept 1755.

LA VÉRENDRYE, FRANÇOIS GAULTIER DE, explorer (b Oct 29, 1715, Sorel, New France [QC]; d July 30, 1794, Ville-Marie [Montreal]). The 3rd son of the La Vérendrye family, François, also known as François Gaultier du Tremblay, was not yet 16 when he left for the West with his father and 2 of his brothers in 1731. After wintering at Kaministiquia (now Thunder Bay, ON), he spent the summer of 1732 building Fort Saint-Charles on Lake of the Woods. He accompanied his father to the Mandan country, in present-day ND, in 1738. He returned to this area a few years later during a 14-month expedition organized by his brother Louis-Joseph, the Chevalier de La Vérendrye. After his father's resignation in 1744, François remained in the West and served under the new commander, Nicolas-Joseph de Noyelles de Fleurimont, whose wife was a niece of La Vérendrye. François was still in the region when his father died in Dec 1749 in Montreal. He returned to Montreal with his brother in 1755, and, on Louis-Joseph's death in 1761, found himself in possession of the family estate. This he surrendered to Louis-Joseph's widow, on condition she give him an annual allowance. François Gaultier de la Vérendrye, unlike his brothers and father, was illiterate, and he lived modestly and unobtrusively. With his death in 1794, the La Vérendrye line ended.

LA VÉRENDRYE, "CHEVALIER" (SIEUR) LOUIS-JOSEPH GAULTIER DE, cartographer, explorer, fur trader (b Nov 9, 1717, Île aux Vaches [just W of present-day Montreal]; d Nov 15, 1761, off Île Royal [now Cape Breton Island, NS]). Louis-Joseph Gaultier de La Vérendrye was the 4th son of explorer Pierre Gaultier de Varennes et de la Vérendrye. Sent to Quebec City in 1734 to learn mathematics and drawing, he left on June 21, 1735, with his father and the Jesuit Jean-Pierre Aulneau for Fort Saint-Charles on Lake of the Woods. Louis-Joseph's first year in the West was marked by the death of his cousin, Christophe Dufrost de la Jemerais, and, a month later, the death of his older brother, Jean-Baptiste Gaultier de la Vérendrye. A party of Sioux (Dakota) killed the latter at Lake of the Woods. With the death of his brother, Louis-Joseph became his father's 2nd-in-command and received the title "Chevalier" ("knight" or "sir"). In Sept 1736, La Vérendrye sent him to re-establish Fort Maurepas at the N end of the Red River just S of Netley-Libau Marsh, which had been abandoned after La Jemerais's death. Louis-Joseph was present at a great council held at Fort Maurepas in March 1737 with **CREE** and Assiniboine chiefs. Louis-Joseph was then sent on an exploratory trip to **LAKE WINNIPEG**, but smallpox (*see* **EPIDEMICS**) among the Cree in that region forced him to return to Fort Saint-Charles. In Oct 1738, after building Fort la Reine, at what is now **PORTAGE LA PRAIRIE**, father and son set out for the Mandan country, in present-day ND.

In April 1739, Louis-Joseph resumed the expedition around Lake Winnipeg to find a site N of Lac des Prairies (lakes **MANITOBA** and **WINNIPEGOSIS**) for a fort, which the Cree in the region had requested. Chevalier spent winter 1741-42 at Fort la Reine preparing to resume explorations into the southwest. He left on April 29, 1742, accompanied by his brother, François, 2 Frenchmen, and some Indian guides. Their 14-month trip would take them as far W as the Big Horn Mountains in Wyoming and S to the Bad and Missouri rivers. As a result of this expedition, La Vérendrye concluded that the route to the Western Sea was not to the SW but to the NW, via the Saskatchewan. With the fall of New France in 1759, the Chevalier prepared for a trip to France to settle some business matters. He set off from Quebec in 1761, aboard the *Auguste*. A month later, on Nov 15, the ship was wrecked on the shores of Cape Breton Island. The Chevalier perished, as did most of the other passengers and crew. Louis-Joseph was married twice; no children were born of these unions. ● LUCIEN CHAPUT

LABOUR FORCE is the total of the adult population, aged 15 and older, available to the labour market at any time. Labour force is determined by the interaction between the number of persons available for work – supply – and the number of jobs available – demand. Labour supply is determined by the size of the population and the fraction of the adult population that chooses to participate in the labour force. From 1976 to 2004, the MB labour force grew at an annual rate of 1%. This growth was due to a combination of increase in the adult population, and a substantially higher female labour participation rate.

MB's working-age population in 2004 was 881,400. Historically, MB's population growth has been adversely affected by out-migration from the province (*see* **POPULATION GROWTH TRENDS**). Between 1993 and 2003, for example, MB had a net average interprovincial out-migration of 3541. In 2004, however, the province lost only 1138 people. The most mobile sector of the population is Manitobans aged 15 to 24 years, with 5% of MB's population in this age group migrating between provinces. To counteract the outflow of working-aged population, MB has relied on **IMMIGRATION** as a major contributor to provincial population and labour force growth. In 2004, 7414 immigrants migrated to MB, a 14% increase from the previous year. While 80% of immigrants called **WINNIPEG** home, both the South Central

The Manitoba Labour Force: 1976 and 2002

YEAR	LABOUR FORCE (000s)		
	TOTAL	MALE	FEMALE
1976	456	281	175
2002	598	321	277

Source: Statistics Canada, The Labour Force Survey

(8%) and Southeast (6%) regions accounted for significant immigration levels.

From 1976 to 2004, the overall labour force participation in MB rose from 61% to 69%, the second-highest rate in Canada behind AB's 73.4%. This increased participation rate was primarily due to a female labour participation rate that grew from 46% to 62%, more than offsetting a small decline in the male participation rate from 77% to 75%. Still, the distribution of occupations chosen by women has changed slowly over time, with 55% of women being employed in sales, service, financial, secretarial, administrative, and clerical occupations in 2004. This compares to 60.5% in the same occupations in 1987. In 2004, 6.6% of all women in the labour force, compared to 5.9% in 1987, were employed in management positions, while 12.4%, compared to 10.2 in 1987, of women were in health-related occupations. Furthermore, 12.3%, compared to 8.3% in 1987, of all women employed were in education, govt, and religion-related occupations.

DEMAND FOR LABOUR: Labour demand depends indirectly on demand for goods and services produced by labour. Employers vary in many ways, including the size of the firm and the industry to which the firm belongs. In 2002, firms that hired 500 or more employees accounted for 49% of employment; firms that hired 100-499 employees accounted for 32% of employment; and firms that hired 20 or fewer employees accounted for 19% of employment. In 1976, the rate of self-employment was 11.6% in MB, whereas in 2002, it was 14.6%. Although self-employment has become more common, Manitobans tend to depend on employment with large firms for their livelihood.

EMPLOYMENT PATTERNS: Employment by industry reflects the industry composition of the overall **ECONOMY**. The MB economy has historically been structured around rural-based agricultural activities. As the economy has modernized, however, the importance of the agricultural sector has declined. Workers have migrated to urban centres, finding employment in other sectors. In 1976, agriculture (excluded the food and drink industries) accounted for 36,100 jobs, or 8.3 % of total employment, whereas in 2002, agriculture accounted for only 30,700 jobs, or 5.4% of total employment.

BUSINESS CYCLE: The MB economy is one of the most stable in Canada. The unemployment

rate is generally lower than the national average, and tends to be less volatile over a business cycle. This stability is attributed to the diverse nature of the economy. Economic activity is spread across a variety of industries, including manufacturing; transportation (*see* **RAILWAYS**); and the **SERVICE INDUSTRY**. No one industry dominates the economy. In 2004, for example, growth in employment was reported across many sectors of the economy. While employment in agriculture and wholesale and retail trade remained steady, there was significant employment growth in high-wage durable manufacturing sectors such as metal products, machinery, and equipment. In addition, the **CONSTRUCTION INDUSTRY**, **FOREST PRODUCTS**, **MINING**, oil and gas, finance (*see* **BANKING**) and real estate, health, education, social services, information, culture and recreation, public administration, and professional services all saw employment growth. Employment, however, fell in non-durable manufacturing sectors such as food, clothing, and pulp and paper, and in transportation, warehousing, hotel industry, and other services.

The steady and balanced growth in the province has led to a steady increase in wages. From 1997 to 2004, average wages in MB rose by 22.2% to $16.76 per hour. Despite this increase in wages, the average hourly wage in MB is 9% below the Cdn average hourly wage. Adjusting for inflation, however, wages in MB rose by 6.7% compared to 2.9% in the rest of Canada from 1997 to 2004, showing that MB has been closing the gap.

WAGES: While the MB economy is known for its balanced and steady growth, not all sectors experienced similar wage increases. Managers, employees in natural and applied sciences and in professional health occupations, and contractors and supervisors in trade and transportation occupations had the largest wage increases from 1997 to 2004. The lowest increases were among childcare and home support workers; those employed in protective services; manufacturing labourers, trades helpers in construction and transportation; retail salespersons; and construction tradespersons. In general, those groups with the highest wages also had the lowest unemployment.

Average wages for women relative to men rose to 87% in 2004 from 81% in 1997. As a percentage

Industrial Distribution of Jobs *Main job: 1976-2002*

INDUSTRY	% OF LABOUR FORCE 1976			2002		
	TOTAL	MALE	FEMALE	TOTAL	MALE	FEMALE
Agriculture	8.3	10.5	4.7	5.4	8.0	2.5
Forestry, Fishing, Mining, Oil, and Gas	1.4	2.1	a	1.0	1.9	a
Utilities	2.2	3.1	0.7	1.1	1.6	0.6
Construction	6.2	9.3	1.3	4.5	7.8	0.7
Manufacturing	12.9	15.5	8.7	12.2	16.5	7.3
Wholesale and Retail Trade	17.1	14.8	20.8	15.3	15.3	15.3
Transportation and Warehousing	8.4	11.7	3.1	6.4	9.5	2.8
Finance Services	5.1	3.6	7.6	5.4	3.7	7.3
Professional Services	3.4	3.2	3.7	7.5	8.0	7.0
Education & Health Services	16.0	8.9	27.6	20.1	8.7	33.2
Other Services	12.2	9.9	16.0	14.7	13.1	16.6
Public Administration	6.6	7.2	5.6	6.2	6.0	6.4

a = less than 0.05%

Source: Statistics Canada, The Labour Force Survey

of men's wages, women's wages in MB were second-highest among all the provinces, exceeding the Cdn average of 83% in 2004. Likewise, by 2004, women's wages in professional health occupations and senior management occupations, which were below those of men in 1997, exceeded men's. Women's wages in several other occupations, such as childcare and health technical/assisting workers, had wages that were almost on par with those of men in similar occupations. Occupations with the lowest relative wages for women were the trades, protective services, and manufacturing.

UNIONIZATION: Unionization rate is the percentage of employees belonging to a union. The unionization rate in MB declined from 37.9% in 1981 to 34.9% in 1998. This compares to a drop in the unionization rate for the whole of Canada from 37.6% to 30.2% over the same period. In both MB and Canada, the fall in the unionization rate stems from declining union membership in the private sector. Though this decline can partly be explained by shifts in employment for industries that have traditionally been highly unionized to industries that have historically resisted unionization, this development has not been fully understood. From 1998 to 2004, however, the unionization rate rose back to 38%. This occurred, in part, due to increased unionization among younger workers, whose union coverage rose from 14% in 1997 to 16% in 2004. Industries and occupations with greater union coverage – utilities, public administration, health care and education – tend to have fewer young workers, but employment in these sectors expanded over this time. ● JAMES TOWNSEND

▶ *See also* **BUSINESS, ECONOMY, UNIONS.**

LAC BROCHET. *See* **BROCHET**

LAC DU BONNET, pop 1009, is a town 110 km NE of **WINNIPEG** along the **WINNIPEG RIVER** and hwy 11. The area was explored in the 1730s by **LA VÉRENDRYE** and was known as Lac du Bonnet after the large "bonnet like" swelling of the river not far from this point. The Lac du Bonnet area was settled by many different nationalities that were attracted by a wide range of economic opportunities in farming, logging, and mining. Swedish, Finnish and Latvians settled on the farm lands E of the Winnipeg River, while the **POLISH, UKRAINIANS** and **GERMANS** settled on the land to the W and S **FRENCH,** from Quebec, came to work the lumber camps; **HUTTERITES** came to take advantage of available land; and the **SCOTS** and **ENGLISH** came to provide many of the services and businesses the community needed. The post office and the railway were established here by 1900, although the town was not incorporated until 1947. Lac du Bonnet has significant ties to **AVIATION**: it was the site of an RCAF airbase from 1926-37; housed the first commercial airbase in MB, and was the site of the country's first official Canada Post airmail flight, in Oct 1927. Although aviation and hydroelectric power plants along the **WINNIPEG RIVER** were once important to the economy, the town is now primarily a service centre for area residents. The town likes to note it has a diverse population made up of 26 nationalities. Lac du Bonnet's picturesque location near 2 **PROVINCIAL PARKS** and many of the province's best hiking trails and angling spots also means that the town benefits from tourism. What used to be a sawmill and a brick works plant have been converted into a water-ski facility. Sitting on the edge of the river, Lac du Bonnet's waterfront is a natural draw, with the riverbank becoming a grandstand for annual Canada Day

celebrations. In the winter, trails attract snowmobilers and an annual ice-fishing derby pulls in fishing enthusiasts. ● GPP

LACROSSE is the oldest organized sport in the province, originating as a recreational and spiritual activity of First Nations people. The game, as it is known today, arose from baggataway, a team game played by Algonquians (**OJIBWAY** and **CREE**) of eastern NA. *Baggataway* comes from an Ojibway word meaning "they bump hips." Plains Cree women of what is now MB also played a lacrosse-style game using tree branches and 2 hide-covered, hair-filled sacs that were bound together by a leather cord. They would use the branches to carry the "ball" and propel it through goals. The Cree called it "the testicle game," owing to the peculiar shape of the "double-ball." The English term for lacrosse comes from *la crosse* ("the crozier"), a French missionary's description of the stick, which reminded him of a bishop's crook.

The European version of field lacrosse was brought W by settlers after MB joined the Dominion. Members of Canada's **MILITARY** formed MB's first lacrosse club in 1871. They played outdoors with teams of 12 players, who passed and threw a hard rubber ball using large sticks fitted with a net, following the rules laid down by eastern Cdn clubs. In 1887, Frederick William Drewry and **JOHN WESLEY DAFOE** presented a silver cup for senior league competition in MB, and the Manitoba Lacrosse Association was founded the following year. The sport was immensely popular, with tense rivalries developing between competing clubs. Some estimates for spectator attendance in 1892 range as high as 10,000.

Despite public support for lacrosse, the frequency of matches began to decrease in the

L

Maroons Athletic Club, 1934

1890s, as rival teams became too quarrelsome to play each other, a situation aggravated by often poor marking of fields, and by the fact that flag posts were used instead of nets. The Manitoba Lacrosse Association dissolved in 1892, though the game continued strongly with the Southern Manitoba Lacrosse League made up of teams in Boissevain, Hartney, Melita, and Souris. In 1896, Edward L. Drewry helped form the Western Canadian Lacrosse Association to revive the sport. At that time, Winnipeg entrepreneur and celebrated Hockey player Donald H. Bain was one of MB's top players.

After going unbeaten on a tour of MB, in 1904 the Winnipeg Shamrocks were sent to the Olympic Games at St. Louis, MO, where lacrosse made its first of 2 Olympic appearances as a full-medal sport. The Shamrocks beat Ontarian Mohawk and US teams, and became the first Cdn team to win an Olympic championship at the sport.

Lacrosse was introduced into Winnipeg schools in 1901, and as a result, the 1920s and '30s saw some of MB's best individual players, such as defenceman Richard Henry "Dick" Buckingham. Lacrosse remained one of the primary sports played by schoolboys until 1929, when the game was dropped from school sports, partly due to rough play but also because of the high cost of lacrosse sticks, which were sold to students at a cost of ¢25. Partly for this reason, the popularity of field lacrosse dropped following WWII.

Box lacrosse or "boxla" later took over as the dominant lacrosse form, largely promoted to make use of empty hockey rinks in summer. It is played indoors with 6 player-teams, and is a game comparable to hockey, though far less popular. The Manitoba Lacrosse Association was incorporated in 1982 and consists of about 1700 members playing on 61 teams. Inter-lacrosse is a non-contact version of the game, which can be played in a gymnasium or outside on a field and is mainly promoted as a school sport. Lacrosse has also seen a resurgence in rural areas of MB, with the formation of leagues in Thompson and Beausejour. ● MICHELLE DOBROVOLNY

LAGIMODIÈRE, Jean-Baptiste,

fur trader (b Dec 25, 1778, Saint-Antoine-sur-Richelieu, QC; d Sept 7, 1855, St. Boniface) was among the first French Canadians to settle permanently in the Red River area. A respected coureur de bois, he made a famed 2900 km winter journey from the Red River Settlement to Ville-Marie (Montreal).

Lagimodière was born on the family farm in QC, where he lived until the death of his mother, when he was 8. The young boy was then sent to Maskinongé, QC, to be raised by an aunt. He went into the Fur Trade in 1799, and spent several years near Grand Portage (in what is now MN), likely as a trader for the NWC. He took a Cree woman known as Josette or Josèphte as a Country-Born wife around 1800. They had at least 2 daughters. He left his family to return to Maskinongé in 1805, where he met and married

Marie-Anne Gaboury on April 21, 1806. He had originally intended to settle in Lower Canada (QC) with his new wife, but by spring, with the urging of his wife, had decided to return to the adventurous life of a coureur de bois. He again headed W, this time accompanied by Marie-Anne, who was determined to stay by her husband's side. They arrived in Fort Daer (now Pembina, ND, near Emerson) in Aug, and their daughter Reine was born there Jan 6, 1807. She was likely the first white child born in the West. The family moved further W in the spring, settling at Fort Augustus (now Edmonton), where Lagimodière began trading with the HBC, the beginning of his long and loyal relationship with the company. In 1811, upon hearing of Lord Selkirk's plans for the Red River Settlement, Lagimodière moved his family to the fork of the Red and Assiniboine rivers. He continued to trade furs, and was hired by Miles Macdonell to organize hunting expeditions, supplying food for the settlers and saving them from starvation in the harsh winter of 1812-13.

Lagimodière arrives in Montreal.

By 1815, life in the Selkirk Settlement had not improved. Provisions were scarce, and the situation was further aggravated by the sometimes-violent confrontations with the rival NWC. HBC agent Colin Robertson decided to send Lagimodière to Montreal with a message for Lord Selkirk, informing him of the numerous problems facing his settlers. Lagimodière and 2 companions set out on Oct 17, 1815, and travelled much of the journey on snowshoes. Successfully managing to avoid capture by NWC agents, Lagimodière reached Montreal on Mar 10, 1816. However, on the return trip, the group was arrested by NWC agents, and brought to Fort William (now Thunder Bay, ON). Their belongings were seized, and they were released to continue their journey, though without food or any means to survive. The group pushed forward, living on boiled moss and small animals, and managed to reach the Red River Settlement in summer 1816. In return for his service, Lagimodière was granted farmland at the mouth of the Seine River, in present-day St. Boniface.

Lagimodière became a prosperous farmer, though he continued accepting expeditions from the HBC. His daughter, Julie Lagimodière, married **Louis Riel Sr.** Their first son was **Métis** leader **Louis Riel.** As of 2006, Lagimodière's Franco-Manitoban and Métis descendants numbered about 50,000, making him the patriarch of what is sometimes referred to as "Manitoba's First Family." • MICHELLE DOBROVOLNY

LAGIMODIÈRE, Marie-Anne. *See* **Gaboury, Marie-Anne.**

LAKE, GOING TO THE. A phrase that epitomizes the MB summer, "going to the lake" is used to describe the escape from urban life to the beach or cottage. In MB in particular, going to the lake has developed into an important socio-cultural phenomenon. Though every province may boast a "cottage country," the abundance of idyllic and relatively affordable lakeside properties in MB has made going to the lake the most common choice for a summertime vacation. In fact, MB has the highest per capita ownership of cottages in Canada, with roughly 35,000 cottages situated in rural municipalities or **Provincial Parks.**

The development of going to the lake dates to the turn of the 20th century, as increased urbanization led growing numbers of city-dwellers to seek refuge from a frenetic metropolitan life in a natural setting. MB's first cottage country, in that the property was primarily for recreational use, can be said to have started around Gull Harbour on **Hecla Island** in 1896. However, remote wilderness areas remained hard to access until **Railway** companies began developing destinations for profitable vacation routes. Such was the case in 1901 when **Sir William Whyte** chose the white sands of **Lake Winnipeg** as the site for a resort. **CPR** lines were running to **Winnipeg Beach** by 1903, with the 50¢ fare including admission to a dance hall. Going to the lake quickly caught on, and by 1920, 13 trains were running along the line, prompting the growth of smaller resort towns such as Matlock and Sandy Hook. Not to be outdone, rival Canadian Northern Railway built a rail line to **Grand Beach** in 1916, developing the site with a hotel, sports facilities, and

a dance hall that was said to be the largest in Canada. In addition to the numerous cottage lots offered at Grand Beach, thousands of vacationers could also overnight cheaply in distinctive, semi-permanent structures made of canvas and timber called "Donaldas."

The properties developed by the rail companies were accessible to people of all race and class. **Victoria Beach**, on the other hand, was developed in 1911 by a group of middle-class investors who turned the area into a tightly controlled and highly segregated "family resort," allowing only well-to-do, Anglo-Saxon property owners until as late as the 1960s. Other lakeside developments included the establishment of "fresh air" camps for children, instilling early on in succeeding generations an appreciation for cottage life.

Later, as automobiles replaced the rails as the main means of travel, cottagers began using highways to go to the lake, opening up Canadian Shield regions like the **Whiteshell** and, into ON, the picturesque Lake of the Woods area, where many Manitobans also own recreational property. Additionally, many Brandonites, as well as Winnipeggers, enjoy Clear Lake in **Riding Mountain National Park.**

Though the mythology surrounding "going to the lake" is often that of sun-filled days by the shore, the reality of growing numbers of vacationers seeking refuge in the same spots has meant many lakeside retreats are losing their rustic charm. Also, MB's growing **Elderly** population often chooses the cottage as a retirement residence, meaning more and more cottages are becoming year-round dwellings, equipped with the noisy amenities of modern life, rather than sanctuaries from the stress of the city. Fortunately, however, MB is known as the land of 100,000 lakes, so there will always be another quiet spot on the water for those willing to travel a little farther. • MICHELLE DOBROVOLNY

LAKE AGASSIZ was the largest of several glacial lakes (*see* **Glaciation**) that covered much of the Prairies starting about 11,000 BC. The huge lake did not exist for long. It probably reached its maximum size about 8000 or 7000 BC. As the ice blocking its drainage retreated northward, so did Lake Agassiz. By about 6000 BC, the lake was gone. **Lakes Winnipeg, Winnipegosis**, and **Manitoba**, as well as **Cedar Lake** and **Lake of the Woods**, are relics of Lake Agassiz.

The glacial lake was named after Jean Louis Rodolphe Agassiz, the 19th-century Swiss-born US geologist who first proposed that glaciers had spread across the northern continents in the geologically recent past. Another US geologist, Warren Upham, was the first to study the

lake in detail. Indicators of the lake's existence are found over an area of more than 500,000 km² in MB, SK, northern ON, ND, and MN. With advances and retreats of the ice front, the lake rose and fell, resulting in overflow in different directions. In the early stages, drainage was to the S into the Mississippi system. Later, outlets opened to the E, leading to the Great Lakes/St. Lawrence system. Later still, overflow was to the NW into the Mackenzie River and ultimately into the Arctic Ocean. Finally, a huge quantity of water (between 150,000 km³ and 163,000 km³) was suddenly released under the ice into **Hudson Bay** and on into the Arctic. This event, and the drainage by the Mackenzie, added enough fresh water to the oceans that the world's climate was affected.

Evidence of Lake Agassiz's existence takes 4 forms: strandlines, which mark former lakeshores; spillways, which carried water from other glacial lakes into Lake Agassiz; deltas, where spillways and rivers entered the lake and dropped sediments; and lake-bottom sediments deposited beyond the immediate lakeshore. Strandlines were formed when the lake remained stable. They take the form of low cliffs eroded into previously deposited glacial sediments; beaches deposited at or near water level; and, possibly, sandbars deposited in shallow water offshore. At its highest, Lake Agassiz extended into the Assiniboine embayment between Pembina Mountain and Riding Mountain. Strandlines of this stage occur along the E of the "mountains," and some poorly defined beaches of this age are found in E **Brandon**. Later the lake stood at a lower level, the Upper Campbell level, at which time a beach was deposited that extends from the US border, NW along the MB Escarpment, and into SK. Known as the Arden Ridge in the Neepawa area, it increases in elevation from S to N due to isostatic rebound (*see* **Glaciation**). Many other strandlines exist along the **MB Escarpment** out into the MB Lowlands. On the east side of Agassiz, strandlines exist in Grand Beach Provincial Park, where they are etched into the glacially deposited Belair moraine. Strandlines are good transport routes; Hwy 352 follows the Arden Ridge, as does Hwy 10 farther N between **Ethelbert** and **Pine River.** Beaches are excellent sources of construction gravel and also played a prominent role in the lives of MB's Aboriginal people as lookout points, routes between campsites, and sources of stone for tools.

Glacial lakes W of MB emptied from higher levels into Lake Agassiz, sometimes quickly – perhaps in a few days – eroding steep-sided, flat-floored spillways. Lakes in SK emptied into Lake Agassiz by the Qu'Appelle and **Assiniboine**

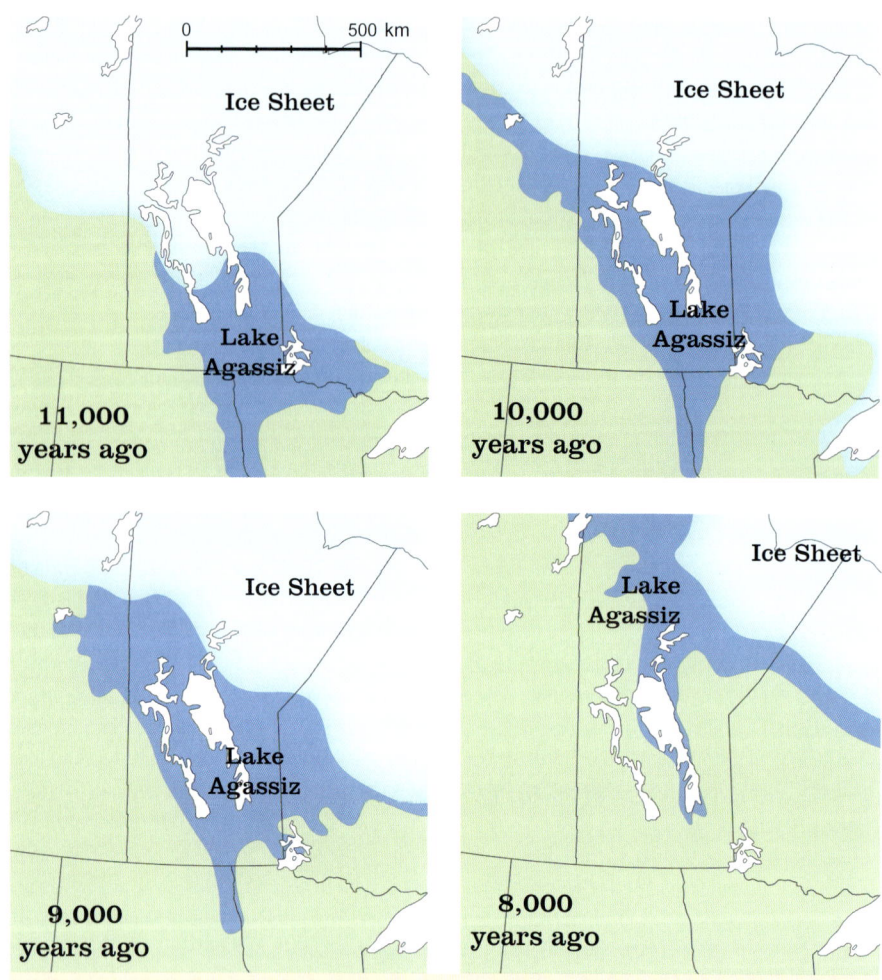

The retreating Lake Agassiz created many of Manitoba's 100,000 lakes.

Lake Manitoba's Steep Rock

above sea level and a maximum depth of 6.3 m. Lake MB discharges through the Fairford River into Lake St. Martin and thence into **LAKE WINNIPEG** by way of the Dauphin River. The mean annual discharge measured at Fairford is 73.7 m³ per second. This 208-km-long NW-to-SE-trending lake is naturally divided into N and S basins at The Narrows. Aboriginal legend states that the drumming of a **MANITOU** or spirit can be heard from the shore of The Narrows, and the **CREE** name for this strait of the spirit, "Manitou-wapow," gives the province's 3rd-largest lake its name.

Lakes **MANITOBA**, Winnipeg, and Winnipegosis, and several smaller lakes in S Manitoba, are remnants of the great glacial **LAKE AGASSIZ**, which covered most of the province between about 11,000 years ago and 6,000 years ago. Between 5000 BC and 1000 BC, the **ASSINIBOINE RIVER** drained into the S basin of Lake Manitoba. Consequently, the drainage basin area (206,200 km²) was about 4 times larger than the current basin. ● GPP

LAKE MANITOBA FIRST NATION, on reserve pop 891, off reserve pop 808, is situated in central MB, along the NW shore of the lower basin of **LAKE MANITOBA,** about 170 km NW of **WINNIPEG**. This first nation signed Treaty 2 in 1871. The Lake Manitoba First Nation is now a member of the Interlake Reserves Tribal Council. The native language of this community is **OJIBWAY**. The Lake Manitoba First Nation has one reserve. Schooling in Lake Manitoba, administered by the First Nation itself, goes from Nursery-Grade 9, and total enrolment for 2003-04 was 85. Road access to the Lake Manitoba First Nation community is available from hwy 6. There is also daily bus service to **GYPSUMVILLE**. The economic foundation for this area is commercial fishing. In Feb 2006, the community hosted the First Nations Agricultural Forum, where Southern MB agricultural ranchers and producers met. Hollywood actor **ADAM BEACH**, perhaps the most recognizable Aboriginal actor in NA, grew up in this community. ● RK

spillways. Similarly, in the south, Lake Regina in SK emptied via lakes Souris and Hind into Lake Agassiz eroding spillways that are now occupied by stretches of the **SOURIS** and **PEMBINA** rivers. Deltas were deposited where spillways and rivers entered the lake. At least 33 have been identified, the largest being the Assiniboine Delta, which is composed of sediment washed down the Qu'Appelle and Assiniboine spillways. This delta, covering an area of 3885 km², has its apex at Brandon and spreads out to the E. Composed of gravel near Brandon and sand farther east, it is a good source of groundwater for small towns and farms. Recently, it has been pumped for irrigation in the Douglas/**CARBERRY** area; the combination of available water and stone-free soils makes for good potato-growing conditions. South of Carberry, delta sands have been blown into dunes – the **CARBERRY SAND HILLS**.

The final pieces of evidence of the lake's existence are sediments – principally fine sand, silt, and clay – that were deposited on what was once the lake floor. These deposits are as much as 50 m thick S of **WINNIPEG** and in some parts of northern MB. Some of the sedimentation took

the form of regular alternations of thin layers of clay and thicker, more coarse-grained layers (termed varved clays). These alternations may represent seasonal deposition, with the coarse-grained layers being deposited in the summer when the lake was open, and fine-grained layers accumulating in quiet conditions during the winter when the lake was frozen. Land exposed when the lake retreated is flat; for example, around **WINNIPEG**, north of **PORTAGE LA PRAIRIE**, and around **DAUPHIN** and **SWAN RIVER**. Seen from the air, the lake floor is crossed by lines from several hundred m to 5 km in length. Icebergs grinding into lake floor sediments when the lake was open may have created some of these. ● JOHN WELSTED

▶ *See also* **DRAINAGE**, **GLACIATION**, **GEOLOGICAL HISTORY**.

LAKE MANITOBA, called Lac des Prairies by **LA VÉRENDRYE**, is the 13th-largest lake in Canada. It has an area of 4659 km², slightly smaller than the entire province of PE. Lake Manitoba drains 54,200 km² of western MB and eastern SK, including the discharge from **LAKE WINNIPEGOSIS**. This shallow lake has an average elevation of 247.5 m

LAKE OF THE PRAIRIES, 100 km W of **Dauphin** in Asessippi Provincial Park, was created in 1968 as the result of the construction of the Shellmouth Dam. The MB govt built the dam on the **Assiniboine River** in order to control **Floods** in W MB. The lake reaches 67 km in length and stretches over the border into Saskatchewan. It covers a 6070 ha (15,000 ac) surface area across the Assiniboine River valley. The dam itself is located at the confluence of the Shell and Assiniboine rivers, at the S end of the lake, about 25 km NNW of **Russell**. The lake is popular for **Sport Fishing** as one of the best-known places in MB to catch **Walleye**. In 2002, Manitoba Conservation restricted fishing with a permit system and catch limits in an effort to preserve populations, and warned of high levels of mercury in walleye. In 2003, the Canada and MB govts agreed on an $8 million joint initiative to upgrade the dam's flood and water supply controls and to compensate landowners for past damages. The project enhanced flow into the Assiniboine to respond to anticipated increases in water usage. Asessippi is the Cree name for Shell River. • GPP

LAKE ST. MARTIN FIRST NATION, on reserve pop 1358, off reserve pop 724, is located 255 km N of **Winnipeg**, N of **Ashern** along hwy 6. Lake St. Martin First Nation is signatory to Treaty 2 and is now a member of the Interlake Reserves Tribal Council. There are 2 reserves located here: the Narrows IR No. 49, and The Narrows IR No. 49A. The native language of Lake St. Martin is **Ojibway**. Education in this community goes from Nursery-Grade 9, and enrolment for the year 2003-04 was 229. Lake St. Martin administers its own schooling. This First Nation community is accessible via all-weather roads. There is also a private runway for flights. The economic foundation of the Lake St. Martin First Nation is agriculture and fishing. In 2006, the community of Lake St. Martin was working to establish a satisfactory water system. The local school was the only building with water; all other buildings and houses had to bring in potable water. • RK

LAKE WINNIPEG was probably named by the English explorer Henry Kelsey who in 1690, may have been the first European to see the "murky waters" of the Manitoba Great Lakes and adopted the Cree Indian name "win-nipi" for the largest of these lakes. Lake Winnipeg is the sixth largest lake in Canada occupying an area of 24,390 km². The lake is estimated to have a maximum depth of 18 m and maintains an average lake level of 217.3 m above sea level. Lake Winnipeg extends 416 km north to south and drains approximately 984,200 km² of land by way of the Saskatchewan,

the Red-Assiniboine, and the Winnipeg River systems. This drainage basin extends from the Front Range of the Rocky Mountains across Alberta, Saskatchewan and Manitoba to the metamorphic uplands of Canadian Shield in Ontario. The drainage basin extends southward along the Red River valley near to the headwaters of the Mississippi River, including large parts of the states of Minnesota and North Dakota. Lake Winnipeg discharges its waters into the Nelson River, which flows north to Hudson Bay at an average annual rate of approximately 2,170 cubic metres per second (m^3 s-1), measured at the Kelsey generating station. Since the construction of a lake-outlet control structure at Jenpeg Manitoba (1976), the mean monthly discharge has been regulated, ranging from a monthly low of 469 m^3 s-1 in July of 1988 to a maximum of 3,360 m^3 s-1 in May of 1986. The control structure maintains lake levels at approximately 217 m above sea level and assures an adequate supply of water for five hydroelectric generating stations on the Nelson River.

Lake Winnipeg lies in a lowland basin that was scoured out of limestone and shale bedrock by continental glaciers during the ice ages. When the glaciers finally melted (about 13,000 years ago) a large lake, Glacial Lake Agassiz, filled the entire basin. Over the next 5000 years the lake drained and exposed a relatively flat lake plain that extends from the Manitoba Escarpment in the west to the rocky edge of the Canadian Shield. Today the exposed lake bottom constitutes the Manitoba Lowlands and is occupied by Lake Winnipeg, Lake Manitoba and Lake Winnipegosis; the Manitoba Great Lakes.

During the 1700's Lake Winnipeg was an important transport link between the Hudson Bay

port of York Factory and the fur-trade hinterlands of the Red-Assiniboine watershed. In 1812 Lord Selkirk's York boats traversed the length of the lake on their way to founding the Red River Colony at the junction of the Red and Assiniboine Rivers. Later the lake gave its name to the settlement and in 1871, Winnipeg became the capital of the new province of Manitoba.

A commercial fishery on Lake Winnipeg began in the early 1800's and has continued since. Initially whitefish, sturgeon and caviar were harvested. By the early 1900, however, the sturgeon/caviar fishery had been severely over exploited and has never recovered. Today Lake Winnipeg has the largest commercial fishery in the province and hatchery programmes support a relatively stable yield of whitefish.

On long and relatively narrow lakes such as Lake Winnipeg interesting wind and wave effects occasionally take place. When the prevailing northerly winds blow along the length of the lake, they exert a horizontal stress on the surface. Surface waters move in the direction of the wind and pile up along the windward south shores – a phenomenon known as a setup or wind tide. Setups greater than 1.00 m above normal lake levels have been recorded along many of southern Lake Winnipeg's recreational beaches, and the associated high waves with their uprush effects have caused considerable storm damage, backshore flooding and shoreline erosion. The highest setups generally occur in the fall when the northerly winds are strongest. If the winds die down suddenly, the waters rush northward, then slosh back and forth in a process called seiching.

The accumulation of the macronutrients nitrogen and phosphorus contribute to the

Lake Winnipeg is the world's 14th largest lake.

eutrophication of lakes and reservoirs. Anthropogenic eutrophication is the unnatural acceleration of the eutrophication process (an increase in nutrient concentrations and organic biomass accompanied by increased levels of productivity in a water system) caused by human activity. Concerns regarding phosphorus loading in Manitoba have been motivated by evidence of serious eutrophication in Lake Winnipeg, specifically satellite images of massive algal blooms of cyanobacteria (blue-green algae) observed in the southern basin. These images and limnological and other data indicate the creation of anoxic zones within the Lake, death of biota and impacts on both commercial fishing and recreation activities.

There are many sources of phosphorous, the bulk of these anthropogenic. One particular source of concern in Manitoba is associated with the very rapid expansion of hog production in the province, specifically the impact of the land-applied manure on the nutrient status of agricultural soils and surface waters. Other major sources of phosphorus to Lake Winnipeg are municipal sewage and industrial effluents; cottages and their associated septic fields; crop fertilization; other livestock operations, particularly those where cattle have access to the riparian zone of streams and lakes; and by atmospheric deposition. Excess nitrogen from the same sources also is being added to the Lake Winnipeg drainage system. At this time, Manitoba has no water quality standards for phosphorous and nitrogen concentrations in surface waters. • R.A. MCGINN/W.H.N. PATON

LAKE WINNIPEGOSIS is MB's 2nd largest lake after **LAKE WINNIPEG**. At 5370 sq km, it is slightly bigger than **LAKE MANITOBA**, into which it flows by way of the Waterhen River. The 195 km long lake drains a 50,000 sq km watershed encompassing the **MB ESCARPMENT** (including **DUCK MOUNTAIN PROVINCIAL PARK** and **RIDING MOUNTAIN NATIONAL PARK**) and part of E Saskatchewan. Tributaries include the Swan, Woody, Red Deer, and Mossy rivers. The two largest islands within its waters are named Spruce and Birch. The lake became part of an important **FUR TRADE** route after **LA VÉRENDRYE**'s 2nd son, Pierre, explored the region. The first Fort Dauphin was built in 1741 at the mouth of the Mossy River on the SW section of the lake, site of present-day **WINNIPEGOSIS**. The communities of **CAMPERVILLE**, Pelican Rapids, and Duck Bay are also located around the lake. Area First Nations include Pine Creek, Sapotaweyak, and Skownan (on nearby Waterhen Lake). It is the 11th largest lake in Canada, and remains important for its **COMMERCIAL FISHING**. The name comes from the

CREE words win-nipi and osis, which combine to mean "little murky waters." • GPP

LALIBERTE, Connie, curler (b Oct 21, 1960, Winnipeg). One of the best curlers to hail from MB, she skipped the first-ever MB women's team to a world title. She won junior provincial titles in 1976 and 1977, and in total has skipped 6 provincial-title winning teams. With a team consisting of her sisters Corinne and Janet, and Chris (Pidzarko-More) Scalena, Laliberte took the 1984 provincial and Cdn title before proceeding to win the women's world championship. She won 2 more Cdn titles, in 1992 and 1995, before retiring from competitive curling in 2000, the same year she was inducted into the Canadian Curling Hall of Fame. • MD

LALONDE, Donny Drew "Golden Boy," boxer (b Mar 12, 1960, Victoria, BC) was the first Manitoban to win a professional boxing title. Lalonde turned to boxing as a means to overcome the physical abuse he suffered as a child. Though his career as an amateur was unremarkable, and he failed to make the 1980 Cdn Olympic team, Lalonde became a successful pro boxer at 19 under the management of Winnipeg promoter Jay Coleman. In 1983, Coleman arranged Lalonde's fight against Roddy MacDonald for the Canadian Professional Boxing Federation's light heavyweight crown. Winning the title in a televised match, Lalonde garnered national attention, known as "The Golden Boy" for his blonde hair and good looks.

After this initial success, Lalonde's career dwindled through the mid-1980s, until he came

under the management of New York promoter David Wolf who arranged a series of high-profile matches for Lalonde. In 1987, he set up a fight with Eddie Davis for the light heavyweight World Boxing Council title. Lalonde won, becoming MB's first world champion boxer. He defended against Leslie Stewart, then saw the peak of his career in 1988 with a Las Vegas fight against Sugar Ray Leonard. Though he lost in the 9th round, the fight earned him over $5 million and fame across NA. Lalonde was made a member of MB's Order of the Buffalo Hunt in 1988. He took time off from fighting in the 1990s to raise a family, but made several comebacks. As of 2006, his record was 38-5-1 with 32 knockouts. • MD

LAMB, Thomas "Tom," aviator, entrepreneur (b June 29, 1898, **GRAND RAPIDS**; d Dec 28, 1969, HI). Lamb was the son of **ENGLISH** immigrant Thomas Henry Peacock Lamb, a schoolteacher-turned fur trader who opened a store in Moose Lake in 1900. Although he never made it past grade 3, the younger Lamb had a vast knowledge of the northern wilderness and was fluent in **CREE**. He married Jean Armstrong when he was 20, and later took over the running of his father's shop. He was a mechanic on flying boats 1921-22, and he hauled the first **WHITEFISH** from MB to market by air in 1932 after seeing a Junkers land on Williams Lake. He also became MB's first flying fur trapper. With the help of his 9 children – all 6 of his sons would fly for the company – the bush pilot's business grew and in 1934, he incorporated northern MB's first airline, Thomas Lamb Airways Ltd. (later Lamb Airways and Lambair). At its peak, the airline had 25 aircraft, including

Donny Lalonde

WINNIPEG FREE PRES

Tom Lamb, 1991 by Leo Mol

several helicopters, and 80 employees. Lamb never lost the bush pilot's entrepreneurial spirit of adventure, summed up in Lambair's motto, "Don't Ask Us Where We Fly: Tell Us Where You Want to Go."

Lamb later retired from flying, concentrating instead on northern cattle ranching. Lamb received an honorary degree from the **U of M** in 1968. He was sometimes called "Mr. North." He died in Hawaii, and his ashes were later scattered over Moose Lake. The airline continued to offer charter, freight, and govt/**HBC** contract flights out of northern communities such as **The Pas**, **Thompson**, and **Churchill** until it folded in 1981 due to recession and to competition from Calm Air. Tom's son, Jack Lamb, chronicles much of the airline's later history in his memoir, *My Life in the North*. A statue of Tom Lamb by **Leo Mol** stands in a downtown Toronto shopping mall, and a Noorduyn Norseman floatplane once flown by Lambair is now part of a memorial to northern pilots in Thompson. ● AJL

▶ *See also* **Aviation**.

LAMPREY is an amazing jawless fish in the family Petromyzontidae, order Petromyzontiformes. The 41 species of lampreys are the last surviving members of an ancient group of jawless fishes originating over 450 mya; the first true lampreys appeared in the fossil record 350 mya (Mississippian period). They display a number of primitive features – lack of jaws, no heart (only a contractile ventral aorta for pumping blood), no paired fins, only a single nostril, and a third eye (pineal). The skeleton is made entirely of cartilage. The body is eel-like, with 7 pairs of gill openings behind the large eye. The mouth is a circular, sucking organ with rows of horny teeth

on the tongue used for rasping off scales and tissue while feeding on the host's blood. Anticoagulants are released by the lamprey to maintain blood flow of the host.

The life cycle of lampreys involves a remarkable pattern of development and migration. Most species remain in freshwater their entire lives, but at least 6 species migrate to and from the sea. The latter group spawns in freshwater, eggs develop into a larva called an ammocoetes, which after 6 years transforms into the adult form, and it then migrates to the sea. Here it attaches to a host fish with its powerful sucking mouth, and feeds on its blood. When sexually mature, it drops off its prey and migrates hundreds of km to its freshwater spawning grounds. After the breeding season, the lamprey dies.

There are 3 species of lampreys in MB, each living its entire life in freshwater. They look very similar and require an expert to ensure identification. Differences are in dental characters, size of the oral disc, and a few other features. The 28 cm Chestnut Lamprey (*Ichthyomyzon castaneus*) is the most-common lamprey and is found in most rivers in the S quarter of the province. The 12 cm Northern Brook Lamprey (*Ichthyomyzon fossor*) is restricted to the Whitemouth River watershed, while the 25 cm Silver Lamprey (*Ichthyomyzon unicuspis*) occurs in the **Red**, **Assiniboine**, **Winnipeg**, Rat and **Nelson** (near **York Factory**) rivers.

Little is known about lampreys specifically in MB. Sexually mature specimens move into larger rivers and spawn in shallow water (30-40 cm) in May and June. A nest is prepared in the gravel by the female, using the mouth to move stones and tail thrusts to clear debris. From 1000-11,000 eggs are laid. Spawned-out, dead individuals are found in late June. The eggs hatch into ammocoetes which burrow into the sand or mud, where they filter-feed on algae, micro-organisms and organic detritus by passing water through basket-like gill structures. The ammocoetes lacks teeth and the eyes are undeveloped. It grows for 4-7 years before transforming at 8-15 cm into the adult, which may lose some weight and length because it does not feed during this period of several months. The new adults (now with enlarged eyes) emerge from the substrate,

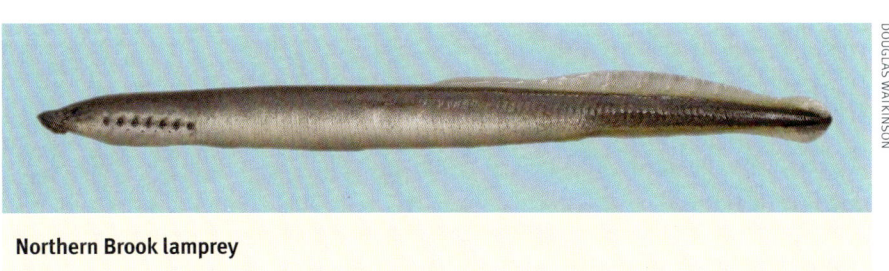

Northern Brook lamprey

L

L

and those of the Chestnut and Silver lampreys attach to a host fish and feed for one season (April to Oct) in the Chestnut and into the winter in the Silver Lamprey. Parasitic lampreys attack many species of fish, selecting a site on the back or side near the pectoral fin. The Northern Brook Lamprey is not parasitic and in fact does not feed at all as an adult; its gut degenerates while the gonads enlarge. Adults spend the winter buried in the substrate and emerge for spawning in the spring. All 3 species spawn only once and then die. • REW

LAMPSHELL is a marine shelled creature in the phylum Brachiopoda, and resembles a clam, but with a quite different internal body plan. The animal is protected by a symmetrical pair of shells or valves (slightly different-sized in the class Inarticulata; same size in the class Articulata), held together by muscles and a hinge. Many species resemble a Roman lamp, hence the common name. Like clams and oysters, the shells are composed of calcium carbonate or calcium phosphate absorbed from the sea water. A muscular stalk anchors the lampshell to a rock or coral. Most species are 5 cm or less. Lampshells feed by sieving plankton from a current of water drawn in by beating waves of fine hairs or cilia lining a pair of body loops next to the mouth. Food particles are trapped in mucous and transferred, like a conveyor belt, to the mouth by the cilia. In most species the sexes are separate, and eggs and sperm are shed into the sea where fertilization takes place.

The distinctively shaped larva (called a trochophore) is propelled through the water, while drifting with the plankton, by means of beating cilia on the creature's 3-lobed body. After only a few days of feeding and growing, the larva sinks to the bottom (from low tide to depths of 3800 m) and develops the reorganized body, shells and stalk, and then takes up a sedentary life style. Known from some of the first fossil-bearing rocks of the Cambrian (600 mya), lampshells reached their greatest diversity (over 30,000 fossil species) around 500 mya . Only 280 species survive today. *Lingula*, from Japan and the S Pacific, holds the remarkable distinction of being the oldest genus of animal with living species, and dates back, relatively unchanged, to over 500 mya. Lampshells are represented in Hudson Bay by 2 species – *Atretia gnomon* and *Hemithiris psittacea* – but others are likely present. Their shells may sometimes be picked up on the shore. • REW, DOF

LANG, Otto Emil, lawyer, politician, (b May 14, 1932, Handel, SK) was a prominent federal Liberal cabinet minister. Lang grew up in SK, the 3rd of 4 children born to German immigrants. He received a BA and LLB from the U of SK, and was selected as a Rhodes Scholar in 1953. He obtained his BCL at Oxford U, and then returned to SK to article. He joined the faculty at the U of SK's College of Law in 1956. In 1961, he became Canada's youngest law dean at the age of 29. He held that position until 1968, when he ran in the federal election and was elected as a Liberal MP. He was appointed minister without portfolio, and the following year was put in charge of the **CANADIAN WHEAT BOARD**, over which he governed until his political defeat in 1979.

Otto Lang, 1975

UMA, TRIBUNE, PERSONALITY FILES

During this time, he introduced a controversial incentive program meant to offset falling prices caused by a wheat surplus, where farmers were paid to take land out of production. His other cabinet posts included Minister of Manpower and Immigration from 1970-72, and Minister of Justice and Attorney General from 1972-79. In 1975, he additionally became Minister of Transport, during which time he combined the passenger services of **CN** and **CP** to form Via Rail as a new Crown corporation. He moved to Winnipeg in 1979, and became exec vice-president of **PIONEER GRAIN COMPANY**, and later president and CEO of Centra Gas until its sale to **MANITOBA HYDRO**. In 1999, he was made an Officer of the Order of Canada. As of 2007, Lang sat on numerous corporate boards, including as director of Investors Group Trust Co. He is married to Madame Justice Deborah McCawley of the Court of Queen's Bench. • MD

LANGRUTH, pop 100, is a hamlet 110 km NE of Brandon on the W shore of **LAKE MANITOBA**. **ICELANDERS** were the earliest immigrants, arriving in the areas around 1885. In 1907, businessmen George Langdon and W. Judson Ruth settled here, and "Langruth" is an amalgamation of their surnames. In the 21st century, Langruth designates itself as the "bird watching capital" of MB; a sculpture of a great blue heron welcomes visitors to 2 bird habitats nearby, Big Grass Marsh and Hollywood Beach. Langruth is a service centre for farmers and winter fishers. And this is where a network to establish rural child care centres throughout in MB began in the 1980s. • GPP

LARCOMBE, Samuel, agronomist, seed grower (b 1851, Axminster, Devonshire, UK; d Oct 20, 1937, **BIRTLE**.) Larcombe came to Canada in 1889, settling at Birtle, where he set out to prove that any vegetable grown in England would also thrive in MB. Later dubbed the "John Bull of Cdn agriculture," he is a member of the MB Agricultural Hall of Fame. In the early 1900s, he began growing grains. He did selection work to develop a new wheat variety in 1917, which he named Axminster, after his hometown. He claimed the variety to be rust-resistant, but it never became popular. However, he won the World Wheat Championship in Peoria, IL, in 1917. Larcombe was so popular that, when his house burned down, grain associates provided him with a new, furnished house. Hundreds travelled by private train to Birtle, where the lieut gov donated a brass tablet inscribed: "This house was built and donated to Samuel Larcombe by his business friends in Winnipeg as an appreciation of his self-denying efforts on behalf of Canadian agriculture." • JIM SHILLIDAY

LARK (family *Alaudidae*) is a small grounddwelling songbird that reaches its greatest variety in Africa and Eurasia. Only one true lark occurs in MB – the Horned Lark (*Eromophila alpes-*

Horned Lark

NICOLE MACPHERSON

tris). It is a widespread species with populations that breed on the Prairies and the tundra, but numbers have declined drastically over the past few decades, possibly reflecting altered agricultural practices on the Prairies and/or the wintering grounds. For many Manitobans, this bird is a harbinger of spring, as it is the earliest returning species. In Feb, the first small flocks appear along roadsides in the south, where they feed on spilled grain and other seeds, and by late Mar, many will be nesting. Fall migration is less obvious, as flocks tend to be small at this time and are not restricted to roadsides. The Western Meadowlark (*Sturnella neglecta*) is not a lark at all, but is related to the BLACKBIRD. ● RUDOLF KOES

LATHLIN, Oscar, politician, CREE leader (b 1951, OPASKWAYAK CREE NATION). He attended high school in CRANBERRY PORTAGE, and after graduating in 1969, accepted a position as a band manager in THE PAS. Lathlin went on to become a member of the boards of the ASSEMBLY OF MANITOBA CHIEFS and the Manitoba Keewatinowi Okimakanak. He worked for the federal govt before being named Swampy Cree Tribal Council's executive director in 1979. In 1985, he was elected chief of his band. Five years later, he was elected as the MLA for The Pas, representing the NEW DEMOCRATIC PARTY.

While in opposition (1990-99), Lathlin spent time as the critic for Northern Affairs. When the NDP under GARY DOER took office in 1999, he became Minister of Conservation. In Sept 2002, he was named Minister of Aboriginal and Northern Affairs, with added responsibility for the administration of *The Communities Economic Development Fund Act*. Lathlin was re-elected in 2003, and continued in his Cabinet post. He won his 5th election in May 2007. ● JT

LAURENCE, Jean MARGARET, author, activist (b July 18, 1926, NEEPAWA; d. Jan 5, 1987, Lakefield, ON) daughter of lawyer Robert Wemyss and Verna Jean (née Simpson), and arguably Canada's finest novelist. Margaret Laurence was a private person who dreaded public occasions, especially if she had to speak. Still, she became one of Canada's most widely read authors. Her work has been translated into several languages and is read and studied around the world. In later life, she vigorously championed human rights and respect for the environment, and attacked censorship and nuclear brinkmanship.

"Peggy," as she was known in her youth, had a challenging life. By age 8, she had lost her mother and father, 2 grandparents, and an uncle. By 10, she had lost several schoolmates in the polio epidemic of 1936. As a child, she moved

from home to home in Neepawa. As an adult, her marriage failed, some of her books were branded immoral, and she had serious health problems. Yet the memoir that she was finishing at the time of her death is joyfully entitled *Dance on the Earth* (1989).

After the death of Laurence's mother, Verna's elder sister, Margaret Campbell Simpson, moved in to take care of Peggy, and married Wemyss. Margaret was an experienced teacher and a booklover who fostered Peggy's love for reading and encouraged her writing. By the age of 7, Peggy was already writing. When Peggy left Neepawa for United College (see U OF W) in WINNIPEG in fall 1944, she continued to be a prize-winning student. She did well in English and pursued writing, contributing poetry, short fiction, and essays to *The Uniter* and *The Manitoban* and working as staff for both publications. In June 1947, she received her BA.

On Sept 13, 1947, Peggy married John Fergus Laurence, a veteran of the RAF and RCAF. While Jack continued his studies in engineering at the U OF M, Peggy wrote for the Communist paper *The Westerner* and then for the short-lived, labour-oriented *Winnipeg Citizen*. When Jack graduated in 1949, they moved to London, UK, and then, in 1950, to British Somaliland (now Somalia), where Jack was employed building earth dams to store water for use in drought. Peggy's first published book, *A Tree for Poverty* (1954), is a collection of her translations of Somali poems and stories, with an introduction to Somali life and literature. *The Prophet's Camel Bell* (1963) is a full account of the Laurences' Somali experiences. Both volumes show how her encounter with a new and strange culture began

a deep transformation of her understanding of herself and the world, and both have been republished with critical commentary, and are highly regarded today.

When Jack's contract was completed in 1952, they returned to London, where Jocelyn was born. By Oct, the family was off to Accra, Gold Coast (now Ghana), where Jack was to oversee the development of a new port and connecting highways at Tema. Here, their son David was born in 1955. Again, the Laurences were immersed in a new and entirely different culture, this time, one suffering critical disruptions, as the colonial Gold Coast was becoming independent Ghana. Out of this new experience, Peggy wrote a series of short stories, several of which won Cdn and US prizes on publication, and her first published novel, *This Side Jordan* (1960), which won the Beta Sigma Phi Award for best first novel by a Cdn author. Most of the short stories she wrote then were collected in *The Tomorrow-Tamer* (1963). Several are reprinted regularly in anthologies of best Cdn short stories.

The Laurences returned to Canada in 1957, and settled in Vancouver for 5 years. Peggy completed her African books and, firmly insisting on becoming Margaret, she started to write the books based on her MB past. Manawaka is a fictionalized Neepawa, and while some of the characters move to Vancouver, Toronto, or the Otonabee River near Peterborough, they are all unmistakably Manitobans whose humanity is universal.

In *The Stone Angel* (1964), Hagar is a confused, proudly respectable 90-year-old woman who finds, too late – like Shakespeare's King Lear – that she has ruined her life and the lives of others, despite her good intentions. In subsequent

Margaret Laurence

PETER TITTENBERGER

novels, the protagonists receive such revelations in time to profit from them. In *A Jest of God* (1966), Rachel Cameron – a lonely, painfully repressed spinster who is dominated by a hypochondriac mother – has a desperate affair. Abandoned by her lover, she thinks that at least she is pregnant, discovers that she has a benign tumour, and leaves Manawaka for Vancouver to risk a new, independent life. Stacey MacAindra – Rachel's married, outgoing sister in *The Fire-Dwellers* (1969) – fears for her children, with the threat of nuclear destruction hanging over normal anxieties, and dreads her uneasiness about her relationship with her husband, but goes to sleep at the end knowing that "Temporarily, they are all more or less okay." Vanessa MacLeod, the hero of the 8 short stories that make up *A Bird in the House* (1970), suffers through the deaths of family members and friends, the apparent doom of the **Métis**, and the tyranny of a grandfather, only to realize that in fighting him, she has been fighting her own nature.

Morag Gunn, the orphaned heroine of the final Manawaka novel, *The Diviners* (1974), is brought up by the despised, uncouth keeper of the nuisance grounds, Christie Logan, and his developmentally challenged wife Prin. They give her security, dignity, and love, and Christie, with his wild **Scots** tales, inspires Morag to become a writer. Her marriage to her English professor fails, and she has a daughter by her old Manawaka Métis friend, Jules Skinner Tonnerre, who dies tragically after he has made Morag and their daughter Pique aware of his heroic Métis heritage in song and story. The usual difficulties between a teenage daughter and her mother are complicated by the challenge of understanding and accommodating 2 distinct heritages with the mainstream culture, and by the threat of racial violence.

Ironically, all the Manawaka fiction was written outside MB. With *The Stone Angel* nearly completed, Margaret separated from her husband and left for England with her children in Oct 1962. She moved to Elm Cottage, Penn, Buckinghamshire, in Dec 1963, where she lived for 10 years. Here, in addition to providing hospitality and encouragement to a procession of budding Cdn writers, she finished *The Stone Angel* and the other Manawaka books, except *The Diviners*, which she completed after her return to Canada. Margaret and Jack were divorced in 1969. As their children approached the end of their schooling, Margaret returned to Canada. She spent 1969-70 as writer-in-residence at the U of Toronto. Then, in 1973, she was appointed as writer-in-residence at the U of Western ON in London, ON, in the fall, and in the spring at Trent U in Peterborough, where she later became

Chancellor. In nearby Lakefield, she bought a house in 1974 and lived there until, following a lengthy illness, in 1987 she quietly made sure that loved ones would not suffer through her protracted dying.

Several of Laurence's works have been successfully adapted for radio and TV. Full-length movies were made of *A Jest of God* (*Rachel, Rachel*) and *The Diviners*; a short of *The Olden Days Coat*; a recording of *Six Darn Cows*; and a distinguished stage version of *The Stone Angel*. Films about Laurence include *Margaret Laurence: First Lady of Manawaka* and *A Writer in the Nuclear Age*. She received the Gov Gen's Award for *A Jest of God* and *The Diviners*. She was made a companion of the Order of Canada in 1971, and received the Molson Prize from the Canada Council for the Arts in 1974. ● WALTER E. SWAYZE

LAVOIE, (Gérard) Daniel, singer/songwriter (b Mar 17, 1949, Dunrea, 45 km SSE **BRANDON**), is one of the few Francophone musicians with origins outside QC or France to gain an international following. Lavoie grew up listening to the classical music adored by his mother, who ensured that her son began learning the piano at a young age. At 14, he left his small Prairie hometown to attend a Jesuit boarding school at St. Boniface College. Immersed in the vibrant Francophone music scene of the 1960s, Lavoie was soon developing his own musical abilities. He started playing saxophone in a rock band, and frequented "Les Cents Nons," in St. Boniface, a popular hangout for French musicians. His musical ambitions were encouraged when, in 1967, he won a national Société Radio-Canada (SRC) singing/songwriting competition.

Daniel Lavoie, 1980

In 1970, Lavoie toured QC. He decided to settle permanently in the province, earning a meagre living by playing piano in cafés and bars. His first recordings gained little attention, but the 1974 single *J'ai quitté mon île* from his debut album *À court terme* became a hit in Brazil, Portugal, and France. He was awarded the QC music industry Félix award for Male Performer of the Year in 1980, and again in 1981 for his album *Aigre doux, how are you?* His greatest success came with the 1983 release *Tension Attention*. The album, full of sensitive and melancholy melodies, earned him 3 Félix awards, in addition to several prestigious awards in France. Through the 1990s, Lavoie continued to record in English and French, but also branched out into theatrical productions and acted in several QC films. He has released 2 children's albums, and written music for singers such as Céline Dion and Nana Mouskouri. ● MICHELLE DOBROVOLNY

LEACH, Reggie Joseph "The Rifle," hockey player (b Apr 23, 1950, **RIVERTON**) was one of the NHL's leading scorers in the 1970s. Raised with 12 siblings by his paternal grandparents, Leach would often ignore his schoolwork to practise 8 hours a day, and by age 13 was playing on a local adult team. He played 2 seasons with the **FLIN FLON BOMBERS** alongside centre **BOBBY CLARKE**, and his 65 goals in the 1969-70 season made him the league's top scorer, earning him an NHL spot with the Boston Bruins. He was with the team for just one season before being traded to the California Golden Seals where he spent an unremarkable 3 years. Meanwhile, his former Bomber teammate Clarke was enjoying a successful career with the Philadelphia Flyers. Clarke believed a little discipline could turn Leach's game around, and urged coach **FRED SHERO** to take on the player. Coming off their 1974 Stanley Cup victory, the Flyers acquired Leach for the 1974-75 season. His discipline subsequently improved, and soon his torrid scoring pace had earned him the nickname "The Rifle." Leach helped the Flyers win their 2nd Stanley Cup in 1975.

The peak of Leach's career, however, came in the 1975-76 season when he scored 19 goals in 16 play-off games, including 5 goals in one game. His record for playoff goals still stands, and though the Flyers were swept by the Montreal Canadiens in the Stanley Cup finals, Leach was awarded that season's Conn Symthe Trophy for playoff MVP. Combined with his 61 regular-season goals, the Riverton Rifle ended Phil Esposito's 6 consecutive years as the top NHL scorer. Leach didn't score more than 34 goals in the ensuing 3 seasons, but made a comeback in the 1979-80 with

Reggie Leach, 1969

50 goals, helping the Flyers set an NHL record by winning 35 consecutive games. He played for the Detroit Red Wings briefly in the 1982-83 season, and then spent 2 years in the minors before retiring. During his 14 NHL seasons, he scored 381 career goals in 934 games. • MD

LEAF RAPIDS, pop 539, is a town 160 km NW of THOMPSON. Situated on the mineral-rich Canadian Shield near the CHURCHILL RIVER, the community was an "instant town" created in 1971 for the Sherritt Gordon Ruttan Mine, which began copper and zinc recovery in 1973. Unlike many other mining towns in MB, a Crown corporation of the provincial govt developed the entire community rather than the mining company. It was designed with full social, cultural, and educational facilities. The "Main Street" or downtown is entirely in one building – the town centre is 210,000 sq ft (19,500 sq m) of insulated, air-conditioned space that houses municipal offices, health centre, hotel, school, library, post office, shopping, restaurant, arena, gymnasium and theatre-auditorium. The community was awarded an award for its distinctive design in 1975. By 1976, the population was 2000. The mine was later absorbed by HUDSON BAY MINING AND SMELTING Co., which closed the operation in 2002. In 2005, determined to survive, the community turned to local resources, and today the economy is based

on tourism – hunting, fishing, and boating. The community is also a service centre for Cree communities of South Indian Lake and Granville Lake. However, the 2006 census showed Leaf Rapids was suffering the classic fate of northern mining towns – the population had declined by 59% from the previous census. In early 2007, Leaf Rapids earned national headlines by becoming the first town in NA to ban plastic bags. Under the municipal bylaw, no retailer in the town is allowed to sell or give away plastic shopping bags. • GPP

LEAFHOPPER is a small (5-9 mm) insect in the family Cicadellida, order Hemiptera, with a thin, streamlined shape and camouflaging striped pattern of colours such as green, blue, red, yellow, or black. Utilizing piercing-sucking mouthparts, they feed on plant juices. Excess sugary sap is sometimes excreted, which is highly attractive to ants and other insects. In fact, ants tenaciously guard leafhopper aggregations to ensure their crop of honeydew. When disturbed while sitting on a leaf, a leafhopper creeps around to the other side of the plant in a attempt to avoid detection. If this proves unsuccessful, the insect suddenly leaps and unfolds its 2 sets of wings and rapidly flies away. Locally abundant on MB trees, shrubs and garden plants is the attractively coloured (green, red and blue) Red-banded Leafhopper (*Graphocephala coccinea*). Courtship calls lead to mating, and the female lays eggs on plant surfaces (often host specific) or inside plant tissues, and these hatch into nymphs which are guarded by the mother. After moulting 4 or 5 times over a month, they reach the adult stage. Summer winds are used effectively to carry swarms of

leafhoppers to new habitats. Over-wintering occurs in either the adult or egg stage, and each individual lives for only a few months. This group is highly diverse, with over 2000 species distributed over Canada and US (10,000 worldwide). Leafhopper fossil history goes back to 115 mya (Early Cretaceous). There are over 170 species known from the Canadian prairies alone, including the common Piglet Bug (*Aphelonema simplex*), so named for its stocky build, bright orange colour, and upturned snout. Some species are highly injurious to crops. • REW

L

LEAH, Vince "Uncle Vince," journalist (b Nov 29, 1913, Winnipeg; d Aug 9, 1993, Winnipeg), had a career that spanned 63 years as a Winnipeg sportswriter. Leah began as a copy boy for the *WINNIPEG TRIBUNE* at the age of 16. He worked his way to sportswriter, and soon found himself actively involved in the games he was

Vince Leah, 1966

Leafhopper preparing to hop

writing about. Leah famously came up with the name for the **Winnipeg Blue Bombers**, based on a reference he made to heavyweight champ Joe Louis, often called the "Brown Bomber." He coached and promoted kids' sports throughout MB, and organized Winnipeg's Excelsior Hockey Club in 1934. He also helped bring Little League Baseball to Canada in 1950. After the *Tribune* folded in 1980, Leah became a columnist for the *Winnipeg Free Press*. He also wrote 8 books on local history. A West Kildonan Recreation Centre and 3 Winnipeg Streets bear his name. Leah was awarded the Order of Canada in 1980. • MD

LEATHERS, Winston, artist, teacher (b Dec 1932, **Miami**; d July 20, 2004, **Winnipeg**) broke new ground with his paintings and prints, continually experimenting with materials and modes of expression. A member of the Royal Canadian Academy of the Arts, he graduated from the School of Art at the **U of M** in 1956; continued his studies in Mexico in 1957; and earned a degree in Art Education in 1958 from the Manitoba Teacher's College. He taught in the Industrial Design Department of the Winnipeg's Technical Vocational High School from 1958-68; and drawing and design in the Environmental Studies Dept of the Faculty of Architecture at the U of M, 1969-93. He received grants and awards for his pioneering printmaking techniques, especially for his use of plastics as a printing medium.

The Prairie landscape and environment are core concerns in his work, with light, colours, and rhythms imbuing his art with energy and movement. Interested in abstraction early in his career, Leathers produced the important *Cosmic Variation Series* of the early 1970s. In subsequent work, he combined elements of abstraction and reality. He created many multiples, prints, and paintings, extending his images beyond any single place or moment. Metallic paints added elements of reflection, and his use of traditional **Japanese** inks and of calligraphic brushwork added poetic and philosophic dimension to his work. Leathers exhibited widely. His work is in many private, corporate and public collections in Canada and internationally. • PATRICIA BOVEY

LEECH is a segmented worm, class Clitellata or Hirudinea, phylum Annelida, identified by its characteristic flattened body and suckers at the mouth and rear end. The body consists of 34 segments, each of which is divided into several rings, and is highly extendible. Leeches are a common inhabitant of ponds, marshes, ditches, slow streams and lakes throughout MB, where they feed on the blood of fish, frogs, turtles and waterfowl, while others engulf insect larvae, snails,

crustaceans and worms. A leech can fast for a year or 2 after a full meal. Like their earthworm (class Oligochaeta) relatives, they are smooth skinned and have no supportive skeleton, but they lack spiny hairs (chaetae) and have a number of sets of eye spots along the back. Leeches range in colour (black, brown, green, reddish, yellow, mottled) and size (1-15 cm). A leech travels by undulating contractions of the elastic and muscular body, or by inch-worming along on its suckers. There are jawed and jawless (with a protrusible proboscis) groups, the former capable of penetrating the victim's skin with a lancet-like jaw apparatus. The wound is then covered by the mouth sucker. The leech's anesthetic and anticoagulant saliva prevents host pain and clotting, allowing blood to be freely ingested.

The leech's stomach pouches are capable of great expansion as they fill with blood; a single meal may weigh up to 5 times the leech's body weight. About 24 freshwater species occur in MB (46 in Canada, 650 worldwide), with *Erpobdella punctata* a common and widespread representative. A leech is an hermaphrodite, producing both eggs and sperm. During copulation, sperm are exchanged (either inserted by a penis or by accepting a sperm package), and the leech deposits the fertilized eggs in a cocoon (clitellum), either maintained in a belt around its body or attached to a submerged rock. Following birth, the young leeches of some species attach to the abdomen of the parent, where they receive some degree of protection for several days, until they become sufficiently strong to fend for themselves. Occasionally a bather will discover a 5-9 cm leech (e.g., *Macrobdella decora*) attached to their skin, and perhaps dozens of tiny detached leeches. This 'bloodsucker' can be removed by gently opening the sucker with a knife, or applying salt or heat. • REW

LEGAL AID has been available in MB to those who cannot afford legal services since 1972, according to the terms of the *Legal Aid Services Act* (LAM), enacted by a unanimous vote of the Legislature in July 1971. Previously, limited legal aid was provided by a handful of lawyers acting *pro bono*. This service was organized by the Law Society of MB's Legal Aid Committee, headed, just before the enactment of LAM, by R. J. Meyers, now a judge of the provincial court of MB. Shortly after the election of **Ed Schreyer**'s govt in 1969, Attorney General Alvin H. Mackling appointed a committee, headed by J. F. Taylor, to research legal aid. The committee was influenced by criticisms of the ON model, especially its emphasis on the delivery of legal aid services by private practitioners (the fee-for-service or "judicare"

model). More positively, the committee looked to the US Legal Services Program – part of Lyndon Johnson's "War on Poverty" – which emphasized neighbourhood- and community-based legal aid clinics employing salaried lawyers. Thus, the committee recommended a mixed system, utilizing both a fee-for-service plan and a neighbourhood-law-office plan. The recommended mixed system was accepted by the govt, coming into force in Dec 1971. The first board, headed by law professor Roland Penner, was appointed in Feb 1972, and the plan formally launched in Sept 1972 with Meyers as its first executive director. The plan's first neighbourhood law office, headed by Norman Larsen, was opened in Oct 1972 on Isabel St in Winnipeg.

Legal Aid Manitoba grew rapidly, with the opening of several neighbourhood offices throughout the province and specialized offices in such areas as Aboriginal law, family law, child protection, and young offenders. The plan covers both civil and criminal matters, and provides duty counsel to provincial and youth courts. Eligibility for legal aid is based on family size and income. The program provides legal aid on a contributing basis for those with incomes somewhat above the statutory guidelines.

A unique feature of the LAM plan is the Public Interest Law Centre (PILC), proposed to the govt by Arne Peltz and created by amendment to the *Legal Aid Services Act* in 1982. PILC represents groups in legal actions relating to such issues as consumer and environmental protection issues, and in opposition to applications for increases in utility rates. Legal Aid Manitoba is funded directly by the MB govt and indirectly by grants made to the province by the federal govt. In addition, LAM receives annual grants from the Manitoba Law Foundation ($1.2 million in 2002-03), part of which helps to fund PILC and the student-run University Legal Aid Centre at the **U of M**. In 2003-04, MB's mixed system for delivering legal aid assisted over 70,000 persons by means of duty counsel attached to various provincial courts, staff lawyers, and lawyers in private practice, to whom, on the application of a client, an area director issues a certificate. • ROLAND PENNER

LEGISLATIVE BUILDING. Located on the N bank of the **Assiniboine River** in **Winnipeg**, about one km W of its confluence with the **Red River**, the Legislative Building is the centerpiece of a 12 ha parcel of land. The seat of MB's govt, the building is an example of Beaux Arts Classic architecture. The predominant material used in the construction is **Tyndall Stone**, quarried exclusively in MB at **Garson** and Tyndall. The base of the building is laid out in the form of the letter H. The building is 3 stories, containing approx 23,255 sq m of space. The dome is 72 m above ground level.

The building was opened on July 15, 1920, the 50th anniversary of MB's entry into Confederation. It was the 3rd building to house MB's legislative assembly. The first, a log building at Main St and McDermot Ave in **Winnipeg**, opened in 1871. Destroyed by fire in 1873, various temporary facilities were used until 1884. At that time, the 2nd building was opened, N of Government House on the present day legislative grounds. It was demolished in 1920.

Legislative Building

In 1911, the MB govt announced a worldwide contest to design a new Legislative Building. English architects Frank Worthington Simon and Henry Boddington III were the winners. By the time it officially opened in 1920, the cost had escalated to more than $9 million, the contractor had been sent to jail and the premier of the day, **Rodmond Roblin**, was forced to resign.

Construction was well underway by the outbreak of WWI in 1914. However, everything ground to a halt in 1915, amidst allegations of shoddy construction, theft of building materials and kickbacks to the Roblin Conservatives. The Conservatives used their majority to forestall any findings of wrongdoing by the Public Accounts Committee. However, the Liberals issued a minority report that accused the govt of fraud. They asked Premier Roblin to set up a commission of enquiry. When he refused, the Liberals petitioned Sir Douglas Cameron, the lt gov. In a rare use of vice-regal power, he forced the government to launch a royal commission.

The commission returned a report that supported the allegations of wrongdoing and Roblin resigned. Criminal charges against him were not pursued, on the grounds of ill health. While contractor Thomas Kelly was convicted of manipulation of govt funds and sentenced to 2 years in jail, all others were exonerated. New tenders were issued in 1917 and the building partially occupied by 1919. The final cost of the MB Legislative Building was more than double that of the AB and SK buildings combined.

It is, nonetheless, an impressive building. The interior design is meant to overawe the senses. MB researcher Frank Albo theorizes that many of the features of the Legislative Building originate with the beliefs of Freemasonry – an old secret fraternity. While this was not uncommon in public buildings constructed at the time, it is interesting to note that the principal architect, Frank Simon, was greatly influenced by Freemasonry. Premier Roblin and many members of his government also belonged to the fraternity.

The intent of the builders, says Albo, was to invoke divine energy and ward off evil. He says the building's numerous statues, engravings and murals embody Masonic symbols. These include Egyptian sphinxes and hieroglyphics; Roman and Greek deities; and a black and white marble star symbolizing the Pole Star. Albo has concluded that the **Golden Boy** represents Hermes Trismegistus – the father of alchemy, and the patron of Freemasonry.

The building's many features have resulted in it being selected for the short list of CBC's Seven Wonders of Canada contest. ● KAREN OMELAN/ SANDY CUSHON

LEHOTSKY, Rev Harry, Baptist minister, activist (b July 26, 1957, New York; d Nov 11, 2006, **Winnipeg**) fought against crime, drugs, and prostitution in Winnipeg's inner city. Lehotsky grew up in Hell's Kitchen, a poor and crime-ridden part of Manhattan. As a teenager, he rebelled against his parents' Christian values, but after winding up in hospital following a drug overdose, Lehotsky reclaimed his Baptist faith. He attended a religious college, graduating with a master's of divinity from the North American Baptist Seminary in 1982. While giving a workshop at a Baptist conference in Niagara Falls, ON, Lehotsky was urged by several pastors to start a congregation in Winnipeg's impoverished inner city. He agreed, and moved to the city with his wife Virginia in 1983. From the basement of their West End home, Lehotsky held Bible study classes, and later small worship services, sometimes with as few as 5 parishioners. He gradually gained a following and founded the local New

Life Ministries, part of the North American Baptist Conference, in 1986. His growing congregation moved into a church on Maryland St. Lehotsky became an outspoken social activist in the community. He was a columnist for the **Winnipeg Sun**, and established several charitable organizations to benefit the West End's low-income residents, including a housing renewal program to buy and renovate derelict buildings and former drug houses. In 2005, he established the Ellice Café & Theatre as a means to bring revenue to the West End. Lehotsky died of cancer in 2006. His funeral attracted 2000 mourners. A mural on Maryland St depicts his work. ● MD

LEISHMAN, William KENNETH, "The Flying Bandit," bank robber (b July 20, 1931, **Treherne**; d Dec 16, 1980, ON). Leishman masterminded the biggest gold heist in Cdn history. Though a serial bank robber, he was also an inherently likeable and charismatic man. Sporting a jovial grin under his pencil-thin moustache, Leishman's amiable appearance belied his lengthy criminal record and kleptomaniac tendencies. He thus became a folk hero, developing a legendary mystique that only grew following his mysterious death.

A product of the Dirty Thirties, Leishman's childhood was spent in impoverished surroundings. His divorced parents took little interest in raising him, and he grew up in the child welfare system before moving in with his grandparents, stern immigrants who worked their grandson hard. He learned early on to be self-sufficient, as well as to disdain figures of authority, and

Mug shot of Ken Leishman on September 3, 1966 after the gold heist.

dropped out of school in grade 7 in order to support himself. He married at 18, but a quiet family life wasn't in store for Leishman. Within the first few months of marriage, he had succumbed to his impulsive nature, stealing furniture from his employer's merchandise stock, which he then offered to his unsuspecting wife as a wedding gift. He was caught, and served 4 months in jail.

Upon his release, Leishman started over, managing to find work as a salesman. Likeable and charming, he was able to turn selling cookware into a profitable career, buying a Cadillac as well as a house for his growing family within 5 years. It was around this time that Leishman first developed an interest in flying, purchasing a small aircraft to fly to customers throughout rural MB. This comfortable life, however, began unravelling in 1957, when his employer went out of business, leaving Leishman jobless.

Unable to support his lifestyle and facing mounting debt, Leishman devised a scheme to rob a bank, not in **Winnipeg**, but Toronto, where authorities wouldn't think to look for the culprit beyond the city's parameters. Leishman booked a passage on a commercial flight, smuggling onboard a handgun that he then used to coax a Toronto bank manager into writing out a cheque for $10,000. Leishman then flew back to Winnipeg the same day, successfully evading any connection with the hold-up. Cordial throughout the robbery, he was dubbed the "Gentleman Bandit" by Toronto newspapers. His confidence bolstered, Leishman attempted another Toronto robbery just 3 months later. However, the 2nd bank manager proved less cooperative and, almost laughing at Leishman's hold-up, apprehended the would-be robber and handed him over to police. When media discovered Leishman's fly-in and fly-out robbery technique, they dubbed him the "Flying Bandit." For his part, far from being shamed, Leishman revelled in the attention.

After serving 4 years at **Stony Mountain Institution**, Leishman was again a free man. However, as a convicted felon, his job prospects were few, and he was left with ample free time to indulge in his passion for flying. Hanging around Winnipeg airport, Leishman learned that shipments of pure gold bullion were being flown in regularly from Red Lake, ON. His imagination took flight. Carefully observing the schedules and security procedures, Leishman devised a plot to steal the gold, enlisting the help of 4 companions. When a large shipment of 12 gold bars, valued at $4 million, arrived at the airport on Mar 1, 1966, Leishman set his plan in motion. Dressed as Air Canada employees, his cohorts nonchalantly loaded up a van with the gold and drove away,

easily carrying out what was then the greatest gold heist in NA history.

An obvious suspect with his previous high profile conviction, Leishman then sealed his fate by bragging about the heist to an undercover RCMP officer. Facing a lengthy sentence, Leishman plotted a daring escape from Stony Mountain. He convinced a group of prisoners to overpower the jail guards, clearing the way for Leishman to flee to **Steinbach** where he hotwired a small plane and flew to the US, making it to Gary, IN, before finally being captured in a dramatic shootout. Leishman, however, was not upset by his arrest: the bold exploits of the "Flying Bandit" made headlines around the world.

Released from prison in May 1974, Leishman slipped into relative anonymity, finding a job flying planes, ironically enough, in Red Lake, the community where the stolen gold had been mined. Nonetheless, residents of Red Lake welcomed Leishman. "Goldfingers," as he was often called by the townspeople, was even elected president of the Red Lake Chamber of Commerce.

But this peaceable existence didn't last long. In 1979, on an air ambulance flight in the midst of a cold winter, Leishman's plane went down. Though fragments of his clothing were later found, his body was never recovered, leading many to wonder if the Flying Bandit could have somehow survived, or if he had perhaps even faked his own death in order start over anew elsewhere.

His biography *The Flying Bandit* by Heather Robertson was published in 1981. A documentary, *Ken Leishman: The Flying Bandit*, was directed by **Norma Bailey** and produced by **Frantic Films** in 2005. ● MICHELLE DOBROVOLNY

LEMMING is a rodent which plays a substantial role in boreal and tundra ecosystems. A lemming's body is compact, with a short tail, ears and limbs and face, which helps prevent heat loss. The coat moults into a remarkably thick pelage in winter, which is pure white in collared lemmings, making them almost invisible on the snow. Four kinds of lemmings have been reported in MB: The Collared Lemming (*Dicrostonyx richardsoni*) inhabits the muskeg and heath ridges of the tundra as far S as the **Churchill** region, where its populations often undergo a 3-5-year cycle, ranging from 0.6-400/ha. These lemmings do not commit suicide, as the myth suggests, but they do die off rapidly from stress of crowding, fighting, exposure, and cessation of breeding.

The periodic crash of lemmings triggers the S emigration of Arctic **Foxes** (desperate for food) deep into the boreal forest of MB. A female Collared Lemming produces 1-3 litters from

April to Sept, with 1-11 young in each. A young female may mate when only 4 weeks old. This species is the only rodent in MB that moults into a white winter coat. It also develops a couple of large claws on the front feet, which aid in digging through crusted snow. One specimen of the Brown Lemming (*Lemmus sibiricus*) showed up on the beach in Churchill many decades ago, but is believed to have been a stowaway on a boat arriving from Nunavut, where the species is abundant. Two species of bog lemmings, looking much like stubby-tailed Meadow Voles, are found in sphagnum moss-heath bogs and sedge fens, where they leave little trails, marked by piles of cut sedge stems and tidy latrines. The Southern Bog Lemming (*Synaptomys cooperi*) occurs in SE MB, while the Northern Bog Lemming (*Synaptomys borealis*) is present throughout the boreal forest. All lemmings are a major food source for northern owls, hawks, foxes, and weasels. ● REW

LEPIDOPTERA is a group of insects, order Lepidoptera, which includes moths, butterflies and skippers. Adults are conspicuous and well known for the many day-flying, brightly coloured species. In addition, the larvae of some species are important pests of cultivated crops. There are at least 53 families in MB, most of which are moths. Adults have 2 pairs of scale-covered wings, which may be large relative to the size of the body. The overlapping scales are responsible for the wing colour (via pigment and light refraction) and patterns. The mouthparts of most species are long and tubular for sucking nectar from floral nectaries, juices of soft fruits, or fermenting sap. The mouthparts are held in a tight coil that springs forward at the front of the face. The antennae are variable: clubbed in butterflies, hooked in skippers, thread-like or feathery in moths. The larvae, or caterpillars, are largely herbivorous, with strong, chewing mouthparts. They live camouflaged on leaves, flowers or stems, hidden underground where they feed on plant roots, enclosed inside plant gall tissue and leaf mines, or burrowed into fruits and woody stems.

Despite various forms of ornamentation, spots and projections, lepidopteran larvae are quite similar in body plan. They are cylindrical, with a well-developed head, 6 hook-like thoracic legs, and a variable number of abdominal prolegs. Many moth species' larvae produce silk, used to construct a refuge and as a means of escape, and to construct a cocoon prior to pupation. Butterflies and skippers do not build a cocoon, but instead have a naked pupa called a chrysalis. MB's fauna is represented by 111 species of butterflies, 33 skippers, and about 600 moths (total

744). Many species of moths remain to be discovered. There are about 5000 lepidopteran species recorded in Canada (actual total may be 7300) and the world total is about 200,000 (14,500 butterflies, 3500 skippers, and 182,000 moths). Lepidopterans first appeared in the fossil record 194 mya (early Jurassic period), but largely diversified 110-90 mya (Cretaceous period) with the radiation of flowering plants (angiosperms) – their main food supply. • TDG, REW

Ambroise-Didyme Lépine

LÉPINE, Ambroise-Didyme, MÉTIS leader (b 1840, St. Vital [now WINNIPEG]; d June 8,1923, St. Boniface), was the son of a French-Cdn father and a MÉTIS mother. From the beginning of the 1869-70 insurrection, Lépine was the military lieutenant and chief enforcer of LOUIS RIEL. He led the armed party that ordered GOV JOHN MCDOUGALL out of the settlement in Oct 1869. He was prominent in the surrenders of JOHN SCHULTZ party in Dec 1869 and of the CHARLES BOULTON party in Feb 1870. It was Lépine who led the Métis horsemen outside UPPER FORT GARRY to capture THOMAS SCOTT and his comrades as they marched back to PORTAGE LA PRAIRIE. Lépine presided at the court martial that tried and convicted Scott, and he pronounced the death sentence. Lépine fled Winnipeg with Riel on the arrival of the WOLSELEY EXPEDITION in 1870.

With Riel, he supported the MB govt at the time of the FENIAN invasion, and he accompanied Riel into exile in the US in 1872. He was subsequently arrested in 1873 and was tried for the murder of Scott in 1874. His defence was that the provisional govt that had executed Scott was a legal govt, and the execution a necessary act. He was found guilty by a jury composed of equal numbers of Anglophones and Francophones. He was originally sentenced to death, but the sentence was commuted to a 2-year prison term. In 1875, he was offered an amnesty by the gov gen, with the provision that he go into exile for 5 years and that he lose his civil rights. Lépine refused to accept the conditions of the amnesty, and served out the full 2-year sentence. • J. M. BUMSTED

LESKIW, Greg, singer/songwriter (b Aug 5, 1946, BRANDON). Leskiw was the son of a well known Brandon-area dance band guitarist, from whom Greg learned how to play guitar. He moved to Shilo at age 10 before arriving in WINNIPEG after high school in 1965 to play in local bands including The Shags, Jamieson Roberts Device, Logan Avenue Comfort Station, and Gettysbyrg Address. In 1969, he joined Bill and Carole Ivaniuk in Wild Rice, where he was spotted by BURTON CUMMINGS of the GUESS WHO. Cummings invited him, along with Kurt Winter, to join the band, replacing guitarist RANDY BACHMAN in June 1970. Leskiw made his Guess Who recording debut on "Hand Me Down World" and his first public appearance July 1 at Montreal's Man and His World Park on Île Sainte-Hélène, followed by a performance on July 4 at the White House. *Share the Land* (1970) included 2 of Leskiw's songs and earned a gold record. *So Long Bannatyne* (1971) and *Rockin'* (1972) featured Leskiw as well, but by the time of the latter's release, his role had diminished, and he left the group in March 1972.

Returning to Winnipeg, Leskiw formed the jazz-influenced Mood Jga Jga with Gord Osland, Hermann Frühm, and Bill Merritt, releasing a self-titled album on WEA Records (1973) and the hit single "Queen Jealousy" before splitting 2 years later. The band would reconvene numerous times over the next 30 years, and released *Boys Will Be Boys* in 1977. Leskiw then formed Crowcuss with ex–Guess Who bassist Bill Wallace, recording a self-titled album (1979) before leaving to record a solo album, *Be My Champion* (1979) under the name LesQ. He then teamed up again with Wallace to form hard rock group Kilowatt, releasing *Kilowatt* (1982) and *Currents* (1984), both produced by ex–Guess Who guitarist Domenic Troiano. Leskiw opened his own Vox Pop recording studio in the 1990s, then formed popular swing jazz trio Swing Soniq with guitarist Greg Lowe and bassist Danny Koulack in 1997, releasing *Moonglow* (1998). Swing Soniq released *Love Wild* (2005), with Richard Moody and Nenad Zdjelar replacing Lowe and Koulack; in 2006, Leskiw released *Hell on Hold* with his new band, the One Eyed Jacks. • JOHN EINARSON

LETELLIER, pop 300, is a community 85 km S of WINNIPEG and 15 km N of the US border, on the Marais River (a small tributary of the RED RIVER) and on Highway 75 and a CN line, near the ROSEAU RIVER FIRST NATION. By the 18th century, French and MÉTIS voyageurs and FUR TRADERS were active in the area. Settlers to the area in the 19th century were predominantly French-speaking Quebecois with smaller numbers of OJIBWAY, though MENNONITES and people from the British Isles came later. These Quebecois came mainly in the 1880s, as there was then a shortage of arable land in that province. The settlers established Letellier as one of several Francophone communities along the RED RIVER. The post office opened in 1880-81. Originally known as Catherine Station – after a local resident, Catherine Wright – the community's name was changed to honour QC politician Luc Letellier de Saint-Just. AGRICULTURE still forms the economic base in this community. Letellier hosts the annual Montcalm Heritage Festival, as well as the annual Letellier Family Ball. • GPP

LÉVEILLÉ, Joseph ROGER, poet, novelist, essayist and visual artist (b Nov 10, 1945, Winnipeg). Léveillé's work has been published in Ontario, Quebec and France as well as in MB. Having studied French literature at the COLLÈGE UNIVERSITAIRE DE ST-BONIFACE, the U OF M and the Sorbonne, he became a TV journalist at Radio-Canada, where he created a popular arts program called *ZigZag*. He has won numerous prizes for his literary work, including the Prix Champlain and the Prix Deschambault, and was one of the inaugural inductees into the Franco-Manitoban *Temple des renommés*. In 2007 he received a Lifetime Achievement Award from the Manitoba Writers Guild. He is the editor of the *Rouge* collection, dedicated to avant-garde writing, at Éditions du Blé.

Greg Leskiw, 1979

L

To date, Léveillé has published 21 books in various genres: novels, poetry, essays and visual works, the latter involving *collage*. Whereas his earlier works reflect the influence of the French Symbolists (the novels *Tombeau*, *La disparate* and *Plage*, and the poetry collections *Oeuvre de la première mort* and *Le livre des marges*), they anticipate the postmodern qualities of his more recent books (the novels *Une si simple passion*, *Le Soleil du lac qui se couche*, *Nosara*, and the poetry collections *Les fêtes de l'infini* and *Fastes*). His *collages* (an enormous poster titled *Extrait*, the magazine-format *Montréal poésie*, and *Pièces à conviction*) explore the boundaries of visual and textual art, exploding traditional notions of genre. Léveillé has also published the most comprehensive work on Franco-Manitoban literature to date, the *Anthologie de la poésie franco-manitobaine*. Léveillé's work has captured the interest of North American and European critics, and has given rise to well over 100 critical essays and reviews as well as to 3 critical volumes and a scholarly thesis. ● ROSMARIN HEIDENREICH

LEVINE, Allan, teacher, author (b Feb 10, 1956, **WINNIPEG**). Educated at the **U OF M** and the U of Toronto, Levine teaches history at St. John's-Ravenscourt School in Winnipeg, and has published several well-regarded books of history and fiction, as well as articles and reviews. *The Exchange: 100 Years of Trading Grain in Winnipeg* (1987) documents the history of the **WINNIPEG COMMODITY EXCHANGE**; *Your Worship: The Lives of Eight of Canada's Most Unforgettable Mayors* was published in 1989; and *Scrum Wars: The Prime Ministers and the Media* (1993) discusses the influence of the media on Cdn politics from Confederation to the present. *Fugitives of the Forest: The Heroic Story of Jewish Resistance and Survival During the Second World War* was short-listed for the McNally Robinson Book of the Year Award in 1998, and won the Yad Vashem Holocaust History Prize in 1999. It was followed in 2002 by *Scattered Among the Peoples: The Jewish Diaspora in Ten Portraits*, and by *The Devil in Babylon* (2006).

Levine is also known to murder mystery fans as the creator of hard-boiled Jewish detective Sam Klein, whose exploits are set in the historic past of Winnipeg, called at one time "the wickedest city in the Dominion." In *The Blood Libel*, Sam investigates a rabbi charged with murdering a Polish girl in Winnipeg's **NORTH END** in 1911; the book was short-listed in 1997 for the Chapters/Books in Canada Award and for the Arthur Ellis First Mystery Novel Award, and won the Manitoba Historical Society Prize for Best Historical Fiction in 2000. The sequel, *Sins of the Suffragette,* in which famed author and women's rights activist **NELLIE MCCLUNG** assists Sam in a 1914 investigation of a suffragette's death, was short-listed for the Carol Shields City of Winnipeg Award in 2001. *The Bolshevik's Revenge* (2002) has Sam struggling to solve the murder of a prominent businessman as the city is engulfed in the turmoil of the 1919 **WINNIPEG GENERAL STRIKE**. ● MILDRED GUTKIN

WINNIPEG FREE PRESS

Leo Lewis

LEWIS, Leo "Lincoln Locomotive," football player (b Feb 4, 1933, Des Moines, IA) had an outstanding 11-year run as halfback for the **WINNIPEG BLUE BOMBERS**. Raised in St. Paul, MN, Lewis started out playing American College football for Lincoln U in Missouri where he still holds many school records. He was drafted into the NFL with the Baltimore Colts following graduation, but found his biggest success as the Blue Bombers' running back. He first joined the Bombers in 1955, though an ankle injury prevented him from playing much of 1956. Over the next 9 years, Lewis was named All-Pro 6 times. His record of 8861 yds rushing remained the best in Bomber history, until he was passed by Charles Roberts in 2007. He had a 29.1 yd average per return, 2nd best in the league, and his 6.6 yds per carry still holds as a CFL record. An injury ended his career in 1966, after which Lewis returned to Lincoln U as the football team's head coach. Lewis is a member of the CFL Hall of Fame. ● MD

LEWIS, Marion Jean, medical researcher (b Windsor, ON, 1925) came to Winnipeg in 1935, graduated from Gordon Bell High School in 1943, trained as a medical laboratory technologist at the Winnipeg General Hospital, and eventually obtained a BA from the **U OF M** in 1960. She joined **HENRY BRUCE CHOWN** in 1944 to form the Winnipeg Rh Laboratory, where she remained her whole career, eventually becoming scientific director in 1977. In 1950, she received additional blood group training at the Lister Institute in London with world-renowned scientists Robert Race and Ruth Sanger. Lewis worked on Rh disease and, along with Chown, also looked at the distribution of blood group genes. Between 1952-61, they visited and tested many Aboriginal populations across Canada, including Stoney (Assiniboine), **CREE**, Siksika (Blackfoot), and Kainai (Blood), as well as Inuit populations in the Arctic. From 1977, Lewis and her colleagues at the Rh Laboratory moved into the field of genetics, becoming internationally renowned for their work on the mapping of blood group genes.

Even though she had only a BA degree, Lewis was appointed an assistant professor in the Dept of Pediatrics at the U of M in 1973, moving through the ranks to professor in 1984. In 1986, she was appointed professor in the Dept of Human Genetics (now Biochemistry and Medical Genetics). Lewis has authored or co-authored more than 100 medical papers. Her awards include the Merit Award from the American Assoc of Physical Anthropologists (1959); the Karl Landsteiner Memorial Award from the American Assoc of Blood Banks (AABB, 1971); and, in 1986, the Teddy Award for Research from the Children's Hospital Research Foundation of Winnipeg. She received a DSc from the **U OF W** (1986); the Medaille de la Ville de Paris (1987); and, in the same year, was made an honorary fellow of the Canadian College of Medical Geneticists. In 1993, she was elected to a fellowship of the Royal Society of Canada, receiving the Emily Cooley Memorial Award from the AABB in 1996, and, on her retirement in that year, was named professor emerita by the U of M. ● JOHN L. HAMERTON

LIBAU, pop. 383, is a community 55 km NE of **WINNIPEG** on Highway 59, on a **CN** line, near **NETLEY-LIBAU MARSH**, and just SW of the **OJIBWAY** community of **BROKENHEAD FIRST NATION**. The post office opened in 1903 and the new town was named Kreiger, after its first postmaster. In 1906, the name changed to Libau after the Liepaja, Latvia (then part of the Russian Empire), whose name means "linden tree." (*Libau* is the German pronunciation for the seaport.) It is believed that ethnic **GERMAN IMMIGRANTS**, **MENNONITES**, and Latvians who had sailed from the port chose Libau's name. **UKRAINIANS**, Poles, and settlers from the British Isles also came to the area to homestead. The community made national news when, in 1967, a group of local residents protested the federal govt's planned move of the post office from one store to another (only a stone's throw away) by kidnaping the local postmaster. The agricultural service industry, including a grain elevator, supports the local economy, as do tourists interested in exploring nearby outdoor sites such as the marsh. Visual artist Don Reichert was born in Libau. • GPP

LIBERAL PARTY OF MANITOBA. The Liberals in MB reach back into the early 1880s. The party initially operated as a loose collection of "provincial rights" candidates in the 1883 provincial election, with Reformer MLA **THOMAS GREENWAY** the unofficial leader. The aim was to defeat **JOHN NORQUAY**'s provincial govt, which was informally connected to PM John A. Macdonald's Conservatives. Greenway's Liberals opposed the National Policy, which included tariffs and the **CPR**'s railway monopoly in MB. The Liberals instead campaigned for settlement and **IMMIGRATION**, provincially chartered **RAILWAYS**, and economic development. Greenway was **ENGLISH** by birth. Before coming to MB, he served as an "Independent Conservative" MP for the ON riding of Fort Huron, until he fell out with Macdonald over trade issues. He moved to MB in 1878 as a land speculator and farm owner.

Sometimes called "Grits" or "Reformers," Greenway's Liberals took power in 1888 with 57% of the provincial vote. In 1890, they revoked the portions of the **MANITOBA ACT** that had guaranteed official bilingualism and public support for **FRENCH**, **ROMAN CATHOLIC** schools. This effectively terminated the delicate arrangements of 1870 between French-speaking settlers, **MÉTIS**, and the English-speaking community. A national political firestorm called the **MANITOBA SCHOOLS QUESTION** ensued, dividing QC-based voters from those in ON. This led to the defeat of Charles Tupper's Conservatives.

The Liberals held power in MB until 1899, when they were defeated by the Conservatives (*see* **PROGRESSIVE CONSERVATIVE** party) led by Macdonald's son, **HUGH JOHN MACDONALD**, and shortly thereafter by **RODMOND ROBLIN**. After Roblin's administration was rocked by scandal, **T. C. NORRIS** brought the Liberals back into power in 1915, weaving together support from a broad coalition of social groupings, including farmers; workers; **PROHIBITIONISTS**; **WOMEN'S RIGHTS** activists; and various urban **REFORM** groups. In part, their success was tied to their forward thinking, but also to a collapse of a scandal-ridden Conservative govt. The Liberals subsequently instituted a number of progressive measures, including voting rights for women and labour reform. However, a

recession following WWI and the **WINNIPEG GENERAL STRIKE** of 1919 discredited the Norris administration. The Liberals were defeated in 1922 by the leaderless United Farmers of Manitoba (UFM), who quickly enlisted **JOHN BRACKEN** as their new premier. The Liberals remained out of power for the remainder of the decade.

In 1932, with the encouragement of federal Liberals, MB Liberals under Murdoch MacKay merged with Bracken's ruling Progressive Party (which had since changed its own name when the UFM withdrew from party politics). The Liberal-Progressives proved unbeatable, with support coming from both urban business interests and rural farmers. In order to present a united front to deal with Ottawa over fiscal relations, as well as due to wartime condition in WWII, Bracken formed an all-party coalition govt. In 1942, Bracken became the new leader of the federal Progressive Conservatives, and thereby vacated the provincial scene.

STUART GARSON succeeded Bracken as the new Liberal-Progressive premier. After Garson left for federal politics in 1948, **DOUGLAS CAMPBELL** became premier and served until 1958. The party under these 3 leaders put forward consistent policies of tight spending and low taxes, as well as antipathy toward organized labour **UNIONS**. The 1958 election, which brought **DUFF ROBLIN** and his PCs to power, would be the last time the "Liberal-Progressive" label would be used in MB.

GILDAS MOLGAT became the new leader in 1961. He faced a 2-front battle with the PCs in the rural areas and the **NEW DEMOCRATIC PARTY** in **WINNIPEG**. He was unable to reverse declining support in the 1966 election, especially among Winnipeg supporters. In 1969, under the brief leadership of Robert ("Bobbie") Bend, **ED SCHREYER**'s NDP encroached further into Liberal urban support, while centre-right rural voters shifted to the PCs. Adding salt to the wound was the defection of St. Boniface MLA Larry Desjardins from the Liberal caucus to sit as a "Liberal-Democrat," and later with NDP. This move allowed the NDP minority govt to hold onto power.

Voting figures illustrate the exchange in fortunes between the Liberals and NDP in the post-Liberal-Progressive era. Between 1962 and 1973, support for the Liberals dropped from 36% to 19%, while the NDP moved from 15% to 42%. Even the sparkling and enigmatic **ISRAEL "IZZY" ASPER**, who became leader in 1970, could not bring the party back to its glory years: in 1973, the party won only 5 seats with 19% of the vote, and Asper resigned in 1975. His successors, Charles Huband and Douglas Lauchlan, led the party into further decline by taking only one seat in 1977, won by **LLOYD AXWORTHY** in Fort Rouge. The party was shut out altogether in 1981. The provincial

party suffered largely because of policies of PM Pierre Trudeau and his federal Liberals that were viewed as unfavourable to the West.

In the 1988 provincial election, **SHARON CARSTAIRS** and her Liberals offered a fresh alternative both to **HOWARD PAWLEY**'s tired NDP govt and to an untested **GARY FILMON**, now leading the PCs. The party moved from "non-party status" to become the Official Opposition by winning 20 seats to the NDP's 12. Some thought the NDP was doomed, but it was not to be. With the exception of **SELKIRK**, the Liberals were confined to Winnipeg, and were unable to produce a province-wide movement. Later, Carstairs appeared to struggle during the tense discussions over the **MEECH LAKE ACCORD**, and then during the 1990 election. The party dropped to 7 seats, while the NDP took 20.

In 1993, Carstairs retired from provincial politics and was appointed to the Senate. The new leader was Paul Edwards, a young MLA and lawyer with a reputation for hard work. In 1995, Edwards resigned after capturing only 3 seats and losing his own. Ginny Hasselfield, an organizer from within the party ranks, took over the leadership in 1996, but was unable to maintain support from 2 members of her own caucus. She stepped down in 1998 to be replaced by Jon Gerrard. Gerrard, a medical doctor, had previously served as an MP for Portage-Interlake (1993-97). The Liberals continue to put forward pragmatic platforms representing the ideological centre, yet they have been unable to break out of their "half-party" status. As of the 2007 provincial election, only 2 Liberals – Kevin Lamoureux and Dr. Gerrard – had seats in the Legislature. • CHRIS ADAMS

LIBRARIES have been part of MB life since the **HUDSON'S BAY COMPANY** sent men to work as traders in **RUPERT'S LAND**, encouraging them to bring favourite books to savour in the cold, long MB winters. "A List of Books belonging to the Red River Settlement" was printed in 1822, listing 74 titles, from practical topics that might be needed in establishing a new culture to the finest literature. Thus, *Tomlin's Law Dictionary* sat beside books on animal husbandry, cooking, botany, and volumes by Shakespeare, Milton, Pope, and Cervantes. The little library received a great boost that year with the death of noted surveyor and explorer **PETER FIDLER**. Fidler's will declared: "All my printed books, amounting to about 500 volumes…I give and bequest to the Governor of the Red River Colony in trust…for the general good of all those colonists settled in the lands of the Earl of Selkirk in Assiniboia."

In 1846, a few eminent citizens started up a subscription library. However, a real push for

395

L

Winnipeg's Millennium Library

a library came with the arrival to the **RED RIVER SETTLEMENT** of LCol John Crofton and his 6th Regt of Foot (the Royal Warwickshire Regt, later Fusiliers). He established a military library for his men, split between the 2 garrisons of **UPPER** and **LOWER FORT GARRY**. Colonel Crofton urged Red River society to set up a library for the good of all, and the Council of Assiniboia passed a resolution to this effect on March 24, 1847. **JAMES CURTIS BIRD**, **ALEXANDER ROSS**, and other citizens convinced the council to support the fledgling library with a grant of $50 (equivalent at the time to about $245). A thousand books from the UK arrived the following summer, although the backers were shocked that they had to pay customs duties on their literary purchases. By 1854, a visiting minister noted approvingly that the library included 2000 volumes, "with a very small proportion of fiction." However, the library began to decline when several of its original proponents moved away.

MB entered Confederation in 1870, and, thanks to the arrival of MB's first lieut gov, a new provincial library was established. To help administer the new province, **ADAMS GEORGE ARCHIBALD** had a library of books suitable for administrative concerns sent to him from the National Library in Ottawa. These titles, combined with Ross's collection, were housed in the provincial secretary's office, and became the basis of MB's Provincial Library, with eminent naturalist Bernard Ross serving as provincial librarian. Unfortunately, a fire in the govt building in 1873 destroyed many precious volumes, so that by 1884, only 400 books were left, 200 from the original Red River Library. The MB Legislative Library still houses the remnants of this collection.

As befits a capital, Winnipeg began to see other libraries spring up. The first university libraries opened up at Manitoba College and St. John's College (*see* **U OF M**) in 1871, and the Manitoba Medical College's Isbister Library opened in 1877. As well, The Historical and Scientific Society founded its own library in 1874. By 1881, the library was housed in Winnipeg's City Hall, with grants from the city and the province to purchase materials. Memberships from subscribers ($5) further sustained the library. Several other associations also organized library services, recognizing that in this frontier province, literacy, and self-education were the way to prosperity and a stable society. Workers at the **CPR** set up a library "to advance the moral and intellectual welfare" of fellow staff. Instrumental in establishing the library was carpenter Jacob Freeman, who had attended the first Conference of Librarians held in London, UK, in 1877.

Throughout the 1880s and '90s, press, labour representatives, and some aldermen agitated for a truly public library, free to all. In 1895, City Council finally agreed to establish a free public library. A grant of $2000 a year was made to establish the library, and the Historical Society transferred 2000 of its books to the new circulating library. By the turn of the 20th century, it was clear that there was not enough room in City Hall for the library to grow, so an appeal was made to US philanthropist Andrew Carnegie. Carnegie had made millions of dollars in the steel industry, and used his wealth to fund libraries around the world. With a grant of $75,000, the Carnegie Library was opened on William Ave in 1905, and expanded, again with Carnegie's help, in 1909. Two more city branches were created in 1915 to serve Winnipeg's rapidly growing population, funded by grants of $35,000 each from the Carnegie Foundation: the Cornish Library, at Cornish and West Gate; and St. John's Library, at Salter and Machray in the **NORTH END**.

While establishing public library service was difficult in Winnipeg, it was more so in rural MB, with its far-flung communities and small municipalities. In 1890, Lady Aberdeen, wife of Canada's gov gen, inspired an association of like-minded women to "collect good and attractive periodicals and other literature and to distribute it in monthly parcels to settlers who apply for it from outlying parts of Canada." These Women's Institutes and reform-minded associations were the driving force for public library service in many towns. In 1899, with the passage of the *Manitoba Library Act*, municipalities were allowed to co-operate to provide library services, and to raise a levy from taxpayers. However, without direction and funding from the province, small communities could seldom raise enough money to provide reasonable library service. The Department of Education operated an open-shelf service out of its Winnipeg textbook bureau, which continues to this day through the province's Public Library Services. Rural inhabitants could mail in requests for books, which were then mailed out. Finally, in the 1950s, the province increased its contributions, which enabled many rural libraries to get started. In the years that followed, and especially in Canada's centenary, 1967, public libraries sprang up in the province. Around Winnipeg, library services began in St. James, St. Vital, St. Boniface, West Kildonan, Fort Garry, and East Kildonan. Regional libraries were established in **BRANDON**, **DAUPHIN**, and **SELKIRK**.

Still, public library service rarely seemed to be in the front of political minds. Through the 1960s and '70s, provincial funding remained static, with MB consistently falling in the lowest national ratings of per capita library funding. In 1977, Winnipeg's old Carnegie Library on William Ave was outgrown, and a new central library, Centennial Library, opened downtown, featuring a sculpture by **TONY TASCONA**. The former William Ave library now houses the City of Winnipeg's **ARCHIVES**. In 1979, the regional libraries around Winnipeg amalgamated to form Winnipeg Public Library.

In the early 21st century, the Winnipeg Public Library – a division of the City of Winnipeg's Community Services Department – renovated its main library. The Millennium Library, as Centennial was renamed, opened in Nov 2005, winning an award for architecture and design and drawing unprecedented numbers of citizens. Outside of Winnipeg, there were 55 library systems with 91 service points, meaning 65% of Manitobans reside in regions with municipal-tax-funded library service. MB Culture, Heritage and Tourism's Public Library Services Branch in Brandon has developed a union catalogue, MAPLIN, to serve these libraries and to encourage resource sharing. With widespread automation of library collections, federal community-based Internet station initiatives, and Internet access to catalogues and databases, the dream of 24-hour library access nears reality. ● LAURA COWIE

▶ *See also* BOOK PUBLISHING, LITERATURE.

LICE is a small (0.5-11 mm) insect in the order Phthiraptera, phylum Arthropoda, characterized by great modifications in body form related to an ectoparasitic way of life. Most species are host-specific, with only 1 or 2 host species. No one is certain when lice first appeared (estimates from 130-300 million years ago), or from what ancestor(s); likely they evolved from bird- and mammal-nest-dwelling bark lice (order Psocoptera). Lice crawl well with their 3 pairs of legs, but cannot jump like fleas. MB species are classified into chewing lice (Mallophaga) and sucking lice (Anoplura), with likely over 300 species represented here (5500 worldwide). Many species remain to be discovered in MB.

MB has 7 families of chewing lice, and all but one are ectoparasites of birds. Species in the remaining family are restricted to mammals, including common parasites of domestic animals. All species are small (except the giant *Laemobothrion* on eagles, hawks, vultures and coots), wingless, and dorso-ventrally flattened, with chewing mouthparts. Most species feed on skin, feathers, and skin secretions, but many also feed on blood. Chewing lice look different from sucking lice, and use different mechanisms for avoiding host grooming activity. They rely on strong mouthparts for obtaining food and also for maintaining their position. They avoid host grooming by being slender and flattened, and by moving rapidly. Some species are well camouflaged, such as the white lice on gulls and Snow Goose. The Pelican Louse (*Piagetiella peralis*) lives inside the pelican's throat pouch, where uses its sharp mandibles to pierce the skin to obtain blood, and to keep from being swallowed along with fish. Clearly, the relationship between lice and their hosts is an old one, and species seldom intrude on each other's territory and resources.

Chewing lice cement their eggs on the feathers or hair of their hosts. The tiny immatures hatch and take up positions on the body, shedding their skins as they grow. Without wings, the lice access new hosts by direct contact, such as host mating, grooming and roosting. Each of MB's species of birds harbours one or more species of chewing lice, however, lice are rarely collected, and so there is little evidence on which species occur here. There are actual MB records for only 37 species, with an additional 36

species known in Canada (4500 worldwide). Many species are yet undescribed, and little is known about most species' life cycles and host interactions. While many species of birds are classified as endangered, none of their ectoparasites have been given similar status. If a bird becomes extirpated or extinct, so do its host-specific parasites. The Passenger Pigeon Louse (*Lipeurus extinctus*) is an example of an extinct MB species of lice.

There are 6 families of sucking lice recorded in MB, all ectoparasites of mammals. They are small and flattened, have piercing and sucking mouthparts. And possess at least one pair of sturdy claws which lock in place around the host's hair follicles. All species feed exclusively on blood, and may be extremely irritating. Females cement their eggs (nits) to body hairs, while the Human Body Louse (*Pediculus humanus corporis*) also lays its eggs among the clothing. From egg to adult may take only 8 days. The Human Head Louse (*Pediculus humanus capitis*) spreads by contact among students, while the Human Crab Louse (*Pthirus pubis*) is spread by sexual contact. Rodents are particularly well-infested with sucking lice, cattle often have 3 species, while horses and dogs also have their own specific species. The formerly common Hog Louse (*Haematopinus suis*) has become rare in MB due to insecticides. This order also includes the only species of insects (family Echinophthiriidae) that are parasitic on marine mammals such as seals in Hudson Bay. There are over 550 species of sucking lice worldwide and 62 in NA, many of which occur in MB. ● TG, REW

LIEUTENANT GOVERNOR is the provincial representative of the British monarch. Appointed by the gov gen on the advice of the PM, the lt gov serves a minimum of 5 years. Nominally, the position ensures the stability and legitimacy of elected govt. However, the modern lt gov mainly fulfills a host of ceremonial duties, among which are the duty to open, prorogue and dismiss the MB Legislative Assembly; appoint and dismiss the premier; swear in the premier and cabinet; read the speech from the throne; select members of the ORDER OF MANITOBA; and give royal assent to provincial legislation and orders-in-council.

In the year's following the establishment of MB as a province, the lt gov did initially hold some political authority, and acted as an agent of federal interests. When PM John A. Macdonald appointed Sir ADAMS ARCHIBALD as the first lt gov, he advised in his letter that, "In your infant society it is necessary that the lt gov should be a paternal despot." Accordingly, Archibald

	Lieutenant Governors	
1st	The Honourable Sir Adams George Archibald	
2nd	The Honourable Alexander Morris	
3rd	The Honourable Joseph Edouard Cauchon	
4th	The Honourable James Cox Aikins	
5th	The Honourable Sir John Christian Schultz	
6th	The Honourable James Colebrooke Patterson	
7th	Sir Daniel Hunter McMillan	
8th	Sir Douglas Colin Cameron	
9th	Sir James Albert Manning Aikins	
10th	The Honourable Theodore Arthur Burrows	
11th	The Honourable James Duncan McGregor	
12th	The Honourable William Johnston Tupper	
13th	The Honourable Roland Fairbairn McWilliams	
14th	The Honourable John Stewart McDiarmid	
15th	The Honourable Errick French Willis	
16th	The Honourable Richard Spink Bowles	
17th	The Honourable William John McKeag, C.M., O.M.	
18th	The Honourable Francis Laurence Jobin	
19th	The Honourable Pearl McGonigal, C.M., O.M.	
20th	The Honourable George Johnson, O.C., M.D.	
21st	The Honourable W. Yvon Dumont, O.M.	
22nd	The Honourable Peter Michael Liba, C.M., O.M.	
23rd	The Honourable John Harvard, P.C., O.M.	

played an influential role in arbitrating disputes between MÉTIS and ON PROTESTANTS. He negotiated land treaties, and also established a 20-man constabulary force to ensure the authority of the Dominion govt in the new province. MB's 2ⁿᵈ lt gov ALEXANDER MORRIS helped establish the U OF M, and promoted responsible govt. Lt gov Joseph Cauchon also exercised his power by reserving a bill for assent by the gov gen which he had deemed unconstitutional, and SIR DOUGLAS CAMERON used his power by threatening to dismiss Premier RODMOND ROBLIN if he did not investigate the allegations of corruption within his administration. Cameron's threat led Roblin to step down as premier.

Notable appointments to the position include Errick French Willis, the first MB-born lt gov, PEARL MCGONIGAL, MB's first female lt gov and YVON DUMONT, MB's first Aboriginal lt gov. While serving, the lt gov resides at Government House, near the Legislature, where the Standard, a blue flag with MB's shield of arms circled by 10 gold maple leaves and surmounted with the crown, flies at all times. Other traditions associated with the position are the vice-regal salute, a musical piece played at ceremonies attended by a lt gov which consists of the opening bars of "God Save the Queen" and a shortened "O Canada." The lt gov also receives a 15-gun royal salute at the opening of the Legislative Assembly, and on official visits to military bases within MB. The title "The Honourable" is conferred to all lt govs for life. • MICHELLE DOBROVOLNY

LITERATURE in MB began with 19th century settlers like Alexander Begg, who published *Dot It Down: A Story of Life in the North-West* in 1871, and William Pennefeather, author of *Thirteen Years on the Prairie* (1892). By the turn of the century, one of the most popular novelists in the British Empire was Ralph Connor (pen-name for the Winnipeg-based clergyman **Charles W. Gordon**), who romanticized the frontier in tales of muscular Christian men and pure uplifting women. **Ernest Thompson Seton** wrote best-selling animal stories. Writers like **Nellie McClung** and E. A. Wharton Gill produced novels that were imitative of standard English fare. Robert J. C. Stead was first to turn, in the 1920s, from popular and formulaic romances of pioneering to realism.

What followed were a number of novels that were realistic portrayals of life in rural MB, with its hardships and the effect of drab routine on the human spirit. The works of **Frederick Philip Grove**, **Douglas Durkin** and **Martha Ostenso**, mostly written in the 1920s, are still regarded as classics of this type. *As for Me and My House*, the highly regarded story of the Depression years in a small prairie town, isn't generally thought of as a MB work, but it was written by Sinclair Ross while he was working at the Royal Bank in Winnipeg. It could be said that **Margaret Laurence**'s powerful Manawaka novels are a culmination of such works, though her fiction offers much more, such as strongly realized female characters, a fine ear for speech patterns, humour, and variations in narrative. **Neepawa**-born Laurence (1926-87) is regarded by many as Canada's finest novelist and her book, *The Stone Angel* (1964), was recently chosen by librarians as the best Canadian novel.

Before the advent of Laurence, however, some MB writers were offering the urban experience as a topic for fiction. In 1956, Adele Wiseman gained national prominence with her first novel, *The Sacrifice*, about immigrant Jewish life

in Winnipeg, and, a year later, John Marlyn published *Under the Ribs of Death*, about Hungarian immigrants in the same city. With Expo 67, Canadians became more interested in home-grown talent, and, at the same time that people like Grove and Stead were being rediscovered, a wider variety of local literature was being nurtured and appreciated. In 1981, the Manitoba Writers' Guild was formed to answer a need for promoting MB books to Manitobans, to make schools more aware of MB books, and to make MB writers more visible in the community.

Martha Ostenso's works are considered classics.

As MB literature matured, it grew more playful and less earnest in the hands of such writers as Jack Ludwig, Helen Levi, **Robert Kroetsch**, **David Arnason** and Dave Williamson. Perhaps the most playful appeared as early as 1947: the spoof biography, *Sarah Binks*, by **Paul Hiebert**. Style became as important to some as substance. One of the finest stylists was **Carol Shields**, who made MB her home from 1980 to 2000. Some of her best books, including the Pulitzer-Prize-winning *The Stone Diaries*, were written in Winnipeg. At once both startling and playful are the novels of Margaret Sweatman, who casts a fresh eye on MB history.

In the last 20 years, Wayne Tefs has been building a strong body of work – 8 novels and a memoir to date. **David Bergen**'s 4 novels, like those of Tefs, are evidence that realism is still very much with us. Linked to the Grove/Stead tradition as well is David Williams, whose *Lacjardin* trilogy deals with social conflict on a prairie

landscape. Recently, Alissa York has emerged as a gifted writer of historical realism.

Many cultures have been represented in MB literature over the years. Gabrielle Roy was born in St. Boniface in 1909 and, though she left in the 1930s, some of her best books (all written in French) deal with her girlhood years in MB. A small group of French-language writers, such as **J. R. Léveillé**, continues to produce lively work and strive to achieve the world-class standard that Roy set. Out of the Aboriginal culture came **Beatrice Culleton**'s *In Search of April Raintree* (1983), which deals with the tragic circumstances faced by a Métis girl when she moves into the city. **Tomson Highway** and Ian Ross are two contemporary playwrights who have achieved success on the national stage through their provocative presentations of Aboriginal people trying to cope with non-Aboriginal society.

A look at what has come out of MB's rich Icelandic culture takes one back all the way to the 1920s and the work of **Laura Goodman Salverson**, whose novel, *The Viking Heart* (1923), has stood the test of time. More recently we have the fiction of **W. D. Valgardson** and the difficult-to-classify work – both fiction and poetry – of Kristjana Gunnars. The ethnic themes dealt with most in MB literature are Mennonite. Armin Wiebe and David Elias have both mined their Mennonite backgrounds for comedy, and **Miriam Toews** has achieved international stature on the strength of her wry third novel about growing up in a small Mennonite MB town, *A Complicated Kindness*. Two of our best poets, Di Brandt and Patrick Friesen, have dealt more seriously – but no less successfully – with their Mennonite heritage and its effect on their lives.

Two poets who lived in MB for only a short time but in many ways influenced the work of others were **Dorothy Livesay**, who founded the journal *CV* and was a prominent social activist, and James Reaney, who taught at the U of M from 1949 to 1956. Reaney not only encouraged many a young writer, he made a name for himself in drama and short fiction as well as poetry. In the last 20 years, other poets whose work has stood out are Dennis Cooley, Catherine Hunter, Jan Horner and Clarise Foster. Hunter has, like social historian **Allan Levine**, also had success in the realm of thriller-writing, a field dominated in the 1970s by journalist Shaun Herron. As we begin the 21st century, the genre seems to be quietly expanding, with lively new work from writers like Alison Preston, David Annandale, Karen Dudley and C. C. Benison. Standing out in the realm of horror/suspense is Susie Moloney, best known for *A Dry Spell*, which attracted Hollywood's attention.

Whether or not James Reaney's short stories, "The Bully" and "The Box Social", have been as influential as they are touted to be, MB has seen some fine short-story writers come and go. **Sandra Birdsell** established herself with 2 volumes of linked stories that showed a knack for crisp, realistic dialogue and an ability to give ordinary people (in Agassiz, a fictionalized Morris) a certain grandeur. Birdsell has since published some notable novels. Don Bailey, also a master of the collection of related stories, wrote prose that was uncluttered, concise and direct, in juxtaposing the tough with the tender. Lois Braun's appealing tales of southern MB drew national attention in the late 1980s. Also notable were Ed Kleiman's wise and witty stories of Winnipeg's North End. Then there were the remarkable post-modernist yarns and hilarious fables of David Arnason. Carol Shields's wisdom and playfulness showed up as well in her short stories as in her longer works. The versatile **Jake Mac-Donald** has shown himself to be equally at home in short fiction, novels and – most recently – in the informal essay or personal memoir, like his much-admired *Houseboat Chronicles*, which evokes the distinctive qualities of the Canadian Shield. Another talented memoirist is Warren Cariou, who also writes fiction.

Western Canada's foremost social historian, **James H. Gray**, was born in Winnipeg and spent his formative years there before embarking on a writing career that produced such ground-breaking books as *Winter Years, Booze* and *Red Lights on the Prairies*. Following in the Gray tradition are J. M. Bumsted, prolific author of MB history, and Brandon's **Fred McGuinness**. MB is also home to the best-selling historian of pop music, John Einarson.

Fiction for young people is another genre that has flourished in MB. Prominent in this field are **Carol Matas**, **Martha Brooks**, Linda Holeman, Diana Wieler, Margaret Buffie, Karmel Schreyer and Duncan Thornton. **Sheldon Oberman** also made his considerable reputation writing books for younger children. Linda Holeman has recently branched out into adult historical fiction with two novels that were published internationally. Two other MB writers who have achieved international success in the historical romance genre are Susan Bowden and Elizabeth Thornton. Brandon's Caron Todd has written romance novels that have sold around the world.

One of the most famous of fantasy fiction writers grew up in MB. A. E. van Vogt (1912-2000) wrote his early fiction for pulp magazines before moving to Hollywood in 1944. Though many of his books were immensely popular, they were seen by some purists as not being science fiction but rather "the hard SF dream" or "rationalized dementia." Two of the more successful present-day fantasy writers are Winnipeg-born **Guy Gavriel Kay** and Steven Erikson.

Though there had been sporadic activity in MB play-writing over the years, a theatrical culture seemed to be developing in the 1980s, and it spawned the work of Alf Silver, at the time the first local playwright in many years to have a play produced by a major theatre company. Since then, there have been works of prairie realism and historical drama by Maureen Hunter and the plays of Bruce McManus that deal with "the blues of the city." Plays exploring identity have come from the aforementioned Tomson Highway and Ian Ross, as well as Joseph Aragon and Brian Drader. Working successfully in the French language are such playwrights as Claude Dorge and Elaine Tugas. For over 25 years, the MB Association of Playwrights has played a role in searching out and nurturing new dramatists. The **Winnipeg Fringe Festival**, founded in 1988, is at present the best place for new playwrights to try out their material. While the festival restricts play length to around an hour, Fringe writers still manage to deal with important issues and attempt diverse forms. Over 100 new works are presented every summer. ● DAVE WILLIAMSON

▶ *See also:* **Aboriginal Literature**, **Book Publishing**, **Poetry**, **Theatre**.

LITTLE, Ken, athlete (b July 30, 1929, Kelowna, BC) excelled provincially in track and field, baseball, hockey, football and curling. Little's athletic accomplishments began as a high school student when he won 6 MB track and field titles between 1946-48. Following graduation, Little played on England's Streatham junior hockey team, which won the Autumn cup and defeated both the US and Cdn hockey teams in exhibition matches in 1952. Upon his return, he helped the Winnipeg Maroons win senior league championships in 1953 and 1954. He was part of the provincial title-winning junior football team in 1949, and helped the St. Boniface Native Sons win 4 senior championships during the 1950s. As a curler, Little won 2 provincial championships in 1964 and 1967. He was inducted into the **Manitoba Sports Hall of Fame** in 1998. ● MD

LITTLE (nee BEND), Olive, baseball player (b May 7, 1917, **Poplar Point**; d Feb 2, 1987, **Winnipeg**), played for the All American Girls Professional Baseball League (AAGPBL) from 1943-45. She received her coaching from her father, Jack Bend, while growing up in Poplar Point. After moving to Winnipeg, Little got her start in league play in 1937, pitching for the Norwood senior women's

Olive Little

softball team. Little's no-hitter games created a stir in Winnipeg media, and she set many league records, averaging 12-14 strikeouts a game in 1940. She then joined the Saskatchewan Royals, where she helped lead the team to a provincial championship victory. Little was scouted by the AAGPBL, the professional women's league which had a brief 2-year life span when many major league players were fighting overseas, and recruited to the Rockford Peaches in Illinois in 1943. Little pitched 4 no-hitters in that time. She retired from play when her husband George Little returned from fighting overseas. ● MD

LITTLE BLACK RIVER FIRST NATION, on reserve pop 676, off reserve pop 261, is 150 km N of **Winnipeg**, on the E shore of **Lake Winnipeg**. It signed Treaty 5 in 1875. It is now a member of the Southeast Tribal Council. The native language of the Little Black River First Nation is **Ojibway**. Besides internal roads, the community has road access via provincial roads. Education, administered by the Southeast Tribal Division for Schools, goes from Nursery-Grade 8, and total enrolment in 2003-04 was 544. Along with several other First Nations, Little Black River has instituted an alternative education program which aims to encourage greater student involvement, academic achievement, and decrease classroom behavioral problems. Fire destroyed the school and the band office in Oct 2006. The economic strength of the Little Black River First Nation is based on wild rice harvesting, commercial fishing, trapping, farming and hunting. As of Aug 2001, this First Nation community has been working on the expansion of an on-reserve truss manufacturing plant. Little

Black River First Nation has also made efforts to protect the area's environment, with work toward improving fish spawning beds, monitoring water composition, and ecological studies. ● RK

LITTLE GRAND RAPIDS FIRST NATION,

on reserve pop 1073, off reserve pop 262, is situated 268 km NE of WINNIPEG, close to the ON border. At the time of signing Treaty 5 in 1875, the Little Grand Rapids people were considered part of the BERENS RIVER FIRST NATION. Due to the differences between the 2 communities, the Cdn govt granted Little Grand Rapids First Nation its own community status in 1930. The local native language is OJIBWAY. There is one reserve here. Schooling in this community goes from nursery-Grade 12, and enrolment for 2003-04 was 262. The Southeast Tribal Division for Schools administers schooling here. This First Nation has an airstrip, where scheduled daily flights are available. The community has no permanent road, but winter roads are set up annually. It is a member of the Southeast Tribal Council. Little Grand Rapids' economic base is fishing, seasonal rice harvesting, and trapping. In 2002, it signed the First Nations Protected Areas Accord with POPLAR RIVER and PAUINGASSI FIRST NATIONS to create a network of protected areas encompassing the ancestral Aboriginal lands, ultimately earning a UN World Heritage site designation. Cornelia Wieman, Canada's first female Aboriginal psychologist, was born and raised in the community of Little Grand Rapids First Nation. ● RK

LITTLE SASKATCHEWAN FIRST NATION,

on reserve pop 661, off reserve pop 372, is situated 255 km N of WINNIPEG. This community signed Treaty 2 in 1871 and is now a member of the Interlake Reserves Tribal Council. The native language is OJIBWAY. Little Saskatchewan First Nation encompasses 2 reserves. This First Nation has all-weather road access and daily bus service. Schooling in Little Saskatchewan goes from nursery-Grade 12, and total enrolment for the year 2003-04 was 239. This community administers education itself. Little Saskatchewan is set in a picturesque environment, with Lake St. Martin, Dauphin River, and Lake Winnipeg all within close proximity. Wildlife in the area includes moose, bears and deer. ● RK

LITTLE SASKATCHEWAN RIVER. The Little

Saskatchewan rises from Lake Audy in Riding Mountain National Park and flows S through Keeseekoowenin First Nation, Elphinstone, Minnedosa, Rapid City, and Rivers to join the Assiniboine River 15 km W of Brandon. It is a misfit stream, its large valley resulting from increased discharges when ice was melting on Riding Mountain at the end of the Ice Age. Terraces, representing former valley floors, occur on the valley side and numerous abandoned meanders, on the valley floor. Peak flow occurs in spring, with a maximum daily discharge of 100 cm^3 per second recorded near Rivers on Apr 15, 1969. Dams are located south of Lake Audy, and at Minnedosa, Rapid City, and Rivers. After the original dam at Minnedosa burst in 1948, flooding parts of the town, a new dam was built in 1953 to maintain Minnedosa Lake. The dam at Rapid City was built for recreational purposes, whereas that at Rivers was built to provide flood protection to Brandon. Another dam that used to exist near the Assiniboine junction was the site of MB's first hydroelectric plant. The existing dams all create reservoirs that are used for recreation.

This waterway was named Saint-Pierre by LA VÉRENDRYE, and the Okanese band of Saulteaux OJIBWAY who later came to the area called it Keeseesatchewan ("Swift-flowing River"), a translation of the Dakota *Mniduzahang* – or, as Alexander Henry called it in 1806, Rapid River – from whence "Minnedosa." Minnedosa Lake was used for the Western Canada Water-ski Championships (1980) and for paddling and rowing events in the Canada Games (1997) and the PAN AM GAMES of 1999. Rivers gets its drinking water from the Little Saskatchewan, which is also used for stock watering and which, in the past, supplied water for steam engines and ice for refrigeration. There is also a history of swimming, skating, curling, and fishing here, and canoeing on the river is popular when spring runoff swells the water level. ● JOHN WELSTED

LIVESAY, Dorothy Kathleen May, poet,

journalist, social activist (b 12 Oct, 1909, WINNIPEG; d Dec 29, 1996, Victoria). The child of a journalist father and a poet/journalist mother, it is no surprise that Livesay wrote poetry throughout her adolescence. After moving to Toronto with her family in 1920, she earned a BA in modern languages at the U of Toronto in 1931 and a Diplôme d'études supérieures at the Sorbonne in Paris in 1932. However, when she returned to Canada, she enrolled in the School of Social Work in Toronto, and was subsequently employed as a caseworker in Montreal, in Inglewood, NJ, and in Vancouver until 1936. She married SCOTTISH-born Duncan Cameron MacNair in 1937, and they had 2 children.

Livesay became interested in the communist movement while in France, and on her return to Canada, she joined the Communist Party because, she said later, no one but them seemed aware of the plight of the common people during the GREAT DEPRESSION, and of the imminent threat of Hitler and Nazism. She also joined the left-wing Progressive Arts Club and other left-wing organizations, and served as regional editor of Vancouver's socialist paper *New Frontier*. Her association with progressive causes continued lifelong.

After the death of her husband in 1959, she worked for UNESCO in Paris and as a teacher in northern Rhodesia (now Zambia) in 1960-63. She completed a master of education degree at the U of BC in 1966, having twice served there as writer-in-residence and instructor in creative writing. At various times over the next decades, she was appointed in that capacity at the Us of NB, AB, Victoria, MB, and Toronto, and at Simon Fraser U.

Livesay published her first book of poetry, *Green Pitcher*, in 1928, at the age of 19, and her second, *Signpost*, in 1932. She won the Gov Gen's Award for poetry or drama in 1944 for *Day and Night*, and again in 1947 for *Poems for People*. In 1947, she was also awarded the Royal Society of Canada's Lorne Pierce Medal for distinguished contribution to Cdn LITERATURE. As world events developed during the 1940s, she broke with official communism, but the interrelationship between societal problems and personal fulfillment remained a constant theme in her writing. *Call My People Home* (1950) indicts the treatment of JAPANESE-Canadians during WWII, and *Right Hand, Left Hand* (1977) combines autobiography with a composite portrait of the Cdn political and social milieu, beginning in the 1930s.

Strongly influenced by the Imagist poetry of the first quarter of the 20th century, and by a range of writers, from Isabella Valency Crawford and Emily Dickinson to D. H. Laurence and W. H. Auden, Livesay published extensively, in chapbooks and collected editions, including such titles as *Selected Poems 1926-56* (1957), *The Unquiet Bed* (1967), *Plainsongs* (1970, rev. 1971), *The Raw Edges: Voices from Our Time* (1981); *Poetry Is Like Bread* (1991). *The Woman I Am*, a selection of poems reflecting women's issues, appeared in 1977 and was reissued in 1991. She published *A Winnipeg Childhood*, a book of fictional memoirs, in 1973, and *Journey With My Selves: A Memoir, 1909-1963* in 1991. Her novella *The Husband* appeared in 1990; and she frequently wrote scripts for CBC radio. She founded the journal *CVII (Contemporary Verse II)* in 1975, and was a founding member of the League of Canadian Poets. Livesay was named to the Order of Canada in 1987, and the Order of BC in 1992. ● MILDRED GUTKIN

LIVESTOCK, Alternative. The MB livestock sector is dominated by cattle farming, hog farming, and **POULTRY** production. However, beginning in the 1990s, livestock producers began to develop alternatives to the "big 3" in an attempt to diversify and find new markets. By 2006, sheep, goats, cervids (**ELK** and **DEER**), and **BISON** had captured some niche markets, and alpacas, raised for their wool and for breeding stock, became an alternative for small farms. Llamas, fierce protectors of smaller animals, were mixed with the smaller alpacas to fend off predators.

Sheep production in MB was popular in the years preceding WWI. The herd inventory hit a high of 340,000 head in 1944, but declined steadily to just 20,000 in 1976. There was a small rebound in interest, along with improved prices, that led to a herd inventory of 84,000 head in 2001. In 2006, MB's sheep industry accounted for just 5.6% of the national flock. Only about 5% of lambs produced in MB are processed in provincially inspected plants; most of the rest go to ON. Exports of live sheep to the US were banned in 2003 with the bovine spongiform encephalopathy (BSE) scare. Wool sales also provide a small income for some producers: in 2004, MB ranchers sold 164,000 kg of sheep and lambs' wool, garnering $71,000 for the MB economy.

Indigenous to MB, bison were at risk of extinction in the 19th and 20th centuries. Breeding of domestic herds began to reverse that trend, and the large ruminants again became a food source. A commercially viable bison herd numbered over 50,000 animals in 2004. MB ranches formed a cooperative to ship bison to the US for slaughter.

Goats are primarily sold in MB for meat. In 2006, the majority of the nannies, bucks, and kids in this fledgling industry were slaughtered in local specialty abattoirs. The meat and hides were sold to buyers across Canada and in the US. Goat milk from the single dairy-goat operation in the province – Oak Island Acres of **ÎLE DES CHÊNES** – was sold to retail outlets in MB or ON, or used in cheese production. ● INGEBORG BOYENS

LIVING PRAIRIE MUSEUM, on the outskirts of **WINNIPEG**, is a grassland prairie preserve of 13 ha (32 ac) with an interpretive centre. Before Europeans arrived, 1 million km² of central NA was comprised of tall grass prairie (*see* **ECOCLIMACTIC REGIONS**). The museum is one of the only places left in NA that can testify to the broad sweep of prairie that once existed. Currently in MB tall grass prairie makes up only 0.0005% of the total landmass. The Living Prairie Museum has more than 160 kinds of prairie plants, and

The Living Prairie Museum preserves the tall grass prairie of yesteryear.

a wide variety of lowland wildlife. The wildlife includes insects such as butterflies and dragonflies; mammals like deer, foxes, jackrabbits, and ground squirrels; and birds such as meadowlarks, savannah sparrows, and bobolinks. The museum's interpretative centre has a panoramic view of the grassland prairie on its 2nd-floor observation deck. Visitors can sign up for guided tours, or can take an independent tour with a self-guided trail brochure. The museum offers school programs, special family agendas, general exhibits, and periodical special event programming. In the last few days of every April, the museum has "Crocus Days," featuring events about MB's provincial flower, the **PRAIRIE CROCUS**. ● REBECA KUROPATWA

LIZARD is a reptile generally not known by the public to inhabit MB, since most lizards are typically creatures of warm climates. However, there is one species in the skink family (Scincidae) that has managed to adapt to MB's great range of temperature. The Northern Prairie Skink (*Eumeces septentrionalis septentrionalis*) ranges from 12-20 cm, including a 10 cm tail. It has a thick, cylindrical body with reduced limbs, and is covered by shiny, smooth and dry scales. Its colour is olive-brown with alternating rows of pale yellow and black longitudinal stripes. In breeding condition, the male's jaws and throat turn orange. The tail of a juvenile is bright blue, likely to draw the attack of a bird away from the camouflaged body. The tail breaks off rather easily when grabbed – an escape mechanism made possible by a weakened junction between 2 tail vertebrae and associated muscles. The tail continues to twitch on the ground for 15 minutes, or in a predator's jaws or beak, causing a momentary distraction while the lizard dashes off to the safety of a burrow. A tail is re-grown, but not to its original length.

The skink inhabits arid, low vegetation covering sand dunes and fields in a small region from the Carberry Sandhills to Neepawa. This population is disjunct, 500 km away from the main range in ND. It likely reached MB 5000-3000 years ago when the climate was warmer and drier. The skink spends most of the time in a shallow burrow or under vegetation or debris. Insects and other small creatures are also attracted to these sites, so they often end up as prey. When cold, the skink is lethargic and moves slowly, but when heated up on a hot day, it moves in rapid short bursts, and if frightened, it speeds off in a blur. This species hibernates in a deep rodent burrow below the frost line for almost 7 months. Remarkably, it can withstand freezing temperatures down to about –6°C for several hours, enabling it to survive an overnight frost. After mating (with internal fertilization), the female lays and broods up to 12 eggs in a nest during May and June. Hatching occurs about 5 weeks later. Sexual maturity is reached at 2 years. ● REW

LLOYD, Gweneth, artistic director, dance teacher (b Sept. 15, 1901, Eccles, Greater Manchester, UK; d Jan 1, 1993, Kelowna, BC) co-founded Canada's first ballet company. Under Lloyd's direction, the Winnipeg Ballet Club would eventually be transformed into the world-renowned ROYAL WINNIPEG BALLET.

Sent to a boarding school in England at the age of 13, Lloyd got her introduction to dance by taking a weekly dancing class. She was determined to make a career out of dancing, but by the time she finished school at 17, she was considered too old, and found little support from her family, who favoured refinement over making "public spectacles." In 1921, Lloyd earned her teaching diploma and was hired to teach a gym program on an island off the coast of France. She renewed her interest in dance when a studio opened nearby. In 1924, she quit teaching and enrolled as a student teacher at the Ginner-Mawer dance school. Later, she opened her own dance school in Yorkshire. Although the school was a success, Lloyd was soon looking for new opportunities.

Gweneth Lloyd, 1967

In 1937, Lloyd travelled to Winnipeg to visit a friend. A year later, she mentioned to former student **BETTY FARRALLY** that she was thinking of moving to Canada. Within a week, their passages were booked and the two women arrived in the spring of 1938, when Lloyd was 36. Within months of their arrival, they founded the Winnipeg Ballet Club, which offered free tuition to students who passed an audition. Lloyd wanted to make ballet accessible to a broad audience, and she succeeded in establishing a small, mobile company that gave diverse performances. During her time with the RWB, Lloyd created 3 dozen ballets, preferring to handwrite her ballets in bed while listening

to music. The repertoire in the corps's first decade consisted almost entirely of Lloyd's creations. Unfortunately, little remains from these ballet scripts, as they were destroyed in a fire.

In 1950, Lloyd left for Toronto, finding it difficult to work with the newly formed board of directors, though she retained the title of director and would return from time to time to mount new ballets. *Shadow on the Prairie* is considered her best. Lloyd taught and directed dance at the Banff Centre School for Fine Arts 1945-56 and at the Royal Conservatory of Music. She also choreographed for opera and television. In 1955, Lloyd was given the largely honorary title of RWB's founding director, though when Farrally left in 1957 after a breach with the board, Lloyd resigned in protest. In 1962, Lloyd and Farrally opened a branch of the Cdn School of Ballet and established branches in Toronto, Lethbridge, and Australia.

For her contributions to dance, Lloyd was awarded the Order of Canada (1977) and the Gov Gen's Performing Arts Award (1992). She also received an honorary doctorate from U of Calgary for making ballet a widely acceptable art form in Canada. • JILL SEXSMITH

LOCAL GOVERNMENT. *See* GOVERNMENT, LOCAL.

LOCHHEAD, Kenneth, painter (b May 22, 1926, Ottawa; d July 15, 2006, Ottawa), was a member of the Regina Five, recipient of the Queen's Golden Jubilee Medal (2002); an LLD from the U of Regina (2001); and the Governor General's Award in Visual Arts (2006). Having studied at Queen's U, The Pennsylvania Academy of Fine Arts and the Barnes Foundation, he became director of the School of Art in Regina in 1950 and administrator of the Norman Mackenzie Art Gallery (1950-1958). He founded the Emma Lake Visiting Artists Workshops in 1955 and was prof of painting at the **U OF M** School of Art (1964-1973); York U (1973-1974) and the U of Ottawa (1975-1989). His work moved from the early representational monumental figures and landscape, to large scale geometric abstractions in the late 1960s, and to the airbrush colour field paintings of the 1970s. Subsequently, he returned to landscape and realism.

He has worked both on canvas and paper, and in each medium his intuitive use of colour and rhythmic expressive line are key characteristics. At times his colour is based on the landscape; others, purely instinctive. He served on many national and regional committees, and exhibited across Canada and the US. He also received many public commissions including the Gander Airport in 1957-58; the Canadian

Chancery Building in Warsaw, the Confederation Centre for the Arts in Prince Edward Island and the Centennial Concert Hall in Winnipeg. In 1970, he received a commission for the Cdn stamp. His work is in many public and private collections including the National Gallery of Canada, The **WINNIPEG ART GALLERY** and the Norman Mackenzie Art Gallery. He has been recognized with an Order of Canada and membership in the Royal Canadian Academy of Artists. His work has also been extensively published including the Mackenzie Art Gallery's *Kenneth Lochhead / Garden of Light*, 2005. • PATRICIA BOVEY

LOCKHART, Wilfred Cornet, educator (b Oct 17, 1906, Dundalk, ON; d Sept 16, 1991, Toronto) was the first president of the **U OF W**. Lockhart was educated at the U of Toronto and the U of Edinburgh. Returning to Canada, he worked at many jobs and served as minister at a number of **UNITED CHURCHES**. In 1955, Lockhart was appointed principal of United College, serving until 1967, when it became **U OF W**. He was the first president and vice-chancellor of the U of W from 1967-71. In 1958, Lockhart touched off the "Crowe Case," the best-known academic freedom case in Canada, when he fired Professor Harry Crowe for writing a "disrespectful and irreligious" private letter, which was sent to Lockhart by mistake; the fallout continued for years. He later served as moderator of the United Church (1966-68). A building at the U of W is named after him. He retired to Toronto and died there. He was the author of *In Such an Age: Younger Voices in the Canadian Church* (1951). • JMB

LOCKPORT, pop 792, is a community 20 km NE of Winnipeg on the **RED RIVER**, in the RM of St. Andrews (*see* **INTERLAKE**). The post office opened in 1894. Originally known as Little Britain, the community was settled mainly by **SCOTS**, **ENGLISH**, and the **COUNTRY-BORN** retired from the **FUR TRADE** at nearby **LOWER FORT GARRY** in the early-to-mid-19th-century, and is the site of **WILLIAM COCKRAN**'s **ANGLICAN** church, St.-Andrew's-on-the-Red, which gives the surrounding RM its name. Later in the 19th century, many other small churches of various denominations were built. Other historic sites in the area include Capt. **WILLIAM KENNEDY**'s house. Some of the province's most exclusive homes are in this region, especially on River Road, which follows the W bank of the Red. Little Britain changed its name after the **ST. ANDREWS LOCK AND DAM** was built there to regulate water levels. Later, the **RED RIVER FLOODWAY**'s entrance was built just to the N of this community. Lockport's economy revolves almost entirely around tourism. In summer, the Red just

UMA, TRIBUNE, PERSONALITY FILES

Locks wide open at Lockport

N of the dam is a popular spot for catfish, **WALLEYE**, and sauger **FISHING**, and a popular place to spot pelicans. Nearby roadside diners/hot dog stands, such as Skinners, attract huge summer crowds. Lockport also hosts an unusual annual children's festival in winter, and many ice fishing huts dot the river as long as weather allows. ● GPP

LOEWEN is Canada's largest manufacturer of wooden windows and doors, and also one of its oldest. The company was founded in 1905, when 22-year-old Russian **MENNONITE** Cornelius Toews Loewen left the family farm near **STEINBACH** and opened a new lumber business on the main street of the MB town. The firm started out selling lumber and millwork products, including windows and doors, and in the 1930s and '40s, it also began producing beekeeping equipment, church pews, and ready-to-move bungalows. During the 1950s and '60s, under the leadership of a 2nd generation of Loewens – Ed, George, and C. P. – the company continued to expand its door and window manufacturing operations. In 1961, it built a 0.53 ha (1.3 ac) door and window factory on the outskirts of the town. At the time, it was the largest factory of its kind on the Prairies. In the 1980s, a 3rd generation of Loewens – Charles, Paul, and Clyde – assumed leadership of the company and began marketing its doors and windows outside Canada.

Although other manufacturers had begun switching to vinyl windows and doors, Loewen opted not only to stick with wooden products, but also to focus exclusively on the upscale residential market. In 1990, it opened its first US branch office, and by the mid-1990s, more than 60% of its yearly revenues came from markets such as the US, Latin America, the UK, and Japan. In 1996, it was named Canada's exporter of the year, and has since continued to expand its presence in export markets. By its centennial year, the company employed more than 1200 workers

at its Steinbach factory, which by then had grown to more than 5.4 ha (13.4 ac) in size. That same year, the company added a weekend production shift at the plant in order to keep up with a growing demand for its products in the US. ● MURRAY MCNEILL

LOGAN, Alexander, politician (b Nov 5, 1841, Point Douglas; d June 23, 1894, **WINNIPEG**). The son of **ROBERT LOGAN** and his 2nd wife, Sarah Smith Ingham, Alexander was born into the **RUPERT'S LAND** "gentry." He was educated at St. John's Collegiate School. He worked in his father's store for several years, then married Maria Lane in 1864. The couple had 8 children. Around 1866, Alex inherited large real estate holdings in Winnipeg and became a land speculator himself. His house, formerly Robert's, was on the W bank of the **RED RIVER**, at 10 George St (the foot of the present Logan Ave, which was named after Alexander. Alexander St is likewise named for him.

Logan was a Winnipeg alderman 1874-78, and a founder of the Winnipeg Board of Trade.

Alexander Logan, 1884

He ran unsuccessfully against Daniel Hunter McMillan for the Legislature in 1880, and was mayor of Winnipeg 1879-80, 1882, and 1884. In that capacity, he – along with other Point Douglas landowners, such as **WILLIAM GOMEZ FONSECA** – helped persuade the **CPR** to have their new national route run through Winnipeg rather than **SELKIRK**. He was influential in creating the aqueduct and **RAILWAY** from **SHOAL LAKE** that still supplies Winnipeg with its drinking water. While he was a popular mayor to begin with, and helped establish Winnipeg as the West's leading city for decades to come, by his last term, the public was wary of his civic spending, and he did not seek re-election for 1885. He made generous contributions to charity, now the Alexander Logan Fund of the **WINNIPEG FOUNDATION**. ● AJL

LOGAN, Robert, businessman, judge (b ca. 1773, UK, d May 25, 1866, **RED RIVER SETTLEMENT**). Apparently the son of a West Indian planter of **SCOTS** extraction who moved to Ville-Marie (now Montreal) in the 1780s, Logan was fluent in both French and English. He started working with the **NWC** in 1801, later moving to a post at what is now Sault Ste. Marie, ON. He married (that is, took as a "country wife") an **OJIBWAY** woman, who is referred to as Mary O'Meara. After many years' work for the NWC without promotion, **COLIN ROBERTSON** convinced him to join the rival **HBC** in 1814. He did, and was stationed at Lac la Pluie (now Rainy Lake, near Fort Frances, ON). In 1819, at **LORD SELKIRK**'s request, Logan came to the **RED RIVER SETTLEMENT** as his agent. He soon became sheriff of **ASSINIBOIA**.

In 1822, shortly after the merger of the 2 rival **FUR TRADING** companies, HBC gov **SIR GEORGE SIMPSON** described Logan, who then lived on the E side of the **RED RIVER**, as the area's "best settler." He became a councillor in the **ASSINIBOIA** court in 1823. In 1825, Logan bought the site of Fort Douglas (already partially ruined), a partially built windmill, and 100 ac (40 ha) of land from the estate of Selkirk, who had died several years before. He built a house at the foot of present-day Logan Ave. Robert ground grain with the windmill, invested in fur business and wholesale, and ran a local general store. He was justice of the peace 1835-39, and again from 1850. Around 1839, after Mary's death, he married an **ENGLISH** widow, Sarah Anne Ingham. Of their 6 children, the most prominent was his son, future **WINNIPEG** mayor **ALEXANDER LOGAN**. Though he had been involved in the **ANGLICAN** cathedral of St. John's, it was likely that Robert was a **PRESBYTERIAN**, as he helped Presbyterians at Red River get their first minister, Reverend John Black, in 1851. ● AJL

LONG PLAIN FIRST NATION, on reserve pop 1708, off reserve pop 1772, is located in the **CENTRAL PLAINS** region of MB, 14 km SW of **PORTAGE LA PRAIRIE**, 100 km W of **WINNIPEG**. It signed Treaty 1 in 1871 and is now a member of the Dakota Ojibway Tribal Council. There are 2 reserves located here: Long Plain IR No. 6, and Long Plain IR No. 6(B). Reserve No. 6 is situated just off of hwy 1 and the secondary reserve is right next to Portage la Prairie. This First Nation community's native languages are **OJIBWAY** and **DAKOTA**. Schooling in this community goes from Nursery-Grade 12, and total enrolment for 2003-04 was 286. Long Plain First Nation community is accessible via all-weather roads. Under the treaty land entitlement program, the federal govt granted this First Nation 45 acres on the outskirts of Portage. Long Plain runs an aggressive development corporation to find economic opportunities in what is virtually an "urban reserve." The Keeshkeemaquah Conference & Gaming Centre (named after Long Plain's first chief) was born from the initiatives of the Arrowhead Development Corporation which showed a profit of $800,000 in 2005. Long Plain has also built a $1.8 million, 50-room office complex here. An Indian Residential School Museum is scheduled to open in 2008. Two prestigious awards, Economic Developer of the Year among Canada's First Nations and Manitoba First Nations Business of the Year have been awarded to Long Plain. This First Nation also has a policy of open audits to avoid the scandals and mistrust that plague some Aboriginal communities. ● RK

LOON (family *Gaviidae*) is represented in MB by 4 species, of which the Common Loon (*Gavia immer*) is best known and most widespread. Perhaps more than any other bird, it represents Canada's wilderness, with its haunting calls carrying through the morning mist on many a lake in cottage country. Loons, and the closely related Grebes, are superficially similar to ducks, but their bodies are more elongated and the bills daggerlike. With feet set far back in the body, they are clumsy on land, but make up for this

Common Loon nesting on edge of Precambrian Lake

with strong flight and great swimming ability. Of the other species, Red-throated Loon (*G. stellata*) and Pacific Loon (*G. pacifica*) are common in summer along the **HUDSON BAY** coast at **CHURCHILL**, while the yellow-billed loon (*G. adamsii*) is an accidental. ● RUDOLF KOES

LORETTE, pop 2200, is a community 25 km SE of **WINNIPEG** on the Seine River in the RM of Taché (*see* **EASTMAN**). **MÉTIS** from French settlements around what is now Winnipeg came to the area in the 1850s. It was then known as Petit Point-des-Chênes ("Little Oak Point"). **ROMAN CATHOLIC** Bishop **ALEXANDRE-ANTONIN TACHÉ** likely renamed the community after a priest or congregant from the parish of Notre-Dame de Lorette in France. After the Dawson Trail came through here in the late 1860s, settlement increased. The post office opened in 1875, and the **RAILWAY** arrived in the early 20th century, though the line has since been abandoned. Francophone Quebecois, **ENGLISH**, **SCOTS**, **IRISH** – and, in the 1930s, Slovaks – moved to the area. Lorette functions as a service centre for surrounding **AGRICULTURE**. Because of its proximity to the capital, affordable housing costs, and low taxes, Lorette also acts as a bedroom community for Winnipeg. In 2006, Lorette was considering incorporating as a village. ● GPP

LOW, Ron Albert, hockey player, coach (b June 21, 1950, **BIRTLE**) had a 30-year career as a player and coach in professional hockey. Low started out playing for the Manitoba Junior Hockey League's Dauphin Kings. He was drafted by the Toronto Maple Leafs in 1970 and, after being bumped around minor league teams, had his first NHL game in 1972. Low was shuffled between the NHL and the CHL before being picked up by the Washington Capitals during the NHL's 1974 expansion draft. After 3 years with the team, he moved to the Detroit Red Wings as backup goalie. Following a brief stint with the Quebec Nordiques, Low reached the pinnacle of his playing career with the Stanley Cup-winning Edmonton Oilers, and then the New Jersey Devils, before finishing his career with the American Hockey League's Nova Scotia Oilers following the 1985-86 season. He stayed on with the team as assistant coach, and was promoted to Edmonton in the same role, winning the Stanley Cup in 1990. Low took a position coaching with the Houston Aeros in the International Hockey League for the 1999-2000 season, following a contract dispute with Oilers' management. From 2000-02 he led the New York Rangers. He coached 423 NHL games over his career, winning 172. As of writing, Low was the goaltending coach and professional scout for the Ottawa Senators. ● MD

LOWE FARM, pop 250, is a community 85 km SSW of **WINNIPEG** on hwy 23 in the RM of Morris. Around 1875, **ENGLISH**-born newspaperman John Lowe – later the federal deputy minister of Agriculture – and his brother James bought 15,000 ac of the land in the Sperling area. In 1889, the Northern Pacific set up a rail line here and in 1894, John Lowe initiated a stock option plan to finance the construction of a water pipeline from the Red River in Morris to what was now called "Lowe Farm" for irrigation. The project failed but the community retained the "Lowe Farm" name. Ontarians, Americans from IL, and later **MENNONITES**, who now form the bulk of the population, succeeded where John Lowe and his various farm managers had failed. A healthy population remained, and a post office opened here in 1901.

In the 2000s, local agriculture consists of grain and oil seed farms with a mix of large hog farms. A bio-mass furnace manufacturing plant has also recently been established. The community's history is detailed in the book *Reflections of Lowe Farm 1899-1999*. Playwright Dean Harder was born and raised in Lowe Farm. There is a small Mennonite community in Mexico also named Lowe Farm, after this community. ● GPP

LOWER FORT GARRY is located on the W bank of the **RED RIVER** about 30 km NE of **WINNIPEG** in **ST. ANDREWS**. It was named in honour of Nicholas Garry, a member of the **HUDSON'S BAY COMPANY**'s governing committee who helped negotiate the merger between HBC and NWC. The HBC began construction of Lower Fort Garry in the fall of 1830 to replace **UPPER FORT GARRY**, which had been damaged by severe flooding in spring 1826. The "Stone Fort," as it was commonly called, was built on higher ground below the rapids at St. Andrew's. Gov **GEORGE SIMPSON** expected Lower Fort Garry to become the new administrative headquarters of the HBC in **RUPERT'S LAND**; however, this role was never fulfilled. In 1835, the HBC rebuilt the Upper Fort at **THE FORKS** of the **RED** and **ASSINIBOINE** rivers (Winnipeg), and it became the centre of political activity in the **RED RIVER SETTLEMENT**. Although some pelts and furs were purchased by the HBC at the Lower Fort, it was not primarily a fur-trading post. Most furs were transported to the fort from neighbouring posts, where they were repackaged and shipped to England via **NORWAY HOUSE** and **YORK FACTORY**. Lower Fort Garry served as an agricultural and industrial supply centre for the HBC, and was a major site for local trade with surrounding Aboriginal communities.

Local settlers sold their surplus farm produce to the HBC, which was used to supply company employees working in northern regions.

STAN MILOSEVIC, WWW.MANITOBAPHOTOS.COM

The Big House at Lower Fort Garry

Receiving produce and foodstuffs from Lower Fort Garry reduced costs for the company, as food no longer had to be shipped from England. It also provided HBC employees with considerably fresher food. For several years after its construction, the Lower Fort also served as a holiday resort for many prominent HBC officers. In the 1840s, the HBC built industrial buildings at the Lower Fort, including a gristmill and sawmill, a brewery and distillery, lime kilns, and a blacksmith's shop. Based on its close proximity to the Red, and its ability to house hundreds of tripmen, Lower Fort Garry became an important trans-shipment post for the HBC.

Although never directly affected by social or political unrest, Lower Fort Garry did house several military contingents while under the direction of the HBC. In 1846, as a response to Gov Simpson's anxiety over the growing number of **Métis** "free traders" in the region and the threat of US aggression as a result of the Oregon boundary dispute, 150 soldiers of the Royal Warwickshire Reg marched into Lower Fort Garry and occupied it for 2 years. Unlike Upper Fort Garry, the Lower Fort did not play a leading role in the **Red River Resistance**. While the majority of the soldiers called into service during the resistance were barracked at the Upper Fort, from Aug 1870 until Apr 1871, 380 members of the 2nd Batt of the QC Rifles were peacefully stationed at Lower Fort Garry.

Shortly after the troops left the fort, the HBC signed a 4-year lease with the new MB govt, making the stone warehouse and its surrounding grounds the site of the first penitentiary in MB. The penitentiary operated under provincial jurisdiction until 1877, when it was taken over by the federal govt and moved to its present site at **Stony Mountain**. The majority of inmates confined at the fort penitentiary had been sentenced to short terms for relatively minor offences, and were usually put to work tending vegetables and livestock or in the prison shoemaking shop.

On July 27, 1871, treaty negotiations began between the **Ojibway** and Swampy **Cree** of MB on the one hand, and the Crown on the other, at Lower Fort Garry. Lt gov Sir **Adams George Archibald** and Weymess Simpson, MP for Algoma, met with an assembly of about 1000 Aboriginals to negotiate the terms of the treaty provisions. After a week of negotiations, Treaty 1 was signed at Lower Fort Garry on Aug 3, 1871. It was the first of 7 treaties to be signed between **First Peoples** and the Crown throughout the 1870s. A plaque commemorating this treaty is in place outside the fort's W gate.

Two years later, Lower Fort Garry became the first training base of the **North West Mounted Police** (NWMP). On Nov 3, 1873, the first 150 recruits were sworn in at the fort. They spent the winter in intensive training, preparing to confront the instability in the N-WTs (present-day SK and AB) fuelled by diminishing animal resources, subsequent Aboriginal and Métis unrest, as well as the presence of the US whisky trade. The NWMP launched their first raid from Lower Fort Garry in Dec 1873 against illegal whisky traders on **Lake Winnipeg**. The raid was a success – 6 men and 45 L (10 UK gallons) of liquor were seized. On June 7, 1873, the NWMP left Lower Fort Garry and began their trek across the Territories, establishing posts along the way. (*See* **Boundary Commission**.)

In 1884, the provincial govt re-leased the old penitentiary building at Lower Fort Garry. However, this time it would serve as a mental asylum, not a penal institution. At both the Lower Fort and the new federal institution at Stony Mountain, mentally ill patients had been confined in the penitentiary. However, this practice was considered both inhumane to the patients and disruptive to the prison population. It was not until 1884 that plans were made to build a new institution at **Selkirk**. The patients remained at Lower Fort Garry until May 1886, when the Selkirk Asylum was finally completed.

After 1886, with the exception of a limited amount of trade, Lower Fort Garry served primarily as a social gathering place for HBC officials and political dignitaries. In 1911, the HBC permanently closed its store, thus ending its active business operations at the fort. In 1913, the newly formed MCC (Motor Country Club) of Winnipeg took a long-term lease on the fort, modernizing many of its facilities. Lower Fort Garry was declared a National Historic Site in 1950, and the following year, the HBC transferred ownership to the federal govt. The Historic Sites Division of the National Parks Branch shared the site with the MCC until 1962, when the club finally gave up its lease. Lower Fort Garry was opened to the public as a National Historic Park in 1963, and extensive restorations of its structures were undertaken in the 1970s. Lower Fort Garry has the largest collection of 19th-century fur trade buildings in Canada, and is the oldest stone fort still intact in NA. ● MICHELLE RYDZ

▸ *See also* **Fur Trade** and **Upper Fort Garry**.

LUMPFISH is a marine fish of the snailfish family Cyclopteridae, order Scorpaeniformes, found in cold waters of the N Pacific, N Atlantic, and Arctic Ocean including Hudson Bay. There are 3 species recorded in Hudson Bay, the largest being the Lumpfish (*Cyclopterus lumpus*) which reaches 58 cm and 9.5 kg. The body is robust and triangular in cross-section, with 7 rows of large tubercles running the length of the trunk. This fish has a remarkable 'sucking disk' on the throat, which incorporates the pelvic fins, and is used to cling to the substrate in the presence of wave action. In April-May, lumpfishes move into shallow water, where the female lays her eggs just below the low-tide line, and leaves the male to fertilize and guard them. In some regions, the eggs are harvested by local people and sold as inexpensive caviar. In the autumn, the adults move back to deeper waters (300 m). The other 2 local species are the Leatherfin and Atlantic Spiny lumpsukers (*Eumicrotremus derjugini* and *E. spinosus*). These interesting marine fishes provide a valuable food source for seals, Beluga, Greenland Shark, Arctic Cod, and sea birds. ● REW

LUNDAR, pop. 881, is a community 110 km NNW of Winnipeg on a **CN** line and on hwy 6, about 15 km E of **LAKE MANITOBA**. **CREE** inhabited the area for many years, and Lundar has a significant **MÉTIS** population. The earliest Europeans to live here were **ICELANDERS** in the 1880s, and the community was founded in 1887 as Swan Lake settlement. Later settlers included Russians, **ENGLISH**, **FRENCH**, and **SCOTS**. A post office opened in 1890, taking the name Lundi, after the Icelandic *lundi* ("puffin," plural *lundar*). The name had changed to Lundar by the 1890s. The economic base here consists of service and retail supporting local farmers and commercial fishing operations, though tourism revenue (particularly related to **WATERFOWL** hunting) also supports the local economy. ● GPP

LUTHERANS are members of a Protestant body that emerged from the 16th-century Reformation in Germany. Lutheranism became the established religion in Norway, Sweden, Denmark, Finland, and Iceland, as well as in most of N Germany. It was also the prevailing religious orientation among the Germans who established themselves in the Baltic countries and who emigrated to Russia and the Austrian territories in Eastern Europe in the 18th century. As a result, early Lutheran development in MB was generally connected with pockets of ethnic settlers who originated from these countries in Europe.

The first Lutherans arrived in what is now MB long before it became a province. They were sailors seeking the Northwest Passage through the Cdn Arctic to the riches of India, part of the **JENS MUNK** expedition sent out in 1619 by King Christian IV of Denmark. An early freeze-up in **HUDSON BAY** forced the expedition to winter near **CHURCHILL**. Among the sailors was a Lutheran clergyman, Rasmus Jensen, who conducted the first recorded Lutheran service in the New World. All but 3 members of the crew, including Jensen, died from scurvy before the expedition was able to head back to Europe.

Later, as MB was being opened up for settlement shortly after becoming a Cdn province, William Wagner, a German Lutheran, was among the early surveyors. Through his efforts, German Lutheran settlers came from the Ottawa Valley to the Ossawa (Berlin) settlement NE of **PORTAGE LA PRAIRIE**. A Lutheran Church/Missouri Synod pastor from MN conducted worship services among them in 1878. By that time, **ICELANDERS** had also arrived to scout for land in MB, with a large contingent of Icelandic Lutherans establishing **NEW ICELAND** at **GIMLI**. In 1876, Rev Paul Thorlaksson (1849-82) arrived to serve them and become the first resident Lutheran pastor in MB.

A fellow Icelander, Jon Bjarnason, arrived the following year and later established the Icelandic Synod with its headquarters in **WINNIPEG** in 1885. Swedes following the US frontier were the next Lutheran group to arrive in MB in the 1880s. In 1883, they asked the officials of their church in MN to send a pastor to Winnipeg.

The early development of the Lutheran Church in MB was often hampered by lack of clergy. No clergymen accompanied the immigrants and the Lutheran bodies in the US did not have enough pastors for their own frontier congregations, much less for the smaller, more-scattered Lutheran settlements in MB. The pressure for pastors increased as the territory W of MB became available for settlement and as German immigrants from Russia and the Austrian Empire began to arrive in large numbers. To serve these immigrants, Trinity Lutheran was organized in Winnipeg on Dec 16, 1888. When its first pastor, Heinrich C. Schmieder, arrived from Philadelphia 2 months later, Trinity became the springboard for the German Lutheran mission work, not only in MB, but in all of W Canada. Congregations resulting from Schmieder's efforts formed the MB Synod of the General Council in 1897. Shortly after he arrived, the Lutheran Church/Missouri Synod resumed its interest in German Lutherans in MB and called Hermann Buegel as its missionary. Georg Gehrke's arrival in 1905 brought a 3rd German Lutheran body, the Ohio Synod, to MB. Winnipeg became the base of operation for both of these bodies as well. Polish Lutherans in W MB near **INGLIS**, Danish Lutherans E of Winnipeg, and Norwegian Lutherans in Winnipeg further contributed to the mosaic of Lutherans in the province.

As Canada and the Lutheran Church developed in W Canada, immigration boards were set up in Winnipeg as the gateway to the West under the auspices of the railways. A bureau for the settlement of Swedish emigrants to Canada was set up in 1915. The Lutheran Immigration Board, a corresponding organization for German immigrants, was established in 1923. Traugott O. F. Herzer of Winnipeg, a former Lutheran Church/Missouri Synod clergyman who worked for the **CPR**, was a key person in the orderly settlement of many new immigrants.

As long as the railway was the dominant method of travel from W Canada to the US, Winnipeg remained the place where broader Lutheran Church meetings generally took place. Winnipeg was the place where representatives of 7 Lutheran bodies active in Canada met to form the Cdn Lutheran Commission for War Service in 1940, a Cdn Lutheran Council in 1945, and the National Committee of the Lutheran World

Federation in 1947. Winnipeg was also the place where the Lutheran bodies established offices that facilitated co-operative work through Cdn Lutheran World Relief (1946), the Cdn Lutheran Council (finally formed in 1952), and its successor body, the Lutheran Council in Canada (1967). Then, in the 1980s, as 2 autonomous churches emerged which encompassed the vast majority of Lutherans in Canada, both of them held constituting conventions and established central offices in Winnipeg: the Evangelical Lutheran Church in Canada (1985) and Lutheran Church – Canada (1988).

While the 2 Lutheran churches are both rooted in the 16th-century Reformation and therefore look alike from the outside, they are different in their basic orientation and emphases in teaching and life. The Evangelical Lutheran Church in Canada, more than twice the size of Lutheran Church – Canada, both nation-wide and in MB, is the product of successive mergers of Lutheran bodies that were initially separated by ethnicity and language. It is the most open to inter-church dialogue and joint work with non-Lutheran church bodies. It is also most concerned about social justice in Canada and in the world. In its passion for inclusiveness, the church admits women as well as men into its ordained ministry. It has also been engaged most strongly in the struggle of how the church should address the issue of homosexuality. Lutheran Church – Canada, historically through its mother church, the Lutheran Church/Missouri Synod, arose as a conservative reaction to the theological indifference of the church in Germany in the 19th century. As a result, it has tended to treasure greater uniformity in theology and practice, thereby taking a more cautious approach to an involvement in Lutheran church mergers as well as joint work with non-Lutheran church bodies.

While it has not remained aloof of social justice issues, strongly favouring, for example, the pro-life position in the debate on abortion, it has encouraged individual action by Christians rather than corporate action by the church bodies. While being open to women serving in various ways in the church, its conservative approach to interpreting the Bible has led it to oppose their admission into the pastoral office and to take a conservative stance on the family.

In MB, the Evangelical Lutheran Church in Canada, headed up by its national bishop, Rev. Ray Schultz, had 60 congregations with about 20,000 members in 2005. Lutheran Church–Canada, headed up by its synodical president, Rev. Ralph Mayan, had 20 congregations with about 5000 members. ● NORMAN J. THREINEN

▸ *See also* **GERMANS**, **ICELANDERS**.

LUXTON, William Fisher, journalist (b Dec 12, 1844, Bampton, Devon, UK; d May 20, 1907, **Winnipeg**). Born to Jane Palmer Luxton (1819-59) and an unknown father, he immigrated to Canada West (now ON) in 1855. He was schooled in St. Thomas (ON), and appears to have worked as a farmer briefly before beginning teaching. He began his journalism career in 1866, founding the *Age* in Strathroy, a community about 40 km W of what is now London, ON. That same year, he married Sarah Jane Edwards of the Township of Lobo, Middlesex Cty, Canada West. They had 8 children. Luxton operated 2 other papers in Southwestern ON before moving in mid-1871 to the **Red River Settlement**, initially to cover the **Red River Resistance** for the *Toronto Globe* (later the *Globe and Mail*), later to teach in the first school under the *Manitoba Schools Act* (*see* **Education, Public**).

William F. Luxton, ca 1884

On Nov 9, 1872, with retired Ontarian farmer John A. Kenny, who became publisher, Luxton began and served as editor of the weekly 4-page **Newspaper** the *Manitoba Free Press* (later the *Winnipeg Free Press*). In a time when newspapers were expected to appeal openly to those of particular political stripes, Luxton's paper initially supported the **Liberal Party** and its values. Though Luxton was a strong supporter of reform and of **John Norquay**, it became increasingly clear that the editor was no party's slave, and the pair later had a falling-out. By July 1874, with the founding of Winnipeg as a city, and thanks to a large influx of primarily Ontarian Liberals, the demand for the paper was such that the *Free*

Press became a daily, also offering the weekly *Free Press Prairie Farmer* for rural Liberals. Among the excellent writers he recruited and helped train was **John Wesley Dafoe**, who would later serve as the paper's editor.

William Luxton helped found the Winnipeg General Hospital (*see* **Health Sciences Centre**) in 1872, served on the Winnipeg Board of Trade, was director of the Agricultural Society 1878-88, and helped found the **Winnipeg Humane Society**. He ran unsuccessfully against **Francis Evans Cornish** for the mayoralty in 1874, though it is unclear whether Cornish was the legitimate winner. Luxton became MLA for Rockwood from 1874-78 and for South Winnipeg 1886-88, and served as Protestant school trustee 1879-82 and school-board chairman 1885-87. A Methodist, he believed in **Prohibition** and in a secular public school system. He also lobbied to abolish **French** as an official language, and argued against the **CPR** monopoly. In what seems a political about-face, he launched editorial opposition to **Thomas Greenway**'s Liberal govt, and, especially, to its anti-Francophone, anti-**Roman Catholic** agenda (*see* **Manitoba Schools Question**). This would prove his undoing, as in Sept 1893, **Donald Alexander Smith**, later Baron Strathcona – to whom Luxton owed money – took control of the paper, though within 5 years it found its way into the hands of **Sir Clifford Sifton**. Luxton started a rival daily within months, but sold it in 1896 and became a reporter for the MN capital's *St. Paul Globe*. After 1901, he came back to MB, where he was inspector of public buildings for the MB govt until he died of a stroke in 1907. Luxton's funeral was among the largest Winnipeg has seen, and an avenue, a school, and a community centre in Winnipeg have all been named for him.
● A.J. LEVIN

LYLETON, pop 155, is an unincorporated community 125 km SW of Brandon, just N of the US border. This area was covered by the glacial Lake Souris, which receded earlier than most of the remainder of what is now MB, so it was the first area in the province to be inhabited by Aboriginal peoples as the Ice Age ended. Though a nomadic people, the **Dakota** have been in this area for thousands of years. Early European immigrants came mainly from the British Isles. The community was named after the first postmaster, Andrew Lyle, on whose premises the post office opened in 1890. The **CPR** established a branch-line terminus here in 1902, which allowed the community to become an important agricultural service centre. The town still has a wooden **Grain Elevator**, and there is a border crossing near here to Antler, ND. NHL forward Marty Murray comes from Lyleton. ● GPP

LYNN LAKE, pop 699, is a mining town about 250 km NW of **Thompson**. The town was situated between and is named after 2 lakes, Lynn and West Lynn, although the former lake was absorbed through mining operations, and only West Lynn remains. The lakes were probably named for Lynn Smith, the chief engineer of Sherritt-Gordon Mines Ltd.

In 1937, concerned about its dwindling copper ore reserves at Sherridon, on Kississing Lake, Sherritt-Gordon Mines Ltd, sent prospectors into the muskeg in search of new ore bodies. In 1941, Austin McVeigh, a lumberjack from ON who had come N in search of gold, was canoeing on Lynn Lake, 200 km N of Sherridon, where he spotted a mineralized outcrop. He chipped a sample, hoping for gold. Instead, he found nickel. Lynn Lake became MB's first nickel **Mining** community, and is known as "The Town That Moved." When the ore in Sherridon was depleted, the town was moved building-by-building over frozen muskeg and rock ridges to Lynn Lake. This process took about 3 years. The first families were relocated there in 1946 and the first shaft sunk in 1948. The post office opened in 1951.

As of 2005, Lynn Lake's mines were inactive, though exploration is ongoing. Lynn Lake is the site of atmospheric and scientific research. Scientists and technicians from around the world are stationed in the town during summer months, and the US's NASA launches balloons that carry equipment used to study the atmosphere and ozone from a base here. Lynn Lake is also a service centre for residents and those in surrounding communities. Tourism plays a key role in the local economy, with numerous lodges and outposts along the lakes and rivers surrounding the town. In summer and fall, anglers, hunters, and outdoor enthusiasts fly into the area, and Lynn Lake calls itself the "Sport Fishing Capital" of MB. Tall **Pine** forests, lakes, rock outcroppings, and large sand and gravel eskers left behind by **Glaciation** define the Lynn Lake landscape. These eskers became historic pathways for First Nations peoples and migrating **Caribou**. Self-guided hiking trails and canoe routes now follow some of these same paths.

Lynn Lake is the birthplace of rocker Tom Cochrane. His parents – Tuck Cochrane, a bush pilot, and Violet Cochrane – were among the town's first residents. Ontarian Lynn Johnston, the creator of the comic strip *For Better or for Worse*, lived here when her career took off in the late 1970s. ● GPP

LYNN, Washington FRANK, artist (b ca 1827, Chelsea [London], UK; d July 20, 1906, Winnipeg). The 2nd son of a surgeon and army officer, Lynn studied at the Royal Academy of Arts,

London, and came to NA in 1861, serving as a *Toronto Globe* reporter covering the US Civil War until 1864. He returned to the UK, finding work publicizing British emigration to Canada with the London-based Canadian Land and Emigration Company. He travelled to the new province of ON in 1868, writing *Farming in Canada* and *Canada: Pamphlets for Working Men* in the UK in 1869. After visiting the US plains and finding them unsuitable for British **IMMIGRANT** farmers, he came to MB in Aug 1872, and decided to remain. He began reporting on the province's conditions to the *Toronto Globe* (later the *Globe and Mail*), and used his artist's training to begin a series of paintings depicting the local culture – primarily landscapes of local forts, with some portraits. His 1872-77 paintings and writings, especially of Métis life, are a unique resource for historians.

Late in 1872, he mounted a campaign against the corruption of the Dominion Lands Office in MB and the **SCRIP** system, singling out Gilbert McMicken and John Stoughton Dennis. While this prodded the govt to introduce some reforms, he was blackballed by the MB establishment, and soon turned to real estate. He married Elizabeth Charlotte Tarren in 1874. The couple had 3 children. Lynn left Winnipeg for St. Paul, MN, in 1878, returned to the UK the following year, and was back in MB in 1885 as a shopkeeper. He ran unsuccessfully for alderman in 1885, 1888, and 1889, became involved in the reform movement, and amassed a small fortune late in life when the T. Eaton Company bought some of his property to build their store on **WINNIPEG**'s Portage Avenue (*see* **EATON'S**). Many of W. Frank Lynn's works, which remain popular with collectors, are in the **WINNIPEG ART GALLERY**, the Glenbow Museum, the **HBC**'s head offices, and in various **ARCHIVES**. ● AJL

LYNX. *See* **CATS**.

LYON, Sterling Rufus, judge, premier (b Jan 30, 1927, Windsor, ON). Lyon was raised in **PORTAGE LA PRAIRIE** and educated in local schools, United College (*see* **U OF W**), and the **U OF M** Law School. He qualified as a lawyer in 1953 and practised as a Crown attorney from 1953-7. He was elected to the MB Legislature in 1958, serving as Attorney General (1958-63, 1966-69). Until he temporarily retired 1969-75, he held several Cabinet positions in the govts of **DUFF ROBLIN** and **WALTER WEIR**. He became leader of the MB **PROGRESSIVE CONSERVATIVES** in 1975 and served as premier 1977-81, giving up the party leadership in 1983. He was appointed to the prov Court of Appeal in 1986.

Lyon's Conservative govt was elected in Oct 1977. At one time associated with the lib-

eral wing of the party, Lyon initiated a program of "acute, protracted restraint." In his first year of office, Lyon established a task force to investigate public programs and expenditures. Lyon's predecessor as leader, **SIDNEY SPIVAK**, chaired the commission. Reporting in 1979, the task force recommended significant reductions in expenditure and public activity. Further, some rent controls were lifted and restrictions on foreign ownership of land were eased.

Sterling Lyon, 1972

In 1979, its 2nd year, the Lyon administration received the report of an inquiry into **MANITOBA HYDRO**. Hydro rates were frozen for a year. A committee to ponder the future of Autopac was established. The Supreme Court of Canada upheld some appeals from Francophones about the status of French in the public institutions of the province, and so remedy had to be provided in the form of an expanded use and availability of the French language. The influential Société Franco-Manitobaine complained that not enough was being done. Thus were sown the seeds of the divisive language politics that would scar MB later, in the early 1980s. (*see* **FRENCH LANGUAGE CRISIS**)

By 1980, the Lyon govt was convinced that, in the absence of any real pull from the national economy, the MB economy was contracting. Lyon's laissez faire approach had not been successful. Yet, while the govt increased spending significantly, it continued to shrink the size of the public sector. More elimination of rent controls took place; the Milk Marketing Board was abolished; and a committee was set up to investigate

the privatization of liquor sales. Like the Autopac committee before it, however, this committee also recommended against major change.

Sterling Lyon was also chairperson of the provincial premiers conference in 1980, and he played a leading role in mobilizing the majority of his fellow premiers against the federal govt's patriation package and, especially, the entrenchment of a Charter of Rights and Liberties. He opposed patriation because he was convinced that PM Trudeau wished to give federal authorities greater power. His position against the Charter was based on his belief that rights and freedoms were the legitimate concern of lawmakers, not courts. He was of the opinion that entrenchment would freeze the cultural and ideological consensus of a particular era in the Constitution. He also argued that the spotty record of the US Supreme Court was a caution against the alleged superiority of judges as guardians of liberty.

The year 1980 saw unparalleled legislative activity. The house sat for 112 days and 98 bills were passed. A major piece of legislation concerned elections: Manitobans would now receive a tax credit for donations to political parties. The Attorney General, Gerald Mercier, also tried to incorporate into the legislation penalties for "misleading statements" during election campaigns, a hopeless if noble proposal that was eventually withdrawn.

In his last year of office, Lyon appeared to retreat significantly from the platform that had initially brought him to power, and to which he had adhered until that point. There was now a 16% increase in public spending. Even more strikingly, the govt seemed to embrace joint private-public ventures to stimulate the economy. Three of these so-called "mega-projects" were considered: the construction of a Western hydro power grid, an aluminum smelter near **TEULON**, and the development of a potash mine near McCauley.

The Lyon govt was defeated in the Nov 1981 election. It was the first MB govt to be thrown out of office after a single term. Lyon had assembled one of the most talented Cabinets in the history of the province, yet it had a singular lack of feel for public relations, and seemed to be indifferent to the public mood. Lyon himself was widely regarded as pugnacious and lacking in personal warmth. The Lyon govt's policy of reducing the size and cost of govt was out of touch with the mainstream and denied the evidence that MB's small economy sometimes needs public stimulus, especially when the national economy is weak. Lyon was later appointed to the MB Court of Appeal. ● GEOFF LAMBERT

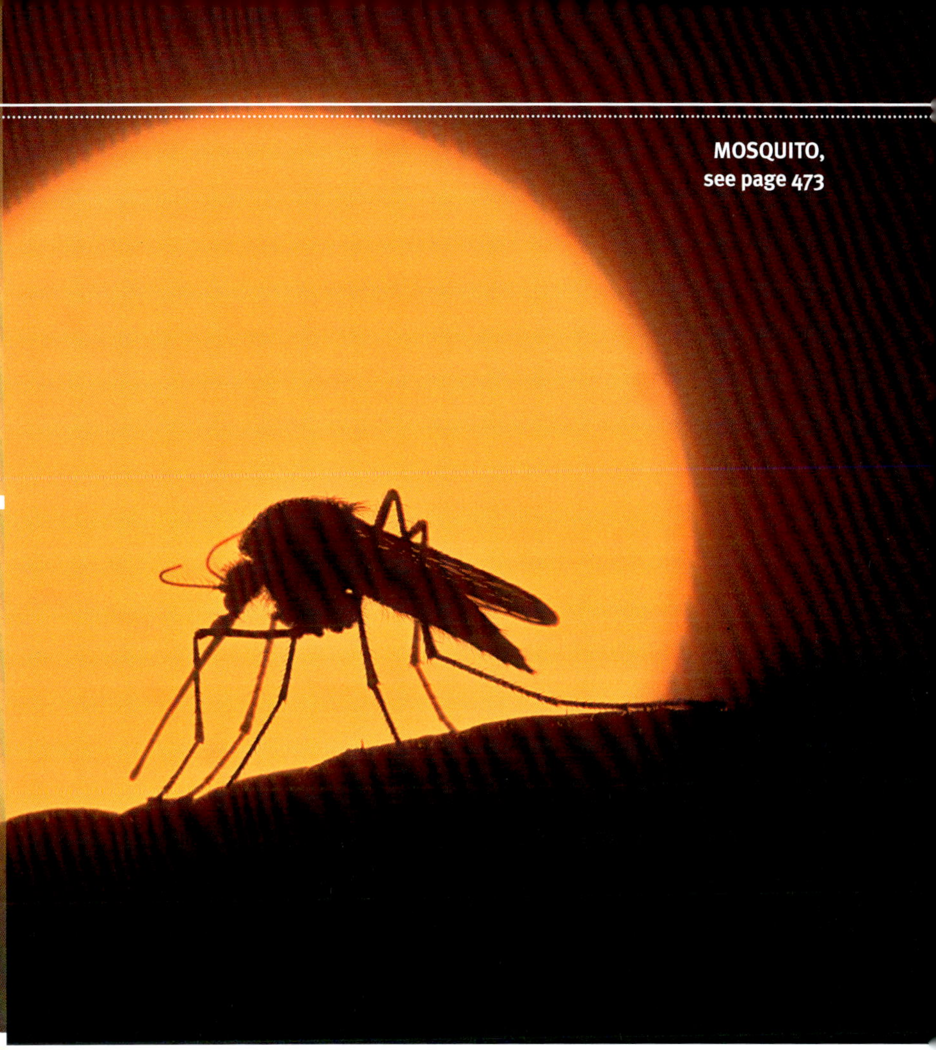

MOSQUITO,
see page 473

M

MCCLUNG, Nellie Letitia (née Mooney), author, social reformer, politician (b Oct 20, 1873, Grey Cty, ON; d Sept 1, 1951, Victoria). McClung, a best-selling author and popular social reformer, was a key figure in the suffrage movement (*see* **WOMEN'S MOVEMENT**) that saw MB become the first Cdn province to grant women the right to vote on Jan 28, 1916. Born Nellie Mooney, she moved to MB from ON when she was 6. Nellie was the youngest of 6 children and grew up on the family farm near Milton, MB. Her mother, Letitia, a strict Calvinist who loved to sing, was 20 years younger than her father. Her father, John, was a more-relaxed **METHODIST**. As a child, McClung was sympathetic to the cause of **MÉTIS** leader **LOUIS RIEL**. She also admired Charles Dickens, who "made the cause of the victims of society his own." This philosophy drove McClung's involvement in public life for the next 50 years. McClung accepted her first teaching position at Hazel School near **MANITOU** before she was 17 years old. While she enjoyed teaching, her ambition to influence the world went well beyond the classroom walls.

After meeting Annie McClung, a local leader in the **REFORM**-minded Women's Christian Temperance Union (WCTU), Nellie became involved in the cause of **PROHIBITION** and suffrage.

ARCHIVES OF MB, PERSONALITY FILES, N7694, 1910

Nellie McClung, 1910

Nellie shared the views of the WCTU that if women could vote, alcohol would be outlawed, and therefore the family violence and poverty that often accompanied alcohol would disappear. Shortly after, she met Annie's son Wesley, a pharmacy student, whom she would marry in 1896. Nellie and Wes McClung moved from Manitou to **WINNIPEG** in 1911 with their 4 children: Jack, Paul, Horace, and Florence. The McClung's 5th child, Mark, would be born later that year. Nellie became involved in women's-suffrage and equal-rights organizations. She was a founding member of the Political Equality League in 1912 and, as a published author (*Sowing Seeds in Danny, The Second Chance*), became a member of the Canadian Women's Press Club.

M McClung was a gifted orator who won over audiences with her logic and a good sense of humour. She travelled throughout Canada, speaking to sold-out audiences on the matter of women's rights to equality. The Political Equality League hosted a public debate on suffrage to rally support for their cause, which drew 1000 people who paid ¢50 each. The Political Equality League also lobbied to bring about improvements in working conditions in factories where thousands of women worked. On one occasion, Nellie McClung and a representative of the Council of Women persuaded MB premier **RODMOND ROBLIN** to accompany them on a tour of sewing factories. They hoped that if he could see the poor lighting, filthy workplaces, and poor sanitation, he would appoint a female labour inspector to improve women's working conditions. No female inspector was hired. In 1914, Nellie McClung and the Political Equality League staged a mock parliament at Winnipeg's Walker Theatre (*see* **THEATRE, C. P. WALKER**) in order to draw attention to their fight for the vote. Nellie McClung assumed the role of female premier, rebuffing a delegation of men who came to plead their case for the vote. The burlesque performance was a hit.

The McClung family moved to Edmonton in Dec 1914 after Wes McClung accepted a promotion. When WWI broke out, Nellie, then 42, was still an ardent pacifist. After her eldest son Jack, 17, enlisted in 1915, her view that the war was evil and that Germany must be stopped grew. She believed that if there had been women of influence in the Reichstag, there would not have been a war. Her views during this time separated her from many of her closest friends, including MB writer **LILLIAN BEYNON**, as well other social reformers, such as **J. S. WOODSWORTH**.

The war did stimulate social reform, however, as women moved in droves into high-paying jobs previously reserved for men. The war also accelerated the prohibitionist cause. It was argued that soldiers were fighting to create a better world and the social fabric of Canada would be improved if liquor were banned. Another goal of the social reform movement – taxation in order to pay for essential public services – took hold during the

war. Govt intervention in society became accepted. Following AB's ban on liquor sales in 1915, other provinces followed, and in 1917, the federal govt prohibited alcohol for the remainder of the war.

In an era when women were not yet permitted to vote or sit in public office, Nellie McClung advocated socialized medicine, equal pay for equal work, and the freedom to choose any career, regardless of sex. Her dream was that Canada would one day be known as the land of "a fair deal." In 1927, she joined **EMILY MURPHY**, Louise McKinney, Henrietta Muir Edwards, and Irene Parlby as a petitioner in the Person's Case. On Oct 18, 1929, that the British Privy Council – then the highest court of appeal in Canada – agreed with the petitioners that women were legally persons, and gave Cdn women the right to run for federal office and to be eligible for federal appointments, including the Senate.

McClung was a Liberal MLA to the AB Legislature from 1921-26. She was the first woman appointed to the board of directors of the **CBC**. She was also the author of 16 books, including adult and teen novels, short stories, and autobiographical accounts. ● PENNI MITCHELL

MCCREARY, pop 522, is a village 60 km SE of **DAUPHIN**, near **RIDING MOUNTAIN NATIONAL PARK**, on hwy 5 and the **CN** main line. The large wildlife population attracted trappers and fur traders to the area in the 18th century. Pioneers – including **ENGLISH**, **UKRAINIAN**, **SCOTS**, and Doukhobors – followed in the late 19th century. Originally known as Chamberlain when the post office opened, then Elliot Station, "McCreary" was chosen in 1899 after William F. McCreary, a surveyor and MP. The village also gives its name to the surrounding RM of McCreary (*see* **PARKLAND**). In 1912, the village became a rail point with a station and **GRAIN ELEVATOR**. The station closed in 1982, though the building now houses a museum. In WWII, **GERMAN** prisoners of war were brought to the area. After the war's end, some stayed, and there is still a **LUTHERAN** church in the area. Businesses that support surrounding agricultural operations form much of McCreary's economy, though the village's school, hospitals, and retailers are also significant. The livestock industry also has a strong presence in the area. McCreary's location near Riding Mountain National Park lends itself to an impressive tourism industry. The surrounding area sees thousands of visitors to the park year-round. Hiking, hunting, fishing, canoeing, and snowmobiling are just a few of the sporting activities residents and visitors enjoy in and around McCreary. Mount Agassiz, 15 km W of the village, was the site of the alpine ski events

at the 1979 Canada Winter Games. Playwright Ian Ross is from McCreary, which also became home to the first licensed taxidermy college in Canada in 1993. ● GPP

MCCREEDY, John "Johnny," hockey player, (b Mar 23, 1917, **WINNIPEG**; d Dec 7, 1979, **THOMPSON**) is the only player in Cdn hockey to have his name on 4 major trophies; the Memorial Cup, the Allan Cup, the World Cup and the Stanley Cup. Though he went on to become a successful businessman, McCreedy grew up in poverty, and was often seen fishing, not for sport, but for food. He began playing hockey with the Winnipeg Monarchs in 1935, and had his first championship win in his sophomore year at the 1937 Memorial Cup. He went on to play for the Trail Smoke Eaters, the team that brought home the 1939 Allan Cup. At that year's World Championship in Switzerland, the team won all 3 of its playoff games, including 7 shutouts. The following season, he played with the Kirkland Lake Blue Devils, and again had his name inscribed on the Allan Cup as part of the championship team. McCreedy played with the Sydney Millionaires for 2 seasons before getting his first chance at the NHL with the Toronto Maple Leafs in the 1941-42 season, helping the team to a Stanley Cup victory. Service in the RCAF during WWII cut his NHL time short, though McCreedy continued to play hockey in the junior leagues as part of RCAF teams. Following his release from service, he played a final season with the Maple Leafs, again winning the Stanley cup, before retiring from play. McCreedy used his money earned from hockey and his veteran credits to put himself through university, earning a BSc in mining engineering. He worked for International Nickel (*see* **INCO LTD**) in Thompson, eventually rising through the company's ranks to become the CEO. ● MD

MACCULLOCH, Todd Carlyle, basketball player (b Jan 27, 1976, **WINNIPEG**). The first Manitoban to play in the National Basketball Association (NBA), he helped the Cdn basketball team qualify for the 2000 Olympics following 12 years of exclusion from the games. MacCulloch attended the U of Washington on a basketball scholarship where he averaged 18.7 pts, 11.9 rebounds, and had a .662 field goal percentage. He led college basketball in field goal percentage for 3 years running. MacCulloch was drafted to the NBA's Philadelphia 76ers in 1999, and was part of the team's reserve roster for 2 seasons before signing on with the New Jersey Nets as the starting centre. In 2000, he also played for the Cdn national basketball team at the Sydney Olympics. After one year with the Nets, he was

WINNIPEG FREE PRESS

Todd McCulloch was the first Manitoban to play in the NBA.

in 1851 due to his distrust of the gov, Maj **WILLIAM COLDWELL**. He became active in the local Church of England as a member of St. John's Cathedral, and helped found Holy Trinity Church. As an old man, he disapproved of **LOUIS RIEL** but took no sides in the **RED RIVER RESISTANCE**, and became a justice of the peace in 1871, after he had retired from all other business. Many of the McDermot daughters married into Red River's elite: Annie married Andrew's business partner and former employee at Norway House, **ANDREW GRAHAM BALLENDEN BANNATYNE**, while daughter Mary Sarah (or Sally) wed HBC gov **WILLIAM MCTAVISH**. By the time of his death, McDermot was deemed the "Wealthiest Man in Manitoba"; employed several servants; entertained generously in his home, Emerald Lodge; and had a reputation for philanthropy. Among other gifts, he provided land for Red River's first post office, on what is now Portage Ave, and for the Winnipeg General Hospital (*see* **HEALTH SCIENCES CENTRE**). His land also included what is now the **LIVING PRAIRIE MUSEUM**. The last surviving original Selkirk settler, he was buried in the St. John's churchyard. ● A. J. LEVIN

M

traded back to Philadelphia, but was forced to retire in 2004 because of a rare hereditary illness, Charcot-Marie-Tooth disease, that causes loss of muscle tissue in the legs and feet. Though his condition forced his retirement from play, MacCulloch remains involved in basketball as a colour commentator for the 76ers. ● MD

MCDERMOT, Andrew, fur trader, philanthropist, merchant, judge (b 1791, Bellanagare House, Roscommon, Ireland; d Oct 12, 1881, **WINNIPEG**). Andrew McDermot was the eldest son of **IRISH** couple Miles McDermot and Catherine (Kitty) O'Connor. Agents of **LORD SELKIRK** convinced McDermot to join the **HBC**, and he sailed from Sligeach (Sligo Town) aboard the *Robert Taylor* in June 1812. Despite a shipboard mutiny, he arrived in late Aug at **YORK FACTORY**. He was soon sent on to various postings, including **NORWAY HOUSE** and **BERENS RIVER**. McDermot, who apparently spoke some Cree, married (or took as a "country wife") a young **MÉTIS** woman, Sarah Mary McNab, around 1814. They appear to have had at least 15 children. After the merger of the HBC with the **NWC** in 1821, he was transferred to the **RED RIVER SETTLEMENT**, about which time he became an **ANGLICAN**. Through his friendship with gov **GEORGE SIMPSON**, McDermot was allowed to undertake various businesses, including **FUR TRADING** independently near **UPPER FORT GARRY** under licence. He was even allowed to set up independent trading posts, as this would help eliminate the threat of US traders from Pembina, ND (*see* **EMERSON**).

McDermot prospered, and in 1839 was made a member of the **COUNCIL OF ASSINIBOIA**. After HBC turned against free traders, McDermot resigned from the council and speculated in land in what would become Winnipeg, and that city's McDermot Ave is named for him. After the 1849 trial of Pierre-Guillaume Sayer, free traders were considered acceptable members of Red River society, and he was made president of the General Quarterly Court of Assiniboia. He resigned this office

ARCHIVES OF MB, PERSONALITY FILES, N12801

Andrew McDermot

MACDONALD, Donald Ian "D. I.," civic administrator, (b Oct 4, 1913, **WINNIPEG**; d Oct 13, 2001, Winnipeg). MacDonald grew up in the Elmwood area, attending Lord Selkirk and St. John's Tech Schools and the **U OF M** and the U of Toronto, graduating from the last with an MA in economics in 1938. He joined the Winnipeg Electric Company, formerly the **WINNIPEG ELECTRIC STREET RAILWAY COMPANY**. His career was interrupted by service as a lieutenant in the RCN in 1944-45. He returned to become the company's assistant manager of transportation. In 1956, MacDonald became director of the new multi-municipality transportation enterprise, the Greater Winnipeg Transit Commission. He was appointed director of Streets and Transit for the Metropolitan Corporation of Greater Winnipeg in 1961. D. I. moved from transportation to civic administration in 1969 when he became the executive director of the Metropolitan Corporation of Winnipeg.

In 1971, with the formation of **UNICITY**, he was appointed the city's first chief commissioner. In the ensuing years, serving until his retirement in 1978, he brought a distinctive and formative vision to the governance and development of the city of Winnipeg. He was a strong supporter of the Trizec initiative at the corner of Portage and Main. In its early years, he became involved with Rossbrook House, working closely with its founder, Sister Geraldine MacNamara and he continued after "Sister Mac's" death to advocate for environmental and social policies that would benefit the inner city, particularly Aboriginal

M

youth. He successfully argued against the building of the Sherbrook-McGregor overpass, which would have bulldozed its course right through the poorest section of the city: With a similar vision of community, MacDonald developed a plan to create an 8 km linear riverbank park centred on **The Forks** and extending along both sides of the **Red River** from Churchill Drive on the S to St. John's Park on the N. His idea was to make the city's rivers accessible to all citizens and to make the river-junction the meeting place it had been in the late 19th century. After his retirement as chief commissioner and after the **CN** East Yards were acquired in accordance with the land-exchange agreement he had negotiated when he was director of Metro, The Forks became a late-20th-century reality. ● DAWNE MCCANCE

MACDONALD, John "Jake," writer, outdoorsman (b Apr 6, 1949, **Winnipeg**) is the author of several best-selling books including the memoir *Houseboat Chronicles* and the teen novel *Juliana and the Medicine Fish*. MacDonald, son of D. I. MacDonald, is one of the few MB authors to make his living exclusively from writing. He supplements his book income with journalism for Canada's top magazines and with radio and film scripts. MacDonald started out working as a fishing guide in northern ON and the NWT. These experiences greatly informed his writing with most of his fiction and non-fiction focusing on the lives of anglers, camp operators and northerners. Combined with his affection for writers like Ernest Hemingway and Jim Harrison, MacDonald's work has a decidedly outdoors and masculine feel. He has won many awards including the 2003 Writer's Trust Award for Non-Fiction. ● R.G. ENFIELD

MACDONALD, Sir Hugh John, lawyer, politician, premier (b Mar, 13, 1850, Kingston, Canada West [ON]; d Mar 29, 1929, **Winnipeg**) served in various public offices in MB. Macdonald was the only surviving son of **Scottish**-born Cdn PM Sir John A. Macdonald and Isabella Clark. He was educated at U of Toronto (BA, 1869), and took part as a Pte in the **Wolseley Expedition** of 1870, against his father's wishes. Macdonald was called to the bar in 1872, and following the death of his wife, returned to Winnipeg in 1882. He set up a law practice with friend J. Stewart Tupper, called Macdonald, Tupper, Tupper, and Dexter. Macdonald fought and achieved the rank of Capt with the **Winnipeg Rifles** during the Northwest Resistance of 1885. He was named Queen's Counsel in 1890, and won election as the Conservative MP for Winnipeg from 1891-93, serving alongside his father until the PM's death.

Hugh John Macdonald, 1900

In 1895, Macdonald built the lavish **Dalnavert**, now a museum and one of Winnipeg's oldest remaining houses (*see* **Manitoba Historical Society**). Macdonald was elected to his former federal seat for 1896-97. He served briefly as minister of the interior in the 1896 Cabinet of PM Sir Charles Tupper (father of J. Stewart), but a Jan 1897 court ruling forced him to resign due to violations by his election workers. During this period, he was closely connected with gov gen Lord Aberdeen. Macdonald was quickly chosen to lead the MB provincial Conservative party in 1897 and in Dec 1899 defeated the **Thomas Greenway** govt to become MLA for South Winnipeg and premier (also Attorney General). In 1900, his govt passed the *Macdonald Act* – alcohol prohibition – before the federal Conservatives came calling again, with some MPs suggesting he could be their future leader. Macdonald agreed to resign as premier (succeeded by **Rodmond Roblin**) to contest the riding of **Brandon** against Liberal Cabinet minister **Clifford Sifton**. He lost, however, and decided to retire from public life and return to practising law.

Macdonald was made a Knight Bachelor in 1913. From 1911-29, he acted as police magistrate for the city of Winnipeg. He sent out 3000 policemen ("the specials") against the striking workers during 1919's **Winnipeg General Strike**, and afterwards called for the deportation of immigrants (*see* **Alien Question**). However, he also became known for his fairness and compassion regarding young offenders. Macdonald often offered homeless criminals temporary shelter in his own home. Shortly after his death, like-minded citizens founded the Sir Hugh John Macdonald Memorial Hostel for adolescent offenders in

a house on Winnipeg's Mountain Avenue. The organization became known as Macdonald Youth Services in 1983, and marked its 75th anniversary in 2005. A Winnipeg junior high school also bears his name. ● JMB/JT

MACDONELL, Miles, army officer, settler (b ca 1767, Scotland; d June 28, 1828, Pointe-Fortune, Upper Canada). Born into a distinguished **Roman Catholic** family with a lengthy military history, Miles Macdonell migrated to the Mohawk Valley of NY in 1773 with his family and about 600 other **Scots**, all members of the Macdonell of Glengarry clan. The Macdonells remained loyal to George III during the US Revolution. After the British defeat, Macdonell emigrated to Osnabrook Township, Upper Canada, where he became a farmer. **Lord Selkirk** visited Macdonell's farm in 1804, and, being impressed with the ex-officer, he attempted to find him employment. Miles was eventually called to London, UK, in 1811 to become the governor of a settlement Lord Selkirk was projecting at **The Forks** of the **Red** and **Assiniboine** rivers, upon a large grant of land he had recently received from the **HBC**.

Miles Macdonell

A hastily recruited collection of young men sailed from Scotland for the **Red River Settlement** in late July 1811. The voyage was delayed and the recruits had to be housed at **York Factory** over the winter of 1811-12. There, they quarrelled amongst themselves. A number were sent back to Scotland; the remainder finally arrived at The Forks on Aug 30, 1812, more than a year after they had left Scotland, and following a lengthy and hazardous journey from York Factory.

Over the next 2½ years, Macdonell faced a series of challenges that would have taxed the ingenuity of most. He needed the loyalty of the settlers, adequate supplies of food, and good relations with the local residents. He was not helped by his employer: Lord Selkirk kept sending fresh settlers, assuming that establishing a settlement in the middle of the wilderness was an easy matter. Moreover, Selkirk insisted that his governor not only had to keep proper books but also charge the settlers for everything he distributed to them. A deft hand would be required to balance all the local inhabitants' needs for food and peace – Miles did not have it.

On Jan 8, 1814, facing famine, he issued his infamous "Pemmican Proclamation" prohibiting the export of provisions from the settlement without a special licence. The fledgling community faced increasing harassment from the mixed-bloods and the Nor'Westers. Miles was ineffective in meeting the challenge, disappearing from the settlement for weeks on end and failing to ensure the support of his settlers. In spring 1815, Nor'Wester **DUNCAN CAMERON** succeeded in inducing most of the settlers to abandon the colony for Upper Canada. Miles surrendered himself to the NWC, in return for promises that his people would not be harmed, and he was taken to QC to stand trial for his "crimes." In spring 1816, Macdonell returned to the West, learning at **LAKE WINNIPEG** of the **SEVEN OAKS INCIDENT**. He hurried E to warn Lord Selkirk, whom he met at Sault Ste Marie (ON), where the earl was leading a party of Swiss mercenaries to Red River. The mercenaries seized Fort William (now Thunder Bay), and Selkirk arrested the partners of the NWC he found there, sending them E for trial. Macdonell subsequently accompanied a party of Swiss soldiers who recaptured Fort Douglas on Jan 10, 1817.

After Lord Selkirk's untimely death, Selkirk's family refused to honour promises of land grants that the earl had made to Macdonell on the grounds that those commitments had been contingent on Macdonell's success. Instead, Lady Selkirk held Macdonell personally responsible for much of the settlement's disastrous history. While most historians do not cast Macdonell as a villain, most agree that he bore some responsibility for the early failure of the Red River Settlement. • HERB MAYS

MCDOUGALL, William, lawyer, politician, lt gov (b Jan 25, 1822, York [Toronto], Upper Canada; d May 29, 1905, Ottawa) helped bring MB into the Dominion of Canada. He was educated at Victoria College, Cobourg, ON. McDougall practised as a lawyer and was admitted to the Canadian Bar in 1862. He was a leading Clear Grit and founder of the semi-weekly *North American*, which was absorbed by the *Globe* (later the *Globe*

and Mail) in 1857. McDougall became an associate of George Brown and entered politics in 1858. He served as provincial secretary in the govt of the Great Coalition of 1864 and attended all the major Confederation conferences. He remained the leading Liberal in the Cdn coalition govt of Sir John A. Macdonald, holding the public works portfolio 1867-69.

McDougall had long advocated westward expansion, and in Dec 1867, he shepherded through Parliament a series of resolutions to incorporate **RUPERT'S LAND** into the Dominion and extend Cdn sovereignty to the Pacific. He and Sir George-Étienne Cartier went to London in 1868 to negotiate the transfer of Rupert's Land from the **HBC** to Canada. He was subsequently appointed the first lt gov of the newly acquired territory, and he was directly responsible for most of the clumsy Cdn actions that galvanized **MÉTIS** hostility in the West. His arrival in the area with a sizeable entourage, including a govt-in-waiting, touched off the 1869 **RED RIVER RESISTANCE**. McDougall never got beyond Pembina, ND (*see* **EMERSON**), although he did briefly set foot on soil N of the 49th parallel. He made a supreme blunder when he issued a proclamation in early Dec that assumed the transfer to Canada had taken place as planned – it had not. He returned to Canada angry, embittered, and humiliated. He was very critical of the *MANITOBA ACT* in the House of Commons in 1870. His political career was not ended by Red River, but he never again held important office. • JMB

MCGONIGAL, Pearl Kathryne, politician, lt gov, (b June 10, 1929, Melville, SK). After working in the banking and merchandising fields, in 1969, Pearl McGonigal was the first woman to be

Pearl McGonigal, 1971

UMA, TRIBUNE, PERSONALITY FILES, 1971

elected to the St. James Assiniboia city council, 2 years before its amalgamation with **WINNIPEG**. From 1971-81, she served Winnipeg city council and enjoyed various roles as the city's deputy mayor, chair of the executive policy committee and member of the Independent Citizen's Election Committee caucus at city hall. In 1981, McGonigal was appointed lt gov of MB, making her the first woman in MB and the 2nd in Canada to receive such an honour. She served in this capacity until 1986. The **U OF M** awarded her an honorary doctor of law degree in 1983. In 1994, she was appointed to the Order of Canada and in 2000, she was awarded the **ORDER OF MANITOBA**. After her political life, McGonigal acted as chair/director of Grace General Hospital and in 2003 received The President's Award from the Winnipeg Press Club and the Royal Military Institute of Manitoba Patriot Award. • RUTH DEGRAVES

MACGREGOR, pop 882, is a village 90 km E of **BRANDON** near the Trans-Canada Highway. In 1881, European settlement – largely **ENGLISH**, **SCOTS**, **IRISH**, and later **MENNONITES** – began in the area. In 1900, the community became known as MacGregor. The gov gen, John Douglas Sutherland Campbell, Marquess of Lorne (later 9th Duke of Argyll), named the village in honour of Scottish minister James MacGregor. In 1948, it was incorporated as a village. Nicknamed the "Heart of the Keystone Province," MacGregor functions as a service centre for the surrounding area, providing health and educational services to surrounding farming families. Locals have also recently established small specialty manufacturing firms. • GPP

MCGREGOR, James Duncan, cattle rancher, politician, lt gov (b Aug 29, 1860, Amherstburg, Essex Cty, Canada West [ON]; d Nov 11, 1935, **BRANDON**). McGregor came to MB in 1877, entering the livestock business in **PORTAGE LA PRAIRIE** and **BRANDON**, and later specializing in breeding Aberdeen Angus cattle. He became a mine inspector for the Yukon (1897-99), then formed Glencarnock Farms in MB, and developed 200,000 ac (81,000 ha) near what is now Medicine Hat, AB. His Aberdeen Angus won the World Grand Championship in Chicago in 1913. He refused to become MB minister of agriculture in 1915, but did agree in 1917 to serve as food controller for the 4 western provinces. He was lt gov of MB 1929-34, and a member of the Manitoba Agricultural Hall of Fame. • JMB

MCGUINNESS, Frederick George "Fred," journalist, author (b Jan 31, 1921, **BRANDON**) is a Brandon journalist and public speaker, known

to many as "the voice of the Prairies." After quitting high school in Grade 9, he got a part-time job as a railway telegraph messenger for the **CPR**. McGuinness finished school after a stint in the navy during WWII. He attended St. Paul's College, and was initially enrolled in pre-med at United College. McGuinness wrote extensively for newspapers around MB and the Prairies, in positions including vice-president and editor of the **Brandon Sun**, and vice-president and publisher of the *Medicine Hat News*. His syndicated column, "Neighbourly News" for the *Brandon Sun*, made him a SW MB fixture. His material appeared frequently on CBC Radio's *Morningside with Peter Gzowski*. McGuinness produced work for the CBC, *Reader's Digest*, and wrote books on popular history. His published work includes *The Wheat City: A Pictorial History of Brandon* (1988) and *Letters From Section 17: A Collection of Morningside Essays* (1999). He also co-wrote histories of MB, including *The Keystone Province: An Illustrated History of Manitoba Experience* (1988) and *Manitoba: The Province and the People* (1987). McGuinness received the Margaret McWilliams Medal for best MB history book in 1985. He also received the **Order of Manitoba** in 2002, and an honorary law degree from **Brandon U**. McGuinness was appointed a Member of the Order of Canada in 2004. In 2007, he resided in Brandon.
 ● AMANDA STEPHENS

MACHRAY, John Alexander, lawyer, academic administrator, embezzler (b Feb 17, 1865, Haddington, East Lothian, UK; d Oct 1933, **Stony Mountain Institution**). John Machray was raised in MB from an early age by his uncle **Robert Machray**, who was **Anglican** bishop of Rupert's Land, and later the first archbishop of Canada. John graduated from St. John's College (*see* **U of M**) in 1884, subsequently taking an MA with first class honours, and a silver medal, at U of M. He then attended the U of Cambridge, receiving a law degree in 1887. Called to the MB bar in 1890, he became a junior partner in the firm of Archibald and Howell in 1899. He became senior partner of Machray and Sharpe when Archibald retired in 1905, a King's Counsel in 1912, and partner of the expanded partnership of Machray, Sharpe, Locke, Parker and Crowley in 1918. He married Emily Florence Drewery, the daughter of one of Winnipeg's leading businessmen, in 1904, and had a daughter, Mary (1905).

Machray parlayed his relationships with his uncle; his uncle's successor, Bishop Samuel Matheson; and his father-in-law, and a demeanour that led people to trust him completely, into a successful career as an investment lawyer. (At

this time, many lawyers made a living by investing and managing other people's money.)

From the beginning, Machray specialized and speculated in **Winnipeg** real estate. He had a reputation for providing high rates of return on investment. What people did not know until the end was that he often paid these high rates by liquidating assets and transferring other investors' money to make the interest payments. His entire investment business was a bookkeeping operation based on Machray's ability to control large sums of investment money, principally that of the U of M, St. John's College, and the diocese of Rupert's Land, while preventing any full audit of his books. It appeared that Machray's firm was bankrupt by 1912, and carried on by employing illicit practices and stonewalling proper audits, continually gambling it would be successful in the future. It wasn't.

According to the Royal Commission, chaired by Chief Justice W. F. A. Turgeon of SK, that investigated Machray in 1932, he had begun raiding the Alexander K. Isbister Trust almost as soon as he acquired management of it in 1901. As for the U of M, Machray's firm acquired its foot in the door in 1906 by offering to manage the funds for less than other bidders, and kept an expanded version of the job over the years by pointing out how inexpensively it worked. From the beginning, auditors of the university accounts complained about bad accounting practices, such as holding out all interest payments until the last day of the fiscal year, thus giving the Machray firm interest-free control of the money for up to a year. But even when the province took over the auditing function in 1917, the auditors did not examine the securities on which the Machray accounts were based. Meanwhile, Machray acquired the financial offices, which meant that there were no real checks on his activities except proper audits that did not come until the end. He became the U of M bursar in 1916 and chancellor in 1924. With both offices, he had consolidated cheque-signing authority solely in his own hands.

Turgeon's commission found the U of M was out $901,175, and loss of interest, or $1,039,438, between 1925 and 1932, though Machray's malfeasance dated at least as far back as 1903. Other clients – mostly the Anglican Church and St. John's College – had lost $1 million. In addition, other large losses were taken on mortgages and agreements for sale; these were never calculated, nor were the losses to the Anglican institutions.

Of the $2 million abstracted from the trust funds, only $301,000 went into Machray's personal account. Over $200,000 went to pay taxes and costs on speculative land. Most of the missing funds went to cover losses on investments, with

the majority of the $782,000 allocated by auditors to the investment account having been used to pay interest on fictional mortgages and to cover up the loss of the principal in trust accounts.

Machray was a man who exuded probity and inspired confidence, and his connections were impeccable. Small investors – especially pious Anglicans – insisted on putting their money in his hands, since he paid good rates of return and they could be sure the money was safe. For many years, Machray dutifully paid the interest out of the proceeds of fresh investment, often secured by fictitious mortgages. The Machray fiasco documented the loose business practices of the era in which John Machray operated. ● J. M. BUMSTED

MCINTOSH, Kathie, swimmer (b Sept 9, 1934, **St. Boniface**), was the first person to swim across **Lake Winnipeg**. Though a vigorous swimmer, she had little formal athletic training, and relied on her stamina and endurance to complete the gruelling swim across the S basin of the lake.

She made her first marathon swim on a dare, crossing Clear Lake while on summer vacation in 1955. Upon hearing that no one had yet made the distance across Lake Winnipeg, 20-year-old McIntosh decided to make the attempt. Though her first effort failed, it nonetheless garnered considerable media attention, and a **Winnipeg** radio station soon after announced a contest to see who would become the first person to swim across MB's largest lake. While 5 male contestants signed up for the swim, McIntosh refrained from officially registering after the **Winnipeg Tribune** offered her money for exclusive story rights if she completed the swim separately.

McIntosh set off from **Grand Marais** on Aug 19, 1955, starting off just down the beach from

Kathy McIntosh, 1955

the official race with a small entourage. Swimming through the cold water at 18 strokes a minute, she maintained her energy through the 29 km swim by eating chocolate bars offered to her on a paddle. After an exhausting 17 hours, she reached the shores of **WINNIPEG BEACH**, collapsing in the sand amidst a cheering mob, who had been told of McIntosh's secret swim after all the official race entrants had given up. Manitobans became enthralled with McIntosh, a stenographer by day, who had triumphed over several strapping men, including an RCAF airman. She became a media darling.

After the hype surrounding her great accomplishment died down, McIntosh taught swimming in Winnipeg to disabled children before marrying and moving to Edmonton. As of writing, she was living in BC, and still competing in Ironman competitions around the world. ● MD

MCINTYRE, Daniel, educator (b 1852, Dalhousie, NB; d Dec 14, 1946, Victoria). McIntyre grew up on a farm before moving to Halifax to attend Dalhousie U. He graduated in 1875 and began a stint as a teacher before returning to university to study law. In 1882, he was named to the NS bar, but moved to **WINNIPEG** to continue his interest in education. After acting as principal of Carlton School, McIntyre became superintendent of all Winnipeg schools in 1885. In his 43 years as superintendent, McIntyre oversaw the transformation of the school system, working closely with **J. B. MITCHELL**. He was responsible for setting education policy – which he based on British Protestant traditions – and officials in other Cdn jurisdictions consulted him. He travelled around NA to survey school building styles and teaching methods, applying his findings to about 50 new schools in Winnipeg. In 1918, after one such trip, McIntyre introduced a plan for junior high schools, a new idea at the time. A pilot program began at Earl Grey School in 1919, and the first MB junior high, Isaac Newton School, opened in 1921. He also created nutritional, medical, dental-care, and English-as-a-second-language programs. The **U OF M** awarded McIntyre an honorary doctorate in 1912, and he was named to the Order of the British Empire in 1935. A Winnipeg high school – Daniel McIntyre Collegiate Institute – was named in his honour in 1923. McIntyre retired from the school board in 1928. A downtown ward of Winnipeg also bears McIntyre's name. ● JOEL TRENAMAN

MCKAY, James, trader, guide, politician (b ca 1825, Edmonton House [Edmonton], NWTs; d Dec 2, 1879, St. James Parish [**WINNIPEG**]). McKay grew up in the **RED RIVER SETTLEMENT** and

began working for the **HBC** in 1853. He spent time as a postmaster and opened trading posts in the US. His **COUNTRY-BORN** heritage – he had a **SCOTS** father and a **MÉTIS** mother – and strong language skills allowed him to establish close relationships with different First Nations groups and with European settlers across the region. A giant of a man, he was an expert guide for HBC gov **GEORGE SIMPSON** and, later, the Palliser Expedition. In 1860, McKay quit the HBC and continued his entrepreneurial activities (chiefly **FUR TRADE** and transportation) on his own. He married and settled along the **ASSINIBOINE RIVER** on property he named Deer Lodge (later part of Winnipeg) in 1859.

James McKay, 1870

His first foray into politics came in 1868, when he was appointed to the **COUNCIL OF ASSINIBOIA**. When the **RED RIVER RESISTANCE** began, McKay refused to take sides and left to spend some time in the US. Generally supportive of the Canadian govt, however, he was named to the first legislative council of MB, serving 1871-76. McKay also served as speaker 1871-74. At the same time, McKay was working on behalf of the federal govt (including as a member of the Council of the North-West Territories), negotiating and acting as interpreter of Treaties 1-3, 5, and 6 (signed 1871-76). He was also minister of agriculture 1874-78 under the govt of **ROBERT DAVIS**, and represented the **LAKE MANITOBA** district in the legislative assembly 1877-78. McKay's land at Deer Lodge was donated during WWI so that a military convalescent hospital – now the Deer Lodge Centre – could be built on the site. ● JOEL TRENAMAN

MCKENNEY, Henry, merchant and founder of **WINNIPEG**. (b ca 1826, Amherstburg, Cty. Essex, Upper Canada [**ON**]; d ca 1886, Washington Territory, US). McKenney was the son of Henry

Henry McKenney, 1872

M

McKenney Sr, a United Empire Loyalist of **IRISH** descent, and Irish-born Elizabeth Reilly, later the mother of Sir **JOHN CHRISTIAN SCHULTZ**. McKenney worked as a storekeeper in his birthplace and married Lucy Stockwell in 1845. The couple had 5 children. McKenney and his elder brother, Augustus, ran a trading post in Minnesota Territory, US, in the 1850s. Henry and his family came to the **RED RIVER SETTLEMENT** in June 1859 by the first steamboat to the settlement, the *Anson Northup*. He soon rented a wooden warehouse from local landowner **ANDREW MCDERMOT**, which he turned into the Royal Hotel, the first hotel in what would become **WINNIPEG**, just N of the present-day intersection of Portage Ave and Main St. McKenney dreamed of establishing a new centre, independent of the **HUDSON'S BAY COMPANY**'s plans for development along what is now Broadway. Though local residents believed it would never succeed, as it was too remote, other businesses soon sprung up in the area, and the hotel became busy enough that McKenney's younger half-brother, John Christian Schultz, came to Red River to help run the hotel.

In 1862, McKenney sold the hotel and opened a dry goods store and fur business at what is now the NW corner of Portage and Main, in a building that quickly acquired the nickname "Noah's Ark." McKenney's vision of a new town centre was realized, and by the time MB entered Confederation, there were dozens of buildings clustered around the intersection. During the **RED RIVER RESISTANCE** of 1869-70, McKenney advocated US annexation of **RUPERT'S LAND**, despite his Loyalist roots, possibly because he owed money from his Amherstburg store. Still, the provisional govt appointed him sheriff in

Feb 1870. Just before MB entered Confederation, he moved to Pembina, ND (*see* **EMERSON**), and soon became its sheriff. He returned to the nascent City of Winnipeg, which he had helped create, in 1874 but moved again in 1876 after finishing last in an election for alderman. He then retired to the US Northwest, after which little is known of him. He died in Washington Territory, probably in late 1886. • AJL

MCKENNITT, Loreena, Celtic-influenced singer/songwriter (b Feb 17, 1957, **MORDEN**). Raised on a livestock farm, Loreena developed an early gift for **MUSIC**, taking the bus every weekend to **WINNIPEG** for piano and voice lessons as a teen. Her final year of school was spent at Balmoral Hall, a private school for girls, following which she began performing in local musical theatre in 1975 at **RAINBOW STAGE**. Her introduction to Celtic music came via the **WINNIPEG FOLK FESTIVAL**, and she began performing at coffeehouses like The Ting on Broadway and the **FORT GARRY HOTEL**'s Drummer Boy Lounge while working in an office at the St. Boniface Stockyards. In 1978, she was a finalist in the CBC *Search for Talent* (later *Search for Stars*) competition, and performed in Toronto. In 1981, again in ON, she auditioned successfully for the Stratford Festival's *The Tempest* (1982) and *The Two Gentlemen of Verona* (1984), and began her recording career in Stratford recording her debut album *Elemental* (1985) in a converted barn for her own Quinlan Road record label. Her instrument of choice was the harp.

Loreena McKennitt, 1977

Busking in Toronto, she sold her albums by hand, releasing *To Drive the Cold Winter Away* in 1987. By 1989's *Parallel Dreams*, she was performing concerts across Canada and in the UK. Signing a distribution deal with Warner Music in 1991 she released *The Visit*, which sold over one million copies. *The Mask and Mirror* (1994) and *The Book Of Secrets* (1997; recorded at Peter Gabriel's UK studio) both sold in the millions, solidifying McKennitt's stature as the queen of Celtic music. Known for her philanthropic work, all proceeds from her 1999 *Live in Paris and Toronto* double CD were donated to the Cook-Rees Memorial Fund for Water Search and Safety, which she founded following the accidental drowning deaths of her fiancé, Ron Rees; his brother, Richard; and friend Gregory Cook. Fiercely independent, McKennitt retains control of her recordings through Quinlan Road Productions. She has won 2 Juno Awards for Best Roots/Traditional Album (1992 and 1994), and a *Billboard* International Achievement Award (1997). In 2004, she was inducted into the Order of Canada. Her worldwide sales total over 13 million. • JOHN EINARSON

MACKENZIE, Gisèle, singer, radio and TV performer, (b Jan 10, 1927, **WINNIPEG**; d Sept. 5, 2003, Burbank, CA). Born Marie Marguerite Louise Gisele LaFleche, MacKenzie studied piano from age 2 before switching to violin. Her professional career began at age 12 with a recital at the Royal Alexandra Hotel in Winnipeg before moving to Toronto to study violin and voice at the Royal Conservatory of Music. While performing for Cdn troops, she met her first husband, bandleader Robert Shuttleworth. Adopting her stage name from her father's 2nd name, MacKenzie starred on CBC radio's *Meet Gisèle* from 1946 to 1950 before moving to New York to work with former Canadian Percy Faith and his orchestra on CBS radio, appearing on *Club 15* and *The Mario Lanza Show*, and appearing as a weekly guest on Jack Benny's radio show in 1953 singing, dueting with Benny on violin or in comedy routines. From 1953 to 57, she was a regular performer on the popular nationally-televised weekly NBC-TV show *Your Hit Parade* followed by *The Gisele MacKenzie Show* for one season.

During this time MacKenzie was one the best-known performers in the US and also appeared on stage in musical productions across the country. She recorded over a dozen albums in her career including *Canada's First Lady of Song* and *Gisele MacKenzie at the Empire Room of the Waldorf Astoria* and enjoyed a hit single in 1955 with "Hard to Get" followed by further hits "Pepper-Hot Baby" and "The Star You Wished Upon Last Night." In

Gisèle MacKenzie, 1953

1963, she returned to TV as a regular guest on *The Sid Caesar Show* while maintaining her singing career in Las Vegas. After moving to Los Angeles in the mid '50s she married and later divorced businessman Robert Klein. MacKenzie went back to TV once again in the 1980s appearing on *MacGyver* and *Murder She Wrote*. She died of colon cancer at age 76. MacKenzie has a star on Hollywood's Walk of Fame. Her brother Georges Lafleche was a well-known Cdn singer and television personality. • JOHN EINARSON

MCKENZIE, Murray, photographer (b Mar 16, 1927, Cumberland House, SK; d Apr 22, 2007, **WINNIPEG**). Murray's **MÉTIS** and **CREE** parents moved the family to the mining community of Sherridon (N of **THE PAS**) when McKenzie was 3. He later moved to The Pas to live with his grandmother. McKenzie contracted **TUBERCULOSIS** at 17 and had a lung removed; however, while confined to a sanatorium, his mother gave him his first camera. He used it to photograph his fellow patients, fostering an interest in photography. He spent time in different areas of the North, finding work **FUR** trapping, **FISHING**, **MINING**, and in **FORESTRY**. He helped produce the first Cree-language radio broadcasts in northern MB, and developed friendship centres in **THOMPSON** and The Pas. Throughout his life, he photographed landscapes, cultural rituals, and gatherings, and is particularly known for his portraits. McKenzie's work was published in the **WINNIPEG FREE PRESS**, the *Toronto Star*, and *Time* magazine, and in 1994 he became the first Aboriginal photographer to exhibit in Europe. • JOEL TRENAMAN

MCKENZIE SEEDS, located in **Brandon**, is Canada's leading supplier of packaged flower and vegetable seeds and gardening products. Albert Edward (A. E.) McKenzie established the company in 1896 as a simple flour, grain, and seed business, but he quickly broadened its scope by aggressively testing new seed varieties and using the latest technologies of the day. He built a massive red-bricked building, which still defines the Brandon skyline and is now designated a MB provincial **Heritage Site**. Incorporated in 1906, A. E. McKenzie Seed Co came to be known as western Canada's greatest seed house, with branches across Canada by 1960. The company has had a long history of social responsibility and commitment to its community. In 1945, McKenzie gave 90% of its shares to the MB govt to facilitate the development of Brandon College (now **Brandon U**), donating the remainder to the govt in 1975. The govt ran the company as a crown corporation until selling it in 1994 to Toronto-based Regal Greetings and Gifts, one of Canada's largest mail-order catalogue companies.

In 2002, ownership of the company returned to Brandon in a deal financed by the MB govt, the City of Brandon, and employees. In late 2006, the Norwegian firm Jiffy International bought McKenzie Seeds. Jiffy is the parent company of Jiffy Ferry-Morse, the largest packet-seed firm in the US. Jiffy International committed to keeping the McKenzie operation in Brandon and to building a new single-storey manufacturing and office facility. In the early 21st century, the company produced many well-known seed brands including

McKenzie, Pike, Thompson & Morgan, and Gusto Italia, which are sold at retailers across Canada. The direct-mail division offers seeds from the McFayden and McConnell catalogues. The company ships to about 5600 Cdn retailers each year, including mass-market retailers, garden centres, and nurseries. According to company estimates, its seeds reach more than 500,000 Cdn homes annually. ● AMANDA STEPHENS

MCLEAN, David "Big Dave," blues singer/songwriter (b Aug 23, 1952, Yorkton, SK). The son of a **Presbyterian** minister, McLean moved to **Winnipeg** at age 8. He began performing in coffeehouses in 1967 playing guitar, harmonica, and washboard. A trip to the Mariposa Folk Festival in 1969 led to his discovery of the blues at a performance by John Hammond Jr. Returning to Winnipeg, McLean performed with the Chicken Flat String Band before forming electric blues bands Black Betty and Crosscut. But he found his real niche as a solo performing artist or in a duo with harmonica player Gord Kidder, working a variety of jobs by day and playing the blues at night in hotel bars like the Occidental, Bell, and Sutherland. He organized regular blues jams at the Bella Vista, the Royal Albert, Times Change, the Marlborough, and the Viscount Gort. His big break came in 1977 when he opening for his hero Muddy Waters at the Centennial Concert Hall. McLean later wrote and performed "Muddy Waters for President" for his hero, who became a personal friend and mentor; the song became the title of McLean's first cassette in 1989 (released

on CD in 1998). McLean released 2 albums for Edmonton-based Stony Plain Records: *For the Blues…Always* (1998, produced by Colin James) and *Blues from the Middle* (2003). McLean has played the Harbourfront Blues Festival in Toronto, as well as blues festivals in Montreal and Ottawa, and smaller Ontarian festivals, such as those of Windsor, London, Stratford, and Thunder Bay. He has also toured Australia. ● JOHN EINARSON

MCLEAN, Ross (b July 19, 1905, **Ethelbert**; d July 26, 1984, Ottawa). While a student at the **U of M**, McLean became interested in movies, joining local and national film societies. Hired as private secretary to Vincent Massey, High Commissioner for Canada to the UK, McLean was shocked by the poor quality of Canadian films shown in England and was largely responsible for hiring John Grierson to study the situation. Grierson's report led to the creation of the **National Film Board of Canada**. When Grierson was hired as first film commissioner in 1939, he quickly hired McLean, who made 3 short WWII-effort documentaries before being named Grierson's assistant in 1941 and deputy in 1943. When Grierson left, McLean was appointed acting film commissioner in 1945. The 'acting' dropped from his title in 1947. Upon leaving the NFB in 1950, he became head of films and visual information at UNESCO in Paris. Returning to Canada in 1957 as a writer and broadcaster, he was a regular contributor to *Saturday Night* and *Canadian Forum* magazines. In 1960, he became research director of the Broadcast Board of Governors, forerunner of the CRTC; and in 1968, he took on the jobs of director of Broadcast Programs Branch and special advisor on policy for the same commission until his 1973 retirement. ● GENE WALZ

MCLEOD, Alan Arnett, war hero (b Apr 20, 1899, **Stonewall**; d June 11, 1918, **Winnipeg**). McLeod was the Royal Flying Corp's youngest and last **Victoria Cross** winner. The son of **Margaret Arnett McLeod**, Alan's military career began at age 15, in Stonewall, with the **Fort Garry Horse** militia, after he tried to join the RFC's cadet wing in Toronto. He was told to wait as he was too young, and enlisted on his 18th birthday, in 1917. He was shipped to England in Aug 1917, joining a bomber squadron in France in Nov, where he was nicknamed "Babe" because of his age. On Mar 27, 1918, McLeod and his observer/gunner, Lt Arthur Hammond, flew army support against a German offensive. Attacked by 8 German fighters, McLeod turned his aircraft to meet them. Both men were hit by enemy fire, but Hammond shot down 4 of the fighters before the bomber burst into flames.

McKenzie Seeds in Brandon

SANDY BLACK

417

McLeod climbed out, and controlled his plane from the wing, sideslipping to keep the flames from himself and Hammond. They crashed and McLeod was thrown clear, but his observer was unconscious and trapped in burning wreckage. With 5 wounds, the pilot crawled to the wreck, worked the badly wounded Hammond free, and, still under enemy fire, dragged him to Allied lines. On Sept 4, now in the uniform of the RAF (which replaced the RFC), McLeod received the VC from King George V. He returned to Winnipeg for hospital treatment, dying of influenza 5 days before the Nov 11 armistice in the 1918 flu pandemic (*see* **EPIDEMICS**). He is buried at Kildonan Presbyterian Cemetery, Winnipeg. ● JIM SHILLIDAY

MCLEOD, Margaret Arnett, historian (b 1877, London, ON; d 1966, **WINNIPEG**). One of Canada's most respected amateur historians, McLeod was born in ON, though her family moved soon after to MB. She was educated in **BRANDON** and Winnipeg, taught school in **STONEWALL**, and married Dr A. N. McLeod. Their son was **ALAN ARNETT MCLEOD**, VC. McLeod was best known for her long introduction to *The Letters of Letitia Hargrave*, which offers a glimpse of the social history of the **RED RIVER SETTLEMENT**. The Champlain Society, a select group of which Hargrave was a member, published the volume in 1947. McLeod's first work was *The Frozen Priest of Pembina*, a story of Oblate Father Joseph Goiffon, published in 1935. Next came *The Bells of Red River*, a 1937 collection of stories originally printed in the **WINNIPEG FREE PRESS**. *The Beaver* printed many of her articles. Her works on MB **MÉTIS** included *Cuthbert Grant of Grantown*. McLeod's *Songs of Old Manitoba* showed that the province has authentic folk songs and dance music. McLeod found the song "Lord Selkirk at Fort William," lost for 140 years, with the help of the director of the department of musicology at the Bibliothèque nationale in Paris. She became a life member of the **MANITOBA HISTORICAL SOCIETY** in 1964. She died, aged 88, in a house fire in her Maryland St home in Winnipeg. ● JIM SHILLIDAY

MCLUHAN, Herbert MARSHALL, academic, media critic (b July 21, 1911, Edmonton; d Dec 31, 1980, Toronto), "the oracle of the electronic age." Although Marshall McLuhan did not live to witness the explosive manifestation of that age at the end of the 20th century, with the advent of the Internet and the personal computer, he gave dramatic expression to the social change underway. Technology, he insisted, fuels social change: "We shape our tools and then our tools shape us." "The new electronic interdependence," he pointed out, "recreates the world in the image

Marshall McLuhan

of a global village," the once-distant corners of Earth indissolubly united; and the concept of a "global village" has become common currency. Moreover, he maintained, "the medium is the message" – that is, the technology of communication informs the information it delivers. This aphorism on the pervasive power of the media is embedded in contemporary discourse. An unflagging critic of popular culture, McLuhan popularized the term "media," by which we designate the various forms of public communication, and proposed an intriguing distinction between "hot" and "cool" media, based on the density of information each conveys and the consequent demand on the reader's, listener's, or viewer's participation.

McLuhan was the son of Herbert and Elsie McLuhan (née Hall). Both were of eastern Cdn stock from, respectively, ON and NS who had come to western Canada before WWI. In 1915, the family moved from Edmonton to **WINNIPEG**, where Marshall attended Gladstone primary school, Earl Grey Junior High, and Kelvin High School. He attended Nassau Baptist Church, now called Trinity Baptist Church on Gertrude Ave. Later, he attended Augustine United and Knox United churches. He entered the **U OF M** in 1928 to study engineering perhaps showing his early interest in technology but switched to English literature the following year and graduated in 1934 with an MA in English literature, going on to the U of Cambridge to take an MA in 1939 and a PhD in 1943. He taught English at the U of Wisconsin and the U of St. Louis and, back in Canada, at Assumption College in Windsor, ON. From 1946 for the rest of his career, he was a member of the faculty of the U of Toronto.

With the publication of *The Mechanical Bride: Folklore of Industrial Man (1951)*, on the

power of advertising to shape public attitudes, and even more with *The Gutenberg Galaxy: The Making of Typographic Man (1962)*, on the sweeping effects of the print revolution, McLuhan became something of a media darling. Quick-witted and the master of the sparkling retort, he was interviewed in print and on radio and television, and was quoted repeatedly. He was on call for lectures and conferences, and he elaborated his views in articles in a variety of publications, with titles such as "Comics and Culture," "The Media Fought the Battle of Jericho," and "Murder by Television." He published *Understanding Media: The Extensions of Man* in 1964, and in 1967, with, Quentin Fiore he published *The Medium Is the Massage: An Inventory of Effects*. The unabashed pun on his much-publicized dictum reiterates that the medium "massages" or shapes its content, and even that media control identifies this "mass age."

During his lifetime, McLuhan received numerous awards and honorary degrees, and was appointed to significant academic and public positions. He founded the U of Toronto's Centre for Culture and Technology and served as director from 1963-79. He was named to the Albert Schweitzer Chair in the Humanities at Fordham U (1967-68), and became a Companion of the Order of Canada in 1970. A convert to Roman Catholicism in 1937, he was awarded a gold medal in 1971 by the president of Italy in recognition of his work as a philosopher of the mass media, and was appointed in 1973 by the Vatican as consultor of the Pontifical Commission for Social Communications.

"I may be wrong," McLuhan once quipped, out of his vast repertoire of quotable quotations, "but I am never in doubt." Ever delighted with the nuances of language, he frequently made his point with rapier wit: "Invention is the mother of necessities," he said. Yet he may seem most arbitrary and idiosyncratic when he is at his most gnomic. Even an admirer may wonder whether the sensory metaphor of "hot" or "cool" best explains media effects; and "Tomorrow is our permanent address" may only be a fanciful restatement of the obvious.

McLuhan's popularity faded in the decades after his death, particularly in academic circles. In his later life, he denounced the electronic media as "a blatant manifestation of the Anti-Christ." Still, in the 21st century, as his perception of the world as global village appears increasingly prescient, his stress on the role played by technology in determining the shape of human history and human lives may well come to be considered a lasting contribution to contemporary thought. ● ALLEN MILLS/MILDRED GUTKIN

MCNALLY ROBINSON BOOKSELLERS is Canada's largest independent bookseller, with 4 large stores in western Canada and one smaller outlet in New York. Owners Paul and Holly McNally got into the bookselling business in 1981, opening a single store in **WINNIPEG**. A separate children's bookstore was subsequently added, along with a wholesale division – Skylight Books – which supplies books to libraries, schools, and institutions. It wasn't until 1996 that McNally Robinson entered the bookselling "big leagues" in Canada, opening the country's largest independent bookstore – a .2 ha (20,000-ft²) outlet in Winnipeg's Grant Park Shopping Centre. The store included a full-service restaurant and a mezzanine children's bookstore. Two years later, the company opened a 0.21 ha (23,000-ft²) bookshop

in Saskatoon, as well as a 700 m² (7500-ft²) store in the Portage Place Shopping Centre in downtown Winnipeg. In 2002, McNally Robinson continued its westward expansion with the opening of a 0.24 ha (26,000-ft²), 3-storey store in downtown Calgary. In Dec 2004, the McNallys' daughter, Sarah, opened a bookshop in New York, and in 2007 the company announced plans to expand into Winnipeg's Polo Park shopping centre and Toronto. The firm has won Bookseller of the Year awards 5 times and Paul has served as president of the Cdn Booksellers Assoc. The company is well known for its sponsorship of Manitoba literary prizes and its support of local and touring authors. ● MURRAY MCNEILL

▶ *See also* **BOOK PUBLISHING**, **LITERATURE**.

MACPHERSON, Stewart, broadcaster (b 1907, **WINNIPEG**; d 1996, Winnipeg). MacPherson travelled to England in 1936 to seek employment as a journalist. After selling shoes for a time, he began covering hockey games for the BBC. This led to more sports assignments, especially boxing. During WWII, MacPherson became the BBC's "Voice from the Air," covering the Blitz and the subsequent bombing of Germany. By 1942 he was one of the most famous journalists in England and won a listeners' poll as British Male Voice of the Year. After the war, he hosted the popular "Twenty Questions" on radio before returning to Winnipeg to join CJAY (later CKY-TV). MacPherson covered politics and read the late-night news. He was also a colour commentator for the early **WINNIPEG JETS** broadcasts. ● GPP

MCRAE, John C. "Big John," police chief (b Mar 4, 1859, Ottawa; d July 19, 1921, **WINNIPEG**) was best known for establishing Winnipeg's

controversial red light district while he headed up the Winnipeg Police 1887-1911. McRae came to Winnipeg at age 20. He joined the police force in 1881 as Const, and was promoted the following year to Sgt, 2nd-in-command of the force. McRae made several high-profile arrests, including that of outlaw Bulldog Kelly, who was wanted on murder charges by the **NORTH-WEST MOUNTED POLICE**, as well as infamous cattle rustler Joe Fant, though Fant ultimately escaped to the US after shooting McRae in the groin. As chief of police, one of the biggest issues McRae had to contend with during his 24-year career was prostitution. Brothels were numerous during Winnipeg's early days as a frontier town, with young, single men making up the majority of the city's population.

JOEL TRENAMAN

John C. McRae

As Winnipeg grew, the brothels – once located on the periphery – became increasingly close to residential neighbourhoods. This proximity, coupled with the growing reform movement, made prostitution an election issue in 1903. Under pressure from new mayor Thomas Sharpe, McRae was forced to lead a series of raids on the brothels. Ultimately, the raids did little to thwart the growing sex trade. Changing tactics, McRae made a deal in 1909 with Winnipeg's leading madam, Minnie Woods, to form a red-light district, officially known as the Point Douglas Segregated Area. The area was located on Rachel (renamed Annabella in 1914) and McFarlane streets, strategically close to the **CPR** station and the downtown. By 1910, the district comprised approximately 50 brothels. A

M

McNally Robinson's Grant Park store in Winnipeg

1911 report, though clearing the police force and McRae of corruption charges, ultimately condemned the district. McRae retired soon after. In 1913, he was awarded the King's Police Medal for meritorious service. When accepting the medal, McRae revealed that the "C" in his name didn't actually stand for anything; he used it to distinguish himself from other McRaes. He is buried in Elmwood cemetery. • MD

M **MACTAVISH (also MCTAVISH), William,** fur trader, politician (b March 29, 1815, Edinburgh; d July 23, 1870, Liverpool, UK) was HBC governor at the time of the **RED RIVER RESISTANCE**. He came to Hudson Bay in 1833 as an apprentice with the **HBC** under the patronage of his uncle, chief factor John George MacTavish. MacTavish worked at **YORK FACTORY** under James Hargrave, soon to be his brother-in-law. In 1857, he moved to the **RED RIVER SETTLEMENT** to take charge of **UPPER FORT GARRY**. He soon married Mary Sarah McDermot, the **MÉTIS**, **ROMAN CATHOLIC** daughter of **ANDREW MCDERMOT**, and sister of **ANNIE MCDERMOT BANNATYNE**. Appointed gov of **ASSINIBOIA** in 1858, he believed the governance of the **FUR TRADE** and the settlement should be separated. Nevertheless, in 1869-70 he was gov of both **RUPERT'S LAND** and **ASSINIBOIA**. His lack of action in the Cdn crisis was partly due to his dislike of politics and his ill health, but also because of his sympathies with the old inhabitants. He believed the locals had a right to a proper arrangement with Canada, and he objected to Cdn imperialism. He criticized Canada for ignoring the inhabitants. From Nov 16, 1869, to Feb 1870, he was virtually (and sometimes actually) imprisoned in Upper Fort Garry by **LOUIS RIEL**, mostly bedridden with advanced **TUBERCULOSIS**. What actions he took were through the agency of his private secretary, J. J. Hargrave (his nephew), and **ANDREW G. B. BANNATYNE**, his brother-in-law. He resigned on Jan 15, 1870. He and his family left for Scotland on May 17, and he died upon disembarking at Liverpool in July. • JMB

MADDIN, Guy, filmmaker (b Feb 28, 1956, **WINNIPEG**). Beginning in 1985 with his debut **FILM** *The Dead Father*, Maddin has directed numerous shorts and 9 feature films, including *The Saddest Music in the World* (2003) and a television ballet, made with many **ROYAL WINNIPEG BALLET** artists, *Dracula: Pages from a Virgin's Diary*. *Dracula* won Maddin an International Emmy for Best Performing Arts Program in 2002. In 2006-07, his feature film *Brand upon the Brain!* was accompanied by live orchestra, narrator, and castrato while playing at the New York, Toronto, and Berlin film festivals. A cult figure revered for

PETER TITTENBERGER

Filmmaker Guy Maddin is the latest arts figure to leave Winnipeg for Toronto

his offbeat humour and retro film style, Maddin has won the prestigious Persistence of Vision Award for lifetime achievement at the San Francisco International Film Festival (2006), the Telluride Silver Medal for life achievement in film (1995), and a US National Film Critics Award for best experimental film for both *Archangel* (1991) and *The Heart of the World* (2001). He is also an author and a freelance film journalist, and has taught film studies courses at the Ontario College of Art and Design in Toronto. In 2007, Maddin's film *My Winnipeg* won top prize at the Toronto International Film Festival. • GENE WALZ

MAFEKING, pop 75, is a community located at the base of the Porcupine Mountain Provincial Park, 150 km NW of **DAUPHIN**. The construction of the railroad in Mafeking, MB took place during the Boer War (1899-1902). During this time, the small town of Mafeking, South Africa, was under attack for over 200 days. Against overwhelming odds, residents managed to defend their town. The post office here in MB opened in 1904. Mafeking attracts many tourists, particularly those interested in hunting and fishing. Since 2006, several lodges have been in operation in the area. Mafeking also plays host to the Jammin' in the Jackpine annual Aboriginal music festival. • GPP

MAGAZINES in MB include a wide range of literary and commercial enterprises. The oldest magazine in MB, *The Beaver*, is also Canada's only popular history magazine. It began as an in-house publication of the **HUDSON'S BAY COMPANY** in 1920. Soon the magazine attracted distinguished writers and historians such as Stephen Leacock, Margaret Mead, Michael Bliss, Donald Creighton,

Desmond Morton, **W. L. MORTON**, and Peter C. Newman. In 1986, the magazine started publishing on a bimonthly schedule. The magazine's focus expanded to include all Canadian history, and the masthead now read "Exploring Canada's History." *The Beaver* became an autonomous entity in 1994 when HBC founded Canada's National History Society as publisher of the magazine. The idea was to make *The Beaver* a popular history magazine accessible to the reading public, with a mix of features, columns, reviews, notes and commentary. The magazine has had only 10 editors, who have included Helen Burgess, Christopher Dafoe and Doug Whiteway.

PRAIRIE GARDEN magazine began as a publication of the Winnipeg Horticultural Society in 1939. Although publication was interrupted during the war years, *Prairie Garden* went on to be western Canada's only gardening annual, generously illustrated and filled with practical gardening information. An average issue contains about 170 pages in a bound format with a 16-page colour insert. The editorial committees over the years have been a who's who of MB horticulture, including academics, senior government employees, and horticulture enthusiasts. *Prairie Garden* has no paid staff except for its editor. The committee, which varies from 9 to 15 members, serves as an editorial staff and meet once a month over dinner in **ASSINIBOINE PARK**. Committees typically include experts such as: a plant pathologist, specialists in water gardens, potatoes, and houseplant care, and a green house expert. The magazine's content is about one-half themed articles and one-half practical gardening tips. Since 1998 the magazine has given out the Prairie Garden Award for Excellence, to honour contributions in horticulture in the prairie region.

CANADIAN DIMENSION, founded in 1963 by **U OF M** economist Cy Gonick, describes itself as "an independent forum for left-wing political thought and discussion." It publishes six times a year. The magazine presents current issues like the environment, feminism, community development, and gender and racial inequality, to a national audience. Originally produced in Gonick's basement, by 1975 an editorial collective took over. Their current banner reads "a magazine for people who want to change the world." Contributing writers have included Judy Rebick, Gregory Baum, Henry Heller, and Leo Panitch.

CONTEMPORARY VERSE 2 is MB's oldest independent literary magazine, and the only poetry quarterly in Canada. It was founded as *Contemporary Verse II* in May, 1975, by **DOROTHY LIVESAY** when she was writer in residence at the U of M. The founding editorial staff included

Steve Buri, Arthur Adamson, and Robert Enright. The original editorial policy was that each issue should include one quarter new Canadian poetry, and three quarters reviews and criticism of Canadian poetry. The Manitoba Arts Council began funding the magazine in 1984; prior to that it was funded directly by Livesay and by the Canada Council. In 1985 the magazine became *CV2*, and was edited by a collective consisting of Pamela Banting, Di Brandt, Jane Casey, and Jan Horner. There was an emphasis on writing by women, and by 1986 the magazine's new subtitle was "a literary journal for men and women." Livesay stepped down as publisher in 1990, when the magazine became incorporated as a non-profit organization. In 2001 the magazine gave Clarise Foster permission to take over the magazine as managing editor. The Manitoba Arts Council approved a 5-year business plan drawn up by Foster and the magazine survived with a new format that emphasizes interviews with contemporary poets as well as Canadian poetry.

PRAIRIE FIRE magazine began its life in 1978 as the Writers' News Manitoba newsletter, which in turn came out of the Winnipeg Writers' Workshop of the early 1970s. Elizabeth Carriere was one of the founders along with her sister Kate Bitney and Andris Taskans, who has remained as editor from 1978 to the present. The Writers' News Manitoba newsletter at first existed largely to agitate for the creation of a writers' guild in the province. Writers such as **GEORGE AMABILE**, Lorna Uher (later Crozier), and Patrick Lane appeared in early issues. The publication's name changed to *Prairie Fire* in 1983. With continued growth, the magazine became an independent non-profit entity in 1989. The magazine featured fiction, poetry, creative nonfiction, and the occasional author interview. *Prairie Fire* began publishing a notable series of special issues in the 1990s, including a special issue on Carol Shields the same year she won the Pulitzer Prize (1995). The magazine has published many notable MB writers before they became nationally known, such as: **DAVID BERGEN, SANDRA BIRDSELL, MIRIAM TOEWS**, Alissa York, and Sylvia Legris. *Prairie Fire* has won numerous honours from the Western Magazine Awards and the National Magazine Awards since the 1990s.

BORDER CROSSINGS is an internationally recognized, quarterly visual arts magazine published in Winnipeg. It began in 1977 as *Arts Manitoba*, edited and to some degree funded by Robert Enright, who would later emerge as an important arts and culture critic for the CBC and other media outlets. The magazine was closely associated with St. John's College professors **DENNIS COOLEY** and **DAVID ARNASON** at the

U of M, who would spawn Turnstone Press in the late 1970s. In 1985, thanks to a special issue that focused on artists in ND and MN, the magazine re-named itself *Border Crossings*, to indicate its cross-disciplinary and international interests. Current editor Meeka Walsh, who took over from Enright in 1992, calls it "a local international magazine." Numerous artists from MB have appeared in *Border Crossings* and gone on to national and international acclaim: Sarah Anne Johnson (whose early photographs were purchased by the Guggenheim), Janet Werner, Karel Funk, and **WANDA KOOP** are just a few examples. The magazine emphasizes lavish colour reproductions of art-work, in-depth artist interviews, essays on visual artists, and a hefty review section. *Border Crossings* has garnered dozens of gold and silver awards from both the National and the Western Magazine Awards.

   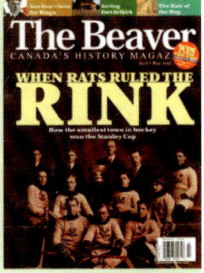  

MB MAGAZINE PUBLISHERS' ASSOCIATION

Magazines published in MB reach an estimated 500,000 readers annually.

HERIZONS is a Canadian feminist magazine published quarterly in Winnipeg. It began as a regional newspaper in 1979, and now boasts a readership of about 7000. Unusually, the magazine does not get operating grants from govt, instead getting revenue primarily from subscriptions and donations. *Herizons* became a magazine

in 1982, and 3 years later launched itself as a national publication. Between 1987 and 1992 it didn't publish, and then, after a large direct mail campaign, relaunched in spring 1992. It is now a successful non-profit organization, edited by Penni Mitchell. The magazine covers issues of interest in the Cdn feminist movement such as health, the environment, the law, politics, and arts and culture. Contributors have included Michele Landsberg, Doris Anderson, and Karen Tulchinsky.

Winnipeg has seen many experimental micro-magazines founded by artists and small collectives. *Midcontinental* magazine was founded by an artists' collective associated with Plug In Gallery in the early 1980s, including Doug Melnyk, Ron Gorsline, Scott Ellis, and Carol Pickering. It featured visual art and experimental writing in an unusual 11x17 format. The magazine was revived in the late 1980s under Rob Ferguson as a city entertainment magazine somewhat similar to the earlier *Winnipeg Magazine* and folded in the early 1990s. Michael Rennie founded a short-lived literary magazine in the 1980s called *Wordloom*. *Dark Leisure*, begun by MB poet Jon Paul Fiorentino, was an experimental literary mag in the late 1990s. *Zygote*, founded by Eva Weidman and Chris Kent, also published literary work in the '90s, folding in 2001. *Tart* magazine began publishing its distinctively designed hipster culture crawl in 1998 with Mariianne Mays and Phil Koch as editors.

Because of its geographic location and low operating costs, Winnipeg has also been home to many trade publications in magazine format. Examples of companies that publish trade magazines include Naylor, Mercury (*Canadian Trucker*, various food services publications), Craig Kelman (*Appraisal Institute*), and Matrix (*Canadian Doctor*). In addition, *Manitoba Business Magazine* has published journalism about the local business community since 1979. ● MAURICE MIERAU

MAIR, Charles, poet and rabble-rouser (b Sept 21, 1838, Lanark, Upper Canada [ON]; d July 7, 1927, Victoria, BC). Mair attended U of Queen's College (now Queen's U) in Kingston, ON, with Sir **JOHN CHRISTIAN SCHULTZ**, but did not graduate. In spring 1868 in Ottawa, he helped organize the secret movement "Canada First." About the same time, he published *Dreamland and Other Poems*, an echo of the **POETRY** of John Keats. He received a patronage appointment from **WILLIAM MCDOUGALL** as secretary for the Cdn mission to London to negotiate the transfer of **RUPERT'S LAND**, but was unable to go. He settled instead for an appointment as assistant on the Cdn road works near **RED RIVER**, and was also named Red

River correspondent of several ON newspapers, including Toronto's *Globe*. His comments about Red River mixed-blood ladies led to his being horsewhipped by **ANNIE BANNATYNE** in Feb 1869, and **LOUIS RIEL** responded in print to his writing.

Mair married a niece of John Schultz and was one of the most active of the pro-Cdn party in Red River in 1869. He was part of the group that surrendered to Louis Riel at John Schultz's house in Dec 1869, but he escaped a month later. He went first to **PORTAGE LA PRAIRIE**, then S to St Paul, travelling E with **DONALD A. SMITH**. He appeared at a number of rallies in ON in 1870 to stir up hostility to Riel and the provisional govt, and testified before the Senate subcommittee in April 1870. Mair later helped found Kelowna, BC, and wrote *Through the Mackenzie Basin* (1908), based upon his work as secretary of the commission that negotiated with Indians there in 1899. He moved to Victoria in 1921. Once a highly regarded Cdn poet, his reputation has slipped into eclipse, at least partly because of the rawness of his Cdn nationalism. ● JMB

MAMMAL is a warm-blooded (homeothermic) vertebrate in the class Mammalia, characterized by a body covering of hair, and which nourish its young with milk produced by paired mammary glands of the female. Mammals evolved from mammal-like reptiles (cynodont therapsids) about 225 mya (Mid-Triassic period). There are 4680 living species worldwide, and an estimated 400,000 species existed in the past. MB is home to a diverse fauna of mammals, due to its large size and position at the centre of NA, and its variety of major plant/animal communities (biomes). Following the last Ice Age, which eliminated almost all life from the province, mammals and other species have been recolonizing MB for only the last 11,000 years. From the Grassland Biome in S MB to the Arctic Tundra and Arctic Marine biomes of the North, mammalian life is present everywhere, sometimes in surprising variety and abundance. Since mammals are notoriously secretive, most people are completely unaware of all but the large and bold species.

Including Humans (*Homo sapiens*), there are currently 86 native species of mammals in MB and 2 introduced species (House **MOUSE** and Brown Rat). Several of these native species arrived here during historical times, such as the Eastern Cottontail, white-tailed **DEER**, and Grey and Fox **SQUIRRELS**. Others, like the Swift **FOX**, Plains **BISON**, Pronghorn, **WALRUS** and Bowhead **WHALE** were extirpated (meaning eliminated from the province, but survive elsewhere) over a century ago from ruthless persecution. Races known as the Plains Grizzly and the Buffalo **WOLF**

were rapidly hunted to extinction with the arrival of Europeans.

Summarizing by families, there are 6 species of shrews, one **MOLE**, 6 **BATS**, one primate, 4 **RABBITS**, 11 squirrels, 2 pocket gophers, one pocket mouse, one **BEAVER**, 17 mice, one **PORCUPINE**, 2 whales, 6 foxes/wolf, 3 **BEARS**, one **RACCOON**, 10 **WEASELS**, 3 **CATS**, 3 **SEALS**, one walrus, 5 deer, one pronghorn, and 2 cattle. Many of these groups and species are covered elsewhere. An analysis by origin/habitat preference reveals the following: 7 species (8% of the fauna) are Arctic Marine, 7 (8%) Arctic Tundra, 23 (27%) Boreal Coniferous Forest, 10 (12%) Eastern Deciduous Forest, 15 (17%) Grassland, and 24 (28%) widespread, occuring in many types of habitats over large regions of NA.

Mammal life also fills a number of strata: 3 species are burrowers that spend almost their entire lives underground (e.g., Star-nosed Mole), 59 are mainly surface dwellers (Arctic Fox), 6 are arboreal (Northern Flying Squirrel), 6 are aerial (Red Bat), 5 often enter freshwater (Water Shrew), and 7 are Marine (Beluga). It is interesting to examine how MB mammals have exploited and partitioned food resources, which help avoid competition: 3 species eat mainly roots (e.g, Plains Pocket Gopher), 2 bark eaters (Porcupine), 26 leaves and buds (mule deer), 11 seeds and fruit (Deer Mouse), 16 arthropods such as insects (Northern Grasshopper Mouse), 19 red meat (American Badger), 5 fish (River Otter), and 4 omnivores, devouring significant amounts of plant and animal material (Black Bear).

We are mammals, and so we can best relate to them and enjoy observing their endless variety of behaviour and habits. Numerous species are important in recreational hunting (from squirrels to Moose), as a source of income through trapping (Canadian Lynx and Red Fox), or as ranched animals for meat (American Bison and American Elk). Sometimes a few species can become a nuisance, such as ground squirrels and pocket gophers eating crops and digging holes in fields, or a beaver taking down valuable trees on private property. A few mammals rarely carry diseases that are transferable to people, such as a Little Brown Bat or Striped Skunk infected with rabies virus, a Deer Mouse carrying hantavirus, or the meat of a Black Bear infected with parasitic worms. With a little knowledge and common sense, people have little to fear and much to enjoy in watching the wild mammals in urban, rural, recreational, and wild areas. ● REW

MAMMOTHS AND MASTODONS were common on the Great Plains and surrounding **SPRUCE** forests of central NA until their extinction 11,000

years ago. They inhabited the green pastures left by receding glaciers (*see* **GLACIATION**) during the warm periods, lasting thousands of years, which occasionally visited the Ice Age. Both animals are believed to have arrived in the western hemisphere by crossing the land bridge between Alaska and Siberia known as Beringia. Mastodons, comparable in size to an elephant, arrived about 15 to 20 mya, and fed on twigs, cones, leaves, and mosses. The woolly or Siberian mammoth belonged to a different family tree, and made its first appearance about 1.7 mya. Mammoths, known for their large spiralling tusks, lived on a diet of Prairie grasses in summer and spruce leaves in winter. Both animals were well insulated by the coarse brown fur that covered their thick layer of fat.

Ice Age elephants roamed the plains.

Remains such as teeth and bone fragments have been found at 15 MB sites. These were likely dredged up by the most recent glacier and deposited out of **LAKE AGASSIZ**. Geologist Henry Youle Hind reported that an **OJIBWAY** hunter knew of a skeleton in the Dauphin Lake area (NE of **DAUPHIN**). Hind himself sighted a mastodon skeleton on the banks of Shell River near **ROBLIN**. Plains Indians venerated these fossils as the bones of Manitou. It is unclear precisely what caused their extinction, but overhunting likely contributed to their demise. ● MD

▸ *See also* **EXTINCT ANIMALS**.

MANDAK LEAGUE is the shortened term for the Manitoba-Dakota Baseball League, which operated 1950-55. The semi-professional league drafted the top ballplayers from MB, ND, and MN, but most notably attracted players from the Negro League in the US, which was in a state of decline following Jackie Robinson's admission into Major League Baseball. MB's **Baseball** teams benefited from the preponderance of former Negro Leaguers who were unable because of racism or who were too old to join the MLB, but were also too young to retire from play. These included Cooperstown Baseball Hall of Fame members Willie Wells, Ray Dandridge, and Leon Day.

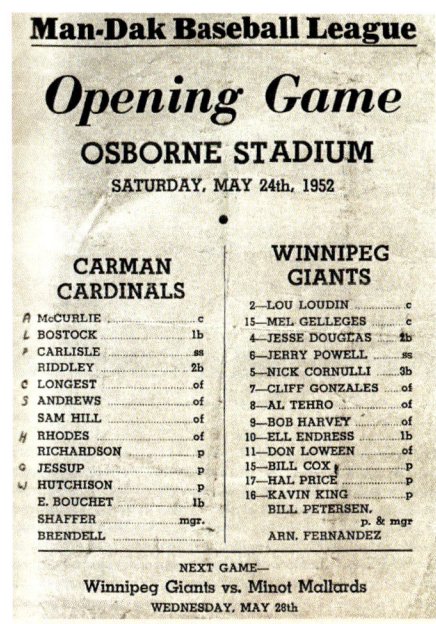

Program for Opening Day 1952 for the Winnipeg Giants

Before the 1950 formation of the ManDak, there was a limit on the number of import players allowed on each Manitoba Senior League (MSL) team. The new league had no such quotas, and offered highly competitive salaries, ranging from $300-$1000 a month, with a cap of $8500 per team.

The ManDak was formed with 3 teams from the MSL: the **Winnipeg** Elmwood Giants (later called the Winnipeg Royals), the **Carman** Cardinals, and the **Brandon** Greys, a powerhouse baseball team that had won both the 1948 and 1949 MSL championships. A new team, the Winnipeg Buffaloes, was started by gambler **Stanley Zedd**, and was comprised entirely of former Negro League players, though it only operated for 2 seasons. Teams from ND included the Minot Mallards and later the Williston Oilers and the Bismarck Barons.

The inaugural season's games were delayed because of the 1950 **Flood** of the **Red River**. Once waters receded, the league opener was an all-star charity game, which raised $2643 for flood victims, with tickets ranging from 50¢ to $1.

New lights were installed at Winnipeg's Osborne Stadium (*see* **Winnipeg Blue Bombers**) for the ManDak teams. The stadium in Carman underwent significant renovations with a new lighting system, purportedly the best in western Canada, at a cost of $22,000. The population of Carman would often double during games, as spectators flocked here to watch former Negro League players.

Soon after its formation, the league began losing money because of the high cost of running the teams, and by 1954, the Elmwood Giants had switched to the Northern League. Also by that time, professional baseball – especially the National League – had started to open up to **Black** players. The remaining MB teams folded in 1955, though the ND teams continued in the US for another 2 years before the ManDak League went under. The league's history was recently chronicled in Barry Swanton's *Mandak League: Haven for Former Negro League Ballplayers, 1950-1957.* ● MICHELLE DOBROVOLNY

▸ *See also* **Walter Lee Gibbons**, **Terry Sawchuk**, **Tony Tascona**, **Armando Vasquez**.

MANIGOTAGAN, pop 160, is a community 150 km NNE of **Winnipeg**, on the mouth of the Manigotagan River on the E shore of **Lake Winnipeg**. The community's name is **Cree** for "bad throat." It is believed an Aboriginal chief was camped by the river when he heard a **Moose** making a peculiar sound. Manigotagan was originally founded to provide access to timber resources in the area. The post office was opened in 1890. Manigotagan is 1 of a 4-community complex that also includes the **Hollow Water Indian Reserve, Seymourville** and Aghaming. Manitgotagan is governed by a mayor and council under *The Northern Affairs Act.* Camping and whitewater **Canoeing** on the Manigotagan River attract tourists to the area which became a **Provincial Park** in 2004. ● GPP

MANIPOGO is reputed to be a mysterious creature living in the depths of **Lake Manitoba**. Manipogo Provincial Park, 45 km NE of **Dauphin**,

bears its name. The legend seems to have arisen around 1910, but the alleged being was named in 1957 after the Ogopogo, a creature said to inhabit BC's Lake Okanagan. Reports over the years have described the Manipogo as black or muddy-brown, and anywhere between 3 and 50 m long. It is said to be snakelike in shape, making it a swift, elusive swimmer. Some say its head is like that of a sheep or horse, and that it has a number of humps.

Enthusiasts of cryptozoology (the study of animals whose existence is unproven) have proposed that the being could be an ancient reptile or whale. This theory suggests that Manipogo is the prehistoric *Basilosaurus*, also called *Zeuglodon cetoides*, due to its apparent similarity to the whale-like creatures that lived 37 to 53 mya. To date, there is no scientific evidence of Manipogo's existence, though believers have documented sightings for decades. In 1962, for example, 2 fishermen snapped a photograph of something odd swimming near their boat. A 1997 report stating that the local RCMP detachment had cornered the animal turned out to be a hoax.

The so-called monster has become a spur to tourism in area communities. The Manipogo Festival is an annual event held the first weekend of March in the lakeside community of **St. Laurent**. Started in 2001, it features **Music**, ice **Fishing**, **Hockey** games, and a parade of Bombardier snow machines. A $1 million prize is offered to anyone who can capture the Manipogo. Manipogo is not to be confused with Winnipogo, a supposed inhabitant of **Lake Winnipegosis**. ● JOEL TRENAMAN

MANITOBA (NAME ORIGIN). Although there is some uncertainty as to the origin of the province's name, in the most likely explanation "Manitoba" is derived from the **Cree** words *manitou* for "Great Spirit" and *wapow* for "strait" or "narrows." In the closely related **Ojibway** language, this meaning would be expressed as *Manitou-baw.*

Could a giant sturgeon be the source of the Manipogo legend?

The reference to the "strait of the Great Spirit" draws on the spiritually significant narrows of **Lake Manitoba**, where waves crashing against the shores of Manitou Island create a sound believed to be the voice or drumbeat of the Great Spirit. Thomas Spence first used the name "Manitoba" in reference to a defined territory with his short-lived Republic of Manitobah. Before a standard pronunciation came into use in the **Red River Settlement**, Manitoba was often pronounced with the stress on the last syllable, as in 'manito-BAH'. In the first List of Rights sent to Ottawa to negotiate the province's entrance into Confederation, **Assiniboia** was the name assigned to the new province. However, **Louis Riel** found the name unappealing, and suggested either North-West or Manitoba be adopted instead. Sir John A. Macdonald chose the latter for its pleasing sound and connection to MB's original inhabitants. ● MD

MANITOBA ACTION COMMITTEE ON THE STATUS OF WOMEN

was instrumental in lobbying for policy changes to improve women's lives throughout the 1970s and '80s. Formed in 1971, MACSW worked through political action, public education, and personal growth to improve attitudes, raise issues, and remove inequalities affecting women in MB. MACSW was formed by a group of women who delivered briefs to the federal Royal Commission on the Status of Women. The commission had been established under PM Pierre Trudeau in 1967, and it released its final report in 1970. MACSW began the work of overseeing the implementation of the report's 167 recommendations and of lobbying federal and provincial govts to comply with it. MACSW was Canada's first provincial committee on the status of women. June Menzies and Jean Carson were the founding members. The group began to research laws in Canada to assess their compliance with UN declarations regarding women's human rights.

The volunteer committee initially held meetings in communities throughout MB to identify issues of concern to women. Among the group's top priorities in the 1970s were equal property rights for women going through a divorce; child support enforcement; and employment equity. The volunteer organization gained stronger footing when the federal govt established the Women's Program in 1973 and MACSW, along with other provincial action committees, received an annual stipend to operate an office. Volunteers continued to do the bulk of the work on various subcommittees that conducted research, lobbied provincial and federal officials, and held demonstrations. They also continued to work in the areas of pension reform, improved welfare, sexual assault, sex-role stereotyping in the workforce and the media, services for battered women, abortion assistance, pornography reform, and extending human rights protection for gays and lesbians. With offices in **Thompson** and **Brandon** as well as Winnipeg, MACSW was the largest feminist group in MB. It continued until the federal govt's Women's Program was closed. By then, an increasing number of specialized women's organizations had already been established. ● PENNI MITCHELL

MANITOBA AGRICULTURAL MUSEUM

was incorporated in 1954 near **Austin**. The museum had its beginnings in an event held for many years on the farm of Don Carrothers. As early as 1948, collectors of old agricultural machinery would bring their steam engines and kerosene tractors, some dating back to the late 19th century, to the Carrothers property. Reliving the memories of fall threshing bees, attendees would feed sheaves of wheat or oats into separators – complicated machines that were the forerunner of the modern combine – and eat traditional harvest suppers. From this event was born the Threshermen's Reunion, which has been held each year since 1954 on the museum grounds.

The location of the museum is itself of historic interest. Three km S of the Trans-Canada Highway at Austin, it occupies land crossed by the 19th-century Fort Ellice Trail, which wound toward the **Carberry Hills** on its way from Winnipeg to MT. As related by Don's brother, Cliff Carrothers, father Tom looked at the map of MB before immigrating from ON and realized the historic significance of the spot he picked for his new farm in MB. Each year on the first day of the Threshermen's Reunion, replica horse-drawn covered wagons lead a vintage parade, having spent several days following what remains of the trail.

With the proceeds from the reunion, museum volunteers acquired and moved examples of buildings onto the museum grounds in the 2 following decades. Today, the museum contains a "village" with a railway station, water tower, and grain elevator; a working vintage telephone switch housed in an original **MTS** switch building; a Masonic lodge, lawyers' office, general store, and post office; an 1880s log house and log schoolhouse; 2 churches; and an elaborate farmhouse – all-original, and filled with original artifacts. There are replicas of a gristmill, a working blacksmith shop, and a livery stable. The original Carrothers farmhouse, once on the periphery of the museum, was incorporated into the village as the museum grew in size to its present 130 ha (320 ac). Ten large pole sheds house the tractor and agricultural equipment collection. The fully enclosed Centennial, Community Ties, Heritage, and MB Amateur Radio Museum buildings contain artifacts and interpretive displays.

The annual 4-day Threshermen's Reunion, held in late July, is home to over 100 Clydesdale horses; a 2-hour vintage parade of agricultural equipment, tractors, trucks, and cars with a special feature each year; a rodeo; the Central Canada Fiddle Festival; and a vintage fashion show. The village is in full operation, as are the sawmill, separators, gristmill, and smithy. The reunion is staffed by over 600 volunteers, who help keep MB's agricultural heritage alive. The Museum is open from May through Sept, and runs a 6-week hands-on program for schoolchildren in May and June, and other special events throughout the summer. ● GERALD DUECK/BARB GFELLNER

Threshing Arena in Austin

MB AGRICULTURAL MUSEUM

MANITOBA ARTS COUNCIL

MANITOBA ARTS COUNCIL (MAC) was established in 1965 to promote development of the arts in the province. MAC is an agency funded through Manitoba Culture, Heritage, and Tourism but operates at arm's length from govt. A 15-member board develops arts policy and presents awards to organizations and individuals working in arts education, literary arts, performing arts, visual arts, Aboriginal arts, and arts development. In 2006 MAC distributed $5,898,760 to 47 different arts organizations and $1,009,452 to 303 individual applicants. Eligibility for MAC funding is based on artistic merit. A peer assessment process is applied to most grants. A multidisciplinary advisory panel, made up of representatives elected by the artistic community, was established in 2002 to assist the board. MAC also employs a small administrative staff as well as program consultants from various artistic disciplines. ● CATHARINA DE BAKKER

MANITOBA CHAMBER ORCHESTRA

MANITOBA CHAMBER ORCHESTRA was founded in 1972 by conductor Ruben Gurevich. Its core of 22 musicians is drawn mainly from the **WINNIPEG SYMPHONY ORCHESTRA**. Additional musicians are added as required. From a debut season of 3 concerts, the MCO now presents 8 concerts at its home base in **WINNIPEG**. Venues have included the **FORT GARRY HOTEL**, Young Street United Church, and Westminster United Church. Over half the music performed by the MCO was composed in the 20th century. The MCO has premiered over 60 new Cdn works for chamber orchestra in recent years. Half of those have been works by MB composers. These include Glenn Buhr, Jim Hiscott and Arthur Polson (concert master of the MCO 1972-87) In addition to numerous MB performances, the MCO has performed in a number of Cdn provinces, at events such as the Guelph Spring Festival and the Calgary Olympics. Through the years, guest artists have included Maureen Forester, James Campbell, Ofra Harnoy, Liona Boyd and Anton Kuerti. Since 1984, the MCO has been a featured performer on CBC II FM, reaching audiences estimated at 3.5 million. ● KAREN OMELAN/SANDY CUSHON

MANITOBA CHAMBERS OF COMMERCE

MANITOBA CHAMBERS OF COMMERCE is MB's largest business lobby group, representing more than 10,000 businesses and 74 communities in the province. The MCC was founded in 1930 to act as the umbrella organization for a small group of autonomous chambers of commerce in communities such as **WINNIPEG**, **BRANDON**, **DAUPHIN**, and **PORTAGE LA PRAIRIE**. The MCC's mandate is to serve as the voice of all MB businesses, big or small, privately or publicly owned, urban or rural-based. Its abilities to be apolitical and to reflect the composition of the province's business community are 2 key aspects of the organization. Among the issues the chamber has addressed over the years are tax, health, and education reforms; infrastructure renewal; labour-related issues, such as provincial minimum wage levels; and enhanced training and employment opportunities for **FIRST PEOPLES**. ● MURRAY MCNEILL

MANITOBA CHILDREN'S MUSEUM

MANITOBA CHILDREN'S MUSEUM opened in 1986 in a renovated warehouse in the Exchange District in **WINNIPEG**. The mandate was to provide a hands-on museum for children aged 2 to 13. In its first year, the museum had over 65,000 visitors, and 500 families became members. In 1988, a second phase opened to the public, doubling the gallery space. However, staff were crammed into an open loft area, and there was no room to grow. So, in 1994, after a $4-million capital campaign, the museum opened in a new, permanent location at **THE FORKS** in an old train-repair facility abandoned when the **CNR** moved its locomotive repairs to other Winnipeg rail yards.

The children's museum has 6 hands-on galleries. The Tree and Me Gallery consists of a 4 m-tall model oak tree and a convincingly realistic underwater beaver dam. The TV Gallery is a real TV studio with video equipment, including cameras and computers. The Wonderworks Gallery demonstrates community infrastructure such as roads, hydro, and water and waste management. For many kids, the highlight of the museum is the 1952 diesel train engine and the 1910 Pullman passenger coach. The bright yellow vintage Volkswagen Beetle is another popular feature, enough so that it has to be re-upholstered every few years.

On top of the hands-on galleries, the museum also houses the original **EATON'S** Santa's Village, which is open from mid-Nov until Jan each year. The "village" illustrates numerous fairy tales with dozens of intricate moving figures in glass display cases. The rest of the year, the area is open as the "Once upon a Time Gallery," and hosts storytelling events for children. The museum offers various drop-in activities on weekends, during school breaks, and during the week for preschool kids. The institution also hosts birthday parties and corporate functions, and a retail store operates within the facility. ● MAURICE MIERAU

MANITOBA CLUB

MANITOBA CLUB has been MB's most exclusive private club since it was founded in July 1874. The Manitoba Club's impressive guest list has included the likes of Mark Twain, the Prince of Wales, and the crown princes of Monaco, Jordan, and Iran. In 2004, the club had 920 members. Its first meetings were held in the old Red River Hall near Main St and McDermot in **WINNIPEG**'s Exchange District. After a fire destroyed the premises mere months later, the club rented a nearby house until 1881, when it moved to a building on Winnipeg's Garry St. In 1902, the club bought land that was once part of **UPPER FORT GARRY** at Broadway and Fort St, and the gov gen, Earl Grey, officially opened the present club there in 1905. The 4-storey, 0.6 ha (60,000-ft^2) club boasts a classic design, original works of art, and antique snooker tables. Once known for its whisky, the club now boasts one of the largest wine lists in western Canada, featuring more than 400 different labels. The club's original purpose was to provide a private refuge for community and business leaders. Once a club for men only, women have been allowed as full members since 1991. Prospective members must be nominated by a current member, with another seconding the referral. Privileges of membership include the use of the restaurant, billiards room, fitness centre, and library. ● JILL SEXSMITH

MANITOBA COLLEGE

MANITOBA COLLEGE. *See* **UNIVERSITY OF WINNIPEG**

MANITOBA ESCARPMENT

MANITOBA ESCARPMENT. This 675 km-long sequence of hills, "mountains," and rock outcrops may be the most distinctive geological feature in MB. It is delineated by the NE edge of 5 uplands: the Pasquia Hills in E central SK and the Porcupine Hills, Duck Mountain, **RIDING MOUNTAIN**, and Pembina Mountain in MB. The Pembina Mountain segment of the escarpment extends into ND as the Pembina Escarpment. The relative relief ranges from a maximum relief of about 425 m in the Duck Mountain segment to about 90 m along the steep scarp face of the Pembina Escarpment. The average relief varies, generally lying between 200 and 350 m. Clearly, the uplands are not mountains; when French fur trader **LA VÉRENDRYE** referred to "mountains" during his explorations along the **ASSINIBOINE RIVER** in 1738, he was probably referring to Pembina Mountain.

The rock sequences that can be observed along the escarpment were deposited in a warm, perhaps 20°C, shallow epicontinental sea (the Western Interior Seaway) that extended from the Mackenzie delta region in the YT/NT area to the Gulf of Mexico during the mid-to-late Cretaceous period (between 112 and 65 mya). The 600 m-thick deposits in MB are believed to represent 2 separate marine incursions (transgression/regressions), the Greenhorn and Niobrara seas. The rocks, predominantly marine shale, interbedded with the occasional sandstone and limestone

M

Riding Mountain segment of the Manitoba Escarpment looking east

layer and over 50 bentonitic layers, are divided into 7 stratigraphic formations or rock layers: the Swan River, Ashville, Favel, Mordon, Shale, Niobrara, Pierre, and Boissevain formations.

Bentonite, cream-to-yellowish-coloured clay layers formed by the alteration of volcanic ash by seawater, are common in the Mordon, Shale, Niobrara, and Pierre formations. The volcanic ash probably came from the ID/MT/southern AB region during periods of intense volcanic activity and settled in the shallow Western Interior Seaway. Bentonite is used in industry for drilling, pelletizing, metal casting, water absorption, grout, and sealing. It was mined in the **Morden/Miami** area in the 1930s.

The Cretaceous deposits of western MB include minute shells (foraminifera), mollusks, and macrovertebrate fossils such as fish bones, scales, and teeth. Mesosaurs and a recently discovered plesiosaur fossils (both large marine reptiles currently displayed at the **Canadian Fossil Discovery Centre** in **Morden**.

The modern configuration of the MB Escarpment is due to pre-glacial fluvial activity, the glaciations of the great Ice Age, and more recent fluvial erosion and lake shoreline development. During the late Tertiary Period (24-4 mya), springs emanating from the Cretaceous-age sandstones of the Dakota group exposed in northwest MN are believed to be the origin of a N-flowing river (the ancestral **Red River**). The river undercut and laterally eroded into the Cretaceous shales of the ancient seabed. The relatively soft cretaceous shale formations were preserved as a western-migrating escarpment during this process because the uppermost rock layer or member of the Pierre Formation, named the Odanah Shales, contains silica, which is more resistant than fluvial erosion than the underlying softer shales. Consequently, these hard shales act as a protective rock cap, and have maintained a relatively steep escarpment face.

While spring sapping and fluvial activity may have initiated escarpment formation, it was the continental glaciers of the ice ages (the Pleistocene Epoch, 2 million years ago to about 8000 BC) that scoured back the face of the escarpment toward the West. Lobes of the advancing glacier flowed up the late Tertiary river valleys (re-entrants), which traversed the escarpment widening the valleys and forming the segmented nature of the modern MB Escarpment. Today, the Assiniboine, Valley, Swan, and Red Deer rivers occupy these re-entrant valleys. When the glaciers began melting around 11,000 BC, the adjacent lowlands filled with the meltwaters of the expanding glacial **Lake Agassiz**. Lake Agassiz persisted for about 5000 years and formed western shorelines along the MB Escarpment. The final drainage of Lake Agassiz, around 6000 BC, into **Hudson Bay** left a broad, flat lake plain: the MB Lowlands or "First Prairie Level," positioned between the MB Escarpment on the west and the Canadian Shield (190-240 km to the E). The MB Great Lakes – lakes Winnipeg, Manitoba, and Winnipegosis, and the Cedar Lake Reservoir – occupy a large portion of these lowlands. ● R. A. MCGINN

▶ *See also* **Geology**, **Glaciation**, **Geography**

MANITOBA FREE PRESS. *See* **Winnipeg Free Press**.

MANITOBA HISTORICAL SOCIETY (MHS)

was founded in 1879 as the Manitoba Historical and Scientific Society by an act of the MB legislature, the first such organization in western Canada. Its founders were Winnipeggers who sought to enrich the intellectual and cultural life of their province. They included city alderman Alexander McArthur, clergyman and professor **George Bryce**, and businessman **Charles Napier Bell**. The MHS was intended to function as a forum for advances in human knowledge, a venue for

publishing research about the province, and it was to function as a library, museum, and archives. Its first years saw the MHS become a chief pillar of the Anglophone cultural elite but, gradually, some functions were taken over by public institutions. The MHS library formed the initial Winnipeg Public **Library**, the MHS archival holdings became the basis of the Archives of Manitoba, and the MHS artifacts were merged into the **Manitoba Museum**. As a result, the MHS declined in importance after 1909. It was rejuvenated for a brief period between the world wars but did not become firmly re-established until after WWII.

Led by historians Margaret McWilliams, **W. L. Morton** and others, the MHS re-emerged as a cultural presence in the province. The society's annual awards for historical writing (named for McWilliams) were introduced in 1955, making them among Canada's oldest literary prizes. It restored and opened **Dalnavert** (the former home of MB premier and judge **Hugh John Macdonald**) as a living museum in 1974 and, a decade later, added the operation of **Ross House** (the first post office in the West) as another museum. In recent years, it has sponsored student essay contests, commemorated farms, businesses, and organizations which existed over 100 years, and published the magazine *Manitoba History*. Its web site is a comprehensive collection of historical materials about MB history. The MHS supports local historical societies and lobbies for the preservation of the province's built heritage.
● J. M. BUMSTED/GORDON GOLDSBOROUGH

MANITOBA HYDRO is the 4th largest electric power utility in the country, generating more than 5500 megawatts of power every year and about $2 billion in revenue. The development of more generating capacity, specifically for the profitable export market, makes the **Crown Corporation** the key source of potential economic development for the province.

In 2006, Manitoba Hydro started construction on the $1.2 billion, 200 MW Wuskwatim generating station and began preparing to build Conawapa, a 1250 MG, $5 billion project. That will bring to 16 the number of hydro generation stations in its portfolio. (The utility also has 2 gas-powered stations.) Virtually all of the power generated from those future sources will end up on the export market. Even without those additional dams Manitoba Hydro was already the country's largest exporter of **Hydroelectricity**, contributing $881 million in sales in 2006 to neighbouring US states and to Ontario and Saskatchewan.

As well as a source of profit for the crown corporation, Manitoba Hydro pays more than

JOEL TRENAMAN

Manitoba Hydro map showing current and proposed generating stations and power lines.

Legend

- Manitoba Hydro generating stations
- Thermal generating stations
- Diesel-supplied communities
- Converter stations
- Control structures
- Diversion channels
- Potential future generating stations
- High Voltage DC transmission lines
- 500-kilo volt transmission lines
- 230-kilo volt transmission lines
- Other transmission lines

of the project and share in the profits for the life of its operation. Manitoba Hydro is negotiating with four other First Nations to allow them to participate in the Conawapa project.

In addition to its mandate to generate hydroelectric power, Manitoba Hydro's $10 billion in assets includes the power transmission infrastructure as well. In 1999 it purchased Centra Gas Manitoba Inc for $245 million becoming the distributor of natural gas and now the one-stop energy supplier for the province. In 2002, it acquired Winnipeg Hydro for more than $250 million completely the aggregation of all of the province's energy distribution assets. The corporation also buys about 100 megawatts of wind power with plans to purchase another 1000 megawatts from third parties by 2017 and integrating it into the power grid.

As part of the Winnipeg Hydro acquisition, Manitoba Hydro agreed to build its new head office in downtown Winnipeg. A 22-storey, 650,000 ft² building on in the heart of downtown **Winnipeg** on Portage Ave is set for commissioning in 2008. It will be one of the most energy efficient buildings of its size in the world. Hydro officials believe that is in keeping with its Power Smart philosophy which encourages and rewards energy conservation with more than 2 dozen programs.

● MARTIN CASH

MANITOBA LIQUOR CONTROL COMMISSION

MANITOBA LIQUOR CONTROL COMMISSION (MLCC), formed in 1923, is a provincial **Crown Corporation** that regulates the sale of alcoholic beverages across the province. It owns and operates 46 liquor stores and licences more than 3000 hotels, lounges, dining rooms, cabarets, private clubs, beverage rooms and beer vendors in MB, plus another 174 liquor vendors that are part of general stores in small towns across the province.

As the sole supplier of beer and alcohol, the MLCC had more than $479.4 million in sales for 2005-06. Profits returned to the provincial treasury that year were $196.2 million, up $11 million from the previous year.

Like many other jurisdictions, **Prohibition** was implemented in MB from 1916 to 1923. In 1924 beer was sold through home delivery only to licensed residents under control of the new provincial Crown corporation and by 1928 licensed premises were allowed to sell beer by the glass for men only. Licences for hotel vendors to sell beer to the public for home consumption started in 1938 but it wasn't until 1956 that the sale of wine, beer, and spirits was permitted to be sold in licensed premises that allowed both men and women.

Regulations continued to be liberalized: legal age was reduced to 18 from 21 in 1970;

$250 million in annual water power rental and other fees directly into the provincial coffers. (But at the same time the corporation carries $6.5 billion in long-term debt.) It employs about 5600 people and is indirectly responsible for another 13,000 jobs. The province uses the utility's profit-generating capacity to set domestic electricity prices at the lowest rates in the country. That serves as a key element of the so-called Manitoba Advantage as promoted by the **NDP** government of **Gary Doer** in 2006.

But this success is not without its challenges. The corporation began diverting flows from the **Churchill River** into the **Nelson River** system in the mid-1970s increasing the power-producing potential of Nelson Rover by 40%. The changes in water flows flooded vast tracts of land

and altered the northern terrain so much so that the traditional way of life for thousands of First Nations people in the North was destroyed. The people from those communities had little-to-say in early hydro development. It took until the late '90s before the utility finally negotiated more than $220 million worth of settlement agreements with several northern First Nations.

Partly to make up for past mistakes Manitoba Hydro has established a more conscientious approach to community involvement in the development of additional power generation. It spent almost a decade negotiating a project development agreement with the **Nisichawayasihk Cree Nation** of Nelson House on whose territory the Wuskwatim dam will be built. The agreement with NCN gives it the right to purchase up to 30%

M

MLCC store in Fort Garry, 1957

private wine stores were licensed in 1994 and 8 of them were in operation in **WINNIPEG** 10 years later; and in 2001 beer vendors, liquor stores and beverage rooms were allowed to open for limited hours on Sundays. In 2004, the people of **STEINBACH** voted in a referendum to allow the sale of alcoholic beverages, ending 30 years of their own version of prohibition.

With 750 direct employees, the MLCC has become a sophisticated retail operator handling more than 3000 different beer, wine and spirits items from 50 different countries. In addition to selling alcoholic beverages, MLCC also is responsible for public education programs on responsible drinking – tackling subjects like underage drinking, fetal alcohol spectrum disorder and various drinking and driving awareness campaigns. ● MARTIN CASH

MANITOBA LOTTERIES CORPORATION (MLC), is the provincial **CROWN CORPORATION** that owns casinos, video lottery terminals (VLTs) and distributes and sells lottery tickets in MB. It got its name and operational mandate in 1993. Prior to that, crown corporations operated and licenced lotteries and casinos dating starting in 1970 when the MB government held its first lottery on the occasion of its centennial year.

Throughout the 1970s, occasional casinos became significant fundraising vehicles for charities and organizations and annual fixtures at events like the Red River Exhibition and the **FESTIVAL DU VOYAGEUR**. In 1984, the Manitoba Lotteries Foundation (precursor to Manitoba Lotteries Corp.) became the sole operator of charitable casinos and opened a semi-permanent casino at the Winnipeg Convention Centre, the first of its

kind in the country. In 1989, that casino moved to the 7th floor of the **FORT GARRY HOTEL** where the Crystal Casino was the country's only permanent full-time casino. It closed in 1999.

Since the late '80s MB has been at the forefront of gambling jurisdictions in the country and has become a significant source of revenue for the provincial treasury. VLTs were introduced first in rural hotels, then in **WINNIPEG** in the early '90s. The Manitoba Lotteries Foundation built 2 fully functioning casinos with table games, VLTs and full-time bingo operations – the McPhillips Street Station and Club Regent – in 1993. They were expanded in 1999 with restaurants, lounges and performance venues. Each has 100 VLTs or slot machines, 30 card tables and bingo.

MLC has avoided many of the controversies that have been associated with organized gambling, however it has not been without its own challenges. Studies have shown that through the first decade of the 21st century MB has among highest rate of problem gamblers in the country. And, in May 2000, then CEO Bill Funk and other senior executives were fired over allegations of unauthorized perks, overspending on expense accounts and the sale of decommissioned vehicles to senior executives at far less than market value.

The MLC has contributed to the establishment of two Aboriginal-owned casinos – the Aseneskak Casino in **THE PAS** which opened in 2002, and the South Beach Casino which opened in 2005 on the **BROKENHEAD FIRST NATION** just N of Winnipeg. MLC owns the VLTs in those casinos and provides technical support to the third party operators. In association with the Western Canada Lotteries Corp the MLC is the sole distributor of lottery tickets in MB and maintains a

dealer network of close to 900 sites. In 2005-06 MLC sold $182 million in lottery tickets including Sport Select sports wagering games. MLC profits flowing to the MB treasury have increased every year since its creation. The contribution to the province topped $270 million in 2005-06. The MLC has about 1800 employees. ● MARTIN CASH

MANITOBA MÉTIS FEDERATION (MMF) is a political organization representing **MÉTIS** people and the **COUNTRY-BORN** in the province. In 1967, a number of Métis attending an annual First Nations and Métis conference sponsored by the Winnipeg Community Welfare and Planning Council realized that they could only make their concerns heard if they had an independent voice. They subsequently met in private and decided to form their own organization. The Manitoba Métis Federation was founded Oct 1, 1967, and incorporated as a non-profit association later that year. Those present at the inaugural meeting – in a sense, the founders of MMF – were Reverend Adam Cuthand, Elizabeth Isbister, Ted Simard, Tom Eagle, and Angus Spence. Cuthand was appointed as the first "voluntary non-paid" president. The first non-elected board of directors was Cuthand, Joe Keeper, and Alfred Disbrowe. The successive presidents of the MMF have been Dr. Adam Cuthand (1960-70), Angus Spence (1970-73), Connie Eyolfson (1973-74), Ferdinand Guiboche (1974-75), Edward Head (1975-76), John Morrisseau (1976-81), Don McIvor (1981-84), **W. YVON DUMONT** (1984-93), Ernie Blais (1993-94), Billyjo DeLaRonde (1994-97), and David Chartrand (1997-writing). As of 2006, the MMF had 9 departments covering everything from housing to justice issues, and 9 other affiliates, such as the Louis Riel Institute and Pemmican Publications. ● FRED J. SHORE

MANITOBA MOOSE. Following the sale and 1996 relocation of the **WINNIPEG JETS**, the Minnesota Moose of the International **HOCKEY** League (IHL) moved N to become **WINNIPEG**'s new professional hockey team. The club debuted at the **WINNIPEG ARENA** during the 1996-97 season, with former Jet Randy Carlyle as head coach and general manager. The team played 5 seasons in the IHL before the league folded due to financial instability.

The Moose and 5 other teams were admitted as expansion franchises to the American Hockey League (AHL) in 2001. They also entered into an affiliation with the Vancouver Canucks of the NHL. The agreement – common for AHL franchises – stipulates that the Canucks place players with the Moose for roster development or injury replacement purposes. Former Canuck

The Manitoba Moose made their debut in the 1996-97 season.

Stan Smyl took over as coach for the next 3 seasons. Craig Heisinger became general manager in 2002.

The Moose moved into the new **MTS CENTRE** in Nov 2004. Randy Carlyle returned to guide the team to a 98-point campaign, and in the 2005 playoffs, the Moose reached the conference finals for the first time, one step away from the Calder Cup championship series. Following the season, Carlyle departed to become head coach of the NHL's Anaheim Ducks, and was replaced by Alain Vigneault for 2005-06. He became head coach of the Canucks in 2006, and another former Jet, Scott Arniel was behind the bench as of the 2006-07 season.

Notable Moose players over the years have included Alex Auld, Brett Hauer, Scott Arniel, Bill Bowler, Brian Chapman, Justin Kurtz, and Brandon Reid, Greg Pankewicz, Wade Flaherty, as well as franchise games and goals leader Jimmy Roy. True North Sports & Entertainment Ltd owns the Moose and also the MTS Centre, with Mark **CHIPMAN** acting as chairman. • JOEL TRENAMAN

MANITOBA MUSEUM. The museum is the largest heritage institution in the province, opened officially in 1970 by HM Queen Elizabeth II. Originally called the Manitoba Museum of Man and Nature, the name was changed in 1996. The museum's reputation is based on its dramatic walk-through exhibits, especially the full-size replica of the *Nonsuch*, whose namesake's 1668-69 voyage led to the founding of the **HUDSON'S BAY COMPANY** (HBC).

The HBC donated its historic collection to the Manitoba Museum in 1994, a collection valued at more than $8 million and which contains more than 10,000 artifacts that cover over 3 centuries of the company's colourful history. This donation is the largest ever to the museum, and has made the museum a world centre for North American **FUR TRADE** research. The permanent HBC exhibit includes the last 13 m **YORK BOAT** to be used; navigational tools; Inuit art; and various trade goods. An 18th-century map of Canada, showing the country carved up into HBC sales regions, says more about Cdn history than many words could. Other notable historical exhibits include "Where Are the Children?" an exhibit on the First Nations experience with residential schools that opened in 2005.

On entering the museum galleries, visitors see a life-size recreation of a 19th-century bison hunt, and a mural of an **OJIBWAY** creation story. The museum is organized in a thematic series of exhibits that correspond to MB's geography. The earth history gallery establishes a geological timeline for the area that is now MB. This gallery contains the world's largest trilobite **FOSSIL**, which was discovered near **CHURCHILL** in 1998. Biome exhibits highlight the North, with an Arctic/sub-Arctic gallery, all the way to the south, with an urban gallery that focuses on historic Winnipeg. Other galleries are devoted to the boreal forest, parkland, and grassland **ECOCLIMACTIC REGIONS**. This organization dramatizes the sweep of MB prehistory and history, covering First Nations, **MÉTIS**, European settlement, and modern economic development.

The urban and *Nonsuch* galleries are the museum's most popular exhibits. The urban gallery recreates Winnipeg in the year 1920. Visitors can explore wooden boardwalks, a vaudeville theatre, and **J. S. WOODSWORTH**'s mission to Winnipeg's poor. A lady of the night prepares herself in a railway hotel, and visitors can see a spectacular stained-glass ceiling in the movie theatre.

The planetarium, 1 of only 5 major ones in Canada, opened in 1968 and became part of the museum in 1972. It features 154 projectors that together create a realistic night sky with more than 9000 stars and planets, viewable from any point on Earth and from any time in the past or future. New technology has brought motion and computer animation to the planetarium, so that current events and recent astronomical discoveries can be part of programs.

The science gallery contains more than 100 exhibits that demonstrate scientific principles. For example, at one exhibit, visitors can build and race boats; the Wave Machine demonstrates pulley and lever systems; and the Tone Memory exhibit tests visitors' ability to hear and recall pitch accurately.

Not all the museum's extensive collection can be displayed at any given time. The heritage collections of the Manitoba Museum include some 1.8 million archaeological artifacts, some dating from 10,000 BC. There is a collection of some 62,000 items relating to social history in the province. In addition, the museum has some 200,000 natural history specimens collected in MB, including 40,000 plant specimens, 9000 geological lots, and thousands of mammal, bird, invertebrate, fish, and amphibian specimens. The museum maintains a professional staff of curators, conservators, and collection managers to ensure proper stewardship of all these materials. The museum also has a library/archives which houses more than 20,000 books. The library is open to the public by appointment.

The Manitoba Museum displays many aspects of the province's past.

More than 100,000 students and their teachers visit the museum each year. The museum conducts group tours, interpretive programs, day camps, even sleepovers and a spring robot competition. The museum depends primarily on the province for funding, but more than 15% of its revenue, the 2nd-largest source, comes from admission fees. The Manitoba Museum is the province's biggest paid tourist attraction. ● MAURICE MIERAU

MANITOBA NATURALISTS SOCIETY (MNS) was founded in 1920 as the Natural History Society (NHS) of Manitoba. Its precursor, the Historical and Scientific Society of Manitoba, was incorporated by provincial act in 1879 and lasted until 1906, publishing a number of papers on the history, ethnology and natural history of MB. It was revived in 1928 as a mainly historical society. The Manitoba Audubon Society formed in 1915 and existed as an amateur birding group until it voted to become part of a new NHS in 1920. Well-known members included Gordon Bell, David Alexander Stewart, V.H. Jackson, R.C. Wallace and Claude William Gray. The NHS compiled the first bird migration data for the province, published an early check-list of MB plants, helped excavate one of the first plesiosaurs at **TREHERNE** and initiated an early (1927-1940) mosquito control program in and around Winnipeg. In 1923, the NHS erected a clubhouse and collecting station at Victoria Beach that still exists, now a cabin for MNS members' use. The NHS was a strong and early advocate for a permanent public museum, pressuring the province to set aside space in the new Winnipeg Auditorium for such a museum. It operated the early museum and provided many of the collections, exhibits, programs as well as honorary curators for the collections. These functions continued until the present **MANITOBA MUSEUM** was formed. In the 2000s, the MNS remains closely associated with the museum.

Membership remained low, at less than 250, until the 1960s when the NHS started to take public positions on conservation and environmental issues. A dynamic president, Lorne Wallace, and others worked hard in the early 1970s to increase the NHS's membership and public voice for the environment. Along with greatly increased membership came a 1971 name change to the Manitoba Naturalists Society (MNS) mainly to distinguish it from the **MANITOBA HISTORICAL SOCIETY**. The MNS now holds bi-monthly natural history lectures and workshops in the winter months and a variety of field trips and outdoor workshops in the summer. It has also contributed its member's expertise

to a wide variety of environmental issues and projects including the Churchill River Diversion, nature trails in Little Mountain Park and the creation of the Clean Environment Committee. The MB Avian Research Committee recently (2003) completed and published the mammoth *Birds of Manitoba* book. The MNS and Zoological Society of Manitoba published a small magazine of natural history articles called first *Zoolog* and then *Manitoba Nature* for many years. In 1973, the MNS took over a cabin on Mantario Lake, in the Back Country Zone of Whiteshell Provincial Park. The Mantario Committee runs an extensive program of summer 5-day wilderness workshops, canoe and hiking trips and winter ski and snowshoe trips out of the cabin and is also involved in the maintenance of the Mantario Trail wilderness hiking route. ● KAREN JOHNSON

MANITOBA OPERA ASSOCIATION was founded in 1969 by A. Kerr Twaddle and 13 others to produce grand opera. It was incorporated in 1970, and one of its first initiatives was to sponsor a **WINNIPEG** performance of the Canadian Opera Company's touring production of *Orpheus in the Underworld*. The Manitoba Opera presented its first self-production, a concert version of Giuseppe Verdi's *Il Travatore*, in 1972. The 2nd production was a staging of *Madama Butterfly* in 1973, directed by Irving Guttman and conducted by Peiro Gamba. The association was offering 3 operas a year by 1975. Productions have included the most popular works of Verdi, Puccini, Mozart, and Donizetti. The opera's productions take place at the Centennial Concert Hall in Winnipeg, and have featured local talents such as Tracy Dahl, Phillip Ens, and Heidi Klassen. Directors and conductors have included Richard Bradshaw, Sonja Frisell, and Irving Guttman. The association operates the Manitoba Opera Chorus, which was directed by Tadeusz Biernacki in 2006. The chorus is supported by the Winnipeg Symphony Orchestra. The opera also works closely with the Manitoba Theatre Centre and the Royal Winnipeg Ballet. The company founded the Orpheus Recital in 1994, which brings some of the world's greatest singers to Winnipeg every year. Since 2002, Manitoba Opera has produced 2 full productions and a concert evening each year. In 2006, Larry Desrochers was the general director and CEO; Tyrone Patterson was the music advisor and principal conductor. The first production of the 2006-07 season was of Johann Strauss's *Die Fledermaus*. ● AMANDA STEPHENS

MANITOBA PRINTMAKERS' ASSOCIATION was formed in the early months of 1984 by a group of **WINNIPEG** printmakers. The group became

an incorporated non-profit corporation in 1985 and moved into a studio space at 114 Market St, Winnipeg, in 1989. The space allowed printmakers from across MB to access machinery and tools to produce any kind of print-based work including intaglio, lithography, and silkscreen. They began to offer classes, and rented private studios. After facing funding difficulties, MPA closed in March 1997. MPA regained its footing in 1998 and reopened. The centre, also now known as Martha Street Studios, relocated to 11 Martha St, where it resided as of 2006. The space now includes a gallery, a residency program, and a retail outlet, where artists can sell their work. ● STACEY ABRAMSON

MANITOBA PROVINCIAL POLICE. The MPP, like the modern Sûreté du Québec and Ontario Provincial Police, was a provincial law enforcement agency responsible for maintaining order in early MB. Lt gov Sir **ADAMS GEORGE ARCHIBALD** founded the MPP's forerunner, the Mounted Constabulary Force, in 1871, with Capt Frank Villiers of the 2nd Quebec Rifles – one of Col Garnet Wolseley's subordinates – filling the role of chief constable. Villiers's force of 24 assumed duties such as supervising the new provincial prison, and patrolling the border when a Fenian raid threatened in late 1871.

Villiers was dismissed after one year, and his deputy and fellow officer, Louis de Plainval, took over the force. Drunken riots were commonplace in early Winnipeg, and the force soon found itself stretched to the limit. De Plainval requested additional funding from the MB govt for more men, uniforms, and supplies, but was rejected, requiring him to decrease his squad to 16. Powerless, de Plainval resigned in 1873 when his officers' horses were taken away. However, De Plainval petitioned PM Sir John A. Macdonald to provide the NWTs with a constabulary similar to the MPP, and so can be partially credited for founding the **NWMP** and its modern successor, the RCMP. By 1874, the MPP consisted of only one man, Richard Powers, due in part to the establishment of the Winnipeg Police Department under **JOHN INGRAM**. Powers was the first MPP member killed on duty while returning a captured fugitive by boat on the **RED RIVER**. The prisoner tried to flee and capsized the boat, drowning both men. Powers was not replaced, and the police service dissolved.

The force re-established itself during the MB-ON boundary dispute of the 1880s. Both provinces claimed Rat Portage (now Kenora, ON), through which the border ran, and stationed a small detachment there. Trouble arose when an MPP man arrested an ON constable for violating

Rare photo of Manitoba Provincial Police detachment

MB's liquor laws; ON authorities retaliated by arresting the entire MB detachment and burning down the MPP jail. Premier **John Norquay** then led an MPP force to Rat Portage, freed his men, and arrested the Ontario Provincial Police. Similar incidents were frequent until ON was finally awarded control of the area.

During the **Winnipeg General Strike**, the city's police force – whose members were largely sympathetic to the strikers – was fired, and the NWMP was called in to control the increasingly volatile crowds. The fear of further police strikes encouraged the provincial govt to strengthen the MPP in 1920. The force grew to 100 men, many of whom were WWI veterans. Detachments were set up in MB's main towns to handle serious crimes. During **Prohibition**, the MPP was largely responsible for chasing rumrunners and bootleggers. After a well-publicized manhunt in 1927, the MPP also arrested serial killer **Earle Nelson**. Financial constraints in the **Great Depression** led to the dismantling of the MPP in 1932, since which time the province has contracted with the RCMP for rural policing services. ● MICHELLE DOBROVOLNY
▶ *See also* **Policing, North-West Mounted Police**.

MANITOBA PROVINCIAL RIFLE ASSOCIA-TION,

formed in 1872, is one of the province's oldest associations. It was formed at a time when **Winnipeg** was a village of 250 people with few stores and no schools, **Railway**, telegraph, or banks. However, this was also a time of discontent and strained relations between European settlers and both the **Métis** and Aboriginal population, and when there was real fear of Fenian invasion. Thus, a rifle association was an important step in national and local defence. An elected officer of the association was **Donald Alexander Smith**, later to become Lord Strathcona. He remained a patron of the association for 40 years.

Annual rifle competitions began Sept 25, 1873. The first trophy was a sterling-silver cup presented by the **HBC**, which is competed for to this day, and is one of the many trophies presented to the association from various companies and individuals. The association's first firing ranges were in St. Boniface, just N of where the cathedral now stands. Over the years, the ranges were relocated – in 1878, to Point Douglas, N of the **CPR** lines; in 1883, to **Stony Mountain**; in 1885, to West Kildonan, N of the present bus barns on Main St in Winnipeg; in 1905, to Sturgeon Creek; and in 1911, to the current St. Charles Rifle Range, just W of Winnipeg. The St. Charles range is now owned by the Air Force's **17 Wing**. In the early days of the association's competitions, it was customary to have a grand opening ceremony. Often, a distinguished lady fired the first shot from a rifle fixed in a rest. In 1877, when the gov gen and his wife, the Countess of Dufferin, attended the competitions, she fired the opening shot.

Many skilled marksmen excelled at competitions over the years. MB teams won many team and individual matches at national championships and numerous individuals competed on the Cdn Bisley team that goes to the annual Commonwealth competitions. In 1909 alone, A. M. Blackburn won the Empire Service Rifle Competition, the Prince of Wales Competition, the Wingrove Trophy, the Birmingham Silver Cup, Martin's Rapid-Fire Cup, and the London Times Cup, all in the UK. The MPRA now mostly consists of civilian members who strive to continue the tradition of the encouragement of safe firearms handling and rifle shooting. ● DORAN SEWELL

MANITOBA PUBLIC INSURANCE CORPOR-ATION

(MPIC or MPI) is the province's publicly owned auto insurance company. It has provided Autopac, a compulsory basic vehicle insurance, to all motorists in MB since 1971 when it was introduced by the **NDP** govt of **Ed Schreyer**. In the late 1960s, many Manitobans believed private insurance companies had failed to provide a reasonable insurance system. Rates were said to be high and unpredictable. Coverage was often inadequate and, for some, almost impossible to obtain at any price. The idea of a public auto insurance monopoly was part of the NDP's platform in the 1969 provincial election. It was politically contentious and drew much opposition. Some critics denounced it as an extreme left-wing initiative. Nonetheless, the NDP govt established MPI, using SK's public insurance as its model.

The new company opened in Nov 1971 with 108 employees and one location in downtown **Winnipeg**. In 2006, it employed about 1700 at 29 sites across the province. In financial year 2004-05, it had an average of 850,000 policies in force, wrote $780 million in premiums, and paid annual costs amounting to $617 million on 253,000 claims. MPI operates MB's universal auto insurance plan as a monopoly and sells optional auto insurance in competition with private insurers. Both types of insurance are distributed through a network of over 300 insurance brokers across the province. Since 1994, all Manitobans injured in collisions anywhere in Canada or the US have been compensated through a no-fault injury protection plan.

Insurance agents protest public insurance legislation, 1970.

MPI sets rates based on the vehicle being driven, where the driver lives, how the vehicle is used and the client's driving record. It does not discriminate based on age, sex, marital status, or any other factor. Customers can acquire optional coverage to lower their deductibles, increase 3rd-party liability, and purchase extra insurance for rental or high-value vehicles. It also operates a Special Risk Extension Insurance business that supports the commercial trucking industry in MB.

In 2004, the govt merged provincial services for driver and vehicle licensing with public auto insurance operations, and MPI now tests and licenses all classes of drivers on behalf of the govt. It also oversees vehicle registration and

M

inspection. Through the Driver Improvement and Control program, it monitors the driving performance of Manitobans to ensure they do not put other drivers at risk. Claims services are available through 18 claim centres in 13 communities across MB. Customers access Driver and Vehicle Licensing services through MPI outlets or independent agents. MPI also works with other road safety partners to instil a safety consciousness in MB. It invests more than $2 million annually in educational programs such as high school driver education. Basic Autopac insurance for automobiles includes the Personal Injury Protection Plan (PIPP). PIPP is based on the premise that, no matter who is at fault, every Manitoban injured in a vehicle collision should receive injury benefits. The program replaced a tort-based court system. In 2004, the public insurer became the first in the North American insurance industry to offer financial incentives aimed at encouraging motorists to purchase anti-theft immobilizers.

MPI contributes to related community programs and invests substantially in bonds and debentures, including many issued by municipalities, school divisions, and health-care jurisdictions. In 2007, it had about $1 billion invested in such financial instruments, out of total assets of about $2.2 billion. ● GPP

MANITOBA SANATORIUM, or the "San" as it was commonly known, was a rest hospital for **TUBERCULOSIS** patients, one of several MB sanatoria in operation in the first half of the 20th century when TB was one of the most dreaded and deadliest of illnesses. Opened in May 1910, the Manitoba Sanatorium was the first such facility in western Canada. Funds were raised for the original 65-bed hospital by the Manitoba Tuberculosis Society and the Manitoba Sanatorium Board, an agency established in 1904 as part of govt efforts to control the spread of the disease. With the first successful treatments, additional wards were soon added, as well as a training school for nurses, and the sanatorium's capacity quadrupled within 15 years of its opening.

The sanatorium was the centre of TB treatment in the province. Located on Pelican Lake near **NINETTE**, it offered a clean environment, fresh air, and good nutrition to TB patients while keeping them isolated from the general public and preventing the spread of the contagious disease. Until antibiotics became available in the 1940s, the "rest cure" remained the only way to treat TB, requiring that patients stay confined to a bed or reclining chair over a convalescence period that often lasted 3-5 years.

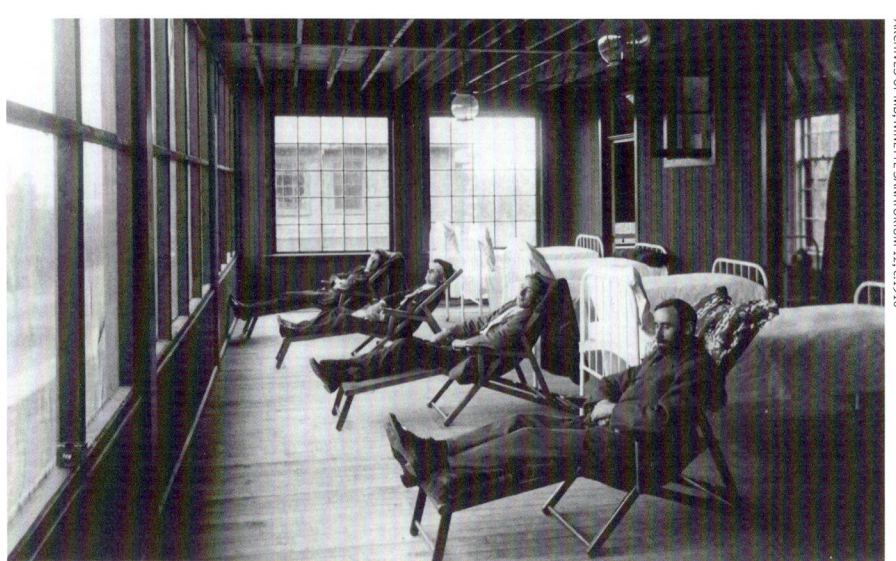

ARCHIVES OF MB, NINETTE SANATORIUM 12, c.1910

Patients "taking the cure" in the men's sleeping pavilion at Ninette Sanatorium, 1910.

The sanatorium's medical superintendent David Alexander Stewart was a leading figure in the fight to eradicate the disease, not only in MB, but across the country. Stewart, who had himself suffered from the disease, stressed prevention through improved living standards as the best means to eliminate the disease, and patients at the sanatorium were required to take classes in hygiene and nutrition. In addition to commissioning numerous studies, Stewart implemented innovative programs through the sanatorium. In 1926, the sanatorium began operating mobile x-ray clinics to test people throughout MB for TB in what was one of the first preventative health programs in Canada. Stewart also persuaded the govt to subsidize the cost of treatment, which was prohibitive to many of MB's TB patients who most often came from the poorest stratum of society.

By the 1960s, improved drugs meant most patients could be treated at home, and MB's sanatoria were closed or converted to other uses. The Manitoba Sanatorium was the last to close its doors in 1972. It was turned into a training centre for mentally handicapped adults, which operated until 2000. ● MD

MANITOBA SCHOOLS QUESTION began as a provincial debate about the funding of public schools in the 1880s, and quickly escalated into a divisive national issue. In 1870, MB entered Confederation with a confessional school system similar to QC's, in which **ROMAN CATHOLICS** and **PROTESTANTS** each had their own autonomous schools and administered them independently of the other. This school system reflected the ethnic and religious equality in the new province but, within a few years, this equilibrium was upset by large-scale Anglo-Protestant **IMMIGRATION** from ON. Complaints were soon voiced concerning the divided nature of the school system and the influence of the Catholic Church in educational matters. In 1888, the provincial **LIBERAL** govt, led by **THOMAS GREENWAY**, introduced amendments to the *School Act* that centralized school administration. The Liberals won a large majority in the election held a short while later, and there were hints that more radical reform would follow. The situation became more volatile in Aug 1889, when D'Alton McCarthy, a Conservative MP from ON, visited MB on a speaking tour. In a passionate speech in **PORTAGE LA PRAIRIE**, McCarthy linked the language and school issues.

Amidst the heightened agitation that followed, the MB govt introduced 2 bills on Feb 12, 1890, that drastically transformed the province's educational system. One bill established a Department of Education headed by a cabinet minister, while the other abolished confessional schools and replaced them with a system of non-sectarian public schools. On Mar 18, another bill, aimed at abolishing the official use of French in the province, was introduced. Catholic Archbishop **ALEXANDRE-ANTONIN TACHÉ** of St. Boniface responded by asking the lt gov of MB to reserve assent to the amendments to the *School Act*. When this request was denied, Taché petitioned the federal govt to disallow the legislation on the grounds that it was unconstitutional. In view of the political ramifications of this matter, the House of Commons unanimously adopted a resolution that the govt seek advice and direction from the courts to avoid making an unconstitutional decision. In the meantime, John K. Barrett, a Catholic ratepayer in **WINNIPEG**, challenged a city by-law compelling him to pay taxes to support the public schools established by the 1890 amendments. The application was dismissed and an appeal was taken before the MB Court of Queen's Bench, where the original decision was upheld. For his part, Taché had the Catholic bishops of Canada petition the gov gen in council, but he was advised that the govt would seek a judicial solution rather than disallow the act.

Since disallowance was an impossible tactic for the govt, Edward Brophy, Barrett's lawyer, appealed to the Supreme Court of Canada, which reversed the Court of Queen's Bench decision. The federal govt, however, believed that the definitive decision should come from the highest court in the Empire, and appealed to the Judicial Committee of the UK's Privy Council (JCPC; until the 1931 *Statute of Westminster*, Canada was legally dependent on the UK). In 1892, that body ruled in favour of the city of Winnipeg and dismissed the appeal. Since the legal challenges had proved prejudicial to Catholic interests, in Sept 1892, Taché brought the grievances of the Catholic minority of MB before the gov gen in council and asked for redress. As with disallowance, redress in the form of remedial legislation would have had serious political ramifications; the govt indicated that it would be bound by the decision of the federal Supreme Court, and the matter was sent to that body. In Feb 1894, the Supreme Court of Canada ruled against the appeal of MB Catholics and the use of remedial legislation. On behalf of the province's Catholics, John Ewart appealed the Brophy case, as it came to be known, to the Privy Council, which ruled in Jan 1895 that the rights of the Catholic minority had been prejudicially affected and that parliament had the right to issue remedial legislation.

The Cdn cabinet met to discuss remedial legislation and, in March 1895, a report of a committee of the privy council recommended that a remedial order be issued. For its part, the govt of MB indicated that it would not obey a remedial order and, consequently, in Feb 1896, a remedial bill was introduced in parliament. Internal problems within the federal Conservative Party, as well as the divisive nature of the legislation, made it impossible to pass the bill before parliament was dissolved. In the subsequent federal election held in Jun, the Liberals under Wilfrid Laurier, campaigning on a policy of "No Coercion," defeated the Conservatives. Negotiations between the federal and MB govts resulted in the Laurier-Greenway Compromise in Nov 1896. This accord permitted religious and bilingual instruction in schools under limited conditions. Archbishop Adélard Langevin of St. Boniface, and much of the rest of the Catholic hierarchy,

regarded the compromise as a gross betrayal of the rights of the Catholic minority, and a measure that fell short of the redress that could have been obtained through remedial legislation. The Catholic clergy openly denounced Laurier and the Liberals, and the PM was forced to appeal to the Vatican to stop these attacks.

Though it started as a provincial matter, the MB Schools Question became a broader issue, echoing the controversy both of **Louis Riel's** execution and of QC's *Jesuit Estates Act* (1888). As the issue evolved in MB, the Legislative Assembly of what was then the NWT also passed amendments limiting the linguistic and educational privileges of French-speaking Catholics. MB's school legislation exacerbated federal/provincial relations as well as the relationship between church and state. It fostered racial and religious prejudices; divided political parties; and heightened partisan politics.

The Catholic community did not escape this division and turmoil. Anglophone **Irish** Catholics in Winnipeg desired a compromise measure and were opposed to the intransigent stance that archbishops Taché and Langevin took. This division precluded a challenge to the legislation abolishing the official use of the French language. In addition, QC nationalists and Francophones in MB entertained different objectives and proposed different policies. In a socio-cultural and historical perspective, the MB Schools Question is a reflection of a debate over the nature of the Cdn identity and the extent of bilingualism and biculturalism in Canada in an age before multiculturalism. ● RAYMOND HUEL

▸ *See also* **French Language Crisis**.

MANITOBA SOCIETY OF ARTISTS.

Founded in 1902, the MSA's self-expressed mandate was "to rectify the lack of recognition in Manitoba for the visual arts." Presidents include artists Hay Stead, Walter Phillips, Alexander Musgrove, Eric Bergman, Georgie Wilcox, **Leo Mol**, Jan Boning, Les Dewar and Gerald Folkerts. From the outset, the MSA was vocal, calling for the founding of a civic art gallery and school of art. Presenting exhibitions since 1903, it maintained activities throughout the **Great Depression** and both world wars. Over the decades the MSA and the **Winnipeg Art Gallery** (WAG) maintained close affiliations. The MSA lobbied for the WAG when finances caused its closure in 1926, and became a sustaining member in 1933 when the WAG moved to the civic auditorium. This relationship fractured in 1975 when the WAG announced it would no longer host MSA exhibitions. The founding of Canadian Artists' Representation (CAR), new arts funding parameters, and new

forms of visual expression, abstraction and new technologies, caused many MSA members to seek to retain more conservative outlooks. Times of survival have been punctuated with those of strong leadership, each witnessing re-evaluations of purpose and place in contemporary art. The MSA continues to present annual juried exhibitions. Publications include *The Manitoba Society of Artists: Artists' Directory 1902-2003*; and Sarah Yates' 1992 publication: *The Manitoba Society of Artists: A History*. ● PATRICIA BOVEY

MANITOBA SPORTS HALL OF FAME AND MUSEUM,

established Feb 24, 1980, is located on the 5th floor of the Bay (**HBC**) store on Portage Ave in downtown **Winnipeg**. The hall and museum's goal is to showcase Manitobans who have made significant achievements in, and efforts to promote and develop, sports in MB. Inductees to the Hall of Fame must have been born in MB, or have been living in MB when that they made a significant contribution to sports in the province. They may have distinguished themselves as athletes, trainers, or founders in individual sports as diverse as archery, shooting, gymnastics, and cycling, and in team sports such as baseball, curling, football, and hockey. The MB Sports Federation started the museum, which is managed by a board of volunteers. Exhibits at the museum deal with a wide range of MB sports themes, such as athletics, softball, baseball, football, curling, hockey, and golf. The 7000 people who visit the museum each year can also see an extensive video, photo, and print sports archive.

The Manitoba Sports Hall of Fame honours sports achievements.

Among the museum's inductees are **Susan Auch**, **Bobby Clarke**, **Bobby Hull**, **Russ Ford**, the **Connie Laliberte** rink, **Vince Leah**, **Leo Lewis**, **Bill Mosienko**, **Terry Sawchuk**, and other pivotal professional, junior, and amateur sports players and teams. ● REBECCA KUROPATWA

MANITOBA STAMPEDE AND EXHIBITION

is the largest professional Cdn rodeo E of AB. It takes place for 4 days in every July in **Morris**. Two local farmers, Bruce McKenzie and Charlie Covernton, and businessman Lyman Sadler founded it in 1963. There had been an agricultural fair in Morris since 1895, but the founders of the modern event wanted to create more of an attraction. Attendance at the stampede peaked within the first decade, when it sometimes attracted over 80,000 people during a 5-day run. At that time the stampede received a lot of media attention and there were no other rodeo events in the region. The marquee events are the rodeo itself, especially the bull ride, and the chuckwagon and chariot racing. Children enjoy watching the "mutton-busting," where kids ride sheep. There are horse shows and fair events that take place outside the grandstand area.

In addition, there is an outdoor stage with all-day entertainment from 8 a.m. to the wee hours. The Manitoba Stampede has evolved into more of a family event, with a petting zoo and a building for face painting, balloon art, and a bubble man. There is also a midway. The stampede is the only rodeo in MB that uses exclusively professional cowboys. It always begins on the Thursday after the end of the Calgary Stampede, so that stock and cowboys, timers, judges, and rodeo clowns can come to MB from AB. The cowboys who compete come from all over Canada, the US, New Zealand, and Australia. Fans who attend are mostly from Winnipeg, but also from the US, and neighbouring provinces. ● MAURICE MIERAU

MANITOBA SUNFLOWER FESTIVAL has been held each year at the end of July in **Altona** since 1964. This southern MB festival offers visitors a free pancake breakfast, parade, midway, entertainment for all ages, carnival, petting zoo, street dancing, baseball tournaments, motorcross racing, as well as a quilt, fashion, and horse show. There is also the Sunflower Queen Contest, a beauty pageant, each year at the festival. Traditional Mennonite food is served at the festival, including kielke – egg noodles – and vareniki – an dumpling similar to perogies. The festival's entertainment includes musical groups from around the province. ● RK

MANITOBA THEATRE CENTRE (MTC). The MTC was born in **Winnipeg** in 1958 from a merger of the amateur Winnipeg Theatre Group and Theatre 77, a semi-professional company founded by **Thomas Hendry** and **John Hirsch**. MTC was the first professional regional **Theatre** in Canada, and it would prove to be the model for other regional theatres across the country. Hendry and Hirsch intended to create a theatre company that would not only produce plays but would also act as the centre of dramatic activity for the community and as the regional theatre for MB, an idea they derived from the work of director Roget Planchon in Villeurbanne, France. Hendry was the company's first general manager, while Hirsch became its first artistic director 1958-66.

MTC's initial mandate consisted of 3 main goals: to develop an annual attendance of 150,000 patrons; to create touring productions that would travel throughout MB and beyond; and to create an educational component of their organization that would engender a taste for theatre in children and students. In 1960, MTC reached its 2nd and 3rd goals by launching both a theatre school and its inaugural provincial tour. At that time, it also opened a 2nd stage, the Studio Theatre, and received its first Canada Council for the Arts grant. That federal granting body would later use MTC as an example for other theatres. All told, MTC's early years were a period of great aspiration and achievement. Hirsch worked zealously to sell the MTC to international actors and directors, leading to several notable productions. For a time, MTC was known informally as "Stratford West" because of the many actors from ON's Stratford Festival of Canada who wintered here. Hendry departed in 1963, and Hirsch followed in 1966, to be replaced by Edward Gilbert.

In 1968, MTC entered a period of transition after losing its home in the Dominion Theatre, demolished to make way for the Richardson Building. This meant MTC was forced to mount productions in the far larger and costlier Centennial Concert Hall. The change in venue not only made it harder to meet ticket-sale quotas; it also made it impossible for Gilbert to stage the sorts of plays he wanted to. He left in frustration after only one season in the Centennial, as did his successor, Kurt Reis (1970-71). But despite difficulties with its main-stage productions, MTC opened a new 2nd stage, the MTC Warehouse on Rupert Ave, in 1969. The MTC Mainstage, at its present home on Market St, was opened the following year, but this new space did not produce a boost in attendance. Gilbert was rehired in 1973 to remedy this situation. He closed MTC's theatre school (which led to the creation of the **Prairie Theatre Exchange**), and began producing seasons of popular plays designed to sell well, though MTC was attacked throughout the 1970s for its conservative programming and for its lack of Cdn content. After Gilbert's 2nd departure in 1975, MTC went through a series of artistic directors in an effort to find a production formula

The rodeo is the marquee event of the Manitoba Stampede and Exhibition.

MB STAMPEDE AND EXHIBITION

that would maintain financial stability while still producing work of artistic merit.

It was not until the 1989 arrival of Steven Schipper that such stability came. Under his direction, the MTC Mainstage maintained a consistent subscription base by producing seasons consisting of Broadway hits, well-known classics, and major new plays from London and New York. To his credit, Schipper has also produced new MB works on the Mainstage, and has cast local actors extensively. The success of the Mainstage has become the foundation that supports MTC's other endeavours. The MTC Warehouse produces a 4-play season of newer and more-daring works, as well as serving as the venue for the set-piece production of MTC's Master Playwrights Festival. Founded in 2001, this annual festival brings together several theatre companies from around Winnipeg to produce works by a major playwright. The first festival was dedicated to the works of Samuel Beckett, with subsequent festivals producing the works of Bertholt Brecht, Harold Pinter, Edward Albee, and QC's Michel Tremblay.

Finally, MTC sponsors the **Winnipeg Fringe Festival**, and is the only major company to support such an event. Created in 1988, the Winnipeg Fringe is among the largest in Canada, with over 130 Manitoban, Cdn, and international theatre companies participating, and ticket sales of over 60,000. It is also generally recognized as one of the best "fringes" in the country. ● DAVID DEGROW

MANITOBA THEATRE FOR YOUNG PEOPLE

(MTYP) was formed in **Winnipeg** out of the Actors' Showcase, an amateur **Theatre** company created in 1965 by Daphne Korol to showcase local talent, which was then incorporated in 1977 under the direction of Tony Pydee. A desire to move into professional theatre led to a conflict over control of the company; it was resolved in 1982 with the induction of Leslee Silverman as artistic director, a position she retained to 2006. From their initial home in the cramped space at 89 Princess St and at the Gas Station Theatre (where their productions were staged), to their new theatre facility at **The Forks** (opened in 1999), the company has maintained a relatively constant level of artistic and popular success. This is due both to the stability provided by Silverman's continued direction, and to the company's constant dialogue with young people in the community.

For their work, the company's productions have been nominated for 2 Chalmers Awards from the Ontario Arts Council (*Comet in Moominland* in 1994 and *Old Friends* in 1998, for which the MTYP won), and Silverman has received both the Governor General's Commemorative Medal and the **Manitoba Arts Council** Arts Award of

Distinction. The company now presents an 8-show season of both touring productions from around the world, and new works by MB playwrights; at least one of the productions tours the province. The MTYP's other main venture is its Theatre School, which is attended by over 1500 students of various ages. Additionally, motivated students have the opportunity to join the MTYP's Young Company, their pre-professional program. ● DAVID DEGROW

MANITOBA WOMEN'S INSTITUTE (MWI).

Originally a home economics society simply known as the "Women's Institute" of the relevant community, it later concentrated on the development of rural communities. The Manitoba Women's Institute was first formed in **Morris** under the name "Ladies Mutual Benefit Societies" in Aug 1910, with 36 members, and was modelled after similar societies in ON. In 1919, with 118 chapters of the popular organization operating in MB, branches from across Canada convened in **Winnipeg** to form the Federated Women's Institutes of Canada. The organization advocated for a wide range of issues. During the 1920s, at a time when the maternal death rate in MB was higher than the national average, MWI sponsored public health classes, and during the **Great Depression**, it provided educational programs on mental health and saving money. In the 1940s, it was the first provincial organization to work with the Cancer Institute in promoting programs to control the disease. It also lobbied for the standardization of children's clothing sizes, and for textile and care labelling on fabric and clothing. The organization established more than 100 rural libraries, and ran "rest rooms," where rural women and children could refresh themselves while visiting town. The **Canadian Costume Museum** has its origins with a MWI fundraising fashion show; in the 1980s, MWI established a college to train and license midwives (*see* **Midwifery**). The MWI motto is "For Home and Country." ● MICHELLE DOBROVOLNY

MANITOBAH, REPUBLIC OF. Before Manitoba was established as a province, a short-lived independent state was founded by Thomas Spence in present-day **Portage la Prairie**. In June 1867, the ambitious Spence approached Portage settlers with a proposal to form an autonomous govt. Spence's plan found some support, as the tiny Portage settlement, located beyond the jurisdiction of the **Council of Assiniboia**, lacked a police force or judicial system. Spence, who was in fact a devoted monarchist, then wrote to Queen Victoria requesting recognition for his independent state, but by Jan 1868 had received

Thomas Spence

no reply He went ahead with his plans to establish the new state regardless. Spence named Portage la Prairie the capital of the new Republic of Manitobah, and became the Republic's president, governing from behind the counter of his general store.

Revenue for the construction of a Manitobah govt house and jail was to be raised by imposing a tax on imports in the settlement. However, enforcing the tax was a problem. When the **HBC** officer flatly refused to pay any tax to the Republic, Spence's council responded with the threat of imprisonment, a largely ineffective tactic as Spence had yet to collect enough taxes to build a jailhouse. His govt was then further discredited by a shoemaker named MacPherson, who charged that Spence's tax revenue was in fact being spent on liquor. In a show of power, Spence then charged MacPherson with treason, and brought him to trial in a log house doubling as a courtroom, with Spence presiding as judge. The trial quickly turned chaotic when MacPherson's supporters attempted to free him; guns were fired, and an all-out brawl ensued, with Spence cowering under a table. Having lost all authority, Spence's Republic collapsed. His term as president of the Republic was officially put to an end when the colonial office in London sent him a letter informing him that his govt had no power. ● MD

MANITOU, pop 718, is a town 125 km SW of **Winnipeg** on hwy 3 in the **Pembina Valley**. **English**, **Scots**, and **Mennonites** settled Manitou. Originally known as Archibald when the post office opened in 1879, the name changed to Manitou in 1889. In both **Cree** and **Ojibway** culture, a manitou is a spirit. A **CPR** point was also established here in 1883. The area's landscape was formed by **Glaciation** in the last Ice Age and later from **Lake Agassiz**. Lake-deposited sediment makes the area's soil very fertile and well suited to agriculture; thus, many retail and service businesses support the surrounding farms. Although the town is also home to govt, health, and educational services, tourism also plays an important role in the local economy, with a golf course and nearby access to the Holiday Mountain downhill ski resort. Manitou's opera house, built in 1930, has been designated as a provincial Heritage Site. In 1890, **Nellie McClung** taught school in Manitou before moving to Winnipeg, and the local high school is named after this pioneer in the **Women's Movement**. ● GPP

MANNING, Frank A., physician, (b March 6, 1946, **Virden**). After earning an MD from the **U of M** in 1970, Manning became a resident in obstetrics and gynecology at the **Health Sciences Centre** in Winnipeg. He continued his training with a fellowship at the Nuffield Institute for Medical Research in Oxford, England, also earning an MSc from U of Oxford. Beginning in the early 1980s, Manning was head of maternal-fetal **Medicine** in the Department of Obstetrics, Gynecology, and Reproductive Sciences at the **U of M**, and practised at HSC. He took up the same position at New York Presbyterian Medical Center, U of Columbia, in 1996. Manning is known as a pioneer in the field of fetal sonography and for the invention and development of the fetal biophysical profile for monitoring the health of the fetus. Manning has also studied in-utero transfusion techniques, Rhesus iso-immunization (*see* **Winnipeg Rh Institute**), and fetal breathing movements. Since 2004, he has been chairman of the Department of Obstetrics and Gynecology at the New York University Hospital and is a faculty member at the Albert Einstein College of Medicine. ● JT

MANTO SIPI CREE NATION (previously known as God's River First Nation), on reserve pop 572, off reserve pop 115, is located on the N shore of God's Lake, 255 km SE of **Thompson**. This community signed Treaty 5 in 1909 and is now a member of the Keewatin Tribal Council. The Manto Sipi Cree Nation's native language is **Cree**. Access to Manto Sipi Cree Nation community is limited to a winter road, a runway, and docks for boats and float planes. Education in this community in a federal school goes from Nursery-Grade

10, and enrolment for the year 2003-04 was 169. The economic foundation of the Manto Sipi Cree Nation is comprised of hunting, fishing, and trapping. ● RK

MAPLE. MB has only 2 native maples, but several introduced ones survive in protected sites in southern areas. Native are the MB maple or box elder tree (*Acer negundo*) and the shrubby mountain maple (*Acer spicatum*). MB maple is the only maple with compound ash-like leaves but can easily be told from ash by its V-shaped pairs of winged seeds and thinner twigs. Reaching nearly 1 m in diameter and 12 m in height on good sites such as river floodplains, it is seldom more than 8 m tall with low, weak, crooked branches on upland sites. It is commonly planted as an ornamental tree and in shelterbelts because it is hardy and fast growing although short-lived. Its sap is less sweet than that of sugar (*A. saccharinum*) or silver maple (*A. saccharinum*), but it is abundant and has been used to make maple syrup and sugar. The wood is too soft and light for much commercial use but is used occasionally in construction and boxes.

Because of the masses of seeds produced by female trees (sexes are separate in many maples), this is the common 'back alley tree' found in **Winnipeg**. MB maple grows naturally in moist areas in the southern part of the province. Its natural northern limit is near Dawson Bay on **Lake Winnipegosis**. Mountain maple is a tall shrub (to 8 m) with typical opposite 3-lobed maple-shaped leaves. It grows on well-drained

Manitoba maple flowers in autumn

ROBERT R. TAYLOR

moist soils under taller trees along streams, lakes and moist hillsides in the southern part of MB, especially E of **Lake Winnipeg**. Its leaves and V-shaped seeds turn bright red in late summer and fall, MB's miniature version of the sugar maple's fall colour. Occasionally planted as an ornamental, it provides food for a variety of animals and birds. Cultivated maples that you might find in Winnipeg and other protected areas include the sugar, silver, and Amur (*A. ginnala*). ● KAREN JOHNSON

MARCEL COLOMB FIRST NATION, on reserve pop 294, off reserve pop 36, is located about 30 km SE of **Lynn Lake**. It is a member of the Swampy Cree Tribal Council. The native language here is Cree. The Marcel Colomb First Nation is a breakaway community from the Mathias Colomb Cree Nation. It became MB's 62nd First Nation in 1999. The members of **Marcel Colomb First Nation** were originally known as the "Tent Village People," a group of families who lived in camps where the town of Lynn Lake now stands. In 1953, several camps were bulldozed to make way for a town site. The Tent Village People remained in camps on the outskirts of town for as long as 30 years, when they were moved to houses within the town. The members of Marcel Colomb First Nation have planned to build a new community on the Black Sturgeon Indian Reserve since it was created in 1990. In 2007, the First Nation was still listed as being "under development." ● RK

MARGARINE DEBATE. Canada's 1886 *Dairy Act* had banned the manufacture, sale, and import of margarine in order to protect the dairy industry. The Supreme Court of Canada overturned the act in 1948, and margarine was allowed in MB markets the following year. Pressured by rural supporters, the MB govt soon passed an act prohibiting the sale of "butter-yellow" margarine by manufacturers. Margarine had instead to be a lardish "ivory" colour, and Manitobans wanting the more appetizing yellow had to colour it themselves – an arduous, time-consuming, and pointless chore. In a 1951 Margarine Referendum, Winnipeggers voted overwhelmingly in favour of lifting the colour ban, but the initiative was nonetheless defeated in the legislature. Though it was widely believed that this was a rural-urban issue, and that a majority of rural Manitobans supported the colour ban, further investigation by **Newspapers** revealed that, at 33¢ a pound (45 kg) for margarine versus 62¢ for butter, the colour ban had an equal amount of opposition outside Winnipeg. The debate led Winnipeg mayor **Stephen Juba** to devise a contest in 1956

Good Luck's flavour is sweeter, fresher!

That's because **Good Luck** is sweet-churned daily!

No other spread can match the wholesome, *spring-sweet* flavour of Good Luck Margarine . . . that special flavour only Good Luck's exclusive sweet-churning can give.

Whatever you try Good Luck on — toast, bread, hot vegetables, pancakes — you'll notice its wonderful difference *immediately*.

Good Luck is good for you and your youngsters. No other spread contains more Vitamin A and wholesome nourishment!

Get wholesome, sweet-tasting Good Luck today. It comes in two popular packages . . . the foil-wrapped, twin-bar package with handy color wafers . . . and the new color-mix bag.

Get **GOOD LUCK**

THE SWEETER, FRESHER MARGARINE!

In 1961, margarine makers in Manitoba finally broke the colour barrier and were allowed to produce butter-yellow margarine.

for the best explanation on why colour should be added to margarine by manufacturers, with the winner receiving a trip to FL. In 1961, **Dufferin Roblin**'s administration at last allowed manufacturers to colour margarine, though it still had to be a shade different than butter. In 1987, the revised *Margarine Act* was repealed. • MD

MARINE ALGAE/SEAWEEDS. Marine algae occur in MB in **Hudson Bay** and along its MB coastline. Unlike freshwater algae, they can tolerate salty water. Algae are simple primitive plants of either a single cell or one cell thickness and without complicated organs like leaves or flowers. 'Seaweeds' are visible large coastal and shallow water marine algae ('benthic') although the tiny microscopic phytoplankton, found in the waters and under the ice of the bay, are much more productive and important ecologically.

Most of the phytoplankton found in the few studies done in Hudson Bay were one-celled diatoms or dinoflagellates, members of the golden-brown algae (Chrysophyceae) and fire algae (Phyrrophyceae) respectively. Dinoflagellates are the alga known to cause toxic 'red tides' in other oceans. None of these species are found in Hudson Bay and there have been no reports of red tides there. Ice algae are mainly diatoms, with some dinoflagellates and green algae (Chlorophyceae), that are found in the bottom 1-5 cm of arctic ice or just under it in the Spring.

From studies done in SE Hudson Bay, most 'seaweeds' or benthic algae belong to the classes of brown algae (Phaeophyceae), red algae (Rhodophyceae) and green algae (Chlorophyceae) in about that order of abundance. Examples of all three classes can be seen growing on rocks or washed up along the shores of the bay. Ice

scours the shoreline and shallow water areas during the winter making it difficult for them to grow there. Little study has been made of the seaweeds in the **Churchill** area but brown algae such as rockweeds (*Fucus* spp.) grown on rocks in the intertidal zone there and kelps (*Laminaria* sp., *Alaria* sp., *Agarum* sp.), some up to 4-5 m in length, are found washed up along beaches. Various red and green (*Ulva lactuca* = 'sea lettuce') algae are also found. Piles of rotting seaweeds, mostly *Fucus* spp., found above the high tide mark along beaches provide food and homes for an amazing number of small invertebrates, mostly crustaceans, as well as being used by local residents as compost for gardens. Polar bears will eat larger seaweeds in the summer.
● KAREN JOHNSON

MARK, Inky, politician (b Nov 17, 1947, Toyshun, China). Inky Mark fled China with his mother and sister in 1955 and settled in **Gilbert Plains.** Before his political life, he worked as a high school teacher, having achieved his BEd at the **U of M**. In 1991, he was elected to **Dauphin** town council and became the town's mayor in 1994. In the federal election of 1997, he ran as a candidate of the Reform Party in the riding of Dauphin-Swan River and became 1 of only 3 Chinese MPs in the House of Commons. When the Reform Party dissolved in 2000 to become the Canadian Alliance, Mark successfully ran in the next general election. He acted as the Alliance Party's parliamentary critic for immigration and helped draft the parliamentary committee's final version of the *Refugee Protection Act* in 2001. That same year, Alliance Party leader Stockwell

Inky Mark was first elected to the House of Commons in 1997.

437

Day undercut Mark's position on the bill in a speech he delivered which supported tighter restrictions against refugee claimants and reduced appeal opportunities for rejected claimants. This caused Mark to join other Alliance MPs in agitating for Day's removal as leader.

Mark left the Canadian Alliance caucus in Sept 2001 to sit as a member of the Democratic Representative Caucus in alliance with the Progressive Conservative Party. He joined the PCs in Aug 2002 and late in 2003, when the Canadian Alliance Party and the Progressive Conservative Party formally merged to create the new Conservative Party, Mark officially joined the new party's caucus. When he was re-elected in the federal election of 2004, Inky Mark was named critic of citizenship and immigration. In Oct 2004, he was named deputy critic of citizenship and immigration and 2 weeks later, was elected to the position of vice-chair of the parliamentary standing committee on citizenship and immigration. Mark was always a maverick; for example, in 2006 flouting govt policy by voting against the Stephen Harper's decision not to hold a plebiscite on the future of the **Canadian Wheat Board**.
● RUTH DEGRAVES

MARLYN, John (a.k.a. Vincent Reid), novelist (b Apr 2, 1912, Nagybeszkerek, Hungary [now Zrenjanin, Serbia]; d Nov 16, 2005, Canary Islands). Brought to **Winnipeg** as an infant, and growing up in that city's **North End**, Marlyn was educated in North End schools and at the **U of M**. He found work during the 1930s in the film industry in England, and returned to Canada before WWII to work as a writer in the Ottawa civil service, teaching creative writing at Carleton U, 1963-67. He later moved to the Canary Islands, where he lived until his death from a heart attack in 2005. Marlyn's first novel, *Under the Ribs of Death* (1957), captures the tensions of the immigrant experience, winning the Beta Sigma Phi First Novel Award. Deprived of the language and cultural identity that sustain his father, his very name now a source of derision, the young protagonist, Sandor Hunyadi, struggles against the humiliation of being an outsider by attempting to assimilate, to become Alex Hunter instead, only to suffer the economic devastation of the **Great Depression**. As a sociological study, the book is an indictment both of the intolerance of the dominant Anglo culture and of its harsh, unforgiving materialism. Marlyn's 2nd novel, *Putzi, I Love You, You Little Square* (1981), is a comically surrealistic comment on the limitations of contemporary society. Marlyn also wrote sci-fi novels pseudonymously as Vincent Reid.
● MILDRED GUTKIN

MARTIAL ARTS were introduced to MB following WWII, and gained in popularity through the 1960s. The first sports clubs dedicated to martial arts in MB started appearing around this time, and offered training in karate, judo, and tae kwon do. There are many different martial arts traditions, and varied styles within each tradition.

Judo originated in Japan, and translates as "the gentle way." Tamotsu "Tom" Mitani was the first judo instructor in MB. Mitani was one of hundreds of **Japanese** Canadians who arrived in MB as a forced migrant during WWII. He established MB's first permanent dojo at a **Military** barracks gym, where he trained **Mamoru "Moe" Oye**. Oye represented MB at the first Cdn championships, held in MB in 1959. Oye became the highest-ranking judoka in the province, and trained many of MB's subsequent judokas, including Mark Berger. Berger is a 4-time national champion, and became the 2nd Canadian to claim an Olympic medal in judo, winning bronze at the 1984 Olympics. There are roughly 600 Judoka and 20 clubs in MB.

Karate also originated in Japan, and translates as "empty hands." There are several different forms practised in MB, but Shotokan is the predominant form. The first karate school in MB opened in 1963, originally as part of the Winnipeg Judo Club. The first karate instructors in MB were Gerald "Jerry" Marr and Richard "Tug" Wilson. In 2006, Marr was the highest-ranking karate instructor in the province. There were about 600 members of Karate Manitoba in that year.

Tae kwon do originated in Korea, and translates as "way of the hands and the feet." Tae kwon do is distinctive for its powerful kicking style, and gained in popularity through the 1970s, when instructors were sponsored by international associations to teach the discipline across NA. Park Jung Tae was one such instructor, and founded the Manitoba Taekwondo Association. There were about 3500 tae kwon do athletes in MB in 2006. ● MD

MARTIN, Joseph, "Fighting Joe," politician, businessman, lawyer (b Sept 24, 1852, Milton, Canada West [ON]; d March 2, 1923, Vancouver), introduced the controversial *Schools Act*, which led to the **Manitoba Schools Question**. Martin was an aggressive orator and political agitator. He is also notable for having served as a **Liberal** in 4 different legislatures. Martin was educated at Toronto Normal School and taught briefly before pursuing a law degree at the U of Toronto. He was called to the MB bar in 1882, and practised in **Portage la Prairie** and **Winnipeg**. He became Liberal MLA for Portage in 1883, and an investor in early **Railways**, later becoming the province's

railway commissioner. This dual position sometimes put Martin in positions of questionable morality, as when the govt granted the company of which Martin was vice-president, the Northern Pacific and Manitoba Railway Company, to build over the **CPR**'s tracks, leading to the **Battle of Fort Whyte**. In the 1888 election, Martin was acclaimed as MLA. In 1890, as Attorney General in the **Thomas Greenway** administration, Martin sponsored the *Official Language Act*, which ended the official use of French in the Legislature and the **Judicial System**. This would remain in place until the **French Language Crisis**, the better part of a century later. At least as vexing to the **French**, **Métis**, and **Roman Catholic** populations – who, several years before, had been the majority in the **Red River Settlement** – was the *Public Schools Act*. This law stopped all public funding of Catholic and French-speaking schools. As odd as it may seem to the modern reader, Martin was also **Reform**-minded, and was an early advocate of the **Women's Movement**.

Joseph Martin, 1883

After a series of disagreements with Greenway, Martin resigned in 1891. He then entered federal politics, running unsuccessfully for the **Selkirk** riding before winning a seat as Winnipeg MP in 1893. Having lost in the 1896 election, Martin moved to Vancouver in 1897, where he practised law, owned extensive real estate, and founded and edited the *Vancouver Guardian* **Newspaper**, which he used to promulgate his ideas and as his personal political mouthpiece. He became a BC MLA in 1898, and served as Attorney General. His legislation there was as nativist as his Manitoban bills, including an

Alien Exclusion Act, preventing **Chinese** people from owning mines in the province. He briefly became premier in 1900 at the request of the lt gov. After a failed bid as an Independent for the Vancouver federal seat, he moved to the UK, where he practised law and was British MP for St. Pancras East, in the London area, 1910-18. After that constituency was abolished, he returned to Vancouver, where he co-founded another newspaper, the *Evening Journal*. • A. J. LEVIN

MARTIN, Patrick "Pat," politician (b Dec 13, 1955 **Winnipeg**). Before his political life, Martin was a miner, carpenter and union leader. Because of his work as business manager of the Manitoba Carpenters Union, vice-president of the Manitoba Federation of Labour, executive member of the Manitoba Trades Council and part of the Winnipeg 2000 Development Committee, worker's rights were always important to Martin. He was first elected to the House of Commons in 1997 representing the riding of Winnipeg Centre for the **New Democratic Party**. Regarded as a solid constituency worker, Martin was re-elected in the general elections of 2000, 2004 and 2006 and has served as vice-chair of the standing committee on access to information, privacy and ethics. He helped underpin the *Federal Accountability Act* by creating tough new measures to fight patronage and is a founding member of the Global Organization of Parliamentarians Against Corruption. For his work for Aboriginal rights in Ottawa, including fighting for compensation for victims of Canada's residential schools, he was honoured with a spirit name by the Assembly of First Nations. • RUTH DEGRAVES

MASON, William Clifford "Bill," filmmaker, canoeist, artist (b April 21, 1929, **Winnipeg**; d Oct 29, 1988, Meech Lake, QC). After employment as a graphic artist and animator at Phillips, **Gutkin** Associates in Winnipeg and at Crawley Films in Ottawa, Mason joined the **National Film Board** in 1962. Working mainly on his own as director, cinematographer, writer, editor, narrator, and even performer, he was among the foremost producers of films on wildlife and the wilderness, especially on **Wolves** and canoeing, and he earned the alias "Mr. Canoe." *Paddle to the Sea* (1965) and *Blake* (1969) were both nominated for Oscars. His feature-length wolf films, *Death of a Legend* (1971), *Cry of the Wild* (1972), and *Wolfpack* (1974), were immensely popular because of their intimate views of wolves, including the birth of cubs; so too was his 4-part series on whitewater canoeing, *Path of the Paddle* (1977). After his final film, *Waterwalker* (1984), about a transcendent canoe trip he made on Lake Superior, he

returned to painting, and published books on nature and the environment. Ten years after his death, a Canada Post stamp honoured Mason. • GENE WALZ

MASTODONS. *See* **Mammoths and Mastodons**.

Jack Matheson, 1967

MATHESON, John "Jack," sports broadcaster (b July 25, 1924, **Winnipeg**), covered sports for the *Winnipeg Tribune* and CJOB in a career that spanned 40 years. Matheson displayed little athleticism as a student at Gordon Bell High School, and instead spent his time reading voraciously. He joined the Cdn navy following his graduation in 1943. After his dismissal from service following the end of WWII, Matheson decided to try his hand at writing. He walked into the office of the *Winnipeg Tribune*, asked for a job, and was immediately put to work covering **U of M** sports. He began writing about the **Winnipeg Blue Bombers** in 1953. His sharp wit and clever style made him a popular *Tribune* columnist, though his critical remarks would occasionally arouse the wrath of players and coaches. After the *Tribune* folded in 1980, he went to work for the CJOB, where he was teamed up with fellow sports broadcasters **Jack Wells** and Bob Irving covering Bombers games. He retired in 1992. • MD

MATHIAS COLOMB CREE NATION (previously known as Pukatawagan Cree Nation), on reserve pop 2227, off reserve pop 926, is situated 819 km NW of **Winnipeg** and 217 km W of **Thompson**. The people of this area signed on to Treaty 6 in 1876, but Mathias Colomb Cree Nation was not formed until 1910. Mathias Colomb, the individual for whom this First Nation is named, left ON and travelled with his family along the river

systems into MB. He settled in the Pukatawagan area of MB, while his family continued on to SK. Mathias Colomb Cree Nation is now a member of the Swampy Cree Tribal Council. There are 2 reserves located here: Pukatawagan IR No. 198, and Highrock IR No. 199.The native language is **Cree**. Education goes from Nursery–Grade 12, and total enrolment for the year 2003-04 was 612. Mathias Colomb administers its own schooling. There is no all-weather road access to this First Nation; a winter road is available only about 3 months per year. So the Mathias Colomb Cree Nation set up its own passenger, cargo and emergency ambulance flight service called Missinippi Airways/Missinippi Air-Care. In the spring of 2002, the Denver-based, short-track rail firm OmniTRAX announced it planned to abandon the Sherridon line from **The Pas**, cutting off all-weather surface access to Mathias Colomb. Fearing the implications of having to depend on air service to bring in supplies, Mathias Colomb combined with **War Lake First Nation** and **Tataskweyak Cree Nation** in April 2004 to create the Keewatin Railway Company to buy out the Sherridon Line. Keewatin would become 1 of just 2 railways in Canada owned and operated by First Nations. Visual Artist, Leonard Bighetti, was born and raised in Mathias Colomb Cree Nation. • RK

MATONABBEE, interpreter, trader, (b ca 1737, **Fort Prince of Wales**; d Aug 1782, Fort Prince of Wales) was a Chipewyan (*see* **Dene**) who led **Samuel Hearne** on his expedition in search of the Coppermine River. Most Dene in Matonabbee's time rarely visited **Hudson Bay Company** posts; conflict with the rival **Cree** nation made trading a dangerous venture. Matonabbee had the advantage of being raised in **Churchill** after his father's early death. Matonabbee's knowledge of Dene, as well as Cree and English, which were spoken at the post, made him a valuable asset to the HBC. Matonabbee became an ambassador between the 2 warring **First Peoples**. By the 1760s, Matonabbee had travelled to the Coppermine River (in what is now NU and the NT) for the HBC. The company then hired Hearne to survey the land. Hearne made 2 unsuccessful attempts at reaching the river before taking on Matonabbee, who insisted on bringing women to help with chores. He was also successful in bringing Hearne to the river because he followed the seasonal movements of **Bison** and **Caribou**, ensuring a food supply. The expedition lasted from 1770-72. Upon his return, the HBC proclaimed Matonabbee the head of the Chipewyan people. He committed suicide in 1782 after a smallpox outbreak amongst his people. • MD

M

Arthur Mauro, 1962

MAURO, Arthur, lawyer, businessman (b 1927, Port Arthur, ON) is a leader in Winnipeg's business community. The son of Italian immigrants, Mauro grew up in ON, and came to MB to study at the **U OF M**. He was active in student politics, and was president of the students' union, and then president of the National Federation of Canadian University Students. He was called to the bar in 1953, and joined the Thorvaldson firm, which later became part of MB's largest law firm **AIKINS**, MacAulay & Thorvaldson. He specialized in transportation and communication law. In 1967, he was appointed chairman of the Royal Commission on Northern Transportation, which was used as a guideline for development in the North. He lectured at the U of M in transportation and communication law, and published a number of papers on the subject. He practised until 1969, and then became a senior exec with Great Northern Capital Corporation. From 1972-76, he was CEO of Transair Ltd. He then joined Investors Group Inc, and was made CEO in 1985.

Mauro has served on a number of major corporate boards, including United Grain Growers and Pacific Western Airlines/Canadian Airlines. He has chaired numerous local community organizations, from the forerunner to the United Way to the **ST. BONIFACE GENERAL HOSPITAL**. In 1991, he was made chancellor at the **U OF M**, a position he held until 2001. He donated $1 million to establish the Arthur V. Mauro Centre for Peace and

Justice at the university. He is an Officer of the Order of Canada and a member of the **ORDER OF MANITOBA**. ● MD

MAXWELL, Fred "Steamer," hockey player (b May 19, 1890, **WINNIPEG**; d Sep 11, 1975, Winnipeg) coached the famous **WINNIPEG FALCONS** hockey team that won the first gold medal in hockey at the 1920 Olympics. His nickname comes from his smooth skating ability. Maxwell started out as a player on the Winnipeg Monarchs team in 1910. His consistent scoring led to a $1500 offer in 1913 to play for the Toronto Blueshirts of the National Hockey Association. Maxwell, highly principled in regards to playing hockey for money, refused the contract, as well as a subsequent $1800 offer to play in the Pacific Coast Hockey League. He chose to stay with the Monarchs, winning the 1915 Allan cup. However, after discovering that some of his teammates had received gifts and money to play for the team, Maxwell retired from play to become the team's coach. He coached the Monarchs for 2 years, then switched to the 1920 Winnipeg Falcons, leading the team to the 1919 Allan Cup, and Canada's first Olympic gold in hockey. He went on to coach the Elmwood Millionaires, The Winnipegs, and the Selkirk Fisherman before joining with the Maroons in the American Association. Maxwell's reputation earned him a lucrative offer to coach for the Toronto Maple Leafs, but again, he turned down the money to remain in Winnipeg. ● MD

Fred "Steamer" Maxwell in a Falcons team photo

MAYER, Charles James, politician, farmer (b April 21, 1936, Saskatoon, SK). Mayer was educated at the U of Saskatchewan and became an agrologist and farmer. Before entering politics, he was president of the Manitoba Beef Growers Association. He was elected to the House of Commons in 1979 for the riding of Portage-Marquette as a member of the **PROGRESSIVE CONSERVATIVE** Party. He was re-elected in 1980 and in 1984 he served in Brian Mulroney's govt as minister of state for the **CANADIAN WHEAT BOARD** until 1987. From 1987-93 he took on the role of minister of state for grains and oilseeds and in 1989 he was named minister of western economic diversification. Mayer was promoted to the position of minister of agriculture in 1993 until the PC govt's defeat that year. In July 2004, he was named chairman of the board for Agronix Inc, an international organic waste management company. In 2005, he was inducted to the Canadian Agriculture Hall of Fame. ● RUTH DEGRAVES

MAYFLY (Fishfly) is a soft-bodied insect in the order Ephemeroptera. Mayflies range from 20-40 mm in length and have 2 pairs of long, clear-to-brownish wings, which are held upright over the body at rest. Common MB species are the burrowing mayflies (*Hexagenia*), with a body length of 25 mm and a wingspan of 50 mm. Their nymphs burrow into sediments to avoid predation by fish. A distinguishing feature of mayflies is the set of 2 or 3 long filaments (cerci) at the end of the abdomen. Remarkably, the adult's mouthparts are undeveloped, and so it survives only a few hours. The adult's sole function is reproduction, which is accomplished in nightly swarms of countless numbers of individuals under optimal conditions. Mass emergence has survival value because local predators are overwhelmed. Mainly in late May or early June, millions of mayflies emerge and swarm from MB lakes and rivers, with hundreds of thousands attracted to lights, under which their dying and dead bodies accumulate in great piles. Cottage screens can be quickly swarmed. Others wash up on shore, their rotting bodies leaving a strong odour for weeks.

During the rise-fall dance, the female selects a male, and the grasping couple retires to a secluded spot to mate. In an hour, the female lays fertilized eggs on the water surface or under submerged stones, and these hatch into elongated, gilled nymphs called naiads. The naiad lives 2-3 years underwater on the bottom or in the mud, feeding on algae and debris, and moulting a number of times as it grows. When mature, the naiad gulps air (filling the digestive tract), crawls out of the water, and sits on a plant stem or rock. It then splits its skin to form a winged, subadult

Mayfly (Fish Fly)

ROBERT R TAYLOR

nymph (subimago) whose legs and reproductive organs complete their growth within a few hours. This stage moults immediately one last time into the adult mayfly.

Mayflies are a major source of food for dragonflies and other insects, fish, birds and bats, and help clean the bottom of waterways. These insects are highly sensitive to water pollution and related loss of oxygen. A mounting ecological problem is the accumulation of heavy metals and toxic chemicals (from industrial products and emissions) in the bodies of mayflies and other organisms, which are then transferred up the food chain in both aquatic and land ecosystems. This group is the oldest-flying type of insect, appearing about 325 mya (Carboniferous period). MB hosts 80 species of 12 families (625 NA species and 2500 worldwide). ● REW, TG

MEADMORE, Marion Ironquill, lawyer, activist (b July 11, 1935, Peepeekis First Nation, SK). She began her professional life by teaching elementary school on the **CREE** reserve. Meadmore then became involved in founding provincial and national Aboriginal organizations, including the National Indian Council (1963), the Native Council of Canada (1968) and the National Indian Brotherhood (now the Assembly of First Nations). She also served as chairperson of **WINNIPEG**'s Indian and **METIS** Friendship Centre (1969). In 1973, she enrolled in law school at the **U OF M**. In 1976, she became the first Aboriginal woman in MB to earn a law degree and, following her call to the Bar in 1977, became Canada's first Aboriginal woman lawyer. She practised law in Winnipeg for several years, but left private practice to focus on organizational work for Aboriginal

Marion Ironquill Meadmore

and urban First Nations groups. She was recognized for her contributions with an Order of Canada in 1984. ● DOUG JOHNSTON

MEDICINE in MB began with the traditional healing methods of First Nations people before the arrival of European settlers (*see* **HOME REMEDIES**). Western medicine arrived with several British doctors and surgeons of the **HUDSON BAY COMPANY** in the 18th century. More than 20 surgeons served at **YORK FACTORY** during that time, the most distinguished being Thomas Hutchings from 1766-73. The earliest doctor known to have practised in the **RED RIVER SETTLEMENT**

was James White, engaged by **LORD SELKIRK** to serve as surgeon to the colony. He landed at York Factory in 1814 and died in 1816 at the **SEVEN OAKS INCIDENT**.

For most of this period, home remedies were the norm. Western medicine truly arrived in 1870-90 with the formation of the Provincial Medical Health Board of MB in May 1871, which became the College of Physicians and Surgeons of Manitoba in 1877. The initial registration was of 46 male doctors; 36 trained in Canada, 6 in Britain, and 2 in the US. The college had the power to admit, censure, and dismiss members, powers that continue to this day. Manitoba Medical College, the first medical school in western Canada, was founded in 1883, its major stimulus coming from potential students who wished to study medicine without having to leave MB. The first dean of the school was James Kerr, trained in Belfast, who had been appointed medical officer of health in Winnipeg for 1882, and the first students were admitted in 1884. Dr. J. Wilford Good, a graduate of the U of Toronto, succeeded him as dean 1887-98, and was the first professor of clinical surgery. The **U OF M** always administered college examinations, and the school formally became part of the U as the Faculty of Medicine in 1919. A major early influence on the school was Henry Havelock Chown, father of **BRUCE CHOWN**. He registered with the College of Physicians of MB in July 1880, leaving in 1882 for further training in the UK. He returned to Winnipeg in 1885 as the first professor of anatomy in the newly formed college, serving as dean there 1900-1917.

Early in the evolution of medical services in MB, the need for improvement in public health and disease surveillance was recognized. Thus, Dr. **GORDON BELL** was appointed provincial bacteriologist and coroner in 1897, and was later named the first professor of bacteriology at the medical college. The Provincial Lab was established under his direction in 1906 at 750 Bannatyne Ave in Winnipeg, and, upon his death in 1923, Fred Cadham, after whom the lab was named, carried on his work. (*See* **CADHAM PROVINCIAL LABORATORY**) In the late 19th and early 20th century, major diseases affecting Manitobans included **TUBERCULOSIS**, scarlet fever, typhoid, and diphtheria. Several outbreaks of smallpox occurred, one of the largest being in 1900. Severe **EPIDEMICS** of poliomyelitis occurred in MB in 1928, 1936, and 1941, but the worst outbreaks occurred in 1952 and 1953, the latter being among the worst suffered anywhere in NA. The Sanatorium Board of MB was established in 1904 and in 1907, David A Stewart was appointed medical superintendent of the Manitoba Tuberculosis Society, becoming superintendent of the new sanatorium at

UMA, TRIBUNE, PERSONALITY FILES, 1970

M

M

Children's Hospital operating room, 1956

Pelican Lake near **NINETTE** in 1910 (*see* **MANITOBA SANATORIUM**).

After WWI, Willis Prowse was dean of the college 1919-28. In 1920, the college was still a small institution, primarily training the next generation of physicians for MB. In 1933, it received a grade of A from the Rockefeller Foundation, 1 of only 3 to be awarded in Canada. Until WWII, the Scottish tradition of didactic teaching prevailed, many professors being either trained at Scottish universities or heavily influenced by those traditions. Psychiatrist Alvin T. Mathers was dean 1931-49. He is, perhaps unfortunately, best remembered for introducing the quota system for selection of medical students in 1933. By 1940, this system was well entrenched, with several lists: a preferred list for Anglo-Saxon, French, and Icelandic male applicants; another of male Jews; another for males of other ethnic backgrounds; and a list for women. Usually only about 12 students were admitted from the non-preferred lists. The U Board of Governors ended this discriminatory system in 1944 after a complaint from a Jewish organization to the education committee of the MB Legislature.

Following WWII, many breakthroughs occurred in medicine, and research became an integral part of the mission of the faculty, due largely to the influence of a few visionary physicians and surgeons. Key among these were: Lennox (Buzz) Bell as dean, 1949-66; **HARRY MEDOVY** and Bruce Chown in paediatrics; **PAUL THORLAKSON**, the power behind the development of polyclinics and the Winnipeg General Hospital (now part of the Health Sciences Centre), and a key player in the development of faculty research; **JOE DOUPE**, hired by Thorlakson and Bell as professor of physiology to develop the Department of Medical Research and to train many of the physicians and clinical researchers who went on to make their names in medicine, both in Winnipeg and elsewhere; Jack Hildes, known for his work during the polio epidemic of the 1950s, who brought medicine to northern MB by developing the Northern Medical Unit; and Morley Cohen and Colin Ferguson, who developed cardiac surgery in MB. **ARNOLD NAIMARK** and **HENRY FRIESEN** developed physiology into a research powerhouse. Naimark became dean in 1972 and president and vice-chancellor of the U of M in 1981. Friesen became president of the Medical Research Council of Canada in 1991, and was instrumental in the founding of the Canadian Institutes for Health Research in 2000.

The Winnipeg and **BRANDON** clinics dominated specialist medicine. The Winnipeg Clinic, under Paul Thorlakson, also served as a stimulus and funding source for research through its Research Foundation, now the Paul H. T. Thorlakson Foundation. Major teaching hospitals were Winnipeg General Hospital, founded in 1872; **ST BONIFACE GENERAL HOSPITAL**, founded by the **GREY NUNS** in 1871; and the Children's Hospital, founded in 1909, expanded and moved to its present site in 1953, and now part of the **HEALTH SCIENCES CENTRE**. These developments were the beginnings of the major biomedical centre that we see today in MB.

Outside Winnipeg, rural hospitals and group practices developed in many parts of the province. **BRANDON** became a major centre for western MB, while **THOMPSON** and **CHURCHILL** developed centres serving northern MB communities. A committee headed by Dean Prowse examined the cancer problem in 1929, and provided the groundwork for the *Cancer Relief Act* (1930). This set up the Cancer Relief and Research Board, renamed the Manitoba Cancer Treatment and Research Foundation in 1957, and CancerCare Manitoba in 1999. The board's early focus on radiation treatment led to the establishment of only the second cobalt unit in Canada in 1953. Under the leadership of Dr. Lyonel Israels, the MB Institute for Cell Biology was established in 1969 to carry out basic and clinical research into the causes and treatment of cancer. The formation of the Department of Family Medicine and Social and Preventative Medicine (now Community Health Sciences), and of the Manitoba Centre for Health Policy, enhanced developments in family medicine, epidemiology, and public health policy.

With the development of medicare in the early 1970s, and increasing costs of universal health care, the organization of medicine began to change. Individual physicians moved to group practice, while local hospital boards managed their own affairs. Regional Health Authorities (RHAs) were established by legislation in the late 1990s, managing health care delivery in 11 regions of the province. The largest of these, the Winnipeg RHA, serves over 600,000 people, while the smallest, Churchill, serves fewer than 1000.

The first half of the 20th century saw little change in medicine in MB, while the second half saw major advances, such as the beginning of the human genome project and the potential to tailor treatments to the specific needs of patients. Deaths from tuberculosis and other infectious diseases and cancer have been reduced. In MB, the work of our forebears has borne fruit, with the development of a major medical centre and a $44.9 million annual research enterprise serving the needs of MB and its citizens. Much work, however, still needs to be done to resolve some of the major challenges facing our health care system in the 21st century. ● JOHN L. HAMERTON

MEDICINE, ALTERNATIVE, or complementary and alternative medicine (CAM) as it is now called, includes treatments or therapies applied in response to medical conditions instead of, or as well as, the conventionally accepted approaches of Western **MEDICINE**.

CAM has become more prominent and accepted in NA because many of its treatments are now considered beneficial under standards of conventional medicine. Many certified practitioners receive much of the same training as medical doctors and go through an accreditation process. However, professional standards are lacking in some branches, and critics often argue that CAM therapies lack a proven biological or physiological basis, or have not been proven as effective as treatments like pharmaceuticals or surgeries.

The **U OF M** Faculty of Medicine is one of the few medical schools in the country to feature an undergraduate Integrative Medicine module to educate 2nd-year medical students about CAM. Dr. Gregory Chernish, who is a family medicine instructor as well as a specialist in acupuncture and traditional **CHINESE** medicine, heads the program.

There are conflicting statistics regarding the use of CAM therapies, but Manitobans tend to use alternative treatments at a rate higher than the national average. A 2006 Fraser Institute national survey found that 59% of Manitobans used one or more forms of alternative or complementary therapy in the previous year. On the other hand, a 2003 StatsCan Canadian Community Health Survey found that 20% of Canadians and 26% of Manitobans had seen an alternative health provider that year.

There are many fields of CAM, but most fit into the categories of **CHIROPRACTIC**, naturopathy, homeopathy, Chinese medicine, mind-body medicine, and energy therapies. Different disciplines share many common techniques, but generally follow the idea of holistic medicine, which places the focus on the treatment of the whole person, including social and psychological factors instead of solely the symptoms of a disease. Many practitioners combine one or more methods. (*See* **MIDEWIWIN**, **MIDWIFERY**, **HOME REMEDIES**.)

Naturopathy refers to drugless treatment of injuries, ailments, or diseases using natural methods or forces such as dietetics, exercise, massage, electrotherapy, and hydrotherapy. MB's

Naturopathic Act makes it 1 of only 4 provinces to regulate the profession. The Manitoba Naturopathic Association registers naturopaths, and in 2007 there were 16, including 3 at the Centre for Natural Medicine Inc. in **WINNIPEG**.

Homeopathy is a form of medicine that began in Germany about 200 years ago. Homeopaths treat illnesses by administering a very small or diluted amount of the illness itself in a chemical or herbal form in order to stimulate the body's own healing mechanisms. There are about 15 centres for homeopathic treatment in Winnipeg.

Chinese Medicine is based on a wide range of concepts developed over thousands of years. One of the best-known treatments, acupuncture seeks to rebalance the body's channels of energy or "Qi" through the insertion of fine needles or the use of heat, pressure, electric current, or rays of light. The Chinese Medicine and Acupuncture Association of Canada lists about 30 members of its MB chapter.

Herbalism is sometimes considered part of Chinese medicine, but has become a field of its own. Herbalists promote the healing properties of plants and their extracts for a wide range of conditions. There are about 10 herbalists in Winnipeg, and stores like **VITA HEALTH** and Aviva Natural Health Solutions sell herbs and natural foods.

The goal of mind-body medicine is to enhance the mind's ability to heal or control the body. Meditation, shamanic healing or counselling, neuro-linguistic programming, hypnotherapy, aromatherapy, and tai chi are some of the therapies offered in MB, and yoga programs have sprung up around the province.

Energy therapies are based on the ideas that the body contains energy fields that influence health. Reiki is a Japanese system where practitioners channel energy through their hands to heal the body through its energy centres. There are 5 MB practitioners registered with the Canadian Reiki Association. Reflexologists apply gentle pressure to specific spots on the feet or hands to promote energy flow or simply relaxation. The Reflexology Association of Canada is based in Winnipeg, and has 30 Manitoban members.

Ayurveda, iridology, osteopathy, and even bloodletting therapy are among the other CAM techniques practised in MB. ● JOEL TRENAMAN

MEDORA, pop 90, is a community located 113 km SW of **BRANDON**. The post office opened in 1890 as Emerald Hill. Its name was changed to Medora Station in 1896; then, in 1915, it was changed to and remained known as Medora.

The community was named in honour of Medora May Campbell, the woman who hosted a group of surveyors during their first survey of the area. Since 2001, the area's economy was supported by oil and agriculture. **MERVIN TWEED**, born in Medora, went on to become a successful businessman and politician. He was elected as the Conservative Party's MP for Brandon-Souris in 2004. ● GPP

MEDOVY, Harry "Hurricane Harry," teacher, author, paediatrician, (b Oct 22, 1904, Russia; d Oct 10, 1995, **WINNIPEG**), moved with his family to Winnipeg at the age of 10 months. He was educated at St. John's High School and graduated from the **U OF M** with a BA (1923) and MD (1928). He won the Chown gold medal in medicine and the Prowse prize for research as a medical student. Following graduation, he did postgraduate training in Winnipeg and at the U of PA, in Philadelphia. Thereafter, Medovy ran a private paediatric practice in Winnipeg, marrying Mary Rosenblat in 1934. The couple had 2 daughters. In WWII, Medovy served in the Royal Canadian Army Medical Corps (1942-45). Following **BRUCE CHOWN**, he was appointed the 2nd full-time head of paediatrics at the U of M and paediatrician-in-chief at the Children's Hospital of Winnipeg from 1954 to 1970. Medovy retired in 1970.

Medovy was an energetic teacher, receiving the nickname "Hurricane Harry" from his tendency to breeze through rounds at high speed. He was an exceptional clinician and diagnostician, showing that blue babies admitted in the 1950s with suspected congenital heart disease were instead suffering from excessive nitrates in the well water used to dilute their formula. His interest in prevention was ahead of the times, and he was an ardent advocate of immunization against childhood infectious diseases such as measles, diphtheria, pertussis (whooping cough), and polio, and of adolescent girls against rubella. He promoted nutritious diets and vitamin supplementation to prevent rickets and scurvy, was an outspoken opponent of cigarette smoking. Medovy was instrumental in establishing the 1959 Children's Hospital of Winnipeg Research Fund, which became the Children's Hospital of Winnipeg Research Foundation in 1971. In 1979, he wrote a history of the Children's Hospital of Winnipeg, *A Vision Fulfilled*.

His many honours include an honorary doctorate from U of M; the first Distinguished Service Award of the MB Medical Assoc; the Ross Medal from the Canadian Paediatric Society; the Distinguished Medical Educator Award from

M

the Professional Assoc of Residents and Interns of MB in 1985; and his appointment as an Officer of the Order of Canada in 1990. Medovy was also an enthusiastic fan of **Music**, and sat on the board of the **Winnipeg Symphony Orchestra**.
● JOHN HAMERTON

MEECH LAKE CONSTITUTIONAL ACCORD.

"Meech" was a controversial agreement entered into by PM Brian Mulroney and the 10 premiers on April 30, 1987. It set off years of constitutional wrangling. The agreement, forged at a conference centre at Meech Lake (about 25 km NW of Gatineau, QC), was designed to get QC's National Assembly to support the 1982 *Constitution Act*. (QC was the only province not a signatory to the repatriated Constitution.) QC's govt under Robert Bourassa co-operated in this, but laid down specific conditions. These became the backbone for the accord agreed to at Meech Lake.

The conditions were several and complicated: QC and the other provinces were to be given additional powers over immigration. Provinces would also be allowed to opt out of new national programs, with financial compensation, if they offered a similar program compatible with "national objectives." As well, provinces were to be given more say in the selection of federal Supreme Court Justices and Senators. But for some critics, especially Manitobans, the main concern became the provision by which an interpretative clause would be added to the constitution delineating the status of QC as a "distinct society." In the end, this clause became the deal-breaker.

All 11 provincial parliaments and legislatures were required to give approval for the accord to become a formal amendment of the Constitution. QC consented on June 23, 1987, beginning the 3-year period within which amendments had to be completed. The federal parliament and 5 provincial legislatures quickly supported the accord.

MB's was not one of them. The Manitoba representative at Meech Lake was **NDP** premier **Howard Pawley**. Little public discussion had preceded his commitment to the accord. At the time, his govt had only a narrow majority. The lone **Liberal** Party MLA, Sharon Carstairs, had been opposed to the pact from the outset. The **Progressive Conservatives** were of mixed outlook. Increasingly, the NDP was uncomfortable with Pawley's original position, and, in late 1987, an open letter by MB NDP notables condemned Meech.

Manitobans raised various objections, which surfaced in formal public hearings. There was concern that the "distinct society" provision granted special status to QC; concern about the

fate of future national programs and the limit on the federal spending power; and resentment among **First Peoples** that their concerns had not been addressed. Senate reform was deemed impossible with the unanimity rule in place, and women's rights were considered to be in jeopardy. Finally, Manitobans criticized the way the agreement had been negotiated, especially the secretiveness of the process and the paucity of politicians involved.

MB acquired a new minority govt after April 1988, led by PC leader **Gary Filmon**. The Liberals now formed the official opposition with 20 seats, largely due to their stance against the pact, while the NDP was reduced to 12 seats. Filmon would need the support of at least 1 of the other 2 parties. He was personally disposed to support the accord, if only as a favour toward PM Mulroney, but his caucus was divided. In Dec, the NDP's new leader, **Gary Doer**, announced his opposition to Meech Lake. Filmon moved gingerly, but events overwhelmed him. On Dec 16, he introduced the accord in the Legislature. Just before this, the Supreme Court had overturned the sign-language provision of QC's Bill 101 (the *Charter of the French Language*), prohibiting non-Francophone commercial signs. After a few days, Bourassa announced his intention to override the Court's decision using the Notwithstanding Clause in the 1982 *Canadian Charter of Rights and Freedoms*. Filmon was now in a pickle. He had indicated support for the accord, yet Manitobans believed QC wanted things its own way in every fashion: a distinct society status in the accord; respect for French language rights outside QC; but within QC, the use of exceptional measures, possibly even additional constitutional powers to ensure French linguistic hegemony over Anglo-Quebeckers. The next day, Filmon withdrew the accord from the Legislature.

Filmon set up an all-party special committee of 6 MLAs, chaired by Wally Fox-Decent of the **U of M**, which began work in March 1989. The task force travelled the province and heard from over 400 individuals and groups. The tone of the presentations was civil, but they were overwhelmingly critical of the accord.

In its Oct 21, 1989 report, the task force recommended against approval of the accord as it was. It proposed the introduction of a "Canada clause" that would recognize First Nations and multiculturalism as well as QC's distinct society; it expressed concern over the effect on women's rights, because of the distinct society clause; and it called for the deletion of the provision that limited federal spending power. The report felt that Senate reform must not require unanimity, and recommended that future constitutional

conferences include representatives from First Nations and the territorial govts. Finally, it called for public hearings before any future constitutional changes.

Time was running out. The June 23, 1989, deadline was fast approaching. MB had yet to agree; even though another dissident province, NB, would soon assent to the accord, NL after April 1989 was governed by an anti-Meech premier, Clyde Wells. Wells recalled his province's assembly to rescind its earlier agreement.

The accord was at a critical point. Mulroney called a first ministers' conference to Ottawa from June 2-8, 1990. Filmon represented MB, though he discussed matters closely with Carstairs and Doer, who were on hand. The atmosphere was charged and fraught with rumour and near-panic. The consensus was to proceed with Meech "as is" but to pursue a later round of constitutional changes that would clarify the distinct-society clause and proceed with Senate reform. All 3 MB representatives supported this outcome, though reluctantly.

Filmon reintroduced the resolution to support the accord on June 12, but because of an oversight regarding the giving of notice of motion, the resolution could only be addressed immediately with unanimous consent. This was denied by **Elijah Harper**, the NDP MLA for **Churchill**, who was by now the voice of an intense campaign by Aboriginal and other groups angered about being overlooked in the Meech Lake process. Further procedural glitches ensued, which delayed matters more, and there was the imminent dilemma of ensuring that there would be time to allow the Legislature to undertake the public hearings that were required by its rules for proposed constitutional amendments. The deadline of June 23 came and went. The legislature was adjourned, and the resolution to agree to the Meech Lake Accord died on the order paper. For good or ill, MB had played, with NL, a definitive role in defeating a major constitutional amendment. ● ALLEN MILLS

MEIGHEN, Sir Arthur, lawyer, prime minister (b June 16, 1874, Anderson, Perth County, ON; d Aug 5, 1960, Toronto) was MB's only prime minister. Meighen was born to **Scots-Irish Presbyterian** parents near St. Mary's, Canada West (now ON). At school, Meighen became a star debater, entering the U of Toronto in 1892. There, Meighen majored in mathematics and – presciently – allowed classmate William Lyon Mackenzie King to take the lead in student politics. After graduation in 1896, he entered a teacher-training program, becoming a teacher the following year. However, Meighen's first posting was traumatic. He disciplined a student who turned out to be the daughter of the chairman of the school board. The chairman entered his classroom and attacked him. Meighen complained to the school board, threatening to resign if the board did not insist that the chairman resign. The board supported its chairman, and Meighen duly resigned.

Arthur Meighen

After teaching proved unsuitable, Meighen headed to MB with a contraption for cleaning dried fruit, for which he had purchased the patent with borrowed money. It proved unprofitable, and Meighen was forced to work to pay off his creditors before studying law. He completed his study in **Portage la Prairie**, remaining there to practise his new profession. He married Isabel J. Cox in 1904, and the couple had two sons and one daughter. In 1908, he unexpectedly won election to the House of Commons as a Conservative. In the House, he became a well-known debater and public speaker, notorious for his partisan destruction in words of any who dared to tangle with him. After a hard campaign, he tripled his majority in Portage in the 1911 election, but was not rewarded with a Cabinet appointment, mainly because the post went to his chief MB rivals, Robert Rogers and William James Roche. However, as one of his party's chief parliamentary strategists, he was soon rewarded with the post of solicitor general.

In WWI, Meighen became well known for his parliamentary defence of the govt's nationalization of the Canadian Northern Railway and of the *Military Service Act*, and for his willingness

to curtail civil liberties: it was Meighen who introduced the *Wartime Elections Act*, which disenfranchised "enemy aliens," in 1917 (*see* **Alien Question**). He became minister of the interior in the wartime Union govt of 1917, and both he and the Unionists won handily in the 1917 election. Meighen was rewarded with the portfolio of the Department of the Interior. After the Armistice, he dominated both the House of Commons and the govt itself while Borden was away at the Versailles Peace Conference. Meighen was no friend of the **Winnipeg General Strike**. He authorized the arrest of its leaders and their subsequent trials for sedition, as well as the repression of radical aliens over the summer of 1919. When Borden stepped down as PM late in 1920, Meighen – who was the favourite of his party's backbenchers – succeeded him. During the brief tenure as PM that followed, Meighen played an important role at the Imperial Conference of 1921, but had few real triumphs. His decision to stake his party's future on a protective tariff was a mistake, and he lost even his own Portage seat in the 1921 election. Another seat was found for him in ON to allow him to rebuild the Conservative Party.

Meighen had many liabilities. He did not speak French well; he continued to defend Canada's subordinate role in the British Empire; he believed in govt by business interests; and he did not understand Mackenzie King's political talents, instead both despising and disparaging his former schoolmate. Still, in the 1925 election, his party won the largest number of seats in the Commons, and he achieved a personal victory in Portage. King refused to resign, however, and Meighen got into trouble over a speech in which he declared he would seek a plebiscite before committing Cdn troops to service abroad. Eventually, King asked the gov gen, Viscount Byng of Vimy, for a dissolution. The gov gen refused to grant one, claiming that Meighen had not been given a chance to govern, creating what would later be known as the King-Byng Affair. Meighen agreed to form a govt. The decision proved ill-advised. Though he avoided automatic resignations of his Cabinet by appointing them without portfolio, he himself had to seek re-election, and was thus not in the Commons to help defend his govt, which was soon defeated. King cleverly based his subsequent campaign on the refusal to grant him a dissolution, and won an easy victory. Meighen resigned from his second term as PM on Sept 26, 1926, and soon took up an appointment with a legal firm in Toronto, moving his family to the ON capital in the process. They never returned to MB.

In Feb 1932, Meighen agreed to accept a Senate appointment and became PM R. B.

Bennett's govt leader in the Red Chamber. After Conservative leader Robert Manion was badly defeated in the election of 1940, the party turned to Meighen in 1941. He agreed to become leader on a platform of coalition govt and conscription. Resigning from the Senate, Meighen ran for the Commons in a by-election in a supposedly safe seat in South York, ON. While the Tory leader won headlines with his speeches on conscription, **CCF** opposition candidate Joseph Noseworthy (the Liberals did not run) campaigned door-to-door against Meighen, accusing him of lacking sympathy for ordinary people and insisting that Meighen had no policies other than conscription, a policy Meighen had favoured in WWI. The former PM was badly defeated and retired finally to private life.

Few federal politicians were afforded as many opportunities at rehabilitation or even complete re-invention, although Arthur Meighen resolutely refused to make any concessions to public opinion. ● J. M. BUMSTED

(l to r) Orest Meleschuk, Dave Romano, John Hanesiak, Pat Hailley

MELESCHUK, Orest & team, curling (1972) took home the world title in one of curling's most infamous moments. Part of the Fort Rouge Curling Club, Meleschuk or "The Big O" and his team competed in MB's curling championship for many years before finally claiming the provincial title in 1972. They went on to win nationally, and represented Canada at the Silver Broom World Championship. Meleschuk and his team finished first in the Silver Broom preliminaries, with 7 wins and no losses. However, in the final game, the Cdn team trailed the US by a 2 pt margin. In order to win the title, Meleschuk would have to use his last rock advantage to force an extra end. He successfully knocked out the counting US stone, but the Cdn stone rolled to the inner edge of the 8 ft ring, making it appear as though Canada had scored only 1 pt. US skip Bob LaBonte became so excited that he jumped up in celebration, slipped on the ice, and accidentally pushed the rock, moving it enough to give the Canadians the pt needed to continue the match. The Canadians then beat the US in the extra end, and took home the world title. Canada's failure to win a world title over the next 7 years eventually was attributed to LaBonte's ire over having so narrowly lost the world crown, and became known as "The Curse of LaBonte." ● MD

MELITA, pop 1111, is a town 134 km SW of **BRANDON** on hwy 3 and on the Antler, a tributary of the Souris River. **ENGLISH**, **SCOTS**, and **IRISH** settlers began to arrive in the area in the 1870s, and dubbed the settlement "Manchester." The Boundary Commission came through shortly afterward. When the post office opened in 1884 and Manchester was put forward as the community's name, the federal govt rejected it, as there was already a post office with this name elsewhere. The **PRESBYTERIAN** Sunday-school superintendent proposed naming the town after Malta (once "Melita"), where the apostle Paul was supposed to have been shipwrecked – the theme of his sermon that Sunday. The name was evidently well-chosen as Melita grew quickly. The railway surveyed the land in 1890, the community was incorporated as a village in 1902 and as a town in 1906. In the 2000s, Melita is a service and retail centre for the area's predominantly large-scale agriculture producers and oil-field workers. Outdoor tourism – including birdwatching and hunting of **WATERFOWL** and **DEER**, are also important to the economy. ● GPP

MENNONITE HERITAGE CENTRE and the associated Centre for Mennonite Brethren Studies, forms the national archives for the 2 largest Cdn **MENNONITE** church denominations: Mennonite Church Canada, and the Canadian Conference of Mennonite Brethren Churches. The Mennonite Heritage Centre has been at the corner of Grant Ave and Shaftesbury Blvd in **WINNIPEG** since 1978, on the campus of the **CMU**. The Centre for Mennonite Brethren Studies moved to Taylor Ave in 2005, from its old home in Elmwood, where it began in 1969.

The Mennonite Heritage Centre's mandate is to collect materials relating to Mennonites in Canada. There are over 600 in-person visits by researchers every year, and more than 250 requests for information a month. The archive includes textual records and some 34,000 photographs, as well as diaries, correspondence, church registers, and organizational material. It has among the most extensive collections of materials on Russian Mennonites from the late 18th century through WWII. Researchers can find everything from genealogical information to memoirs documenting pioneer life, wartime experiences, and the struggles of refugees and immigrants. The collection includes the Canadian Mennonite Board of Colonization Records from 1923-65, and a microfilm collection of civic records from Odessa and St. Petersburg covering the period 1789-1941. In addition to the archives, the facility also helps administer a large rare book collection on Mennonite historical topics, and houses the Walter Loewen Manuscript Collection of medieval Gregorian chant manuscripts and books.

The archive traces its beginning to the appointment of a church archivist in 1933. Until the founding of the Canadian Mennonite Bible College (CMBC), which was absorbed by CMU, in the late 1940s, the archive was in private hands. The collection was housed with CMBC throughout the 1960s and '70s. With the erection of the distinctive A-frame building in 1978, a formal archive was established. Lawrence Klippenstein served as the founding historian and archivist of the Mennonite Heritage Centre from its opening until his retirement in 1997, followed by Ken Reddig 1997-99. Alfred Redekopp has been the director since.

Herb Giesbrecht was the founding archivist of the Centre for Mennonite Brethren Studies (CMBS) in 1969. In 1979, the archive moved into a slightly larger space, though staff joked that the basement space consisted of "catacombs" because of crowding and problems with environmental controls. In 1991, Abe Dueck became director of the centre, taking over from Reddig; 2 years later, the collection was significantly damaged as a result of heavy rain and a sewer backup. In 2000, the archive moved out of the basement into a former administrative area of the church-run college (Mennonite Brethren Bible College). The CMBS contains over 1200 boxes of material including conference, congregational, and personal papers; 23,000 photographs; and some 700 periodical titles. There are also maps, audio recordings, and a video collection.

Like many church archives, genealogical researchers frequently consult the CMBS. It contains a microfilm collection of Cdn church baptismal and membership records that go from the late 19th century to 1978. It also houses an important collection of hymnbooks and **MUSIC** manuscripts, the Benjamin and Esther Horch Music Collection. ● MAURICE MIERAU

MENNONITES in MB are part of a religion that includes 1.3 million adults in 65 countries, with 128,000 members in Canada. According to the 1991 Census, 66,000 Manitobans identified themselves as Mennonite. In MB, they are organized into 12 conference groups, and dozens of independent congregations. In addition, tens of thousands of people of Mennonite background do not relate to any Mennonite church. MB's Mennonites are represented in virtually all occupations, professions, trades, unions, and political parties. They are major contributors to charities, and active in volunteering their time for many projects. Theologically, Mennonites span a wide range from conservative to evangelical and liberal. Mennonites are one of the significant faith-based groups in MB.

EARLY HISTORY: The Mennonite story began as part of the 16th century Anabaptist religious reformation. Influenced by both Catholics and Protestants, Mennonites differed from both in that they practised adult baptism, separated church and state, and were pacifist. Considered dangerous to the established order because these views disrupted the prevailing state/church assumptions, they were persecuted and fled to areas where they were tolerated. Two branches of Mennonites formed – one in the Netherlands and northern Germany, and a 2nd in Switzerland and southern Germany. Hutterites, who are closely related to Mennonites in origin and belief, organized communal groups in Moravia and Hungary. Mennonites in southern Europe fled to PA in the 17th century, and on to ON after the US Revolution. In northern Europe, some found refuge in the Vistula River region of Poland, and, in the 18th century, in Russia. In 1874, when Russian reforms threatened Mennonites' beliefs, $1/3$ moved to MB.

IMMIGRATION: The 7000 Mennonites who immigrated in the 1870s were promised ample land, their own schools, exemption from military service, and the right to affirm instead of swearing the oath to the Crown. During the 1920s, after the establishment of Communist rule in the USSR threatened Mennonite communities, an additional 21,000 migrated to Canada, of whom about 6000 settled in MB. After WWII destroyed Mennonite communities in Ukraine, Germany and Poland, more than 7000 refugees from these areas came to Canada. Some settled in MB, primarily in **WINNIPEG**.

When Mennonites arrived in MB in the 1870s, they were some of the first settlers on the open Prairie. They established more than 100 semi-communal villages on land E and W of the **RED RIVER** reserved for them by the federal govt. A few also located near **ROSENORT**. By the early 20th century, many of the villages had dissolved, with residents moving their houses and barns onto their own land. Only about 25 villages survived. The 1920s **IMMIGRATION** from the USSR resulted in new Mennonite communities being formed throughout MB. After WWII, increased mechanization of farm work caused Mennonites to move to Winnipeg, and to towns and

at the **U of W**, and a developing seminary program are additional post-secondary institutions.

COMMUNITY: From the earliest days, Mennonites established organizations to serve community needs. The most important such organizations were the orphans' bureaus. They administered the estates of orphans and widows, accepted deposits, and made loans. The bureaus also saw to the care and education of orphans. Fire insurance organizations protected against losses and enforced safety standards. In the 1920s and '30s, Mennonites built hospitals when govts were not yet in a position to do so, and set up health insurance systems to make care affordable for local residents. When the orphans' bureaus collapsed during the **GREAT DEPRESSION**, they were replaced by numerous community-based **CREDIT UNIONS**. After WWII, Mennonites established more than about 25 personal-care, retirement, and supportive-housing facilities, as well as Eden Mental Health Centre in Winkler. Most of these facilities now serve locals, whether Mennonites or not.

Mennonites' emphasis on peace leads to their rejection of military service. Since before Confederation, Canada exempted from military service Mennonites and Amish, a traditional Anabaptist group mostly located in the US and in ON that is often regarded as a subgroup of Mennonites. This exemption was reaffirmed when Mennonites came to Canada from Russia in the 1870s. In WWI, Mennonites were exempted based on group affiliation; in WWII, they had to individually present their case for conscientious objector status. In WWII, more than 60% of men eligible for military service chose to become conscientious objectors.

In response to the humanitarian needs caused by the war, Mennonites formed relief, immigration, and service organizations that were amalgamated into Mennonite Central Committee (Canada) in 1964. Its provincial branch is Mennonite Central Committee (MB). MCC has become the most important Mennonite service and relief agency, addressing both international and local needs. MB Mennonites were instrumental in organizing thrift stores and the Canadian Foodgrains Bank, both of which began as subsidiaries of MCC. There are active local MB chapters of Mennonite Disaster Service (MDS) and Mennonite Economic Development Associates (MEDA). MDS responds to disaster situations throughout NA with volunteers and finances; MEDA provides expertise and financial assistance to local entrepreneurs around the world, especially in developing countries.

ARTS AND CULTURE: MB Mennonites have established many community newspapers, historical periodicals, academic journals, and

Traditional Mennonite home with barn attached

smaller cities such as **WINKLER**, **MORDEN**, **ALTONA**, **GRUNTHAL**, and **STEINBACH**. About ⅓ of MB Mennonites live in Winnipeg at present, forming 42 congregations. In recent years, new Mennonite churches have formed in Winnipeg and northern MB, consisting of Korean, **CHINESE**, Latin American, Laotian, **ABORIGINAL**, and other peoples. In addition, people from other ethnic and religious backgrounds have joined established Mennonite churches.

EDUCATION: Mennonites see education as important for passing on their faith from one generation to the next (*see* **EDUCATION, PRIVATE**). After arriving in MB, Mennonites organized primary schools, both public and private. The first secondary school, now called the Mennonite

Collegiate Institute (MCI), in **GRETNA**, was established in 1891 with Henry H. Ewert as principal. For about 15 years, the school was accredited provincially to train teachers for Mennonite primary schools. When the provincial govt closed all Mennonite private and bilingual public schools in the 1920s and enforced instruction in English only, some Mennonites emigrated to Mexico and Paraguay. Those who remained in MB responded by organizing Bible schools, colleges, and high schools. At present, Mennonites operate more than 20 private primary, high schools, and colleges. Three colleges – Menno Simons, Concord, and Canadian Mennonite Bible College – amalgamated in 2000 to form the CMU. Steinbach Bible College, the chair in Mennonite Studies

Mennonite Heritage Village Museum in Steinbach

denominational papers. Creative writing has flourished since the 1930s, initially in German and Low German (Plattdeutsch). Since the 1960s, most of the creative writing has been in English. Indeed, some would say MB writing is now dominated by authors of Mennonite descent. Some of the notable authors are **Patrick Friesen**, Di Brandt, **David Bergen**, and **Miriam Toews**.
 ● JOHN J. FRIESEN

MENTAL HEALTH POLICY in MB focuses both on the treatment of mental illness and the promotion of mental health. Mental illness refers to a variety of diagnosable mental disorders, health conditions characterized by alterations in thinking, mood, or behaviour. In Canada, mental illness is the single largest category of disease. Up to 20% of the population will experience a mental illness at some point in their lives, 1 in 3 will suffer from a severe and persistent mental illness, and 1 in 8 will actually be hospitalized. Promoting mental health is a central part of the policy of the health care authorities in MB.

As well as pursuing these general goals, mental health policy in MB has responded to historical influences, legislative and financial initiatives, service system experiences and, more recently, influences from advocacy organizations. Early Cdn provincial mental health policies, with the exception of QC, found expression in provincial mental health acts based largely on British mental health law and this continued until the mid-1960s. Early mental health acts addressed issues that still define modern mental health legislation such as involuntary admission criteria, involuntary admission procedures, treatment authorization and rights and safeguards.

Mental health policy and legislation in MB began to change in the late 1960s. The terminology and designations changed, from terms such as "insane" and "lunatic asylum" to "mentally disordered" and "hospital." Committal criteria were clarified as were the initial involvement of the courts in involuntary admissions and also the introduction of voluntary admissions. More consideration was given to the patient's human rights and the availability of appeal mechanisms and leave provisions. Since 1960, 3 major reports addressing mental health reform in MB have influenced public policy. These reports, in turn, reflected changes in the legal environment because of the Charter of Rights, and influences from the service system and the advocacy environment.

The Charter supported the growth of a strong citizen advocacy environment based on a human rights perspective. Significant improvements in the medical and psychological treatment of severe mental disorders have resulted in great changes

to the options available to anyone with psychological/psychiatric difficulties. Chief amongst these is the availability of effective treatments that allow persons previously confined to institutions to live and receive treatment in the community.

These trends have been reflected in all the major reviews of mental health policy in MB in the past 30 years. In 1960, the Progressive Conservative government of **Duff Roblin** commissioned the Adamson Report, the primary thrust of which was to recommend the establishment of a "system of regional hospitals and psychiatric teams oriented to community delivery." In 1973, the new NDP government of **Ed Schreyer** commissioned the Clarkson Report, which reaffirmed the recommendations of the Adamson Report and added an emphasis on community care, the development of professional services beyond those provided by psychiatrists and the drafting of a new mental health act. This time the government committed itself to action in the department of health's paper, *Mental Health Programs in Manitoba* (1975), which stated that it would expand the number of mental health workers, reduce in-patient beds, establish "appropriate local governance" and emphasize accountability and measures for program evaluation.

Despite this, the government failed to implement many of the proposed initiatives of the department's policy paper. The number of workers redeployed and the nature of their work as well as the community-based initiatives were not altered substantially. Also, the implementation of community-based initiatives and evaluation mechanisms were not developed. In 1978,

another Progressive Conservative government, that of **Sterling Lyon**, recommended that the mental health policy should "re-affirm the thrust to de-institutionalization and the provision of community-base services," along with the establishment of an appropriate authority.

These issues were addressed yet again in the Pascoe Report (1983), commissioned by the **Howard Pawley** NDP government, which laid out 19 principles for mental health services which emphasized human rights and the move toward consumer empowerment, local community-based treatment, interdisciplinary approaches, local authorities and higher accountability as well as recommendations for an organizational and financial structure to support them.

Since then there has been substantial movement toward these policy objectives as reflected in government documents such as *Vision for the Future: Guiding Principles and Policies for Mental Health Service Providers* (1990) which included the fundamental principle that "mental health services shall augment and reinforce helping networks in the community such as family, friends, clergy and self-help groups as well as other government departments and agencies." As well the document, *Building the Future of Mental Health Services in Manitoba, (1992)* was developed which emphasized the principle that "local citizens, consumers and communities shall participate in the planning, development and delivery of mental health services to community members."

In 1997, Regional Health Authorities were established, and with them came a change in the

The Selkirk Mental Health Centre continues to house patients.

GLENN MARQUEZ

responsibility for the provision of services. Manitoba Health, the overarching govt department, is responsible for co-ordinating planning related to mental health services, working with the 11 regional health authorities (RHAs). RHAs have operational responsibility for mental health services including planning, delivery, and ongoing management of the services. • BARRY MALLIN

MENTORING ARTISTS FOR WOMEN'S ART

(MAWA) was formed as a response to the lack of representation that women artists had in the MB arts community. Founding members Peter Krowina, Paula Newman, Harry Symons and Diane Whitehouse worked with a women's advisory committee in 1983 to examine ways to provide professional development to women artists in the province. The group hired Andrea Philp to make their recommendations a reality, and in Aug 1984, Manitoba Artists for Women's Art was formed. The organization developed a program in which established senior artists were paired up with emerging artists for a year-long mentorship. By 2007, 154 women had gone through the program. In Sept 1990, the Manitoba Artists for Women's Art became its own independent organization, and the name changed to Mentoring Artists for Women's Art. MAWA's mandate is to "encourage and support the intellectual and creative development of women in the visual arts by providing an ongoing forum for education and critical dialogue". The programming has grown to include workshops, monthly lectures, a mentor-in-residence program and Aboriginal, rural and remote member initiatives. The organization has grown to have over 400 local, national and international members. It was the first organization to move into Winnipeg's newly revitalized North Main area, in the former Norman's Meat building on Main St. • STACEY ABRAMSON

MERASTY, William George "Billy," actor

(b May 16, 1960, BROCHET). Growing up in a large CREE-speaking family, Merasty lived off-reserve near the BARREN LANDS FIRST NATION. Like his uncles, writer TOMSON HIGHWAY and dancer René Highway, he took an interest in the arts, but was more influenced by the Cree storytelling tradition. Merasty attended high school in CRANBERRY PORTAGE, SWAN RIVER, and BRANDON, graduating in 1978. He moved to Toronto at age 18, and in 1983, enrolled in a summer theatre program. Immediately afterward, he began a long association with Native Earth Performing Arts Inc of Toronto, an Aboriginal theatre, dance, and music company founded in 1982.

Merasty's debut film role was in *Justice Denied: The Donald Marshall Story* (1989), the

Billy Merasty has appeared in numerous stage, film, and television productions.

story of the wrongfully convicted Mi'kmaq man. He had parts in Atom Egoyan's *Exotica*, Denys Arcand's *Stardom*, and Terrence Malick's *The New World*. He was cast in the title role for *Elijah*, the story of ELIJAH HARPER, scheduled for 2007. His many television roles have included Canadian shows *This Is Wonderland*, *Liberty Street*, and *The Red Green Show*, as well as the US miniseries *Into the West*. In addition to his 25 stage acting and a similar number of screen credits, as of 2006, Merasty wrote the play *Fireweed* (debuting in 1992), and was working on his 2nd, *Godly's Divinia: A Love Story*, for 2007. Merasty has also spoken openly about being queer or two-spirited (an Aboriginal belief that individuals can embody both genders). He presented on the subject at the U OF M in 2005. • JOEL TRENAMAN

MERCREDI, Ovide William, lawyer, CREE

leader (b Jan 30, 1946, GRAND RAPIDS). The former grand chief of the Assembly of First Nations grew up on the GRAND RAPIDS FIRST NATION, and attended high school in THE PAS. While studying at the U OF M, Mercredi helped form the first Native Students' Association in Canada. He graduated with his law degree in 1977, specializing in constitutional law, and in 1979 began to practise in The Pas. In 1982, he went on to work for the Assembly of First Nations (AFN) in Ottawa as a legal advisor and later vice-chief. He also represented the AFN at the United Nations on a number of occasions. In 1991, he became national chief of the organization. He was re-elected in 1994, but lost the position to PHIL FONTAINE in 1997.

Mercredi helped organize Aboriginal opposition to the proposed MEECH LAKE ACCORD, particularly in association with the ASSEMBLY OF MANITOBA CHIEFS. He was heavily involved in the discussions leading up to the Charlottetown Accord, advocating for Aboriginal self-rule. While chief, he also presented to the United Nations in New York and Geneva; led a delegation to the State of Chiapas, Mexico, to meet local Indigenous peoples; and initiated programs to address HIV/AIDS, family violence, and economic conditions on reserves. He co-wrote *In the Rapids: Navigating the Future of First Nations*, released in 1993.

Mercredi went on to lecture as a member of the Faculty of Native Studies at Laurentian U in Sudbury, ON, and has received honorary degrees from St. Mary's and Bishop's universities. Mercredi returned to MB, and in June 2005 was elected chief of Grand Rapids First Nation. He also became grand chief of the Swampy Cree Tribal Council, an umbrella group for 8 MB First Nations communities. • JOEL TRENAMAN

METCALFE, E. Bennett "Ben," journalist,

environmentalist (b Oct 31, 1919, WINNIPEG; d Oct 14, 2003, Shawnigan Lake, BC). Greenpeace co-founder Metcalfe left Winnipeg in his teens and made his way to England, where he joined the Royal Air Force. He was first posted to India and later fought in North Africa during WWII. Following the war, Metcalfe became a journalist in France, and in 1951 returned to Canada to work for the *WINNIPEG FREE PRESS*. He went on to write for the *Vancouver Province* and work as a broadcaster. In the 1960s, Metcalfe and his wife founded a public relations company and in 1969 began working on campaigns for environmental causes, recognizing their potential to raise public awareness. He was among the founders of the Greenpeace Foundation in 1971 and became the organization's first chairman. Fellow Winnipeg journalist BOB HUNTER became the first Greenpeace president in 1973. Metcalfe was particularly passionate in his opposition to nuclear weapons, and in 1972 hired future movement leader David McTaggart to help guide a boat protesting French weapons testing in the South Pacific. Metcalfe stepped back from the movement in the mid-1970s when Greenpeace's focus shifted. He retired to Vancouver Island and returned to writing, and in 1985 published the biography *A Man of Some Importance: The Life of Roderick Langmere Haig-Brown*. • JT

METEORITE STRIKES have occurred at least

4 times in MB, as evidenced by craters formed by the impact. WEST HAWK LAKE, the deepest lake in MB, formed in a crater left after a meteorite

M

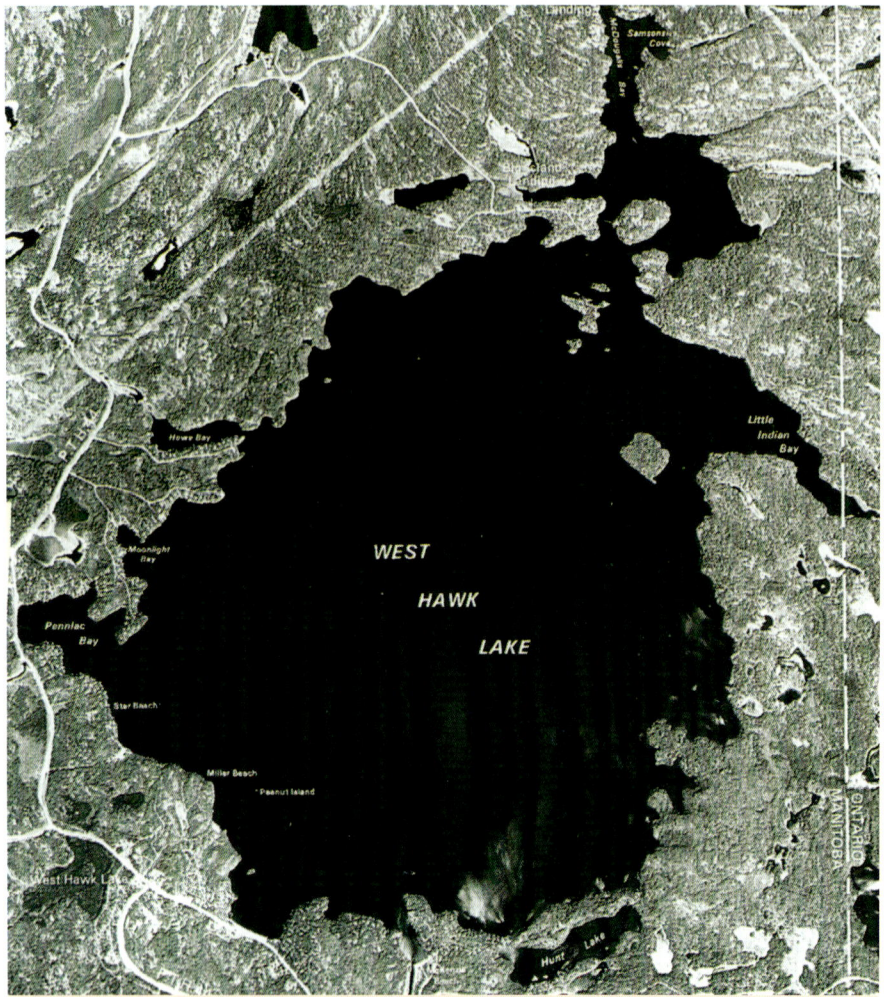

West Hawk Lake in Whiteshell Provincial Park is the end result of a meteorite strike 150 mya.

struck about 150 mya. Hundreds of millions of years before that, in the late Ordovician or early Silurian period, a smaller crater struck near Highrock Lake, 140 km NE of **FLIN FLON**. NW of Lake St. Martin there is a Permian Age crater which is 23 km in diameter and more than 300 m deep. This crater is filled with debris from the impact, including a layer of purplish, lava-like rock solidified from a molten state. Iridium-dating technology allows scientists to date meteorite strikes with considerable accuracy, but this procedure does not work for comet impacts. Another crater lies under the E part of **LAC DU BONNET**, but its age is unknown. ● MD

METHODIST CHURCH began in the 18th century by John Wesley as a revival movement within the Church of England and had become established as a separate denomination by the end of that century. Methodism was first brought to MB in 1840 when the **HBC** co-sponsored missionaries of the British Wesleyan Society to minister in several widely scattered posts. The Rev James Evans, stationed at **NORWAY HOUSE**, was the

superintendent of this group. In 1846, Evans left Norway House amid charges of sexual impropriety and thereafter the British Wesleyan missions declined. However, Evans left one significant legacy – the syllabic system he developed for writing the **CREE** language allowed the Bible to be translated into Cree and became the standard Cree orthography until it was superseded by Roman orthography in the 20th century.

A renewed effort was initiated by the Wesleyan Methodist Church in Canada (after 1874 the Methodist Church of Canada), when in 1868 Rev George Young was sent to what would become **WINNIPEG**. Young founded a mission that was to become Grace Church in 1871 and preached extensively around the new province. Thereafter, Methodist churches were established in many of the cities and towns of the agricultural frontier. Missions to Aboriginal people were also established in northern MB. In 1883, the territory was raised to conference status and the Conference of Manitoba and the North West was divided into 6 districts: Brandon, Pembina and Turtle Mountain, Portage la Prairie, Winnipeg, Saskatchewan

and Regina. As settlement progressed further, organizational changes took place. In 1884, the several branches of Methodism in Canada united as the Methodist Church.

During the period 1870-1925, the church established institutions in order to serve particular needs in its education and outreach activities. In 1888, classes began at Wesley College in Winnipeg which offered study in arts in affiliation with the **U OF M**. In 1894, the college began the independent granting of degrees in theology. Wesley College merged with Manitoba College in 1938 to become United College and in 1967 United College became the U of W.

Starting in 1892, Winnipeg's All Peoples Mission provided not only traditional church services but also a range of social and recreational services to immigrant families. The church also co-operated with the federal govt in running **RESIDENTIAL SCHOOLS** for Aboriginal children in Brandon (1889, first an industrial school and later a residential school); and Norway House (1900) and also ran day schools in various northern Aboriginal communities. In 1894, the Methodist General Conference upheld tradition by refusing to ordain women and refusing to allow women to hold office on church courts. That same year, an order of deaconesses was created that gave women a role, albeit limited, in the ministry of the church. In MB, deaconesses worked in mission settings undertaking teaching, nursing or social work or a combination of those roles. During WWI a shortage of ministers opened the way for deaconesses to conduct Sunday services and other pastoral duties. The long-standing role of women in doing practical work in support of the church's missionary efforts resulted in the formation of missionary societies at the congregational level. Local units of the Woman's Missionary Society (WMS) were formed starting in 1881 and the Manitoba Conference Branch of the WMS was created in 1895. The WMS, along with other women's groups of the period, became a forum for women to learn organizational skills and to collectively address issues outside the sphere of their own homes.

The practice of Methodism during this period continued to be based, at least nominally, on the rules first set out by Wesley in 1743. Methodists were to seek a holy life by doing no harm and avoiding evil of every kind; doing good of every possible sort and, as far as possible, to every person; attending all church ordinances including public worship and the public reading of scripture; communion; family and private prayer; personal Bible study; and fasting or abstinence. In the face of strong secularizing forces, it became difficult to maintain the more abstemious aspects of Wesley's program. However, when the Methodist Church joined in forming the United Church of Canada in 1925 it carried into the new church firm convictions for maintenance of the Sabbath day and for abstaining from alcohol and gambling.

Mainstream Methodism emphasized personal sin and personal salvation but also good works. Influenced by theological currents from Germany, Britain and the US, some Cdn Protestants, particularly younger urban clergy, began to think that it was the church's proper mission to help in redeeming society as a whole from its social and industrial ills and that the church must strive to achieve the Kingdom of God in this world not the next. Salem Bland of Wesley College along with the Rev William Ivens and the Rev **J. S. Woodsworth** were leading figures on the radical edge of this movement which came to be known as the "social gospel." Their views,

which centred on a fundamental critique of the capitalist economy, put them squarely at odds with the powerful businessmen who led church and college boards. While their tenure within the church became increasingly uncomfortable, both Ivens and Woodsworth left the ministry of their own volition. Whether Bland's political views had any role in his dismissal by the Wesley College board in 1917 – ostensibly the result of a reorganization of the faculty following several years of deficits – continues to be debated. By 1920, most of the more radical social gospel leaders had ceased to pursue their goals from within the church. Moderate social gospellers remained and their agenda became one of the strands woven into church union in 1925.

The Methodist Church had responded to the challenge of expanding into the Canadian West by co-operation in certain areas with other Protestant churches. Out of these experiences

came a movement to unite the Methodist, Presbyterian and Congregational churches in Canada into one new denomination. Sentiment in favour of union was strong in MB where in the 1921 census 610,100 people described themselves as Methodists. The vote conducted in each congregation resulted in all MB Methodist congregations voting to join in forming the **United Church of Canada** in 1925. With the formation of the new church the Methodist Church ceased to exist.
● CATHERINE MACDONALD

MÉTIS. European involvement in NA after 1492 took many forms. In the North, the driving force was the chase for fur, which dictated a less destructive intrusion into Aboriginal lands than what was practised in Central and South America. Throughout **Fur Trade** country – from the Great Lakes to the Rocky Mountains, and far into the northern boreal forests – the 'Indians' were left more or less unchanged so that they could continue to trap for furs unmolested, save that the European traders often moved into Aboriginal communities in order to increase productivity. Inevitably, the Europeans were sometimes assimilated by the First Nations, despite their plans to the contrary. These men formed relationships with First Nations women, often of long duration, and their offspring became the foundation of the Métis people. Though many such children became part of their mothers' people, in western Canada a group of them began to develop a separate identity that was not **Cree** or **Ojibway** or **Dene**, nor was it *Canadien*, **Scots**, or **English**. Rather, they became "the people who own themselves" (from the Cree, *oteepaymsoowuk*) – the "New People" also known as the Métis. The term Métis means "mixed" in French. Other terms that have been used to refer to them include Bois-Brûlé (from the Ojibway term *wissakodewinini*, meaning burnt-wood people), half-breed, **Country-Born**, mixed-blood, **Michif**, chicot, mountain men, and Rupertslanders.

The early origins of the Métis (up to 1750) occurred in the Great Lakes area and were concentrated on small local fur trade depots – places where traders from New France lived year-round, in frequent contact with First Nations people and economically interdependent with them. In the fur trade depots, neither the French males nor the Aboriginal women were dominant and, separated from their respective communities for much of the year, they had to compromise on cultural matters: thus the process of Métissage ("mixing") was begun. Here some of the cultural features of the Métis were created: their characteristic dress, blending European and Aboriginal elements and including the bright woven sash (*ceinture*

Fort Rouge Methodist Church (built in 1910) is now known as Crescent Fort Rouge United Church.

fléchée); the Michif language, a blend of French nouns and mostly Cree verbs; and, over time, the self-identification as a distinct group. These early "proto-Métis" gradually formed their own social, economic and political institutions as well. As the fur trade depot system spread to the Plains, the Métis moved with it, gradually integrating themselves into the equestrian bison-hunting economy that had developed since the European introduction of the horse. Bison pemmican became the mainstay of the western fur trade and the dominant factor in Métis economic development, since the Métis became major providers of bison pemmican to the trading companies.

The Métis Nation was born in what was later to be known as western Canada. The development of a new nation anywhere on the planet is not a common occurrence, even in colonial settings. In most situations of intermarriage between peoples, the children tend to blend in with the people of one parent or the other. Métis national development was relatively rapid, taking less than two hundred and fifty years from origins to the present. It was forged partly in situations of conflict, beginning with the Pemmican Wars, a vicious and sometimes bloody trade war between the **HBC** and **NWC** that raged from 1780-1821. In this case the Métis were major players on both sides. When the war ended in an amalgamation of the 2 companies in 1821, the reorganized HBC that emerged discharged many employees, among them a good many Métis. These individuals often became "free traders," selling furs independently in defiance of the HBC, mainly to US buyers. In fact, this was the reason for

the Métis's Cree appellation, *oteepaymsoowuk* ("the people who own themselves"), a term distinguishing them from servants of the company. This occupation sparked another important conflict for the Métis, a battle with the HBC over the right to trade fur in the area the company called "Rupert's Land." Throughout the early 1800s, the Métis challenged the Hudson's Bay Company's claimed trade monopoly through active free trading and defending their rights in court. By 1850, the Métis had effectively defeated the HBC's monopoly. (*see* **SAYER TRIAL**)

The years between 1821-70 have been called the "golden years" of the Métis Nation, a period when they were centred in Red River and able to develop and expand relatively unhindered. They continued to carve out economic and social niches for themselves and defend their pemmican-based economy against opponents. Another pivotal conflict was the clash with the **DAKOTA** over the right to hunt bison on the plains, settled through the Battle of Grand Coteau in 1851, in which the Métis defeated a much larger force of Dakota warriors. In these years, their incipient national organization, based on the bison hunt, underwent rapid growth to become the foundation of their nation and political systems. When the Métis hunted bison, an elected council organized the hunt, maintained discipline, and ensured that no one went out to hunt on their own, stampeding the bison away to the loss of everyone in the camp. Thus the Métis initiated and practised the cultural mechanisms by which they managed their communities.

But the most important and fateful conflicts the Metis faced were those with the Dominion of Canada, beginning with the **RED RIVER RESISTANCE** of 1869-70. By resisting being annexed to Canada without their consent, the Red River Métis were able to negotiate their right to enter the new country as a province instead of a territory, as well as to secure cultural protection in the form of French language and Catholic schooling rights. These rights were enshrined in the Manitoba Act, passed by the federal government in 1870, which created the province of MB. Thus, Métis leadership and political determination led to the establishment of the province with a decided role set aside for the Métis people. Although not all Métis in Red River supported the 8-month resistance led by **LOUIS RIEL**, overall the process furthered the Métis sense of nationhood.

Unfortunately, the rights guaranteed in the *Manitoba Act* were not scrupulously upheld once English Canadians had actual control of the territory. Instead, from 1870-72 the Métis faced a reign of terror at the hands of the Red River Expeditionary Force, which had been sent out by Canada to put down the resistance of 1869-70. This army arrived after the parties had negotiated a settlement, but its volunteers were eager to punish the Métis. Thus, in the province of MB's first 2 years, arson, sexual assault and violence against Métis people were the order of the day. At the same time, Canada reneged on the constitutional deals made in the *Manitoba Act* and the Métis rapidly lost control of their homes, lands and the 1.4 million ac (.57 million ha) of land promised in Section 31 of the *Manitoba Act*. Incoming non-Aboriginal settlers received the best lands at the Métis's expense. Between 1870-78, the Métis were overwhelmed by a wave of largely Ontarian settlers from the East who were hostile to both their Catholic faith and their French language. With the loss of their home base, the Métis were forced to disperse across the west, into the north and, in some cases, into the US. By 1880, the Métis were no longer a force in MB and were rapidly becoming marginalized across western Canada.

Many Métis who left MB migrated to the area around Batoche, in the "North-West Territories" (now SK), to make a fresh start. It was here that their last battle with Canada occurred, best known today as the Northwest Rebellion of 1885. This ill-fated uprising, led by a much-changed Louis Riel and supported by only about 300 of the area's 1500 Métis, was quickly crushed by 8000 troops rushed out to the West on the new **CPR** transcontinental railway. After Riel's trial and hanging in 1885, the Métis were dispossessed once more. Their homes were plundered

A Métis ox-cart train, 1870

and burned by the victorious Cdn troops, and the Métis were relegated to the crown lands of the West. In some cases, they were forced to live on road allowances so that they could be near employment as cheap farm labour on land that they once had owned. The rapidly enforced dispersal throughout their former homeland left the Métis in poverty, while the 1885 uprising tainted them for decades as "traitors" and "worthless halfbreeds." To survive, many suppressed their Métis origins and heritage, passing as French Canadians or other non-Aboriginal settlers. Some Métis social practices and traditions were retained, but many more were lost. The 'Forgotten Years' which followed were marked by the concentration on individual survival, which was all that was left to them.

It was not until the 1960s that the Métis began the long road back to national status, in a changed political climate that made it safer to identify as Métis once more. When they finally began to reformulate their culture, they faced many problems, not the least of which was the changed nature of their membership. For example, some northern communities that featured English-speaking, Protestant heritage, along with Aboriginal, began to identify themselves as Métis rather than country-born. There were several historic developments: Métis leader Yvon Dumont was appointed lt gov of MB; the Métis community of St. Laurent was featured in the Smithsonian museum in Washington DC.

In the process of cultural reformulation, the Métis turned to those Elders who still remembered the old ways and, in so doing, they rebuilt the basic structures of their Nation. They also began a political process in an attempt to reverse the land loss and resulting impoverishment they had suffered in the 19th century. At the time of writing, a Métis-initiated lawsuit concerning the 1.4 million ac promised in the *Manitoba Act* was again before Canadian courts.
● FRED J. SHORE / ROBIN JARVIS BROWNLIE

METRO WINNIPEG (Metropolitan Corporation of Greater Winnipeg) came into existence in 1960. By the 1950s, the 19 Winnipeg-area municipalities were a patchwork of different governance arrangements, marked by disorderly growth and an infrastructure crisis. Of particular concern was water availability: East Kildonan, West Kildonan, Fort Garry, St. James, and Tuxedo all depended on the water pumps of the central city of Winnipeg, and Winnipeg was less than enthusiastic about maintaining the necessary water pressure. The provincial govt responded by appointing the Greater Winnipeg Investigating Committee, which reported in 1959, advocating

Metro advertised its services in 1961.

a 2-tier metropolitan govt with authority for various metropolitan-wide services and for infrastructures such as transit, mosquito control, and major thoroughfares.

The *Metropolitan Winnipeg Act* became law in 1960 and mandated a metro govt of 10 councillors, each elected from a wedge-shaped district. In retrospect, this may have been Metro Winnipeg's downfall, as the Metro and its component municipalities were permanently locked in conflict. Winnipeg mayor Stephen Juba was particularly hostile to the Metro Corporation, and argued vociferously in favour of total amalgamation. The hostility between the 2 levels of govt reached a point of absurdity in 1970, when both the City of Winnipeg and the Metro Corporation independently submitted proposals to the federal govt for the construction of a new convention centre. The citizens of Winnipeg also opposed the Metro structure in favour of amalgamation in a 1964 referendum. Metro's failure was sealed by the amalgamation of area municipalities to form Unicity in 1972.

While Metro Winnipeg was undoubtedly a political failure, it did resolve the infrastructure crisis of the 1950s. Water pumping capacity was vastly increased, eliminating shortages in the suburbs. New thoroughfares, such as Grant Ave, connected the suburbs to the city core. New buses were purchased, and the transit system's finances were underwritten by area-wide taxation. Perhaps most importantly, Metro Winnipeg acted as an intermediary stage between the political fragmentation and inertia of the 1950s, and the total amalgamation of 1972. ● CHRIS LEO/MATTHEW MULAIRE

MIAMI, pop 400, is an unincorporated community 100 km SW of Winnipeg in the Pembina Valley. The area was originally settled by English, Scots, and Mennonites and established as Thompsonville – after William Thompson, early settler and first postmaster. (The RM is called Thompson.) By late 1878, the govt changed the community's name to Miami, after the Algonquian-speaking people of the same name from SW of Lake Erie in what is now the US. The name is not related to Miami, FL. A branch-line Railway point with a grain elevator was established here in 1889. In the 2000s, the community functions as a service centre for the surrounding agricultural area, with a K-12 school and a medical clinic. The Miami Railway Station Museum, in one of the oldest structures left in southern MB, is situated between 2 working tracks. Miami has a strong spirit of volunteerism, with the volunteer fire department for the RM and a volunteer responder unit for the local health centre. There is also a tradition of sports in the community with curling ice, a skating and hockey rink, and a covered grandstand that hosts the annual agricultural fair and rodeo. The Miami Pioneer Museum boasts vertebrae and head bones from prehistoric mammals. On Christmas Eve 2005, Miami was hit by a mass theft in which all of the community's 44 street signs were stolen. The signs were never recovered nor were the thieves found. ● GPP

MICHIF. This unique language – also called Métis Creole – evolved in parts of what is now western Canada when First Nations women and French fur traders lived close to fur depots,

M

isolated from both French and Aboriginal communities. Evenly matched and needing to co-operate to make the depots work, the inhabitants could not force culture or language on their partners. Instead, they collaborated to create a new, common language, usually a combination of French and, for the most part, **CREE**, though there may be elements of Assiniboine, **DENE**, and other tongues. There are also Michif languages today based on Middle/Classical French and Saulteaux (**OJIBWAY**) in places like **ST. LAURENT**.

Michif has caused many linguists sleepless nights. Being part French and part **CREE**, it has 2 parents and not the one parent common to the "family tree" model of language. Nouns are taken from the European language, while verbs come from the Aboriginal people. People who speak Michif – generally **MÉTIS** – rarely know the 2 source languages. It is also not a standard "mixed" language: it combines both parent languages with separate sounds, morphological endings, and syntactic rules. There are, to all intents and purposes, 2 languages in 1. This is what upsets linguists.

No other place on the globe has reported a language like Michif. Unfortunately, it is threatened with extinction, as the number of fluent speakers in the US and Canada is in steady decline. In an effort to save and revitalize the language, Métis people have created lessons and a pronunciation guide and are teaching it to young people. The language is the subject of a 1997 book, *A Language of Our Own: The Genesis of Michif, the Mixed Cree-French Language of the Canadian Métis* (Oxford University Press). ● FRED J. SHORE

MIDDLECHURCH, pop 3400, is an ex-urban community 20 km N of **WINNIPEG** along the W side of the **RED RIVER** in the RM of West St. Paul (*see* **INTERLAKE**). In 1825, an Anglican parish called Middlechurch was established here, and the area settled by **SCOTS** and **ENGLISH**. Middlechurch was so named because of its midpoint location between 2 other Anglican churches, St. John's Cathedral in Winnipeg, and St. Andrew's Church, from which the RM of St. Andrews takes its name. More recently, **UKRAINIANS**, **GERMANS**, Poles, and **ITALIANS** have come to the area. The Middlechurch post office opened around 1870 and closed in 1963. In 1904, a rail line went from Winnipeg through Middlechurch and **LOCKPORT** to **SELKIRK**. Just before WWI, a **CPR** line was added from here to **STONEWALL**. In 1937, the service was curtailed and, in 1939, abandoned outright. Today, most residents of the RM live in Middlechurch, and due to its proximity to Winnipeg, Middlechurch has become the site of extensive housing development for residents who work in the nearby city. ● GPP

MIDEWIWIN, or Grand Medicine Society, is a highly organized, formal association of Indigenous healers that, according to tradition, originated among ancestral Ojibway on the Atlantic seaboard many generations ago. It was likely introduced into MB in the late 1700s by Ojibway moving W with the **FUR TRADE**. The roots of the Midewiwin lie in pre-contact Woodland culture, but its full development drew impetus from the effects of disease, depopulation, and threats to Aboriginal economic, political, and religious systems brought on by the arrival of the Europeans. The strong influence of the Midewiwin is one reason the Ojibway historically resisted the inroads of Christianity.

The Midewiwin is a closed group that provides training in traditional **MEDICINE**. Its membership (*mideg* or *kitchimidewiwak*) includes both men and women – and in some cases, children – and is obtained by a 3-phase process of application, preliminary instruction, and formal initiation at a semi-annual or annual communal gathering. It is principally devoted to securing health and good life (*bimaadiziwin*) for its members, and to the maintenance of the spiritual, physical, and emotional well being of the community. The ability to heal is given to the *mideg* by spiritual beings, and their responsibility is to share this gift for the benefit of all. One source notes that "Midewiwin" most correctly translates as "Society of Good-Hearted Ones" or "The Resonance," the latter referring to the distinctive sound of water drums used during ceremonies.

Under the leadership of their "priests," Midewiwin practitioners are able to acquire and increase their healing powers by passage through 4 to 8 stages, or degrees. Some individuals can achieve as many as 16 levels of learning. Advancement from one degree to another involves intensive periods of instruction in numerous rituals and in the use of medicinal remedies, quests for spiritual knowledge, and special initiation ceremonies. In addition to formal instruction, knowledge is also acquired through personal vision quests. The priests are conversant in Ojibway history, cosmology, and cosmography, and these are embodied in teachings codified in pictographic designs incised on sacred birch bark scrolls. These mnemonic devices are used in the instruction of individual *midé* candidates, and at communal ceremonies, when traditional teachings are recounted to the assembly of participants. Midewiwin motifs also appear as rock paintings in selected locales on the Canadian Shield. (*see* **PETROFORMS**.)

Members of the Midewiwin carry out their functions both privately and communally. Their approach to healing is holistic, and treatments accordingly address the mind, body, and spirit of individual patients. The principal communal ceremony of the society is a Grand Medicine Feast, a public gathering held each year in late spring and/or early autumn. Feasts are held in a large, specially built rectangular lodge (*midewigan*) constructed of poles and saplings. Midewiwin practitioners employ ritually prescribed sacred objects during the ceremonies, including animal-hide medicine bags representing various degrees of membership; seashells, including cowrie (*Cypraea montea*); rattles; water drums; and ceremonial pipes. The sacred plants of tobacco, cedar, sage, and sweetgrass are also used. Spiritual offerings include tobacco and other material goods, some of which are gifts for the priests in return for their services. Observances, which extend over a period of several days, include continuous prayer and, during the first days of celebration, the retelling of the traditional Creation story, deeds of the culture hero Nanabozho, origins of the Midewiwin, and migration stories of the Ojibway. The beginnings and functions of the 7 original clans (*odoidaymiwug* – Bear, Bird, Crane, Fish, Hoof, Loon, and Martin), which provide the people with their roles in the order of creation, are recounted. The mandates, responsibilities, and associated strengths of the various clans are the fabric of indigenous Ojibway society, and as such also have their place in the functioning of the Midewiwin. During the final days of the ceremony, candidates are initiated into the appropriate degrees. Throughout the duration of the Medicine Feast, those in attendance partake of specially prepared communal meals.

While the *Indian Act* never banned the celebration of the Midewiwin outright, missionaries and Indian agents acting on behalf of the Department of Indian Affairs discouraged its practice. However, the ceremonial redistribution of goods ("Giveaways"), as practised at the Grand Medicine Feasts, did contravene federally imposed restrictions until 1951. Giveaways were considered to be impoverishing, and the prayer offerings of material goods wasteful and incompatible with European-Cdn values of individualized property ownership and material progress. Traditional healers were undermined, and the rich knowledge of medicinal remedies and healing methods which had been used for generations were dismissed by the authorities as "quackery."

Persistent missionary activity and the **RESIDENTIAL SCHOOL** system also served to discourage membership in the Midewiwin. Despite these challenges, elements of it have prevailed, and the society has been revitalized in several different forms in keeping with local traditions. Recently, syncretic expressions of the Midewiwin have been developed by combining traditional teachings with Christian symbols and beliefs. Today, the sounding of the holy water drum calls together members of the Society of the Good-Hearted Ones to use their healing gifts for the benefit of all. Increasingly, **Ojibway** people from all callings, including professionals, are returning to the teachings of the Midewiwin. Their lives are guided by a strict code of ethics based on wisdom, love, respect, courage, honesty, humility, and truth, and which are grounded in centuries of ancient sacred teachings. ● KATHERINE PETTIPAS/LEO PETTIPAS

MIDGE (marshfly) is a type of small (1-10 mm), mostly non-biting fly in the family Chironomidae. The adult midge has a thin, mosquito-like body, the wings are held to the side when at rest, and the male has large feathery antennae. Adult midges are short lived, only a few days to a week, and feed on honeydew and plant nectar. At dusk, the males form mating swarms, usually over a particular piece of ground or tall structure. These can be a nuisance if a person becomes engulfed in the cloud. Adult midges are sometimes attracted to lights at night in astonishing numbers. At Delta Marsh, massive mating swarms look like columns of smoke above the treed beach ridge. Females fly into a swarm of males, where copulation takes place. The female leaves the swarm to lay eggs on water and these hatch soon after. The larval stage resembles a small worm, but with an obvious head capsule. The larvae of some species are blood-red due to the presence of oxygen-carrying hemoglobin in the body fluids. Most of the life cycle is spent in the larval stage, which can last from several weeks to many years, depending on the species, habitat conditions, and latitude. Midge larvae can be found in silken tubes in soft-bottom substrates, burrowed into aquatic plants, or free-living on bottom.

Midges are present in almost all types of aquatic habitats. One species (*Metriocnemus knabi*) is specialized to live in pitcher plants (Sarracenia purpurea). Midge larvae feed on a variety of microscopic foods, and can be herbivores, detritivores (eating organic debris), and predators. Midges overwinter as larvae, which in some species can tolerate freezing. Larval and adult midges are consumed by other invertebrates, fish, birds and bats. High densities of songbirds at Delta Marsh are attributed to the abundance of adult midges that originate from Lake Manitoba and the marsh. Over 100 species occur there, and larval densities in the bottom

mud have been found be as high as 16,000/m². About 135 genera and 480 species are known in Canada, and about 300 species are found in MB. Midges evolved from a lineage of insect whose adults had a diet of vertebrate blood or insect fluids (hemolymph) about 210 million years ago (Late-Triassic period). They are known from a wealth of well-preserved fossils in lake sediments and amber. ● DW, REW

MIDWIFERY has existed in MB for a long time. It was traditional in First Nations communities long before modern Western medicine. However, over the 20th century, physicians displaced midwives, replacing a notion of the childbearing cycle as normal and natural with a model of pregnancy and childbirth as high-risk medical conditions. During this period, the practice of midwifery in Canada was neither legal nor officially recognized. While midwifery was never entirely eliminated, particularly in remote, northern areas, the few women providing these services operated in a legal grey zone. Unfortunately, Canada was the last developed country to recognize or regulate midwifery, a calling that had long history in both the UK and France.

Over the 1970s and '80s, feminists and others challenged obstetricians' monopoly on childbearing. The women's health movement lobbied extensively to make midwifery legal and accessible, and to integrate it into MB's public health system. In 2000, the passage of MB's *Midwifery Act* allowed the practice to evolve from an "underground" practice to a legitimate, self-regulating profession based on respect for pregnancy as a state of health and the view of childbirth as a normal physiological process. The act defines midwives as "primary health care providers" able to care for women during pregnancy, to conduct normal spontaneous vaginal deliveries, and to care for infants up to 6 weeks after birth. MB was the 4th Cdn province to legislate midwifery, after ON, QC, and BC. (NT and NU both allow for midwives, and AB and SK have since passed similar legislation.) The midwifery model of care in MB specifies that midwives are autonomous providers offering continuity of health care; respect for a woman's choice of birth settings; and collaboration with other health professionals. Midwives in the province recognize that there should be 2 attendants at each birth. The act also establishes a self-regulating governing body known as the College of Midwives of MB, with whom midwives must be registered before practising. The college has established a rigorous registration process to test midwifery competencies skills, and experience.

In 2005, MB had 29 practising midwives and about 15,000 births. There is a severe shortage of midwives, particularly outside Winnipeg. Unlike ON, QC, and BC, MB has not established a postsecondary midwife training program, though the **Aboriginal** Midwifery Education Program was scheduled to open in **The Pas** and **Norway House** in Sept 2006. ● SUSAN PRENTICE

MIGRATION is the repeated movement of an organism between 2 areas in response to changes in the environment, often related to temperature and availability of food resources. Migration is sometimes confused with immigration, which is the one-way movement into a region, and emigration, the movement out of a region. Dragonflies often emigrate long distances, but do not return to their home pond. Likewise, jellyfish and other creatures drift on the currents into **Hudson Bay** in summer but do not exit, completing their lives there. And one of the most-widely publicized migrations – that of the lemming – is in reality emigration, for the rodents are stressed by over-population into dispersing to new unoccupied territories, and never return.

Numerous examples of true migration may be found in many kinds of animals. As examples, zooplankton (small animals suspended in the water) in both fresh and marine waters undergo daily vertical migrations (e.g., 1-50 m) in response to light level – downward in the day, and back up during the night. The **Monarch Butterfly** may travel 130 km/day (assisted by winds) and up to 1900 km in late summer from S MB to roost by the millions in trees in the Mexican highlands, although it is the succeeding generations that make the return trip in spring. Numerous species of hawkmoths (family Sphingidae) migrate in the spring from S and central US into MB to reproduce, and they and/or their offspring return S to avoid the winter. Fishes, both freshwater and marine, make annual migrations to favourite feeding or natal breeding grounds, some like Arctic Char moving between marine and freshwater. The Tiger Salamander migrates overland several km in the spring to breed in a pond, while the Plains **Garter Snake** spends the summers feeding in the marshes and fields (e.g., **Inwood**), only to return to the same sinkhole for hibernation by fall.

The all-time record holder for long-distance migrants – the Arctic Tern – migrates 35,000 km roundtrip, breeding in N MB and the High Arctic and wintering in Antarctica. The Hoary, Red and Silver-haired bats migrate up to 1000 km S to winter in the S US, while the Little Brown Bat may migrate only 200 km between its summer home range in SE MB to hibernating caves in the

RUDOLF KOES

The Arctic Tern holds the record for long-distance migration.

INTERLAKE. Barren-ground **CARIBOU** travel about 700 km between the summer breeding grounds on the barrens of Nunavut to the forest-tundra woodland and forests of central MB for the winter. Up until the great herds of **BISON** and Pronghorn were decimated by the late 19th century, both species migrated up to 500 km into S MB for the summer and back into the Dakotas for the winter, although some apparently remained here year-round. The Beluga and Bowhead **WHALES** migrate S from the Arctic Ocean into Hudson Bay each summer, and depart N again before freeze-up. Several species of seals display the same pattern of movements.

There are countless variations on the theme of migration, some merging into short-range travels. Examples of elevational migration are rare due to MB's relatively flat landscape. Usually species take specific routes or flyways on their migration, and not always the most-direct N-S path. MB is on both the Central and Atlantic flyways of birds. While some species travel only at night, others prefer the day, or travel both day and night. Movements may be halted by poor weather, and storms frequently blow migrants way off course. In fact, the Nene or Hawaiian Goose (*Branta sandvicensis*) evolved from a few errant Canada Geese migrating along the Pacific coast of NA. Many birds await favourable winds before resuming the next flight leg, and waterfowl in particular fly in V patterns – both traits designed to conserve energy. There are numerous examples of astounding feats of migration. Snow Geese can fly at altitudes up to 6100 m to locate strong winds, and there is a recorded instance of a large flock of these geese departing

from the High Arctic and reaching the Gulf of Mexico in 2 days, with only a brief stopover in James Bay.

Many people enjoy watching bird migrations, such as the fall warblers in **ASSINIBOINE PARK** in **WINNIPEG** and along the S shore of **LAKE WINNIPEG**. Signs of spring are the appearance of the Horned Lark along roadways as early as late Feb, Western Meadowlark in mid-March, and soon after, American Robin in farms and city yards. Many birders converge in April to the Pembina Hills near Windygates and the **ST. ADOLPHE** Bridge on the **RED RIVER** to witness the spectacular return of hawks and eagles (often over 400 raptors per day). The cost of migration is high, both in terms of energy expenditure and loss of life (depleted fat reserves, accidents, predation, bad weather, becoming lost). However, this instinctive behaviour is widespread in the animal kingdom, so the advantages in finding new unoccupied breeding territories, with a rich food supply and breeding cover, confers over-riding advantages for species survival. ● REW

MIKI, Arthur Kazumi "Art," citizenship judge, educator, community activist, (b 1936, Vancouver) is known for his work to promote improved race relations and to increase awareness of **HUMAN RIGHTS** issues in Canada. In 1942, when Miki was 5 years old, his family was forcibly removed from Vancouver to **STE. AGATHE** to work on a **SUGAR BEET** farm. In 1944, the family moved to **WINNIPEG**'s North Kildonan and Miki attended his first **ENGLISH**-speaking school. He went on to receive his BSc from the **U OF W** in 1968, a BEd in 1969, and his MEd in 1975 from the **U OF M**.

Miki, brother to author **ROY MIKI**, subsequently became a teacher and principal in Winnipeg schools for 29 years.

Miki became active in cultural organizations, especially in the **JAPANESE** Canadian community. He became president of the National Association of Japanese Canadians in 1984, and led the negotiations that achieved a 1988 settlement for Japanese Canadians interned during WWII. He served as the first vice-chair of the Canadian Race Relations Foundation that was established as part of the redress settlement. Miki was also the exec dir of the Organization for Co-operation in Overseas Development and a board member of several organizations, including director of the Manitoba Japanese Canadian Cultural Centre. He is the author of the book *Japanese Canadian Redress Legacy: A Community Revitalized* (2003).

CHERYL MIKI

Art Miki has increased awareness of human rights issues.

Miki dabbled in politics when he ran for the **LIBERAL PARTY** in the 1993 federal election, coming within 100 votes of winning. He was appointed Citizenship Judge for MB and SK in 1998. Miki has received numerous awards, including an Exceptional Contribution Award from the Manitoba Federal Council. In 1991, Miki received the Order of Canada, and in 1999 he received an honorary doctorate from the U of W. ● AMANDA STEPHENS

MIKI, Roy Akira, poet, writer, activist (b Oct 10, 1942, **STE. AGATHE**), was born during WWII on a sugar beet farm where his parents had been relocated by the Cdn govt as part of the *War Measures Act*. As a 3rd-generation **JAPANESE** Canadian, this wartime experience profoundly affected his life. Roy grew up in **WINNIPEG**, graduating from the **U OF M** in 1964 with a BA in English. A year later, he became involved with the Toronto folk **MUSIC** scene, and his first published poems began to appear in literary journals. Miki subsequently earned a MA from Simon Fraser U and a PhD from the U of BC. Miki has taught English at Simon Fraser U since 1975, and edits *West Coast Line*. Miki's experiences inspired his involvement in the redress movement, which in 1988 successfully won compensation from the federal govt for interned and relocated Japanese Canadians. He chronicles this struggle in the non-fiction books *Justice in Our Time: The Japanese Canadian Redress Settlement* (1991) and *Redress: Inside the Japanese Canadian Call for Justice* (2005). However, Miki is probably best known for his poetry, in which he explores issues of authority, identity, and family history, as in *Saving Face: Poems Selected, 1976-1988* (1991), *Random Access File* (1995), and *Surrender* (2001), for which he won the Gov Gen's Award for poetry. ● JILL SEXSMITH

MILGAARD, David, wrongfully convicted (b July, 1952, Winnipeg). Milgaard's **WRONGFUL CONVICTION** is one of the most infamous cases in Cdn history. He spent 23 years in prison for the murder of Gail Miller in Saskatoon. Born in **WINNIPEG**, Milgaard moved to SK as a child. A free-spirited teenager, at age 16 Milgaard went on a road trip with some friends, and happened to be passing through Saskatoon on the day of Miller's murder. Under mounting public pressure to find the young woman's killer, police zeroed in on Milgaard. He was tried and convicted of the murder in 1970, largely on the basis of contradictory witness testimony. Milgaard refused to admit guilt for the crime, though his adamant claims of innocence meant he was denied a chance for early parole. His mother Joyce Milgaard fought tirelessly for her son's release throughout the more than 2 decades he was incarcerated, mainly at **STONY MOUNTAIN PENITENTIARY**. Milgaard's lawyer David **ASPER** finally succeeded in having a review of his case ordered, and the SK govt released Milgaard in 1992, though he wasn't fully exonerated by DNA evidence until 1997. Serial rapist Larry Fisher was subsequently convicted of Miller's murder in 1999. The SK govt then issued a formal apology and $10 million in compensation to Milgaard. In 2004, an inquiry was launched to examine the case. The final report had not been released as of writing. Milgaard's story is detailed in the book *When Justice Fails: The David Milgaard Story* (1992) by Carl Karp and Cecil Rosner. ● MD

MILITARY IN MANITOBA

By P. D. Hatton, Bruce Tascona, Fred McGuinness, and Carl A. Christie

M

The military in Manitoba, as with the rest of Canada, has a rich history. That history can be divided into 3 eras: an era of no formal military presence; an era of military presence brought in from abroad; and an era of contributing to the Cdn military. Army units have had the longest history in the province, with navy and air force becoming significant in the 20th century.

AM, WINNIPEG - BUILDINGS - BUSINESS- RADIGER, C.W. 1, N1252

Soldiers parading on Main Street, Winnipeg, ca 1872

OVERVIEW: Before the **RED RIVER RESISTANCE** and MB's entry into Confederation through the **RUPERTSLAND TRANSFER**, there was little formal military involvement in the area. Actions that would now be classed as military were performed by various individuals rather than by professional soldiers. This was true whether the conflicts were between different Aboriginal groups, such as the Battle of Grand Coteau between **DAKOTA** and **MÉTIS** in 1851; or skirmishes between different tribes, such as ongoing disputes – usually over horses – between the Plains **CREE** and the Dakota; or between **FUR TRADE** groups, such as **PIERRE-ESPRIT RADISSON**'s capture of a **FORT** on the **NELSON RIVER** at **HUDSON BAY** in 1682; or between white and Aboriginal people, such as the **SEVEN OAKS INCIDENT** of 1816. This style of "military" presence was eventually replaced by various regimental troops imported to MB.

As European **IMMIGRATION** grew, the British (and later the Cdn) govt began to show military interest in the area. **LORD SELKIRK** hired Swiss mercenaries to help protect his **RED RIVER SETTLEMENT**. Later, a few **ENGLISH** units, such as the Chelsea Pensioners – a group of UK Army veterans so named because their distinguished service allowed them to be domiciled at the

Royal Hospital Chelsea in London – would be sent by the **HBC** to oversee the peace, but their presence was sporadic. In reaction to the Red River Resistance of 1869-70, the Cdn govt decided to establish an army presence in the new province. This was originally a collection of British Imperial soldiers and militia volunteers from ON and QC known as the Manitoba Field Force, under the command of Col Garnet Wolseley. This force did not see any action, however, as **Louis Riel** fled and his **Provisional Government** melted away upon the arrival of the troops. However, from then on, there was a continuous military presence in the Red River/**Winnipeg** area.

A 3rd stage of military development in MB began in the late 19th century, when local militia units were formed. They not only met MB's needs but eventually also made significant contributions to Canada's military requirements overseas. In 1884, Wolseley – charged with raising the Siege of Khartoum in Sudan – recruited **York Boat** rivermen from MB to crew the transport boats travelling up the Nile. During the 1885 North West Resistance in what is now SK, several MB-based units (including the newly formed batt that would become the **Royal Winnipeg Rifles**) rode W to help defeat the Métis irregulars. In 1899, many Manitobans fought in the Boer War in South Africa.

Camp Hughes, 1916

In WWI, MB was particularly noteworthy for its contribution. Almost 55,000 volunteers from Manitoba served in the military – about 12% of the total Cdn force, at a time when MB had about 6% of the national population. Almost half of all eligible Manitoban males signed up – by far the highest rate of any province. In addition, those who served did so with distinction. By the end of the war, MB boasted 15 of 70 Cdn **Victoria Crosses**, including 3 by men from one street in Winnipeg, Pine St (*see* **Valour Road**). Training took place on a large scale at Camp Hughes, located near Shilo, which boasted the 2nd-largest population in MB during the war. Complete with an entire trench system, Camp Hughes trained thousands of troops and prepared them for action in Europe.

In WWII, Manitobans again rose to the challenge, with 75,000 enlistees, approaching 50% of eligible males. A significant contribution to the war effort, however, was also found at home. Canada agreed to create schools to train air personnel in the **British Commonwealth Air Training Plan**, and MB was a key player. A total of 18 units trained thousands of men and women from around the world, in every trade from pilot and navigator to wireless operator and air gunner. The flat terrain and the sunny weather made MB an ideal location for aircrew training.

After WWII, troops dispersed back to their homes, bringing a wealth of experiences from around the world to the province. During the Cold War, the defence of NA involved an intricate web of radar stations to warn of potential bomber and missile attacks to the continent. In the 1950s and '60s, radar stations at **Beausejour**, Bird (NE of Gillam), **Cranberry Portage** and **Gypsumville** were part of the MB contribution to the Pinetree and Mid-Canada lines.

The military has been required in MB during peacetime, too. During the great **Floods** of the **Red River** in 1950 and 1997, the CF was called upon to aid in aerial surveillance, rescue work, building sandbag dikes, communications, and in many other needs. During the 1997 flood, over 8500 CF members from across Canada assisted, making it the largest peacetime military operation in Cdn history to that date.

Today, MB has 3 regular force locations. In Air Command, 17 Wing, among the larger air bases in Canada and the home of 1 Canadian Air Division Headquarters (the HQ for all CF operational flying in Canada), is in Winnipeg. **CFB Shilo** is home of the 1st Regt, **Royal Canadian Horse Artillery**, and the 2nd Batt, **Princess Patricia's Canadian Light Infantry** (who were serving in Afghanistan, as of writing). The 3rd, Southport Airport at Portage la Prairie, is a civilian/military partnership that houses 3 Canadian Forces Flying Training School, which provides primary flying training, helicopter, and multi-engine training for the CF. With these, and the naval reserve unit HMCS *Chippewa* and air reserve, as well as the militia units scattered throughout the province, there is no doubt that Manitobans will continue to make great contributions to the defence of Canada. ● P. D. HATTON

ARMY. Army activities for many years consisted entirely of volunteer militia units based around MB that would expand or contract, or be completely reorganized, based on the level of perceived threat to the province or nation.

THE FENIAN RAID, 1871: By summer 1871, MB's political troubles following entrance into Confederation had barely subsided when an old threat resurfaced. In late Sept, the US consul in Winnipeg informed lt gov **Adams George Archibald** about the presence of Fenian leader John O'Neill in Pembina, Dakota Territory (now ND). The Fenians were an organization dedicated to the capture of Canada in order to trade it for an independent Ireland. The Fenians' strategy was to take advantage of the troubles that had plagued the Red River Settlement in previous years. However, unknown to O'Neil, this was not the **Assiniboia** of 1869, with its many grievances. By 1871, the local population had resolved many of their complaints.

The Dominion govt established a small force of regular troops, consisting of 2 service companies of rifles, under the command of Maj A. G. Irvine.

AM, FENIAN RAID 6, N10050

Provisional Battalion leaving Fort Garry in search of Fenians, 1871

These were created from the volunteers of the 1st Ontario and 2nd Quebec batts, which came W with the **WOLSELEY EXPEDITION** of 1870. On hearing that the Fenians were near Pembina, the Cdn govt decided to raise another expeditionary force under Maj Thomas Scott. With the onset of winter looming, no guarantee could be made, however, that the relief force would arrive before the freeze-up of rivers and lakes in northwestern ON. With that in mind, Archibald and Irvine realized they would have to confront this threat with local resources. On Oct 2, 1871, Archibald authorized Irvine to recruit and organize local companies of militia within the province. Overnight, volunteers stepped forward to form the 1st active militia corps.

The Fenians invaded Canada on Oct 5, 1871. They crossed over the border at Emerson, capturing the HBC fort. Upon hearing the news, Irvine's unit left Upper Fort Garry. They travelled to the Scratching River (now **MORRIS**) when word reached them that the US army had already taken decisive measures and entered Canada to arrest the Fenians. It was rumoured Americans were being held hostage, and this had forced the US army to act. After the threat evaporated, the volunteers were soon disbanded.

MANITOBA'S VOLUNTEER MOVEMENT, 1872-84: MB was gazetted as Military District 10 on Oct 16, 1871, with LCol Osborne Smith as its 1st commanding officer. A month later, the 2nd Red River Expedition finally arrived at Upper Fort Garry. This small force took up its duties as both police and military garrison in the district.

The lessons of the Red River Resistance and the Fenian Raid of 1871 were clear to Osborne Smith. To meet any future crisis in the province a force of active militia should be organized. Using the Fenian Raid as a guideline, Smith determined that the local militia forces should be authorized as follows: 2 troops of cavalry (mounted infantry), on demi-battery, and 9 companies of infantry. From the beginning, it was apparent that the raising of this authorized number of militia corps would never be achieved. The local populace felt a sense of security with the arrival of the regular Dominion Forces, which was reinforced by the creation of the **NORTH-WEST MOUNTED POLICE** in 1873. By 1872, only one troop of cavalry, the demi-battery, and 4 companies had been organized.

Training was the responsibility of the local company commander. All too often local officers lacked appropriate certificates of qualification. The result was that units could only perform the simplest of drill and manoeuvres. Between 1871-74, training was held annually at the local corps headquarters. The economic depression of 1874-75 limited the resources available, with the City Corps, whose instruction cost less, being trained annually whilst the Rural Corps only trained every 2 years. Since most of the units were designated "rural," this policy resulted in a low standard of efficiency.

To ensure the political situation of MB would remain stable, regular troops brought in from eastern Canada in 1871 – and subsequently each year afterward – were formed into Canada's first regular infantry batt. This unit was composed of 17 officers and 300 men billeted at **LOWER FORT GARRY**, **UPPER FORT GARRY**, and Fort Dufferin, under the command of LCol Irvine. When the creation of the **NORTH-WEST MOUNTED POLICE** took place the next year, many of the original volunteers to this force came from the Provisional Batt.

The NWMP provided a sense of security to the European settlers. By 1875, only a company of infantry and an artillery battery of the original militia volunteer companies established in 1872 were on the active list. However, the Little Bighorn debacle of 1876 in the Montana Territory saw the arrival of Lakota Sioux refugees throughout western Canada. This led to a wave of insecurity, which, combined with the 6-fold growth in population since 1870, made it necessary to create more units of militia.

The commanding officer, LCol C. F. Houghton, neglected these new companies – his energies were focused on the creation of an infantry batt within the district.

MILITIA, 1883-1902: By 1883, settlers from ON and QC were quickly filling up the open spaces of MB. The rapid growth meant that MB was inheriting many of the institutions long established in the older parts of the country, including the Cdn militia. Canada at the time possessed a small regular army backed by a large militia consisting of citizen soldiers. In 1883, the citizens of Winnipeg petitioned the govt in Ottawa to create an infantry batt. This new military unit was created using the existing Winnipeg Infantry Company to form the nucleus of the 90th Winnipeg Batt of Rifles (later to become the **ROYAL WINNIPEG RIFLES**). Apart from the 90th, the Winnipeg Field Battery, the Kildonan Infantry Company, and the Winnipeg Troop of Cavalry remained as effective militia units in Military District 10. A permanent school of Mounted Infantry was organized in 1883 in Winnipeg, which became "B" Squadron, Royal Canadian Dragoons in 1892.

The Royal Winnipeg Rifles earned their nickname (Little Black Devils) at the Battle of Fish Creek during the Northwest Rebellion of 1885

THE NORTHWEST REBELLION, 1885: In March 1885, the Métis under **LOUIS RIEL** fought and beat the NWMP and their volunteers in the skirmish at Duck Lake (in what is now SK). As the crisis deepened, the govt mobilized many corps and regts throughout eastern Canada. However, it would take several months before their presence would be felt. The 90th Batt and the Winnipeg Field Battery were ordered mobilized for active service soon after Duck Lake. These 2 units would receive their baptism of fire at the battle of Fish Creek and would later take part in the siege and battle of Batoche.

Within days of their departure in early April, 2 new infantry batts were organized – officers from some of the existing local militia companies were authorized to form the 91st Winnipeg Batt of Infantry under LCol Scott – the former commander of the 2nd Red River Expedition of 1871. The Kildonan Infantry Company formed 1 Company of the 92nd Winnipeg Batt of Light Infantry under the command of LCol Osborne Smith – the former commander of Military District 10. This battalion would become part of the Alberta Field Force under BGen Strange. It undertook a long, arduous march from Calgary to Edmonton, then took part in the campaign to subdue Big Bear and his followers. This campaign culminated in the battle of Frenchman's Butte. The existing Winnipeg Troop of Cavalry was mobilized and served on the lines of communications of MGen Middleton's column during the Rebellion. A provisional corps of mounted troops was organized by Maj CHARLES BOULTON from the Russell/Birtle district to be known as Boulton's Mounted Infantry Corps. This unit served as scouts and mounted infantry for Middleton's column, and was present at the battles of Fish Creek and Batoche.

Following the Northwest Rebellion, the infantry units that were raised provisionally for the crisis were absorbed into the militia. This reorganization of the Cdn militia in MB continued throughout the 1890s.

THE SOUTH AFRICA (BOER) WAR, 1899-1902: When war in South Africa broke out, the militia units in MB consisted of the following corps: The Winnipeg Field Battery, 90th Winnipeg Rifles, "A and B" Troops, Manitoba Dragoons. Volunteers from the 90th and the Manitoba Dragoons in 1899 formed "A" Company, Royal Canadian Regt. This outfit made up Canada's 1st contingent in the war. It was present and key at the battle of Paardeburg – the 1st notable victory for the British in the Boer War. Successive contingents left Canada, the most notable being the first Canadian Mounted Rifles (later to be known as the Royal Canadian Dragoons). The Manitoba Dragoons formed "B" Troop of this regt. Later, the Manitoba Dragoons contributed to the 2nd Canadian Mounted Rifles and 5th Regt of Canadian Mounted Rifles. The Winnipeg Field Battery contributed volunteers to the Royal Canadian Field Artillery contingents.

1902-14: Following the general departure of British troops from NA, 5 regts of cavalry were created: 12th Manitoba Dragoons (1903), 18th Manitoba Mounted Rifles (1907), 20th Border Horse (1908), 32nd Manitoba Horse (1912), and the 34th Fort Garry Horse (1912). In addition to cavalry, 4 more regts of infantry were formed: 99th Manitoba Rangers (1908), 100th Winnipeg Grenadiers (1908), 79th QUEEN'S OWN CAMERON HIGHLANDERS OF CANADA (1910), 106th Winnipeg Light Infantry (1912). A militia artillery battery was established in 1912 known as 36th St. Boniface Independent Battery CFA. In 1914, the 14th Field Artillery Brigade CFA was established in Winnipeg when the 38th Winnipeg Field Battery CFA was brigaded with the 13th Winnipeg Field Battery CFA. Miscellaneous units were also created to provide some balance in the District's organization: 2 Field Troop, Canadian Engineers (1912), 11th Company Canadian Army Service Corps (1905), 18th Company Canadian Army Service Corps (1912) all were located in Winnipeg.

The Permanent Regular Forces were expanded as well, the Royal Canadian Mounted Rifles became known as the Lord Strathcona Horse (Royal Canadians). This regt would have a link with Winnipeg until after WWII when it moved to Calgary. "C" Battery, Royal Canadian Horse Artillery was a component of the Winnipeg Garrison and is now a regular army unit stationed at CFB Shilo under the name 1st Regt, Royal Canadian Horse Artillery.

In 1910, a 120-mi² area for military training was established at Sewell Camp (today's CFB Shilo). For the next 4 years, thousands of militiamen would gather from SK, NW ON, and MB to train in manoeuvres and drill at Sewell. Armouries were built in many communities – the Minto and McGregor armouries were built in Winnipeg, while Brandon, Portage la Prairie, Virden, Dauphin, and Minnedosa had armouries built in their communities.

WWI, 1914-18: With the outbreak of war, the federal Minister of Militia and Defence, Col Sam Hughes, initiated a new mobilization scheme whereby militia regts were not to be mobilized, but rather drafts of volunteers from each unit would be sent to the newly created Canadian Expeditionary Force (CEF).

Initially, the Winnipeg garrison gathered at Camp St. Charles in Aug 1914 waiting for orders. By the end of Aug, volunteers from every corps and regt within the province boarded special trains destined to Camp Valcartier. Arriving in Sept, Manitobans helped formed the following units of the 1st Canadian Contingent: The 12th Manitoba Dragoons provided a contingent to the 5th "Western Cavalry" Infantry Battalion CEF. The 18th Manitoba Mounted Rifles, 20th Border Horse, 32nd Manitoba Horse and 34th Fort Garry Horse formed the 6th Canadian Infantry Battalion CEF. The 90th Regt, Winnipeg Rifles, formed the nucleus of the 8th Canadian Infantry Battalion CEF. The 99th Manitoba Rangers provided approximately 200 men to this battalion. The 106th Winnipeg Light Infantry along with a Calgary regt formed the 10th Canadian Infantry Battalion CEF. The 100th WINNIPEG GRENADIERS along with SK regts formed the 11th Canadian Infantry Battalion CEF. The 79th Camerons formed a double company of the 16th Canadian Infantry Battalion. The militia regts were not the only organizations to help form units for the CEF; social organizations and ethnic groups helped raise new battalions for overseas service.

Manitoban regts served with valour at various battles on the Western Front. The 90th Winnipeg Rifles were sent to Ypres in April 1915 where they were among the first battalions to suffer a poison gas attack from the Germans. Despite high casualties, the Rifles drove off the attack, thereby beginning a tradition of never losing a trench to the enemy. The Queen's Own Cameron Highlanders of Canada also served with distinction, with Winnipeg's 43rd Battalion being awarded 18 battle honours. In 1917, the FORT GARRY HORSE engaged in one of the last successful cavalry engagements, overrunning a German machine gun nest and incurring heavy losses.

THE INTER-WAR YEARS, 1920-39: Once the Great War had ended, the CEF was disbanded and the defence of the country was returned to the Cdn militia. The permanent force garrison was expanded with the creation of the infantry regt of the Princess Patricia's Canadian Light Infantry (PPCLI). Later, with the formation of the 2nd Batt, PPCLI, the town of Tuxedo became a military garrison town with the former agricultural college being purchased by the govt. The Osborne Barracks near Broadway was closed and a new Fort Osborne Barracks was established in Tuxedo. This suburb of Winnipeg lost its status as a military garrison community in 2005 when the Kapyong Barracks, formerly known as Fort Osborne, was closed. One of the most notable changes was the increase in supporting arms units. The Great War had taught the military the need to increase the units of the Army Service Corps and the artillery. In 1935, several regts were disbanded and converted to artillery, creating the 26th Field Brigade RCA (today the 26th Field Regt) based out of Brandon. In 1934, the training camp of Camp Hughes, near CARBERRY, was closed and all its buildings moved to the nearby CNR siding known as Camp Shilo.

WWII, 1939-45: The frantic efforts to mobilize seen in the Great War were not to materialize with the coming of WWII. There was a methodical plan for raising the military units to go on active service. Apart from sending MB's regts to war, the main focus was on training the newly expanded Canadian Army.

Manitoba units went on to win many battle honours. The first unit to see action was the Winnipeg Grenadiers, who in 1941 were sent – against British PM Winston Churchill's advice – to strengthen the British garrison at Hong Kong. The UK, Indian, and Cdn troops were overrun by the Japanese in Dec, with the Grenadiers losing 130 in the battle, including Victoria Cross winner JOHN ROBERT OSBORN. The survivors spent a horrific 4 years in POW camps, with a large number dying in the camps. Meanwhile, on the European front, in Aug 1942, the Camerons took part in the ill-fated raid on Dieppe, France. Of 503 Camerons participating in the raid, 346 were casualties. The unit rejoined battle action in July 1944 and fought its way through France and Holland, ending up – with the rest of the Canadian Army – in northern Germany. The regt won 21 battle honours during WWII. The Royal Winnipeg Rifles led the charge on Juno Beach, Normandy, on D-Day. After heavy losses, they went on to help take the port city of Caen and continued up the French coast to Holland, where they cleared the Scheldt in vicious fighting with SS units. They then participated in the invasion of Germany, crossing the Siegfried Line in spring 1945. The Fort Garry Horse, as part of the 2nd Armoured Brigade, also took part in D-Day and in the subsequent advance up the French coast. Largely using under-gunned Sherman tanks, the Garries had to take out bigger Panther and Tiger tanks. This they did, in addition to providing much-needed infantry support.

THE COLD WAR, 1946-90: After WWII, the reserve (militia) units of MB turned their focus to nuclear war. A National Survival Strategy directed the reserves to assist civil administrations in the event of war. There was a brief but bloody flare-up when Canada sent the 2nd Batt PPCLI as part of Canada's UN contribution in Korea. The "Patricias" fought in several engagements, including the unit's most significant battle, near Kapyong, in April 1951. They helped hold back a Chinese/North Korean offensive that had breached UN lines and was headed for the South Korean capital, Seoul. After Korea, the growth of NATO and the Warsaw Pact, with their focus on nuclear deterrence, made the relevance of the reserves questionable. A period of downsizing occurred during the 1960s, especially after unification of the CF in 1968, when many proud regts were disbanded. The only remaining MB reserve regts as of writing were the Royal Winnipeg Rifles, the Queen's Own Cameron Highlanders, and the Fort Garry Horse. Today, the old Military District 10 is known as the 38th Brigade Group. It encompasses all the reserve army units in MB, NW ON, and SK.

SINCE 1991: Since the collapse of communism, peacekeeping and peacemaking have become the new doctrine of the Army. MB's reserve units have taken on new life, as they have sent volunteers on every recent mission of the Army, including to Kosovo and other parts of the former Yugoslavia, and to Afghanistan. ● BRUCE TASCONA

NAVY. The first recorded naval battle off what is now MB took place in 1697, when 4 French vessels under the command of Sieur Pierre LeMoyne d'Iberville took on a small British fleet near York Factory. After defeating the British, d'Iberville forced the surrender of York Factory, interrupting for a brief period the HBC's hegemony over the northern **FUR TRADE.**

Up to and including WWI, there was no official naval establishment in MB, but some Manitobans served in the UK's Royal Navy. There was a courtesy arrangement under which volunteers could go through the introductory process in Winnipeg before being dispatched to the UK. Domestic naval service began in MB in 1923 with the formation of the "Winnipeg Company, Royal Canadian Navy Volunteer Reserve," which soon was renamed "Winnipeg Division, RCNVR." The first premises were minimal, with one small office and one classroom in the MacGregor Armoury. There were several temporary relocations in the next few years before the Navy moved into a warehouse on Ellice Ave, which served until a permanent home was established at 1 Navy Way. It was during the division's stay on Ellice when Manitobans first heard of a "vessel" named the *Chippewa*. On Nov 1, 1941, those barracks on Ellice were christened *HMCS Chippewa*. To insiders, this was a "stone frigate:" it would never go to sea, but in all other aspects, it was a full-fledged ship of the line.

Even before it was commissioned, Winnipeg's Navy establishment scored a major success with its corps of Sea Cadets. Within only a few years, it had 550 men in uniform, reportedly the largest complement of this type in the Commonwealth. Documents from that period state that the objective was to create self-confidence in boys in their formative years, and not merely to direct recruits to the permanent force. The service accomplished its goal through instruction in seamanship, communications, and the important business of learning to work co-operatively.

Ships Honouring Manitoba Places

NAME OF VESSEL	SERVED	TYPE
HMCS *Assiniboine* (1)	1939-46	Destroyer
HMCS *Assiniboine* (2)	1956-88	Destroyer
HMCS *Brandon* (1)	1941-45	Corvette
HMCS *Brandon* (2)	1999-	Coastal Defence
HMCS *Dauphin*	1941-45	Corvette
HMCS *Morden*	1941-45	Corvette
HMCS *Portage*	1943-58	Minesweeper
HMCS *St. Boniface*	1943-46	Minesweeper
HMCS *The Pas*	1941-45	Corvette
HMCS *Transcona*	1942-45	Minesweeper
HMCS *Winnipeg* (1)	1942-46	Minesweeper
HMCS *Winnipeg* (2)	1995-	Frigate

MANITOBA NAVAL STATIONS: Winnipeg's naval activities expanded dramatically with the outbreak of WWII. About 7660 recruits were given their primary training in Winnipeg before being sent off to the Atlantic or Pacific for more-specialized training. During WWII, it was estimated that of the 100,000 members of the Cdn Navy, 40% were from the Prairies. Few of these sailors had seen the sea before enlisting. For generations, youths in Prairie cities and towns, and on Prairie farms, had looked E and W and dreamed of ships and the sea. Prairie sailors joined their counterparts from other parts of the nation in one of the great battles of WWII, protecting the Atlantic shipping lanes in order that more troops, food, and *matériel* could be transported to a beleaguered Europe.

Even though MB is a Prairie province, its citizens have volunteered for naval service in surprising numbers. Manitobans served with distinction during WWII in every aspect of the war at sea: Atlantic, Pacific, Mediterranean, and the Murmansk run. In his book *The History of the Naval Reserve in Winnipeg*, Mark Nelson lists the names of 98 officers, men, and women, who were decorated for services "beyond the call of duty."

In June 1942, naval authorities in Ottawa issued a general call for women to join the Women's Royal Canadian Naval Service, or WRCNS, as it was originally described. This title was soon amended to WRENS. Previously, women could enlist, but only as nursing sisters. Jane White, of Winnipeg, was the first Manitoban to enlist in the first class of nursing sisters. In the same week in which Ottawa issued its call for women to join the Navy, the recruiting officer in Winnipeg, Lt (N) E. R. Hyman, announced he wanted to enlist women aged 18-45 who had no children and no dependents. Within a year, *Chippewa* was recruiting more women into the WRENS than any of the other 18 Cdn shore stations.

Security of the nation is the first purpose of the armed services, but also important is aid to civil authorities. Winnipeg's WRENS and Wardroom Wives played a pivotal role in 1950 when MB suffered a severe flood. They helped house more than 400 flood refugees in *Chippewa* and fed thousands more working on dike-building gangs. The WRENS organized

M

461

150 women into 3 shifts in the ship's galley. Every 4 hours, they distributed 180 L (40 UK gal) of soup and 15,000 sandwiches.

In 1995, the Cdn Navy launched the HMCS *Winnipeg*, one of the newest class of battle frigates. Many MB men and women continue to serve on that ship and others. Despite the lack of a base on Hudson Bay and MB's distance from Atlantic and Pacific saltwater ports, the province maintains proud naval traditions. ● FRED MCGUINNESS

AIR FORCE. Canada's Air Force has significantly influenced the life and development of MB; similarly, the province has played an important role in the history of the service.

In 1920, when the Canadian Air Board and the fledgling Canadian Air Force (CAF) staged the first trans-Canada flight, Winnipeg marked the halfway point in the series of individual hops between Halifax and Vancouver. Here, the civil aviation section of the Air Board and its flying boats handed over to the uniformed pilots of the CAF and their landplanes for the rest of the trip. Taking almost 50 hours in the air and spread over 10 days, this venture marked a significant achievement – a team of pilots and support staff using half a dozen planes demonstrated the peacetime potential of the new invention, which had already played such a crucial role in WWI.

AM. C.J. GINGRAS COLLECTION 91

Bristol Bolingbroke aircraft, Bombing and Gunners School, RCAF Station, McDonald, Manitoba, 1944

During WWI, Manitobans had distinguished themselves among the 20,000 Canadians who served in the British flying services, the RFC and the Royal Naval Air Service (later amalgamated as the RAF). WILLIAM "BILLY" BARKER of DAUPHIN and ALAN MCLEOD of STONEWALL each won a VICTORIA CROSS, the Empire's highest award for gallantry. Winnipegger ACmdre Redford "Red" Mulock commanded the formation charged with bombing Berlin, something that only the Armistice prevented from happening.

In 1920, a federal Order-in-Council created the Canadian Air Force as a small militia-style organization. Its pilots – all war veterans – aided the civil sector by dusting crops with insecticides, spotting for forest fires, flying Indian Dept agents to isolated posts, and aerially photographing stretches of wilderness to help prepare maps of uncharted portions of Canada. Flying out each spring from Winnipeg to seasonal bases in locales such as VICTORIA BEACH, LAC DU BONNET, and NORWAY HOUSE, CAF pilots and mechanics then flew on to even-more-temporary – or sometimes nonexistent – facilities throughout the NORTHERN region. This important work continued after the CAF became permanent and "Royal" in 1924.

WWII: When WWII erupted in 1939, the 3 Canadian services together numbered fewer than 10,000 officers and men. The RCAF made up about 4100 of this total. Initial mobilization gave little hint of what the war years would bring; by 1944, the RCAF would grow to about 210,000. Winnipeg's RCAF Reserve unit – designated 112 (Army-Co-operation) Squadron in 1939, ended the war as 402 (City of Winnipeg) Squadron, having played a valued role in the liberation of Europe.

Upon the outbreak of war, the govt jumped on a request from the UK that Canada train airmen for the Commonwealth's air forces, as it had in Borden, ON, in WWI. To PM Mackenzie King, this offered a war of "limited liability" to avoid the carnage of another Western Front. Before the ink had even dried on the BRITISH COMMONWEALTH AIR TRAINING PLAN agreement, Department of Transport surveyors crossed Canada identifying potential airfield sites for the Dept of National Defence. Each of the 9 provinces – NL did not enter Confederation until 1949 – saw BCATP facilities opening by the early 1940s. In MB, a dozen communities had Air Force training units within their boundaries or nearby. Winnipeg, Brandon, and Portage la Prairie each hosted 2 or more bases. Fully 216 airmen from many countries died in MB as part of the BCATP. They are memorialized in Winnipeg's Garden of Memories, opposite **17 WING**'s southern gate, as well as by a statue on Memorial Blvd near the Legislature. Many citizens thus got used to military funerals, as well as to social events with the young men training nearby, along with their graduation at "wings parades." The wartime development of Air Force stations changed life for local civilians almost as much as the war itself changed the lives of military personnel. The BCATP stations were self-contained, complementing and competing with nearby communities. With the interchange between base and town, many young women connected – often permanently – with the handsome young men in uniform.

Manitobans flocked to recruiting centres to enlist in the RCAF, as well as the Army, the RCN, and the Merchant Navy. Therefore, many – such as **ANDREW MYNARSKI**, who won the province's 3rd air VC – did not live to see the end of the war and are today memorialized in the Manitoba Geographical Names Program. The province remembers at least 1760 individual air force men and women in this manner; most died during WWII, and a few during WWI or since 1945.

POST-WAR: Immediately after the war, the govt set the RCAF's establishment at just over 12,000 and left air defence to RCAF reserve squadrons, such as No. 402, flying out of Stevenson Field, as Winnipeg's airport was then known. Air training took place at Portage la Prairie, Macdonald, Gimli, Winnipeg, and Rivers (with the latter's Joint Air Training Centre closing, somewhat ironically, at the same time the Armed Forces were unified in 1968). Other old wartime stations fell into neglect or were taken over by civilians for other, primarily commercial, uses.

The Cold War brought an increase in strength and more training; a large influx of students from new allies after the creation of NATO in 1949 exposed several provinces, including MB, to a renewed international influence. The threat posed by the USSR also meant closer co-operation between Canada and the US. Two of the 3 northern radar-warning lines had stations in MB – **BIRD** and **CRANBERRY PORTAGE** on the Mid-Canada Line, and **BEAUSEJOUR** and **GYPSUMVILLE** on the Pinetree Line. For half a century, the arrangements for continental air defence have been enshrined in the NORAD agreement. Today, NORAD has its Canadian Region headquarters, co-located with the Air Force's operational heart, in the Bishop Building at 17 Wing Winnipeg – also home to a number of Air Command schools and squadrons, including 402 Squadron. ● CARL A. CHRISTIE

▶ *See also* AVIATION, WESTERN CANADIAN AVIATION MUSEUM.

MILLAN, Lorri, performance artist, (b Nov 11, 1965, North Bay, ON). Millan began collaborating with fellow artist **Shawna Demspey** in 1989 in an artistic partnership that would see them produce countless influential works. Since their initial video *We're Talking Vulva* – a hilarious look at the apparently frightening world of the female anatomy – they subsequently found international acclaim. Many works by Millan and Dempsey are seminal in the history of North American performance, including the video *Homogeneity and the Dress Series*. In 1995, their book *In the Life* saw Millan grace the cover of a faux-*Time* magazine, and star in the accompanying video, *A Day in The Life of a Bull Dyke*. Millan and Dempsey began to take their unique brand of work into artist-run centres, and to various school and organizations in the form of lectures and performances. Recent installation-based performances, such as *Scentbar* and *Grocery Store*, studied the effects of consumerism and urban gentrification, respectively. As of writing, their continuing performance work had seen the 2 travel across the world, clad in tan park-ranger uniforms, educating the masses about the delicate nature of lesbian ecosystems. Their performance – and the accompanying book – is a commentary on heterosexist notions of what is natural. Videos and documentation of their performance works are held in several private collections and in both the National Gallery of Canada and the **Winnipeg Art Gallery**.
● STACEY ABRAMSON

MILLER, Colleen, rower, (b Dec 12, 1967, **Dunnotar**), captured 3 world titles in lightweight rowing. Miller won her first competitions at the Royal Canadian Henley Regatta in 1990, winning gold in the Lightweight Single Sculls and the Women's Open Coxed Four, as well as silver in the Lightweight Straight Four. In 1992, with partner Michelle Darville, Miller took home a silver medal at the World Championship, though the pair failed to qualify for the 1992 Olympics at trials where lightweight had not yet been distinguished as a category. The following year, Miller was successfully paired with ON native Wendy Wiebe. They went on to win 3 consecutive world titles from 1993-95. The team was a favourite to win at the 1996 Olympics, when the lightweight category was introduced as a separate race, but only placed 7th as Wiebe was ill with the flu. Miller then retired from competitive rowing, though she continued involvement in the sport with Rowing Canada. ● MD

MILLIPEDE is a multi-segmented, cylindrical arthropod in the class Diplopoda, related to centipedes (class Chilopoda) and that superficially resembles a worm or insect. There are numerous unique characteristics, such as 2 pairs of legs per segment, which may number from 9-375 pairs in various species. In spite of all these legs, a millipede travels slowly, the legs moving in coordinated waves which pass along the body. None has wings, as do most insects. Millipedes also lack compound eyes, but simple eyes (ocelli) are present, which function only to determine light levels. Millipedes range in size from 2 mm-30 cm (a fossil species reached 1.8 m), but MB species are under 3 cm long. Many species can roll into a tight defensive ball when disturbed, and secrete toxic substances (e.g., hydrogen cyanide, glomerin) that repel, paralyze, or poison predators such as ants, spiders, toads and mice. Some species of millipedes can immobilize ants with grappling-hook bristles. The body wall of most species is strengthened by being impregnated with calcium carbonate. As they ram and wedge their way through soil or creep along crevices, they demonstrate great sensitivity to scents, touch and vibration, and small changes in humidity and temperature via specialized nerve receptors in the antennae, feet, mouthparts and skin. Millipedes are found under bark, in the leaf litter, under rotting logs, and under stones, and are mainly active at night, when the humidity is higher, for unlike insects, they loose moisture readily through their unwaxed body surface (cuticle) and uncloseable breathing pores (spiracles).

Mating is stimulated by touch and pheromones, the male transfers sperm via modified legs, and the female lays her fertilized eggs in the soil. These hatch into a legless pupal stage with only several segments, followed by a series of moults as it grows, adding additional pairs of legs each time. Almost all species feed on plant material (mostly dead, but some living) with their strong jaws. Since millipedes are often abundant, they are significant recyclers (detritivores) – breaking down plant tissue into soil nutrients, ready for absorption by plant roots. Some species live up to 12 years. There are only 3 species recorded in MB (all in the S) – *Underwoodia iuloides* (10 mm), *Oriulus venustus* (26 mm), and *Aniulus garius* (20 mm). To date, 62 species have been recorded in Canada (including 20 introduced from Eurasia), and 11,000 species worldwide. Millipedes appeared in the fossil record 385 million years ago (Early Devonian period). ● REW

MINING AND MINERALS industries produce a variety of materials that have significantly influenced the lives of Manitobans. Consumer goods that require metal products range from motor vehicles and computers to water purification systems and jewellery. Metals are derived from minerals such as chalcopyrite for copper (Cu), sphalerite for zinc (Zn), pentlandite for nickel (Ni), tantalite for tantalum (Ta), pollucite for cesium (Cs), spodumene for lithium (Li), and also from native metals such as gold (Au) and silver (Ag). Millions of tonnes of ore deposits containing these minerals formed as a result of geological processes that occurred on the seafloor or deep within Earth's crust billions of years ago.

Over the last 100 years, MB's mining industry has resulted in more than 70 mines in the North, plus railways, roads and airports. Together, they have given rise to today's mining communities: **Flin Flon, Snow Lake, Lynn Lake, Leaf Rapids** and **Thompson** in the N and Bissett in the S. MB currently has 6 producing mines and 2 operating smelters and refineries (at Flin Flon and Thompson). The main metals produced are Cu, Ni, Zn, Au and Ta. Spin-offs from the mining industry in tourism, forestry and hydro-electricity have further strengthened the provincial economy.

The province's **Geology** controls the distribution of mineral deposits in MB. Many mines are located in greenstone belts – composed of metamorphosed volcanic rocks. For example, the copper and zinc deposits at Flin Flon and Lynn Lake were formed as ancient volcanoes erupted on the seafloor, while gold deposits at Snow Lake, Lynn Lake and Bissett were emplaced much later in the geological history of these areas, after the volcanic rocks were formed and subsequently folded and faulted. Most of MB's nickel deposits, by contrast, are located in the Thompson Nickel Belt, within the collisional boundary between the ancient Superior Province and the younger Trans-Hudson Orogen.

Mining for metals in MB has a rich history, dating back hundreds of years when aboriginal people mined hematite and yellow ochre (both forms of iron oxide) for use as pigments. In the early 1800s, salt was an important commodity for the fur trade industry. Salt from brine springs along the W side of **Lakes Manitoba** and **Winnipegosis** became the first commercially developed mineral in MB. Commercial salt operations continued in MB until 1978. In 1901, the first economic development of gypsum deposits occurred when the Manitoba Union Mining Company erected a crushing and calcining mill on Portage Bay.

At the turn of the century, gold was being separated by hand from small veins throughout SE MB. Gold was first discovered at Rice Lake in 1911 near the present-day community of Bissett. The first underground mining operation,

M

Postcard of early Thompson mine site

the Penniac Reef Mine, was located near Falcon Lake and produced several gold bars in 1913 and 1914. This was followed shortly thereafter by the development of small gold mines near Snow Lake (1917–1918), and the Mandy Cu-Zn Mine at Flin Flon (1916). The advent of large-scale industrial mining activity dates back to the early 1920s with the development of the Flin Flon mining complex and the San Antonio gold mine in the Rice Lake area. Several small underground gold mining operations were developed on Gods Lake and Island Lake in the 1930s, and Cu-Zn mines in Sherridon followed soon after. The first commercial shipment of lithium minerals in Canada was made from the Pointe du Bois district in 1937. In the late 1940s and late 1950s nickel was discovered at Lynn Lake and Thompson respectively. Inco's nickel discovery in 1956 resulted in the first fully integrated nickel operation in MB, where ore is mined, concentrated, smelted, and refined in one complex.

Today, metal mining activity is primarily centered on the Cu, Zn, and Ni mining camps in the Flin Flon–Snow Lake and Thompson regions. Mining operations at Flin Flon have been sustained for over 80 years and new discoveries are still being made. The new 777 mine at Flin Flon came into production in 2003 and will help sustain mining activity in the region to at least 2013. Inco's Thompson operation continues to produce approximately 100 million pounds of nickel per year. Tantalum, lithium and cesium are mined at Bernic Lake. Gold mining operations at Lynn Lake, Snow Lake and Bissett have been suspended due to depleted reserves and poor market conditions. The Ruttan Mine at Leaf Rapids, a former Cu-Zn producer that produced feed for

the smelting and refining complex in Flin Flon, closed in 2002.

The Paleozoic rocks of the Williston Basin contribute to MB's mineral industry through mineral products such as crushed dolomitic limestone for aggregate, building stone (**TYNDALL STONE**), dolomite (potential for magnesium metal), and high-calcium limestone for cement. Sodium chlorate, derived from subsurface deposits of salt, are used as a whitening agent for the pulp and paper industry. Potash, an essential component of fertilizer, is also a potential product. Gypsum (for wallboard) is an important mineral product from rock formations of the Mesozoic Era. Sand and gravel from glacial deposits are used in the construction industry.

The metals mining industry in MB annually contributes approximately $1 billion to the Manitoba economy, representing approximately 3% of the provincial Gross Domestic Product. Mining is the 2nd largest primary resource sector of the MB economy with metals responsible for approximately 11% of the province's total exports. ● RIC SYME

MINIOTA, pop 969, is a community 85 km WNW of **BRANDON** along hwy 83 near the **ASSINIBOINE RIVER**. The post office was opened in 1885 as Parkisimo and the community incorporated in 1899 with the arrival of the **CPR**. The name was changed to Miniota in 1900. A Grand Trunk (*see* **CN**) railway point was established here one mi (1.6 km) apart from the CPR station. "Miniota" is a **DAKOTA** Sioux word meaning "plenty of water," perhaps referring to the Assiniboine. The community took its name from the former Miniota Cty, now the RM of Miniota (*see* **WESTMAN**),

established around 1884. The economy is supported by agriculture. For recreation, residents enjoy a community hall and arena complex, 3 museums and walking trails. Miniota has been granted numerous awards for beautification. ● GPP

MINITONAS, pop 538, is a town 120 km NNW of **DAUPHIN** on hwy 10. "Minitonas" comes from the **CREE** for "isolated water hill," referring to nearby hills to the S. Minitonas also gives its name to an RM in the **PARKLAND** Region. This, the first settlement in the Swan River Valley, was first known as "Tent Town." Around 1900, local settlers anticipated the extension of the **RAILWAY** through the area, and created a makeshift village that would entice the railway planners to pass through the area. "Tent Town" featured all the amenities of a typical community of the era, such as a land titles office, 2 **IMMIGRATION** halls, churches, and a schoolroom. When the railway surveyed Minitonas and **SWAN RIVER** in 1899, the residents of "Tent Town" quickly settled into the nearby permanent settlement of Minitonas. **GERMANS** as well as **UKRAINIANS**, Czechs, and others of Slavic origin immigrated into the area in the 1920s. The town also has a significant **MÉTIS** community. Minitonas, which was incorporated as a town in 1948, is a service centre that supports surrounding logging and agricultural operations. Tourism is also significant, as the town is 30 km N of **DUCK MOUNTAIN PROVINCIAL PARK** and close to the Porcupine Hills. ● GPP

MINK (*Mustela vison*) is a member of the weasel family Mustelidae and is found along watercourses, lakes and wetlands in all areas of MB. It can be observed hunting anytime, and is often so intent on investigating interesting odours that it ignores the presence of people. When cornered by a larger predator, a mink is a ferocious contender, growling and biting with great speed. Its main prey, the Muskrat, is no match for its adversary, in spite of the rodent's impressive incisors. No small creature is safe from the mink's voracious appetite – mice, frogs, insects, birds, crayfish and worms. Like the Striped Skunk, the Mink has a powerful smell, the result of large musk glands in the anal region, with which it marks its territory of up to 5 km of shoreline. Mating (which can be a violent affair) occurs from March to April, and after a gestation period of 40-75 days (including a period when the embryos pause in developing), an average of 5 (2-10) young are born in May in a den underground or in a hollow log. They grow quickly on their mother's milk and begin learning to hunt at only 7 weeks. They depart to set up their own territories by the autumn. The Mink's coat is so dense and soft, its excellent insulation allows the animal to be active in the coldest weather and when swimming in ice-cold water. Mink can dive to a depth of 6 m and travel 30 m before coming up for air. Mink pelts have often dominated the fur market, supplementing the income of many a northerner. • REW

MINNEDOSA, pop 2474, is a town 50 km N of **BRANDON** on the Little Saskatchewan and Minnedosa rivers, on the **CPR** main line, and at the junction of hwys 10 and 16. The area was known as Tanner's Crossing in the 1860s, as the first European settler here, John Tanner, operated a ferry service across the Little Saskatchewan River, as well as a general store. The post office opened here in 1876 as Little Saskatchewan, after the river. The name became Hallsford in 1880 and Minnedosa in 1882, after the river, whose Dakota name, *Mniduzahan*, means "rapid water." The area was reputed to be inhospitable and lawless, though this changed with the establishment of a NWMP outpost in 1875, the laying of CPR tracks, and the arrival of additional **ENGLISH**, **SCOTS**, and **IRISH** settlers, and later **UKRAINIANS**, **GERMANS**, **POLES**, and Swedes. The town of Minnedosa was incorporated in 1883.

Residents and visitors enjoy Lake Minnedosa. Created by a dam and spillway on the Little Saskatchewan River, the lake is lined with cottages, a sandy beach, and a campground. The lake is also home to the Minnedosa Rowing Centre, a world-class **ROWING** facility that hosts several regional and national events, and was home to the rowing, canoeing and kayaking events in the 1999 **PAN AMERICAN GAMES**. Each year, the shores of Lake Minnedosa come alive with music with the Classic Rock Weekend Festival. The weekend event attracts thousands of fans to camp and enjoy the music.

The town's most famous citizen is probably **ISRAEL ASPER**, founder of the **CANWEST GLOBAL** empire, and son of the operators of Minnedosa's movie theatre. Minnedosa's weekly *Tribune*, founded 1883, is among the oldest newspapers in western Canada. Retail and services aimed at surrounding agricultural operations form the town's economic base, though govt and manufacturing both have a presence in the town. As of writing, Husky Energy was moving forward with plans to develop a new $145 million ethanol plant. • GPP

MINNOW is a fish in the cyprinid family, and forms the most-dominant group of fishes in MB with 26 native and 2 introduced species – the Common Carp (*Cyprinus carpio*) and Goldfish (*Carassius auratus*). There are 2010 species

in this family worldwide. Minnows have exceptional hearing as a result of an unusual auditory apparatus formed from several front vertebrae and ribs connecting the inner ear to the swim bladder. The jaws lack teeth, but food is ground up by several rows of teeth lining the 5th pharyngeal arch (back of the gill chamber). Other distinguishing characters are cycloid scales (overlapping, smooth and disc-like) and no adipose fin (mid-back behind the dorsal fin). The local fauna consists of 3 minnows, 13 shiners, 5 chub, and 5 dace – all small species (4-23 cm). Most have exacting habitat requirements related to water depth, current, and type of bottom. They are a dependable source of food for predatory fish, birds and insects. Representative and prominent MB species are detailed below:

Lake Chub (*Couesius plumbeus*) is a large minnow reaching up to 23 cm. It is blue-grey to black above, silver below. During the spawning season, both sexes develop what are called nuptial tubercles on the head, and the male may have a splash of bright red on the bases of the pectoral and pelvic fins and corners of the mouth. It is a cool-water species, occupying depths from 15 cm to 178 m. It is found in streams, rivers, and lakes throughout the N 2/3 of the province (mainly absent from the Red and Assiniboine watersheds). It moves to shallow waters for spawning from April to June, where water temperatures surpass 14°C. Lake Chub is often abundant, so it is an important prey item for Northern Pike, Walleye, and Lake Trout. The female lays about 500 eggs, not bothering to make a nest or to defend her brood. The young feed on plankton and graduate to insects and small fish, maturing in year 3 or 4. This species lives up to 5 years, and many die after spawning.

Emerald Shiner

Emerald Shiner (*Notropis atherinoides*) is a slender species occuring abundantly in lakes and rivers as far N as **CHURCHILL** and **YORK FACTORY** (absent from tundra waters). It is mainly silvery, sometimes with an iridescent emerald band along the sides. It is usually present in large schools, far offshore in summer and moving into the shallows in the autumn, where it is often observed along shorelines and around docks. The schools over-winter in deep waters. This species can tolerate turbid rivers like the Red and Assiniboine. It spawns in mid-water at night from June to Aug.

in warm waters (21-24°C), with the eggs (up to 2000) sinking to the bottom. Hatching occurs in about 24 hours, and the fry feed near the surface on microorganisms in the plankton, changing over to insects as they grow larger (max. 10 cm). Longevity is 3 years. Numbers are known to be highly variable from year to year. Along with the Spottail Shiner (*Notropis hudsonius*), this shiner is used heavily for bait, with most specimens taken in the lower Red River and adjacent Lake Winnipeg. Due to abundance and near-surface activity, the Emerald Shiner is dominant in the diet of most fish and birds such as terns, gulls, and cormorants.

Northern Redbelly Dace (*Phoxinus eos*) is a small minnow averaging 5 cm and closely related to the Finescale Dace (*Phoxinus neogaeus*). In fact the 2 species occasionally interbreed to form fertile hybrids, resulting in specimens challenging to identify, and remarkably, all-female clonally reproducing females in some populations in E Canada. It prefers quiet boggy creeks, streams and ponds (clear or stained brown with tannins) in 2 distinct regions – in the W, in the watersheds of the Souris River and lakes Dauphin and Manitoba (but not in the lakes), and in the E, in watersheds E of the Red River and South Basin of **LAKE WINNIPEG**. It is attractively coloured olive, brown or black above and silvery below. During the breeding season (June to Aug.), 4-5 rows of nuptial tubercles appear on the throat area, the fins turn yellowish, and the spawning male takes on a brilliant red colour on the undersides, punctuated by a black lateral line. Courting groups of one female and several males seek out a mass of algae, and release and fertilization of eggs occurs inside the green mass of filaments. The eggs hatch in 8 days at water temperatures over 20°C. This species feeds on algae, micro-organisms, organic debris and insect larvae. The life span is 3 years.

Fathead Minnow (*Pimephales promelas*) is a common species throughout the S half of the province, reaching the Upper **NELSON** and **HAYES** rivers. Reaching a maximum of 9 cm, it is dark olive or brown above and silvery on the underside. Its variable colour and presence or absence of a dark lateral band result in frequent misidentification. It can live in a wide variety of aquatic habitats from large, clear lakes and rivers, turbid streams, saline or bog ponds, and even stagnant water. It prefers the cover of aquatic plants. Its ability to live in waterbodies that experience low-oxygen levels (especially during the winter) enable it to invade water-retention ponds, dugouts, ditches, and pools cut off from regular flows of rivers, often in the company of the Brook Stickleback (*Culaea inconstans*). The spawning season extends from May to July in water temperatures above 16°C. The male develops nuptial tubercles on the snout and a spongy pad on the forehead. The male selects a site in shallow water, with a sand or mud bottom, and constructs a cavity nest under some object like a submerged tree branch or rock. He then stimulates one or several ripe females to release their eggs, which after fertilization, float up and stick to the underside of the nest cover. The male aggressively chases other fish away from the nest site, using the rough tubercles on the snout. Females may lay eggs in the nests of several males. Few individuals survive beyond 2 years. This species is a bottom and mid-water feeder, accepting vegetation, insect larvae (especially mosquito) and detritus. Due to its presence in almost all bodies of water, it is an important item in the diet of many fish and predatory birds. Its adaptiveness makes it a useful species for research, such as determining water quality and toxicity of pollutants. It is also a popular baitfish. ● REW

MITCHELL, Coulson NORMAN, VICTORIA CROSS winner (b Dec 11, 1889, **WINNIPEG**; d Nov 17, 1978, Montreal) graduated from the **U OF M** as an engineer. He enlisted in 1915 as a signaller in an engineer field troop, sailed to Britain with a railway construction unit, and was promoted to Lt, then to Capt on his arrival in France. He worked with tunnelling companies until posted to first Tunelling Company, 4th Batt, Canadian Engineers, in 1918, as an explosives expert. On June 8 of that year, the objective was the capture of Cambrai, Nord–Pas de Calais, France. Moving ahead of the infantry, Mitchell's small unit was to prevent the enemy from blowing up a vital bridge over the Canal de l'Escaut. He succeeded, after engaging in hand-to-hand fighting with the enemy, killing 3 and capturing 12, and removing several explosive charges. His VC is the only one ever awarded to a Cdn engineer. Norman Mitchell returned to Winnipeg to practise civil engineering, and served in the militia, going overseas again as an engineer in WWII for the RCE. He eventually rose to the rank of LCol. After the war, he joined a Montreal engineering firm. A Montreal branch of the Royal Canadian Legion was renamed Norman Mitchell VC Branch in 1965. He died in Montreal and was buried in the Field of Honour Cemetery (Champ d'honneur), in Pointe-Claire, QC. ● JIM SHILLIDAY

MITCHELL, James Bertram "J. B.," school architect, soldier, policeman (b 1852, Gananoque, Canada West [ON]; d Nov 1945, **WINNIPEG**). At the age of 14, Mitchell joined the Cdn militia, becoming a Cpl at 18. He served in ON before

leaving to study architecture at the Montreal Institute of Art. In 1873, however, Mitchell joined the newly formed **NORTH-WEST MOUNTED POLICE**. His division was sent W, encountering hardships across the Prairies. Mitchell was a signatory to Treaty 6 in 1876, and left the NWMP in 1877 for Winnipeg. In the 1885 North-West Resistance, he fought **MÉTIS** forces.

In 1888, Mitchell was elected to the Winnipeg School Board, and in 1892, was named architect and commissioner of school buildings and supplies. He worked with board superintendent **DANIEL MCINTYRE** to build the city's school system in an era of rapid population growth. Mitchell designed 48 schools, nearly all of them named after heroes of the British Empire. His designs included a basic interior plan with a range of styles for exteriors. Mitchell emphasized comfort and safety, as his schools became known for their advanced heating, ventilation, and fire-escape systems. Mitchell served in WWI, commanding the 78th Infantry Batt and the 100th Batt, CEF (better known as the **WINNIPEG GRENADIERS**) 1912-20, earning the rank of Col and the honorary rank of BGen. In 1939, he was honoured with an invitation to meet King George VI and Queen Elizabeth.

J. B. Russell School, built in 1956, was reopened and renamed École J. B. Mitchell School – an English/French-immersion elementary school – in 1991. Mitchell's son, Ross Mitchell (1880-1972), was a prominent MB doctor and historian. ● JOEL TRENAMAN

MITE is an abundant and ecologically diverse group of minute, joint-legged (arthropod) animals in the subclass Acari. Due to their small

size (.08-16 mm) and cryptic nature, MB mites are poorly known, and most people are completely unaware of their existence. They are a challenge for even scientists to collect and research. Unlike most other arachnids (e.g., spiders), their oval body is not separated into 2 units – a cephalothorax and abdomen. The jaws (chelicerae) are pincer-like for chewing or sucking. Species have 1-4 pairs of legs with 6 or 7 segments. Having evolved over 400 mya (Devonian period), the group has successfully integrated in almost all possible habitats, from the treetops to 10 m underground, freshwater ponds to the ocean depths, deserts and hot springs to mountain tops. One m² of MB forest litter can easily harbour over one million mites of 200 species, and they remain active throughout the year, even under the snow. A pond or stream can support over 75 species. Mites can disperse great distances by sailing on silk threads like spiders, or hitchhiking on moths, birds and bats. Their life cycles are highly complex, involving as many as 6 stages within 2 weeks after hatching from the egg. In some species, the number of stages may be reduced, and in some remarkable cases, all developmental stages occur within the mother.

Mites are extraordinarily important in the soil, breaking down organic matter, feeding on soil plant debris, fungi and microscopic animals, and contributing to soil fertility and structure. Mites also feed on various parts of living plants, and may become serious pests. The Spider Mite (*Tetranychus urticae*) is a common problem for horticulturalists and home gardeners. The Flour Mite (*Acarus siro*) has also adapted to the grain-storage ecosystem and can cause great losses. Other species are beneficial by attacking

Mite

harmful aphids, other insects, and roundworms. Many people will have seen the large, Red Freshwater Mite (*Limnochares americana*) swimming in a pond, without realizing that this juvenile stage feeds on the blood of aquatic insects and molluscs. Many species of mites inhabit the bodies of vertebrates – the skin surface, hair follicles (Human Follicle Mite, *Demodex folliculorum*), on the surface of feathers and hair, inside feather quills, and in the respiratory tract feeding on body fluids, cell debris, or micro organisms. There are also many species of predatory mites that feed on other small invertebrates in soil, in nests of birds and mammals, in water, and on the surfaces of plants. There are tiny mites that are parasitized by even smaller mites. Homes are rich feeding grounds for House Dust Mites (*Dermatopagoides farinae* and *D. pteronyssinus*), which perform the useful task of devouring our continuously shed skin cells (5-10 g per week), but may cause serious allergies in Humans. Water mites are excellent indicators of water quality. It is difficult to estimate the numbers of MB species, but there are at least 1000 (35,000 worldwide and over one million yet unnamed). Mites appear in the fossil record by 375 million years ago (Early Devonian period). ● TDG, REW

MOFFAT COMMUNICATIONS LTD.

MOFFAT COMMUNICATIONS LTD. was a MB-based company that owned cable and TV networks across NA, known primarily in MB for having started CKY-TV. The company's origins lie in Depression-era SK where Lloyd Moffat turned an amateur radio station into a successful commercial operation. Moving to **Winnipeg** in 1949, Moffat purchased a radio station license, and took over the call letters CKY, formerly used by the forerunner to the CBC. The station eventually grew to include a series of FM stations, and expanded into television in 1960 with Winnipeg's first privately owned TV station. Originally known as CJAY, it was 1 of 8 stations nationwide that amalgamated into the national network CTV in 1961.

By the time Randall Moffat, the son of Lloyd Moffat, took over the company in 1964, it was operating TV and radio stations across western Canada. Through the 1970s, CKY broadcasts extended to cover virtually all of MB, gaining entry into the **Brandon** market in 1972 after reaching a deal with rival Western Manitoba Broadcasters Ltd. (*see* **Craig Media Inc**). Moffat Communications also ran the public access channel Winnipeg Videon Inc, which ran a series of popular local shows such as *Math with Marty* and *The Pollock & Pollock Gossip Show*.

Through the 1990s, attempts to expand the company's interests into the lucrative Toronto market failed. Looking westward, the company sold its radio stations to finance the purchase of 25 cable systems in AB. It also launched Lifestyle Television Ltd in 1995, which ran the Winnipeg-based Women's Television Network. Nonetheless, Moffat Communications was struggling to compete in an increasingly consolidated media business. Its broadcast interests were sold to CTV in 1997, and in 2000 the company in its entirety was bought by Shaw Communications Inc., ending 50 years of Moffat Communications broadcasts in MB. After the sale, Randy Moffat donated $100 million to the **Winnipeg Foundation**, the largest individual donation to a community foundation in Cdn history. ● MD

MOL, Leonid Molodozhanyn "Leo," artist (b Jan. 15, 1915, Polonne, Khmelnytskyi, Ukraine). Mol is a master sculptor, some of whose work appears in the Leo Mol Sculpture Garden in **Winnipeg**'s **Assiniboine Park**. The sculpture garden is the largest in NA to feature the work of a single artist, and has more than 300 bronzes, ceramics, paintings, and drawings on permanent display. Mol learned to work with clay from his father in Poland, and by the time he began formal art studies, he was already an experienced clay modeller. Mol studied at the Leningrad (now the Imperial) Academy of Arts, in what is now St Petersburg, from 1936-40, and continued his studies in Berlin and The Hague. He originally wanted to study painting, but his true calling as a sculptor was undeniable. In Dec 1948, Mol and his wife Magareth, whom he had married in 1943, left the USSR and came to MB, where his career as a sculptor blossomed. Mol's work has been commissioned around the world – his sculptures can be found as far away as Argentina, Washington, DC, and Rome. For his artistic contributions, Mol was made an Officer of the Order of Canada in 1989. In 2002, he was honoured by having his sculpture *Lumberjacks* featured on a Cdn postage stamp. His life inspired the documentary *Leo Mol in Light and Shadow* (1993). ● JILL SEXSMITH

MOLE, STAR-NOSED (*Condylura cristata*) is the only true mole (family Talpidae) found in the province. It is an eastern NA species, reaching its western limit in S MB. Seldom seen, its only signs are push-ups of soil or cores of earth running along the ground in meadows or bogs, revealing where the animal deposited earth from its underground home. Occasionally a housecat will capture and bring home a mole, but it is rarely eaten due to its musky odour. People usually confuse this animal and its sign with the more-common pocket gophers (rodent family Geomyidae), ground squirrels (rodent family Sciuridae), or shrews (insectivore family Soricidae). The mole's adaptations to a burrowing lifestyle are many and fascinating, such as strong wide hands with robust claws for digging, reduced eyes and ears, plush black fur that lies in any direction, and a scaly touch-sensitive tail which is used for feeling the burrow walls (especially when moving

Early photo of Leo Mol in his studio.

backwards), as a rudder while swimming, and also for fat storage. However, the most unique feature is the nose, encircled with 22 pink, touch-sensitive tentacles, which along with the snout whiskers detect prey in the soil or stream-bottom. The mole does not hesitate to enter water, even under ice, its thick fur insulating the body from the frigid cold for several minutes. The mole is active for periods day and night, on the surface or underground, hunting over a home range of about half a ha. When it comes across prey (worm, insect, snail, or salamander), it is crushed quickly by the mole's battery of 44 sharp-edged teeth. With a ravenous appetite, it consumes $1/3$ of its 50-g weight each day (sometimes twice its weight). Like other insectivores, the mole has a high metabolic rate. In May or June, 2-7 young are born, with a life span of 3 years. ● REW

MOLGAT, Gildas L., politician (b Jan 25, 1927, STE. ROSE DU LAC; d Feb. 28, 2001, Ottawa). Molgat was educated at the **U OF M** and received his honours degree in commerce in 1947. He served with the reserve **ROYAL WINNIPEG RIFLES** for 20 years. However, Molgat is best known for a political career that spanned 5 decades. It began in 1953 when he was elected to the MB legislature as a Liberal Progressive for the riding of Ste. Rose. When his party lost the 1958 election, Molgat maintained his seat and he was easily re-elected in 1959, 1962, 1966, and 1969. **DOUGLAS CAMPBELL** resigned as leader of the **LIBERAL** party in 1961 and Molgat was selected to replace him. He became the first francophone Liberal party leader in the province, acting as leader of the opposition to Tory premiers **DUFF ROBLIN** and **WALTER WEIR**. He held this position until he retired in 1969.

PM Pierre Trudeau appointed him to the Cdn senate in 1970. As a senator, he was active in constitutional reform, co-chairing the special joint committee on the constitution of Canada in 1971. In the late 1980s, he was chair of the senate committee on the **MEECH LAKE CONSTITUTIONAL ACCORD** and chair of the senate task force on Meech Lake and the Yukon and Northwest Territories. He was heavily involved in the business of the senate; in 1983, he acted as chair on the committee on senate reform. That same year, he was elected deputy speaker of the senate and re-elected in 1988. From 1991-1993, he served as deputy opposition leader in the upper house. One of the most colourful moments in his career came during that time when the Liberals tried to derail the Mulroney govt's Goods and Services Tax. Liberal senators used noisemakers to disrupt senate business – Molgat played a kazoo. Throughout his career, Molgat also served on the boards of more than a dozen community organizations

in MB. He was the founding chairman of the **ST. BONIFACE GENERAL HOSPITAL** Research Foundation. Under PM Jean Chrétien, Molgat became deputy govt leader. He was appointed speaker of the senate in 1994 and enjoyed that post until just before his sudden death of a stroke in 2001. ● RUTH DEGRAVES

MOLLUSC is a major group of animals in the phylum Mollusca, which includes snails, clams, mussels, chitons, squid, octopus, and nautilus. Most molluscs are protected by a hard calcareous shell secreted by the mantle (a membranous extension of the body wall) from dissolved minerals in the water and from food. Though highly compressed, the unsegmented body consists of a head (with mouth, brain and sense organs), visceral mass (with digestive, urinary and reproductive tracts), and the foot (a muscular organ used for locomotion). Some molluscs (e.g.. snails) feed by rasping off particles of vegetation with a ribbon-like organ called the radula, others (clams) filter vast quantities of water with their siphons for minute forms of life, while others (squids) are aggressive predators taking large prey like fish. This group has been enormously successful in number of species, population sizes, distribution, and individual longevity, ever since they appeared over 600 million years ago (Proterozoic era). The hard shell preserves so well that a wealth of mollusc fossils is known – 35,000 fossil species have been described, but many thousands of others existed.

About 100,000 species are living today. Remarkably, 102 marine species of molluscs have been recorded in the **HUDSON BAY** Arctic Marine Ecosystem of MB, and additional ones will no doubt be discovered. Included here are 51 species of snails (class Gastropoda), 47 clams, mussels and scallops (Pelecypoda), 3 chitons (Polyplacophora) and one tusk shell (Scaphopoda). There are 25 species of freshwater clams and mussels and 43 freshwater and land snails. The total mollusc fauna for MB currently totals 170 species, and could reach 180 with further investigation. Molluscs provide an important source of food for a wide array of creatures, including Walrus, Raccoon, Mink, fish, frogs and shorebirds. They were a major source of food for prehistoric peoples and are still utilized (both wild and cultivated stocks) right up to the present time. Certain molluscs may be parasites of fish, and others are parasitized by disease organisms like the Giant Liver Fluke. They also play a significant role in ecosystems through their filtering and cleansing of aquatic and marine environments. ● REW, EP, DBS

▸ *See* **CLAMS, SNAILS.**

MONARCH BUTTERFLY (*Danaus plexippus*) is an insect in the family Nymphalidae, order Lepidoptera. It is the best-known of MB and NA insects, and is readily identified by its striking orange and black pattern. It is a strong flyer with a wingspan of 9-11 cm. After mating, the female Monarch lays eggs singly on several species of milkweeds, including Common and Showy milkweeds (*Asclepias syriaca* and *A. viridiflora*, respectively). The eggs hatch and develop into large (7 cm) white, black and yellow caterpillars. When mature, they enter the pupal stage inside a beautiful gold and green chrysalis. The adults emerge 3-6 weeks after the egg stage. The Monarch and the slightly smaller Viceroy (*Limenitis archippus*) provide a dramatic example of protection gained from mimicry – in this case called Mullerian mimicry, since both species are to some degree distasteful to predators. Birds readily learn that these butterflies are poor choices as food, since attempts to eat them result in prompt rejection or regurgitation. This unpalatability results from a battery of toxic chemicals (e.g., steroidal cardiac glycosides called cardenolides) stored in its body, acquired by the caterpillar when devouring milkweed. Here is the most-notable example of an insect overcoming powerful plant defensives and in turn using these plant toxins to deter predation by insect-eating birds. Experienced birds equate the warning colour pattern of the Monarch and Viceroy to bitter taste and vomiting, and hence leave these butterflies alone.

Monarchs are also famous for their impressive migration between S Canada to the S US and Mexico, much like migratory birds and bats. Hanging in bunches from trees, the adults pass the winter hibernating in immense colonies (numbering in the millions) at about 30 surviving sites in southern Central America and in Oyamel Fir (*Abies religiosa*) forests (3000 m elevation) in the Mexican Highlands W of Mexico City, where temperatures remain a few degrees above freezing. In late winter they emerge from hibernation and begin a mass migration N, taking advantage of S winds. With the warming temperatures of spring, they mate and lay eggs on milkweed. While these adults perish en route, their progeny continue the N flight through the spring and early summer, arriving in S MB from mid-May to late June. The number of Monarchs reaching southern Canada varies from year to year, depending on winter survival and weather conditions. These immigrants produce a new generation during the summer, and under warm conditions, a second generation may occur. Beginning in late Aug and Sept, MB-born individuals undertake the astonishing migration

Monarch butterfly

ROBERT R. TAYLOR

. In 1987, they decided to enter the **GARMENT INDUSTRY** by designing and manufacturing a line of beachwear and casual pants. All designing and manufacturing was done out of their parents' basements. For the following 2 summers, they sold their merchandise from a booth at **GRAND BEACH**, where their flag-embroidered sweatshirts became popular. In 1989, the brothers were awarded the Small Business Achiever Award by Winnipeg's *Uptown Magazine*. After the brothers completed undergraduate degrees in May 1990, they incorporated the business and started full-time company operations. The company had no structured hierarchy, and the brothers operated in an informal, team-oriented atmosphere.

The founders of Mondetta Clothing

In late 1991, Mondetta expanded from its Winnipeg locations into ON, QC, and the Maritimes. The company since expanded to more than 800 stores throughout Canada, the US, Sweden, Italy, the Netherlands, Japan, and the UK. The company also has offices in Hong Kong and China. In 2003, Mondetta moved into performance wear and activewear with its MPG (Mondetta Performance Gear) brand. Mondetta supplied jackets for the 2005 Juno Award ceremonies' swag bags. As well, Cdn **CURLING** teams were clothed in Mondetta during the 2006 Winter Olympics. Ash Modha now serves as the president and CEO of Mondetta Clothing Company, and in 2001 was appointed to the MB premier's Economic Advisory Council. In Oct 2006, Mondetta Charity Foundation Inc., a registered charity (*see* **NON-PROFIT SECTOR**) separate from Mondetta Clothing, was launched to provide support for children in Africa suffering from HIV/AIDS and poverty. As of writing, the Mondetta Clothing Company's head office remained in Winnipeg. ● AMANDA STEPHENS

MONNIN, Alfred Maurice, lawyer, judge (b March 6, 1920, **WINNIPEG**). Monnin graduated from **COLLÈGE UNIVERSITAIRE DE SAINT-BONIFACE** in 1939 and from 1942-45 served both in Canada and Europe during WWII. He graduated from the

---

of 2500-3800 km to the Mexican hibernation sites. How they navigate and survive the rigours of flight are unknown; individuals too weak or worn to fly perish in late fall. Sadly, illegal logging at the hibernation sites, and human development and agricultural practices (pesticides and herbicides) in Mexico, US, and Canada will eventually threaten this remarkable species. ● REW, ARW

MONARCH INDUSTRIES LIMITED is a privately owned **WINNIPEG** company that manufactures a variety of water pumps, hydraulic cylinders, cement mixers, and custom iron castings for the retail, agriculture-equipment, and construction-equipment markets. Founded in 1935 as Monarch Machinery, the company operated for many years out of a 1.2 ha (130,000-ft^2) former horse barn on Erin St before moving in late 2001 to a 1.6 ha (170,000-ft^2) manufacturing facility in SE Winnipeg. In addition to its Winnipeg head office and manufacturing plant, Monarch also owns and operates a .7 ha (75,000 ft^2) foundry in **WINKLER**, where it melts scrap metal to produce iron castings, both for its use and to sell

to other manufacturers. Because it sells its products all over NA, the company also has distribution centres and an extensive parts-and-service network scattered throughout the continent. In 1995, Monarch was named 1 of Canada's 50 Best Managed Companies, and in 2003, it was named Manitoba Exporter of the Year by the Canadian Manufacturers and Exporters. ● MM

MONDETTA CLOTHING COMPANY was founded in **WINNIPEG** by 2 sets of brothers, Amit and Raj Bahl, and Ash and Prashant Modha. Both families immigrated to Winnipeg from East Africa in the early 1970s, though they are of **SOUTH ASIAN** heritage. The name Mondetta is based on the French word for world "monde" combined with the Latin suffix "etta," which means small. Their apparel line focuses on the theme of international awareness and globalization, and features products such as sweatshirts, T-shirts, golf shirts, leather goods, and golf bags for corporations including Sony, BMW, **PALLISER FURNITURE**, and the Winnipeg Airports Authority. The pairs of brothers got their start by operating a small business selling cards and stationery while at the

M

U OF M law school in 1946, and was in private practice until his appointment to the Court of Queen's Bench in 1957. He was elevated to MB's Court of Appeal in 1962, and became Chief Justice of MB in 1983. Monnin retired from the Court of Appeal in 1990. Lured out of retirement in 1998, he oversaw a provincial govt inquiry into the INTERLAKE VOTING SCANDAL, a vote-splitting scandal in 3 rural MB ridings during the 1995 election. The Monnin Inquiry, as it became known, resulted in a finding that PROGRESSIVE CONSERVATIVE Party organizers were guilty of inducing at least one candidate to enter the election campaign under an Aboriginal-interests-party banner in order to split the NEW DEMOCRATIC PARTY's vote. Monnin's famous line from the hearings – "In all my years on the bench, I have never encountered as many liars in one proceeding as I did in this inquiry" – has survived both the scandal and the inquiry. In 1990, Monnin was named an Officer of the Order of Canada, and in 2000, he became a Member of the ORDER OF MANITOBA. ● DOUG JOHNSTON

Jack Montgomery, 1972

MONTGOMERY, John Douglas "Hollywood Jack," Crown attorney (b July 29, 1927, Salisbury [Harare], Southern Rhodesia [Zimbabwe]; d Dec 7, 2004, WINNIPEG), was a prominent Winnipeg prosecutor. The son of missionary parents, Montgomery grew up in Toronto and attended law school at Osgoode Hall, and at the U OF M. He was called to the Manitoba Bar in 1960 and articled with the firm Filmore and Riley. He joined the MB Department of Justice in 1962, eventually serving as MB's chief prosecutor, and worked closely with many city police officers. He was appointed QC in 1971. Later, he became the director of criminal prosecutions and general counsel in the department. His flamboyant

personality and silver hair earned him the nickname "Hollywood Jack." He retired in 1998. He wrote 3 books: *She Was Only Three: The Trials of John James Jr.*; *Trials & Errors: The People vs. Brian Gordon Jack*; and *Beyond Redemption: The People vs. Lucas and Bender*. ● MD

MOONEY, Patrick Roy "Pat," environmentalist (b Feb 24, 1947, BRANDON), is one of the world's pre-eminent experts on genetic diversity in agriculture. He grew up in WINNIPEG's River Heights neighbourhood. Mooney was stricken with Stargardt's disease – a rare hereditary illness – at age 12, and is now blind. After dropping out of Kelvin High School to attend a UN youth seminar in Vienna, Mooney worked as a consultant for the UN Food and Agriculture Organization. He also spent time in development projects in Asia, Africa, and Latin America. In 1977 – together with BC-born, Scandinavian-based Cary Fowler, and Hope Shand, a North Carolinian – Mooney began publicizing the loss of plant genetic resources, and lobbied for plans to conserve biological and agricultural diversity. His *Seeds of the Earth: A Private or Public Resource?* (1979) raised the issues of monoculture and of ownership of crop hybrids by mega-corporations, an issue that affects notably the CANOLA industry in MB. In 1984, he co-founded Rural Advancement Foundation International (RAFI), whose name changed in 2001 to Erosion, Technology, and Concentration Group (ETC Group). ETC Group addresses the effects of new technologies on rural communities around the world. Originally headquartered in Winnipeg, the organization relocated to Ottawa in 2004, as did Mooney. ETC also has offices in NC and in Mexico. Mooney has authored or co-authored several books on the politics of biotechnology and biodiversity. He received the Swedish Right Livelihood Award in 1985, and the American Giraffe Award, given to those who "stick their necks out." ● AMANDA STEPHENS

MOOSE (*Alces alces*) is the largest-surviving member of the deer family Cervidae, and is found right across northern NA and Eurasia in boreal and montane coniferous forest. The species first appeared in the fossil record of Europe 200,000 years ago, and it spread to NA 20,000 years ago over the Bering Land Bridge, formed during the last Ice Age. It is native to all regions of the province, but reaches its greatest abundance in the boreal coniferous forest. Due to habitat loss, hunting, and disturbance, it is now absent around towns and cultivated areas of SW MB. The Moose looks ungainly, but is wonderfully adapted for a life in northern forests. It can

travel long distances before tiring, and for short periods can reach a speed of 56 km/hr. Its long legs help it to wade through deep snow and it is an excellent swimmer. In fact, the moose often feeds on aquatic plants and has been known to dive several m to feed.

ROBERT R. TAYLOR

Bullmoose in autumn

Males average 450 kg (females 350 kg), with a maximum of 600 kg. Moose have no upper incisors, so buds and bark are stripped off by using the tough upper lip and the lower incisors. A truly high-fibre diet is essential to maintain health, and 20 kg of plant material are devoured in a day, but may reach 3 times this in the autumn in preparation for the lean winter period. Bacteria in the gut break down the tough cellulose, enabling the moose to extract nutrients from this otherwise hard-to-digest food. The annual breeding season or rut occurs from Sept to Nov, and bulls become aggressive during this time. Each animal may mate with several partners, since no harem is maintained as in American Elk. Moose are afflicted by a deadly brain parasite introduced by White-tailed deer, when the latter expanded into former Moose range. The current estimate for MB is over 30,000. ● REW, VC

MORDEN, pop 6571, MB's 9th largest town, is located 100 km SW of WINNIPEG and 25 km N of the US border on hwy 3. The first white settlers, Alvey Morden and his family, left Walkerton, ON, to come here in 1874. By 1878, there were 3 post offices in the district, Morden, Nelson and Mountain City, all competing for the railway and the settlers it would bring. In 1882, the CPR decided to put its Pembina line across the Mordens' land. By 1890, hardly a building remained in Nelsonville and Mountain City and Morden was a thriving community. It was incorporated as a village in 1895 and a town in 1903.

Its location in the centre of particularly rich agricultural land attracted settlers and services. MENNONITE homesteaders, who had great success farming the fertile soil, arrived. Their descendants now make up half of the town's population. Other prominent groups to come to Morden were

TOWN OF MORDEN, MAN

Two views of Morden in 1888.

ENGLISH, **DUTCH**, **SCOTS**, and **IRISH**. In the 21st century, the town continues to expand, thanks to an emphasis on community development and aggressive policies to attract continued immigration. Morden's advantage is a mix of urban-type services and jobs with a relaxed rural charm. In 2004, *Harrowsmith Country Life* magazine rated Morden the "Best in Country Living." As a manufacturing, retail, and agricultural-service centre, Morden is home to 3M Canada and **BÜHLER INDUSTRIES** plants and has a significant federal and provincial govt presence, including regional headquarters for **MANITOBA HYDRO** and **MTS**, and an Agricultural Canada Research Station. The town also hosts the Corn and Apple Festival, the Back Forty Folk Festival, and the Morden International Triathlon each year. The **CANADIAN FOSSIL DISCOVERY CENTRE** contains Canada's largest collection of Marine Reptile fossils that point back to 80 million years ago when the area was covered by a sea which stretched S to what is now the Gulf of Mexico. The town is also home to the province's **BASEBALL** Hall of Fame. Singer **LOREENA MCKENNITT**, businessman **JOHN BÜHLER**, and scientist **HENRY FRIESEN** all come from Morden. Morden enjoys a healthy rivalry with nearby **WINKLER**. • GPP

MORDEN CORN AND APPLE FESTIVAL.
The festival has taken place each Aug in **MORDEN** since 1988. It was started up by a small group of local artists who set up an assortment of pottery, glassworks, paintings, sculptures, and other artworks. By 2006, the festival had grown considerably, with about 45,000 attendees a year. A petting zoo, face painting, and entertainers are available for young visitors. For adults, there is a free **MUSIC** ranging from country to rock 'n' roll. Local farmers and gardeners sell their produce at a fresh market. The festival features free locally produced corn and apple cider. • RK

MORMONS. The Church of Jesus Christ of Latter-day Saints (Mormon) began in upstate New York in 1830. Founded on the teachings and revelations of Joseph Smith Jr, the Church claims to be the true restoration of primitive Christianity, complete with priestly authority, continuing prophetic revelation, and modern scripture, particularly the Book of Mormon.

Intensely persecuted for their religious convictions, the "Saints" moved W to IL, where Smith was martyred in 1844. Beginning in 1846, the Church migrated to the Rocky Mountains under Brigham Young. As part of his gathering and colonization efforts, the Mormon presence in eastern Canada – early Mormon missionaries had proselytized in Upper Canada, now ON, as early as 1832 – dwindled dramatically. By 1861,

the Census counted only 74 Latter-day Saints in Canada West (later ON). Meanwhile, Mormon settlements sprang up all over Utah Territory and the inter-mountain US West.

Charles Ora Card was dispatched to western Canada in 1886-87 to establish a new settlement free from the anti-polygamy raids in Utah Territory and the anti-Mormon hysteria of the time. Card successfully formed a small Mormon colony on Lee's Creek, 50 km SW of Lethbridge. The Mormon presence soon grew from a few hundred settlers near Cardston, AB (as the community became known), to almost 10,000. In 1911, AB missionaries fanned out from Cardston to SK and MB to the E, and BC to the W. Gradually, Latter-day Saints became respected for their hard work and industry, building an economy based on ranching, sugar beet farming, and canal building.

Mormon missionaries were in MB almost from its beginning. Thomas Brandley laboured among his **MENNONITE** relatives in 1884, while Jacob Johnson worked with his **ICELANDIC** kin in 1893. Charles Ora Card sent missionaries E from Cardston to **WINNIPEG** and **BRANDON** throughout the 1890s. While a "Sister Williams" was the first known Manitoban convert (1897), the first family to join the Church was the Cornelius de Winter family, baptized in the **RED RIVER** in Winnipeg in 1901. The Winnipeg branch of the church, formed in 1910, was the first in western Canada outside AB. Since the turn of the 20th century, the church has actively proselytized more or less continuously with steady, if modest, success.

As of writing, a single stake – an entity comparable to a diocese – served the spiritual needs of approximately 3000 Mormons in MB. While membership is concentrated in Winnipeg, wards and branches are scattered over a vast territorial expanse stretching from the nickel-**MINING** city of **THOMPSON** to **DAUPHIN**, **BRANDON**, **SELKIRK**, and other more-southerly communities.

A distinctly Christian faith, the Church of Jesus Christ of Latter-day Saints believes in the Holy Bible and the Book of Mormon; faith in God the Eternal Father and in His Son, Jesus Christ, and His infinite atonement; repentance; baptism by immersion for the remission of sins; and the companionship of the Holy Ghost. In addition, it believes in the separation of church and state, and in the literal Second Coming of Jesus Christ and his ultimate return not only to the Jerusalem of old but also to a New Jerusalem yet to be established in NA. Church teachings emphasize such virtues as fidelity in marriage between a man and a woman, family togetherness, personal accountability and integrity, and obedience to civil and religious law. Whereas its former practice of plural marriage ceased in 1890, its belief in temple-centred eternal marriages continues as a hallmark doctrine. Latter-day Saints also live by the Word of Wisdom, a health code that encourages good dietary habits, exercise, and the avoidance of tobacco, illicit drugs, tea, and coffee, as well as alcohol. The Latter-day Saints are also well known for believing in baptism for the dead, in life after death, and in family exaltation, and are well known for promoting genealogical research. The worldwide Latter-day system of family-history centres has benefited Canadians of all faiths for many years. ● RICHARD E. BENNETT

MORRIS, pop 1673, is a town 60 km SSW of **WINNIPEG** in the **RED RIVER VALLEY** at the meeting point of the Morris and **RED** rivers, on **CN** and **CP** lines and on hwy 75. **FRENCH FUR TRADERS** were attracted to the area as early as the 18th century because of the location's opportune position along the Red. By 1801, 2 fur-trading stations were established. By 1869, oxcarts began to carry more settlers to the area, and the town grew. A post office and **RAILWAY** points were established here in 1874. Morris was originally known as Scratching River after the nearby waterway of that name, now the Morris River. The river was so named (and previously called Rivière-aux-Gratias in French, or "Prickly River") because of a prevalence of thorn bushes nearby. In 1881, the name changed to honour **ALEXANDER MORRIS**, first Chief Justice of the Court of Queen's Bench and 2nd lt gov of MB. The town was incorporated in 1883, and is composed primarily of **MENNONITES** and **GERMANS** as well as people of **ENGLISH**, **DUTCH**, **SCOTS**, French, and **MÉTIS** extraction. The Red River's repeated **FLOODING** has left the Morris area covered in rich river silt: consequently, the area possesses some of the best agricultural soils in the world, and agriculture, particularly hog farms, form the economic base nearby. Morris residents have also had to contend with recurrent **FLOODING**, however. After the 1950 flood, a dike was constructed to reduce risk of future flood damage, though an improved dike later had to be constructed. Morris serves principally as a retail and service centre for surrounding farms, but has a diversified economy, with other industries including govt agencies as well as manufacturing. Morris hosts the **MANITOBA STAMPEDE AND EXHIBITION**, one of the province's largest attractions. ● GPP

MORRIS, Alexander, lawyer, judge, politician (b March 17, 1826, Perth, Upper Canada [ON]; d Oct 28, 1889, Toronto). Born of **SCOTS PRESBYTERIAN** parents, Morris was educated in Scotland at Madras College, St. Andrews, and at the U of Glasgow. He became fluent in French, then

Engraving of Alexander Morris, 1872.

emigrated to Canada and studied law in Kingston under John A. Macdonald. He attended the U of Queen's College (now Queen's U, in Kingston, ON), and then graduated from McGill. Morris was an early Cdn imperialist, publishing *Canada and its Resources* in 1855, and in his 1858 lecture "Nova Britannia: Or, British North America, Its Extent and Future," he predicted Confederation and transcontinental railway expansion. He was an early advocate of the annexation of **HBC** territories and, as Conservative MLA and MP from Lanark from 1861-72, a leading Father of Confederation. He was appointed minister of inland revenue in 1869. When he retired from federal politics in 1872 due to ill health, he specifically requested to be sent to MB as a judge, where "the work would be light" and he "could be of use."

He served as the first chief justice of the Court of Queen's Bench of MB, and acted as administrator of MB and the NWTs when **SIR ADAMS ARCHIBALD** departed in Oct 1872. He once described his court as a "bear garden" because of differing French and English practices. He regarded it as fortunate that the legislature had adopted English practice and English law. He "quietly enforced both" until appointed lt gov of the province and the NWT in Dec 1872. As lt gov, he continued Archibald's insistence on responsible govt and supported the foundation of the **U OF M**. His administration in MB failed, however, to preserve **MÉTIS** lands in that province, and he himself was an active investor and speculator. After he stepped down as lt gov, he attempted to enter MB politics by running as MP from **SELKIRK**, losing by 10 votes to **DONALD A. SMITH**. In 1880, he

published a book entitled *The Treaties of Canada with the Indians of Manitoba and the North-West Territories*. He was in ill health for many years before his death. The town of **MORRIS** is named for him. ● JMB

MORTON, William Lewis "W. L.," educator, historian (b Dec 13, 1908, **GLADSTONE**; d Dec 7, 1980, Medicine Hat, AB) wrote numerous essays and books on MB and Cdn history. W. L. Morton was educated at St. John's College (*see* **U OF M**) and Oxford U, where he was a Rhodes Scholar. He returned to the U of M in 1942, where he was head of the history department from 1950-64. In 1964, he went to Trent U, in Peterborough, ON to become master of Champlain College and Vanier Professor of history. After retirement in 1975, he returned to the U of M, where he taught until his death. Morton began his historical work on the West with a collaboration with his sister, Margaret Morton Fahrni, *Third Crossing: A History of the Town and District of Gladstone in the Province of Manitoba* (1946). He then produced *The Progressive Party in Canada* (1950, rev ed, 1967). Beginning in the mid-1950s, Morton entered into a decade of prodigious output that moved him from being a regional to a national historian. In 1956, he published 2 lengthy introductions to collections of documents: *The London Correspondence Inward from Eden Colvile 1849-52* and

W. L. Morton, 1963

Alexander Begg's "Red River Journal" and Other Papers Relative to the Red River Resistance of 1869-70. A year later, he published his seminal history of the province, *Manitoba: A History* (1957, rev. 1967). He founded the Manitoba Record Society, editing its first volume, *Manitoba: The Birth of a Province*, in 1965. His collected essays have been compiled in *Contexts of Canada's Past: Selected Essays of W. L. Morton* (1980). Morton was considered a "red Tory." ● JMB

MOSAKAHIKEN CREE NATION (previously known as Moose Lake First Nation), on reserve pop 1203, off reserve pop 467, is located 470 km NW of **WINNIPEG**, 58 km SE of **THE PAS**. It relies on The Pas for many of its services. The native language here is Cree, and the community signed Treaty 5 in 1875. It is a member of the Swampy Cree Tribal Council. Schooling in this community goes from Nursery-Grade 9, and total enrolment for the year 2003-04 was 341. The Frontier School Division administers education. There are a total of 5 reserves in the Mosakahiken Cree Nation, the most populous of which is Moose Lake. Road access includes all-weather roads from The Pas. There are also docks for boat and float planes. The economic foundation for this Cree Nation is derived from fishing, hunting, and logging. Mosakahiken Cree Nation felt the negative impact of the Grand Rapids Hydro project. When it was built in 1963, the generating station and dam caused serious flooding in the area, depleting the region's moose and waterfowl populations. And local residents reported more incidents of crime, illness, and substance dependency. Mosakahiken signed an agreement with Manitoba Hydro in 1990 to direct more than $7 million to the community as compensation. **TOM LAMB**, who started Lamb Air, lived in the neighouring off-reserve community of Moose Lake. ● RK

MOSIENKO, Billy "Mosie," hockey player, (b Nov 2, 1921, **WINNIPEG**; d July 9, 1994, Winnipeg) scored 3 goals in 21 seconds, setting a hat trick record that is unlikely to ever be broken. Mosienko came from humble beginnings, growing up with 14 siblings in Winnipeg's **NORTH END**. He skated for the Tobans and the Sherburn Athletic Club before playing his first junior season with the Winnipeg Monarchs in 1939-40. At 18, he signed with the Chicago Black Hawks, splitting his time between the major and minor leagues over the next 2 years. His career was briefly interrupted by military service during WWII. He returned to the NHL for the 1943-44 season, and was signed on full-time with the Black Hawks. He played in 5 All-Star games over the course of his 14 years

in the NHL, and had 258 goals and 282 assists in 711 games. In 1945, he was awarded the Lady Byng Trophy for sportsmanship.

Mosienko's most memorable moment came on Mar 23, 1952, in a game against the New York Rangers. The Rangers were leading the Black Hawks 6-2 in the 3rd period. Lined up for a face-off, centre Gus Bodnar won the draw and passed the puck to Mosienko, who skated swiftly around the Rangers' defenceman on the right side and scored with a wrist shot. Following the subsequent centre-ice puck drop, Bodnar and Mosineko repeated a virtually identical play, and Mosienko again beat goalie Lorne Anderson. Only 11 secs had passed between goals. The Rangers and Black Hawks lined up for a 3rd time. Bodnar again won the draw, but changed tactics, passing the puck to leftwinger George Gee. Gee skated up the ice and slid the puck to Mosienko, who deked Anderson and netted his 3rd goal in 21 secs. The Black Hawks completed the comeback, winning 7-6. Mosie's record for the fastest 3 goals still stands.

Billy Mosienko

He finished his playing days with the Winnipeg Warriors, signing on for the 1955-56 season and leading the team to the Western Hockey League championship, before taking on coaching duties in 1960. He was named Manitoba's Athlete of the Year in 1957. He retired from the ice in 1959, taking over coaching duties for the Warriors for one year before moving on to other Winnipeg minor hockey teams. He opened a bowling alley on Winnipeg's north Main St. A Winnipeg hockey arena is named in his honour. Mosienko was inducted into the Hockey Hall of Fame in 1965. ● MD

MOSQUITO is an insect in the family Culicidae, order Diptera – a type of fly highly modified for a parasitic mode of life. The group evolved 130 million years ago (Early Cretaceous period); the Canadian Amber Mosquito (*Paleoculicis*

minutus) is known in amber dated 75 million years old. A male mosquito has a pair of feathery antennae while the females are sparsely haired. There are 4 larval stages and a non-feeding pupal stage. Under ideal conditions (water and high temperatures), development from egg to adult may be completed in as little as 6 days. People often ask why there are so many mosquitoes in MB. The answer lies in species abundance, adaptive diversity, and perfect living conditions over the entire low-lying, often wet, province. For example, one ha of muskeg in northern MB can produce over 10 million mosquitoes in the few brief months of summer. There are nearly 50 species of mosquitoes recorded for MB, each one with its own unique way of life, and categorized according to its breeding habits.

Snowmelt species represent the most predictable group of nuisance mosquitoes. The Snow Mosquito (*Aedes communis*) is found in northern forests and is able to fly when the ground is still covered with **SNOW**. In most cases, females lay their eggs in late spring to early summer along the margins of depressions holding the remnants of pools that had filled from melting snow. The eggs will not hatch until they have been exposed to an extended period of low temperatures. This mechanism guarantees that the eggs will overwinter and develop the following spring, when pools form. Some species hatch at very low temperatures, and the larvae are present in pools even when ice forms on the surface each night. The larvae of these species are dark coloured and form dense aggregations on sunny days in the shallows, thereby collectively absorbing infrared (heat) energy from the sun. Larval development is thus accelerated with elevated temperature. The larvae pupate after several weeks, and the adults emerge and fly off to mate. Females of most species take a blood meal from a host and then return to a pool edge to deposit their eggs. A few species are able to lay one small batch of eggs without a prior blood meal, thus guaranteeing that there will be another generation. To lay additional eggs, though, they are dependent on having additional nutrients from blood. Snowmelt species form the first sign of mosquito activity in spring.

Summer flood water mosquitoes are those species whose females also lay their eggs on the sides of pools and ditches, but once the eggs mature, they hatch as soon as they are flooded from summer thunderstorms. The larvae experience much higher temperatures in summer and develop rapidly into adults. However, since these pools are generally temporary, many immatures are left stranded and perish. These species require blood to lay eggs and feed once or several times, laying a batch of about 100 eggs after each meal. Consequently, there are 3 or 4 generations each summer. Although flood-water mosquitoes emerge in vast numbers, not all flooded eggs hatch with one rainfall, so there are always more eggs lying in wait to take advantage of the next heavy rain. As the days of summer begin to shorten, the eggs respond by entering a stage of dormancy, and once this happens, they must be exposed to low temperatures for many weeks (i.e., winter) before they will hatch. These mosquitoes are not set back by occasional years of drought, since they can survive in the debris at the sides of the pools for several years, until it rains sufficiently to flood them. These species often lay their eggs in the ideal breeding habitat of roadside ditches, which occur throughout most of southern MB. Adults also disperse widely on the prairie winds, another reason cities and towns are overwhelmed with these pests, even after fogging with control agents.

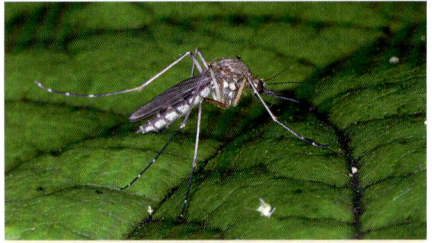

Mosquitoes need water to flourish.

Wetland mosquitoes consist of a few species that lay their eggs in the more permanent standing water of wetlands. One species (*Coquilletidia perturbans*) has extraordinary larvae and pupae which attach themselves to the roots and stems of emergent aquatic plants such as cattails. While other species of mosquitoes rise to take air at the surface, this species draws air from the tissues of the plant, so they have no need to come to the surface. The adults are among the most-aggressive and savage biters, and make themselves known to any creature in the marsh as it gets dark in mid-summer.

Container-breeders are several species that traditionally lay eggs exclusively in long-lasting pools or tree-holes. A consequence of this habit is that they have switched to standing water in artificial containers, such as bird baths, eavestroughs, abandoned wading pools, catch basins, rain barrels, and used tires. They are seldom abundant enough to be considered a serious nuisance, and some species bite mainly birds, but because of their ability to serve as vectors of pathogenic organisms that infect humans, horses, and wildlife, they warrant careful consideration. *Culex tarsalis* is just such an example. This species breeds in permanent and semi-permanent pools,

and is occasionally found in artificial containers, though not as frequently as the bird-feeding species, *Culex restuans*. *Culex tarsalis* is of particular importance because it is believed to be the primary vector for Western Equine Encephalitis and West Nile Virus to humans in MB. It feeds readily on birds, which is where it acquires the virus, but it also feeds avidly on large mammals, acting as a bridge vector, carrying these viral pathogens from the bird reservoir to humans.

There is one container-breeder, of no concern as a pest, but fascinating because of its unusual habitat. The Pitcher Plant Mosquito (*Wyeomyia smithii*) is found exclusively in the cupped leaves of the carnivorous Purple Pitcher Plant, which grows in acid bogs as far N as THE PAS. The water held in these leaves acts as a trap for unwary insects, which drown in the water and eventually decay, their nutrients then being absorbed by the plant. Among the drowned insects swim the larvae of the Pitcher Plant Mosquito. The adults never take blood, and always lay their eggs in the leaves of the pitcher plant. To overwinter, the larvae enter dormancy and freeze inside the block of ice within a leaf, only to regain their activity and growth again in the spring when the thawing ice releases them. ● TDG

MOSS ANIMAL or ectoproct is a small, primitive creature in the phylum Bryozoa that usually lives in colonies, and forms a crust or branching structure in freshwater or marine habitats. While resembling a coral, it is more complex internally. An individual in the colony is called a zooid, whose body is enclosed in a protective tunic made of either chitin (a protein found also in insect skeletons) or calcium carbonate. This sheath is continuous with other members of the colony. An extension of the body, called a lophophore, extends from the top of the tunic and contains the mouth surrounded by a number of tentacles. Bryozoans feed by capturing microorganisms with their ciliated tentacles, and in turn are grazed upon by sea urchins and fish. Bryozoans prefer hard surfaces rather than unstable muddy or sandy sediments for attachment, and are more prevalent at depths over 30 m (max 8200 m). To date, 46 species have been recorded in Hudson Bay, but others remain to be discovered. Common species include *Celleporella hyalina*, *Cysticella saccata* and *Myriapora subgracila*. The species *Eucratea loricata* has been found at 160 m depth in the bay. Remarkably, 20 species were recorded growing on large blades of kelp algae (*Laminaria*) that washed up on shore at Churchill.

Freshwater bryozoans are all members of one family (Phylactolaemata), which includes a number of species in the genera *Cristatella*,

Plumatella and *Fredericella*, distributed widely across Canada and the world. The number of freshwater species in MB is unknown. *Pectinella magnifica* colonies, which may be found growing on a submerged tree branch, can reach the size of a basketball, although each zooid is only 1 mm long. Bryozoans reproduce asexually by budding, or sexually – some species shedding both eggs and sperm into the water, while others capture floating sperm with their tentacles to fertilize eggs maintained in brood chambers. In some species, the colony dies each winter and regenerates in spring from surviving cell masses (statoblasts), which can withstand freezing and drying for long periods. Fossil bryozoans have been found in MB in limestone rocks formed 475 mya (Ordovician period), but the group likely first evolved over 500 mya (Cambrian period). There are more than 4000 species of living bryozoans world-wide. ● REW

MOTH is a mainly nocturnal insect closely related to butterflies, from which they differ in both physical appearance and behaviour. The antennae of butterflies are smooth and either swollen at the ends or posses a small hook, while moth antennae are usually covered in hairs and appear feathery, without a noticeable hook or swollen tip. At rest, a moth often holds its front wings over the hindwings, roof-like over the body. A moth's body also tends to be stouter and is covered in dense tufts of hair, or has a furry appearance, while a butterfly's body is almost smooth. Most moths become active at night, but there are over 20 species of day-flyers in MB, some of which are mistaken for butterflies. Many moths posses a long tongue-like proboscis used for obtaining nectar from flowers at night, and consequently are important pollinators.

Many MB moths are small (<3 cm wing width) and drab grey, brown, and black. There are also brightly coloured species, some with wing spans up to 16 cm, including several native species related to the silk moth from China, such as the pale-green Luna Moth (*Actias luna*), the orange and black Cecropia Moth (*Hyalophora cecropia*), and the Polyphemus Moth (*Antheraea polyphemus*), with multi-coloured eyespots containing window-like membranes. The sphinx or hawkmoth family Sphingidae contains species mistaken for hummingbirds because of their large size, rapid flight, and hovering ability in front of flowers during the day and at dusk, while sipping nectar with their long (>3 cm) tongues. The White-lined Sphinx (*Hyles lineata*), with a 9 cm wingspan, is a common species found from S MB to Latin America. Its large colourful caterpillars feed on many kinds of crops, and the adults are frequently attracted at night to house lights.

Moth reproduction often involves the release by the female of chemical attractants (pheromones), which the male detects with its sensitive antennae. In a remarkable display of homing ability, males fly towards the female's location by following the plume of scent molecules drifting in the air. Moths go through 4 developmental stages – egg, larva (caterpillar), pupa (cocoon), and adult. The larvae or caterpillars are herbivorous, with strong chewing mouthparts. Species feeding on plant surfaces are remarkably camouflaged in colour pattern and posture, others hide underground where they feed on plant roots, or are enclosed inside plant galls or leaf mines, or burrow into fruit and stems. Despite various forms of ornamentation, spots and projections, the larvae are similar in body plan – cylindrical, with a well-developed head, 6 hook-like thoracic legs, and a variable number of prothoracic prolegs. Many species produce silk used by the larvae during active growth, or to construct a cocoon prior to pupation. A cocoon is made up of many silk strands interwoven with caterpillar hairs and sometimes soil debris. Certain MB moths do not form a complete cocoon, and the almost-bare pupa is buried in the soil or wrapped in plant leaves. Most MB moths spend the winter in either the egg stage, or as a bare pupa, or a pupa within a cocoon. There is usually one generation per year, although some species may have up to 3, depending on the length of summer and harshness of winter.

In MB, many moths lay eggs singly on plant leaves and their caterpillars are solitary feeders, causing minor damage to their food plants. A few species are serious pests of crops (e.g., canola), trees and gardens, and these feed gregariously and may be cyclic in nature. The Spruce Budworm Moth (*Choristoneura fumiferana*) gradually builds up in large numbers, defoliating thousands of hectares of spruce and fir trees in MB. An outbreak may last for up to 8 years before predators, parasites, weather and other factors cause the population to crash and then remain absent for years. Outbreaks of the Forest Tent Caterpillar (*Malacosoma disstria*) result in millions of large furry blue caterpillars defoliating trees in the spring (new leaves appear in July). The green and grey Cankerworm Moth caterpillar (*Alsophila pometaria*) defoliates elm and ash trees in June, and then descends on silken threads, trying to reach the soil to pupate. Vegetable gardeners are familiar with the brown, grub-like larvae of cutworm moths (family Noctuidae), which emerge from the soil at night to damage tomatoes and other succulent plants.

Most MB species are native and spend their entire life cycle here, but others such as hawk-moths migrate here each spring from S and central US. The latter cannot survive a MB winter, but reproduce here during the summer, and they and/or their offspring return S in the fall. Moths have been affected by habitat destruction and chemical poisoning (pollutants and pesticides). The Luna Moth, while still common in MB, is now classified as endangered in some regions.

Moths form one of the largest lineages of plant-eating organisms in the world, and play important roles in natural ecosystems and in urban areas. They serve as pollinators and a food source for other insects, birds, mammals and parasites. Moths are closely related to caddisflies (order Trichoptera), likely having evolved from a common ancestor by 200 million years ago (Early Jurassic period). The oldest lepidopteran is *Archaeolepis mane*, known from 190 million years old fossils. Moths became prominent by 100 million years ago (Middle Cretaceous period). Over 500 species are recorded in MB, but could reach 600 with future field studies (over 11,000 in NA, and 183,000 worldwide). ● ARW, REW

MOTOR COACH INDUSTRIES (MCI) is NA's largest intercity **Bus Manufacturing** firm, with production plants in **Winnipeg** and Pembina, ND, adjacent to **Emerson**. MCI also has 6 sales centres, 7 support service centres, and more than 2000 employees. Its customers include charter and tour operators, scheduled-service and line-haul operators, transit agencies, and conversion companies. MCI began as an auto repair shop (Fort Garry Motor Body and Paint Works Ltd). Fort Garry got into the bus-making business in 1933, when founder Harry Zoltok came up with a design for an 11-passenger bus and began producing the new vehicle. In 1941, Zoltok changed the company's name to Motor Coach Industries, selling a 65% stake in the company to Greyhound of Canada 7 years later. A decade after the majority sale, Greyhound acquired the remaining 35% and transformed MCI from a small, regional player into a leading intercity bus manufacturer with the development of the first 12 m (40-ft) motor coach, which it called the MC-6.

MCI continued to improve upon its original product with the subsequent introduction of several other new models. In 1994, MCI was sold to Grupo Dina, of Mexico City, which continued to develop new models, including a new luxury coach. In 1999, Grupo Dina sold a majority of MCI to an NY-based private equity firm, JLL (Joseph, Littlejohn & Levy). In 2003, with the North American intercity-bus industry still reeling from a dramatic decline in tourist travel following the Sept 11, 2001, terrorist attacks, MCI shut down its production plant in Mexico and shifted that work to Winnipeg, where its workers had agreed to accept wage cuts and other concessions. It invested $40 million US in the expansion of its Winnipeg production plant, and in March 2005, unveiled a new version of its D-series coach, which has become the most popular coach on the continent. ● MURRAY MCNEILL

▶ *See also* **Bus Manufacturing**.

M

Building a bus in 1955.

MOUNT CARMEL CLINIC, named after a Biblical mountain on Israel's Mediterranean coast, was the first community health centre in Canada. The **Winnipeg** clinic is recognized across the country as a model for holistic community health care. Over the years, the clinic has gained popularity among **North End** and Point Douglas residents for its non-judgemental services and its attention to physical, spiritual, emotional, and mental well-being.

Mount Carmel was created by impoverished European **Jews** in North Winnipeg. Although hospitals had provisions for caring for the poor, the ethnicity of each patient had to be documented and printed in newspapers for statistical purposes. Concerned by the perception that they were overusing these free services, the Jewish community established the clinic in 1926 in a house on Pritchard Ave. As needs grew, the clinic moved to 120 Selkirk Ave in 1929. By the late 1940s, with the **Great Depression** over and area Jews prospering, there was less call for the clinic's services. In 1948, when **Anne Glass Ross** was hired as a nurse, the clinic saw only 3 or 4 patients a day. Mount Carmel needed to adapt. Under Ross's leadership, the clinic focused on serving local people rather than a religious group. She was not satisfied merely to provide services, and sought actively to assess and to respond to community needs. She believed in a holistic approach to medical treatment. This approach – then unorthodox – emphasized addressing socioeconomic causes of poor health, and curing disease, where possible, instead of simply treating symptoms.

Initially, govt- and volunteer-run clinics were reluctant to refer patients to Mount Carmel. As doctors started regularly to volunteer there in the 1960s – after the introduction of medicare in 1969, usually donating much of their govt-set fees to the clinic – patients could be referred to the clinic instead of a hospital. While it was illegal at the time, the clinic still took a lead role in providing **Abortions**; and when the pill was first available in 1960, the clinic was among the few places to make the new form of birth control available. Women who were pleased with the quality of care at their clinic often recommended Mount Carmel to male as well as female relatives and friends. Thus, while some thought that medicare would spell the end of the clinic, patients came in growing numbers, many of them part of the 1950s/'60s influx of **First Peoples** to the city. People from the various waves of immigration from around the world would also make up much of the clientele.

As the clinic's patients changed, so did its programming. Mount Carmel began offering various new programs, most notably a day hospital where children needing treatment could attend by day, returning home at night. Other programs included free milk for pregnant women; a daycare; counselling; a pharmacy offering discounted or free prescription drugs to those who could not afford the full price; and, in 1964, free dental care. By the 1970s, with the additional services and with an average of between 125 and 150 patients a day, the clinic was much too small. Ross sought to obtain the funds necessary to relocate. In 1974, the govt passed the *Mount Carmel Clinic Act*, officially recognizing the clinic as a body. This, and Ross's concerted efforts, paved the way for the clinic's 1982 move to a purpose-built location at 886 Main St. Here the clinic continues to adapt and expand, with a teen clinic, a parenting support program, Sage House (an outreach and health centre on Argyle St for women in the sex trade), and diabetes and hepatitis-C clinics, among other programs. As of writing, the clinic was planning an expansion to an adjacent building on Main St. • A.J. LEVIN

MOUSE is an enormously successful group of rodents found worldwide and throughout MB, in all natural land habitats as well as agricultural fields and even inside buildings. Since the province has such a diversity of terrestrial habitats (prairie to tundra), it is only natural that it harbours a rich fauna of mice – 19 in fact, including 3 introduced species. Through sheer numbers, these small mammals play a major role in converting plant material into animal life – a feature counted on by a hoard of predators, from fish and reptiles to birds and mammals. They transport and bury seeds that often germinate, and devour prodigious numbers of insects injurious to trees and other plants. Their burrowing activities turn over and aerate the soil, improving its fertility and drainage. In fact, if mice suddenly disappeared, most land ecosystems would be greatly affected. People walk right past mice all the time when hiking, even within cities and towns, but they are seldom seen, since an obvious mouse would quickly be spotted and eaten by a hawk, fox or cat. Although a few kinds are active for periods day and night, most prefer the cover of darkness for their above-ground activities of foraging for food and potential mates, and dispersing to new home ranges. When the early settlers arrived in the **Red River** Valley, their crops were devoured not only by **Grasshoppers** but also by legions of mice. They still cause enormous losses to the agricultural industry, through eating young plants and mature seeds.

The Olive-backed Pocket Mouse (*Perognathus fasciatus*) is so distinct that it is given its own family (Heteromyidae). It is a tiny

White-footed mouse

(10 gram) rodent with fur-lined cheek pouches, which it uses like a shopping cart to carry seeds, as it searches dry sandy prairie and grain fields. The next 3 species are called jumping mice (Family Dipodidae) on account of their remarkable hopping ability using their long hind legs, and long tail for balance. The Meadow (*Zapus hudsonius*) and Western (*Zapus princeps*) jumping mice are found in meadows and dry prairie, respectively, while the Woodland Jumping Mouse (*Napaeozapus insignis* – meaning 'woodland nymph with big feet') is a rare inhabitant of streambanks in mixed forest in extreme SE MB. All 3 have beautiful yellow or orange sides, brown or black backs, and white bellies. These appealing and delicate little creatures double their weight in fat stores by Oct and then hibernate 1-2 m underground for 7 months of the year; they are among the most-profound mammalian hibernators in the world.

The remaining mice are all closely related and form the family Muridae. The Northern Grasshopper Mouse (*Onychomys leucogaster*) is the powerfully built bully of the mouse world, eating mostly seeds and insects, but is not beyond devouring other small animals when offered the chance. It can whistle loudly like a miniature wolf standing over its prey. It is rare and found in only a few isolated localities in dry prairie of SW MB. Its close relative – the dainty Deer Mouse (*Peromyscus maniculatus*) – is one of the most-abundant mammals in MB and all NA, and abounds in habitats from the grasslands through all types of forest and shrub cover. It has a charming face (for a mouse), with big bulging eyes, enormous ears, and a snoutful of whiskers. Recently it has been found to harbour a hantavirus, which has claimed the lives of a few people in rural MB.

Next come a host of voles – a term used for short-tailed mice gathered into their own subfamily. The Northern Red-backed Vole (*Clethrionomys rutilus*) lives in shrubby tundra in the far N of MB, while the Southern Red-backed Vole (*Clethrionomys gapperi*) occurs in forests and shrubs everywhere but the tundra region. Four kinds of lemmings have been reported here. The Collared Lemming (*Dicrostonyx richardsoni*) cycles in enormous numbers on the tundra, while one specimen of the Brown Lemming (*Lemmus sibiricus*) showed up in Churchill many decades ago, but is believed to have been just a stowaway on a boat arriving from farther up the coast of Hudson Bay, where it is abundant. The 4-year crash of lemmings and voles is what triggers the famous S migration of Arctic Foxes (desperate for food) deep into the forest zone of MB. Two species of bog lemmings (with only stubs for tails) are typically found in bogs and fens, where they leave little trails in the moss and sedge, marked by piles of cut stems and tidy latrines. The Southern Bog Lemming (*Synaptomys cooperi*) is restricted to SE MB, while the Northern Bog Lemming (*Synaptomys borealis*) occurs widely in boreal forest bogs. Both are important prey for owls, hawks and weasels. The Heather Vole (*Phenacomys intermedius*) is a rare inhabitant of boreal forest and willow shrubs, while the Meadow Vole (*Microtus pennsylvanicus*) is widespread and abundant in meadows, marshes and grasslands. This is the species that sometimes takes up residence in people's lawn, and turns up at the doorstep in the cat's mouth. The Prairie Vole (*Microtus ochrogaster*) is a rare, grizzled species found on arid-prairie hilltops, such as occur in the Carberry Sandhills. The Chestnut-cheeked Vole (*Microtus xanthognathus*) is a robust (170-gram) vole but also an enigma – it has been found only once in the province, in a small temporary colony (almost a century ago) near York Factory. The Muskrat (*Ondatra zibethicus*) is a large and highly specialized, aquatic member of this family (*see* **Muskrat**).

Lastly, 2 exotic species – the House Mouse (*Mus musculus*) and Norway or Brown Rat (*Rattus norvegicus*) – arrived for the first time (but not the last) with the early explorers and settlers. These incredibly adaptable Eurasian rodents have spread around the world with the assistance of people, and have been responsible for devouring and contaminating vast food sources, as well as harboring several deadly diseases. Fortunately, their numbers are controllable with appropriate hygiene and pest-control methods. Most are unable to survive outside in MB winters, and must find winter shelter in buildings. ● REW

MTS ALLSTREAM is the 3rd largest telecommunications company in Canada with annual revenues of about $2 billion. It is the dominant local and long distance telephone provider in MB and has about 50% of the cellular telephone and high speed Internet business in the province and about 30% of the digital television market in Winnipeg. Its Allstream division is the 2nd largest provider of sophisticated enterprise telecommunications service to business customers across the country.

The company's roots in MB go back to the late 1870s where the booming **Red River** community was site of some of the most enthusiastic early users of the new technology. MB's public telephone system was the very first to become government owned and one of the last on the continent to be privatized. Manitoba Government Telephones was formed in 1908 when the province paid $3.3 million for the Bell Telephone Company's operations in the province. Ostensibly it was done in response to public outcry over unruly competition that ensued after Alexander Graham Bell's patent expired in 1893. There were 700 employees at the time.

It was briefly in the radio business, owning what would become CKY until the early postwar year when it was forced to sell after federal legislation was passed preventing provincial governments from owning radio stations. In 1933 the provincial govt shut down its telephone department converting it to a crown corporation and changing its name to Manitoba Telephone System. It had 1000 employees at the time.

Through the mid-to-late 20th century, the relatively small Cdn telecommunications company tried to develop external markets. In the 1980s it formed a consulting division, called MTX to provide technical services to Saudi Arabia. That venture ended in controversy with losses approaching $30 million.

The crown corporation was wracking up sizeable debts through the 1990s. Although the PC government of **Gary Filmon** had told voters it would not privatize MTS, concerns mounted about the telco's relative ability to keep up with rapidly changing technology and its commitment to provide service throughout Manitoba's sparsely populated north country.

M

Manitoba Telephone System operators in 1974

UMA, TRIBUNE, MANITOBA TELEPHONE SYSTEM, JEFF DE BOOY PHOTO, 50A-3704-18, 1974

A privatization strategy began in 1996 with financial advisors recommending a full public offering of shares to raise capital. As part of the process the province would assume about $400 million of the crown corporation's debt in exchange for equity. Argument over the privatization of MTS produced some of the most rancorous debates ever seen in Cdn govt. At one point Filmon challenged an **NDP** opposition member to a fight outside the house.

M An initial public offering of shares took place on Jan 7, 1997 producing unprecedented stock market activity among Manitobans who were able to buy shares on an instalment plan. The offering raised $910 million. Investors paid $13 per share in 1997. Since then prices went as high as $53 in the spring of 2004 and have rarely traded below $40 since then.

Ten years later it remained a hot button topic for the NDP government of **Gary Doer** who, notwithstanding the fact it was not their stated intention, would regularly warn voters that if the Tories were again elected they might attempt a similar end-run to privatize **Manitoba Hydro**.

In the summer of 2004 MTS shocked the national telecommunications industry by buying Allstream, the former AT&T Canada, for $1.7 billion. It meant that MTS was no longer exclusively a regional player. The company then changed its name to MTS Allstream. It also resulted in the acrimonious ending of a relationship with mighty Bell Canada. MTS sold its stake in a joint venture called Bell West for $645 million and settled a lawsuit with Bell for $75 million.

Through the 1990s and the first decade of the new century the company reduced its workforce from about 5,200 to 3,600 at the beginning of 1997. Ten years later its MB workforce was down to 2,900. MTS weathered the increasingly competitive marketplace storms including the introduction of cable telephones. It was a NA trailblazer as one of the first telephone companies to offer television service. Four years after launching the service in 2003 it was providing digital television service to 30 per cent of the Winnipeg market. Through the latter part of the first decade of the new century MTS continues to be a take-over target of larger telcos like Bell, Telus, or Rogers. • MARTIN CASH

MTS CENTRE is a multi-purpose facility located in downtown **Winnipeg**. It opened in Nov 2004, replacing the **Winnipeg Arena** as the primary **Hockey** and large concert venue in MB. True North Sports & Entertainment Ltd owns and operates the building, and also assumed ownership of the **Manitoba Moose** in 2003 to act as its main tenant. It seats up to 15,015 for hockey and **Curling**, and can accommodate more than

The MTS Centre opened in downtown Winnipeg in 2004.

16,000 for concerts. Mark Chipman acts as chairman, and Jim Ludlow as president and CEO.

Although citizens and govt officials had debated the need for a new city facility since the 1970s, no plan materialized before the relocation of the **Winnipeg Jets** in 1996. In the late 1990s, the long-time focus on the revitalization of the downtown core area along with the remaining appetite for a new hockey arena led to renewed negotiations between the city, led by Mayor **Glen Murray,** and a group of investors. When **Eaton's** vacated their historic storefront in 1999, the building remained unoccupied and that land was chosen as the preferred arena site. A deal between the 3 levels of govt and the True North group was signed in May 2001. The proposed demolition of the square block to make way for the new construction was controversial, however. A group called Save the Eaton's Building Coalition filed provincial and federal court challenges to halt the project, motivated by the belief that the building was a heritage structure that should be converted for alternative mixed uses. A smaller group called Winnipeg's Arena Quest raised concerns that the planned structure would not be adequate for the city's needs. In March 2002, the Supreme Court of Canada dismissed the coalition's appeal, and the demolition proceeded.

The total capital cost of the arena was $133.5 million, with $93 million in private money from investors like the **Crocus Investment Fund**,

Osmington Inc, Centara Corporation, the **Chipman Family**'s Megill-Stephenson Company Ltd, a consortium of MB and SK **Credit Unions**, and the Workers Compensation Board of Manitoba. The federal, provincial, and civic govts contributed a total of $40.5 million. Denver, CO architectural firm Sink Combs Dethlefs, along with Winnipeg's Number Ten Architectural Group, were responsible for the design. It was known as the True North Centre until late 2003, when MTS paid $7 million to secure 10 years of naming rights.

Since 2004, the MTS Centre has hosted hundreds of events, including all Manitoba Moose games, the 2007 World Women's Hockey Championships, the 2006 American Hockey League all-star game, the 2005 Juno Awards, and concerts by the likes of Eric Clapton, Pearl Jam, The Tragically Hip, the Red Hot Chili Peppers, and Crosby, Stills, Nash & Young. • JOEL TRENAMAN

MTX SCANDAL dominated the MB legislature for months in 1986. In its efforts to make sales, MTX, a subsidiary of **MTS** set up telecommunications operations to Saudi Arabia, ignored basic Cdn human rights by discriminating against **Jews** and women, even allowing flogging of its Saudi employees. The subsidiary also managed to lose $27 million before it was shut down.

MTX had been set up in the early 1980s. However, it was **Howard Pawley**'s **NDP** govt that took the brunt of the blame in 1986. **Progressive**

CONSERVATIVE communications critic Don Orchard mounted a sustained and effective attack on the govt using the legislative assembly's Public Utilities Committee to exploit the issue with a series of damaging revelations about MTX's alleged financial, ethical, and human rights foibles. To get the Saudi contract, the NDP govt had apparently bowed to Saudi Arabian customs and agreed to prohibit MTX from hiring women and Jews. Several MTX employees were flogged in July 1983 for working during prayer hours and for allowing a woman in their office. More serious, however, was evidence that MTX had been paying bribes to Saudi businesses and that it had invested large sums of money in SADL, a heavily indebted Saudi company it half-owned.

The PCs demanded a judicial inquiry, charging that the minister, the govt, the cabinet's economic development committee, and govt appointees on the MTS board were all incompetent and ignored repeated warnings that the venture was in serious financial trouble. The govt responded with an RCMP investigation of possible criminal wrongdoing, a managerial review by Coopers and Lybrand (now part of the international accounting firm PricewaterhouseCoopers), and the involvement of the Canadian Human Rights Commission. Five senior MTS executives were ultimately fired, and MTS president Gordon Holland resigned. ● GPP

MUDMINNOW is a fish in the Mudminnow family Umbridae, and is related to the **PIKE**. The Central Mudminnow (*Umbra limi*) is a robust, 10-15 cm, olive-brown species with a short snout, flattened head, and rounded caudal fin. It occurs N to The Pas and W to the Souris River, preferring slow-moving streams, bogs, swamps and pools with dense beds of vegetation. It has the unusual capability of breathing atmospheric oxygen at the surface, using its air bladder for gaseous exchange. This feature enables the species to live in water with low levels of dissolved oxygen, which may develop in its habitat in summer (temperatures may rise to 30°C in stagnant

water) or under the ice. Mudminnows move into the shallows and up into springs to spawn from May to June when water temperatures reach 13°C. Following fertilization, from 200-2300 sticky eggs are attached to aquatic plants and are then abandoned. Hatching occurs in about 6 days and the young quickly retreat into the bottom ooze when startled. They travel into deeper water when they reach about 3 cm. Males become sexually mature at 2 years and females at 3 years at a length of 5-7 cm. Longevity is at least 4 years. The Central Mudminnow feeds on small aquatic organisms such as crustaceans, insects and snails in mid-water and on the bottom, and takes mainly small fish during the winter. ● REW

MULDREW, Cecil "Cec," educator, activist (b June 30, 1923, WINNIPEG; d Sept 6, 2004, Winnipeg), was known across Canada as a campaigner for peace. Both of Muldrew's parents were schoolteachers, and he followed their example, graduating from Manitoba Normal School in 1941. He then joined the RCAF, serving in India. Upon his return, Muldrew married and went on to attain degrees in science and education, whereupon he taught for 34 years, including an almost-20-year stint as a school principal. He was politically involved, serving as secretary of the Winnipeg Teachers Association and president of the Science Teachers Association, besides being a lifelong supporter of the **NDP**, receiving that party's Pioneer Award for 50 years of volunteering. Muldrew was active in the **UNITARIAN** Church, and championed goodwill organizations such as the UN, UNICEF, the Red Cross, Veterans Against Nuclear Arms, Scouts Canada, and the United Way. In 1995, he was honoured with the Global Citizenship Award. In 1998, he received the Peace Award from Project Peacemakers, and, in 1999, the YMCA Peacemaker of the Year Award. ● RK

MULTIPLE SCLEROSIS (MS) is a degenerative disease of the nervous system, and its prevalence in MB is among the highest of any region in the world. Symptoms may include visual disturbances,

loss of sensation, fatigue, pain, loss of balance, muscle weakness, and alterations in bladder and bowel function. These symptoms arise due to degeneration of the "insulation" (called myelin sheath) surrounding neurons in the brain and spinal cord, causing disordered transmission of signals within our nervous system. MS is the most common primary neurological condition of young adults. The peak age of onset of MS symptoms is around 30, but symptoms may occur much earlier or later in life. Women are affected about twice as often as men. MS causes a heavy burden to the people who have it, their families, and society, with estimated lifetime costs of $1.6 million per case in Canada (1998).

The term "multiple" refers to the many areas of inflammation and demyelination that can occur within the nervous system, as well as to the repeated attacks of neurological symptoms that can occur over time. The term "sclerosis" refers to scarring that occurs within the brain and spinal cord as the disease progresses. Symptoms vary markedly between people. In many cases, the condition follows a relapsing/remitting pattern, whereby the symptoms may disappear for variable lengths of time, and then recur again. In others, the disease may get progressively more severe (chronic progressive), or may go into remission initially with subsequent progressive deterioration (secondary progressive pattern). Several categories of drugs may be used to treat MS and its symptoms. Powerful new therapies called disease-modifying agents became available in 1993, and have reduced the symptoms and disability for many people with MS.

It is not yet known what factors cause the autoimmune system to attack the myelin sheaths of the nervous system. It has long been suspected that MS occurs much more commonly farther from the Equator. A classic study performed by K. B. Westlund and L. T. Kurland, published in 1953, demonstrated that the prevalence of MS in Winnipeg was several times that in New Orleans. An increasing S-to-N gradient in MS rates has since been confirmed in most regions of the northern hemisphere, with Canada and Northern European countries having the highest documented rates of MS. Currently, there are an estimated 3000 with MS in MB. Several reasons are suggested for the higher prevalence of MS in northern regions. There is genetic susceptibility to MS – it tends to occur more frequently in close relatives of those with the disease – with those of Caucasian ancestry, and particularly Scottish, English, and Northern European ancestry, being at highest risk; and many Manitobans have these ancestries. Scientists also believe that some environmental factors directly or indirectly

M

Mudminnow

DOUGLAS WATKINSON

related to a colder climate may play a role. For example, inadequate levels of vitamin D in the body (due to insufficient dietary intake or limited sun exposure during winter) may put people at increased risk of MS. Finally, the frequency and age at which people are exposed to certain viruses may differ in colder climates.

The Multiple Sclerosis Society of Canada was founded in 1948 to help find a cure and to provide services to people with the disease and their families. Over 60% of all research in Canada is funded by the society. The MB division of the society, established in 1981, provides services and programs for people living with MS across the province. Consisting of 4 chapters, the MB division offers support, education, information, social action, recreational activities, and self-help and support groups. ● LAWRENCE ELLIOTT

MUNK, Jens Eriksen, Danish/Norwegian explorer (b June 3, 1579, Barbo, Norway; d June 24, 1628, Copenhagen), the first European explorer to produce a complete map of **Hudson Bay**. Raised in Jutland, Denmark, Munk became a sailor, going as far afield as Brazil, and rose to the rank of Capt in the Danish Navy. Munk had distinguished himself in the Swedish War (1611-13), and had experience in Arctic sailing to the area of Novaya Zemlya, Russia. Thus, King Christian IV sent Munk in search of the Northwest Passage. He set sail in May 1619 with 2 vessels, *Enhjørningen* ("The Unicorn") and *Lamprenen* ("The Lamprey"), heading NW toward Greenland. He was in sight of the western shore of Davis Strait by July 8, but was prevented from landing by ice and fog. Munk then mistakenly sailed into Frobisher Bay, thinking it was Hudson Strait. He realized his error, and then sailed S to reach the strait, which he called *Fretum Christian* (Latin for "Christian Strait"). He sailed along the N shore, and anchored at a place he called "Rinsund" to speak with the either First Nations or Inuit inhabitants and to shoot **Caribou**. Munk claimed the land for Denmark, calling it Nova Dania ("New Denmark"). He continued through Ungava Bay before eventually entering Hudson Bay on Aug 25 near Digges Island. Munk named the bay "Novum Mare Christian," Latin for the "New Christian Sea."

At the time of Munk's voyage, only the S of the bay had been named Hudson's Bay after **Henry Hudson**, while the western part was "Button's Bay," after Adm Sir Thomas Button. Munk's map of Hudson Bay was the first to treat the water body as a whole. Upon entering the bay, Munk sailed SW to anchor at a spot later called Cape Churchill, about 60 km E of the present Town of **Churchill**. As it was already late Sept, Munk was

forced to winter in the estuary of the **Churchill River**, which he named Munkenæs, "Munk's Bay." His expedition was the first to winter in the Churchill area, and his crew included a minister, who performed the first **Lutheran** service in what is now MB. However, without adequate provisions of fruits and vegetables, 61 of Munk's crew died of scurvy. Munk had planned to resume his search for the Northwest Passage in the spring, but instead sailed home with his 2 surviving crewmen in *Lamprenen* on July 16, 1620. He published *Navigatio Septentrionalis*, an account of his expedition, in 1624. ● MD

MUNRO, William Grant, animator, actor, documentarian, editor, cinematographer (b April 25, 1923, **Winnipeg**). Producer/director Norman McLaren recruited Grant Munro to join the newly formed **Film** animation department at the **National Film Board** of Canada in 1944. Except for several intervals of employment around the world, he worked there until his retirement in 1988. An irrepressible raconteur, Munro's main claim to fame was his collaborative work with McLaren, especially on the Oscar Award–winning pixillation film *Neighbours* (1952) and on *Canon* (1964). Munro also worked with other animators, as well as producing and directing animated films and documentaries on his own, most notably *The Animal Movie* (1966); *See You in the Funny Papers* (1983), a film portrait of comic-strip creator Lynn Johnston, formerly of **Lynn Lake**; and *McLaren on McLaren* (1983). ● GENE WALZ

MURAKAMI, Takashi, chef, humanitarian (b Apr 2, 1949, Akita, Japan), came to Calgary from Japan to work as a chef in 1970. In 1975, Murakami moved to **Winnipeg**, and has worked ever since at the exclusive St. Charles Country Club as executive chef. Murakami became involved in professional culinary competitions, and coached Culinary Team Canada to a world championship title in 1984. The same year, Murakami won the Manitoba Restaurant Association Award, was given honorary membership with the international Escoffier Club. Today, Murakami is considered among Canada's top chefs.

Murakami's impressive abilities in the area of culinary arts are matched with his generosity and his efforts to strengthen community. He spends much time mentoring youth in the art of cooking, and has worked with Share Our Strength Winnipeg (SOS), raising funds for hunger relief and nutritional-education programs. For his contributions to nutrition, Murakami received the Order of Canada award in 2005. ● RK

MURDERBALL (wheelchair rugby) started in 1977 with a group of **Winnipeg** quadriplegic athletes. Duncan Campbell, sometimes called the sport's "quadfather," was a **Hockey** player before breaking his neck in a diving accident. Looking for a way to regain some of his former athleticism, he would often throw around a **Volleyball** while in rehab with Gerry Terwin, Chris Sargent, Randy Dueck, and Paul Lejeune. A rough-and-tumble game developed, involving full wheelchair contact, and was dubbed "murderball." The game grew into a strategic sport after **U of M** professor Ben Harnish wrote the first game book, and the possibility of corporate sponsorship persuaded the team to switch the sport's name to the less aggressive-sounding "wheelchair rugby."

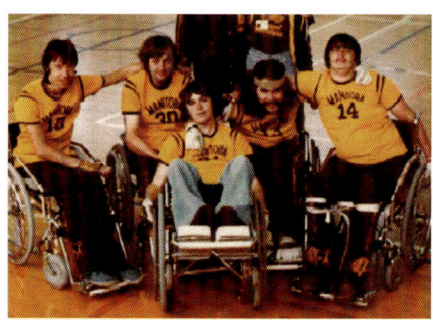

The original 5 "murderball" players

Though it incorporates a scoring system similar to rugby, wheelchair rugby also involves a hockey-like strategy, and fouls similar to basketball. It is played on a hardwood court by 2 teams of 4 players who are graded on their balance and mobility to ensure a fair competition. Glue is applied to the athletes' hands to help with ball control. Cdn wheelchair rugby championships were first held in Winnipeg in 1979, and a US team was formed in 1981. The sport became internationally recognized as a demonstration event at the 1996 Atlanta Paralympic Games, and became a full-medal sport in the 2000 Sydney Games. Its popularity further increased with the release of the US documentary film *Murderball* in 2005. ● MD

MURPHY, Cal, coach (b Mar 12, 1932, **Winnipeg**). As head coach and general manager, Murphy led the **Winnipeg Blue Bombers** to some of their best seasons through the 1980s and early '90s. Born in Winnipeg, Murphy moved to Vancouver as a child. He played football at UBC, followed by a brief professional career with the BC Lions. He then coached high school football before gaining a position at Vancouver College in 1960, leading the team to an undefeated season against some of the top US schools on the

Cal Murphy

West Coast. He moved on to coach at several US universities before returning to the CFL in 1974 with the BC Lions. Moving on as assistant coach for the Montreal Alouettes and then the Edmonton Eskimos, Murphy led 6 consecutive Grey Cup-winning teams. He was hired as the Bombers' head coach in 1983, ushering in a tremendous decade for the club, and putting an end to a 22-year Grey Cup dry spell with the 1984 victory. Murphy was awarded the Annis Stukus Trophy in both 1983 and 1984 as Coach of the Year. Taking over as general manager, with Mike Riley as head coach, Murphy brought the team 2 more Grey Cup victories in 1988 and 1990.

Following heart surgery in 1992, Murphy saw the Bombers to 2 more Grey Cup games before the Bombers began to slide, culminating with a 1996 playoff 68-7 defeat to the Edmonton Eskimos. Murphy left the Bombers the following season to coach for the Saskatchewan Roughriders. He became an NFL scout for the Indianapolis Colts in 2001. ● MD

MURPHY, Emily Gowan "Janey Canuck," feminist, writer (b March 14, 1868, Cookstown, ON; d Oct 27, 1933, Edmonton) was a leader in the fight for women's suffrage. Born Emily Ferguson, Murphy was educated at Bishop Strachan School in Toronto. Murphy had established herself as a writer and journalist before she accompanied her clergyman husband to **Swan River** in 1903. The couple lived there until 1907, Emily collecting the material that would become *Janey Canuck in the West* (1910). She also served as literary editor of the *Winnipeg Tribune* 1904-12. Joining with like-minded women in the West and especially in **Winnipeg**, she was active in the **Women's Movement**. She subsequently moved to Edmonton, where she became a Juvenile Court judge and leader of the move to recognize female Senators. Under the pseudonym "Janey Canuck," Murphy wrote 3 books of essays and travel accounts, while under her own name she exposed the drug trade in *The Black Candle* (1922). ● JMB

MURPHY, William Arthur "W. A.," grain merchant, goose hunter (b Sept 11, 1884, **Carberry**; d 1968, Hobe Sound, FL). A prominent businessman and community leader, W. A. Murphy also helped save the Giant Canada goose (*Branta canadensis maxima*) from extinction. He was born on a farm near Carberry, and was educated at St. John's College (*see* **U of M**). He was one of the founders of the Reliance Grain Company in 1910, which grew to operate more than 250 grain elevators throughout MB. He was also president of the Winnipeg General Hospital (*see* **Health Sciences Centre**) from 1941-65.

Murphy's most enduring contribution to the province, however, was in preserving a rare species of goose that otherwise would have died out. An avid hunter, Murphy converted his ranch at Marshy Point on **Lake Manitoba** into a goose sanctuary in 1947. He nursed a flock of 11 wild goslings taken from Island Park in **Portage la Prairie**. Unaware that the birds were in fact a rare breed of Canadian geese believed to be extinct, he released them into his marshland, and the flock grew to 100 birds. Murphy would often boast of the unusually large size of the birds inhabiting his property.

In 1962, while tagging geese on a lake near the Mayo Clinic in Rochester, MN, scientist Harold Hanson discovered that the average weight of one flock was nearly twice as much as that of the largest geese of other flocks. Hanson concluded that the geese must be the Giant Canada goose and, excited about his discovery, Hanson tracked the large birds to Murphy's refuge. Upon hearing that his geese were in fact an endangered species, Murphy increased his efforts to protect the flock, which eventually grew to 55,000 birds, making Marshy Point the largest privately owned bird sanctuary in the world. Murphy became a devoted conservationist, and served as director of the North American Wildlife Foundation for 2 decades. ● MD

MURRAY, Andy, Hockey coach, (b Mar 3, 1951, **Souris**). Following successful coaching stints at the amateur, professional, and international levels, Murray was named the head coach of the NHL's St. Louis Blues in Dec 2006. Murray attended **Brandon U**, earning BA and BEd degrees by 1974. That year he also became an assistant coach with the school's Bobcats hockey team. That experience helped him become head coach of the Brandon Travellers of the Manitoba Junior Hockey League in 1976, a team that had featured future NHLers **Glen Hanlon** and Dave Semenko earlier in the decade. Murray returned to coach the Bobcats from 1978-81, winning a league championship in his final year. His success saw him recruited to coach in Europe, and from

1981-87 he brought the Cdn style to teams in the Swiss league. The Hershey Bears of the American Hockey League hired him as an assistant coach in 1987, and Murray went on to hold the same position with the Philadelphia Flyers (1988-90), Minnesota North Stars (1990-92), and the Winnipeg Jets (1993-95).

His international hockey résumé continued to grow in the late 1990s. Murray served as the head coach of the Cdn national team from 1996-98, and was an assistant on the 1996 silver medal-winning World Cup of Hockey team. He has coached Canada to a combined 9 gold medals at Spengler Cup and world championship tournaments (most recently in 2007), and was an associate coach during the 1998 Olympic Games. The 1998-99 season saw Murray travel between Germany and Minnesota. He was the general manager of Koln, and the head coach of US high school powerhouse Shattuck-St. Mary's. In June 1999, the Los Angeles Kings made him their head coach, and he compiled a franchise-record 215 wins during nearly 7 seasons before his dismissal in March 2006. Murray also holds an MSc in sports management, is co-owner of the Salmon Arm Silverbacks of the British Columbia Junior Hockey League, and in 2006 contributed to Hockey Manitoba's National Coach Mentorship Program. ● JOEL TRENAMAN

MURRAY, Glen, politician (b Oct 26, 1957, Montreal) was Winnipeg's most colourful and controversial mayor since **Stephen Juba**. Murray was raised in the Montreal neighbourhoods of Notre Dame de Grace and Rosemont, and was educated at CÉGEP John Abbott College and at Concordia U. He left Concordia in his final year to take a job in communications with Canada Post.

In 1984, he transferred to Winnipeg. His public involvement began with volunteer work at a community clinic, and in 1987, he left Canada Post to become education co-ordinator of the Village Clinic, serving people with HIV/AIDS. Two years later, he ran successfully for Winnipeg's city council, and was re-elected in 1992 and 1995. He had been elected initially as a member

Glen Murray

of a left-liberal reform group called Winnipeg into the Nineties (WIN). Elected Winnipeg's 41st mayor in 1998, he was the first openly gay mayor of any major Cdn city.

Murray's primary challenge as mayor was to balance his left-leaning philosophies with a business-oriented city hall. His initial appointments to the executive policy committee (EPC), council's most influential committee, included only 2 of his left-leaning colleagues together with 4 right-wingers. Within 2 years, he had demonstrated his political mettle by keeping the business community onside, while appointing all of his left-leaning colleagues, and only 2 right-wingers, to EPC, and marginalizing the right-wingers most troublesome to him.

There followed a flurry of activity. Murray solidified his standing by delivering a 2%-a-year cut to property tax. He then breathed life into a longstanding but desultory effort at revitalizing of the commercial heart of the city by creating an economic development agency, CentreVenture, that gained credibility through intelligent leadership, strong support from the business community, tax credits, and govt funding. At the same time, he oversaw the formulation of the Winnipeg Housing Policy, which, with the help of substantial contributions from other levels of govt, had seen marked improvements in some of Winnipeg's more threatened neighbourhoods.

Murray was not universally lauded. He took a sharp turn when he repudiated an election promise to save the 8-storey downtown **EATON'S** building, and instead oversaw its demolition and replacement with the **MTS CENTRE**. He also earned mixed reviews when he pushed for the development of a pedestrian bridge with a restaurant at the centre over the **RED RIVER** to **ST. BONIFACE**, and the bridge itself, later named Esplanade Riel after **LOUIS RIEL**, was commended for its landmark design by some and derided by others.

Murray's policies were always on the knife's edge between his longstanding ideology and political necessity. He was controversial. His supporters – who, by this time, were more likely to be centrists or liberals rather than leftists – saw him as bringing a welcome infusion of visionary leadership to the city. His detractors on city council and in the provincial govt, however, said he was *too* visionary and criticized him for ineffectively implementing his own ideas.

Murray also made an appearance on the national stage, often tied to NGOs such as the Federation of Canadian Municipalities, of whose Big City Mayors Caucus he was chair. His venture into tax cuts had convinced him that Canada's cities needed access to a revenue source more likely to grow with the economy than property taxes. He

showed his political skills by defining the quest for more revenues as a venture into charter cities and urban autonomy, enlisting urban visionary Jane Jacobs (1916-2006) as a supporter. For a time, Murray was the primary spokesperson for cities on the national stage, and his timing was right, because cities were making an appearance on the national agenda, especially after Paul Martin became PM. Murray's campaign had some limited success when the Martin govt agreed to share gas taxes with cities and municipalities.

Murray's career as mayor came to an abrupt end in 2004, when he resigned to make an unsuccessful bid for a seat in the House of Commons in Charleswood-St James. Had he won, it was widely assumed that he would have been appointed to Cabinet. However, he was defeated and soon moved to Toronto, where he accepted a position as Visiting Fellow at Massey College, U of Toronto and formed his own consulting company.
● CHRISTOPHER LEO/MATTHEW MULAIRE

MUSÉE SAINT-BONIFACE. *See* **ST. BONIFACE MUSEUM**.

MUSHROOMS/TOADSTOOLS. Mushrooms are the best known of the thousands of kinds of fungi that occur in MB. Fungi are parasitic (living off other living things) or saprophytic (living off of dead organic matter) organisms that cannot make their own food because they have no chlorophyll. Most of their living matter is

made up of microscopic cells or tiny filaments, only their reproductive spore-producing structures are usually visible. Fungi range from yeasts that produce beer and wine to smuts and rusts and blights on trees and crops to the molds on oranges and apples. They cause severe damage to trees and crops and are responsible for several nasty human diseases ranging from 'athlete's foot' to blastomycosis. Fungi, along with bacteria, are the most important groups of decomposers. They are needed to break down dead organic matter to its basic parts so that its nutrients can be recycled to new living things. Mushrooms are simply the fleshy, usually above ground, sexual fruiting bodies of the higher fungi, the Ascomycetes (Sac Fungi) and Basidiomycetes (Club Fungi). Most mushrooms are produced by Club Fungi but the common Spring morel mushrooms (*Morchella* spp.) are members of the Sac Fungi.

MB probably has nearly 1000 different kinds of mushrooms but there is no complete list available. They come in all sizes, many shapes and some vivid colours. Toadstools are simply poisonous mushrooms. There is no simple or easy way to tell a poisonous from an edible mushroom! You can't tell by colour, smell or shape and can't remove poisons by drying or boiling in water with or without a silver spoon! The only way you can tell an edible mushroom is to identify it down to its exact species/kind, using a reliable field guide – or the expertise

CHARLES SHILLIDAY

Wild mushroom, Turtle Mountain Provincial Park

of a mycologist or someone that has collected them for years and is still alive. Even commonly edible mushrooms can make someone allergic or sensitive to them ill. When trying a new wild mushroom, one should always eat only a small bit and keep a specimen in case of a bad reaction. You need to carefully compare the mature mushroom with its description in a good guide and make a 'spore-print' to determine its species. Most mushrooms have a distinct cap and stem. The underside of the cap may have pores, small holes like the esteemed edible cepe or Steinpilz (*Boletus edulis*) or 'gills', lines coming out from the central stem, like the common field mushroom (*Agaricus campestris*) sold in stores or the deadly destroying angel (*Amanita virosa*).

Choice and commonly collected edible MB mushrooms include the early (mid-May to mid-June) morel (*Morchella esculenta*) which has a triangular 'wrinkled' top and grows in aspen woods and the honey mushroom or 'pipanky' (*Armillaria mellea*), Steinpilz (*Boletus edulis*) and spicy chanterelle (*Cantharellus cibarius*) beloved of **UKRAINIANS** and other European immigrants. Others include 'puffballs', mushrooms that have no cap and stem. These include one of the largest mushrooms in MB, the giant puffball (*Calvatia gigantea*) which can reach nearly the size of a soccer ball. Inky cap (*Coprinus atramentarius*), a common white mushroom of yards and meadows, breaks down into a slimy black mess but is edible when young if not eaten with alcohol. It contains a toxin that reacts with alcohol in some people. Many MB mushrooms are found around the world, especially in Europe and Asia.

Although most mushrooms are not deadly, many could make you quite sick. The ones that are deadly, members of the genus *Amanita* and others, will kill you very unpleasantly. By the time the symptoms appear, often 24-48 hours after eating them, it is usually too late for successful treatment. Many deadly mushrooms are very beautiful. The destroying angel (*Amanita virosa*) is a beautiful pure white mushroom that sometimes grows under evergreens in **WINNIPEG** yards. The 'magic mushroom' (*Amanita muscaria*) has white 'spots' on a bright red or yellow (more common in MB) cap. Found occasionally in coniferous forests, its toxins are hallucinogenic and have been used in religious and other ceremonies around the world.

MB's mushrooms are a varied and colourful lot and can be appreciated for their beauty as well as their edibility. They are most common in moist woods or bogs and in years of high rainfall.

● KAREN JOHNSON

MUSIC IN MANITOBA
By Lawrence Jones and John Einarson

M

Music in all its forms has played an important part in the daily lives of Manitobans. From the spiritual aspects of First Nations drum ceremonies to the spirited revelries of the **RED RIVER JIG** to the local community centres that spawned international superstars like **THE GUESS WHO**, MB has long been a musical hotbed.

EARLY MUSIC: Little of MB's earliest music was set down. The Orkadians of the **HUDSON'S BAY COMPANY** and immigrants to **LORD SELKIRK**'s **RED RIVER SETTLEMENT** brought **SCOTS** songs. **MÉTIS** sang **FRENCH** songs like "Les raftsmen" brought by voyageurs from QC, some of which trace back to France. In the 19th century, **PIERRE FALCON** had a talent for writing songs about local events, such as the **SEVEN OAKS INCIDENT**; Métis carried these across the West, and many still exist in modern editions. Both groups liked fiddle music, and while they shared tunes, distinct Scottish and Métis fiddle styles survive. At dances, fiddles might be joined by the sounds of accordion, harmonica, Jew's harp, and "mouth reels" – oral imitations of instrumental sounds.

Many of the European settlers who arrived after MB joined Confederation in 1870 came with instruments – especially the piano. Transport was arduous, by **YORK BOAT** and **RED RIVER CART**, but pianos were essential to pioneer women hoping to recreate civilized living. Near the piano, stacks of sheet music, song albums, and hymnbooks served family and neighbourly singsongs. Preferences included folk songs, excerpts from operetta, and popular and comic songs like "My Grandfather's Clock," "Roamin' in the Gloamin'," or "Who Put the Overalls in

Musical broadcast from the Fort Garry Hotel, 1930

Mrs. Murphy's Chowder?" Omnibus anthologies printed favourite classics by Bach, Beethoven, and Mendelssohn alongside "Listen to the Mockingbird" and "Maple Leaf Rag," and, for Sunday use, variations on popular hymn tunes. The violin remained popular, as, unlike the piano, it was easily carried. As a violin, it could play solos with piano, guitar, or accordion, or carry the tune in singsongs; as a fiddle, it provided dance music.

CHURCH: The church was another stimulus to music-making. While certain **PRESBYTERIANS**, **MENNONITES**, and others forbade instruments in worship, most churches embraced them. Reporting from **BIRTLE** in 1888, a correspondent writes:

M

On my arrival in 1882, I found only one miserable little melodeon and two pianos in the whole place. In 1883, our Methodist friends advanced a step and invested in a very fair reed organ, the English church people shortly after following suit. The same year witnessed a large increase in the town, not only of musical instruments, but of talent…. The town could then boast of seven organs and eight pianos. Toward the end of this year we organized the *Birtle Musical and Dramatic Club…*

HALLS AND COMMUNITY CENTRES: Public performance is central to music, and by 1912, most communities had a concert hall or **THEATRE**. Still serving are **MANITOU**'s Opera House, **VIRDEN**'s Auditorium Theatre, **DAUPHIN**'s Vernon Watson Arts Centre, and, in **WINNIPEG**, the Playhouse and Walker theatres. In the 1960s, concert halls honouring Canada's Centenary were built in Winnipeg and **BRANDON**. Smaller concerts are held at Eva Clare Hall at the **U OF M**, Lorne Watson recital hall at **BRANDON U**, Eckhardt-Gramatté Hall at the **U OF W**, and the Muriel Richardson Auditorium at the **WINNIPEG ART GALLERY**. Mennonite Brethren Collegiate Institute's Jubilee Auditorium in the Elmwood area of Winnipeg, **CMU**'s Laudamus Hall, and facilities in **FLIN FLON**, **MINNEDOSA**, **PORTAGE LA PRAIRIE**, **GRETNA**, and **MORDEN** have raised the standards of venues for performance.

CONCERTS: In rural MB, travelling shows presented something for everybody: magic acts, comic sketches, and recitations mingled with music: handbells, musical glasses, fancy fiddling, novelty piano solos such as "Kitten on the Keys," and even musical saws. Winnipeg hosted famous performers and entertainers, including **VAUDEVILLE** acts: the Marx Brothers met Charlie Chaplin there in 1921. The Women's

Elks Jazz Band, 1922

Winnipeg Symphony Orchestra

M

Musical Club of Winnipeg, founded in 1894, has staged ambitious annual concert seasons since 1899. Universities in Winnipeg and Brandon are active concert presenters.

SINGERS AS CELEBRITIES: Canada's first international star, soprano Emma Albani, during a cross-Canada tour, performed in Winnipeg and Brandon in 1897. So did Nellie Melba in 1923, ending her programs, as always, with "Home Sweet Home." In 1911, Winnipeg pianist Fred Gee organized a recital by violinist Mischa Elman. Encouraged by success as a sponsor for soprano Amlita Galli-Curci in 1927 (attendance 7200), he formed Celebrity Concerts Canada. Gee's Celebrity Concerts brought famous musicians to Winnipeg, and later to Brandon and other centres in MB and across the Prairies. After Gee moved his Winnipeg concerts into the new 4000-seat Civic Auditorium – now home to the Provincial **ARCHIVES** – in 1932, subscribers grew to 3500. This made it the largest concert series in NA at the time. Among hundreds of performers, some are legends: singers Schumann-Heink and Chaliapin; pianists Hofmann, Lhevinne, and Rachmaninoff; violinists Kreisler and Heifetz.

MUSICAL THEATRE: The musical comedies of W. S. Gilbert and Arthur Sullivan were popular from the 1880s into the 1960s, staged by amateurs and professionals. Operettas by Victor Herbert, Sigmund Romberg, Rudolf Friml, Franz Lehár, and Emerich Kálmán enlarged the repertoire. Local performers dominated the calendar at halls and theatres. Singers trained in school and church took the stage in operettas. The great tenor Jon Vickers learned via this route, moving from Prince Albert, SK, through Flin Flon, Brandon, Winnipeg, and Toronto to the world's capitals. Since the 1960s, Broadway musical shows have replaced operettas on local stages. In Brandon, Marjorie Johnson directed the Brandon Opera Society in annual productions from the mid-1920s to 1940, while Stuart Schultz, head of the Brandon Mental Hospital (*see* **MENTAL HEALTH**), also produced and directed musicals, drawing on the talents of patients, staff, and community. Many towns – for example, Flin Flon's Glee Club – produced operettas and musicals from the '50s through the '60s. In 1999, Flin Flon musicians drew national attention with the production of a home-grown musical, *Bomber Town* (revived 2001), a celebration of the

city and of its **HOCKEY** team. Book and music are by Mark Kolt, who continues with new projects. In the capital, Danny Shur's musical *Strike!* (2003, revised 2006) treated the 1919 **WINNIPEG GENERAL STRIKE**. Full-length **OPERAS** appeared sporadically: in **ST. BONIFACE**, the Societé lyrique staged operas from 1935 into the '50s. Celebrity Concerts occasionally presented touring companies, including Charles Wagner and Boris Goldovsky. During the '50s and '60s, the Canadian Opera Company toured the nation, giving recitals in Winnipeg and Brandon. The Manitoba Opera Company's professional performances began in 1968, at the new Centennial Concert Hall.

EDUCATION: At first, private instruction was the only way to learn music. To raise the standards of this instruction, and to advocate a stronger role for music in education, Eva Clare and others created a Registered Music Teachers' Association. In 1920, they succeeded in persuading the province to grant high school credit for music as an optional subject, offered through private instruction. The curriculum made use of the examinations conducted by the Toronto (later Royal) Conservatory of Music. Eva Clare then lobbied for the formation of a Western Board of Music, linking the U of M, U of Saskatchewan, and U of Alberta (1936). Provincial departments of education set uniform standards for the High School Music Option, evaluated through Western Board's examinations. In 1997, the administration of the Western Board of Music merged with that of the U of Western Ontario Conservatory, and now conducts examinations as Conservatory Canada. Vocal music dominated the curriculum in schools where music was taught. *The Manitoba School Song Book* (1940, Ethel Kinley, editor) was distributed to every school, though its use in smaller schools was haphazard. Music was included in teacher training at MB's Normal Schools, but teachers without other musical experience often omitted the subject. Since 1923, the Manitoba Schools Orchestra, now the Winnipeg Youth Orchestra, has provided extracurricular orchestral experience for high school musicians. Instrumental music entered the school curriculum in the '50s and '60s, with pioneer programs in **SWAN RIVER** and in Winnipeg's Elmwood and Technical Vocational schools. Instrumental programs dominate music in secondary schools, many staffed by graduates of Brandon U and the U of M. Organizations for music education are the

Manitoba Music Educators Association (1959) and its subgroups: instrumental and choral directors, and specialists in Carl Orff and Zoltán Kodály. Postsecondary music training was available for a time at Brandon College (*see* **BRANDON U**), where Dr. William Lewis Wright (director of music 1907-47) and his faculty offered advanced diploma programs, attracting students from across Canada; this ended with the financial constraints of the **GREAT DEPRESSION**. Director Lorne Watson introduced degree programs at Brandon U (BMus, 1963; MMus, 1981); Leonard Isaacs and Dale Lonis did likewise at the U of M (BMus, 1964; MMus 2003). CMU and Providence College in Otterburne also grant BMus degrees.

CHOIRS: Church choirs; oratorio choirs (as early as 1903 in Winnipeg and Brandon); and choirs with French, **GERMAN** (Mennonite), **UKRAINIAN**, **JEWISH**, **ICELANDIC**, Norwegian, as well as British focus have been vital in MB's musical life. In Winnipeg, the Men's Musical Club (1915-86) was an energetic force: from its first venture, a Male Voice Choir, it moved on to manage the **WINNIPEG PHILHARMONIC CHOIR**, setting up a Junior Male Voice Choir and a Juvenile Boys Choir; and co-operate with other choral organizations. Large companies – notably **EATON'S**, **HUDSON'S BAY**, and **GREAT-WEST LIFE** – also formed employee choirs. The Winnipeg Choristers began national CBC radio broadcasts in the 1940s, 1st directed by W. H. Anderson, then by Filmer Hubble. On Hubble's death in 1969, these broadcasts morphed into national CBC TV's long-running *Hymn Sing* show. The Winnipeg Singers is successor to these professional broadcasting choirs. Amateur choral societies have been organized in many communities, when leaders are available. An ambitious example is the 80-voice Flin Flon Community Choir. Under Crystal Kolt, this choir has performed major works with the Saskatoon Symphony. MB's university and high school choirs win national awards. Youth choirs in western, central, and eastern MB tour their regions each year. Choir programs for children thrive in Brandon, **STEINBACH**, and Winnipeg. In 1998, choral enthusiast Richard Loewen established the Foundation for Choral Music in Manitoba with a $1-million endowment. The Manitoba Choral Association (1976) and other groups can apply for support from this fund.

RADIO AND TELEVISION: In the 1930s, the Manitoba Telephone System (*see* **MTS ALLSTREAM**) opened stations CKY in Winnipeg and CKX in Brandon. Both carried programs supplied by the CBC (1932, 1936) as well as by local musicians. When MTS was regulated out of broadcasting, CKY and CKX were privatized, and in 1948, the CBC opened CBW Manitoba. In 1948, the national Crown broadcaster set up the CBC Winnipeg Orchestra, directed by Eric Wild. The presence of its musicians made it possible to form a **WINNIPEG SYMPHONY ORCHESTRA**, directed by Walter Kaufmann. CBC Winnipeg also broadcast lighter music under directors like Richard Seaborn, Neil Harris, and Bob McMullin. Among several shows, *Prairie Schooner* offered weekly national broadcasts, featuring a variety of standards alongside folk and country music.

FAMOUS MANITOBANS: Manitoba musicians who have enjoyed national and international careers include singers **DEANNA DURBIN**, **GISÈLE MACKENZIE**, and Wally Koster in early popular music; in classical, Mary Morrison, Morley Meredith, Norman Mittelmann, **TRACY DAHL**, Valdine Anderson, Philip Ens, and Hugh Russell; violinists Frederick Grinke and **JAMES EHNES**; cellists Zara Nelsova, Lorne Munroe, and Eric Wilson; and pianists Diedre Irons and Emmanuel Ax. Composers from or active in MB include Harry Freedman, Barbara Pentland, **CHESTER DUNCAN**, Robert Turner, David Matthews, Sid Robinovich, Jim Hiscott, Patrick Carrabré, David R. Scott, and Jocelyn Morlock. In **NEEPAWA**, Remi Bouchard's many pieces have enriched the life of piano students. A composer with an international reputation, **SOPHIE-CARMEN ECKHARDT-GRAMATTÉ**, lived in Winnipeg from 1953 until her death in 1974. A national competition named for her,

emphasizing the performance of Cdn music, has been held in Brandon annually since 1976.

The high levels of musical activity described here, and the accomplishments of institutions and individuals, are out of proportion to MB's population. The province's contributions to the arts are known and valued internationally. ● LAWRENCE JONES

POPULAR MUSIC: At the dawn of the 1960s, few could have imagined that as the decade unfolded, MB would produce some of the greatest musical talents in the country, and plant the seeds for continued successes in the following decades. By the end of the millennium, Manitoban recording artists, both those born and those making their start from here, would account for over 100 million records, albums and singles, sold worldwide – a staggering figure for a provincial population of barely a million. For a time, the province on the whole, and Winnipeg in particular, was regarded as the rock 'n' roll capital of Canada. Geographic isolation dead centre in the mid-continent has often been cited as the reason for the plethora of renowned musicians, groups, singers, and songwriters emerging from MB, creating an insular music environment that fostered and supported local talent.

BIRTH OF POP: While the province had produced popular music entertainers of the 1950s – including Gisèle MacKenzie and her brother, George LaFlèche; **JULIETTE**; Lucille Starr; and folksinger **OSCAR BRAND** – these artists had to leave the province in order to find fame. That would soon change. With baby boomers reaching their teens as rock 'n' roll hit its stride by the early 1960s, Winnipeg stood poised for a rock 'n' roll revolution. Emerging from more than 50 neighbourhood community clubs scattered throughout the city was a raucous sound generated by more than 250 rock bands by the middle of the decade. Teenagers flocked every weekend to hear local groups like The Deverons (featuring a young **BURTON CUMMINGS**), The Shondels, The Crescendos, The Galaxies, The Squires (led by **NEIL YOUNG**), The Quid, The Jury, and Chad Allan & the Reflections. Local radio stations promoted the dances and played recordings by local bands. It was a mini-Liverpool driven by the beat emanating from the community clubs.

From this fertile milieu would emerge the **GUESS WHO** – Chad Allan, **RANDY BACHMAN**, Jim Kale, Garry Peterson, and Bob Ashley – who defied

Mood Jga Jga, 1975

the odds by scoring a national number-one record with their cover of Johnny Kidd & the Pirates' "Shakin' All Over" in March 1965. In doing so, they became Canada's first nationally recognized rock stars. By summer, the record had breached *Billboard*'s coveted Top 30, selling upward of 200,000 copies as the group toured across the US. In the wake of "Shakin' All Over," major record labels rushed to sign other local groups like The Eternals, The Fifth, The Luvin' Kind, The Mongrels, and The Shondels. Encouraged by the Guess Who's success, Neil Young took his Squires to Toronto before heading S to Los Angeles to form Buffalo Springfield with Stephen Stills, and, later Crosby, Stills, Nash & Young. Neil Young subsequently launched a meteoric solo career.

By 1969, Burton Cummings was fronting The Guess Who (the band added 'The' at this time) as they again stormed the pop charts, earning 5 gold records in less than 2 years, including a *Billboard* #1 with "American Woman." In 1970, they were the top-selling singles artists in the world, and would continue to enjoy international acclaim for their self-styled "Wheatfield Soul" until their 1975 breakup.

Randy Bachman left The Guess Who in 1970 and after a few tries reached the top of the album and singles charts with Bachman-Turner Overdrive, one of the biggest-selling bands on the mid-'70s. Cummings launched his own solo career in the latter '70s, notching up an impressive string of gold records. Cummings also branched off into movies and television.

Other MB artists drew inspiration from these early successes. While the community club scene had dried up by the early '70s, pubs, coffee-houses, and nightclubs became launching pads for the likes of singer/songwriter Rick Neufeld (whose "Moody Manitoba Morning" became a hit for The Bells), Graham Shaw, Dan Donahue, Robbie McDougall, and contemporary Christian star **STEVE BELL**. Pub rock and the Manitoban phenomenon of the **SOCIAL** flourished in the '70s and '80s with Harlequin, Streetheart, Queen City Kids, Mood Jga Jga, and The Pumps (later Orphan) providing the soundtrack. At the same time, an energetic New Wave/punk club scene centred around Winnipeg's Royal Albert and Wellington hotels, and in clubs like The Pyramid and Tom Tom Club, spawned **BIF NAKED**, Personality Crisis, Propagandhi, The Fuse, The Fixx, Chocolate Bunnies From Hell, Popular Mechanix, and, later, the internationally acclaimed quartet **THE WEAKERTHANS**.

Beginning in 1974 and still operating out in **BIRD'S HILL PARK** each July as the premier annual outdoor concert in NA, the **WINNIPEG FOLK FESTIVAL** gave folk, blues, and world-music artists such as **HEATHER BISHOP**; folk artist Connie Kaldor; and bluesman Big Dave McLean their first break. Later groups to get their start at the Folk Fest include The Duhks, Alana Levandoski of the small community of Kelwood, just E of **RIDING MOUNTAIN NATIONAL PARK**; klezmer specialists Finjan; The Wyrd Sisters; and folk trio The Wailin' Jennys.

From Main St's funky Blue Note Café in the early '90s came the **CRASH TEST DUMMIES**, led by the distinctive voice of Brad Roberts. They would go on to sell over 7 million records. In their wake were hard-rockin' acts like The Watchmen, Combo Combo, and the New Meanies. Singer/songwriter **CHANTAL KREVIAZUK** bypassed the conventional route to stardom, signing a $1-million recording contract solely on the strength of her early demos. She has since become one of NA's more respected songwriters, providing tunes for pop-rock icons Avril Lavigne and Gwen Stefani.

BEYOND ROCK 'N ROLL: Despite a well-earned reputation as the heart of Cdn rock 'n' roll, MB has produced an eclectic mix of musicians and performers crossing a variety of music genres, the result perhaps of the provinces multicultural character. Morden's **LOREENA MCKENNITT** is the top-selling Celtic-based recording artist in the world, with sales nearing 15 million. Christian rapper **FRESH I. E.** has been nominated for 2 coveted

Grammy Awards and several other honours. Hip-hop group Mood Ruff have earned acclaim across the country. Americana roots and blue-grass-influenced artists like Nathan and D-Rangers have earned praise worldwide for their unique blending of styles. Country music has remained a mainstay, both in rural MB and in Winnipeg, with dozens of recording artists notching up hit records, including **DOC WALKER**; **AMANDA STOTT** from Brandon; **OAKBANK**'s Foster Martin Band; Stu Clayton, from Manitou; **ROBLIN**'s Tara Lyn Hart; fiddler extraordinaire Andy Dejarlis; Cindi Cain; Farmer's Daughter; Angela Kelman; and Rhonda Hart.

A thriving Aboriginal Music scene, initially centred on Winnipeg's Indian & Métis Friendship Centre in the latter '60s, fostered artists such as C-Weed's Errol Ranville, Shingoose, singer/actor **TOM JACKSON**, and later Eagle & Hawk. Long-time singer/songwriter and TV star **RAY ST. GERMAIN** has championed his roots in songs like "The Métis." MB's many francophone communities have produced renowned artists such as singer/songwriter sensa-

Eagle & Hawk

tion **DANIEL LAVOIE**, Hart Rouge, and Marcel Soloudre. MB leads the way in children and family entertainers, beginning with beloved performer **FRED PENNER**, one of the most recognized children's entertainers in the world, followed by **AL SIMMONS**, Heather Bishop, Jake Chenier, Aaron Burnett, and Just Kiddin'. The jazz world was set on its ear by Winnipeg-based guitar genius **LENNY BREAU**, while other jazz artists like Dave Young, Ron Paley, Greg Lowe, Flin Flon's Jennifer Hanson, **GREG LESKIW**'s Swing Soniq, and Walle Larson remain influential and popular.

No longer isolated, the province continues to produce world-class talent. By building on the remarkable accomplishments of those before them and eschewing trends, MB artists continue to chart their own course and make highly distinctive and original music. ● JOHN EINARSON

Big Dave McLean

M

Muskrat is Canada's most important fur-bearing animal.

ROBERT R. TAYLOR

MUSKRAT (*Ondatra zibethicus*) resembles a giant mouse, and is actually a member of the same family Muridae. It averages 1 kg but can reach 2 kg. The tail is 24 cm long, flattened vertically, and is used like a rudder when swimming. Propulsion is achieved by paddling of the large webbed and bristled hind feet. Like many other aquatic creatures, the Muskrat has an enormous distribution – covering the entire province and extending from the Arctic Ocean to the US-MEX border. Almost any body of water (fresh and brackish) may be home to this adaptable species. Its thick, luxurious coat insulates against cold air and water, and is responsible for the Muskrat being the most important fur-bearing animal on the continent, with millions of pelts sold annually. The animal receives its name from the odour of its anal musk glands. This scent is deposited around the lodge and along trails through the marsh, advertising the animal's residency to other muskrats. Populations may show great fluctuations over the years, from 1-150/ha. Under pressure of high numbers, Muskrats engage in fierce battles, biting with their long, razor-sharp incisors. At this time, many succumb from bites and infections, or are driven out into unsuitable habitats where they are usually picked off by predators. This species builds its den in a bank, but if none is available, it creates several 1 m-high lodges out of mud and marsh plants, which may also serve as a source of food if necessary during the winter. The Muskrat does not hibernate, but continues to swim under the ice for succulent roots of cattail and other plants. It must remain alert to avoid predators such as the Mink, Red Fox, hawks and owls. An average of 7 young occur in each of 2 litters during the summer, and life expectancy is 3 years in the wild (10 in captivity). ● REW

MUSSELS. *See* CLAMS.

MYNARSKI, Andrew Charles "Andy," RCAF VC winner in WWII (b Oct 14, 1916, WINNIPEG, MB; d June 12, 1944, near Cambrai, Nord-Pas de Calais, France), was the son of Polish immigrants to the NORTH END of WINNIPEG. He was educated at King Edward and Isaac Newton schools and at St. John's Technical School. He worked as a leather cutter before joining the ROYAL WINNIPEG RIFLES, enlisting in the RCAF in Nov 1941. In 1942, he graduated from an RCAF school in MacDonald as a mid-upper gunner. He went overseas with 419 Squadron in Dec 1942. In a night raid on a Cambrai target, his Lancaster bomber was attacked by a Luftwaffe Junkers 88 and set afire. Set to bail out, he saw that rear gunner Pat Brophy was trapped in his turret, and made his way through flames, his parachute and clothing soon on fire, to try and release his friend. Brophy urged Mynarski to jump, which he finally did, after saluting Brophy. Ground observers saw flames as he came down. Found by French troops, he died of his burns soon after, though Brophy survived to tell the tale. Mynarski is buried in Méharicourt Cemetery, Picardie, France. PO Mynarski's VC is on display at **17 WING**, Air Command HQ, Winnipeg. A school and a park in Winnipeg were named after him, as was a local Royal Cdn Legion branch. A Lancaster in the Cdn Warplane Heritage Museum in Hamilton, ON, similar to the one Mynarski flew in, is dedicated to his memory. A statue of Mynarski also stands at Durham Tees Valley Airport, near Darlington, Durham, UK, and his name is inscribed on the RCAF monument in University Ave in downtown Toronto. ● JIM SHILLIDAY

Andrew Mynarski

NONSUCH,
see page 501

NAIMARK, Arnold, physician, educator, administrator (b 1933, **WINNIPEG**). A high-profile leader in the medical and academic fields, Naimark grew up in **NORTH END** Winnipeg. He graduated from St. John's High School and decided to pursue **MEDICINE** at the **U OF M**, graduating in 1957 with his BSc (Med) and MD. Naimark then earned a MSc in 1959 and underwent specialized training in internal medicine. In 1963, he began his career as an academic with an appointment as assistant professor of medicine and physiology, also at the U of M. Naimark became a full professor in 1967, and the dean of the faculty of medicine in 1971. He held that post until 1981, when he was chosen to succeed Ralph Campbell as the U of M's president and vice-chancellor. From 1983-93, Naimark chaired the North Portage Development Corporation, and also led the national Association of Universities and Colleges of Canada from 1987-89. In 1991, he was named an officer of the Order of Canada.

Following a 15-year tenure as U of M president, in 1996 Naimark was named the director of the university's Centre for the Advancement of Medicine, a medical education and research organization. In Dec 1998, he compiled a report for the Hospital for Sick Children of Toronto concerning a controversial Apotex Inc pharmaceutical trial

that touched off a wide-ranging debate about the relationships between industry and science. Researcher Nancy Olivieri, after finding that the drug Deferiprone could potentially be detrimental to patients, released the information publicly in violation of her confidentiality agreement with the company. Her action led to disputes with the hospital, and lawsuits between her and Apotex. Naimark's report found faults with the conduct of all of the involved parties.

Naimark has also worked with national bodies such as the Canadian Health Services Research Foundation, the Canadian **BIOTECHNOLOGY** Advisory Committee, the Association of Canadian Medical Colleges, the Canadian Institute for Advanced Research, and the Canadian Physiological Society. In 2003, he was named to the **ORDER OF MANITOBA**, and in 2005 was appointed to a 3-year term as the chair of Health Canada's Science Advisory Board. As of 2007, Naimark was also a member of the boards of Medicure Inc and CancerCare Manitoba, and the principal of Naimark Consulting. • JT

NANTON, Sir Augustus Meredith, banker (b May 7, 1860, Toronto; d April 24, 1925, Toronto) was a prosperous businessman. He left school at age 13 and worked his way up in the banking business. He came to **WINNIPEG** in 1883 as resident

Augustus Meredith Nanton, 1911

Entrance to the Narcisse Snake Dens

N

partner of Osler, Hammond and Nanton, investment bankers, and oversaw the financing of 4 railways in the 1890s. By 1900, he was on the boards of dozens of corporations and associations. His home in Winnipeg was called Kilmorie. He was president of the Manitoba Patriotic Fund during WWI, and was knighted in 1917 for his war work. During the **Winnipeg General Strike**, he personally patrolled his grounds at Kilmorie because of threats against him, and an arsonist burnt down his barn at Rosser. He returned to Toronto in 1924 to become president of the Dominion Bank. He was buried in Winnipeg. ● JMB

NAPINKA, pop 100, is a community located in SW MB about 120 km SW of **Brandon**, and 30 km from the SK and US borders. It is located in the RM of Brenda on the historic Boundary Trail that was an important route for all early settlers moving W from **Winnipeg** and for the "March West" by the **North-West Mounted Police**. Napinka was also on the **CPR** line that runs through the area. The people who settled here were largely **English** and **Scots**, coming from ON. The community was established in 1890, and became incorporated as a village in 1902. The Napinka School, a solid structure made of fieldstone, was built in 1896 – a testimony to the village's confidence in the future. However, the school was closed in 1968. Now one of the last remaining schoolhouses of its kind in the area, it acts as a drop-in centre. Administratively, the village became part of the RM in the late 1980s so that sewer and water systems could be put in place. Like many other small towns, Napinka has suffered from rural depopulation. The economic base of the area continues to be agriculture, however in 2007 most Napinka residents travelled to nearby Melita for services. ● GPP

NARCISSE, pop 37, is a community 100 km NNW of Winnipeg. Narcisse was settled in 1914 and named for Narcisse Leven, a former leader of the nearby **Jewish** ghost town of **Bender Hamlet**. A rail line, established here in 1916, is no longer in use. The Jewish population has entirely disappeared from the area, and most locals now are of **Ukrainian** background. In 2000, Narcisse suffered a near-fatal blow when the last general store closed. Narcisse's economic base is agriculture and tourism, as the Narcisse Snake Dens are close by. Each year around May, spectators come to witness tens of thousands of red-sided **Garter Snakes** emerge from their winter dens to mate – the highest concentration of reptiles anywhere in the world. ● GPP

NATIONAL FILM BOARD (NFB) was founded May 1939 as a panel of 8 people charged with co-ordinating and overseeing the federal govt's filmmaking agencies. The NFB soon became a studio responsible for all govt film production and distribution. By 1941, under the first film commissioner John Grierson – the man who coined the term "documentary" – the NFB was making dozens of films a year and employed as many as 600 people in Ottawa alone. While many of these films were meant as propaganda for the wartime effort, the overall mandate was to show Canada to Canadians, and Canadians to the rest of the world. After the war, the NFB struggled to find its niche, but it has since made animated and fiction films as well as documentaries. In the 1970s, regionalization established film production offices from coast to coast, giving rise to provincial film industries nationwide. Throughout its existence, the NFB has supported local and independent filmmakers, making it easier for female and Aboriginal filmmakers, for example, to find their cinematic voices.

Many Manitobans contributed to the establishment and have helped fuel the success of the

Stuart Legg and John Grierson discuss their next NFB production

NFB. MB politician **Ross McLean**, also a founding member of the National Film Society, convinced the Liberal govt to hire John Grierson to study the state of filmmaking in Canada, leading to the proclamation of a *National Film Act*. When Grierson was named film commissioner, McLean became his assistant, briefly replacing Grierson upon his departure. **Joseph Thorson**, Liberal-Progressive MP for Selkirk and minister for national war services, took over responsibility for the NFB in 1941 and personally initiated some films, including *Iceland on the Prairies*. Fellow **Icelandic**-Manitoban Gordon Adamson set up the alternative film circuits that gave Canadians an opportunity to view their country's films.

During WWII, several Manitobans went to Ottawa to join the NFB, including 2 women who had a significant influence on the kinds of films made there. Margaret Ann Bjornson turned her job as researcher on *Iceland on the Prairies* into a full-time position as researcher, editor, and chief assistant to UK-born documentary-maker Stuart Legg on the World in Action series. Gudrun Parker (née Bjerring) made a film in **Starbuck** called *The People's Bank* (1943) and one about the annual music festival in Winnipeg called *Listen to the Prairies* before turning her attention to films for mothers and children, and films meant to provoke discussion regarding social, political, and ethical issues. She also helped husband and fellow **U of M** graduate Morten Parker to produce *City in Siege*, about the 1950 flood, and *The Stratford Adventure*, about the founding of the Shakespeare Theatre in Stratford, ON. Winnipeggers Stanley Jackson and **Grant Munro** joined the NFB during WWII and enjoyed long, productive careers there,

Munro serving as one of famed animator Norman McLaren's chief assistants, as well as a director in his own right. One of the most important Manitobans to work for the NFB began with a modest film about an aging immigrant who cleaned the streetcar tracks along Portage Ave; *Paul Tomkowicz: Street-Railway Switchman* (1954) became a prototype of the candid eye movement and a model for cinéma-vérité films around the world. Filmmaker Roman Kroitor became a leading member of the NFB's famed Unit B, and was 1 of the 3 people who invented the IMAX film system.

A prairie production office was established in Winnipeg in 1974 with Jerry Krepakevich, Michael Scott, Ches Yetman, and Joe McDonald serving as regional producers. What made this office more successful than its other regional counterparts was a determination to produce fiction and animated films as well as documentaries. As a result, Allan Kroeker became a much-respected maker of short fiction based on Cdn and especially prairie writers; **Norma Bailey** developed into one of western Canada's best all-around directors; **Richard Condie** and **Cordell Barker** created animated films nominated for Academy Awards; and **John Paskiewich** emerged as one of Canada's best documentary filmmakers. Among the more noteworthy films created by the NFB in MB during the past 25 years are: *Something Hidden: A Portrait of Wilder Penfield* (director Bob Lower, 1981); *Ted Baryluk's Grocery* (John Paskiewich, 1982); *In the Fall* (Allan Kroeker, 1984); *The Big Snit* (Richard Condie, 1985); *Daughters of the Country* (Norma Bailey, 1987); *The Cat Came Back* (Cordell Barker, 1988); *The Last Winter* (Aaron Kim Johnston, 1989); and *A Kind of Family* (Andrew Koster, 1992). • GENE WALZ

NATIONAL HISTORIC SITES are considered places of importance in Cdn history. As of 2005, more than 1500 places, persons, and events had been designated "national historic sites" by the Cdn govt. Of these sites, 52 are in MB, including the **Inglis** elevators, **Fort Prince of Wales**, and **The Forks**. Similar to municipal and provincial heritage sites, a national designation helps protect the site's integrity. National historic sites represent thousands of years of human history under 5 broad themes: peopling the land, governing Canada, developing economies, building social and community life and expressing intellectual and cultural life. The designation process is made on a case-by-case basis in accordance with specific evaluation criteria and guides. A board convenes biannually to review applications and the entire process between application and designation may take up to 2 years to complete. • JS

NATIONAL MICROBIOLOGY LABORATORY

(NML) at the Canadian Science Centre for Human and Animal Health in **Winnipeg** is Canada's only facility to operate at Biological Safety Level 4, the world's highest standard. The NML opened in 2000, and employs about 220. Its host facility, the Canadian Science Centre for Human and Animal Health, is also home to the National Centre for Foreign Animal Disease. The scientific director of the NML is Winnipeg-born researcher **Francis Plummer**, and the deputy director is former head of the department of pharmacology and therapeutics in the faculty of medicine at the **U of M**, Gary B. Glavin.

The Public Health Agency of Canada mandates the lab to identify, control, and prevent the spread of infectious diseases. The level-4 designation allows many of Canada's most highly trained researchers to work with the most dangerous airborne, incurable human and animal pathogens, such as viral haemorrhagic fevers (Ebola, Marburg, and Lassa fever), as well as viruses like hantavirus and influenza. However, researchers also work with less-dangerous agents in open, or level-1, environments. Security systems control access to the building but also emphasize biological containment using intensive airlocks, airtight rooms, filters, and sterilization processes. The NML also features storage for about 250,000 genomic DNA samples for research. In 2006, the majority of the samples came from patients with Alzheimer's disease.

The NML is split into 4 major research departments. The bacteriology and enteric diseases program studies biological threats of both natural and terrorist-induced source, and works with public health authorities to prevent and control **Epidemics** of food-borne and other illnesses.

*A scene from **Totem: The Return of the G'Psgolox Pole**, directed by Gil Cardinal*

NATIONAL FILM BOARD

N

National Microbiology Laboratory in Winnipeg

The host genetics and prion disease program examines transmissible spongiform encephalopathies: these are neurological illnesses such as Creutzfeldt-Jakob disease, bovine spongiform encephalopathy, and chronic wasting disease.

The viral diseases division works to identify new pathogens as well as to look at blood-borne, respiratory, and sexually transmitted infections. The zoonotic diseases and special pathogens program focuses on illnesses shared by or transmitted between humans and other animals, such as severe acute respiratory syndrome and West Nile virus. In April 2006, NML microbiologist Heinz Feldmann and a research team reported a successful vaccine for monkeys against Marburg virus, on the heels of Steven M. Jones's promising discovery of an Ebola vaccine in 2005. Both projects are associated with the US Army Medical Research Institute of Infectious Diseases, of Fort Detrick, MD, and are examples of the continuous research undertaken by the scientists at the NML. • JOEL TRENAMAN

NATURAL RESOURCES TRANSFER AGREEMENT. When MB was created in 1870 out of the **RUPERTSLAND TRANSFER**, it and the NWTs – unlike pre-existing provinces ON, QC, NS, and NB – were denied jurisdiction over public lands and resources. Instead, the federal department of the interior controlled the lands and resources of MB, and, in 1905, with the establishment of AB and SK, of those provinces as well. This arrangement was novel, since in the British legislative system, self-governing entities held powers over lands and resources. The federal govt compensated the prairie provinces for the loss of the beneficial interests in lands and resources with

annual per capita subsidy payments. Still, for years, the loss of resources was a matter of much grievance for prairie populists, who regarded the situation as "colonial."

In 1913, prairie premiers Sir **RODMOND ROBLIN**, Walter Scott (SK), and Arthur Lewis Sifton (AB) petitioned the federal govt for the transfer of the lands and resources. By the 1920s, the federal govt was willing to cede control, but without compensation payouts or a continuation of annual subsidies. The prairie provinces argued they were entitled to compensation. In particular, MB premier **JOHN BRACKEN** sought significant payment from the federal govt. PM William Lyon Mackenzie King convinced Bracken to agree to a royal commission to consider compensation. The commission report of May 30, 1929, laid the basis for a compromise that would become 1930's Natural Resources Transfer Agreement (NRTA): MB agreed to a payment of $4.5 million in compensation for the loss of the beneficial interest in resources spanning a 60-year period.

Once the compensation question was settled, the other necessary terms of the agreement were negotiated. The central purpose of the agreement was to put the prairie provinces "in a position of equality with the other provinces of Confederation with respect to the administration and control of its natural resources." Nonetheless, the agreement included protection for a variety of existing land tenures that had been granted by the federal govt. Of lasting significance, several First Nation interests (*see* **ABORIGINAL RIGHTS**) received constitutional protection under the NRTA. On Dec 14, 1929, the govts of MB, AB, and Canada signed natural resource agreements that were later enacted by provincial and federal

GLENN MARQUEZ

legislation. SK did not play a significant role in shaping the content of the NRTA, and later negotiated its agreement separately.

The NRTA was no ordinary statute: in fact, in order to transfer the lands and resources, the *British North America Act*, now know as *Constitution Act*, had to be amended. Before 1982, amendments to the Constitution required passage through the British Commons and House of Lords. With very short notice, the UK Parliament amended the *BNA Act* (formerly 1867-1916, then 1867-1930). This legislation received Royal Assent on July 10, 1930, in time for MB's Jubilee anniversary. The legal and legislative process leading up to the transfer of resources entailed a complex interplay of federal/provincial relations, and Mackenzie King proved very adept at resolving a decades-old problem that had caused much complaint. While the events and processes that resulted in the transfer of resources to the prairie provinces have passed largely unnoticed, issues relating to the litigation of Aboriginal rights continue to arise from the NRTA even today. • FRANK J. TOUGH

NATURE CONSERVANCY OF CANADA is Canada's leading conservation organization whose goal is the permanent protection of ecologically sensitive and valuable landscapes across Canada. Non-profit, science-driven, and non-confrontational, NCC works through partnerships with individuals, corporations, foundations, other conservation organizations, and govt agencies to preserve key areas of habitat and the wildlife dependant on them. Scientifically evaluated and Board-approved properties are either purchased outright, or a conservation easement is purchased, in which the landowner agrees to maintain the habitat for wildlife in perpetuity.

The primary areas of focus are the last remnants of the Tall-grass Prairie Ecosystem in SE MB, the Aspen Parkland/Prairie Transition around the Riding and Duck Mountains, and the Mixed-grass Prairie/Sandhills Ecosystem in SW MB. Formerly extending from S MB to Texas, the Tall-grass Prairie has been eliminated by agriculture and other developments, leaving less than 0.5% surviving in small patches. Canada's only representative piece is conserved in the Tall-grass Prairie Preserve (E of the **RED RIVER**) by NCC and its partners. Home to over 1000 species of vertebrates, invertebrates and plants, it also harbours Canada's sole populations of the vulnerable Plains Pocket Gopher and the endangered Western Prairie Fringed Orchid, as well as the Sandhill Crane, American Elk, and other prominent species. Less than 5% of Mixed-grass Prairie and 10% of Aspen Parkland remain in MB. Consequently, NCC is

The Nature Conservancy of Canada protects ecologically sensitive landscapes.

conserving interconnected parcels of lands S of Riding Mountain National Park (breeding grounds for large **Mammals**, **Waterfowl**, and migratory **Birds**) and S of **Duck Mountain Provincial Park** and Forest, providing a broad corridor for the interchange of wildlife between the 2 mountain ranges. Each year hundreds of ha of wildlife habitat are added to the program, and managed for the benefit of all wildlife. ● MMB, REW

NATYNCZYK, LGen Walter John "Walt," soldier (b Oct 29, 1957, **Winnipeg**), Vice Chief of the Defence Staff, was also the deputy commanding general III US Corps and Multi-National Corps in Iraq in 2004. Born in Winnipeg to a family of **Polish** and **German** heritage, Natynczyk enlisted in 1975, and trained at Victoria's Royal Roads Military College and at the Collège militaire royal de Saint-Jean, graduating in 1979. He was posted to the Royal Canadian Dragoons at CFB Lahr, West Germany, where he served as both a troop commander and staff officer. In 1983, he became squadron commander of the Royal Military College. Later in the 1980s, he went through a succession of appointments, including with the UN peacekeeping force in Cyprus. In 1994-95, as a LCol, he headed UN force operations staff in south western Bosnia and served at the UN mission headquarters in Zagreb. He returned to serve in the VCDS organization prior to commanding his regt, the Dragoons, based in Petawawa, ON, 1996-98.

Promoted to Col in 1998, he served in the National Command Element in Bosnia prior to being appointed director of operations at National Defence Headquarters, planning Canada's participation in the NATO campaign in Kosovo. In 2001, he attended the US Army War College at Carlise Barracks, PA prior to becoming deputy commander

of the US Army's IIIrd Corps at Fort Hood, TX in 2002. When the corps deployed to Iraq, he became deputy commander of the Multi-National Corps in Iraq from 2004-05. Natynczyk also became a MGen in 2004. In 2005, Natynczyk headed both the Land Force Doctrine and Training System and the Canadian Forces Transformation Team; the latter was responsible for reshaping Canada's military. In 2006, Natynczyk was promoted to LGen and became vice chief of the defence staff. He also heads the Defence Advisory Group for Persons with Disabilities. Among his honours are Commander of the Order of Military Merit, the Meritorious Service Cross, and the Canadian Forces Decoration, and he is an Officer of the US's Armed Forces Legion of Merit. ● AJL

NEEPAWA, pop 3298, is a town 60 km NE of **Brandon** on **CN** and **CP** lines and on hwy 16. In

the late 19th century, settlers from the British Isles as well as **Poles**, **Ukrainians**, and Hungarians came to the area. In 1882, the first post office opened here with the name Clydesdale, though Neepawa is the older name, apparently coming from the **Cree** word for "plenty." As lilies are grown commercially in the area, the town bills itself the "Lily Capital of the World," and these flowers are much in evidence during the annual Neepawa and Area Lily Festival. Politician John Andrew Davidson, a founder of the town, is buried here. His tombstone came to be known as the "Stone Angel," and was a muse of renowned local writer **Margaret Laurence**. She came from Neepawa and fictionalized it as the town of Manawaka in her writings. Her home is now a museum. Though the museum, various festivals, and the nearby **Trans-Canada Trail** draw tourists to the picturesque town, the economy here depends mainly on serving surrounding agricultural operations; on food processing; and on a forest products facility. ● GPP

NELSON, Earle "Strangler," serial rapist, murderer (b 1898, San Francisco, CA; d Jan 13, 1928, **Winnipeg**) went on a murderous spree that ended in Winnipeg. Little is known of his early life. He was expelled from school in grade 2, could not keep a job, and complained of pains in his head and of "spells." He spent some time in a mental institution. According to police, his career of violence began in San Francisco in 1926, when his first female victim was raped and strangled. He allegedly repeated the same modus operandi more than 20 times across the US as far E as Philadelphia, becoming in the process notorious as the "Gorilla Strangler." His trail of violence ended in Winnipeg in 1927 with 2

Neepawa's historic railway station

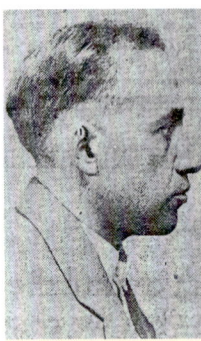

N

Mug shot of Earle "Strangler" Nelson at Winnipeg's Central Police Station, 1927

killings in early June, one of a 14-year-old flower girl and the other of a 27-year-old housewife. Captured near Wakopa (25 km SE of **Boissevain**) on June 15, 1927, after Canada's largest manhunt, he escaped when his guard left the **Killarney** town hall lockup to find matches. He was subsequently recaptured and taken for trial to Winnipeg. Tried only for the death of the housewife, Nelson was hanged 7 months later at the Vaughn St jail in Winnipeg. He never confessed to any of the crimes, and the link to the US deaths was purely circumstantial. • JMB

NELSON RIVER, 644 km long, rises at the NE corner of **Lake Winnipeg** and empties into **Hudson Bay** S of **Churchill** near the site of **York Factory**. Once a primary fur trade route, it has become MB's most important river for **Hydroelectric Power** development.

The Nelson flows NNE from Playgreen Lake near **Norway House**, and then through Cross, Sipiwesk, Split, and Stephens lakes. Its watershed includes the Burntwood River – which runs through **Thompson** – and the Grass River, as well as waterways like the **Red, Assiniboine** and **Saskatchewan** rivers that feed **Lake Winnipeg**. The Cree name for the river is Keche Sipi, or Great River. British naval officer (later admiral) Sir Thomas Button, who was sent after **Henry Hudson** to search for the Northwest Passage, first mapped the W shore of Hudson Bay in 1612. Button named the area New Wales. Though he did not explore further upstream, Button dubbed the river while wintering at its mouth after his late shipmaster Robert Nelson. **Pierre Radisson** later called it Rivière Bourbon for the **French**. In 1684, **HBC** Gov George Geyer established York Factory at Marsh Point, a small peninsula separating the Nelson from the mouth of the **Hayes River**. Both rivers acted as important routes for the **Fur Trade**, though the Hayes became the more prominent corridor.

The Nelson is the province's most suitable river for hydro dam construction, due to its gradual drop and an immense natural volume that has been supplemented by a diversion of the **Churchill River**. **Manitoba Hydro** built its first Nelson dam at Kelsey in 1960, and later developed Jenpeg, Kettle Rapids, Long Spruce, and Limestone. In 2006, at least 6 more dam ventures remained under consideration on the Nelson alone. • JT

NERVE-WINGED INSECT is an insect characterized by 2 pairs of wings that are prominently veined in a net-like pattern. Neuropterans include a number of interesting families in MB, including lacewings (family Chrysopidae), mantidflies (Mantispidae), and antlions (Myrmeleontidae). The Green Lacewing (*Chrysoperla plorabunda*) is a common, long-winged, golden-eyed insect (20 mm) seen in meadows, which provides a valuable service in controlling insect pests like aphids on cultivated plants. A most-unusual anti-predator feature is the presence of hearing organs in the large wing veins, which are sensitive to the echo-locating calls of hunting bats. The organs also serve in courting communication – species-specific coded messages arising from vibrating the abdomen. It lays its eggs suspended by white silk threads underneath leaves. Mantidflies resemble miniature (25 mm) preying mantids, with mobile heads, large compound eyes, and greatly enlarged raptorial front legs for catching insects. The Brown Mantidfly (*Climaciella brunnea*) is widespread in grasslands and forest-edge habitats. It attaches its eggs to leaves by mean of long stalks. There is a single species of antlion in MB (*Brachynemurus abdominalis*) – an ungainly night-time flyer, described as "a helicopter about to crash." The adult has a long (35 mm), thin body and looks like a delicate damselfly, and not at all like its larva – a wide, flattened creature with huge jaws that lurks in its burrow in sandy areas ready to ambush passing ants and other insects. Nerve-winged insects are represented by about 100 species in Canada, likely over half of which occur in MB (and 5000 species worldwide). The group arose as early as 290 mya (Early Permian period). • REW, TG

NETLEY-LIBAU MARSH, at 26,000 ha (64,000 ac), is the largest freshwater coastal wetland in MB, and among the largest in Canada. It lies along the S shore of **Lake Winnipeg**, separated from the lake by a 25 km-long series of barrier islands. The marsh consists of a complex of shallow lakes, lagoons, and channels. The **Red River** passes through the marsh on its way to the lake, branching into 3 main channels before emptying into Lake Winnipeg. Netley Marsh lies on the W side of the river and Libau Marsh on the E.

Openings in the barrier islands (currently 11) allow water exchange between Lake Winnipeg and Netley-Libau Marsh. Strong lake winds can result in significant fluctuations, sometimes exceeding one m in water levels on the marsh.

Netley-Libau Marsh provided resources for early Aboriginal people, including the **Peguis First Nation** in the 1800s, and subsequently for **Lord Selkirk**'s settlers. The vicinity developed into an important recreational and agricultural area through the 20th century. Its importance has much to do with the abundant **Fish** and wildlife that occur in the marsh. It has been recognized internationally as major habitat for nesting, staging, and moulting **Waterfowl**. It is also used for recreational activities such as **Hunting, Fishing,** boating, bird watching, and ecotourism. Bird Studies Canada and the Canadian Nature Federation have recognized the marsh as one of the province's 38 important bird areas. Abundant species that use the marsh for nesting or during **Bird Migration** include Red-winged blackbird (*Agelaius phoeniceus*), Yellow-headed blackbird (*Xanthocephalus xanthocephalus*), Franklin's gull (*Larus pipixcan*), Western grebe (*Aechmophorus occidentalis*), Black-crowned night heron (*Nycticorax nycticorax*), Sandhill crane (*Grus canadensis*), and several duck and goose species. The marsh also provides spawning, nursery and feeding habitat for many fish species from Lake Winnipeg and the Red River.

Over 90% of the marsh is publicly owned, including a 1073 ha (2650-ac) game bird refuge. Still, the ecological integrity of Netley-Libau Marsh is under threat. Introduction of exotic species, such as purple loosestrife (*Lythrum salicaria*) and common carp (*Cyprinus carpio*), has altered the structure of the marsh. The Red, which drains an enormous area and supports large urban centres, is a source of **Pollution** in the form of phosphates, nitrates, pesticides, and herbicides. Erosion of uplands that formerly divided the marsh into smaller units has lead to the creation of large, open, wind-swept bays that have lost their fundamental marsh character. Dredging of a channel into Netley Lake in 1913 has permitted greater inflow of polluted water from the Red. As a result, the marsh is not as effective a purifier of pollutants flowing through the Red River into Lake Winnipeg. Habitat for fish and wildlife has been compromised from loss of aquatic plants and uplands that provide cover, habitat diversity, and breeding sites. • DALE WRUBLESKI/GORDON GOLDSBOROUGH

NEVILLE, Anita, politician (b July 22, 1942, **Winnipeg**) received her BA in political science from the **U of M**. Before entering political life, she worked as an economic consultant for the province of MB, as director of Workforce 2000, for the Winnipeg Core Area Initiative and Employment Training Program and was also involved in the Law Society of Manitoba. From 1986-2000, she served as school trustee and chair of the Winnipeg School Board. She lost an attempt at a provincial seat when she ran as a **LIBERAL** candidate in the MB election of 1995. She succeeded in pursuing her political career, however, in 2000, winning the federal seat of Winnipeg-South Centre. Under the govt of Paul Martin, she served as parliamentary secretary to the minister of Cdn heritage and the minister responsible for the status of women. She was re-elected in 2004 and 2006, appointed Opposition critic for Indian affairs and northern development and chair of the national Liberal women's caucus. ● RUTH DEGRAVES

NEW BOTHWELL, pop 530, is a community 45 km SSE of **WINNIPEG**. It had its beginnings in the 1870s with the **MENNONITE IMMIGRATION** to MB, and may have first been called Kronstal or Osterwick. The original name of the modern community was Bothwell, but to avoid confusion with a town of the same name in ON, residents here agreed to rename it New Bothwell. The community is in the heart of what was the province's **DAIRY** belt. A local **CO-OPERATIVE** dairy set up a cheese plant in 1936 which has become Bothwell Cheese, a widely-known, artisan cheese maker that in 2007 produced more than 30 varieties and 1200 lbs (544 kg) of cheese every day (*see* **FOODS & BEVERAGES, MANITOBAN**). Although Bothwell Cheese still draws its milk from surrounding farms, hog production (*see* **PORK INDUSTRY**) was becoming more significant to the area in the early 2000s than dairy farming. In the community itself, there is a K-Grade 9 school, a store, and a community centre with skating rinks and ball diamonds. New Bothwell is the hometown of ultimate fighting competitor and mixed martial artist Joe Doerksen, and Mennonite poet Audrey Poetker-Thiessen. ● GPP

NEW DEMOCRATIC PARTY (NDP) was founded in 1961 in Ottawa as a joint effort of the **CO-OPERATIVE COMMONWEALTH FEDERATION** (CCF) and the Canadian Labour Congress. The leadership of the 2 moved to form a new party with the hope that it would gain more electoral support than the CCF. The NDP began as a moderate democratic socialist party and, although it has never formed a govt or even been the Official Opposition at the national level, it has formed govts in the provinces of MB, SK, BC, and ON, as well as YT.

In its early years, 2 individuals figured prominently in the federal NDP – **TOMMY DOUGLAS** and **STANLEY KNOWLES**. Both immigrated to MB and enrolled as students at Brandon College (*see* **BRANDON U**), where they became immersed in the theology of the social gospel. Both worked as preachers: Douglas in **CARBERRY, SHOAL LAKE, STRATHCLAIR,** and **AUSTIN,** before becoming a Baptist minister in SK; Knowles in **RAPID CITY, RESTON,** and **WINNIPEG BEACH** before becoming a United Church minister in Winnipeg.

ARCHIVES OF MB, PERSONALITY FILES, 1957

Russ Paulley was the NDP's first leader in Manitoba.

Douglas served as the CCF premier of SK for 17 years and became known as the father of medicare. In 1961, he was elected as the first national leader of the NDP. Douglas was succeeded by David Lewis in 1971, and later by Ed Broadbent, Audrey McLaughlin, Alexa McDonough, and Jack Layton. Knowles served a total of 38 years as MP for Winnipeg North Centre and gained a reputation as the parliamentarian who best knew Parliament's rules and procedures and as a fighter for improvements to Old Age Security, the Canada Pension Plan, and other pension benefits.

Some of the other well-known NDP MPs from MB have included **DAVID ORLIKOW**, a former municipal and provincial politician who represented Winnipeg North for 26 years; **EDWARD SCHREYER,** who was elected to Parliament twice in the 1960s; and **BILL BLAIKIE,** who has represented constituencies in northeast Winnipeg and Transcona since 1979 and who ran for the federal leadership in 2003.

At the provincial level, the last CCF leader in MB, **RUSS PAULLEY,** also became the first NDP leader. Under Paulley, the NDP increased its support; but while a majority of its party memberships were held in rural MB, most of its MLAs and the party leadership were from Winnipeg. Paulley was replaced, in 1969, by Edward Schreyer. He led the party in one of the most critical elections in MB's history. Support for the NDP went from 23% in 1966 to over 38% in 1969, and the party won 28 of the 57 seats in the Legislature.

Schreyer had formed an electoral coalition that drew heavy support from ethnic and religious minorities and included the working class neighbourhoods in north Winnipeg and Brandon, and most of northern MB. With the coming of Schreyer's govt, the NDP has been the dominant electoral coalition in the province, ruling MB more than half the time since 1969. Higher income ridings in south Winnipeg and rural communities in southern MB, which had dominated the province's politics for most of its first century, continued to elect Conservatives.

Schreyer's govt, the first NDP govt in Canada, remained in office for more than 8 years, during which it introduced public automobile insurance, amalgamated all the municipalities in Winnipeg into one **UNICITY**, and brought in a more progressive tax system, including the elimination of medicare premiums.

In 1981, after only one term in office, the Progressive Conservatives under **STERLING LYON** were defeated by the NDP, led by **HOWARD PAWLEY**, a former member of the Schreyer cabinet. The Pawley govt held office until 1988 and was known for its labour legislation and its support of govt services in French.

In 1999, the NDP was elected again in MB, this time under **GARY DOER**. One of his most important acts was to drastically reform election financing legislation to eliminate financial contributions from corporations and trade unions. Doer led the NDP to its greatest election victory ever, in 2003, when it won over 49% of the popular vote and elected 35 MLAs, including some from south Winnipeg ridings that had never before elected NDP MLAs. This was the beginning of 3 successive majority wins for Doer.

By the beginning of the 21st century, the NDP had dropped any pretense of being a socialist party, although the federal party is still a member of the Socialist International. In provinces like MB where it has had its greatest electoral success, the NDP has become a broadly based coalition of the political left. ● JAMES MCALLISTER

NEW FLYER INDUSTRIES is one of NA's largest heavy-duty transit-**Bus Manufacturing** companies, producing more than ⅓ of all such buses sold each year in Canada and the US. New Flyer began in 1930 as Western Auto & Truck Body Works. In 1937, Western Auto began building intercity buses, and was renamed Western Flyer Coach Ltd 11 years later. Western Flyer continued to operate as a small manufacturer of intercity buses, producing an average of 30 vehicles per year until 1968, when it switched to making local transit buses. Although it was able to find customers for its new products, the company struggled financially, and in 1971, the provincial Crown agency Manitoba Development Corporation (MDC) took it over and renamed it Flyer Industries, Ltd. Flyer continued producing transit and trolley buses for the Cdn and US markets, and in 1978 introduced its first 11 m (35-ft) model. In 1986, MDC sold Flyer to the den Oudsten family of the Netherlands, which renamed it New Flyer Industries. The den Oudsten family also owned a bus manufacturing company in the Netherlands, and the factory there was instrumental in helping New Flyer to modernize its production plant and to add low-floor and articulated buses to its offerings. Under the den Oudstens, New Flyer also expanded its operations into the US, opening an assembly plant in CA in 1987.

Over the next 12 years, the assembly plant relocated several times, first to Grand Forks, ND, then to Crookston, MN, and finally to St. Cloud, MN. In the 1990s, the company also began experimenting with more environmentally friendly alternative-fuel buses, starting with buses running on hydrogen fuel cells and on compressed natural gas in 1994, followed by liquid natural gas buses, and, in 1999, a diesel-electric hybrid bus. Other new models were later added, including a suburban bus; a 3-axle, high-floor model; and a new low-floor model called the Invero, featuring composite materials and electronic controls, which made it lighter, easier to maintain, and less costly to operate. Despite its successes with alternative-fuel buses, New Flyer ran into financial difficulties and changed hands twice between Mar 2002, when KPS Special Situations Fund acquired it from the den Oudsten family, and Dec 2003, when KPS sold it to 2 New York private equity firms – Harvest Partners and Lightyear Capital. In Mar 2005, New Flyer solidified its position as NA's leading producer of hybrid-fuel buses with the sale of the first gasoline-electric buses. The firm went on to record 3 $100 million-plus orders in 2006, adding 130 workers, bringing the total to just fewer than 1500. ● MURRAY MCNEILL

NEW ICELAND (Nýja-Ísland), a unique settlement in what is now MB, was established as an Icelandic reserve on the shores of **Lake Winnipeg** in 1875. The first **Icelanders** to make their way here were scouts from ON and WI seeking land for group settlement. With them was John Taylor, Dominion Icelandic agent. Finding the Red River Valley devastated by grasshoppers, this group explored the W shore of Lake Winnipeg which in the 1870s lay beyond the northern boundary of MB. At the group's request, 12 townships – together with Big Island ("Mikley," now **Hecla Island**) – were set aside for Icelandic settlement. Dubbed New Iceland, this reserve was within the District of Keewatin in Canada's NWTs, and was thus under direct jurisdiction of the Dominion govt. Contrary to popular lore, at no time did New Iceland claim or hold the status of "republic," which would have run counter to the spirit and letter of the settlement's close relationship with the Cdn govt. The settlers did, however, organize a local govt with a constitution and by-laws for administering local affairs.

The first settlers bound for New Iceland arrived in **Winnipeg** via Duluth, MN, and the **Red River** in fall 1875, many of them from the failed settlement at Kinmount, ON, NNW of Peterborough. The eventful landing of this group at Willow Point (S of Gimli) aboard flatboats on Oct 21, 1875, and the subsequent hardships of their

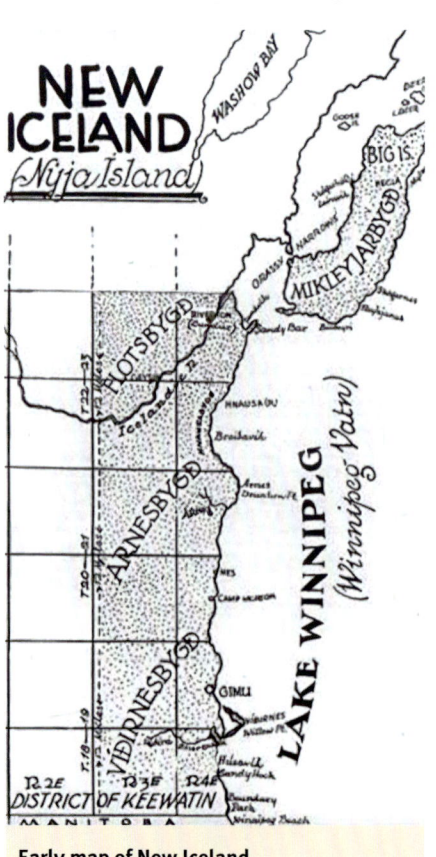

Early map of New Iceland

first winter at Gimli are now the stuff of legend. Remarkably, despite primitive conditions and a scurvy outbreak that winter, the settlers established a school for the teaching of English. In 1876, some 1200-1400 additional immigrants known as the "Large Group" arrived directly from Iceland. Many of this group were from E Iceland, where entire districts had been devastated by ashfall from the volcano Askja. These settlers claimed virtually all suitable homesteads along 80 km of lakeshore, from Boundary Creek (**Winnipeg Beach**) to Gull Harbour on Hecla Island.

New Iceland included 4 administrative districts: Viðinesbyggð (Willow Point Community), Árnesbyggð (River Point Community), Fljótsbyggð (River Community), and Mikleyjarbyggð (Big Island Community). Three town sites were surveyed: Gimli, Sandvik (**Sandy Bar**), and **Lundur** (Icelandic River/**Riverton**). Post offices and small business centres were subsequently established at Husavik, Nes, **Arnes**, Hnausa, Geysir, Isafold (Howardville), and Hecla.

The original settlers' dreams were dashed by repeated misfortune and tragedy. Over winter 1876-77, smallpox ravaged the settlement. **Mosquitoes** and heavy rain hampered early attempts at **Agriculture** in this poorly drained and heavily wooded area, and religious feuds between the supporters of Rev. **Jón Bjarnason** and Rev. Páll Þorláksson (**Paul H. T. Thorlaksson**) spoiled community spirit. Widespread disillusionment prompted an exodus to Dakota Territory in 1878-79. Severe **Floods** in 1880 then sounded a virtual death knell for New Iceland. Even many "Loyalists" abandoned their homesteads. Mindful of the Cdn govt's generosity, however, this group moved to the "Argyle Settlement" (**Baldur/Glenboro**) in SW MB, thus remaining in Canada. By 1881, only a small core of settlers remained in New Iceland around an ambitious sawmill and transportation enterprise operating on the Icelandic River. **Sigtryggur Jónasson** and his business partner **Friðjón Friðriksson Frederickson** are credited with sustaining New Iceland through this critical time. A new influx of immigrants from Iceland arrived in 1883, repopulating New Iceland and rekindling community life. In 1885, settlement expanded W into the Geysir district and N into Isafold. After 1900, the Árdal (now Ardal), Framnes, and Víðir (Vidir) districts formed still farther up the Icelandic River. New Iceland was incorporated into the province of MB in 1881, and in 1887, the settlers adopted municipal govt. Public education was introduced in 1889. New Iceland's reserve status, however, was not officially abolished until 1899.

A map in Gimli's New Iceland Heritage Museum shows the routes of early settlers.

Though agriculture was slow to take root in New Iceland, the **FISHING INDUSTRY** on Lake Winnipeg provided seasonal employment, as did logging, wood cutting, navigation, and winter freighting. Success in **GRAIN** growing during the late 1880s prompted renewed land clearing, and with the advent of machinery and rising prices during WWI, agriculture in New Iceland took a forward leap that resulted in the establishment of some of MB's finest farms. The arrival of the **RAILWAY** at Gimli (1906), Ardal/Arborg (1910), and Riverton (1914) sparked new economic activity, as these railheads served vast northern areas. Tourism also became significant to the local economy around 1900, and today, what was New Iceland's shoreline is prime recreational and residential real estate. The area's Icelandic heritage now blends with other cultures, but still thrives and attracts widespread attention each Aug with **ÍSLENDINGADAGURINN** (the Icelandic Festival) at Gimli. ● NELSON GERRARD

NEWSPAPER ROW housed **WINNIPEG**'s 3 daily **NEWSPAPERS** at the turn of the 20th century. The *Winnipeg Telegram*, **WINNIPEG TRIBUNE**, and the *Manitoba Free Press* (*see* **WINNIPEG FREE PRESS**) were all situated near the corner of Albert St and McDermot Ave. City residents would often congregate on the corner to hear the latest news, either posted on the walls or shouted through megaphones from the office windows. Tension among the Conservative *Winnipeg Telegram*, the anti-**CPR** *Winnipeg Tribune*, and the Liberal *Free Press*, which boasted the highest circulation in the community, often ran high. However, in the summer of 1907, the 3 papers banded together to protest the monopoly of Canadian Pacific Telegraph, which sold mostly US wire stories, and founded their own system of national and international correspondents under the Western Associated Press, the forerunner to the Canadian

The Telegram Building, 244 McDermot Avenue, 1910

Press wire service. Newspaper Row disappeared when the dailies either folded or moved to larger premises elsewhere. ● MD

NEWSPAPERS have been important sources of information in MB since 1859, when the ***NOR'-WESTER*** was established in the village not yet called **WINNIPEG**. This newspaper and its rival, *The Red River Pioneer*, were both suppressed in 1869 by **LOUIS RIEL**, who understood the political value of controlling the press. Riel authorized the publication of the *New Nation*, which first appeared on Jan 1, 1870, but it soon annoyed him

with pro-US agitation, and was also briefly closed down. After the entrance of MB into Confederation, many short-lived weekly newspapers were published in and around Winnipeg. One of these, the *Manitoba Free Press* (later the **WINNIPEG FREE PRESS**), went daily in 1874, thus establishing the Winnipeg newspaper community as the centre of the daily paper in MB. Other places, like **BRANDON** and **PORTAGE LA PRAIRIE**, would also eventually establish dailies – by 1912, Brandon had 3, each of which produced a weekly version – but the major cut-throat competition was in the big city, where 10 dailies and 22 weekly

497

Winnipeg Tribune, July 18, 1931

N

and semi-monthly newspapers had been started before 1884. Only 1 daily and 4 weeklies survived into 1885.

Winnipeg controlled the province's press until 1877, when weekly newspapers outside the city began to appear (the Morris *Standard* and the Icelandic *Framfari*). Beginning in 1881, the number of new rural newspapers kept pace with the expansion of settlement. Between 1881 and 1887, 43 rural weeklies and 4 dailies were established. Every railhead town had to have its newspaper, with 2 or 3 sometimes competing for the same local market. Competition was often caused by the need for local political parties to have their own newspaper and their editorial voice to fight the heavily partisan elections of the day. Daily newspapers came and went, and were joined by specialist papers, including ethnic newspapers, mostly published in Winnipeg, at first for circulation among the Icelandic and German communities, and later among Slavic and Eastern European peoples as well. By 1914, some of these papers had adopted radical editorial lines. In 1913, Louis Philip Adélard Langevin, Archbishop of St. Boniface, founded *La Liberté*, which exists to this day. The *Manitoba Free Press* absorbed several competitors in the 1880s. However, the *Daily Tribune* (see **WINNIPEG TRIBUNE**), which would prove to be a long-term competitor, started up in 1890. From virtually the beginning, the *Free Press* was the newspaper of record, covering domestic and foreign affairs and devoting much attention to what was happening in the

Empire. The heyday of the *Free Press* was during the ownership of the **SIFTON** family and the editorship of **JOHN WESLEY DAFOE**, which covered nearly the first half of the 20th century. The *Tribune* concentrated mainly on local news in and around metropolitan Winnipeg; most people thought its local sports coverage far superior to that in its rivals.

The explosion in ethnic newspapers matched the growth in Winnipeg before 1914. Over 20 such papers were started in Winnipeg before WWI, representing most of the major ethnic communities, and more joined them afterward. Other new developments included the appearance of local newspapers in suburban Winnipeg and the emergence of regional newspapers designed for the rural farm audience. Some of the farm papers were weekly editions published by the 3 Winnipeg dailies with "Farmer" in the title – the *Telegram* had joined the *Free Press* and the *Tribune* between 1898 and 1920 as a consciously Tory voice. In 1908, the **UNITED GRAIN GROWERS** first produced the *Grain Growers' Guide*, designed to circulate across the western Prairies, although published in Winnipeg. The "GGG" would serve as the political voice of the farmer for many years. It joined several other similar papers: *The Nor'-West Farmers and Farm and Home* (1882), and The *Farmer's Advocate and Home Journal* (1890), published in Winnipeg for the Western farm audience. The number of rural failures and mergers continued to run high up to WWI. There were too many newspapers and not enough

market to support them. The **GREAT DEPRESSION** was hard on newspapers of all kinds, and many collapsed or merged.

From 1940, the newspaper picture in MB remained relatively stable. One exception occurred in 1948, when the left-leaning *Winnipeg Citizen* was founded as a co-operative daily, owned by 13,000 shareholders. The *Citizen* was an outgrowth of an earlier newspaper produced during the 1919 **WINNIPEG GENERAL STRIKE**, but despite the presence of **MARGARET LAURENCE** as radio critic, it lasted for only 13 months, defeated by an undeserved reputation for being Communist-dominated. The *Tribune* was closed in 1980, a victim of national chain shuffling, and was soon replaced by a tabloid, the **WINNIPEG SUN**, which covered the same local market as the *Trib*, but in more sensationalist fashion and with a much smaller circulation. The *Free Press* became by far the most dominant newspaper voice in the province. The only other provincial daily with any widespread regional circulation is the **BRANDON SUN**, though there are 3 other dailies in MB. Rural and suburban weeklies, foreign-language and ethnic papers, and specialized papers (such as the *Winnipeg Real Estate News*) still continue. ● J. M. BUMSTED

NICKEL, Grace, ceramic artist, (b June 18, 1956, **ALTONA**) has received international critical acclaim for her hand-built clay sculptures. She graduated with her BFA from the **U OF M**'s School of Art in 1980, and has held residencies in Banff, AB, Perth, Australia, and Tainan County, Taiwan. Her sconces, tiles, and pillars are made from paper clay. Her forms are from antiquity and nature, and she adds decorative detail with clay slips and by carving into the wet clay. At times, she includes glass and fabric, the glass and light evoking hope and inspiration. The clay, from the earth, is the ground; and her symbols and images, leaves, plants and butterflies, are drawn from nature. Together these materials and symbols allude to ancient traditions and architectural history, simultaneously creating personal spaces. The scale of her ceramics, especially her pillars, stretches the technical capacity of clay. The columns refer to human beings and the sconces represent the spirit. Her installations thus connect the dichotomies of the inner and spiritual self to material history and traditions. Her work has been exhibited in Canada, Taiwan, the US, Australia, Japan and Hong Kong and is represented in public and private collections in Canada, including The **WINNIPEG ART GALLERY**; the US; Europe and Taiwan. She has received the Manitoba Arts Council Major Arts Award, Canada Council Craft Award, and the Bronze Award at the 2nd International Ceramics Competition in Japan in 1989. Publications include The Winnipeg Art Gallery's *Grace Nickel/A Quiet Passage*, 2002 and *Ceramics Monthly*, January 2007. In 2007, she was named to the National Society of Artists and was inducted into the Royal Canadian Academy of Arts. • Patricia Bovey

NICKNAMES. For a young political entity, MB, and many of its cities and areas, are rich in nicknames. Some time shortly after 1870, MB became known as the "Postage Stamp Province," because the newly formed Cdn province was a square of 36,075 km² whose shape seemed like that of an early stamp. Partly for the shape of the expanded province in 1912, which resembled a builder's stone arch, and partly because it was at the centre of NA, it became the "Keystone Province." This nickname has survived, and gives the **Keystone Centre** in **Brandon** its name. The province is sometimes called "Land of 100,000 Lakes," though it is unclear whether MN's sobriquet "Land of 10,000 Lakes" predates this. Residents are occasionally called "'Tobans" by other Cdns.

Winnipeg's nicknames have often said more about its living in the shadows of larger centres than about the city itself. Sometimes called "River City," Winnipeg also became known – not altogether aptly – as the "Chicago of the North" in the 1910s, when it was a boomtown, a rail centre, and the 3rd-largest city in Canada. Because of its rapid expansion, the MB capital was also called "Mushroom City." Around the same time, Winnipeg also acquired the title "Gateway to the West." Often called "The 'Peg," MB's largest centre is also known widely as "Winterpeg" – on average, its winters are the 2nd-coldest of any city of more than 500,000 people, behind Ulan Bator in Mongolia. Despite the cold winters, the city enjoys the dubious reputation of being the "Slurpee Capital of Canada." High homicide rates and low civic pride have also inspired the epithets "Murder Capital of Canada," "Murderpeg," and "Killerpeg." To rural Manitobans and those in much of northern ON, Winnipeg is simply "the City." U of Toronto philosophy professor, and former Winnipegger, Mark Kingwell calls Winnipeg "Plague City" – in honour of its **Mosquitoes**, canker worms, **Floods**, **Epidemics**, and so forth – though Torontonians referred to their city by this name after the World Health Organization issued a warning regarding severe acute respiratory syndrome (SARS) there in 2003. A few local features have their own nicknames, notably the **Red River Floodway**, called "Duff's Ditch" in honour of premier **Duff Roblin**.

Most smaller MB towns have some sort of nickname that boosters hope will make the community stand out. **Lynn Lake** is known as "The

Town That Moved," though many communities relocated as the **Railway** made its way across Canada. **Churchill** is "Polar Bear Capital of the World"; **Thompson** is the "Hub of the North"; and **Altona** is the "Sunflower Capital of Canada." Brandon is generally called the "Wheat City," though some have termed it the "Paris of the Prairies," a less-apt moniker that is moreover claimed by both Calgary and Saskatoon. • A. J. Levin

Nielsen's speed and capable hands were an asset to the Bombers.

NIELSEN, Ken, football player, (b May 10, 1942, Hanna, AB) was one of the **Winnipeg Blue Bombers'** most popular receivers. Nielsen started playing football in high school, and starred for the U of Alberta while studying dentistry. He started playing for the Bombers in 1965, and set a CFL record that season when he caught a 109-yd pass from **Ken Ploen** in the Western Final, helping get the team to the Grey Cup. In the 1968-69 season, he was voted the most popular Blue Bomber by fans in a contest. He won the Schenley Award as the CFL's top Canadian in 1968. Over 5 years with the Bombers, Nielsen caught 280 passes for 4340 yds. A neck injury ended his career prematurely in 1970. Nielsen remained in Winnipeg where he set up a dental office. • MD

NINETTE, pop 192, is a community 50 km SSE of **Brandon** at the N end of Pelican Lake, part of the **Souris River** system, on hwys 18 and 23. Assiniboines occupied the area for many centuries, with European, primarily **English**, **Scots**, and **Irish**, settlement beginning late in the 19th century. The community name, a diminutive of "Nina," probably derives from the heroine of a Victorian novel. A post office opened in 1883, and the Northern Pacific and Manitoba **Railway** was built through in 1899. In the early 20th century, **Tuberculosis** (TB) was the most lethal communicable disease worldwide. In 1910, the 65-bed **Manitoba Sanatorium** – a govt-funded project of the Manitoba Tuberculosis Society – opened here. By the 1920s, this convalescence centre was regarded as a model for TB care. With the advent of antibiotics, and especially penicillin and its variants, sanatoriums were no longer necessary. Thus, the Ninette Sanatorium as it was also known, closed in 1972. Retail and services catering to surrounding farms now form the economy here, though the abundant **Waterfowl** on aptly named Pelican Lake offer tourists wildlife-watching, fishing and **Hunting** opportunities. In winter, snowmobiling is popular, and the community boasts a variety of festivals and fairs in summer. • GPP

NISICHAWAYASIHK CREE NATION (previously known as Nelson House Cree Nation), on reserve pop 2807, off reserve pop 1451, is situated 72 km W of **Thompson** and 813 km N of **Winnipeg**. This community signed Treaty 5 in 1908. Nisichawayasihk Cree Nation administers its own education programs. Schooling in Nisichawayasihk goes from Nursery-Grade 12, and enrolment for 2003-04 was 766. The native language of this community is Cree. There are 4 reserves here. Transportation for this area is available via an all-weather road from **Thompson**. Boat and float plane-equipped docks, Grey Goose Bus Lines, and taxi service is also available. The economic base for the Nisichawayasihk Cree Nation is hunting, fishing, and trapping. It is an independent First Nation; therefore it is not a member of any Tribal Council. After being affected by hydro developments on the **Nelson River** system, this is 1 of 5 First Nations that is party to the **Northern Flood Agreement**.

Mercury contamination has had a very severe impact on Nisichawayasihk, poisoning fish and drinking water, and even the land. Wild game in the area began to move on to other regions. Many social and health problems in the community arose due to this environmental change, such as depression, substance abuse, and crime. However, the Nisichawayasihk Cree Nation has agreed to become a partner in **Manitoba Hydro's** next proposed development. In June 2006, 63% of voters in the First Nation gave the okay to spend $28 million, along with a $56 million loan, in return for a 33% share in the proposed Wuskwatim hydroelectric project, 35 km SE of the community. Although the generating station will flood about 37 ha, Nisichawayasihk Cree Nation hopes there will be significant job and revenue benefits to the First Nation. The Clean Environment Commission was holding hearings in early 2007 to assess the environment implications of the $1 billion project.

In Feb 2004, THOMPSON approved the conversion of a portion of Nishichawayasihk-owned property in the city to treaty land. This agreement was one of the first times that privately owned land bought by a First Nation people, was recognized as an urban reserve. As of Dec 2005, the O-PIPON-NA-PIWIN CREE NATION (OPCN) officially broke away from the Nisichawayasihk Cree Nation. ● RK

NIVERVILLE, pop 2464, is a town 20 km S of **WINNIPEG,** on a **CPR** line and the E edge of the **RED RIVER VALLEY**. Regular **FLOODING** of the **RED RIVER** has made this area rich in silt, and therefore ideal for farming. **GERMAN** immigration agent **WILLIAM HESPELER** brought a group of **MENNONITE** settlers to Niverville in 1873, making it the first Mennonite settlement in the new province of MB. Mennonites remain the predominant group, with smaller populations of **ENGLISH, ICELANDERS, SCOTS, FRENCH,** and **IRISH,** among others. Hespeler also built western Canada's first **GRAIN ELEVATOR** in Niverville. The roots of this town are based in agricultural support and manufacturing. Niverville was named after Chevalier Joseph Claude Boucher de Niverville, the successor of **LA VÉRENDRYE** as manager of French **FUR TRADING** posts in the Northwest. The post office opened in 1879, and Niverville was incorporated in 1887 as a village, becoming a town in 1993. Unlike many other MB agricultural service centres, Niverville has grown significantly in past decades, partly as a bedroom community for Winnipeg. The local **CREDIT UNION** is also a major employer. In 2007, Niverville was working on constructing a $6-million Heritage Centre, which was to house medical, commercial, and recreational services, as well as a seniors' residence. ● GPP

NOLAN, Bob, singer/songwriter, actor (b April 13, 1908, **WINNIPEG;** d June 16, 1980, Los Angeles). Born Clarence Robert Nobles, he changed his name to Nolan moving to CA in 1929. There, he joined the Sons of the Pioneers singing group with Roy Rogers and Tim Spencer in 1933. They released their first recordings in 1935, and later

starred on national radio with *Lucky U Ranch*. That year he appeared in his first feature film, *The Old Homestead*. Over the next 2 decades, Nolan appeared in over 90 movies, often alongside Rogers or with the group, including *Rio Grande* (1950) with John Wayne. He was also the singing voice of actor Ken Maynard for *In Old Santa Fe*. Nolan left the Sons of the Pioneers in 1949, releasing his first solo album in 1953 before rejoining the group 1955-58. He is credited with writing over 1200 songs in his career, including "Tumbling Tumbleweeds" and "Cool Water".

He is honoured in the Cowboy Hall of Fame (1971); the Nashville Songwriters Hall of Fame (1971); the Hollywood Walk of Fame, with a star for the Sons of the Pioneers (1976); a designation as US "national treasures" (for the Sons of the Pioneers) at the Smithsonian Institute (1977); and the Country Music Hall of Fame in Nashville (1977). He also received a BMI (Broadcast Music Industry) award for his song writing (1972). Nolan was also inducted posthumously into the Canadian Country Music Hall of Fame (1993), the Western Music Hall of Fame (1994), and the Canadian Songwriters Hall of Fame (2005). ● JOHN EINARSON

NON-PROFIT SECTOR is the section of the **ECONOMY** comprised of organizations that do not distribute profits to any set of owners. The members of these organizations' boards of directors volunteer; therefore, the sector can also be called the voluntary sector. As a complement to the public and for-profit private sectors, the non-profit sector also is called the "3rd sector" of the economy. A subset of the non-profit sector is the charitable sector, which is made up of organizations called charities that hold registered-charity status under Cdn tax law. In addition to having volunteer boards of directors, many non-profit organizations rely heavily on the contributions of volunteer labour, and of public donation.

MB's non-profit sector is large and vibrant. MB has one of the largest non-profit sectors in Canada per capita, superceded only by the NT and SK. MB consistently ranks among the top-3 provinces for volunteer participation. Some unique features characterize MB's non-profit sector. Although the province's population is only about 1.1 million, there are almost 6500 non-profit organizations. In addition, MB's population includes large groups of distinct populations, including indigenous groups such as **WINNIPEG's** urban Aboriginal population; religiously based groups, such as the worldwide Mennonite Central Committee, which is headquartered in the city (*see* **MENNONITES**); and culturally defined groups – for example, the province is home to

large Eastern European, Finnish, and Filipino communities, all of which have traditions of community cohesion and providing "for the common good" of their society. These cultural influences in MB provide a setting in which a variety of non-profit organizations might be expected to flourish. Indeed, MB has a history of grassroots initiatives and strong social activism.

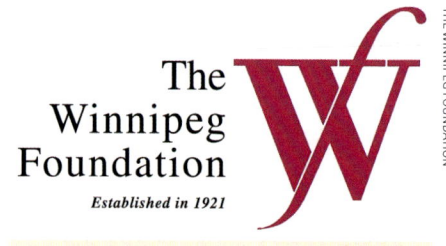

The **Winnipeg Foundation** is Canada's 2nd-largest community foundation.

The non-profit sector in MB, as elsewhere, is varied. Organizations range from large universities and hospitals to small local clubs that assemble for social occasions. Organizations in the sector share a commitment to improving the lives of some segment of the population. These organizations are the cornerstones in creating and maintaining civil society, as they provide people with a way to interact, co-ordinate, and mobilize around shared interests or community needs.

Non-profits in MB, like those around the world, tend to rely heavily for funding on govts, foundations, and contributions from the for-profit sector. In 1997, the Canadian Centre for Philanthropy, now called Imagine Canada, found that MB charities receive about 55% of their revenue from govt, with charities across Canada averaging 60% reliance on govt funding. Two provincial foundations, the United Way and the **WINNIPEG FOUNDATION,** contribute significantly to the sector. The Winnipeg Foundation was the first community foundation established in Canada (in 1921), and remains Canada's 2nd-largest community foundation.

Even as there is increasing recognition of the role that non-profits play in building society, this sector faces increasing hostility through legislation. Erratic govt funding and irregular and frequent program changes within govt departments have led the sector to a state where few jobs are secure and chronic social needs cannot be addressed on a sustained basis. While the aging of a large part of MB's population may lead to greater volunteerism, the monetary contribution of govt will remain essential in ensuring that MB's non-profit sector can continue to strive to improve the lives of Manitobans into the future. ● LAURA BROWN/ELIZABETH TROUTT

NONSUCH was the sailing ship in which **Médard Chouart des Groseilliers** made the first successful **Fur Trading** expedition to **Hudson Bay**, opening up commerce in what would later be MB and leading to the establishment of the **HBC**.

Planning for Groseillers's historical voyage began in 1666, after he and **Pierre Radisson** convinced a syndicate of **English** businessmen and courtiers, including Prince Rupert, that Hudson Bay provided a quicker route to the fur riches of NA's interior rather than the existing voyageur canoe routes from the Northwest to what is now QC. The expedition required small vessels that could be hauled ashore during winter, away from damaging ice, but which were sturdy enough to survive the harsh Atlantic crossing. The *Nonsuch*, built in Wivenhoe, Essex, England, in 1650, was suited to the task. She was a 50-ton ketch – a sailing ship like a sloop but that is rigged with a second mast or mizzen-mast behind the main mast – measuring 16.2 m across the deck and 11.3 m along the keel. She was likely named after Nonsuch Palace, Surrey, an estate Henry VIII built for Anne Boleyn in 1538, or after a number of Royal Navy ships of this name, the earliest dating to 1584. Though the *Nonsuch* was originally a merchant vessel, she saw service in the Royal Navy before being purchased by timber merchant Sir William Warren, who sold the ship to Groseilliers's backers for £290 (about $1410 in 1870's currency) in March 1668.

The *Nonsuch* set out from Gravesend, Kent, England, on June 3, 1668. Aboard were Groseilliers, Capt Zachariah Gillam, 2 mates, a surgeon, and a crew of 7 or 8 men. A 2nd ketch in which Radisson sailed, the *Eaglet*, was also part of  the expedition, but was forced to turn back after being damaged in a storm. The *Nonsuch* weathered the storm, crossing the Atlantic in 44 days, touching land at Labrador Aug 1, 1668, before continuing on to Hudson Bay. Groseilliers anchored for the winter at the mouth of the Rupert River in the SE part of the James Bay in late Sept. The crew established Charles Fort (later Rupert House, now Waskaganish, QC), building a stockade and a small dwelling. With the onset of spring, they were able to trade with roughly 300 Swampy **Cree** who came to the fort; once the ice was sufficiently melted, the *Nonsuch* embarked on her return voyage, arriving in England on Oct 10 with a large cargo of furs valued at £1400 (equivalent to about $6810 in 1870). Though not enough to cover the expense of the voyage, the cargo nonetheless proved that Hudson Bay was a viable trade route, and King Charles II signed a Royal Charter for the HBC less than a year later. The subsequent fate of the *Nonsuch* is unknown.

To commemorate its 300th anniversary, the HBC commissioned a *Nonsuch* replica. This was built in Appledore, Devon, UK, from authentic period materials. After her completion in 1968, she sailed to various Cdn and US saltwater and freshwater ports, covering about 14,000 km. In fall 1973, the *Nonsuch* was shipped overland from the West Coast to the **Manitoba Museum**, where it remains. The replica is likely the museum's most popular exhibit. ● A. J. LEVIN

NORQUAY, John, politician, MB premier (b May 8, 1841, **St Andrews**; d July 5, 1889, **Winnipeg**), was a prominent politician in **Red River**. Of mixed-blood ancestry (*see* **Country-Born**), he attended St. John's Collegiate School and became a school teacher before he began farming at High Bluff and **Fur Trading** on **Lake Manitoba**. Although not actively involved in the **Red River Resistance**, at one point he served as a messenger from the Anglophone mixed-bloods to **Louis Riel**. High Bluff elected him as its MLA by acclamation late in 1870, and after he moved to St. Andrews, he represented that constituency

Nonsuch **replica in the Manitoba Museum**

N

from 1874 until his death. He was a prominent **Anglican**, active in the diocese and in the St. John's Collegiate School.

John Norquay, 1878

Like many leading mixed-bloods, he was a veritable giant of a man, over 1.8 m (6 ft) tall and weighing over 135 kg (300 lbs). He spoke several languages, including **English**, **French**, **Cree**, and **Ojibway**. In the Legislature, he assumed the leadership of a major bloc of Anglophone mixed-bloods, becoming Minister of Public Works and of Agriculture in 1871. In 1875, he was acknowledged as leader of one of the Anglophone factions in the province – the mixed-bloods – which had an equal number of legislative seats (8) to the Francophones and also to the new settlers from ON. In 1878, he became premier, presiding over a province that was growing rapidly and shifting demographically toward Anglophone Protestants. Politics centred around **Railways**, with all Manitobans seeking a share of the **CPR**'s hoped-for competitors. Ottawa disallowed MB railway charter legislation in 1882. The rail controversy eventually brought Norquay down in 1887, when he was unable to find financing for the Red River Valley Railway, which was intended to link Winnipeg with the US, and (with the assistance of PM Macdonald) ended up with a shortfall in the province's books. Norquay was known as one of the province's finest speakers. He died unexpectedly in the summer heat of 1889. • JMB

NORRIE, William "Bill," lawyer, politician (b Jan 21, 1929, **St. Boniface, MB**). As a Rhodes Scholar in 1953, Bill Norrie attended Queen's College at Oxford U and returned to the **U of M** to complete his law degree in 1955. He practised law for a number of years before he entered municipal politics as a trustee of the Winnipeg School Board from 1965-71. Elected to the city of **Winnipeg**'s council in 1971, he served on the executive policy committee and as deputy mayor in 1977. That same year, he was appointed Queen's Counsel. Norrie became mayor of Winnipeg in 1979 and continued in that role until 1992. In the municipal election of 1983, he set a record for the largest numbers of votes ever given to a mayoral candidate in the city. After stepping down as mayor, he resumed his law practice and served on a number of boards including the **Winnipeg Foundation** and the Winnipeg Arts Advisory Council, acted as Honorary Consul-General of Japan for MB, chaired the successful 1993 Jimmy Carter Work Camp building blitz, and chaired the MB School Divisions/District Boundaries Review Commission. In 1995, he was inducted to the **Assiniboine Park** Citizen's Hall of Fame. Named chancellor of the U of M in 2001, he was honoured again when their new facility at 485 Selkirk Ave was dedicated as William Norrie Centre. He was the recipient of the Order of Canada and the **Order of Manitoba**. • RUTH DEGRAVES

NORRIS, Tobias Crawford "T. C.," premier, businessman (b Sept 5, 1861, near Brampton, ON; d Oct 29, 1936, Toronto) was one of MB's most significant political figures. From 1915-22, he was premier of MB, and his first govt, in office 1915-20, was among the most progressive in the province's history.

Norris moved from ON to MB in the late 1880s or early 1890s and purchased land near Griswold, 40 km WSW of **Brandon**. He had become primarily a livestock auctioneer by the time he was a prominent politician in the early 20th century. From his earliest days in Griswold, Norris was a low-tariff Liberal. In the 1896 provincial election, he ran for the **Liberal** party in the Lansdowne constituency, in which Griswold was located. He won the seat, won it again in the 1899 election, lost it in 1903, but regained it in 1907, and was re-elected in 1910. By then, he was one of the most prominent Liberals in the province. After the 1907 election, he became leader of the provincial party.

Between 1910 and 1915, Norris and other Liberals worked hard to discredit the governing Conservative Party (see **Progressive Conservative** party) led by **Rodmond P. Roblin**. By 1914, the Liberals were growing in popularity, but there was little reason to think they might soon form a govt. Then, early in 1915, an investigation

by a Royal Commission established that the Conservatives had accepted kickbacks from contractors on the new **Legislative Building**. The Roblin govt resigned in disgrace; Norris was asked to form a govt, and did. He then quickly called an election, and his party won 42 of the province's 49 seats.

Over the next 5 years, the Norris govt would change the province. It provided significantly more money than had been allocated previously to Public Education, to the **U of M**, to health care facilities and programs, to assistance for vulnerable women and children, to the provincial road system, and to factory inspection. It also was responsible for legislating a number of significant reforms. Women were given the right to vote, as well as to hold provincial and municipal offices (see **Women's Movement**). A *Mothers' Allowance Act* was adopted. School attendance became compulsory.

Many political changes were also introduced. Among them was a system of preferential voting in **Winnipeg** for provincial elections. A Civil Service Commission was established to allocate govt jobs more on merit and less on party allegiance. Another political reform was the *Initiative and Referendum Act* (1916). It was declared unconstitutional, but the Norris govt used non-binding referenda to ascertain public opinion on 2 different **Prohibition** measures. The first of these measures was the 1916 legislation that allowed for sale of only very low-alcohol beverages; the 2nd, passed in 1920 after the federal govt had given provinces the power to do so, prohibited importation of alcoholic beverages from outside MB. Among other pieces of legislation were several to improve working conditions for wage earners, as well as a *Minimum Wage Act* that applied to female employees, and, after the 1919 **Winnipeg General Strike** of 1919, an act that established a Council of Industry to inquire into labour disputes, wages, and working conditions. Almost all these measures had the support of farmers and rural people, and additional ones were introduced specifically in the interests of these groups. Legislation was introduced to encourage co-operation among municipalities to create hospitals. Assistance was given to municipalities in providing **Hydroelectric** power. The *Noxious Weeds Act* was improved. Purchasers of farm machinery were protected against inaccurate claims of salesmen. Several different pieces of legislation helped to make loans available to farmers at low rates of interest. In summary, the Norris govt of 1915-20 passed "enlightened and courageous" measures, as **W. L. Morton** said in his history of the province. It was also scandal-free. Moreover, Norris himself was very popular personally. However, during its term, his activist govt offended many people.

The strongest opponents of the Norris administration by 1920 were members of minority ethnic groups. Manitobans of **French**, **German**, **Ukrainian**, Russian, and **Polish** background resented the 1916 legislation that made English the sole language of instruction in schools, as they did later regulations designed to make public schools more effective agents of "Canadianization." Most of the ethnic minorities also were unenthusiastic about Prohibition and woman's suffrage. Finally, many minorities resented the fact that in 1917, the Norris administration had supported a Union govt at the federal level. This meant it supported conscription as well as the different measures passed federally to eliminate rights and privileges of people born in enemy territory. In 1919, a time when "foreigners" became associated not only with disloyalty during the recent war but also with labour unrest, the Norris govt even established an Alien Investigation Board to identify people the federal govt might wish to deport (*see* **Alien Question**).

Among other enemies of the Norris Liberals were those made during the 1919 Winnipeg Strike. Norris had adopted a "neutral" attitude toward this labour confrontation, but the province dismissed employees who joined the walkout. For this and for other reasons, it was criticized for supporting a federal govt that trampled on workers' rights. On the other hand, some rural Manitobans and Winnipeg businessmen resented the neutral attitude, interpreting it as a failure to oppose decisively an attempted revolution.

Norris's Liberals had reason to expect opposition from organized labour and members of minority groups, but not from Protestant **English** and **Scots** farmers, a group that Norris's govt had bent over backward to satisfy. However, Manitoban farmers, like those across the country, had become convinced that political parties frustrated democracy. By 1920, they were suspicious of anyone associated with a party. So were many others in the province, and to satisfy them, 67 "independent" candidates ran in the provincial election – in a normal MB provincial election, there might be 5 or 10. Most of the independents were backed either by labour organizations or a local chapter of the United Farmers of Manitoba (UFM). Some of the farm candidates represented resentful ethnic groups, but most had no important criticisms to make of the Norris administration. They simply wanted to help establish a new era of non-partisan govt that would be even more open and democratic than that Norris had led.

The results of the 1920 election surprised almost everyone. Norris and the Liberals took 21

seats; farm candidates, 12; labour candidates, 11; Conservatives, 7; and other independents, 4. Candidates who were neither Liberals nor Conservatives received nearly 1 of every 2 votes, whereas in earlier provincial elections since the 1890s they had received perhaps 1 in 10. In MB, as elsewhere in Canada just after WWI, voters turned to new parties or to independent candidates.

After this election, the Norris Liberals still controlled more seats than any other party or group, so a new minority govt was formed. It was not successful, however. Very little important legislation was passed, mostly because none of the opposition groups or parties could be counted on for support. Furthermore, a national post-war depression, especially in **Agriculture**, meant that it was difficult to maintain the new programs and commitments that the 1915-20 administration had introduced. The conclusion many people came to was that, since 1915, the Liberals had brought in desirable but not affordable programs and policies.

T. C. Norris, 1915

ARCHIVES OF MB, PERSONALITY FILES

In 1922, the minority govt fell, and in the election that followed, Norris and the Liberals were criticized for extravagance and for the legislative inactivity of the previous 2 years. The UFM decided to field many more candidates in this election, and to do so as a provincial organization rather than at the level of individual constituencies. Moreover, a group of Winnipeg businessmen, motivated primarily to reduce govt expenditures, formed a Progressive Party to run candidates who, if elected, would work with

the UFM. The UFM/Progressive candidates took 28 seats, a slight majority. Meanwhile, the Liberals took 8 seats; the Conservatives, 7; the labour candidates, 6; and independents, 6. The new, leaderless UFM/Progressive majority soon found a leader in **John Bracken**, principal of the U of M's Agricultural College. Bracken became premier.

Norris remained MLA for Lansdowne until 1928 – he resigned his seat to run unsuccessfully in the '25 federal election, then regained it in a by-election – and leader of the provincial Liberal Party and Leader of the Opposition until 1926. When he resigned as party head, he and other Liberals knew that he would soon receive a federal appointment. Had he been married, and had he been wealthy, he might have been named MB's lt gov. However, long-time Liberal Theodore Arthur Burrows received the appointment instead. A vacant Senate seat from the West had a prior claimant. Finally, in 1928, the King govt appointed Norris to the federal Board of Railway Commissioners. As a member of the **Railways** board, he was a useful voice for the West. He remained on the Board until around his 75th birthday, in Sept 1936. He was in very poor health by this time, and died about a month later in Toronto. • MORRIS MOTT

NORTH END of Winnipeg. The North End, which is bounded by Main, Jarvis, McPhillips, and Inkster, has 2 distinct halves with quite separate personalities. While its northern section has long been a pleasant middle-class area, the south part is notably grittier, having been developed in the late 19th century as a housing ghetto for a mixed population of European **Immigrants** (mainly **Germans**, **Poles**, **Jews**, and **Ukrainians**) who journeyed to the epicentre of the continent and laboured here in the vast Weston **CPR** rail yards. Most of the workers employed by the railway, 5000 strong at its highpoint, dwelt close by in rickety tenements and small houses on narrow lots; this shabby part of the North End came to be known as "Babel." Despite this poverty, or perhaps because of it, the North End has also produced an extraordinary number of talented writers, performers, scientists and politicians.

During its major growth periods, which ended after WWII, waves of new immigrants helped make the North End a lively place despite the relative poverty of its inhabitants. Selkirk Ave was established by the 1870s as the main commercial venue. It came to feature department stores like Oretski's, specialty food shops, busy diners, 2 movie houses, and the city's first steam bath, Obee's, built in 1914 (just off Selkirk on Manitoba Ave). This facility was no doubt much appreciated in a time before every home had a bathroom with hot water on tap. The

The North End's heyday occurred in the late 1960s and early '70s. Suddenly, all the socially devalued trappings of immigrant heritage became mainstream and even chic, thanks in part to the mosaic model of ethnic co-existence promoted by PM Trudeau. The multicultural North End achieved a kind of mythic status then, giving rise in 1970 to Winnipeg's internationally recognized **Folklorama**, a summer "celebration of difference" promoting ethnic foods, colourful costumes, and artistic performances.

After this apotheosis, increasingly affluent 2nd- and 3rd-generation offspring of the original migrants started moving to the suburbs in the latter 1970s and through the '80s, seeking larger houses on greener streets, leaving the North End bereft of vitality. For Sale signs, boarded-up businesses, and other urban eyesores came to dominate the neighbourhood's streetscapes. Some Eastern European favourites survived, including Kelekis Restaurant, Alycia's (a "perogy palace"), and City Bread; but despite such holdouts, as the crime rate started to climb, the North End's movement to entropy might have seemed unstoppable.

However, such neighbourhoods, created to welcome refugees and aliens, have long existed worldwide; and the rhythm of different immigrant groups moving in and out is a familiar one. At this point, the North End has been around for more than a century and now houses a new demographic, including an influx of **Filipinos** and a growing population of First Nations people. Historic edifices like Obee's have been revitalized as housing complexes; St. John's High School is now planning its 100th reunion; and Kelekis continues to draw customers for its shoestring fries. The North End is also frequently featured, both as character and background, in **Film** (including, most recently, *Stryker* by Winnipeg *auteur* Noam Gonick), **Literature**, and other cultural products coming out of Winnipeg. This venerable neighbourhood lives on in locals' hearts and minds as an icon of what it means to be united through difference. ● RYSZARD DUBANSKI

NORTH WEST COMPANY (NWC, Nor'Westers) was an organization of merchants that was a major participant in the **Fur Trade** 1779-1821. Unlike its major competitor, the **Hudson's Bay Company** (HBC), the NWC was not a chartered company but a syndicate of trading firms and individuals formed in order to eliminate competition amongst themselves; to pool resources, the better to compete with rivals; to influence govt policy. Primarily managed by **Scots** based in Montreal, the original partnership was divided into 16 shares.

Motorists on the Slaw Rebchuk bridge are welcomed to the North End by a sign on an autobody shop. The venerable socialist slogan "People before profit" also appears.

neighbourhood also supported many community halls, houses of worship of different denominations, and benevolent associations.

Not surprisingly, given their turbulent Old World history, most North Enders promoted a left-wing radicalism in their "brave new world." For example, the Ukrainian Labour Temple at MacGregor and Pritchard was the birthplace of the **Winnipeg General Strike** of 1919, in which virtually the entire workforce of the city walked off the job. In 1928, the People's Co-op started up, offering "Marxist milk" for home delivery, low cost gas stations, and the like. The strike also inspired **Joe Zuken**, the longest-serving **Communist** politician in NA. Widely lauded as an honourable defender of the needy and downtrodden – active even through the McCarthyism of the late 1940s and the 1950s, era – Zuken was elected and re-elected to the school board for 20 years, and then as city councillor from 1961 until his retirement in 1983.

The original inhabitants of the North End toiled at low-end jobs, struggling to save enough to get their children educated. They sent their offspring mostly to independent grade schools, and thousands of these youngsters wound up at St. John's on Salter St, the city's oldest high school. Sometimes called "High School of the Stars," this institution celebrated its 75th birthday in 1985 with a gala reunion of more than 4000 at the downtown convention centre. Alumni include a disproportionate number of famous entertainers – **Burton Cummings**, **Monty Hall**, CBC journalist Larry Zolf, and singer Morley Meredith of New York's Metropolitan Opera – as well as scientists, such as nuclear physicist **Louis Alexander Slotin** of the Manhattan Project and **U of M** president **Arnold Naimark**; sports figures like football tight end Norman Hill, also a neurosurgeon at the Mayo Clinic; and other notables, including academic-turned-US-senator Samuel Ichiye "S. I." Hayakawa.

In the early years, the NWC could usually absorb or eliminate its competition and prosper. Competition from **FREE TRADERS** made it clear that an even-more-consolidated organization was required. Therefore, in winter 1783-84, the NWC created a new, enduring partnership principally controlled by Simon McTavish and the Frobisher brothers, Benjamin and Joseph. Despite this, powerful opposition remained. Gregory, McLeod, and Co., mainly backed by John Ross, provided serious competition between 1784-87. When Ross was murdered, Gregory and McLeod made the decision to amalgamate with the Nor'Westers in 1787. This amalgamation brought entrepreneurs like William and Simon McGillivray into the NWC. Angry with Simon McTavish's insistence on promoting relatives instead of more experienced traders, a group of men led by Forsyth, Richardson and Co., created the New Northwest Company or XY Company in 1798 to oppose the NWC. When Simon McTavish died, the 2 groups reconciled and merged in 1804.

Willaim McGillivray led the North West Company during the apex of its operations.

The NWC's main competition continued to come from the HBC. The NWC men, who had a personal stake in the prosperity of the company, proved more-adventurous explorers than their HBC counterparts. For instance, Peter Pond reached Lake Athabasca in 1778; Alexander Mackenzie followed the Mackenzie River to its mouth in 1789, and in 1793, he crossed the Rocky Mountains and reached the Pacific Coast; in 1808, Simon Fraser discovered what became known as the Fraser River; and in 1811, David Thompson explored the Columbia River to its mouth. These discoveries helped the NWC gain

control of nearly 80% of the North American fur trade by 1795, and they stood on the verge of taking over their major competitor. They had become so aggressive that they were even negotiating transit rights through HBC territory and purchasing large quantities of their rival's stock. Any takeover was ruled out, however, when **ANDREW WEDDERBURN COLVILE** and **LORD SELKIRK** assumed leadership of the HBC in 1807.

On June 13, 1811, the HBC granted Lord Selkirk the colony of **ASSINIBOIA**, which included 300,000 km^2 of land surrounding present-day city of **WINNIPEG** (between **LAKE WINNIPEG** and the headwaters of the **RED RIVER**). Selkirk, who held substantial HBC stock and who had many influential friends in England, saw NA as an ideal place to settle dispossessed farmers from the UK. Selkirk had attempted colonies in PE and Upper Canada (now ON), and in 1812 planned to establish an agricultural colony at Red River. The proposed settlement sent shockwaves through the NWC ranks and they were determined to stop the proposed colony from becoming established.

The Red River played a key role in the Nor'Westers' system and the proposed settlement at Red River had the potential to halve the NWC's transportation and provisioning networks. **PEMMICAN** had become vital to the men of the NWC, due to the extended trade of the company, and the **MÉTIS** settlements at Red River specialized in making it. Without pemmican, the NWC men would have had to spend ½ of their travelling time securing food. With the colony, an offshoot of the HBC right in the middle of the NWC operations, the 2 halves of the NWC would not be able to survive. The settlement also angered the Métis, who depended on trade with the NWC and saw agricultural settlements as a direct assault on their way of life. Despite numerous efforts by both the Métis and the NWC men to harass the colonists, the settlement remained. The situation further deteriorated when HBC gov **MILES MACDONELL** issued the **PEMMICAN** Proclamation in 1814, which prohibited the sale of the dried food staple to the traders.

Between 1815 and 1819, there were repeated battles between the men of the 2 companies. Among these was the **SEVEN OAKS INCIDENT**, where Métis leader **CUTHBERT GRANT** was intercepted by Red River gov **ROBERT SEMPLE** on June 19, 1816. An altercation took place and 21 settlers, including Semple, died. The continued hostilities took their toll on the Nor'Westers, impairing their business and getting them involved in numerous costly court battles. Not all NWC partners supported William McGillivray's aggressive measures against the HBC. By 1820, strong forces were moving toward a solution to the conflict. As

both companies lobbied Britain for support, the Colonial Office worked toward a swift settlement to the conflict. In 1821, a deal was finally struck which granted exclusive trade to the HBC and to William McGillivray, **SIMON MCGILLIVRAY**, and Edward Ellice in a coalition designed to placate all parties. A Deed Poll designated 53 field officers – 32 NWC, 21 HBC – as shareholding chief factors and chief traders, under the control of HBC govs William Williams and **GEORGE SIMPSON**.

The resentment of the Métis based on the encroachment of the Europeans at Red River did not disappear easily. Métis discontent continued in the region setting the stage for the **RED RIVER RESISTANCE** and the creation of MB as a province in 1870. • COLIN OAKES

NORTH WEST COMPANY, INC, The. This company is the largest retail chain operating in remote northern communities in Canada and AK, with a network of 181 stores trading under the names Northern, NorthMart, AC Value Centre, Quickstop, and Giant Tiger. It is also one of the world's longest continuing enterprises, tracing its roots back to the **NORTH WEST COMPANY** of 1779, when a group of fur traders formed the company and began developing a network of forts and trading posts across what would later become Canada. During its storied history, the company has undergone several ownership and name changes. In 1821, it merged with its once-bitter **FUR-TRADING** rival and operated for the next 166 years as the Fur Trade Department, and later the Northern Stores Division, of the **HUDSON'S BAY COMPANY**. In 1987, the Northern Stores Division was purchased by a group of investors that included 415 of the division's employees, and 3 years later, the new owners changed the company name back to The North West Company. Headquartered in **WINNIPEG**, the firm had 4552 employees in Canada and 736 in Alaska as of 2004. It is the largest employer of Aboriginal people in Canada outside of the federal govt. • MURRAY MCNEILL

NORTH-WEST MOUNTED POLICE (NWMP; ROYAL NWMP, 1904-1920; RCMP, 1920-present). Canada's national police force was created in 1873 to maintain law and order in the immense area outside the newly formed province of MB designated as the NWTs (1870-1905). PM Sir John A. Macdonald envisioned a force that would combine the mobility of the mounted riflemen that the Union used effectively against the Confederates in the US Civil War with the organizational structure and civil responsibilities of the Royal Irish Constabulary. MacDonald wanted the force to establish friendly relations with **FIRST PEOPLES** and to be the advance guard of

505

Mounted
Constable

Winter
Dress

Walking Out
Dress

Full Dress (officer)

The NWMP had uniforms for different seasons and occasions.

N

settlement. Through imperialistic and authoritarian control, he hoped to avoid the armed conflict associated with expansion that the US had experienced.

An 1873 act and order-in-council provided provisions for the creation of the NWMP with duties to preserve peace, prevent crime, and apprehend criminals. Officers were required to act as court orderlies, jailers, customs officers, and escorts for prisoners. Two officers sitting in court had the powers of a magistrate, an unusual but necessary requirement in the sparsely populated NWTs. Recruits had to speak both English and FRENCH. Service was for 3 years, at the end of which, they received a land grant of 160 ac (65 ha) in the NWTs.

The first recruits arrived at LOWER FORT GARRY in late Oct with no uniforms of their own and few supplies. The force of around 150 men paraded into the fort on Nov 3, 1873, and acting commissioner Lt Col W. Osborne Smith swore the men in, and service in the NWMP officially began. The recruits were divided into divisions and they received quarters from the HUDSON'S BAY COMPANY. The quarters consisted of a barracks to house "B" division, and a 3-storey warehouse in which "A" and "C" divisions lived. Officers were housed in the attic of the company's "Big House," and stables were constructed within the fort. The first patrol left the fort on Dec 10, 1873, to investigate reports of illegal whisky trading on LAKE WINNIPEG, then outside the MB border. Six

days later, the NWMP's permanent commissioner, George Arthur French, arrived at the fort and was appalled at the conditions of the force. He began a rigorous training schedule throughout the winter, ordered more stores and equipment, and pressed the govt for more recruits to bring the force up to 300. As well as training, the men attended dances, skating parties, and even had a rifle contest with the military. The new force wore red-coloured coats because of the long-standing respect that the Aboriginals had for the red-coated British.

On Jun 19, 1874, the force from Fort Garry met new recruits from Toronto at Fort Dufferin, near EMERSON, in what was to be the first and only time in its history that the entire NWMP was gathered in one place. The next night, a violent thunderstorm struck the area, and 250 horses stampeded. On July 8, 1874, the force left on the "March West" destined for the aptly named whisky post "Fort Whoop-Up" (officially Fort Hamilton), near what is now Lethbridge, AB. Twenty-two men were left behind at Dufferin, while 6 remained at Fort Garry.

In 1875, in order to establish more efficient communications between Fort Garry and Ottawa, temporary detachments were opened in MB at Palestine (GLADSTONE), Tanner's Crossing (MINNEDOSA), and Shell River. These posts, however, were all closed within the year. Also in 1875, a detachment was built at SHOAL LAKE. This was the only NWMP detachment in MB 1876-83, except for a training depot opened in Winnipeg in 1883. The Shoal Lake detachment was closed in 1885. That same year, the MB govt requested that NWMP patrols investigate reports of horse rustling. The NWMP acceded after reminding MB that this was a provincial responsibility. Patrols were spread out between MANITOU, Clearwater, Wakopa, DELORAINE, and Sourisford, without finding any cases of horse theft.

In 1888, the NWMP extended their patrols into MB along the 49TH PARALLEL, at the request of the Department of Customs and Interior, with headquarters established at MORDEN. Border detachments in MB were opened until 1894 at Deloraine, BOISSEVAIN, KILLARNEY, Wakopa, Pembina (now in ND; see EMERSON), Manitou, Windygates, Snowflake, CRYSTAL CITY, Clearwater, CARTWRIGHT, and Sourisford (near MELITA). These detachments collected customs duties, wood permits, and issued *laissez-passers* to people crossing the international border. By the early 1900s, detachments were established in northern MB (then the District of Keewatin in the NWT) at CHURCHILL, YORK FACTORY, Split Lake, Port Nelson, and THE PAS.

In 1904, in recognition for its services, King Edward VII added the prefix "Royal" to the title of the NWMP, and they became the Royal North-West Mounted Police. In 1912, MB's boundaries were extended northward, but the RNWMP continued to patrol the area as they had before. In 1916, 18 detachments were opened in southern MB, with headquarters at Emerson and a sub-district headquarters at Boissevain, in order to patrol for pro-GERMAN elements attempting to enter Canada to stir up unrest. In 1918, the RNWMP gave up provincial policing rights in northern MB. From 1919 to 1932, the force's role in MB was to only enforce federal statues. (*See* MANITOBA PROVINCIAL POLICE.)

During the WINNIPEG GENERAL STRIKE of 1919, the city's mayor appealed to the RNWMP to assist in the troubles, as the local police force was sympathetic to the strikers. Thus, 54 mounted police rode into an illegal parade, killing one civilian. The General Strike highlighted the need for a federal police force when local militia or authorities could not be counted upon, and on Feb 1, 1920, the RNWMP joined with the Dominion Police and became the RCMP. Today the RCMP is in charge of policing most parts of rural MB. • ALLAN NEYEDLY

▸ *See also* JUDICIAL SYSTEM, POLICING.

NORTHERN FLOOD AGREEMENT was signed in 1977 between the federal govt, the govt of MB, MANITOBA HYDRO, and the Northern Flood Committee. This committee represented 5 CREE nations in northern MB: NORWAY HOUSE CREE NATION, YORK FACTORY FIRST NATION, Split Lake (now TATASKWEYAK CREE NATION), Nelson House (now NISICHAWAYASIHK CREE NATION), and Cross Lake First Nation (now PIMICIKAMAK CREE NATION). The need for this agreement arose from the rapid pace and dramatic effects of HYDRO-ELECTRIC POWER development in northern MB in the 1960s and '70s.

In 1957, the first hydro project in northern MB commenced at Kelsey on the NELSON RIVER. Shortly thereafter (1960-68), the first export-oriented northern hydro project was undertaken at GRAND RAPIDS, where the Saskatchewan River flows into LAKE WINNIPEG. While this project was still under construction, the provincial govt and Manitoba Hydro decided to proceed with an even-larger integrated plan of northern hydro development. By means of the CHURCHILL RIVER Diversion, 85% of the Churchill's flow was to be blocked at Missi Falls on South Indian Lake, turning that lake into a vast reservoir covering 837 km², the spillover of which would be redirected by a channel into the Rat River/Burntwood system. These rivers would then bring the increased water flow

into the Nelson. It was along the Nelson River that MB's new generation of hydro dams would be built.

Meanwhile, many viewed the relocation of the people of South Indian Lake, and the destruction of local FUR TRAPPING and of the FISHING INDUSTRY – a direct result of lake levels rising 3 m – as an unmitigated disaster. It was clear to the people of the Norway House, York Factory, Split Lake, Nelson House, and Cross Lake First Nations – who knew that their communities would be affected next –that some sort of action had to be taken.

The catalyst for action came in winter 1973-74, when Nelson House was informed that they could expect a 10 m rise in the level of their lake. In April 1974, the leaders of Nelson House convened a meeting with the 4 other Cree nations. At this meeting, held in THOMPSON, the Northern Flood Committee (NFC) was formed. With support from some faith-based organizations, notably the Inter-Church Task Force, this committee spent the next 3 ½ years attempting to work out an agreement with the govt and Manitoba Hydro that would safeguard their interests. However, the NFC was negotiating from a position of weakness, as there was no chance of stopping the planned projects: from the govt's and Manitoba Hydro's perspective, all necessary action to get proper approvals had already been taken. When the final terms of the NFC were released, it did seem that the govt of MB and MB Hydro had made some serious concessions. For example, anyone adversely affected by the projects would be liable for compensation, to be determined by an arbitrator. There was also a provision calling for land exchange at the rate of 4 ac (1.6 ha) of replacement land for every 1 ac (0.4 ha) of reserve land flooded, as well as promises concerning safe supplies of drinking water, and new and improved infrastructure for affected communities. Most promising of all was Schedule E, which dealt with development planning for the 5 communities. Section 2 of this schedule outlined the intention to create development and joint-action programs for the eradication of mass poverty and mass unemployment; and to improve physical, social, and economic conditions as well as transportation.

From the outset, the NFA was controversial. The NDP govt of EDWARD SCHREYER was badly divided over the agreement. Natural Resources Minister SIDNEY GREEN refused to sign it, while the premier was committed to moving forward with the deal. The govt subsequently fell, and the new PROGRESSIVE CONSERVATIVE administration of STERLING LYON signed the agreement in Dec 1977, with the 5 affected communities

ratifying arrangement early in 1978. This, however, was only the beginning of the controversy surrounding the NFA. While some viewed the NFA as a contract aimed at compensating for losses caused by flooding, others interpreted it more broadly, seeing it as a treaty, and therefore having much greater significance in constitutional law. Regardless of any confusion concerning the document's exact legal status, it is clear that most attempts to hold MB Hydro and the provincial govt accountable to the terms of the agreement to the satisfaction of the affected First Nations were fruitless. The Royal Commission on Aboriginal Peoples (1996) and the Inter-Church Inquiry into Northern Hydro Development (2001) both agreed that the implementation of the NFA had been a failure. Instead of an agreement that guaranteed co-operation on a series of vital matters, the NFA had become a vehicle for rancorous disputes, few of which were resolved. By the early 1990s, the Northern Flood Committee had lost faith in the NFA, and its members began negotiating what were originally called comprehensive implementation agreements – referred to as master implementation agreements (MIA) – for each community. These, too, are highly controversial agreements, for while they specify money and other aid awarded to the individual First Nations to a greater extent, they also call for the full extinction of rights under both Treaty 5 and the NFA. Nonetheless, by 2006, all but the Pimicikamak Cree Nation had signed an agreement of this kind. • JIM MOCHORUK

▸ *See also* DRAINAGE, FLOODS, HYDROELECTRIC POWER

NORTHERN LIGHTS. *See* AURORA BOREALIS.

NORTHERN REGION, also called Nor-man, is 1 of 8 administrative and tourist regions of the province. MB's largest region, it encompasses about ¾ of the province's total landmass to the N of PARKLAND, INTERLAKE, and EASTMAN.

The district's terrain varies widely. S of FLIN FLON, an imaginary E-to-W line marks the transition to the Canadian Shield landscapes of the North (*see* PHYSIOGRAPHIC REGIONS). The Precambrian rock also dominates the E side of LAKE WINNIPEG, where boreal forest remains undisturbed by major road construction. In the far N, the Shield gives way to the tundra of the HUDSON BAY Lowlands. In the SW corner is the AGRICULTURAL land of the SASKATCHEWAN RIVER Valley. Tens of thousands of LAKES dot the landscape, with the largest being part of Lake Winnipeg and all of LAKE WINNIPEGOSIS. Powerful rivers – including the NELSON, HAYES, CHURCHILL, and Saskatchewan – cross the territory.

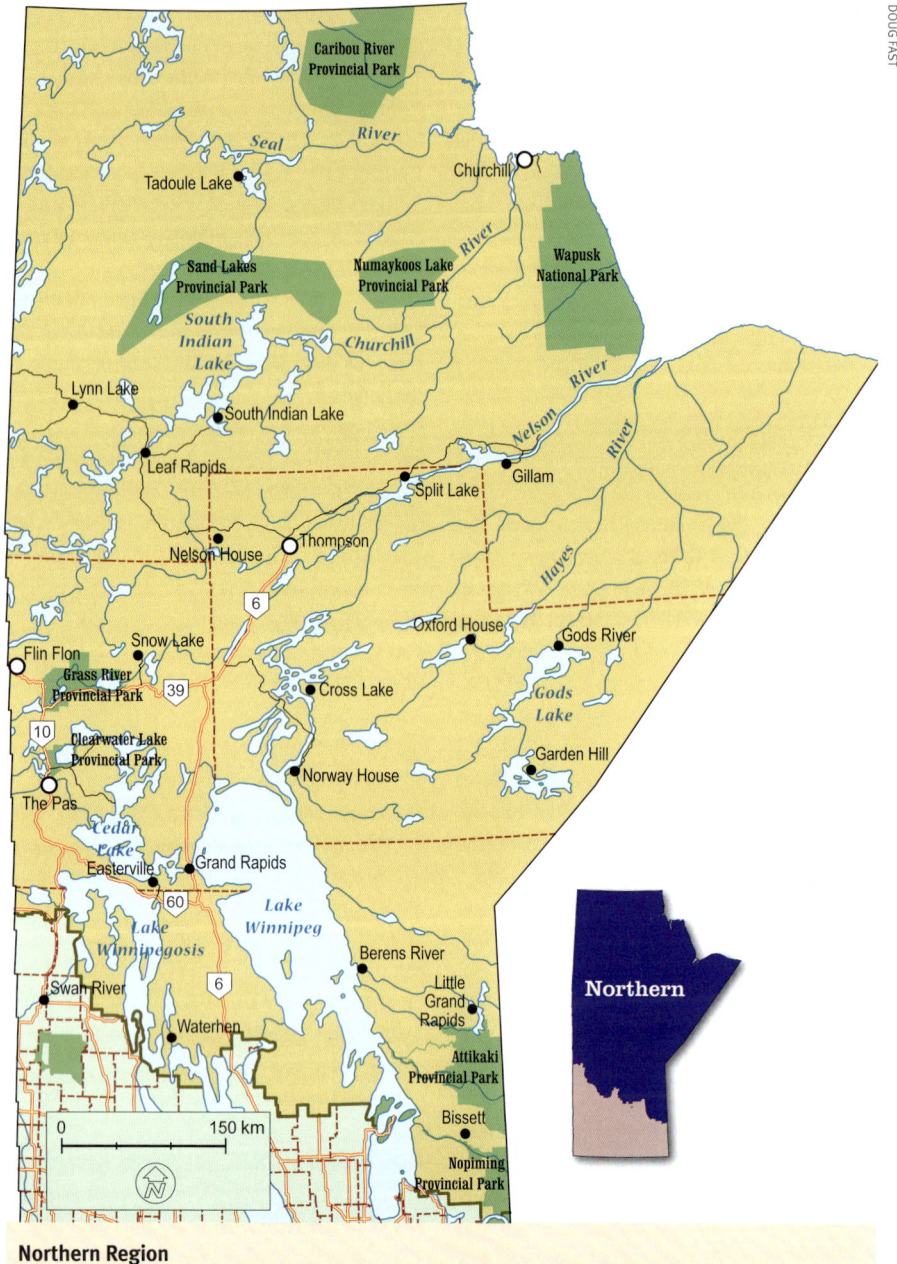

Northern Region

challenges for the area's predominantly Aboriginal populace (*see* **NORTHERN FLOOD AGREEMENT**). Despite these ongoing **MANITOBA HYDRO** developments, a lack of employment is among the region's largest challenges. ● JOEL TRENAMAN

NORTHERN MANITOBA TRAPPER'S FESTIVAL,

held in the 3rd week in Feb in **THE PAS**, celebrates the customs of northern pioneering trappers. One of the oldest festivals in MB, it began in 1916 (with breaks only during WWI and the **GREAT DEPRESSION**). This festival grew out of the desire of those in the **FUR TRADE** to publicize trapping and trading opportunities. The main attraction at this festival is the "World Championship Dog Race," whose winners include **ÉMILE ST. GODARD**, Swanson Highway, and Raymond and Kevin Cook. It begins at the **SASKATCHEWAN RIVER**, runs along the Carrot River, then going through the **CRANBERRY PORTAGE**, **FLIN FLON**, and Cumberland House areas. Until 1976, the race occurred at 3 times, over 3 consecutive days, at 70 km intervals. Beginning in 1976, the distance was extended to 150 km. The winner of the race was determined according to the participants' best race times.

Two prominent festival contests are the Fur Queen beauty contest – which inspired a book by **TOMSON HIGHWAY** – and the King Trapper Contest, which began in 1955. The King Trapper is chosen based on 21 events that reflect historical fur trappers' daily lives, including moose and goose calling, tree felling, wood chopping, canoe packing, axe throwing, muskrat skinning, fish filleting, and trap setting. Other festival activities are the children's shows, arts and crafts show, seniors' activities, the talent show, and a beard-growing contest. ● REBECA KUROPATWA

NORTHLANDS DENE FIRST NATION (pre-

viously known as Lac Brochet First Nation), on reserve pop 796, off reserve pop 139, is located on the N shore of Lac Brochet, about 200 km N of **LYNN LAKE.** This First Nation community signed Treaty 10 in 1906, and its native language is **DENE**. The **SAYISI DENE FIRST NATION** was part of the Northlands Dene. However, the 2 groups spoke different Dene dialects and practised different Christian faiths. In the mid-1950s, the 2 communities were separated through govt land claim settlements. The Northlands Dene First Nation is a "break-away" community itself. In the early 1970s, community strife prompted a large proportion of Brochet First Nation to move N and become the **BARREN LANDS FIRST NATION**. Northlands Dene is a member of the Keewatin Tribal Council. It administers its own education. Schooling in Northlands goes from Nursery-Grade

Most of MB's First Nations communities are in the North, and Aboriginal peoples are the majority. For thousands of years, groups of Swampy **CREE** were found nearly throughout the region, with the **DENE** peoples concentrated in the NW. MB's first European settlers came down the Hayes River from **HUDSON BAY**, including the **LORD SELKIRK**'s group that founded the **RED RIVER SETTLEMENT**.

Unlike the other provincial regions, the sparsely populated North is not made up of a network of adjoining rural municipalities. The sole exception is the RM of Kelsey (named after **HENRY KELSEY**), near **THE PAS**. Aside from incorporated cities, towns, and First Nations reserves, community councils govern local areas under MB's *Northern Affairs Act*. Most of the wilderness

territory is Crown land under the direction of the provincial govt.

MINING once was, and in some cases still is, the driving economic force of settlements at **LYNN LAKE**, **LEAF RAPIDS**, **THOMPSON**, **SNOW LAKE**, and Flin Flon. **TOURISM** is especially important to **CHURCHILL**, with fly-in **SPORT FISHING** and hunting lodges scattered across the region. Other key industries tend to be resource-based, and include **FORESTRY**, **MANUFACTURING**, **FUR TRAPPING**, and **TRANSPORTATION**. **FISHING** (both sport and commercial) is significant economically and culturally. MB's **HYDROELECTRIC** industry employs hundreds across the region, in both dam-building and power-generating capacities; as of 2006, the Nelson River had 5 power dams, the Saskatchewan, one. These dams have reshaped the region's landscape, and presented

12, and total enrolment for the year 2003-04 was 199. There is one reserve located here. Access to the Northlands Dene First Nation community consists of an occasional winter road, boat and float plane-equipped docks, and a runway for air travel. This First Nation's economic foundation is fishing, hunting, and trapping. ● RK

NORWAY HOUSE (pop 456) is a non-treaty community sharing its name with the neighbouring **NORWAY HOUSE CREE NATION**, 450 km N of Winnipeg, on the **NELSON RIVER**. First settled by Norwegian labourers in the early 1800s, it was an important centre in the **HBC FUR TRADE**. Here, furs and goods were gathered and shipped out. In the 21st century, a mayor and council govern the community. The federal govt funds treatment and public health nursing services to the Norway House Cree Nation, while provincial services are provided to residents of the town of Norway House and to First Nations people living off reserve. There is a community fire hall here, federal hospital, 3 community health workers, and ambulance service. A regional service and transportation centre, Norway House's economy is also based on trapping, **FISHING**, and **WILD RICE** harvesting. Activities include **FISHING**, **HUNTING**, boating, **CURLING**, **HOCKEY**, and **BASEBALL**. There is a shopping mall, several restaurants, a bank, and a dental clinic. It is served by 2 small airlines. ● GPP

NORWAY HOUSE CREE NATION, on reserve pop 4822, off reserve pop 1570, is located 450 km N of **WINNIPEG**, at the junction of the **NELSON RIVER** and Playgreen Lake. This Cree Nation received its name from Norwegian labourers recruited to build the **HUDSON'S BAY COMPANY** post here in 1814. Until the 1950s, people residing in the Norway House Cree Nation lived mainly in scattered housing, without electricity, telephone service, or road access. Today, all of these services have been established. Norway House is now one of the largest communities in the North and one of the biggest and most prosperous First Nations in MB. It is closely affiliated with the non-status community of **NORWAY HOUSE**. This Cree Nation signed Treaty 5 in 1875. It has 3 reserves making up nearly 8000 ha. The Norway House Cree Nation has all-weather road access. There is also an airstrip, taxi service, boat and float plane docks, and a summer ferry service.

There is a 16-bed hospital in Norway House, a community health unit, 3 community health workers and a personal care home. The Norway House Cree Nation has its own private radio station. The economic base for this community is **FORESTRY**, **FISHING**, **HUNTING**, trapping, govt services, and commercial businesses. It is an independent First Nation; therefore it is not a member of any Tribal Council. In the summer of 2006, members forced the resignation of the chief and council,

forcing a general election. Education in 3 Norway House schools goes from Grade 3-Grade 12, and enrolment for 2003-2004 was 1410. The Frontier Division administers schooling. Norway House was severely affected by **MANITOBA HYDRO** developments and covered by the **NORTHERN FLOOD AGREEMENT**. Actress and MP **TINA KEEPER** was born in the community. Runner **JOE KEEPER,** a 5000 and 10,000 m Olympian, was also a member of the reserve. The community hosts an annual **YORK BOAT** race that draws contestants from around the province. ● RK

N

NOR'-WESTER was the earliest newspaper to exist in MB, or anywhere else in western Canada. The newspaper was the dream of 2 young Canadians, William Buckingham and **WILLIAM COLDWELL**. The pair departed St. Paul, MN, by ox team for **UPPER FORT GARRY** in the **RED RIVER SETTLEMENT** on Sept 28, 1859. The 2 were experienced journalists whom Toronto *Globe* editor George Brown encouraged to head W to start a newspaper in the isolated settlement, which was then just coming to the attention of Canada. In their wagon, Cunningham and Coldwell carried a Hoe Washington Super-Royal Model press that they had purchased at St. Paul. Less than 5 weeks later, on Nov 1, 1859, they reached Red River, barely ahead of the snow cover. They set up shop in a small building at the corner of Main St and Water in a village that was not yet called Winnipeg. On Dec 7, 1859, the **COUNCIL OF ASSINIBOIA** passed a resolution granting free postage to all newspapers. The young editors brought out the first issue of their newspaper, the *Nor'-Wester*, Dec 28, 1859, to take advantage of outgoing mail heading for Pembina, ND, and eventually St. Paul. Most of the issues of the newspaper Buckingham and Coldwell sent out (via US mail) were addressed to other newspapers in the US and in eastern Canada. Soon, a constant return flow of newspapers was heading to their tiny office, to be used to provide international coverage for the *Nor'-Wester*.

The newspaper would not only help to connect Red River to the world; it would also provide a record of events and an active effort to influence them. Especially in its earlier years, the *Nor'-Wester* sought to be a paper of record for the settlement. Later historians accused the *Nor'-Wester* of writing what most Canadians (as opposed to most Red River residents) wanted to hear. In his 1869 survey of the area, Bishop **ALEX-ANDRE-ANTONIN TACHÉ** described the newspaper as "almost entirely supported by the English-speaking population." The newspaper was purchased and briefly edited by **JOHN CHRISTIAN SCHULTZ**, a contentious and opinionated businessman from Canada, and then Walter Bown, a local dentist.

CHARLES SHILLIDAY

A picturesque island near Norway House

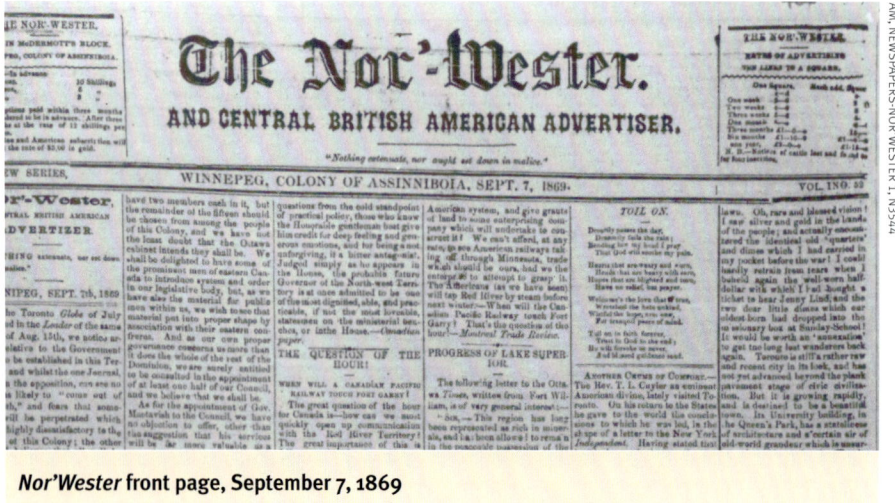

Nor'Wester front page, September 7, 1869

Neither had any journalistic experience: both were partisan Cdn annexationists. **LOUIS RIEL** stopped the publication of the *Nor'Wester* in early Dec 1869, and the life of the oldest Cdn newspaper W of ON was silenced, although their presses were subsequently used for printing proclamations of the provisional govt and temporary newspapers. ● J. M. BUMSTED

NOTRE DAME DE LOURDES, pop 619, is a Franco Manitoban village 110 km ESE of **BRANDON**. **LA VÉRENDRYE** is said to have passed through here in around 1738. A trading post was established soon after. Quebecois settlers began arriving here around the 1880s. The village was named after Notre Dame de Lourdes ("Our Lady of Lourdes"), formerly Lourdes, France, where a 14-year-old peasant girl claimed to see an apparition of the Virgin Mary in 1858. In the 1880s, the **ROMAN CATHOLIC** order of the Canons Regular of the Immaculate Conception, and, later, the Canonesses Regular of the Five Wounds of Our Saviour, ministered to the community's needs. In 1891, settlers from France, Belgium, and Switzerland began arriving here as well, thanks to the efforts of Dom Paul Benoît. The vast majority of the village's population is of **FRENCH** descent, with small populations of **ENGLISH**, **SCOTS**, and **IRISH** origin. The village museum chronicles both the Chanoinesses and the early settlers. The post office opened here in 1892 and the village was incorporated in 1963. Lourdéons remain staunchly French – as evidenced by the local **NEWSPAPER**, *L'Écho de Notre-Dame* – and Catholic. In 1954, the populace set up a grotto, modelled after a work in the village's French namesake, in tribute to their Patron's protection of village youth during the 1946-47 polio **EPIDEMIC**. The bilingual village offers health, education, and community services (Notre Dame's largest employment sectors) in both official languages.

The diverse economy is largely based on various services to surrounding **AGRICULTURAL** operations, and on **TRUCKING**. ● GPP

NYGÅRD, Peter J., clothing designer, tycoon, (b 1943, Finland) is the CEO and chairman of one of the most successful apparel manufacturers in NA, Nygård (International). In 1952, his parents emigrated from Finland to **DELORAINE,** where the family lived in very humble circumstances without electricity or water. They moved to **WINNIPEG** when Nygård was a teenager, and he graduated from Glenlawn Collegiate in 1958. He received his BSc and BA from the U of ND. Nygård worked at the Winnipeg **EATON'S** in the early 1960s and rose to a managerial position. He left Eaton's to buy into an apparel company,

which he took over and renamed Nygård in 1967. The company began as a simple sportswear manufacturer, but has become a multi-million-dollar organization with 200 retail and production centres and 12,000 employees around the world.

Although company headquarters have moved to Toronto, Nygård continues to have close ties with MB. He was a founder of the Manitoba Fashion Institute in 1968 and has remained an executive member since. Nygård contributed $25,000 to the construction of Nygård Park which opened in Deloraine in 2002. He has also acted as president of Canadian Ladies Fashion since 1986. Nygård has been the recipient of numerous awards, including the City of Winnipeg's Community Service Award (1986), the Government of Canada's Commemorative Medal Award (1993), the AIM All Star Award for international excellence in manufacturing (1998), and the Queen Elizabeth II Golden Jubilee Medal (2003). In 2007, he announced plans for a major expansion of retail outlets in both Canada and the US.

Nygård is one of Canada's best-known bachelors, honing an outrageous image of the hedonistic celebrity. He took up permanent residence in the Bahamas in 1975 at a lavish beachside home he designed, complete with a fake mountain, replica Mayan pyramid, and shark pool. Despite his flamboyant lifestyle, he has also taken on charitable causes, most notably breast cancer. He is a sponsor of the Nygård International Molecular Biology Breast Cancer Research Unit and Breast Cancer Tumour Bank in the Manitoba Breast Cancer Research Centre. ● AMANDA STEPHENS

Peter Nygård's portrait is front and centre in a mural on the company's Market Avenue building.

ORCID (YELLOW LADYSLIPPER),
see page 515

O

O-CHI-CHAK-KO-SIPI FIRST NATION (previously known as Crane River First Nation), on reserve pop 512, off reserve pop 339, is situated on the N side of **LAKE MANITOBA**, 364 km NW of **WINNIPEG**. The O-Chi-Chak-Ko-Sipi First Nation's native language is **OJIBWAY**, and it signed Treaty 2 in 1871. It is a member of the West Region Tribal Council. Schooling in this community goes from Nursery-Grade 8, and total enrolment for the year 2003-04 was 126. O-Chi-Chak-Ko-Sipi First Nation administers its own schooling. There is one reserve located here: Crane River IR No. 51. There is all-weather road access available to the O-Chi-Chak-Ko-Sipi First Nation, along with bus and taxi service and a runway. The economic foundation of this First Nation community is bison and elk ranching and commercial fishing. ● RK

O-PIPON-NA-PIWIN CREE NATION, on reserve pop 896, off reserve pop 203, is the newest First Nation community in MB, and its 63rd. It came into existence on Dec 22, 2005. It is 130 km NW of **THOMPSON,** and 750 km NW of **WINNIPEG** at South Indian Lake. Most of the members of the O-Pipon-Na-Piwin Cree Nation (OPCN) were formerly part of the **NISICHAWAYASIHK CREE NATION**. This newly formed Cree Nation was in

negotiations for over a decade to separate from Nisichawayasihk. The people of Nisichawayasihk Cree Nation were generally supportive of the O-Pipon-Na-Piwin Cree Nation's search for independence. Under O-Pipon-Na-Piwin's official status, it received more than 11,000 ha in 20 parcels around Southern Indian Lake. The O-Pipon-Na-Piwin Cree Nation was one of the northern communities most severely affected by **HYDRO** developments. Mercury contamination of Southern Indian Lake had a very severe impact, rendering fish and drinking water poisonous. Many social and health problems like depression, substance abuse, and crime arose. In 2007, the proposal to build the Wuskatim dam and generating station was a contentious issue that loomed over this new First Nation community. ● RK

OAK. MB is the only Prairie province to host the sturdy, long-living oak (Bur Oak: *Quercus macrocarpa Michx*). This magnificent tree, which can live 300 years and rise to a height of 40 m, is found in solitary pockets throughout S MB. It can also grow in conjunction with dominant species like **ASPEN** or **ELM**. Early settlers often encountered stands of bur oak on the MB prairie, which led to a plethora of place names such as **OAK BLUFF**, **OAK LAKE**, **OAKBANK**, etc. The

On the Canadian prairies, the oak is found only in Manitoba.

GREGG SHILLIDAY

bur oak comes in many shapes and sizes but is usually noted for its twisting, gnarled limbs and straight trunk. It has a very hard wood that can be used for flooring and furniture. It also makes excellent firewood. Leaves are alternate, deciduous, broadest at the top, with deep lobes. They are among the most easily recognized of tree leaves. Bark is yellow-brown with deep furrows. Many animals (and some humans) enjoy the autumn acorns dropped by the tree. These tasty fruit/nuts are half-covered by a fringed cup. The bur oak is indigenous to MB but rarely extends farther N than the **INTERLAKE**. • GPP

OAK BLUFF, pop 250, is a community 15 km SW of **WINNIPEG**, near hwys 2 and 3. The first settlers to come to Oak Bluff were mainly of **ENGLISH** and **SCOTS** origin, arriving between 1887 and 1891. The Oak Bluff post office was established in 1890. A **CPR** line opened here in 1901, and with a **GRAIN ELEVATOR**, the community became an **AGRICULTURAL** service centre. Soon after in 1910, American settlers also began arriving in this area. In 1960, the provincial *Metropolitan Winnipeg Act* (*see* **METRO WINNIPEG**) gave control of zoning to Winnipeg. Since 1960, Oak Bluff has seen a tenfold increase in population. The economy remains tied to surrounding farms, but its commuter population has grown considerably. • GPP

OAK HAMMOCK MARSH is a 36 km² Wildlife Management Area 30 km N of **WINNIPEG**, near **STONY MOUNTAIN**. It is a remnant of the former St. Andrews Bog, which extended N from the edge of present-day Winnipeg to **TEULON**, covering approximately 47,000 ha. In 1896, St. Andrews Bog became part of the first **DRAINAGE** district established in western Canada. Through the building of ditches, initially by hand and later by steam- and gas-powered dredges, the bog was converted to farmland, and only 60 ha of the original **WETLANDS** remained.

According to a fanciful explanation for the origin of this large wetland's name, in the early 1870s, settlers from **LOWER FORT GARRY** and **ST. ANDREWS** gathered for community picnics on an oak-covered knoll bordering "The Bog" and relaxed in hammocks; its owner, **SCOTS** settler Adam MacDonald, called the heavily treed knoll "Oak Hammock," and eventually the name was adopted for the whole area when a post office opened. The story that picnickers relaxed in hammocks is unlikely, though they may have done so during severe floods, if they were forced to camp on these drier knolls until the waters receded. A more probable origin for the place name is that it derives from *hummock*, a raised stand of trees.

In the late 1960s and early '70s, the provincial government acquired much of the current marsh from landowners with help from the federal govt. With the assistance of **DUCKS UNLIMITED CANADA**, Manitoba Conservation built earthen dikes to restore a small portion of the original marsh. When construction was complete in spring 1973, the restored marsh and surrounding upland areas were officially designated as the Oak Hammock Marsh Wildlife Management Area (WMA). The WMA is currently 3,581 ha in size with 32 km of dikes. The marsh is divided into 6 units or cells, in which water levels can be managed independently. In 2001, Oak Hammock Marsh was designated as an Important Bird Area (IBA), with global significance for **SHOREBIRDS** and national significance for 2 tern species (*see* **GULLS AND TERNS**), black terns (*Chlidonias niger*) and Forster's terns (*Sterna forsteri*). Along with **DELTA MARSH**, Oak Hammock Marsh is the only wetland in MB that has been designated a "Wetland of International Significance" under the international Ramsar Convention of 1971.

The marsh supports a rich biodiversity, including 300 hundred species of **BIRDS**, and numerous **MAMMALS**, **FISH**, **AMPHIBIANS**, **REPTILES**, and **INVERTEBRATES**. Each fall, upwards of 400,000 **WATERFOWL** use the marsh as a migratory stopover. The WMA has a variety of habitats, including wetland, tall-grass prairie, lure crops, nesting cover, wet meadow, aspen/oak forest, willow bluffs, and creeks (*see also* **ECOCLIMACTIC REGIONS**).

The Oak Hammock Marsh Conservation Centre, which opened in 1992, contains the national headquarters of Ducks Unlimited Canada. The interpretive centre offers programs and exhibits dedicated to increasing public awareness and knowledge of the values of wetland ecosystems throughout NA, and gathering public support for their conservation. • PAULA GRIEEF/ DALE WRUBLESKI/GORDON GOLDSBOROUGH

OAK LAKE, pop 359, is a town 50 km W of **BRANDON**, on the Trans-Canada Highway and a **CPR** line, just S of the **ASSINIBOINE RIVER**. The town's name was taken from a lake by the same name, 15 km SW of the town, formerly the site of an **HBC** post. There was also a **NWC** post in the area. Though this area was home to the **DAKOTA**, and possibly other First Nations, for millennia, **MÉTIS**, attracted

A boardwalk view of Oak Hammock Marsh

STAN MILOSEVIC, WWW.MANITOBAPHOTOS.COM

by the trade in **Bison** robes, lived here early in the 19th century. French-speaking Belgian and Quebecois settlers replaced them later in the century, and subsequent European migrants included **English**, **Irish**, **Scottish**, **Mennonite**, and Polish people. The **Oaks** from which the lake and town take their name made this a popular stopping point for **Red River Cart** treks, as the vehicles often needed repair. In 1881, the CPR main line came through what would become the town, then called Flat Creek. Oak Lake was incorporated as a town in 1907, and is a services and goods provider for surrounding agricultural operations. **Tourism** to the area is also a significant revenue source, and many local 19th-century buildings are protected Heritage Sites. Diplomat and businessman **Maurice Strong** was born here. ● GPP

OAK RIVER, pop 125, is an unincorporated community 50 km NW of Brandon. The hamlet is named after a nearby river. In the early 1880s, a railway survey in the area attracted **English**, **Scots** and **Irish** settlers, but the **CPR** ran its main line to the S through **Brandon**. A branch line was built in 1889 and abandoned in the 1900s. The post office was built in 1879. Today, it is a service and retail centre for local grain and cattle operations, and site of RM of Blanshard offices. **Victoria Cross** winner **Alexander Picton Brereton** and former **Winnipeg Jets** coach John Paddock were born in Oak River. ● GPP

OAKBANK, pop 2075, is an ex-urban community 15 km E of **Winnipeg**. A post office was established here in 1880, when the settlement was known as Sunnyside. After a rail spur was connected to the main **CPR** line in 1906, settlers came from several European countries. In the 2000s, Oakbank has an RCMP detachment and is an agricultural service and retail centre, a bedroom community for Winnipeg, and an educational centre for the surrounding area. Lyncrest Airport houses a locally constructed, early 1930s Pietenpol airplane. Ukrainian residents annually hold a Malanka celebration on New Year's Eve of the Julian calendar. ● GPP

OAKBURN, pop 92, is a community 75 km SSW of **Dauphin** at hwys 45 and 21 and on a **CN** line. The post office opened in 1882, and in 1906, a rail line was built in the area which operated until the late 1990s. It was previously called Oak River after a nearby waterway of this name. **Scots** settlers appear to have renamed the community, as "burn" is Scottish dialect for "creek." **Ukrainian** homesteaders soon followed, though many died in a 1899 scarlet fever **Epidemic**. A monument marks the mass grave site of the victims. The

surrounding Prairie pothole lands are popular with **Waterfowl** hunters and wildlife enthusiasts. Oakbank also attracts tourists because of its proximity to **Riding Mountain National Park** and to numerous Ukranian heritage sites. ● GPP

OBERMAN, Sheldon, author, teacher (b May 20, 1949, **Winnipeg**; d Mar 26, 2004, Winnipeg). Born and brought up in the vibrant ethnic diversity of Winnipeg's **North End**, Oberman attended St. John's High School and then the **U of W**, working in summer as a door-to-door-salesman; in a drug store; as a cinema usher; and as a railway porter. Graduating with a BA, he backpacked in Europe and North Africa, worked in a kibbutz in Israel, and spent a year on scholarship at the U of Jerusalem, then returned home to earn a B.ed.

Sheldon Oberman wrote for both children and adults.

He began a teaching career, first at **Altona**, and then, for 20 years, at Joseph Wolinsky Collegiate in north Winnipeg.

Oberman's writing for both children and adults – which received many honours and was shortlisted for many more – mirrors his responsiveness to many cultures and his interest in the transmission of tradition from generation to generation. *The Always Prayer Shawl* (1994) reflects his Jewish background, as does *The Hanukkah Light* (1997), while *The Wisdom Bird: A Tale of Adam and Sheba* (2000) draws on both African and Jewish legend. *The Shaman's Nephew* (1999) records the stories of **Inuit** tradition, as told to Oberman by one of the last Inuk to use the traditional Northern way of life; the book was shortlisted for the Gov Gen's Award. *Island of the Minotaur* (1999) retells the Cretan myths of ancient Greece, and *The Lion in the Lake* offers an entertaining bilingual French/English alphabet book. Oberman died in Winnipeg, aged 54, of cancer. ● MILDRED GUTKIN

ODJIG, Daphne, artist (b Sept 11, 1919, Wikwemikong Indian Reserve, Manitoulin Island,

Odjig with *The Frog Spirit*, 1968

ON). Influenced by her father and grandfather, the **Métis** painter showed artistic ability at a young age. However, it wasn't until Odjig left the reserve, got married, and moved to BC that she started painting regularly. She relocated to Northern MB with her 2nd husband, Chester Beavon, in the early 1960s, and was inspired by the plight of **Cree** communities displaced from their flooded land.

In 1972, she was part of a **Winnipeg Art Gallery** exhibition that also featured **Jackson Beardy** and Alex Janvier. Following the show the 3 helped found the Professional Native Indian Artists Association, also called the Indian Group of Seven or Woodlands Group of Seven. Odjig was the sole woman in the group. Also in 1972, Odjig and her husband opened a gallery on Donald St in Winnipeg, providing a rare venue for Aboriginal artists. They sold the gallery (which became the Wah-sa Gallery) in 1976 and returned to BC, where Odjig began to plan a mural that she would paint for the Canadian Museum of Civilization (then the Museum of Man) in 1978.

The self-taught Odjig is known for her work on Aboriginal myths, legends, and politics, but her style is also heavily influenced by cubism. In 1986, she was invited to Paris to participate in a Picasso memorial painting with only 3 other artists. That same year, she was appointed to the Order of Canada. She published an autobiography, *A Paintbrush in My Hand*, in 1992, and received a National Aboriginal Achievement Award in 1998. She has been the recipient of a number of honorary doctorates. The Winnipeg Art Gallery exhibited *Daphne Odjig: Four Decades of Prints* in spring 2006. ● JOEL TRENAMAN

OGNIWO POLISH MUSEUM SOCIETY, located on Main St in **Winnipeg**, is the only **Polish** museum in western Canada. Senior Polish community members founded the museum in 1984. Today, younger generations have begun to step forward, taking up a greater role in managing the non-profit museum. The museum offers guided tours and workshops on how to make traditional Polish handicrafts. The museum's rotating collections and exhibits focus on themes related to Polish **Immigration** to Winnipeg and MB from the early 1800s onward. There are artifacts of MB Polish pioneers, exhibits informing visitors about the various provincial Polish organizations, and displays that illustrate, through period clothing, archival photos, and folk arts and crafts, the essence of the Polish community's folklore, customs, and heritage. ● RK

OJIBWAY (also Saulteaux, Anishinabe) constitute a large, numerous, and far-flung Aboriginal nation whose people live throughout southern and central MB, as well as much of ON, southern SK, and several US states. Like other **First Peoples**, they have inhabited this continent for thousands of years, spending much of that time around the Great Lakes. They were traditionally a woodland hunting and gathering people who lived on large and small game, roots and plants, and especially fish, a very plentiful resource until commercial fishing began. The Ojibway speak an Algonquian language with different regional dialects that are mutually comprehensible. The term "Ojibway" comes from their own language and refers to "puckering," apparently a description of their moccasin style. The Ojibway are also known as Anishinabe, meaning "the first people" in their own language, and as Saulteaux, from the French "saulteurs," referring originally to the Ojibway of the rapids at present-day Sault Ste Marie.

Their migration to the area that became MB began in the 2nd half of the 18th century, as Ojibway from around western Lake Superior established villages in the Rainy River region, then around Lake of the Woods, and subsequently in the **Red River** Valley. These lands had more abundant animals than the Ojibway's depleted home territories and would allow them to maintain their pre-eminent place in the **Fur Trade**. The devastating smallpox epidemic of 1780-83 further fuelled the westward movement, as grief-stricken survivors abandoned the places where they had lost so many family members. This migration caused conflict with the eastern **Dakota**, who occupied these territories. There were several decades of warfare that tapered off only as the Dakota moved out onto the plains. By

contrast, the **Cree** and Assiniboine of the Red River Valley welcomed the Ojibway as allies who would strengthen them as they recovered from the horrific depopulation of the smallpox.

The Ojibway who followed **Chief Peguis** signed the first western treaty in 1817 with **Lord Selkirk**, permitting white settlement around the Red and **Assiniboine Rivers** in return for annual tobacco payments. Ojibway were also signatories to Treaties 1, 2, 3, 4, and 5, covering parts of MB. Under these treaties, they received about 30 reserves in the south of the province and around **Lakes Winnipeg** and **Manitoba**. Though they are relative newcomers to the prairies and parkland, the Ojibway are prominent and influential, especially in the cultural and political spheres. They have produced major national leaders such as **Ovide Mercredi** and **Phil Fontaine** and have played a central role in the development of **Winnipeg**'s urban Aboriginal community with its well-established social and political institutions. ● ROBIN JARVIS BROWNLIE

O'KELLY, Christopher Patrick John, **Victoria Cross** winner (b Nov 18, 1895, **Winnipeg**; d 1922, Lac Seul, ON. O'Kelly was a St. John's College undergraduate (*see* **U of M**) when he joined the 144th Batt, CEF, later transferring to the 52nd. Leading a company as an Acting Capt in Passchendaele, Belgium, during fierce fighting over an 18-hour period in Oct 1917, he took 284 prisoners, captured 21 machine guns and 6 pillboxes. He was promoted to Capt and rejoined the Winnipeg Rifles in 1921 with the rank of Maj. While prospecting at Lac Seul, ON, about 50 km NW of Sioux Lookout, his canoe was caught in a storm. His body was never found. His VC is in the Cdn War Museum. ● JIM SHILLIDAY

OLD DUTCH FOODS INC. was founded in St. Paul, MN, in 1934 and expanded into Canada in 1954 with the creation of a new Cdn division, Old Dutch Foods Ltd., based in **Winnipeg**. The US and Cdn divisions operate as separate entities, although both are owned by the Aanenson family of Minneapolis. In addition to its main production facility in Winnipeg, the Cdn operation also has 2 potato chip plants in AB. It also operates an online store to serve customers outside its regular distribution area. Although it started out producing 3 varieties of potato chips – regular, barbeque, and onion and garlic – the company now manufactures 10 different varieties, including the original 3, as well as salt and vinegar, dill pickle, ketchup, cheddar and sour cream, and roasted garlic and cheddar. As of mid-2004, Old Dutch employed a total of about 1000 people in Canada, including about 170 in Winnipeg. ● MM

OPASKWAYAK CREE NATION, on reserve pop 2983, off reserve pop 1948, is situated 620 km NW of **Winnipeg** on hwy 10, near **The Pas**. First Nations people here signed Treaty 5 in 1876. In the 21st century, Opaskwayak Cree Nation is a prosperous and independent-minded First Nation. Its concerted effort to gain greater autonomy in the management of band affairs began in 1968 when the federal dept of Indian Affairs allowed the band to take over a small portion of its financial and administrative services. By 1969, the First Nation had its first welfare administration. Over the years, Opaskwayak assumed the administration of other programs. By the late 1990s, the band employed 800 people during the summer, and 550 during the rest of the year. This community is the 2nd biggest employer in the area, and is an economic leader among MB First Nation communities.

In 1984, this community became the first in Canada to successfully negotiate a gaming license with a province. The resulting Aseneskak Casino, which is a joint venture with the Swampy Cree Tribal Council, and the Kikiwak Inn are key employers in this First Nation. Opaskwayak also has its own ONC Blizzard Junior A Hockey Team, a member of the Manitoba Junior Hockey League. The native language of this community is Cree. It is a member of the Swampy Cree Tribal Council. There are 17 parcels of land under this First Nation's jurisdiction. Education in the Opaswayak Cree Nation, administered by the First Nation's own education authority, goes from Nursery-Grade 12, and total enrolment for 2003-04 was 854. There is an airport located just N of **The Pas**; Grey Goose Bus Lines and VIA Rail provide service N and S, daily. There is an RCMP detachment in The Pas, but Opaswayak employs 6 First Nation constables on reserve. The **Opaskwayak Indian Days** is a festival that takes place here every Aug. **The Pas** Trapper's Festival is hosted both in this First Nation community and in The Pas. **Oscar Lathlin,** a cabinet minister in **Gary Doer**'s **NDP** govt was born and raised in the Opaskwayak community. ● RK

OPASKWAYAK INDIAN DAYS is an annual, weeklong festival that has been held in Aug in **The Pas** for over 40 years. The Opaskwayak Indian Days festival celebrates the traditions of the **Cree** culture and community, and is hosted by the **Opaskwayak Cree Nation**. Festival highlights include the Western Cdn Square Dance Championships, the Miss Opaskwayak Indian Days Pageant, and canoe races ("the Canoe Classic"). Some of the major competitions offer $20,000 or more in prize money. All together, the festival has over 28 activities for visitors to select from. Traditional events, a family fun night, seniors' events, teen dances, the "Tightest Jeans Contest," alcohol-free socials, and the "Tootsie Contest," are just some of the entertainment at hand. Visitors can learn how to perform goose and moose calls. Traditional foods, such as moose stew and bannock, are available for attendees. ● RK

ORCHIDS, NATIVE. MB has 36 native orchid species, with 2 varieties, several hybrids, and many colour forms. Canada has only 64 species. Orchids are among our most beautiful wildflowers. While many people know the large showy and yellow lady's slippers, or perhaps the endangered small white lady's slipper or western prairie fringed-orchid, there are many lovely smaller species. They range in size from the large pink-and-white-flowered showy lady's slipper, near one m tall, to the tiny greenish twayblades and adder's-mouths often under 10 cm tall. Flower colours range from bright pinks and yellows through white to inconspicuous greens and browns. Some kind of orchid grows everywhere in MB but they are most common and abundant in bogs and moist areas in the SE. Their blooming season is from late May through Sept with most blooming in June or July. Orchids have very specialized and intricate flowers and are considered among the most highly evolved plants. Their flowers are designed to attract insect pollinators, and only one or a few closely

ROBERT R. TAYLOR

The Venus Ladyslipper is one variety of native orchid.

Native Orchids of Manitoba

ORCHID SPECIES NAME AND STATUS	ORCHID COMMON NAME	HABITAT
Amerorchis rotundifolia [common]	small round-leaved orchid	bogs, wet tundra
Arethusa bulbosa [rare]	dragon's-mouth	bogs, fens
Calopogon tuberosus [rare]	grass-pink	bogs, fens
Calypso bulbosa [uncommon]	fairy-slipper	coniferous forest
Coeloglossum viride [common]	long-bracted orchid, frog orchid	prairies, mixed forest
Corallorhiza maculata var. maculata [rare]	spotted coral-root	mixed to dry forest
Corallorhiza maculata var. occidentalis [common]	western spotted coral-root	mixed to dry forest
Corallorhiza striata [uncommon]	striped coral-root	moist forest
Corallorhiza trifida [common]	early coral-root	moist forest to tundra
Cypripedium acaule [uncommon]	moccasin-flower	pine forest, rocks, bogs
Cypripedium arietinum [rare]	ram's-head lady's slipper	conifer forest, bogs
*Cypripedium candidum [endangered]	small white lady's slipper	prairie, ditches
Cypripedium parviflorum var. makasin [common]	northern small yellow lady's slipper	prairie, forest, bogs
Cypripedium parviflorum var. pubescens [common]	large yellow lady's slipper	prairie, forest, bogs
Cypripedium passerinum [uncommon]	sparrow's-egg lady's slipper	moist gravel or sand
Cypripedium reginae [uncommon]	showy lady's slipper	forest, bogs, fens
Goodyera repens [common]	lesser rattlesnake-orchid	conifer forest, bogs
Goodyera tesselata [common]	checkered rattlesnake-orchid	conifer forest
Liparis loeselii [uncommon]	Loesel's twayblade	fens, ditches, ands other moist places
Listera borealis [very rare]	northern twayblade	conifer forest
Listera cordata [uncommon]	heart-leaved twayblade	conifer forest, bogs
Malaxis monophyllos [rare]	white adder's-mouth	conifer forest, bogs
Malaxis paludosa [very rare]	bog adder's-mouth	conifer forest, bogs
Malaxis unifolia [rare]	green adder's-mouth	conifer forest, bogs
Platanthera aquilonis [common]	northern green bog-orchid	moist forest, wet areas
Platanthera dilatata [uncommon]	white bog-orchid	fens
Platanthera hookeri [rare]	Hooker's rein-orchid	dry conifer forest
Platanthera huronensis [common]	tall green bog-orchid	widespread
Platanthera lacera [very rare]	ragged fringed-orchid	conifer bogs
Platanthera obtusata [common]	blunt-leaved rein-orchid	moist forest and tundra
Platanthera orbiculata [uncommon]	round-leaved rein-orchid	moist conifer forest
*Platanthera praeclara [endangered]	western prairie fringed-orchid	tall-grass prairie
Platanthera psycodes [very rare]	small purple fringed-orchid	moist deciduous forest
Pogonia ophioglossoides [rare]	rose pogonia	fens, disturbed areas
Spiranthes lacera [uncommon]	slender ladies'-tresses	dry forests and rock
*Spiranthes magnicamporum [endangered]	Great Plains ladies'-tresses	tall-grass prairie
Spiranthes romanzoffiana [common]	hooded ladies'-tresses	open and disturbed sites

* listed as Endangered by MB and/or Canada

related insects usually pollinate each species. These range from **Mosquitoes** and fungus gnats (for the tiny twayblades and adder's-mouths) to large bumblebees (*see* **Bees**) and night-flying **Moths** for the lady's slippers and western prairie fringed orchid. Orchid seeds are the smallest known and contain no food supply. They are produced in the thousands and millions and can be carried by wind to sites far from the parent plants. They depend on "hooking up" with an underground fungus for their germination and survival. This is why they are so hard to grow and transplant, as the fungus requires specific soil conditions to prosper. Orchids should never be picked or transplanted for this reason, because many of them are rare and some endangered, and because some, such as lady's slippers, can cause skin irritation. ● KAREN JOHNSON

ORDER OF MANITOBA (OM) is the highest provincial honour that can be bestowed on an individual who is or was a long-time MB resident. Established under lt gov Peter Liba in 1999, the Order "recognizes individuals who have demonstrated excellence and achievement in any field of endeavour, benefiting in an outstanding manner the social, cultural or economic well being of Manitoba and its residents." Like other provincial orders, the OM was incorporated into the Order of Precedence for Canadian Orders, Declarations and Medals through order-in-council, and is approved by the gov gen. Outstanding Manitobans were once recognized with the Order of the Buffalo Hunt, established in 1957, at the discretion of the premier. Since the establishment of the OM, the Order of the Buffalo Hunt has been primarily awarded to Manitobans who have achieved success outside the province.

With the exception of the inaugural year's 20 recipients, a maximum of 12 OMs are granted each year. Nominations are made to the secretary of the Order of Manitoba Advisory Council. Any Manitoban with Cdn citizenship can be nominated, with the exception of federal and provincial politicians still in office, and judges serving in any court. The OM is not given posthumously or to groups or organizations.

The appointment is selected by a council of 7 individuals, including the Chief Justice of Manitoba (or the Chief Justice of the Court of Queen's Bench), the clerk of the executive council, and the president of the **U of M**, **U of W**, or **Brandon U**. The 4 remaining members are appointed to a 3-year term by the lt gov, one of whom serves as chairperson. After reviewing all nominations, the council makes recommendations to the lt gov, who is Chancellor of the Order. The appts are announced each year on or around May 12, the

date that the *Manitoba Act* was passed in 1870. The installation ceremony is held on or close to July 15, the day that MB entered Confederation. Members are presented with a medal that resembles a **Crocus**, bearing the shield of MB's coat of arms set underneath the Crown. Members use the post-nominal OM after their name. ● MD

ORLIKOW, David, politician (b April 20, 1919, **Winnipeg**; d Jan 19, 1998, Winnipeg). Raised in the **North End**, he was educated at the Workman's Circle School, St. John's High School, and the **U of M**, where he studied pharmacy. He was elected a school trustee in 1945, beginning an unbroken 43-year political run that graduated to Winnipeg City Council, then the **Legislature**, and finally Parliament. In the process, he won 18 consecutive elections, including 9 to the House of Commons, where he sat as an **NDP** champion from 1962 until his defeat in 1988. He described himself as a "right-wing Social Democrat" and had little patience with the doctrinaire wing of the NDP. ● JMB

ORTHODOX CHRISTIANS, who follow the Byzantine rite, in differentiation to **Roman Catholics**, began arriving in MB in the late 19th century. At the 2001 Census, there were 15,645 in the province. At the start, they were identified by their ethnic origin: Bukovynians, **Ukrainians**, Russians, Greeks, Romanians, and Serbians. More-recent immigrants have been of Egyptian (Coptic) and Ethiopian origin. Through marriage and conversion over the past few decades, other ethnic backgrounds are now represented. Nevertheless, most Orthodox jurisdictions in Canada continue to maintain their ethnic origins in their titles. The first jurisdiction to delete the ethnic designation in order to become fully North American was the Russian Orthodox Church; it was proclaimed self-governing and became the Orthodox Church in America/Archdiocese of Canada in 1970.

Original Russian Orthodox Christians in MB included people of several ethnic backgrounds: Bukovynian, Ukrainians, Russians, and Belarusians. The Bukovynians came first, settling in the Stuartburn area (30 km E of **Dominion City**) in 1896, and building the province's 1st Orthodox church a year later – St. Michael's in Gardenton. Priests of the Russian Orthodox Mission of America served this church, which now an historic site. The first Orthodox church in **Winnipeg** was Holy Trinity Sobor, on Manitoba Ave. Bishop Tikhon, the future Patriarch of Moscow and now a saint, consecrated it in 1904. From 1908 to 1910, the Russian Orthodox Mission in Canada was administered by Archimandrite Arseny

Holy Ghost Ukrainian Greek Orthodox Church, Tolstoi MB, 1977

Chakhovtsov. He became bishop of the diocese 1926-36, and his missionary efforts resulted in his becoming the first Cdn Orthodox saint. St. Arseny Orthodox Christian Theological Institute continues his work.

Greek Orthodox Christians arrived in MB in 1898. By 1912, they had formed an association called "Annunciation," and shortly thereafter purchased a Winnipeg house to serve as church, school, and social hall. Under the leadership of Father Anthony Mavromaras, a church on Westminster and Furby, purchased in 1955, was supplanted by the present St. Demetrios Church, at the corner of Shaftesbury and Grant. The 5 Romanian Orthodox churches in MB trace their origins back to 1901, when 4 families emigrated to Lennard, a small community 25 km N of **Russell**. Two years later, they built a sod church named St. Elijah, after the farmer who donated the property, Elie Burla. It was replaced in 1908, and again in 1952, by more-permanent structures. Unique among Romanian Orthodox churches is St. George's in Winnipeg, the first to offer services in English. Serbs came to **Flin Flon** in 1912 to work the mines, and then to Winnipeg 16 years later. With the increasing numbers of immigrants beginning after WWII, they eventually formed a parish of their own in 1972.

In 1918, former Ukrainian Greek Catholics left that church and formed what is now the Ukrainian Orthodox Church of Canada, headquartered in Winnipeg. Over the years, immigrants from Bukovynia and Ukraine have swelled their numbers, and several parishes have been established throughout the province, the most important being the Holy Trinity Cathedral of Winnipeg. From 1951 to 1972, the ruling bishop was His Beatitude Metropolitan Ilarion, who translated the Bible into Ukrainian. During his time,

St. Andrew's College was constructed on the **U of M** campus. It now houses a Faculty of Theology and the Centre for Ukrainian Canadian Studies.

African immigration increased in the 1970s and 1980s, with Coptic Orthodox Christians establishing their present home at St. Mark's Church in 2005, and Ethiopian Orthodox Christians establishing a parish on Mountain Ave in Winnipeg in 2000. Their parish priest also provides services for a mission parish in **Brandon**. • MIRONE KLYSH

OSBORN, John Robert, Victoria Cross winner, (b Jan 2, 1899, Norfolk, UK; d Dec 19, 1941, Hong Kong). Osborn served with the Royal Navy Volunteer Reserve in WWI. He subsequently moved to Canada, farmed in SK, then worked for the **CPR** in **Winnipeg**. Osborn joined the **Winnipeg Grenadiers** in 1933. He was called to active service in Sept 1939 as a company SgtMaj in the 1st Batt. Osborn was serving in Hong Kong when the Japanese invaded in 1941. On Dec 19, he and his company were engaged in hand-to-hand combat with the enemy, who lobbed hand grenades into their position on Mt Butler. Osborn kept picking them up and throwing them back, until he realized one would explode before he could return it. He shouted "Duck, lads!" and threw himself on top of the grenade, dying in the explosion. His VC – the 1st awarded to a Cdn in WWII and the only VC connected to the Battle of Hong Kong – is in the Cdn War Museum in Ottawa, and a statue commemorates his actions in Hong Kong Park. • JIM SHILLIDAY

OSBORNE, Helen Betty, murder victim (b July 16, 1952, **Norway House**; d Nov 12, 1971, **The Pas**). Her tragic death brought about MB's **Aboriginal Justice Inquiry**. Born to **Cree** parents,

Helen Betty Osborne

she was locally educated before being sent to the residential school Margaret Barbour Collegiate in The Pas in 1969. On Nov 12, 1971, 4 males in a car abducted her. She was subsequently sexually assaulted, beaten, and stabbed many times with a screwdriver. Although the identity of her killers was known to many people in The Pas, no arrests were made until 1986. The trial of 2 accused men took place in 1987, and 2 others were granted immunity in return for their testimony – with national media following it closely. Only one of the accused, Dwayne Johnston, was convicted. This case, along with the shooting of **J. J. Harper**, prompted the MB govt in 1988 to begin an inquiry into the treatment of Aboriginal people under the province's criminal justice system. • JMB

OSTENSO, Martha, author (b Sept 17, 1900, Haukeland, Bergen, Norway; d Nov 24, 1963, Seattle). The Ostenso family emigrated to NA in 1902, living in MN and ND before moving to **Brandon** in 1915 and to **Winnipeg** in 1917. Ostenso taught in a rural school in MB for a year, then studied English at the U of M. In 1922, she followed her English professor, **Douglas Leader Durkin**, to New York, where and the 2 lived together, marrying in 1943 after the death of Durkin's first wife, who had refused him a divorce. After attending Columbia U, Ostenso returned briefly to Winnipeg in 1923-24, and published with a NY publisher an enthusiastically hailed first novel, *Wild Geese*, in 1925. Of 15 subsequent novels, most of them based on MB farm life, the most successful was the 1943 Literary Guild Award winner, *O River, Remember*. Recent feminist criticism has paid attention to the depiction of women in these novels as strong and sexual beings. However, there have been some reservations as to their authorship. While all the novels were published under the name of Martha Ostenso, they appear, from copyright information and other evidence, to have been a collaborative effort with Durkin, also a novelist.

Nevertheless, *Wild Geese*, set in rural MB and based on Ostenso's own year of teaching, is considered a significant landmark in the development of the school of "Prairie realism," similar to the works of **Sinclair Ross** and **Frederick Philip Grove**. Breaking with the traditional romanticism that portrayed life in the Cdn West as the heroic triumph of human courage over the challenges of nature, the male protagonist, in the novel's own words, is "as harsh, as demanding, as tyrannical as the very soil from which he drew his existence," and his obsession with land ends in his own destruction.

Ostenso and Durkin later spent some time writing scripts in Hollywood where they were

friends with stars like Douglas Fairbanks and Mary Pickford. They then moved to the Minnesota cottage country around Brainerd. Ostenso died in 1963 of cirrhosis of the liver. • MILDRED GUTKIN

OSTRY, Bernard Abraham "Bernie," civil servant, administrator (b June 10, 1927, Wadena, SK; d May 24, 2006, Toronto), was the chair and CEO of TVOntario, ON's public broadcaster. Ostry was born in Wadena, 185 km E of Saskatoon, and grew up in **Flin Flon** until he was sent to **Winnipeg** to attend Hebrew school. The family later settled in Winnipeg's **North End**, a block away from **Sylvia Ostry** (née Knelman), Ostry's future wife. Ostry received his BA from the **U of M**, and did graduate work in international history at the London School of Economics (LSE). While in England, he became an unpaid aide of Krishna Menon, then India's High Commissioner to the UK. Ostry helped Menon draft the 10-point peace plan that eventually ended the Korean War. Ostry also co-authored *The Age of Mackenzie King: The Rise of the Leader* (1955).

While in England, Ostry was reunited with Knelman; they married in 1956. After teaching at the LSE, Ostry moved to Ottawa in the 1960s and began his career in broadcasting at the CBC and in the public service, hosting the show *Nightline*. He worked in numerous ministries and departments at a senior level throughout the 1970s. Following a brief stint in Paris, he returned to ON, becoming the province's Deputy Minister of Industry and Trade. He served in provincial govt throughout the early 1980s, before he was appointed chair and CEO of TVOntario in 1985. Ostry remained with the broadcaster until late 1991, when a provincial auditor's report detailed questionable expense claims, whereupon he resigned. Ostry received honorary doctorates from the U of M, the U of Waterloo, and York U. He was awarded a Commemorative Medal for the 125th Anniversary of Confederation (1992), and was elevated shortly before his death from Officer of the Order of Canada (1988) to Companion. • AMANDA STEPHENS

OSTRY, Sylvia, economist, public servant (b June 3, 1927, **Winnipeg**), became the first woman deputy minister in the Cdn govt in 1975. Ostry, born Sylvia Knelman, was raised in a **Jewish** community in Winnipeg's **North End**. After attending public schools, Ostry studied medicine at the U of M before switching to McGill U, where she completed a MA (1950), followed by a doctorate from the U of Cambridge and McGill U (1954). While in the UK, she married **Bernard Ostry**, whom she had met at school in Winnipeg. They had 2 sons, Adam and Jonathan.

Ostry began her career as a lecturer and assistant professor before becoming Canada's chief statistician in 1972. She thereupon held numerous positions in the federal govt, including Deputy Minister of International Trade, and acted as Canada's ambassador for Multilateral Trade Negotiations and the PM's personal representative for the G7 Economic Summit (1985-88). Ostry has also acted as head of the Economics and Statistics Department of the Organisation for Economic Co-operation and Development in Paris and as the chairwoman of the U of Toronto's Centre for International Studies. In 1987, she was the recipient of the federal govt's Public Service Outstanding Achievement Award. In 1990, Ostry was named a Companion of the Order of Canada; the following year, she was named a Fellow of the Royal Society of Canada. Ostry has received 18 honorary doctorates from across Canada, and has more than 80 publications to her credit. Since 1997, Ostry has acted as the Distinguished Research Fellow at the U of Toronto's Munk Centre for International Studies. ● AMANDA STEPHENS

OTTER, RIVER (*Lutra canadensis*) is an aquatic member of the weasel family Mustelidae, order Carnivora, and is characterized by a sleek, streamlined body, a thick, muscular tail, remarkably high level of activity year-round, and a seemingly playful nature. The otter formerly inhabited most MB waterways, from grassland and forests to the edge of the barren-ground tundra. Susceptible to over-trapping, water pollution and disturbance, it is now absent from agricultural and developed areas. With a ravenous appetite, the otter pursues even the fastest fish, and frogs, snails, clams and other underwater life, as well as mice, chipmunks and snakes on land. Generally solitary, an otter patrols a large home range, sometimes travelling 100 km, and easily covering

15 km in a day. Paddling with all 4 legs, its supple body is propelled, seal-like, through the water at speeds up to 12 km/h. It may also swim upside down or in a spiral. The animal's curiosity is endless, as it investigates any unusual object, or plays with a pebble or floating stick for many minutes. They communicate with each other with whistles, chirps, snorts and chuckles, both above and under the water. Females become sexually mature at 3 years, but males are usually unable to compete for a female until 5 years old. The mating season in MB occurs from March to May, but the 1-6 embryos cease developing until early the following spring, and then grow over an additional 50 days until birth – a full year after conception. The father is driven away until the young are 6 months of age. Few wild otters survive 14 years, but captives can reach up to 23 years. ● REW

OWLS (family Strigidae) have forward-facing eyes, which give them a "wise" look. Besides their excellent binocular vision, they have superb hearing. Many species hunt almost exclusively by sound, and can find their prey under a blanket of snow or in the deep of night. Eleven species of typical owls occur in MB (The barn owl, *Tyto alba*, belongs to a different family). Of these, the Burrowing Owl, or "ground owl" (*Athene cunicu-*

laria), has been almost extirpated. Pesticides (see **POLLUTION**) and habitat loss have resulted in its current endangered status. Widespread is the Great Horned Owl (*Bubo virginianus*), a fierce predator that may take prey as large as a whitetail jackrabbit (*Lepus townsendi*). Of similar size is the Snowy Owl (*Nyctea scandiaca*), which is frequently seen perched on hay bales or utility poles in winter. Three species of particular interest to birders visiting from elsewhere are the boreal owl (*Aegolius funereus*), the northern hawk owl (*Surnia ulula*), and the **GREAT GREY OWL** (*Strix nebulosa*). The latter is MB's Provincial Bird Emblem. ● RUDOLF KOES

OYE, Mamoru "Moe," judo master, coach (b April 1, 1937, Ucluelet, BC) is MB's only 8th-degree black belt in judo. The **JAPANESE** Cdn learned judo from Tamotsu Mutani, who taught at the RCMP barracks in the late 1940s. Oye represented the province at the first Cdn Judo Championships held in MB in 1959, and was hired by the following year as a judo instructor at the **U OF M**. He has trained more than 60 black-belt students in MB, among them 3 Olympians. Oye was inducted into the Judo Canada Hall of Fame in 1996 and the Manitoba Sports Hall of Fame in 2000. ● MD

River Otter

Saw Whet Owl in nest

PRAIRIE CROCUS,
see page 553

P

PAGTAKHAN, Dr. Rey D., politician, physician (b Jan 7, 1935 Manila, Philippines). Before Pagtakhan immigrated to Canada in 1968, he received his Doctor of Medicine from the U of Philippines. He completed his residency and fellowship at the Washington University Medical Centre/St. Louis Children's Hospital and his Master of Science from the **U of M**. Lecturer for the medical faculty at the **U of M** starting in 1971, he became a full professor of pediatrics and child health in 1985. From 1971-1988, he worked as a pediatric respirologist at the Winnipeg Children's Hospital and served as director of the Manitoba Cystic Fibrosis Centre and president of the Manitoba Pediatric Society. In 1986, he was elected as a **Winnipeg** school trustee and served for 2 years. Pagtakhan successfully ran for the **Liberal Party** in the riding of Winnipeg North in the 1988 and 1993 federal elections, becoming the first Filipino-born Canadian to be elected to the House of Commons. Returned in 1997 in the redistributed riding of Winnipeg North-St. Paul, he served as parliamentary secretary to PM Jean Chretien.

After the federal election of 2000, Pagtakhan was appointed to cabinet and served as secretary of state (Asia-Pacific) until 2002. He was named to the post of minister of veteran affairs and senior minister for MB in 2002 and served on the cabinet committees on economic union, social union and govt communications and was chair of the standing committee on citizenship and immigration and on human rights and the status of persons with disabilities as well as the western and northern federal Liberal caucus. As senior minister for MB, he brought about funding for the expansion of the **Red River Floodway** and the proposed Canadian Museum for Human Rights. In 2002-2003, he acted as secretary of state (science, research and development). PM Paul Martin appointed Pagtakhan minister of western economic diversification in Dec 2003 and in this capacity he served on the cabinet committees of domestic affairs and Aboriginal affairs. While in this position he announced funding for the Winnipeg based International Centre for Infectious Diseases. When he lost in the 2004 general election to New Democrat **Judy Wasylycia-Leis**, he returned to private life and his medical practice and went on to be director of the Global College at the **U of W**. ● RUTH DEGRAVES

PALEO PERIOD. In the history of MB, the Paleo, or Paleoindian, Period is considered to be the earliest era of human activity. It coincided with the final recession of the Laurentide glacier and the growth and demise of meltwater lakes that had formed along the edge of the ice sheet, all of which governed the progress of human colonization of the regional landscape (*see* **GLACIATION**). By 9200 BC, small bands of early First Nations, identified by archaeologists as "Clovis" hunter-gatherers based on the distinctive style of their spear points, were making inroads into what is now the extreme SW of MB. The environment consisted of a mosaic of shrub tundra and **SPRUCE**-dominated forest/woodland capable of supporting such big game species as muskox (*Ovibos moschatus*) and **CARIBOU** (*Rangifer* spp.), as well as the now-extinct **MAMMOTH** (Mammuthus primigenius), western **BISON** (*Bison occidentalis*) and elk-moose (*Cervalces scotti*). These Clovis people adapted to, and expanded their territories in lockstep with, the recession of the ice front as far N as **DUCK MOUNTAIN**. However, high water levels during the Lockhart Phase of **LAKE AGASSIZ** prevented their eastward movement beyond the **MANITOBA ESCARPMENT**.

Between 9000 BC and 8000 BC, Aboriginal groups known by their "Folsom," "Midland," and "Goshen" points moved into western MB. This ongoing inmigration from the S and W was accelerated after 8000 BC, when grassland and deciduous parkland quickly replaced the open spruce forest, and *Bison occidentalis* became the predominant big-game animal species across the region. New generations of Plains-adapted ("Plano") peoples – identifiable by the diagnostic "Agate Basin," "Hell Gap," "Alberta," "Scottsbluff," and "Eden" styles of projectile points and the distinctive "Cody" knife – expanded their hunting territories to include southwestern MB. Their southern origins are indicated by their extensive use of Knife River Flint from western ND. This material was replaced by the abundant and locally available **SWAN RIVER** Chert once they had familiarized themselves with the MB countryside and its resources. The low-lying terrain E of the escarpment, meanwhile, was flooded by the Emerson Phase meltwaters of Lake Agassiz, and was therefore uninhabitable.

The gradual "retreat" of the glacier continued across the northern half of the province between 7500 BC and 5500 BC. Lake Agassiz underwent its final recession, and drought conditions became ever more pronounced on the high plains to the south. These factors encouraged and/or facilitated the occupation of the Manitoba Lowlands and adjacent Canadian Shield (*see* **PHYSIOGRAPHIC REGIONS**) during this 2000-year interval. Archaeologists identify people making inroads into southern MB at the time by "AgateBasin-like," "Angostura," "Frederick," and "Manitoba" point types, the latter showing signs of incipient side-notching whereby the point was

firmly secured to the end of the wooden shaft. The precise parallel-horizontal flaking patterns manifested on Scottsbluff and Eden points gave way to the delicate parallel-oblique ("ribbon") finish of the Angostura and Frederick forms. In southeastern MB, the generalized lanceolate points and trihedral adzes of the "Caribou Lake Complex" reflect a continuing big game **HUNTING** tradition within a partially forested boreal landscape.

Paleo Period dart points

Late Plano peoples, whose forebears had long been oriented toward prairie and parkland environments, penetrated the Shield country of northwestern MB via the well-drained end moraines, eskers and fossil Agassiz beaches. Their occupation of the boreal woodland ecozone with its resident populations of caribou, **MOOSE** (*Alces alces*), bison and a wide range of smaller game is expressed in the occasional discovery of "Northern Plano" projectile points within the **CHURCHILL RIVER** drainage basin. • LEO F. PETTIPAS

▸ *See also* **ARCHAEOLOGY, ARCHAIC PERIOD, GEOLOGY, WOODLAND PERIOD.**

PALEY, Ron, musician, composer, recording artist (b Nov 20 1950, **WINNIPEG**). Paley is one of MB's most respected and busiest musicians. Paley graduated from the **U OF M**'s Faculty of Music in 1972 followed by a year at the prestigious Berklee School of Music in Massachusetts. His studies there were interrupted by an offer to tour with the Buddy Rich Big Band on bass, followed by a stint touring and recording with Woody Herman's Big Band. With Herman, Paley recorded 3 albums, one backing Frank Sinatra. In 1975, he returned to Winnipeg performing in clubs and concerts fronting ensembles and big bands including the nationally renowned Ron Paley Big Band as well as doing studio work and arranging, appearing on hundreds of sessions. From 1976 to '86 he served as director of the U of M stage band and performed at Expo 86. Paley was music director for CBC TVs *Jerry and Ziz* in 1979 and CKND's *Friday Night Live* in 1987. He has recorded 3 albums: 1977's Juno award-

nominated *Boxton*, *Ron Paley Big Band Jazz Rocks & Swings* in 1986, and *The Big Band Dance Album* in 1987. Paley has had over 25 of his big band and symphony compositions published and has worked with the **WINNIPEG SYMPHONY ORCHESTRA**. • JOHN EINARSON

PALLISER FURNITURE LTD is Canada's largest household furniture manufacturing company. Palliser can trace its beginnings to 1944, when founder A. A. DeFehr launched a 2-person operation out of his **WINNIPEG** home. Called A. A. Manufacturing Ltd, the company started out producing wooden ladders, stepping stools, and ironing boards at the rate of about 3 items per day. Its first factory was a converted chicken coop that DeFehr rented for $12 a month, but by the time he retired in the late 1970s, the family business had mushroomed to 4 production plants producing about 1000 pieces of furniture a day. The company changed its name to Palliser Furniture in 1980, when the family decided to amalgamate its 2 Winnipeg operations – A. A. DeFehr Manufacturing and Comfort Furniture – together with its 2 Alberta companies – Towne Hall Furniture and Rocky View Industries – to create one giant company. By the time the company celebrated its 60th year in business in 2004, it was operating production plants in 4 different countries; had a chain of 195 retail stores and store-within-a-store galleries operating under the name EQ3 in Canada and the US; and boasted more than 4200 employees and nearly $500 million in annual sales. Employment at its Winnipeg factories reached its peak in 2002 at more than 3800. By early 2005, it had declined to about 2800 because of technological changes within its manufacturing operations and the transfer of some production work to its factory in Mexico. The company remains privately owned, with the founder's son, **ARTHUR DEFEHR**, serving as its president and chief executive officer. • MURRAY MCNEILL

PALLISTER, Brian William, politician (b July 6, 1954 **PORTAGE LA PRAIRIE**). Pallister earned his university degree at Brandon U in arts and education. A member of the **PROGRESSIVE CONSERVATIVE** party, he served from 1992-1997 in the MB legislature, representing the riding of Portage la Prairie. He was the minister of govt services in **GARY FILMON**'s administration, helping MB become a leader on balanced budget legislation. In early 1977, he stepped down to prepare for his first federal campaign and was nominated a PC candidate that year. He lost in the 1997 federal election to Reform candidate Jake Hoeppner. Pallister campaigned for the PC federal party leadership in 1998 on a right-wing platform designed to win

back voters who had left the Tories for Reform. He finished 4th on the first ballot, yet declined to endorse another candidate. Pallister left the PCs and joined the Alliance party in 2000 and won his new party's nomination for Portage-Lisgar. In the general election of 2000, Pallister was elected to the House of Commons and served on the opposition benches. Stephen Harper formed the new Conservative Party in 2003 and Pallister supported him and joined the party. In 2004, the Liberals were reduced to a minority govt and a re-elected Pallister was named critic for national revenue, Canada Post, the Royal Canadian Mint and Aboriginal affairs. He gained national prominence in Sept 2005 when he drew attention to apparent spending irregularities by the CEO of the Mint. After a review, auditors found no such irregularities but Pallister believed the review was incomplete. He was re-elected in 2006 and Harper appointed him to the finance committee and his peers elected him as chair. At 6'8", Pallister is the tallest MP in the House.
● RUTH DEGRAVES

PAN AMERICAN GAMES

PAN AMERICAN GAMES (also Pan Am Games). This sporting event for the western hemisphere is held every 4 years in the summer preceding the Summer Olympic Games. WINNIPEG has twice hosted the Games, largely because of the volunteerism of city residents.

FIFTH PAN AMERICAN GAMES, 1967: Critics claimed that Winnipeg was too small to host an international event, but mayor **STEPHEN JUBA** ignored the naysayers and, in 1958, organized a committee to examine the possibility of making a bid for the Games. The initial 1959 bid failed, but Winnipeg was encouraged by a positive response from the Pan American Society Organization (PASO), and a successful bid 4 years later secured the 1967 Games for Winnipeg. **JAMES DALY** was instrumental in the process, overseeing both delegations to PASO and fostering Winnipeg support by speaking publicly an average of 150 times a year over 5 years. He also had to convince reluctant Latin American PASO contingents to overlook the cost of travelling so far N.

The V Games were held from July 23 to Aug 6, and had 2361 athletes from 29 countries competing in 19 sports. It was the largest amateur sporting event to be held in NA at the time. **W. CULVER RILEY** was the volunteer chairman of a management committee responsible for organizing the mainly grassroots operation. This committee enlisted the help of over 9000 volunteers with a plea for "Total Community Involvement." Roughly 1000 **MILITARY** personnel looked after transportation and protocol.

Opening the 1967 Pan Am Games

HRH Prince Philip presided over the opening ceremony, with 22,000 people attending despite thundershowers. A team of 15 Cdn Aboriginal runners carried the torch from St. Paul, MN, to Winnipeg, running the 805 km (500 mi) distance at an average of 16 km/hour (10 mi/hour), though a white athlete was ultimately chosen to bring the torch into the stadium, later inciting charges of racism. During the ceremony, political tensions became evident as Cuban athletes sang revolutionary songs, consequently inciting jeers from the US delegation. Nonetheless, a festive atmosphere was maintained throughout the games. A cabaret at Fort Osborne featured nightly go-go dancing, and dozens of Winnipeg girls volunteered as dance partners for the primarily male athletes.

Prominent athletes in attendance included British Columbian swimmer Elaine "Mighty Mouse" Tanner and US swimmer Mark Spitz. The number and high position of women officials and referees was unprecedented for an international competition. For example, Winnipeg's Marilyn Redekop became the first female official at an international-level men's **VOLLEYBALL** match.

The games brought in just over $1 million in total revenue, though the longest-lasting benefit to the city was the construction of numerous sports facilities, such as a velodrome, a track-and-field stadium at the **U OF M**, and the $2.9-million Pan Am Pool, which was the 3rd-largest in the world at the time of its completion. The **RED RIVER FLOODWAY**, inundated with 3180 l (700 ga) of water, was temporarily turned into a sporting venue for rowing events. The games were lauded as an organizational success by the International Olympic Committee, which awarded organizers the Olympic Cup.

THIRTEENTH PAN AMERICAN GAMES, 1999: Don MacKenzie, head of the Manitoba Sports Federation, spearheaded Winnipeg's 2nd bid for the Games. He led a small contingent to the 1987 Indianapolis Pan Am Games in order to appraise the event. After Winnipeg hosted a successful 1990 Western Canada Summer Games, MacKenzie co-chaired the bid process for the Pan Am Games in 1992. The Winnipeg delegation won the Canadian Olympic Association's support, and the city was then chosen over Santo Domingo, Dominican Republic, and Bogotá in the PASO selection process. MacKenzie won over PASO officials by emphasizing Winnipeg's reputation for volunteerism established at the 5th instalment of the Games 32 years earlier.

The Games were held from July 23 to Aug 8, and had 8949 athletes from 42 nations competing in 41 sports. Sandy Riley, nephew of 1967 Pan American Games Society chairman Culver Riley, took over the reins as volunteer chairman of the 1999 Pan American Games Society, with MacKenzie serving as CEO. With a budget of $141 million, including $28 million in corporate sponsorship, it was acclaimed Canada's largest sporting and cultural event, and had roughly 20,000 volunteers, distinguishable by their salmon-coloured shirts.

HRH The Princess Royal (formerly known as Princess Anne) opened the games at a ceremony attended by roughly 40,000 spectators. In an effort to redress the perceived discrimination of the V Games, 7 of the Aboriginal runners who had carried the torch in 1967 brought it into the stadium. **TANYA DUBNICOFF** carried in the Cdn flag, and racquetball champion Sherman Greenfeld swore in the athlete's oath. Nightly concerts at **THE FORKS** went on throughout the games, attracting an estimated 30,000 people.

The games were also a financial success for Winnipeg, bringing in a total profit of $8 million. This included $3 million in revenue from merchandise featuring the Pan Am mascots – a wood duck and a parrot. Sales of 464,000 tickets generated over $11 million.

The XIII Games had its share of drama, including 3 failed drug tests, one of which brought about the revocation of the Cdn roller hockey team's gold medal; and 5 political defections from visiting athletes. Some notable athletic moments include Winnipeg-born runner Graham Hood winning gold in the 1500-m event, bringing a capacity crowd at University Stadium to their feet, and the silver medal win of the Cdn 4 × 100 relay team, led by sprinter Donovan Bailey. The win somewhat redeemed the star athlete from the controversy surrounding the $200,000 he accepted in payment from the Pan Am Games Society. The Cdn medal count of 196 remained, as of writing, the highest at any Pan Am Games. An estimated 400 million viewers watched the Games, with the CBC airing 50 hours of coverage. New facilities constructed for the XIII Games include the $8.6-million Investors Group Athletic Centre, CanWest Global Park, and an artificial-turf venue for field hockey. The closing ceremony drew roughly 23,000 people, and saw THE GUESS WHO reunite for their first performance since 1983. ● MICHELLE DOBROVOLNY

Paquin, Anna. Born in ST. BONIFACE, Paquin gained worldwide attention by winning an Academy Award at the age of 11 for her role in the 1993 film *The Piano*. She is the 2nd-youngest Oscar winner in history, and has since gone on to star in many Hollywood films, including roles as Rogue in all 3 *X-Men* movies and in the MB-filmed *Blue State*, shown above. ●

PARISIEN, Norbert, victim (b 1814, RED RIVER SETTLEMENT; d Mar 4, 1870, Red River). Born in the West, little is known of Parisien before his capture as a "spy" by the Portage expedition of 1870 on its way to Kildonan. Held overnight at the Kildonan Church, Parisien escaped, seized a gun, and fatally wounded Hugh John Sutherland,

who came upon him inadvertently on horseback. Parisien attempted to get away across the ice, but was soon captured and was treated very roughly by the crowd of men who had gone after him. He died a few weeks later, apparently of head wounds suffered in the scuffle on the ice. Ironically, the date of his death was the same day as the execution of THOMAS SCOTT. Parisien was sometimes included (with Thomas Scott and Hugh John Sutherland) as one of the few casualties of the RED RIVER RESISTANCE. MÉTIS supporters often attempted to place his death on one side of a balance sheet that put Thomas Scott on the other side. ● JMB

PARKLAND, named for DUCK MOUNTAIN PROVINCIAL PARK and RIDING MOUNTAIN NATIONAL PARK, both found in the area, is one of the province's 8 administrative regions. Located W of LAKE MANITOBA and LAKE WINNIPEGOSIS extending to the MB/SK border, Parkland covers a 28,000 km² area directly N of the WESTMAN REGION and S of Cedar Lake. It encompasses 22 rural municipalities.

Dominating the national and PROVINCIAL PARKS (including the abovementioned as well as Asessippi) and the PROVINCIAL FORESTS that bear their names, the Porcupine, Duck, and Riding mountains make up part of the Southwestern Uplands (*see* PHYSIOGRAPHIC REGIONS) and are the defining features of the region. The ASSINIBOINE RIVER Valley extends into the SW corner of the district, where the Shellmouth Dam created the artificial LAKE OF THE PRAIRIES.

Though TOURISM – both to the many outdoor attractions and to such sights as the INGLIS GRAIN ELEVATORS – is important to the economy. AGRICULTURE and related industries form the dominant sector. DAUPHIN is the largest population centre, while SWAN RIVER, ROBLIN, GRANDVIEW,

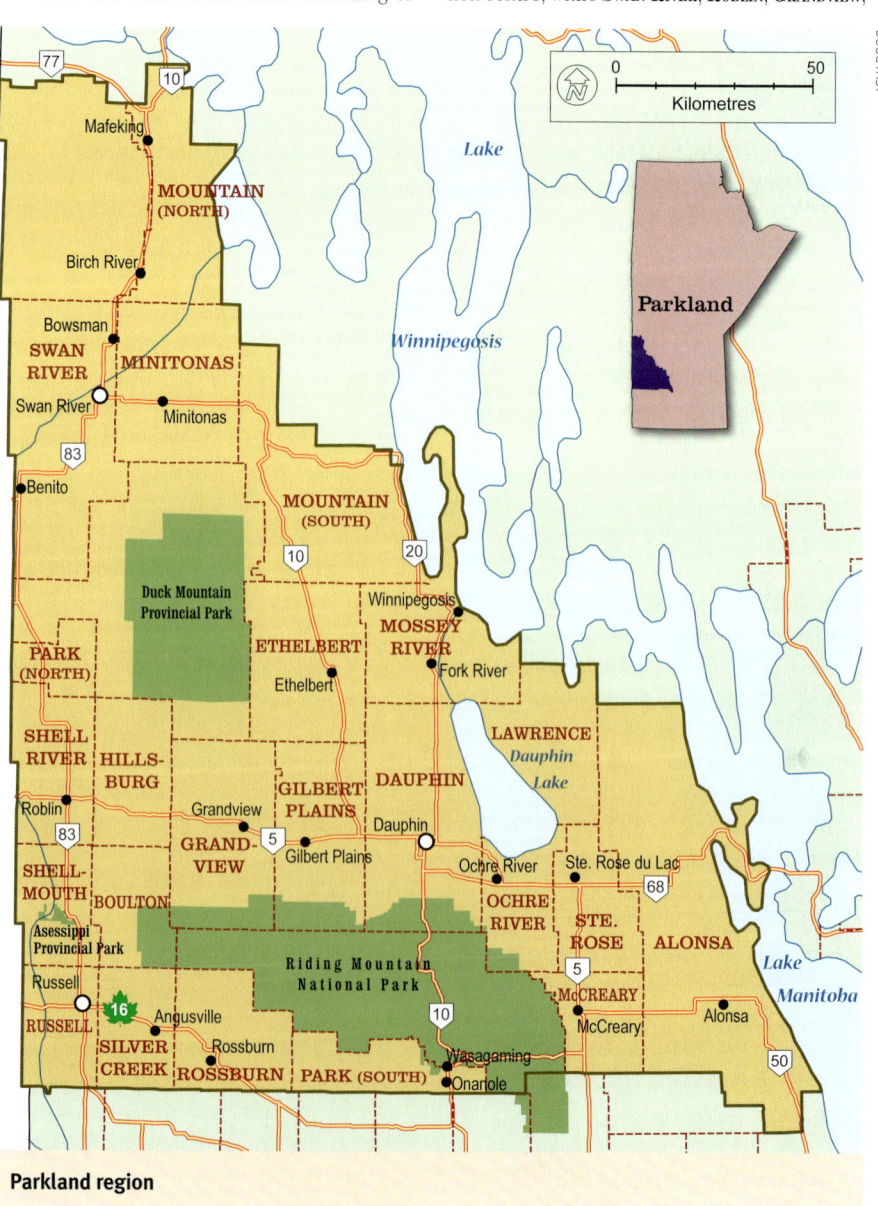

Parkland region

RUSSELL, and STE. ROSE DU LAC are also in the vicinity. FIRST NATIONS communities in Parkland include EBB AND FLOW, WAYWAYSEECAPPO, WUSKWI SIPIHK, and TOOTINAOWAZIIBEENG.

Historically, Plains CREE and Assiniboine groups would have frequented the area, mainly to hunt BISON. Today, about 30% of current Parkland residents name UKRAINIAN as part of their ethnic background, the largest regional concentration in MB. From the 1890s until WWI, a major wave of IMMIGRATION from what is now western Ukraine brought predominantly farmers to MB. In 2001, Parkland's population was about 44,000.
● JOEL TRENAMAN

PASKIEVICH, John, filmmaker and photographer (b Apr 24, 1947, Linz, Austria), to parents displaced by WWII, came to Canada as a young boy. After studies in sociology and anthropology at the U OF M and U OF W, he went to Europe, then returned to study photography and film at Ryerson Polytechnic in Toronto, graduating in 1973. His first book, *A Place Not Our Own*, photographs of NORTH

John Paskievich

END WINNIPEG (1978), was followed by *Waiting for the Ice-Cream Man: A Prison Journal* (1978) and *Urban Indians* (1980), both in collaboration with writer Larry Krotz. Paskievich returned to Europe for his book *A Voiceless Song: Photographs of Slavic Lands* (1983). Paskievich's first film, *Ted Baryluk's Grocery* (1982), marked the transition from his first medium to his next and confirmed his relationship with the NATIONAL FILM BOARD of Canada. The 10-minute movie, composed of black and white still photographs, documents a Winnipeg neighbourhood grocery store and poignantly expresses the relationship between the immigrant owner and a daughter reluctant to carry on the business. The film serves as a template for Paskievich's ongoing concerns: displacement, the clash of cultures, the struggle to assert spiritual values in a materialist and globalized culture.

In his films since, Paskievich has sought out other people and stories: a disenfranchised farmer (*The Price of Daily Bread*, 1985), the adherents of an archaic Russian orthodoxy (*The Old Believers*, 1989), an immigrant Winnipeg photographer (*The Actor*, 1990), Inuit stone carvers (*Sedna: The Making of a Myth*, 1992), Czech youth who emulate North American Aboriginal culture (*If Only I Were an Indian*, 1995), Europe's maligned Rom (*Gypsies of Svinia*, 1998), and his generation's own Ukrainian heritage (*My Mother's Village*, 2001). More recently, Paskievich has examined stuttering (*Unspeakable*, 2006) from a variety of viewpoints including his own experience. ● HOWARD CURLE

PATERSON GLOBALFOODS INC, formerly N. M. Paterson & Sons Ltd, is a WINNIPEG-based, family-owned conglomerate whose holdings include Paterson Grain, a Winnipeg grain-handling company; Growers International Organic Sales Inc., which is one of Canada's leading exporters of certified organic cereal grains; NutraSun Foods Ltd., a Regina-based flour mill; FeedMax, a KILLARNEY feed mill; Truck Freight International, a Winnipeg-based grain transportation company; PTC Construction Ltd., a Winnipeg construction company whose specialties include the building of inland grain terminals; and Australia-based Global Grain Australia Pty Ltd. Launched in Winnipeg in 1908 by Norman M. Paterson, the company began as N. M. Paterson and Co. Ltd., but changed its name to N. M. Paterson & Sons Ltd. after the founder's son, Donald Paterson, and his nephew, John Paterson, joined the company following WWII. On Jan 1, 2005, the name was changed again to Paterson GlobalFoods Inc. to reflect the global nature of the company's current operations – it exports to 47 countries worldwide – and its long-term strategic plan to become a bigger player in the food sector. ● MURRAY MCNEILL

PATRICK FAMILY is a family of successful athletes who have played hockey and football at the professional level.

STEPHEN PATRICK, SR, football player, politician (b Mar 24, 1932, GLENELLA). Over 13 seasons on the WINNIPEG BLUE BOMBERS, Patrick appeared on 4 Grey Cup-winning teams. He first played football with the Winnipeg Light Infantry, and then joined the Bombers as a defensive middle guard. He was named All-Star in 1958 and 1959, and was captain from 1961-64. In addition to his football career, Stephen Sr founded Patrick Realty Ltd. in 1955. In 1962, he entered provincial politics, elected as MLA for the Assiniboia area. He was re-elected 4 times. He was inducted into the MANITOBA SPORTS HALL OF FAME in 1988. He is a member of MB's Order of the Buffalo Hunt, and a recipient of the Canada Centennial Award for Public Service.

STEPHEN PATRICK, JR, hockey player (b Feb 4, 1961, WINNIPEG) played in the NHL from 1980-86. He grew up in St. James, and was a noted athlete in high school. At 6'4" and over 200 lbs, he was often referred to as "Big Steve." He played for the BRANDON WHEAT KINGS in the 1979-80 season, and then was drafted to the Buffalo Sabres, 20th overall in the first round. He was traded to the New York Rangers in 1984, and the Quebec Nordiques the following season. He retired from hockey to help his father run the family business, taking over as president. He became one of the top real estate brokers in Winnipeg.

JAMES PATRICK, "JEEP," hockey player (b June 14, 1963, Winnipeg). James had a successful and lengthy career as a defenceman in

PETER TITTENBERGER

the NHL. He played hockey for the U of North Dakota, helping the school's team win the 1981-82 National Collegiate Athletic Association championship. He was named the Western Collegiate Hockey Association's Freshman of the Year in 1982. He was a 1st-round draft pick, 9th overall, for the New York Rangers in 1981. As part of Canada's national team, James went to the 1984 Sarajevo Olympics, and in 1987 played in the Canada Cup. He set a record with 40 games played for the Canadian team. James left the Rangers in the 1993-94 season, briefly playing with the Hartford Whalers before joining the Calgary Flames for 4 seasons. He signed with the Buffalo Sabres for the 1998-99 season. He retired in 2005, having played in the NHL for 21 seasons with 1280 games and 639 pts. As of writing, he was the assistant coach for the Sabres. • MD

PAUINGASSI FIRST NATION, on reserve pop 524, off reserve pop 37, is about 280 km NE of **WINNIPEG** and 24 km N of Little Grand Rapids. In 1875, **LITTLE GRAND RAPIDS FIRST NATION** from which the Pauingassi First Nation branched off, signed Treaty 5. In 1988, Pauingassi was given reserve status, and in 1991, became a separate First Nation. The native language of this First Nation community is **OJIBWAY**. Education in this community goes from Nursery-Grade 9, and total enrolment for the year 2003-04 was 573. The Southeast Tribal Division for Schools administers schooling. The Pauingassi First Nation IR is this nation's only reserve. It is a member of the Southeast Tribal Council. Although winter roads are constructed each year, this isolated community does not have permanent road access. There is an airstrip about 24 km S of Pauingassi at Little Grand Rapids. However access to the airstrip is limited to float plane or boat in the summer or by snow machine in the winter. When the annual spring thaw or freeze up is underway, access to this First Nation community is only possible by helicopter. The Pauingassi First Nation economy is based on wild rice, fishing, and trapping. Unfortunately, the community has seen its share of hard times, with suicide rates and solvent sniffing making the headlines in the 2000s. Along with **POPLAR RIVER** and **LITTLE GRAND RAPIDS FIRST NATIONS** on the E side of **LAKE WINNIPEG** and the Pikangikum First Nation in ON, Pauingassi is involved in an effort to protect a swath of the boreal forest by designating it a UNESCO World Heritage site. • RK

PAULLEY, Andrew Russell "Russ," politician (b 1909, **WINNIPEG**; d May 19, 1984, Winnipeg) was born in the Weston district of Winnipeg. Upon his marriage in 1938, he moved with his bride to Transcona, where he spent the remainder of his life. He worked in the **CNR** shops before entering politics, first as mayor of Transcona and then in 1953 as **CO-OPERATIVE COMMONWEALTH FEDERATION** (later **NDP**) member of the MB legislature. He served as Transcona's MLA in the Legislature from 1953-78. He was leader of the MB CCF from 1959-69, and later served as Minister of Labour in the govt of **EDWARD SCHREYER** 1969-77. For 10 years, he was rector's warden of St. George's **ANGLICAN** Church in Transcona, and he was a past master of the Grand Lodge of MB. • JMB

PAWLEY, Howard Russell, premier, (b Nov 21, 1934, Brampton, ON), served as MB's 19th premier 1981-88. He led the **NDP** of MB 1979-88. The son of Russell Pawley and Velma Leone (née Madill), Pawley studied at United College (*see* **U OF W**) before entering the **U OF M** Law School. He was called to the bar and practised law in **SELKIRK**. He married Adele Schreyer, a cousin of **EDWARD SCHREYER**, in 1960. They have 2 children.

In 1957, Pawley was elected head of the provincial **CCF**. After contesting 3 provincial and 2 federal elections unsuccessfully, Pawley was elected as an MLA in 1969. He served in the Cabinet of Edward Schreyer, the first **NDP** premier of MB, as Minister of Municipal Affairs (1969-76) and, more briefly, of Government Services (1969). Pawley's most enduring legacy was the introduction of public automobile insurance – Autopac legislation – in the face of a well-financed opposition by the insurance industry. He was the first chair of the **MB PUBLIC INSURANCE CORP**, an institution that has come to be a well-accepted part of the provincial identity. Pawley stepped down from that role to serve as Attorney General (1973-77).

In 1977, the Schreyer govt fell to **PROGRESSIVE CONSERVATIVE** leader **STERLING LYON**. With Schreyer's appointment to the post of gov gen in 1979, Pawley took over the party, initially on an ad hoc basis and later formally in a party convention. The election of 1981 saw Pawley become premier at a time of economic recession and job loss: the election was fought largely on the economic and employment situation of the province. Pawley's success turned largely on convincing MB voters that promised Conservative economic mega-projects were unlikely to materialize.

The Pawley govt featured a record number of women in the Cabinet. Pawley appointed former party leadership rival Muriel Smith to be deputy premier. Other prominent women in the Pawley Cabinet included Maureen Hemphill in Education and Mary Beth Dolin in Labour. Key economic ministers in the Pawley govt included Vic Schroeder, who served in Finance; Eugene Kostrya, who served in Urban Affairs, Culture, and Finance; Jay Cowan, who served in Northern Affairs; and Wilson Parasiuk, who served in Energy and later in Health.

The major crisis of Pawley's first term of office was the **FRENCH LANGUAGE CRISIS**. The situation started with an English-only traffic ticket issued to **GEORGES FOREST**, a Francophone Manitoban, in 1983. Efforts to amend legislation to recognize the right of French-language service rights polarized public opinion and caused a dramatic drop in support for Pawley's govt. Eventually, due to an impasse in the Legislature and broad public opposition – some fomented by unsavoury groups – the Pawley govt dropped its proposed constitutional amendment.

Howard Pawley, 1979

For the balance of its first term, the Pawley govt focused on job creation and economic development. The economic downturn of 1982 caused a sharp deterioration in employment levels and in provincial finances. Pawley responded by accelerating development of **HYDROELECTRIC POWER** installations, moving ahead with the Limestone Generating Station on the **NELSON RIVER**. As well, the MB Jobs Fund was created. A strong emphasis was placed on the inclusion of **FIRST PEOPLES** in employment and other benefits derived from northern development. Ministers Parasiuk and Cowan played a large role in implementing these programs.

Other notable accomplishments of the Pawley govt included the amendment of the *Manitoba Human Rights Act* to prohibit discrimination based on sexual orientation. MB was the first province to ban such discrimination. Changes were also made to laws and structures affecting children. The Winnipeg Children's Aid Society was devolved to local agencies. Out-of-country ADOPTION of Aboriginal children was ended after a judicial review by Edwin Kimelman. Other reforms included comprehensive workplace health and safety legislation and the introduction of pay equity legislation for the public sector.

The Pawley govt participated with Winnipeg mayor BILL NORRIE and federal cabinet minister LLOYD AXWORTHY on 3 initiatives that helped reshape Winnipeg. These were the Winnipeg Core Area Initiative, the North Portage Development, and redevelopment of THE FORKS. Together with Provincial Urban Affairs Minister Eugene Kostrya, they brought forth a mini-renaissance for downtown Winnipeg and its rivers and riverbanks. The redevelopment of the historic Forks at the junction of the RED and ASSINIBOINE rivers has profoundly restored Winnipeg's sense of itself as a city. Other measures were aimed at bringing people back to live in the core area of the city, partially reversing the damage done by movement of residential populations to the suburbs.

In 1986, the Pawley govt was re-elected with a reduced majority. Three new ministers joined Pawley's Cabinet: JUDY WASYLYCIA-LEIS, who would eventually move to federal politics and a seat in the House of Commons; ELIJAH HARPER, an OJIBWAY-CREE chief from Red Sucker Lake, who would bring about the failure of the MEECH LAKE ACCORD; and future premier GARY DOER.

Pawley's 2nd term saw a major overhaul of the accountability of MB Crown corporations. Triggered by a debacle at the phone company, MTS, (*see* MTX SCANDAL) the reforms culminated in the *Crown Corporations Public Review and Accountability Act* (1988). However, the term was overshadowed by significant and unpopular increases in MPI premiums. The loss of long-serving Health Minister LARRY DESJARDINS also weakened the Pawley govt's support base. Two years later, long-time NDP backbencher and former Speaker Derek James "Jim" Walding voted against his govt's budget. The defeat of the budget triggered an election in 1988, in which GARY FILMON's Conservatives defeated Pawley's govt.

Following his defeat both as premier and as MLA for Selkirk, Pawley ran unsuccessfully in the federal riding of Selkirk in 1988. He then left politics and MB, and taught political science at the U of Windsor in Windsor, ON, until his retirement in 2000. Pawley was inducted into the Order of MB (2001) and the Order of Canada (as an Officer, 2003). ● MICHAEL DECTER

PEAK OF THE MARKET is one of Canada's premier grower-owned vegetable suppliers. Formed in 1942, the co-operative has more than

6 decades of experience in growing vegetables and marketing them domestically and internationally. The co-operative and its more than 60 member-growers employ more than 1000 people and contribute more than $50 million a year to the MB ECONOMY. The member-growers produce more than 120 different varieties of vegetables, and their use of environmentally controlled storage facilities enables them to store some of their produce – such as beets, potatoes, cabbage, and carrots – for long periods. That, in turn, has enabled Peak of the Market to become a year-round supplier of produce, shipping its products across Canada and into a variety of export markets such as the US, Europe, Asia, Latin America, and the Caribbean. The period from 1994 to 2005 represented a series of record-breaking sales years for the marketer. In 1999, the organization was named one of Canada's 50 best-managed companies – a designation it gained again in 2000 and in 2001. In 2002, Peak of the Market also received a MB Quality Award, and the following year it was presented with a Community Builder Award by the Winnipeg Chamber of Commerce. ● MURRAY MCNEILL

PEANUT WORM is a strange, peanut- or sausage-shaped marine creature in the small phylum Sipuncula, found in HUDSON BAY. It is characterized by a mouth with feeding tentacles, and covered externally with bumps or spines. The body is not segmented, and the slender front section constantly moves in and out of the plump posterior part. A pair of primitive eyes (ocelli) are present. Peanut worms borrow into the sea-bottom sand or mud, or hide under rocks or inside a shell, generally in the intertidal zone or in shallow water, although some species have been found in other oceans at depths of over 5000 m. They may spend their entire life at one spot, or move if necessary. The gut is U-shaped, with the anus opening on top near the head. Circulatory and respiratory systems are also lacking, but the body fluid carries nutrients and oxygen. Food consists of organic detritus captured from the sediment or floating in the water by a cilia-mucus system. Interestingly, about 10% of nutrient requirements are absorbed directly through the thin cuticle body wall. Sexes are separate, releasing their sperm or eggs into the sea. The fertilized eggs develop into free-swimming larvae called trochophores, which float in the plankton, eat other tiny creatures, and disperse great distances before sinking and transforming into the sessile adult. Remarkably, the peanut worm can also regrow not only a missing tentacle, but even half of its body by a natural process called fission. Each half then grows the missing part of the

organism. So far, 4 widespread species have been collected and identified from Hudson Bay (e.g., *Golfingia lilljeborgi*), and additional ones await discovery in future studies. Only 320 species of peanut worms exist worldwide, all of which are marine. Most are around 10 cm long (max 72 cm). This is a primitive group which arose over 530 mya (Early Cambrian) and is likely related to annelid worms (phylum Annelida). ● REW

Bert Pearl, 1972

PEARL, Bert, entertainer (b Feb 2, 1913, WINNIPEG; d June 17, 1986, Hollywood, CA) was successful in show business. He attended Aberdeen School and St. John's High School before taking a pre-medical course at the U OF M on an Isbister Scholarship. He moved to Toronto during the GREAT DEPRESSION to earn money to continue medical training, and found work with the CBC. He formed the Happy Gang, a radio musical troupe, in 1937. He was the "Gang's" star and emcee for over 20 years in Canada and the US. In 1959, he went to Hollywood to write for Jimmy Durante. He later served as musical director for GISELE MACKENZIE. Pearl was also well known as a pianist, appearing in nightclubs and with the WINNIPEG SYMPHONY ORCHESTRA. He is a member of the Order of the Buffalo Hunt. ● JMB

PEEBLES, Phillip James Edwin, professor, cosmologist (b April 25, 1935, St. Boniface) is considered the world's leading theoretical cosmologist. His work has furthered the understanding of the formation of galaxies, and he popularized the theory of dark matter. Peebles grew up in St. Vital, and his father was a book-keeper at the **Winnipeg Grain [Commodity] Exchange**. Mechanically-minded as a child, he built radio receivers for a hobby, but his passion for science didn't take hold until studying physics at the **U of M**. Encouraged by some of his professors, he then chose to pursue particle physics, and was accepted as a graduate student at Princeton U.

Working under his advisor Richard Dicke, Peebles' became increasingly interested in cosmology, later choosing it as his main field of study. In 1965, the research Peebles compiled for his post-doctoral thesis allowed him to develop predictions of the existence of cosmic microwave background radiation (CMBR), further proof of the Big Bang theory. Peebles accurately predicted that this diffuse radiation would be detectable at microwave frequencies. Though CMBR was then discovered in a fluke by 2 other scientists, it was Peebles who gave an accurate analysis of the phenomena. Among his many other contributions, Peebles developed calculations for statistical descriptions of the structure of the universe. His first book *Physical Cosmology* was published in 1971, and largely established cosmology as a specific branch of physics. He was named Albert Einstein Professor of Science at Princeton U in 1984. He has received honourary degrees from numerous universities, including U of T as well as his alma mater U of M. He has received both the Eddington medal and the gold medal from the Royal Astronomical Society. An asteroid is named after him, 18242 Peebles. • MD

PEGUIS, Chief, (b ca 1774, Sault Ste Marie [ON]; d Sept 24,1864, **Red River Settlement**) led a band of his people to the Red River area around 1800. **Lord Selkirk**'s settlers found a good friend in Peguis, who used his relationship with the settlement to cement his claims to the land his people had earlier occupied. Peguis assisted the settlers in retreating from Red River after the **Seven Oaks Incident** in 1816, and he helped Selkirk's Des Meuron soldiers in recapturing Fort Douglas in Jan 1817. Later in 1817, Lord Selkirk made a treaty with him, and after 1855, he received an annual pension from the **HBC**. In 1832, missionary **William Cockran** persuaded Peguis and a few of his people to settle in a community just N of present-day Selkirk, which by 1836 was known as St. Peter's. He was baptized into the **Anglican** Church in 1840, giving up 3 of his 4 wives to do so. He took the name William King, and his children used the last name Prince (among his descendants is **Tommy Prince**). In 1860, he protested to the Aborigines' Protection Society that he had

Chief Peguis

been deprived of land he had never formally surrendered; the case was not resolved until after his death. **Colin Inkster** recalled him as "short in stature, with a strong, well-knit frame, and the voice of an orator." His nose had been bitten off in a fracas around 1802, and he was often known as "Chief Cut-Nose." • JMB

PEGUIS FIRST NATION, on reserve pop 3408, off reserve pop 4646, is the largest First Nation in MB, both in terms of its population and its land area. It is located 170 km N of **Winnipeg** on the Fisher River. There are 9 reserves in total on the Peguis First Nation, making up 30,700 ha, although most of the population is in IR 1B. Peguis IR 1C, on the W shores of Fisher Bay, is used for a student summer camp. Reserve 1A is used as a fishing station.

This First Nation's history is marred by its forced relocation from its original reserve, the St. Peter's Reserve north of **Selkirk**. The original reserve, provided in Treaty 1 in 1871, gave the Peguis First Nation prime agricultural land on both sides of the lower Red River. Despite **Chief Peguis**'s earlier friendship to the **Red River Settlers**, new immigrants from ON worked for years to get rid of a reserve in their midst. Their efforts paid off in 1907 when the First Nation was moved N to swampy, unproductive land in the **Interlake**. Elders called it "the land that no one wants." Since the relocation, Peguis First Nation has had repeated problems with spring flooding from the Fisher River. In 2007, the community was voting on whether to accept a $64 million compensation offer from the provincial govt – the largest treaty land settlement deal in MB history.

Peguis First Nation has all-weather roads, with bus and taxi service. Schooling in this community goes from Nursery-Grade 12, and total enrolment for the year 2003-04 was 941. Peguis First Nation administers its own education. Employment levels have risen and conditions have improved over the years with the establishment of local businesses and housing that includes apartment buildings, senior housing and personal care units.

Peguis First Nation is a member of the Interlake Reserves Tribal Council. Residents are largely the **Cree** and **Ojibway** descendants of Chief Peguis and his band. Peguis' descendants commemorate their heritage each July with a Treaty Days Celebration and Powwow. Canada's longest-serving elected band chief, Louis Stevenson, was ousted in March 2007 after 26 years in power. • RK

PELICAN (family *Pelecanidae*) is represented in MB by only one species, the American White pelican (*Pelecanus erythrorhynchos*), a huge white bird with black wingtips and an enormous orange pouched bill. It may come as a surprise to learn that more of these fish-eaters breed in MB than anywhere else. Their colonies are located on reefs and islands in many of our larger Lakes, but they wander widely in search for food. Particularly good spots to watch feeding flocks are at the **Lockport** dam. • RUDOLF KOES

PEMBINA VALLEY is a provincial designation for the region covering the S-central portion of MB. Immediately SW of **Winnipeg**, it is bounded by the US border, to the S; **Westman**; **Eastman**; and, to the N, **Central Plains**. The region takes its name from the Pembina River; *Pembina* is an Anglicization of a **Cree** word for the highbush cranberry (*also see* **Emerson**).

In the E, the MB lowlands of the **Red River** Valley feature fertile black soils. However, the area is prone to **Floods**, as the Red and the Morris River, alongside their tributaries, often top their banks, inundating farmland across a wide area. In the W, the soil becomes more sandy leading up to the **Manitoba Escarpment**, which formed the shoreline of ancient **Lake Agassiz**.

RURAL MUNICIPALITIES in Pembina Valley

Argyle	Dufferin
Lorne	Louise
Montcalm	Morris
Pembina	Rhineland
Roblin	Roland
Stanley	Thompson

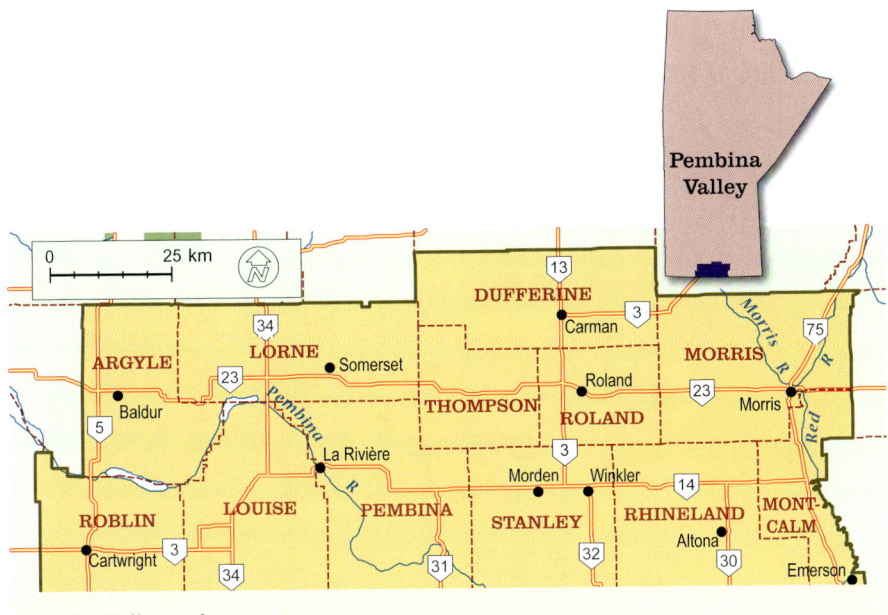

Pembina Valley region

Pembina Valley includes 12 municipalities and some of the fastest-growing communities in the province. Both **Winkler** and **Morden** experienced close to 10% growth during each of the 3 Census periods from 1991 to 2006. Other major centres include **Altona**, **Emerson**, **Morris**, and **Carman**. More than 50,000 people inhabit the region. The economy remains dominated by **Agriculture** and related services, but it has diversified, mostly due to a boom in light Manufacturing.

Dakota natives would likely have been most prominent in the area, but there is also evidence of Assiniboine people and of a Plains **Cree** presence, especially at **Pilot Mound**. In the late 18ᵗʰ century, **Fur Trade** settlements began along the Red River near the site of present-day Morris. Russian **Mennonites** journeyed farther W to live near Winkler as early as 1874. Waves of **German** (often meaning Mennonite) **Immigration** to the region occurred in the early 20ᵗʰ century and following WWI. In the 1996 Census, 44% of residents listed German as part of their heritage. ● JOEL TRENAMAN

PEMMICAN is a mixture of fat, jerky, and, when possible, dried fruit. Pemmican was an ideal food for First Nations people and, later, **Métis** and European **Fur Traders**, as it was easy to transport; was high in protein; and, because of the properties of the fat, could last for years. It was also a way to avoid spoilage of meat after a hunt, and to preserve food for times of scarcity. Aboriginal people, initially women, made pemmican by drying the meat in the sun or over a fire, then pounding it together with fruits and with fat or tallow, usually with a rock. The fat

generally came from marrow, and was generally extracted by boiling split bones.

The word *pemmican* is derived from a **Cree** term meaning "fat mixture," though its use was by no means confined to Cree people. The Cree and **Ojibway** typically mixed Saskatoons, blueberries, or the native wild red currant (*Ribes triste*) into their pemmican, in season. The **Dene** also had a version, and the quality of the Assiniboines' pemmican was regarded as excellent. Their fellow Siouan speakers, the **Dakota**, called this *wasna*, and often mixed dried chokecherries, and sometimes corn, in with the fat and meat. Even the Inuit have a similar food, *akutaq* ("mixture"), also referred to as "Inuit ice cream."

In what is now southern MB, **Bison** was the meat of choice. One cow typically yielded a 20 kg (45 lb) standard bag of pemmican, while a bull yielded twice that amount. Elsewhere, **Deer**, **Moose**, and **Caribou** meat were used, but the bison form is best remembered and most closely associated with MB's history. While it could be eaten raw, the women of the **Red River Settlement** cooked their pemmican in 2 forms: *rubaboo*, also known as burgoo, was made by adding pemmican in a sort of porridge, often with whatever vegetables, grains, or other ingredients were available; *rowshow* consisted of shredded pemmican mixed with flour and water, then panfried. Pemmican was primarily an emergency food source for much of the Red River Settlement's European populace, as it had a strong odour and was hard to chew, but voyageurs in fur brigades were said to consume just over 1 kg (2.5 lbs) per person each day. Such was the demand for this food among the Métis that when **HBC** gov **Miles Macdonell** issued the infamous Pemmican

Proclamation, it triggered mass protest, culminating in **Cuthbert Grant**'s siege of several **HBC** forts and in the **Seven Oaks Incident**. ● A. J. LEVIN

PENIS WORM is a cylindrical, phallic, unsegmented marine creature in the small phylum Priapulida found worldwide in cold marine waters. This group contains truly ancient and bizarre creatures ranging in size from 5mm-30cm. The body is supported by hydrostatic pressure and consists of a trunk with a large forward proboscis and a rear appendage. The trunk, ending in the anus, is encircled with numerous indented rings, and with wart-like nodules on the posterior ones. The large (1/3 body length) retractable, club-shaped proboscis, has many longitudinal rows of fine spines, and houses the mouth. The penis worm can move slowly by means of waves of muscular contractions (peristaltic action). Small species and young individuals eat bacteria and organic detritus in the mud or sand of the sea floor, but larger ones are predatory and swallow whole prey such as annelid worms or even their own kind.

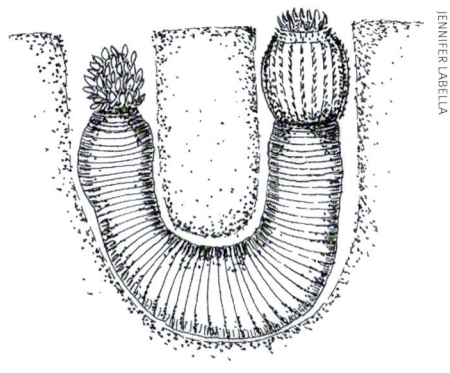

Penis Worm

The sexes are separate, with external fertilization in large species and internal in small ones. Fertilized eggs hatch into planktonic larva which drift for a few days to a month before settling on the bottom and metamorphosing into an adult. Only 2 species have been found in **Hudson Bay** – the 10 cm long, cream-coloured Tailed Priapulid Worm (*Priapulus caudatus*) and *Priapulus humanus*. Another species (*Halicryptus spinulosus*) occurs in Hudson Strait and will likely also be found off MB shores. The Tailed Priapulid Worm occurs in both Arctic and Antarctic seas, a remarkable bipolar distribution. Penis worms are found in or on mud or sandy sediments, usually below the low-tide mark and to depths of 500 m. They are tolerant of fluctuating salinity, low oxygen levels, and can withstand lack of food for long periods. Penis worms are represented today by only 17 surviving species, but many others existed back to 520 mya (Mid-Cambrian period). ● REW

P

PENNER, Donald Wills, physician, (b Jun 8, 1918, Rosthern, SK; d 2004, **WINNIPEG**). A nationally recognized pathologist, Penner gained prominence before he had even completed medical school, as he founded and operated MB's first blood bank in 1941. Upon receiving his MD from the **U OF M** in 1942, Penner facilitated the first laboratory measurement of blood-alcohol levels of emergency room patients, while still an intern. His research led him to campaign for laws against drinking and driving and to restrict smoking.

Penner trained in New York under George Papanicolaou, the inventor of the "pap smear" test to detect cervical cancers. When he returned to MB, Penner introduced the examination – and also techniques of cytology (microscopic cell analysis) – to the medical system. He also developed diagnosis and testing standards for the practices in MB, and helped do the same for the College of American Pathologists. Late in his career, from 1988-98, Penner lived in Kenya and helped establish clinical pathology and cytotechnology programs at the U of Nairobi.

The Canadian Association of Pathologists named a set of awards after Penner in 1977. In 1995 he received the Manitoba Medical Association's Distinguished Service Award, and the Canadian Medical Association's highest honour, the F.N.G. Starr Award. In 1998, he became a member of the Order of Canada. Penner also served as a school board trustee for 29 years. The Dr. D.W. Penner School in Winnipeg's Louis Riel School Division bears his name. ● JOEL TRENAMAN

PENNER, Fredrick Ralph "Fred," children's songwriter, actor (b Nov 6, 1946, **WINNIPEG**) is a well-loved children's entertainer who has been performing sold-out shows to children and their parents for 25 years. He has gained popularity for his unique storytelling abilities, which combine music and comedy with an emphasis on positive values. Penner started composing songs and taught himself guitar from an early age. Though he had no formal musical training, he played folk music in high school and university, obtaining a BA in economics and psychology from the **U OF W**, intending to become an economist. Penner came to realize the healing potential of music for children through his experiences with his sister, who had Down's syndrome, and from his 2 years working with disabled children after graduation. In the 1970s, Penner performed as a folk singer, with rock bands, in a musical comedy act, and as a character actor in productions at **RAINBOW STAGE**. He toured with **ALBERT WILLIAM "AL" SIMMONS** 1973-76.

In 1977, Penner started a children's dance company with choreographer Odette Heyn, whom

Fred Penner

he would later marry. The couple has 4 children. At one concert, an audience member, impressed with Penner's talent and charisma, offered to pay to produce Fred's album. The result of this was *The Cat Came Back* (1979), the album that launched Penner's career and established him as one of the leading children's entertainers in NA. He hosted the national CBC children's show, *Fred Penner's Place* (1984-97), which also ran in the US on Nickelodeon (1989-97). In 1987, Penner and his manager established the Oak Street Music label to issue and reissue children's and contemporary folk recordings. Collectively, his CDs have sold close to one million copies and have been nominated for 8 Juno Awards. He and his Cat's Meow Band continue to perform throughout the continent, singing in French and Spanish as well as English. Penner has also adapted several of his songs into children's books. He was made an Officer of the Order of Canada in 1992, and received an honorary doctorate from the U of W in 1995. ● JILL SEXSMITH

PENNER, Jacob, municipal politician (b Aug 12, 1880, Ukraine; d Aug 28, 1965, **WINNIPEG**) came to MB in 1904 and taught school in **GRETNA**. He subsequently moved to Winnipeg where he worked as a florist and an accountant. He helped found the Socialist Party of Canada in 1905 and the Social Democratic Party a few years later. He joined the Communist Party in 1921 and was its national chair in 1958. In 1934, he was elected to the Winnipeg City Council as a **NORTH END** Communist, serving almost continuously until 1961. He insisted that his chief concern was to protect "those on the lower rung of the social ladder," and was particularly noted for his advocacy of low-rental housing. ● JMB

PENNER, Roland, law professor, politician (b July 30, 1924, **WINNIPEG**), was called to the bar and began private law practice in 1961, specializing in criminal and civil litigation. In 1972, while a professor of law at the **U OF M**'s law faculty (1968-81), he became the founding chair of the **LEGAL AID SOCIETY** of Manitoba, an office he occupied until

1978. The son of Communist city councillor Jacob Penner, Roland was elected as a **NEW DEMOCRATIC PARTY** MLA in 1981 and again in 1986. While in govt, he held the offices of Attorney General; Minister of Consumer and Corporate Affairs; chair of the Treasury Board; Minister Responsible for Constitutional Affairs; and Minister of Education. He returned to the Faculty of Law in 1988, serving as its dean (1989-94). He remained a professor of law, as of writing. He became a Member of the Order of Canada in 2000, and was cited for his contributions to legal aid, access to justice, and human rights. ● DOUG JOHNSTON

PERCH is a fish (*Perca flavescens*) in the Perch family Percidae (order Perciformes), which also includes 9 other native fishes in MB – **WALLEYE** [Pickerel] (*Sander vitreus*), Sauger (*Sander canadensis*), Logperch (*Percina caprodes*), and 6 species of darters (Etheostoma and Percina species). The Yellow Perch has a deep and robust body, and an attractive greenish-yellow colour. A lateral pattern of 7 green or brown, tapered bars offer camouflage while this predatory fish lurks in weeds. There are sharp, stiff spines in the dorsal, anal and pelvic fins, and the jaws have pads with small teeth used for grasping slippery prey fish. This perch commonly reaches 30 cm and 340 g (max 40 cm and 2 kg), but with food shortage, adults may be only half this size. The range in MB includes most rivers and lakes as far N as **CHURCHILL**, but it is absent from the tundra region. It is uncommon in the **RED** and **ASSINIBOINE** rivers, likely due to heavy turbidity, and also the current in the Red. It often congregates around structures in the water, such as logs, dense vegetation, or docks, where it is frequently caught by anglers. It is also taken commercially. This species spawns in May or June, as soon as water temperatures surpass 6C. Travelling into shallow water, the female releases long (up to 2.1 m by 10 cm wide), folded, gelatinous strands of eggs (2000-110,000), which are fertilized by one or more attending males. No nest is prepared. The semi-buoyant strands break up in the waves or current and snag around vegetation. Hatching in 10 days, the transparent fry devour tiny plankton and soon graduate to insects and then small

Yellow Perch

fish by autumn. Longevity is up to 11 years. The Yellow Perch plays a significant role in freshwater ecosystems due to its wide distribution and abundance, often occuring in schools up to 200 individuals. • REW

PEREGRINE, David (b David Alan Evans), dancer, actor (b Sept 19, 1954, Ottawa; d June 7, 1989, near Anderson, AK) obtained international recognition as a ballet dancer in 1980 after winning bronze medals at world competitions in Japan and Bulgaria, both times partnering with prima ballerina **Evelyn Hart**, with whom he often had a strained working relationship.

Peregrine got his start as a ballet dancer in Ottawa and later studied with David Moroni at the **Royal Winnipeg Ballet**. He made his professional debut as a member of the RWB corps de ballet in 1975, becoming a soloist in 1978 and principal dancer in 1980. Peregrine was a frequent guest with ballet companies throughout Europe and NA. He performed in classical and modern ballets, giving performances that were often described as noble. Roles for which he earned critical acclaim include Romeo in *Romeo and Juliet*, the Prince in *Swan Lake*, and Jamie Paul in *The Ecstasy of Rita Joe*. He and Hart won Norbert Vesak a gold medal for his choreography of the pas de deux "Belong," from *What to Do Till the Messiah Comes* (1973). Peregrine and Hart would perform this piece regularly. David made his professional acting debut at the **Manitoba Theatre Centre** in 1982. The 1989 MTC production of *Frankenstein* played an indirect role in his death. The production, set in the Arctic, inspired Peregrine to explore the region for himself. His light aircraft crashed in the Alaska Range about 160 km S of Fairbanks, AK, some time around June 7, 1989. Peregrine, his brother, and a friend were killed in the accident. • JILL SEXSMITH

PERIMETERITIS is an affliction widespread among Winnipeggers that disables their abilities to cross the Perimeter Highway, and, in extreme cases prevents them from even recognizing that life exists outside the boundaries of the city of **Winnipeg**. The Perimeter Highway encircles the capital, and with it about 60% of the province's population in 1% of its area. Suggested treatment: in mild cases, take a trip outside the Perimeter to places such as the Spirit Sands or **Inglis Grain Elevators**; or hold a meeting in **Portage la Prairie** or in **Brandon**. In severe cases, residence outside Winnipeg is required. • GPP

PETERSFIELD, area pop 1300, is a community 50 km NE of **Winnipeg**, by Netley Creek, on hwy 9. European settlement began about 1803, when the **North West Company** built a post near the present community. A decade later, their rivals, the **HBC**, constructed a fort nearby. Settlement was sparse until a rail line was built. A post office subsequently opened in 1908. Close to **Netley-Libau Marsh**, Petersfield functions largely as a vacation and bedroom community for **Selkirk** and Winnipeg. Naturalist and scenic charter cruises are available. • GPP

STAN MILOSEVIC, WWW.MANITOBAPHOTOS.COM

Petroforms turtle

PETROFORMS are systematic patterns, such as geometric or animal figures, formed in outline by the placement of boulders or cobbles. These features are particularly common in the **Whiteshell Provincial Park** area known as Manito Ahbee (the place where the Great Spirit sits). They occur in large clusters on rock surfaces called boulder mosaics, such as Bannock Point and Tie Creek, or as isolated items, such as turtles, at portages. These mosaics also include snakes and geometric forms. On the western plains, human, **Bison**, and geometric forms, medicine wheels, and sacred circles occur. At least 2 sacred circles resembling giant teepee rings are known in western MB. Petroforms are located at sacred sites that represent teachings for the spiritual, mental, and physical healing of people. • C. GORDON HILL

▸ *See* **Ancient Aboriginal Art**, **Midewiwin**

PETROLEUM and its derivatives – from gasoline to plastics – are essential to our modern way of life. In MB, petroleum products are derived from oil produced in the very SW part of the province

UMA, TRIBUNE, WINNIPEG-GENERAL, 70-6473-40

Shell refinery, Winnipeg, 1975

from sedimentary rocks millions of years old. The petroleum industry is an important part of the economy in SW MB and provides direct employment for 300-350 people and indirect employment for an additional 350-450. Landowners, owners of oil and gas rights, local govt, and the province all benefit from petroleum industry expenditures in the province. There are 13 oil fields and 169 non-confidential oil pools in the province. MB's crude oil production is equivalent to about a quarter of the province's refined petroleum product requirements.

In 2006, 478 new wells were dug, a 34% increase over the previous record year of 1951. Even though MB is now producing 20,000 bbls a day, it is still far behind the 1.5 millions bbls a day produced by Alberta.

MB's oil production occurs in the SW, along the NE flank of the Williston Basin, part of the Phanerozoic sequence of rocks. The Williston Basin discovery well was drilled in the Daly Field in 1951; 2 years later, the **Virden** Field was discovered. Almost 80% of the province's cumulative oil production comes from these 2 fields. The province has produced a total of 36.8 million m^3 of oil as of 2005, and has estimated remaining recoverable oil reserves of 4.3 million m^3. The first horizontal well was drilled in MB in 1991. The longest horizontal well in province extends over 1353 m horizontally through the oil-bearing formation. Horizontal wells, because of their increased reservoir exposure, are typically more productive than vertical ones. Currently, 33.6 % of MB's oil production comes from horizontal wells. Oil produced in MB is transported by interprovincial pipeline to oil refineries in the US Midwest and in ON. • MICHAEL BENARROCH/JOHN FOX

▸ *See* **Geology**, **Hydroelectric Power**, **Pollution**

PHARMACEUTICAL INDUSTRY. The pharmaceutical industry in MB, as opposed to pharmaceutical retailing (or drugstores), has a long history is this province.

HISTORY: Before the development of modern drugs, Aboriginal peoples used local plants and herbs for therapeutic use, as with the **Ojibway Midewiwin** who used such treatments as part of a holistic approach to medicine. Many of these practices were then incorporated by early European settlers into **Home Remedies**, which remained the primary method of treating ailments until improved transportation reduced the cost of bringing drugs into the **Red River Settlement**. MB saw its first wholesale and retail drug store in 1873, though for many years, mail-order catalogues and travelling medicine shows remained the primary retailers of pharmaceuticals to MB's scattered rural population.

P Unlike today's pharmacists, most early druggists were both drug retailers and manufacturers, concocting medicines right behind the storefront counter. To regulate the drugs produced in such shops and safeguard public health, industry regulation became necessary. In 1878, the Manitoba Pharmaceutical Association became the body responsible for regulating drug labelling, though control later shifted to govt. The druggist profession also became more standardized in the province with the establishment of the Manitoba College of Pharmacy in 1899, now a faculty at the **U of M**.

The industry itself was gradually shifting, as certified pharmacists increasingly took on the role of drug dispensers rather than manufacturers, and production moved from the druggist shop to the factory. One of MB's first wholesale operations was the Bole Drug Company, which merged with drug companies from across Canada in 1905 to form the National Drug and Chemical Company of Canada Ltd. By the 1940s, few drug companies remained as the industry became increasingly consolidated in order to take advantage of the economies of scale afforded by large operations. Consolidation allowed for increased investment in R & D, though today private companies still rely on partnerships with govt and universities to fund costly initiatives. MB has several institutions involved in research: the National Research Council's Institute for Biodiagnostics, the Canadian Science Centre for Human and Animal Health, and the U of M. These research centres bolster a growing pharmaceutical industry, increasingly linked to **Biotechnology**, and employing 1300 people with revenue of $445 million in 2006.

MANUFACTURING: The pharmaceutical industry in MB is centred around 4 major drug manufacturers: Biovail Corporation in **Steinbach**, **Vita Health** Products Inc, a subsidiary of Leiner Health Products Inc, and **Cangene** along with its majority shareholder, Apotex Fermentation Inc. Apotex's Winnipeg operation is Canada's largest facility involved in the fermentation of microorganisms, a crucial process in the manufacture of antibiotics.

Of the major companies, Toronto-based Apotex is the sole generic drug manufacturer. The other 3 major companies are defined, in industry terms, as "research-based," meaning they sell patented drugs under a brand name. Patented drugs, such as the MB-developed pregnancy drug WinRho (*see* **Winnipeg Rh Institute**) and the antidepressant Wellbutrin XL, are a contentious subject in the pharmaceutical industry. While brand name drug manufacturers claim patent protection is needed to regain investments made into R & D, generic manufacturers argue that patents only allow large corporations to maintain high prices on life-saving drugs.

INTERNET RETAILING: Canada's highly profitable but controversial online pharmaceutical industry is centred in MB. Based on the mass cross-border sale of prescription medications to the US, the beginnings of the industry date to 2000, when an enterprising **Minnedosa** pharmacist, Andrew Strempler, started selling nicotine gum over the Internet, capitalizing on the huge discrepancies between US and Cdn prices. He soon established MediPlan Pharmacy, Canada's first cross-border online pharmacy. Selling primarily to US seniors, the company was an immediate success, and by 2003 had moved from its original small backroom operation into a $1-million, 1858 m² (24,000 ft²) distribution centre in **Niverville**.

More than 100 online pharmacies across Canada were soon in operation, comprising an industry valued at half a billion dollars. The sector was strongly based in MB, with more than 70 pharmacies operating in the province, employing roughly 20% of MB's 1500 pharmacists. However, ongoing legal battles with pharmaceutical corporations and a new drug plan introduced in the US in 2006 curtailed cross-border sales. Business was so affected that MediPlan closed in 2006, selling off its Niverville warehouse. Nonetheless, some companies did manage to survive through consolidation. As of 2007, there were 20 online pharmacies left in MB, filling roughly 2 million prescriptions a year to US customers. ● MICHELLE DOBROVOLNY

PHILLIPS, Walter Joseph, artist, educator (b Oct 25, 1884, Barton-upon-Humber, Lincs., UK; d July 5, 1963, Victoria, BC) was a fine watercolourist in the English tradition. The son of a Primitive Methodist minister, he moved with his family from manse to manse. At age 14, he was enrolled in Bourne College (near Birmingham) and at Birmingham's Municipal School of Art. In 1901, he became an assistant instructor at Yarmouth College, then emigrated to the Transvaal (South Africa) for 5 years. By the time of his return, Philips was committed to being an artist. With his wife and baby, he immigrated to **Winnipeg** in 1912, choosing the city "for no particular reason." He soon found a job at St. John's Technical High School, and he began sketching and exhibiting with **LeMoine FitzGerald** and Cyril Barraud. When the latter joined the CEF in 1917, Phillips acquired his press, plates, paper, and tools, enabling him to fulfill a lifelong ambition to make prints.

He and his family spent a year in England in 1924-25 to enable him to improve his technique, particularly with woodcut blocks, and he acquired a reputation as the nation's finest woodcut artist. Economic conditions in Winnipeg in the 1930s were as hard on Phillips as on any other artist, and he was anxious to leave. Election to full membership in the Royal Canadian Academy did not alleviate his fear that he was "getting older and getting nowhere" in a "more moth-eaten" city. Life seemed little more than a constant scramble for survival. In 1940, he began a 20-year run of teaching in the summers at the Banff School of Art, and a year later he accepted a position teaching at Calgary's institute of Technology and Art. Finances improved and he built a house at Banff, to which he moved in 1948. He and his wife later moved to Victoria. His woodcuts fetch astounding prices, though he still has not made his way into the first rank of Cdn artists, not least because his exquisite miniature landscapes did not shout their emotions. ● JMB

PHORONID WORM is a sessile, tubular marine creature in the phylum Phoronida, also known as a Horseshoe Worm due to the shape of feathery tentacles at the front end of the body. These function in food gathering, respiration and defense. The animal lives inside a chitinous tube buried in the sand or mud, or attached to a rock, from the low-tide mark down to 400 m, although they are most abundant in shallow water. The unsegmented body is long (species range from 0.5 mm to 45 cm), thin, and cylindrical. The double row of tentacles form a spiraled crescent (called a lophophore), with the mouth inside. Cilia on the tentacles move a current of water carrying food particles, which become trapped in mucus and then are directed by beating cilia to the mouth. Food passes into the U-shaped gut and wastes exit via the anus not far from the mouth.

W. J. Phillips, 1954

UMA, TRIBUNE, PERSONALITY FILES (CPR PHOTO)

The body fluids carry oxygen-bearing hemoglobin – the same molecule on human red-blood cells. These worms are hermaphrodites, their gametes being shed into the sea to be fertilized. The larva (called an actinotrocha) of most species floats away in the plankton, while a few species brood and protect the larva among the tentacles. The larva captures food with its tentacles, and 20 days after fertilization it descends to the sea floor where it undergoes radical metamorphosis in only 30 minutes. The new adult quickly secretes its protective tube. Other options for reproduction are splitting (fission) or budding. This group is represented in Hudson Bay by one species, which has not yet been identified. Only 15 species of these marine wormlike animals remain alive, with a worldwide distribution. Early ancestors of phoronid worms can be traced back 400 million years ago (Devonian period). • REW

PHOTOGRAPHY in MB long precedes the creation of the province, and remains an important hobby, art, and business. This article will concentrate mainly on the art and business aspects of photography.

EARLY HISTORY: In 1857, the Cdn govt sent an expedition into the West, primarily to establish a route for immigrants between Lake Superior and the **RED RIVER SETTLEMENT**. Known formally as the Assiniboine and Saskatchewan Exploring Expedition and informally as the Dawson-Hind Expedition, it was led by Henry Youle Hind, a professor of chemistry and geology from Trinity College (now part of the U of Toronto), and surveyor/engineer **SIMON JAMES DAWSON**. Notably, this was the first expedition in Canada to make use of photography. The photographer employed to document this adventure was Humphrey Lloyd Hime, who made some of the best-known early photographs of landscape in MB. Hime's image, *The Prairie, on the Banks of the Red River, Looking South* (1858) is the definitive Prairies photograph. It shows a lone human skull in the foreground of an otherwise empty landscape extending outward to a flat horizon under a featureless sky. This image has become a Prairie stereotype, highlighting the wide-open space and seemingly limitless expanses. Hime's views of prairie topography reached an international audience when they were published in *The Illustrated London News*.

In the 1870s, an A. Barnard visited Winnipeg and bartered photographs for supplies. Other early photographers in MB included itinerants such as Charles Cavilier and Joseph Langevin, who opened a photography gallery and became the first photographers in western Canada to make *carte-de-visite* (small prints mounted on

Cathedral of St. Boniface and Nunnery on the Banks of Red River, 1858 by Humphrey Lloyd Hime

cardboard) portraits. As settlement of the West increased, other photographers followed, and by 1879, 3 were listed in the **WINNIPEG** city directory. In 1887, noted Montreal photographer William McFarlane Notman (1826-91) photographed in the West. The best known of his photographs from this period are his images of the recently completed Winnipeg-to-Vancouver section of the **CPR**.

Other early photographers in MB were members of the Geological Survey of Canada (GSC). One of these expeditionary photographers was Dr. Robert Bell, who subsequently became acting director of the GSC. In the 1870s and 1880s, he used the recently introduced dry-plate technology to produce views of Winnipeg's Main St. As a proven and effective illustrative tool, photography was used extensively in brochures and newspapers to entice prospective immigrants to the Prairies. One such MB example was the brochure *Gladstone and District*, published by the Gladstone Board of Trade in 1906, which featured images by a J. Jessup.

DEVELOPMENT AS A BUSINESS AND AN ART: Women occupied a significant place in the early development of commercial photography in Manitoba. By 1890, there were 5 known professional women photographers in the province, one of whom was Rosetta E. Carr, whose specialty was portraits of children. Carr opened her studio, called the American Art Gallery, in Winnipeg in 1883, maintaining an active photographic business until her retirement in 1897. Among the men, the most notable was **LEWIS B. FOOTE**, who

photographed in Winnipeg 1902-57. In the period 1907-28, he worked with a partner, George James. Foote's images record the construction of significant examples of Winnipeg architecture and document numerous social and historical events such as "Bloody Sunday," which ended the **WINNIPEG GENERAL STRIKE** of 1919. Substantial collections of photographs by both Carr and Foote are held by the Archives of Manitoba.

Commercial photography thrived in MB. One of the oldest graphics firms in Canada, Toronto-based Brigdens, opened a branch in Winnipeg in 1914 to produce the W Cdn edition of the **EATON'S** catalogue. Brigdens hired many local artists and photographers to work on a variety of projects that reflected the social history of MB. The CPR also employed photographers. In 1929, Nicholas Morant joined the CPR's Winnipeg press bureau and worked for over 50 years on assignments as a "special photographer." His work combines the best of industrial and fine art photography. Morant's photographs received international attention through their publication in magazines such as *Time*, *Look*, *Life*, and *The Saturday Evening Post*. Another CPR employee, Mickey Potoroka, worked as a public-relations representative in Winnipeg after WWII. His photographs document the expansion of the **RAILWAY** in the Cdn West.

The development of amateur photography in MB took place largely through camera clubs. The Winnipeg Camera Club (WCC) was formed in 1892 and, in keeping with the time, encouraged

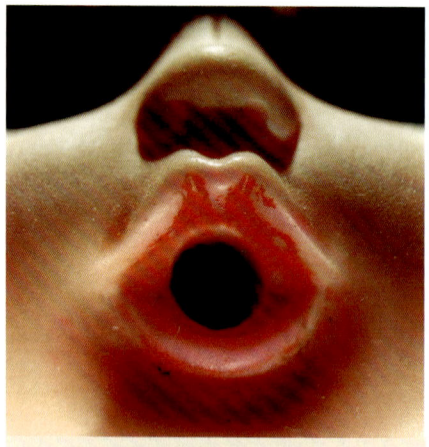

Doll Mouth (Black Eyes) by Diana Thorneycroft

P

a Pictorialist aesthetic. Among its more notable early members were W. Rowe Lewis and Egon Ratibor. The club distinguished itself by winning the championship plaque at the Festival of the Empire Competition in the UK in 1912. As with many other Canadian camera clubs, further development of the WCC was disrupted by the outbreak of WWI. A successor, the Manitoba Camera Club (MCC), was formed in 1932, and in 1935 featured an exhibition of western Canadian pictorial photography. The MCC continues to meet in Winnipeg to this day.

By the 1970s and 1980s, art photography was well established across Canada. Notable in MB in this period were portrait photographers Cal Bailey and Michaelin McDermott, as well as **John Paskievich** and David Barbour, whose work could be called "social documentary." Significant in the development of photography as art was the **Winnipeg Art Gallery**, which maintains a substantial collection of contemporary photography. The WAG has mounted numerous exhibitions of MB photographers, including David Appel, David Barbour, Scott MacEachern, John Paskievich, and, more recently, **Diana Thorneycroft** and William Eakin. Winnipeg art journal *Border Crossings* has been a strong advocate of photography by contemporary Manitobans.

THE PRESENT: Another major influence on art photography in the province has come from the School of Art's photography program at the U of M, headed by David McMillan. Other photography instructors have included: Susan Close, William Eakin, Rosalie Favell, Larry Glawson, and Bruce Kirton. Former students of this undergraduate program include: Sarah Ann Johnston, Laura Letinsky, Meera Singh, and Lisa Stinner.

Other venues in which to see art photography in MB include Winnipeg's Platform Gallery (formerly Floating Gallery), Ace Art Gallery,

and the Plug In Institute of Contemporary Art. Contemporary art photographers active in MB include Sarah Crawley, William Eakin, Richard Holden, David McMillan, Sarah Anne Johnston, Lisa Stinner, Sheila Spence, and Dominque Rey. The 2006 *SuperNova* exhibition at the Winnipeg Art Gallery highlighted emerging artists, including photographers Richard Hines, Talia Potash, and Meera Singh. • SUSAN CLOSE

PHYSIOGRAPHIC REGIONS in MB are the product of 3.5 billion years of geological history. Because of that history, present-day MB can be divided into 4 distinct physiographic or topographical regions – the Precambrian Shield, the Hudson Bay Lowlands, the Manitoba Lowlands, and the Southwest Uplands. Rocks of the Precambrian Shield underlie the entire province, but 40% of this ancient basement is covered by younger formations that accumulated underwater. **Fossils** found in rocks in MB were clearly deposited under an ancient ocean. They contain small marine invertebrates (ancestors of clams, corals, and insects), as well as giant marine reptiles that have only been found near **Morden** (*see* **Canadian Fossil Discovery Centre**). MB's physiographic regions reflect both the nature of the ancient basement as well as the effects of the Pleistocene **Glaciation**, the last major surface-shaping event in MB's long history.

PRECAMBRIAN SHIELD: The Precambrian, Laurentian, or Canadian Shield is exposed in a relatively level though hummocky terrain with plenty of rock outcrops. In the central part of the shield, the Nelson trough slopes seaward, giving the waters of the Churchill, Nelson, and Hayes rivers an exit into the sea. In northwestern MB, the surface of the shield is hilly with plenty of rock outcrops, eskers, and drift ridges that rise up to 100 m above the valley bottoms.

The rocks that make up the shield were formed over about 3.5 billion years. At first, there were just volcanic islands in a large Precambrian ocean. Some of those started as rift valleys under the sea, where the so-called "black smokers" – geysers spewing hot gases with large volumes of valuable metals – periodically formed among the volcanic piles. Examples of those that survived erosion are **Flin Flon**, **Snow Lake**, **Leaf Rapids**, and **Lynn Lake**. Later on, the volcanic deposits were involved in a collision of continents and were elevated into mountains. Molten rock or magma that normally underlies mountains at great depth precipitated deposits of titanium near **Cross Lake** and the rare metals lithium, cesium, and tantalum near **Lac du Bonnet**. These metals have many uses in the pharmaceutical industry and in high-tech

manufacturing, including batteries, aircraft, cellular phones, atomic clocks and wristwatches, and computers. Shield rocks have also a potential for diamonds and other gems. Where ancient continents once collided, lavas poured out from great depths, bringing deposits of nickel. This was the unique environment where the **Thompson** nickel belt formed. At that time, the group of mountains running from Flin Flon to **Churchill** was probably the tallest ever on Earth. We know this because their rocks exposed on the surface today formed as deep as 15 km below Earth's surface. Older mountains spread over the rest of the province.

HUDSON BAY LOWLANDS: The Hudson Bay Lowlands is an undulating plain of subdued relief and low elevation. The region is blanketed with marine clays and has been elevated up to 150 m due to glacial rebound. Strandlines marking former beaches are the major elements of relief. The **Churchill River** and the **Nelson** have cut major banks, 18 to 50 m tall, into the till and bedrock. Erosion by the continental ice sheet has altered the drainage creating a multitude of swamps, lakes, and streams. Oil exploration has provided much information on the sedimentary layers that make up the Hudson Basin. The layers get thicker toward the centre of Hudson Bay. On the MB shore of the bay, these sedimentary rock layers are about 900 m thick and should reach about 2 km thick under the bay.

During the Paleozoic era, between about 450 and 250 mya, parts of the province were under a tropical sea, and marine life flourished – something like the Bahamas Banks of today. Eventually, the sea animals, which included corals, clams, crinoids, and cephalopods, became preserved as fossils in limestone such as the renowned **Tyndall stone**; near Churchill, the world's biggest trilobite was discovered in limestone. At least once during this time, the ocean dried up. In its place, thick accumulations of salt, Potash, and gypsum formed. Today, these formations are buried below the surface. Groundwater brings some of these chemicals to the surface in the salt springs around **Lake Winnipegosis**. There, salt was the first resource to be commercially produced in MB. Salt springs can also be exploited locally as spas that bring soothing to sufferers of arthritis, psoriasis, and a host of other ailments.

Shortly after the Paleozoic era ended, a 4 km²-large meteor left a monstrous crater in the **Interlake**, the largest in western Canada. Seawater eventually filled the crater and deposited gypsum when it dried up. The town of **Gypsumville** lies in the middle of this meteorite crater.

MANITOBA LOWLANDS: The Manitoba Lowlands region is underlain principally by gently dipping Paleozoic strata. It is the flattest part of the province. The lowlands lie SW of the Precambrian Shield and are bounded on the W by the steep rise of the **MANITOBA ESCARPMENT**, a preglacial feature. The rise in the land is generally less than 8 m high. The Saskatchewan, **RED**, and **ASSINIBOINE** rivers drain the region, and the principal lakes are **WINNIPEG**, **WINNIPEGOSIS**, and **MANITOBA**, all remnants of **LAKE AGASSIZ**. South of these lakes, bedrock is deeply buried beneath the silty clays of what was Lake Agassiz. This makes the region one of the richest for farming in Canada. In the last 8,000 years since the Pleistocene ice sheet melted, the exposed Paleozoic limestone has developed sinkholes and small caves. Before the Ice Age, these caves would have been much bigger, but the ice gouged them away.

SOUTHWESTERN UPLANDS: Mesozoic rocks and Pleistocene moraine deposits underlie the Southwestern Uplands. The Porcupine, **DUCK**, and **RIDING** mountains, whose eastern margins form the Manitoba Escarpment, are separated in turn by broad gentle valleys, the work of rivers much larger than the present misfit streams. The surface of these mountains, which rise up to 500 m above the MB Lowlands, is a flat plateau. Bedrock is exposed along the escarpment face, but on the plateau, it is covered by a great thickness of glacial deposits. ● MICHAEL ISSIGONIS

▸ *See* **ECOCLIMATIC REGIONS**, **GEOLOGY**, **GLACIATION**.

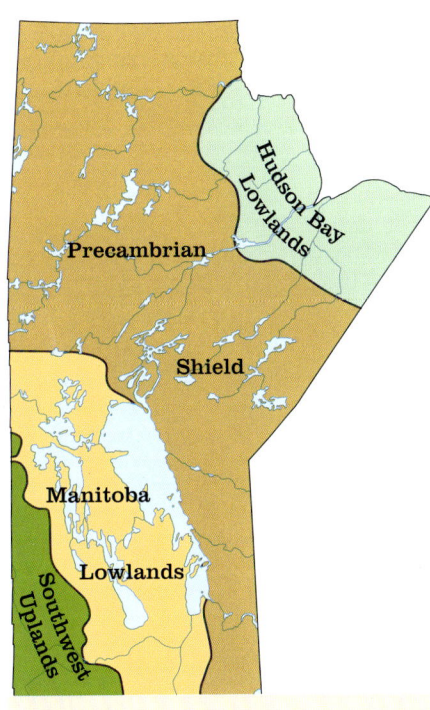

Physiographic Regions Map

PICKEREL. *See* **WALLEYE**

PICKERSGILL, John Whitney "Jack," federal cabinet minister, historian (b June 23, 1905, Wyecombe, Norfolk Cty, ON; d Nov 14, 1997, Ottawa) worked on Parliament Hill for over 30 years. He moved when young to a MB homestead. He graduated from the **U OF M** with a BA in 1927, moving on to the U of Oxford to study history. In 1929, he accepted a lectureship at Wesley College (*see* **U OF W**) in **WINNIPEG**, and he taught history there until 1937, when he wrote the civil service examination and finished first. He was appointed to the PM's Office, and remained there until 1949, rising to become Clerk of the Privy Council in Louis St. Laurent's govt. Pickersgill was one of the most ardent supporters of Newfoundland's entry into Confederation in 1949. With Joey Smallwood's assistance, he ran for Parliament for the riding of Bonavista-Twillingate in 1949, serving in Parliament until 1967. He held several cabinet portfolios (Minister of Citizenship and Immigration, and Transportation Minister) before arranging his own appointment as chair of the Transport Commission, which he, as Minister, had created. He retired from that post in 1975. Pickersgill was an active writer on politics and political biography, as well as a memoirist. ● JMB

PICTOGRAPHS are images sketched by **FIRST PEOPLES** on vertical rock faces along rivers and lakes in the forested areas of the MB shield in eastern and northern MB. They are also found in adjacent areas of northwestern ON and northeastern SK. They are made by applying a mixture of red ochre and **FISH** oil, particularly **STURGEON**, with a brush. Many could only have been made while in a canoe but others can be reached by standing or kneeling on a ledge.

These images are simple outline sketches of many symbols or icons. These include hands, animals such as **MOOSE**, **ELK** and **BISON**, spiritual beings such as Thunderbirds and people or shamans with spiritual power lines emanating from their mouths or heads, and a variety of geometric forms. These images are usually portrayed as simple but powerful stick figures. (*See* **ABORIGINAL SPIRITUALITY**.)

First Nations elders have identified some sites as the doorways to the living areas of the Maymaygwashi, or little people, living behind the rock surfaces. Unlike humans, these little people can penetrate the solid rock surfaces and even paddle their canoes through the rock faces. It has been suggested that some sites represent expressions of hunting magic to insure success in the hunt.

Pictograph sites are considered to be sacred by traditional First Nations peoples. Many still leave small gifts of tobacco or other items when they visit or pass a site. These sites have been referred to as rock art sites (*see* **ANCIENT ABORIGINAL ART**), but a more suitable term might be "sacred symbol sites."

The ages of these sites are unknown. They begin sometime in the Precontact Period perhaps as early as the Middle or Late Woodland periods (*see* **WOODLAND PERIOD**), based on the ages of nearby campsites. At least a few were produced during the **FUR TRADE** Period because they show canoes with flags and/or long-barrelled guns. ● E. LEIGH SYMS

P

PIERSON, pop 230, is an unincorporated village in the RM of Edward, 8 km E of SK, 19 km N of the US border. The village welcomed a **CPR** line and a post office in 1891. The community was named after Jean L. Pierson whose Amsterdam, Holland, company financed the railway spur line through the settlement. When the station closed in 1971, much of its furniture and equipment was sent to the Amsterdam head office in appreciation of the company's role in helping to settle the area. Pierson is a service centre, and mixed farming is still the primary economic activity. There are 2 churches, 2 elevators, community hall, seniors' lodge, fitness centre, doctor's office, bank, and a variety of businesses. The community supports a library and a theatre group. Each summer, more than 2000 persons attend the Pierson Carnival of Crafts, one of the biggest such sales in MB. The Pierson area is noted for wildlife, with many eastern and western bird varieties. ● GPP

PIKE is a fish in the Pike family Esocidae (order Esociformes) of which there are 2 species represented in MB – the Northern Pike (*Esox lucius*) and the Muskellunge (*Esox masquinongy*). The head and body of these species are streamlined (with dorsal and anal fins placed posteriorly), as befitting predators that ambush prey at great speed. The Northern Pike is olive with numerous pale-yellow spots or diagonal bars, and dark-brown fins. The colour and pattern create excellent camouflage as the fish lurks motionlessly, often among weeds. The lower jaw is lined with substantial fangs and smaller teeth appear in areas on the roof of the mouth. The pike has an enormous range that covers the entire province. It prefers cool and clear water of lakes and large rivers without much current. Maximum size recorded in MB is 150 cm and 17.2 kg. This species begins spawning in rivers and streams as soon as the ice clears (water temperature of 4-11°C) in April in the S, and May in the N. Courted by one or 2 smaller males, the female seeks a site with dense vegetation. Rolling over intermittently with the males, she releases an

Northern Pike

P average of 32,000 (max. 600,000) adhesive eggs, which are fertilized by the male's milt and then stick to plants and the bottom. The eggs hatch in 12 days. One study estimated a mortality rate of eggs and fry at 99.8% – hence the adaptiveness of producing such large numbers of eggs. Fry feed on tiny animals in the plankton but graduate to insects larvae and small fish in only a few weeks. Frogs, leeches, crayfish, muskrats and birds also enter the diet. In Southern populations, males become sexually mature in 2-3 years, females in 3-4, while in the N where growth is slower, maturity is reached at 5 and 6 years respectively. Maximum life span also varies with water temperature – 10-12 years in the S and 24-26 years in the N. A top-level predator of aquatic ecosystems, the Northern Pike is a valued game and commercial species.

The Muskellunge is similar to the Northern Pike, but is brownish-olive with dark blotches or bars (white on the belly), and there are technical differences in scales and pores on the head. It is native in MB only in the Winnipeg River system, although it has been introduced to lakes in the **Riding** and **Duck Mountains** and has spread to **Lake Manitoba**. The "muskie" grows larger than the Northern Pike, with MB records of 106 cm and 16 kg. It is Canada's second-largest freshwater fish (after Lake Sturgeon), with maximum size reaching 183 cm and 45 kg. It is believed to spawn in May (water temperatures 10-16°C) – several weeks later than pike, and possible the larger pike fry devour such numbers of smaller muskie fry that this factor may limit the spread of the latter species in MB. The Muskellunge is also more specific in habitat requirements, and is found only in larger rivers and lakes. Growth is rapid, up to 30 cm by Nov. Females grow faster and larger, some reaching 30 years old. A large female can produce 265,000 eggs a season. Hybridization between the Muskellunge and Northern Pike occurs infrequently. Catching a record muskie is the aim of many anglers. • REW

PILOT MOUND, pop 676, is a town 100 km SE of **Brandon** on hwy 3, near the Pembina River. The town takes its name from a nearby land formation of the same name, so called because the 35 m-high **Ancient Mound** was used as a guiding landmark for First Nations peoples. While most geologists say a natural gas explosion created this landform, some claim the distinctive topography is due to **Glaciation**. The mound is steeped in Aboriginal lore. In 1908, archaeologists unearthed evidence that the Mound Builders – early Aboriginal people – were active here thousands of years ago. According to local oral tradition, **Bison** hunters from the **Red River Settlement** massacred about 600 **Dakota** people in the area in Sept 1854. Two Dakotas were allowed to survive so they could relate the events to their people. The slain warriors were supposed to have been buried in a mass grave at the W side of the mound, and Dakota visit the mound every Sept to honour their ancestors.

In 1878, permanent settlers of European origin, primarily people of **English**, **Scots**, and **Irish** stock from ON, came here to farm grain. A post office opened in 1880. The following year, a small community, including a school and bank, was built atop Pilot Mound's namesake hill. Later in the 1880s, the community moved several km SE of the mound – which locals now call "Old Mound" – to where the **CPR** came. The area grew quickly, and soon **Grain Elevators** stood along the railway. Later settlers included **French** and **Ukrainians**, and **Beef Cattle Farming** soon joined grain production as a major industry in the area. In the 21st century, Pilot Mound still acts as a service center for surrounding farms. "Black Jack" Stewart, hockey player, and **Paul Hiebert**, author of *Sarah Binks* – a satire of an imaginary SK poet and of the academics who study her – were born and raised here. Alexander Gordon Craig, founder of **Craig** Broadcasting, also lived in Pilot Mound. • GPP

PIMICIKAMAK CREE NATION (formerly known as Cross Lake First Nation), on reserve pop 4825, off reserve pop 1772, is located about 190 km S of **Thompson**, 520 km N of **Winnipeg**, on the shores of the **Nelson River**, where it meets with Cross Lake. Pimicikawak signed Treaty 5 in 1875; the native language here is Cree. There are a total of 7 reserves in this First Nation community, although the primary population is in Cross Lake IR No. 19. The Pimicikamak Cree Nation administers its own schooling, from Nursery-Grade 12. Total enrolment for the year 2003-04 was at 1583. It is an independent First Nation, so it is not a member of any tribal council.

The Pimicikamak Cree Nation is 1 of the 5 First Nations that was signatory to the **Northern Flood Agreement**. The community of Pimicikamak experienced some of the most severe fluctuations in water levels under the effects of hydroelectric development. The Jenpeg Power Dam was built about 15 km upstream of the First Nation. Commercial fishing, trapping, and hunting, the economic foundation for Pimicikamak Cree Nation, have been hugely disrupted by flooding. The challenges continue. In July 2006, a state of emergency was declared at Pimicikamak Cree Nation when the community's nursing station was closed for all medical services except for emergencies, and all other health care services are only available by travelling to Thompson or Winnipeg. This community has an all-weather road to Pipestone Lake, but is essentially dependent on winter roads and air service.

Eric Robinson, MLA and cabinet minister in **Gary Doer**'s govt, was born in the community. Prominent native musician Ernest Monias also comes from the Pimicikamak Cree Nation community. • RK

PINAWA, pop 1500, is a community 100 km ENE of **Winnipeg** along the **Winnipeg River** near **Whiteshell Provincial Park**. The area was long occupied by Cree peoples, who gave the area the name, *pinnowok* – referring to how calm the channel seemed to be compared to the fast-running waters of the **Winnipeg River**. The name was subsequently anglicized as "Pinawa." The Winnipeg Electric Street Railway Company (*see* **Winnipeg Street Railway**) built a dam here in 1906 to generate **Hydroelectric** power – the first in the province – for the capital's streetcars. The population grew around the power industry, and in 1910, a post office opened. The generator remained in operation until 1951, a few years

Pinawa's suspension bridge

before Winnipeg's streetcar service was discontinued. Residents then left "Old Pinawa," the townsite built around the original dam, en masse. With the building of a new planned community, "New Pinawa," in the early 1960s by Atomic Energy of Canada Ltd (AECL) to accompany the Whiteshell Nuclear Research Establishment – the post office reopened.

AECL, a federal Crown agency, was the dominant employer here for decades, attracting scientists from across the world. Pinawa thus became significantly more educated and more ethnically diverse than its location would otherwise suggest. In 1998, AECL decided to decommission the Whiteshell facility, a process of downsizing that could take 20 years. In an effort to diversify its economy, the town began promoting its broadband Internet access. By 2006, 60 home-based businesses had started up in the community. Newcomers were also attracted by lifestyle amenities such as access to fishing, an excellent **GOLF** course and the nearby provincial park. Nevertheless, the community's population fell nearly 10% from 1996 to 2001. ● GPP

PINAYMOOTANG FIRST NATION (previously known as Fairford First Nation), on reserve pop 1124, off reserve pop 1543, is located 240 km NW of **WINNIPEG**, on Lake St. Martin. The native language here is **OJIBWAY**, and the Pinaymootang First Nation community signed Treaty 2 in 1871. There is one reserve situated on this land, called Fairford IR No. 50. An all-weather road via hwy 6 services the community. Schooling, administered by the Fairford School Board and the Interlake Reserves Tribal Council, goes from Nursery-Grade 12, and total enrolment for the year 2003-2004 was 85. The economic foundation of Pinaymootang First Nation is ranching, fishing, trapping, and hunting. It is a member of the Interlake Reserves Tribal Council.

This was the site of a **HBC** trading post in the 19th century. Anglican Church missionaries, from Fairford, England, subsequently built a mission here in 1851. The community was first known as Partridge Crop, but David Anderson, the bishop of **RUPERT'S LAND**, changed the name to Fairford. This is a picturesque setting, featuring one of MB's favourite **SPORT FISHING** spots just down from the Fairford Dam, which joins Lake Manitoba and Lake St. Martin on the Fairford River. A **CN** railway bridge, built in 1912, can be swung out of the path of larger boats. The First Nation celebrates Treaty Days every summer. ● RK

PINE. MB has 3 native species of pine **TREES**, the common jack pine (*Pinus banksiana*), rare red or Norway pine (*P. resinosa*) and the even

rarer white pine (*P. strobus*). All are evergreen softwood conifer (cone-bearing) trees. Manitobans tend to call all evergreen trees '**SPRUCE**' or 'pine' but they are actually quite easy to tell apart. Pines always have their needle leaves in clusters rather than singly along the twigs as do spruce and fir. Jack pine and red pine have stiff needles in bundles of 2. Jack pine's are short (2-4 cm long) and twisted, red pine's longer (7-17 cm) and straight. White pine has long (5-12 cm) soft needles in bundles of 5. Jack pine cones are small (3-5 cm), yellow, curved, and glossy, with a coating of natural high-temperature glue and remain on the tree. Those of red pine are larger (3-6 cm), nearly square and shed each year. These 2 pines need lots of sun and are fire-adapted, with thick bark and cones that only open at high temperatures. They survive, or are the first colonizers, after fires that leave bare mineral-rich soil, perfect for the germination and growth of the rain of winged seeds released from their cones.

White pine has long (to 15 cm) slender cones that are shed each year and is not fire-resistant. It is at the eastern edge of its natural range and found on only a few sites in SE MB. In eastern Canada and the US it grew so tall and straight that the British Crown reserved it for masts for its sailing ships. Red Pine is found naturally on a few sites in SE MB and on the E end of Black Island in **LAKE WINNIPEG** and is planted in forest reserves and as an ornamental elsewhere. Neither red nor white pine is economically important other than as local lumber or firewood in MB. Jack pine is the common 'scrub' pine of sandy and rocky areas throughout MB, reaching N to Kettle Rapids on the **NELSON RIVER**. Often bent and twisted in shape, especially in open areas, it is seldom used for lumber or for firewood because of its high pitch and knot content. It is an important source of wood for paper products and oriented strand board, providing about 30% of MB's forest harvest. **FIRST PEOPLES** used its needles, bark, and pitch for various medicinal and other uses and the wood for a few purposes. **PORCUPINES** enjoy the bark and red **SQUIRRELS** harvest and store the cones for their small edible seeds. Scot's pine (*Pinus sylvestris*) is a common introduced tree found as an ornamental and in older forestry plantations. It has 4-8 cm long stiff needles in bundles of two and distinctive smooth orange-red bark on the upper part of older trunks. ● KAREN JOHNSON

PINE CREEK FIRST NATION, on reserve pop 1217, off reserve pop 1402, is located about 437 km NW of **WINNIPEG**. Pine Creek First Nation is adjacent to the S border of **CAMPERVILLE**. The native language here is **OJIBWAY**, and Treaty 4

was signed in 1874. There are 2 reserves located on Pine Creek: Pine Creek IR No. 66A and Treaty Four Reserve Grounds No. 77. It is a member of the West Region Tribal Council. Pine Creek First Nation administers schooling from Nursery-Grade 11 in a new 16-room school. Enrolment for the year 2003-04 was 233. This First Nation can be accessed by all-weather roads, via hwy 20 from **DAUPHIN**. Grey Goose Bus Lines provides daily service to the community. The economic foundation of the Pine Creek First Nation is trapping, hunting, and **FISHING**. ● RK

PIONEER GRAIN is a subsidiary of Winnipeg-based James Richardson International, which in turn is the largest subsidiary of **JAMES RICHARDSON & SONS, LIMITED**. Pioneer is Canada's largest private grain company, providing western Canada producers with grain handling, grain marketing, and logistical services. As well, it sells crop input products such as herbicides and fertilizers. Pioneer, which is headquartered in Winnipeg, traces its roots back to 1857, when James Richardson, a Kingston, Canada West (ON), tailor, began accepting grain as payment for the tailoring services he provided to some of his cash-strapped farm customers. From there, he began buying and selling grain on a regular basis, and eventually he left the tailoring business to concentrate his time and efforts on developing his fast-growing grain merchandising operations. The business later expanded from ON into western Canada, and Pioneer Grain Company Limited was established in 1913 as a wholly owned subsidiary to manage the parent company's grain elevator network in the region. At its peak, Pioneer Grain owned several hundred such facilities in western Canada. As of 2005, it still had more than 60, including 8 in MB. It also owned or partly owned 2 grain-handling terminals in BC. ● MURRAY MCNEILL

PIPER, "Rowdy Roddy," wrestler (b Apr 17, 1954, Saskatoon). Piper, whose real name is Roderick George Toombs, has made a name for himself as an often-maligned personality in US wrestling entertainment. As a child, Piper moved all over Canada because of his father's work with **CN** Rail. After being expelled from a Toronto junior high school, Piper moved to **WINNIPEG** where got his start wrestling in 1973. His success in Winnipeg's amateur wrestling rings led to his 1975 Los Angeles wrestling debut as the "Masked Canadian." He remained in the National Wrestling Alliance through the late 1970s before entering the ring as "Roddy Piper" in the World Wrestling Federation during its expansion throughout NA in 1984. Piper, whose new persona reflected his Scottish descent, became famous for his interview segments called "Piper's Pit," as well as his trademark "sleeper" hold, a move where he would incapacitate opponents by tightly holding their neck between his bicep and forearm.

He served as interim WWF president in 1996 before moving to the World Champion Wrestling organization, which was amalgamated into the WWF in 2001. In 2000, Piper was let go at the age of 46, and filed a lawsuit claiming age discrimination. His autobiography "In the Pit with Piper: Roddy Gets Rowdy" was published in 2002, and he made a brief return to the WWF, which had changed to the WWE, in 2003 but was subsequently fired for making negative comments about the wrestling industry. His fame as a wrestler led to other opportunities in the entertainment industry, and Piper has appeared in over 30 movies over the course of his career. • MD

PISCHKE, Garth, VOLLEYBALL player, (b Aug 12, 1955, WINNIPEG) is a well-known figure on MB volleyball courts. Pischke first started playing while attending Bruce Junior High, and continued on at Silver Heights High School. His success on the varsity team earned him a spot on 3 MB junior teams, all of which won Cdn championships, with Pischke named as MVP in 1973. He was selected for the Cdn Olympic team while still in his grade 12 year, and went to the 1976 Montreal Olympics. He later played for both the U OF W and the U OF M volleyball teams, playing on all together 3 Canadian Interuniversity Athletic Union championship teams, and twice winning MVP.

After retiring from play on the university court, he played professionally in the US for 3 seasons. Pischke earned rookie of the year in his first season, and the league's MVP in his 2nd

Garth Pischke has had an outstanding career as a volleyball player and coach.

season. Upon his return to Winnipeg, Pischke coached the U of M Bison's volleyball team. At the end of the 2005-06 season, his 26th season as head coach, Pischke had coached the Bisons to 1080 wins and 18 Conference titles, where he was named Top Coach 8 times. He led the team to 9 Canadian Interuniversity Athletic Union championships, where he was named Top Coach 6 times.

In 26 years, Pischke's Bisons qualified for the National Championships 25 times, earning 22 CIAU medals (9 gold, 9 silver, and 4 bronze), finishing 4th twice and 5th once. Pischke made a brief playing comeback with the Cdn Olympic Team, joining them at the 1984 Los Angeles Olympics. The Cdn team finished 4th, which, as of writing, remains the national team's highest ranking in Olympic competition. He took over coaching duties for the national team from 1996-2000, and then returned to his coaching position at the U of M. In 2000, Pischke was named Canada's Best Male Volleyball Player Ever by Volleyball Canada Magazine. He has been inducted into Volleyball Canada's Hall of Fame, the **MANITOBA SPORTS HALL OF FAME**, and the Canadian Olympic Hall of Fame. • MD

PITBLADO, Isaac, lawyer (b 1867, Glenelg, NS; d Dec 6, 1964, WINNIPEG) was educated at Dalhousie U and the **U OF M**, where he earned his BA in 1886 and MA in 1893. He received an honorary LLD from Dalhousie in 1919. Pitblado came to Winnipeg in 1882 and was called to the Manitoba Bar in 1890. A prominent lawyer, he was president of the Manitoba Law Society 1917-20. He also served as registrar of the U of M 1893-1900. Regarded as an expert on the intricacies of **RAILWAY** freight rates and grain marketing, he served on a number of Royal Commissions. He was a member of the **CITIZEN'S COMMITTEE OF 1000** in the **WINNIPEG GENERAL STRIKE**. An avid golfer and curler, he was president of the Manitoba Curling Association in 1910-11. • JMB

PLOEN, Ken, football player (b June 3, 1935, Lost Nation, IA) was a popular quarterback during the glory days of the **WINNIPEG BLUE BOMBERS** through the late 1950s and early 60s. Ploen started out as a college quarterback for the Iowa Hawkeyes, leading them to a 1957 Rose Bowl victory. Riding this wave of success, he joined the Bombers for the 1957-58 season. Ploen was remarkable for his ability both on offence and defence. In 1959, he was named All-Western and set a new franchise record with 10 interceptions on defence. He also excelled as a quarterback, bringing the Bombers to Grey Cup victory in 1961 when he scored the winning touchdown in the final game against the Hamilton Tigercats

Kenny Ploen, 1965

in the first and only Grey Cup game to go into overtime. In 1965, Ploen set a new CFL record when he threw a 109 yd pass to **KEN NEILSEN**. He was selected that year as All-Canadian quarterback, and received the Air Canada Award for most popular player. Ploen retired in 1967, with 1080 completions over 1916 passes attempted for 16470 yds, including 119 touchdown passes. He is a member of the Canadian Football Hall of Fame. He continued to live in **WINNIPEG** following his retirement from the Bombers. • MD

PLUM COULEE, pop 725, is a town 90 km SSW of **WINNIPEG** on hwy 14 and on the Plum Coulee River – a small tributary of the **RED RIVER** – after which the town is named. Plum Coulee is among the few places in MB that has true prairie (see **PHYSIOGRAPHIC REGIONS**), and was mainly occupied by Siouan peoples before European contact. The **CPR** came here around 1884, which sparked migration from Russian **MENNONITES**, who still constitute the vast majority of the population. **AGRICULTURE** was and remains the primary pursuit, and a flour mill was built here in 1890, the same year a post office opened. Plum Coulee was incorporated as a village in 1901, and a town in 1915. Plum Coulee is the birthplace of Saidye Rosner, later Saidye Bronfman, wife of Jewish liquor magnate Samuel Bronfman (see **BRONFMAN FAMILY**), and the Samuel and Saidye Bronfman Family Foundation has contributed to town renewal projects such as landscaping a park and developing a beach. Other recent local initiatives have included the transformation of the town's **Grain Elevator** into a multipurpose centre. **Tourist** attractions include the annual Plum Coulee Sports Day in June; Plum Fest in Aug; Perogie Fall Supper in Sept and Christmas tree lighting ceremonies in Nov. Plum Coulee is also home to the Plum Coulee Express hockey team. The infamous **"Bloody Jack" Krafchenko** lived near Plum Coulee and robbed a local bank branch in 1913. • GPP

PLUMMER, Francis Allen "Frank," medical researcher (b Dec 2, 1952, **Winnipeg**). An internationally recognized AIDS researcher and microbiology expert, Plummer graduated from Shaftesbury High School in Winnipeg in 1969 and entered the **U of M**. After completing his medical degree in 1976 under the tutelage of **Allan Ronald**, he continued his training in internal **Medicine** and infectious diseases at the U of Southern California, the US's Centers for Disease Control (Atlanta), and the U of Nairobi. At the Kenyan posting, he completed a year-long fellowship in 1981.

In 1984, Plummer returned to Nairobi, spending the next 16 years at the World Health Organization's Collaborating Centre for Research and Training in Sexually Transmitted Diseases, studying STDs and HIV/AIDS. Plummer began surveying the incidence of acquired immune deficiency syndrome amongst Kenyan prostitutes. In 1985, 2/3 of the 500 women in the study were infected with HIV or AIDS, at a time when some questioned whether heterosexual women could contract HIV at all. By 1988, he discovered that a small group of the women had not contracted the virus despite a history of exposure. The women seemed to have a natural immunity, pointing to the potential for a vaccine.

In Sept 2000, Plummer returned to Winnipeg to serve as scientific director general of Health Canada's **National Microbiology Laboratory**. In 2001, he became the U of M Distinguished Professor of Medicine and Medical Microbiology, as well as associate professor of Community Health Sciences. He was also named the Canadian Institutes of Health Research's Canada Research Chair in Resistance and Susceptibility to Infections. Plummer was appointed director general of the Centre for Infectious Disease Prevention and Control in Ottawa in 2003, and is chief scientific advisor of the Public Health Agency of Canada.

As head of the Winnipeg microbiology laboratory, Plummer did extensive research into severe acute respiratory syndrome (SARS) in 2003 and '04. He was part of the team that identified the coronavirus believed to be the cause of the outbreak. He later questioned that explanation after finding that only 40% of Cdn SARS patients had the virus, while others who had the coronavirus had no symptoms of SARS. His findings contradicted the conclusions of the World Health Organization (WHO).

Also known for his colourful personality, Plummer has received a number of honours, including from the Medical Research Council of Canada, the **Winnipeg Rh Institute**, the American Venereal Disease Association, the American College of Surgeons, and, in June 2005, both the **St. Boniface Hospital** Research Foundation international award and an honorary doctorate from the U of Calgary. Further recognition came in June 2005, when the Bill and Melinda Gates Foundation's Grand Challenges in Global Health program gave Plummer a 5-year, $8.3-million US (Ca $9,775,000) grant to continue his studies on Kenyan prostitutes and work toward a vaccine.

In July 2006, Plummer was elected to the Royal Society of Canada. He has also been a member of the American Society of Clinical Investigation and of the Association of American Physicians, and has served as an advisor and consultant to the govts of Kenya, India, and Lesotho; to the World Bank and the WHO; and to the US National Academy of Sciences. • JOEL TRENAMAN

POCKET GOPHER is a cylindrical, subterranean rodent in the family Geomyidae (meaning earth-mouse), represented in MB by 2 species. Both are largely unknown to the public except farmers that have to deal with them in their fields and pastures. They are often referred to as **Moles**, because they leave a series of large earthen mounds on the surface. Moles, however, leave a volcano-shaped mound while pocket gophers leave more of a horseshoe shape. The gophers' entrances are almost always plugged with earth, which distinguishes their burrows from those of other animals, which are left open. The larger is the Plains Pocket Gopher (*Geomys bursarius*) with a chocolate-brown pelage and males weighing 260g (females 225g). Its only distribution in

Northern Pocket Gopher

MB (and in Canada) is the small area of former tall-grass prairie between the Roseau River and the MN border. It prefers easy tunnelling in rich black or sandy loam, and when abundant (18/hectare), it has been known to turn over 10 tonnes of soil/hectare/year. The smaller Northern Pocket Gopher (*Thomomys talpoides*) is brownish-grey, weighs 150g (females 125g), and inhabits meadows, shrub-grassland, and even open woodland, including gravelly soil. Its range is more extensive – to the limit of grassland and aspen parkland in SW and SC MB. In places where both occur, the larger and more aggressive Plains species forces out the Northern one.

These are among the few mammals that spend almost their entire life underground, and this existence is possible through some remarkable adaptations – powerful front limbs with stout claws and huge incisor teeth (with a fold-behind flap of skin to keep earth out of the mouth) for burrowing, tiny eyes and external ears (normal-sized ones would be of little use and would be in the way), short plush fur, loose skin to enable tight turns, a touch-sensitive tail for backing up, and spacious fur-lined cheek pouches for transporting food (e.g., succulent roots) back to the living chambers. With constant wear, the incisors and claws exhibit astonishing replacement growth of 0.5-1 mm/day. Pocket gopher females often survive 5 years, while males seldom live 3, perhaps the result of their highly pugnacious nature. When one male happens to burrow into the home of another, a fight almost always ensues, frequently with mortal wounds. Rarely, when feeding, dispersing, or flooded out, a pocket gopher will travel on the surface, which explains how their bones appear occasionally in the pellets of owls. Their lifestyle of avoiding the surface life has proven successful, for the group has been around for over 36 million years on the NA plains and western mountains. • REW

PODOLAK, Mitch, arts organizer (b Sept 21, 1947, Toronto, ON). Best known locally as the co-founder of the **Winnipeg Folk Festival**, Podolak began producing folk **Music** concerts at Toronto's Bohemian Embassy Coffee House when he was just 16, learning from Don Cullen. In the early years of his lifelong commitment to **Communism** and social activism, Podolak came to **Winnipeg** in 1968 to act as a field organizer for the League For Socialist Action, an international movement committed to Trotskyism.

Podolak worked in **Broadcasting** as a CBC Radio documentary maker, contributing to the programs CBC Tuesday Night, Between Ourselves, Five Nights, and This Country In The Morning. In 1973, inspired by ON's Mariposa Folk Festival,

P

Mitch Podolak, 1975

he decided that Winnipeg should host a similar festival as a centennial project. CBC colleagues Walter Unger and Paul Mills were instrumental in the festival's development, as was architect and **THEATRE** buff Colin Gorrie (later a children's festival producer). They amassed enough money and political support to hold the first Winnipeg Folk Festival one year later. Podolak remained the festival's artistic director until 1986.

Many of the other Cdn folk festivals are marked with Podolak's influence. He also founded the Vancouver Folk Music Festival (1978), The Travelling Folk Festival & Goodtime Medicine Show, and The Stan Rogers Folk Festival, and has worked alongside the organizers of the successful Edmonton, Calgary, Victoria, and Owen Sound events. The 1980 Toronto Folk Festival and 1998 World Next Door Festival in Winnipeg were not so successful, however. In 1976, Podolak founded Barn Swallow Records, using his personal savings and a bank loan to finance and release the first 2 albums of Cdn folk legend Stan Rogers. In 1987, he founded Winnipeg's West End Cultural Centre, a community institution that remains the primary live folk music venue in the city.

Podolak remains a festival consultant, most recently with the Northern Lights Borealis Festival in Sudbury, ON, The Roots and Blues Festival in Salmon Arm, BC, and the Ottawa Folk Festival. He manages The Walnut Street Music Company and Home Routes, both based in Winnipeg. Mitch's son Leonard is a member of successful music group **THE DUHKS**. • JT

POETRY in MB was at first the terrain of writers better known for their fiction, drama, or politics, including **CHARLES MAIR** and **LOUIS RIEL**, and later

FREDERICK PHILIP GROVE, **MARTHA OSTENSO**, **DOUGLAS DURKIN**, and **PAUL HIEBERT**. The publication and recognition of poetry in MB, however, came into its own in the 1970s. Until that time, there had been writers and readers of poetry in the province, but no local publishing outlets beyond newspapers and self-publication. **DOROTHY LIVESAY** and **MIRIAM WADDINGTON** were probably the first distinguished poets to come from MB. Though they wrote about MB or from their experiences of it, tellingly, they both left and achieved recognition elsewhere, as did Grove, Durkin, and Ostenso. In a culture as mobile as Canada's, where poets write about, or where their compasses point, is as important as where they were born. Numerous other poets have written from this place and were born here and left, including **PATRICK FRIESEN**, Douglas Burnett Smith, Marilyn Bowering, Rhea Tregebov, Andy Patton, Dale Zieroth, John Paul Fiorentino, Sylvia Legris, **ROY MIKI**, and Darren Wershler-Henry. Many others lived in MB for a while, such as James Reaney, Roy Daniells, Marie Annharte Baker, Birk Sproxton, Méira Cook, and Kristjana Gunnars, to name a few.

Poetry audiences in NA are small and specialized, typically being well educated, urban, and middle class or better off. In the '70s, many of these conditions were in place for the first time. Furthermore, interest in national identity stemming from both Canada's and MB's centennials had awakened interest in Manitoban and Cdn literature. In MB, 2 new presses that published poetry were founded – the Four Humours Press (started by Myron and Susan Turner) in 1974, and Turnstone Press (started by faculty at St. John's College, **U OF M**) in 1975. More recently, poets have found venues for publication in Pemmican Publications, Signature Editions, and

The Muses' Company. Also crucial to the development of poets and poetic publications was the formation of a provincial granting body, the **MANITOBA ARTS COUNCIL**, in 1975.

The role of the universities, in particular the **U OF M**, where the faculty has included distinguished poets (**DENNIS COOLEY**, **GEORGE AMABILE**, Kenneth MacRobbie, and **ROBERT KROETSCH**), was important both in developing new poets and in cultivating an audience for poetry. In 1968, Amabile and Turner started MB's earliest magazine devoted to contemporary poetry and poetry criticism, *Far Point* (later *Northern Light*, 1974-85). Dorothy Livesay, when writer-in-residence and later professor at the U of M, started the quarterly *CVII* (*Contemporary Verse II*, 1975-) along with supporters such as Robert Foster and Robert Enright. Writing groups have been a popular form of support for both poets and readers; the group known as W3 started the newsletter *Writers News Manitoba* in 1978, which then became *Prairie Fire* (1983-) under the editorship of Andris Taskans. Along with *CV2* (which *CVII* became), it continues to publish fledgling and established MB poets. *Prairie Fire* currently runs the annual, national Bliss Carman Poetry Award competition.

Maurice Mierau is one of the younger generation of MB poets.

The **MENNONITE** tradition has provided MB with a rich and varied body of poetic work in which poets both document and resist their cultural roots. Patrick Friesen was the first to appear, encouraged by Livesay and published by Turnstone Press in 1976. He was followed by Di Brandt, Audrey Poetker, John Weier, and Sarah Klassen, among others. Immigration has also brought MB rich new voices and perspectives through poets such as Maara Haas and Uma Parameswaran. MB's **ABORIGINAL WRITING**, which dates back to Riel, now includes poets such as **CREE** writers Duncan Mercredi and Doug Nepinak (1960-2005); and Emma LaRoque; **MÉTIS** poet Joanne Arnott; and **OJIBWAY** artist/poet Marvin Francis (1955-2005). Many MB poets write out of an urban, literate experience: Kate Bitney, **U OF W** professor Catherine Hunter, Jan Horner, and Patrick O'Connell (1944-2005), for example. Many poets of the younger generation, such as Barbara Schott, Todd Bruce, Lori Cayer and Maurice Mierau, write poetry that is informed by contemporary critical theory. Weier and Jim Tallosi are examples of poets who are particularly drawn to the natural world in their writing.

The myriad voices and styles of contemporary MB poetry reflect the diversification, urbanization, and increased global outlook of the province as a whole. As a highly literate genre, poetry will continue to face challenges. The effects that digital and electronic media will have on the form are still unclear, but publication and performance has been vibrant here for the last 4 decades, and, with luck will remain so. ● JAN HORNER

▸ *See also* **BOOK PUBLISHING**, **LITERATURE**.

POGUE CARBURETOR is a MB invention that reputedly ran automobiles 320 km on 4½ l of gas, or 200 mi to the gallon. The existence of the carburetor, named after its inventor Charles Nelson Pogue of **MINITONAS**, remains disputed, as it was never put to market. However, it is known that, beginning in 1928, Pogue conducted many experiments from his **WINNIPEG** garage in an effort to build a vapour carburetor which would heat gas before entering the engine cylinder, thereby reducing the amount required for combustion. With the backing of financier W. J. Holmes, the Pogue Carburetor Company filed 13 patents in the US and Canada. In 1936, one of Pogue's carburetors was fitted into a V8 coupe, and some reports claimed that tests run by automobile companies proved the astounding gas mileage. Little else is known of the carburetor, though local newspapers at one point reported that 3 models had been stolen from Pogue's shop. The headlines, which played on the incredible fuel efficiency of the stolen carburetors, caused something of a media sensation, and cash-strapped consumers of the Dirty Thirties eagerly awaited news of the efficient device. When the missing carburetors were never recovered, many speculated that big oil companies were behind the theft. Pogue left Winnipeg in the late 1930s for Montreal, where he ran an oil filter company, and nothing more was heard of his carburetor. ● MD

POISON IVY (*Toxicodendron radicans* (L.) Kuntze) is the "leaves of 3, let it be" menace of the plant world that causes the most allergic skin reactions in people. Symptoms range from none (in non-sensitive people) to a mild itch to severe rashes with blisters to the "itch from Hell." They are caused by urushiol, a toxic oil released by breaking any part of the plant. This oil sticks easily to skin or anything else it touches, including shoes, tools, and pets' fur. Burning the plant releases urushiol in smoke, which, if it lands on skin or is breathed into the lungs, can cause severe, even life-threatening, allergic reactions. Poison ivy is widespread in moist areas in S MB. It can be recognized by its glossy-green, 20-to-40 cm-tall, 3-parted, deeply toothed leaves in summer; its bright red-orange leaves in autumn; and a stalk of small white-ridged berries in winter. Poison ivy is often mis-called "poison oak" in MB, but true poison oak and poison sumac, related but taller and woodier plants, are not found this far north. Only humans are allergic to these plants; **DEER**, **RABBITS**, and **MUSKRATS** eat the leaves, while birds such as **CROWS** eat the fruit with impunity. ● KAREN JOHNSON

POISONOUS PLANTS. MB has 2 kinds of native plants that would be likely to cause serious harm to most people if eaten. A much larger number could cause mild to severe discomfort, especially if you happened to be allergic to that particular plant. **POISON IVY** will cause allergic skin reactions in many people and other plant such as nettles (*Lapportea dioica* and *Urtica dioica*) and some **ORCHIDS** (especially lady's-slippers) are known to cause similar reactions.

The most poisonous native plants in MB are 3 species of water hemlocks (*Cicuta maculata*, *C. bulbifera*, and *C. mackenzieana*) and baneberry (*Actea rubra*). *Cicuta* is considered the most-poisonous group of plants in NA. Water hemlocks are members of the carrot family (Apiaceae), and grow in marshy and wet places throughout MB. They have divided leaves; have clusters of small white flowers from a single point, like those of dill, carrot, or parsley; and are common in roadside ditches in July and Aug. All parts of the plant are poisonous, especially the roots, and they have a strong, disagreeable smell. A marble-sized bite will kill a human. *Cicuta* is closely related to the European true hemlock (*Conium* spp.), which killed Socrates. Baneberry grows in moist woods in the southern ¾ of MB. It is a common member of the buttercup family (Ranunculaceae) with divided dark-green leaves and an upright stalk of shiny either red or white berries. The berries appear in the late summer and people sometimes mistake them for edible ones. Aboriginal peoples used baneberry to treat various stomach and reproductive tract problems. Plants are poisonous because of the strong chemicals they contain and many of these chemicals are useful drugs in small amounts. Most of our present-day drugs originally came from plant or fungi sources.

Some plants families are more likely to contain poisonous chemicals than others. Avoiding them will prevent most plant-related poisonings. Families like the buttercup (Ranunculaceae), carrot (Apiaceae), bean (Fabaceae), arum (Araceae), potato/tomato (Solanaceae), dogbane (Apocynaceae), spurge (Euphorbiaceae), sunflower (compositae) and lily (Liliaceae) are most likely to cause problems. Several families have both edible and poisonous berries and fruits. The rose family (Rosaceae) has many edible plants, but the twigs and seeds of plums, apples, and cherries are poisonous. The heath family (Ericaceae) produces blueberries and cranberries but also has the poisonous Labrador tea, bog-laurel and *Rhododendron* spp. The honeysuckle family (Caprifoliaceae) contains the edible high-bush cranberry and nannyberry (*Viburnum* spp.), and the poisonous elderberry (*Sambucus pubens*) and snowberrys (*Symphoricarpos* spp.). Other native plants to avoid include Canada yew (*Taxus canadensis*) and both native and introduced bittersweets (*Celastris scandens* and *Solanum dulcamara*). ● KAREN JOHNSON

POLES first moved into the **RED RIVER SETTLEMENT** in 1817, as part of the military escort to **LORD SELKIRK**. By 1895, there were over 1000 Poles in **WINNIPEG**. Mass **IMMIGRATION** of Poles, in response to Sir **CLIFFORD SIFTON**'s campaign to settle the Cdn Prairies, only occurred from 1896 until WWII. It drew on immigrants from the Russian and Austrian areas of partitioned Poland. The largest Polish settlements in MB were in Winnipeg, **HADASHVILLE**, Polonia, Wisla, and **BRANDON**. However, Poles were often sent to areas avoided or abandoned by other settlers, as heavy physical labour and harsh conditions did not seem to discourage them. Indeed, thrift and perseverance characterized the Poles who colonized MB, and who contributed to the development of the province.

By the early 20th century, Winnipeg had become the centre of Polish life in MB. Immigrants established several voluntary organizations that still operate today: the Holy Ghost Fraternal Aid Society (1902), the Polish Gymnastic Association – Sokol (1906), and the Polish Fraternal Aid Society of St. John Cantius (1918). These provided a safety net for immigrants and aid for widows, the sick, and the unemployed. The oldest Polish **ROMAN CATHOLIC** church in MB, Holy Ghost, dates from 1898; its priests established the first Polish-language school and published the *Gazeta Katolicka* ("Catholic Weekly"). In 1907, the Polish National Catholic Church was established, offering the Catholic liturgy in Polish. The weekly **NEWSPAPER** *Czas* ("Time") was

Sokol parade float on MB Legislature grounds, July 1, 1927

set up in 1914, serving as an important vehicle to connect immigrants and to present news from both Poland and Canada.

By 1916, there were 16,751 Poles in MB. Although these early arrivals were mainly peasants and unskilled workers, they actively maintained cultural and historical traditions they brought from Poland. Their national consciousness was reflected when they organized the Polish Batt, which fought in France and Poland during WWI. Providing military and financial help for Allied forces, the immigrants made a significant contribution to Cdn society.

MB played a major role in the formation of the Canadian Polish Congress. In Winnipeg, in 1932, the Union of Polish Societies in Canada was founded under the guidance of the Polish consul here. This association, which unified the activities of the community across Canada, was transformed into Canadian Polish Congress in 1944. The role of the CPC was vital in persuading the Cdn govt to admit Polish political refugees after WWII. These included Polish veterans of the UK's Royal Army in Europe, members of displaced persons camps, as well as children from an orphanage in Tanganyika (now Tanzania). Between 1946 and 1947, Canada admitted 4527 Polish immigrants, several hundred of whom settled in MB. Especially prominent among these was CPC president Bernard Dubienski, who presented the case of postwar immigrants at a special Senate Committee meeting. In 1973, in recognition of outstanding achievements and service to his community and humanity, Dubienski was awarded the Order of Canada. Another exceptional person of the time was Mary Panaro, who worked tirelessly on behalf of refugees and immigrants. As a member of the Welfare Council of Winnipeg, she helped bring Polish refugees to Canada. Panaro, known as "International Mother," helped found the International Centre of Winnipeg. Her many achievements were also recognized with the Order of Canada in 1983. The contribution of Poles to the Cdn effort in WWII reached its zenith in the person of PO **Andrew Mynarski**, a

Winnipeg-born son of Polish immigrants. Mynarski was posthumously awarded the **Victoria Cross**.

Post-WWII immigrants included professionals and skilled workers who left Poland during the war and who could not return to their birthplaces in Eastern Poland, which had been incorporated into the USSR. This group found a new home in Canada, bringing fresh ideas and strengthening the existing community. Their experience as soldiers and strong political opponents to **Communism** gave rise to the Polish Combatants' Association Branch 13, an organization promoting cultural and national consciousness. This same wave of immigration fostered an expansion in the structure of community with the establishment of "Polish Study Funds" at the **U of M**; the founding of the Radio Polonia station and the Polish Museum Ogniwo; the building of the Copernicus Telescope in the Winnipeg Planetarium (*see* **Manitoba Museum**) and the erection of a monument on Copernicus Hill in the **Duck Mountains** – both named after famed Polish astronomer Mikołaj Kopernik – among others. It was characteristic of this group that upon arrival, they immediately took their place in the labour force, creating social and economic networks that helped them establish new lives. A further important contribution was their children: a second generation of Polish Cdn citizens, the majority of whom attained higher education and became active in the Polish community and in Cdn society as a whole.

The late 1970s and the 1980s brought to MB a large number of immigrants who fled Poland because of political oppression and economic hardship. Highly educated professionals as well as skilled labourers, they enriched Cdn society. This group – the so-called "Solidarity (Solidarność) immigration" – was distinguished by its rapid assimilation and active participation in the intellectual and political life of Canada. Through public demonstrations, the local TV Polonika, and other special events, the association Friends of Solidarity in Winnipeg kept immigrants, and society as a whole, informed of the oppression endured by opponents of Communism. From

the 1990s on, the Solidarity immigration has shared with Cdn society its fascination with Polish cultural and artistic achievements. The Polish Arts Festival has introduced Winnipeg audiences to accomplished artists from Polish culture, adding unique facet to MB's multicultural society. ● MAGDALENA BLACKMORE

POLICING. Until 1870, part-time volunteers, mostly military pensioners who had been brought from the UK to serve in exchange for free land, policed **Rupert's Land**. These volunteers became known as the "Ulster Volunteers," and were mandated not only to deal with unruly and intoxicated persons, but also to keep the property of the **HBC** safe and secure. After 1870, the Hudson Bay Territory was turned over to the Dominion of Canada, becoming the 5th province. From that moment, with a continuing growth in population, policing became more militarized and structured. The Mounted Constabulary Force, established under the command of Capt Frank Villiers from the 2nd Quebec Rifles, was the first police presence. The force was made up of 10 soldiers who had come with Villiers, as well as 10 local men. Required to work 7 days a week for low wages, members of the Mounted Constabulary Force policed the entire province, a daunting task in those early days.

Winnipeg Police wearing buffalo coats, 1963

In 1873, the **North-West Mounted Police**, later to become known as the RCMP, moved into MB as part of PM Sir John A McDonald's plan to preserve the West from the influence and control of the US and ensure the orderly settlement of the Prairies. Initially, 150 recruits were sent to MB. The province can claim to be the birthplace of the RCMP, since it was in MB that the first NWMP post was established, at Fort Dufferin, near present-day **Emerson**. The first headquarters was established near **Swan River**, and the first arrest ever made by the NWMP was by a group from **Lower Fort Garry** who apprehended a group of whisky traders near **Gimli**. The most famous "original" member, Supt Sir Samuel Benfield Steele, is buried in Saint John's Cemetery in **Winnipeg**. The coming of the NWMP gradually saw it take over much of the responsibilities of the Mounted Constabulary Force, and though the latter force continued to exist until the 1930s, their role in Manitoba's history is of limited significance.

By 1874, population along the **Red** and **Assiniboine** rivers had grown to nearly 2000 people. With the growth of both the population and crime, and the establishment of the city of Winnipeg, one of the first acts of the new city council was to appoint the city's first police chief, John Ingram, and 2 constables, whose early work was mainly to deal with "morality" offences. As Winnipeg became a boomtown, the municipal force expanded substantially. By the mid-1880s, the force had grown to 34, and by 1907 – with the city's population climbing to 115,000 – the police force had 90 members.

By 1912, as land development and settlement continued, additional police departments were created in rural communities. The **Great Depression** and WWII, however, brought challenges to the provincial policing community: the economy turned downward and crime escalated throughout the province. After the war, returning soldiers contributed to the steady growth of numbers of police at a time when crime was increasing to an unprecedented level. In 1972, the Winnipeg area alone contained 14 separate police departments. In 1974, soon after **Unicity**, they merged into one, becoming the largest police department in MB with 921 members.

Today, there are 14 separate police agencies in MB communities. Along with the Winnipeg Police Service and RCMP, there are police forces in **Altona**, **Brandon**, East St. Paul, **Morden**, **Rivers**, **Ste. Anne**, **Victoria Beach**, and **Winkler**, alongside the rural municipalities of Whitehead, Springfield, and St. Clement, though as of 2006, the future of the Rivers service was doubtful. The Dakota Ojibway Police Service is unique in MB; the Brandon-based outfit investigates crime and enforces legislation in 5 First Nations in the S and W parts of the province. The RCMP provide federal and First Nations policing through 50 host and standalone detachments with more than 900 regular members, and over 250 civilian members and public servants in Manitoba.

Long gone are the whisky traders and wagon trains. Police find themselves in an ever-more-complex environment. Changing demographics and social attitudes – especially to do with the growth and urbanization of Aboriginal peoples, geography, multiculturalism, terrorism, and huge technological advances – all require police to be trained to an unprecedented level of sophistication. • GORD SCHUMACHER

POLITICS IN MANITOBA
By Allen Mills

Manitoba's political system arose out of nothing, yet eventually it became a sophisticated, developed liberal democracy. The province was conceived in rebellion and, in 1919, its capital underwent a general strike unparalleled in Cdn history. Nevertheless, for most of its existence, MB has followed a politics of profound placidity and caution.

BEGINNINGS: In 1868, the **Hudson's Bay Company**'s **Rupert's Land** had been surrendered to the Cdn govt (*see* **Rupertsland Transfer**) After the resistance of 1869-70, MB emerged as a province with the proclamation of the *Manitoba Act* of 1870. An expanding central-Cdn state, aided by immigrants from ON, had large, imperial plans for the new area: MB would have provincehood but would not control Crown lands (*see* **Natural Resources Transfer Act**). By the *Dominion Lands Act* of 1872, the geometric surveying of the land into sections and its distribution to immigrants – ignoring both existing signs of human habitation by **First Peoples** and the seigneurial lot system of the **Red River Settlement** – presaged the dominant economic strategy of **Agricultural** settlement. For Indigenous peoples, the **Cree**, **Ojibway**, **Dakota**, and, in the north, the **Dene**, the onset of Canada's empire was especially destructive. Loss of land made the buffalo hunt impossible, though **Bison** had all but disappeared by the end of the 1870s. "Indians," as the First Nations were then called, were to be controlled through treaties and reserves. Between 1871 and 1875, the federal govt concluded several treaties in the lands within the original boundaries of MB. Administrative and cultural control was further consolidated through the *Indian Act* (1876).

Gov George Simpson

Few politicians have a chance to construct a new social order on a blank slate – or so it seemed to the earliest governors. Where there were people and traditions – all Indigenous – they were disregarded. First Nations had pursued a time-honoured existence as communitarian, egalitarian societies, primarily following a semi-nomadic gathering and hunting culture with limited agriculture. They possessed their own politics and faith, but the new governors were hostile or, at best, indifferent to these. Aboriginal people were to be sequestered on reserves managed by the central govt, and, it was intended, assimilated to Anglo-Saxon, Christian standards through **Residential Schools** and other techniques.

Initially, the **Métis** in the Red River Settlement fared better. The **Red River Resistance** led by **Louis Riel** had ensured through the *Manitoba Act* that the new province would at least include language, educational, and religious rights consistent with a population that was largely French-speaking and **Roman Catholic**. But the Métis and **Country-Born**, with a population of only 10,000, were quickly submerged by incoming, mainly Ontario settlers. The settlers were deeply British and Protestant, and avidly supported both Canada's and

Britain's empires. They brought to their new habitat a version of Upper Canadian Grit liberalism, with its rustic, frontier sense of freedom. Hard work and piety toward a Protestant God were their lodestars, as were thrift, frugality, and self-reliance. In their minds, govt should keep its distance, and economics should be
left to private initiative. Increasingly by the 1880s, the demographic balance was tipping in favour of the British-Ontarians. The Métis were outnumbered, and had – either through negligence or malfeasance – lost or never received the lands promised them under the *Manitoba Act* (*see* SCRIP). Twenty years after 1870, they would lose their language and educational rights, too.

P At the outset, MB's electoral system had a property-based franchise and public voting. The area of the Postage Stamp Province (see NICKNAMES) was initially 36,075 km² – a small fraction of the current size – and the electorate's numbers were minuscule. In the first election, in Dec 1870, just over 1000 men voted. Only in 1888 was there universal male vote by secret ballot. Parties did not dominate early politics, and political independents were numerous, but by the mid-1880s, political parties had become more evident. Initially, a group cohered around JOHN NORQUAY, premier from 1878-87, in support of the federal govt of Sir John A. Macdonald. But there were many grievances about the terms of Confederation: the paucity of financial subsidies from Ottawa, the loss of Crown lands to the central govt, the CPR monopoly, freight rates, and, especially

after 1879, the protective tariff. Opposition to the federal govt and what was called its National Policy cohered around THOMAS GREENWAY, premier from 1888 to 1900, and this became the nucleus of the LIBERAL PARTY.

Greenway's govt entrenched the new Protestant, anglophone hegemony of the farmers. In 1890, his govt eradicated bilingual rights in the JUDICIAL SYSTEM and the Legislature, as well as the separate-schools rights of Catholics and, by implication, of francophones (*see* MANITOBA SCHOOLS QUESTION). The new enduring cultural order was now in place: MB would be a transplanted facsimile of ON. The values of British-Ontarian farmers would dominate govt at least until DUFF ROBLIN's triumph in 1958, and through a process of cultural osmosis, they extended throughout the province and to the present.

Liberals and Conservatives (*see* PROGRESSIVE CONSERVATIVE PARTY) alternated in power until 1922 in partisan rotation under strong premiers: Norquay, Greenway, Sir RODMOND ROBLIN (premier 1900-15), and TOBIAS NORRIS (premier 1915-22). Apart from the vote for the Patrons on Industry in 1896, the 2 parties divided the electoral spoils roughly equally. The average vote for the Conservatives between 1883 and 1915 was 45%, with 49% for the Liberals.

The political-cultural order established after 1890 had nonetheless to absorb rapid changes. In 1891, a province mainly of agriculturalists had a population of 152,500. Thirty years later, there were 610,000, an astounding increase. WINNIPEG, which had had all of 100 souls in 1870, had 210,000 citizens by 1921, already ⅓ of the provincial total. Before 1891, the preponderance of IMMIGRATION had been ENGLISH, SCOTS, and IRISH Protestants from ON and the British Isles. After 1897, the new immigrants came in large numbers from eastern Europe. The latter spoke no English, and in religion were either ORTHODOX or Catholic Christians, or were JEWISH. The young province now confronted the question of the integration of what some contemporaries called an "alien" influx (*see* ALIEN QUESTION).

WORKERS: The main consequence of the new immigration was the emergence of Winnipeg as a significant industrial centre with a multi-ethnic work force. Milling, RAILWAYS, metal shops and ironworks, and the GARMENT INDUSTRY provided the foundation of a working class. A new class brought new politics. W. L. MORTON made famous the idea that immigrants seized by a utopian vision inhabited Canada's West. There were few established institutions in MB at the time, and the province seemed a blank slate on which every conceivable idea could be written. If farmers in the freedom of the new land could construct their own version of a perfect society, why couldn't labourers? Before WWI, Winnipeg was a veritable garden of earthly political delights. On a summer's evening, many street-corner evangelists held forth in Market Square, preaching US economist Henry George's land-values taxation, REFORM, free trade, votes for women (*see* WOMEN'S MOVEMENT), co-operativism, SOCIALISM, and COMMUNISM.

Equally important were the technological changes underway. The railway came to the province – initially the Lake Manitoba Railway and Canal Company line in 1878, then the national CPR line in 1882 – followed by the telegraph. Print technology was significant from the beginning, producing a vibrant local NEWSPAPER market. HYDROELECTRIC construction, mainly on the WINNIPEG RIVER after 1881, provided energy for the new factories and workshops. By early in the 20th century, there were mass-produced automobiles, movies, and powered aircraft. Radio followed in the 1920s, and, after 1940, the self-propelled combine harvester along with efficient, dependable tractors. The last, especially, led to extensively mechanized agricultural production, which in turn led to ever-larger farms.

Though farmers had their complaints, especially with Ottawa, MB's first major crisis of the 20th century was the WINNIPEG GENERAL STRIKE in May-June 1919. Workers had perceived being treated unjustly as early as

Members of Manitoba's first Legislative Assembly, 1870

Original design for the Manitoba Legislature

the 1890s. The Winnipeg Labour Party formed in 1896, and in 1900, Arthur Puttee became Canada's first Labour MP, representing Winnipeg. In 1902, the Marxist Socialist Party of Manitoba appeared, and in 1908, the Social Democratic Party. By the eve of WWI, workers complained of low wages, job insecurity, lack of **Union** recognition, overcrowded housing, and inadequate **Public Health** standards. War added many other tensions, including inflation and rising ethnic antagonism. By 1917, there was the revolutionary model of a worker-controlled state in the USSR. At the same time, the UK's Labour Party offered an impressive example of the democratic pursuit of socialist power. Across western Canada, and especially in Winnipeg, trade union leaders and socialists were working on radical strategies like the One Big Union. The explosion produced by all this was the General Strike in Winnipeg, which spilled over into the **Brandon General Strike**.

The meaning of the Winnipeg strike was controversial at the time and continues to be, still occasioning fights among historians. At root, it was about what would eventually become straightforward issues, such as a living wage and union recognition. Other notions of the era's heady atmosphere were mixed into the strike, however, including revolution and industrial syndicalism. These were implied by the impending formation of the One Big Union and by the workers' militancy. However one characterizes the strike, its goals could not be seen as conventionally political and parliamentary, and so the labour disruption did little to advance the

agenda of a worker-oriented political party. Before 1919, political power had resided in the hands of an informal alliance of primarily English south Winnipeg businessmen and farmers in SW MB. The workers radically challenged this establishment, but the socio-economic power base stood firm: all 3 levels of govt brusquely put down the strike, with the help of the Royal **North-West Mounted Police**. The workers were defeated.

After the strike, the workers' political movement split finally asunder, though not immediately. For a moment, it seemed that the fallout from the strike would not be submission and fragmentation, but consolidation and progress. The 1920 provincial election seemed a political breakthrough of sorts. A loose coalition of labourites and socialists gained over 20% of the overall vote, and won 42% of the vote in Winnipeg, where Dixon topped the polls. Thereafter, however, things fell apart. Some socialists joined the Communist Party after its founding in 1921. With a voting base of around 7000 predominantly **Ukrainian** and Jewish voters in the **North End**, the Manitoba Communist Party had an MLA for much of 1936-58. Another group consolidated itself around Fred Dixon and **J. S. Woodsworth** and the Independent Labour Party (ILP). The latter espoused a parliamentary form of socialism and avoided talk of revolution. In time, the **Co-operative Commonwealth Federation** (CCF) would emerge out of this group. It in turn gave birth to the **New Democratic Party** (NDP) in 1961.

Though Woodsworth, and, in time, A. A. Heaps were elected as MPs, and ILP MLAs such as Dixon, **JOHN QUEEN**, and Marcus Hyman performed yeoman's service in the Legislature, the vote of the Left slipped back. In 1922, it fell to 16%, and in 1927 declined below 10%. Many immigrant voters feared reprisals after the strike, especially deportation or job loss, and abandoned support of the Left. In 1945, the CCF did poll a significant provincial vote – by which time MB-raised **TOMMY DOUGLAS** had become CCF premier of SK – but things fell back again until **ED SCHREYER**'s electoral breakthrough of 1969. Of course, always weighing heavily against the power of the Left in MB was the longstanding under-representation of urban areas in what was a decidedly rurally-biased **ELECTORAL SYSTEM**.

FARMERS: Liberal individualism and a belief in the autonomy of the independent producer marked the transplanted Ontarian Grittism of MB. Govt must intervene to dismantle privileges and special favours, Liberals believed, but thereafter, the market should govern the terms of trade. As producers in an economic hinterland with control concentrated in central Canada, MB's farmers had their share of grievances, but Prairie utopianism also ran through the farmers' mind, as it did for the labourer. The period 1880-1920 was the veritable high-water mark of the newly educated common man and woman. For farmers and workers, it was a time of widespread literacy, which is everywhere considered a crucial condition for democracy.

Free trade was one of the radical ideas affirmed by the farmers. So was the rejection of political parties, which were seen as venal, self-serving instruments of privileged interests. The voice of the people was to be liberated through measures such as the initiative-and-recall and group govt. Land-value taxation and graduated income taxes were bruited, as was co-operativism. The Manitoba Grain Growers' Association had been formed in 1903, and advanced many of these ideas. For the moment, it functioned as a civil-society movement and stayed out of partisan politics. Norris's first Liberal govt of 1915-20 had depended on extensive farmer support and carried forward many reform ideas: a *Temperance Act* (*see* **PROHIBITION**), a school-attendance act, votes for women, and the abolition of bilingual teaching.

Perhaps Norris's government was too reformist, or maybe WWI had brought special problems for farmers, but his support eroded. Indeed, farmers faced several hurdles in the war, including a shortage of farm labour and the uprooting of traditional political loyalties over the national issue of Conscription. In any event, while the events of 1919-20 were turning points around which history failed to turn for the Left, not so for the farmers' movement and for the electoral system in general. In Jan 1920, the United Farmers of Manitoba decided to engage in independent political action. Its popular support in the provincial election that year was modest (14%), but 2 years later, it had grown to a substantial 33%, and won 28 seats. It was the largest bloc in the Legislature, and was therefore entitled to form a govt. It was, however, leaderless. In a moment of stupendous improvisation **JOHN BRACKEN**, principal of the Manitoba Agriculture College, was persuaded to take over as leader and premier and was conveniently parachuted into the vacant seat of **THE PAS**. (Elections in the northern ridings were then held in the early summer, later usually than the southern seats.) Under Bracken and for the next decades, MB operated with what could be considered either a multi-party electoral system or a party-less one: the agrarian-oriented premier continually sought ways to preside over a non-partisan coalition govt.

Bracken was an immigrant from ON (like every MB premier since 1870 except John Norquay) an agronomist and college official without political experience. Bracken pursued economic development in the **NORTH** through a railway to **FLIN FLON** and the opening of a mine there, and

A triumphant Howard Pawley

encouraged hydroelectric development, as on the **WINNIPEG RIVER** at the Seven Sisters site, W of **PINAWA**. Mainly, however, he governed according to farmers' policy of disdain for partisan politics, what was called "party-ism." Govt was to be a sort of grand committee of everyone. He brought the Liberals into a coalition in 1932, and Social Credit entered in 1936. Echoing his federal counterparts during WWII, he presided over an all-party coalition that included the CCF and the Conservatives. Otherwise, the agrarian ethos predominated in his administration's pinched, sober conviction that govt must live within its means and balance the books. Fundamentally, Manitoba Grittism was, in the full flood of its independent political triumph, all about small govt and non-partisanship. Bracken's coalition govts – and that of Stuart Garson 1943-48 – bought the province through the **GREAT DEPRESSION** and WWII through simple endurance and persistence rather than imaginative **SOCIAL POLICY**.

MODERN POLITICS: By 1945, provincial politics cried out for reform and modernization. Population growth had accelerated after the inertia of the 1930s, increasingly concentrated in and around Winnipeg. The capital was already beginning to assume its present identity as a city-state that demographically and, perhaps, politically dominated the province. Farmers' votes continued to be the bedrock of successful govts, but such influence as they exerted did not stem the **RURAL AND REMOTE DEPOPULA-TION** that continues to this day. The under-representation of Winnipeg was by now close to scandalous. In 1952, 228,000 urban voters elected 17 MLAs, while 224,000 rural voters returned 40 MLAs. The formal require-ments of universal adult suffrage had been in place since 1916, when women were given the franchise, and were completed in 1952, when First Nations people received the provincial vote. But without political-party competition to energize the process, and without redistribution in favour of the urban voter, democracy seemed largely redundant.

The agent of political reform was Winnipeg car dealer Duff Roblin, grandson of the famed Sir Rodmond. Duff Roblin took the **PROGRESSIVE CONSERVATIVES** (PCs), as they had been renamed in 1946, out of the coalition in time for the 1953 election and re-established the dynamic of partisan politics. His eventual success was greatly aided, though inad-vertently, by the last Liberal-Progressive premier of the coalition period,

Douglas Campbell (premier 1948-58). In 1957, Campbell had introduced electoral reform and established an independent electoral commission. The gerrymandering of constituencies ended, and a rational process was put in place for periodic redistribution of seats. In 1958, Roblin (premier 1958-67) won a large electoral victory and set about a major reshaping of the province's infrastructure and institutions.

Roblin's 1958 victory was the result of a widespread increase of support throughout the province. The PCs made a major breakthrough in remote constituencies, and doubled their vote in the urban areas from 26,000 to 55,000. In the farming countryside, their vote went up substantially too, from 30,000 to over 54,000. However, the urban vote now carried much more weight. Roblin governed in a more modern style, almost social democratic in its demeanour. His was an activist government that saw the state itself as a positive economic and social force. Under his administration, a massive initiative was undertaken to build hydro stations on the **Nelson River**. The state was useful, too, in building the **Red River Floodway** to protect Winnipeg from the perennial **Floods** of the **Red River**. He also promoted the then-new concept of joint public-private business ventures through the Manitoba Development Fund. Funding for the enlarged provincial apparatus came partly through a new provincial sales tax in 1966, though Roblin would never recover from the unpopularity of this tax.

Winnipeg came increasingly into its own, and with galloping economic affluence and the suburbanization of the city after WWII, a growing urban middle class came to be a crucial base of political support. A hint of cosmopolitanism entered MB's public life, and there was the cultural revolution of the 1960s. Old, submerged animosities were overcome. The outsider status of Jews, Ukrainians, and **Mennonites** was ceasing. After Roblin, the inheritor of this new cosmopolitan identity was **Ed Schreyer** (premier 1969-77) and his NDP, who, in 1969, came to power for the first time.

In 1969, the NDP was an even more urban political force than Roblin's PCs had been. Its city support was at 87,000, almost 3 times its support in the countryside. It was also successful in the North. The social bastions of Schreyer's triumph were the working-class districts of the **North End** and central Winnipeg, and a band of constituencies in poorer farming areas running diagonally from **Dauphin** through the **Interlake** to **Lac du Bonnet**. His was, in effect, a class-based govt, but with a bias toward centrist politics that allowed it electoral success in middle-class urban ridings such as St. Vital and St. James. This was a crucial strategic dimension of winning a legislative majority: the historic, hidden injuries of class, albeit now expressed mutedly, were now embodied in an explicitly social democratic government that took seriously the ideas of reform and innovation. Autopac and **Unicity** were early examples of this ethos.

Sterling Lyon's 1977 triumph represented a return to the simpler political economy of an agrarian liberalism, of smaller govt and a dependence on the market. What later came to be called neo-liberalism in the hands of PM Thatcher in the UK and president Reagan in the US had been anticipated by Lyon in MB between 1977-81. Since then, PCs have behaved more in the tradition of Duff Roblin, and the NDP more in the cautious tradition of Schreyer's 2nd govt of 1973-77.

The main casualty of this new political order has been the Liberals. In 1953, the Liberal-Progressives had garnered 39% of the vote. By 1969, support for the Liberal Party was down to 24%, and by the 1981 election, it all but disappeared, bottoming at 7%. No longer having to answer for their Trudeau-led federal cousins after Mulroney's PC triumph in 1984, and riding the anti-**Meech Lake Accord** wave of the late 1980s, they came back from the dead under Sharon Carstairs in 1988 and 1990. But they have not been successful in displacing either the PCs or the NDP as one of the 2 major provincial parties since the mid-1990s.

MB now has a 2-party-dominant system with the PCs and NDP regularly winning, between them, close to 90% of the popular vote. **Gary Filmon** (premier 1990-99) ran a moderate govt with a tilt to business and the market, and **Gary Doer** (1999-) has run a modestly reformist administration with a tilt to the trade unions and the public sector. Both parties vie for the support of moderate, middle-class opinion. Everything is done cautiously, and financial rectitude is supremely important. Urban voters have now come into their own only to discover that they, too, have been affected by Grit values blown in from the countryside.

CONCLUSION: MB began its political history with a blank slate. First Nations peoples were dismissed and the Métis quickly pushed aside. Farmers and the urban business class ruled the roost for much of the time. Industrial workers and the new immigrants from Europe challenged this dominance in 1919 but to little avail. Left to their own devices, the leadership of the province have often done little but sustain a liberal status quo. Yet there has been sufficient opposition and political pluralism, especially since 1958, to create an impetus for a social democratic-like reform. (PCers would prefer to think of it as "Red Tory-ism.")

MB has become a mature liberal democracy with universal, democratic rights, a transparent electoral commission, an independent civil service commission, healthy political debate and a minimally generous welfare state. Its civil society of interest and advocacy groups, religious and ethnic organizations, as well as its business community, farmers' organizations, trade unions and free media, all together minister to the maintenance of a democratic order.

Even the narrow cultural dominance of the ON Grit inheritance has been compromised. Official bilingualism has been re-instated in the legislature and in the courts, and there is a practical multiculturalism and multilingualism in the schools. In 2007, the Métis were waiting to hear the outcome of their court case to seek restitution for their lost or nugatory land entitlements of the early 1870s and the descendants of the First Nations of 1870 have been increasingly effective in asserting their claims to self-govt. In provincial politics, Aboriginal people have played an increasing role through the NDP in the governance of the province. These eventualities have brought the province full circle. Politics in MB has arrived where it began. •

UMA, TRIBUNE, MANITOBA - ELECTIONS, JIM WILEY PHOTO, 50-3526-20

Provincial election ballot boxes stored in a basement hallway of the Legislative Building, 1977

545

POLLARD BANKNOTE LTD. is one of only 3 companies in the world to manufacture instant-win, break-open lottery tickets. With 5 production plants in NA (3 in Canada and 2 in the US), the **WINNIPEG**-based firm has the capacity to produce 12 billion scratch tickets and 4 million pull-tab lottery tickets per year. As of mid-2005, it was supplying lottery tickets and other lottery-related products and services, including promotional games, ticket vending machines, and lottery management services, to 45 lotteries around the world. The firm had 5 facilities with 1200 employees.

Pollard Banknote traces its roots back to 1907, when Winnipeg businessmen Oliver Pollard and George Saults launched a commercial printing operation. For the first 70 years, Saults & Pollard printed everything from catalogues to business cards, moving to stock and bond certificates in 1974. In 1977, the company began specializing in security printing by producing cheques for local banks, followed soon after by lottery tickets. By 1983, the company had ceased printing bank cheques in order to concentrate on its burgeoning lottery-ticket business. Two years later, it changed its name to Pollard Banknote in an attempt to diversify into printing currency. As the lottery-products arm of the business grew, the company continued to build and to acquire additional production plants, and gave up on attempts to print banknotes. In 2002, Pollard launched its own lottery in Puerto Rico, and by 2004, annual sales had grown to $171.9 million, of which 90% was for government-controlled lotteries. In Aug 2005, the privately owned firm became a publicly traded company by converting to an income trust. The move raised an estimated $50 million, which its owners – primarily the Pollard family of Winnipeg – planned to use to cash in on some of their holdings. However, the Pollard family retains a controlling majority of the firm. • MURRAY MCNEILL

POLLUTION. The province, and especially **ECONOMIC** activity, is associated with a variety of developments that affect air, soil, and water quality. Southern MB, where people are concentrated (mostly in urban areas), sustains the greatest environmental consequences and habitat destruction. In northern MB, mines, smelters, and **HYDROELECTRIC** projects affect large land areas. Scientists recognize many broad categories of pollution, including air, water, soil, light, sound, and radioactive pollutions. These are sometimes further subdivided into point-source pollution – those that originate from single sources, such as oil spills or carbon emission from coal-fired generating plants – and non-point-source pollution, which comes from multiple or diffuse sources.

AIR POLLUTION: Air pollution takes many forms, notably smog and greenhouse gases, which are responsible for climate change by weakening the ozone layer. The thinner stratospheric layer of ozone allows greater amounts of ultraviolet light (100-400 nm wavelengths) to reach Earth's surface, causing ever-increasing surface temperatures, more cancer-causing radiation, and intolerable conditions for many species. In MB, global warming will likely lead to the extinction of Arctic species such as polar bears by 2050, and possibly sooner. MB's greenhouse-gas emissions consist of carbon dioxide (more than 50% of the total) and nitrous oxide (more than 25%), with the remainder comprised primarily of methane and fluorocarbons, but also carbon monoxide. More than 50% of total greenhouse gases in MB come from combustion of fossil fuels associated with transportation, including cars and **AVIATION**; **MANUFACTURING**, especially of plastics; commercial, institutional and residential sources, such as the burning of natural gas for heating; the **PETROLEUM** industry; and fossil-fuel use in **AGRICULTURE**, **FORESTRY**, and **MINING**. An additional 33% of greenhouse gas originates from agricultural sources, including cattle, manure, and microbial activity of agricultural soil. Other sources include chlorofluorocarbons in propellants and refrigerants, though these have been banned and slowly promise to become less of a problem. As well, industrial processes, organic solvents, forest fires, land clearing, and waste management (landfills, incinerators, wastewater treatment) are also sources of air pollution.

More than 50% of greenhouse gases in MB are associated with the combustion of fossil fuels

Another problem for air quality is smog, a toxic suspension of particulates, greenhouse gases, and ground-level ozone often visible as a yellow-grey miasma on the horizon. Smog, usually worst in summer, causes widespread death and health problems, as well as billions of dollars of annual lost revenue in highly industrialized places around the southern Great Lakes such as southern ON, MI, OH, and NY. Because of strong prevalent winds and relatively low population densities in MB and areas immediately surrounding it, smog is relatively rare here. As well, unlike AB, SK, ON, NB, and other Cdn jurisdictions, MB relies highly on **HYDROELECTRIC** rather than fossil-fuel energy sources. Fourteen of MB's power generating stations are **HYDROELECTRIC** and supply 98% of MB's electricity; 2 thermal stations operate, at **BRANDON** (which burns coal and natural gas) and **SELKIRK** (which has used natural gas since 2002). In 2005, MB embarked on wind-turbine pilot projects for energy export. Diesel generating stations, once used through many areas of the province, are now scarce. Air quality in MB is regularly monitored for 5 parameters in Winnipeg and Brandon. Most urban air pollution originates from fossil fuel combustion. Pollutant levels within MB cities are among the lowest in Canada, and rate as "good" more than 90% of the time.

When sulphur dioxide and nitrogen oxides are converted in the atmosphere to sulphuric and nitric acids, these can precipitate as acid rain or dust (dry acid deposition). The largest sources of sulphur dioxide in MB are smelters, accounting for more than 95%. Also responsible are fossil-fuel combustion and the **FORESTRY** industry. Sulphur dioxide is monitored at 6 locations near the 2 smelters. Other air-quality issues include odorous industrial emissions and facilities such as feedlots, large hog farms, and sewage lagoons. The vast majority of atmospheric ammonia in MB originates from agriculture through volatilization of inorganic fertilizers and manure.

WATER AND SOIL POLLUTION: In SW MB, irrigation brings groundwater with high total dissolved solids to the surface, aggravating soil salinity. Excessive salt levels can lead to contamination of both groundwater and aquifers. Sources of aquifer contamination include compromised well casings, surface spills, leaching from manure, sewage lagoons, landfills, failed septic fields, mining process water and tailings ponds, and groundwater heat exchange pumps. Gravel pits and other excavations near or below the water table (for example, the **RED RIVER FLOODWAY**) may funnel surface pollutants to groundwater. Intractable groundwater and soil pollution may also originate from industrial sites. Only a small proportion of sewage effluent is disinfected in MB before it is released to surface waters. Fecal coliform (especially *Escherichia coli*) measurements in the **RED RIVER** N of Winnipeg often exceed guidelines. Excessive coliform levels are responsible for beach closures in summer, for permanent boil-water advisories for wells in rural areas, and for closure of public wells in some cottage communities.

Nutrient (nitrogen and phosphorus) inputs to surface water have been increasing, resulting in aesthetic and public health concerns arising from algal blooms, especially in **Lake Winnipeg**. These algae thrive on phosphates, many of which originate from various household and industrial soaps and detergents. These blooms cause fish kills through oxygen depletion, and produce potentially lethal toxins. A MB govt 1998 survey found detectable toxin levels in ⅔ of treated municipal water. Nutrient sources in MB include municipal sewage and septic effluent, cottage wastewater, livestock waste, chemical fertilizer runoff, stubble burning, forest fires, land clearing, clear-cutting, pulp and paper mills, and mine drainage. Draining of wetlands has severely impaired natural detoxification and nutrient absorption within watersheds.

Herbicide and pesticide use is widespread in domestic, aesthetic, and agricultural settings, though as of writing, Brandon had passed a law prohibiting merely cosmetic use of biocides. Chemical weed control in parks, golf courses, and on rights-of-way of roadways, **Railway** lines, and power transmission lines is conducted by municipal and provincial departments, and by corporations. In N MB, herbicide use on permafrost accelerates melting and ground destabilization. Water in the Red River downstream of Winnipeg often contains as many as 30 times the 2,4-D (a common herbicide) as upstream. Urban centres also have programs for mosquito larviciding and fogging, which may contribute to lung disease and potentially some cancers, and which can be lethal for a variety of birds and small mammals.

An extensive array of minerals is mined in MB. Mining is associated with toxic effluents containing high concentrations of metals and other elements (including iron, arsenic, copper, nickel, zinc, lead, cadmium, manganese, antimony, aluminum, cobalt, strontium, and selenium) as well as high levels of total dissolved solids from mineshafts and process water. Process chemicals may escape to surface waters. Some entire lake basins have been appropriated as permanent process waste repositories. Effluents, sampled by the operators, are regulated by federal Metal Mining Effluent Regulations (2002). However, the majority of lead, zinc, and aluminum in MB is derived from air pollution. Although most leaded fuels were discontinued during the early 1970s (CAN still imports leaded racing fuels), roadside soils and vegetation continue to retain elevated amounts of the substance.

Environmental concerns from landfills relate to air quality; leaching of various compounds,

Water pollution can interfere with recreational enjoyment of Manitoba lakes.

including heavy metals, to groundwater (particularly from numerous older sites throughout MB); and inundation of sites within the Red River floodplain during seasons of flooding. Nearly 200 active and inactive disposal grounds are less than 1.5 km from a municipal water supply source, or are in contact with aquifers that supply wells. Since the establishment of the 1991 Waste Disposal Ground Regulation, many rural landfills in MB have been decommissioned, and waste collection sites have been centralized. The Manitoba Product Stewardship Program supports recycling of paper, glass, steel, aluminum, and recyclable plastics. The Manitoba Tire Stewardship Board was created in 1993 to reduce tire accumulation in landfills. Depots operate at various communities to collect hazardous materials.

Stagnation associated with large water reservoirs promotes microbial methylation of inorganic mercury into highly toxic methyl mercury, which bioaccumulates in animals. This has created hardship for **First Peoples**, especially **Cree**, communities, where fish have been a dietary staple and economic mainstay. At Southern Indian Lake, mercury levels in walleye and northern pike have exceeded Cdn marketing and export thresholds.

Crude oil extraction in SW MB is associated hydrogen sulphide and volatile hydrocarbons. Petroleum products account for hundreds of contaminated sites in MB that have required remediation. Fuel from industrial plants may contaminate underground aquifers and render

them unpotable. Underground fuel storage tanks at service stations may leak for years before the problem is discovered. While tank registration became mandatory in 1976, and aging underground tanks are replaced routinely, the location of many abandoned installations is unknown. In northern areas, leakage and spills have occurred from aboveground tanks. MB operates a program for waste-oil recycling. Still, only a portion of waste oil is recovered. ● EVA PIP

POLSON, Arthur, violinist, composer, conductor, (b Vancouver, Mar 2, 1934; d Vancouver, Feb 25, 2003). Polson studied violin in Vancouver with his father, with Joy Calvert and Gregori Garbovitsky, and with Louis Persinger in California and New York. He was a member of the Vancouver Symphony Orchestra 1954-62, giving the Cdn premiere of Shostakovich's Concerto No. 1 in 1958; concertmaster of the Victoria Symphony Orchestra 1962-64; concertmaster of the **Winnipeg Symphony Orchestra** 1966-86, **Manitoba Chamber Orchestra** 1970-86 and CBC Winnipeg Orchestra 1966-75. He conducted the WSO and CBC Orchestra frequently, in subscription, educational and tour concerts. He also led the Winnipeg Youth Orchestra 1966-72 and the Greater Winnipeg Schools Orchestra. Returning to Vancouver in 1986, he played as co-concertmaster of the CBC Radio Orchestra and the Vancouver Opera Orchestra and conducted the Vancouver Youth Symphony Orchestra 1986-2003. Polson led the VYSO on international tours and recorded CDs with them. Throughout his career, he performed in chamber groups (including Cassenti Players and Festival Players of Canada) and as a soloist in concerts and on radio and television. He composed more than 100 works, including chamber pieces and concertos, many created on commission from orchestras and soloists. • DON ANDERSON

POPLAR RIVER FIRST NATION,

on reserve pop 1093, off reserve pop 270, is situated E of **Lake Winnipeg** at the Poplar River, and about 340 km N of **Winnipeg**. The native language of this community is **Ojibway**, and it signed Treaty 5 in 1875. It is a member of the Southeast Tribal Council. Poplar River First Nation offers schooling from Nursery-Grade 12, and enrolment for 2003-04 was 322. There is one reserve located on the Poplar River First Nation land. Poplar River has no permanent access road – just a winter road from Pine Dock, just N of Berens and Poplar Rivers, where there is an all-weather road. This isolated community's economic base is trapping and **Fishing**.

In an effort to protect the pristine boreal forest setting, Poplar River First Nation has been working with Pikangikum in ON, and **Pauingassi**, and **Little Grand Rapids First Nations** in MB since 2002 to safeguard ancestral lands by seeking a UNESCO World Heritage listing. Poplar River resident Sophia Rabliauskas was awarded the Goldman Environmental Prize in early 2007 for her efforts to protect the unspoiled wilderness from the effects of logging to the S and hydroelectric development to the N. She was the first Cdn Aboriginal woman and one of only a handful of Canadians to win the award, given to just one person from each of the world's inhabited continents each year. • RK

POPLAWSKI, Joe "Pop," Football

player, (b Aug 2, 1957, Edmonton, AB) was one of the **Winnipeg Blue Bombers**' star players during the 1980s. Poplawski, an all-around athlete in high school, was offered scholarships to several American universities, but opted to stay in his native Alberta and play for the U of Alberta Golden Bears. He was named the Canadian Interuniversity Athletic Union's All-Star Receiver in 1977 and, though the Edmonton Eskimos had originally signed Poplawski, his contract was traded to the Bombers after he refused to close the door on his NFL options, angering Eskimos' management.

A clutch receiver, Poplawski joined the Bombers in 1978 and played an incredible first season. His performance earned him the Jackie Parker Trophy for Outstanding Rookie in the West and the Schenley Outstanding Rookie Award. He was also named that year's CFL

WINNIPEG FREE PRESS

Joe Poplawski won 2 Schenley Awards.

All-Western Wide Receiver. Poplawksi went on to play for the league's All-Canadian team 5 times. His career highlight was the 1984 Bombers' Grey Cup victory, the first the team had won in 22 years. Poplawski received his 2nd Schenley Award in 1986, and was named the Manitoba Sportswriters and Sportscasters Association Athlete of the Year, after which he retired with career totals of 549 receptions for 8341 receiving yds. He was inducted into the Canadian Football Hall of Fame in 1998. He continues to live in **Winnipeg** with his family. • MD

POPULATION TRENDS

in MB reflect a gradual decline over more than the last 100 years. In the 2006 census, MB had a population of 1,148,401 in a territory of 649,950 km². Although this accounted for only 3.6% of the Canadian total, it ranked fifth among the provinces and territories. Since its birth, population growth in MB has varied over time and in geographical distribution.

EARLY COLONIZATION: The early colonization of **Rupert's Land** by Upper Canadian and European people began with the fur trade and was continued at the initiative of **Lord Selkirk**. By the 1850s, the new settlements accounted for more than 10,000 persons along the **Red** and **Assiniboine** rivers. During the last quarter of the 19th century, immigrants to the new province increased progressively, coming mainly from ON and the US. They were later joined by French immigrants from PQ, Mennonites from Russia, Icelanders, along with many others. Consequently, MB's population surged to over 150,000 within two decades of its joining Confederation.

LIBERALIZATION OF IMMIGRATION: In order to satisfy the economic needs of the country before WWI, Canada's national immigration

policy was liberalized, resulting in a steady increase in number of immigrants to MB. The increase continued in the first 2 decades of the 20th century: from 255,211 in 1901 to 610,118 in 1921. Most of the province's arable land was taken up between 1896 and 1914. Simultaneously, the population inflow acted as a catalyst to **Winnipeg**'s immigrant-based economy. Between 1901 and 1913, the city grew from 42,000 to over 150,000, and for the first time 1/3 of the provincial population lived in Winnipeg.

THE DEPRESSION AND WARS: The 1930s and early 1940s were disappointing for MB in terms of environmental, economic, and demographic conditions. Crop failures, the collapse of the Manitoba Cooperative Wheat Producers, and the **Great Depression** created an economic crisis with massive unemployment and declining wages. Largely due to deliberate measures to stop new international immigrants by the fed gov, MB's population grew by only 4% during the period 1931-41. During the period 1941-51, MB's population did not grow much (just 6.4%) due to 2 major factors: first, the war-based industrial boom in Canada was concentrated mainly in ON, and second, the natural-resource richness of BC gave it an advantage over MB to attract young adults.

POST-WAR BABY BOOM: The post-war fertility boom and a more liberal immigration policy, especially in accepting refugees from war-affected Europe, contributed to a national population growth of 30.2% and provincial growth of 18.7% during the period 1951-1961. However, this surge did not last due to several significant social, economic, and geographical factors – such as preference for the nuclear family, the economic shock from the Middle East oil crisis in the mid-1970s, and setbacks in agriculture from international competition. Along with other parts of Canada, MB experienced a decline in the fertility level below the replacement level throughout the 1970s and 1980s; crude birth rate fell from 18 live births per year (per 1,000 population) in 1971 to as low as 16 live birth in 1980. Significant population change through both emigration and immigration into MB but with a very limited net increase has become the norm in recent decades. The slow natural increase along with emigration resulted in only a 7.2% net increase of population for the period 1961-71, and as little as a 3.8% increase for the period 1971-81.

SLOW GROWTH: Since 1981, supported by an economic recovery triggered by federal and provincial fiscal policies and management, the baby boomers have reversed the trend of declining fertility. The number of live births increased from 16.1 per 1,000 in 1981 to 17.0 in 1987. However, this resurgence did not last long as the

Provincial & National Population Trends

MB			CANADA		
Year	Population	% Change	Population	% Change	MB's % of the national population
1901	255,211	—	5,371,315	—	4.8
1911	461,394	80.8	7,206,643	34.2	6.4
1921	610,118	32.2	8,787,499	21.9	6.9
1931	700,139	14.8	10,376,786	18.1	6.7
1941	729,744	4.2	11,506,655	10.9	6.3
1951	776,541	6.4	14,009,429	21.8	5.5
1961	921,686	18.7	18,238,247	30.2	5.1
1971	988,247	7.2	21,568,311	18.3	4.6
1981	1,026,241	3.8	24,343,181	12.9	4.2
1991	1,091,942	6.4	27,296,859	12.1	4.0
2001	1,119,583	2.5	30,007,094	9.9	3.7
2006	1,148,401	2.6	31,612,897	5.4	3.6

number of live births dropped to as low as 11.6 per 1,000 in 2002, and is unlikely to create long-term overall population growth. Emigration, both from farms and from Winnipeg, along with the slow natural increase have created new challenges for MB in keeping its population stable. During the 1991-2001 decade, MB's population remained virtually stagnant, with only 2.5% growth.

Historically, Winnipeg played a pivotal role, as the "gateway to western Canada," in transforming the economic and political landscape of MB. Since the mid-20th century more than half of the province's population has lived in this urban agglomeration. With a population size of 661,730, the city contained 60% of the province's population in 2001. With increased diversification of nonagricultural economy on the one hand, and the uncertainty of the farm economy on the other, many people have left their traditional place of rural residence and moved to, or closer to, the major city – Winnipeg – and along the Pembina valley of S MB. Thus, newer patterns of rural-urban population distribution, characterizing by major concentrations in and around Winnipeg, are emerging through rearrangement and redistribution of existing settlements in the province.

Presently, the nuclear-family structure is a well-established norm, and "multiple-member family living" disappearing rapidly. Data from the censuses indicate that not only did the proportion of children (younger than 15 years) decline between 1961 and 2001 but their absolute numbers also decreased significantly. This means that in the coming decades the number of children entering MB's labour force will be much lower than at present, while the proportion of the elderly will expand further, a result of reduced mortality. Such changing demographic conditions will affect all spheres of MB's economy and society. ● C. EMDAD HAQUE

PORCUPINE (*Erethizon dorsatum*) is such an unusual rodent that it is placed in its own family Erethizontidae. It is widespread in NA, from the N treeline of Canada and Alaska to nothern Mexico, and occupies all land habitats of MB. This distribution is remarkable considering its ancestors originated in tropical South America. The subspecies inhabiting the boreal and mixed forests have black and white hairs, while the Prairie subspecies is a beautiful yellow and black. There are other porcupine relatives in Central and South America, as well as unrelated porcupines in the Old World (family Hystricidae). Its success is due mainly to two adaptations – an effective defensive armour of sharp quills (stiff, barbed guard hairs) and the ability to survive on shrub and tree bark, buds and conifer needles, with the help of cellulose-digesting bacteria and protozoa in the gut. Weighing an average of 18 kg,

this large rodent is a slow but sure climber, using its strong limbs and claws.

Surviving on an energy-poor diet, the porcupine is relatively inactive, and often remains in the same tree for days, similar to the sloths of South America. It usually deposits its droppings at one site – often in a hollow tree trunk. When it is time to travel to another area to feed, it waddles along slowly, ever ready to raise its quills against any predator that comes to investigate. It cannot throw its quills, but it readily flips its tail into the nose of its antagonist, and the shock and pain are often sufficient to drive the unsuspecting predator away. The quills may work their way through the victim's body over many weeks, and can cause death should they strike some vital organ. The Great Horned Owl, Fisher and Cougar are adept at flipping the Porcupine over to expose its undefended belly. The male first

ROBERT R. TAYLOR

Sharp quills provide effective protection for the porcupine.

courts a female, and then mounts her carefully, both partners keeping their quills down to avoid injury. About 210 days after copulation, one young, weighing 400 g, is born in summer. Porcupines can live to 17 years in the wild. • REW

PORK INDUSTRY in MB has undergone many changes since the **Red River** Valley was first settled in the early 1800s. With the loss in 1995 of the **Crow Rate** and the advantages it provided for grain producers, hog production has expanded dramatically throughout southern MB. Since that time, both production and processing have expanded in numbers and distribution throughout the province. In 1986, 1.8 million pigs were marketed from farms in MB. In 2006, there were about 1.2 million people living in MB and 8.8 million hogs were marketed – more than 4 times the number in 1986, making MB the largest hog-producing province in Canada. In 2007, MB accounted for more than ¼ of total Cdn production. Manitobans only consume about 8% of what is produced in the province. According to the department of agriculture, hog production was the most valuable agricultural sector in MB in terms of value of production ($792 million), employment (17,000 jobs), and economic spinoffs ($2 billion) in 2003. In fact, the hog sector was the primary reason that MB outpaced the rest of Canada in diversification according to the 1996 and 2001 Agricultural Census.

The number of farms with pigs however, is declining. In 1976, there were 6069 farms with hogs, but the numbers fell steadily since then – 3563 in 1986, 2064 in 1996, and 1280 in 2006. The result is concentrated production on fewer farms, most particularly with the trend towards confined animal feeding operations or CAFOs. There are several reasons for the increased production on fewer farms, including transition out of wheat production with the loss of the Crow Rate transportation subsidy, provincial support for developing the sector, emerging global markets for pork, elimination of the hog marketing monopoly, and developments in the pork processing sector.

In 2007, MB had a slaughter capacity of almost 7 million pigs per year. Adding to existing pork processing plants in Neepawa and Winnipeg, Maple Leaf Meats constructed a state-of-the-art pork processing plant in Brandon that began production in 1999. This plant has the capability to process 45,000 pigs per week in one shift. There are proposals to add a 2nd shift that would double production to 90,000 per week. In 2007, the first shift employed about 1150 workers. A 2nd shift would require another 1000 employees.

The hog sector is not without controversy. Manitoba established a Hog Marketing Board in 1965 at a time when processing was concentrated in the city of Winnipeg. It was a divisive decision when the **Progressive Conservative** administration under **Gary Filmon** abolished the board that had been created by an earlier Conservative govt, arguing that an open market would give producers more options and make the province more attractive to processors. Sure enough, in 1998, Maple Leaf Foods announced it would build a processing plant in Brandon. Soon after, both AB and SK followed MB's lead, eliminating their hog marketing boards. Processing capacity increased in those provinces as well.

In 2007, Manitoba had an annual slaughter capacity of almost 7 million pigs.

MANITOBA PORK COUNCIL

However, there are concerns about concentrating production on larger farms with fewer operations. Adding to this issue, is that only 1/3 of farms are 'farrow to finish' operations, which means farms that raise pigs from birth until they are sold to market. In the 21st century, the trend is for operations to specialize, either in the birth to weanling phase or in the 'fattening' stage where weanlings are raised until sold. The need for 2 barns to raise a hog means increased transportation issues, community, and environmental concerns. Based on experiences in the US, there are also concerns about 'corporate control' in the sector. The MB govt department acknowledges that while individual farmers and Hutterite colonies represent part of the increased production in the province, 'production companies' have played a significant role. Increased production has also given rise to complaints from rural residents living near hog operations about noise, dust and smell. Some also argue that focusing on one commodity such as pork makes the agricultural sector vulnerable in the same way wheat was in past generations.

But the biggest concern about increased hog production is that it may pollute waterways and aquifers. Phosphorus – mainly found in detergents, fertilizers and human and animal waste – has been blamed for algae on **Lake Winnipeg**, which could choke out aquatic life. Many place the blame on the pork industry. However, others argue that MB is different from other hog production areas like NB, ON, and QC, in that it has a large land base for facilities, feed production, and spreading of manure. The Clean Environment Commission (CEC) began holding hearings in early 2007 to assess the industry's sustainability.

In 2007, it was unclear whether further expansion of the MB pork industry would be encouraged. Maple Leaf had resolved to centre its Prairie processing at its Brandon plant. It had announced funding to increase sewage treatment capacity, a necessary step to expanding to a second shift and thereby doubling production. However, in late 2006, the MB govt put a moratorium on future hog barn construction until the CEC final report was in. That ban was partially behind the decision of 2 of the 3 partners of another pork processing plant proposed for Winnipeg to pull out. At the time of writing, the future of that proposal was uncertain. If there is increasing processing in the province, there will surely be a need for more hogs. However, with continued uncertainties in the grain and oilseed sectors, diversifying into hog production will likely remain an option for many MB farmers. • DOUG RAMSEY

PORTAGE LA PRAIRIE, pop 12,728, is MB's 4th largest city. It is located 70 km W of **Winnipeg**, S of **Lake Manitoba**. It is on the Trans-Canada and Yellowhead hwys, on both the **CN** and **CP** main lines, and is served by **Via Rail**. The name is of French origin, and means prairie portage (for the portage route that runs from the **Assiniboine River** to **Lake Manitoba**). In the early days it was known variously as Meadow Portage, Plain Portage or simply The Portage. It was an important historical site with ancient Aboriginal trails criss-crossing the area. These trails, useful to fur traders and early explorers, later also served missionaries and incoming settlers who walked with packs on their backs or led laden carts with perhaps a cow in tow and children trailing alongside. As early as 1739, **La Verendrye** built the 2nd of 2 forts he called Fort la Reine. (The first was located near **Poplar Point**). The fort here served as a trading post as well as being the centre of La Verendrye and his sons' western explorations. La Verendrye's successors subsequently abandoned the fort about 1751 after trouble with marauding First Nations and the fort later was looted and burned. Soon after, the French govt ceded this area to the UK, and it became part of **Rupert's Land**. The site of the fort is now a museum that includes a replica of the fort and serves as the tourist bureau for the area.

About 1780, a Roman Catholic Mission with a log chapel was established on the island at

Portage la Prairie. The **North West Company** operated a fort in the area, at least until 1821 when it amalgamated with the **HBC**. But it remained for Archdeacon William Cochrane of **Red River** to bring about the first real settlement. He brought with him a dozen or more English-speaking settlers and their families. In 1853, he opened a mission to the First Nations people. The first Anglican Church was built in 1853 near the Assiniboine River at Pratt's Landing and the first school soon followed. A post office was set up in 1870, and Portage was incorporated as a town in 1880. With the building of a women's jail here in 1906 (now the Women's Correctional Institute), population increased, and Portage was incorporated as a city the following year.

With some of the most fertile soils in the West, farming was the draw for much early settlement in the area. In the 21st century, Portage remains an agricultural service centre, as well as a retail and service magnet for surrounding rural areas. Portage is the heart of a large agricultural area, growing grains, beans and other vegetables, spices and some of the best potatoes in the country. McCain Foods and **Simplot** each operate large potato processing plants here. A Potato Festival is held each August. There are also numerous fruit and U-pick farms in the area.

Portage la Prairie has seen significant development since its beginnings. What used to be a "slough," a semi-dry offshoot of the river, has been developed into Crescent Lake with water sports. "Island Park" features an 18-hole golf course, horseracing track, ball diamonds, deer and bird pens, arboretum, maze, picnic areas, tennis courts, and a water park. Recreational

features include **Manitobah Republic** Park's 11 soccer fields, 9 ball diamonds, 2 beach volleyball courts, and a football/rugby field. The Portage and District Terrriers Hockey Club, with both the Memorial Cup and the Centennial Cup to its credit, enjoys a 40-year history in Portage. The new Portage la Prairie City Library and the William Glesby Performing Arts Centre and Art Gallery have added to the cultural life of Portage. Two senior centres contribute to the activities and well being of the older population. The Canadian Senior Games were held here in late summer 2006. Three shopping malls include major retail outlets, and a variety of specialty stores offer high quality goods. Employment opportunities also include the Manitoba Development Centre, Agassiz Youth Centre, Women's Correctional Institute, various government departments and other small businesses and ventures. For 50 years, Portage was home to a Canadian Air Force base. When the base was closed in 1990, Southport Aerospace Centre Inc. was established as a non-profit development venture to attract and manage aerospace initiatives. Famous people from Portage la Prairie include **Arthur Meighen** and **Sterling Lyon**. •
HELEN MULLIGAN

PORTUGUESE immigration to MB began in 1952, though Portugal's world-renowned navigators reached and explored what is now NL long before Columbus reached the New World in 1492. The earliest **Immigrants** to Canada were not destined for MB, but as they searched for work, many chose the **Railways**. As this was mainly seasonal work, some settled down for the winter in

nearby cities while laid off. A number of these workers migrated to cities, especially **Winnipeg**, and sought work in other sectors such as the **Garment Industry**, **Construction**, and the trades. Those who were married sent for their wives and children and remained in Winnipeg to raise their families. These people formed the base of the Portuguese community in the city, and they joined to maintain the Portuguese language and traditions while integrating into Cdn society. The ensuing proliferation of more formal Portuguese organizations such as associations, cultural centres, businesses, social clubs, sports teams, and religious organizations, arose from the early and informal social gathering of immigrant workers looking for support and camaraderie in an unfamiliar New World as well as in response to the organizing efforts of other ethnic groups and the overarching acceptance of multiculturalism in Winnipeg. The Portuguese pavilion was among the first to participate in **Folklorama**, which was established in 1974.

Canada stopped actively recruiting labourers from Portugal in 1958, but family member sponsorship brought a steady flow of Portuguese immigrants to major urban centres like Toronto and surrounding area, Montreal, Winnipeg, and Edmonton. The decade between 1966 and 1976 registered the highest number of arrivals in MB, with entries peaking in 1971 at 657 immigrants; followed by 637 in 1974 and 623 in 1973. Immigration fell off after that, but the Portuguese community in Winnipeg remains strong owing to ongoing cultural, religious, and familial ties to Portuguese communities around the world, including mainland Portugal, the Azores, and Madeira.

With over 95% of all Portuguese considering themselves **Roman Catholic**, it is no surprise that the church is often the focal point of the community. The church also provides a social opportunity through the yearly celebration of important feast days such as *Espirito Santo* (Holy Spirit), *Santo Cristo* (Holy Christ), *Nossa Senhora da Fatima* (Our Lady of Fatima), and *Santo Antonio* (St. Anthony). More secular holidays are also observed, such as the wine-harvest feast known as *São Martinho*, or St. Martin's, when local winemakers are encouraged to bring their homemade wine to annual tastings in Winnipeg, in keeping with traditional wine-tasting festivals in Portugal. The Portuguese also celebrate *25 de Abril* (April 25), marking a bloodless coup in which a half-century dictatorship was overthrown in 1974. Portugal Day is celebrated on June 10 of every year and, in Winnipeg, marks the inauguration of a week-long *Semana de Portugal* (Portugal week), with events celebrated at the 3 largest Portuguese cultural and social

Island Park in Portage la Prairie

551

P

"Lucky roosters" at the 2006 Portugal Folklorama pavilion

organizations in Winnipeg: the Portuguese Association of Manitoba (and Portuguese Cultural Centre); the *Casa do Minho* Portuguese Centre; and, the *Centro Cultural Açoriano*. The Portuguese community in Winnipeg has a number of other social, cultural and sport organizations as well, including the Portuguese Non-Profit Housing Corporation, and affiliation in the Portuguese Canadian National Congress.

The Portuguese also celebrate Carnival (Fat Tuesday), as do many Catholic societies in Europe and in Latin America. Occurring in the first week before the start of Lent, celebrations are held in the various cultural organizations around the city, with prizes awarded for the most original masks and best costumes. Christmas and New Year's Eve feasts are very important as well in providing community members with the opportunity to renew ties with friends and family and with the "Portuguese" Roman Catholic Church in Winnipeg – Imaculada Conçeicão (Immaculate Conception).

With only one language – Portuguese – and no significant dialects beyond regional accents, both *Açorianos* (from the Azores) and *Continentais* (mainland Portuguese) are fiercely proud of their ethnic and national origin. *Saudade* is an uniquely Portuguese expression and emotional complex that has no English equivalent, but which is said often by the Portuguese to express their feelings in literature, dance and song – particularly the *fado*, which is referred to as the Portuguese blues. Along with the church, another pillar of the Portuguese community in Winnipeg is the family. Despite modern social pressures exerted upon traditional notions of family, mother,

father, and children still stand together as a solid unit in a complex social structure that includes the church, the ethnic social and cultural organizations, as well as the larger community. In Winnipeg, over 10,000 respondents in the last national Census gave their ethnicity as Portuguese, which ranked 20th in a list of over 80 ethnic origins.

The Portuguese are adaptable, and have worked hard to integrate with the mainstream and become Cdn, while at the same time maintaining a fierce loyalty to Portugal and local expressions of their homeland in the community. It is this duality – perhaps borne of a long-rooted, historical tendency to explore, navigate and settle in foreign lands – that makes the Portuguese so much at home wherever they settle. ● SALLY CORREIA/AUGUST BAIROS

POSNER, Barry Innis, physician, researcher (b 1937, **WINNIPEG**). After receiving his MD from the **U OF M** in 1961, Posner undertook postgraduate residency at the Winnipeg General Hospital (*see* **HEALTH SCIENCES CENTRE**), the Massachusetts Institute of Technology, and the New England Medical Center. Posner's first major appointment was as a biochemistry research associate at the National Institutes of Health in Bethesda, MD. In 1970, he moved to Montreal to accept positions at the Royal Victoria Hospital and the McGill U Faculty of **MEDICINE**, and in 1979, he became director of the Polypeptide Hormone Laboratory, a full professor in the Department of Medicine, and senior physician at the hospital. Later in his career, Posner also held roles as professor in the McGill U Department of Anatomy

and Cell Biology, and from 1996-2002 was physician-in-chief at the Sir Mortimer B. Davis Jewish General Hospital, also in Montreal.

Posner's internationally recognized research focuses on the genetics of diabetes, and also how pancreatic peptide hormones – insulin and insulin-like growth factors – act on cells. He has secured numerous grants, including funding from the Medical Research Council of Canada and the National Cancer Institute, as well as a $16.2 million Genome Canada grant for his research group to work on identifying the genes related to type-2 diabetes. By 2006, Posner had authored or co-authored more than 275 scientific articles, and had been the recipient of numerous awards, including his 1991 election as a fellow in the Royal Society of Canada, and a 1999 appointment as an Officer of the Order of Canada. ● JOEL TRENAMAN

POULTRY FARMING. The poultry industry in MB has changed dramatically since its inception. What was once a case of keeping backyard flocks for home consumption is now an industry dominated by highly specialized commercial enterprises that supply a largely urban marketplace. Unlike many other sectors of **AGRICULTURE**, poultry production has been protected from radical fluctuations in price and demand by supply-management systems introduced in Canada in the 1960s and early '70s. Supply management ensures a fair price for farmers and a domestic market for production – MB poultry farms now produce 98% of local market demands. Only 3% of total production is exported.

From 1990-2006, the number of producers in MB declined from 136 to 18, yet consumer demand increased dramatically over the same period, resulting in a 60% increase in quotas for the remaining farms. The majority of the 40.4 million kg of finished chicken produced in 2005 was raised on farms in southeastern MB. In the 21st century, chicken and turkey production dominate the MB poultry industry. Breeding stock, selected for the quality and quantity of meat, is primarily imported from the US and housed in MB hatcheries. Most chickens and turkeys raised in the province are processed at 2 packing plants, one in **WINNIPEG**, the other in Blumenort. A small plant in **NIVERVILLE** processes halal chickens for the Muslim market.

In 2005, MB was home to 58 turkey producers, 6 breeder farms, and one of the largest turkey hatcheries in western Canada. Demand for whole turkeys peaks in Oct and Dec. The rest of the year, consumer demand shifts to cut-up turkey. This supply-managed industry produced 1.4 million birds in 2005, or 10 million kg. Turkey parts that Manitobans shun

– feet, tails, and some drumsticks and wings – are exported. Although MB's goose industry declined from about 150,000 domestic birds in 1968 to about 60,000 in 2001, it is still among the largest in Canada. In the early 21st century, annual production of geese and ducks was valued at less than $1 million.

The poultry industry regulates the amount of space required for each bird, so flock sizes vary with the type of bird raised. There are no caged poultry flocks in MB. In 2006, EPIDEMICS of avian influenza, especially strain H5N1, remained a threat to poultry operations worldwide, but MB was still free of the virus. Future expansion of the poultry sector is expected as the industry supplies new markets for processed products. ● Anne Cote ▸ *See* EGG FARMING.

PoW CAMPS. MB had 2 prisoner of war camps during WWII. While across Canada, 34,000 German PoWs were held at the request of the British govt, just 450 PoWs stayed in MB, all volunteers who had offered their service for work camps located deep in the wilderness at Whitewater Lake in RIDING MOUNTAIN NATIONAL PARK and Cache Lake in present-day DUCK MOUNTAIN PROVINCIAL PARK. Though PM Mackenzie King had initially resisted plans to put the PoWs to work, believing the effort required to force labour from German soldiers would exceed the value, a fuel shortage eventually prompted the govt to offer a daily 50 cent wage to PoWs willing to cut cordwood. Regulations authorizing the employment of PoWs were officially introduced on May 10, 1943, and volunteers were recruited from the main camps in AB. The work camps for PoWs in MB were constructed, somewhat ironically, by MB conscientious objectors forced into alternative work service.

Although park officials at Riding Mountain were initially wary of bringing PoWs into MB's forests, concerned that the presence of Nazi soldiers would frighten off summer campers, the PoWs soon proved a non-threatening and even congenial group, who were appreciative of the natural beauty of their surroundings. Furthermore, the camps had all the necessary amenities to provide the PoWs with a comfortable existence, including bunkhouses equipped with washrooms, a dining hall, and small hospital. Notably, the camps lacked fences or guard towers, and camp boundaries were instead defined by a red blaze marked on a ring of trees encircling the camp. The red paint was a rather insubstantial barrier, leaving the PoWs free to wander beyond the parameters on nature walks or even to attend social events in nearby communities. Few escape attempts were made, as the PoWs had little reason to leave the ease of life at the camp.

While the PoWs spent part of the day cutting cordwood for fuel, they also had ample leisure time, which they often spent outdoors playing sports, or even building dug-out canoes for fishing. In the camp's entertainment room, they could play cards, darts and Ping-Pong. At Riding Mountain, the rec room even had a piano, which the PoWs would gather around for sing-a-longs while drinking hooch provided by friendly camp staff. Though the PoWs ate well, and were not subject to the same rationing as Cdn civilians, they also bred and raised pigs to make the traditional food of their homeland, such as bratwurst. Though one prisoner died in an unfortunate accident while felling a tree, most of the PoWs found camp life quite enjoyable, and many returned to MB in the years following the war for visits, or even to settle permanently. ● MICHELLE DOBROVOLNY

POWERVIEW-PINE FALLS, pop 1400, is 120 km NE of WINNIPEG, next to the Sagkeeng First Nation, on the S bank of the WINNIPEG RIVER. On May 1, 2005, the 2 adjacent communities of Powerview and Pine Falls amalgamated.

Pine Falls was believed to be the last privately owned mill community in Canada. It was established in 1925 when the paper industry started, and the RAILWAY came here in 1926. John D. McArthur brought the paper company to its fruition, and it is now owned and operated by Tembec Industries Inc. Powerview was incorporated as a village in 1951. Early on, Powerview had been known as Tin Town because it was built up around the community of Pine Falls with mill and construction workers' homes. The Pine Falls Generating Station came online in 1952, and was the last HYDROELECTRIC dam to use the abundant flows of the WINNIPEG RIVER.

The community's central economic backbone is the hydro and paper industry. The region attracts outdoor-sports enthusiasts, SPORT FISHERMEN, and hunters. During the Labour Day weekend, Powerview-Pine Falls holds its annual 4P (Power, Paper, Peas, and Pickerel) Festival, the title of which refers to the community's economic strengths, as well as 2 of its major natural resources – commercial PICKEREL fishing and St. Georges peas. ● GPP

POWWOWS. The contemporary powwow developed from traditional forms of singing, drumming, and DANCE and includes dances and songs exchanged among First Nations across the Prairies. Some northern communities also hold a variation of the powwow or attend a celebration at southern locales. Many of the more northerly Prairie peoples trace the origins of their powwow to the Grass Dance or "Sioux Dance" that they adopted from the Siouan peoples.

Several types of powwows are celebrated throughout MB. While some are small, local affairs, the type most familiar to the public are the large intertribal gatherings that occur primarily in summer. The larger powwows are intended to promote understanding, appreciation, and respect for Aboriginal heritage among Aboriginal as well as non-Aboriginal people. Through the sharing of traditional forms of MUSIC, dance, and prayer, participants gather in a spirit of fellowship and are encouraged to connect with the values of their cultural traditions and to carry these lessons into the future. At these powwows, dance and drumming competitions take place in different categories, including traditional dance, jingle dress dance, fancy shawl dance, and fancy feather dance. The outfits of the dancers are exquisitely decorated with both traditional and contemporary items. Traditional drumming, often referred to as the "heartbeat of the Nation," accompanies the dances.

Both music and dance are, in essence, forms of prayer, and are deeply imbued with the spirituality of First Nations cultures. At many powwows, other ceremonies occur, such as the honouring of war veterans and other worthy community members. The powwow continues to serve as a force of unity, pride, and regeneration in many MB First Nations communities. ● KATHERINE PETTIPAS ▸ *See also* SUN DANCE.

PRAIRIE CROCUS (*Anemone patens*) is the provincial flower of MB. The province's schoolchildren chose the prairie crocus as MB's provincial floral emblem; the western red lily (*Lilium philadelphicum* L.), SK's floral emblem, was 2nd. The bill making the flower MB's emblem received Royal Assent March 16, 1906.

Not a true crocus but a member of the buttercup or crowfoot family, it is closely related to other wild and tame anemones. True crocuses (*Crocus* spp.) grow naturally around the

Prairie crocus clump

Mediterranean and have been introduced throughout much of Europe. True crocuses were the first spring flowers seen in their homelands, so European **Immigrants** naturally called the first ones they saw here "prairie crocuses." Prairie crocuses push their fuzzy flower buds up even through snow: the fuzz is believed to provide insulation to the early flowers. Their purple-to-almost-white flowers are made up of 5-8 sepals, the outer ring of flowerlike parts. Like other anemones, they lack true petals and have many separate central pollen- and seed-producing parts (stamens and pistils). Each seed has a long, feathery tail to help wind carry it to a new area. The seed heads are almost as beautiful as the flowers, and fields of them are often called "prairie-smoke." Another name, "pasque flower," refers to their usual blooming time near Easter. **First Peoples** used its fresh leaves to treat rheumatism and neuralgia; its crushed leaves for poultices; smelled pulverized leaves to alleviate headaches; and made decoctions from roots to treat lung problems. The plant contains strong chemicals that irritate the skin and mucous membranes and which can produce blisters. It should be handled with care and never eaten.

Although greatly diminished in numbers by habitat destruction, the prairie crocus is not endangered in MB. It grows on sunny, dry soils throughout much of southern MB, reaching the N end of **Lake Winnipeg**. You can still see it in the dozens and hundreds on dry, sandy areas in western MB; under Jack **Pines** in **Provincial Forests** and **Provincial Parks** in SE MB; and at the **Living Prairie Museum** in Winnipeg. It is almost impossible to transplant the flower; collecting and planting seeds, or buying it from a local wild plant garden centre, are better if you wish to grow it, and will leave the wild populations to maintain our provincial flower. ● KAREN JOHNSON

PRAIRIE DOG or gopher are terms that many people in MB use indiscriminately when referring to several kinds of ground squirrels (see **Squirrels**). In fact, the Black-tailed Prairie Dog (*Cynomes ludovicianus*) is an entirely different animal that lives in the mixed- and short-grass plains from S SK and ND S to Mexico. While occasionally stated as having occurred in S MB, there is no evidence that it reached this far to the NE during the historical period. Around 5000 to 3000 years ago, when the climate of MB was considerably warmer and drier than now, it is quite possible that this Prairie Dog spread into the SW corner of the province. There are two captive colonies on exhibit in MB – the **Assiniboine Park Zoo** and the **Fort Whyte Centre** – where they are a popular attraction because of their interesting

BARTLEY KIVES

Prairie dog surveys surroundings

and entertaining antics. The species displays complex social behaviour adapted for colonial life. Before the advent of widespread agriculture, these colonies extended for many hundreds of km², and included millions of individuals. ● REW

PRAIRIE THEATRE EXCHANGE (PTE) originated from the Manitoba Theatre Workshop, a group formed in 1972 under director Colin Jackson and Charles Huband to replace the Manitoba Theatre School, the Manitoba Theatre Centre's educational branch. The group changed its name to Prairie Theatre Exchange in 1981 to mark both its expansion into professional **Theatre** and its establishment of a regular season of productions. This new theatre would become the main alternative theatre in MB, catering to audiences dissatisfied with the fare provided by the **Manitoba Theatre Centre**. PTE would also become the major producer of local playwrights.

PTE's first 2 seasons under artistic director Gordon McCall were relatively successful, and included the first production of Albertan George Ryga's *The Ecstasy of Rita Joe* with Aboriginal actors and characters. Under Kim McCaw (artistic director 1983-91), PTE began to produce seasons consisting entirely of Cdn work, with an emphasis on the Prairies and on new local writers. In 1989, the company relocated from its home in the Grain Exchange Building into a newly built theatre on the 3rd floor of Portage Place Mall. PTE continued to produce new Cdn work, including the premiere of Ian Ross's Governor General's Award–winning *fareWel* in 1996.

The change in location, however, as well as 4 seasons of edgier theatre under artistic director Michael Springate (1991-95) precipitated a downturn in subscription. This was only remedied by a move toward seasons of better-known works under artistic director Allen MacInnis (1995-2003). The present artistic director, Robert Metcalfe, has attempted to strike a balance, producing seasons of both new works and recognized plays. PTE also runs a theatre school, which teaches over 700 students each year and offers workshops in core-area schools, and leases its 2nd studio theatre (the Colin Jackson) to outside companies. ● DAVID DEGROW

PRATT, Walter "Babe," hockey player, (b Jan 7, 1916, **Stony Mountain**, MB; d Dec 16, 1988, Vancouver) had 15 championship wins in a 26-year hockey career in the NHL and junior leagues. Pratt started out as a prolific minor league hockey player in Winnipeg, though his nickname "Babe," after Babe Ruth, is rooted in his early childhood years spent on a baseball diamond. He real passion was hockey, and by 1933 Pratt was playing on 5 local teams, each of which won that year's championship in their respective league. As a 17-year-old playing in the amateur hockey league for the Kenora Thistles, Pratt led the league in scoring. He was drafted by the New York Rangers in 1935. Paired with Ott Heller on defence, Pratt let in just 17 goals in 48 games during the championship season of 1941-42, but it was after being traded to the Toronto Maple Leafs halfway through the 1942-43 season that his playing really began to gain attention. The 1943-44 season saw Pratt earn 57 points in 50 games, setting a new NHL record. He won that year's Hart Memorial Trophy, though the honour is rarely bestowed upon defensive players. His record remained undefeated for 21 years. Pratt remained on the West Coast as a coach before becoming part of the Vancouver Canucks as the club's goodwill ambassador in 1970, where he remained until he died after suffering a heart attack while watching a hockey game. He is a member of the Hockey Hall of Fame. • MD

PREGNANT MARE'S URINE (PMU), used for menopause therapy, was a significant agricultural industry in MB from the late 1960s to 2003. The bottom fell out of this sector when the National Institutes of Health in the US reported in 2002 that the hormone therapies derived from the estrogren-rich urine from pregnant mares caused women taking the drugs more danger than benefit. Along with the other Prairie provinces, MB was the focus of the industry because of the location of a pharmaceutical plant in **BRANDON**. In 2003, the industry had 248 ranches, 200 in MB. The industry was a flash-point for the animal rights movement as thousands of pregnant mares were confined for about 6 months of the year, with their urine chanelled into collection devices. The offspring of the PMU mares were routinely sold into the slaughter market. Ayerst Organics, a division of Ayerst Pharaceuticals and the sole buyer of PMU, discontinued many of its contacts with farmers when doctors cut back their prescriptions. By 2006, there were only 73 PMU ranches across the Prairies, with 55 in MB. • ANNE COTE

PRESBYTERIAN CHURCH. Presbyterianism first came to MB when the Canada Presbyterian Church sent Rev. John Black to the **RED RIVER SETTLEMENT** in 1851. Kildonan Church, the stone church the settlers then built in 1854, was the first Presbyterian church in western Canada. A provincial historic site, it still stands though its congregation now worships in a newer building. It was not until 1870, when immigration to MB began in earnest, that the Presbytery of Manitoba and the North West was created. In 1884, the Presbytery was raised to synod status and the new synod divided into 3 presbyteries: **WINNIPEG, BRANDON** and Rock Lake. Further organizational changes took place as settlement of the West continued. In 1875, all the Cdn Presbyterian churches united to form the Presbyterian Church in Canada (PCC).

The challenge of establishing churches and filling pulpits along the homesteading frontier caused the church to create the office of superintendent of Home Missions. James Robertson, who had been the first minister of Knox Church in Winnipeg, became the first superintendent in 1881 and from his base in Winnipeg he travelled the new territory by train and horse setting up new congregations and missions, recruiting missionaries and giving oversight to new congregations and mission stations.

Presbyterians valued education and particularly valued an educated clergy. In 1871, **GEORGE BRYCE** was sent West to found a Presbyterian college. Manitoba College, as it was named, occupied an imposing building completed in 1882 on Ellice Ave in Winnipeg where studies in arts were offered in affiliation with the **U OF M** and theological degrees were granted independently starting in 1883. Manitoba College and Wesley College cooperated for a period and, following the creation of the **UNITED CHURCH OF CANADA** in 1925, formally merged to form United College in 1938.

The PCC was a partner with the federal govt in running residential schools for Aboriginal children in **BIRTLE**, (1883) and **PORTAGE LA PRAIRIE** (1886). Support for the schools additional to that provided by govt came from the Woman's Foreign Missionary Society (WFMS).The church retained responsibility for the Birtle school after church union in 1925 but the federal govt took it over in 1969 and closed it shortly thereafter. The church also ran long-standing missions to the **DAKOTA** Sioux on the **BIRDTAIL** and Oak Lake First Nation reserves for which it retained responsibility after the 1925 union.

The role of women's groups in the funding and provisioning of the church's missionary efforts cannot be understated. The first local WFMS auxiliary in MB was formed in 1884. In 1903, the national Women's Home Missionary Society (WHMS) was formed which in MB funded school-homes for **UKRAINIAN** immigrant children

St. Paul's Presbyterian Church, Brandon, 1910

P

at **Teulon**, **Ethelbert** and **Sifton**. In 1914, the WFMS and the WHMS merged to form the Women's Missionary Society (Western Division).

While the Westminster Confession of Faith of 1646 continued to be the basic faith statement of Canadian Presbyterianism, the Calvinist theology underlying this statement came under siege in the 19th century while at the same time liberal theology began to make headway among Cdn theologians. The emphasis of the Westminster Confession on the utter sinfulness of human nature and the distance between humans and God became less palatable in an increasingly secular age. **Charles Gordon** of St. Stephen's Church in Winnipeg, writing popular novels under the pen name Ralph Connor, brought a new mellower Presbyterianism to Cdn readers and did much to popularize liberal theological views.

Serious discussions leading to the union of the Presbyterian, Methodist and Congregational churches began in 1902 and culminated in 1925 with the creation of the **United Church of Canada** (UCC). Of the 21 Presbyterian congregations in Winnipeg and 3 in Brandon, only one congregation in each city elected to remain Presbyterian. However, 15 rural churches, including **Selkirk** and Kildonan, voted to stay out of the union. The "continuing Presbyterians" were formed into a reorganized Synod of Manitoba and Northwestern Ontario with Presbyteries of Winnipeg, Brandon and Superior. In Winnipeg the members who had not voted for union from the Augustine, St. Stephen's, Knox and Westminster churches combined to form a new Presbyterian congregation, First Presbyterian Church, which moved into its new building on the corner of Picardy Place and Canora St in 1927. The new Winnipeg congregations of St. James and Norwood were also formed in 1925 as was First Presbyterian in Portage la Prairie.

The 1921 census reported 138,201 Presbyterians in MB. The 1931 figure of 55,720 showed the significant loss of members to the UCC. Nevertheless, in succeeding years new congregations were formed in Winnipeg (Westwood, St. Vital, St. David's, Korean) Brandon (Southminster), **Thompson** and **Flin Flon** but the church suffered the same drop-off in membership experienced by other traditional Protestant churches in Canada after 1971 which has caused church closures and amalgamations, particularly in rural areas.

While important to the church's efforts, women remained in subsidiary roles until late in the 20th century. An order of deaconesses was approved in 1908 but women were barred from ordination and from election as elders. Finally in 1966, the PCC approved the ordination of women and allowed their election as elders. In 1989, Coleen Gillanders became the first woman

ordained in the Synod of Manitoba and Northwestern Ontario.

In the 2001 census, 9,365 Manitobans described themselves as Presbyterian. In spite of its smaller membership, the church is still active. In 2006, the sod was turned iin Winnipeg for Endiiaang (Place of Hope), a transition centre for Aboriginal people sponsored by the Presbyterian Winnipeg Inner City Missions and funded by 3 levels of government. The same year in SW Winnipeg, a new congregation was formed that hoped to build a new church on the corner of McGillivray Boulevard and Post St in the community of Whyte Ridge. ● CATHERINE MACDONALD

PRINCE, Thomas George "Tommy,"

war hero (b Oct 25, 1915, **Petersfield**; d Nov 25, 1977, **Winnipeg**) was Canada's most decorated Aboriginal war veteran. Prince grew up on the **Brokenhead Ojibway First Nation**, 1 of 11 children born to Harry and Arabella Prince. He was a descendant of **Chief Peguis**, and of Chief William Prince, who led the Ojibway-Manitoba contingent of Nile voyageurs. Prince attended Elkhorn Residential School until grade 8, when his family could no longer afford to support his studies. Though skilled as a hunter and marksman, Prince's lack of formal education meant he had to apply several times before being accepted into the army in June 1940. He spent 2 years as a sapper with the Royal Canadian Engineers, and was then selected for the elite first Special Service Force.

Prince was a fearless soldier, known for many daring exploits. In Italy in 1944, Prince

Tommy Prince, 1952

AM, PERSONALITY FILES, N197

was spying on a German camp when his phone line was severed by shellfire, preventing him from relaying intelligence to his unit. Disguising himself as a farmer, Prince walked into the field to fix the line, in full view of the enemy soldiers. He calmly repaired the break, resuming communication and helping his unit destroy 4 German positions, so effectively that the SSF became known among the Germans as the Devil's Brigade. Later that year, while stationed in France, Prince snuck behind enemy lines to locate an enemy encampment. He then returned to his own force to lead the battalion in an attack that resulted in the capture of 1000 German soldiers. In acknowledgement of his heroism, Prince was then summoned to Buckingham Palace where King George VI awarded him the MM and, on behalf of the US president, the Silver Star.

After the war, Prince was active in fighting for First Nations' treaty rights as chairman of the Manitoba Indian Association. However, he was so discouraged by the discrimination he faced in negotiations with govt that he took a job as a lumberjack in Pine Falls. When the govt called for troops for the Korean War, Prince enlisted with the 2nd Battalion **PPCLI**, joining the 27th Commonwealth Brigade in battle in 1951. Prince was as daring as ever, leading men on nighttime snatch patrols to infiltrate enemy positions, despite a painful arthritic knee. On his 2nd tour of duty in 1952, Prince's patrol came under fire, and though he had been wounded himself, he managed to carry a fallen man on his shoulders back to camp. He was awarded Korean, Canadian Volunteer Service and United Nations Service medals. In total, Prince earned 10 medals and decorations over the course of his military career. After his honourable discharge in 1953, Prince returned to MB, but had difficulty adjusting to civilian life. He fathered 5 children, and worked odd jobs until the mid-1960s. Alcoholism ultimately overtook his life, and he was often seen wandering around the Main St strip in Winnipeg. Few remembered him as a war hero until his death, when media began retelling the stories of his war days. 500 people attended his funeral. He is buried in Brookside cemetery. ● MD

Princess Patricia's Canadian Light Infantry

(Second Battalion), or 2 PPCLI, is a mechanized infantry battalion based at **CFB Shilo** near **Brandon**. Comprised of roughly 600 soldiers, many members of 2 PPCLI have seen recent duty in Afghanistan. Although the regiment was first created in Ottawa in 1914 (named after the daughter of the Governor General at the time), the Manitoba-based Second Battalion was not formed until 1950.

PPCLI's primary vehicle, the LAV (Light Armoured Vehicle) III in Afghanistan.

HISTORY: 2 PPCLI was created as part of Canada's UN commitment to the Korean War and the unit was quickly trained and dispatched to the Korean peninsula. Its most memorable action was fought at Kapyong in April, 1951. Along with other allied soldiers, 2 PPCLI held back a Chinese assault aimed at the capital city of Seoul. The battalion was consequently awarded the United States Presidential Unit Citation. After the war, the unit served in numerous capacities in Alberta, Manitoba, Germany and Cyprus. The battalion moved its base to Tuxedo in 1970 at the new Kapyong Barracks. In 1993 as part of the United Nations Protection Force in Croatia, 2 PPCLI was involved in a violent battle near the town of Medak, for which they were the first recipients of the Commander-in-Chief's Unit Citation. 2 PPCLI also served with the NATO Stabilization Force in Bosnia-Hercegovina in 1997, 2001 and 2003. Recent domestic operations have included the 1997 Manitoba flood, the 1998 Quebec ice storm, the 2002 Kananaskis G-8 Summit and the 2003 BC forest fires. In 2004, after much public debate, 2 PPCLI moved from Winnipeg to CFB Shilo. Since 2002 the battalion has, on a rotating basis, provided soldiers for active duty in the dangerous Kandahar region of southern Afghanistan. ● BRUCE TASCONA

PRINTING INDUSTRY. This sector consisted of 215 printing and related support companies in MB in 2006, accounting for roughly 3.9% of the total Cdn industry output. Most of these companies are small firms; however, MB is also home to a few international corporations that grew out of small commercial presses, which once served local needs for printed material. Large companies such as **FRIESENS** Corporation and **POLLARD BANKNOTE LTD.** have benefited from MB's mid-continental location, but have also prospered by developing specialties apart from general commercial printing. In 2005, printing shipments were valued at $445 million, with exports at $189.48 million.

The industry's beginnings can be traced to 1841, when missionary James Evans printed the *Cree Syllabic Hymn Book*, using a crude hand press with wood-carved moulds, and a **CREE** typeface made from the lead linings of old tea boxes. The roughly 100 copies were printed with a soot-based ink onto **BIRCH** bark in a slow and laborious process. Printing with paper and printer's ink would have been an expensive undertaking for early settlers, as all the supplies had to be shipped in. In 1858, **GRIFFITH CORBETT** brought the first printing press to the **RED RIVER SETTLEMENT**, as a means to publish his views on the settlement's annexation as a British Crown colony. In 1859, **WILLIAM COLDWELL** and William Buckingham transported a printing press in a **RED RIVER CART** to start the *NOR-'WESTER*, establishing the first commercial printing in the West. With new machinery facilitating mass production, most MB communities soon had at least one printing press in operation, generally for the publication of a daily or weekly **NEWSPAPER**. Printing at this time required the labour of many different craftsmen, and printers' **UNIONS** were some of the first to organize. The Winnipeg Typographical Union, established 1881, was among western Canada's first labour unions.

PPCLI

In the early 20th century, most of Winnipeg's commercial presses were located on or near **NEWSPAPER ROW**. Thomas William Taylor ran the most-mechanized of these shops, boasting the West's first paper-rolling machines. A Winnipeg street honours Taylor. Some of these printers also served MB's increasingly multiethnic demographic. National Publishers Ltd., originally established as a **UKRAINIAN** bookstore, later printed books in several different languages for new immigrants. Most of the printing shops in this area closed in the recession following WWI. The industry has seen steady growth and continued consolidation since the 1950s, including the merger of 2 local printers to form Stovel-Advocate Press Ltd., the company that printed the first **HARLEQUIN** novels. ● MD

PRITCHARD, William Arthur "Bill," labour leader (b Apr 3, 1888, Salford, England; d Oct 23, 1981, Los Angeles, CA). Born in England, he was educated at Swinton and attended night classes at the Royal Institute of Technology and the Manchester School of Technology. He immigrated to Vancouver in 1911 and quickly became a socialist leader. He edited the *Western Clarion* from 1914 to 1917 and led the BC contingent to the Calgary Western Labour Conference in March 1919 that founded the One Big Union. He arrived in **WINNIPEG** on 10 June 1919 with James Farmer and was soon involved in the **WINNIPEG GENERAL STRIKE**. A warrant was issued for his arrest, and he was captured in Calgary and put on trial for sedition with other leaders singled out by the federal government. He defended himself and was sentenced to one year in prison. His *Address to the Jury* was published in 1920. He then returned to Vancouver, where he was elected to the Burnaby council in 1928 and chosen reeve in 1930. He also became president of the Union of British Columbia Municipalities. After the death of a daughter in 1938 he moved to Los Angeles, where he became active in the Socialist Party of America. ● JMB

PROCH, Don, sculptor (b 1944, Hamilton, ON) is best known for his complex sculptures and masks with which he depicts the Prairie landscape, combining the past and the future. His 1972 inaugural exhibition at The **WINNIPEG ART GALLERY**, *The Legend of Asessippi* included unique silverpoint drawings, sculptures, assemblages, and prints, each reflecting new visual vocabulary, view points and subject matter. Proch has continued to develop this unique iconography and combinations of materials, hand built and high tech, creating multiple layers of intersecting personal and universal references. His masks, grain elevators, The *Pincushion Man*

P

DON PROCH

Great Plains Mask, 1984 (Private Collection, Regina) by Don Proch

PROGRESSIVE CONSERVATIVE PARTY OF MANITOBA. MB's PC Party enjoys the distinction of being the only Conservative party in the Cdn West never to disappear or to be shut out of the legislature. Candidates calling themselves "Conservative" first contested the provincial election of 1879. **John Norquay**, who served 1878-87, is sometimes regarded as the first Conservative premier, though his govt included both Conservatives and Liberals (*see* **Liberal Party**). In 1883, Conservatives ran in every seat where there was a contest. In those early days, individual candidates more or less wrote their own platform. In 1899, the party became an official entity offering a unified platform to the electorate. Manitoba Conservatives have been inclined to keep close to the centre and have mainly eschewed radical ideas. This moderation may well explain why the party has held power for 47 of the years from 1883 to writing, and was in a coalition for another decade. For much of their history, they have been able to rely on the support of **English** and **Irish** Protestants, and, more recently, businesspeople and **Mennonite** farmers in southern MB and south **Winnipeg**.

Sir **Rodmond Roblin** assumed the leadership in 1899, taking over as premier after Sir **Hugh John Macdonald**'s brief time in office in 1900. Roblin's was an active, progressive administration. He showed goodwill to Francophones not long after the divisive **Manitoba Schools Question**; proved an able advocate for the province in federal-provincial issues; and was responsible for establishing both **Manitoba Hydro** and **Manitoba Telephone** as public entities, as well as founding new agricultural and technical colleges, setting up a Workers' Compensation board, building rail lines, and settling the provincial boundaries. Roblin was the 2nd-longest-serving premier of MB; only **John Bracken** has surpassed his nearly 15 years on the job. However, his reputation was sullied by 2 events: he was an unrepentant opponent of the **Women's Movement**, and his govt was disgraced and fell from power in 1915 as a consequence of a scandal involving kickbacks, bribes, and other form of corruption. The Conservative Party spent the next 43 years in the political wilderness.

Progressive Party of Manitoba leader John Bracken dominated early-mid-century politics in MB. Adopting a variety of labels, including "Coalition," he stayed in power 1922-42, and was the only premier in Canada to retain office through the **Great Depression**. The Conservatives, after having enjoyed something of a revival in the 1920s under Fawcett Taylor, joined the coalition 1940-50, led by Errick French Willis. The party held on to its electoral base, but remained a long way

and *Asessippi Tread* are all major works. Many have rough elements, giving a sense of fragility and vulnerability.

His combinations of unlike materials, metal, mirrors, clay, graphite, and nickel oxides, and his use of colour, coupled with images of Prairie landscapes and skies, create thought-provoking, evocative works which are as elegant as they are unsettling. Beautiful yet disconcerting, he layers rural and urban images with personal and regional references. In many he includes images relating to Aboriginal cultures, history, and land.

Proch graduated with a BFA from the **U of M**'s School of Art in 1966, beginning his career as a teacher. He has received many awards, including 'A' grants from both the Canada Council and the Manitoba Arts Council. His work has been shown in many Cdn and US galleries and is represented in public and private collections, including The Winnipeg Art Gallery, the Art Gallery of Ontario, the Canada Council Art Bank and the National Gallery of Canada. It has been published in *Border Crossings* (1990) and a number of exhibition catalogues. ● PATRICIA BOVEY

from office. In 1943, "Progressive" was added to the party's name following Bracken's insistence that the federal Conservative Party change to the Progressive Conservatives when he became that party's leader in 1942. The party's "Young Turks," led by Sir Rodmond's son, **DUFFERIN ROBLIN**, successfully insisted that the "Progressive" Conservatives pull out of the coalition in 1950, and they fought the June 1953 election as an independent entity. Roblin took over the leadership of the PC Party in 1954, posing a formidable challenge to the established regime of Liberal-Progressive premier **DOUGLAS CAMPBELL**, heir and successor to Bracken. The PCs defeated Campbell's govt in 1958, earning a minority. Roblin would remain premier for a year before calling an election, going on to win 3 majorities.

There was more "progressive" than "conservative" in Roblin's approach. Just about every area of govt activity underwent an infusion of cash and new ideas. New construction took place, and the province began to shake off its Depression mentality. His crowning achievement, however, was the construction of the **RED RIVER FLOODWAY**, often referred to as "Duff's Ditch." Roblin quit the premiership in 1967 to run, unsuccessfully, for the national leadership of the PCs. A funeral director from **MINNEDOSA**, **WALTER WEIR**, succeeded him. Weir's selection was an assertion of power by the party's rural, conservative wing against its urban, red-Tory element. Weir put the brake on reform and resisted some important federal measures such as medicare. In 1969, he gambled on an early election, losing to the newly formed **NEW DEMOCRATIC PARTY OF MANITOBA** led by the young **EDWARD SCHREYER**. Since that election, the

Liberal Party has typically finished 3rd behind the Conservatives and NDP.

Weir was quickly replaced by **SIDNEY SPIVAK**, a former Cabinet minister, Harvard U graduate, and **JEWISH** liberal. Spivak did better than expected in the 1973 election, capturing only 25,000 fewer votes than the victorious NDP, but his status as a Red Tory (and, possibly, his religion) did not go down well with his party's largely rural base. So, after a searing and bitter battle in 1975, he was replaced as leader by **STERLING LYON**. Lyon, who was raised in **PORTAGE LA PRAIRIE**, had long, close ties with the rural parts of the province; and although he had been the candidate many party liberals tipped to succeed Duff Roblin in 1967, by now he was regarded as a right-winger. In the election of 1977, he campaigned on a platform of "acute, protracted restraint," meaning less govt, lower taxes, and fewer bureaucrats. During his time in office, too, he chaired the Premiers' (now First Ministers') Conference when PM Trudeau was actively pursuing repatriation of the Constitution and the entrenchment of a Charter of Rights and Freedoms. Lyon was articulate in his opposition to the Charter. Some even say he briefly considered joining QC in rejecting the revised constitution. Lyon's prescription for MB – fuelling the private sector by reducing govt – was unsuccessful. By the 1981 election, in fact, he was promoting large, publicly funded infrastructure projects. Still, in that year, he became the first and only premier in the 20th century to lose power after a single term. Always popular within the party (if not outside; highly intelligent, his abrasive personality sometimes

alienated people), he was allowed to pick his own time to resign, which he did in 1983.

Lyon's successor, **GARY FILMON**, was of Eastern European descent; a university gold medallist; an engineer and businessman; moderate; and upwardly mobile. He led the party to a minority govt in 1988. As befits an engineer, he was intensely practical. It was also said that, "like Teflon," nothing ever clung to him. He was a hugely popular figure in a party that, federally, was suffering decline under Brian Mulroney. Filmon was premier for 11 years, winning majorities in 1990 and 1995. Throughout, he harnessed the province's resources carefully. Although serving at a time when "neo-conservatism" was in full flower, he seemed to have a gentler touch than his contemporaries. Perhaps his most significant achievement was the passage of Balanced Budget Legislation. He also took pride in the fact that his govt raised no significant tax throughout its time in office. He was defeated by **GARY DOER** in 1999. In 2000, he was replaced by rural-SK-born but Winnipeg-based moderate, **STUART MURRAY**, who was in turn succeeded by **HUGH McFADYEN**, also a Winnipegger, in 2006. ● GEOFF LAMBERT

PROHIBITION, the move to ban the manufacture and sale of all alcoholic products, flourished in MB, as it did throughout Canada, in the early decades of the 20th century. It became provincial law 1916-22. Organized temperance movements to restrict alcoholic beverages through private and individual reform began in the **RED RIVER SETTLEMENT** in the 1850s, but they did not immediately lead to attempts to legislate on the sale or distribution of drink. Nevertheless, by the closing years of the 19th century, the growth of unsettled social conditions led to campaigns by organizations like the Manitoba Prohibitory League, founded in 1892, for total prohibition. That same year, the provincial legislature passed a bill authorizing a plebiscite on the "liquor question." This began a series of popular votes on the matter of liquor control, administered by both the federal govt (in 1898 and 1920), and by the province in 1902, 1916, 1923, and 1927.

Prohibition was a reform sponsored chiefly by **EVANGELIST** Protestants and by women's organizations such as the Woman's Christian Temperance Union (WCTU). Members of various other religions (including **ROMAN CATHOLICS**, **UKRAINIAN CATHOLICS**, **ANGLICANS**, **JEWS**, and the Orthodox Church) often opposed Prohibition, because wine is an integral part of their services. In 1898, pressure led the federal Liberal govt of Sir Wilfrid Laurier to authorize a national referendum on Prohibition. As a province, only QC defeated the measure in the vote, but the tally

Sidney Spivak supporters, Manitoba PC Leadership Convention, 1975

was so close nationally – the "yes" votes outnumbered the "no" votes by only 13,687 – that Laurier was able to evade action by arguing that the majority was insufficient. Attempts to introduce provincial legislation, both before and immediately after the 1898 plebiscite, were met by a govt insistence that Prohibition was beyond the powers of a province under the *British North America Act*. At the same time, local communities could ban liquor with local licensing laws ("local option"), including forbidding the public sale of beer. Most of MB was "dry" for years under such regulations. But the new Conservative govt of Sir **HUGH JOHN MACDONALD** passed the *Temperance Act* (1900), drafted by Sir **JAMES ALBERT AIKINS**, which did not deal with the import or export of liquor but did outlaw its sale in the province. The legislation was declared unconstitutional by the Cdn Supreme Court on Feb 23, 1901, but the Judicial Committee of the British Privy Council later upheld the act's legality. However, a provincial referendum in 1902 saw Prohibition defeated by more than 7000 votes: the reformers were divided, while the liquor interests were well organized.

A still to make homebrew in a home on Boyd Avenue, Winnipeg, 1922

After 1902, Prohibition was kept alive by the emergence of social problems exacerbated by liquor, and a second temperance movement began with the formation of the Moral and Social Reform Council of MB in 1907. The reformers came increasingly to support the **LIBERAL PARTY OF MANITOBA**, helping to defeat the **RODMOND ROBLIN** govt in 1915. The new Liberal govt under **T. C. NORRIS** implemented a new referendum on Macdonald's act, which passed by a 24,000 majority in 1916. Two years later, a federal order-in-council produced national Prohibition, a reform that seemed initially to work, partly because the chief consumers of excess were away in the military. When the soldiers returned, many problems arose over enforcement of the liquor bans, ranging from blatant avoidance of the law through smuggling to abuse of prescription drugs.

In 1921, the Moderation League of MB was formed to oppose Prohibition. Opponents had found a new strategy in the advocacy of govt regulation and control of the sale of liquor, which was implemented in a pioneer *Liquor Control Act* in 1923 later imitated by other provinces. A subsequent plebiscite in 1927 opened the door to the sale of beer by the glass, although it permitted local option. The provincial govt never returned to banning the sale of alcoholic beverages throughout the province, although at the end of the 20th century, it ceased attempting to enforce a public monopoly and permitted the sale of wine in carefully regulated private shops. The last community in MB to make the public sale of alcoholic beverages through licensing illegal was **STEINBACH**. Several local referenda in that predominantly **MENNONITE** community were held, and in 2003, Steinbach overturned the liquor ban. • J. M. BUMSTED

▸ *See* **BRONFMAN FAMILY**, **BREWERIES**.

PROTOZOA is a huge group of mostly unicellular life demonstrating a wonderful array of forms and representing a major part of the kingdom Protoctista. Other members of this kingdom are the Red Algae (phylum Rhodophyta), Brown Algae (Phaeophyta), and Green Algae (Chlorophyta) – the latter being prominent in both freshwater and marine environments of MB. These algal groups used to be called plants (kingdom Plantae), but they are now known to be sufficiently distinct to be placed in the Protoctistans. Algae are often colonial and are among the earliest and most-important life forms on earth – as food for countless creatures, absorbing vast quantities of carbon dioxide, and producing much of the oxygen in the atmosphere.

Protozoans were formerly included in the animal kingdom (Animalia), because many types are mobile (with beating cilia or a whip-like flagellum) and they devour other micro-organisms. The true relationships of most of these groups remain controversial, as could be expected with life forms having characteristics shared (and sometimes being ancestral to) higher organisms such as plants and animals. Remarkably, protozoans are able to perform all the body functions carried out by advanced multi-cellular organisms. They may contain one or more nuclei in the cell. These organisms more than compensate for their microscopic size by sheer numbers and adaptiveness, and are members of all ecosystems and food webs, as well as contributing to immense sedimentary deposits of soil on land, freshwater and marine environments. Some are important disease agents, such as malaria-causing *Plasmodium*.

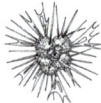  

JENNIFER LABELLA

Examples of protozoa

There are over 50,000 named species and a debatable number of surviving phyla of protozoans. At least 27 phyla have been recognized, with dominant ones being the foraminiferans (phylum Granulreticulosa), radiolarians (Actinopoda), silicoflagellates (Chrysomonada), dinoflagellates (Dinomastigota), ciliates (Ciliophora), and diatoms (Diatoms). *Paramecium* (a ciliate) and *Amoeba* (a rhizopod) are well-known protozoans found in pond water and used in laboratories. The diatoms (with 10,000 species) are important members of the plankton in all fresh and marine waters. Via photosynthesis, they form the basis of aquatic food webs, and contribute indirectly to terrestrial ones as well. Much remains to be discovered about protozoan diversity and their ecological roles in all MB habitats. • REW

PROVENCHER, Joseph-Norbert, ROMAN CATHOLIC bishop, politician (b Feb 12, 1787, Nicolet, Canada [QC]; d June 7, 1853, St. Boniface). The son of Jean-Baptiste Provencher and Élisabeth Proulx, Provencher came from a large farming family of limited means. He had to wait for the opening of a free primary school in Nicolet to begin his studies at age 14. After attending college, he was ordained as a priest Dec 21, 1811. Provencher ministered in several parishes, where his humility, receptiveness, and apostolic zeal caught the attention of Joseph-Octave Plessis, Bishop of Quebec. In 1818, Bishop Plessis suggested that Provencher go to the fledgling **RED RIVER SETTLEMENT** to establish the Roman Catholic Church in western Canada. On May 19, 1818, Provencher, accompanied by Father Sévère-Joseph-Nicolas Dumoulin and seminarian Guillaume Edge, left Ville-Marie (Montreal) by canoe, arriving at Fort Douglas on July 16. Measuring 1.93 m (6 ft 4 in) and wearing clerical garb, Provencher caused quite a stir amongst the local population. On their arrival, the missionaries set to work, performing 72 baptisms in less than 2 weeks. With the help of their voyageurs, they began building a small house that would serve as the priests' residence and chapel on a 12 ha (30 ac) lot on the E shore of the Red River, opposite the mouth of the **ASSINIBOINE**, given to the missionaries by **LORD SELKIRK**. On Nov 1, 1818,

AM. L. B. FOOTE COLLECTION 662, N2262

the chapel was consecrated with St. Boniface as the patron. Provencher also founded a boys' Latin school that would later evolve into the **Collège Universitaire Saint-Boniface.**

Two years after his arrival, Provencher returned to Lower Canada (later QC), where he was ordained bishop. On his return to Red River in 1822, he was informed by the **HBC** that the mission of Pembina (see **Emerson**), built by Dumoulin, would have to be abandoned because it was on US territory. Discouraged, Dumoulin returned to Lower Canada while Provencher helped the **Métis** from Pembina settle at **St. François Xavier**, along the Assiniboine River. Although Provencher was sent to evangelize the Aboriginal peoples, most of his time was spent ministering to the growing Métis population. He tried to encourage **Agriculture** and ranching, bringing seed and livestock from Lower Canada and the US. He taught school to some of the Métis boys of the colony, whom he hoped might embrace the priesthood. In 1829, he opened a school for girls in St. Boniface, and in 1838, he set up an "industrial school" to teach weaving, using **Bison** wool. By the 1830s, the Catholic Church was well established among both Europeans and Métis living along the Red and Assiniboine rivers, with Provencher as their leader.

In Feb 1835, Provencher was invited to sit as a member of the **Council of Assiniboia,** the local govt put in place by the HBC. Two years later, he was admitted as a councillor, and in 1845, served as a member of the finance committee.

Joseph-Norbert Provencher

In spite of the many gains, Provencher felt that the growing needs of the mission required additional help. By 1843, of the 13 missionaries that had come to help Provencher, only 4 were still at Red River. In 1843, he left for Lower Canada and Europe, hoping to find some religious congregations willing to help with the long-term apostolic work in the Northwest. During this trip, he persuaded the **Grey Nuns** of Ville-Marie (Montreal) to send some sisters to Red River. Four Sisters of Charity arrived at Red River in 1844. In France, Provencher met Bishop (later Saint) Charles-Joseph-Eugène de Mazenod, the founder of the Congregation of the **Oblate Missionaries of Mary Immaculate.** Two Oblates, one of them **Alexandre-Antonin Taché,** Provencher's successor, came to Red River in 1845. In 1847, the Diocese of the North-West was established with Provencher as its bishop; the name was changed to the Diocese of Saint-Boniface in 1851. Bishop Provencher, known as the "Giant of the West," died June 7, 1853. The mission entrusted to him 35 years before had been fulfilled. With its twin-spired cathedral, bishop's palace, and Grey Nuns' convent, which doubled as a hospital, the former mission of St. Boniface was now firmly established. ● LUCIEN CHAPUT

PROVINCIAL FORESTS are areas of Crown land set aside by the govt for logging and recreation. Provincial forests differ from **Provincial Parks** in that their main purpose is to provide a regular source of products for the **Forestry** industry.

MB Natural Resources manages the areas according to the *Forest Act* and Forest Management License Agreements with companies. The agreements usually include reforestation quotas. "Annual Allowable Cut" restrictions stipulate that the number of trees cut must balance out with the number grown. Sand, gravel, and peat moss extraction occurs in some areas. **Hunting,** cross-country **Skiing, Snowshoeing,** snowmobiling, berry picking, hiking, **Sport Fishing,** birdwatching, and scientific research also take place in the forests.

Beginning in 1895, the Canadian govt created timber reserves in MB as a means of managing forests that could be logged for building materials and fuel. It was a practical way of preventing homesteaders from clearing trees for profit or trying to create farmland in areas with unsuitable soils. In 1930, the federal govt allowed the province partial control of its resources under the *Natural Resources Transfer Agreement.* A year later, the province established forest reserves at Spruce Woods, Duck Mountain, Porcupine Mountain, Sandilands, and the Whiteshell. The provincial forest designation was applied in the 1970s. The idea remained the same throughout:

to ensure a supply of timber on land that cannot be converted for other uses.

Land in provincial forests must receive Protected Area status in order to prohibit logging and **Mining,** as well as **Petroleum,** natural gas, and **Hydroelectric Power** development. Only the Bell and Steeprock canyons in Porcupine Provincial Forest and Douglas Marsh in Spruce Woods had been given the protected status as of late 2006, however.

The 1988 *Forest Act* lists 15 provincial forests covering a total area of about 22,000 km^2. Spruce Woods, Duck Mountain, Porcupine, Sandilands, Cormorant, Agassiz, Belair, Northwest Angle, Turtle Mountain, Whiteshell, Cat Hills, Brightstone Sand Hills, Moose Creek, Wampum, and Swan-Pelican. Some of these forests contain provincial parks within their boundaries. The most popular for recreation activities are Sandilands, Whiteshell, and Duck Mountain. The latter is also the largest forest, at 3770 km^2. Wampum is the smallest, covering 10 km^2. ● JOEL TRENAMAN

PROVINCIAL PARKS are designated land areas dedicated to the preservation of natural and cultural resources, the provision of recreation opportunities, and, in some cases, resource development. The province's Dept of Conservation provides oversight in accordance with the *Provincial Park Lands Act.* By 2006, 80 provincial parks had been created, of which Sand Lakes Provincial Park (831,000 ha) and Caribou River Provincial Park (764,000 ha) were by far the largest. The smallest is Woodridge Provincial Park (0.8 ha). **Birds Hill,** Grand Beach, and St. Malo receive the most visits each year, thanks to their proximity to **Winnipeg.** The **Whiteshell** is also popular, as is **Duck Mountain.**

The federal govt's *Natural Resources Transfer Agreement* turned over control of "excess" Crown lands to MB in 1930. The provincial govt began to establish conservation partnerships with different communities. One of the first projects was the rehabilitation of Saskatchewan River Delta marshes and **Muskrat** habitats that were suffering from low water levels. Trappers in **The Pas** region were becoming destitute due to decreasing game populations. In 1931, the province began to create forest reserves, the precursors to **Provincial Forests** and parks. In 1960, the **Dufferin Roblin** govt passed the *Provincial Parks Act,* providing the process for park creation and management. The idea was to set aside areas for recreation. The first provincial parks were established in 1961, and designations continued throughout the decade. Motivated by movements for environmental awareness and preservation, the *Provincial Park Lands Act* was adopted in 1972. This 2nd act emphasized a mandate of ecological and cultural conservation.

More recently, the 1997 System Plan for Provincial Parks confirmed boundaries and split existing parks into 4 categories: Wilderness, Natural, Recreation, and Heritage. About 70% of parkland is designated as Wilderness, primarily for preservation. Natural parks combine protection, recreation, and resource extraction. Heritage parks are smaller areas focused on promoting and safeguarding important cultural sites, such as CAMP MORTON. Manitoba Parks administers management plans that last 5-10 or more years for each park, as required by law. These determine zoning and land-use objectives (there are 6 land-use categories), and are subject to an ongoing review process and public consultation.

Land in parks remains open to resource development – including logging and mining – unless it has been classified as Wilderness or designated under the 1993 Protected Areas Initiative (revised in 2000). Forty-four parks, as well as separately designated smaller areas, have been protected in whole or part since the initiative began in 1990 in response to the World Wildlife Fund Canada's Endangered Spaces Campaign. In its first 15 years, protected areas increased from 350,000 ha to more than 5.4 million ha (or about 8% of the province). There are

also 21 ecological reserves that are designed to preserve specific ecosystems on Crown land from any development or recreational use.

Popular recreation uses include camping, hiking, wildlife viewing, SWIMMING, canoeing, SKIING, snowmobiling, and other forms of TOURISM. Cottage development in parks is so popular that the provincial govt instituted a cottage-lot draw process in the late '90s in order to deal with overwhelming demand. The govt allows long-term land leases in most parks. Several NGOs monitor MB govt administration of parks and advocate for environmental protections. These include the Canadian Parks and Wilderness Society, Manitoba Wildlands, Manitoba Eco-Network, Manitoba Naturalists Society, Manitoba Future Forest Alliance, and the MB chapter of the Western Canada Wilderness Committee. The latter group has particularly criticized successive govts for allowing logging and resource extraction; all have lobbied for more protected areas and completely development-free parks. ● JOEL TRENAMAN

PROVISIONAL GOVT. *See* RED RIVER RESISTANCE

PSEUDOSCORPION is a tiny (3-8 mm) relative of spiders, mites and scorpions (class Arachnida) and acquires its name from a pair of

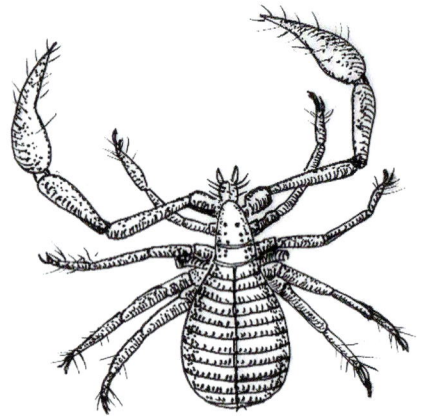

Pseudoscorpions look threatening, but they are harmless.

venomized pincers that closely resemble those of a scorpion; however, no scorpion-like tail is present. Perfectly harmless to people, it preys on mites, springtails, ants and other small creatures in the soil and leaf litter, under bark and stones, and in bird and mammal nests. Species have 4 sets of legs, 2, 4, or no eyes, and rely mainly on the sense of touch to navigate. Little is known about these creatures in MB, but a few species have been discovered so far. *Microbisium brunneum* occurs in sphagnum bogs in boreal forest and forest-tundra N to Churchill, *Microbisium parvulum* and *Mundochthonius rossi* are found in woodland litter, and the cosmopolitan *Chelifer cancroides* is commonly present in barns, homes and other buildings (moist sites like sinks, bathtubs, basement walls), where it preys on book lice and house mites. These little creatures are often brought into homes with firewood. Pseudoscorpions may be incredibly abundant in some areas and totally absent in others. They may disperse to new sites by hitching a ride on larger animals like beetles, flies, wasps, bees, birds or mice. They reproduce sexually, producing about 2-dozen young, butmales are so scarce in some species that parthenogenesis is suspected. They live from 6 months to 3 years. There are a total of about 20 species in MB, with 55 in Canada, 350 in NA and over 3000 worldwide. These creatures have special significance because they were among the first colonizers of land, and have been found in deposits as old as 380 million years ago. ● REW

PUBLIC FINANCE deals with the income and expenditure policies of government. It looks at the relationship between revenues and expenditures, their trends, and their effects on other economic variables and on the economy in general. Within the Cdn confederation, public finance also deals with the federal/provincial fiscal relations.

Tranquil summer scene in Whiteshell Provincial Park

Total Government Revenues and Expenditures for the Province of Manitoba:
Selected years (Millions of $)

YEAR	GPP	REVENUES	% OF GPP	EXPENDITURE	% OF GPP
1941	402.2	19.9	4.9	18.2	4.5
1951	1,164.3	46.0	3.9	42.4	3.6
1961	1,893.0	118.0	6.2	137.2	7.2
1971	4,097.0	535.7	13.1	521.0	12.7
1981	12,800.0	2,690.4	21.0	2,937.9	22.9
1991	23,741.0	4,917.5	20.7	5,241.5	22.1
2001	35,219.0	6,900.0	19.6	6,779.3	19.2
2004	40,265.0	7,571.0	18.8	7,472.0	18.6

Major Sources of Revenues and their Percentages of Total Revenues:
Selected years (Millions of $)

YEAR	TOTAL TRANSFERS	%	CORPORATE INCOME TAX	%	PERSONAL INCOME TAX	%	GENERAL SALES TAXES	%
1961	42.6	36.1	1.3	1.1	n/a	n/a	n/a	
1971	163.6	30.5	34.7	6.5	119.4	22.3	73.3	13.7
1981	853.7	31.7	118.9	4.4	529.7	19.7	269.0	15.9
1991	1,670.1	33.9	185.8	3.8	1,211.1	24.6	610.0	12.4
2001	2,209.6	32.0	303.4	4.4	1,649.6	23.9	976.5	14.1
2004	2,447.2	32.3	313.0	4.1	1,788.2	23.6	1,154.3	15.2

Major Types of Expenditures and their Percentages of Total Expenditures:
Selected Years (Millions of $)

YEAR	HEALTH	%	EDUCATION	%	SOCIAL SERVICES	%	DEBT CHARGES	%
1961	30.7	22.4	35.0	25.5	11.9	8.7	n/a	n/a
1971	139.8*	26.8	180.3	34.6	58.9*	11.3	47.46	9.1
1981	782.7	26.7	653.9	22.3	376.2	12.8	360.9	12.3
1991	1759.3	33.6	956.9	18.3	589.2	11.2	558.3	10.7
2001	2,685.90	39.6	1,485.5	21.9	812.3	12.0	390.6	5.8
2004	3,161.3	42.3	1,648.1	22.0	912.8	12.2	238.7	3.2

* Author's estimate

The *Canadian Constitution Act* was founded on the assumption that the main role of govt, both federal and provincial, is to maintain law and order and to facilitate the orderly function of the market. When MB joined Confederation in 1870, the size and scope of govt activity in the province was limited. The provincial govt's main revenue sources were licence fees and other direct charges, plus transfers from Ottawa. Most of the province's expenditures went toward health and **EDUCATION**.

The constitution gave the federal govt the power to raise tax revenues by any mode, while restricting the provincial govts to raising funds only by means of direct taxation. At the same time, a much larger share of spending power went to the federal govt. For these reasons, the tax and expenditure arrangements between federal and provincial govts were controversial from the outset. It was not until the early 1940s,

when the federal and provincial govts entered into a tax agreement, that provincial govts began to consolidate their fiscal positions. Out of the ashes of the *Wartime Tax Agreements*, under which provinces turned over all taxing powers to the federal govt, rose a series of negotiated tax agreements between Ottawa and the provinces known collectively as the *Tax Rental Agreements* (TRA). These arrangements took place during 1947-52, 1952-56, and 1957-61. The 1957-61 *Tax Sharing Agreement* and the 1962-66 *Tax Collection Agreement* (TCA) largely determined the system that continues to operate in Canada. Under this agreement, provinces are allowed to determine their own tax rates, providing their tax base conforms to federal law.

In 1901, total govt revenues in MB amounted to just $1,008,653, with federal subsidies as the principle revenue source, while expenditures were $988,251. With increased population,

urbanization, and standard of living, the overall size of govt and its role in the economy has expanded over time. In particular, total revenues as a percentage of gross provincial product (GPP) rose from only 4.9% in 1941 to 18.8% in 2004. At the same time, govt expenditures as a percentage of GPP rose from a low of 4.5% in 1941 to a relatively high 18.6% in 2004. These trends clearly indicate the increase in demand for publicly provided goods and services, and the need for the govt of MB to raise additional revenues to meet these rising demands.

Until the 1960s, the majority of revenues received by the provincial govt came in the form of federal transfers. Since 1961, this source of revenue has remained steady, while the other 3 major sources of revenue (personal income tax, corporate income tax, and general sales taxes) have grown as a proportion of the provincial budget: as of 2004, transfer payments from Ottawa account for about 30% of provincial revenues. As the federal govt allowed provinces to access additional tax revenue sources, such as sales taxes, the govt of MB has increased its reliance on other revenue sources. In 2004, around half of the MB govt's revenues came from different tax sources. In particular, corporate income tax as a percentage of total tax revenues, after reaching a high of 6.5% in 1971, has remained within the 4% range. Personal income tax revenue has oscillated around 22% to 24% range of total revenues. MB's personal income tax was based on the basic federal tax until 1999 where the rate was 48.5%. Starting in 2000, MB has introduced its own personal income tax rate and base. The personal income tax bases and rates for MB in 2004 ranged from 10.9% for an income less than $30,544 to 17.4% for incomes of more than $65,000 a year. The relative share of general sales tax has risen from around 13.3% to 15.2% during the period reported. There are 2 main reasons for this relative increase in revenue from general sales tax. First, the retail sales tax rate was raised from 5% to 7%; also, MB's economy has enjoyed healthy growth, resulting in increased sales and tax revenues.

The major expenditures for the govt of MB come in 3 areas: health, education, and social services made up 76.5% of total govt expenditures in 2004. Health spending as a percentage of total expenditures has risen from a low of 22.4% in 1961 to a high of 42.3% in 2004. The sharp increase in health expenditures since 1991 is due to the changes made in federal/provincial transfer arrangements and what has come to be known as the "offloading" of costs of services to the provinces by the federal govt. In addition, the higher costs of providing health services and an aging population have contributed to this sharp increase. Expenditures on education relative to total expenditures have remained relatively constant at just over 20%. Relative spending on social services have followed a mild upward trend from 8.7% in 1961 to 12.2% in 2004.

Another source of govt expenditures are debt charges related to the interest payments the govt of MB makes on its accumulated debt. From the early 1980s until the early 1990s, when interest rates were close to historical highs, it cost the govt of MB more than 10% of its total expenditures to finance its debt. Fortunately, interest rates fell since the early 1990s, lowering the cost of debt financing for MB to 3.2% of total expenditures in 2004. All the above trends point to a relatively stable ECONOMY and budgeting system that has characterized govt finances in MB.
● SOHRAB ABIZADEH

PUBLIC HEALTH POLICY seeks to improve and maintain the health of all citizens through community-based intervention emphasizing illness prevention and health promotion. In MB, these efforts have, in many ways, come full circle since 1876, when the fledgling province's first public health legislation required that all infants be vaccinated against smallpox by 3 months of age. In 1877, the Department of Agriculture, Immigration, Statistics, and Health appointed a provincial health superintendent, and local govts were required to hire a health officer during outbreaks of communicable disease. The first extended *Public Health Act* was passed in 1890, and in 1893, MB's first permanent Board of Health was established within the Department of Agriculture. A separate Department of Health and Public Welfare was created in 1928. Since then, the department has undergone several name changes, and responsibility for services other than health was ultimately transferred to a separate govt department.

Rather than provide direct services, MB's early boards of health supervised local health departments and provided technical advice to local authorities during disease outbreaks. WIN-NIPEG established the province's first local health department in 1882, appointing its first full-time health officer in 1900. Development of public health services in the rest of the province was much slower. Sparse populations and a small tax base precluded the provision of permanent services in these areas. Grants from the Rockefeller Foundation supported the establishment of full-time health units in the Winnipeg areas of St. James/St. Vital in 1928 and in BRANDON-Cornwallis in 1929. A 3rd full-time health unit opened in St. Boniface in 1934, but the ravages

of the Dirty '30s precluded further development of the province's public health system. In 1945, the MB Health Plan attempted to extend full-time public health services throughout the province by providing participating municipalities with ²/₃ of the funding necessary to establish local health units. The provincial health department assumed total responsibility for the development of public health policy throughout the province (except in Winnipeg), co-ordinated all public health programs, and provided technical as well as financial support to local health units. Although the plan called for the establishment of 26 local health units, by 1959, only 13 full-time health units were in operation, covering 45% of the province and more than 80% of its population. By 1972, the province was divided into 7 health regions providing public health programs under the direct control of the provincial health department. In 1999, responsibility for public health programs was transferred from the provincial health department to 12 (now 11) newly created provincial regional health authorities (RHAs). During this period, Winnipeg's formerly autonomous civic health department was transferred to the Winnipeg RHA.

In the late 19th and early 20th centuries, public health policy emphasized the control of communicable diseases such as smallpox, typhoid fever, and TUBERCULOSIS; the development of sanitary infrastructures and programs in populated areas; and the regulation of food production, particularly meat and milk. The Sanatorium Board of MB administered tuberculosis-control programs, but policy development for the control of other communicable diseases was the responsibility of MB's health department. The province's first clinic for sexually transmitted diseases opened in Winnipeg in 1918. Childhood immunization became a priority in the 1920s after the introduction of effective vaccines against diphtheria and pertussis (whooping cough). In the early 1950s, MB experienced several severe poliomyelitis EPIDEMICS, which ended only after the introduction of Jonas Salk's vaccine in 1955. For the most part, childhood immunization programs have been publicly funded to ensure maximum uptake of available vaccines. A growing list of communicable diseases evolved throughout the 20th century in response to improved treatments, new vaccines, and new infectious agents

Health education programs were introduced in the early 20th century. The Margaret Scott Nursing Mission and the Victorian Order of Nurses employed visiting nurses to pioneer child welfare, school health, occupational health, and maternal health programs within the province, particularly in Winnipeg. By

the end of WWII, the province had taken over these programs. MB's first public health nurses (PHNs) were hired by Winnipeg's health department in 1913 to staff its newly established tuberculosis control and child welfare programs. MB became the first Cdn province to employ PHNs when it established its public health nursing program in 1916. Under the 1945 MB Health Plan, these nurses were reassigned from their work in unorganized regions of the province to staff the newly established units. Health education programs also expanded during this era to include early detection of non-infectious diseases such as cancer, cardiovascular disease, and diabetes.

However, this focus changed after the publication of the federal govt's *A New Perspective on the Health of Canadians*, also called the "Lalonde Report" (1974). While acknowledging that human biology, lifestyles, the environment, and the health care system all influenced human health, this report argued for a fundamental refocusing of the health care system from cure to health promotion. Initially, public health policies and programs emphasized individual lifestyle modification, but subsequent knowledge development in public health has focused on the role that social, economic, and environmental factors play in determining human health. In theory, policy development shifted from a sole emphasis on individual risk factors to the development of programs that address issues such as poverty, sex, racism, and environmental contamination, and which modify the complex health risks experienced by vulnerable populations such as women, Aboriginal peoples, immigrants, sex trade workers, and youth. While public health programs are currently the responsibility of individual RHAs, the provincial Health Department plays a leadership role in the organization and financing of the system. Unfortunately, the public health sector continues to suffer from significant underfunding, receiving less than 5% of the total funding allocated to health care in the province.

Communicable disease control programs have once again returned to centre stage in the early 21st century. The resurgence of tuberculosis; the emergence of new infections such as HIV/AIDS, severe acute respiratory syndrome (SARS), and *Escherichia coli* O157:H7; the increased threat of imported diseases; and the anticipated next influenza pandemic, as well as the threat of avian influenza H5:N1, have all forced the development of new protocols and programs to protect the public's health. ● MARION MCKAY

▶ *See also* HOME CARE, MEDICINE, MOUNT CARMEL CLINIC.

Q

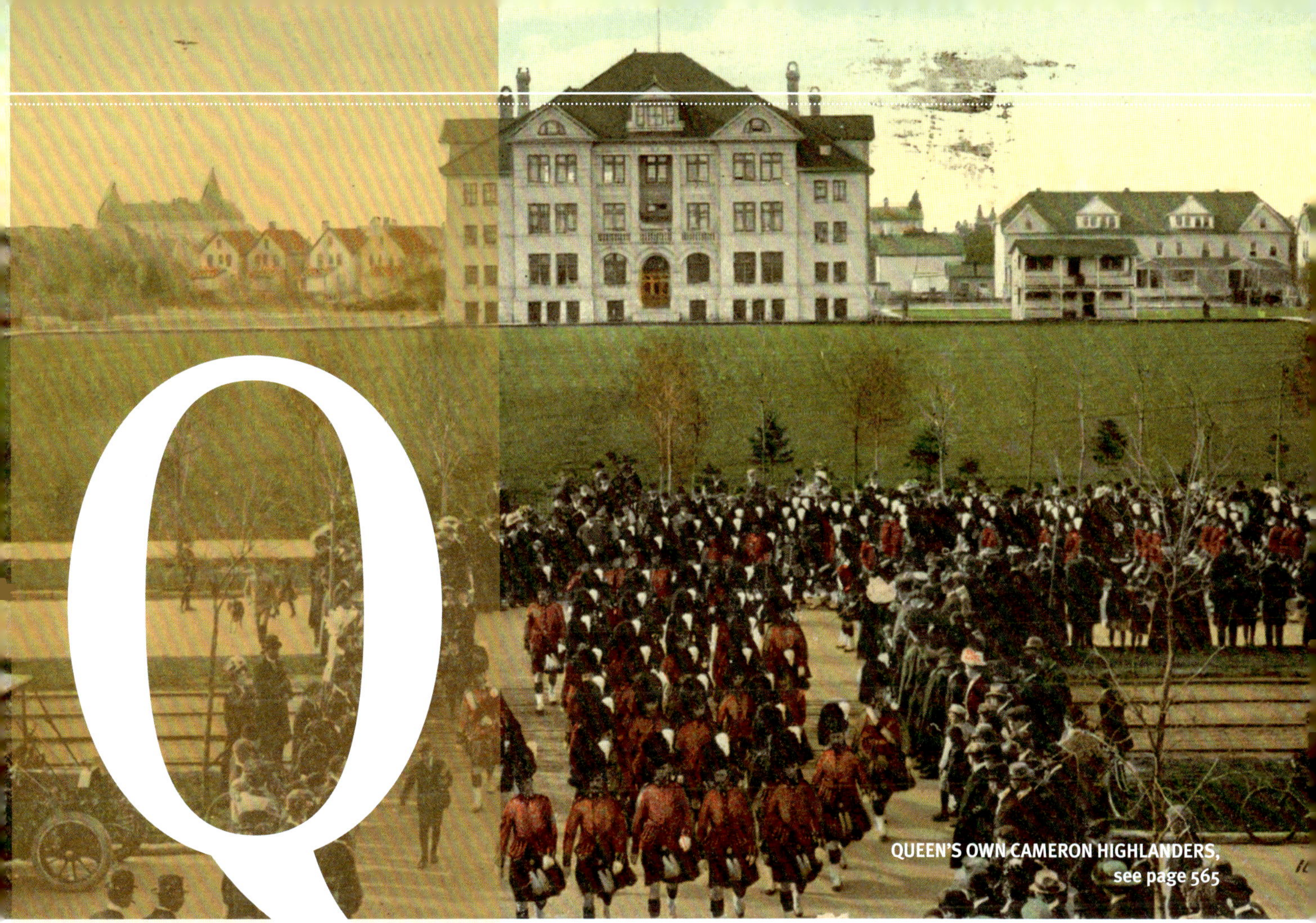

QUEEN'S OWN CAMERON HIGHLANDERS, see page 565

QUEEN, John, politician (b Feb 11, 1882, Lanarkshire, UK; d July 14, 1946, **Winnipeg**) was a **Socialist** mayor of Winnipeg. Born to a **Scots** family of Plymouth Brethren, he came to Winnipeg in 1906 and, although a cooper by trade, was employed as a driver of a horse-drawn delivery wagon. He was a member of the Social Democratic Party, co-founder of the Winnipeg Socialist Sunday School, as well as business agent and advertising manager for the *Western Labor News*. He was Winnipeg alderman for Ward 5 from 1916-19. He served as chair of a meeting at the Walker Theatre (*see* **Theatre**) of Dec 22, 1918, which passed several radical resolutions. He was arrested on June 17, 1919, by the Mounties (*see* **North-West Mounted Police**) on charges of sedition connected with the **Winnipeg General Strike**, defended himself, and was sentenced in 1920 to one year in prison. He was a MLA from 1920-32. He served as mayor of Winnipeg for 7 one-year terms (1935-36 and 1938-42). While mayor, Queen once famously hosted a visit to Winnipeg by the King and Queen of England, as well as PM Mackenzie King. • GPP

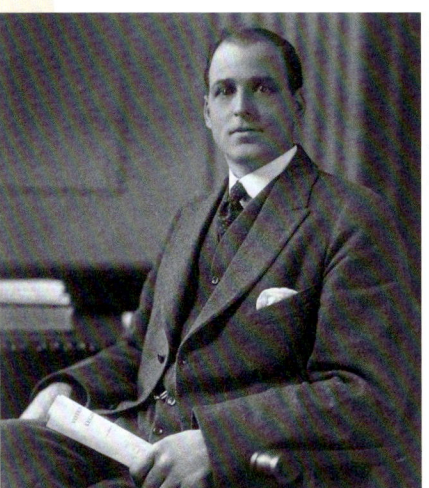

AM, PERSONALITY FILES, N14996

John Queen, ca 1921

QUEEN'S OWN CAMERON HIGHLANDERS OF CANADA, THE. A reserve infantry regiment currently attached to the 38th Brigade Group of the Canadian Army. This military unit was formally known as the following:

- 79th Highlanders of Canada (1910)
- 79th Cameron Highlanders of Canada (1910)
- Cameron Highlanders of Canada (1920)
- Queen's Own Cameron Highlanders of Canada (1923)
- Queen's Own Cameron Highlanders of Canada (Motor) (1954)

- Queen's Own Cameron Highlanders of Canada (1958-present)

HISTORY: The Camerons in 1914 originally contributed a large company of volunteers to the 16th Battalion CEF. This battalion went overseas with the First Canadian Division and was instrumental at the Second Battle of Ypres in stalling the German attack. At this battle, the Germans deployed poison gas – the 16th suffered terrible casualties but the enemy attack was repulsed. One member, Lt **ROBERT SHANKLAND**, won the Victoria Cross. In 1915 and 1916 – the regt raised two more infantry battalions as reinforcements to the Canadian Expeditionary Force, namely the 174th and 179th Infantry Battalions CEF.

In September 1939, the regt was mobilized for active service. Most notably, in August 1942, the regt participated in the ill-fated raid on Dieppe, suffering 50% casualties. In 1944, the Camerons took part in the Normandy campaign a participated in most actions of the First Canadian Army until V-E Day.

After WWII, the Camerons remained active in the Canadian Reserves. Today, members of the regiment have participated in peacekeeping operations and active operations with the Canadian Army.

Victoria Cross Recipient: Lt Robert Shankland DCM, October 23, 1917 • BRUCE TASCONA

QUINZHEE is a snow hut or dome shelter made from soft, unconsolidated snow (*Api*). It was one of the major technological advances discovered by early northern-forest people, on a par with the Inuit igloo made from blocks of hard, consolidated snow (*Upsik*) of the tundra. The quinzhee enabled the Athapaskan (**DENE**) people to become masters of winter in the taiga (N coniferous forest) – to travel, hunt, and sleep in comfort within their home range in winter. A quinzhee is based on several characteristics of the taiga: continuously very cold and stable winter weather, little wind, and a snow cover at least 25 cm thick. The result is a snow profile that has a steep temperature gradient from about -5 or $-8°C$ at its base, to whatever the ambient air temperature is at the surface, say $-30°C$. The basics of quinzhee construction are as follows.

Using mittens, a snowshoe, or a shovel, scoop up snow into a pile by working in a circle, so that this action mixes the cold upper and warm lower snow particles. Molecules from the warmer snow crystals immediately attach themselves to the colder ones. "Sintering" or hardening of the snow mixture begins to take place almost immediately. Continue scooping around and around the pile until it reaches about 2.5 m in height and 3 m in diameter. With a snowshoe or tree branch, round off the top of the cone to make a dome. It is important not pack the structure, even with your hands. A quinzhee's strength arises from the freezing together of tiny ice crystals, and packing only serves to break these bonds and actually weakens the structure. The colder the weather, the quicker the dome consolidates. At ambient -30°C, the dome will be self-supporting after one hour. The next step is to make a tunnel into the base of the dome on the downwind side. The tunnel must be only big enough to pull out scoops of the interior snow. Do not dig or break out chunks, but just scoop out loose snow. Slide your body into the tunnel and begin to burrow upward toward the top of the dome. When you can see weak blue light filtering through the wall and ceiling, they are a satisfactory thickness (about 20 cm).

Proceed by removing the snow down to the ground. The inside space at the base should have a diameter of about 2.5 m. Continue by smoothing the inside of the dome and removing all snow until the ground is exposed, thus allowing heat from the earth to flow up into the living space. The tunnel can be closed from the inside with a rucksack or piece of cardboard. What has been accomplished is enlargement of the *"pukak"* space – the home of voles and shrews. The quinzhee will now remain at -5 to $-8°C$, no matter how cold the outside air becomes. There is no need for any other heat source, such as a pressure stove or lantern. These present a hazard of carbon monoxide poisoning, undetectable until it is too late. A candle offers sufficient light. Knowledge of building a quinzhee has undoubtedly saved many lives over the millennia, and remains an indispensable method of escaping life-threatening winter conditions in an emergency. • WOP

FESTIVAL DU VOYAGEUR

Quinzhees with a designer touch at the Festival du Voyageur

LOUIS RIEL *(statue by Miguel Joyal)*, see page 585

RABBITS AND HARES are members of the rabbit family (Leporidae), which feature elongated hind limbs for rapid bounding; long ears, which gather sounds and assist with the control of body temperature; and soft fur over the entire body. These mammals were once thought to be related to rodents, but this resemblance is due to similar eating and ecological habits. They are herbivores, with some interesting adaptations for handling large amounts of plant material. A blind sac at the end of the small intestine, called the cecum (related to our appendix), holds food material for a period for further digestion with the help of bacteria. Soft cecal pellets are then eliminated as feces, but these are eaten and mixed with new green food, and additional nutrients (e.g., B vitamins) are absorbed. Finally, hard feces are passed and abandoned. Hares and rabbits are major prey for a host of avian and mammalian predators. In response, their reputation for reproduction is legendary, for they can produce several annual litters, each with up to 8 young. Hares try to outrun predators, have a 40-50-day gestation period, and give birth to well-developed, furred young. Rabbits take alternate strategies of quickly seeking refuge, have a short gestation of 30 days, and give birth to young that are

poorly developed, blind and naked. There are 4 species represented in MB.

ARCTIC HARE (*Lepus arcticus*): is a large (5 kg), stocky animal of the tundra with a dense white coat in winter, which moults into a grey coat in snow-free months (but remains white year-round in the High Arctic). Occupying the extreme NE corner of MB, it continues farther N than any other mammal – including all the major Arctic islands and Greenland. During the short summer it fattens on forbs, grasses and low shrubs, and during winter, it barely subsists by digging through crusted snow with the front feet and sharp claws to reach dormant vegetation. A single litter of 5 (1-8) young is usually produced in June, but a few females have a second litter in Aug under favourable conditions. Homes ranges can vary from 4-20 ha, with only the immediate nest area defended by the female. The hare remains motionless on the approach of a wolf, fox, or person, relying on its remarkable camouflage to avoid detection, but it will bound away at 40 km/hr if alarmed, sometimes using repeated hops on the hind feet to gain greater height and view of the pursuer.

SNOWSHOE HARE (*Lepus americanus*): is a 1.5 kg inhabitant of coniferous and deciduous forests, with an attraction to recent burns and alder-willow swamp, where its foods of herbaceous plants and shrub bark and buds are plentiful. Where dwarf shrubs occur, it can even extend out onto the prairie and tundra. Mating begins in late March, with several males pursuing a female. Chasing and urinating are part of the courtship and competing males may box and kick fiercely with their clawed feet to gain the right to copulate with the female. About 37 days later she gives birth to 1-8 young in a nest which is little more than a depression on the ground. After a few days she stashes her offspring separately under cover, visiting them only to nurse, thereby ensuring that at least some of her young avoid predation from foxes, weasels, lynx, and raptors. However, in spite of a camouflaged coat and ability to bound away at 40 km/hr, the Snowshoe Hare still remains the most important food item for most of these carnivores. Several litters are possible, and one female may produce up to 20 offspring by Sept. When conditions are positive, hare numbers build up to a peak about every 10 years, but crash thereafter for reasons still not entirely understood. The maximum lifespan is 5 years, but most individuals survive only one year.

WHITE-TAILED JACK RABBIT (*Lepus townsendi*): is double the size (4 kg) of the Snowshoe Hare, and has even longer ears. It first invaded S MB in 1881, with the first specimen collected at Boissevain. It has slowly spread as far N as Victoria Beach and the S Interlake. Sustained by abundant food from agriculture (especially corn, alfalfa and clover), this species has become common, and in some years it is not unusual to find 50 in a grain field. It is a master at remaining undetected, and even moults its coat in the autumn from brown to white. To escape extremely cold the jack rabbit burrows into a snow bank, and waits for fairer weather to return. Mating occurs from late Feb to July, leading to 2 or 3 litters, each with 1-8 young. The new-born are fully furred, with eyes open, and begin to move about within hours. Growing rapidly on their mother's milk, they nibble tender plants at 3 weeks, and are independent in 4 weeks. Adult size is attained by 14 weeks, and they first breed the following spring. This species is capable of withstanding prairie heat and drought – allowing the body temperature to rise to 41°C (thus preserving water from evaporative cooling), radiating heat through the big ears, and producing concentrated urine and dry feces.

EASTERN COTTONTAIL (*Sylvilagus floridanus*): only arrived in MB from MN in 1912, with the first record at Emerson. Settlement and agriculture created such ideal deciduous forest-edge conditions that it spread to the SW corner

Cottontail rabbits are often unwelcome visitors in gardens.

of MB within 2 years, and by 1940 it reached Winnipeg and Dauphin. It has now become a pest in people's yards even in the heart of towns and cities, being particularly fond of ornamental and vegetable plants. It is a wonder that it can persist here in the face of continual predation by dogs and cats, and the poisoning of lawns with weed- and mosquito-killing chemicals. This is the smallest of MB rabbits, weighing 1.3 kg. It remains brown throughout the year, although it moults in both spring and fall. The Cottontail receives its name from its tail, which is brown above and white below. Young Cottontails are occasionally found by people when cutting their lawn, since the mother makes a nest in the grass for her 1-12 offspring, which are born naked and blind. A female averages about 21 young per year (3 litters) at the latitude of MB. • REW

RACCOON (*Procyon lotor*) and close family relatives (Procyonidae) originated in Mesoamerica, but only the raccoon has spread to Canada. During the early settlement years, this species was rare in the hills and river valleys of extreme S MB. After about 1940, however, it showed a remarkable increase in numbers and range, reaching **DELTA** in 1949. Occupying the aspen parkland and mixed woods, it began to appear in the boreal forest, with records as far N as Norway House. Two tagged individuals were found to disperse over 275 km in MB. This range expansion was no doubt supported by agriculture and

Raccoons are cute but they can be pests.

buildings (i.e., food and shelter), which greatly improved the chances of winter survival. The Raccoon begins mating from mid-Feb on, with most births occuring in May and early June. An average of 4 (2-8) young are weaned by 12 weeks and they remain with their mother until the following spring. Now highly dependent on grain, the omnivorous raccoon also devours insects, frogs, crayfish, birds' eggs, berries, and nuts. Since few tree dens of sufficient size are available in MB forests, the animals usually retreat to the burrows of other species, and to home basements and attics. Fall is a period of high activity, as the animals attempt to gain as much body fat as possible. With decreasing temperatures and the appearance of snow, they enter a deep sleep in a sheltered place (communal denning is common), but not true hibernation, since they maintain their normal body temperature. Juvenile mortality from freezing, disease, and starvation is high during this period, with some losing over 50% of their weight. An adult weighs about 8 kg in summer. This adaptable "masked bandit" is now a common sight and sometimes a pest in city yards, parks, and rural areas. • REW

RACQUET SPORTS such as squash and racquetball are played on courts in private clubs, university gyms, and a few commercial facilities in MB. Squash, played with a long-handled racquet and a spongelike ball, is the older sport. It began in MB after the Winnipeg Squash Racquet Club opened in 1909, and was later played at the Winnipeg Winter Club, which opened in 1929. MB's first professional squash instructor was Charles Ives, who began offering lessons in 1934 and taught at **WINNIPEG** squash clubs for more than 4 decades. The first Manitoban to win a Cdn championship was Henry Thiessen in 1982. Gene Turk, the Cdn team coach since 1991, won his first MB title in 1977, and was one of the province's top players until retiring from play in the early 1990s. There are 24 singles and 2 doubles courts in MB, with about 2000 players. Winnipeg has hosted the Canadian Open Squash Championships twice, in 1975 and 1996.

The relatively new sport of racquetball was developed in the US in the early 1950s. Originally called "paddle racquets," it resembles a combination of squash and handball. Racquetball is played with a rubber ball and short-handled racquet and using the floor, ceiling, and left and right walls in play. Early racquetball enthusiasts in MB were mainly **U OF M** and **U OF W** athletes who used university handball courts before racquetball courts were built at Court Sports in the early 1970s. The Manitoba Racquetball Association was formed in 1971. In 1979, racquetball was

Canadian Northern to Hudson Bay Junction (formerly Etoimami; after 1947, simply Hudson Bay) in SK. From this point, a branch line was built back into MB, and reached THE PAS in 1908. The CNoR refused to build N of The Pas without substantial assistance from Ottawa. The federal govt then undertook to build the rest of the line from The Pas to a port on Hudson Bay. In 1912, the govt decided that the terminus of the line should be at Port Nelson, at the mouth of the NELSON RIVER. From 1913-17, govt contractors constructed 530 km of the line NW from The Pas to within 145 km of the bayside community. In Dec 1917, wartime shortages of labour and materials halted construction. The CNR took over operation of the Hudson Bay Railway in 1923. On the recommendation of a British consulting engineer, the govt decided in 1927 that the line should end at CHURCHILL rather than Port Nelson. In 1928-29, the CNR finished the last section of the line to Churchill, some 810 km from The Pas. The govt completed the building of port facilities at Churchill in 1931. Grain was now shipped from Churchill to Europe, but only in the short late-summer period of open navigation through Hudson Strait. Most of the prairie grain crop was still shipped to Europe via the Lakehead/St. Lawrence River route.

The Hudson Bay Railway and the CNR played a significant role in the development of MINING in northern MB. In 1953, the CNR built a 230 km branch line from Sherridon Lake on the Hudson Bay Railway to LYNN LAKE, to enable Sherritt Gordon to develop a nickel operation. In 1957, the CNR put in a 50 km branch line to THOMPSON to facilitate the development by INCO of a new nickel mining, smelting, concentrating, and refining complex there. That was the end of major railway construction in MB, as changing economics and the widespread use of motor vehicles led to a policy of branch-line abandonment. ● JOHN A. EAGLE

RAINBOW STAGE, Canada's longest-running outdoor summer theatre was established in 1954 at KILDONAN PARK in WINNIPEG by James Duncan, with the support of Thomas Hodgson, Winnipeg's Superintendent of Parks. In its first summer, the theatre presented a variety show directed by Duncan. In summer 1955, Duncan directed a performance of Lerner and Loewe's *Brigadoon*. The 1956 season of the summer theatre was comprised of Irving Berlin's *Annie Get Your Gun*, directed by Duncan and Syd Perlmutter; *The Wizard of Oz*, directed by JOHN HIRSCH; Thornton Wilder's *Our Town*, directed by Hirsch and Moray Sinclair; and Cole Porter's *Kiss Me, Kate*, directed by Peggy Green.

Rain, Douglas. Born in 1928 in WINNIPEG, Rain was primarily a Shakespearian stage actor. He starred in various roles at the MANITOBA THEATRE CENTRE but is most famous for his role as the voice of HAL 9000 in Stanley Kubrick's iconic film *2001: A Space Odyssey*, as well as the sequel *2010*. ●

After its initial triumphs, operating under a series of bold but unsuccessful directors and general managers, Rainbow Stage found itself plagued by recurrent financial difficulties. This problem seemed to resolve itself under the leadership of Jack Shapira from 1966-87. Shapira pursued a policy of producing 2 well-known musical-comedy classics each summer, with a cast that including established Cdn stars and local semi-professionals and amateurs. For over 21 years, Shapira's shows sold out at Rainbow Stage. The stage and auditorium were renovated and improved, and the summer theatre became one of Winnipeg's most stable theatre institutions. Then, in one of 1988's more shocking developments, Shapira was convicted of embezzling $381,000 from the theatre, and was sentenced to 18 months.

Shapira's successor, Jack Timlock, was not able to match Shapiro's record of box-office success, and Timlock resigned in 1992, leaving the theatre in poor financial shape. Since that time, Rainbow Stage, under changing leadership, has continued to shuttle between seasons with small surpluses and seasons saddled by worrisome deficits. A perpetual public debate rages over whether a theatre that produces old-fashioned commercial musicals can in fact be seen as doing culturally relevant work. For the most part, funding agencies have been unwilling to support Rainbow Stage, leaving it more dependent on box-office receipts than competing non-profit theatres.

After a deficit-ridden 2005 summer season, Rainbow Stage announced the adoption of an expanded, year-round, subscription-based season for the coming year. This experiment was abandoned in Nov 2005 after box-office failure. In 2007 the company put on 2 shows and announced plans to continue as long as possible. ● REG SKENE

RAPID CITY, pop 424, is a town 30 km N of BRANDON, on the LITTLE SASKATCHEWAN RIVER. European settlement began in the 1870s, at which time the community had several names, including Farmers' Crossing; Prairie City, and Ralston's Colony, after Jon Ralston, an Ontarian who led a group of settlers here. The post office opened in 1879. Prairie College (an ancestor of Brandon U) was established here in 1880, and the community incorporated as a town in 1883 as Rapid City, around the time a **CPR** branch line came here. *Rapid* originated with the swift Little Saskatchewan, once known as the Rapid River. As railways lost ground to the automobile, Rapid City's population waned. In the 21st century, the economy is concentrated on service and retail support of nearby agriculture, though the elementary school is among the larger employers in town. In summer, the town boasts both an agricultural fair and a rodeo. The town is also home to MB's first natural fish ladder, associated with a recreational dam on the Little Saskatchewan, and a fishing derby occurs here in March. Writer FREDERICK PHILIP GROVE lived here from 1922-29, during which time he was the school's principal. STANLEY KNOWLES also lived here. ● GPP

REARDON, Kenny, hockey player, (b April 1, 1921, WINNIPEG) had a long career playing defence and, after retiring from play, working in the executive for the NHL's Montreal Canadiens. He first played hockey growing up in Winnipeg, helping Clifton Community Club win the city's playground championship in 1931 and 1932. He was with the East Kildonan Bisons for their Bantam Championship wins in 1933 and 1943, and played for the Winnipeg Monarchs when they won the Juvenile City Championship the following year. Reardon signed with the Canadiens in

R

1940, playing for 2 years before enlisting in the army during WWII where he played on military teams, winning the 1943 Allan Cup as part of the Ottawa Commandos. Reardon served overseas, and rejoined the Canadians upon his return in 1945. He played another 4 seasons before retiring from play, in large part because of the many injuries he had sustained from his aggressive style of play. He became part of the Canadiens' executive, working as a talent scout and team manager over farm teams before eventually becoming vice-president. He is a member of the Hockey Hall of Fame. • MD

REAY, William T. "Billy," athlete, coach (b Aug 21 1918, **WINNIPEG**; d Sept 23, 2004, Madison, WI), was a Montreal Canadiens centreman and the long-time coach of the Chicago Blackhawks. Reay got his start in MB's junior **HOCKEY** leagues, playing with the East Kildonan Bisons of the Manitoba Midget League, the Elmwood Maple Leafs Juvenile Team, and the St. Boniface Seals of the Manitoba Junior Hockey League. He was part of the Memorial Cup-winning Seals in 1938.

The Detroit Red Wings signed Reay in 1939 and assigned him to Omaha of the American Hockey Association for 2 seasons. He then took a role as player/coach of the senior league Quebec Aces, leading them to 2 Allan Cup championships. Reay made his NHL debut in 1943, but was traded to the Montreal Canadiens in 1945 after playing only 4 total games with the Red Wings. He went on to win Stanley Cups in 1946 and 1953, his first and last seasons with the Canadiens. He was often the centreman for Maurice "Rocket" Richard.

After 479 games, Reay retired from the NHL and became player/coach of the Victoria Cougars

MB SPORTS HALL OF FAME & MUSEUM, MS1999.42.1

Billy Reay coached the Blackhawks for 14 seasons.

of the Western Hockey League from 1953-55. He gained other minor league experience before the Toronto Maple Leafs named him their head coach for 2 seasons, 1957-59. It was in 1963 when Reay began his stint with the Blackhawks that he made his mark. He was known as a responsive "players' coach" in an era when nearly all NHL bench bosses took an authoritarian approach. With his trademark red fedora, Reay led the Blackhawks to the finals 3 times (1965, 1971, 1973), but lost all 3, including 2 close series to the Canadiens. He coached Hall of Fame Chicago players Stan Mikita, **BOBBY HULL**, and Glenn Hall during his 14 seasons, accumulating a franchise-record 516 wins. Fired in 1976, Reay's NHL coaching record of 542-385-175 left him with the 6th most wins in league history. He was one of a few individuals to ever capture Memorial Cup, Allan Cup, and Stanley Cup titles, and was inducted into the **MANITOBA SPORTS HALL OF FAME** in 1996. • JOEL TRENAMAN

RECORDING INDUSTRY. MB may have a reputation for producing some of this country's best-known recording artists, but launching a recording career from here has not always been easy. In the 1950s and '60s there were few recording facilities available and national exposure was slim. In **WINNIPEG**, Arbuthnot Studios and Inland Broadcasting offered 1 and 2-track recording equipment as did CBC studios and radio stations CKY and CKRC. The province's earliest pop and jazz recordings emanated from these facilities including **RAY ST. GERMAIN's** "She's A Square", The Balladeers' "I Want A Girl," Portage la Prairie's Gary Cooper, and the first recordings by **NEIL YOUNG, BURTON CUMMINGS** and **RANDY BACHMAN**. In Dec 1964, the fledgling **GUESS WHO** cut their breakthrough single "Shakin' All Over" at CJAY TV's broadcast studio using one microphone and a monophonic tape recorder. However, a number of local musicians and singers made the trek either to Minneapolis's Kay Bank Studios or recording facilities in Toronto to lay down tracks. It was not until Century 21 Studios on King Edward St opened in 1969 by the Hildebrand and Paley brothers of popular rock band The Eternals that Winnipeg boasted a professional quality multi-track facility, initially featuring 8-track recording boosted to 16 and upwards from there.

Following the national success of the Guess Who's "Shakin' All Over," record labels were keen to sign up and record local artists. National labels such as Quality, London, Columbia and Warners released recordings by local acts including The Jury, The Fifth, The Shondels, The Luvin' Kind, Justin Tyme and Next while several homegrown labels like V Records (specializing in the polka

recordings of popular duo Mickey & Bunny until Neil Young's Squires became their lone foray into local rock 'n' roll), Eagle Records (run by Charlie Ward out of Selkirk Ave's Country Music Centre), Franklin Records (operated by Hungry I Agency's Frank Weiner) and labels set up by bands or managers themselves such as Syntax Records, TCP (featuring Fred 'BTO' Turner's earliest recordings with The Pink Plumm) and Nafro Records. Local record producers like CJAY TV personality Bob Burns, CKRC and later Century 21's Harry Taylor, Century 21's Ralph Watts, CKY's Darryl Burlingham, and Guess Who guitarist **RANDY BACHMAN** produced recordings for many local artists. Bachman and Mongrels' manager Lorne Saifer ran SaBaLoRa Productions, writing and recording many local acts including The Mongrels and Sugar & Spice.

Over the next 3 decades, recording artists including **CRASH TEST DUMMIES**, Harlequin, **THE WATCHMEN**, **CHANTAL KREVIAZUK**, The Pumps, **THE WEAKERTHANS**, country bands **DOC WALKER** and the Foster Martin Band, opera star **TRACY DAHL**, classical violinist **JAMES EHNES**, Grammy-nominated rap artist **FRESH I.E.,** award-winning family entertainers **FRED PENNER** and **AL SIMMONS**, and Christian contemporary singer/songwriter **STEVE BELL** launched successful recording careers from MB. More studios sprang up to meet the increased demand including jazz drummer Wayne Finucan's self-named recording facility (first in his Mercury Bay home before relocating to Sargent Ave), Roade Recording on Grosvenor Ave, VoxPop in Fort Garry operated by ex-Guess Who guitarist **GREG LESKIW**, Ness Michael's Sunshine Records (Platinum/Gold Studios) on Selkirk Ave, and God of Thunder studio owned by Crash Test Dummies' Brad Roberts.

Created in 1987 to fund, promote and assist local recordings, the Manitoba Audio Recording Industry Association (MARIA) has become a major player in fostering a thriving industry in the province. Together with the jointly federal and provincially funded Cultural Industries Development Office (1987), later renamed Manitoba Film and Sound, over a quarter of a million dollars annually is made available for local artists to make recordings. Today, a number of top notch recording facilities can be found in Winnipeg such as MidCanada Productions, Mid Ocean Studio (owned and operated by Steve Bell and partner Dave Zeglinski), Private Ear Recording (operated by The Cheer's Lloyd Peterson), Platinum/Gold Studios (where writer/producer Danny Shur works), Lenny Milne's Bedside Studios, Channels Audio (formerly Finucan Studios), Lion's Den Recording (operated by Juno Award-winning producer Dan Donahue), Maddock

Studio, and locally-owned independent record labels and production companies including Arbor Records, G7 Records, Sunshine Records, Signpost Music (Steve Bell), Mother of Pearl Records (Heather Bishop), Oak Street Records (Fred Penner), Norm Dugas Productions, CBG Artist Management (CHRIS BURKE-GAFFNEY), Groove Jungle, Choral Recording Services, Allen Hunnie Audio, and Burning Circus Media (Glen Willows of Harlequin). In the new millennium the province continues its reputation for producing uniquely talented and successful recordings and recording artists. • JOHN EINARSON

RED RIVER has played an important role in MB's settlement, transportation, trade, and culture. It rises in Lake Traverse on the SD-MN border, at the confluence of the Bois de Sioux and Otter Tail rivers. It is not known as the Red until it flows through Fargo, ND and is joined by the Sheyenne River. From there it runs N for 877 km with a 70 m drop, emptying by way of a wide delta (NETLEY-LIBAU MARSH) into LAKE WINNIPEG. .

OJIBWAY tribes were said to call it Pisquoqummeewee Sibi and the CREE referred to it as Miscousipi or Mikwakumewesepe, both meaning "red water river," due to its red clay bottom, or from some accounts, due to the blood spilled from previous battles. French explorers deemed it the Rivière Rouge shortly after the arrival of LA VÉRENDRYE in 1734. The ASSINIBOINE RIVER joins the Red at THE FORKS in WINNIPEG, where Fort Rouge was built in 1738. French and MÉTIS began to live along the river nearby. The first STEAMBOAT to navigate the river did so in 1859. The *ANSON NORTHUP* travelled up the Red from Fort Abercrombie (in what would later become ND). In Winnipeg's KILDONAN PARK, commemorative plaques were unveiled in 1961 to mark the event.

The river has had a tremendous impact on area residents due to a history of spring FLOODS in the Red River Valley. However, the river valley also has rich topsoil, a remnant of glacial LAKE AGASSIZ. After a catastrophic flood in 1950, the govt of DUFF ROBLIN initiated the construction of the RED RIVER FLOODWAY in the 1960s to protect Winnipeg from future floods of similar magnitude. It proved its worth in the 1997 flood. Water quality remains one of the main issues related to the river and its watershed. The city of Winnipeg and other communities release high volumes of toxins and sewage into the river system. In Sept 2002, a broken valve at a Winnipeg treatment plant led to the release of 427 m³ of raw, unfiltered sewage into the Red.

In the early 2000s, the MB govt tried to stop the govt of ND from developing an outlet to drain

The Red River watershed extends all the way to South Dakota.

the oft-flooding Devil's Lake into the river system by way of the Sheyenne River. It raised concerns about high levels of salts, arsenic, boron, phosphorous and mercury, as well as foreign FISH species and diseases in the water that would reach already polluted Lake Winnipeg. In addition to taking legal action in US courts, MB unsuccessfully pushed for the dispute to be settled by the commission administering the INTERNATIONAL BOUNDARY WATERS TREATY. The outlet began operating in 2005, though an agreement was reached to filter the lake's outflow, and to undertake further study. As of late 2006, high sulphate levels in the Sheyenne had kept the diversion closed (under state regulations), preventing any significant outflows into the Red. The river passes near or through a multitude of MB communities, including EMERSON, ROSEAU RIVER FIRST NATION, MORRIS, LOCKPORT, and SELKIRK. • JOEL TRENAMAN

RED RIVER CARTS. The earliest Red River carts were brought to the Northwest around 1800 by **NWC** trader ALEXANDER HENRY, who taught the locals at Pembina how to build a cart in the style of the ones used in Scotland. Having proved their usefulness on the prairie, the oxcart trains grew in popularity, until cart trains of 2500 plied the trail from the RED RIVER SETTLEMENT to MN in 1869.

The carts were simple constructions made with readily available materials, and required only basic tools, such as axes, saws, screws, augers, and drawknives. The axle was made from hard MAPLE, which had no give; the hubs

Red River Cart at Lower Fort Garry

were **Elm**, which was not easily split; the felloes (or rim) were made of ash, which could be bent into a curve; and the oxen's bow was made from ash or **Oak**, which could be boiled and pressed into shape. Since the cart was made entirely out of wood, repairs could be made anywhere. Oxen were preferred to horses as draft animals because they could haul more weight. Some carts had strands of rawhide (called babiches) wrapped around the 2 wheels to serve as a rudimentary tire.

R   The infamous screech made by the carts was the result of wood scraping against wood in the axle. No grease was used, as it would only have trapped dust in the axle and shortened its life. The screech gave the carts the nickname of "Northwest fiddle." The Red River cart could also serve as a makeshift raft: an oiled cloth or hide would be wrapped around the wheels, which would then be fastened to the bottom of the cart. The cart could then be rowed or poled over water. For a small vehicle, the carts could carry enormous amounts – up to 550 kg (1200 lbs). The carts were used for everything from hauling meat and hides during the annual **Métis Bison** hunts to bringing woodstoves into the Red River Settlement from MN. • MD

RED RIVER COLLEGE in **Winnipeg**, named after the river that largely defines the city, has nearly 40,000 full- and part-time students enrolled in a diverse range of 110 diploma, certificate, and apprenticeship programs. The college favours a practical, hands-on approach to education.

The college's roots trace back to the Industrial Vocational Education Centre, established in the 1930s. At the height of the **Great Depression**, founders started evening programs at a barebones facility at 331 Henry Ave in Winnipeg to help train unskilled and unemployed youth in the trades. The college was subsequently housed in several locations, including on Ellice Ave and in an automotive plant on Portage Ave. The centre's success led to federal govt support in 1938 and marked what is considered the official beginning of the college. Initial offerings included carpentry, sheet metal working, and power engineering. The college also offered training to troops going overseas as well as those returning from WWII. By 1948, the majority of veterans had been retrained, and the centre opened to the public under the name Manitoba Technical Institute (MTI). Training at MTI – the first public higher vocational school in the province – focused on providing marketable skills in the trades and in industrial and business fields.

In 1963, in anticipation of increasing demand for this training in the wake of the Baby Boom, the college built a new campus on Notre Dame Ave, serving 2000 students. In 1968, the college expanded its mandate, creating an arts-and-sciences complex called the Manitoba Institute of Applied Arts. Programs in the fields of communications, hospitality services, and graphic design marked MTI's departure from a purely technical curriculum. Shortly after, MTI changed its name to Red River Community College. By 1970, the college had almost 10,000 full- and part-time students, and it continued to grow, reaching 25,000 in 1985. Demand for programs by students unable to attend classes on campus led to continuing- and distance-education programs, and from 1985-92, a succession of regional centres opened up in smaller communities such as **Portage la Prairie**, **Selkirk**, **Gimli**, **Steinbach**, and **Winkler**.

Notre Dame campus of Red River College

In 1998, the name was again changed, to Red River College of Applied Arts, Science, and Technology. New course offerings prepare workers for careers in the **Aerospace** (at the Stevenson Aviation & Aerospace Training Centre), confectionery, **Construction**, and **Trucking** industries, among others. In 2003, the college completed the redevelopment of a group of buildings in Winnipeg's Exchange District (preserving the historic façades), creating its Princess Street Campus where 2000 students are now enrolled in media, **Information and Communications Technology**, and business-related programs. • GPP

RED RIVER EXHIBITION. The annual **Winnipeg** exhibition takes place every June at the **Assiniboia Downs** racetrack. The exhibition started in 1952, and has had many homes over the years. Initially at the Osborne Stadium/Amphitheatre complex, where the **Great West Life** headquarters now stand, the "Ex" soon moved to the Polo Park Race Track, then to the Winnipeg Stadium (now Canad Inns Stadium), the **Winnipeg Arena**, and the Winnipeg Velodrome facilities, which were demolished in 1998. In 1997, the Exhibition moved to its present location at the Assiniboia Downs fairground. The Red River Exhibition attracts more than 200,000 visitors each year. It features a popular midway, with a wide variety of rides, games, and foods; stage performances; children's programs; talent shows; opening-day fireworks; and artist, agriculture, historical, and educational exhibits. • RK

RED RIVER FLOODWAY is a 47 km excavated channel that allows floodwaters from the **Red River** to be diverted around the eastern edge of **Winnipeg**, permitting river levels within the city to be maintained at or below minimum **F0lood** levels. At a cost of $63 million, it was the largest and most-critical component of the flood control system for Winnipeg implemented in the 1960s by the govt of premier **Duff Roblin**.

The floodway begins just S of the St. Norbert neighbourhood on the S edge of Winnipeg and rejoins the Red at **Lockport**, 10 km SE of **Selkirk**. Flow into the floodway and the division of streamflow between the floodway and the river channel through the city is regulated by a control structure built into the river channel just downstream of the floodway inlet. The structure contains 2 wedge-shaped gates. Under normal conditions, the gates are submerged, and the entire flow of the river is allowed to pass down the river through the city. When discharge threatens to exceed minimum flood levels within the city, the gates are raised, constricting the flow through the openings and creating a partial dam across the river. The raising of the gates elevates the water level upstream of the structure to a height above the lip of the floodway's inlet, and water flows naturally into it. This division of flow begins when river discharge reaches 840 m^3 per second. Dikes extending to the E and W prevent water from bypassing the structure. On the E, the dike formed part of the floodway channel embankment; to the W, the dike extended S and W for a distance of 34 km. At the floodway outlet near Lockport, a concrete structure was built to dissipate excess energy in the floodway water and prevent erosion of the natural river channel.

The original floodway was 115-165 m wide at the bottom and 215-305 m wide at the top, with an average depth of 9 m; in the Birds Hill area, where the terrain was somewhat higher, the depth of excavation reached 20 m. Construction of the floodway began in 1962 and was completed in 1968. In addition to the excavation of 75 m^3 of earth (about 40% of the amount dug for the Panama Canal), it involved the relocation, reconstruction, or modification of a dozen railway and highway bridges; oil and gas pipelines; 6 hydro transmission lines; 2 branches of the Winnipeg aqueduct; and even the construction of a siphon under the floodway to maintain flow in the Seine River within Winnipeg. In 1967, when

STAN MILOSEVIC, WWW.MANITOBAPHOTOS.COM

Duff Roblin on a floodway bridge, 1969.

Winnipeg first hosted the **Pan Am Games**, a portion of the partially completed excavation hosted the rowing events.

Under severe flood conditions, the floodway was designed to convey up to 1700 m³ per second around Winnipeg. In the most serious emergencies, this could be increased to about 2800 m³ per second. The overall protection scheme, of which the floodway was the most important component, was designed to protect Winnipeg from floods of up to about 4800 m³ per second, which at the time it was constructed, corresponded to a 1-in-160 year event. The late 20ᵗʰ century, however, saw a remarkable series of floods that provided an immediate demonstration of the system's value. The floodway was used to prevent small-scale flooding in 1969, the first spring after its completion, and in many years thereafter. Most of these events were relatively small, but in 1974 and 1979, floods of 1950 magnitude were controlled with little damage within Winnipeg. By 1980, the system had prevented more than $1 billion in damages, and this amount was increased substantially in 1996 when what otherwise could have rivalled the 1950 flood was easily managed.

The original decision to construct the floodway had been controversial because of its prohibitive cost, or preferences by some for alternative schemes. The floodway became known as "Duff's Ditch," after the premier; whatever skepticism may have been implied in the original use of this term, however, was quickly converted to great affection as the value of the project became apparent. By far the most dramatic demonstration of its value came in 1997 when the "Flood of the Century" pushed the capabilities of the entire control system to its limits and focused national attention on the floodway. At the flood's peak on May 4, the floodway carried 1840 m³ per second – without it, flooding within Winnipeg would have been catastrophic. Much of the city would have required evacuation, and estimates of the damages might have ranged into the billions of dollars.

By the end of the 20ᵗʰ century, the increased frequency of flooding had reduced the level of protection for Winnipeg from a 1-in-160 year event to about 1-in-90 years. The narrow escape from the 1997 flood demonstrated the need to increase the level of protection for Winnipeg even further, to encompass events even beyond the historic 1826 flood, which had an estimated discharge 40% greater than that of 1997. After extended negotiations between the provincial and federal govts over cost sharing, engineering studies, environmental assessments, and public hearings, work began in summer 2005 to widen the original floodway by up to 110 m, involving excavation of an additional 34 million m³ of earth. Together with improvements to the diking and the control and outlet structures; modifications to utility, pipeline, and bridge crossings; and changes to drainage systems and the Seine River siphon, the enlarged channel increased the floodway capacity from 1700 m³ per second to 4000 m³ per second, providing protection for Winnipeg from floods of up to a 1-in-700-year magnitude. ● W. F. RANNIE

RED RIVER JIG. The jig is a distinctly MB dance, originating from the **Powwows** of Plains tribes and from the folk dances of **Scots** and **Irish**. It became the central feature of the social gatherings of the early days of the **Red River**

Settlement. To the tune of energetic fiddling, a man and a woman would face each other about 2 m apart and stand on tiptoes. They would shuffle forward and back with flourishes and fancy steps, depending on the skill of the performer. When one or the other partner dropped out, a fresh dancer would take his or her place. Dancing would sometimes continue until dawn, which often led to the consumption of a great deal of liquid refreshment. ● RK

RED RIVER RESISTANCE (also known as the Red River Rebellion). This movement saw residents of the **Red River Settlement** prevent the Cdn govt in 1869-70 from assuming control of the **Rupert's Land** territory it had purchased from the **Hudson's Bay Company (HBC)**. Its leadership, headed by **Louis Riel**, established a provisional govt that negotiated an agreement with Canada guaranteeing rights and admission to Confederation as the province of MB. Whether to call this movement a "resistance" or a "rebellion" depends on one's view as to its legitimacy. The Cdn govt maintained that it was a rebellion against the HBC's valid govt, while most MB historians have viewed the situation as being much more complex.

The govt of the United Province of Canada coveted the western territory of the HBC as a region for the expansion of settlement and economic activity. After the establishment of Confederation in 1867, the new Cdn govt quickly passed legislation for the takeover of the West, and terms were negotiated with the HBC, who constituted the govt of Red River – with the approval of the UK govt – for the transfer in 1868, to take effect in Sept 1869, though this was later postponed until Dec 1869. None of the 3 govts involved – Canada's, the UK's, or the HBC's – bothered to consult with the inhabitants of the Red River region, or to inform local representatives of the HBC either about the transfer or about Cdn policy for the territory. The residents, many of whom were wholly or partially First Nations or **Métis**, and who were largely **Roman Catholic** and Francophone, learned of their future by reading the Cdn newspapers, which told them that Canada would govern Red River as a colony under appointed officials – most of them Anglophone Protestants from the East – and without any recognition of local rights.

Canada sent in a party in 1868 before the official transfer to construct a road to the settlement, and dispatched another mission that same year to survey land in the settlement in advance of new immigration into the region. Cdn politician Joseph Howe, whose Cabinet portfolio included the new territory, visited Red River unofficially in

PUBLIC NOTICE TO THE INHABITANTS OF RUPERTSLAND.

The President and Representatives of the French-speaking population of Rupert's Land in Council, ("the Invaders of our rights being now expelled") already aware of your sympathy, do extend the hand of friendship to you our friendly Inhabitants, and in doing so invite you to send twelve Representatives from the following places, viz.

St. Margret's 1. Headingly 1. St. James 1, St. Mary's 1, Kildonan 1, St. Paul's 1, St. Andrew's 1, St. Clement's 1, St. Peter's 1, Town of Winnipeg 2 in order to form one body with the above Council consisting of twelve members to consider the present political state of this Country, and to adopt such measures as may be deemed best for the future welfare of the same.

A meeting of the above Council will be held in the Court House at Fort Garry on Tuesday the 16th day of November at which the invited Representatives will attend.

Winnipeg Nov. 6th 1869.

By order of the President,
LOUIS RIEL,
Sect.

Notice to the Inhabitants of Rupert's Land, 1869

early Oct. He was surprised to discover that the settlement had a formal govt and a legal system, but he did not speak to any representatives of the **French** population. Two days after Howe's arrival, a surveying party working not far from **The Forks** was stopped by a band of 18 Métis, headed by Louis Riel, the son of one of Red River's Francophone leaders. The Métis began organizing to prevent the Cdn govt, headed by **William McDougall** as lt gov-in-waiting, from entering the territory of the settlement. McDougall was forcibly kept S of the border by an armed group of Métis led by **Ambroise-Didyme Lépine** at the end of Oct, and on Nov 2, a larger armed group led by Riel would occupy **Upper Fort Garry** unopposed. Riel, serving as secretary of the Métis National Committee, spent Nov attempting in formal meetings to bring the English-speaking mixed-bloods (**Country-Born**) to support the Métis in their resistance, with neither complete success nor total failure. In the end, the meeting produced a Bill of Rights acceptable to both sides, but no agreement on strategy. Lt gov McDougall issued a proclamation on Dec 1, taking over the territory

and ordering those loyal to Canada to take up arms to oppose the Métis, but nothing much came of this effort. In early Dec, the Métis surrounded a house owned by Dr. **John Christian Schultz**, leader of the Canadian Party in the settlement, and captured 45 adult men who had barricaded themselves inside. Riel then issued a "declaration of the people" on Dec 8, and 2 days later proclaimed a provisional govt to replace the HBC, which was still in control of Red River, as the Cdn govt had refused to accept the transfer while the territory was in a rebellious state. Riel wanted to negotiate with Canada, but could find no one in the settlement authorized to discuss terms with the Métis. He eventually held an open-air meeting with **Donald Alexander Smith** who had been sent by Canada to calm the settlement but had no power to deal with the resistors. Smith could promise nothing, but suggested that the people of Red River meet in convention and decide what they wanted to demand from Canada. That meeting, involving 40 elected delegates from both language groups, met at the end of Jan.

After considerable debate, this convention produced another list of rights delegates were to take to Canada. Before the delegates could leave Red River, however, the first lot of prisoners was released and another lot taken. One of the prisoners was an Irish-born Cdn and Orange Lodge member, **Thomas Scott**, who angered his captors to the point where they brought him before a court, found him guilty of rebellion against the provisional govt, and summarily executed him on Mar 4, 1870. Scott's execution seemed to change the dynamic with Canada, particularly after the Canada First Party used the execution to stir up Protestant ON against Riel and the Métis. The Cdn govt refused to meet with the Red River delegates officially, and privately negotiated an arrangement that resulted in the drafting of the *Manitoba Act*, passed by Parliament May 12, 1870. Canada's major concessions were the provision of several million ha of land for the settlement of Métis claims – though the govt has still never made good on these promises – and the acceptance of Riel's demand for provincial status for Red River, limited to its existing boundaries and now named **Manitoba**. The Cdns made noises about an amnesty for Riel and the other rebel leaders, but they refused to put anything in writing. The supposed satisfaction of the demands of Red Riverites through the *Manitoba Act* made possible the dispatch of the **Wolseley Expedition** to impose order on the new province. When that expedition arrived in Winnipeg on Aug 24, Riel and his provisional govt fled the scene and became fugitives from justice. ● J. M. BUMSTED

RED RIVER SETTLEMENT

RED RIVER SETTLEMENT (or Colony). The colony at **The Forks** of the **Red** and **Assiniboine** rivers was first seriously suggested in 1811 by the **Hudson's Bay Company (HBC)** directors, who were looking for a haven for retired employees. **Lord Selkirk** (Thomas Douglas, 5th Earl of Selkirk), who was a company director, was persuaded to organize the settlement in return for a land grant from the company of 300,000 km² of unsettled territory, covering huge areas of what is now MB, MN, ND, SK, and MS, as well as parts of MT, SD, and AB. Neither Selkirk nor any of the other directors had ever visited the HBC lands. Thus, they had no real idea of the difficulty posed by the winter climate; nor had they an idea of the travel requirements, which consisted of up to 3 months by sea from Britain to **Hudson Bay**, and 3 or more months of travel over inland waters in **York Boats** to the proposed site of the settlement.

When the HBC's **Fur Trade** rival, the **North West Company (NWC)**, opposed the land grant, Selkirk became more stubborn about pressing

Sketch of the Red River Settlement, believed to have been drawn by Lord Selkirk in 1817

ARCHIVES OF MANITOBA

aheadl with the project. He sent **Miles Macdonell** and a party of recruits – most of them intended to remain in the W for only 3 years to prepare the way for further settlers – to Hudson Bay in 1811. This first party, which arrived at the Forks in Aug 1812, set the pattern for a series of disastrous journeys by the early settlers – most of them Highland **Scots** – in 1812, 1813, and 1814. Macdonell was unable to feed and house the new arrivals, and in 1814 attempted to resolve the food problems by issuing the *Pemmican Proclamation*, forbidding the export of foodstuffs from the region without a licence. This proclamation assumed sovereignty over a region disputed by the North West Company. In 1815, the Norwesters succeeded in persuading most of the settlers to move to Upper Canada. A small remnant of loyalists were joined later in the year by the new governor of the territory, **Robert Semple**, and by another party of immigrants. In 1816, the settlers clashed with the local Métis – the infamous **Seven Oaks Incident** – and the settlement was again dispersed, to be reconstituted by forces loyal to Lord Selkirk and, in 1817, by Selkirk himself.

After 1817, Red River had little more trouble with the fur trade war. Problems shifted to the natural environment, with prairie fires and grasshopper infestations exacerbated by isolation and an inability to find a market for crops. In 1818, the first **Roman Catholic** priests arrived in the settlement, and in 1820, the first **Anglican** minister. In 1821, the last large contingent of settlers from Europe arrived in the form of a party of nearly 200 Swiss recruited by the Selkirk estate. A major **Flood** in spring 1826 devastated the settlement, and drove many of the European settlers S into the US. They were gradually replaced by people of mixed descent unable to find a future in the fur trade after the merger of the HBC and the NWC.

By the early 1840s, the Selkirk estate had sold its interest in the settlement to the HBC,

which reorganized Red River as the District of **Assiniboia**, ruled by an appointed governing council and a Court of Quarterly Session. In 1839, **Adam Thom** became the first judge in the court, with the title of "recorder." He subsequently prepared a law code for the settlement.

Increasingly, talented young people of mixed descent began exceeding the local employment opportunities. One result was a party of outward migration to the Oregon Territory in 1841; another was the rise of local Free Traders competing with the HBC. The company managed to convince the UK govt to station regular troops (the 6th Royal Regt of Foot) in the settlement in 1846, ostensibly to protect the border against US incursions, but mainly to keep local law and order. The regulars were subsequently withdrawn, and were replaced in 1848 by a contingent of retired soldiers called the Chelsea Pensioners. In 1849, in a tense local trial, trader Guillaume Sayer was found guilty of infringing the HBC monopoly, but was released by the court unsentenced. After 1849, authorities tried to improve relations with the Métis, appointing Catholic spiritual leader Reverend **Alexandre-Antonin Taché** and others to the **Council of Assiniboia**, and generally seeking local support. By the early 1850s, forces in Canada West, which became ON, were beginning to eye the region as prime for expansion, and a Select Committee of the House of Commons in 1857 recommended that Red River eventually be annexed by Canada.

The external world swiftly arrived in Red River in 1859, a year in which a steamboat first landed in the settlement, a newspaper (the ***Nor'-Wester***) was established, and the first organized postal system begun. During the 1860s, there was much political agitation from newly arrived immigrants from Canada, and, in the wake of Cdn Confederation, resolutions in the young Parliament for the purchase of **Rupert's Land**. During famine conditions that began in 1868, the Cdns began road-building and surveying activities

in advance of the negotiation of the transfer of Red River and the Indian Territories to Canada negotiated in 1869. The stage was set for the **Red River Resistance** of 1869-70. ● J. M. BUMSTED

RED SUCKER LAKE FIRST NATION, on reserve pop 786, off reserve pop 110, is located 709 km NE of **Winnipeg**, on the NE shore of Red Sucker Lake, close to the ON border. The Red Sucker Lake First Nation community signed Treaty 5 in 1909, and its native languages are **Ojibway** and **Cree**. It is a member of the Island Lake Tribal Council. Until 1969, Red Sucker Lake, along with **St. Theresa Point**, **Wasagamack**, and **Garden Hill First Nations**, was one unified community known as the Island Lake Band. The Red Sucker Lake First Nation has one reserve. This is an isolated First Nation dependent on air service and a winter road to Garden Hill. The First Nation administers schooling from Nursery-Grade 12. Enrolment for the year 2003-04 was 200. The economic foundation for Red Sucker Lake is commercial fishing and trapping.

Elijah Harper, Aboriginal politician and social activist, was born and raised in Red Sucker Lake First Nation. The Red Sucker Lake non-treaty community (pop 33) is on 2 islands close to the First Nation of the same name. ● RK

REEVE, Gordon, sculptor, (b March 30, 1946, Chatham, ON) received his BFA from Cranbrook Academy of Art and his MFA from Rhode Island School of Design. He has been a professor of sculpture at the **U of M**'s School of Art since 1976. In addition to working as a sculptor, he was also a documentary film maker from 1987-96. He made *Moment of Light the Dance of Evelyn Hart* with the **National Film Board** in 1992. He creates his sculptures in steel, bronze and wood, producing abstract forms and large-scale constructions. He rhythmically marks the surfaces of the materials combining linear details with the macro scale. Reeve has received a number of commissions and competitions. His work includes *Justice* (1985), the major stainless steel, outdoor public work at the Manitoba Law Courts Building, and (2004), a large stainless steel work that draws its inspiration from the landscape and the prairie light at **Friesens** printers in **Altona**. Mounted on a concrete pad *Luna*, incorporates an emerald glass casting, which, coupled with the sweeping manner and pattern in which Reeve has worked the surface of the metal, gives the piece a sense of fluidity and depth. Other commissions include the major work at the provincial building in **Dauphin** (1979); a piece in Framingham, MA (1973); and *The Sharon Screens* at the Sharon Home, Winnipeg (1999-2000). ● PATRICIA BOVEY

R

REFORM in MB was a catch-all phrase that covered efforts to improve and ameliorate social, political, and economic conditions. It began in the 1840s with the first temperance movement, but it was not until the 1890s that reform coalesced as a movement. Reforms – and reformers – split into 3 general tendencies. One was concerned with social reform, which usually focused on urban problems and was thus largely confined to **Winnipeg**. Another focused on political change, based either on popular democracy centred outside the framework of parliamentary govt, or on the egalitarian redistribution of goods and opportunities. A third tendency was to see the adoption of free trade as a panacea for all the province's problems. Many specific reforms and tendencies originated outside the province, often in the UK or the US, but had acquired local emphases and interpretations.

From the close of the 19th century, and then sporadically during WWI, reform initiatives included women's suffrage and improvement in women's legal status (*see* **Women's Movement**); direct legislation; **Prohibition**; flat versus progressive taxation; sanitation and **Public Health**; the social gospel; and the eugenics movement. A series of coalitions among these movements occurred, so that almost all eventually merged into a single movement. Provincially, reformers came increasingly to support the **Liberal Party of Manitoba**, largely because the Conservative govt of 1899-1915 (*see* **Progressive Conservative Party of Manitoba**) built a large part of its electoral success on blatant appeals to the Francophone/**Roman Catholic** and immigrant vote, to which was added a loyalty vote from the older population based on unabashed flag-waving. The provincial support of the Francophones was ironic, given the association of the federal Liberal Party with Sir Wilfrid Laurier and QC; nevertheless, the Conservatives became increasingly tarnished by scandal and by internal division over tough political and social issues.

During this period, MB's population changed substantially in numbers, in composition, and in geographic location. Particularly noteworthy was the growth in the numbers of people not part of the "founding" ethnic groups of the province who dominated the settlement of MB in the decades after 1870 – the **French**, **Scots**, **English**, and **Irish**, often from ON, usually **Anglican**, **Methodist**, **Presbyterian**, or **Baptist**. The newcomers came especially from southern and eastern Europe, spoke different languages, and were of various, usually non-Protestant, religious affiliations. (*See* **Immigration**) Although some came to MB to become farmers, most of the new arrivals settled in the cities, especially Winnipeg, and the percentage of **Rural** inhabitants in the province fell from 72% to 56% between the 1901 and 1911 Censuses. At the same time, farming, notably grain cultivation, flourished.

Winnipeg had its own problems, with thousands of newcomers unadjusted to their new environment. The resulting situation caused the British Protestants – themselves a new majority, as the province had been mainly **French** and largely **Métis** until recently – to feel threatened and to become involved in various social-reform initiatives to shore up their deteriorating position of power and authority. Not all reformers were motivated by self-interest, however. Many were genuinely horrified by the conditions that they sought to change. But most reformers saw their crusade as a moral one, and many were also patronizing about their efforts, making little effort to involve the subjects of their action as agents in their own improvement.

By 1915, the Liberal Party had taken over a sufficient number of the reformers' planks to produce an electoral victory at the polls, and the new **T. C. Norris** govt spent the remainder of WWI implementing several of the more prominent items in its platform, such as the vote for women and the reduction of alcohol consumption. The Great War itself would provide a major impetus for the national success of much progressive reform advocated in MB, such as women's suffrage (which led to MB being the first province to give women the vote in 1916), Prohibition, and graduated tax levies. At the same time, the waging of the war badly divided the federal Liberal Party, and in the postwar period, most agrarian reformers in the province abandoned the provincial Liberals, joining the United Farmers of Manitoba instead. ● J. M. BUMSTED

REICHERT, Don, painter, photographer and digital media artist, (b Jan 11, 1932, **Libau**) graduated from the **U of M** School of Art in 1956, continuing his studies at the Insituto Allende in Mexico (1957-58). Widely travelled across Canada and Europe, Reichert is primarily an abstract artist, embracing expressionism, geometric abstraction, and the seemingly more spontaneous "splatter" abstractions. The formal complexities and rich variety of the landscape, rocks, water, the cosmos and sky are the subjects in his work. He explores both the macro and micro aspects, blending his personal response with geological history and the enormity of the landscape. Texture and pattern are constant in his work. He often incorporates elements of nature and the granite rock formations directly by placing his canvas on the ground, applying his paint outdoors, finishing them in the studio.

In the 1980s, he included photographs in his paintings, sometimes painting over them, always intuitively creating organic images depicting light, movement, solidity, and the momentary. Subsequent computer paintings furthered these themes. He taught at the U of M from the mid-1960s until his retirement. Public and private collections include The **Winnipeg Art Gallery** (WAG), the National Gallery of Canada, The Art Gallery of Ontario, the Canada Council Art Bank, and the Montreal Museum of Fine Art. Exhibitions include the WAG (1960, 1969, 1974, 1995), The Beaverbrook Art Gallery (1962) and the Canadian Embassy in Washington DC (2004). Publications include *Don Reichert; A Life in Work,* (WAG 1995) *Headcount: An Installation and Related Work by Don Reichert* (Glenn Allison: Art Gallery of Southwestern Manitoba 1992), and *Don Reichert: Paintings from the Land* (WAG 1983). ● PATRICIA BOVEY

REIMER, David, gender reassigned test case, (b Aug 22, 1965, **Winnipeg**; d May 4, 2004, Winnipeg). The tragic story of David Reimer has been studied by sexologists throughout the world. After suffering a botched circumcision, he was castrated and raised as a girl alongside his identical twin. This presented an exact control match

Redwood Bridge Reconstruction 2006-02-01, inkjet on canvas, 91 x 218 cm by Don Reichert

for the study of the development of gender differences. Reimer's sex change, however, proved to be misguided, and had devastating consequences for the Reimer family.

The decision to rear Reimer as a girl was made on the advice of Dr. John Money, a leading US sexologist who was seeking to establish proof of his theory that gender differences are learned rather than innately defined. In 1966, presented with an infant Reimer and his irrevocably damaged penis, Money saw an opportunity to test his theory and told Reimer's parents that their son would have a better chance at a fulfilled life as a girl. Reimer was consequently castrated and renamed Brenda. Following Money's instructions, Brenda remained ignorant of his real gender.

Money closely monitored the development of the twins over the course of their childhood, and published numerous articles in scientific journals about what he termed the "John/Joan Case." Noting "Brenda's" feminine qualities in comparison to his twin brother, he declared the gender experiment a success, and his conclusions became widely accepted by the medical establishment as proof that nurture does indeed take precedence over nature in establishing gender identity.

Money's analysis, however, was wrong. In reality, the experiment was an unmitigated failure, and "Brenda" was never able to conform to a female role. He was teased throughout his school years for his oddly masculine features, and led an anguished existence until the age of 14 when his parents finally told him of his gender reassignment. Upon hearing the truth, "Brenda" immediately rejected his forced femininity. Adopting the name David, he underwent an operation to remove the breasts that had developed as a result of hormone treatment and, with surgical procedures vastly improved since his birth, was able to have a penis reconstructed.

As an adult, Reimer lived an anonymous, blue-collar existence in Winnipeg. He married a single mom, raised a family, and remained silent on what had been done to him. No one knew the truth of the "John/Joan Case" until Dr. Milton Diamond followed up on Money's experiment in 1997. Shocked to find that, far from having developed into a normally socialized woman, Brenda had in fact been traumatized by the gender reassignment, Milton publicly challenged Money's supposedly successful case. In an effort to prevent similar gender reassignments, Reimer then went public with his story in 2000 in the book *As Nature Made Him: The Boy Who Was Raised as a Girl* by John Colapinto. However, Reimer's own life was forever scarred by the trauma of his early years. Following a string of personal tragedies, including the suicide of his twin brother, Reimer committed suicide in 2004. ● MICHELLE DOBROVOLNY

REIMER EXPRESS LINES LTD is one of Canada's largest **Trucking** firms, primarily operating as a less-than-truckload (LTL) carrier. LTL means instead of hauling large quantities of goods for one customer at a time, as is the case with truckload carriers, a Reimer tractor/trailer unit typically carries an average of 100 kg of goods for 20-50 customers at a time as it travels from an original shipping terminal to a destination city. The **Winnipeg**-based firm got its start in 1952, when **Steinbach** teen D. S. Reimer, who had been hauling goods between Winnipeg and Steinbach for his family's general store and feedmill operation, also started hauling goods for other people on a for-hire basis. He named his new company Reimer Express Lines, set up a head office in Winnipeg, and began transporting goods between the MB capital and Windsor, ON. As the business flourished, he added overnight freight service between Winnipeg and NW ON, then Winnipeg and Montreal. Once the company had established a foothold in the East, it began expanding its operations into the rest of western Canada by acquiring existing trucking firms in SK, AB, and BC. Today, Reimer Express Lines hauls goods throughout Canada, the US, and Mexico. In addition to its LTL operations, it also offers expedited transportation services through its Fast as Flight, direct-to-customer operations, and service to different points within the province through its Reimer Express Manitoba operation. As well, a school it launched in 1970 to train drivers for its own operations – the Reimer Express Driver Training Institute Inc. – subsequently expanded to train drivers for other trucking firms as well. Reimer Express Lines remained a family-owned business until 1997, when it was purchased by the largest long-haul trucking firm in the US, Roadway Express Inc., of Akron, OH. Despite the change in ownership, the company remains headquartered in Winnipeg, and founder D. S. Reimer continues to serve as the firm's chairman. ● MURRAY MCNEILL

REINFELD, pop 700, is a community 100 km SW of **Winnipeg**, just one km E of Winkler. It is a mainly Mennonite community, first settled in the 1890s. The community has a church called the Old Colony Church. The Reinfeld community is named for the German word meaning "clean field." Like Winkler and other southeast MB communities, Reinfeld experienced significant growth between the 2001 and 2006 Census. The RM of Stanley, which surrounds Winkler and includes Reinfeld, grew by 24% to 6367. ● GPP

RENNIE, pop 100, is a community 180 km E of **Winnipeg** on the edge of the **Whiteshell Provincial Park**. Rennie's landscape is a mix of both prairie and pine forest. The Alfred Hole Goose Sanctuary and visitor centre is near Rennie. The community opened "Rennie River Leisure" in 2005 to serves as a marine, snowmobile, and ATV service and parts facility for the surrounding area. As well, the Whiteshell Trappers Museum is in Rennie. In Feb, Rennie hosts an annual Winter Fun Carnival, and in July the community holds a Children's Festival. ● GPP

Painted Turtles

REPTILE is a prominent group of scaly-skinned, 4-legged land animals that evolved from amphibians about 325 million years ago (Carboniferous period). It includes the lizards, snakes, turtles and crocodilians. Key to reptilian development were the features of internal fertilization and the amniote egg with a protective, hard or leathery shell and embryonic membranes – a feat that freed these animals from having to return to water to lay eggs. This 'invention' was of the utmost importance to humans, since it made possible the evolution of both birds (class Aves) and mammal-like reptiles (subclass Synapsida, flourishing 280-195 million years ago) and ultimately the entire mammal line, including our order, the Primates, and our species *Homo sapiens*. Remarkably, there are still a few mammals around (Monotremes like the Duck-billed Platypus) that continue this egg-laying tradition. Reptiles are ectothermic, meaning they are dependant on heat from their surroundings (augmented by basking in sunlight) to maintain their body temperature in a range within which they can function. Consequently, MB's few species of reptiles must be able to rapidly carry out their life processes (e.g., growing and reproducing) from late spring to early fall, and then to enter hibernation for the 7 cold months.

Reptiles have a dry, either rough or smooth, skin or shell. They feed on insects, worms, fish, and carrion, and the Snapping Turtle can on occasion also capture and devour small birds and mammals. MB's reptile fauna consists of 8 species (Canada has 42) – 2 turtles, one lizard,

R

and 5 snakes. These are the Common Snapping Turtle (*Chelydra serpentina*), weighing up to 16 kg and capable of biting ferociously; Western Painted Turtle (*Chrysemys picta*), with a wonderful pattern of red and yellow on the plastron or belly shell; Northern Prairie Skink (*Eumeces septentrionalis*), which is found only in an isolated pocket of sandy soil in the Carberry Sandhills area; Northern Redbelly Snake (*Storeria occipitomaculata*), only 16 cm long and with a reddish-orange belly; Western Plains Garter Snake (*Thamnophis radix*), a yellow and black snake of the grasslands; Red-sided Garter Snake (*Thamnophis sirtalis*), which prefers woodlands, has blotches of red on the sides, and is famous for its hibernating dens holding the largest concentrations of snakes in the world; Plains Hognose Snake (*Heterodon nasicus*), which has an upturned snout for digging through the sand and specializes on a diet of toads; and Smooth Green Snake (*Opheodrys vernalis*), a thin and delicate little lime-green and yellow snake of the grasslands. All these species reach their northern limit of their ranges in S MB. • REW

REPUBLIC OF MANITOBAH. *See* MANITOBAH, REPUBLIC OF.

RESIDENTIAL SCHOOLS existed in Canada between 1892 and 1960, although a few of the schools remained open until the 1980s. With the support of federal funding, the schools were operated by the ANGLICAN, ROMAN CATHOLIC, PRESBYTERIAN, and UNITED churches. First Nations children between the ages of 6 and 15 were removed from their parents and communities and institutionalized in facilities, often far from their homes or reserves. They were separated from their Indigenous cultural influences, were forbidden to speak their own languages, and often suffered from harsh treatment, poor living conditions, emotional stress, and sexual abuse. Today, even those who view their experience positively still recall the trauma of being separated from their families and cultures.

In MB, the earliest boarding school experiment was introduced in the RED RIVER SETTLEMENT by Reverend John West under the sponsorship of the Anglican-based Church Missionary Society. During his service as a chaplain to the HUDSON'S BAY COMPANY, 1820-23, West boarded a few Aboriginal children from other areas for purposes of instruction and to foster the development of an Aboriginal ministry in NA. By 1833, the school was closed; however, it was the precursor of residential schools. While various church denominations ran mission schools, it was not until the treaties were negotiated in

the 1870s that support for Aboriginal schooling became a federal responsibility.

Recognizing the need to adapt to the growing presence of European Cdns on their traditional lands, many Aboriginal leaders wished to ensure that their children would have a secure and meaningful place in a fast-changing world. By requesting educational support, however, they did not intend to surrender political self-determination nor their right to retain their cultural identities. First Nations leaders expected the federal govt to build and operate day schools on the newly created reserves. However, the govt and churches favoured an education system that imposed assimilation. It was their belief that the children could be best prepared for integration into Cdn society by isolating them from the influences of their parents and home communities.

By the late 1890s, there were 4 industrially oriented boarding schools in MB, where trades such as blacksmithing, shoe-making, harness-making, and commercial printing were taught. There were also 4 boarding schools offering academic education. At least 17 residential schools operated in the province for varying lengths of time between 1874 and 1980. Although "status Indians," as defined in the *Indian Act of Canada*, formed the majority of attendees, MÉTIS children were also accepted, often to boost school enrolment figures in order to increase funding.

Until the 1950s, instruction in residential schools was based on a "half-day system." Ideally, students would spend half the day in classroom study, and the other half learning work skills that they would need in order to earn a living in the Euro-Cdn economy. Daily chores included making beds, cleaning and scrubbing the dormitories, assisting with meals, sewing, and laundry. Outdoor work involved tending gardens, caring for livestock, helping with harvests, cutting wood, and even hunting. While residential schools did

provide various levels of training in domestic skills for girls, and prepared boys for lives as farmers, fishermen, labourers, and the trades, such as carpentry, in practice, the exploitation of child labour was integral to the operation of many of the schools.

Over the same period, the federal govt realized that the original objectives of the residential school system were not being met. Most children left the schools with substandard education and skills, and found that they were suspended between two worlds, ill prepared to enter mainstream Cdn society, and equally at a loss in their home communities. The enduring legacy of the residential school system is felt to this day. An educational policy that has been termed "ethnocide" (an imposed process intended to result in the eradication of a people's culture) has had effects spanning generations of residential school survivors, their children and grandchildren, and their communities.

Demands for public acknowledgement and compensation increased as more residential school survivors shared their stories of the devastating effects of emotional, physical, and sexual abuse. In response, the federal govt and some of the churches involved issued public apologies. Some former students are seeking redress through the criminal justice system. In its 1996 report, the Royal Commission on Aboriginal Peoples brought the trauma and devastation experienced by former residential school students to national attention. The commission not only recommended public apologies to school survivors, but also called for a public inquiry and compensation.

In 1998, the federal govt released a *Statement of Reconciliation* that included an apology to those who were physically or sexually abused. In addition, funding was granted for the creation of the Aboriginal Healing Foundation in support

Aboriginal children at Birtle Residential School, 1925

of healing initiatives across Canada. Three years later, the Department of Indian Residential Schools Resolution Canada was established to manage and bring resolution to abuse claims. In 2003, the National Resolution Framework was introduced and included a litigation process, a commemoration program, and an alternative dispute resolution (ADR) process. The latter is a voluntary, culture-based, holistic way of providing abused students with options to settle claims outside of court.

In 2005, the Assembly of First Nations, under the leadership of National Chief **PHIL FONTAINE**, was party to an agreement-in-principle to provide monetary remuneration and other forms of support for residential school survivors. However, there were concerns that the agreement failed adequately to address and resolve outstanding issues, and to compensate for lost childhoods.

In MB, a unique initiative by the **LONG PLAIN FIRST NATION** will ensure that the history of residential schools in Canada is not forgotten. Built in 1916, the former **PORTAGE LA PRAIRIE** Indian Residential School, now called the Rufus Prince Building, was designated a Provincial Heritage Site in 2005. In 2006, planning was underway for the development of the Indian Residential School Museum of Canada at the site. Its purpose will be to raise public awareness by sharing the historical legacy of residential schools with all Cdns, and to support healing initiatives. • KATHERINE PETTIPAS, WITH ELDER ANN CALLAHAN

RESTON, pop 300, is an unincorporated community 90 km SW of **BRANDON,** on hwy 2. It was named by Scots who came here in the late 1800s from Reston, Berwickshire. A **CPR** station and a post office were established in 1890. Today, Reston is primarily a service and retail centre for surrounding agricultural operations. It has a historical museum. • GPP

RHODES, Donnelly (b Donnelly Rhodes Henry), actor (b Dec 4, 1937, **WINNIPEG**), has appeared in over 100 television series in his 40-year career. Rhodes is the son of playwright Ann Henry, and has an actor brother, Tim Henry. Rhodes was born and raised in Winnipeg, and trained to be a Parks Canada warden. He joined the Royal Canadian Air Force (*see* **MILITARY**) as an airman-mechanic before he began acting. Rhodes studied at the **MANITOBA THEATRE CENTRE** and was a member of the first graduating class of Montreal's National Theatre School. Rhodes made his professional stage debut as Stanley in *Death of a Salesman*. He spent a season at ON's Stratford Festival, and worked on several programs at the CBC. Rhodes became a contract

Donnelly Rhodes, 1960

player for Universal Pictures in the US. His first Hollywood role was in *Alfred Hitchcock Presents*. Rhodes has appeared on TV non-stop since 1965. Rhodes's best-known roles were on *The Young and the Restless* (1973-75), *Soap* (1978-81), *Danger Bay* (1984), *Da Vinci's Inquest* (1998-2005), and *Battlestar Galactica* (2004-06). Rhodes was a 4-time Gemini Award nominee. In 2002, he won a Gemini Award for Best Performance by an Actor in a Continuing Leading Dramatic Role for his work on *Da Vinci's Inquest*. As of writing, he divided his time between Los Angeles and Vancouver. • AMANDA STEPHENS

RIBBONWORM is a type of worm found in marine and fresh waters as well as land habitats. This strange group is remarkable in that it ranges from one mm to 60 m in length, making it one of the longest animals on Earth; however, the body is so elastic that the same ribbonworm can contract to 30 m. Most species are under 20 cm. Many resemble a leech or fluke, creeping by means of tiny hairs called cilia, aided by mucous, although others can swim. A ribbonworm was among the earliest creatures to have evolved a gut with both mouth and anus. The group includes predators, herbivores, scavengers and parasites. The predatory species feed on protozoans, insects, crustaceans, worms and molluscs, tracking them down by following their scent trail. The ribbonworm then rapidly everts a large proboscis (operated by a muscle generating hydrostatic pressure),

which engulfs the prey or winds around it, while a sharp structure (stylet) repeatedly stabs it into submission. A retractor muscle then transfers the food item to the mouth. Other species simply suck the victim's juices. They generally hide in the sand, mud or algae of shallow waters, or under stones. They may reproduce by sexual (externally fertilization) or asexual (splitting or fission) means, and a few species are hermaphrodites. The larvae swim and are the main way species disperse to new areas. Over 1500 species have been named worldwide, but scientists expect the total to reach 3000. The majority of Canada's species (<100) inhabit the 3 coastlines, including several kinds in **HUDSON BAY**. A freshwater species of *Prostoma* (formerly named *P. rubrum*) is widespread in NA and MB, and is found among filamentous algae and plant roots. • REW

RICHARD, Mary, **MÉTIS** community leader, politician (b June 7, 1940, **CAMPERVILLE**). One of the founders of **WINNIPEG**'s Indian and Métis Friendship Centre in the 1960s, Richard became executive director of the organization and is known as a pioneer of the friendship-centre model. Richard became known for her commitment to the restoration and protection of Aboriginal languages in the 1980s. As director of the MB Association for Native Languages, she created retention programs and education kits for universities and schools.

An interest in politics led Richard to a role working with **GARY FILMON**'s govt on its Urban Aboriginal Strategy, and in 1997, she joined Winnipeg's North Main Task Force as co-chair. The committee examined social problems in the **NORTH END**, with Richard backing the idea of an Aboriginal business district. Richard went on to become president of the Aboriginal Council of Winnipeg. In 1999, she ran for the provincial **PROGRESSIVE CONSERVATIVE PARTY** in Point Douglas, finishing 3rd. In 2000, she switched parties to be the Liberal candidate in the federal riding of Winnipeg North Centre, finishing 2nd to the NDP's **JUDY WASYLYCIA-LEIS**.

As chair of the Neeginan Development Corporation, Mary helped found the $2.8-million, Winnipeg Development Agreement–funded Circle of Life Thunderbird House in 2000, based on a 30-year-old idea of the Indian and Métis Friendship Centre. Richard became the CEO and president. She also acted as an elder, working to develop social support systems, including programs to help people fight addictions and to leave the sex trade and gangs (PaaPiiWak program). Richard has also been a board member of **THE FORKS** North Portage Partnership, a member of the Manitoba Round Table on Sustainable Development,

R

and part of the Heritage Council of Manitoba. She was named to the Order of Manitoba in 2000, and received a National Aboriginal Achievement Award in 2003 for her community development work. In 2007, Richard lived in ON. • JT

RICHARDSON, Robert Lorne, journalist, politician (b June 28, 1860, Balderson, Canada West; d Nov 6, 1921, Winnipeg). Educated in Lanark County, ON, Richardson joined the *Globe* in Toronto. He came to **WINNIPEG** in 1882, founding the *Manitoba Sun*, which was absorbed by the *Manitoba Free Press* (later the **WINNIPEG FREE PRESS**) in 1889 while Richardson was city editor. Five weeks later, he founded the **WINNIPEG TRIBUNE**, and divided his attention between journalism and politics. Under Richardson, the *Tribune's* primary point of view was anti-**CPR**. He was elected to the federal Parliament as a **LIBERAL** for Lisgar in 1896. After a dispute with the Liberals, Richardson held his seat as an independent in the 4 following elections in other constituencies. He broke the streak in 1917, when he was elected Unionist Party of Canada member for Springfield. He was an orator and known for his sense of humour, which he displayed in a column titled "The Major." He published 2 novels, *Colin of the Ninth Concession: A Tale of Pioneer Life in Eastern Ontario* (1903) and *The Camerons of Bruce* (1906). • JIM SHILLIDAY

RICHARDSON, William "Bill," radio broadcaster, author (b Sept 11, 1955, **WINNIPEG**). Richardson is a humorist, writer, and the host of several CBC Radio programs. He received his BA from the **U OF W** in 1976, and completed his Master of Library Sciences at UBC in 1980. Before beginning his work as a writer and broadcaster, Richardson worked as a children's librarian for 6 years. He began his broadcasting career in 1992 as a summer replacement program host. In 1997, he became the host of his own show, *Richardson's Roundup*. His columns have appeared in *The Globe and Mail*, *Western Living Magazine*, *The Vancouver Sun*, and *Georgia Straight*. Richardson is also the author of a dozen books, including the 1994 book *Bachelor Brothers' Bed and Breakfast* which won the Stephen Leacock Medal for Humour. His books include picture books and novels for young adults, as well as the books *Scorned and Beloved: Dead of Winter Meetings with Canadian Eccentrics*, and *Waiting for Gertrude*. His novel for young readers, *After Hamelin*, won the Silver Birch Award in ON in 2000. He has moderated CBC's *Canada Reads* since 2003. Richardson received an Honorary Doctor of Law from the U of W in 1998. In 2007, he lived in Vancouver. • AMANDA STEPHENS

Top Left to Right: Founder James Richardson 1819-1892; George A. Richardson (2nd President) 1852-1906; Senator Henry W. Richardson (3rd President) 1855-1918; James Armstrong Richardson (4th President) 1885-1939; Agnes M. (Richardson) Benidickson (Director) 1920-2007; The Honourable James A. Richardson (Chairman 1966-68) 1922-2004;

Bottom left to Right: Muriel S. Richardson (5th President) 1890-1973; Carolyn (Richardson) Hursh (Chairman 2000 -); Hartley T. Richardson (7th President, 1993-); Kathleen M. Richardson (Director) and George T. Richardson (6th President)

RICHARDSON FAMILY is made up of some of Winnipeg's most prominent and affluent citizens, known for their business and philanthropic endeavours. The family's wealth comes largely from private ownership of James Richardson & Sons, Limited. The international holding company began as a one-man grain merchandising business, and has since expanded to include operations in agriculture and food processing, oil and gas exploration, real estate, and financial services. The Richardsons are regarded as patrons of Winnipeg arts and culture, having made substantial philanthropic contributions to support the development of numerous arts organizations and charities. In 1957, the Richardson Century Fund was established to manage the company's charitable donations, renamed the Richardson Foundation in 2000.

JAMES RICHARDSON, businessman, tailor (b Oct 6, 1819, Aughnacloy, Northern Ireland; d Nov 15, 1892, Kingston Township, Upper Canada) started the one-man enterprise that would become the largest grain-exporting firm in the British Commonwealth. James immigrated with his family to Upper Canada in 1822 or 1823. Orphaned at a young age, he was apprenticed as a tailor and opened a shop in Kingston Township in 1844. James often accepted grain as payment, leading to the establishment of his grain trading firm in 1857. The company expanded

quickly, and soon needed to source more grain. James began exploring the vast potential for grain production in MB. In 1883, his company exported the first bushel of western wheat overseas. Upon James' death, his son George Algernon Richardson took over the company, overseeing the construction of the first country grain elevator in Neepawa in 1890. George Richardson died in 1906. His brother Henry Richardson became the third president of the company at age 50.

JAMES ARMSTRONG RICHARDSON, SR, business exec, aviation pioneer, entrepreneur (b Aug 25, 1885, Kingston, ON; d June 26, 1939, Winnipeg) took over after his uncle Henry's death and greatly expanded the Richardson family's holdings. He made entrepreneurial ventures into the fledgling airline and broadcast industries, and relocated JRSL headquarters from Kingston to Winnipeg, establishing the family's influential position in MB. He was educated at Queen's U, and entered the family business in 1906 following the death of his father George A. Richardson. James Sr. was one of the most powerful grain merchants on the Winnipeg Grain Exchange (*see* **WINNIPEG COMMODITY EXCHANGE**). He became the vice president of JRSL in 1912, and president in 1919.

In 1926, James Sr started Western Canada Airways Limited to develop the mining potential in the Cdn shield, starting out with a single Fokker Universal aircraft. WCA quickly began acquiring other aircrafts and, in 1930, joined with several small air services to form Canadian Airways Limited, Canada's first national airline. James Sr. envisioned a single airline that would provide coast-to-coast transportation and mail service. However, his plans were thwarted by the formation of Trans-Canada Airlines in 1937, a rival federal govt-owned air service that soon dominated the air transport industry. The same year he started WCA, James Sr received a license to operate a radio station in SK, becoming one of the Prairie's first private broadcasters. The station was prohibited from operating in Winnipeg until 1933, after the federal govt had vetoed MB's radio licensing arrangement that gave MTS a monopoly on radio broadcasts. The Winnipeg station operated under the name CJRC, and provided farmers with crop reports, grain prices, and weather updates. James Sr was a director of numerous companies, including the CPR, the Canadian Bank of Commerce, Great-West Life Assurance Co, International Nickel, National Trust and Canadian Vickers. He was also a president of the Winnipeg Grain Exchange. He died suddenly at the age of 54. For his role in Canadian aviation, Richardson was recognized through the renaming of Winnipeg's International Airport as James Armstrong Richardson International Airport, the first private citizen to ever receive such an honour.

MURIEL SPRAGUE RICHARDSON, businesswoman, volunteer leader (b March 26, 1890, Belleville ON; d Jan 8 1973, Winnipeg) was the first Cdn woman to lead a major corporation. She was also known for her volunteer work, establishing the family's tradition of quiet philanthropy. Muriel arrived in Winnipeg at the time of her marriage in 1919. She became president of JRSL following the death of her husband James Sr. In addition to running the company, Muriel was active in the war effort during WWII, volunteered with several community organizations, and served on the board of regents at United College from 1940-51. She established the Richardson Foundation in 1957, and was an honorary chair on many local and national charities. She was awarded an honorary degree from the **U OF M** in 1958. She retired as president of JRSL in 1966, leaving the company to her children: James, George, Kathleen and Agnes.

JAMES ARMSTRONG RICHARDSON, JR, politician, business executive (b March 28, 1922, Winnipeg; d May 17, 2004, Winnipeg) was a voice for western interests in Ottawa as a minister in Pierre Trudeau's cabinet. He attended St. John's-Ravenscourt School and then Queen's

U, graduating with a BA in political science and economics. He entered the RCAF in 1943, and logged over 1000 hours on air force patrol in the North Atlantic, earning several medals. He joined the family company upon leaving the service. James Jr enjoyed sailing, and represented western Canada at the Olympic trials in 1948. In 1949, he married Shirley Anne Rooper of Surrey, UK. At 32, James Jr became the youngest director to have been appointed at the CIBC. He was also a director of Inco, Investors Group, HBC, and CPR. He was chairman and CEO of JRSL from 1966-68, and then resigned to enter federal politics. He was elected to represent Winnipeg South 3 times, and his influence helped bring the Royal Canadian Mint to Winnipeg. He served in Trudeau's cabinet for 10 years, as minister without portfolio in 1968, and then as minister of supply and services from 1969-72. After the 1972 election, beating PC Sterling Lyon by 1266 votes, he was appointed minister of national defence, but resigned in protest over language policies. He crossed the floor in 1978 to sit as an independent, and then left politics in 1980 to returned to work in the family company. James Jr helped found the Canada West Council. His career as a politician and businessman earned him several awards, including the Queen Elizabeth II Silver Jubilee Medal in 1975.

GEORGE TAYLOR RICHARDSON, business executive (b Sept 22, 1924, Winnipeg) built the first modern skyscraper in Winnipeg. He entered the family business after graduating from the U of M in 1946, becoming vice-president in 1954 and president in 1966. The company's most visible symbol, the Richardson Building in downtown Winnipeg, was built in 1969. George could often be seen piloting the family's helicopter to the top of the skyscraper on his way to and from work. George also oversaw the merger of Richardson Securities, a financial subsidiary of JRSL, with Greenshields Inc in 1982. Richardson Greenshields became the largest privately owned investment and contracts dealer in Canada, at its peak employing more than 700 investment advisors in 70 offices worldwide, serving over 400,000 clients with assets under management of $18 billion under administration.

George has served on many corporate boards, including Dupont Canada, Canada Packers, Inco, Tundra Oil & Gas Ltd. George also served as Vice-President of the CIBC and chairman of Great-West Life Assurance Co. He was the first Cdn-born governor of the HBC, a position he held from 1970-82. George's philanthropic endeavours included supporting the Health Sciences Centre Foundation and the U of M, where he served on the board of governors from 1955-66. He helped

found the Manitoba Museum (then the Manitoba Museum of Man and Nature), and was instrumental in bringing the Nonsuch replica to the museum. He retired in 2000. He is a member of the Order of Manitoba, and was made a member of the Order of Canada in 2002. His wife Tannis is also a member of the Order of Canada.

KATHLEEN M. RICHARDSON, philanthropist (b 1928) served as a director of James Richardson & Sons, Limited for 53 years and is also recognized as a patron of the arts in MB. She is most well known for her support of the RWB. Since the 1950s, her generous contributions have helped the dance company maintain its reputation as one of NA's premier dance companies. She was president of the RWB from 1957-61, and has been honorary chair since 1963. She has earned numerous awards and honours for her philanthropy, including the Edmund C. Bovey award for support of the arts as well as the Distinguished Alumni Award from the U of M. In 1994, Kathleen became a companion of the order of Canada. She is a past member of the Manitoba Arts Council, Winnipeg Art Gallery, and the Pan Am Games Society. Through the Kathleen M. Richardson Foundation, she has also financially supported the Winnipeg Symphony Orchestra, the Manitoba Theatre Centre, Contemporary Dancers of Canada and the Prairie Theatre Exchange. Already a member of the Order of Canada, she was made a member of the Order of Manitoba in 2005.

HARTLEY T. RICHARDSON, business executive (b 1954, Winnipeg) has served as president and CEO of JRSL since 1993. He graduated from the U of M with a commerce degree, and joined the family firm in 1978. He has held several positions within the grain and real estate operations of JRSL. In 1993, he became president of the company, succeeding his father, George. In 2003, Hartley expanded the company's interests into financial management with the launch of Richardson Financial Group which operates two distinct divisions, Richardson Capital Limited, focused on private equity investing, and Richardson Partners Financial Limited, which provides money management for high net worth clients. He is a director of CPR Ltd, Railpower Technologies Corp, BA Energy, Angiotech Pharmaceuticals Inc, Neuromed Technologies Inc and SemBioSys Genetics, Inc. He is chairman of the Business Council of Manitoba, and vice-chairman of the Canadian Council of Chief Executives. He was awarded an honorary doctorate from the U of M in 2004 and, in 2007, he was awarded membership to the Order of Canada.
● MICHELLE DOBROVOLNY

RICHER, pop 500, is a community 55 km ESE of **WINNIPEG** on the Trans-Canada Highway. Settlement began after the Dawson Trail passed through here, an event remembered in the name of the local weekly, *The Dawson Trail Dispatch*. The community was originally called St-Juliende-Chambord, and was renamed Richer after a local politician after the post office opened in 1900. The economic foundation of Richer is service and retail support for the nearby **FORESTRY** industry, though it is also a bedroom community for **STEINBACH** and Winnipeg, and there is an elementary school here. **TOURISM** is also important, with several campgrounds in the area. Snowmobiling and hunting are also popular activities here. • GPP

RIDD, John Carl "King Carl," academic, activist, **BASKETBALL** player (b Aug 17, 1929, **WINNIPEG**; d Mar 29, 2003 Winnipeg). An outstanding basketball player through the 1940s and '50s, Ridd was leading scorer for the **U OF M** team from 1947-51. He was a member of the 1952 Cdn Olympic team, and in 1954, was the leading scorer for the Winnipeg Paulins when they won the national championship. At that year's World Basketball Championships in Brazil, Ridd was the only Canadian selected to the All-Star team. He was inducted into the Canadian Basketball Hall of Fame in 1980 and the **MANITOBA SPORTS HALL OF FAME** in 1983. Offered a professional contract by the Milwaukee Hawks of the National Basketball Association in the 1950s, Ridd turned it down to pursue an academic career, including a MA from the U of M in English (1956), a bachelor of divinity from United College (1963; *see* **U OF W**), and a doctorate in religion and literature from Drew U in Madison, NJ (1977).

An ordained minister in the **UNITED CHURCH**, he served the **EMERSON/DOMINION CITY** charge from

Carl Ridd

1958-63. In 1966, Ridd returned to Winnipeg to establish and head the Department of Religious Studies at the new U of W. Ridd became known for his signature course, Religious Quest in the Modern Age, which he taught over his 3 decades at the U, introducing thousands of students to broader existential questions. In 1972, he recorded 5 lectures of this course to be broadcast on the CTV network. He won the Robson Award for Excellence in Teaching from U of W in 1973, and in 1989, was awarded the Clarence Atchison Award for Excellence in Community Service.

Outside the classroom, Ridd was a tireless activist and community lobbyist, in areas such as human rights, economic and social justice, ecology, Muslim-Christian dialogue, and the well-being of the inner city. He was involved in the struggle for justice of the people of Central America, and travelled to El Salvador in 1982 as a member of the Inter-Church Committee on Human Rights. He was one of the founders of Project Peacemakers, a local justice and peace group, and volunteered at Augustine Oak Table, the inner-city community ministry of his church, Augustine United. He was a member of the Manitoba Environmental Council from 1980-85, and chaired the Manitoba Energy Council from 1983-88. In 2003, he was posthumously honoured with the **JOSEPH ZUKEN** Citizen Activist Award, and was inducted into the Citizen's Hall of Fame at **ASSINIBOINE PARK** for his public affairs, volunteer, and professional work in 2004. A lover of words and etymology, and a prolific writer, Ridd also authored hundreds of articles and addresses on a wide range of topics, including literature, culture, religion, social and political life, economics, athletics, nuclear waste disposal, and ethics.

Ridd retired from U of W in 1995, and for the next 8 years, coached basketball at Rossbrook House, an inner-city drop-in centre; edited *The Eye-Opener*, a 4-page quarterly on economics, ecology, and community; and remained an outspoken advocate of peace and justice concerns. Just weeks before his death, he spoke at a large rally in downtown Winnipeg opposing the Iraq War. • BRENDA SUDERMAN

RIDDELL, Clayton Howard, oil baron, geologist (b July 13, 1937, **TREHERNE**). Chairman, CEO, and founder of the oil and gas company Paramount Resources Ltd, Riddell made his fortune in the lucrative AB oil sands. He is one of the richest Cdn oil barons. His origins, however, are modest. The son of a mailman, Riddell entered the oil business after graduating with a BSc in geology from the **U OF M** in 1959. He worked as an exploration geologist for Standard Oil of California until 1969, when he struck out on his

own as an independent energy consultant. With his background in earth sciences, Riddell was able to correctly perceive the potential for shallow gas exploitation in the Devonian sub-crop of northeastern AB, an area previously thought to rich in bitumen only. Riddell drilled his first well in the region in 1976, uncovering billions of cubic feet of natural gas, and earning him a fortune. His company Paramount went public in 1978, and expanded into areas of western AB as well as the NWT. As of 2007, he was continuing to head up the company, making him one of Canada's longest-serving CEOs of an energy company. Following his $10 million donation in 2005 to the U of M, the university's faculty of Environment, Earth, and Resources was renamed in his honour. He is a co-owner of the Calgary Flames as well as several Calgary restaurants. He also breeds horses on his 192 ha ranch in AB. • MD

RIDING MOUNTAIN NATIONAL PARK was set aside by the federal govt for summer recreation and tourism. At different times, however, it has also hosted a **PoW** camp, the legendary faker and conservationist **GREY OWL**, and a relief work camp during the **GREAT DEPRESSION**.

Before its establishment as a national park, Riding Mountain was home to **CREE** and Assiniboine peoples. Europeans started exploring and trading on the plains around Riding Mountain in the early 18th century, around the same time **OJIBWAY** migrated from the Great Lakes to the area. By the beginning of the 19th century, the area was surrounded by **FUR TRADING** posts. Horseback was the easiest way to explore the rugged terrain for furs and game, and the earlier name of Fort Dauphin Hill was changed to Riding Mountain.

A century and a half of exploitation had a dire effect on the animal population in the Riding Mountain area, with predator species such as otter, marten, and wolverines (*see* **WEASELS**) disappearing completely. In 1922, Riding Mountain became a game reserve and the hunting and trapping of animals was prohibited. Extensive research programs on **WOLVES** and black **BEARS** have since been established in the park. These apex predators are among 60 mammal species indigenous to the park, including **COYOTES**, **BEAVERS**, and **LYNX**. The park also houses 260 of the 380 **BIRD** species normally found in the province.

Settlers from eastern Canada, Europe, and the US represented the next wave to establish themselves on the plains around Riding Mountain after the railway reached **BRANDON** in 1881. Their use of wood for buildings, **RAILWAYS**, and firewood were hard on the environment and toward the close of the 19th century, those living

Clear Lake at Riding Mountain

in the highland resettled and the area was made into a forest reserve.

Riding Mountain was the first national park in MB, officially recognized in 1930 and opened in 1933. The quick pace of development during the park's first decade can be credited to make work initiatives the govt established in the 1930s as a way of employing the large labour force that was out of work during the depression. Riding Mountain had the largest relief camp of all the national parks with over 1200 men assigned to various projects between 1934 and 1935.

In the **GREAT DEPRESSION**, many of the major roads, parking areas, and buildings were constructed as make-work projects. Among other jobs, the golf course was cleared, the telephone system extended and the foundation for a museum was built. Each relief worker was paid only $5 per month. Aid during the Depression also took the form of funding through the public works construction act. A large portion of these funds were used to construct buildings in the park. Many of the craftsmen who were hired to design and construct these buildings were Swedish immigrants who had settled in the vicinity of the park. Their expertise in log and stone construction and had great influence over the style of architecture used for park buildings.

During WWII, federal funding was redirected in support of the war effort, and the park's development was not a priority. A fuel shortage brought on by the requirements of the war left many Canadians dependent on cordwood. To alleviate hardship, Riding Mountain was made accessible once again to **RURAL** communities for the cutting of firewood. Also during WWII, **GERMAN** prisoners were held at Whitewater Lake from 1943-45. Due to its remoteness, Riding Mountain was considered an ideal place to have a prisoner-of-war camp. With

450 German soldiers, captured in North Africa, the camp was one of the largest of its kind in Canada. Though no walls or fences enclosed it, escape was considered unlikely. The German soldiers were also used as firefighters in light of the shortage of manpower in Canada. Some were even billeted with nearby farmers, and made lasting friendships with the families they lived with and worked for.

Riding Mountain National Park is the 2nd-oldest national park in Canada and maintains its original purpose as a scenic spot for summer recreation. Within the park's 2979 km² there are features numerous hiking trails, lakes, campgrounds, a golf course, **BISON** reserve, horseback riding trails, and panoramic views of the prairie.
● JILL SEXSMITH

RIDLEY INC is one of NA's largest manufacturers and distributors of feeds and health products for livestock and poultry. The company, which maintains dual headquarters in **WINNIPEG** and Mankato, MN, was formed in 1994 when Ridley Corporation Limited, Australia's largest commercial stockfeed manufacturer and salt producer/refiner, purchased Winnipeg-based Feed-Rite, one of western Canada's largest feed suppliers. Three years after acquiring Feed-Rite, which was founded in 1939 by businessman Cyril A. Anderson, Ridley expanded into the US with the acquisition of one of that country's oldest feed milling operations, Hubbard Milling Company of Mankato. That was followed 3 years later by the acquisition of another major US livestock feed manufacturer – the Wayne Feeds Division of the ContiGroup of Companies. Two more companies were added in 2002 with the acquisition of McCauley Bros., a manufacturer of equine feeds and nutritional supplements in Versailles, KY, and Saskatoon-based Shamrock Feeds Ltd.

Shamrock, which also manufactured livestock feed, was subsequently integrated into the company's Feed-Rite operations. As of early 2005, Ridley owned and operated 41 production plants in NA and employed about 1000 people. ● MM

RIEL, Louis David, visionary, **MÉTIS** leader, (b Oct 22, 1844, **ST. BONIFACE**; d Nov 16, 1885, Regina) was born in the **RED RIVER SETTLEMENT** to a leading Francophone family. His father, **LOUIS RIEL SR**, a SK-born miller, was a powerful spokesman for the Métis during the 1840s in their ongoing struggle with the **HUDSON'S BAY COMPANY**. His mother, Julie Lagimodière, was the daughter of **JEAN-BAPTISTE LAGIMODIÈRE**, voyageur and founder of what would become St. Boniface, and **MARIE-ANNE GABOURY**, the first European woman to settle in the W.

The young Riel's Aboriginal ancestry was minimal, perhaps one-eighth, but he grew up speaking **CREE**, and he always thought of himself as a Métis. A bright child, Louis attended school from the age of 7, and at 13 was among a group of young men picked by Bishop **ALEXANDRE-ANTONIN TACHÉ** to go to QC to prepare for holy orders. He initially did well in Montreal, but a combination of events – the death of his father in 1864; a love affair that was ended by her parents who disapproved of their daughter marrying a Métis; and concerns about the priesthood – unsettled him, and he returned via the US to Red River in 1869.

Riel first came to the attention of the public with a letter (signed "L. R.") published in the QC newspaper *Nouveau Monde* defending Red River and the Métis from criticisms by recent arrival **CHARLES MAIR**. A few months later, he met with Lt Col John Stoughton Dennis (father of Col John Stoughton Dennis Jr), the chief surveyor for the Cdn govt, which was then in the process of annexing the former **HBC** territory of **RUPERT'S LAND**. He asked for information on behalf of "his brethren the half-breeds," and obviously was not satisfied by the answers. A few days later, he was apparently one of "Two Métis" who drafted a letter to the QC newspaper *Le Courrier de Saint-Hyacinthe* complaining that the Cdn survey was illegal and disregarded local opinion.

On Oct 11, 1869, Riel headed a group of 18 mixed-bloods who blocked a survey team on the property of André Nault. From this point on, HBC authorities viewed Riel as the spokesman for the Métis, although officially the leader of the opposition was a carpenter named John Bruce. When a meeting was held on Oct 20, the National Committee of the Métis of Red River named Riel its secretary. This meeting formally ordered **WILLIAM MCDOUGALL**, the man chosen by Canada to be the new lt gov of the annexed territories, to remain

585

out of them. Riel and Bruce travelled around Red River, attempting to raise support for their resistance to Cdn annexation without a negotiation of terms based on resident rights. The **COUNCIL OF ASSINIBOIA** refused to support them, deciding instead to sit on its hands.

On Nov 2, the Métis council seized **UPPER FORT GARRY**, meeting no resistance from the HBC. The Métis then invited 12 representatives from the Anglophone community to meet with 12 Métis on Nov 16 to negotiate. At this meeting, which lasted for some days, Riel did most of the talking, attempting to convince the Anglophones to join the Métis in keeping out the Canadians unless gov McDougall agreed to confirm existing land rights and recognize **ABORIGINAL RIGHTS**. This "Council of 24" met sporadically without agreement through Nov, while Riel consolidated the Métis power locally.

On the morning of Dec 7, Riel and his armed horsemen forced the surrender of more than 40 Canadians barricaded in the house of Dr. **JOHN CHRISTIAN SCHULTZ**. The prisoners were sent to Upper Fort Garry. A day later, John Bruce and Riel issued a proclamation refusing to recognize the authority of Canada, and establishing a provisional govt on Nov 24. The provisional govt was publicly proclaimed at **THE FORKS** on Dec 10. In hindsight, Riel might have been better advised to take over the govt of the HBC, which was still technically the legal authority in Red River; still, he had brought the settlement to the point of full-blown resistance without the loss of a single life. Riel now needed to persuade Canada to negotiate with the provisional govt on the basis of the pre-existing rights of the residents. While he sought to bring this about, he had to provide the settlement with effective govt under a better system than martial law and defend it against hostile Aboriginals. The chief problem with negotiation was the need to find somebody authorized to negotiate. Several Cdn emissaries were present in the settlement, but none had real authority to deal with the rebels.

While Riel attempted to bring Anglophones into his govt, a group of prisoners, headed by Mair, Schultz, and a young Irish-born Cdn named **THOMAS SCOTT**, all escaped from Upper Fort Garry. A Toronto reporter expelled from the settlement by Riel offered a nasty and negative portrait of Riel that appeared in the Eastern newspapers, even insulting his appearance.

During various meetings, Riel proved unable to maintain a solid front among the Métis, and he accused those who opposed him of being "traitors." Riel's loss of temper appeared to be a result of not getting his own way, and much of his subsequent behaviour through Feb and early March seems to have been motivated by pique and frustration at not being able to get people to do as he wanted. He put the dying gov McTavish under armed guard and threatened to shoot him. Riel would escalate this sort of behaviour over the weeks ahead.

A serious threat to the peace of Red River came from an armed party from **PORTAGE LA PRAIRIE**, which marched through Winnipeg to Kildonan to meet up with several other armed parties. They demanded the release of the prisoners, and, when that was achieved, marched back through Winnipeg only to be captured by the Métis outside the walls of Upper Fort Garry. Riel became ill at the end of Feb, and he increasingly threatened the prisoners. The culmination of this process was the trial and punishment meted out to Scott, who had been a prisoner in Dec (and escaped) and was captured again in Feb. Exactly what Scott did was never clear, but he clearly aggravated Riel and the Métis guards. He was charged with a series of offences and tried by an informal court with irregular proceedings, which sentenced him summarily to be shot on March 5. That sentence was carried out, despite much pleading for Scott's life by local clergymen and others, probably because Riel thought a statement of firmness was required, and Scott was an unimportant stranger. "We must make Canada respect us," Riel told **DONALD A. SMITH**.

Scott's execution changed entirely both the nature of the **RED RIVER RESISTANCE** and the subsequent career of Louis Riel. It shocked the Red River community, enabled the govt of PM Sir John A. Macdonald to treat the provisional govt as violent rebels, and forced Riel and his associates into years of exile in the US as accused murderers. Shooting Scott was Riel's first serious miscalculation, but it was one from which he never recovered. Informal negotiations between Canada and the delegates of the provisional govt were carried on in Ottawa in the spring of 1870, and resulted in the *Manitoba Act*, which created the small province of Manitoba and set aside 565,000 ha (1,400,000 ac) of land for the Métis, though they have still never received this land. The provisional govt's negotiators had been instructed not to continue discussion without the previous concession of a complete amnesty for the insurgents, but allowed themselves to be fobbed off with informal promises rather than a guarantee. As a result, Riel and his closest lieutenants found themselves fugitives from justice, not leaders of the new administration.

The period 1870-75 was one of much anguish for Riel. His efforts were chiefly devoted to gaining an amnesty and to attempting to protect the place of the Métis in the new province.

He spent most of these years in the US. Given his popular support, both in MB and in QC, Ottawa could not afford to take him into custody; but hostility to him in ON prevented any resolution of his situation. He was elected as an Independent to the Cdn Parliament 3 times, but could never take his seat. The arrest and trial of his lieutenant **AMBROISE-DIDYME LÉPINE** for the murder of Scott – a jury found Lépine guilty – finally forced the administration of PM Alexander Mackenzie to pass amnesty legislation for Riel and his colleagues in 1875. Part of the conditions involved Riel living in exile for 5 years. Riel responded to the conditional amnesty by suffering a series of nervous breakdowns and spending some months in mental asylums in QC. He had a series of religious experiences – though never a "vision" – and became obsessed with his religious mission as prophet of a new Christianity.

Louis Riel, 1876

When Riel recovered his health, he moved to MT, married, and took US citizenship, apparently intending to make a new life, teaching school for a living. But he was unable to refuse an invitation in 1884 to return to the Northwest to lead another resistance – this one of white settlers, Aboriginals, and Métis – against the Cdn govt. He successfully organized a petition to the Cdn govt that was sent to Ottawa in mid-Dec 1884, but which Sir John A. Macdonald ignored. In Mar 1885, Riel announced the formation of a new provisional govt. In late March, at Duck Lake in what is now SK, the Métis led by Gabriel Dumont defeated a contingent of **NORTH-WEST MOUNTED POLICE** and a handful of Anglophone settlers. As the presence of the settlers demonstrated, Riel was unable to unite opposition to Canada as he had in 1870. The resistance would be led solely by armed Métis and a few

Aboriginal leaders, who operated without much co-ordination against a large Cdn force that arrived eventually from the E. The rebels were easily defeated at the Battle of Batoche, SK. Riel surrendered on May 15 and was brought to trial for high treason in Regina.

The highly politicized trial of Riel became part of his legend. The Crown focused on Riel in order to act with leniency against his associates. Riel's lawyers wanted to defend him on grounds of insanity – the preponderance of medical opinion at the trial insisted that he was mad – but Riel refused to accept this defence and explicitly argued against it before the jury, although he was still having inner religious experiences. He convinced the jury of 6 that he was sane, and was found guilty with a recommendation for mercy. The presiding magistrate ignored the recommendation (a guilty verdict of high treason carried a mandatory death sentence) and sentenced him to death by hanging. Despite considerable public pressure from his supporters in both the US and Canada, Sir John A. Macdonald's govt chose to carry out the execution. Riel might have been saved, had the US govt chosen to intercede on behalf of one of its citizens. The US refused to plead for his life, however, and Riel was hanged on Nov 16, 1885, in Regina. • J. M. BUMSTED

RIEL, Louis (Sr) (b 1817, SK, d 1864, **RED RIVER SETTLEMENT**) **MÉTIS** leader, father of **LOUIS RIEL JR**. Born at Ile-a-la-Crosse in what is now SK, he went east to Lower Canada with his family in 1822 and was educated there as a wool carder. At age 21 he joined the **HBC** at Rainy River, where he served from 1838 to 1840. He later returned to Lower Canada for a brief spell with the Oblates, but he left the order for want of a sense of vocation. When he came west to Red River, he married Julie, the daughter of **JEAN-BAPTISTE LAGMODIÈRE** and **MARIE-ANNE GABOURY**. He supported the free traders within the Metis, and also insisted that the **COUNCIL OF ASSINIBOIA** have Métis representation and that the courts of Red River employ French. He was less successful in business; a textile mill that he opened with equipment purchased in the East failed in the late 1850s. • JMB

RIEL, Sara, nun (b Oct 11, 1848, **ST. BONIFACE**; d Dec 27, 1883, Île-à-la-Crosse, SK). Sara Riel was one of the first Métis to join the **GREY NUNS**. She was the daughter of **LOUIS RIEL SR** and Julie Lagimodière, and the sister of **LOUIS RIEL**. She had a profound influence on her brother as revealed through their many correspondences which document an intimate friendship based on their shared devotion to the **ROMAN CATHOLIC** faith. In

1871, she joined a group of missionaries destined for Île-à-la-Crosse, the birthplace of her father. She suffered a near-death experience the following year after coming down with pneumonia. Overcoming her illness through prayer to Sister Marie-Marguerite, Riel then changed her name to honour her patron saint. This caused some confusion among family members, who would refer to her alternately as Sister Sara or Marguerite-Marie. • MD

RIEL DIET was the alimentary regime followed by MB's founding father, **LOUIS RIEL**, a devout **ROMAN CATHOLIC** whose strict religious convictions permeated his eating habits. Riel's ascetic approach to food is well-documented as he often makes mention of his diet in his personal journals, particularly in the section titled "Prophetic Admonitions" in which he chastises himself for eating too much. Though Riel's abstemious diet was likely the result of his rigid morality, he also complained of a weak stomach, and may have preferred foods that would alleviate his digestive issues. He would often cook blood into his broth in order to fortify himself, and recommended bean soup, ripe peas and corn as foods to be favoured by those seeking to improve their constitution. Peas especially were thought by Riel to add to his physical and spiritual strength. Alcohol, of course, was something in which Riel rarely, if ever, indulged. His rather Spartan diet was followed up to his final moments; for the last meal before his execution, Riel requested only 3 eggs accompanied by a glass of milk. • MD

RILEY, Martin, BASKETBALL player, (b May 8, 1955, **WINNIPEG**) helped revive Cdn basketball during the mid-1970s when public interest in the sport was at an all-time low. Riley attended Sisler High School where, as captain of the Spartans squad, he led the team to a MB record-setting no-loss season and a provincial championship. The 5'11" point guard earned a spot on the Cdn team following that year's triumph, though the national team's future looked grim as the federal govt contemplated whether to continue funding a national basketball team. Then Riley's performance at the 1976 Montreal Olympics led to a 4th place finish for the Cdn team, which secured the govt's support for the national basketball program. That same year, he played for the **U OF M** Bisons as they won the national championship, receiving the Mike Moser Trophy for top player. He played professionally in Argentina during the 1980-81 season, before returning to MB to coach the U of M team from 1981-84, and then working in the basketball programs of several Winnipeg high schools. • MD

RILEY FAMILY. The Riley family is one of MB's oldest and most influential business families, with longstanding ties to Canada's insurance and brewing industries, as well as sports.

ROBERT THOMAS RILEY, insurance exec (b July, 1851, Beverley, UK; d July 1944, **WINNIPEG**. As one of the founders of Great-West Life Assurance Company (*see* **GREAT-WEST LIFECO INC**.), Riley was one of **WINNIPEG**'s most successful businessmen, though he came from modest beginnings. Born to Quaker parents, he attended school until the age of 16, and then worked as a civil servant. His father had some involvement in shipping news, and published a paper called the *Maritime Gazette*. He also owned a small interest in UK's *Daily Telegraph and Courier*, a newspaper which would again come into the family's possession in 1985, when it was purchased by Riley's great-grandson, media mogul Conrad Black.

Riley, an ambitious and energetic man, quickly became bored with work in Britain's War Office. He left the UK at the age of 22, and spent several years in ON. He moved to Winnipeg in 1881, and was involved in real estate as well a number of other business ventures. He was elected to public office as a Winnipeg councillor in 1887, and had many connections within the city's business community. In addition to Great-West Life, Riley was involved in the establishment of the Northern Trusts Company, Northern Mortgage Company, and Canadian Fire Insurance Company. Riley strongly believed in the future of his adopted city. As part of the directorate of the Union Bank, Riley successfully initiated plans to have its headquarters moved to Winnipeg.

CONRAD STEPHENSON RILEY, rower, businessman (b Aug 25, 1875, at sea on *S.S. Ontario*; d Nov 20, 1960, Winnipeg) was a prominent insurance exec, and also an accomplished athlete. He led a Winnipeg rowing crew to victory at the world's most prestigious rowing event, the Henley Royal Regatta in the UK.

Riley, who was born at sea on his mother's return voyage from a trip to her native UK, grew up in Winnipeg. An avid sportsman, he joined the Winnipeg Rowing Club in 1893, and became an accomplished rower. In 1902, Riley and the WRC crew competed in the US championship in Philadelphia, where they won both the intermediate and the senior eights events. Bolstered by this success, the WRC then sent a crew to the Henley Royal Regatta in 1904. With Riley in bow position, the WRC crew placed 2nd, losing only to an elite Cambridge crew. In 1910, the WRC crew entered the Henley again, this time defeating a favoured UK team in the preliminaries before claiming victory over a crew from

587

Germany, and becoming the first Canadians to win the Stewards' Challenge Cup. Their success continued in 1912 at the National Association of Amateur Oarsmen Regatta, where the WRC crew set a record by winning every race. Other notable competitions include a race against the American Harvard team for the Henley's Grand Challenge Cup, where the WRC crew narrowly lost by ¾ of a length. In total, Riley won 7 American sweep oar championships over the course of his athletic career. He rowed his last race at age 70. He was inducted into Canada's Sports Hall of Fame in 1974, and the Manitoba Sports Hall of Fame in 1982.

Conrad Stephenson Riley

Riley served in the artillery division during WWI. As a businessman, he built on his father's success. Riley was director not only of Great-West Life Assurance, but the Royal Bank, Winnipeg Electric Company, Beaver Lumber Company, and Montreal Trust. By the 1940s, media were listing him as one of 50 men in control of Cdn finances. His daughter Jean Elizabeth Riley was married to beer baron George Montegu Black Jr.

WILLIAM CULVER RILEY, insurance exec (b June 21, 1907, Winnipeg, d 1970, Ottawa) was a visionary businessman who spearheaded the campaign for a new football stadium and hockey arena in Winnipeg in the 1950s. Raised in Winnipeg, Riley was an avid rower like his father Conrad Riley. He attended McGill U, and then returned to Winnipeg to work in his father's firm, the Canadian Fire Insurance Company. During

WWII, he served with the Royal Canadian Ordnance Corps, rising through the ranks to become LCol. He was awarded the Order of the British Empire for his service.

As president of the Winnipeg Football Club in the 1950s, Riley initiated plans to replace Winnipeg's only major sports facilities, the Amphitheatre Rink and Osborne Stadium, which were falling apart and failed to meet the needs of Winnipeg's growing population. The new stadium was completed in 1953, and the arena in 1955. As president of Winnipeg Enterprises Corporation, Riley oversaw construction of the Polo Park stadium-arena sports complex, and maintained ownership as landlord. He was a commissioner on the Flood Cost-Benefit Study from 1956-58, and was president of the organizing committee for the 1967 PAN AM GAMES. He was a director for the Royal Bank, Great-West Lifeco Inc, Dominion Bronze, Union Oil, and Southam Press. For his work as an organizer and chairperson, Riley was inducted into the Manitoba Sports Hall of Fame in 1981.

HUGH SANFORD "SANDY" RILEY, business exec (b 1951 Montreal) was born in Montreal, but maintained close ties with his Winnipeg family, including his uncle William Culver Riley. He graduated from Queen's U, and then Osgoode Hall Law School. He was a member of the national sailing team from 1972-80, competing in the 1976 Olympics. After several years as a lawyer in Winnipeg, he spent some time working in Toronto and Montreal before eventually returning to Winnipeg as president and CEO of Investors Group Inc.

As head of Canada's largest mutual fund distributor from 1992-2001, Riley built up the company's assets from $10 billion to $75 billion, overseeing the $4-billion acquisition of MacKenzie Financial Corporation. He was chairman of the 1999 Pan Am Games and the United Way Campaign. He is closely tied with the Richardson Family, and helped to establish financial divisions of the family's business with Richardson Capital and Richardson Partners Financial. He has received many awards for his contributions to the Winnipeg community, including the MB Lieutenant Governor Award in 2002. He is a member of the Order of Canada, as well as the Order of the Buffalo Hunt. As of 2007, he was president of Richardson Financial Group, and chancellor of the U of W. He is also a member of several corporate boards including Molson Coors Brewing Company and The North West Company.
• MICHELLE DOBROVOLNY

RINDISBACHER, Peter, artist (b April 12, 1806, Eggiwil, Switzerland; d Aug 12, 1834, St. Louis, MO) depicted many MB First Nations people in his artwork. He came with his family,

German-speaking LUTHERANS, to the RED RIVER SETTLEMENT in 1821. He became a clerk for the HBC, but supplemented the family income with his watercolour painting, mainly of life around the settlement. Word of his talent spread, and he received commissions from as far away as London, often filling them by making traced copies of his own works and finishing them in watercolour. Robert Pelly had oil copies made in England of some of his works, and colour lithographs of these were sold without remuneration to the artist. Most of Rindisbacher's subjects were the Aboriginal people of the settlement, rather than his own people. The Rindisbachers and other Swiss fled the colony after the flood of 1826, re-establishing themselves in the US. Rindisbacher went to WI and later to St. Louis, where he became a successful artist. He died of cholera. A collection of his work, given to St. John's College (see U OF M), was later sold to the Provincial Library and Archives. • JMB

RINGETTE was originally conceived as a less-aggressive women's alternative to HOCKEY. Though it resembles hockey, it is played with a straight stick and rubber ring, and has no intentional body contact. It was developed in ON during the 1960s; MB was the 2nd province to adopt the sport, with the first team organized in 1967. A 3-team league was developed in 1970, and the Manitoba Ringette Association (MRA) was formed in 1973. The first invitational tournament was held in WINNIPEG the following year. The MRA joined the Manitoba Sports Federation in 1976, bringing increased organization and funding for the sport's development. A rural team was organized that year in MIAMI. In 1978, ringette was introduced to the Manitoba Winter Games. The first Cdn Ringette Championship was held in Winnipeg in 1979. A Winnipeg team travelled to Finland that year, and was the first Cdn team to play the sport in Europe. By 1981, there were 182 teams in MB, comprising 2355 players. The Debs of Fort Richmond, coached by Garry Johnson, was the first MB team to win the Cdn championship. The St. James Ringette Association introduced ringette to the USSR in 1985. The Manitoba Ringette Hall of Fame was established in 1990. TANYA DUBNICOFF, known for her success in cycling, played ringette as a teenager, and was at the first World Ringette Championships in 1990. Though player numbers began declining slightly in MB through the 1990s, the sport continued to spread through NA, and the national sports channel TSN broadcast the 1995 Canadian Ringette Championships from Winnipeg. CLARA HUGHES and Jennifer Botterill (see BOTTERILL FAMILY) also played ringette before moving on to SPEED SKATING and hockey, respectively. • MD

RITCHOT, Abbé Noël-Joseph, priest, political advisor (b Dec 25, 1825, L'Assomption, Lower Canada [QC]; d March 16, 1905, St. Norbert). Father Ritchot arrived at the **RED RIVER SETTLE-MENT** in early June 1862. Bishop **ALEXANDRE-ANTO-NIN TACHÉ** soon appointed him as the parish priest of the predominantly **MÉTIS** parish of St. Norbert (now at the very S of **WINNIPEG**). Over the summers of 1866 and 1867, Ritchot also established the Qu'Appelle Mission in what is now SK. Ritchot developed a strong respect for the Métis, which was atypical of many of the other clergy of the period.

During summer 1869, he played a critical role in helping legitimize and guide the militant Métis movement that rose to counter the **RUPERT'S LAND TRANSFER** of their homeland to the new Dominion of Canada by the **HUDSON'S BAY COMPANY**. Troubled by the arrogance and land speculation of several Canadians already in the Red River Settlement either privately or as officials from Canada, many Métis grew concerned that their collective and individual rights would be ignored by a new Ottawa-based regime. As the militants met and grew more organized under the eventual leadership of **LOUIS RIEL**, Ritchot hosted the leaders in his home, kept minutes of their meetings, and worked closely with Riel, who regarded the clergyman as his principal advisor. Eventually, Richot was elected by the Métis of St. Norbert as one of their representatives to the Métis National Council of which John Bruce was the president and Riel the secretary. When the main camp and headquarters of the militants moved from St. Norbert to **UPPER FORT GARRY** following its seizure on Nov 2, Ritchot became more discreet in his role as militant and advisor as Riel united most of the settlement under a provisional govt.

His importance to the movement was confirmed when the elected representatives of the Red River Settlement chose him as 1 of the 3 delegates sent to Ottawa at Canada's request to negotiate a peaceful resolution to the **RED RIVER RESISTANCE** based on a Bill of Rights prepared by the provisional govt. Ritchot emerged as the leader of the delegation and the man whom Canada had to satisfy, if the UK's demand for a peaceful settlement was to be met. Ritchot's "journal" of those discussions is the only known record of those negotiations. Canada eventually agreed to the demands for provincial status, bilingualism, separate schools, and the guarantee of existing land holdings, also promising to distribute 1.4 million ac (5665 km²) of land to the children of the MB Métis in recognition of their **ABORIGINAL RIGHTS**. Not noted in the *MANITOBA ACT*, however, were a variety of other understandings, the

most important of which was the promise made to Ritchot by John A. Macdonald and George-Étienne Cartier that Canada would lobby the Crown in favour of a general amnesty for Riel and for all others who may have committed offences during the troubles. Ritchot's private and public support of the merits of the *Manitoba Act* led directly to the peaceful acceptance of Confederation by Riel and by the population of Red River.

When the arrival of the **WOLSELEY EXPEDITION** in Aug 1870 signalled not the quiet transfer of authority anticipated by Riel but the beginning of several weeks of intimidation, beatings, and worse by the volunteer soldiers from ON, it became clear to Ritchot and the others the spirit of conciliation had not taken root in the minds of those in Red River and Canada who regarded the Red River Resistance as nothing less than high treason punctuated by the "murder" of **THOMAS SCOTT**. With Riel and the other Métis leaders forced into hiding and exile, leadership of the Métis fell to newly arrived **FRENCH** Canadians such as **JOSEPH ROYAL**, **JOSEPH DUBUC**, **MARC-AMABLE GIRARD**, and others. As the old practices of Red River were replaced by what the historian **W. L. MORTON** described as the "triumph of Ontario Democracy," Ritchot became the oracle through which defenders of French and Métis rights sought to understand the meaning and intentions of the *Manitoba Act* and what had been agreed to in the Ottawa negotiations.

For his part, Ritchot returned several times to Ottawa to press the govts of both Macdonald and PM Alexander Mackenzie to honour the promises of amnesty, security of land tenure, and the equitable distribution of the 1.4 million acres to the Métis. As demonstrated by such events as the **SCRIP** issue, the **MANITOBA SCHOOLS QUESTION**, and the century-long battle over **FRENCH** language rights, MB ceased to be a hospitable place for the Métis, the French language, and the **ROMAN CATHOLIC** faith. Even though Riel was granted a conditional amnesty in 1874, many of the Métis moved away from the new province with most ending up in SK. Ritchot had no involvement in what became the 1885 North West Rebellion, but certainly understood that the roots of Riel's and Métis frustration were found in the unfulfilled promises of the *Manitoba Act* he helped negotiate. As late as 2006, MB Courts were still dealing with issues related to Métis land claims based on the *Manitoba Act*, with Ritchot's notes considered pivotal evidence. Ritchot's role in MB history was not well known until recently, but a National Historic Sites and Monuments plaque dedicated to his efforts now shares pride of place next to the statue of Louis Riel on the grounds of the MB Legislative Building. ● PHILIPPE MAILHOT

RITER HAMILTON, Mary, artist, (b 1873, Teeswater, ON; d 1954, Vancouver, BC) is best-known for painting more than 350 stark scenes of WWI battlefields. Born Mary Riter, she moved to Clearwater, MB as a small child. She married Charles W. Hamilton in 1889 and they moved to Port Arthur, ON, where Charles became a leading merchant. At the age of 23, following Charles's death, Mary returned to MB. She opened a china painting school, which became very successful. Riter Hamilton studied briefly in Toronto before travelling to Europe to continue her education. By 1909, her work began to achieve success and recognition; her painting *Les Pauvres* was displayed in The Salon, earning acceptance by the French Academy. The work was later shown at the Panama-Pacific Exhibition in San Francisco in 1915. Mary Riter Hamilton returned to Winnipeg in 1911, and brought with her a collection of nearly 150 oils and watercolours that went on display at several galleries. She hoped to go overseas as an artist during WWI, but that work was not open to a woman. So she painted Cdn landscapes during the war, donating them to aid in fundraising activities. In 1919, she was finally commissioned to produce paintings of French battlefields for reproduction in a veteran's magazine *Gold Stripe*. She spent the years from 1919-1922 living alone in France in a tin hut alongside the Chinese workers hired to clear the western front of the debris of war, bury the dead and restore some sort of order to the land. These battlefield paintings were exhibited in both Vancouver and Victoria as well as being published in the magazine. Hamilton returned once again to Winnipeg in 1925, now blind in one eye due to a 1923 illness. She refused to sell any of her battlefield paintings, and instead donated 227 of her works to the Canadian Public Archives in 1925. She died in Vancouver at the age of 81, and was buried in Port Arthur next to her husband. ● AMANDA STEPHENS

RIVERS, pop 1193, is a town 30 km NW of **BRANDON**, on hwy 25. Conceived when the Grand Trunk Pacific Railway was being planned and a division point was required, the town was named in 1908 after the railway's president, Sir Charles Rivers-Wilson. Settled mainly by people of **ENGLISH**, **SCOTS**, **IRISH**, and **UKRAINIAN** descent, the community had grown to village size by 1911 and was incorporated as a town in 1913. In 1940, a major RCAF and BCATP base – #1 Central Navigation School – was set up nearby with 30 hangars and support facilities. The population soared. The base was closed at war's end, reopened in 1950 as a joint-service training base, then closed permanently in 1971, which resulted in a major local depression.

In 1972, the federal department of Indian and Northern Affairs took control of the former base and converted it to the Oo-Za-We-Kwun Centre for Aboriginal job training. This closed in 1980. The base was subsequently bought by Hangar Farms Ltd, a swine farrowing operation, and one of the area's most prominent employers. Today, Rivers is a bedroom community for Brandon. It has a K-6 school, high school, 16-bed hospital, and fire and police protection. The railway station has been designated a heritage site. ● GPP

R **RIVERTON,** pop 537, is a village 125 km N of **WINNIPEG** on the Icelandic River, between hwy 8 and **LAKE WINNIPEG**, and just SW of **HECLA/** Grindstone Provincial Park. Though small, Riverton is among the more storied MB villages. Long known to First Nations and used as a stopping-place along a canoe route, the area is near where the Whitemud River, as the Icelandic was then known, discharges into Lake Winnipeg. By the 18th century, Europeans were active in the **FUR TRADE** in this area, and in 1863, the **HBC** set up a trading post at nearby Grassy Narrows. Permanent European settlement came in 1876, when **ICELANDERS** came to **NEW ICELAND** which would later become part of MB. The Icelanders rechristened the Whitemud River as the Icelandic River and used the same name for their New Iceland Reserve. During this time, the community's post office address was Icelandic River. The settlement grew rapidly, with large numbers of immigrants from Iceland arriving over the next 20 years.

When the New Iceland govt was abandoned in 1883, a municipal administration was established. By 1900, other groups – from Austria, Ukraine and Hungary – began settling in what had been the reserve. In anticipation of the railway's arrival, the community of Lundi moved many of its businesses across the river and renamed the community "Riverton" in 1924. The vast tracts of lumber and pulp wood, the growing agricultural production, and the fish industry helped bring the railway to Riverton in 1924, which attracted continued immigration. Riverton was incorporated as a village in 1951. With improved road access, the railway was abandoned. The village took over the **CPR** grounds establishing a heritage centre in the station. Along with its transportation theme, it recognizes the contributions of early founders **SIGTRYGGUR JÓNASSON**, Johann Briem, **GUNNSTEINN EYJÓLFSSON**, **FRIÐJÓN FRIÐRIKSSON**, **GUTTORMUR "GUTTI" JÓNSSON GUTTORMSSON** and many others. There is also a large Aboriginal population in Riverton, primarily of **OJIBWAY** and **MÉTIS** ancestry. From those ranks came **HOCKEY'S REGGIE LEACH**, once the winner of the NHL's Conn Smythe Trophy. ● GPP

ROBERTSON, Colin, fur trader (b ca July 23-27, 1783, Perth, UK; d Feb 4, 1842, Montreal). Robertson entered **NWC** service around 1803. He left the NWC in 1809, and sailed for London with an introduction to the HBC's London Committee. He advocated an active push into the Athabasca Territory with Cdn voyageurs. This proposal was rejected at the time, and Robertson went into trade in Liverpool. He submitted a revised plan in 1814, which was accepted with him in charge. His motto was "When among Wolves, Howl." He understood the need for the flamboyant gesture, and often made it. In the **RED RIVER SETTLEMENT**, he seized **FORT GIBRALTAR** from the NWC, and returned it only under conditions. He subsequently disagreed with gov **ROBERT SEMPLE** over strategy for defending the settlement, and went back to the UK at the end of 1816. He returned to Ville-Marie (now Montreal) to stand trial for the Fort Gibraltar business, and was acquitted. He then organized his Athabasca venture, eventually collecting 27 canoes and 190 men. The strategy was successful and brought the NWC to the bargaining table with the HBC. He was made a chief factor in the reorganized HBC in 1821, but HBC gov **GEORGE SIMPSON** did not like him. Simpson and Robertson contested over the latter's effort to introduce his mixed-blood wife into **RED RIVER** society. Simpson forced Robertson to plan retirement. Before he could retire, however, he had a stroke, and therefore did not leave the Company officially until 1840. He died in Canada West (QC) shortly after election to the Canadian Legislative Assembly. ● JMB

ROBERTSON, Joe Duncan, trapper, conservationist, writer (b Aug 8, 1913, Fork River, MB) has received over 25 awards and citations for his work in wildlife conservation, including the Order of Canada in 2007. In 1927, a 14-year-old Joe joined his father on the trap line E of **THE PAS** along the Minago River. A decade later, he spent a winter alone, with a tent and a dog team, trapping along the Seal River N of Churchill. Despite just a Grade 4 education, Joe kept diaries of his adventures, which he self-published in *From Prairie to Tundra* and other books. He worked for Manitoba Conservation from 1940-76, except for the 3 years he served with the RCAF in WWII. While working for the govt in the 1940s, he set up the first registered trap lines in the province and helped introduce licensed hunting. He led the campaign in the 1950s that saved the barren ground caribou from over-hunting and wolf predation. He ran MB's predatory control program in the 1950s and '60s. He has long argued that treaty hunting rights threaten wildlife populations, when combined with modern technology like all-terrain vehicles and high-powered rifles. He founded the Fort Dauphin Museum, and is a founding member of the Manitoba Archaeological Society. In his later years, he made and taught others to tan hides, make moccasins, and rawhide-webbed snowshoes, for which he earn the **OJIBWAY** name, Net Awa Gimos Sed (Snow Shoe Walker). ● BILL REDEKOP

GLENN MARQUEZ

Riverton's railway station, 2007

ROBINSON, Eric, politician (b Feb 5, 1953, NORWAY HOUSE). After spending his early years at the Jack Rivers RESIDENTIAL SCHOOL in Norway House, Robinson (also known as Ka-Kee-Nee Konee Pewonee Okimow) lived at GRAND RAPIDS, CROSS LAKE, and CHURCHILL. He is a CREE member of the CROSS LAKE FIRST NATION. He went on to work as a broadcaster and producer for the CBC Radio program *North Country*, based in Churchill and THOMPSON, and for Native Communications Incorporated (*see* BROADCASTING). He founded the Native Media Network, and in 1985 co-wrote a book, *Infested Blanket: Canada's Constitution and the Genocide of Indian Nations*.

Following the resignation of ELIJAH HARPER, Robinson won a 1993 by-election to become the NDP MLA for Rupertsland. He was named critic for the Native Affairs ministry and the ABORIGINAL JUSTICE INQUIRY (for which he had worked as a researcher). When the NDP formed a govt in 1999, Robinson became Minister of Aboriginal and Northern Affairs, and helped create the Aboriginal Justice Implementation Commission. In Sept 2002, he moved to the Culture, Heritage, and Tourism portfolio, and was also responsible for Sport and Recreation. Robinson continued in that post following the 2003 election, and like OSCAR LATHLIN, won his 5th election in 2007. Robinson has served on the board of Thompson's Ma-Mow-We-Tak Friendship Centre, and in 2006, volunteered for a number of justice-related causes, including the John Howard Society, the Aboriginal Court Worker Program, and spiritual and reconciliation services in prisons. ● JT

ROBLIN, pop 1818, is a town 90 km W of DAUPHIN, on a CN line, at the junction of hwys 5 and 83, and just E of the SK border and LAKE OF THE PRAIRIES. Farmers initially settled what is now the Roblin area in the 1880s. The diverse populace includes people of UKRAINIAN, ENGLISH, SCOTS, IRISH, MENNONITE, FRENCH, POLISH, OJIBWAY, CREE, and MÉTIS origin. The RAILWAY came to this area in 1903. In 1904, when a post office opened, the community was called Goose Lake after a water body of that name near the town. The name was changed to Roblin, after premier RODMOND ROBLIN, later that year. Roblin incorporated as a village in 1913 and became a town on May 1, 1962. The town, which likes to call itself the "Jewel of the Parkland," functions primarily as an agricultural service centre, but also has the benefits of FORESTRY, retail, EDUCATION, and health care. Popular TOURIST destinations in the area include the Asessippi Provincial Park and Duck Mountain Provincial Park. FISHING, HUNTING, and SNOWMOBILING all draw tourists to the area. Other local attractions include the manmade Lake of the Prairies, the Frank Skinner Arboretum Trail (named after horticulturist FRANK LEITH SKINNER), and the Keystone Pioneer Museum. Roblin's big annual events are the Agricultural Society's Annual Fair and the Pro Modified Demolition Derby. Peter Stasiuk, a UKRAINIAN CATHOLIC bishop, was born here. ● GPP

ROBLIN, Charles DUFFERIN "Duff," businessman, premier (b June 17, 1917, WINNIPEG). Some of Roblin's ancestors were active in the political life of Upper Canada (now ON) before Confederation, and he is the grandson of Sir RODMOND ROBLIN, MB premier 1900-15. Duff attended Winnipeg public schools, and St John's College School, and studied at the U OF M and the U of Chicago. He was a WCdr in the RCAF 1940-45.

vertical text: AM, PERSONALITY FILES, N19416

Duff Roblin, 1957

Roblin's early political career largely coincided with the beginning of the modern era in MB govt and politics. The changes associated with his years in office were driven mainly by a general post-war desire for innovation. Demographic changes, for example, produced a shift in political power and priorities away from a long-standing, almost exclusively rural/agrarian focus, to one encompassing both Winnipeg and the North. This, however, was augmented by a new govt which was active rather than reactive, and which understood the social and economic implications of these changes.

After WWII, Roblin's political views and agenda were shaped by what he saw as the stifling effects of the coalition govt through which the Progressive Party of Manitoba had governed, either alone or with allies, from 1922 onward. The coalition's end in 1950 created the opportunity to restore parliamentary party govt to MB, and the possibility of revitalizing the provincial Conservative party, which had not formed a govt since it was beset by scandal in 1915. From his election as an MLA in 1949, as an independent Conservative opposed to the coalition, through to his election as party leader in 1954, Roblin was pre-eminently the catalyst for these developments. He is usually credited with the rebuilding of the provincial Conservative party, which was as much an act of creation as it was of restoration, so much did it embody Roblin's values and outlook.

The new party was conservative in many respects, particularly in its commitment to the values of parliamentary govt and in its understanding of the rate at which change could be brought about; yet, in policy, it provided one of the most progressive govts in Manitoba's history. Paradoxically, its arrival after more than 35 years of conservative govt by Progressives heralded, with appropriate caution, 9 years of progressive govt by Conservatives. Elected as a minority govt in 1958, they were re-elected in 1959 with a substantial majority and were further re-elected in 1962 and 1966.

In contrast with the previous govt's cautious, pay-as-you-go approach to public finances, Roblin saw the use of the power and resources of the state as a major tool in modernizing the province. He argued that public spending in areas such as EDUCATION, training, MEDICINE, welfare, and economic development was a form of investment that would strengthen the economy and create the reward of increased prosperity. This perspective was familiar to other Cdn jurisdictions of the era, but the contrast with the approach of the previous govt could hardly have been greater.

Education was the govt's highest priority, and encompassed reorganization of the primary school system; the establishment of 3 new community colleges (*see* ASSINIBOINE COMMUNITY COLLEGE, RED RIVER COLLEGE, and Keewatin College); and substantial increases in educational spending, including spending on existing universities, and the establishment, in 1967, of 2 new ones in Winnipeg (U OF W) and Brandon (BU). Industrial and tourist development, another priority, was reflected in the creation of a development fund; extra funds for construction and reconstruction of roads and highways; the establishment of CROP INSURANCE and new credit facilities for those engaged in AGRICULTURE; the establishment of conservation, farm management, and statistics divisions in the department of agriculture; and the initiation of new forest management

R

R

measures and the employment of people to undertake the program; and a research program for Manitoba fisheries.

Social policy recognized individual need as a suitable basis for reform and enlargement. These needs were reflected in the construction of a rehabilitation and convalescent hospital; new additions to the PORTAGE LA PRAIRIE and SELKIRK hospitals for mental diseases; expanding prisoner probation services; a reformed *Mothers' Allowance Act*; aid for needy old-age pensioners; changes in child ADOPTION laws; and action to increase the number of medical technicians, practical nurses, and health units in the province.

In 1960, the Roblin govt established a 2nd-tier METRO WINNIPEG govt over the 13 existing municipalities of greater Winnipeg. This was assigned responsibility for services that crossed existing municipal boundaries, such as transport. It also addressed, through a shared services arrangement between the public and separate school systems, one of the unresolved and lingering issues flowing from the MANITOBA SCHOOLS QUESTION. Among its initially controversial initiatives was the decision, to proceed with the building of the RED RIVER FLOODWAY with funding help from PM John Diefenbaker's govt. The later positive consequences of what came to be known as Duff's Ditch effectively banished most criticism of its high cost. The Roblin govt's last years were marked by public anger over the introduction of a sales tax, and was followed by a public inquiry into the CHURCHILL FOREST INDUSTRIES (CFI) project even though little money was actually dispersed during Roblin's administration.

The Roblin govt has been viewed, not least by several later premiers of differing political stripes, as the most influential since WWII. Duff Roblin is credited with the restoration of the party system, wherein partisan competition came to be driven by substantively differing views on policy and the role of govt. In this, and in the modernization of MB and its govt, Roblin substantially altered the agenda and the nature of political discourse in the years that followed.

In 1967, Roblin was a candidate for the leadership of the federal Progressive Conservative Party, in succession to John Diefenbaker, but he lost to Robert Stanfield. He resigned as premier in Nov 1967 and was a candidate in the 1968 federal election in Winnipeg South Centre, but was defeated by a combination of Trudeaumania and public unhappiness over the MB sales tax. He ran for Parliament again in 1974, in Peterborough, ON, and was again defeated. In 1978, he was appointed to the Senate, and served in the Mulroney Cabinet as govt leader in the Senate 1984-86. He retired from the Senate in 1992. ● WILLIAM NEVILLE

ROBLIN, Sir Rodmond Palen, businessman, premier (b Feb 1, 1853, Sophiasburg, Canada West (ON); d Feb 16, 1937, Hot Springs, AR) Roblin was born in 1853 in Prince Edward Co, in what is now ON, into a United Empire Loyalist family. Educated at the METHODIST Albert College, in Belleville, ON, Rodmond Roblin managed his family's farm for a short time before deciding to emigrate to MB. He had married Agnes Demill 2 years before making his first exploratory trip to the West in 1877. With his brother-in-law, he opened a general store in what is now CARMAN and soon engaged in grain buying and making loans to his farmer neighbours. He also became involved in local politics, serving as reeve and chair of the school board before running unopposed as Liberal MLA for Dufferin. He was to continue as a MLA for most of the next 27 years.

Rodmond Roblin, 1915

By 1889, Roblin's expanding grain business led him to move to WINNIPEG. Roblin was one of the founding members of the WINNIPEG GRAIN EXCHANGE, and, in 1897, he and several partners formed the Dominion Elevator Company (*see* GRAIN ELEVATORS), of which he was the president. However, it was as a politician that Roblin decided to spend the most productive years of his life. He was a great platform speaker and a combative debater who could wound and humiliate his opponents, and he made many enemies as a result.

Roblin broke with THOMAS GREENWAY's Liberals over their policy of removing the special status of MB's Francophone population, and because he did not support Greenway's RAILWAY policy, an unsuccessful attempt to lower freight rates by creating a rival for the dominant CPR.

In early 1890, Roblin was elected as leader of the tiny Conservative opposition in the MB legislature. In 1899, he stepped down as leader so that the popular Sir HUGH JOHN MACDONALD, son of Canada's first PM, could lead the party in the general election of that year. Macdonald was able to form a govt, but after only a year, he resigned to run, unsuccessfully, in the federal elections of 1900, and Roblin became premier. He would lead the Conservatives to majority govts in 4 elections – 1903, 1907, 1910, and 1914 – before resigning in disgrace over the LEGISLATIVE BUILDING scandal in 1915.

One of Roblin's most important accomplishments was providing effective competition for the CPR. In Feb 1901, he announced that he had signed an agreement with the Northern Pacific Railway to lease all the lines they controlled in MB – 570 km of track – for 999 years. The province would pay $210,000 a year to begin with, and the rate would climb to $300,000 over 30 years. A short time later, he announced that the lines were in turn leased to Canadian Northern Railway, at the time a small railway just setting out on a decade of expansion. CNoR gave the province control of freight rates in return for provincial guarantees of its construction bonds. This meant that Roblin's govt had the power to set freight rates below those of the CPR, and it did so, forcing the older railway to reduce its rates in turn. By these actions, Roblin accomplished what Western politicians had been trying to do for decades, and broke the monopoly of CPR in the West.

The Roblin govt's liquor policy was not as successful. The evils of drink were widely condemned at the time and the temperance movement – supported by many REFORM leaders, including clergy, politicians, and leaders of the WOMEN'S MOVEMENT, including NELLIE McCLUNG – was a significant political force in MB. Premier Macdonald's provincial govt had passed a *Prohibition Act* in June 1900, whose constitutionality was tested in the courts all the way to the UK Privy Council. But when he became premier, Roblin announced that there would be a provincial referendum before the act was proclaimed. The temperance side lost this plebiscite, and their outrage over what they characterized as Roblin's betrayal never abated. They continued to oppose him to the end of his career. Still, Roblin, being a wise politician and a good METHODIST, maintained that he was a temperance man. His approach was to control the liquor business with regulations and to leave PROHIBITION up to individual municipalities, which could hold referendums on the question and ban liquor, if voters preferred. During his time in power, the *Liquor*

Act regulations were continually strengthened; regulated beer parlours replaced the old open saloons of MB's early days; and liquor sales were strictly controlled.

Roblin was, except for women's suffrage, in tune with the progressive ideas of his time. He was a "bricks and mortar progressive" who saw a large role for govt in the development of the provincial **Economy**. He favoured public ownership of utilities, as did many other Cdn politicians at the time, and Roblin created the first govt-owned telephone system in Canada (*see* **Manitoba Telephone Systems**), in the process extending service into **Rural** areas where private companies refused to go. Acceding to the wishes of the Grain Growers movement (*see* **United Grain Growers**), he set up a govt-owned country elevator system, forcing his old colleagues at the Winnipeg Grain Exchange to accept the Grain Growers Grain Company, a co-operative enterprise, as a member of the exchange. He introduced taxes on corporations and his govt pursued an ambitious program of public works, building roads, bridges, and public buildings like the Agricultural College, many courthouses, and the new Legislative Building. His Minister of Public Works made sure that the Conservative Party benefited from all these public projects, and it was over kickbacks on the contracts for the Legislative Building that Roblin and his govt were hounded out of office in 1915.

Corruption was a fact of life in Cdn politics at the time and the Roblin administration used all the common methods such as collecting kickbacks from contractors and misappropriating govt funds in order to buy votes and finance election campaigns. But a reform spirit was sweeping through Canada, and voters were in no mood to tolerate the blatant corruption practised by the old-fashioned party machines. In 1915, it was proven that the contractor Thomas Kelly had overcharged the province for work on the new Legislative Building and paid the surplus to the Tory Party. The Conservatives resigned and, in the election of Sept 1915, were reduced to 5 seats. Roblin and 2 of his ministers were indicted. It was an ignominious end for a govt that had been one of the most active and successful in MB's history.

Roblin was premier of MB for 15 years, and he and his ministers created much of the infrastructure that served the province throughout the 20th century. His many accomplishments are now largely overshadowed by the Legislative Building scandal and by his steadfast opposition to female suffrage. After his resignation in 1915, he was charged and brought to trial, although the charges were later dropped. He went back to the grain business, acting again as president of Dominion Elevators, and he operated a business called Consolidated Motors in partnership with his sons. He died while on holiday in Hot Springs, Arkansas, in winter 1937. ● JIM BLANCHARD

ROBSON, Hugh Amos "H. A.," lawyer, politician, judge (b Sept 9, 1871, Barrow-in-Furness, UK; d July 9, 1945, **Winnipeg**). Born in England, Robson immigrated as a child to the then-NWTs that later became SK. He practised law in Regina, and became NWT's first attorney-general, before joining the law firm of Sir **James A. M. Aikins** in Winnipeg in 1899. He was appointed to MB's Court of King's Bench in 1910, but resigned from the bench in 1912 to become the province's first public utility commissioner. In 1919, he chaired a royal commission of inquiry into the causes and effects of the **Winnipeg General Strike**, which had occurred earlier the same year. He apportioned blame for the strike and massive civil unrest that followed equally between employers who failed to bargain collectively with unions and socialist ideologues who exploited workers' legitimate grievances. He was chosen leader of the **Liberal Party** in 1927 and elected MLA that year. He was appointed a judge of the Court of Appeal in 1930, and Chief Justice of the Court of King's Bench in 1944. His tenure as Chief Justice was short; he died suddenly, likely of a heart attack, the next year. Robson was a legal-education pioneer, early advocating that lawyers' professional training be integrated with university post-secondary education. He was a prime mover in the **U of M** and Law Society of Manitoba joint initiative to create the Manitoba Law School in 1914. The U of M Faculty of Law building, "Robson Hall," is named after him. His grandson, Paul Robson, is a former player and GM for the **Winnipeg Blue Bombers** and is now CEO of the **Red River Exhibition**. ● DOUG JOHNSTON

ROCKOLA, David Cullen, businessman, jukebox innovator (b 1897, **Virden**; d Jan 28, 1993, Chicago, IL). The son of a Virden blacksmith, Rockola left home at 14, working his way around western Canada and making his way to Toronto. He ended up in Chicago around the age of 22, and found work in the slot-machine business as a mechanic. In 1927, he started his own company, Rock-Ola Manufacturing Corporation. In June 1929, Rockola made an immunity deal to testify before a grand jury about mob-related companies for whom he had illegally altered slot machine payouts. His testimony helped expose a large crime syndicate involving police officers and politicians. However, he continued to produce his own slot machines following the trial.

Millions rocked to tunes on the Rock-ola.

In 1932, Rockola created his first pinball machine, "Juggle Ball," and in 1934 he acquired a design for a mechanism that allowed for the automatic storage and play of records: the jukebox. He fought and won a patent lawsuit filed by competitor Wurlitzer. By 1936, Rock-Ola was said to have 1000 employees producing vending, slot, and pinball machines, weigh scales and jukeboxes. Wurlitzer, Seeburg, and AMI companies were the original jukebox industry leaders, but the Rock-Ola brand eventually became the standard. The Rock-Ola factory converted to arms manufacturing during WWII, producing M-1 rifles for the US Army.

In 1954, the company introduced the "Tempo," a 45 rpm-record jukebox (which replaced the old 78 rpm records). The design reflected the rock n' roll culture of the time and paved the way for Rock-Ola's greatest market success, with Rock-Ola jukeboxes found in burger joints and bars across NA. In 1992, Rockola sold the jukebox line to Antique Apparatus Company of CA, and in 1993, he died at the age of 96. ● JOEL TRENAMAN

ROGERS, Edith, social **Reformer** (b ca 1876, **Norway House**; d April 12, 1947, **Winnipeg**). The daughter of D. C. McTavish, chief factor of the **HBC**, she was the first woman to be elected to the MB **Legislature** in 1920, representing Winnipeg. She was an active advocate of the *Child Welfare Act*. A Liberal, she was re-elected in 1922 and 1927. During WWI, she had been very involved in volunteer work, and was particularly

Edith Rogers

active in social-welfare work. She served as the only woman on the Winnipeg General Hospital Board (*see* **HEALTH SCIENCES CENTRE**), and was secretary of the Central Council of the Battalion Auxiliaries. She moved to ON in 1942. • JMB

ROLAND, pop 350, is a community 16 km N of Winkler. The post office opened as Lowestoft in 1884, named after the community's first postmaster, William H. Lowe. The community was renamed Roland in 1889, after early settler and lumberman, Roland MacDonald. Canada's **4-H** got its start in Roland, and the community has a museum devoted to 4-H history and activities. Area residents are noted for growing large pumpkins, and this has been recognized in the Guinness Book of World Records. A pumpkin fair is held each Oct. • GPP

ROLLING RIVER FIRST NATION, on reserve pop 499, off reserve pop 402, is situated 6 km SW of Erickson, about 65 km N of **BRANDON**, and about 245 km NW of **WINNIPEG**. The native language of this community is **OJIBWAY**, and it signed Treaty 4 in 1874. It is a member of the West Region Tribal Council. Education in Rolling River First Nation, administered by the community, goes from Nursery-Grade 12, and total enrolment for the year 2003-04 was 113. There are 2 reserves located on the Rolling River First Nation land: Rolling River IR No. 67, and Treaty Four Reserve Grounds No. 77. The Rolling River First Nation community has all-weather road access with bus service to nearby **ERICKSON**. The economic base of this community is agriculture – particularly **BEEF CATTLE** farming. Situated in the heart of MB's beef country, Rolling River put land into hay production, selling what it does not use on the Internet. • RK

ROMAN CATHOLIC CHURCH. The first Roman Catholics in MB were French fur traders and explorers during the late 18th century. Then in 1812, convinced that religion was the foundation on which to build a peaceful and prosperous **RED RIVER SETTLEMENT**, gov **MILES MACDONELL**, petitioned the bishop of QC for clergy to serve the several hundreds of French Catholic fur traders as well as German Catholic mercenary soldiers (the **DES MEURONS**) among the **LORD SELKIRK** settlers. And so it was that Catholic priests arrived at Red River in June 1818 and were provided with land E of the Red River by Lord Selkirk. **JOSEPH-NORBERT PROVENCHER**, Vical-General of the mission, saw to the construction of a log building to contain both a priests' residence and a chapel, which he dedicated to **ST. BONIFACE**. The name soon came to be applied to the small French Catholic settlement growing up around the church on the E bank of the **RED RIVER** at its juncture with the **ASSINIBOINE**. Meanwhile, Provencher's 2 companions had located among the French Canadians and Catholic Métis who lived among the **BISON** herds at Pembina where they built a small school, a chapel, and a small residence.

With the merging of the rival fur trading companies **HBC** and **NWC** in 1821, a measure of peace came to the Red River valley. With the establishment of peace, more settlers came west, many of them Catholics seeking the sacramental ministry of their church. Given the immense distance between Red River and PQ, the West needed its own bishop. And so, in 1822, Provencher was consecrated as coadjutor Bishop of Quebec for the North-West – the vast territory west of the Great Lakes and north to Hudson Bay and beyond – with a Catholic population of less than 1000. In 1823, Provencher established the first school in St. Boniface which by 1827 was the first secondary school in Red River. It would become St. Boniface College (*see* **COLLEGE UNIVERSITAIRE DE SAINT BONIFACE**), one of the founding colleges of the U of M in 1877.

By 1844, Grey Nuns from Montreal reached St. Boniface. They soon opened a hospital and school for 80 girls in what is today the **ST. BONIFACE MUSEUM**. The 4 secular priests in the territory at the time devoted themselves almost exclusively to the salvation of the Aboriginal population and were seldom available to the white population. Accordingly, Provencher secured the service of the Oblates of Mary Immaculate (a new religious order, founded in 1816) to work as missionaries in his vast territory. One of the first 2 Oblates to arrive in Red River was **ALEXANDER-ANTONIN TACHÉ**. These 2 were followed by a large number who spread across the Cdn West.

When Bishop Provencher died in 1853, he was succeeded by Taché. The diocese of the North-West, which changed its name to St. Boniface in 1854, boasted a stone twin-towered cathedral (1839), Bishop's house, and the large log convent/hospital of the Grey Nuns. The Catholic population, more than 1100 at that time, was served by 4 secular priests and 7 Oblate missionaries. The vast size of the diocese led to the appointment in 1859 of a coadjutor or auxiliary Oblate bishop, Vital Grandin.

In 1871, the *Manitoba Schools Act* created a dual school system based on the principle that public money would be used for the support of separate, denominational schools under the control of the appropriate English Protestant or French Catholic section of a provincial board of education. At the time, 17 French Catholic schools enrolled 639 pupils and the enrolment in 16 English Protestant schools totalled 816. Just 20 years later, there were 629 Protestant schools with 18,850 pupils but only 90 Catholic schools with 4364 pupils. So it is not surprising that, in 1890, the Manitoba Legislature passed 2 bills: one abolished the official use of French in the legislature, provincial courts, and the civil service of MB and the 2nd bill created a system of non-denominational schools administered by a provincial govt dept of education which allowed for the use of languages other than English only under certain conditions.

Archbishop Taché served notice of his intention to fight to regain the rights and privileges lost by the French and Catholic population. And, in 1895, the govt of Canada issued an order to MB requiring the provincial govt to enact legislation restoring to Roman Catholics the rights and privileges which were denied by the legislation of 1890. However, the remedial order was never carried out and the **MANITOBA SCHOOLS QUESTION** remained a source of contention for years.

By 1900, more than 1000 **POLISH** Catholic immigrants had settled in Winnipeg's **NORTH END** and Holy Ghost parish was erected, served by 2 Polish Oblate priests. After 1904 they also ministered to a new **GERMAN** parish (St. Joseph's). Rapid growth of the **UKRAINIAN** community in the town of **DAUPHIN**, lead to the creation of St. Viator's parish in 1905 (served initially by the Clerics of St. Viator). Until the coming of the railway, most Catholics in MB were of French or Aboriginal descent and the clergy, with few exceptions, were from QC or France. By 1906, however, a growing Irish immigrant population expressed their dissatisfaction with diocesan services provided to English-speaking Catholics. Their petition did not come as a surprise since MB had a turbulent past of French-English conflict and new tensions had already arisen as Eastern Europeans and the English-speaking Irish. The Irish asked Archbishop Langevin for more English-speaking parishes served by clergy whose first language was English, an English-speaking Catholic College for their sons, and the establishment of an English-speaking Diocese of Winnipeg with its own Bishop.

Archbishop Langevin responded that he was securing land for 2 more English-speaking parishes in Winnipeg and that he supported the idea of a new English-speaking College but had no money to build or staff it. When, a year later, there were still no new parishes, the Irish petitioners contacted the Apostolic Delegate to Canada (appointed by the Pope) to express their concerns. An exchange of letters with the Apostolic Delegate, culminating in a 1908 "order" that the Archbishop create the promised parishes "in spite of all difficulties," led to the opening of St. Edward the Confessor parish in western Winnipeg and St. Ignatius Loyola parish in Fort Rouge.

UMA, TRIBUNE, ROMAN CATHOLIC CHURCH, GORDON AIKMAN PHOTO, 59-4915-89, 1977

St. Malo Catholic Church was founded in 1890. The statue was erected to celebrate the 65th anniversary.

Bishop Langevin died in June, 1915. On Dec 4, the Apostolic Delegate announced the creation of the new Archdiocese of Winnipeg (about ⅓ of the area of MB, a sizable portion of the existing Archdiocese of St. Boniface) and its first Archbishop, Alfred Arthur Sinnott, was installed on Christmas Eve, 1916. Statistics from 2005 list 155,000 MB Catholics as belonging to the Archdiocese of Winnipeg. They were served by 65 diocesan priests (14 retired), 22 priests who are members of Religious Orders, 122 Religious Order Sisters, and 18 Deacons. There are 70 parishes and 22 missions in the diocese.

In 1910, the Vicarate Apostolic of Keewatin was erected with Ovide Charlebois OMI as Vicar. Fifteen years later, the Vicarate joined with the Inuit mission to form the Prefecture Apostolic of Hudson Bay, In 1967, the original Keewatin Vicarate became the archdiocese of Keewatin-The Pas with Paul Dumouchel OMI as its Archbishop. In 1986, he was succeeded by Peter Sutton OMI. Following Archbishop Sutton's retirement in 2006, Sylvain Lavoie, OMI became Archbishop of the 45,000 Catholics living in 49 parishes (served by 16 priests) spread throughout this vast missionary territory.

The story of the Ukrainian Archeparchy of Winnipeg is intimately tied to the history of Ukrainian settlement in Canada. Although individual Ukrainians immigrated to Canada earlier, it was in 1891 that the first group of Ukrainians arrived in MB. Virtually all of the Ukrainians who settled in the Cdn West passed through Winnipeg where they were welcomed into existing Catholic churches. Initially they were associated with the Church of the Immaculate Conception, later contributing to the building of Holy Ghost church intended to serve both Polish and Ukrainian Catholics.

It was only in April 1897, that the first Ukrainian priest Father Nestor Dmytriv travelled from the US to MB with the express purpose of ministering to Ukrainian Catholics in the province. Two years later, Father Damascin Polivka came to Winnipeg from Europe to establish a Ukrainian church building offering the sacred liturgy as it had been celebrated in the Ukraine. The first Ukrainian bishop, Nykyta Budka arrived in Canada in Dec 1912. His successor, Basil Ladyka, was ordained as a bishop in 1929. In 2003, there were 29,740 Ukrainian Catholics in MB, served by 51 priests and 15 deacons. Only 21 of more than 125 Ukrainian Catholic parishes had resident pastors. Nov 3, 2006 marked the 50th anniversary of the establishment of the Ukrainian Catholic Metropolitanate in Canada.

Results of the Canadian census in 2006 indicate that the population of MB was 1,119, 583, of which 323,690 were Roman Catholic. ● DAVID CREAMER

RONALD, Allan Ross, physician, researcher (b Aug 24, 1938, PORTAGE LA PRAIRIE). One of a group of distinguished Manitoban medical researchers, Ronald graduated from the U OF M with his MD in 1961, the same year as diabetes researcher BARRY POSNER. He spent the next 7 years training at the Winnipeg General Hospital (see HEALTH SCIENCES CENTRE), the U of Washington, the U of Maryland, and in Lahore in internal MEDICINE, infectious diseases, and microbiology.

In 1968, the U OF M recruited Ronald to head its infectious disease unit in the faculty of medicine, beginning a long career at the institution. He went on to be full professor and chair of the medical microbiology department from 1976-85, chair of the internal medicine unit from 1985-90, and the faculty's associate dean of research from 1993-1999. In addition to his academic responsibilities, Ronald also served first as head of clinical microbiology and later physician-in-chief at the Health Sciences Centre from 1985-90, and then head of infectious diseases at the ST. BONIFACE GENERAL HOSPITAL (SBGH) from 1991-95.

A 1975 outbreak of chancroid in WINNIPEG spurred Ronald's interest in sexually transmitted diseases (STDs). In 1979, he was a founding member of the World Health Organization's research and training program in sexually transmitted diseases jointly based at the U of M and U of Nairobi, where he conducted HIV/AIDS research alongside specialists like FRANK PLUMMER. One of Ronald's main contributions to the program was the training of more than 70 Kenyan doctors while acting as a visiting professor at the Kenyan centre. Ronald also took on a similar role at the U of Hong Kong from 1998 to 2002, after which he also retired from the U of M.

As of early 2007, Ronald remained a distinguished professor emeritus at the U of M, a visiting professor at Makerere U in Kampala, Uganda, chair of the World Health Organization's Diagnostics Committee for Tropical Diseases and Tuberculosis, and scientific director of the National Collaborating Centre on Infectious Diseases. He was also a board member of the Academic Alliance for AIDS Care and Prevention in Africa (a public-private partnership backed by Pfizer Inc that includes the distribution of AIDS drugs).

Ronald has authored or co-authored more than 400 publications, and also acted as president of the International Society for Infectious Diseases and as a governor of the American College of Physicians. His work has been recognized with many awards, including the Order of Canada (1994), a fellowship from the Royal Society of Canada, the Canadian Medical Association's F. N. G. Starr Award, SBGH's International Award (2005), and an honorary DSc from the U OF W (2006). ● JOEL TRENAMAN

ROOS, Noralou Preston, health researcher, (b Apr 21, 1942, WINNIPEG). An innovator in health-care policy research, Roos was educated at Stanford U (BA with honours in 1963) and the Massachusetts Institute of Technology, where she earned a PhD in 1968. Roos was co-founder of the Manitoba Centre for Health Policy (MCHP), based at the U OF M. She was one of the first researchers

595

in NA to use regular administrative data to uncover patterns and trends in health care: analyzing information to determine the level of system use among different populations, and the effects of funding cuts on health outcomes, for example.

During her career, Roos has also been an associate of the Canadian Institute for Advanced Research, a health scientist through the National Health Research and Development Program, a member of the Prime Minister's National Forum on Health, served the Board of Directors of the Medical Research Council, and helped establish the Canadian Institutes for Health Research. Roos became a Canada Research Chair in Population Health in 2001 and was appointed a member of the Order of Canada in 2004. As of 2007, she remained a professor in the U of M Faculty of MEDICINE's Department of Community Health Sciences, and MCHP director emeritus and senior researcher. ● JT

RORKETON, pop 114, is a hamlet situated 80 km NE of DAUPHIN, in the RM of Lawrence. The community sits between LAKE MANITOBA and Lake Dauphin, and it is the largest community in Lawrence. The Rorketon post office opened its doors in 1921. And the hamlet was named after an early settler, G. A. Rorke. Rorketon became established in Dec 1921, and the community's CN line was completed in 1924, but was closed in 1974. The MANIPOGO sea monster has been said to have been seen in the Rorketon area. Rorketon's economic foundation is the service industry and agriculture. The community functions as the main service centre for nearby communities. ● GPP

ROSEAU RIVER ANISHINABE FIRST NATION, on reserve pop 1115, off reserve pop 996, is a community situated approx 20 km N of the US-Canada border, and 92 km S of WINNIPEG. The native language here is OJIBWAY, and it signed Treaty 1 in 1871. There are 2 reserves here: Roseau River IR No. 2 and the Roseau Rapids IR No. 2A; of which, the Roseau River community is the main population centre. Roseau River Anishinabe First Nation is a member of the Dakota Ojibway Tribal Council. This First Nation is accessible from hwy 75. Schooling in this community, self-administered, goes from Nursery-Grade 12. Enrolment for 2003-04 was 234. This First Nation's economy is based on cattle grazing, agriculture, and residential development ● RK

ROSENORT, pop 600, is a community 40 km SE of WINNIPEG, and on the Morris River. Thirty-one Russian MENNONITE families settled the community in 1874, establishing Rosenort as a farming community. In 1879, a windmill from STEINBACH was purchased for $1500, dismantled and then erected in Rosenort. Rosenort was evacuated during the 1997 FLOOD, but suffered little damage. Nevertheless, the community subsequently built up its ring dike. In the 2000s, the community was home to several large manufacturing companies like Westfield Industries, which builds grain augers, and Landmark Feeds, Western Canada's leading livestock and poultry feed supplier. Rosenort has its own airport, a K-12 school and the largest independent credit union in the province. The Rose Lane Tea House, open from April to Dec, is a popular draw. ● GPP

ROSS, Alexander, fur trader, historian (b May 9, 1783, Morayshire, UK; d Oct 23, 1856, RED RIVER) came to MB to make his fortune in the FUR TRADE. Born in Scotland, he arrived in Lower Canada (now QC) in 1804, and worked as a schoolmaster there and in Glengarry, Upper Canada (ON). In 1810, he signed on as a clerk with the Pacific Fur Company and sailed aboard the *Tonquin* for the Pacific Northwest, arriving in March 1811 to help establish Fort Astoria. He went to the NWC when it took over the Pacific Fur Company in 1813, working mainly in the interior until his forced retirement to RED RIVER in 1825. In the settlement, he farmed and traded. Although GEORGE SIMPSON did not like him, he gradually acquired positions of responsibility. He became sheriff of ASSINIBOIA in 1835, and a councillor of Assiniboia a year later. As sheriff and head of the Volunteer Corps of 60 men used as a police force, he refused to enforce the fur trade monopoly of the HBC. His demeanour was pedantic, and in later years he was known in the settlement as the "the Professor." In 1850, he and a number of other judges and magistrates refused to continue their work while gov William Caldwell remained in office. He fought for years to create a PRESBYTERIAN church in the settlement. In his later years, he wrote 3 autobiographical books, *Adventures on the Columbia* (1849), *The Fur Hunters of the Far West* (1855), and *The Red River Settlement* (1856). This made him the pre-Confederation Northwest's most prolific author, and its finest, as well. He may also have written the novel *Selma: A Tale of the Sixth Crusade* (1839). ● JMB

ROSS, Anne Glass, health administrator, activist (b 1912, WINNIPEG; d 1998, Winnipeg), is credited with expanding the MOUNT CARMEL CLINIC in Winnipeg's NORTH END into a major health clinic, recognized across Canada and the US as a model for holistic health care. Ross, a controversial figure, was often in conflict with govt, doctors, and politicians as she lobbied for money, support, and free services for the clinic. Ross attended

Anne Ross helps a client.

United College (*see* U OF W) and the U OF M. She studied nursing at Winnipeg General Hospital, and psychiatric nursing in New York. She then married Bill Ross, leader of the MB Communist Party and brother of Joe Zuken. In 1948, she became Mount Carmel's first full-time employee. As her role grew, so did the scope of the clinic. She worked tirelessly to expand services, including counselling, ABORTIONS, and day care. Ross wrote 3 books: *Pregnant and Alone* (1978); *Teenage Mothers, Teenage Fathers* (1982); and *Clinic with a Heart: The Story of Mount Carmel Clinic* (1998). Her life inspired the documentary *Anne Ross: Rebel with a Cause* (2000). ● JS

ROSS, Charlotte (Whitehead), physician (b July 15, 1843, Darlington, UK; d Feb 21, 1916, WINNIPEG) came to Montreal with her parents in 1847. She completed the medical course at the Women's Medical College in Philadelphia in 1875. When her husband, David Ross, came W to build the railway, the family settled in WHITEMOUTH, in territory disputed between MB and ON. Special

Ross family portrait, Charlotte seated with baby on right, ca 1889

legislation was introduced to enable her to practise in MB but was not passed. She continued to practise for many years, although she was never formally licensed by the Manitoba College of Physicians and Surgeons. She moved to Winnipeg in 1916, and died there. The Charlotte W. Ross Gold Medal in obstetrics was first awarded by the Manitoba Medical College (*see* **U OF M**) in 1917. • JMB

ROSS, James SINCLAIR, author (b Jan 22, 1908, Shellbrook, SK; d Feb 20, 1996, Vancouver). The youngest of 3 children, his parents separated when he was 7, and Ross's childhood was spent on a succession of SK farms where his mother worked as housekeeper. He left school after grade 11 to work for the Royal Bank of Canada, and earned his living thereafter as a teller in various small towns before moving to **WINNIPEG** in 1933. In contrast to another SK-born writer, W. O. Mitchell, who had instant success with his 1947 *Who Has Seen the Wind*, Sinclair Ross's first novel, *As for Me and My House,* was published in 1941 to largely indifferent reviews. However, Ross's debut has since become a much-studied icon of Prairie realism. Set on the drought-stricken Prairies during the **GREAT DEPRESSION**, the novel captures the essential nature of the genre, its arid landscape mirroring the lives of its protagonists as sterile and frustrated, and small-town society as mean-spirited and oppressive. The story's bleak defeatism may reflect its author's own experience during most of his lifetime, his inability to acknowledge his homosexuality openly in the climate of the time, and his failure to achieve recognition for his literary efforts.

Ross worked at the craft of writing since early adulthood. He published his first short story in 1934; and after the unenthusiastic reception of *As for Me and My House*, he continued to write, though this was interrupted by 4 years of war service, 1942-46, as an ordnance clerk in the Cdn Army. However, the war brought him to London, UK, and wider horizons, including some encounters with British and US intellectuals and a memorable lecture by T. S. Eliot. Then he returned briefly to Winnipeg before obtaining work at the Royal Bank in Montreal, where he was employed until 1968. Upon retiring, he lived for a time in Greece and then in Spain, until ill health forced him back to Canada, to Montreal. He died in Vancouver at the age of 88. Ross was awarded the Order of Canada in 1992 and the SK Lifetime Achievement Award in 1993. • MILDRED GUTKIN

ROSS, Malcolm Mackenzie, academic, critic (b Jan 2, 1911, Fredericton; d Dec 4, 2002, Halifax). A distinguished scholar of English literature, Ross was a graduate of the Us of NB, Toronto,

and Cornell, and became a superb teacher and an influential commentator on Cdn life and letters. After serving during WWII on the **NATIONAL FILM BOARD** and the **CANADIAN WHEAT BOARD**, he joined the English Department of the U of M. In an interview toward the close of his career, he remembered his classes there as "the most exciting run of students" he had ever had: writers **MARGARET LAURENCE**, **ADELE WISEMAN**, Jack Ludwig, and **PATRICIA BLONDAL**; actor **DOUGLAS RAIN**; painter **WILLIAM KURELEK**; **ROLAND PENNER** (later Attorney General of MB); and others who became leaders in education, business, and govt across Canada. He published *Milton's Royalism* in 1943, and *Poetry and Dogma* in 1954; the latter work, he explained later, developed out of his 17th-century course in MB. From 1950 until his retirement in 1982, he taught successively at Queen's U, U of Toronto, and Dalhousie U. Ross was a founding member of ACUTE, the Association of Canadian University Teachers of English, and an officer of the Canada Council for the Arts, the Royal Society of Canada, and the Humanities Association. As editor of the *Queen's Quarterly* and general editor of the reprint series *New Canadian Writing*, to which he contributed several introductions, as well as in such publications as *Our Sense of Identity* (1954), *The Arts in Canada* (1958), and *The Impossible Sum of Our Traditions* (1986), he articulated a vibrant sense of Cdn identity from an interdisciplinary historical, literary, and social perspective. • MILDRED GUTKIN

ROSS HOUSE MUSEUM is a log house made almost entirely of hand-carved oak timber in the Point Douglas area of **WINNIPEG**. It is owned and operated by the **MANITOBA HISTORICAL SOCIETY** (MHS). The house's structure is an exemplar of Red River frame buildings, a style of construction popular in this region. Begun in 1852, and built by William and Jemima Ross, **ALEXANDER ROSS** – William's father – provided the plot of land on which it was built. William was the postmaster for the **COUNCIL OF ASSINIBOIA** in 1855. The house was thus used as a residence for the Ross family, and as a post office. It was the first post office W of Thunder Bay, ON, other than those owned by the **HUDSON'S BAY COMPANY**. In 1949, the MHS and the City of Winnipeg gained ownership of the house and relocated it to Higgins Ave, across from the former **CANADIAN PACIFIC RAILWAY** station, now the Aboriginal Centre of Winnipeg. In 1984, it was moved one final time to a city park on Meade St N in Point Douglas. The museum is important because it gives a glimpse not only into the lives of the Ross family and the day-to-day happenings of 1850s farmstead life, but also a view into how early post offices operated. • RK

ROSSBURN, pop 568, is a town 155 km NW of **BRANDON**, 300 km NW of **WINNIPEG**, on the SW corner of **RIDING MOUNTAIN NATIONAL PARK**. Rossburn was first settled by **ENGLISH** and **SCOTS** in 1879. The community was named Rossburn after the Ross family, the first settlers in the area. After the arrival of the first pioneers, Rossburn took shape as a small village. The second wave of immigration came from Poland and Ukraine in 1899, and the construction of the railway around the turn of the century furthered development. In 1913, Rossburn became incorporated as a town.

The Rossburn area provides a variety of recreation options and destinations for those travelling on hwy 45, including the national park and Deep, Arrow and Rossman lakes. Recent subdivisions at Gundy and Rossman Lakes have offered more than 100 building lots, attracting new residents from England, the US and Canada. For 3 days every summer, Rossburn hosts quarter-horse racing on its track. Rossburn has undertaken inventive steps to maintain its population. In 1993, Rossburn advertised in the *Toronto Sun*, promising a low-stress country lifestyle and low-cost real estate. The promotions blitz attracted hundreds. By 2007, 7 families were still in town and Rossburn was trying a more strategic and less high-profile attempt to entice newcomers. The **WAYWAYSEECAPPO FIRST NATION** is about 5 km W of Rossburn. Provincial politician Len Derkach was born in Rossburn. • GPP

ROTHSTEIN, Marshall E., lawyer, judge (b Dec 25, 1940, **WINNIPEG**). Rothstein practised law in Winnipeg 1966-92, and for over 20 of those years was a lecturer in transportation and contract law at the **U OF M**'s law faculty. He served as chair of MB's Commission on Compulsory Retirement in the early 1980s, and in 1991, he chaired the federal Ministerial Task Force on International Air Policy. He became a judge of the Federal Court of Canada, Trial Division, in 1992, and was elevated to the Federal Court of Canada, Appeal Division (now the Federal Court of Appeal) in 1999. Marshall became a justice of the Supreme Court of Canada on March 1, 2006, an appointment that made legal and political history. His appointment was confirmed only after a hearing before Parliament's ad hoc committee to review a nominee for the Supreme Court of Canada, the first time a parliamentary committee publicly vetted and questioned a nominee to the Supreme Court. • DOUG JOHNSTON

ROTIFER is a cylindrical, microscopic (averaging 70-500 μm), multicellular animal sometimes called a Wheel Animal due to the revolving wheel-like organs at the anterior end. Lined with rows of fine hairs (cilia), these wheels are used to row the animal through the water and to sweep plankton (e.g., crustaceans, bacteria) and detritus into the mouth, where the jawed pharynx grinds up the food particles. About 2500 species are known worldwide, with the majority being freshwater forms; some are marine and terrestrial. There are likely 40-50 species present in MB. Rotifers are extremely numerous in aquatic habitats from ditches to deep lakes (40-500/l), in the sediments, on surfaces of aquatic plants and rocks, and in shoreline mud and sand (1.2 million/l). Terrestrial species occur in damp moss hummocks, on arboreal lichens, and in decomposing leaf litter. *Cephalodella gibba* is a common resident in the water of the pitcher plant (*Sarracenia purpurea*) of MB bogs. Many species are free-swimming or floating, but most remain attached by a "foot" with several "toes." Almost all rotifers in a sample are females, which usually reproduce by parthenogenesis (asexually); males are rare or unknown for most species, and the few that have been discovered are much smaller than the female, degenerate, and live for only a couple of days – long enough to supply females with sperm. Females survive for 5 days to 6 weeks. Eggs may hatch inside the female or they may be released to float away, buoyed up by a droplet of oil. Winter or resting eggs sink to the bottom. The cysts of a few species are capable of reviving after being dried for decades, and cysts carried along with dust in the wind may be dispersed around the globe. Rotifers play significant roles as omnivores and scavengers at the microscopic level of the food chains of most food webs, and are devoured by larger creatures like crustaceans and fish fry. Fossils have been found back to 30 million years ago (Oligocene period). ● REW

ROUNDWORM is an unsegmented, cylindrical and tapering worm, generally around 1-2 mm long (range of .2 mm to 9 m in whale parasites). Relatively simple in anatomy, many are so thin-walled that they are translucent, with organs clearly visible. Most either suck or engulf food items, and there are rasping teeth in the mouth cavity. They literally swarm in all habitats in MB, from grassland, forest and tundra soils, freshwater from puddles to deep lakes and rivers, and in the marine sediments of Hudson Bay. There are herbivorous, carnivorous, scavengers, and parasitic forms on both plants and animals. Examples of the latter are the 35 cm Ascaris worm (*Ascaris lumbricoides*) in humans, the 100 cm Giant Kidney Worm (*Dioctophyme renale*) in pet dogs, and the Brain Worm (*Parelaphostrongylus tenuis*) of white-tailed deer, which causes no disease in its normal host, but causes fatal disease

in **Moose**, **Elk**, **Caribou** and mule **Deer**, where their ranges overlap with white-tails. In fact, it appears that every kind of plant and animal has roundworms that feed on them.

Some life cycles of roundworms are highly complex, often involving a change in environments. The carnivorous kinds devour small animals such as **Rotifers**, segmented worms, and tardigrades. Many species feed on fungi and plants, and some cause damage to crops like potatoes. Most species reproduce by having both males and females, but others are parthenogenic and males are rare or unknown. Eggs may be remarkably resistant to drying and temperature extremes, and can survive for several decades. The larvae undergo 4 moults before reaching the adult stage. Aquatic and marine species cannot swim, but work their way, bending side-to-side, through the upper 2 cm of the bottom ooze. They can be incredibly abundant, especially in lake mud and sewage (where oxygen level is low), often numbering over $100,000/m^2$, with 5-150 species represented in one sample. A decaying apple may contain 90,000 roundworms. There are an estimated half-million species worldwide, and likely several thousand in MB. Roundworms play prominent roles in all ecosystems, and are useful indicators of soil health, responding negatively to poor tillage, fertilizer, and pesticide practices. This ancient group, traceable back 400 million years ago (mid-Paleozoic era), remains largely unstudied. ● REW

ROWING involves propelling a boat along the water with oars. Though similar to indigenous **Canoeing**, today's sport of rowing was brought to MB by the **English**. The sport, which originated in 1715 as a race between watermen on the Thames, was later adopted by the British upper class, and, consequently, **Winnipeg**'s wealthy residents introduced competitive rowing to MB waterways. Among the founders of rowing were cousins **George Frederick Galt** and John Galt Jr, who had moved here from ON to oversee the expansion of the family's mercantile business. The Galts began rowing on the **Red River**, and founded the Winnipeg Rowing Club in 1881, which was incorporated in 1883, with **John Norquay** serving as club patron. The club had its first international competition in 1886 at Lake Minnetonka, MN, put on by the North Western International Rowing Association. The WRC took home the NWIRA competition's first championship, which is still held annually between rowing clubs within MB, SK, ON, and MN.

In 1914, the NWIRA was presented with a championship cup from the founder of the Lipton Tea brand, Sir Thomas Lipton, which is now awarded annually to the Grand Aggregate

champion. In 1910, **Conrad Riley** led a Winnipeg crew to victory at the Stewards Challenge Cup in the UK, to become the first non-UK crew to win the Stewards Challenge Cup (for a crew of 4 without coxswain) at the Henley Royal Regatta. In 1912, Riley again led a Winnipeg crew to victory, winning every event at the US National Association for Amateur Oarsmen's Regatta championship. The WRC disbanded during WWI and WWII, which hampered the athletic achievements of rower **Theodore Dubois**, who won numerous NA events but who was thwarted from ever reaching the Olympics. The WRC continues to train athletes who compete at an international level, most recently 3-time World Champion **Colleen Miller**. In MB, **Pinawa**'s Rowing and Sailing Club and Winnipeg's Prairie Fire Rowing Club are primarily devoted to recreational rather than competitive rowing. ● MD

ROY, Gabrielle, author, (b March 22, 1909, **St. Boniface**; d July 13, 1983, Quebec) is one of Canada's most influential 20th-century **French** authors. The youngest of Léon and Mélina Roy's 11 children, Gabrielle Roy spent the first 29 years of her life in St. Boniface, graduating from the Académie Saint-Joseph in 1929, the year her father died. After teaching for a year in **Rural** MB, she was offered a permanent teaching position in St. Boniface at Provencher School; among her students was a young **Antonio "Tony" Tascona**. Living with her mother in the house built by her father in 1905 at 375 rue Deschambault in 1905, she participated in the cultural life of the city, primarily with the theatre company Le Cercle Molière. During that time, she also published several short works of fiction in English and in French in newspapers in **Winnipeg**, Montreal, and Toronto, including "The Jarvis Murder Case: A Prize-winning Short, Short Story" in the **Winnipeg Free Press** in 1934. After working in a school in northwestern MB during the summer of 1937, Gabrielle Roy left St. Boniface that fall to study drama in England and France. In Europe, Roy wrote articles for the French journal *Je suis partout*. She also sent articles to Canada for publication in the Franco-Manitoban weekly *La liberté et le patriote*, and the Catholic *North West Review*.

WWII forced her to return to Canada in 1939. She decided to stay in Montreal, and tried to earn a living with her writing. For the next 6 years, she worked as a freelance reporter while writing her first novel about life in a working-class neighbourhood of Montreal during WWII. *Bonheur d'occasion* was published in 1945, 2 years after the death of her mother. The novel became an immediate success. When its English translation appeared in 1947, as *The Tin Flute*, all of Toronto was abuzz; finally, "the great Canadian novel" had been written. The success was also financial. The English translation became a selection of the Literary Guild of America in New York, and Universal Pictures bought the film rights for $75,000, of which 90% went to the author. Although the film was never produced, *The Tin Flute* gave the new author financial stability for the rest of her life and allowed her to undertake a writer's life without financial worries. In 1947, she received France's Prix Fémina for *Bonheur d'occasion*, and the Gov Gen's Award for the English translation *The Tin Flute*.

Gabrielle Roy, 1951

Also in 1947, Gabrielle Roy married a young MB doctor, Marcel Carbotte, in St. Vital, now part of Winnipeg. The newlyweds left for Europe and stayed in France for the next 3 years. While there, Gabrielle started writing her first "Manitoban" novel, *La petite poule d'eau* (*Where Nests the Water Hen*), which was published in 1950 when she returned to Canada. In 1952, Roy and Carbotte moved to Quebec, and in 1957, they bought a summer home at Petite-Rivière-Saint-François, QC, 100 km NE of the provincial capital. Gabrielle spent all her summers until her death there. Also that same year, Gabrielle Roy received a 2nd Gov Gen's Award, this time for the English translation of *Rue Deschambault* (*Street of Riches*), her 2nd "MB" novel, issued in 1955. Several other of the 13 books published during her lifetime were inspired by her MB years. They include *La Route d'Altamont* (*The Road past Altamont*) and articles in *Fragiles lumières de la terre* (*The Fragile Lights of Earth*).

Throughout her career, Roy received many literary awards, including a 3rd Gov Gen's Award

in 1978 for her last novel, *Ces enfants de ma vie* (*Children of My Heart*). She was the first woman to become a fellow of the Royal Society of Canada (1947), and was made a Companion of the Order of Canada in 1967. Gabrielle Roy died July 13, 1983, of heart failure. Her husband Marcel Carbotte died July 8, 1989. They had no children. Between 1997-2003, Roy's birthplace in St Boniface was restored and turned into a museum, the Maison Gabrielle Roy. ● LUCIEN CHAPUT

ROYAL, Joseph, lawyer, politician (b May 7, 1837, Repentigny, Lower Canada [QC]; d Aug 23, 1902, Montreal) was arguably the most important **FRENCH** politician of his generation in MB. Born in Lower Canada to poor parents, he was educated by the Sulpicians and the Jesuits. He articled in law with George-Étienne Cartier's firm in 1857 and became an active journalist, in 1858 founding *L'Ordre*. In 1867, he helped create *Le Nouveau Monde*, and he was editing the **NEWSPAPER** in 1869 when the **RED RIVER RESISTANCE** began. He printed much material favourable to the **MÉTIS**, and soon came to the attention of Bishop **ALEXANDRE-ANTONIN TACHÉ**, who was on the lookout for Francophone professionals for the new province. He founded *Le Métis* in **ST. BONIFACE** in 1871 and opened a law practice with **JOSEPH DUBUC**.

Royal was soon one of the leaders of the Francophones in MB, with his finger in almost every possible pie. He was elected MLA for **ST. FRANÇOIS XAVIER** West in 1870, was chosen first Speaker of the House in 1871, and soon became Provincial Secretary. He later also served as Minister of Public Works and as Attorney General. He was a member of the team defending **AMBROISE-DYDIME LÉPINE** in the notorious murder trials of 1873-74. He was a consistent supporter of the Métis and their cause (including an amnesty for **LOUIS RIEL** and Lépine), anxious to incorporate them in a Francophone bloc in the Legislature. **JOHN NORQUAY** eventually forced him out of the govt in 1879, and he soon shifted to the federal scene, where he became Conservative MP for Provencher, retaining the seat in 1882 and 1887. In 1888, he was named lt gov for the NWTs, but he was uncomfortable with the loss of French rights during his term of office, which ended in 1893. He hoped to become a Senator but was never nominated. In his last years, he worked as a journalist in Montreal. ● JMB

ROYAL ART LODGE was formed by **MARCEL DZAMA**, Michael Dumontier, Drue Langois, Jonathan Pylypchuk, Adrian Williams and Neil Farber in 1996. The group attended classes together at the **U OF M**'s School of Art, where they began to work as a collective at the "lodge" studio space

in Winnipeg's Exchange District every Wednesday. The group began working collaboratively on drawings, dolls, paintings, videos. They also worked on music together through such acts as Albatross, Jeffery and Humphrey and Eyeball Hurt and the Medicine. Credited with the rebirth of interest in contemporary art in Winnipeg, their crude, black humour-laden works have collectively exhibited around the world at venues such as The Drawing Centre (New York City), Museum of Contemporary Art (Los Angeles) and the Atelier Gallery (Vancouver). The 2003 touring exhibition and publication *Ask the Dust* was published and organized by The PowerPlant (Toronto). They have gone on to receive much international critical recognition with the help of the now high profile work of Dzama. The group sometimes included outside members such as siblings Hollie Dzama and Miles Langois, though it is currently comprised of Dumontier, Dzama and Farber. Farber and Dumontier currently live and work in Winnipeg, while Dzama resides in New York City. ● STACEY ABRAMSON

ROYAL CANADIAN HORSE ARTILLERY (1st Regiment). 1 RCHA is based in **CFB SHILO**, along with the 2nd Battalion of the **PRINCESS PATRICIA CANADIAN LIGHT INFANTRY**. The artillery regt provides indirect fire support to the 1st Canadian Mechanized Brigade Group in various theatres around the world.

HISTORY: The First Regiment of the RCHA is the oldest unit in the Canadian Forces. The regt was formed in 1871, and stationed at Kingston and Quebec City. The unit saw action during the North-West Rebellion, the Boer War, both WW1 and WW11, and the Korean War. In July, 1992, the artillery unit was moved to CFB Shilo. The RCHA's main weaponry was upgraded to 105mm howitzers. Several natural disasters, including the Quebec ice-storm and the 1997 Red River flood, led to personnel being posted in rescue duties around the country. As well, the regt continued to be deployed to the world's hotspots, including Bosnia and Afghanistan. ● BRUCE TASCONA

ROYAL CANADIAN MINT is the federal Crown corporation responsible for producing and distributing Canada's coins. Though the RCM is headquartered in Ottawa, all the country's circulation coins are produced at the Mint's state-of-the-art production facility in **WINNIPEG**. The 15,000 m² facility, designed by architect **ÉTIENNE GABOURY**, opened in 1976, and is considered to be among the most modern and innovative coin-production facilities in the world. Its original production plant in Ottawa – which took over

Cdn coin operations from the UK's Royal Mint in 1908 – now produces only collector coins, Maple Leaf bullion, and medals. Winnipeg was selected for the Royal Canadian Mint's circulation currency plant location, because it is close to the geographic centre of Canada. This makes it the most convenient location from which to transport circulation coins to all areas of the country.

The Winnipeg plant, which as of mid-2005 had a full-time staff of about 230, not only produces more than one billion coins a year for Canada, but also competes against other mints for international contracts to produce coins and coin blanks for other countries. Over the past 25 years, it has produced coinage products for more than 60 nations, including New Zealand, Australia, Thailand, Bangladesh, and the United Arab Emirates. To produce 300 million $2 coins, 2 rapid presses were built in the Winnipeg plant in 1996, enabling the coins to be made in a record 9 months. Early in the 21st century, it developed a new, patented technology enabling it to manufacture coins using steel blanks instead of the more costly nickel blanks. In 2005, the Mint undertook an $18-million expansion of its Winnipeg facility, which more than doubled production capacity and enabled it to add the colour yellow to the coins it manufactures. Besides minting all regular circulation Cdn coins, the mint is also a popular tourist attraction, with visitors, especially children, coming from across NA for guided tours. • MURRAY MCNEILL

ROYAL CANADIAN MOUNTED POLICE. See NORTH-WEST MOUNTED POLICE.

ROYAL MANITOBA WINTER FAIR, one
of Canada's largest agricultural events, occurs annually at the end of March in the KEYSTONE CENTRE in BRANDON. The week-long fair offers many western Cdn agricultural, entertainment, livestock, and equestrian attractions. The Provincial Exhibition of Manitoba, established in 1882, gave birth to the Brandon Agricultural Society, which, in Oct 1882, began holding various farm-animal and grain contests. This became known as the Manitoba Summer Fair. In March 1908, the first Manitoba Winter Fair came into existence. On July 12, 1970, HM Queen Elizabeth established patronage to the winter event, and it was thus dubbed the Royal Manitoba Winter Fair. The fair's aim is to encourage livestock sales, breeding lines, and animal care awareness. The horse sales are the most popular attraction. The fair features many shows and contests, such as the heifer scramble, where children try to catch a running calf; the 8-horse wagon pull; and the equestrian and draughthorse contests.

Children's entertainment and fiddling contests are also regular features of the fair. At the Royal Farmyard, visitors can learn about alpacas and miniature horses, and can watch agricultural stage demonstrations. Visitors can see the inner workings of a grain elevator, plants, and interactive and innovative school projects, are available to visitors at the fair's Seed Show. The fair attracts about 130,000 visitors, and has over 300 commercial exhibit spaces. Currently, the Provincial Exhibition of Manitoba runs 3 annual fairs: the Manitoba Summer Fair, the Royal Manitoba Winter Fair, and the Manitoba Livestock Expo (instituted in 1974). • RK

ROYAL WINNIPEG BALLET (RWB) is MB's
leading artistic export. The WINNIPEG company's history has sealed its reputation as one of NA's oldest and finest ballet troupes. In addition to staging groundbreaking new works and celebrated productions of classics, the RWB has been the matrix for the careers of such ballet stars as ARNOLD SPOHR, Mark Godden, Norbert Vesak, Brian Macdonald, DAVID PEREGRINE, and prima ballerina EVELYN HART.

The Winnipeg Ballet Club, formed in 1939 by GWENETH LLOYD and BETTY FARRALLY, became Canada's first professional ballet in 1949. The troupe gave a command performance for HRH Princess Elizabeth (now HM Queen Elizabeth II) in 1951, and received Royal patronage from the newly crowned Queen, the first such ballet company in the Commonwealth. By 1953, the RWB, as it had just become, had already completed its inaugural national tour, and embarked on the first tour of the US by a Cdn ballet company. In 1957, the RWB received its first grant from the Canada Council for the Arts, and in 1958, Arnold Spohr was appointed artistic director. In 1959,

the RWB gave another command performance for HM Queen Elizabeth II and HRH the Duke of Edinburgh.

After Spohr's 1988 retirement, dancer Henny Jurriens became artistic director, though he died in a car accident in 1989. André Lewis then became interim artistic director until Australian John Meehan assumed the role in 1990. In 1993, Meehan left the RWB, to be replaced by dancer and choreographer William Whitener. After Whitener left the RWB in 1995, Lewis became permanent artistic director.

Famed American choreographer Agnes de Mille brought her choreography to the company in 1961. She was later known as the RWB's "fairy godmother" after the elevating effect she had on the already famous troupe. Throughout the 1960s, the RWB hosted stars from Russia's Bolshoi Ballet; in 1973, Mikhail Baryshnikov gave RWB audiences his first performance with partner Gelsey Kirkland after defecting from the USSR.

The company's General (now called Recreational) and Professional Division schools have developed many of the RWB's – and Canada's – best ballerinas and danseurs. In 1962, former RWB principal dancer Jean McKenzie opened the General Division School, and in 1970, former principal dancer David Moroni established the RWB's new professional division, which would become a centre for excellence in dance training. In 1996, the RWB School's Professional Division celebrated its 25th Anniversary with nearly 200 young dancers on stage in a full-length *Don Quixote*.

Outstanding new works of choreography the RWB has staged include: the company's first original full-length ballet, *Rose Latulippe* (Macdonald, 1966); *The Ecstasy of Rita Joe* (Vesak, 1971); *Belong Pas de Deux* (Vesak, 1980); a new staging of *Swan Lake* (Galina Yordanova, 1987);

Students at the RWB School

The Big Top: A Circus Ballet (Jacques Lemay, 1986); *Anne of Green Gables* (Lemay, 1989); and *The Messiah* (Mauricio Wainrot, 2006). International firsts for the company include: first Cdn company to represent Canada at the British Commonwealth of the Arts, in 1965; first Cdn company to tour the Caribbean, in 1966; first Cdn company to tour Israel. Despite a legacy of touring, the RWB maintained its presence in Winnipeg as well, whether on its home stage at the Manitoba Centennial Concert Hall, or at Ballet in the Park, its gift to Winnipeg audiences since 1972.

The company's 1964 appearance at US dancer Ted Shawn's MA-based Jacob's Pillow Dance Festival was another international breakthrough; since then, awards and recognition for the RWB have poured in. Brian Macdonald, company choreographer in 1964, won a gold medal in Paris for his *Aimez-vous Bach?* In 1968, the RWB became the first Cdn company invited to the Concours international de danse de Paris (Paris International Dance Competition), where it gathered 2 golds – one for Best Company, and another to Christine Hennessy for Best Female Interpretation.

However, the gold and bronze that principal dancers Peregrin and partner Hart won in 1980 at the World Ballet Concours in Osaka, Japan – they would reverse the honours at the International Ballet Competitions in Varna, Bulgaria, later that year – cemented the company's reputation and made Hart a star on the world stage. In 1989, RWB dancer Mark Godden received the Clifford E. Lee Choreography Award from the Banff Centre. He followed this up with top honours at the 14th International Ballet Competition in Varna in 1990, and took 2nd prize for new choreography at the 1991 International Ballet Competition in Helsinki. Godden became the RWB's resident choreographer in 1990.

The company and its principals have been the subject of documentaries such as 1992's *Moment of Light: The Dance of Evelyn Hart*, a 50-minute movie by Winnipeg filmmaker Gordon Reeve. To date, the most successful film treatment has been of Godden's original work *Dracula* – a hit for the company in Canada, the US, and Europe. **Guy Maddin**'s 2002 silent film *Dracula: Pages from a Virgin's Diary* featured the RWB's star dancers, and won an International Emmy Award and glowing reviews from US publications such as the *New Yorker*, *Boston Globe*, *Washington Post*, and from European critics.

In 1988, the RWB built their current home at 380 Graham Ave in Winnipeg. The complex includes 10 dance studios (one of them a performance studio), a physiotherapy room,

administrative and production offices, a box office, a wardrobe department, and the Royal Winnipeg Ballet School's Professional and Recreational divisions. A special portable "sprung" floor, designed to reduce injuries to dancers and to enable them to jump higher, was built in 2005 for the company's home stage in Winnipeg. In addition to appealing to Manitobans, the company continues to tour internationally, playing to sold-out houses. ● GARTH A. BUCHHOLZ

ROYAL WINNIPEG RIFLES (1883-Present). A reserve infantry regiment in the city of Winnipeg attached to 38th (Reserve) Brigade Group. Its motto is "Hosti Acie Nominati" (named by the enemy in battle). This military unit at different times was formally known as the:

- 90th Battalion of Winnipeg Rifles (1883)
- 90th Regiment Winnipeg Rifles (1900)
- The Winnipeg Rifles (1920)
- The Royal Winnipeg Rifles (1935-Present)

HISTORY: Volunteers, including their commanding officer Lt. Colonel **William Nassau Kennedy**, took part in the 1884 relief of Khartoum. They served as boatmen conveying Gen Garnet Wolseley's troops up the Nile.

In March 1885, the 90th was mobilized and sent to the Northwest Territories to help put down the Riel Rebellion. It was the first infantry unit to arrive in the district and was part of General Frederick Middleton's column. Its baptism of fire was at the Battle of Fish Creek (April 23) and bore the brunt of the fight. It later took part in the siege and battle of Batoche. Afterwards the unit received its nickname "Little Black Devils" because of their "dark green uniforms." A Métis prisoner made the comment "we know who the redcoats are but who are those Little Black Devils?"

In 1914, the 90th Regiment formed the nucleus of the 8th Battalion Canadian Expedition-

ary Force (CEF) of the First Canadian Division. The 8th Battalion was present at the 2nd Battle of Ypres April 1915 where it was instrumental in stalling the attack where poison gas was used for the first time in the war. It proudly claims that the 8th "never lost a trench." The 8th Battalion suffered over 6000 casualties in WWI and the unit had three Victoria Cross recipients.

The regt was raised again for active service in June, 1940. It became a unit of the 7th Infantry Brigade, 3rd Canadian Division. It did not see action until June 6, 1944 when the Devils took part in the Normandy landing. It fought continuously until VE Day.

Today the Royal Winnipeg Rifles remains an active part of the Canadian Forces reserves providing personnel to peacekeeping and military missions.

Victoria Cross Winners:

Company Sergeant Major F. Hall, April 24, 1915
    (2nd Battle of Ypres)
Corporal A Brereton, August 9, 1918 (Amiens)
Corporal F Coppins, August 9, 1918 (Amiens)
● BRUCE TASCONA

RUGBY arrived in MB with British settlers in the late 1870s, with soldiers at **Winnipeg**'s Osborne Barracks, near the site of the present **Legislative Building**, forming the first official clubs around 1876. In 1879, the Winnipeg Rugby Football Club was formed; Canadians used the terms *football* and *rugby* more or less interchangeably in the 19th century, though *football* – in full, Association Football – more often referred to **Soccer**, as it does in the modern UK. Cdn **Football** evolved from rugby union, a version of a sport derived from soccer at Rugby school in the UK. Rugby league, another branch of rugby, is a primarily professional version most popular in Northern England, Australia, and New Zealand. Union rugby predominates through much of the Commonwealth, including Africa,

90th Battalion, later Royal Winnipeg Rifles, who served at Fish Creek and Batoche, 1885

much of the Pacific, and in Western and Central Europe, though Australians and New Zealanders play this form too. League rugby is seldom, if ever, played in MB.

By 1885, there were enough rugby teams in MB to have a fixture list. Rugby union was the preferred sport at Wesley and St. John's colleges (*see* **U OF W** and **U OF M**). The **NORTH-WEST MOUNTED POLICE** formed rugby teams, as did several athletic clubs. The various clubs came together under the Manitoba and Northwest Rugby Union in 1891. In the early 20th century, the famous New Zealand All Blacks visited Winnipeg to play exhibition games, and NHL player Art Ross formed a rugby team in **BRANDON** around this time. Another rugby league, the Western Canada Rugby Football Union, formed in 1911 with teams from MB, AB, and SK. Winnipeg real estate agent Hugo Ross donated a championship cup, but the union was short-lived and ended with the outbreak of WWI. Though the Gov Gen, Albert Henry George, 4th Earl Grey, donated the Grey Cup for the top Cdn amateur rugby team in 1909, a MB team did not appear in the cup final until 1925, when the Winnipeg Tigers lost to a far-superior Ottawa team.

"English Code" rugby was revived again with the influx of UK immigrants during the 1920s. Winnipeg had 8 teams in 1928: North Kildonan All Blacks, Grain Exchange, the Garrison, Hebrews, Wanderers, Collegians, Marlboros, and Sherburn Athletic. Some of these teams played exhibition games against colleges in ND. The Americanized version of rugby, now known as American football, originated when Montreal's McGill U introduced league rugby to Harvard U in 1874. In the intervening half-century, though, it developed along separate lines, introducing innovations such as scrimmages, downs, and, most dramatically, the forward pass. Initially, when Winnipeg teams played those from ND, ½ game would use American rules, the other, the Cdn code. As time wore on, Canada gradually ceded to US practices, leading to rule changes, the most notable being the introduction of the forward pass in 1929. This led to a schism between modern Cdn football, as promoted by the Canadian Rugby Football Union (the predecessor of Football Canada), and the Rugby Union of Canada, formed that year by purists who wished to maintain the old rules.

After the Winnipeg Rugby Football Club, formed in 1930 (*see* **WINNIPEG BLUE BOMBERS**), adopted the "US" (Cdn football) form, it predominated. By the onset of WWII, organized rugby was virtually non-existent in MB, and only UK and Commonwealth servicemen stationed here under the **BRITISH COMMONWEALTH AIR TRAINING PLAN** played matches. In 1944, a touring

Australian military team played one such exhibition match against a New Zealand side at Osborne Stadium, the Blue Bombers' home field. NATO servicemen similarly organized games while training in MB from 1949 until the program's closure in 1955.

Rugby was revived in 1960 with the founding of the Winnipeg Rugby Club, mainly by expatriates from other Commonwealth nations. Later called the Wanderers, the club was alone in Winnipeg until the founding of the rival Wasps in 1965, which led to the organization of the Manitoba Rugby Union that year. Soon after, in 1968, MB joined the Canadian Rugby Union. In 1973, 10,000 spectators watched the Manitoba Selects play the Welsh rugby champions at Winnipeg (now **CANAD INNS**) Stadium. The Manitoba Rugby Union, which became Rugby Manitoba in 1997, has survived, partly because of the 1973 adoption into Cdn schools of rugby, and because of the sport's expansion in the late 1970s to include women's teams. In 1985, the city of Winnipeg opened Maple Grove Rugby Park, featuring 5 full-sized pitches. The park hosted its first National Rugby Championship Festival in 2003. There are currently 11 rugby teams in MB. ● MICHELLE DOBROVOLNY

RUPERT'S LAND was a vast political and geographical unit that was defined by the Hudson Bay drainage basin and which existed from 1670 to 1870. In 1670, a small group of merchants lead by Prince Rupert, Count Palatine of the Rhine, but more importantly, the "dear and beloved" cousin of English king Charles II received a charter to incorporate the **HUDSON'S BAY COMPANY**. As an act of Royal prerogative of the British Crown, the HBC charter claimed sweeping authority. Since in the British Crown had no specific geographical knowledge from which to delineate boundaries of the HBC lands from other European territorial claims in NA, the language of the charter shrewdly stated: "grant unto them and their successors the sole trade and commerce of all those seas, straits, bays, rivers, lakes, creeks and sounds, in whatsoever latitude they shall be, that lie within the entrance of the straits, commonly called Hudson's Straits, together with all the lands, countries and territories upon the coasts and confines of the seas, straits, bays, lakes, rivers, creeks and sounds aforesaid, which are not now actually possessed by any of our subjects, or by the subjects of any other Christian Prince or State..."

Simply put, the charter granted property and monopoly trading rights to all the lands drained by rivers flowing into **HUDSON BAY** and Hudson Strait. This was done at the pleasure of the Crown. According to the charter, the

HBC grant of Rupert's Land was good unless it conflicted with the possession of other Europeans. The charter did not contemplate the sovereignty or property rights of the Aboriginal peoples occupying the lands that would become known as Rupert's Land. In modern terms, Rupert's Land extended from southern AB to NU's Baffin Island. Periodically, the HBC claim was challenged: by France during periods of imperial rivalry; from trade competitors such as the **NORTH WEST COMPANY**; and in the 19th century, by determined **MÉTIS FREE TRADERS**. In the mid-19th century, the HBC charter came under sharp attack and its ability to command the population at the **RED RIVER SETTLEMENT** slipped. Following drawn out negotiations involving Colonial Office authorities, Canadian cabinet ministers, and HBC officials, and only with the apparent resolution of the issues that gave rise to the **RED RIVER RESISTANCE**, the HBC's control over the North-Western Territory and Rupert's Land was transferred to the Dominion of Canada on July 5, 1870. ● FRANK J. TOUGH

RUPERT'S LAND TRANSFER, July 15, 1870, was the outcome of a legal and legislative process that resulted in the transfer of **RUPERT'S LAND** and the NWTs from the control of the **HUDSON'S BAY COMPANY** to the newly formed Dominion of Canada. This vast territory included the original grant provided by the HBC Charter of 1670 (the Hudson Bay basin) and the NWTs (the Mackenzie River basin) amounting to about 6.47 million km[2]. Together, these 2 territories are referred to as the HBC Territory. This transaction can be described as the largest real estate deal in history and was carried out without the involvement of the inhabitants of the region.

Negotiations between the HBC and Canada dragged out between 1863 and 1868. Progress towards the transfer accelerated with the Confederation of British North American colonies. Section 146 of the *British North America Act*

Signing of the Hudson's Bay Company Charter by Charles II on May 2, 1670

(1867) provided for the admission of Rupert's Land and the Northwestern Territory into the federation. Between Oct 1868 and March 1869, serious negotiations occurred between the HBC directors and Canada, represented by PM Sir John A. Macdonald's Cabinet ministers, George Étienne Cartier and William MacDougall. Senior UK Colonial Office officials served as intermediaries.

During the negotiations, HBC sought several forms of compensation for the surrender of its rights, including a large cash payment, a large land grant, and royalties from future mineral wealth. The position taken by the Cdn delegates disputed entirely the HBC claim. The ministers argued that the Crown should not purchase what it already possessed, claimed that the HBC was obstructing the progress of imperial policy, and rejected the suggestion that future revenues from lands and resources could compensate the company. Since the parties were far from an agreement, Colonial Office Secretary Lord Granville proposed the terms of a settlement on an accept-or-reject basis – the HBC surrenders its charter, Canada pays the HBC £300,000 ($1.46 million), the HBC receives 50,000 ac (20,235 ha) around its posts and 5% of the Fertile Belt, land titles issued by the HBC would be confirmed, and the HBC would not face exceptional taxation. With some reluctance, both the Cdn and HBC negotiators agreed to Granville's ultimatum. After the decisive intervention of area residents that culminated in the **RED RIVER RESISTANCE**, and following the passage of the *Manitoba Act* (1870), an Order in Council of June 23, 1870, was issued.

While the compensation made to the HBC did not satisfy many of its shareholders, in the long run, the HBC was able to benefit from the terms of the surrender. Between 1905 and 1922, the company's dividend rate paid to shareholders ranged from 20 to 50%, in a large part due to the success of its land sales. Net profits of $96,366,021 (in constant dollars) were generated by land sales between 1891 and 1931. For MB, because of the terms of the surrender, the HBC had acquired 1,279,965 ac (5180 km²) by 1930; by comparison, only 559,301 ac (about 2263 km²) had been granted as Indian reserves. • FRANK J. TOUGH

RURAL AND REMOTE MANITOBA. Statistics Canada defines urban as places that have more than 1000 people living within a density of more than 400 people per sq km. All else is considered rural. Thus 'rural' is defined by default, illustrating the importance given to 'urban' in Canada. The corresponding definition of "rural and small town" is any community with fewer than 10,000 inhabitants. In 1871, in the first Canadian Census with MB as a province, only

Rural Population in Manitoba and Canada

YEAR	% RURAL MANITOBA	% RURAL CANADA
1871	96	81
1891	73	69
1911	57	55
1931	55	46
1951	43	38
1971	31	24
1991	28	23
2001	28	20
2006	29	20

4% of the population was considered urban (see table). However, by 1951, more Manitobans were considered urban than rural: in this way MB lagged behind the nation as a whole, which first exceeded 50% urban population in 1931. Since 1951, the proportion of people living in rural MB has continued to decline, stabilizing at 28% since the 1986 Census. In fact, the proportion of Manitobans living in rural areas has been between 28 and 33% since 1966. By comparison, the proportion of Canadians classified as rural has been less than that for MB in each Census since 1871 and as of 2006, only 20% of Canadians or 1 in 5 (about 6 million) were classified as rural.

Rural depopulation has been a factor in all provinces and territories in Canada, particularly since the **GREAT DEPRESSION** of the 1930s. Nowhere is this depopulation greater than in agricultural communities, which are particularly characteristic of SK and MB. This has been true since the foundation of the province and is still the case today. The 2001 farm population in Manitoba was 68,130, a decline of 15% percent from the previous (1996) Census. The number of farms in MB fell from 21,074 in 2001 by 9.6% to 19,054 in 2006. Thus, while *rural* populations have stabilized in Manitoba (29%), farm populations continue to decline. If it were not for the factor of the Hutterian population, which accounted for 9075 (13%) of the 68,130 people living on farms in 2001, this decline would have been much greater. An outflow of city dwellers into rural areas ("the urban fringe") has also had an effect, particularly around **WINNIPEG**, but also around the smaller centres. Although leading to larger rural populations in these areas, and thus a larger tax base, these migrants have been a source of conflict as their lifestyles are often at odds with those of the pre-existing farmers. This ex-urban migration mirrors a national trend where rural populations close to urban centres grew by 4.7% from 2001 to 2006 but remote rural populations fell by .1%.

Significantly, 60% of Manitobans live in the Census Metropolitan Area of Winnipeg, the capital city. This creates a unique provincial population distribution. Outside of Winnipeg, the next three largest communities are **BRANDON** in the southwest (41,511), **THOMPSON** in the mid-north (13,446), and **PORTAGE LA PRAIRIE** in south-central MB (12,728). Each of these 3 act as a regional service centre with hospitals and other private and public services. In addition, Brandon and Thompson have post-secondary institutions (**ASSINIBOINE COMMUNITY COLLEGE** and **BRANDON UNIVERSITY** in the "Wheat City," and **UNIVERSITY COLLEGE OF THE NORTH** in Thompson). All other communities other than **STEINBACH** have fewer than 10,000 people and thus are classified as "rural and small town" by Statistics Canada.

While the southern rural region is dominated by restructuring agricultural patterns, most of its communities are within 2 hours of either Winnipeg or Brandon, and their selection of services is very much negatively influenced by this proximity. The northern remote region is also dominated by restructuring industries, in this case forestry, fishing and mining. Within these economic sectors, people tend to live in communities that were at least at one time classified as urban (e.g., **THE PAS, LEAF RAPIDS, THOMPSON,** and **CHURCHILL**). Even so, transportation and access to services continue to be major issues, particularly to those living outside of the few larger centres. Further, technological changes in industries such as forestry tend to result in less employment.

There are 63 First Nations' communities in MB. Of these, only 18 have populations of more than 1000 people. However, none of these meet the density requirement as First Nation boundaries tend to be larger in area than the traditional nodal mining and agricultural settlements of MB. For example, **NORWAY HOUSE** had a population of 4,071 people in 2006. However, given the area of the reserve is 73 sq km, the population density is only 55.6 people per sq km. Because the density aspect of the definition is not met, Norway House would be considered rural by the Statistics Canada definition. These issues are interesting because the population growth rate of Aboriginal people is greater than non-Aboriginal in MB. A trend such as this could be seen as a stabilizing demographic and economic factor in specific rural areas.

Rural depopulation needs to be assessed in light of the structure of these larger central places across the province. Winnipeg is the undisputed primate city, with Brandon being the 2nd largest urban place with 40,000 people. What is unique about MB is that while there were 23 communities in 2001 with populations of more than 2000, there were 30 communities that had populations between 1000-2000 people, 14 of which are First Nations communities.

The future of 'rural' in MB is a series of question marks. Can growth in the rural residential population adjacent to urban centres continue to partially balance off declines in the farm population, and if so is this really rural? Can the mining sector in the north – especially LYNN LAKE and LEAF RAPIDS – rebound? Finally, will a new rural demographic balance be achieved through increasing numbers of HUTTERITES, Aboriginals, and recent immigrants? • DOUG RAMSEY

RUSSELL, pop 1428, is a town 100 km SW of DAUPHIN, 20 km SW of RIDING MOUNTAIN NATIONAL PARK. The HBC was active in the area, as the nearby ASSINIBOINE RIVER was crucial to the fur trade for 200 years. However, Europeans did not settle the area until 1880, when settlers came by Red River cart to the surrounding valleys. A post office N of the current townsite – originally called Shell River, after the tributary of the Assiniboine near there – opened that year. In 1889, the burgeoning agricultural community, which grew around a CPR point, changed its name to Russell, possibly after Lindsay Russell, who surveyed much of this area. Also that year, a campus of DR. BARNARDO'S SCHOOL FOR BOYS opened. This program saw British orphans coming to Canada to work on farms. The Russell campus closed in 1908, but the charity has left its mark on the region. The Barnardo Home building is now a museum.

Russell was incorporated as a town in 1913. In the 21st century, Russell is still an agricultural service and retail centre, catering to surrounding grain and oilseed operations and cattle farms. The elimination of the CROW'S NEST PASS AGREEMENT and the Western Grain Transportation Subsidy has allowed Russell to benefit from increased beef cattle production. A giant statue of a bull stands on the southern approach to Russell as a recognition of the town's agricultural roots. The statue is locally dubbed "Arthur the Bull," in honour of Art Kinney, Russell's mayor from 1975-80 and the founder of the community's longstanding Beef and Barley Festival.

Since the creation of the Shellmouth Dam and the manmade LAKE OF THE PRAIRIES WNW of here in the 1960s, Russell has seen increased outdoor tourism in the form of sport fishing, water skiing, boating, and swimming. Russell is situated in the scenic Parkland region, with its rolling hills and beautiful valleys. The nearby Asessippi Ski Area and Winter Park also draws travellers to the area. In addition to the Beef and Barley Festival in Oct – the town's main annual celebration – Russell hosts Yamchinka Ukrainian Dance Competition and 21 other annual festivals. Russell also hosted the National Fly Fishing Championship in 2003. In the 1990s, Russell entered into a tax-sharing agreement with the surrounding RM of Russell, becoming the first municipality in MB to sign such a deal.

In late 2006, Russell unveiled 2 sets of massive wooden arches across its Main St. They are a symbol of a concerted effort by the town to atttract increased tourism – an initiative that began with an information trip to Leavenworth, WA, a small town that was on the brink of extinction before it re-invented itself as one of the top destinations in the nortrhwestern US. Team Canada's volleyball centre Kerri Ann Buchberger was born here, water skiing champion Kole Magnowski is from Russell, and the NHL's Theoren Fleury once lived in the area. • GPP

RUSSELL, John Hamilton Gordon, architect (b Nov 5, 1862, Toronto; d Feb 7, 1946, WINNIPEG). Born to SCOTS parents, he was educated at the Model School of Toronto before apprenticing as an architect. He worked as an architect in the US until 1893, when he came to Winnipeg, where he opened an office in 1895. He designed the McArthur Building, the Trust and Loan Building, and the Great West Permanent Loan Building, as well as the Westminster and Knox churches. He served as president of the Royal Architectural Institute of Canada in 1912-13. He was also a vice-president of the Manitoba Provident Mortgage Company. He was a director of the Rotary Club. • JMB

RUSSELL, Robert Boyd "R. B.," labour leader, socialist (b Oct 31, 1888, Glasgow, UK; d Aug 2, 1964, WINNIPEG) was a leading figure of the WINNIPEG GENERAL STRIKE. He came to Canada in 1911. A member of the Socialist Party of Canada, he was not active in labour's opposition to WWI or to conscription. Leader of the International Association of Machinists Local 122 in 1919, he was a main leader of the Winnipeg General Strike and a member of the Central Strike Committee. He was arrested on June 17, 1919, and 2 months later became secretary-treasurer of the

R. B. Russell, a leader in the Winnipeg General Strike

Winnipeg Labor Council formed by the One Big Union. Russell was the only member of the 15-person Central Strike Committee charged with seditious libel. His trial began Nov 25, 1919, and the verdict of guilty was delivered on Dec 23, 1919. The court was not sympathetic to Russell's insistence that he was only acting as a paid agent of the strikers, and sentenced him to 2 years in prison. His appeal to the Manitoba Court of Appeal was unanimously dismissed, the court finding that his actions amounted to a seditious conspiracy. He tried to appeal to the British Judicial Committee of the Privy Council, but failed because the matter was held to be a criminal, rather than civil, one. He subsequently successfully defended the One Big Union against a COMMUNIST Party takeover, but was unable to win elected office. He held on through the GREAT DEPRESSION as secretary of the OBU in Winnipeg. A junior vocational school in Winnipeg was named after him in 1966. • JMB

RUTTAN, John "Jack," hockey player, (b Apr 5, 1889, WINNIPEG; d Jan 7, 1973 Winnipeg) was an influential player in Winnipeg's early amateur hockey teams. Starting in 1905, Ruttan's first 3 hockey seasons were spent with 3 different championship-winning teams; the Armstrong Point and Rustler Club juvenile teams, and the St. John's College team. He graduated to senior hockey in 1909, playing for the Manitoba Varsity team that also won its league championship. His most successful season came with the 1912-13 Winnipeg Hockey Club that won that season's Allan Cup. After the end of his playing days, Ruttan coached senior teams in Winnipeg. He is a member of the Hockey Hall of Fame. • MD

STEAMBOATS,
see page 656

S

ST. ADOLPHE, pop 1070, is a community 20 km S of **WINNIPEG** on the **RED RIVER** and hwy 75. The Crow Wing Trail ran through here on its way from Ridgeville (just NE of **EMERSON**) to the **RED RIVER SETTLEMENT**. The primarily Francophone community of **MÉTIS/FRENCH** descent was originally called Pointe Coupée ("Cut Point"), but was renamed St. Adolphe after local resident Adolphe Turner, who funded much of the construction of the community's **ROMAN CATHOLIC** church. In June 1869, a Cdn survey party came to the St. Adolphe area to prepare for the entry of **ASSINIBOIA** into Confederation. Local Métis protested by removing and burning the survey stakes. Though the population is still primarily French, **MENNONITES** also later came to the area. Today, St. Adolphe is an agricultural service centre. With its location on flat land near the Red, St. Adolphe is vulnerable to **FLOODING**, and was affected in the floods of 1950, 1979, and 1997, among others. While St. Adolphe does not draw significant revenues from tourism, it does feature a cornfield maze each fall as well as a winter carnival. ● GPP

STE. AGATHE, pop 500, is a community 30 km S of Winnipeg on hwy 75. Founded by **MÉTIS**, and settled later by Quebecois, Ste. Agathe was initially called Pointe Grouette. **LOUIS RIEL** bought a lot here in 1871, and sold part of it in 1873. The settlement was renamed by a priest after the Laurentians town of Sainte-Agathe-des-Monts. A post office opened in the 1870s, and a railway line followed in 1888. A ferry across the **RED RIVER** was established in 1871. When a bridge was completed in 1960, ferry service ceased, and in 1988 the bridge was named after Riel. Ste. Agathe is on relatively high ground, but was damaged by Red River **FLOODING** in 1950 and hard-hit by the 1997 flood, which resulted in the construction of a $4.2 million dike. The Red River Valley Flood Interpretive Centre chronicles the Red's flooding history. In the 2000s, agriculture is the dominant industry here. Festivals in this largely bilingual centre include a winter carnival and, in summer, Cheyenne Days, named after the **STEAMBOAT** *Cheyenne*, which sank here in 1875. Ste. Agathe had high hopes for new economic development in 1998 when European investors built a $60 million canola crushing plant that was supposed to extract canola oil without chemicals. It took until 2005, and new ownership, for the world's largest chemical-free canola crushing plant to open. ● GPP

ST. AMANT is a non-profit organization dedicated to assisting persons with physical and

605

mental disabilities. In 1931, the **Grey Nuns** opened a facility on River Rd in **Winnipeg** to treat **Tuberculosis** patients. In 1959, the focus shifted to helping children with disabilities. It was given the name St. Amant Centre in 1974, in tribute to dedicated employee Béatrice St. Amant.

The organization retains the spiritual values of its founders as part of the Catholic Health Network (which also includes Sara Riel, the Taché Centre, and the **St. Boniface General Hospital**), but receives most of its funding from the Winnipeg Regional Health Authority and provincial Department of Family Services and Housing.

The original facility, now called River Road Place, is a 216-bed residence for children and adults, and offers respite, short, and long-term care. Since 1977, St. Amant has operated a community residential program that in 2007 cared for 150 clients in more than 50 locations. Other initiatives include a community support outreach program to train caregivers of people with disabilities; preschool childcare; a school; and adult literacy education. In 1997, the St. Amant Research Centre was created, and in 2002, the organization launched a behaviour analysis project to treat children with autism. The St. Amant Association allows parents and community members to have input on organizational policies. In Oct 2006, the 15th annual St. Amant Conference attracted 450 attendees to discuss developmental disabilities and autism. ● JOEL TRENAMAN

ST. ANDREW'S LOCK AND DAM, in **Lockport**, on the **Red River**, was created to make river navigation possible from **The Forks** in **Winnipeg**, over the St. Andrews Rapids, to **Lake Winnipeg**. In 1900, work began on the Caméré curtain dam, a style named after the French engineer who pioneered this design. The Lockport dam, which is movable and can raise its floodgates, is the only Caméré curtain type in NA, and the world's largest. The vast quantity of mud and stone dug at the site was used to create a park-like artificial island S of the dam, where wildfowl often gather. The dam and lock were opened in July 1910 by PM Sir Wilfrid Laurier. The site was declared a **National Historic Site** in 1995. ● GPP

STE. ANNE, pop 1534, is a town 25 km SE of **Winnipeg**, on hwy 12. **French** and **Métis** settled the area from the mid-1850s. Oak timber was supplied from here for construction of the **Roman Catholic** cathedral in St. Boniface. At first, the community was called Pointe des Chênes, becoming Sainte-Anne-des-Chênes in 1891. Ste. Anne was on the Dawson Trail, used by travellers from eastern Canada, and had an **HBC** post starting in 1872. A rail spur connected the settlement to the main CPR line in the late 1800s, bringing British settlers, and then **Mennonites**. Ste Anne is mainly bilingual, and was incorporated as a village in 1967 and as a town in 1997. It mainly is a bedroom community for Winnipeg, although it offers local services and retail and health care and education are significant employers. Dawson Trail Days and the Ste.Anne Winter Carnival attract visitors. ● GPP

ST. BONIFACE is the first permanent **French Catholic** settlement in western Canada. Its founding dates back to the arrival of Father **Joseph-Norbert Provencher** at the **Red River Settlement** on July 16, 1818 after a 60-day canoe trip from Montreal. Sent by Quebec's Bishop Plessis at the request of **Lord Selkirk**, Provencher's mission was to evangelize the **First Peoples** of the West and to minister to the **Métis** and French Canadians living at Red River. Feeling unworthy for the mission, Provencher told his Bishop that it would take a missionary of the calibre of a Saint Boniface to succeed. On Nov 1, 1818 Provencher inaugurated a chapel on the east side of the **Red River**, across from the mouth of the **Assiniboine River** and the future **Upper Fort Garry**, on a 22 acre (12 hectare) parcel of land given to the Church by Lord Selkirk with Boniface, the English martyr who established the German Catholic Church in the 8th century, as the mission's patron saint.

In 1829, Provencher opened a school for girls in St. Boniface. In 1838, he set up an "industrial school" to teach weaving using the wool from the bison. With the arrival of the Sisters of Charity of Montreal (**Grey Nuns**) in 1844, and the Oblate Missionaries in 1845, other institutional buildings were built, including, the Grey Nuns' convent, the largest oak log structure still in existence in NA and **Winnipeg**'s oldest building. By 1853, the year of Provencher's death, a cathedral with its famous twin spires, a Bishop's Palace and the Grey Nuns convent which doubled as a hospital, gave St. Boniface the appearance of being a bustling enclave in the middle of the Prairies.

In 1870, the year of MB's entry into Confederation, the parish of St. Boniface, population 813, stretched on both sides of the Red River, with 330 Métis living in St. Boniface West (Fort Rouge ward) and 483 Métis and French Canadians living in St. Boniface East (St. Boniface ward). And except for the core of Catholic institutional buildings, St. Boniface was a rural parish whose residents were established on parish river lots. The first "urban" development occurred in 1874, when the diocese subdivided land it owned north of the actual Provencher Blvd and sold building lots to newly arrived French Canadians.

During the 1870s St. Boniface seemed to be destined to a bright future as a transportation hub. The first steam locomotive, the ***Countess of Dufferin***, arrived in St. Boniface in Oct 1877 aboard the steamboat *Selkirk*. The St. Paul & Manitoba Railroad link from St. Boniface to Pembina in the USA was completed in Dec 1878. For the next several years, St. Boniface would have two railway stations, one East of the Seine River, and one on Provencher Blvd which was also the western end of the Dawson Road. When it came time to build a railway bridge on the Red River, St. Boniface interests lobbied unsuccessfully to locate the bridge at the foot of Provencher Blvd. However with the construction of the Louise Bridge at Point Douglas in 1880, train traffic arrived directly in Winnipeg bypassing St. Boniface.

The first municipal government was created in 1880. In 1883, the northern part of the municipality was separated from the RM and

St. Andrews Locks, ca 1950

The Esplanade Riel provides a dramatic entrance to St. Boniface.

incorporated as the town of St. Boniface. Called the "Village," this is the first francophone urban municipality in western Canada. Its 1,449 residents (1886 Census) were overwhelmingly Catholic (93%) and francophone (83%). However, contrary to the 1870 parish of St. Boniface which was 85% Métis, the new "Village" was French Canadian: only 32% of the residents were born in MB and only 10% were Métis. Over the next 25 years, this French Catholic "Village" would become the bilingual city of St. Boniface.

The phenomenal growth of the city of Winnipeg at the beginning of the 20th century stimulated the growth of St. Boniface. MB's fourth largest urban municipality in 1886, St. Boniface was the third largest city 20 years later, behind only Winnipeg and Brandon. In the late 1880s, the Norwood Improvement Company, formed largely of CANADIAN PACIFIC RAILWAY directors, acquired land in St. Boniface south of Marion Street which was subdivided and sold as building lots, creating a new suburb called Norwood, settled primarily by English-speaking people. French-speaking immigrants from Europe and immigrants who did not speak English or French also settled in St. Boniface at the turn of the 20th century. The Club Belge (Belgian Club), founded in 1905, built its clubhouse on Provencher in 1908. Polish and Ukrainian residents would do the same. Most ethnic groups would also have their own church and parish.

In 1908, the town of St. Boniface became the city of St. Boniface. The new city annexed the part of the RM of St. Vital located East of the Seine River, thus regaining all the territory of the 1870 St. Boniface East Red River Parish. It is an indication of the changing face of St. Boniface that by 1912, the city had elected its first non-francophone mayor, Thomas Berry.

Less stringent municipal bylaws enticed some industries, such as meat packing, to locate in St. Boniface. After WWII, the population of St. Boniface was 21,613 (1946 Census). The boom years that followed and its proximity to Winnipeg fuelled suburban growth. With the extensive Windsor Park development in the early 1960s, and the Southdale area after 1965, the population grew over the next 20 years, reaching 45,370 people by 1969. With the creation of Unicity in 1971, the city of St. Boniface, against its will, was amalgamated to the city of Winnipeg along with the 11 other municipalities of the Greater Winnipeg area. The name of the former city lives on as a bilingual municipal ward of Manitoba's capital. In 2001, 46.5% of the 45,600 residents of the St. Boniface municipal ward were Catholic, and 32% were bilingual (English and French). Most of the Franco-Manitoban provincial associations are headquartered in St. Boniface, which is still seen as the capital of francophone MB. ● LUCIEN CHAPUT

ST. BONIFACE COLLEGE. *See* COLLÈGE UNIVERSITAIRE DE SAINT-BONIFACE.

ST. BONIFACE GENERAL HOSPITAL (SBGH) is MB's 2nd-largest health care facility. It is a major centre for acute care, research, and teaching, and has become MB's hub for cardiac care. In 2006, it featured more than 180 departments spread out in 7 buildings on an 8 ha campus, and maintained 553 beds supported by more than 4000 staff as well as 340 doctors with admitting privileges. About 14,000 surgeries take place each year.

The Sisters of Charity of Montreal (GREY NUNS), who had arrived at the RED RIVER SETTLEMENT from Canada East (QC) in 1844, established the hospital in 1871. The first infirmary W of ON, the Hôpital Saint-Boniface was a 4-bed unit located on the E bank at THE FORKS of the RED and ASSINIBOINE rivers in St. Boniface, where the modern facility remains. At the hospital's founding, the new govt of MB provided a $500 grant.

In 1877, the sisters purchased a 10-bed house, and residential quarters were added to allow

24-hour care. In the 1880s, the hospital gained its first doctor, Théogène Fafard, and moved again to a 60-bed building. A formal nursing school opened in 1897, though nurses had been trained on-site since 1891. Building expansions and technological upgrades occurred frequently in that era, including operating rooms, a pharmacy, and a maternity ward in 1900. In the 1920s, St. Boniface's status as a teaching hospital received a boost when an agreement was reached with the **U OF M** to train medical students. A new residence allowed the hospital to train up to 200 students at once. The School of Nursing was in operation until 1997, when responsibility shifted to the U of M.

The hospital performed the province's first cardiac surgery in 1959. SBGH was the first in the world to use an Eindhoven heart X-ray machine in 1966, and opened Canada's first palliative care unit in 1974. With the help of $13 million from the SBGH Foundation, the hospital's groundbreaking research centre opened in 1987. With almost 250 employees and a $7-million annual budget, the centre has conducted research on infectious diseases, family medicine, nephrology, cardiology, clinical nursing, and cancer. NARANJAN DHALLA and ROBERT EARL BEAMISH were prominent researchers in the cardiovascular department. The foundation also provided $4 million for the purchase of MB's first MRI machine in 1990; 2 more units were added in 1999. The hospital increased its reputation as a research nucleus with the 1998 launch of the Centre for Research on Diseases of the Aging, and the 2003 completion of the I. H. Asper Clinical Research Institute, MB's first facility able to administer clinical trials of new treatments (*see* IZZY ASPER). The Winnipeg Regional Health Authority (WRHA) moved to consolidate all cardiac surgery at SBGH by early 2007. The Bergen Cardiac Sciences Centre was completed in late 2006. MB Health also committed $30 million for further heart-surgery capital expansion, due to be completed in 2009.

The original religious and FRENCH influences remain factors in the hospital's governance,

From its simple origins, St. Boniface Hospital has grown into an impressive complex.

though in 2000 the Grey Nuns of MB transferred authority and ownership of their health-care institutions (which also included Sara Riel, Taché Centre, and the **St. Amant Centre**) to the Catholic Health Corporation of MB, which in turn created the Catholic Health Network. The hospital's mission refers to a "special responsibility" to francophones. There has been a focus on bilingualism initiatives, including a 2004 plan to hire more French-speaking doctors and other staff. The SBGH board also works with the WRHA, and is affiliated with the U of M as a clinical teaching site, as well as through research partnerships. Dr. Michel Tétreault has served as SBGH president and CEO since Jan 2005, and in 2006, former **Progressive Conservative Party** leader Stuart Murray took on that role for the research foundation. • JOEL TRENAMAN

ST. BONIFACE MUSEUM (also Musée Saint-Boniface). The museum was founded in **St. Boniface** in 1967, and is based in the former **Grey Nuns'** convent along the E bank of the **Red River** near **The Forks** in **Winnipeg**. On the urging of Bishop **J. P. Provencher**, the Sisters of Charity built the site in the 1840s, and ran in it the oldest hospital, girls' school, and orphanage in the Cdn West. The building, made primarily of oak using the Red River frame technique (*see* **Architecture**), is among the oldest in Winnipeg. Likely the oldest surviving oak building in NA, the convent became a **National Historic Site** in 1958.

The museum displays about 2300 items, though the entire collection consists of almost 10 times that number of pieces. These include paintings, prints, photographs, musical instruments, everyday articles such as snowshoes, and some effects of **Louis Riel**'s. Collections are focused on the arrival of missionaries and the Sisters to the area; the history of St. Boniface, of **French** and **Métis** in MB; Riel, the **Red River Resistance**, and the Northwest Resistance; and pioneer life. The museum houses reconstructions of a workshop; a Métis hunting camp; a spinning room; dining, working, and sleeping quarters; and a kitchen. The museum displays religious objects and vestments in its chapel, including the first church bell in western Canada, which **Lord Selkirk** gave the convent. In front of the museum sits a bronze bust of Riel, sculpted in 1989 by artist Réal Bérard of **St-Pierre-Jolys**. • AMANDA STEPHENS

ST. CLAUDE, pop 588, is a village on hwy 2, 80 km W of **Winnipeg**. **French** immigrants from St-Claude, France, settled here in the 1880s, followed by French-speaking **Métis**, Swiss, and Belgians. A spur line connected the community to the main CPR line in 1892, and a post office

opened the next year. St. Claude became a village in 1963, the same year architect **Étienne Gaboury** designed the Roman Catholic St. Claude's Church. In the 21st century, agriculture is the primary business in this bilingual centre. The milk processing plant here is one of the largest in MB. And St. Claude is home to the Manitoba **Dairy** Museum. An 1895 jail is now a museum and tourist office. • GPP

ST. EUSTACHE, pop 300, is a community 35 km NW of **Winnipeg**. It was first established and settled in 1885 by **Roman Catholic** missionaries. It was linked to the railway and opened a post office in the late 1880s. Many early settlers were **Métis** hunters, and St. Eustache took the name of the patron saint of hunters. The parish church has one of the largest carillons in western Canada; Charles Aimé Halpin, former Catholic Archbishop of Regina, was born and ordained here. The surrounding area is primarily agricultural, includes several **Hutterite** colonies. • GPP

ST. FRANCOIS XAVIER (formerly Grantown), pop 508, RM pop 1024, is a community 30 km W of **Winnipeg** on hwy 26. The municipality is long and narrow, stretching for about 50 km along the **Assiniboine River**, with the village area located at the site of the originial first settlement. Though the area had been occupied by Assiniboine for hundreds of years, the earliest permanent settlement here was in 1824, when inhabitants of **Pembina**, many of who were **Métis** and relatives of **Cuthbert Grant**, followed Grant to the White Horse Plains. The community was therefore known as Grantown. That same year, Grant saw to the establishment of a **Roman Catholic** parish, Saint-François-Xavier. This parish, named after a Jesuit missionary, is the second oldest Catholic parish in MB. Grant, who was among the largest landowners in **Rupert's Land**, also provided amenities such as a mill for the settlers. A working replica of Grant's flourmill now stands on Sturgeon Creek in **Winnipeg**, where Grant had earlier built a mill.

Though Grant worked hard to enable locals to pursue subsistence **Agriculture**, early Grant-owners were largely engaged in **Bison** hunting, and produced **Pemmican** and buffalo robes for **Red River** settlers. Together with **Cree** and **Ojibway** groups, Grant and many Métis here worked to repel **Dakota** attacks on the Red River settlement. This culminated in several huge battles including, in 1851, a decisive victory at Grand Coteau (ND). So famed were the Métis of Grantown as warriors that US Gen James Dickson came here attempting to recruit them for an "Indian Liberation Army" around 1836-37. After Grant's death in 1854, the parish name gradually took hold, primarily when

The landmark White Horse on the Trans-Canada Highway near St. Francois Xavier

non-Métis **French** settlers and smaller numbers of other Europeans came to the area. Grant was buried under the altar of the church, a singular honour. However, with the later destruction of the church in a fire, Grant's gravesite remains unknown. Though St. Francois Xavier serves partially as a bedroom community of Winnipeg, agriculture is still pursued in the area, and the community offers a range of retail and services. There is a small airport here as well as a credit union, giftshop and tea house, manufacturing plants, and the elementary community school which draws students from Elie and St. Eustache as well as the students who reside in the RM. • GPP

ST. GERMAIN, Ray, country singer/songwriter, broadcaster, actor (b July 29, 1940, St. Boniface). St. Vital-raised St. Germain, a **Métis**, began his professional career at age 16 with Hal Lone Pine and Betty Cody's *CKY Caravan* show as an Elvis Presley sound-alike, touring the province in one of the very first rockabilly shows. Teaming with Lone Pine Jr (**Lenny Breau**), St. Germain cut his first single, "She's a Square" (1959) – probably **Winnipeg**'s first rock 'n' roll record. That same year, he won **CBC**'s *Talent Caravan* and performed in Toronto. A 3-year stint hosting CBC Winnipeg's weekly *Music Hop Hootenanny* solidified St. Germain's reputation as a national performer. He recorded the show's theme, "Raise a Ruckus Tonight," as a single in 1964. In 1970, he hosted *My Kind of Country* for CBC-TV and later *Ray St. Germain Country* and *Big Sky Country* on CKND (*see* **CanWest Global**), running nationally for 14 years. His 2 daughters, Chrystal and Cathy, were regular performers on the show.

St. Germain wrote and recorded "The Métis" (1979), earning him the Aboriginal Order of Canada (1985) and a place on the Aboriginal Wall of Honour (1998). Other honours include membership in the Canadian Country Music Hall of Fame as well as the Manitoba Annual Country Award for Entertainer of the Year, Song of the Year, Male Vocalist of the Year, Recording Artist of the Year, and the Lifetime Achievement Golden Award (1978-85). He is a program manager and drive-home DJ for Native Communications Incorporated (*see* **Broadcasting**) in Winnipeg, and hosts *The Road Show* and *Métis Hour ×2* as well as *Rhythms of the Métis* on the **Aboriginal Peoples Television Network** (APTN). He is the voice of the bear on the APTN children's series *Tipi Tales*. • JOHN EINARSON

ST. GODARD, Emile, dogsled racer (b Aug 15, 1905, **St. Boniface**; d Mar 26, 1948, **The Pas**). At the height of the popularity of dogsledding in the 1920s and '30s, Canada's top racer was Emile St. Godard, a farm boy from The Pas. He started racing in 1925, winning in his first attempt at The Pas Dog Derby, a gruelling event that lasted 4 days and covered 320 km. He won the next 4 derbies consecutively up to 1929. With his lead dog Toby, a greyhound-husky cross to whom St. Godard was extremely devoted, he won 28 international races, on average racing 2400 km per season. His greatest rival was US dogsledder Leonard Seppala. The adversaries had their ultimate face-off at the 1932 Lake Placid Olympics, where dogsledding was briefly introduced as a demonstration sport. St. Godard won the gold medal, beating Seppala, who thereafter refused to race St. Godard. By 1934, St. Godard had married and retired from racing, having over the course of his career won 40 dogsledding trophies. He later ran a farm in the Carrot River Valley. He was entered into Canada's Sports Hall of Fame in 1956, the only dogsled racer to have been inducted. • MD

ST. LAURENT, pop 1454 (RM), is a community 80 km NW of **Winnipeg**, on the S end of **Lake Manitoba**, on hwy 6. A **Roman Catholic** parish named Saint-Laurent was first established here in 1857 by Oblate missionaries. **Métis** arrived after the 1870 **Red River Resistance** and after flooding of the **Red River** in 1874. In the 1800s, locals supported themselves through **Bison** hunting, ranching, **Fishing** and trapping. Early in the 1900s, Ukrainians and French Canadians from QC also settled here. However, St. Laurent retained a strong Métis identity. Even in the 21st century, the **Michif** language – a patois of Cree and French – is still spoken here. The St. Laurent Métis culture is profiled in an exhibit at the Smithsonian Institution in Washington, DC.

The community is different from many small towns and villages in MB in that it is based on the early parish lot system along the lake rather than early settlement and a railway point. St. Laurent is spread out along a 13-km stretch; there is no Main St. here, no grid roads.

In the 2000s, the economy relies on services and retail to nearby agricultural operations, and has meat- and fish-packing plants. Waterfowl hunting and sport fishing, including ice fishing on the lake, attract tourists. Commercial ice fishing is important, the community claiming to have the largest assembly of commercial snow machines in the province. The **Manipogo** Festival, named after a mythical lake monster, is held annually, as is the summer Métis Days. In 2007, the community was planning on developing an environmentally-friendly biomass heating system for its public buildings. **Yvon Dumont**, who served as the **Manitoba Métis Federation** president and MB's **Lt Gov** from 1993 to 1999, comes from St. Laurent. The 2006 Census showed significant population grown for the RM of St. Laurent over the 2001 count – 24.1%. • GPP

ST. LAZARE, pop 265, is a village 125 km NW of **Brandon** and 125 km SW of **Dauphin**, along the **Assiniboine River**, 15 km E of the SK border, on a **CN** line, and on hwys 41 and 42. The community was named by a missionary Rev. Father Jules Decorby after the railway station in France from which he departed when he left for Canada in 1867. St. Lazare was located close to the site of the former **Fur Trading** post Fort Ellice and the Carlton Trail. Settled largely by **French**, **Métis**, and **English**, this bilingual, largely **Roman Catholic** community became a village in 1950. Manufacturing and potash extraction are the main economic activities here, though the school is among the larger employers, and diverse **Service** and **Retail** operations cater to a wide area outside the village. Festivals include the annual Ride for Hope, at the site of the old **HBC** and **NWMP** fort; a winter carnival (March); and Pioneer Days (Civic Holiday weekend). In the early 2000s, the village and the RM had expropriated the Fort Ellice site and were in the process on doing work. They also bought a building on the village's main street and were establishing an interpretive centre. • GPP

ST. MALO, pop 900, is 65 km SSE of Winnipeg on the Rat River and on hwy 59. The initially Francophone community was formed in the mid-19th-century decades after **NWC Fur Trader** Charles Chaboillez came here. It was apparently named after Louis Malo, an early resident here; according to tradition, a nearby priest jocularly referred to the settlement as "St. Malo" after him,

and the name stuck. However, it is more likely that, like nearby La Rochelle, St. Malo took its title from a northern French town of the same name. France's St. Malo is named for a Welsh student of St. Brendan who was later canonized. The community is primarily of **Roman Catholic** and **French/Métis** descent, though the surrounding area was colonized by **Mennonites**. The earliest church was built in 1890, the same year the post office opened. The church subsequently burnt down, but a replica of the old "chapel House (Maison-Chapelle) has been built – this new building houses a French/Métis interpretation centre, restaurant and gift shop. **Agriculture** forms much of the economy here, though **Tourism** to a nearby provincial park and lake is an important revenue source. The St. Malo Summer Festival also draws tourists to a soapbox derby and to strongman competitions. • GPP

ST. PIERRE-JOLYS, pop 839, is a village 50 km SSE of **Winnipeg** on hwy 59 near the Rat River. Part of the 19th-century Crow Wing Trail linking **Upper Fort Garry** with St. Paul (now MN), the area was initially settled by **French**-speaking people, including **Métis** and Quebecois. English settlers later came here in smaller numbers, as well. Father **Noël-Joseph Ritchot** and **Joseph Dubuc** both helped with St. Pierre's founding. The Breton-born Father Jean-Marie Jolys started a parish and encouraged many QC families to move here. In 1922, the post office added the name "Jolys" to "St. Pierre" to recognize the 40 years of Father Jolys as parish priest, but it was only in 1977 that the village was officially named St. Pierre-Jolys.

The **Roman Catholic** faith has been inextricably linked to the settlement's growth, and a former convent of the Sisters of the Holy Names is now the village's museum. Though the post office opened in 1879, St-Pierre-Jolys only incorporated as a village in 1947. **Agriculture** was the dominant industry here, primarily **Dairy Farming** and **Livestock.** However, in the 21st century, local businesses, services, and hospitality are important sectors for the life of the community. There are also 3 schools, a hospital, and a sizable **RCMP** detachment here. Tourism is also important to the village: the former Crow Wing here is now part of the **Trans-Canada Trail**, and St-Pierre-Jolys hosts several popular festivals, such as the Cabane à sucre (maple syrup festival) in April; the signature **St. Pierre-Jolys** Frog Follies – the only frog-jumping contest in Canada; and a Festival of Lights in Dec. Bilingual St. Pierre-Jolys has collaborated with nearby **St. Malo** on several ventures, including a newsletter, a trade show, and a **Hockey** league. • GPP

STE. ROSE DU LAC, pop 995, is a town 40 km SE of **Dauphin** on hwy 5. In 1889, **Métis** from St. Vital (now part of Winnipeg) settled here. Quebecois, Belgians, **French**, and later **English** and **Germans** arrived soon after. The Oblates of Mary Immaculate set up a **Roman Catholic** mission here. A post office opened in 1894. Initially called St. Rose, the "du Lac" was added later, referring to Dauphin Lake. The village was incorporated in 1920; it became a town in 1998. An RCMP detachment opened here in 1932. Ste. Rose, now less than 1/3 bilingual, is the most-northerly "French" town in MB, and is still predominantly Catholic. The town offers health care, education, and retail services for a large trading area. Ste. Rose du Lac is the self-described "cattle capital of MB" with 10% of the province's beef herd close by. Hoof N' Holler Days – a cattle auction, rodeo, and barn dance – is held each Thanksgiving weekend. Cattle auctions, as well as baseball and softball, draw visitors to town. There is a grotto here that is a stone replica of the Lourdes, France grotto where the Virgin Mary is said to have appeared in 1858. A former railway station is now a fire hall. • GPP

ST. THERESA POINT FIRST NATION, on reserve pop 3027, off reserve pop 213, is situated 467 km NE of **Winnipeg**. The native languages of this community are **Ojibway** and **Cree**. The St. Theresa Point First Nation signed Treaty 5 in 1909; in the 2000s it was a member of the Island Lake Tribal Council. Education, administered by St. Theresa Point, goes from Nursery-Grade 12, with enrolment for 2003-04 at 954. There are 3 reserves located here: Cantin Lake IR, Mukwa Narrows IR, and St. Theresa Point IR. The isolated community is accessible only by winter road and air. Indian and Northern Affairs launched a plan to improve water and sewer infrastructure at St. Theresa Point in 2003. • RK

SALAMANDER is a type of amphibian characterized by a long, thin body and tail, slimy skin, and an aquatic larval stage. Unlike frogs, they have reduced legs (with no claws on the toes), and a number of furrows (costa) running vertically on the sides. Most spend their lives underground or under bark and dead leaves, where they hunt for worms and insects, but during the breeding season (usually in spring), they instinctively head for pools to mate. While courting (displaying and rubbing), the male deposits a sperm package on the pond bottom and the female accepts it into her cloaca, where her eggs are then fertilized internally (not externally as in frogs). These are then laid and attached to vegetation or on the pond bottom until they hatch into larvae with gills for gaseous exchange underwater, and broad tails used for swimming. Feeding on small aquatic life, the larvae continue growing for several months and then transform into the land-dwelling adult, starting with the emerging front legs (unlike frogs which begin with the hind legs) and absorption of the gills. Certain species remain aquatic as adults. There are 3 species of salamanders in MB.

By far the largest salamander (and amphibian) in the province is the Mudpuppy (*Necturus maculosus*), which may reach 30-43 cm. It is greyish-brown with large feathery red gills, and dwells in SE rivers (including the Red, Assiniboine, and Winnipeg) and lakes (S Lake Winnipeg). Most people have no idea that such a creature exists here, although it is not uncommon in rocky shallows of lakes in cottage country. Occasionally taken on hook and line, people are astonished to see what they have caught. The animal may be active all year round in deep water (i.e., 12 m). This species mates in the fall, and the female lays up to 100 eggs the following spring. The adult retains the larval form, complete with gills, and never ventures on land.

ROBERT R. TAYLOR

Red-backed salamander

The Grey Tiger Salamander (*Ambystoma tigrinum diaboli*) is stocky (with 11-14 costa), 18-33 cm long, and grey-green with variable black markings. There are half-a-dozen subspecies across NA with remarkably different bold patterns. It is common in grassland, aspen parkland, and farm fields of S and W MB, especially where potholes, sloughs and ditches provide ideal breeding habitat. In April and early May, great numbers begin their migration in search of a breeding pond, and unfortunately countless thousands are killed along highways on rainy nights. The adult is a voracious feeder, snapping up and swallowing any creature it can stuff into its wide mouth, from beetles and worms to frogs and baby mice. With the arrival of cold weather in Oct, these salamanders either dig their own burrow, or use that of another animal (ground squirrel or pocket gopher) and hibernate below the frostline for the next 6 months. Individuals may survive over 12 years in the wild, and up to 20 years in captivity.

The Blue-spotted Salamander (*Ambystoma laterale*) is a thin, delicate, 10-14 cm creature, black with beautiful light-blue spots, and 12 costal grooves. It is night active and highly secretive, so is seldom seen, although it can be common in mixed woods with ponds in extreme SE MB. Individuals may be discovered by lifting logs or stones. It hunts through the leaf litter for worms, insects, spiders, snails and millipedes. Even before pond ice has completely thawed in late April, these tiny salamanders emerge from hibernation in the soil near ponds, the males arriving first to set up territories. Remarkably, they swim around in this cold water at night, searching for aquatic life to eat, and a mate. If molested, it secretes a foul substance from its back and tail, which may repulse the predator (e.g., bird or shrew). Loss of habitat and erosion from forestry and peat farming, and mining pollution are a threat to this species. • REW

SALISBURY HOUSE RESTAURANTS OF CANADA LTD, known unofficially as "Sal's," is MB's oldest and largest restaurant chain. Ralph Erwin, an Oklahoman who visited **Winnipeg** as a member of a touring theatre group, founded the company in 1931. Erwin decided that the MB capital needed a coffee shop/restaurant where theatregoers could stop in after a show, so he borrowed $235 and opened a 10-seat coffee shop on Fort St just S of Portage Ave. He named it Salisbury House, after Salisbury steak, and called the hamburgers on the menu "Nips," both because they were a portion of a Salisbury steak and because he didn't like the word *hamburger*. The Fort St restaurant was followed by several more "Sal's" at other downtown Winnipeg locations, including Kennedy St just S of Portage, the corner of Broadway and Osborne St, and the corner of Portage and Spence St. In the decades that followed, the chain continued to grow to the point where, in the 1970s, it boasted more than 30 outlets in MB. In 1979, Erwin sold the chain to the Montreal-based Steinberg grocery store chain, which operated it for 11 years before selling it to another Montreal company, Interaction Restaurants.

Interaction retained ownership of the chain until 2001, when it sold it to a group of Winnipeg investors which included Protos International, a local holding company which owned Maple Leaf Distillers; **The Guess Who** lead singer **Burton Cummings**; former **Winnipeg Jets** player Thomas Steen; Dickie Dee Ice Cream owner Earl Barish; and **Winnipeg Goldeyes** baseball team owner (and future Winnipeg mayor) **Sam Katz**. Katz later sold his interest in the company, and in 2004, the **Tribal Councils Investment Group**, a Winnipeg-based consortium of 7 MB First

The original "Little Red Roof" Salisbury House on Portage Ave.

Lárus Guðmundsson and Ingibjörg Guðmundsdóttir. In 1913, Laura married a struggling immigrant Norwegian railwayman, George Salverson. Laura Goodman Salverson experienced firsthand the physical hardship and spiritual alienation of the newcomers to the crude new western frontier. She had learned English only at the age of 10, when she first went to school, and had worked as a domestic servant, but she was determined to hold a career as a writer in English. At a time when intellectual life in Canada was just beginning to emerge from colonial subservience to British culture, Salverson's work represents an early appearance of the non-British ethnic writing that was to enrich the country's literature. She was encouraged by members of the newly founded Canadian Authors Association, and in 1922, her short story "Hidden Fire" won first prize in a contest for the best rendition of life on the Prairies, sponsored by the Women's Canadian Club of Regina. Her first novel, *The Viking Heart* (1923), traces in almost documentary fashion the story of the Icelandic arrival in **GIMLI**, and it earned Salverson instant popularity.

Writing partly out of economic necessity, to supplement the inadequate family income, she published 2 more novels and more than 100 short stories and other works during the years before WWII, and her autobiography, *Confessions of an Immigrant's Daughter,* won a Gov Gen's Award in 1939, as did her novel *The Dark Weaver* in 1937. Although Salverson's work marks a significant development in western Cdn fiction, her essential purpose was rather the celebration of Norse tradition and Icelandic values over the meagre spiritual life of the world around her, and an affirmation of the importance of the Icelandic role in the history of NA. A strong vein of social protest runs through her writing, against the injustices perpetrated by society on its weaker members, and most particularly against its prejudiced contempt for the immigrant. After WWII, she had little interest in the experimental techniques then coming into literary fashion, and published little. The recent advent of feminist criticism has to an extent revived interest in her work. ● MILDRED GUTKIN

Nations councils, also became part owners of the chain. As of early 2006, Salisbury House had 20 restaurants in Winnipeg and one in **HEADINGLEY**. Its Winnipeg outlets included a 91-seat restaurant and lounge, which opened in summer 2005, on the new, $22-million pedestrian bridge over the **RED RIVER**, the Esplanade Riel. The company beat out several other contenders for the right to set up shop on the bridge. That angered some St. Boniface residents and community leaders, who wanted an eatery they felt would better represent French culture and cuisine.

In 2006, Protos executives David Wolinsky and Costas Ataliotis, who spearheaded the drive to return the restaurant chain to MB ownership, were removed as officers and directors of the numbered company, 4328796 Manitoba Ltd, which owns 80% of the restaurant chain. Barish was elected as the firm's president and CEO. The changes were made to stave off receivership and to put the operation back on a solid financial footing. ● MURRAY MCNEILL

SALT SPRINGS. Natural salt or saline springs, pools, marshes, and near-shore waters occur in MB along the W shore of **LAKE WINNIPEGOSIS**, especially in the Dawson Bay/Bell River Bay area ("Salt Point"). The salinity of these waters comes from the underground flow of water through Middle Devonian–age salt deposits, or a dense pool of brines in the centre of the geological Williston Basin. Surface waters enter these deposits from as far away as MT, producing pressure that eventually (over 900 to 2000 years) forces the

saline waters, often with associated helium gas, to surface. Salt levels or salinities in Dawson Bay can reach 36%, while marshes and saline pools range from 8-61%. Higher salinities create a near-sterile environment in which only a few hardy bacteria can grow and erode rocks into weird and wonderful shapes. A central area of bare soil, often bright yellow or orange in colour from the bacteria, is surrounded by a spring that often has bubbles of helium gas coming up through the water. As water flows farther away from the spring, it mixes increasingly with freshwater and becomes less salty. Eventually, it reaches a low-enough salt concentration that plants and animals that normally live only along sea-coasts, such as those of **HUDSON BAY** or the Gulf of Mexico, can survive. These plants form a ring of salt marsh that gives way to freshwater marsh as the saline water becomes increasingly diluted. Salt marsh plants found on these sites include seaside plantain (*Plantago maritima*), sea blite (*Suaeda depressa*), and several salt-tolerant grasses. Marine invertebrates include various species of ostracodes, rotifers, and foraminifera, such as *Jadammina macrescens*, *Miliammina fusca*, and *Polysaccammina ipohalina*. Most of these marine plants and animals probably came in on the feet and beaks of migratory **BIRDS**. ● KAREN JOHNSON

SALVERSON, Laura Goodman, author (b Dec 9, 1890, **WINNIPEG**; d July 13, 1970, Toronto). Laura was the child of impoverished and culturally isolated **ICELANDIC** immigrants to Canada,

SAND LANCE is a slender fish in the family Ammodytidae, 20-25 cm long, and with long dorsal and anal fins. It is an iridescent blue-green to bronze on the back, and white on the undersides. The Northern Sand Lance (*Ammodytes dubius*) is common in shallow waters (usually 5-20 m, occasionally to 90 m) and estuaries in Hudson Bay, preferring a sandy or gravel bottom. When not feeding (mainly during the day), schools often burrow into the sand, even above the

611

low-tidal zone, thereby avoiding predators and strong tidal currents. The fish are able to survive for hours in the sand, when there is limited water for respiration. They may make short passages from rest areas to feeding grounds, but do not travel to deeper, warmer water when temperatures fall in winter, as do many other fish species. The sand lance matures after age 2 and spawns on sand in shallow water during the winter months. The eggs fall to the bottom where they stick to sand grains. Hatching just prior to spring break-up of the ice, larvae rise to surface waters to feed on plankton for several weeks, providing an important food source for other predators. Larvae are particularly abundant in the Nelson River estuary, less so in the Churchill River estuary. When about 30 mm long, they develop into juveniles with adult colouration, and descend to the bottom where they remain for the remainder of their lives (max 9 years). The Sand Lance feeds on many kinds of small organisms, especially copepods (e.g., *Calanus finmarchicus*), which they pursue as the crustaceans rise from the depths with the fading evening light. This species is highly important in the diet of predatory fish, seabirds, and marine mammals. • DBS, FOC, REW

SANDY BAR (Sandvik), an 80 ac (267.9 ha) "ghost town" on the W shore of **Lake Winnipeg**, 120 km N of **Winnipeg**. The place derives its name from the prominent sand point 4 km to the N, near **Riverton**. Immortalized in the poem "Sandy Bar" by Icelandic Cdn poet **Guttormur Jónsson Guttormsson** of Riverton, this site is symbolic of the smallpox epidemic that befell the Icelandic pioneers of 1876. The arrival of **Icelanders** at Sandy Bar is also commemorated in composer Hallgrímur Helgason's cantata *Sandy Bar*, performed in 1975 to honour 100 years of Icelandic settlement in MB.

Originally a winter encampment used by the Sandy Bar Saulteaux, a semi-nomadic **Ojibway** group associated with the **Peguis First Nation** at St. Peter's, Sandy Bar is also known as the burial site of Betsey Ramsay, wife of John Ramsay, an Aboriginal hunter. Remembered as a friend to the early Icelandic settlers, John Ramsay provided the newcomers with meat and taught them local hunting and fishing techniques. Ramsay's appearance in the dreams of Icelandic craftsman Trausti Vigfússon prompted the placement of a picket fence around Betsey Ramsay's grave at Sandy Bar about 1908. This historic burial site, marked by a single marble headstone dating from 1877, is also the resting place of several Icelandic pioneers and children, as well as of John Ramsay himself. Today, the events associated with Sandy Bar serve as a

model for inter-racial compassion and co-operation in the face of shared adversity.

One of 3 original townsites in **New Iceland**, Sandy Bar was surveyed into streets and lots in 1877. The scene of some early commerce and an attempt to establish a fish cannery in 1884, it nevertheless failed to develop into a village, largely because of its proximity to **Lundur** (Icelandic River/Riverton) and the erosion of its harbour during high water around 1900. As a result, Hnausa to the S was selected as the site for a govt dock. Today, though undeveloped and often inaccessible, Sandy Bar is visited by tourists familiar with the **Poetry**, **Music**, and legend inspired by this historic MB site. • NELSON GERRARD

SANDY BAY FIRST NATION, on reserve pop 3324, off reserve pop 1948, is a community located on the W shore of **Lake Manitoba**, approx 90 km NW of **Portage la Prairie** and 165 km NW of **Winnipeg**. It signed Treaty 1 in 1871. This nation is a member of the Dakota Ojibway Tribal Council. There is one reserve located here. The Sandy Bay First Nation has all-weather road access. Education, administered by Sandy Bay itself, goes from Nursery-Grade 12, and enrolment for the year 2003-04 was 904. In 2007, 90% of the residents of this First Nation could speak **Ojibway**, and this community's cultural practices are still well upheld. Late in the summer, the community holds a traditional powwow. The economic base for the Sandy Bay First Nation is based on trapping and commercial fishing. The community's proximity to both Portage and Winnipeg also means economic opportunities are close by. • RK

SANFORD, pop 761, is a farming and bedroom community 35 km SW of **Winnipeg**, on hwy 3. A new trail from the city, in 1887, encouraged many families to settle here. In 1891, a post office was established and called Mandan, a local Indian name. The name Sanford was adopted in 1906. In the 2000s, there are regional schools here, municipal fire and rescue services, a church, stores, restaurants, credit union and farm supply outlets. Recreational facilities include an indoor arena and ball diamonds. William James Parker (1896-1971), a farmer named to the Manitoba Agricultural Hall of Fame and who served as president of the Manitoba Pool Elevators in the early 1940s, was born and raised in Sanford. • GPP

SAPOTAWEYAK CREE NATION, on reserve pop 954, off reserve pop 969, is N of **Lake Winnipegosis** about 450 km N of **Brandon**. The native language of this First Nation is **Cree**, and it signed Treaty 4 in 1874. It is a member of the Swampy Cree Tribal Council. Sapotaweyak Cree

Nation has 4 reserves: Shoal River IR No. 65A, Shoal River IR No. 65B, Shoal River IR No. 65F, and Treaty Four Reserve Grounds No. 77. Shoal River IR No. 65A is the main occupied community, while Shoal River IR No. 65F is unoccupied. Education in this First Nation community goes from Nursery-Grade 8, and total enrolment for the year 2003-04 was 351. Sapotaweyak Cree Nation administers its own schooling. This community is accessibly by all-weather road, via hwy 10 from **Swan River**. The community's economic foundation is logging, trapping, cattle ranching, and fishing. • RK

SAULTEAUX. *See* **Ojibway.**

SAWCHUK, Terrance Gordon "Ukey," goaltender, (b Dec 28, 1929, **Winnipeg**; d May 31, 1970, New York) was one of the greatest goalies in NHL history. Sawchuk first played goal at the age of 10, taking over the goalie pads of his teenage brother who had died suddenly of a heart attack. He displayed early on a high threshold for pain, which later on saw him through the innumerable injuries he sustained in net. Over the course of his career, he received 400 stitches for cuts to his face. At the age of 12, he badly injured his right arm during a rugby game, but let it go untreated. Doctors discovered 2 years later that Sawchuk had actually broken the limb, which had healed poorly and was left 2 inches shorter than his left arm.

Sawchuk played in Winnipeg junior leagues before turning professional at 17. As a minor league player, he was named rookie of the year in the United States Hockey League, and then the American Hockey League. He graduated

Terry Sawchuk, 1961

UMA, TRIBUNE, PERSONALITY FILES

An important technical development at the cyclotron laboratory involved the winding and formation of electric quadrupole magnets for use in the laboratory. Originally, such magnets had been purchased from the US where an industrial coil maker had supplied the product. As the laboratory grew and new facilities were required, it was found that the purchased items were no longer built within the tolerances and specifications supplied. They also could not be delivered for almost 2 years. The on-site workshops at the laboratory then manufactured a prototype electromagnet to the required specifications, within a few months, and from that time constructed such items in-house. This ability was born of necessity, but later, with sufficient local capability on-site, the magnet-building know-how of the laboratory was transferred to a tool and die firm, K & S Tool & Die, in downtown Winnipeg, thanks to a grant of $112,500 from the provincial govt's Technical and Commercialization Program. This company then set up a manufacturing arm as Canadian Electromagnetics, which is still in operation. Further, the physics workshops, in collaboration with this company constructed the first sextupole magnet for use at the colliding beam HERA facility near Hamburg in Germany as part of the Cdn contribution to the international effort there. The completed article is shown with the initials of K & S Tool & Die, and the U of M clearly displayed. The technical ability to tackle such projects became invaluable to the laboratory, and to the spin-off company involved.

Various joint projects of a technical or analytical nature, outside the normal research programs of the laboratory, included joint projects with Martin Marietta Aerospace Company and Oak Ridge National Laboratories in Tennessee, and the construction of equipment for the TRIUMF laboratory in Vancouver on the West Coast of Canada. The construction of heliostats for solar research, and the analysis of the protein content in grain, were additional projects tackled by members of the laboratory which applied features of the science used or developed in the cyclotron group for environmental studies and purposes.

THE WHITESHELL ORGANIC COOLED REACTOR *(WR-1):* Water, either ordinary or heavy, has disadvantages as a coolant in a nuclear power reactor. At the temperatures needed for efficient generation of power, the water exerts a high pressure, which increases rapidly with temperature. In pressure-tube reactors, a balance has to be struck between the coolant temperature and the thickness of the pressure tube. Increasing the temperature increases the pressure and thus a thicker pressure tube is needed. The higher temperature permits a higher thermodynamic efficiency, but the thicker tube captures more neutrons. The balance results in a lower efficiency than that obtained in coal- or oil-burning plants. These problems have now been overcome in the CANDU system. However, a proposal to build a test reactor, cooled by organic liquid, as the centrepiece of a nuclear research establishment in MB was approved in 1960. The establishment was named the Whiteshell Nuclear Research Establishment (WL). Construction of the reactor began in 1963 and criticality was achieved in 1965. The reactor was called WR-1.

The decision to establish WL was made because the Chalk River Laboratory (CRL), in Ontario, was at an ideal size for an applied laboratory of its type and further expansion there would be counterproductive. So a company townsite was established at Pinawa, analogous to Deep River for CRL and about the same distance from the plant at Whiteshell. The major programs in which WL took a lead role over the years have been in the development and promotion of the organic-cooled CANDU power-reactor concept, reprocessing for advanced-CANDU fuel cycles, CANDU reactor safety research and development (R&D), and

AECL facility at Pinawa before closure

waste management. At the same time, it has contributed to the majority of the other AECL R&D programs. The laboratory is currently being decommissioned, but its significance remains.

THE SLOWPOKE ENERGY SYSTEM: Because of its large area and sparse population, Canada had a need for economical off-grid electricity and remote steam production. In 1964, AECL established a small group at Whiteshell to see if a small nuclear reactor could be developed to meet this need. A Chalk River physicist who had been attached to the Whiteshell group then, returned to Chalk River with an idea for a research reactor which could operate unattended and be used by universities, hospitals and research institutes for teaching, activation analysis and the production of small quantities of short-lived radioisotopes. A reactor with intrinsic safety features was licensed for unattended operation even in large population centres where the universities, hospitals, and research institutes were located. The design was developed through 1968 and 1969, and in 1970, the first prototype commenced operation. The reactor was named SLOWPOKE for "safe, low-power critical experiment." Seven SLOWPOKE research reactors were eventually sold: 5 to Canadian universities, 1 to the U of the West Indies in Jamaica, and 1 to the Saskatchewan Research Council in Saskatoon.

THE INVENTION OF A CERENKOV VIEWING DEVICE (CVD): In vacuum the speed of a high-energy particle approaches that of light. Hence when this particle enters a transparent solid, in which the speed of light is much less than it is in vacuum, the particle initially travels with a speed exceeding that of light. In the rapid slowing-down process, it emits a blue-violet radiation, called Cerenkov radiation, which is concentrated in the forward direction and well explained by Maxwell's electromagnetic theory of light. An individual fast particle, when incident on clear plastic, emits sufficient light to activate a photomultiplier. This arrangement, called a Cerenkov counter, serves for the detection of very energetic electrons and protons. The study of Cerenkov light then led to the development of the CVD technology at WL by the innovative modification of image intensifier technology developed by the military for night vision. It has since been used extensively by the International Atomic Energy Agency (IAEA) for confirming the disposition of spent fuel, for non-proliferation purposes, and a visit to the used fuel bay in the storage pool at Point Lepreau CANDU 6 nuclear power station in New Brunswick, for example, can be useful in understanding the nature and relevance of Cerenkov light to used fuel assessment.

OTHER INNOVATORS: Over the years, many local scientists have contributed to applied science and innovation in the province of MB. Some notable researchers, scientists, and innovators include:

Dr. **BALDUR STEFANSON**, Faculty of Agricultural and Food Sciences, U of M, is known as the "Father of Canola," He conducted research that turned rapeseed oil, an industrial oil, into canola, an edible oil. Canola is now the largest cash crop in western Canada, replacing wheat, and is worth over $1 billion to the economy of the West every year.

Dr. **JOHN BOWMAN** (in conjunction with the late Dr. **BRUCE CHOWN**), Faculty of Medicine, U of M, is recognized internationally for his pioneering work in virtually eliminating infant deaths from Rh disease. He developed a method of preventing Rh-negative women from having an immune reaction against their babies, which could lead to miscarriages. Dr. Bowman's work has significantly advanced the quality of medical care mothers-to-be and infants receive worldwide.

Dr. **HENRY FRIESEN**, Faculty of Medicine, U of M, discovered the human pituitary hormone *prolactin*. He has carried out research on the human growth hormone, which made successful replacement therapy in hormone deficient children possible. He was the winner of the 2001 Wightman Award, given by the Gairdner Foundation to a Canadian who

has demonstrated outstanding leadership in medicine and medical science for "his leadership to Canadian medical research and especially for leading to the establishment of the Canadian Institutes of Health Research," The Gairdner Foundation recognizes the world's top medical research scientists via the Gairdner International Awards.

Dr. **NARANJAN DHALLA**, St. Boniface Hospital Research Centre, is recognized as a world leader in heart research. His research has led to the discovery of a number of compounds that could have significant health benefits for cardiovascular and diabetes patients.

Dr. Geoff Hicks, Manitoba Institute of Cell Biology, is co-leader of the Canadian component of the International Knockout Mouse Project. He and his team of international collaborators will create a library of genetic mutations in mouse cells that will provide a powerful tool to further new treatments on cancer and hereditary diseases. The impact of this project is expected to be on the same scale as that of the sequencing of the human genome project itself.

Dr. Sabine Mai, Manitoba Institute of Cell Biology, identified a protein that may be responsible for the disruption of chromosomes that lead to the onset of cancer. This discovery could lead to the development of an early diagnostic tool, or new cancer therapies.

Dr. Robert Hill, Department of Plant Science, Faculty of Agricultural and Food Sciences, U of M, was the first to discover a receptor for a plant hormone called abscisic acid (ABA) which is essentially a survival hormone that is involved in a plants response to many environmental stresses. The receptor protein discovered is FCA which is involved in the plant's transition from a juvenile to a reproductive stage. The discovery, published in *Nature* (Jan 19, 2006) is a major leap forward in understanding plant growth and development. The findings are of particular significance to agriculture and forestry, especially in the Canadian climate where the response to cold, drought, salt and timing of germination and flowering are all regulated by this hormone.

Dr. Frank Hawthorne, Department of Geological Sciences, U of M, has established a new field that links the arrangement of atoms in the crystal structure of a mineral to its occurrence in the Earth. He has developed a new appreciation for the geochemical processes that underlie the formation of crystals.

Dr. **ALLAN RONALD**, Faculty of Medicine, U of M, is one of this country's foremost microbiologists, who helped establish Canada's clinical specialty in infectious diseases at the U of M. He has significantly advanced HIV/AIDS prevention programs in Africa and the understanding of HIV transmission. Dr. Ronald was the winner of the 2006 Wightman Award for "his leadership in developing the specialty of clinical infectious disease in Canada and for his exceptional international contribution in Africa."

Dr. **FRANCIS "FRANK" PLUMMER**, Scientific Director General, National Microbiology Laboratory, in 1988, discovered a natural immunity to AIDS in a group of Kenyan women which suggested that a vaccine could be eventually developed. He is one of the world's leading specialists on HIV/AIDS and his research has significantly expanded knowledge of AIDS.

Dr. Stephen Jones and Dr. Heinz Feldmann, National Microbiology Laboratory, produced the first vaccine system that has proven 100% effective in protecting monkeys against infection from Ebola and Marburg, 2 of the world's deadliest viruses. The vaccines are safe and effective in the animal model and show potential for use in humans.

Dr. Ken Standing and Dr. W. Ens, Department of Physics and Astronomy, U of M, are recognized around the world for their use of mass spectrometry in the advanced study of proteomics.

Finally, although wheat-rye hybrids date back to 1875, it was only in 1953 that the first NA triticale breeding program was initiated, at the U

National Research Council Centre for Biomedical Technology on Ellice Avenue, Winnipeg

of M. According to Dr. E. N. Larter, triticale (× *Triticosecale* Wittmack) is still a minor crop in Canada; however, production is gradually increasing as better cultivars (commercial varieties) are developed. Triticale grain is used either as a human food or as a livestock feed. Relative to wheat, triticale grain is high in lysine, a component of protein required by humans and most other animals for normal growth and development. Hence, triticale is expected to assume an increasingly important role as a food grain in regions in which cereal crops already constitute the main dietary source of protein.

SMARTPARK AT THE U OF M: Following some 2 decades of debate, and comprehensive analysis of the need and potential for a research park on the campus, the first building to be erected on Smartpark, as it is now called, welcomed its tenants in Jan 2002. This building, identified as 135 Innovation Dr, was a 30,000-ft^2 (2800-m^2) office/computer laboratory multi-tenant facility, was followed rapidly by completion of the **Cangene Corporation**'s 76,000-ft^2 (7050-m^2) expansion program, and then by 137 Innovation Dr, an incubator, computer laboratory, multi-tenant facility. The start of construction of the Richardson Centre for Functional Foods and Neutriceuticals in 2004 then pointed the way to major development in the next phase of the Smartpark development.

Some residents of Smartpark have taken considerable advantage of their proximity to the research university and employed graduate students to work on projects related to their master's or doctoral programs on-site. Park tenants include:

- Profitmaster Canada, whose flagship product is its Enterprise Resource Planning (ERP) software solution program, has employed graduate students in Computer Science as it attempts to become the IT department of its clients across Canada.
- Monteris Medical, which has developed an automated system with the potential to provide a minimally invasive surgical option that has several advantages over the current methods of performing laser interstitial thermal therapy. Only the tissue in the defined treatment volume is treated, and the normal tissue surrounding it is protected.
- RTDSs – named after real-time digital simulators, a fully digital electromagnetic transient power system simulator used to conduct closed-loop testing of physical devices. The simulator allows the user to investigate the effects of disturbances on power system equipment and networks to prevent outages or complete failure. Because the solution is real time, the simulator can be connected directly to power system control and protective relay equipment.

- Iders, a university spin-off firm that has developed and manufactured the GUIDE A07 single board computer for Guide Systems. The firm has manufactured and jointly developed the fibre Bragg grating (FBG) sensor interrogation unit with ISIS Canadian that is being used to measure the stress on Taylor Bridge in Headingly, the Confederation Bridge (PEI), the Gentilly 1 Nuclear Reactor Containment Structure, as well as the Golden Boy and Provencher pedestrian bridge, in Winnipeg. Here we have several made in Manitoba solutions to local problems.
- Wolftrax has developed a family of innovative micronutrients using a proprietary formulation process, exclusive to the business. It also operates a Remote Pharmacy that can fill on the consumer's behalf, while maintaining a consistent filling process throughout an integrated organization.
- Cangene Corporation – Rh Pharmaceuticals, the business that commercialized the discoveries made by Drs. John Bowman and Bruce Chown in the 1950s. The scientists developed a method of preventing Rh-negative women from having an immune reaction against their babies. Rh Pharmaceuticals was purchased by Toronto-based pharmaceutical firm Apotex in 1990, then in 1995 Rh went public and took the name Cangene. It is now listed on the Toronto Stock Exchange and is 82%-owned by Apotex. It is an anchor tenant of the Smartpark at the U of M.

FUTURE INNOVATION: The word *innovation*, deriving from the Latin *innovare*, "to renew," implies the introduction of something new, such as a device, an improved version of an existing model, or on occasion the specifics of an original invention. Innovation is the driving force in practical economic progress, and typically arises from the direct application of existing science to a new and specific problem.

MB, as a province, is well positioned to take advantage of the skills and expertise of its citizens through the stimulation of applied science and innovation. Successive provincial govts through the Department now called Industry, Trade, and Mines, have encouraged local research, development, and demonstration, through the funding of technology transfer, and assistance with the incubation of emerging businesses. The research park at the U of M is now playing a prominent role in this respect.

There are 2 groups of skilled scientists that are essential to the burgeoning of a culture of innovation in MB. Firstly, there are the many qualified scientists and engineers who have developed an understanding of the needs of business and industry, and have the vision to apply the knowledge they possess to new challenges. Secondly, with so many trained scientists and technically qualified people in the province, there are those who can act as interpreters of new science to the community.

Almost as important as the ability to discover or apply existing science directly is the appreciation of new science discovered by others elsewhere in the global environment in which we live. To have a feeling for and understanding of new discovery and its relevance to the solution of local problems, is a massive asset for any community, and in MB the number of such people is comfortably large. So, while the generation of new science, and the application of science in general are vitally important, as we move forward, the existence of a vibrant pool of highly educated scientists who understand the relevance of discoveries elsewhere is also of great importance. Scientists with an immediate field of interest, whether in agriculture, medicine, engineering, virology, biology or physics, will, of course, continue to be essential to further innovation as we move forward together. MB is a balanced microcosm of world science, and has many of the early characteristics of a future Silicon Valley. Innovation is becoming rampant here, and the future is bright. ●

Mary Scorer, 1975

SCORER, Mary, bookseller, publisher (b 1911, Newcastle, UK; d 1988) came to Canada aged 3. Educated in **Winnipeg**, she worked as a secretary for Purity Flour for many years. During WWII, she went to Britain as an ambulance driver, then worked for an English publisher after the war. She returned to Canada in 1950, and worked at **Eaton's** book department from 1950-59, and then opened her own bookstore in 1959. She established Peguis Publishers in 1967 (now Portage & Main Press), which was MB's first full-time **Book Publishing** company. At Peguis, Scorer published many books on MB history. The bookstore initially financed the publishing, but she gradually moved full-time into the publishing business and sold the bookstore to other parties. She was named YWCA Woman of the Year in 1982 and was inducted into the Order of the Buffalo Hunt in 1984. An annual prize for the best book by a MB publisher is named in her honour. ● JMB

SCORPIONFLY is a bizarre-looking insect with an elongated body (12-26 mm) and legs, exceptionally long, downward-directed beak (rostrum), and enlarged tip of the abdomen (in the male) that swells and turns up over the back menacingly like a scorpion's tail. It is harmless to humans, since it cannot sting or bite. The 2 pairs of prominent wings are camouflaged with black patches and bands. A pair of large compound eyes as well as 3 simple eyes (ocelli) are present, indicative of good eyesight associated with a predatory lifestyle. Several species are found in SE MB (e.g., *Panorpa helena* and *Bittacus strigosus*) in moist forests, where they either prey or scavenge on live or dead insects and other small creatures. These insects have been seen raiding spider webs of caught prey, somehow avoiding detection by the owner. They are usually observed standing on or hanging from a leaf. Courtship is an elaborate affair, with the males releasing pheromones to attract females, and a nuptial gift by the male is a prerequisite for mating acceptance by the female. Eggs are laid in the soil and the caterpillar-like larvae devour both plant and dead animal material with their large mandibles. Pupation occurs in the ground. Many kinds of insects, small mammals and birds feast on scorpionflies. There are about 40 species in Canada, 550 worldwide. Snow scorpionflies (family Boreidae), which live in and feed on moss, emerge in spring to walk around on the snow. These 5 mm dark insects have not yet been discovered in MB, but they may occur here. The order appeared in the fossil record 144 million years ago (Jurassic period). ● REW, TDG

SCOTS are one of the key ethnic groups to have shaped MB. The Scots' roots in the province can be traced back to the early days of the **Fur Trade** in NA. The first employees of the **Hudson Bay Company** (HBC), established in 1670, came mainly from the Orkney Islands off the N coast of Scotland. These hardy Scots manned isolated trading posts as factors, and would later promote the use of **York Boats**, favoured by the HBC to transport furs and supplies along its water routes in MB. These boats helped create the company's distinct advantage over its rival company, the **North West Company** (NWC), established in 1779, whose employees navigated the waters of Canada's interior in much smaller canoes. Besides the Orkadians, other noteworthy Scots were associated with the fur trade. Simon Fraser (1776-1862) and Sir Alexander Mackenzie (1764-1820), through their extensive expeditions into northwestern NA, would contribute significantly to the exploration and expansion of Canada. Sir **George Simpson** was gov of the HBC just after its merger with the NWC.

The fact that these early recruits of the fur trading companies were exclusively male would, through time, add to the richness of the demographic diversity in the province of MB. Once in NA, many of these Scotsmen took First Nations women as their country wives or "femmes du pays." These were associations not merely of convenience, but of necessity. The Aboriginal women taught the Scottish fur traders much about the skills required to survive in the harsh environment in this part of the continent and served as important liaisons between Aboriginal and fur trader. Without the support of Aboriginal peoples, there likely would have been a much diminished fur trade, in terms of both operational efficiency and geographical expansion. Another outcome of this relationship would be the development of a sizable Scots **Country-Born/Métis** culture in MB. This unique culture would evolve to combine distinctive features of both Aboriginal and Scots traditions.

Scottish tenant farmers made their way to Manitoba in the 1920s.

The St. Andrews Society celebrated Winnipeg's 75th Anniversary in 1949.

Adversity and human injustices in the Highlands of Scotland after the failed Jacobite Rebellion of the 1740s contributed in large part to the further exodus of Scots from their homeland to NA. **Lord Selkirk** persuaded the HBC to grant him a huge tract of land – almost 5 times the size of Scotland – in the **Red River Valley**. Selkirk imagined a **Red River Settlement** ("**Assiniboia**," as he called it) where crops could be grown and livestock raised, to supply the fur traders and to serve as a place of retirement for HBC employees.

In summer 1812, the first party of about 100 Scottish settlers arrived at **The Forks** in a fleet of York boats. In June 1814, another party of 83 settlers, the Sutherlanders, from Kildonan, Isle of Arran, in Scotland's Hebrides, arrived with their leader, Archie MacDonald. They were settled on 100 ac (40-ha) lots with a river frontage of 3 chains (roughly 75 m) downstream from Point Douglas. The settlers paid £10 (equivalent to $48.60 at the time) per head and 5 shillings (a little over $1.20 then) per ac. In return, they received their transportation and one year's provisions. The notion of free transportation must have come back to haunt them, as they made the 34 portages from **York Factory** to the settlement with their York boats.

The ongoing conflict between the HBC and the NWC resulted in a slow start to Selkirk's colony. This situation was further exacerbated by poor crop yields and by acrimony between the **Métis** and the new settlers. The Métis feared the settlers would disrupt their way of life. The tension between the two groups came to a head in 1816 at the **Seven Oaks Incident**. More than 20 of the settlers were killed during this encounter. **Cuthbert Grant**, the leader of the Métis, was the son of a Métis mother and Scots father. Although Grant's loyalties may have seemed divided during this battle, he would, in later years, help the new settlers at Red River by thwarting attacks from wandering Dakota bands. In spite of these setbacks as well as **Floods**, the little colony of settlers at Red River eventually took root.

Many other Scots made important contributions to the region that would eventually become MB. Duncan McRae was a stonemason from Stornoway in the Scottish Hebrides. He was employed by the HBC in 1837 and arrived in the Red River Settlement the same year. Some of his major undertakings include **Upper Fort Garry**, St. John's Cathedral, Kildonan Church, Kennedy House, **Lower Fort Garry**, and St. Peter's Church. James Ross established Red River's first newspaper, the *Nor'-wester*, in 1859. Kirkcaldy-born Sir **Sandford Fleming** – also the inventor of standard time and of the first adhesive postage stamp – was the chief engineer for the CPR. Sir Sandford advocated that the railway cross the **Red River** on the higher, less-flood-prone land near **Selkirk**, rather than near The Forks. This turned out to be a prophetic judgment, given **Winnipeg**'s vulnerability to flooding.

Through the late 19th and 20th centuries, Scots continued to migrate to MB, many having particular skills in fields as diverse as medicine, education, and engineering. In the 2001 Census, 195,575 Manitobans claimed Scottish heritage, making the Scots the 4th-largest population group in the province. Scots have taken their place within the broad mosaic of ethnic groups that now typifies MB, but Scottish traditions are still in evidence in the province. Many public and private ceremonies today are replete with the music of the highland bagpipe, Scotland's national instrument. Other evidence of Scottish heritage exists in the form of the Highland Games in Selkirk; historical buildings along the Red River; displays in the **Manitoba Museum**; and the Scottish **Folklorama** Pavilion. It is evident that the Scots have made a most important and lasting contribution to the creation and growth of the province of MB. ● DUNCAN ALLAN

SCOTT, Margaret Elizabeth, (née Ruttan Boucher), charity worker (b July 28, 1855, Colborne, Canada West [ON]; d Aug 1, 1931, **Winnipeg**) advocated health care for Winnipeg's needy at the turn of the 20th century. Scott lost her husband, William, in 1881, and arrived in Winnipeg in 1886, where she worked at the Dominion Land Office. There she acquired a reputation as an expert stenographer. She began her charity work at the **Anglican** Holy Trinity Church, where she helped with parish activities, later organizing a facility for delinquent young women. She likewise founded a lumberyard to employ jobless men. A devout Christian, she relinquished paid work to spend more time helping the poor, even moving into the Winnipeg Lodging and Coffee House – an early form of a soup kitchen that the downtown church operated – on Lombard St in order to be closer to the needy. She received funding for her work through private patrons, who furnished her with a pony and cart for her daily visits to the poor.

In 1904, Winnipeggers renamed her charity the Margaret Scott Nursing Mission, an interdenominational facility to provide nursing care. The facility cared for 7000 needy individuals in 1905. The staff expanded the following year, with funding secured from the city. A children's department was added in 1911, principally to combat **Epidemics** such as typhoid. The mission's visits numbered 28,830 by 1913, and the newly formed **Winnipeg Foundation** donated money to the Scott in 1922 and '25. Scott was also instrumental in having "district nursing" added to the nurses' training program at the Winnipeg General Hospital (*see* **Health Sciences Centre**). She was dubbed the "Angel of Poverty Row," and inspired Toronto's Scott Mission, founded in 1941 to care for that city's poor. During WWII, the Margaret Scott Mission withdrew from the field of **Public Health**, as the newly arrived **Victorian Order of Nurses** filled this role. Margaret Scott School (1920-89), on Winnipeg's Alfred Ave, was named for her. ● MICHELLE DOBROVOLNY

Execution of Thomas Scott outside the walls of Upper Fort Garry

SCOTT, Thomas, adventurer, (b ca 1842, probably Clandeboye, Co. N Ireland; d March 4, 1870, **RED RIVER SETTLEMENT**). Scott seems to have had a **PRESBYTERIAN** upbringing in Clandeboye and some education. He came to Canada in the early 1860s, likely to join his brother Hugh in Toronto. He served briefly in the Hastings Batt of Rifles at Stirling, ON.

In 1869, Thomas Scott decided to head W. Shortly after arriving in **RED RIVER** that summer, Scott took a job with the Cdn road-building crew headed by John Allan Snow. Snow had experienced considerable trouble over the construction of the road from ON to **UPPER FORT GARRY**, both within the settlement and on the site. Scott apparently led a 3-day strike against Snow, which concluded with the strikers – Scott at their head – marching 27 km (17 mi) to Snow's office on Oct 1 to demand pay both for the time they had worked and for the time they had been on strike. Snow was prepared to pay the former, but not the latter. The men seized Snow and threatened to "duck" him. Snow paid up, but then had warrants issued against four of the men for aggravated assault.

Scott was given 30 days to pay a fine of $4 (nearly $20 at the time), his counsel Joseph Coombs acting as security for the payment. Alexander Begg observed that the case had been badly handled by the defence.

All sorts of descriptions of Scott's behaviour after the Snow incident appeared after his death, including some suggesting confrontations between Scott and **LOUIS RIEL**, but none can be independently confirmed. He was one of a delegation of 3 sent by those in Sɪʀ **JOHN CHRISTIAN SCHULTZ**'s house to negotiate with Riel on Dec 7, 1869; he was subsequently held by Riel as a prisoner at Upper Fort Garry. There is no evidence that Scott was a troublemaker on this occasion. However, he and others escaped on Jan 9, 1870, by digging for nights at the windows of Upper Fort Garry with penknives, finally removing the iron bars and fleeing at 3:00 am.

Scott went to **PORTAGE LA PRAIRIE**, where he helped encourage the Portage attempt of Feb 1870 to free the remaining prisoners by marching to Kildonan and joining other Cdn parties there. On the way to Kildonan, he and Capt. **C. A. BOULTON** searched the house of a Riel relative looking for the Métis leader. Scott was captured Feb 17, 1870, with others returning to Portage. While in custody, he clearly antagonized his Métis captors, as he was sentenced to death by a Métis tribunal on Mar 3, 1870, for breaking his parole and for insubordination and rebellion against the provisional govt.

Scott had made no such promises to his captors, having escaped from imprisonment rather than being released, and none of the charges seemed to warrant a death sentence. He may have been loud and prejudiced against Riel and his guards, but he was not accused of any horrendous crimes until after his death

Scott was executed by firing squad the next day, becoming a martyr for Protestant Ontarians. Only after his death did anyone in Red River learn that he had been an Orangeman, and only after his death did Riel and other Métis describe his transgressions, the accounts – none of which could be confirmed by independent witnesses – becoming more strident and detailed over time. Scott's death – regarded by the Cdn govt as murder – was held to be the central transgression committed by Riel and the Métis during the **RED RIVER RESISTANCE**.

A resolution of the Orange Lodge in the Toronto *Globe* called for the govt to avenge "Brother" Scott's death, but there is no evidence – even in the Métis-inspired accounts – that Scott had any anti-Catholic sentiment. Scott appears to have been not so much a leader of the Cdn party as the wrong man in the wrong place at the wrong time. • J. M. BUMSTED

SCRIP was a paper certificate that gave holders the right to claim land or, sometimes, money in lieu of land. First used 1875-79 to distribute lands promised under Section 31 of the *Manitoba Act* to the **MÉTIS** and **COUNTRY-BORN**, scrip was unconstitutional as the act promised land, not paper. Dependent children received scrip worth 240 ac (100 ha) or $240, while heads of households and spouses received scrip for 160 ac (65 ha) each. Non-Aboriginal settlers who lived in the **RED RIVER SETTLEMENT** before 1870 also received the same benefits. The 1885 scrip was worth 240 ac or $240 and was only for Métis/Country-Born people who were born in **RUPERT'S LAND** before 1870 and who were not residents of the 1870 boundaries of the "postage-stamp" province of MB.

Although scrip was meant to provide the Métis with land, fraud and violence in MB after 1870 prevented most settlement Métis from holding on to their homes and land, and they sold the scrip to fund relocation. The lands that were to be claimed by scrip were also far from traditonal Métis homes. The fraudulent management of the scrip distribution in the 1870s is the basis for a court case brought by the **MANITOBA MÉTIS FEDERATION** against the federal and provincial govts. • FRED J. SHORE

SCULPIN is a fish in the Sculpin family Cottidae, which are bottom-dwellers with a bizarre appearance. They are mostly 5-20 cm, stout, tapered fish with 2 separated dorsal fins. These are large-headed fish with wide jaws and prominent eyes placed high on the head. Sculpins are partly scaled or scaleless, and some species have knobs on the head or rows of prickles along the sides. Various species have spines, but no MB species have associated venom glands. This is mainly a family of marine fishes, occurring in polar and temperate seas of both hemispheres. Most species prefer shallow water, but others are found at depths of over 1000 m. There are 8 marine species in **HUDSON BAY** near MB, and 4 freshwater species in the province. Several species in both categories enter estuaries on occasion, to feed or to spawn.

All 4 freshwater sculpins occur from the Winnipeg River watershed to the NW through lakes and rivers in the boreal forest region, with the Slimy Sculpin (*Cottas cognatus*) having the broadest range, including the tundra. Perhaps the most interesting is the Deepwater Sculpin (*Myoxocephalus thompsoni*) found in MB's deepest lakes (West Hawk, George, Athapapuskow and Reindeer). A marine glacial relict, this species evolved recently from populations of the marine Fourhorn Sculpin (*M. quadricornis*), which became trapped in glacial lakes S of the Laurentide Glacier. As this vast glacier retreated over the last 18,000 years, these sculpins were able to survive by withdrawing to deep lakes, and becoming a new freshwater species. Reaching a length of 24 cm, it feeds on insect larvae and crustaceans such as *Mysis relicta* (a mysid) and *Pontoporeia affinis* (an amphipod) – also glacial relicts, originating from former marine or brackish ancestors. Due to its inaccessible habitat (depths to 366 m), little is known of breeding habits; spawning likely occurs from July to Aug, with parental care of eggs and young.

The Hudson Bay sculpins play significant roles as predators and as food for shorebirds, seals, Beluga and local people. The Fourhorn Sculpin has 4 bony knobs on the head, and is found from deep water to estuaries. The Shorthorn Sculpin (*M. scorpius*) is common and one of the largest sculpins, averaging 30 cm (max 90 cm). It is found in coastal waters (including the Churchill River estuary) from the intertidal zone in summer to a depth of 100 m in winter. It sits motionless on the bottom and darts forward to gulp down fish, crabs, shrimp, and worms. The sexes look different, the male being slimmer, with more prickles on the sides, and its belly turns bright red with white spots during the breeding season. Spawning occurs from Nov to Feb in schools, and fertilization is external. The sticky eggs clump and sink to the bottom or attach to vegetation. The larvae feed in the drifting plankton near the surface and reach 2 cm by June. Sexual maturity is attained at a length of 15 cm. ● REW

SEAL is a marine mammal evolved from a bear-like carnivore 23 million years ago in the N Pacific. Three species of true seals (family Phocidae, order Carnivora) occur regularly along the MB coast and live in **HUDSON BAY** year-round – the Ringed, Bearded, and Harbour. Two others, the Harp Seal and Hooded Seal, are rare summer migrants from the Arctic and N Atlantic oceans. The Walrus (*Odobenus rosmarus rosmarus* – the Atlantic subspecies) is also native to Hudson Bay, but now rarely approaches the MB coastline

(*see* **WALRUS**). They have a streamlined body and short limbs modified as flippers – the hind ones used for propulsion, the front for steering. Many other adaptations have evolved for swimming, diving and communicating underwater.

RINGED SEAL (*Pusa hispida*) – the smallest of the Arctic seals – is by far the most abundant seal in Hudson Bay (1.7/km² around Churchill). Adults average 65 kg and 125 cm long, and sport a pattern of rings on the coat. A recent estimate for the W coast of Hudson Bay is 141,000, and over ¼ million total for Hudson and James bays. Due to its abundance and occupation of pupping dens for many weeks, this seal is the most-important prey of the Polar Bear. In winter this seal maintains a series of breathing holes through relatively stable land-fast ice, as well as over pressure ridges out in the centre of the Bay. It is at one of these holes that the female excavates a den in the packed snow cover, in which to give birth. This species usually reproduces annually, but only about half of the females in the Bay breed each year – perhaps due to difficulty in finding sufficient food. The pup is born from March to April and lives in the snow den for 1-2 months. The fasting mother returns to nurse the pup for 6 weeks, keeping the breathing hole open with her claws and teeth. If discovered by a bear or fox, the mother attempts to lead the pup away underwater to another den some distance away. Decreased snow depth (<32 cm) and therefore thinner dens has resulted in increased susceptibility of attack by bears, and this factor appears responsible for the significant drop in pup recruitment in the last 25 years. The Ringed Seal may travel over 1300 km over the course of

a year, in search of concentrations of prey and preferred ice conditions. Important food items are fish (cod and sculpins), shrimp, and invertebrates lying on the bottom. It is solitary, unlike several other seal species in the Arctic. Most live about 18 years (max 43 years).

BEARDED SEAL (*Erignathus barbatus*), often called 'square-flipper' due to its shape of the fore-flippers, is a large seal (weight 300 kg, max 380 kg, 240 cm length; sexes the same size). A recent estimate of the W Hudson Bay population is 12,000, but only 1980 (0.2/km²) close to Churchill. This species has no colour pattern on the body, has long white whiskers, and may swim with its back exposed. A widespread seal in the Arctic Ocean, it is restricted in Hudson Bay to regions with abundant invertebrates on the sea floor, where it may hunt alone or in small groups. Favoured food species are mussels, shrimp, sea cucumbers, and fish such as Arctic Cod and sculpins. The strong claws and stiff touch-sensitive whiskers help in detecting creatures in the soft sediment. In summer the seals haul out on shore or reefs, sometimes in the company of Harbour Seals. As the mating season approaches in March and April, the male sings underwater to attract females and to establish a territory. Mating occurs from April to May, right after some females give birth. A single pup, weighing 36 kg, is born on the pack ice every second year, rarely 2 years in a row. The pup can swim immediately and is nursed for only 12-18 days before it is abandoned and must feed itself on crustaceans, although it may accompany its mother for several weeks longer. Like other species of seals, it matures sexually

S

Bearded Seal near Churchill

around the age of 6 years. It may live 31 years in captivity.

HARBOUR SEAL (*Phoca vitulina*) occurs along most of Canada's coasts (except the central Arctic) and can be identified by small size (60 kg, max 111 kg, and 15 cm length for both sexes) and numerous blotches on a dark back. The population size along the W coast of Hudson Bay is unknown, but likely is less than 12,000. This species has been heavily hunted for centuries, and so it is uncommon in many areas of previous abundance. It is especially susceptible to over-hunting because it hauls out in groups on favourite rocky shores or swims in shallow estuaries such as the Churchill and Seal rivers. This species is most unusual in that some individuals congregate in estuaries and migrate in summer up certain rivers (following fish runs) on both sides of Hudson Bay, in Quebec (including a landlocked freshwater population in Upper and Lower Seal lakes), Nunavut (Thleiwaza), and MB – 55 km up the Churchill and on the Seal River to Shethanei and Stony lakes, 230 km inland. The breeding season runs from July to Sept (immediately after completing lactation from last year's offspring, and the single pup (weighing 12 kg) is born on shore or a rocky reef (or occasionally underwater if stormy) in May or June. It must have the strength to swim before the next tide comes in. If separated, it has a remarkable homing instinct to find its home rookery. The mother may support the pup on her shoulders. She nurses the pup for 2-5 weeks before it is independent. The diet includes both marine and freshwater fishes, crustaceans, and other invertebrates. It may undertake long journeys, some as far as 1475 km. This species is presently being studied in MB by researchers of the Canadian Wildlife Service and University of Alberta.

HARP SEAL (*Phoca groenlandica*) is common in the N Atlantic and some enter Hudson Strait as soon as ice opens in spring while on migration to the NW. Small numbers continue S into Hudson Bay for the summer and may turn up anywhere from June to Oct (5 months) during their search of food – mainly fish and crustacean. They leave the Bay in the fall before freeze-up. This species was likely more common and widely distributed in Hudson Bay in the past. It averages 135 kg (max 180 kg), is 170 cm long, and has a blue-grey coat highlighted by a black head and saddle across the shoulders and flanks.

HOODED SEAL (*Cystophora cristata*) is also found in the N Atlantic and Arctic oceans, and while on spring migration N, a few enter Hudson Bay and remain here from July to Sept. It prefers deep waters to feed, so it is seldom seen by people. Reports exist in the estuary of the Kaskattama River in MB in 1955 and on the coast of James Bay, Ontario. Males average 300 kg (max 400 kg), females 160 kg, and reach a maximum length of 300 cm. ● REW, DBS, FOC

SELANNE, Teemu "Finnish Flash," hockey player, (b July 3, 1970, Helsinki, Finland) was one of the most popular players of the **WINNIPEG JETS** NHL team. Selanne gained the attention of NHL scouts while playing junior hockey in Finland. He was drafted by the Jets in 1988, playing in the NHL for the first time in the 1992-93 season. His prolific scoring revived the lackluster team, and made him a fan favorite. He scored 76 goals and 56 assists in his first season, earning him the Calder Trophy for best rookie and beating out the previous NHL rookie record of 53 goals. His following season was cut short because of an ankle injury, though he still scored 26 goals in the 51 games he played, and the Jets plummeted to last place in the NHL. Following the NHL lockout in the 1994-95 season, Selanne was traded to the Anaheim Mighty Ducks. He helped lead the Ducks to their first Stanley Cup in 2006-07. Though he played just 4 seasons with the Jets, Selanne remains one of the most popular former Jets. ● MD

SELKIRK, pop 9515, is a city 34 km N of **WINNIPEG** on hwy 9, on the W side of the **RED RIVER**. The Selkirk area was settled in the early 1800s by **SCOTS** and **IRISH IMMIGRANTS** who arrived under the auspices of **LORD SELKIRK,** with the hope of establishing new and better lives for their families. These original "Selkirk Settlers" were helped to cope with harsh **WEATHER** and challenging living conditions by **CHIEF PEGUIS** and his **OJIBWAY** band members. When it was announced in 1874 that the new transcontinental railway (*see* **CPR**) would cross the Red at Selkirk – which stands on higher ground than Winnipeg and is therefore less prone to **FLOODS** – Selkirk had an opportunity to become the "Gateway to the West." However, intensive lobbying by **WINNIPEG** politicians saw federal officials change the plans so the railway would pass through that city. The town of Selkirk was incorporated in 1880, named in honour of Lord Selkirk, and Selkirk became a city in 1998.

In the late 1800s and early 1900s, agriculture and **COMMERCIAL FISHING** played important roles in Selkirk's economy. Its proximity to **LAKE WINNIPEG** allowed Selkirk to become an important harbour on the Red River system, and marine transportation and other related businesses

were major contributors to the community. In 1886, the provincial asylum for the insane opened, the predecessor to the present-day Selkirk Mental Health Centre (*see* **MENTAL HEALTH**). The steel industry became a major employer in the community around 1913 with the opening of the Manitoba Rolling Mills (giving Selkirk its "Steeltown" **NICKNAME**). Manufacturing, particularly steel-related, continues to be the major source of private-sector jobs, while the Lord Selkirk School Division and the Mental Health Centre are the largest public-sector employers.

Selkirk is well known as a hockey town, and local residents are avid supporters of the Selkirk Steelers (Junior A) and the Selkirk Fishermen (Junior B). The city boasts 2 arenas – the aging Selkirk Arena on Jemima St, and the much newer Selkirk Recreation Complex, with a spectator capacity of 3000 that is exceeded in MB only by Winnipeg's **MTS CENTRE** and **BRANDON**'s **KEYSTONE CENTRE**. A large statue of a **CATFISH** (named "Chuck the Channel Cat") at the S entrance to the city signifies Selkirk's claim to be the "Catfish Capital of North America." **RECREATIONAL FISHING** attracts tourism, as do Selkirk Park, the annual Triple S Fair and Rodeo, the Highland Gathering, and the Selkirk Marine Museum.

Proximity to Winnipeg has traditionally had advantages and disadvantages for Selkirk. A 30-minute drive on a 4-lane paved highway has attracted residents who work in Winnipeg but prefer the lower property taxes and "small-town" friendliness of Selkirk, as well as enabling residents of Winnipeg to seek employment in Selkirk.

STAN MILOSEVIC, WWW.MANITOBAPHOTOS.COM

"Chuck the Channel Cat" greets visitors to the City of Selkirk.

The same ease of access, however, has been an ongoing concern for local merchants, who find potential customers attracted to Winnipeg retailers. There has been a significant decline in the success of local businesses in Selkirk's traditional downtown shopping areas of Main St and Manitoba Ave. In the early 21st century, however, a newer shopping district, complete with plenty of free parking and some of the same national and international retailers that previously necessitated a drive to Winnipeg, was established in the NW area of the city. This attracted shoppers not only from Selkirk, but also from the surrounding communities of St. Andrews and St. Clements (*see* **INTERLAKE**), as well as increasing local employment opportunities. • RUSS GOURLUCK

SELKIRK, (Lord) 5th Earl of, colonialist, politician, author (b Thomas Douglas, June 20, 1771, St. Mary's Isle, near Kirkcudbright, Dumfries and Galloway, UK; d Apr 8, 1820, Pau, France). The 7th and youngest son of **SCOTS** peer Dunbar Hamilton Douglas, 4th Earl of Selkirk, Lord Selkirk came unexpectedly into his titles (also Baron Daer and Shortcleuch) because of the early deaths of his elder brothers. He was educated at the U of Edinburgh, and spent considerable time in Paris during the French Revolution. Because of one notoriously radical brother, Basil William Douglas, Lord Daer, who was responsible for bringing Thomas Paine to the UK in 1792, and a brother-in-law (Sir James Hall, 4th Baronet) who was a leading geologist and geophysicist, Selkirk was on familiar terms with many of the leading *philosophes* of the revolutionary period. He always regarded himself as a "political economist" who sought to harmonize the obvious need for social reform with both personal self-interest and imperial utility. His was an almost solitary voice in Britain in support of emigration to the British colonies. Between 1796 and 1801, when he witnessed the results of uprooting people in the Highland clearances, as well as the aftermath of a revolution in Ireland in 1798 that had been brought on largely by religious strife, Selkirk became convinced that colonizing North American lands with his oppressed and disadvantaged countrymen was the ideal remedy. He believed the colonies would benefit, the colonial promoter would benefit (either with public approbation or personal profit), and the nation would rid itself of unwanted people who might otherwise turn to crime or revolution. Selkirk's best-known book, *Observations on the Present State of the Highlands of Scotland* (1805), made a persuasive case for the advantages of emigration to both colonies and the mother country, at the same time as it criticized the Highland landlords for their lack of adequate calculation of their own best interests.

Selkirk first proposed to lead a party of Irish rebels to LA. When the British govt rejected this plan, he turned to PE, buying land from proprietors and recruiting more than 800 Highlanders as settlers. Selkirk hoped to use PE to prove his theory on emigration: Highlanders could be transported to NA and successfully transplanted in agrarian circumstances. In July 1803, Selkirk set sail with his Highland emigrants for PE and arrived in Aug. This settlement was only one of a number planted in British North America by Highland Scots in the period 1801-03, as several thousand emigrants departed for the New World from the Hebrides and adjacent mainland. Leaving his settlers in Sept, Selkirk travelled from Halifax to Boston; to York (Toronto), Upper Canada; and then to Ville-Marie (Montreal), where he learned much about the **FUR TRADE** from fellow Scots. While in Upper Canada, he was granted in excess of 1200 ac (485 ha) of land for settlers in an area, chosen by him, on Lake St. Clair, which he called Baldoon (near present-day Wallaceburg, ON). He visited and made plans for this site in Jun 1804, and settlers soon followed. On his way home in July, he visited his Prince Edward Islanders and found them well established. Early the following year he learned that Baldoon had proved an expensive failure, partly because the swampy area was a breeding ground for disease-bearing **MOSQUITOES**, but chiefly because its manager had no intention of supervising the settlement personally, and could never find reliable resident agents. Selkirk came to regard the unscrupulous behaviour of agents as part of the "American disease," and never did find a solution.

Both the PE and Upper Cdn schemes were dwarfed by the sheer audacity of Selkirk's last and largest promotion: the establishment of a colony in **RUPERT'S LAND**, at **THE FORKS** of the **RED** and **ASSINIBOINE** rivers, roughly on the site of the present city of **WINNIPEG**. To facilitate this venture, Selkirk and his family gained a substantial financial interest in the **HUDSON'S BAY COMPANY (HBC)**, which at the time was at a serious disadvantage in its rivalry with the QC-based **NORTH WEST COMPANY (NWC)**. In 1811, Selkirk received a grant from the HBC of 116,000 mi^2 (300,000 km^2) covering much of present-day MB, ND, SK, and MN, as well as small portions of AB, SD, and MT. **MILES MACDONELL** was named the first gov of **ASSINIBOIA**, as the territory was called, in June 1811. On July 26, he and the first colonists left for **HUDSON BAY**, arriving two months later at **YORK FACTORY**. After wintering on the **NELSON RIVER** until the break-up of ice toward the end of June

1812, Macdonell and his party did not arrive at the junction of the Red and Assiniboine until Aug 30. The colony quickly ran afoul of the NWC, which from its base at Fort Gibraltar employed the Red River region as the source of **PEMMICAN** for the provisioning of its traders on the vast inland canoe routes. In 1813, Selkirk nearly persuaded the UK govt to finance the recruiting, equipping, and transporting to the Red River of a Highland Regiment to be commanded by himself. The scheme had won ministerial approval, but at the last minute was vetoed by the commander-in-chief, the Duke of York. Selkirk was reduced to sending to the Red River Settlement, at his own expense, people for the regiment recruited from the estates of the Duke of Sutherland.

Thomas Douglas, 5th Earl of Selkirk

When the Selkirk settlers were forced to rely on **BISON** meat and pemmican for food, Gov Macdonell proclaimed that pemmican could not be exported from the region without his permission. This action, which endangered the pemmican supply to the northwestern Athabasca country of the North West Company, led its local leaders to resort to aggressive opposition. The settlement was nearly dispersed in 1815, and experienced disaster at the **SEVEN OAKS INCIDENT** a year later. Selkirk learned of Seven Oaks on July 25, 1816, at Sault Ste. Marie, Upper Canada (ON), while on his way to Red River with a small flotilla of soldier-settlers and boatloads of arms and supplies. He made his way to Fort William (now Thunder Bay, ON), the headquarters of the North West Company, seized it, made some arrests, and occupied it for the winter. On May 1 of the following year, he left for Red River, where he remained until Aug. He then departed for Upper Canada. Legal charges brought against him by the NWC and the associated court proceedings as well as ill health combined to produce Selkirk's departure from Canada later in the year.

Selkirk died in Pau, Aquitaine, France, in 1820, and was buried in the nearest Protestant cemetery, in nearby Orthez. He was virtually bankrupt, although he had succeeded in placing before the British public a powerful set of arguments about emigration and colonization that gained much acceptance in the years after the Battle of Waterloo. He had insisted that the usual policy of govt – "to take no charge whatever of emigrants, even of those who embark for our own colonies, but to leave to every one to provide for himself as best he can" – was a mistake. Selkirk was a proponent both of govt involvement in emigration and settlement as an imperial matter, and of the development of colonial land by large landholders as an investment. In both respects, he anticipated the future. ● J. M. BUMSTED

SEMPLE, Robert, colonial official (b Feb 26, 1777, Boston; d June 19, 1816, **Red River Settlement**) was involved in the **Seven Oaks Incident**. Born to Loyalist parents in MA, he travelled widely at the time of the Napoleonic Wars as a merchant (and, probably, as a British spy), producing a number of travel books and a novel, *Charles Ellis, Or the Friends* (1807). In 1815, **Lord Selkirk** named him gov of **Assiniboia**, and he arrived at **York Factory** in Aug 1815 with settlers from Sutherlandshire, Scotland. At

Robert Semple, ca 1800

Red River, he soon ran into conflict with **Colin Robertson**, who persisted in calling him "Mr. Simple." Robertson found him both too conciliatory and too contemptuous of the **Métis**. In the Seven Oaks Incident, he was killed leading a party of armed settlers (20 of whom also died) by a group of Métis under **Cuthbert Grant** at the area known as Frog Plain (or Seven Oaks) on June 19, 1816. Lord Selkirk and the **HBC** always referred to this skirmish as a "massacre," although evidence of who was the aggressor and what actually happened at Seven Oaks is not at all conclusive. Although a number of the Grant party were tried in Upper Canada (ON) for murder on Selkirk-initiated indictments, none was ever convicted. ● JMB

Ernest Thompson Seton

SETON, Ernest Thompson, naturalist, artist, author (b Ernest Evan Thompson, Aug 14, 1860, South Shields, Tyne & Wear, UK; d Oct 23, 1946, Seton Village, Santa Fe Cty, NM). Widely regarded as one of the world's great naturalists, Seton and his family emigrated to ON when he was a child. He showed an early flair for drawing, and after earning a gold medal in a competition in Toronto, he won a scholarship in 1879 to attend the Royal Academy of Arts in the UK. Ill health forced him back to Canada, and in 1881, he moved to MB to join 2 of his brothers on their homestead near **Carberry**. Here, his talent as an artist combined with his keen powers of observation to produce some of his greatest work as a naturalist. *Mammals of Manitoba* was published in 1886, and *Birds of Manitoba* in 1891. These volumes led to his appointment

as naturalist for the govt of MB in 1892, a position he held until his death. Among Seton's discoveries were the MB nesting grounds of Connecticut **Warblers**.

With the 1898 publication of *Wild Animals I Have Known* – which has never been out of print – he became internationally famous. In addition to his books, he wrote some 10,000 scientific and popular articles. Seton had met Lord Baden Powell, the founder of the Scouts movement, while overseas. Together, they founded Boy Scouts of America. Seton wrote the first manual and was the first Chief Scout, but disagreed with Powell's militaristic approach, leaving the organization in 1915.

Carberry is home to The Seton Centre, a museum dedicated to his work; an Ernest Thompson Seton Institute is headquartered in **Winnipeg** and in Los Angeles; a city park is named after him in Toronto; and museums devoted to him are at the Philmont Scout Ranch, near Cimarron, NM, and at Seton Castle in Santa Fe. ● DOUG ALLEN

SEVEN OAKS GENERAL HOSPITAL is the primary health-care institution servicing the northern portion of the city of Winnipeg and surrounding communities. It operates under the direction of the Winnipeg Regional Health Authority in association with a Board of Trustees.

The first patient was admitted on Jan 14, 1981, nearly 20 years after councillor **Joseph Zuken** first addressed city council in 1962 regarding the need for a hospital in the **North End**. In 1968, Zuken and then-mayor of West Kildonan Saul A. Miller formed the Inter-Municipal Hospital Committee to help lobby the provincial government for support and funding. The hospital was incorporated in 1970, and during the following decade a diverse coalition of local politicians served on its Board of Trustees, notably **Abe Yanofsky**, Olga Fuga, Charles Bachman and Joseph Cropo. The board, which Zuken chaired until 1981, continued to negotiate with **Ed Schreyer**'s govt, eventually securing funding in 1975 for a $32 million, 336-bed, acute-care facility.

The hospital's unique design incorporates hexagonal ward layouts that situate patients much closer to nursing stations compared to traditional models with their long hallways. Smith Carter and Partners earned a premier's Design of Merit award for the architectural plan. An early controversy saw the govt-mandated closure of the underutilized Obstetrics Unit in late 1983, due to the small number of births. Despite the objection of the board, labour and delivery services were relocated to the **Health Sciences Centre**. During the 1980s, the hospital continued to open more beds and streamline policies while achieving modest budget surpluses. In an era of overall cuts to health-care spending, in 1994, GARY FILMON's govt proposed closing the hospital's emergency as a cost-saving measure. A community-based campaign entitled "Save the Oaks" included a number of public rallies in opposition to the idea, and the govt relented.

In 1996, the hospital opened the Wellness Institute, an award-winning facility dedicated to education, fitness and health promotion with an emphasis on cardiac rehabilitation. It was the first of its kind in Canada, and was funded by retained hospital surpluses and a lengthy capital campaign. The 7400 m² space attracts a membership of more than 6000, and features programs like weight management, nutrition counselling, smoking cessation. Seven Oaks General Hospital celebrated its 25th anniversary in 2006 as a 275-bed facility that employs approx 1500 and accommodates more than 30,000 visits per year to an emergency department that was undergoing an $11 million expansion in 2007. ● JOEL TRENAMAN

SEVEN OAKS HOUSE MUSEUM, at 115 Rupertsland Ave E in the West Kildonan area of WINNIPEG, was the home of SCOTS settler John Inkster, and is one of the oldest dwellings in MB. This log house recreates conditions in the 19th-century RED RIVER SETTLEMENT. "Orkney Johnny," born in 1799, was a free trader and merchant, and organized a post office and store after building his log house. The restored home, now a museum, was apparently called Seven Oaks House because of its proximity to Seven Oaks Creek,

Seven Oaks House Museum, 2007

a small tributary of the RED RIVER that was once lined with 7 large oak trees, near the site of the SEVEN OAKS INCIDENT. Inkster built a mill on this creek in 1856.

Although the house was made mainly of wood, Inkster himself laid a stone foundation/cellar. This foundation is particularly well crafted, as it is held together by the cut of the stone alone. Because of FLOODING by the Red in 1852, construction on the house had to be stopped, though the 2-storey, 9-room house was completed the next year. The last occupant, Mary Inkster, a daughter of John, died here in 1912: her spirit is said still to haunt the place. The now-defunct city of West Kildonan gained control of the grounds shortly thereafter, and full ownership of the house and its outbuildings in 1952. It began restorations to the property, and the Seven Oaks House Museum opened its doors to the public on July 2, 1958. Displays include many of the Inksters' personal effects and furniture pieces, as well as letters and records written by members of the family. ● AJL

SEVEN OAKS INCIDENT (also known as the Battle of Seven Oaks). The 1816 event is one of the most prominent in MB's history. Historians disagree about the facts of the incident: who fired the first shot; whether the bodies of the fallen were mutilated; whether the event should be termed a "massacre," "battle," or "incident;" and wherein its significance lies. However, most concur that the historical significance of this engagement resides in its usefulness as an ideological weapon in the arsenal of warring cultures competing for prairie lands.

The Seven Oaks Incident has been appropriately viewed as the boiling-over of the rivalry between the HUDSON'S BAY COMPANY (HBC) and the NORTH WEST COMPANY (NWC) for dominance in the trade with interior First Nations groups, primarily the CREE, in the region of RUPERT'S LAND. By 1800, MÉTIS employees of the NWC began to settle along the banks of the RED and ASSINIBOINE rivers. In 1812, they were joined by transplanted SCOTS crofters in LORD SELKIRK's colony. These Scots were granted lands by the HBC, partly as a bulwark against perceived encroachments by the NWC. Questioning the authority of the HBC to grant these lands to the Selkirk settlers, the Métis regarded the colonists as interlopers from the outset.

Seven Oaks resulted from a succession of confrontations, beginning with an 1814 proclamation by gov MILES MACDONELL prohibiting the export of PEMMICAN from the RED RIVER SETTLEMENT without his approval. Macdonell was concerned about food shortages, but the

NWC viewed his proclamation as an attempt to sabotage its pemmican trade. The Métis hunters, who procured BISON for the company, refused to accept Macdonell's authority under the HBC charter to take actions to curtail their economic activities. Several conflicts followed, marking a general deterioration in relations between the HBC and Selkirk settlers, on the one side, and the NWC and the Métis settlers, on the other.

In 1815, Macdonell resigned as gov and was replaced by ROBERT SEMPLE. The hostilities quickly escalated in March 1816, with the HBC's seizure, and later destruction, of the NWC's FORT GIBRALTAR at THE FORKS. Thus prevented from moving their pemmican to The Forks for trans-shipment to their headquarters at Fort William (now Thunder Bay, ON), the Métis under CUTHBERT GRANT occupied the HBC post of Brandon House in May 1816, then escorted a pemmican brigade down the Assiniboine toward The Forks. When this party was observed passing Fort Douglas on June 19, 1816, Semple precipitously led a party of 20 HBC employees and Selkirk settlers out from the fort to intercept them. Semple's men were on foot, already at a disadvantage to the mounted Métis; they also lacked the skills of marksmanship that were prevalent among the Métis.

The events that followed have been much debated and discussed. Members of the Selkirk and HBC side alleged that the Métis started firing and carried out an unprovoked massacre, then looted and mutilated the bodies; the Métis party disputed these assertions. Notwithstanding the witnesses' disagreement on various issues, the meticulous reconstruction of the facts of the event by William Bachelor Coltman (the principal commissioner appointed to investigate Seven Oaks and other violent episodes of the fur companies' rivalry) provided the most comprehensive and balanced account of the event.

From the eyewitness accounts, it appears that a member of Semple's party fired the first shot, perhaps by accident. This shot precipitated a general fusillade, in which Semple and 20 of his men were killed along with one member of the Métis party. Following the battle, Lord Selkirk led a force that seized the NWC's principal base at Fort William, also reoccupying Fort Douglas. A period of extensive litigation followed, culminating in the merger of the 2 companies in 1821.

The Seven Oaks Incident inspired 2 traditions. In the first instance, the Métis victory became enshrined in folklore in the song "Chanson de la Grenouillère," by PIERRE FALCON, which celebrated it as a defining moment in the birth of their nation. The Francophone historiography continued into the 20th century in works by Auguste-Henri de Trémaudan and Louis-Arthur

Dramatized portrayal of Seven Oaks Incident by C. W. Jefferys

Prud'homme. In the Red River era, writing on Seven Oaks was roughly balanced between the ethnocentric judgements of **ALEXANDER ROSS** and the more pluralistic accounts of Donald Gunn and Joseph James Hargrave.

The 2nd – and the dominant – tradition arises from the Anglophone settlers, mainly from ON, or their descendants, who identified with the Selkirk settlers and HBC forces. This group of historians rewrote the history of the incident as a "massacre" of the Semple party by Métis aggressors – an interpretation that served a specific ideological purpose. As newcomers who had recently displaced the Métis, **FRENCH**, and First Nations, the settlers from Upper Canada/ON saw the legitimacy of their claim to Western lands as challenged by the **RED RIVER RESISTANCE** of 1869-70 and the Northwest Resistance of 1885. In this context, Anglo-Cdn historians felt the need to secure a bloodline to the early colonial period. They found the desired nexus by adopting the Selkirk settlers, the only available full-blooded European settlers from the early 19th century, as imagined ancestors in the West. Their interpretation formed part of a developing narrative of the region's past as a struggle between forces of "civilization" and "savagery," in which Seven Oaks served as a useful demonstration of how their ancestors had overcome presumed forces of darkness.

The characterization of Seven Oaks as a "massacre" continues in encyclopedia, popular, novelistic, and even some academic accounts. These versions demonstrate the strength and resilience of historical fabrication. Fortunately,

in the last decades, and in the wake of the provincial centennial, several scholarly treatments have presented a more nuanced account of the event, though it has been hard to wean Anglo-Manitobans from the old interpretation. • LYLE DICK

SEYMOURVILLE, pop 135, is 70 km from Pine Falls, in MB's Precambrian Shield country. The community started out as a co-operative, (what Statistics Canada classified as an "Unorganized Territory"), on Sept 10, 1970; and about 20 years later, on Jan 10, 1990, transformed itself into part of a group of 4 communities (along with Manigotagan, the Hollow Water Reserve, and Aghaming). The Manitoba Model Forest project (a forum that focuses on climate change), in 2003, took place in Seymourville, which is where the northern region of this project is situated. This forum started up in 1992, and is 1 of 11 that are spread out in different locations across Canada. The community of Seymourville's water source is **LAKE WINNIPEG**. The topography of this region is comprised of granite-gneissic rock, with little soil cover. The economic foundation of Seymourville is fishing, logging, trapping, wild rice harvesting, and tourism. • GPP

SHACK, Sybil Francis, educator, author (b Apr 1, 1911, **WINNIPEG**; d Jan 22, 2004, Winnipeg). Born in the family home behind a **NORTH END** grocery store, Shack entered the **U OF M** on an Isbister Scholarship at the age of 14, graduating with a BA in 1929. A year at Normal School earned her a teaching certificate, but she was unable to find a placement. She worked for 2

years in a variety of stopgap jobs, tutoring, marking papers, writing for newspapers, and serving as a substitute teacher. A full-time school position finally materialized in **FOXWARREN**. She taught for 3 years there and in **SHOAL LAKE**, and then was admitted to teach in the Winnipeg school system. A decade later, Shack returned to the U of M, to take the Gold Medal in Education in 1945 and an MEd in 1946. Subsequently, she studied educational administration at the Ontario College of Education. Her distinguished career as principal of several Winnipeg schools began in 1948 at Sargent Park School and ended in 1976 with her retirement from Kelvin High School.

Shack was an advocate for women's rights, writing numerous books and articles in which she examined the changing role of women in education and business. She was the author of several noteworthy books, including *Armed With a Primer* (1965); *The Two-Thirds Minority* (1973), on women in education; and *Saturday's Stepchildren* (1977), on Cdn women in business. A president of the Canadian Civil Liberties Association; a member of the Advisory Board of the Centre on Aging at the U of M and of the Manitoba Judicial Council; and a frequent broadcaster on CBC radio and television, Dr. Shack received numerous awards. She was named a member of the Order of Canada and Provost of the Buffalo Hunt in 1984,

Sybil Shack, 1966

received a Manitoba Human Rights Achievements Award in 1995, and was enrolled in the Winnipeg Citizens' Hall of Fame in 1996. Shack's papers are deposited in the **Archives** of the U of M.

As a footnote to a career in pursuit of humanist ideals, Sybil Shack and her parents became the foster family of the noted theatre producer **John Stephen Hirsch** on his arrival in Canada in 1947 as a teenager in flight from a Nazi-devastated Europe. • MILDRED GUTKIN

SHAKESPEARE IN THE RUINS (SIR) is MB's longest-running professional Shakespearean theatre company. The company's productions require audiences to follow the actors as they move about. The actors will at times "break the 4th wall," interacting with the audience. In 1993, the ruins of a 100-year-old Trappist monastery in St. Norbert, at the very S of **Winnipeg**, inspired founding members of SIR to stage their first show outdoors. Surrounded by the crumbling monastery walls, the company performed before students in an effort to make Shakespeare more accessible. Armed with only a small grant, founding members planned the production as a one-time event. In 2002, the company relocated to Lagimodière-Gaboury Historic Park in Winnipeg. Leaving the monastery was a move that allowed the company to explore new locations and promenade theatre in innovative ways. For example, in 2002, SIR staged *Romeo and Juliet* on the rooftop of a downtown Winnipeg multi-storey parking lot. SIR subsequently moved indoors, to the conservatory in **Assiniboine Park**. Besides producing plays, SIR offers professional development workshops and apprenticeships that allow emerging artists to work alongside established artists. • JILL SEXSMITH

SHAMATTAWA FIRST NATION, on reserve pop 1241, off reserve pop 21, is situated 1277 km N of **Winnipeg**, and 365 km E of **Thompson**. The Shamattawa First Nation community signed Treaty 5 in 1910, and its native language is **Cree**. There is one reserve located in the community. It is a member of the Keewatin Tribal Council. Shamattawa initially functioned as an outpost to **York Factory**, and in 1934 it became an independent post. In the 21st century, Shamattawa First Nation's schooling goes from Nursery-Grade 11, and total enrolment for the year 2003-04 was 327. This First Nation administers its own education. It is an isolated community, dependent on winter road access, air access and water access in the summer. Shamattawa relies on trapping and fishing; Unemployment and poverty are endemic. The Shamattawa First Nation found itself in national headlines in 1986 and 1992 for its addiction

problems and again in 2004 after a rash of suicides. As of Jan 2005, Indian and Northern Affairs Canada was trying to improve the water and sewer quality infrastructure conditions in the community. • RK

Remy Shand's debut album, recorded in his parents' Garden City condo in Winnipeg, sold more than 750,000 copies.

SHAND, Remy, soul/pop singer/songwriter (b Oct 14, 1977, **Winnipeg**). Released in 2002, newcomer Shand's debut album *The Way I Feel* became a pop sensation, reaching number one across Canada, selling over 750,000 copies worldwide, and earning praise from the likes of Elton John. Shand began writing the songs at age 19, recording in a home studio in his parent's Garden City home in 2001, playing all the instruments himself. Released on the Motown Records soul label in the US, the album boasted the mellow funk/soul hit singles "Take A Message," "The Way I Feel," and "Rocksteady," earning the fledgling recording artist 4 Grammy nominations for Best Male R&B Vocal Performance, Best Traditional R&B Vocal Performance, Best R&B Song, and Best R&B album; 2 Prairie Music Awards for Best Pop Recording and Best Producer (2003); and a Juno Award for Best R&B Recording (2002). He toured NA and appeared on *The Tonight Show* and *Live with Regis and Kelly*. In 2004, he married Winnipeg singer Maiko Watson and began recording his follow-up album, *Day in the Shade*. Shand later returned to his school, St. John's High, to donate $10,000 to its music program. • JOHN EINARSON

SHANKLAND, Robert, Victoria Cross winner (b 1887, Ayr, UK; d Jan 20, 1968, Vancouver). A **Scots**-born Winnipegger (living on Pine St, later renamed **Valour Rd**), he was a 30-year-old Lt in the 43rd (Cameron Highlanders of Canada) Batt in WWI. On Oct. 26, 1917, at Passchendaele,

Belgium, he distinguished himself while leading his men to overrun an enemy position, holding it despite counterattacks. He also served in WWII, retiring with the rank of LCol. In 1946, Shankland left the forces to became secretary of a securities firm in Vancouver, where he lived for the rest of his life. • JIM SHILLIDAY

SHARK, GREENLAND (*Somniosus microcephalus*) is a huge (max 7 m and 2.25 tonnes), greyish-brown shark (family Somniosidae) common in Hudson Strait and reported occasionally in **Hudson Bay**. Due to its secretive habits, it is likely more common than suspected along the MB coast. Occurring in Arctic and North Atlantic waters, it has been found as deep as 2000 m and in temperatures from 1-12°C. It hunts in near dark, relying on its keen sense of smell rather than sight. In fact, even its small eyes are compromised by a 6 cm parasitic copepod crustacean (*Ommatokoita elongata*) attached to the cornea of its eyes. Clues for navigation are smell, sound, salt concentration, current, temperature, pressure and electromagnetism. Rivalling the Great White Shark (*Carcharodon carcharias*) in size, it tends to be sluggish, but can put on a burst of speed to capture seals, fish, squid and sea birds. It can suck in fish from one m away, and does not hesitate to scavenge whale carcasses, which it locates by smell from many kms away. Large chunks of flesh are torn out with the sharp teeth and powerful jaw muscles. It tends to feed near the surface in winter and descends to the depths in summer.

During the mating act, the male flushes his spermatophores along a groove in the clasper and into the oviduct of the female. Months later, about a dozen soft-shelled eggs (goose-egg size) hatch within the mother shark's uterus, the pups gaining nutrients only from the yolk sac (i.e., no placental support). At birth, the 38 cm pups are fully developed (ovo-vivipary) and capable of survival on their own. In such a cold environment, this species grows very slowly. Longevity is unknown but is lengthy. This shark is harvested locally for meat, oil and hides. Although the fresh meat is toxic (due to urea and other natural chemicals), it may be eaten safely when dried. The Inuit formerly used the sharp teeth (50 in each jaw) for knives, and the rough skin (covered in tough denticles of dentine) for mukluks. Sharks have been major predators for over 400 million years (Silurian period). • REW

SHARP, Mitchell William, economist, public servant, politician (b May 11, 1911, **Winnipeg**; d March 19, 2004, Ottawa). The son of **Scots** immigrants, Sharp studied at the **U of M** and the London School of Economics. Following his studies, the Winnipeg grain firm **JAMES RICH-ARDSON & SONS, LIMITED** employed him as an economist. Sharp joined the federal finance department in 1942. In 1947, he took part in the negotiations that led to Newfoundland's entry into Confederation. Sharp moved to the department of trade and commerce in 1951 as associate deputy minister. In 1958, he left the civil service to become vice president of Brazilian Traction Light & Power Company. Sharp resigned in 1962 to enter federal politics as a **LIBERAL** candidate. Narrowly defeated in the 1962 election, he was successful in the April 1963 election.

Mitchell Sharp, 1965

UMA, TRIBUNE, PERSONALITY FILES

Sharp was named minister of trade and commerce in the cabinet of PM Lester B. Pearson. From 1965-68, he served as minister of finance. In 1968, Sharp ran for the leadership of the Liberal party. The day before the convention however, he withdrew in favour of the eventual winner, Pierre Trudeau. From 1968-74, he was secretary of state for external affairs and deputy prime minister. Sharp resigned from Parliament in 1978. He returned as personal advisor to PM Jean Chretien following the 1993 general election. In his personal life, Sharp was an avid and accomplished pianist. He once claimed that the greatest moment of his life was a benefit concert where he performed with the Toronto Symphony Orchestra. ● KAREN OMELAN/SANDY CUSHON

SHAY, Jennifer, naturalist, conservationist, educator (b March 27, 1930, Kingston-upon-Hull, UK), promoted conservation, ecology, and protection of the environment from the late 1950s

onward, long before these causes were popular. Born in Hull, UK, as Jennifer Walker, she did an honours BSc at Bedford College, U of London, then worked as assistant director of the Field Studies Council at Flatford Mill Field Centre, Essex. She came to Canada in 1957, earning an MSc and PhD in botany at the **U OF M**. Her doctorate was on the effects of falling water levels on the vegetation of **DELTA MARSH**. Spurred by the lack of field stations for biological and ecological studies in MB, she then established the U of M's Delta Marsh Biological Field Station almost single-handedly, and served as its director for 20 years. She continued her research on marsh ecology and the giant reed grass (*Phragmites* spp.), then worked on the present and past ecology of Crete with her archaeologist husband, Tom Shay. She was a professor in the U of M's Department of Botany, and taught courses in the Department of Landscape Architecture for many years. She received the institution's Dr. and Mrs. H. H. Saunderson teaching award in 1992, a year before her retirement.

Shay's numerous conservation activities have included work on the original *Ecological Reserves Act* for MB; research on the effects of military training at **CFB SHILO** on the surrounding short-grass prairie projects with the International Biological Programme and the Nature Conservancy of Canada; involvement in protesting the 1966-77 diversion of the **CHURCHILL RIVER** for **HYDROELECTRIC** power; and extensive involvement with the Manitoba Naturalists Society. She has received many honours and awards provincially and federally, most notably Member (1998) then Officer (2000) of the Order of Canada. Her papers are now in the U of M's **ARCHIVES**. ● KAREN JOHNSON

SHERO, Fred Alexander "The Fog," hockey coach (b Oct 23, 1925 **WINNIPEG**; d Nov 24, 1990, Philadelphia). Shero was a successful coach, known for introducing an extremely physical style of hockey to the NHL. He led the Philadelphia Flyers, including MB players **REGGIE LEACH** and **BOBBY CLARKE**, to 2 consecutive Stanley Cup victories in 1974 and 1975. The son of Russian immigrants, Shero grew up in Winnipeg's **NORTH END** where he started out in boxing, winning the Cdn Bantamweight Boxing Championship at 13. He attended the **U OF M** for 2 years before serving in the navy during WWII, where he played hockey for the military team. Shero also continued to box competitively, and was later offered $10,000 to turn professional. However, he was also offered a contract with the New York Rangers, and opted to play hockey instead, against the advice of his father who said that hockey players

are unemployed by the time they hit 30. He started his first season with the Rangers in 1947. He was a mediocre defenceman, and played just 3 seasons in the NHL before being relegated to the minor leagues, where he played from 1951-58.

It was as a coach that Shero left his mark in hockey. He first started coaching while still a player for the Shawinigan Cataracts in the 1957-58 season, leading the team to that year's Ontario Hockey League Championship win. Over his 13 years coaching in the minors, Shero had 6 championship wins, and placed either 2nd or 3rd in the seasons that his team failed to secure a trophy. He was promoted to the NHL in 1971, taking over the Philadelphia Flyers. He saw his greatest success in his 7 years with the Flyers. Under his aggressive coaching style, the Flyers became known the "Broad Street Bullies," and through their intimidating tactics, won consecutive 1974 and 1975 Stanley Cup wins, earning Shero the 1974 Jack Adams Award for Coach of the Year. Unhappy with the Flyers' performance in the 1977-78 season, Shero resigned and briefly took over the New York Rangers. Shero spent the 1980s as a radio analyst for the New Jersey Devils, with a brief stint coaching hockey in Europe. In addition to raising the level of aggression in hockey, Shero's impact on the NHL can still be seen in other practices he introduced after studying Soviet hockey, such as hiring an assistant coach and installing complex playing systems. ● MD

SHIELDS, Carol (b June 2, 1935, Oak Park, IL; d July 16, 2003, Victoria, BC). The much-loved Manitoba novelist was born Carol Warner in the Chicago suburb of Oak Park, the same place Ernest Hemingway had been born many years earlier. Her parents were Robert and Inez Warner, and she had an older brother and sister, twins Robert and Barbara, born 1933. Carol attended Nathaniel Hawthorne School and Ralph Waldo Emerson School in Oak Park and graduated from Oak Park High School in 1953. From 1953 to 1957, she took arts at Hanover College in Hanover, IN. In 1955-56, she was an exchange student at the U of Exeter, UK. Over the Christmas 1955 season, she opted to take a British Council–sponsored study holiday in Aberfoyle, Stirling, UK. There she met Donald Hugh Shields, an engineering graduate of the U of SK who was in Scotland on an Athlone Fellowship. They married in 1957, after Carol graduated from Hanover with her BA.

In the next 11 years, Don's work as an engineer, and his post-graduate studies, took them to Vancouver, Toronto, Manchester, Toronto again, and Ottawa. Their 5 children were born during this period: John (1958, Toronto), Anne (1959, Toronto), Catherine (1962, Manchester, UK), Margaret (1964, Toronto), and Sara (1968, Ottawa). While living in Ottawa between 1967 and 1978, Carol became a Cdn citizen and did post-graduate work in English at the U of Ottawa, receiving her MA in 1975. Her first published book was *Others* (1972), a collection of **POETRY**, followed by another, *Intersect* (1974). In 1976, her *Susanna Moodie: Voice and Vision*, a critical work based on her master's thesis, appeared. That work is a key to some of the effects and preoccupations that run through Shields's fiction. Her first novel, *Small Ceremonies*, was published that same year. The quiet, low-key episodes in the book showed her ear for lifelike dialogue, and her eye for the nuances of character that show up in the small events of quotidian living. The book received the Canadian Authors Association Award for best novel. She taught English and creative writing at the U of Ottawa 1976-78, and her 2nd novel, *The Box Garden*, was published in 1977. The family moved to Vancouver in 1978, and Shields taught at the U of BC, publishing her 3rd novel, *Happenstance*, in 1980.

That same year, Don took a position as head of civil engineering at the **U OF M**, and the Shieldses moved to **WINNIPEG**, where they would spend the next 20 years. This was not only the longest they lived in any one city; it was also a period of unusual productivity for Carol, who not only became an active member of the local writing community, but also achieved international acclaim. For most of this time, she taught English at the U of M. Her 4th novel, *A Fairly Conventional Woman*, was published in 1982 as a companion to *Happenstance*; where the earlier novel presents a few days in the life of Jack Bowman while his wife Brenda is away at a convention, the latter book shows what Brenda does over the same timeframe. (The 2 were eventually published in a single volume under the title *Happenstance*.) In 1983, Shields's radio drama, *Women Waiting*, won first prize in a CBC competition. Two years later, her short story "Mrs. Turner Cutting the Grass" won a National Magazine Award, and her first collection of stories appeared under the title *Various Miracles*. At the same time, Shields worked on 2 stage plays, one in collaboration with Winnipeg's **DAVE WILLIAMSON**, *Anniversary*; the other was a play of her own, patterned after A. R. Gurney's *The Dining Room*, called *Departures and Arrivals*. She cut *Anniversary* to one act to take advantage of the new interest in lunchtime theatre, and it was produced as *Not Another Anniversary* by Toronto's Solar Stage in 1986.

Her riveting novel *Swann: A Mystery* was published in 1987, winning the Arthur Ellis Award for Best Canadian Mystery. That was followed in 1989 by a 2nd collection of short stories, *The Orange Fish*. A year later, she received the Marian Engel Award, given annually to a distinguished female Cdn writer in mid-career. During this time, she was collaborating by mail with BC novelist Blanche Howard, and in 1991, their epistolary novel, *A Celibate Season*, was published. The following year saw the appearance of her wise and witty novel *The Republic of Love*. So pleasant is her depiction of Winnipeg, the *New York Times* reviewer, Elinor Lipman, wanted to head there on the next plane. A 3rd collection of Shields's poetry, *Coming to Canada*, came out the same year.

Early in 1993, her charming stage play about bridge-playing women, *Thirteen Hands*, premiered in Winnipeg. That fall marked the publication of her magnum opus, *The Stone Diaries*. This whimsical story of the life of MB-born Daisy Goodwill won the Gov Gen's Award for fiction; because of Carol's dual citizenship, it was also eligible for prestigious US awards, of which it won 2 in 1995: the National Book Critics' Circle Award and the Pulitzer Prize. That same year, Winnipeg hosted the first presentation of her play *Fashion Power Guilt and the Charity of Families*, written with her daughter Catherine. While continuing to teach English at the U of M, Shields was named chancellor of the **U OF W** in 1996, a year that also saw a revised 2-act version of an earlier collaboration, *Anniversary*, open in Winnipeg. Her 1997 novel, *Larry's Party*, explored the tribulations of a contemporary young man; it went on to win the lucrative Orange Prize.

In fall 1998, Shields was diagnosed with breast cancer, but that only temporarily interrupted her production of significant work. She and Don moved to England for a year in 1999 and, upon their return in 2000, they took up residence in Victoria. Her 3rd collection of short stories, *Dressing Up for the Carnival*, was published, and, a year later, her biography of a writer with whom she is often compared, Jane Austen, appeared as part of the "Penguin Lives" series. That book won her the Charles Taylor Prize for Literary Non-Fiction. The same year, she and Winnipeg's Marjorie Anderson edited a collection of personal essays by 35 different women entitled *Dropped Threads: What We Aren't Told*. This collection, documenting the life experiences that women were previously forbidden to talk about, proved to be wildly popular, staying on the *Globe and Mail*'s bestseller list for nearly 2 years. A 2nd collection of *Dropped Threads* essays, subtitled *More of What We Aren't Told*, was published in

spring 2003. A 3rd collection, edited by Anderson alone, appeared in 2006.

The year 2002 saw the publication of Shields's novel, *Unless*, one that celebrates a happy marriage – like her own – while at the same time challenging present-day society for not taking women seriously. The novel, which is also about writing fiction, emphasizes the importance of characters' occupations – this fascination with people's jobs runs through all her work. *Unless* was nominated for many major awards. Also in 2002, her 4 plays were published in a single volume called *Thirteen Hands and Other Plays*. She later adapted *Unless* for the stage with the help of her daughter, Sara Cassidy; it was produced posthumously by the Canadian Stage Company (Toronto) and by others.

Shields was in Victoria working on a new novella when she succumbed to cancer on July 16, 2003. "Segue," a segment of this work, was included in *The Collected Stories*, which appeared in 2004. Shields was a member of the Royal Society of Canada, was inducted into the Order of Canada (1998) and Order of Manitoba (2001), and was named Winnipeg Citizen of the Year (2001). She also received honorary doctorates from Carleton U, Concordia U, U of Ottawa, U of Victoria, and several others. ● DAVE WILLIAMSON

SHIPLEY, Nancy Evelyn "Nan," author, (b Nov 6, 1902, Glasgow, Scotland; d Jan 23, 1990, **WINNIPEG**). Born and raised Nancy Somerville, she moved with her husband George Shipley to Winnipeg in the 1920s. She became known for her writing and for her support of Aboriginal and Métis cultures. Shipley organized MB's first Aboriginal crafts sales centre in 1959 and focused her writing on Aboriginal and Métis women. She wrote many short stories and articles and 14 books, including children's stories, historical studies, and one biography. Her first book was called *Anna and the Indians* (1955) and has been reprinted multiple times. Her best known works are *Frances and the Crees* (1957), *The Railway Builders* (1965), *The James Evan Story* (1966), and *Churchill: Canada's Northern Gateway* (1974). Shipley also hosted a weekly TV program in 1974-1975 at CKND Winnipeg. She was elected Woman of the Year by the Women's Advertising and Sales Club of Winnipeg in 1965. Shipley's papers, including several unpublished works, were donated to the **U OF M**, the U of Southern Mississippi, and the Archives of MB. ● AMANDA STEPHENS

SHOAL LAKE, pop 801, is a town 85 km NW of **BRANDON** on the N end of a lake of the same name; on hwy 16. The town takes its name from

S

the shallow lake it stands by. A small **NORTH-WEST MOUNTED POLICE** contingent came to the area in 1874, associated with their march W from **FORT DUFFERIN** along the **BOUNDARY COMMISSION** trail. They established a post at the S end of the lake. With the arrival of the **RAILWAY** at the N end of the lake in 1885, the townsite moved. English people settled here, as did smaller numbers of **SCOTS**, **IRISH**, and **GERMANS**. The town was incorporated in 1909.

There is still an RCMP detachment here, and the Official Museum of the North-West Mounted Police chronicles the long history of police presence in Shoal Lake, as well as the lives of pioneers here. Service and **RETAIL** support for **AGRICULTURE** now constitute the bulk of the local economy, though the lake itself draws tourism in the form of **HUNTING** and **FISHING**, and the Feb winter festival, Thunder and Ice, attracts many visitors. Thanks to Shoal Lake's recycling and composting program, begun in 1991, the town has the highest rates of household recycling in Canada. • GPP

SHOREBIRDS (families Recurvirostridae and Scolopacidae) form a large group of small-to-medium-sized birds that are mostly associated

with the edges of water bodies, mudflats, or grasslands, where they feed on a variety of invertebrate matter. Some 42 species have been known to occur in MB, of which one, the Eskimo Curlew (*Numeneus borealis*), is probably extinct.

The Killdeer (*Charadrius vociferus*) may be the most familiar. This noisy bird is commonly found in open areas and is one of our spring migrants. It is closely related to the Piping Plover (*Charadrius melodus*), which is endangered due to human disturbance at the wide, sandy beaches it needs. A few pairs have managed to hang on at Grand Beach Provincial Park.

Among the most difficult birds to identify are the so-called "peeps" – small, active brownish shorebirds that rarely allow one a long look. Much easier to identify is the American Avocet (*Recurvirostra americana*), with is black, white, and pink plumage, and upturned bill. The American Woodcock (*Scolopax minor*) is a crepuscular bird, meaning it is most active at dawn and dusk. It delivers its odd spring display-flight in clearings in wooded areas of the southeast. Although several species breed in the southern part of the province, most migrate N to **CHURCHILL** or beyond to nest. • RUDOLF KOES

American Avocet

SHORTT, Angus Henry, wildlife artist, naturalist (b Sept 25, 1908, Belfast, N Ireland; d Jan 8, 2006, **WINNIPEG**) dedicated his life to painting Prairie birds, wildlife, and landscapes. His family emigrated from Ireland in 1911, and Shortt's passion for birds and artistry developed early in his life in western Winnipeg. He trained at **BRIGDENS'** graphic arts training program at the Winnipeg School of Art, and began his career working in Winnipeg and New York museums and doing early etchings for catalogues and museum dioramas. Shortt started his career with **DUCKS UNLIMITED CANADA** in 1939; he continued his work there until his retirement in 1973. His waterfowl artwork was internationally renowned for its detail, and he was commissioned to paint hundreds of waterfowl paintings for people throughout NA, SA, Europe, and Australia. In 1963, Shortt was the commissioned designer for the 15 cent Canada Geese stamp for the Canadian Post Office. Aside from his thousands of paintings, Shortt also took many photographs of flowers, and these were used in annual catalogues for the T&T Seed Co. He was a long-time member and lecturer at the Natural History Society of Manitoba, and was an active participant in the Winnipeg Horticultural Society. Shortt also wrote a column called Wild Wings that was published in the **WINNIPEG TRIBUNE** and *Marsh World*. In 2003 his autobiography, *My Life With Birds* was published. Shortt had a lake named after him in 1945, and received numerous awards for his painting, including the Centennial Gold Medal of Remembrance from the **MANITOBA HISTORICAL SOCIETY** (1970), the Art Award for contributions to preservation of North America's Wildlife Heritage by Ducks Unlimited Canada (1981), and the Queen's Commemorative Medal for her Golden Jubilee from the province of MB in 2002. Shortt died at the age of 97. • AMANDA STEPHENS

SHREW is a member of an ancient group of mammals (family Soricidae, order Insectivora) which gave rise about 70 million years ago (Late Cretaceous period) to our own early ancestors – the Primates. Like bats, shrews are capable of communicating and possibly echo-locating with high-frequency sounds, well above our range of hearing. Shrews have a remarkably long, thin nose and head, enabling them to squeeze through narrow spaces in the ground and leaf litter. The eyes are reduced, so shrews rely on acute senses of smell and touch (with hairs and long whiskers) to navigate through their tunnels and on the surface. They exhibit an astonishingly high rate of metabolism, which demands a high food intake – up to their own body weight daily of insects, worms, snails, spiders, and some plant material.

Heart rates of up to 1200 beats/minute have been recorded. With such a fast pace of living, the average shrew lives only one year, although some of the larger species may survive for 2 or even 3 years. Surprisingly, shrews do not hibernate, and must continue to search for food in the litter under the snow. They maintain body heat with a thick winter coat, however an insulating snow cover is also essential for their survival in MB.

There are 6 species of shrews in the province, all graded in size from the smallest Pygmy Shrew (*Microsorex hoyi*), at 3 grams a challenger for the world's smallest mammal, the 4 g Masked (*Sorex cinereus*), 6 g Dusky (*Sorex monticolus*), 7 g Arctic (*Sorex arcticus*), 15 g Water (*Sorex palustris*); and 18 g Short-tailed Shrew (*Blarina brevicauda*). This gradation in body size affords a partial separation of different-sized prey species, lessening competition among shrew species inhabiting the same area. There is scarcely a grassland, forest, and tundra habitat in all MB that does not support at least 1 or 2 species, and some prime habitats, such as spruce swamp, may have 5 species. Although shrews are active for short periods both day and night, most people are completely unaware of their presence. They have made a specialty out of being secretive – an essential ability considering the great many birds, mammals and other predators that hunt them. Populations often occur at 10 individuals/ha, but can reach over 120. With such abundance, they play a critical predatory role and help prevent outbreaks of insects destructive to forests.

Shrews are fascinating members of the local fauna. The Short-tailed Shrew is credited with a poisonous saliva, which may assist in demobilizing active prey such as a mouse, or paralyzing snails for future meals. The Water Shrew has stiff bristles along the sides of the feet which trap air bubbles while the animal scampers across the surface of a pond or stream. It seems to be equally at home on land or underwater, and has been seen diving after minnows and digging in the substrate to find insect larvae. Shrews are aggressive and are armed with 32 sharp teeth, so they generally avoid each other. They come into breeding condition periodically from April to Sept, and 20 days after mating, 2-11 young are born in an underground nest. • REW

SIEMENS, Jacob John, farm leader (b May 23, 1896, **ALTONA**; d July 12, 1963, **WINNIPEG**) organized agricultural co-operatives in MB. He was educated at the **MENNONITE** Educational Institute, and at the Manitoba Normal School. He was an active member of the **CO-OP** Movement, and helped found over 30 co-ops in the region. An advocate of agricultural education, he organized

the Rhineland Agricultural Institute for youth training in 1937, and helped found the Western Co-operative College at Saskatoon. During WWII, he advocated the growth of **SUNFLOWERS** and marketed the idea of extracting oil from them, eventually organizing Co-op Vegetable Oils Ltd. in Altona. He is a member of the Manitoba Agricultural Hall of Fame. • JMB

SIFTON, pop 250, is a community 50 km W of Brandon. In the middle of the 1890s, **UKRAINIAN** pioneers began settling in this area. Sifton gets its name from then-minister of interior Sir **CLIFFORD SIFTON,** who believed eastern European farmers were well suited to establish communities in western Canada. The community of Sifton has a church called the Russian Orthodox Holy Resurrection Church that has been in existence since 1926, when Bishop Vladyka Arseny came to build it. Regular church services dwindled in the middle of the 1980s. Today however, it is 1 of 3 Russian Orthodox churches remaining in rural MB. In 2003, the church was vandalized. This incident brought the people of Sifton and nearby communities to work together and repair the church. Since 2005, the church stands on new foundation, and has been designated a municipal heritage site. The **ORTHODOX CHURCH** of Canada has further made it a tradition to have an annual pilgrimage to the church. Sifton is the place where Canada's 1950s Mary Maxim sweater fashion-wear got its start. This company went on to become an international mail order business. There is a spinning wheel atop a cairn in town, a reminder that this community had once been the heart of woollen milling in MB. This industry is what saw the town through the Depression. In 1949, a fire destroyed many businesses on the town's Main St. Agriculture is Sifton's economic backbone. • GPP

SIFTON, Sir Clifford, publisher, politician (b March 10, 1861, London, Canada West [now ON]; d April 17, 1929, New York) was an owner of the ***WINNIPEG FREE PRESS***. He was educated at Victoria College in Cobourg, ON, (1880), and was called to the Manitoba Bar in 1882. He practised law in **BRANDON** and was MLA for North Brandon from 1888-96, serving as attorney general and minister of education from 1891-96. He was responsible for dealing with the federal govt over the **MANITOBA SCHOOLS QUESTION**, and was a constant opponent of the principle of separate schools. He was subsequently Liberal MP for Brandon from 1896-1911, and served as minister of the interior and superintendent-general of Indian Affairs 1896-1905. He is associated with an aggressive **IMMIGRATION** policy that brought many settlers, including those from eastern Europe, to

Clifford Sifton, 1892

AM, PERSONALITY FILES, N19972

the Prairie region. Although he broke with the Liberals over reciprocity in 1911, as owner of the *Manitoba Free Press* (later *Winnipeg Free Press*), he continued to have an influential voice in Cdn affairs, and was knighted Jan 1, 1915. He is buried in Toronto. • JMB

SIGFUSSON, Svein Olafur, athlete, businessman (b 1912, **LUNDAR**, d 1992, **WINNIPEG**). Sigfusson was an outstanding athlete, winning a bronze medal in the discus at the 1950 British Empire Games. He was also a Cdn champion hammer thrower. He won 9 MB championships and 9 Cdn championships in the years he competed in the Amateur Athletics Union. For many years he ran a transportation company in northern MB, which operated on a road system of 3,500 miles; most of this road system had been developed by Sigfusson. The company employed over 400 people, nearly half of whom were Aboriginal. He received the Manitoba Centennial Medal in 1970, the Order of Canada in 1974, and was elected to the Manitoba Sports Hall of fame in 1982. In 1992 he published *Sigfusson's Roads*, describing his northern transportation network. • JMB

SIKHS first arrived in MB in the mid-1950s. That was a time when MB faced an extreme shortage of educators. All immigration offices abroad had instructions to recruit and fast track applicants who were teachers. Severaal Sikh teachers and professors at the **U OF M** arrived from India and the UK via this initiative. The number of Sikh immigrants rose further in the mid-1960s, when family members came to join the teachers.

During the 1960s, MB became known in India and in other countries where Sikhs resided as a welcoming place for newcomers. In this decade, more professionals – doctors, architects, engineers, and professors – arrived here. When Canada relaxed the rules of immigration in the 1970s and problems in Africa, notably Uganda, caused trades and business people to flee; a large percentage of these immigrants were Sikhs.

The Sikh religion is rooted in equality, human rights, helping others, and supporting social causes. Sikh scriptures preach respect for all human beings, protection of weak and disfranchised members of society, and promoting community causes. Giving donations for worthy causes is mandatory for Sikhs. The main belief in Sikhism is that all religions are good and all paths lead to the same God. Sikhs do not believe in a living Guru. They accept the teachings of 10 Gurus which are contained in the holy book, *Sri Guru Granth Sahib Ji*. These teachings reflect on the place of human beings in the universe and provide guidelines for every day life. Sikh priests, Gianis, are allowed to marry; women are accorded equal status in Sikhism and can perform all religious ceremonies.

The Sikh religion is very young, only 500 years old and is founded in rebellion against injustices at that time. Sikhs were ordained as soldiers to fight against injustice and the rulers who were exploiting others. As protectors of the weak, Sikhs became a warrior nation and prescribed a way of life appropriate for a solider. Sikhs were required to keep 5 K's – kesh, kara, kutcha, kirpan, and kanga. Sikh men must cover their hair (kesh) with turbans to act as protective gear for the head; they must wear a steel bracelet (kara), as a reminder of purity and connection to God; special underwear (kutcha)must be worn to maintain dignity at all times; they must carry a small sword (kirpan), to protect self and others from injustice, and a comb (kanga) must be carried as a symbol of cleanliness. Sikh symbols have been recognized and accepted in much of Cdn culture. For example, baptized Sikhs who maintain 5 K's are allowed to wear turbans and small swords in RCMP and other professions. Baptized students are allowed to wear small kirpans to school, as a symbol of their Sikhism.

Over the past 40 years or so, Sikhs have strongly established their identity in MB. In Winnipeg, there are 8 places of worship called Gurdwaras meaning Houses of God. They are built with 4 quadrants for community activities. Every weekend, prayers are held in each of them. And on Sunday, each Gurdwara has a communal meal called langar at lunch time. One does not have to be a Sikh to participate in prayers or the meal.

The only requirement is that visitors remove their shoes and cover their heads.

In 2007, there were over 6000 Sikhs in the province. They were primarily found in the medical, academic and business fields. In transportation, the taxi cab business is primarily owned and operated by Sikhs. MB Sikhs have been recognized for their contributions to the broader community with awards such as the Order of Canada and the **Order of Manitoba**. ● TEJ BAINS

SILL, THOMAS, accountant, philanthropist (b 1905, **Winnipeg**, d 1986, Winnipeg). Thomas Sill attended St. John's High School in **North End** Winnipeg. He then went on to study accountancy and graduated as chartered accountant in 1927. During the **Great Depression** he began investing in the recovering stock market. These investments proved successful and would eventually become the financial basis for the Thomas Sill Foundation. Sill also founded the MB accounting firm now known as Sill Streuber Fiske & Company. He was a member of the Rotary Club of Winnipeg, and an avid curler who lead his team to the 1933 Tucker Trophy. Upon his death in 1986, Sill instructed that his fortune be used to create a charitable foundation. The Thomas Sill Foundation is now the largest private charitable foundation in the province. ● CATHARINA DE BAKKER

SIMARD, Raymond, politician (b March 8, 1958, **Ste. Anne**), received his BA at the **College Universitaire de Saint-Boniface** and a degree in commerce at the **U of M**. As a businessman and consultant, he was founding president and CEO of Riel Economic Development Corporation and president and co-owner of Simard Solutions. He also oversaw the creation of the Riel Tourism Bureau. In a by-election of 2002, Simard was selected as the **Liberal** candidate in the riding of St. Boniface and won a seat in the House of Commons. In a riding with a significant French-Canadian population, he has supported Francophone concerns in Canada. When he was re-elected in the 2004 election, he was appointed parliamentary secretary to the minister for internal trade, minister responsible for official languages, and deputy leader of the govt caucus. He also served as associate minister of national defence. From March 2003, he has chaired the MB federal Liberal caucus and in 2004, was chair of the northern and western caucus and the Liberal caucus for official languages minority communities. Simard was returned in the 2006 election and appointed deputy whip of the opposition and associate critic of the western economic diversification/ Pacific gateway portfolio. ● RUTH DEGRAVES

SIMMONS, Albert William "Al," entertainer, musician, author, actor (b Sept 5, 1948, **Winnipeg**), combines song, dance, magic, and a wacky sense of humour in performances that have delighted children and adults for more than 25 years. Encouraged by his parents to explore performing, Simmons began staging shows for family and friends in his backyard. He earned his first ¢5 as a performer after playing "Oh Susanna" on the harmonica with his nose. His father, an eccentric collector, inspired Simmons's love of gadgets. He works many crazy props, such as a ukulele made out of a toilet seat, into his shows.

Al Simmons and friends, Winnipeg International Children's Festival, 2007

In 1969, Simmons began entering talent contests, singing, dancing, and doing comedy. Before becoming a full-time performer, Simmons worked for **Manitoba Hydro**, at a gas station, and as a clown for birthday parties and department stores. At 21, he quit Manitoba Hydro to form his first musical comedy group, Just Us Three (later Out to Lunch). From 1973 to 1976, he toured Canada with **Fred Penner** in Kornstock; the pair knew each other from their time in the Royal Canadian Air Cadets.

Simmons and his wife Barbara co-starred in the 36-episode CTV series *All for Fun* (1981-83). He had a show at Vancouver's Expo 86, made guest appearances on *Sesame Street*, and ran for the federal Rhinoceros Party (1963-93), whose only platform was zaniness. In 1987, Penner offered Simmons a recording contract with his Oak Street Records. The result was the **Vaudeville**-sounding *Something's Fishy at Camp Wiganishie* (1992). Simmons has since issued several other children's CDs, which have been nominated for 3 Juno Awards; in 1996, Simmons won the Juno for *Celery Stalks at Midnight*. Simmons has also performed with the **WINNIPEG SYMPHONY ORCHESTRA** and **MANITOBA CHAMBER ORCHESTRA**, and has toured the US, Australia, Hong Kong, Japan, and the Caribbean. The opera *Il Pollo Diavollo*, for which Simmons wrote the libretto, premiered at the New Music Festival in 1997, featuring **TRACY DAHL** as the soprano. Simmons's children's book *Counting Feathers* was published that same year. Simmons is an ambassador for UNESCO, and in 2004-05, played "Frog" in Winnipeg and Edmonton performances of *A Year with Frog and Toad*, a musical based on the work of US writer Arnold Lobel. ● JOHN EINARSON

SIMPLOT CANADA LIMITED is a Cdn subsidiary of the Boise, ID-based agricultural firm J. R. Simplot Company. Simplot entered the MB market in 1961 when it purchased an old **BRITISH COMMONWEALTH AIR TRAINING PLAN** airport hangar in **CARBERRY** and converted it into a potato processing plant that produced frozen french fries. The company – which has had a separate Cdn division headquartered in **BRANDON** since 1966 – made another major investment in the MB market 4 years later with the opening of a new $30-million fertilizer complex in Brandon. The complex included different production plants that produced a variety of types and grades of fertilizer. In addition to the production plants, the complex also included bagging and bulk loading facilities, a variety of storage facilities, and a major research laboratory. In the years since its inception, the Brandon complex has undergone major expansions and upgrades. The company's potato processing operations also have undergone some major changes. In 1986, Simplot and Nestlé Canada Inc joined forces to create a new joint venture (Midwest Food Products Inc) to run the Carberry plant. Midwest ran the plant until 1998, when the partners sold it to french-fry giant McCain Foods. Simplot remained out of the potato processing business in MB until 2003, when it opened a new $120-million plant in **PORTAGE LA PRAIRIE**. When it opened, it was among of the most advanced french-fry processing plants in the world, producing 450,000 kg of french fries a day, almost exclusively for restaurant chains such as McDonald's and KFC. ● MM

SIMPSON, Sir George "The Little Emperor," **HBC** governor, (b 1786, Loch Broom, UK; d Sept 7, 1860, Montreal). Simpson was born outside wedlock to an unknown mother. His father, also named George, was the son of Calvinist minister Thomas Simpson of Avoch, 10 km N of Inverness, Scotland. At some stage, he was taken to his grandfather's home in Dingwall, Ross-shire, where his aunt, Mary Simpson, was responsible for his care and education.

George Simpson later went to London to work in his uncle's sugar brokerage firm. One of the partners there was **ANDREW WEDDERBURN COLVILE**, a director of the **HUDSON'S BAY COMPANY**'s London committee since 1810. Colvile's tenure began just as clashes between the **NORTH WEST COMPANY** and HBC intensified, especially in the **RED RIVER SETTLEMENT**. The rivalry between the 2 companies became particularly bitter around 1818-19, in the aftermath of the **SEVEN OAKS INCIDENT**. **COLIN ROBERTSON**, a HBC leader, had been arrested. There were bench warrants against HBC gov William Williams for his arrest of Nor'Westers, which might have necessitated his removal from **RUPERT'S LAND**. To help secure its position, the HBC committee decided a back-up manager was necessary. Colvile offered the position of gov-in-chief to George Simpson at an annual salary of $600 (about $2900 at the time).

In March 1820, with only 5 days' notice, Simpson sailed to New York, where he took a steamboat to Albany and then travelled overland to what would become Montreal. As soon as canoe travel was practicable, he left following the usual **FUR TRADERS'** route, arriving at Rock Depot (later Gordon House), at Whitemud Falls on the **HAYES RIVER**, some time in July. Gov Williams appointed Simpson temporarily in charge of Athabasca.

The Athabasca district was a good testing ground for the newcomer. Simpson's main concern was survival: there was the perennial shortage of pemmican, and the men were often on short rations. He quickly grasped the lack of discipline among the officers and men, the disastrous effects of alcohol, and the dire need to economize. On his way out of Athabasca in spring 1821, Simpson learned that the HBC and NWC had amalgamated. The amalgamation, under the name of the HBC, resulted in a fur trade monopoly not only in Rupert's Land but also in the Pacific Northwest interior and the Oregon Territory. Simpson's long and successful career with the HBC was about to begin.

Travelling at his usual relentless pace, Simpson arrived at **YORK FACTORY** in 1825 in time to board the company's annual ship for London to report to the committee. In Feb 1826, gov Williams was recalled to London, and Simpson became gov of both the Northern and Southern Departments, making him the HBC's chief representative in NA. He established his headquarters at Lachine (now part of Montreal), thus giving him access to a commercial centre, and quicker access to London.

Gov. Simpson on inspection trip

S

Simpson returned to Rupert's Land unmarried, and in 1828, journeyed to the HBC's District of New Caledonia, W of the Rocky Mountains and N of the Columbia Valley, roughly corresponding to what is now BC. He inspected the Fraser River as a practicable alternate route to the coast, but decided that the canyons and waterfalls were too great a hindrance. After wintering at Fort Vancouver, he returned to Rupert's Land in spring 1829. He spent most of winter 1829-30 in London. There he met 18-year-old Frances Simpson, daughter of his uncle Geddes Simpson. They were married on Feb 24, 1830, and left for NA shortly thereafter.

During his early years in the company's service, Simpson had formed liaisons with First Nations and **Métis** women, and had several children with them. He had little emotional attachment to these women, and used them primarily for the fulfilment of his personal gratification. Among the best known of these "country wives" was Margaret Taylor, who accompanied Simpson on his 1828 voyage to the Columbia. For him, marriage was not a consideration, but Taylor waited with 2 children for Simpson to return to **Red River** in 1830, only to be told that he had married Frances Simpson. However, he did find husbands for his discarded lovers, provided for the children financially, and found positions for his sons in the fur trade.

The Simpsons lived in the Red River Settlement from 1830 to 1833. It was a miserable experience for both of them. The gov was not well, and the social strains of his former liaisons weighed heavily on his wife. The Simpsons' first child, born in Sept 1831, died the following April. It was a devastating period for them, as Frances had had a difficult pregnancy. She did not recover her health, and in 1833, Simpson took her to London to be with her family. She never returned to Red River.

By the mid-1830s, Simpson was well ensconced in Montreal society. His knowledge of the fur trade was unrivalled, and he had melded the NWC and HBC officers into a strong working coalition. There were no serious competitors; fur prices were good; and the company was profitable. From 1825 until years after Simpson's death, dividends never fell below 10%. In 1839, the company rewarded Simpson with the title of gov-in-chief.

In the 1850s, Simpson's travels lessened, but he maintained a strong interest in the HBC and in public affairs. He investigated the shipping of goods by rail, instead of the **York Boat** route from **Hudson Bay**, and in 1857 appeared before a select committee of the British House of Commons when it investigated the renewal of the HBC's licence for exclusive trade.

Shortly after entertaining the Prince of Wales (later King Edward VII), Simpson died of a stroke or brain haemorrhage. He was buried in Mount Royal Cemetery, Montreal, beside his wife. Simpson's investments in **Railways** and mines had contributed to his substantial wealth. He left an estate of over £100,000 ($487,000 at the time), and the legacy of being the supreme architect of the 19ᵗʰ-century fur trade. ● SHIRLEE SMITH

SIMPSON, Homer, nuclear technologist, beer drinker (b ca 1955, **Winnipeg**). One of the leading citizens of Springfield USA, Homer Simpson has been uncharacteristically silent about his origins. His mentor, Matt Groening, says Homer is a Canadian and was named after Matt's own father, who was born in Winnipeg. In various episodes of the popular series, there have been references to Winnipeg, especially in regard to cheap drugs. In May of 2003, the city of Winnipeg declared Homer Simpson an honorary citizen. Due to prior commitments, Homer was unable to attend the ceremony at city hall with mayor **Glen Murray**. Homer is married to Marge (*nee* Bouvier), and they have 4 children, son Bart, and daughters Lisa, Maggie, and Jessica. ● GPP

SINCLAIR, Murray, lawyer, judge (b Jan 24, 1951, **Selkirk**). After growing up on the **Ojibway** and **Cree** St. Peter's Indian Reserve (now **Peguis First Nation**) N of Selkirk, Sinclair was named valedictorian and athlete of the year upon his 1968 graduation from Selkirk Collegiate. He went on to become vice-president of the **Manitoba Métis Federation**, and an assistant to the MB Attorney General (then **Howard Pawley**), in the 1970s, before entering the **U of W**. Sinclair moved on to the **U of M** and graduated with a law degree in 1979. He articled in Selkirk and was called to the bar in 1980. As a practising lawyer, he specialized in criminal and civil litigation, as well as Aboriginal issues, becoming particularly well regarded for his work on the latter. He also served as counsel for the Manitoba Human Rights Commission.

In March 1988, Sinclair began an appointment as associate chief judge of the Provincial Court of Manitoba (*see* **Judicial System**), becoming MB's first Aboriginal judge (there had been Aboriginal judicial officials prior to 1870, but not judges). Only a month later, he was chosen to head up the **Aboriginal Justice Inquiry** alongside co-commissioner **Alvin C. Hamilton** (then associate chief justice of the Court of Queen's Bench). He was also in charge of the Paediatric Cardiac Surgery Inquest, an examination of the deaths of 12 children who died following surgery at the

Health Sciences Centre in 1994, and authored the 516-page report released in late 2000. Sinclair was named a justice on the Court of Queen's Bench in Jan 2001.

Murray Sinclair

Sinclair began teaching Aboriginal issues in 1981, and is an adjunct professor of law at the U of M. He has received a National Aboriginal Achievement Award (1994), as well as 3 honorary degrees. He serves on the advisory board of the *Indigenous Law Journal*, and is a 3ʳᵈ-degree member of the **Midewiwin** (Grand Medicine) Society. ● JOEL TRENAMAN

SIOUX. *See* **Dakota**.

SIOUX VALLEY DAKOTA NATION, on reserve pop 1377, off reserve pop 833, is situated about 45 km W of **Brandon**. The **Assiniboine River** runs through this region. The native language of this community is **Dakota**, and this First Nation was officially established in 1873. The Sioux Valley Dakota Nation is a member of the Dakota Ojibway Tribal Council. This is 1 of 5 First Nation communities in MB that has been allowed to develop a casino. Schooling in Sioux Valley Dakota Nation goes from Nursery-Grade 9, and enrolment for 2003-04 was 401. Sioux Valley administers its own education. There are 2 reserves located on the Sioux Valley land: Sioux Valley IR No. 58, and Fishing Station IR No. 62A. The Sioux Valley Dakota Nation community has easy access to the southern MB hwy system. The primary economic base for this First Nation, beyond the casino, is farming. Sioux Valley Dakota Nation signed the first self-govt agreement in MB. It has been negotiating with the federal govt since 1988. In May 2004, the First Nation established its own local circuit court. ● RK

SISSONS, Melrose, lawyer, activist (b 1887, PORTAGE LA PRAIRIE; d Sept 26, 1973, WINNIPEG). Following graduation with a BA from the U OF M in 1911, having won the gold medal in history and political economy, she became the first woman in MB to apply to study law. However, as the province's *Law Society Act* did not include women within its definition of "persons" eligible to practise law, she was compelled to take her case to the provincial legislature to amend the act. The legislation was amended in 1912. In 1915 she and another woman, Winnifred Wilton, became the first women called to the Bar in MB. She practised in Portage la Prairie until 1917, when she married lawyer Earl Stuart Everall and they took up residence in MCCREARY. Following marriage she never resumed the practice of law. However, she remained active in numerous organizations – the UNITED CHURCH OF CANADA, the WOMEN'S INSTITUTE and hospital aid. The U of M's Faculty of Law maintains a bursary endowed jointly in her and Wilton's names. ● DOUG JOHNSTON

SKATING, FIGURE, originally called "fancy skating," can be traced back to the mid-19th century as a favourite MB winter pastime. Hundreds of people strapped blades to boots, and glided across a lake or river. In WINNIPEG, they traced figures and executed simple dance steps, often to the strains of live band music, on the ASSINIBOINE RIVER. In 1887, this nationally popular activity led to the founding of the Amateur Skating Association of Canada, renamed the Canadian Figure Skating Association (CFSA, 1939) and, in 2000, Skate Canada.

Construction of indoor ice rinks in MB commenced in Winnipeg in 1893, with the McIntyre, built near the corner of Portage and Main, and the Olympic Rink in 1922 at 480 Charles St. Built in 1909, on the present site of GREAT-WEST LIFE's headquarters (Whitehall Ave and Osborne St), the Amphitheatre was originally a horse show building. It was converted in 1912 to an ice rink and was home to figure skaters until 1955. In 1942, the Amphitheatre was the only artificial ice rink in Canada between Winnipeg and Toronto.

In the wake of rink building, the early 1920s saw the formation of ice skating clubs. The Winnipeg Skating Club held its inaugural carnival in a building that is now the site of HMCS Chippewa. In 1929, the Winnipeg Skating Club became the Winnipeg Winter Club (WWC), with "fancy skating sessions" held on Wednesday evenings and Sunday afternoons. In 1930, the WWC hosted the Canadian Figure Skating Championships. In 1942, the WWC sold its building at 51 Smith St to the Royal Canadian Navy for $256,000, investing the proceeds to help the war effort and to

build at its present location on River Ave. The WWC has continuously offered members instruction in compulsory figures (until the event was eliminated in most of the world in 1990); free skate; dance; pairs; and CFSA/Skate Canada testing. The Figure Skating Club of Greater Winnipeg was formed in 1942 and later incorporated as the Ice Club of Greater Winnipeg. By spring 1946, membership in the Ice Club exceeded 300, with many more figure skaters at the Assiniboine Club and the WWC. Figure skating was fostered at most of the community clubs.

Rupert Whitehead, who between 1924 and 1934 won numerous national figure skating titles, was instrumental in the development of the sport throughout MB. During the 1940s and early '50s, Rupert travelled by bus to organize clubs, instruct skaters, and produce ice shows. During this era, many other MB skaters went on to perform in professional ice shows such as Ice Capades, compete in Western Canadian Championships, and become skating instructors. Others responsible for the development of figure skating outside of Winnipeg were Lorne Carter, of PORTAGE LA PRAIRIE, and Doreen "Dodie" Wardle, who in 1941 started the FLIN FLON Figure Skating Club. At a national level, MB-born Mary Rose Thacker-Temple won 3 Cdn championships, and was named Canada's Female Athlete of the Year in 1939 and 1941.

In the 1960s, all skating clubs were encouraged to join the CFSA in order to offer input into the development of the National Skating Test (NST) Program; access and train qualified judges; and obtain funding for competitors. The Manitoba Section, previously part of the Prairie Section, became autonomous in 1968, with Anne Doherty as chairperson. (In 2000, the Manitoba Section's name was changed to Skate Canada–Manitoba.) Becoming part of CFSA afforded opportunities for skaters to compete in interprovincial and national competitions, and in Canada Winter Games. After the 1967 PAN AM GAMES, the Manitoba Sports Federation was formed, with figure skating as one of the original sport members. Growth continued into the '70s throughout MB, with over 100 clubs affiliating with the MB section and CFSA. Figure skating established an administrative office in Winnipeg in 1978 to serve the needs of this growing sport. Figure skating reached its peak in the 1980s, with many skaters competing and winning at central divisional, Canadian, and Junior World titles, as well as qualifying for Worlds and the Olympics. Skaters were training year-round, on and off the ice, often moving outside the province to supplement their training. Highly qualified national and international coaches came to MB to conduct

seminars on all aspects of skating. Membership in MB clubs was at an all-time high, often rivalling that of larger centres in eastern and western Canada. Volunteers took active roles at the national level in administration and judging.

During the '90s, membership in the sport began to decline due to costs, societal trends, and competition from other activities. More options, including girls' HOCKEY and ringette, were available to young people. Skating has now come full circle. There are fewer skaters and therefore fewer competing at higher levels. Smaller clubs are amalgamating to control costs and to utilize the coaches and volunteer base more effectively. Skaters are again training for the love of the sport. ● LOIS HOWARD, PEARL HUMENNY, GAIL McLEOD

SKATING, SPEED is an event at which MB athletes have succeeded internationally since the competitive version of the sport hit NA. Seventeen WINNIPEG skaters been made the Speed Skating Canada Hall of Fame; no other city has more than 5 skaters inducted.

Skating has been a popular recreation in MB since the 1870s, though before the development of artificial rinks, public skating in Winnipeg was done on a section of the RED RIVER kept clear of snow at the foot of Burrows Ave. Victoria Skating Rink – the city's first indoor rink built on land, rather than a frozen water body – was erected in 1875. The first record of a timed skate in MB is from 1877, when CHARLES NAPIER BELL skated along the Red from Winnipeg to SELKIRK in 2 hrs and 15 mins. Winnipeg's Auditorium Rink, built in 1898 with an ice surface of 60 m by 25 m and a spectator capacity of 2000, was an impressive structure for its time, and soon became the city's venue for skating competitions. Jack McCulloch was the first MB speed skater to gain international renown. He won numerous Cdn and international titles, including the World Championship in 1897, before turning professional and touring across Canada. He is also credited with the development of the tube skate, which had a hollow metal cylinder placed above the blade for added strength without extra weight.

Through the early 20th century, MB skaters won few titles, as competitive speed skating came to a standstill when conflicts over professionalism led to the severance of the Amateur Speed Skating Association of Canada from the national amateur-sports umbrella organization. In the years leading up to WWI, national competitions were held erratically, and were marred by infighting between different speed skating groups. Amateur competition was re-established in 1920, when the Cdn indoor championships were held in Winnipeg,

Speed skaters train outside despite snow and frigid temperatures.

and won by local resident Mike Goodman, who also played with the **Winnipeg Falcons**.

As **Hockey** became increasingly popular, it largely eclipsed speed skating in most Cdn provinces. However, skating remained comparatively strong in MB, with about 450 speed skaters racing in weekly meets at Winnipeg's 5 clubs. **Newspapers** touted the city as one of NA's top for speed skating, rivalled only by Minneapolis and Chicago. **Frank Stack** was the top speed skater in MB at this time, with a record-setting win at the 1930 North American championship, and then one of Canada's first Olympic medals in speed skating at the 1932 Winter Olympics at Lake Placid, NY. In 1946, Stack and Eileen Whalley, also from Winnipeg, won the Cdn outdoor championships for men and women; Whalley also won that year's North American title.

Canada failed to produce any Olympic medals in speed skating in 1948 (the games were cancelled in 1940 and 1944 because of WWII). The drought ended in 1952, when Gordon Audley won bronze in Oslo. Through the 1960s, Doreen McCannell set 31 Cdn records. At the first Canada Winter Games, in 1967, the gold-medal wins of McCannell and fellow Manitoban Robert Boucher – under the training of the team coach and Doreen's father, Donald McCannell – made MB the highest-scoring province in speed skating events.

The following year, Boucher became the first Cdn speed skater to race the 500 m in under 40 sec. In 1968, Winnipeg skaters claimed the Cdn Metric Style Championships when McCannell and Peter Williamson won the women's and men's titles. At the 1971 Canada Winter Games, MB again had the best provincial standing in the sport.

Sylvia Burka was one of the world's top speed skaters through the 1970s, with 40 national records. In 1976, Burka won the International Skating Union's overall title in senior competition, while fellow Winnipegger Elizabeth Appleby took 2nd place in 3 junior events. **Susan Auch**, the top female speed skater through the 1980s, has given the main skating oval where Winnipeg skaters train her name. Competitive speed skaters nowadays train in the off-season as cyclists, which is why speed skater **Clara Hughes** is 1 of 4 Canadians to have won an Olympic medal in summer and winter games. Many leading skaters from MB, such as **Cindy Klassen**, now train in Calgary. As of writing, Klassen's 6 Olympic medals are the most any Cdn athlete has won. • MD

SKIING is a popular recreational winter sport that arose in Scandinavia and Russia. Though MB's predominantly flat topography is most suited to cross-country skiing, downhill skiing is

popular, primarily on artificial slopes. Ski jumping, which collectively with cross-country forms Nordic skiing, was the oldest form practised here, though the least suitable to MB.

Scandinavian **Immigrants**, who built MB's first ski jump on the E bank of the **Red River** near **Winnipeg**'s Provencher Bridge, introduced ski jumping or "ski-soaring" to the province. Soon after, in 1912, the first MB ski organization – the Winnipeg Ski Club (WSC) – was founded. **Snowshoeing** remained more common, as it was difficult and expensive to travel to ski slopes or trails outside the city, and as of 1928, the WSC had just 32 members. With limited hills and few practitioners, early skiers here rarely differentiated between forms of the sport. Thus, Doug Groff was a provincial champion in downhill, slalom, cross-country, and jumping events. Jumping remained the predominant recreational form, though. The first indoor ski-jumping exhibition in Canada was held at the Winnipeg Civic Auditorium (see **Archives**) in 1948, and introduced the activity to roughly 10,000 spectators. Winnipeg at one time had 2 towers designated for ski jumping, but interest in jumping declined in the 1960s.

Downhill (or alpine) and cross-country skiing became more popular as improved transportation made travel outside cities easier. The **CPR** and **CNR** ran weekend trains to downhill slopes such as **La Rivière** and Snow Valley from the late 1930s until 1953, though WWII put a temporary end to the trains. With an increase in skiers' numbers, a 2nd Winnipeg club was established in 1938; each club had about 500 skiers. The sport gained wider recognition in MB when Mary Ruttan of Winnipeg won the Cdn slalom championship in 1939. The provincial ski organization, Manitoba Ski Zone, grew to include 16 member clubs.

By the late 1960s, cross-country and alpine ski were regarded as distinct, and MB housed separate cross-country and downhill ski associations. In 1961, a downhill ski facility was opened on a former Winnipeg landfill, commonly called "Garbage Mountain" though officially named Westview Park, but was closed after only a few ski seasons when grooming machines caused some of the underlying garbage to shift, resulting in a small landslide. The WSC ran a separate downhill facility at its clubhouse through the 1970s, but a fire in 1981 led to financial difficulty, and the eventual dissolution of the WSC in 1989. Altogether, about 15 downhill or alpine areas, such as Asessippi and La Rivière, have been developed for skiing throughout the province.

A surge in the popularity of cross-country during the 1970s led to the establishment of the Jackrabbit Program in 1975, an instructional

Alpine skiing appeals to Manitobans of all ages who like small hills.

course developed by MB skiers to introduce children to cross-country skiing. The successful program was later adopted by the national cross-country ski organization. In the mid-1980s, the skating technique in cross-country skiing was brought to MB, and the wide-legged, diagonal stride is popular among competitive skiers such as Lindsay Gauld, a 5-time champion of the US Mora Loppett and the original owner of Olympia Cycle and Ski in Winnipeg. The Manitoba Loppet, the province's longest-running ski race, has been held annually in **PINAWA** since 1976. About 35 cross-country ski clubs in MB maintain local trails in **PROVINCIAL PARKS** such as **GRAND BEACH** and **WHITESHELL**. ● MD

SKINNER, Frank Leith, horticulturist (b May 5, 1882, Rosehearty, Aberdeenshire, UK; d Aug 27, 1967, Dropmore, MB). After coming to Canada in 1895, Skinner worked on his **SCOTS** family's farm at Dropmore (25 km S of **ROBLIN** and just W of **LAKE OF THE PRAIRIES**) before establishing his own homestead in 1900. He began to teach himself about horticulture in 1911 when he spent the winter on Vancouver Island reading books about Asian plants.

Skinner returned to MB and started a garden on his farm in order to experiment with hybrid varieties of native and non-native plants suitable to the soil and **CLIMATE**. In 1924, he was able to sell seeds and stock from what had become known as "Skinner's Nursery." He was recognized for creating a number of unique hybrids, including strains of ornamental fruit **TREES**, **POPLARS**, willows, basswoods, and **SPRUCE**, as well as flowers-chrysanthemums, lilacs, roses, primroses, and lilies. Skinner accumulated plants during trips around the world and bred them with others in

his garden. His quick-growing trees were often used to plant shelterbelts on MB farms. In total, he introduced 248 species of plants to the Prairies, including 144 improved varieties.

In 1943, Skinner was made a member of the Order of the British Empire, and in 1947, he received an honorary doctorate from the **U OF M**. He also accumulated many horticultural awards, including a number of international citations. The Frank Skinner Arboretum Trail near Roblin, developed in 1994, bears his name, as does the Skinner Memorial Library at the U of M. He published his autobiography, *Horticultural Horizons: Plant Breeding and Introduction at Dropmore, Manitoba*, in 1967. ● JOEL TRENAMAN

Frank Leith Skinner, 1932

SKOWNAN FIRST NATION (previously known as Waterhen First Nation), on reserve pop 658, off reserve pop 523, is situated on the SW shore of Waterhen Lake, about 280 km N of **WINNIPEG**. The native language of this community is **OJIBWAY**, and it signed Treaty 2 in 1871. It is a member of the West Region Tribal Council. There is one reserve situated in Skownan First Nation: Waterhen IR No. 45. There is all-weather road access to the community. Schooling in this First Nation goes from Nursery-Grade 12, and total enrolment for the year 2003-04 was 126. The West Region Tribal Council administers education. Since 2004, this First Nation community has arranged for a group of grades 5 and 6 students to come to Winnipeg's **RED RIVER COLLEGE**, and learn about various professions, such as stock brokering, journalism, electronic engineering, and computer programming. The economic foundation of this community rests on its wood bison establishment project. ● RK

SKUNK, STRIPED (*Mephitis mephitis*) is a member of the weasel family Mustelidae (order Carnivora) that is instantly recognizable to people by sight or scent. The animal can accurately spray its smelly secretion from the anal glands for up to 3 m and the mist can reach targets 5 m away. Unfortunately, skunks are attracted to roadside ditches for hunting and denning, with the result that they are frequently killed by vehicles. After having evolved and deployed (for 34 million years) one of the most effective anti-predator chemical defences in the animal world, species of skunks have not had time to alter their ineffective strategy of facing down fast-moving vehicles. The smell is not the only reason to stay clear of a skunk – an occasional individual harbours rabies which is transferable to a human via a bite. From the N treeline of MB to Mexico, the Striped Skunk occupies a great variety of habitats, from coniferous and deciduous forests to prairie and desert. It thrives even within city limits. It eats both plants and small animals, with mice and insects predominating in the diet.

Mating occurs in March and April and the 2-10 young are born in May. The young are capable of spraying musk from their anal glands at only 4 weeks. They nurse in the underground den until an age of 6-8 weeks, then join the mother during nightly forays. The white stripe along the back shines like a beacon in the moonlight and helps keep the family together. The young skunks observe the best locations to seek refuge and to find favourite food sources. The mother may even demonstrate how to rid a beetle of its repellant spray before eating it by rubbing it in the dust. By autumn, the family disperses and they pass the winter in underground dens, where they enter a deep sleep (but not true hibernation). They live off their fat reserves, losing from $\frac{1}{3}$ to $\frac{2}{3}$ of their body mass by emergence in late March or April. • REW

SLOTIN, Louis Alexander, scientist (b Dec 1, 1910, WINNIPEG; d May 30, 1946, Los Alamos, NM) was a gifted physicist who died as a result of his work with nuclear fission. Born in Winnipeg's NORTH END, he attended St. John's Technical High School and the **U OF M**, winning the gold medal in chemistry and physics and completing an MSc in 1933. He received his PhD in biochemistry from the U of London in 1936. He was also an amateur boxer. He became a research associate at the U of Chicago, working on an atom-smashing cyclotron. He began work in the Metallurgical Laboratory of the Manhattan Project in Chicago in 1942, and moved to Los Alamos in Dec 1944. Slotin became an expert at hand-assembling the core of atomic bombs, and it was an accident during the process of assembly that led to his death. In order to save his colleagues, he terminated a connection in a bomb core, and as a result exposed himself to a fatal dose of radiation. Slotin's tale is told in the 1955 novel *The Accident* by Dexter Masters. • JMB

SLUG is a gastropod mollusc in the class Gastropoda (phylum Mollusca) which lacks a conspicuous external shell. It has a vascular mantle for gaseous exchange, and usually has 2 pairs of tentacles, with eyes on the larger, posterior pair. It travels by means of wave-like contractions of the muscular foot and a film of mucus, which allows a gliding motion. Some species can hang and descend from plants on a mucus thread without falling. Mostly nocturnal, slugs may emerge during the day in wet weather. They shelter in leaf litter or under rocks, logs and boards, and return to their favourite food sources and cover using their sense of smell. Slugs occupy various habitats, but the presence of organic matter, availability of cover, and moisture are important factors.

Slugs play important ecological roles as detritivores and decomposers, consuming fungi, leaf litter, and other decaying material, as well as living plants. Slugs are primarily hermaphroditic (carry both sex organs) and some species display complex and unique courtship behaviours during which individuals exchange sperm. The eggs are laid singly or in groups in protected moist sites. The lifespan of most slugs is less than a year. Since the area over which they range is very limited, they must rely on passive dispersal by other animals and humans to reach new habitats. Their

natural predators include beetles, amphibians, reptiles, birds, and small mammals such as shrews and squirrels. To deter predators, some species exude unpleasant odours when threatened. Slugs frequently become pests in gardens (e.g., on tomatoes) and greenhouses. Those most responsible for damage are introduced species that have arrived into NA with shipments of foreign produce, horticultural goods, or soil; native slugs do little or no damage. In the garden, protection may be provided by barriers of diatomaceous earth, wood ashes, seaweed mulch, strips of copper, or petroleum jelly dusted with table salt. Traps may be constructed using stale beer in shallow containers, or distributing pieces of rind or rotting board under which they can collect. Native and exotic slugs of MB have not been surveyed. • EP

SMALL BUSINESS makes up the largest proportion of MB's business sector. About 75,414 – or 97% of – MB business establishments are small businesses, similar to the national average. About 96% of the business establishments in WINNIPEG and NORTHERN regions are small businesses, while small businesses constitute 99% of businesses in the remaining regions.

"Small business" has a dizzying array of definitions. Businesses have been categorized by size based on the value of annual sales or shipments, annual gross or net revenue, the size of assets, and the number of employees. Complicating matters further, many institutions define a "small business" based on their own needs. For example, the Export Development Corporation defines a small or "emerging" exporter as a firm with export sales under $1 million. The most common basis for defining small business is the number of employees. Between 0 and 49 employees is the most common standard for categorizing small business in MB, and echoes the international definition. Included in this grouping are "indeterminate establishments" – incorporated or unincorporated businesses that do not have a workforce for which payroll remittances are made to the Revenue Canada. The workforce for indeterminate establishments may consist of contract workers, part-time employees, family members, and/or owners. MB's small businesses are predominately of the indeterminate category (55%), while 25% employ 1-4 people, 9% employ 5-9, 7% employ 10-19, and 5% employ 20-49.

In 2003, small business contributed 23% of Manitoba's gross domestic product (GDP). This compares favourably to the Cdn average for small business (24%). The contribution small business made to MB's GDP dropped by 1% from 1993 to 2003. This was part of a trend; during this period, 7 provinces saw a drop in the contribution

small business made to GDP. Future trends are for increased contribution of small business to the ECONOMY; a rise in the number of "micro-businesses" (establishments with fewer than 5 employees); increased self-employment; and growing roles of "greying entrepreneurs" (55 years of age or older), women, and FIRST PEOPLES in small business. • DAN OVERALL

DOUGLAS WATKINSON

The capelin, native to Hudson Bay

SMELT is a fish in the smelt family Osmeridae (order Osmeriformes, class Osteichthyes) represented in MB by 2 species. The Capelin (*Mallotus villosus*) is a native marine species found in Hudson Bay, while the introduced Rainbow Smelt (*Osmerus mordax*) is a schooling, freshwater and anadromous (enters brackish or saltwater to feed in summer) species along all 3 Canadian marine coastlines. Following illegal introductions in MN and NW ON, the Rainbow Smelt dispersed into the Winnipeg River (prior to 1991), Lake Manitoba, Dauphin River, Nelson River N to its estuary with Hudson Bay, and then N along the coast and into the mouth of the Churchill River. Long and slender, it resembles a young trout. Its body is translucent and iridescent greenish or purple above and silvery below. This species grows to up to 33 cm, but MB specimens have been under 22 cm. Spawning occurs soon after ice break-up in April (water temperature over 4°C) and mature individuals move onto lake reefs or into streams, where eggs (8000-70,000) are shed and fertilized. Hatching occurs in about 20 days, and the young feed on plankton such as crustaceans. After attaining a length of 15 cm, they add small fish of other and their own species to their diet. Maturing at 3 years, they can live for 6 years. This species has been implicated in the decline of other species such as Emerald Shiner and Lake Whitefish. It has now become an important addition to the diet of other large fish, such as Walleye and Lake Trout. Scavengers like gulls quickly devour washed-up smelts that die following spawning. There is evidence that native fish eating smelt accumulate higher levels of fat and mercury. (*see* CAPELIN) • REW

SMITH CARTER ARCHITECTS AND ENGINEERS INC. provides design services in architecture, engineering, planning, and interior design. The company's WINNIPEG office was established in 1947 and has grown into a 150-person organization specializing in fitness facility and health services design. The firm has worked on community and corporate gym facilities, pools and spas, ice rinks, racquet courts, climbing walls, and fitness studios. It has also completed renovation projects for YMCA-YWCAs in Winnipeg, the Wellness Institute at SEVEN OAKS GENERAL HOSPITAL, and other facilities in MB and across the country. Since its inception, Smith-Carter has been involved in either an architectural or engineering capacity in all of the major healthcare centres in Winnipeg, including several projects for Cancer-Care Manitoba. Current design projects include redevelopment of the YMCA-YWCA Winnipeg South Branch, the creation of a corporate fitness centre for GREAT-WEST LIFE, and a renovation of the Asper Jewish Community Campus. Smith Carter is also collaborating on the building of the MANITOBA HYDRO headquarters in downtown Winnipeg. ● CATHARINA DE BAKKER

SMITH, Donald Alexander, first Baron Strathcona and Mount Royal, Businessman, politician (Aug 6, 1820, Forres, Scotland, UK, d Jan 21, 1914, London, UK). Born in Scotland, he joined the HBC in 1838, serving mainly in Labrador 1848-68, where he was promoted to chief trader (1852) and chief factor (1862). In 1869 he was appointed a special commissioner to RED RIVER [SETTLEMENT] to deal with the recalcitrant MÉTIS. Arriving in late December, he spent most of his stay in Red River under house arrest, but did manage to meet with the people in public assembly on 19-20 January 1870, where he encouraged the rebels to call the Convention of Forty to present their demands to Ottawa. Although the mission was officially successful, the Canadian

government privately felt he had failed, since his real assignment had been to bribe the rebels into complete submission.

Smith then became chief commissioner for the HBC, serving until 1874 when he became land commissioner for the company. In 1883 he became a director and in 1889 governor of the HBC; by this time he was its largest stockholder. During his years as commissioner, Smith spent much time in MB. He served as MLA from WINNIPEG from 1870 to 1874, and as MP from SELKIRK from 1871; his break with Sir John A. Macdonald in 1873 helped lead to the fall of the govt. He was frequently criticized for election corruption. He later served as Montreal West MP from 1887 to 1896, retiring when he was appointed Canadian high commissioner in London, a post he held until his death. Smith used his HBC position to make shrewd investments in other endeavours, including RAILWAYS, and his involvement in the CPR gave him the right to drive the last spike in 1886. He became a pillar of the Bank of Montreal and had his hand in all sorts of business activities. Raised to the peerage in 1897, in 1898 he raised, equipped, and maintained a unit of mounted rifles (Lord Strathcona's Horse) for service in the South African War. In later years he received innumerable honours from government and the private sector. He died in London. ● JMB

SMITH, Joy Ann, politician, teacher, author (b Feb. 20, 1947 DELORAINE). For 21 years, Joy Smith worked as a teacher, writing several best-selling books about education – *Lies My Kid's Teacher Told Me* and *Tools of the Trade*. Owner of Gem Records for a period of time, Smith was nominated for MB's Woman Entrepreneur of the Year. She became part of the political world as a PROGRESSIVE CONSERVATIVE and in 1999 she was elected to the MB legislature for the south-central constituency of Fort Garry and was the PC critic for education, justice and intergovernmental affairs. She also served on the MB Taskforce for Building Sustainable Communities. As justice critic, Smith spoke against a bill which provided adoption rights to same-sex couples in MB. She felt the proposed legislation was flawed and maintained the bill discriminated against married man-woman couples. In 2003, Smith lost in her riding to a NDP candidate. In the federal election of 2004, she won a seat as a PC candidate in the north Winnipeg riding of Kildonan-St. Paul. She was named MB caucus chair and took a seat on the Conservative Party's Planning and Priorities Committee. Smith made up part of the Canadian delegation to the Ukraine in 2004 to observe in the court-ordered repeat of the second round of voting the Ukraine Presidential election. In 2006,

committee peers elected Smith as vice-chair of the standing committee on the status of women in 2006. ● RUTH DEGRAVES

SNAIL is a mollusc in the class Gastropoda (phylum Mollusca) generally with a calcareous spiral shell. Snails are predominantly marine, but numerous freshwater and terrestrial species have evolved to occupy practically every habitat on earth. They glide over surfaces on a thin bed of mucous by means of muscular contractions of a single large foot, and explore their environment with tentacles and eyes. Freshwater snails consist of 2 subclasses: Prosobranchia have gills, while the Pulmonata must come periodically to the surface to breathe air using a modified lung. In most prosobranchs the sexes are separate, and the shell opening can be sealed with a tough trapdoor (operculum). Pulmonates lack an operculum and are hermaphroditic (ovary and testis in the same body). While most snails lay eggs, one rare prosobranch, the Brown Mystery Snail (*Campeloma decisum*) of E MB, gives birth to live young; this species is parthenogenetic (eggs develop without fertilization) and MB populations are all females. All other MB prosobranchs are small and live about one year. While most pulmonates also live about one year, some individuals of larger species, such as the Great Pond Snail (*Lymnaea stagnalis*), or the Tadpole Snail (*Physa gyrina*), may survive up to 3 years in S MB. Freshwater snails feed on algae, aquatic plants and organic detritus. In MB, birds and fish are important predators of freshwater snails.

In MB, 43 species of freshwater snails have been recorded, with SE MB showing the highest species diversity. There are 2 species of freshwater limpets (*Ferrissia*) that grow up to 3 mm. *Marstonia gelida* is an extinct Pleistocene (within 2 million years ago) prosobranch whose shells still occur in beach drift along lakeshores. The 4 most-common freshwater MB snails are: Great Pond Snail, Tadpole Snail, Larger Eastern Ramshorn (*Helisoma trivolvis*), and Common Stagnicola (*Stagnicola elodes*). Snails are good indicators of ecological health, and unfortunately some species have become rare or extirpated. The Showy Pond Snail (*Bulimnea megasoma*), up to 5 cm long, has shown a major decline. The endemic (only world range), 12 mm Lake Winnipeg Physa (*Physella winnipegensis*) is endangered and barely survives, with a few small populations living on rocks exposed to heavy wave action. Eggs are laid in the spring in gelatinous clusters on the undersides of rocks. Its lifespan is a year. Threats are removal of rocks from beaches, use of chemicals to kill algae, and pollution. Abundance and species richness

Donald Alexander Smith

of freshwater-snail communities have declined significantly in MB since the 1970s, associated with many factors – pollution from industry, municipalities, agriculture, mining, algaecides, and fuel spills, as well as from wetland drainage, increased ultraviolet light, logging, dams, disturbance from watercraft, shoreline alteration, and climate change.

Land snails are found in all MB habitats, but abundance and diversity increases with moisture and calcium availability. They feed on organic matter in the soil, fungi and plants. In winter they hibernate under leaf litter, stones or logs. During drought, they seal the shell opening with a hardened mucous wall (epiphragm) and enter a dormant state (aestivation) which may last several years. Most MB species are small (2-10 mm) such as *Vallonia*, *Discus*, and *Zonitoides*, however the largest species, *Succinea ovalis*, can grow to >20 mm and is common in deciduous woods.

Marine snails are represented in MB waters of Hudson Bay by at least 52 species (e.g., *Acmaea*, *Lepeta*, *Margarites*, *Boreotrophon*, *Buccinum*). More than 100 species of marine snails have thus far been recorded in Canadian Arctic waters, occupying habitats ranging from the intertidal zone (e.g., Periwinkles like *Littorina*) to very deep water. They breathe by means of gills and may be herbivorous or carnivorous. While most have coiled shells, those of limpets are cap-shaped. ● EP, REW

SNAILFISH is a small group of marine fishes (family Liparidae, order Scorpaeniformes) living in cold waters in both hemispheres. Shallow-water species are remarkable for 'sucking disk' on the outside of the throat, which incorporates the pelvic fins, and is used to cling to the substrate in the presence of wave action. The body is tadpole-like with a large head, and the skin lacks scales. The 155 species in the family live from tide pools to great depths of 7500 m. They range in size from 5-77 cm and up to 11 kg, but most are much smaller. There are 4 species recorded in Hudson Bay. The Kelp Snailfish (*Liparis tunicatus*) lives in kelp beds, while the Sea Tadpole (*Careproctus reinhardti*) is a deepwater species occuring down to 1250 m. The Gelatinous Snailfish (*Liparis fabrichii*) often selects a muddy bottom and acquired its name because its skin is loose and gelatinous. The Variegated or Dusky Snailfish (*Liparis gibbus*), usually found on the bottom around 100-200 m, is being investigated to find out how it and its relatives resist freezing in water temperatures several degrees below 0°C. It is known that antifreeze proteins/polypeptides (AFPs) are produced in the skin, and glycoproteins (AFGPs) in the liver, which bind to

ice crystals forming in the plasma or tissues and inhibit further crystallization and prevent cell damage. Snailfish are commonly eaten by seals, cod and sea birds. ● REW, DBS

SNAKE is a readily recognizable animal in the order Squamata (class Reptilia) characterized by a long thin body covered in dry scales, lack of legs, and unusual mode of movement by slithering along the ground or in trees. Perhaps it is this last feature that startles most people and makes them frightened of snakes. A snake is generally well camouflaged and therefore seldom seen until it suddenly bolts into action at close range. However this fear may lay far deeper in our psyche. Both snakes and spiders are at the top of the list of venomous creatures in Africa where humans evolved, and so it is quite possible that our ancestors developed an instinctive fear of these creatures through natural selection. Fortunately, there are no poisonous snakes in MB, although such species do occur in adjacent provinces and states. The family of snakes represented in MB is the colubrids (Colubridae), which includes 78% of all the world's snake fauna. Snakes have been evolving and adapting to local conditions around the world for over 125 million years. With such unusual lifestyles, they demonstrate a number of fascinating abilities and habits. Being 'ectothermic' (i.e., cold-blooded), they require warm environmental temperatures to remain active, and so they frequently bask in the sun or lay on a warm surface like exposed bedrock. Some, like garter snake, are capable swimmers and can reach distant islands or cross rivers and ponds.

The vitally important physiological capability of hibernating for the 6-7 months of cold weather makes possible their existence in the province. They cannot survive freezing, so it is

imperative that they instinctively retreat in the autumn to animal burrows, anthills, or cracks in rocky sites like limestone sinkholes that descend below the frostline. Since snakes continue to grow slowly their entire life, they moult their skin periodically, which may be rubbed off in one or several pieces, unlike a human which sloughs off skin cells continuously. Even the transparent eye scale comes away at this time. Snakes have no moveable eyelids, and external ears are also lacking, but sounds, such as vibrations from the approach of prey or a predator, are detected through the body. The forked tongue slides out to pick up scent particles in the air or on objects, and then is retracted and thrust into a special smell-sensitive sac (Jacobson's organ) in the roof of the mouth. The front of the upper jaw and the back of both jaws are loosely hinged to allow the swallowing of relatively large prey items, since a snake cannot bite off pieces of food. All the organs are elongated to accommodate the body shape. Snakes are active predators on insects, worms, frogs, toads, and rodents. They are relished by a host of predatory birds like hawks and herons, and carnivorous mammals. Their protection lies in their camouflage pattern, while remaining motionless, and sliding rapidly for the cover. Snakes are represented in MB by 5 species:

NORTHERN REDBELLY SNAKE (*Storeria occipitomaculata*), only 16-25 cm long and brown with a reddish-orange belly, is a retiring little snake discovered only by those rare people that go around looking under boards and other debris, or who stop and examine roadkilled creatures. Reaching the NW periphery of its range in the S of the province, it inhabits meadows, bogs, fens and marshes where it hunts beetles, ants, earthworms, and slugs. The 1-18 young hatch

Redbelly snakes hide under debris.

internally in the female and are born alive and ready to wander off from Aug to Sept. Sexual maturity is reached in 2 years and life expectancy is 10 years. It seems to have a preference for hibernating in large numbers (over 100 have been discovered) under an anthill, sometimes in the company of other snakes.

SMOOTH GREEN SNAKE (*Opheodrys vernalis*) is a rare, delicate, lime-green and yellow snake measuring less than 50 cm. It is restricted to the S grasslands, where it is challenging to spot in the grass. Its numbers have been greatly reduced due to habitat destruction and pesticides from agriculture. It feeds on insects like grasshoppers. From 5-15 eggs are laid in July and these hatch in less than a month.

PLAINS HOGNOSE SNAKE (*Heterodon nasicus*) is light brown with dark-brown patches, and has an upturned snout like a shovel, useful for burrowing through the sand. This species is another 'glacial relict' in MB – left behind from a larger and contiguous range with populations farther S in the Dakotas. It is found only in extreme SW MB in sandhills around Carberry, Wawanesa, Lauder and Oak Lake. It specializes on a diet of toads, and so it must be immune to the toxins produced in the toad's many skin glands. Although the toad may attempt to foil the attack by bloating up with air, the snake's teeth soon puncture and deflate the body, and the fate of the toad is sealed. There is some evidence that the snake's salivary glands contain a mild venom which destroys the victim's red blood cells. This species seldom feigns death by rolling over on its back, as does its close relative, the Eastern Hognose (*H. platyrhinos*). Up to 11 eggs are laid in July, and hatching occurs about 8 weeks later.

WESTERN PLAINS GARTER SNAKE (*Thamnophis radix haydeni*) is a yellow and black snake of the grasslands. *Red-sided Garter Snake* (*Thamnophis sirtalis parietalis*) prefers mixed and boreal coniferous woodlands in the S half of the province, has blotches of red on the sides, and is famous for its hibernating dens holding apparently the largest concentrations of snakes in the world. MB and other far-N populations of these snakes are unusual in that they are freeze tolerant for some hours and at several degrees below the freezing point, which enables them to survive exposure to overnight frosts in fall and spring, when they are not protected in their deep hibernacula. A number of limestone sinkholes in aspen parkland near NARCISSE and INWOOD offer the snakes ideal winter quarters (unless there is flooding), while nearby fields and marshes are rich feeding grounds for frogs and insects from spring to autumn. Some snakes are known to

have travelled 18 km away and returned for denning in the fall. Watching thousands of snakes (up to 10,000) emerge from the pits after the ground has thawed in May, with dozens forming mating balls (many males after each larger female), is one of Nature's spectacles – a scene that has drawn researches and tourists from afar, and numerous documentaries and magazine features. Females give birth to an average of 16 (maximum 60) live young in late summer and fall. Maximum life span is 12 years. The commercial harvest of the snakes in MB for biological-supply companies was halted in 1989. ● REW

SNOW ECOLOGY is the study of the inter-relationships of plants and animals with the physical attributes of snow. Snow is precipitation of frozen water vapour in the form hexagonal flakes, formed high in the atmosphere. It covers MB for 5-7 months of the year, depending on the latitude and snow accumulation. The English language has few words when it comes to describing the various forms and formations of snow, but for N FIRST PEOPLES, whose lives depended on this knowledge, the multiple manifestations of snow have given rise to a rich vocabulary. The few terms used here are adapted from the Kovakmiut People of Alaska.

Nowhere is snow more fascinating for researchers and integral to the local ecology than in the N coniferous forest or taiga, which covers half the land area of MB. The snow cover here is remarkably uniform in thickness and fluffiness. The forest acts as a wind break so as the snow accumulates, the individual flakes lie just as they fall, and are not tumbled and broken by wind. Such a snow cover exists in 2 phases: snow covering the ground is called *api*, while snow caught and retained by trees is *qali*. Around the base of each coniferous tree is a bare area called *qamaniq*. As the *api* layer increases, the lighter and broad-footed Snowshoe Hare may run on the surface, while the heavy Grey Wolf flounders. Moose are able to wade through moderate snow depths on their stilt-like legs, but will also "yard" in protected sites and keep to broken trails to conserve energy.

Qali affects the arboreal activities of the Red and Flying squirrels, Marten, Canada Jay, chickadees, redpolls and crossbills. During periods of heavy *qali* accumulation, birds fly to windy hilltops where *qali* is less thick on the branches. *Qali* may become so heavy that it breaks tree limbs, which can affect forest succession. As branches fall to the forest floor, their build-up kills a patch of lichen-feather moss on the floor. This dead vegetation makes a good seed-bed for deciduous trees and shrubs such as birch,

aspen and alder. The cycle of qali-breaks of coniferous trees and appearance of deciduous growth is a major cause of the mosaic pattern of the taiga so visible from the air.

The snowflakes that accumulate on the forest floor soon undergo physical changes, caused by heat and moisture flowing up from the earth. Molecules of water depart from the thin tips of the relatively warm, bottom-most snowflakes, and as this process continues, a subnivean (under the snow) space begins to form. These errant water molecules reattach themselves to the colder flakes above, but now they form pyramids around a central spike. Groups of pyramids, as large as 10-15 mm across, create fragile columns with empty spaces between them. This layer is called *pukak* and may be 10 cm or more thick. The heat differential of -5 to -8°C of the earth, to perhaps -30°C at the snow surface, is the pump that causes and maintains *pukak*.

The *api* is crucial to the winter survival of small mammals, hibernating frogs, nestling Western Painted Turtles, and many kinds of invertebrates. Were it not for the insulating properties of *api*, these species would be killed by exposure to much-lower temperatures, and hence would not be part of MB's fauna. In autumn, before the *api* reaches a depth of 15 cm, the presence of small mammals (voles, mice and shrews) is evident by the pattern of tracks and runways on the snow surface. After the *api* reaches a thickness about 20 cm, these signs disappear as the mammals abandon the surface and occupy the *pukak*. This thickness of snow results in the forest floor becoming isolated from the fluctuations in ambient air temperature – the true onset of winter for plants and small creatures. Before this occurs, MB may experience plummeting temperatures and cold rains which soak the fur and nests of small mammals. Without the protective insulation of either thick, dry fur or a deep snow cover, small mammals suffer cold stress, which can lead to a massive die-off. In the spring, melting snow and cold weather again test the survival abilities of small wildlife. Without a regular supply of these creatures, predatory animals such as weasels, Marten, Fisher, and owls could not survive either. Consequently, the complex boreal food web and even the fine-fur industry could not exist without the all-important *api*.

About half the land area of MB is treeless, or with scattered trees or groves. The N section of this landscape is called the tundra and forest-tundra, while the S is prairie (steppe), forest-steppe, and aspen parkland. In these open regions, the snow cover is markedly affected by wind. Snowflakes are rolled along the ground, and the broken fragments travel some distance before

S

coming to rest. With constant wind speed and direction, the needle-like fragments creep slowly in groups over the snow in an arrowhead shape, like a small sand dune. Above the drifts, the air is full of moving snow fragments which over many years can abrade and shape plants like willow and spruce. When the wind dies down, the snow fragments freeze in place together and the drift hardens, reaching 100s of g/cm^2, which affects animal movements and ability to feed. Caribou must work hard to scrape away packed snow with hooves and muzzle to reach plants below.

Topography also affects snow cover on the tundra and prairie. Snow blows off hilltops and accumulates in hollows. Muskox and caribou seek the former for easier access to food, while lemmings, Ermine, Arctic Fox, Arctic Hare, Spruce Grouse, and ptarmigan seek shelter by burrowing into the latter. Deep drifts or *zaboi* may not melt completely until well into the summer, so that the growing season of plants is progressively shorter toward the deep centre. A large boulder or steep bank on the tundra can cause wind-eddy currents to scoop out a hollow in the snow, which may be the only sites where the ground or vegetation lies exposed. Rock and Willow ptarmigan, Snow Bunting, Hoary, and Common redpolls, and other migrants congregate for precious food items and grit for their gizzards.

On the Prairies, clumps of shrubs and trees accumulate deep drifts downwind, which are important sites for White-tailed Jack Rabbit burrows, providing shelter from exposure to the elements and from predation from the Great-horned Owl, Red Fox and Coyote. On Hudson Bay, and on lakes and streams, a cover of snow may help prevent the formation of deep ice (often over 1 m), which protects from freezing creatures living in the shallows (e.g., Leopard Frog); however, sunlight and oxygen are also cut off from these aquatic ecosystems, the latter sometimes causing asphyxiation of fish and other life. The fauna of MB demonstrates abundant evidence of a long evolutionary adaptation to the multiple characteristics and challenges of snow, but much remains to be discovered about this relationship. • WOP, REW

SNOW LAKE, pop 837, is a town 125 km E of **FLIN FLON** on the E shore of Snow Lake. Though situated on early fur-trading routes, the area was not settled by Europeans until the late 1940s, when mineral deposits were found here. The townsite for Snow Lake was laid out in 1945 after the Howe Sound Exploration Co Ltd decided to develop a gold mine. The "company" town was incorporated in 1947. The mine closed in 1958 and Snow Lake would have become a ghost town

if Hudson's Bay Mining and Smelting Co Ltd (HBMS) had not begun mining copper and zinc in the area. In the mid-1980s, HBMS had 6 mines in production; in 2007, that number was down to one. Like other mining towns, Snow Lake's population has been variable. It swelled to a peak in the 1970s, and dropped as area mines closed. Snow Lake lost 25% of its population between 1991 and 2001 and numbers fell by another 400 people by the 2006 Census. There is a small airport, school, and clinic/nursing station here. The retail and service centre's outdoor activities draw visitors. A suspension bridge spans Wekusko Falls. The Aurora Borealis Arts Council has attracted performances by the **MANITOBA THEATRE CENTRE** and the **ROYAL WINNIPEG BALLET**. The annual Winter Whoot, in early March, features snowmobile races and other winter contests. Nearby **PETROGRAPHS** date from 500 AD. • GPP

SNOWSHOEING originated thousands of years ago – and is still used – as a means of winter travel for **FIRST PEOPLES**. European fur traders quickly adopted snowshoes. Snowshoeing was first taken up as a recreational sport in Montreal during the mid-19th century, and then travelled W where long Prairie winters quickly made it a favourite pastime. By 1900, competitive snowshoeing was an immensely popular sport in **WINNIPEG**.

The city's earliest snowshoe club was formed in 1878, with **ANDREW G. B. BANNATYNE** serving as president. It became the St. George's Snow Shoe Club in 1880. By winter 1886-87, there were 3 Winnipeg snowshoe clubs with a total membership nearing 1000. In 1910, the Manitoba Snowshoe Association (MSA) was formed. Though WWI greatly diminished most other sport activity, the MSA continued to hold championships

in 1915 and 1916, with entrants from the militia (*see* **MILITARY**) and the Boy Scouts. Women were also frequent entrants in competitions. In 1920, about 600 snowshoers took part in the YMCA's club hike, though it was the last time newspapers covered the event, as **HOCKEY** became MB's dominant winter sport. From 1933-40, track and field athlete Eric Coy competed in snowshoe events as a means of winter training, and set numerous Cdn and world records.

Today snowshoeing is an increasingly popular recreational activity in MB, and is regarded as an ideal aerobic workout for winter, especially when combined with cross-country ski poles. • MD

SOCCER is a shortened term for "Association Football," and is known in most of the world simply as "football." **ENGLISH** immigrants brought modern soccer to MB, and the sport had become well established in **WINNIPEG** and surrounding **CPR** towns by the 1880s. The Manitoba Football Association was founded in 1896, and the province played a prominent role in developing the sport nationally. MB teams were some of the first to tour across Canada. In 1898, a team from **CARBERRY** toured ON, followed by the Winnipeg Shamrocks in 1902. The Dominion of Canada Football Association (DCFA), forerunner to the Canadian Soccer Association, was formed in 1912 with Winnipeg's J. D. Pratt serving as honorary president. At the first annual meeting, held in Winnipeg in 1913, the gov gen – Prince Arthur, Duke of Connaught and Strathearn – gave the association the Connaught Cup for national competition. The first national championship was then organized, and Winnipeg teams claimed the Connaught Cup 3 years running: the Norwood Wanderers won in

CPR Ladies' Snowshoe Club, 1922

was earlier known in French as the Saint-Pierre. Rising in southeastern SK, it flows into the US, then back into Canada, south of Coulter. From the US border, it flows NE to **Souris**, then SE to a point N of Margaret, where at "the elbow," it bends sharply to the NE to join the **Assiniboine** near Treesbank. It receives several minor tributaries – the Antler, Gainsborough, Jackson, Plum, and Elgin creeks. Principal settlements near the river are **Melita**, **Hartney**, Souris, and **Wawanesa**. South of Coulter and between Melita and Souris, it meanders across the floors of glacial lakes Souris and Hind. Downstream from Souris, it flows in a gorge, increasing in depth below the elbow, where it cuts through the Tiger Hills. Near Wawanesa are several incised meanders, one of which surrounds the village. Maximum discharge occurs in spring, with low flow in summer. Dams in SK and ND, as well as in MB – 2 near Melita and one near Napinka, Hartney, Souris, and Wawanesa – have modified discharge, but spring floods still occur, as they did in 1976 and 1999. Water is extracted for municipal supply at Souris and Wawanesa, and for irrigation. The International Joint Commission (*see* **International Boundary Waters Treaty**) oversees withdrawal of water in SK and ND, requiring ND to deliver, to the best of its ability, 0.566 m³/sec (20 ft³/sec) to MB between Jun and Oct. Canoeing is popular in spring, with spectacular scenery in the Sours River Bend Wildlife Management Area at and below the elbow. ● JOHN WELSTED

SOUTH ASIANS

SOUTH ASIANS are one of the largest ethnic minorities in MB, with East Indians contributing the largest share. After the **Filipino**, **German**, and **Chinese** communities, East Indians are the next most represented ethnic minority in MB and **Winnipeg**. South Asians live or originate in the Indian Subcontinent, namely India, Bangladesh, Pakistan, Sri Lanka, Nepal, Bhutan, Maldives, and the British Indian Ocean Territory.

South Asians are a diverse group, comprising people of many ethnicities, language families, and religious denominations. The beginnings of the South Asian community in Canada are found in the early 20th century, with the arrival in BC of a handful of Sikhs from the Punjab Province of India. In 1908, the govt imposed an **Immigration** regulation known as the "continuous journey" requirement. This regulation, stipulating that arrivals would have to possess tickets booked from ports in their native state, was aimed at halting South Asians' migration to Canada. As a result, until the mid-1960s, South Asians arrived in Canada sporadically and in small numbers. In 1967, the Cdn immigration policy established objective criteria, such as age, education, and pre-arranged employment, to select immigrants to Canada. This resulted in increasing numbers of South Asian immigrants. While ON, BC, AB, and QC, have been the preferred destinations for most South Asians, the MB's South Asian community has also increased substantially since the 1960s. The Census reports that an average of 2-300 Indians lived in MB between the 1910s and the 1960s. In 1971, the number of Indians living in the province was over 1100, while a decade later, it was already over 2500. The 2001 Census counts more than 6400 South Asian immigrants in MB, of which more than 6100 declared an East Indian ethnicity. There are indications the South Asian community in MB will continue to expand. In 2005, India and Pakistan have been the 3rd and 10th immigrant-source countries in MB. About 95% of South Asians living in MB reside in Winnipeg, consistent with the behaviour of this ethnic group nationally.

The South Asian community has contributed significantly to MB economically, socially, and politically. The Punjabi-speaking community – the dominant East Indian group here – has had representatives in the Legislative Assembly for decades. Gulzar Cheema was a **Liberal** MLA 1988-93, later also serving as a BC MLA. In 2003, Bidhu Jha won elections as MLA for the Radisson constituency. East Indians have also given MB many social leaders. Haroon Siddiqui, a **Muslim** from Brandon, was a **Newspaper** editor at the *Brandon Sun* before he moved to the *Toronto Star*. Shahin Siddiqui has been a well-known spokesperson of the conservative Muslim community. South Asians have also contributed to MB's economy. Sham Joshi, a trained veterinarian, started a firm called Feed-Rite with 2 other Canadian colleagues. This animal-feed business has grown into a multi-million-dollar venture, with plants in Winnipeg, **Portage la Prairie**, the US, and China. Raj Pandey, owner of APR Industries, a business specializing in fireplaces and heating stoves, recently donated $1.5 million to the Hindu Society of Manitoba toward construction of a **Hindu** temple and community centre. Another important contributor to this enterprise is Daya Gupta, a Winnipeg eye doctor.

South Asians are represented in many industries. The Punjabi-speaking group, although concentrated in non-professional occupations (taxi drivers, factory workers, and small- business ownership), has been economically successful. Most South Indians tend to concentrate in professional occupations. The many Sri Lankan Tamil refugees often work in the **Garment Industry** or other non-skilled occupations.

South Asian communities have been active in cultural activities. The India School of Dance, Music, and Theatre has been popular for more than 25 years. Many of its graduates are popular Cdn artists. An example is the well-known **Dance** and drama group Manohar. South Asians are present in **Folklorama**, with separate pavilions for Sri Lankans of Tamil origin and East Indians. An annual East Indian festivity is the celebration of Diwali – a festival of lights – at the Winnipeg Convention Centre, with the participation of many politicians. There are also many ethnic social organizations, such as the Bitchra (Bengali Association), Gujarati Association, Tamil Association, Bangladeshi Association. Various South Asian groups – including Hindus from India, **Buddhists** from Sri Lanka, and Muslims from India, Pakistan, and Bangladesh – have their own ethno-religious prayer places. The Sikh community alone has 8 Gurudvaras (temples). ● SHIVA HALLI/RADUCA BUZDUGAN

SPALL, Robert

SPALL, Robert, soldier, **Victoria Cross** winner (b Mar 5, 1890, Ealing, Suffolk, UK; d Aug 12, 1918, Parvillers-le-Quesnoy, Somme, France), moved with his family to **Winnipeg** when he was 2 years old. Spall was employed in a city office when WWI broke out. He enlisted in the 90th **Royal Winnipeg Rifles**, later transferring to the **Princess Patricia's Canadian Light Infantry**. He was a Sgt leading a patrol when it was isolated from the regiment by enemy troops. Twice, Spall grabbed a Lewis machine gun, climbed over the trench parapet, and faced the advancing enemy soldiers, firing on them. He turned the enemy back, saving his platoon, but was killed by enemy fire. His VC is held by the Military Museums in Calgary. ● JIM SHILLIDAY

SPARROW

SPARROW (family Emberizidae) is a small, ground-dwelling bird that uses its stubby beak to feed on seeds in winter and insects in summer. Most sparrows have a drab-brownish, streaky plumage. Thirty species are on the MB list. Although a few, such as the Dark-eyed Junco (*Junco hyemalis*) and snow bunting (*Plectrophenax nivalis*), may linger in winter, most spend that season in the southern US or Mexico. The most widespread is the Savannah Sparrow (*Passerculus sandwichensis*), which sings its buzzy, insectlike song in grasslands and other open areas. Perhaps better-known is the White-throated Sparrow (*Zonotrichia albicollis*), a common migrant and feeder visitor throughout the S. Cottagers in the boreal forest (*see* **Ecoclimactic Regions**) are familiar with its cheery "Oh, Sweet, Canada, Canada, Canada" song. The first nest of the closely related Harris's sparrow (*Zonotrichia querula*) was not found until 1930, at **Churchill**. Like so many other grassland

S

Harris's Sparrows were first found in Manitoba in 1930.

species, Baird's Sparrow (*Ammodramus bairdii*) and the Chestnut-collared Longspur (*Calcarius ornatus*) have declined greatly and are now restricted to the SW. Once common as far E as Winnipeg, these species have not been able to cope with the loss of their native prairie habitat. An unrelated invasive species is the house or English sparrow (*Passer domesticus*), a native to the Old World. Since its 19th-century introduction to NA, the aggressive species has displaced native birds such as the Eastern bluebird.
● RUDOLF KOES

SPECIALTY CROPS. MB farmers grow a range of crops, often referred to as "specialty crops," grown in small amounts but returning a higher value than traditional grains or oilseeds. MB is second only to PE in potato area planted, with production going to french fry processing plants in **PORTAGE LA PRAIRIE** and **CARBERRY**. Sunflowers are grown for cooking oil, confectionery, and for bird seed. MB produces a variety of edible beans such as navy, pinto, and black beans. Other crops include lentils, peas, rye, and buckwheat. MB farmers produce between 150,000 and 250,000 acres of corn per year, with production used as livestock feed or by the Diageo distillery in **GIMLI**. In the late 1990s, soybean production began to grow in some areas, especially the Red River Valley. Mustard seed was introduced into MB in 1952 and quickly expanded into an export crop with markets around the globe including the US, Australia, France and Belgium. In the last few years, mustard makers in Dijon, France have been importing MB and prairie mustard seed for their famous Dijon mustard. Exports include a small percentage of finished products, prepared mustard and mustard flour. MB is the 2nd largest producer of mustard seed in Canada next to SK.
● JOHN MORRISS

SPECIES is a discrete group of organisms that can be diagnosed on the basis of certain specialized features, and that had a common ancestor and unique evolutionary history. In determining what is a species, scientists use evidence from morphology (physical features), behaviour, ecology, genetics, biochemistry, and possible hybrid status. While many species are clear-cut, others are challenging to define, which should be expected in a natural world so full of complex variation and evolutionary transition in time and space. The next lower level of classification, sometimes used in this Encyclopedia, is the subspecies, which describes species variation in identifiable subpopulations, occuring in distinct ranges over often-large geographic areas. The development of new research techniques (e.g., DNA analysis) may well revise the definition of what constitutes species, and will result in lumping or splitting numerous species as currently recognized. Where available, the currently known species (and sometimes higher estimates of various animal groups (taxa) are given for MB, Canada, and the world. In only a few well-known groups (e.g., mammals) is the total number of representatives known with any assurance. The total number of all living species in MB is wide open to conjecture (perhaps over 1 million). (*see* **BIODIVERSITY**). ● REW

SPEED SKATING. *See* **SKATING, SPEED**.

SPEERS, Robert James "R. J." or "Jim," horseman (b 1882, Toronto; d July 19, 1955 **WINNIPEG**) established a thoroughbred racing empire in the Cdn prairies. At the age of 18, Speers moved to Battleford, SK, where he set up a grain and livestock operation, which eventually grew to include 6 grain elevators. While selling cattle in Winnipeg, he was asked by a local racing group if he would finance their operations. Although an enthusiastic gambler, Speers said he would only become involved in racing if the "crooks, bookies and touts" were forced out. He then moved to Winnipeg in 1920, and then lobbied the MB govt to pass the province's first Horse Racing Legislation Act, which passed in 1925. He organized his first race meet at River Park in 1922, and built Whittier Park in 1924, obtaining the land on a 99-year lease for the price of $1. He opened Polo Park a year later, as well as Chinook park in Calgary. In 1926, Speers formed the Prairie Thoroughbred Breeders and Racing Association, which led to only thoroughbred horses being allowed to race in MB. That same year, Speers established Whittier Park Stock Farms at **ST. BONIFACE**, which later relocated to a 10,000 acre farm near **BRANDON**. Speers' vast fortune withstood the **GREAT DEPRESSION**; during this period, he even imported into MB what was then the largest consignment of thoroughbreds ever brought into Canada. In 1939, he developed the first mechanical starting gate to be used on a recognized racetrack in NA, garnering the attention of Queen Elizabeth and King George VI upon their visit that year. He imported breeding stock from some of the most fashionable English and American bloodlines, and was considered Canada's leading breeder from 1946-51. ● MD

SPENCE, Thomas. *See* **MANITOBAH, REPUBLIC OF**.

SPERLING, pop 100, is a community 60 km SW of **WINNIPEG**, via hwy 3. First settled in the 1880s, mostly by people from southern ON, it was called Mariposa. The name Sperling was adopted in 1901, after a financial firm associated with Morden and the Northwestern railway. The first school was established in 1897. Presbyterian and Methodist churches founded in 1899 and 1903 became the United Church in 1924. The Catholic Church was in service from 1935 to 1972. The Mennonite Bretheren Church was located about 10 km SE and served from 1932-67. Sperling thrived through the first half of the 20th century with an area pop of about 300 and a full slate of commercial businesses. Today, Sperling is mainly residential, with one major manufacturing business, Sperling Industries Ltd. A community hall

RICHARD DE MAY

in the arena is the centre of social activity. The local cemetery is the site of an annual Ancestors' day held each June to honour community members who have passed away. Sperling managed to weather the rise and fall of the Prairie grain industry, maintaining its wooden grain elevator. In 2007, the co-op board was trying to find a new owner for the last co-operatively-owned wooden grain elevator in MB. • GPP

SPIDER is a predacious arthropod of the order Araneae (class Arachnida or Pycnogonida) with 2 body parts (called the prosoma and opisthosoma or abdomen) attached by a narrow stalk, 4 pairs of legs, and no antennae or wings (insects have 3 body parts, 3 pairs of legs, 2 antennae, and most are winged). The arachnids (spiders, mites, ticks, scorpions) occur in astounding numbers worldwide, with over 80,000 species described, 35,000 of which are spiders; the total number of spider species is estimated at 175,000. Spiders range in body size from 0.37 mm to 9 cm, the largest being the Goliath Tarantula (*Theraphosa leblondi*) of South America, with a legspan of 26 cm. They are all predatory, injecting digestive juices into their prey and sucking up the liquefied remains. Venom comes in 2 types – neurotoxins affecting nerves and muscles (causing paralysis and even death), and cytotoxins, which break down tissues (potentially resulting in death, or slow-healing wounds and scars). Spiders make silk for egg cases, nurseries, lining tunnels, trap doors, snares, safety draglines, and ballooning on the wind. While many species live only 1 year, other species can reach 30 years. Spiders originated over 400 million years ago (Devonian period) and remain important components of all the world's terrestrial ecosystems. They are increasingly being examined in biodiversity and other research.

Spiders have received little attention in MB. The most-recent survey recorded 528 species in 23 families. The Red River Valley (including Winnipeg) is host to over 293 species. It is estimated that over 700 species are native to MB. Major families are Linyphiidae with 193 species and Lycosidae with 45. Faunal associations are arctic/subarctic, boreal, eastern deciduous forest, grassland, and several species are introduced. Another MB study recorded a rich 82 species in a S taiga bog and 39 in a N taiga bog (16 species shared). Due to MB's central location, it has about 50% of Canada's spider fauna represented, which currently stands at 1309 species, but is estimated at 1400.

Spiders are common in all MB terrestrial habitats, even in crops, yards, and inside homes and other buildings. All have venom to immobilize and begin digestion of their prey, but there are no truly dangerous native species in MB. However, Black Widow Spiders (e.g., *Latrodectus mactans*; family Theridiidae) and a few other highly venomous species occur in other provinces and states, and not infrequently are imported accidentally into MB with shipments of fruit (e.g., from Florida and California) or other goods. The females of Black Widows (5 NA species are known) pose a significant threat (the smaller males cannot bite), with a neuro-venom rated 15 times more toxic than rattlesnake venom. Fortunately, only minimal venom is injected with a bite, so that fewer than 1% of cases are fatal. These spiders are instantly recognizable by the black, rounded body (13 mm long), highlighted on the abdomen by a red or orange, hour-glass-shaped pattern.

An interesting family represented in MB is the jumping spiders (Salticidae), with 35 species, averaging only 6 mm in length, but brightly coloured mimics of flowers, where they usually sit waiting to pounce on incoming insects. They have binocular vision like humans with 2 of their 8 eyes enlarged and situated on the front of their face. Examples are *Evarcha hoyi* in mixed forests and meadows, and *Habronattus altanus* on the prairies. The wolf spiders (family Lycosidae) are large (10-22 mm), hairy, fast-moving predators with strong jaws and good eyesight. Typical species are *Geolycosa missouriensis* of sand dunes and plains, and *Pardosa xerampelina* of mixed forests, riverbanks and beaches. The females of this family carry their egg sac by attaching it to their spinnerets.

Fall is a time when spiders seem to appear from nowhere and enter houses or spread webs across windows and doors. Orbweavers (family Araneidae) are most noticeable at this time, as most species lay their eggs in the fall and the female's abdomen can be quite large prior to making the egg sac. Common species include *Araneus gemmoides* and *Araneus trifolium*. Another group of spiders common around buildings is the funnelweb spiders (family Agelenidae). These spiders produce the easily recognized funnel-shaped web, and the MB species are typically most active in the fall as they look for mates prior to winter. Examples include *Agelenopsis utahana* and *Agelenopsis actuosa*. While the cold winters of MB kill off many spiders, some remain active under an insulating blanket of snow, where temperatures usually range from -3 to -10C. Dwarf sheet-web weavers (family Linyphiidae) such as the Hammock Spider (Pityohyphantes costatus) have been found active down to -8C. These are the most numerous winter-active spiders, but there are others including juveniles of summer-active species. Occasionally these spiders appear on the surface of the snow when the air is around 0˚C.

There are no NA spiders that are fully aquatic, but some could be described as semi-aquatic – hunting along beaches, mud flats, rocky shores, and even dashing out on the water surface to capture stranded prey or creatures inhabiting the surface film. In MB, there are 4 species of dock spiders (family Pisauridae), which are

Spiders are found throughout Manitoba but none are dangerous to humans.

capable of diving below the surface and remaining submerged for over 45 minutes while hunting for insects and small fish. On land, the female protects her egg case by carrying it in her fangs, later attaching it to a shore plant with a nursery web, where the spiderlings emerge. Two species (*Dolomedes scriptus, D. tenebrosus*) can grow to a body length of 25 mm with a leg span of 6 cm, making them the largest spiders in MB and Canada. Many cottagers are only too familiar with these 2 species, as they commonly take up residence under any shelter along the water's edge. • REW, DJW

SPIRIT SANDS. *See* **Carberry Sand Hills**.

SPIVAK, Sidney Joel, Lawyer, businessman, politician, (b May 23, 1928, **Winnipeg**; d July 8, 2002, Winnipeg) received his law degree from the **U of M** in 1951. He also attended Harvard U, receiving a Master of Laws degree in 1952. From 1966-1979, Spivak represented the **Progressive Conservatives** as MLA for the River Heights riding in Winnipeg. He served under Premiers **Duff Roblin, Walter Weir** and **Sterling Lyon**, holding a variety of cabinet positions. In 1971, Spivak defeated **Harry Enns** to become leader of the PC party. He was leader of the official opposition from 1971-1975. When **Ed Schreyer** and the **New Democratic Party** won the 1973 provincial election, some PC party members blamed Spivak. Considered a Red Tory, Spivak was often at odds with the right wing of the caucus and the party. In 1975, Sterling Lyon beat him at a leadership convention. In the 1977 election, Lyon and the PCs defeated Schreyer and the NDP, giving Spivak another chance to serve in cabinet. However, he chose to resign his seat to run in the 1979 federal election. He lost to **Liberal Lloyd Axworthy**.

A strong supporter of Israel, Spivak was involved in organizations such as B'nai Brith, Jewish National Foundation and the Canada-Israel Committee. Spivak served on the board of governors of the U of M and as a director of St. Boniface Hospital. He was also chairman of the

Refugee Assistance Committee, resettling Vietnamese boat people in Winnipeg. PM Brian Mulroney appointed his wife, Mira Spivak, (b July 12, 1934), a long-time party organizer and school trustee, to the Canadian Senate in 1986. • KAREN OMELAN/SANDY CUSHON

SPLIT LAKE CREE FIRST NATION. *See* **Tataskweyak Cree Nation**.

SPOHR, Theodore "Arnold," dancer, choreographer (b Dec 26, 1927, Rhein, SK) led the **Royal Winnipeg Ballet** as artistic director for 30 years. For his innovative and daring approach to choreography, he is credited for helping the organization attain its current position as one of Canada's most internationally acclaimed performing ensembles. Born in a small community about 50 km NE of Yorkton, SK, Spohr received dance training in London, UK; New York; and Hollywood. He got his start as a professional dancer in 1945 with the Winnipeg Ballet, where he performed for 9 years, eventually becoming a principal dancer. In 1957, he was appointed the interim artistic director, becoming permanent artistic director in 1958.

After a fire destroyed the RWB studios, including choreographic records, sets, scores, and costumes, in Jun 1954, Spohr was determined to restore and revitalize the company. During his travels, Spohr sought out interesting choreographers to help develop the company's repertoire of short ballets that would please varied audience tastes. Under his direction, the company had numerous successful national and international tours, and the RWB developed a reputation as an accessible ballet company, willing to perform in communities both large and small. During Spohr's tenure, the RWB also began to mount full-length classical ballets. Spohr helped to direct the summer school at the Banff Centre for Continuing Education. After leading the RWB through decades of outstanding achievement, Spohr retired in 1988, though he retains an advisory role at RWB as artistic director emeritus. For his accomplishments in the arts, he was inducted into the Order of Canada as an Officer (1970), and was later promoted to Companion (2004). He was also the recipient of the Gov Gen Performing Arts Award (1998). • JILL SEXSMITH

SPONGE is a simple, yet multi-cellular aquatic animal (class Desmospongiae, phylum Porifera) which grows into an asymmetrical colony, but with no distinct separation of individuals. A supporting structure is made of the tough protein collagen, strengthened by tiny calcareous or siliceous needles (spicules). A sponge forms a cup, mat or crust on rocks, plants, branches and other stable objects, mostly in shallow (usually <2m; seldom to 50 m) standing or running water. They range from 1 cm² to 40 m², and 1 mm to 4 cm thick, but the underlying layers are likely dead cells from previous years' growth. The thin-walled body consists of 2 types of cells – collar cells serving digestive and sperm-generating functions, and amoebocytes which produce eggs and spicules. Water containing algae, bacteria and debris is swept into the hollow interior of the sponge by hairs (flagella) on the collar cells distributed around numerous pores (ostia) on the sponge surface. Food items are trapped in mucous or simply engulfed, and the water leaves through one or more vents. Of about 5000 living species of sponges, most are tropical and marine. Only one of several freshwater families (Spongillidae) is found in MB and NA freshwaters. They are common in clean ponds, lakes and rivers, but are seldom

Sidney Spivak 1975 (L), Mira Spivak 1971 (R)

Arnold Spohr, 1958

UMA, TRIBUNE, PERSONALITY FILES

noticed because of their camouflaging shape and colour (green, yellow or brown) and resemblance to algae. In fact, green algae may live in the cells of the sponge. Sponges reproduce by both asexual (from buds or broken pieces) and sexual means (some species are hermaphrodites; in others the sexes are separate). A highly resistant resting stage (gemmule) is produced, which can withstand repeated freezing and drying. There are several species of freshwater sponges in MB – *Spongilla lacustris*, *Eunapius fragilis* and *Ephydatia muelleri* – and likely a few more will be discovered. One species of marine sponge (*Hymeniacidon heliophila*) is known from Hudson Bay near MB, and other species have been collected, but are as yet unidentified and unstudied. Sponges are among the most-primitive of the living phyla, found in fossils of great antiquity – 700 million years old (Neoproterozoic period). • REW

SPRAGUE, pop 300, is located 185 km SE of **Winnipeg**, near the Sandilands Provincial Forest and is the gateway to NE Minnesota. The community got its name from Daniel Eames Sprague, a friend of the Prince of Wales, who was awarded a timber grant in the area around 1885. The railway came to Sprague in 1900. The first school, which was one-room, was built in 1917. It was renovated into a 4-room school, and has since been built up to a 14-room institution. The first hotel was constructed in 1926. The community has 3 churches: Sprague Baptist, Peniel Full Gospel, and the Roman Catholic Church. The local post office services the communities of Sprague, Vassar, South Junction, and Middlebro. Each August, Sprague hosts a celebration called Western Fest. MB's eastern-most border crossing is located in Sprague. • GPP

SPRINGTAIL is a primitive, minute (1-9 mm), wingless type of insect in the class Collembola (phylum Uniramia), which happens to be one of the most-common animals in MB, yet people seldom notice them. It is a hunchbacked creature characterized by a forked spring mechanism on the abdomen, formed by the partially joined 4th or 5th appendages, which fits into a catch plate on the 3rd. When released, the spring (furcula) strikes the ground with a force sufficient to catapult the insect 1-30 cm through the air at speeds up to 970 m/sec, thereby escaping attack. The head bears either chewing or sucking mouthparts, a number of eyes (often 8), and a pair of antennae. A tube-like structure (collophore) is used to adhere the springtail to a surface, but it also serves other functions – water transport, excretion, respiration, and produces a lubricant

for grooming the legs. The body may be spindly to lumpy, smooth, scaly, or hairy, and either brightly or somber coloured. Crawling on 3 pairs of legs, springtails literally swarm in the soil (50,000-400,000/m²), down to a depth of about 150 cm. They occur in almost all habitats of the world (even in Antarctica), but are particularly abundant in damp soil and leaf litter, and often occur in moist places in the home. A few species congregate on top of the snow in spring and are consequently called 'snowfleas,' while others live on plants, at the surface of ponds (feeding on algae), or in sand and mud beaches of lakes, rivers, and the intertidal zone of Hudson Bay. Although incredibly abundant in both species and numbers of individuals, the life history of most springtails is unknown. There are no estimates of the number of species found in MB, but likely over 200 exist (so far 675 in Canada and US, 8000 worldwide). They are an important component at lower levels of the food web, feeding on plants, fungi and organic debris, and in turn are preyed upon by other small creatures in the soil (e.g., worms) and in water (e.g., fish fry). Occasionally they may damage seedlings of garden plants and commercial crops, examples being the Garden Springtail (*Bourletiella hortensis*) and the Lucerne Flea (*Sminthurus viridis*). This is an ancient form of animal life, known as far back as 400 million years ago (Devonian period). • REW, TDG

SPRUCE. MB has 2 species of native spruce, black (*Picea mariana*) and white (*Picea glauca*). Both are evergreen, softwood coniferous (cone-bearing) trees. They, along with tamarack (*Larix laricina*), are the most widespread trees in the boreal forest zone and occur throughout MB except for the far NE arctic and SW prairie areas. White spruce is the provincial tree of MB and prefers moist but well-drained soils. Large trees grow on the sand hills in SW MB, outside of the normal range. Spruce trees are often planted as shelterbelt throughout southern MB. Spruce forms the twisted 'krumholz' trees near **Hudson Bay** at **Churchill** but usually it has a broad triangular shape. Especially large and beautiful trees grow in **Riding Mountain National Park**. Black spruce is the characteristic evergreen tree of bogs and other wet acid areas, often growing with the deciduous tamarack. It is smaller and narrower than white spruce and often has a distinct cluster of branches ('crow's nest') near its tip.

While Manitobans tend to call all evergreen needle-leaved trees 'pines' or 'spruces', they are easy to tell apart. Pines have their needles in bundles of 2 or more, while spruces and firs have them singly along their twigs. Spruce needles

The White Spruce is the provincial tree of Manitoba.

are 4-sided, stiff and sharp while fir needles are flat and soft, with 2 white lines underneath. Black and white spruce can be difficult to tell apart but you can usually identify them by their habitat, twigs and cones. Young white spruce twigs are thick and smooth at their tips. Black spruce twigs are thinner and covered with tiny rust-coloured hairs between the needles. Their cones are smaller (1.5-3 cm long) and nearly round while those of white spruce are 2.5-5 cm long and twice or more as long as wide. Native peoples used the pitch, bark, needles, roots and wood of both spruces for a wide variety of purposes. Early Europeans made 'spruce beer' from the young twigs in spring. The 2 spruces make up about 40% of MB's annual forest harvest. Most of the wood is used for pulp and turned into paper products. Some white spruce is used locally as lumber, black spruce usually being too small and twisted for this purpose, and both are used as firewood. The cones of both spruces are the main source of food for red squirrels. The non-native Colorado Blue Spruce (*Picea pungens*) is often seen in ornamental plantings in southern MB. It has much longer cones than either native spruce. • KAREN JOHNSON

SQUIRREL is a prominent group of rodents in the family Sciuridae (order Rodentia) found almost worldwide. While most people know that there are several kinds of squirrels living in MB, there are actually 10 species represented here. In the grassland are 3 short-tailed ground squirrels – Richardson's (*Spermophilus richardsonii*)

ROBERT R. TAYLOR

which is sandy in colour; Thirteen-lined (*S. tridecemlineatus*), smaller and yellow with brown stripes; and Franklin's (*S. franklinii*), grey and preferring shrubs nearby. There are 4 long-tailed tree squirrels found in both deciduous and coniferous forests, including the Red Squirrel (*Tamiasciurus hudsonicus*), reddish, common and noisy; Grey Squirrel (*Sciurus carolinensis*), large, common in towns, and first invading S MB in 1930 (introduced by people); Fox Squirrel (*Sciurus niger*), invading around 1970 from ND, and resembling the Grey, but with a rusty belly and black-tipped tail hairs; and the Northern Flying Squirrel (*Glaucomys sabrinus*), secretive, nocturnal, greyish-brown, and with a flattened, feather-like tail. The largest local member is the Woodchuck or groundhog (*Marmota monax*), which is found from the prairies to open spruce-tamarack woodland reaching as far N as York Factory on **HUDSON BAY**. It inhabits the edges of meadows and roadways, retreating with a loud, quivering whistle to its underground burrow on the approach of a predator. The Arctic Ground Squirrel (*Spermophilus parryii*) inhabits the gravel ridges along the coastal tundra N of Churchill. It was only discovered in MB in 1973, by the author. Finally, there are 2 species of chipmunks – the smaller Least Chipmunk (*Eutamias minimus*) widespread in shrubs and deciduous and coniferous forests, and the larger, rusty-rumped Eastern Chipmunk (*Tamias striatus*), which is found only in deciduous forests and shrubs of S MB.

While the tree squirrels remain active through the winter, the ground squirrels, chipmunks, and Woodchuck are profound hibernators, remaining underground for half the year or longer. Several m below the surface, these rodents experience a remarkable reduction in metabolism, and breathing and heart rates, barely surviving until their biological clock and the warming soil trigger their release back to activity and a life in the sun. The males generally emerge 2 weeks before the females, coming into reproductive condition and mating with each female as she becomes active. This ability to pass such a lengthy unfavourable season, while food resources are inaccessible, is instrumental in these species being able to live in Canada. While the chipmunks and tree squirrels offer people an interesting opportunity to observe wildlife in their yards, park, or cottage, the ground squirrels and Woodchuck may become serious problems. They devour much grain and vegetables, compete with domestic stock for forage, and on occasion harbor disease – Richardson's Ground Squirrels W of MB have been known to harbour fleas that carry plague. However, they play

Noisy Red Squirrels are the bane of dogs.

significant roles in prairie and meadow ecosystems, and are preyed upon by legions of predators – particularly birds and mammals. Certain species, such as the endangered Ferruginous Hawk and the American Badger, concentrate on ground squirrels for food, and would likely disappear from MB were it not for the great numbers of these squirrels.

The Richardson's Ground Squirrel (commonly called "gopher") is an abundant and highly visible animal of the Prairies, 28 cm long and weighing 400 g. Before an adult enters hibernation (as early as July for some), it can weigh up to 655 g including a thick layer of fat. The diet consists of leaves, seeds and roots of hundreds of plant species, as well as insects (like grasshoppers) and carrion. The mating season lasts from late March through April, with both sexes taking several partners. About 22 days later, 3-13 young are born in a grass-lined underground nest. Young appear aboveground in May and June, and disperse 3-10 km during the summer. They must grow quickly, devouring prodigious amounts of food to ensure a sufficient fat reserve to survive the upcoming hibernation period, usually beginning in Sept or Oct. Life expectancy is 2 years, but 6 years is possible. This species demonstrates complex social behaviour, utilizing many kinds of gestures, calls (some ultrasonic) and scents in their communication. The home range is small, usually less than 1 ha and the burrow system extends 4-15 m and descends over 2 m deep, well below the frost line. Population density is often 1-5/ha, but can reach 27/ha. Main predators are hawks,

weasels, foxes and badger, and many are killed along highways by vehicles.

The Red Squirrel (weighing 200 g) is a noisy and bold creature commonly found in coniferous forest, since it specializes in extracting and eating the seeds of spruce and pine cones. In fact it is one of the few mammals that can make a living in Jack Pine forest and dwarf White Spruce woodland of the forest-tundra transition – both meagre environments. In MB, it can also occur in deciduous forest and oak-aspen savanna, where its rounded summer nest of grass and leaves can be seen built in the fork of a tree branch. In winter the squirrel usually nests underground, but its sign of tracks and middens of cone scales can be observed in the snow over its 1.5 ha home range. Defending its caches of seeds, dried berries and fungi is critical to its survival during the lean months of winter, which explains why the squirrel frequently patrols its territorial borders and announces its ownership with chirring calls and chirps. An unwary competitor (even a Grey Squirrel 3 times its weight) is quickly attacked with the resident's sharp incisors, and sent on its way. The 2 sexes come together briefly to mate in April or May, and 1-8 young are born 35 days later; a few females produce a second litter in Aug. While most individuals survive only a couple of years, they may reach 10 years in captivity. **HAWKS**, **OWLS**, **CANADIAN LYNX**, American Marten and Fisher are dependant on this species as predominant prey, but it takes lightning speed on the ground or in the trees to capture a Red Squirrel. ● REW

SS *Princess* on Lake Winnipeg

SS PRINCESS. The *Princess* was a **STEAMBOAT** christened in Aug 1881 by the gov gen, John Douglas Sutherland Campbell, Marquess of Lorne, to honour his wife, Princess Louise, 4th daughter of Queen Victoria. Despite her auspicious launch, the *Princess* sank while crossing **LAKE WINNIPEG** on Aug 26, 1906, resulting in 6 deaths, including that of the skipper, John Hawes. On her 400-km voyage from Warren Landing, about 30 km S of **NORWAY HOUSE**, to **SELKIRK**, she carried a crew of 10 with 11 passengers and a full cargo of fish. The *Princess* started taking on water after winds shifted. When efforts to bail out the water proved futile, Hawes became paralysed by fear, and only agreed to run for the lee of nearby George's Island after his mate pressured him to do so. With wind and water tearing at the stricken ship, the engine failed, and the *Princess* was swept broadside. Towering waves of nearly 8 m crashed down, sending the smokestack to the bottom of the hull. Just as the ship was breaking in half, 14 survivors piled into the yawl, pulling a woman and her baby from the water as the strong winds pushed them from the sinking wreckage. As dawn came, the survivors were still unable to put back into the wind for a rescue mission, though they could hear the singing of the doomed crew and passengers until the last remnants of the *Princess* foundered. ● AJL

STACK, Frank, speed skater (b Jan 1, 1906, **WINNIPEG**; d Jan 25, 1987, Winnipeg) won Canada's first Olympic medal in speed skating, establishing MB's medal-winning tradition in the sport. Stack's father had him skating competitively at the age of 13, though finding a suitable training facility at the time was no easy task. Training on the **RED RIVER** in West Kildonan, Stack had to clear away the snow himself before practicing. His first major wins came in 1931 when he won the US National Outdoor Championship and the Senior Men's title at the World Indoor Championships in Chicago, establishing a world record in the 5 mi race. In total, he won the Cdn championship 6 times. Representing Canada at the 1932 Lake Placid Olympics, Stack earned a bronze medal in the 10,000 m. He was named to the 1936 Olympic team as well, but couldn't secure the funding needed to attend. As the Olympics were cancelled during WWII, Stack didn't have a chance to compete again until the 1948 Olympic Winter Games at St. Moritz, Switzerland, where he placed 6th in the 500 m. He attended the 1952 Oslo Olympics as both a coach and an athlete. Stack enjoyed competitive skating, and at the age of 60 he competed in the National Indoor Speed Skating Championship. He was inducted into the Canada's Sports Hall of Fame in 1974. ● MD

STANDARD AERO LIMITED is a leading international supplier of aircraft-engine maintenance, repair, and overhaul services. Headquartered in **WINNIPEG**, the company got its start in 1911 when local businessmen Charles Pearce and William Bucknell founded Standard Machine Works. Initially, the company specialized in repairing and overhauling rebuilt automotive engines. However, in the late 1920s, it expanded into the repair and overhaul of aircraft engines, and subsequently changed its name to Standard Aero Engine Works. In the 1960s, it began overhauling turboprop and turboshaft engines, and in 1978 changed its name to Standard Aero Limited to reflect the fact it did more than just repair and overhaul aircraft engines. Today, the company has 3 primary operating divisions – a commercial services division in Winnipeg, which repairs and overhauls engines used in regional and business planes and helicopters; a govt services division in San Antonio, TX, which works on engines for govt and military planes and helicopters; and an energy division in Tilburg, Netherlands, which provides maintenance and repair services for industrial gas turbines and power packages used in the energy, oil and gas, and marine industries. As of 2004, the company employed more than 2600 people in 6 different countries, including about 1250 in Winnipeg, and had reported sales of $786.6 million US. That same year, the company also underwent another ownership change when Doughty Hanson, a UK equity firm, sold it to another UK-based equity firm – The Carlyle Group – for $670 million US. ● MM

STARBUCK, pop 350, is a community located 32 km W of **WINNIPEG**, by the La Salle River in the RM of MacDonald. Farmers first settled this area in the 1870s. The railway arrived in 1881. The railway contractor named the station "Starbuck," after a village by the same name in Minnesota. In 1884, the **CPR** took over construction of the railway line that later became known as the CPR's **SOURIS** line. By 1909, Starbuck had become a booming agricultural community thanks to its grain elevator storage capacity and its twice-a-day passenger rail service. The community had 2 general stores, a butcher, blacksmith, a bank, and a hotel. In the 21st century, the passenger train service may have stopped, but Starbuck has the amenities of a larger town, including shops, 3 churches, an elementary school, a recreation centre, plus an 18-hole golf course. Given that the community is only a 20-minute drive to Winnipeg, many residents commute. ● GPP

STARKELL, Don, paddler, adventurer (b Dec 7, 1932, **WINNIPEG**) paddled from Winnipeg to Brazil, setting a Guinness Book world record for the world's longest canoe trip. From an early age, Starkell enjoyed testing his physical limits, once swimming across **LAKE WINNIPEG** on a whim. Starkell went on his first major canoe trip at the age of 34 when he entered and won the Centennial Trans-Canada canoe race.

After planning for years to go on a canoe trip to Brazil, Starkell set off with his 2 sons on June 1, 1980 in a 21-ft-long canoe, which weighed over 450 kg when loaded with supplies and food. To reach the Amazon, the group had to paddle down the **RED RIVER**, Mississippi River, Intecoastal Waterway, Orinoco River, and Rio Negro. The journey was fraught with difficulties. Starkell and his sons endured dehydration, severe sunburn, and near starvation. They were robbed, jailed and, in one terrifying incident, almost executed by Central American bandits. Unwilling to continue on the dangerous trip, Starkell's youngest son returned home after reaching Mexico. Starkell and his eldest son continued on, arriving in Belem, Brazil, on May 2, 1982. It took nearly 2 years to reach the Amazon, and Starkell and his son had paddled approximately 20,000 km.

Starkell's adventures did not end there. In 1984, he cycled from Winnipeg to PEI. After paddling from Vancouver, BC, to Ketchikan, AK, in

655

1986, Starkell dreamt up the idea of making the world's longest kayak trip through the Cdn Arctic. He made 3 attempts to complete the 4800 km journey from **Churchill** to Tuktoyaktuk, NT, coming within kms of his destination in the last try before succumbing to frostbite. Starkell has written 2 books about his adventures: *Paddle to the Amazon* (1987) and *Paddle to the Arctic* (1995). Over the course of his life, Starkell has paddled the circumference of the Earth 3 times. ● MD

STEAD, Robert James Campbell, author (b Sept 4, 1880, Middleville, ON; d Jun 26, 1950, Ottawa), has been identified with the "Prairie Realism" mode in Cdn literature. Though born in ON's Ottawa Valley, he grew up in **Cartwright** from the age of 2, and edited the Cartwright weekly newspaper then the **Crystal City** *Courier* before moving to Calgary in 1912. Perhaps in recognition of the attention his writing drew to the abundance promised by the Cdn West, he was appointed publicity director for the colonization branch of the **CPR** in 1913, and publicity director for the federal department of immigration and colonization in 1919, becoming director of publicity for the federal department of mines and resources 1936-46. He was elected president of the Canadian Authors Association in 1923.

Initially, Stead published several volumes of intensely patriotic verse, such as *The Empire Builders and Other Poems* (1908). His subsequent novels, set on the Cdn Prairies, similarly extolled British ideals of loyalty and fortitude in the lives of the homesteaders, and attracted a wide popular audience. Nonetheless, though these tales of achievement through dedication and high spiritual integrity have been compared to the robust romanticism of Ralph Connor, works such as *Grain* (1926) offer a perceptive and realistic account of pioneer hardship, of isolation and loneliness, and of the daily details of homesteader existence. ● MILDRED GUTKIN

STEAMBOATS were the primary means of transportation for goods and people on the **Red River** in the 1860s and '70s, until the arrival of the **CPR**. Though first run commercially in NA at the start of the 19th century, they only began operating in what is now MB in 1859, after the US govt allowed **HBC** goods to be carried through the US, thanks to prodding from Sir **George Simpson** When the bulk of traffic shifted from **Hudson Bay** to the railhead at St. Paul, MN, the Chamber of Commerce in St. Paul offered a reward of $1000 (USD) to anyone who would launch a steam vessel on the Red River and sail it to **Upper Fort Garry**. MN hotelier Anson Northup agreed to do it for double the reward. He disassembled his small vessel,

named the *North Star*, and dragged it 240 km overland from the headwaters of the Mississippi to the Red, a task requiring 60 men, 26 oxen, and 17 horses. In 1859, the new boat, renamed *Anson Northup*, sailed to the **Red River Settlement**. Her 100-hp boilers burnt a cord of wood an hour.

The HBC steamer *International*, which the company bought in 1862 to ferry trade goods, brought many hundreds of settlers to MB. On July 31, 1874, 50 families of Russian **Mennonites** landed; in 1875, she brought more than 270 **Icelanders**. At 42 m, bow to stern; a beam of 8 m; and a 6 m draft, she was the largest of the Red River steamers.

To handle shallow Prairie rivers, steamboats were often equipped with spars and tackle forward of the mast. Aground, a spar would be lowered through rings on the side of the hull, with a tackle attached to the top, leading down through a turning block to the capstan. The hull was lifted slightly, and engines were run either to clear or back off the obstacle. Steamers were usually loaded more heavily at the head, so that when the bow cleared, the craft would not hang up amidships. In this way, the craft might "walk" or "grasshopper" over obstacles. Other steamers and paddlewheelers that plied the more shallow **Assiniboine River** depended on this system.

In 1871, the American govt decided that only US-registered ships could carry freight on US waterways and across the border. The *SS International*, of British registry, was put out of business for the time being. James Hill, the Cdn transportation baron who made his fortune in the US Northwest, decided to get into the burgeoning Red River trade. He commissioned the construction of a new ship, the *Selkirk*, a smaller version of the grand Mississippi riverboats, ushering in the golden age of Red River shipping. The Red River Transportation Company, owned by St. Paul, MN, businessman Norman Kittson, was the dominant force on the Red River, operating the *Dakota*, *Cheyenne*, and *Alpha* steamboats. In 1874, a syndicate of MB and St. Paul businessmen formed the Merchants International Steamboat Line in an effort to drive down freight rates. The following year, they launched the *Manitoba* and the *Minnesota*, but after one year, these ships were sold to the Red River Transportation Company, now backed by the HBC.

In 1877, the *Selkirk* brought by barge MB's first locomotive, the *Countess of Dufferin*. The arrival of the railway signalled the end of the steamboats on the Red River. While traffic continued for a few years, railways were now the preferred method to move goods and people. The last commercial steamer run, by the *Grand Forks*, arrived in **Winnipeg** June 7, 1909. By 1912,

extraordinarily dry **Weather** had lowered water levels to make passage impossible for even shallow-draft steamers, though freighters and pleasure steamers continued for decades on **Lake Winnipeg** and the lower Red. ● MICHELLE DOBROVOLNY

▸ *See also* **SS *Princess*.**

Thomas Steen's entire NHL career was with the Winnipeg Jets.

STEEN, Thomas, **Hockey** player (June 8, 1960, Tockmark, Sweden). One of the most popular players to don the jersey of the **Winnipeg Jets**, Steen was a creative, hard-nosed, 2-way centre that spent his entire 14-year NHL career with the team. At the age of 15, Steen played junior hockey with the Grums IK club before jumping to Elitserien (Swedish Elite League) teams Leksands in 1976, and later Farjestads. The Jets selected him in the 5th round (103rd overall) of the 1979 NHL entry draft, just after the NHL accepted the team from the World Hockey Association (WHA). The WHA Jets had been successful in large part because of Swedish players Anders Hedberg, Ulf Nilsson, and Lars-Erik Sjöberg.

Steen made his NHL debut during the 1981-82 season, scoring 44 points in 73 games as a rookie, though the Calder Trophy-winning, 103-point rookie performance of **Dale Hawerchuk** garnered far more attention. His breakthrough 84-point season helped the Jets to their best record ever in 1984-85, but it was in 1988-89 that Steen seemed to enter his prime. His career best 88 points were followed by 3 injury-filled campaigns, though he managed well more than a point-per-game average in each. He was a co-captain of the team from 1989-91, and played his final season in 1994-95. Steen's jersey #25 was retired during an emotional ceremony at the **Winnipeg Arena** on May 6, 1995, making him only the 2nd Jet to be honoured in this manner (after **Bobby Hull**). He finished with 817 career points, and holds the franchise records for most games played (950) and most assists (553).

Steen also played for his country during 3 world junior championships, 3 world championships (winning silver medals in 1981 and 1986), and the 1981, 1984, and 1991 Canada Cup tournaments. Following his retirement from the NHL, Steen returned to Europe to play in the Deutsche Eishockey Liga (Germany's top league). He suited up for the Frankfurt Lions in 1995-96 and then Eisbaren (Berlin Polar Bears) from 1996-97 until his retirement in 1999.

Since leaving the game as a player, Steen has remained involved in hockey, including serving as an assistant coach for Swedish team Vastra Frolunda, a scout for the Minnesota Wild, and operating a hockey school in Orsa, Sweden. His **Winnipeg**-born son Alexander Steen was a first-round draft choice of the Toronto Maple Leafs, and began his NHL career with the team in 2005. ● JOEL TRENAMAN

STEFANSSON, Baldur Rosmund, agricultural researcher (b Apr 26, 1917, Vestfold; d Jan 3, 2002, **Winnipeg**). Often referred to as the "father of **Canola**," Stefansson grew up on a family farm started by his parents, pioneering **Icelanders**. He served in WWII before studying **Agriculture** at the **U of M**. He earned a diploma in 1949, and a BSc in 1950. He finished an MSc 2 years later, and began teaching in the department of plant science. Stefansson completed his PhD in 1966.

At Agriculture Canada, Stefansson worked with Keith Downey on oilseed research and breeding that transformed rapeseed, a mustard-like plant whose oil was used industrially, into edible **Canola** by reducing levels of erucic acid, a fatty acid that is potentially harmful if ingested in large amounts, and bitter compounds called glucosinolates. Stefansson registered the first canola variety, Tower, in 1974. Canola has since become very widely planted, and is used for animal feed and food oil. Stefansson continued to work on better hybrids and varieties of canola until he retired in 1986. He was made an Officer of the Order of Canada in 1985, and received the **Order of Manitoba** in 2000. ● JOEL TRENAMAN

STEINBACH, pop 11,066, MB's 6th-largest city and among its fastest-growing centres, is 50 km SE of **Winnipeg** on hwy 12. The city's name means "Stone Stream" in German, and was so named in 1874 – probably after Steinbach,

Ukraine – when about 20 **Mennonite** families of the "Kleine Gemeinde" came here to farm. This movement – later known as the Evangelical Mennonite Church and the Evangelical Mennonite Conference – was a smaller, more rigorous form of the Anabaptist faith which arose in Imperial Russia. Later, adherents to the other major strands of Mennonite belief came to Steinbach from various places – including Paraguay. Smaller numbers of **English** and of **German Lutheran** settlers came here as well. A post office opened in 1884, though the **Railway** never passed through – atypically, in this part of the province.

Education is important, with several schools, the Steinbach Bible College, and a campus of **Red River College**. The economy is diverse, and has been throughout the city's history. **Garment Manufacturing** once employed many locals. Tourism, principally to the Mennonite Heritage Village Museum and to the Pioneer Days festival, is significant. Manufacturing – including **Loewen Windows** – makes up a portion of Steinbach's economic base, but the largest industry is **Retail** (especially automobile sales) and **Service** support for surrounding **Agriculture**. The **Pharmaceutical Industry** also has a presence here in manufacturer **Biovail Corp**.

Award-winning novelist **Miriam Toews** was born here. Also from Steinbach are Albert Driedger, a former MB cabinet minister, and poet **Patrick Friesen**. The city's *Carillon* has among the highest circulations of weekly **Newspapers** in MB. ● GPP

Baldur Stefansson, 1975

Steinbach's Mennonite Heritage Village

STEINBERG, David, comedian, director, actor, writer, (b Aug 9, 1942, **Winnipeg**) was the youngest person to guest-host Johnny Carson's *Tonight Show*, and is 2nd only to Bob Hope in number of appearances on the program. Born and raised in Winnipeg's **North End**, Steinberg was the son of a Romanian rabbi, and, like US **Jewish** comedian Jackie Mason, was initially interested in theology. However, he lost interest in the rabbinate as a vocation after seeing Lenny Bruce perform. Steinberg moved to IL as a teenager to attend the U of Chicago, where he majored in English literature. While there, Steinberg joined the Second City comedy troupe. After a few years, he decided to perform solo. Steinberg's comedy routines revolved around his childhood and youthful rebellion against religion. Although he briefly wanted to be an actor, and performed in several Broadway productions in the late 1960s, his fame came from comedy. Steinberg appeared on *The Smothers Brothers Comedy Hour* in 1967, even contributing to the show's cancellation because of his irreverent "sermons."

He later hosted a successful CBS comedy variety series called *The David Steinberg Show*. This program launched the careers of many famous Cdn comedians, including John Candy and Martin Short. Steinberg had his directorial feature-film debut with *Paternity* (1981), starring Burt Reynolds, and directed an episode of *Newhart*. Steinberg was successful in TV, directing, acting, and executive-producing many episodes of *Designing Women*. Steinberg has also directed episodes of *Mad About You*, *Seinfeld*, *Friends*, and *Curb Your Enthusiasm*. Steinberg has released 4 solo comedy albums, and has directed over 300 commercials. He won 2 Emmy Awards for his writing on Oscar telecasts in the early 1990s. Steinberg has won almost every award in advertising, including 2 Clio Awards and the Silver Lion Award at the Cannes Lions International Advertising Festival. Steinberg was inducted into Canada's Walk of Fame in 2003. In 2002, Steinberg returned to his hometown to perform in the **CBC Winnipeg Comedy Festival**. In 2005-06, he created and hosted the talk show *Sit Down Comedy with David Steinberg* for the TV Land network. Steinberg was also the show's executive producer. ● Amanda Stephens

STEINKOPF, Helen, nurse, activist (b 1918, Chicago; d May 23, 2005, **Winnipeg**) worked for 55 years on behalf of those living with mental disabilities. The mother of a child with Down's syndrome, she endeavored to improve the quality of life of challenged people by pioneering group homes. As part of her commitment, she was instrumental in founding the Manitoba Marathon, which has raised millions of dollars for group homes since its inception in 1979.

Steinkopf focused much of her attention on Continuity Care, an organization dedicated to helping families plan a safer and more secure future for relatives living with a disability. She also advocated for tax deductions for the parents of Down's syndrome children who would have to continue supporting their children into adulthood. Before moving to Winnipeg from Chicago in 1947, Steinkopf practised nursing. She was the wife of MB politican **Maitland Steinkopf** She died while on the telephone seeking support for the Continuity Care Endowment Fund. ● JS

STEINKOPF, Maitland, Lawyer, politician (b Sept 10, 1912, **Winnipeg**; d Nov 22, 1970, Winnipeg). Steinkopf graduated in law from the **U of M** in 1936. As a student, he had organized the athletic board of control and was vice-president of the students' union. He succeeded his father Max as honorary consul for Czechoslovakia in 1937. During WWII, he served in the army. In 1962, he was elected MLA for River Heights, serving as provincial secretary and minister of public utilities. He was chair of the Manitoba Centennial Corporation from 1963 until his death. He also served as chair of a Special Committee of the Legislative Assembly on consumer credit in 1966. ● JMB

STEPHENSON, Sir William Samuel, "Intrepid," spy, soldier, entrepreneur, inventor (b Jan 11, 1896, or Jan 23, 1897, **Winnipeg**; d Jan 31, 1989, Paget, Bermuda). Stephenson's life is shrouded in mystery, making him a perplexing subject for biographers. What is known is that, from humble Winnipeg roots, Stephenson rose through the **Military**, became prominent in commerce, and headed British counterespionage in the western hemisphere during WWII.

William was likely born to a **English** father named Stanger and an Icelandic mother first-named Sarah. According to this view, after his father, possibly also William, died, Sarah passed William to the Icelandic **Immigrant** Stephensons for informal adoption. The Stephenson (originally Stefánsson) family appear to have lived on Point Douglas's Syndicate St in Winnipeg. William's adopted father is sometimes referred to as Vigfús or Vilhjálmur, though it is unlikely that the spy was the son of Arctic explorer Vilhjálmur Stefánsson. Rolls list a Lt W. H. Stephenson, presumed to be the adoptive father, as having succumbed to "enteric" (typhoid) in South Africa in 1902 while serving with the Canadian Scouts. However, other accounts claim the elder Stephenson died in 1900, and several Cdn Stephensons served in the Boer War and survived, including a William James Stephenson of the 5th Regt., Canadian Mounted Rifles, from **Portage la Prairie**. Adding to the confusion, at least 2 Cdn Stangers died in the war.

Young William seems to have left school after grade 6 to work as a telegraph operator and possibly also in a lumberyard. By other accounts, he attended Argyle High School, though Winnipeg had no school by that name until years later. After WWI broke out, Stephenson enlisted as a Pte either with the 101st Battery, Royal Canadian Engineers, or more likely with the 101st Batt, CEF (later folded into the Winnipeg Light Infantry). After basic training on the Prairies, he was sent to France, where he worked his way up to the rank of Sgt. After damaging his lungs in a German mustard-gas attack, Stephenson transferred out of the trenches, learned to fly, and transferred to the Royal Flying Corps, where he became Lt (and later a Capt). Despite the RFC pilots' sobriquet "20-Minuters," for their supposed life expectancy once airborne, Stephenson achieved at least 12 kills over France and undertook valuable surveillance flights. He was awarded the Military Cross, the Distinguished Flying Cross, and several French honours. In summer 1918, toward the end of the war, Stephenson was shot down and was taken prisoner by German forces. If accounts are to be believed, it was in this POW camp that Stephenson found his penchant for intrigue, supplying British GHQ, particularly RAdm Sir William "Blinker" Hall of British naval intelligence, with valuable information on the prison and on German operations.

After the war, Stephenson reputedly returned to Winnipeg to set up a hardware business, but when this failed, he left for England. There, and possibly at the **U of M**, he seems to have studied radio communication, an abiding interest: as a teenager, he is supposed to have built a radio transmitter and receiver set. However, he may also have acquired his knowledge of radio transmission while working as a telegraph operator. Whatever the source of this expertise, Stephenson was credited with developing the first wireless photograph transmission system – the ancestor of the fax machine. According to tradition, Stephenson's first transatlantic message transmitted with this technology was a photograph of his wife, Mary French Simmons, the daughter of a Tennesseean tobacco nabob; the pair had married in 1924, apparently after a visit by Stephenson to the US. Thanks to the proceeds of his invention, Stephenson purchased a firm that manufactured radios, then a new medium. Stephenson became a millionaire by age 30, diversifying into the film, television, and aircraft industries, and into coal mining, steel fabrication, and oil refining. In connection with his aviation enterprise, Stephenson may also have been associated with the development of the Supermarine (Vickers) Spitfire fighter.

Most elements of the stories of Stephenson's interwar years are inconsistent, and the young inventor's sudden success and wealth could have been staged – a cover to give industrial credentials to a man who was already spying for His Majesty. Stephenson expressed early concern over the rise of Nazism in Germany, probably because, as a steel merchant, he was aware of the Axis power's military buildup – a violation of the treaty ending WWI – after Hitler's rise to power.

William Stephenson

After WWII broke out, Stephenson became involved more or less immediately in co-ordinating covert activities, and may have helped secure a Nazi encryption machine. When Winston Churchill became PM in 1940, he appointed Stephenson head of the British Security Co-ordination, an arm of MI-6 headquartered in the still-neutral US. From New York's posh 5th Ave, Stephenson oversaw British espionage for the Americas, using as a cover the office of British Passport Officer. There he had the telegraphic address and codename "Intrepid." He soon hired a large number of Cdn women to staff the office, and who became key participants in both espionage and counter-espionage activities in NA.

Much of Stephenson's work at this time was kept and remain secret, leading to endless speculation about the exact role Stephenson played. Stephenson is supposed to have been involved in persuading the US public and govt to join WWII through propaganda and other means. He was instrumental in the establishment of a new US intelligence service, the Office of Strategic Services (OSS, predecessor to the Central Intelligence Agency) under US MGen William J. "Wild Bill" Donovan; he broke codes, monitored and censored messages, and undertook cloak-and-dagger operations against Axis countries. Stephenson may also have operated as a courier between the US president Roosevelt and PM Churchill, and he was almost certainly linked to the assassination of several Axis agents operating in NA. The former aviator was pivotal in the training of hundreds of Allied agents, establishing Camp X at the boundary between Whitby and Oshawa, ON, E of Toronto. Stephenson is supposed to have run afoul of J. Edgar Hoover, director of the Federal Bureau of Investigation, but the US administration clearly valued Stephenson's contribution, as he received the Presidential Medal for Merit, the highest US civilian award at the time, in 1946. For his services to the Empire, King George VI knighted Stephenson.

Stephenson's postwar activities are decidedly more straightforward than his earlier years, though even there, tantalizing clues stop short of revealing the man's full story; speculation centres in particular on his role, if any, in the Cold War. In 1946, Sir William moved to Jamaica, where he developed a cement plant. With former spy colleague Bill Donovan, Stephenson co-founded the New York–based British American Canadian Corporation (later the World Commerce Corporation), a trading company – and possibly a cover for secret agents – involved in redeveloping countries destroyed by the war through the Marshall Plan. Sir William sat on several Cdn boards, retiring to Bermuda in 1968, remaining there until his death in 1989.

In the Caribbean, Stephenson likely met former British spy Ian Fleming, who made annual visits to Jamaica from the end of WWII. Fleming later wrote a series of spy books with James Bond as the protagonist. Agent 007's exploits, though pure fantasy, were probably partly inspired by Stephenson, though by other accounts, the Manitoban served as the model for the character M. Attempts to unravel the real Bill Stephenson from the false have only prompted more questions. UK-born Cdn writer William Stevenson wrote 2 bestsellers about Stephenson: *A Man Called Intrepid* (1977) and *Intrepid's Last Case* (1983). The former of these was made into a miniseries in 1979, with David Niven playing

the role of Stephenson. *Goldeneye: The Secret Life of Ian Fleming*, a 1989 film based on a John Pearson book, cast Australian Ed Devereaux as Sir William. An earlier biography by IRISH-born Harford Montgomery Hyde, *The Quiet Canadian* (1962, published in the US as *Room 3603*) conflicts with these accounts; Bill MacDonald's *The True Intrepid: Sir William Stephenson and the Unknown Agents* (Vancouver: Raincoast, 2001) offers yet another perspective on the man's life. MacDonald's book inspired an hour-long TV documentary. In fairness to his biographers, the clever spy probably perpetuated falsehoods; Stephenson often used deliberate ruses, and was occasionally "seen" simultaneously on 2 different continents. The spy is also said to have suffered a stroke that may have impaired his memory, making some of his assertions suspect.

Besides his many military honours, Stephenson was inducted into the Order of Canada in 1979, and received honorary degrees from the U OF M and the U OF W. He established a $100,000 scholarship fund at the U of W. In 1982, he was made honorary Col Commandant of the Intelligence Branch of Canada's AIR FORCE. Sir William gave his name to a Winnipeg library branch, and to a school near where Camp X once stood in Whitby, ON. A bronze statue of "Intrepid" was erected before the LEGISLATIVE BUILDING in 1999; in 2000, a Canada Post stamp honoured this most mysterious of Winnipeggers. It is a pity that Stephenson's many contributions were not recognized during his lifetime, and remain poorly understood today. ● A. J. LEVIN

STEVENSON, Frederick J. "Stevie," air ace, pioneer bush pilot (b Dec 2, 1896, Parry Sound, ON; d Jan 5, 1928, THE PAS), grew up in WINNIPEG and at 18, left Wesley College (see U OF W) to join 196th University Batt, transferring to the Royal Flying Corps in 1917. In France, he destroyed 18 enemy aircraft and 3 observation balloons. By the end of WWI, he was a Capt, and held the Distinguished Flying Cross and the Croix de Guerre. Post-war, he ferried peace conference diplomats between London, UK, and Paris, and served as an RAF flying instructor in Russia.

In 1920, Stevenson joined the Canadian Aircraft Company in Winnipeg as a pilot, flying widely in MB and SK, contracting with towns for aerobatic exhibitions and short flights for passengers. For 2 years, he flew for the Ontario Provincial Air Service, then joined Western Canada Airways Ltd., flying heavy equipment in open-cockpit Fokker Universal aircraft from a base along the HUDSON BAY RAILWAY, often in severe winter conditions. These flights aided in the selection of CHURCHILL as an ocean terminus,

S

Frederick Stevenson in 1928 at The Pas

and marked the beginning of large-scale freighting by air in Canada.

In 1928, Stevenson died in a crash during a test flight out of The Pas. Months later, Winnipeg and the RM of St. James opened an airport W of the city, unveiling a plaque stating: "This aerodrome is named Stevenson Field in dedication to the late Captain F. J. Stevenson of Winnipeg, Canada's Premier Commercial Pilot." The airport was renamed Winnipeg International Airport in 1958, but the plaque still is on display. Stevenson is buried in nearby Brookside Cemetery. • JIM SHILLIDAY

STICK-INSECT, NORTHERN is a walkingstick insect of the family Heteronemiidae (order Cheleutoptera or Phasmatodea) represented by only one species in the province – *Diapheromera femorata*. It is found only in deciduous forest in extreme SC MB. The body is narrow and cylindrical, the abdomen ends in 2 paired filaments (cerci), wings are absent, and there are 3 pairs of long, slender legs which can break off easily as an escape mechanism (regenerated only by the nymph at the next moult). The antennae are slender and nearly as long as the body. Its colour is variable, ranging from grey, green or brown (males are usually brownish). The insect's shape and colour result in a remarkable degree of camouflage as it sits motionless during the day like a twig on a leaf or stem, usually high in the crown. If discovered, it feigns death. The male may reach 75 mm, the female 95 mm. The Northern Stick-insect feeds on the leaves of oak, hazel, and rose at night (mainly between 15:00 to 03:00 hours). If individuals become dislodged by the wind and fall to the ground, their instinct

is to climb back up to the tree crown. As adults mature in Aug-Sept, each female secretes sex pheromones which attract male suitors. The successful male mounts the female and fends off other males during the mating act, remaining coupled for many hours. Several hundred fertilized eggs (resembling plant seeds) are released by the female in Sept, which drop into leaf litter. They remain dormant there over winter and spring, then hatch from mid-June to mid-July. The nymphs are replicas of the adult form (i.e., no larval stage) and undergo 4-6 nymphal stages while growing in size before reaching the adult stage in Aug or early Sept. Although this species is the most-common stick-insect across NA, it is too rare and restricted in range in MB to cause damage to trees, but such injury has been reported in ON and in the US. Over 2500 species (some with wings) of stick-insects have been described, and several tropical species are the longest insects alive (max 56 cm). Most are arboreal but some live on the ground. • REW

STICKLEBACK, is a small (3-5 cm) fish in the family Gasterosteidae (order Gasterosteiformes) characterized by a row of 3-9 spines along the back. It is related to the bizarre seahorses and

The Brook Stickleback thrives in clear, cold waters.

pipefishes of tropical marine waters, with whom it shares the habit of the male tending the young. At the beginning of the breeding season in June or July, the male stickleback changes colour and constructs and guards a tunnel-shaped nest of plant debris, glued together with a kidney secretion. Through an elaborate courtship dance, he entices 1-7 successive females to lay their eggs in the nest, which he then quickly fertilizes. Another nest may be constructed while the eggs are developing. He keeps the eggs oxygenated and clean from silt by fanning with his fins and expelling water from his mouth, and aggressively drives away potential predators, even those larger than himself. He remains on guard until the fry disperse. Maximum lifespan is 3.5 years. The main food items are insects, crustaceans, fish eggs and fry, and algae. These small fish are important prey items for larger fish and birds. There are 3 species native to MB. The Brook Stickleback (*Culaea inconstans*) lives in clear, cold, weedy pools, streams, bogs, and retention ponds and ditches, where it is sometimes collected by youth and researchers to maintain in aquaria. It is found all over the province except the tundra. The Ninespine Stickleback (*Pungitius pungitius*) occurs in large rivers, stream and lakes all over the province, except in the grassland region. Populations along the coast of Hudson Bay may live in marine waters, but return to freshwater to spawn (anadromous). The Threespine Stickleback (*Gasterosteus aculeatus*) is the rarest and most localized of the 3 species, and occurs in migratory populations (anadromous) along the coast of Hudson Bay, as well as non-migratory, fully freshwater populations in lakes on the tundra. Due to their abundance and accessibility, sticklebacks are important in the diet of many fish and birds. • REW

STOCK, Sarah, wrestler (b Mar 4, 1979, WINNIPEG). Though virtually unknown in NA's wrestling circuit, Stock has made a name for herself as a *luchadora* or lady wrestler in Mexico's *lucha libre*. She attended St. John's-Ravenscourt, and received a chemistry degree from the U OF M. Though she had planned to study medicine, Stock developed an interest in fighting, initially as a kick boxer. When she didn't get as many fights as she had hoped for, Stock began looking to other contact sports for matches. In Dec 2001, she began training with the Winnipeg promotion Top Rope Championship Wrestling. Just 5 weeks into her training, Stock made her professional debut with Can-Am Wrestling, winning her first title in 2002. She went on to wrestle in several independent promotions throughout NA. Looking for opportunities to advance her career,

Sarah Stock, *luchadora*

Imaginal Expression, Detail 2, 2004, multimedia installation: 4 computer-controlled video projections, 14.63 x 2.74 m, by Reva Stone

S

Stock took advantage of her trainer's connections in the thriving wrestling circuit in Mexico, and jumped at the chance to join the *lucha libre*, a popular form of entertainment wrestling in Mexico where a wrestler's status is closely tied to their masked identity. In mask matches, a *luchadora* wins only after unmasking her opponent.

Adopting the stage name Dark Angel, Stock was the Lucha Libre Feminil Juvenil champion in 2003. In 2004, she switched to the Consejo Mundial de Lucha Libre (CMLL), one of the top Mexican promotions, where her skill and sex appeal brought her matches against some of Mexico's top *luchadoras*. Her muscular physique also won her the title in the CMLL's first female body building contest. Stock then won the first women's mask match at Arena Mexico, one of Mexico's oldest arenas, becoming the first female wrestler to unmask her opponent in the historic facility. ● MD

STONE, Reva, artist (b Aug 21, 1944, **Winnipeg**) received her BA from the **U of M** in 1968, and returned to the school in 1985 where she received her BFA. In 1990, she began her work with digital media with the work *Legacy*, which examined the gender stereotyping of children's toys. Since then, Stone has shown in various venues around the globe including Ottawa, Italy and Rotterdam. Her new media works and computer-based installations examine the effects between technology, the human body and the mind, and the interaction between them. She has participated in several residencies with such organizations as the Banff Centre for the Arts and the Art Gallery of Surrey. In 2004, a survey of her work entitled *Displacement* was exhibited at the **Winnipeg Art Gallery**, and in June 2007 Stone was inducted into the Royal Canadian Academy of Artists. She currently lives and practises in Winnipeg. ● STACEY ABRAMSON

STONEFLY is a 3-50 mm, aquatic, yellow or brown, soft-bodied insect in the order Plecoptera (class Insecta) with transparent wings that fold over the back. Although it is capable of flight, the insect prefers to retreat on its sturdy legs. It has 2 or 3 eyes (ocelli) and long segmented antennae. At least 40 species in 7 families have been recorded in MB (over 300 species in Canada, 485 NA, 2000 worldwide). While most species have wide distributions, others are highly localized, like *Capnia manitoba*, described in one spring near Treesbank in 1924, and recently found again in springs draining into the **Assiniboine River**. Stoneflies are an important component of aquatic ecosystems because of their enormous abundance and great value as a major food item in the diets of fishes, amphibians and birds. First Nations peoples used to prepare them for food, and fishing enthusiasts have long used the larvae (up to 9 cm long) as bait. Depending on the species, aquatic nymphs are plant eaters, detritus eaters, or predators on small creatures. Stoneflies are remarkable for their courtship rituals in which the male attracts females by sounds produced by drumming the abdomen on the ground. In other species, the 2 sexes alternate sounds in a kind of duet. The fertilized female then lays her egg mass in cool, clean water; the nymphs are intolerant of warm, poorly oxygenated, or polluted water. The gilled nymphs take refuge under debris or rocks. They require 2 or 3 years to complete their development, moulting over 25 times as they enlarge. Most adults have biting mouthparts, but many species do not feed, and so live only a few days, while others graze on algae and may survive for up to a month. This ancient group of insects appeared over 300 mya (Carboniferous period). ● REW, TDG

STONEWALL, pop 4376, is a town 30 km NW of **Winnipeg**. Listed as MB's 12th-largest urban centre, the 2006 census noted Stonewall was the province's 4th-fastest growing town, thanks largely to it being a "bedroom" or commuter community for Winnipeg. However, the town's economy is vibrant, based on a "business park" with a number of non-manufacturing/non-industrial businesses. There are 3 banks and a credit union, a district hospital, a variety of elderly-person housing, an RCMP detachment, and 2 large grocers.

The area was originally known by local Aboriginals as Thunder Hill. It was first settled in 1873 by **Samuel Jacob Jackson**, who donated the land that would become the townsite, and designed the street plan. The area's first major economic engine was limestone quarrying, which began in the 1880s, with several quarries. In 1904, one quarry employed 150 men producing building

661

S

Draw kilns at Stonewall Quarry Park

Amanda Stott

stone, 30 million l of lime, and 36,000 m³ of limestone rubble. Another shipped 2 trainloads of stone a day to Winnipeg. This activity ended in 1965. However, kilns from that era, just visible above the horizon, are the town's symbol in the 2000s. Many of Stonewall's significant buildings are made with limestone, including the town hall, post office, **ANGLICAN** Church, and the CIBC Building. Since the 1980s, an annual celebration on the main street has been the 3-day Quarry Days.

Stonewall was incorporated as a town in 1908. In 2001, half the town's population was under 45 years of age. Many residents work in Winnipeg. It also is a popular retirement location. From 2000 to 2006, 168 single-dwelling houses were built. In 2007 there was a 25-year space availability for 1100 more homes. The town, and nearby **OAK HAMMOCK MARSH**, are tourist attractions. A sports complex houses an arena, **CURLING** rink, skateboard facility, and has 5 soccer pitches. There are 9 **BASEBALL** diamonds at Fines Field (the 1999 **PAN AM GAMES** venue), which host national and western Cdn baseball championships each year. Quarry Park offers a museum, interpretive centre, and a walking trail. Kinsmen Lake, built in 1956, is popular with adults and children. McLeod House, where **VICTORIA CROSS** winner **ALAN ARNETT MCLEOD** lived, became a period tearoom early in the 21st century. Stonewall is no longer considered a farm-industry centre, but an annual agricultural fair is held S of town. ● JIM SHILLIDAY

STONY MOUNTAIN, pop 1757, is a community 25 km N of **WINNIPEG** on hwy 7. One of MB's earliest settlements, it is on a rise of 3 hills 1.5 km across and 20 m high. It was a refuge during 1852 **RED RIVER FLOODING**. Construction of the first federal penitentiary in western Canada, **STONY MOUNTAIN INSTITUTION**, was begun in 1874, partly to house prisoners held at Lower Fort Garry since the 1870 uprising. Made of local stone and bricks, it was finished in time to receive prisoners from the

1885 Riel Rebellion. The warden, Col Samuel Bedson, kept **BISON** that became the foundation herd for most of the bison populations on the continent today. British, Metis, and French settlers came to the community from the **RED RIVER SETTLEMENT**. A post office was established in 1873. The community was named Stony Mountain in 1880. The Stony Mountain Ski Area, which opened in 1966, has 6 runs and 2 lifts for skiing and snowboarding. The economy rests on the penitentiary, **BRISTOL AEROSPACE** rocket plant, and services and retail stores catering to agriculture. Stony Mountain has a fire department, curling rink, recreation centre, and elementary school. Hockey legend **WALTER "BABE" PRATT** was born here. ● GPP

STONY MOUNTAIN INSTITUTION, with the adjacent Rockwood Institution, is the only federal prison in MB. Located in the community of **STONY MOUNTAIN**, "Stony" is a medium-security institution for men. The penitentiary has space for 546 inmates. The facility opened in 1876, originally to house First Nations inmates. Chief Big Bear and Poundmaker were 2 well-known early inmates. Other inmates have included the wrongfully convicted Thomas Sophonow and David Milgaard. The prison gained media attention when it was seen in the television movie *Hard Time: The David Milgaard Story*. The prison also appeared in the film *Capote*, acting as a stand-in for Kansas State Penitentiary.

Stony Mountain Institution has featured frequently in the media in the first decade of the 21st century because of a significant problem with "drug-tossers," people who throw drugs over the prison gates for inmates to pick up and sell inside. In 2006, the penitentiary gained further attention when the Correctional Service of Canada banned indoor cigarette smoking in federal penitentiaries, and Stony Mountain took the ban a step further by prohibiting inmates from having matches or cigarette lighters. ● AMANDA STEPHENS

STOTT, Amanda, singer, entertainer (b May 6, 1982, **BRANDON**), is a successful pop/country and western performer. She started singing in a church choir at the age of 3. Stott's father is a musician, and together with her drummer brother, a family band was formed. She was performing on the festival and fair circuit in Canada by age 11, and drew attention at the 1994 **DAUPHIN COUNTRYFEST**. Stott signed with Warner Music Canada in 1999 and released a self-titled album the following year. She was nominated for a Juno Award for Best New Solo Artist in 2001, as well as the Rising Star Award, Outstanding Country Recording, and Outstanding Album for her debut. Her sophomore album, *Chasing the Sky*, appeared in 2005. Stott co-wrote over half the songs on this release. Stott's best-known singles are "Black Is Black"; "Paper Rain," which reached number-1 on the Canadian Top 40 Chart; "Homeless Heart"; and "She'll Get Over It." In 2006, Stott was featured as a singer in the travelling Cirque du Soleil show *Delirium*, and toured Canada and the US. ● AMANDA STEPHENS

STOUGHTON, Jeff, curler (b July 26, 1963, **WINNIPEG**) is a 2-time Brier winner and a world champion. Stoughton grew up in Winnipeg's Fort Garry neighbourhood, just a block from Wildewood **CURLING** Club where he threw his first rock at the age of 14. Coming from a family that often curled recreationally, Stoughton showed early promise. His first provincial title came in 1988, and he also won that year's Cdn mixed curling title. By 2007, Stoughton had won a total of 8 provincial titles in both mixed and men's curling, though he retired from mixed curling competition following his 1994 provincial win, opting to concentrate on men's competitions.

Stoughton is known for his "spin-o-rama," a move where he spins his entire body around while throwing the rock, which he does to amuse fans on unimportant shots. His greatest triumph came in 1996, when his team lost just 2 games on their way to a Cdn title, and were defeated only once en route to a world championship. He continues to curl from Charleswood Curling Club. His 2007 championship marked the 6th time that a MB curler has defended his provincial title. ● MD

STOVEL, LGen Richard Carlton, soldier (b March 31, 1921, **WINNIPEG**). Born and raised in Winnipeg and educated at the **U OF M**, Stovel joined the RCAF in 1940. After getting his wings later that year, Stovel trained aviators at a pilot school in Trenton, ON, and at Uplands, in the Ottawa area. He also flew WWII missions in Europe, most often in the speedy two-engine Mosquito. By 1944, he was a WCdr. After the war, he served as at Western Air Command Headquarters, in Vancouver. He trained at the US army's Adjutant General's Staff School (Carlisle Barracks, PA), and took various staff officer positions, including a NATO posting. In 1954, as a GCapt, he took command of the new RCAF station (now CFB) in Cold Lake, AB, home to the Avro CF-100 fighter jet. In 1958, he was posted to the newly opened North American Air Defence (now NORAD) Command Headquarters in Colorado Springs, CO, remaining as Deputy Director of Plans and Policy until 1962. In 1963, he was made ACmdre and became Chief of Staff of first Air Division in France. On the unification of the Forces in 1968, he became a MGen, and in 1969 was Deputy Chief of Operations and Reserves for the amalgamated **MILITARY**. He then served as Canada's Defence Attaché to the US. In 1974, he became LGen, and finished his career as Deputy Commander-in-Chief of NORAD. Stovel retired from the military in 1976. ● AJL

STRATHCLAIR, pop 100, is a community about 110 km NNW of **BRANDON**. The original settlement, The Bend, emerged N of the present community on a meandering bend of the **LITTLE SASKATCHEWAN RIVER** at the intersection of numerous overland trails near an **HBC** trading post. The rolling hills, cultivated farmland, and multitudes of sloughs S of The Bend presented a stark contrast to the wooded parklands to the N. By the mid-1870s, the area had been surveyed, and a section-township-range grid was in place for future homesteaders. Early settlers included **ENGLISH** and **IRISH**, and following an influx of **SCOTS**, The Bend was renamed Strathclair, a combination of the Scottish word *strath*, "valley," and *clair*, after an area surveyor. After the arrival of the railway, a new town was constructed at Strathclair Station, 6 km S of The Bend, later referred to as "Old Strathclair." Later, **UKRAINIANS** and **POLES** settled in the area. Though early residents were decimated by a scarlet fever **EPIDEMIC**, (New) Strathclair had grown into a robust and thriving farm community by the early 20th century. Since the glory years of the mid-1950s, Strathclair, like many Prairie farm **SERVICE** towns, has experienced a steady decline. As of writing, the community was developing a new commercial/industrial park in an attempt to shore up the economy. ● GPP

STRATHCONA, first BARON. *See* **SMITH, DONALD ALEXANDER**.

STRONG, Maurice Frederick, businessman, diplomat, environmentalist (b April 29, 1929, **OAK LAKE**). Born to impoverished parents Frederick Milton and Mary Fyfe Strong, Strong ran away from home as a teenager, initially to Vancouver, and then taking a job at a remote **HBC FUR TRADING** post. In 1947, he came to **WINNIPEG**, where he worked for **JAMES RICHARDSON & SONS, LIMITED** before getting involved in the **PETROLEUM INDUSTRY**, where he appears to have made a substantial fortune. In 1951, Strong married. He travelled extensively in Africa and Europe, and later moved his Cdn base from Winnipeg to a cottage at Lost Lake, in the Kawarthas district N of Peterborough, ON. By the 1960s, he had become involved with the federal Liberal party. This, coupled with his business ties, led to many positions of importance for Strong, among them the Power Corporation of Canada, the Canadian International Development Agency, Petro-Canada, and Ontario Hydro. Since 1970, with 2nd wife Hanne Marstrand Strong, he had extensive real estate dealings in the US Southwest, notably in and around Crestone, CO, where Hanne was from. The pair separated in the early 1990s, though by 2006 had not divorced. Strong's land holdings extended to Costa Rica, where he headed a UN postsecondary institution.

Though tied to the oil sector, Strong is an environmentalist, and has worked at least since the 1960s to bring environmental issues to the fore. Involved with World Wildlife Fund Canada, the UN Conference on the Human Environment (Stockholm, 1972), the 1992 Rio de Janeiro Earth Summit, and the 1997 Kyoto Accord, he also chaired the Earth Council Federation and, in 2006, wrote the book *The Earth Charter in Action: Toward a Sustainable World* (KIT Publishers). Strong's environmental papers are on deposit with Harvard U.

Strong's work with and for the UN has been extensive, including stints as Undersecretary-General; as UN envoy to North Korea; and as special advisor to 2 secretaries-general, Boutros Boutros-Ghali and Kofi Annan. He has sometimes been criticized for conflict of interest at the UN, with implications that he was involved with the scandal-ridden Oil-for-Food program in Iraq. Strong has also been criticized as a New Ager because of Crestone's "alternative lifestyle" community, while some US reporters have labelled Strong a closet **COMMUNIST** – despite his considerable wealth – largely because of his dealings in North Korea and China.

Strong was inducted into the Order of Canada in 1999, was made a Privy Councillor, and holds the **ORDER OF MANITOBA**, as well as numerous honorary degrees. He is also a fellow of both the Royal Society (UK) and the Royal Society of Canada. Strong accompanied gov gen Adrienne Clarkson on her 2003 tour of Finland, Iceland, and Russia. As of writing, Strong's latest interest appeared to be in fostering trade between Canada and China. ● A. J. LEVIN

STUBBS, Eva, sculptor, (b April 20, 1925, Budapest, Hungary) emigrated to Canada with her family in 1944. Stubbs graduated from the **U OF M**'s School of Art in 1957 and taught art in Montreal and Winnipeg, turning to full-time studio work in 1974. She was Visiting Artist at Lakehead U (1989) and in Oakland California (1982). She was elected to the Royal Canadian Academy of Art in 1995. Working in clay and bronze, her work focuses on human relationships and the place of the human being in history and the wider world. Monumental in scale, some of her works are comprised of stacked sections, simultaneously conveying conflicting sensibilities of human strength and fragility. Suggesting past civilizations, they are also contemporary understandings of the human psyche and changing social patterns of 'family.' While seemingly solitary, the figures in her installations are dependent on each other. The mother-and-child theme recurs, underlining her hope for the humanity's future. Her painterly, textured and subtly coloured surfaces are

S

PHOTO BY ERNEST MAYER

Family, clay, 2002, approx. 1.8 m, by Eva Stubbs

sensitive; the firing cracks suggestive of archaeology and geology. Important exhibitions and publications include *Memories for the Future*, The **Winnipeg Art Gallery** (1987), and that with **Caroline Dukes** in Budapest in 1993. Her work has been published in *Arts Manitoba* (1985); *Prairie Fire* (1986); *Women Artists News*, 1984 and *Artswest*, 1982. Collections include The Winnipeg Art Gallery, Manitoba Arts Council Art Bank, Museum of Fine Art Budapest, the U of M, and private and corporate collections in Canada, the US, Barbados, Germany, Japan and England. Commissions include the Winnipeg Real Estate Board, U of M Law Faculty and the **Manitoba Public Insurance Corporation**. • PATRICIA BOVEY

STUBBS, Lewis St. George, lawyer, judge, politician, (b June 14, 1878, Turks and Caicos; d May 12, 1958, **Winnipeg**). Stubbs abandoned his studies at the U of Cambridge to fight in the Boer War, 1900-01. After his military service, he emigrated to Winnipeg in 1902 and was called to the bar of MB in 1906. In 1908, he moved to **Birtle**, where he practised law for 14 years. Appointed to the County Court in 1922, he was the first judicial appointment of newly elected Liberal PM Mackenzie King. In 1929, Stubbs was elevated to senior judge of that court. Stubbs's judicial career stumbled after the 1929 *The McDonald Will* litigation that involved 2 wills with different sets of beneficiaries. The case was a cause célèbre, and Stubbs's judgments put him in conflict with judges of both the Court of King's Bench and the Court of Appeal. When Stubbs's orders were reversed by the higher courts, he organized a rally at Winnipeg's Walker Theatre (*see* **Theatre**) and spoke publicly against the decisions of his fellow judges. The subsequent 3 years saw several complaints of judicial misconduct lodged by MB's attorney general with the federal dept of justice. Following a 1933 Federal Commission of Inquiry into Stubbs's judicial conduct, he was removed from the bench by an Order-in-Council. He returned to private practice in Winnipeg, and in 1936, ran as an independent in the election. He swept the polls, winning election as an MLA with the greatest majority ever recorded in MB. He won re-election in 1941 and 1945. • DOUG JOHNSTON

STUBBS, Roy St. George, lawyer, judge, author (b Sept 6, 1907, **Winnipeg**; d June 6, 1995, Winnipeg) worked for the **Winnipeg Tribune** before attending the **U of M** (LLB, 1936). He served in the RCAF 1941-45. After years of family law practice, in 1970 he was appointed senior judge of the juvenile and family court, serving until his retirement in 1982. He published a number of books, including *Lawyers and Laymen* (1939), *Men in Khaki* (1941), *Prairie Portraits* (1954) and *Four Recorders of Rupertsland* (1967). He was also an ardent advocate of the work of the **Icelandic** poet **Guttormur Jónsson Guttormson**, who became the subject of his last book, *In Search of a Poet* (Peguis, 1975). • JMB

STURGEON (class Osteichthyes) is an ancient group of fishes of the family Acipenseridae (order Asipenseriformes) which appeared in the fossil record 150 million years ago (Late Jurassic period). They look like giant creatures of ages past, with a shark-like tail fin, heavy scales along the sides of the tail, and an elongated snout armed with 4 barbels and an under-slung mouth. It uses its touch- and chemically sensitive barbels to local food items in the bottom muck, and its protrusible mouth to vacuum in creatures like insects, crayfish and algae. Teeth are lacking. The largest fish ever recorded from MB waters was a 3 m, 185 kg Lake Sturgeon (*Acipenser fulvescens*), taken in the Roseau River in 1903. This giant species was once abundant in all major rivers and lakes from the Red River in the prairies N to the Seal and Churchill rivers on the tundra. However, over a century of over-fishing by commercial companies and anglers, the devastating effects of hydroelectric dams, and mounting pollution have placed it in the endangered category in MB, although this fact has yet to be recognized officially. Reintroductions have been attempted on several occasions to help bolster remaining stocks, but complete protection of the stocks, restoration of breeding grounds and migratory routes, and a clean-up of water quality are all prerequisites to ensure this remarkable species continues to survive in the province. Other reasons for this fish's drastic decline are its slow growth rate and long time to reach sexual maturity (over 25 years) and failure to breed every year. The capture of each prized large specimen means a further blow to the species' survival, leaving behind the dwindling populations of subadults. Females may live over a century and can produce over 3 million eggs each spawning season, so recovery of populations is feasible with appropriate management. • REW

STUTSMAN, Enos, frontier lawyer, speculator (b Feb 14, 1826, IN; d Jan 24, 1874, Pembina, ND). As the first practising lawyer in the **Red River Settlement**, Stutsman had considerable political influence. He proved himself in many instances to be a charismatic and persuasive man, though he failed in his attempts to convince **Louis Riel** that the Red River Settlement should join with the US.

Stutsman's life was coloured by a significant challenge: born without legs, he relied on a pair of short crutches to help him walk on the end stumps of his limbs. This made Stutsman a rather notable character, though it otherwise seems to have figured relatively little in his life. His early years were spent in IL. He was a schoolteacher, and then worked as a court clerk in the Dakota Territory, during which time Stutsman studied law on his own. He passed the state bar in 1851, dabbled in real estate, and was active in politics. While serving as an elected representative in the Dakota Territory legislature from 1862-73, Stutsman was appointed a US agent at Pembina, bringing him into the affairs of the Red River Settlement. In 1868, as the only practising lawyer within 800 km, Stutsman was hired to defend Red River settler Alex McLean in his murder trial. Stutsman gave a remarkable performance in the Quarterly Court of the **Council of Assiniboia**. Judge Black, who also served as the trial's prosecutor, was ill-prepared for the presence of an actual defence attorney in his courtroom. With little challenge to Stutsman's arguments, McLean was easily acquitted.

With numerous land speculations in the region, Stutsman stood to gain personally from Red River annexation to the US, and worked his way into Louis Riel's inner circle in order to push forth this aim. Though his efforts were in vain, he nonetheless had some influence on the leader, evident in Riel's draft of the provisional govt's List of Rights, the first 4 clauses being identical to those written by Stutsman a month prior in a proposed bill of rights for the Dakota Territory. Soon after MB entered the Dominion of Canada, Stutsman's left MB. His biography *Attorney for the Frontier: Enos Stutsman* by Dale Gibson was published in 1984. • MD

The Lake Sturgeon is becoming an endangered species.

SUCKER is a medium- to large-sized (30-70 cm) group of fish of the family Catostomidae (order Cypriniformes), comprising 7 species in MB, and whose combined ranges cover the entire province. They are known by colourful names like Bigmouth Buffalo (*Ictiobus cyprinellus*), Golden Redhorse (*Moxostoma erythrurum*) and Quill-back (*Carpiodes cyprinus*). These are robust and deep-bodied fish with a downward-directed mouth. They typically lack teeth in the jaws, but can still grind up food items (insect larvae and crustaceans) using a paired row of small teeth on the arches at the rear of the gill chamber, which work against a hardened pad on the back of the throat (pharynx). The most-abundant and widely distributed species is the White Sucker (*Catostomus commersoni*). It plays a dominant role in the aquatic food chain, feeding on a host of bottom-dwelling creatures and plankton, and in turn, being the most-important food item for predatory commercial and game fishes. Due to it prevalence in MB's 'Great Lakes,' the White Sucker is also valued for human consumption, joining other suckers in the manufacture of fish cakes and canned fish. A large part of its success lies in its ability to thrive in almost all kinds of aquatic habitats, including gravel, sand and mud substrates in lakes, rivers, ponds and even bogs. It prefers gravel substrates for spawning, and may travel several-dozen km up-stream to reach a preferred site, beginning in mid-April when water temperatures reach 10°C. Up to 150,000 eggs are broadcast by the female, fertilized by the male, and then drift downstream until they stick to the bottom. Maximum age for various species is 14-20 years. ● REW

SUGAR BEET INDUSTRY. Farming of the sugar beet (*Beta vulgaris altissima*) was once a significant industry in MB. The beets were grown mostly SW of Winnipeg, especially around **PLUM COULEE**, and processed at a factory in Winnipeg's Fort Garry neighbourhood. A sugar beet is a different subspecies of *Beta vulgaris* – a species that includes the red beet, the chard, and the mangel-wurzel – but closely resembles a giant parsnip, with an average length of 30 cm and a weight of 0.5-1.0 kg.

Though all plants produce sugar through photosynthesis, the amount in a sugar beet is comparatively high at 14-17% (cabbage leaves and turnip roots, for comparison, each have less than 3%). The sugar is extracted by slicing the beet into thin strips, and placing them through a diffuser, which sluices away the sugar as a dark, grey juice. The raw juice is cleansed with lime and carbon dioxide before being filtered and evaporated into concentrated syrup. Sugar

crystals are then formed by boiling the syrup in large drums and mixing in a fine sugar slurry. The crystals are spun and dried before packaging. Roughly 18 kg of sugar beets produce a 2.3 kg bag of granulated sugar.

It took years of research and development to establish a viable sugar industry in MB. The Selkirk Settlers tried to grow beets in Kildonan in the 1840s, and in 1880, there is a record of the provincial **AGRICULTURE** minister awarding a prize for growing sugar beets. Test plots run by the provincial govt in the early 20th century were discouraging, resulting in beets with low sugar content, but the Manitoba Agriculture College (*see* **U OF M**) continued research. When the **GREAT DEPRESSION** hit, the provincial govt was eager to develop new crops as global demand for wheat plummeted. With the govt providing farm machinery on loan, and abundant cheap labour, sugar beet farming was one of the few profitable crops in the early 1930s. A plant in ND processed the beets, following a 1930 agreement that allowed sugar to be shipped back to MB duty-free. One of the largest and most-successful plantations in MB was a 13 ha (32 ac) plot at **HEADINGLEY** Penitentiary, which had a high average yield of 26.7 tonnes/ha (10.6 UK tons/ac) of beets, compared to the plantation at the St. Norbert Trappist Monastery, which yielded 9.24 tonnes/ha (3.68 tons/ac). The fledgling industry was stalled in 1933 when the ND plant stopped processing MB beets due to opposition from US farmers, who believed Manitoban crops were cutting into their profits.

The industry revived in 1940, when a MB processing plant was opened, largely financed by a **GERMAN** businessman seeking to reinvest capital beyond the control of the Nazi regime. WWII further bolstered the industry as the federal govt began to stress the production of sugar within Canada to lessen dependence on increasingly expensive imports. In its first year, the Manitoba Sugar Company signed contracts with 1119 farmers, who grew 80.8 km² (31.2 mi²) of beets.

The labour required to cultivate sugar beets was arduous, and the workers found in sugar beet fields were often in the direst situations. The federal govt brought **JAPANESE** Cdn workers to MB sugar beet farms throughout WWII, thus lessening the numbers being held at internment camps in the BC interior while filling a farm labour shortage brought on by the war. By 1942, over 1000 Japanese Canadians had arrived in MB. They were forbidden from taking any other employment during beet growing season, and were forced to live in small dwellings provided by farmers or in prefabricated houses offered by the Manitoba Sugar Company for $245.

German POWs held in MB also provided labour. Following their return to Germany at the end of the war, new labour was found among European displaced persons who lived in the barracks just vacated by the Germans prisoners.

The sugar industry was profitable, and when the Manitoba Sugar Company was sold to BC Sugar in 1955, it was producing 22% of Canada's beet sugar and nearly 75% of the sugar consumed in MB. As foreign immigration dwindled in the 1950s, beet farmers began looking to First Nations communities for labour. By 1959, 800 Aboriginal people were working on sugar beet farms, mostly from the reserves in MB's Interlake region. Farmers would often drive N with trucks to transport workers to their farms in southern MB. The demand for cheap labour fell when a new type of seed requiring less maintenance was introduced to MB in the late 1960s. In 1968, there were roughly 600 sugar beet farmers. The Manitoba Sugar Company was renamed Rogers Sugar Ltd in 1995, growing 109 km² (42 mi²) of beets valued at $40 million. It supplied over 70% of sugar in MB. As more than ½ of the plant's sugar was exported to the US, the introduction of heavy import tariffs in the US on Cdn sugar led to the plant's closure in 1997, and the end of the sugar beet industry in MB. ● MICHELLE DOBROVOLNY

SUN DANCE is one of the most sacred and powerful ceremonies still celebrated among First Nations residing on the northern prairies. In MB, it is observed primarily by the **DAKOTA** and Plains **OJIBWAY**, but some northerly groups have either adopted the ceremony or participate at southern locales. Although its true origin is undocumented in the historical records, the ceremony likely evolved into its classic "high plains" form during the period 1800-83. Its rapid spread is attributed to the acquisition of the horse and the availability of substantial bison herds that enabled large gatherings of people. The Ojibway adopted the Sun Dance from the Plains **CREE** who in turn received it from their Assiniboine allies.

Historically, the ceremony was the high point of the plains sacred year and was held in the early summer when the land was lush with new grass and replete with large herds of bison. It was a time when people who lived and hunted in smaller groups throughout the winter now came together. Traditionally, large Sun Dance gatherings lasted for a number of weeks, depending on the availability of food. At these gatherings, many other types of smaller ceremonies were conducted. It was a time for marriages, the renewal of old alliances and the forging of new ones, council meetings, feasting, storytelling, dancing, gambling, horseracing, and visiting.

The focus of these assemblies however, was on the performance of the Sun Dance itself, which served to reinforce political and cultural identity and such cherished values as courage, respect, fidelity, co-operation, generosity, and wisdom. All of these qualities were prerequisites for living in balance with the natural universal order of things and for one's spiritual, emotional, and physical well-being.

The popularized term "Sun Dance" is derived from Europeans observing the sun-gazing rituals of Oglala Lakota celebrants. Indigenous names for the ceremony generally refer to the abstinence from food and water by those who have vowed to dance – hence the use of the term "Thirst Dance" by some First Nations.

The ceremony is generally held at designated sacred sites near the time of the summer solstice. The sponsorship of a Sun Dance is a major undertaking, and earlier in the winter, sponsors and participants who have vowed to dance take part in a number of rituals to prepare themselves.

The Sun Dance lodge is a distinctive structure, and its construction involves several important rituals that are performed according to generations of sacred teachings. It is a circular structure that contains the "sacred tree" or Sun Dance pole at its centre along with an altar for holy objects. The tree is forked, and a sacred Thunderbird nest is built at the apex. It marks the centre of the world, and throughout the ceremony it connects humans with the spiritual elements of earth and sky and serves as a channel for prayer. For 4 days, celebrants who have pledged to participate in the dance offer themselves in prayer and make various forms of personal sacrifices such as fasting from food and water. Some take part in a "piercing" ritual that involves self-mortification.

One of the events occurring at all ceremonies, including the Sun Dance, was the holding of "Giveaways" or the redistribution of food and valued material goods. Traditionally, dressed animal hides, blankets, clothing, European trade goods and horses were given away. This practice, including the spiritual offering of material goods, came under criticism from missionaries and the federal government in the 1880s. Today, more contemporary goods are distributed or offered.

With the signing of the prairie treaties in the early 1870s and attempts to settle First Nations peoples on their respective reserves, travel to Sun Dance gatherings off the reserve and the content of the ceremony were viewed as impediments to the policy of "civilizing the Indian." Both the federal govt and missionaries supported the regulation of Indigenous expressions

of spirituality and other forms of cultural expressions as necessary for the transformation of First Nations peoples into mainstream Canadians. In addition, spiritual offerings of material goods and "giveaways" or redistribution of goods to those in need or as remuneration for a service were also considered objectionable behaviours on the grounds that the practices impoverished the contributors.

The Sun Dance itself was not banned in Canada but its practice was certainly discouraged. In 1895, a section of the *Indian Act* was revised to outlaw the "giving away of goods" at all festivals, dances, or ceremonies that were viewed by the authorities as objectionable. The pass system that required people to apply to their Indian Agents for permits to travel off their reserves was also used to discourage participation in ceremonies. In response, community leaders challenged the legitimacy of the regulations and the manner in which they were implemented that often went beyond the law. In addition, they practised some of their ceremonies "underground", altering times and location, and revised the content of the Sun Dance to comply with the terms of the act.

Historical evidence in the form of govt reports, Aboriginal petitions, oral history and anthropological fieldwork, indicates that while ceremonial life was interrupted by official repression, some form of the Sun Dance persisted in many communities. The 2 decades following 1918 were extremely stressful for most reserve residents struggling to survive under devastating conditions including racial discrimination, the separation of family members through the **RESIDENTIAL SCHOOL** system, poverty, and depopulation from disease such as **TUBERCULOSIS** and influenza. In the absence of federal health programs, many community members continued to look to their own traditional methods of healing, especially the powerful Sun Dances, for support.

The rise of a national sense of awareness by returning war veterans, many of whom were former residential school students, from the world wars led to the evolution of political organizations and demands for change. As early as 1919, the League of Indians of Canada insisted on the rights of Aboriginal people to retain their indigenous values, cultural identity and customs. Petitions sent to Ottawa raised the issue of human rights, and religious freedom was a key objective of many of the lobbyists. In 1945, the Cdn govt appointed a joint committee of the Senate and House of Commons to review the *Indian Act* and its administration. A number of representations were made by Aboriginal leaders, and the "freedom of religious worship" was raised. However, it was never specifically discussed by the committee, and when the

new version of the Indian Act was drafted in 1951, those sections prohibiting certain ceremonial practices and other forms of cultural expression off reserves were simply removed.

The govt's regulation of plains ceremonial life and the forced conversion of many Aboriginal children through the **RESIDENTIAL SCHOOL** system remain important historical symbols of the colonial repression of Canada's Indigenous peoples. In spite of this history, the Sun Dance has been revived and even adopted by new groups. It remains a powerful force in many lives today.
● KATHERINE PETTIPAS

SUNFLOWERS (*Helianthus annuus*), among the few food crops native to Canada, form a small but significant sector of MB's **AGRICULTURE**. Roughly 85-90% of Canada's total sunflower crop grows in the province, with MB growers harvesting an average of 50,6000 ha (125,000 ac) a year, producing about 200,000 tonnes of seed. Most sunflower crops grow in southern MB, where a relatively long, dry growing season and fertile soil are ideal for cultivating the species.

The sunflower is a tall, broad-leafed plant indigenous to the Central Plains of NA. It usually reaches 1.25-1.75 m. It is noted for its large, golden flowers. Sunflowers are heliotropic: the face of the flower moves with the Sun from E to W over the course of the day. All sunflowers grown in MB are hybrids, developed to improve production in different climates or to increase the seed's oil content. Though **FIRST PEOPLES** grew sunflowers as a crop as long ago as 1000 BC, commercial Cdn sunflower production began in the early 1940s. The confectionery industry uses most of the crop. The grey-and-white-striped confectionery seeds can be either roasted and bagged as a snack food, or dehulled for use in baking. About

As much as 90% of Canada's sunflower crop is grown in Manitoba.

40% of the sunflower crop is the smaller, all-black oilseed variety, which is crushed and processed into oil. This oil can be used in the production of margarine and mayonnaise. There are no crushing facilities in MB, and only confectionery seeds are processed within the province. Both types of seed are also used in birdfeed. A closely related plant, the Jerusalem artichoke or sunchoke (*H. tuberosus*), is also native to MB. It grows easily with little care, and is sometimes grown for its potato-like rootstock. • MD

SWALLOWS (family Hirundinidae) are small, slender songbirds that catch their insect prey on the wing. They arrive from their wintering grounds in Apr or May, and most have departed by early Sept. Six species occur regularly in MB, while another is accidental. The Barn Swallow (*Hirundo rustica*) is readily familiar to rural residents, as the species commonly nests in barns, deserted buildings, and culverts. In the open countryside, Tree Swallows (*Tachycineta bicolor*) can easily be attracted to nestboxes placed along fence lines, while the **Mosquito**-eating purple martin (*Progne subis*) frequently occupies multi-compartment birdhouses. Elaborate structures have been erected for this species in **Gimli, Beausejour, Neepawa, Boissevain**, and other towns. Cliff Swallows (*Petrochelidon pyrrhonota*) nest colonially under bridges, while bank swallows (*Riparia riparia*) excavate their nest-burrows in riverbanks. • RUDOLF KOES

SWAN LAKE FIRST NATION, onreserve pop 691, off reserve pop 492, is located about 135 km SE of **Brandon**, and 175 km SW of **Winnipeg**. The native language of this community is **Ojibway**, and Treaty 1 was signed in 1871. It is a member of the Dakota Ojibway Tribal Council. There are 2 reserves located in the Swan Lake First Nation community: Swan Lake IR No. 7, and Indian Gardens IR No. 8. The Swan Lake First Nation people have all-weather road access to the southern MB hwy network. Schooling, administered by Swan Lake First Nation, goes from Nursery-Grade 12. Total enrolment for the year 2003-2004 was 125. The economic foundation of Swan Lake is bison and elk production, cow calf operations, potato, and cereal grain farming. • RK

SWAN RIVER, pop 3859, MB's 13th largest community, is a town 135 km NW of **Dauphin** and 25 km E of the SK border on the river of the same name. **English** explorer **Henry Kelsey** was likely the first European to the area, passing through here about 1690. Within 100 years, European **Fur Traders** were active in the region. Both the **NWC** and **HBC** had **Forts** near here, and Englishman David Thompson passed through the Swan River Valley in 1797. The river, from which the town takes its name, probably comes from an older Aboriginal name. The river is in turn named for nearby Swan Lake, a water body between the town and **Lake Winnipegosis**, out of which the Swan flows. The lake's name probably refers to the now-extirpated

flocks of trumpeter swans that used to congregate here. Though Swan River is farther N than many Manitoban agricultural centres, the land is suited to various crops. Homesteaders, including **English, Ukrainians, Irish, Scots, French,** and **Germans**, initially came to the area around 1897 to farm. In 1905, the railway came here, and settlers continued to pour in. Three years later, population had grown to the point where Swan River incorporated as a town. In the 21st century, Swan River continues to function as an agricultural support centre offering **Retail** and services to surrounding farms. However, **Forestry** and govt services such as **Health Care** and **Education** are significant employers. **Tourism** is also important, as Swan River's natural scenery placement between the Duck and Porcupine mountains makes the area suitable for outdoor pursuits such as **Hunting, Fishing,** and wildlife watching. Swan River also hosts the Northwest Round-up and Exhibition in late July, and a stampede/harvest celebration in Aug. • GPP

SWANS. *See* **Waterfowl**.

SWEAT LODGE, often referred to as a "purification lodge," has long been used by Aboriginal peoples in MB. There are various rituals associated with sweat lodge that are invoked and performed according to its purpose at the particular time of use. The sweat lodge occupies a sacred place within Indigenous culture and connects humans with all the beings of the universe. Its main purpose is to foster spiritual, mental, and physical well-being, and is often used to prepare the individual for participation in other ceremonies such as the **Sun Dance** or a personal vision quest.

The low, dome-shaped sweat lodge is constructed of willow poles and covered with hides or canvas. The entrance generally faces the east. In the centre of the lodge is a pit to which heated rocks are conveyed from a hearth outside of the structure. The rocks are the sacred "Grandfathers," the oldest of all the relations. During the ceremony, water is splashed on the rocks to produce steam, and prayers are offered by celebrants who are seated around the Grandfathers. Often, herbs are mixed in with the water and the four sacred plants – sage, cedar, tobacco and sweetgrass – are used. The sweat lodge is sacred and is considered to symbolize a mother's womb; the celebrants' re-emergence into the outside world as they leave the lodge is likened to being reborn. • KATHERINE PETTIPAS

SWIFTS (family *Apodidae*) are small non-perching birds that spend most of their lives in the air. Superficially similar but not related to **Swallows**, swifts have cigar-shaped bodies with

Tree swallows are attracted to nestboxes.

LARRY DE MARCH

S

Chimney Swift in its nest

sickle-like wings. They are represented in MB by only one species, the chimney swift (*Chaetura pelagica*), a greyish bird that occurs in summer through most of the southern half of the province, especially over cities and towns and near water. The chimney swift – a distant relative of **HUMMINGBIRDS** – has a high-pitched, single-noted chattering call, often heard as it flies, in bat-like fashion, hunting for small insects. It takes its name from its habit of building nests on vertical structures such as chimneys.

SWINTON, George, teacher, artist, academic (b April 17, 1922, Vienna, Austria; d April 22, 2002, **WINNIPEG**) was a renowned authority on Inuit Art. Swinton studied economics and political science in Vienna (1936-1938) before coming to Canada in 1939. He served 5 years in the Canadian Intelligence Corp of the Cdn army before attaining citizenship in 1944. Swinton completed his BA at McGill U in 1946 and then took courses at the Montreal School of Art & Design from 1946-1947 and the Art Students' League of New York from 1949-1950. Prior to joining the **U OF M**'s faculty in 1954, he was the curator at the Saskatoon Art Centre, an instructor at Smith College, and Artist-in-Residence at Queen's U. Swinton was also director of the **WINNIPEG ART GALLERY**. He held his position on the faculty of the U of M's School of Art for 20 years, until he left in 1974 to join Carleton U's faculty as a professor of Canadian Studies and Art History until 1985. Aside from academia, Swinton was also the art critic for the *Winnipeg Tribune* from 1954-1958, and hosted the CBC television series "Art in Action" from 1959-1962. He wrote numerous articles on Inuit Art, as well as 4 books, including *Eskimo/Sculpture/Esquimade* (1965), *Sculpture of the Eskimo* (1972), and *Almost Poems* (2001). His own artwork is

displayed in the National Gallery of Canada, the Vancouver Art Gallery, and the WAG. He received numerous awards for his work, including the Centennial Medal (1967), Professor Emeritus from Carleton U (1986), and an honorary degree from the U of M (1987). In 1979, Swinton was made a Member of the Order of Canada. He continued to promote Inuit art until his death in 2002. • AMANDA STEPHENS

SWYSTUN (SWISTUN), Michael, circus performer, farmer (b Nov 14, 1901, Olha, MB; d July 16, 1980, Olha) was once billed as "The Strongest Man in the World" while touring with the famous Ringling Brothers' Barnum and Bailey Circus. Born in a *budda*, a thatched-roofed dwelling built by his **UKRAINIAN** parents, Swystun overcame the drudgery of pioneer life by

entertaining his small community with magic tricks. Naturally charismatic, his commanding presence was bolstered by his gargantuan size. He eventually discovered that he could lift bags of grain with his teeth, and performed this trick so many times that his jaw became strong enough to bend iron bars.

Swystun's unique talents earned him a spot with the Barnum and Bailey circus during the summer of 1923. He spent several happy months travelling through NA, seeing the world beyond Olha for the first time, but his circus career was cut short when he received a telegram telling him to return home for the harvest. Though he obeyed his family's demand, Swystun was not content to settle for a dull life of farm work, and continued to perform magic tricks in his hometown under the title "Swistun the Magician, Master of 42 Tricks and Illusions." In one incident, having hypnotized several local ladies, Swystun convinced them that they were wading through deep water so that they scandalously lifted up their skirts. Some such tricks were caught on film in a 1980 documentary about his life, including one where Swystun astounds film crews by pushing a 7-in spike into the back of his head and pulling it out through his nose.

Swystun's hypnotic and magical abilities, whether real or imagined, caused him to be shunned by his superstitious neighbours, who considered it a form of devilry. He became something of an outcast in Olha, and took to restoring the *buddas* he remembered from his youth. He lived to a ripe old age, beating cancer 4 times and, he claimed, surviving a heart attack by willing his heart to beat again. • MICHELLE DOBROVOLNY

Mike Swystun could bend steel bars on his teeth.

THOMPSON,
see page 679
Mural of Robert Bateman wolf sketch

TACHÉ, Alexandre-Antonin, ROMAN CATHOLIC archbishop, colonialist, writer (b July 23, 1823, Rivière-du-Loup, QC; d June 22, 1894, ST. BONIFACE). Taché was the 3ʳᵈ of 5 children born to Charles Taché and Louise Henriette de la Broquerie, in a small settlement near the St. Lawrence River. Taché studied at the Collège de Saint-Hyacinthe, then studied theology at the Grand séminaire de Ville-Marie, in what is now Montreal, before entering the noviciate of the Oblates of Mary Immaculate in Longueuil, Canada East (QC), in 1844. The following year, he was sent to assist Bishop JOSEPH-NORBERT PROVENCHER in the RED RIVER SETTLEMENT. Taché was the first French Canadian Oblate in western Canada, and the first Oblate to be ordained in that region. After his ordination, Taché served in the St. Boniface region before being sent to Île-à-la-Crosse, SK, in 1846, where he was responsible for ministering to a large area that stretched from Lac Ste. Anne, AB, to Rcindeer Lake. While there, Taché learned the Chipewyan language (he had already learnt OJIBWAY). In 1850, Taché was named coadjutor bishop of the North-West; bishop, upon the death of Provencher in June 1853; and the first archbishop of the Ecclesiastical Province of St. Boniface in 1871.

During the RED RIVER RESISTANCE, the federal govt asked Taché to act as its mediator, and

Alexandre-Antonin Taché, 1890

he was instrumental in negotiating a peaceful settlement, along with ABBE RICHOT, that culminated in the creation of the province of MB. Unfortunately, he was unable to obtain a complete amnesty for all participants in the insurrection, and always maintained that the govt had broken its promise to him. The outcome of the amnesty question, and problems associated with the distribution of the "Half-Breed Grant," convinced many MÉTIS that Taché had betrayed their interests. This sentiment was reinforced by Taché's failure to censure the govt for executing LOUIS RIEL in 1885.

As the old order based on the **Bison** hunt and **Fur Trade** gave way to sedentary **Agricultural** settlement, Taché promoted **French** Catholic immigration to MB. As a French Canadian, Taché regarded MB as a "sister province" to QC. Thus, he urged his native province to support his colonization ventures to ensure a strong French Catholic presence in national affairs, and to demonstrate that Canada was bilingual and bicultural. His views on the importance and necessity of a Catholic education led him to establish what would become the **Collège Universitaire Saint-Boniface**. Given the fusion between language and religion among French Canadians, Taché zealously guarded and defended the linguistic and educational rights of French-speaking Catholics in MB and the NWTs. When these privileges were threatened, he wrote numerous tracts and pamphlets defending his concept of a bilingual and bicultural nation and the necessity of maintaining the agreements entered into in 1867 and 1870. Taché's prolific writings are characterized by a polemical style that identifies an injustice, contradicts the assertions of opponents, and proposes a solution based on justice and equity.

As an ecclesiastical and religious superior, one of Taché's main preoccupations was to obtain the material and human resources that his large missionary diocese required. An astute businessman, Taché purchased land in St. Boniface in advance of settlement and later sold it at a significant profit. He invested his surplus capital at a good rate of interest and with first-class sureties. Taché also established an elaborate network of agents in France, the UK, the US, and Canada to oversee the ordering of supplies and their distribution to missions in the diocese. Since the Oblate General Administration in France could never supply enough personnel, Taché was constantly occupied with recruiting clergy for his missions. Personnel problems were compounded as the number of settled parishes increased. This was exacerbated by Taché's managerial style, which was autocratic and haughty. He was unable to effectively delegate authority, rarely explaining his decisions or seeking the advice of those who served under him. Taché's main concern was the accomplishment of institutional objectives, and not the feelings of the individuals whose efforts worked toward those goals. Despite his lack of interpersonal skills, Taché had a charisma that created a strong bond even among those who were negatively affected by his actions.

Despite his many years in western Canada, Taché always remained a Québécois, and his nationalist vision and political convictions reflected those of his birthplace. He attempted to replicate QC society in MB and the North-West by encouraging French Catholic immigration and by seeking constitutional guarantees for the French language and the Catholic faith. Unlike QC, however, the French soon became a minority in the North-West and MB; this placed them in a vulnerable position with respect to their rights. QC contributed to this state of affairs by refusing to support Taché's colonization projects, even undermining them. Taché was often at odds with the nationalists of QC, who did not share his vision of a bilingual and bicultural nation and who had their own parochial political agendas.

When **English** and **Scots** Protestants became the dominant element in MB, the school and linguistic rights of the French and Catholic elements were rescinded by legislation in MB and the NWTs, and Taché's eloquent protests against the violation of sacred accords fell on deaf ears. His categorical stand on the **Manitoba Schools Question** was not shared by **Irish** Catholics in Winnipeg who wanted a compromise measure similar to that which had been adopted in parochial schools in the US.

Taché's career coincides with some pivotal events in the history of western Canada: the fur trade era; the Red River Resistance and the subsequent North-West Resistance; the settlement frontier; and the debate over language and schools. Taché suffered from ill health in his last years, compounded by delays in having his successor appointed. As a missionary and bishop, Taché left an indelible imprint on the Catholic Church in western Canada. He was an enigmatic personality, but his actions were beyond reproach: he was motivated by a strong sense of duty and service to God and country. ● RAYMOND HUEL

TAIGA BIOLOGICAL STATION is an off-campus Institute and field station of the **U of M** situated 2 km N of Wallace Lake, in the boreal forest of SE MB. It is accessible only by canoe, skis, or snowmobile. Founded in 1973 by boreal ecologist Dr. William O. Pruitt, Jr., its mission is to study the ecology of animals and plants of the taiga under natural conditions. Hundreds of young and advanced students and volunteers have experienced the wonders of the taiga at this remote and undisturbed site. Research studies conducted here have included the ecology of snow, the effects of fire on plant succession, Woodland **Caribou**, **Grey Wolf**, Fisher, American Marten, **Beaver**, small mammals (30-year annual census), **Owls**, **Woodpeckers**, **Spiders**, lichens, and vegetational mapping. ● WOP

TAIT, James Edward, soldier, **Victoria Cross** winner, (b May 17, 1886, Dumfries, UK; d Aug 11, 1918, Amiens, France), son of James Bryden Tait and Mary Johnstone Tait, was educated in Scotland, emigrated to **Winnipeg**, and joined the 78th Batt, Manitoba Regiment, in 1915. A Lt during the attack on Vimy Ridge, April 9, 1916, he was wounded while all the other company officers were killed. Still, he led his men on to an enemy position, then, unable to walk, directed his company until it had captured the post, whereupon he crawled back to his own lines. For his leadership and bravery, he was awarded the VC. Months later, in a similar battle, he was wounded by an exploding shell, and continued to direct his men until he died. The officer was buried at Fouquescourt British Cemetery, Somme, France, and his VC is on display at Calgary's Glenbow Museum. ● JIM SHILLIDAY

TANNER, John "Falcon" Jr., guide, interpreter, author (b ca 1780, KY; d ca July 1846, near Sault Ste. Marie, Canada West [ON]), was a white settler who was taken captive and raised by **Ojibway** and other Algonquian peoples. Virginian clergyman-turned-farmer John Tanner Sr was John's father. John's mother died when he was 2. The boy lived with his siblings, his half-siblings, and his remarried father and his stepmother in what is now Elkhorn City, KY, near Cincinnati. There was then a climate of mutual hostility between the Shawano (Shawnee) and the Americans. In this atmosphere, a small Shawano party kidnapped Tanner from his father's homestead about 1789. Many First Nations at that time kidnapped people to replace relatives lost in combat or to disease.

Tanner's Shawano family named the boy "Shashawa(s)nebase," which can mean either "Falcon" or "Swallow." Initially, Tanner stayed in a Shawano village near what is now Saginaw Bay, MI. Facing rough treatment at the hands of his stepfather Manitoukeezik, Tanner was nevertheless well treated by his stepmother and stepsisters. Manitoukeezik happily sold the boy to a relative, Odawa (Ottawa) chief Netnokwa of L'Arbre Croche, MI. Netnokwa and her husband, Tagiiwinini, "The Hunter," proved kind foster parents, though Tagiiwinini died before long. In 1795, Netnokwa, many other Odawas, and Tanner relocated to what is now MB. Tanner adapted to the Ojibway lifestyle and faith, becoming a skilled hunter and trapper. From 1804-12, he also joined several Ojibway parties that fought the **Dakota**. In 1800, Falcon married Miskwabunokwa, "Red Sky of Morning," and they had several children. Tanner and Miskwabunokwa parted ways by 1810, by which time he married Theresa Lavallee.

Tanner lived near **The Forks** when **Lord Selkirk**'s **Red River Settlement** was established.

By this time, he spoke little English and could barely recall his birth name. He remained neutral in the **HBC** dispute with the **NWC**, though he worked as a guide to lead Selkirk's mercenaries from Fort William (Thunder Bay) to Fort Douglas (**WINNIPEG**) in 1816. The earl became greatly interested in Tanner's story, and helped him contact his Kentuckian family. Tanner met with his original family in KY in 1817. Tanner also disliked the family of his 2nd wife, and this combination prompted him to consider a European way of living. After returning to Red River, he attempted to move his Aboriginal family S with him to KY, but one of Tanner's children died en route. Tanner reached KY in 1819, but could not adjust easily to a European lifestyle. In 1823, he returned N, and tried to reclaim his children from his first marriage, but his wife refused to surrender them. In 1824, he moved to Michilimackinac (Mackinac Island, MI), where he worked as an interpreter for the American Fur Company and for US Indian Agent Henry Schoolcraft. His 2nd wife joined him, but Theresa – who had become a **ROMAN CATHOLIC** – did not go with him.

In 1830, with the assistance of US army doctor Edwin James, Tanner wrote a memoir of his life with the Ojibway. This autobiography, *A Narrative of the Captivity and Adventures of John Tanner* (also called *The Falcon*), gives a vivid, detailed account of Indian life, as well as of the changes to it brought about by colonization. Tanner's eldest son, Picheto Tanner, was a prominent Ojibway war chief; Picheito's eldest son, John "Gambler" Turner – also a chief, as many subsequent Tanners have been – refused to sign the **TREATY** that formed **WAYWAYSEECAPPO FIRST NATION**, forming instead **GAMBLERS FIRST NATION**. Many Tanners settled in the **RIDING MOUNTAIN** area, and **MINNEDOSA** was originally called "Tanner's Crossing" after "Falcon's" grandson, also named John Tanner (1839-1932). • AJL

TASCONA, Antonio "Tony," (b March 16, 1926, **ST. BONIFACE**; d May 28, 2006, **WINNIPEG**). Known as the "Godfather of Manitoba Art," Tony's work is represented in public, private, and corporate collections across Canada and in Japan. His exhibition record of group and solo shows is impressive. The 2nd-youngest of a large family, Tascona was proud of his Sicilian heritage and his St. Boniface roots. Writer **GABRIELLE ROY**, an early teacher, made a lasting impression on him. In 1946, soon after leaving the **MILITARY**, Tascona enrolled at the Winnipeg School of Art through the Veteran's Affairs program, and later left his semi-professional **BASEBALL** career with the **MAN-DAK LEAGUE** to undertake fine-art studies. Earning his diploma in 1950, he continued studying art in 1951 at the School of Art, newly part of the **U OF M**, where Joseph Plaskett and William McCloy were important and influential teachers. Tascona became particularly interested in the colour and abstraction theories of Hans Hoffman, in the work of British artist Wyndham Lewis and his colleagues in the Vorticism movement, and in Mexican muralist Diego Rivera.

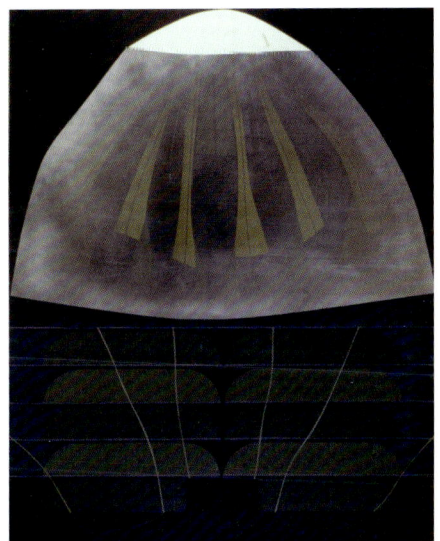

WAG, PHOTO BY ERNEST MAYER

Black Madonna, **acrylic/aluminum painting, 152 x 122 cm, 1999, by Tony Tascona**

Tascona was among the first generation of artists to both study and lead their professional lives in Winnipeg. On graduation, he worked as an electroplating mechanic in the aerospace industry at **TRANS-CANADA AIRLINES** (later Air Canada) 1953-70, primarily in Winnipeg, but he was posted to Montreal for several years. While there, he became friends with many Quebecois contemporary artists, including Minimalist Abstract painters Louis Comtois, Serge Tousingnant, and Guido Molinari. In the early 1970s, after completing the major commissions in the new Winnipeg Centennial Concert Hall, he chose to devote his full-time and creative energies to his art.

Tascona's work falls into 3 general phases – the early work and Natural Abstraction, 1953 to the mid-1960s; Geometric Abstraction, from 1965 through the 1970s; and Organic Abstraction in the 1980s and 1990s. Tascona's colour sense and facility with line were evident as a student. Paintings, prints, and resin sculptures and installations were the primary focus of his artistic practice until he was hospitalized in the 1990s. He then rediscovered drawing, finding it a liberating and engaging medium. This later focus on drawing lead him back to organic forms and the combination of organic and geometric elements.

His early period, Natural Abstraction, includes *Winter Landscape* (1961). Mixing sand with lacquer to create a grainy surface shows his early interest in surface textures. In its colour and composition, he has conveyed the tones of the MB winter landscape and the vast spaces and movement. The shapes show his interest in biological forms, with the human lungs and heart becoming seed pods blowing across the landscape.

While in the aerospace industry, he developed the artistic use of resins and plastics. Always inventively experimenting with non-traditional materials, he developed new techniques and special effects of texture and light. He built reliefs in aluminum, on which he poured multiple layers of acrylic lacquer, creating the smooth, almost silky effect of enamel as seen in *Inverted Apex*, 1969. The large abstractions, with angular forms and intersecting directional lines of force, characterize the Geometric Abstraction period. Many are bold in colour – including yellows, oranges, and blues – while some are almost monochromatic. Others, like *Inverted Apex*, have contrasting colours, referring to farm machinery. These geometric abstractions seemingly extend beyond the picture frame, like mechanical continuums, and include wheels and various elements from technology, fusing his interests in technology, science, and art.

Organic Abstraction, his 3rd period, introduces the organic elements of earlier years into the geometric abstractions of the 2nd period. He became increasingly spiritual in this phase, as in the *Black Madonna* series of the mid-1990s; this work was inspired by a trip to Sicily in 1990. The enigmatic, ominous quality of these works is compelling and thought-provoking. Tascona had no particular dogma or religion, though, but rather a deep understanding of the spiritual roots of many cultures.

A prolific artist, he created in several media simultaneously. Tascona intuitively "orchestrated" his art, systematically "building" works rich in juxtapositions of seemingly incongruous elements. In each medium, he controlled the colours and forms. He often embedded other forms and shapes in the resin pieces that were created by pouring the resins in layers. The results include the large translucent installations such as that at the Fresh Water Institute in Winnipeg, depicting plankton as seen through a microscope, and the *Chains of Being*, showing the relationship between modern medical research and the body explored in the resin lozenges descending the atrium at **ST. BONIFACE HOSPITAL**. Like his processes for paintings and resins, his drawing approach was slow and personal. Using both coloured pencils and acrylic inks, and high quality papers, he added colours

T

layer by layer. He developed his own methods of working dark colours into dark papers, at times using a pointillist technique and varying concentrations of dots and shifting colour ranges, sometimes adding silver ink, to convey the refraction of the light through particles in the air. Inspired by the open spaces, organic forms, light, and horizons, the Prairie underlies all his work. His compositions were not preconceived; the abstracted forms flowed and grew as each work developed, becoming visual "transformations" of his thoughts and subconscious feelings. These abstracted essences, or syntheses, are the elements of place and geology, the moods, and sensibilities, each work imbued with his particular insights and spirit, embodying the colours, rhythms, and structures of the land. Combining past and present experiences, he achieved a balance between solid rootedness and organic fluidity. Whatever the medium, his works are strong, evocative, powerful, and reflective, at times almost mystical.

His legacy is significant in his own work, in his support and encouragement to other artists, and through the bursary he established at the U of W for the study of Cdn art history. Tascona was a member of the Royal Canadian Academy (1973), the board of trustees of the National Gallery of Canada, and the board of governors of the **WINNIPEG ART GALLERY**. He was a member of the Order of Canada (1996), and received a **U OF W** honorary doctorate (1994). • PATRICIA BOVEY

TATASKWEYAK CREE NATION (previously known as Split Lake Cree Nation), on reserve pop 2169, off reserve pop 851, is located 120 km NE of **THOMPSON**. Tataskweyak signed Treaty 5 in 1908. It is now a member of the Keewatin Tribal Council. The people's native language is **CREE**. Education in this First Nation goes from Nursery-Grade 12, and total enrolment for 2003-04 was 588. The Tataskweyak Cree Nation administers its own schooling. Tataskweyak has 3 reserves. All-weather road access is available. The economic foundation is seasonal trapping and commercial fishing.

Affected by flooding caused by hydro development, this Cree Nation is a signatory to the **NORTHERN FLOOD AGREEMENT**. As of Aug 2002, **MANITOBA HYDRO** and the Tataskweyak Cree Nation have agreed to go ahead with a planned expansion of the community's water treatment plant to resolve long-standing water quality concerns. Along with Mathias Columb and **WAR LAKE FIRST NATIONS**, Tataskweyak jointly operates the Keewatin Railway Company which took over the northern rail line between Sherritt Junction and Lynn Lake. • RK

TAYLOR, Andrew, engineer, explorer, historian (b 1907, Edinburgh; d Oct 8, 1993, **WINNIPEG**). This noted Arctic and Antarctic explorer immigrated with his **SCOTS** family to Winnipeg in 1911. Taylor graduated from the **U OF M** in 1931 with a BSc in civil engineering and took a position as a surveyor, working mostly in **NORTHERN MB**. In 1933, he moved to **FLIN FLON**, becoming the municipal engineer. He was responsible for initiating many of the community's early infrastructure projects.

Taylor enlisted in the Army during WWII, but saw no action before transferring to the UK's Royal Navy in 1943 to take part in a secret mission. The expedition travelled to Antarctica, surveying the region for 3 years. In the latter 2 years, Taylor took charge, becoming the only Cdn ever to lead an Antarctic mission. After the war, Taylor returned to the Army to a position at the engineering directorate in Ottawa. He participated in a joint US/Cdn mission to the Queen Elizabeth Islands in the northern Arctic. Taylor earned his MA and PhD in geography from the Université de Montréal in the early 1950s, and contributed to research on the operation of **MILITARY** equipment in cold weather. He retired from the Army in 1952 and became a private contractor. In 1956, he worked for the US's air force in **CHURCHILL**, helping lay out the Distant Early Warning system, a line of Cold War radar stations extending from AK to Baffin Island designed to detect incoming bombers.

Taylor moved back to Winnipeg in the early 1960s and started an engineering consulting firm with an additional office in Ottawa. He specialized in town planning, highway construction, and **MINING** surveys in the Northern Region. He also helped survey the **RED RIVER FLOODWAY**. In 1970, Taylor retired as an engineer and opened the Antiquarian Book and Art Gallery. He also wrote extensively about the North, though he is best known for indexing the British Parliament's reports on 19th-century Arctic exploration – the "Blue Books" – beginning in the 1950s. Taylor was named an Officer of the Order of Canada in 1986, and was received an honorary doctorate from the U of M in 1991. • JOEL TRENAMAN

TAYLOR, Hannah, child philanthropist (b Jan 18, 1996, **WINNIPEG**) started The Ladybug Foundation Inc. when she was just 7 years old, making her the youngest advocate for the homeless in Cdn history. The Ladybug Foundation is a registered **NON-PROFIT** organization aimed at raising awareness and funding for homeless people by working alongside existing charities to provide food, shelter, and clothing. In 2005, Taylor's foundation was credited with directly and indirectly raising $500,000 through donation, sponsorship,

sales of scarves decorated with a ladybug motif, and the distribution of coin jars painted to resemble ladybugs. At the age of 6, Hannah, the 3rd child of Bruce and Colleen Taylor of Winnipeg, saw a man eating out of a garbage can. She began to ask about homelessness, and soon, with the help of teachers, friends, classmates, and family members, she began collecting spare change in ladybug jars for Siloam Mission, a Winnipeg charity that assists hundreds of homeless people each day by providing food and clothing. Taylor is a bug lover, and many European cultures believe that ladybug beetles bring good luck. Despite suffering congenital heart problems, Taylor has spoken to thousands of people, including some of Canada's top executives and politicians, on the topic of homelessness. • JILL SEXSMITH

TAYLOR, Robert R., photographer, writer (b June 16, 1940, Toronto, ON) is a well-known photographer with more than 40 years of experience. He has conducted nature tours in the Cdn Arctic in search of animals and plant-life. For more than 20 years, he has taught photography workshops in **CHURCHILL** and elsewhere. Taylor has also conducted numerous African photo-safaris. His enthusiasm, love of nature, and photography skills have made him a sought-after guide, teacher, and lecturer. His photography has appeared in 11 books and numerous magazines including *Equinox, The Beaver, Life,* and *Canadian Geographic*. His own award-winning book, *The Manitoba Landscape: A Visual Symphony*, was a Cdn bestseller, and was reprinted 5 times. His other books include *The Edge of the Arctic: Churchill and the Hudson Bay Lowlands, The Edge of the Arctic: Churchill and the Hudson Bay Region, The Great Grey Owl: On Silent Wings,* and *Manitoba: Seasons of Beauty*. In 1978, he was accepted into the prestigious Royal Canadian Academy of Arts, one of few photographers to receive this honour. • JS

TECHNOLOGY in MB has been influenced by the province's geographic and economic position, located between ON, with its dominance in manufacturing, and AB, with its rapid expansion of resource industries. MB's **ECONOMY** reflects this somewhat ambiguous status. It has a relatively well developed **MANUFACTURING** sector for a western province, as well as an important resource sector; but unlike AB and, to a lesser extent, SK, MB's resource wealth lies in **HYDROELECTRICITY** rather than fossil fuels. A 3rd factor is MB's emerging role as a research centre in the biomedical and life sciences. These economic, geographic, and, to an extent, political realities have helped direct MB's technological priorities.

Manufacturing remains central to MB's economy, employing 71,000 workers and accounting for 14% of the provincial GDP. The manufacturing sector is diverse, but several industries stand out as technological frontrunners. **Winnipeg** is NA's largest centre for **Bus Manufacturing**, with 2 dominant firms, **Motor Coach Industries** and **New Flyer**. These companies are researching more energy-efficient forms of urban and inter-urban public transportation New Flyer has been working to develop alternative power sources, such as natural gas, hydrogen, and hybrid engines, for urban buses for the North American market.

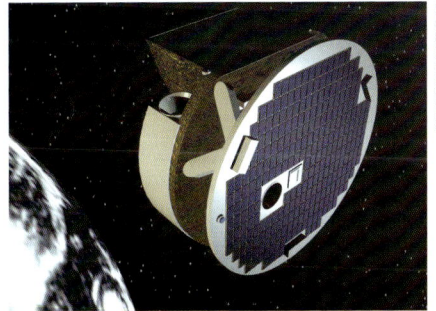

Artist's rendering of the SCISAT satellite, manufactured in Winnipeg by Bristol

MB's **Aerospace** industry is the 3rd-largest in Canada, with over $1 billion in annual sales. The province is home to a variety of manufacturing, repair, overhaul, and service firms. Manufactured products include composite aircraft assemblies, advanced alloy engine components, and spacecraft systems. The 4 leading companies are **Bristol Aerospace**, **Boeing Canada**, **Standard Aero Ltd**, and Air Canada Maintenance. The industry directly employs over 5000 workers and exports 80% of its output.

The electronics industry in the province is vibrant. The closely related computer or information technology (IT) industry comprises manufacturing and service companies that store, manipulate, and transmit information. Compared to other parts of Canada, where large companies dominate, MB's IT industry is largely composed of **Small Business** and medium-sized companies. One of the most successful is Vansco Electronics, which employs 600 people and which specializes in the manufacture of custom electronic and electro-mechanical products. **Manitoba Telecom Services**, primarily involved in the Communications Industry, has over $1 billion in revenue and more than 3500 employees, and is MB's leading information provider. It has played a vital role in supporting industrial development by implementing an advanced telecommunications infrastructure, with high-speed Internet access available to more than 85% of its MB locations. One IT group that has taken advantage of the advanced communications environment is the technical help-desk industry. Nearly 1000 Manitobans work to provide technical help-desk support services for IT applications.

Hydroelectricity represents MB's greatest resource for future development. The province is already a leader in long-distance electrical transmission, and MB obtains 95% of its power from this form of energy. **Manitoba Hydro**, Canada's 4th-largest energy utility, produces more than 5000 mW of electricity from 14 hydro generating stations annually. There is an equivalent amount of untapped hydroelectric potential, largely in northern MB's **Nelson** and **Churchill** rivers. MB plans to translate its hydro resources and technological experience into an economic advantage in a post-fossil-fuel world. The image of hydroelectricity as a clean and green form of energy is open to question, however. Past hydro developments in MB have caused **Floods** and other environmental damage and disruption of First Nations communities. Proposed dams on the drawing board have been designed to reduce environmental depredation, and have involved a process of consultation with affected First Nations. Through the Energy Development Initiative, MB hopes to diversify its position by promoting a variety of alternative energy sources, such as ethanol, hydrogen, and biomass. The St. Leon Wind Energy Project, backed by private and public financing, was slated in 2005 to become among the largest and most technologically advanced wind farms in Canada.

Biotechnology and the life sciences represent an area of growing significance for MB. This has been largely due to the success of research efforts in the agricultural and biomedical sciences, and the potential for synergy between the 2 fields. The province has long been a centre for research in plant, animal, and even aquatic sciences in the prairie environment. More recently, MB has gained a reputation for success in medical research, especially in the area of communicable diseases. The result has been a proliferation of university programs, research institutes, govt laboratories, and biotech companies that have started up or expanded to take advantage of MB's expertise in the life sciences. The federal govt has recognized this expertise by establishing prestigious research laboratories in Winnipeg. These include the **Canadian Science Centre for Human and Animal Health**, and the National Research Council's **Institute for Biodiagnostics**. By the early 21st century, the research component of MB's life sciences sector was critical to its growth and viability. More than $120 million is spent annually on research and development in this field, which supports more than 1800 technical staff employed in 20 research institutes. The industrial component is also expanding. There are 37 biotechnology companies that employ more than 1600 people, and manufacture a variety of **Pharmaceutical**, nutritional, and agricultural products. Five companies – **Cangene**, Biovail, Apotex, Monsanto, and Vita Health – dominate this sector.

Other technologically competitive manufacturers include the **Garment Industry**, the 3rd-largest in Canada, and the printing industry, with success stories including **Altona**-based **Friesens Corporation**, one of Canada's largest book printers.

Geographic and economic realities, such as a diversified economy balanced between natural resource, manufacturing, and service industries, have played a leading role in shaping MB's technological priorities. Hydroelectric potential represents MB's main hope for future resource development. Other developments, especially those in biotechnology and the life sciences, will require investment in human resources, particularly in post-secondary education. Like hydroelectricity, they also pose important questions of future environmental sustainability and human well-being. ● JOEL NOVAK

TELPNER, Eugene Louis "Gene," journalist, entrepreneur, philanthropist, pilot (b Jun 1, 1920, Omaha; d May 9, 2005, **Winnipeg**). Telpner was a prominent Winnipeg journalist whose career spanned more than 60 years. After studying journalism at the U of NE, he joined the *Omaha World-Herald* as a copyboy, also writing for US television shows. In WWII, Telpner served in the US air force, achieving the rank of Capt. On a 1944 mission over Brunswick, Germany, his plane was shot down, forcing him to parachute. On landing, he suffered injuries, was captured, and was held for 13 months in Stalag Luft 1, Barth, Germany. After the war's end and his discharge, Telpner married Fritzi Schuckett, whom he had met while visiting an aunt in **Winnipeg** when he was a teenager. The couple settled in Omaha, moving to Winnipeg a few years later, and had 3 children. After his move, Telpner worked as a journalist for 30 years, frequently interviewing Hollywood personalities. He worked as an arts and entertainment writer, bowling columnist, news analyst, and media panellist. He worked for 14 years with the **Winnipeg Free Press** and 13 years with the **Winnipeg Tribune**. After the *Tribune* closed in 1980, Telpner joined the **Winnipeg Sun** as an associate editor and a columnist. Telpner founded the local chapter of the Variety Club, a fundraising organization for children's charities, and received many awards for his charity work. Telpner died, aged 84, in a Winnipeg nursing home after suffering from Alzheimer's disease. Many of Telpner's papers are on deposit with the **ARCHIVES** at the **U OF M**. • AJL

TERNS. *See* **GULLS**.

TENNIS is the familiar singles or doubles game played on courts, a descendant of the French indoor game jeu de paume, also called real (or court) tennis. The game can be played on courts made of clay or other surfaces as well as grass.

Tennis was a fashionable sport among the elite of MB at the beginning of the 20th century, and was played primarily in private clubs. The Manitoba Lawn Tennis Assoc began operating in 1880, with many of its members also belonging to the Winnipeg Lawn Tennis Club. By 1890, there were roughly 25 tennis courts in **WINNIPEG**. Plum Creek (*see* **SOURIS**), **BIRTLE**, and **OAK LAKE** also had clubs. Games were held daily at the Winnipeg Lawn Tennis club, starting with a tea in the early evening before 3 hours of tennis, and closing the affair with a small dinner. It was one of the few sports in which women could play dressed in full-length skirts. Women were considered "tea members" of the Winnipeg club. They only received full membership rights in 1935.

One of MB's most prominent tennis clubs was in **MINNEDOSA**, which hosted an annual open tournament that attracted players from all over MB. By 1910, a provincial championship was well established. As the sport grew more popular, churches and municipal govts also built tennis courts. In 1915, Winnipeg churches formed their own tennis league, and in 1920, the Cdn lawn tennis championship was held in Winnipeg. Lawn tennis began to decline as the British way of life became less pervasive in MB, and the game became more of a competitive sport than a social event. Tennis Manitoba, formed in 1974, now governs all aspects of the sport in the province. • MD

TERMITE is an insect in the order Isoptera (class Insecta) characterized by a soft, pale body, broad waist connecting thorax to abdomen, and highly developed social behaviour in colonies of 100s to 7 million. MB currently has no native species of termites, with cold temperatures preventing a successful invasion, but this will likely change soon with global warming. There are 41 species in NA. The Eastern Subterranean Termite (*Reticulitermes flavipes*) was accidentally introduced in a load of lumber to a few buildings in Winnipeg during the 1980s, but with control applications it appears not to have spread. This most widespread species in E and central NA

causes over $50 million of structural damage to buildings annually. With the aid of protozoa, bacteria and fungi in the gut, termites feed on dead wood and fungi, eventually turning sound timber into powder. Tunnels may reach 20 m. A colony is often composed of several million individuals, consisting of a king, queen, winged reproductives (young kings and queens), soldiers and countless workers – all with different form and functions, but interdependent. There are 6 nymphal stages, lasting 2 years. When conditions are right in the spring (above 20C), the winged reproductives emerge and swarm in large numbers, mating and then dispersing to found new colonies. The reproductive potential is astounding, with the large queen producing over 2000 eggs per day over a 25-year lifespan. • REW

TEULON, pop 1058, is a town 60 km N of **WINNIPEG** and 20 km W of **LAKE WINNIPEG** on hwy 7 and on a **CPR** branch line. Teulon was incorporated as a village Jan 4, 1919, and as a town in 1997. CPR inspector Charles C. Castle, who played a prominent role in bringing the railway line to the area, dubbed the community "Teulon," his wife's maiden name. Teulon was first home to **SCOTS**, **UKRAINIAN** and **ICELANDIC** settlers. In the 21st century, significant employers within Teulon include the hospital and medical care facilities, as well as a goose processing plant that makes goose down pillows, blankets, jackets and also prepares meat for market. Teulon is home to elementary and secondary schools, as well recreation facilities that include an indoor arena and curling club, and a community park that offers baseball diamonds, soccer pitches, a campground, and a museum. Teulon's annual festivals, notably the Veselka Ukrainian Dance Festival, the Teulon Pumpkin Festival, and the Agricultural Fair, also serve as tourist attractions. • GPP

THANADELTHUR, "The Slave Woman," interpreter (b ca 1697; d Feb 7, 1717, Fort York) assisted in peace talks between the warring **CREE**

and **DENE** (Chipewyan) Nations. A Dene by birth, Thanadelthur was captured by Cree in 1713 and forced into slavery. She learned of useful trade goods, unavailable to her people for fear of attack while travelling, that the Cree obtained from the **HUDSON'S BAY COMPANY**. In Nov 1714, she escaped to the HBC post at **YORK FACTORY**. The fort's gov, James Knight, saw that Thanadelthur – whom he called "Slave Woman" – could be of help as an interpreter and negotiator, as she spoke both Cree and Dene. She subsequently accompanied HBC servant William Stuart and a party of 150 Cree on a peace mission. While most of the mission gave up the task following the murders of 5 Denes, Thanadelthur persisted, and convinced her people to set aside their arms. Gov James Knight described her as being of "great Courage." • MD

THE PAS, pop 5589, is MB's 10th largest community. It is located 120 km SSE of **FLIN FLON**, on the **SASKATCHEWAN** River near its confluence with the Pasquia and Carrot Rivers; on hwy 10; 35 km E of the SK border. The Woodland **CREE** and later the Swampy Cree long inhabited the area, making it one of the oldest settled sites in northern MB. The Pas is located at a point where the Saskatchewan River Delta narrows and breaches a prominent glacial ridge, "The Pas Moraine." The name "The Pas" is derived from the Cree word *wapasquia*, or *opasquia*, meaning "rising tree line." The adjacent **OPASKWAYAK CREE NATION** takes its name from the same word; over time, this was shortened to "The Pas." The first European to the area was **HENRY KELSEY** in 1690, and ill-fated Arctic explorer Sir John Franklin twice visited here in the 1820s. In 1748, the sons of **LA VÉRENDRYE** founded a **FRENCH FUR TRADING** post, Fort Paskoyac (also named for the river) here. Several years later, this area saw what is believed to be the first grain cultivated in what is now western Canada, planted by the fort's commander, Capt Louis, Chevalier de la Corne. In 1774, the **HBC** built nearby Cumberland House

Winner of the Ladies' Dog Race, Trappers Festival, 1953, The Pas

(just W of the SK border), and the area subsequently served as a meeting place between Cree, French, **Métis**, and **English** trappers. In 1840, the first **Anglican** mission was established, led by Cree catechist Henry Budd, who in 1853 became the first Aboriginal minister of the Church of England in North America.

The steamboat era began at The Pas in 1874 with the arrival of the HBC's SS *Northcote*. The railway reached The Pas in 1908 through the lobbying efforts of Herman Finger, a US lumberman who went on to create The Pas Lumber Company and became the first mayor of the town when it was incorporated in 1912. With the coming of the railway, word spread of the abundant opportunities in the area in lumbering, mining and agriculture, and people were drawn to the area. Mining claim-stakers headed N to prospect, and over the next decades, the area proved rich in minerals, leading to the expansion of this community, and the creation of others.

The **Hudson Bay Railway**, still a significant employer here, was built from The Pas to **Churchill** starting around the same time, though it took until 1929 to complete the line. In 1906, the federal govt bought the townsite from the local Swampy Cree, who moved just N of the river to what is now the Opaskwayak Cree Nation (OCN). The town's population of 500 upon incorporation in 1912 tripled within one year, with the arrival of people of various backgrounds. The most prominent groups remain the **Cree**, French, **Scots**, and English, though **Ukrainians**, **Germans**, and **Irish** form large minorities. The town continued to grow until the last quarter of the 20th century, since which time it has declined, shrinking 6% (from 6166 to 5975) between 1991-2001.

To the earlier industries of forestry/pulp and paper – with Tolko Industries Ltd. the biggest employer in the town, making both kraft paper and lumber – and agriculture – primarily grains and oilseeds – The Pas has added commercial **Fishing**, **Tourism**, govt services, and **Transportation**. For this last reason, The Pas calls itself the "Gateway to the North." The former Keewatin College, now the **University College of the North**, is based here as well as in **Thompson**. Hunters come here for the massive flocks of **Waterfowl**, and other forms of outdoor tourism, such as **Canoeing** and **Angling**, are popular. Other attractions are the **Northern Manitoba Trapper's Festival**, founded 1916; the Sam Waller Museum, located in a courthouse built that same year; **Opaskwayak Indian Days**; and the nearby provincial park. Despite the town's divided nature – part Euro-Canadian town, part Cree reserve – everyone backs the OCN Blizzard, a highly competitive junior **Hockey** team. ● AJL

THEATRE IN MANITOBA
By Reg Skene

Theatre in Manitoba began in **Winnipeg** in the early 1870s. Officers of local army garrisons regularly produced plays, and civilian amateurs staged *tableaux vivants* on literary themes and presented such well-known romances as Boucicault's *The Colleen Bawn* and such farcical melodramas as *Ten Nights in a Barroom*. American railways brought freight and passengers to Fargo, ND, where steamboats took them to Winnipeg, and US professional performers soon began finding their way north by this route.

DAN SKWARCHUK COLLECTION

The brochure for the 1907 opening of the Walker Theatre emphasized its fireproof construction.

A new Winnipeg City Hall was built on Main St in 1876 with a 500-seat second-story auditorium and a real stage – the settlement's most satisfactory theatre to that date. In 1877, the first professional touring ensemble, the Cool Burgess Repertory Company appeared at Winnipeg's City Hall Theatre. In 1878, a rail link was built between Winnipeg and Pembina, ND, adjacent to **Emerson**, giving access to the MB capital without need for steamboats. Eugene McDowell's company took advantage of this new route, as did the troupes of actress-managers Katy Putnam and Phosa McAllister.

In 1883, City Hall was judged structurally unsound and was demolished, destroying Winnipeg's first real theatre. A new place of entertainment was opened that year, the Princess Opera House, on Princess St at Ross. The Princess was leased to William Seach and Charles Sharp, former building contractors. Sharp booked an impressive range of US touring shows through a St. Paul agent. Attractions at the Princess included the noted Shakespearean actor Thomas Keene; the 15-year-old "boy tragedian" Walker Whiteside; character comedian Dan Sully; and actor-playwright William Gillette. The Princess Opera House was destroyed by fire May 1, 1892.

Seach continued booking the St. Paul-based program at the Bijou Theatre, a converted concert hall at Notre Dame Ave and Adelaide, controlled by Confederation Life. At the end of 1896, Seach resumed his partnership with Sharp, and they briefly managed a converted meeting hall on Main St. South until that building was destroyed by fire on Jan 17, 1897. Seach and Sharp then remodelled a warehouse on McDermot Ave between Main and Albert, opening it Apr 15, 1897, as the Grand Opera House.

THE WALKER ERA: In January 1897, Confederation Life announced plans to convert the Bijou into a fully modern playhouse, and to seek a new manager for it in the US. The manager they found was **C. P. WALKER** of the Fargo Opera House. Charles H. Wheeler, architect and drama critic of the *WINNIPEG TRIBUNE*, was put in charge of the theatre conversion. Walker leased the building for 9 years, and opened it Sept 6, 1897, as the Winnipeg Opera House.

This acquisition provided Walker with a flagship theatre for the Red River Valley theatre circuit he and his brothers had been assembling. With theatres at Winnipeg; Fargo, Grafton, and Grand Forks, ND; and Crookston and Fergus Falls, MN, the Walker brothers had access to a potential audience large enough to qualify them as an affiliate of the New York Theatre Syndicate, an organization formed in 1895 to gain monopoly control of US theatrical touring. Syndicate affiliation enabled Walker to book the core of his season directly from New York and his competitors soon found their source of bookings in St. Paul rapidly drying up. Seach and Sharp tried for a time to use stock companies to compete with Walker's New York attractions. The most ambitious of these was the company of Harold Nelson, Toronto elocution-teacher-turned-tragedian, who was keen to establish a classical repertoire on the Prairies. Nelson developed shows at the Grand and then toured them through western Canada. Within 3 years, Seach and Sharp were driven out of business, closing their theatre and selling the building to the *Tribune* newspaper. Nelson transferred his operation to the Winnipeg Theatre where Walker financed his productions and sponsored his Western tours. Walker also mounted tours of his own, producing shows in Winnipeg and booking them into the growing number of theatres he controlled on Canada's Prairies.

It wasn't just C. P. Walker's syndicate connection or his aggressive management style that allowed him to gain monopoly control of Winnipeg theatre by 1900. He was backed by a remarkable publicity and public relations operation created and managed by his wife. Harriet Walker was a competent journalist, a talented musical comedy actress, a skilled theatre director, and an imaginative publicist. She compiled all the press releases for the Red River Valley circuit and, innocent of concern for conflict of interest, wrote under a pseudonym a column of theatre commentary in *Town Topics*, Winnipeg's weekly society newspaper. *Town Topics* was owned and edited by Charles Handscomb, drama critic of the *Manitoba Free Press* (later *WINNIPEG FREE PRESS*), and close friend of C. P. Walker. Less supportive of the Walker operation was Charles H. Wheeler, *Tribune* drama critic and architect of the Winnipeg Opera House conversion and sharply hostile to Walker was R.L. Richardson, editor of the *Winnipeg Tribune*.

In Dec 1903, the Syndicate's Iroquois Theatre in Chicago was burned. The fire killed 602 audience members. Civic officials closed unsafe theatres across the US and Richardson, in his editorial columns, led a campaign to close Walker's wooden, second-storey theatre, and put Walker himself out of business. The Winnipeg Theatre was clearly a firetrap, but Walker managed to hold off civic action on the issue until a new fireproof theatre on Smith St at Notre Dame could be built. The new playhouse, the Walker Theatre, officially opened Feb 18, 1907.

The Walker Theatre offered the Syndicate's best programming. Walker Theatre audiences saw 2 recent Broadway shows most weeks, a pattern broken at intervals by the presentation by leading US companies of repertoires of Shakespeare, Modern Drama, Grand Opera and Musical Comedy. Such international stars as Olga Nethersole, Mrs. Patrick Campbell, Viola Allen, and John Drew became familiar to Winnipeg audiences through their appearances on the Walker stage. Walker lost his theatre monopoly Dec 1904 when vaudeville came to Winnipeg, with the opening of the Dominion Theatre on Portage Ave. East. A second vaudeville house, the Bijou, on Main St. south of William, opened in 1906. Theatrical stock became a strong competitor in 1906 when W. B. Lawrence came from Cleveland OH with a permanent stock company for the Winnipeg Theatre. By WWI, 2 additional vaudeville houses had opened in Winnipeg, the Orpheum Theatre, on Fort St. (1911), and the Pantages Theatre, on Market St. (1914). When Pantages vaudeville left the Market St. theatre in 1923, another stock company was installed there and the name of the theatre was changed from the Pantages to the Playhouse.

By the end of WWI, the theatre situation had changed considerably. Increased costs and a flight of US capital from live theatre to movies had depleted the supply of US touring shows. An all-Cdn syndicate, Trans-Canada Theatres Limited, was attempted to build an east-west system of Cdn tours by British theatrical companies. Walker leased the Walker Theatre to this corporation in Nov 1919, but within 3 years, the venture collapsed and Walker was forced to resume management of his theatre. For the rest of the decade, Walker imported leading British companies and arranged tours in co-operation with other Cdn theatre managers. In 1930 Famous Players Corporation, a subsidiary of Paramount Pictures, issued an edict forbidding the managers of their theatres to book any live shows on their stages. Famous Players was protecting their parent company's investment in talking pictures. Since Famous Players Corporation controlled all the theatres in key Cdn cities, financially viable theatre tours in Canada became impossible. C.P. Walker tried to keep the Walker Theatre open by creating a stock company, but he soon had to accept defeat and close it down.

EARLY PLAYWRITING, AMATEUR THEATRE, AND NON- THEATRE: The first professionally produced play set in MB was *The Big Boom*, written by 19-year-old Charles Hanscomb, then a junior reporter, and presented at the Princess Theatre in 1886 by a visiting repertory company. In 1910, C. P. Walker booked 2 musical farces by local playwright/composer Stanley Adams, *Quits* and *Dolly Denton's Doings*, at the Walker Theatre.

In 1907, when Gov Gen Earl Grey sponsored the first Music and Drama Festival in Ottawa, the Earl Grey Trophy was won by the Winnipeg Dramatic Club with a production of "The Release of Allan Danvers," written by their director, Major James Devine and 2 newspaper reporters, Ernest Beauford and Wilson Blue. The Earl Grey Trophy was awarded to the Winnipeg Opera Society for their production of "The Chimes of Normandy" directed by Harriet Walker. The following year, back in Ottawa, the trophy was won by Col W. K. Chandler's Winnipeg company, The Strollers, with a production of Shaw's "You Never Can Tell." After her stint as a musical-comedy director, Harriet Walker turned her attention

Winnipeg Little Theatre cast, 1936

Leaders of the Community Players made a concerted effort to draw into their fold the members of ethnic amateur groups in the city, particularly those of Icelandic, Jewish and French-speaking groups. Close attention was given to theatrical materials from the various cultural communities in establishing the program of the Community Players. LE CERCLE MOLIÈRE, which was to become one of Canada's most respected French-language theatres, was founded in St. Boniface in 1925, and co-operation between Le Cercle Moliere and the Community Players was particularly close in the late 1920s. Prominent members of the Community Players were John Craig, Nancy Pyper, Edith Sinclair, O. A. Eggertson (a strong promoter of Icelandic culture), and Lady Margaret Tupper, all of whom acted and directed. Painters Lemoine Fitzgerald and W. J. Phillips were active in designing and decorating sets.

In 1930, when commercial touring abruptly stopped, the Community Players engaged John Craig as a paid full-time director. Craig renamed the organization the Winnipeg Little Theatre and reshaped its artistic strategy to capture the mainstream audience left behind when the commercial theatre collapsed. His production of Ibsen's "A Doll's House" (Mar 1931) starring Nancy Pyper, and his "Othello" (August 1932) starring George Waight, achieved national critical notice and drew large houses locally.

By the end of the 1920s, amateur theatre had grown in MB to the extent that a system of play festivals on the British seemed the appropriate next step. The Extensions Service of the Department of Agriculture and the Women's Institute were eager to back such a project and the membership of the Winnipeg Little Theatre was prepared to provide artistic and organizational leadership. The Manitoba Drama League was founded in 1931 and immediately attracted 90 theatre groups from every part of the province. The MDL gave support and practical aid to amateur companies, organizing regional festivals and providing adjudicators for them. After the founding of the Dominion Drama Festival in 1932, through the efforts of Lord Bessborough and others, MDL activities were merged with those of the DDF, and a co-ordinated system of festivals was created. This system stayed in place until the death of the DDF in the 1970s.

In 1933, the Winnipeg Little Theatre moved from their theatre at Main and Selkirk to the Dominion Theatre, now vacant and owned by grain merchant and financier James Richardson. Rent was set at a nominal rate. Disputes soon broke out between Craig and Lady Tupper, a powerful Little Theatre member who had been instrumental in gaining the new venue. Craig wanted to develop the Little Theatre into a professionally oriented theatre, with high production standards and a program geared to the tastes and interest of the local audience. Lady Tupper favoured development of an idealistic amateurism closely aligned with Gov Gen Lord Bessborough's plans for a Dominion Drama Festival. Lady Tupper withdrew from the Little Theatre organization and established the Players' Guild, a company devoted to Shakespeare, Celtic opera, verse drama, ethnic dance plays, and "high art," establishing herself as a formidable force in the councils of the Dominion Drama Festival. John Craig's 1936 production of Henrik Ibsen's *Peer Gynt*, with Esse Ljungh in the title role, drew an audience in excess of 3 000, but box-office success was his undoing. Audience response to Craig's work led the Richardsons to realize that the Dominion could once again become a commercially viable and rent-yielding theatre. In the summer of 1936, they summoned a company of young Toronto actors under the direction of John Holden to bring stock operation at the Dominion Theatre that fall. Finding themselves without a theatrical home, Craig's Little Theatre company mounted 2 productions in rented Orpheum facilities, but when a deficit developed the Board of the Little Theatre disbanded that

to theatre activities at the U of M. From 1915 to 1921, she directed a string of polished shows at the university, all the while providing workshops in acting and play production.

By the 1920s, MB was filled with amateur theatre groups. **BRANDON** had an active and competent amateur theatre association, as did most smaller rural MB communities. The Brandon Operatic Society was as active and musically adept as their sister organization in Winnipeg, a city where they were often invited to perform. Particularly impressive was the amateur theatre produced in the province in languages other than English. From the early 1900s, Icelandic communities, in the **INTERLAKE** region and in Winnipeg, had produced Icelandic-language plays, retelling traditional Icelandic stories, and commenting on social and economic conditions of Icelandic immigrants. Culturally and politically aware Ukrainian amateurs regularly produced in Winnipeg's North End, tradition-based theatre in their own language, and striking examples of a more radical, socially oriented theatre of protest. There had been an active amateur Yiddish theatre in Winnipeg from 1904, performing at the Queen's Theatre on Selkirk Ave, a venue which also hosted visiting theatre companies from the professional Yiddish touring circuits in the US. French language theatre on classical lines had been present since the 1890s both in St. Boniface and rural francophone communities, promoted by religious teachers and amateur lay groups interested in preserving the French language and culture.

THE COMMUNITY PLAYERS: In 1921, at about the time Trans-Canada Theatres was floundering, 2 Winnipeg lawyers, H. A. V. Green and Alan Crawley, founded the Winnipeg Community Players. The organization was a reaction against the shallowness and cynicism of commercial theatre, and a response to the idealism of the amateur Little Theatre movement then sweeping NA and Europe. Members were largely from Winnipeg's young professional class – doctors, lawyers, teachers, engineers, and their families. The first performances were given at the Dominion Theatre, but the amateur company soon found a home in a small refurbished "pop" vaudeville house at the corner of Main St and Selkirk Ave, in Winnipeg's North End.

T

organization. The Holden Players continued at the Dominion Theatre until the outbreak of WWII when the male members of the company joined the Canadian Forces. Lady Tupper's Players' Guild dissolved shortly after the Winnipeg Little Theatre, and Lady Tupper turned her attention to the needs of the Winnipeg Ballet Club.

REVIVAL OF THE WINNIPEG LITTLE THEATRE: In 1948, George Brodersen and Robert Jarman re-established the Winnipeg Little Theatre. Initial members were theatrical academics, professional radio actors, former members of Winnipeg's pre-war theatre organizations, and U of M students wishing to become professional theatre workers. Productions were staged at the city-owned Playhouse Theatre. Four plays a year were produced, directed by the most theatrically experienced members of the organization. Other groups rented the Playhouse as well, among them the Winnipeg Dramatic Society, the Teachers' Dramatic Society, and the Winnipeg Repertory Theatre. Semi-professional theatre groups soon emerged, notably the Actor's Guild, founded and run by Robert Jarman's daughter Peggy Green, the Junior League Children's Theatre, and the Musical Comedy Guild.

Among the ambitious younger members of the Winnipeg Little Theatre was JOHN HIRSCH, a Jewish Hungarian war orphan who came to Winnipeg in 1948. John mastered English, earned a BA from the U of M, founded a puppet troupe, and wrote plays for the Junior League Children's Theatre. He acted at every opportunity and longed for an opportunity to direct. In Apr 1953, Jarman, by then full-time managing producer of the Little Theatre, was stricken by a fatal heart attack while adjudicating a play festival at Pilot Mound. Hirsch was appointed to succeed him. In the 1953-54 season, Hirsch created a sensation with productions of William Saroyan's "The Time of Your Life" and Jean Giraudoux's "The Enchanted." Peggy Green, through her teaching and directing, had by this time established a company of actors in Winnipeg, eager to begin professional work. Hirsch made brilliant use of them. At the conclusion of the 1953-54 season Hirsch left Winnipeg for London, UK, pursuing more formal theatre studies. In the summer or 1956 Hirsch was recalled to Winnipeg by James Duncan, then attempting to establish Rainbow Stage, an outdoor summer theatre at KILDONAN PARK. The 1956 season of the summer theatre consisted of *Annie Get Your Gun*, directed by Duncan and Syd Perlmutter, "The Wizard of Oz", directed by John Hirsch, "Our Town", directed by Hirsch and Moray Sinclair, and "Kiss Me Kate", directed by Peggy Green. That fall, Arthur Zigouras, a graduate of the Yale School of Drama, became the paid, full-time Artistic Director of the Winnipeg Little Theatre. A search for a permanent theatrical home for the organization uncovered the fact that the Dominion theatre was once more on the market. An anonymous donor, a member of the Richardson family, purchased the Dominion for the Winnipeg Little Theatre. In the summer of 1957, Duncan summoned Hirsch once again. His staging of *Chu-Chin-Chow* was a critical and box-office success, and Hirsch's reputation as a theatrical miracle-worker in Winnipeg was secure.

In fall 1957, Hirsch and Tom Hendry, with a company of the actors who had worked with them at Rainbow Stage, founded Theatre 77, a professional company that rented the Dominion Theatre from the Winnipeg Little Theatre in the periods between the Little Theatre's own shows. In the 1957-58 season, Theatre 77 and Winnipeg Little Theatre presented alternate shows on the Dominion Theatre stage.

BIRTH OF MTC: In the spring of 1958, Zigouras resigned as Little Theatre Artistic Director and the board of the Little Theatre invited the leaders of Theatre 77 to a meeting. The 2 organizations were brought together into a single administrative framework to be known as the MANITOBA THEATRE CENTRE. The Winnipeg Little Theatre would remain

Interior of Prairie Theatre Exchange during rehearsal

amateur and Theatre 77 would operate as a professional company. Hendry became the MTC administrator, and Hirsch kept on as director of Theatre 77, MTC's professional division. Zara Shakov, from New York, was hired as the director of the amateur Little Theatre productions. At the end of the first season Hirsch became over-all Artistic Director of the Manitoba Theatre Centre. By 1962, MTC was a unified, professional organization, paying minimum equity rates, and no amateur aspects remained in its operations. MTC was adopted as the model for Canadian regional theatres, the first in a string of such theatres established across Canada.

Hirsch resigned in 1966 and was replaced by Eddie Gilbert. When the Richardsons demolished the Dominion Theatre in 1968 to make way for a Portage and Main Development, MTC was temporarily homeless. In 1970, MTC moved into a new main-stage facility on Market St, east of the Playhouse Theatre. After a chaotic period marked by abrupt terminations of artistic directorship, Steven Schipper was appointed Artistic Director of MTC in 1989. In the years since his appointment, Schipper's leadership has kept the theatre financially solvent by presenting a program marked by carefully quality control. A second MTC theatre, the Warehouse, presents plays more daring and experimental than those offered on the main stage. MTC has an active outreach program and conducts regular tours throughout the province.

OTHER IMPORTANT PROFESSIONAL THEATRES: PRAIRIE THEATRE EXCHANGE, originally an offshoot of the MTC Theatre School has developed into an important alternative theatre. The organization began in an old building in Winnipeg's Exchange District but in 1989 moved to new facilities in the Portage Place Shopping Mall. Actors' Showcase, founded in 1965 by Daphne Korol, was transformed into a Children's theatre by succeeding artistic director, Tony Pydee. In 1982, when Leslie Silverman became Artistic Director the name of the organization was changed to Manitoba Theatre for Young People. Under Silverman's leadership it has gained a reputation as a remarkable theatre for children, specializing in child-advocacy and educational drama. MTYP has its own theatre building and education complex in Winnipeg's Forks development. •

THICKET PORTAGE, pop 200, is a community 45 km SW of Thompson, on the Hudson Bay Railway line to Churchill. It formerly was known as Franklin, after Arctic explorer Sir John Franklin. "Thicket Portage" is an English version of a **CREE** name. Though the railway is the only all-year ground transportation, there is an airstrip here, and the community has a winter road. Electrical service was supplied in 1997 with completion of a 95 km transmission line connecting to the provincial grid. The $4.5 million project employed some town residents. The economic base is **FORESTRY**, **COMMERCIAL FISHING**, and trapping. ● GPP

THIN AIR. *See* **WINNIPEG INTERNATIONAL WRITERS FESTIVAL**.

Adam Thom, 1838

THOM, Adam, polemicist, judge (b Aug 30, 1802, Brechin, Angus, UK; d Feb 21, 1890, London, UK) was a controversial judge. Thom first tried to find a career in London, then came to Canada in 1832 to make his way in journalism. He published several pamphlets and, from 1836-38, he was editor of the *Montreal Herald*. In 1836, he attacked the French-Canadian party in the legislature in a pamphlet called *Anti-Gallic Letters*. He began to read law, and he was called to the bar of Lower Canada in 1837. At first a critic of the Durham mission, Thom became a secretary to Lord Durham and an advisor on the famous Durham Report. At least one obituary claimed that Thom was responsible for most of Durham's document. While in London, Thom met **GEORGE SIMPSON**, who offered him the job as the recorder (judge) of **RUPERT'S LAND**. He arrived in the **RED RIVER SETTLEMENT** in spring 1839. His eyesight was bad, his **FRENCH** virtually non-existent, his knowledge of the law dubious and his attitude

toward ethnic minorities not good. Moreover, Thom saw himself as an advocate for the **HBC**. In his court, he ran roughshod over the constitution of the settlement, hanging an Indian in 1845 despite an act of Parliament requiring all capital cases to be tried in Canada. In 1843, he heard a lawsuit against him brought by Anne Rothney, one of his own servants, and refused to order the jury's verdict against him. His most notorious cases were the **SAYER TRIAL** and **FOSS-PELLY CASE**. In the first, he lost the confidence of the Francophone community, in the second, the confidence of the Anglophone. On the positive side, he did prepare in 1851 an extensive report on the state of the law in Red River. Thom remained for 4 years after his replacement as judge, and then in 1854 retired to Edinburgh. ● JMB

THOMPSON, pop 13,446, is a city 275 km ENE of **FLIN FLON**, nestled along the Burntwood River. Now MB's 3rd-largest city, being slightly larger than **PORTAGE LA PRAIRIE**, Thompson sprang into being almost over night after an important ore body was discovered in 1956. **INCO LTD** built the mine, mill, smelter, refinery, and town services, and agreed to provide financial assistance toward **MANITOBA HYDRO**'s Kelsey Generating Station and toward a **RAILWAY** spur line which

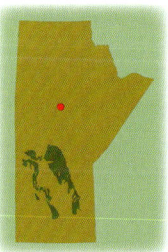

would connect with **CN**'s Bay Line near **THICKET PORTAGE**. Plans were laid for a community of 8000, which was named for the company's chair, John F. Thompson.

In lieu of taxes, the company agreed to pay 55% of the community's operating expenses annually. As of writing, residents still did not pay for their water usage, with all mineral rights underneath belonging to Inco. Following that initial agreement, in early winter 1957, a total of 1000 round trips were made by 150 men on 24 diesel-powered tractor trains hauling supplies and equipment over frozen rivers, lakes, and muskeg from Thicket Portage to the new townsite. The tractor train, dubbed "The Snowball Express," greatly helped with railway construction. The "Last Spike" ceremony was held on Oct 20, 1957. The Thompson Inco project – at the time, the largest capital project ever undertaken in MB – resulted in the development of the world's first fully integrated nickel **MINING** and processing complex. Despite Inco's significant contributions toward establishing the community, the agreement between the company and the province of MB clearly laid out that this was not to be a "company town," and as such laid the foundation for individual and commercial private development. Thompson's first home, occupied by Roy and Elsie McGinnis, was built in 1958, and in 1961, western Canada's first enclosed shopping centre was completed in the downtown core. By 1965, the population had grown to 8500,

Instant housing development in Thompson, 1958

and Thompson was incorporated as a town. In 1970, in the presence of the Royal family, the town became a city, population 20,000.

Today, Thompson is known as "The Hub of the North," and for good reason. With its paved roads and highways, scheduled daily air service, and railway system, it is the regional trade and service centre of northern MB. Both federal and provincial govts use Thompson as a base of operations for their work in northern MB. As a regional hub, Thompson has all of the services and amenities one would expect in a larger urban centre, including shopping malls, swimming pools, bowling lanes, a curling club, library, skating rinks, and athletic fields. The city's Millennium Trail, built in 2001, is a 15 km hiking/ bike loop around the city. The trail runs along the Burntwood – a large tributary of the Rat River – through boreal forest (see ECOCLIMACTIC REGIONS) and parks, featuring stops at the zoo, the King Miner commemorative statue, and the Heritage North Museum. Thompson's Spirit Way, slated to be completed in 2007, is a walking and biking route that overlaps the Millennium Trail in 2 sections, and features 18 points of interest with historical, cultural, geological, industrial, artistic, and scenic perspectives. A highlight of the Spirit Walkway is a 10-storey replica of a sketch of a wolf by BC artist Robert Bateman. The mural was painted by Charles Johnston, a professional WINNIPEG muralist.

As Thompson is set in Canadian Shield country, with its coniferous forests and pristine lakes, and with transportation links to numerous SPORT FISHING lodges, TOURISM and other outdoor-attraction operators are important to the city's ECONOMY. Thompson boasts a golf course, cross-country ski trails, downhill skiing, snowboarding, and a biathlon range. Just S of the city, Paint Lake Provincial Recreational Park offers sand beaches, shaded picnic grounds with playground equipment, a campground, cottages, a large marina, boat rentals, and an abundance of fishing. Snowmobiling is also extremely popular, with more than 300 km of groomed trails between Thompson and Sasagiu Rapids. Sasagiu Rapids is about 75 km S of Thompson on Highway 6.

Thompson has a strong Aboriginal presence, which participates in the city's economic, cultural, social, and artistic development. More than half of the NORTHERN REGION'S off-reserve status First Nations people reside in Thompson. In 2004, city council gave its approval to NISICHA-WAYASIHK CREE NATION (NCN) to convert a parcel of NCN-owned property within Thompson to treaty land, thereby creating an urban reserve.

Since 1956, Inco has been Thompson's largest employer. Various levels of govt employ the

2nd-highest concentration of Thompsonites. The 3rd-largest employer is the aviation sector, and the 4th is the School District of Mystery Lake. Accessibility, combined with occasionally frigid winter temperatures, has been good for business. The Ford Motor Company began extreme-cold testing of its vehicles here in the 1980s, established a permanent test site in 1997, and added a 2nd test track in 2005. ● ANITA DAHER

THOMPSON, Susan Ann, politician (b Apr 12, 1947, WINNIPEG). In 1971, Thompson attained her BA at the U OF W before working in retailing in Calgary, Montreal and Winnipeg. In 1980, she took over the family business, Birt Saddlery, which she owned and operated for 15 years. She became the first female mayor of Winnipeg, serving 2 terms from 1992-98. Thompson's first term was difficult, as she was a political newcomer and had to navigate the political structures at city hall. However, in her second term, she found her footing and was able to use the knowledge she had gained to win substantial change in the upper levels of the civic bureaucracy, including the abolition of the board of commissioners. She also oversaw the city's response to the biggest crisis to hit Winnipeg in the 20th century – the flood of 1997. Following her public life in Winnipeg politics, Thompson was named Canada's Consul General in Minneapolis, MN, the first woman to be appointed to the post in its 30-year history. In 2003, she returned to Winnipeg to assume the position of CEO of the University of Winnipeg Foundation. ● RUTH DEGRAVES

THORKELSSON, Ione, glass installation artist (b April 20, 1947, WINNIPEG) grew up in ASHERN, studied ARCHITECTURE at the U OF M (1965-1969), and established her first private studio in 1973, moving to ROSEISLE in 1979. Exploring the many

effects and properties of glass, she creates both translucent and opaque pieces using various techniques, particularly blowing and casting, at times combining them. Her internationally acclaimed blown vases, perfume bottles and paper weights are rich in their layers and colours of glass. Blowing gives her complete control over her shapes and forms; with casting she has control over the surface and textures. She draws her subjects for her sculptures and installations from the beauty and fragility of the natural world casting birds, insects and bones in glass. Thorkelsson then assembles her 'specimens,' fusing elements from different sources to create new, imaginary species. By combining techniques and fusing the vertebrae of one being with the skull or foot of another, she achieves a true sense of mystery, giving her creations a permanence in the material generally deemed 'fragile.' She presents her fantastic imaginary vertebrae, birds' wings, tree trunks, and skeletons as artifacts and museum 'specimens.'

Her work has been exhibited across Canada, the most recent including, *Ossuary 501* (Toronto 2006); *Arboreal Fragments* (WAG 2006); *Tropocene* (Toronto 2004). Her work is in public and private collections including The WINNIPEG ART GALLERY, the Canadian Museum of Civilization, Canadian Clay and Glass Museum, Canada Council Art Bank, Rideau Hall, Ottawa. She has received many commissions and grant awards and has been written about widely including: *Fragments & 2 partial reconstructions: Everything we know about the Tropocene*, (Clay and Glass Museum 2004); *Ione Thorkelsson: New Work and Retrospective*, (WAG 1998); *The Unwilling Bestiary*, (with Lea Littlewolf Turnstone Press, 1998). In 2007, Thorkelsson was inducted into the Royal Canadian Academy of Arts. ● PATRICIA BOVEY

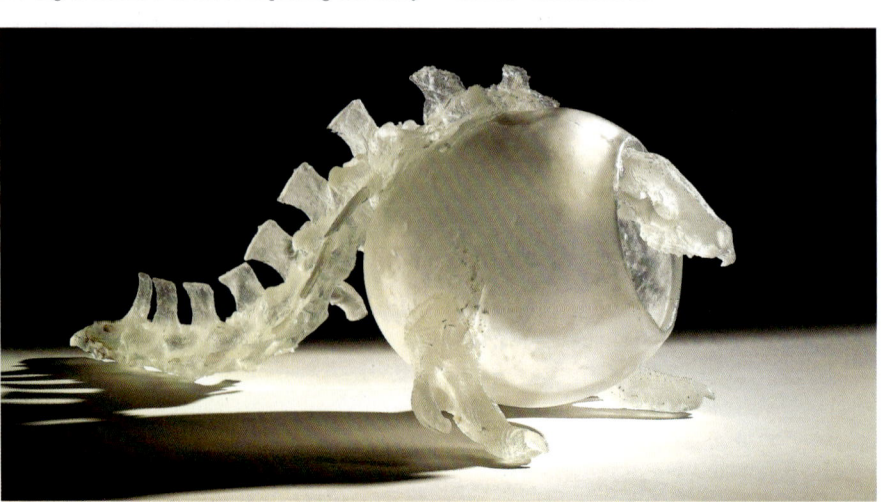

Spine Animal, glass, 22 x by 47 x 30 cm, 1998, by Ione Thorkelsson

WAG 2005-51

THORLAKSON, Paul Henrik Thorbjorn "Dr. Thor," surgeon, administrator, teacher (b Oct 5, 1895, Park River, ND; d Oct 19, 1989, WINNIPEG). Born in the US, Thorlakson grew up in SELKIRK and enrolled in the Manitoba Medical College (later absorbed by the U OF M) in 1914. He volunteered for military service in 1916 and graduated as a doctor in 1917. He initially practised in SHOAL LAKE before taking postgraduate studies in surgery in the UK. On returning to MB, Thorlakson joined Neil John MacLean to form the MacLean-Thorlakson Clinic – the forerunner of the Winnipeg Clinic – in 1926. By 1937, the practice had expanded so much that Thorlakson purchased a property on the corner of St Mary Ave and Vaughan St, which became the site of the city's first multi-specialty group practice, the present Winnipeg Clinic. He was appointed to the first Medical Research Committee of the National Research Council of Canada in 1938 (forerunner of the Medical Research Council of Canada) at the invitation of Sir Frederick Banting and helped form the Western Regional Committee on Medical Research of the Council. He was also the founder and the first president of the MB Institute for the Advancement of Medical Education and Research, later the Winnipeg Clinic Research Institute.

Thorlakson was a vigorous promoter of medical research, which he believed was essential for exemplary medical care, and of medical education in all, even underdeveloped, regions of the country. He pioneered group medicine in Canada and became an international authority on the subject; was an initiator of the first comprehensive scheme for insured physician services in MB; and promoted the concept of the Manitoba Medical Centre, which later became the HEALTH SCIENCES CENTRE in Winnipeg. He was appointed as professor and department head of surgery at the U of M and Winnipeg General Hospital in 1946, but his interest in education was not confined to medicine. He was president of the MB Division of the Canadian Conference on Education, and played an active role in MB's system of higher education, including establishment of a chair in Icelandic studies at the U of M. Moreover, he was chancellor of the U of W 1969-78.

"Dr Thor" received many awards and honorary degrees from Cdn and Icelandic institutions. In 1951, he was appointed to the Íslenzka Fálkaorða (Icelandic Order of the Falcon) by that govt. He was appointed a Companion of the Order of Canada in 1970, and was inducted into the Winnipeg Citizen's Hall of Fame in 1990. An art gallery at U of M is also named after him. He is the subject of a 1986 biography by Thomas Albert John "Jack" Cunnings, *The Saga of Dr. Thor*, and his papers are archived by the U of M. ● JOHN HAMERTON

Martyrdom of Captain Canuck, digital photograph, 102 x 127 cm, 2005, by Diana Thorneycroft

THORNEYCROFT, Diana, artist, (b 1956, Claresholm, AB), is internationally known as a challenging imagemaker. Her provocative works, which often deal with violent or menacing subject matter, have been shown across Canada and the US, and also in Edinburgh, Moscow, Tokyo, and Sydney. Thorneycroft received her BFA from the U OF M in 1979, and her MA in Art from the U of Wisconsin-Madison in 1980. Her photography and multi-media works are often surrounded in controversy. For example, in the late 1990s she provoked outrage in Winnipeg when she nailed dead rabbit carcasses to trees. In her *Doll Mouth Series* of photographs (2004-2005), she drew out issues of voyeurism, sexuality and socialization with images of glossy baby doll lips and tiny wet tongues. Thorneycroft's exhibits also include *The Body, its lesson and camouflage* (2000-2002) and *Martyr's Murder* (2003-2005). Thorneycroft has received numerous awards for her work, including an Established Artist grant form the Canada Council, several Senior Arts Grants from the MANITOBA ARTS COUNCIL, and a Fleck Fellowship from the Banff Centre for the Arts. Her work is displayed in private, corporate, and museum collections throughout Canada, the US, and Russia, including The WINNIPEG ART GALLERY and the Canadian Museum of Contemporary Photography in Ottawa. Thorneycroft has been the subject of national documentaries for the CBC in both radio and television. Her work was published with interviews in the book *Diana Thorneycroft: The body, its lessons and camouflage* (2000). In 2007,

she worked in Winnipeg as an associate professor at the U of M's School of Art. ● AMANDA STEPHENS

THORSON, Charles Gustav "Cartoon Charlie," cartoonist (b Aug 29, 1890, WINNIPEG; d Aug 7, 1966, Vancouver), worked as a political cartoonist for Winnipeg NEWSPAPERS, including both ICELANDIC papers – *Heimskringla* and *Lögberg* – and the *Grain Growers Guide* as well as a graphic designer at BRIDGENS of Winnipeg for EATON'S catalogues. He also designed

Charles Thorson created Punkinhead for Eaton's.

the uniform for the **Winnipeg Falcons**. Charlie Thorson left Winnipeg in 1934 to try his hand in the nascent animation industry in CA. He was immediately hired by Walt Disney and worked at Disney Studios for 2 years on many short films and the studio's first feature, *Snow White and the Seven Dwarfs*. Although many people worked on the creation of the title character, Thorson claimed he designed her to look like the Icelandic girlfriend – waitress Kristín Sölvadóttir – he had left behind in Winnipeg. The resemblance is, in fact, striking. Thorson's knack for designing cute animals and children made him a much-sought-after employee; he moved from Disney to Harman-Ising, MGM, Warner Bros., Fleischer Brothers, Terrytoons, Columbia Screen Gems, and finally to George Pal Studios. In the process, he helped create some of the most popular and endearing creatures of that animated-movie era, including the prototype for Bugs Bunny. When he wore out his welcome in the US industry, he returned to Canada, working in the advertising business before moving to children's book publishing. His first book, *Keeko*, went into 9 editions and prompted a sequel, *Chee Chee and Keeko*. He also created the Eaton's character Punkinhead, illustrating the first 3 Christmas booklets, and designed Elmer the Safety Elephant, a national icon for children's safety. • GENE WALZ

THORSON, Joseph Thorarinn, politician, judge, professor (b March 15, 1889, **Winnipeg**; d July 5, 1978, Ottawa) was born to **Icelandic** immigrants, Sigriður Thorarinsdottir and Stefan Thorðarson, and was a brother to Disney animator **Charles Thorson**. A Rhodes Scholar, he served overseas during WWI as captain of the 223rd division and the head of security in a French POW camp from 1916-1919. He became the first dean of the **U of M**'s Faculty of Law before his election as Liberal MP for Winnipeg South Centre from 1926-1930, and again for **Selkirk** from 1935-1942. He served as a delegate to the League of Nations in 1938 and also became minister of National War Services from 1941-2. Thorson served as president of the Exchequer Court of Canada, the forerunner of the Federal Court of Canada (1942-1964) and as co-founding delegate and president of the Canadian chapter of the International Commission of Jurists, an organization devoted to the legal defence of human rights. Known as a headstrong man, Thorson narrowly escaped with his life when he was shot twice after resisting a robbery at an ICJ conference in Brazil the age of 73. In 1972 his opposition to the principles behind the Official Languages Act resulted in a landmark Supreme Court decision in which he gained the right to sue the federal government

Joseph Thorson, 1976

as an individual. Interestingly the OLA itself had been drafted by his own son, deputy minister of justice Donald Thorson. Joseph published a popular book on his opposition to the legislation in 1973 entitled *Wanted: A Single Canada* but eventually withdrew his case. • LAURIE K. BERTRAM

THORSTEINSON, Arni, real estate entrepreneur (b Oct 14, 1948, Rosetown, SK) is president and owner of Shelter Canadian Properties Ltd., one of the largest apartment and condominium managers in the country. Shelter manages 100 multi-unit rental, condominium, commercial, and hotel properties, comprised of over 8000 suites and nearly 28 ha (69 ac) of commercial space. Thorsteinson is also the founder and CEO of 2 publicly traded real estate income trusts (REITs) – Huntingdon and Lanseborough – and is a director of a 3rd, Whiterock. All the companies other than Whiterock are based in **Winnipeg**.

Thorsteinson received a Bachelor of Commerce degree from the **U of M**. He was a central figure in real estate investment and development in Winnipeg during the 1980s and '90s, with his companies managing significant renovations to heritage buildings in the downtown. In the low-interest-rate era of the early 21st century, Huntingdon and Lanseborough REITs were among the most active buyers in the western Canadian real estate market. Thorsteinson has also been an important fundraiser for the MB **Progressive Conservatives** and has long had ties to the provincial and federal Conservative parties. Thorsteinson was a former corporate finance executive who helped raise money for the original CanWest Capital Corp., the entity that Cdn business titans **Izzy Asper** and **Gerry Schwartz** started as partners in the late 1970s. He has remained a director of Schwartz's Onex Corp for many years, and an investor in Asper's **CanWest Global Communication Corp**, the eventual heir of CanWest Capital. • MARTIN CASH

THRIP is a flea-like insect in the order Thysanoptera (class Insecta) characterized by small

size (0.5-15 mm), slender shape, and 2 pairs of fringed (with hairs or cilia) wings folded over the back. The legs end in claws or an extrusible bladder which aid the insect in clinging to surfaces. The mouthparts consist of a single mandible used to bite into plant tissues (a few species are predatory on mites and scale insects) and a feeding tube for sucking plant juices. Certain species, such as the Grain Thrip (*Limothrips cerealium*), can seriously damage crops with their feeding activities. They may also transmit bacterial, fungal and wilt-virus diseases to vegetable crops like tomatoes. Thrips can cause havoc in greenhouses and gardens, especially when populations erupt with warm, moist conditions after a cold spell. These insects may appear everywhere – in the air, on flowers, shrubs and trees, and even in swimming pools where they drown in such numbers that they foul the water. They are capable of biting the skin and can make sitting in the garden or park most unpleasant. They can fly for hours and on landing, they crawl quickly with their abdomen curled over the back. While reproduction is usually bisexual, fertilized eggs develop into females, while unfertilized ones become males. Males may fight over females. In some species, females can reproduce without mating and males are unknown. There are 2 larval and 2-3 pupa-like stages before moulting into the adult. The life cycle takes only 3 weeks, so many generations are produced from spring to fall. About 59 species occur in MB (110 named species in Canada, and an expected total of over 250; 600 in NA and 5500 worldwide). Thrips are known from 220-million years old fossils (Triassic period). • REW, TDG

THRUSHES (family *Turdidae*) and their relatives include what many consider the best songbirds of NA. Familiar to most Manitobans is the American robin (*Turdus migratorius*),

The Hermit Thrush is a melodic songbird.

a fine songster in its own right, but perhaps none sounds more magical than a hermit thrush (*Catharus guttatus*) in the quiet evening of a boreal forest (*see* ECOCLIMACTIC REGIONS). Eastern bluebirds (*Sialia sialis*) and mountain bluebirds (*S. curricoides*) are small, sparrow-sized thrushes that can be attracted to nest boxes in the appropriate habitat. The Spruce Woods area is particularly favoured by them. Closely related are the *Mimidae* ("mimic family"), represented in the province by the grey catbird (*Dumetella carolinensis*), the brown thrasher (*Toxostoma rufum*), and, rarely, the northern mockingbird (*Mimus polyglottos*). These birds have a highly varied song repertoire, frequently mimicking other species. • RUDOLF KOES

THUNDERSTORMS roll across MB skies frequently every summer, most often in July. Spectacular displays of lightning and deafening thunderclaps can be both awe-inspiring and terrifying. The complex electrical activity that occurs during storms can produce lightning bolts that carry up to 100 million V of electricity – one million times more powerful than the current running through houses.

Of all areas in Canada, southern MB experiences the greatest number of nocturnal lightning flashes. Within southern MB, the SW corner is a lightning hotspot. Lightning causes almost half of all forest fires in the province, and can cause widespread power outages, damage buildings, and kill people and livestock. On April 22, 1932, 52 wild geese (*see* WATERFOWL) died in a morning thunderstorm near ELGIN. A resident watched the flock as they plunged to earth after a lightning flash and roar of thunder. After they were inspected and deemed edible, the geese were distributed among townsfolk. • SHELLEY PENZIWOL

TICK is a small (1.5-6.5 mm when unfed), flat, parasite of the order Metastigmata (class Arachnida) related to spiders, mites and scorpions. There are 2 types of ticks – soft (family Argasidae) and hard (family Ixodidae) – the latter being far more important for public health. There are no records of soft ticks in MB, apart from the occasional Spinose Ear Tick (*Otobius megnini*) brought in by people who have travelled to the S US, but there are at least 15 species of hard ticks recorded here, including several which do not persist in the province, but which are brought in by migrating birds or human travellers. Occasionally, exotic species of hard ticks arrive on snakes or lizards imported for the pet trade. Worldwide there are over 850 species. Ticks appeared in the fossil record around 50 million years ago (Eocene period), but they may have evolved as early as 250 million years ago (Permian period).

These 8-legged creatures are familiar pests to those frequenting the outdoors in summer, when they crawl onto the body of people and other animals to take a blood meal by piercing the skin with their sharp mouthparts. They detect movement (shadows) and carbon dioxide from passing hosts, and climb aboard using their spiny legs and claws. They crawl around until they find an appropriate place to attach. Ticks are most common in grass and low shrubs – habitats that facilitate ticks finding a succession of hosts, such as mice, deer and cattle. The Wood Tick (*Dermacentor variabilis*) requires 3 hosts. Males need a little blood to survive, but a female must fill her abdomen by remaining attached for a week or more. The male transfers a sperm package to the female, who stores it until she is ready to lay 3000-10,000 eggs on the ground or in the nest or burrow of the host; then both adults die. The eggs hatch into tiny 6-legged larvae and these

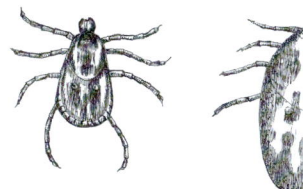

Wood tick (left) and engorged wood tick (right)

attach to a passing host, take a blood meal, and then moult to an 8-legged nymph. The nymph takes a blood meal and then moults to the adult stage. Ticks at various stages can live for years awaiting the arrival of the next host. Depending on the species, a tick may spend its entire life on one host; for example, the Winter Moose Tick (*Dermacentor albipictus*). Most tick species drop off each host to moult to the next stage. The Wood Tick does this, and must wait in the grass for a new host before it can get a blood meal and resume development. Its life cycle takes 2 years to complete, the first winter spent as a larva, and the second winter as an adult.

After mosquitoes, ticks are the most important group of arthropods as vectors of pathogens to humans, domestic animals and wildlife. The Wood Tick can cause paralysis in animals when the feeding female injects a potent toxin that acts on the nervous system. Other species of ticks (e.g., Rabbit, Rodent, Dog, and Bird ticks) can transfer the bacterial disease Tularemia. A recent threat in MB is the appearance of the Deer Tick (*Ixodes scapularis*), which may transmit Lyme's Disease, the bacterial agent being *Borrelia burgdorferi*. Ticks can transmit viruses (Tick-borne Encephalitis, Powassan Encephalitis), bacteria (Ehrlichiosis), rickettsiae (Rocky Mountain Spotted Fever), and protozoans (Babesiosis). Many people also suffer severe sensitivity to tick bites, or acquire secondary bacterial infections. Some species of ticks found in W Canada and the US are also known to cause Tick Paralysis – the toxic response to the tick's saliva resulting in paralysis or death, if the tick is not removed in time.

Personal protection is by far the most-effective means of avoiding tick bites and tick-borne infections. If ticks are present, tuck pant legs into the socks to keep ticks on the outside of clothing. Ticks are more-easily discovered on light-coloured clothes and with short hair. Repellent on socks and pant legs is also helpful. After a day of tramping in the field, check carefully for ticks, especially at the hairline. If you find an attached tick, grasp it gently with tweezers or fingers, and pull it out, using gradual, steady pressure. Do not squeeze, smash, twist, burn, or smother them

A dramatic Manitoba thunderstorm illuminates the sky.

in petroleum jelly or mineral oil, all of which may cause the tick to regurgitate saliva into the wound. Even if you have been attacked by an infected tick, the sooner you remove it, the less likely you are to be infected. ● TDG, REW

TILLENIUS, Clarence Ingwall, artist, naturalist, (b Aug 31, 1913, Sandridge, MB) is known for his paintings and dioramas of wildlife. Tillenius studied nature since his childhood and devoted his lifetime to painting all species of Canadian wildlife. His subjects range from Yukon grizzlies to Newfoundland caribou to the bison of the Prairies. Tillenius worked on farms and pulpwood plants in central, western and northern MB and ON throughout the 1930s until he lost his right arm in a 1936 CNR construction accident. He was still determined to capture wildlife on canvas, and so he returned to **WINNIPEG** in 1937 and began to study with Alex Musgrove. By 1940, Tillenius was illustrating magazine covers for the *Country Guide* and *Beaver* magazines, and was illustrating for US nature magazines. He painted a series of paintings of Canada's wildlife and wilderness landscapes in 1954 that are now grouped together at the Assiniboine Park Pavilion Gallery in Winnipeg.

Tillenius also travelled extensively across Canada and throughout Europe to study painting and diorama creation, and to study animals in their natural habitats. He was featured in exhibitions in the Canadian Museum of Nature in Ottawa and in the Whyte Museum of the Canadian

Clarence Tillenius, 1966

Rockies in Banff. Tillenius is well-known for his 18 wildlife dioramas, created for the provincial museums of BC, AB, MB, and the National Museum of Canada. For the **MANITOBA MUSEUM** in Winnipeg, Tillenius created a diorama depicting a Red River Buffalo Hunt (1970). He is the author/illustrator of several books, *Sketch Pad out-of-doors* (1956), *Days of the Buffalo* (1998), and *Tillenius* (1998). He was a founding member of the Society of Animal Artists in New York and the Society of Wildlife Art of the Nations (SWAN) in England. Tillenius received an Honorary Doctorate from the **U OF W** in 1970, the **ORDER OF MANITOBA** in 2003, and became a Member of the Order of Canada in 2005. He is a Fellow Emeritus of the Explorers Club headquartered in New York, and a Fellow of the National Geographic Society of England. In 2007, Tillenius lived and worked in Winnipeg. ● AMANDA STEPHENS

TIME SCALE is a set of time periods of Earth's history developed to assist with the placement of geological events and biological evolution. Geologists study rocks and minerals, while paleontologists examine fossil life preserved in the rocks, amber and other materials. Both fields incorporate vast periods of time, going back to the very formation of Earth. Over the last couple of centuries, accumulated evidence from many sources has enabled scientists to generate a relatively accurate time scale, based on major geological events. Earliest forms of life (bacteria and blue-green algae) evolved at the beginning of the Precambrian Era, which is dated at 3.8 billion years ago. The first animals, simple invertebrate forms, appeared in the late Precambrian, perhaps about 600 million years ago. Then, in only 70 million years of the Cambrian Era (570-500), there was literally an explosion of life forms, including many bizarre "experimental" types. By the end of this era, all the main animal lines that exist today had appeared, but none conquered the land until the Silurian Period of the Paleozoic Era (440 million years ago). Throughout all this unimaginable time, the region now occupied by MB underwent remarkable changes, including mountain building (higher than the Himalayas) to sea and freshwater submergence, and glacial to tropical climates. Scientists are just commencing on the road of discovery of MB's rich geological and biological heritage. ● REW

TOAD is an amphibian of the order Salientia (class Amphibia) represented in MB by 4 species in 2 families – Pelobatidae for the Spadefoot, and Bufonidae for the other 3 species. These lumpy, short-legged creatures are seen more often at night, but may be out hunting during the day as

well. They sit motionless until an insect or worm moves within range, and then with a speedy lunge of the body, the sticky tongue shoots out of its gaping mouth and snares and retracts the prey. Quite distinct from frogs, the skin of toads is dry and bumpy – the latter containing glands that produce distasteful and toxic chemicals. This protective strategy confers considerable safety from attack by many kinds of predators, including careless dogs, which may die from the experience.

The American Toad is found in mixed forests in SE Manitoba.

The Plains Spadefoot (*Scaphiopus bombifrons*) is a fascinating, 3-6 cm creature, almost comical in appearance, with ghostly colour, bulging gold eyes, fat stubby limbs, and a tough spur on each hind foot with which it digs backward into the soil. This is a seldom-seen species since it is active only in the dark, and comes to the surface briefly to feed and breed. It is also very rare, with fewer than 10 specimens from 3 locations in sandy soils in extreme SW MB. Noted for its remarkable breeding habits in temporary pools of rainwater, it does not attempt to reproduce during years of drought, since it requires that heavy rains fill nearby ponds and ditches during relatively warm weather from May to July. Instinctively knowing when conditions are right, the night air is filled with their snoring-like calls – 'wrrk' – which announces their presence and readiness to mate. From 1000-2500 eggs are laid, which hatch in 2-7 days. When tadpoles are abundant in pools that are rapidly drying up, an amazing body change occurs in certain individuals. While most tadpoles continue to feed frantically on algae, plants and tiny animals, a few transform into cannibals with great jaws for chewing on their dead and living siblings. The extra nutrients greatly speed their development and increases their chance of reaching maturity before the water dries up. Transformation from egg to toad may take as little as 21 days – a remarkable adaptation for an arid environment. Hundreds disperse at the same time and take up their new homes centred around a few burrows. Because it is so rare and localized, and its habitats have been greatly disturbed and poisoned by agriculture, this species should be declared endangered.

The 3 *Bufo* species include the American Toad (*Bufo americanus*), found in mixed forests of SE MB; the Canadian Toad (*Bufo hemiophrys*), in grassland, aspen parkland, and boreal forests; and the Great Plains Toad (*Bufo cognatus*), rare and discovered only recently along the ND border in extreme SW MB. Due to its rarity and degree of disturbance of its prairie habitat, the Great Plains Toad should be classified as endangered. There is some evidence that the Canadian Toad may be a subspecies of the American Toad, likely having evolved separately for a period, and then coming together again along a hybridization zone in extreme SE MB. The habits and life history of all 3 species are similar. Soon after the ice has disappeared from ponds and ditches in the spring, the toads emerge from hibernation and commence their trilling calls to attract a mate, which continues from April to June. The male grasps the larger female from the back, under her front legs, and holds on securely for many hours to prevent her escape and the advances of other males. He then externally fertilizes her 4000-8000 eggs as they are expelled in gelatinous strings in shallow water. The eggs hatch in 3-10 days and the tadpoles eat algae and other tiny pond life. The tadpoles transform into little terrestrial toads in July. After the breeding season, toads may travel some distance from water to feed. An adult fills its stomach with insects once a night and then retires to digest the meal. Toads are surprisingly good at digging (with the hind feet) into the soil, and have been found at depths of over 1.2 m – a skill used to avoid predators, cold snaps, and in preparation for hibernation in Oct. Toads have a great variety of sense organs, many similar to ours, but others we lack, such as a taste-smell organ in the roof of the mouth, and moisture-sensitive cells in their feet. Toads may live a surprising 31 years. • REW

TOEWS, Miriam, author (b 1964, **STEINBACH**). Brought up in the Mennonite community of Steinbach, Toews left town at the age of 18 for the wider world first of Montreal, then of London and Europe. Returning to take a BA in film studies at the **U OF M** and a BA in journalism at the U of King's College, Halifax, she worked in Winnipeg as a freelance journalist, writing for the CBC as well as for national and international magazines. Toews's first novel, *The Summer of My Amazing Luck* (1996), is a comic portrayal of life on the edge of poverty for a single mother; it was shortlisted for the Stephen Leacock Memorial Medal for Humour and the **McNALLY ROBINSON** Book of the Year Award. It also earned

Miriam Toews has won numerous awards for her writing.

Toews the **JOHN HIRSCH** Award for Most Promising Manitoba Writer. Her 2nd novel, *A Boy of Good Breeding* (1998), about life in a small town, won the McNally Robinson Award. *Swing Low: A Life* (2000), Toews's moving memoir of her father's struggle with bipolar disorder, won both the McNally Robinson Award and the Alexander Kennedy Isbister Award for Non-Fiction. In *A Complicated Kindness* (2004), Toews turned her wry humour and her sharp but compassionate insight on to the internal tensions of a fundamentalist religious community. A much-lauded contender for the Giller Prize, the book won the Gov Gen's Literary Award for fiction, as well as the CBC's 2006 Canada Reads competition. • MILDRED GUTKIN

TOEWS, Victor "Vic," politician, lawyer (b Sept 10, 1952 Filadelfia, Paraguay). Toews' Mennonite family moved to MB in 1956. After taking an undergraduate degree at the **U OF W**, he earned his law degree at the **U OF M** in 1976 and became a member of the bar in 1977. As crown attorney with the provincial ministry of justice for over a decade, he was promoted to director of constitutional law for MB in 1987 and in this capacity advised the MB government on the **MEECH LAKE ACCORD**. After his appointment as Queen's Counsel in 1991, he spent the next 4 years as associate counsel for **GREAT WEST LIFE** Assurance and then took a leave of absence in 1995 when he entered political life. He joined the **PROGRESSIVE CONSERVATIVES** in 1989 and first campaigned in the 1990 provincial election but lost to the NDP incumbent. When he narrowly won in the N Winnipeg constituency of Rossmere in 1995, he was appointed to **GARY FILMON**'s cabinet as the minister of labour. By June 1997, Toews was promoted to minister of justice and attorney general. He quickly earned a reputation as a law and order man and was one of the most prominent figures in the Filmon govt. The PCs were defeated in the provincial election of 1999 and Toews was not re-elected in his riding. In 2000, Toews joined the Alliance Party and won the

riding of Provencher in the federal election and was appointed justice critic in the opposition shadow cabinet. In Stephen Harper's bid for leadership of the newly formed Conservative Party of Canada, Toews worked as the MB organizer. He was easily returned in the general election of 2004 and retained as justice critic in the parliament that followed. When the Conservatives won a minority government in the 2006 federal election, Toews was appointed to cabinet as Canada's minister of justice and attorney general. In a cabinet shuffle Jan 4, 2007, he was made president of the treasury board. • RUTH DEGRAVES

TOLSTOI, pop 75, is situated 97 km S of **WINNIPEG**, off hwy 59 in the RM of Franklin. The community came into being in 1880, and was started up by settlers of Ukrainian descent. Tolstoi is home to the Holy Ghost Ukrainian Orthodox Church, which was constructed in 1927. But in the 21st century, Tolstoi is best known as the location of the Manitoba Tall Grass Prairie Preserve, the largest stretch of tall-grass prairie still left in the province. The 2000 ha preserve has a variety of animals, as well as over 150 kinds of plants, including many that are endangered. • GPP

TOOTINAOWAZIIBEENG TREATY RESERVE FIRST NATION (formerly known as Valley River First Nation), on reserve pop 577, off reserve pop 639, is located alongside the S side of **DUCK MOUNTAIN PROVINCIAL PARK**, 398 km NW of **WINNIPEG**. The Tootinaowaziibeeng Treaty Reserve First Nation signed Treaty 4 in 1874. The native language here is **OJIBWAY**. Schooling in Tootinawaziibeeng goes from Nursery-Grade 12, and is self-administered. This First Nation houses 2 reserves: Valley River IR No. 64A, and Treaty Grounds No. 77. Tootinaowaziibeeng is accessible by all-weather roads. The economic base for Tootinaowaziibeeng is farming. • RK

TOURISM provided nearly $1.4 billion in revenue, or 3.9% of GDP, for MB's economy in 2003. The industry provided an estimated 17,100 directly related jobs – about 3% of the labour force of province. MB's tourism industry is primarily regional, with 62% of revenues coming from the province's own residents. A smaller percentage of the revenue, 20%, is earned from visitors from the rest of Canada, with only 18% of revenue being generated by visitors from outside the country – 14% from the US and just 4% from overseas visitors.

The most important sources of revenue for the MB tourism industry are entertainment ($293 million), cultural/heritage ($202 million), and adventure/outdoor tourism ($190 million), such

T

as **Sport Fishing**, hunting, and **Golf**. Most of the employment in the sector is in accommodations (24%), restaurants and food services (23%), and transportation (18%). The tourism industry is diverse and fragmented, consisting mainly of small to medium operators. There are, for example, more than 18 major tour operators in the province; 12 airlines providing access to MB; 9 small within-province carriers; and more than 500 accommodation facilities.

Much of the attraction of tourists to MB centres on the adventure travel and eco-tourism. A diverse geography provides a natural environment for the adventure travel and eco-tourist sectors. Among the highlights are 62,000 km² of pristine boreal forest (*see* **Ecoclimactic Regions**) on the E side of **Lake Winnipeg**; canoeing on Seal and Bloodvein rivers; the "Polar Bear Capital of the World," **Churchill**; more than 100,000 freshwater **Lakes**; and 150 **Parks** and top-quality resorts. Fly-in fishing resorts and hunting lodges are also popular.

MB also benefits from the province's many cultural and heritage attractions, with the province's population representing diverse cultures with their own festivals, from **First Nations** and Francophones to **Scots** and **Ukrainians**. There are over 130 museums and 100 annual festivals throughout the province. Among the highlights are **Folklorama**, **St. Boniface**, the **Royal Winnipeg Ballet**, the **Winnipeg Folk Festival**, and the **International Peace Gardens**. In addition to such regular attractions, the industry benefits from a highly skilled labour force and high-quality infrastructure.

After an increase of 11.1% in 2002, tourism was adversely affected in 2003 by global events such as fears of terrorism and resulting tightened security; war in Iraq and elsewhere; and threat of some infectious diseases (SARS, BSE, and West Nile virus). Combined with the rapid appreciation of the Canadian dollar relative to the US dollar, the industry recorded a decline of 4.6% in overnight direct entries, and an 8.1% decline in same-day entries, from the US to MB in 2003. However, MB performed slightly better than the rest of Canada overall, with international overnight travel to Canada as a whole declining by 13%, compared to 5% in MB.

To develop and promote tourism, the govt of MB created Travel Manitoba, an industry-led Crown agency responsible for tourism marketing, visitor information services, product development, research, and public information. ● GABRIEL DRAGAN

TOVEY, Bramwell, conductor, musician, composer (b July 11, 1953, Ilford, UK) led the **Winnipeg Symphony Orchestra** from 1989 to 2001,

making him the orchestra's longest-serving **Music** director. Tovey is known for his versatility and for conducting a range of works across the musical spectrum. In 1992, his commitment to exploring New Music led to his co-creating Winnipeg's **New Music Festival**, now considered one of the premiere New Music events in NA. Under Tovey's direction, the festival premiered more than 250 works from a range of international and Canadian composers.

Tovey left Winnipeg in 2000 to join the Vancouver Symphony as artistic director. In 2002, he also started work as chief conductor and music director of the Luxembourg Philharmonic Orchestra. He has worked as a guest conductor with numerous orchestras, including the New York Philharmonic, Toronto Symphony, and Montreal Symphony. When not conducting, Tovey, an adept jazz pianist, performs regularly. Tovey has received many awards, including Member of the Order of MB (2000) and the Canada 125th Anniversary Medal. He holds honorary doctorates from the **U of W** and **U of M**, and in 2003, he won a Juno Award for Best Classical Composition for his *Requiem for a Charred Skull*. ● JS

TOWN, Thomas, runner, (b Aug 7, 1893, Nottingham, UK; d March 29, 1957, **Winnipeg**) won 8 Cdn titles in short and long distance running. Town immigrated to **Brandon** from his native UK in 1910. Having already won national junior championships in England, Town soon dominated the running events in his adopted country, winning his first time at MB's 3-mi championship. His first Cdn title came in 1919 at the 5-mi championship in Ottawa. At the following year's championships in Montreal, Town won both the 5-mi and the 5000-m races. He qualified to represent Canada at the 1920 Antwerp Olympics, but failed to win any medals after injuring his ankle while training on the arduous oversea voyage. In Winnipeg in 1921, he again won the 5-mi, as well as the 3-mi, beating legendary MB runner **Joe Keeper**. The following year he won the 5 mi in Calgary, and finished his racing days with 2 Cdn titles in the 880 yd and 1-mi. Although Town qualified to compete in the 1924 Paris Olympics, he again missed his chance at an Olympic medal as the Dominion Track and Field Association couldn't find the funds to sponsor the trip. ● MD

TRACK AND FIELD. *See* **Athletics**.

TRAILS AND ROADS, Early. Before the advent of the **Railway** and the automobile, what is now MB was mostly navigated in summer through waterways – canoes, and later by **York Boats**

and **Steamboats,** or by foot and later horseback. In winter, dogsledding was often the preferred means of transport, though snowshoes and travois were used as well. Snowshoers could follow frozen-over waterways for part of the winter, but footpaths allowed for travel in all 4 seasons.

All Aboriginal peoples in what is now MB were at least semi-nomadic, and an extensive network of trails – whose evidence is substantiated by both archaeological evidence and oral tradition – criss-crossed the continent. Some of these paths date from thousands of years ago, and may have been created by large animals such as **Bison**, herds of which Aboriginal hunters would follow. Some trails also led to landmarks or to places of great spiritual significance, such as the formation for which **Pilot Mound** is named.

While these routes served in part to access sacred sites and sources of game, fish, and ripe plants, the trail network was also intended for seasonal migration of groups; to communicate with neighbouring villages; and to participate in trade. The trade network of early NA was extensive, allowing for exchange of minerals and metals, tools, flints (*see* **Ancient Aboriginal Technology**), cowrie shells, jewellery, pelts, and so forth. Even peoples of widely divergent ancestry and language could trade through Plains Sign Language, an elaborate lingua franca of gestures. At certain times of year, even members of traditionally rival groups might trade with each other.

Trails were often indicated with waymarks such as bent trees. Paths often took advantage of natural topography, as, for example, eskers caused by **Glaciation**, but generally followed upland routes to avoid swampy or buggy areas. Furthermore, paths often followed the lee side of slopes to mitigate the effects of bad weather.

After European contact, as the **Fur Trade** radically transformed Aboriginal society to depend more on trade especially of **Beaver** pelts with Europeans, some of these routes became more prominent while others fell into disuse. For example, the La Vérendrye Trail traces the route of **La Vérendrye**. By the early 19th century, some of these paths were noted on maps, but inexact cartography makes the location of some of these routes a mystery. The **U of M**'s **Archives** house **Nan Shipley**'s collection of maps of many of these Western routes.

European immigrants to NA often used First Nations trails as settlement routes, as did the **Boundary Commission** and, later, the **NWMP**. The Crow Wing Trail wound from the **Red River Settlement** along the E bank of the **Red River** down to St. Paul, Minnesota Territory (later MN), in the mid-19th century, crossing the US border in the Pembina/Fort Dufferin (**Emerson**)

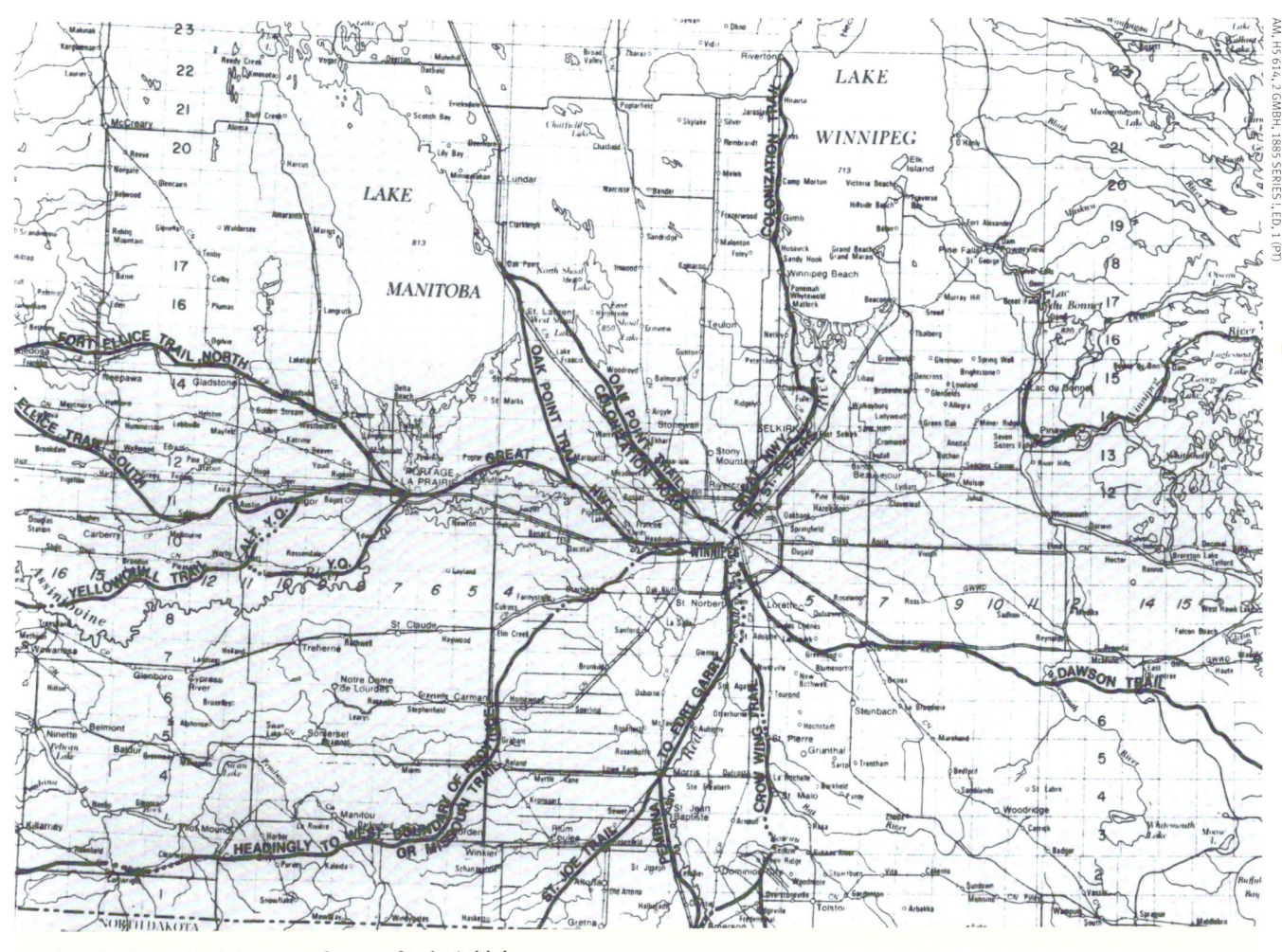

Early trails determined the route of many of today's highways.

AM. H5 614, 2 GMBH. 1885 SERIES I, ED. 1 (PT)

area. **RED RIVER CARTS** widened these trails, many of which would become highways. The Yellowhead Highway, known in **WINNIPEG** as Portage Ave, arose as part of a system of overland routes from the Upper Fort to **PORTAGE LA PRAIRIE** and eventually to the **HBC**'s Fort Edmonton (now Edmonton) and beyond. Winnipeg's Main St similarly was a route from the Upper Fort to **LOWER FORT GARRY**. Other early paths survive in whole or in part as trails for skiing, snowmobiling, or hiking; parts of the **TRANS-CANADA TRAIL** are former First Nations pathways, as is Winnipeg's Wellington Cres.

While Europeans took ready advantage of existing routes, some created their own, as the **MENNONITES** apparently did with the Post Road. Most notable among these new routes was the Dawson Trail (or Rd) from the head of Lake Superior (modern Thunder Bay, ON) to **UPPER FORT GARRY**. With the impending **RUPERT'S LAND TRANSFER**, engineer **SIMON DAWSON** led 1857-58 expeditions to Red River and beyond into the NWTs to scout a route for a roadway. In late 1868, a party that included John Snow and **CHARLES MAIR** began surveying an 850 km road to aid in

the annexation of the Northwest by Canadians (and, especially, Ontarians). The road, the first to link ON with the Cdn Prairies, cut through the **WHITESHELL** area and through **STE. ANNE**, and still exists, in part, as forestry roads and recreational trails. Much of this route was a "corduroy road" – an unpaved roadway made over marsh or muskeg by laying logs side by side. ● A.J. LEVIN

TRANS-CANADA AIR LINES (TCA; now Air Canada), created as a federal Crown corporation in Apr 1937 through an act of Parliament by then-Transport Minister C. D. Howe, was Canada's national and international air carrier. TCA officials divided the airline into 2 divisions: an eastern division at Montreal, to handle everything from the Atlantic to **WINNIPEG**; and a western division at Winnipeg, to cover the area between that city and Vancouver. Operational headquarters and the main overhaul base were at Stevenson Field (Winnipeg International Airport), since Winnipeg was conveniently in the centre of the continent. The city remained a major player in the TCA picture until 1949, when TCA moved its operational headquarters

to Montreal. From TCA's perspective, this was a logical move, since Montreal had become the terminus for the Atlantic, Caribbean, New York, and Tampa, FL, services, and was closer to Ottawa, where the corporation had many dealings.

By 1957, the centre of the **AVIATION** industry had also shifted east. The early 1960s were boom times for aviation. TCA decided to move from the UK-built turboprop Vickers Viscount 700s to an all-jet fleet to remain competitive, and they built a Montreal base to service those jets. This spelled the end of the Winnipeg base as an overhaul centre. The decision set off a storm of protests from Winnipeg businesses, MB's TCA employees, and local MPs, who viewed it as a further blow to Winnipeg's economy and reputation. In 1964, TCA became Air Canada, to better reflect its international routes. In 1969, CAE Industries Limited of Montreal, a high-tech aviation electronics firm, purchased the Air Canada complex at Winnipeg International Airport. CAE received the contract to service the Viscounts until they were retired in the early 1970s.

In 1974, with a federal election looming, growing unrest in the West, and declining

employment at CAE, Winnipeg MP **JAMES RICH-ARDSON** suggested that Air Canada should either buy the Winnipeg base back from CAE or build a new hangar to house its **BOEING** 727s when they came into service. To placate the West, the federal govt agreed to finance the construction of a new maintenance hangar in Winnipeg. In 1977, Air Canada moved into the new hangar, built on the opposite side of the airport to its original complex. In 1983, CAE sold the former TCA complex to the **WESTERN CANADIAN AVIATION MUSEUM**. Though Winnipeg remained a pilot base for another decade, and Air Canada erected a large cargo facility at the airport and a modern office building in the city's downtown, the glory years of Air Canada in Winnipeg were over. In 1989, Air Canada was privatized, and by the start of the 21st century, the airline was no longer using its large cargo building in Winnipeg, the pilot base was gone, and the number of flights originating and terminating in Winnipeg was reduced.
● SHIRLEY RENDER

TRANS-CANADA TRAIL. This Atlantic-to-Pacific recreational trail will be more than 18,000 km long when finished, making it the longest in the world. Construction on the trail began in 1992 as a heritage project to commemorate Canada's 125th birthday. Initially slated for completion by 2000, as of writing, the Manitoba Recreational Trail Assoc (MRTA) estimated the trail to be completed, or nearly so, in 2007. The MB portion of the trail is managed by the volunteer-based MRTA, with the provincial govt providing $2.65 million in funds. Volunteer associations connected with the MRTA

raise additional funding. The first significant length of the Trans-Canada Trail registered in MB was the Rossburn Subdivision, an abandoned rail line purchased from **CN**. As of 2006, there were 869 km of operational trail in MB, with pavilions in **WINNIPEG**, **EMERSON**, **ROBLIN**, and at **WEST HAWK LAKE**. The trail is built along existing routes, on abandoned **RAILWAY** lines and **EARLY TRAILS AND ROADS**, and through Crown land. When complete, there will be 1300 km of trail in MB. ● MD

TREE NURSERIES supply **TREES** for landscaping, as opposed to silviculture operations, which grow trees for reforestation. Roughly 20 nurseries in MB grow trees that are sold within the province, as well as in AB, SK, and some parts of ON and the northern US.

The industry in MB has its origins with the first Prairie settlers, as a largely treeless prairie landscape necessitated the construction of shelterbelts to protect homesteads and gardens. While early shelterbelt trees were transplanted from natural stands along riverbanks, this small supply was not enough to cover the vast Prairies, and the Cdn govt shipped in a half-million trees from ON in the 1880s. Most of these did not survive, but the success of early MB nurseries – such as one established in 1874 on Alexander Stevenson's farm in **MORDEN**, and the Patmore Nursery established in **BRANDON** in 1883 – demonstrated that tree cultivation on the Plains was possible. The federal govt then established experimental nurseries in Brandon in 1888 and Morden in 1915; trees grown there were widely distributed to settlers. Regardless of govt promotion, by the

early 20th century, most MB communities had a nursery of some kind to supply a growing demand for urban landscaping and tree-lined boulevards. These operations were often combined with the commercial selling of produce and livestock. Through the 1940s, door-to-door salesmen often travelled through rural MB selling nursery stock, but retail selling later returned to nurseries and commercial garden centres. The Manitoba Nurserymen's Association, formed in 1957, later becoming Landscape Manitoba.

The nursery industry in MB has developed many new hybrids in response to the need for hardy plants suited to MB's climate. Dr. **FRANK LEITH SKINNER**, who opened Skinners Nursery in Dropmore (a community 30 km SSW of **ROBLIN**) in 1910, bred many new varietals by crossing native plants with hardy seeds he had gathered from travels abroad, such as the Dropmore **ELM**, for which he used Siberian seeds. In 1926, Stevensons' Evergreen Nursery in **MORRIS** further diversified MB tree stocks by growing the first evergreens at a Prairie nursery. Poplar and ash remain the most-common trees grown in MB nurseries, since these species can withstand both cold winters and drought.

Numerous technological developments have led to improved production in nurseries. Irrigation systems came into use in the 1960s, allowing growers to maintain steady moisture levels despite seasonal variations, and refrigeration allowed nurseries to extend storage periods. The most-significant development came in the 1980s, when container-grown trees became increasingly common, replacing bare-root production. ● MD

TREEHOPPER is a small (10 mm) insect in the family Membracidae (order Hemiptera) evolved from leafhoppers and closely related to cicadas and aphids. There are 41 species known in MB (over 100 in Canada). Treehoppers have been found in amber dated over 40 million years ago (Eocene period). With an elongated, triangular shape, they are usually coloured green or brown, which offers excellent camouflage. The front of the body (prothorax) often ends in sharp defensive spines, which easily penetrate the mouth of a predator (and a bare foot if stepped on). Treehoppers are likely to be regurgitated by birds attempting to swallow such prickly prey. Some species have great flaring shields extending above the back, making the individual appear much larger, and this may look different in the 2 sexes. With piercing-sucking mouthparts, they feed on plant juices. When disturbed while sitting on a leaf, the insect leaps and rapidly unfolds its wings and flies away with great speed. Locally common examples on poplar and shrubs is the

Trans-Canada Trail

Buffalo Treehopper (*Ceresa alta*). Hundreds can be present among the leaves of a large tree. The male attracts a female with a courting call, and after mating, the female deposits her eggs into plant tissues, where they remain over winter. As soon as plant buds begin to grow in spring, the eggs hatch and the nymphs feed on plant juices with their sucking mouthparts. As they grow larger over the next month, they moult 5 times. The female may remain nearby to guard her brood. This aggregation attracts the attention of ants, which are anxious to feed on the excess sugary sap released by the treehoppers via a terminal tube. Rather than harming their hosts, the ants vigorously defend the treehoppers – an interesting association that benefits both groups. • REW

TREES, NATIVE. Although MB is called a prairie province, most of it is covered by a thick green blanket of trees. They even extend out along rivers and other moist areas into the southwestern grasslands and on protected sites into the northeastern arctic zones. Trees allow people to live comfortably in most of MB. They provide oxygen, shade and clean air to the entire province as well as heat, shelter, tools, jobs, medicines and food. Their beauty and usefulness has caused them to be regarded as sacred by many cultures. As the glaciers of the last Ice Age pretty well scraped MB's surface flat, all of the trees here have migrated into it over the past 11,000 years and are still moving into and northwards within MB. Although MB has only 26 known kinds of native trees, there are millions of them in the central boreal forest and mixed woods (deciduous and coniferous) areas. Because of MB's severe growth-limiting climate, trees don't reach the huge sizes here that they do on Canada's E or W coast. But individuals can still become large and beautiful on protected sites such as river valleys or in the **Riding Mountain** area. The province maintains a listing of exceptionally large heritage trees.

Trees are woody plants which have single stems/trunks greater than 10 cm in diameter and are taller than 5 m. They are usually divided into 2 main types: conifers/softwoods and deciduous/hardwoods. Conifers produce their seeds in cones and usually have evergreen needle leaves and soft wood; spruces and pines are good examples. Deciduous trees have harder wood, produce their seeds in proper dry or wet fruits and shed their leaves every fall. MB has 7 regular conifers, 18 deciduous hardwoods and 1 deciduous conifer softwood. Evergreen conifers include 2 spruces, one fir, 3 pines, 1 cedar and the deciduous conifer tamarack. Deciduous trees include 1 maple, 1 oak, 4 poplars, 1 willow, 1 ironwood, 2 ash, 1 mountain-ash, 1 elm, 2 birches, 1 basswood or linden , 1 hackberry and 2 wild plums.

White **Spruce** was proclaimed MB's provincial tree in 1991. White and black spruce, tamarack and jack pine are the most broadly distributed conifers and the most common trees of the boreal forest. White spruce and tamarack form the arctic treeline, the northern limit of trees in the far NE corner of MB.

Bur **Oak** forms the southern treeline where forests give way to grasslands. Cold temperatures and permafrost prevent the growth of trees in the N while drought and fires keep them out of the southern grassland areas. White and red pine are found naturally only in the SE corner of MB, although red pine is widely planted elsewhere. The most beautiful stand of remaining red pine occurs on the E end of Black Island in **Lake Winnipeg**. Balsam fir is found on moist well-drained soils throughout the boreal forest while eastern white cedar occurs mainly on moist sites in the central **Interlake** and southeastern MB.

Aspen (white poplar), balsam poplar and the birches have the broadest distribution for deciduous trees, mostly within the boreal forest. Eastern cottonwood, white elm, basswood,

Trees of Manitoba

COMMON NAME	SCIENTIFIC NAME	TYPE	RANGE IN MB (NATURAL)	ABUNDANCE
Balsam Fir	Abies balsamea	Conifer/softwood	N to Hayes R.	Common
Black Spruce	Picea mariana	Conifer/softwood	Missing SW	Abundant
Eastern White Cedar	Thuja occidentalis	Conifer/softwood	SE & Central Interlake	Locally common
Jack Pine	Pinus banksiana	Conifer/softwood	South	Abundant
Red/Norway Pine	Pinus resinosa	Conifer/softwood	SE Corner	Uncomm.
White Pine	Pinus strobus	Conifer/softwood	Far SE Corner	Rare
White Spruce	Picea glauca	Conifer/softwood	Missing far NE and SW	Abundant
Tamarack/Larch	Larix laricina	Deciduous conifer/softwood	Missing SW	Abundant
Alaska Paper Birch	Betula neoalaskana	Deciduous/hardwood	Missing far N	Common
Aspen/White Poplar	Populus tremuloides	Deciduous/hardwood	Missing NE corner	Abundant
Balsam/Black Poplar	Populus balsamifera	Deciduous/hardwood	Missing far NE corner	Abundant
Basswood/Linden	Tilia americana	Deciduous/hardwood	S river valleys	Uncomm.
Black Ash	Fraxinus nigra	Deciduous/hardwood	SE quarter	Occas.
Bur/Scrub Oak	Quercus macrocarpa	Deciduous/hardwood	S third	Common
Canada Plum	Prunus nigra	Deciduous/hardwood	SE	Occas.
Eastern Cottonwood	Populus deltoides	Deciduous/hardwood	S quarter	Common
Eastern Mountain-ash	Sorbus decora	Deciduous/hardwood	S half	Occas.
Green Ash	Fraxinus pennsylvanica	Deciduous/hardwood	S two/fifths	Common
Hackberry	Celtis occidentalis	Deciduous/hardwood	Delta, Oak L.	Very Rare
Ironwood	Ostrya virginiana	Deciduous/hardwood	SE	Rare
Large-toothed Aspen	Populus grandidentata	Deciduous/hardwood	Far SE	Rare
MB maple/Box Elder	Acer negundo	Deciduous/hardwood	S half	Common
Paper/White Birch	Betula papyrifera	Deciduous/hardwood	Missing far N	Abundant
Peach-leaf Willow	Salix amygdaloides	Deciduous/hardwood	S one-fifth	Common
White/American Elm	Ulmus americana	Deciduous/hardwood	Originally S two-fifths	Occas.
Wild Plum	Prunus americana	Deciduous/hardwood	SE	Occas.

Manitoba maple (box elder), green and black ash and peach-leaf willow form the flood plain forests along southern MB rivers. Mountain maple, mountain-ash and the plums occur on moist sites throughout parts of southern MB, the plums restricted to more southerly sites usually on basic soils. Bur oak is MB's only native oak, occurring on dry well-drained sites throughout the southern 1/3 of the province. Large-toothed aspen, ironwood and hackberry occur in only a few moist spots in southern MB. Fire is part of the natural cycle in the boreal forest and helps form the southern treeline. Several trees are well adapted to this fire regime especially jack pine and aspen. Jack pine needs full sun and its cone-scales are glued together with a substance that only melts in the heat of a forest fire. This releases thousands of tiny winged seeds onto the nice bare mineral soil after a fire. Aspen has underground stems that usually survive a fire and quickly produce new saplings. • KAREN JOHNSON

TREHERNE, pop 646, is a town 95 km SE of **BRANDON** on hwy 2. In the 1870s, **ENGLISH**, **MENNONITES**, **UKRAINIANS**, and **POLES** settled here. The community was named after early settler George Treherne. A post office opened in 1880 and a **CPR** branch line arrived in 1886. The town was incorporated in 1948. Treherne terms itself the "Gateway to Tiger Hills," referring to a raised landscape that forms a scenic background to the town and surrounding farms. The origin of the name is uncertain, one theory being that early settlers applied the name after seeing cougars in the hills. Service and retail support for farm operations is the main economy, with health and education facilities employing many. There is a pioneer museum with a significant gun collection. The gothic revival **UNITED CHURCH** is designated a municipal heritage site. • GPP

TRIBAL COUNCILS INVESTMENT GROUP OF MANITOBA INC. is the largest **FIRST NATIONS** investment company in Canada. The company was formed in 1990 when the 7 Tribal Councils in MB, representing 55 First Nations communities and more than 92,000 people, each invested $25,000 to form a single corporate entity to invest in business opportunities on their behalf. TCIG's primary goal is to obtain a high rate of return on its investments. One of its first investments was to acquire Arctic Beverages, the Pepsi-Cola Canada Inc. bottling franchise for northern Manitoba, northern SK, NW ON, NU, and Baffin Island. By early 2005, TCIG had amassed an investment portfolio of more than $40 million. Their assets included all or part of 15 different companies, including: Rupertsland Holding Inc., an Aboriginal-owned company which owns a substantial

stake in the **NORTH WEST COMPANY**; First Nations Bank of Canada, an affiliate of TD-Canada Trust (*see* **BANKING**); First Canadian Health Management Corporation Inc., a health-benefit claims processing service; Exchange Industrial Group Income Trust, which owns MB-based Perimeter Aviation Ltd.; **SALISBURY HOUSE OF CANADA LTD.**; Maple Leaf Distillery, a sister company of Salisbury House and MB's largest Canadian-owned distillery; Protos International, the Winnipeg-based parent company of Salisbury House and Maple Leaf Distillery; **STEINBACH**-based Big Freight Systems Inc., the 12th-largest **TRUCKING** firm in MB; Bieber Securities Inc., a **WINNIPEG**-based full-service stock brokerage firm; the **MANITOBA MOOSE**; the **MTS CENTRE**; and First Canadian Fuels Inc., a fuel distribution company which TCIG and Domo Gasoline Corporation formed in 2005 to distribute fuel to bulk-fuel retailers in First Nations communities in MB. • MURRAY MCNEILL

TRIFUNOV, James, wrestler, (b July 18, 1903, Jarovac, Serbia; d June 27, 1993 **WINNIPEG**) was an Olympic medallist and 10 time Cdn wrestling champion. Trifunov first immigrated to Regina before eventually settling in Winnipeg, where he worked at the ***WINNIPEG FREE PRESS***. He won his first Cdn wrestling title in 1923, and went on to compete at the 1924 Paris Olympics. At the 1928 Amsterdam Olympic Games, he won a bronze medal, and a gold medal in the Bantamweight Division at the 1930 British Empire Games. After retiring from competition in 1932, Trifunov remained active in the sport as a coach for the Cdn national wrestling team. He served 25 years as president of the Manitoba Amateur Wrestling Association. He was made a member of the Order of Canada in 1981. • MD

TRIGGS, Donald, vintner, (b April 29, 1944, **TREHERNE**), grew up on a farm and graduated with a BSc from the **U OF M** in 1966. Triggs met his wife, Elaine, while in school and the 2 were married once Triggs finished his first degree. He earned his MBA at the U of Western Ontario in 1968. Triggs managed the North American market of John Labatt's Ridout Wines until 1989, when he and friend Allan Jackson teamed up to buy out all of Labatt's wine interests in Canada. They named their new company Jackson-Triggs wines. Soon after, prestigious Cdn winery Inniskillin Wines was purchased by Jackson-Triggs, further boosting the company's portfolio. In 1993, Jackson-Triggs merged with T. G. Bright. & Co. and Vincor International was established. The growth of the company continued, with the Jackson-Triggs name becoming a line of wines with

a $10 million production facility in the Niagara region of ON. Vincor purchased wineries across the US, New Zealand and Australia, and in 2006, the company was taken over by wine and spirits producer/marketer Constellation Brands – the world's largest wine company by volume. Once the Constellation acquisition was completed, Triggs opted to resign immediately from the company he had worked so hard to build. Today, Vincor is Canada's largest wine producer, as well as the world's 8th largest producer and distributor of wine and related products by revenue, with more than 10,000 employees worldwide. Pinot noir is Don Triggs' favourite grape. • TAMMY MARLOWE JOHNSON

TROTZ, Barry, hockey coach (b July 15, 1962, **WINNIPEG**). A long-serving coach of the NHL's Nashville Predators, Trotz grew up in **DAUPHIN** before pursuing his hockey dream with the Regina Pats of the Western Hockey League (WHL). Following his 4-year major junior career, Trotz played one season for the **U OF M** Bisons in 1983-84. He stayed on for the 1984-85 season as an assistant coach of the team before taking over as general manager and coach of the Manitoba Junior Hockey League's Dauphin Kings for 2 seasons. Trotz returned for one year as head coach of the Bisons during 1987-88, while also acting as a part time amateur scout. In 1988, the NHL's Washington Capitals hired him first as a regional scout and then chief western scout. Trotz began his coaching career at the professional level with the Baltimore Skipjacks of the American Hockey League in 1991. The team became the Portland Pirates in 1993, and Trotz was the head coach for 4 seasons, winning a league championship and coach of the year award in 1994-95. The expansion Nashville Predators made him the franchise's inaugural head coach in Aug 1997, and Trotz went on to set an NHL record as a team's longest serving first coach. He has also acted as an assistant coach for team Canada at the 2002 and 2003 world championship tournaments, winning a gold medal in 2003 along with fellow Manitoban **ANDY MURRAY**. • JOEL TRENAMAN

TROUT is a group of fishes in the family Salmonidae (order Salmoniformes) which plays a prominent role in the freshwater and marine waters of the province. Some species spend their entire lives in freshwater, while others have some populations that live in the marine waters of Hudson Bay (where food resources are richer) and return to freshwater to over-winter and to spawn. These fish are characterized by a streamlined body and the presence and placement of a number of spineless fins. There are 8 native members

DOUGLAS WATKINSON

The Brown Trout was introduced to challenge anglers.

(Cisco, Shortjaw Cisco, Lake Whitefish, Round Whitefish, Arctic Grayling, Arctic Char, Brook Trout, and Lake Trout) and 4 exotics, introduced to provide sport opportunities for anglers (Rainbow Trout, Cutthroat Trout, Kokanee, and Brown Trout). This family prefers cold, clear, highly oxygenated waters, and so, most species live in the colder, N portion of the **HUDSON BAY** drainage system. Several species (e.g., Lake Trout and Lake Whitefish) are sought after by both the commercial-fishing industry and by anglers in MB. A few representative species follow.

ARCTIC GRAYLING (*Thymallus arcticus*) is an attractive fish growing to a length of 44 cm and features an enormous, flag-like dorsal fin. Its appearance, excellent eating, and occurrence in picturesque, fast-moving streams are responsible for the Grayling being rated as a prime target for anglers. It is truly an arctic species, inhabiting streams, rivers, and lake shallows across the tundra region of MB. It is frequently the only large species in many of these N waterways. It shuns the estuaries along the coast of Hudson Bay, where salt water works its way upstream. Its main predators are Northern Pike and Lake Trout. Spawning occurs in May and June, once water temperatures surpass 3°C. Males maintain a territory, but no nest is constructed, the fertilized eggs simply dropping to the gravel bottom. The diet consists of insects and small fish. Grayling may live to 7 years.

ARCTIC CHAR (*Salvelinus alpinus*) has one of the most fascinating life histories of any MB fish, due partly to its annual migrations from marine to freshwater water (i.e., amphidromous). From **YORK FACTORY** northward, it inhabits rivers discharging into Hudson Bay and its offshore marine waters, and indeed continues northward throughout the Arctic Ocean all the way to N Greenland. In MB, some populations travel to the Bay to feed during the warmer months, and return in Sept to freshwater, either to spawn and/or to over-winter. Other populations remain in lakes and deep pools in rivers year-round. In waters of sufficient depth to remain unfrozen,

but under the cover of ice, the female creates a nest in the gravel at a site guarded by the male. After several bouts of egg deposition and fertilization, the female covers the eggs with gravel by thrusting her tail fin, and a new generation begins. Requiring temperatures from 0-3°C, the eggs develop over the winter and hatch in April. After about 5 years, and when about 20 cm long, the young migrate to the Bay for the first time. Full size (85 cm) is attained in 20 years, but a few individuals reach 40 years of age. The Char is a mainstay in arctic ecosystems, as food for other fish, diving birds, seals, and the Inuit. The species is also a great attraction for sports-fishing enthusiasts.

LAKE TROUT (*Salvelinus namaycush*) is a predatory species restricted to deep, cold (0-10°C), well-oxygenated lakes of the Pre-Cambrian Shield, and so is absent from the SW corner of the province. It prefers water around 10°C in summer, and consequently descends to 12-53 m to find this temperature. Spawning begins in Oct with the male cleaning off a boulder or bedrock (with the fins, body and snout) at depths of 1-36 m and in water ranging from 9-14°C. A pair or a number of males and females may spawn together in the cover of darkness, a large female depositing about 18,000 eggs. The fertilized eggs fall and stick on the bottom, and hatch 5 months later in March. Sexual maturity is attained in about 6 years in the S, but up to 13 years in the N, since the rate of growth is slowed in colder waters. Maximum longevity is 23 years. The largest recorded MB specimens were 126 cm long and 46 kg. This species is highly prized by anglers and commercial fishers. ● REW

TRUCKING is a key component of MB's economy. A recent study estimated the industry generated about 33,000 direct and indirect jobs in the province and about $1.2 billion in annual revenues. Another indication of the industry's effect on the economy is that, according to the Manitoba Trucking Association, 95% of all of

the merchandise moved within the province is moved by truck.

Although the number of for-hire trucking firms can fluctuate from year to year, the MTA estimates there were about 430 companies operating in the province in 2006. Between them, they paid out between $600 million and $650 million a year in wages and benefits, and operated an estimated 14,000 power units (trucks) and 18,000 trailers.

Most of the province's trucking companies are national or international carriers, meaning they haul goods outside the province. About 10 to 12 of them are larger operators with more than 150 trucks. They include companies such as **REIMER EXPRESS LINES**, Bison Transport Inc., Paul's Hauling Ltd/Gardewine Group., TransX Ltd., Big Freight Systems Inc., Kleysen Transport Ltd., Arnold Bros. Transport Ltd., Penner International Inc., and Payne Transportation Inc. However, while some larger trucking companies are headquartered here, MB's trucking industry is still relatively small by national standards, accounting for 5% of the annual revenues generated of Cdn industry.

The local industry can trace its roots back to the early 20th century, shortly after the arrival of automobiles in the provincial capital, **WINNIPEG**. By 1910, motor trucks were reported to be gaining a strong foothold in towns and cities in the province. Three years later, 2 employees from the Canadian Motor Company made the first interprovincial truck run in western Canada when they hauled a truckload of bedding and bedsprings from Winnipeg to Regina in 4 days. However, it wasn't until the latter stages of WWI – when a shortage of **RAILWAY** freight cars in the US forced many American businesses to start buying large trucks to haul their goods from city to city – that the motor trucking industry came of age in NA. US automobile manufacturers began churning out more trucks to meet the growing demand, and more of those vehicles wound up in Winnipeg.

In 1919, MB's first regularly scheduled trucking company, Rural Motor Transports Limited, began operations. It hauled produce and freight between Winnipeg and **POPLAR POINT**, but lasted less than a year before going out of business. However, other trucking firms continued to spring up, and their numbers continued to grow throughout the 1920s and '30s. By the outbreak of WWII, more than 460 were operating in the province. That period from the early 20th century to 1939 later came to be referred to as the industry's pioneering phase.

The post-war period saw Canada's railways also expand into the trucking business, further increasing existing tensions between these competing sectors. The 1950s and '60s was a period of unprecedented growth for the trucking industry. By the start of the 1970s, it was big business in the province, boasting more than 5000 employees and greater than $50 million in assets. By then, the trend also was toward larger trucking firms because it was thought they would be better able to meet the many challenges the industry faced. Those challenges included soaring fuel costs and a shortage of experienced drivers.

The 1980s and '90s were another period of dramatic change for the industry, as new free-trade agreements among Canada, the US, and Mexico began to alter truck traffic patterns within Canada dramatically. Fewer goods were being hauled E to W; instead, more product was flowing N and S between Canada and its new NAFTA partners.

Deregulation of the MB trucking industry in 1994 also caused major changes. It meant MB trucking firms could haul anything anywhere and charge whatever the market would bear, rather than have their rates dictated by provincial regulatory agencies. It also fuelled further consolidation within the industry, with even some of the province's oldest and largest trucking firms getting caught up in the ongoing shift toward ever-larger trucking operations. Some of the more notable examples of this were the 1997 purchase of Reimer Express by US-based Roadway Express Inc.; the 1998 acquisition of Atomic Transport by AB-based TCT Logistics Inc.; and the 2006 sale of Kleysen Transport to another AB trucking conglomerate, The Mullen Group Income Fund.

Some of the same problems that plagued the industry in the 1970s, such as soaring fuel costs and a shortage of drivers, remain major challenges for the industry in the first decade of the 21st century. Also added to the list were tougher **Pollution**-control standards for the industry, and increased security measures at Canada-US border crossings. • MURRAY MCNEILL

TUBERCULOSIS (TB), primarily an infectious lung disease that was formerly known as "consumption," was the leading cause of death in Canada in 1900. Although the disease is largely under control today, TB is still a significant problem in MB's northern **First Nations** communities, where poor nutrition and congested housing encourage its spread.

Even though the pathogen that causes TB – *Mycobacterium tuberculosis* – was identified in 1882, there was no cure for the disease until the 1960s, when effective drug treatment became widely available. The only TB treatment for most of the 20th century was supervised bedrest in sanatoriums, or specialized TB hospitals. Patients were secluded and given "rest therapy," which consisted of bedrest, improved nutrition, and various forms of lung surgery.

The ON govt opened the Muskoka Sanatorium in 1897, and the pressure was on MB to build a similar facility. In 1904, MB passed an *Act Respecting a Sanatorium for Consumptives* (TB patients), which led to the building of the MB Sanatorium at **Ninette**. By 1928, legislation was broadened to make the Sanatorium Board of MB responsible for TB treatment in the province. The act was unique in Canada, and made the Sanatorium Board the first provincial non-governmental organization.

Soon the "San Board," as people called it, operated a central TB registry and a clinic in Winnipeg, mobile chest and X-ray clinics, a sanatorium with hundreds of beds in Ninette, and 4 other medical facilities that treated TB patients. The Ninette Sanatorium, as it was informally called, began operating in 1910 on the shores of Pelican Lake, with Dr. David A. Stewart as the founding medical director.

By the 1950s, improved public health and TB drugs started to empty sanatorium beds. The govt became reluctant to fund the mostly empty TB hospitals at **Brandon**, Clearwater Lake, and Dynevor. While the Ninette San had 400 beds and 24 buildings in the 1950s, it, too, entered a period of decline.

In 1972, Jack Cunnings, executive director of the San Board at the time and later author of a book on Dr. **Paul Thorlakson**, presided over the controversial closing of the Ninette San. The timing was determined by the retirement of the board's key medical staff. Closing the San was painful, since it touched the lives of many Manitobans over its 62-year existence. Also, it was the major employer in Ninette, and the largest enterprise of the board. However, the San Board needed to become a community health organization to survive the decline in TB rates.

In 1975, the Sanatorium Board opened a new division called the MB Lung Association, the name by which most Manitobans have known it since. The Board continues to operate a TB control program under contracts with the province and the federal govt. Dr. Earl Hershfield, who took over as medical director in 1967, modernized the TB control program by standardizing drug regimens, centralizing control and monitoring, and treating the disease within the larger medical system rather than in separate institutions. Hershfield went on to a long career as an internationally recognized TB consultant,

Canadian National Express truck and drivers, 1920

The Sanatorium Board of Manitoba sent mobile x-ray units around the province to screen for TB, including this one in 1963.

researcher, and teacher, retiring from the San Board in 2003.

While TB is now under control in Canada, with a rate of about 5 active cases per 100,000 people, 2 million people still die of the disease every year worldwide. In Canada, TB remains a serious problem in 3 population areas: new immigrants who are foreign-born and from countries with high rates of TB; homeless people in urban areas; and First Nations people, especially those in remote communities. Even though MB Aboriginal people suffered with TB at a disproportionately high rate throughout the 20th century – thanks to poverty, poor nutrition, and RESIDENTIAL SCHOOLS – it took almost 30 years before the San Board provided TB hospitals for this community. When they did, the facilities were segregated and were inferior to what other Manitobans used. In present-day MB, with 12% of the population being First Nations or Aboriginal, periodic outbreaks in this community are an ongoing concern. ● MAURICE MIERAU

TUNICATE is a most unusual, soft-bodied group of marine organisms sometimes referred to as a urochordates (subphylum Urochordata, phylum Chordata). It is of keen interest because it is related to the ancestor of all higher animals (chordates), including humans. They present a strange mixture of chordate characteristics, such as a series of segmented muscles along the trunk, a notochord or supporting rod down the back, and a hollow, dorsal nerve chord in the free-swimming larval stage, but these features are lost in the transition to the sessile, invertebrate-like adult. There are several classes of these sea animals, with 16 species of sea squirts or ascidians (class Ascidiacea) and 2 species of larvaceans (class Larvacea or Appendicularia) occuring in MB marine waters. Most sea squirts (e.g., *Boltenia echinata*) attach by means of a stalk to rocky (occasionally muddy) substrates in the intertidal (littoral) zone. Interestingly, the larvaceans remain in the larval form – a tiny (5-50 mm), transparent, tadpole-like creature, which spends its life in the plankton community, drifting in the currents (e.g., *Fritillaria borealis*).

The body is protected by a protein-cellulose 'house', which is shed periodically as the creature grows and its feeding net becomes clogged. All tunicates are filter feeders. Sea squirts have an incurrent and excurrent siphon, and wave hair-like cilia to drive currents of food-laden water past sticky-mucus surfaces on what is called a pharyngeal basket, and then into a U-shaped gut for digestion. The larvaceans move water with muscular tail movements, and minute creatures and food particles are trapped in a fine, gelatinous mesh. The water currents also bring in oxygen and remove wastes. Tunicates are hermaphrodites (with both testis and ovary) and may reproduce sexually (eggs fertilized in the sea or in a brood pouch), or asexually by budding. The larva of sea squirts eventually sinks to the bottom and attaches to the substrate, where it develops a barrel-shaped, tough tunic around its body.

Sea squirts may occur singly (e.g., body about 25 mm high and 10 mm wide) in some species, or in packed colonies produced by budding, which resemble a crust or sponge (e.g., 15 cm wide). Although 18 species have been found in Hudson Bay near MB, many others have been reported in James Bay and Hudson Strait, so numerous other species will no doubt be added to the MB fauna. This is an ancient group traceable back 540 million years (Early Cambrian period). ● REW

TURTLE is a reptile (order Testudines, class Reptilia) characterized by a protective outer shell composed of bony scutes covered with plates of keratin (same material as our nails). The evolution of the shell has served turtles well, for they have been perpetual members of many of the world's ecosystems for over 230 million years (Triassic period). The upper shell is called the carapace; the lower, the plastron. Restriction by the shell has compressed the body into a short and wide shape. Obviously, as the turtle grows, the shell's bony minerals must be continually reabsorbed and re-deposited, while the horny scutes become worn and are replaced. Most turtles are able to withdraw their head, tail, and stubby legs in line with the shell, which offers protection from the bites of most predators. Turtles lack teeth, but can bite off food with their sharp-edged jaws, and a few species defend themselves by biting. Turtles are protected in MB, and should never be collected or disturbed in any way. The following 2 species are found here.

WESTERN PAINTED TURTLE (*Chrysemys picta belli*) of the Water Turtle family Emydidae, is an attractive reptile with an intricate pattern of red, yellow and black on the plastron, the purpose of which is unknown. The head and legs are black with bright-yellow lines. Occupying permanent waterways from the prairies to the boreal coniferous forest, its N limits have yet to be determined (about the S half of MB). It is occasionally seen crossing a road or basking on a log or boulder at the water's edge – a pastime it appears to enjoy for hours at a time, soaking up infra-red radiation (warming rays) from the sun. Average size is 25 cm long, with females somewhat larger than males. It accepts a wide variety of plants (60% of the diet) and animals, from crustaceans to frogs and fish. Up to 20 eggs are laid during June in a nest excavated by the female's spade-like hind feet. She selects a well-drained site with sand or gravel, usually not far from the water's edge. Eggs hatch in about 90 days, and most of the juvenile turtles remain underground in the nest overwinter, where remarkably they can withstand freezing down to –10°C. Some may hatch in the spring. The young turtles dig their way to the surface and instinctively head for the nearest watercourse. Adults hibernate in the mud at the bottom of deep ponds and rivers. This turtle can survive 12 years in the wild. A related species – the Red-eared Turtle (*Chrysemys scripta*) of the SE United States – is the species commonly sold in pet shops. This captive should not be released into the wild, for it will perish during the winter and may introduce foreign disease and parasites into the province.

COMMON SNAPPING TURTLE (*Chelydra serpentina*), family Chelydridae, is a bizarre creature, prehistoric in appearance, with a massive head and saw-tooth tail. The carapace has 3 longitudinal ridges, but these become less distinct as the animal ages, and the entire surface is often covered in a thick carpet of algae, adding to the animal's already excellent camouflage. The plastron is remarkably reduced, which lightens the weight of the turtle and permits room for greater expansion of fat deposits around the thighs. The largest turtle recorded from MB (near Sperling) measured 53 cm long and weighed 18 kg, but fat specimens may attain more than double this weight. This 'snapper' should never be handled, particularly large ones, for they do not hesitate to lunge and bite ferociously, and can cause considerable damage to a hand before letting go. This species is widely distributed in streams, rivers, lakes and ponds throughout the S third of the province. Being highly aquatic, it only leaves the water to emigrate to a new watercourse, locate a mate during the breeding season in spring, or to lay eggs. People occasionally see

a Snapping Turtle laying eggs in a hole dug in gravel road. Many of these clutches, containing 20-85 leathery, round eggs, are excavated and devoured by raccoons, foxes and other predators. Eggs are usually laid in June and hatch in late Aug or Sept – the rate of development depending on temperature. Some eggs laid in late summer may overwinter, although some likely fail to survive due to freezing. A hardy survivor, it lives for up to 60 years, even in rivers in cottage country and cities like Winnipeg, although most people are unaware of its presence. It hibernates in the muddy substrate of deep water from Oct to March. It feeds on fish, frogs, crustaceans, and any animal it comes across (including ducklings), live or dead, as well as aquatic plants (36% of the diet). ● REW, WDP

TWEED, Merv, politician, (b Aug 6, 1955, **MEDORA**). Educated at **BRANDON U,** Tweed began his career in politics in the early 1990s at the municipal level serving as councilor and deputy reeve in the RM of Brenda. In 1995, 1999 and 2003, he was elected to the MB legislature as a **PROGRESSIVE CONSERVATIVE** in Turtle Mountain. During his time as a MLA, Tweed was the PC critic for most provincial Crown corporations. In govt, he acted as parliamentary assistant to a number of ministers before being appointed minister of industry, trade and tourism in Gary Filmon's administration. When Filmon's govt fell to the NDP in 2003, Tweed was nevertheless re-elected handily. When federal Conservative MP **RICK BOROTSIK** announced his retirement in

2004, Tweed resigned his provincial seat and won the PC nomination in the federal riding of Brandon-Souris. He won that seat in the House of Commons in June 2004. Tweed was re-elected in the 2006 general election and named chairman of the standing committee on transport. ● RUTH DEGRAVES

TYNDALL, pop 560, is a community 45 km NE of **WINNIPEG** at the conjunction of hwys 12 and 44. The community was probably named after 19th-century **IRISH** physicist John Tyndall. The **CPR** came here in 1877, though the line has since been abandoned. Home to a few businesses and a school, Tyndall is often grouped together with neighbouring **GARSON**. As **TYNDALL STONE** was shipped from here by rail, it was named after Tyndall, despite the fact that this limestone has always been quarried at Garson. ● GPP

TYNDALL STONE is a grey to buff-mottled limestone that is quarried at **GARSON**, 37 km NE of Winnipeg. It belongs to the Selkirk Member of the **RED RIVER** Formation, dated from 445-447 million years old (Late Ordovician period). Tyndall Stone has been quarried in the Garson area since 1895; similar stone was quarried after 1832 near Lower Fort Garry along the Red River. This stone has long been called Tyndall Stone because it was shipped from **TYNDALL**, near Garson. It can be seen in many buildings in the Winnipeg area, including the **MB LEGISLATIVE BUILDING** and the **WINNIPEG ART GALLERY**, and in several other important buildings in Canada such as the Parliament Buildings in Ottawa, the Canadian Museum of Civilization in Gatineau, and the Empress Hotel in Victoria. Tyndall Stone was deposited as lime sediment in a warm, shallow inland sea at a time when what is now S MB was slightly S of the equator. The darker mottles are considered to be burrows made by shrimp-like animals moving through the mud of the ancient seafloor. The burrows are darker because they are made of dolomite (calcium magnesium carbonate), while the surrounding material is limestone (calcium carbonate). Tyndall Stone contains a diverse array of fossils, the most common being receptaculitids – an extinct group of uncertain affinities, possibly calcareous green algae (commonly called sunflower corals). The second-most abundant are the solitary rugose or horn corals. Other common groups include stromatoporoid sponges, colonial corals, brachiopods (lamp shells), bryozoans (moss animals), gastropods (snails), cephalopods (relatives of squids and octopus), crinoids (sea lilies), trilobites (extinct relatives of crabs and insects), and conodonts (microscopic jaw elements of fish-like chordates). ● GY

ROBERT R. TAYLOR

The Snapping Turtle is prehistoric in appearance.

UPPER FORT GARRY,
see page 705

U

UKRAINIAN CULTURAL AND EDUCATION-AL CENTRE OF WINNIPEG (in Ukrainian "Oseredok," meaning "nexus" or "hub"). Oseredok was founded in 1944 as a way to preserve **UKRAINIAN** culture in Canada, since so much of Ukraine had been destroyed or looted during WWII. Today, the centre houses a museum, archive, art gallery, library, and boutique, and delivers programming. It is located in downtown **WINNIPEG** in a structure originally built by the British and Foreign Bible Society in 1912. The Bible Society overestimated the size of its mission in western Canada, however, and the Children's Aid Society occupied most of "Bible House" from 1913 to 1957. The Ukrainian National Publishing Company purchased the building in 1949, and called it the "New Pathway Building" after their newspaper. Various Ukrainian Cdn organizations had offices in the building, but most moved to Toronto by the mid-1950s. The New Pathway building was largely vacant until 1971, when Oseredok moved from its original Main St location to the two top floors. When the *New Pathway* newspaper moved to Toronto in the 1970s, the centre bought the whole building and took over all 5 floors.

The museum houses thousands of artifacts, including religious icons, needlework, Easter eggs (*pysanka*), wood carvings, musical instruments,

and items from Cdn pioneer days. The collection was first put together for MB's centennial year, 1970, when it was displayed at the MB legislature and then the **MANITOBA MUSEUM**. The Centre has the largest archive of Ukrainian holdings outside Ukraine, and is frequently consulted by professional researchers from all over the world. The papers of many Ukrainian Cdn leaders are housed here, including those of Mykhailo Seleshko, a founding member of the militant Organization of Ukrainian Nationalists (OUN). The records of various associations, including the Ukrainian Canadian Congress, are housed in the centre, with about 80% of the material related to Ukrainians in Canada.

The centre's art gallery displays the work of Ukrainian Canadian and Ukrainian artists, both contemporary and traditional, in icons, sculpture, and paintings. The centre's art collection is used for research, in-house exhibits, and loans to other Cdn galleries. There are more than 40,000 books and periodicals in the centre's library, with collections of children's books, folklore, music, and rare books, and reference materials in Ukrainian and English. A boutique offers embroidered shirts and blouses, T-shirts, music recordings, videos, materials for learning Ukrainian, Easter egg kits, original artwork, and many gift items.

695

Programming at the centre covers workshops on making traditional painted Easter eggs, lectures, and language classes. • MAURICE MIERAU

UKRAINIANS began a major **IMMIGRATION** to the Prairies from W Ukraine between 1890 and 1914. At that time, central and eastern Ukraine was part of the Czarist Russian Empire, while W Ukraine was mostly under the Austro-Hungarian Empire or Romanian rule. The first rural settlements in MB were established in 1896 in Stuartburn and Terebowla in the **DAUPHIN** area. It is estimated that Ukrainians opened up 4 million ha (10 million ac) or 40% of Canada's Prairie land.

In the 1890s, Ukrainians were known by regional names such as Ruthenians, Rusyns, Carpatho-Rusyns, Galicians, Lemkos, and Bukovinians. Because they arrived with Austro-Hungarian documents, or, later Polish ones, some were also labelled "Austrian" or "Polish." Whatever they were called, these settlers arrived as farmers and labourers, in possession of little wealth but eager to work the land. Not all were as illiterate and destitute as depicted in some histories. The quick establishment of churches, reading societies, theatre groups, schools, publishing houses, and newspapers indicates the cultural level of the pioneers.

WINNIPEG played a major role in Ukrainian Cdn life. From the 1890s to the beginning of WWI, the hub for new arrivals was that city's downtown **CPR** station. From there, the new arrivals dispersed across western Canada, though some stayed in the city. Frank Yaciw, son of Wasyl and Mary Yaciw, b in Winnipeg on Feb 14, 1893, was the first native-born Cdn of Ukrainian descent. The headquarters for the numerous cultural, social, professional, and academic organizations were – and often still are – in the capital of MB. The Metropolitans and Consistories of both the Ukrainian Greek **ORTHODOX CHURCH** of Canada and of the Ukrainian **CATHOLIC CHURCH** are in Winnipeg. *Kanadiysky Farmer* was the first Ukrainian-language newspaper published in Canada (1903). In 1904, the first Ukrainian book, the *Christian Catechism*, was printed, also in Winnipeg. The first Ukrainian-language bookstore opened in the city in 1905.

A Ukrainian strain of early-ripening **WHEAT**, Red Fife (in Ukrainian, "Halychanka"), was brought to the Prairies via Scotland in 1842. Red Fife and the Marquis variety – a cross first made 50 years later between Halychanka and an Indian variety, Hard Red Calcutta – became the foundation of wheat farming in western Canada.

With the outbreak of WWI and the federal govt's *War Measures Act* (1914), some immigrants were considered "enemy aliens" because they had emigrated from Austro-Hungary. Of the 8579 individuals interned, over 5000 were Ukrainian. Another 80,000, the majority of them Ukrainians, were obligated to register as "enemy aliens." The internees became forced labourers in infrastructure development. In MB, there was an internment receiving station operating at Fort Osborne in Winnipeg (1914-16), and an internment camp at the **BRANDON** Agricultural Exhibition Building (*see* **ROYAL MANITOBA WINTER FAIR**). At the same time, Ukrainian Canadians enlisted and served in Canada's armed services during WWI. After the war, Ukrainian workers played a major role in the **WINNIPEG GENERAL STRIKE** of 1919.

The 2nd major immigration occurred between the 2 wars (1919-39). About 70,000 Ukrainians from W Ukraine (then under Polish rule) arrived in Canada. In MB, the new settlers joined the earlier generations of Ukrainian Canadians. This period also saw the establishment of new associations, such as the Ukrainian National Federation, the Ukrainian Self-Reliance League, and the Brotherhood of Ukrainian Catholics.

During WWII, about 40,000 Ukrainian Canadians served in the Forces overseas. They aided Ukrainian displaced persons, refugees, political prisoners of concentration camps, and forced labourers and *Ostarbeiters* ("eastern workers") of wartime Germany. Members of Winnipeg Branch 141, one of the largest Ukrainian branches of the Royal Canadian Legion in Canada, played a significant role in this during and after the war.

The 3rd wave of Ukrainian immigrants arrived in Canada from the end of the war to the early 1950s. They were mostly political refugees who would not return to what was now Soviet Ukraine. Many were professionals and members of the intelligentsia. They formed new organizations, such as the Canadian League for the Liberation of Ukraine, the Ukrainian Youth Association of Canada, and Plast Ukrainian Youth Association. New waves of highly qualified economic and professional immigrants have come to Manitoba beginning with the 1980s to the present.

The Ukrainian Canadian Congress (to 1989, the Ukrainian Canadian Committee), was founded in Winnipeg in 1941 and is the umbrella organization for Ukrainians across Canada. The Ukrainian Canadian Foundation of Taras Schevchenko – named after the nation's great poet – was established in 1963, is affiliated with the Congress, and supports the promotion and advancement of Ukrainian culture in Canada. Both organizations are headquartered in Winnipeg. One group not represented by the UCC is the pro-Communist Assoc. of United Ukrainian Canadians, formerly the Ukrainian Labour-Farmer Temple Assoc., founded in 1918.

In science, cardiologist Jaroslaw Barwinsky was the first doctor in Winnipeg to insert a pacemaker in 1962. Isydore Hlynka, cereal chemist at the Grain Research Laboratory in Winnipeg, was the founding president of the Ukrainian Canadian Foundation of Taras Shevchenko, and a columnist in the newspaper *Ukrains'kyi Holos*. ("Ukrainian Voice"). Peter Kondra, animal geneticist, was the first to investigate the hatching quality of commercial feed for poultry breeders in MB, resulting in changes to feed sources. **HARRY WASYLYK** of Winnipeg co-invented the disposable garbage bag in 1950.

In govt, Peter Liba served as **LT GOV** 1999-2004. Benjamin (Bohdan) Hewak was Chief Justice of the Court of Queen's Bench for 17 years. Ukrainians have been active at the local, provincial, and federal levels. In 1911, Theodore

Ukrainian family harvesting, 1920

Skill and patience are needed to create Ukrainian Easter Eggs.

FOLKLORAMA - CANADA'S CULTURAL CELEBRATION; WHERE TO LOOK PHOTOGRAPHY

Stefanyk was elected as Winnipeg's first Ukrainian city councillor. The first Ukrainian MLA was Taras Ferley, elected in 1915. Nicholas V. Bachynsky served as MLA for a record 34 years (1922-58). In 1956, STEPHEN JUBA, Cdn-born son of Ukrainian pioneers, was the first non-Anglo-Saxon mayor of Winnipeg, and the longest-serving one (21 years). Slaw Rebchuk was another longstanding Winnipeg politician.

Three of the "fathers" of the 1971 Multiculturalism Policy of Canada – Isydore Hlynka, J. B. Rudnyckyj, and Paul Yuzyk – were Ukrainian Manitobans, along with Bohdan R. Bociurkiw of AB. Though official multiculturalism in Canada can be traced back to a speech by PM Sir Wilfrid Laurier, the 1971 policy moved this country from being bicultural to being multicultural. In 1963, Rudnyckyj was appointed to the Royal Commission on Bilingualism and Biculturalism. He submitted a separate statement to the commission regarding Canada's multicultural, rather than bicultural, society. Hlynka presented the submission to the commission from the Ukrainian Canadian Committee, indicating that Canada was multicultural and multilingual. Historian and professor Paul Yuzyk represented MB in the Senate for 23 years, and was the first Ukrainian to sit in the Red Chamber. He stated the policy that Canada was not a bilingual but multicultural nation in his maiden speech in 1964.

Ukrainians have notably influenced the arts in MB and Canada. The internationally renowned sculptor and artist LEO MOL (Leonid Molodoshanin) is known for his monuments and stained glass. Also well known is artist Roman Iwan Kowal. WILLIAM KURELEK, who grew up in STONEWALL, depicted realistic scenes of Cdn life, especially pioneer times and growing up on the Prairies, in his paintings. Painter and book illustrator Peter Kuch was the editorial cartoonist of the *WINNIPEG FREE PRESS* for 28 years (1952-80). Bill Lobchuk was influential in Prairie arts through his Great Western Canadian Screen Shop (1969-79). The mixed-media works of DON PROCH are in numerous private and corporate collections. Roman Rozumnyj is known internationally for his painting and interior architecture.

In LITERATURE, MUSIC, and DRAMA, Maara Lysechko Haas, Paul Grescoe, playwright Ted Galay, and producer, playwright, and composer Danny Schur are prominent MB figures. Singers and actors Joanne Karasevych, ED EVANKO, Tamara Gorski, actor MIMI KUZYK, ON Stratford Festival director Andrey Tarasiuk, child prodigy violinist Donna Grescoe, singers Juliette Sysak Cavazzi, Alexis Kochan, and RANDY BACHMAN (a Dobrinsky on his mother's side) and singer-songwriter CHANTAL KREVIAZUK have enriched the MB and Cdn cultural scenes. Cecil Semchyshyn was the founder of Folklorama. ROMAN KROITOR is a member of the NATIONAL FILM BOARD OF CANADA and recipient of many international awards. Slawko Klymkiw is executive director of network programming, CBC, and Ed Huculak is publisher of the *WINNIPEG SUN*. Nestor Burtnyk, a native of ETHELBERT and a graduate of the U of M, was a pioneer in computer animation, developing the y-frame animation technique for which, with Marcelle Wien, he received the Academy Award (1997) for technical achievement. Mary Maximchuk of SIFTON achieved fame with her Mary Maxim sweaters. A National Research Council engineer, and a recipient of many awards including the Member of the Order of Canada, Burtnyk contributed to the development of the Canadarm through his robotics and image processing work.

In sports, the Hockey Hall of Fame includes 2 Ukrainian Manitobans, goalie TERRY SAWCHUK and right-winger BILLY MOSIENKO. Steve Patrick Sr., a WINNIPEG BLUE BOMBER, is in the MB Sports Hall of Fame. Curling champions include OREST MELESCHUK and Ed Werenich.

The MB govt provided a bilingual PUBLIC EDUCATION system from 1897 to 1916, which included a Ukrainian school system. In 1979, the English-Ukrainian Bilingual Program was established, which operates in 10 schools among 6 school divisions. Immaculate Heart of Mary School (formerly St. Nicholas School), founded 1905 in Winnipeg, continues to be operated by the Sister Servants of Mary Immaculate. At the U OF M, a Department of Slavic Studies was established in 1949. Department heads were Jaroslav Rudnyckyj, Jaroslav Rozumnyj, and Myroslav Shkandrij. The mission of the Centre for Ukrainian Canadian Studies, founded at the U of M in 1981, is to create, preserve, and communicate knowledge relating to Ukrainian Cdn culture and scholarship. The Slavic Collection at the U of M Libraries, the 2nd-largest in Canada, has major Ukrainian holdings. The Ukrainian Academy of Arts and Sciences (formerly the Ukrainian Free Academy of Sciences, UVAN) moved to Winnipeg from Europe in 1949.

Building on the foundation established by the Ukrainian pioneers to MB, cultural organizations have continued their work in the province. The Ukrainian Cultural and Educational Centre – Oseredok, founded in 1944 in Winnipeg, continues to be a major national institution. The Oleksander Koshetz Choir, the Rusalka Ukrainian Dance Ensemble, and the Hoosli Ukrainian Folk Ensemble are some of the hundreds of performing groups in MB.

Since 1965, CANADA'S NATIONAL UKRAINIAN FESTIVAL in DAUPHIN has grown into the largest Ukrainian cultural festival in NA. Other summer festivals take place in Gardenton, TEULON, and

Winnipeg Beach. In Winnipeg, 2 Ukrainian pavilions – Kyiv and Lviv – participate in Folklorama.

The 2001 Census of Canada lists 157,655 individuals of Ukrainian origin in MB, with 102,635 in Winnipeg (about 10% of the city's population), making Ukrainians the 2nd-largest group in MB. Even after intermarriage, most Ukrainians have maintained varied connections to their cultural heritage. Annual and family customs and traditions, foods, folk arts, music, and fine arts are part of general MB life. After more than a century, they are no longer a minority immigrant group, but an integral part of MB.
● ORYSIA TRACZ

UNICITY began in 1972, a result of the **New Democratic Party**'s rise to power under **Edward Schreyer**. In its first term in office, the NDP launched an ambitious amalgamation of the 12 municipalities of **Metro Winnipeg** under what conservative local politicians fearfully referred to as One Big Govt (a reference to the planned One Big Union of the **Winnipeg General Strike**).

Unicity was originally the brainchild of Meyer Brownstone, a high-ranking civil servant in the SK govt from the 1940s until its defeat in 1964. Brownstone, who was equally committed to social justice and a grassroots version of parliamentary democracy, sought to design a local govt structure that reflected these beliefs. He sought to design a municipal version of parliamentary govt on the UK model, but with additional features to ensure greater openness to grassroots participation. The Unicity executive would consist of a mayor elected by council, and who would therefore be responsible to council in the same way that the PM is responsible to the House of Commons. Brownstone assumed that this structure would motivate party politics at the local level.

The centralization of power inherent in Unicity was to be ameliorated by a 50-member council – unusually large by Cdn standards – elected by wards. The council would presumably be capable of providing intensive representation at the neighbourhood level. Two other features of Unicity, community committees and resident advisory groups (RAGs), were to take Unicity's institutions beyond parliamentary democracy-by-delegation to grassroots participation in political decision-making. Brownstone's vision was never realized. Even in the process of passage, the provincial govt abandoned the idea of a mayor elected by Council, thereby removing much of the rationale for forming political parties.

The 50-member council was reduced to 30, and then to 15. Community committees, consisting of the members of council from each of the old municipalities – Charleswood, North Kildonan, Tuxedo, West Kildonan, Transcona, St. James–Assiniboia, Fort Garry, Old Kildonan, East Kildonan, St. Vital, and **St. Boniface** – retained some authority in their respective areas, but their powers were whittled down, while the number of community committees was reduced from 12 to 5. RAGs, which were chosen by popular votes at the community level, were to play an advocacy role before community committees, but the concept proved largely unworkable in practice. In short, the idea of a local parliamentary govt enhanced by citizen participation did not survive the rough-and-tumble of local and provincial politics. Unicity has often been pronounced a failure, and the name itself has fallen into disuse.

However, enhancement of local democracy was only 1 of 3 three major objectives of Unicity. The other 2 – tax equalization and political centralization – have proven more lasting and influential. There was growing pressure in the 1960s to reshape municipal politics, as the central city of Winnipeg was the main supplier of services to a burgeoning metropolitan area, while most new development, and the tax revenues it brought, occurred in municipalities surrounding the city. Through political centralization of the entire metropolitan area under a single municipal govt, and equalization of municipal taxes, the provincial govt put the new city of Winnipeg in a position to ensure coherent management of the city's further growth, and rational, equitable expansion of municipal services and infrastructure. A survey of the growth that has taken place since then suggests that the city did not use its powers wisely, however; and many question whether single jurisdictions are in fact preferable to various smaller ones.

The modern history of Winnipeg's representative and administrative institutions reads like an obituary for Unicity. The Board of Control, which headed the Unicity administration, has been abolished and replaced by a single chief administrative officer (CAO). The mayor, still popularly elected rather than being responsible to Council, as Brownstone had intended, has become among the most powerful municipal executives in Canada. He chairs the executive policy committee (EPC), the equivalent of a Cabinet, and appoints its members, 4 of whom he simultaneously appoints as chairs of Council's standing committees. Additionally, the mayor's term is now 4 rather than 3 years.

Still, Unicity provided the foundation on which Winnipeg's institutions have since been built. On that ground alone, it cannot entirely be dismissed as a failure. Furthermore, Unicity has influenced municipal govt design in ON, QC, and NS, all provinces that went through a rash of amalgamations in the 1990s and early 21st century. Today, a large, amalgamated central city dominates the typical Cdn metropolitan area, a sharp contrast with much-more-fragmented US metropolitan areas.

In 2002, the **NDP** govt of **Gary Doer**, introduced the *City of Winnipeg Charter Act*, a revision of the former *City of Winnipeg Act* encom-passing an ambitious devolution of power from provincial to municipal govt. Whether this results in a "downloading" of services onto municipalities without a concomitant ability to raise taxes is unclear; it is appropriate, though, that the term *Unicity* has been laid to rest, because its underlying concepts are unrecognizable in Winnipeg's current governance.

Even Unicity's genuine successes – municipal centralization and tax equalization for the metropolitan area – have become artifacts in the wake of a fresh round of urbanization in formerly rural municipalities surrounding the city. In the 21st century, much of the metropolitan area's growth is slipping beyond Winnipeg into surrounding areas, including that of **Headingley**, which seceded from the city in 1993. Winnipeg is again the overburdened and overtaxed central city, rapidly losing control of the growth of the metropolitan area. ● CHRIS LEO/MATTHEW MULAIRE

UNIDENTIFIED FLYING OBJECTS (UFOs) have had a long and colourful history in MB. The first recorded sighting of an unusual aerial object over MB took place long before it was even a province. In autumn 1792, explorers David Thompson and Andrew Davy were camped on the shore of Landing Lake, near what is now **Thicket Portage**, and were startled to see a "meteor of globular form…larger than the Moon." The object seemed to come directly toward them, descending as it flew, and "when within 300 yards [275 m] of us, it struck the River ice, with a sound like a mass of jelly, was dashed in innumerable luminous pieces and instantly expired." The next morning, when they went to see the hole it should have made in the ice, they were surprised to find no markings whatsoever.

Between then and writing, more than 1000 sightings of UFOs have been recorded in MB, most during the past 50 years. These range from simple sightings of what are known as nocturnal lights to more sensational and detailed reports of apparently physical flying saucers and their occupants – the "close encounters." Among the former are the hundreds of reports of Charlie Redstar, the playful, reddish light seen by many Manitobans during the summers of 1975 and 1976 near **Carman**. In July 1975, so many curiosity-seekers lined the rural farm roads in the evenings, hoping to catch a glimpse of the mysterious object heralded in the news, that there were traffic jams at 2:00 am on some mornings in local highways.

Included in the close encounters is the remarkable claim of Stefan Michalak near Falcon Lake in 1967. On May 20, he had been doing some amateur prospecting N of the Trans-Canada Highway and had stopped to have lunch. He was surprised to see 2 red, glowing saucer-shaped objects, one of which descended and seemed to land on a flat rock face nearby. It changed colour from red to orange to white and, eventually, silver, possibly cooling, and remained there long enough for Michalak to make a sketch of the craft and approach it warily on foot. Bright lights emanated from the object, and a door opened in its side, from which Michalak could hear high-pitched voices. Thinking the saucer was an American military craft, he bravely strode to the door and said, "Okay, Yankee boys, having trouble? Come on out and we'll see what we can do about it." The voices abruptly ceased and Michalak realized it might be a foreign craft, so he hailed the occupants in German, Russian, and Polish, but to no avail. Suddenly, the door shut, the craft rotated, and a grille or exhaust

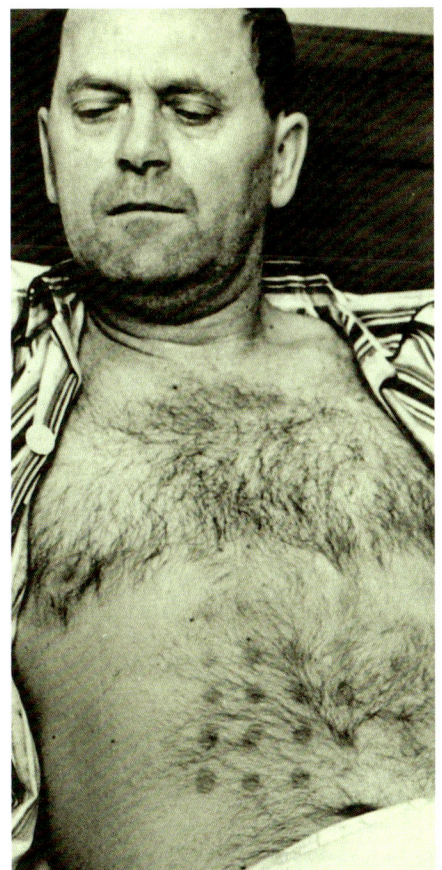

Stefan Michalak displays burn marks he attributed to UFO encounter.

vent now faced him. A blast of hot gas shot out, engulfing Michalak and setting his clothes on fire. The object ascended and flew off, leaving its injured and dazed witness to find his way back to civilization. Official investigations by RCMP, the US air force, and civilian organizations could not fully explain Michalak's experience. The case is listed by the US air force in its *Scientific Study of Unidentified Flying Objects* as "unexplained," although one of the study's investigators, Roy Craig, believed the case to be a hoax.

Civilian UFO investigation and discussion groups have formed and dissipated in MB. Most notable was the Canadian Aerial Phenomenon Research Organization (CAPRO), created in the late 1960s and which dissolved in the 1970s. It published a national newsletter that at one time had a circulation in the thousands and a national readership. In 1976, Ufology Research of Manitoba (UFOROM) was initiated as an association of independent investigators and researchers. It still exists today, and may be the longest-running Cdn UFO group, though it is not open to the public.

National polls have found that an amazing 10% of the Cdn population claim to have seen UFOs. In MB alone, more than 100,000 people have had UFO experiences. According to the 2004 Cdn UFO Survey, produced and published by UFOROM, nearly 900 UFO sightings were reported in Canada that year, of which 112 were in MB. Investigators have found that only a comparative handful of cases each year have no explanation, of the order of a few percentage points. The other reports are misidentifications of ordinary objects, or contain insufficient information to conduct proper investigations. Even so, there are enough unexplained UFO cases every year that UFOROM advocates further scientific study of the phenomenon, whatever its cause or causes.
● CHRIS RUTKOWSKI

UNIONS in MB have faced many of the same pressures and challenges experienced by labour organizations in the rest of Canada. Nonetheless, some distinctive features exist in the province, largely due to the occupational and industrial composition of the workforce, but also because of legislative differences.

In the aftermath of the 1919 **WINNIPEG GENERAL STRIKE**, union membership in the country declined, largely because of anti-labour legislation that, in its most-extreme form, saw union leaders charged under sedition laws. Despite many colourful political events – including the rise of the **CO-OPERATIVE COMMONWEALTH FEDERATION** (CCF) and the formation of many **COMMUNIST**-led unions – the high unemployment rates

of the **GREAT DEPRESSION** forestalled unionization. It was not until WWII that nationwide organizing drives among workers in manufacturing industries, such as automobile and steel, brought an upturn in union membership. In MB, this trend was most apparent in the successful organization of the **BEEF PROCESSING** Industry. A 2nd wave of post-WWII unionization occurred in the 1960s, when provincial and federal govt workers won collective bargaining rights.

Since the early 1980s, however, unionization has been in decline. Between 1981 and 2004, union membership as a percentage of the workforce fell in both Canada (from 37.6 to 30.6%) and in MB (from 37.9 to 35.4%). The decline was caused by several factors, most importantly, a shift away from traditionally unionized, industrial, blue-collar jobs toward occupations in the service sector that have proved difficult to unionize. Compounding this shift is the growth in key service industries of large corporations that have assumed a determined anti-union stance. Wal-Mart and McDonald's are well-known examples. These trends are probably responsible for the discrepancy between the unionization rates in the commercial sector (at 20%) and public sector (61%). MB's high proportion of public-sector workers has meant that the labour movement has fared relatively well during these difficult times. The province is now 2nd only to NL in unionization. An important corollary of the increasing prominence of public-sector unions is the growing percentage of women in the labour movement. Over half of unionized workers in the province are women, a significant change from the male-dominated days of the immediate postwar period.

Of the roughly 167,000 union members in MB, nearly 90,000 are concentrated in 5 large public sector unions: the Manitoba Govt and General Employees Union (MGEU, 32,000), the Canadian Union of Public Employees (CUPE, 24,000), The Manitoba Teachers' Society (MTS, 16,000), the Manitoba Nurses Union (MNU, 11,000) and the Public Service Alliance of Canada (PSAC, 10,000). Amalgamation has occurred within both the commercial and public sectors, notably among several industrial unions that suffered a loss in membership in the early 1980s. Today the United Food and Commercial Workers (UFCW, 16,000) and the Canadian Autoworkers (CAW, 10,000) are the largest unions outside of the public sector, with the CAW carrying out the most determined efforts to unionize workers outside of its traditional automobile and aerospace industries as well as into the public sector. This consolidation has often resulted in more effective service for union members, particularly in

Union Density in workforce, Manitoba and Canada

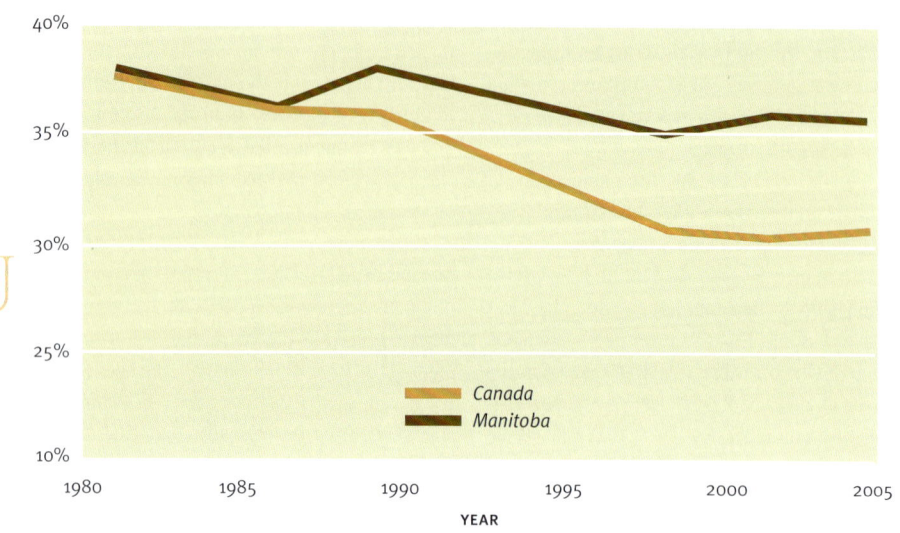

rural and northern areas, where populations are scattered.

Most union locals in the province are affiliated with the Manitoba Federation of Labour (MFL). The MFL was created by the Canadian Labour Congress (CLC) to advance the political and economic interests of organized labour. The CLC regulates its member unions over such important matters as jurisdiction, and has an important lobbying role for issues of both national and international scope. Some of the longstanding divisions within the labour movement have subsided due to the growing predominance of national public-sector unions, although the increasing prominence the CAW has created political frictions.

Another reason for the relative success of the MB labour movement is that, since the late 1960s, the **NEW DEMOCRATIC PARTY** (NDP) has formed the provincial govt 6 times. The NDP has roots in organized labour and, when, in govt, has been more sympathetic toward unions. Notwithstanding this relationship, labour has yet to realize its longstanding goal of achieving legislation that would ban the use of replacement workers, often called "scabs," during a strike or lockout. Changes to the *Labour Relations Act* in the late 1980s through the 1990s – including the requirement of over 60% support for certification of a union in a workplace; the need for unions to file annual financial statements to the Manitoba Labour Board (MLB); the right of union members to inspect financial records; and the ability of employers to prevail upon the Minister of Labour to force a vote on any proposed collective agreement – have also caused frustration. In 2000, the NDP govt enacted legislation that

forbade unions and corporations from contributing to election campaigns, a change that was greeted with some ambivalence by labour.

Unions have obtained some legislative concessions, however. In particular, the MLB can impose initial contracts if a newly certified union local and an employer cannot negotiate one. This can be beneficial when the employer seeks to forestall union representation at the bargaining table. Experiences in provinces where labour boards lack this power suggest that it is useful in averting work stoppages. If parties are negotiating with respect to an existing collective agreement, final offer selection is available, and is intended to promote reasonable expectations by the parties. MB also has progressive Workplace Safety and Health legislation. Workers have the right to refuse unsafe work, thereby placing greater onus on employers to demonstrate that their workplaces are safe. The legislation also mandates workplace health and safety committees that include both management and union representatives. These legislative initiatives have likely contributed to the peaceful industrial relations prevailing in the province at writing, at which time work stoppages due to lockout or strike were at low levels. In 2005, for instance, there were only 5 work stoppages (2 due to lockouts and 3 due to strikes) involving 800 workers – a far cry from the militant days on the 1970s.

Whatever success the MB labour movement has achieved, it still faces many challenges. Foremost is the need to appeal to younger workers, many in part-time, service occupations, in a manner relevant to the economic, political, and social priorities of these workers. At the same time, key sectors of the economy, such as financial

services (*see* **BANKING**), have largely resisted unionization. Developing the capacity to respond to these challenges is necessary if the labour movement in MB is to remain an important and progressive force in the province. ● HUGH GRANT/LISA MCGIFFORD

UNITARIANISM is a liberal religious tradition with roots in 19th-century New England Congregationalism (*see* **UNITED CHURCH OF CANADA**) and Transcendentalism, although its ultimate origins lie in the Radical Reformation of the 16th century, also the origin of **MENNONITES** and **HUTTERITES**. Historically, Unitarians affirmed to unity of God, the humanity of Jesus, and "the brotherhood of man." No longer a distinctly Christian denomination, present-day Unitarianism affirms the essential worth and dignity of persons, the unfettered search for truth and meaning, and respect for the interdependent web of all existence. It embraces religious humanism and the wisdom found in all world religions.

Unitarianism in MB first appeared among **ICELANDIC** immigrants who were dissatisfied with the doctrines of the Icelandic Evangelical Lutheran Synod. After 5 years of missionary work, Reverend Björn Pétursson and his wife, Jennie E. McCaine Peterson, organized the First Icelandic Unitarian Church of Winnipeg on Feb 1, 1891. The congregation erected its first chapel the following year. Rev. Rögnvaldur Pétursson assumed the ministry of the First Icelandic Unitarian Church of **WINNIPEG** in 1903. Six years later, he became field secretary for the Icelandic churches by the American Unitarian Assoc (AUA). Under his leadership, which lasted until 1940, Unitarian churches were centres of Icelandic cultural activities as much as they were centres of liberal religion.

In 1904, the first English-speaking Unitarian congregation, All Souls Unitarian Church, was organized by Rev. H. F. M. Ross, a former **PRESBYTERIAN** minister and journalist, and Arthur W. Puttee, Canada's first Labour MP. During the ministry of Horace Westwood (1912-19), All Souls Church emerged as one of the spiritual centres of labour politics in the city. Westwood was 1 of 2 ministerial delegates to the Winnipeg Trades and Labour Council and a frequent contributor to city newspapers, especially the **WINNIPEG TRIBUNE** and *The Voice*. He left the city on the eve of the **WINNIPEG GENERAL STRIKE** of 1919, having fallen out of favour with the labour movement after criticizing the firefighters for joining the previous year's strike. All Souls Church entered a period of decline until Philip M. Petursson arrived as its minister in 1929, changing its name to the Unitarian Church of Winnipeg.

In the early 1930s, the Unitarian Church of Winnipeg vacated its building and began meeting at First Federated Church. Philip M. Petursson was installed as minister of the Federated Church in 1935, serving both the English- and Icelandic-speaking congregations, which remained separate until 1943, when they merged to form a single, bilingual congregation. By the 1960s, the congregation was known simply as the Unitarian Church of Winnipeg. In 1994, it reincorporated as the First Unitarian Universalist Church.

The GIMLI Unitarian Church is the only congregation remaining from among those that followed Reverend Magnús Skaptason out of the Lutheran Synod in 1891. After a period of inactivity, it was reorganized in 1903 and erected its landmark building in 1905. By mid-century, the church had entered a period of decline and once again became dormant. In 1994, the church was revived as a summer congregation. The ARBORG Unitarian Church was organized in 1923 as the Icelandic Federated Church and had a church built 3 years later. It is the only rural congregation to maintain relatively continuous activity from its founding until present. In addition to the congregations already mentioned, churches were organized and built in 6 localities: ARNES, LUNDAR, Mary Hill, Oak Point, Otto (SHOAL LAKE), and RIVERTON.

A women's society was established at the Winnipeg church in 1904, with the pioneer suffrage leader MARGRÉT BENEDICTSSON as its first president. Similar societies were established in other congregations and, in 1926, these societies organized the Western Canada Alliance of Unitarian Women. In 1937, the Alliance, led by María Björnson of Arborg, established the Federated Fresh Air Camp at Hnausa to provide outdoor vacations for needy children from Winnipeg, although its work eventually expanded to include children from across the province. Following WWII, the camp was used primarily for church-related events until the 1960s, when it became available to various non-profit organizations.

Since the 1950s, the Icelandic dominance of MB's Unitarians has steadily declined but has been replaced by a more culturally diverse mix of adherents. Sociologically, Unitarians are highly educated and predominantly from the middle class, with a disproportionate number employed in the public sector. There are presently 3 Unitarian congregations in MB, located in Winnipeg, Arborg, and Gimli. Their combined membership totals 286 adults and 145 children. ● STEFAN M. JONASSON

UNITED CHURCH OF CANADA (UCC) was created in 1925 by the union of the METHODIST CHURCH, the Congregational Union of Canada and

about 70% of the membership of the PRESBYTERIAN CHURCH. On its formation, it became the largest Protestant denomination in Canada. MB was a centre of support for the new church with all of the Methodist and Congregational congregations and all but 17 of the Presbyterian congregations voting to go into the UCC. UCC records in 1931 cited 54,317 members in the province.

The new church's organizational structure borrowed from its founding denominations. The "provincial" unit of administration was the conference; conferences were to be divided into presbyteries, presbyteries were to be made up of pastoral charges (the official name for local congregations). Manitoba Conference was organized into 9 presbyteries in 1925: Superior, Rock Lake, CARMAN, PORTAGE LA PRAIRIE, BRANDON, BIRTLE, DAUPHIN and LAKE WINNIPEG. Over the years, presbyteries have changed and amalgamated so that in 2006 they are: Northland, Assiniboine, Agassiz, Winnipeg, SELKIRK and Cambrian. In 1981, at the request of the church's Native Elders' Council, Keewatin Presbytery was established as an Aboriginal presbytery in MB. In 1988, the All Native Circle Conference (ANCC) was formed as an Aboriginal conference to be made up of presbyteries located in several provinces. Keewatin Presbytery joined the new conference and the conference headquarters were established in Winnipeg.

The union meant change for the former Methodist and Presbyterian colleges in Winnipeg. After a period of cooperation, MB and Wesley

colleges formally merged as United College in 1938. United College continued to offer study in arts in affiliation with the U OF M and granted theology degrees independently. At least in its early years, the theology taught was little changed from the pre-1925 era in which most of its professors had begun their careers. An Old Testament scholar of international reputation, William C. Graham, who became president of the college in 1938, concentrated on improving the quality of teaching both in arts and theology and himself taught Old Testament.

The church's first years were difficult. Depression and war caused a significant reduction in givings. MB's portion of national church funds for missions declined from $1.2 million in 1928 to about $.5 million in 1942. Local church leaders worried that the expected revival in religious commitment had not materialized. Ministers were hard to find, particularly for rural charges, and the church had little presence in the suburbs of cities where its primarily middle-class members were living in increasing numbers. The lack of ministers in rural and northern congregations added impetus to the movement to ordain women, a measure that was approved in 1936. The first woman ordained in MB Conference was Marguerite Corner in 1942. In spite of the difficulties of this time, membership continued to increase slowly.

The new church continued the institutional structures through which the women of its founding denominations had contributed

Westminster United Church, Maryland Avenue, Winnipeg

money and provisions to missionary efforts. The Woman's Missionary Society (WMS) was formed in 1926. The WMS was structured with a Dominion Board, conference branches, presbyterial societies and affiliated Canadian Girls in Training (CGIT) groups. Parallel in structure to the WMS was the Woman's Association (WA) which was the successor of the ladies aid groups at the congregational level. In 1962 the WMS and the WA were replaced by one new organization, the United Church Women (UCW).

In Winnipeg, the church inherited a group of unco-ordinated central city missions from its founding denominations: All Peoples Mission, Maple St, Point Douglas, Robertson Institute and Maclean Mission. These missions provided religious, educational, recreational and social services in their neighbourhoods. Originally the missions served an impoverished immigrant population but the focus shifted to the urban Aboriginal population that moved in as waves of immigrants moved out to other areas of the city. At the same time more social services began to be provided by govts and by the 1960s the church had become critical of the paternalism of its former approach in these missions, leading to debate about its role in the inner city. The era of decreased membership and funding after 1967 saw a rationalization of city missions and eventual closure of Maple St, Point Douglas, Maclean and Robertson.

The UCC co-operated with the federal govt in running residential schools for Aboriginal children at Norway House, Brandon and Portage la Prairie until the government took over responsibility for the schools in 1969. The church has been involved in on-going litigation with former students over incidents of physical and sexual abuse and the loss to students of their language and culture. In 1998, the church formally apologized to former students and First Nations communities for the pain and suffering that resulted from the church's involvement in the residential schools system.

Following WWII, new churches were built in suburban Winnipeg, Brandon and Portage la Prairie and in the new resource towns of Flin Flon, Sherridon, The Pas, Lynn Lake and Snow Lake. The post-war baby boom increased family attendance and a healthy economy improved the church's givings. But like other traditional Protestant denominations, the UCC has experienced a steady decline in membership since the mid-1960s. The church's MB statistics showed membership peaking in 1966 at 81,616; by 2005 the figure had fallen to 42,088. Many churches were forced to close or amalgamate and the closure rate has been especially high in rural pastoral charges, where a decline in population compounded the problem.

In 1967, United College became the U of W. The university retained a faculty of theology but changes following a reorganization of the church's seminary programs on the Prairies meant the faculty no longer prepared candidates for UCC ministry. It continued to offer postgraduate degrees to ministers and others interested in theological study as well as programs in marriage and family therapy. In recent years, while retaining its relationship with the UCC, the faculty has participated in a multi-denominational consortium that prepares candidates for ministry in the participating denominations.

While it has been buffeted from the outside by the surging fundamentalism of the 1990s and 2000s, the UCC has held fast to its tradition of liberal theology though not without cost. The church's determination in the 1970s to use inclusive and gender neutral language in its prayers and hymns and its 1988 decision to ordain homosexual persons alienated more conservative members and may have increased the already steady decline in its numbers. As the UCC matured, other theological currents – particularly Barthian neo-orthodoxy in the 1940s and 1950s and liberation theology in the 1960s – have challenged and modulated its theology. But it proudly remains a bastion of liberal Protestantism with its inheritance of engagement in social and human rights issues and openness to new ideas. ● CATHERINE MACDONALD

UNITED GRAIN GROWERS

UNITED GRAIN GROWERS was among Canada's first farmer-owned grain co-operatives. It began in 1906 in Winnipeg when a group of western Cdn grain growers formed the Grain Growers Grain Company. Its role was to market the grain they grew, and in Sept of that year, it received its first railcar-load of grain. In 1917, GGG and another Western-based co-operative, Alberta Farmers Co-operative Elevators Company, merged to form United Grain Growers Limited. UGG had an eastern division based out of Winnipeg, and a western division that operated out of Calgary. UGG continued to operate as a farmer-owned co-operative until 1993, when it became a publicly traded company. In Nov 2001, UGG merged with another Winnipeg-based farmers' co-operative, Agricore Limited, to form the country's largest grain company, **Agricore United,** which subsequently was taken over by SaskPool in 2007. ● MM

UNIVERSITY COLLEGE OF THE NORTH

(UCN) is a post-secondary educational institution designed to serve the Northern Region of MB. Created in June 2004 by an act of the legislature, UCN combined the pre-existing vocational and trades programs of Keewatin Community College with new university-level academics. The primary goal was to improve access to culturally sensitive education as a means of improving social and economic development in the North. The unique institution offers about 30 different diplomas and certificates in areas like business administration, computer programming, service industries, and building trades, but also degree programs including a bachelor of arts and a bachelor of nursing. UCN has 2 main campuses, in The Pas and Thompson, as well as regional teaching locations in Churchill, Cross Lake, Easterville, Flin Flon, Nelson House, Norway House, Pukatawagan, Split Lake, St. Theresa Point, and Swan River. UCN is administered by a governing council which appoints the president, as well as a learning council (academic matters) and a council of elders. It also carries out joint programs with Brandon U, the U of M, and the U of W under an initiative called Inter-Universities Services. In March 2007, the province announced $17 million in new funding for a resource library and student services centre in The Pas, as well as additional teaching centres in Grand Rapids and Oxford House. During the 2006-07 academic year, UCN and its 250 staff members served 2400 students. ● JOEL TRENAMAN

UNIVERSITY OF MANITOBA (U of M) is MB's largest university and the oldest in western Canada. It is the province's only research-oriented comprehensive university offering undergraduate, master's, doctoral, continuing education, and professional programs (*see* Education, Post-Secondary). The majority of its 26,000 students (2006-07 enrolment) are based at the university's 274-ha Fort Garry campus in S Winnipeg.

HISTORY: The 1877 establishment of the U of M was spearheaded by Lt Gov Alexander Morris and 3 church-affiliated colleges: St. John's College (Anglican), Manitoba College (Presbyterian), and St. Boniface College (Roman Catholic). The Methodist Wesley College was amalgamated in 1888. Church leaders like Alexandre-Antonin Taché operated their colleges with the help of provincial funds, remaining in charge of instruction while the university became the official degree-granting body. The non-religious Manitoba Medical College also came on board in 1882.

The 1900 amendment of the *University of Manitoba Act* accredited the organization as a teaching entity in its own right, and 6 scientists, including Gordon Bell, began instruction at a small downtown Winnipeg campus in 1904. Other colleges continued to join the U of M fold over the years, including professional pharmacy

AM, UNIVERSITY OF M - FORT GARRY SITE

University of Manitoba, 1930

and agricultural schools, St. Paul's, **BRANDON**, St. Andrews (**UKRAINIAN** Orthodox), and **W. L. MORTON**'s University College. Wesley and Manitoba colleges merged and later become the **U OF W**, and Brandon College became **BRANDON U**.

After much debate, the university's present location was decided on in 1913 after the provincial govt agreed to donate 55 ha S of Winnipeg along the **RED RIVER** next to the new Agricultural College (another plan had proposed an **ASSINIBOINE PARK** location). A larger location and increasing enrolments led to the gradual establishment of various faculties and departments, and the university completed its move to the new site in 1929. In 1915, student enrolment numbered 1000, including 155 women. The most significant period of enrolment increases occurred in the late 1960s and 1970s, the result of the "baby boom" demographic trend.

ADMINISTRATION & ACADEMICS: The university's corporate affairs are managed by a 23-member Board of Governors, while a Senate oversees academic matters. Emöke J.E. Szathmáry is to serve as U of M president until July 2008. She was preceded by **ARNOLD NAIMARK**. The chancellor is the titular head. **JOHN W. DAFOE**, **VICTOR SIFTON**, **SAMUEL FREEDMAN**, **HENRY DUCKWORTH**, **ARTHUR MAURO**, and **WILLIAM NORRIE** are among those to have held the position. The university operated with a $437 million budget for the 2007-08 year (about 60% of which comes from the province), and employed about 4900 academic and 4200 support staff.

The University of Manitoba Students' Union (since 1919), the Graduate Students' Association, as well as faculty and college councils, provide student representation. U of M publications include the *Bulletin* (administration news), *On*

Manitoba (an alumni magazine), the *Manitoban* (the primary student newspaper since 1914), and the *Gradzette* (graduate student magazine). The University of Manitoba Press specializes in **BOOK PUBLISHING**.

In 2007, there were 24 faculties and schools at the U of M ranging from **ARCHITECTURE** and law to fine arts and human ecology. Current satellite campuses include **COLLÈGE UNIVERSITAIRE DE SAINT-BONIFACE**, featuring instruction

in **FRENCH**; the Bannatyne campus attached to **HEALTH SCIENCES CENTRE**, home of the dentistry, dental hygiene, medical rehabilitation, **MEDICINE**, and (beginning in 2008) pharmacy programs. The Fort Garry campus features 6 residences with a combined capacity of more than 1200 students.

RESEARCH: The U of M is home to 36 on-campus institutes and centres, and $140 million worth of research was conducted in 2005-06. The university's most notable historical and contemporary applied research programs include: Rh factor research leading to the creation of a preventative antibody (*see* **WINNIPEG RH INSTITUTE**); the 1974 development by **BALDUR STEFANSSON** and Keith Downey of the first edible **CANOLA** plant, which subsequently became a $30-billion-a-year international industry (*see* **GRAINS**); the Institute of Cardiovascular Sciences led by **NARANJAN DHALLA**; an infectious diseases program under **ALLAN RONALD**; an international program in HIV/AIDS research (*see* **FRANK PLUMMER**); and power systems and electrical engineering.

The university's Smartpark Development Corporation created a 40-ha research park in 1999 as an on-campus base for companies in the **INFORMATION AND COMMUNICATIONS TECHNOLOGY**, engineering, **BIOTECHNOLOGY**, and agricultural sectors. The main tenants are **CANGENE CORPORATION**, BASF, Monsanto, and Monteris Medical Inc. The

JOEL TRENAMAN

U of M students take a break with a frisbee in front of the Tier Building.

$25 million **RICHARDSON** Centre for Functional Foods and Nutraceuticals supports researchers working to derive new products from crops.

SPORTS: U of M athletics programs have produced many successful athletes and teams. Football, hockey, curling, and basketball tournaments were the first to take place in the 1880s and 1890s. The contemporary **BISON** sports program is best known for the perennial success of its men's and women's volleyball teams in Canadian Interuniversity Sport competitions (led by respective coaches **GARTH PISCHKE** and Ken Bentley). The U of M is also home to the Canadian national volleyball teams. The current primary sports facility, the Investors Group Athletic Centre, was built for use during the 1999 **PAN AMERICAN GAMES**.

RECENT DEVELOPMENTS: In 1999, the **NDP** govt instituted a tuition fee "freeze" and rebate program, preventing universities from raising tuition fees without the consent of students. Since that time, provincial funding increases failed to keep pace with the U of M's budgetary demands, leading to debates between those who advocate for more affordable tuition fees, and those who charge that funding limits reduce the quality of the university's academic programs and infrastructure. The pharmacy, law, dentistry, and engineering programs have secured student-supported fee increases to offset rising costs, and the university has raised fees for international students in an attempt to raise funds. Student politicians have generally opposed the moves.

The U of M has had to face questions about its reputation and overall quality of education over the years. The annual *Maclean's* magazine Canadian university issue consistently placed the university at or near the bottom of if its rankings in a number of significant categories, including entrance standards. Administrators have aggressively defended the institution, often pointing out that their students have secured more Rhodes scholarships (Oxford) than any other university in western Canada over the last 30 years. In Sept 2006, the U of M and 11 other universities ended their participation in the study due to objections regarding the magazine's research methods.

In June 2007, the administration announced the $10 million purchase of the adjacent 49-ha Southwood Golf and Country Club, to be used for unspecified future development.

NOTABLE U OF M ALUMNI: Many of MB's prominent citizens attended the U of M, including **MELROSE SISSONS**, **MITCHELL SHARP**, **JOSEPH DOUPE**, Alfred Monnin, **WILLIAM KURELEK**, Israel **ASPER**, Kathleen **RICHARDSON**, **IVAN EYRE**, **HENRY FRIESEN**, **MARSHALL MCLUHAN**, **LLOYD AXWORTHY**,

PHIL FONTAINE, **OVIDE MERCREDI**, **JOHN HOPPS**, and **BRIAN DICKSON**. • JOEL TRENAMAN

UNIVERSITY OF WINNIPEG (U of W) is MB's 2nd-largest university. The primarily undergraduate institution is known for its small classes, accessible faculty, and downtown **WINNIPEG** location. During the 2006-07 session, the U of W was the academic home of more than 9300 students, 330 faculty, and 800 staff (*see* **EDUCATION**, **POST-SECONDARY**).

HISTORY: The **PRESBYTERIAN CHURCH** established Manitoba College, a founding college of the **U OF M**, in 1871. In 1888, the **METHODIST CHURCH** formed Wesley College. Both colleges occupied various sites until 1896, when Wesley College found a permanent home on Portage Ave in its landmark sandstone building (Wesley Hall). In 1910, U of M professor Daniel Wilson circulated a pamphlet making a case for an independent liberal arts college that would focus on smaller classes and individual instruction, thus planting the philosophical seed for the new university. In 1931, Manitoba College moved to the Wesley site, and in 1938, the 2 merged to become United College. The university received its provincial charter in 1967, but the *University of Winnipeg Act* was not passed until 1998. The present-day campus developed around Wesley Hall with the addition of various structures, including: Sparling Hall (1912), Bryce, Ashdown, and Manitoba Halls (1950s), Graham Hall and Riddell Hall (1962).

ADMINISTRATION & ACADEMICS: The university is governed by a 36-member Board of Regents and a Senate which oversees academic matters. Reflecting its roots, the board includes

10 representatives from the **UNITED CHURCH OF CANADA**. The institution's operating budget for 2007-08 is $96 million. The University of Winnipeg Students' Association has represented students since 1972, and has often focused on advocating for lower tuition fees.

As of 2007, the U of W offered over 800 courses in more than 40 different subject areas with a focus on liberal arts, **SCIENCE**, theology, and **EDUCATION**. Conflict resolution and international development studies, offered in conjunction with Global College and Menno Simons College (*see* **CANADIAN MENNONITE UNIVERSITY**), is one of the signature programs. The U of W also specializes in urban and inner-city studies, in conjunction with the Institute of Urban Studies, and features a strong **THEATRE** and film department (*see* **FILMMAKING**). Pre-professional studies, joint professional programs with **RED RIVER COLLEGE** (including communications and environmental studies), and continuing education course options are also popular. Though the university is not oriented to graduate studies, the U of W does offer a theology master's and 3 joint master's degrees in concert with the U of M (history, public administration, and religion).

The school is considered one of western Canada's finest undergraduate universities, placing well in the controversial *Maclean's* guide to Cdn universities. The Collegiate at U of W is Canada's only on-site high school offering Senior 2, 3 and 4 programs to about 550 students each year. The U of W has a solid athletics program, especially for a small university, with the Wesmen volleyball and basketball teams among the country's most successful.

Manitoba College, 1895, precursor to U of W

Wesley Hall, U of W

RECENT DEVELOPMENTS: In 2004, **LLOYD AXWORTHY**, a U of W alumnus and Canada's former foreign affairs minister, became president, helping to raise the school's profile. At the same time, the university has recently enjoyed its highest-ever enrolments. In 2007, the U of W was moving ahead with a substantial campus redevelopment plan, in association with a $60 million capital campaign. A $3.5 million donation by the **RICHARDSON** family was earmarked to help build a college for environmental studies, and was followed by a $3 million pledge from **CANWEST GLOBAL COMMUNICATIONS CORP** for the construction of a $5.5 million centre for theatre and film. A $3.2 million expansion of the athletics-oriented Duckworth Centre (*see* **HENRY DUCKWORTH**) was set to open in late 2007.

Notable U of W alumni include **SUSAN THOMPSON**, **DAVID BERGEN**, **THOMAS AXWORTHY**, **GUY MADDIN**, **STERLING LYON**, **WILLIAM NORRIE**, **FRED PENNER**, and **ART MIKI**. ● JOEL TRENAMAN

UPPER FORT GARRY was located at the forks of the **ASSINIBOINE** and **RED RIVERS** on the N bank of the Assiniboine. In 1822, the HBC moved the company's headquarters from deteriorating Fort Douglas to the former NWC-controlled Fort Gibraltar, which had been acquired a year earlier through the merger of the HBC and NWC companies. Fort Gibraltar was subsequently renamed Fort Garry (also called Fort Garry I), in honour of Nicholas Garry, a member of the HBC's London Committee, who later served as deputy governor of the company. In 1826, Fort Garry was severely damaged by spring flooding. In response to the near destruction of the fort, HBC Gov **GEORGE SIMPSON** authorized the construction of **LOWER FORT GARRY**, on much higher ground, approx. 30 km N on the banks of the Red River near **SELKIRK**. Although Simpson intended the Lower Fort to be the new headquarters of the company, Fort Garry continued to be the commercial and population centre of the **RED RIVER SETTLEMENT**. As a result, in 1835, the HBC rebuilt Upper Fort Garry (the 'Upper' was added to distinguish it from Lower Fort Garry), and it became the administrative centre for the company and the seat of civil govt for the district. What remained of Fort Garry I was used as part of an experimental farming operation. It was subsequently leased to a local settler, and when damaged again by flooding in 1852, it was demolished.

Built slightly to the W of its predecessor, the new Upper Fort Garry was constructed of stone walls approx. 5 m high, with 4 large bastions capable of housing a canon at each corner. Among the buildings enclosed within its walls were the governor's house, the chief factor's residence, a general store, a fur store, the officers' quarters, a pemmican store, and a barracks. A liquor store was also located just outside the south wall of the fort. Initially, a court house and jail were also built within the fort; however, their existence inside the fort was considered both inconvenient and dangerous, and in 1843, it was decided that these buildings would be abandoned and a new jail would be erected outside the NW wall of the fort.

Upper Fort Garry was the administrative, judicial, and economic centre of **RUPERT'S LAND**. All roads within the settlement radiated out from the fort and therefore, whoever had control of the fort had control over the region. Upper Fort Garry was also the site of hospitality and social gathering for visiting and resident officers, explorers, scientists, authors, and other travellers of note passing through the territory. In 1853, as a result of increased trading, the area of the fort was extended at the N end. In an attempt to reduce the cost of this extension, the HBC used wood instead of stone in its construction. Considering the use of wood to be an affront to the integrity of the fort and its dominance within the settlement, Chief Factor Alexander Hunter Murray designed a proper stone gate for the new N wall.

Upper Fort Garry is best known as the main setting of the Red River Resistence of 1869-70. On Nov 2, 1869 **LOUIS RIEL** and 120 of his Métis guards peacefully took possession of the fort, which they occupied until Riel was forced to flee its gates in Aug 1870. During this time, several key events took place inside the walls of the fort, including the establishment of Riel's provisional

Upper Fort Garry

govt, the imprisonment of invading Cdn soldiers, and the subsequent execution of **Thomas Scott**. In 1882, amid a great land boom, the HBC sold Upper Fort Garry and the land upon which it rested. Unoccupied, the fort quickly fell into disrepair, and by 1883, it had been dismantled in order to facilitate the straightening of Main St. Some of the limestone and other building materials from the fort were used in the construction of new buildings along the quickly expanding streets of **Winnipeg**. The governor's residence was sold for $100 and subsequently used for firewood. The N gate is all the remains of Upper Fort Garry. In 1897, the HBC gifted the gate to the city of Winnipeg with the promise that it would forever remain a park. As of 2007, a group of prominent Winnipeggers were trying to convince the city of Winnipeg to allow for a major interpretive centre to be developed around the gate. ● MICHELLE RYDZ

URBAN PLANNING is the process by which communities attempt to control and design development in their physical environments. Issues falling within the scope of urban planning are grouped under 2 categories: those involved in thinking ahead to accommodate city growth, and issues that focus on the already built-up areas. The rationale for urban planning is that a controllable future offers more promise and quality of life than the alternative.

The progressive reform movement in the US, with its attacks on political corruption; housing reform movements in several countries; the British "Garden City" movement of Ebenezer Howard; and the UK's Town Planning movement of the late 19th century all influenced the development of urban planning in MB. Charles Hodgetts, advisor to the Canadian Commission of Conservation from 1910-22, introduced such planning ideals to MB. He appointed Thomas Adams, an eminent British planner, to help initiate planning studies in many cities, **Winnipeg** included. Adams was keenly aware of the unhealthiness of housing and neighbourhood infrastructure, and drew on Garden City principles – including balanced land use and green corridors – to incorporate better standards of city design. His work stimulated the development of comprehensive development plans for the city, and resulted in interesting garden suburbs, such as Armstrong Point.

Public Health issues in Winnipeg were also a factor. A 1904 report described the filthy conditions of many Winnipeg neighbourhoods. Conditions near the **CPR** tracks were squalid, with outdoor toilets along the streets draining into ditches, creating long open latrines. There were 6500 outdoor toilets in Winnipeg, many along Portage Ave and Main St. Especially in the **North**

End, conditions were oppressive. From 1900-05, over 400 people died in typhoid **Epidemics**, a death rate higher than any other city in NA or Europe. These conditions prompted the introduction in Winnipeg of a City Planning Commission in 1911.

Reform-minded leaders, such as **J. S. Woodsworth**, also introduced elements of social policy to urban planning. Woodsworth, superintendent of **All Peoples' Mission**, went well beyond traditional religious practices to highlight such policy. His 1913 study indicated that a normal standard of living in Winnipeg required a family income of $1200 annually, although many labourers received less than $600. He pressed on Winnipeg's City Council the need to improve health and building by-laws, municipal housing, fair wage schedules, and public works programs.

Law is an important aspect of urban planning. MB law addresses planning in various statutes, principally *The Municipal Act* (1880), the *Planning Act* (1911, revised 1976) the *Provincial Land Use Policies Act* (1980), the *City of Winnipeg Act* (1873), and the *Sustainable Development Act* (1998). All seek to ensure planning for orderly growth and development.

The province also actively provides planning services and advice, particularly outside the City of Winnipeg; the capital is allowed more flexibility to undertake its own planning within broad provincial guidelines. However, as land use and planning issues became more complex, the province created a Department of Municipal Affairs in 1959 to provide professional planning services to smaller municipalities. Today, the govt provides expanded planning services through the Community Land Use and Planning Services Division of the Department of Intergovernmental Affairs.

With the substantial growth of cities after 1945, govt began efforts to improve the level of planning education. The Canada Mortgage and Housing Corporation provided funding to sponsor degree-granting programs at universities, and a City Planning Program began at the **U of M** in 1949. The Manitoba Professional Planners Institute (MPPI) represents MB's professional planners, handles membership applications and services, and is responsible for enforcement of professional conduct in the profession. MPPI works with the Canadian Institute of Planners (CIP) to advocate for more effective planning, and innovative thinking. The Urban Development Institute (UDI) represents the land development industry, promoting well-planned communities and maintaining planning ethics in the industry.

As the population and tax base of some municipalities outside Winnipeg declined,

and as Winnipeg grew beyond its original municipal jurisdictions, the province encouraged the development of planning districts, under which municipalities joined to plan on a regional basis. In the Winnipeg area, a 2-tier metropolitan govt, **Metro Winnipeg**, was introduced in 1960. In this system, a metropolitan corporation planned for regional services for 13 municipal jurisdictions, while individual municipalities planned for local services. When lack of municipal co-operation reduced the effectiveness of planning, the province legislated a single-tier govt on Jan 1, 1972, amalgamating all the municipalities into the **Unicity** jurisdiction.

Since the 1970s, urban planning has focused largely on revitalizing Winnipeg's older, inner-city residential areas and the downtown. Planning models used in this ongoing effort – under such initiatives as Core Areas I and II and Neighbourhoods Alive! – introduced a more-comprehensive approach to urban planning, expanding from traditional views of land use to incorporate social, health, economic, and educational considerations. ● TOM CARTER

URBAN SHAMAN GALLERY is one of the largest contemporary Aboriginal galleries in Canada. It had its roots in the 1970s when a group of Aboriginal artists formed in Winnipeg, calling themselves the Indian Group of Seven. It was from this group composed of **Daphne Odjig**, Norval Morrisseau, **Jackson Beardy**, Carl Ray, Joseph Sanchez, Eddy Cobiness and Alex Janvier that Aboriginal artists began to be seen as artists and not simply as craftsmen and women. Springing off of this movement and heading into the 1980s, efforts were made to increase the profile of Aboriginal artists in Winnipeg which saw the creation of the Aboriginal Arts Group. Louis Ogemah took this movement one step further after an internship at aceart-inc, an **Artist-Run Centre**, in 1996. Alongside fellow Winnipeg artists Leah Fontaine, John Schneider and Liz Barron, Ogemah founded Urban Shaman Gallery in January 1996 at 90 Albert St. In 2004 the gallery received the very first Community Award for the Arts from the Manitoba Foundation for the Arts, Inc. The gallery's quarterly publication, *Conundrum*, was replaced in 2005 with an online version. The gallery's vision is stated as being "a shape shifting site that presents cutting edge aboriginal art with integrity, while remaining firmly rooted in diverse aboriginal cultures." After several moves, the gallery, located at 290 McDermot Ave in 2006, has continued to grow and is the only one of its kind in MB. ● STACEY ABRAMSON

VALOUR ROAD,
see page 708
Valour Road Memorial

VALGARDSON, William Dempsey "W. D.," author (b May 7, 1939, **Winnipeg**). Valgardson grew up in the **Icelandic** fishing community of **Gimli** and began to write **Poetry** in a creative writing class at United College (*see* **U of W**). He received a teaching certificate from the **U of M**, and taught for a year at Transcona Collegiate, went north to teach at **Snow Lake** and then at **Pinawa**, taking correspondence courses in writing from the U of ND. An encounter with the work of Ontario poet Al Purdy made him aware of a specifically Canadian voice in **Literature**, and his own output of poetry increased enormously. He earned an MFA on scholarship at the U of IA, and taught creative writing at the U of Victoria starting in 1974. Valgardson's first collections of adult short stories, *Bloodflowers* (1973); *God Is Not a Fish Inspector* (1975); and *Red Dust* (1976) brought him positive critical attention. His first novel, *Gentle Sinners* (1980), won the Books in Canada First Novel Award. He has also published 2 volumes of verse, *In the Gutting Shed* (1976), and *The Carpenter of Dreams* (1986). In 1992, his novel *The Girl with the Botticelli Face* won the Ethel Wilson Award for Fiction. Turning to children's fiction, Valgardson won the Mr. Christie's Book Award in 1995 for *Thor;* his short story, "The Chicken Lady," from *Garbage Creek*

and Other Stories (1997), received the Canadian Authors Association's Vicky Metcalf Short Story Award; and he was nominated for the 1999 Gov Gen's Award and the Sheila A. Egoff Children's Book Prize for *The Divorced Kids' Club and Other Stories*. ● MILDRED GUTKIN

VALKO, Andrew, painter, (b 1957 Prague, Czechoslovakia) moved to Canada at 12 with his family following the 1968 Soviet invasion. He received his diploma in graphic design and applied arts from **Red River College** and subsequently studied woodblock printmaking in Japan with master printmaker Toshi Yoshida. He was elected to the Royal Canadian Academy of Arts in 1994. His hyper-realistic drawings and paintings, (acrylics on hardboard) are narratives of 1950s and 1960s transitory places and spaces – motels, drive-in theatres and swimming pools. Valko presents private relationships of the moment; anonymous, disquieting and not nostalgic. In these familiar settings, he usually includes 'new technologies' – a camcorder or TV and remote control – each being a lens for seeing, and each intensifying the pathos of the disconnection between the self-absorbed figures. Valko's light is eerie, the colours magnifying the green TV light, the motel signs and street lights. The movies he portrays are

Movie Channel, 1995, acrylic on wood, 60 x 89 cm, by Andrew Valko

franchise was likely inspired by Van Vogt's first published sci-fi story, "Black Destroyer" (1939). Another 1939 Van Vogt story, "Discord in Scarlet," became the hit movie *Alien* (1979). The film's producers paid a small settlement to Van Vogt for recycling his concept. The political conflicts of some of his novels bore a distinct resemblance to those of the Cdn Prairies in the 1930s. Perhaps because of his Mennonite background, Van Vogt was obsessed with pseudo-science and self-help fads with religious trappings. The first of these was Dianetics, the "science of mental health" according to founder L. Ron Hubbard. Van Vogt knew Hubbard as a fellow pulp writer, and directed Hubbard's Dianetic Research Foundation 1950-53. When Dianetics grew into the Church of Scientology, Van Vogt broke with Hubbard. His other major interest was "General Semantics," an eccentric self-help system that gave rise to Van Vogt's "Null-A" novels. ● MAURICE MIERAU

romances, of heroes and nostalgia, further contrasting illusionary Hollywood with the reality of his figures' disconnect. Cool and seemingly clinical, the works underline larger societal issues. In making the works, Valko scores the board, carving it and creating ridges, then applies the paint smoothly and precisely, creating multi-layers of paint, reflecting the multi-layers of meaning. Valko has exhibited across Canada, including The **Winnipeg Art Gallery**, Art Gallery of Greater Victoria, the **U of W**, and in Japan, Seattle, San Francisco and Taiwan. His work is in public and private collections including the Canada Council Art Bank, MB govt, **U of M**, and many corporate collections. He has received a Manitoba Arts Council A grant and his work has been widely published including the *New Yorker*, *Border Crossings*, and with Michelle Berry in *Postcard Fictions*, (Key Porter Books, 2001). ● PATRICIA BOVEY

VALOUR ROAD is the **Winnipeg** street that was renamed in honour of the 3 **Victoria Cross** winners from WWI who had lived on it: **Frederick William Hall**, **Leo Clarke**, and **Robert Shankland**. What was once Pine St was the only road in the British Empire known to have had 3 VC recipients. A bronze plaque is mounted on a street light at the corner of Portage Ave and Valour Rd, and in 2005, the city built a small square on the street as further recognition of the soldiers' bravery. ● GPP

VAN HELLEMOND, Andy, NHL referee (b Feb 16, 1948, **Winnipeg**) was one of the NHL's longest-serving officials. After playing junior **Hockey**, Van Hellemond got his start in 1968 refereeing Western Hockey League games in Winnipeg. After 2 years, the NHL signed up the young referee,

and at 23, Van Hellemond had his first chance to officiate an NHL game. Over the next 25 seasons, Van Hellemond was named the NHL's #1 referee 14 times consecutively. During that time, he refereed 1475 regular season games, 227 playoff games and 19 Stanley Cup finals, all of which stand as league records. Van Hellemond was also one of the first officials to wear a helmet in 1984, as the increased size and speed of players had made refereeing a risky occupation. Towards the end of his career, he served as president of the NHL Officials Association. Van Hellemond oversaw his last NHL game in 1996, and took on an executive position with the East Coast Hockey League. He was inducted into the Hockey Hall of Fame in 1999. Following the 2000-01 season, he returned to the NHL as the director of officiating, but resigned in 2004 following allegations that he had borrowed money from on-ice officials in return for playoff postings. ● MD

VAN VOGT, Alfred Elton "A. E.," writer (b Apr 26, 1912, Edenburg, near **Gretna**; d Jan 26, 2000, Hollywood, CA). During the late 1940s and early '50s, Van Vogt was the most popular science-fiction writer in the world, outselling luminaries such as Isaac Asimov and Robert Heinlein. Van Vogt was born in a small village just E of Gretna to a **Mennonite** family. His father, a lawyer, moved the family to SK and later to **Winnipeg**, where Van Vogt attended Kelvin High School. As a teenager, Van Vogt started to write fiction using a how-to book from the library called *The Only Two Ways to Write a Short Story*. Van Vogt moved to Los Angeles in 1944, where he lived the rest of his life, achieving fame for his 85 science-fiction novels and short-story collections. The *Star Trek*

VARDALOS, Antonia Eugenia "Nia," actor, screenwriter (b Sept 24, 1962, **Winnipeg**) wrote and starred in the most successful independent film of all time. Vardalos grew up in Winnipeg, and got her start in acting at **Rainbow Stage**. She attended Ryerson U's School of Acting. While in Toronto, Vardalos joined Second City, an improvisational comedy-theatre troupe best known for its association with the TV series *SCTV*. She transferred to IL to perform with Chicago's Second City troupe. There she won Chicago's Jeff Award for Best Actress. In 1993, Vardalos returned to Winnipeg to marry fellow Second City actor Ian

Nia Vardalos at the Globe Theatre in Portage Place, Winnipeg

Gomez at St. Demetrios Greek Orthodox Church. The 2 moved to Los Angeles, where Vardalos won guest spots on several TV series, such as *The Drew Carey Show* (1997), *Boy Meets World* (1999), and *Curb Your Enthusiasm* (2000). In 2000, she composed a one-woman play based on her marriage to Gomez. The play was nominated for an Ovation Award for Best New Play in Los Angeles. Actress Rita Wilson attended a performance, and Wilson's husband, Tom Hanks, proposed turning the script into a film. As of writing, *My Big Fat Greek Wedding* (2003) was among the highest-grossing independent films and romantic comedies ever. It was produced for $5 million US and made more than $210 million US. Vardalos was nominated for a Golden Globe for her performance and for an Academy Award for screenwriting. She won an Independent Spirit Award for Best Debut Performance. The film spawned a short-lived TV spin-off, *My Big Fat Greek Life* (2003). Vardalos also wrote and acted in the 2004 film *Connie and Carla*. In 2006, Vardalos and her husband lived in southern CA.
● AMANDA STEPHENS

VÁSQUEZ, Armando (aka "Bus Quinn"), **BASEBALL** player (b Aug 20, 1919, Güines, Cuba) was a star left-handed pitcher and infielder for the **BRANDON** Greys in the Manitoba Senior League and the **MANDAK LEAGUE**. Known as a good fielder, Vásquez played for the New York Cubans from 1944-48. He was recruited to the Brandon Greys in the Manitoba Senior League in 1948, originally playing under the name "Bus Quinn." In his Brandon debut year, he went to a 10-1 record and batted .324, helping the team – whose roster included **TONY TASCONA** – win that year's Manitoba Senior League championship. The Greys took the league title the following year as well, with Vásquez pitching for a 12-1 record and batting .323. **WALTER LEE GIBBONS** also played for the Greys that year. In 1950, the team joined with 3 other MB teams and one ND team to form the semi-pro ManDak League, where he faced many of his former Negro League teammates. Vásquez had a win in his only recorded decision and batted .244 with one homer and 27 RBI. The Greys finished 2nd in the ManDak in 1950. They won the championship the following year, with Armando hitting a respectable .279 and functioning mainly as a 1st baseman. For 1952, Vásquez left Brandon, ending his career in a Mexican ball league. He was inducted into **MORDEN**'s Manitoba Baseball Hall of Fame in 2006. ● MD

VAUDEVILLE entertained Manitobans in the last decades of the 19th century and through the first quarter of the 20th century, as it did people all over NA. It was, however, an entertainment limited to those lucky enough to live in the province's larger centres on **RAILWAY** lines.

The traditional vaudeville bill was a variety show consisting of 9 acts that could include singers, musicians, dancers, comedians, jugglers, or acrobats, and a short comic or dramatic sketch. Once movies had been invented, the vaudeville bill would also include a short moving picture. The acts were arranged to grab the audience's attention and to work up to the climax of the headline act, the second-last on the bill.

When establishments, called variety theatres, appeared in **WINNIPEG**, they were a response to the population growth that followed the real estate boom of the early 1880s. These variety theatres flourished in Winnipeg from 1882 to 1885. During this period, the Royal Theatre, the Théâtre Comique, the Victoria Theatre, the Board of Trade Varieties, and the Britannia Music Hall offered vaudeville shows, liquor sales, and perhaps a chance to meet the female performers, who in some of these establishments were expected to socialize with the audience, which was almost exclusively male.

Winnipeg City Council passed laws to rid the city of the variety theatres. The campaign against these theatres was supported by citizens in the liquor trade, who saw the theatres as competition, and citizens, many connected to the **REFORM** movement, who believed the theatres were immoral and bad for Winnipeg's reputation as a good place in which to settle and invest.

The Orpheum on Fort Street offered 2 vaudeville shows a day.

It was not until after 1900 that vaudeville reappeared in Winnipeg as respectable family entertainment. Conditions had changed so as to make local businessmen think that offering vaudeville to Winnipeggers would be profitable. The economy had revived and Winnipeg's population had begun to grow again. Centralized booking for vaudeville acts and theatre circuits for them to tour on had developed. By 1914, the 3 circuits that dominated vaudeville in the US West were operating in Winnipeg.

The Unique, which was opened in Dec 1903 at 529 Main St, was one of the first theatres to specialize in vaudeville. It was opened by John A. Schuberg, or Johnny Nash, which was his professional name. Before opening the Unique, Nash had been exhibiting moving pictures in a tent. Because early films were not attractive enough to provide an evening's entertainment, Nash, like other theatre owners, combined movies with live acts. Admission to the Unique was 10¢ for a matinee, and 15¢ for the evening show. At these prices, and with 5 shows a day, the Unique was offering small-time vaudeville. The following year, G. A. and V. C. Kobold, who were dealers in real estate, opened the Dominion Theatre at 175 Portage Ave with the hope of giving Winnipeggers big-time vaudeville. On Jan 15, 1906 Nash, with his father-in-law, Fred Burrows, opened a 2nd theatre, the Bijou, at 489 Main St.

To obtain acts for their theatres, Winnipeg theatre managers tried to connect their theatre to a circuit of vaudeville theatres in the US. Nash had a booking agreement with the Unique Theatre in Minneapolis. Eventually Nash and Burrows controlled a circuit of 7 theatres in Canada and the US Midwest. In 1907, Nash transferred control of his circuit to the Sullivan and Considine circuit. In Feb 1906, the manager of the Dominion was able to announce that the Dominion would be affiliated with the Orpheum chain, which had a reputation for booking first-class talent at high salaries. In 1909 W. B. Lawrence, the manger of the Dominion, was booking acts through William Morris, an independent circuit based in New York. In 1910, Lawrence also brought William Morris vaudeville to the Walker Theatre when a dispute between US booking agencies made it difficult for C. P. Walker to obtain touring companies for his theatre.

In 1909, Morris Beck, the manager of the Orpheum circuit, announced that his firm would build its own theatre in Winnipeg, and he bought land at 283 Fort St. The Orpheum opened on Mar 13, 1911. It presented 2 shows a day with an admission price ranging from 10¢ to 75¢.

The Pantages vaudeville chain was the last of the Western circuits to be established in

Winnipeg. W. B. Lawrence, as managing director of the Pantages, oversaw the construction and operation of the Market St. theatre. The Pantages opened on Feb 8, 1914, offering 3 shows a day for 10¢ to 50¢. Since Winnipeg was at the eastern edge of the Pantages circuit, it was in Winnipeg where acts would be evaluated and their place on the bill determined before they were sent W.

Theatre managers vied with one another to obtain the best acts and boasted in their advertising of their ability to book European acts. During vaudeville's heyday Winnipeggers saw Sarah Bernhardt, W. C. Fields, and Ruth St. Denis at the Orpheum and Charlie Chaplin in the Fred Karno Company's *A Night in an English Music Hall* at the Dominion.

In the early 1930s, vaudeville supplied by the large US circuits ceased to be the dominant popular entertainment in NA. The successful addition of sound to moving pictures led to films replacing vaudeville. Thus in 1929, the Orpheum was offering a continuous show with fewer live acts and a longer movie. This was the beginning of the end of vaudeville in Winnipeg. Remnants of it appeared in movie theatres like the Capital, which mixed live entertainment with movies, and at the Beacon Theatre, which presented shows with local talent.

Smaller centres in MB probably had a taste of vaudeville, but not of the scale that Winnipeggers enjoyed at the Orpheum. The proprietors of the Arcade in the **NORTH END** of Winnipeg opened an Arcade Theatre in **BRANDON** in 1905. Brandon's Princess Theatre, later renamed the Orpheum, was described as a vaudeville theatre; however, it was also a venue for touring companies. ● CAROL BUDNICK

▸ *See also* **THEATRE**.

VERGARA, Héctor Osvaldo, referee, sports administrator (b Dec 15, 1966, Chile), is the first Cdn official to referee in 2 World Cup **SOCCER** matches. He emigrated from Chile in 1978 and got his start refereeing minor games in Winnipeg. Vergara graduated from the **U OF M** with a recreation studies degree in 1992, and was a sports administrator at the 1999 **PAN AMERICAN GAMES**. Vergara has officiated at more than 90 international matches – more than any other referee – including 9 games (among them, the bronze-medal match) in the 2002 World Cup. He also officiated at the 2004 Olympics in Athens. One of his most controversial games was a 2005 World Club Championship match in Japan between the UK's Liverpool Football Club and São Paulo Futebol Clube, where he called back 3 goals by the Liverpool team, incurring the wrath of that team's fans. Vergara's position at the 2006 World Cup required

FIFA officials to bend the rules; officiating crews are supposed to work together for 4 years preceding the games, but after one of Vergara's crew was injured, potentially eliminating his chance at officiating, FIFA found another crew for Vergara to work with. His team went on to become the 1st crew of referees to officiate 5 games together at a single World Cup. Héctor's wife, Joanne Vergara, is also active in sports as a Paralympic swimmer, and set 6 world records and won 6 gold medals at the 1988 and 1992 Paralympic Games. Vergara is the chief administrative officer of the Manitoba Soccer Association. ● MD

VICTORIA BEACH, pop 227, is a cottage resort community about 100 km NNE of **WINNIPEG** on **LAKE WINNIPEG**, whose population in summer reaches upward of 10,000 people. The resort was developed by the Victoria Beach Investment Company, a land syndicate that in the first decade of the 20th century acquired control of the entire peninsula on which the beach is located. C. W. N. Kennedy, of the provincial land titles office, who headed the syndicate, had visions of creating an exclusive, rustic, English-village-style cottage community at the beach. Unfortunately, "exclusivity" meant that access and ownership were barred to **JEWS**, though "restricted" now refers to bans on motor vehicles. Originally, the only access was by boat, but in 1913, the syndicate successfully negotiated an agreement with the CNoR, giving the railway 50% ownership of the newly formed Victoria Beach Company. This led to completion of a branch line to the beach in 1916. The VBC successfully negotiated the creation of the Municipality of Victoria Beach in 1919, and in 1968, the company's assets were turned over to the municipality. Although Kennedy's vision was never fully realized, some of its elements survive, with the settlement boasting a lack of popular entertainments, superior quality cottages on wooded lots and winding, unpaved lanes. ● JOHN SELWOOD

VICTORIA CROSS (VC). This medal, awarded to military personnel for acts of valour, was first issued by Queen Victoria – after whom the honour is named – during the Crimean War of 1854-55. All VCs have been awarded by the UK sovereign, and are cast from bronze cascabels of 2 cannon that were captured from the Russians at the siege of Sevastopol, the last great battle of the Crimean War. The cascabel is a large knob at the rear of cannon, to which ropes were secured when the artillery piece was being handled. During WWI, metal from guns captured from the Chinese during the Boxer Rebellion was also used. What's left of the only remaining cascabel, weighing slightly more than 1 kg, is stored in a vault in the UK. About

List of Manitoban VC Winners:

William "Billy" Barker
Alexander Picton Brereton
Leo Clarke
Frederick William Hall
Alan Arnett McLeod
Coulson Norman Mitchell
Andrew Charles Mynarski
Christopher Patrick John O'Kelly
John Robert Osborn
Robert Shankland
Robert Spall
James Edward Tait

80-85 medals could be cast from this source. London, UK-based Hancocks & Co. (Jewellers) Ltd. has been responsible for the production of all 1354 VCs awarded, 95 to Canadians, 12 of which went to Manitobans. In addition, at least 7 VC recipients were non-Manitobans fighting with MB-based regts when they earned the medal. Australia, Canada, and New Zealand have each introduced their own honours system, replacing British medals such as the Military Cross with their own awards; but each country has kept the Victoria Cross as their highest honour. The Cdn Victoria Cross, instituted in 1993 but never awarded as of 2005, is inscribed in Latin ("Pro Valore") rather than English ("For Valour"). ● JIM SHILLIDAY

▸ *See also* **VALOUR ROAD**.

VINCENT, Arthur James, grain merchant, (b Dec 13, 1913, Toronto; d Nov 10, 1998, **WINNIPEG**). Vincent spent his early years in Toronto, and, after the sudden death of his father, moved to Copper Cliff, ON, 10 km SW of Sudbury, to take up employment with the International Nickel Company. He earned his pilot's licence in Sudbury, and began commercial flights with Dominion Airways in Noranda, QC, eventually joining the Royal Canadian Air Force before WWII broke out. He took on the position of instructor, holding supervisory positions at various bases in Canada, before being posted overseas to the Empire Central Flying School in Hullavington, Wilts., UK. In 1943, he returned to Canada as chief instructor of the **BRITISH COMMONWEALTH AIR TRAINING PROGRAM**, and in the same year was promoted to WCdr. He was awarded the Air Force Cross. After the war, Vincent moved to **WINNIPEG** to begin his career in the grain business. He managed the Prairie **GRAIN ELEVATORS** of Reliance Grain Company, before becoming president of Smith, Vincent & Company, a position he held from 1958 to his death. He was one of the pioneers in opening the Chinese market for Canadian grain. An unfailing supporter of the arts, Vincent was a regular donor to the **WINNIPEG ART GALLERY**, the **MANITOBA**

THEATRE CENTRE, and the WINNIPEG SYMPHONY ORCHESTRA. He helped finance the Children's Theatre at the WAG, and the aquarium at the Fort Whyte Centre (*see* FORTWHYTE ALIVE). In 1986, he received the Distinguished Service Award from the U OF M. • DOUG ALLEN

VIRDEN, pop 3010, Mb's 15th largest town, is 70 km W of BRANDON, at the junction of the Trans-Canada and hwy 83, on the CPR main line, and near Bosshill Creek, a small feeder of Gopher Creek, itself a tributary of the ASSINIBOINE RIVER. Though the Virden region was long known to and occupied by Assiniboines, ENGLISH, SCOTS, IRISH, and Americans settled late in the 19th century, primarily attracted by free land. When the CPR arrived and a post office was established – both around 1882 – the community's name became Manchester, likely after William Drogo Montagu, 7th Duke of Manchester, who held substantial CPR stock. As another MB community had already registered that name, the name was promptly changed to Virden. The origin of this name remains unclear.

Virden, which became a town in 1904, remained a farming centre for the better part of a century, and housed a BRITISH COMMONWEALTH AIR TRAINING PLAN base and air force station in the 1940s. PETROLEUM was discovered around here in 1951. An oil well was drilled and capped here in 1956; 50 years later, as of writing, the area was home to about 1100 active oil wells, and services and retail catering to this industry easily dominated the economy. EDUCATION, health, and various other govt agencies also have strong presences in Virden's diverse economy, and some farming, primarily livestock, still occurs. The Manitoba Oil Museum and Hall of Fame is fittingly in this town, as is a museum/art gallery in the former CPR station. The station building, like the grand Virden Municipal Building and Auditorium – the oldest opera house in western Canada – is a provincial heritage site. The town also keeps its connection to the land alive through a summer rodeo and an agricultural fair. The arts and the outdoors are also important here, and Virden was home to the first GOLF course in MB. BASEBALL also has a long history here, and disgraced former Chicago "Black" Sox shortstop Swede Risberg played here in 1929.

This pretty town's many celebrated citizens have included LILA ACHESON WALLACE, co-founder of *Reader's Digest*; Dr. Ballard, the maker of specialty pet foods; jukebox magnate DAVE ROCKOLA; Trevor Hurst (born Hayhurst), lead singer of Econoline Crush; Saskatchewan Court of Appeal Justice D. A. McNiven; Terry McLean, wildlife artist; and MLA Avis Gray. • GPP

VISUAL ART IN MANITOBA
By Patricia Bovey

V

Manitoba, and especially its capital WINNIPEG, has been a vibrant hub of visual arts in Canada since the early 19th century. Through the province's history, MB artists have created work in many media, and developed modes of expression and unique visual responses to the landscape, to peoples, to social and political issues, and to the changing intellectual milieu. The resulting rich body of work, portraying all aspects of the province, has contributed significantly to the scope and depth of Cdn art, and Manitoban artists have been in the forefront of many new artistic departures.

EARLY HISTORY: Art in what is now MB developed quickly and benefited from diverse elements and international cultures. The long visual traditions of First Nations peoples (*see* ABORIGINAL ANCIENT ART), including porcupine quill work, bark biting, and PETROFORMS, significantly influenced the European artists who arrived in the area in the 19th century. In every period of its history, MB has welcomed IMMIGRANTS from many countries, each group bringing its own artistic traditions and training, and contributing new perspectives and aesthetics. For long periods, MB's artistic traditions were rooted in Britain and continental Europe. By the 1880s to the early 20th century, some MB artists had trained in US art schools; more recently, the cultural roots of MB's artists have expanded widely.

Most consider that the earliest non-Aboriginal art in what is now MB started in 1821, with the arrival of PETER RINDISBACHER. However, there is evidence of earlier work, including an engraving after a sketch by Samuel Hearn of FORT PRINCE OF WALES (ca 1769); a watercolour sketch by H. J. Robertson of FORT GIBRALTAR, dated 1804; and an engraving after a sketch by LORD SELKIRK of Fort Douglas in 1817. Other such sketches were certainly done by early FUR TRADERS and explorers but have not survived. Formal documenting of art history here begins in 1821 with the "Itinerant Era" and the union of the HUDSON'S BAY COMPANY and the NORTH WEST COMPANY. This union brought permanent settlement to the area, including a Swiss group, among whom was 15-year-old Peter Rindisbacher. They stayed for 5 years. Fascinated by his new surroundings, he painted many portraits of Aboriginals, both alone and engaged in traditional pursuits and in treaty signings. He also recorded Europeans in the region. The sensitivity and ability with which he portrayed his subjects suggests he had some art training.

Lionel Lemoine Fitzgerald

Most early itinerant artists passed through the region as members of exploratory parties. Sir George Back (1796-1878) accompanied John Franklin on 2 Arctic expeditions and did some particularly interesting detailed topographical sketches. Others include important artists like PAUL KANE; William Hind, (1833-89); Frederick A. Verner (1836-1928); and William Armstrong (1822-1914).Their subjects included landscape, which obviously was different from what they had seen before, and the daily life of Aboriginal and European peoples in RUPERT'S LAND. Constantly travelling, they faced many challenges. They were limited in materials because they had to be carried over land, water, and rugged portages, and, as noted in artists' diaries, much was lost in accidents. Materials had to be portable, and thus light and small. Art was done after hours when camp was set up, or during travel breaks, so artists also had to use quick, fast-drying techniques. Therefore, most of the early works were done in watercolour or pencil, usually on paper rather than board or canvas. Paul Kane and Frederick Verner executed many exquisite watercolour sketches and drawings that capture the feeling of the vastness of the Prairies and the MB sky. These works on paper are fresh and confident, and became the basis for larger oil paintings done later in their Toronto studios. The oils, painted in indoor light and on a dark ground rather than white paper, are heavy in feeling, losing some of their freedom in translation from the on-site sketches.

V   In the late 1850s and the 1860s, at least 2 major Canadian artistic triumphs were realized in MB. Hind executed the first oil painting outdoors on location, and photographer Humphrey Lloyd Hime overcame many hazards and problems to take a significant number of landscape and portrait photographs. Hind worked in watercolour and oil, also illustrating his diaries. His oil paintings, in contrast to Kane's, are small and exude a freshness, capturing the sensibilities of Prairie light, colour, and space. His winter scenes are particularly successful. His subjects are local, as with *Breaking a Road in Manitobah* and *Horse Drinking at an Ice Hole* (both ca 1870). The directness and crispness of these works, which were painted on a light ground, suggest they were done on the spot, and not translated later from a sketch. The photographs by Humphrey Hime, recording the expedition in 1858 led by Henry Youle Hind, also breathe of the individuality of the artist. His compositions and subjects, the **CREE** and the **RED RIVER SETTLEMENT**, are handled in a personal and sensitive manner. Capturing the depth of the sitter, he also portrays the expansive space, with a dominant landmark providing a focal point. The problems of setting up the complex and necessary photographic equipment, glass plates, chemicals, and bulky apparatus, were great, especially given the elements of nature.

Engineer William Armstrong also left important pictorial accounts of the places he saw. **W. FRANK LYNN**, a well-trained commercial artist, is considered the first resident painter in MB. He, too, painted the place and contemporary activities, executing a number of paintings of **THE FORKS** and HBC **FORTS**. *The Dakota Boat* proves his capability in the treatment of composition and the handling of colour. The tonal shading in the sunset and the group in the foreground combine in a strong composition, leading the eye through space from the central group, across the river to the fort, and on to the evening sky. Several of Lynn's paintings were displayed in Winnipeg hotels, and a number of versions of his more-typical scenes exist. Like Rindisbacher, he received commissions for his more-popular works, enabling him to earn a living as a commercial artist. Constantin Nicolas Tauffenbach (1829-90) adopted MB as his home in the early 1880s. An itinerant artist and postmaster, he travelled within the new province – MB joined Confederation in 1870 – painting works of, and for, regional churches. While his creations are naive and at times stiff, they exhibit knowledge of painting.

AFTER CONFEDERATION: Winnipeg incorporated in 1873, with the first council assuming office in Jan 1874. The province, especially the new city, witnessed rapid population growth, flourishing business, and a blossoming cultural scene. Organizations were founded, exhibitions presented, and art classes begun. The Winnipeg Women's Art Association's and the **VIRDEN** Fair were important facets of this burgeoning art scene. The 1893 Virden Fair included a special section for fine arts and crafts, and subsequent **AGRICULTURAL** fairs in the mainly agrarian province became the major exhibition venues for artists. Exhibitions were reviewed in the press and often produced catalogues listing artists and entries. Founded in 1894, the Winnipeg Branch of the Women's Art Association's, which

worked to promote interest in art in Canada, provided shared studios and models, encouraged art in all media, and developed collections of Western art, including Aboriginal work. The association also organized exhibitions and sales of local, national, and international work, presented lectures, and promoted art education curriculum. Artist Mary Riter Hamilton led the Winnipeg Women's Art Association. Immediately following WWI, she painted battle sites in France, for which she was awarded the French order of the Palmes académiques and became the first Cdn officer of the Académie française. Artists in the Winnipeg Women's Art Association studied with prominent international artists, including James Abbott McNeill Whistler in Paris and William Merritt Chase in New York, and thus expanded and modernized the sensibilities, techniques, and approaches in the work of MB artists. Other new influences were **ENGLISH** artists John Ruskin and William Morris.

The Manitoba Society of Artists was founded in 1903 to encourage and foster art in the province. By then, the press noted the shift of the community from pioneer life to a centre of business, bringing a corresponding appreciation for art. The coming of the **RAILWAY** was another tremendous impetus for creative development. Artists working for the **CPR** stopped in Winnipeg to exhibit their work, and shipping art from Chicago or Toronto became easy, enabling the Women's Art Association to sponsor many travelling exhibitions. New buildings, including Winnipeg's Carnegie Library, likewise transformed the city, positively affecting education and the arts. The Women's Art Association also worked for the establishment of an art gallery, but was turned down by City Council. Citizen leaders in the Industrial Bureau, the precursor of the Chambre of Commerce, finally founded the **WINNIPEG ART GALLERY** (WAG) in 1912, making it the first civic art gallery in Canada. The Winnipeg School of Art opened in 1913. With growing interest in art, teachers, artists, and architects arrived from England, Scotland, and eastern Canada, and business became increasingly intent on creating a thriving arts scene to ensure a good quality of life. Among those who arrived 1912-14 were Valentine Fanshaw (1878-1940), later art teacher at Winnipeg's Kelvin High School; artist Donald MacQuarrie, who became the WAG's first curator; Alexander Musgrove (1882-1952), who became the first head of the Winnipeg School of Art; and Arnold Brigden, who in 1914 founded **BRIGDENS** of Winnipeg Ltd., the commercial engraving and advertising company for **EATON'S** and the employer of many artists. Artist **WALTER PHILLIPS** arrived in 1913, and Eric Bergman (1893-1958), who joined Brigden's Ltd., came in 1914. **CHARLES COMFORT** (1900-94) was another prominent MB artist who worked at Brigdens. Each of these became local leading figures in the visual arts.

Marion Hope Nelson Hooker arrived as a bride to **SELKIRK** in 1907. A trained artist, she did many paintings of the Selkirk area as well as portraits, some of her favourite subjects being First Nations chiefs. She gave her sitters a keen perception, as seen in *William Berens, Chief of the Saulteaux* (1932). Her work is the result of yet another development of the art of the province at the turn of the 20th century – the art of portraiture, which gained

Pauline Boutal

increasing momentum with the commissioning of official portraits. The contributions in portraiture at the turn of the 20th century by Victor A. Long (1866-1938) and Nicholas de Grandmaison (1892-1978) were significant. De Grandmaison is especially known for his pastel portraits of Aboriginal leaders, while Long was the master of many official portraits in Winnipeg and through the province. Other subjects of increasing importance early in the 20th century include scenes of Winnipeg. A prime example, *Main Street* (1912) – a watercolour by naive painter E. J. Hutchins is full of the precise details of the city's architecture and streetscapes.

AFTER WWI: The 1920s and '30s were important years of artistic growth. **LIONEL LEMOINE FITZGERALD** joined the faculty of the Winnipeg School of Art in 1924, the year Frank Johnston (1888-1949), a former member of the Group of Seven, became its principal. FitzGerald succeeded him as principal, serving 1929-49. During these years, the nationalist ideas of the Group of Seven swept the country. Frank Johnston introduced Group of Seven influences to his students, many of whom embraced them, as did some artists working at Brigden's. FitzGerald joined the Group in 1932, exhibiting with them on several occasions. During this time, FitzGerald was perhaps the best-known MB artist. Working in oil, pencil, watercolour, and ink, he had complete mastery of his subject, the Prairie landscape (winter and summer), still-lifes, and views from his window. These were done in various styles – naturalistic, abstract, impressionistic, and pointillist. FitzGerald's concept of space was powerful, as seen in his portrayals of Prairie sky and fields, as in *Summer Afternoon – the Prairie* (1921) and *Potato Patch, Snowflake* (1925). His abstractions of the 1950s developed from realism, an important work being *Abstract in Green and Gold* (1954), with its subtle treatment of colour, depth, and receding movement of the various planes.

While the Group of Seven was exploring and painting the Cdn landscape, MB artists initiated Canada's interest in abstract painting, and a number of the mid-century Cdn movements had their roots in Winnipeg initiatives. Writer and painter **BERTRAM BROOKER**, who lived for a time in **NEEPAWA** and who subsequently moved to Toronto, adopted abstraction with *Sounds Assembling* (1927) and *Alleluia* (1928), making him the first abstract painter in Canada. The strong geometric yet rhythmic colours reflect his love of music and fascination with motion pictures. He and FitzGerald entered into a long, mutually influential, correspondence detailing many of their thoughts about art and their work. FitzGerald, though primarily a realist, turned to abstraction in the early 1950s, and Brooker embraced realism for a period in the 1930s and '40s. Meanwhile, Fritz Brandtner (1896-1969) explored cubist experiments of form, work that would not be nationally accepted until after WWII, by which point he had moved to Montreal. Winnipeg artists, like Montreal's Beaver Hall Group, were also concerned with social issues in their work. Immigration to MB in the 1930s and '40s was high, many coming from Eastern Europe, especially **UKRAINIANS**. Alison Newton (1890-1967) portrayed people of various ethnic diversities at work, as in *Grading Onions, Near Gonor* (ca 1940). Georgie Wilcox (1889-1970), depicted new technologies, as in *Western Industries Steel Pour, Vulcan Iron Works, Winnipeg* (ca 1939).

AFTER WWII: In 1950, the Winnipeg School of Art joined the **U OF M**. Its programs and student base expanded significantly. In the 1950s and '60s, the school hired faculty from various parts of the US, from Canada, and from farther afield, bringing new contemporary concerns to Winnipeg. William McCloy, and later Richard William, arrived from the US to head the school. Austrian-born artist **GEORGE SWINTON** (1917-2002) came to Winnipeg from the US in 1954 to teach painting, and there became an early "discoverer," supporter, and author on the subject of Inuit art. Robert Bruce, a painter and muralist, joined the faculty in 1955.

IVAN EYRE, a former School of Art student, was hired to teach painting in 1959. Continuing his own work in painting, printmaking, drawing, and sculpture, Eyre created large surrealistic canvases, and mythological, imaginative figurative pieces and landscapes. Other artists hired have included **KEN LOCHHEAD**, who came in 1964. He was a member of the Regina Five and a leader in both geometric abstraction, as in *Sky Location* (1967), and colour field painting, typified in his *Colour Coaster* (1973). He later returned to figurative painting, but he was a consummate colourist throughout as well as a highly regarded teacher. Don Reichert, an abstract painter who graduated from the School of Art in 1956 and undertook further studies in Mexico, was hired to teach painting in 1964. These individuals, along with other members of the faculty, created a lively dynamic. Many also had studios in the heart of the city, creating energy there, too. In 1951, **FERDINAND ECKHARDT**, an Austrian art historian, arrived in Winnipeg as director of the WAG, a position he held until his retirement in 1974. These years were exciting and Winnipeg became a truly dynamic centre for Cdn art. From 1955 through 1970, the WAG held the important annual Winnipeg Show, a national juried exhibition of contemporary art. Introducing Winnipeg to the ideas and artistic expressions from across Canada, it showcased the work of Winnipeg artists in a national context. The Canada Council for the Arts was founded in 1957. Through travel and production grants to artists, the professionalism of the visual arts in MB grew exponentially. Internationalism, New York, and colour field painting became major interests.

PETER TITTENBERGER

Ivan Eyre

From the 1960s to the present, Winnipeg has been home to many other significant artists who also had truly successful careers. Those include **TONY TASCONA** (1926-2006) and **BRUCE HEAD** (b 1931), both of whom are nationally known for their paintings, sculptures, and prints. Both have done many public art commissions, and both developed their own visual language. Tascona worked with new materials, mainly resins and enamels, and built his abstract paintings and installations, drawing his ideas from nature. Head, a painter and sculptor, is inspired by the landscape. He is a colourist, interested in textures, and often includes stencils and cut-outs in his vivid and detailed large works. In 1971, the WAG opened its new, exciting triangular building designed by **PORTUGUESE** architect Gustavo da Roza. The gallery building has since become a focal point of the Winnipeg art scene. That same year, CARFC, a national artists' collective, held its first meeting in Winnipeg, with the goal of ensuring artists' copyrights and lending and exhibitions rights. In this period, the formation of artist-run spaces, Plug In Institute of Contemporary Art, and various commercial galleries also energized artists and art connoisseurs, providing more opportunities to present and see work.

PRINTMAKING: Printmaking came to the fore in the late 1960s and '70s through the Screen Shop, founded in 1968 by printmaker and painter Bill Lobchuk (b 1941). Winnipeg had been a printmaking hub in earlier years with Walter Phillips, a woodblock print master, and Eric Bergman, a master of wood engraving, both renowned across the country for their work. The Screen Shop, however, was a successful group endeavour, active through the 1970s and '80s, providing technical expertise to artists. In addition to assisting individual artists, it produced several group portfolios. **WINSTON LEATHERS**, a professor at the U of M's Faculty of Architecture, had already greatly influenced Cdn printmaking through his experiments with new techniques and materials, achieving textured effects by printing on a variety of supports, including glass and wax paper. Also a painter, Leathers's work was inspired by the landscape and horizon lines. Using unique calligraphic brushwork and metallic paints, his interest extended to cosmic variations and night skies. Printmaker Ted Howorth (b 1943), another participating artist at the Screen Shop, broke new ground in printmaking through his research and experiments with new inks and photography. The Martha Street Studio, lead by artist Sheila Spence, has been a critically important centre for contemporary printmaking in Winnipeg since the 1990s, providing equipment, workshops, and exhibition spaces to members.

SCULPTURE: Sculpture in MB had its beginnings in the public statuary at the **LEGISLATIVE BUILDING**, including the "**GOLDEN BOY**," set a high artistic standard. It was, however, in the 1950s and '60s that sculpture gained more prominence. A major figure in MB sculpture in the late 20th century was **LEO MOL**, whose traditionally based bronzes are in **ASSINIBOINE PARK**. With his *Asessippi Tread* (1972), Don Proch (b 1944) marked exciting new departures. Exploring the interaction of human action in, and on, the landscape, he developed Plains imagery on his sculptures of helmets and **GRAIN ELEVATORS**, using his 3-dimensional pieces as canvases. His Prairie sensibilities and the juxtapositions he created are rich and compelling. Eva Stubbs, working in clay and bronze, creates life-size figures and families with carefully modulated surfaces rich in texture and subtle in colour. Her work examines human relationships and interactions. **AGANETHA DYCK** creates domestic-based work with her bees dripping beeswax over carefully chosen objects, such as shoes, purses, and clothes. Recent sculpture graduates are also gaining North American acclaim, including Linda Richardson, student of sculptor and teacher Gordon Reeves of the School of Art. Public art thrived in the 1970s, and is again, with the recent passing of the City of Winnipeg Public Art Policy.

CONTEMPORARY ARTISTS: MB art continues to expand in every field of creation – painting, drawing, printmaking, installation work, ceramics, sculpture, performance art, and video. Artists working in the early 21st century continue the traditions of exploration and experimentation, discovering new artistic boundaries. The number of professional MB artists continues to grow, and includes far more than can be mentioned here. **ESTHER WARKOV**, with her unique insights and observations into quotidian routines, has developed an innovative technique of tearing, folding, and rolling paper on which she has drawn and shaded forms. Her works capture the real and the imaginary, and her personal imagery of mirrors and a variety of other everyday objects, as seen in many of her works from the 1960s on, fuse in *The House of Tea* (1997-98), which portrays the imaginary life of a woman. This large, 3-dimensional work is inventive and particularly important in Cdn art. Hungarian-born **CAROLINE DUKES** brought not only her artistic roots, but also many personal and historical memories, all of which inspired her strong, compelling canvases. Current painters include internationally known **ELEANOR BOND** and **WANDA KOOP**. Bond has painted large-scale imaginary cities seen from disquieting perspectives, which become metaphors for the uncertainties created

Steve Gouthro

by technological, post-industrial societies. Koop, a strong colourist, explores issues of memory and landscape, as seen in *Site Lines* (1999), to create imagery through recognizable places, evoking either calm or angst through colour. Realist **ANDREW VALKO**; abstract painter Diane Whitehouse; landscape realist and performance artist Bill Pura; and **STEVE GOUTHRO**, who was interested in the environment in the work at the Selkirk Steel Mill, are only some painters enriching the visual energy of modern MB.

First Nations artists are also doing significant work and gaining international acclaim. Painter **ROBERT HOULE** addresses many of the wrongs done to Aboriginal peoples in poignant works such as *Sandy Bay* (1998-99); **COLLEEN CUTSCHALL**, painter and installation artist, teaches at **BRANDON U**; and **MÉTIS** photographer Rosalie Favell explores personal and cultural relationships and identities in contemporary society and popular culture. They are only some of the major Aboriginal artists carrying on the rich traditions and foundations set by **JACKSON BEARDY**.

Installation art and photography thrive, at times fused, and at others as standalone works. **DIANA THORNEYCROFT** combines both to create disquieting, thought-provoking, controversial, works questioning social structures and meaning. David MacMillan's photographic works in the *Chernobyl Series* and Richard Holden's *Garden Series* are other important examples of the contemporary insights and expressions of MB artists. Performance art, another critical aspect of the MB art scene since 1969, is presented by a number of artists, including **SHAWNA DEMPSEY** and **LORI MILLAN**. New technologies are the focal point in the work of artists like **REVA STONE**, who explores how technology reorders the human body and memory in interactive works such as *Carnevale* (2000-02) and *Imaginal Expressions* (2004). Working in large-scale glass architectural installations, Warren Carther creates works based on geological structures and environmental concerns, pointing to the dichotomies in the contemporary world. His work crosses boundaries of technology, nature, and culture, and he has won many national and international commissions, such as *Prairie Boy's Dream* in **INVESTORS GROUP**'s Winnipeg headquarters.

MB's position as a critical and vibrant centre in Cdn visual arts is unquestioned, and has been since art began here in 1821. The landscape is compelling; the relative geographic isolation is both an advantage and disadvantage; and the energy and insights, the abilities and commitment, of MB's artists, past and present, working in all media is unparalleled. Today, coincidentally, Mentoring Artists for Women's Art has picked up the traditions of the Winnipeg Women's Art Association of 100 years ago. Many new directions in Cdn art emanated from the "Keystone Province" in the past 1½ centuries of creativity by artists from many diverse backgrounds. All embraced this place, finding new visual vocabularies to express its many facets. •

V

A Halfcast and his Wife and Child, ca 1825, by Peter Rindisbacher

Horse Drinking from an Ice Hole, oil on canvas on academy board, ca 1863, by William Hind

V

Dakota Boat, by W. Frank Lynn

Sounds Assembling, oil on canvas, 1928, by Bertram Brooker

St Clements Church, engraving, 1931, by Marion Nelson Hooker

V

Telea Polephemus, wood engraving on paper, 1939, by H. Eric Bergman

V

Sky Location, acrylic on canvas, 354 x 205 cm, 1967, by Ken Lochhead

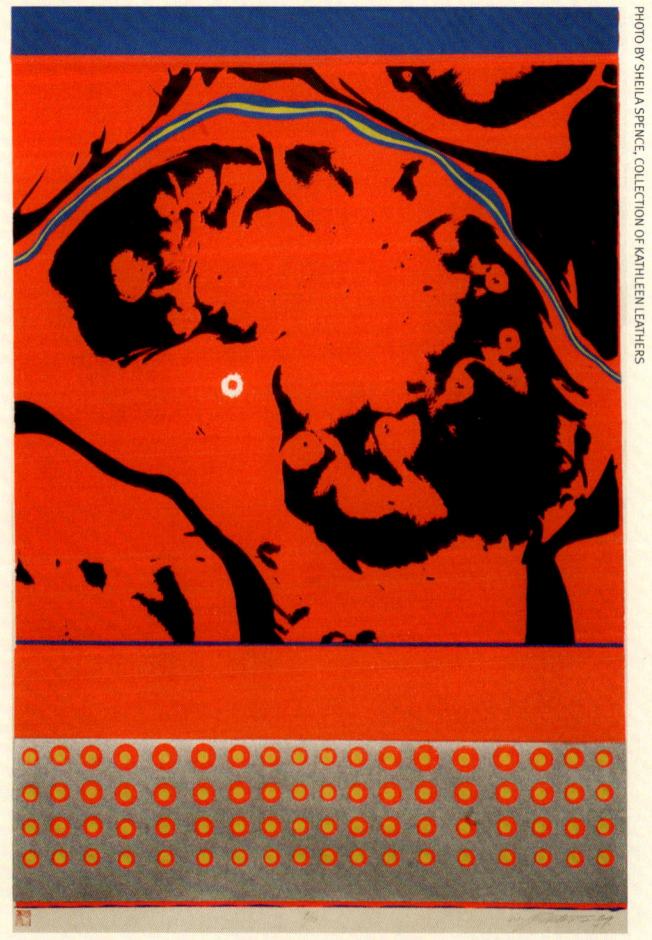

Nocturnal Landscape, serigraph, 61 x 43 cm, 1969, by Winston Leathers

Untitled (Airplane), acrylic, rhoplex on plywood, 224 X 366 cm, 1983, by Wanda Koop

V

Untitled: Grain Elevator, Silkscreen, 1985, by Bill Lobchuk

V

Rockclimbers Meet with Naturalists on the Residential Parkade, oil on unstretched canvas, 244 x 373 cm, 1989, by Eleanor Bond

Sand Bank, acrylic on canvas, 142 x 142 cm, 1996, by Ivan Eyre

V

Sleeping Giant, acrylic on canvas, 2003, by Bruce Head

VITA, pop 300, is a community 90 km SSW of **Winnipeg**, 15 km N of the US border, and just E of a tributary of the Roseau River, in the RM of Stuartburn (*see* **Eastman**). **Ukrainians** settled here in the early 20th century and named the community Szewczenko (or Shevchenko), after 19th-century Ukrainian artist and writer Taras Schevchenko. Other settlers included **English** and **Mennonites**. In 1908, a year after the post office, federal officials forced a name change to Vita – Latin for *life* – against the wishes of many townspeople. The local school retains the name Shevchenko, however. Vita is a retail and service centre for surrounding farms, though some Vitans commute to nearby **Steinbach**. Former **NDP** Cabinet Minister MaryAnn Mihychuk was born here. ● GPP

VITA HEALTH is a chain of health-food stores that started in **Winnipeg** and grew to become Canada's leading vitamin manufacturer. Started in 1936, it began as a mail-order company selling herbs and patented medicines, and was the first health food business in western Canada. It was founded by **German**-born **Immigrant** Gerhard Wilhelm Seier (b Jan 16, 1908, Raesfeld [Nordrein-Westfalen], Germany; d May 10, 2006, Winnipeg), who got his start in the natural remedy business working as a salesman for a Minneapolis company selling herbal bed-wetting formulas. Seier subsequently took courses in herbology and iridology. Most of Vita Health's initial customers were European immigrants, though the business soon grew to include a broader clientele. A Vita Health store, including one of Winnipeg's first vegetarian restaurants, was opened in 1940 in the Curry Building on Portage Ave. Initially, all the herbal formulas were sold as tea, but in the mid-'60s Seier began selling the herbal remedies in tablet form. He started manufacturing the tablets himself in 1973 in rented facilities in **Selkirk**. A Vita Health production facility in Winnipeg was built in 1975. In 1979, Seier transferred control of the company to his children to focus on farming: over the course of his life, Seier operated 2 mink ranches, a cattle operation, and a trout farm, and, in the 1990s, he raised ostrich.

In 1997, Vita Health Company was sold to US-based Leiner Health Products, though Seier's son-in-law, John Holtmann, bought back the MB retail stores the following year in order to keep the retail operations as a family business. The retail stores, operating under the name "Vita Health Natural Food Stores of Manitoba," have 7 stores in Winnipeg and 1 in **Steinbach**, with a total of 50 employees. The Leiner subsidiary, under the name "Vita Health Products Inc.," continued to grow, taking control of BC-based Stanley Pharmaceuticals in 1999. This acquisition doubled VHP Inc.'s sales volume. With a 20,000-m² manufacturing facility, Vita has become a key player in MB's growing **Biotechnology** sector, and is Canada's largest manufacturer of private and generic label vitamins and over-the-counter medicines. With roughly 400 employees, it produces more than 500 products and ships 5 billion pills a year to Wal-Mart, Costco, ON-based national chain Loblaws, and Shoppers Drug Mart. ● MD

VOLLEYBALL was born in 1895, the brainchild of William Morgan, director of the YMCA in Holyoke, MA. He based it on the popular German game "Faustball" but reworked the rules considerably. In 1900, volleyball crossed the border into Canada's YMCAs, and regular inner-city competitions were staged in Ottawa, Montreal, and Toronto. While the sport spread through the US, Russia, and the Orient before WWI, it remained dormant in Canada. By the end of WWII, worldwide interest in the game had grown so much that the International Volleyball Federation was formed.

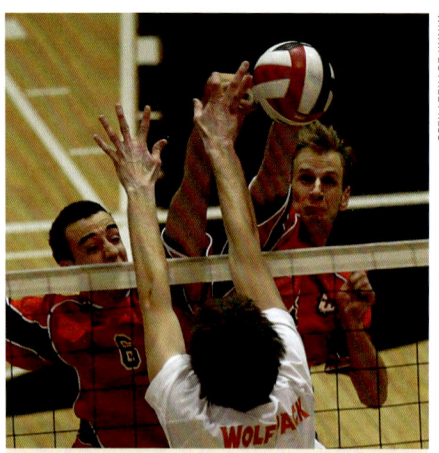

Winnipeg Wesman in action

Volleyball began in MB as a recreational summer program offered by **Winnipeg** schools around the time of WWI. The YMCA was instrumental in providing time and space for the sport after the summer playground leagues finished. They, along with the YMHA (*see* **Jews**) and city fireman, organized a league complete with local championships and tournaments, with the YMCA donating spoons, cups, and medals to the winners. The YMCAs also ran noon-hour house-league programs. In 1928, **Virden**-raised MLA (and future Saskatchewan Court of Appeal Justice) Donald Alexander McNiven, who was dedicated to YMCA work, donated a trophy. Every spring, teams from the 3 Prairie provinces competed for McNiven's trophy. The tournament was usually staged in Winnipeg, **Brandon**, and Regina. The Winnipeg YMCA Rovers dominated in the early years, winning in 1928-33 and 1935-38. In later years, the Winnipeg YMCA Comets, Eagles, Redskins, and Kids would take over as dominant men's teams in the province, in western Canada, and into the US.

In 1953, the first MB Provincial Open Men's tournament was held, and in 1957, the Greater Winnipeg Men's Volleyball League was formed. In 1963, the Manitoba Secondary Schools Athletic Assoc (MSSAA) was established, and the Vincent Massey Trojans won the first high school championship in both the boys' and girls' categories.

MB continued to be a dominant province in the sport of volleyball throughout the 1970s and '80s, winning medals annually at the various national and western Canadian Championships. The men's and women's volleyball programs of both the **U of M** and **U of W** have been among the most successful national programs for the last 35 years, winning over 26 national titles, though **CMU** and **Red River College** often field strong teams as well. Since the first Canada Games in 1967, MB has only missed the volleyball medals once, in 1983, when only the women competed, coming in 4th. Today, MB teams continue to perform well at national and western Cdn championships, winning numerous medals.

MB has also been recognized for its presence at the national level. MB hosted its 1st national championship in 1964 with the Senior Open, and as of writing, continued to host either a Western or a Canadian Championship each year. The province also hosted the National Men's Team 1974-77 and the National Women's Team 1992-96, and housed both the men and women's programs at the Team Canada Volleyball Centre from 1997 to writing.

The Manitoba Volleyball Association incorporated in 1977, and has since been the governing body overseeing all aspects of the sport in the province. The MVA runs programming for recreational and elite athletes from youth to senior. Along with the indoor game, many opportunities are available in the outdoor game: beach volleyball has become very popular around the world, and is growing considerably in MB, as it is elsewhere in Canada. ● GREG JARVIS

Sometimes volleyball can be a contact sport

The skyline of downtown WINNIPEG, see page 743

WABOWDEN, pop 497, is a community 105 km SSW of **THOMPSON** on Setting Lake and on the **HUDSON BAY RAILWAY**. The area was used by **CREE** people long before Europeans arrived here, and became a common stopover in the **FUR TRADE** era, as it was located between **CROSS LAKE** and the **HBC**'s Nelson House, both important to the voyageurs' canoe routes as well as Aboriginal dogsled routes. The lake on which Wabowden stands was called Setting Lake because these goods canoes would "set" (rest) along its shores in poor **WEATHER**. The **RAILWAY** passed through here around 1914, whereupon this community was called Mile 137, referring to its 220 km distance from the S terminus at **THE PAS**. With the establishment of a rail link, the community grew, and the HBC built a post here in the early 1920s. The community name was changed to Wabowden in 1928 after the railway point name, which honoured W. A. Bowden, the chief engineer of the federal Dept of Railways and Canals. Soon after, **FORESTRY** became – and remains – the economic base here. **MINING** was important from the 1950s to the 1970s, but several mines closed in the latter decade. Other Wabowden area enterprises include **COMMERCIAL FISHING**, trapping, and **TOURISM**, including hunting outfitters and **SPORT FISHING** lodges. The Feb **DOGSLED** races are also a popular tourist draw. Though Via Rail offers passenger service here 3 times a week, like many other northern centres, Wabowden's population has declined since the 1970s. • GPP

WADDINGTON, Miriam Dworkin, poet (b Dec 23, 1917, **WINNIPEG**; d Mar 3, 2004, Vancouver). Waddington's parents were eastern European **JEWISH** immigrants; her father operated a kosher meat-curing business on Selkirk Ave in Winnipeg's **NORTH END**, and she attended Machray School as well as the Yiddish-language I. L. Peretz School. The family moved to Ottawa when Miriam was entering her teens, but, as she explained later, the fishing and resort town of **GIMLI** remained her "most beloved place in all of Canada," and Winnipeg stayed in her mind, she said, "like a poem, and its rhythms linger in my blood like snow songs." Waddington received a BA from the U of Toronto and an MA in social work from the U of PA, and practised in Montreal and Toronto during the 1940s and 1950s as a caseworker. She had been writing since she was a small child, and, in addition to her professional responsibilities, she taught creative writing courses. In 1964, she was appointed to the English Department of the newly opened York U. She continued there until her 1983 retirement.

Coming of age in the social turmoil of the **GREAT DEPRESSION**, the Spanish Civil War, and WWII, Waddington remained concerned with progressive movements, and was an ardent advocate of women's writing and women's rights. Her poetry, with its sensitive evocation of both the Prairie landscape and the inner landscape of female experience, is considered a significant component of Modernist Cdn writing. • MILDRED GUTKIN

WALBY, Chris, football player, (b Oct 23, 1956, **WINNIPEG**) spent 16 seasons as an all-star offensive tackle with the **WINNIPEG BLUE BOMBERS**. Walby first played football with the Winnipeg Rods, where he gained the attention of scouts from Dickinson State U in ND. After graduating, Walby was drafted by the Montreal Alouettes in 1981, and played just 5 games before switching to the Bombers. His achievements led to numerous awards: CFL All-Star honours 9 times, Western All-Star 4 times, and Eastern All-Star 7 times. He won the Schenley Award in 1987, and the CFL Award for most outstanding lineman in 1993. The Bombers won 3 Grey Cups during Walby's time with the team. He retired in 1996, and made an unsuccessful run at provincial politics before becoming a colour commentator for CBC. He was inducted into the CFL Hall of Fame in 2004. • JT

WALKER, Corliss Powers "C. P.," impresario (b Sept 19, 1853, Poultney, VT; d Sept 24, 1942, **WINNIPEG**) was the owner of Winnipeg's Walker Theatre. He moved to Winnipeg in 1897 as a theatrical impresario, and began with the Bijou

Theatre as part of his Red River Valley Theatre Circuit, which was connected with a New York syndicate and possessed several theatres in ND. Walker's venues made it possible for him to bring touring companies to Winnipeg and the adjacent US for major runs. He developed the luxurious Walker Theatre (1906) in conjunction with Montreal architect Howard Colton Stone. It staged many popular productions including Ben Hur, complete with horses and chariots. • JMB

WALLACE, Lila Bell, publisher (b Dec 25, 1890, **VIRDEN**; May 8, 1984, Mount Kisco, NY) helped start *Reader's Digest* magazine. The daughter of a **PRESBYTERIAN** minister, Wallace was educated at the U of Oregon, graduating in 1917 with a BA in Germanic languages and literature, after which she worked as a social worker in the eastern US. In 1921, in Pleasantville, NY, she married DeWitt Wallace, who at the time was trying to sell his idea of a "digest" that would condense various magazine articles in one publication. Failing to find an interested publisher, the couple decided to print the magazine themselves. Operating initially from a basement office in New York's Greenwich Village, the Wallaces printed the first *Reader's Digest* in 1922. Circulation of the magazine grew quickly, from 1500 in 1922 to 200,000 in 1929 and to tens of millions at its peak in the 1950s. The magazine became known for its positive, upbeat content aimed at middle-class householders, though during the height of its popularity during the Cold War, it often served as a medium for anti-Communist propaganda. Wallace was a noted philanthropist, and most of her fortune was donated to various causes following her death. • MD

WALLEYE or pickerel (*Sander vitreus*) is the largest Cdn member of the perch family (Percidae). It is usually yellow to green on the upperparts, sometimes with black mottling, but can be quite variable in colour. The mouth has rather large fang-like teeth. Its elongate body usually ranges from 35-50 cm (record 99 cm in the **RED**

RIVER) and up to 10 kg. Males mature at 2-4 years (when over 28 cm), females 3-6 years (over 36 cm). Courtship begins at temperatures of only 1°C, but spawning occurs in small groups after spring breakup (mid-April to late May), when temperatures reach 4-11°C. At night, eggs (up to 600,000 from a large female) are released, fertilized and dispersed over rocky bottoms (no nest is formed) and then they are abandoned. The eggs hatch within 12-18 days and the fry feed on plankton, insects and crustaceans the first year, graduating progressively to larger fish from the second year on. The Walleye is found in large rivers and lakes throughout MB, except the extreme North and East. Its full range is enormous, occupying most of the boreal and deciduous forest regions of NA, where it prefers deep, clear waters, and avoids strong currents. Walleye schools often occur with other species, such as Yellow Perch and Northern Pike. Movements in summer range from 5-8 km, and individuals remain active and feeding through the winter and are often caught by ice fishers. Predators are mainly Northern Pike, large catfish and anglers. Walleye are often cannibalistic with smaller individuals. This species may possibly reach 20 years in cold, N waters. This is MB's and Canada's most-valuable inland-species of fish, prized by anglers, and subsistence and commercial fisheries. • REW

WALRUS (*Odobenus rosmarus*) is a type of seal so different that it has its own family (Odobenidae). It is instantly recognizable by its huge bulk (Atlantic males weigh 850-1750 kg; females 650 kg) supported by flippers, the tusks (canines averaging 36 cm, max 60 cm), and formation of herds (the sexes usually segregated). The tusks mainly signify dominance status, but are also used as a weapon and ice pick when hauling out. The animal keeps warm with a 5 cm thick skin and 15 cm layer of blubber. It may utilize a coastline or sea-ice for hauling-out to rest, preferably near mollusk beds in waters generally less than 100 m deep (but up to 180 m). Most feeding on clams and other invertebrates occurs

C. P. Walker, 1907

The Walleye is prized by anglers

at depths of 10-80 m, while submerged for up to 24 minutes. It roots on the bottom for prey with its stout whiskers (about 450). The Walrus can consume 40 kg of food, and then it may fast for a week. As **Hudson Bay** freezes in Nov, they keep holes open in the ice over preferred feeding beds by pushing the ice with their heads, but eventually they must retreat to an open shore lead. The mating season occurs from Dec to March, and the female produces a calf only once every 3 years (gestation 16 months) in early summer. The calf weighs about 60 kg and is weaned in 2 years, and becomes sexually mature at 6 years. The Polar Bear and Human are the main predators of Walrus. Maximum life span is 35 years in the wild, 40 in captivity. This species was originally common in both Hudson and James bays, and it still occurs in N and E Hudson Bay and in James Bay (total population 4450). Historical records reveal it occurred all along the MB coast, but it was largely exterminated over a century ago. Small herds are still seen on occasion in this area (e.g., 6 animals in 1954 at Churchill), but the species cannot reclaim lost territory in MB waters because of uncontrolled hunting and disturbance from boat traffic. The Walrus evolved from eared seals 10 million years ago (Miocene period). • REW

UMA, TRIBUNE, PERSONALITY FILES

Harry Walsh, 1976

WALSH, Harry, lawyer (b Aug 14, 1913, Old Kildonan [near **Winnipeg**]) is MB's longest-practising lawyer, with a career spanning nearly 70 years. The son of **Jewish** immigrants from the Russian Empire, Walsh initially earned money by selling newspapers on the corner of River and Osborne in Winnipeg. He received his BA from the **U of M** in 1932, earning the $125 tuition for law school by working in a chocolate factory, where he was paid $5 for a 50-hour workweek. Upon graduation, Walsh articled with Edward James McMurray, KC, and was called to the Manitoba Bar in 1937. He established Walsh, Micay and Company that same year, which later grew to employ 27 lawyers. Upon learning that Winnipeg's elite Blackstone Club didn't accept Jewish members, Walsh helped form the Jessel Club for Jewish lawyers, and was founder and first president of the Manitoba **Legal Aid** Society. He was named a QC in 1953. He has chaired several national legal committees, most notably chairing the committee that led to the abolition of capital punishment in Canada in 1976. In 2000, he was named one of MB's top 10 lawyers of the 20th century. His son, Paul Victor Walsh, is also a lawyer and a QC. • MD

WANLESS, pop 183, is a community 45 km NNW of **The Pas** on hwy 10, 30 km E of the SK border and just E of the system that feeds into the **Saskatchewan River**. The **Hudson Bay Railway** came through here in 1927, and was completed to **Flin Flon** and Sheridon in 1928. The community expanded during the **Great Depression** years when the govt offered homesteaders property in the area. The community took its name in 1919 from a **Mining** financier Jack Wanless, who was a prominent businessman from The Pas. Although he never lived in Wanless, he gave generously toward ensuring an education for children in the community. Tourism and logging are the primary industries in the area and the community boasts 2 fishing and hunting lodges on Rocky Lake. Theodore Dupas and his family owned and operated the first commercial fish camp on the lake in the 1920s and a bay is named in his honour. Wanless is centrally located with Clearwater Lake and other good fishing lakes nearby. Snowmobiling is also popular in winter with groomed trails that run through the community. Along with **Roblin**, Wanless boasts the most snowfall in MB. It bills itself as "the snow capital of MB." Wanless, recognized as one of the province's most northerly agricultural areas, once grew registered timothy and alfalfa seed and was home to a **U of M** experimental farm. • GPP

WAPUSK NATIONAL PARK, MB's 2nd and newest national park, lies along the SW shore of **Hudson Bay**. The park was established in 1996 to encourage the preservation of the delicate Hudson/James Bay Lowlands. *Wapusk* (or *wabusk*) is the **Cree** word for "white bear." The name is fitting, as the park protects an area in which the endangered polar bear can birth and raise its young. The bears come inland between mid-July and early Aug, when the bay ice breaks up. Pregnant bears dig dens and give birth in late-Nov to early Dec. The rest of the bears begin to move NW along the coast, returning to the bay once the winter ice has formed. Continuous permafrost lies beneath the surface of most of the park's 11,475 km^2. The landscape is predominantly treeless tundra or low **Arctic Plants**, such as cotton grass and sedges. Wapusk also represents the deepest layer of peat in NA. Water lies everywhere in this poorly drained region and covers half of the land's surface in lakes, bogs, streams, and rivers. Beach ridges are a prominent feature and break the consistent look of the landscape. The area is also characterized by diverse vegetation and species of plants that are rare for this latitude. Particularly significant are the wetland communities and plant species associated with the boreal forest (*see* **Ecoclimactic Regions**) at the northern limits of its range. Inuit, Cree, and **Dene** have all inhabited the Wapusk area for thousands of years. Traditional land use by these groups and other locals continues under the agreement to establish a park. In 2005, use of the land included gathering **Berries**, deadwood, and flowers, as well as hunting **Caribou**. Treaty Indians continue to exercise their Aboriginal and Treaty rights to hunt, trap, and fish in the park. Although several commercial tour operators are authorized to provide services in the road less park, access to most areas in Wapusk is limited. • GPP

WAR LAKE FIRST NATION, on reserve pop 125, off reserve pop 110, is located at **Ilford**, 40 km SE of Split Lake, 688 km N of **Winnipeg**. Most of the originating members of the War Lake First Nation branched off of the **Tataskweyak Cree Nation**, and some came from the **Fox Lake Cree Nation**. War Lake is a member of the Keewatin Tribal Council. The native language here is **Cree**. There is one reserve situated on the War Lake First Nation land, called Mooseocoot. The War Lake community has winter road access to York Landing, Split Lake, and Ilford at which there is an airstrip. The first nation is also on the Bay line, which provides passenger rail service to **Thompson** and **Churchill**. War Lake First Nation schooling goes from Nursery-Grade 8, and enrolment for 2003-04 was 18. The Keewatin Tribal Council administers education. Along with Mathias Columb and Tataskweyak First Nations, War Lake jointly operates the Keewatin Railway Company, which took over the northern rail line between Sherritt Junction and Lynn Lake. The economic base at War Lake First Nation is trapping and commercial **Fishing**. ● RK

CHRISTIAN ARTUSO

Yellow-rumped Warblers arrive early and leave late.

WARBLERS, or wood-warblers (family Parulidae), are among the most colourful birds found in NA. Their brilliant plumages, ranging from flame-orange and bright yellow to deep blue and jet-black, more than make up for what they lack in vocal ability. Some 25 species breed regularly in the province, while another 10 occur occasionally. They are small, slender birds, with short, pointed beaks, and feed almost exclusively on insects. The greatest variety during the breeding season is found in the boreal forest (*see* **Ecoclimactic Regions**), but during migration, they may show up anywhere. **Winnipeg's Assiniboine Park** is a notable hotspot during late May and from early Aug to mid-Sept. They winter mostly in Central and South America. Some of MB's notable species include the Yellow Warbler (*Dendroica petechia*), with highest breeding densities noted anywhere in its range at the **Delta Marsh** beach ridge, and Connecticut Warbler (*Oporornis agilis*), which ranks in the top 10 of "most-wanted" species by birders on the continent. The commonest species on migration, and generally the earliest to arrive and the latest to depart, is the Yellow-rumped warbler (*D. coronata*). ● RUDOLF KOES

WARKOV, Esther, artist, (Oct 12, 1941, **Winnipeg**) attended the **U of M**'s School of Art, leaving in her 3rd year to start painting. A successful figurative painter, Warkov soon embraced surrealism and modernism, developing a highly personal visual vocabulary and creative methodology. She turned solely to creating 3-dimensional narrative drawings and installations from the 1980s onwards. Warkov's **Jewish** heritage and **North End** Winnipeg roots have continuously provided her with material; so too has her vivid imagination. She combines historical references, images from popular culture and daily life, particularly scenes from the bus window, and her highly complex, intense personal symbols. Some symbols have universal meanings; others are invented for her own purposes. Her work is complicated, beautiful and compelling.

Warkov develops stories in many, such as in *The House of Tea* (1997-98), with the headless female figure suspended above the casket filled with objects and references of the woman's life. The dress and every surface of the coffin are covered with exquisite, minute details, drawn, torn, cut and curled, the fragments reassembled and pasted together. Mirrors, flowers, spoons, books, pens etc. all add to the memory of the woman's life. These large 3-dimensional drawings/installations are fragmented worlds, enigmatic and dreamlike, but often with a dark side. They always pose unanswerable questions. A member of the Royal Canadian Academy of Art, Warkov has exhibited nationally and internationally, her first solo exhibition being in 1964 at The **Winnipeg Art Gallery** and later in 1972, 1985-86; 1998-99; the National Gallery of Canada 2000, and London, ON, Regina, Toronto and Montreal with group exhibitions in France, the US and across Canada. Her work is in public, corporate and private collections including the National Gallery of Canada, the Vancouver Art Gallery, The WAG, and the Canada Council. It has been widely published, including *Magic Off Main: The Art of Esther Warkov*, (Beverly Rasporich, U of Calgary Press, 2003). ● PATRICIA BOVEY

WARREN, pop 750, is a community 40 km NW of **Winnipeg** on hwy 6 near hwy 67. Those of **English**, **Scots**, and **Irish** stock primarily settled the area. A post office opened here in 1882 as Hanlan, apparently after Ontarian rower Ned Hanlan. The railway (later **CN**) came through in 1905, and the community was renamed after A. E. Warren, a railway executive. Although Warren is a retail centre for the surrounding farms, it also functions as a bedroom community for the province's capital. The elementary and secondary schools are also substantial employers. The community benefits from a tourist steam-locomotive **Railway** excursion from just W of Winnipeg, the Prairie Dog Central. As Warren is at the end of the trip, and passengers have a layover here, locals organized the West Interlake Trading Company both to sell crafts and foods to the rail passengers and to entertain them. In the early 21st century, the local **Grain Elevator** escaped demolition, mainly because of the tourist presence. The Warren area also features a golf course and the V. Gross Doll Museum, with a collection of thousands of dolls and vintage toys. ● GPP

WARREN, Peter William, journalist, radio personality (b Oct 2, 1941, London, UK). Warren began his journalistic career in England, later becoming a reporter for several Cdn daily **Newspapers**, including the *Calgary Herald*, the *St. John Telegraph-Journal*, and the **Winnipeg Tribune**, where he became city editor. He was best known in **Winnipeg** as the host of the call-in

THE WAG, 2000-86, PHOTO BY ERNEST MAYER

The House of Tea, 1997-98, graphite, charcoal pencil, conte crayon, pastel on handcoloured barrier white paper, 213 x 152 x 244 cm, by Esther Warkov

radio show *The Action Line* on CJOB from 1971 to 1998 (*see* **Broadcasting**). Warren's on-air manner was abrupt, outspoken, and no-nonsense; two of his trademark declarations were "Let's get right down to business" (to begin a show) and "Get on with it" (to divert callers who attempted social niceties like "How are you?").

Peter Warren, 1969

Listeners to the highly popular radio program respected his compassion for the disadvantaged and for victims of injustice. When Warren was inducted into the Order of the Buffalo Hunt (*see* **Order of Manitoba**) in 1998, then-premier **Gary Filmon** described him as "a champion of the average citizen." Manitobans admired Warren's involvement in raising millions of dollars for flood victims and for ensuring that senior citizens didn't run out of food during a Winnipeg blizzard. He was one of the first journalists to help Thomas Sophonow, **David Milgaard**, and James Driscoll make the public aware of their **Wrongful Convictions**. Warren's pugnacious style might have been honed by his brief stint as a professional boxer in his early adulthood.

Peter Warren's journalistic accomplishments include provocative interviews with 10 Cdn PMs. Pierre Trudeau described being interviewed by Warren as "worse than Question Period." His many dramatic achievements include having 4 escaped convicts give themselves up on the air. In 1997, the Western Association of Broadcasters named him Broadcaster of the Year, and he was inducted into the Canadian Association of Broadcasters' Hall of Fame in 1999.

After announcing his "retirement" in 1998, Warren moved to Victoria, BC and soon became host of a syndicated weekend call-in show that ran from 1998 to March 2006 on the Corus Radio Network, establishing his still-unmatched record as NA's longest-running radio talk show host. In 2007, Warren's website continues to offer his services as an investigator "on behalf of victims seeking closure, but not publicity, to cases involving sexual abuse, medical mistreatment, even murder." ● RUSS GOURLUCK

WASAGAMACK FIRST NATION, on reserve pop 1486, off reserve pop 128, is located on the W shore of Island Lake, 607 km NE of **Winnipeg**. This First Nation community used to be a part of the Island Lake Band, which was comprised of 3 other communities, including **Garden Hill**, **St. Theresa Point**, and **Red Sucker Lake** (all of which are now independent First Nation communities). The Wasagamack First Nation signed Treaty 5 in 1909 and is now a member of the Island Lake Tribal Council. The native languages here are **Ojibway** and **Cree**. Schooling in this isolated First Nation goes from Nursery-Grade 12, and total enrolment for the year 2003-04 was 480. Wasagamack administers its own education. There are a total of 3 reserves on Wasagamack land: Feather Rapids IR, Naytawunkank IR, and Wasagamack IR. The community depends on winter road access from St. Theresa Point, which maintains a runway. The community's economic foundation is commercial trapping and **Fishing**. ● RK

WASAGAMING, is a community 60 km S of **Dauphin** in the southern part of **Riding Mountain National Park** on Clear Lake. At an elevation of 615 m, Wasagaming, a seasonal resort town, sees its summer population swell to several hundred cottage dwellers, and many park workers and businesspeople. The number of summer visitors fluctuates considerably but may exceed 10,000 on peak weekends. With cabins and cottages, as well as businesses and park services, largely closed during the winter, it has virtually no winter resident population and only sporadic day visitors. Wasagaming originated as a recreational campground and as a site of early summer cottages during the early 20th century. The townsite was surveyed in 1931, and additional lakeside cottages were built even before Riding Mountain National Park was officially opened in 1933. Today, Wasagaming consists of: a compact commercial core with about 35 summer businesses, 250 prestigious cottage lots, some 520 cabin lots, 510 camping sites, Parks Canada buildings, and a RCMP station. The special character of

Wasagaming consists not only in its historical development and functional orientation, but also in its administration, land and building regulations, and the aspirations and activities of its seasonal summer population. While Wasagaming is a federally-administered national park town, the adjacent RM of Park, with Onanole as its commercial and administrative centre, falls under provincial and municipal jurisdiction. While Wasagaming and Onanole have some different planning objectives, the recent years have been characterized by a greater co-operation and by a sharing of responsibilities and services, as well as by a harmonization of conservation efforts and development goals. ● CHRIS STADEL

WASKADA, pop 208, is a village 100 km SW of **Brandon**, 10 km N of the US border, in the SW of the province. The village takes its name from the Siouan language. The **NWMP** passed by Waskada on their **Boundary Commission** march, and European settlers – primarily of **English**, **Scots**, **Irish**, and **French** heritage – were here by the 1880s. In 1889, the Waskada and North-Eastern Railway Co. was formed to connect to Waskada from points E, though like many other early branch-line **Railways**, it was bought out by 1901, though **CP Rail** now operates the branch line here. Waskada became a village in 1949. The economy is based on support for agriculture, and has 2 **Grain Elevators**, though petroleum extraction also occurs in the area. Local festivals here are the Borderfest Party in the Park, in late July, and the harvest-time Threshing Days festival. Nearby outdoor tourist attractions include Turtle Mountain Provincial Park and Lowe Natural Heritage Area. ● GPP

WASP is an insect of the order Hymenoptera which also includes the ants, bees and sawflies. Characteristics of the group are wings with few veins, fore- and hind-wings connected by hooks (hamuli), and the first segment of the abdomen is fused to the last segment of the thorax. The thin 'wasp waist' characterizes the suborder Apocrita – including true wasps and parasitic wasps. Another characteristic of wasps and bees is the venom-injecting sting. Wasps have complete metamorphosis – egg, several larval stages, pupa, and adult. Wasps can be traced back 185 million years ago (Early Jurassic period), and several of the earliest thread-waisted wasps (family Sphecidae) are known from fossil amber collected on the shores of Cedar Lake, MB. Distinctive species (*Lisponema singularis*, *Archisphex crowsoni* and *Procleptes carpenteri*) from this site date back to 140-70 mya (Cretaceous period). The hymenopterans form a huge

W

There are 15 species of wasps in Manitoba.

© ROY ELLIS CARMAN MB

group of over 11,000 species in Canada (280,000 estimated species in 106 families worldwide). Several prominent MB families of wasps are highlighted below.

BRACONID WASPS (family Braconidae) are among the most diverse families with over 4000 species in Canada, but 80% of these are undescribed or unrecorded. Most of these tiny wasps are internal parasites of other insects. The female stings the host, causing temporary paralysis, and inserts 1 or more eggs inside the body cavity. When the eggs hatch, the larvae consume the host's tissues, eventually killing the host (i.e., parasitoidism). Many species are solitary parasitoids, with only a single larva per host. Some species of *Chelonus* wasps lay their eggs inside the egg(s) of the host, however, the *Chelonus* eggs remain dormant until the host larva nears maturity. The parasitoid then hatches, grows quickly, and kills its host. Other braconids have larvae that are external parasites of other insects such as a caterpillar, which is slowly consumed by a mass of maggot-like larvae. These eventually spin beautiful golden or silver pupal cocoons, attached to the skin of their emaciated host.

ICHNEUMON WASPS (family Ichneumonidae) are a large group of parasitic wasps which attack other insects. There are an estimated 7000 species in Canada, only 2000 of which have been described. They range from 3 mm-7.5 cm. Species of *Megarhyssa* are intimidating because of their large size and outlandish ovipositor, which may exceed the length of their 5 cm-long body. They are common in all parts of MB. The adults of some *Ophion* species are the large, orange wasps that commonly visit lights on a summer night. Bizarre *Megarhyssa* and *Rhyssa* species, with their 7-10 cm-long ovipositors, attack siricid wood wasp larvae. They are able to detect chemicals released by symbiotic fungi associated with the siricid larva, seeking refuge under several cm of wood. The female wasp locates the larva and then uses the sharp tip of the ovipositor to force the entire length of the structure through the wood to reach its host, without ever actually seeing it. The female then forces an egg down the ovipositor and onto the lost larva. The whole process may take 30 minutes. Many species (e.g., *Banchus flavescens*) have been used as biological-control agents to reduce numbers of Bertha Armyworms (*Mamestra configurata*).

CHALCID WASPS (superfamily Chalcidoidea) are small (.2-8 mm) wasps and are black and yellow, metallic green, blue, or bronze. There are 15 families, but an unknown number of species in MB (over 1300 in Canada). Some species, which attack the eggs of horse flies, are only 0.2 mm long. *Trichogramma semblidis* has been found to destroy large numbers of eggs of the deer fly (*Chrysops aestuans*). Some chalcidoids are plant feeders but most species are parasitoids. There are even species that are parasitoids of other parasitoids (hyperparasitoidism).

CUCKOO WASPS (family Chysididae) are little jewels with the 25 species in MB being metallic green, greenish-blue, or bronze. Parasitoids of solitary bees and wasps, the female lays an egg on the host larva or prepupa while the nest burrow is still under construction by the parent, or after the provisioning parent has left the scene. The cuckoo wasp larva then completely consumes its host. Some cuckoo wasp females are heavily armoured, and often have deep pits into which is directed the sting of an irate parent that has returned home to find the intruder. Most cuckoo wasps have a characteristic defensive posture they use when they are caught – they roll into a ball, and there is little damage that the host parent can inflict.

VELVET ANTS (family Mutillidae) resemble ants but are parasitic wasps, the females of which are wingless. These wasps are covered with dense hairs of various colours, including rusts, orange, red, black and white. The males may not resemble the females; in fact, the sexes of some species are probably described as separate species (rearing or mating experiments are needed). At least 6 species have been recorded in MB, and likely over 17 occur here; *Dasymutilla asopus* is a prominent species in S MB. Velvet ants are common in sandy areas (e.g., Carberry Sandhills), with solitary bees and wasps commonly affected hosts. The female can deliver a scintillating sting, while the males are harmless.

SPHECID WASPS (family Sphecidae) include common species like mud daubers and thread-waisted wasps, but most are small and retiring. There are about 100 species in MB, all of which capture either insects or spiders as prey for their young. The female delivers paralyzing stings and then transports the immobilized prey to the nest site, where she deposits an egg on or near her prize. There are species that construct organ-pipe-style nests of wet mud, while others like the large, greenish sand wasps (*Bembix* species), dig their nests in sand banks. The largest sphecid wasp across Canada is the Cicada Killer (*Sphecius speciosus*) which provisions its nests with cicadas.

SPIDER WASPS (family Pompilidae) include 40 MB species, females of which all attack spiders. They are either black or blue-black, some with white or orange/red markings. These are the commonly observed wasps that display incessant bobbing of the body and wings as they search the ground. The female wasp crawls down into the burrow of the spider to deliver a powerful sting, and may then use the spider's own burrow in which to rear its young.

POTTER AND MASON WASPS (family Eumenidae) use mud or clay in nest construction, carried to the site in the female wasp's mandibles. They are common in MB, with about 24 species. Some species are twig and hole nesters, and their larvae are provided with caterpillars. *Eumenes* species build clay pots anchored to branches. The female stings caterpillars and stuffs them into the pot through the narrow opening at the top. Before sealing the pot with more mud, she suspends a single egg by a slender thread.

YELLOW JACKETS AND HORNETS (family Vespidae) are annoying for their habit of collecting sweet liquids (soft drinks and rotting apples) and meat scraps in late summer and fall. They may be aggressive and are responsible for numerous deaths in Canada each year. Some people succumb to anaphylactic shock following a painful sting, while others have fatal automobile accidents when stung. There are 15 species recorded for MB, including an irritating European introduction (*Vespula germanica*). Most hornets and yellowjackets are social, living in carton nests constructed in trees and shrubs or in underground cavities. Some species, such as the Bald-faced Hornet (*Dolichovespula maculata*) capture insects as food for their larvae, while others are scavengers and are fond of meat. In the fall, when the colony may reach several thousand workers, the social cohesion of the colony begins to fail, and as the males are produced, these wasps become aggressive and sometimes attack people. Not all species are so aggressive. *Polistes* species (which build small nests) may be safely brushed aside. ● TDG, RBW

WASYLYCIA-LEIS, Judy, politician (b Aug. 10, 1951 Kitchener, ON) earned a BA in political science and French from the U of Waterloo, and an MA in political science from Carleton U in 1976. She unsuccessfully sought election to the legislative assembly in ON in 1977, 1980, and 1981. During this period she served as exec assis to federal NDP leader Ed Broadbent, as well as the party's Women's Organizer. After moving to Winnipeg, she worked as exec assis to premier **HOWARD PAWLEY**. In 1986, she was elected to the MB legislature representing the St. John's riding. She was appointed to cabinet as Minister of Culture, Heritage and Recreation, where she was responsible for the Status of Women. After Pawley's govt was defeated in 1988, she served as the NDP critic for family services and the status of women, and later as the health critic and deputy leader. She resigned her seat in 1993 to seek federal election. She was defeated in Winnipeg North by **REY PAGTAKHAN**. In 1997, she tried again and was elected in the Winnipeg North Centre riding. After the riding was re-distributed, she defeated Pagtakhan in the 2004 federal election. Wasylycia-Leis has earned a reputation for outspokenness. During the 2006 conflict between Israel and Hezbollah, Wasylycia-Leis caused controversy within her party when she visited Israel with fellow Winnipeg NDP MP, **PAT MARTIN**.
● CARSON JEREMA

WASYLYK, Harry, inventor, entrepreneur (b Nov 8, 1904, **WINNIPEG**; d Sept 20, 1995, Winnipeg) Wasylyk worked in his family's fruit cannery in WWII, but developed an interest in plastics after the war. A **SOCIALIST**, he ran for the CCF for Springfield in the 1949 federal election and for MLA for St. Clements in the 1950 election, both times finishing 2nd. Around 1950, Wasylyk co-invented the plastic garbage bag. (Two other Cdn inventors – Larry Hansen, an employee of Union Carbide in Lindsay, ON, and Toronto-based Frank Plomp – worked on the garbage bag simultaneously but independently.) Wasylyk made the bags from low-density polyethylene (LDPE-4), a manmade organic polymer first synthesized from petroleum in 1942. At the time, he was researching products for the Winnipeg General Hospital (now the **HEALTH SCIENCES CENTRE**), for whom he was making plastic hospital gloves. The hospital needed bags that would not spill their potentially hazardous contents, but which were cheap to produce. Initially, only the hospital used the bags, which Wasylyk produced in his house. This, like the cannery, was a family operation, and he recruited nephews and other relations to help his business. Harry later set up a plant to mass-produce the bags. After Union Carbide bought his operation, they manufactured Glad Garbage Bags – the first commercial application of Wasylyk's product – for the public starting around

rotated text: UMA, TRIBUNE, PERSONALITY FILES

Harry Wasylyk, 1958, inventor of green garbage bag

1969. Unfortunately, what seemed to be a boon for the Boomer housewife has taken its toll on the environment. Plastic has replaced biodegradable products, such as wood, cloth, and paper, in most of the world. As very few organisms digest plastics, the bags may sit for thousands of years before they completely break down. ● AJL

WATCHMEN, THE, hard rock recording artists formed in south **WINNIPEG** neighbourhoods of River Heights and Tuxedo in the late 1980s. By 1992, the lineup had solidified around Danny Greaves (vocals), Joey Serlin (guitar), Sammy Kohn (drums) and Peter Loewen (bass) and began performing their driving brand of original music, composed by the writing team of Greaves and Serlin, in local clubs. Years of steady travelling resulted in a reputation as a hard-working band, landing them a recording contract with MCA Canada. Their debut album, *McLaren Furnace Room* (1993) was named for their rehearsal space in the basement of a downtown Winnipeg hotel. Loewen was replaced by Ken Tizzard from Toronto prior to recording their 2nd album *In The Trees* (1994), their best selling album featuring hit single and perennial crowd favourite "Boneyard Tree." *Brand New Day* (1996) failed to emulate the platinum status of their previous release but the band continued to enjoy popularity on the road. Signed to Capital Records in 1998, they released *Silent Radar* enjoying a hit single in Canada and Australia with "Stereo". Kohn left before their final album, 2001's double album *Slo-motion* which offered a sharp change in style to more electronic music. With limited success, the band folded in 2003 and the members, now all Toronto-based, scattered to other groups. ● JOHN EINARSON

WATER BEAR or tardigrade is a type of microscopic arthropod, which takes its name from its plump, bearlike shape (also known as a water piglet). It is so unusual that it is sometimes given its own phylum status. A water bear consists of only 5 segments, the first forming a 'head,' while the remaining ones each bear a pair of legs, ending in several claws. It moves slowly with a

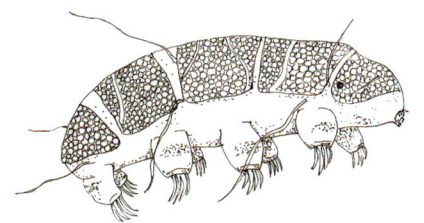

rotated text: JENNIFER LABELLA

The Water Bear's name reflects its unusual shape.

lumbering gait. While it has a brain, eyespots, digestive, excretive and muscular systems, lacking are circulatory and respiratory systems. Water bears are found in land, freshwater and marine ecosystems, with a favoured habitat of moss and lichen (on the ground, trees and rocks), sand, and leaf litter; basically anywhere there is moisture. When conditions become unsuitable, such as desiccation or freezing, it enters a reversible dormant state (crytobiosis) so profound that in experiments, water bears have recovered from exposure to -253°C, +151°C, X-rays, vacuum, and 6000 atmospheric pressure. They obtain nourishment by piercing cell walls of bacteria, algae, moss, lichen, roundworms, and other small creatures by means of sharp stylets in the mouth. It then sucks up the prey's juices. There are males and females, and after mating, 1-30 eggs are laid, which develop into little water bears (no larval stage). An amazing discovery is that the total number of cells in the body is set at birth. Over 50 species are known to date in Canada, and likely more than half of these widespread species will be found to inhabit MB. Over 400 species are known worldwide. These amazing little animals are dispersed around the world on wind currents. An extinct species of water bear (*Beorn leggi*) was found in amber from Cedar Lake, MB, which is famous for the pieces of amber (yellow-brown, fossilized conifer resin) washed up on the shore. This species apparently became entombed about 125 mya (Cretaceous period), and has been found nowhere else. • REW

WATER LILIES. MB has 2 species of yellow water lilies (*Nuphar variegata* and *N. microphylla*), 3 species of white water lilies (*Nymphaea odorata*, *N. tetragona*, and *N. leibergii*), and a closely related rare water plant called water shield (*Brasenia schreberi*). All of their flowers open only late in the morning, on sunny days. Both yellow water lilies (also called spatterdock, cow-lily, and yellow pond-lily) are common in ponds and other quiet waters in the southern ¾ of MB. They have oval floating leaves that are divided on one side and waxy yellow flowers. Their leaves and huge floating stems are eaten by **BEAVERS**, **MUSKRATS**, and **MOOSE**, and were used medicinally by **FIRST PEOPLES**. The large white water lily (*N. odorata*) is the largest and the least-common of our 3 species. It is found only in a few lakes around **WHITESHELL PROVINCIAL PARK**, such as Lily-Pond Lake, and the west-central part of MB. Its fragrant white flowers are up to 12 cm wide, and the nearly round floating leaves reach 20 cm in width. The other 2 species, called pygmy or small white water lilies, are more widespread but have much smaller flowers and leaves. The rare water

White Water Lilies are less common in Manitoba than the yellow variety.

shield has small (8 cm) round leaves with no divisions and small (2 cm) purple flowers. It is found only in a few places (such as Lily-Pond) in the Whiteshell area of SE MB. • KAREN JOHNSON

WATER SKIING. Soon after its invention – apparently by the teenaged Ralph Samuelson at Lake Pepin, MN, in 1922 – this activity spread to MB. The earliest recorded water skiing in the province occurred in the late 1920s at a **LAC DU BONNET** resort. In 1932, a picture of a water skier appeared in the ***WINNIPEG FREE PRESS*** with the caption "Introducing Water-Skiing: A New

Aquatic Sport." In 1945, Dr. William Reid of **SELKIRK** was the first Manitoban to make a pair of water skis. Made from plywood, they measured 2.4 m (7 ft by 12 in) long. For foot bindings, he used a pair of size-5 shoe rubbers, which were small enough for his size-10 feet to create suction hold. Though ingenious, the cumbersome skis did little to advance the sport's popularity. The skis are now housed in the Water Ski Museum in Selkirk. Reid's descendants continued to develop the sport; his son, Ian Livingstone Reid, formed the Selkirk Seals Water Ski Club in 1952. The club, still active today, has produced champion

Water skiing in the Whiteshell, 1952

water skiers such as Ian's son, Bruce Reid, winner of 19 Cdn titles. Both Ian and Bruce Reid are members of the **MANITOBA SPORTS HALL OF FAME**.

Similar water-skiing clubs were also established in the early 1950s at Betula Lake and at Lake Minnewasta near **MORDEN**, leading to the formation of the Manitoba Water Ski Association in 1953. It was the first provincial water-skiing organization in Canada, and consisted of nearly 100 members from 8 clubs. Among these 8 was **MINNEDOSA**'s Mallards Club, which earned fame when member Vailla Hogan became the first Cdn woman to win a gold medal in an international competition in 1966. The Winnipeg Water Ski Club was also formed in 1956, but it soon dissolved in the early 1960s, as the **RED RIVER** became too polluted (*see* **POLLUTION**).

MB's first provincial tournament was held in 1954, using a 25 hp Johnson outboard engine on a 4.9 m (16 ft) aluminum Aeroliner boat. By comparison, a typical boat today would have a 320-hp inboard engine and would measure more than 6 m. Most of the skis at the first tournament were homemade and the skiers self-taught. The most complicated trick performed was a 360° turn, a novice stunt by today's standards. The Cdn championship was held in MB for the first time in 1962, with Manitobans taking 3 national titles. The province continues to be among the country's most active in the sport, earning MB the Province of the Year award 4 times from Water Ski and Wakeboard Canada. In 1998, the Manitoba Water Ski Association opened the artificial Lake Shirley, which is where the provincial team trains, in the South Transcona area of **WINNIPEG**. Manitoba Water Ski has grown to include 11 clubs with roughly 150 members. ● MD

WATER SPORTS. Recreational swimming and aquatic games have long been popular in MB, a province boasting 100,000 lakes. Of course, water sports were a summertime activity until the arrival of indoor swimming pools, with the first being the YMCA pool in Winnipeg in 1900. Pools were also considered a means to promote public hygiene, and the city of Winnipeg began running public facilities in 1912 with the opening of the Pritchard Avenue Public Baths, offering rented bathing suits for 10¢. Indoor facilities were also an important development in that they promoted water sports through swimming lessons and the organization of games such as water polo.

Social taboos against nudity waned through the 1930s, and water sports accordingly gained in popularity as swimmers were allowed to don less cumbersome suits that increased mobility and athleticism. Swimming was also one of few sports considered acceptable for women. One of

MB's first aquatic stars was diver Judy Moss, who earned fame across Canada after winning a gold medal at the 1934 British Empire Games, despite almost missing the event due to lack of funds. The financial hardships of the **GREAT DEPRESSION** also prevented Winnipeg's Albert Ford, a national champion, from participating in the 1936 Berlin Olympics. Bob Hamerton then became the first male swimmer from MB named to a Cdn Olympic team. Though national record-setting swimmer Catherine (nee Kerr) Gordon and western Cdn 1-mi champion Ethel (nee Gilbert) Bieber qualified for the Olympics in 1939, they both missed out on their chance at competing with the outbreak of WWII. MB's Russell Saunders was the 1939 Cdn 3 m diving champion, though he is better known for his career as a Hollywood stuntman, having worked in over 100 movies. Interestingly, he was also the model for Salvador Dali's 'Christ of St. John of the Cross.'

Notable long-distance swimmers from MB include Claudia McPherson, who at 17 years of age became the youngest person to complete the celebrated English Channel Crossing in 1963, and Vivian (nee King) Thompson, a successful amateur swimmer who established numerous records through the 1940s. In 1956, she crossed **LAKE WINNIPEG** in a record 8 hours and 40 min, beating the time previously set by **KATHIE MCINTOSH**, the first person to successfully cross the lake.

Synchronized swimming was introduced to MB in the late 1940s as an offshoot of Royal Life Saving Society skills, under the auspices of the Canadian Amateur Swimming Association (CASA). As the sport grew, it developed into its own executive and national organization, separating from CASA in the mid-1950s. In fact, all water sports were collectively administered by CASA until 1966 when Vaughan Baird, a prominent MB lawyer and the chairman of the national diving organization, helped bring each sport into separate divisions of aquatic sports, leading to the establishment of provincial sports divisions for swimming, diving, synchronized swimming and water polo.

Winnipeg did not have a regulation-size pool until the Pan Am Pool was built for the 1967 **PAN AMERICAN GAMES**. The pool was at the time considered the finest diving facility in Canada, and was also the site of the Aquatic Hall of Fame and Museum of Canada until 2006, when the museum was closed. The Pan Am Games were an important milestone for water sports in MB as they opened the door for numerous officials, including Marjorie Simpson, Gerry Land, Laura Ealing and Karen Land, to judge at international meets. The Pan Am Pool also provided a superior

training facility for MB divers such as Pan Am and Commonwealth Games gold medallist Janet Nutter in the 1970s, as well as Mike Mourant, who competed at the 1984 Los Angeles Olympics.

Swimming is an ideal means to increase the mobility of people with visual impairments, and MB is home to 2 notable Paralympic swimmers: Tim McIsaac, who became the world's first blind swimmer to tumble turn in the 1970s, a technique previously only used by sighted swimmers, and **KIRBY COTE**, a Paralympic gold medallist.

Through the 1980s, Cindy Caeser and Canada Games gold medallist Jennifer Land were both named to national teams, and competed internationally at meets such as the Swiss Open, the Austrian Open, and the French Open. In the 2000s, MB continued to show a strong presence with swimmers such as Rhiannon Leier ranking among Canada's top swimmers. ● VAUGHAN BAIRD/GPP

WATERFOWL (family Anatidae) are well represented in MB, with 41 species occurring here. Swans, geese, and ducks make up this family. Swans are large, white birds with long necks. The only common member of this group in the province is the Tundra Swan (*Cygnus columbianus*), which gathers in large flocks on fields in spring or at certain lakes, such as Whitewater, in fall. Both it and the trumpeter swan (*C. buccinator*) suffered great losses in the 18th and 19th centuries due to the quill trade. The latter species was believed to be nearly extinct early in the 20th century, but reintroduction programs have aided it in making a gradual comeback, and a few nests are now found annually in **RIDING MOUNTAIN NATIONAL PARK** and **DUCK MOUNTAIN PROVINCIAL PARK**.

Geese are intermediate in size between swans and ducks. An abundant species is the Canada Goose (*Branta canadensis*), which can be found nesting throughout the province, even in cities and towns near waterbodies. Huge flocks gather each fall at **OAK HAMMOCK MARSH**, **FORT WHYTE CENTRE**, and elsewhere in MB. Cackling Geese (*B. hutchinsii*, formerly *B. canadensis minima* and other subspecies) are now largely regarded as a separate species to the larger Canada Geese. They migrate to and from northern breeding grounds in large flocks. Snow geese (*Chen caerulescens*) are also abundant during migration, especially in the west, but breed in MB only in the La Pérouse Bay vicinity, E of **CHURCHILL**.

Ducks are often divided into 2 groups, based on their feeding habits. Those that gather food at the surface of the water are the "dabblers" or "puddle ducks," while the "diving ducks" find most of their food well-below the surface.

W

Trumpeter swans neared extinction a century ago.

Common "dabblers" include the Mallard (*Anas platyrhynchos*) and the Blue-winged Teal (*A. discors*), while common diving ducks are Lesser Scaup (*Aythya affinis*) and Common Goldeneye (*Bucephala clangula*). One diving duck, the Canvasback (*Aythya valisineria*), has been studied extensively at **DELTA MARSH** and inspired the classic book *The Canvasback on a Prairie Marsh* (1981) by H. Albert Hochbaum. Although many species of ducks nest province-wide, a few, such as common eider (*Somateria mollissima*) and long-tailed duck (*Clangula hyemalis*), are restricted to the vicinity of Hudson Bay.

The Prairie provinces, and adjacent states, host a large percentage of the continent's breeding waterfowl population, hence the apt moniker "Duck Factory of NA" for this region. Although habitat losses due to conversion of prairie to agricultural land and drainage of potholes have greatly reduced the overall number of birds in the past 150 years, impressive concentrations can still occur at our marshes and lakes. Notable areas to see such spectacles include Whitewater Lake, Delta Marsh, **OAK HAMMOCK MARSH**, the pothole region around **MINNEDOSA**, and the mouth of the **CHURCHILL RIVER**. ● RUDOLF KOES

WATERHEN, pop 389, is a community 85 km NW of **DAUPHIN**, on the Waterhen River, between Waterhen Lake and **LAKE MANITOBA**. Novelist **GABRIELLE ROY**'s first book on MB, *La Petite Poule d'Eau (Where Nests the Water Hen)*, is set in this community, where Roy taught school in 1937. The area has a large Aboriginal population, mainly concentrated in the **SKOWNAN FIRST NATION**. Waterhen relies on commercial **FISHING**,

CATTLE FARMING, and fur trapping. There are several hunting and sport fishing lodges in the area. A free-roaming herd of wood **BISON** is maintained near the community as part of the Waterhen Wood Bison Project. ● GPP

WATSON, James KEN, curler (b Aug 12, 1904, **MINNEDOSA**; d Jul 26, 1986, **WINNIPEG**) was the first Cdn curler to skip his team to 3 Brier championships. Watson moved to Winnipeg at 12, and started curling at 15. As a day job, Watson worked as a schoolteacher in the 1920s, and then joined the insurance company Crown Life from 1944 until his retirement in 1983. Watson entered his first Manitoba Bonspiel in 1923. He curled with St. John's Club, before switching to Strathcona Club in 1931, where he remained throughout his competitive career. Watson is known for improving the slide delivery, after having discovered that sliding was easier if he removed the rubber sole of his shoe, which not only gave greater distance but also helped balance. This technique became known as the "Winnipeg Slide."

Using this improved long slide, Watson went on to win 32 major bonspiels, including 7 grand aggregates, in 1939 and consecutively between 1942-47. He had a career Brier record of 25 and 2, winning the Tankard in 1936, 1942 and 1949. Only 3 other curlers have matched Watson's number of wins. Watson was an important figure in the development of curling. In 1939, he established the first MB high school Bonspiel, and then helped organize the Canadian School Curling Championships. He was instrumental to the development of the Scotch Cup, forerunner to the World Curling Championships. He wrote

instructional articles on curling for newspapers across the country, and wrote 4 books on curling, including *Ken Watson on Curling*, published in 1950, which sold 150,000 copies. He was inducted into the Canadian Sports Hall of Fame in 1969, and the Canadian Curling Hall of Fame in 1973. In 1978, he was the first recipient of the World Freytag Award, given by the World Curling Federation. Watson was awarded the Order of Canada in 1975. ● MD

WAWANESA, pop 516, is a village 30 km SE of **BRANDON** along the **SOURIS RIVER** near its junction with the **ASSINIBOINE RIVER**, and on hwy 2. European settlers, predominantly **ENGLISH** and **SCOTS**, came to this region during the 1870s and 1880s. Wawanesa was previously called Sipiweske, "light through the trees," but was rechristened Wawanesa, either from an older Dakota name for the area meaning "place without snow," or from the **OJIBWAY** word for "whippoorwill." The Northern Pacific **RAILWAY** (later absorbed by **CNR**) and 2 grain elevators came here in 1890. **ALONZO FOWLER KEMPTON** (who enjoyed an occasional sipiweske) started Wawanesa Mutual Insurance Company, one of the biggest insurance companies in Canada, here in 1896. The company is still technically headquartered here, although the working headquarters are in **WINNIPEG**. Wawanesa incorporated in 1909, and absorbed much of the population of adjacent ghost towns such as Methven and Souris City. While the village's eponymous insurance firm is the largest employer, agriculture is Wawanesa's economic base. Among other ventures here is a recent geothermal home-heating station, the first in the province. Tourist attractions in and around the pretty village include the Sipiweske Museum; **CURLING** and harness races; and the **CRIDDLE**-Vane Homestead Provincial Park. ● GPP

WAWANESA INSURANCE, which includes the Wawanesa Mutual Insurance Company and Wawanesa Life Insurance Co., is one of Canada's largest insurance firms. Although its working headquarters are in **WINNIPEG**, the head office remains in the tiny southwestern village of **WAWANESA**. That's where the company got its start in 1896, when area resident **ALONZO FOWLER KEMPTON**, local farmer Alex Naismith, and 19 other farmers joined to create a new policyholder-owned insurance company that could provide affordable insurance coverage for their steam-powered threshing machines. As the company's list of policyholders grew, Wawanesa Insurance expanded its products to include coverage for homes, commercial dwellings, and automobiles. By the 1930s, it was selling insurance across

WEASEL

Wawanesa Mutual's Head Office, 1948

Canada, and in 1961, it expanded into life insurance with the formation of the Wawanesa Life Insurance Co. In 1974, Wawanesa also became the first Cdn general insurance company to enter the US market when it opened an office in San Diego, CA, to serve markets in CA and OR. Today, the company's Cdn insurance products are distributed by more than 1300 independent insurance brokers scattered through every province except QC, where products are sold through the company's own agents. In 2000, US rating firm A. M. Best Co. rated Wawanesa Mutual one of the top-5 property and casualty insurance providers in Canada. ● MURRAY MCNEILL

WAYWAYSEECAPPO FIRST NATION, on reserve pop 1337, off reserve pop 944, is situated on the SW corner of **RIDING MOUNTAIN NATIONAL PARK**, 144 km NW of **BRANDON** and 351 km NW of **WINNIPEG**. The native language here is **OJIBWAY**, and Treaty 4 was signed in 1874. Waywayseecappo is an independent First Nation; therefore it is not a member of any Tribal Council. Waywayseecappo First Nation administers its own schooling – Nusery-Grade 12, and total enrolment for the year 2003-04 was 403. Waywayseecappo First Nation includes 2 reserves: Waywayseecappo First Nation and Treaty Four Reserve Grounds No. 77. Waywayseecappo First Nation has all-weather road access. The community is made up of a very young population, with the majority of the residents under the age of 29, and only about 2% of the population over the age of 65. Waywayseecappo's economic base is agriculture. This First Nation runs the Waywayseecappo Gaming Centre, situated in the Birdtail valley, and the Waywayseecappo Inn, located in the First Nation community ● RK

WEAKERTHANS, THE, indie rock group, were formed in **WINNIPEG** in 1997 by guitarist/singer/songwriter John K. Samson and guitarist Stephen Carroll, both from Kelvin High School, and drummer Jason Tait. The Weakerthans emerged from the underground punk music scene that thrived in Winnipeg in the 1980s. Their debut album, *Fallow* (1997), was released on Propagandhi's G-7 label, with the band touring Europe twice in support of it. Bassist John Sutton joined for *Left and Leaving* (2000). The album was nominated for a Juno Award for Best Independent Recording, and won 2 Prairie Music Awards (for Independent Recording and for Video of the Year,

John K. Samson of the Weakerthans onstage at the Pyramid Cabaret

2001). Signing with US-based Epitaph Records, the more ambitious *Reconstruction Site* (2003) also earned a Juno nomination and featured their ironical anthem "One Great City" about Winnipeg. The album garnered rave reviews in the UK's *New Musical Express* and in *Playboy* magazine, and earned a Western Canada Music Award (2004). Sutton left the group in 2005. Samson also co-operates Arbeiter Ring, a left-leaning **BOOK PUBLISHER** based in Winnipeg. ● JOHN EINARSON

WEASEL is a carnivorous animal of the family Mustelidae with an ancient lineage arising 32 mya (Oligocene period), and well represented in MB with 10 species. Interestingly, they demonstrate different niches, habitats, and body sizes, which permit broad exploitation of their environments while helping to avoid direct competition. In the weasels proper, the males are about ⅓ larger than the females, which enables the pair to handle a considerable range of prey. With this significant overlapping of species' sizes, some specimens of weasels become hard to identify. The largest is the Long-tailed Weasel (*Mustela frenata*), weighing 225 g, and found in the prairie and aspen parkland of extreme SW MB. It is a relatively rare animal and little is known about its life history, although it likely differs little from its smaller relatives. It feeds on ground squirrels, rabbits, mice, birds, and other small creatures. The Short-tailed Weasel or Ermine (*Mustela erminea*), at 80 g is far-more common and occurs all across MB and indeed over most of the N Hemisphere. Like the other 3 weasels, it changes its brown summer coat to a white winter pelage, with only the black-tipped tail, nose and eyes remaining black. Its movements are fast and furious as it hunts – diving down mouse burrows, leaping over grass or boulders, and climbing into bushes. The Least Weasel (*Mustela nivalis*), at 45 g, is no bigger than the mice and shrews it preys upon, and in fact it is the world's smallest member of the order of Carnivores. It may be distinguished from the 2 larger weasels by its relatively short tail. It occurs all across the province (including city parks) in grassland, forests and tundra, and also most of Eurasia and even N Africa. Although seldom seen, it is present in most areas and contributes significantly to controlling populations of rodents.

The other members of MB's weasel family are not what most people would think of as related to weasels. They are the secretive American Marten (*Martes americana*), Fisher (*Martes pennanti*), and Wolverine (*Gulo gulo*) of boreal coniferous and mixed forests, the playful River Otter (*Lutra canadensis*) of the waterways,

733

Short-tailed weasels are found thoughout Manitoba.

ROBERT R. TAYLOR

W Mink (*Mustela vison*) of wetlands and rivers, American Badger (*Taxidea taxus*) of the prairies, and Striped Skunk (*Mephitis mephitis*), which ranges through prairie and forests almost to the treeline. Most of these well-known species are treated in detail under their names. The Black-footed Ferret (*Mustela nigripes*), at 575 g, is currently found on the short- and mixed-grass prairies of AB and SK and to the S in the US, but has never been recorded in MB, although it sometimes appears on faunal lists. It is feasible that during the warm-dry period of 5000 to 3000 years ago, this species may have expanded its range into the SW section of the province. It is among NA's most-endangered species, and is just now recovering in numbers through captive breeding and release programs led by zoos. It is dependant on several species of prairie dogs and ground squirrels for food and burrows. ● REW

WEATHER in MB, often a topic of conversation, varies from hour to hour, from day to day, and from season to season. Weather refers to the state of the atmosphere – heat or cold, wetness or dryness, calm or wind, clearness or cloudiness – and is measured by temperature, pressure, humidity, cloud cover, wind speed and direction, precipitation, and fog. In MB, extreme weather events, including **Blizzards**, **Thunderstorms**, and **Windstorms**, occur frequently. **Climate**, in comparison, refers to long-term patterns created by daily weather conditions.

Equipped with thermometers and barometers, employees of the **Hudson's Bay Company** made many of MB's earliest weather observations as the **Fur Trade** moved inland from the **Hudson Bay** coast. The Meteorological Service of Canada (MSC), established in 1871 as a dominion-wide weather survey system, began monitoring weather in 1872 at St. John's College (*see* **U of M**) in **Winnipeg**, 2 km N of the junction of the **Red** and **Assiniboine** rivers. James Stewart, the **Red River Settlement**'s first druggist, was making weather observations as early as 1871; soon after, the **Criddle Family** was keeping a similar log near **Wawanesa**.

For more than a century, weather observers measured and described current weather conditions. As the province continued to grow, so did the need for weather "probabilities" or forecasts. Produced by the MSC, the first official weather forecast for MB and the Northwest was published in the *Manitoba Daily Free Press* (later the *Winnipeg Free Press*) on Aug 26, 1891. On that day, residents were told to expect "winds west to north; a few local showers, but mostly fair, cool weather with a danger of frost."

Today, several organizations monitor and forecast the weather for agricultural purposes, transportation, flood forecasting, forest fire preparedness, and for other needs. Specialized monitoring and forecasting tools, including automated weather stations, lightning detection sensors, Doppler radar, and weather satellites, allow meteorologists to connect Manitobans with timely, meaningful weather information. Understanding weather, and being prepared for it, is key to living in the sometimes-harsh and notoriously variable climate of MB. ● SHELLEY PENZIWOL

WEIR, Walter C. premier, mortician (b Jan 7, 1929, High Bluff; d April 17, 1985, **Minnedosa**) had the shortest MB premiership of the 20th century, barely more than 2 years. He suffered the misfortune of representing rural conservative values at a time – the 1960s – when the province and the country were moving in radical and exciting new directions.

AM. PERSONALITY FILES

Walter Weir, 1969

Son of a grain buyer, Weir was educated in High Bluff and **Portage la Prairie**. In 1953, he moved to Minnedosa, where he owned a funeral parlour until 1963. Weir was active politically in Minnedosa, and became its **Progressive Conservative** MLA in 1959. He became minister of municipal affairs in 1961; of public works in 1962; and of highways in 1967. When the free-spending **Duff Roblin** resigned the premiership in 1967 to run for the federal party leadership, Weir – who was popular with his Cabinet colleagues because of his fiscal restraint – became the new party leader, and therefore premier, at a Nov convention.

Weir's govt fought reforms proposed by the federal Liberals, such as official bilingualism

Wind storms can be destructive episodes of Manitoba summers.

WINNIPEG FREE PRESS

and constitutional reform, and was also faced with controversy surrounding **Manitoba Hydro**'s proposed flooding of South Indian Lake, which would force the relocation of the area's **First Nations** community. Nonetheless, feeling confident after Tory victories in 3 of 4 by-elections, Weir called an early election in 1969, but was defeated by the **New Democratic Party** led by **Edward Schreyer**.

Weir maintained his seat but left politics in 1971 and moved shortly thereafter to ON, returning to Minnedosa in 1976. Though he served on several govt boards and committees under the govt of **Sterling Lyon**, he never ran for office again. He died at home in Minnedosa in 1985. Weir was the last of the rural-based premiers of MB that had long dominated provincial politics. ● R.G. ENFIELD

WELLS, John Hampson "Cactus Jack," sports broadcaster (b May 13, 1911, Moose Jaw, SK; d May 24, 1999, **Winnipeg**) was a pioneer in Cdn sports broadcasting. After his father's contracting business failed, Wells was forced to quit grade 8 to support the family. He moved to Saskatoon, where he worked as a clerk for the **CPR**. Though he had no experience in broadcasting, Wells applied for a job at a local radio station on a bet. He was offered the job and, by 1939, was a regular staff announcer. In 1941, Wells moved to Winnipeg where he worked at CJRC, later CKRC, covering the **Winnipeg Blue Bombers**. When

Jack Wells, 1959

Wells was given exclusive rights to the games at Osborne Stadium, he left CKRC to freelance his broadcasts. In 1954, at a time when TV sports broadcasting was still in its infancy, he signed a contract with CKY giving them exclusive rights to his broadcasts, and became the highest paid broadcaster in western Canada. Adopting the colourful name "Cactus Jack," Wells was one of the first nationally recognized sportscasters. His TV work ended in the 1970s, after which Wells moved to CJOB where he worked as a commentator well into his 80s. While covering Bomber football games, Wells came up with the "Happy Honker Award," where he would select a Blue Bomber player to be saluted by honking cars around the city. ● MD

WERBENIUK, William Alexander "Big Bill," professional snooker player (b Jan 14, 1947, **Winnipeg**; d Jan 20, 2003, Vancouver) found fame in the UK as a top snooker player, at one time ranking 8th in the world. His love for snooker, a billiards game similar to pool, developed at an early age while hanging out in Pop's Billiards, a Winnipeg gaming hall owned by his **Ukrainian** grandfather. By the age of 12, Werbeniuk was beating all the local champs at pool. He won his first NA snooker championship in 1973, and held the title until 1976. He then moved to the UK, where snooker is particularly popular, and lived out of a converted bus that he used to get to tournaments all over the country.

Werbeniuk became notorious for his heavy drinking during competitions, at one game famously downing 28 pints of lager and 16 whiskies over the course of 11 frames. He claimed the drinking alleviated hand tremors caused by a hereditary disease, and received a medical certificate approving his beer drinking, which allowed him to offset the cost of the alcohol against income tax. His irreverent sense of humour, beer drinking and snooker-playing antics made him popular with British fans. Extremely overweight, he once split his trousers along the backside seam while struggling to reach a ball on the table at a 1980 World Cup game. However, his weight did not prevent Werbeniuk from achieving status as a top snooker player; in 1982, Werbeniuk helped the Cdn team take the World Cup title. Werbeniuk retired from professional playing in the early 1990s over a dispute with the World Professional Billiards and Snooker Association about a banned prescription drug he was taking for his hand tremors. He returned to Canada, where heart problems eventually ended his life. ● MICHELLE DOBROVOLNY

WESLEY COLLEGE. *See* **University of Winnipeg**.

WEST, Michael, neurosurgeon, (b Aug 28, 1948, **Winnipeg**). West completed medical school at the **U of M** and proceeded to complete his surgical internship at the **Health Sciences Centre**. He specialized in neurosurgery and after his training he was awarded a Medical Research Council Fellowship and completed a PhD in physiology in 1980. In San Francisco, he studied brain and pituitary tumor surgery and went on to complete another fellowship in London, Ontario in cerebrovascular surgery. Further training in the area of pediatric neurosurgery took him to Chicago. He worked at Winnipeg's HSC from 1981-1996 and introduced computer-guided stereotactic surgery. After a 4-year period in Cleveland, OH, West was asked to return in 2000 to rebuild the Neurosurgery Program in Winnipeg. With $4.7 million, the Neuro program became one of the most advanced programs in NA. He has introduced more state-of-the-art technology, including the Gamma Knife (the Perfexion system) making Winnipeg the first in Canada to have this technology. West is author of over 55 scientific publications and is chair of the Specialty Committee in Neurosurgery of the Royal College of Physicians and Surgeons of Canada. ● RUTH DEGRAVES

WEST HAWK LAKE, about 140 km E of **Winnipeg** on the ON border, is one of the largest and most-visited lakes in **Whiteshell Provincial Park**. At 111 m, it is the deepest lake in MB. That and its clarity – as well as sunken curiosities, including a telephone booth and intentionally submerged bathtubs – make it a prime location for MB dive clubs and for businesses focused on scuba diving. The immediate area is also rich in mineral deposits. In fact, core samples from speculative lakebed drilling, beginning in 1965, spurred scientific research at the lake. Geologists believe a large **Meteorite** crashed here about 100 million years ago, causing a crater with a diameter of 2.4 km. The impression later filled with water, forming a lake 3.6 km across, believed to be caused either by the regression of **Lake Agassiz,** or by an ancient extension of nearby Lake of the Woods. The West Hawk Museum incorporates displays on this geological heritage. The lake is popular for cottage development, camping, **Sport Fishing**, hiking, and related recreational activities. The terrain is characteristic of the Canadian Shield (*see* **Physiographic Regions**). ● JOEL TRENAMAN

WEST NILE VIRUS. *See* **Insect Control**.

WESTEEL LIMITED is one of Canada's oldest agricultural companies and among the world's largest manufacturers of steel-sided grain bins and other steel storage tanks. Its round, yellow-topped Westeel-Roscoe grain bins have become a fixture on the Cdn Prairies and can be found in farmyards as far away as Australia and New Zealand. Founded in **WINNIPEG** in 1905 by W. J. McMartin, the company was initially called Winnipeg Ceiling and Roofing Company. Its building products were used in such landmark buildings as the Banff Springs Hotel and Toronto's Maple Leaf Gardens. It wasn't until the 1920s that the company began making steel-sided grain bins. In the ensuing years, a variety of other steel products were added to its burgeoning product list, including road culverts, road signs, metal garages, and storage tanks for holding substances such as fertilizer, seed, sand, and fuel and other petroleum products.

After the acquisition of a rival steel grain-bin manufacturer, Roscoe Metal Products, in the mid-1960s, the company's primary focus became the production of storage tanks for agricultural and industrial uses. Over its history, the company has changed names and owners a few times. It became Western Steel Products Limited in 1921, which was later shortened to Westeel Products Limited and then to just Westeel. In 1980, Toronto-based Jannock Limited acquired a majority stake in the company. Three years later, it amalgamated its road construction-drainage division with Armco Canada Ltd., and 3 years after that, it merged its building products, farm roofing, and siding division with ON-based Vic Metal Inc. to form Vic West Steel Inc. That allowed the company to focus solely on producing steel storage products, and in 1990, it began marketing its storage products around the world. By 2005, it had sold more than 500,000 of its grain bins worldwide. In 2003, the company became a wholly owned subsidiary of Oakville, ON-based Vicwest Corporation. In addition to its 12,100-m² plant in Winnipeg, the company has production facilities in Regina, Saskatoon, and Olds, AB, as well as distribution centres in St-Simon, QC, and Fargo, ND. ● MURRAY MCNEILL

WESTERN CANADA AVIATION MUSEUM

(WCAM), a charitable non-profit organization incorporated in 1974, grew at the hands of 6 founding members, including Gordon Charles Emberely, to one of Canada's largest aviation museums. WCAM is 1 of 6 provincially designated "Special Theme" museums, and has the best collection of bush aircraft in the world. The 24 or more aircraft regularly on exhibit reflect the history of aviation development in MB and Canada. Examples range from bush planes to transport, military, and commercial craft, such as the most complete 46-passenger Vickers Viscount in the

Vintage Viscount aircraft at the Western Canada Aviation Museum

world. WCAM also houses many unique aircraft, such as Canada's first helicopter (built in MB by the **FROEBE** brothers); the Avrocar ("flying saucer"); a replica of the Junkers JU-52/1M ("Flying Boxcar"); the Vickers Vedette Flying Boat; and the Fokker Super Universal. WCAM has one of the largest aviation library/archival holdings in Canada and the largest photographic collection of Cdn women in aviation, and other holdings, such as the **BLACK BRANT** rocket made in **WINNIPEG** by **BRISTOL AEROSPACE**; aircraft models; and aviation-themed paintings. WCAM's current site at Winnipeg International Airport is the original 1938 **TRANS CANADA AIR LINES** (later Air Canada) operational headquarters and base. It is 8450 m² (91,000 ft²), including 3715 m² (40,000 ft²) of exhibit space, a gift shop, an interactive children's area, restoration shops, observation "Flight Deck," multi-purpose rooms, and exhibits/photo/library/archives workshops. Over 200 volunteers are involved in every aspect of the museum. Income is generated mainly by the museum's internal efforts. WCAM offers tour guides, travelling exhibits, and programming such as the Take Flight Education Program and Summer Camps. ● SHIRLEY RENDER

WESTERN GLOVE WORKS LTD. is a privately owned, **WINNIPEG**-based firm that designs and manufacturers blue jeans and other cotton clothing. The firm was founded in 1921 by the grandfather and 3 great uncles of the current generation of owners, which include 2 sets of brothers – Bob and Michael Silver and their cousins, Don and Norm Stern. As its name suggests, Western Glove started by making work gloves. However, in the early 1950s, it switched to making jeans and cotton clothing such as double-knit slacks and leisure suits. It wasn't until the 1970s, when jeans

went from being work apparel to fashion apparel, that Western Glove's sales took off. In addition to making private-label brands for a variety of other companies, the firm began designing and manufacturing its own brand of jeans, Ziggy. In 1988, it acquired an ON company that owned the Cdn rights to produce Wrangler and Calvin Klein jeans, and it began making those as well.

Today, Western Glove still makes private-label brand jeans for other companies, though it no longer owns the Cdn rights to Wrangler or Calvin Klein. As well, it designs and manufacturers 3 of its own upscale brands of jeans – Silver, Jag, and 1921 – which it sells throughout Canada, the US, Japan, and Europe. In 2007, it announced a deal to make a new brand of high-end jeans endorsed by ex-Spice Girl Victoria Beckham. Although it used to make all of its products in Winnipeg, the bulk of Western Glove's manufacturing is now done in lower-cost developing countries such as Mexico, China, and Bangladesh. As a result, its Winnipeg staff has declined from a peak of nearly 1300 to about 280 in 2005. Remaining staff performs mainly head-office and corporate functions, such as administration, merchandising, and marketing. Although the Winnipeg facility also continues to produce small quantities of clothing, it is used primarily as a test-marketing facility, or to produce items the company needs to get to market in a hurry. ● MURRAY MCNEILL

▸ *See also* **GARMENT INDUSTRY**.

WESTMAN is 1 of 8 MB regions named by the provincial govt. There are 38 rural municipalities within the district, which is in the SW corner of the province, S of **PARKLAND**, and W of **CENTRAL PLAINS** and **PEMBINA VALLEY**. The area also borders SK to the W and ND to the S. The **ASSINIBOINE**

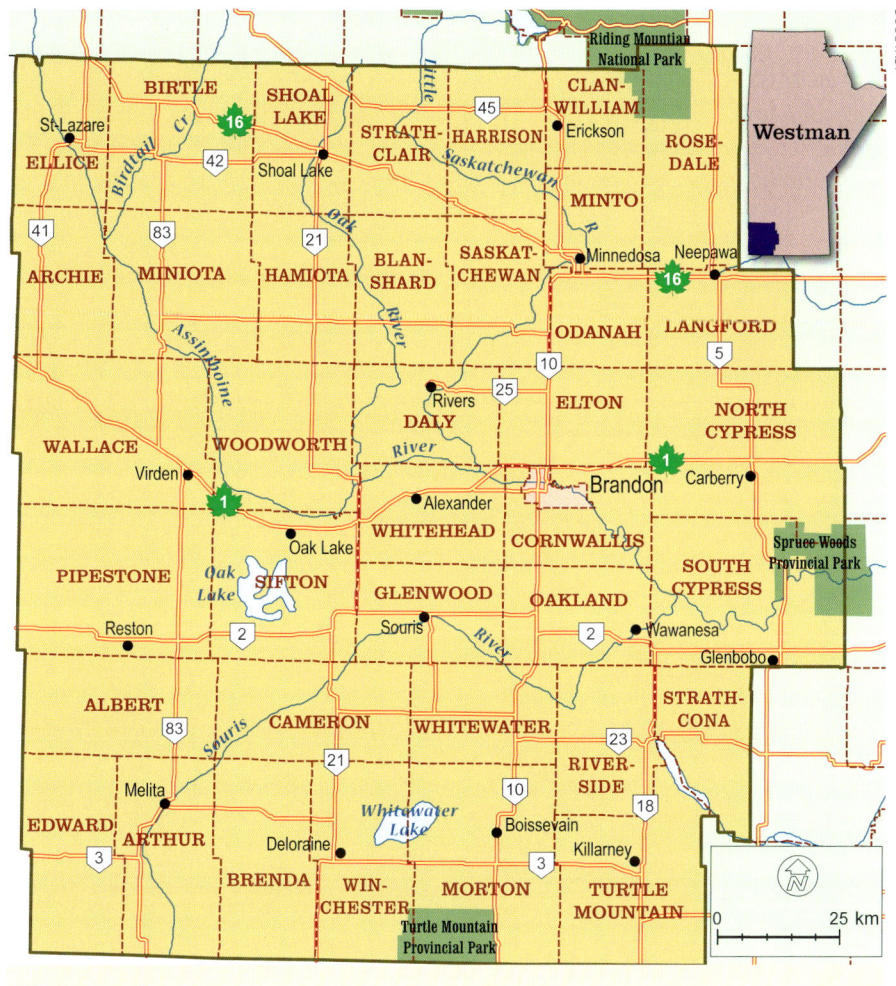

Westman region

Westman

SHILO and an Internet pharmacy in Minnedosa are important employers. Rising oil prices have led to increased exploration and production in the Virden area. The provincial govt is focused on promoting the construction of biodiesel and ethanol plants in the area. • JOEL TRENAMAN

WETLANDS have 3 main characteristics: (1) persistent water, usually less than 2 m deep, so the soil is saturated for some portion of the plant growing season; (2) soils whose chemistry reflects low oxygen levels due to water saturation; and (3) plants with specific adaptations that allow them to thrive in these water and soil conditions. Within this definition, 5 primary types of wetlands occur in MB. Two types, bogs and fens, are characterized by at least 30 cm of peat (partially decomposed plants and animals), whereas 3 types – marshes, swamps, and shallow open water – have little or no peat. Wetlands cover roughly 233,000 km², or about 41% of MB's land area, the highest percentage of any Cdn province. Over 90% of MB's wetlands are peatlands, ½ of which are underlain by permafrost, mostly in the northern part of the province above LAKE WINNIPEG and in the boreal forest (*see* ECOCLIMACTIC REGIONS) along the E side of the lake.

Bogs are wetlands that receive their entire water supply from rainfall and snowmelt, so they tend to have low nutrients and productivity, characterized by mosses and, if some cases, small, stunted trees and shrubs. The high acidity in many bogs retards decomposition, producing deposits of peat that may be several m deep in the S of the province. In practice, peat is non-renewable as its rate of growth is typically 1 mm a year. Commercial peat harvesting occurs in southeastern MB. In northern parts of the province, the shifting of ice buried in the peat leads to the formation of large polygonal tiles on the landscape, the tiles being separated by shallow moats of water that thaw during the short summer. Bogs are found throughout northern MB, and in a few isolated locations in southern Manitoba.

Fens are peatlands that, unlike bogs, are in contact with groundwater. Consequently, they tend to be less acidic, and higher in nutrients and productivity. Their vegetation consists of grass meadows, shrubs, and trees. Patterned fens occur in northern Manitoba where groundwater flow leads to the creation of shallow water pools (flarks) separated by narrow uplands (strings). Fens are found throughout central and northern MB, and in some parts of southeastern MB.

Swamps are wetlands where the dominant vegetation consists of deciduous or coniferous trees. The tree species are tolerant of periodic flooding so they tend to grow slowly. Swamps are

and SOURIS rivers flow E across Westman, but there are few lakes to be found here compared to other regions of the province. The landscape is mostly flat, except for the slight elevations of the MANITOBA ESCARPMENT and gentle river valley depressions. At 27,000 km², the area is about the same size as Parkland, but has more than double the population (about 103,000 in 2001). KILLARNEY, MINNEDOSA, NEEPAWA, and VIRDEN are regional hubs, but BRANDON, MB's "Second City," is the focal point. First Nations communities include GAMBLER, KEESEEKOOWENIN, ROLLING RIVER, BIRDTAIL SIOUX, SIOUX VALLEY, and CANUPAWAKPA DAKOTA.

For thousands of years, Assiniboine clustered along the river of the same name, hunting BISON and foraging. DAKOTA were also present farther S. Following the 1872 *Dominion Lands Act* and treaties with Aboriginal groups signed during the 1870s, a flood of IMMIGRANTS began to arrive W of the RED RIVER SETTLEMENT/WINNIPEG. ENGLISH, SCOTS, and IRISH settlers from ON, as well as Americans, were the first to make the journey, and their descendants remain the majority in Westman today.

The regional economy remains rooted in AGRICULTURE, but has diversified over the past 2 decades. A hog-processing plant in Brandon is the single largest employer, although CFB

RURAL MUNICIPALITIES in Westman

Albert	Archie
Arthur	Birtle
Blanshard	Brenda
Cameron	Clanwilliam
Cornwallis	Daly
Edward	Ellice
Elton	Glenwood
Hamiota	Harrison
Langford	Miniota
Minto	Morton
North Cypress	Oakland
Odanah	Pipestone
Riverside	Rosedale
Saskatchewan	Shoal Lake
Sifton	South Cypress
Strathclair	Strathcona
Turtle Mountain	Wallace
Whitehead	Whitewater
Winchester	Woodworth

relatively rare in MB, being found in west-central MB, west of **Lake Winnipegosis**, and in southeastern parts of the province.

Marshes are non-peat-forming wetlands where the dominant vegetation consists of mixtures of reeds, rushes, or sedges that emerge from the water, and "pondweeds" and other plants living underwater. Marshes are found throughout MB, but are especially numerous in southern parts of the province. Southwestern MB contains numerous depressions formed during the last glaciation that have since filled with water. These "pothole" marshes are mostly small (less than 60 ha) and shallow (less than 2 m). Their water budgets are dominated by evaporation, precipitation, and surface runoff. They vary from ephemeral basins, which are wet for only a few weeks in the spring, to permanent basins that lack water only in severe drought years. More-permanent basins typically support an abundant assemblage of emergent and submersed plants, which provide food and nesting and staging habitat for migratory **Waterfowl**, as well as amphibians, small **Fish**, and furbearing **Mammals**.

Coastal marshes are associated with lake boundaries. There are numerous coastal marshes in MB, by virtue of the many **Lakes** in the province, especially the "Great Lakes." Two of the largest coastal marshes in NA are in MB – **Netley-Libau Marsh**, at the S end of Lake Winnipeg, and **Delta Marsh**, on the south end of **Lake Manitoba**. Coastal marshes provide spawning and nursery habitat for commercially important fish species that eventually disperse into the lakes. They also provide spring and fall aquatic **Bird Migration** and staging habitat, particularly for waterfowl. Coastal marshes are often the initial sink for terrestrial runoff and eroded soil, as well as human-created wastes such as pesticides, metals, fertilizers, acids, and domestic and industrial sewage.

The shallow open water wetland type, sometimes known locally as ponds or sloughs, are standing bodies of water where there are few, if any, emergent plants, though submersed plants and algae may occur. They are usually shallower than lakes. They are found on the lowlands adjacent to Hudson Bay and in southwestern MB.

MB wetlands have long been perceived as worthless. However, scientific evidence now points to their numerous ecological and economic benefits. In the **Red River Valley**, for instance, wetlands comprised over 11% of the land cover in the 1870s and only about 0.1% in the mid-1990s. This loss occurred because of intensive **Agriculture**, in which wetlands were drained to provide farmland (*see* **Oak Hammock Marsh**). Runoff from spring snowmelt now occurs more rapidly,

so that floods are shorter but crest higher, causing more catastrophic damage. The retention of water on the landscape for longer periods reduces the extent and severity of soil erosion and limits input of soil-associated nutrients and other chemicals into water. Gradual seepage of water from wetlands into the ground recharges aquifers, which provide water for consumption and irrigation in much of southern Manitoba. Abundant plant growth in wetlands provides food for animals, and wetlands are home to many endemic and endangered species. The attraction of wildlife to wetlands enhances local aesthetics and property values, and provides opportunities for recreation and education. Wetlands are able to break down environmental pollutants because of their high biological activity. Artificial wetlands are therefore being created in MB to remove nutrients, sediments, pathogens, and contaminants from wastewater. Finally, peatlands and, possibly, other wetlands store more carbon that they release, so they can help mitigate climate change due to accumulation of greenhouse gases in the atmosphere.

Agriculture, including **Drainage**, peat harvesting, and livestock grazing, most commonly causes wetland damage in MB. Other threats to wetlands include invasion by exotic species such as common carp (*Cyprinus carpio*) and purple loosestrife (*Lythrum salicaria*); alteration of natural flow patterns and vegetation cover by dredging, water level management, and large-scale forestry; residential and industrial expansion leading to wetland drainage; and melting of permafrost under northern peatlands due to climate change and reservoir construction for **Hydroelectric** power development. Wetlands have no formal protection status in MB, although 2 well-known wetlands, Delta Marsh and Oak Hammock Marsh, have been designated as "Wetlands of International Significance" under the global Ramsar Convention largely for their importance in providing habitat for waterfowl.

● GORDON GOLDSBOROUGH / DALE WRUBLESKI

WHALE is a marine mammal in the order Cetacea. Whales in MB may come as a surprise to some readers, considering that the S of the province lies at the very centre of NA. However, the NE corner of MB boasts an Arctic Marine Ecosystem in **Hudson Bay**, which receives influxes of fauna and flora from Arctic and Atlantic waters. While no whales over-winter in ice-covered regions of the bay, the arrival of spring brings in several species of migrating whales. The **Beluga** or White Whale (*Delphinapterus leucas*) spends the summer along MB's coasts and estuaries, while the Bowhead (*Balaena mysticetus*) and

Orca or Killer Whale (*Orcinus orca*) regularly enter N Hudson Bay and on occasion migrate as far S as MB. There is even a 1990 record of a stray Minke Whale (*Balaenoptera acutorostrata*) at Button Bay near Churchill. The Narwhal (*Monodon monoceros*) population in N Hudson Bay is estimated at 1800, and while there are no records of its occurrence along the MB coastline, it likely has appeared here on occasion and could turn up in the future. Several dead specimens have been carried in the current S to the Ontario coastline.

Bowhead Whale is a large (17-20 m and 60-100 tonnes), bluish-black, slow-swimming whale of Arctic waters. The skull is a massive 5 m long and the tail flukes measure 8 m wide. The animal's huge bulk confers several advantages for living in frigid water – storing oxygen for long dives, accumulating extra blubber for insulation and energy reserves, and providing a low surface-to-volume ratio, which reduces heat loss. The 6-m-long mouth holds a huge tongue and about 720, 3-4-m-long, narrow whalebone or baleen plates (made of keratin like our nails), which are used to strain zooplankton (mainly copepod crustaceans) and small fish from the water. To concentrate this fine food, the whale swims upward in ascending circles while releasing air from the lungs, creating a spiralling curtain of bubbles that concentrates the zooplankton. During the brief summer period of abundant food supplies, the whale processes 1000-2500 kg of food per day. A 4-m-long calf is born about every 3 years in early spring, a year after mating. Sexual maturity is reached in 20 years, and the potential life span is well over 200 years, making it by far the longest-living vertebrate animal in the province. Inuit, American and European whalers sought the Bowhead for its oil (processed from the blubber), baleen, and meat. Commercial whalers reported killing 572 Bowheads from NW Hudson Bay from 1765 to 1915, almost exterminating the species from these waters..

Orca or Killer Whale traditionally migrates into N Hudson Bay in small numbers each summer to feed on seals, Beluga and fish. One individual was photographed and shot in 1978 in Baker Lake, Nunavut, and occasional sightings exist further S along the coast to Churchill, and along the QC coast of Hudson Bay. It was likely more common before the advent of commercial hunting and human disturbance. Interestingly, there are observations by fishers and scientists that Orcas are on the increase (about 30 individuals in recent years) in Hudson Bay, probably due to the decreasing Arctic ice and longer ice-free-season in the Bay from global warming. This strikingly patterned black and white species reaches a maximum of 9 m for males and

7.7 m for females. The dorsal fin of males can be 1.8 m high, and it often folds to one side. Maximum weight is around 8000 kg. Both sexes reach sexual maturity by 15 years. Mating occurs from May to July and the female produces a calf about every 5 years (gestation 12-17 months). Life expectancy is 30 years for males (max 50) and 50 years (max 80) for females. Sadly, there are probably fewer than 200 Orcas left in all Canadian waters. They are susceptible to pollution, loss of food resources from human overfishing, disturbance, accidents (entrapment in nets and oil spills), and formerly overhunting.

● REW, DBS, FOC

▸ *See also* **BELUGA**.

WHEAT had its beginnings in MB when the Selkirk Settlers arrived in 1812. They sowed wheat they brought with them from UK along the **RED** and **ASSINIBOINE** rivers. They were the first people to plant wheat in the West. However, those early years of farming were difficult. After the mid-1800s, the early farmers abandoned the soft White Russian and Club varieties for Red Fife, which was more suited to the Prairies. Red Fife was seen as the wonder wheat of the country. And MB became the king of the wheat-producing Prairies. By 1890, wheat acreage yielded 10 million bushels.

HISTORY: In the early years, the amount of wheat grown barely exceeded local demand. The export economy began on Oct 21, 1876, when the first shipment of wheat from western Canada left **WINNIPEG** by Red River steamer. Bound for Toronto were 857 bushels of Red Fife at 85 cents per bushel, for use in ON as seed. In 1879, the **CPR** reached Winnipeg and wheat immediately began to flow E to the Lakehead and Montreal. In 1884, the first export of wheat by an all-Canadian route left Brandon. One thousand bushels of Red Fife travelled by rail to Port Arthur, by lakeboat to Owen Sound, by rail to the E coast and then by ship to Glascow, Scotland. The entire journey took 21 days. The burgeoning wheat economy was intrinsically tied to **IMMIGRATION**. In 1896, 17,000 immigrants arrived in the West, the next year 32,000. Many were from the US where Canada had opened 9 offices and displayed the hard wheat that had been grown with relative success on the Prairies. Soon MB became a big wheat-producing province, and in 1887 the **WINNIPEG GRAIN EXCHANGE** was established. Millions of bushels of wheat were traded daily, and the city became internationally known as a NA commodity center.

By the end of WWI, MB and the rest of western Canada had become the "bread basket of the British Empire." In the last half of the 1920s, the

CHARLES SHILLIDAY

Wheat field west of La Riviere

area of improved land on the Prairies increased to 25 million ha and wheat production was between 300-500 million bushels a year, 40% of the world's export market. The wheat economy brought employment and benefit to Canadians far beyond farm fields – jobs in the railways, lake and ocean shipping, elevator operation, milling, baking, banking, administration, manufacture of farm machinery and other essentials, distribution, sales. The wheat economy was well established in a complex structure of grain production, handling, and grading systems when the **GREAT DEPRESSION** of the 1930s hit. The federal govt and the Cdn people were forced to reconsider their reliance on the competitive market for agricultural exports. And the demand for Cdn wheat fell even further as Hitler's armies invaded former customers. The land continued to produce – 1942 saw the biggest wheat crop ever at 550.7 million bushels. However, the golden years of Canada's wheat economy were over.

WHEAT STRAINS: Despite its success, Red Fife was not early maturing, and fell victim to early frosts and disease like smut, which fills the kernel with black dust. The country's scientists searched for varieties more suitable to the prairie climate. At the Agassiz experimental farm in BC, plant scientist Percy Saunders crossed Red Fife in 1882 with various imported early-ripening varieties, including an Indian parent, Hard Red Calcutta. From a single head of this cross, the descendant Marquis was isolated in 1903 in Ottawa and proven in 1907 at the Brandon experimental farm. Exhibiting Marquis seed in New York, SK grower Seager Wheeler was crowned "World Wheat King" in 1911, projecting the new wheat strain into the limelight. But Marquis

was unstable, tending to revert to type. Wheeler developed a stable strain he named Marquis 10B, probably not realizing how important it would be to development of the West, and to the pocketbooks of the East. Marquis 10B became the dominant Canadian wheat and remained so until after WWII. In the 1930s, the first rust-resistant wheat varieties were developed: Thatcher (which would end the era of Marquis domination), Apex and Renown. Their significance to western wheat-growing equalled the development of Marquis 2 decades earlier. Newer varieties of winter wheat, sown in the fall and then emerging from dormancy, have also become more popular. Durum wheat, used for pasta or couscous, is grown in the hotter, drier climate of SW MB. Though drought and early frost conditions on the Prairies present challenges for grain production, the long days, cool nights and relatively dry climate are ideal to produce high-quality hard red spring wheat. The strong gluten and high protein in this type of wheat are ideal for high-rising NA-type breads, and overseas buyers often buy hard wheat to blend with their softer domestic varieties. Western Canada is justified in claiming it grows the world's best wheat. Records of the 54 world championship competitions held from 1911 to 1968 show that Cdn exhibitors won the top title 49 times; western Canadian exhibitors, 48 times, including MB's Samuel Larcombe from Birtle, in 1917.

In the early 21st century, wheat remained a dominant crop for MB farmers, although in 2004 farmers earned $597 million from canola compared to $540 million for wheat. The repeal of the **CROW'S NEST** subsidy also resulted in more specialty crops being grown. In 2007, wheat

W

acreage was down 10% from the previous year to its lowest level in 37 years. Wheat is still important in MB, but the days of wheat being "king" are over. • JIM SHILLIDAY/JOHN MORRISS

▸ *See also* **CANADIAN WHEAT BOARD**.

WHITE BIRD, Dennis, politician (b **ROLLING RIVER FIRST NATION**). An educator for 7 years before entering politics, White Bird served as chief of Rolling River 1980-98. During his tenure, he was able to negotiate a **TREATY** for his First Nation with the provincial and federal govts, gaining 19,000 ha (46,950 ac) of land. He moved on to become Assembly of First Nations regional chief (1998-2000), working on treaty issues and measures to protect Aboriginal languages. White Bird was elected grand chief of the **ASSEMBLY OF MANITOBA CHIEFS** (AMC) in Aug 2000. He joined the opposition to PM Chrétien's controversial legislation, Bill C-19 (*Fiscal Relations Act*) and to the *First Nations Governance Act* (Bill C-7). He resigned from the AMC in May 2005 to take the lead role at the Manitoba Treaty Relations Commission, an independent organization mandated to improve research and public education on treaty issues and to facilitate discussion or negotiation. • JT

WHITE BUFFALO is a Plains Bison (*Bison bison bison*) and a member of the cattle family Bovidae. While normally dark brown, reddish, or black, white individuals have been known from the past and several are currently alive. Exceedingly rare, a white buffalo may arise from several genetic factors. An albino lacks the ability to produce the dark pigment melanin and consequently the skin and eyes appear pink. Albino buffalos usually die after a few years, evidence of other physiological problems. A few individuals have been reported that are born white and remain so, usually showing some honey colour on the shoulders and head. Since the few surviving Bison herds in the 1800s were exposed to cattle and occasionally interbred, there is also the possibility that a buffalo may be born white from carrying cattle genes. In March of 2006, the **ASSINIBOINE PARK ZOO** acquired a male white buffalo calf named Blizzard from a large herd in the United States. This rare animal was added to the collection due to its great significance to local First Nations and Métis peoples. The symbolism of the white buffalo began over 2000 years ago among the Lakota People of the N Plains, with the appearance of the White Buffalo Calf Woman. This legend tells of a benevolent spirit in the form of a White Buffalo calf, which changed into a young maiden. Visiting the village to offer gifts, teachings, prayers,

and a ceremonial pipe, she promised to return someday to rejuvenate the people's spirituality. She departed the village and rolled over on the ground, turning progressively into a brown, red, yellow, and finally a white calf. • REW

WHITEMOUTH, pop 170, is a community 85 km E of **WINNIPEG**, on the Whitemouth River, at hwy 11/44, and on the **CP** main line. A post office opened here in 1880, and the railway came in 1919. The current economy centres on farming, with Whitemouth acting as a service and retail centre for nearby agricultural operations. Tourist attractions in the area include a municipal museum, and outdoor visitors pass through on their way to Whiteshell Provincial Park (just E of here) and to several nearby **PROVINCIAL FORESTS**. The Whitemouth River, after which the community is named, is also a tourist draw, offering good whitewater rafting, kayaking, and canoeing. **CHARLOTTE ROSS**, the first female doctor in MB, lived here 1881-1912, and a local monument commemorates this. Annual events in the community include Sports Days, Heritage Days, curling bonspiels, Christmas craft sales, flea markets, Homecoming Week and a Gospel Music Jamboree. • GPP

WHITESHELL PROVINCIAL PARK, in E MB, is characterized by more than 2700 km² of protected lakes, rivers, and Precambrian Shield (*see* **GEOLOGY** and **PHYSIOGRAPHIC REGIONS**). The park offers some of the finest hiking trails in the province. "Whiteshell" is believed to come from the small white cowrie or "Megis" shells found in the area, which **OJIBWAY** teachings say breathed life into the first human. Rock alignments called **PETROFORMS**

in the park are a major attraction. These rock formations occur in the shape of snakes, turtles, humans, and various geometric shapes. The builders and the first people to use the petroforms have not been identified, though it is believed that an Algonquin-speaking people from whom the Ojibway are descended made them. These petroforms were used as part of healing rituals that are still performed by Ojibway.

ARCHAEOLOGY shows that the area was inhabited as long ago as 6000 BC. Europeans, members of **LA VÉRENDRYE**'s expedition, first arrived in Whiteshell in 1733. This marked the beginning of the **FUR TRADE** era. The discovery of gold near Keewatin in the early 1900s sparked a wave of activity in the area, just as Manitobans started to appreciate Whiteshell's potential as a recreational area. The first summer cottages were built in the **WEST HAWK**, **FALCON LAKE**, Nora Lake, and Florence Lake areas in the 1920s. These areas attracted the most interest, as they could be accessed from passing trains. Jurisdiction over the province's natural resources was transferred to the MB govt in 1930. A year later, the province established the Whiteshell Forest Reserve.

The development of roads marked the beginning of a new era for the Whiteshell. Road construction took place as part of the govt's initiatives during the **GREAT DEPRESSION**. The roads in the Whiteshell were built for access but also to support firefighting efforts. In 1961, a **PROVINCIAL PARK** was created for recreational use and to preserve the Manitoba Lowlands **PHYSIOGRAPHIC REGION**. In the autumn, most vacationers leave the park and the **WILD RICE** that fills the lakes and banks of the Whiteshell River is harvested.

Peaceful scene along the Whiteshell River

The rice is harvested as a person poles a canoe through the rice field while a 2nd bends the stalk into the canoe and knocks the ripe grains off with a picking stick. Whiteshell Provincial Park is also popular in the winter for snowmobiling, snowshoeing, and cross-country skiing. • JILL SEXSMITH

WIEBE, Armin, author, teacher (b 1948, **ALTONA**). An instructor in creative writing at **RED RIVER COLLEGE** in **WINNIPEG**, Wiebe taught for many years in schools throughout MB and the NT, and has served as writer-in-residence in Saskatoon and **DAUPHIN**. He is a founding member of the MB Writers' Guild. Wiebe's first novel, *The Salvation of Yasch Siemens* (1984), set in the fictional **MENNONITE** village of Gutenthal, echoes the vocabulary and the rhythms of his characters' Plattdeutsch (Low German) speech patterns in a comic account of the Mennonite milieu; it was shortlisted for the Books in Canada First Novel Award, and the Leacock Medal for Humour. His 2nd and 3rd novels, *Murder in Gutenthal: A Schneppa Kjnals Mystery* (1991) and *The Second Coming of Yeeat Shpanst* (1995), return to the same engaging scene, as do some of his short stories. Wiebe's contact with First Nations culture during his teaching experience in the Tlicho (Dogrib) community of Lac la Martre, NT, provides the different background for his 2003 novel, *Tatsea*. A drama of survival in the Cdn subarctic of the 18th century, the book won the **MCNALLY ROBINSON** Book of the Year Award and the **MARGARET LAURENCE** Award for Fiction. • MILDRED GUTKIN

WIEBE, Cornelius W., country doctor, politician (b Feb 18, 1893, **ALTONA**; d July 12, 1999, **WINKLER**). Wiebe was educated at Wesley College (*see* **U OF W**), the **U OF M**, and the Manitoba Medical College, graduating in 1924. Wiebe began to practise medicine in Winkler in 1925 and did not officially retire until 1978. In this time, he delivered more than 6000 babies, often after journeys by sleigh to farm homes. He served as **LIBERAL** MLA for **MORDEN** and Rhineland 1932-36, the first **MENNONITE** in MB's **LEGISLATURE** and its longest-lived member. He founded Bethel Hospital in Winkler in 1935, also establishing a school for mentally challenged children there. Wiebe served on the Winkler School Board 1929-53, and was a life member of the province's Liberal Party. He was also involved in provincial medical organizations, serving as president of both the Manitoba College of Physicians and Surgeons (1945-46) and the Manitoba Medical Association (1952-53). Shortly before his death in Winkler in 1999, Wiebe was awarded the Order of Canada,

the oldest person so honoured. He was buried in Winkler. Wiebe is the subject of at least 2 profiles: Mavis Reimer's full-length biography *Cornelius W. Wiebe, A Beloved Physician: The Story of a Country Doctor* (Hyperion, 1983) and a shorter 1984 profile in the *Canadian Bulleton of Medical History* by C. Stuart Houston. • AJL

WILD RICE (*Zizania palustris* and *Z. aquatica*), or *manomin* ("good berry") in **OJIBWAY**, is an annual aquatic grass that grows in marshlands along the shores of rivers and streams, and in the shallows of calm **LAKES**. The nutty-tasting seeds are found in south-eastern MB, around the Great Lakes, and farther E in northern NA. It is the only "cereal" native to MB. *Z. palustris* grows in 2 main regions in MB: the eastern Whiteshell area (*see* **EASTMAN**), and NW of **THE PAS**. *Z. aquatica* occurs only in the former range. Both are mainly cultivated from natural bodies of water, usually by First Nations people who then sell the crop to wild rice companies. These companies, of which there were 8 in MB in 2006, then process the grain. Since the grains ripen throughout the season, crops must be picked as many as 8 times.

Wild rice, high in B-vitamins and amino acids, is a traditional food staple for the **CREE** and especially the Ojibway, who originally harvested it by hand, drying it over a fire before hulling the grain. These Algonquian groups also used the plant for medicinal purposes. Drying decreases water content from 60% to less than 10%, giving wild rice its distinctively dark colour. At the industry's peak in the 1980s, wild rice was valued at about $22/kg; as of 2006, prices had dropped to about $5/kg because of an increase in cultivated paddy rice in the US, the main export market. Japan and Western Europe also import large amounts of the foodstuff. Annual production depends on the stability of water levels, but MB generally accounts for 25% of Canada's wild rice crop. • MD

WILLIAMS, Esten Kenneth, lawyer, author (b 1889, Parkhill, ON; d April 28, 1970, Surrey, BC) was a MB chief justice. He was called to the ON bar in 1911, then came to **WINNIPEG**. During the **WINNIPEG GENERAL STRIKE**, he was a member of the **CITIZENS' COMMITTEE OF 1000**. After joining the Aikins law firm (later Aikins, MacAulay and Thorvaldson; *see* **JAMES ALBERT MANNING AIKINS**), Williams began teaching at the Manitoba Law School, later part of the **U OF M**, where he was known for his severe countenance. He helped draft the Canadian Bar Association's canon of legal ethics in 1920, and published a law textbook the following year that was used in virtually all Cdn law schools. In 1930, he drafted MB's

E. K. Williams, 1961

Highway Traffic Act, the first motor-vehicle statute in Canada, though he himself did not drive. He became a trustee at the Manitoba Law School in 1937. Williams was part of the committee that drafted new rules for the MB Court of King's Bench (*see* **JUDICIAL SYSTEM**) in 1939. He served as chief counsel for the Royal Commission on Espionage, which investigated the allegations of Soviet defector Igor Gouzenko, but his recommendations received criticism from civil rights activists. He was appointed chief justice of the MB Court of King's Bench in 1946. As a judge, he was known for his scholarly knowledge of the law and for his forensic abilities. He was a traditionalist, and introduced coloured gowns and sashes for judges in 1949. Between 1947-51, he oversaw 5 murder trials, sentencing all the convicted men to hang. He was made chair of the board of trustees at the Manitoba Law School in 1947. Ill health caused his early retirement in 1962. The law library at the U of M is named in his honour. • MD

WILLIAMSON, Dave, teacher, author (b July 18, 1934, **WINNIPEG**). Having earned a BA and a BEd at the **U OF M**, Williamson became advertising manager of The Bay (*see* **HBC**), and then joined **RED RIVER COLLEGE** in Winnipeg as an instructor in advertising, communications, and creative writing. Until his retirement, he worked as dean of business and applied arts at Red River.

He has also served from 1986-89 as president of the MB Writers' Guild, as well as chair of the Writers' Union of Canada in 1992-93. A freelance book reviewer and columnist, he has published a collection of short stories, *Accountable Advances* (1994), has written a play, *Anniversary* (1998) in collaboration with **CAROL SHIELDS**, and has co-edited *Beyond Borders: An Anthology of New Writing from Manitoba, Minnesota, Saskatchewan, and the Dakotas* (1992). He has published 4 novels: *The Bad Life* (1975), *Shandy* (1980), *Running Out* (1987), and *Weddings* (1992). His most recent publication, *Author! Author!* (2000), is a memoir of his encounters with famous writers who have influenced his work.
● MILDRED GUTKIN

WIND POWER. Often touted as a new eco-friendly "alternative" to fossil fuels, wind power is actually one of the oldest forms of energy to be harnessed for human use, early examples ranging from kites and sail boats to wind and **FLOUR MILLS**. Moreover, prior to the expansion of rural electrification systems that used **HYDROELECTRIC POWER**, small wind turbines were often the only source of electricity for remote MB farms.

Though an inexhaustible energy supply, wind power is subject to changing strength and

WINNIPEG FREE PRESS

Wind power turbines stand 80 m tall with 41 m blades, near St. Leon

seasonal variation, making it unsuitable to meet a continuous energy demand. When conventional reliance on hydrocarbons came into question as a result of the oil crisis of the 1970s, in addition to growing concern over pollution, the Cdn govt began considering wind power as a supplemental energy source. An experimental wind turbine was installed in **CHURCHILL** in 1981 as part of a federal program to test MB's capacity for wind power. Costs at the time were still largely prohibitive, however, and the province's first wind farm, wasn't established until 2005 at St. Leon (150 km SW **WINNIPEG**). Consisting of 63 turbines, standing 80 m-tall with 41 m-long blades, the privately-owned wind farm has a capacity of 99 MW, power that is purchased by **MANITOBA HYDRO** to be absorbed into the province's energy grid. The farm provides enough energy for approximately 41,000 homes.

MB will likely see several wind farms in the near future, with roughly 50 anemometers located throughout the province to determine ideal locations for future farms. The high cost of fossil fuel energy in northern MB makes wind power particularly attractive for this region. Wind farms, however, can present a fairly lucrative project for rural landowners throughout the province, bringing in additional wind-rights payments while interfering very little with agricultural usage of land. Manitoba Hydro is planning to have developed 1000 MW of wind power capacity in MB by 2010, though this number still represents just a fraction of the province's total energy needs. Canada's wind resources remain, as a whole, vastly under-exploited. ● MD

WINDSTORMS, including both tornadoes ("twisters") and straight-line winds, can be the most powerful and destructive kinds of **WEATHER** events to occur in MB. Tornadoes, named for their swiftly rotating winds, occur about 9 times per year in the province. The tornado season runs from April to Sept, with July being the month with the greatest frequency. Most common in southern MB, tornadoes have also been reported in boreal forest areas, over water, and even in the north. Damaging tornadoes in MB have included:

- **KILLARNEY**, Sept 10, 1942. An evening tornado struck during the midst of a promising harvest. In total, 7 homes and 16 barns were destroyed. Several people were injured, and cattle and horses were also injured and killed. **GRAIN** stooks were lifted from a field and later fell from the sky during heavy rain.
- **VITA**, June 19, 1955. Residents of Vita were out enjoying a late Sunday afternoon base-

ball game in their new ballpark when rain and hail forced cancellation of the game in the 7th inning. People scattered for shelter just in time. At 4:30 p.m., a violent tornado struck the community, almost wiping it off the map. Twenty homes, a store, garages, a school, and a church were destroyed. Amazingly, no one was killed.

- Rosa (15 km SE of **ST-MALO**), July 18, 1977. An evening tornado, so strong that it stripped trees of their bark and tore pavement from the highway, destroyed 3 farms near the community of Rosa. In one case, a homeowner and his wife were killed when their home was ripped from its foundation and carried several hundred m.
- Gull Lake, Aug 5, 2006. Farms, homes, cottages, and trailers were damaged or destroyed by a tornado that struck the Gull Lake area, several km E of the **BROKENHEAD OJIBWAY FIRST NATION**, on a busy long weekend. A lodge near Pointe du Bois on an island in the **WINNIPEG RIVER** system was completely demolished. Several people were injured, and one woman was killed.

Tornadoes that pass over lakes can pick up water, causing waterspouts. On Aug 8, 1984, several waterspouts were observed heading E across the S basin of **LAKE WINNIPEG**. As the waterspouts reached the shore, they disappeared into the clouds, and heavy rain fell for a brief period. No damage was reported from this wondrous display.

Straight-line windstorms, sometimes called derechos (from the Spanish for "straight") or plough winds, can also exhibit a destructive nature. Unlike tornadoes, which have relatively narrow paths of destruction, straight-line winds can cause damage over large areas with sustained wind speeds well in excess of 100 km/hour. The winds can also persist for an hour or more, making damage more severe due to both the strength and duration of the wind. Damaging straight-line windstorms in MB have included:

- **PORTAGE LA PRAIRIE**, June 23, 1922. Considered one of MB's worst windstorms, a wide area from Portage la Prairie to **WINNIPEG** experienced the wind's fury in the early hours of June 23rd. Numerous homes and businesses were destroyed, telephone poles and trees were snapped in half, and crops were cut off level with the ground. In some cases, fire played a role in the thorough destruction. Five people across southern MB were killed, with many more injured.
- **GROSSE ISLE**, Sept 5, 1996. Nineteen hydro towers toppled in an early morning straight-line wind event that travelled from **MARQUETTE** to East **SELKIRK**.

WINNIPEG FREE PRESS

Surveying the damage after a wind storm

W

Winnie and Harry Colebourn

In addition to toppling hydro towers, the wind damaged **TREES**, grain bins, and crops.

- **ELIE,** June 2007. The strongest tornado in Cdn history struck the town, but amazingly no-one was hurt.
  - SHELLEY PENZIWOL

WINKLER, pop 9106, is a city 100 km SW of Winnipeg on a **CPR** line, at the junction of hwy 32 and hwy 14, and 20 km N of the US border. Winkler is MB's 7th largest city and had among the fastest-growing populations in the province, expanding nearly 25% from 1991-2001 and another 14.6% from 2001-06. Originally part of the Western Mennonite Reserve, the area had its beginnings in 1874 when the area was settled by a mass migration of **MENNONITES** from Russia. Winkler is named for Valentine Winkler, a lumber entrepreneur and politician who convinced the CPR to build a spur line here in 1892. On April 7, 1906 Winkler was incorporated as a village.

In the 1950s, local leaders were worried about economic stagnation and set up an aggressive economic development corporation. That began a long period of supporting new business start-ups, such as trailer-maker Triple E and a number of light manufacturing companies. On April 7, 1954, Winkler reincorporated as a town; in April 2002, it became a city. In that year, Winkler saw a record 55 new businesses established. In the 21st century, the economy here is diverse, including strong manufacturing, finance, retail, and service components, mostly in support of local Mennonite **FARMS**. There are 4 industrial parks in

Winkler, with plans in 2006 for a 5th. In 2006, about 90% of all businesses in Winkler were established by local entrepreneurs. The city's population was broad, with 35 flags flying at Winkler's civic centre to represent a nationality of those making the city their home. The Thresherman's Museum, just W of town, and the annual Harvest Festival and Exhibition draw tourists to the city. Poet **DI BRANDT** was born here, and long-time area doctor **CORNELIUS W. WIEBE** spent most of his life in Winkler. ● GPP

WINNIE-THE-POOH, author A.A. Milne's legendary bear of 'very little brain,' is **WINNIPEG**'s most famous namesake. The British writer's honey-loving character was in fact named after a Cdn black bear called "Winnipeg" which was the hometown of her owner, Cpt Harry Colebourn. A veterinarian and member of the **FORT GARRY HORSE**, Colebourn was on a train from Winnipeg to Valcartier, QC, en route to WWI in Europe when he acquired the cub during a stopover near White River, ON. "On train all day. Bought bear $20," reads the Aug 24, 1914, notation in his diary. Colbourn purchased the cub from a hunter who had shot and killed her mother. The officer took Winnipeg (Winnie for short) with him to England. The orphan slept under his cot and quickly became a favourite among the men and eventually became the regiment's mascot.

When the troops were ordered to France, Colebourn decided to leave Winnie behind and entrusted her to the London Zoo, where she quickly became a hit with the zoo's visitors, including author Milne and his son Christopher Robin. When Colbourn returned from the war he decided to leave Winnie at the zoo. The bear continued to delight children of all ages until its death in 1934. Newspapers around the world

– including the **WINNIPEG FREE PRESS** – ran her obituary. Over the decades, however, Winnipeg forgot about its connection with the bear until it was rediscovered some 50 years after her death. Somewhat starved for positive tourism draws, Winnipeg now celebrates its connection with the world's most famous bear. A full-scale campaign is impossible, however, as long as the Disney Corp. zealously protects its copyright on Winnie images. Nonetheless, a bronze statue of Cpt Colebourn (his son Fred posed for it) stands near the entrance of **ASSINIBOINE PARK** and an oil portrait of Winnie-the-Pooh by original illustrator Ernest H. Shepard is on display in the park's pavilion, forever linking the famous bear to the city that provided her name. ● HEIDI GRAHAM

WINNIPEG (pop 633,451) is unique amongst Cdn cities, outside of Atlantic Canada, in that there is no counter-balancing community of comparable size in the province. Consequently, for many people, Winnipeg and MB are virtually inter-

changeable. This has sometimes led to resentment outside the city and a parochial view from within. Nonetheless, Winnipeg's relative isolation has resulted in a hardy self-reliance and a flourishing cultural scene. One of the city's main challenges is adjusting to its new role as a slow-growth city after years of trumpeting itself as "The Gateway to the West."

Portage and Main, 1882

EARLY HISTORY: Winnipeg was not incorporated until 1872. The earlier **Red River Settlement** was spread for many miles along the **Red** and **Assiniboine** rivers. The first settlers below the **HBC**'s **Upper Fort Garry** were newcomers to the Red River Settlement from ON. They were attracted by what was expected to be a booming community, especially after the North West was taken over by Canada. The first to build was **Henry McKenney**, who constructed a building on the edge of the **HBC** land reserve at the point where the tracks along the rivers intersected. This would later become the fabled corner of Portage and Main. The local newspaper *The Nor'-Wester* first included the name "Winnipeg" on its masthead on Feb 24, 1866, after **Lake Winnipeg**. The lake's name comes from the **Cree** for "murky waters."

By the time of the **Red River Resistance** in 1869, a little village had sprung up around McKenney's site. It consisted of a hotel and a few houses and huts, some of them dispensing alcoholic beverages and some providing a few rooms for lodgers. There was one small eating establishment run by a pensioner. Tradesmen also operated out of buildings which served as their homes. There was a watchmaker, harnessmaker, a sleigh builder, a tailor, 2 butchers, a baker, and a shoemaker. Walter Bown had a dental office from 1866. One house was occupied as a school by the Sisters of Charity, connected to the Oblate mission in **St. Boniface**. **Andrew McDermot** had put up a steam-mill, which served both as gristmill and sawmill. Three of the buildings served as churches on Sunday. **Methodist** missionary George Young and his family used their home for services. Knox Church, at the corner of present Portage and Fort, was used by the **Presbyterians**. The **Anglicans** employed Red River Hall, built by McDermot – which was a long building with several shops and a meeting hall

on the upper storey – although their cathedral was a few km downriver.

The village played a prominent role in the Resistance, serving as the administrative capital of Red River under **Louis Riel**'s provisional govt, and turning naturally into the capital of the new province of MB. A. G. B. Bannatyne in 1871 sold his home on McDermot Ave just east of Main St to the provincial govt for use as a Legislature. The building, a substantial log structure, burnt to the ground in 1873. As newcomers rushed into the province, virtually every day saw the founding of a new institution or the appearance of a new service. The residents first called for incorporation in February 1872, and the MB Assembly passed legislation to that effect in early 1873.

INCORPORATION, 1873-86: After incorporation, the city began to grow. There were 2 kinds of investors – private land entrepreneurs and the HBC – and a rivalry over the location of public buildings, which would influence business district development. The private investors won. The breakthrough came when Winnipeg interests won a struggle with Selkirk over the location of the railway crossing of the Red River. The federal govt gave the crossing to Winnipeg in April 1879, providing the city built the bridge. This decision led to the founding of the Winnipeg Board of Trade. Another struggle ensued over the bridge's location, and the winner was the North End, with the bridge being built at Louise St. Once this location was settled, the real estate boom of the early 1880s could begin. Toronto and Montreal money moved into Winnipeg, and sales of urban land were brisk in 1880 and 1881. In 1882, Upper Fort Garry was torn down by the HBC to make room for downtown residential development. A bust in 1882 bankrupted many, but the boom had defined the commercial district around Portage and Main and Market Square. Residential sections moved away from this area, and a residential class

structure began to emerge. Wealthier residents lived in the district developed by the HBC W of Fort St. and S of Portage, as well as in Fort Rouge, Armstrong's Point, and St. John's around the cathedral. A shantytown sprang up in the north end near the rail yard and the CPR depot, known as "New Jerusalem" or the "Foreign Quarter." Another area for the poor, this one of long standing, was on the flats around the Forks.

Manufacturers entered the city, led by the Ogilvie Mill in 1882 and the CPR shops in 1883. Wholesale distributors, mainly branches of eastern houses, flourished. This period saw the establishment of cultural amenities such as the Manitoba Club (1874), the Manitoba Scientific and Historical Society (1875), the Manitoba Curling Club (1876), and the U of M (1877). In that same year, both the Manitoba Law Society and the Manitoba College of Physicians and Surgeons were founded, and the Winnipeg General Hospital settled in a permanent site in 1883. A red-light district around Colony St was moved W of the city limits in the summer of that year. A Winnipeg regiment, the Royal Winnipeg Rifles, was founded by William Nassau Kennedy in 1883, and would serve at Batoche, SK, in 1885. A new city hall, a masterpiece of Victorian gingerbread, was completed in 1885. By 1886, Winnipeg had a population of about 25,000.

CHICAGO OF THE NORTH, 1886-1913: By 1886, many observers had begun referring to Winnipeg as the "Chicago of the North" because of the rapidity and extent of its growth. The years 1886-1913 were the glory years of Winnipeg. The rapidity of settlement in southern MB (and farther W) and the success of the cultivation of wheat inevitably made Winnipeg, with its rail links throughout the province and region, into the wheat marketing capital of the Cdn West. In 1885, William Van Horne had convinced the federal govt to introduce a new grading system for grain, and in 1887 the Grain and Produce Exchange was established. Within a year it had established a call market and within another year a western board of grain examiners. As well as serving as the marketer of grain, Winnipeg also became the centre of the Western wholesale trade, a position given a boost by a 15% discount given by the railways to goods shipped W by city firms. By 1890, 80 wholesale firms were doing business worth $15 million annually from their Winnipeg base. Winnipeg was part of "a mighty empire." It had a polyglot population, dominated by people of British stock from ON and the British Isles, who comprised the city's middle and upper classes. The "foreign element" made up the rest of the population. The elite consisted of no more than 400 people. The Manitoba Club catered to this small clientele. The

ENGLISH controlled the civil service, the SCOTS the police force, the IRISH the fire department. The non-Anglos were for the most part relegated to low status jobs in construction and in the railway shops, although a growing JEWISH community had rapidly become acculturated. There was residential segregation: the North End was foreign, except the St. John's area, while a "vestigial family compact" lived in the south and western parts of the city (Ward 2, around Dulnavert; Point Douglas, Winnipeg Centre, Armstrong Point).

The downtown was dominated by Chicago-style buildings, characterized by a dominant repetition of vertical arches and of recessed spandrel members. A rich cultural and artistic life had grown up, led by the Historical and Scientific Society of MB, which was an affiliate of the Royal Society of Canada and had been instrumental in founding the Winnipeg public library. The people of Victorian Winnipeg were joiners, belonging to secret societies and fraternal organizations, church groups, political party organizations, ethnic groups, sports clubs, and militia units. Some of these had female auxiliaries attached. The ethnic societies (St. Andrew's Society, the Sons of England, the Orange Lodges) had large memberships. Other organizations, like the Masons, were more exclusive. The Sons of England had 5 local lodges and was led by Anglican ministers. The Orange Lodge was proud of the fact that it (unlike other secret societies) was Christian; it fought for a national school system in MB. Enthusiasm for the monarchy was whipped up by ritual and procession. Sports were important, not least as a cultural link to the empire. As a mark of the compatibility of Cdn and Imperial, sports were both those of empire (CRICKET and RUGBY) and those of Canada (HOCKEY and LACROSSE).

Winnipeg had many churches and its social consciousness had not yet secularized. Winnipeg also had many denominations, but was dominated by Anglicans, Presbyterians, and Methodists. These churches all had strong mission outreaches to the newcomers and the aboriginals. Clergymen also were the local intellectuals. Like all Victorian cities, Winnipeg was fascinated by war. The city had supported Col GARNET WOLSELEY in the Sudan, fought Riel at Batoche, and was the home of 4 of Canada's 26 urban militia battalions in 1897. The 4 units were well-known and popular, frequently parading down city streets. Winnipeg also had a garrison feel. The drill hall and Fort Osborne Barracks were prominent landmarks. Military, school cadet, and boys' brigades trained regularly. On special Sundays, Winnipeg churches saw military uniforms and music. Most leading politicians held military offices. The local press kept the public informed of the wars of the empire. Duty in defence of the empire was the call, and it would in 1914 lead to a flood of enlistments for overseas service. After 1900, a huge influx of immigration to the city brought thousands of British, but even larger numbers from Eastern Europe who settled uncomfortably in the North End. The city more than tripled in population between 1896 and the Great War, and much local employment was generated building housing and business facilities for this expansion, including a range of large retail establishments such as EATON'S and the Hudson's Bay Company along Portage Ave. The building boom came to an end in the year before the war began.

THE WAR AND THE STRIKE, 1914-20: WWI returned prosperity and full employment to Winnipeg. Thousands of young men were taken out of the work force and put in Europe's trenches, while the city benefited to some extent from wartime demand for munitions and other weapons. The federal govt insisted on holding the line on wages, while the cost of living shot up substantially. Many in the ranks of organized labour opposed conscription in 1916 and 1917. A precursor of the WINNIPEG GENERAL STRIKE of 1919 occurred in 1918, when civic employees went on strike for higher wages and middle-class volunteers did their jobs until the strike was settled. The 1919 strike solved nothing, while making the many ethnic, social, and political divisions in the city painfully obvious. The psychological legacy of the strike on Winnipeg's residents was and is incalculable.

REACHING A PLATEAU, 1920-45: After a period of economic slowdown caused by the inability of Europe to be able to afford Canada's grain and raw materials, which led to the collapse of the markets in these commodities, prosperity returned to Winnipeg for the remainder of the 1920s. It was to some extent an artificial boom, created by an increase in personal consumption and indebtedness, but the era saw increased employment within the city in both the wholesale and retail sectors, as well as in manufacturing. JAMES A. RICHARDSON, who had come W in 1919 to take control of his family's Winnipeg operations, demonstrated what an imaginative and energetic entrepreneur could do when he opened Richardson Securities in 1925 and organized Western Canada Airways in 1926. Unfortunately, Richardson was virtually alone in providing innovative leadership within the city's business community; most Winnipeg businessmen were not interested in adventurous business opportunities, and the increasing external competition to the city from other forms of transportation besides railways and other Prairie cities became manifest when the international depression struck in 1930. For nearly a decade, Winnipeg became a city of unemployed workers who stood in line for various relief handouts and waited for work, which sometimes came. The contraction of the wholesale trade created hundreds of square metres of empty warehouse space which was never again filled, and the rundown seediness of the warehouse district slowly began to spread into other parts of the downtown area, which after 1926 (when the HBC's square-block-size department store was completed) experienced no new construction for many years. The closest new construction came to Portage Ave was on Vaughan St near the Legislative Building, where a new Civic Auditorium was built with public funds in the

By the early 1900s, Portage and Main was the commercial centre of Winnipeg.

POSTCARD COURTESY DAN SKWARCHUK

W

Winnipeg's skyline, 2007

but was no longer a national force; many head offices departed Winnipeg, and the city survived partly by supplying its own people with goods and services. Ethnics in the city became gradually more economically and politically successful, as well as more dominant numerically, and in 1956 an ethnic mayor – **STEPHEN JUBA**, of **UKRAINIAN** origin – was elected. By 1970, ethnicity could be celebrated as a positive feature, in a week-long festival called **FOLKLORAMA** that became an annual fixture on the calendar. A few years earlier, in 1967, the city had surprised itself by hosting a highly successful meeting of the Pan-American Games. This event and various centennial celebrations brought a resurgence of new construction into the city, much of it providing the physical infrastructure for a veritable renaissance of cultural activity in the city. Nevertheless, the major trend continued to be dispersal of the population into the suburbs, occurring with virtually no long-term planning. The first major shopping mall opened at Polo Park in 1959, and was the first of many such centres with adequate parking that lured shoppers away from the downtown centre. The only effort to counter these decentralizing forces was the formation of Metropolitan Winnipeg in 1960, amalgamating 7 cities, 5 suburban municipalities, and one town, with the City of Winnipeg at the centre, as a secondary tier of administration. It was not entirely successful, but was followed in 1972 by the controversial formation of **UNICITY** by provincial fiat. Unicity made possible an integrated administration of an integrated Winnipeg, but could not entirely eliminate all the structural problems that beset the city.

AFTER UNICITY, 1972-PRESENT: One of the key problems facing Unicity was the increasing deterioration of Winnipeg's urban core. A series of initiatives over many years attempted to deal with the problem by restoring life to the downtown city – a hockey arena was even built downtown in the early years of the 21st century to replace an earlier arena by Polo Park – but without much visible effect. The reality was that the downtown had become an area of large buildings and larger parking lots where almost nobody lived. Beyond the downtown itself could be seen the decaying of many of its surrounding neighbourhoods and those extending into the North End. Not surprisingly, these areas attracted the generations of newcomers who entered the city, especially after 1970. Two trends worked in tandem. One was the migration of many First Nations people from rural reserves into the city, drawn by economic opportunity and the availability of health care facilities. In 1970, Winnipeg had contained only a few thousand Aboriginal

depths of the Depression. With an ending of massive immigration into MB after 1919, the population size of the city stabilized and during 1931-36 even declined. This allowed the city's ethnic groups to become better integrated into the community, thus reducing ethnic tensions, but it also brought a permanent end to Winnipeg's great growth spurt. Like the size of the population, municipal politics stabilized into a contest between the city's older population of the south end (and their business allies) versus the ethnics and organized labour of the north end; the business party usually won.

POSTWAR RESURGENCE, 1946-71: The senior division of the **U OF M** had moved to the southern suburbs in the early 1930s, thus setting the pace for a move away from the downtown core which characterized the postwar period. Winnipeg foundered in the years immediately after the war. The major event was the great flood of 1950. Such periodic inundations were ended, it was thought, with the construction of the Red River Floodway in the 1960s. Population growth slowed to a snail's pace, comparing unfavourably with that of other Cdn and Prairie urban centres. The city continued as a local economic centre,

people. By 2006, it was the home of about 55,000 Aboriginals, more than in any city in Canada. The concentration of Aboriginals in a relatively few wards in the city's centre was regarded by many as the city's most important social problem. The second trend was the shift in the origins of Cdn immigrants from Europe and NA to countries in Latin America, Africa, and Asia. This new population brought a considerable expansion of ethnic diversity to the city, including new restaurants and food shops. But it also brought what many held to be new kinds of criminal activity, including the emergence of urban gangs, many of them ethnically organized, and the beginning of street violence. Winnipeg became the "Murder Capital of Canada," and had high incidences of crimes against property.

The less pessimistic pointed out that the newcomers were no different than those of earlier generations; both sought opportunities to improve their way of life by taking up residence in the city. Like previous new arrivals, these would gradually acculturate and become part of the mainstream. In the process, they might even bring into being new notions of tolerance and cultural diversity, as well as adding their energy to urban improvement. Only time would tell. By 2007, Winnipeg seemed to have accepted its role as a 2nd-tier city in Canada, one incapable of supporting "major-league" sports activity. Winnipeggers boasted of the city's many cultural amenities – especially internationally recognized artists like **Carol Shields, The Guess Who, Guy Maddin,** and the **Royal Winnipeg Ballet** – and had, for the most part, stopped agonizing over the limited influence the city now exercised in the modern world. ● J. M. BUMSTED

WINNIPEG AQUEDUCT, in full, the Greater Winnipeg Water District Aqueduct and Railway, is a pipeline and **Railway** that brings **Winnipeg** its drinking water from Shoal Lake, at the ON border. An ambitious project for its time, the aqueduct follows a 137 km-long route through muskeg, forest, and granite. Before the construction of the aqueduct in 1915, "watermen" on ox carts used to haul untreated water from the **Red** and **Assiniboine** rivers, delivering it by barrel around the city. Then the city switched to artesian wells, which produced unreliable if not dangerously polluted water. The aqueduct was first conceived in 1912, after typhoid **Epidemics** had killed hundreds of Winnipeg residents, and it became necessary that the city's malodorous, contaminated water be replaced if Winnipeg's growth were to continue. US engineer Charles Slichter gave the city 3 options: drill new water wells N of Winnipeg; build a pipeline to the **Winnipeg River**; or build

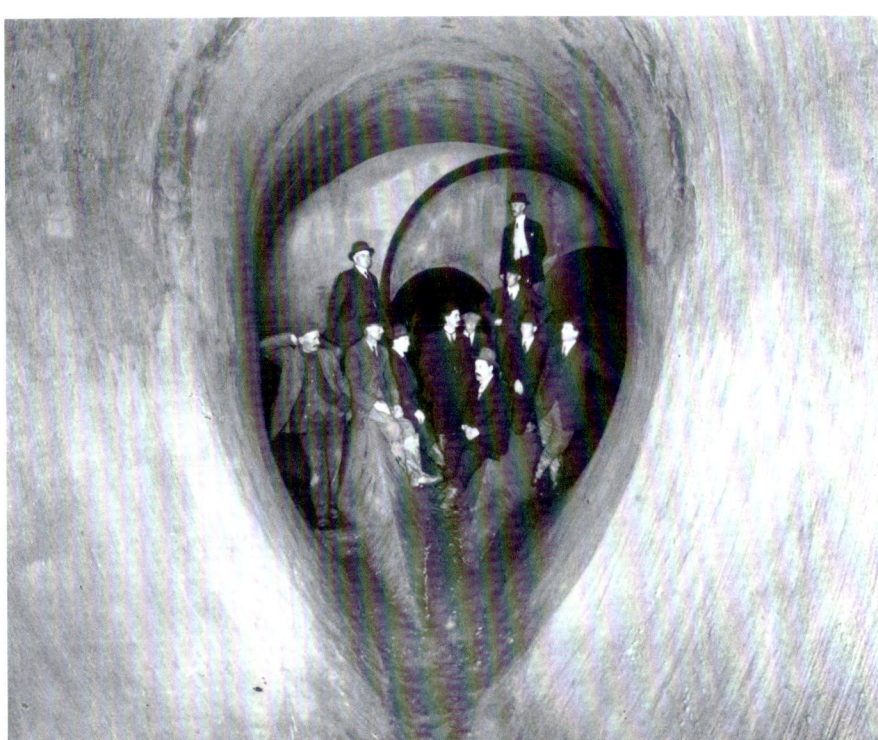

The Winnipeg Aqueduct carries water from Shoal Lake.

an aqueduct to Shoal Lake, a much purer water source. While the 1st and 2nd options were less expensive, they were still unreliable. Though the Shoal Lake scheme was initially rejected by city council because of its cost, Winnipeg residents supported the idea, and elected Thomas Deacon mayor in 1913 on a Shoal Lake platform. Deacon held a plebiscite, and the Shoal Lake plan won by a landslide. Construction on the supporting railway began in 1914, with work on the aqueduct starting the following year.

The aqueduct was built underground, below the frost line. In cross-section, it was a dome-shaped concrete shell mounted on a concrete floor, or "invert." The sections of pipe were poured into concrete forms and coupled together with copper expansion joints to allow for changes in temperature. The higher elevation of Shoal Lake meant that gravity would carry it to the city. At the Seine River and the Red, tunnels were drilled down into bedrock 25 m below the riverbed, and then lined with pre-cast sections of concrete pipe 3 m in diameter. Builders had to contend with difficulties such as the muskeg "soup" that flowed into the ditch while excavating, soft gumbo that caused the heavy pipe to sag and crack, and forest fires that burned off the aqueduct's insulating blanket of earth. The aqueduct began operating on April 6, 1919. The total cost of the project was $17 million, and the aqueduct is still in use. It channels up to 385 million L of water per day. ● MD

WINNIPEG ARENA was the city's primary high-capacity indoor sporting and concert facility for half a century. Following the construction of the **Winnipeg Stadium**, the non-profit **Winnipeg** Enterprises Corporation announced plans in 1953 to build and operate a neighbouring arena with a $2 million loan from the city. Completed in 1955, with a capacity of 9500 seats, it was touted as one of the best **Hockey** facilities in Canada or even NA. The new building replaced the (Shea's) Amphitheatre (1909), a rink on the downtown site that would later be occupied by **Great-West Lifeco**'s operations.

The Winnipeg Warriors of the Western Professional Hockey League played at the arena from 1955-61. The arena also played host to game 3 of the 1972 Soviet Union-Canada Summit Series, one month before the Oct 1972 debut of the **Winnipeg Jets**, then a World Hockey Association (WHA) franchise. The WHA Jets played in the arena from 1972-79.

In the latter half of the 1970s, debates raged about whether Winnipeg needed a new arena and who would pay for it. A number of proposals from the Jets owners, local business people, and the city were considered and rejected, including plans for facilities near **The Forks** and as part of downtown Winnipeg's North Portage redevelopment. In Sept 1978, city council approved $3.5 million of public funds for a 6000-seat expansion, and in Jan 1979, the Jets signed an 8-year lease, 2 months before the WHA-NHL merger brought the team into the NHL. Other notable events held there over the years included the World **Curling** Championships, the Labatt Brier, the World Junior Hockey Championships, the **Pan American Games** and hundreds of concerts by Canadian and international artists.

After the Jets were sold and departed Winnipeg in 1996, the **Manitoba Moose** became the building's primary tenant. The arena's doors were finally closed in Nov 2004 to make way for the newly built **MTS Centre**. The City of Winnipeg considered proposals for redevelopment of the facility, including an indoor water park, but in a controversial move, city officials decided to pay to demolish the building and sold the land to Ontrea Inc. for retail development. Explosives (200 kg worth) and demolition machines destroyed the building, sometimes referred to as the "old barn," on March 26, 2006. ● JOEL TRENAMAN

WINNIPEG ART GALLERY, THE, (WAG), MB's pre-eminent public gallery, opened Dec 16, 1912 at the Industrial Bureau with an inaugural exhibition of 250 works by members of the Royal Canadian Academy. The import of opening Canada's first civic art gallery was marked by the attendance of the lt gov and three 3 RCA members, Maurice Cullen, Homer Watson and Frederic Challoner. The impetus for the gallery came from citizens and business, the Women's Art Association having created interest and developed community artists through their initiatives since 1880. The gallery's official founders were business leaders, W. Bulman, the president of the Industrial Bureau, an early version of the Chambre of Commerce, James McDiarmid, George Wilson and Mayor R. D. Waugh. As an amateur artist, McDiarmid was the driving force. He presided over the gallery until the end of WWI and in 1913 Donald MacQuarrie became the first curator. The gallery consistently presented British, Dutch and Cdn exhibitions.

In 1913, the **Winnipeg School of Art** was established and the gallery and school of art were incorporated in 1923 by a special act of the MB govt. By the mid-1920s, however, the financial support from the Industrial Bureau had ended. The gallery was forced to close in 1926. The WAG Association was formed, joined by the Manitoba Society of Artists, to actively promote the value of a civic gallery. During its closure, the WAG's collection was held in trust by the school of art. Scottish artist, Alexander Musgrove, (head of the school 1913-1921) was instrumental in obtaining space for the gallery in the new civic auditorium in 1932. It re-opened with an exhibition from the National Gallery of Canada. The auditorium was

the WAG's home until its new building, designed by Gustavo da Roza, opened in 1971.

Musgrove, curator from 1932-49, organized a full exhibition program and started children's art classes. He was followed by Alvin Eastman who arrived in 1950 and Austrian art historian, **Ferdinand Eckhardt**, director from 1953-74, who led the gallery to new levels. The Women's Committee, (Volunteer Committee), was founded in 1951 to support and raise money for acquisitions and programs. In 1954, they inaugurated the annual juried, national Winnipeg Show. Over 16 years, it had tremendous impact on contemporary art, show-casing the best, including many Winnipeg artists. The exhibition became a biennial in 1962; the last held in 1970. The

Volunteer Committee also undertook initiatives in art education, and still run the Gallery Shoppes and Art Rental. During the 1960s and 1970s, MB govt support grew and the staff expanded with the move to the new building. In 1962, the validity of the gallery was affirmed in an act of the legislature.

The mandate of the WAG from the outset has been to collect, exhibit, preserve and interpret the works of contemporary and historic art, local, national and international, including all media, and photography, ceramics and decorative arts. The collection, over 22,500 works including the major Inuit collection, is one of the most important in Canada. WAG publications and exhibitions have been critical for the development of

Winnipeg Art Gallery

Cdn art. Successive directors, staff and boards of governors have each made significant contributions, building on previous visions, developing collections, exhibitions and programs, presenting MB artists' work at home and world-wide, while bringing international treasures to Winnipeg, including art of Vincent Van Gogh, (1962 and 1999), the Hermitage (1976), and American art from the Walker in Minneapolis (2004). A founding member of the Western Canadian Art Circuit in the 1950s, the WAG has toured exhibitions ever since. At the forefront of many new departures in art education and access, the WAG partnered in the pioneer virtual exhibition *Panoramas: The North American Landscape in Art* with the Canadian Museum of Civilization, the Smithsonian and the Museo Nacional de Arte in Mexico City (2001) and continues to play a vibrant role in an exhilarating visual arts community. ● PATRICIA BOVEY

WINNIPEG BEACH, pop 800, is a town 80 km N of **WINNIPEG**. It is one of the largest summer resorts on the W side of **LAKE WINNIPEG**. In 1900, Sir **WILLIAM WHYTE**, president of the **CPR**, acquired land there. The beachfront was subsequently developed as a major vacation and recreation spot incorporating a hotel, boardwalk, dance hall, Ferris wheel, roller coaster, and other entertainments typical of seaside towns. For many years, it was Winnipeggers' most popular summer resort, with the CPR running daily excursions carrying up to 40,000 passengers up to the beach and many Winnipeg firms holding their employees' picnics there. Evening "moonlight specials" and "daddy trains"

also serviced the resort throughout the summer. After WWII, the resort declined in popularity as Winnipeggers turned elsewhere for their recreation. Some of the facilities burned down, the popular beachfront entertainments disappeared, and **RAILWAY** passenger service was discontinued in 1961. However, the cottages have been maintained, with numbers of them used by several generations of families. Many cottages are being upgraded for year-round use and some Winnipeg Beach residents now commute into the city daily. In 1968, the govt created a provincial park at the beachfront and began a rehabilitation program, leading to restoration of the boardwalk in the 1990s. The popular TV program *Falcon Beach* was filmed here. ● GPP

WINNIPEG BLUE BOMBERS (officially the Winnipeg Football Club), known initially as the Winnipeg Rugby Football Club and by the unfortunate nickname of the "Winnipeg Winnipegs," was formed on June 10, 1930, by the union of several Winnipeg **RUGBY** teams dating to the 1880s. They wore green and white, and elected Dick Mahoney as their first president. However, the new team quickly adopted what would become Cdn **FOOTBALL** rules, influenced by US innovations to the rules of their version of rugby. By 1933, under the guidance of Joe Ryan, the Winnipegs amalgamated with another local team, the St. Johns Tigers, and adopted blue and gold as their colours, and changed their name to the 'Pegs. Soon after, they moved into a new home, the 6000-seat Osborne Stadium in the shadow of the **LEGISLATIVE BUILDING**. The amalgamation

brought together a talented group that included local stars such as Andy Currie, Lou Mogul, Arni Coulter, Rosy Adelman, and Herb and Tommy Mobberley, along with US players like Carl Cronin, Greg Kabat, and Russ Rebholz. In 1933, the 'Pegs made a losing appearance in the Grey Cup semi-final against the Toronto Argonauts. By 1935, and with the addition of more star players such as Eddie James, Bob Fritz, Bert Oja, Bud Marquardt, Herb Peschel, and the famed **FRITZ HANSON**, the Winnipegs were a power in Cdn football. On December 7, 1935, they became the first Western team to win the Grey Cup. Hanson, who sported a variety of nicknames such as the "Galloping Ghost" and the "Perham Flash," had a phenomenal day, returning punts for more than 300 yd (275 m) as the Winnipegs defeated the Argos 18-12.

In that 1935 season, people started referring to the team as the "Blue Bombers." **WINNIPEG TRIBUNE** sportswriter **VINCE LEAH** was enamoured with the exploits of US heavyweight-boxing champion Joe Lewis, the "Brown Bomber." While watching the powerful "Winnipegs" perform, Leah decided they bore a resemblance to Lewis, and he started calling them the "Blue Bombers." The name stuck, and in 1936, the team officially registered its name as the Blue Bombers. The Bombers would go on to play in 4 more Grey Cup games in the next 5 years, losing in 1937 and 1938 but defeating the Ottawa Rough Riders 8-7 in 1939. In 1941, they took home the cup in an 18-16 victory, again over the eastern Riders. The punting exploits of Art Stevenson in '39 and Ches McCance in '41 played key roles in those victories.

WWII dominated the next few years, though the patriotically named Winnipeg RCAF Bombers made several Cup appearances. When regular play resumed in 1945, the Blue Bombers – with a mainly local cast that included Mel Wilson, Wilf Daniels, Harry Hood, Rube Ludwig, Bud Irving, and Moe Simovitch – made it back to the Grey Cup game, but were shellacked 35-0 by Hall of Fame back Royal Copeland and the Argos. In 1946, Copeland and Joe Krol, collectively the "Gold Dust Twins," did much of the damage as the Argos again dealt the Bombers a Grey Cup defeat, this time 28-6. In 1947, for a 3rd year in a row, the Argos had Winnipeg's number, although this time the Bombers had to endure a heartbreaking 10-9 loss. All told, the Bombers made a staggering 10 Grey Cup appearances 1935-47, winning 3 and losing 7. 1948 and '49 were tough years for the Bombers as they posted bleak 3-9 and 2-12 records, respectively, but the 1950s would bring football glory back to Winnipeg.

The early part of that decade was the "Indian" **JACK JACOBS** era. At a time when the CFL's

A warm summer day at Winnipeg Beach

STAN MILOSEVIC, WWW.MANITOBAPHOTOS.COM

roots in rugby emphasized running above all else, the famed Cherokee quarterback – who came to the Bombers from the NFL – brought a style of offence that emphasized the passing game, which created a new level of excitement among fans. Jacobs didn't play for long, but such was his effect that when he retired in 1954, he was given much of the credit for the construction of a beautiful new home for the Bombers, Winnipeg Stadium. With thousands of fans clamouring to see Jacobs, Osborne Stadium became obsolete and Winnipeg (now Canad Inns) Stadium, which the Bombers moved into in 1953, was referred to as "The house that Jack built."

What is often referred to as the golden age of Blue Bomber football began in 1957, when management had the wisdom and persuasive powers to convince one of their tight ends to take over the coaching reins. The man's name was Harry Peter "Bud" Grant, and when Grant retired from play at age 29 and assumed the head-coaching duties from departed Bud Sherman, it didn't take long for him to establish a CFL dynasty. The Bombers went 12-4 in Grant's rookie year before losing the Grey Cup game, but they captured the cup the next 2 years, going on to win 4 CFL titles over a 5-year span. Those teams featured some of the great players in Bomber history, including **KEN PLOEN**, Leo Lewis, Buddy Tinsley, Ernie Pitts, Frank Rigney, Ron Latourelle, Cornell Piper, Ed Kotowich, Herb Gray, Steve Patrick (*see* **PATRICK FAMILY**), Gord Rowland, Norm Rauhaus, and Henry Janzen, to name a few. Some of the more memorable Grey Cup games were also written into the CFL history books during the Grant era, including the 1962 Fog Bowl at Toronto's Exhibition Stadium. That game had to be extended over 2 days when a thick fog rolled in from Lake Ontario, making it impossible for players to see. The Blue Bombers ended up winning 28-27. When Grant left to become head coach of the Minnesota Vikings of the NFL after the 1966 season, his teams had won 102 regular season games and lost only 56, and the Bombers made 6 Grey Cup appearances, winning 4, in his 10-year tenure.

The Bombers went through some lean years after Grant left. With most of the great players from the '50s and '60s retired or past their prime, Grant's successor, Joe Zaleski, couldn't produce a winner, nor could Jim Spavital, who followed Zaleski at the helm. Things started to turn for the better when GM Earl Lunsford hired Bud Riley as head coach in 1974, and Riley brought in a young quarterback from Birmingham, AL, named Ralph "Dieter" Brock. Brock would go on to become one of the great passing QBs in CFL history, winning back-to-back MVP Awards in 1980 and 1981. Still, Brock couldn't deliver the Bombers a Grey Cup,

Milt Stegall scoring his 138th touchdown on July 27, 2007 to set a new CFL record

and it wasn't until **CAL MURPHY** took over as Blue Bomber head coach in 1983, following the departure of Ray Jauch, that Winnipeg's fortunes again took off. Brock was traded to the Hamilton Tiger Cats for Tom Clements during that 1983 season, and Clements led an immensely talented Bomber team to a lopsided 47-17 Grey Cup win over his former team-mates in frigid Commonwealth Stadium in Edmonton. This, the first Grey Cup game held in a western city other than Calgary or Vancouver, ended a 22-year Bomber Grey Cup drought. That Bomber team included future Hall of Famers such as Willard Reaves, **JOE POPLAWASKI**, **CHRIS WALBY**, James Murphy, Stan Mikawos, Rick House, Jeff Boyd, Ken Hailey, Trevor Kennerd, and Bob Cameron, to name a few.

The CFL moved the Bombers to the Eastern Division in 1987 when the Montreal Concordes (formerly the Alouettes) folded, but the team continued to succeed. Murphy became the full-time general manager, and hired Mike Riley, Bud's son, as head coach. Over the next 4 years, the Bombers won 2 more Grey Cups. In 1988, the Bombers upended the BC Lions 22-21 in Ottawa with quarterback Sean Salisbury, receiver James Murphy, and punter Bob Cameron playing starring roles. Riley's 2nd Grey Cup came in 1990,

when QB Tom Burgess and linebacker Greg Battle were instrumental in Winnipeg's 50-11 rout of Edmonton in Vancouver.

The early 1990s featured additional success and 2 more Grey Cup appearances, albeit losing ones, in 1992 and 1993. With Matt Dunigan calling the signals and receivers such as Gerald Wilcox, David Williams, and Alfred Jackson, the Bombers were a high-scoring squad. But in the 2nd and final year of a failed expansion sojourn into the US, the Bombers' fortunes began to decline. And when they suffered a 68-7 loss to Edmonton in the 1996 playoffs, Murphy was fired after 14 years as the man in charge of the Bombers. That move led to even leaner times, as the Winnipeg franchise reached rock bottom under Jeff Reinebold, going 4-14 and 3-15 in 1998 and '99.

When Dave Ritchie was hired as head coach in 2000, the pendulum swung back the other way. Ritchie slowly restored the Bombers to respectability, and by 2001, with QB Khari Jones, running back Charles Roberts, and slotback Milt Stegall leading the way, the Bombers returned to the Grey Cup final for the first time in 8 years. Coming off a 14-4 regular season, the Bombers were prohibitive favourites against an 8-10 Calgary team, but Wally Buono's Stampeders shocked a huge crowd at Olympic Stadium in Montreal, upsetting the Bombers 27-19. The years 2002 and 2003 produced 13- and 11-win seasons, but by 2006, Ritchie was gone, and so was the man who had replaced him, Jim Daley; Doug Berry had taken over the Bombers' head-coaching chores.

In 2005, the Winnipeg Football Club celebrated its 75th year of existence. Another high point for the team came in July 2007 when Milt Stegall became the all-time CFL touchdown scorer. Three-quarters of a century of Cdn football in Winnipeg produced 24 Grey Cup appearances, 10 victories, and a legacy of great players and memorable moments that has made the Blue Bombers an integral part of the fabric of Winnipeg. ● BOB IRVING

WINNIPEG BRANCH, WOMEN'S ART ASSOCIATION.

Founded in 1894, this association was a significant force in developing the visual arts in **Winnipeg**. Its aims were "to promote and encourage more general interest in art in Canada and to foster the mutual help and cooperation of women who were either serious artists or lovers of art." Their activities included shared studios and models, the presentation of exhibitions of MB, Cdn and international artists. They also made significant advancements in art education in school curricula and presented lectures by artists and international art historians. Given Winnipeg's geographic isolation the Winnipeg Women's Art Association created connections with the East and New York providing artists important contacts. Their work and outspokenness was vital in developing the impetus for the founding of both The **Winnipeg Art Gallery** and the School of Art. The association also developed a collection of MB art, including First Nations, and they recognized the multicultural dimensions in the area's artistic activities. The association was a victim of its own success, discontinuing its meetings in 1916-17 and suspending its activities in 1917-1918. Its work had been assumed by the new organizations, but the scope of the activities of the Women's Art Association established the benchmark for the mandate of The Winnipeg Art Gallery. While the association had become redundant, its legacy is at the root of the vibrancy of subsequent arts activity in Winnipeg. ● PATRICIA BOVEY

WINNIPEG CHAMBER OF COMMERCE

is the leading voice for the Winnipeg business community. The Chamber is older than the city of Winnipeg, having been incorporated as the Winnipeg Board of Trade by an act of the legislature on March 8, 1873, which was some 6 months before Winnipeg became incorporated as a city.

Its goal is to ensure the views of business are heard on the major issues of the day, and to lobby govts for legislative and policy changes that will help ensure the future health and prosperity of the local business community. Some of the changes the chamber has lobbied for in recent years include health and education reforms, proposed changes to provincial labour laws, the extension of Sunday shopping hours in Winnipeg, the removal of provincial rent controls, tax reforms, increased funding for infrastructure renewal and downtown revitalization, enhanced education, training and employment opportunities for Aboriginals, and the reduction of govt bureaucracy and red tape. In addition to its role as a voice for business, the chamber also provides a variety of programs, services, and benefits for its members. They include a group insurance plan, discounts with local merchants, education programs, and a variety of breakfast, luncheon, and dinner events designed to educate, entertain, and provide networking opportunities for Chamber members. As of mid-2005, more than 1600 businesses and organizations were members of the Winnipeg Chamber. ● MURRAY MCNEILL

WINNIPEG COMMODITY EXCHANGE

is the only exchange in Canada where contracts on agricultural commodities are traded. Contracts currently traded on the exchange are futures and options on canola, flaxseed, domestic feed **Wheat**, and domestic feed barley. The WCE is the world's leading exchange for the trading of canola contracts. The exchange is now in the Commodity Exchange Tower on Main St near Portage Ave.

The commodity futures and options market provides the grain industry with pricing information and allows producers, processors and resellers the opportunity to hedge the risk associated with unexpected price changes. The role of the WCE is to provide the facilities and rules of trade for member firms, called participants, which trade on the exchange. Non-members can buy or sell exchange contracts through a participant called a futures commission merchant.

The exchange was formally opened on December 7, 1887. It was initially called the Winnipeg Grain and Produce Exchange and was in the basement of Winnipeg City Hall. Created by a group of local grain merchants as an unincorporated trade association, the WCE was to provide a central location and set of rules for members to trade agricultural commodities. In the early years, the exchange operated as a cash and forward contracts market. Commodities were purchased for immediate delivery or for future delivery with contract terms such as delivery date, delivery place, commodity grade, and quantity set as part of the negotiation between buyer

A busy day in 1937 on the Grain Exchange trading floor

and seller. Since these forward contracts were not standardized and did not involve a third party guarantee, traders could not easily liquidate their positions and were subject to default risk (the risk that the other contracting party would not fulfill their obligations).

Futures contracts on wheat, oats, and flaxseed were introduced in 1904. Futures contracts, which are standardized, involve mechanisms to reduce default risk and are guaranteed by the exchange's clearinghouse. The introduction of futures contracts made trading less risky, and made entering and exiting contract positions much easier. This greatly contributed to the expansion of activity at the exchange. The rapid growth of both trading and exchange membership in the early years necessitated moves to larger facilities. In 1892, the exchange moved from City Hall to the first "Grain Exchange" building at 164 Princess St. In 1899, a new Exchange Building was officially opened at 160 Princess. In 1908, the exchange was reorganized and renamed as the Winnipeg Grain Exchange and moved into a new Grain Exchange Building at the corner of Rorie St and Lombard Ave. The exchange remained in this building until 1980, when it moved to its current location.

From its inception through much of the first half of the 20th century, the exchange played an important role in the development of both Winnipeg and agriculture in Canada. In addition to marketing western Cdn grains to the rest of the world directly, the exchange campaigned for improved transportation facilities and for an effective national system of grain inspection. The exchange was also integral to Winnipeg's early development as a centre for agribusiness and the financial services industry. The importance of the WCE was diminished in the 1940s, when the **Canadian Wheat Board** was given a monopoly in the marketing of wheat and assumed a primary role in the marketing of oats and barley. In 1974, however, there was a partial return to more open markets and the WCE was able to start trading futures on domestic feed grains (wheat, oats, and barley).

In 1972, the exchange's name was changed to the Winnipeg Commodity Exchange to reflect the introduction of gold futures trading (the world's first gold futures market). Options contracts were first traded at the exchange in 1979. Since its original inception, the exchange has seen derivatives trading come and go on a variety of underlying commodities and securities, including various grains, cattle, potatoes, gold, silver, treasury bills, and Govt of Canada bonds. The WCE is recognized by the Manitoba Securities Commission as a self-regulatory organization. On Dec 20, 2004, open

outcry trading on the exchange floor was replaced with a trading system in which buy and sell orders are matched by computers. This made the WCE the first commodity futures exchange in NA to convert fully to electronic trading. ● STEPHEN C. ALFORD/GADY JACOBY

WINNIPEG CONTEMPORARY DANCERS

(WCD) has been MB's premier modern dance company for more than 40 years. As one of the oldest professional modern dance companies in Canada, WCD produces avant-garde dance shows that challenge both artist and audience. The company uses new and existing works to display their cutting-edge approach.

The company was founded in Feb 1964 with an inaugural performance at the **U of M**. Invitations to perform followed, and the company gained local prominence. Founder **Rachel Browne** initially served as the company's instructor, choreographer, dancer, tour planner, fundraiser, publicist, and artistic director. In July 1965, WCD appeared on CBC TV's *Across the Nation* program to present selections from their repertoire. Extensive performances throughout MB coupled with CBC television specials helped propel the company forward. That year also marked their first season as a touring company. The Contemporary Dancers became the first modern dance company to receive financial support from the Canada Council for the Arts in 1967, though the start-up years were marked by financial struggles.

In 1972, Browne and Faye Thompson founded the School of Contemporary Dancers and Apprentice Program. Under their direction, the school has developed into one of the leading modern dance performance training programs in Canada producing numerous dance artists, choreographers, and teachers who have established distinguished careers in the field of contemporary dance. The school became a separate corporation in 1995.

In 1973, international choreographers began to work with the company and touring opportunities followed the next year. WCD has given performances throughout Canada, the US, and Mexico. Also in 2003, the troupe moved from its rented facility in an Osborne Village church into the newly renovated Crocus Building. As of 2005, Winnipeg Contemporary Dancers had garnered a surplus, and the company was on its way to getting their financial house in order. ● JILL SEXSMITH

WINNIPEG CONVENTION CENTRE (WCC)

is Winnipeg's largest convention facility, generating millions of dollars a year in financial

benefits to the local economy through delegate spending and tax revenues. Opened in 1974, and controlled and funded jointly by the city and the province, the 14,865-m² (160,000-ft²) facility can handle conventions of up to about 2000 people and receptions or dinners for up to 5000 guests. In 2002, the 3-storey structure underwent a $6.6-million facelift, which included removing its original Tyndall stone cladding and replacing it with composite-metal wall panels, giving it a sleeker look and improved protection against Winnipeg's extreme climate. The makeover also included a redesigning and replacing of the 2nd-level windows along 2 sides of the building. In 2005, the upgraded facility was voted one of Canada's favourite convention or meeting facilities by Cdn meeting planners. That same year, the WCC commissioned a market feasibility study to determine if a major expansion of the facility was warranted, and if it was, how big it should be. Two years earlier, the WCC's board had called for either govt funding or the creation of a new hotel tax to finance an $80-million expansion, arguing the existing centre was too small to attract major conventions. The proposed expansion would have included the construction of a 3-storey, "mirror" facility on the S side of York Ave, which would be connected to the main building by a 3rd-floor skywalk. It also would have included ballrooms on the first 2 floors, a 3rd-floor exhibition hall, street-level retail space, a 3-storey parking lot, and a 2-level underground garage. However, the proposal was put on hold after encountering stiff opposition from the city's hotel industry. ● MURRAY MCNEILL

WINNIPEG FALCONS were a storied MB team which won hockey's first Olympic gold in 1920. Formed in 1909, the team of mainly **Icelandic** players was unable to play in the Winnipeg Hockey League (WHL) because of ethnic prejudice. Undeterred, they created the Manitoba Hockey League (MHL) with 4 other teams and played independently. The Falcons performed poorly in their first season, but won the MHL championship of 1914-15. The Falcons disbanded during WWI, when many of the players joined the 223rd ("Scandinavian Canadian") Batt in **Winnipeg**, though many of them still played together in the Winnipeg Patriotic League. They regrouped for the 1919-20 season under the management of **Fred Maxwell** and with **Frank Fredrickson** serving as team captain. After winning the MHL championship, the Falcons then had to play against the rival WHL's **Selkirk** team in order to determine which team would go on to the Allan Cup. The Falcons won 6-5 in overtime. Then the Falcons surprised many by going on to beat

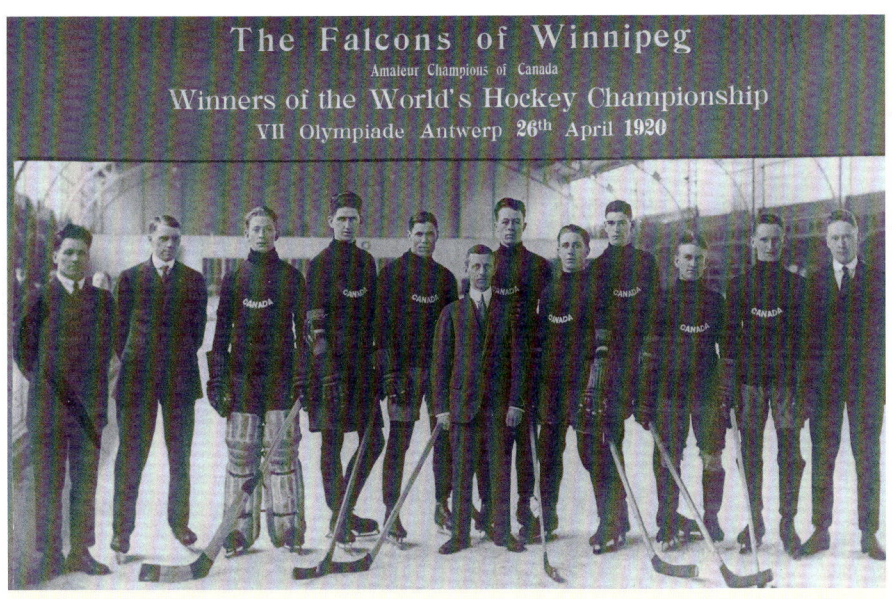

The Falcons of Winnipeg
Amateur Champions of Canada
Winners of the World's Hockey Championship
VII Olympiade Antwerp 26th April 1920

Winners of hockey's first Olympic Gold Medal.

the favoured U of Toronto Varsity Blues in a 2-game, total-goal series with scores of 8-3 and 3-2. As a result, they were chosen to represent Canada at ice hockey's Olympic debut in Antwerp. They beat Czechoslovakia 15-0, the US 2-0, and Sweden 12-1 en route to their Olympic gold victory on April 26, 1920. A half-day holiday was proclaimed in Winnipeg upon their return, and the players were each awarded a gold watch. In the following season, after some of the best players went to professional clubs, the Falcons fared less well, and eventually dissolved in the early 1930s. In 2006, the 1920 team was inducted into the Canadian Sports Hall of Fame. ● MD

WINNIPEG FILM GROUP (WFG) is a non-profit organization founded in 1974 by a group of independent filmmakers that encourages filmmakers to develop their skills at making, producing, distributing, and screening independent films. The WFG exhibits films in **WINNIPEG** in partnership with Cinamatheque, which is MB's only independent art-film house. The WFG has established itself as one of the most respected film organizations in Canada. Many Manitobans in the film industry, including **NORMA BAILEY** and **GUY MADDIN**, have received support and training from the WFG at some point. In 2005, the 4 departments of the WFG included education and training; production; distribution; and exhibition. Located in the Artspace (formerly Galt) Building in the Exchange District, the WFG offers workshops year-round to assist those interested in developing their skills as writers, producers, directors, or crew. WFG offers funding to qualified applicants; production and editing equipment at a reduced cost; an artist-in-residence program;

and opportunities to work on other filmmakers' shoots. With the help of the WFG's distribution department, members have their work submitted to festivals and galleries around the world. Members' films have been shown and have received critical acclaim from as far away as Switzerland, Germany, India, and Australia. ● GENE WALZ

WINNIPEG FOLK FESTIVAL is the largest folk **MUSIC** festival in NA, drawing 50,000 fans for a 4-day weekend every July to **BIRDS HILL PROVINCIAL PARK**, 20 km NE of **WINNIPEG**. The festival has become an important cultural event, helping to launch the careers of many local and Cdn musicians. The festival began in 1974 as a

free event intended to be a one-time celebration of Winnipeg's centennial. Co-founded by **MITCH PODOLAK**, Ava Kobrinsky, and Colin Gorrie, there were about 50 acts on 4 stages, with 22,000 people attending. Admission at the first festival was free, and all performers were paid the same amount, reflecting Podolak's idealism. Performers at the inaugural festival included Bruce Cockburn, Sylvia Tyson, Mimi Farina, and Murray McLaughlin. None of these performers were famous at the time. There were 14 volunteers, recruited from among Podolak's and Gorrie's friends. Since 2000, there have been about 1800 volunteers at every WFF, and the festival has long charged admission, attracting music lovers with relatively prominent performers.

Rosalie Goldstein succeeded Podolak as artistic director of the festival in 1986. She widened the definition of folk music at the festival to include world music, jazz, rock, dub poetry, and even punk. Pierre Guérin became the next artistic director for the 1992 festival. A former roots musician himself, Guérin took the festival back to more traditional programming, although the world music and electric instruments have stayed. Rick Fenton, a former CBC radio music producer, followed Guérin as artistic director from 2001-04. In 2004, the festival hired Chris Frayer as director of music programming; he previously held the same position with the **JAZZ WINNIPEG FESTIVAL** and the West End Cultural Centre in Winnipeg.

Virtually all notable MB musicians who play music with some folk flavour have appeared at the WFF. Some of the Manitobans to grace the festival's stages include **HEATHER BISHOP**; the **CRASH TEST DUMMIES**; the **DUHKS**, featuring Mitch

Moving to the music at the Folk Festival, 2004

Podolak's son, Leonard; Eagle and Hawk; Elias, Schritt, and Bell; Fubuki Daiko; **TOM JACKSON**; Alana Levandoski; **LOREENA MCKENNITT**; Mood Jga Jga; **FRED PENNER**; and the Wailin' Jennys, among others. For some of these musicians, their appearance at the festival was a milestone that helped launch their careers.

Cdn performers such as Bruce Cockburn, Connie Kaldor, Stan Rogers, and Spirit of the West have been popular with festival audiences over the years. Internationally-known performers at the festival have included the Buena Vista Social Club, Billy Bragg, Mary Chapin Carpenter, Elizabeth Cotton, Ani DiFranco, Stéphane Grappelli, Ladysmith Black Mambazo, Leon Redbone, Buffy Sainte-Marie, Pete Seeger, and Doc Watson. From the first year, when CBC Radio's Peter Gzowski acted as co-host, CBC radio has recorded performances at the Festival and done live broadcasts of the Sunday evening programs. National Public Radio in the US also broadcasted WFF performances in 1988 and 1990.

The festival has grown immensely since 1974. The operating budget of the festival has been more than $2 million since 2000. A 2001 study showed that the festival generates over $16 million in MB, of which more than $14 million is spent in Winnipeg. In recent years, 7 stages on the festival site accommodate more than 250 artists throughout the daytime. Once evening falls, the focus shifts to the main festival stage, where everyone gathers for a smorgasbord of music from all over the world: bluegrass, Celtic, rock, world beat, and so on. The festival's audience reflects a greater age range than it did in the 1970s, going all the way from young children to seniors. Daytime activities include a family area and a stage dedicated to children's performers.

The long-term success of the WFF has made it a model to other events across the country, such as the Edmonton and Vancouver folk festivals. The organization has recognized expertise in areas like operational and volunteer management. Other festivals have also adopted their "Young Performers Program," which provides youth between 14 and 25 with mentoring by festival performers. Canada's Environmental Choice Program made the festival the first event of its kind to be certified as a "Green Event" in 1997. This was in recognition of the festival's efforts to be environmentally sensitive, such as by washing over 12,000 reusable plates on-site during the festival weekend.

The festival is a not-for-profit charitable organization. There have been years of deficits and red ink, largely caused by heavy rain during the summer festival; but since 2000, the organization has been close to self-sustaining, generating

almost 80% of its budget through ticket and merchandise sales. Less than 10% of funding comes from govt sources, with the remainder coming from various fundraising and sponsorship activities. The organization has operated a retail music store since 1982, and runs concerts in the city outside the WFF season. ● MAURICE MIERAU

WINNIPEG FOUNDATION, THE, was established in 1921 with a gift of $100,000 from **WILLIAM FORBES ALLOWAY**. The first community foundation in Canada, The Winnipeg Foundation is a collection of permanently endowed funds. These endowments generate interest that is distributed in the form of grants to charitable organizations serving the citizens of MB – primarily those living in **WINNIPEG**. Alloway, an entrepreneur and prominent local banker, was a community philanthropist who wished to provide ongoing support for the city in which his business prospered. Together, Alloway and his wife Elizabeth contributed more than $2 million to the Foundation during their lifetimes and through their estates. In 1922, The Winnipeg Foundation made its first grants to community organizations, distributing $6,000. Alloway's original gift to the Foundation was followed in 1924 by "The Widow's Mite," an anonymous gift of three gold coins, each valued at five dollars. This second gift has come to symbolize the spirit of philanthropy and of the Foundation – that it's the act of giving, rather than the size of the gift, that is important.

In 1930, Peter Lowe, an employee at Alloway and Champion Bank, became the Foundation's first executive director, after acting as secretary, on a volunteer basis, since its establishment. (Over its 85-year history, the Foundation has had just four other executive directors – Hugh Benham, Alan Howison, Dan Kraayveld and Richard Frost.) By 1931, ten years after it was established, the Foundation's annual granting reached almost $40,000, which helped address community need caused by the Depression. The Winnipeg Foundation has always been able to

respond to both ongoing needs and community crises, including the 1950 flood and the polio outbreak a few years later.

Over the next decades, the Foundation's grant-making scope continually expanded and the Foundation supported a number of major initiatives: **MANITOBA MUSEUM**, Volunteer Manitoba, Fort Whyte Centre (*see* **FORTWHYTE ALIVE**) and the United Way, as well as projects addressing the Aboriginal population, seniors, the inner-city and recreation needs. To celebrate the Foundation's 75th anniversary in 1996, a bronze bust of Alloway was sculpted by **LEO MOL**; it appears in the sculpture gardens in **ASSINIBOINE PARK**.

By the turn of the last century, the scope of programming and grant-making was dramatically changing. The Winnipeg Foundation established its successful Youth in Philanthropy initiative, the largest program of its kind in Canada. A number of other special programs were launched including the Centennial Neighbourhood Project, the Literacy for Life Fund and administrative support for MB's other community foundations. In 2001, The Winnipeg Foundation received a stunning gift of $100 million from the **MOFFAT** family, the largest gift ever made to a Canadian community foundation. Its largest grant commitment came two years later when $6 million was pledged for the Canadian Museum for Human Rights. By its 85th anniversary year in 2006, the Foundation had granted more than $170 million to a wide range of charities in Winnipeg, supporting hundreds of projects annually in the areas of: community service, education, health, environment, heritage, arts and culture, and recreation.

In 2007, The Winnipeg Foundation describes itself as "Your Centre for Community Philanthropy" because of its active effort to create a stronger philanthropic climate in Manitoba. The Foundation holds 1800 endowment funds, has assets totalling more than $400 million and distributes over $17 million in annual grants. There are now 39 community foundations in MB alone, more than 150 across Canada and

W. F. Alloway's cheque established The Winnipeg Foundation in 1921.

hundreds more worldwide. The Winnipeg Foundation is a leader in this international community foundation movement. • RICHARD FROST

WINNIPEG FREE PRESS is MB's oldest and largest daily newspaper. Originally *The Manitoba Free Press,* the newspaper was founded in 1872 to provide information to the residents of the burgeoning frontier town of **WINNIPEG**. Its founders were newspaperman **WILLIAM FISHER LUXTON**, who came to MB to cover the **RED RIVER RESISTANCE** for the *Toronto Globe,* and retired farmer John A. Kenny, the paper's first publisher. The *Free Press* struggled to survive in those early years, but its fortunes changed in 1898 when federal Liberal Cabinet minister Sir **CLIFFORD SIFTON** bought it and subsequently hired **JOHN WESLEY DAFOE** to be its editor. Dafoe went on to become a trusted advisor to several Cdn Liberal PMs, and his talent,

reputation, and influence helped to establish the *Free Press* as one of the country's leading newspapers. While its local news coverage slowly became more important over the years, the *Free Press*'s main claim to fame was its editorial pages. Editors and writers like Shaun Herron, F. S. Manor, Peter McLintock and John Wesley's grandson, John Dafoe, kept the *Free Press* in the national eye.

For many decades, the home of the daily was a 6-storey red-brick building at 300 Carlton St (hence the nickname, The Old Lady of Carlton St). In 1991, the newspaper abandoned the downtown and moved to its current home – a state-of-the-art, $150-million printing plant on Mountain Ave. The paper was owned at that time by Toronto-based Thomson Newspapers Corporation, which had acquired it and 8 other Cdn daily newspapers in 1980 from the Sifton-family-owned FP Publications.

Ten years after the paper moved to Mountain Ave, Thomson sold it and a sister paper, the **BRANDON SUN**, to a newly formed company (FP Canadian Newspapers Limited Partnership). The company is owned by Winnipeg businessman Bob Silver, a co-owner of Winnipeg jeans manufacturer **WESTERN GLOVE WORKS LTD.**, and his cousin Ronald Stern. Since acquiring the 2 newspapers, FP Canadian Newspapers has been converted into an income trust (FP Newspapers Income Fund), with the income fund being entitled to 49% of the distributable cash of FP Canadian Newspapers. The company also has added 5 Winnipeg weeklies to its publishing operations under its subsidiary Canstar Community News Ltd – *The Metro, The Herald, The Lance, The Times,* and *The Headliner.* In 2005, the subsidiary that was created to run the weekly newspaper operations, Canstar also acquired 2 other Winnipeg publications – *Uptown,* a free weekly entertainment magazine, and *The Prime Times,* a twice-monthly paper aimed at readers aged 50 years and older.

Today's *Free Press* is regarded as an innovator in Cdn journalism. As an independent, the newspaper can attempt things that a chain paper might not. For example, in 2006 the *Free Press* converted its front page to simply pictures and headlines in an effort to improve street box sales. The experiment worked. Now newspapers from around NA are studying the *Free Press* and some will no doubt copy the innovation. • R. G. ENFIELD

▸ *See also* **NEWSPAPERS**, *WINNIPEG TRIBUNE.*

WINNIPEG FRINGE FESTIVAL started in 1987 to provide alternative **THEATRE** and performance at low prices to a large audience. There is no other event where Winnipeggers can see improvisational comedy, Shakespeare, TV parodies, Theatre of the Absurd, circus acts, cutting-edge plays, dance, with local talent filling out half the roster. The festival runs in July every year for 12 days, making it the longest fringe festival in NA. The festival is part of the international fringe theatre movement, which gives every conceivable kind of performer non-juried access to venues and audiences. Fringe festivals began in Edinburgh in 1947. By 2004, there were 18 such festivals in Canada, with Edmonton having the country's largest and oldest event.

The Winnipeg Fringe Festival was co-founded by Rick McNair, then the artistic director of the **MANITOBA THEATRE CENTRE**, and Larry Desrochers, later to become the executive director of **MANITOBA OPERA**. In its inaugural year, the "Fringe" took in about $64,000 through 5 venues. In 2004, it collected more than $400,000 in box office revenues and held performances in 24 sites, most of them in **WINNIPEG**'s historic Exchange

The *Manitoba Free Press* reported on events around the world.

The Fringe at Old Market Square in 2007

District. The Winnipeg Fringe stays in line with the shoestring-budget approach of all fringe festivals. Ticket prices are capped at $8 a seat. The festival relies heavily on a volunteer contingent of more than 700, rather than hiring a large staff. Volunteers billet many out-of-town performers. Winnipeg Fringe audiences are famous for putting up with at least a few venues that lack air-conditioning and comfortable seating.

Like other fringe festivals, the Winnipeg Fringe tries to promote local performing artists while also bringing new international artists to town. Performers are accepted on a non-juried first-come, first-served basis, and all ticket revenues go to the artists. The festival's mandate is to ensure that at least half of the performances are by Manitobans, another 30% by other Canadians, and the final 20% by international performers. There are self-managed performance companies that travel to fringe festivals all over Canada and internationally. The bulk of the international performers come from the UK, but there have also been performers from France, Ireland, South America, Japan, Australia, and New Zealand. Noted performers at past Winnipeg Fringe Festivals include Ian Ross, English Suitcase, Three Dead Trolls in a Baggie, T. J. Dawe, and Ross Macmillan. ● MAURICE MIERAU

WINNIPEG GENERAL STRIKE. WWI finally ended on Nov 11, 1918. In its wake, both Cdn and US fears of a Bolshevik-inspired uprising led to increased efforts to control radicalism at home. At the same time, the federal govt demobilized hundreds of thousands of soldiers as quickly as it could transport them home. The immediate post-war time saw inflation and unemployment running rampant; Reds were suspected under

every bed; and in 1918, the Spanish influenza pandemic (*see* **EPIDEMICS**) struck. In the period immediately after the "War to End All Wars," **WINNIPEG** was caught up in both the menace and the exhilaration of peace, which played themselves out through the Winnipeg General Strike.

The labour disputes at the heart of the Winnipeg General Strike occurred in the city's metal fabrication and **CONSTRUCTION** industries. The situations within the 2 industries in 1919 were different. The metal fabrication industry had to adjust to new peacetime conditions without govt weapons contracts, while the construction sector was gearing up for a building boom deferred by the war. In both industries, labour regarded the key issue as employer recognition of the right to collective bargaining through **UNION** organizations selected by and held to be acceptable to workers themselves.

In the metal industry, management was prepared to deal with individual craft unions, but not with an umbrella organization that included outside unions, such as the railway ones. The ironmasters insisted that their understanding of collective bargaining was the commonly accepted one, and this insistence was at least arguable. The metalworkers sought to move to a different form of collective bargaining, by industry instead of by particular unions within the industry. This new version had been recognized in the ship-building industry in Vancouver in 1918 under wartime conditions. In the construction trades, the Winnipeg Building Trades Council (BTC) was attempting in 1919 to assert for the first time a similar industry-wide responsibility for negotiations with the employers in the Builders Exchange. The builders admitted that they liked the idea of being able to settle with everyone

at once, but insisted that they simply could not afford the wage demands being made by the BTC. The issue became centred around collective bargaining, because the Builders Exchange refused to negotiate with the BTC unless their 10¢-an-hour, across-the-board wage offer was accepted. The Building Trades Council went on strike May 1, and was joined by the Metal Trades Council a day later. Labour unrest in Winnipeg was hardly confined to these 2 industries, however. All workers in the city felt threatened by an inflation that had put real income in jeopardy; buying power had been constantly eroded in Winnipeg by inflation since 1910; and many industries were seeking to organize.

The Building Trades Council and the Metal Trades Council both took their disputes to the Winnipeg Trades and Labour Council, the umbrella organization for labour organizations of the time, looking for support. The Winnipeg TLC, after some debate, agreed to distribute ballots authorizing a general strike (often called a general "sympathy" strike) in support of BTC and MTC demands. The recognition of collective bargaining – the basic issue – was in no sense simple. But an industry-wide conception of collective bargaining, as presented in Winnipeg in 1919, had not yet become the standard anywhere in NA, except perhaps in the Vancouver shipyards.

To achieve what were, for 1919, advanced labour objectives, the Winnipeg labour movement turned to general strike as a tactical weapon. General strikes had long been used in Europe as the ultimate weapon in the class struggle. The general strike involved a near-total withdrawal of services to topple the capitalistic state, and many European syndicalists would insist that without a revolutionary intent there could be no genuine general strike. In British and North American labour history, the general strike was a part of an attempt to find new sources of advantage in labour disputes. Obviously, simultaneous withdrawal of services by masses of workers could potentially become an effective labour weapon, as opposed to a political one, if it could be executed without seriously threatening the political fabric. One way of limiting the damage might be by defining the period of the withdrawal of services. The problem here was that if society could survive the defined period of the general strike – perhaps by viewing it as a general holiday – it was not likely to be effective. The general strike had to have consequences for the public to accomplish anything.

Unfortunately, it was all too easy to confuse syndicalist general strikes with pragmatic general strikes, particularly when the Cdn labour movement simultaneously appropriated much of the terminology and rhetoric of syndicalism. In the years after 1900, Canada experienced a substantial influx of immigrants from Europe, particularly from the industrial centres of the UK and Ireland, and from eastern and central Europe. These people were familiar with new views of unionism and new ideologies of the class struggle; were militant and articulate; and were far less committed to traditional trade unionism, particularly as worked out in unions dominant in the US. The Great War had politicized labour because the traditional party system did not work well under the conditions of concentrated hypernationalism that then prevailed. Labour became an umbrella movement for opposition to the war policies of the govt, especially after the western Liberals had joined the Conservatives in a Union govt in 1917. Conscription, govt by order-in-council, and the suppression of dissent were some of the issues. As the war ended, labour was more overtly political than it had ever been, and that some circles had taken over the vocabulary if not the intentions of the European Left, which had apparently achieved a great success in Russia.

It is probably true that the Central Strike Committee – as its members always claimed – had no real intention of violently overthrowing established govt. If intending such an overthrow is the only definition of *revolution*, then these men were not revolutionaries. At the same time, it would be a mistake to see the strike as nothing more than a traditional labour action. The subsequent govt prosecutions of the "strike leaders" for seditious conspiracy tended to force everyone into a defensive position about the strike's intentions. The protestations of innocence have obscured the point that many of those involved

in the strike clearly did believe in the need for radical social and economic change, including the elimination of capitalism.

Winnipeg in 1919 was a city divided – socio-economically, ethnically, geographically, and along class lines. Curiously, one of the critical class divisions was not ethnic, but among those residents of the city usually regarded as homogeneous, those of British origin. The British community neatly divided into 2 camps: the business elite and the labour elite. The 2 groups lived in different parts of the city and would continue their battles for a generation after the strike. By 1919, the business leadership and the middle class that supported its values (and often sought access into its ranks) had come to reside chiefly in selected districts of the southern and western parts of the city, mainly – although not exclusively – S of the Assiniboine River and W of the Red River. E of the Red was the Franco-Manitoban municipality of St. Boniface. Like the business elite, Winnipeg's labour aristocracy lived together in the few districts in the city that were inhabited by skilled workers. Most of these districts were near major railway yards, which served as the employment magnets for the skilled. The principal districts included Fort Rouge, in the SW section of the city; St. John's, in the S part of the North End; Weston; and much of the West End. Houses in these areas were smaller than in the residential areas of the businesspeople, but each had its own small yard and was sturdily built. There was also a growing "third force" in Winnipeg after the turn of the century, in the persons of new immigrants, mainly Ukrainians, Poles, and Jews. The new immigrants lived almost exclusively in the North End of Winnipeg.

Many within the Cdn govt became persuaded that agitators among the immigrants – some of whom were attached to the Left – would infect Cdn labour and, especially, demobilized veterans with their radical ideas.

As it played out, the Winnipeg General Strike was not merely a work stoppage. It was a series of popular demonstrations within the framework of a large-scale general strike. By spring 1919, Winnipeg had thousands of former troops within its boundaries, most of them unemployed and at loose ends. The mass intervention of the returned soldiers in the public events of the strike at the end of May greatly changed its character. Up to the active involvement of the veterans, the strike had been a relatively quiet affair, with little evidence that the large crowds might have potential for violence. After the veterans were involved, large-scale, increasingly volatile public demonstrations became the norm. The most important veteran intervention came on July 21, in response to the federal govt's arrests, on June 16-17, of leading figures among the strikers. The soldiers determined to mount a parade, desperate last-minute efforts on the part of the authorities to prevent it. "Bloody Saturday" went ahead as scheduled. Although the events of this day would produce some of the dominant images of the strike in the public memory, particularly the charge by the Royal North-West Mounted Police on horseback into the crowd, they were decidedly anti-climatic. Whether the strike and the activities of the soldiers can be separated into distinct compartments remains an interesting, probably irresolvable question.

The crowd on June 21 contained many women. Until recently, the role of women in the strike had generally been neglected. In most of the literature about the strike, women have appeared only briefly in supportive and supporting roles, mainly as the helpmeets of various strike leaders. We only now begin to appreciate the extent to which women were active strikers, and one female labour leader of the time – Helen Armstrong – has emerged as a major figure. Contemporary photographs of crowd scenes during the strike often contain a smattering of women in formal dress. An especially large number turned out for "Ladies' Day" at Victoria Park on Jun 12. Many women strikers occupied seats of honour near the front platform, and at the conclusion of a speech by J. S. Woodsworth calling for the emancipation of women and the equality of the sexes, the females shouted together, "We'll fight to the end!" There were women in the crowd on Main St on the afternoon of "Bloody Saturday," despite Mayor Charles Gray's warning to women and children to stay off the streets. Several

Anti-strike war veterans gather for a rally in June, 1919.

women were injured that day in the melee, and 4 were arrested.

The strike was viewed ambivalently outside MB's major centres, especially in rural communities. BRANDON staged a short-lived sympathy strike known as BRANDON GENERAL STRIKE. Contrary to the conventional wisdom of most historians, which has seen the farmer community as almost universally hostile to the strike, the response of the farmer and rural newspapers in MB was mixed. Both sympathy for workers and hostility to the concept of a general strike was widespread. How these contradictory sentiments would influence farmer/labour co-operation was another matter.

The strike was opposed by many private citizens in Winnipeg and by all 3 levels of govt. From the perspective of the strikers, all opposition seemed far more monolithic and co-ordinated – even conspiratorial – than was probably the case. The secretive, even furtive, behaviour of the CITIZENS' COMMITTEE OF 1000 in 1919 brought upon itself much of the opprobrium it has received. The Citizens' Committee was organized at a meeting on May 15, 1919. Leaders of the Winnipeg Board of Trade, the Winnipeg branch of the Canadian Manufacturers Association, and the Manitoba Bar Association spearheaded it. It represented a ruling-class and middle-class opposition to a working-class threat. The Citizens' Committee appears to have devoted itself early on to attempting to keep essential services running.

The Winnipeg General Strike is one of the most heavily researched incidents in Cdn history. The verdict of history has been favourable to the strikers. That approval began, perhaps, with the findings of a Royal Commission headed by H. A. ROBSON that acknowledged that the strike had been held for traditional labour issues and was not intended to foment revolution. It blamed the troubles on a small group of Socialist agitators. By implication, the response of the federal govt – to arrest and try the leaders for seditious conspiracy – was an over-reaction. ● J. M. BUMSTED

WINNIPEG GOLDEYES. The first WINNIPEG baseball team known as the Goldeyes commenced play in 1954. Owned by Mark Danzker and Max Freed, it acted as the "class-C" affiliate of the Major League Baseball (MLB) St. Louis Cardinals from 1954-64, and played at the WINNIPEG STADIUM. TERRY HIND was the team's only general manager and helped the team win Northern League (NL) titles in 1957, 1959, and 1960. The Cardinals ended the arrangement following the 1964 season. The Goldeyes resurfaced for one season in 1969, when they acted as the Kansas City Royals' affiliate in the NL.

Professional baseball returned to Winnipeg in Nov 1993 when the NL (resurrected prior to the 1993 season by Miles Wolff) approved the sale of the Rochester Aces franchise to SAM KATZ along with Winnipeg Enterprises Corp. and partners Jeff and Syd Thompson. The name Goldeyes was chosen in a public contest. In 1994, under the guidance of General Manager John Hindle and Manager Doug Simunic, the team had a won-loss record of 43-37 and won its only league championship (as of 2007) in its first year. Like its predecessor, the team played at the WINNIPEG STADIUM.

In 1996, Katz became the Goldeyes' sole owner. Simunic was replaced as manager by former MLB manager Hal Lanier, who led the team to winning records in 9 of his 10 seasons at the helm. In 1999, the Goldeyes moved to the new CANWEST GLOBAL PARK near THE FORKS, averaging more than 6000 fans per game. Andrew Collier took over as GM in 2001, and in 2003 the ballpark underwent an expansion. That year the club made the playoffs for the 10th consecutive season, and averaged more than 7000 fans per game.

The Goldeyes have been one of the NL's successful teams on and off the field, reaching the league finals 7 times in first 10 years. They have consistently tallied the highest attendance in the league and been among the highest drawing minor league teams in NA. Even though the quality of competition in the NL is quite low, major league teams had signed 6 Goldeye players since 1994. The NL reached a high of 18 teams in 2002, but had retracted to 8 for the 2006 season, which also saw former Goldeye pitcher Rick Forney became the team's manager. ● JOEL TRENAMAN

WINNIPEG GRENADIERS, THE, is a reserve infantry regiment formed in 1908, reduced to nil strength and placed on the supplementary order of battle in 1965. The unit was formally known as:

- 100th Regiment Winnipeg Grenadiers (1908-20)
- The Winnipeg Grenadiers (1920-36)
- The Winnipeg Grenadiers M.G. (1936-46)
- The Winnipeg Grenadiers (1946-65)
- The Winnipeg Grenadiers Cadet Corps (1965-Present)

HISTORY: The 100th Regt Winnipeg Grenadiers formed the nucleus of the 11th Batt CEF at Camp Valcartier by providing 630 officers and men. The 11th Battalion went overseas in Oct 1914 with the First Canadian Contingent. Once in England, the unit became a reinforcement battalion for the first Canadian Division. The 11th Reserve Battalion CEF (as it was known) received drafts from Canada and provided reinforcements to the Canadian Corps 1915-18. In 1915, the 100th Winnipeg Grenadiers was authorized to raise an infantry battalion for overseas service known as the 78th Battalion CEF. This unit became part of the 12th Infantry Brigade of the 4th Canadian Division. Two members of the 78th, Lt J. E Tait and Lt S. L. Honey, won the Victoria Cross.

In Sept 1939, the Winnipeg Grenadiers were mobilized for active service in WWII. In May 1940, the Grenadiers were sent to garrison Jamaica and Bermuda. In late Oct 1941, the regt returned to Canada to reorganize. The unit left for the Orient to become part of the ill-fated Hong Kong Defence Force. On Dec 8, 1941, the

The Goldeyes in action at CanWest Global Park

Winnipeg Grenadiers celebrate their release from a Hong Kong PoW camp.

Japanese attacked Hong Kong and, as a result, the Grenadiers were the first unit of the Canadian Army to go into to action. For three weeks the Grenadiers fought against great odds and were forced finally to surrender on Christmas Day. The regt was annihilated – every member was killed, wounded or taken prisoner. One member, CS-M J.R. Osborn, won the Victoria Cross.

After the fall of Hong Kong, the Winnipeg Grenadiers were reorganized in Canada and became part of the 13th Infantry Brigade Group. In May, 1944 the Winnipeg Grenadiers were sent overseas to England as reinforcements to the Canadian Army. The Winnipeg Grenadiers had another batt, known as the 2nd Battalion **Winnipeg Grenadiers**, which served in the Reserve Army. In 1965, the regt was placed on the supplementary order of battle and became dormant. Today, only the cadet corps remains to perpetuate the memory of the Winnipeg Grenadiers.

Victoria Cross Awards:

Lieutenant J. E. Tait MC
      August 8-12, 1918
Lieutenant S. L. Honey DCM MM,
      September 27- October 2, 1918
Company Sergeant Major J. R. Osborn
      December 19, 1941

● BRUCE TASCONA

WINNIPEG HUMANE SOCIETY, THE, (WHS)

has focused on the treatment, protection, and welfare of animals throughout MB for more than a century. In 1894, just 2 decades after **Winnipeg**'s incorporation as a city, a group of citizens formed a society to work on alleviating suffering. They were a cross-section of Winnipeg society, including businessmen, lawyers, politicians, clergymen, and **Reform**-minded women. (In the days before universal suffrage, becoming part of a formally constituted board of directors was the only political involvement women could have.) Originally,

the Winnipeg Humane Society was designed for the protection of women and children, as well as animals. Within the next decade, child welfare organizations had begun to form, and the society focused its resources to protect animals from suffering and to promote their welfare and dignity. Over the past century, the society has become a well-known community service organization helping both animals and the people who care about them, and has done this with a volunteer board of directors at the helm.

The Winnipeg Humane Society, originally housed on Charlotte St, used to routinely inspect slaughterhouses and tried to ensure the proper treatment of horses, then the most common form of transportation in the city. Later, the society,

and the animals it protected, was located on the main floor of a house at 1057 Logan Ave, while Sally Warnock, the society's secretary, lived upstairs. She led the work of the society for more than 30 years until her death in 1957, and is remembered through "Aunt Sally's Farm" at the **Assiniboine Park Zoo**.

In 1968, after several years with no facility to care for the animals, the Winnipeg Humane Society completed its shelter at 5 Kent St. The society evolved into a multi-service animal shelter offering a safe haven for unwanted animals as well as offering a multitude of other animal services. The role of the society expanded so dramatically that the facility on Kent began to burst with animals. As of writing, the society was to move into a new facility on Hurst Way in 2007.

In the early 21st century, the Winnipeg Humane Society housed an average of 9000 homeless animals each year. The core functions of the society included finding homes for those animals; providing spay and neuter services; conducting humane inspections to ensure animal welfare; conducting educational presentations to school-age children; rescuing injured animals from the city streets; and advocating for the humane treatment of all animals throughout MB, including farm animals, wildlife, and domestic pets. Donations and fees raised through animal adoptions and kennelling services finance the work of the society.

● VICKI BURNS

The Winnipeg Humane Society's second home was on Logan Avenue.

W

Children's Festival performance, 2006

WINNIPEG INTERNATIONAL CHILDREN'S

FESTIVAL, held annually in June, is the premier summer event in MB for families with elementary-school-aged children. Musicians Gord Osland and Bill Merritt, together with **MITCH PODOLAK**, who also started the **WINNIPEG FOLK FESTIVAL**, founded the festival in 1982.

The first festival was held in 1983 at **ASSINIBOINE PARK**, where 1700 paid admission to see 20 performing artists. For the next 6 years, the festival was held at **KILDONAN PARK**, where the event grew rapidly but parking was limited. In 1990, the festival moved to **THE FORKS**, and in 1995, the festival changed its format, charging a single admission for all shows rather than charging for each performance, as it had previously. By the 1990s, the festival had grown to a paid attendance between 20,000 and 25,000, more than 10 times the box office of its inaugural year. The budget reached $750,000. The volunteer corps doubled to more than 700. By 2004, there were about 120 performances over 4 days.

The festival features musicians, singers, dancers, storytellers, clowns, face painters, and roving performers. Children can take part in activities and games like a talent show contest; there are also concessions and a general store. Most of the performances take place in tents on the banks of the **RED RIVER** at The Forks, giving the event the atmosphere of an old-fashioned circus. Some of the notable performers who have appeared at the Children's Festival include: **FRED PENNER**; **AL SIMMONS**; Rocki Rolletti; Jake Chenier; Raffi; Sharon, Lois, and Bram; Robert Munsch; Utah Phillips; and Australia's Flying Fruitfly Circus. Local storytellers like Jamie Oliviero cut their teeth with young audiences at the

Festival. Two-thirds of the audience is from the public; the remaining third comes from schools and daycare groups who bus in from all over MB, northern ON, MN, and ND.

During the public school system's spring break at the end of March, the Children's Festival runs an event called the Festival of Fools, letting frustrated parents and their housebound children blow off some steam. This event includes more than 40 shows, with international artists, clowns, and what amounts to a free preview of the Children's Festival to come.

Since 1997, the Children's Festival has run a community initiative called the Circus and Magic Partnership (CAMP), whose goal is to teach circus skills to inner city and at-risk youth. Every year the program gives lessons in tightrope walking, flying trapeze, aerial aerobatics, unicycling, illusions, sleight of hand, and juggling skills to about 250 kids. It was inspired by similar programs in inner-city Detroit and in London, UK. The circus program tours to 2 northern communities in MB each year, training local adults to deliver the program and donating circus gear to each community. The circus program has expanded to Kenora; Saskatoon; and London, ON, and won crime prevention awards from the federal and provincial departments of justice. The Circus and Magic Partnership is the only organization to win both the premier's and the mayor's volunteer service awards in a single year. • MAURICE MIREAU

WINNIPEG INTERNATIONAL WRITERS

FESTIVAL (or Thin Air) was founded in 1997 by *Prairie Fire* editor Andris Taskans, Manitoba Writers' Guild executive director Robyn Maharaj, and **U OF W** professor Mark Morton. Volunteers

put on the first festival; all subsequent ones have employed regular staffers. This festival was created to promote **POETRY** and **LITERATURE**, literacy, education, local, national and international writers, and to connect readers and writers. Writers who have graced the festival stage include Manitobans **DAVID ARNASON**, **SANDRA BIRDSELL**, **DI BRANDT**, and **DAVID BERGEN**; and Canadians such as Margaret Atwood, George Elliott Clarke, and Susan Musgrave. In 1998, the festival hired their first general manager, acquired charitable status, and added the title "International" to its name. The festival has a Francophone segment, the "Foyer des écrivains," representing Franco-Manitobans such as **J. R. LÉVEILLÉ**, Québécois writers, and Francophone writers from Africa and elsewhere. Since 2001, the CanWest Global Performing Arts Centre at **THE FORKS** has been the central location for the festival, where it holds its symposiums, readings, and lectures. The festival also annually presents an Aboriginal authors' rural tour, "Words on Wheels." In 2003, the title "Thin Air" was added to the festival's title, and the federal govt began partially to fund the festival. Thereupon, the festival expanded to having presentations and events held at school stages, and an "Afternoon Book Chat" series held at participating **McNALLY ROBINSON** café venues. The festival presents a wide variety of writing styles among 50 authors, celebrating genres like mystery, **JEWISH**, East Coast, and social satire. • RK

WINNIPEG JETS. A hockey team based in the city from 1967-96, the Jets began as a major junior club active in the Western Canada Junior Hockey League (now the Western Hockey League) a league that also included MB teams like the **BRANDON WHEAT KINGS** and the **FLIN FLON BOMBERS**. Owned by **BEN HATSKIN**, the junior version of the Jets was part of the WCJHL from 1967-73 before the franchise was renamed the Winnipeg Clubs, and in 1976, the Monarchs.

1970s: Hatskin (with lawyer Saul Simkin) purchased a $25,000 franchise in the newly created World Hockey Association (WHA) in 1971. The league's 12 teams helped put up money for Hatskin to sign superstar **BOBBY HULL** away from the NHL's Chicago Black Hawks. The NHL tried unsuccessfully to block the move in the courts. On June 22, 1972, Winnipeggers gathered at Portage and Main for a ceremony to mark Hull's $1 million signing bonus. The Jets went on to play their first game in Oct of that year, defeating the New York Raiders 6-4. They finished the season with a record of 43-31-4. In the years following, the Jets were one of hockey's most entertaining teams. Their success can be attributed to the innovative recruitment of quality European players, especially Hull's Swedish linemates Ulf Nilsson and Anders Hedberg (they were called the "Hot Line"), and defenceman Lars-Erik Sjöberg. NHL veteran defenceman **Ted Green** added a physical presence, and Joe Daley was solid in goal.

Nicknamed "The Golden Jet," in 1975 Hull scored 50 goals within the first 50 games, a feat that had only been accomplished by Maurice Richard in the NHL 30 years earlier. Hull went on to score 77 times that season. The Jets won their first WHA championship (Avco Cup) in May 1976, defeating the Houston Aeros. They triumphed again in 1978 and also 1979 – the WHA's last year of existence. Another highlight came in Jan 1978 when the Jets became the first club team to defeat the Soviet Union's top national team.

Off the ice, however, the Jets were in financial trouble from the start. The team lost money in each of its first 2 years, and Hatskin talked about selling. In 1974, businessmen Bob Graham and James Burns, as well as lt gov Jack McKeag organized a community ownership rescue plan modelled after the structure of the **Winnipeg Blue Bombers**. A fundraising campaign raised more than $600,000 of the $2.3 million purchase price. Debates surrounding a new or expanded arena began in 1975, and city council battles over the issue would continue on and off for the next 20 years. In Feb 1978, a group of investors called 8 Hockey Ventures Inc – led by Michael Gobuty and the Shenkarow brothers (Barry and Martin) – purchased the effectively bankrupt team. In Sept, city council approved a $3.5 million, 5000-seat expansion of the then 10,000-seat **Winnipeg Arena**. League-wide financial woes forced the WHA to fold at the close of the 1979 season.

In that same year, largely due to the effective lobbying of Jets GM John Ferguson, the NHL reluctantly admitted the Jets (and 3 other WHA teams) after stripping them of all but 2 players.

1980s: The Jets plummeted to the bottom of the standings in their first 2 NHL seasons, winning less than half of their games and failing to make the playoffs. But on Aug. 13, 1981, another important signing took place after the Jets landed top draft pick **Dale Hawerchuk**. The rookie forward didn't disappoint, racking up 103 points in his first season and leading the Jets to the NHL playoffs for the first time. Some of the decade's other notable Jets included Morris Lukowich, Serge Savard, Dave Babych, Brian Hayward, Randy Carlyle, Paul MacLean, **Thomas Steen**, and Teppo Numminen. Steen's No. 25 was later retired by the franchise, joining Hull's No. 9. The team's best ever season came in 1984-85 when their 96 points placed them 4th overall. In the post-season, Jets fans picked up on a technique of the rival Calgary supporters, and began wearing white to games. The "white-out" playoff tradition was born. Throughout the 1980s, the Jets owners fought with Winnipeg Enterprises Corporation over control of the arena's revenues and lease agreement. Enterprises bought 36% of the team in 1985, injecting millions of dollars into the team. The deal gave WEC an option to purchase the Jets in the event of an outside offer, but only if they committed to covering the team's losses.

1990s: GM Mike Smith shook up the team in 1990 when he traded captain and fan-favourite Hawerchuk to Buffalo for offensive defenceman Phil Housley, who would become key to the success of yet another Scandinavian star. The 1992-93

season saw the arrival of **Teemu Selanne**, the "Finnish Flash." Selanne scored 76 goals and 132 points, establishing rookie records for both goals and points in a Calder Trophy-winning performance. However, the Jets lost in the first round to Vancouver, a typical story for a team that only made it to the 2nd stage of the Stanley Cup playoffs twice in its history. That season was also the rookie year for young standouts Alexei Zhamnov and Keith Tkachuk. Future league stars Nikolai Khabibulin and Shane Doan followed on their heels.

The economics of NHL had been changing over a number of years, with rising salary budgets outpacing revenue streams. Owners around the league made new building construction the priority. Debate over doing the same in Winnipeg surfaced again in 1989, though the arena was rarely full. A number of arena and multiplex proposals surfaced in the following years, touting sites at **The Forks**, **Assiniboia Downs**, adjacent to the city's **Convention Centre**, and even on the existing Winnipeg Arena property. These were joined by a series of controversial reports and studies regarding the team's viability.

In 1991, a new Interim Operating Agreement brought the govt of MB on board to share the cost of all of the team's losses and granted the city and province a $32 million purchase option valid until June 1994. The deal helped renew the debate over the suitability of govt subsidies to a private business. A group called Thin Ice was established in Oct 1993 in opposition to public funding for the Jets and a new arena. About the same time, MB business leaders formed Manitoba Entertainment Complex Inc. (including members of the **Richardson** and **Riley** families) and later Spirit of Manitoba (spearheaded by **Israel Asper**), part of continuing efforts to secure private investment for the team. Neither group could deliver enough concrete corporate support, despite increasing commitments from govt to fund a new building. During spring 1995, a series of public rallies and $13.5 million of fundraising by Operation Grassroots to "Save Our Jets" was too little too late. In Oct 1995, American businessmen purchased the team from Shenkarow and his partners and made plans to relocate the franchise to Phoenix, AZ at the end of the 1995-96 season. Attendance slumped that season, as fans were resigned to the loss of their team. The Jets played their final game in front of a sold-out, frenzied crowd on Apr. 28, 1996, falling 4-1 to the Detroit Red Wings.

2000s: The idea that Winnipeg could once again be home to an NHL franchise is often discussed in the city. Internet campaigners and other boosters point to the success of the **Manitoba Moose**, the **MTS Centre**, and the NHL salary cap

Triumphant Jets with the AVCO Cup, 1976

as reasons why a team could return. However, many of the factors leading to the Jets' departure still loom large – a lack of prospective ownership, a small facility, and the unstable economics of major league hockey. ● JOEL TRENAMAN

WINNIPEG MUSIC COMPETITION FESTIVAL INC

WINNIPEG MUSIC COMPETITION FESTIVAL INC was first held in 1918, making it one of the longest-running music festivals in NA. The festival syllabus includes several classes of competition for solo voice, duets, trios and choirs, as well as solo instruments, chamber groups, bands, and orchestras. Major trophies include the Rose Bowl for senior vocal classes and the Aikins Memorial Trophy for senior instrumental classes. Choral competition figures significantly, with leading high school and community choirs vying for the Lord Tweedsmuir Memorial Trophy. The record for most consecutive wins of this trophy belongs to the St. Stephen's Broadway Choir Church, which held the Tweedsmuir from 1941-62.

Initially known as the Manitoba **MUSIC** Competition Festival, the festival was for many years run by the now defunct Men's Music Club, a group founded in 1915 made up of Winnipeg businessmen devoted to promoting musical talent. As the festival was the first from Canada to join with the Federation of British Music Festivals, it for many years held a tradition of hiring predominantly British adjudicators, among them **LEONARD ISAACS** who later became a director at the **U OF M**'s School of Music. Past competitors of

the festival who went on to some renown include **TRACY DAHL**, **CHANTAL KREVIAZUK**, and **LOREENA MCKENNITT**. ● MD

WINNIPEG PHILHARMONIC CHOIR. The choir has played an integral part in MB's **MUSIC** scene for more than 85 years and is considered one of MB's most active choirs. The philharmonic choir has on average 80 full-time singers, and with the addition of part-time/associate members, there can be 150 or more singers depending on the repertoire requirements. The choir's repertoire includes oratorios, masses, cantatas, and choral symphonies. The choir has also commissioned and performed original works. WPC was founded in 1922 and ran initially as an independent body until 1929 when administrative duties were taken over by the Men's Music Club. In 1959, the WPC became a performing arm of the **WINNIPEG SYMPHONY ORCHESTRA**, a joint agreement that lasted for 10 years. In 1982, the WPC became independent again with its own board of directors. The board is composed of elected volunteers but the choir employs a music director and an executive director. To finance its operations, the choir relies on concert revenue, performance fees, fundraising projects, private and corporate donations, and public grants. As part of its regular season, the WPC performs 3 times in addition to special public, private and benefit performances throughout the year. Each year the WPC tours to at least one community in rural MB giving its first performance in **THOMPSON** in 1999.

The WPC has worked with other choirs including the Greater Grand Forks Symphony Orchestra, the MB Youth Orchestra, and the Salvation Army Band. The WPC performed at Expo '86 in Vancouver. To celebrate its 75th anniversary, the WPC gave a performance at Carnegie Hall. ● JS

WINNIPEG POLICE MUSEUM is situated in the Winnipeg Police Training Academy (Allard School), at 130 Allard St, in Winnipeg. Its artifacts date as far back as 1874, and the archives include records from the 1880s onward. The museum itself has been in operation for over 125 years. The museum's collection includes everything from early ID cameras, criminal mug shots, glass negatives, hand-written record books, original bomb suits and police shields, X-ray machines, bomb robots, and early radar equipment. It also has antiquated firearms and handcuffs, and bulletproof vests – with bullet imprints on them – that have saved the lives of officers. The museum has a section dedicated to honouring the "special constables" of the 1919 **WINNIPEG GENERAL STRIKE**. This section has displays of special constable armbands and badges, period photographs, and batons. Another visitor draw is the display devoted to **EARLE "STRANGLER" NELSON**, a US serial killer who terrorized NA until he was captured in MB in 1927. As well, a 1911 Winnipeg **NORTH END** E-Division holding cell has been reconstructed and set up on display at the museum. Such jails were used in Winnipeg until 1966. The museum also houses a large artifact section, including restored cars such as a 1925 REO Patrol Wagon, and a 1978 Harley-Davidson police motorcycle and sidecar. ● REBECA KUROPATWA

WINNIPEG RH INSTITUTE is a private, non-profit institute founded in 1969 to support and encourage research and development of blood-related products. The lab was co-founded by **HENRY BRUCE CHOWN**, **JOHN BOWMAN**, **MARION LEWIS**, and David Bowles. In the early 1940s, Chown and Bowman developed a treatment and, ultimately, a prevention for Rhesus disease – also known as Rh disease, hemolytic disease, or hydrops fetalis – that goes under the trade name WinRho. Rh disease affects unborn and newborn babies and can result in jaundice, anaemia, and death. Initially, their work involved testing the blood of all pregnant women in MB as well as attending the births of all babies born to Rh-negative mothers. This work often required performing autopsies on babies. The development of the antibody WinRho, licensed in 1980, is credited with the prevention of Rh disease in 98.3% of all cases. This figure represents an estimated 200 lives saved each year in Canada alone. Chown

In 1950, eager students competed in the Music Festival at the Winnipeg Auditorium.

and Bowman's research led to the establishment of Winnipeg company Rh Pharmaceuticals. Rh Pharmaceuticals was purchased by Toronto-based Apotex in 1990, and went public in 1995, taking the name CANGENE. Cangene sells the WinRho product in 35 countries with reported sales of $157 million in 2004. In 2005, the institute was the major supplier in the Cdn market. In Oct 1983, the institute unveiled a plasma fractionation facility on the U OF M campus, incorporated as the Winnipeg Plasma Laboratory. This facility is considered among the most modern such plants in the world, capable of processing 75,000 l of plasma a year. The plasma lab makes Canada self-sufficient in the processing of blood products. The Winnipeg Rh Institute also participates in research programs with the U of M and the Red Cross, and contributes to the study and treatment of haemophilia. In 2005, the institute was carrying out research and development of new blood products. ● JS

▸ *See also* PHARMACEUTICAL INDUSTRY.

WINNIPEG RIVER flows NW from its rise at Lake of the Woods in western ON before draining into LAKE WINNIPEG near PINE FALLS. It is known for its role in the FUR TRADE and as a modern source of HYDROELECTRIC POWER. It is 813 km long from its head of the Firesteel River when including its course as the Rainy River, but is known as the Winnipeg River for about 225 km from a dam E of Kenora, ON. The watershed encompasses 136,000 km² and includes the Bird, Lee, Whitemouth, and English rivers.

It was the main canoe route W from Lake Superior for FIRST PEOPLES and became the key to developing the fur trade in what would become MB. Pierre la Vérendrye's son, Jean-Baptiste la Vérendrye (*see* LA VÉRENDRYE family), was the first recorded European to navigate the river. The HBC and the NWC both built FORTS along its banks – especially near Lake Winnipeg – in competition for furs until 1821. In those days, the river was known for the rapids and falls that required 26 portages to complete the full trip. In the late 19th and early 20th centuries, the river's powerful flow, a 106 m drop, and relatively accessible location led to extensive hydroelectric development on both sides of the provincial border. The Winnipeg General Power Company began the PINAWA Dam in 1902 before amalgamating with the Winnipeg Electric Street Railway in 1904. The dam was closed in 1951 and made into a PROVINCIAL PARK. The city of Winnipeg formed Winnipeg Hydro in 1906, leading to decades of competing projects on the river. In 2006, MANITOBA HYDRO operated 6 dams on the river that generated 583 mW.

Scene along the Winnipeg River

The river runs through WHITESHELL PROVINCIAL PARK, widening to form Nutimik, Eleanor, Dorothy, and Margaret lakes (popular for cottaging and recreation). PETROFORMS occur near its confluence with the Whiteshell River. The communities of Pinawa, POWERVIEW, and LAC DU BONNET are located farther downstream. ● JOEL TRENAMAN

WINNIPEG STADIUM, or CANAD INNS Stadium as it has been called since 2001, is the city's largest outdoor sports facility. Best known as the home of the WINNIPEG BLUE BOMBERS football team, it opened in 1953. The community-owned Bombers had been playing in Osborne Stadium, but had been attracting capacity crowds based largely on the success of quarterback JACK JACOBS. The new stadium was often referred to as

"The House that Jack Built," though much of the credit goes to then-Bombers president William "Culver" Riley (*see* RILEY FAMILY).

In 1952 the province passed legislation to create the Winnipeg Enterprises Corporation (WEC), a non-profit organization that would build and manage sports facilities. The members included BRIAN DICKSON and Riley, with the latter as chairman. The WEC immediately began plans to construct the $500,000, 17,000-seat stadium, and 2 years later, the WINNIPEG ARENA. Public funding paved the way for both projects.

The SW corner of the structure was converted for use by the WINNIPEG GOLDEYES BASEBALL team in 1954, and remained that way until 1984 when the Bomber offices were added. The re-born Goldeyes played in the stadium's NW corner from 1994 until the completion of **Can-West Global Park**. Other renovations took place in 1971 (addition of upper decks) the late 1980s (artificial field, seating), and then in advance of the 1999 **Pan American Games** (seating, sound, scoreboard). The changes brought the seating capacity for football up to 29,503.

The stadium has also been home to the Winnipeg Rifles football team, and concerts by the likes of The Rolling Stones, Pink Floyd, U2, and Paul McCartney. Ceremonies and events of the Pan American Games were held there in 1967 and 1999, as were Canadian Football League Grey Cup championships in 1991, 1998 and 2006.

In 2004, WEC transferred the control of Canad Inns Stadium to the Winnipeg Football Club board of directors. Talk of a new facility for the team began immediately, with a proposed site near **Assiniboia Downs**. The plan stalled, and in early 2007 the Bombers made a public appeal for other proposals. A Canad Inns plan suggested a $500 million domed stadium development in St. Boniface, and a David Asper-backed (*see* **Asper Family**) scheme offered a $120 million open stadium at the current Polo Park site with his company assuming private ownership of the team. Both propositions would also require govt funding. In June 2007, the Bombers board approved a letter of intent to pursue exclusive negotiations with Asper's group. ● JOEL TRENAMAN

WINNIPEG STREET RAILWAY COMPANY

was the operator of Canada's first electric transit system, and was started by **Albert William Austin**. The son of a wealthy Toronto businessman, Austin arrived in **Winnipeg** in 1880 and saw the need for a horse-drawn street **Railway** system such as Toronto had had since the 1860s. In 1881, with support from prominent local investors **J. W. Ashdown** and Hugh Sutherland, Austin organized the Winnipeg Street Railway Company, and negotiated a 20-year franchise to own and operate the system from the city. The first track was laid along the W side of Main St, N to the new City Hall at William Ave. Austin ordered 4 rail cars seating 24 passengers from New York, and imported 20 horses from ON. Headquarters were established on Assiniboine Ave between Fort and Garry streets. A test run took place on Oct 20, 1882. The operation was deemed successful, and new track was laid from City Hall N to the **CPR** station at Higgins, and W on Portage Ave to Kennedy St. In winter, the cars were outfitted with runners to cope with the inevitable buildup of ice and snow on the tracks.

As the city continued to expand in all directions, Austin realized that the horse-drawn system would be unable to meet increasing

Opening of the Winnipeg Electric Street Railway, Sept. 5, 1892

demand. In 1888, Austin travelled to Richmond, VA, after hearing reports of an electric street railway. He returned to Winnipeg, convinced that electric trolley cars were the way to the future. Nervous about this new technology, city council hedged, finally agreeing to allow Austin to test the new system across the **Assiniboine River** in sparsely populated Fort Rouge. The tests were successful, and Winnipeg's first electric streetcar, manufactured in Canada, arrived via CPR flatcar in Nov 1890. Austin was so confident of his system that he did not wait for spring to test it. On Jan 27, 1891, before a large crowd of curious onlookers, the car made its first run from the S side of the Main St Bridge, up River Ave to Osborne St, and back again. The original run proving successful, Canada's first commercial electric street railway went into regular service the following day. By the next year, a rival firm, the Winnipeg Electric Street Railway Company, had begun operations, and Austin sold his operation to them in 1894. In 1904, the new company added **Hydroelectric Power** interests and became known as Winnipeg Electric Railway, and in 1924, simply Winnipeg Electric Company. ● MD

WINNIPEG SUN

is Manitoba's 2nd-largest daily **Newspaper**, printed in tabloid style with an average daily circulation of about 45,000. The newspaper was founded after the demise of the **Winnipeg Tribune**, which shut down unexpectedly in Aug 1980 after 94 years. A small and diligent group of former *Tribune* workers, motivated by the sudden termination, dedicated themselves

to providing readers with an option to the **Winnipeg Free Press**. With this in mind, the *Winnipeg Sun*'s first issue hit newsstands just 3 months after the *Trib's* closure, in Nov 1980. The paper originally published 3 times a week – Monday, Wednesday, and Friday. Within a year of its debut, the *Sun* earned the designation of "fastest growing newspaper in Canada." Publication on Tuesdays and Thursdays was added in Feb 1982, and a Sunday edition appeared in March of that year. The "S'Paper," a word used by the *Winnipeg Sun* to describe its new Saturday paper, debuted in April 1992 to complete the 7-day news cycle. Cdn communications and printing conglomerate Quebecor purchased the *Winnipeg Sun* in 1983, and over the next 15 years, the newspaper went through a number of different visual and editorial incarnations. Quebecor merged with Sun Media Corporation in 1999 and the *Winnipeg Sun* became part of a national Sun chain that includes similarly styled papers in Ottawa, Calgary, Edmonton, and Toronto. Today, the *Winnipeg Sun* is known for its focus on breaking news, local crime, in-depth sports, cheeky political editorials, and the daily photograph of a bikini-clad Sunshine Girl (and, for a time, a similarly dressed Sunshine Boy). ● TAMMY MARLOWE JOHNSON

WINNIPEG SYMPHONY ORCHESTRA

(WSO) gave its first concert on Dec 16, 1948. As far back as 1880, Winnipeggers had made short-lived attempts to establish an orchestra. However, it was not until after WWII that the CBC announced that it intended to found a broadcasting orchestra in the city. Local **Music** groups banded together to plan the simultaneous creation of an orchestra to give public concerts. In 1947, the Winnipeg Civic Music League established a stock company, the Winnipeg Symphony Orchestra Ltd. Through public sales and private donations, it raised funds to launch a financially stable orchestra.

Walter Kaufmann was chosen as the first conductor. He gave the fledgling orchestra a foundation in the standard classics. In 1958, Victor Feldbrill, only the 2nd Cdn-born conductor to lead a major orchestra, succeeded him. Feldbrill expanded the WSO's concert schedule; took the orchestra on its first tours, to ON, SK, and the northern US; and programmed a significant amount of Cdn and Modern music. He placed the orchestra's players under contract for the first time. George Cleve succeeded Feldbrill in 1968, launching the orchestra's residency in its newly built home, the Manitoba Centennial Concert Hall. Piero Gamba arrived as music director in 1971. He brought in many renowned guest soloists, made albums with the WSO for CBC Records, and took the orchestra to Carnegie Hall in Mar 1979. By that time, ticket sales had been falling for several seasons. In July 1980, the WSO faced an accumulated deficit of more than $700,000. The entire board of directors resigned and Gamba left, and the MB govt took control of the orchestra. Conductor Kazuhiro Koizumi was music director 1983-89. The orchestra continued to make recordings for the CBC and began playing music by MB composers. The subscription base grew to more than 10,000, and by 1984, the deficit had been erased.

Bramwell Tovey served as the WSO's artistic director from 1989 until 2001. He played an active role in the musical community and presided over special concerts marking the orchestra's 50th anniversary. In 1992, he and composer-in-residence Glenn Buhr spearheaded the risky venture of a New Music Festival. It drew international recognition. The WSO maintained a balanced budget through the early 1990s. As the millennium approached, continued financial challenges resulted in a new deficit. A deadlock in contract negotiations led management to lock out the musicians for the first time on Dec 13, 2001. A settlement arranged by a govt-imposed mediator resulted in a resumption of the season on Jan 16, 2002, and an increase in musicians' representation in running the organization.

Russian-born Andrey Boreyko became music director in 2002. His 4 seasons witnessed strong artistic growth, but by 2003, renewed decreases in sales swelled the accumulated deficit to more than $3 million. Support from all levels of govt, and a 15% wage reduction for the musicians, resulted in a budget surplus of $100,000 on the 2003/04 season. In 2005, the 65-member orchestra had an annual budget of $6 million. Its 36-week season included 12 pairs of classics concerts, 6 Musically Speaking programs, 7 Pops, and 5 children's programs, plus elementary school concerts, special concerts, 4 concerts in **Brandon**, run-outs to rural MB, and the New Music Festival. The WSO performs for Manitoba **Opera**, the **Royal Winnipeg Ballet**, and **Rainbow Stage**, and its musicians form the nucleus of the **Manitoba Chamber Orchestra**.

The WSO's guest artists have included Isaac Stern, Pierre Monteux, Itzhak Perlman, Mstislav Rostropovich, Vladimir Ashkenazy, David Oistrakh, Van Cliburn, Sir Yehudi Menuhin, Jacqueline du Pré, Glenn Gould, Sir John Barbirolli, Yo-Yo Ma, Charles Dutoit, Kirill Kondrashin, and Jean-Pierre Rampal. Concertmasters have been Richard Seaborn (1948-60), Lea Foli (1960-66), Arthur Polson (1966-86), and Gwen Hoebig (1987-). The orchestra's pops concerts have featured such noteworthy performers as Arthur Fiedler, Mitch Miller, Henry Mancini, Mel Tormé, Doc Severinsen, and Ethel Merman. Children's concerts have been a regular feature of the WSO's schedule, presenting family entertainers both local (**Fred Penner**, **Al Simmons**) and national (Shari Lewis). Local amateur performers of many musical genres and ethnic origins have appeared with the orchestra. The WSO performs annual educational concerts for thousands of elementary school children. It gives concerts in such city venues as parks, churches, and shopping malls. • DON ANDERSON

WINNIPEG TOILERS. The **Winnipeg** team, formed Oct 5, 1910, dominated MB's **Basketball** scene from the 1920s into the early 1930s, winning the provincial championship 13 times. The Toilers, so called to represent the idea of hard work, perseverance, and courage, were also the first MB team to win a Cdn championship, winning the top national prize in 1926, 1927, and 1932. In 1933, a series was arranged with the Tulsa Oilers, the US champions. Billed as the "World's Basketball Championship," it was to be a home-and-home series, with 2 games in Tulsa and 2 in Winnipeg. Unaccustomed to US rules, the Toilers lost both games in Tulsa, 32-13 and 41-19. Tragically, on the flight back to Winnipeg on March 31, their plane crashed in a wheat field near Neodesha, KA. Two of the team's brightest young stars, Mike Shea and Joe Dodds, were killed, and the rest suffered broken bones and shattered dreams. The team never recovered from this tragedy, and disbanded in 1937. The Toilers' memory is preserved in the Toilers Memorial Park in Fort Garry. • MD

WINNIPEG TRIBUNE was one of western Canada's oldest newspapers when it suddenly ceased publication in 1980. It had first emerged after the turmoil of the mid-1880s when **Winnipeg** was a hotbed of newspapermen looking for a cause. Anyone with a "slashing pen" set up a newspaper. Few survived for long. From this editorial melange, 2 publications would engage in perpetual warfare: the *Tribune*, established in 1890, and the *Manitoba Free Press* (later the **Winnipeg Free Press**) started 18 years earlier.

Robert Lorne Richardson and Duncan Lloyd McIntyre pooled funds in 1890 and for $7000 bought the printing press and building of the defunct *Manitoba Sun* (which had been absorbed by the *Free Press*), founding the *Tribune*. (Ninety years later, the *Tribune*'s presses would be sold and the building torn down by the *Free Press* owner, preventing rebirth of a newspaper there.) Throughout its existence, the *"Trib"* was 2nd in circulation to the opposition *Free Press*, but often considered the leader in local newsgathering. Richardson's feuding with the "other paper" would foster an esprit de corps amongst *Tribune* scoop-happy reporters that lasted for the life of the newspaper.

As editor, Richardson initiated a lively political duel with the *FP* in 1890, supporting the **Thomas Greenway** govt, which the other daily opposed. Political alignments eventually were switched and, by the mid-20th century, the *Tribune*'s leaning was strongly Conservative. At a provincial Progressive Conservative meeting and dinner in Winnipeg in the early 1950s, the *Tribune*'s chief Legislature reporter covered the occasion from the party leader's head table. A top editor could receive a prime patronage appointment when Conservatives were in power in Ottawa.

One service to Cdn journalism delivered by the *Tribune*, in an unusual alliance with the *Free Press* and the *Telegram* (later absorbed by the *Tribune*), was the institution of their own newsgathering service – the Western Associated Press, in 1907. Before then, all Cdn newspapers paid CP Telegraphs for dissemination of news, mainly from US sources, and the Winnipeg newspapers rebelled when rates were doubled and coverage of Cdn events was dumped. The WAP spread throughout Canada's West, and evolved after 5 years into the Canadian Press, a co-operative newswire service that included every major newspaper in the country in its membership.

The *Tribune* was bought by William Southam in 1920. The Southam chain allowed complete

THE WINNIPEG TRIBUNE

FINAL EDITION

Red Rises Here, Floods Near Selkirk

Elm Park Blockade Disputed

Country Phones Severed

TWO DEAD IN FLOODS; RED ENTERS EMERSON

2 Feet Water In Town

Red Tide Rises

The *Tribune* was noted for its extensive coverage of local news.

policy autonomy for its newspapers. The *Tribune*'s newsroom was considered a school for journalists, attracting wandering aspirants from as far away as the UK, South Africa, and the US. Many would go on to be editors-in-chief and managing editors at news organizations across the country. Outstanding graduates included **RALPH ALLEN**, war correspondent, author, historian, magazine editor, and **JIM COLEMAN**, sports icon, Canada's first sports journalist with a nationally syndicated column and named to 5 sports "halls of fame." Some well-known *Tribune* writers were Victor V. Murray, columnist; **ROBERT HUNTER**, later a founder of Greenpeace; **VINCE LEAH**, sports; **GENE TELPNER**, entertainment; Val Werier, natural environment and heritage columnist; and **JACK MATHESON**, sports. Sports editor Matheson, noted for his "tell it like it is" writing style, put heavy emphasis on curling and **WINNIPEG BLUE BOMBERS**' football.

In the mid-1970s, Southam's charged head-on at the *Free Press*, financing a remake of the *Tribune*'s design and content, hiring a New York specialist who introduced modular layout of its page columns, and innovating a Saturday Lifestyle section, a comic book and free classified want ads. *Tribune* circulation experienced unprecedented growth, climbing from a low of 66,000 to more than 100,000 near decade's end. However, these gains did not come without a cost to both the *Trib* and the *Free Press*. The owners of the 2 newspapers saw a growing sea of red ink: one of the papers had to go.

When the *Tribune* was shut down in 1980, it gave Thomson's *Free Press* a free hand in Winnipeg. Toronto-based Thomson closed the *Ottawa Citizen*, leaving Southam the Ottawa market. A Royal Commission and the courts subsequently absolved the newspaper chains of complicity. • JIM SHILLIDAY

WINNIPEG VICTORIAS. *See* **HOCKEY, ICE.**

WINNIPEGOSIS, pop 621, is a village 60 km N of **DAUPHIN**, along the shores of **LAKE WINNIPEGOSIS**, at the mouth of Mossy River (sometimes spelled "Mossey"), and on hwy 20. Initially called Mossy River in 1896 when a post office opened here, the name was changed to Winnipegosis, after the river, 2 years later. Winnipegosis became a village in 1915. The **CN** once came here, but the line was abandoned in the 1970s. **CREE** had been in the area for centuries, before French **FUR TRADERS** arrived. Winnipegosis was the site of the original Fort Dauphin, built around 1741 by **LA VÉRENDRYE** and named for the French dauphin at the time, Louis Ferdinand. Over the years, **FORESTRY** and **COMMERCIAL FISHING** gradually replaced trapping, and **ICELANDIC**, British, **UKRAINIAN, POLISH, MENNONITE,** and **FRENCH** settlers came to the area in the late 19th and early 20th century. These groups still make up most of the pop of Winnipegosis. The village is primarily a service and retail centre for surrounding ranches, though the largest employers are the local hospital and school division. Outdoor activities are also important to the region. • GPP

WINPAK LTD. is among NA's largest manufacturers and distributors of plastic packaging and plastic packaging machines for the protection of food, beverage, and dairy products, as well as some pharmaceutical applications. Founded in 1977 by Nastola, Finland, plastic-packaging giant Wihuri Oy Wipak and mutual fund giant **INVESTORS GROUP INC**, Winpak began with a single manufacturing plant in **WINNIPEG**. Two years later, a group of 12 senior managers and the Federal Business Development Bank also acquired stakes in the company, although the FBD and Investors Group subsequently sold their interests in the firm when it became publicly traded in 1986. In the years since its inception, Winpak has helped to fuel its growth by acquiring other plastic-packaging operations in NA. By early 2005, the company owned and operated 10 production plants in NA, including 2 in Winnipeg. Its annual revenues had grown from about $4 million in its first year to nearly $400 million in 2004. • MURRAY MCNEILL

WINTER BIRDS that weather out the tough MB season number about 100 species. Winter is defined here as the period from Dec through Feb, based on actual conditions, not what the calendar says. Many birds linger in the province into early Dec, and succumb to the elements soon thereafter, but dozens of species are well adapted to survive the winter season here.

PETER TAYLOR

Evening Grosbeaks are known as "winter finches."

Most **GROUSE** and their allies are non-migratory, and find a plentiful supply of buds and seeds to live on. In addition, our native species, such as ptarmigans, Ruffed Grouse (*Bonasa umbellus*), and Sharp-tailed Grouse (*Tympanuchus phasianellus*), have fully feathered, fringed toes that allow them to walk on snow with ease. Only a few diurnal **HAWK** species winter here in numbers, most notably the Northern Goshawk (*Accipiter gentilis*) and the Merlin (*Falco columbarius*). In contrast, most **OWLS** remain behind; winter often provides the best opportunities to see these intriguing birds as they hunt voles or other prey. Most **WOODPECKERS**, too, can find enough natural food here during winter, as do ravens and magpies, nuthatches, and chickadees.

The "winter **FINCHES**" comprise a group of small, seed-eating birds that are most easily seen in winter as they visit feeders. Redpolls (*Carduelis* spp.) and Pine Grosbeaks (*Pinicola enucleator*) arrive from northern breeding grounds, crossbills may frequent conifers when the cone crop is good, and Evening Grosbeaks (*Coccothraustes vespertinus*) form noisy flocks at the edge of the boreal forest (*see* ECOCLIMACTIC REGIONS). At times, Pine Siskins (*Carduelis pinus*) and American goldfinches (*C. tristis*) may also linger, but numbers fluctuate from year to year, as is the case with most of the other species in this group. Urban areas and farmyards are the strongholds of rock pigeons (*Columba livia*), European starlings (*Sturnus vulgaris*), and house sparrows (*Passer domesticus*), all exotic species that were released in NA in the 19th century and are now among our commonest birds.

Feeding birds has become a popular hobby for many Manitobans. Winter provides a great opportunity to get close-up views of woodpeckers, nuthatches, chickadees, and winter finches. Some people feel that feeding is detrimental to the birds, but our native species find enough other food to balance their diets, and in some cases, a well-stocked feeder may help a lingering "half-hardy" species survive the season.

Black sunflower seeds are the food of choice for most species, while sparrows and some finches prefer millet or Niger thistle (also known as Nyjer) seed. Seed mixes are not recommended. Suet provides high-energy food for woodpeckers, nuthatches, and chickadees. Feeders are best placed 2-3 m from cover – close enough to allow birds a nearby hiding place, but far enough to prevent squirrels from jumping onto them – and at a height of at least 1.5 m to protect from cats.

Two winter endeavours involving amateur birdwatchers throughout NA are Christmas Bird Counts (CBCs) and Project Feeder Watch. CBCs originated over a century ago and take place between Dec 14 and Jan 5; most large MB communities conduct them. Project Feeder Watch has a more recent origin. It is co-ordinated by the Cornell Lab of Ornithology and Bird Studies Canada. ● RUDOLF KOES

WINTER ROADS (or ice roads), found in all provinces and territories except NS and PE, are seasonal snow and ice roads that are connected to and reach beyond MB's all-weather highway network. There are 2 principal components of MB's winter-road system, one E of LAKE WINNIPEG, the other in the more northerly reaches of the province. In 2005, the total length of the system was about 1600 km, less than half the 4000 km total during the late 1960s. The roads E of Lake Winnipeg are rarely usable for more than 50 days between mid-Jan and mid-Mar, depending

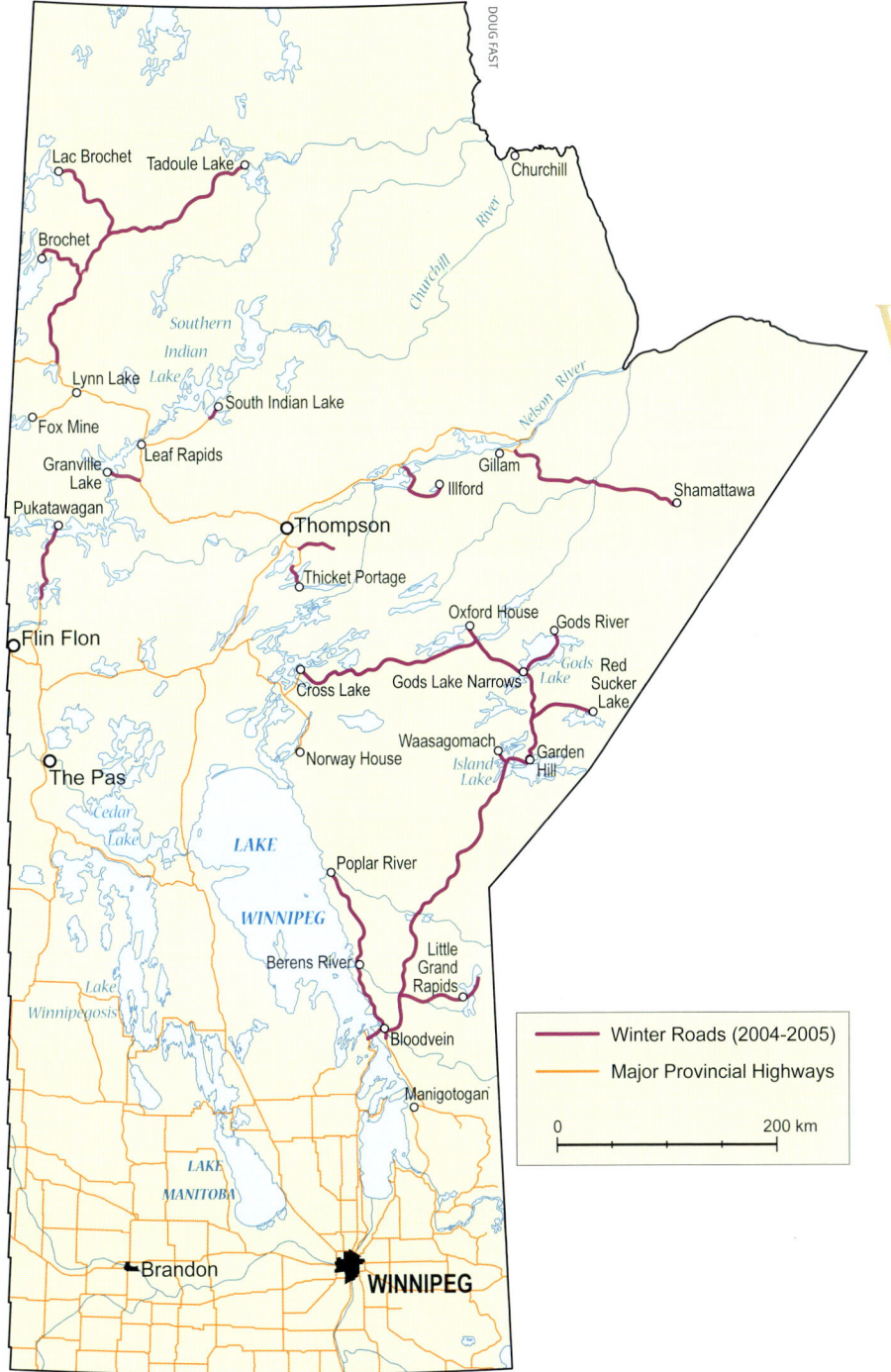

Winter roads in northern Manitoba

on WEATHER conditions and construction delays. In 1998, these routes did not open at all. Winter roads in northern MB are usually open somewhat longer. During their limited operating period, winter roads provide land access for otherwise isolated, predominantly First Nations communities.

In MB, winter roads date back at least to the early 1940s, when tractor trains were used to supply winter fishing camps on some of the province's northern LAKES and, in turn, transport the catch to collection points for shipment to markets across NA. The early roads were largely the creation of the Sigfusson Brothers Transportation Company, which hauled freight on them until 1972 (*see* TRUCKING INDUSTRY). In 1971, the provincial govt took over the construction and maintenance of winter roads. At present, First Nations-run companies, under the direction of the Department of Transportation and Govt Services, carry out much of the work. Annual

W

Winter roads provide access to isolated Manitoba communities.

construction begins with an aerial reconnaissance of the routes, which don't change much from year to year. If the weather has been sufficiently cold for frost penetration and water freeze-up, construction can begin in Dec; however, in recent years, thanks to climate change, a Jan start has been typical. Since these roads are located in wilderness areas, considerable care is taken to minimize potential damage to the natural environment. For example, as few trees as possible are removed, and provincial govt policy does not permit the destruction of beaver dams.

There are 2 types of winter road: snow roads and ice roads. The former traverse swamp or muskeg mainly, although they also cross "dry ground" and bedrock "ridges" of the **Canadian** Shield. The first step in their construction is to clear the right-of-way and level the road base as much as possible. Snow is not permitted to become too deep because it serves as ground insulation and retards frost penetration. When frost has penetrated 15 cm, tracked vehicles up to the size of small bulldozers build up and compact the snow. As the compacted snow thickens to about 20 cm, heavy graders, often pulling log or steel I-beam drags, continue the compacting and levelling. This process is repeated many times before a road is ready. The typical width of a completed snow road is 9 m.

Ice roads cross frozen lakes and are about 60 m wide so the pressure of vehicular weight is spread; otherwise a narrow strip of ice would be vulnerable to collapse. Ice roads must be at least 70 cm thick to support large, fully loaded trucks. When lake ice thickness reaches at least 25 cm, light equipment can be used to clear snow from the designated route in order to accelerate the

rate of ice formation. With continuous ice thickening, progressively heavier equipment is used to keep the surface bare. Speed on ice roads, particularly that of heavy trucks, is limited, often to about 15 km/hr, because the weight and forward motion of traffic cause wave action beneath the ice. Too much wave action can buckle the ice. As a result, the 400 km trip between Manigotogan and Island Lake takes about 12 hours.

A variation on the ice road is the ice bridge, essentially an ice road across a stream. Whereas ice roads on lakes rely mainly on natural ice, ice bridges are commonly created artificially by flooding the crossing and letting the water freeze. This process strengthens the stream crossing and raises the ice bridge closer to road level, thus reducing the grade of descent and ascent. It should be noted that ice formed by surface flooding has about half the load-bearing capacity of natural ice. Winter roads enable isolated communities to be supplied with most of their yearly needs of bulk goods, as long as roads are open long enough. Groceries, building materials, machinery, and fuels are among the principal types of commodities shipped in 1000 or more truckloads. Air transport is the year-round alternative, except for communities along the eastern shoreline of Lake Winnipeg, which are able to rely on the water link to **Selkirk**, because the lake is ice-free for more than half the year. Some goods, particularly foodstuffs, are flown in throughout the year, but the cost by air is about 10 times that by truck.

MB's winter roads are open to the public; thus, in addition to their role in moving freight, they encourage seasonal contacts among residents of communities on the network. Moreover,

travel to and from places throughout most of the province is possible because the winter roads are temporary extensions of the province's highway system. The length of the winter road network is being reduced as the system of all-weather roads expands, but some routes will no doubt continue to function for many years. The role these roads have had in providing seasonal access to and from isolated communities in MB for more than 60 years is testimony to their importance. ● RICHARD H. FOSTER

WISEMAN, Adele, author (b, 1928, **Winnipeg**; d June 1, 1992, Toronto). *The Sacrifice,* Wiseman's first novel, won the 1956 Gov Gen's Award for fiction, climaxing her long, determined drive to achieve professional standing as a writer. Born to a close, working-class **Jewish** family in Winnipeg's **North End**, she attended St. John's High School as well as Jewish secular schools, and graduated in English from the **U of M**. Then, in order to enable her to continue writing, she worked as a social worker in London, UK; as a teacher in the Overseas School in Rome; and, returning to Winnipeg, as a lab technician and as secretary to the **Royal Winnipeg Ballet**. Following the success of her first novel, Wiseman spent 3 years in New York on a Guggenheim Fellowship, and another 2 years in London. She then taught for several years in Montreal at Sir George Williams U, Macdonald College, and McGill U, and was awarded a Canada Council for the Arts grant to devote herself full-time to writing. Moving to Toronto, she served at various times as writer-in-residence at the U of Toronto, Concordia U, Trent U, and the U of Western ON, and she led the summer workshops in creative writing at the Banff School of Fine Arts. *The Sacrifice* and Wiseman's subsequent novel, *Crackpot* (1974), have been admired for their deeply mythological use of cultural material, and her account of her mother's doll-making in *Old Woman at Play* (1978) provides a poignant insight into nature of creativity. Wiseman also published plays, a collection of essays, a children's story, and critical articles and reviews. Together with her life-long friend, **Margaret Laurence**, she is considered a significant member of the "3rd wave" of western Cdn women writers. ● MILDRED GUTKIN

WITTMEIER, Bonnie, gymnast (b Sept 15, 1966, **Winnipeg**) was an elite athlete. She trained at the Winnipeg Panthers Gym Club, and then at the Winnipeg Gymnastic Centre. At the 1979 Canada Games, Wittmeier won 3 gold and 1 silver medal. She competed internationally, and placed 5th all-around at the Pacific Rim Championships. Moving into senior competition, she then qualified as second alternate for the 1980 Olympic team, though the team did not see competition as the Games were boycotted. She won bronze in all-around at the 1981 national championship, and then competed at the world championship where she finished in 34th place. She was the 1982 Cdn champion, and ranked 25th at the world championships the following year. At the 1984 Los Angeles Olympics, Wittmeier placed 13th all-around. In 2007, she lived in Vancouver, BC. • MD

WOLF, GREY (*Canis lupus*) is a large member of the canid or dog family found originally over a vast range from southern Mexican to the High Arctic, and across Eurasia from the Arctic coast south to Arabia, India and China. It has been persecuted for thousands of years due to fear of attack and predation on livestock. It is now absent from developed and agricultural regions, including SW MB, but the species is still found elsewhere in the province, including the spruce-pine-aspen forests only 100 km E of Winnipeg. The male weighs about 50 kg (max 80 kg); females slightly less. Total length is 180 cm, including a 45 cm bushy tail. The thick fur, consisting of long guard hairs and dense underfur, is a blend of brown, grey, and black. The wolf is occasionally confused at a distance with the more-common coyote (*Canis latrans*), but the latter is considerably smaller and slimmer at 18 kg.

Wolves often commence hunting in the early evening, travelling up to 30 km before retiring. Home range is determined by prey abundance and terrain. Generally detecting prey by scent (up to 3 km away), wolves approach and size-up the situation, watching carefully for signs of prey weakness or injury. The wolf is designed to run down its exhausted prey over long distances (hence its long legs and great stamina), and often hunts in family packs averaging 8 members. Such combined efforts permit the successful capture of large, dangerous prey such as Elk and Moose. Pack members bite down with powerful jaws on the legs, flanks and shoulders of prey (avoiding strikes of the antlers and front hooves), which soon succumbs to shock and loss of blood. With 42 strong teeth, the wolf slices off hunks of meat and organs and swallows them whole as fast as possible, instinctively ensuring a share of the food in order of dominance. A strict hierarchy is maintained in the pack, reinforced by gestures (baring of fangs) and voice (howl, growl, whimper). While some wolves pair off and maintain a close bond for many years, other lone individuals come together only during the breeding season in early spring. About 63 days after mating, an average of 6 young are born in a den. By 3 weeks they begin playing around the entrance, with the mother remaining close, and the family being supplied with fresh and regurgitated food by the non-breeding members of the pack. Full grown by 10 months, the subadults reach maturity in 2 years, breed for the first time at 3 years, and live up to 10 years (18 years in captivity). • REW

WOLFE, Bernie, politician (b Nov 19, 1922, **WINNIPEG**). Wolfe was educated at United College (*see* **U OF W**) where he studied Liberal Arts. In the early 1950s, he established a real estate and insurance company called, Ernst, Little, Wolfe and by 1957, he became president of the **MANITOBA CHAMBERS OF COMMERCE**. Wolfe sat on the council of the Metropolitan Corporation of Greater

Winnipeg from 1960-65 and again from 1967-71 as a representative of Transcona. He supported the amalgamation of Winnipeg in the early 70s and in 1971 was elected to city council under **UNICITY**. As a founding member of the Independent Citizen's Election Committee, he became its unofficial leader in 1974. From 1972-74, he also sat on the executive policy committee. Mayor **STEPHEN JUBA** appointed him deputy mayor in 1974 and he held that post until 1977. That year, Transcona erected the Bernie Wolfe Community School in his honour. In 1978, he became a founding member of Heritage Winnipeg and was its president for 5 years. He was appointed to the Canadian Transport Commission in Ottawa and served until his retirement in 1987. He received the Order of Canada in 2001, and for his ongoing dedication to Heritage Winnipeg, he was given an honorary award in 2003. • RUTH DEGRAVES

WOLSELEY EXPEDITION was a joint UK/Cdn military expedition to the **RED RIVER SETTLEMENT** in 1870, allegedly to assert British authority and sovereignty over the territory in the wake of the **RED RIVER RESISTANCE**. The expedition was initially planned before it was clear that Red River could be pacified, although the planning continued as the May 1870 *Manitoba Act* made its way through the legislative process.

The Cdn govt realized that it would have to reach Red River by the traditional **FUR TRADE**/voyageur route, and it ordered boats for this service early in 1870. The British insisted that they would supply and pay for no more than 250 regular troops only if the legitimate demands of the residents of Red River were satisfied, which pressured the Cdn govt to settle with the resistant **MÉTIS**. The British commander of the force would be Col Garnet Wolseley, an **IRISH**-born career soldier who had served in Burma, the Crimea, India, and China, before being posted to Canada in 1861. Immediately upon the gov gen's assent to the *Manitoba Act* on May 12, Ottawa formally established 2 batts of volunteer militia.

From the beginning, the expedition was contentious, since many could not see any need for it. The troops were embarked for the West in May, setting up a temporary headquarters at Prince Arthur's Landing, near what is now Thunder Bay, ON. A disagreement over whether a wagon road constructed over the winter was ready for use resulted in Wolseley ordering the boats to be used to transport the troops to be brought up the Kakabeka Falls via the Kaministiquia River. This was an arduous journey that made the expedition unnecessarily difficult. Having successfully transported boats, men, and supplies up the Kaministiquia, the expedition began its water

Wolves usually hunt in family packs.

ROBERT R. TAYLOR

W

route W on July 16. Although boats occasionally got lost on the journey, little real difficulty was experienced by the expedition. One soldier was wounded by his own revolver, but the expedition met no resistance and reached Fort Alexander, at the head of the **WINNIPEG RIVER**, by early Aug. Wolseley led his regulars into the **RED RIVER** and toward what would later be known as **WINNIPEG** on Aug 22. He approached the village at the head of an invading army, and both the commander and his men were disappointed that Métis leader **LOUIS RIEL** and his govt had apparently fled rather than standing to fight. For his part, Riel had expected to hand over the settlement to Wolseley without any trouble, and he was startled that the settlement was being forcibly "liberated." Because Riel had not fired a shot, martial law was not proclaimed, and the senior officer of the **HBC** in what had hitherto been the **COUNCIL OF ASSINIBOIA** was recognized as governor until the arrival of the new civilian lt gov.

Wolseley treated his campaign as an important lesson for rebels, and most of his contemporaries in Canada and the UK agreed. Wolseley would build a subsequent military career – culminating in a term as commander-in-chief of the British Army – on his Red River 'victory'. He quickly turned authority over to the Cdn volunteers, who arrived in Winnipeg on Aug 27, and took his regulars back to ON. Another body of volunteers would depart from Lake Superior for Red River in late Oct 1870 to reinforce the garrison, using the road Wolseley had rejected. This 2nd expedition was designed to help protect against a feared **FENIAN** invasion which had, however, fizzled out before its departure. The 2nd

expedition arrived in Winnipeg on Nov 18 after a 28-day overland march, providing evidence to the US of Canada's determination to defend its new territory. A number of MB's future leaders, such as **WILLIAM FORBES ALLOWAY**, arrived as volunteers with the 2 military expeditions of 1870 and 1871. ● J.M. BUMSTED

WOLVERINE (*Gulo gulo*) is a member of the weasel family Mustelidae and has rightly earned a reputation as a fierce and powerful predator and scavenger. It is capable of driving off a black bear from a carcass, despite its much-smaller size (15 kg). It often avoids being trapped, while removing bait and caught furbearers. Its powerful jaws and determination enable it to break large-mammal bones to extract the marrow, earning it the title of 'hyena of the North.' With incredible endurance, it may gallop for hours without tiring while it roams the boreal forest, forest-tundra, or the barren-ground tundra. Covering up to 10-50 km in a day, it traverses a home range of up to 2000 km^2 over the course of a year. The Wolverine is solitary, generally respecting the territories of other individuals, which are marked with scent and urine. Females come into heat for a few days from March to Oct, which attracts males. After mating, the fertilized eggs cease development until Jan or March, and 5 weeks later (March to early April) 2-6 young are born in a den in a snow bank, rocky crevice, or underground. Following 10 weeks of nursing, the offspring begin to eat regurgitated meat brought home by the mother. They are independent by winter, after learning how to find and catch prey. This species has survived for 17 years in zoos, but

does not approach this lifespan in nature. Disturbance from resource extraction, over a century of trapping pressure, loss of prey (ie, Woodland caribou), occasional poisoning programs, and a low reproductive rate have combined to keep populations well below traditional levels. MB is one of its last strongholds in NA, but it is rare even here and is endangered in E Canada. ● REW

WOMEN'S INSTITUTE. *See* **MANITOBA WOMEN'S INSTITUTE.**

WOMEN'S MOVEMENT. The women's movement has been a significant force for social and legal **REFORM** in MB for more than a century. MB women were the first in Canada to receive the right to vote, and several key women who gained renown in the province, including **NELLIE MCCLUNG** and **E. CORA HIND**, became nationally famous. The women's movement in NA is characterized by 2 periods or waves. The first wave began in the late 1800s and centred on establishing fundamental legal rights including the right of married women to hold property in their own name, the right to have custody of children following divorce, the right to vote and the right to attend university. The second wave began in the early 1960s as the women's movement galvanized around issues such as birth control, divorce reforms, daycare, sexual assault, and workplace discrimination. The implementation of public policy measures to end discrimination and achieve women's equality continued throughout the 1980s and 1990s.

THE FIRST WAVE (LATE 19TH CENTURY): Equal suffrage, the effort of women to gain the right to vote, was first taken up by MB's temperance movement (*see* **PROHIBITION**). The MB chapter of the Women's Christian Temperance Union (WCTU), established in 1886, held the central belief that alcohol led directly to violent crimes against women and children. Tales of violent, alcoholic husbands who squandered meagre family earnings on alcohol were common in communities throughout the province, and the WCTU galvanized thousands of women to sign petitions demanding the vote. The temperance union maintained that a plebiscite on banning liquor sales would pass if women could vote. The WCTU helped to popularize the idea of equal suffrage in rural areas, and later, in conjunction with urban women's organizations, worked to bring about legal reforms to eliminate other laws that discriminated against women.

At a time of no radio or television, printed newspapers were the chief source of information. The first suffrage newspaper in Canada was published in 1892 in **GIMLI**. *Freja* (which means

The Wolseley Expedtion followed an old voyageur route to Red River.

"woman" in Icelandic) was edited by **Margret Benedictsson**, an **Icelander** and member of the Gimli Suffrage Association. *Freja* became an outspoken 40-page monthly newspaper focused on helping "unhappily married women and unfortunate girls" by supporting initiatives leading to improved social conditions. A growing community of suffrage organizations existed in Winnipeg in 1911 when Nellie McClung moved from **Manitou** to Winnipeg. The MB Equal Suffrage Club, the Canadian Women's Press Club, and the Political Equality League, of which McClung was a founding member, acted together to petition the Conservative govt of MB premier Sir **Rodmond Roblin** for the vote. He steadfastly and resolutely refused to support women's suffrage, maintaining that equal suffrage would destroy families. Roblin gained notoriety for declaring, "Nice women don't want the vote."

Nevertheless, support for the suffrage movement grew. Women in rural communities were galvanized by reading articles in the *Grain Growers' Guide*, which had taken up the cause for women's suffrage. **Lillian Beynon** and her sister **Francis Beynon** edited the women's pages of the *Guide*. In addition to recipes and household tips, they printed letters on birth control and gave advice on how to organize women's groups in rural communities. Support for suffrage also extended to the labour newspaper *The Winnipeg Voice*. The Canadian Women's Press Club drew prominent women writers like E. Cora Hind, hired by the *Manitoba Free Press* in 1901, to lend their name to the suffrage cause and toured the province to gain additional support. While the vote symbolized women's equality efforts, other issues were important to the social reformers. For example, Nellie McClung of the Council of Women persuaded Premier Roblin to tour Winnipeg sewing factories, where a largely female workforce toiled long hours in hot, dimly lit, poorly ventilated, unsanitary "sweatshops." The women wanted the premier to appoint a female factory inspector. He refused. Working class women continued to support the vote as a means to improve their low pay and poor working conditions.

During WWI, women entered the workplace in greater numbers, in many cases to replace the men who had gone overseas. The sight of women of all classes participating in Canada's war effort also changed public opinion of women's capabilities. Public opinion was further galvanized in their favour when, in Jan 1914, a mock parliament was held at the Walker Theatre. In it, members of the Political Equality League reversed gender roles on stage to mock politicians who refused to grant women the vote. A delegation of men entered the stage appealing for the vote

Women voiced their views on a wide range of issues.

only to be informed by "premier" McClung that: "Politics unsettles men, and unsettled men mean unsettled bills – broken furniture, broken vows and divorce." The play was a huge success.

Two years later, on January 28, 1916, the new Liberal govt in MB under **T. C. Norris** passed a bill to enfranchise women, the first of its kind in Canada. Thanks to last minute lobbying by the Beynon sisters, the bill also gave women the right to be elected as members of the legislature. MB women were the first in Canada to win the provincial franchise. Most Cdn provinces and the federal govt followed suit within the next 2 years.

LEGAL AND SOCIAL REFORMS: Once the vote was secured, women's efforts turned to other social reforms. One early victory was the *Mothers' Allowance Act* of 1916, which gave poor mothers financial assistance if her children were "neglected" because of the death, insanity, imprisonment, or disability of their father. It was the first public welfare program in the province.

By then, women had made inroads into professions which previously barred women. **Charlotte Ross** was the first woman to practise medicine in MB; in 1912, **Melrose Sissons** and Winifred Wilton became the first female lawyers. Kate Simpson Hayes, women's editor of the *MB Free Press* in 1899, was elected president the Canadian Women's Press Club in 1906. The CWPC served as Canada's professional association of female journalists and supported equal suffrage.

All employed women were economically disenfranchised under MB law when they married. A bill passed in MB in 1871 stated that a married woman's earnings belonged to her husband, unless he was "cruel, insane, drunken or neglectful," in which case the court entitled her to her own earnings, as well as those of her dependent children. Further, the 1885 *Manitoba Real Property Act* stipulated that when a woman property owner got married, she was required to obtain a new title bearing her husband's name.

771

The same year, under the *Devolution of Estates Act*, a wife's right to an automatic share of her husband's estate (dower rights) was abolished in MB. In 1918, MB women finally won back their dower rights, giving them the right to veto any transaction involving their homestead. Wives were guaranteed a minimum share in the estate of their husbands.

The *Married Women's Protection Act* of 1900 permitted the wife of a "cruel, drunken or irresponsible" husband to ask for a court order freeing her from her obligation to live with him, barring him from her residence and allowing the court to award her custody of their children and demanding that he pay her support. MB law still held that "as a rule the father shall have custody and control of his infant children." Courts would generally grant the mother custody if the father was dead, provided that she hadn't committed adultery. It was not until 1922 that the *Child Welfare Act* gave mothers equal rights to the custody and control of children under 21.

LABOUR FORCE REFORM: Another focus for early feminists was equality in the workplace. Following WWI, women represented more than 20% of the labour force in MB. The Women's Labour League, established to secure better wages in the largely un-unionized female work sector, succeeded in pushing the MB govt to pass the first *Minimum Wage Act* in 1918. In the time leading up to the 1919 **WINNIPEG GENERAL STRIKE,** women continued to work to improve their work conditions. **HELEN ARMSTRONG**, affectionately known as "Ma," was an outspoken labour activist and president of the Women's Labour League. The WLL organized soup kitchens for striking workers. As well, women workers played a leading role in the strike itself. On May 14, 1919, the day before the general strike was scheduled to begin, 'bread and cake' workers – mostly women, walked out to enforce their wage demands, shutting down all but one of the city's confectionery plants. At 7:00 the next morning on May 15, Winnipeg's "Hello Girls" (telephone operators) unplugged their switchboards and abandoned their posts, 4 hours before the work stoppage planned by the strike committee. While the employers won the strike, the spirit for labour reform, including women's rights, remained firmly on the public agenda in MB.

In 1920, **EDITH ROGERS** (Liberal) became the first woman elected to the MB legislature, a post she held for 12 years. Although women were starting to make strides in provincial legislatures, a 1876 ruling in British common law held that: "Women are persons in matters of pains and penalties, but are not persons in matters of rights and privileges." A group of women known as The Famous Five (including Nellie McClung) petitioned the Canadian courts for a ruling on the matter in what became known as the Person's Case. When the Canadian court agreed with the British common law, the women appealed to the British Privy Council which, on October 18, 1929 ruled that women were "persons" under the *British North America Act* and qualified for federal appointments, including the Senate. Despite the ruling, it was not until the 1960s that MB women were elected or appointed to the Senate and House of Commons.

THE SECOND WAVE: In 1963, Betty Friedan's book, *The Feminine Mystique* galvanized a new generation of women to address "the problem that had no name." The book sold a million copies in its first year of publication. Two years later, Margaret Atwood's *Edible Woman* was published, echoing similar themes of women's powerlessness, though in a fictional setting.

As a new wave of social reforms gained momentum, the Canadian Federation of University Women and the Fédération des femmes de Québec tried – unsuccessfully – to convince the federal govt of Lester Pearson to establish a royal commission to study the status of women in Canada. In MB, June Menzies and Jean Carson became founding members of a MB ad-hoc committee on the status of women. The group met with **THELMA FORBES**, the first female speaker of the provincial legislature, with the hopes of convincing the MB govt to establish a provincial commission on women. The govt declined and so members of the ad hoc group created their own women's commission and travelled the province to meet with women in order to document issues of discrimination. A committee was formed around each group of concerns. In Ottawa, a Royal Commission on the Status of Women was finally established in 1969 and headed by broadcaster Florence Bird. Each of the MB committees of the ad hoc women's group delivered a brief to the Royal Commission. Menzies, Carson and other women officially formed the MB Action Committee on the Status of Women (MACSW) in 1971. MACSW was an influential lobbying organization for the next 20 years.

By 1968, divorce laws had been changed to include rape and marital breakdown as grounds of divorce and in 1969, PM Pierre Trudeau legalized birth control for the first time, saying that "govt had no place in the bedrooms of the nation." However, the release of the report of the federal Royal Commission on the Status of Women in Nov 1970 would transform Canadian society over the next 30 years. The recommendations called for legalized abortion, affirmative action, the elimination of "occupation sex-typing," removal of discrimination based on marital status in work, equality in education for girls, family life education, divorce reform, measures to promote equal partnership in marriage, changes to the *Indian Act* and policies to end discrimination against single mothers.

In MB, the efforts of the women's movement led to several public services. By the mid-1970s, women's crisis shelters were being formed across the country to provide shelter to battered women and their children. Osborne House in Winnipeg, was one of the first, opening its doors in 1974. Two years later, 244 families stayed in shelter and 239 women and children were turned away due to lack of space. By 1991, there were 31 agencies in MB dealing with the wife abuse, and 10 residential shelters for women and children. Ikwe-Widdjitiwin, of Winnipeg, was incorporated as the province's first shelter for Aboriginal women in 1985. Eight other residential shelters were established throughout the province by 1992.

In the early 1970s, information on birth control and **ABORTION** was not widely available in MB. A group of Winnipeg women established the Pregnancy Information Service and its volunteers provided phone counselling and information on obtaining abortions. At that time, women were required to obtain permission for the procedure from a hospital therapeutic abortion committee. Pregnancy Information Service later became the Women's Health Clinic, an organization that continues to provide counselling on unplanned pregnancy, but has branched out to provide women-specific health programs such as smoking cessation, counselling on eating disorders, and women in menopause. Many of the clinic's programs have become templates for other women's health centres across Canada. Montreal-based Dr. Henry Morgentaler challenged the Criminal Code provisions governing **ABORTION**s repeatedly during the 1970s. In May 1983, he opened an abortion clinic in Winnipeg, which was raided shortly after on 2 occasions that saw staff charged and equipment seized. Eventually, the private clinic re-opened, and the Winnipeg Regional Health Authority later purchased its assets. The WHRA authorized the Women's Health Clinic to set up a satellite clinic to provide publicly insured abortions in 2005.

By the mid-1970s, women had become a visible presence in the workforce. Many were demanding to be hired in non-traditional areas such as police, firefighting, and trades. Women's Institutes, active for 50 years, advanced issues of importance to rural and farmwomen. Jean Folster of **NORWAY HOUSE** became the first female First Nations chief elected in MB in 1971. By 1980, 7 women MLAs represented 14% of the seats

1917, he embraced a more emphatically political perspective, believing that only an elected socialist party would bring justice to working people, the poor, and farmers. Part of the abiding Christian influence on Woodsworth was his pacifism, a movement to which he claimed to have been converted in 1906. The crisis of his association with established institutions, religious and otherwise, came, predictably, over war and violence. In Dec 1916, he publicly spoke out against Canada's involvement in WWI. He was fired from his job and went to Gibson's Landing, BC, for one last attempt at serving as a Methodist minister. The following year, he resigned from the church and worked as a longshoreman on the docks of Vancouver.

J. S. Woodsworth

He now refined his conception of political action living among left-wing people associated with the new BC Federated Labour Party. He embraced the model of the British Labour Party and its manifesto, "Labour and the New Social Order," and preached a politics of socialist economics, democratic electoral action, and transformative change. His life of activism took him on many speaking trips in the Prairies on behalf of the Non-Partisan League and the Labour Church. On one such trip, he arrived in Winnipeg in the middle of spring 1919, the time of the WINNIPEG GENERAL STRIKE. He took the workers' side. When some of the leaders were arrested, he helped edit the strikers' newspaper. Though arrested and charged with seditious libel, his case was never brought to trial. His renown helped catapult him into the House of Commons, however, and in Dec 1921, he was the successful

candidate for the Independent Labour Party of MB in Winnipeg Centre. He was successful in 5 succeeding elections until his death.

Woodsworth was a tireless speaker and agitator for a nationally based democratic socialism. Like writer Edward Bellamy, he believed that through technological innovation, industry was moving in the direction of ever-larger scale and efficiency. Increased manufacturing productivity made it possible to imagine a society that would provide material sufficiency for all. The fruits of industry would be captured by labour parties of workers and farmers, which would win power through electoral means and thereafter plan a co-operative commonwealth of equality for all. Internationally, Woodsworth was fearful of the continuing role of imperialism, and he agitated for a democratic league of nations. He was for a long time dismissive of the League of Nations, believing it to be a league of imperialist powers. He also worried that it might resort to force in its pursuit of collective security.

The culmination of Woodsworth's political life was the founding of the CO-OPERATIVE COMMONWEALTH FEDERATION in Regina in 1933, the first truly national and enduring party of socialism in Canada He was its first and its most important leader. Woodsworth was mainly a practical politician who sought to bring about as much immediate change as possible. He was, then, a gradualist who sought small increments of change, if that was all that was on offer. The sole exception to this pragmatism was his stance against violence and war; on that topic, he was a perfectionist and unbending. Force was never justified, he believed, even on behalf of just causes or in pursuit of collective security. He thus defied his country and his party in protesting the declaration of war against Nazi Germany in Sept 1939.

Woodsworth was one of the most significant politicians to emerge from MB. His influence on 20th-century Canadian politics was immense, from the founding of the CCF to his constant action for a more egalitarian society. When he entered Parliament, he was convinced that Canada was poised to become a socialist society. Reality was more recalcitrant, and the CCF elected few MPs, never winning more than 10% of the national vote. Woodsworth's main success was as a lobbyist on behalf of causes to which other political parties could give their agreement. The model of this was his pressure for an old-age pension program in 1926, at a time when PM Mackenzie King and the Liberals needed labour's support. So was initiated a major part of what would become the welfare state in Canada. Socialism was not attained but Canadians' social welfare was significantly advanced. • ALLEN MILLS

House wrens often nest in gardens.

WRENS (family Troglodytidae) are small, insect-eating songbirds characterized by brownish plumage and a tail that is often raised above the back. They are quite secretive, creeping through shrubbery or reeds, but they betray their presence through loud song. Four species occur here regularly, while an additional 2 have been seen occasionally. Most familiar to the casual observer is the House Wren (*Troglodytes aedon*), which nests readily in gardens. Like some of its relatives, it has the habit of destroying eggs of other species by pecking them, a trait that does not endear it to most. • RUDOLF KOES

WRONGFUL CONVICTIONS. MB has acquired an unfortunate reputation for questionable murder prosecutions after the wrongful convictions of James Driskell and Thomas Sophonow. In a recent case yet to be resolved as of writing, the conviction of Kyle Unger has also been called into question. The infamous case of David Milgaard, who was wrongfully convicted in a SK trial, also has close ties to MB.

While wrongful convictions are the result of serious flaws in the justice system, they also serve to highlight where judicial reform needs to take place. For example, the convictions of both Sophonow and Driskell were in part based on unreliable testimony from jailhouse informants. While paying such informants for testimony was once considered acceptable procedure for Crown counsel, the 2001 judicial inquiry into Sophonow's wrongful conviction led the MB justice dept to revise its policy. The province has adopted some of the most stringent regulations in Canada regarding the use of jailhouse informants.

Faulty and inadequate forensic testing has been another key factor in wrongful convictions. Prior to the widespread use of DNA analysis, hairs found at crime scenes were often microscopically analysed by a forensic scientist,

W

James Driskell was exonerated after 13 years of imprisonment.

leaving room for human error. Both Driskell and Unger were falsely placed at crime scenes through this method, and later cleared when more precise DNA analysis showed that the hair had been wrongly matched. Microscopy has since been discredited by many forensic experts as a flawed method for analysing hair, and in MB a forensic hair review committee was established in 2003 to re-examine convictions based wholly or partly on such evidence.

THE DRISKELL CASE: James Driskell spent 13 years in jail for the murder of Perry Dean Harder. He grew up on the periphery of criminal subculture in Winnipeg's tough **NORTH END** neighbourhood. Prior to his murder conviction, Driskell ran a garage on Main Street. His problems with the law began in 1989, when Driskell and his friend Harder were arrested and charged with possession of stolen property, accused of cutting up stolen vehicles for parts in Driskell's shop. Days before his 1990 trial was to begin, Harder went missing. His body was found 3 months later. Police believed Driskell had motive to silence his co-accused, and arrested him a month later.

At his 1991 trial, the only physical evidence linking Driskell to the crime were 3 hairs found in his van, which had been identified as Harder's using hair microscopy. The Crown's case also relied on jailhouse informants Reath "Ray" Zanidean and John Gumieny, who had both been paid for their testimony. At Driskell's trial, however, Zanidean perjured himself by saying that he had not received any kind of compensation. Crown attorneys then failed to disclose to defence that the witnesses were in fact receiving payment,

and that Zanidean had lied in court. Driskell was subsequently convicted of first degree murder. Driskell appealed, but was denied a new trial in 1992. Media reports questioning Driskell's conviction led to an internal review of the Harder murder investigation. Though the report found several flaws with the investigation, it was not released to the public, despite its value to Driskell's defence team in forming an appeal.

In 2002, DNA testing on the hairs found in Driskell's van showed beyond doubt that they did not belong to Harder. Driskell was then released pending a federal review of his case, and was finally exonerated in 2005 when the fed justice minister quashed his conviction. The MB govt subsequently launched its investigation into Driskell's case. As of writing, Driskell was awaiting settlement of a $20 million civil suit he launched against those involved in his conviction.

THE SOPHONOW CASE: Thomas Sophonow spent nearly 4 years in prison for the murder of Barbara Gayle Stoppel. Though he was acquitted in 1985, Sophonow remained under a shadow of guilt until his exoneration in 2000. On the night of Dec 23, 1981, 16-year-old Stoppel was found unconscious in the bathroom of the donut shop where she worked as a waitress. She died in hospital 6 days later. Under immense public pressure to find the murderer of a young girl, police quickly zeroed in on Sophonow as a suspect. Though a Vancouver resident, Sophonow had been in Winnipeg on the night of the murder, and matched the description of a man seen at the crime scene. In what was later proven to be misleading evidence, police also linked the twine used to strangle Stoppel to a manufacturer on the

West Coast. Most of the case against Sophonow, however, was based on the testimony of several jailhouse informants, including one inmate with a perjury conviction on his lengthy record who had served as an informant in 9 other trials.

Sophonow was tried 3 times for Stoppel's murder. In his first trial, the jury was unable to reach a unanimous verdict. He was tried again, found guilty, but won on appeal. Sophonow was then prosecuted a 3rd time, again found guilty, but then released after the verdict was overturned in his 1985 appeal. The Supreme Court then ruled that the Crown could not try Sophonow's case again. Sophonow had already by then spent 45 months in prison. In 2003, following his full exoneration, Sophonow received $2.6 million compensation from govt. Stoppel's murder remains unsolved.

THE UNGER CASE: Kyle Unger spent 14 years in prison for the June 1990 rape and murder of 16-year-old Brigitte Grenier at an outdoor rock concert in **ROSEISLE**. MB's forensic evidence review committee established in 2004 that the single hair used to place Unger at the crime scene was in fact not his, and the remaining basis for his conviction, primarily jailhouse informant testimony and a controversial confession made to undercover RCMP, has since come under close scrutiny. Unger was released from prison in 2005 and, as of writing, his case was awaiting federal review. • MICHELLE DOBROVOLNY

WUSKWI SIPIHK FIRST NATION, on reserve pop 179, off reserve pop 403, is a community on the NE shore of Swan Lake, W of **LAKE WINNIPEGOSIS**, and about 560 km NW of **WINNIPEG**. The people of Wuskwi Sipihk First Nation originated from the Sapotaweyak Cree Nation community, but separated in Sept 1982. They signed Treaty 4 in 1874; the community is now a member of the Swampy Cree Tribal Council. The native language of Wuskwi Sipihk is **CREE**. Schooling in this First Nation goes from Nursery-Grade 8, and enrolment for 2003-04 was 106. Wuskwi Sipihk First Nation administers its own education. This First Nation land houses 4 reserves, including: Swan Lake IR No. 65C, Wuskwi Sipihk First Nation IR No. 1, Wuskwi Sipihk First Nation IR No. 2, and Treaty Four Reserve Grounds No. 77. There is all-weather road access. The economic foundation for Wuskwi Sipihk First Nation is trapping and fishing. This community co-owns Aseneskak Casino (along with other First Nations, including **CHEMAWAWIN FIRST NATION**, **GRAND RAPIDS FIRST NATION**, **MOSAKAHIKEN CREE NATION**, **OPASKWAYAK CREE NATION**, **SAPOTAWEYAK CREE NATION**, and the Swampy Cree Tribal Council Inc.). This casino opened Feb 2002, and is located in the Opaskwayak Cree Nation. • RK

XYZ

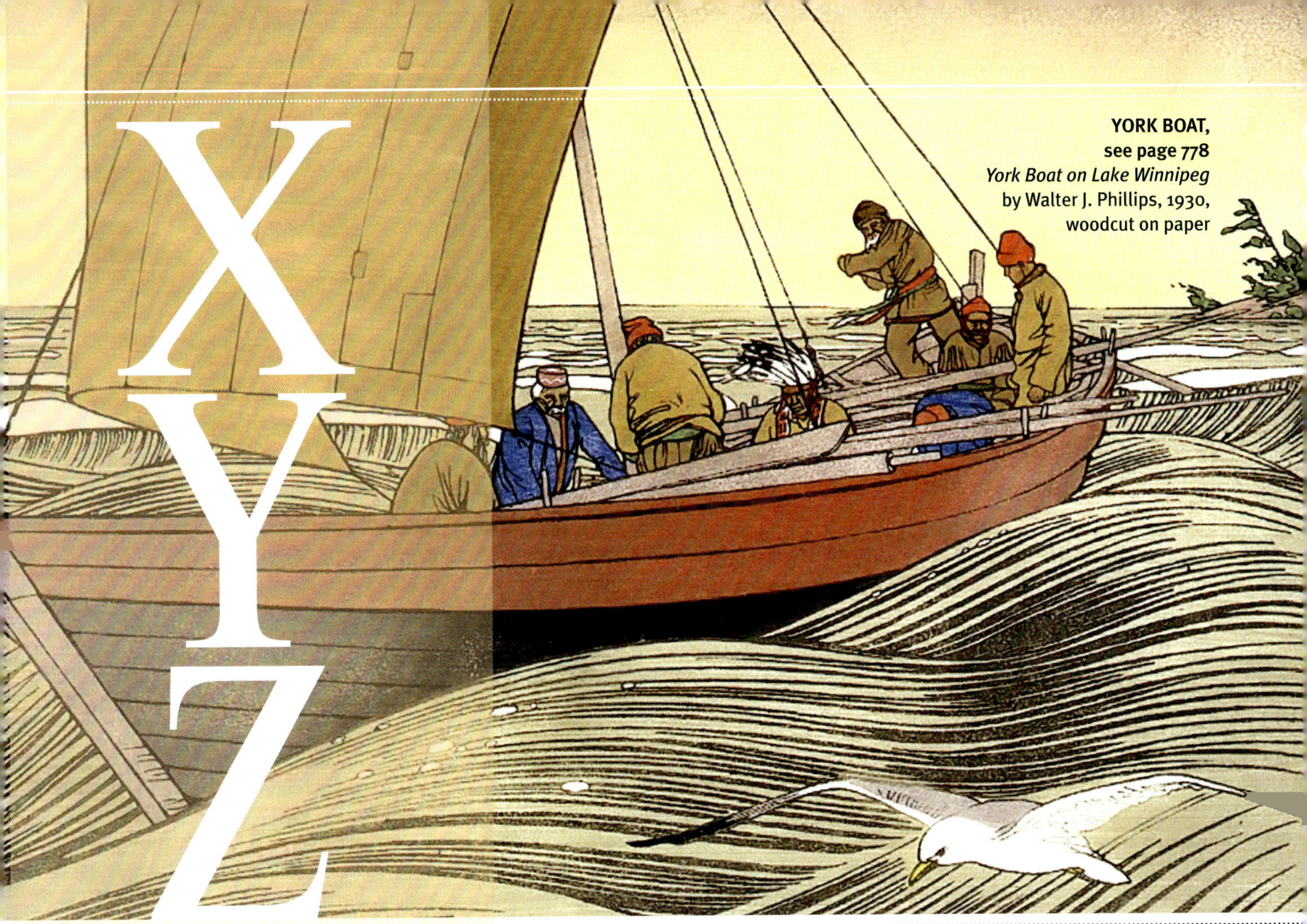

YORK BOAT,
see page 778
York Boat on Lake Winnipeg
by Walter J. Phillips, 1930,
woodcut on paper

YANOFSKY, Daniel Abraham "Abe," chess champion, civic politician (b Mar 26, 1925, Brody, Poland; d Mar 5, 2000, **Winnipeg**) was a chess child prodigy and Canada's first grandmaster. He remains 1 of only 3 Canadians to hold the title. He was a prominent civic politician in Winnipeg for over 20 years. Yanofsky moved to Winnipeg from Poland as an infant. He learned to play chess at the age of 8. By the age of 12, he was the provincial champion, ranking 4th in Canada. His father died when he was 13, leaving Yanofsky with the responsibility of providing for his family. He was forced to attend public night classes while working day jobs, but still managed to compete in chess tournaments, and qualified for the Cdn team that went on to the 1939 world team championships in Argentina, where Yanofsky was awarded a special prize for best score on Board 2. In 1946, he beat the world champion Mikhail Botvinnik. He played in many European tournaments, and won the 1953 British championship. He won the Cdn title 8 times, and became Canada's first Grandmaster in 1964. Yanofsky was awarded the Order of Canada in 1972. Outside chess, Yanofsky served in the Royal Canadian Navy during WWII, after which he studied law at Oxford U before returning to Winnipeg, where he set up a law practice with his brother. As a politician, Yanofsky was mayor of the city of West Kildonan from 1961-70, and then served on Winnipeg's city council following **Unicity** until his retirement from politics in 1986. He was also pivotal in the development of the **Seven Oaks General Hospital**, serving for many years on its Board of Trustees. • MD

YELLOW QUILL, Chief (Ozawekwun), Aboriginal leader (b 1821; d 1910, Indian Gardens Reserve [near **Rathwell**]). Little is known of

AM, PERSONALITY FILES

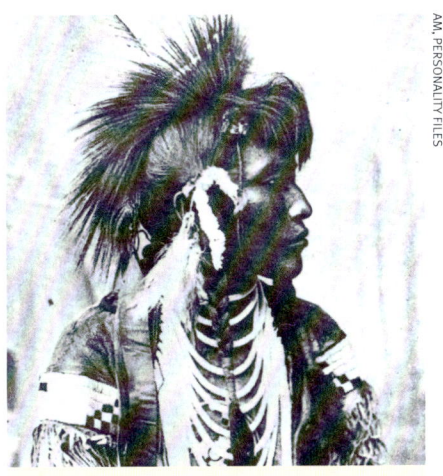

Yellow Quill

his early life, but he was reputed one of the best hunters in the **RED RIVER SETTLEMENT**. Not a hereditary chief, around 1860 he was "clothed" by the **HBC** as chief of the mixed Ottawa and **OJIBWAY** band that claimed the land around **PORTAGE LA PRAIRIE**. He did not take an active role in the negotiations for Treaty 1 at **LOWER FORT GARRY** in Aug 1871, and subsequently was more willing to agree to govt proposals than were his councillors. He selected the Swan Lake Reserve 7 for his band in 1876, but he was unable to convince many of his people to follow him. Instead, the band remained at Hamilton's Crossing and was rejoined by Yellow Quill. In 1890, he opposed provincial attempts to enforce game laws against the Aboriginal people of MB. After his death, the federal govt in 1913 agreed to establish a reserve at Hamilton's Crossing, known as Indian Gardens Reserve No. 8. Yellow Quill was highly respected by govt agents, and his leadership eventually came to be accepted by his people. ● JMB

YEOMANS, Amelia, physician, suffragist (b 1842; d 1913). Born in Canada into a civil service family, she married Dr. Augustus Yeomans, who died in 1878. After his death she decided to join her daughter Lillian in medical studies at Michigan State University, and she graduated in 1883. Lillian Yeomans took up medical practice in **WINNIPEG** in 1882 and was joined by her mother a year later although Amelia was not licenced until 1885. Amelia became an active practitioner of "social medicine" in the city's tenement districts, speaking out for better working conditions, housing reform, and the eradication of venereal disease through an ending of prostitution. She helped found the **WINNIPEG HUMANE SOCIETY** in 1894. She quickly came to see alcohol as the symbol of the deterioration of society, becoming a leader of the Woman's Christian Temperance Union and its president in 1896-97. Reform would not be possible without the enfranchisement of women, she believed. She thus acted the part of premier in the mock parliament organized by the WCTU in 1893 and helped demonstrated in favour of the suffrage in 1894, subsequently leading in the founding of the Equal Franchise Association, which was committed to empowering women. Yeomans joined her daughters in Calgary in 1906 in semi-retirement. ● JMB

YORK BOAT was a small inland vessel used by the **HBC** in the **FUR TRADE**, first built around 1750 and predominantly based in **YORK FACTORY**, the main HBC depot on **HUDSON BAY**. Modeled after the sturdy fishing boats of the Orkney Islands, the birthplace of most HBC traders, the York boat

was well-suited to navigating the treacherous, often ice-ridden waters of MB. Its main benefit, however, was that even the smallest York boats could carry more than 2700 kg of goods – twice the capacity of the canoes paddled by the voyageurs of the rival **NWC** – while the largest could carry up to 5440 kg.

Constructed at stations situated along principle trade routes, the York boat became, by the late 18th and through much of the 19th century, the HBC's primary method of freighting goods, and impressive brigades of the double-ended, open vessels were a common sight throughout the Northwest, from James Bay to Fort Chipewyan in present-day AB. Of course, a heavy York boat was not well suited to a portage, presenting a significant drawback as overland transport was often unavoidable. The HBC overcame this by having trails cut through the dense brush of the wilderness, so that York boats could thus be passed relatively easily over rolled logs laid along the trails. The traces of these tramways can still be seen in northern MB, particularly on the Robinson Portage along the Hayes River.

Rowing a York boat was extremely laborious. With an average length of 12.6 m, reaching 9.1 m to the keel with an inside depth of .9 m, the hefty vessel required the strength of 6-8 oarsmen (tripmen), each working an oar 6 m in length and weighing over 11 kg. Rowing was so arduous a task that the oarsmen would have to engage the entire bulk of their bodies, standing up to push the oar forward and sitting to pull the stroke through, an action that was repeated up to 16 hours a day. This heavy workload was mercifully eased on open waters like **LAKE WINNIPEG**, provided the good fortune of a strong wind blowing in a favourable direction, which allowed the men to utilize a square sail erected on an attachable mast.

By the early 1870s, the declining strategic importance of York Factory to the HBC, as well

as the development of systems of **RAILWAYS** and steamboats (*see* **STEAMBOATS**), led to the gradual abandonment of the York boat. Though its days as an important commerce vessel have long since passed, the York boat has not fallen entirely into disuse: fleets of the historic boats can still be seen during York Boat Days, an annual festival held in **NORWAY HOUSE**. ● MICHELLE DOBROVOLNY

YORK FACTORY was the foremost **HUDSON BAY** trading and administrative post for the **HBC**, located on the N shore of the **HAYES RIVER**, about 9 km from the coast (250 km SE of **CHURCHILL**). Named for the Duke of York and sometimes called York Fort, the first structure was established in 1684 after a previous attempt near the mouth of the **NELSON RIVER** (Port Nelson) proved unsuccessful.

The **FRENCH** captured the fort in 1694 and again in 1697, renaming it Fort Bourbon. The 1713 Treaty of Utrecht returned it, and control of Hudson Bay trading, to the **ENGLISH**. James Knight and **HENRY KELSEY** built a replacement structure in 1715. The **FUR TRADE** flourished during the 18th century with the HBC using Aboriginal middlemen, and York Factory surpassed **FORT PRINCE OF WALES** to become the HBC's most important Hudson Bay post. After the French burnt the fort in 1782 and the site flooded in 1788, the location was moved upstream, leading to the construction of the octagonal stone and wood post known as York Factory III. In the late 1700s, as the fur trade shifted S, the HBC faced tough competition from Montreal-based traders that had established forts on **LAKE WINNIPEG**. The HBC responded with their own inland posts. Goods were now shipped back and forth from York Factory via long, difficult **YORK BOAT** trips.

Beginning in 1810, when it became the headquarters of the HBC's Northern Department, York Factory was the company's regional

York boat at Lower Fort Garry

base of operations, an important storage centre, and the sole **RUPERT'S LAND** entry point for European immigrants until the 1850s. At that time, the outpost featured about 50 buildings and had grown into a settlement of hundreds, including large numbers of **CREE** traders. Shortages of food and firewood, competition from the **NORTH WEST COMPANY**, and the emergence of cheaper, easier southern transportation routes contributed to its decline, however, and by 1880 the factory was but a depot. The HBC closed it down completely in 1957, and transferred it to the govt of Canada in 1968. Today, York Factory is a 102 ha national historic site. Two buildings remain standing among the ruins, including the wooden HBC depot (1831) that is said to be the oldest structure still standing on permafrost.
• JOEL TRENAMAN

YORK FACTORY FIRST NATION, on reserve

pop 452, off reserve pop 620, is located about 100 km SSE of **CHURCHILL**, and 110 km NE of **THOMPSON** at York Landing. The people of this First Nation were originally from **YORK FACTORY**, a community that was located on the N shore of the **HAYES RIVER**, approx 9 km inland from the Hudson Bay coast. During the fur trade in the 18th and 19th centuries, a fur trading post was active here. By 1730, this post had become the **HBC'S** most important post on **HUDSON BAY**, with the highest trading volume. By the 1850s, success of the fort reached its peak, but by the 1870s, it was in decline. The HBC finally closed its doors at York Factory in 1957, leaving fur trading history and Aboriginal peoples behind. When the post and store were shut down, the Cree peoples from around York Factory were relocated more than 200 km inland to an area on Split Lake that is now known as York Landing. The community at York Landing did not receive reserve status until 1989, naming itself York Factory First Nation.

This small First Nation is a signatory to Treaty 5 in 1910 and is now a member of the Keewatin Tribal Council. There is one reserve located on the land of York Factory First Nation, called York Landing IR. Its native language is **CREE**. The First Nation offers schooling from Nursery-Grade 12, and enrolment for 2003-04 was 143. This isolated community is accessible via a winter road and summer ferry from nearby Split Lake. A runway is maintained in the community for essential air travel and supplies. Life here was disrupted again by flooding due to hydro development in the 1960s-70s. York Factory is 1 of 5 First Nations party to the **NORTHERN FLOOD AGREEMENT**. The economic base of York Factory First Nation in the 21st century is hunting and trapping. • RK

YOUNG, Alexander "Scott," journalist, author (b April 14, 1918, **CYPRESS RIVER**; d June 12, 2005, Kingston, ON). Young was best known as a journalist and prolific author of 45 fiction and non-fiction books. His books include *Neil and Me* (1984), a memoir about his relationship with his rock 'n' roll son **NEIL YOUNG**. Scott Young attended Kelvin High School in **WINNIPEG** and got his start as a journalist with the **WINNIPEG FREE PRESS**. After the paper refused to give him a raise, he moved to Toronto, where he worked for the Canadian Press as a war correspondent in London 1942-43. He wrote for the *Globe and Mail* as a sports columnist 1957-69 and 1971-80. He also worked for *Maclean's* and the *Toronto Telegram*. Young enjoyed particular success as a short story writer, publishing 75 stories. • JS

YOUNG, Neil Percival, rock musician, singer/songwriter (b Nov 12, 1945, Toronto). The son of noted journalist/author **SCOTT YOUNG** and *Twenty Questions* TV-show panellist Edna "Rassy" Ragland, Neil Young moved with his mother to **WINNIPEG** in Aug 1960 after his parents' divorce, as his grandparents lived in Winnipeg and in rural MB. Young's interest in music was kindled at Earl Grey School, and later Kelvin High School, where he took up guitar and met musical partner Ken Koblun, the 2 forming a succession of local bands beginning with The Jades. He made his first recording – "The Sultan," with "Aurora" on the B-side – with his new band The Squires at radio station CKRC's studios in 1963. After 3 years on the community-club circuit, Young relocated to Port Arthur (now Thunder Bay), ON, in early 1965, where he met US guitarist/singer Stephen Stills before heading to Toronto to be a folksinger. When fame eluded him there, he joined rock group The Mynah Birds – managed by John Craig Eaton of **EATON'S** fame – and fronted by Rick James, later a funk singer. In March 1966, Young and bass player Bruce Palmer drove a 1953 Pontiac hearse to CA, meeting up again with Stills and guitarist/singer Richie Furay in a Los Angeles traffic jam, forming Buffalo Springfield with them the same night. The group became stars of the Sunset Strip clubs, scoring a hit with Stills's protest anthem "For What It's Worth" in 1967. Young quit the band 3 times before it finally folded in 1968. Thereupon, he launched a stellar solo career while simultaneously recording and touring with Crazy Horse and Crosby, Stills, Nash & Young. By 1970, the latter had become the most-successful group in America after appearing at the Woodstock Festival and releasing multi-million-selling albums *Déjà Vu* (1970) and *Four Way Street* (1971). The protest song "Ohio," written and sung by Young, became their greatest hit of 1970.

Over the next 3 decades, Young released more about 25 acclaimed albums – including *After the Gold Rush* (1970), *Harvest* (1972), *On the Beach* (1973), *Tonight's the Night* (1975), *Rust Never Sleeps* (1979), *This Note's for You* (1988), *Freedom* (1989), *Ragged Glory* (1990), *Harvest Moon* (1992), *Sleeps with Angels* (1994), *Prairie Wind* (2005), and *Living with War* (2006) – earning a reputation as one of rock music's most iconoclastic and influential mavericks. Among his best-known songs are "Sugar Mountain," "Cinnamon Girl," "Down by the River," "Southern Man," "After the Gold Rush," "Heart of Gold," "Helpless," "The Needle and the Damage Done," "Comes a Time," "Lotta Love," "Harvest Moon," and "Rockin' in the Free World." Young has also dabbled in filmmaking, with the self-produced/directed *Journey Through the Past* (1974), *Rust Never Sleeps* (1979), *Human Highway* (1982), *Berlin* (1983), *Year of the Horse* (directed by Jim Jarmusch, 1997), *Greendale* (2004), and *Heart of Gold* (directed by Jonathan Demme, 2006).

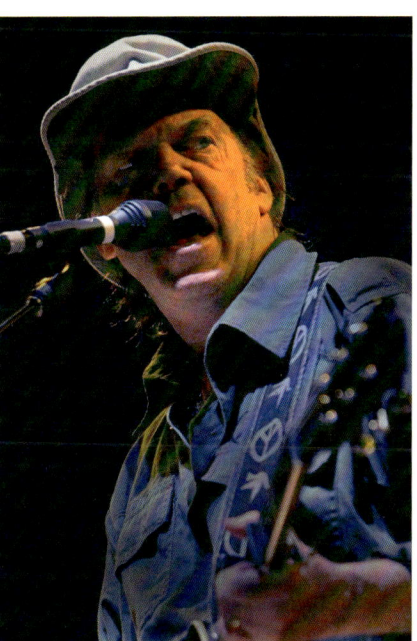

Neil Young began his musical career in Winnipeg.

An environmental and social activist, Young helped found Farm-Aid and the Bridge School, performing annually at benefits for both, as well as supporting cerebral palsy research – his 2 sons, Zeke and Ben, were born with the disease. Young has been outspoken in his anti-war stance. Young lives on Broken Arrow, a sprawling ranch in northern CA, with 2nd wife Pegi (with whom he has a daughter, Amber). Inducted into the Canadian Music Hall of Fame in 1982, Young is also in the Rock 'n' Roll Hall of Fame, won Juno Awards for Album of the Year (1994) and

Male Vocalist of the Year (1995), and has been nominated for an Academy Award (*Philadelphia*, 1994). Despite living in CA since 1966, Young continues to be inspired by MB, as in his 2005 *Prairie Wind* album and the *Heart of Gold* film. ● JOHN EINARSON

ZEDD (ZARAWIECKI), Stanley, racketeer, sports organizer (b 1899, Ukraine; d May 26, 1969, **WINNIPEG**). Using profits from illegal gambling, Zedd helped launch a MB-Dakota baseball league (*see* **MANDAK LEAGUE**) that attracted many star players from the former US Negro League and brought top-level **BASEBALL** to MB. Zedd immigrated to Winnipeg from the Ukraine at the age of 10. His family anglicized their last name to avoid discrimination, but as a poor immigrant living in the **NORTH END**, Zedd's opportunities remained limited. He started running illegal craps games in the 1930s, renting out private homes in which to hold the all-night games. Gamblers from all over the city were soon flocking to Zedd's high-rolling games. At the peak of his business, he was making up to $3000 a night, and had become a minor celebrity in the North End.

Stanley Zedd

In 1950, Zedd jumped at the opportunity to bring in talented players from the recently folded US Negro league to play for the new ManDak League. With his profits from gambling, Zedd was able to form a team made up entirely of the highly paid and highly talented former Negro league players. Called the Winnipeg Buffaloes, the team won the first ManDak league championship. However, their glory was short-lived, as Zedd shut the "Buffs" down in the 1952 season after many of his star players were lured to the Toronto Maple Leafs AAA ball club. Zedd continued to organize bookie operations and crap games through the 1950s. He also opened a restaurant across from the former Polo Park racetrack. Though police often turned a blind eye to his illegal gambling operations, public pressure resulted in increased raids on

Zedd's games, putting an end to his most profitable bookie operation, which dealt with bets across NA. Zedd racked up 12 gambling convictions over his life, most of which led to fines, though he did serve 2 months in jail. Eventually, his own gambling habits left Zedd impoverished. ● MD

ZUKEN, Joseph, municipal politician (b Dec 12, 1912, Gorodnize, Ukraine; d March 26, 1986, **WINNIPEG**). Zuken came to Canada with his family in 1914 and grew up in Winnipeg's **NORTH END**, attending St. John's High School. He graduated as a lawyer in 1936 from the **U OF M**, but was unable to gain employment, not because of his **JEWISH** roots but because of his **COMMUNIST** affiliations. He taught Yiddish for 6 years and eventually opened his own law office. He was active in the Progressive Arts Club and New Theatre (*see* **THEATRE**) in the 1930s. Zuken began his political career as a school trustee, serving on the Winnipeg School Board from 1942-62. He then became one of Winnipeg's longest-serving councillors,

from 1962 to his retirement in 1983. He ran unsuccessfully for mayor in 1979; the prospect of a North American city electing a Communist mayor became an international story.

Although he was a Communist, Zuken was immensely popular. Called both a "gadfly" and the conscience of city council, Zuken was noted for his concern for the underdog, and never voted for a city budget because he claimed they did not help the poor and unemployed. He was a supporter of low-rental housing and a champion for the development of the **SEVEN OAKS GENERAL HOSPITAL**. He took on the dominant group at city council for its decision to ban street-level pedestrian traffic at Winnipeg's most famous intersection at Portage and Main. The Joseph Zuken Memorial Association and the Manitoba Historical Society unveiled a plaque in 2006 honouring Zuken at an inner-city park, which is also named for Zuken. He was also the subject of a biography by Doug Smith, *Joe Zuken, Citizen and Socialist* (Lorimer, 1990). ● AJL

Joe Zuken, centre, and Bill Norrie in a mock sparring match during the 1979 mayorality campaign.

CONTRIBUTORS

Sohrab Abizadeh
Stacey Abramson
Chris Adams
Gary Adams
Stephen C. Alford
Doug Allen
Duncan Allan
Don Anderson
Trevor Anderson
David Arthurs
Ralph Bagley
August Bairos
H. H. Barber
Judith Hudson Beattie
Michael Benarroch
Richard E. Bennett
Margaret Bertouilli
Mary M. Birt
Magdalena Blackmore
Danny Blair
Jim Blanchard
Hazel Bochinski
Patricia Bovey
Peter Bowes
Ingeborg Boyens
Laura Brown
Kevin Brownlee
Robin Jarvis Brownlie
Garth Buchholz
Carol Budnick
J. M. Bumsted

Vicki Burns
David Butterfield
Raduca Buzdugan
Linda Cantiveros
Francis M. Carroll
Tom Carter
Martin Cash
Lucien Chaput
Bruce Cherney
Carl A. Christie
Susan Close
R. H. Collett
Tim Corkery
Sally Correia
Anne Côté
Laura Cowie
David Creamer
Vince Crichton
Howard Curle
Sandy Cushon
Anita Daher
Catharina de Bakker
Ruth DeGraves
David DeGrow
Michael Decter
Teji Dedi
Lyle Dick
Michelle Dobrovolny
Gordon Dodds
Gabriel Dragan
Leo Driedger

Joseph Du
Ryszard Dubanski
Gerald Dueck
John A. Eagle
Derreck Eberts
Renate Eigenbrod
John Einarson
Lawrence Elliott
Roy Ellis
R. G. Enfield
Jane Evans
John Everitt
Doug Fast
Judy Flynn
Richard H. Foster
Kimberly Francey
Gerald Friesen
John J. Friesen
Alexander Freund
Richard Frost
Terry D. Galloway
Nelson Gerrard
Barbara Gfellner
Ryan Gibson
Gordon Goldsborough
Barry Gosnell
Russ Gourluck
Heidi Graham
Hugh Grant
Allan Gray
Paula Grieef

Mildred Gutkin
Shiva Halli
John L. Hamerton
John Hamilton
Al Handford
C. Emdad Haque
Caron Hart
P. D. Hatton
Raymond M. Hébert
Richard Henley
C. Gordon Hill
Jan Horner
Lois Howard
Raymond Huel
Bob Irving
Michael Issigonis
Gaby Jacoby
Greg Jarvis
Carson Jerema
Karen Johnson
Douglas J. Johnston
Lawrence Jones
Paula Kelly
Trevor Kennerd
Dave Kerr
Bartley Kives
Mirone Klysh
Rudolf Koes
Peter Kulchyski
Rebeca Kuropatwa
Rhéal C. Lafrenière

Geoff Lambert
Frederick A. Leighton
Chris Leo
A. J. Levin
Allan Levine
James McAllister
Dawne McCance
Jake MacDonald
Kerri McDonnell
Lisa McGifford
R. A. McGinn
Fred McGuinness
Marion McKay
Jasper McKee
Brad McKenzie
Valerie McKinley
Shauna MacKinnon
Murray McNeill
Philippe Mailhot
Christopher Malcolm
Barry Mallin
Tara Maltman
Atish Maniar
George Manson
Tammy Marlowe Johnson
Herb Mays
Maurice Mierau
Keiko Miki
Allen Mills
Stan Milosevic
Penni Mitchell

Tom Mitchell
Jim Mochoruk
T. Kent Morgan
John Morriss
Saeed Moshiri
Morris Mott
Matthew Mulaire
Steven T. Nagy
William Neville
Allan Neyedly
Glen Nicoll
Joel Novak
Colin Oakes
Karen Omelan
Dan Overall
Leigh Patterson
Roland Penner
Shelley Penziwol
Diane Perreault
Katherine Pettipas
Leo F. Pettipas
Eva Pip
Mechyslava Polevychok
Susan Prentice
William B. Preston
Brenda Prosken
Vic Pruden
William O. Pruitt
Doug Ramsey
W. F. Rannie
Nolan Reilly

Shirley Render
Cecil Rosner
Wendy Ross
Rob Roughley
Mark Ruml
Frances Russell
Chris Rutkowski
Michelle Rydz
Keith A. P. Sandiford
Dennis Schellenberg
Gord Schumacher
Gladwyn Scott
Geoff Scott
John Selwood
Doran Sewell
Jill Sexsmith
Charles Shilliday
Gregg Shilliday
Jim Shilliday
Fred J. Shore
Reg Skene
Doug Smith
Geoffrey C. Smith
Shirlee Smith
Wally Sopiwnyk
Chris Stadel
Gary T. Steiman
Amanda Stephens
D. Bruce Stewart
Taz Stewart
Allen Sturko

Brenda Suderman
Walter E. Swayze
Ed Sweeney
Gerri Sweet
E. Leigh Syms
Brian Sumner
Bruce Tascona
Robert Taylor
Lorna Tergesen
Paul G. Thomas
Norman J. Threinen
Frank J. Tough
James Townsend
Orysia Tracz
Joel Trenaman
Elizabeth Troutt
Tessa Vanderhart
David J. Wade
Ted Wakefield
Gene Walz
William Watkins
John Welsted
A. Richard Westwood
Jeremy Wiebe
Dave Williamson
Nelson Wiseman
W. Scott Wright
Robert E. Wrigley
Dale Wrubleski
Graham Young
Scott Young

CONTRIBUTOR ABBREVIATIONS

AJL – Adam J. Levin, Associate Editor, Great Plains Publications

ARW – Dr. A. Richard Westwood, Associate Professor, Department of Biology and Department of Environmental Studies, University of Winnipeg.

DBS – D. Bruce Stewart, Head, Arctic Biological Consultants.

DJW – David J. Wade, Insect Control, City of Winnipeg.

DW – Dale Wrubleski, Ducks Unlimited Canada.

EP – Dr. Eva Pip, Department of Biology, University of Winnipeg.

FAL – Dr. Frederick A. Leighton, Executive Director, Canadian Cooperative Wildlife Health Centre, Western College of Veterinary Medicine, University of Saskatchewan.

FOC – Fisheries and Oceans Canada (used with permission).

GPP – Great Plains Publications staff

GY – Dr. Graham Young, Curator of Geology and Paleontology, The Manitoba Museum.

JMB – J. M. Bumsted, Professor of History, University of Manitoba

JS – Jill Sexsmith, writer, Great Plains Publications

JT – Joel Trenaman, Assistant Editor, Great Plains Publications

LP – Leigh Patterson, Ducks Unlimited Canada.

MAF – Manitoba Agriculture and Food (used with permission).

MC – Manitoba Conservation.

MD – Michelle Dobrovolny, Senior Writer, Great Plains Publications

MM – Murray McNeill, Business Reporter, *Winnipeg Free Press*

MMB – Mary M. Birt, Nature Conservancy of Canada, Manitoba Region.

RCL – Rhéal C. Lafrenière, Business Development Specialist and Provincial Apiarist, Manitoba Agriculture, Food and Rural Development Initiatives.

RE – Roy Ellis, Manitoba Agriculture and Food.

REW – Dr. Robert E. Wrigley, Curator, Assiniboine Park Zoo.

RK – Rebeca Kuropatwa, writer, Great Plains Publications

TDG – Dr. Terry D. Galloway, Department of Entomology and Associate Curator of J.B. Wallis Museum of Entomology, Faculty of Agricultural and Food Sciences, University of Manitoba.

VC – Vince Crichton, Manager of Game, Fur and Problem Wildlife, Manitoba Conservation.

WBP – Dr. William B. Preston, retired Curator, Lower Invertebrates and Invertebrates, Manitoba Museum.

WOP – Dr. William O. Pruitt, Jr, Professor Emeritus, Zoology Department, University of Manitoba.

WW – William Watkins, Manitoba Conservation.

RECOMMENDED READING

BOOKS AND MAGAZINES/JOURNAL ARTICLES

GENERAL:

Bumsted, J. M. *A Dictionary of Manitoba Biography* Winnipeg: University of Manitoba Press, 1999.

Canadian Who's Who. Toronto: University of Toronto Press, 2007.

Casselman, Bill. *Casselman's Canadian Words*. Toronto: Copp Clark, 1995.

Cook, Ramsay and Réal Bélanger. *Dictionary of Canadian Biography*. Toronto: University of Toronto Press/ Presses de l'Université Laval, 2000.

Donnelly, Murray. *Dafoe of the Free Press.* Toronto: Macmillan Canada, 1968.

Kurnarsky, Larry. *Famous and Fascinating Manitobans*. Winnipeg: FACE Publications, 1982.

Marsh, James H., ed. *The Canadian Encyclopedia*. Edmonton: Hurtig Publishers Ltd., 1988.

Rutkowski, C. and Dittman, G., eds. *The 2004 Canadian UFO Survey*. Winnipeg: UFOROM, 2005.

Wishart, David J., ed. *Encyclopedia of the Great Plains*. Lincoln: Univ. of Nebraska Press, 2004.

ARCHAEOLOGY:

Berry, Susan and Jack Brink. *Aboriginal Cultures in Alberta: Five Hundred Generations*. Edmonton: The Provincial Museum of Alberta, 2004.

Dyck, Ian. "The Prehistory of Southern Saskatchewan." In *Tracking Ancient Hunters: Prehistoric Archaeology in Saskatchewan*, edited by H.T. Epp and I. Dyck, 63-139. Saskatoon: Saskatchewan Archaeological Society, 1983.

Flynn, Catherine M. "*Cultural Responses to the Medieval Warm Period on the Northeastern Plains: The Example of the Lockport Site (EaLf-1)."* Masters thesis, Winnipeg: University of Manitoba, 2002.

Flynn, Catherine and E. Leigh Syms. "Manitoba's First Farmers." *Manitoba History* 36, (1996): 4-11.

Hamilton, Scott and B.A. Nicholson. "Ecological Islands and Vickers Focus Adaptive Transitions in the Pre-contact Plains of Southwestern Manitoba." *Plains Anthropologist* 44, (1999): 5-26.

Hodder, Ian, ed. *Archaeological Theory Today*. Cambridge: Polity Press, 2002.

Karklins, Karlis. *Trade Ornament Usage Among the Native Peoples of Canada: A Source Book.* Ottawa: National Historic Sites Parks Service/Environment Canada, 1992.

Lenius, Brian J. and David M. Olinyk. "The Rainy River Composite: Revisions to Late Woodland Taxonomy." In *The Woodland Tradition in the Western Great Lakes: Papers Presented to Elden Johnson*, edited by Guy E. Gibbon. Minneapolis: University of Minnesota Publications in Anthropology No. 4 (1990): 77-112.

McGhee, Robert. *The Last Imaginary Place: A Human History of the Arctic World.* Gatineau/Toronto: Canadian Museum of Civilization and Key Porter Books, 2004.

Nicholson, B.A. "Ceramic Affiliations and the Case for Incipient Horticulture in Southwestern Manitoba." *Canadian Journal of Archaeology* 14 (1990): 33-60.

Nicholson, B. A., D. Wiseman, S. Hamilton and S. Nicholson. "Climatic Challenges and Changes: A Little Ice Age Period Response to Adversity – the Vickers

Focus Forager/Horticulturalists Move On." *Plains Anthropologist* Memoir 38 Vol. 51, No. 199 (2006): 253-280.

Pettipas, Leo F., ed. *Studies in Manitoba Rock Art: I. Petroforms.* Papers in Manitoba Archaeology, Miscellaneous Paper No. 14 (second edition). Winnipeg: MB Department of Cultural Affairs and Historic Resources, 1983.

————. *Introducing Manitoba Prehistory*. Papers in Manitoba Archaeology, Popular Series No. 4. Winnipeg: Department of Culture, Heritage, and Recreation. Government of Manitoba, 1983.

Pettipas, Leo F. *Aboriginal Migrations: A History of Movements in Southern Manitoba*. Winnipeg: Manitoba Museum of Man and Nature, 1996.

Rempel, G. "The Manitoba Mound Builders: The Making of an Archaeological Myth, 1857-1900." *Manitoba History*, 28 Fall (1994): 12-18.

Rajnovich, Grace. *Reading Rock Art: Interpreting the Indian Rock Paintings of the Canadian Shield*. Toronto: Natural Heritage/Natural History Inc., 1994.

Steinbring, Jack. "Aboriginal Rock Painting Sites in Manitoba." *Manitoba Archaeological Journal* Vol. 8 (1998): Nos. 1&2.

Syms, E. Leigh. *Aboriginal Mounds in Southern Manitoba: An Evaluative Overview*. Manuscript Report Series No. 323, Ottawa: Parks Canada, 1978.

Syms, E. Leigh, Ed Winters and C. Gordon Hill. *The Initial Glimpse of an Exciting Heritage Record: Bruneau Lake Site #6 (GfLm-3)*. Winnipeg: The Manitoba Museum, 2004.

Three Fires Society, Roseau River Chapter. *An Anishinabe Understanding of the Petroforms in Whiteshell Provincial Park.* Parks Branch, Winnipeg: MB Department of Natural Resources, 1990.

Wright, James V. "A History of the Native People of Canada," Vols. I–III, *Mercury Series*, Archaeology Paper 152, Gatineau: Canadian Museum of Civilization, 1995.

ARTS, CULTURE, SOCIETY, EDUCATION, ETHNICITY, AND RELIGION:

Adamson, Arthur. *Arthur Adamson: A Celebration*. Winnipeg: J. Gordon Shillingford Publishing Inc., 2006.

Allen, Richard, ed. *Religion and Society in the Prairie West*. Regina: Canadian Plains Research Centre, 1974.

Anderson, Carol. *Rachel Browne: Dancing Toward the Light*. Winnipeg: J. Gordon Shillingford, 1999.

Balan, Jars. *Salt and Braided Bread: Ukrainian Life in Canada.* Toronto: Oxford University Press, 1984.

Bedford, A. Gerald. *The University of Winnipeg: A History of the Founding Colleges*. Toronto: University of Toronto Press, 1975.

Boon, T. C. B. *The Anglican Church from the Bay to the Rockies: A History of the Ecclesiastical Province of Rupert's Land and Its Dioceses. From 1820 to 1950*. Toronto: Ryerson Press, 1962.

Boughton, Noelle. *Margaret Lawrence, A Gift of Grace: A Spiritual Biography.* Toronto: Women's Press, 2007.

Bumsted, J. M. *The University of Manitoba: An Illustrated History*. Winnipeg: University of Manitoba Press, 2001.

Butcher, Dennis L. et al. *Prairie Spirit: Perspectives on the Heritage of the United Church of Canada in the West*. Winnipeg: University of Manitoba Press, 1985.

Butterfield, David, and Maureen Devanik Butterfield. *If Walls Could Talk: Manitoba's Best Buildings Explored and Explained*. Winnipeg: Great Plains Publications, 2000.

Canadian Museum of Civilization. *Art and Ethnicity: the Ukrainian Tradition in Canada*. Hull, QC: Canadian Museum of Civilization, 1991.

Carrington, Philip. *The Anglican Church in Canada: A History*. Toronto: Collins, 1963.

Cavaick, Wemyss. *Uprooted Heather: A Story of the Selkirk Settlers*. Vancouver: Mitchell Press, 1967.

Chiel, Arthur A. *The Jews in Manitoba: A Social History*. Toronto: University of Toronto Press, 1961.

Dafoe, Christopher. *Dancing Through Time: The First Fifty Years of Canada's Royal Winnipeg Ballet*. Winnipeg: Portage & Main Press, 1990.

Einarson, John. *Made in Manitoba: A Musical Legacy*. Winnipeg: Great Plains Publications, 2005.

Ewanchuk, Michael. *Pioneer Profiles: Ukrainian Settlers in Manitoba*. Winnipeg: M. Ewanchuk, 1981.

————. *Reflections and Reminiscences: Ukrainians in Canada, 1892-1992*. Winnipeg: M. Ewanchuk, 1995.

———. *Vertical Development: A New Generation of Ukrainian Canadians*. 2 vols. Winnipeg: M. Ewanchuk, 2000-02.

Ferguson, Barry, ed. *The Anglican Church and the World of Western Canada*. Regina: Canadian Plains Research Centre, University of Regina, 1991.

Friendly, M., and J. Beach. *Early Childhood Education and Care in Canada, 2004*. Toronto: Child Care Resource and Research Unit, University of Toronto, 2005.

Friesen, Rhinehart. *A Mennonite Odyssey*. Winnipeg: Hyperion Press, 1988.

Gaboury-Diallo, Lise, Rosmarin Heidenreich, and Jean Valenti (eds). *J.R. Léveillé par les autres*. Saint-Boniface: Éditions du Blé, 2005.

———. *J.R. Léveillé: plaisirs du texte et textes de plaisir*. Winnipeg: Presses universitaires de Saint-Boniface, 2007.

Gutkin, Harry. *Journey into Our Heritage: The Story of the Jewish People in the Canadian West*. Toronto: Lester & Orpen Dennys Ltd., 1980.

Heidenreich, Rosmarin. *Paysages de désir. J.R. Léveillé: Réflexions critiques*. Ottawa: Éditions l'Interligne, 2005.

Hughes, Kenneth James. *Contemporary Manitoba Writers: New Critical Studies*. Winnipeg: Turnstone Press, 1990.

Hughes, Lesley. *We Chose Canada: Eleven Profiles from Manitoba's Mosiac*. Winnipeg: Aivilo Press, 2005.

Isaacs, Leonard. *Five Lives in One* (Selected Memoirs). Hubbards, NS: Good Cheer Publishing, 1998.

Kaye, Vladimir J., ed. *Dictionary of Ukrainian Canadian Biography: Pioneer Settlers of Manitoba, 1891-1900*. Toronto: Ukrainian Canadian Research Foundation, 1975.

Kaye, Vladimir J. and J. B. Gregorovich, eds. *Ukrainian Canadians in Canada's Wars*. Toronto: Ukrainian Canadian Research Foundation; Winnipeg: Distributed by Ethnicity Books, 1983.

Kelly, Paula. *For the Arts: A History of the Manitoba Arts Council*. Winnipeg: Manitoba Arts Council, 1995.

Keywan, Zonia. *Greater Than Kings: Ukrainian Pioneer Settlement in Canada*. Montreal: Harvest House, 1977.

Kordan, Bohdan S. and Luciuk, Lubomyr Y. *A Delicate and Difficult Question: Documents in the History of Ukrainians in Canada, 1899-1962* (Builders of Canada Series, no. 3). Kingston, ON: Limestone Press, 1986.

Krijff, J. Th. J. *100 Years Ago: Dutch Immigration to Manitoba in 1893*. Windsor, ON: Electa Press, 1993.

La Frenière, Roger, and Jacques Rollier. *Le Cercle Molière: Cinquantième anniversaire*. Winnipeg: Éditions du blé, 1975.

Lane, Brian M. *Hal Foster: Prince of Illustrators and Father of the Adventure Strip*. Clinton, NJ: Vanguard Productions, 2001.

Lester, Tanya. *Women Rights Writes: Some Herstorical Profiles of Western Canadian Writers*. Winnipeg: Lilith Publications, 1985.

Lindal, W. J. *The Icelanders in Canada*. Ottawa: National Publishers, 1967.

Little, Ada S. *Dogtown to Dauphin*. Winnipeg: Watson & Dwyer, 1988.

Lohrenz, Gerhard. *The Mennonites of Western Canada*. Winnipeg: G. Lohrenz, 1974.

Longfield, Kevin. *From Fire to Flood: A History of Theatre in Manitoba*. Winnipeg: Signature Editions, 2001.

Lupul, Manoly R., ed. *A Heritage in Transition: Essays in the History of Ukrainians in Canada*. Toronto: McClelland & Stewart in association with the Multiculturalism Directorate, Dept. of the Secretary of State, and the Canadian Government Publishing Centre, Supply and Services Canada, 1982.

———. *Visible Symbols: Cultural Expression Among Canada's Ukrainians*. Edmonton: Canadian Institute of Ukrainian Studies, University of Alberta, 1984.

McCarthy, Martha. *To Evangelize the Nations: Roman Catholic Missions in Manitoba, 1818-1870*. Winnipeg: Manitoba Culture, Heritage and Recreation, Historic Resources, 1990.

Machray, Robert A. *Life of Robert Machray, Archbishop of Rupert's Land*. London: Macmillan, 1909.

Manitoba Japanese Canadian Citizen's Association. *The History of Japanese Canadians in Manitoba*. Winnipeg: Manitoba Japanese Canadian Citizen's Association, 1996.

Marnoch, James. *Western Witness: The Presbyterians in the Area of the Synod of Manitoba, 1700-1885*. Winnipeg: Watson & Dwyer, 1994.

Martynowych, Orest T. Ukrainians in Canada: the formative period, 1891-1924. Edmonton: Canadian Institute of Ukrainian Studies Press, 1991.

Marunchak, Mykhailo H. *The Ukrainian Canadians: A History*. 2nd ed. Winnipeg: Ukrainian Academy of Arts and Sciences in Canada, 1982.

Mitchell, Estelle. *The Grey Nuns of Montreal and the Red River Settlement 1844-1984*. Montreal: Grey Nuns, 1986

Morton, W. L. *One University: A History of the University of Manitoba 1877-1952*. Toronto: McClelland & Stewart, 1957.

Mycak, Sonia. *Canuke Literature: Critical Essays on Canadian Ukrainian Writing*. Huntington, NY: Nova Science Publications, 2001.

Neufeld, William. *From Faith to Faith: The History of the Manitoba Mennonite Brethren Church*. Winnipeg: Kindred Productions, 1989.

Peel, Bruce. *Early Printing in the Red River Settlement 1859-1870 and Its Effects on the Riel Rebellion*. Winnipeg: Peguis Publishers, 1974.

Pitman, Bonnie. *150 Years of Art in Manitoba*. Winnipeg: Winnipeg Art Gallery, 1970.

Poonwassie, Deo H., and Anne Poonwassie. *Adult Education in Manitoba: Historical Aspects*. Mississauga, Ont.: Canadian Educators' Press, 1997.

Powers, Lyall H. *Alien Heart: The Life and Work of Margaret Laurence*. Winnipeg: University of Manitoba Press, 2003.

Prentice, S. "Manitoba's Childcare Regime: Social Liberalism in Flux." *Canadian Journal of Sociology.* (2004): 193-207.

Rempel, John D. *Atlas of Original Mennonite Villages and Homesteaders of the Mennonite East Reserve, Manitoba*. Altona, MB: J. Rempel and W. Harms, 1988.

———. *Atlas of Original Mennonite Villages, Homesteaders, and Some Burial Plots of the Mennonite West Reserve, Manitoba*. Altona, MB: J. Rempel and W. Harms, 1990.

Ricard, François. *Gabrielle Roy: A Life*. Translated by Patricia Claxton. Toronto: McClelland & Stewart, 2001.

Rotoff, Basil. *Monuments to Faith: Ukrainian Churches in Manitoba*. Winnipeg: University of Manitoba Press, 1990.

Roy, Gabrielle. *Enchantment and Sorrow: An Autobiography*. Toronto: Lester & Orpen Dennys, 1987.

Rozumnyj, Jaroslav. ed., with Oleh W. Gerus and Mykhailo H. Marunchak. *New Soil, Old Roots: the Ukrainian Experience in Canada*. Winnipeg: Ukrainian Academy of Arts and Sciences in Canada, 1983.

Semple, Neil. *The Lord's Dominion: The History of Canadian Methodism.* Montreal & Kingston: McGill-Queen's University Press, 1996.

Todaschuk, Sylvia, and Stephen Walter Mical. *Winnipeg's Folklorama: Canada's Cultural Celebration*. Winnipeg: Folk Arts Council of Winnipeg, 2001.

Wilson, Keith, and James B. Wyndels. *The Belgians in Manitoba*. Winnipeg: Peguis Publishers, 1976.

Wyman, Max. *Evelyn Hart: An Intimate Portrait by Max Wyman*. Toronto: McClelland & Stewart, 1991.

———. *The Royal Winnipeg Ballet: The First Forty Years*. Toronto: Doubleday Canada, 1978.

Yuzyk, Paul. *The Ukrainians in Manitoba: A Social History*. Toronto: University of Toronto Press, 1953.

ECONOMY, BUSINESS, INDUSTRY, AND LABOUR:

Anderson, Charles W. *Grain: The Entrepreneurs*. Winnipeg: Watson & Dwyer, 1991.

Bellan, Ruben. *Winnipeg's First Century: An Economic History*. Winnipeg: Queenston House, 1978.

Bennett, Richard E. *History of the Great-West Life Assurance Company*. Winnipeg: The Great-West Life Assurance Company, 1992.

Canada Press Club. *The Multilingual Press in Manitoba*. Winnipeg: Canada Press Club, 1974.

Coates, Ken. *The Keystone Province: An Illustrated History of Manitoba Enterprise*. Burlington, ON: Windsor Publications, 1988.

Dyck, John. *Crosstown Credit Union Limited: Serving the Mennonite Community – The First Fifty Years, 1944-1994*. Winnipeg: Crosstown Credit Union Ltd., 1993.

Honey, Janet and Brian Oleson. *A Century of Agriculture in Manitoba: A Proud Legacy.* Winnipeg: Credit Union Central Manitoba, 2006.

Jones, Robert H. *Building Futures: A History of Investors Group*. Winnipeg: Investors Group, 1993.

Kuz, Tony, ed. *Winnipeg 1874-1974: Progress and Prospects*. Winnipeg: Manitoba Dept. of Industry and Commerce, 1974.

Levine, Allan. *The Exchange: 100 Years of Trading Grain in Winnipeg*. Winnipeg: Peguis Publishers, 1987.

————. *From Winnipeg to the World: The CanWest Global Story*. Winnipeg: CanWest Global Communications, 2002.

McDonnell, Greg. *Wheat Kings: Vanishing Landmarks of the Canadian Prairies*. Erin, ON: Boston Mills, 1998.

MEDTP Inc. *Currents of Change: Métis Economic Development*. Winnipeg: Pemmican Publications, 1986.

Neville, William. *Raising the Standard: A History of the Institute of Chartered Accountants of Manitoba 1886-1986*. Winnipeg: The Institute of Chartered Accountants of Manitoba, 1986.

Render, Shirley. *Double Cross: The Inside Story of James A. Richardson and Canadian Airways*. Vancouver: Douglas & McIntyre, 1999.

Smith, Doug. *Let Us Rise! An Illustrated History of the Manitoba Labour Movement*. Vancouver: New Star Books, 1985.

FIRST NATIONS, ABORIGINAL, INUIT, AND MÉTIS:

Aboriginal Justice Inquiry – Child Welfare Initiative (2005). *A Profile of Child and Family Services, Authorities and Agencies*. Winnipeg: Government of Manitoba.

Ahenakew, Alice. *They Knew Both Sides of Medicine: Cree Tales of Curing and Cursing, Told by Alice Ahenakew*. Edited and translated by H. C. Wolfart and Freda Ahenakew. Winnipeg: University of Manitoba Press, Publications of the Algonquin Text Society, 2000.

Ahenakew, Edward. *Voices of the Plains Cree*. Edited by Ruth Matheson Buck. Toronto: McClelland & Stewart, 1973.

Angel, Michael. *Preserving the Sacred: Historical Perspectives on the Ojibwa Midewiwin*. Winnipeg: University of Manitoba Press, 2002.

Baraga, Friedrich. *A Dictionary of the Ojibway Language*. (reprint) St. Paul: Minnesota Historical Society, 1992.

Bloomfield, Leonard. *Plains Cree Texts*. New York: American Ethnographic Society Publications No. 16, 1934.

Bowsfield, Hartwell. *Louis Riel: Rebel of the Western Frontier or Victim of Politics and Prejudice*. Toronto: Copp Clark, 1969.

Brown, Jennifer S. H. *Strangers in Blood: Fur Trade Company Families in Indian Country*. Vancouver: University of British Columbia Press, 1980.

———— and Jacqueline Peterson, eds. *The New Peoples: Being and Becoming Métis in North America*. Winnipeg: University of Manitoba Press, 1985.

———— and Robert Brightman. *"The Orders of the Dreamed": George Nelson on Cree and Northern Ojibwa Religion and Myth, 1823*. Winnipeg: University of Manitoba Press, Publications of the Algonquin Text Society, 1988.

Budd, Henry. *The Diary of Henry Budd 1870-1875*. Edited by Katherine Pettipas. Manitoba Record Society Publications Vol. 4. Winnipeg: Hignell, 1974.

Bussidor, Ila. *Night Spirits: The Story of the Relocation of the Sayisi Dene*. Winnipeg: University of Manitoba Press, 1997.

Campbell, Martia. *Halfbreed*. Toronto: McClelland & Stewart, 1973.

Carlson, Paul H. *The Plains Indians*. College Station: Texas A&M University Press, 1998.

Castel, Robert J. *Castel's English-Cree Dictionary and Memoirs of the Elders: Based on the Woods Cree of Pukatawagan, Manitoba*. Brandon: Brandon University Northern Teacher Education Program, 2001.

Cerbelaud-Salagnac, Georges. *La Révolte des métis: Louis Riel, héros ou rebelle?* Vancouver, Montreal: HMH, 1971.

Coates, Ken, and Fred McGuinness. *Aboriginal Land Claims in Canada: A Regional Perspective*. Newmarket, ON: Addison-Wesley, 1992.

Collins, Joseph Edmund. *The Story of Louis Riel the Rebel Chief*. Toronto: J. S. Robertson & Bros., 1885.

Comeau, Pauline, and Aldo Santin. *The First Canadians: A Profile of Canada's Native People Today*. Toronto: James Lorimer & Co., 1990.

Davidson, W. M. *The Life and Times of Louis Riel*. Calgary: Albertan Publishing, 1951.

Dickason, Olive P. *Canada's First Nations: A History of Founding Peoples from Earliest Times*. Toronto: McClelland & Stewart Inc., 1992.

Elias, Peter Douglas. *The Dakota of the Canadian Northwest: Lessons for Survival*. Winnipeg: University of Manitoba Press, 1988.

Erasmus, Peter. *Buffalo Days and Nights*. Calgary: Glenbow Institute, 1976.

Flanagan, Thomas, ed. *Louis "David" Riel: "Prophet of the New World."* Rev. ed. Toronto: University of Toronto Press, 1996.

———. *Métis Lands in Manitoba*. 1991.

——— and Claude Rocan. *Rebellion in the North-West: Louis Riel and the Métis People*. Toronto: Grolier, 1984.

———. *Riel and the Rebellion: 1885 Reconsidered*. Saskatoon: Western Producer Prairie books, 1983.

Frémont, Donatien. *The Secretaries of Louis Riel: Louis Schmidt (1870), Henry Jackson, Philippe Garnot*. Translated by Solange Lavigne. Prince Albert, Sask.: Les éditions Louis Riel for La Société canadienne-française de Prince Albert, ca. 1885.

Friesen, John W. *The Cultural Maze: Complex Questions on Native Destiny in Western Canada*. Calgary: Detselig Enterprises, 1992.

Giraud, Marcel. *Le métis canadien*. Paris: Institut d'ethnologie, 1945.

Grant, Agnes. *James McKay: A Métis Builder of Canada*. Winnipeg: Pemmican Publications, 1994.

———. *A School on Each Reserve: Aboriginal Education in Manitoba*. Brandon: Brandon University Northern Teacher Education Program, 2001.

Grisdale, Alex, and Nan Shipley. *Wild Drums: Tales and Legends of the Plains Indians*. Winnipeg: Peguis Publishers, 1974.

Hallett, Bruce. *Aboriginal People in Manitoba 2000*. Winnipeg: Human Resources Development Canada, 2001.

Hallowell, A. Irving. *The Ojibwa of Berens River, Manitoba: Ethnography into History*. Toronto: Harcourt Brace Jovanovich, 1992.

Hamilton, A.C., and C.M. Sinclair. *Report of the Aboriginal Justice Inquiry of Manitoba*. Winnipeg: Aboriginal Justice Inquiry of Manitoba, 1991.

Harring, Sidney L. *White Man's Law: Native People in Nineteenth-Century Canadian Jurisprudence*. Toronto: University of Toronto Press, 1998.

Hull, Jeremy. *Aboriginal People and Social Classes in Manitoba*. Winnipeg: Canadian Centre for Policy Alternatives, 2001.

Indian Tribes of Manitoba. *Wahbung: Our Tomorrows*. Winnipeg: Indian Tribes of Manitoba, 1971.

Johnston, Basil H. *Indian School Days*. Toronto: Key Porter, 1988.

———. *The Manitous: The Spiritual World of the Ojibway*. New York: HarperCollins, 1995.

———. *Ojibway Heritage*. New York: Columbia University Press, 1976.

Kimelman, E. *No Quiet Place* (Final Report of the Review Committee on Indian and Métis Adoptions and Placements). Winnipeg: Manitoba Community Services, 1985.

Krotz, Larry. *Indian Country: Inside Another Canada*. Toronto: McClelland & Stewart, 1990.

———. *Urban Indians: The Strangers in Canada's Cities*. Edmonton: Hurtig Publishers, 1980.

Lacombe, Father Albert, O.B. *Dictionnaire de la langue des Cris*. Montreal: C. O. Beauchemin & Valois, 1874. (Available online at http://www.canadiana.org.)

Lavallée, Guy Albert Sylvestre. *The Metis of St. Laurent, Manitoba: Their Life and Stories, 1920-1988*. Winnipeg: G. Lavallée, 2003.

Lussier, Antoine S., ed. *Louis Riel and the Métis*. Winnipeg: Pemmican Publications, 1988.

Lytwyn, Victor P. *Muskekowuck Athinuwick: Original People of the Great Swampy Land*. Winnipeg: University of Manitoba Press, 2001.

MacEwan, Grant. *Métis Makers of History*. Saskatoon: Western Producer Prairie Books, 1981.

Mandelbaum, David. *The Plains Cree*. New York: Anthropological Papers of the American Museum of Natural History, 1940.

Manitoba Historic Resources Branch. *Ancient Traders in Southern Manitoba*. Winnipeg: Manitoba Culture, Heritage and Recreation, Historic Resources, 1989.

Martel, Gilles. *Le Messianisme de Louis Riel*. Waterloo, ON: Wilfred Laurier University Press, 1984.

Miller, J. R. *Big Bear (Mistahimusqua): A Biography*. Toronto: ECW Press, 1996.

———. *Singwauk's Vision: A History of Native Residential Schools*. Toronto: University of Toronto Press, 1996.

———. *Skycrapers Hide the Heavens: A History of Indian-White Relations in Canada*. Toronto: University of Toronto Press, 1989.

Milloy, John Sheridan. *A National Crime: The Canadian Government and the Residential School System, 1879 to 1986*. Winnipeg: University of Manitoba Press, 1999.

———. *The Plains Cree: Trade, Diplomacy, and War, 1790 to 1870*. Winnipeg: University of Manitoba Press, 1990.

Morrison, Sheila Jones. *Rotten to the Core: the Politics of the Manitoba Métis Federation*. Winnipeg: Hignell, 1995.

Morton, Desmond. *The Queen v. Louis Riel: Canada's Greatest State Trial*. Toronto: University of Toronto Press, 1974.

Nelson, George. *"The Orders of the Dreamed": George Nelson on Cree and Northern Ojibwa Religion and Myth, 1823*. Winnipeg: University of Manitoba Press, 1988.

Osler, E. B. *The Man Who Had to Hang*. Toronto: Longmans Green, 1961.

Peers, Laura L. *The Ojibwa of Western Canada, 1780-1870*. St. Paul: Minnesota Historical Society Press, 1995.

Penman, Sarah, ed. *Honor the Grandmothers: Dakota and Lakota Women Tell Their Stories*. St. Paul: Minnesota Historical Society, 2000.

Pettipas, Leo. *Aboriginal Migrations: A History of Movements in Southern Manitoba*. Winnipeg: Manitoba Museum, 1996.

Pond, Samuel W. *Dakota Life in the Upper Midwest*. St. Paul: Minnesota Historical Society, 2002.

Priest, Lisa. *Conspiracy of Silence: The Riveting Real-life Account of The Pas Murder and Cover-up that Rocked the Nation*. Toronto: McClelland & Stewart, 1989.

Quan, Holly. *Native Chiefs and Famous Métis: Leadership and Bravery in the Canadian West*. Canmore, AB: Altitude Publishing Canada, 2003.

Ray, A. J. *Indians in the Fur Trade: Their Role As Trappers, Hunters, and Middlemen in the Lands Southwest of Hudson's Bay*. Toronto: University of Toronto Press, 1974.

Riel, Louis. *Collected Writings/Écrits complètes*. 5 Vols. Edited by George F. G. Stanley. Edmonton: University of Alberta Press, 1985.

———. *The Diaries of Louis Riel*. Edited by Thomas Flanagan. Edmonton: Hurtig Publishers, 1976.

Saint-Aubin, Bernard. *Louis Riel: Un destin tragique*. Montreal: La Presse, 1985.

St-Onge, Nicole J. M. *Saint-Laurent, Manitoba: Evolving Métis Identities, 1850-1914*. Regina: Canadian Plains Research Centre, 2004.

Sanders, Douglas E. *Aboriginal and Treaty Rights in Manitoba*. Vancouver: Aboriginal Justice Inquiry, 1990.

Sawchuck, Joe. *The Métis of Manitoba: Reformulation of an Ethnic Identity*. Toronto: Peter Martin Associates, 1978.

Sealey, D. Bruce, and Antoine S. Lussier. *The Métis: Canada's Forgotten People*. Winnipeg: Manitoba Métis Federation Press, 1975.

Sealey, Margaret, and Bruce Sealey. *Six Métis Communities*. Winnipeg: Manitoba Métis Federation Press, 1974.

Siggins, Maggie. *Riel: a Life of Revolution*. Toronto: HarperCollins, 1994.

Sinclair Jr., Gordon. *Cowboys and Indians: The Shooting of J. J. Harper*. Toronto: McClelland & Stewart, 1999.

Sprague, D. N. *Canada and the Métis, 1869-1885*. Waterloo, ON: Wilfrid Laurier University Press, 1988.

Stanley, G. F. G. *The Birth of Western Canada: A History of the Riel Rebellions*. London: Longmans, Green, & Co., 1936.

Stanley, George F. G. *Louis Riel*. Toronto: Ryerson Press, 1963.

Stonechild, Blair, and Bill Waiser. *Loyal till Death: Indians and the North-West Rebellion*. Calgary: Fifth House Publishers, 1997.

Sutherland, Donna G. *Peguis: A Noble Friend*. St. Andrews, MB: Chief Peguis Heritage Park Inc., 2003.

Trémaudan, Auguste-Henri de. *Hold High Your Heads: History of the Métis Nation in Western Canada*. Translated by Elizabeth Maguet. Winnipeg: Pemmican Publications, 1982.

Turner, C. Frank. *Across the Medicine Line: The Epic Confrontation between Sitting Bull and the North-West Mounted Police*. Toronto: McClelland & Stewart, 1973.

Vennum, Thomas. *Wild Rice and the Ojibway People*. St. Paul: Minnesota Historical Society, 1988.

Ward, Donald B. *The People: A Historical Guide to the First Nations of Alberta, Saskatchewan, and Manitoba.* Saskatoon: Fifth House, 1995.

Wiebe, Rudy, and Bob Beal (ed.). *War in the West: Voices of the 1885 Rebellion.* Toronto: McClelland & Stewart, 1985.

Wilson, Stan. *Opasquiak: The Pas Indian Reserve.* Toronto: Holt, Rinehart, and Winston, 1973.

Woodcock, George. *Gabriel Dumont: The Métis Chief and His Lost World.* Edmonton: Hurtig Publishers, 1976.

GOVERNMENT, POLITICS, LAW, AND JUSTICE:

Anderson, Frank. *Outlaws of Manitoba.* Aldergrove, BC: Frontier Publishing, 1971.

Brownstone, Meyer, and T. J. Plunket. *Metropolitan Winnipeg: Politics and Reform of Local Government.* Berkeley, CA: Univ. of California, Institute of Governmental Studies and Institute of International Studies, 1983.

Dafoe, John Wesley. *Clifford Sifton in Relation to His Times.* Toronto: Macmillan, 1931.

Doern, Russell. *The Battle over Bilingualism: The Manitoba Language Question, 1983-85.* Winnipeg: Cambridge Publishers, 1985.

Elections Manitoba. *Statement of Votes for the 38th Provincial Election.* 2003.

Gerrard, Jon. *Battling for a Better Manitoba: A History of the Provincial Liberal Party.* Winnipeg: Heartland, 2006.

Hamilton, A. C., and C. M. Sinclair. *Report of the Aboriginal Justice Inquiry of Manitoba.* 2 vols. Winnipeg: Manitoba Public Inquiry into the Administration of Justice and Aboriginal People, 1991, 1999.

Harrop, G. Gerald. *Advocate of Compassion: Stanley Knowles in the Political Process.* Hantsport, NS: Lancelot Press, 1984.

Hébert, Raymond M. *Manitoba's French Language Crisis: A Cautionary Tale.* Montreal/Kingston: McGill Queen's University Press, 2004.

Hull, Jeremy. *The Political Economy of Manitoba.* Regina: Canadian Plains Research Centre, University of Regina, 1990.

Knowles, Stanley. *The New Party.* Toronto: McClelland and Stewart, 1961.

McAllister, James A. *The Government of Edward Schreyer: Democratic Socialism in Manitoba.* Kingston/Montreal: McGill-Queen's Univ. Press, 1984.

Mann Trofimenkoff, Susan. *Stanley Knowles: The Man from Winnipeg North Centre.* Saskatoon: Western Producer Prairie Books, 1982.

Mills, Allen. *Fool for Christ: the Political Thought of J. S. Woodsworth.* Toronto: University of Toronto Press, 1991.

Peden, Murray. *Hearken to the Evidence.* Stittsville, ON: Canada's Wings, 1983.

Redekop, Bill. *Crimes of the Century: Manitoba's Most Notorious True Crimes.* Winnipeg: Great Plains Publications, 2002.

Roblin, Duff. *Speaking for Myself: Politics and Other Pursuits.* Winnipeg: Great Plains Publications, 1999.

Stubbs, Roy St. George. *Four Recorders of Rupert's Land: A Brief Survey of the Hudson's Bay Company Courts of Rupert's Land.* Winnipeg: Peguis Publishers, 1967.

Templeman, Jack. *From Force to Service: The Winnipeg Police Service – A Pictorial History.* Calgary: Bunker to Bunker Books, 1998.

Willie, Richard Allan. *"These Legal Gentlemen": Lawyers in Manitoba, 1834-1900.* Winnipeg: Legal Research Institute of the University of Manitoba, 1994.

Wiseman, Nelson. *Social Democracy in Manitoba: A Political History of the CCF-NDP.* Winnipeg: University of Manitoba Press, 1983.

HISTORY AND GEOGRAPHY:

Adam, G. Mercer. *The Canadian North-West.* Toronto: Rose Publishing, 1885.

Aiken, Don. *It Happened in Manitoba: Stories of the Red River Province.* Calgary: Fifth House, 2004.

Beal, Bob, and Rod Macleod. *Prairie Fire: The 1885 North-West Rebellion.* Edmonton: Hurtig Publishers, 1984.

Begg, Alexander. *History of the North-West.* 3 vols. Toronto: Hunter, Rose & Co., 1894-95.

Bell, Charles N. "The Old Forts of Winnipeg." In *A Thousand Miles of Prairie: The Manitoba Historical Society and the History of Western Canada*, edited by Jim Blanchard, 192-217. Winnipeg: University of Manitoba Press, 2002.

____, *Local History in Manitoba*. Winnipeg: Historical and Scientific Society of Manitoba, 1976.

Berger, Carl, and Ramsey Cook, eds. *The West and the Nation: Essays in Honour of W. L. Morton*. Toronto: McClelland & Stewart, 1976.

Berry, Virginia C. *A Boundless Horizon: Visual Records of Exploration and Settlement in the Manitoba Region, 1624-1874*. Winnipeg: Winnipeg Art Gallery, 1983.

Bickle, Ian. *Turmoil and Triumph: The Controversial Railway to Hudson Bay*. Calgary: Detselig Enterprises, 1995.

Bohi, Charles. *Canadian National's Western Depots*. Toronto: Railfare Enterprises Ltd., 1977.

Bryce, George. *Manitoba: Its Infancy, Growth, and Present Condition*. London: Low, Marston, Searle & Rivington, 1882.

———. *Canada: An Encyclopaedia of the Country*. Vol. 1, Toronto: The Linscott Publishing Company, 1898.

———. *A History of Manitoba: Its Resources and People*. The Canadian History Company, 1906.

———. *The Remarkable History of the Hudson's Bay Company*. Toronto: W. Briggs, 1900.

Buchner, Anthony P., ed. *Geographical Names of Manitoba*. Winnipeg: Manitoba Conservation, 2001.

Bumsted, J. M. *Flood of the Centuries: A History of Flood Disasters in the Red River Valley 1776-1997*. Winnipeg: Great Plains Publications, 1997.

———. *The Manitoba Flood of 1950: An Illustrated History*. Winnipeg: Watson & Dwyer Publishing Ltd., 1993.

———. *Thomas Scott's Body and Other Essays on Early Manitoba History*. Winnipeg: University of Manitoba Press, 2000.

———. *Trials and Tribulations: The Red River Settlement and the Emergence of Manitoba, 1811-1870*. Winnipeg: Great Plains Publications, 2003.

Douglas, Robert. *Place Names of Manitoba*. Ottawa: Geographic Board of Canada, 1933.

Edwards, William G. *Stony: A History of Manitoba Penitentiary (Stony Mountain Institution)*. Stonewall, MB : Interlake Publishing, 2004.

Fleming, Howard A. *Canada's Arctic Outlet: A History of the Hudson Bay Railway*. Berkeley, CA: University of California Press, 1957.

Friesen, Gerald. *The Canadian Prairies: A History*. Toronto: University of Toronto Press, 1984.

———. *River Road: Essays on Manitoba and Prairie History*. Winnipeg: University of Manitoba Press, 1996.

Gill, Edward Anthony Wharton. *An Irishman's Luck: A History of Manitoba*. 1914.

Gourluck, Russ, *A Store Like No Other: Eaton's of Winnipeg*. Winnipeg: Great Plains Publications, 2004.

———. *Going Downtown: A History of Winnipeg's Portage Avenue*. Winnipeg: Great Plains Publications, 2006.

Gray, James H. *The Winter Years: The Depression on the Prairies*. Toronto: Macmillan, 1966.

Gutkin, Mildred and Harry Gutkin. *Profiles in Dissent: The Shaping of Radical Thought in the Canadian West*. Edmonton: NeWest Press, 1997.

Haig, Kennethe M. *Brave Harvest: The Life Story of E. Cora Hind*. Toronto: Thomas Allen, 1945.

Ham, Penny. *Place Names of Manitoba*. Saskatoon: Western Producer Prairie Books, 1980.

Healy, W. J. *Women of Red River: Being a Book Written from the Recollections of Women Surviving from the Red River Era*. Winnipeg: Peguis Publishers, 1967.

Higgitt, W. L. *Opening up the West: North-West Mounted Police Reports, 1874-1881*. Toronto: Coles Publishing, 1973.

Hislop, Mary. *The Streets of Winnipeg*. Winnipeg: T. W. Taylor Co., 1912.

Hollihan, Tony. *Disasters of Western Canada: Courage Amidst the Chaos*. Edmonton: Folklore Publishing, 2004.

Holm, Gerald F. and Anthoney P. Buchner, eds. *A Place of Honour: Manitoba's War Dead Commemorated in its Geography*. Winnipeg: Manitoba Geographical Names Program, 2003.

Huck, Barbara. *Crossroads of the Continent: A History of the Forks of the Red and Assiniboine Rivers*. Winnipeg: Heartland Associates Inc., 2003.

Huck, Barbara et al. *Exploring the Fur Trade Routes of North America*. Winnipeg: Heartland Associates Inc. 2002.

Hume, Mary, ed. *Brandon: A Prospect of a City*. Brandon: City of Brandon, 1982.

International Joint Commission. *Living with the Red: A Report to the Governments of Canada and the United States on Reducing Flood Impacts in the Red River Basin*. Ottawa, International Joint Commission, 2000

Jackel, Susan, ed. *A Flannel Shirt and Liberty: British Emigrant Gentlewomen in the Canadian West, 1880-1914*. Vancouver: University of British Columbia Press, 1982.

Jackson, James A. *The Centennial History of Manitoba*. Toronto: McClelland & Stewart, 1970.

Leah, Vince. *West of the River: The Story of West Kildonan*. Winnipeg: Vince Leah, 1970.

McKenzie, N. M. W. J. *Men of the Hudson's Bay Company*. Fort William (Thunder Bay), ON: Times-Journal Press, 1921.

Manitoba Library Association. *Pioneers and Early Citizens of Manitoba: A Dictionary of Manitoba Biography from the Earliest Times to 1920*. Winnipeg: Peguis Publishers, 1971.

Meyer-Oakes, W., ed. *Life, Land, and Water*. Winnipeg: University of Manitoba Press, 1961.

Morton, W. L. *Manitoba: A History*. Toronto: University of Toronto Press, 1957 (2nd ed. 1967).

Paterson, Edith. *Tales of Early Manitoba from the "Winnipeg Free Press."* Winnipeg: Winnipeg Free Press, 1970.

———. *Tales of the Early West*. Winnipeg: Hignell Printing, 1978.

Peterson, Murray. *Winnipeg Landmarks*. Toronto: Watson & Dwyer, 1995.

Ray, Arthur J. "History and Archaeology of the Northern Fur Trade," *American Antiquity* 43, no. 1 (Jan. 1978): 26-34.

Rich, E. E. *The Fur Trade and the Northwest to 1857*. Toronto: McClelland & Stewart Ltd., 1967.

Ross, Alexander. *The Fur Hunters of the Far West*. Norman, OK: University of Oklahoma Press, 1978. Originally published 1855.

Ross, Alexander. *The Red River Settlement, Its Rise, Progress, and Present State*. Minneapolis, Ross and Haines, 1957. Originally published 1856.

Rudnyckyj, Jaroslav Bohdan. *Manitoba Mosaic of Place Names*. Winnipeg: Canadian Institute of Onomastic Sciences, University of Manitoba, 1970.

———. *Mosaic of Winnipeg Street Names*. Winnipeg: Canadian Institute of Onomastic Sciences, University of Manitoba, 1974.

Russenholt, E. S. *The Heart of the Continent: Being the History of Assiniboia, the Truly Typical Canadian Community*. Winnipeg: Macfarlane Communication, 1968.

Rutkowski, C. *Unnatural History: True Manitoba Mysteries*. Winnipeg: Chameleon Publishers, 1993.

Shilliday, Gregg, ed. *Manitoba 125: A History* (Vol 1-3). Winnipeg: Great Plains Publications, 1993.

Shipley, Nan. *Road to the Forks: A History of the Community of Fort Garry*. Winnipeg, Stovel-Advocate Press, 1970.

Stone, Ted. *The Story Behind Manitoba Names : How Cities, Towns, Villages, and Whistle Stops Got Their Names*. Calgary: Red Deer Press, 2006.

Van Kirk, Sylvia. *Many Tender Ties: Women in Fur Trade Society*. Norman, OK: University of Oklahoma Press, 1983.

Vorst, Charlotte van de. *Making Ends Meet: Farm Women's Work in Manitoba*. Winnipeg: University of Manitoba Press, 2002.

Warkentin, John. *The Mennonite Settlements of Southern Manitoba*. Steinbach: Hanover Steinbach Historical Society, 2000.

Warkentin, John, and Richard I. Ruggles. *Historical Atlas of Manitoba: A Selection of Facsimile Maps, Plans, and Sketches from 1612 to 1969*. Winnipeg: Manitoba Historical Society, 1970.

Weir, Thomas R., ed. *Atlas of Manitoba*. Surveys and Mapping Branch, Dept. of Natural Resources, Province of Manitoba, 1983.

Welsted, John, John Everitt, and Christoph Stadel, eds. *Brandon: Geographical Perspectives on the Wheat City*. Regina: Canadian Plains Research Centre, 1988.

———— (ed.). *The Geography of Manitoba: Its Land and Its People*. Winnipeg: University of Manitoba Press, 1996.

Williams, W. H. *Manitoba and the North-West*. Toronto: Hunter, Rose & Co., 1882.

SCIENCE, MEDICINE, NATURE, AND TECHNOLOGY:

Aitchison-Benell, C. W. and C. D. Dondale. "A Checklist of Manitoba Spiders (Aranae) with notes on geographic relationships." *Naturaliste canadien* 117 (1990): 215-237.

Ames, Doris, et. al. *Orchids of Manitoba: A Field Guide*. Winnipeg: Native Orchid Conservation Inc., 2005.

Arnett, R.H. Jr., and R.L. Jacques, Jr., 1981. *Simon and Schuster's Guide to Insects*. New York: Simon and Schuster Inc., 1981.

Banfield, A.W.F. *The Mammals of Canada*. Toronto: University of Toronto Press, 1974.

Bezener, Andy, and Ken De Smet. *Manitoba Birds*. Edmonton: Lone Pine, 2000.

Borror, D.J. and R.E. White. *The Field Guide to the Insects*. Boston: Houghton Mifflin, 1998.

Boschung, H.T. Jr., J.D. Williams, D.W. Gotshall, D.K. Caldwell, and M.C. Caldwell. *The Audubon Society Field Guide to North American Fishes, Whales, and Dolphins*. New York: Alfred A. Knopf, 1983.

Bousquet, Y., ed. *Checklist of Beetles of Canada and Alaska*. Ottawa: Agriculture Canada & Ministry of Supply and Services Canada, 1991.

Buddle, Chris. "A primer on pseudoscorpions and taxonomic status in Canada." In *Newsletter of the Biological Survey of Canada (Terrestrial Arthropods)*, vol 24, no. 1 (2005): 12-16.

Burton, Maurice, ed. *The New Larousse Encyclopedia of Animal Life*. New York: Hamlyn, 1980.

Capinera, J.L., R.D. Scott, and T.J. Walker. *Field Guide to Grasshoppers, Katydids, and Crickets of the United States*. Ithaca, NY: Cornell University Press, 2004.

Carey, Brad. *The Birds of Manitoba*. Winnipeg: Manitoba Naturalists Society, 2003.

Carey, Brad et al. *Finding Birds in Southern Manitoba*. Winnipeg: Manitoba Naturalists Society and Brandon Naturalists Society, 2006.

Carr, Ian. *Manitoba Medicine: A Brief History*. Winnipeg: University of Manitoba Press, 1999.

Carter, R.T. *An Annotated Catalogue of the Formicidae (ants) of Manitoba*. Unpub. Manuscript, University of Manitoba, Department of Entomology, 1992.

Chartier, Bonnie. *A Birder's Guide to Churchill, Manitoba*. Colorado Springs, CO: American Birding Association, 1994.

Clifford, H.F. *Aquatic Invertebrates of Alberta*. Edmonton: University of Alberta Press, 1991.

Conant, R., and J.T. Collins. *A Field Guide to the Reptiles and Amphibians of Eastern and Central North America*. Boston: Houghton-Mifflin Co., 1998.

Cook, F. R. *Introduction to Canadian Amphibians and Reptiles*. Ottawa: National Museum of Natural Sciences, 1984.

Covell, C.V. Jr,. *A Field Guide to the Moths of Eastern North America*. Boston: Houghton-Mifflin Co., 1984.

Cunnings, T. A. J. *The Saga of Dr. Thor, Paul H. T. Thorlakson, CC, MD: A Biography*. Winnipeg: University of Manitoba Press, 1986.

Deyrup, M. *Florida's Fabulous Insects*. Tampa, FL: World Publications, 2000.

Downie, N.M, and R.H. Arnett. *The Beetles of Northeastern North America*. Gainesville, FL: The Sandhill Crane Press, 1996.

Edge, Fred. *The Iron Rose: The Life of Dr. Charlotte Ross*. Toronto: University of Toronto Press, 1991.

Ferguson, Colin. *One Hundred Years of Surgery 1883-1983*. Winnipeg: Peguis Publishers, 1983.

Froom, B. *Amphibians of Canada*. Toronto: McClelland and Stewart, 1982..

Godfrey, W.E. *The Birds of Canada*. Bull. No. 203. Ottawa: National Museum of Canada, 1966.

Grimaldi, David, and Michael S. Engel. *Evolution of the Insects*. New York: Cambridge University Press, 2005.

Hackett, F. J. Paul. *A Very Remarkable Sickness: Epidemics in the Petit Nord, 1670-1846*. Winnipeg: University of Manitoba Press, 2002.

Hay, Rankin K. *Neurosurgery and Neurological Science in Manitoba, 1884-1984*. Winnipeg: R. K. Hay, 2003.

Hinks, David. *The Fishes of Manitoba*. Winnipeg: Manitoba Department of Mines and Natural Resources, 1943.

Holldobler, B, and E.O. Wilson. *Journey to the Ants: A Story of Scientific Exploration.* Cambridge, MA: Belknap Press of Harvard University Press, 1994.

Hopps, John A. *Passing Pulses – The Pacemaker and Medical Engineering: A Canadian Story*. Ottawa: Publishing Plus Limited, 1995.

Ives, W.G.H., and H.R. Wong. *Tree and Shrub Insects of the Prairie Provinces*. Edmonton: Canadian Forestry Service, 1988.

Johnson, Dan L. *Band-winged, Spur-throated and Slant-faced Grasshoppers of the Canadian Prairies and Northern Great Plains*. Arthropods of Canadian grasslands No. 7-9. Ottawa: Agriculture and Agri-Food Canada, 2001-2003.

———. *Grasshopper Identification and Control Methods*. Ottawa: Agriculture and Agri-Food Canada, 2006.

Johnson, Derek, et. al. *Plants of the Western Boreal Forest and Aspen Parkland*. Edmonton: Lone Pine, 1995.

Johnson, Karen L. *Wildflowers of Churchill and the Hudson Bay Region*. Winnipeg: University of Manitoba Press, 1987.

Kershaw, Linda J. *Manitoba Wayside Wildflowers*. Edmonton: Lone Pine, 2003.

Klassen, P. *The Butterflies of Manitoba*. Winnipeg: Manitoba Museum of Man and Nature, 1989.

Laberry, R.A., P.W. Hall, and J.D. Lafontaine. *The Butterflies of Canada*. Toronto: University of Toronto Press, 1998.

Lange, I.M., *Ice Age Mammals of North America*. Missoula, MT: Mountain Press, 2002.

Levi, H.W., L.R. Levi, and H.S. Zim. *Spiders and Their Kin (Golden Guide)*. New York: St. Martin's Press, 2002.

Macdonald, D., ed. *The Encyclopedia of Mammals*. Oxfordshire: Andromeda Oxford Ltd., 2001.

McDougall, D., ed. *The History of Pharmacy in Manitoba, 1878-1953*. Winnipeg: Manitoba Pharmaceutical Association, 1954.

Manitoba Naturalists Society. *The Birds of Manitoba*. Winnipeg: Manitoba Avian Research Committee, 2003.

Manitoba Resources Branch. *Dr. Frank Leith Skinner*. Winnipeg: Manitoba Historic Resources Branch, 1981.

Margulis, L. & Schwartz, V. *Five Kingdoms; An Illustrated Guide to the Phyla of Life on Earth*. New York: W.H. Freeman & Company, 1988.

Marshall, Stephen A. *Insects: Their Natural History and Diversity*. Richmond Hill, ON: Firefly Books, 2006.

Medovy, Harry. *A Vision Fulfilled: The Story of the Children's Hospital of Winnipeg 1909-1973*. Winnipeg: Peguis Publishers, 1979.

Meinkoth, Norman A. *The Audubon Society Field Guide to North American Seashore Creatures*. New York: Alfred A. Knopf, 1981.

Merritt, R.W., and K.W. Cummins, eds. *An Introduction to the Aquatic Insects of North America*. Dubuque, IA: Kendall/Hunt, 1996.

Mierau, Maurice. *Memoir of a Living Disease: The Story of Earl Hershfield and Tuberculosis in Manitoba and Beyond*. Winnipeg: Great Plains Publications, 2004.

Milne, Lorus, and Margery Milne. *The Audubon Society Field Guide to North American Insects and Spiders*. New York: Alfred A. Knopf, 1980.

Nikula, B., Jackie Sones, Donald Stokes, and Lillian Stokes. *Stokes Beginner's Guide to Dragonflies and Damselflies*. Boston: Little, Brown and Co., 2002.

O'Toole, Christopher, ed. *Firefly Encyclopedia of Insects and Spiders*. Richmond Hill, ON: Firefly Books, 2002.

Pearson, D.L., C.B. Knisley, and C.J. Kazilek. *A Field Guide to the Tiger Beetles of the United States and Canada*. New York: Oxford University Press, 2006.

Penziwol, Shelley. *Storm Signals: A History of Weather in Manitoba*. Winnipeg: Great Plains Publications, 2004.

Peterkin, Audrey, and Margaret Shaw. *Mrs. Doctor: Reminisces of Manitoba Doctors' Wives*. Winnipeg: Prairie Publishing, 1976.

Preston, W.B. *The Amphibians and Reptiles of Manitoba*. Winnipeg: Manitoba Museum of Man and Nature, 1982.

Preston-Mafham, R. and K. *Insects and Other Invertebrates*. Animal fact files. Chartwell Books, 2005.

Reimer, Mavis. *Cornelius W. Wiebe: A Beloved Physician*. Winnipeg: Hyperion, 1983.

Resh, V.H. and R.T. Carde. *Encyclopedia of Insects*. Burlington, MA: Academic Press, 2003.

Scott, J.A. *The Butterflies of North America*. Stanford, CA: Stanford University Press, 1986.

Scott, W.B., and E.J. Crossman. *Freshwater Fishes of Canada*. Bull. 184. Fisheries Research Board of Canada, 1973.

Seton, Ernest Thomas. *Fauna of Manitoba*. 1916.

Smith, Douglas Grant. *Pennak's Freshwater Invertebrates of the United States: Porifera to Crustacea*. Toronto: John Wiley and Sons, 2001.

Stebbins, R.C. *Field Guide to Western Reptiles and Amphibians*. Boston: Houghton-Mifflin, 2003.

Steward, D.B., and W.L. Lockhart. *An Overview of the Hudson Bay Marine Ecosystem*. Can. Fish. Aquat. Sci. 2586, 2005.

Stewart, David B. *Holy Ground: The Story of the Manitoba Sanatorium at Ninette*. Killarney, MB: J. A. Victor David Museum, 1999.

Stewart, Kenneth W. and Douglas A. Watkinson. *The Freshwater Fishes of Manitoba*. Winnipeg: University of Manitoba Press, 2004.

Teller, J.T., ed. *Natural Heritage of Manitoba*. Winnipeg: Manitoba Museum of Man and Nature, 1984.

Thorpe. E. L. M. *The Social Histories of Smallpox and Tuberculosis in Canada (Culture, Evolution, and Disease)*. Winnipeg: University of Manitoba, Department of Anthropology, 1989.

Tudge, C. *The Variety of Life – A Survey and a Celebration of All the Creatures That Have Ever Lived*. New York: Oxford University Press, 2000.

Vandervoort, Julie. *Tell the Driver: A Biography of Elinor F.E. Black, M.D.* Winnipeg: University of Manitoba Press, 1992.

Vickery, V.R., and D.K. McE. Kevin. *The Grasshoppers, Crickets, and Related Insects of Canada and Adjacent Regions*. The Insects and Arachnids of Canada, Part 14. Publ. 1777, Research Branch, Agriculture Canada, 1985.

Weber, L. *Spiders of the North Woods*. Duluth, MN: Kollath-Stensaas, 2002.

White, R.E. *A Field Guide to the Beetles of North America*. Boston: Houghton-Mifflin, 1983.

Wrigley, R.E. *Manitoba's Big Cat – The Story of the Cougar in Manitoba*. Winnipeg: Manitoba Museum of Man and Nature, 1982.

———. *Mammals in North America*. Winnipeg: Hyperion Press Ltd, 1986.

Wrigley, R.E., ed. *Animals of Manitoba*. Winnipeg: Manitoba Museum of Man and Nature, 1974.

———. *Polar Bear Encounters at Churchill*. Winnipeg: Hyperion Press, 2001.

SPORTS, LEISURE, AND RECREATION:

Carpenter, David. *Fishing in the West*. Saskatoon: Western Producer Prairie Books, 1984.

Fatsis, Stefan. *Wild and Outside: How a Renegade Minor League Revived the Spirit of Baseball in America's Heartland*. New York: Walker Publishing, 1996.

Humber, William. *Diamonds of the North: A Concise History of Baseball in Canada*. Toronto: Oxford University Press, 1995.

Leah, Vince. *A History of the Blue Bombers*. 1979.

Ling, Nils. *True Blue: The Inside Look at a Championship Season*. Winnipeg: Wordsnorth Communications, 1984.

Maxwell, Doug. *Canada Curls: The Illustrated History of Curling in Canada*. Vancouver: Whitecap Books, 2002.

Mott, Morris, and John Allardyce. *Curling Capital: Winnipeg and the Roarin' Game, 1876 to 1988*. Winnipeg: University of Manitoba Press, 1989.

Silver, Jim. *Thin Ice: Money, Politics, and the Demise of an NHL Franchise*. Halifax: Fernwood, 1996.

Swanton, Barry. *The ManDak League: Haven for Former Negro League Ballplayers, 1950-1957*. Jefferson, NC: McFarland & Co., 1996.

PERIODICALS

The Beaver. The Hudson's Bay Co./Canada's National Historic Society, 1920-

Border Crossings.

Canadian Dimension. 1963-

Herizons.

Manitoba Archaeological Journal. Manitoba Archaeological Society.

Manitoba Business. 1978-

Manitoba History. Manitoba Historical Society, 1980-

Manitoba Nature Magazine. Manitoba Naturalists Society and the Zoological Society of Manitoba. 1972-1982.

Prairie Fire. Prairie Fire Press Inc.

ELECTRONIC RESOURCES

Canadian Encyclopedia Online. Historica Foundation. http://www.thecanadianencyclopedia.com

Dictionary of Canadian Biography Online. University of Toronto/Université Laval. http://www.biographi.ca

Eagle Feather: Celebrating First Nation Achievers in Manitoba. Indian and Northern Affairs Canada. http://www.ainc-inac.gc.ca/mb/eglfthr/EF6/ef6_e.html

Encyclopedia of Music in Canada. Historica Foundation. http://www.collectionscanada.ca/emc/index-e.html

Global Anabaptist Mennonite Encyclopedia Online. Mennonite Historical Society of Canada et al. www.gameo.org

Manitoba Community Profiles. Government of Manitoba. http://www.communityprofiles.mb.ca/

Statistics Canada. Government of Canada http://www.statcan.ca/

IMAGE ACKNOWLEDGEMENTS

Great Plains Publications is grateful to the organizations and individuals who provided images to illustrate the entries in the *Encyclopedia of Manitoba,* including the following:

Archives of Manitoba (Sharon Foley, Christopher Kotecki)
Ron Blakey
Patricia Bovey
Roy Ellis
Doug Fast
Folk Arts Council of Winnipeg Inc. (Kiersten Drysdale, Debra Fehr)
Janet Honey
Bartley Kives
Rudolf Koes
Jennifer LaBella
Manitoba Museum (E. Leigh Syms)
Manitoba Sports Hall of Fame and Museum Inc. (Andrea Reichert, Gloria Romaniuk)

Manitoba Water Stewardship (Alf Warkentin)
Glenn Marquez
Stan Milosevic
Charles Shilliday
Robert R. Taylor
Peter Tittenberger
Joel Trenaman
University of Manitoba Archives and Special Collections (Brett Lougheed, Lewis St. George Stubbs, Shelley Sweeney)
Douglas Watkinson
Western Canada Aviation Museum (Shirley Render)
Winnipeg Free Press (Jon Thordarson)
Winnipeg Goldeyes Baseball Club (Jonathan Green)
Winnipeg Art Gallery

ABBREVIATIONS IN IMAGE CREDITS

AM = Archives of Manitoba

UMA = University of Manitoba, Department of Archives and Special Collections.

UMA, Tribune = University of Manitoba, Department of Archives and Special Collections, *Winnipeg Tribune* Collection Due to space limitations, credits for images from the news files (boxes 20 to 75) in this collection do not include these preliminary collection identifiers: PC18-A81-12. For example, the full citation PC18-A81-12-31-1244-6 is abbreviated to 31-1244-6, (the box, file, and photo numbers respectively).

IMAGE COPYRIGHTS

Attempts were made until press time to locate current copyright holders of images used in this publication and to obtain permission for their use. The publisher welcomes clarifications and corrections from rights holders. Images from the *Winnipeg Tribune* Collection are © University of Manitoba and are reproduced with permission.

INDEX

799